© 2004 Freddie Mac

better tomorrow.

hope.

an opportunity.

potential.

Bringing America a brighter future.

home.

At Freddie Mac, our goal remains unchanged — the expansion of housing opportunities throughout the United States. And together, we will remain inspired by the shared vision of building a brighter future. www.FreddieMac.com

Freddie Mac

We make home possible℠

ANUARIOHISPANO-HISPANICYEARBOOK

PUBLISHER
Juan Ovidio Zavala

EDITOR
Angela E. Zavala

ASSOCIATE PUBLISHER
John Zavala

PRODUCTION
Ramón Palencia-Calvo
Joyce K. Rono

**GOVERNMENT RELATIONS
& CIRCULATION**
Jess Quintero

**ADVERTISING & PUBLIC
RELATIONS**
Evelyn Day
Robert James

RESEARCH
Christina M. Azores
Fredalyn Bardaje
Judy Mwangi
Alka Singh

CONTRIBUTING EDITORS
Shane M. Barney, MA, MPA
Aimée Winegar
Stephen J. Winegar

DESIGN
Caruso Creative, LLC

ADVERTISING SALES
Mongoose Atlantic, Inc.
For advertising inquiries, call
(212) 968-0196 or email
yearbooks@mongoosemedia.com

Trademark No. 78159159
Library of Congress Control No: 87-64-1284
Call Main No. HD2346.u 52 W 352
ISSN: 1067-330X
ISBN:0-9656545-8-3

ANUARIO HISPANO-HISPANIC YEARBOOK
is an annual publication of
TIYM Publishing Company, Inc.

Angela E. Zavala, President & CEO

An 8(a) Certified Company
DUNS:161904669

TIYM Publishing Company

HEADQUARTERS

6718 Whittier Avenue
Suite 130
McLean, Virginia 22101
USA

Tel: (703) 734-1632

Fax: (703) 356-0787

E-mail: tiym@tiym.com

Web Site: www.tiym.com

**AnuarioHispano.com
HispanicYearbook.com**

TIYM Publishing Company, Inc. is a current 8(a) certified business, qualified as a Small Disadvantaged Business (SDB) under the SBA's Office of Small Disadvantaged Business Certification and Eligibility.

DISTRIBUTION NETWORK
Circulation 150,000

Distributed to some of the groups and organizations listed in this edition:
• Federal & State Employment Offices
• Private Sector Employment Contacts
• Private Sector Minority Business Contacts
• US Marines, Army, US Coast Guard, Air Force and Navy Recruiting Stations
• Hispanic Organizations, Publications & Media

Throughout the United States:
• US Senate and House of Representatives
• US Institutions of Higher Education
• US Department of Defense
• High Schools
• Libraries
• The Congressional Hispanic Caucus
• Sponsors of the ANUARIO HISPANIO-HISPANIC YEARBOOK
• Retail Outlets in Association with the Independent Publishers Group (IPG)

At Conferences and Conventions:
• Association of American Chambers of Commerce in Latin America
• Adelante! San Antonio
• American Council on Education
• HAPCOA
• Minority Business Development Agency (MED WEEK)
• National Association of Bilingual Education (NABE)
• National Council of La Raza
• G.I. Forum
• Ser-Jobs for Progress
• US Hispanic Chamber of Commerce
• New York State Federation of HiCOC
• Mexican American Chamber of Commerce
• NALEO
• National Society of Hispanic MBAs

International:
• US Embassies around the World
• Argentina, Mexico, Panama, Paraguay, and Spain, as well as to other Latin American countries, on an individual basis.

THE WHITE HOUSE

WASHINGTON

January 24, 2005

I send greetings to readers of the Anuario Hispano - Hispanic Yearbook.

Across our country, Hispanic Americans have contributed to the vitality, success, and prosperity of our Nation. They have helped shape our country's character and enhanced the diversity that makes America strong. Since 1986, the Anuario Hispano - Hispanic Yearbook has served the Hispanic community by providing valuable information on employment, business, and educational opportunities.

My Administration remains committed to broadening opportunities for all Americans and building a future where every person can realize the promise of America. In 2002, I set a goal of increasing the number of minority homeowners by at least 5.5 million by the end of the decade. We are making good progress -- having added nearly 1.9 million minority homeowners so far. Through the No Child Left Behind Act of 2001, we are also working to improve minority achievement and ensure that schools are serving every student.

I join all Americans in recognizing the accomplishments of Hispanic Americans, and I commend those dedicated to strengthening the Hispanic-American community. The warmth and vitality of the Hispanic culture are great gifts to America and are a part of the unique fabric of our country.

Contents

HISPANIC: An American citizen or resident of Spanish or Latin-American descent.*

LATINO: A person of Latin-American or Spanish-speaking descent.*

HISPANICS OR LATINOS are those people who classified themselves in one of the specific Spanish, Hispanic, or Latino categories listed on the Census 2000 questionnaire -"Mexican, Mexican Am., Chicano," "Puerto Rican", or "Cuban" -as well as those who indicate that they are "other Spanish/Hispanic/Latino." Persons who indicated that they are "other Spanish/Hispanic/Latino" include those whose origins are from Spain, the Spanish-speaking countries of Central or South America, the Dominican Republic or people identifying themselves generally as Spanish, Spanish-American, Hispanic, Hispano, Latino, and so on. Origin can be viewed as the heritage, nationality group, lineage, or country of birth of the person or the person's parents or ancestors before their arrival in the United States.**

*Source: The Random House Dictionary of English Language. 2nd edition.

**Source: US Census Bureau.

Indice

2005/2006

ANUARIO HISPANO

Néstor Kirchner, Presidente de la República Argentina

El libro sobrevive a la palabra oral y la trasciende, la conjuga, la comparte, la reproduce, la esparce, la perdura, y la hace llegar incluso allí donde muchas veces los medios tecnológicos mas sofisticados no pueden hacerlo.

Y en cualquiera de sus formatos -en este caso, como anuario- es un objeto de arte. Un instrumento de comunicación de ayer, de hoy y de siempre, que no ha podido ser superado en su sencillez, su accesibilidad, su universalidad.

Lo digo como lector y como Presidente: Así como en todo anuario esta presente en la cotidianeidad, recíprocamente la vida misma, corregida y aumentada, enriquecida, profundizada, lo esta en él.

Seguramente por eso Jorge Luis Borges decía que se imaginaba el paraíso en forma de biblioteca.

Por eso, señores responsables de esta edición, mi total beneplácito con la presentación del "ANUARIO HISPANO - HISPANIC YEARBOOK" que ustedes realizan por primera vez en la Argentina.

Y mi agradecimiento: a través de estas líneas, que me ofrecen la oportunidad de enviar el más cordial saludo a mis compatriotas radicados en los Estados Unidos, a la comunidad hispana y al pueblo estadounidense todo.

Nos sentimos legítimamente orgullosos de la contribución que la comunidad argentina viene realizando en los más diversos ámbitos culturales de los Estados Unidos: el científico, el intelectual, el económico, el artístico.

Como -citando una vez más a Borges- "dar es recibir", la sociedad estadounidense, fiel a su vocación abierta y pluralista, no vaciló en reconocer dicho aporte argentino y en acoger a sus artífices en su seno.

Históricamente, la Argentina ha sido asimismo un proverbial faro de atracción para hombres y mujeres que buscaron en su suelo un futuro mejor.

En la actualidad estamos trabajando para volver a poner de pie esa Argentina, y honrar así una tradición que fue, es y será una de las "señas particulares visibles" de nuestra idiosincrasia.

Nuestro país volverá a constituir la tierra promisoria que buscaron y encontraron nuestros mayores, abierta a todos los hombres y mujeres de buena voluntad que quieran realizarse aquí como personas y ciudadanos del mundo. No nos importó antes ni nos importará ahora su origen y procedencia: sólo les pediremos una coherencia sin fisuras con los valores democráticos y pluralistas que compartimos con los Estados Unidos.

Valores que sustenta, para terminar, la propia comunidad argentina a través de la mas fructífera colaboración en los diversos lugares del exterior donde reside, y por supuesto en los Estados Unidos. Y a la que debemos la imagen de un pueblo emprendedor, inteligente y dinámico, capaz de contribuir, desde los hechos, a una mayor comprensión mutua entre los pueblos.

A un acercamiento interactivo que estoy seguro de que esta publicación que ustedes presentan ayudará a acrecentar.

Por eso apoyamos con verdadero entusiasmo la elección de nuestro país para el lanzamiento del Anuario en la región del MERCOSUR.

Porque coincide con el impulso de mirar hacia delante recuperado por esta nueva Argentina que estamos llevando a cabo con el esfuerzo de todos. Y también y muy especialmente con el de los compatriotas que viven fuera del país, pero que llevan este anhelo muy adentro, haciéndolo suyo desde los hechos cotidianos.

Néstor KIRCHNER
Presidente de la Nación

Desde España seguimos con mucho interés y satisfacción la continuidad y el desarrollo de un proyecto como el del Anuario Hispano, a cuyos responsables les transmito mi más cordial felicitación. El Anuario constituye una obra indispensable que ha logrado ofrecernos un inventario completo de la pujante comunidad hispana en los Estados Unidos a la que España, por razones obvias, se siente muy vinculada.

A un español nada de lo hispano le es ajeno. Los españoles somos los hispanos del otro lado del Atlántico. Somos los hispanos europeos.

Hay muchos factores que vinculan a España con los Estados Unidos, muchas razones por las que queremos que nuestras relaciones de todo tipo se enriquezcan y profundicen. Entre ellas, una muy poderosa es la existencia en este país de una comunidad con la que los españoles compartimos lengua, cultura e historia.

España desea incrementar sus relaciones con la comunidad hispana en Estados Unidos, desea conocerla mejor y desea emprender proyectos conjuntos para beneficio mutuo. Proyectos sin duda en el área económica, pero también en la educativa, en la cultural o en la científica.

Hace ya años que las relaciones entre Latinoamérica y España han dado un salto cualitativo. Ya no son sólo los vínculos históricos y culturales los que unen a nuestras sociedades. Las relaciones económicas han pasado también a un primer plano. España es hoy el segundo inversor extranjero en Latinoamérica y ha unido su propia prosperidad al desarrollo en equidad del Continente.

Esa profundización de relaciones con el hemisferio debe contar sin duda con los Estados Unidos. Y dentro de los Estados Unidos, debe contar con una población hispana emergente, que cada vez más asume funciones de alta responsabilidad en el gobierno y en la sociedad de ese gran país y que por derecho propio también pertenece a la gran familia hispana del mundo.

Nosotros no sólo observamos el crecimiento cuantitativo de la comunidad hispana. También queremos saber más de las dinámicas nuevas a que está dando lugar, como la afirmación de los valores hispanos, la relación permanente con los países de origen y el papel tan relevante que la comunidad hispana puede desempeñar en las relaciones entre los Estados Unidos, América Latina y España.

Pero hoy debemos celebrar la extraordinaria aportación del Anuario, que en su nueva edición certifica con su contenido la pujanza de la comunidad hispana. Se trata de un instrumento imprescindible para todos los que deseamos trabajar en estrecho contacto con esa comunidad. Muchas gracias por su trabajo.

José Luis Rodríguez Zapatero

Translation on p 208

Letter from the Editor

I t is hard to believe that we commenced work on the 1st edition of the ANUARIO HISPANO-HISPANIC YEARBOOK twenty years ago. Back then, in 1985, the Hispanic American community was not seen as an attractive market, and in fact, some questioned its potential, notwithstanding the eye-opening population projections. Fortunately, we identified a niche and stuck with it, witnessing first-hand the shift in attitudes and perceptions toward the U.S. Hispanic market over the years.

Ms. Georgette M. Dorn addressing guests during the launching of the 2004 edition of the ANUARIO HISPANO-HISPANIC YEARBOOK at the Library of Congress.

Today, the importance of the Hispanic American community is irrefutable. Political parties customize their campaigns, in order to attract potential voters from the largest minority group and be well-positioned for future demographic change. Corporate America is becoming fully bilingual, speaking Spanish not only in ads, but also within the organization. And the media have embraced Hispanic athletes, artists and entertainers, some of who have transcended ethnicity to become authentic American icons.

Hopefully, this edition reflects the richness and prominence of the Hispanic community. As you may have already noticed, we have realized numerous changes for this edition – both in terms of content and design – always with the purpose of providing relevant, accurate, and useful information for and about Hispanics. In this edition, you will find our much-utilized listings of Hispanic organizations, publications, and media outlets, which have been greatly enhanced. Also, for the first time, we have included interviews with prominent Hispanic Americans, as well as new population data.

We thank the many individuals and organizations that have supported and encouraged our efforts over the past two decades, and we look forward to continuing our work with the Hispanic community.

Affectionately,

Angela E. Zavala
Editor

From left to right: Col. Angie Salinas, U.S. Marine Corps, Angela E. Zavala, U.S. Senator Ken Salazar, and Hector Garza, President of the National Council for Community and Education Partnerships.

Interview

SENATOR MEL MARTINEZ

Mel Martinez came to Florida from his native Cuba at age fifteen as a part of "Operation Peter Pan," a humanitarian program led by the Catholic Church that helped over 14,000 Cuban children escape Communist Cuba. Mel lived with foster families for four years until he and his family were reunited in Orlando. Mel graduated from Bishop Moore High School in Orlando and then received his undergraduate and law degrees from Florida State University. Eager to give back to the community that had provided opportunities for him, Mel became involved in various youth, business, and civic organizations. Mel served on numerous boards including: Chairman of the Orlando Housing Authority, Chairman of the Orlando Utilities Commission, Vice Chairman of Catholic Charities, and many others. He even shared his love of baseball by coaching Little League.

AHHY In your opinion, what is the greatest challenge facing the Hispanic community?

Martinez A quality education and the opportunity to succeed professionally must be available to all Americans.

As a Cuban-American growing up here in the U.S., my education was my most valuable asset. In the coming years, we must ensure that each and every individual — both children and adults — have access to a first-rate education.

Continued on 10

AHHY How does the Republican Party speak to the needs and interests of Hispanics? What do you think your party needs to do in order to attract a larger share of the Hispanic vote?

Martinez Not only do Hispanic Americans share many Republican values, but Hispanic American leaders represent a group of the Republican Congress as well. There are seven Hispanic members of Congress and two Hispanic members in the President's Cabinet. Generations of Hispanic-Americans know the oppression of a socialist or communist society and immigrate to America in search of freedom. Recognizing the Republican value system and the ideals of individualism and less government as important priorities, Hispanic Americans are gradually aligning themselves with a realistic ideology.

AHHY Hispanics have typically voted Democratic. In recent years, However, there has been a steady trend for an increasing number of Hispanic voters to vote republican. What factors do you believe have lead to this shift?

Martinez Hispanics identify with the fundamental Republican beliefs, but mainly realize that less government allows them more personal choices.

AHHY What has been the U.S. Hispanic community's greatest achievement in recent years?

Martinez There is not just one great accomplishment, but the combination of many successes for the Hispanic community – achievements that no one would have dreamed of many years ago. Just this year, Alberto Gonzales was confirmed as U.S. Attorney General, Carlos Gutierrez was appointed as U.S. Secretary of Commerce and the first two Hispanic-American senators were elected in more than twenty-five years.

More Hispanics are involved in the political process than ever before, allowing for the voice of the Hispanic American community to be heard.

Additionally, more Hispanics own homes than ever before in history and Hispanics are embracing the opportunity for entrepreneurship that has been provided by the American Dream Downpayment Act, and the Blueprint for the American Dream.

AHHY How have your experiences as a Cuban immigrant helped you to understand the challenges that newcomers to our country encounter? How were you able to overcome these challenges?

Martinez Yes. Coming here from Cuba alone, I was forced to learn the ways of this country on my own. It was difficult to communicate, and I was frustrated by the preconceived ideas that Americans possessed about Hispanics. However, I was determined and didn't give up. My determined attitude and perseverance brought me to where I am today.

The language and accent barriers can present challenges. I had difficulty pronouncing common English words and names, but I put my embarrassment aside and boldly practiced until I mastered the language.

AHHY As the first Cuban American Senator, do you feel you have a unique responsibility toward the Hispanic community nationwide?

Martinez I have an incredible responsibility to serve as a role model, an example and an illustration of the possibilities that lie ahead for Hispanics nationwide. By embracing the fundamental values of our great country, the American Dream can become a reality.

AHHY What advice would you give to young Hispanics interested in entering politics or public service?

Martinez If you work hard and play by the rules, anything is possible.

AHHY What impact, if any, do you believe the controversy in Florida surrounding the close Presidential election of 2000 had on minority voter participation in the recent 2004 election?

Martinez The 2000 election was intense, continuing on for several weeks. As a result, Americans realized the importance of their duty to vote as citizens of this country. People throughout the nation expressed more of a desire to be involved in the political process by promoting our country's democratic values.

THE SECRETARY OF THE NAVY
WASHINGTON, D.C. 20350-1000

TO THE ANUARIO HISPANO - HISPANIC YEARBOOK 2005

Congratulations on another terrific edition of the Anuario Hispano. This yearbook again highlights the vital contributions to peace and progress made by Hispanic Americans and our friends around the world. This important reference guide has helped connect business and government leaders and build relationships around the globe since 1986.

Once again, the United States Navy and Marine Corps Team is pleased to be a part of this publication. I am especially proud of the thousands of Hispanic Sailors and Marines who proudly serve the cause of freedom. From Admiral David Glasgow Farragut - the son of a Spanish immigrant, to The Honorable Edward Hidalgo, a former Secretary of the Navy, to the current Sergeant Major of the Marine Corps, Sergeant Major John L. Estrada, the Navy-Marine Corps Team is resplendent with those of Hispanic ancestry. The men and women who wear the cloth of our Nation are not only in the Navy and Marines Corps, they are the Navy and Marine Corps. These great men and women represent our core values of Honor, Courage and Commitment and their contributions have, and continue to, strengthen the very fiber of America.

The impressive achievements and service of Hispanic men and women throughout our history have greatly contributed to our legacy and the greatest Navy the world has ever known.

CONGRESSMAN ROBERT MENENDEZ

Congressman Bob Menendez has made a stellar and rapid rise to the highest levels of influence in the U.S. House, and the highest levels of prominence in American political life. Today, Bob Menendez is the Chairman of the Democratic Caucus. He is the third-ranking Democrat in the U.S. House, the highest ranking Hispanic in Congressional history, and the only Hispanic ever elected to a leadership position, in either chamber, by either party. In addition to being the first Democratic House Member from New Jersey elected to a Leadership post, he is also the youngest member of the elected Democratic Leadership. Previously, Menendez served two consecutive terms as the Vice Chairman of the Democratic Caucus.

Congressman Menendez is also a former State Assemblyman, State Senator, and an attorney in private practice. He received his B.A. from St. Peter's College in Jersey City and his law degree from Rutgers University. He was raised in Union City and currently resides in Hoboken. He has two children, Robert and Alicia.

AHHY In your opinion, what is the greatest challenge facing the Hispanic community?

Menendez I think that the greatest challenge facing the community is our effort to continue to achieve high education levels, which means high economic advances. When we still have over fifty percent of our children who do not graduate from high school and only a small percentage of Hispanic Americans have a college degree, compared to the rest of American society, that obviously limits social mobility and economic opportunities. That is why I believe that education, in that respect — at both of those levels — is our greatest challenge. Education unlocks economic opportunity, which is fundamental to the progress of Hispanics.

AHHY As the highest-ranking Hispanic in Congressional history, what unique responsibility do you feel towards the Hispanic community?

Menendez Very often at leadership meetings of my party, or bipartisan leadership meetings in the House, or in leadership meetings with the Senate, or even at the White House, I am the only Hispanic who is sitting at the table, by virtue of my elected leadership position. So, therefore, I feel an enormous responsibility to put forth the issues and the agenda of our community, even when we are talking about issues like how we respond to the 9-11 Commission Report. I have spent most of the last several days dealing with the immigration components of that bill, to ensure that we do those things that are necessary to avoid terrorists using our immigration laws, but do not hurt the legitimate individuals from trying to gain asylum, obtaining citizenship, permanent residency, or the reunification of families. That is an example of how my being at the table in these discussions, by virtue of my leadership, provides me with a unique opportunity, and also a great responsibility, to the broader Hispanic community to make a case about our issues and how our concerns come to bear on these broader issues. So if we are talking about education: How do we deal with the fact that fifty percent of Hispanic children don't finish high school? How do we deal with the fact that the fastest rate of growth among small business are among Latino-owned businesses? How do we create access to capital for them? How do we ensure that we can bring millions of people from our community who are in an undocumented status of some form, to full participation in American society? And those are just a few examples. Finally, although they are not in leadership positions, I hope to be joined in this effort by the two U.S. senators of Hispanic descent. But there will still be times, by virtue of my leadership role, that I will be the only Hispanic voice at the table. That is both a privilege and a great responsibility, and I try to do the best that I can.

AHHY What role will the Hispanic community play in shaping the general direction of the country?

Menendez A huge role. Beyond the fact that we are the largest minority in the country today, I think what is more important than the numbers is the impact we are having. We have a trillion dollar domestic marketplace which will grow dramatically. We are younger by a decade than the rest of the population. So as the rest of America ages, it will increasingly depend upon us for the quality of their lives. As I always say, some of us, as dishwashers, will be cleaning a knife in a kitchen that someone used, while another person will be holding a surgeon's knife in an operating room. And how well educated and trained that Hispanic American surgeon is at that time is going to be incredibly important to the health care of all Americans. Within the next fifty years, we are going to be twenty-five percent of all of the nation's schoolchildren, which means that the competitive future of the nation is going to increasingly depend upon how well-educated and well-trained we are. And that's not just for us as a community, but for the nation as a whole. Our community has already made an enormous impact on the culture of this country. You cannot play major league baseball and remove all the Hispanic players from it; in fact, without the Hispanic and African-American players, there wouldn't be much major league baseball left. We have

> "We [the Hispanic community] are affecting all parts of American culture: economically, socially, culturally, and also in terms of the nation's competitive future, and access to twenty-one countries in the world. We are going to be the natural ambassadors; we are going to continue to make a huge impact, I believe."

introduced soccer in this country and it's growing exponentially. Our artists in music, movies, and television are growing dramatically in numbers and influence. So we are affecting all parts of American culture: economically, socially, culturally, and also in terms of the nation's competitive future, and access to twenty-one countries in the world. We are going to be the natural ambassadors; we are going to continue to make a huge impact, I believe.

AHHY You were instrumental in the establishment of the "New Partnership for America's

Continued on 14

Future." How can Hispanic-Americans expect to benefit from this initiative?

Menendez The Partnership for America's Future is, in essence, the core values that the Democratic Party in the House of Representatives believes in and advocates for. Our community will most certainly be very enriched by that partnership, should we be able to succeed in moving elements of that partnership forward. It talks about a world class education for every child in this country and having both the high standards and the resources to ensure that. It talks about expanding access to health care. And when you have nearly fourteen to fifteen million Hispanic Americans who have no health care coverage whatsoever, and many more who have inferior health care coverage, that is critical. It talks to Hispanic seniors in this country by saying that not only do we want to ensure retirement security, but health care security, and that means a very good prescription drug program where you never have to choose between putting food on the table, keeping a home, and having access to life saving medication. It talks about security, and we understand that our community also shares the concern about security and has also contributed a great deal to the security of this country by the very significant number of men and women of Hispanic descent who wear the uniform of the United States, serving in the Armed Forces. So it talks about security and how we achieve greater security at home and a better relationship with the rest of the world. It is about prosperity, opportunity, security, responsibility, and a sense of community. And in all of those elements, the Hispanic community obviously will greatly benefit from what the partnership offers.

AHHY What advice would you give to young Hispanics interested in entering politics or public service?

Menendez I would say, first: Get a good education because in order to enter public service at any level of government, in which the issues increasingly get so much more difficult and complex, a good foundation in fundamental abilities, analytical thinking, and problem-solving, regardless of what the issue is, is going to be incredibly important. So get a good education. Certainly there are many ways to serve, and there are many ways to start serving early, and I would certainly advocate that they find ways to be of service to other people in their own communities, in their own states, and of course, ultimately, in the nation and around the world. And finally, understand that public service is about sacrifice; if you think it is a glamorous life, then you are mistaken. If you want to get into public service because it is your calling, and because your satisfaction is going to come because you are able to change the course of events for the better, then by all means, come. But if you're thinking that you are going to either make money or that it is glamorous, go make money or go and become a movie star instead.

AHHY President Roosevelt once referred to Latin America as the "backyard of America." How would you refer to Latin America today and what is the future of U.S. – Latin American relations?

Menendez Well, I think President Roosevelt had it wrong, and I see Latin America in terms of its hemispheric integration with the United States. That is both in the national interest and national security interests of the United States, and ultimately, it will be in the national interest and national security interests of the countries of Central and South America as well. That also means that the greater progress

we make on economic integration, the greater opportunities that we create for economic success in Latin America, the greater political stability will exist in the hemisphere, and the greater security will exist in the hemisphere. I am the Ranking Democrat on the Western Hemisphere Subcommittee of the International Relations Committee, and probably one of the few "Latin Americanists" in the Congress to focus their attention on Latin America. I view this as a symbiotic, important relationship that needs to move increasingly toward integration for the national interest and security of the United States and the other countries in the hemisphere, and I believe that we are on that course, and it will take time and there will be challenges, but we are on that course.

AHHY Today in Argentina fifty percent of the population is living under poverty. How would you encourage them to be optimistic with this situation, especially when it appears that President Bush has other priorities?

Menendez I hope that, for example, my legislation, which has had bipartisan support but has not moved, will in the next congress move forward. It is for economic and social development for the Americas. It changes or refocuses our policy toward Central and Latin America with an emphasis on understanding that it is in the United States national and security interest to help with the economic and social development of the Americas. If we make investments in education, healthcare, economic development, and transparent judicial systems, then we improve the quality of life for Latin Americans. When we do that, it creates greater political stability and economic opportunities, and therefore, peace and progress in the hemisphere. It will expend about 2.5 billion dollars over the next five years to both the USAID and the IDB, and we think that would be the greatest amount of money spent in over a generation in Latin America by the United States. We would work in combination with both the countries as well as the non-governmental organizations to achieve these goals in education, health care, economic development, and judicial transparency and professionalism. It would change a policy that just simply engages in trade and believes that trade alone will improve the nature of the hemisphere's standing, when

we understand that nearly fifty percent of the people who live in the southern hemisphere are below the poverty level, and trade alone will not improve the standards of those individuals. So we must match trade with social and economic investment, and when we do that as was noted in the last Summit of the Americas, with this whole issue of the alleviation of poverty, the division of poverty in Latin America between those who are very wealthy and those who are not, can be addressed in order to have greater stability. I hope that legislation will make it through the next Congress. I hope the President will endorse it. I heard what the United States said at the summit of Monterrey. Now we need to act on it.

HISPANIC AMERICAN Population

According to the 2000 Census, the Hispanic population increased from 22.4 million in 1990 to 35.6 million in 2000. As of July 1, 2003, the estimated Hispanic population of the United States was 39.9 million. The Hispanic population is projected to grow from 35.6 million to 102.6 million between 2000 and 2050. The Hispanic community's share of the nation's population would nearly double from 12.6 percent to 24.4 percent (Fig. 1).

In 2002, 40.2 percent (fifteen million) of the Hispanic population in the United States was foreign-born (Fig. 2). Among the foreign born Hispanic population, 52.1 percent entered the United States between 1990 and 2002, and only 7.3 percent of them had become citizens by 2002 (Fig. 3). The states of Hawaii and Montana had the smallest proportion of foreign-born Hispanics in their total population while California, Texas, and Florida had the largest number.

The Hispanic population is younger than the U.S. population. In 2002, 35.7 percent of Hispanics in the U.S. were under the age of eighteen. The median age was 25.9 compared with 35.3 for the United States as a whole, and Mexican descendants had the lowest median age for all Hispanic groups (Fig. 4). In 2000, more than one person in eight that lived in the United States was of Hispanic origin. According to the Selig Center

FIG 1. Projected Population of the United States, by Race and Hispanic Origin: 2000 to 2050 (As of July 1, 2003. Resident population.)

POPULATION IN THOUSANDS	2000	2010	2020	2030	2040	2050
POPULATION TOTAL	**282,125**	**308,936**	**335,805**	**363,584**	**391,946**	**419,854**
White alone	228,548	244,995	260,629	275,731	289,690	302,626
Black alone	35,818	40,454	45,365	50,442	55,876	61,361
Asian Alone	10,684	14,241	17,988	22,580	27,992	33,430
All other races	7,075	9,246	11,822	14,831	18,388	22,437
Hispanic (of any race)	**35,622**	**47,756**	**59,756**	**73,055**	**87,585**	**102,560**
White alone, not Hispanic	195,729	201,112	205,936	209,176	210,331	210,283

PERCENT OF TOTAL POPULATION	2000	2010	2020	2030	2040	2050
TOTAL	**100.0**	**100.0**	**100.0**	**100.0**	**100.0**	**100.0**
White alone	81.0	79.3	77.6	75.8	73.9	72.1
Black alone	12.7	13.1	13.5	13.9	14.3	14.6
Asian Alone	3.8	4.6	5.4	6.2	7.1	8.0
All other races	2.5	3.0	3.5	4.1	4.7	5.3
Hispanic (of any race)	**12.6**	**15.5**	**17.8**	**20.1**	**22.3**	**24.4**
White alone, not Hispanic	69.4	65.1	61.3	57.5	53.7	50.1

Source: U.S. Census Bureau, 2004, "U.S. Interim Projections by Age, Sex, Race, and Hispanic Origin," www.census.gov/ipc/www/usinterimproj, Internet Release Date: March 18, 2004.

for Economic Growth at the University of Georgia, by 2009, nearly one person out of every six living in the United States will be of Hispanic origin. Projections by the Congressional Hispanic Caucus Institute state that by 2030, U.S. Latinos will represent twenty-six percent of the eighty-three million U.S. youth.

The Hispanic population consists of a wide-cross section of diverse nationalities with Mexicans making up the largest group followed by Puerto Ricans and Cubans. Salvadorans are the largest Central American group and Colombians, the largest South American group (Fig. 5 & 6). Hispanics are more concentrated in the West or South with regional distribution ranging from 44.2 percent in the West to 7.7 percent in the Midwest (Fig. 7). As of July 1, 2003 population estimates, the top ten states by Hispanic population are California, Texas, Florida, New York, Illinois, Arizona, New Jersey, Colorado, New Mexico, and Georgia (Fig. 8).

FIG 2. Foreign-Born Population by Sex, Citizenship Status, Year of Entry, Hispanic Origin, and Race: March 2002 (Numbers in thousands)

Citizenship status and year of entry	Total		Hispanic origin and race [1]					
			Hispanic		Non-Hispanic, White		Non-Hispanic, Other	
	Number	Percent	Number	Percent	Number	Percent	Number	Percent
Total	32,453	100.0	15,058	100.0	7,245	100.0	10,150	100.0
1990-2002	15,781	48.6	7,842	52.1	2,906	40.1	5,034	49.6
1980-1989	7,960	24.5	3,851	25.6	1,204	16.6	2,904	28.6
1970-1979	4,605	14.2	2,077	13.8	965	13.3	1,563	15.4
Before 1970	4,107	12.7	1,288	8.6	2,170	29.9	649	6.4
Naturalized citizen								
Total	11,962	100.0	3,781	100.0	3,642	100.0	4,539	100.0
1990-2002	2,002	16.7	570	15.1	545	15.0	886	19.5
1980-1989	3,584	30.0	1,150	30.4	644	17.7	1,790	39.4
1970-1979	3,069	25.7	1,116	29.5	669	18.4	1,283	28.3
Before 1970	3,307	27.6	944	25.0	1,784	49.0	579	12.8
Not a citizen								
Total	20,491	100.0	11,278	100.0	3,602	100.0	5,611	100.0
1990-2002	13,779	67.2	7,271	64.5	2,361	65.5	4,147	73.9
1980-1989	4,376	21.4	2,702	24.0	560	15.6	1,114	19.9
1970-1979	1,536	7.5	961	8.5	295	8.2	280	5.0
Before 1970	799	3.9	344	3.0	386	10.7	69	1.2

[1] *Hispanic refers to people whose origin is Mexican, Puerto Rican, Cuban, South or Central American, or other Hispanic/Latino, regardless of race.*

Source: U.S. Census Bureau, Current Population Survey, March 2002, Ethnic and Hispanic Statistics Branch, Population Division. Internet Release date: June 18, 2003

FIG 3. U.S. Citizenship of the Foreign-Born Hispanic Population by Year of Entry: 2002

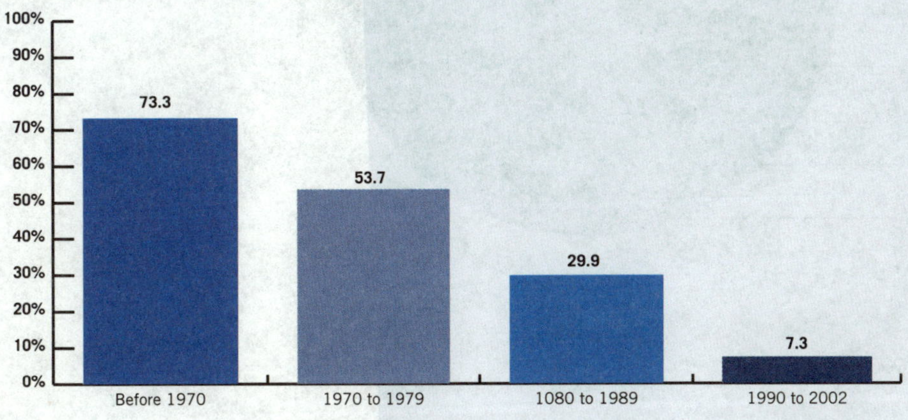

Source: U.S. Census Bureau, Annual Demographic Supplement to the March 2002 Current Population Survey.

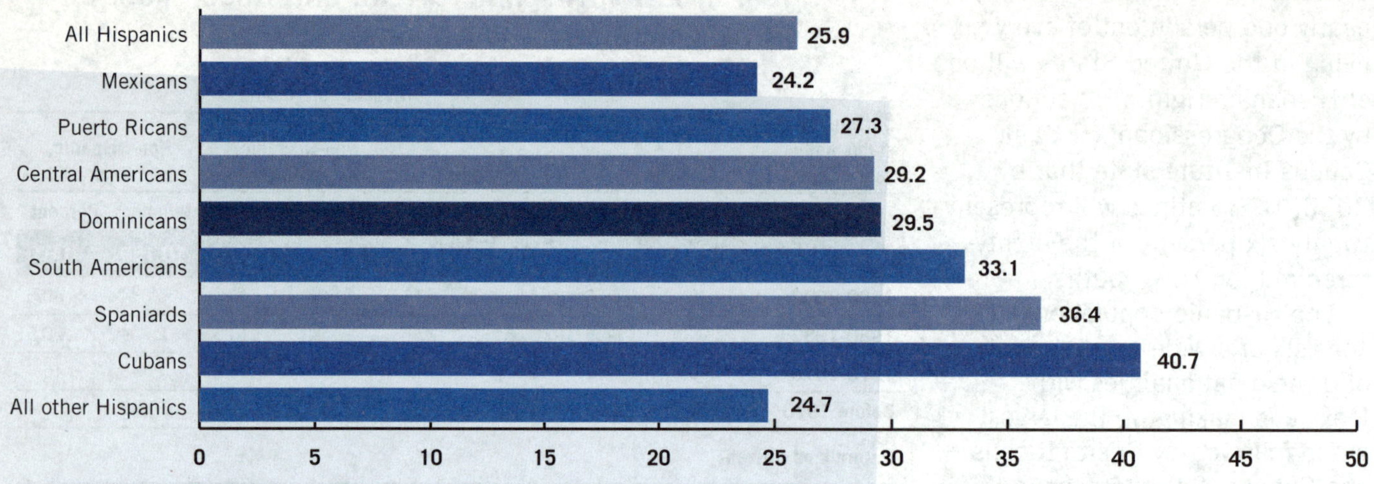

Source: U.S. Census Bureau, 2000 Census.

FIG 5. Percent Distribution of the Hispanic Population by Type: 2000

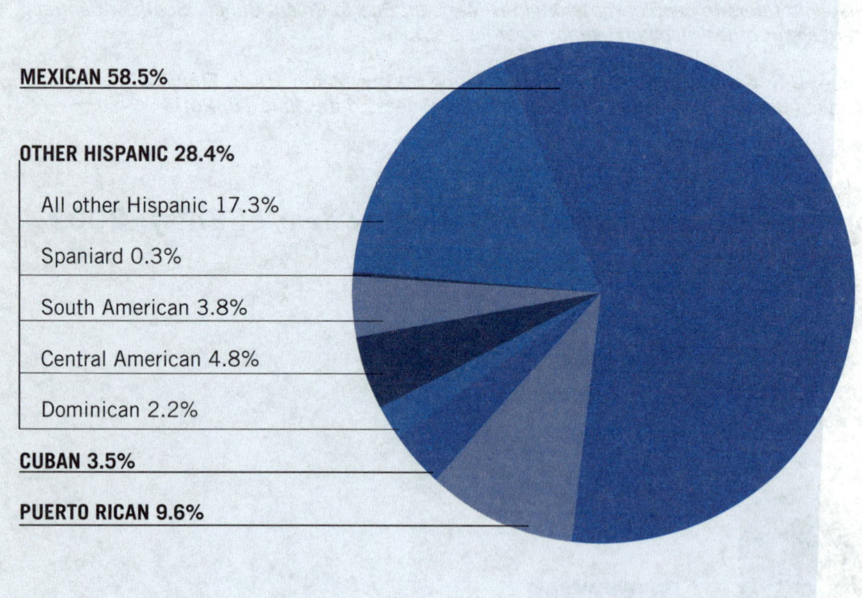

Source: U.S. Census Bureau, 2000 Census.

FIG 6. Hispanic by Type: 2000

	Number	Percent
HISPANIC OR LATINO ORIGIN		
Total Population	281,421,906	100.0
Hispanic or Latino (of any race)	35,305,818	12.5
Not Hispanic or Latino	246,116,088	87.5
HISPANIC OR LATINO BY TYPE		
Hispanic or Latino (of any race)	35,305,818	100.0
Mexican	20,640,711	58.5
Puerto Rican	3,406,178	9.6
Cuban	1,241,685	3.5
Other Hispanic or Latino	10,017,244	28.4
Dominican (Dominican Republic)	764,945	2.2
Central American (excludes Mexican)	1,686,937	4.8
Costa Rican	68,588	0.2
Guatemalan	372,487	1.1
Honduran	217,569	0.6
Nicaraguan	177,684	0.5
Panamanian	91,723	0.3
Salvadoran	655,165	1.9
Other Central American	103,721	0.3
South American	1,353,562	3.8
Argentinean	100,864	0.3
Bolivian	42,068	0.1
Chilean	68,849	0.2
Colombian	470,684	1.3
Ecuadorian	260,559	0.7
Paraguayan	8,769	0
Peruvian	233,926	0.7
Uruguayan	18,804	0.1
Venezuelan	91,507	0.3
Other South American	57,532	0.2
Spaniard	100,135	0.3
All other Hispanic or Latino	6,111,665	17.3
Checkbox only, other Hispanic	1,733,274	4.9
Write in Spanish	686,004	1.9
Write in Hispanic	2,454,529	7.0
Write-in Latino	450,769	1.3
Not elsewhere classified	787,089	2.2

Source: U.S. Census Bureau, Census 2000.

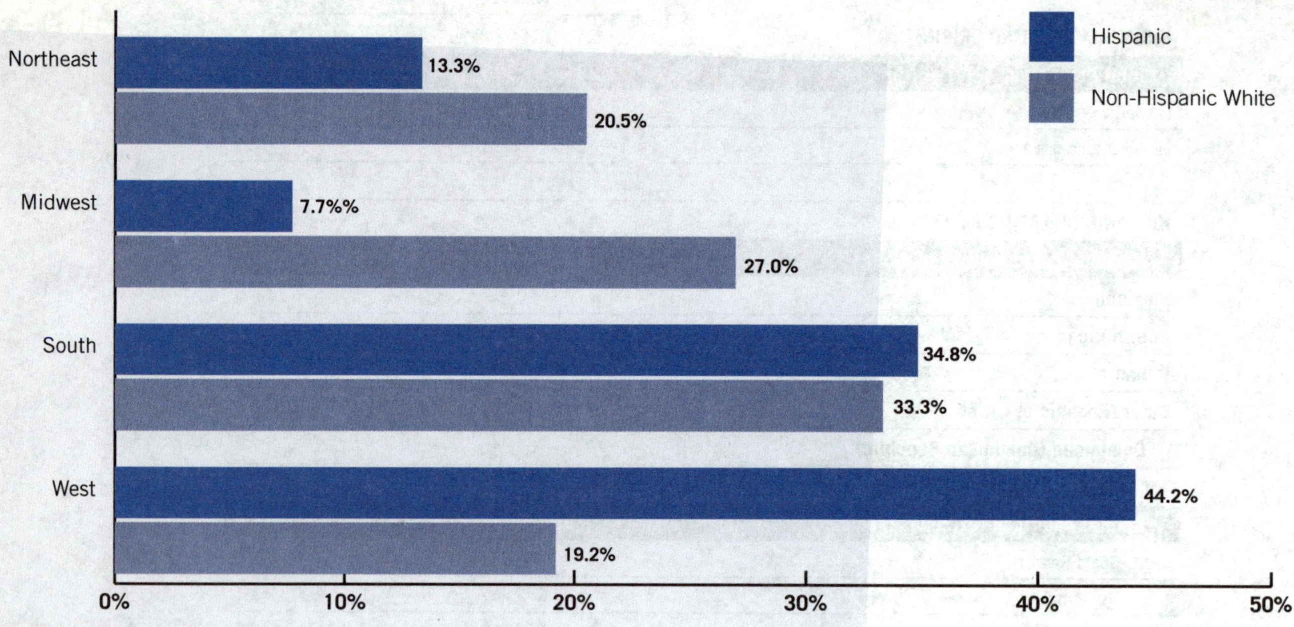

Source: U.S. Census Bureau, Annual Demographic Supplement to the March 2002 Current Population Survey.

FIG 8. Top 10 States by Hispanic Population (July 1, 2003)

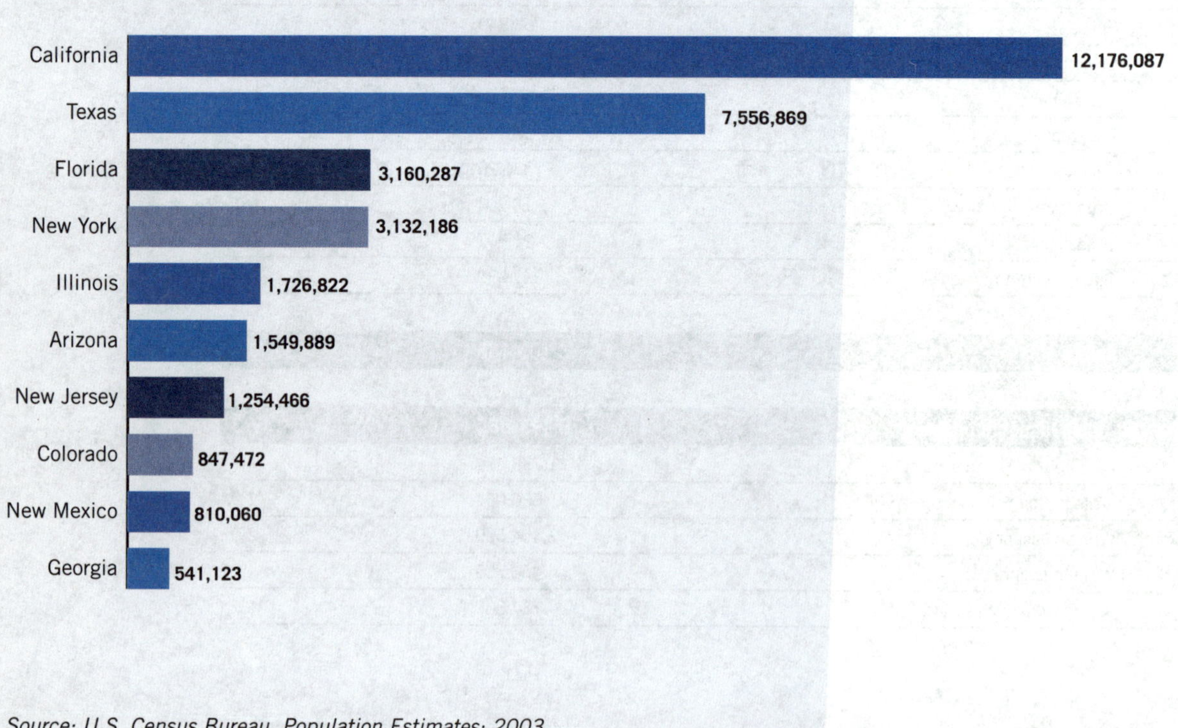

Source: U.S. Census Bureau, Population Estimates: 2003.

**A Message From the Chief of Staff of the United States Army
To the Hispanic-American Yearbook 2005**

Congratulations on the nineteenth edition of the Hispanic-American Yearbook. Our Army shares the goals of TIYM Publishing to inform the Hispanic-American community about the personal growth, opportunity, diversity and teamwork that the various organizations featured in this book can offer.

Hispanic-Americans have long been a proud part of our Army's history, all the way back to the War of Independence. Our ranks have included distinguished Hispanic-American patriots who served in units such as the New Mexico Volunteers, the Rough Riders under President Theodore Roosevelt and the Women's Army Corps during World War II. These pioneers enjoy an esteemed legacy in our history, and they are honored by Hispanic Soldiers serving in our Armed Forces today.

We believe today's American Soldier is the embodiment of the best of the American spirit, regardless of race, creed or gender. While diversity in our force fosters ingenuity and new ideas, we all live under one set of shared ideals: the seven Army values of loyalty, duty, respect, selfless service, honor, integrity and personal courage.

Service to our Nation is both an honor and a responsibility, one that requires self-sacrifice. Soldiers today serve in difficult conditions in far-away places, so that other Americans may sleep soundly. They bring security where there was chaos, hope where there was despair. We are proud of our accomplishments over the last three years in liberating 46 million people from tyranny and oppression. Our success has come at a high cost, and we mourn the loss of our fallen comrades in arms, but they have not died in vain. We know America is worth fighting for, and each day we are further weakening the terrorists' ability to harm our Nation.

On behalf of our Army, I salute the achievements of Hispanic-Americans who contribute so much to our society while strengthening our Nation for future generations.

Sincerely,

PETER J. SCHOOMAKER
General, United States Army
Chief of Staff

JAN 2 4 2005

The United States Air Force is proud to participate in this year's edition of the Anuario Hispano-Hispanic Yearbook. This is an important reference guide for Hispanic and non-Hispanic Americans alike.

The Air Force has a proud Hispanic heritage with contributions to air and space power ranging from military leaders like Lieutenant General Elwood Quesada, whose 9th Fighter Command cleared the skies over Normandy on D-Day, and Captain Manuel Fernandez, one of America's top three aces in the Korean War, to today's senior civilian leaders like Mr. Michael Montelongo, Assistant Secretary for Financial Matters and Comptroller, and Mr. Michael Dominguez, Assistant Secretary for Manpower and Reserve Affairs.

Recruiting and developing leaders like these are top priorities for us. Air and space power requires a highly skilled, diverse, educated, and technologically superior force, both military and civilian. Diversity is critical to maintaining the flexibility and adaptability needed to sustain our air and space dominance. It is a vital source of strength and resilience within our ranks that keeps us the world's preeminent air and space power.

We need men and women who are a cross-section of American culture – all races, religions, social, and economic, those with technical and creative skills, and those with knowledge of languages, cultures, and an appreciation of history. We need scientists, engineers, doctors, nurses, accountants, and many others, both military and civilian. This variety of perspectives results in greater insight and creativity. This is our investment in the future.

This investment runs from the newest Airmen to the most senior leaders. We are committed to ensuring diversity at all levels. The innovation that comes with diversity improves our ability to fly and fix airplanes, to employ air and space power, and ultimately, to defend America. Furthermore, we know that our Air Force is fundamentally your Air Force – America's Air Force. We should reflect the people and values of the country we protect and serve.

On behalf of the men and women of the United States Air Force, we congratulate you and wish you the very best in the year ahead.

John P. Jumper
General, USAF
Chief of Staff

Peter B. Teets
Acting Secretary of the Air Force

Hispanics are seen to play a major role in both local and national elections by both the Republican and Democratic parties. This is mainly due to the rapid growth of the Hispanic population. According to exit polls from CNN and NBC (both use the National Election Pool), in the 2004 elections, fifty-three percent of Hispanics voted for Democrat nominee John Kerry while forty-four percent of Hispanics voted for President Bush (Fig. 1). Hispanics accounted for eight percent of the vote nationally according to the same exit poll.

The Hispanic Business News estimated that 10.2 million Hispanics were registered to vote on November 2, and of that number, slightly more than 7.6 million cast their ballots. This accounted for 1.2 million more Hispanic voters than in the November 2000 Presidential elections.

Among the Hispanics who registered to vote in the 2000 elections, seventy-nine percent of them voted. This represented nearly six million votes. Although the voting rate for the Hispanic population did not change significantly from the 1996 and 2000 elections, the number of Hispanic voters increased by about twenty percent. In comparison to the African-American population that had a similar population size to the Hispanic population, African-Americans had more eligible voters (twenty-three million compared to thirteen million Hispanic eligible voters) in 2000 (Fig. 2). This was largely due to the large number of Hispanics who were not citizens, and those who were too young to vote.

Hispanics will continue to play a larger role in future elections because of an increasing number of native-born Hispanics who will expand the pool of potential Hispanic voters. Since 2000, an average of 425,000 native-born Hispanics have turned eighteen years old and become eligible to vote according to a 2004 report by the Pew Hispanic Center.

This survey also shows that education, economy, healthcare, terrorism, and immigration, among other issues, were important to registered Hispanics in the 2004 elections (Fig. 3). However, there are barriers that many Hispanics face that prevent them from actively engaging in the political process. This includes language, immigration and citizenship status, educational attainment, and voting.

According to a U.S. Census report, there is significant statistical correlation between educational attainment and voting rates. People with a bachelor's degree are more likely to vote compared to those who have not finished high school (Fig. 4). With only eleven percent of Hispanics obtaining a bachelor's degree, this impacts their voting or political participation.

FIG 1. Vote by Race, Election 2004

Vote by Race	BUSH		KERRY	NADER
TOTAL	2004	¹2000	2004	2004
White (77%)	58%	+4	41%	0%
African-American (11%)	11%	+2	88%	0%
Latino (8%)	44%	+9	53%	2%
Asian (2%)	44%	+3	56%	*
Other (2%)	40%	+1	54%	2%

Source: CNN.com, Exit polls, Election 2004.

¹ *The 2000 column represents the difference in the number of percentage points — either an increase or decrease — between the 2004 exit poll responses and the responses in 2000 to the Voter News Service exit polls. The 2000 column applies only to President Bush.*

* *No respondents (The percentage of the White and African-American population who voted for Nader was rounded to zero).*

FIG 2. Reported Voting and Registration by Citizenship, Race, and Hispanic Origin: November 1996 and 2000 (Numbers in thousands)

Characteristic	Total population				Citizens				Registered	
	Total	Citizen	Reported registered	Reported voted	Percent reported registered	90 percent C.I. (±)[1]	Percent reported voted	90 percent C.I. (±)[1]	Percent reported voted	90 percent C.I. (±)[1]
2000										
Total, 18 years and over	**202,609**	**186,366**	**129,549**	**110,826**	**69.5**	**0.3**	**59.5**	**0.3**	**85.5**	**0.3**
Race and Hispanic origin										
White	168,733	157,291	110,773	95,098	70.4	0.3	60.5	0.4	85.8	0.3
White non-Hispanic	148,035	144,732	103,588	89,469	71.6	0.4	61.8	0.4	86.4	0.3
Black	24,132	22,753	15,348	12,917	67.5	1.1	56.8	1.2	84.2	1.1
Asian and Pacific Islander	8,041	4,718	2,470	2,045	52.4	2.7	43.3	2.7	82.8	2.9
Hispanic (of any race)	**21,598**	**13,158**	**7,546**	**5,934**	**57.3**	**2.0**	**45.1**	**2.0**	**78.6**	**2.2**
1996										
Total, 18 years and over	**193,651**	**179,935**	**127,661**	**105,017**	**70.9**	**0.3**	**58.4**	**0.3**	**82.3**	**0.3**
Race and Hispanic origin										
White	62,779	153,057	110,259	91,208	72.0	0.3	59.6	0.4	82.7	0.3
White non-Hispanic	145,343	142,597	104,101	86,604	73.0	0.3	60.7	0.4	83.2	0.3
Black	22,483	21,486	14,267	11,386	66.4	1.2	53.0	1.2	79.8	1.2
Asian and Pacific Islander	6,775	3,865	2,210	1,741	57.2	3.0	45.0	3.0	78.8	3.3
Hispanic (of any race)	**18,426**	**11,209**	**6,573**	**4,928**	**58.6**	**2.2**	**44.0**	**2.2**	**75.0**	**2.5**

Source: U.S. Census Bureau, Current Population Survey, November 2000 and 1996.

[1] *This figure added to or subtracted from the estimate provides the 90-percent confidence interval.*

FIG 3. Top Issues For Determining the Latino Vote

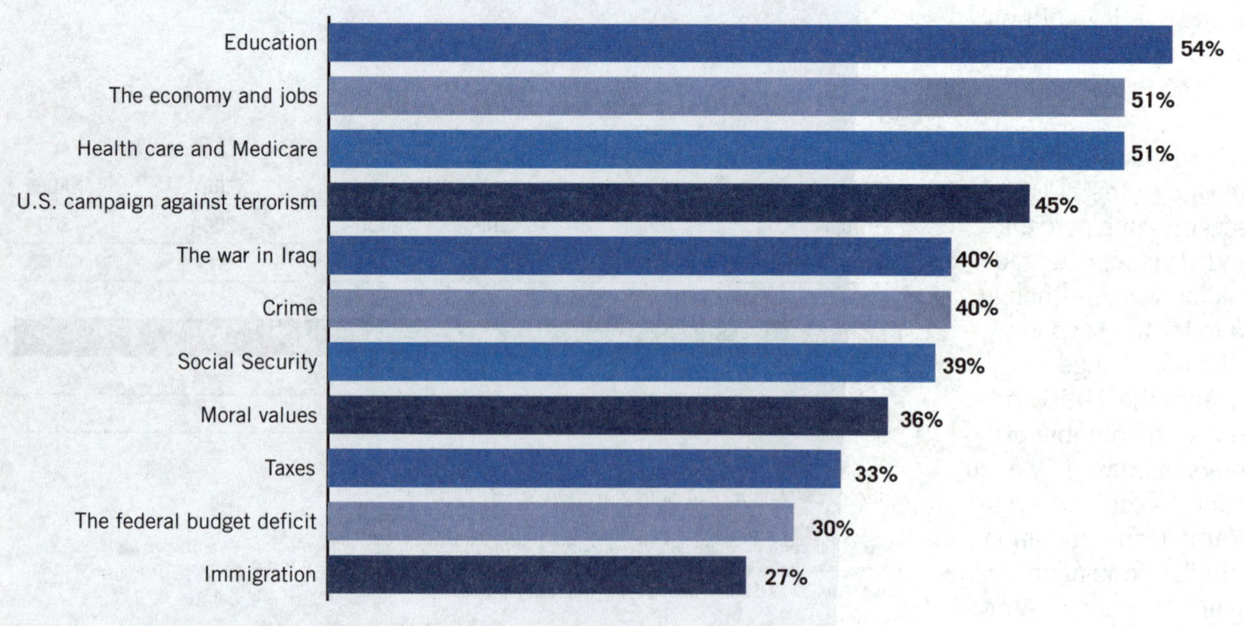

Source: Pew Hispanic Center/Kaiser Family Foundation National Survey of Latinos: Politics and Civic Engagement, July 2004 (conducted April – June 2004).

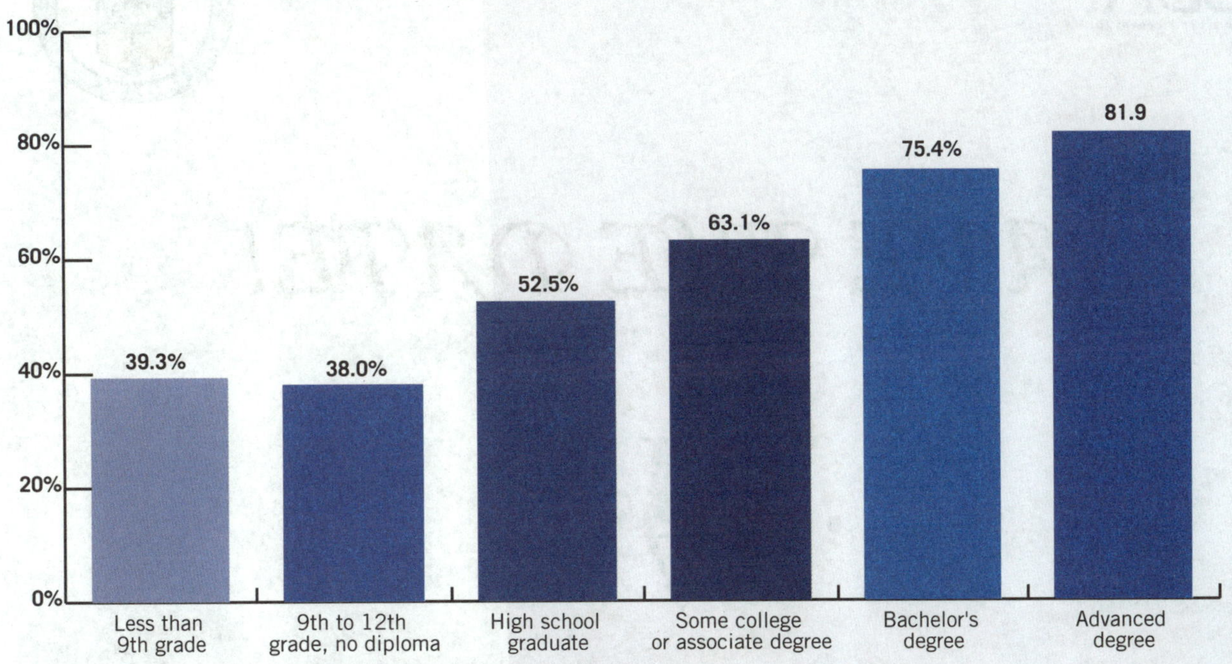

Source: U.S. Census Bureau, Current Population Survey, November 2000.

SAVE THE DATE!

National Minority Enterprise Development (MED) Week 2005 Conference
"The Art of the Deal: Making It Happen"

Sponsored by the U.S. Department of Commerce's Minority Business Development Agency, in collaboration with the U.S. Small Business Administration and their respective public and private sector partners.

WASHINGTON, DC
SEPTEMBER 12-14, 2005

KEY HIGHLIGHTS OF NATIONAL MED WEEK 2005 INCLUDE:

- **WHITE HOUSE BREAKFAST SERIES**
- **INFORMATION VENUES & WORKSHOPS**
- **EMERGING BUSINESS LEADERS SUMMIT**
- **BUSINESS EXPO**
- **NETWORKING RECEPTIONS**
- **INFORMATIVE LUNCHEONS**
- **AWARD CEREMONIES**
  AND MUCH MORE!

Be sure to register early!

Conference Registration: 1-877-MED Week (1-877-633-9335)
Website: **www.medweek.gov**

UNITED STATES DEPARTMENT OF COMMERCE
Minority Business Development Agency
Washington, D.C. 20230

FEB 8 2005

Greetings:

The Minority Business Development Agency (MBDA) is pleased to support TIYM in the publication of the *2005 ANUARIO HISPANO* and we appreciate the opportunity to send our best wishes to all its readers.

As the only federal agency created to foster the establishment and growth of minority businesses in the United States, MBDA works closely with many of the business, government and non-profit resources featured in this YEARBOOK. It is a delight to be among friends and to further the economic well being of the Hispanic community.

MBDA is proud that the growth of minority owned businesses over the past several years has exceeded those of all U.S. firms, both in number of firms and revenues. In fact, of the three million plus minority firms in the U.S., **nearly 1.2 million businesses are owned by U.S. Hispanics and, together, these firms employ 1.4 million people and produce $186.3 billion in revenues.** New figures from the U.S. Census will be available in a MBDA report, *"The State of Minority Business"* and I am optimistic we will see an increase in Hispanic business enterprises. However, MBDA is cognizant of the U.S. Census Bureau's projections that indicate 90 percent of the U.S. population growth through 2050 will be in minority communities. That is why President Bush and the Department of Commerce have made minority business enterprises a *national priority*.

We believe that by becoming major shareholders in the American economy and society, minority entrepreneurs create and share wealth, and in the process improve the quality of life for those with whom they work and the community at large. The pursuit of opportunity is what the American dream has always been about and MBDA's goal is to foster an environment that grows the number and size of minority businesses in the United States. MBDA does this by leveraging public and private sector partnerships to help minority entrepreneurs obtain access to capital, procurement and contract opportunities, technical assistance and business development services.

Thank you Angela Zavala, and everyone at TIYM, for your dedication to building a nation that is strong, proud, productive and inclusive. We value your work and your collaborative spirit. MBDA wishes you continued success with the *HISPANIC YEARBOOK*.

Sincerely,

Ronald N. Langston
National Director

Hispanic U.S. Senators

MEL MARTINEZ
U.S. Senator, Florida (R)

Mel Martinez came to Florida from his native Cuba at age fifteen as a part of "Operation Peter Pan," a humanitarian program led by the Catholic Church that helped over 14,000 Cuban children escape Communist Cuba. Mel lived with foster families for four years until he and his family were reunited in Orlando.

Mel graduated from Bishop Moore High School in Orlando and then received his undergraduate and law degree from Florida State University. Upon graduating from Law School, Mel returned to Orlando - the community that adopted him years earlier - and went to work with a private law firm.

Eager to give back to the community that had provided opportunities for him, Mel became involved in various youth, business and civic organizations. Mel served on numerous boards including: Chairman of the Orlando Housing Authority, Chairman of the Orlando Utilities Commission, Vice Chairman of Catholic Charities, and many others. He even shared his love of baseball by coaching Little League.

In 1998, Mel was elected to serve as Mayor of Orange County Florida — one of the state's largest counties. He quickly earned a reputation as a bold leader, a tax-cutter, and a champion of law enforcement and education.

President George W. Bush nominated Mel to serve in his Cabinet as the nation's twelfth Secretary of Housing and Urban Development. After serving three years as the HUD Secretary, He returned to Florida to seek the Republican nomination for the United States Senate.

Mel was elected to the United States Senate on November 2, 2004, and is the first Cuban-American ever elected to the U.S. Senate.

Mel and his wife of thirty-four years, Kitty, have three children and two grandchildren, and are active members of St. James Cathedral Parish in Orlando.

Ken Salazar was elected to the United States Senate in November 2004 as Colorado's thirty-fifth United States Senator after serving six years as Colorado Attorney General.

Ken is a fifth generation Coloradan born on March second, 1955, and is one of eight brothers and sisters. He and his family have been farmers and ranchers in the San Luis Valley since before Colorado was a state.

Ken attended St. Francis Seminary, graduated from Centauri High School in Conejos County in 1973, received a political science degree from Colorado College in 1977 and his law degree in 1981 from the University of Michigan. Salazar also received honorary doctorates of law from Colorado College in 1993 and the University of Denver in 1999.

Ken has been a farmer and rancher in the San Luis Valley, natural resources lawyer, and small business owner much of his life. He and his wife have owned radio stations in Pueblo and Denver and own and operate a Dairy Queen in Westminster, Colorado. In addition to being Colorado Attorney General, he has served as chief legal counsel to the Governor, executive director of the Department of Natural Resources, and chairman of the Rio Grande Compact Commission. Ken also practiced water, environmental, and public lands law for eleven years in the private sector.

As executive director of the Department of Natural Resources, Ken protected Colorado's water and crafted reforms for mining, and oil and gas operations to provide greater public and environmental protections. He also co-authored the constitutional amendment creating Great Outdoors Colorado (GOCO), led the successful campaign for its passage, and served as the first chairperson of the Great Outdoors Colorado Board. GOCO is the most successful land conservation effort in modern Colorado history. In addition, Salazar created the Youth in Natural Resources program for thousands of Colorado's youth to work and learn about Colorado's natural resources.

As Colorado's 36th Attorney General, Ken led efforts in Colorado to fight crime, address youth and family violence, combat fraud against the elderly, and protect Colorado's environment.

He has served on many boards and commissions including the Colorado Water Conservation Board, the Peace Officers Standards and Training Board (Chair), and selection committees for United States Attorney and Federal District Court judges. He is currently a member of the American Farmland Trust President's Council and the Board of Trustees of Colorado College in Colorado Springs.

Ken currently serves on the Senate Committees on Agriculture, Nutrition and Forestry, Energy and Natural Resources, and Veterans Affairs.

Ken and his wife, Hope, have two teenage daughters, Melinda and Andrea. His older brother John Salazar was elected to the United States Congress in November 2004 from Colorado's 3rd Congressional District.

Hispanic U.S. Representatives

JOE BACA

Congressman (D - 43rd District, California)

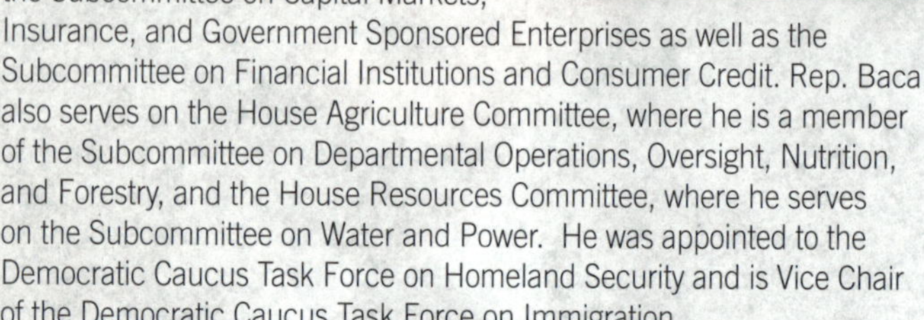

Representative Joe Baca (43rd District, California) was elected to the United States House of Representatives on November 16, 1999, i a special election. He was elected to his second full two-year term on November 5, 2002, to serve in the 108th Congress. He represents San Bernardino County.

In the 108th Congress, Rep. Baca sits on the influential House Financial Services Committee, where he is a member of the Subcommittee on Capital Markets, Insurance, and Government Sponsored Enterprises as well as the Subcommittee on Financial Institutions and Consumer Credit. Rep. Baca also serves on the House Agriculture Committee, where he is a member of the Subcommittee on Departmental Operations, Oversight, Nutrition, and Forestry, and the House Resources Committee, where he serves on the Subcommittee on Water and Power. He was appointed to the Democratic Caucus Task Force on Homeland Security and is Vice Chair of the Democratic Caucus Task Force on Immigration.

Congressman Baca was born in Belen, New Mexico in 1947. He moved with his family to Barstow, California, when he was a young boy. He is a Vietnam War-era veteran, serving in the U.S. Army as a paratrooper with both the 101st and the 82nd Airborne Divisions from 1966-68. He left with the rank of Specialist E-4. Following his military service, Rep. Baca earned his bachelor's degree in sociology from California State University-Los Angeles. He worked for fifteen years in community relations with General Telephone and Electric.

In 1989, he and his wife, Barbara, began their own business, Interstate World Travel, in San Bernardino. They have four children: Joe Jr., Jeremy, Natalie, and Jennifer.

XAVIER BECERRA

Congressman (D - 31st District, California)

First elected to the House of Representatives in 1992, Rep. Becerra is the only member from Southern California currently serving on the powerful House Committee on Ways and Means. His committee is responsible for formulating our nation's tax, Social Security, Medicare, trade, and welfare laws.

Rep. Becerra currently serves on the Trade and Social Security subcommittees. He is a member of the Congressional Hispanic Caucus (CHC) where he served as Chairman during the 105th Congress (1997-98). He currently serves as the Chairman of the CHC's Telecommunications and Technology Task Force as well as Vice Chair of the 289-member Congressional Diabetes Caucus. The Congressman is also a member of the Executive Committee of the Congressional Asian Pacific American Caucus. At the international level, he serves as Vice Chairman of the U.S.-Korea Interparliamentary Exchange.

Rep. Becerra is the son of working-class immigrant parents and was the first in his family to graduate from college. In 1980, Rep.

Becerra earned his Bachelor of Arts in Economics from Stanford University. He was awarded his Juris Doctorate from Stanford Law School in 1984. Rep. Becerra is married to Dr. Carolina Reyes. They are the proud parents of three young daughters: Clarisa, Olivia and Natalia. The Becerra family resides in the Los Angeles neighborhood of Eagle Rock.

HENRY BONILLA

Congressman (R - 23rd District, Texas)

Congressman Henry Bonilla is fifty years old and has two children: Alicia, age nineteen and Austin, age fifteen. Henry was born in San Antonio, attended South San Antonio High School, and earned a Bachelor of Journalism degree from the University of Texas at Austin in 1976.

Henry's election in 1992 marked the first time a Hispanic Republican was elected to Congress from Texas. At the beginning of his first term, he was chosen to serve on the House Appropriations Committee, a position not held by a Republican freshman in more than twenty-five years. He currently serves as chairman of the Appropriations Subcommittee on Agriculture, and is also a senior member of the Subcommittee on Foreign Operations, and the Subcommittee on Defense.

Henry was selected by President George W. Bush and the Republican National Committee (RNC) to serve as co-chairman of the 2000 and 2004 Republican National Conventions. As a co-chair, Henry emceed the week-long national televised events, delivered major speeches, and oversaw both formal nominations of Bush. In addition to his role as a co-chair, Henry was tapped as an adviser to President Bush's campaign and co-chairman of the RNC's Victory 2000 effort. Henry also served as chairman of Texas Victory 2002, the state-wide Republican re-election campaign, which focused on voter turn-out and registration efforts.

HENRY CUELLAR

Congressman (D - 28th District, Texas)

Henry Cuellar was sworn in as United States Congressman for the 28th District in Texas in January 2005, previously serving as the Texas Secretary of State and a fourteen year member of the Texas Legislature. Congressman Cuellar was most recently appointed to serve on the House Agricultural Committee.

As Texas Secretary of State and State Representative, Henry Cuellar made his mark as a champion of education, healthcare, and in creating a strong, diversified Texas economy.

Congressman Cuellar received his Associate degree in Political Science, Summa Cum Laude, from Laredo Community College. He then attended Georgetown University in Washington, D.C. for his bachelor's degree in Foreign Service, graduating Cum Laude. He later earned a law degree from the University of Texas at Austin. Congressman Cuellar studied at the Universidad Pan Americana in Mexico City and then earned a Masters in International Trade at Texas A&M International University. He also holds a Ph.D. in Government from UT Austin.

Congressman Cuellar and his wife, Imelda, have two daughters: Christina Alexandra and Catherine Ann.

LINCOLN DIAZ-BALART

Congressman (R - 21st District, Florida)

Lincoln Diaz-Balart received a degree in international relations from New College of Florida, in Sarasota, and also obtained a diploma in British politics in Cambridge, England. He received his law degree from Case Western Reserve University in Ohio.

In 1992, Diaz-Balart was elected to the United States House of Representatives from Florida's 21st Congressional District, which encompassed much of western Miami-Dade County. He served as a member of the House Foreign Affairs Committee during his first term, working to preserve the special U.S. - Israel relationship while also striving to protect United States' national security. In 1994, Lincoln Diaz-Balart became the first Hispanic in U.S. history to be named to the powerful Rules Committee. The Rules Committee, composed of only nine members of the majority party and four from the minority, decides which legislation may reach the House Floor and what amendments may be debated. Diaz-Balart was named Vice-Chairman of the Sub-Committee on the Rules of the House.

Congressman Diaz-Balart lives in Miami with his wife, Cristina, and their two sons: Lincoln and Daniel.

MARIO DIAZ-BALART

Congressman (R - 25th District, Florida)

Congressman Mario Díaz-Balart was born in Ft. Lauderdale, FL, on September 25, 1961. He attended the University of South Florida in Tampa to study Political Science before beginning his public service career as an aide to then City of Miami Mayor Xavier Suarez in 1985. Díaz-Balart was elected to the Florida House of Representatives in 1988 where he served until 1992.

In 2002, Díaz-Balart was elected to the U.S. House of Representatives to represent Florida's 25th Congressional district. The district encompasses the western portion of Miami-Dade County, a large part of eastern Collier County and a segment of Monroe County. He serves on the Budget Committee and the Transportation and Infrastructure Committee. While only in his first term, Díaz-Balart has already made his presence known. He has worked in conjunction with Senate Majority Leader Bill Frist in support of Miguel Estrada's judicial nomination. He helped found the Congressional Hispanic Conference and the Washington Waste Watchers.

Díaz-Balart has deep roots in politics. One of his three older brothers, Lincoln, represents Florida's 21st Congressional District and his father Rafaél served as the Majority Leader in Cuba's House of Representatives before the communist revolution. Díaz-Balart's uncle and grandfather also served in the Cuban House.

LUIS G. FORTUÑO

Congressman (R - Puerto Rico)

Congressman Fortuño was sworn in to his first term in the U.S. House of Representatives, as the first Republican elected to Congress representing Puerto Rico, in January of 2005. Before coming to Congress, Mr. Fortuño was a partner at the San Juan law firm of Correa, Collazo, Herrero, Jiménez & Fortuño since 1998 specializing in corporate finance, real estate and general corporate counseling. Having practiced law since 1985, he entered public service in 1993 after being appointed by the Governor as Executive Director of the Puerto Rico Tourism Company and President of the Hotel Development Corporation. He became Puerto Rico's first Secretary of the Department of Economic Development and Commerce the following year. As such, Mr. Fortuño served on numerous government boards of directors, including the Government Development Bank for Puerto Rico. He returned to the private practice of law early in 1997.

Fortuño was recently re-elected by the Republican Party of Puerto Rico's General Assembly to continue serving as National Committeeman, a position he has held since 2001. In 1996, he served on the Platform Committee at the Republican National Convention, where he participated as a member of the Platform Committee and was successful in including the support for self-determination and eventual statehood for Puerto Rico in the Party Platform.

On November 9, 2003, Luis Fortuño became the official candidate for Puerto Rico's only seat in Congress for the New Progressive Party, after obtaining an overwhelming 62% of the votes in a four-way race in the party primary.

Mr. Fortuño earned a bachelor's degree from the School of Foreign Service at Georgetown University and obtained his Juris Doctor (JD) from the University of Virginia Law School. He is married to attorney Lucé Vela and has three children.

CHARLIE A. GONZALEZ
Congressman (D - 20th District, Texas)

Charles A. Gonzalez is currently in his fourth term in the United States Congress as the Representative from the 20th Congressional District of Texas.

Congressman Gonzalez is a member of the New Democrats and the Congressional Hispanic Caucus. As a Freshman in the 106th Congress, Congressman Gonzalez was elected Vice President of his class. Since 1999, Congressman Gonzalez has served as a Texas Regional Whip for the Democratic Caucus and as Chair of the Hispanic Caucus Civil Rights Task Force.

In January 2004, Congressman Gonzalez was appointed to the House Energy and Commerce Committee where he serves on the Subcommittee on Telecommunications and the Internet, the Subcommittee on Commerce, Trade, and Consumer Protection, and the Subcommittee on Environment and Hazardous Materials.

Congressman Gonzalez previously served on the Select Committee on Homeland Security, the House Financial Services Committee, and the House Small Business Committee.

Charles Gonzalez is a San Antonio native. A graduate of Thomas A. Edison High School in San Antonio, Gonzalez received a Bachelor of Arts degree in Government from the University of Texas at Austin and then received a Juris Doctorate degree from St. Mary's School of Law in San Antonio.

Charles A. Gonzalez is one of eight children of the late Congressman Henry B. Gonzalez and Bertha Gonzalez. His father served as United States Congressman representing the 20th District from 1961-1998.

RAUL M. GRIJALVA
Congressman (D - 7th District, Arizona)

Raúl M. Grijalva has dedicated much of his life to the people of Southern Arizona, and on January 7, 2003, was sworn in as the first congressman for the newly created 7th Congressional District.

Raúl was born in Tucson, Arizona in 1948. His father was a bracero, who emigrated from Mexico in 1945 to help offset the loss of skilled American ranch hands serving in World War II. Raúl's parents stressed the importance of education to their three children, and it was that encouragement that led Raúl to his career into life-long public service.

During his tenure as a member of the Pima County Board of Supervisors, Raúl set a tone on many community issues, such as health care, children and families, the environment, and working families. Raúl serves on the Committee on Education and Workforce, with seats on the Education Reform Subcommittee and the Employer-Employee Relations Subcommittee, and the Committee on Resources, with seats on the National Parks, Recreation and Public Lands Subcommittee and the Water and Power Subcommittee. In addition, Raúl is also the chair of the House Democratic Environmental Task Force.

Raúl and his wife Ramona have been married for over thirty years, and they have three daughters: Raquel, Adelita, and Marisa Grijalva. His family has lived and worked in District 7 their entire lives. The contributions of the Grijalva family to the betterment and quality of the community are a career and lifelong commitment.

LUIS GUTIERREZ
Congressman (D - 4th District, Illinois)

During his six terms in the U.S. House, Congressman Luis V. Gutierrez has worked to establish himself as an effective legislator and energetic spokesman on behalf of his constituents in Illinois' Fourth District. At the same time, Gutierrez' tireless leadership championing the causes of the Latino and immigrant communities has led to greater responsibilities within the U.S. Congress and has earned him widespread acclaim throughout the country— culminating in his selection as the most admired Latino leader in the country, according to a recent nationwide survey.

As a member of the House Veterans Affairs Committee, he helped pass landmark legislation to provide priority health care to veterans of the Persian Gulf War during his first term and was awarded by the Vietnam Veterans of America as "Legislator of the Year." During 1999, he passed legislation to ensure that women veterans receive treatment and care for incidents of sexual abuse that occurred while they were in the military.

Mass transit issues have also played a prominent role in Gutierrez' agenda. He secured federal authorization for a $315 million project to reconstruct the aging Douglas Branch of the Chicago Transit Authority's Blue Line, the "L" route which runs through the southwest side and suburbs in his district. He also introduced legislation offering tax credits to commuters who use public transit on a full-time basis. Gutierrez joined community and business leaders to implement creative ridership incentive programs and to press for the restoration of full service on the CTA.

Gutierrez was born in Chicago on December 10, 1953. He graduated from Northeastern Illinois University in 1975 and worked as a teacher, social worker, community activist, and city official until his 1986 election as Alderman from the city's 26th ward. In the Chicago City Council, he led the fight for affordable housing, tougher ethics rules, and a law to ban discrimination based on sexual orientation. He and his wife Soraida have two daughters: Omaira and Jessica.

RUBÉN HINOJOSA
Congressman (D - 15th District, Texas)

In Congress, Rubén Hinojosa is regarded as a champion for the disadvantaged and has distinguished himself as a strong advocate for education, housing, and economic development. His primary goal in Congress has been to reduce the chronic unemployment rate in regions of the district. By focusing on developing a highly educated, well-trained workforce, modernizing the local infrastructure including roads and highways, and creating new job opportunities, Congressman Hinojosa has been instrumental in bringing unemployment rates to record lows. Congressman Hinojosa serves on three House committees: Committee on Education and the Workforce, Committee on

Financial Services, and Committee on Resources. He formerly served on the Committee on Small Business.

As chairman of the Education Task Force for the Congressional Hispanic Caucus, Congressman Hinojosa ensures that federal education policy never loses sight of the youngest and fastest growing population in the country—Hispanic Americans. By focusing on a group of proven federal education programs that are critical to the Hispanic community, often referred to as the Hispanic Education Action Plan (HEAP), Hinojosa has helped to secure dramatic increases in resources that target Hispanic communities. The HEAP programs have grown from just under $8.5 billion in 1998 to over $15 billion for 2004.

During the 108th Congress, Congressman Hinojosa was appointed to the House Resources Committee where he successfully passed legislation to modernize a variety of irrigation systems throughout South Texas in order to save substantial water currently lost through evaporation and seepage. Over the years, he has obtained $7 million in federal investments to complete these critical upgrades. Congressman Hinojosa also believes that innovative solutions are needed to relieve long-term water shortages that hinder sustained growth. He is working with the Corps of Engineers to find new sources of water for the region and to explore bringing floodwaters from chronic flood-zones like Houston to the Rio Grande Valley. He also continues the fight to bring Mexico into compliance with the 1944 water treaty by repaying its debt that currently stands at over 1.5 million acre feet.

ROBERT MENENDEZ

Congressman (D - 13th District, New Jersey)

Through a decade in the U.S. House of Representatives, Congressman Bob Menendez, who represents New Jersey's 13th Congressional District along the Hudson River and overlooking the Statue of Liberty, has made a stellar and rapid rise to the highest levels of influence in the U.S. House and the highest levels of prominence in American political life. Today, Bob Menendez is the Chairman of the Democratic Caucus, elected by his colleagues on November 14, 2002.

In that post, Bob Menendez is the third-ranking Democrat in the U.S. House, the highest-ranking Hispanic in Congressional history, and the only Hispanic ever elected to a leadership position, in either chamber, by either party. In addition to being the first Democratic House Member from New Jersey elected to a Leadership post, he is also the youngest member of the elected Democratic Leadership. Previously, Menendez served two consecutive terms as the Vice Chairman of the Democratic Caucus.

Also a former State Assemblyman and State Senator—where he was the author of New Jersey's landmark bias crime law, and New Jersey's telecommunications reform act—and an attorney in private practice, Congressman Menendez received his B.A. from St. Peter's College in Jersey City, and his law degree from Rutgers University. He was raised in Union City and currently resides in Hoboken. He has two children: Robert and Alicia.

GRACE FLORES NAPOLITANO

Congresswoman (D - 38th District, California)

Grace Flores Napolitano was first elected to Congress in 1998. She is currently serving her third term, representing California's 38th District, having won reelection with seventy-one percent of the vote. Her Los Angeles County-based district covers several cities and communities in the S   and San Gabriel Valley areas.

Congresswoman Napolitano is the Ranking Member of the Water and Power Subcommittee and also serves on the Energy and Mineral Resources Subcommittee. She is an avid promoter of conservation, water recycling, desalination, and sound groundwater management and storage to address Southern California's need for adequate water quality and supply. Her legislative effort to begin removal of a huge uranium tailings pile at the banks of the Colorado in Moab, stands out as a major accomplishment. This pile has posed a danger to the health of more than twenty-five million people living in Southern California and six other states who rely on the Colorado River for drinking water.

The Congresswoman was born and raised in Texas. She began her political career as a member of the Norwalk City Council, winning her first election in 1986 by a mere 28 votes. Four years later she won re-election by the highest margin of votes recorded in city history. In 1989, Napolitano was elevated by her council colleagues to serve as Mayor. During her council tenure, she focused much of her attention on providing access to constituents and on redevelopment and transportation issues to address the city's need for jobs and a more diversified economic base.

Grace is currently married to Frank Napolitano, a retired restaurateur and community activist. They reside in Norwalk, California and take great pride in their five grown children and fourteen grandchildren.

SOLOMON ORTIZ

Congressman (D - 27th District, Texas)

The Honorable Solomon Ortiz was elected to Congress in 1982 following a Congressional redistricting that created the 27th District of Texas: a new seat along the Gulf Coast of South Texas. Congressman Ortiz ran for Congress on a platform of bringing jobs to South Texas and increasing the focus on access to education for South T   who live in an area of the country with traditionally high unemployment rates.

Congressman Ortiz joined the Army at age sixteen to help support his family. In the army, he earned his GED and received advanced military police training. Returning to South Texas, he was elected County Constable in 1964. In 1968, he was elected to County Commissioners Court. In 1976, he was elected Nueces County Sheriff.

In Congress, Congressman Ortiz turned his love of law enforcement into a love of lawmaking. He was assigned to the House Armed Services Committee and the House Merchant Marine and Fisheries

Committee (today, the House Resources Committee). Four military bases in the Coastal Bend area and the historic tug of war over water and other natural resources in the American west make these committee assignments uniquely suited to South Texas. Congressman Ortiz' specialty is defense policy, particularly issues facing the readiness of the U.S. armed forces. He is currently the Ranking Democrat on the House Armed Services Security Committee's Subcommittee on Readiness. He is also Chair of the Congressional Hispanic Caucus Task Force on Arts & Entertainment.

Congressman Ortiz' diplomatic ability and bipartisan efforts have earned him countless awards, including the Latin American Leadership Award, National Security Leadership Award, National Hispanic Business Advocate, and National Association for Free Trade Zones Man of the Year Award.

ED PASTOR
Congressman (D - 4th District, Arizona)

In the 108th Congress, Ed Pastor has served twelve years in Congress. He represents the 4th Congressional District of Arizona (a new district that is the result of redistricting). He formerly represented the Second Congressional District. Currently, he serves on the House Appropriations Committee, and serves on three Subcommittees: the Subcommittee of Energy and Water Development; the Subcommittee of Transportation, Treasury, Postal Service, and General Government; and the Subcommittee on the District of Columbia.

Ed also serves on the Democratic Steering and Policy Committee. In addition, Ed continues serving as one of four Chief Deputy Whips in the Democratic Leadership, an appointment he received during the 106th Congress. He formerly served on the Committee on Standards of Official Conduct, also known as the Ethics Committee, during the 107th Congress. During the 104th Congress, Ed was Chairman of the Congressional Hispanic Caucus (CHC). His two-year term ended in January 1997, but he remains an active member of the CHC. He also was named by the Democratic Leadership to the party's eight-member Leadership Advisory Group.

Ed was elected to the Maricopa County Board of Supervisors in 1976 and went on to serve three more terms before resigning in May of 1991 to run for Congress. On August 13, Ed became the Democratic nominee from Arizona's Second District, and was elected on September 24. He was sworn into office on October 3, 1991. Prior to his election as Supervisor, Ed was a member of Governor Raul Castro's staff. He also taught chemistry at North High School, and served as deputy director of the Guadalupe Organization Inc.

Ed is married to Verma Mendez Pastor, an education consultant. The couple has two daughters, Yvonne and Laura, and two grandchildren, Alexis and Francisco.

SILVESTRE REYES
Congressman (D - 16th District, Texas)

Representative Silvestre Reyes, now in his fourth term, became the first Hispanic to represent the 16th District of Texas in the U.S. House of Representatives in 1996.

After serving his country in Vietnam, Reyes decided to devote his life to public service. In 1969, Reyes began his career with the U.S. Immigration and Naturalization Service (INS). He was Assistant

Regional Commissioner for five years in Dallas, where he had direct responsibility for administering a budget program exceeding $100 million for a thirteen state area.

Reyes is a member of the House Armed Services Committee and the House Permanent Select Committee on Intelligence. As a member of the Armed Services Committee, he serves as the Ranking Member of the Strategic Forces Subcommittee and as a member of the Subcommittee on Readiness. As a member of the Intelligence Committee, Reyes serves on the Subcommittee on Terrorism and Homeland Security and the Subcommittee on Human Intelligence, Analysis, and Counterintelligence. He has also served on the House Veterans' Affairs Committee.

He holds an Associates Degree in Criminal Justice from El Paso Community College and attended the University of Texas at Austin and El Paso. He is married to Carolina Gaytan Reyes, and they have three children: Monica, Rebecca and Silvestre, Jr. He is also the proud grandfather of Amelia and Mateo Silvestre.

ILEANA ROS-LEHTINEN
Congresswoman (R - 18th District, Florida)

The first Hispanic woman elected to the United States Congress, Ileana Ros-Lehtinen was born in Havana, Cuba on July 15, 1952, and came to the United States with her family fleeing communist aggression when she was seven years old. She earned her Bachelor's and Master's degrees from Florida International University and her Associate in Arts degree from Miami-Dade Community College. She has also been bestowed an honorary Doctor of Pedagogy Degree from Nova Southeastern University. She is presently working on her doctoral dissertation in higher education from the University of Miami.

Ros-Lehtinen currently serves on the International Relations and Government Reform Committees as well as on the Subcommittee on the Western Hemisphere. She is also a Member of the Subcommittee on Wellness and Human Rights. Ros-Lehtinen is the first Hispanic woman to chair a subcommittee. As Chair of the Subcommittee on Middle East and Central Asia, she has become a leading figure shaping foreign policy.

Ros-Lehtinen has spent most of her adult life committed to enhancing the lives of others: the disabled, the elderly, our veterans, the homeless, and students. She thrives at her job and it shows. Congresswoman Ros-Lehtinen and her husband, Dexter Lehtinen, the former U.S. Attorney for the Southern District of Florida have four children, their daughters, Amanda and Patricia, and his two, Douglas and Katharine, plus four dogs and one cat.

LUCILLE ROYBAL-ALLARD
Congresswoman (D - 34th District, California)

Congresswoman Roybal-Allard maintains a busy schedule working out of her offices in Washington, D.C. and Los Angeles, CA. The Congresswoman represents the 34th Congressional District, which includes downtown Los Angeles, East Los Angeles, and nine southeast cities of Los Angeles County. A political pioneer, in 1992, Congresswoman Roybal-Allard became the first Mexican-American woman elected to Congress. Before that, she represented the 56th Assembly District of California for six years.

As a Member of the House Appropriations Committee, one of the most powerful and distinguished committees in Congress, she spends much of her time attending hearings and meetings. She is the first Latina in U.S. history to be appointed to the Appropriations Committee, which controls the purse strings of the federal government. The Congresswoman serves on two influential subcommittees–the Subcommittee on Homeland Security and the Subcommittee on Labor, Health and Human Services, and Education. As a member of these two subcommittees, Congresswoman Roybal-Allard oversees funding of the new Department of Homeland Security, U.S. Citizenship and Immigration Services, Coast Guard, U.S. Customs Service, Department of Labor, Department of Health and Human Services, and Department of Education.

Congresswoman Roybal-Allard was born and raised in Boyle Heights, California. She is the eldest daughter of Lucille Beserra Roybal and retired Congressman Edward R. Roybal, a Member of Congress for 30 years. The 1965 graduate of the California State University at Los Angeles is married to Edward T. Allard, III. Together, they have four children: Ricardo, Lisa, Angela, and Guy Mark, and four grandchildren: Diego and Santiago Olivarez, and Tyler and Abby Allard.

JOHN SALAZAR

Congressman (D - 3rd District Colorado)

Born a fifth generation Coloradoan, John Salazar (3rd District, Colorado) is the third of eight children raised on a small farm in Colorado's San Luis Valley. John's family arrived in Southern Colorado in the mid-1860's and settled an area called Los Rincones. For six generations, the Salazar family has farmed and ranched the same land outside of the small town of Manassa.

John graduated from Centauri High School (La Jara, CO), and in 1973, he joined the United States Army. After serving in Heidelberg, Germany, Salazar received an honorable military discharge in 1976. Following his service, John enrolled at Adams State College in Alamosa, Colorado where he received a Bachelor's Degree in Business (1981).

On November 2nd, 2004, John Salazar was elected and sent to the United States House of Representatives to proudly represent the 3rd District of Colorado. The district is comprised of twenty-nine counties stretching from Otero County in the East to Moffat County in Northwest Colorado. Upon arrival, John was appointed to sit on the powerful House Transportation and Infrastructure Committee, which among other things has jurisdiction over the nation's highway and transit programs, water resources development, and aviation.

John and his wife, Mary Lou, have been married for twenty six-years. The couple has three sons: Jesus, Esteban, and Miguel and one grandson: Charlie.

LINDA SÁNCHEZ

Congresswoman (D - 39th District, California)

Congresswoman Linda Sánchez was sworn into office on January 7, 2003 to represent the newly created 39th Congressional District of California.

Sánchez's service is historic as she joins her sister Loretta (D–Garden Grove) in the U.S. House. They are the first sisters and the first women of any relation to ever serve in Congress.

Sánchez serves on the Judiciary Committee, which considers all legislation pertaining to judiciary and to civil and criminal judicial reform. Specifically, the committee reviews issues such as civil liberties, constitutional amendments, immigration, naturalization, and protection of trade and commerce against unlawful restraints and monopolies. The Committee also has jurisdiction over the U.S. Department of Justice as well as federal aid to local law enforcement. Congresswoman Linda Sánchez also serves on the Committee on Government Reform, which has oversight over all federal government activities and serves as the watchdog to prevent waste, fraud, and abuse of taxpayer dollars. Additionally, she serves on the Small Business Committee.

Linda Sánchez is the sixth of seven children born to immigrant parents from Mexico. Born in the City of Orange, she attended public schools before graduating from the University of California, Berkeley, where she earned a Bachelor of Arts in Spanish Literature with an emphasis in Bilingual Education. After working her way through undergraduate school as a bilingual aid and "English as a Second Language" instructor, she attended law school at U.C.L.A., graduating and passing the bar exam in 1995. During her legal studies at U.C.L.A., Linda interned with the Honorable Judge Terry Hatter, Jr., Chief Justice of the Central District Court. She also spent a summer working for the National Organization for Women Legal Defense and Education Fund (NOW LDEF) in New York City. After law school, she practiced law in the areas of appellate law, civil rights, and employment law.

LORETTA SÁNCHEZ

Congresswoman (D - 47th District, California)

Congresswoman Loretta Sánchez represents the 47th Congressional District of California. She began her congressional career in November 1996, and is serving her fifth term in the House of Representatives. Loretta is known for two things: accessibility and collaboration. Those traits have served her well, both in Washington and in Orange County. She travels to her home district from Washington each week to do work in the community and meet with constituents. Loretta has focused much of her time on issues such as education, public safety and crime reduction, economic development, and protections for our senior citizens.

Loretta attended Chapman University in Orange, California, where she was selected in January 2002 to serve as the university's first

Latina member of the Board of Trustees. She received her bachelor's degree in economics in 1982 (voted "Business Student of the Year"), and then entered American University in Washington, D.C. to obtain her master's in Business Administration with an emphasis on finance, which she received in 1984. Congresswoman Sánchez is the ranking woman of the House Armed Services Committee. Her seat on this panel helps her bring jobs to Orange County's growing high-tech industrial base. Loretta was instrumental in requiring the Department of Defense to include the City of Palmdale, California when it investigates cost alternatives for Joint Strike Fighter production. She has served on the Terrorism Panel of this Committee, where she joined other Members to investigate intelligence progress and terrorist threats to the United States.

JOSÉ E. SERRANO
Congressman (D - 16th District, New York)

U.S. Representative José E. Serrano represents the 16th Congressional District of New York, in the Bronx. He serves on the exclusive House Appropriations Committee as Ranking Minority Member on the Subcommittee on Commerce, Justice, State, and the Judiciary, and as a senior member of the newly created Appropriations Subcommittee on Homeland Security. Serrano is also currently one of three Vice Chairs of the Democratic Steering and Policy Committee, which is the body that makes committee assignments for all Democratic Representatives and advises the Democratic Leader on policy.

Born in Mayagüez, Puerto Rico on October 24, 1943, Serrano moved to the Bronx with his family when he was a young boy. From 1964-66, Serrano served in the 172nd Support Battalion of the U.S. Army Medical Corps. After an honorable discharge from the Army, he returned to the Bronx and worked in a bank and as a school administrator before his election to the New York State Assembly in 1974.

Congressman Serrano was first sworn in as a Member of the U.S. House of Representatives in March 1990 after he won a special election in what was then New York's 18th Congressional District. He was subsequently reelected to serve a full term in the 102nd Congress in November of that year. Following a statewide decennial redistricting in 1992, he has continued to represent the Bronx from its 16th Congressional District. Serrano is now the most senior Member of Congress of Puerto Rican descent.

HILDA L. SOLIS
Congresswoman (D - 32nd District, California)

First elected to Congress in 2000, Congresswoman Hilda L. Solis is serving her third term in the U.S. House of Representatives. She represents the 32nd Congressional District of California, which encompasses the San Gabriel Valley and parts of East Los Angeles.

Congresswoman Solis serves on the powerful House Energy and Commerce Committee becoming the first Latina to serve on this committee. She is the Ranking Member of the Environment and Hazardous Materials Subcommittee and is part of the Energy and Air

Quality Subcommittee. Solis is also Democratic Chair of the Congressional Caucus on Women's Issues, Chairwoman of the Congressional Hispanic Caucus' Task Force on Health, and a Regional Whip for Southern California. Her priorities include protecting the environment, improving the quality of health care and fighting for the rights of working families.

Congresswoman Solis graduated from California State Polytechnic University, Pomona in 1979, and earned a Masters degree in Public Administration from the University of Southern California in 1981. She worked in the Carter White House Office of Hispanic Affairs and was later appointed as a management analyst with the Office of Management and Budget in the Civil Rights Division.

Congresswoman Solis is a lifetime resident of the San Gabriel Valley and currently resides in the city of El Monte with her husband Sam, a small business owner. Her parents and her six siblings continue to be a great source of inspiration to Congresswoman Solis.

NYDIA VELÁZQUEZ
Congresswoman (D - 12th District, New York)

Congresswoman Nydia M. Velázquez has made history several times during her tenure in Congress. In 1992, she was the first Puerto Rican woman elected to the U.S. House of Representatives. In February of 1998, she was named Ranking Democratic Member of the House Small Business Committee, making her the first Hispanic woman to serve as Chair or Ranking Member of a full committee in the history of the House.

Given her achievements, her roots are humble. She was born in Yabucoa, Puerto Rico–a small town of sugar-cane fields–in 1953 and was one of nine children. Velázquez started school early, skipped several grades, and became the first person in her family to receive a college diploma. At the age of sixteen, she entered the University of Puerto Rico in Rio Piedras. She graduated magna cum laude in 1974 with a degree in political science. After earning a Master's degree on scholarship from N.Y.U., Congresswoman Velázquez taught Puerto Rican studies at C.U.N.Y's Hunter College in 1981.

In 1992, after months of running a grassroots political campaign, she was elected to the House of Representatives to represent New York's 12th District. Her district, which encompasses parts of Brooklyn, Queens, and the Lower East Side of Manhattan is the only tri-borough district in the New York City congressional delegation. Encompassing many diverse neighborhoods, it is home to a large Latino population, with pockets of Polish communities, and parts of Chinatown.

ARIZONA

SENATE

Richard Miranda (D-13th District)
Phoenix Office
1700 W Washington #310
Phoenix, AZ 85007
Tel: (602) 926-5911 Fax: (602) 417-3171
Email: rmiranda@azleg.state.az.us
Web: www.azleg.state.az.us

Linda Aguirre (D-16th District)
Phoenix Office
1700 W Washington #213
Phoenix, AZ 85007
Tel: (602) 926-3830 Fax: (602) 417-3145
Email: laguirre@azleg.state.az.us
Web: www.azleg.state.az.us

Rebecca Rios (D-23rd District)
Phoenix Office
1700 W Washington #315
Phoenix, AZ 85007
Tel: (602) 926-5685 Fax: (602) 417-3167
Email: rrios@azleg.state.az.us
Web: www.azleg.state.az.us

Jorge Luis Garcia (D-27th District)
Phoenix Office
1700 W Washington #311
Phoenix, AZ 85007
Tel: (602) 926-4171 Fax: (602) 417-3162
Email: jgarcia@azleg.state.az.us
Web: www.azleg.state.az.us

Victor Soltero (D-29th District)
Phoenix Office
1700 W Washington #312
Phoenix, AZ 85007
Tel: (602) 926-5342 Fax: (602) 417-3169
Email: vsoltero@azleg.state.az.us
Web: www.azleg.state.az.us

HOUSE OF REPRESENTATIVES

Steve Gallardo (D-13th District)
Phoenix Office
1700 W Washington #329
Phoenix, AZ 85007
Tel: (602) 926-3392 Fax: (602) 417-3013
Email: sgallardo@azleg.state.az.us
Web: www.azleg.state.az.us

Martha Garcia (D-13th District)
Phoenix Office
1700 W Washington #127
Phoenix, AZ 85007
Tel: (602) 926-5830 Fax: (602) 417-4123
Email: mgarcia@azleg.state.az.us
Web: www.azleg.state.az.us

Robert Meza (D-14th District)
Phoenix Office
1700 W Washington #331
Phoenix, AZ 85007
Tel: (602) 926-3425 Fax: (602) 417-3114
Email: rmeza@azleg.state.az.us
Web: www.azleg.state.az.us

David M. Lujan (D-15th District)
Phoenix Office
1700 W Washington #124
Phoenix, AZ 85007
Tel: (602) 926-5829 Fax: (602) 417-3115
Email: dlujan@azleg.state.az.us
Web: www.azleg.state.az.us

Ben R. Miranda (D-16th District)
Phoenix Office
1700 W Washington #323
Phoenix, AZ 85007
Tel: (602) 926-4893 Fax: (602) 417-3116
Email: bmiranda@azleg.state.az.us
Web: www.azleg.state.az.us

Pete Rios (D-23rd District)
Phoenix Office
1700 W Washington #322
Phoenix, AZ 85007
Tel: (602) 926-5761 Fax: (602) 417-3023
Email: prios@azleg.state.az.us
Web: www.azleg.state.az.us

Amanda Aguirre (D-24th District)
Phoenix Office
1700 W Washington #332
Phoenix, AZ 85007
Tel: (602) 926-4430 Fax: (602) 417-3024
Email: aaguirre@azleg.state.az.us
Web: www.azleg.state.az.us

Manuel Alvarez (D-25th District)
Phoenix Office
1700 W Washington #318
Phoenix, AZ 85007
Tel: (602) 926-5895 Fax: (602) 417-3025
Email: malvarez@azleg.state.az.us
Web: www.azleg.state.az.us

Olivia Cajero Bedford (D-27th District)
Phoenix Office
1700 W Washington #338
Phoenix, AZ 85007
Tel: (602) 926-5835 Fax: (602) 417-3027
Email: ocajerob@azleg.state.az.us
Web: www.azleg.state.az.us

Linda Lopez (D-29th District)
Phoenix Office
1700 W Washington #321
Phoenix, AZ 85007
Tel: (602) 926-4089 Fax: (602) 417-3029
Email: llopez@azleg.state.az.us
Web: www.azleg.state.az.us

Tom Prezelski (D-29th District)
Phoenix Office
1700 W Washington #330
Phoenix, AZ 85007
Tel: (602) 926-3424 Fax: (602) 417-3129
Email: tprezels@azleg.state.az.us
Web: www.azleg.state.az.us

CALIFORNIA

SENATE

Deborah Ortiz (D-6th District)
Capitol Office
State Capitol #5114
Sacramento, CA 95814
Tel: (916) 445-7807 Fax: (916) 323-2263
Web: http://democrats.sen.ca.gov/senator/ortiz

District Office
1020 N St. #576
Sacramento, CA 95814
Tel: (916) 324-4937 Fax: (916) 327-8754

District Office
5951 Birdcage Center Ln. #145
Citrus Heights, CA 95610
Tel: (916) 961-1482 Fax: (916) 961-1148

Liz Figueroa (D-10th District)
Capitol Office
State Capitol #4061
Sacramento, CA 95814
Tel: (916) 445-6671 Fax: (916) 327-2433
Web: http://democrats.sen.ca.gov/senator/figueroa

District Office
43801 Mission Blvd. #103
Fremont, CA 94539
Tel: (510) 413-5960 Fax: (510) 413-5965

Abel Maldonado (R-15th District)
Capitol Office
State Capitol #4082
Sacramento, CA 95814
Tel: (916) 445-5843 Fax: (916) 445-8081
Email: senator.maldonado@sen.ca.gov

District Office
1356 Marsh St.
San Luis Obispo, CA 93401
Tel: (805) 549-3784 Fax: (805) 549-3779

District Office
100 Paseo de San Antonio #206
San Jose, CA 95113
Tel: (408) 277-9461 Fax: (408) 277-9464

Dean Florez (D-16th District)
Capitol Office
State Capitol #5061
Sacramento, CA 95814
Tel: (916) 445-4641 Fax: (916) 327-5989
Web: http://democrats.sen.ca.gov/senator/florez

District Office
2550 Mariposa Mall #2016
Fresno, CA 93721
Tel: (559) 264-3070 Fax: (559) 445-6506

District Office
1800 30th St. #350
Bakersfield, CA 93301
Tel: (661) 395-2620 Fax: (661) 395-2622

Richard Alarcon (D-20th District)
Capitol Office
State Capitol #4035
Sacramento, CA 95814
Tel: (916) 445-7928 Fax: (916) 324-6645
Web: http://democrats.sen.ca.gov/senator/alarcon

District Office
6150 Van Nuys Blvd. #400
Van Nuys, CA 91401
Tel: (818) 901-5588 Fax: (818) 901-5562

Gilbert Cedillo (D-22nd District)
Capitol Office
State Capitol #5100
Sacramento, CA 95814
Tel: (916) 445-3456 Fax: (916) 327-8817
Web: http://democrats.sen.ca.gov/senator/cedillo

District Office
617 S Olive St. #710
Los Angeles, CA 90014
Tel: (213) 612-9566 Fax: (213) 612-9591

Gloria Romero (D-24th District)
Capitol Office
State Capitol #313
Sacramento, CA 95814
Tel: (916) 445-1418 Fax: (916) 445-0485
Web: http://democrats.sen.ca.gov/senator/romero

District Office
149 S Mednik Ave. #202
Los Angeles, CA 90022
Tel: (323) 881-0100 Fax: (323) 881-0101

Martha Escutia (D-30th District)
Capitol Office
State Capitol #5080
Sacramento, CA 95814
Tel: (916) 327-8315 Fax: (916) 327-8755

District Office
12440 E Imperial Hwy. #125
Norwalk, CA 90650
Tel: (562) 929-6060 Fax: (562) 929-0366

Nell Soto (D-32nd District)
Capitol Office
State Capitol #4074
Sacramento, CA 95814
Tel: (916) 445-6868 Fax: (916) 445-0128
Web: http://democrats.sen.ca.gov/soto

District Office
822 N Euclid Ave.
Ontario, CA 91762
Tel: (909) 984-7741 Fax: (909) 984-6695

District Office
505 S Garey Ave., 2nd Fl.
Pomona, CA 91766
Tel: (909) 469-9935 Fax: (909) 469-9206

District Office
357 W 2nd St. #1
San Bernardino, CA 92401
Tel: (909) 381-3832 Fax: (909) 381-0739

Denise M. Ducheny (D-40th District)
Capitol Office
State Capitol #4081
Sacramento, CA 95814
Tel: (916) 445-6767 Fax: (916) 327-3522
Web: http://democrats.sen.ca.gov/senator/ducheny

District Office
637 3rd Ave. #C
Chula Vista, CA 91910
Tel: (619) 409-7690 Fax: (619) 409-7688

District Office
1224 State St. #D
El Centro, CA 92243
Tel: (760) 335-3442 Fax: (760) 335-3444

District Office
53990 Enterprise Way #14
Coachella, CA 92236
Tel: (760) 398-6442 Fax: (760) 398-6470

ASSEMBLY

Alberto Torrico (20th District)
Capitol Office
P.O. Box 942849
Sacramento, CA 94249-0020
Tel: (916) 319-2020 Fax: (916) 319-2120
Email: assemblymember.torrico@assembly.ca.gov
Web: http://democrats.assembly.ca.gov/members/a20

District Office
39510 Paseo Padre Pkwy. #280
Fremont, CA 94538
Tel: (510) 440-9030 Fax: (510) 440-9035

Joe Coto (23rd District)
Capitol Office
P.O. Box 942849
Sacramento, CA 94249-0023
Tel: (916) 319-2023 Fax: (916) 319-2123
Email: assemblymember.coto@assembly.ca.gov
Web: http://democrats.assembly.ca.gov/members/a23

Simon Salinas (28th District)
Capitol Office
P.O. Box 942849
Sacramento, CA 94249-0028
Tel: (916) 319-2028 Fax: (916) 319-2128
Email: assemblymember.salinas@assembly.ca.gov
Web: http://democrats.assembly.ca.gov/members/a28

District Office
100 W Alisal St. #134
Salinas, CA 93901
Tel: (831) 759-8676 Fax: (831) 759-2961

Nicole Parra (30th District)
Capitol Office
P.O. Box 942849
Sacramento, CA 94249-0028
Tel: (916) 319-2030 Fax: (916) 319-2130
Email: assemblymember.parra@assembly.ca.gov
Web: http://democrats.assembly.ca.gov/members/a30

District Office
601 24th St. #A
Bakersfield, CA 93301
Tel: (661) 334-3745 Fax: (661) 334-3796

Hanford Office
321 N Douty St. #B
Hanford, CA 93230
Tel: (559) 585-7170 Fax: (559) 585-7175

Juan Arambula (31st District)
Capitol Office
P.O. Box 942849
Sacramento, CA 94249-0031
Tel: (916) 319-2031 Fax: (916) 319-2131
Email: assemblymember.arambula@assembly.ca.gov
Web: http://democrats.assembly.ca.gov/members/a31

District Office
Hugh Burns State Bldg.
2550 Mariposa Mall #5031
Fresno, CA 93721
Tel: (559) 445-5532 Fax: (559) 445-6006

Pedro Nava (35th District)
Capitol Office
P.O. Box 942849
Sacramento, CA 94249-0035
Tel: (916) 319-2035 Fax: (916) 319-2135
Email: assemblymember.nava@assembly.ca.gov
Web: http://democrats.assembly.ca.gov/members/a35

District Office
101 W Anapamu St. #A
Santa Barbara, CA 93101
Tel: (805) 564-1649 Fax: (805) 564-1651

Cindy Montanez (39th District)
Capitol Office
State Capitol #3013
Sacramento, CA 95814
Tel: (916) 319-2039 Fax: (916) 319-2139
Email: assemblymember.montanez@assembly.ca.gov
Web: http://democrats.assembly.ca.gov/members/a39

District Office
11541 Laurel Canyon Blvd. #C
Mission Hills, CA 91345
Tel: (818) 838-3939 Fax: (818) 838-3931

Dario Frommer (43rd District)
Capitol Office
P.O. Box 942849
Sacramento, CA 94249-0043
Tel: (916) 319-2043 Fax: (916) 319-2143
Email: assemblymember.frommer@assembly.ca.gov
Web: http://democrats.assembly.ca.gov/members/a43

District Office
620 N Brand Blvd. #403
Glendale, CA 91203
Tel: (818) 240-6330 Fax: (818) 240-4632

Fabian Nunez (46th District)
Capitol Office
P.O. Box 942849
Sacramento, CA 94249-0046
Tel: (916) 319-2046
Email: assemblymember.nunez@assembly.ca.gov
Web: http://democrats.assembly.ca.gov/members/a46

District Office
320 W 4th St. #1050
Los Angeles, CA 90013
Tel: (213) 620-4646

Hector de La Torre (50th District)
Capitol Office
P.O. Box 942849
Sacramento, CA 94249-0050
Tel: (916) 319-2050 Fax: (916) 319-2150
Web: http://democrats.assembly.ca.gov/members/a50

Jenny Oropeza (55th District)
Capitol Office
P.O. Box 942849
Sacramento, CA 94249-0055
Tel: (916) 319-2055 Fax: (916) 319-2155
Email: assemblymember.oropeza@assembly.ca.gov
Web: http://democrats.assembly.ca.gov/members/a55

District Office
1 Civic Plaza Dr. #460
Carson, CA 90745-2243
Tel: (310) 518-3324 Fax: (310) 518-3508

Rudy Bermudez (56th District)
Capitol Office
P.O. Box 942849
Sacramento, CA 94249-0056
Tel: (916) 319-2056 Fax: (916) 319-2156
Email: assemblymember.bermudez@assembly.ca.gov
Web: http://democrats.assembly.ca.gov/members/a56

District Office
12501 E Imperial Hwy. #210
Norwalk, CA 90650
Tel: (562) 864-5600 Fax: (562) 863-7466

Ed Chavez (57th District)
Capitol Office
P.O. Box 942849
Sacramento, CA 94249-0057
Tel: (916) 319-2057 Fax: (916) 319-2157
Email: assemblymember.chavez@assembly.ca.gov
Web: http://democrats.assembly.ca.gov/members/a57

Industry Office
13181 Crossroads Pkwy. North #160
Industry, CA 91746
Tel: (626) 961-8492

Ron Calderon (58th District)
Capitol Office
P.O. Box 942849
Sacramento, CA 94249-0058
Tel: (916) 319-2058
Email: assemblymember.calderon@assembly.ca.gov
Web: http://democrats.assembly.ca.gov/members/a58

District Office
400 N Montebello Blvd. #100
Montebello, CA 90640
Tel: (323) 838-5858

Gloria Negrete-McLeod (61st District)
Capitol Office
P.O. Box 942849
Sacramento, CA 94249-0061
Tel: (916) 319-2061 Fax: (916) 319-2161
Web: http://democrats.assembly.ca.gov/members/a61

District Office
4959 Palo Verde St. #100B
Montclair, CA 91763
Tel: (909) 621-2783 Fax: (909) 621-7483

Joe Baca, Jr. (62nd District)
Capitol Office
P.O. Box 942849
Sacramento, CA 94249-0062
Tel: (916) 319-2062 Fax: (916) 319-2162

Email: assemblymember.baca@assembly.ca.gov
Web: http://democrats.assembly.ca.gov/members/a62

District Office
201 North E St. #205
San Bernardino, CA 92401
Tel: (909) 388-1413 Fax: (909) 388-1176

Lori Saldana (76th District)
Capitol Office
P.O. Box 942849
Sacramento, CA 94249-0076
Tel: (916) 319-2076 Fax: (916) 319-2176
Email: assemblymember.saldana@assembly.ca.gov
Web: http://democrats.assembly.ca.gov/members/a76

Juan Vargas (79th District)
District Office
678 3rd Ave. #105
Chula Vista, CA 91910-5844
Tel: (619) 409-7979 Fax: (619) 409-9270
Email: assemblymember.vargas@assembly.ca.gov
Web: http://democrats.assembly.ca.gov/members/a79

Bonnie Garcia (R-80th District)
Capitol Office
State Capitol Bldg. #2002
Sacramento, CA 95814
Tel: (916) 319-2080 Fax: (916) 319-2180

District Office
1430 Broadway #8
El Centro, CA 92243
Tel: (760) 336-8912 Fax: (760) 336-8914

District Office
68-700 Avenida Lalo Guerrero #B
Cathedral City, CA 92234
Tel: (760) 321-8522 Fax: (760) 321-8410

COLORADO

SENATE

Abel Tapia (D-3rd District)
Capitol Office
200 E Colfax
Denver, CO 80203
Tel: (303) 866-4878
Email: abel.tapia.senate@state.co.us
Web: www.state.co.us/gov_dir/leg_dir/senate/members/sen03.htm

Valentin J. Vigil (D-32nd District)
Capitol Office
200 E Colfax #271
Denver, CO 80203
Tel: (303) 866-2964
Email: val.vigil.house@state.co.us
Web: www.state.co.us/gov_dir/leg_dir/house/members/house32.htm

Paula Sandoval (D-34th District)
Capitol Office
200 E Colfax
Denver, CO 80203
Tel: (303) 866-2931
Email: paula.sandoval.senate@state.co.us
Web: www.state.co.us/gov_dir/leg_dir/senate/members/sen34.htm

HOUSE OF REPRESENTATIVES

Fran Coleman (D-1st District)
District Office
200 E Colfax #271
Denver, CO 80203
Tel: (303) 866-2966
Email: fran.coleman.house@state.co.us

Michael Garcia (D-42nd District)
Capitol Office
200 E Colfax #271
Denver, CO 80203
Tel: (303) 866-3911
Email: michael@michaelgarcia.info
Web: www.state.co.us/gov_dir/leg_dir/house/
members/house42.htm

Dorothy Butcher (D-46th District)
District Office
200 E Colfax #271
Denver, CO 80203
Tel: (303) 866-2968
Email: dorothy.butcher.house@state.co.us

Rafael Lorenzo Gallegos (D-62nd District)
District Office
200 E Colfax #271
Denver, CO 80203
Tel: (303) 866-2916
Email: rafael.gallegos.house@state.co.us

CONNECTICUT

HOUSE OF REPRESENTATIVES

Minnie Gonzalez (D-3rd District)
Capitol Office
Legislative Office Bldg. #4115
Hartford, CT 06106-1591
Tel: (860) 240-8585
Email: minnie.gonzalez@cga.ct.gov

District Office
97 Amity St.
Hartford, CT 06106
Tel: (860) 236-9654

Evelyn C. Mantilla (D-4th District)
Capitol Office
Legislative Office Bldg. #3802
Hartford, CT 06106
Tel: (860) 240-8585
Email: evelyn.mantilla@cga.ct.gov

District Office
36 Charter Oak Pl.
Hartford, CT 06106
Tel: (860) 246-0385

David Aldarondo (D-75th District)
Capitol Office
Legislative Office Bldg. #4000
Hartford, CT 06106-1591
Tel: (860) 240-8585
Email: david.aldarondo@cga.ct.gov

District Office
107 Draher St. #3
Waterbury, CT 06708-3566
Tel: (203) 759-7600

Juan Candelaria (D-95th District)
Capitol Office
Legislative Office Bldg. #4010
Hartford, CT 06106-1591
Tel: (860) 240-8585
Email: juan.candelaria@cga.ct.gov

District Office
82 Elliott St.
New Haven, CT 06519

Lydia N. Martinez (D-128th District)
Capitol Office
Legislative Office Bldg. #4005
Hartford, CT 06106-1591
Tel: (860) 240-8585
Email: lydia.martinez@cga.ct.gov

District Office
1137 Pembroke St.
Bridgeport, CT 06608

Felipe Reinoso (D-130th District)
Capitol Office
Legislative Office Bldg. #4014
Hartford, CT 06106-1591
Tel: (860) 240-8585 Fax: (860) 240-0067
Email: felipe.reinoso@cga.ct.gov

District Office
P.O. Box 839
Bridgeport, CT 06601

DELAWARE

HOUSE OF REPRESENTATIVES

Joseph E. Miro (R-22nd District)
Capitol Office
Carvel State Office Bldg., 820 N French St.
Wilmington, DE 19801
Tel: (302) 577-8723

District Office
P.O. Box 1401
Dover, DE 19903
Tel: (302) 744-4123

FLORIDA

SENATE

Alex Diaz de la Portilla (R-36th District)
Capitol Office
Senate Office Bldg. #314, 404 S Monroe St.
Tallahassee, FL 32399-1100
Tel: (850) 487-5109
Email: portilla.alex.web@flsenate.gov

District Office
1555 SW 8th St.
Miami, FL 33135-5218
Tel: (305) 643-7200 Fax: (305) 643-7202

Alex Villalobos (R-38th District)
Capitol Office
Senate Office Bldg. #330, 404 S Monroe St.
Tallahassee, FL 32399-1100
Tel: (850) 487-5130
Email: villalobos.alex.web@flsenate.gov

District Office
2350 Coral Way #202-A
Miami, FL 33145-3500
Tel: (305) 222-4160

Rodolfo Garcia, Jr. (R-40th District)
Capitol Office
Senate Office Bldg. #302, 404 S Monroe St.
Tallahassee, FL 32399-1100
Tel: (850) 487-5106
Email: garcia.rudy.web@flsenate.gov

District Office
7475 W 4th Ave.
Hialeah, FL 33014-4327
Tel: (305) 364-3191

HOUSE OF REPRESENTATIVES

John Q. Quinones (R-49th District)
Capitol Office
1301 The Capitol, 402 S Monroe St.
Tallahassee, FL 32399-1300
Tel: (850) 488-9240

District Office
101 N Church St., 3rd Fl., Kissimmee City Hall
Kissimmee, FL 34741-5054
Tel: (407) 935-3777

Bob Henriquez (D-58th District)
Capitol Office
313 House Office Bldg., 402 S Monroe St.
Tallahassee, FL 32399-1300
Tel: (850) 488-9460

District Office
4221 N Himes Ave. #102
Tampa, FL 33607-6228
Tel: (813) 673-4673

Rafael Arza (R-102nd District)
Capitol Office
204 House Office Bldg., 402 S Monroe St.
Tallahassee, FL 32399-1300
Tel: (850) 488-1683

District Office
14645 NW 77th Ave. #104
Hialeah, FL 33014-2569
Tel: (305) 827-2720

Gustavo A. Barreiro (R-107th District)
Capitol Office
221 The Capitol, 402 S Monroe St.
Tallahassee, FL 32399-1300
Tel: (850) 488-9930

District Office
1454 SW 1st St. #100
Miami, FL 33135-2203
Tel: (305) 643-7324

Rene Garcia (R-110th District)
Capitol Office
210 House Office Bldg., 402 S Monroe St.
Tallahassee, FL 32399-1300
Tel: (850) 487-2197

District Office
3814 W 12th Ave.
Hialeah, FL 33012-4126
Tel: (305) 827-2767

Marco Rubio (R-111th District)
Capitol Office
317 The Capitol, 402 S Monroe St.
Tallahassee, FL 32399-1300
Tel: (850) 488-4092

District Office
6427 SW 8th St.
Miami, FL 33144-4813
Tel: (305) 442-6939

David Rivera (R-112th District)
Capitol Office
417 House Office Bldg., 402 S Monroe St.
Tallahassee, FL 32399-1300
Tel: (850) 488-7897

District Office
2450 SW 137th Ave. #205
Miami, FL 33175-6312
Tel: (305) 227-7630

District Office
3301 E Tamiami Trail #305, Collier County
Admin. Bldg.
Naples, FL 34112-3972
Tel: (239) 434-5094

Carlos Lopez-Cantera (R-113th District)
Capitol Office
1401 The Capitol, 402 S Monroe St.
Tallahassee, FL 32399-1300
Tel: (850) 488-4202

District Office
2300 Coral Way #111
Miami, FL 33145
Tel: (305) 442-6877

Anitere Flores (R-114th District)
Capitol Office
1003 The Capitol, 402 S Monroe St.
Tallahassee, FL 32399-1300
Tel: (850) 488-2831

District Office
1321 SW 107th Ave. #205-C
Miami, FL 33174-2523
Tel: (305) 227-7626

Juan Carlos J.C. Planas (R-115th District)
Capitol Office
317 House Office Bldg., 402 S Monroe St.
Tallahassee, FL 32399-1300
Tel: (850) 488-3616

District Office
8532 SW 8th St. #280
Miami, FL 33144-4054
Tel: (305) 442-6800

Marcelo Llorente (R-116th District)
Capitol Office
308 House Office Bldg., 402 S Monroe St.
Tallahassee, FL 32399-1300
Tel: (850) 488-5047

District Office
13701 SW 88th St. #201
Miami, FL 33186-1309
Tel: (305) 273-3200

Julio Robaina (R-117th District)
Capitol Office
405 House Office Bldg., 402 S Monroe St.
Tallahassee, FL 32399-1300
Tel: (850) 488-6506

District Office
6741 SW 24th St. #19
Miami, FL 33155-1766
Tel: (305) 442-6868

Juan C. Zapata (R-119th District)
Capitol Office
218 House Office Bldg., 402 S Monroe St.
Tallahassee, FL 32399-1300
Tel: (850) 488-9550

District Office
13550 SW 88th St. #150
Miami, FL 33186-1541
Tel: (305) 273-3288

GEORGIA

SENATE

Sam Zamarripa (D-36th District)
Capitol Office
121 E State Capitol
Atlanta, GA 30334
Tel: (404) 463-8054 Fax: (404) 657-3248
Email: sam@zamarripa.com

District Office
P.O. Box 7850
Atlanta, GA 30357

HOUSE OF REPRESENTATIVES

Pedro Marin (D-66th District)
Capitol Office
Legislative Office Bldg. #611
Atlanta, GA 30334
Tel: (404) 656-0314
Email: marinstatehouse@aol.com
Web: www.marinstatehouse.com

District Office
2625 Ridge Brook Trail
Duluth, GA 30096
Tel: (770) 416-8465

David S. Casas (R-68th District)
Capitol Office
Legislative Office Bldg.
18 Capitol Square #611
Atlanta, GA 30334
Tel: (404) 656-0314
Email: dcasas@legis.state.ga.us

District Office
P.O. Box 283
Lilburn, GA 30048-0283
Tel: (770) 931-8033 Fax: (770) 931-8839

HAWAII

SENATE

Lorraine R. Inouye (D-1st District)
Capitol Office
Hawaii State Capitol #201, 415 S Beretania St.
Honolulu, HI 96813
Tel: (808) 586-7335 Fax: (808) 586-7339
Email: seninouye@capitol.hawaii.gov

IDAHO

HOUSE OF REPRESENTATIVES

Elmer Martinez (D-29th District)
District Office
8209 W Portneul Rd.
Pocatello, ID 83204
Tel: (208) 232-4532
Email: emartine@house.state.id.us

ILLINOIS

SENATE

Antonio Munoz (D-1st District)
Capitol Office
124 Capitol Bldg.
Springfield, IL 62706
Tel: (217) 782-9415

District Office
2021 W 35th
Chicago, IL 60609
Tel: (773) 869-9050 Fax: (773) 869-9046

Miguel del Valle (D-2nd District)
Capitol Office
321-A Capitol Bldg.
Springfield, IL 62706
Tel: (217) 782-5652

District Office
4150 W Armitage Ave.
Chicago, IL 60639
Tel: (773) 292-0202 Fax: (773) 292-1903

Martin A. Sandoval (D-12th District)
Capitol Office
118 Capitol Bldg.
Springfield, IL 62706
Tel: (217) 782-5304

District Office
4843 W Cermak Rd.
Cicero, IL 60804
Tel: (708) 656-2002 Fax: (708) 656-7608

Iris Y. Martinez (D-20th District)
Capitol Office
M106 Capitol Bldg.
Springfield, IL 62706
Tel: (217) 782-8191

District Office
3024 N Pulaski Rd.
Chicago, IL 60641
Tel: (773) 283-7000 Fax: (773) 283-2507

HOUSE OF REPRESENTATIVES

Susana Mendoza (D-1st District)
Capitol Office
200-1S Stratton Office Bldg.
Springfield, IL 62706
Tel: (217) 782-7752 Fax: (217) 782-8917

District Office
2500 S Millard
Chicago, IL 60623
Tel: (773) 277-7711 Fax: (773) 277-6196

Edward J. Acevedo (D-2nd District)
Capitol Office
109 Capitol
Springfield, IL 62706
Tel: (217) 782-2855 Fax: (217) 782-7762

District Office
2439 S Oakley
Chicago, IL 60608
Tel: (773) 843-1200 Fax: (773) 523-9900

William Delgado (D-3rd District)
Capitol Office
264-S Stratton Office Bldg.
Springfield, IL 62706
Tel: (217) 782-0480 Fax: (217) 557-9609

District Office
4150 W Armitage Ave.
Chicago, IL 60639
Tel: (773) 292-0202 Fax: (773) 292-1903

Cynthia Soto (D-4th District)
Capitol Office
288-S Stratton Office Bldg.
Springfield, IL 62706
Tel: (217) 782-0150

District Office
2615 W Division
Chicago, IL 60622
Tel: (773) 252-0402 Fax: (773) 342-3860

Michelle Chavez (D-24th District)
Capitol Office
252 W Stratton Office Bldg.
Springfield, IL 62706
Tel: (217) 782-8173

District Office
2138 S 61st St.
Cicero, IL 60804
Tel: (708) 863-1766 Fax: (708) 863-1768

Maria Antonia Berrios (D-39th District)
Capitol Office
200-3S Stratton Office Bldg.
Springfield, IL 62706
Tel: (217) 558-1032

District Office
2058 N Western Ave.
Chicago, IL 60647
Tel: (773) 235-3939 Fax: (773) 278-2541

Linda Chapa LaVia (D-83rd District)
Capitol Office
235-E Stratton Office Bldg.
Springfield, IL 62706
Tel: (217) 558-1002 Fax: (217) 782-0927

District Office
8 E Galena Blvd. #240
Aurora, IL 60506
Tel: (630) 264-6855 Fax: (630) 264-6752

INDIANA

HOUSE OF REPRESENTATIVES

John Aguilera (D-12th District)
District Office
200 W Washington St.
Indianapolis, IN 46204
Tel: (800) 382-9842

KANSAS

HOUSE OF REPRESENTATIVES

Louis Ruiz (D-32nd District)
Capitol Office
2914 W 46th Ave.
Kansas City, KS 66103

Tel: (913) 262-1634 Fax: (913) 262-1634
Email: ruiz@house.state.ks.us

Tom Sawyer (D-95th District)
District Office
1041 S Elizabeth St.
Wichita, KS 67213
Tel: (316) 265-7096 Fax: (316) 529-4678
Email: sawyer@house.state.ks.us

Mario Goico (R-100th District)
Capitol Office
1254 N Pine Grove Ct.
Wichita, KS 67212
Tel: (316) 721-3682 Fax: (316) 721-3682
Email: goico@house.state.ks.us

Delia Garcia (D-103th District)
Capitol Office
400 W Central #1006
Wichita, KS 67204
Tel: (316) 371-2242
Email: garcia@house.state.ks.us

MARYLAND

SENATE

Alex Mooney (R-3rd District)
Capitol Office
James Senate Office Bldg. #402
110 College Ave.
Annapolis, MD 21401-1991
Tel: (410) 841-3575 Fax: (410) 841-3193
Email: alex_mooney@senate.state.md.us

Philip C. Jimeno (D-31st District)
Capitol Office
James Senate Office Bldg. #101
110 College Ave.
Annapolis, MD 21401-1991
Tel: (410) 841-3658 Fax: (410) 841-3586
Email: philip_jimeno@senate.state.md.us

HOUSE OF REPRESENTATIVES

Ana Sol Gutierrez (D-18th District)
District Office
Lowe House Office Bldg. #219
84 College Ave.
Annapolis, MD 21401-1991
Tel: (410) 841-3181 Fax: (410) 841-3053
Email: ana_gutierrez@house.state.md.us

Victor R. Ramirez (D-47th District)
District Office
Lowe House Office Bldg. #203
84 College Ave.
Annapolis, MD 21401-1991
Tel: (410) 841-3326 Fax: (410) 841-3239
Email: victor_ramirez@house.state.md.us

MASSACHUSETTS

SENATE

Jarrett T. Barrios (D)
Capitol Office
State House #309
Boston, MA 02133
Tel: (617) 722-1650 Fax: (617) 722-1323
Email: jarrett.barrios@state.ma.us
Web: www.mass.gov/legis/member/jtb0.htm

HOUSE OF REPRESENTATIVES

Cheryl A. Rivera (D-10th District)
Capitol Office
State House #26
Boston, MA 02133
Tel: (617) 722-2080
Email: cheryl.rivera@state.ma.us
Web: www.mass.gov/legis/member/car1.htm

Jeffrey Sanchez (D-15th District)
Capitol Office
State House #146
Boston, MA 02133
Tel: (617) 722-2575
Email: rep.jeffreysanchez@hou.state.ma.us
Web: www.mass.gov/legis/member/j_s1.htm

William Lantigua (D-16th District)
Capitol Office
State House #437
Boston, MA 02133
Tel: (617) 722-2425
Email: rep.williamlantigua@hou.state.ma.us
Web: www.mass.gov/legis/member/w_l1.htm

MICHIGAN

SENATE

Valde Garcia (R-22nd District)
Capitol Office
P.O. Box 30036
Lansing, MI 48909-7536
Tel: (517) 373-2420 Fax: (517) 373-2764
Web: www.senate.michigan.gov/gop/senator/
garcia

HOUSE OF REPRESENTATIVES

Lee Gonzales (D)
District Office
N-0898 House Office Bldg.
Lansing, MI 48909-7514
Tel: (517) 373-7515 Fax: (517) 373-5817
Email: leegonzales@house.mi.gov

MINNESOTA

HOUSE OF REPRESENTATIVES

Carlos Mariani (D-65th District)
Capitol Office
203 State Office Bldg., 100 Rev. Dr. Martin
Luther King Jr. Blvd.
St. Paul, MN 55155
Tel: (651) 296-9714
Email: rep.carlos.mariani@house.mn

NEBRASKA

SENATE

Ray Aguilar (R-35th District)
Capitol Office
State Capitol #1008
Lincoln, NE 68509
Tel: (402) 471-2617 Fax: (402) 479-0935
Email: raguilar@unicam.state.ne.us
Web: www.unicam.state.ne.us/senators/
district35.htm

NEVADA

SENATE

Bob Coffin (D-10th District)
District Office
1139 5th Pl.
Las Vegas, NV 89104-1413
Tel: (702) 384-9501 Fax: (775) 684-1427
Email: bcoffin@sen.state.nv.us

HOUSE OF REPRESENTATIVES

Genie Ohrenschall (D-12th District)
District Office
1124 S 15th St.
Las Vegas, NV 89104-1740

Tel: (702) 384-5992
Email: gohrenschall@asm.state.nv.us

NEW HAMPSHIRE

HOUSE OF REPRESENTATIVES

Hector M. Velez (D-12th District)
Capitol Office
269 Central St.
Manchester, NH 03103-4745
Tel: (603) 647-8683
Email: hector.velez@leg.state.nh.us

Carlos E. Gonzalez (R-17th District)
Capitol Office
P.O. Box 154
Manchester, NH 03105-0154
Tel: (603) 645-4375 Fax: (603) 645-4375
Email: carlosgonzalez@webtv.net

NEW JERSEY

ASSEMBLY

Nilsa Cruz-Perez (D-5th District)
District Office
800 Cooper St. #525
Camden, NJ 08102
Tel: (856) 541-1251 Fax: (856) 541-3415

Joseph Vas (D-19th District)
District Office
276 Hobart St.
Perth Amboy, NJ 08862
Tel: (732) 324-5955 Fax: (732) 324-1879

Eric Munoz (R-21st District)
District Office
203 Elm St., 1st Fl.
Westfield, NJ 07090
Tel: (908) 232-3673

District Office
57 Union Pl. #310
Summit, NJ 07901
Tel: (908) 918-0414 Fax: (908) 918-0275

Wilfredo Caraballo (D-29th District)
District Office
371 Bloomfield Ave., 2nd Fl.
Newark, NJ 07107
Tel: (973) 350-0048 Fax: (973) 350-0951

Albio Sires (D-33rd District)
District Office
303 58th St.
West New York, NJ 07093
Tel: (201) 854-0900 Fax: (201) 854-4818

Nellie Pou (D-35th District)
District Office
100 Hamilton Plz. #1403-05
Paterson, NJ 07505
Tel: (973) 247-1555 Fax: (973) 247-1550

NEW MEXICO

SENATE

Ricardo Martinez (D-5th District)
Capitol Office
P.O. Box 934
Espanola, NM 87532
Tel: (505) 753-8027

Carlos R. Cisneros (D-6th District)
Capitol Office
P.O. Box 1129
Questa, NM 87556
Tel: (505) 586-0873
Email: carlos.cisneros@state.nm.us

Pete Campos (D-8th District)
Capitol Office
500 Raynolds Ave.
Las Vegas, NM 87701
Tel: (505) 454-5700
Email: petecampos@newmexico.com

Linda M. Lopez (D-11th District)
Capitol Office
9132 Suncrest SW
Albuquerque, NM 87121
Tel: (505) 831-4148

James G. Taylor (D-14th District)
District Office
3909 Camino Del Valle SW
Albuquerque, NM 87105
Tel: (505) 986-4862
Email: jamesg.taylor@nmlegis.gov

Nancy Rodriguez (D-24th District)
Capitol Office
1838 Camino La Canada
Santa Fe, NM 87501
Tel: (505) 983-8913

Bernadette M. Sanchez (D-26th District)
Capitol Office
7712 Ranchwood NW
Albuquerque, NM 87120
Tel: (505) 884-5404

Ben D. Altamirano (D-28th District)
Capitol Office
1123 Santa Rita St.
Silver City, NM 88061
Tel: (505) 538-3525

Michael S. Sanchez (D-29th District)
Capitol Office
3 Bunton Rd.
Belen, NM 87002
Tel: (505) 865-0688

Cynthia Nava (D-31st District)
Capitol Office
3002 Broadmoor
Las Cruces, NM 88001
Tel: (505) 882-6200
Email: cynthia.nava@state.nm.us

Mary Jane M. Garcia (D-36th District)
Capitol Office
P.O. Box 22
Dona Ana, NM 88032
Tel: (505) 523-0440
Email: maryjane.garcia@state.nm.us

Phil A. Griego (D-39th District)
Capitol Office
P.O. Box 10
San Jose, NM 87565
Tel: (505) 988-2233
Email: phil.griego@state.nm.us

Dianna J. Duran (R-40th District)
Capitol Office
909 8th St.
Tularosa, NM 88352
Tel: (505) 439-2716
Email: dianna.duran@state.nm.us

HOUSE OF REPRESENTATIVES

Kandy Cordova (D-7th District)
District Office
613 Frederico Blvd.
Belen, NM 87002
Tel: (505) 864-1483

Fred Luna (D-8th District)
District Office
1651 Los Lentes NE
Los Lunas, NM 87031
Tel: (505) 865-7426

Henry Kiki Saavedra (D-10th District)
District Office
2838 2nd St. SW
Albuquerque, NM 87102
Tel: (505) 242-9582

Rick Miera (D-11th District)
District Office
1011 Forrester NW
Albuquerque, NM 87102
Tel: (505) 843-6641

Ernest H. Chavez (D-12th District)
District Office
1531 Severo Rd. SW
Albuquerque, NM 87105
Tel: (505) 877-5416
Email: ernestc@aol.com

Daniel P. Silva (D-13th District)
District Office
1323 Canyon Trail SW
Albuquerque, NM 87121
Tel: (505) 831-2185

Miguel P. Garcia (D-14th District)
District Office
1118 La Font Rd. SW
Albuquerque, NM 87105
Tel: (505) 450-2455
Email: miguel.garcia@state.nm.us

Harriet Ruiz (D-16th District)
District Office
4901 El Aguila NW
Albuquerque, NM 87120
Tel: (505) 831-1009

Edward C. Sandoval (D-17th District)
District Office
5102 12th St. NW
Albuquerque, NM 87107
Tel: (505) 344-8449
Email: edward.sandoval@state.nm.us

Sheryl Williams Stapleton (D-19th District)
District Office
P.O. Box 25385
Albuquerque, NM 87108
Tel: (505) 986-4774
Email: williams_sm@aps.edu

Al Park (D-26th District)
District Office
1840 Dakota NE
Albuquerque, NM 87110
Tel: (505) 986-4234

Lorenzo A. Larranaga (R-27th District)
District Office
7716 Lamplighter NE
Albuquerque, NM 87109
Tel: (505) 986-4215

Joni Marie Gutierrez (D-33rd District)
District Office
208 N Miranda
Las Cruces, NM 88005
Tel: (505) 986-4234
Email: jonig@zianet.com

Mary Helen Garcia (D-34th District)
District Office
5271 State Hwy. 28
Las Cruces, NM 88005
Tel: (505) 526-6608

Antonio Lujan (D-35th District)
District Office
429 1/2 San Pedro
Las Cruces, NM 88001
Tel: (505) 556-1657
Email: alujan@zianet.com

Andy Nunez (D-36th District)
District Office
P.O. Box 746
Hatch, NM 87937
Tel: (505) 267-3451

Manuel G. Herrera (D-39th District)
District Office
300 N. Franey St.
Bayard, NM 88023
Tel: (505) 537-5577 (h)

Nick L. Salazar (D-40th District)
District Office
P.O. Box 1076
San Juan Pueblo, NM 87566
Tel: (505) 667-0362

Debbie A. Rodella (D-41st District)
District Office
P.O. Box 1074
San Juan Pueblo, NM 87566
Tel: (505) 665-0075
Email: debbie.rodella@state.nm.us

Roberto J. Gonzales (D-42nd District)
District Office
6193 NDCBU
Taos, NM 87105
Tel: (505) 751-1467

Jim Trujillo (D-45th District)
District Office
1901 Morris Pl.
Sante Fe, NM 87505
Tel: (505) 438-8890
Email: jimtrujillo@msn.com

Ben Lujan (D-46th District)
District Office
05 Entrada Celedon y Nestora
Santa Fe, NM 87506
Tel: (505) 455-3354

Luciano Varela (D-48th District)
District Office
1709 Callejon Zenaida
Sante Fe, NM 87501
Tel: (505) 982-1292

Gloria C. Vaughn (R-51st District)
District Office
503 E 16th St.
Alamogordo, NM 88310
Tel: (505) 986-4453

Joseph Cervantes (D-52nd District)
District Office
2610 South Espina
Las Cruces, NM 88001
Tel: (505) 526-5600
Email: cervanteslaw@zianet.com

Jose A. Campos (D-63rd District)
District Office
1050 S. 10th St.
Santa Rosa, NM 88435
Tel: (505) 472-3361
Email: Josephs@plateautel.net

Hector H. Balderas (D-68th District)
District Office
P.O. Box 88
Wagon Mound, NM 87752
Tel: (505) 986-4254
Email: hectorbalderas@msn.com

W. Ken Martinez (D-69th District)
District Office
P.O. Box 730
Grants, NM 87020
Tel: (505) 287-8801
Email: wken.martinez@state.nm.us

Richard D. Vigil (D-70th District)
District Office
P.O. Box 456
Ribera, NM 87560
Tel: (505) 421-1104

NEW YORK

SENATE

Martin Malave Dilan (D-17th District)
Capitol Office
606 Legislative Office Bldg.
Albany, NY 12247
Tel: (518) 455-2177
Email: dilan@senate.state.ny.us

District Office
786 Knickerbocker Ave.
Brooklyn, NY 11207
Tel: (718) 573-1726

Jose M. Serrano (D-28th District)
District Office
Albany, NY 12247
Tel: (518) 455-2795
Email: serrano@senate.state.ny.us

Ruben Diaz, Sr. (D-32nd District)
Capitol District
304 Legislative Office Bldg.
Albany, NY 12247
Tel: (518) 455-2511
Email: diaz@senate.state.ny.us

District Office
1750 Westchester Ave.
Bronx, NY 10472
Tel: (718) 892-7513

Efrain Gonzalez, Jr. (D-33rd District)
Capitol Office
711-B Legislative Office Bldg.
Albany, NY 12247
Tel: (518) 455-3395
Email: gonzalez@senate.state.ny.us

District Office
1780 Grand Concourse, 1st Fl.
Bronx, NY 10457
Tel: (718) 299-7905

ASSEMBLY

Jose R. Peralta (39th District)
District Office
82-11 37th Ave.
Jackson Heights, NY 11372
Tel: (718) 458-5367
Email: peraltj@assembly.state.ny.us

Albany Office
LOB 528
Albany, NY 12248
Tel: (518) 455-4567

Felix Ortiz (51st District)
District Office
404 55th St.
Brooklyn, NY 11220
Tel: (718) 492-6334
Email: ortizf@assembly.state.ny.us

Albany Office
LOB 542
Albany, NY 12248
Tel: (518) 455-3821

Vito J. Lopez (53rd District)
District Office
434 S 5th St.
Brooklyn, NY 11211
Tel: (718) 963-7029
Email: lopezv@assembly.state.ny.us

Albany Office
LOB 943
Albany, NY 12248
Tel: (518) 455-5537

Phil Ramos (6th District)
District Office
1010 Suffolk Ave.
Brentwood, NY 11717
Tel: (631) 435-3214
Email: ramosp@assembly.state.ny.us

Albany Office
LOB 820
Albany, NY 12248
Tel: (518) 455-5185

Adam Clayton Powell IV (D-68th District)
District Office
107 E 116th St.
New York, NY 10029
Tel: (212) 828-3953
Email: powella@assembly.state.ny.us

Albany Office
Legislative Office Bldg. 527
Albany, NY 12248
Tel: (518) 455-4781

Adriano Espaillat (72nd District)
District Office
210 Sherman Ave. #A
New York, NY 10034
Tel: (212) 544-2278
Email: espaila@assembly.state.ny.us

Albany Office
LOB 652
Albany, NY 12248
Tel: (518) 455-5807

Peter M. Rivera (76th District)
District Office
1262 Castle Hill Ave.
Bronx, NY 10462
Tel: (718) 931-2620
Email: riverap@assembly.state.ny.us

Albany Office
LOB 826
Albany, NY 12248
Tel: (518) 455-5102

Jose Rivera (78th District)
District Office
2488 Grand Concourse #416
Bronx, NY 10458
Tel: (718) 933-2204
Email: riveraj@assembly.state.ny.us

Albany Office
LOB 536
Albany, NY 12248
Tel: (518) 455-5414

Naomi Rivera (80th District)
Albany Office
LOB 637
Albany, NY 12248
Tel: (518) 455-5844

Carmen E. Arroyo (84th District)
District Office
384 E 149th St. #608
Bronx, NY 10455
Tel: (718) 292-2901
Email: arroyoc@assembly.state.ny.us

Albany Office
LOB 734
Albany, NY 12248
Tel: (518) 455-5402

Ruben Diaz, Jr. (85th District)
District Office
1163 Manor Ave.
Bronx, NY 10472
Tel: (718) 893-0202
Email: diazr@assembly.state.ny.us

Albany Office
LOB 419
Albany, NY 12248
Tel: (518) 455-5514

Luis M. Diaz (86th District)
District Office
2488 Grand Concourse #310-11
Bronx, NY 10458
Tel: (718) 933-6909
Email: diazl@assembly.state.ny.us

Albany Office
LOB 921
Albany, NY 12248
Tel: (518) 455-5511

NORTH CAROLINA

SENATE

Tom Apodaca (R-48th District)
District Office
1127 Legislative Bldg.
Raleigh, NC 27601-2808
Tel: (919) 733-5745
Email: toma@ncleg.net

HOUSE OF REPRESENTATIVES

Daniel F. McComas (R-19th District)
District Office
506 Legislative Office Bldg.
Raleigh, NC 27603-5925
Tel: (919) 733-5786
Email: dannym@ncleg.net

OREGON

HOUSE OF REPRESENTATIVES

Sal Esquivel (R-6th District)
Capitol Office
900 Court St. NE H-485
Salem, OR 97301
Tel: (503) 986-1406
Email: rep.salesquivel@state.or.us
Web: www.leg.state.or.us/esquivel

Interim Office
28 Quince St.
Medford, OR 97501

Billy Dalto (R-21st District)
Capitol Office
900 Court St. NE H-291
Salem, OR 97301
Tel: (503) 986-1421
Email: rep.billydalto@state.or.us
Web: www.leg.state.or.us/dalto

PENNSYLVANIA

HOUSE OF REPRESENTATIVES

Angel Cruz (D-180th District)
Capitol Office
2749 N 5th St.
Philadelphia, PA 19133
Tel: (215) 291-5643 Fax: (215) 291-5647

District Office
117-A E Wing
Harrisburg, PA 17120-2020
Tel: (717) 787-1407 Fax: (717) 783-8536

RHODE ISLAND

SENATE

Juan M. Pichardo (D-2th District)
District Office
229 Atlantic Ave.
Providence, RI 02907
Tel: (401) 222-4278
Email: sen-pichardo@rilin.state.ri.us

HOUSE OF REPRESENTATIVES

Anastasia Williams (D-9th District)
District Office
32 Hammond St.
Providence, RI 02909
Tel: (401) 272-8135
Email: rep-williams@rilin.state.ri.us

Grace Diaz (D-11th District)
District Office
45 Adelaide Ave.
Providence, RI 02907
Tel: (401) 467-8413
Email: grace@gracediaz.com

Edwin R. Pacheco (D-47th District)
District Office
46A Spring St.
Pascoag, RI 02859
Tel: (401) 567-0382
Email: rep-pacheco@rilin.state.ri.us

SOUTH CAROLINA

HOUSE OF REPRESENTATIVES

Gloria Arias Haskins (R-22nd District)
Capitol Office
2435 E North St.
Greenville, SC 29616
Tel: (864) 292-7239
Email: gah@scstatehouse.net

District Office
326-D Blatt Bldg.
Columbia, SC 29211
Tel: (803) 734-2978

TENNESSEE

HOUSE OF REPRESENTATIVES

Dolores R. Grensham (R-94th District)
District Office
3515 Country Club Rd.
Somerville, TN 38068
Email: rep.dolores.gresham@legislature.state.tn.us

Nashville Office
106 Mar Memorial Bldg.
Nashville, TN 37243-0194
Tel: (615) 741-6890

TEXAS

SENATE

Mario Gallegos, Jr. (D-6th District)
Capitol Office
P.O. Box 12068, Capitol Station
Austin, TX 78711
Tel: (512) 463-0106 Fax: (512) 463-0346

District Office
2205 Clinton Dr.
Galena Park, TX 77547
Tel: (713) 678-7080 Fax: (713) 678-7080

District Office
3411 Irvington Blvd.
Houston, TX 77009
Tel: (713) 227-0607 Fax: (713) 227-5075

District Office
5425 Polk St. #1101
Houston, TX 77023
Tel: (713) 923-7575 Fax: (713) 923-7676

Gonzalo Barrientos (D-14th District)
Capitol Office
P.O. Box 12068, Capitol Station
Austin, TX 78711
Tel: (512) 463-0114 Fax: (512) 463-5949

Frank L. Madla (D-19th District)
Capitol Office
P.O. Box 12068, Capitol Station
Austin, TX 78711
Tel: (512) 463-0119

District Office
1313 SE Military Dr. #101
San Antonio, TX 78214
Tel: (210) 927-9464 Fax: (210) 922-9521

District Office
103 W Callaghan
Fort Stockton, TX 79735
Tel: (432) 336-2173

District Office
480 S Americas Ave. #A-1
El Paso, TX 79907
Tel: (915) 791-0119 Fax: (915) 791-0121

Juan Hinojosa (D-20th District)
Capitol Office
P.O. Box 12068, Capitol Station
Austin, TX 78711
Tel: (512) 463-0120 Fax: (512) 463-0229

District Office
612 Nolana #410B
McAllen, TX 78504
Tel: (956) 972-1841 Fax: (956) 686-8462

District Office
400 SPID #101
Corpus Christi, TX 78405
Tel: (361) 299-2788 Fax: (361) 299-2824

Judith Zaffirini (D-21st District)
Capitol Office
P.O. Box 12068, Capitol Station
Austin, TX 78711
Tel: (512) 463-0121

District Office
1407 Washington St.
Laredo, TX 78042
Tel: (956) 722-2293 Fax: (956) 722-8586

District Office
12702 Toepperwein Rd. #214
San Antonio, TX 78233
Tel: (210) 657-0095

Leticia Van de Putte (D-26th District)
Capitol Office
P.O. Box 12068, Capitol Station
Austin, TX 78711
Tel: (512) 463-0126

District Office
3718 Blanco Rd. #2
San Antonio, TX 78212
Tel: (210) 733-6604 Fax: (210) 733-6605

Eddie Lucio, Jr. (D-27th District)
Capitol Office
P.O. Box 12068, Capitol Station
Austin, TX 78711
Tel: (512) 463-0127 Fax: (512) 463-0061

District Office
7 North Park Plz.
Brownsville, TX 78521
Tel: (956) 548-0227 Fax: (956) 548-0440

District Office
500 S Kansas
Weslaco, TX 78596
Tel: (956) 968-9927 Fax: (956) 447-0583

HOUSE OF REPRESENTATIVES

Dora Olivo (D-27th District)
Capitol Office
P.O. Box 2910 #EXT E2.806
Austin, TX 78768
Tel: (512) 463-0494 Fax: (512) 463-1403

District Office
P.O. Box 2130
Missouri City, TX 77459
Tel: (281) 208-8806 Fax: (281) 208-8826

District Office
2440 Texas Pkwy. #102
Missouri City, TX 77459

Ryan Guillen (D-31st District)
Capitol Office
P.O. Box 2910 #EXT E2.210
Austin, TX 78768
Tel: (512) 463-0416 Fax: (512) 463-1012

District Office
500 E Gravis
San Diego, TX 78384
Tel: (361) 279-7344 Fax: (361) 279-2129

Vilma Luna (D-33rd District)
Capitol Office
P.O. Box 2910 #CAP 4S.03
Austin, TX 78768
Tel: (512) 463-0484 Fax: (512) 463-8090

District Office
4525 Gollihar #200
Corpus Christi, TX 78411
Tel: (361) 854-9816 Fax: (361) 852-0665

Abel Herrero (D-34th District)
Capitol Office
P.O. Box 2910 #EXT E2.816
Austin, TX 78768
Tel: (512) 463-0462 Fax: (512) 463-9545

Yvonne Gonzalez Toureilles (D-35th District)
Capitol Office
P.O. Box 2910 #EXT E2.716
Austin, TX 78768
Tel: (512) 463-0645 Fax: (512) 463-5896

Kino Flores (D-36th District)
Capitol Office
P.O. Box 2910 #CAP GN.10
Austin, TX 78768
Tel: (512) 463-0704 Fax: (512) 463-5364

District Office
2023 N Conway
Mission, TX 78572
Tel: (956) 584-8999

District Office
118 S Cage Blvd., 1st Fl.
Pharr, TX 78577
Tel: (956) 782-7284 Fax: (956) 782-7285

Rene Oliveira (D-37th District)
Capitol Office
P.O. Box 2910 #CAP 4N.10
Austin, TX 78768
Tel: (512) 463-0640 Fax: (512) 463-8186

District Office
855 W Price Rd. #22
Brownsville, TX 78520
Tel: (956) 542-1828 Fax: (956) 542-1618

Jim Solis (D-38th District)
Capitol Office
P.O. Box 2910 #CAP GN.08
Austin, TX 78768
Tel: (512) 463-0606 Fax: (512) 463-1077

THE DEPARTMENT OF JUSTICE EMPLOYMENT OPPORTUNITIES

- ATTORNEYS
- CRIMINAL INVESTIGATORS
- SPECIAL AGENTS
- CORRECTIONAL OFFICERS
- CLERK TYPISTS
- SECRETARY STENOGRAPHERS
- PARALEGAL SPECIALISTS
- DEPUTY U.S. MARSHALS
- COMPUTER SPECIALISTS/SCIENTIST AND MANY OTHER ADMINISTRATIVE AND TECHNICAL POSITION

The Department of Justice employs over 101,000 persons throughout the Nation, foreign countries, and in U.S. Territories. Through its thousands of lawyers, investigators, agents and support staffs, the Department plays a key role in protecting against crime; in ensuring healthy competition of business; in safeguarding the consumer; in enforcing civil rights laws. The Department also plays a significant role in protecting citizens through its efforts in areas of prosecution and rehabilitation of offenders and represents the Government in legal matters generally, rendering legal advice and opinions upon request to the President and to the Heads of Executive Department and agencies.

For more information about career opportunities, please visit our website at

www.USDOJ.GOV/JMD/EEOS

United States Department of Justice
An Equal Opportunity Employer

District Office
1418 E Tyler #6
Harlingen, TX 78550
Tel: (956) 421-4120

Armando Martinez (D-39th District)
Capitol Office
P.O. Box 2910 #EXT E1.312
Austin, TX 78768
Tel: (512) 463-0530 Fax: (512) 463-9473

District Office
800 W Railroad St., Bldg. W4 #G3
Weslaco, TX 78596
Tel: (956) 447-9473 Fax: (956) 447-8683

Aaron Pena (D-40th District)
Capitol Office
P.O. Box 2910 #EXT E1.512
Austin, TX 78768
Tel: (512) 463-0426 Fax: (512) 463-0043

District Office
1108 S Closner
Edinburg, TX 78539
Tel: (956) 383-7444 Fax: (956) 383-7379

Veronica Gonzales (D-41st District)
Capitol Office
P.O. Box 2910 #EXT E2.302
Austin, TX 78768
Tel: (512) 463-0578 Fax: (512) 475-1700

Richard Raymond (D-42nd District)
Capitol Office
P.O. Box 2910 #EXT E2.902
Austin, TX 78768
Tel: (512) 463-0558 Fax: (512) 463-6296

District Office
City Hall, 3rd Fl., 1110 Houston St.
Laredo, TX 78040
Tel: (956) 753-7722 Fax: (956) 753-7729

Juan Escobar (D-43rd District)
Capitol Office
P.O. Box 2910 #CAP E2.704
Austin, TX 78768
Tel: (512) 463-0666 Fax: (512) 463-1765

District Office
P.O. Box 2910
Austin, TX 78768
Tel: (512) 463-0666

Eddie Rodriguez (D-51st District)
Capitol Office
P.O. Box 2910 #EXT E2.412
Austin, TX 78768
Tel: (512) 463-0674 Fax: (512) 463-5896

District Office
P.O. Box 2910
Austin, TX 78768
Tel: (512) 463-0674

Pete Gallego (D-74th District)
Capitol Office
P.O. Box 2910 #CAP 4S.05
Austin, TX 78768
Tel: (512) 463-0566 Fax: (512) 263-9408

District Office
P.O. Box 777
Alpine, TX 79831
Tel: (432) 837-7383 Fax: (432) 837-1153

Chente Quintanilla (D-75th District)
Capitol Office
P.O. Box 2910 #EXT E1.218
Austin, TX 78768
Tel: (512) 463-0613 Fax: (512) 463-1237

District Office
120 N Horizon #A-112
El Paso, TX 79927
Tel: (915) 859-3111 Fax: (915) 859-3120

Norma Chavez (D-76th District)
Capitol Office
P.O. Box 2910 #EXT E2.214
Austin, TX 78768
Tel: (512) 463-0622 Fax: (512) 478-6755

District Office
6070 Gateway East
El Paso, TX 79905
Tel: (915) 778-9960

Paul Moreno (D-77th District)
Capitol Office
P.O. Box 2910 #CAP 1W.09
Austin, TX 78768
Tel: (512) 463-0638 Fax: (512) 463-5896

District Office
2314 Montana
El Paso, TX 79903
Tel: (915) 544-0789

Elvira Reyna (R-101st District)
Capitol Office
P.O. Box 2910 #CAP GN.11
Austin, TX 78768
Tel: (512) 463-0464 Fax: (512) 463-1492

District Office
18601 LBJ Freeway #700
Mesquite, TX 75150
Tel: (972) 279-7030 Fax: (972) 279-9554

Rafael Anchia (D-103rd District)
Capitol Office
P.O. Box 2910 #EXT E1.316
Austin, TX 78768
Tel: (512) 463-0746 Fax: (512) 463-5826

Roberto Alonzo (D-104th District)
Capitol Office
P.O. Box 2910 #EXT E2.910
Austin, TX 78768
Tel: (512) 463-0408 Fax: (512) 463-1817

District Office
351 W Jefferson Blvd. #600, Lot 124
Dallas, TX 75208
Tel: (214) 942-7104 Fax: (214) 942-8104

Trey Martinez Fischer (D-116th District)
Capitol Office
P.O. Box 2910 #EXT E2.710
Austin, TX 78768
Tel: (512) 463-0616 Fax: (512) 463-4873

District Office
1910 Fredericksburg Rd.
San Antonio, TX 78201
Tel: (210) 737-7200 Fax: (210) 737-6700

Carlos Uresti (D-118th District)
Capitol Office
P.O. Box 2910 #EXT E1.306
Austin, TX 78768
Tel: (512) 463-0714 Fax: (512) 463-1448

District Office
1114 SW Military Dr. #103
San Antonio, TX 78221
Tel: (210) 932-2568

Robert Puente (D-119th District)
Capitol Office
P.O. Box 2910 #CAP 4N.07
Austin, TX 78768
Tel: (512) 463-0452 Fax: (512) 463-1447

District Office
2823 E Southcross
San Antonio, TX 78223
Tel: (210) 532-8899

Mike Villarreal (D-123rd District)
Capitol Office
P.O. Box 2910 #EXT E2.510
Austin, TX 78768
Tel: (512) 463-0532 Fax: (512) 463-7675

District Office
1809 Blanco Rd.
San Antonio, TX 78212
Tel: (210) 734-8937 Fax: (210) 734-0356

Jose Menendez (D-124th District)
Capitol Office
P.O. Box 2910
Austin, TX 78768
Tel: (512) 463-0634 Fax: (512) 463-7668

District Office
7121 U.S. Hwy 90 West #240
San Antonio, TX 78227
Tel: (210) 673-3579 Fax: (210) 673-3816

Joaquin Castro (D-125th District)
Capitol Office
P.O. Box 2910 #EXT E1.318
Austin, TX 78768
Tel: (512) 463-0669 Fax: (512) 463-5074

District Office
6502 Bandera #106
San Antonio, TX 78238
Tel: (210) 684-6896 Fax: (210) 684-6945

Joe E. Moreno (D-143rd District)
Capitol Office
P.O. Box 2910 #EXT E1.212
Austin, TX 78768
Tel: (512) 463-0614 Fax: (512) 463-5896

District Office
1026 Mercury Dr.
Houston, TX 77029
Tel: (713) 675-8596 Fax: (713) 675-8599

Rick Noreiga (D-145th District)
Capitol Office
P.O. Box 2910 #EXT E2.718
Austin, TX 78768
Tel: (512) 463-0732 Fax: (512) 463-5896

District Office
2900 Woodridge #305
Houston, TX 77087
Tel: (713) 649-6563 Fax: (713) 649-6454

Jessica Farrar (D-148th District)
Capitol Office
P.O. Box 2910 #CAP GW.04
Austin, TX 78768
Tel: (512) 463-0620 Fax: (512) 322-0641

District Office
P.O. Box 30099
Houston, TX 77249
Tel: (713) 691-6912 Fax: (713) 691-3363

UTAH

HOUSE OF REPRESENTATIVES

Ross I. Romero (D-25th District)
Capitol Office
W030 State Capitol Complex
Salt Lake City, UT 84114
Tel: (801) 538-1029
Email: rossromero@utah.gov

Mark A. Wheatley (D-35th District)
Capitol Office
W030 State Capitol Complex
Salt Lake City, UT 84114
Tel: (801) 538-1029
Email: markwheatley@utah.gov

WASHINGTON

SENATE

Margarita Prentice (D-11th District)
Capitol Office
316 John A. Cherberg Bldg.
Olympia, WA 98504-0411
Tel: (360) 786-7616 Fax: (360) 786-1999
Web: www1.leg.wa.gov/senate/prentice

HOUSE OF REPRESENTATIVES

Mary Skinner (R-14th District)
District Office
434 John L. O'Brien Bldg.
Olympia, WA 98504-0600
Tel: (360) 786-7810
Web: www1.leg.wa.gov/house/skinner

Phyllis Kenney (D-46th District)
District Office
330 John L. O'Brien Bldg.
Olympia, WA 98504-0600
Tel: (360) 786-7818
Web: www1.leg.wa.gov/house/kenney

District Office
12345 30th Ave. NE #E
Seattle, WA 98125
Tel: (206) 368-4491

WISCONSIN

HOUSE OF REPRESENTATIVES

Pedro A. Colon (D-8th District)
Capitol Office
P.O. Box 8952
Madison, WI 53708-8953
Tel: (608) 267-7669
Email: rep.colon@legis.state.wi.us

WYOMING

HOUSE OF REPRESENTATIVES

Floyd A. Esquibel (D-44th District)
District Office
1222 W 31st St.
Cheyenne, WY 82001
Tel: (307) 638-6529 Fax: (307) 632-6518
Email: fesquibel@house.wyoming.com

Artistic/Literature

SANDRA BENITEZ
Writer

Sandra Benitez has spent her life moving between the Latin American culture of her Puerto Rican mother and the Anglo-American culture of her father. She was born March 26, 1941 in Washington D.C., one of a pair of identical twins. Her sister, Susana, died just thirty-seven days after their birth. A year later, her father, who worked for the U.S. State Department, was assigned to Mexico, where her sister, Anita, was born. Not long after, the family transferred with him to El Salvador and this is where Sandra lived for most of the next twenty years. In Latin America, she learned that life is frail and capricious; that people can find joy in the midst of insurmountable obstacles; that, in the end, it is hope that sustains.

When Benitez reached high school age, her parents, in part to "Americanize" her, sent Sandra to her paternal grandparents' modest dairy farm in northeastern Missouri. She attended Unionville high school, returning each summer to El Salvador. In Missouri, she saw the back-breaking work and quiet self-reliance required to extract a living from the land and its animals. She learned that life is what you make it; that satisfaction comes from a job well done; that, in the end, it is steadfastness that leads to goals accomplished and dreams realized.

In 1980 she began to write fiction. It was not until thirteen years later that her first book, *A Place Where the Sea Remembers*, set in Mexico, was published. It won wonderful reviews and a number of prizes including the Barnes and Noble Discover Award, the Minnesota Book Award, and selection as a finalist for the *Los Angeles Times'* First Fiction Award. Her second book, *Bitter Grounds*, set in El Salvador, won an American Book award and a nomination for Great Britain's prestigious Orange Prize. Both books, and her third as well, have been published in more than half a dozen languages.

Sandra's third novel, *The Weight of All Things*, also set in El Salvador, tells the heart-breaking story of a nine-year-old boy caught up in a vicious civil war. While it won no awards, it garnered plenty of praise from reviewers. Her latest novel, *Night of the Radishes* draws on her unique bi-cultural background. In it, a Minnesota woman, plunged into depression by a series of family tragedies, finds a long-lost brother and redemption in the mystical atmosphere of Oaxaca, Mexico. The book was published by Hyperion in January, 2004.

Sandra's work has earned her nearly two dozen honors, awards, and grants, and she is much in demand as a teacher and speaker. In 1997, she was selected as the University of Minnesota Edelstein-Keller Distinguished Writer in Residence. In 1998 she did the Writers Community Residency for the YMCA National Writer's Voice program. In the spring of 2001 she held the Knapp Chair in Humanities as Associate Professor of Creative Writing at the University of San Diego. Other teaching residencies include Bread Loaf Writers Conference, Flight of the Mind, the University of Minnesota Split Rock Arts Program, and Hamline (Minn.) University.

Sandra is the recipient of the 2004 National Hispanic Heritage Award Honoree for Literature.

Benitez has lectured at colleges, high schools and professional organizations coast to coast. All of her first three novels, but especially *A Place Where the Sea Remembers*, are used extensively in classrooms through the country and are book group favorites as well.

Benitez lives with her husband, Jim Kondrick, in

Edina, Minnesota and has completed her first non-fiction book, *Bag Lady: How one Woman Turned the Sow's Ear of a Chronic Disease into the Silk Purse of a Fulfilling Life*. The book is an account of Sandra's thirty year struggle with ulcerative colitis, and her acceptance of the ileostomy surgery that changed her life.

JOHN LEGUIZAMO
Actor

A multi-faceted performer and Emmy Award winner, John Leguizamo has established a career that defies categorization. With boundless energy and creativity, his work in film, theatre, television, and literature covers a variety of genres, continually threatening to create a few of its own.

Recently, Leguizamo traveled to France to promote *Cronicas*, an Un Certain Regard selection at the 2004 Cannes Film Festival. *Cronicas* also screened at the 2004 Toronto Film Festival. Written and directed by Sebastien Corduro and produced and financed by Alfonso Cuaron's Monsoon Entertainment, *Cronicas* follows a popular TV reporter, (Leguizamo), who is willing to sacrifice everything to get the story of a notorious serial killer.

Next up for Leguizamo is the fourth installment of writer/director George Romero's *Night of the Living Dead* series. The zombies have taken over the earth and the survivors have barricaded themselves inside a walled city to keep out the living dead. As the wealthy hide out in skyscrapers and chaos rules the streets, the rest of the survivors must find a way to stop the evolving zombies from breaking into the city. Also starring in the film with Leguizamo are Dennis Hopper, Simon Baker, and Asia Argento. Universal Pictures will release the film in 2005.

Leguizamo recently completed work on the remake of John Carpenter's 1976 film *Assault on Precinct 13* with Laurence Fishburne, Ethan Hawke, Gabriel Byrne, Brian Dennehy, Maria Bello, and Drea de Matteo, and directed by French filmmaker Jean-Francois Richet.

Leguizamo just finished shooting *The Honeymooners* in Ireland with Cedric the Entertainer, Mike Epps, Regina Hall, Gabrielle Union, and Eric Stoltz. Directed by John Shultz, Paramount Pictures will release *The Honeymooners* in 2005.

Leguizamo also recently filmed *The Alibi* directed by Kurt Matilla and Matt Checkowski for Summit & Endgame Entertainment and will star opposite Steve Coogan and Rebecca Romijn-Stamos. The independent film tells the story of Ray Elliott (Coogan) who runs a successful business providing alibis for men and women who cheat on their spouses. Leguizamo plays Hannibal, the fierce gang-banger but tortured soul, who preys on Ray to find information about his former lover. James Marsden, Selma Blair, Sam Elliot, James Brolin, Jon Polito, and Jaime King also co-star.

Leguizamo's forthcoming projects also include *Sueño*, the story of Antonio (Leguizamo) a talented musician from Mexico who pursues his dream of becoming a singer in Los Angeles. The early 2005 Screen Gems release also features Elizabeth Pena and Nestor Serrano.

Leguizamo has also signed on to reprise his voice role as Sid, the Sloth for the *Ice Age* sequel.

Leguizamo was last seen in HBO's *Undefeated*, his feature directorial debut. Scripted by Frank Pugliese from a story by Leguizamo and Kathy DeMarco, the film is a drama about a young Latino boxer dealing with love and career success.

Leguizamo's filmography includes Franc Reyes' *Empire*, co-starring Peter Sarsgaard, Denise Richards and Isabella Rossellini, Jonas Akerlund's *Spin*, with Jason Schwartzman, Mena Suvari and Brittany Murphy, Baz Luhrmann's *Moulin Rouge*, starring Nicole Kidman and Ewan McGregor (ALMA nomination, Best Supporting Actor), *Ice Age*, Spike Lee's *Summer of Sam*, Seth Zvi Rosenfeld's *King of the Jungle* (ALMA nomination, Best Lead Actor), the cult hit *Spawn*, Baz Luhrmann's *William Shakespeare's Romeo and Juliet*, and *Dr. Doolittle*. For his performance as a sensitive drag queen in *Too Wong Foo: Thanks For Everything, Julie Newmar*, opposite Patrick Swayze and Wesley Snipes, Leguizamo garnered a Golden Globe nomination for Best Supporting Actor.

In 1991, Leguizamo created an off-Broadway sensation as the writer and performer of his one-man show, *Mambo Mouth* in which he portrayed seven different characters. He received Obie, Outer Critics Circle and Vanguardia awards for his performance. The play's HBO special led to his first television comedy special, Comedy Central's *The Talent Pool*, for which he received a CableACE Award.

Leguizamo's second one-man show, *Spic-O-Rama*, had an extended sold-out run in Chicago at the Goodman and Briar Street theaters before opening in New York. The play received numerous accolades including the *Dramatists*' Guild Hull-Warriner Award for Best American Play and the Lucille Lortel Outstanding

Achievement Award for Best Broadway Performance. Leguizamo received the Theatre World Award for Outstanding New Talent, as well as a Drama Desk Award for Best Solo Performance. *Spic-O-Rama* also aired on HBO, receiving four CableACE Awards.

Freak, Leguizamo's third one-man show, ended a successful run on Broadway in 1998. Billed as a "Semi-Demi-Quasi-Pseudo Autobiography." *Freak* was described as "scathingly funny" (*The New York Times*). Along with the Tony Award nominations for Best Play and Best Performance by a Leading Actor in a Play, Leguizamo won the Drama Desk and the Outer Critic's Circle Awards for Outstanding Solo Performance. A special presentation of *Freak*, directed by Spike Lee, aired on HBO and earned Leguizamo the Emmy Award for Outstanding Performance in a Variety or Music Program as well as a nomination for Outstanding Variety, Music, or Comedy Special.

On television, Leguizamo starred with Ray Liotta in HBO's *Point of Origin* and in ABC's mini-series, *Arabian Nights* where he played both The Ring Genie and the The Lamp Genie in the literary classic. In January 1995, Leguizamo set a precedent by creating and starring in the first Latin comedy/variety show, the Emmy award-winning, *House of Buggin* for FOX.

Raised in New York City, Leguizamo studied acting with Lee Strasberg and Wynn Handman at New York University. He was the recipient of the 2002 ALMA Award for Entertainer of the Year.

CARLOS SANTANA
Musician

At the beginning of a new century and the dawn of a new millennium, Carlos Santana is at the pinnacle of a remarkable recording and performing career. Carlos' music has spanned five decades, outlasted countless musical trends, sold more than fifty million albums, played live to upwards of thirty million fans, and garnered countless awards and honors, including a 1998 induction into the Rock 'n Roll Hall Of Fame. For over thirty years, Santana has been tirelessly creating his own unique fusion of passionate, guitar-powered music, creatively blending potent rock 'n roll with blues-driven elements, sensuous Afro-Cuban rhythms, and infusions of numerous other global music idioms. Long before 'World Music' was coined as a phrase, Santana was making it and popularizing it-perhaps even defining it and ever since Carlos and his band exploded onto the stage with an electrifying performance at the original 1969 Woodstock Festival, the world has indeed been listening.

Carlos Santana's latest album release, *Supernatural,* the 36th of his career, spotlights a legendary artist at the peak of his powers. *Supernatural* has sold in excess of ten million copies, and has been officially certified 'Dectillion Platinum' - Diamond Status by the R.I.A.A. It won nine Grammys at the 42nd Annual Grammy Awards in February 2000, including Album Of the Year, Best Rock Album, Record Of The Year and Song Of The Year, for *Smooth*, Santana's unforgettable collaboration with alternative-rock favorite Matchbox Twenty's Rob Thomas. In 1999, anyone on the planet with a radio couldn't help but feel the sultry groove of this Latin flavored, mid-tempo rock masterpiece. Carlos explains that "Some songs are just like tattoos for your brain...you hear them and they're affixed to you"-'Smooth' proved its staying power with a record 12 consecutive weeks at #1 on Billboard's Hot 100 chart, making it the longest running #1 single of 1999.

This most recent success is a tremendous high point of an artistic journey that began some fifty years ago in the Mexican village of Autlan, where at age five, Carlos was introduced to 'traditional music' by his father Jose, an accomplished mariachi violinist. The family moved to the border boom town of Tijuana in 1955, where Carlos seriously took up guitar, studying and emulating the sounds of B.B. King, John Lee Hooker, T. Bone Walker, and other greats he heard on the radio. As much as he was inspired by the early training he received from his father in traditional musical form and theory, Carlos soon realized his dream was to break free and play rock 'n roll. He began performing with local bands like The T.J.s, adding his own personal flair to the popular songs of the 1950s. As he continued playing with different bands up and down the bustling 'Tijuana Strip,' Carlos Santana began to hone his considerable skills and invent his inimitable sound.

In 1961, he moved stateside to San Francisco, joining his family, who had relocated there the previous year. Destiny had most certainly brought Carlos to the right place at the right time, planting him smack in the middle of the burgeoning and hugely influential Bay Area music scene as well as in an era-defining melting pot of cultural, political, and artistic change. In this climate, Carlos continued to evolve his unique, genre-bending style, and in 1966, he took his music to the people with the debut performance of the Santana Blues Band. For the next two years, the group was swept up in a whirlwind of acclaim and popularity that carried them from the boards of Bill Graham's historic Fillmore West to the main stage at the epochal Woodstock 'Peace, Love, Music' Festival, where on August 16, 1969, the Santana band's gale-force Latin-flavored rock was delivered to the masses.

Today, millions of fans, new and old, enjoy the work of this extraordinary musician, both through his extensive catalogue repertoire and via the phenomenal impact of *Supernatural* and its accompanying world tour. Just as Carlos Santana brought the work of Latin music icon Tito Puente to a new generation of rock fans in 1970, he now completes the circle by introducing his massive world music following to an exciting line-up of rock, pop, and hip hop personalities via Supernatural's dynamic roster. More than three decades into his career, Carlos Santana is more vital and relevant than ever, one of the biggest musical forces on the planet. His work unites our global village, transcending cultural, genre, and language barriers. Its soul-stirring celebration of life, spirit, brotherhood, and diversity is as powerful as its creator's magical guitar virtuosity. Carlos Santana is a jubilant 21st century man, and like the new century, he is just getting started.

BUSINESS

IRMA B. ELDER
Owner of the Elder Automotive Group

Irma Elder refers to herself as a "truly multi-cultural person." Born in Xicotencalt, Mexico, she moved with her family to Florida as a teen, speaking only a few words of English.

Later, while on vacation, she met James Elder and in 1963, they were married and moved to Michigan. They opened Troy Ford in April of 1967 with Mr. Elder running the business and Mrs. Elder at home raising their three children. In November 1983, James Elder died suddenly, leaving his wife to take over the reigns of the business. She became a trailblazer of sorts, the first woman to own a Ford dealership in the greater Detroit area.

Since that time, the dealership has undergone many changes, the most notable being its name change to Elder Ford in order to keep it more closely associated with the family name. Today, the Elder Automotive Group has grown to encompass not only Elder Ford, but also Aston Martin Jaguar of Troy (the number one Jaguar Dealership in the world in volume of automotive sales), Saab of Troy (the number one Saab Dealership in the United States in volume of automotive sales), Signature Ford-Lincoln-Mercury-Jeep of Owosso, Signature Ford of Perry, and Aston Martin Jaguar of Tampa, Florida. The latter dealership opened in early 2002 with much acclaim for its innovative design as well as its sales accomplishments and awards during the first year of operation.

Mrs. Elder's success is evident not only in the impressive growth of her companies but also in the recognition she continues to receive. Elder Automotive Group consistently ranks in the top ten of *Hispanic Business Magazine*'s top 500 Hispanic-owned corporations (the only female-owned corporation in the top ten). In addition, she is one of the highest ranking women in Working Woman Magazine's Top 500 Women in the country.

Irma Elder has received an abundant amount of civic awards and is in constant demand as a speaker, particularly to women's groups. She feels a great responsibility to the women of today's society and works tirelessly to convey her positive message to them. She firmly believes that women can achieve significant accomplishments. They may have a few more obstacles to overcome in pursuit of their goals, but with perseverance, success is within their reach.

Her numerous board activities cover a broad spectrum of interest and purpose. She is a former board member with groups as diverse as the Chicago Branch of the Federal Reserve Board and Lear Corporation and currently with the more local Northwood University and Oakland Family Services. The magnitude of her involvement in business and community activities make Irma Elder one of the country's most visible and dynamic community leaders.

FERNANDO ESPUELAS
Chairman and CEO of VOY, LLC

Fernando Espuelas is the Chairman and CEO of VOY, LLC, a company focused on building a cultural bridge between Latinos and the mainstream through media platforms including cable television, music, television programming, film, publishing, and internet. VOY's core brand message is that self-empowerment and optimism are the keys to success and personal fulfillment.

With a long history of building globally-recognized brands and a strong advocate of empowering and connecting Latinos, Espuelas co-founded and was formerly Chairman and CEO of StarMedia Network, a pioneering internet media company for Spanish- and Portuguese-speaking audiences worldwide. At StarMedia, he was responsible for building a network that has broken national barriers to become the most recognized internet brand in Latin America, serving twenty-five million people worldwide. Espuelas raised $500 million dollars for the company in a combination of private and public offerings.

Espuelas' visionary leadership has earned him worldwide recognition. *Time Magazine* honored him as one of the "Leaders of the Millennium," and he was recognized as a "2000 All-Star" business leader by *Crain's New York Business magazine*. The *World Economic Forum* includes him among its elite "Global Leaders of Tomorrow," and he was also a recipient of *Latin Trade Magazine*'s prestigious Bravo award. He received a *New York magazine* Award in 1999. Espuelas is a coveted speaker in the United States, Latin America, and Europe on topics related to opportunities in the Latin American and U.S. Hispanic markets. He has also received extensive broadcast, print, and online coverage throughout the world.

Espuelas has a history of linking and integrating Spanish-and Portuguese-speaking communities. He was the Managing Director of Marketing Communications for AT&T Caribbean and Latin America. Prior to AT&T, Espuelas held various senior positions at Ogilvy & Mather in both the United States and Latin America. Espuelas' career also includes positions at other advertising agencies such as Lowe & Partners and Wunderman Worldwide.

BETSY SILVA HERNANDEZ
Chief Diversity Strategist of Freddie Mac

Betsy Silva Hernandez is Freddie Mac's Chief Diversity Strategist. In this role, she oversees the development and implementation of a corporate-wide diversity strategy that integrates and aligns the senior management's diversity vision with business initiatives.

Prior to joining Freddie Mac, Betsy served as Founder and President of Silva Hernandez Consultants, an international minority-owned consulting firm specializing in strategic diversity, organizational development, coaching, career development, and related seminars and conferences. Among the companies she consulted to are Unilever, United States Postal Service, Colgate Palmolive, and Sara Lee Corporation.

Previous to founding Silva Hernandez Consultants, Betsy was Vice President of Diversity and Work-Life for American Express Company. In this pivotal role, Betsy was the corporation's chief diversity and work-life strategist. She partnered with a line of business professionals throughout the world, to develop a comprehensive global strategy to support the company's efforts in these critical areas. Betsy designed and implemented strategic plans that included the revitalization of the Corporate Executive Diversity Council, the creation of a Corporate Diversity Scorecard, the design, pilot, and roll-out of a Diversity Leadership Skills workshop, and the regeneration of the corporation's Work-Life initiative. Under Betsy's direction and leadership, Working Mother's awarded American Express the prestigious "Ten Best Companies for Working Mothers" (2002).

In addition, Betsy was Director of Workforce Diversity for Sara Lee Branded Apparel, a division of Sara Lee Corporation based in Winston-Salem, North Carolina. As Director of Workforce Diversity, she served as a consultant to the company's executive team on diversity strategies and leadership. She had corporate-wide responsibility for furthering the strategic design, development, and implementation of diversity and work-life initiatives at the domestic level. On the international level, the development of the organization's diversity strategy for the countries of Central America, Mexico, Dominican Republic, Costa Rica, and Puerto Rico were crafted under Betsy's careful guidance and leadership.

Betsy is currently a Board Member for Plays for Living in New York City. Previously, Betsy was a Board Member for the Winston-Salem, North Carolina Urban League and a commissioner for the Winston-Salem, North Carolina Human Relations Commission. She has served as Chair of the Hispanic League of the Piedmont Triad and is a co-founder of the Hispanic League.

She is a frequent guest speaker on topics that include: U.S. Latinos/Hispanics, managing personal and professional change, career development, strategic workplace diversity, balancing the demands of work and personal life, and women in the workplace. She has been a guest speaker at the National Hispanic MBA Conference, Conference Board Diversity Council,

Conference Board Diversity Workshops, Working Women's Annual Diversity Conference, Catalyst Awards Conference, RJ Reynolds Tobacco Diversity Conference, Raytheon's Women's Conference and various community organizations.

Betsy received her Bachelor of Business Administration degree in Accounting and a Master's degree in Business Administration from the Inter-American University in San German, Puerto Rico. She is certified as a Myers-Briggs analyst, certified in the world's leading multi-rater (360 degree feedback) instrument, Profilor, and is a graduate of Leadership Winston-Salem.

JOHN C. LOPEZ
Chairman of Lopez Foods, Inc.

John C. Lopez was born and raised in Glendale, Arizona and attended Northern Arizona University and the American Institute of Banking.

From 1978 to 1992, John C. Lopez and his family-run operation grew from one to four McDonald's restaurants in the Los Angeles area, where his operations had annual sales of approximately $8 million and 175 employees.

On January 2, 1992, after the sale of his restaurants in Los Angeles, John C. Lopez purchased Normac Foods located in Oklahoma City, Oklahoma, where he was elected Chairman and Chief Executive Officer. On November 27, 1995, he changed the company name to Lopez Foods, Inc. This marked the dawning of a new era in the company's relationship to its customers and the community in which it operated.

Today, Lopez Foods, Inc. is a "state of the art" meat processing plant that supplies all-beef hamburger patties, pork breakfast sausage, and Canadian-style bacon to the McDonald's restaurant system, and supplies a variety of meat products to Wal-Mart Stores and Sam's Club.

John's major achievement at Lopez Foods has been the "McDonaldization" of the company's culture. Through implementation of a Total Quality Management philosophy and commitment to viable goals, action plans, and accountability, Lopez Foods has become a benchmark in the meat processing industry. And in recognition, *Hispanic Business Magazine* named Lopez its 2002 "Entrepreneur of the Year" from fifteen finalists representing the nation's foremost Latino-owned businesses.

As of 2004, Lopez Foods employs over 800 associates throughout its corporate headquarters and two plants located in Oklahoma City, Oklahoma and Columbus, Nebraska; and its annual sales exceed $400 million. Over 300 associates operate the Oklahoma City facility around the clock, making the company one of the city's major employers—and with production of approximately 200 million pounds per year. It is also one of the city's leading manufacturers.

John and his wife Patricia have three married daughters and two married sons. John's strong belief in a healthy family life is echoed in the direction he leads Lopez Foods and the path in which he leads his own family. Daughters Kathy Thorley, Kristy Berdin, and Karen McWilliams are McDonald's owners/operators in the Oklahoma and Texas regions. His oldest son, John Patrick, is Assistant Vice President of Operations; and youngest son, Dave Lopez, is Assistant Vice President of Purchasing.

John is proud of Lopez Foods' association with McDonald's and the "ketchup" that runs through the veins of his entire family. He feels fortunate to be a supplier to the McDonald's and Wal-Mart systems and looks forward to continuing these enduring relationships.

Communication/Media

LINDA CHAVEZ
President of the Center for Equal Opportunity

Linda Chavez is president of the Center for Equal Opportunity, a non-profit public policy research organization in Sterling, Virginia. She also writes a weekly syndicated column that appears in newspapers across the country, is a political analyst for FOX News Channel, and hosts a nationally syndicated, daily radio show on Liberty Broadcasting. Chavez authored *Out of the Barrio: Toward a New Politics of Hispanic Assimilation* (Basic Books 1991), which the *Denver Post* described as a book that "should explode the stereotypes about Hispanics that have clouded the minds of patronizing liberals and xenophobic conservatives alike." *National Review* described Chavez's memoir, *An Unlikely Conservative: The Transformation of an Ex-Liberal* (Basic Books 2002), as a "brilliant, provocative, and moving book." Chavez's latest book, *Betrayal: How Union Bosses Shake Down Their Members and Corrupt American Politics* (Crown Books, 2004), describes how unions divert hundreds of millions of dollars into political campaigns, often without their members' knowledge or permission and the public policy consequences that ensue. In 2000, Chavez was honored by the Library of Congress as a "Living Legend" for her contributions to America's cultural and historical legacy. In January 2001, Chavez was President George W. Bush's nominee for Secretary of Labor until she withdrew her name from consideration.

Chavez has held a number of appointed positions, among them Chairman, National Commission on Migrant Education (1988-1992); White House Director of Public Liaison (1985); Staff Director of the U.S. Commission on Civil Rights (1983-1985); and she was a member of the Administrative Conference of the United States (1984-1986). Chavez was the Republican nominee for U.S. Senator from Maryland in 1986. In 1992, she was elected by the United Nations' Human Rights Commission to serve a four-year term as U.S. Expert to the U.N. Sub-commission on the Prevention of Discrimination and Protection of Minorities.

Chavez was also editor of the prize-winning quarterly journal *American Educator* (1977-1983), published by the American Federation of Teachers, where she also served as assistant to AFT president Al Shanker (1982-1983) and assistant director of legislation (1975-1977).

Chavez serves on the Board of Directors of ABM Industries, Inc., as well as on boards of several non-profit organizations. She is a member of the Council on Foreign Relations and was Co-Chair of the Council's Committee on Diversity (1998-2000).

Chavez was born in Albuquerque, NM, on June 17, 1947, received a Bachelor of Arts degree from the University of Colorado in 1970. She is married and is the mother of three sons. She currently lives in Reston, Virginia.

GISELLE FERNANDEZ-FARRAND
Television Journalist and Producer

As one of television's most seasoned young journalists, Giselle Fernandez-Farrand is president of her own production company, Skinny Hippo Productions. There she develops programs for cable network television and has several projects in the developmental stage, all on subjects close to her heart.

Most recently, Fernandez co-anchored the KTLA Morning News on Tribune's KTLA WB5 in Los Angeles. Fernandez is also working on more episodes of her successful talk show, "Café Olé with Giselle Fernandez." In association with SiTV and Baruch Entertainment, Fernandez is taking her up-beat show to English-language stations in an attempt to bring more Latino-themed programming to mainstream television.

Fernandez is also launching her own maverick Internet company designed to meet the specific needs of Latinas on-line in America. In conjunction with Creative Artists Agency and the founding partners of the very successful Inktomi.com and Consorio.com, she plans to launch an exciting gateway for the empowerment of the Latin woman. SoyMujer.com will be an all-purpose bi-lingual destination. She also sponsors LAStories.com where people can share stories about life in Los Angeles.

Known over the past decade for her coverage of international news stories and major events, Fernandez has made significant contributions to the CBS and NBC networks. Among her numerous posts, Fernandez anchored NBC's weekend edition of the "Today Show" and Sunday edition of the "NBC Nightly News." She also handled special and foreign assignments for the NBC network. Prior to that, Fernandez served at CBS News substituting for Paula Zahn on "CBS This Morning," Dan Rather on the "CBS Evening News" and Connie Chung on the "CBS Weekend News." Additionally, Fernandez was a regular contributor to CBS "Sunday Morning," "Face the Nation" and "48 Hours." Her coverage of international news stories and interviews with global leaders garnered this news veteran five Emmy Awards.

In a brief three-year departure from serious reporting, Fernandez, known for her unique style of interviewing, co-hosted "This Week in History," a one-hour weekly documentary series profiling famous people and events in history on A&E Network's History Channel and profiled Hollywood's a-list celebrities as co-host of NBC's nightly entertainment news magazine, "Access Hollywood." From Barbra Streisand to Sharon Stone to Robert Redford and Tom Cruise, Fernandez was a favorite and highly regarded as one of the finest interviewers in Hollywood. In the words of Oprah Winfrey after a Fernandez profile, the talk show Queen summed it up best with, "She's a magical girl."

Born in Mexico and raised in Southern California, Fernandez is the daughter of a Jewish mother and renowned Mexican flamenco dancer father. Her ethnic heritage inspired her to refer to herself as the original "Kosher Burrito." As a young child touring Mexico with her mother, who was researching a doctoral thesis in Mexican folklore, Fernandez developed her passion for journalism. Rich with knowledge and filled with excitement, the experience of exploring Mexican pueblos and gathering mystical stories inspired her to pursue a career in journalism.

Majoring in journalism at Sacramento State University in northern California, Fernandez landed her first on-air job in Pueblo, Colorado following graduation. Through the years, she has anchored and reported in top positions in Los Angeles, Chicago, and Miami before being elevated to a career in network news in New York.

Away from the cameras, Fernandez is busy covering her other passions. She actively lectures on the subjects of Latina empowerment, health and fitness, spas, and alternative approaches to medicine and healing. She has been a guest editor for both *Shape* and *Living Fit* magazines and writes feature articles on the latest in the fields of health and fitness.

A Children's Hospital Los Angeles board of trustees member, Fernandez is also very active with several charities that raise money and awareness for breast cancer research, education, and treatment. She is an active supporter of "Revlon's Run/Walk for Women" and for the second year is spokesperson for "Race For The Cure," an annual event benefiting the Susan G. Komen Breast Cancer Foundation. Fernandez is also a member of the Smithsonian National Board for Latino Initiatives and an active champion in the Latino community. In addition, she supports the Children's Hospital of Los Angeles and the Beit Issie Shapiro Foundation, a charity which helps developmentally disabled children in Israel.

Fernandez is an avid collector of Latin American art and the work of famous women photographers.

Her passion for researching the lives of daring dames and maverick women throughout history is evident not only in her extensive library but also at her own web site, DaringDames.com. She herself is an amateur photographer and filmmaker. Her passions also include running, hiking with her dogs and tennis. Fernandez splits her time between Los Angeles and Fiji and lives with her husband, John Farrand, former CEO of Panavision, Inc.

HERB SCANNELL
President of the MTV Networks Group

Herb Scannell is MTV Networks Group President and President, Nickelodeon Networks. In this position, Mr. Scannell is a member of the MTV Networks Management Committee and plays a lead role in the overall management of the company.

Mr. Scannell is responsible for all creative and business operations at Nickelodeon, the number one kid's entertainment brand; Nickelodeon's digital television offerings Noggin/The N, Nickelodeon Games and Sports and NickToons Television; TV Land, the highest rated cable network to launch within the past eight years; and the first network for men, Spike TV. Additionally, Mr Scannell oversees Paramount Parks and Viacom Consumer Products.

Under Mr. Scannell's leadership, Nickelodeon has been the number one-rated cable network for over nine consecutive years in total day ratings. He has successfully led Nickelodeon's continuing innovations in original TV programming for kids and expanded Nickelodeon's brand into feature films, consumer products, magazines, online, and live theatrical shows. Nickelodeon now reaches over 283 million homes in 162 territories around the world and provides kids programming in 30 different languages. Honored with numerous awards, including NAMIC Vision, Imagen, Parent's Choice, and The Peabody Award, Mr. Scannell and Nickelodeon received acclaim by critics and advocates for its continued leadership and groundbreaking commitment to diversity with shows such as *Dora The Explorer, The Brothers Garcia, Little Bill and Romeo!*

Nickelodeon is the preeminent producer of original programming for kids on television. In 1996, Mr.

Scannell secured a $350 million investment in original animation for Nickelodeon, which resulted in the construction of Nicktoons Studio in Burbank, CA, the first animation studio constructed in Los Angeles in thirty-five years. Mr. Scannell also commissioned the creation of a digital animation studio in New York City, NY to compliment Nickelodeon's studio facilities in Orlando, FL and Hollywood, CA. The results of this investment have been a string of the most popular animated kids' shows in TV history, including *Rugrats* to *Dora the Explorer, Jimmy Neutron, Boy Genius, Hey Arnold!, The Fairly Odd Parents* and the number one kids show in television, *SpongeBob SquarePants*.

In 1996, following the runaway popularity of Nick at Nite, Mr. Scannell successfully launched TV Land, a 24-hour network dedicated to Classic TV. TV Land has proven to be one of cable television's most successful network launches. Now seen in more than eighty-five million homes, TV Land's broad mix of sitcoms, westerns, variety shows, and drama have made the network a consistent top ten network. In 2004, Mr. Scannell oversaw TV Land's slate of new, original programming such as *Still Brady…After All These Years* and the *Top 10 series*, making it the channel's most watched year ever.

Mr. Scannell has continued Nickelodeon's tradition of innovation in expanding the company's portfolio into digital television by launching Noggin, a commercial-free educational network which also includes the N, its night time block for teens; Nick Games & Sports, a channel devoted to kids play; and Nicktoons TV, a channel featuring 24-hours of animation from Nickelodeon's award-winning library. With his leadership, Nickelodeon has become the most popular provider of kids' entertainment in the online world, reaching more kids (6-12) through nick.com than any other entertainment online provider.

Prior to his appointment as President in February 1996, Scannell served as Executive Vice President for Nickelodeon Network and U.S. Television. In that position, he oversaw the management and strategic direction of the Nickelodeon and Nick at Nite cable television networks. Additionally, he engineered the development of the network's popular Nicktoons animated series and Nick Jr., the network's weekday pre-school programming block.

Before joining Nickelodeon, Scannell was Director of Program Promotion for Showtime/The Movie Channel, developing promotional campaigns for *The Honeymooners*: *The Lost Episodes*, for which he won a number of CTAM awards and BPME awards, including "Best Campaign."

Scannell holds a Bachelor of Arts degree in English and History from Boston College. He and his wife, Sarah, reside in Manhattan with their daughters: Caroline and Isabella.

Community

JUAN GONZALEZ
President of The National Association of Hispanic Journalists (NAHJ)

Juan Gonzalez, the new president of NAHJ, has been a professional journalist for twenty-five years and a staff columnist at the *New York Daily News* since 1987. He has covered a wide range of national and international events, including the U.S. invasion of Panama, political troubles in Mexico and the Caribbean, the 1992 Los Angeles riot, and the 1999 Seattle protests against the World Trade Organization. His columns on inner city problems, race relations, and the labor movement have won him numerous awards, including the 1998 George Polk Award for commentary.

His work has appeared in scores of publications, including *Mademoiselle, The Nation, The Source*, and *Hispanic Magazine*. He is also a co-host of Pacifica Radio's daily morning news magazine, *Democracy Now*, and a visiting professor in public policy at Brooklyn College of the City University of New York and has twice been named to *Hispanic Business* magazine's annual list of the nation's 100 Most Influential Hispanics. In 2004, he received the Hispanic Heritage Award for Leadership.

He was a founding member of NAHJ and is considered one of the founding fathers of Unity, Journalists of Color. Throughout his career, he has also been an active member of the Newspaper Guild, having chaired the strike committees of the 1985 strike at the *Philadelphia Inquirer* and *Daily News*, and the 1990-91 strike at the *New York Daily News*. Before entering journalism, Gonzalez was already well-known in the Latino community as a founder of the Young Lords, a 1960s Puerto Rican civil rights group, and as a president of the National Congress for Puerto Rican Rights.

Born in Ponce, Puerto Rico, he grew up in New York City and graduated from Columbia University where he was a leader of the 1968 Columbia student strike against the Vietnam War and university racism.

ROBERTO SURO
Director of the Pew Hispanic Center

Roberto Suro is director of the Pew Hispanic Center, a Washington-based research and policy analysis organization. The Center is a project of the University of Southern California Annenberg School for Communication, where Suro is on the faculty as a research professor. The Center was founded in July, 2001 with support from the Pew Charitable Trusts. Through public opinion surveys and a variety of research projects, the Center serves as a source of non-partisan information on the rapid growth of the Latino population and its implications for the nation as a whole.

A former journalist, Suro has nearly thirty years of experience writing on Hispanic issues and immigration. He is author of *Strangers Among Us: Latino Lives in a Changing America*, (Vintage) as well as numerous reports, articles, and other publications regarding the growth of the Latino population. During his career in journalism Suro worked for *TIME Magazine*, *The New York Times*, *The Washington Post* and other publications. He worked extensively in Washington, did tours as a domestic correspondent in Chicago and Houston and was posted as a foreign correspondent in Latin America, Europe, and the Middle East. He is a graduate of Yale University (BA, 1973) and Columbia University (MS, 1974).

research at UC Santa Barbara. Before joining UC Santa Barbara in 1996, she was chief scientist at NASA from 1993 to 1996, serving as the primary scientific advisor to the NASA administrator and the principal interface between NASA headquarters and the broader scientific community. Córdova headed the department of astronomy and astrophysics at Pennsylvania State University from 1989 to 1993 and served as deputy group leader of the Space Astronomy and Astrophysics Group at the Los Alamos National Laboratory from 1979 to 1989.

Córdova's scientific career contributions have been in the areas of observational and experimental astrophysics, multi-spectral research on X-ray and gamma ray sources, and space-borne instrumentation. She has published nearly 140 scientific papers, is the winner of NASA's highest honor, the Distinguished Service Medal, and was recognized as a 2000 Kilby Laureate, a prestigious award honoring an individual for contributions to society through science, technology, innovation, invention, and education, which was named for the internationally acclaimed inventor of the integrated circuit, Nobel Laureate, Jack St. Clair Kilby.

The oldest of twelve children, Córdova attended high school in La Puente, Calif., east of Los Angeles. She then entered Stanford University, where she graduated cum laude with a bachelor's degree in English and, among other activities, conducted anthropology field work in a Zapotec Indian pueblo in Oaxaca, Mexico. She attained a Ph.D. in physics from the California Institute of Technology in 1979.

Córdova is married to Christian J. Foster, a science educator, and has two teenage children: Anne-Catherine and Stephen.

Education

FRANCE A. CÓRDOVA
Chancellor of the University of California, Riverside

Chancellor Córdova assumed her duties as the seventh chancellor of the University of California, Riverside on July 1, 2002. Prior to joining UC Riverside, Córdova, a nationally recognized astrophysicist, served as professor of physics and vice chancellor for

DR. GLORIA G. RODRIGUEZ
Founder, President and CEO of AVANCE

Dr. Gloria G. Rodriguez is the founder, president and CEO of AVANCE, Inc. In 1973, as a former schoolteacher, she founded a nonprofit organization that would help low-income parents get their children, birth to three years of age, ready for school as a means of reducing the high dropout rate among Latinos. AVANCE's successful proven model and Dr. Rodriguez have received tremendous national and local recognition. AVANCE has been featured in the

New York Times (4 times), including two editorials, *ABC World News Tonight*, *Good Morning America*, *McNeil Lehrer News Hour*, and included in three First Ladies books (Barbara Bush, *First Teachers*; Hillary Clinton, *It Takes a Village*, and Rosalyn Carter, *Helping Someone with Mental Illness*.) AVANCE has been visited by Prince Charles and First Lady Barbara Bush. Dr. Rodriguez was featured in *Parade Magazine*, received the Parent Action Award from *Parent's Magazine*, was included in *Working Mother's Magazine* as one of twenty-five influential working mothers; was included several times as one of 100 leading Hispanics in *Hispanic Business Magazine*; was inducted in the Texas Hall of Fame; received the Attitude Award by Life Time Television, the Distinguish Service to Education Award from the National Association of School Principals and in 2004 received the Hispanic Heritage Award in Education at the Kennedy Center in Washington, DC. In San Antonio, Dr Rodriguez was named Woman of the Year for the San Antonio Light, was inducted into the San Antonio, Edgewood Hall of Fame and Leadership San Antonio Hall of Fame. She also received the Maldef Award, the Sr. Benetia Award and the Avenida Guadalupe Award. Dr. Rodriguez is the author of *Raising Nuestros Niños*: *Bringing Up Latino Children in a Bicultural World* by Simon and Schuster. Her works are included at the Eugene Barker Center on Texas History at UT of Austin.

Dr. Rodriguez has her Ph.D. in Early Childhood Education from UT of Austin, is married to Salvador C. Rodriguez and is the mother of three children.

Government

R. ALEXANDER ACOSTA

Assistant Attorney General
U.S. Department of Justice Civil Rights Division

R. Alexander Acosta was selected by President Bush, and confirmed by the Senate, to serve as Assistant Attorney General for the Civil Rights Division of the United States Department of Justice on August 22, 2003. The Civil Rights Division is responsible  for enforcing federal civil rights statutes, including those statutes that prohibit discrimination on the basis of race, sex, disability, religion, and national origin in education, employment, credit, housing, public accommodations and facilities, voting, and certain federally funded and conducted programs.

Prior to his service as Assistant Attorney General, Mr. Acosta was selected by President Bush, and confirmed by the Senate, as a Member of the National Labor Relations Board ("NLRB"), an independent federal agency responsible for administering and interpreting the National Labor Relations Act, the principal private-sector national statute regulating labor relations. Mr. Acosta has also served as Principal Deputy Assistant Attorney General in the Civil Rights Division.

A native of Florida, Mr. Acosta earned his bachelor's degree from Harvard College and his law degree from the Harvard Law School. After graduation, he served as a law clerk on the U.S. Court of Appeals for the Third Circuit and then worked at the Washington office of the Kirkland and Ellis law firm, where he specialized in employment and labor issues.

Mr. Acosta is the first Hispanic to serve as an Assistant Attorney General at the Department of Justice. He is a 2004 recipient of the Arab American Anti-Discrimination Committee Michigan's Distinguished Leadership Award, the 2003 Mexican-American Legal Defense and Education Fund's Excellence in Government Service Award, and the 2003 DC Hispanic Bar Association's Hugh A. Johnson, Jr. Memorial Award. He has also taught several classes on employment law, disability-based discrimination law, and civil rights law at the George Mason School of Law.

ANNA ESCOBEDO CABRAL

Treasurer
US Department of the Treasury

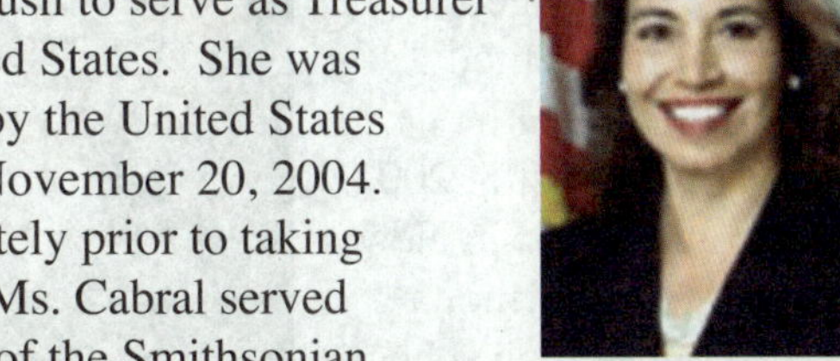

Anna Escobedo Cabral was nominated on July 22, 2004, by President Bush to serve as Treasurer of the United States. She was confirmed by the United States Senate on November 20, 2004.

Immediately prior to taking this office, Ms. Cabral served as Director of the Smithsonian Institution's Center for Latino Initiatives, where she led a pan-institutional effort to improve Latino representation in exhibits, and public programming among the Institution's nineteen museums, five research centers, and the National Zoo. From 1999 to 2003, Ms. Cabral served as President and CEO of the Hispanic Association on Corporate Responsibility, a non-profit organization headquartered in Washington, DC, which partners with Fortune 500 companies to increase Hispanic representation in employment, procurement, philanthropy, and governance. Under her leadership, the organization published a best practices series, and instituted a partnership with Harvard Business School to provide executive training programs in Corporate Governance Best Practices to community leaders.

From 1993 to 1999, Ms. Cabral served as Deputy Staff Director for the United States Senate Judiciary Committee under Chairman Orrin G. Hatch. The Committee's jurisdiction ranges from oversight of the Department of Justice and our nation's criminal and drug enforcement laws to approving federal judicial nominations, and it includes review of immigration, antitrust, patents and trademark, and technology-related legislation. In addition, she simultaneously served as Executive Staff Director of the U.S. Senate Republican Conference Task Force on Hispanic Affairs, a position she held since 1991. Ms. Cabral managed this task force of twenty-five senators dedicated to ensuring that the concerns and needs of the Hispanic community are addressed by Congress through legislation.

A native of California, Ms. Cabral majored in Political Science from the University of California, Davis, and earned a Master's degree in Public Administration with an emphasis in international trade and finance from the John F. Kennedy School of Government at Harvard University.

Ms. Cabral and her husband Victor have four children: Raquel, Viana, Catalina, and Victor Christopher.

VICE ADMIRAL RICHARD H. CARMONA, M.D., M.P.H., F.A.C.S.
United States Surgeon General

Vice Admiral Richard H. Carmona was sworn in as the 17th Surgeon General of the United States Public Health Service on August 5, 2002.

Born and raised in New York City, Dr. Carmona dropped out of high school and enlisted in the U.S. Army in 1967. While enlisted, he received his Army General Equivalency Diploma, joined the Army's Special Forces, ultimately becoming a combat-decorated Vietnam veteran, and began his career in medicine.

After leaving active duty, Dr. Carmona attended Bronx Community College of the City University of New York, where he earned his associate of arts degree. He later attended and graduated from the University of California, San Francisco, with a Bachelor of Science degree (1977) and medical degree (1979). At the University of California Medical School, Dr. Carmona was awarded the prestigious gold headed cane as the top graduate. He has also earned a Masters of Public Health from the University of Arizona (1998).

Dr. Carmona has worked in various positions in the medical field including paramedic, registered nurse, and physician. Dr. Carmona completed a surgical residency at the University of California, San Francisco, and a National Institutes of Health-sponsored fellowship in trauma, burns, and critical care. Dr. Carmona is a Fellow of the American College of Surgeons, and is also certified in correctional health care and in quality assurance.

Prior to being named Surgeon General, Dr. Carmona was the chairman of the State of Arizona Southern Regional Emergency Medical System, a professor of surgery, public health, and family and community medicine at the University of Arizona, and the Pima County Sheriff's Department surgeon and deputy sheriff.

Dr. Carmona has also held progressive positions of responsibility as chief medical officer, hospital chief executive officer, public health officer, and finally chief executive officer of the Pima county health care system. He has also served as a medical director of police and fire departments and is a fully-qualified peace officer with expertise in special operations and emergency preparedness, including weapons of mass destruction.

Dr. Carmona has published extensively and received numerous awards, decorations, and local and national recognition for his achievements. A strong supporter of community service, he has served on community and national boards and provided leadership to many diverse organizations.

Military

BRIGADIER GENERAL JOSEPH V. MEDINA
Commander, Expeditionary Strike Group Three

Brigadier General Medina received his commission in 1976, following graduation from the United States Naval Academy. He holds a Bachelor of Science (Physics) and a Master of Science (Systems Management) from the University of Southern California.

Upon completion of The Basic School, Quantico, VA, he was assigned to the 5th Marine Regiment, 1st Marine Division. He served as a Rifle Platoon Commander, Assistant Adjutant, Company Commander for Company F, 2nd Battalion, 5th Marines, and culminated this tour as the Headquarters Company Commander, 5th Marines. He transferred in April 1980 to 3rd Marine Division in Okinawa, Japan, and was assigned to 2nd Battalion, 4th Marines as the Battalion Adjutant and later as Company Commander, Company F.

Returning from Okinawa in May 1981, he reported to Marine Corps Recruiting Station, Seattle, WA, where he served as Executive Officer. Following this assignment, he completed Amphibious Warfare School as an Honor graduate in May 1985 and was transferred to 3rd Battalion, 5th Marines, 1st Marine Division. He served as Company Commander, Weapons Company from June 1985 to January 1987 until reassignment as the Battalion S-3/Operations Officer until July 1988.

In July 1988, then Major Medina joined the Naval ROTC unit at Penn State University as the Marine Officer Instructor/Associate Professor of Naval Science. In August 1991, he reported to the Marine Corps Command and Staff College as a student.

Upon completion of school as a distinguished graduate in June 1992, he was reassigned to the staff of The Basic School where he served as the Company Commander for two Basic Officer Courses. Upon selection to Lieutenant Colonel, he was assigned as the Instructional Group Chief/Chief Instructor. During October 1994, he transferred to 2nd Marine Division, where he was initially assigned to the G-3/Operations Section. In May 1995, he assumed command of 3rd Battalion, 2nd Marine Regiment. During his tour as Battalion Commander, the battalion deployed to Guantanamo Bay, Cuba in Support of JTF-160 for Operation SEA SIGNAL in 1995 and to Okinawa, Japan as part of the Unit Deployment Program in 1996. Upon relinquishment of his command in February 1997, he was reassigned as Executive Officer, 2nd Marines until being transferred to the NATO Defense College, Rome, Italy in August 1997.

Upon graduation from the NATO Defense College in February 1998, he was transferred to Headquarters, U.S. European Command where he was assigned as Contingency Plans Branch Chief, J3 Directorate. With the onset of the Kosovo Crisis, he simultaneously served as Chief, Kosovo Plans Group for Operations NOBLE ANVIL/ALLIED FORCE and JOINT GUARDIAN from August 1998 until June 1999. Upon his promotion to Colonel in June 1999, he was assigned as the Chief, Operational Plans Division (J35), Operations Directorate. He was transferred to Marine Corps Recruiting Command at Quantico, VA in January 2000, as the G-3, Enlisted Recruiting Operations & Plans. He assumed command of the 3rd Marine Regiment in June 2001, and served as Commander, SPMAGTF-3 for four HCAXs and RIMPAC-02 during this period. He was advanced to Brigadier General in November 2003, and assumed command of the newly established Expeditionary Strike Group Three (ESG-3). Brigadier General Medina is currently deployed with ESG-3 to the CENTCOM AOR in USS ESSEX (LHD 2) serving as Commander, Task Force 58, operating in the North Arabian Gulf in support of Operation IRAQI FREEDOM.

Brigadier General Medina's personal decorations include: Defense Superior Service Medal, Legion of Merit, Defense Meritorious Service Medal, Meritorious Service Medal with two gold stars, Joint Service Commendation Medal, and the Navy Commendation Medal with two Gold Stars.

Science

DAVID E. HAYES-BAUTISTA, PH.D
Professor of Medicine, UCLA

Dr. David Hayes-Bautista is internationally recognized for his research on the culture and health of Latinos, focusing on the dynamics and processes of the health status of that population. One important outcome of his growing body of work, and a significant contribution to the field of medicine, was his establishment of the UCLA Center for the Study of Latino Health and Culture (CESLAC). CESLAC houses Dr. Hayes-Bautista's research and provides a significant resource for training medical students, health care providers, and public health officials to manage the care of Latino patients effectively, efficiently, and economically. The energetic and inspirational professor teaches a section of the Doctoring course and one on Health in the Latino Population for our medical students. He is also the director of the UCLA/Drew Center of Excellence for Minority Medical Education, which is dedicated to increasing the number of minority physicians in clinical and academic careers. In addition to those responsibilities, Dr. Hayes-Bautista serves on a number of important University, national, regional, local, and international bodies. He has an important voice in the national and statewide dialogue concerning the provision and access to health care. Dr. Hayes-Bautista is also the faculty advisor for the UCLA/Drew chapter of the Latino Medical Student Association, the pre-medical group Chicanos/Latinos for Community Medicine (CCM), and he is a senior advisor to the California Latino Medical Association.

To date Dr. Hayes-Bautista has produced over eighty publications, including books, monographs, peer-reviewed articles, and editorials. His work has appeared in a variety of medical journals including *Family Medicine*, the *American Journal of Public Health*, *Family Practice*, *Academic Medicine* and *Salud Publica de Mexico*. He has authored over forty proposals for funded research projects. In addition, he has given over 680 presentations to medical and lay communities and to government agencies concerned with our nation's health care delivery system. Dr. Hayes-Bautista has received more than fifty commendations for his work. These include the City of Los Angeles Mayor's Award, the March of Dimes Viva Los Ninos Award, the Lifetime Achievement in Health Sciences Eagle Award, and the Surgeon General's Hispanic/Latino Health Initiative Certificate.

Dr. Hayes-Bautista, a graduate of the University of California, Berkeley, earned his Master's in 1971 and his Doctorate in Medical Sociology from the University of California, San Francisco in 1974. He came to UCLA from U.C. Berkeley School of Public Health to head the UCLA Chicano Studies Research Center in 1986. He joined the faculty of the UCLA School of Medicine in 1987. Dr. Hayes-Bautista is married to Maria Hayes-Bautista, RN, MPH who is a principal staff associate of CESLAC. They are the proud parents of one daughter, Catalina, and one son, Diego.

OLGA M. DOMINGUEZ
Deputy Assistant Administrator, Office of Management Systems (NASA)

Olga Dominguez is the Deputy Assistant Administrator for the Office of Management Systems in Washington DC. As the Deputy, she provides support to the Assistant Administrator and the NASA Administrator on leadership, management oversight, guidance, and coordination of institutional management systems, processes, and facilities for environmental, real property, logistics, aircraft, management controls, and ISO 9001. Ms. Dominguez is a member of the Department of Defense Joint Group on Pollution Prevention, representing NASA's interests within this forum and in the international community. Previously at NASA, she was the Director of the Environmental Management Division. As director, she was responsible for establishing Agency environmental policy and guidance, developing, advocating, and managing Agency-level environmental budgets, and providing support to the NASA Administrator on environmental issues. She joined NASA Headquarters in 1990 and became a member of the United States of America Senior Executive Service in 1998. Previously, she directed the Environmental Program for the Navy's David Taylor Research Laboratories and was a lead enforcement inspector for the State of Maryland's Department of the Environment and the Prince Georges Health Department.

Ms. Dominguez has received several medals and awards since coming to NASA. They include the Presidential Award for Leadership in Energy Management from President Bush in 2001; Stennis Space Centers Frontline Award; NASA's Cooperative External Achievement Award; NASA's Medal for Outstanding Leadership; she was named as one of "The 80 Elite Hispanic Women" by the *Hispanic Business* magazine in April of 2002; and she received the President's Meritorious Executive Rank award in 2002.

Ms. Dominguez's educational background includes a Bachelor of Science in Fish and Wildlife Management with emphasis in Zoology. She brings over twenty-four years of experience in environmental management spanning local, state, and federal governments. Ms. Dominguez's career has spanned many levels and challenges including enforcement, design, audit, oversight, budget development and advocacy, development of field and corporate level policy and guidance, process reengineering, and leadership. She and her family reside in Annapolis, MD

MARIO J. MOLINA
Professor

Mario J. Molina, a professor at the Massachusetts Institute of Technology who won the 1995 Nobel Prize in Chemistry for his role in elucidating the threat to the Earth's ozone layer of chlorofluorocarbon gases, or CFCs, will join the faculty at the University of California, San Diego.

Molina, UCSD's sixteenth Nobel Prizewinner, will be a professor in UCSD's Department of Chemistry and Biochemistry and in the Center for Atmospheric Sciences at Scripps Institution of Oceanography when he arrives on July 1. He will join a group of leading atmospheric chemists at UCSD that includes Paul Crutzen, who shared the 1995 Nobel Prize in Chemistry with Molina and F. Sherwood Rowland of UC Irvine for their work on the chemistry of atmospheric ozone.

Molina, a native of Mexico whose early research with Rowland convinced governments around the world to eliminate CFCs from spray cans and refrigerators, has focused much of his recent research on the chemistry of air pollution in the lower atmosphere. He has been working with collaborators from other countries, most notably colleagues in Mexico City, on assessing and mitigating the air pollution problems of rapidly growing cities around the world.

"Mario Molina has provided us with the means to become more responsible stewards of our global environment," said Marsha A. Chandler, Acting Chancellor of UCSD. "Environmental research is a major strength of UCSD, one that is pursued across many disciplines. And Mario Molina's atmospheric chemistry research programs in Mexico and other countries will help to strengthen UCSD's collaborations around the world."

Born in Mexico City, Molina received a bachelor's degree in chemical engineering from the Universidad Autónoma de México in 1965, a postgraduate degree in 1967 from the University of Freiburg in West Germany and a doctorate in physical chemistry in 1972 from UC Berkeley. As a postdoctoral researcher in 1974 at UC Irvine, he was a co-author with Rowland of a paper in the journal *Nature* that detailed their research on the threat to the ozone layer in the stratosphere of CFCs, then widely used as propellants in spray cans and as refrigerants in refrigerators.

He held teaching and research positions at UC Irvine, the Universidad Nacional Autónoma de México and the Jet Propulsion Laboratory at the California Institute of Technology before arriving at MIT in 1989 as a professor in the Department of Earth, Atmospheric and Planetary Sciences, and the Department of Chemistry. He was named MIT Institute Professor in 1997. He is a member of the National Academy of Sciences, the Institute of Medicine and the Pontifical Academy of Sciences. He has served on the U.S. President's Committee of Advisors in Science and Technology, the Secretary of Energy Advisory Board, National Research Council Board on Environmental Studies and Toxicology, and on the boards of U.S.-Mexico Foundation of Science and other non-profit environmental organizations.

Sports

LISA FERNANDEZ
Olympic Gold Medalist Pitcher for the U.S. Women's Softball Team

Lisa Fernandez is a three-time Olympic gold medalist pitcher for the U.S. women's softball team (2004, 2000, 1996) and regarded as the world's best all-around player. Currently a member of the Women's Sports Foundation's Board of Trustees (elected 2002), Fernandez led the U.S. national team to the 6-0 win over Canada in the gold-medal game of the 2003 U.S Cup. In 2003, she also took home gold at the Pan American Games. She won the gold medal at the 2002 U.S. Cup and at the 2002 women's softball world championship with the U.S. national team. Fernandez played for the Women's Professional Softball League gold team for the "Tour of Fastpitch Champions" in 2001. In 2000, she was ranked in *Sports Illustrated* for Women's list of "All-Time Greatest Female Athletes." In 1999, she won gold medals at the Pan American Games, the Canada Cup, and the USA softball women's national team festival, where she led all pitchers with thirty-three strikeouts in twenty-one innings. In 1998, Fernandez helped lead the U.S. national team to its fourth consecutive win at the International Softball Federation (ISF) women's world championship. She also led the California Commotion to its third straight victory in the Amateur Softball Association women's major fastpitch national championship. It was in the same year she received the U.S. Olympic Committee's Top 10 Athlete of the Year Award. Fernandez was also a member of the gold-medal-winning North Team at the 1995 U.S. Olympic Festival and, that same year, played on the team that finished second in the Canada Cup. She won gold medals at the 1994 and 1990 ISF Women's World Championship as well as at the 1993 Intercontinental Cup and the 1992 Women's

World Challenge. At the University of California-Los Angeles (UCLA), Fernandez was a four-time All-American (1993, 1992, 1991, 1990) and pitched the softball team to two NCAA titles (1992, 1990). Fernandez received the 1994 Sportswoman of the Year Award (Team) from the Women's Sports Foundation. She was a three-time recipient of the Honda Award for softball (1993, 1992, 1991) and also earned the 1993 Honda-Broderick Cup, presented to the most outstanding collegiate female athlete. Also in 1993, Fernandez was named the NCAA Athlete of the Year. She remains active in softball and motivational skills camps and clinics and has worked with the Cancer Foundation/Bone Marrow Testing Foundation and the Rescue Mission/Salvation Army. She served as a member on the Women's Sports Foundation's Athletes Council of the National Advisory Board (1994 -1999). Fernandez is an assistant softball coach at UCLA, featured in the Women's Sports Foundation book *SuperWomen: 100 Women - 100 Sports*. and the educational program GoGirlGo!

The United States Postal Service
CAREER EMPLOYMENT INFORMATION

As one of the nation's largest employers, the United States Postal Service enjoys a workforce rich in talents, abilities, and skills. We strive to make the Postal Service a great place to work and a great place for our customers to do business.

CAREER POSTAL EMPLOYMENT BENEFITS:

- **Competitive Salary**
- Paid Vacations
- **Retirement**
- Affordable Health Insurance
- **Paid Holidays**
- On-the-job Training
- **Sick Leave**
- Life Insurance
- **Promotion Opportunities**

For information on Postal employment opportunities, products, and services, visit our website @ *www.usps.com*

WE ARE AN EQUAL OPPORTUNITY EMPLOYER

U.S. Department of Labor

Join The Team
Working for the 21st Century

The Department of Labor is committed to the recruitment, development and retention of a diverse workforce that is:
- highly competent
- innovative
- focused on results and service to America's workers

The U.S. Department of Labor
is planning to hire:

Accountants/Auditors	Pension Law Specialists
Computer Specialists	Safety and Occupational
Economists	Health Specialists
Industrial Hygienist	Worker's Compensation
Investigators	Claims Examiners
Mathematical Statisticians	Workforce Development
Pension Benefits Advisors	Specialists

For specific information about DOL vacancies visit our website:
http://www.jobs.dol.gov
or write: U.S. Department of Labor
Room C-5522, Dept. OWPD
200 Constitution Avenue, N.W., Washington, DC 20210

An Equal Opportunity Employer

Federal and State Employment Offices
Oficinas de empleos federales y estatales

ALABAMA

AGRICULTURE, DEPT. OF
Southeast Region
1504-C Hwy. 31 South
Bay Minette, AL 36507
Carolyn King, HEPM
Tel: (251) 937-3297 X3
Fax: (251) 580-0026
Email: carolyn.c.king@al.usda.gov
Web: www.usda.gov

AIR FORCE, DEPT. OF THE
Maxwell AFB
42 MSS/DPC, 50 Lemay Plz., South
Maxwell AFB, AL 36112-6334
Tel: (334) 953-6558 Fax: (334) 953-6040

ARMY, DEPT. OF THE
US Army Recruiting Battalion Montgomery
775 McDonald St., Bldg. 1510 MAFB
Gunter Annex, AL 36114-6629
Tel: (334) 271-3059

**EQUAL EMPLOYMENT OPPORTUNITY
COMMISSION**
Birmingham District Office
1130 22nd St. South #2000
Birmingham, AL 35205
Bernice Williams-Kimbrough, Director
Tel: (205) 212-2100 Fax: (205) 212-2105
Web: www.eeoc.gov

NAVY, DEPT. OF THE
Navy Recruiting District, Montgomery
2400 President South Dr.
Montgomery, AL 36116
Tel: (334) 279-8543

USMC Recruiting Station, Montgomery
2853 Fair Ln., Bldg. G #64
Montgomery, AL 36116-1698
Tel: (334) 647-3110 Fax: (334) 647-3115
Web: www.marines.com

POSTAL SERVICE
Alabama District
351 24th St. North
Birmingham, AL 35203-9989
April Williams, Diversity Development
Specialist
Tel: (205) 521-0256 Fax: (205) 521-0935
Email: april.m.williams@usps.gov
Web: www.usps.com

ALASKA

AGRICULTURE, DEPT. OF
Forest Service
P.O. Box 21628
Juneau, AK 99802
Teddy Castillo, HEPM
Tel: (907) 586-8886 Fax: (907) 586-7931
Email: tcastillo@fs.fed.us
Web: www.fs.fed.us

AIR FORCE, DEPT. OF THE
Eielson AFB
354 MSS/DPC, 3125 Wabash Ave. #1
Eielson AFB, AK 99702-1720
Tel: (907) 377-2345 Fax: (907) 377-5115

Elmendorf AFB
3 MSS/DPC, 8517 20th St. #203
Elmendorf AFB, AK 99506-2400
Tel: (907) 552-4575 Fax: (907) 522-3221

NAVY, DEPT. OF THE
USMC Recruiting Sub-Station, Anchorage
800 E Diamond Blvd.
Anchorage, AK 99515
Tel: (907) 271-6473
Web: www.marines.com

ARIZONA

AIR FORCE, DEPT. OF THE
Davis-Monthan AFB
355 MSS/DPC, 5260 Granite St.
Davis-Monthan AFB, AZ 85707-3018
Tel: (520) 228-3844 Fax: (520) 228-3037

Luke AFB
56 MSS/DPC, 7883 N Litchfield Rd. #1172
Luke AFB, AZ 85309-1514
Tel: (623) 856-7761 Fax: (623) 856-3968

ARMY, DEPT. OF THE
US Army Recruiting Battalion Phoenix
1 N 1st St. #400
Phoenix, AZ 85004-2357
Tel: (602) 254-1981/253-2105

**EQUAL EMPLOYMENT OPPORTUNITY
COMMISSION**
Phoenix District Office
3300 N Central Ave. #690
Phoenix, AZ 85012-2504
Susan Grace, Acting Director
Tel: (602) 640-5000   Fax: (602) 640-5071
Web: www.eeoc.gov

**GOVERNOR'S OFFICE OF EQUAL
OPPORTUNITY**
State of Arizona
1700 W Washington Ave. #156
Phoenix, AZ 85007
Patti Campbell, Equal Employment
Opportunity Specialist
Tel: (602) 542-3711 Fax: (602) 542-3712
Email: pcampbell@az.gov
Web: www.governor.state.az.us

INTERIOR, DEPT. OF THE
Bureau of Indian Affairs
Western Region, Personnel Office
400 N 5th St., 12th Fl.
Phoenix, AZ 85004
Merle Zunigha, Personnel Officer
Tel: (602) 379-6739 Fax: (602) 379-4966

NAVY, DEPT. OF THE
Navy Recruiting District, Phoenix
P.O. Box 25368
Phoenix, AZ 85002
Tel: (602) 256-6026

USMC Recruiting Station, Phoenix
215 N 7th St. #101
Phoenix, AZ 85034-1012
Tel: (602) 256-0618 Fax: (602) 256-0618
Web: www.marines.com

POSTAL SERVICE
Arizona District
1441 E Buckeye Rd. #100
Phoenix, AZ 85034-4128
Pascual J. Torres, Hispanic Program
Specialist
Tel: (602) 223-3636 Fax: (602) 307-1323
Email: ptorres@email.usps.gov
Web: www.usps.com

Arizona District
4949 E VanBuren
Phoenix, AZ 85026
Aidea Murrieta-Penn, Diversity
Development Specialist
Tel: (602) 225-5451 Fax: (602) 225-5432
Email: aidea.d.murrietapenn@usps.com
Web: www.usps.gov

ARKANSAS

AGRICULTURE, DEPT. OF
South Central Region
2510 N Hervey #F
Hope, AR 71801-8419
Rose Webb, HEPM
Tel: (501) 301- 3174 Fax: (870) 777-3284
Email: rose.webb@ar.usda.gov
Web: www.ar.nrcs.usda.gov

AIR FORCE, DEPT. OF THE
Little Rock AFB
314 MSS/DPC, 1255 Vandenberg Dr. #227
Little Rock AFB, AR 72099-5052
Tel: (501) 987-3212 Fax: (501) 987-3212

**DEPARTMENT OF FINANCE AND
ADMINISTRATION**
State of Arkansas
Office of Administrative Services
P.O. Box 2485
1515 Bldg. #101
Little Rock, AR 72203
Jenette Manno, Manager of Human
Resources
Tel: (501) 371-6009 Fax: (501) 683-2174
Email: jenette.manno@dfa.state.ar.us
Web: www.dfa.state.ar.us

**EQUAL EMPLOYMENT OPPORTUNITY
COMMISSION**
Little Rock Area Office
820 Louisiana St. #200
Little Rock, AR 72201
Kay Klugh, Director
Tel: (501) 324-5060 Fax: (501) 324-5991
Web: www.eeoc.gov

NAVY, DEPT. OF THE
Navy Officer Recruiting Station, Fayetteville
4201 N Shilo Dr. #1285E
Fayetteville, AR 72703

Navy Officer Recruiting Station, Little Rock
1520 Riverfront Dr. #200
Little Rock, AR 72202

USMC Recruiting Sub-Station, Jonesboro
1311 Stone St.
Jonesboro, AR 72401
Tel: (870) 935-5380
Web: www.marines.com

POSTAL SERVICE
Arkansas District
420 Natural Resources Dr.
Little Rock, AR 72205-9001
Judy E. Gurkin, Diversity Development
Specialist
Tel: (501) 228-4263 Fax: (501) 228-4249
Web: www.usps.com

CALIFORNIA

AGRICULTURE, DEPT. OF
Food, Nutrition and Consumer Service
550 Kearny St. #400
San Francisco, CA 94108
Dominic Pagano, Hispanic Employment
Program Coordinator
Tel: (415) 705-1322 Fax: (415) 705-1364
Email: dominic.pagano@fns.usda.gov
Web: www.fns.usda.gov

550 Kearny St. #400
San Francisco, CA 94108
Jesus Mendoza, Jr., HEPM
Tel: (415) 705-1336 Fax: (415) 705-1364
Email: jesus.mendoza@fns.usda.gov
Web: www.fns.usda.gov

Forest Service
Mendocino National Forest
825 Humboldt Ave.
Willows, CA 95988
Lupe Hernandez, Human Resources
Specialist

Tel: (530) 934-1110 Fax: (530) 934-1109
Email: ghernandez01@fs.fed.us
Web: www.fs.fed.us

AIR FORCE, DEPT. OF THE
Beale AFB
9 MSS/DPC
17581 Warren Shingle Rd. #200
Beale AFB, CA 95903-1533
Tel: (530) 634-2234 Fax: (530) 634-2239

Edwards AFB
95 MSS/DPC, 36 N Wolfe Ave.
Edwards AFB, CA 93524-1470
Tel: (661) 277-4616 Fax: (661) 277-9531

Los Angeles AFB
61 MSS/DPC, 325 Challenger Way #1020
El Segundo, CA 90245-4677
Tel: (310) 363-1793 Fax: (310) 363-5334

March AFB
452 MSG/DPC, 1351 Graeber St. #105
March AFB, CA 92518-1723
Tel: (909) 655-4076 Fax: (909) 655-4671

Onizuka Air Station
21 SOPS/DPC
1080 Lockheed Martin Way #117
Sunnyvale, CA 94089-1233
Tel: (408) 752-3619 Fax: (408) 752-6541

Travis AFB
60 MSS/DPC, 540 Airlift Dr.
Travis AFB, CA 94535-2406
Tel: (707) 424-2268 Fax: (707) 424-1746

Vandeburg AFB
30 MSS/DPC, 1031 California Blvd. #B-110
Vandeburg AFB, CA 93437-6252
Tel: (805) 606-5846 Fax: (805) 606-0763

ARMY, DEPT. OF THE
US Army Recruiting Battalion Los Angeles
5051 Rodeo Rd. Rm. 2087
Los Angeles, CA 90016-4793
Tel: (323) 293-5209

US Army Recruiting Battalion Sacramento
2880 Sunrise Blvd. #230
Rancho Cordova, CA 95742-6549
Tel: (916) 638-0970/3093

US Army Recruiting Battalion Southern California
27401 Los Altos #330
Mission Viejo, CA 92691-6316
Tel: (949) 367-1159

EMPLOYMENT DEVELOPMENT DEPARTMENT
State of California
EEO Office
800 Capital Mall, MIC-49
Sacramento, CA 95814
Bob Polk, Chief
Tel: (916) 654-8434 Fax: (916) 654-9371

ENERGY, DEPT. OF
Human Resources
Berkeley Site Office
Lawrence Berkeley National Lab
1 Cyclotron Rd. M/S 937-600
Berkeley, CA 94720
William Elkins, Human Resources Manager
Tel: (510) 486-7950 Fax: (510) 486-4710
Email: welkins@lbl.gov
Web: www.lbl.gov

ENVIRONMENTAL PROTECTION AGENCY
Region 9
75 Hawthorne St. AIR-5
San Francisco, CA 94105
Matthew Salazar, HEPM
Tel: (415) 972-3982
Email: salazar.matt@epa.gov
Web: www.epa.gov

EQUAL EMPLOYMENT OPPORTUNITY COMMISSION
Fresno Local Office
1265 W Shaw Ave. #103
Fresno, CA 93711
Michelle Narddlla , Director
Tel: (559) 487-5793 Fax: (559) 487-5053
Web: www.eeoc.gov

Los Angeles District Office
255 E Temple St., 4th Fl.
Los Angeles, CA 90012
Olophius E. Perry, Director
Tel: (213) 894-1000 Fax: (213) 894-1118
Web: www.eeoc.gov

Oakland Local Office
1301 Clay St. #1170-N
Oakland, CA 94612-5217
Joyce Hendy, Director
Tel: (510) 637-3230 Fax: (510) 637-3235
Web: www.eeoc.gov

San Francisco District Office
350 The Embarcadero #500
San Francisco, CA 94105-1260
H. Joan Ehrlich, Director
Tel: (415) 625-5600 Fax: (415) 625-5609
Web: www.eeoc.gov

San Jose Local Office
96 N 3rd St. #200
San Jose, CA 95112
Adria Boetig, Acting Director
Tel: (408) 291-7352 Fax: (408) 291-4539
Web: www.eeoc.gov

INTERIOR, DEPT. OF THE
Bureau of Reclamation
Human Resources
2800 Cottage Way, M/C MP500
Sacramento, CA 95825
Tyrone Long, Personnel Management Specialist
Tel: (916) 978-5482 Fax: (916) 978-5496
Email: tlong@mp.usbr.gov
Web: www.usbr.gov/mp

JUSTICE, DEPT. OF
Bureau of Alcohol, Tobacco, Firearms and Explosives
3120 W March Ln. #2C
Stockton, CA 95219
Roger Isquierdo, HEPM
Tel: (925) 479-7656
Email: roger.isquierdo@atf.gov
Web: www.atf.gov

LABOR, DEPT. OF
Employment and Training Administration
Office of Youth Programs and Job Corps
71 Stevenson St. #1015
San Francisco, CA 94105-2970
Ernie Priestly, Regional Director
Tel: (415) 975-4680 Fax: (415) 975-4715

NAVY, DEPT. OF THE
12th Marine Corps District Headquarters
3074 Hochmoth Ave.
San Diego, CA 92140-5191
Tel: (619) 542-5519 Fax: (619) 542-5520
Web: www.marines.com

Naval Reserve Recruiting Command Area Pacific
960 N Harbor Dr.
San Diego, CA 92132-5000
Tel: (619) 532-3157

Navy Recruiting District, Los Angeles
5051 Rodeo Rd.
Los Angeles, CA 90016
Tel: (800) 252-1588

Navy Recruiting District, San Diego
33055 Nixie Way
San Diego, CA 92147

Tel: (619) 524-6683

USMC Recruiting Station, Los Angeles
5061 Rodeo Rd. #201
Los Angeles, CA 90016-4794
Tel: (213) 294-3679 Fax: (213) 294-0415
Web: www.marines.com

USMC Recruiting Station, Orange County
1921 E Alton Ave. #150
Santa Ana, CA 92705
Tel: (949) 261-0331 Fax: (949) 261-9039
Web: www.marines.com

USMC Recruiting Station, San Diego
2221 Camino del Rio South #212
San Diego, CA 92108-3610
Tel: (619) 688-1508 Fax: (619) 688-1509
Web: www.marines.com

USMC Recruiting Sub-Station, Sacramento
3870 Rosin Ct. #110
Sacramento, CA 95834
Tel: (916) 646-6980 Fax: (916) 646-9610
Web: www.marines.com

USMC Recruiting Sub-Station, San Francisco
620 Central Ave., Bldg. 2E
Alameda, CA 94501-3406
Tel: (510) 865-8336 Fax: (510) 865-6432
Web: www.marines.com

POSTAL SERVICE
Oakland District
1675 7th St. #306
Oakland, CA 94615-9512
Elmira A. Walton, Diversity Development Specialist
Tel: (510) 874-8665 Fax: (510) 433-7643
Email: ewalton@usps.gov
Web: www.usps.gov

Oakland District
1675 7th St. #329
W. Sacramento, CA 95799-0060
Yolanda Marquez, Hispanic Program Specialist
Tel: (916) 373-8115
Web: www.usps.gov

Sacramento District
3775 Industrial Blvd #3001
San Diego, CA 92199-9002
Hector Baca, Hispanic Program Specialist
Tel: (858) 674-0256 Fax: (858) 674-2711
Email: hector.baca@usps.gov
Web: www.usps.gov

San Diego District
11251 Rancho Carmel Dr. #162
San Diego, CA 92199-9002
Hector Baca, Hispanic Program Specialist
Tel: (858) 674-0256 Fax: (858) 674-2711
Email: hector.baca@usps.gov
Web: www.usps.gov

San Francisco District
P.O. Box 885348
San Francisco, CA 94188-5348
Abel E. Sanchez, Diversity Development Specialist
Tel: (415) 550-5710 Fax: (415) 550-5283
Email: asanche4@email.usps.gov
Web: www.usps.com

Santa Ana District
15421 Gale Ave.
City of Industry, CA 91747-9347
Norma Diaz, Diversity Development Specialist
Tel: (626) 855-6354 Fax: (626) 855-6696
Email: normadiaz@usps.com
Web: www.usps.com

Santa Ana District
15421 Gale Ave.
City of Industry, CA 91715-9347
Christina Sandoval, Hispanic Program Specialist
Tel: (626) 855-6351 Fax: (626) 855-6696

Email: christina.sandoval@usps.gov
Web: www.usps.gov

Van Nuys District
28201 Franklin Pkwy.
Santa Clarita, CA 91383-9994
Alex Hernandez, Hispanic Program Specialist
Tel: (661) 775-7055 Fax: (661) 775-7190
Email: tyrone.d.washington@usps.gov
Web: www.usps.gov

TREASURY, DEPT. OF THE
Internal Revenue Service, EEO and Diversity Office
Southern California Territory
24000 Avila Rd. M/S1515
Laguna Niguel, CA 92677
Chéri L. Blair, EEO Specialist/HEPM
Tel: (949) 389-4407 Fax: (949) 389-5016
Email: cheri.l.blair@irs.gov

Southern California Territory
24000 Avila Rd. M/S1515
Laguna Niguel, CA 92677
Lorretta Ceja, EEO Assistant/Alternative HEPM
Tel: (949) 389-4282

COLORADO

AGRICULTURE, DEPT. OF
Forest Service
Rocky Mountain Region (R-2)
Civil Rights Unit
740 Simms Ave.
Golden, CO 80401
Angela Baca, Equal Employment Specialist
Tel: (303) 275-5343 Fax: (303) 275-5502
Email: abaca@fs.fed.us

Rocky Mountain Research Station
240 W Prospect Rd.
Fort Collins, CO 80526-2098
Mary E. McDonough, HEPM
Tel: (970) 498-1167 Fax: (970) 498-1158
Email: mary.mcdonough@fs.fed.us
Web: www.fs.fed.us

Tech Support
Job Corp Field Office, Region 2
740 Simms Ave.
Golden, CO 80401
Bob Gonzales, HEPM
Tel: (303) 275-5468 Fax: (303) 275-5475
Email: bgonzales@fs.fed.us
Web: www.fs.fed.us

Natural Resources and Conservation Service
655 Parfet St. #E200C
Lakewood, CO 80215-5517
Herman Garcia, HEPM
Tel: (720) 544-2814 Fax: (720) 544-2962
Email: herman.garcia@co.usda.gov
Web: www.nrcs.usda.gov

AIR FORCE, DEPT. OF THE
Air Force Space Command Headquarters
HQ AFSC/DPC, 150 Vandenberg St. #1105
Peterson AFB, CO 80914-4450
Tel: (719) 554-3611 Fax: (719) 554-3441

Buckley AFB
460 MSS/DPC, 18401 E A-Basin, Bldg. 606
Buckley AFB, CO 80011-9542
Tel: (303) 677-6378 Fax: (303) 677-6383

Peterson AFB
21 MSS/DPC, 135 Dover St. #1057
Peterson AFB, CO 80914-1142
Tel: (719) 556-4775 Fax: (719) 566-6228

Schriever AFB
50 MSS/DPC, 210 Falcon Pkwy. #217
Schriever AFB, CO 80912
Tel: (719) 567-5778 Fax: (719) 567-2832

USAF Academy
10 MSS/DPC, 8034 Edgerton Dr. #100
USAF Academy, CO 80840-2215
Tel: (719) 333-2125 Fax: (719) 333-3741

ARMY, DEPT. OF THE
US Army Recruiting Battalion Denver
1600 Sherman #400
Denver, CO 80203-1620
Tel: (303) 894-9804/9819

ENERGY, DEPT. OF
Denver Regional Office
1617 Cole Blvd.
Golden, CO 80401-3393
Steve Palomo, HEPM
Tel: (303) 275-4838 Fax: (303) 275-4830
Email: steve.palomo@ee.doe.gov
Web: www.nrel.gov

Golden Field Office
1617 Cole Blvd.
Golden, CO 80401
Victor Candelaria, CPPA, OPMO/HEP
Manager
Tel: (303) 275-4717 Fax: (303) 275-4790
Email: victor.candelaria@go.doe.gov
Web: www.go.doe.gov

Western Area Power Administration
P.O. Box 281213
Lakewood, CO 80228-8213
Teresa Garcia, HEPM
Tel: (720) 962-7035 Fax: (720) 962-7041
Email: garcia@wapa.gov
Web: www.wapa.gov

Civil Rights and Diversity Management
Rocky Flats Field Office
10808 Hwy. 93, Unit 9
Golden, CO 80403
Ricky Newton, Equal Employment Manager
Tel: (303) 275-4718 Fax: (303) 966-8083
Email: ricky.newton@go.doe.gov
Web: www.rf.doe.gov

EQUAL EMPLOYMENT OPPORTUNITY COMMISSION
Denver District Office
303 E 17th Ave. #510
Denver, CO 80203
Francisco J. Flores, Jr., Director
Tel: (303) 866-1300 Fax: (303) 866-1085
Web: www.eeoc.gov

HOUSING AND URBAN DEVELOPMENT, DEPT.
Office of Fair Housing & Equal Opportunity
Denver HUD Office
1670 Broadway, 23rd Fl.
Denver, CO 80202
Ann Muniz, HEPM
Tel: (303) 672-5430 X1372
Fax: (303) 672-5026
Email: ann_muniz@hud.gov
Web: www.hud.gov

INTERIOR, DEPT. OF THE
Bureau of Reclamation
Diversity Equal Opportunity
P.O. Box 25007
Federal Center Bldg. 67, #D-7511
Denver, CO 80225
Hector Salazar, Diversity Manager
Tel: (303) 445-2658 Fax: (303) 445-6384
Web: www.usbr.gov

Human Resources
P.O. Box 25007
Denver, CO 80225-0007
Laurie Johnson, Manager
Tel: (303) 445-2656 Fax: (303) 445-6349
Email: ljohnson@do.usbr.gov

Geological Survey, Personnel Office
Central Region

P.O. Box 25046
Denver, CO 80225-0046
Deborah M. Douglas, Human Resources
Officer
Tel: (303) 236-9562 Fax: (303) 236-5582
Email: ddouglas@usgs.gov
Web: www.usgs.gov

National Park Service
Intermountain Region, Office of Human
Resources
P.O. Box 25287
Denver, CO 80225-0287
John Crowley, Assistant Regional Director
Tel: (303) 969-2506 Fax: (303) 969-2785
Email: john_crowley@nps.gov
Web: www.nps.gov

NAVY, DEPT. OF THE
Naval Reserve Recruiting Command Area West
791 Chambers Rd. #502
Aurora, CO 80011-7152
Tel: (303) 361-0631 Fax: (303) 361-0648

Navy Recruiting District, Denver
225 E 16th Ave.
Denver, CO 80203
Tel: (303) 866-1984

USMC Recruiting Station, Denver
1600 Sherman St. #500
Denver, CO 80203-1609
Tel: (303) 832-3730 Fax: (303) 832-3780
Web: www.marines.com

POSTAL SERVICE
P.O. Box 172000
Denver, CO 80217-2000
Roger R. Ramirez, Hispanic Program Specialist
Tel: (303) 853-2118
Web: www.usps.gov

HOMELAND SECURITY, DEPT. OF
US Coast Guard
USCG Recruiting Office Hartford
William Cotter Bldg., 135 High St. #G-5
Hartford, CT 06103
Tel: (860) 240-4260 Fax: (860) 240-4302
Email: rdavidson@cgrc.uscg.mil
Web: www.gocoastguard.com

USCG Recruiting Office New London
Fleet Bank Bldg., 260 S. Frontage Rd. #202
New London, CT 06320-2641
Tel: (860) 444-4947/48/49 Fax: (860) 444-4946
Email: dmerrill@cgrc.uscg.mil
Web: www.gocoastguard.com

NAVY, DEPT. OF THE
USMC Recruiting Sub-Station, Bridgeport
4490 Main St.
Bridgeport, CT 06606
Tel: (203) 365-8423
Web: www.marines.com

USMC Recruiting Sub-Station, Hartford
233 Pearl St.
Hartford, CT 06103
Tel: (860) 493-6572
Web: www.marines.com

USMC Recruiting Sub-Station, New Haven
157 Orange St.
New Haven, CT 06510
Tel: (203) 789-4484
Web: www.marines.com

USMC Recruiting Sub-Station, Norwich
372 W Main St.
Norwich, CT 06360
Tel: (860) 885-2992
Web: www.marines.com

USMC Recruiting Sub-Station, Waterbury
2457 E Main St.
Waterbury, CT 06705
Tel: (203) 759-2095
Web: www.marines.com

POSTAL SERVICE
Connecticut District
141 Weston St.
Hartford, CT 06101-9632
Karen Kucharczyk, Diversity Development
Specialist
Tel: (860) 524-6137 Fax: (860) 524-6446
Web: www.usps.gov

Northeast Area Office
6 Griffin Rd. North
Windsor, CT 06006-7050
Juan L. Cruz, Hispanic Program Specialist
Tel: (860) 285-7227 Fax: (860) 285-1203
Email: juan.l.cruz@usps.gov
Web: www.usps.gov

Northeast Area Office
6 Griffin Rd. North
Windsor, CT 06006-7110
Michelle D. Collins, Senior Diversity
Program Coordinator
Tel: (860) 285-7012 Fax: (860) 285-1203
Email: michelle.d.collins@usps.gov
Web: www.usps.gov

AGRICULTURE, DEPT. OF
East Region
1221 College Park Dr. #100
Dover, DE 19904
Georgia Brock, HEPM
Tel: (302) 678-4160 Fax: (302) 678-0843
Email: georgia.brock@de.usda.gov
Web: www.usda.gov

AIR FORCE, DEPT. OF THE
Dover AFB
436 MSS/DPC, 520 Main Gate Way
Dover AFB, DE 19902-5520
Tel: (302) 677-4640 Fax: (302) 677-4667

NAVY, DEPT. OF THE
USMC Recruiting Sub-Station, Dover
1300 S Dupont Hwy.
Dover, DE 19901
Tel: (302) 674-4191
Web: www.marines.com

AGENCY FOR INTERNATIONAL DEVELOPMENT
Office of Equal Opportunity Programs
1300 Pennsylvania Ave. NW #RRB-2.09-082, Ronald Reagan Bldg.
Washington, DC 20523-2901
Gloria Blackwell, Equal Employment
Specialist
Tel: (202) 712-0376 Fax: (202) 216-3524
Web: www.usaid.gov

AGRICULTURE, DEPT. OF
1400 Independence Ave. SW, #209-A
Washington, DC 20250
John Curina, Deputy Assistant Secretary for
Administration
Tel: (202) 720-3291 Fax: (202) 720-2191
Email: john.curina@usda.gov
Web: www.usda.gov

Agricultural Marketing Service
1400 Independence Ave.
SW #3074, South Bldg.
Washington, DC 20250

Constance T. Bails, Director of Civil Rights
Tel: (202) 720-3980 Fax: (202) 690-0476
Email: constance.bails@ams.usda.gov
Web: www.ams.usda.gov

Agricultural Research Service
1400 Independence Ave.
SW #3552, South Bldg.
Washington, DC 20250
Korona Prince, Director of Civil Rights
Tel: (202) 720-6161 Fax: (202) 690-0109
Email: kprince@ars.usda.gov
Web: www.ars.usda.gov

14th & Independence Ave. SW #3914
Washington, DC 20250
Maria Goldberg, Executive Director/Hispanic
Serving Institutions National Program
Tel: (202) 720-6506 Fax: (202) 720-5336
Email: mgoldberg@ars.usda.gov
Web: www.ars.usda.gov

Cooperative State Research, Education, and Extension Service
800 9th St. SW #1230, Waterfront Ctr. Bldg.
Washington, DC 20250
Curtiland Deville, Director of Civil Rights
Tel: (202) 720-2700 Fax: (202) 720-6954
Email: cdeville@csrees.usda.gov
Web: www.csrees.usda.gov

Economic Research Service
1800 M St. NW #N5058
Washington, DC 20036-5831
Nydia Suárez, National HEPM
Tel: (202) 694-5259 Fax: (202) 694-5884
Email: nrsuarez@ers.usda.gov
Web: www.ers.usda.gov

1800 M St. NW #4152
Washington, DC 20036-5831
Joyce Key, Director of Civil Rights
Tel: (202) 694-5005 Fax: (202) 694-5757
Email: jkey@ers.usda.gov
Web: www.ers.usda.gov

Farm and Foreign Agricultural Service
Farm Service Agency (FSA)
1400 Independence Ave.
SW, #0509, South Bldg.
Washington, DC 20250
John Toles, Director of Civil Rights
Tel: (202) 401-7220 Fax: (202) 401-7100
Email: john.toles@usda.gov
Web: www.fas.usda.gov

Farm Service Agency (FSA)
1280 Maryland Ave.
SW #580B, Portal Bldg.
Washington, DC 20024
Sean Clayton, National HEPM
Tel: (202) 401-7215 Fax: (202) 401-7100
Email: sean.clayton@wdc.fsa.usda.gov
Web: www.fsa.usda.gov

Foreign Agricultural Service (FAS)
1400 Independence Ave.
SW #6630, South Bldg.
Washington, DC 20250-1034
Jorge L. Hazera, National HEPM
Tel: (202) 690-3518 Fax: (202) 720-1378
Email: jorge.hazera@fas.usda.gov
Web: www.fas.usda.gov

Risk Management Agency (RMA)
1400 Independence Ave.
SW #3059, South Bldg.
Washington, DC 20250-0801
Tanya Ahmed, National HEPM
Tel: (202) 690-2684 Fax: (202) 690-2818
Email: ahmed.tanya@wdc.usda.gov
Web: www.rma.usda.gov

Farm Service Agency
1280 Maryland Ave. SW, #580-B
Washington, DC 20250
Carmen Martinez, Director of Civil Rights
Tel: (202) 401-7220 Fax: (202) 401-7100

Email: carmen.martinez@usda.gov
Web: www.usda.gov

Forest Service
201 14th St. SW #4-SW
Washington, DC 20250
Kathleen Gause, Director of Civil Rights Staff
Tel: (202) 205-1585 Fax: (202) 690-1025
Email: kgause@fs.fed.us
Web: www.fs.fed.us

Grain Inspection, Packers, and Stockyards Administration
1400 Independence Ave.
SW #0623, M/S 3602
Washington, DC 20250
Eugene Bass, Director of Civil Rights
Tel: (202) 720-0216 Fax: (202) 690-0609
Email: eugene.bass@usda.gov
Web: www.usda.gov/gipsa

Marketing and Regulatory Programs
Agricultural Marketing Service (AMS)
1400 Independence Ave.
SW #3074, South Bldg.
Washington, DC 20250-0206
Kenneth R. Johnson, Affirmative
Employment Manager
Tel: (202) 720-0583 Fax: (202) 690-0476
Email: kennethr.johnson@usda.gov
Web: www.ams.usda.gov

Office of Civil Rights
1400 Independence Ave. SW #326-W
Washington, DC 20250
Sadhna G. True, Director of Civil Rights
Tel: (202) 720-5212 Fax: (202) 720-0953
Email: sadhna.true@usda.gov
Web: www.usda.gov

Office of Human Resources Management
1400 Independence Ave. SW #316-W,
Jamie L. Whitten Bldg.
Washington, DC 20250
Alicia Rodriguez, HEPM
Tel: (202) 690-0640 Fax: (202) 720-7138
Email: alicia.rodriguez@usda.gov
Web: www.usda.gov

Office of Civil Rights/ECTAD
1400 Independence Ave. SW, M/S 9403
Washington, DC 20250-9403
Harry R. Salinas, Departmental HEPM
Tel: (202) 401-1416 Fax: (202) 690-2345
Email: harryr.salinas@usda.gov
Web: www.usda.gov

Office of Operations
1400 Independence Ave.
SW #S-314, South Bldg.
Washington, DC 20250
Pamela G. Carter, National HEPM
Tel: (202) 720-2874 Fax: (202) 690-2604
Email: pamela.carter@usda.gov
Web: www.usda.gov

Research, Education and Economics
Cooperative State Research, Education, and
Extension Service (CSREES)
800 9th St. SW #1230,
Waterfront Center Bldg.
Washington, DC 20024
Richard G. Chavez, Equal Opportunity
Specialist
Tel: (202) 690-2051 Fax: (202) 720-6954
Email: rchavez@csrees.usda.gov
Web: www.csrees.usda.gov

National Agricultural Statistics
Service (NASS)
1400 Independence Ave.
SW #4117, South Bldg.
Washington, DC 20250-2000
Rafael Sánchez, National HEPM
Tel: (202) 720-8257 Fax: (202) 720-9013
Email: rsanchez@nass.usda.gov
Web: www.nass.usda.gov

Risk Management Agency
1400 Independence Ave.
SW #3053, M/S 0801, South Bldg.
Washington, DC 20250
Bill Buchanan, Director of Civil Rights
Tel: (202) 690-6068 Fax: (202) 690-2496
Email: bill.buchanan@usda.gov
Web: www.rma.usda.gov

1400 Independence Ave.
SW #6709, South Bldg.
Washington, DC 20250
Tonya Ahmed, National Special Emphasis
Program Manager
Tel: (202) 690-2684 Fax: (202) 690-2496
Email: tonya_ahmed@usda.gov

Rural Development
Office of Civil Rights
1400 Independence Ave. SW #0344
Washington, DC 20250-0703
Jacqueline Micheli, National HEPM
Tel: (202) 692-0099 Fax: (202) 692-0008
Email: jacqueline.micheli@usda.gov
Web: www.usda.gov

AIR FORCE, DEPT. OF THE
Headquarters
HQ USAF/DPPF
1040 Air Force Pentagon #4E235
Washington, DC 20330-1040
Colleen Corcoran, Affirmative Action
Program Manager
Tel: (703) 693-2699 Fax: (703) 695-4083
Email: corcoranc@pentagon.af.mil

Office of Civilian Personnel
HQ 11 WG/DPC, 1460 Air Force Pentagon
Washington, DC 20330-1460
Tel: (703) 697-3127 Fax: (703) 693-5392

CENTRAL INTELLIGENCE AGENCY
Diversity Plans & Programs
Rm. 1A1116-OHB
Washington, DC 20505
Fran Edelan, HEPM
Tel: (703) 482-2011 Fax: (703) 482-2036

COMMERCE, DEPT. OF
Bureau of the Census
EEO Division
4700 Silver Hill Rd. #1229, Bldg. 3
Washington, DC 20233-1912
Roy Castro, Chief
Tel: (301) 763-2853 Fax: (301) 457-1160
Email: roy.p.castro@census.gov
Web: www.census.gov

Office of Civil Rights
14th & Constitution Ave. NW #6012
Washington, DC 20230
Clarissa Lara, EEO Manager
Tel: (202) 482-8189 Fax: (202) 482-5375
Email: clara@doc.gov
Web: www.commerce.gov

CORPORATION FOR NATIONAL AND COMMUNITY SERVICE
Office of Civil Rights and Inclusiveness
1201 New York Ave. NW #7110
Washington, DC 20525
Jonathan Williams, Director
Tel: (202) 606-5000 X309 Fax: (202) 565-2816
Email: dc@cns.gov
Web: www.americorps.org

DEFENSE, DEPT. OF
Defense Intelligence Agency
Bldg. 6000
Washington, DC 20340
Ivan Nunez-Barreiro, Chairman of HEPM
Tel: (202) 231-8254 Fax: (202) 231-8181

Office of Diversity Management and Equal
Opportunity
Bolling AFB, Bldg. 6000 #D4-938
Washington, DC 20340
Susan Sternard-Basel, Acting Deputy Chief
Tel: (202) 231-8178 Fax: (202) 231-3865
Email: susan.sternad-basel@dia.mil

Office of Deputy Assistant Secretary of Defense for Equal Opportunity
4000 Defense Pentagon #3A272
Washington, DC 20301-4000
Charmaine Collins, Diversity Manager
Tel: (703) 695-0107 Fax: (703) 695-4619
Email: charmaine.collins@osd.mil

ENERGY, DEPT. OF
Corporate Human Resources, NE 50.1
1000 Independence Ave. SW #4E-040
Washington, DC 20585
Jeffrey Vargas, National HEPM
Tel: (202) 586-3039 Fax: (202) 586-3294
Email: jeffrey.vargas@hq.doe.gov
Web: www.energy.gov

Energy Information Administration, EI-30
1000 Independence Ave. SW #2H-055
Washington, DC 20585
Barbara Hall, HEPM
Tel: (202) 586-4482 Fax: (202) 586-0552
Email: bhall@eia.doe.gov
Web: www.eia.doe.gov

Environmental Management, EM-13
1000 Independence Ave. SW
Washington, DC 20585
Jeff Vargas, HEPM
Tel: (202) 586-3039 Fax: (202) 586-0293
Email: jeff.vargas@em.doe.gov
Web: www.em.doe.gov

Fossil Energy, FE-422
1000 Independence Ave. SW #3G-063
Washington, DC 20585
Casimiro Izquierdo, HEPM
Tel: (202) 586-9353 Fax: (202) 586-7919
Email: casimiro.izquierdo@hq.doe.gov

Office of Science SC-5
Office of Planning & Analysis
1000 Independence Ave. SW SC-5
Washington, DC 20585
William J. Valdez, Director/HEPM
Tel: (202) 586-9942 Fax: (202) 586-7719
Email: bill.valdez@science.doe.gov
Web: www.science.doe.gov

ENVIRONMENTAL PROTECTION AGENCY
Office of Civil Rights
1200 Pennsylvania Ave. NW, M/C 1201A
Washington, DC 20460
Melissa Rodriguez, National HEPM
Tel: (202) 564-7273 Fax: (202) 501-1836
Email: rodriguez.melissa@epa.gov
Web: www.epa.gov

EQUAL EMPLOYMENT OPPORTUNITY COMMISSION
Washington Field Office
1801 L St. NW #100
Washington, DC 20507
Dana Hutter, Acting Director
Tel: (202) 419-0700 Fax: (202) 419-0740
Web: www.eeoc.gov

EXECUTIVE OFFICE OF THE PRESIDENT
Office of Administration
EEO Office
725 17th St. NW #2200
Washington, DC 20503
Linda Sites, Director for EEO
Tel: (202) 395-3996
Email: linda.sites@oa.eop.gov

EXPORT-IMPORT BANK OF THE U.S.
EEO and Diversity Programs Office
811 Vermont Ave. NW
Washington, DC 20571
Sherry Beyers, Acting Director
Tel: (202) 565-3591 Fax: (202) 565-3595
Email: sherry.beyers@exim.gov
Web: www.exim.gov

Human Resources
811 Vermont Ave. NW #771
Washington, DC 20571
Elliott Davis, Director of Personnel
Tel: (202) 565-3316 Fax: (202) 565-3627
Email: elliott.davis@exim.gov
Web: www.exim.gov

FEDERAL BUREAU OF INVESTIGATION
Office of Equal Employment Affairs
935 Pennsylvania Ave. NW
Washington, DC 20535
Az Mercado, Hispanic Employment
Program Manager
Tel: (202) 324-2349 Fax: (202) 324-3976
Email: wizmom21@aol.com
Web: www.fbi.gov

FEDERAL DEPOSIT INSURANCE CORPORATION
Office of Diversity and Economic Opportunity
801 17th St. NW #1220
Washington, DC 20434-0001
Rolando Esparza, EEO Specialist/HEPM
Tel: (202) 416-2451 Fax: (202) 416-2486
Email: resparza@fdic.gov
Web: www.fdic.gov

FEDERAL ELECTION COMMISSION
Equal Employment Opportunity Office
999 E St. NW #436
Washington, DC 20463
Patricia Brown, EEO Director
Tel: (202) 694-1228 Fax: (202) 219-3880
Email: eeo@fec.gov
Web: www.fec.gov

FEDERAL HOUSING FINANCE BOARD (FHFB)
Department of Human Resources
1777 F St. NW #105
Washington, DC 20006
David Lee, Human Resources Officer
Tel: (202) 408-2514 Fax: (202) 408-2530
Web: www.fhfb.gov

FEDERAL MARITIME COMMISSION
Office of the General Counsel
EEO
800 N Capitol St. NW #1052
Washington, DC 20573
Alice M. Blackmom, Director
Tel: (202) 523-5806 Fax: (202) 523-4224
Email: aliceb@fmc.gov
Web: www.fmc.gov

FEDERAL MEDIATION & CONCILIATION SERVICE
Human Resources
2100 K St. NW, 7th Fl.
Washington, DC 20427
Dan Ellerman, Director
Tel: (202) 606-5460 Fax: (202) 606-4216
Email: dellerman@fmcs.gov
Web: www.fmcs.gov

FEDERAL RETIREMENT THRIFT INVESTMENT BOARD
Personnel Office
1250 H St. NW
Washington, DC 20005-3952
Natasha Bailey, Director of Personnel
Tel: (202) 942-1600 Fax: (202) 942-1674
Web: www.frtib.gov

FEDERAL TRADE COMMISSION
Human Resources
600 Pennsylvania Ave. NW #723
Washington, DC 20580
Janet Silva, Director
Tel: (202) 326-2344 Fax: (202) 326-2328
Email: jsilva@ftc.gov
Web: www.ftc.gov

FIRE DEPARTMENT
District of Columbia
1923 Vermont Ave. NW #201 South
Washington, DC 20001
Frederica Smith, EEO Officer/Diversity
Program Manager
Tel: (202) 673-3320 Fax: (202) 462-0807
Email: frederica.smith@dc.gov
Web: www.dc.gov

GOVERNMENT ACCOUNTABILITY OFFICE
Recruitment Office
441 G St. NW #1165
Washington, DC 20548
Sally Jaggar, Director
Tel: (202) 512-6808 Fax: (202) 512-2539
Web: www.gao.gov

GOVERNMENT PRINTING OFFICE
Customer Services
732 N Capitol St. NW
Washington, DC 20401
James C. Bradley, Managing Director
Tel: (202) 512-0111
Email: jbradley@gpo.gov
Web: www.gpo.gov

HEALTH AND HUMAN SERVICES, DEPT. OF
Administration for Children and Families
901 D St. SW, Aerospace Bldg., 6th Fl. West
Washington, DC 20447
Carl Montoya, Intergovernmental Affairs
Tel: (202) 205-8557 Fax: (202) 401-5727
Email: cmontoya@acf.hhs.gov
Web: www.acf.dhhs.gov

EEO Programs Group
200 Independence Ave. SW #536E
Washington, DC 20201
Bonita V. White, Esq., Director
Tel: (202) 690-6555 Fax: (202) 690-8328
Email: bonita.white@hhs.gov
Web: www.os.dhhs.gov

**Office of the Secretary and Administration
on Aging**
Office of EEO
HHH Bldg., 200 Independence Ave.
SW #709-D
Washington, DC 20201
David Shorts, Manager
Tel: (202) 619-1564 Fax: (202) 619-0823
Email: david.shorts@hhs.gov

HOMELAND SECURITY, DEPT. OF
Animal & Plant Health Inspection Services
1400 Independence Ave.
SW #1133, South Bldg.
Washington, DC 20250
Anna P. Grayson, Director, Civil Rights
Tel: (202) 720-6312 Fax: (202) 720-2365
Email: anna.p.grayson@usda.gov
Web: www.aphis.usda.gov

U.S. Coast Guard Headquarters
Civil Rights Office
2100 2nd St. SW #2400
Washington, DC 20593
Meghan Collins, Affirmative Employment
Program Manager
Tel: (202) 267-0037 Fax: (202) 267-4282
Email: mcollins@comdt.uscg.mil
Web: www.uscg.mil

US Customs and Border Protection
EEO
1300 Pennsylvania Ave. NW #3.3-31
Washington, DC 20229
Christopher Rodriguez, EEO Specialist
Tel: (202) 344-1481 Fax: (202) 344-1476
Email: christopher.rodriguez1@dhs.gov
Web: www.dhs.gov

HOUSING AND URBAN DEVELOPMENT, DEPT. OF
Office of EEO
451 7th St. SW #2134
Washington, DC 20410
Linda Bradford, Deputy Director
Tel: (202) 708-3362 Fax: (202) 401-2843
Web: www.hud.gov

INTERIOR, DEPT. OF THE
Bureau of Indian Affairs
Office for Equal Opportunity Programs
1849 C St. NW, M/S 3039
Washington, DC 20240
Grace Sine, Acting Director
Tel: (202) 208-2475 Fax: (202) 208-4742

Bureau of Land Management
Office for Equal Opportunity
1849 C St. NW, M/S 5541
Washington, DC 20240
Michelle Stroman, EEO Officer
Tel: (202) 208-1565 Fax: (202) 208-6893
Web: www.blm.gov

Bureau of Reclamation
Office of the Commissioner
1849 C St. NW #7060-MIB
Washington, DC 20240-0001
Janice Johnson, Chief of Administrative
Services
Tel: (202) 513-0522 Fax: (202) 513-0310
Email: jjohnson@usbr.gov
Web: www.usbr.gov

National Park Service
Employment Office
1849 C St. NW #2328
Washington, DC 20240
Mary Plumley, Human Resource Manager
Tel: (202) 354-1975 Fax: (202) 219-1786
Web: www.nps.gov

National Capital Region
1100 Ohio Dr. SW
Washington, DC 20242
William Nieto, Jr., HEPM
Tel: (202) 619-7020 Fax: (202) 619-7496
Email: william_nieto_jr@nps.gov
Web: www.nps.gov

National Capital Region, Department of
Human Resources
1100 Ohio Dr. SW
Washington, DC 20242
Kym Elder, Special Emphasis Recruitment
Officer
Tel: (202) 619-7246 Fax: (202) 619-7244
Email: kym_elder@nps.gov
Web: www.nps.gov

Office for Equal Opportunity
1201 Eye St. NW
Washington, DC 20005
Dianne Spriggs, Director
Tel: (202) 354-1852 Fax: (202) 371-1449
Web: www.nps.gov

WAFO Area, Office of Human Resources
1201 Eye St. NW, 12th Fl. #2653
Washington, DC 20005
Ella Drummond, Recruitment Coordinator
Tel: (202) 354-1996 Fax: (202) 371-1762
Web: www.nps.gov

INTERIOR, DEPT. OF THE
Office of Equal Opportunity
1849 C St. NW, M/S 5214
Washington, DC 20240
Sharon Eller, Director
Tel: (202) 208-5693 Fax: (202) 208-6112
Email: sharon_eller@ios.doi.gov

Office of Surface Mining
Office for Equal Opportunity
1951 Constitution Ave. NW #138
Washington, DC 20240
James E. Joiner, Chief
Tel: (202) 208-5897 Fax: (202) 219-3109
Email: jjoiner@osmre.gov
Web: www.osmre.gov

Office of Equal Opportunity
1951 Constitution Ave. NW #138
Washington, DC 20240
Diane Wood-Medley, HEPM
Tel: (202) 208-2997 Fax: (202) 219-3109
Email: dwood@osmre.gov
Web: www.osmre.gov

INTERNATIONAL BROADCASTING BUREAU
Office of Civil Rights
330 C St. SW #1086, Switzer Bldg.
Washington, DC 20237
Delia L. Johnson, Director
Tel: (202) 619-5151 Fax: (202) 260-0406
Email: djohnso@ibb.gov
Web: www.ibb.gov

JUSTICE, DEPT. OF
Executive Office for US Attorneys
EEO Office
1331 Pennsylvania Ave. NW #524
Washington, DC 20530
Juan E. Milanes, Assistant Director
Tel: (202) 514-3982 Fax: (202) 305-1431
Email: juan.milanes@usdoj.gov
Web: www.usdoj.gov

Federal Bureau of Prisons
Discriminations, Complaints and Ethics
320 1st St. NW #770
Washington, DC 20534
Carlos V. Rivera, Diversity Manager
Tel: (202) 307-3175 Fax: (202) 514-9650
Web: www.bop.gov

Headquarters
Office of EEO
1110 Vermont Ave. NW #620
Washington, DC 20530
Carmen Mendez, EEO Program Manager
Tel: (202) 616-4812 Fax: (202) 616-4823
Web: www.usdoj.gov/jmd/eeos

LABOR, DEPT. OF
Bureau of Labor Statistics
Division of Human Resources
2 Massachusetts Ave. NE #4280
Washington, DC 20212
Dorothy Wigglesworth, EEO Officer
Tel: (202) 691-6604 Fax: (202) 691-6610
Email: wigglesworth_d@bls.gov
Web: www.bls.gov

Employment Standards Administration
Equal Employment Opportunity Unit
200 Constitution Ave. NW #C-3315
Washington, DC 20210
Kate Dorrell, Director
Tel: (202) 693-0024 Fax: (202) 693-1455
Email: dorrell.kate@dol.gov
Web: www.dol.gov

International Labor Affairs
Economic Affairs
200 Constitution Ave. NW #S5325
Washington, DC 20210
Ana Maria Valdes, HEPM
Tel: (202) 693-4918 Fax: (202) 693-4880
Email: valdes-ana@dol.gov

Occupational Safety & Health Administration
EEO Office
200 Constitution Ave. NW #N-3425
Washington, DC 20210
Betty Gillis-Robinson, Director
Tel: (202) 693-2150 Fax: (202) 693-1626
Email: betty.gillis-robinson@osha.gov
Web: www.osha.gov

Office of Civil Rights
EEO Office
200 Constitution Ave. NW #N-4123
Washington, DC 20210
Linda Blumner, EEO Specialist
Tel: (202) 693-6513 Fax: (202) 693-6505
Email: blumner-linda@dol.gov
Web: www.dol.gov

**Office of the Assistant Secretary for
Administration and Management**
Business Operation Center/EEO Office
200 Constitution Ave. NW #S1509A
Washington, DC 20210
Milton Blount, EEO Manager
Tel: (202) 693-4031 Fax: (202) 219-5138
Email: blount-milton@dol.gov
Web: www.dol.gov

Office of Workforce Planning and Diversity
200 Constitution Ave. NW #C5520
Washington, DC 20210
Sara Clemente, HEPM
Tel: (202) 693-7635 Fax: (202) 693-7729
Email: clemente.sara@dol.gov

LIBRARY OF CONGRESS
Human Resources
101 Independence Ave. SE #LM-645
Washington, DC 20540
Rafael Landrau, Director of Workforce
Tel: (202) 707-5627 Fax: (202) 707-1454
Web: www.loc.gov

MERIT SYSTEM PROTECTION BOARD
EEO Office
1615 M St. NW
Washington, DC 20419
Janice Pirkle, Director
Tel: (202) 653-6180 Fax: (202) 653-7130
Email: equalopportunity@mspb.gov
Web: www.mspb.gov

METROPOLITAN POLICE DEPARTMENT, OFFICE OF POLICE RECRUITING
District of Columbia
#6 DC Village Ln. SW, Bldg. 1A
Washington, DC 20032
Capt. Kevin Anderson, Director
Tel: (202) 645-0445 Fax: (202) 645-0444
Web: www.mpdc.dc.gov

NATIONAL AERONAUTICS AND SPACE ADMINISTRATION (NASA)
300 E St. SW, Code EI
Washington, DC 20546
Mike Torres, HEPM
Tel: (202) 358-0937 Fax: (202) 358-3336
Email: mtorres@nasa.gov
Web: www.nasa.gov

NATIONAL ENDOWMENT FOR THE ARTS
Civil Rights/EEO Office
1100 Pennsylvania Ave. NW #219
Washington, DC 20506
Angelia Richardson, Director
Tel: (202) 682-5454 Fax: (202) 682-5553
Email: richarda@arts.endow.gov
Web: www.arts.endow.gov

Human Resources
1100 Pennsylvania Ave. NW #627
Washington, DC 20506
Craig McCord, Director
Tel: (202) 682-5405 Fax: (202) 682-5666

Email: mccordc@arts.endow.gov
Web: www.arts.endow.gov

NATIONAL ENDOWMENT FOR THE HUMANITIES
Administrator Services
1100 Pennsylvania Ave. NW #202
Washington, DC 20506
Willie V. McGhee, Jr., EEO Officer
Tel: (202) 606-8233 Fax: (202) 606-8243
Email: wmcghee@neh.gov
Web: www.neh.gov

Office of Human Resources
1100 Pennsylvania Ave. NW #418
Washington, DC 20506
Timothy Connelly, Director
Tel: (202) 606-8415 Fax: (202) 606-8656
Email: tconnelly@neh.gov
Web: www.neh.gov

NATIONAL LABOR RELATIONS BOARD
Office of EEO
1099 14th St. NW #6300
Washington, DC 20570
Robert Poindexter, Director
Tel: (202) 273-3891 Fax: (202) 273-4473
Email: robert.poindexter@nlrb.gov
Web: www.nlrb.gov

NATIONAL MEDIATION BOARD
Office of Arbitration Services
1301 K St. NW #250 East
Washington, DC 20572
Roland Watkins, Director/HEPM
Tel: (202) 692-5055 Fax: (202) 692-5086
Web: www.nmb.gov

NAVY, DEPT. OF THE
Computer and Telecommunications Command
1014 N St. SE, #1
Washington, DC 20374-5050
Issac Oliver, Command Deputy EEO Officer
Tel: (202) 685-1879 Fax: (202) 433-2653

Navy Internal Programs Division
Nebraska Ave. Complex
4255 Mt. Vernon Dr. #17100
Washington, DC 20393-5445
Reno Pivirotto, Executive Director
Tel: (202) 764-2840 Fax: (202) 764-2835
Email: reno.pivirotto@navy.mil
Web: www.navy.mil

Office of Naval Intelligence
Office of the Director
4251 Suitland Rd. #2A129
Washington, DC 20395-5720
Benjamin Stepens, Acting Command Deputy EEO Officer
Tel: (301) 669-5119 Fax: (301) 669-3991

Secretariat/HQ Human Resources Office
2 Navy Annex #2052
Washington, DC 20370-5240
Rhonda L. Woods, Command Deputy EEO Officer
Tel: (703) 693-0202 Fax: (703) 693-1333
Email: rhonda.woods@navy.mil

OFFICE OF BILINGUAL EDUCATION
District of Columbia
Division of Special Programs
Roosevelt Administrative Unit,
13th & Upshur St. NW
Washington, DC 20011
Elba Garcia, Interim Director
Tel: (202) 576-8850 Fax: (202) 576-8859

OFFICE OF HUMAN RIGHTS
District of Columbia
441 4th St. NW #570 North
Washington, DC 20001
Kenneth L. Faunders, Director
Tel: (202) 727-4559 Fax: (202) 727-9589

Web: www.ohr.dc.gov

OFFICE OF LATINO AFFAIRS
District of Columbia
2000 14th St. NW, 2nd Fl.
Washington, DC 20009
Gustavo Velazquez, Director
Tel: (202) 671-2825 Fax: (202) 673-4557
Email: gustavo.velazquez@dc.gov
Web: www.ola.dc.gov

OFFICE OF MANAGEMENT AND BUDGET
Energy Science & Water Division
725 17th St. NW #8025
Washington, DC 20503
Cynthia Vallina, HEPM
Tel: (202) 395-3634 Fax: (202) 395-1086
Email: cynthia_vallina@omb.eop.gov

OFFICE OF PERSONNEL
District of Columbia
441 4th St. NW #300S
Washington, DC 20001
Lisa Marin, Director
Tel: (202) 442-9600 Fax: (202) 727-6827
Email: lisa.marin@dc.gov
Web: http://dcop.dc.gov

OVERSEAS PRIVATE INVESTMENT CORPORATION
Human Resources Management
1100 New York Ave. NW
Washington, DC 20527
Larry Mentzer, HEPM
Tel: (202) 336-8529 Fax: (202) 408-9853
Web: www.opic.gov

PEACE CORPS
American Diversity Program
1111 20th St. NW, 8th Fl.
Washington, DC 20526
Shirley Everest, Manager
Tel: (202) 692-2137 Fax: (202) 692-2131
Email: severest@peacecorps.gov
Web: www.peacecorps.gov

Office of Diversity Recruitment
Volunteer Recruitment and Selection
1111 20th St. NW, 6th Fl.
Washington, DC 20526
Wilfredo Sauri, Director
Tel: (202) 692-1819 Fax: (202) 692-1801
Email: wsauri@peacecorps.gov
Web: www.peacecorps.gov

POSTAL SERVICE
Diversity Development
475 L'Enfant Plz. SW #3901
Washington, DC 20260-3901
Jacquelyn Padrón, National Hispanic Program Specialist
Tel: (202) 268-6446 Fax: (202) 268-4263
Email: jacqueline.padron@usps.gov
Web: www.usps.com

475 L'Enfant Plz. SW #3821
Washington, DC 20260-5610
Lolita Mancheno-Smoak, Manager, HQ & Field Programs
Tel: (202) 268-6610 Fax: (202) 268-6573
Web: www.usps.com

475 L'Enfant Plz. SW #3821
Washington, DC 20260-3821
Chester Cross, Manager/Affirmative Employment Program
Tel: (202) 268-7456 Fax: (202) 268-6573
Email: chestersjr.cross@usps.gov
Web: www.usps.com

PUBLIC SCHOOLS, OFFICE OF HUMAN RESOURCES MANAGEMENT
District of Columbia
Central Operations
825 N Capitol St. NE, 6th Fl.

Washington, DC 20002
Tony Demasi, Director
Tel: (202) 442-4080 Fax: (202) 442-5315
Email: tony.demasi@k12.dc.us
Web: www.k12.dc.us

SMALL BUSINESS ADMINISTRATION
Office of EEO
409 3rd St. SW #4600
Washington, DC 20416
Rose Trujillio, Assistant Administrator for EEO/CRC
Tel: (202) 205-6750 Fax: (202) 205-7580
Email: rosetrujillio@sba.gov
Web: www.sba.gov

Personnel Services Division
409 3rd St. SW #5300
Washington, DC 20416
Richard Drechbiel, Director
Tel: (202) 205-6605 Fax: (202) 205-6802
Web: www.sba.gov

SMITHSONIAN INSTITUTION
Office of Equal Employment and Minority Affairs
750 9th St. NW #8100
Washington, DC 20560-0921
Pauline Fletemeyer, Special Emphasis Program Manager
Tel: (202) 275-0151 Fax: (202) 275-0160
Web: www.si.edu

Office of Human Resources and Recruitment
750 9th St. NW #6100, MRC 912
Washington, DC 20560-0912
Darnell Caldwell , Chief Executive Resources Branch
Tel: (202) 275-1055 Fax: (202) 287-2015
Web: www.si.edu

STATE, DEPT. OF
2401 E St. NW
Washington, DC 20522-0108
Harby Issa, HR Specialist/Hispanic Coordinator
Tel: (202) 261-8122 Fax: (202) 261-8842

TRANSPORTATION, DEPT. OF
Bureau of Transportation Statistics
400 7th St. SW #3430, M/S K-5
Washington, DC 20590
Paula Robinson, National HEPM/ Administrative Officer
Tel: (202) 366-3103 Fax: (202) 366-3640
Email: paula.robinson@bts.gov
Web: www.bts.gov

Federal Aviation Administration
Office of Civil Rights
400 7th St. SW
Washington, DC 20590
Carlos Manduley, HEP Manager
Tel: (202) 385-8127 Fax: (202) 366-6028
Web: www.faa.gov

Federal Motor Carrier Safety Administration
Office of Civil Rights
400 7th St. SW
Washington, DC 20590
Carmen Sevier, HEPM
Tel: (202) 366-4330 Fax: (202) 366-3375
Email: carmen.sevier@fmcsa.dot.gov
Web: www.fmcsa.dot.gov

Federal Railroad Administration
1120 Vermont Ave. NW #RRS-12, M/S 25
Washington, DC 20590
Francisco Gonzalez, National HEPM
Tel: (202) 493-6076 Fax: (202) 493-6478
Email: f.gonzalez@fra.dot.gov
Web: www.fra.dot.gov

Federal Transit Administration
400 7th St. SW #9100
Washington, DC 20590

Eugene Jenkins, HEPM
Tel: (202) 366-0793 Fax: (202) 366-3475
Email: eugene.jenkins@fta.dot.gov
Web: www.fta.dot.gov

Maritime Administration
400 7th St. SW
Washington, DC 20590
Celia Luck, HEPM
Tel: (202) 366-3581 Fax: (202) 366-6988
Email: celia_luck@marad.dot.gov
Web: www.marad.dot.gov

National Highway Safety Administration
400 7th St. SW #6128
Washington, DC 20590
Phyllis D. Alston, HEPM
Tel: (202) 366-8046 Fax: (202) 366-1746
Email: palston@nhtsa.dot.gov
Web: www.nhtsa.dot.gov

Office of the Secretary
Human Resources Operations
400 7th St. SW #2225, M/S SVC-190
Washington, DC 20590
Frances Brown, Special Emphasis Program Manager
Tel: (202) 366-5809 Fax: (202) 366-3733
Email: frances.brown@tasc.dot.gov
Web: www.dot.gov

Departmental Office of Civil Rights
400 7th St. SW #5414A, M/S 32
Washington, DC 20590
Milton Belardo, Departmental HEPM
Tel: (202) 366-9450 Fax: (202) 366-7717
Email: milton.belardo@ost.dot.gov
Web: www.dot.gov

St. Lawrence Seaway Development Corporation
400 7th St. SW #5424
Washington, DC 20590
Mary Hollomon, Special Emphasis Program Manager
Tel: (202) 366-0091 Fax: (202) 366-7147
Email: mary.e.hollomon@sls.dot.gov
Web: www.seaway.dot.gov

TREASURY, DEPT. OF THE
Bureau of Alcohol Tobacco and Firearms
650 Massachusetts Ave., NW, #8210
Washington, DC 20226
Dora Silas , HEPM
Tel: (202) 927-7760 Fax: (202) 927-8835

Bureau of Engraving and Printing
EEO Office/Employee Counseling Services
14th & C St. SW #639-17 PD
Washington, DC 20228
Arthur W. Hicks, Chief/EEO Officer
Tel: (202) 874-2460 Fax: (202) 874-3311
Email: arthur.hicks@bep.treas.gov
Web: www.bep.treas.gov

Comptroller of the Currency
250 E. St., SW M/S 2-6
Washington, DC 20219
Ruby Thomas, Director, EEO Program
Tel: (202) 874-5360 Fax: (202) 874-5629
Email: ruby.thomas@occ.treas.gov

250 E St., SW M/S 2-6
Washington, DC 20219
Irene Sandate, Supervisor EEO Specialist
Tel: (202) 874-5360 Fax: (202) 874-5629
Email: irene.sandate@occ.treas.gov
Web: www.occ.treas.gov

Financial Management Services
Hispanic Employment Advisory Committee
401 14th St. SW
Washington, DC 20227
Norina Carpeteiro, Chair
Tel: (202) 874-6599 Fax: (202) 874-6965
Email: norina.carpeteiro@fms.treas.gov
Web: www.fms.treas.gov

Internal Revenue Service
1111 Constitution Ave. NW #2326
Washington, DC 20224
Sonia DaCosta, Servicewide HEPM
Tel: (202) 927-9929 Fax: (202) 622-6776
Web: www.irs.gov

US COMMISSION ON CIVIL RIGHTS
Human Resources Division
624 9th St. NW #510
Washington, DC 20425
Myrna Hernandez, Human Resources
Specialist
Tel: (202) 376-8364 Fax: (202) 376-7577
Email: mhernandez@usccr.gov
Web: www.usccr.gov

US GOVERNMENT PRINTING OFFICE
EEO Office
732 N Capitol St. NW #C-709, M/S EO
Washington, DC 20401
David Ware, HEPM
Tel: (202) 512-0641 Fax: (202) 512-0521
Email: dware@gpo.gov
Web: www.gpo.gov

VETERANS AFFAIRS, DEPT. OF
Office of Diversity Management & EEO
810 Vermont Ave. NW
Washington, DC 20420
Brenda A. Martin, EEO Specialist
Tel: (202) 501-1970 Fax: (202) 501-2145
Email: brenda.martin@mail.va.gov
Web: www.va.gov/dmeeo

WHITE HOUSE
Office of Management and Budget
725 17th St., NW, #8026
Washington, DC 20503
Claudia Magdalena Abendroth, Program
Examiner
Tel: (202) 395-6827 Fax: (202) 395-5836

Public Liaison
Old Executive Office Bldg. #186
Washington, DC 20502
Daniel Garza, Associate Director
Tel: (202) 456-2380 Fax: (202) 456-2130

FLORIDA

AGRICULTURE, DEPT. OF
Southeast Region
750 S Military Trail #G
West Palm Beach, FL 33415
Gregorio Cruz, HEPM
Tel: (561) 683-2285 X106 Fax: (561)
683-8205
Email: gregorio.cruz@fl.usda.gov
Web: www.usda.gov

Natural Resources and Conservation Service
Palm Beach Soil & Water Conservation
District
750 S Military Trail #G
West Palm Beach, FL 33415-3963
Gregorio Cruz, Florida Hispanic Emphasis
Program Manager
Tel: (561) 683-2285 X106 Fax: (561)
863-8205
Web: www.pbswcd.org

AIR FORCE, DEPT. OF THE
Eglin AFB
96 MSS/DPC, 310 W Van Matre Ave. #157
Eglin AFB, FL 32542-6825
Tel: (850) 882-3325 Fax: (850) 882-2941

Homestead AFB
482 SPTG/DPC, 29050 Coral Sea Blvd.
Box 79
Homestead AFB, FL 33039-1299
Tel: (305) 224-7061 Fax: (305) 224-7049

Macdill AFB
6 MSS/DPC, 8011 Tampa Point Blvd. #4
Macdill AFB, FL 33621-5321
Tel: (813) 828-2694 Fax: (813) 828-3696

Patrick AFB
45 MSS/DPC, 1138 Jupiter St.
Patrick AFB, FL 32925-3303
Tel: (321) 494-5238 Fax: (321) 494-6741

Tyndall AFB
325 MSS/DPC, 445 Suwannee Rd. #247
Tyndall AFB, FL 32403-5538
Tel: (850) 283-3203 Fax: (850) 283-8222

ARMY, DEPT. OF THE
US Army Recruiting Battalion Jacksonville
1851 Executive Center Dr. #130
Jacksonville, FL 32207-2350
Tel: (904) 396-2673/2451

US Army Recruiting Battalion Miami
The Augusta Bldg.,
8685 NW 53rd Terr. #200
Miami, FL 33166-4611
Tel: (305) 591-1833

US Army Recruiting Battalion Tampa
3350 Buschwood Park Dr. #140
Tampa, FL 33618-4447
Tel: (813) 935-5657/8955

EQUAL EMPLOYMENT OPPORTUNITY COMMISSION
Miami District Office
1 Biscayne Tower, 2 S Biscayne Blvd. #2700
Miami, FL 33131
Federico Costales, Director
Tel: (305) 536-4491 Fax: (305) 536-4011
Web: www.eeoc.gov

Tampa Area Office
501 E Polk St. #1000
Tampa, FL 33602
Manuel Zurita, Director
Tel: (813) 228-2310 Fax: (813) 228-2841
Email: manuel.zurita@eeoc.gov
Web: www.eeoc.gov

FEDERAL MEDIATION & CONCILIATION SERVICE
South Region
345 Lake Lynda Dr. #122
Orlando, FL 32817
Sergio A. Delgado, Director
Tel: (407) 382-6598 Fax: (407) 382-3727
Email: sdelgado@fmcs.gov
Web: www.fmcs.gov

NAVY, DEPT. OF THE
Naval Reserve Recruiting Area Southeast
5850 T.G. Lee Blvd. #210
Orlando, FL 32822-4437
Tel: (407) 856-4424 Fax: (407) 856-4424

Navy Recruiting District, Miami
8523 53rd Terr., Savannah Bldg. #201
Miami, FL 33166-4521
Tel: (954) 845-0101

USMC Recruiting Station, Ft. Lauderdale
7820 Peters Rd. #E109
Plantation, FL 33324-4006
Tel: (954) 452-0223 Fax: (954) 474-5461
Web: www.marines.com

USMC Recruiting Station, Jacksonville
3728 Phillips Hwy. #229
Jacksonville, FL 32207
Tel: (904) 858-9698 Fax: (904) 399-1994
Web: www.marines.com

USMC Recruiting Station, Orlando
5886 S Semoran Blvd., Air Business Ctr.
Orlando, FL 32822
Tel: (407) 249-5870 Fax: (407) 249-5880
Web: www.marines.com

POSTAL SERVICE
Central Florida District
P.O. Box 999994
Mid Florida, FL 32799-9994
Erica D. Mann, Hispanic Program Specialist
Tel: (407) 333-8460 Fax: (407) 444-3020
Email: erica.d.mann@usps.gov
Web: www.usps.com

Central Florida District
P.O. Box 999237
Mid-Florida, FL 32799-9237
Annie P. Seabrooks, Diversity Development
Specialist
Tel: (407) 333-4892 Fax: (407) 333-8467
Email: annie.p.seabrooks@usps.gov
Web: www.usps.gov

North Florida District
P.O. Box 40005
Jacksonville, FL 32203-0005
Mary L. Alston, Diversity Development
Specialist
Tel: (904) 858-6575 Fax: (904) 858-6633
Email: malston@email.usps.gov
Web: www.usps.gov

South Florida District
2200 NW 72nd Ave. #204
Miami, FL 33152-9461
Dorothy (Dottie) Johnson, Diversity
Development Specialist
Tel: (305) 470-0622 Fax: (305) 470-0647
Web: www.usps.com

Sun Coast District
2203 N Lois Ave. #1070
Tampa, FL 33607-7170
Regla M. Watts, Diversity Development
Specialist
Tel: (813) 354-6023 Fax: (813) 877-8656
Email: rwatts@email.usps.gov
Web: www.usps.gov

GEORGIA

AGRICULTURE, DEPT. OF
Southeast Region
P.O. Box 8
Monroe, GA 30655-0008
Jose Pagan, Acting HEPM
Tel: (770) 267-1359 Fax: (770) 267-7276
Email: jose.pagan@ga.usda.gov
Web: www.usda.gov

Forest Service
Southern Region/Civil Rights Office
1720 Peachtree Rd. NW #866S
Atlanta, GA 30309
Debra Harrell Wilfred, Director
Tel: (404) 347-7358 Fax: (404) 347-0356
Web: www.fs.fed.us

AIR FORCE, DEPT. OF THE
Air Force Reserve Command Headquarters
DPCS
1000 Marchbanks Rd.
Robins AFB, GA 31098
Phyllis Ross, Human Resources Specialist
Tel: (478) 327-1339 Fax: (478) 327-0530
Email: phyllis.ross@afrc.af.mil
Web: www.afrc.af.mil

Dobbins AFB
94 MSG/DPC, 1430 1st St. #1128
Dobbins AFB, GA 30069-5010
Tel: (678) 655-4966 Fax: (678) 655-4837

Moody AFB
347 MSS/DPC, 3010 Robinson Rd.
Moody AFB, GA 31699-1518
Tel: (229) 257-3047 Fax: (229) 257-3573

Robins AFB
78 SPTG/DPC, 215 Page Rd. #326
Robins AFB, GA 31098-1662
Tel: (478) 926-3805 Fax: (478) 926-6249

ARMY, DEPT. OF THE
US Army 2nd Recruiting Brigade
Southeast Region
1295 Hood Ave.
Forest Park, GA 30297-5104
Tel: (404) 469-3192/3194

US Army Recruiting Battalion Atlanta
2400 Herodian Way #490
Smyrna, GA 30080-8500
Tel: (770) 951-2815/2834

CENTERS FOR DISEASE CONTROL & PREVENTION
Human Resources Management Office
4770 Buford Hwy. M/S K15
Atlanta, GA 30341
Ramona Ramsey, HEPM/Human Resources
Management Consultant
Tel: (770) 488-1894 Fax: (770) 488-1991
Web: www.cdc.gov

ENERGY, DEPT. OF
Southeastern Power Association
1166 Athens Tech Rd.
Elberton, GA 30635-6711
Joel Seymour, HEPM
Tel: (706) 213-3810 Fax: (706) 213-3884
Email: joels@sepa.doe.gov
Web: www.sepa.doe.gov

EQUAL EMPLOYMENT OPPORTUNITY COMMISSION
Atlanta District Office
100 Alabama St. SW #4R30
Atlanta, GA 30303
Bernice Williams-Kimbrough, Director
Tel: (404) 562-6800 Fax: (404) 562-6909
Web: www.eeoc.gov

Savannah Local Office
410 Mall Blvd. #G
Savannah, GA 31406-4821
Lynn Jordan, Director
Tel: (912) 652-4234 Fax: (912) 652-4248
Email: lynn.jordan@eeoc.gov
Web: www.eeoc.gov

FEDERAL RESERVE BANK
Human Resources/EEO
Atlanta Region
1000 Peachtree St. NE
Atlanta, GA 30309-4470
Mary Kepler, Director
Tel: (404) 498-8500 Fax: (404) 498-8997
Web: www.frbatlanta.org

HOMELAND SECURITY, DEPT. OF
Federal Law Enforcement Training Center
Facilities Management Division Bldg. 200
Glynco, GA 31524
Luz Sánchez, Engineer/HEPM
Tel: (912) 267-2839 Fax: (912) 267-3056
Web: www.fletc.gov

INTERIOR, DEPT. OF THE
Geological Survey, Personnel Office
Southeast Region
3850 Holcomb Bridge Rd. #160
Norcross, GA 30092
Kevin Scott, Director
Tel: (770) 409-7751 Fax: (770) 409-7771
Email: kscott@usgs.gov
Web: www.usgs.gov

National Park Service
Southeast Region, Office of EEO and
Diversity Programs
100 Alabama St. SW, 1924 Bldg., 5th Fl.

Atlanta, GA 30303
Gwen Evans, Special Emphasis Program
Manager
Tel: (404) 562-3103 X562
Fax: (404) 562-3269
Email: gwen_evans@nps.gov
Web: www.nps.gov

LABOR, DEPT. OF
Atlanta Regional Office
Personnel Office
61 Forsyth St. SW #6B50
Atlanta, GA 30303
Mike Watt, Personnel Manager Specialist
Tel: (404) 562-2008 Fax: (404) 562-2050

Employment and Training Administration
South East Job Corps
61 Forsyth St. SW #6T95
Atlanta, GA 30303
Wenomia Person, Outreach Coordinator
Tel: (404) 562-2382 X125
Fax: (404) 562-2396
Email: wperson@doleta.gov
Web: www.doleta.gov

NAVY, DEPT. OF THE
Navy Recruiting District, Atlanta
2400 Herodian #400
Smyrna, GA 30080
Tel: (770) 612-4384

USMC Recruiting Station, Atlanta
6855 Jimmy Carter Blvd. #2600
Atlanta, GA 30071
Tel: (770) 246-9029 Fax: (770) 246-0636
Web: www.marines.com

POSTAL SERVICE
Atlanta District
P.O. Box 599390
Duluth, GA 30026-9390
Beverly Allen Stokes, Diversity Development
Specialist
Tel: (770) 717-2992 Fax: (770) 717-2993
Web: www.usps.gov

South Georgia District
451 College St. #414
Macon, GA 31213-9800
Alberta Lawson, Diversity Development
Specialist
Tel: (478) 752-8494 Fax: (478) 752-8685
Web: www.usps.com

SMALL BUSINESS ADMINISTRATION
Disaster Personnel Office-Disaster Area 2
1 Baltimore Pl. #300
Atlanta, GA 30308
Keka Wessmen, Personnel Officer
Tel: (404) 347-3771 Fax: (404) 347-5487

SOCIAL SECURITY ADMINISTRATION
Civil Rights and EO Office
Atlanta Region
61 Forsyth St. SW., 22T-64
Atlanta, GA 30303
Herberto Sanabria, Director
Tel: (404) 562-1387 Fax: (404) 562-1395

GUAM

AIR FORCE, DEPT. OF THE
Andersen AFB
36 MSS/DPC, Unit 14001 Box 13
APO, AP 96543-4001
Tel: (671) 366-2378 Fax: (671) 366-2378

HAWAII

AGRICULTURE, DEPT. OF
West Region
USDA-FSA 300 Ala Moana Blvd. #5-112
Honolulu, HI 96850
Rueben Flores, HEPM
Tel: (808) 541-2600 X136
Fax: (808) 541-2648
Email: rueben.flores@hi.usda.gov
Web: www.usda.gov

AIR FORCE, DEPT. OF THE
Hickam AFB
15 MSS/DPC, 655 Vickers Ave.
Hickam AFB, HI 96853-5398
Tel: (808) 449-1230 Fax: (808) 449-3685

Hickam AFB
HQ PACAF/DPF, 25 E St. #D208
Hickam AFB, HI 96853-5411
Tel: (808) 449-1961 Fax: (808) 449-5518

**EQUAL EMPLOYMENT OPPORTUNITY
COMMISSION**
Honolulu Local Office
P.O. Box 50082
300 Ala Moana Blvd. #7-127
Honolulu, HI 96850-0051
Timothy A. Riera, Director
Tel: (808) 541-3120   Fax: (808) 541-3390
Web: www.eeoc.gov

NAVY, DEPT. OF THE
Navy Officer Recruiting Station, Honolulu
733 Bishop St.
Honolulu, HI 96813

USMC Recruiting Sub-Station, Honolulu
1221 Kapiolani Blvd. #107
Honolulu, HI 96814
Tel: (808) 591-6677
Web: www.marines.com

IDAHO

AGRICULTURE, DEPT. OF
Forest Service
Coeur d'Alene River Ranger District
Idaho Panhandle National Forests
Coeur d'Alene, ID 83815
Irene Nipp, HEPM
Tel: (208) 556-5107 Fax: (208) 765-7307
Email: inipp@fs.fed.us
Web: www.fs.fed.us

AIR FORCE, DEPT. OF THE
Mountain Home AFB
366 MSS/DPC, 366 Gunfighter Ave. #190
Mountain Home AFB, ID 83648-5298
Tel: (208) 828-6683 Fax: (208) 828-6597

ENERGY, DEPT. OF
Idaho Operations Office
850 Energy Dr. M/S 1235
Idaho Falls, ID 83401
José L. Elizondo, HEPM
Tel: (208) 526-0965 Fax: (208) 526-7246
Email: elizonjl@id.doe.gov
Web: www.id.doe.gov

INTERIOR, DEPT. OF THE
Bureau of Reclamation
Pacific Northwest Region, Human
Resources
1150 N Curtis Rd. #100
Boise, ID 83706-1234
Max Gallegos, Human Resources Officer
Tel: (208) 378-5140 Fax: (208) 378-5023
Email: mgallegos@pn.usbr.gov
Web: www.usbr.gov/pn

National Interagency Fire Center
Human Resources
3833 S Development Ave.
Boise, ID 83705-5354
Sandy Tripp, Personnel Management
Specialist
Tel: (208) 387-5627 Fax: (208) 387-5723
Web: www.nifc.gov

ILLINOIS

AGRICULTURE, DEPT. OF
Midwest Region
233 S Soangetaha Rd.
Galesburg, IL 61401
Barb Lutrell, HEPM
Tel: (309) 342-5138 X117
Fax: (309) 342-9246
Email: barb.lutrell@il.usda.gov
Web: www.usda.gov

AIR FORCE, DEPT. OF THE
Scott AFB
HQ AMC/DPC, 100 Heritage Dr., Rm. 106
Scott AFB, IL 62225-5002
Tel: (618) 229-7901 Fax: (618) 229-0221

Scott AFB
375 MSS/DPC, 201 E Winters St.
Scott AFB, IL 62225-5037
Tel: (618) 256-3914 Fax: (618) 256-2553

ARMY, DEPT. OF THE
US Army Recruiting Battalion Chicago
P.O. Box 130
Sheridan US Army Reserve Ctr., Bldg. 142
Highland Park, IL 60035-7130
Tel: (847) 266-1359/1360

**DEPARTMENT OF COMMERCE AND
COMMUNITY AFFAIRS**
State of Illinois
620 E Adams St.
Springfield, IL 62701
Victoria Benn-Rochelle, EEO/Affirmative
Action Manager
Tel: (217) 524-2997 Fax: (217) 524-0189

ENERGY, DEPT. OF
Chicago Operations Office,
New Brunswick Laboratory
9800 S Cass Ave., Bldg. 350
Argonne, IL 60439
Maria E. Morales-Arteaga, HEPM
Tel: (630) 252-5435 Fax: (630) 252-6256
Email: maria.morales@ch.doe.gov
Web: www.ch.doe.gov

Chicago Operations Office,
Office of the Manager
9800 S Cass Ave., Bldg. 201
Argonne, IL 60439
Sara J. Brunson, Diversity Manager
Tel: (630) 252-2321 Fax: (630) 252-2315
Email: sara.brunson@ch.doe.gov
Web: www.ch.doe.gov

**EQUAL EMPLOYMENT OPPORTUNITY
COMMISSION**
Chicago District Office
500 W Madison St. #2800
Chicago, IL 60661
John P. Rowe, Director
Tel: (312) 353-2713   Fax: (312) 886-1168
Web: www.eeoc.gov

FEDERAL RESERVE BANK
Human Resources/EEO
Chicago District Office
230 S LaSalle St.
Chicago, IL 60604-1413
Catherine M. Cummings, EEO Officer

Tel: (312) 322-5322 Fax: (312) 322-5332
Web: www.chicagofed.org

LABOR, DEPT. OF
Employment and Training Administration
Office of Youth Programs and Job Corps
Federal Bldg. #676, 230 S Dearborn St.
Chicago, IL 60604
Donna Kay, Regional Director
Tel: (312) 596-5489 Fax: (312) 596-5471
Email: dkay@doleta.gov
Web: www.doleta.gov

Office of the Solicitor
230 S Dearborn St., 8th Fl.
Chicago, IL 60604
Rafael Alvarez, HEPM
Tel: (312) 353-1144 Fax: (312) 353-5698
Email: alvarez-rafael@dol.gov

NAVY, DEPT. OF THE
**Naval Reserve Recruiting Command Area
Central**
2834B Green Bay Rd., Bldg. 3400, #266
Great Lakes, IL 60088-5709
Tel: (847) 688-2548

Navy Recruiting District, Chicago
3400 Patten Rd. #300
Ft. Sheridan, IL 60037
Tel: (847) 688-2024

USMC Recruiting Station, Chicago
1700 S Wolf Rd.
Des Plaines, IL 60018
Tel: (847) 803-0128 Fax: (847) 803-8374
Web: www.marines.com

POSTAL SERVICE
Central Illinois District
6801 W 73rd St.
Bedford Park, IL 60499-9311
Sharon Murphy, Diversity Development
Specialist
Tel: (708) 563-7343 Fax: (708) 563-7638
Email: sharon.t.murphy@usps.gov
Web: www.usps.gov

Chicago District
433 W Harrison St., 4th Fl.
Chicago, IL 60607-9998
Esmeralda Dominguez, Hispanic Program
Specialist
Tel: (312) 983-8014 Fax: (312) 983-8033
Web: www.usps.com

Great Lakes Area Office
244 Knollwood Dr., 4th Fl.
Bloomingdale, IL 60117-3050
Jaime Claudio , Senior Diversity Program
Coordinator
Tel: (630) 539-8338 Fax: (630) 539-7095
Web: www.usps.com

Northern Illinois District
500 E Fullerton Ave.
Carol Stream, IL 60199-9601
Marquetta Tisdell, Diversity Development
Specialist
Tel: (630) 260-5203 Fax: (630) 260-5841
Email: mtisdell@email.usps.gov
Web: www.usps.gov

Northern Illinois District
500 E Fullerton Ave.
Carol Stream, IL 60199-9601
Efren Anguiano, Hispanic Program
Specialist
Tel: (630) 260-5213 Fax: (630) 260-5625
Web: www.usps.com

RAILROAD RETIREMENT BOARD
844 N Rush St. #844
Chicago, IL 60611-2092
Lynn Cousins, Director of EEO
Tel: (312) 751-4942 Fax: (312) 751-7179

Email: lynn.cousins@rrb.gov
Web: www.rrb.gov

TRANSPORTATION, DEPT. OF
Federal Highway Administration
19900 Governors Dr. #301
Olympia Fields, IL 60461
Deborah J. Martinez, HEPM
Tel: (708) 283-2339 Fax: (708) 283-3501
Email: deborah.martinez@fhwa.dot.gov
Web: www.dot.gov

INDIANA

AIR FORCE, DEPT. OF THE
Grissom ARB
434 SPTG ARW/DPC,
Bldg. 596, #204 Warthog Dr.
Grissom ARB, IN 46971-5000
Tel: (765) 688-4836 Fax: (765) 688-4833

ARMY, DEPT. OF THE
US Army Recruiting Battalion Indianapolis
9152 Kent Ave.
Indianapolis, IN 46216
Tel: (317) 549-0338/1738

EQUAL EMPLOYMENT OPPORTUNITY COMMISSION
Indianapolis District Office
101 W Ohio St. #1900
Indianapolis, IN 46204
Danny G. Harter, Director
Tel: (317) 226-7212 Fax: (317) 226-7953
Web: www.eeoc.gov

NAVY, DEPT. OF THE
Navy Recruiting District, Indianapolis
9152 Kent Ave., Bldg. 401 #352
Indianapolis, IN 46216
Tel: (317) 554-0701

Navy Reserve Center Indianapolis
3010 White River Pkwy.
Indianapolis, IN 46208
Tel: (317) 921-2024
Email: d2s20007@cnrrc.nola.navy.mil

USMC Recruiting Station, Indianapolis
9152 Kent Ave., Bldg. 401, 2nd Fl.
Indianapolis, IN 46216-2036
Tel: (317) 554-0504 Fax: (317) 554-0514
Web: www.marines.com

Greater Indiana District
3939 Vincennes Rd.
Indianapolis, IN 46298-9855
Patricia A. Proctor, Diversity Development Specialist
Tel: (317) 870-8562 Fax: (317) 837-8686
Email: patricia.proctor@usps.gov
Web: www.usps.gov

IOWA

ARMY, DEPT. OF THE
US Army Recruiting Battalion Des Moines
210 Walnut St., Federal Bldg. Rm. 557
Des Moines, IA 50309-2108
Tel: (515) 280-7401

NAVY, DEPT. OF THE
Navy Officer Recruiting Station, Iowa City
400 S Clinton St.
Iowa City, IA 52240

USMC Recruiting Station, Des Moines
4725 Merle Hay Rd. #209
Des Moines, IA 50322-1983
Tel: (515) 253-9347 Fax: (515) 252-6237
Web: www.marines.com

KANSAS

AGRICULTURE, DEPT. OF
Natural Resources Conservation Service
North Plains Region
320 N Jefferson St.
Wilmington, KS 67152
Mary Hainsworth, HEPM
Tel: (620) 326-2612 Fax: (620) 326-7971
Email: mary.hainsworth@ks.usda.gov
Web: www.nrcs.usda.gov

AIR FORCE, DEPT. OF THE
McConnell AFB
22 MSS/MSC, 57798 Leavenworth St. #4
Mc Connell AFB, KS 67221-3614
Tel: (316) 759-4332 Fax: (316) 759-4139

EQUAL EMPLOYMENT OPPORTUNITY COMMISSION
Kansas City Area Office
Gateway Tower II, 4th & State Ave., 9th Fl.
Kansas City, KS 66101
George R. Dixon, Director
Tel: (913) 551-5655 Fax: (913) 551-6957
Web: www.eeoc.gov

NAVY, DEPT. OF THE
USMC Recruiting Sub-Station, Dodge City
2601 Central Ave.
Dodge City, KS 67801
Tel: (316) 227-8151
Web: www.marines.com

USMC Recruiting Sub-Station, Meridian
2201 Hwy. 39 North
Meridian, KS 39301
Tel: (601) 693-6777
Web: www.marines.com

USMC Recruiting Sub-Station, Olathe
115 S Clairborne Ave.
Olathe, KS 66062
Tel: (913) 782-9040
Web: www.marines.com

USMC Recruiting Sub-Station, Overland Park
8153 Santa Fe Dr.
Overland Park, KS 66204
Tel: (913) 341-4080
Web: www.marines.com

USMC Recruiting Sub-Station, Topeka
5967 SW 29th St.
Topeka, KS 66614
Tel: (785) 271-1067
Web: www.marines.com

USMC Recruiting Sub-Station, Tupelo
3885 N Gloster St. #B
Tupelo, KS 38804
Tel: (662) 842-7734
Web: www.marines.com

USMC Recruiting Sub-Station, Wichita
614 N West St.
Wichita, KS 67203
Tel: (316) 943-8132
Web: www.marines.com

KENTUCKY

ARMY, DEPT. OF THE
US Army 3rd Recruiting Brigade
Upper Midwest Region
Bldg. 6580
Fort Knox, KY 40121-2726
Tel: (502) 626-1030/1041

US Army Cadet Command, ROTC
Public Affairs Office
Fort Knox, KY 40121-5610
Tel: (502) 624-8149

EQUAL EMPLOYMENT OPPORTUNITY COMMISSION
Louisville Area Office
600 Dr. Martin Luther King, Jr. Place #268
Louisville, KY 40202
Marcia Hall-Craig, Director
Tel: (502) 582-6082 Fax: (502) 582-5895
Web: www.eeoc.gov

NAVY, DEPT. OF THE
Navy Reserve Center Lexington
151 Votech Rd.
Lexington, KY 40511
Tel: (859) 422-8767
Email: d2s20010@cnrrc.nola.navy.mil

USMC Recruiting Station, Louisville
600 Martin Luther King Jr. Pl. #221
Louisville, KY 40202-2269
Tel: (502) 582-6607 Fax: (502) 582-6604
Web: www.marines.com

LOUISIANA

AGRICULTURE, DEPT. OF
National Finance Center
13800 Old Gentilly Rd.
New Orleans, LA 70129
Donald Lewis, Director, Civil Rights
Tel: (504) 426-6221 Fax: (504) 426-9710
Email: donald.lewis@usda.gov
Web: www.nfc.usda.gov

Natural Resources Conservation Service
South Central Region
4274 Front St.
Winnsboro, LA 71295
Donna Remides, HEPM
Tel: (318) 435-7328 Fax: (318) 435-7436
Email: donna.remides@la.usda.gov
Web: www.nrcs.usda.gov

AIR FORCE, DEPT. OF THE
Barksdale AFB
2 MSS/DPC, 345 Davis Ave. West #223
Barksdale AFB, LA 71110-2073
Tel: (318) 456-4502 Fax: (318) 456-3808

ARMY, DEPT. OF THE
US Army Recruiting Battalion New Orleans
4400 Dauphine St., Bldg. 602-2C
New Orleans, LA 70146-1699
Tel: (504) 678-8531/8533

ENERGY, DEPT. OF
Strategic Petroleum Reserve
900 Commerce Rd. East
New Orleans, LA 70123
Jorge Aguinaga, HEPM
Tel: (979) 230-2201 Fax: (979) 230-2308
Email: jorge.aguinaga@spr.doe.gov
Web: www.spr.doe.gov

EQUAL EMPLOYMENT OPPORTUNITY COMMISSION
New Orleans District Office
701 Loyola Ave. #600
New Orleans, LA 70113-9936
Manuel Zurita, Acting Director
Tel: (504) 589-2329 Fax: (504) 589-6861
Web: www.eeoc.gov

INTERIOR, DEPT. OF THE
Minerals Management Service
Personnel Office
1201 Elmwood Park Blvd., M/S 2620
New Orleans, LA 70123
Vanessa Matthews, Human Resources Specialist
Tel: (504) 736-2884 Fax: (504) 736-2478
Email: vanessa.matthews@mms.gov
Web: www.mms.gov

NAVY, DEPT. OF THE
Navy Recruiting District, New Orleans
4400 Dauphine St.
New Orleans, LA 70146
Tel: (504) 678-5520

USMC Recruiting Station, New Orleans
4400 Dauphine St.,
Bldg. 602 NSA 602-2-C
New Orleans, LA 70146-6500
Tel: (504) 678-5095 Fax: (504) 678-5660
Web: www.marines.com

POSTAL SERVICE
Louisiana District
701 Loyola Ave. #10021
New Orleans, LA 70113-9813
Hedy H. Duplessis, Diversity Development Specialist
Tel: (504) 589-1283 Fax: (504) 589-1467
Email: hduples1@email.usps.gov
Web: www.usps.gov

MAINE

ARMY, DEPT. OF THE
US Army Recruiting Battalion New England
33 Canam Dr.
Topsham, ME 04086-1117
Tel: (207) 725-8637

HOMELAND SECURITY, DEPT. OF
US Coast Guard
USCG Recruiting Office Portland
Brighton Avenue Plz., 1041 Brighton Ave.
Portland, ME 04101-1042
Tel: (207) 761-4307/3921
Fax: (207) 874-6058
Email: dhodgdon@cgrc.uscg.mil
Web: www.gocoastguard.com

NAVY, DEPT. OF THE
Naval Reserve Center Brunswick
500 Sewall St.
Brunswick, ME 04011
Tel: (207) 921-1534
Email: d5s20005@cnrrc.nola.navy.mil

USMC Recruiting Sub-Station, Bangor
667 Hogan Rd., Maine Sq. Mall #7
Bangor, ME 04401
Tel: (207) 942-5138
Web: www.marines.com

POSTAL SERVICE
Maine District
P.O. Box 7800
Portland, ME 04104-7800
Debbie Woods, Diversity Development Specialist
Tel: (207) 828-8400 Fax: (207) 828-8447
Web: www.usps.gov

MARYLAND

AGRICULTURE, DEPT. OF
Food Safety and Inspection Service (FSIS)
Office of Civil Rights
5601 Sunnyside Ave. #2-1134, M/S 5261
Beltsville, MD 20705
Sylvia Holguin Bourn, National HEPM
Tel: (301) 504-7751 Fax: (301) 504-7746
Email: sylvia.bourn@fsis.usda.gov
Web: www.fsis.usda.gov

5601 Sunnyside Ave. M/S 5261, #1134-A
Beltsville, MD 20705-5000
Steven Newbold, Director of Civil Rights
Tel: (301) 504-7748 Fax: (301) 504-7746

Marketing and Regulatory Programs
Animal and Plant Health Inspection
Service (APHIS)
4700 River Rd. #92-5C17
Riverdale, MD 20737
Terry A. Henson, National HEPM
Tel: (301) 734-5555 Fax: (301) 734-3698
Email: terry.henson@aphis.usda.gov
Web: www.aphis.usda.gov

Natural Resources Conservation Service
5601 Sunnyside Ave. #1-1123
Beltsville, MD 20705-5000
Andrew Johnson, Director of Civil Rights
Tel: (301) 504-2182 Fax: (301) 504-2175

ARMY, DEPT. OF THE
Baltimore District Corps of Engineers
10 S Howard St. #9500
Baltimore, MD 21201
Marie O. Johnson, EEO Officer
Tel: (410) 962-4556 Fax: (410) 962-2416
Email: marie.johnson@usace.army.mil
Web: www.usace.army.mil

US Army 1st Recruiting Brigade
Northeast Region
4550 Llewelyn Ave.
Fort George Meade, MD 20755-5380
Tel: (301) 677-2380/2378

US Army Recruiting Battalion Baltimore
Bldg. 4550, Rm. 245
Fort George G. Meade, MD 20755-5390
Tel: (301) 677-7034/7029

**CENTERS FOR DISEASE CONTROL &
PREVENTION**
National Center for Health Statistics
Office of EEO
3311 Toledo Rd., 4th Fl.
Hyattsville, MD 20782
Linda J. Adams, Equal Employment Officer
Tel: (301) 458-4636 Fax: (301) 458-4041
Email: lca9@cdc.gov
Web: www.cdc.gov

COMMERCE, DEPT. OF
**National Institute of Standards and
Technology**
100 Bureau Dr. M/S 1740
Gaithersburg, MD 20899-1740
Luis Jimenez, Jr., Diversity Program
Manager
Tel: (301) 975-5562 Fax: (301) 975-5387
Email: luis.jimenez@nist.gov
Web: www.nist.gov

Office of Civil Rights
100 Bureau Dr., M/S 1740
Gaithersburg, MD 20899-1740
Mirta-Marie M. Keys, Director
Tel: (301) 975-2042
Email: mirta-marie.keys@nist.gov
Web: www.nist.gov

**National Oceanic and Atmospheric
Administration**
Office of Civil Rights
1305 EastWest Hwy. #12222, Bldg. SSMC4
Silver Spring, MD 20910
Al Corea, Director
Tel: (301) 713-0500 X114
Fax: (301) 713-0983
Email: alfred.a.corea@noaa.gov
Web: www.noaa.gov

DEFENSE, DEPT. OF
Defense Security Service
Office of Diversity Management
881 Elkridge Landing Rd.
Linthicum, MD 21090
Lori A. Simmons, EEO Director
Tel: (410) 865-2477 Fax: (410) 865-3438

Email: oaaeop.questions@mail.dss.mil
Web: www.dss.mil

**National Imagery and Mapping Agency
(OEE/D-119)**
4600 Sangamore Rd.
Bethesda, MD 20816-5003
Deborah Dominique, EEO Specialist/HEPM
Tel: (301) 227-7870 Fax: (301) 227-2428
Email: deborahdominique@nga.mil
Web: www.nga.mil

**EQUAL EMPLOYMENT OPPORTUNITY
COMMISSION**
Baltimore District Office
City Crescent Bldg., 10 S Howard St., 3rd Fl.
Baltimore, MD 21201
Marie M. Tomasso, Director
Tel: (410) 962-3932 Fax: (410) 962-4270
Web: www.eeoc.gov

HEALTH AND HUMAN SERVICES, DEPT. OF
Centers for Medicare and Medicaid Services
Office of Equal Opportunity and Civil Rights
7500 Security Blvd. #N2-21-13
Baltimore, MD 21244-1850
Angela Davis Putty, Affirmative
Employment/Special Emphasis
Tel: (410) 786-5112 Fax: (410) 786-9549
Email: angela.davis@cms.hhs.gov
Web: www.cms.hhs.gov

Office of Equal Opportunity and Civil Rights
7500 Security Blvd. #N2-22-17
Baltimore, MD 21244-1850
Patricia Lamond, Director
Tel: (410) 786-5110 Fax: (410) 786-9549
Email: plamond@cms.hhs.gov
Web: www.cms.hhs.gov

Office of Equal Opportunity and Civil Rights
7500 Security Blvd. #N2-22-07
Baltimore, MD 21244-1850
Richard E. Torres-Estrada, HEPM/Equal
Employment Opportunity Specialist
Tel: (410) 786-0018 Fax: (410) 786-9549
Email: rtorresestrada@cms.hhs.gov
Web: www.cms.hhs.gov

**Health Resources and Services
Administration**
5600 Fishers Ln. #14-A27
Rockville, MD 20857
Darío Prieto , HEPM
Tel: (301) 443-0331 Fax: (301) 443-7898
Email: dprieto@hrsa.gov
Web: www.hrsa.gov

Office of Minority Health
Resource Center
1101 Wooton Pkwy. #650
Rockville, MD 20852
José T. Carneiro, Project Director
Tel: (301) 251-1797 Fax: (301) 251-2160
Email: jcarneiro@omhrc.gov
Web: www.omhrc.gov

Program Support Center
Office of EEO
5600 Fishers Ln. #16A-54
Rockville, MD 20857
Kay Nitta, HEPM
Tel: (301) 443-1144 Fax: (301) 443-1145
Email: knitta@psc.gov
Web: www.psc.gov

Office of EEO
5600 Fishers Ln. #16A-54
Rockville, MD 20857
Donald L. Inniss, Director
Tel: (301) 443-1972 Fax: (301) 443-1145
Email: donald.inniss@psc.hhs.gov
Web: www.os.dhhs.gov

**Substance Abuse and Mental Health
Services Administration**
EEO/Civil Rights Office
Parklawn Bldg., 5600 Fishers Ln. #16A44
Rockville, MD 20857
Carlos O'Kieffe, EEO Project Manager
Tel: (301) 443-2112 Fax: (301) 443-2118
Email: carlos.o'kieffe@psc.hhs.gov
Web: www.samhsa.gov

**NATIONAL AERONAUTICS AND SPACE
ADMINISTRATION (NASA)**
Goddard Space Flight Ctr., M/C 120
Greenbelt, MD 20771
Dan Krieger, HEPM
Tel: (301) 286-7913 Fax: (301) 286-0298
Email: dan.krieger@nasa.gov
Web: www.nasa.gov

NAVY, DEPT. OF THE
Naval Reserve Center Baltimore
Ft. McHenry
Baltimore, MD 21230-5392
Tel: (410) 547-1915
Email: d5s20006@cnrrc.nola.navy.mil

USMC Recruiting Station, Baltimore
6845 Deerpath Rd., Dorsey Business Ctr.
Oakridge, MD 21075
Tel: (410) 379-5709 Fax: (410) 379-5209
Web: www.marines.com

USMC Recruiting Station, Frederick
5112 Pegasus Ct.
Frederick, MD 21704-8303
Tel: (301) 668-2025 Fax: (301) 668-2036
Web: www.marines.com

NUCLEAR REGULATORY COMMISSION
Office of Human Resources
11555 Rockville Pike
Rockville, MD 20852
Peggy A. Etheridge, Senior Recruiter
Tel: (301) 415-2294 Fax: (301) 415-3818
Email: pae@nrc.gov
Web: www.nrc.gov

POSTAL SERVICE
Baltimore District
900 E Fayette St. #327
Baltimore, MD 21233-9989
Thomasine A. Adams, Diversity
Development Specialist
Tel: (410) 347-4265 Fax: (410) 234-8260
Email: thomasine.a.adams@usps.gov
Web: www.usps.gov

TREASURY, DEPT. OF THE
Financial Management Service
Office of Equal Opportunity and Diversity
3700 East West Hwy. #133
Hyattsville, MD 20782
Paul M. Curran, Director
Tel: (202) 874-8330 Fax: (202) 874-8660
Email: paul.curran@fms.treas.gov
Web: www.fms.treas.gov

EEO
3700 Eastwest Hwy. #133
Hyattsville, MD 20782
Paul Curran, Director
Tel: (202) 874-8330 Fax: (202) 874-8660
Email: paul.curran@fms.treas.gov
Web: www.fms.treas.gov

AIR FORCE, DEPT. OF THE
Hanscom AFB
66 SPTG/DPC, 20 Schilling Cr.
Hanscom AFB, MA 01731-2800
Tel: (781) 377-2723 Fax: (781) 377-7084

Otis ANGB
Granville St. #24
Otis ANGB, MA 02542-5028
Tel: (508) 968-4333 Fax: (508) 968-4660

Westover AFB
439 SPTG/DPC, 100 Lloyd St. S. Wing #106
Westover AFB, MA 01022-1843
Tel: (413) 557-2871 Fax: (413) 557-3474

**EQUAL EMPLOYMENT OPPORTUNITY
COMMISSION**
Boston Area Office
475 Government Ctr.
Boston, MA 02203
Robert L. Sanders, Director
Tel: (617) 565-3200 Fax: (617) 565-3196
Web: www.eeoc.gov

HOMELAND SECURITY, DEPT. OF
US Coast Guard
USCG Recruiting Office Boston
Capt. John Foster Williams Bldg., 408
Atlantic Ave. #548
Boston, MA 02110-3350
Tel: (617) 565-8656 Fax: (617) 565-8460
Email: wslauenwhite@cgrc.uscg.mil
Web: www.gocoastguard.com

US Coast Guard
USCG Recruiting Office Springfield
New Federal Office Bldg.,
1550 Main St. #110
Springfield, MA 01103-1422
Tel: (413) 785-0324/22
Fax: (413) 785-0326
Email: tryan@cgrc.uscg.mil
Web: www.gocoastguard.com

LABOR, DEPT. OF
Employment and Training Administration
Office of Youth Programs and Job Corps
JFK Federal Center Bldg. #E-350
Boston, MA 02203
Joseph Semansky, Regional Director
Tel: (617) 788-0197 Fax: (617) 788-0189

NAVY, DEPT. OF THE
Naval Reserve Center Quincy
85 Sea St.
Quincy, MA 02169
Tel: (617) 753-4669 Fax: (617) 753-4642
Email: d5s20001@cnrrc.nola.navy.mil

Navy Recruiting District, New England
495 Summer St.
New England, MA 02210
Tel: (800) 792-9099

USMC Recruiting Station, Springfield
105 East St.
Chicopee Falls, MA 01020
Tel: (413) 594-2033 Fax: (413) 594-9815
Web: www.marines.com

TRANSPORTATION, DEPT. OF
Research & Special Programs Administration
Volpe National Transportation Systems Ctr.
55 Broadway DTS-802
Cambridge, MA 02142
María Caminos-Medina, HEPM
Tel: (617) 494-2340 Fax: (617) 494-3334
Email: caminos@volpe.dot.gov
Web: www.volpe.dot.gov

AGRICULTURE, DEPT. OF
Midwest Region
3001 Coolidge Rd. #250
East Lansing, MI 48823
Jessica Modert, HEPM
Tel: (517) 324-5264 Fax: (517) 324-5171
Email: jessica.modert@mi.usda.gov

Web: www.usda.gov

AIR FORCE, DEPT. OF THE
Selfridge ANGB
127 WG/DPC, 29553 George Ave., Bldg. 303
Selfridge ANGB, MI 48045-5399
Tel: (586) 307-4791 Fax: (586) 307-4123

ARMY, DEPT. OF THE
US Army Recruiting Battalion Great Lakes
Holiday Office Park North,
6545 Mercantile Way #11
Lansing, MI 48911-5974
Tel: (517) 887-5782

**EQUAL EMPLOYMENT OPPORTUNITY
COMMISSION**
Detroit District Office
477 Michigan Ave. #865
Detroit, MI 48226
James R. Neely, Jr., Director
Tel: (313) 226-4600   Fax: (313) 226-4610
Web: www.eeoc.gov

INTERIOR, DEPT. OF THE
National Park Service
Sleeping Bear Dunes National Lake Shore
9922 Front St.
Empire, MI 49630
Gale Purifoy, Personnel Management
Specialist
Tel: (231) 326-5134 Fax: (231) 326-5382
Email: gale_purifoy@nps.gov
Web: www.nps.gov

NAVY, DEPT. OF THE
Navy Recruiting District, Michigan
1155 Brewery Park Blvd. #320
Detroit, MI 48207
Tel: (313) 259-1004

Navy Reserve Center Detroit
Bldg. 1410, 25154 Plattsburg
Selfridge ANGB, MI 48045-4911
Tel: (586) 307-6638 Fax: (586) 307-6985
Email: d2s20008@cnrrc.nola.navy.mil

USMC Recruiting Station, Lansing
6845 Mercantile Way #12
Lansing, MI 48911-5972
Tel: (517) 882-1892 Fax: (517) 882-1793
Web: www.marines.com

USMC Recruiting Station, Troy
580 Kirts Blvd. #307
Troy, MI 48084-4141
Tel: (248) 269-9210 Fax: (248) 269-9286
Web: www.marines.com

POSTAL SERVICE
Detroit District
1401 W Fort St., 10th Fl.
Detroit, MI 48233-9998
Alzana Braxton, Diversity Development
Specialist
Tel: (313) 226-8131 Fax: (313) 226-8005
Email: abraxton@email.usps.gov
Web: www.usps.gov

Greater Michigan District
P.O. Box 999997
Grand Rapids, MI 49599-9997
Susan Pfeifer, Diversity Development
Specialist
Tel: (616) 776-6139 Fax: (616) 336-5381
Email: susan.d.pfeifer@usps.gov
Web: www.usps.gov

MINNESOTA

ARMY, DEPT. OF THE
US Army Recruiting Battalion Minneapolis
BHW Federal Bldg. #3700, 1 Federal Dr.
Fort Snelling, MN 55111-4007

Tel: (612) 725-3122/3123

**EQUAL EMPLOYMENT OPPORTUNITY
COMMISSION**
Minneapolis Area Office
Towle Bldg., 330 S 2nd Ave. #430
Minneapolis, MN 55401-2224
Cornelius Sheppard, Acting Director
Tel: (612) 335-4040 Fax: (612) 335-4044
Web: www.eeoc.gov

NAVY, DEPT. OF THE
Navy Recruiting District, Minneapolis
6020 28th Ave. South
Minneapolis, MN 55450
Tel: (612) 725-0414

USMC Recruiting Station, Twin Cities
Bishop Henry Whipple Federal Bldg.,
1 Federal Dr. #450
Fort Snelling, MN 55111-4080
Tel: (612) 725-3229 Fax: (612) 725-3232
Web: www.marines.com

POSTAL SERVICE
Northland District
P.O. Box 645001
St. Paul, MN 55164-5001
Andrew S. Fisher, Diversity Development
Specialist
Tel: (651) 293-3716 Fax: (651) 293-3000
Email: andrew.s.fisher@usps.gov
Web: www.usps.gov

MISSISSIPPI

AIR FORCE, DEPT. OF THE
Columbus AFB
14 MSS/DPC, 680 7th St. #254
Columbus AFB, MS 39710-6801
Tel: (601) 434-2635 Fax: (601) 434-2652

Keesler AFB
81 MSS/DPC, 500 Fisher St. Rm. 213
Keesler AFB, MS 39534-2547
Tel: (228) 377-3889 Fax: (228) 377-1732

ARMY, DEPT. OF THE
US Army Recruiting Battalion Jackson
Howie Bldg., 3780 I-55 N Frontage Rd.
Jackson, MS 39211-6323
Tel: (601) 366-0895

**EQUAL EMPLOYMENT OPPORTUNITY
COMMISSION**
Jackson Area Office
100 W Capitol St. #207
Jackson, MS 39269
Benjamin Bradley, Director
Tel: (601) 965-4537   Fax: (601) 965-5272
Web: www.eeoc.gov

NAVY, DEPT. OF THE
Naval Reserve Center
434 Rosenbaum Ave.
Meridian, MS 39309
Tel: (601) 679-7105 Fax: (601) 679-8609
Email: d3s20013@cnrrc.nola.navy.mil

POSTAL SERVICE
Mississippi District
P.O. Box 99987
Jackson, MS 39205-9987
Fannie B. Smith, Diversity Development
Specialist
Tel: (601) 351-7251 Fax: (601) 351-7504
Email: fannie.b.smith@usps.gov
Web: www.usps.gov

MISSOURI

AGRICULTURE, DEPT. OF
Midwest Region
P.O. Box 199
Marble Hill, MO 63764
Michael Squires, HEPM
Tel: (573) 238-2028 X3
Fax: (573) 238-3315
Email: mike.squires@mo.usda.gov
Web: www.usda.gov

National Information Technology Center
8930 Ward Pkwy.
Kansas City, MO 64114
William Morales, HEPM
Tel: (816) 823-2409 Fax: (816) 926-6754
Email: william.morales@nitckc.usda.gov
Web: www.usda.gov

AIR FORCE, DEPT. OF THE
Jefferson Barracks ANGS
NGB-HR-Eastern Center, 44 Johnson Rd.
St. Louis, MO 63125-4193
Tel: (314) 260-8724

Whiteman AFB
509 MSS/DPC, 509 Spirit Blvd. #104
Whiteman AFB, MO 65305-5021
Tel: (660) 687-6475

ARMY, DEPT. OF THE
US Army Recruiting Battalion Kansas City
10300 NW Prairie View Rd.
Kansas City, MO 64153-1350
Tel: (816) 891-8721/8729

US Army Recruiting Battalion St. Louis
Robert Young Bldg.
1222 Spruce St., 10th Fl.
St. Louis, MO 63102-2815
Tel: (314) 331-4131/4145

DEFENSE, DEPT. OF
National Imagery and Mapping Agency
EEO Office
3838 Vogel Rd., M/S L11
Arnold, MO 63010
Margaret Brown, Deputy Director
Tel: (314) 263-4442 Fax: (314) 263-4252

**EQUAL EMPLOYMENT OPPORTUNITY
COMMISSION**
St. Louis District Office
Robert A. Young Federal Bldg., 1222
Spruce St. #8-100
St. Louis, MO 63103
Lynn Bruner, Director
Tel: (314) 539-7800 Fax: (314) 539-7894
Web: www.eeoc.gov

FEDERAL RESERVE BANK
Human Resources/EEO
Kansas City Region
925 Grand Blvd.
Kansas City, MO 64198-0001
Debra Bronston, Assistant VP
Tel: (816) 881-2463 Fax: (816) 881-6742
Web: www.kc.frb.org

NAVY, DEPT. OF THE
9th Marine Corps District Headquarters
3805 E 155 St., Bldg. 710
Kansas City, MO 64147-1309
Tel: (816) 843-3924 Fax: (816) 843-3984

Navy Recruiting District, Kansas City
10306 Prairie View Rd.
Kansas City, MO 64153
Tel: (816) 880-1105

Navy Recruiting District, St. Louis
1222 Spruce St., 10th Fl.
St. Louis, MO 63103
Tel: (314) 331-4296

USMC Recruiting Station, Kansas City
10302 NW Prairie View Rd.
Kansas City, MO 64153
Tel: (816) 891-2564 Fax: (816) 891-6590
Web: www.marines.com

USMC Recruiting Station, St. Louis
1222 Spruce St. #10.311
St. Louis, MO 63103-2817
Tel: (314) 331-4018 Fax: (314) 331-4017

POSTAL SERVICE
Gateway District
1720 Market St. #3011
St. Louis, MO 63155-9756
Glenda Fields, Diversity Development
Specialist
Tel: (314) 436-3868 Fax: (314) 436-6424
Email: gfields@email.usps.gov
Web: www.usps.com

Mid-America District
315 W Pershing Rd. #509B
Kansas City, MO 64108-9994
Rita Hamilton, Diversity Development Specialist
Tel: (816) 374-9131 Fax: (816) 374-9487
Web: www.usps.com

MONTANA

AGRICULTURE, DEPT. OF
Forest Service
Northern Region (R-1)
P.O. Box 7669
Missoula, MT 59807
Nate Thomas, HEPM
Tel: (406) 329-3568 Fax: (406) 329-3124
Email: nthomas@fs.fed.us
Web: www.fs.fed.us

Natural Resources Conservation Service
North Plains Region
30 Lower Valley Rd.
Kalispell, MT 59901
Angel Rosario, HEPM
Tel: (406) 752-4242 X104
Fax: (406) 752-4879
Email: angel.rosario@mt.usda.gov
Web: www.usda.gov

AIR FORCE, DEPT. OF THE
Malmstrom AFB
341 MSS/DPC, 7215 Goddard Dr.,
Bldg. 1191 Rm. 123
Malmstrom AFB, MT 59402-6857
Tel: (406) 731-4644 Fax: (406) 731-4464

INTERIOR, DEPT. OF THE
Bureau of Indians Affairs
Rocky Mountain Region,
Personnel Office
316 N 26th St.
Billings, MT 59101
Sharon Limberhand, Personnel Officer
Tel: (406) 247-7956 Fax: (406) 247-7902
Web: www.doi.gov

Bureau of Reclamation
Great Plains Region
P.O. Box 36900
Billings, MT 59107-6900
Sue McCannel, Personnel Officer
Tel: (406) 247-7699 Fax: (406) 247-7741
Web: www.usbr.gov/gp

NAVY, DEPT. OF THE
Navy Officer Recruiting Station, Butte
100 E Broadway, Finlan Hotel
Butte, MT 59701

POSTAL SERVICE
Big Sky District
841 S 26th St.
Billings, MT 59101-9437

Leslie Denny, Diversity Development Specialist
Tel: (406) 657-5660 Fax: (406) 657-5788
Web: www.usps.gov

NEBRASKA

AGRICULTURE, DEPT. OF
North Plains Region
100 Centennial Mall North, Federal Bldg.
#152, MS 36
Lincoln, NE 68508
Karl Hipple, HEPM
Tel: (402) 437-5351 Fax: (402) 437-5336
Email: karl.hipple@mssc.nrcs.usda.gov
Web: www.usda.gov

AIR FORCE, DEPT. OF THE
Offutt AFB
55 MSS/DPC, 106 Peacekeeper Dr. #2N3
Offutt AFB, NE 68113-4015
Tel: (402) 232-8164 Fax: (402) 232-5679

EQUAL OPPORTUNITY COMMISSION
State of Nebraska
P.O. Box 94934
Lincoln, NE 68509-4934
vacant, Executive Director
Tel: (402) 471-2024 Fax: (402) 471-4059

INTERIOR, DEPT. OF THE
National Park Service
Midwest Region, Office of Human Resources
601 Riverfront Dr.
Omaha, NE 68102-4226
Carol Solnosky, Human Resources Specialist
Tel: (402) 661-1650 Fax: (402) 661-1737
Email: carol_solnosky@nps.gov
Web: www.nps.gov

NAVY, DEPT. OF THE
Navy Recruiting District, Omaha
6910 Pacific St. #400
Omaha, NE 68106
Tel: (402) 558-7909

NEVADA

AIR FORCE, DEPT. OF THE
Nellis AFB
99 MSS/DPC, 4475 England Ave. #120
Nellis AFB, NV 89191-6526
Tel: (702) 652-9294 Fax: (702) 652-5579

ARMY, DEPT. OF THE
US Army 6th Recruiting Brigade
Western Region
4539 N 5th St.
North Las Vegas, NV 89031
Tel: (702) 639-2071/2072

DEPARTMENT OF EMPLOYMENT TRAINING AND REHABILITATION
State of Nevada
Human Resources Office
500 E 3rd St.
Carson City, NV 89713
Ruth Jones, Human Resources Manager
Tel: (775) 684-3923 Fax: (775) 684-3927
Web: http://detr.state.nv.us

INTERIOR, DEPT. OF THE
Bureau of Reclamation
Lower Colorado Region, Personnel Office
P.O. Box 61470
Boulder City, NV 89006-1470
Robert W. Johnson, Regional Director
Tel: (702) 293-8411 Fax: (702) 293-8416
Web: www.usbr.gov

NAVY, DEPT. OF THE
Armed Forces Reserve Center Las Vegas
Navy Reserve, Area III
5095 Range Rd., Nellis Air Force Base
Las Vegas, NV 89115
Tel: (702) 632-1468
Email: d7s200011@cnrrc.nola.navy.mil

USMC Recruiting Sub-Station, Carson City
777 E Winnie Ln. #3
Carson City, NV 89706
Tel: (775) 883-2404
Web: www.marines.com

USMC Recruiting Sub-Station, Reno
394 E Moana Ln. #2
Reno, NV 89502
Tel: (775) 829-8911
Web: www.marines.com

POSTAL SERVICE
Nevada Sierra District
1001 E. Susset Rd. #2207
Las Vegas, NV 89199-9421
Maggi Lara, Hispanic Program Specialist
Tel: (702) 361-9586
Web: www.usps.com

NEW HAMPSHIRE

NAVY, DEPT. OF THE
USMC Recruiting Station, Portsmouth
875 Greenland Rd. #A9
Portsmouth, NH 03801-4123
Tel: (603) 436-0598 Fax: (603) 436-7196
Web: www.marines.com

POSTAL SERVICE
New Hampshire District
955 Goffs Falls Rd.
Manchester, NH 03103-9994
Harry H. Figueroa, Diversity Development Specialist
Tel: (603) 644-3890 Fax: (603) 644-3896
Email: hfiguero@email.usps.gov
Web: www.usps.com

NEW JERSEY

AGRICULTURE, DEPT. OF
Natural Resources Conservation Service
854 S Whitehorse Pkwy. #3
Hammonton, NJ 08037
Edwin Muniz, HEPM
Tel: (609) 561-3223 x16
Email: emuniz@nj.usda.gov
Web: www.usda.gov

AIR FORCE, DEPT. OF THE
McGuire AFB
305 MSS/DPC, 2903 McGuire Blvd.
McGuire AFB, NJ 08641-5000
Tel: (609) 754-5698 Fax: (609) 754-5719

ARMY, DEPT. OF THE
US Army Recruiting Battalion Mid-Atlantic
Lakehurst Naval Air Station, Hwy. 547,
Bldg. 120, 1st Fl.
Lakehurst, NJ 08733
Tel: (732) 323-7380/7376

EQUAL EMPLOYMENT OPPORTUNITY COMMISSION
Newark Area Office
1 Newark Ctr., 21st Fl.
Newark, NJ 07102-5233
Corrado Gigante, Director
Tel: (973) 645-6383 Fax: (973) 645-4524
Web: www.eeoc.gov

HOMELAND SECURITY, DEPT. OF
US Coast Guard
USCG Recruiting Office Atlantic City
1333 New Rd. #8
Northfield, NJ 08225-1202
Tel: (609) 484-8260 Fax: (609) 484-9471
Email: glopez@cgrc.uscg.mil
Web: www.gocoastguard.com

US Coast Guard
USCG Recruiting Office Newark
Peter Rodino Federal Bldg.,
#143-A, 970 Broad St.
Newark, NJ 07102-2596
Tel: (973) 645-2635 Fax: (973) 645-2641
Email: wmarks@cgrc.uscg.mil
Web: www.gocoastguard.com

NAVY, DEPT. OF THE
Naval Reserve Center Fort Dix
5994 New Jersey Ave.
Fort Dix, NJ 08650-7810
Tel: (609) 723-6582 Fax: (609) 723-4832
Email: d5s20008@cnrrc.nola.navy.mil

USMC Recruiting Station, New Jersey
201 Hwy. 34 S, Bldg. C38
Colts Neck, NJ 07722
Tel: (732) 866-2937 Fax: (732) 866-1219
Web: www.marines.com

POSTAL SERVICE
Central New Jersey District
21 Kilmer Rd.
Edison, NJ 08099-9998
Jaya Bhambhwani, Diversity Development Specialist
Tel: (732) 819-3675 Fax: (732) 819-3889
Web: www.usps.com

Northern New Jersey District
494 Broad St.
Newark, NJ 07102-9998
Florina Cordero, Diversity Development Specialist
Tel: (973) 468-7203 Fax: (973) 468-7254
Email: fcordero@email.usps.gov
Web: www.usps.com

NEW MEXICO

AIR FORCE, DEPT. OF THE
Cannon AFB
27 MSS/DPC, 110 E Sextant Ave. #2038
Cannon AFB, NM 88103-5326
Tel: (505) 784-4845 Fax: (505) 784-4849

Holloman AFB
49 MSS/DPC, 681 2nd St., Bldg. 222
Holloman AFB, NM 88330-8060
Tel: (505) 572-3588 Fax: (505) 572-7114

Kirtland AFB
377 MSS/DPC, 1451 4th St. SE
Kirtland AFB, NM 87117-5625
Tel: (505) 846-9548 Fax: (505) 846-6675

ENERGY, DEPT. OF
Energy, Minerals and Natural Resources
New Mexico State Parks Division
1220 S Saint Francis Dr.
Santa Fe, NM 87505
Faye Barela, Personnel Officer
Tel: (505) 476-3375 Fax: (505) 476-3361
Email: fbarela@state.nm.us

National Nuclear Security Administration
Albuquerque Operations Office
P.O. Box 5400
Albuquerque, NM 87185-5400
Donald J. García, HEPM
Tel: (505) 845-5878 Fax: (505) 284-7078
Email: dgarcia@doeal.gov
Web: www.doeal.gov

EQUAL EMPLOYMENT OPPORTUNITY COMMISSION
Albuquerque Area Office
505 Marquette NW #900
Albuquerque, NM 87102
Georgia M. Marchbanks, Acting Director
Tel: (505) 248-5201 Fax: (505) 248-5239
Web: www.eeoc.gov

INTERIOR, DEPT. OF THE
Bureau of Indian Affairs
Southwest Region, Personnel Office
P.O. Box 26567
Albuquerque, NM 87125
Karen Parrish, Personnel Officer
Tel: (505) 563-3170 Fax: (505) 563-3040
Web: www.doi.gov

NAVY, DEPT. OF THE
Navy Officer Recruiting Station, Albuquerque
4565 San Mateo Northeast #F34
Albuquerque, NM 87109

USMC Recruiting Station, Albuquerque
5338 Montgomery Blvd. NE #30
Albuquerque, NM 87100
Tel: (505) 248-5280 Fax: (505) 248-5278
Web: www.marines.com

POSTAL SERVICE
Albuquerque District
500 Marquetta Ave. NW #782
Albuquerque, NM 87102-9994
Ana De Antonio, Hispanic Progran Specialist
Tel: (505) 346-8817
Web: www.usps.com

NEW YORK

AIR FORCE, DEPT. OF THE
Niagara Falls ARS
914 AW/DPC, 2720 Kirkbridge Dr.
Niagara Falls ARS, NY 14304-5001
Tel: (716) 236-2203 Fax: (716) 236-2202

ARMY, DEPT. OF THE
US Army Recruiting Battalion Albany
21 Aviation Rd.
Albany, NY 12205-1131
Tel: (518) 438-5536/1615

US Army Recruiting Battalion Syracuse
The Atrium, 2 Clinton Sq. #230
Syracuse, NY 13202-1042
Tel: (315) 479-8534

ENERGY, DEPT. OF
Schenectady Naval Reactors
P.O. Box 1069
Schenectady, NY 12301
Calvert Bowie, HEPM
Tel: (518) 395-6373 Fax: (518) 395-6078
Email: bowiec@kapl.doe.gov
Web: www.kapl.gov

EQUAL EMPLOYMENT OPPORTUNITY COMMISSION
Buffalo Local Office
6 Fountain Plz. #350
Buffalo, NY 14202
Elizabeth Cadle, Director
Tel: (716) 551-4441 Fax: (716) 551-4387
Web: www.eeoc.gov

New York District Office
33 Whitehall St.
New York, NY 10004
Spencer H. Lewis, Jr., Director
Tel: (212) 336-3620 Fax: (212) 336-3622
Web: www.eeoc.gov

FEDERAL RESERVE BANK
Human Resources/EEO
Head Office
33 Liberty St., 7th Fl.
New York, NY 10045-0001
Renoka Singh, EEO Officer
Tel: (212) 720-6434 Fax: (212) 720-8787
Web: www.ny.frb.org

HOMELAND SECURITY, DEPT. OF
U.S. Coast Guard
USCG Recruiting Office Bronx
46 Westchester Square
Bronx, NY 10461
Tel: (718) 904-8585 Fax: (718) 904-1900
Email: pgladding@cgrc.uscg.mil
Web: www.gocoastguard.com

US Coast Guard
USCG Recruiting Office Albany
324 Northern Blvd., Loudon Plz.
Albany, NY 12204-1028
Troy Timmons, Recruiter in Charge
Tel: (518) 465-6182 Fax: (518) 465-6319
Email: ttimmons@cgrc.uscg.mil
Web: www.gocoastguard.com

US Coast Guard
USCG Recruiting Office Brooklyn
7810 Flatlands
Brooklyn, NY 11236
Tel: (718) 251-1636 Fax: (718) 251-1660
Email: tharris@cgrc.uscg.mil
Web: www.gocoastguard.com

US Coast Guard
USCG Recruiting Office Long Island
747 Wantagh Ave., Wantagh Plz.
Wantagh, NY 11793-3133
Dana Jewett, Recruiter in Charge
Tel: (516) 796-3340 Fax: (516) 796-3344
Email: djewett@cgrc.uscg.mil
Web: www.gocoastguard.com

US Coast Guard
USCG Recruiting Office Manhattan
Battery Park Bldg., 1 S St. #109
New York, NY 10004-1466
Tel: (212) 668-7036/7219/7873
Fax: (212) 668-7866
Email: kbrathwaite@cgrc.uscg.mil
Web: www.gocoastguard.com

US Coast Guard
USCG Recruiting Office Queens
116-18 Queens Blvd.
Forest Hills, NY 11375
Richard McCusker, Recruiter in Charge
Tel: (718) 793-4962
Email: rmccusker@cgrc.uscg.mil
Web: www.gocoastguard.com

NAVY, DEPT. OF THE
Naval Reserve Recruiting Center Brooklyn
Floyd Bennett Field
Brooklyn, NY 11234-7097
Tel: (718) 258-0324 Fax: (718) 258-0780

Navy Recruiting District, Buffalo
300 Pearl St. #200
Buffalo, NY 14202
Tel: (716) 551-5816

Navy Recruiting District, New York
1975 Hempstead Trnpk.
East Meadow, NY 11554
Tel: (800) 451-8758

USMC Recruiting Station, Albany
40 Buffington St., Bldg. 403
Watervliet, NY 12189-4050
Tel: (518) 266-6120 Fax: (518) 266-6110
Web: www.marines.com

POSTAL SERVICE
Albany District
30 Old Karner Rd.
Albany, NY 12288-9291
Josephine Grimes, Diversity Development
Specialist
Tel: (518) 452-2219 Fax: (518) 512-4525
Email: jgrimes1@email.usps.gov
Web: www.usps.com

Long Island District
P.O. Box 7700

Islandia, NY 11760-9997
Betsy Diaz, Diversity Development
Specialist
Tel: (631) 582-7478 Fax: (631) 582-7595
Email: betsy.diaz-konstanzer@usps.gov
Web: www.usps.gov

New York Metro Area Office
142-02 20th Ave. #318
Flushing, NY 11351-0600
Zaidee Vazquez, Hispanic Program Specialist
Tel: (718) 321-5857
Web: www.usps.com

Westchester District
1000 Westchester Ave. #3130
White Plains, NY 10610-9411
Enid M. Samuels, Diversity Development
Specialist
Tel: (914) 697-7102 Fax: (914) 697-7152
Email: esamuels@email.usps.gov
Web: www.usps.com

Western New York District
1200 William St. #304
Buffalo, NY 14240-9431
Donna C. Biro, Diversity Development
Specialist
Tel: (716) 846-2484 Fax: (716) 846-2407
Email: donna.c.biro@usps.gov
Web: www.usps.com

SMALL BUSINESS ADMINISTRATION
Office of Disaster Assistance-Disaster Area 1
360 Rainbow Blvd. South, 3rd Fl.
Niagara Falls, NY 14303-1192
Gina Koop, Personnel Management
Specialist
Tel: (716) 282-4612 Fax: (716) 282-6151

Regional Personnel Office
Region II (NY, NJ, PR, VI)
26 Federal Plz. #3108
New York, NY 10278
Viola McCoy, Administrative Officer
Tel: (212) 264-3254 Fax: (212) 264-7753

NORTH CAROLINA

AIR FORCE, DEPT. OF THE
Pope AFB
43 MSS/DPC, 384 Maynard St. #8
Pope AFB, NC 28308-2372
Tel: (910) 394-2418 Fax: (910) 394-4269

Seymour Johnson AFB
4 MSS/DPC, 1570 Wright Bros. Ave. #400
Seymour Johnson AFB, NC 27531-2469
Tel: (919) 722-0117 Fax: (919) 722-0107

ARMY, DEPT. OF THE
US Army Cadet Command, ROTC
Eastern Region
Attn: Public Affairs Office
Fort Bragg, NC 28307-5000
Tel: (910) 396-9415

US Army Recruiting Battalion Raleigh
Cypress Bldg., 3117 Poplarwood Ct. #218
Raleigh, NC 27604-1041
Tel: (919) 872-9147/3441

**EQUAL EMPLOYMENT OPPORTUNITY
COMMISSION**
Charlotte District Office
129 W Trade St. #400
Charlotte, NC 28202
Reuben Daniels, Jr., Director
Tel: (704) 344-6682 Fax: (704) 344-6734
Web: www.eeoc.gov

Greensboro Local Office
2303 W Meadowview Rd. #201
Greensboro, NC 27407
Michael A. Whitlow, Director

Tel: (336) 547-4188 Fax: (336) 547-4032
Web: www.eeoc.gov

NAVY, DEPT. OF THE
Navy Recruiting District, Raleigh
801 Oberlin Rd.
Raleigh, NC 27605
Tel: (919) 831-4158

NORTH DAKOTA

AGRICULTURE, DEPT. OF
North Plains Region
P.O. Box 5638
Fargo, ND 58105
Manuel Matos, HEPM
Tel: (701) 231-7562 Fax: (701) 231-7861
Web: www.usda.gov

AIR FORCE, DEPT. OF THE
Grand Forks AFB
319 MSS/DPC, 226 Steen Blvd., Bldg. 101
Grand Forks AFB, ND 58205-6338
Tel: (701) 747-5029 Fax: (701) 747-3067

Minot AFB
5 MSS/DPC, 300 Summit Dr. #222
Minot AFB, ND 58705-5038
Tel: (701) 723-1986 Fax: (701) 723-4228

OHIO

AIR FORCE, DEPT. OF THE
Air Force Material Command Headquarters
AFMC/DPC
4375 Chidlaw Rd. #N208
Wright-Patterson AFB, OH 45433-5006
Stacy Zaire, HEPM
Tel: (937) 257-4137 Fax: (937) 257-3928
Web: www.wpafb.af.mil

Wright Patterson AFB
HQ AFMC/DPC, 4375 Chidlaw Rd. #6
Wright Patterson AFB, OH 45433-5006
Tel: (937) 257-2806 Fax: (937) 257-3928

Wright Patterson AFB
88 MSG/DPC, 4040 Ogden Ave.
Wright Patterson AFB, OH 45433-5763
Tel: (937) 257-1249 Fax: (937) 257-2389

Youngstown ARS
910 AW/DPC, 3976 King Graves Rd. #4
Vienna, OH 44473-5904
Tel: (330) 609-1382 Fax: (330) 609-1097

ARMY, DEPT. OF THE
US Army Recruiting Battalion Cleveland
1240 E 9th St. #1269
Cleveland, OH 44199
Tel: (216) 802-1409

US Army Recruiting Battalion Columbus
New Federal Bldg., 200 N High St. #114
Columbus, OH 43215-2483
Tel: (614) 469-2343/2345

ATTORNEY'S GENERAL OFFICE
State of Ohio
EEO Office
30 E Broad St., 16th Fl.
Columbus, OH 43215-3428
Alethea Botts, Director
Tel: (614) 466-8911 Fax: (614) 728-7582
Web: www.ag.state.oh.us

ENERGY, DEPT. OF
Ohio Field Office
P.O. Box 66
Miamisburg, OH 45342
Ronald Berry, HEPM
Tel: (937) 865-4836 Fax: (937) 847-8352
Email: ronald.berry@ohio.doe.gov

Web: www.ohio.doe.gov

**EQUAL EMPLOYMENT OPPORTUNITY
COMMISSION**
Cincinnati Area Office
550 Main St., 10th Fl.
Cincinnati, OH 45202
Wilma L. Javey, Director
Tel: (513) 684-2851 Fax: (513) 684-2361
Web: www.eeoc.gov

Cleveland District Office
1660 W 2nd St. #850
Cleveland, OH 44113-1412
James R. Neely, Jr., Director
Tel: (216) 522-2003 Fax: (216) 522-7395
Web: www.eeoc.gov

FEDERAL RESERVE BANK
Human Resources/EEO
Cleveland District
P.O. Box 6387
Cleveland, OH 44101-1387
Karen Connors, EEO Specialist
Tel: (216) 579-2000 Fax: (216) 579-3198
Web: www.clevelandfed.org

NAVY, DEPT. OF THE
Naval Reserve Center Cleveland
1089 E 9th St.
Cleveland, OH 44114
Tel: (216) 861-3406
Email: d2s20005@cnrrc.nola.navy.mil

Navy Recruiting District, Ohio
200 N High St. #609
Columbus, OH 43215
Tel: (614) 469-6672

USMC Recruiting Station, Cleveland
7261 Engle Rd. #110
Middleburg Heights, OH 44130-3479
Tel: (440) 243-4010 Fax: (440) 243-3247
Web: www.marines.com

POSTAL SERVICE
Cincinnati District
1623 Dalton St. #423
Cincinnati, OH 45234-9431
Jo Ann Hutton, Diversity Development
Specialist
Tel: (513) 684-5250 Fax: (513) 684-5240
Email: jhutton@usps.gov
Web: www.usps.gov

Cleveland District
2200 Orange Ave. #238
Cleveland, OH 44101-9431
Gloria M. Jennings, Diversity Development
Specialist
Tel: (216) 443-4235 Fax: (216) 443-4879
Email: gloria.m.jennings@usps.gov
Web: www.usps.gov

Columbus District
850 Twin River Dr.
Columbus, OH 43216-9402
Deborah O'Neal, Diversity Development
Specialist
Tel: (614) 722-9629 Fax: (614) 722-9649
Email: doneal@email.usps.gov
Web: www.usps.com

OKLAHOMA

AIR FORCE, DEPT. OF THE
Altus AFB
97 MSS/DPC, 308 N 1st St.
Altus AFB, OK 73523-5001
Tel: (580) 481-7537 Fax: (580) 481-6812

Tinker AFB
72 MSG/DPC, 3001 Staff Dr. #1AH190B
Tinker AFB, OK 73145-3014
Tel: (405) 739-3334 Fax: (405) 739-7453

Vance AFB
71 MSS/DPC, 246 Brown Pkwy. #124
Vance AFB, OK 73705-5011
Tel: (580) 213-7260 Fax: (580) 213-7589

ARMY, DEPT. OF THE
US Army Recruiting Battalion Oklahoma City
300 N Meridian #200N
Oklahoma City, OK 73107-6538
Tel: (405) 947-6449/6459

ENERGY, DEPT. OF
Southwestern Power Administration
1 W 3rd St. #3300
Tulsa, OK 74103
Carlos E. Valencia, HEPM
Tel: (918) 595-6707 Fax: (918) 595-6656
Email: carlos.valencia@swpa.gov
Web: www.swpa.gov

EQUAL EMPLOYMENT OPPORTUNITY COMMISSION
Oklahoma Area Office
210 Park Ave. #1350
Oklahoma City, OK 73102
Joyce Davis Powers, Director
Tel: (405) 231-4911 Fax: (405) 231-4140
Web: www.eeoc.gov

INTERIOR, DEPT. OF THE
Bureau of Indian Affairs
Southern Plains Region, Personnel Office
P.O. Box 368
Anadarko, OK 73005
Carla Chappabitty, Acting HR Officer
Tel: (405) 247-6673 X218
Fax: (405) 247-3920

NAVY, DEPT. OF THE
Naval Reserve Center Oklahoma City
5316 Douglas Blvd.
Oklahoma City, OK 73150-9702
Tel: (405) 733-3368
Email: d3s20002@cnrrc.nola.navy.mil

USMC Recruiting Station, Oklahoma City
5924 NW 2nd St. #1000
Oklahoma City, OK 73127
Tel: (405) 787-0618 Fax: (405) 495-6821
Web: www.marines.com

POSTAL SERVICE
Oklahoma District
3030 NW Expressway St. #1042
Oklahoma City, OK 73198-9807
Eugene Talley, Diversity Development Specialist
Tel: (405) 553-6217 Fax: (405) 553-6107
Email: eugene.talley@usps.gov
Web: www.usps.gov

OREGON

AGRICULTURE, DEPT. OF
Forest Service
P.O. Box 3623
Portland, OR 97208-3623
Robert Alvarado, HEPM
Tel: (503) 808-2901 Fax: (503) 808-2469
Email: ralvarado@fs.fed.us
Web: www.fs.fed.us

Pacific Northwest Region Office
P.O. Box 3623
Portland, OR 97208-3623
April Willson, EEO Officer
Tel: (503) 808-2818 Fax: (503) 808-2210
Email: awillson@fs.fed.us
Web: www.fs.fed.us

AIR FORCE, DEPT. OF THE
Portland IAP
939 ARW/DPC, 6801 NE Cornfoot Rd.,
Bldg. 300

Portland IAP, OR 97218-2797
Tel: (503) 335-4615 Fax: (503) 638-4614

ARMY, DEPT. OF THE
US Army Corps of Engineers
Portland District
333 SW 1st Ave.
Portland, OR 97204-3495
Ismael Caballero, HEPM
Tel: (503) 808-4325 Fax: (503) 808-4329
Email: ismael.caballero@usace.army.mil
Web: www.usace.army.mil

US Army Recruiting Battalion Portland
6130 NE 78th Ct.
Portland, OR 97218-2853
Tel: (503) 256-1436/1433

ENERGY, DEPT. OF
Bonneville Power Administration
P.O. Box 3621
Portland, OR 97208
Lidia Navarro, HEPM
Tel: (503) 230-5587
Web: www.bpa.gov

INTERIOR, DEPT. OF THE
Bureau of Indians Affairs
Northwest Region, Personnel Office
911 NE 11th Ave.
Portland, OR 97232-4169
Jeannie Cooper, Personnel Officer
Tel: (503) 231-6710 Fax: (503) 231-6110

Bureau of Land Management
Oregon State Office, EEO Office
333 SW 1st Ave.
Portland, OR 97208-2965
Karen Bell, EEO Manager
Tel: (503) 808-6341 Fax: (503) 808-6108
Web: www.or.blm.gov

NAVY, DEPT. OF THE
Navy Recruiting District, Portland
Airport Business Ctr., 7028 NE 79th, Bldg. 2
Portland, OR 97218
Tel: (503) 258-2017

USMC Recruiting Station, Portland
1220 SW 3rd Ave. #519
Portland, OR 97204-2888
Tel: (503) 326-3016 Fax: (503) 326-3024
Web: www.marines.com

OFFICE OF THE GOVERNOR
State of Oregon
Affirmative Action
155 Cottage St. NE
Salem, OR 97310
Peggy C. Ross, Director
Tel: (503) 378-3544 Fax: (503) 378-3139
Web: www.governor.state.or.us

PENNSYLVANIA

AGRICULTURE, DEPT. OF
Natural Resources and Conservation Service
East Region
1 Credit Union Pl. #340
Harrisburg, PA 17110-2993
Noel Soto, HEPM
Tel: (717) 237-2173 Fax: (717) 237-2338
Email: noel.soto@pa.usda.gov
Web: www.usda.gov

AIR FORCE, DEPT. OF THE
Pittsburgh IAP-ARS
911 AW/DPC, 2475 Defense Ave.
Pittsburgh IAP-ARS, PA 15108-4403
Tel: (412) 474-8530 Fax: (412) 474-8535

Willowgrove ARS
913 SPTG/DPC, 1051 Fairchild St.
Willowgrove ARS, PA 19090-5203

Tel: (215) 443-1035 Fax: (215) 443-1945

ARMY, DEPT. OF THE
US Army Recruiting Battalion Harrisburg
M Ave., Bldg. 54 #11
New Cumberland Army Depot
New Cumberland, PA 17070-5099
Tel: (717) 770-6721/7252

US Army Recruiting Battalion Pittsburgh
Wm. Moorhead Federal Bldg., Rm. 1404,
1000 Liberty Ave.
Pittsburgh, PA 15222-4197
Tel: (412) 395-5879/5786

BOARD OF PROBATION AND PAROLE
Commonwealth of Pennsylvania
1101 S Front St.
Harrisburg, PA 17104-2522
LeDelle Ingram, EO Specialist
Tel: (717) 787-6897
Email: lingram@state.pa.us
Web: www.state.pa.us

COMMUNITY AND ECONOMIC DEVELOPMENT, DEPARTMENT OF
Commonwealth of Pennsylvania
Personnel Office
400 North St.,
Commonwealth Keystone Bldg.
Harrisburg, PA 17120
Darren McNoldy, Director
Tel: (717) 720-1426 Fax: (717) 787-6939
Email: dmcnoldy@state.pa.us
Web: www.state.pa.us

CORRECTIONS, DEPARTMENT OF
Commonwealth of Pennsylvania
Office of EEO
P.O. Box 598
Camp Hill, PA 17001-0598
Raphael Cheike, Director
Tel: (717) 975-4905 Fax: (717) 731-7115
Web: www.cor.state.pa.us

DEFENSE LOGISTICS AGENCY
Defense Supply Center Philadelphia
700 Robbins Ave.
Philadelphia, PA 19111
Carlos Deno, Jr., HEPM
Tel: (215) 737-5738 Fax: (215) 737-2520
Email: carlos.deno@dla.mil
Web: www.dla.mil

DEPARTMENT OF BANKING
Commonwealth of Pennsylvania
Office of Human Resources
333 Market St., 16th Fl.
Harrisburg, PA 17101
Cheryl Dondero, Director
Tel: (717) 787-4129 Fax: (717) 705-5492
Email: cdondero@state.pa.us
Web: www.state.pa.us

DEPARTMENT OF COMMUNITY AND ECONOMIC DEVELOPMENT
Commonwealth of Pennsylvania
EEO Office
Keystone Bldg., 4th Fl.
Harrisburg, PA 17120
Brenda Longacre, Human Resources Analyst
Tel: (717) 346-7786
Email: blongacre@state.pa.us
Web: www.state.pa.us

DEPARTMENT OF PUBLIC WELFARE
Commonwealth of Pennsylvania
Bureau of Equal Opportunity
H & W Bldg. #223
Harrisburg, PA 17105
Merry Grace Majors, Director
Tel: (717) 787-1146 Fax: (717) 772-4366
Email: mmajors@state.pa.us
Web: www.state.pa.us

ENERGY, DEPT. OF
National Energy Technology Center
P.O. Box 10940, M/S 922-105
Pittsburgh, PA 15236-0940
Nancy Vargas, EEO Diversity Officer
Tel: (412) 386-4654 Fax: (412) 386-4604
Email: nancy.vargas@netl.doe.gov
Web: www.netl.doe.gov

Pittsburgh Naval Reactors
P.O. Box 109
West Mifflin, PA 15122-0109
Ed Rose, HEPM
Tel: (412) 476-7204 Fax: (412) 476-7573

EQUAL EMPLOYMENT OPPORTUNITY COMMISSION
Philadelphia District Office
The Bourse Bldg., 21 S 5th St. #400
Philadelphia, PA 19106
Marie M. Tomasso, Director
Tel: (215) 440-2600 Fax: (215) 440-2632
Web: www.eeoc.gov

Pittsburgh Area Office
Liberty Ctr., 1001 Liberty Ave. #300
Pittsburgh, PA 15222-4187
Eugene V. Nelson, Director
Tel: (412) 644-3444 Fax: (412) 644-2664
Web: www.eeoc.gov

FISH AND BOAT COMMISSION
Commonwealth of Pennsylvania
1601 Elmerton Ave.
Harrisburg, PA 17110
Bernard Matscavage, Personnel Officer
Tel: (717) 705-7820 Fax: (717) 705-7802
Web: www.fish.state.pa.us

GENERAL SERVICES, DEPARTMENT OF
Commonwealth of Pennsylvania
Office of EO
Finance Bldg. #402C
Harrisburg, PA 17120
Annette Allen, Director
Tel: (717) 787-9995 Fax: (717) 705-0788
Email: aallen@state.pa.us
Web: www.state.pa.us

HISTORICAL AND MUSEUM COMMISSION
Commonwealth of Pennsylvania
Human Resources
300 North St.
Harrisburg, PA 17120
Jane Peyton, Director
Tel: (717) 772-2839 Fax: (717) 783-2839
Web: www.phmc.state.pa.us

HOMELAND SECURITY, DEPT. OF
US Coast Guard
USCG Recruiting Office Philadelphia NE
Roosevelt Shopping Ctr., 2327 Cottman Ave. #48
Philadelphia, PA 19149
Tel: (215) 331-2788 Fax: (215) 473-8956
Email: mhoward@cgrc.uscg.mil
Web: www.gocoastguard.com

US Coast Guard
USCG Recruiting Office Philadelphia West
7567 Haverford Ave., Haverford Ave. Shops
Philadelphia, PA 19151
Tel: (215) 473-8497/8943
Fax: (215) 473-8956
Email: mhoward@cgrc.uscg.mil
Web: www.gocoastguard.com

HUMAN RELATIONS COMMISSION
Commonwealth of Pennsylvania
Human Relations
301 Chestnut St. #300
Harrisburg, PA 17101
Richard Fairfax, Director
Tel: (717) 787-4410 Fax: (717) 214-0584
Web: www.phrc.state.pa.us

INSURANCE DEPARTMENT, BUREAU OF ADMINISTRATION
Commonwealth of Pennsylvania
Human Resources Office
1326 Strawberry Square
Harrisburg, PA 17120
Kathy Culbertson, Director
Tel: (717) 705-4194 Fax: (717) 705-3873
Email: kculbertson@state.pa.us
Web: www.state.pa.us

INTERIOR, DEPT. OF THE
National Park Service
Northeast Region, Office of Human
Resources, Staffing Division
200 Chestnut St., 3rd Fl.
Philadelphia, PA 19106
Delores Dyer, Special Emphasis Program
Manager
Tel: (215) 597-7067 Fax: (215) 597-5747
Email: delores_dyer@nps.gov
Web: www.nps.gov

LABOR AND INDUSTRY, DEPARTMENT OF
Commonwealth of Pennsylvania
Office of Equal Opportunity
L & I Bldg. #514
Harrisburg, PA 17120
Autro Heath, Jr., Acting Director
Tel: (717) 787-1182 Fax: (717) 772-2321
Email: aheath@state.pa.us
Web: www.state.pa.us

LABOR, DEPT. OF
Employment and Training Administration
Office of Youth Programs and Job Corps
170 Independence Mall West, The Curtis
Center #815 East
Philadelphia, PA 19106-3315
Lynn Intrepidi, Regional Director
Tel: (215) 861-5501 Fax: (215) 861-5520
Email: lintrepidi@doleta.gov
Web: www.doleta.gov

LIQUOR CONTROL BOARD
Commonwealth of Pennsylvania
Northwest Office Bldg. #408
Harrisburg, PA 17124
Kathy Blatt, Equal Opportunity Specialist
Tel: (717) 705-6958 Fax: (717) 705-6218
Email: mblatt@state.pa.us
Web: www.lcb.state.pa.us

MILITARY VETERANS AFFAIRS, DEPT. OF
Bureau of Administrative Services
EEO Office
Ft. Indiantown Gap, Bldg. S-0-47
Annville, PA 17003-5002
Kristie L. Smith, Director
Tel: (717) 861-8796 Fax: (717) 861-2932

MILK MARKETING BOARD
Commonwealth of Pennsylvania
Agriculture Bldg. #110, 2301 N Cameron St.
Harrisburg, PA 17110
Timothy Moyer, Chief of Support Services/
Personnel
Tel: (717) 787-4231 Fax: (717) 783-6492
Email: tmoyer@state.pa.us
Web: www.mmb.state.pa.us

NAVY, DEPT. OF THE
Navy Recruiting District, Philadelphia
700 Robbins Ave., Bldg. 2D
Philadelphia, PA 19111
Tel: (215) 697-3984

Navy Recruiting District, Pittsburgh
1000 Liberty Ave. #713
Pittsburgh, PA 15222
Tel: (412) 395-6824

USMC Recruiting Station, Harrisburg
Bldg. 54, #5
New Cumberland, PA 17070-5003

Tel: (717) 770-6659 Fax: (717) 774-5886
Web: www.marines.com

USMC Recruiting Station, Pittsburgh
1000 Liberty Ave. #1512, William S.
Moorehead Federal Bldg.
Pittsburgh, PA 15222-4179
Tel: (412) 395-5815 Fax: (412) 395-4766
Web: www.marines.com

OFFICE OF ADMINISTRATION
Commonwealth of Pennsylvania
Bureau of Equal Employment Opportunity
Finance Bldg. #222
Harrisburg, PA 17120
LaMonte Williams, Director
Tel: (717) 783-1130 Fax: (717) 472-3302
Web: www.state.pa.us

POSTAL SERVICE
Erie District
2709 Legion Rd.
Erie, PA 16515-9741
Wendy Nelson-Smith, Diversity
Development Specialist
Tel: (814) 678-6574 Fax: (814) 836-7215
Email: wnelsons@email.usps.gov
Web: www.usps.gov

Harrisburg District
1425 Crooked Hill Rd.
Harrisburg, PA 17107-0041
Bobbi Reid, Diversity Development
Specialist
Tel: (717) 257-5380 Fax: (717) 257-2152
Email: breid1@email.usps.gov
Web: www.usps.com

Philadelphia District
P.O. Box 7237
Philadelphia, PA 19101-7237
Belinda Kelley, Diversity Development
Specialist
Tel: (215) 895-8040 Fax: (651) 406-5549
Web: www.usps.com

Pittsburgh District
1001 California Ave. #2358A
Pittsburgh, PA 15290-9600
Clarissa A. Scott-Jones, Diversity
Development Specialist
Tel: (412) 359-7510 Fax: (412) 359-7535
Email: clarissa.scott-jones@usps.gov
Web: www.usps.gov

PUBLIC TELEVISION NETWORK
Commonwealth of Pennsylvania
EEO Office
24 Northeast Dr.
Hershey, PA 17033
Jane M. Staver, EO Specialist
Tel: (717) 534-1502 Fax: (717) 533-4236
Email: jstaver@state.pa.us
Web: www.pptn.state.pa.us

SECURITIES COMMISSION
Commonwealth of Pennsylvania
Personnel Office
Eastgate Office Bldg., 2nd Fl.
Harrisburg, PA 17102-1410
Margaret Hivner, Director
Tel: (717) 783-4689
Email: mahivner@state.pa.us
Web: www.state.pa.us

STATE CIVIL SERVICE COMMISSION
Commonwealth of Pennsylvania
P.O. Box 569
Harrisburg, PA 17108-0569
Cynthia Rodriguez, HEPM
Tel: (717) 787-6652 Fax: (717) 787-5731
Email: cyrodrigue@state.pa.us
Web: www.scsc.state.pa.us

STATE, DEPT. OF
North Office Building, Room 306
Harrisburg, PA 17120
Harold Conrad, Director of Human
Resources
Tel: (717) 787-6604 Fax: (717) 783-0630
Email: hconrad@state.pa.us
Web: www.state.pa.us

STATE POLICE COMMISSION
Commonwealth of Pennsylvania
EEO Office
1800 Elmerton Ave.
Harrisburg, PA 17110
Sergeant Martin Henry, Director
Tel: (717) 787-7220 Fax: (717) 705-2185
Email: marthenry@state.pa.us
Web: www.state.pa.us

TREASURY, DEPT. OF THE
105 Finance Bldg.
Harrisburg, PA 17120-0018
Linda Zuvich, Director of Human Resources
Tel: (717) 787-5979 Fax: (717) 787-3026
Email: lzuvich@state.pa.us
Web: www.state.pa.us

PUERTO RICO

AGRICULTURE, DEPT. OF
Caribbean Area
P.O. Box 5100
San German, PR 00683-5100
Carlos Hernandez, Outreach Coordinator
Tel: (787) 264-1912 X7796
Fax: (787) 264-1917
Email: carlos.hernandez@pr.usda.gov
Web: www.pr.nrcs.usda.gov

Forest Service
UPR Experimental Station Grounds,
Botanical Garden
Jardin Botanico Sur, 1201 Calle Ceiba
San Juan, PR 00926
Elizabeth Hernandez, HEPM
Tel: (787) 766-5335 Fax: (787) 766-6302
Email: ehernandez@fs.fed.us
Web: www.fs.fed.us

NAVY, DEPT. OF THE
USMC Recruiting Sub-Station, Puerto Rico
Buchanono Office Ctr. #104, Carr. 165 KM
06, Puebloviego
Guaynabo, PR 00966
Tel: (787) 273-1115
Web: www.marines.com

OFFICE OF PERSONNEL MANAGEMENT
San Juan Service Center
Torre de Plaza las Americas #1114,
525 F.D. Roosevelt Ave.
San Juan, PR 00918
Luis Rodriguez, Director
Tel: (787) 766-5620 Fax: (787) 766-5598
Email: sanjuan@opm.gov
Web: www.opm.gov

RHODE ISLAND

EQUAL OPPORTUNITY OFFICE
State of Rhode Island
1 Capitol Hill
Providence, RI 02908
A. Vincent Igliozzi, Administrator
Tel: (401) 222-3090 Fax: (401) 222-6391

HOMELAND SECURITY, DEPT. OF
US Coast Guard
USCG Recruiting Office Providence
380 Westminster Mall

Providence, RI 02903-3246
Tel: (401) 421-1291 Fax: (401) 528-4371
Email: sharrison@cgrc.uscg.mil
Web: www.gocoastguard.com

SOUTH CAROLINA

AGRICULTURE, DEPT. OF
Southeast Region
P.O. Box 528
St. Matthew's, SC 29135
Monica Franklin, Regional HEPM
Tel: (803) 874-3337 Fax: (803) 874-2820
Web: www.usda.gov

AIR FORCE, DEPT. OF THE
Charleston AFB
437 MSS/DPC, 101 E Hill Blvd. #503
Charleston AFB, SC 29404-5021
Tel: (843) 963-4501 Fax: (843) 566-4482

Shaw AFB
20 MSS/DPC, 504 Shaw Dr.
Shaw AFB, SC 29152-5028
Tel: (803) 895-2655 Fax: (803) 895-1677

ARMY, DEPT. OF THE
US Army Recruiting Battalion Columbia
Strom Thurmond Federal Bldg., 1835
Assembly St. Rm. 733
Columbia, SC 29201-2491
Tel: (803) 765-5640

ENERGY, DEPT. OF
Savannah River Operations Office
P.O. Box A
Aiken, SC 29802
Roberto González, Co-Chair, National
HEPM Advisory Council
Tel: (803) 208-8175 Fax: (803) 725-5833
Email: roberto.gonzalez@srs.gov
Web: www.srs.gov

Savannah River Operations Office
P.O. Box A
Aiken, SC 29801
Alicia Gibbons, HEPM
Tel: (803) 725-7648 Fax: (803) 725-8856
Email: alicia.gibbons@srs.gov
Web: www.srs.gov

EQUAL EMPLOYMENT OPPORTUNITY COMMISSION
Greenville Local Office
301 N Main St. #1402
Greenville, SC 29601-9916
Patricia B. Fuller, Director
Tel: (864) 241-4400 Fax: (864) 241-4402
Web: www.eeoc.gov

MINORITY BUSINESS DEVELOPMENT CENTER
South Carolina State Wide
1515 Richland St.
Columbia, SC 29201
Greg Davis, Director
Tel: (803) 779-5905 Fax: (803) 779-5915

NAVY, DEPT. OF THE
Naval Reserve Center Columbia
513 Pickens St.
Columbia, SC 29201-4198
Tel: (803) 256-7167 Fax: (803) 156-7096
Email: d4s20007@cnrrc.nola.navy.mil

USMC Recruiting Station, Columbia
9600 2 Notch Rd. #17
Columbia, SC 29223
Tel: (803) 788-8788 Fax: (803) 699-0489
Web: www.marines.com

POSTAL SERVICE
Greater South Carolina District
P. O. Box 929801
Columbia, SC 29292-9801
Mary Ellen Padin, Diversity Development
Specialist
Tel: (803) 926-6429 Fax: (803) 926-6434
Email: maryellen.padin@usps.gov
Web: www.usps.gov

SOUTH DAKOTA

AGRICULTURE, DEPT. OF
North Plains Region
P.O. Box 1258
Pierre, SD 57501-1258
Colette Kessler, HEPM
Tel: (605) 224-2476 Fax: (605) 224-6615
Email: colette.kessler@sd.usda.gov
Web: www.usda.gov

Natural Resources Conservation Service
P.O. Box 1258
Pierre, SD 57501-1258
Colette M. Kessler, Hispanic Special
Emphasis Program Manager/
Communications Specialist
Tel: (605) 224-2476 Fax: (605) 224-6615
Email: colette.kessler@sd.usda.gov
Web: www.sd.nrcs.usda.gov

AIR FORCE, DEPT. OF THE
Ellsworth AFB
28 MSS/DPC, 1000 Ellsworth St. #2300
Ellsworth AFB, SD 57706-4700
Tel: (605) 385-2484 Fax: (605) 385-2194

PERSONNEL BUREAU
State of South Dakota
500 E Capitol Ave.
Pierre, SD 57501
Jeff Bloomberg, Attorney
Tel: (605) 773-3148 Fax: (605) 773-4344

TENNESSEE

AGRICULTURE, DEPT. OF
Southeast Region
420 W Morris Blvd. #340
Morris Town, TN 37813
Paul McQuaede, HEPM
Tel: (423) 586-0321 Fax: (423) 586-9914
Web: www.usda.gov

AIR FORCE, DEPT. OF THE
Arnold AFB
656 ABS/DPC, 100 Kindel Dr. #C314
Arnold AFB, TN 37389-3314
Tel: (615) 454-5477 Fax: (615) 454-7899

ARMY, DEPT. OF THE
US Army Recruiting Battalion Nashville
2517 Perimeter Place Dr.
Nashville, TN 37214
Tel: (615) 871-4172

ENERGY, DEPT. OF
Oak Ridge Operations Office
P.O. Box 2001
Oak Ridge, TN 37831
Leon F. Duquella, HEPM
Tel: (865) 576-9755 Fax: (865) 576-1665
Email: duquellaf@oro.doe.gov
Web: www.oro.doe.gov

EQUAL EMPLOYMENT OPPORTUNITY
COMMISSION
Memphis District Office
1407 Union Ave. #621
Memphis, TN 38104
Danny G. Harter, Director
Tel: (901) 544-0115   Fax: (901) 544-0111
Web: www.eeoc.gov

Nashville Area Office
50 Vantage Way #202
Nashville, TN 37228-9940
Sarah L. Smith, Director
Tel: (615) 736-5820   Fax: (615) 736-2107
Web: www.eeoc.gov

NAVY, DEPT. OF THE
Naval Reserve Center Memphis
5722 Integrity Dr., Bldg. N-930
Millington, TN 38128
Tel: (901) 874-5056   Fax: (901) 874-5841
Email: d4s20006@cnrrc.nola.navy.mil

Navy Recruiting District, Nashville
640 Grassmere Park #104
Nashville, TN 37211
Tel: (615) 332-0824

USMC Recruiting Station, Nashville
2519 Perimeter Place Dr.
Nashville, TN 37214
Tel: (615) 627-1526 Fax: (615) 736-2201
Web: www.marines.com

POSTAL SERVICE
Tennessee District
811 Royal Pkwy.
Nashville, TN 37229-9771
Sheila Baskins, Diversity Development
Specialist
Tel: (615) 872-5693 Fax: (615) 885-9374
Web: www.usps.com

TEXAS

AGRICULTURE, DEPT. OF
South Central Region
P.O. Box 1006
Zapata, TX 78076-1006
Zaragoza Rodriguez, III, HEPM
Tel: (956) 765-6911 Fax: (956) 765-9625
Email: zaragoza.rodriguez@tx.usda.gov
Web: www.usda.gov

Natural Resources and Conservation Service
South Central Region
P.O. Box 6567
Fort Worth, TX 76115-3400
Humberto Hernandez, National Resource
Manager
Tel: (817) 509-3225 Fax: (817) 509-3279
Email: hhernandez@ftw.nrcs.usda.gov
Web: www.usda.gov

AIR FORCE, DEPT. OF THE
Air Force Personnel Center
HQ AFPC/DPCFD,
Recruitment Services Center
Randolph AFB, TX
Customer Service Representatives
Tel: (800) 699-4478 Fax: (210) 527-2377

HQ AFPC/DPKR, Air Force Intern Programs
Randolph AFB, TX 78150-4759
Tel: (210) 565-2286
Web: www.afpc.randolph.af.mil/cp/recruit

Brooks AFB
311 ABG/DPC, 3105 North Rd. #C
Brooks AFB, TX 78235-5358
Tel: (210) 536-3535 Fax: (210) 536-5351

Dyess AFB
7 MSS/DPC, 417 3rd St. #110
Dyess AFB, TX 79607-1517
Tel: (915) 696-2391 Fax: (915) 696-4213

Goodfellow AFB
17 MSS/DPC, 305 Flightline Ave.
Goodfellow AFB, TX 76908-3216
Tel: (915) 654-3325 Fax: (915) 654-3825

Lackland AFB
37 MSS/DPC, 1760 Patrick St. #1
Lackland AFB, TX 78236-5226
Tel: (210) 671-3905 Fax: (210) 671-3910

Laughlin AFB
47 MSS/DPC, 155 Arkansas, Rm. 169
Laughlin AFB, TX 78843-5230
Tel: (830) 298-5299 Fax: (830) 598-5917

Randolph AFB
HQ AETC/DPC
Randolph AFB, TX 78150-4308
Tel: (210) 652-7725 Fax: (210) 652-4809

Randolph AFB
12 MSS/DPC, 550 D St. East #2
Randolph AFB, TX 78150-4308
Tel: (210) 652-7725 Fax: (210) 652-4809

Sheppard AFB
82 MSS/DPC, 426 5th Ave. #3
Sheppard AFB, TX 76311-2927
Tel: (940) 676-6677 Fax: (940) 676-1819

ARMY, DEPT. OF THE
US Army 5th Recruiting Brigade
South-Central Region
P.O. Box 8277
Bldg. 2064, Fort Sam Houston,
Wainwright Station
San Antonio, TX 78208-0277
Tel: (210) 221-1900/0176

US Army Recruiting Battalion Dallas
1350 Walnut Hill Ln. #150
Irving, TX 75038-3025
Tel: (972) 756-0842

US Army Recruiting Battalion Houston
1919 Smith St. #1529
Houston, TX 77002
Tel: (713) 209-3220/3222

US Army Recruiting Battalion San Antonio
1265 Buck Rd., Bldg. 2003
Fort Sam Houston, TX 78234-5034
Tel: (210) 295-0624/0626

ENERGY, DEPT. OF
Strategic Petroleum Reserve
P.O. Box 2276
Freeport, TX 77542-2276
Jorge Aguiñaga, HEPM
Tel: (979) 230-2201 Fax: (979) 230-2308
Email: jorge.aguinaga@spr.doe.gov
Web: www.spr.doe.gov

EQUAL EMPLOYMENT OPPORTUNITY
COMMISSION
Dallas District Office
207 S Houston St., 3rd Fl.
Dallas, TX 75202
Mike Fetzer, Director
Tel: (214) 253-2700 Fax: (214) 253-2720
Web: www.eeoc.gov

El Paso Area Office
300 E Main Dr. #500
El Paso, TX 79901
Robert Calderon, Director
Tel: (915) 534-6700 Fax: (915) 534-6701
Web: www.eeoc.gov

Houston District Office
1919 Smith St. #600 & 700
Houston, TX 77002-8049
Mike Fetzer, Director
Tel: (713) 209-3320 Fax: (713) 209-3381
Web: www.eeoc.gov

San Antonio District Office
5410 Fredericksburg Rd. #200
San Antonio, TX 78229
Pedro M. Esquivel, Director
Tel: (210) 281-7600   Fax: (210) 281-7690
Web: www.eeoc.gov

FEDERAL RESERVE BANK
Human Resources/EEO
Dallas Region
2200 N Pearl St.
Dallas, TX 75201
Tyrone Gholson, EEO Officer
Tel: (214) 922-6000
Web: www.dallasfed.org

HOMELAND SECURITY, DEPT. OF
Bureau of Customs and Border Protection
Human Resources
2301 S Main St.
McAllen, TX 78503
Cynthia Garcia, Personnel Specialist
Tel: (956) 984-3813 Fax: (956) 984-3990
Web: www.customs.ustreas.gov

INTERIOR, DEPT. OF THE
National Park Service
San Antonio Missions National
Historical Parks
2202 Roosevelt Ave.
San Antonio, TX 78210-4919
Karen Steed, Human Resources Specialist
Tel: (210) 534-8875 X240
Fax: (210) 534-1106
Email: karen_steed@nps.gov
Web: www.nps.gov/saan

JUSTICE, DEPT. OF
Attorney's Office
601 NW Loop 410 #600
San Antonio, TX 78216-5597
Tina Gomez, HEPM
Tel: (210) 384-7372 Fax: (210) 384-7322
Email: tina.gomez@usdoj.gov
Web: www.usdoj.gov

LABOR, DEPT. OF
Employment and Training Administration
Office of Youth Programs and Job Corps
525 Griffin St. #403
Dallas, TX 75202
Jose de Olivares, Regional Director
Tel: (214) 767-2114 Fax: (214) 767-2148
Email: jmdeolivares@doleta.gov
Web: www.doleta.gov

NAVY, DEPT. OF THE
Naval Reserve Recruiting Command Area
South
1564 Headquarters Ave.
Ft. Worth, TX 76127-1564
Tel: (817) 782-6131/69

Navy Recruiting District, Dallas
6440 N Beltline Rd. #150
Irving, TX 75063
Tel: (972) 714-8300

USMC Recruiting Station, Dallas
207 S Houston St. #146
Dallas, TX 75202
Tel: (210) 655-3480 Fax: (210) 655-3489
Web: www.marines.com

USMC Recruiting Station, Ft. Worth
3313 W Pioneer Pkwy.
Pantego, TX 76013
Tel: (817) 303-0993 Fax: (817) 303-7450
Web: www.marines.com

USMC Recruiting Station, Houston
701 San Jacinto St. #240, US Customs
House
Houston, TX 77002
Tel: (713) 718-4284 Fax: (713) 227-2535
Web: www.marines.com

USMC Recruiting Station, San Antonio
1265 Buck Rd. #MC
Fort Sam Houston, TX 78234-5034
Tel: (210) 295-1018 Fax: (210) 295-0498
Web: www.marines.com

OFFICE OF THE GOVERNOR
State of Texas
P.O. Box 12428
Austin, TX 78711
Edna Henderson, Director of Human
Resources
Tel: (512) 463-1740 Fax: (512) 463-8464

POSTAL SERVICE
Dallas District
951 W Bethel Rd.
Coppell, TX 75099-9460
Martina M. Jubera, Hispanic Program
Specialist
Tel: (972) 393-6185 Fax: (972) 393-6198
Email: mjubera@email.usps.gov
Web: www.usps.com

Fort Worth District
4600 Mark IV Pkwy.
Fort Worth, TX 76161-9100
Arlene Sanchez, Hispanic Program
Specialist
Tel: (817) 317-3311 Fax: (817) 317-3320
Web: www.usps.com

Fort Worth District
4600 Mark IV Pkwy.
Fort Worth, TX 76161-9100
Linda A. Brantley, Diversity Development
Specialist
Tel: (817) 317-3333 Fax: (817) 317-3320
Web: www.usps.com

Houston District
1002 Washington Ave. #228B
Houston, TX 77002-9421
John Martinez, Hispanic Program Specialist
Tel: (713) 226-3186 Fax: (713) 226-3567
Web: www.usps.com

Rio Grande District
1 Post Office Dr.
San Antonio, TX 78284-9425
Maricela G. Rivas, Hispanic Program
Specialist
Tel: (210) 368-5512
Web: www.usps.com

Southwest Area Office
P.O. Box 225459
Dallas, TX 75222-5459
Vickie Tovar, Senior Diversity Program
Coordinator
Tel: (214) 819-8736 Fax: (214) 819-8956
Email: vickie.a.tovar@usps.gov
Web: www.usps.gov

SMALL BUSINESS ADMINISTRATION
Disaster Assistance-Disaster Area 3
14925 Kingport Rd.
Ft. Worth, TX 76155
Kandye Wells, Personnel Officer
Tel: (817) 868-2300 Fax: (817) 684-5621

SOCIAL SECURITY ADMINISTRATION
Greater Houston Area
7324 SW Frwy. #500
Houston, TX 77074
Andrew Hardwick, Metropolitan Public
Affairs Specialist
Tel: (713) 219-5636 X3039
Fax: (713) 219-5650
Email: andy.hardwick@ssa.gov

TREASURY, DEPT. OF THE
Bureau of Engraving and Printing
9000 Blue Mound Rd.
Ft. Worth, TX 76131
Frank Martinez, HEPM
Tel: (817) 847-3900 Fax: (817) 847-3706

VETERANS AFFAIRS, DEPT. OF
Veterans Administration Hospital
Voluntary Services

3600 Memorial Blvd.
Kerrville, TX 78028
Nick Villanueva, HEPM
Tel: (830) 792-2580 Fax: (830) 792-2659
Email: nicholas.villanueva@med.va.gov

WORKFORCE COMMISSION
State of Texas
Human Resources
101 E 15th St. #230
Austin, TX 78778-0001
Jan Thomas, Director
Tel: (512) 463-2314 Fax: (512) 463-2832
Web: www.twc.state.tx.us

UTAH

AGRICULTURE, DEPT. OF
West Region
1860 N 100 East
North Logan, UT 84341
John Hardman, HEPM
Tel: (435) 753-5616 X23
Fax: (435) 755-2117
Web: www.usda.gov

Forest Service
324 25th St. #4411, Federal Bldg., HR&S
Ogden, UT 84341
Sherry L. Neal, EEO Specialist
Tel: (801) 625-5806 Fax: (801) 625-5722
Email: slneal01@fs.fed.us
Web: www.fs.fed.us

AIR FORCE, DEPT. OF THE
Hill AFB
00-ALC/DPC, 6053 Elm Ln.
Hill AFB, UT 84056-5819
Tel: (801) 777-5504 Fax: (801) 777-0587

ARMY, DEPT. OF THE
US Army Recruiting Battalion Salt Lake City
2830 S Redwood Rd.
Salt Lake City, UT 84119-4708
Tel: (801) 974-9518/9519

DEPARTMENT OF COMMUNITY AND ECONOMIC DEVELOPMENT
State of Utah
State Office of Hispanic Affairs
324 S State St. #500
Salt Lake City, UT 84111
Tony Yapias, Director
Tel: (801) 538-8755 Fax: (801) 538-8678
Email: tyapias@utah.gov
Web: http://dced.utah.gov/hispanic

NAVY, DEPT. OF THE
Navy Officer Recruiting Station, Salt Lake City
2835 S Redwood
Salt Lake City, UT 84119

USMC Recruiting Station, Salt Lake City
Metro Business Park, 1279 W 2200 S
Bldg. #A
West Valley City, UT 84119-1471
Tel: (801) 954-0412 Fax: (801) 645-7129
Web: www.marines.com

POSTAL SERVICE
Salt Lake City District
1760 W 2100 South
Salt Lake City, UT 84199-2922
Pania Heimuli, Diversity Development
Specialist
Tel: (801) 974-2922 Fax: (801) 974-2975
Email: pania.heimuli@usps.gov
Web: www.usps.gov

VIRGINIA

AGRICULTURE, DEPT. OF
Southeast Region
Woodstock Service Ctr., 505 N Main St. #102
Woodstock, VA 22664
Jim Snyder, HEPM
Tel: (540) 459-5735 Fax: (540) 459-8364
Web: www.usda.gov

Food, Nutrition and Consumer Service
813 Sledgehammer Dr.
Fredericksburg, VA 22405
Carmen Zamora Nordlund, President of
USDA Chapter of Hispanic Organizations
Leadership Alliance
Tel: (703) 305-7480 Fax: (540) 899-3887
Email: carmen.nordlund@fns.usda.gov

3101 Park Center Dr. #942
Alexandria, VA 22302
Michael Watts, Director, Civil Rights
Tel: (703) 305-2195 Fax: (703) 305-2832
Email: michael.watts@fns.usda.gov
Web: www.fns.usda.gov

Civil Rights Division/Alternative Dispute
Resolution & Special Emphasis Program
3101 Park Center Dr. #942B
Alexandria, VA 22302
Candace SP Johnson, Program Manager
Tel: (703) 305-2215 Fax: (703) 305-2832
Email: candace.johnson@fns.usda.gov
Web: www.fns.usda.gov

3101 Park Center Dr. #520
Alexandria, VA 22302
Jacqueline Rodriguez, National HEPM
Tel: (703) 305-0414 Fax: (703) 305-2196
Email: jackie.rodriguez@fns.usda.gov
Web: www.fns.usda.gov

National Appeals Division (NAD)
3101 Park Center Dr. #1100
Alexandria, VA 22302
Ethel M. Dancy, National HEPM
Tel: (703) 305-1601 Fax: (703) 305-2825
Email: ethel.dancy@usda.gov
Web: www.nad.usda.gov

AIR FORCE, DEPT. OF THE
Langley AFB
HQ ACC/DPC, 114 Douglas St. #214
Langley AFB, VA 23665-2773
Tel: (757) 764-7621 Fax: (757) 764-5667

Langley AFB
1 MSS/DPC, 4 Nealy Ave. #119
Langley AFB, VA 23665-2096
Tel: (757) 764-6243 Fax: (757) 764-2266

ARMY, DEPT. OF THE
Fort Myer, EEO Office
Bldg. 203 #215
Fort Myer, VA 22211-1199
Vacant, EEO Specialist
Tel: (703) 696-3544 Fax: (703) 696-8588

Headquarters
2531 Jefferson Davis Hwy., 8th Fl.
Arlington, VA 22202-3905
Deborah Muse, Director of EEO
Tel: (703) 602-6357 Fax: (703) 602-3491
Email: deborah.muse@hqda.army.mil

**Military Traffic Mgmt. Command,
Headquarters**
200 Stovall St. #12S71
Alexandria, VA 22332-5000
Ana L. Colon, EEO Director
Tel: (703) 428-2105 Fax: (703) 428-3318
Email: colona@sddc.army.mil

**Office of the Assistant Secretary of the Army
from Manpower**
EEO Agency
1941 Jefferson Davis Hwy.,
Crystal Mall #4, #207
Arlington, VA 22202-4508
Delia Trimble, Manager/Hispanic
Employment Program
Tel: (703) 602-5368
Email: delia.trimble@hqda.army.mil
Web: http://eeoa.army.pentagon.mil

US Army Cadet Command, ROTC
Public Affairs Office, Bldg. 56 Patch Rd.
Fort Monroe, VA 23651-5000
Tel: (757) 788-4610

COMMERCE, DEPT. OF
Patent & Trademark Office
Office of Civil Rights
600 Dulany St. #7D-09A
Alexandria, VA 22312
Patricia Gail Boylan, Director
Tel: (571) 272-8095 Fax: (571) 273-0154
Email: patricia.boylan@uspto.gov
Web: www.uspto.gov

DEFENSE, DEPT. OF
Commander in Chief, US Atlantic Fleet N1CP
1562 Mitscher Ave. #250
Norfolk, VA 23511-2487
Tel: (757) 836-0497 Fax: (757) 836-3844
Web: www.marines.com

**Defense Contract Audit Agency,
Headquarters**
8725 John J. Kingman Rd. #2135
Ft. Belvoir, VA 22060
Vicky O'Donnell, EEO Director
Tel: (703) 767-1240 Fax: (703) 767-1228

National Guard Bureau
EEO Division
1411 Jefferson Davis Hwy.
Arlington, VA 22202
Phyllis Brantley, HEPM
Tel: (703) 607-0782 Fax: (703) 607-0790
Email: brantleyp@ngb.ang.af.mil

Office of the Inspector General
EEO Office
400 Army Navy Dr. #336
Arlington, VA 22202
Cassandra Johnson, Director
Tel: (703) 604-9710 Fax: (703) 604-0044
Email: cjohnson@dodig.osd.mil
Web: www.dodig.osd.mil

Washington Headquarters Services
EEO Office
1777 N Kent St.
Arlington, VA 22209
Renee Coates, Assistant Director
Tel: (703) 588-0451 Fax: (703) 588-7555
Web: www.pentagon.mil

EQUAL EMPLOYMENT OPPORTUNITY COMMISSION
Norfolk Area Office
Federal Bldg., 200 Granby St. #739
Norfolk, VA 23510
Herbert Brown, Director
Tel: (757) 441-3470 Fax: (757) 441-6720
Web: www.eeoc.gov

Richmond Area Office
830 E Main St., 6th Fl.
Richmond, VA 23219
Gloria L. Underwood, Director
Tel: (804) 771-2200 Fax: (804) 771-2222
Web: www.eeoc.gov

INTERIOR, DEPT. OF THE
Bureau of Land Management
Eastern State Office
7450 Boston Blvd.
Springfield, VA 22153-3121
Lynda Nix, EEO Manager
Tel: (703) 440-1593 Fax: (703) 440-1609
Email: lynda_nix@es.blm.gov
Web: www.blm.gov

Fish & Wildlife Service
Directorate of Civil Rights
4501 N Fairfax Dr. #201
Arlington, VA 22203
Pedro De Jesus, EEO Manager
Tel: (703) 358-2552 Fax: (703) 358-2030
Email: pedro_dejesus@fws.gov
Web: www.fws.gov

Office for Diversity and Civil Rights, Office
for Equal Opportunity
4501 N Fairfax Dr., 2nd Fl.
Arlington, VA 22203
Tracy Thompson, Officer
Tel: (703) 358-1724 Fax: (703) 358-2030
Email: tracy_thompson@fws.gov
Web: www.fws.gov

Forest Service, Jefferson National Forest
Human Resources
5162 Valley Pointe Pkwy.
Roanoke, VA 24019
Laura Germaine, Personnel Manager
Tel: (540) 265-5245 Fax: (540) 265-5250
Web: www.fs.fed.us

Minerals Management Service
EEO Division
381 Elden St. M/S 2900
Herndon, VA 20170
Rosa Thomas, EEO Specialist
Tel: (703) 787-1314 Fax: (703) 787-1601
Email: rosa.thomas@mms.gov
Web: www.mms.gov

Office of Equal Opportunity
381 Elden St. M/S 0400
Herndon, VA 22070
Patricia Callis, Chief
Tel: (703) 787-1313 Fax: (703) 787-1601
Email: patricia.callis@mms.gov
Web: www.mms.gov

US Geological Survey
12201 Sunrise Valley Dr. M/S 602
Reston, VA 20192-0002
Lynne Sendejo, HEPM
Tel: (703) 648-4868 Fax: (703) 648-4445
Email: lsendejo@usgs.gov
Web: www.usgs.gov

Office for Equal Opportunity
12201 Sunrise Valley Dr., 602 National Ctr.
Reston, VA 22092
Alesia Pierre-Lois, Chief
Tel: (703) 648-7770 Fax: (703) 648-4445
Web: www.usgs.gov

JUSTICE, DEPT. OF
Drug Enforcement Administration
EEO Staff
600 Army Navy Dr. #E11275
Arlington, VA 22202
vacant, EEO Manager
Tel: (202) 307-8895 Fax: (202) 307-8942

LABOR, DEPT. OF
Mine Safety and Health Administration
Office of Diversity, Outreach & Employee
Safety
1100 Wilson Blvd. #2514
Arlington, VA 22209-3939
Michael Thompson, Director
Tel: (202) 693-9880 Fax: (202) 693-9881
Email: thompson.michael@dol.gov
Web: www.msha.gov

Office of Diversity, Outreach & Employee
Safety
1100 Wilson Blvd. #2122
Arlington, VA 22209-3939
Ellen Gee, HEPM
Tel: (202) 693-9899 Fax: (202) 693-9856
Web: www.msha.gov

NATIONAL CREDIT UNION
ADMINISTRATION
EEO Programs Office
1775 Duke St. #3019
Alexandria, VA 22314
Marilyn Gannon, Director
Tel: (703) 518-6325 Fax: (703) 518-6681
Email: eeomail@ncua.gov
Web: www.ncua.gov

NATIONAL SCIENCE FOUNDATION
Office of Equal Opportunity Programs
4201 Wilson Blvd. #255S
Arlington, VA 22230
Ronald D. Branch, Director
Tel: (703) 292-8020 Fax: (703) 292-9072
Email: rbranch@nsf.gov
Web: www.nsf.gov

NAVY, DEPT. OF THE
Navy Recruiting District, Richmond
411 E Franklin St.
Richmond, VA 23219
Tel: (804) 771-2001

USMC Recruiting Station, Richmond
9210 Arboretum Pkwy. #220
Richmond, VA 23236-3472
Tel: (804) 272-0458 Fax: (804) 272-0535
Web: www.marines.com

OFFICE OF PERSONNEL MANAGEMENT
Norfolk Service Center
Federal Bldg., 200 Granby St. #500
Norfolk, VA 23510-1886
F. Alan Nelson, Director
Tel: (757) 441-3373 Fax: (757) 441-6280
Email: norfolk@opm.gov
Web: www.opm.gov

POSTAL SERVICE
Northern Virginia District
8409 Lee Hwy.
Merrifield, VA 22081-9996
Julie Lane, Diversity Development Specialist
Tel: (703) 698-6614 Fax: (703) 204-3004
Email: jlane3@email.usps.gov
Web: www.usps.gov

WASHINGTON

AIR FORCE, DEPT. OF THE
Fairchild AFB
92 MSS/DPC, 220 W Bong St.
Fairchild AFB, WA 99011-8524
Tel: (509) 247-8324 Fax: (509) 247-3235

McChord AFB
62 MSS/DPC, 100 Main St. #1047
McChord AFB, WA 98438-1109
Tel: (253) 982-2340 Fax: (253) 982-3213

ARMY, DEPT. OF THE
US Army Cadet Command, ROTC
Western Region
Attn: Public Affairs Office
Fort Lewis, WA 98433-7100
Tel: (253) 967-7473

US Army Recruiting Battalion Seattle
P.O. Box 3957
4735 E Marginal Way South
Seattle, WA 98124-3957
Tel: (206) 764-3599

ENERGY, DEPT. OF
Richland Operations Office
P.O. Box 450, M/S H6-60
Richland, WA 99352
Paul Hernández, HEPM
Tel: (509) 376-2209 Fax: (509) 376-3661
Email: paul_r_hernandez@rl.gov
Web: www.hanford.gov

Office of Regulatory Compliance and
Assurance Division
Richland Operations Office
P.O. Box 550 #H6-60
Richland, WA 99352
Paul R. Hernandez, HEPM
Tel: (509) 376-2209 Fax: (509) 376-3661
Email: paul_r_hernandez@orp.doe.gov
Web: www.orp.doe.gov

EQUAL EMPLOYMENT OPPORTUNITY
COMMISSION
Seattle District Office
Federal Office Bldg., 909 1st Ave. #400
Seattle, WA 98104-1061
Jeanette M. Leino, Director
Tel: (206) 220-6883   Fax: (206) 220-6911
Web: www.eeoc.gov

LABOR, DEPT. OF
Employment and Training Administration
Office of Youth Programs and Job Corps
1111 3rd Ave. #800
Seattle, WA 98101-3212
Ernest Priestley, Associate Regional Director
Tel: (206) 553-7938 X8057
Fax: (206) 553-4009
Email: epriestley@doleta.gov
Web: www.doleta.gov

NAVY, DEPT. OF THE
Navy Officer Recruiting Station, Spokane
1330 N Washington #3700
Spokane, WA 99201

Navy Recruiting District, Seattle
2901 3rd Ave.
Seattle, WA 98121
Tel: (800) 832-0258

USMC Recruiting Station, Seattle
4735 Marginal Way South,
Federal Ctr. South
Seattle, WA 98134-2335
Tel: (206) 762-1645 Fax: (206) 763-1194
Web: www.marines.com

POSTAL SERVICE
Seattle District
415 1st Ave. North
Seattle, WA 98109-9997
Eric Colon, Hispanic Program Specialist
Tel: (206) 442-6203 Fax: (206) 378-2537
Web: www.usps.gov

SOCIAL AND HEALTH SERVICES,
DEPARTMENT OF
State of Washington
Aging & Adult Services Administration-State
Unit on Aging
P.O. Box 45600
Olympia, WA 98504-5600
Patty McDonald, Diversity Program
Manager
Tel: (360) 725-2559 Fax: (360) 438-8633
Email: mcdonpm@dshs.wa.gov

WEST VIRGINIA

ARMY, DEPT. OF THE
US Army Recruiting Battalion Beckley
21 Mallard Ct.
Beckley, WV 25801-3615
Tel: (304) 252-0422

INTERIOR, DEPT. OF THE
National Park Service
Harpers Ferry Center, EEO Office
P.O. Box 50
Harpers Ferry, WV 25425
Magaly M. Green , EEO Manager
Tel: (304) 535-6003 Fax: (304) 535-6080
Email: magaly_green@nps.gov
Web: www.nps.gov

NAVY, DEPT. OF THE
USMC Recruiting Station, Charleston
4216 St. Route 34
Hurricane, WV 25526-9788
Tel: (304) 757-5028 Fax: (304) 346-0469
Web: www.marines.com

TREASURY, DEPT. OF THE
Bureau of Public Debt
200 3rd St.
Parkersburg, WV 26106
Cheryl D. Adams, EEO Officer
Tel: (304) 480-6527 Fax: (304) 480-6074
Email: cheryl.adams@bpd.treas.gov
Web: www.publicdebt.treas.gov

WISCONSIN

AGRICULTURE, DEPT. OF
Midwest Region
6515 Watts Rd. #200
Madison, WI 53719-2726
Kent Pena, HEPM
Tel: (608) 662-4422 X274
Fax: (608) 276-5890
Email: kent.pena@wi.usda.gov
Web: www.usda.gov

ARMY, DEPT. OF THE
US Army Recruiting Battalion Milwaukee
310 W Wisconsin Ave. #600
Milwaukee, WI 53203-2211
Tel: (414) 297-4596/1193

DEPARTMENT OF EMPLOYMENT
RELATIONS
State of Wisconsin
P.O. Box 7855
Madison, WI 53702
Demetri Fishers, Affirmative Action Division
Tel: (608) 266-5709 Fax: (608) 267-1020

EQUAL EMPLOYMENT OPPORTUNITY
COMMISSION
Milwaukee District Office
310 W Wisconsin Ave. #800
Milwaukee, WI 53203-2292
Chester V. Bailey , Director
Tel: (414) 297-1111 Fax: (414) 297-4133
Web: www.eeoc.gov

NAVY, DEPT. OF THE
Navy Officer Recruiting Station, Milwaukee
2810 Crossroads Dr. #1700S, Plz. 1
Milwaukee, WI 53707

USMC Recruiting Station, Milwaukee
310 Wisconsin Ave. #480
Milwaukee, WI 53203-2216
Tel: (414) 297-3838 Fax: (414) 297-1017
Web: www.marines.com

WYOMING

AIR FORCE, DEPT. OF THE
FE Warren AFB
90 MSS/DPC, 7305 Randall Ave.
FE Warren AFB, WY 82005-3905
Tel: (307) 773-2061 Fax: (307) 773-2720

Private Sector Employment Opportunities
Oportunidades de empleo en el sector privado

ARIZONA

HONEYWELL, INC.
1944 E. Sky Harbor Cr.
Phoenix, AZ 85034
Kathi Winter, Director of Human Resources
Tel: (602) 365-2203 (602) 365-2640
Email: kathi.winter@honeywell.com
Web: www.honeywell.com/careers

CALIFORNIA

AMERICAN PRESIDENT LINES LTD.
Headquarters
1111 Broadway Ave.
Oakland, CA 94607-5500
ATTN: Human Resources
(510) 272-8000 Fax: (510) 272-7421
Web: www.apl.com

AMGEN, INC.
Headquarters
1 Amgen Ctr. Dr.
Thousand Oaks, CA 91320-1799
Ted Bagley, Director of Human Resources
Tel: (805) 447-7396 Fax: (805) 447-1010
Web: www.amgen.com

APPLE COMPUTER, INC.
1 Infinite Loop
Cupertino, CA 95014
Shelly Hulffer, Director of Human Resources
Tel: (408) 974-2852
Email: college@apple.com
Web: www.apple.com/jobs/

ATLANTIC RICHFIELD COMPANY (ARCO)
Headquarters
4 Centerpoint Dr.
La Palma, CA 90623
Dan Place, Human Resources Advisor
Tel: (714) 670-5122 Fax: (714) 670-5326
Web: www.arco.com

BAE SYSTEMS
5140 W. Goldleaf Cir.
Los Angeles, CA 90056
Marylin Conderan, Manager of Human Resources
Tel: (323) 298-6300
Web: www.na.baesystems.com

BECHTEL CORPORATION
Headquarters-Staffing Support Center
50 Beale St.
San Francisco, CA 94105-1895
ATTN: Human Resources
Tel: (415) 768-1234 Fax: (415) 768-9038
Email: employna@bechtel.com
Web: www.bechtel.com

CHEVRONTEXACO CORPORATION
Worldwide Headquarters
6001 Bollinger Canyon Rd.
San Ramon, CA 94583
ATTN: Human Resources
Tel: (925) 842-1000
Web: www.chevrontexaco.com

FRESQUEZ & ASSOCIATES
P.O. Box 721238
San Diego, CA 92172
Ernesto Fresquez, Principal
Tel: (858) 538-4424 Fax: (858) 538-4449
Email: ernesto@fresquez.com
Web: www.fresquez.com

HEWLETT PACKARD CORPORATION
Employment Response Center
3000 Hanover St.
Palo Alto, CA 94304-1185
ATTN: Human Resources
Tel: (650) 852-8473 Fax: (650) 857-5518
Web: www.jobs.hp.com

KAISER FOUNDATION HEALTH PLAN, INC.
Regional Office
1950 Franklin St.
Oakland, CA 94612
ATTN: Human Resources
Tel: (510) 987-4806
Web: www.kaiserpermanente.org

LEVI STRAUSS & COMPANY
1155 Battery St.
San Francisco, CA 94111
ATTN: Human Resources
Tel: (415) 501-6000 Fax: (415) 501-7112
Web: www.levistrauss.com/careers/

LOCKHEED MARTIN
1111 Lockheed Martin Way,
Dept. 350S Bldg.154
Sunnyvale, CA 94089
Vanessa Williams, Equal Opportunity Manager
Tel: (408) 742-8346
Email: jobs.lmc@lmco.com
Web: www.lmco.com

MARSHALLS REGION 6 OFFICE
424 Executive Ct. North
Fairfield, CA 94534
ATTN: Human Resources
Tel: (707) 864-8044 Fax: (707) 864-8088
Web: www.tjx.com

MCKESSON CORPORATION
1 Post St.
San Francisco, CA 94104
Ralph Dechabert, Manager of Affirmative Action
Tel: (415) 983-9454 Fax: (415) 983-9113
Web: www.mckesson.com

MEDIAN PERSONNEL SERVICES, INC.
23361 El Toro Rd. #107
Lake Forest, CA 92630
Cecile Enojado, Employment Specialist
Tel: (949) 770-2728 Fax: (949) 770-1509
Email: workforce2@aol.com

MOTOROLA, INC.
6450 Sequence Dr.
San Diego, CA 92121
Lori Russen, Manager of Human Resources
Tel: (800) 445-3620 Fax: (858) 404-2556
Web: www.mot.com

NESTLÉ USA, INC.
800 N. Brand Blvd.
Glendale, CA 91203
ATTN: Corporate Recruiting
Tel: (818) 549-6000
Web: www.nestlejobs.com

NORTHROP GRUMMAN
Headquarters
1840 Century Park East
Los Angeles, CA 90067
Sandra Evers-Manly, Director of EEO & Diversity
Tel: (310) 553-6262
Web: www.northgrum.com

ORACLE CORPORATION
Diversity Manager
500 Oracle Pkwy.
Redwood Shores, CA 94065
ATTN: Human Resources, Jane Robertson
Tel: (650) 506-7000 Fax: (650) 506-7200
Web: www.us.oracle.com

PACIFIC BELL
A Division of SBC Communications
140 New Montgomery
San Francisco, CA 94105
ATTN: HR Dept., Executive Offices
Tel: (800) 303-3000 Fax: (415) 896-0264
Web: www.sbc.com/careers

PACIFIC GAS & ELECTRIC CORPORATION
P.O. Box 770000
San Francisco, CA 94177
ATTN: Human Resources
Tel: (415) 973-7000 Fax: (415) 973-1366
Web: www.pge.com

SILICON GRAPHICS, INC.
Headquarters
1500 Crittenden Ln.
Mountain View, CA 94043
ATTN: Human Resources
Tel: (650) 960-1980 Fax: (650) 933-0908
Web: www.sgi.com

SONY PICTURES ENTERTAINMENT
10202 W. Washington Blvd.
Culver City, CA 90232
Sussane Criley, Head of Human Resources
Tel: (310) 244-4000 X4334
Fax: (310) 244-2626
Email: sussane_criley@spe.sony.com
Web: www.sonypicturesjobs.com

SUN MICROSYSTEMS, INC.
10 Network Cr.
Menlo Park, CA 94025
Candy Castleberry, Manager of Corporate Diversity
Tel: (408) 404-8586 Fax: (408) 276-8333
Web: www.sun.com

T.J. MAXX
PACIFIC REGIONAL OFFICE-PRO
2151 Michelson Dr. #200
Irvine, CA 92612-1311
ATTN: Human Resources
Tel: (949) 752-8716 Fax: (949) 752-0140
Web: www.tjmaxx.com

TACO BELL
17901 Von Karman Ave.
Irvine, CA 92614
ATTN: Human Resources
Tel: (949) 863-4500 Fax: (949) 863-3980
Web: www.yumcareers.com

THE WELLA CORPORATION
6109 DeSoto Ave.
Woodland Hills, CA 91367
ATTN: Human Resources
Tel: (818) 999-5112
Email: Jobs@wellacorp.com
Web: www.wellausa.com

TOYOTA MOTOR SALES, USA, INC.
19001 S. Western Ave.
Torrance, CA 90501
ATTN: Human Resources
Tel: (310) 468-4000 Fax: (310) 618-7816
Email: resumes@toyota.com
Web: www.toyota.com

COLORADO

COORS BREWING COMPANY
Placement Center
P.O. Box 4030
Golden, CO 80401
ATTN: Human Resources
Tel: (303) 279-6565 Fax: (303) 277-6132
Web: www.coorsjobs.com

QWEST
1801 California St.
Denver, CO 80202
ATTN: Human Resources-Occupational Staffing
Tel: (303) 896-4675 Fax: (303) 992-1724
Email: staffing@qwest.com
Web: www.qwest.com

STORAGETEK CORPORATION
1 StorageTek Dr.
Louisville, CO 80028-0001
Connie Fulmer, EEO Specialist
Tel: (303) 673-4837
Email: connie_fulmer@storagetek.com
Web: www.stortek.com

CONNECTICUT

AETNA, INC.
151 Farmington Ave.
Hartford, CT 06156
ATTN: Human Resources
Tel: (860) 273-0123
Web: www.aetna.com

GENERAL ELECTRIC
3135 Easton Turnpike
Fairfield, CT 06828
Debb Elam, Diversity Manager
Tel: (203) 373-3574 Fax: (203) 373-2342
Web: www.gecareers.com

PITNEY BOWES
1 Elmcroft Rd.
Stamford, CT 06926-0700
Peter Castillo, Director of Staffing
Tel: (203) 351-7849 Fax: (203) 351-6759
Email: peter.castillo@pb.com
Web: www.pitneybowes.com

THE TRAVELERS COMPANIES
A Member of Citigroup
1 Tower Sq.
Hartford, CT 06183-7060
Diana Gale, Associate Staffing Consultant
Tel: (860) 277-0111 Fax: (860) 277-1970
Web: www.stpaultravelers.com

UNITED TECHNOLOGIES CORPORATION
1 Financial Plz., 4th Fl.
Hartford, CT 06101
Oswald Reid, Work Force Diversity Director
Tel: (860) 728-7000
Web: www.utc.com

XEROX CORPORATION
Supplier Diversity
800 Long Ridge Rd.
Stamford, CT 06904
Dan Robinson, Manager
Tel: (585) 422-2295
Web: www.xerox.com/supplierdiversity

DELAWARE

ASTRAZENECA
Headquarters
P.O. Box 15437
Wilmington, DE 19850-5437
ATTN: Human Resources
Tel: (302) 886-3000 Fax: (302) 886-2972
Web: www.astrazeneca.com

DUPONT
Headquarters-Diversity & Work Life
1007 Market St.
Wilmington, DE 19898
Sandra Bowe
Tel: (302) 774-1000
Web: www.dupont.com

MBNA AMERICA
International Headquarters
1100 N. King St.
Wilmington, DE 19884-0244
ATTN: Personnel
Tel: (888) 884-6262 Fax: (302) 432-3367
Web: www.mbnacareers.com

DISTRICT OF COLUMBIA

AMERICAN ASSOCIATION OF HEALTH PLANS
601 Pennsylvania Ave. NW #500
Washington, DC 20004
Debbie Manning, Head of Human Resources
Tel: (202) 778-3200 Fax: (202) 9554397
Web: www.ahip.org

CITIBANK
1775 Pennsylvania Ave. NW
Washington, DC 20006
ATTN: Human Resources
Tel: (202) 429-7760
Web: www.citibank.com

CITIBANK/CITICORP
Mid-Atlantic Region
1101 Pennsylvania Ave. NW #10
Washington, DC 20004
Alyson Klug, Manager of Human Resources
Tel: (202) 879-6817 Fax: (202) 508-4512
Web: www.citibank.com

EDISON ELECTRIC INSTITUTE
701 Pennsylvania Ave. NW, 3rd Fl.
Washington, DC 20004-2696
Jennifer Vick, Human Resources Assistant
Tel: (202) 508-5487 Fax: (202) 508-5503
Email: jvick@eei.org
Web: www.eei.org

EDISON ELECTRIC INSTITUTE
Employment and Human Resources Services
701 Pennsylvania Ave. NW, 3rd Fl.
Washington, DC 20004-2696
Louis Smoak, Manager
Tel: (202) 508-5635 Fax: (202) 508-5503
Web: www.eei.org

EQUITY RESEARCH CORPORATION
5 Thomas Cr. NW
Washington, DC 20005
Miriam I. Cruz, President
Tel: (202) 387-3331 Fax: (202) 797-1344
Email: equityrc@aol.com

FANNIE MAE
3900 Wisconsin Ave. NW
Washington, DC 20016-2892
ATTN: Human Resources and Training
Tel: (202) 752-7000
Web: www.fanniemae.com

NUCLEAR ENERGY INSTITUTE
1776 I St. NW #400
Washington, DC 20006-3708
Olga Zamora, Manager of Human Resources
Tel: (202) 739-8000 Fax: (202) 785-4019
Email: omz@nei.org
Web: www.nei.org

RIGGS NATIONAL BANK OF DC
Career Services
1512 Connecticut Ave. NW
Washington, DC 20036
ATTN: Human Resources
Tel: (301) 887-4400 Fax: (202) 835-5616
Web: www.riggsbank.com

THE WASHINGTON POST
1150 15th St. NW
Washington, DC 20071
Martha Lequeux, Director of Human Resources
Tel: (202) 334-7174
Web: www.washingtonpost.com

TOM BROWN & COMPANY, INC.
1090 Vermont Ave. NW #800
Washington, DC 20005-4905

Mona Brown, VP of Human Resources
Tel: (202) 393-7755 Fax: (202) 393-7758
Email: tbrownco@aol.com

WORLD DATA, INC.
1015 18th St. NW #710
Washington, DC 20036
Robert Dick, VP Human Resources
Tel: (202) 785-6800 Fax: (202) 785-8850
Email: resumes@worlddata.com
Web: www.worlddata.com

FLORIDA

AERO SIMULATION, INC.
4450 E. Adamo Dr. #501
Tampa, FL 33605-5941
Robert Rodriguez, Director of Human Resources
Tel: (813) 628-4447 Fax: (813) 628-8404
Email: r_rodriguez@aerosimulation.com
Web: www.aerosimulation.com

AIRBORNE EXPRESS
1200 S. Pine Island Rd. #600
Plantation, FL 33324
ATTN: Human Resources Recruiting
Tel: (800) 225-5345
Web: www.airborne.com

BURGER KING
Staffing Department
5505 Blue Lagoon Dr.
Miami, FL 33126
Tel: (305) 378-3000 Fax: (305) 378-3516
Web: www.burgerking.com

DHL WORLDWIDE EXPRESS
Corporate Headquarters
1200 S. Pine Island Rd.
Plantation, FL 33324
ATTN: Human Resources
Tel: (954) 888-7000
Web: www.dhl-usa.com

MARSHALLS REGION 3 OFFICE
12801 W. Sunrise Blvd.
Sunrise, FL 33323
ATTN: Human Resources
Tel: (954) 858-1768 Fax: (954) 846-8753
Web: www.tjx.com

RYDER SYSTEM
3600 NW 82nd Ave.
Miami, FL 33166
Lisa Fisher, Recruiter
Tel: (305) 593-3726 Fax: (305) 500-5909
Email: careers@ryder.com
Web: www.ryder.com

GEORGIA

BANK OF AMERICA
Headquarters
600 Peachtree St. NE, Atlanta Plz. Bldg.
Atlanta, GA 30308
Gerri Thomas, Diversity Executive
Tel: (404) 607-6140 Fax: (404) 607-6113
Email: gerri.thomas@bankofamerica.com
Web: www.bankofamerica.com

BELLSOUTH CORPORATION
Headquarters
1155 Peachtree St. NE
Atlanta, GA 30309-3610
Rochellle Stockett, Director of Diversity
Tel: (404) 249-4158 Fax: (404) 249-3245
Web: www.bellsouth.com/employment

COCA COLA COMPANY
1 Coca Cola Plz. NW
Atlanta, GA 30313

Pegui Mariduena, Director of Global Diversity
Tel: (404) 676-2121 Fax: (404) 515-2999
Web: www.cocacola.com

MARSHALLS DECATUR
Distribution Center
2300 Miller Rd.
Decatur, GA 30035
ATTN: Human Resources
Tel: (770) 808-4703 Fax: (770) 808-4725
Web: www.tjx.com

PFIZER, INC.
Southeast Region
400 Perimeter Ctr. Ter. #1000
Atlanta, GA 30346
ATTN: Human Resources
Tel: (770) 551-5950
Web: www.pfizer.com

T.J. MAXX
SOUTHEAST REGIONAL OFFICE-SERO
1600 Parkwood Cr. #610
Atlanta, GA 30339
ATTN: Human Resources
Tel: (770) 980-1114 Fax: (770) 980-1972
Web: www.tjmaxx.com

UNITED PARCEL SERVICE
55 Glenlake Pkwy. NE
Atlanta, GA 30328
Gary Wheeler, Director of EEO & Diversity
Tel: (404) 828-4267 Fax: (404) 828-6440
Email: garywheeler@ups.com
Web: www.upsjobs.com

US FOOD SERVICE
7950 Spence Rd.
Fairburn, GA 30213
Cathy M. Wofford, VP of Human Resources
Tel: (770) 774-8300 Fax: (770) 774-8505
Web: www.usfoodservice.com

IDAHO

BOISE CASCADE CORPORATION
P.O. Box 50
1111 W. Jefferson St.
Boise, ID 83728-0001
ATTN: Human Resources
Tel: (208) 384-6161 Fax: (208) 384-7189
Web: www.bc.com

ILLINOIS

ALLSTATE INSURANCE COMPANY
Employment Selection Team
2775 Sanders Rd.
Northbrook, IL 60062
Joan Crockett, Manager
Tel: (847) 402-1142
Web: www.allstatecareers.com

AMERITECH INTERNATIONAL
Headquarters
225 W. Randolph Rd., 18th Fl.
Chicago, IL 60606
Doug Alexander
Tel: (312) 609-6224
Web: www.ameritech.com

BANK ONE CORPORATION
131 S. Dearborn St., 4th Fl.
Chicago, IL 60603
Lupe William, Human Resources Recruiter
Tel: (312) 385-7394
Web: www.bankone.com

BAXTER INTERNATIONAL, INC.
Global College Relations
1 Baxter Pkwy.
Deerfield, IL 60015

Mike Tucker, Senior VP of Human Resources
Tel: (847) 948-2000 Fax: (847) 948-2964
Web: www.baxter.com

BP CORPORATION
Headquarters
28100 Torch Pkwy.
Warrenville, IL 60555-3938
ATTN: Human Resources
Tel: (630) 420-5111
Web: www.bpamoco.com

CATERPILLAR, INC.
100 NE Adams St.
Peoria, IL 61629
ATTN: Corporate Employment Services
Tel: (309) 675-1000 Fax: (309) 675-4332
Web: www.cat.com

GE CAPITAL FINANCE COMPANY
500 W. Monroe St., 19th Fl.
Chicago, IL 60661
Diana McGrawlin
Tel: (312) 441-7010 Fax: (312) 441-7360
Web: www.hellerfin.com

HOUSEHOLD FINANCE CORPORATION
961 Weigel Dr.
Elmhurst, IL 60126
Roberta Cacioppo, Human Resources Assistant
Tel: (630) 617-7000 Fax: (630) 617-7442
Email: rmcacioppo@household.com
Web: www.householdfinance.com

HYATT HOTELS CORPORATION
200 W. Madison Ave.
Chicago, IL 60606
Carrie Novak, Associate Director of Human Resources
Tel: (312) 750-1234 Fax: (312) 920-2350
Web: www.hyatt.com

INTERNATIONAL SOFTWARE CONSULTING
Corporate Office
1699 E. Woodfield Rd. #200
Schaumburg, IL 60173
ATTN: Human Resources
Tel: (847) 619-5005 Fax: (847) 969-9097
Web: www.isc-software.com

MCDONALD'S CORPORATION
1 McDonald's Plz.
Oak Brook, IL 60523
Kevin Bradley, Director of Diversity Initiatives
Tel: (630) 623-3000 Fax: (630) 623-7232
Email: kevin.bradley@mcd.com
Web: www.mcdonalds.com

REXAM
Headquarters
8770 W. Bryn Mawr Ave.
Chicago, IL 60631-3655
Margaret Steinhagen, Recruiter
Tel: (773) 399-3000
Web: www.rexam.com

SEARS, ROEBUCK & COMPANY
3333 Beverly Rd.
Hoffman States, IL 60179
David Roudi, College Relations
Tel: (847) 286-3595 Fax: (847) 286-8310
Email: droudi@sears.com
Web: www.sears.com

SMURFIT-STONE CONTAINER CORPORATION
Corporate Headquarters
150 N. Michigan Ave.
Chicago, IL 60601
Patty Olsen, Manager of Human Resources
Tel: (312) 580-4875 Fax: (312) 649-4332
Web: www.smurfit-stone.com

STATE FARM INSURANCE COMPANIES
Corporate Employment Center
2205 E. Washington St.
Bloomington, IL 61710
ATTN: Human Resources
Tel: (309) 735-1700 Fax: (309) 735-1723
Web: www.statefarm.com

T.J. MAXX
MID-WEST REGIONAL OFFICE-MWRO
3501 W. Algonquin Rd. #330
Rolling Meadows, IL 60008
ATTN: Human Resources
Tel: (847) 818-1734 Fax: (847) 818-1995
Web: www.tjmaxx.com

TENNECO AUTOMOTIVE, INC.
500 N. Field Dr.
Lake Forest, IL 60045
Barbara Kluth, Executive Director of Human Resources
Tel: (847) 482-5000 Fax: (847) 482-5295
Web: www.tenneco-automotive.com

UNITED AIRLINES
P.O. Box 66100
Chicago, IL 60666
ATTN: Human Resources
Tel: (888) 825-5627 Fax: (847) 700-6958
Web: www.united.com

INDIANA

DO GROUP SYSTEMS INC.
2701 Industrial Park
Elkhart, IN 46516
ATTN: Human Resources
Tel: (574) 293-0624 Fax: (574) 294-1906
Web: www.centercore.com

T.J. MAXX - EVANSVILLE
Distribution Center-Human Resources
3301 Maxx Rd.
Evansville, IN 47711-2905
ATTN: Human Resources
Tel: (812) 424-0932 Fax: (812) 465-4852
Web: www.tjmaxx.com

KANSAS

SPRINT CORPORATION
6200 Sprint Pkwy.
Overland Park, KS 66251
JIm Kissinger, Senior Vice President of Human Resources
Tel: (913) 794-1303 Fax: (913) 523-9669
Web: www.sprint.com/hr

KENTUCKY

KFC
Public Affairs for Diversity
1441 Gardiner Ln.
Louisville, KY 40213
ATTN: Staffing Department
Tel: (502) 874-8300 Fax: (502) 874-8662
Web: www.kfc.com/careers/

MAINE

BATH IRON WORKS
Employment Department
700 Washington St.
Bath, ME 04530
Nancy Fortin
Tel: (207) 442-3555 Fax: (207) 442-1919
Email: employment@gdbiw.com
Web: www.gdbiw.com

MARYLAND

BGE
Headquarters
750 E. Pratt St.
Baltimore, MD 21202
ATTN: Human Resources
Tel: (410) 783-2800
Email: careers@constellation.com
Web: www.bge.com

CHEVY CHASE BANK
7501 Wisconsin Ave.
Bethesda, MD 20814
Russ McNish, Director of Human Resources
Tel: (240) 497-4600 Fax: (240) 497-4688
Web: www.chevychasebank.com

COUNTER TECHNOLOGY, INC.
4733 Bethesda Ave. #800
Bethesda, MD 20814
Jennifer Cramb, Manager of Human Resources
Tel: (301) 907-0127 Fax: (301) 907-6997
Web: www.countertech.com

GIANT FOOD, INC.
6524 Landover Rd.
Landover, MD 20785
ATTN: Human Resources
Tel: (301) 322-7441
Web: www.giantfood.com

HONEYWELL TECHNOLOGY SOLUTIONS, INC.
Organizational Development
7000 Columbia Gateway Dr.
Columbia, MD 21046
Rose Boehm, Learning & Diversity Manager
Tel: (410) 964-7259 Fax: (410) 964-7498
Email: rose.boehm@honeywell-tsi.com
Web: www.honeywell-tsi.com

MARRIOTT CORPORATION
10400 Fernwood Rd.
Bethesda, MD 20817
ATTN: Staffing Resources
Tel: (301) 380-1200 Fax: (301) 380-2111
Web: www.marriott.com

SUNTRUST BANK, INC.
14401 Sweitzer Ln.
Laurel, MD 20707
Desare Marshall, Human Resources Representative
Tel: (301) 497-3591 Fax: (301) 497-3585
Web: www.suntrust.com

MASSACHUSETTS

A.J. WRIGHT
Headquarters
550 Cochituate Rd.
Framingham, MA 01701
ATTN: Human Resources
Tel: (508) 390-4000 Fax: (508) 390-4011
Web: www.tjx.com

A.J. WRIGHT
Distribution Center-Human Resources
350 Commerce Dr.
Fall River, MA 02720
Grace McDonnel, Recruiter
Tel: (508) 730-2027
Web: www.tjx.com

COMPUTER SCIENCES CORPORATION
275 Second Ave.
Waltham, MA 02451
ATTN: Human Resources
Tel: (781) 890-7446 Fax: (781) 890-1208
Web: www.csc.com

GETRONICS
Headquarters
290 Concord Rd.
Billerica, MA 01821-4130
Marty Levin, Recruiting Director
Tel: (978) 625-4359 Fax: (978) 625-3077
Email: martin.levin@getronics.com
Web: www.getronics.com

HOMEGOOD'S DISTRIBUTION CENTER
71 Hampden Rd.
Mansfield, MA 02048
Nora Crowley, Manager of Human Resources
Tel: (508) 337-3381 Fax: (508) 261-2833
Web: www.tjx.com

HOMEGOOD'S HOME OFFICE
770 Cochituate Rd.
Framingham, MA 01701
ATTN: Human Resources
Tel: (508) 390-3886 Fax: (508) 390-3850

LIBERTY MUTUAL INSURANCE GROUP
Employees Relations Dept.
175 Berkeley St.
Boston, MA 02116
ATTN: Human Resources
Tel: (617) 357-9500 Fax: (617) 357-5616
Email: careers@libertymutual.com
Web: www.libertymutual.com/careers/

LOTUS DEVELOPMENT CORPORATION
A Division of IBM
1 Rodgers St.
Cambridge, MA 02142
Sheilla Scott, Diversity Manager
Tel: (617) 693-4252
Email: shiela_scott@us.ibm.com
Web: www.lotus.com

MARSHALLS REGION 1 OFFICE
60 Mall Rd. #300
Burlington, MA 01803
Virginia Coyne
Tel: (781) 273-4033 Fax: (781) 229-9924
Web: www.tjx.com

POLAROID CORPORATION
Staffing, Learning & Development
1265 Main St.
Waltham, MA 02451
Abby Lassus, Human Resources Associate
Tel: (781) 386-2000 Fax: (781) 386-3925
Web: www.polaroid.com

REEBOK INTERNATIONAL, LTD.
1895 JW Foster Blvd.
Canton, MA 02021
Susanne Sammoneli, Diversity Development
Tel: (781) 401-5000 Fax: (781) 401-7402
Web: www.reebok.com

T.J. MAXX - WORCESTER
Distribution Center-Human Resources
135 Goddard Memorial Dr.
Worcester, MA 01603
ATTN: Human Resources
Tel: (508) 797-8667 Fax: (508) 791-0911
Web: www.tjmaxx.com

THE MARMAXX GROUP
Staffing Department
770 Cochituate Rd.
Framingham, MA 01701
Doug Systrom, Vice President
Tel: (508) 390-6842 Fax: (508) 390-2486
Web: www.tjx.com

THE TJX COMPANIES, INC. Headquarters
770 Cochituate Rd.
Framingham, MA 01701
Bruce Margolis, EVP of Human Resources
Tel: (508) 390-3541 Fax: (508) 390-2486
Web: www.tjx.com

MICHIGAN

COMPUWARE CORPORATION
1 Campus Martius
Detroit, MI 48226
ATTN: Human Resources
Tel: (800) 267-4884 Fax: (877) 873-6784
Email: compuware.recruiting@compuware.com
Web: www.compuware.com

DAIMLER CHRYSLER CORPORATION
Daimler Chrysler Corporation
Auburn Hills, MI 48326-2766
ATTN: Human Resources
Tel: (248) 512-2187
Web: www.daimlerchrysler.com

DOW CHEMICAL
2020 Dow Ctr.
Midland, MI 48674
ATTN: Human Resources
Tel: (989) 636-1000
Web: www.dow.com

FORD MOTOR COMPANY WORLDWIDE
Henry Ford II World Center,
1 American Rd. #224
Dearborn, MI 48126
Jeff Hustick, Human Resources Associate
Tel: (888) 621-1723
Web: www.mycareer.ford.com

GENERAL MOTORS CORPORATION
300 Renaissance Ctr.
Detroit, MI 48265-3000
Kathleen Barclay, VP of Human Resources
Tel: (313) 556-5000 Fax: (248) 696-7300
Web: www.gm.com

K-MART INTERNATIONAL
Headquarters
3100 W. Big Beaver Rd.
Troy, MI 48084
Janet Delecke, VP of Human Resources
Tel: (248) 463-1000
Web: www.kmart.com

KELLOGG COMPANY
P.O. Box 3599
1 Kellogg Sq.
Battle Creek, MI 49016-3599
ATTN: Human Resources
Tel: (269) 961-2000
Web: www.kelloggs.com

TRW
Headquarters
12025 Tech Ctr. Dr.
Livonia, MI 48150
ATTN: Human Resources
Tel: (734) 266-2600 Fax: (734) 266-5702
Web: www.trw.com

MINNESOTA

3M COMPANY
Staffing Resource Center
3M Ctr. Bldg.
St. Paul, MN 55144-1000
Jene Washington, Manager of Workforce Diversity
Tel: (651) 733-7587 Fax: (651) 733-3572
Email: gwashington@mmm.com
Web: www.mmm.com

ALLIANT TECHSYSTEMS
Headquarters
5050 Lincoln Dr.
Edina, MN 55436-1097
Becky Bridgeman, Staffing Personnel
Tel: (952) 351-3000 Fax: (952) 351-3009
Web: www.atk.com

NORTHWEST AIRLINES
Headquarters
2700 Lone Oak Pkwy. M/S A1415
Eagan, MN 55121-1534
ATTN: Human Resources
Tel: (612) 726-3600 Fax: (612) 726-2524
Email: nwajobs@nwa.com
Web: www.nwa.com

MISSOURI

ANHEUSER-BUSCH, INC.
Corporate Staffing
1 Busch Pl.
St. Louis, MO 63118
Joe Castellano, Head of Human Resources
Tel: (314) 577-2000 Fax: (314) 577-9859
Web: www.anheuser-busch.com/overview/diversity.html

HALLMARK CARDS
Corporate Staffing Center
P.O. Box 419580
2501 McGee M/D 112
Kansas City, MO 64141
ATTN: Human Resources
Tel: (816) 274-5111
Email: hcorp01@hallmark.com
Web: www.hallmark.com

MONSANTO COMPANY
800 N. Lindbergh Blvd.
St. Louis, MO 63167
ATTN: Human Resources
Tel: (314) 694-1000

NEBRASKA

MUTUAL OF OMAHA
Mutual of Omaha Plz.
Omaha, NE 68175
Molly Brinker, Human Resources Consultant
Tel: (402) 342-7600 Fax: (402) 351-3026
Email: careers@mutualofomaha.com
Web: www.mutualofomaha.com

NEVADA

S.I.R., INC.
P.O. Box 10206
Zephyr Cove, NV 89448
Raymond C. Ramos, President
Tel: (775) 588-2226 Fax: (775) 588-2226
Email: sirinc@earthlink.net

T.J. MAXX - LAS VEGAS
Distribution Center
4100 E. Lone Mountain Rd.
Las Vegas, NV 89081
ATTN: Human Resources
Tel: (702) 643-4033 Fax: (702) 643-2436
Web: www.tjmaxx.com

NEW JERSEY

AMERADA HESS CORPORATION
Headquarters
1 Hess Plz.
Woodbridge, NJ 07095
Walter C. Vertreace, Manager/Corporate EEO
Tel: (732) 750-6408 Fax: (732) 750-6678
Email: wvertreace@hess.com
Web: www.hess.com

AT&T CORPORATION
Headquarters
1 AT&T Way #412

Bedminster, NJ 07921
ATTN: Human Resources
Tel: (908) 221-4191
Web: www.att.com/

AVIS
Headquarters
6 Sylvan Way
Parsippany, NJ 07054
Darlin Stewart, EEO Director
Tel: (973) 496-3500
Web: www.avis.com

GOYA FOODS, INC.
100 Seaview Dr.
Secaucus, NJ 07096
ATTN: Human Resources
Tel: (201) 348-4900 Fax: (201) 348-6609
Web: www.goya.com

HOFFMANN-LA ROCHE, INC.
340 Kingsland St.
Nutley, NJ 07110
ATTN: Human Resources
Tel: (973) 235-5000 Fax: (973) 235-6500
Web: www.rocheusa.com/career/index.asp

JOHNSON & JOHNSON
1 Johnson & Johnson Plz.
New Brunswick, NJ 08933
ATTN: Human Resources
Tel: (732) 524-0400 Fax: (732) 214-0332
Web: www.jnj.com/careers

LUCENT TECHNOLOGIES
Corporate Headquarters
600 Mountain Ave.
Murray Hill, NJ 07974
Ethel Batten, VP of Recruiting
Tel: (908) 582-8500 Fax: (908) 508-2576
Web: www.lucent.com

METROPOLITAN LIFE INSURANCE COMPANY
Tenpark Ave.
Morristown, NJ 07962
Stuart Cook, VP Human Resources
Tel: (973) 355-4000 Fax: (973) 355-4333
Web: www.metlife.com

PFIZER, INC.
Northeast Region
400 Interpace Pkwy., Bldg. C
Parsippany, NJ 07054
Everett Brown, Recruiting Manager
Tel: (973) 541-5900 Fax: (973) 541-6394
Web: www.pfizer.com/pfizerinc/career

PRUDENTIAL FINANCIAL
751 Broad St.
Newark, NJ 07102
Billie Divine, Associate Manager of Administration
Tel: (973) 367-4833
Web: www.prudential.com

T.J. MAXX
MID-ATLANTIC REGIONAL OFFICE-MARO
1000 Atrium Way
Mt. Laurel, NJ 08054
ATTN: Personnel
Tel: (856) 787-1071 Fax: (856) 787-1084
Web: www.tjmaxx.com

TELCORDIA TECHNOLOGIES
A SAIC Company-Human Resources
444 Hoes Ln.
Piscataway, NJ 08854
Linda Villa, VP
Tel: (732) 699-2800 Fax: (732) 336-4167
Email: villali@telcordia.com
Web: www.telcordia.com

TETRATECH SW
1000 The American Rd.
Morris Plains, NJ 07950

Kevin McDonald, Executive Director of Human Resources
Tel: (973) 630-8000 Fax: (973) 630-8111
Web: www.fwenc.com

TOYS "R" US
Headquarters
1 Geoffrey Way
Wayne, NJ 07470-2030
ATTN: Human Resources
Tel: (973) 617-3500
Web: www.toysrus.com

NEW MEXICO

SANDIA NATIONAL LABORATORIES-ENERGY SECTOR
Staff and General Employment
1515 Eubank SE
Albuquerque, NM 87123
ATTN: Staffing Depatment
Tel: (505) 845-0011 Fax: (505) 284-6262
Email: empsite@sandia.gov
Web: www.sandia.gov

NEW YORK

AMERICAN EXPRESS CORPORATION
World Financial Center
200 Vessey St.
New York, NY 10285
Linda Hassan, Director Global Diversity Recruitment
Tel: (212) 640-2000 Fax: (212) 640-0368
Web: www.americanexpress.com

AVON PRODUCTS, INC.
Avon Global Human Resources
1251 Ave. of the Americas
New York, NY 10020
Ros Bennett, Director of Diversity
Tel: (212) 282-7536 Fax: (212) 282-6893
Web: www.avoncareers.com

BAE SYSTEMS
450 Pulaski Rd.
Greenlawn, NY 11740-1606
Mary Rothe, Human Resources Representatives
Tel: (631) 262-8196 Fax: (631) 262-8446
Web: www.na.baesystems.com

BRISTOL-MYERS SQUIBB COMPANY
P.O. Box 5335
345 Park Ave.
New York, NY 10154
Stacy Gibson, Diversity Program Manager
Tel: (212) 546-4000 Fax: (212) 605-9628
Email: stacy.gibson@bms.com
Web: www.bms.com/career/data

COLGATE-PALMOLIVE COMPANY
300 Park Ave.
New York, NY 10022
ATTN: Human Resources
Tel: (212) 310-2000 Fax: (212) 310-2106
Web: www.colgate.com

CONSOLIDATED EDISON
4 Irving Pl.
New York, NY 10003
Claude Trahan, VP of Human Resources
Tel: (212) 460-4600 Fax: (212) 228-9439
Web: www.coned.com

EASTMAN KODAK COMPANY
Training and Acquisition
343 State St.
Rochester, NY 14650-1139
Eleanor Lathan
Tel: (585) 724-3249 Fax: (585) 724-9416
Email: eleanor.lathan@kodak.com
Web: www.kodak.com

GIRLS SCOUTS OF THE USA
Staffing & Diversity
420 Fifth Ave.
New York, NY 10018-2798
Iris Ruiz, Initiative Specialist
Tel: (212) 852-5095 Fax: (212) 852-6514
Email: iruiz@girlscouts.org
Web: www.girlscouts.org

H.B.O.
1100 Ave. of the Americas
New York, NY 10036
Paula Cornier, Executive Assistant of
Human Resources
Tel: (212) 512-5731
Email: paula.cornier@hbo.com
Web: www.hbo.com

IBM CORPORATION
Global Work Force Diversity
North Castle Dr.
Armonk, NY 10504
Ted Childs, VP
Tel: (914) 765-5900 Fax: (914) 765-5290
Email: tedchilds@us.ibm.com
Web: www.ibm.com

JP MORGAN CHASE
Headquarters
270 Park Ave.
New York, NY 10017
ATTN: Human Resources
Tel: (212) 270-6000 Fax: (212) 638-7421
Web: www.jpmorganchase.com

MERRILL LYNCH
4 World Financial Ctr.
New York, NY 10080
Terry Kassel, Senior VP of Human
Resources
Tel: (212) 449-8808 Fax: (212) 449-8809
Email: terry_kassel@ml.com
Web: www.ml.com/careers

METRO-NORTH COMMUTER RAILROAD
Employment Department
347 Madison Ave., 4th Fl.
New York, NY 10017
Diana Tucker, Manager
Tel: (212) 340-2159 Fax: (212) 340-4970
Email: tucker@mno.org
Web: www.mta.nyc.ny.us

NEC USA, INC.
8 Corporate Ctr. Dr.
Melville, NY 11747
ATTN: Human Resources
Tel: (631) 753-7000
Web: www.nec.com

NEW YORK LIFE INSURANCE COMPANY
51 Madison Ave. #3200
New York, NY 10010
ATTN: Human Resources
Tel: (212) 576-7000
Web: www.newyorklife.com

PEPSICO, INC.
Global Diversity and Community Affairs
700 Anderson Hill Rd.
Purchase, NY 10577
Paula Banks, Senior Vice President
Tel: (914) 253-2000 Fax: (914) 253-2070
Email: paula.banks@pepsi.com
Web: www.pepsijobs.com

PFIZER, INC.
235 E. 42nd St.
New York, NY 10017
ATTN: Human Resources
Tel: (212) 573-2323
Web: www.pfizer.com

PLANNED PARENTHOOD FEDERATION OF AMERICA
434 W. 33rd St.
New York, NY 10001
Desiree Bunch, VP of Human Resources
Tel: (212) 261-4644 Fax: (212) 261-4361
Web: www.plannedparenthood.org

REVLON
237 Park Ave.
New York, NY 10017
Barbara Jettmara
Tel: (212) 527-4000 Fax: (212) 527-4995
Web: www.revlon.com

VERIZON COMMUNICATIONS
Corporate Office
1095 Ave. of the Americas
New York, NY 10036
ATTN: Personnel
Tel: (212) 395-2121
Email: hr.helpline@core.verizon.com
Web: www.verizon.com/careers

NORTH CAROLINA

BURLINGTON INDUSTRIES, INC.
3330 W. Friendly Ave.
Greensboro, NC 27410
Bob Garren, Manager of Human Resources
Tel: (336) 379-2000
Web: www.burlington.com

T.J. MAXX - CHARLOTTE
Distribution Center
14300 Carowinds Blvd.
Charlotte, NC 28273
ATTN: Human Resources
Tel: (704) 588-9222 Fax: (704) 583-7743
Web: www.tjmaxx.com

OHIO

BORDEN CHEMICAL, INC.
180 E. Broad St.
Columbus, OH 43215
ATTN: Human Resources
Tel: (614) 225-4000
Web: www.bordenchem.com

DISCOVER CARD SERVICES, INC.
6500 New Albany Rd.
New Albany, OH 43054
ATTN: Human Resources
Tel: (614) 283-1569
Web: www.discovercard.com

GOODYEAR TIRE & RUBBER COMPANY
1144 E. Market St.
Akron, OH 44316-0001
Ingram Brown, Manager of Human
Resources
Tel: (330) 796-2121 Fax: (330) 796-2222
Web: www.goodyear.com

PROCTER & GAMBLE
P.O. Box 599
Cincinnati, OH 45202
ATTN: Diversity Recruiting
Tel: (513) 983-1100
Web: www.pg.com/careers

OREGON

QWEST
421 SW Oak St. #130
Portland, OR 97204
Chas Fleenor, Manager of Staffing
Tel: (503) 464-1872 Fax: (503) 242-3147
Web: www.qwest.com

PENNSYLVANIA

ALCOA
Headquarters
201 Isabella St.
Pittsburgh, PA 15212-5858
ATTN: Human Resources
Tel: (412) 553-4545 Fax: (412) 553-4498
Web: www.alcoa.com

GLAXOSMITHKLINE
P.O. Box 7929
1 Franklin Plz.
Philadelphia, PA 19101-7929
ATTN: Human Resources
Tel: (215) 751-4000
Web: www.gsk.com

MARSHALLS PHILADELPHIA
Distribution Center-Human Resources
2760 Red Lion Rd.
Philadelphia, PA 19114
Sonya Medley, Manager of Human
Resources
Tel: (215) 856-0449 Fax: (215) 961-1793
Web: www.tjx.com

SHAW ENVIRONMENTAL & INFRASTRUCTURE, INC.
2790 Mosside Blvd.
Monroeville, PA 15146
Dennis Papciak, Recruiter
Tel: (412) 372-7701 Fax: (412) 858-3973
Web: www.shawgrp.com

T.J. MAXX - PITTSTON
Distribution Center
4000 Oldfield Blvd.
Pittston, PA 18640
Heide Ellen, Manager
Tel: (570) 603-2800 Fax: (570) 603-5858
Web: www.tjx.com

UNITED STATES STEEL CORPORATION
600 Grant St.
Pittsburgh, PA 15219-2800
Don DiGirolamo, Manager of Human
Resources & Development
Tel: (412) 433-1121 Fax: (412) 433-6762
Web: www.uss.com

SOUTH CAROLINA

CHEM-NUCLEAR SYSTEMS
140 Stoneridge Dr.
Columbia, SC 29210
Sandra Payne, Manager of Human
Resources
Tel: (800) 925-1592 Fax: (803) 799-4470
Web: www.chemnuclear.com

DENNYS
203 E. Main St. Box P-5-11
Spartanburg, SC 29319
Patricia Parker, Senior Human Resources
Manager
Tel: (864) 597-7073 Fax: (864) 597-7457
Web: www.dennys.com

FLUOR DANIEL
100 Fluor Daniel Dr.
Greenville, SC 29607
Lea Tores, Manager of Human Resources
Tel: (864) 281-4400 Fax: (864) 281-4938
Web: www.fluor.com

TENNESSEE

FEDERAL EXPRESS
P.O. Box 727
Memphis, TN 38194
ATTN: Human Resources
Tel: (901) 369-3600
Web: www.fedex.com/us/careers

INTERNATIONAL PAPER COMPANY
6400 Poplar Ave.
Memphis, TN 38197
Allie Bond, Director of Diversity &
Compliance
Tel: (901) 419-9000 Fax: (901) 419-1236
Email: allie.bond@ipaper.com
Web: www.internationalpaper.com

TEXAS

AIR LIQUIDE AMERICA CORPORATION
2700 Post Oak Blvd. #1800
Houston, TX 77056
ATTN: Human Resources
Tel: (713) 624-8000 Fax: (713) 624-8190
Web: www.airliquide.com

AMERICAN AIRLINES
American Airlines Human Resources
P.O. Box 619616
M/D 5257
DFW Airport, TX 75261
Deborah Johnson, VP Human Resources
Tel: (817) 967-2661
Web: www.aa.com

APACHE CORPORATION
2000 Post Oak Blvd. #100
Houston, TX 77056
Beverly Malke, Human Resources Assistant
Tel: (713) 296-6000 Fax: (713) 296-6479
Email: beverly.malke@apachecorp.com
Web: www.apachecorp.com

BOY SCOUTS OF AMERICA
1325 W. Walnut Hill Ln.
Irving, TX 75015-2079
Iran Smith, Head of Human Resources
Tel: (972) 580-2000 Fax: (972) 580-7818
Web: www.scouting.org

CENTEX CORPORATION
Administration
3100 McKinnon St., 7th Fl.
Dallas, TX 75201
David Preston, VP Human Resources
Tel: (214) 468-4700 Fax: (214) 468-4250
Email: dpreston@ccgmail.com
Web: www.centex.com

CHASE BANK OF TEXAS
Diversity Program
712 Main St., 12th Fl. East
Houston, TX 77002
Ernest Smith, Director
Tel: (713) 216-4312 Fax: (713) 216-2385
Email: ernest.smith@chase.com
Web: www.chase.com

DELL COMPUTER CORPORATION
One Dell Way
Round Rock, TX 78682
ATTN: Global Diversity
Tel: (512) 338-4400 Fax: (512) 728-0572
Web: www.dell.com/

FRITO LAY
7701 Legacy Dr.
Plano, TX 75024-4099
ATTN: Human Resources
Tel: (972) 334-7000 Fax: (972) 334-2019
Web: www.fritolay.com

H-E-B GROCERY COMPANY
4326 Kostoryz Rd.
Corpus Christi, TX 78415
Mayda Garcia, Recruiter
Tel: (210) 938-8000

Email: garcia.mayda@heb.com
Web: www.heb.com

HERMAN HOSPITAL
6411 Fannin St., 4th Fl.
Houston, TX 77030
Cecilia Rodriguez, Senior Office Assistant
Tel: (713) 704-3514 Fax: (713) 704-6192
Email: cecilia_rodriguez@mhhs.org
Web: www.mhhs.org

HEWLETT-PACKARD CORPORATION
Corporate Diversity
P.O. Box 692000
M/S 110701
Houston, TX 77269-2000
Terri Alexander, Director
Tel: (281) 514-2119 Fax: (281) 514-9107
Web: www.hp.com

HILTON HOTELS CORPORATION
2050 Chennault Dr.
Carrollton, TX 75006
Stan Heatley, Manager of Human
Resources
Tel: (972) 770-6100
Web: www.hilton.com

J.C. PENNEY COMPANY
6501 Legacy Dr.
North Plano, TX 75024
ATTN: Employment Services
Tel: (972) 431-2300 Fax: (972) 431-2320
Email: apply@jcpenney.com
Web: www.jcpenney.com

LOCKHEED-MARTIN
Professional Staffing
P.O. Box 748
Fort Worth, TX 76101
Grace Jones, Senior Manager
Tel: (817) 935-5400 Fax: (817) 935-5402
Web: www.lockheedmartin.com

MARSHALLS
Region 5 Office
8500 Freeport Pkwy. #350
Irving, TX 75063
Sam Sutton, Manager of Human Resources
Tel: (214) 596-0204 Fax: (214) 492-2209
Web: www.tjx.com

MARY KAY CORPORATE
Headquarters
16251 N. Dallas Pkwy.
Addison, TX 75001
ATTN: Corporate Recruiting
Tel: (972) 687-6300
Web: www.marykay.com

PFIZER, INC.
Gulf Coast Region
7 Village Cr. #500
Westlakes, TX 76262
Cory Littlepage, Human Resources
Manager
Tel: (817) 491-8400 Fax: (817) 491-8443
Web: www.pfizer.com

PIZZA HUT
Headquarters
14841 N. Dallas Pkwy.
Dallas, TX 75254
ATTN: Human Resources
Tel: (972) 338-7700 Fax: (972) 338-6869
Web: www.yumcareers.com

RAYTHEON-SYSTEMS, INC.
Garland Division
1200 S. Jupiter
Garland, TX 75041
Tim Harris, Director of Human Resources
Tel: (972) 272-0515 Fax: (972) 205-4598
Email: tim_b_harris@raytheon.com
Web: www.rayjobs.com

SBC COMMUNICATIONS INC.
Workforce Diversity and Employee Ethics
130 E. Travis #4-R-8
San Antonio, TX 78205
Norma L. Gonzales, Executive Director
Tel: (210) 351-2868
Email: ng5520@txmail.sbc.com
Web: www.sbc.com

SHELL OIL COMPANY
910 Louisiana St.
Houston, TX 77002
Cari Wilkins, Director of Attraction and
Recruitment
Tel: (713) 241-5997 Fax: (713) 241-6844
Email: cari.wilkins@shell.com
Web: www.shell.com

T.J. MAXX
SOUTHWEST REGIONAL OFFICE - SWRO
8500 Freeport Pkwy. #350
Irving, TX 75063
ATTN: Human Resources
Tel: (972) 870-0215 Fax: (972) 870-0437
Web: www.tjx.com

TEXAS INSTRUMENTS, INC.
Headquarters
12500 TI Blvd.
Dallas, TX 75243
Terry Howard, Director of Diversity Program
Tel: (214) 480-2800
Web: www.ti.com

TGI FRIDAY'S, INC.
Part of Carlson Restaurants Worldwide,
Inc.
4201 Marsh Ln.
Carrollton, TX 75007
Lucy Finger, Corporate Recruiter
Tel: (972) 662-5400
Email: careers@crww.com
Web: www.fridays.com

THE SOUTHLAND CORPORATION/7-
ELEVEN
P.O.Box 711
Dallas, TX 75221-0711
Janice McCasland, Human Resources
Assistant
Tel: (214) 828-7011 Fax: (214) 828-7561
Web: www.711.com

VALERO ENERGY CORPORATION
1 Valero Way
San Antonio, TX 78249-1112
ATTN: Human Resources
Tel: (210) 345-2000 Fax: (210) 345-2646
Web: www.valero.com

WASTE MANAGEMENT FEDERAL
SERVICES, INC.
1001 Fannin St. #4000
Houston, TX 77002
Michelle Buenavidez, Human Resources
Assistant
Tel: (713) 512-6200 Fax: (713) 512-6299
Web: www.wastemanagement.com

VIRGINIA

ALMA CONSULTANT SERVICES
5130 N. 24th St.
Arlington, VA 22207
Alma Riojas, President
Tel: (703) 241-0835

BBT&T
6400 Arlington Blvd.
Falls Church, VA 22042
ATTN: Human Resources

Tel: (703) 241-4866 Fax: (703) 531-2862
Web: www.firstvirginia.com

BOOZ ALLEN & HAMILTON
8283 Greensboro Dr.
McLean, VA 22102
ATTN: Human Resources
Tel: (703) 902-5000 Fax: (703) 902-3022
Email: recruiting_feedback@bah.com
Web: www.bah.com

CIRCUIT CITY STORES, INC.
Staffing and Career Resources
Department
9950 Mayland Dr.
Richmond, VA 23233
Cindy Smith, Recruitment Manager
Tel: (804) 527-4000 X8246
Fax: (804) 527-4086
Web: www.circuitcity.com

DIVERSITYWORKS, INC.
800 Third St.
Herndon, VA 20170
ATTN: Human Resources
Tel: (703) 707-9797 Fax: (703) 707-9590
Web: www.diversityworksinc.com

3225 Gallows Rd.
Fairfax, VA 22037
ATTN: Human Resources
Tel: (703) 846-3000
Web: www.exxonmobil.com

GENERAL DYNAMICS CORPORATION
2941 Fairview Park Dr. #100
Falls Church, VA 22042-4513
Walter Oliver, Director of Human Resources
Tel: (703) 876-3000 Fax: (703) 876-3550
Web: www.gd.com

J.C. PENNEY COMPANY - DISTRICT OFFICE
8350 Sudley Rd.
Manassas, VA 20109
Rob Arnold, District Manager
Tel: (703) 530-0336
Web: www.jcpenney.com

MARSHALLS BRIDGEWATER
Distribution Center-Human Resources
701 N. Main St.
Bridgewater, VA 22812
Bill Scullion, Head of Human Resources
Tel: (540) 828-5161 Fax: (540) 828-5118
Web: www.tjx.com

MCI
22001 Loudon County Pkwy.
Ashburn, VA 20147
Holley Waldron, Senior Staff Specialist
Tel: (800) 677-6580 Fax: (703) 886-0088
Web: www.mci.com

MITRE CORPORATION
Quality of Work Life Division
7515 Colshire Dr.
McLean, VA 22102-7508
William Allbright, Director of Human
Resources
Tel: (703) 883-6000 Fax: (703) 883-6538
Web: www.mitre.org

PEROT SYSTEM GOVERNMENT SERVICES
1800 N. Beauregard #200
Alexandria, VA 22311
ATTN: Human Resources
Tel: (703) 560-9477 Fax: (703) 933-2639
Web: www.psgsevents.com

PHILIP MORRIS U.S.A.
P.O. Box 26603
Richmond, VA 23261
ATTN: Human Resources
Tel: (804) 274-2000
Web: www.philipmorris.com

RATNER COMPANIES
Headquarters
2815 Hartland Rd.
Falls Church, VA 22043
ATTN: Human Resources
Tel: (703) 698-7090 Fax: (703) 876-2897
Web: www.ratnerco.com

T.J. MAXX
MID-SOUTH REGIONAL OFFICE-MSRO
205 Van Buren St. #120
Herndon, VA 20170
ATTN: Human Resources
Tel: (703) 481-5337 Fax: (703) 481-6419
Web: www.tjmaxx.com

TURNER CONSTRUCTION COMPANY
3865 Wilson Blvd. #300
Arlington, VA 22203
Beverly Harris, VP of Diversity
Tel: (703) 841-5200 Fax: (703) 841-4559
Web: www.turnerconstruction.com

UNIDYNE CORPORATION
A Titan Corporation
2740 Ells Mere Ave.
Norfolk, VA 23513
ATTN: Human Resources
Tel: (757) 963-1326
Web: www.titan.com/unidyne/

UNISYS CORPORATION
8008 W. Park Dr.
McLean, VA 22102
ATTN: Human Resources
Tel: (703) 556-5000 Fax: (703) 556-5172
Web: www.unisys.com

USAIR, INC.
2345 Crystal Dr. Crystal Park Four
Arlington, VA 22227
Tujuanna Williams, Director of Diversity &
Work Life
Tel: (703) 872-7447 Fax: (703) 872-7410
Email: tujuanna_williams@usairways.com
Web: www.usairways.com

WASHINGTON GAS
Human Resources
6801 Industrial Rd.
Springfield, VA 22151
Connie Morris
Tel: (703) 750-1000 Fax: (703) 750-7593
Web: www.washgas.com

WASHINGTON

BOEING SATELLITE SYSTEMS
7755 E. Marginal Way South
Seattle, WA 98108
ATTN: Human Resources
Tel: (800) 254-1591
Email: employmentoperations@boeing.com
Web: www.boeing.com

NORDSTROM
1617 6th Ave. #500
Seattle, WA 98101
Jammie Baugh, Manager of Human
Resources
Tel: (206) 628-2111 Fax: (206) 303-5819
Web: www.nordstrom.com

WISCONSIN

MILLER BREWING COMPANY
Diversity Affairs
3939 W. Highland Blvd.
Milwaukee, WI 53208
Danae Davis, Director
Tel: (414) 931-3456
Web: www.millerbrewing.com

Public Sector Minority Business Opportunities
Oportunidades de negocios minoritarios en el sector público

AGRICULTURE, DEPT. OF
Natural Resources Conservation Service
3381 Skyway Dr.
Auburn, AL 36830-6443
Lynn Thomas, Contracting Officer
Tel: (334) 887-4507 Fax: (334) 887-4551
Email: lynn.thomas@al.usda.gov
Web: www.al.nrcs.usda.gov

COMMERCE, DEPT. OF
Minority Business Development Agency, Birmingham Minority Business Opportunity Committee
710 20th St. North
Birmingham, AL 35203
Andrew Mayo, Administrative
Tel: (205) 254-2799 Fax: (205) 254-7741
Email: ajmayo@ci.birmingham.al.us
Web: www.birminghammboc.com

DEFENSE, DEPT. OF
US Air Force, 42nd Contracting Squadron/LGC-Air Education and Training Command, Small Business Office
50 LeMay Plz. S.
Maxwell AFB, AL 36112-6334
Gladys Johnson, Small Business Specialist
Tel: (334) 953-5457 Fax: (334) 953-2453
Email: gladys.johnson@maxwell.af.mil
Web: www.maxwell.af.mil

US Air Force, HQ Standard Systems Group/AQP-Air Force Materiel Command, Small Business Office
490 E. Moore Dr., Gunter Annex
Maxwell AFB, AL 36114-3004
Rosa Shanon, Small Business Specialist
Tel: (334) 416-5415
Email: rosa.shanon@gunter.af.mil
Web: www.selltoairforce.org

US Army Engineer & Support Ctr., Small Business Office
4820 University Sq.
Huntsville, AL 35816-1822
Judy Griggs, Small Business Specialist
Tel: (256) 895-1179 Fax: (256) 895-1049
Email: Judy.K.Griggs@hnd01.usace.army.mil
Web: www.hnd.usace.army.mil

NATIONAL AERONAUTICS & SPACE ADMINISTRATION (NASA)
Marshall Space Flight Ctr.
M/S PS01
Huntsville, AL 35812
Stanley McCall, Field Installation Small/Minority Business Specialist
Tel: (256) 544-0254 Fax: (256) 544-5851
Email: stanley.e.mccall@nasa.gov
Web: www.hq.nasa.gov

M/S PS10
Huntsville, AL 35812
David Brock, Small Business Specialist
Tel: (256) 544-0267 Fax: (256) 544-5185
Email: david.e.brock@nasa.gov
Web: www.nasa.gov

AGRICULTURE, DEPT. OF
Forest Service, Contracting Office
P.O. Box 21628
Juneau, AK 99802-1628
Mark Phillipp, Supervisory Contracting Officer
Tel: (907) 586-7902 Fax: (907) 586-7090
Email: mphillipp@fs.fed.us
Web: www.fs.fed.us/r10/

COMMERCE, DEPT. OF
Minority Business Development Agency, Alaska Statewide County Minority Business Development Ctr.
122 1st Ave. #600
Fairbanks, AK 99701
Loyd Allen, Project Director
Tel: (907) 452-8251 Fax: (907) 459-3851
Email: lallen@tananachiefs.org
Web: www.mbda.gov

DEFENSE, DEPT. OF
US Air Force, 343rd Contracting Squadron/CC-Pacific Air Forces, Small Business Office
3112 Broadway Ave. #5B
Eielson AFB, AK 99702-1887
Sharon Cobb, Small Business Specialist
Tel: (907) 377-4183
Email: sharon.cobb@eielson.af.mil
Web: www.eielson.af.mil

US Air Force, 3rd Contracting Squadron/CC-Pacific Air Forces, Small Business Office
10480 22nd St.
Elmendorf AFB, AK 99506
Della Simmons, Small Business Specialist
Tel: (907) 552-1419
Email: della.simmons@elmendorf.af.mil
Web: www.elmendorf.af.mil

VETERANS AFFAIRS, DEPT. OF
Northwest Network, Alaska VA Healthcare System & Regional Office
2925 DeBarr Rd.
Anchorage, AK 99508-2989
Sandra Magers, Small Business Specialist
Tel: (907) 257-6945 Fax: (907) 257-6711
Email: Sandra.Magers2@med.va.gov
Web: www.va.gov/osdbu

COMMERCE, DEPT. OF
Minority Business Development Agency, Arizona Statewide Minority Business Development Ctr.
255 E. Osborn Rd. #202
Phoenix, AZ 85012
Izzy Gonzalez, Project Director
Tel: (602) 248-0007 Fax: (602) 279-8900
Email: izzyg@azhcc.com
Web: www.mbda.gov

DEFENSE, DEPT. OF
CECOM Acquisition Ctr., SW Operations
Attn.: AMSEL-IE-SB,
Greeley Hall #3212, Bldg. 61801
Fort Huachuca, AZ 85613-5300
Chuck Collins, Small Business Advisor
Tel: (520) 538-7870 Fax: (520) 533-0360
Email: charles.collins@netcom.army.mil

US Air Force, 355th Contracting Squadron/LGC-Air Combat Command, Small Business Office
3180 S. Craycroft Rd.
Davis-Monthan AFB, AZ 85707-3522
Joanne Squire, Small Business Specialist
Tel: (520) 228-3131 Fax: (520) 228-7834
Email: joanne.squire@dm.af.mil
Web: www.dm.af.mil/355cons2/355cons.htm

US Air Force, 56th Contracting Squadron/CC, Small Business Office
14100 W. Eagle St.
Luke AFB, AZ 85309-1217
Ken Barborak, Alternate Small Business Specialist
Tel: (623) 856-7179 X265
Fax: (623) 856-4969
Email: ken.barborak@luke.af.mil
Web: www.luke.af.mil

US Air Force, 56th Contracting Squadron/CC-Air Education and Training Command, Small Business Office
14100 W. Eagle St.
Luke AFB, AZ 85309-1217
Teresa Hendrix, Small Business Specialist
Tel: (623) 856-7179 X223
Fax: (623) 856-4969
Email: teresa.hendrix@luke.af.mil
Web: www.luke.af.mil

VETERANS AFFAIRS, DEPT. OF
Northern Arizona VA Healthcare System
3601 S. 6th Ave.
Tucson, AZ 85723
Carlene S. Rush, Acquisition Manager/Small Business Specialist
Tel: (520) 629-4610 Fax: (520) 629-1817
Email: carlene.rush@med.va.gov
Web: www.va.gov/osdbu

VA Medical Ctr.
500 Hwy. 89 N.
Prescott, AZ 86313
James Waterman, Small Business Specialist
Tel: (520) 629-4623 Fax: (520) 629-1817
Email: james.waterman@med.va.gov
Web: www.va.gov/osdbu

650 E. Indian School Rd. M/C 90C
Phoenix, AZ 85012
Pat Amidon, Small Business Specialist
Tel: (602) 212-2163 Fax: (602) 212-2155
Email: pat.amidon@med.va.gov
Web: www.phoenix.med.va.gov

DEFENSE, DEPT. OF
US Air Force, 314th Contracting Squadron/CCD-Air Education and Training Command, Small Business Office
642 Thomas Ave.
Little Rock AFB, AR 72099-5019
Ray Blevis, Small Business Specialist
Tel: (501) 987-3836 Fax: (501) 987-6624
Email: ray.blevis@littlerock.af.mil
Web: www.littlerock.af.mil

VETERANS AFFAIRS, DEPT. OF
Arkansas Veterans Healthcare System
1100 N. College Ave.
Fayetteville, AR 72703
Donna Lenz, Small and Disadvantaged Business Specialist
Tel: (479) 444-5035 Fax: (479) 444-5031
Email: donna.lenz@med.va.gov
Web: www.va.gov/osdbu

Central Arkansas VA Healthcare System, John L. McLellan Memorial Veterans Hospital
2200 Fort Roots Dr., Bldg. 41 #202
North Little Rock, AR 72114
Michael D. Barger, Small Business Specialist
Tel: (501) 257-1047 Fax: (501) 257-1055
Email: mike.barger@med.va.gov
Web: www.va.gov/osdbu

AGRICULTURE, DEPT. OF
Agricultural Research Service
800 Buchanan St.
Albany, CA 94710
Jack Nelson, Procurement/Property Officer
Tel: (510) 559-6016 Fax: (510) 559-6023
Email: jnelson@pw.ars.usda.gov

Forest Service, IBET Province
100 Forni Rd.
Placerville, CA 95667
Kathryn Griffin, Contracting Officer
Tel: (530) 622-5061 Fax: (530) 621-5297
Email: kgriffin@fs.fed.us

Tahoe National Forest, 631 Coyote St.
Nevada City, CA 95959-2250
Alan James, Contracting Officer
Tel: (530) 478-6121 Fax: (530) 478-6126
Email: amjames@fs.fed.us
Web: www.fs.fed.us/r5/tahoe/

Natural Resources Conservation Service
430 G St. #4164
Davis, CA 95616
Brian Hallet, Administrative Services Officer
Tel: (530) 792-5675 Fax: (530) 792-5795
Email: Brian.Hallet@ca.usda.gov
Web: www.usda.gov

COMMERCE, DEPT. OF
Minority Business Development Agency, East Los Angeles County Minority Business Development Ctr.
5271 E. Beverly Blvd.
Los Angeles, CA 90022
Sal Carlos, Project Director
Tel: (323) 726-4072 Fax: (323) 721-9794
Email: scarlos@elambdc.org
Web: www.mbda.gov

San Francisco Regional Office
221 Main St. #1280
San Francisco, CA 94105
Linda Marmolejo, Deputy Regional Director
Tel: (415) 744-3001 Fax: (415) 744-3061
Email: LMarmolejo@mbda.gov
Web: www.mbda.gov

West Los Angeles County Minority Business Development Ctr.
3550 Wilshire Blvd. #905
Los Angeles, CA 90010
Ramesh N. Swamy, Project Director
Tel: (213) 368-1450 Fax: (213) 368-1451
Email: rswamy@usc.edu
Web: www.mbda.gov

DEFENSE, DEPT. OF
Defense Contract Management Command West
18901 S. Wilmington Ave., Bldg. DH2
Carson, CA 90746
E. Renee Deavens, Director of Small Business
Tel: (310) 900-6025 Fax: (310) 900-6029
Email: renee.deavens@dcma.mil
Web: www.dcma.mil/DCMAHQ/dcma-sb/index.htm

Fleet & Industrial Supply Ctr., San Diego
937 N. Harbor Dr., M/C 260
San Diego, CA 92132
Gary Thomas, Small Business Specialist
Tel: (619) 532-3439 Fax: (619) 532-2575
Email: gary.p.thomas@navy.mil

Naval Air Warfare Ctr. Weapons Division
Naval Air Warfare Ctr.
Code 00K000D, 1 Administration Cir.
China Lake, CA 93555-6001
Pam Lochhead, Small Business Officer
Tel: (760) 939-2712 Fax: (760) 939-2712
Email: pamela.lochhead@navy.mil
Web: www.nawcwpns.navy.mil

Space and Missile Systems Ctr.
2420 Bela Way #1467
El Segundo, CA 90245-4692
Edward Whatley, Small Business Specialist

Tel: (310) 363-2855 Fax: (310) 363-1189
Email: edward.whatley@losangeles.af.mil
Web: www.losangeles.af.mil

US Air Force, 30th Space Wing/BZ-Air Force Space Command, Small Business Office
806 13th St., Bldg. 7015 #113
Vandenberg AFB, CA 93437-5228
Charles Painter, Small Business Specialist
Tel: (805) 605-7265 Fax: (805) 606-5662
Email: Charles.Painter@vandenberg.af.mil
Web: www.vandenberg.af.mil

S Air Force, 452nd LSS/LGC-Air Force Reserve Command, Small Business Office
1940 Graeber St.
March ARB, CA 92518-1650
Mary Boswell, Small Business Specialist
Tel: (909) 655-3116 Fax: (909) 655-3772
Email: mary.boswell@march.af.mil
Web: www.selltoairforce.org

US Air Force, 60th Air Mobility Wing/LGC-Air Mobility Command, Small Business Office
350 Hangar Ave., Bldg. 549
Travis AFB, CA 94535-2632
John Clarke, Director
Tel: (707) 424-7713 Fax: (707) 424-8456
Email: John.Clarke@travis.af.mil
Web: www.public.travis.amc.af.mil/pages/60cons/

US Air Force, 9th Contracting Squadron/LGC-Air Combat Command, Small Business Office
6500 B St. #101
Beale AFB, CA 95903-1712
Sandy Turzak, Small Business Specialist
Tel: (530) 634-2872 Fax: (530) 368-3311
Email: sandra.turzak@beale.af.mil
Web: www.beale.af.mil

US Air Force, Flight Test Ctr./BC-Air Force Materiel Command, Small Business Office
30 N. Wolfe Ave., Bldg. 1609
Edwards AFB, CA 93524-6351
Donna L. Thomason, Director
Tel: (661) 277-3640 Fax: (661) 275-9652
Email: donna.thomason@edwards.af.mil
Web: www.edwards.af.mil

US Air Force, Space and Missile Systems Ctr./BC-Air Force Space Command, Small Business Office
155 Discoverer Blvd. #2017
El Segundo, CA 90245-4962
Charles R. Willett, Director
Tel: (310) 363-2855 Fax: (310) 363-1189
Email: charles.willett@losangeles.af.mil
Web: www.losangeles.af.mil/SMC/BC/home.htm

ENERGY, DEPT. OF
Lawrence Berkeley National Laboratory, Procurement
1 Cyclotron Rd. #937-0200
Berkeley, CA 94720
David T. Chen, Team Leader
Tel: (510) 486-4506 Fax: (510) 486-4380
Email: DTChen@lbl.gov
Web: www.procurement.lbl.gov

Oakland Operations Office, Lawrence Livermore National Laboratory, University of California
P.O. Box 5012
700 E. Ave.
Livermore, CA 94561
Stan Howell, Small Business Program Manager

Tel: (925) 422-8997 Fax: (925) 422-3253
Email: howell6@llnl.gov

Oakland Operations Office, Stanford Linear Accelerator Ctr.
2575 Sand Hill Rd., M/S 01
Menlo Park, CA 94025
Small Business Liason
Tel: (650) 926-3556 Fax: (650) 926-2000

Stanford Linear Accelerator Ctr.
2575 Sand Hill Rd.
Menlo Park, CA 94025
Robert S. Todaro, Purchasing Officer
Tel: (650) 926-2425 Fax: (650) 926-2000
Email: rocker@slac.stanford.edu

ENVIRONMENTAL PROTECTION AGENCY
Region IX, Office of Small and Disadvantaged Business Utilization
75 Hawthorne St. (PMD-1)
San Francisco, CA 94105
Joe Ochab, Officer
Tel: (415) 972-3761 Fax: (415) 947-3556
Email: ochab.joe@epa.gov
Web: www.epa.gov/region09/

75 Hawthorne St. (PMD-8)
San Francisco, CA 94105
Barbara Bycsek, Contracting Specialist
Tel: (415) 972-3716 Fax: (415) 947-3558
Email: Bycsek.Barbara@epa.gov
Web: www.epa.gov/osdbu

GENERAL SERVICES ADMINISTRATION
Pacific Rim & Northwest/Artic Regions
450 Golden Gate Ave.
San Francisco, CA 94102-3400
Antoinette B. Brady, Regional EEO Officer
Tel: (415) 522-2711 Fax: (415) 522-2710
Email: antoinette.brady@gsa.gov
Web: www.gsa.gov

NATIONAL AERONAUTICS & SPACE ADMINISTRATION (NASA)
Ames Research Ctr.
M/S 241-1
Moffett Field, CA 94035-1000
Thomas J. Kolis, Field Installation Small/Minority Business Specialist
Tel: (650) 604-4690 Fax: (650) 604-4646
Email: t.kolis@nasa.gov
Web: www.hq.nasa.gov

Dryden Flight Research Ctr.
P.O. Box 273
M/S D-1422
Edwards, CA 93523-0273
Robert Medina, Field Installation Small/Minority Business Specialist
Tel: (661) 276-3343 Fax: (661) 276-2904
Email: robert.medina@nasa.gov
Web: www.hq.nasa.gov/office/codek

Jet Propulsion Laboratory
M/C 249-104
Pasadena, CA 91109
Margo Kuhn, Field Installation Small/Minority Business Specialist
Tel: (818) 354-5722 Fax: (818) 393-1978
Email: margo.p.kuhn@jpl.nasa.gov
Web: www.hq.nasa.gov

Jet Propulsion Laboratory, Business Opportunity Office
M/C 190-205
Pasadena, CA 91109
Tom May, Manager
Tel: (818) 354-2121 Fax: (818) 393-1746
Email: thomas.h.may@jpl.nasa.gov
Web: acquisition.jpl.nasa.gov

Jet Propulsion Laboratory, NASA Management Office
M/C 180-802K
Pasadena, CA 91109

Dora Huff, Field Installation Small/Minority Business Specialist
Tel: (818) 354-6315 Fax: (818) 354-6051
Email: dora.s.huff@nasa.gov
Web: www.hq.nasa.gov

TREASURY, DEPT. OF THE
Internal Revenue Service, Western Area Field Office
333 Market St. M:P:F:W, #1400
San Francisco, CA 94105
Jan Janson, Small Business Specialist
Tel: (415) 848-4716 Fax: (415) 848-4711
Email: jan.janson@irs.gov
Web: www.treas.gov

333 Market St. M:P:F:W, #1400
San Francisco, CA 94105
Mark S. Pfeiffer, Small Business Specialist (alternative)
Tel: (415) 848-4716 Fax: (415) 848-4711
Email: Mark.S.Pfeiffer@irs.gov
Web: www.treas.gov

VETERANS AFFAIRS, DEPT. OF
Sierra Pacific Network, VA Central California Healthcare System
2615 E. Clinton Ave.
Fresno, CA 93703
Pamela Mondrey, Small Business Specialist
Tel: (650) 849-0570 Fax: (650) 849-0332
Email: pam.mondrey@med.va.gov
Web: www.va.gov/osdbu

VA Medical Ctr.
5901 E. 7th St., Bldg. 149 VA Network Business Ctr.
Long Beach, CA 90822
Wayne Keen, Small Business Specialist
Tel: (562) 826-8154 Fax: (562) 826-5828
Email: wayne.keen@med.va.gov
Web: www.long-beach.med.va.gov

COLORADO

AGRICULTURE, DEPT. OF
Agricultural Research Service, Northern Plains Area
2250 Ctr. Ave., Bldg. D #S-310
Ft. Collins, CO 80526-8119
Richard Jansen, Supervisory Contract Specialist
Tel: (970) 492-7017 Fax: (970) 492-7031
Email: dick.jansen@ars.usda.gov
Web: www.ars.usda.gov

Forest Service, Procurement Technology, Central Administrative Zone
240 W. Prospect Rd.
Fort Collins, CO 80526
Katherine Padilla, Procurement Technician
Tel: (970) 498-1285 Fax: (970) 498-1045
Email: kpadilla@fs.fed.us
Web: www.fs.fed.us

Natural Resources Conservation Service
655 Parfet St. #E200C
Lakewood, CO 80215
Tony K. Doxtater, Contract Specialist
Tel: (720) 544-2826 Fax: (720) 544-2962
Email: Tony.Doxtater@co.usda.gov

USDA Forest Service, Rocky Mountain Acquisition Service Team
P.O. Box 25127
Lakewood, CO 80225
Joy Bartlett, Procurement Analyst
Tel: (303) 275-5556 Fax: (303) 275-5453
Email: jlbartlett@fs.fed.us
Web: www.fs.fed.us

COMMERCE, DEPT. OF

Minority Business Development Agency, Denver Minority Business Development Ctr.
3840 York St. #230B
Denver, CO 80211
Sara Fuentes, Director
Tel: (303) 455-3099 Fax: (303) 455-3076
Email: sfuentes@dmbdg.com

National Oceanic and Atmospheric Administration, Mountain Administrative Support Ctr., Acquisition Management Division
325 Broadway, M/C 3
Boulder, CO 80305-3328
Janet Clark, Small Business Specialist
Tel: (303) 497-6320 Fax: (303) 497-3163
Email: jan.clark@noaa.gov
Web: www.noaa.gov

DEFENSE, DEPT. OF
US Air Force, 10 ABW/LGC, Small Business Office
8110 Industrial Dr. #200
USAF Academy, CO 80840-2315
Sherry Pittinger, Director
Tel: (719) 333-4561 Fax: (719) 333-4404
Email: sherry.pittinger@usafa.af.mil
Web: www.usafa.af.mil/lg/lgc/sb

US Air Force, 21st Contracting Squadron/LGC-Air Force Space Command, Small Business Office
700 Suffolk St.
Peterson AFB, CO 80914-1200
Jim Redd, Small Business Specialist
Tel: (719) 556-4669 Fax: (719) 556-4321
Email: Jim.Redd@peterson.af.mil
Web: www.spacecom.af.mil/21cons/index.htm

US Air Force, 50th Contracting Squadron
210 Falcon Pkwy. #2116
Schriever AFB, CO 80912-2116
Detrice Shields, Small Business Specialist
Tel: (719) 567-3805 Fax: (719) 567-4974
Email: detrice.shields@schriever.af.mil
Web: www.schriever.af.mil

US Air Force, 821 SPTS/LGC-Air Force Space Command, Small Business Office
320 N. Beaver Creek, M/S 70
Buckley AFB, CO 80011
Theo Watson, Small Business Specialist
Tel: (720) 847-6745 Fax: (720) 847-6443
Email: Theo.Watson@buckley.af.mil
Web: www.buckley.af.mil

ENERGY, DEPT. OF
Golden Field Office
1617 Cole Blvd.
Golden, CO 80401
Stephanie Carabajal, Small Business Program Manager
Tel: (303) 275-4911 Fax: (303) 275-4788
Email: stephanie.carabajal@go.doe.gov
Web: www.go.doe.gov

Golden Field Office, National Renewable Energy Lab
1617 Cole Blvd.
Golden, CO 80401-3393
Nancy Gardner, Small Business Development Liaison
Tel: (303) 384-7335 Fax: (303) 384-7310
Email: nancy_gardner@nrel.gov
Web: www.nrel.gov

1617 Cole Blvd., M/S 1632
Golden, CO 80401-3393
Victoria Nosal, Small Business Program Manager
Tel: (303) 275-3120 Fax: (303) 275-3109
Email: victoria_nosal@nrel.gov
Web: www.nrel.gov

Office of River Protection, CH2M Hill Companies
9191 S. Jamaica St.
Englewood, CO 80112
Willie T. Franklin III, Small Business Program Manager
Tel: (720) 286-2274 Fax: (720) 286-9121
Email: wfrankli@ch2m.com

Western Area Power Administration
12155 W. Alameda Pkwy.
Lakewood, CO 80228
Judy Madsen, Small Business Program Manager
Tel: (720) 962-7154 Fax: (720) 962-7161
Email: madsen@wapa.gov

ENVIRONMENTAL PROTECTION AGENCY
Region VIII, Office of Small and Disadvantaged Business Utilization
999 18th St. #500, M/C TMS-G
Denver, CO 80202-2466
Maurice Velasquez, Officer
Tel: (303) 312-6862 Fax: (303) 312-6685
Email: velasquez.maurice@epa.gov
Web: www.epa.gov/osdbu

GENERAL SERVICES ADMINISTRATION
Small Business Utilization Ctr., Rocky Mountain Region
P.O. Box 25006, 8AB
Denver Federal Ctr. Bldg. 41 #234
Denver, CO 80225
Pennie Estrada, Director
Tel: (303) 236-7409 Fax: (303) 236-7552
Email: pennie.estrada@gsa.gov
Web: rmrbsc.gsa.gov

VETERANS AFFAIRS, DEPT. OF
Denver Distribution Ctr. (905)
P.O. Box 25166
Denver, CO 80225-0166
Patrick Harvey, Small Business Specialist
Tel: (303) 914-5180 Fax: (303) 914-5189
Email: Patrick.Harvey@med.va.gov
Web: www.va.gov/osdbu

VA Health Administration Ctr.
300 S. Jackson St. #444
Denver, CO 80206-9020
James Davis, Small Business Specialist
Tel: (303) 331-7556 Fax: (720) 889-2387
Email: James.Davis@med.va.gov
Web: www.va.gov/osdbu

VA Medical Ctr.
1055 Clermont St.
Denver, CO 80220
Susan Penn, Small Business Specialist
Tel: (303) 393-2846 Fax: (303) 393-2860
Email: susan.penn@med.va.gov
Web: www.va.gov/osdbu

2121 North Ave.
Grand Junction, CO 81501
Denise Boren, Contract Specialist
Tel: (970) 263-5004 Fax: (970) 244-7721
Email: denise.boren@med.va.gov
Web: www.va.gov/osdbu

VETERANS AFFAIRS, DEPT. OF
VA Medical Ctr.
950 Campbell Ave.
West Haven, CT 06514
Bruce Fortuna, Small Business Specialist
Tel: (203) 937-3881 Fax: (203) 937-4347
Email: bruce.fortuna@med.va.gov
Web: www.va.gov/osdbu

DEFENSE, DEPT. OF
US Air Force, 436 CONS/LGCD
639 Atlantic St. #204
Dover AFB, DE 19902-5639
Thelma Gabrielson, Contracting Specialist
Tel: (302) 677-2184 Fax: (302) 677-5105
Email: Thelma.Gabrielson@dover.af.mil
Web: public.dover.amc.af.mil

VETERANS AFFAIRS, DEPT. OF
Stars & Stripes Healthcare Network, VA Medical Ctr. & Regional Office
1601 Kirkwood Hwy.
Wilmington, DE 19805
Toni A. Wilson, Small Business Specialist
Tel: (302) 633-5371 Fax: (302) 633-5377
Email: toni.wilson@med.va.gov
Web: www.va.gov/osdbu

AGRICULTURE, DEPT. OF
Agricultural Marketing Service, Poultry Division
1400 Independence Ave.
SW #3941-S M/S 0260
Washington, DC 20250
Mark Thomas, Agricultural Marketing Specialist/OSDBU Coordinator
Tel: (202) 720-7693 Fax: (202) 720-5871
Email: mark.thomas@usda.gov
Web: www.ams.usda.gov

CPB, Fruit & Vegetable Programs
1400 Independence Ave. SW M/S 0239
Washington, DC 20250
Michelle Warren, Contract Specialist
Tel: (202) 720-4517 Fax: (202) 720-2782
Email: Michellee.Warren@usda.gov
Web: www.ams.usda.gov

Livestock & Seed Division
1400 Independence Ave. #1566 S. Bldg.
Washington, DC 20250
Ondray James, Small Business Specialist
Tel: (202) 720-7117 Fax: (202) 720-3001
Email: ondray.james@usda.gov

Agricultural Research Service
1280 Maryland Ave. SW #580C
Washington, DC 20250
Anthony S. Wimbush, Contracting Specialist
Tel: (202) 720-3998 Fax: (202) 720-3987
Email: awimbush@ars.usda.gov
Web: www.ars.usda.gov

Farm Service Agency, Contracting and Acquisitions Management Division
1280 Maryland Ave. SW #6957
Washington, DC 20024
Scott P. Cook, Small Business Coordinator
Tel: (202) 720-7349 Fax: (202) 690-0689
Email: Scott.cook@wdc.usda.gov
Web: www.fsa.usda.gov/amb

Farm Service Agency, Procurement & Donations Division
1400 Independence Ave.
SW #5754S, M/S 0551
Washington, DC 20013
Lisa Brown, Coordinator
Tel: (202) 720-0956 Fax: (202) 690-1809
Email: lisa_brown@wdc.fsa.usda.gov

Forest Service, Acquisition Management Branch
P.O. Box 96090, #706, Rosslyn Plz. East
Washington, DC 20090-6090
James G. McDonald, Director of Small Business Outreach
Tel: (703) 605-5144 Fax: (703) 605-5100
Email: jmcdonald04@fs.fed.us

Natural Resources Conservation Service, Administrative Services Division
1400 Independence Ave. SW #0106
Washington, DC 20250
Terry Kirby, NRCS Small Business Coordinator
Tel: (202) 720-8758 Fax: (202) 720-2899
Email: terry.kirby@usda.gov
Web: www.nrcs.usda.gov

Office of Communications, Resources Management Staff
1400 Independence Ave. SW #434-A,
Jamie L. Whitten Bldg.
Washington, DC 20250
Terry Logan, Financial Management Specialist
Tel: (202) 720-3118 Fax: (202) 690-1131
Email: Terry.Logan@usda.gov
Web: www.usda.gov

Office of Operations, Procurement Division
300 7th St. SW #377, Reporters Bldg.
Washington, DC 20250
Sandra Turner, Contracting Officer
Tel: (202) 720-4674

Office of Procurement & Property Management / POD
300 7th St. SW #367, Reporters Bldg.
Washington, DC 20024
Richard Storie, Procurement Analyst/Coordinator
Tel: (202) 720-3211 Fax: (202) 720-4529
Email: Richard.Storie@usda.gov
Web: www.usda.gov

Office of Small and Disadvantaged Business Utilization
400 Independence Ave. SW #1566-S
Washington, DC 20250
James E. House, Director
Tel: (202) 720-7117 Fax: (202) 720-3001
Email: house.jamese@usda.gov
Web: www.usda.gov/osdbu

400 Independence Ave. SW #1566-S
Washington, DC 20250
Sherry Cohen, Women Business Representative
Tel: (202) 720-7117 Fax: (202) 720-3001
Email: sherryr.cohen@usda.gov
Web: www.usda.gov/osdbu

400 Independence Ave. SW #1566-S
Washington, DC 20250
Stella Hughes, Veteran Business Representative
Tel: (202) 720-7117 Fax: (202) 720-3001
Email: stella.hughes@usda.gov
Web: www.usda.gov/osdbu

Office of the Inspector General, Contracts and Procurement Branch
1400 Independence Ave. SW #40-E,
Jamie L. Whitten Bldg.
Washington, DC 20250
Tina Jones, Coordinator
Tel: (202) 720-5931 Fax: (202) 690-1282
Email: tmjones@oig.usda.gov

Rural Business Cooperative Service
1400 Independence Ave. SW #5801A
Washington, DC 20250
John Rosso, Administrator
Tel: (202) 690-4730 Fax: (202) 690-4737
Email: john.rosso@usda.gov
Web: www.usda.gov

Rural Development
1400 Independence Ave. SW, M/S 0741

Washington, DC 20250-0741
Rodney Harrison, Contract Specialist
Tel: (202) 692-0017 Fax: (202) 692-0235
Email: rodney.harrison@usda.gov
Web: www.rurdev.usda.gov

COMMERCE, DEPT. OF
Minority Business Development Agency
14th & Constitution Ave. NW #5053
Washington, DC 20230
Ronald N. Langston, National Director
Tel: (202) 482-5061 Fax: (202) 501-4698
Email: RLangston@mbda.gov
Web: www.mbda.gov

Office of Small and Disadvantaged Business Utilization
14th & Constitution Ave. NW,
Herbert C. Hoover Bldg. #6411
Washington, DC 20230
La Juene Desmukes, Acting Director
Tel: (202) 482-1472 Fax: (202) 482-0501
Email: Ldesmukes@doc.gov
Web: www.commerce.gov/osdbu

Office of the Secretary, Office of Acquisition Management
14th & Constitution Ave. NW #H6521
Washington, DC 20230
Frank J. Krempa, Small Business Specialist
Tel: (202) 482-0997 Fax: (202) 482-4988
Email: fkrempa@doc.gov
Web: www.oamweb.osec.doc.gov

US Census Bureau, Procurement Office
4700 Silver Hill Rd. #G-314
Washington, DC 20233-0001
Jacqueline V. Wilson, Small Business Specialist
Tel: (301) 763-1864 Fax: (301) 457-1785
Email: jacqueline.v.wilson@census.gov
Web: www.census.gov

COMMODITY FUTURES TRADING COMMISSION
Office of Financial Management
1155 21st St. NW
Washington, DC 20581
Steven Grossman, Deputy Director for Procurement Operations and Policy
Tel: (202) 418-5192 Fax: (202) 418-5529
Web: www.cftc.gov

1155 21st St. NW
Washington, DC 20581
Nicholas Graham, Contracting Officer
Tel: (202) 418-5191 Fax: (202) 418-5414
Email: ngraham@cftc.gov
Web: www.cftc.gov

DEFENSE, DEPT. OF
Military Sealift Command, Small Business Office
914 Charles Morris Ct. SE, Bldg. 210
Washington Navy Yard, DC 20398-5540
Dave B. Grove, Associate Director
Tel: (202) 685-5554 Fax: (202) 685-5515
Email: david.grove@navy.mil
Web: www.msc.navy.mil

US Air Force, 11th Contracting Squadron/LGCB, Small Business Office
110 Luke Ave.
Bolling AFB, DC 20032-0305
Everett Carter, Director Specialist
Tel: (202) 767-8086 Fax: (202) 404-7006
Email: Everett.Carter@bolling.af.mil
Web: www.bolling.af.mil

US Air Force, Office of Small and Disadvantaged Business Utilization
SASSB, 1060 Air Force, The Pentagon
Washington, DC 20330-1060
Joseph Diamond, Director
Tel: (703) 696-1103 Fax: (703) 696-1170

Email: joseph.diamond@pentagon.af.mil
Web: www.selltoairforce.org

SASSB, 1060 Air Force, The Pentagon
Washington, DC 20330-1060
Sara Mitchele, Women Business Representative
Tel: (703) 696-1103 Fax: (703) 696-1170
Email: Sara.Mitchele@pentagon.af.mil
Web: www.selltoairforce.org

US Army Corps of Engineers, Small Business Office
441 G St. NW, 3rd Fl.
Washington, DC 20314-1000
Judith Blake, Director of Small Businesses
Tel: (202) 761-0725 Fax: (202) 761-4609
Web: www.hq.usace.army.mil/hqhome/

US Army Office of Small and Disadvantaged Business Utilization
106 Army Pentagon #3B #514
Washington, DC 20310-0106
Tracey L. Pinson, Director
Tel: (703) 697-2868 Fax: (703) 693-3898
Email: tracey.pinson@hqda.army.mil
Web: www.sellingtoarmy.info

US Navy, Office of Small and Disadvantaged Business Utilization
720 Kennon St. SE #207 Navy Yard
Washington, DC 20374-5015
Nancy Tarrant, Director
Tel: (202) 685-6485 Fax: (202) 685-6865
Email: nancy.tarrant@navy.mil
Web: www.hq.navy.mil/sadbu

720 Kennon St. SE #207 Navy Yard
Washington, DC 20374-5015
Paulette Widmann, Deputy Director
Tel: (202) 685-6490 Fax: (202) 685-6865
Web: www.hq.navy.mil/sadbu

EDUCATION, DEPT. OF
Office of Small and Disadvantaged Business Utilization
400 Maryland Ave. SW #7048, PCP
Washington, DC 20202-0521
Marcella Coverson, Procurement Analyst
Tel: (202) 245-6300 Fax: (202) 245-6304
Email: marcella.coverson@ed.gov
Web: www.ed.gov

ENERGY, DEPT. OF
Energy Efficiency & Renewable Energy, EE 3.2
1000 Independence Ave. SW
Washington, DC 20585
Turnetta Cook, Small Business Program Manager
Tel: (202) 586-9288 Fax: (202) 586-9652
Email: Turnetta.Cook@ee.doe.gov
Web: www.eere.energy.gov

Energy Information Administration, EI-20
1000 Independence Ave. SW
#2H055- EI20
Washington, DC 20585
Gwenne Goodwin, Small Business Program Manager
Tel: (202) 586-6307 Fax: (202) 586-0552
Email: ggoodwin@eia.doe.gov
Web: www.eia.doe.gov

National Nuclear Security Administration
1000 Independence Ave. SW
Washington, DC 20585
Gary Lyttek, Small Business Program Manager
Tel: (202) 586-8304 Fax: (202) 586-7535
Email: nnsa.smallbusiness@nnsa.doe.gov
Web: www.nnsa.doe.gov

Office of Congressional and Intergovernmental Affairs, CI-3
1000 Independence Ave. SW #8G096
Washington, DC 20585
Laura Brown, Small Business Program Manager
Tel: (202) 586-5524 Fax: (202) 586-0230
Email: laura.brown@hq.doe.gov
Web: www.doe.gov

Office of Counter Intelligence, CN-1
1000 Independence Ave. SW #8F089
Washington, DC 20585
Sharon Steffe, Procurement and Budget Specialist
Tel: (202) 586-5218 Fax: (202) 586-0551
Email: sharon.steffe@cn.doe.gov
Web: www.doe.gov

Office of Economic Impact and Diversity
1000 Independence Ave. SW #5B-148
Washington, DC 20585
Yosef Patel, Deputy Director
Tel: (202) 586-7377 Fax: (202) 586-5488
Email: yosef.patel@hq.doe.gov
Web: www.doe.gov

Office of Science, Energy Research, SC-64
1000 Independence Ave. SW #SC-64
Washington, DC 20585
Martin P. Rubenstein, Procurement Analyst, Grants and Contracts
Tel: (301) 903-4946 Fax: (301) 903-4194
Email: martin.rubenstein@science.doe.gov
Web: www.sc.doe.gov

Office of Security and Emergency Management, SP 1.12, GTN C-379
1000 Independent Ave. SW
Washington, DC 20585
David R. O'Connell, Procurement Advisor
Tel: (301) 903-4124 Fax: (301) 903-6081
Email: david.o'connell@hq.doe.gov
Web: www.vm1.hqadmin.doe.gov

Office of the Inspector General, IG-12
1000 Independence Ave. SW #5D-031
Washington, DC 20585
Gloria Jennings, Small Business Program Manager
Tel: (202) 586-1930 Fax: (202) 586-7851
Email: gloria.jennings@hq.doe.gov
Web: www.ig.doe.gov

ENVIRONMENTAL PROTECTION AGENCY
Contracts & Management Division
1200 Pennsylvania Ave. NW M/C 3903R
Washington, DC 20460
Lupe Saldaña, Officer
Tel: (202) 564-5353 Fax: (202) 565-2467
Email: saldana.lupe@epa.gov
Web: www.epa.gov

Office of Small and Disadvantaged Business Utilization
1200 Pennsylvania Ave. NW M/C1230A
Washington, DC 20460
Jeanette L. Brown, Director
Tel: (202) 564-4100 Fax: (202) 501-0756
Email: brown.jeanettel@epa.gov
Web: www.epa.gov/osdbu

EXECUTIVE OFFICE OF THE PRESIDENT
Office of Small and Disadvantaged Business Utilization
#148 Eisenhower Executive Office Bldg.
17th & Pennsylvania Ave. NW
Washington, DC 20503
John Strub, Director
Tel: (202) 395-7669 Fax: (202) 456-6512
Web: www.whitehouse.gov

FEDERAL COMMUNICATIONS COMMISSION

Office of Communications Business Opportunities
445 12th St. SW #4A-624
Washington, DC 20024
Karen Beverly, Consumer Industry Affairs Specialist & Assistant for Management
Tel: (202) 418-0990 Fax: (202) 418-0235
Email: karen.beverly@fcc.gov
Web: www.fcc.gov/ocbo

445 12th St. SW #4A624
Washington, DC 20554
Carolyn Flemming Williams, Director
Tel: (202) 418-0990 Fax: (202) 418-0235
Email: carolyn.williams@fcc.gov
Web: www.fcc.gov/ocbo

FEDERAL DEPOSIT INSURANCE CORPORATION
Division of Administration, Acquisitions Services Branch, Headquarters
550 17th St. NW #PA1700-4002
Washington, DC 20429
Ann Bridges Steely, Associate Director
Tel: (202) 942-3010 Fax: (202) 942-3544
Email: ASteely@fdic.gov
Web: www.fdic.gov/buying

FEDERAL TRADE COMMISSION
Acquisition Office
600 Pennsylvania Ave. NW #H-706
Washington, DC 20580
Jean Sefcheck, Women Business Representative
Tel: (202) 326-2258 Fax: (202) 326-3529
Web: www.ftc.gov/procurement

GENERAL SERVICES ADMINISTRATION
Office of Enterprise Development
1800 & F St. NW #6029
Washington, DC 20405
Felipe Mendoza, Associate Administrator
Tel: (202) 501-1021 Fax: (202) 501-2590
Email: Felipe.Mendoza@gsa.com
Web: www.gsa.gov/oed

Small Business Utilization
1800 F St. NW #6029
Washington, DC 20405
Elizabeth Ivey, Women Business Representative
Tel: (202) 501-1021 Fax: (202) 501-2590
Email: liz.ivey@gsa.gov
Web: www.gsa.gov/oed

Small Business Utilization Ctr.
7th & D St. SW #1050 WCAB
Washington, DC 20407
Shaunta Johnson, Director
Tel: (202) 708-5804 Fax: (202) 205-2872
Email: shaunta.johnson@gsa.gov
Web: www.gsa.gov

HEALTH & HUMAN SERVICES, DEPT. OF
Office of Small and Disadvantaged Business Utilization
200 Independence Ave. SW #517D
Washington, DC 20201
Debbie Ridgely, Director
Tel: (202) 690-7300 Fax: (202) 260-4872
Email: debbie.ridgely@hhs.gov
Web: www.hhs.gov/osdbu

HOMELAND SECURITY, DEPT. OF
Customs and Border Protection, National Office
1300 Pennsylvania Ave. NW #1310
Washington, DC 20229
William Bickelman, Small Business Specialist
Tel: (202) 927-0278 Fax: (202) 927-1190
Web: www.cbp.gov

Federal Emergency Management Agency, Financial and Acquisitions Management Division/ Flood Fire and Mitigation Branch Office
500 C St. SW #350
Washington, DC 20472
Brenda Thomas, Small Business and Disadvantaged Utlization Specialist
Tel: (202) 646-4584 Fax: (202) 646-3846
Email: brenda.d.thomas@dhs.gov
Web: www.dhs.gov

US COAST GUARD
2100 2nd St. SW #2606
Washington, DC 20593
Phyllis Miriashtiani, Small Business Program Manager
Tel: (202) 267-1172 Fax: (202) 267-4011
Email: pmiriashtiani@comdt.uscg.mil
Web: www.dhs.gov

US Customs Service, National Office, Procurement Division
1300 Pennsylvania Ave. NW #1310
Washington, DC 20229
William Bickelman, Small Business Specialist
Tel: (202) 344-1168 Fax: (202) 344-1190
Email: william.bickelman@dhs.gov
Web: www.customs.gov

US Secret Service, Procurement Division
950 H St. NW
Washington, DC 20332
Marcia Rodrigues, Small Business Specialist
Tel: (202) 406-6129 Fax: (202) 406-6801
Email: Marcia.Rodrigues@usss.dhs.gov
Web: www.ustreas.gov/usss

HOUSING & URBAN DEVELOPMENT, DEPT. OF
Office of Small and Disadvantaged Business Utilization
451 7th St. SW #3130
Washington, DC 20410-1000
A. Jo Baylor, Director
Tel: (202) 708-1428 Fax: (202) 708-7642
Email: A._Jo_Baylor@hud.gov
Web: www.hud.gov

INTERIOR, DEPT. OF THE
Office of Small and Disadvantaged Business Utilization
1849 C St. NW #2252
Washington, DC 20240
Robert W. Faithful, Director
Tel: (202) 208-3493 Fax: (202) 219-2131
Web: www.doi.gov/osdbu

INTERNATIONAL TRADE COMMISSION
Facilities Management, Procurement Division
500 E. St. SW #414
Washington, DC 20436
Jonathan Brown, Director
Tel: (202) 205-2741 Fax: (202) 205-2337
Email: Jonathan.Brown@usitc.gov
Web: www.usitc.gov

JUSTICE, DEPT. OF
Bureau of Alcohol, Tobacco and Firearms, Acquisition & Property Management Division
650 Massachusetts Ave. NW #3290
Washington, DC 20226
Grace Foster, Small Business Specialist
Tel: (202) 927-8332 Fax: (202) 927-7311
Email: grace.foster@atf.gov
Web: www.usdoj.gov

Bureau of Prisons, National Contracts & Policy
320 1st St. NW #5006

Washington, DC 20534
Lenard Foust, Small Business Administrator
Tel: (202) 307-0985 Fax: (202) 616-1146
Email: len.g.foust@usdoj.gov
Web: www.usdoj.gov

Federal Bureau of Investigation, Construction and Laboratory Unit
935 Pennsylvania Ave. NW #1B015
Washington, DC 20525-0001
Julie Hammond, Small Business Specialist
Tel: (202) 324-0569 Fax: (202) 324-0570
Web: www.usdoj.gov

Justice Management Division
1331 Pennsylvania Ave. NW #1000
Washington, DC 20530
Ken Freeman, Procurement Services Staff
Tel: (202) 307-1971 Fax: (202) 307-1931
Email: kenneth.h.freeman@usdoj.gov
Web: www.usdoj.gov

Office of Detention Trust
1331 Pennsylvania Ave. NW #1210
Washington, DC 20530
Lori A. Ray, Small Business Representative
Tel: (202) 353-4601 Fax: (202) 353-4611
Email: lori.ray@usdoj.gov
Web: www.usdoj.gov

Office of Justice Program
810 7th St. NW #3621
Washington, DC 20531
Raymond German, Small Business Representative
Tel: (202) 307-0613 Fax: (202) 307-0086
Email: raymond.german@ojp.usdoj.gov
Web: www.usdoj.gov

Office of Small and Disadvantaged Business Utilization
1331 Pennsylvania Ave. NW #1010
Washington, DC 20530
Romona Glover, Director
Tel: (202) 616-0521 Fax: (202) 616-1717
Web: www.usdoj.gov/jmd/osdbu

US Marshals Service, Procurement Office
#932 CS3
Washington, DC 20530-1000
Elizabeth Howard, Small Business Specialist
Tel: (202) 307-9349 Fax: (202) 307-9695
Email: elizabeth.howard@usdoj.gov
Web: www.usdoj.gov

LABOR, DEPT. OF
Office of Small Business Programs, Procurement Services Ctr.
200 Constitution Ave. NW #C2318
Washington, DC 20210
Frederick Trakowski, Small Business Advisor
Tel: (202) 693-6465 Fax: (202) 693-6485
Email: trakowski-frederick@dol.gov
Web: www.dol.gov

NATIONAL AERONAUTICS & SPACE ADMINISTRATION (NASA)
NASA Headquarters, Office of Small and Disadvantaged Business Utilization, Code K
300 E St. SW #9K70
Washington, DC 20546-0001
Shirley Perez, Program Manager for Aero-Space Technology
Tel: (202) 358-0640 Fax: (202) 358-3261
Email: shirley.perez@nasa.gov
Web: www.hq.nasa.gov

300 E St. SW #9K70
Washington, DC 20546-0001
Thomas V. Green, Special Assistant for Procurement

Tel: (202) 358-2403 Fax: (202) 358-3261
Email: tgreen@bolg.public.hq.nasa.gov
Web: www.hq.nasa.gov

300 E St. SW #9K70
Washington, DC 20546-0001
Eleanor N. Chiogioji, Ph.D, Program Manager for Education
Tel: (202) 358-2088 Fax: (202) 358-3261
Email: echiogioji@nasa.gov
Web: www.hq.nasa.gov

SMITHSONIAN INSTITUTION
Office of Equal Employment and Minority Affairs
P.O. Box 37012
Victor Bldg. #8100 MRC921
Washington, DC 20013-7012
Rudy D. Watley, Supplier Diversity Program Manager
Tel: (202) 275-0157 Fax: (202) 275-2055
Email: watleyr@si.edu
Web: www.si.edu

STATE, DEPT. OF
Office of Small and Disadvantaged Business Utilization
A/SDBU, SA-6 #L500
Washington, DC 20522-0602
Durie N. White, Operations Director
Tel: (703) 875-6822 Fax: (703) 875-6825
Email: whitedn@state.gov
Web: www.state.gov/m/a/sdbu

A/SDBU, SA-6 #L500
Washington, DC 20522-0602
Patricia B. Culbreth, Women-Owned Business Representative
Tel: (703) 875-6881 Fax: (703) 875-6825
Email: culberthpb@state.gov
Web: www.state.gov/m/a/sdbu

TRANSPORTATION, DEPT. OF
Federal Aviation Administration, Small Business Utilization Office
800 Independence Ave. SW #715
Washington, DC 20591
Fred Dendy, Small Business Program Analyst
Tel: (202) 267-8881 Fax: (202) 493-4380
Email: fred.dendy@faa.gov
Web: www.faa.gov

Federal Highway Administration
400 7th St. SW #4404
Washington, DC 20590
Frank Waltos, Small Business Specialist
Tel: (202) 366-4205 Fax: (202) 366-3705
Email: frank.waltos@fhwa.dot.gov
Web: www.fhwa.dot.gov

Federal Railroad Administration, Office of Acquisition and Grants Services, (RAD-30)
1120 Vermont Ave. #6125
Washington, DC 20005
Illona Williams, Director
Tel: (202) 493-6130 Fax: (202) 493-6171
Email: illona.williams@fra.dot.gov
Web: www.fra.dot.gov

Federal Transit Administration
400 7th St. SW
Washington, DC 20590
Dale Johnson, Small Business Specialist
Tel: (202) 366-2512 Fax: (202) 366-3808
Email: Dale.Johnson@fta.dot.gov
Web: www.fta.dot.gov

Maritime Administration
400 7th St. SW #7310
Washington, DC 20590
Rita Thomas, Small Business Specialist
Tel: (202) 366-2802 Fax: (202) 366-3237
Email: rita.thomas@marad.dot.gov
Web: www.marad.dot.gov

National Highway Traffic Safety Administration
400 7th St. SW #5301
Washington, DC 20590
Lamont Norwood, Small Business Specialist
Tel: (202) 366-8573 Fax: (202) 366-9555
Email: lamont.norwood@nhtsa.dot.gov
Web: www.nhtsa.dot.gov

Office of Small and Disadvantaged Business Utilization
400 7th St. SW #9414
Washington, DC 20590
Sean M. Moss, Director
Tel: (202) 366-1930 Fax: (202) 366-7228
Email: sean.moss@ost.dot.gov
Web: www.osdbuweb.dot.gov

400 7th St. SW #9414 M/S S40
Washington, DC 20590
Pat Hodge, Women Business Representative
Tel: (202) 366-1930 Fax: (202) 366-7228
Email: Pat.Hodge@ost.dot.gov
Web: www.dot.gov

Research and Special Programs Administration
400 7th St. SW #7104
Washington, DC 20590
Nauman Ansari, Small Business Specialist
Tel: (202) 366-5513 Fax: (202) 366-7974
Email: nauman.ansari@rspa.dot.gov
Web: osdbuweb.dot.gov/index.html

TREASURY, DEPT. OF THE
Bureau of Engraving and Printing
14th & C Sts. SW #708A-06
Washington, DC 20228
Kimberly Witcher, Small Business Specialist
Tel: (202) 874-2451 Fax: (202) 874-2200
Email: kimberly.witcher@bep.treas.gov

Comptroller of the Currency, Acquisitions
AQS 4-13 250 E. St. SW
Washington, DC 20219
Karen Galloway, Small Business Specialist
Tel: (202) 874-4567 Fax: (202) 874-5625
Email: karen.galloway@occ.treas.gov
Web: www.treas.gov

Departmental Offices, Procurement Office
1425 New York Ave. #2100
Washington, DC 20220
Dan Alderman, Small Business Specialist
Tel: (202) 622-6539 Fax: (202) 622-2343
Email: dan.alderman@do.treas.gov
Web: www.treas.gov

Financial Management Service
#456B 401 14th St. SW
Washington, DC 20227
Bonnie Stokely, Small Business Specialist
Tel: (202) 874-6784 Fax: (202) 874-7275
Email: fms.sb@fms.treas.gov
Web: www.treas.gov

Office of Thrift Supervision, Procurement Services
1700 G St. NW, 3rd Fl.
Washington, DC 20552
Douglas Mason, Small Business Specialist
Tel: (202) 906-7624 Fax: (202) 906-5748
Email: douglas.mason@ots.treas.gov
Web: www.treas.gov

US Mint
801 9th St. NW
Washington, DC 20220
Crystal Johnson, Small Business Specialist
Tel: (202) 354-7421 Fax: (202) 756-6514
Email: cfjohnson@usmint.treas.gov
Web: www.treas.gov

US Secret Service, Procurement Division
950 H St. NW
Washington, DC 20223
Robert Petrosky, Branch Chief
Tel: (202) 406-6940 Fax: (202) 406-6801
Email: rpetrosky@usss.treas.gov
Web: www.usss.treas.gov

US AGENCY FOR INTERNATIONAL DEVELOPMENT
Office of Small and Disadvantaged Business Utilization, Minority Resource Ctr.
1300 Pennsylvania Ave. NW #7.8E,
Ronald Reagan Bldg.
Washington, DC 20523-7800
Rhoda Isaac, Women Business Representative
Tel: (202) 712-1500 Fax: (202) 216-3056
Email: risaac@usaid.gov
Web: www.usaid.gov

1300 Pennsylvania Ave. NW #78E,
Ronald Reagan Bldg.
Washington, DC 20523-7800
Marilyn Marton, Director
Tel: (202) 712-1500 Fax: (202) 216-3056
Email: mmarton@usaid.gov
Web: www.usaid.gov/business

US POSTAL SERVICE
Supplier Diversity
475 L'Enfant Plz. SW #4320
Washington, DC 20260-4320
Janice B. Williams-Hopkins, Program Manager
Tel: (202) 268-4101 Fax: (202) 268-7288
Email: janice.b.williams-hopkins@usps.gov
Web: www.usps.com

VETERANS AFFAIRS, DEPT. OF
Acquisitions Operations and Analysis Service
810 Vermont Ave. NW
Washington, DC 20420
Melissa Powell, Small Business Specialist
Tel: (202) 273-8769 Fax: (202) 273-7448
Email: melissa.powell@mail.va.gov
Web: www.va.gov/osdbu

Office of Small and Disadvantaged Business Utilization
810 Vermont Ave. NW
Washington, DC 20420
Scott F. Denniston, Director
Tel: (202) 565-8124 Fax: (202) 565-8156
Email: scott.denniston@mail.va.gov
Web: www.va.gov/osdbu

810 Vermont Ave. NW
Washington, DC 20420
John Blake, Small Business Specialist
Tel: (202) 565-5784 Fax: (202) 565-4921
Email: john.blake@mail.va.gov
Web: www.va.gov/osdbu

VA Medical Ctr.
50 Irving St. NW
Washington, DC 20422
Joan F. VanMiddlesworth, Small Business Specialist
Tel: (202) 745-8000 X8413
Fax: (202) 745-8465
Email: joan.vanmiddlesworth@med.va.gov
Web: www.va.gov/osdbu

Veterans Benefits Administration
810 Vermont Ave. NW M/C 20S2
Washington, DC 20420
Patricia Stanford, Director of Acquisition
Tel: (202) 273-6818 Fax: (202) 275-1283
Web: www.va.gov/osdbu

FLORIDA

COMMERCE, DEPT. OF
Minority Business Development Agency, District Office
51 SW 1st Ave. #1314 Box 25
Miami, FL 33130
Business Development Specialist
Tel: (305) 536-5054 Fax: (305) 530-7068
Web: www.mbda.gov

Miami/Ft. Lauderdale Minority Business Development Ctr.
3050 Biscayne Blvd. #201
Miami, FL 33137
Andrew Byer, Small Business Specialist
Tel: (786) 316-0888 Fax: (786) 316-0090
Email: abyer@mbdcsouthflorida.org
Web: www.mbdcsouthflorida.org

3050 Biscayne Blvd. #201
Miami, FL 33137
John Rivera, Project Director
Tel: (786) 316-0888 Fax: (786) 316-0090
Email: jrivera@mbdcsouthflorida.org
Web: www.mbdcsouthflorida.org

Satellite Office
3800 W. Broward Blvd. #101
Ft. Lauderdale, FL 33313
Ricardo Martinez, Small Business Specialist
Tel: (954) 660-7601 Fax: (954) 587-3703
Email: rmartinez@mbdcsouthflorida.org
Web: www.mbdcsouthflorida.org

Orlando Minority Business Opportunity Committee
6880 Lake Eleanor Dr. #104A
Orlando, FL 32809
Malik Ali, Executive Director
Tel: (407) 245-6062 Fax: (407) 857-8647
Email: malik@fmsdc.org
Web: www.nmsdcfl.com

DEFENSE, DEPT. OF
US Air Force, 16th Contracting Squadron/LGC-Air Force Special Operations Command, Small Business Office
P.O. Box 9190
Hurlburt Field, FL 32544-9190
Ron Siniscalchi, Small Business Specialist
Tel: (850) 884-5376 X1250
Fax: (850) 884-2001
Email: Ron.Siniscalchi@hurlburt.af.mil
Web: www.selltoairforce.org

US Air Force, 325 Contracting Squadron/CC-Air Education and Training Command, Small Business Office
501 Illinois Ave. #5
Tyndall AFB, FL 32403-5526
Norma Myers, Small Business Specialist
Tel: (850) 283-3670 Fax: (850) 283-1222
Email: norma.myers@tyndall.af.mil
Web: www.selltoairforce.org

US Air Force, 45th Space Wing/BZ (AFSPC), Small Business Office
1201 Edward H. White II St.
Patrick AFB, FL 32925-3237
Linda Sherod, Small Business Specialist
Tel: (321) 494-2207 Fax: (321) 494-5599
Email: linda.sherod@patrick.af.mil
Web: www.patrick.af.mil

US Air Force, 482 LSS/LGC-Air Force Reserve Command, Small Business Office
29050 Coral Sea Blvd.
Homestead ARS, FL 33039-1299
John Marshburn, Small Business Specialist
Tel: (305) 224-7474 Fax: (305) 224-7055

Email: john.marshburn@homestead.af.mil
Web: www.selltoairforce.org

US Air Force, 6th Air Refueling Wing/LGC (AF)-Air Mobility Command, Small Business Office
2606 Brown Pelican Ave.
MacDill AFB, FL 33621-5000
Judy Hall, Director of Contract Operations
Tel: (813) 828-4752
Email: hallj@macdill.af.mil
Web: public.macdill.amc.af.mil/6contracting.html

US Air Force, Air Armament Ctr./BC-Air Force Materiel Command, Small Business Office
205 W. D Ave. #449
Eglin AFB, FL 32542-6863
Marcia A. Smith, Director of Small Business Office
Tel: (850) 882-2843 X2
Fax: (850) 882-4836
Email: marcia.smith@eglin.af.mil
Web: www.eglin.af.mil/org-busopp.htm

US Air Force, HQ AFSOC/PKM-Air Force Special Operations Command, Small Business Office
100 Bartley St.
Hurlburt Field, FL 32544
Ron Siniscalchi, Small Business Specialist
Tel: (850) 884-2376 Fax: (850) 884-1250
Email: Ron.Siniscalchi@Hurlburt.af.mil
Web: www.selltoairforce.org

US Special Operations Command
7701 Tampa Point Blvd.
Tampa, FL 33621-5323
Karen Para, Small Business Specialist
Tel: (813) 828-7549 Fax: (813) 828-7504
Web: www.socom.mil

US Naval Air Warfare Ctr. Aircraft Division, Small Business Office
12350 Research Pkwy. M/C 253C
Orlando, FL 32826-3224
Argentina V. Thompson, Deputy of Small Business
Tel: (407) 380-8253 Fax: (407) 380-4487
Email: argentina.thompson@navy.mil
Web: www.ntsc.navy.mil

NATIONAL AERONAUTICS & SPACE ADMINISTRATION (NASA)
Kennedy Space Ctr.
M/C OP-CIAO
Kennedy Space Ctr., FL 32899
David A. Wansley, Field Installation Small/Minority Business Specialist
Tel: (321) 867-7346 Fax: (321) 867-8599
Email: david.a.wansley@nasa.gov
Web: www.hq.nasa.gov

M/C OP-CIAO
Kennedy Space Ctr., FL 32899
Ember Smith, Small Business Specialist
Tel: (321) 867-7312 Fax: (321) 867-7999
Web: www.nasa.gov

VETERANS AFFAIRS, DEPT. OF
VA Medical Ctr.
10,000 Bay Pines Blvd.
St. Petersburg, FL 33708
Karen S. Beaty, Small Business Specialist
Tel: (727) 398-6661 X5575
Fax: (727) 398-9536
Email: karen.beaty@med.va.gov
Web: www1.va.gov/visn8/baypines/

1201 NW 16th St.
Miami, FL 33125
Gwendolyn Moore, Chief of Procurement
Tel: (305) 575-7000 X3221
Fax: (305) 575-3266

Email: gwen.moore@med.va.gov
Web: www1.va.gov

1601 SW Archer Rd.
Gainesville, FL 32608-1197
Susan Little, Small Business Specialist
Tel: (386) 755-3016 X2095
Fax: (386) 758-3211
Email: susan.little@med.va.gov
Web: www.va.gov/osdbu

P.O. Box 33207
7305 N. Military Trail
West Palm Beach, FL 33410-6400
Dinora Bruno, Small Business Specialist
Tel: (561) 422-8262 X6511
Fax: (561) 422-6507
Email: dinora.bruno@med.va.gov
Web: www1.va.gov

13000 Bruce B. Downs Blvd.
Tampa, FL 33612
Cathy Tridlides, Small Business Specialist
Tel: (813) 972-7515 Fax: (813) 972-7572
Email: Cathy.Tridlides@med.va.gov
Web: www.va.gov/osdbu

GEORGIA

AGRICULTURE, DEPT. OF
Agricultural Research Service, South Atlantic Area
P.O. Box 5677, College Station Rd.
Athens, GA 30604
Mary LaRue, Supervisory Procurement Analyst
Tel: (706) 546-3532 Fax: (706) 546-3444
Email: laruem@saa.ars.usda.gov
Web: www.saa.ars.usda.gov

Natural Resources Conservation Service, Georgia State Office
Federal Bldg. #200, 355 E. Hancock Ave.
Athens, GA 30601
Holli Kuykendall, Acting State Administrative Officer
Tel: (706) 546-2272 Fax: (706) 546-2120
Email: holli.kuykendall@ga.usda.gov
Web: www.nrcs.usda.gov

Federal Bldg. #225, 355 E. Hancock Ave.
Athens, GA 30601
Carolyn Adams, Contracting Officer
Tel: (706) 546-2280 Fax: (706) 546-2157
Email: carolyn.adams@ga.usda.gov
Web: www.nrcs.usda.gov

COMMERCE, DEPT. OF
Minority Business Development Agency, Atlanta Regional Office
401 W. Peachtree St. NW #1715
Atlanta, GA 30308
Robert Henderson, Regional Director
Tel: (404) 730-3300 Fax: (404) 730-3313
Email: rhenderson@mbda.gov
Web: www.mbda.gov

Minority Business Development Ctr.
760 Spring St. NW
Atlanta, GA 30332-0640
Donna Ennis, Project Director
Tel: (404) 894-2096 Fax: (404) 894-1192
Email: donna.ennis@edi.gatech.edu
Web: www.georgiambdc.org

DEFENSE, DEPT. OF
US Air Force, 347th Contracting Squadron/CC-Air Combat Command, Small Business Office
4380B Alabama Rd.
Moody AFB, GA 31699-1793
Ailene B. Duff, Small Business Specialist/Director of Business Operations
Tel: (912) 257-4706 Fax: (229) 257-2638

Email: ailene.duff@moody.af.mil
Web: www.moody.af.mil

**US Air Force, 94 CONF/LGC,
Small Business Office**
1538 Atlantic Ave.
Dobbins ARB, GA 30069-4824
Linda K. Lewis, Chief of Contracting
Tel: (678) 655-4981 Fax: (678) 655-5612
Email: linda.lewis@dobbins.af.mil
Web: www.selltoairforce.org

**US Air Force, Warner-Robins Air
Logistics Ctr./BC-Air Force Materiel
Command, Small Business Office**
180 Page Rd.
Robins AFB, GA 31098-1600
James A. Lovett, Jr., Director
Tel: (478) 926-5873 Fax: (478) 926-2929
Email: jim.lovett@robins.af.mil
Web: www.robins.af.mil/smallbusiness/
index.htm

**ENERGY, DEPT. OF
Southeastern Power Administration**
1166 Athens Tech Rd.
Elberton, GA 30635-6711
Francis Deal, Small Business Program
Manager
Tel: (706) 213-3825 Fax: (706) 213-3884

**ENVIRONMENTAL PROTECTION AGENCY
Region IV, Office of Small and
Disadvantaged Business Utilization,
Minority Business Enterprise/ Women
Business Enterprise**
61 Forsyth St. SW
Atlanta, GA 30303-8960
Rafael Santamaria, MBE/WBE Coordinator
Tel: (404) 562-8110 Fax: (404) 562-8370
Email: santamaria.rafael@epa.gov
Web: www.epa.gov/osdbu

**HEALTH & HUMAN SERVICES, DEPT. OF
Ctr. for Disease Control and Prevention,
Procurement and Grants Office**
2920 Brandywine Rd. #1142
Atlanta, GA 30341
Curtis L. Bryant, Small Business Program
Manager
Tel: (770) 488-2806 Fax: (770) 488-2828
Email: ckb9@cdc.gov
Web: www.cdc.gov

**HOMELAND SECURITY, DEPT. OF
Federal Law Enforcement Training Ctr.,
Office of Small and Disadvantaged
Business Utilization, Procurement
Division**
Bldg., #93 #143 1131 Chapel Crossing Rd.
Glynco, GA 31524
Beverly Nesmith, Small Business Specialist
Tel: (912) 267-2449 Fax: (912) 280-5343
Email: beverly.nesmith@dhs.gov
Web: www.fletc.gov

**TREASURY, DEPT. OF THE
Internal Revenue Service, Southeast
Area Field Office**
2888 Woodcock Blvd. #300
Atlanta, GA 30341
Pat Hewitt , Small Business Specialist
(alternate)
Tel: (404) 338-9205 Fax: (404) 338-9203
Email: Patricia.Hewitt@irs.gov
Web: www.treas.gov

2888 Woodcock Blvd. #300
Atlanta, GA 30341
Lori Johnson, Small Business Specialist
Tel: (404) 338-9204 Fax: (404) 338-9203
Email: Lori.Johnson@irs.gov
Web: www.treas.gov

US POSTAL SERVICE

Atlanta District, Diversity Office
P.O. Box 599390
North Metro, GA 30026-9390
Barbara A. Danzy, Diversity Development
Specialist Manager
Tel: (770) 717-2992 Fax: (770) 717-2999
Email: Barbara.A.Danzy@usps.gov
Web: www.usps.gov

**VETERANS AFFAIRS, DEPT. OF
VA Medical Ctr.**
One Freedom Way
Augusta, GA 30904
Cindy Rogers, Procurement Analyst
Tel: (706) 481-6724 Fax: (706) 481-6741
Email: cindy.rogers2@med.va.gov
Web: www.va.gov/osdbu

HAWAII

**COMMERCE, DEPT. OF
Minority Business Development Agency,
Honolulu Minority Business
Development Ctr.**
1088 Bishop St. #2506
Honolulu, HI 96813
Jean Williams, Project Director
Tel: (808) 521-6221 Fax: (808) 524-3313
Email: jean@mbdc-honolulu.com
Web: www.mbdc-honolulu.com

**DEFENSE, DEPT. OF
US Air Force, 15th Contracting
Squadron**
90 G St.
Hickam AFB, HI 96853-5320
Jim Watanabe, Small Business Specialist
Tel: (808) 449-6860 X103
Fax: (808) 449-7026
Email: james.watanabe@hickam.af.mil
Web: www.hickam.af.mil

IDAHO

**AGRICULTURE, DEPT. OF
Forest Service**
1249 S. Vinnell Way #200
Boise, ID 83709
Diana Early, Procurement Assistant
Tel: (208) 373-4150 Fax: (208) 373-4197
Email: dearly@fs.fed.us

**DEFENSE, DEPT. OF
US Air Force, 366th Contracting
Squadron/CCD-Air Combat Command,
Small Business Office**
366 Gunfighter Ave. #498
Mountain Home AFB, ID 83648-5296
Marilyn Lemmon, Small Business Specialist
Tel: (208) 828-3106 Fax: (208) 828-6132
Email: marilyn.lemmon@mountainhome.
af.mil
Web: www.mountainhome.af.mil

**ENERGY, DEPT. OF
Idaho Operations Office**
1955 N. Fremont Ave.
Idaho Falls, ID 83401-1221
Trudy A. Harmel, Small Business Program
Manager
Tel: (208) 526-9519 Fax: (208) 526-5548
Email: harmelta@id.doe.gov
Web: www.id.doe.gov

**VETERANS AFFAIRS, DEPT. OF
VA Medical Ctr.**
500 W. Fort St.
Boise, ID 83702-4598
Amanda Glade, Purchasing Agent
Tel: (208) 422-1000 X1363 Fax: (208)
422-1139
Email: Amanda.Glade@med.gov
Web: www.va.gov/osdbu

ILLINOIS

**AGRICULTURE, DEPT. OF
Agricultural Research Service,
Midwestern Area**
1815 N. University St.
Peoria, IL 61604
Rebecca Holzinger, Area Procurement
Officer
Tel: (309) 681-6618 Fax: (309) 681-6683
Email: rholzinger@mwa.ars.usda.gov
Web: www.mwa.ars.usda.gov

**COMMERCE, DEPT. OF
Chicago Minority Business
Development Ctr.**
1 E. Wacker Dr.
Chicago, IL 60601
Steven Maduly-Williams, Project Director
Tel: (312) 755-8889 Fax: (312) 755-8891
Email: smwilliams@chiventures.org
Web: www.mbda.gov

**Minority Business Development Agency,
Chicago Minority Business Opportunity
Committee**
1 E. Wacker Dr. #1200
Chicago, IL 60601
Tracye E. Smith, Executive Director
Tel: (312) 755-8880 X15
Fax: (312) 755-8890
Email: tsmith@cmbdc.org
Web: www.cmbdc.org

**Minority Business Development Agency,
Chicago Regional Office**
55 E. Monroe St. #1406
Chicago, IL 60603
Eric Dobyne, Regional Director
Tel: (312) 353-0182 Fax: (312) 353-0191
Email: EDobyne@mbda.gov
Web: www.mbda.gov

**DEFENSE, DEPT. OF
US Air Force, 375th Contracting
Squadron/(AMC) (AF) Air Mobility
Command, Small Business Office**
201 E. Winters St., Bldg. 50
Scott AFB, IL 62225-5015
Garth Sanginiti, Small Business Specialist
Tel: (618) 256-9322 Fax: (618) 256-2649
Email: garth.sanginiti@scott.af.mil
Web: www.selltoairforce.org

**US Air Force, AMC Contracting Flight/
LGCF-Air Mobility Command, Small
Business Office**
507 Symington Dr. #W202
Scott AFB, IL 62225-5015
Cathy Simpson, Small Business Specialist
Tel: (618) 256-9995 Fax: (618) 256-5724
Email: Cathy.Simpson@scott.af.mil

**US Air Force, Contract Airlift Division/
DOY-Air Mobility Command, Small
Business Office**
H2 AMC/A34Y 402 Scott Dr. 3A1
Scott AFB, IL 62225-5302
Rodney D. Gilbert, Small Business
Specialist
Tel: (618) 229-2459 Fax: (618) 256-8316
Email: rod.gilbert@scott.af.mil
Web: www.public.amc.af.mil/business/
smallbiz/newsbpg.htm

**ENERGY, DEPT. OF
Argonne National Laboratory,
Procurement Department**
9700 S. Cass Ave., Bldg. 201
Argonne, IL 60439-4873
Diana Thompson, Small Business Liaison
Officer
Tel: (630) 252-6920 Fax: (630) 252-4517
Email: dlthompson@anl.gov

Chicago Operations Office
9800 S. Cass Ave.
Argonne, IL 60439
Larry Thompson, Small Business Program
Manager
Tel: (630) 252-2711 Fax: (630) 252-5045
Email: larry.thompson@ch.doe.gov
Web: www.ch.doe.gov

**Chicago Operations Office, Fermi
National Accelerator Laboratory**
P.O. Box 500
Batavia, IL 60510
Joe Collins, Small Business Program
Manager
Tel: (630) 840-4169 Fax: (630) 840-2457
Email: jcollins@fnal.gov
Web: www.fnal.gov

**ENVIRONMENTAL PROTECTION AGENCY
Region V, Office of Small and
Disadvantaged Business Utilization**
77 W. Jackson Blvd., M/C 10J
Chicago, IL 60604-3507
Sharon Green, Officer
Tel: (312) 353-5661 Fax: (312) 353-9096
Email: green.sharon@epa.gov
Web: www.epa.gov/region09/

**GENERAL SERVICES ADMINISTRATION
Small Business Utilization, Region V**
230 S. Dearborn St. #3718
Chicago, IL 60604
Beverly Coley, Small Business Specialist
Tel: (312) 353-1100 Fax: (312) 886-9893
Email: beverly.coley@gsa.gov
Web: www.gsa.gov

**VETERANS AFFAIRS, DEPT. OF
VA Healthcare System, VA Medical Ctr.**
333 E. Huron St.
Chicago, IL 60611
Michael J. Cunningham, Small Business
Specialist
Tel: (414) 902-5407 Fax: (414) 902-5440
Email: michael.cunningham@med.va.gov
Web: www.va.gov/osdbu

VA National Acquisition Ctr.
P.O. Box 76
Hines, IL 60141
Jay McLain, Small Business Specialist
Tel: (708) 786-5154 Fax: (708) 786-5223
Email: jay.mclain@med.va.gov
Web: www.va.gov/osdbu

INDIANA

**COMMERCE, DEPT. OF
Minority Business Development Agency,
Northwest Indiana Minority Business
Opportunity Committee**
504 Broadway St. #337
Gary, IN 46402
Lucia Dotson, Executive Director
Tel: (219) 886-9572 Fax: (219) 881-4999
Email: ldotson@nimboc.com
Web: www.nimboc.com

US Census Bureau, Procurement Office
1201 E. 10th St. #149, Bldg. 66
Jeffersonville, IN 47132
Connie Smith, Chief
Tel: (812) 218-3351 Fax: (812) 218-3937
Email: connie.smith@census.gov
Web: www.census.gov

**DEFENSE, DEPT. OF
US Air Force, 34 LG/LGC-Air Force
Reserve Command, Small Business
Office**
448 Mustang Ave.
Grissom AFB, IN 46971-5320

Patricia Craddock, Small Business Specialist
Tel: (765) 688-2801 Fax: (765) 688-2803
Email: patricia.craddock@grissom.af.mil
Web: www.selltoairforce.org

HOMELAND SECURITY, DEPT. OF
Customs and Border Protection,
Regional Office
P.O. Box 68905
6026 Lakeside Blvd.
Indianapolis, IN 46278
Beverly Tyree, Small Business Specialist
Tel: (317) 298-1180 Fax: (317) 298-1344
Web: www.ready.gov

STATE OF INDIANA
Dept. of Administration, Indianapolis
MBDC
402 W. Washington St. #W-469
Indianapolis, IN 46204
Ronalda Minnis, Deputy Comissioner
Tel: (317) 232-3061 Fax: (317) 233-6921
Email: RMinnis@idoa.state.in.us
Web: www.in.gov/idoa/minority

VETERANS AFFAIRS, DEPT. OF
Northern Indiana Healthcare Systems
2121 Lake Ave.
Ft. Wayne, IN 46805
Robert Nash, Small Business Specialist
Tel: (260) 426-5431 Fax: (260) 460-1336
Email: robert.nash@med.va.gov
Web: www.va.gov/osdbu

VA Medical Ctr.
1481 W. 10th St.
Indianapolis, IN 46202
Craig Earles, Small Business Specialist
Tel: (317) 554-0000 X2740
Fax: (317) 554-0200
Email: craig.earles@med.va.gov
Web: www.va.gov/osdbu

IOWA

ENERGY, DEPT. OF
Chicago Operations Office, Ames
Laboratory
Iowa State University, 211 TASF
Ames, IA 50011
Connie Heim, Small Business Program
Manager
Tel: (515) 294-4191 Fax: (515) 294-6166
Email: heimc@ameslab.gov
Web: www.ameslab.gov

VETERANS AFFAIRS, DEPT. OF
Central Plains Health Network, VA
Medical Ctr., Contracting Office
601 Hwy. 6 West
Iowa City, IA 52240
Patricia K. Parker, Contracting Officer
Tel: (319) 338-5081 Fax: (319) 339-7121
Email: patricia.parker@med.va.gov
Web: www.va.gov/osdbu

VA Medical Ctr.
1515 W. Pleasant St.
Knoxville, IA 50138
Steven Ethell, Small Business Specialist
Tel: (641) 828-5043 Fax: (641) 828-5083
Email: steven.ethell@med.va.gov
Web: www.va.gov/osdbu

KANSAS

DEFENSE, DEPT. OF
US Air Force, 22nd Air Refueling Wing/
LGC-Air Mobility Command,
Small Business Office
53147 Kansas St. #102

McConnell AFB, KS 67221-3606
Edward W. Harvell, Small Business Specialist
Tel: (316) 759-4505 Fax: (316) 759-4507
Email: ed.harvell@mcconnell.af.mil
Web: www.selltoairforce.org

ENVIRONMENTAL PROTECTION AGENCY
Region VII, Office of Small and
Disadvantaged Business Utilization
901 N. 5th St.
Kansas City, KS 66101
Chester Stovall, Officer
Tel: (913) 551-7549 Fax: (913) 551-7579
Email: stovall.chester@epa.gov
Web: www.epa.gov/osdbu

VETERANS AFFAIRS, DEPT. OF
VA Medical Ctr.
4101 S. 4th St., Traffic Way
Leavenworth, KS 66048
Marcus A. Clayton, Small Business Specialist
Tel: (913) 758-4281 Fax: (913) 758-6495
Email: marcus.clayton@med.va.gov
Web: www.va.gov/osdbu

KENTUCKY

AGRICULTURE, DEPT. OF
Natural Resources Conservation
Service
771 Corporate Dr. #210
Lexington, KY 40503-5479
Connie McKinney, Contract Specialist
Tel: (859) 224-7395 Fax: (859) 224-7393
Email: connie.mckinney@ky.usda.gov

VETERANS AFFAIRS, DEPT. OF
VA Medical Ctr.
800 Zorn Ave.
Louisville, KY 40202
Robert Hubert, Small Business Specialist
Tel: (502) 287-4000 X55312
Fax: (502) 287-6225
Web: www.va.gov

LOUISIANA

AGRICULTURE, DEPT. OF
National Finance Ctr.
13800 Old Gentilly Rd.
New Orleans, LA 70129
Deidre V. Phillips, Head of Contracting Support Team
Tel: (504) 426-0281
Email: deidre.phillips@usda.gov
Web: www.nfc.usda.gov

Natural Resources Conservation
Service
3737 Government St.
Alexandria, LA 71302
Ralph E. Broome, Contracting Officer
Tel: (318) 473-7781 Fax: (318) 473-7831
Email: ralph.broome@la.usda.gov
Web: www.la.nrcs.usda.gov

DEFENSE, DEPT. OF
US Air Force, 2nd Contracting
Squadron/CCD-Air Combat Command,
Small Business Office
841 Fairchild Ave. #205
Barksdale AFB, LA 71110-2271
Connie Shirley, Small Business Specialist
Tel: (318) 456-6940 Fax: (318) 456-2629
Email: connie.shirley@barksdale.af.mil
Web: www.barksdale.af.mil

ENERGY, DEPT. OF
Strategic Petroleum Reserve, Project
Management Office

900 Commerce Rd. E.
New Orleans, LA 70123
Geralyn "Geri" Champagne-Funk, Small Business Program Manager
Tel: (504) 734-4766 Fax: (504) 818-5766
Email: geralyn.champagne@spr.doe.gov
Web: www.spr.doe.gov

Strategic Petroleum Reserves Project
Management Office, Dyn McDermott
Petroleum Operations Co.
850 S. Clearview Pkwy.
New Orleans, LA 70123
Steven E. Haines, Diversity Subcontracting Program Manager
Tel: (504) 734-4394 Fax: (504) 818-5394
Email: steve.haines@spr.doe.gov
Web: www.spr.doe.gov

VETERANS AFFAIRS, DEPT. OF
VA Medical Ctr.
P.O. Box 69004
Alexandria, LA 71306-9004
Herman Chelette, Small Business Specialist
Tel: (318) 473-0010 X2239
Fax: (318) 483-5063
Email: herman.chelette@med.va.gov
Web: www.va.gov/osdbu

1601 Perdido St.
New Orleans, LA 70112
Denise Smith, Small Business Specialist
Tel: (504) 589-5280 Fax: (504) 589-5289
Email: denise.smith3@med.va.gov
Web: www.va.gov/osdbu

Veterans Integrated Service Network,
VA Medical Ctr.
510 E. Stoner Ave.
Shreveport, LA 71101-4295
Terry Galbraith, Chief of Acquisitions & Material Management
Tel: (318) 424-6034 Fax: (318) 424-6078
Email: terry.galbraith@med.va.gov
Web: www.va.gov/osdbu

MAINE

VETERANS AFFAIRS, DEPT. OF
VA Medical Ctr.
1 VA Ctr.
Togus, ME 04330
Kathleen Burnham, Small Business Specialist
Tel: (207) 623-5717 Fax: (207) 621-7325
Email: kathy.burnham@med.va.gov
Web: www.va.gov

MARYLAND

AGRICULTURE, DEPT. OF
Agricultural Research Service
10300 Baltimore Blvd. BARC-WEST,
Bldg. 003 #329
Beltsville, MD 20705
Michael Wyckoff, Supervisory Procurement Analyst
Tel: (301) 504-7019 X452
Fax: (301) 504-5009
Email: wyckoffm@ba.ars.usda.gov
Web: www.ba.ars.usda.gov

Agricultural Research Service
5601 Sunnyside Ave., M/S 5124
Beltsville, MD 20705-5124
Dennis Foley, Contract Specialist
Tel: (301) 504-1704 Fax: (301) 504-1717
Email: dfoley@ars.usda.gov
Web: www.afm.ars.usda.gov

Food Safety and Inspection Service,
Procurement and Property Branch

5601 Sunnyside Ave. #5320,
Beltsville Office Facility
Beltsville, MD 20705-5230
Diane Furr, Contrating Specialist
Tel: (301) 504-4211 Fax: (301) 504-4276
Email: Diane.Furr@usda.gov

FSIS, ASD, AAS
5601 Sunnyside Ave., M/S 5230
Beltsville, MD 20705-5230
Madonna Langley, Contracting Officer
Tel: (301) 504-4228 Fax: (301) 504-4276
Email: madonna.langley@usda.gov
Web: www.fsis.usda.gov

USDA-ARS-AFM-FD-FCB
5601 Sunnyside Ave., M/S 5124
Beltsville, MD 20705-5124
Regina Herchak, Procurement Analyst
Tel: (301) 504-1179 Fax: (301) 504-1187
Email: rherchak@ars.usda.gov
Web: www.afm.ars.usda.gov/fd/FCB.htm

COMMERCE, DEPT. OF
Minority Business Development Agency,
National Capital Minority Business
Opportunity Committee
4640 Forbes Blvd. #200
Lanham, MD 20706
Nicola Shaw, Executive Director
Tel: (301) 429-2168 Fax: (301) 429-8762
Email: nshaw@ncmboc.com
Web: www.ncmboc.com

National Institute of Standards &
Technology, Acquisitions & Assistance
Division, Small Business Office
100 Bureau Dr., Bldg. 301 #B-129
Gaithersburg, MD 20899-3570
Henry M. Levy, Small Business Specialist
Tel: (301) 975-6343 Fax: (301) 975-8884
Email: henry.levy@nist.gov
Web: www.nist.gov

National Institute of Standards &
Technology, Acquisitions & Assistance
Division
100 Bureau Dr.,
Bldg. 301 #B-129,
M/S 3570
Gaithersburg, MD 20899
Phyllis Bower, Chief of Acquisition Division
Tel: (301) 975-6348 Fax: (301) 926-0628
Web: www.nist.gov

National Institute of Standards &
Technology, Acquisitions & Logistic
Division
100 Bureau Dr., Bldg. 301 #B-147
Gaithersburg, MD 20899-3570
Barbara Camp, Procurement Analyst
Tel: (301) 975-6338 Fax: (301) 975-6319
Email: barbara.camp@nist.gov
Web: www.nist.gov

COMMERCE, DEPT. OF
National Oceanic and Atmospheric
Administration, Acquisition & Grants
Management, OFA, Acquisition
Management Division
1305 East-West Hwy. #7604
Silver Spring, MD 20910
Gary Rice, Director
Tel: (301) 713-0839 X190
Fax: (301) 713-0809
Email: gary.rice@noaa.gov
Web: www.rdc.noaa.gov

1305 East-West Hwy. Bldg. 4
Silver Spring, MD 20910-3281
Robert Ransom, Head of Contracting
Tel: (301) 713-0820x108
Fax: (301) 713-0809
Email: Robert.Ransom@noaa.gov

Web: www.rdc.noaa.gov

1315 East-West Hwy. #10100
Silver Spring, MD 20910
Dick Bennett, Director
Tel: (301) 713-3478 x170
Fax: (301) 713-4155
Email: Dick.Bennett@noaa.gov
Web: www.rdc.noaa.gov

National Oceanic and Atmospheric Administration, Acquisition & Grants Office, National Weather Service, Acquisitions and Management Division
1325 East-West Hwy., SSMC2 #1530
Silver Spring, MD 20910
Tel: (301) 713-3405 Fax: (301) 713-1024
Web: www.rdc.noaa.gov

National Oceanic and Atmospheric Administration, Acquisition & Grants Office
1335 East-West Hwy. #6300
Silver Spring, MD 20910
Helen Hurcombe, Director
Tel: (301) 713-0325 Fax: (301) 713-1974
Email: helen.hurcombe@noaa.gov
Web: www.rdc.noaa.gov

COMMERCE, DEPT. OF
US Census Bureau, Procurement Office
4700 Silver Hill Rd. #G-314
Suitland, MD 20746
Michael Palensky, Chief
Tel: (301) 763-1818 Fax: (301) 457-1785
Email: michael.l.palensky@census.gov
Web: www.census.gov

DEFENSE, DEPT. OF
Naval Air Warfare Ctr. Aircraft Division, Small Business Office
21983 Bundy Rd., Bldg. 441
Patuxen River, MD 20670-1127
Estella Balmaceda, Deputy for Small Business
Tel: (301) 757-9087 Fax: (301) 757-9093
Email: Estella.Balmaceda@navy.mil
Web: www.navair.navy.mil

US Air Force, 89th Airlift Wing/LGC-Air Mobility Command, Small Business Office
1419 Menoher Dr.
Andrews AFB, MD 20762-6500
Sandra Foster, Small Business Specialist
Tel: (301) 981-6509 Fax: (301) 981-6538
Email: sandra.foster@andrews.af.mil
Web: public.andrews.amc.af.mil/index.asp

US Army Aberdeen Proving Ground, Office Small Business
Attn.: AMSRD-SB, Aberdeen Proving Ground, Bldg. E-4455
Aberdeen, MD 21010-5424
John Rasmusen, Small Business Officer
Tel: (410) 436-3136 Fax: (410) 436-7744
Web: www.sbccom.army.mil

HEALTH & HUMAN SERVICES, DEPT. OF
Agency for Healthcare Research and Quality, Office of Small and Disadvantaged Business Utilization
540 Gaither Rd.
Rockville, MD 20850
Jacquelyn Carey, Acting Small Business Program Manager
Tel: (301) 427-1780 Fax: (301) 427-1740
Email: jcarey@ahrq.gov
Web: www.ahrq.gov

Ctrs. for Medicare & Medicaid Services
7500 Security Blvd. M/C C2-21-15
Baltimore, MD 21244-1850
Joanne Day, Small Business Specialist
Tel: (410) 786-5166 Fax: (410) 786-9922
Web: cms.hhs.gov

Ctrs. for Medicare & Medicaid Services, OICS/Acquisition and Grants Group, Acquisition Support and Policy
7500 Security Blvd. M/C C2-21-15
Baltimore, MD 21244-1850
Sharon McKinney, Small Business Program Manager
Tel: (410) 786-5162 Fax: (410) 786-9088
Email: smckinney@cms.hhs.gov
Web: cms.hhs.gov

Food & Drug Administration, Office of Facilities, Acquisition and Central Services
5600 Fishers Ln. #12A43 M/C HFA630
Rockville, MD 20857
Ron Loube, Small Business Program Manager
Tel: (301) 827-7031 Fax: (301) 827-7233
Email: rloube@oc.fda.gov
Web: www.fda.gov

Health Resources & Services Administration, Office of Equal Opportunity & Civil Rights
5600 Fishers Ln. #13A-03 Parklawn Bldg.
Rockville, MD 20857
Steve Zangwill, Small Business Adviser
Tel: (301) 443-2750 Fax: (301) 443-8254
Email: szangwill@hrsa.gov
Web: www.hrsa.gov

Indian Health Service, Office of Management Support
12300 Twinbrook Pkwy. #450-A
Rockville, MD 20852
Nelia K. Holder, Small Business Specialist
Tel: (301) 443-1480 Fax: (301) 443-0929
Email: nholder@hqe.ihs.gov
Web: www.ihs.gov

National Cancer Institute, Office of Small and Disadvantaged Business Utilization
6120 Executive Blvd. #6038,
Executive Plz. South
Bethesda, MD 20892
Joseph Bowe, Small Business Program Manager
Tel: (301) 435-3810 Fax: (301) 480-0309
Email: jb166i@nih.gov
Web: www.nih.gov

National Institutes of Health, Small Business Office
6100 Executive Blvd. #6D05, M/S 7540
Bethesda, MD 20892-7540
Diana Mukitarian, Chief
Tel: (301) 496-9639 Fax: (301) 480-2506
Email: sbmail@od.nih.gov
Web: sbo.od.nih.gov

Program Support Ctr., Division of Acquisition Management
5600 Fishers Ln. #5C-26, Parklawn Bldg.
Rockville, MD 20857
Linda Danley, Small Business Specialist
Tel: (301) 443-1715 Fax: (301) 443-7593
Email: linda.danley@psc.hhs.gov
Web: www.psc.gov

Substance Abuse & Mental Health Services Administration, Office of Small and Disadvantaged Business Utilization
5600 Fishers Ln. #13-99
Rockville, MD 20785
Vivian C. Kim, M.A., Small Business Program Manager
Tel: (301) 443-8843 Fax: (301) 443-0839
Email: vivian.kim@samhsa.hhs.gov
Web: www.samhas.gov

NATIONAL AERONAUTICS & SPACE ADMINISTRATION (NASA)

Goddard Space Flight Ctr.
M/C 210
Greenbelt, MD 20771
Gilberto Del Valle, Procurement Analyst
Tel: (301) 286-8136 Fax: (301) 286-1746
Email: gilberto.delvalle-1@nasa.gov
Web: procurement.nasa.gov

M/C 210
Greenbelt, MD 20771
Rosa Acevedo, Procurement Analyst
Tel: (301) 286-4679 Fax: (301) 286-0237
Email: Rosa.E.Acevedo@nasa.gov
Web: procurement.nasa.gov

NUCLEAR REGULATORY COMMISSION
Office of Small Business and Civil Rights
11545 Rockville Pike, M/S T2F18
Rockville, MD 20852
Mauricio Vera, Small Business Program Manager
Tel: (301) 415-7160 Fax: (301) 415-5953
Email: mxv@nrc.gov
Web: www.nrc.gov/who-we-are/small-business.html

11545 Rockville Pike, M/S T2F18
Rockville, MD 20555
Corenthis B. Kelley, Director
Tel: (301) 415-7380 Fax: (301) 415-5953
Email: cbk@nrc.gov
Web: www.nrc.gov

SOCIAL SECURITY ADMINISTRATION
Office of Small and Disadvantaged Business Utilization
1710 Gwynn Oak Ave.
Baltimore, MD 21207-5279
Wayne Mcdonald, Director
Tel: (410) 965-7467 Fax: (410) 965-2965
Email: wayne.mcdonald@ssa.gov
Web: www.ssa.gov/oag

1710 Gwynn Oak Ave.
Baltimore, MD 21207
Pat Bullock, Small Business Specialist
Tel: (410) 965-9457 Fax: (410) 965-2965
Email: pat.bullock@ssa.gov
Web: www.ssa.gov/oag

TREASURY, DEPT. OF THE
Internal Revenue Service National Office
Constellation Ctr.,
5th Fl. A:P:P 6009 Oxon Hill Rd.
Oxon Hill, MD 20745
Jodie L. Paustian, Small Business Specialist
Tel: (202) 283-1350 Fax: (202) 283-1529
Email: Jodie.L.Paustian@irs.gov
Web: www.procurement.irs.treas.gov

DEFENSE, DEPT. OF
US Air Force, 439th LSS/LGC-Air Force Reserve Command, Small Business Office
250 Airlift Dr.
Westover ARB, MA 01022-1525
Michael LaFortune, Small Business Specialist
Tel: (413) 557-3508 Fax: (413) 557-2017
Email: michael.lafortune@westover.af.mil
Web: www.selltoairforce.org

US Air Force, Electronic Systems Ctr./ BC-Air Force Materiel Command, Small Business Office
275 Randolph Rd.
Hanscom AFB, MA 01731-2818
Bill Donaldson, Small Business Specialist

Tel: (781) 377-4973 Fax: (781) 377-3015
Email: bill.donaldson@hanscom.af.mil
Web: www.herbb.hanscom.af.mil

US Army Soldiers Systems Ctr., Biological and Chemical Command, Small Business Office
258 Kansas St.
Natick, MA 01760-5008
David Condon, Small Business Specialist
Tel: (508) 233-4995 Fax: (508) 233-4676
Email: david.condon@natick.army.mil
Web: www.natick.army.mil/soldier/business

ENVIRONMENTAL PROTECTION AGENCY
Region I, Office of Small and Disadvantaged Business Utilization
John F. Kennedy Federal Bldg.,
1 Congress St.
Boston, MA 02203
Sharon Molden, Officer
Tel: (617) 918-1062 Fax: (617) 918-1909
Email: molden.sharon@epa.gov
Web: www.epa.gov/osdbu

GENERAL SERVICES ADMINISTRATION
Small Business Utilization, Region I
O'Neill Federal Bldg.,
10 Causeway St. #901
Boston, MA 02222
France A. Lopez, Small Business Director
Tel: (617) 565-8100 Fax: (617) 565-8101
Email: france.lopez@gsa.gov
Web: www.gsa.gov

VETERANS AFFAIRS, DEPT. OF
VA Medical Ctr.
150 S. Huntington Ave.
Boston, MA 02130
Marianne Leblanc, Small Business Specialist
Tel: (617) 232-9500 X5535
Fax: (617) 278-4546
Email: marianne.leblanc@med.va.gov
Web: www.va.gov/osdbu

200 Springs Rd.
Bedford, MA 01730
Richard Terramagra, Contract Specialist
Tel: (781) 687-2368 Fax: (781) 687-2661
Email: richard.terramagra@med.va.gov
Web: www1.va.gov

421 N. Main St.
Leeds, MA 01053
Douglas Brown, Small Business Specialist
Tel: (413) 582-3093 Fax: (413) 582-3119
Email: douglas.brown2@med.va.gov
Web: www.va.gov/osdbu

AGRICULTURE, DEPT. OF
Natural Resources Conservation Service, State Office
3001 Coolidge Rd. #250
East Lansing, MI 48823
Bonnie Kilgore, Contract Specialist
Tel: (517) 324-5243 Fax: (517) 324-5287
Email: bonnie.kilgore@mi.usda.gov
Web: www.mi.nrcs.usda.gov

VETERANS AFFAIRS, DEPT. OF
Aleda E. Lutz VA Medical Ctr.
1500 Weiss St.
Saginaw, MI 48602
Joseph Roberts, Small Business Specialist
Tel: (989) 497-2500 X3806
Fax: (989) 791-2221
Email: Joseph.Roberts@med.va.gov
Web: www.va.gov/osdbu

VETERANS AFFAIRS, DEPT. OF
VA Medical Ctr.

2215 Fuller Rd.
Ann Arbor, MI 48105
Brenda M. Johnson, Small Business Specialist
Tel: (734) 769-7100 X5246
Fax: (734) 213-3833
Email: brenda.johnson3@med.va.gov
Web: www.va.gov/osdbu

5600 W. Dickman Rd.
Battle Creek, MI 49016
Linda J. Cunic, Small Business Specialist
Tel: (269) 966-5600 X3075
Fax: (269) 966-5518
Email: linda.cunic@med.va.gov
Web: www.va.gov/osdbu

MINNESOTA

AGRICULTURE, DEPT. OF
Forest Service, North Central Research Station
1992 Folwell Ave.
St. Paul, MN 55108
Cindy Johnson, Group Leader, Acquisitions Manager
Tel: (651) 649-5203 Fax: (651) 649-5285
Email: cjohnson06@fs.fed.us
Web: www.fs.fed.us

1992 Folwell Ave.
St. Paul, MN 55108
Carol A. Hulstrom, Contract Specialist
Tel: (651) 649-5201 Fax: (651) 649-5285
Email: chulstrom@fs.fed.us
Web: www.fs.fed.us

DEFENSE, DEPT. OF
US Air Force, 934 LG/LGC-Air Force Reserve Command, Small Business Office
760 Military Hwy.
Minneapolis, MN 55450-2100
Darcee Copus-Sabart, Small Business Specialist
Tel: (612) 713-1432 Fax: (612) 713-1425
Email: darcee.copus-sabart@minneapolis.af.mil
Web: www.selltoairforce.org

VETERANS AFFAIRS, DEPT. OF
VA Medical Ctr.
4801 Veterans Dr.
St. Cloud, MN 56303
Wendy Hoeschen, Small Business Specialist
Tel: (320) 255-6307 Fax: (320) 255-6341
Email: wendy.hoeschen@med.va.gov
Web: www1.va.gov

VA Medical Ctr. (618/90C)
1 Veterans Dr.
Minneapolis, MN 55417
Linda Kelly, Small Business Specialist
Tel: (612) 725-2183 Fax: (612) 725-2072
Email: linda.kelly2@med.va.gov
Web: www.va.gov/osdbu

MISSISSIPPI

AGRICULTURE, DEPT. OF
Agricultural Research Service
P.O. Box 225
Stoneville, MS 38776
Terry Krutz, Procurement Realty Specialist
Tel: (662) 686-5361 Fax: (662) 686-5373
Email: tkrutz@ars.usda.gov
Web: www.ars.usda.gov

Forest Service, R8/R9 Western Operations Ctr., Procurement
A.H. McCoy Federal Bldg. #1141,

100 W. Capitol St.
Jackson, MS 39269-1199
Byron Brown, Procurement Officer
Tel: (601) 965-4391 X155
Fax: (601) 965-4391
Email: bbbrown@fs.fed.us
Web: www.fs.fed.us

Natural Resources Conservation Service
A.H. McCoy Federal Bldg. #1321,
100 W. Capitol St.
Jackson, MS 39269
Matleaner B. Spann, State Administrative Officer
Tel: (601) 965-5183 Fax: (601) 965-4940
Email: matleaner.spann@ms.usda.gov
Web: www.ms.nrcs.usda.gov

COMMERCE, DEPT. OF
National Oceanic and Atmospheric Administration, National Data Buoy Ctr., Program Support Division
Bldg. 1100 #360
Stennis Space Ctr., MS 39529-6000
Dennis E. Morris, Small Business Specialist/ Small Purchases
Tel: (228) 688-1706 Fax: (228) 688-3153
Email: Dennis.Morris@noaa.gov
Web: www.noaa.gov

DEFENSE, DEPT. OF
US Air Force, 14th Contracting Squadron/CC-Air Education and Training Command, Small Business Office
555 7th St. #113
Columbus AFB, MS 39710-1006
Neo Cole, Small Business Specialist
Tel: (662) 434-7802 Fax: (662) 434-7764
Email: neo.cole@columbus.af.mil
Web: www.columbus.af.mil/Cons/welcome.htm

US Air Force, 81st Contracting Squadron/CCB-Air Education and Training Command, Small Business Office
310 M St. #102
Keesler AFB, MS 39534-2147
Linda Falks, Small Business Specialist
Tel: (228) 377-3131 Fax: (228) 377-9775
Email: linda.falks@keesler.af.mil
Web: www.selltoairforce.org

NATIONAL AERONAUTICS & SPACE ADMINISTRATION (NASA)
John C. Stennis Space Ctr., Procurement Office
M/C DA30
Stennis Space Ctr., MS 39529-6000
Jane Johnson, Small & Minority Business Specialist
Tel: (228) 688-3681 Fax: (228) 688-1141
Email: jane.johnson@ssc.nasa.gov
Web: www.ssc.nasa.gov

VETERANS AFFAIRS, DEPT. OF
VA Medical Ctr.
1500 E. Woodrow Wilson Dr.
Jackson, MS 39216
Brenda Stewart, Small Business Specialist
Tel: (601) 364-1361 Fax: (601) 364-1346
Email: brenda.stewart@med.va.gov
Web: www.va.gov/osdbu

VA Medical Ctr., Acquisitions
400 Veterans Blvd.
Biloxi, MS 39531
Kenneth W. Johns, Small Business Specialist
Tel: (228) 563-2692 X2692
Fax: (228) 563-2675
Email: kenneth.johns@med.va.gov
Web: www.va.gov/osdbu

MISSOURI

AGRICULTURE, DEPT. OF
Farm Service Agency
6501 Beacon Dr. M/S 8698
Kansas City, MO 64133
Betty Kunkel, Small Business Specialist
Tel: (816) 926-3295 Fax: (816) 823-4034
Email: bakunkel@kcc.usda.gov
Web: www.fsa.usda.gov/mo/

Farm Service Agency, Kansas City Commodity Office
P.O. Box 419205 M/S 8748
Kansas City, MO 64141-6205
Todd Shuck, Contract Officer
Tel: (816) 823-1114 Fax: (816) 823-1804
Email: tashuck@kcc.usda.gov
Web: www.fsa.usda.gov

6501 Beacon Dr., M/S 8738
Kansas City, MO 64133
Austen Merrick, Chief, Export Operations Division
Tel: (816) 926-6715 Fax: (816) 823-1640
Email: admerrick@kcc.usda.gov

National Information Technology Ctr.
8930 Ward Pkwy.
Kansas City, MO 64114
Regina Allen, Procurement Specialist
Tel: (816) 926-2719 Fax: (816) 926-2804
Email: regina.allen@usda.gov

COMMERCE, DEPT. OF
National Oceanic and Atmospheric Administration, Acquisition Management Division
601 E. 12th St. #1756
Kansas City, MO 64106
Sharon Webster Tyson, Small Business Specialist
Tel: (816) 426-7267 X222
Fax: (816) 426-7530
Email: Sharon.K.Tyson@noaa.gov
Web: www.ofa.noaa.gov

DEFENSE, DEPT. OF
US Air Force, 509th Contracting Squadron/CCV-Air Combat Command, Small Business Office
727 2nd St. #124A
Whiteman AFB, MO 65305-5344
Bill Krause, Small Business Specialist
Tel: (660) 687-3641 Fax: (660) 687-5418
Email: william.krause@whiteman.af.mil
Web: www.whiteman.af.mil/509cons/509cons.html

ENERGY, DEPT. OF
Albuquerque Operations Office, Honeywell Federal Manufacturing & Technologies, LLC
P.O. Box 419159, Dept. 626, M/S 0C44
Kansas City, MO 64141-6159
C. J. Warrick, Small Business Program Manager
Tel: (816) 997-2874 Fax: (816) 997-5063
Email: cwarrick@kcp.com
Web: www.kcp.com

GENERAL SERVICES ADMINISTRATION
Small Business Utilization, Region VI
1500 E. Bannister Rd.
Kansas City, MO 64131
Lois Phillips, Small Business Specialist
Tel: (816) 926-7203 Fax: (816) 823-1167
Email: lois.phillips@gsa.gov
Web: www.r6.gsa.gov

MONTANA

DEFENSE, DEPT. OF
US Air Force, 341st Contracting Squadron/LGC-Air Force Space Command, Small Business Office
7015 Goddard Dr.
Malmstrom AFB, MT 59402-6863
Mark Roush, Small Business Specialist
Tel: (406) 731-4017
Web: www.malmstrom.af.mil

VETERANS AFFAIRS, DEPT. OF
VA Medical Ctr.
P.O. Box 187
Fort Harrison, MT 59636
Daniel Herrera, Procurement Analyst
Tel: (406) 447-7305 Fax: (406) 447-7916
Web: www.va.gov/osdbu

NEBRASKA

DEFENSE, DEPT. OF
US Air Force, 55th Contracting Squadron/CCD-Air Combat Command, Small Business Office
101 Washington Sq.
Offutt AFB, NE 68113-2107
Cindy Beyer, Small Business Specialist
Tel: (402) 232-5676 Fax: (402) 232-6375
Email: cindy.beyer@offutt.af.mil
Web: www.offutt.af.mil

VETERANS AFFAIRS, DEPT. OF
VA Medical Ctr.
2201 N. Broadwell Ave.
Grand Island, NE 68801
Leigh Porter, Small Business Specialist
Tel: (308) 382-3660 X7915
Fax: (308) 385-2712
Email: leigh.porter@med.va.gov
Web: www.va.gov/osdbu

NEVADA

DEFENSE, DEPT. OF
US Air Force, 99th Contracting Squadron/CC-Air Combat Command, Small Business Office
5865 Swaab Blvd.
Nellis AFB, NV 89191-7063
George Salton, Small Business Specialist
Tel: (702) 652-4003 Fax: (702) 652-5405
Email: george.salton@nellis.af.mil
Web: www.selltoairforce.org

ENERGY, DEPT. OF
Yucca Mountain Site Characterization Office
P.O. Box 364629
Las Vegas, NV 89036
Birdie Hamilton Ray, Director/Contracting
Tel: (702) 794-5886 Fax: (702) 794-5557
Email: birdie_hamilton-ray@ymp.gov
Web: www.ocrwm.doe.gov

NEW HAMPSHIRE

DEFENSE, DEPT. OF
Naval Shipyard, Purchasing Division
Portsmouth Naval Shipyard M/C 530SB
Portsmouth, NH 03801-2590
Michael Levesque, Deputy for Small Business
Tel: (207) 438-1630 Fax: (207) 438-1251
Email: levesquemj@mail.ports.navy.mil
Web: www.ports.navy.mil

VETERANS AFFAIRS, DEPT. OF

VA Medical Ctr.
718 Smyth Rd.
Manchester, NH 03104
Richard Marino, Contracting Specialist
Tel: (603) 624-4366 X6506
Fax: (603) 626-6577
Email: Richard.Marino@med.va.gov
Web: www1.va.gov

NEW JERSEY

COMMERCE, DEPT. OF
Minority Business Development Agency, New Jersey Statewide Minority Business Development Ctr.
744 Broad St. #1812
Newark, NJ 07102
Lorraine Kelsey, Project Director
Tel: (973) 297-1142 Fax: (973) 297-1439
Email: LKelsey@newjersey-mbdc.com
Web: www.newjersey-mbdc.com

DEFENSE, DEPT. OF
Naval Air Warfare Ctr. Aircraft Division, Small Business Office
Hwy. 547 Code Air-09c4
Lakehurst, NJ 08733-5082
Patricia Kohanyi, Deputy for Small Business
Tel: (732) 323-7535 Fax: (732) 323-2908
Email: patricia.kohanyi@navy.mil
Web: wingspan.navair.navy.mil

US Air Force, 305th Air Mobility Wing/ LGC-Air Mobility Command, Small Business Office
2402 Vandenberg Ave.
McGuire AFB, NJ 08641-1712
Lidija Erazo, Small Business Specialist
Tel: (609) 754-5929 Fax: (609) 724-3735
Email: lidija.erazo@mcguire.af.mil
Web: public.mcguire.amc.af.mil/

US Army Armament Research, Development & Engineering Ctr.
Attn.: AMSTA-AR-SB
Picatinny Arsenal, NJ 07860-5000
Richard A. Burdett, Small Business Specialist
Tel: (973) 724-4106 Fax: (973) 724-3002
Email: rburdett@pica.army.mil
Web: www.pica.army.mil

US Army Communications-Electronic Command, SADBU
HQ-CECOM, Attn.: AMSEL-SB
Fort Monmouth, NJ 07703-5005
Kevin Loesch, Chief, Small Business
Tel: (732) 532-4511 Fax: (732) 532-8732
Email: kevin.loesch@mail1.monmouth.army.mil
Web: www.sadbu.cecom.army.mil/sadbu

NEW MEXICO

COMMERCE, DEPT. OF
Minority Business Development Agency, New Mexico Statewide Minority Business Development Ctr.
718 Central Ave. SW
Albuquerque, NM 87102
Anna Muller, Project Director
Tel: (505) 843-7114 Fax: (505) 242-2030
Email: inso@nedainc.net
Web: www.mbda.gov

DEFENSE, DEPT. OF
US Air Force, 27 LGC/CD-Air Combat Command, Small Business Office
511 N. Torch Blvd.
Cannon AFB, NM 88103-5109

Eddie West, Small Business Specialist
Tel: (505) 784-2321 Fax: (505) 681-2322
Email: Eddie.West@cannon.af.mil
Web: www.cannon.af.mil

US Air Force, 49th Contracting Squadron/COV-Air Combat Command, Small Business Office
1210 Forty Niner Ave.
Holloman AFB, NM 88330-7908
Francis Eggert, Small Business Specialist
Tel: (505) 572-3048 Fax: (505) 572-5456
Web: www.holloman.af.mil

US Air Force, AFRL/VS, Small Business Office
2000 Wyoming Blvd. SE, Bldg. 20604
Kirtland AFB, NM 87117-5060
Joan Fulkerson, Small Business Specialist
Tel: (505) 846-8515 Fax: (505) 846-4919
Email: joan.fulkerson@kirtland.af.mil
Web: www.de.afrl.af.mil

US Air Force, HQ AFOTEC/Air Force Operational Test and Evaluation Ctr., Small Business Office
8500 Gibson Blvd. SE
Kirtland AFB, NM 87117
Sherry Freeman, Small Business Specialist
Tel: (505) 846-5627 Fax: (505) 846-2414
Email: sherry.freeman@afotec.af.mil
Web: www.afotec.af.mil

US Army White Sands Missile Range, Small Business Office
Bldg. 143 Crozier St.
White Sands Missile Range, NM 88002
Ron Taft, Small Business Advisor
Tel: (505) 678-1401 Fax: (505) 678-3883
Email: taftr@wsmr.army.mil
Web: www.wsmr.army.mil/docpage/docpage.htm

ENERGY, DEPT. OF
Albuquerque Operations Office, Los Alamos National Laboratory
P.O. Box 1663 M/S P201
Los Alamos, NM 87545
Teresa Trujillo, Small Business Program Manager
Tel: (505) 667-4410 Fax: (505) 667-9819
Email: tere@lanl.gov
Web: www.lanl.gov

Albuquerque Operations Office, Sandia National Laboratories
P.O. Box 5800 M/S 0201
Albuquerque, NM 87185-0201
Julia DeLaCruz, Business Consultant
Tel: (505) 844-9869 Fax: (505) 844-7468
Email: jdelacr@sandia.gov
Web: www.sandia.gov/supplier

Albuquerque Operations Office, Westinghouse TRU Solutions, Waste Isolation Pilot Plant
P.O. Box 2078
Carlsbad, NM 88220
Bob Prentiss, Small Business Program Manager
Tel: (505) 234-3264 Fax: (505) 234-3196
Email: bob.prentiss@wipp.ws
Web: www.wipp.ws

National Nuclear Security Administration, Service Ctr.
P.O. Box 5400
Albuquerque, NM 87185
Greg Gonzales, Small Business Program Manager
Tel: (505) 845-6182 Fax: (505) 845-4210

Email: ggonzales@doeal.gov
Web: www.doeal.gov

NEW YORK

AGRICULTURE, DEPT. OF
Natural Resources Conservation Service
441 S. Salina St. #354
Syracuse, NY 13202
Laureen M. Eipp, Contract Specialist
Tel: (315) 477-6522 Fax: (315) 477-6560
Email: laureen.eipp@ny.usda.gov
Web: www.ny.nrcs.usda.gov

COMMERCE, DEPT. OF
Minority Business Development Agency, Manhattan/Bronx Minority Business Development Ctr.
350 5th Ave.
New York, NY 10118
Lora Trimingham, Assistant Director
Tel: (212) 947-5351 Fax: (212) 947-1506
Email: LTrimingham@manhattan-bronx-mbdc.com
Web: www.manhattan-bronx-mbdc.org

Minority Business Development Agency, New York Regional Office
26 Federal Plz. #3720
New York, NY 10278
Heyward Davenport, Regional Director
Tel: (212) 264-3262 Fax: (212) 264-0725
Email: HDavenport@mbda.gov
Web: www.mbda.gov

Queens/Brooklyn Minority Business Development Ctr.
90-33 160th St.
Jamaica, NY 11432
Earl Francis, Project Director
Tel: (718) 206-2255 Fax: (718) 206-3693
Email: jbrc@jbrc.org
Web: www.mbda.gov

90-33 160th St.
Jamaica, NY 11432
Timothy H. Marshall, President/CEO
Tel: (718) 206-2255 Fax: (718) 206-3693
Email: tmarshall@jbrc.org
Web: www.jbrc.org

Williamsburg (Brooklyn) Minority Business Development Ctr.
12 Heyward St.
Brooklyn, NY 11211
Deborah Charnas, Project Director
Tel: (718) 522-5620 Fax: (718) 522-5931
Email: oda@odabdc.org
Web: www.odabdc.org

DEFENSE, DEPT. OF
US Air Force, 914th AW/LGC-Air Force Reserve Command, Small Business Office
2720 Kirkbridge Dr.
Niagara Falls, NY 14304-5001
Barbara Mansfield, Small Business Specialist
Tel: (716) 236-2216 Fax: (716) 236-2357
Email: barbara.mansfield@niagarafalls.af.mil
Web: www.selltoairforce.org

US Air Force, AFRL IFB-Air Force Materiel Command, Small Business Office
26 Electronic Pkwy.
Rome, NY 13441-4514
Janis Norelli, Small Business Specialist
Tel: (315) 330-3311

Email: norellij@rl.af.mil
Web: www.if.afrl.af.mil/div/IFK/bc-main.html

ENERGY, DEPT. OF
Chicago Operations Office, Brookhaven National Laboratory
50 Brookhaven Ave., Bldg. 355
Upton, NY 11973
Jill Clough-Johnston, Small Business Program Manager
Tel: (631) 344-3173 Fax: (631) 344-5878
Email: clough@bnl.gov
Web: www.bnl.gov

Ohio Field Office, West Valley Nuclear Services Company
10282 Rock Springs Rd.
West Valley, NY 14171-9799
Lynn Whiting, Small Business Utilization Officer
Tel: (716) 942-4477 Fax: (716) 042-4110
Web: www.wvnsco.com

Schenectady Naval Reactors Office
P.O. Box 1069
Schenectady, NY 12301
Marie Pastor, Small Business Program Manager
Tel: (518) 395-6375 Fax: (518) 395-6390
Email: smbus@snrmail.kapl.gov

ENVIRONMENTAL PROTECTION AGENCY
Region II, Office of Small and Disadvantaged Business Utilization
290 Broadway, 29th Fl.
New York, NY 10007-1866
Otto Salamon, Officer
Tel: (212) 637-3417 Fax: (212) 637-3518
Email: salamon.otto@epa.gov
Web: www.epa.gov/osdbu

Small Business Utilization, Region II
26 Federal Plz. #18-110
New York, NY 10278
Colleen Pappas, Small Business Specialist
Tel: (212) 264-1236 Fax: (212) 264-2760
Email: colleen.pappas@gsa.gov
Web: www.gsa.gov

TRANSPORTATION, DEPT. OF
Saint Lawrence Seaway Development Corporation
P.O. Box 520
180 Andrews St.
Massena, NY 13662-0520
Linda M. Harding, Contracting Officer
Tel: (315) 764-3244 Fax: (315) 764-3268
Email: linda.harding@sls.dot.gov
Web: www.osdbuweb.dot.gov

TREASURY, DEPT. OF THE
Internal Revenue Service, Northeast Area Field Office
290 Broadway
New York, NY 10007-1867
Deborah Paulin-Foster, Small Business Specialist
Tel: (212) 436-1481 Fax: (212) 436-1849
Email: deborah.e.foster@irs.gov
Web: www.treas.gov

290 Broadway
New York, NY 10007-1867
Pamela King-Doran, Small Business Specialist
Tel: (212) 436-1481 Fax: (212) 436-1849
Email: pamela.k.doran@irs.gov
Web: www.treas.gov

VETERANS AFFAIRS, DEPT. OF
VA Medical Ctr.
130 W. Kingsbridge Rd.
Bronx, NY 10468
Tony Palma, Small Business Specialist

Tel: (718) 584-9000 X4332
Fax: (718) 741-4704
Email: Tony.Palma@med.va.gov
Web: www.va.gov/osdbu

3495 Bailey Ave.
Buffalo, NY 14215
Cherie Widger-Kresge, Supervisory Contract
Specialist/NCA Contract Manager
Tel: (716) 862-6388 Fax: (716) 862-8893
Email: cherie.widger-kresge@med.va.gov
Web: www.va.gov/osdbu

NORTH CAROLINA

COMMERCE, DEPT. OF
Minority Business Development Agency,
Raleigh/Durham/Charlotte Minority
Business Development Ctr.
114 W. Parrish St.
Durham, NC 27701
Dan Stafford, Director of Information
Technology and Compliance
Tel: (919) 287-3198 Fax: (919) 688-8478
Email: dstafford@ncimed.com
Web: www.mbda.gov

114 W. Parrish St., 5th Fl.
Durham, NC 27702
Andrea Harris, Executive Director
Tel: (919) 956-8889 Fax: (919) 688-7668
Email: andreah@ncimed.com
Web: www.ncimed.com

DEFENSE, DEPT. OF
US Air Force, 23rd Contracting
Squadron/LGC-Air Mobility Command,
Small Business Office
1443 Reilly Rd. #C
Pope AFB, NC 28308-2896
Leslie L. Crawley, Small Business Specialist
Tel: (910) 394-6244 Fax: (910) 394-7040
Email: leslie.crawley@pope.af.mil
Web: public.pope.amc.af.mil

US Air Force, 4th Contracting
Squadron/CD-Air Combat Command,
Small Business Office
1695 Wright Bros Ave.
Seymour Johnson AFB, NC 27531-2459
Lavern Miller, Small Business Specialist
Tel: (919) 722-5411 Fax: (919) 722-5414
Email: sba@seymourjohnson.af.mil
Web: www.seymourjohnson.af.mil/4fwunits/
msg/cons/default.htm

HEALTH & HUMAN SERVICES, DEPT. OF
National Institute of Environmental
Health Sciences, Acquisitions
Management Branch, OM
P.O. Box 12874, M/D NH-02
Research Triangle Park, NC 27709
Small Business Program Manager
Tel: (919) 541-0377 Fax: (919) 541-5117
Web: www.niehs.nih.gov

NORTH DAKOTA

DEFENSE, DEPT. OF
US Air Force, 319th Air Refueling
Wing/LGC-Air Mobility Command, Small
Business Office
575 6th Ave., Bldg. 418
Grand Forks AFB, ND 58205-6436
Marsha Alberts, Small Business Specialist
Tel: (701) 747-5256 Fax: (701) 747-4215
Email: marsha.alberts@grandforks.af.mil
Web: public.grandforks.amc.af.mil

US Air Force, 5th Contracting
Squadron/LGC-Air Combat Command,
Small Business Office

211 Missile Ave.
Minot AFB, ND 58705-5027
Dwight Slotto, Small Business Specialist
Tel: (701) 723-4188 Fax: (701) 723-4172
Email: dwight.slotto@minot.af.mil
Web: www.minot.af.mil

VETERANS AFFAIRS, DEPT. OF
Fargo VA Medical/Regional Office Ctr.
2101 Elm St.
Fargo, ND 58102
Small Business Specialist
Tel: (701) 232-3241 Fax: (701) 239-3705
Web: www.va.gov/osdbu

OHIO

AGRICULTURE, DEPT. OF
Natural Resources Conservation
Service
200 N. High St. #522
Columbus, OH 43215
Barbara S. Clayton, Contracting Specialist
Tel: (614) 255-2502 Fax: (614) 255-2548
Email: barbara.clayton@oh.usda.gov
Web: www.oh.nrcs.usda.gov/

COMMERCE, DEPT. OF
Ohio Statewide Minority Business
Development Ctr.
7162 Reading Rd. #630
Cincinnati, OH 45237-3844
Onnie R. Martin, Executive Director
Tel: (513) 631-7666 Fax: (513) 631-7613
Email: omartin@ohiostatewidembdc.org
Web: www.ohiostatewidembdc.org

DEFENSE, DEPT. OF
US Air Force, 910 CONF/LGC
3976 King Graves Rd. #31
Youngstown ARS, OH 44473-5931
Jacqueline Rogers, Small Business
Specialist
Tel: (330) 609-1155 Fax: (330) 609-1042
Email: jacqueline.rogers@youngstown.
af.mil
Web: www.selltoairforce.org

US Air Force, Aeronautical Systems
Ctr./BC-Air Force Materiel Command,
Small Business Office
2196 D St. #109
Wright-Patterson AFB, OH 45433-7201
Teresa Rendon, Small Business Specialist
Tel: (937) 255-5322
Email: teresa.rendon@wpafb.af.mil
Web: www.wpafb.af.mil/pk

US Air Force, Air Force Research
Laboratory-Air Force Materiel
Command, Small Business Office
1864 4th St. #225
Wright-Patterson AFB, OH 45433-7132
Patricia Deschaine, Small Business
Specialist
Tel: (937) 904-7130 Fax: (937) 656-9619
Email: patricia.deschaine@afrl.af.mil
Web: www.afrl.af.mil

US Air Force, Contracting Division/BCO-
Air Force Materiel Command, Small
Business Office
1940 Allbrook Dr. #3
Wright-Patterson AFB, OH 45433-5309
Mary Jones, Small Business Specialist
Tel: (937) 257-2324 X4506
Email: mary.jones@wpafb.af.mil
Web: www.wpafb.af.mil/bc

ENERGY, DEPT. OF

Ohio Field Office
175 Tri-County Pkwy.
Springdale, OH 45246
Lisa G. Kosko, Small Business Program
Manager
Tel: (513) 246-0101 Fax: (513) 246-0226
Email: lisa.kosko@ohio.doe.gov
Web: www.ohio.doe.gov

Ohio Field Office, Battelle Memorial
Institute
505 King Ave.
Columbus, OH 43201
Warren K. Weaver, Small Business Officer
Tel: (614) 424-4515 Fax: (614) 424-6311
Email: weaverwk@battelle.org
Web: www.battelle.org

Ohio Field Office, CH2M HILL Mound,
Inc.
1 Mound Rd.
Miamisburg, OH 45343
Don Liepold, Small Business Program
Manager
Tel: (937) 865-3074 Fax: (937) 865-3816
Email: Liepda@doe-md.gov
Web: www.doe-md.gov

Ohio Field Office, Fluor Fernald
P.O. Box 538704
Cincinnati, OH 45253
Gwen Jones, Small Business Liaison
Tel: (513) 648-5151 Fax: (513) 648-5176
Email: gwendolyn.jones@fernald.gov
Web: www.fernald.gov

Ohio Field Office, RMI (Earthlink)
1800 E. 21st St.
Ashtabula, OH 44004
Mushammad Shakoor, Manager, Contract
Administration
Tel: (440) 993-2044 Fax: (440) 993-2819
Email: mushammad_shakoor@rmies.com
Web: www.earthlinetech.com

ENVIRONMENTAL PROTECTION AGENCY
Contracts & Management Division
26 W. Martin Luther King Dr.
Cincinnati, OH 45268
Norman G. White, Officer
Tel: (513) 487-2024 Fax: (513) 487-2004
Email: white.norman@epa.gov
Web: www.epa.gov

NATIONAL AERONAUTICS & SPACE
ADMINISTRATION (NASA)
Glenn Research Ctr.
M/C 3-9
Cleveland, OH 44135
Sunil Dutta, SDB/HBCU/OMI Program
Manager
Tel: (216) 433-8844 Fax: (216) 433-2946
Email: sunil.dutta-1@nasa.gov
Web: www.hq.nasa.gov

M/C 500-313
Cleveland, OH 44135
Carl L. Silski, Field Installation Small/
Minority Business Specialist
Tel: (216) 433-2786 Fax: (216) 433-5489
Email: carl.l.silski@nasa.gov
Web: www.hq.nasa.gov

VETERANS AFFAIRS, DEPT. OF
VA Medical and Regional Office Ctr.
(541/90C)
10000 Brecksville Rd.
Brecksville, OH 44141
James F. Gates, Small Business Specialist
Tel: (440) 526-3030 X7440
Fax: (440) 838-6052
Email: james.gates@med.va.gov

Web: www.va.gov/osdbu

VA Medical Ctr.
17273 State Route 104
Chillicothe, OH 45601
Sharon Kempton, Small Business Specialist
Tel: (740) 773-1141 X7011
Fax: (740) 772-7008
Email: sharon.kempton@med.va.gov
Web: www.va.gov/osdbu

3200 Vine St.
Cincinnati, OH 45220
Joseph Boggs, Small Business Specialist
Tel: (513) 475-6336 Fax: (513) 475-6500
Web: www1.va.gov

4100 W. 3rd St.
Dayton, OH 45428
Jodi Cokl, Chief Acquisition Management
Tel: (937) 268-6511 X3388
Fax: (937) 262-5974
Email: jodi.cokl2@med.va.gov
Web: www.va.gov/osdbu

VA Outpatient Clinic (757/90C)
543 Taylor Ave.
Columbus, OH 43203-1278
Richard T. Hardy, Small Business Specialist
Tel: (614) 257-5520 Fax: (614) 257-5526
Email: richard.hardy@med.va.gov
Web: www.va.gov/osdbu

OKLAHOMA

COMMERCE, DEPT. OF
Minority Business Development Agency,
Oklahoma City Minority Business
Development Ctr.
4205 Lincoln Blvd. #109
Oklahoma City, OK 73105
Nancy Alexander, Project Director
Tel: (405) 962-1623 Fax: (405) 962-1639
Email: nhalexander@lunet.edu
Web: www.mbda.gov

DEFENSE, DEPT. OF
US Air Force, 38th EIG ATT.: Small
Business Office
Hilltop Rd. Bldg. 4064
Tinker AFB, OK 73145-2713
Karen Nobles, Small Business Specialist
Tel: (405) 734-9394 Fax: (405) 734-1615
Email: karen.nobles@tinker.af.mil
Web: www.tinker.af.mil

US Air Force, 71st FTW/CVC-Air
Education and Training Command,
Small Business Office
246 Brown Pkwy. #205
Vance AFB, OK 73705-5037
Thomas Patton, Small Business Specialist
Tel: (580) 213-7565 Fax: (580) 213-6397
Email: Thomas.Patton@vance.af.mil
Web: www.selltoairforce.org

US Air Force, 97th Contracting
Squadron ATT.: Small Business Office
303 J Ave., Bldg. 302
Altus AFB, OK 73523-5132
Michael Pierce, Small Business Specialist
Tel: (580) 481-7320 Fax: (580) 481-7472
Email: michael.pierce@altus.af.mil
Web: www.altus.af.mil

US Air Force, DynCorp, Local Purchase,
Vance Support Division
273 Scott Rd. #123
Vance AFB, OK 73705-5514
Jerry D. Cornwell, Small Business Specialist
Tel: (580) 213-7174 Fax: (580) 213-6047

Email: jerry.cornwell@vance.af.mil
Web: www.selltoairforce.org

US Air Force, OC-ALC/BC
3001 Staff Dr. #1AG85A
Tinker AFB, OK 73145-3009
Michael Yort, Small Business Director
Tel: (405) 739-2601 Fax: (405) 739-7085
Email: michael.yort@tinker.af.mil
Web: www.tinker.af.mil

**US Air Force, Oklahoma City Air
Logistics Ctr.-Air Force Materiel
Command, Small Business Office**
3001 Staff Dr. #1AG84A
Tinker AFB, OK 73145-3009
Carole Wanish, Small Business Specialist
Tel: (405) 739-5242 Fax: (405) 739-7085
Email: Carole.Wanish@tinker.af.mil
Web: www.tinker.af.mil

**US Air Force, Oklahoma City Air
Logistics Ctr.-Air Force Materiel
Command, Small Business Office**
3001 Staff Dr. #1AG84A
Tinker AFB, OK 73145-3009
Renaye Tyce, Small Business Specialist
Tel: (405) 739-2604 Fax: (405) 739-7085
Email: Renaye.Tyce@tinker.af.mil
Web: www.tinker.af.mil

**ENERGY, DEPT. OF
Southwestern Power Administration**
1 W. 3rd St.
Tulsa, OK 74103
Gary Bridges, Small Business Program
Manager
Tel: (918) 595-6659 Fax: (918) 595-6656
Email: gary.bridges@swpa.gov
Web: www.swpa.gov

**VETERANS AFFAIRS, DEPT. OF
VA Medical Ctr.**
1011 Honor Heights Dr.
Muskogee, OK 74401
Small Business Specialist
Tel: (918) 680-3616 Fax: (918) 680-3852
Web: www.va.gov/osdbu

VA Medical Ctr., Contracting Office
921 NE 13th St.
Oklahoma City, OK 73104
Danny M. Drennan, Small Business
Specialist
Tel: (405) 270-0501 X5110
Fax: (405) 270-5115
Email: danny.drennan@med.va.gov
Web: www.va.gov/osdbu

OREGON

**AGRICULTURE, DEPT. OF
Forest Service, Region 6**
Deschutes National Forest,
1645 Hwy. 20 East
Bend, OR 97701
Dan Parazoo, Contract Specialist
Tel: (541) 383-5550 Fax: (541) 383-5544
Email: dparazoo@fs.fed.us
Web: www.fs.fed.us/r6/centraloregon/

Mt. Hood National Forest, 16400
Champion Way
Sandy, OR 97055
Lois Tate, Contract Specialist
Tel: (503) 668-1768 Fax: (503) 668-1763
Email: ltate@fs.fed.us

Ochoco National Forest, 3160 NE 3rd St.

Prineville, OR 97754
Jeanette Young, Contract Specialist
Tel: (541) 416-6533 Fax: (541) 416-6661
Email: jayoung@fs.fed.us
Web: www.fs.fed.us/r6/centraloregon

P.O. Box 520
Rogue River National Forest-Siskiyou
Medford, OR 97501
John Owen, Supervisory Contract Specialist
Tel: (541) 858-2209 Fax: (541) 858-2224
Email: jowen@fs.fed.us
Web: www.fs.fed.us

Umatilla National Forest,
2517 SW Hailey Ave.
Pendleton, OR 97801
Gary Dillavou, Contract Specialist
Tel: (541) 278-3841 Fax: (541) 278-3845
Email: gdillavou@fs.fed.us
Web: www.fs.fed.us

P.O. Box 10607
Willamette National Forest
Eugene, OR 97440
Maurica Owen, Contract Specialist
Tel: (541) 225-6325 Fax: (541) 225-6220
Email: mowen@fs.fed.us

**ENERGY, DEPT. OF
Bonneville Power Administration**
P.O. Box 3621 M/S CK1
Portland, OR 97208
Nancy Faber, Small Business Program
Manager
Tel: (503) 230-7414 Fax: (503) 872-7936
Email: nkfaber@bpa.gov
Web: www.bpa.gov/corporate

**VETERANS AFFAIRS, DEPT. OF
VA Medical Ctr.**
3710 SW US Veterans Hospital Rd. M/C
P4CONT
Portland, OR 97239
Guin Peterson, Small Business Specialist
Tel: (503) 402-2865 Fax: (503) 402-2914
Email: Guinevere.Peterson@med.va.gov
Web: www.va.gov/osdbu

VA Roseburg Healthcare System
913 NW Garden Valley Blvd.
Roseburg, OR 97470-6513
Terry Albertus, Small Business Specialist
Tel: (541) 440-1000 X44250
Fax: (541) 440-1276
Email: terry.albertus2@med.va.gov
Web: www.va.gov/osdbu

**VA Southern Oregon Rehabilitation Ctr.
and Clinics**
8495 Crater Lake Hwy.
White City, OR 97503
Katherine A. Baughman, Small Business
Specialist
Tel: (541) 826-2111 X3213
Fax: (541) 830-3511
Email: kathy.baughman@med.va.gov
Web: www1.va.gov

PENNSYLVANIA

**AGRICULTURE, DEPT. OF
Agricultural Research Service, North
Atlantic Area**
600 E. Mermaid Ln.
Wyndmoor, PA 19038
Eileen LeGates, Supervisor, Procurement
Analyst
Tel: (215) 233-6551 Fax: (215) 233-6558
Email: elegates@naa.ars.usda.gov
Web: www.naa.ars.usda.gov

**COMMERCE, DEPT. OF
Minority Business Development
Agency, Philadelphia Minority Business
Development Ctr.**
105-107 N. 22nd St., 1st Fl.
Philadelphia, PA 19103
Marjorie Anderson, Project Director
Tel: (215) 496-9100 X117
Fax: (215) 496-0980
Email: manderson@milligancpa.com
Web: www.mbda.gov

**DEFENSE, DEPT. OF
Fleet & Industrial Supply Ctr.,
Philadelphia Detachment**
Small Business Office M/C 09B Bldg. 600
Philadelphia, PA 19112-5082
Gerald Furey, Small Business Specialist
Tel: (215) 697-9555 Fax: (215) 697-9554
Email: Gerald.Furey@navy.mil
Web: www.nor.fisc.navy.mil

**Naval Inventory Control Point, Small
Business Office**
700 Robbins Ave. Bldg. 1
Philadelphia, PA 19111-5098
Nina Evans, Small Business Specialist
Tel: (215) 697-4950 Fax: (215) 697-2986
Email: phil_sadbusphiladelphia@navy.mil

**US Air Force, 911th AW/LGC-Air Force
Reserve Command, Contracting Office**
Pittsburgh IAP-ARS, 2375 Defense Ave.
Coraopolis, PA 15108-4495
Dan Lucci, Small Business Specialist
Tel: (412) 474-8119 Fax: (412) 474-8410
Email: Daniel.Lucci@pittsburgh.af.mil
Web: www.afrc.af.mil/911aw/

**US Air Force, 913th LG/LGC-Air Force
Reserve Command, Contracting Office**
Willow Grove ARS, 1051 Fairchild St.
Willow Grove, PA 19090-5203
Joseph Madden, Small Business Specialist
Tel: (215) 443-1057 Fax: (215) 443-1956
Email: joseph.madden@willowgrove .af.mil
Web: www.afrc.af.mil/913aw/

**US Navy Inventory Control Point, Small
Business Office**
P.O. Box 2020
5450 Carlisle Pike M/C 006
Mechanicsburg, PA 17055-0788
Helen Katz, Small Business Specialist
Tel: (717) 605-6625
Web: www.navicp.navy.mil

**ENERGY, DEPT. OF
National Energy Technology Laboratory**
P.O. Box 10940
Pittsburgh, PA 15236-0940
Larry R. Sullivan, Small Business Specialist
Tel: (412) 386-6115 Fax: (412) 386-6137
Email: Larry.Sullivan@netl.doe.gov
Web: www.netl.doe.gov

**Pittsburgh Naval Reactors Office,
Bechtel Bettis Atomic Power
Laboratory, Bechtel Bettis, Inc.**
P.O. Box 79
West Mifflin, PA 15122-0079
Elaine Scott, Small Business Program
Manager
Tel: (412) 476-6003 Fax: (412) 476-7320
Email: smallbizinfoCtr.@bettis.gov
Web: www.bettis.gov

**ENVIRONMENTAL PROTECTION AGENCY
Region III, Office of Small and
Disadvantaged Business Utilization**
1650 Arch St.
Philadelphia, PA 19103
Romona McQueen, Officer
Tel: (215) 814-5155 Fax: (215) 814-5108

Email: McQueen.Romona@epa.gov
Web: www.epa.gov/osdbu

**VETERANS AFFAIRS, DEPT. OF
VA Medical Ctr.**
1111 E. End Blvd.
Wilkes Barre, PA 18711
George Dath, Small Business Specialist
Tel: (570) 821-7222 Fax: (570) 821-7277
Email: George.Dath@med.va.gov
Web: www.va.gov/osdbu

135 E. 38th St.
Erie, PA 16504-1596
Susan Lang, Small Business Specialist
Tel: (814) 860-2091 Fax: (814) 860-2990
Email: susan.lang@med.va.gov
Web: www1.va.gov

1400 Black Horse Hill Rd.
Coatesville, PA 19320
Duane E. Trotter, Chief of Acquisitions
Tel: (610) 383-0227 Fax: (610) 383-0235
Email: duane.trotter@med.va.gov
Web: www.va.gov/osdbu

2907 Pleasant Valley Blvd.
Altoona, PA 16602-4377
Jean Gelbke, Small Business Specialist
Tel: (814) 943-8164 X7233
Fax: (814) 942-9253
Email: Jean.Gelbke@med.va.gov
Web: www.va.gov/osdbu

325 New Castle Rd.
Butler, PA 16001
Sharon Leszczynski, Small Business
Specialist
Tel: (724) 287-4781 X2523
Fax: (724) 477-5026
Email: sharon.leszczynski@med.va.gov
Web: www.va.gov/osdbu

VA Medical Ctr. (N125)
1700 S. Lincoln Ave.
Lebanon, PA 17042
Ben Grogg, Acquisition Manager
Tel: (717) 228-5939 Fax: (717) 228-5936
Email: benjamin.grogg@med.va.gov
Web: www.va.gov/osdbu

VA Pittsburgh Healthcare Systems
7180 Highland Dr. M/C 04A-H
Pittsburgh, PA 15206
Linda Glancey, Small Business Specialist
Tel: (412) 365-5436 Fax: (412) 365-5444
Email: Linda.Glancey@med.va.gov
Web: www.va.gov/pittsburgh/highland.htm

PUERTO RICO

**COMMERCE, DEPT. OF
Minority Business Development
Agency, Puerto Rico Minority Business
Development Ctr.**
406 Capitan Espada St.
San Juan, PR 00918
Teresa Berrios, Project Director
Tel: (787) 753-8484 Fax: (787) 753-0855
Email: teresaberrios@mbdcpr.com
Web: www.mbdcpr.com

**Puerto Rico Minority Business
Opportunity Committee**
530 Ponce de Leon Ave.,
Atrium Office Ctr. #320
San Juan, PR 00901
Jeanette S. Trevino, Project Director
Tel: (787) 289-7880 Fax: (787) 289-7850
Email: jeannette@puertoricomboc.com
Web: www.puertoricomboc.com

VETERANS AFFAIRS, DEPT. OF
VA Medical Ctr. (B03)
10 Casia St.
San Juan, PR 00921-3201
Elisa Cruz, Small Business Specialist
Tel: (787) 641-2948 Fax: (787) 781-8721
Email: elisa.cruz@med.va.gov
Web: www.va.gov/osdbu

RHODE ISLAND

DEFENSE, DEPT. OF
Naval Undersea Warfare Ctr.,
Small Business
NUWC Bldg. 11 M/C 00SB
Newport, RI 02841-1708
David Rego, Small Business Advocate
Tel: (401) 832-1766 Fax: (401) 832-4820
Email: regodj@npt.nuwc.navy.mil
Web: www.npt.nuwc.navy.mil

VETERANS AFFAIRS, DEPT. OF
VA Medical Ctr.
830 Chalkstone Ave.
Providence, RI 02908
James M. Gunn, Small Business Specialist
Tel: (401) 457-3035 Fax: (401) 457-3079
Email: james.gunn@med.va.gov
Web: www.va.gov/osdbu

SOUTH CAROLINA

COMMERCE, DEPT. OF
Minority Business Development Agency,
South Carolina Statewide Minority
Business Development Ctr.
1515 Richland St.
Columbia, SC 29201
Greg Davis, Director
Tel: (803) 779-5905 X28
Fax: (803) 779-5915
Email: Busdev@scmbdc.com
Web: www.scmbdc.com

DEFENSE, DEPT. OF
Naval Facilities Engineering Command,
Southern Division, Code 09J,
Small Business Office
P.O. Box 190010
North Charleston, SC 29419-9010
Robin Brown, Small Business Specialist
Tel: (843) 820-5935 Fax: (843) 820-5935
Email: robin.brown1@navy.mil
Web: www.efdsouth.navfac.navy.mil

US Air Force, 20th Contracting
Squadron/CC-Air Combat Command,
Small Business Office
305 Blue Jay St.
Shaw AFB, SC 29152-5004
Judith Croxton, Director of Business
Operations
Tel: (803) 895-6834 Fax: (803) 895-6019
Email: Judith.Croxton@shaw.af.mil
Web: www.shaw.af.mil

US Air Force, 437th Airlift Wing/LGC-
Air Mobility Command, Small Business
Office
101 E. Hill Blvd.
Charleston AFB, SC 29404-5021
Donna R. Barber, Small Business Specialist
Tel: (843) 963-3328 Fax: (843) 963-5880
Email: donna.barber@charleston.af.mil
Web: www.437contracting.charleston.af.mil

ENERGY, DEPT. OF
Savannah River Office of Contracts
Management

P.O. Box A
Bldg. 730-B #2250
Aiken, SC 29802
David W. Hepner, Sr., Business Advocate/
Development Manager
Tel: (803) 952-9354 Fax: (803) 952-9452
Email: david.hepner@srs.gov

Savannah River Operations Office,
Westinghouse Savannah River Co.
Bldg. 730-4B #226
Aiken, SC 29802
Margaret Rhone, Director of Supply
Development
Tel: (803) 952-9991 Fax: (803) 952-6159
Email: margaret.rhone@srs.gov
Web: www.srs.gov

Wackenhut Services, Inc., Savannah
River Site
P.O. Box W
Aiken, SC 29802
Lorri Wright, Procurement Administrator
Tel: (803) 952-7598 Fax: (803) 952-6020
Email: lorri.wright@srs.gov

VETERANS AFFAIRS, DEPT. OF
Ralph H. Johnson VA Medical Ctr.
(534/90CFO)
109 Bee St.
Charleston, SC 29403
Cindy Rogers, Procurement Analyst
Tel: (706) 481-6724 Fax: (706) 481-6741
Email: cindy.rogers2@med.va.gov
Web: www.va.gov/osdbu

SOUTH DAKOTA

AGRICULTURE, DEPT. OF
Natural Resources Conservation
Service
Federal Bldg., #308 220 4th St. SW
Huron, SD 57350
Joe Volesky, Contract Specialist
Tel: (605) 352-1169 Fax: (605) 352-1187
Email: joe.volesky@sd.usda.gov
Web: www.sd.nrcs.usda.gov

DEFENSE, DEPT. OF
US Air Force, 28th Contracting
Squadron/LGCD-Air Combat Command
1000 Ellsworth St. #1200
Ellsworth AFB, SD 57706-4904
Larry Bulman, Director of Business
Operations
Tel: (605) 385-1719 Fax: (605) 385-1726
Email: lawrence.bulman@ellsworth.af.mil
Web: www.ellsworth.af.mil

VETERANS AFFAIRS, DEPT. OF
VA Black Hills Healthcare System
(FIN-20)
113 Comanche Rd.
Ft. Meade, SD 57741
Neil Ondriezek, Small Business Specialist
Tel: (605) 347-7027 Fax: (605) 720-7029
Email: neil.ondriezek@med.va.gov
Web: www.va.gov/osdbu

TENNESSEE

DEFENSE, DEPT. OF
US Air Force, Arnold Engineering
Development Ctr./BC-Air Force Materiel
Command, Small Business Office
100 Kindel Dr. #A332
Arnold AFB, TN 37389-1332
Alan Fudge, Small Business Specialist
Tel: (931) 454-4406 Fax: (931) 454-7330
Email: alan.fudge@arnold.af.mil

Web: www.arnold.af.mil/aedc/contracting/
smallbus.htm

ENERGY, DEPT. OF
Oak Ridge National Laboratory
P.O. Box 2008, M/S 6419
Oak Ridge, TN 37831-6419
Will Minter, Small Business Program
Manager
Tel: (865) 574-9803 Fax: (865) 576-0096
Email: minterwd@ornl.gov
Web: www.ornl.gov

Oak Ridge Operations Office
P.O. Box 2001
Oak Ridge, TN 37381-8501
Freda H. Hopper, Small Business Program
Manager
Tel: (865) 576-9430 Fax: (865) 576-9188
Email: hopperfh@oro.doe.gov
Web: www.oro.doe.gov

Oak Ridge Operations Office, Bechtel
Jacobs Company, Supplier Advocate
Office
E. Tennessee Technology Park, Hwy. 58,
M/S 7596, Bldg. K-1007
Oak Ridge, TN 37831-7596
McArthur Moore, Small Business Program
Manager
Tel: (865) 576-3847 Fax: (865) 241-9330
Email: mzo@bechteljacobs.org
Web: www.bechteljacobs.com

Oak Ridge Operations Office, Oak Ridge
Associated Universities
P.O. Box 117
Oak Ridge, TN 37381-0117
John Bennett, Procurement Manager
Tel: (865) 241-4887 Fax: (865) 576-9385
Email: bennettj@orau.gov
Web: www.orau.gov

Oak Ridge Operations Office,
Wackenhut Services, Inc., Oak Ridge
Team
161 Mitchell Rd.
Oak Ridge, TN 37830
Rose Weaver, Small Business Program
Manager
Tel: (865) 276-9270 Fax: (865) 276-9318
Email: weaverr@wsi-or.net

Oak Ridge Operations, Socioeconomic
Programs, Acquisition and Asset
Management
P.O. Box 2009, MS 6501
BWXT Y-12, LLC
Oak Ridge, TN 37831-6501
Spencer E Rollins, Small Business Program
Manager
Tel: (865) 576-2090 Fax: (865) 576-3664
Email: rollinsse@y12.doe.gov
Web: www.y12.doe.gov

UT-Battelle
P.O. Box 2008 M/S 6293
One Bethel Valley Rd.
Oak Ridge, TN 37831
Al Guidry, Operations Manager
Tel: (865) 241-4161 Fax: (865) 576-6645
Email: guidrya@ornl.gov
Web: www.ornl.gov

VETERANS AFFAIRS, DEPT. OF
VA Acquisition Service Ctr. (VISN 9/90)
3410 Lebanon Pike
Murfreesboro, TN 37129
Patricia McKay, Chief of Acquisitions
Management
Tel: (615) 867-6091 Fax: (615) 867-5429
Email: Patricia.McKay@med.va.gov
Web: www.va.gov/osdbu

VA Medical Ctr.
3400 Lebanon Pike
Murfreesboro, TN 37129
William Dunn, Small Business Specialist
Tel: (615) 867-6096
Web: www.va.gov/osdbu

TEXAS

AGRICULTURE, DEPT. OF
Agricultural Research Service,
Southern Plains Area
7607 Eastmark Dr. #230
College Station, TX 77840
Michael C. Downing, Area Procurement &
Realty Officer
Tel: (979) 260-9446 Fax: (979) 260-9413
Email: mdowning@spa.ars.usda.gov
Web: www.spa.ars.usda.gov

COMMERCE, DEPT. OF
Minority Business Development Agency,
Dallas Regional Office
1100 Commerce St. #726
Dallas, TX 75242
John F. Iglehart, Regional Director
Tel: (214) 767-8001 Fax: (214) 767-0613
Email: jiglehart@mbda.gov
Web: www.mbda.gov

Dallas/Ft. Worth/Arlington/ Minority
Business Development Ctr.
545 E. John Carpenter Frwy. #100
Irving, TX 75062
Joseph Newton, Project Director
Tel: (214) 688-1612 Fax: (214) 688-1753
Email: jnewton@dmbdc.com
Web: www.mbda.gov

El Paso Minority Business Development
Ctr.
5959 Gateway Blvd. W. #425
El Paso, TX 79925
Jose Rocha, Project Director
Tel: (915) 774-0626 Fax: (915) 774-0680
Email: EPNeda@aol.com
Web: www.nedainc.net

Houston Minority Business Development
Ctr.
2900 Woodridge St. #310
Houston, TX 77087
Milton Thibodeaux, Director
Tel: (713) 644-0821 Fax: (713) 644-3523
Email: mthibodeaux@gacompanies.com
Web: www.mbda.gov

San Antonio Minority Business
Development Ctr.
501 W. Durango Blvd.
San Antonio, TX 78207
Fletcher M. Parks, Director
Tel: (210) 458-2480 Fax: (210) 458-2481
Email: fparks@utsa.edu
Web: www.mbda.gov

South Texas Minority Business
Opportunity Committee
2412 S. Closner St. #160
Edinburg, TX 78539
Pedro Salazar, Project Director
Tel: (956) 292-7535 Fax: (956) 292-7561
Web: www.coserve.org

DEFENSE, DEPT. OF
US Air Force, 12th Contracting
Squadron
395 B St. W. #2
Randolph AFB, TX 78150-4525
Estella Calvillo, Small Business Specialist
Tel: (210) 652-5460 X3064
Fax: (210) 652-4673

Email: estella.calvillo@randolph.af.mil
Web: www.randolph.af.mil/12ftw/12lg/
12cons/

US Air Force, 17th Contracting Squadron/CC-Air Education and Training Command, Small Business Office
210 Schertz Blvd.
Goodfellow AFB, TX 76908-4705
Philip Kirby, Small Business Specialist
Tel: (325) 654-3821 Fax: (325) 654-5052
Email: philip.kirby@goodfellow.af.mil
Web: www.goodfellow.af.mil

US Air Force, 301 MSG/LGC-Air Force Reserve Command, Small Business Office
1710 Burke St. #100, NAS/JRB
Ft. Worth, TX 76127-6200
Nancy Audelo, Small Business Specialist
Tel: (817) 782-7315 X237
Fax: (817) 782-5371
Email: nancy.audelo@carswell.af.mil
Web: www.selltoairforce.org

US Air Force, 311th Human Systems Wing/BC-Air Force Materiel Command, Small Business Office
8046 Crouch Rd.
Brooks AFB, TX 78235-5366
Mary Urey, Small Business Specialist
Tel: (210) 536-4348 Fax: (210) 536-4363
Email: mary.urey@brooks.af.mil
Web: www.brooks-smallbusiness.com

US Air Force, 37th Contracting Squadron/CC-Air Education and Training Command, Small Business Office
1655 Selfridge Ave.
Lackland AFB, TX 78236-5253
Arthur Dinwiddie, Small Business Specialist
Tel: (210) 671-2852 Fax: (210) 671-0674
Email: Arthur.Dinwiddie@lackland.af.mil
Web: www.Lackland.af.mil

US Air Force, 47th Contracting Squadron/LGCD-Air Education and Training Command, Small Business Office
171 Alabama Ave. Bldg. 7
Laughlin AFB, TX 78843-5102
Jesús N. Martinez, Small Business Specialist
Tel: (830) 298-5641 Fax: (830) 298-4178
Email: jesus.martinez@laughlin.af.mil
Web: www.laughlin.af.mil

US Air Force, 7th Contracting Squadron/CC, Small Business Office
381 3rd St.
Dyess AFB, TX 79607-1581
William Banks, Small Business Specialist
Tel: (325) 696-2285
Email: william.banks@dyess.af.mil
Web: www.dyess.af.mil

US Air Force, 82nd Contracting Squadron/LGC-Air Education and Training Command, Small Business Office
136 K Ave. #1
Sheppard AFB, TX 76311-2746
Tandy Weaver, Small Business Specialist
Tel: (940) 676-4138 Fax: (940) 676-7829
Email: tandy.weaver@sheppard.af.mil
Web: www.sheppard.af.mil

US Air Force, AETC Contracting Squadron/LGCA-Air Education and Training Command, Small Business Office
2021 1st St. W., Bldg. 853
Randolph AFB, TX 78150-4302
Floyd Taylor, Small Business Specialist
Tel: (210) 652-3660 Fax: (210) 652-7665

Email: floyd.taylor@randolph.af.mil
Web: www.randolph.af.mil

ENERGY, DEPT. OF
BWXT Pantex
P.O. Box 30020
Pantex Plant
Amarillo, TX 79120
Marilyn Daves, Small Business Program Manager
Tel: (806) 477-3850 Fax: (806) 477-3839
Email: mdaves@pantex.com
Web: www.pantex.com

ENVIRONMENTAL PROTECTION AGENCY
Region VI, Office of Small and Disadvantaged Business Utilization
1445 Ross Ave., 12th Fl. #1200
Dallas, TX 75202-2733
Debora N. Bradford, Officer
Tel: (214) 665-7406 Fax: (214) 665-7284
Email: bradford.debora@epa.gov
Web: www.epa.gov

GENERAL SERVICES ADMINISTRATION
Office of Small Business Utilization, Region VII
819 Taylor St. #1E13A
Fort Worth, TX 76102
Willie Heath, Jr., Director
Tel: (817) 978-0800 Fax: (817) 978-0440
Email: willie.heath@gsa.gov
Web: www.gsa.gov

NATIONAL AERONAUTICS & SPACE ADMINISTRATION (NASA)
Johnson Space Ctr.
M/C BA
Houston, TX 77058
Jeffrey Cullen, Small Business Advocate
Tel: (281) 483-0248 Fax: (281) 483-5100
Email: Jeffrey.M.Cullen@nasa.gov
Web: www.nasa.gov

Johnson Space Ctr., Space Station Program Office
M/C BD3
Houston, TX 77058
Cheryl Harrison, Field Installation Small/Minority Business Specialist
Tel: (281) 483-3734 Fax: (281) 483-4326
Email: cheryl.a.harrison@nasa.gov
Web: www.hq.nasa.gov

TREASURY, DEPT. OF THE
Internal Revenue Service, Mid-States Area Field Office
4050 Alpha Rd., M/SRO 1800
Dallas, TX 75244-4203
Jeff Schraeder, Small Business Specialist
Tel: (972) 308-1637 Fax: (972) 308-1928
Email: Jeff.L.Schraeder@irs.gov
Web: www.treas.gov

VETERANS AFFAIRS, DEPT. OF
South Texas Veterans Healthcare System (671/90C)
7400 Merton Minter Blvd.
San Antonio, TX 78229
Frank M. Caraballo, Chief Purchasing/Contracting
Tel: (210) 617-5152 Fax: (210) 617-5255
Email: frank.caraballo@med.va.gov
Web: www.va.gov/osdbu

VA Automation Ctr.
1615 E. Woodward St.
Austin, TX 78772
Dave W. Peterson, Small Business Specialist
Tel: (512) 326-6020 Fax: (512) 326-6028
Email: david.peterson@mail.va.gov
Web: www.va.gov/osdbu

VA Healthcare System (138/90C)
5001 N. Piedras St.
El Paso, TX 79930-4211
Daniel Portillo, Small Business Specialist
Tel: (915) 564-6112 Fax: (915) 564-6109
Email: daniel.portillo@med.va.gov
Web: www1.va.gov

VA Medical Ctr.
300 Veterans Blvd.
Big Springs, TX 79720-5500
Beverly Atwell, Small Business Specialist
Tel: (432) 264-4866 Fax: (432) 264-4887
Email: Beverly.Atwell@med.va.gov
Web: www.va.gov/osdbu

4500 S. Lancaster Rd. M/C90C
Dallas, TX 75216
Donald Knight, Chief of Acquisitions
Tel: (214) 857-0028 Fax: (214) 857-0027
Email: knight.donald@gsa.gov
Web: www.va.gov/osdbu

6010 Amarillo Blvd. W.
Amarillo, TX 79106
Robert Auffrey, Small Business Specialist
Tel: (806) 354-7845 Fax: (806) 354-7875
Email: robert.auffrey@med.va.gov
Web: www.va.gov/osdbu

VA Medical Ctr. (580/90C)
2002 Holcombe Blvd.
Houston, TX 77030-4298
Linda B. Dean, Small Business Specialist
Tel: (713) 794-7405 Fax: (713) 794-7869
Email: linda.dean@med.va.gov
Web: www.va.gov/osdbu

UTAH

AGRICULTURE, DEPT. OF
Forest Service, R-4 Acquisition Management
324 25th St.
Ogden, UT 84401
Carleen Ashbaker, Supervisory Contract Specialist
Tel: (801) 625-5137 Fax: (801) 625-5365
Email: cashbaker@fs.fed.us

Forest Service, State of Utah
2222 W. 2300 S.
Salt Lake City, UT 84119
Jo Lippire, Head Contracting Officer
Tel: (801) 975-3444 Fax: (801) 975-3483
Email: jlippire@fs.fed.us
Web: www.fs.fed.us/r4/

DEFENSE, DEPT. OF
US Air Force, OO-ALC/BC
6038 Aspen Ave., Bldg. 1289
Hill AFB, UT 84056-5805
Marsha Peterson, Management Assistant
Tel: (801) 777-4143
Email: marsha.peterson@hill.af.mil
Web: contracting.hill.af.mil/newcontracting/Opportunities/SmallBusiness/SmallBusiness.asp

VETERANS AFFAIRS, DEPT. OF
VA Salt Lake City Healthcare System (04A)
500 Foothill Blvd.
Salt Lake City, UT 84148
Brenda Alverson, Small Business Specialist
Tel: (801) 584-1201 Fax: (801) 584-2506
Email: brenda.alverson@med.va.gov
Web: www.va.gov/osdbu

VERMONT

VETERANS AFFAIRS, DEPT. OF
VA Medical and Regional Office Ctr.
215 N. Main St.
White River Junction, VT 05009
Suzanne Rybczyk, Small Business Specialist
Tel: (802) 295-9363 X5790
Fax: (802) 296-5103
Email: susanne.rybczyk@med.va.gov
Web: www.va.gov/osdbu

VIRGINIA

AGRICULTURE, DEPT. OF
Food and Nutrition Services, Administrative Services Division
3101 Park Ctr. Dr. #228
Alexandria, VA 22302
Sabrina Mathis, Contracting Officer
Tel: (703) 305-2268 Fax: (703) 305-2071
Email: Sabrina.Mathis@fns.usda.gov
Web: www.fns.usda.gov

3101 Park Ctr. Dr. #220
Alexandria, VA 22302
Patricia Palmer, Branch Chief, Contract Operations
Tel: (703) 305-2250 Fax: (703) 305-2071
Email: Patsy.Palmer@fns.usda.gov
Web: www.fns.usda.gov/fncs/

Forest Service
Rosslyn Plz. E #706 1621 N. Kent St.
Arlington, VA 22209
James G. McDonald, Small Business Coordinator
Tel: (703) 605-5144 Fax: (703) 605-5100
Email: jmcdonald04@fs.fed.us
Web: www.fs.fed.us

COMMERCE, DEPT. OF
National Oceanic and Atmospheric Administration, Eastern Administrative Support Ctr., Acquisition & Grants Management, Acquisition Management Division
200 Granby St.,
Norfolk Federal Bldg, 8th Fl. #815
Norfolk, VA 23510
Jack O. Salmon, Chief
Tel: (757) 441-6893 Fax: (757) 441-3786
Email: Jack.O.Salmon@noaa.gov
Web: www.rdc.noaa.gov

200 Granby St.,
Norfolk Federal Bldg, 8th Fl. #815
Norfolk, VA 23510
Michele A. McCoy, Small Business Specialist
Tel: (757) 441-6879 Fax: (757) 441-3786
Email: Michele.A.Mccoy@noaa.gov
Web: www.easc.noaa.gov

Patent & Trademark Office, Office of Procurement
2011 Crystal Dr., Crystal Park 1 #810
Arlington, VA 22202
Muriel A. Brown, Small Business Liaison
Tel: (703) 305-8370 Fax: (703) 305-8294
Email: muriel.brown@uspto.gov
Web: www.uspto.gov

2011 Crystal Dr., Crystal Park 1 #810
Arlington, VA 22202
Michael Anastasio, Director
Tel: (703) 305-8419 Fax: (703) 305-8294
Email: Michael.Anastasio@uspto.gov
Web: www.uspto.gov

Patent & Trademark Office, Office of Procurement, Information Technology Branch
2011 Crystal Dr., Crystal Park 1 #810
Arlington, VA 22202
Kate Kudrecwicv, Branch Chief
Tel: (703) 305-8219 Fax: (703) 305-8294
Email: Kate.Kudrecwicv@uspto.gov
Web: www.uspto.gov

Patent & Trademark Office, Office of Procurement, Services & Support Branch
2011 Crystal Dr., Crystal Park 1 #810
Arlington, VA 22202
Page Etzel, Division Chief
Tel: (703) 305-8579 Fax: (703) 305-8294
Email: page.etzel@uspto.gov
Web: www.uspto.gov

DEFENSE, DEPT. OF
Defense Advanced Research Projects Agency, Small and Disadvantaged Business
3701 N. Fairfax Dr., CMO-SBIR
Arlington, VA 22203-1714
Connie Jacobs, Small Business Advocate Program Manager
Tel: (703) 526-4162 Fax: (703) 696-9781
Email: cjacobs@darpa.mil
Web: www.darpa.mil

Defense Commissary Agency
1300 E. Ave.
Fort Lee, VA 23801-1800
Michele Templeman, Small Business Specialist
Tel: (804) 734-8138 Fax: (804) 734-8619
Email: michele.templeman@deca.mil
Web: www.commissaries.com

Defense Contract Management Agency, Office of Small and Disadvantaged Business Utilization
6350 Walker Ln. DCMA-OCA
Alexandria, VA 22310
Barbara J. Little, Director of Small Business
Tel: (703) 428-0787 Fax: (703) 428-3578
Email: smallbusiness@hq.dcma.mil
Web: www.dcma.mil

Defense Energy Support Ctr., Small Business
8725 John J. Kingman Rd. #4950
Fort Belvoir, VA 22060-6222
Kathy S. Williams, Associate Director
Tel: (703) 767-9400 Fax: (703)767-9446
Email: kathy.s.williams@dla.mil
Web: www.desc.dla.mil

8725 John J. Kingman Rd. #4950
Fort Belvoir, VA 22060-6222
Temple Ferrell, Small Business Specialist
Tel: (703) 767-9681 Fax: (703)767-9446
Email: Temple.J.Ferrell@dla.mil
Web: www.desc.dla.mil

Defense Logistics Agency, Office of Small and Disadvantaged Business Utilization
8725 John J. Kingman Rd.
Ft. Belvoir, VA 22060-6221
Thomas D. Ray, Director
Tel: (703) 767-1662 Fax: (703) 767-1670
Email: thomas.ray@dla.mil
Web: www.dla.mil/db

8725 John J. Kingman Rd. #1127-DB
Ft. Belvoir, VA 22060-6221
Thomas Ray, Director
Tel: (703) 767-1662 Fax: (703) 767-1670
Email: thomas.ray@dla.mil
Web: www.dla.mil/db

8725 John J. Kingman Rd. #2533
Ft. Belvoir, VA 22060-6221
Patricia A. Cleveland, Women Business Representative
Tel: (703) 767-1652 Fax: (703) 767-1670
Email: patricia.cleveland@dla.mil
Web: www.dla.mil/db

Fleet & Industrial Supply Ctr.
1968 Gilbert St. #600 M/C 04 Bldg. 143
Norfolk, VA 23511-3392
Linda Owen, Deputy for Small Business
Tel: (757) 443-1435 Fax: (757) 443-1355
Email: linda.owen@navy.mil
Web: www.nor.fisc.navy.mil

Naval Facilities Engineering Command Atlantic
6506 Hampton Blvd.
Norfolk, VA 23508-1278
Barbara N. Taylor, Deputy for Small Business
Tel: (757) 322-4430 Fax: (757) 322-4611
Email: barbara.n.taylor@navy.mil
Web: www.navfac.navy.mil

Naval Surface Warfare Ctr., Commander Dahlgren Division
17320 Dahlgren Rd.
Dahlgren, VA 22448-5100
Robert E. Ashley, Jr., Deputy for Small Business
Tel: (540) 653-4806 Fax: (540) 653-7088
Email: robert.e.ashley@navy.mil
Web: www.nswc.navy.mil

Office of Small and Disadvantaged Business Utilization
1777 N. Kent St. #9100
Arlington, VA 22209
Frank Ramos, Director
Tel: (703) 588-8631 Fax: (703) 588-7561
Email: frank.ramos@osd.mil
Web: www.acq.osd.mil/sadbu

1777 N. Kent St. #9100
Arlington, VA 22209
Linda Oliver, Deputy Director
Tel: (703) 588-8631 Fax: (703) 588-7561
Email: linda.oliver@osd.mil
Web: www.acq.osd.mil

1777 N. Kent St. #9100
Arlington, VA 22209
Peg Meehan, Women Business Representative
Tel: (703) 588-8631 Fax: (703) 588-7561
Email: peg.meehan@osd.mil
Web: www.acq.osd.mil

US Air Force, 1st Contracting Squadron/ LGCD-Air Combat Command, Small Business Office
74 Nealy Ave. #100
Langley AFB, VA 23665-2088
Linda S. Greaves, Small Business Specialist
Tel: (757) 764-3246 Fax: (757) 764-7706
Email: linda.greaves@langley.af.mil
Web: www.langley.af.mil/1msg/1cons/ lgcs_business.shtml

US Air Force, ACC Contracting Sq/CCD- Air Combat Command, Small Business Office
130 Douglas St. #400
Langley AFB, VA 23665
Della Shelton, Small Business Specialist
Tel: (757) 764-4286 Fax: (757) 764-9773
Email: della.shelton@langley.af.mil
Web: www.selltoairforce.org

US Air Force, AFOSR/PK
4015 Wilson Blvd. #713
Arlington, VA 22203-1977

Maj Larry Bradbury, Small Business Specialist
Tel: (703) 696-5904 Fax: (703) 696-9733
Email: larry.bradbury@afosr.af.mil
Web: www.afosr.af.mil

US Marine Corps, Regional Contracting Office NE
3250 Catlin Ave.
Quantico, VA 22134-5000
Greg Flaherty, Deputy Director
Tel: (703) 784-1921 Fax: (703) 784-3597
Email: gregory.flaherty@usmc.mil
Web: www.usmc.mil

ENERGY, DEPT. OF
Oak Ridge Operations Office, The Southeastern Universities Research Association
Thomas Jefferson National Accelerator Facility, 12000 Jefferson Ave.
Newport News, VA 23606
Danny Lloyd, Small Business Program Manager
Tel: (757) 269-7121 Fax: (757) 269-7121
Email: lloyd@jlab.org
Web: www.jlab.org

INTERIOR, DEPT. OF THE
US Fish & Wildlife Service, Division of Contracting & General Services
4401 N. Fairfax Dr. #210-A
Arlington, VA 22203
James W. McKoy, Jr., Business Utilization & Development Specialist
Tel: (703) 358-2225 Fax: (703) 358-2264
Email: jim_mckoy@fws.gov
Web: www.doi.gov

JUSTICE, DEPT. OF
Drug Enforcement Administration, Office of Procurement
700 Army-Navy Dr. #W-5140
Arlington, VA 22202
Vernon Carter, Small Business Specialist
Tel: (202) 307-4921 Fax: (202) 307-4877
Web: www.usdoj.gov

NATIONAL AERONAUTICS & SPACE ADMINISTRATION (NASA)
Langley Research Ctr.
M/S 134
Hampton, VA 23681-2199
Vernon Vann, Small Business Specialist
Tel: (757) 864-2456 Fax: (757) 864-9299
Email: archer.v.vann@nasa.gov
Web: www.osdbu.nasa.gov

Langley Research Ctr.
M/S 134
Hampton, VA 23681-0001
Randy Manning
Tel: (757) 864-6074 Fax: (757) 864-2502
Email: randy.a.manning@nasa.gov
Web: www.hq.nasa.gov

Wallops Flight Facility Goddard Space Flight Ctr.
M/C 244.1
Wallops Island, VA 23337
Lisa B. Hall, Procurement Analyst
Tel: (757) 824-1420 Fax: (757) 824-1974
Email: lisa.b.hall@nasa.gov
Web: www.nasa.gov

NATIONAL SCIENCE FOUNDATION
Office of Small and Disadvantaged Business Utilization
4201 Wilson Blvd. #527
Arlington, VA 22230
Donald Senich, Director

Tel: (703) 292-7082 Fax: (703) 292-9055
Email: dsenich@nsf.gov
Web: www.nsf.gov

VETERANS AFFAIRS, DEPT. OF
National Cemetery Administration Operations Support Ctr., Centralized Contracting Division (402D3)
5101 Russell Rd.
Quantico, VA 22134
Joseph C. Kepple, Small Business Specialist
Tel: (703) 441-4000 Fax: (703) 441-3070
Email: jck@cem.va.gov
Web: www.cem.va.gov

VETERANS AFFAIRS, DEPT. OF
VA Medical Ctr.
100 Emancipation Dr.
Hampton, VA 23667
Nancy Bailey, Small Business Specialist
Tel: (757) 728-3113
Email: nancy.bailey@med.va.gov
Web: www1.va.gov/midatlantic/facilities/ hampton.htm

VA Medical Ctr. (04E)
1201 Broad Rock Blvd.
Richmond, VA 23249
Kevin Buser, Small Business Specialist
Tel: (804) 675-5489 Fax: (804) 675-5502
Email: Kevin.Buser@med.va.gov
Web: www.va.gov/osdbu

WASHINGTON

AGRICULTURE, DEPT. OF
Forest Service, Region 6
Colville National Forest, 765 S. Main St.
Colville, WA 99114
Cathy E. Van Alyne, Contracting Specialist
Tel: (509) 684-7114 Fax: (509) 684-7280
Email: cvanalyne@fs.fed.us
Web: www.fs.fed.us/r6/colville/

Mt. Baker-Snoqualmie National Forest, 21905 64th Ave. W.
Mountlake Terrace, WA 98043-2278
Elizabeth Waits, Purchasing Agent
Tel: (425) 744-3338 Fax: (425) 744-3336
Email: ewaits@fs.fed.us
Web: www.fs.fed.us/r6/mbs/

Okanogan National Forest, 1240 S. 2nd Ave.
Okanogan, WA 98840-3275
Kris Bellini, Contract Specialist
Tel: (509) 826-3072 Fax: (509) 826-3789
Email: kbellini@fs.fed.us
Web: www.fs.fed.us/r6/okanogan/

Olympic National Forest, 1835 Black Lake Blvd. SW #A
Olympia, WA 98512-5623
Mile Sutherland, Contract Specialist
Tel: (360) 956-2471
Email: msutherland@fs.fed.us

Wenatchee National Forest, 215 Melody Ln.
Wenatchee, WA 98801
Carl Erickson, Contract Specialist
Tel: (509) 664-9316 Fax: (509) 664-9281
Email: cerickson@fs.fed.us
Web: www.fs.fed.us/r6/wenatchee/

COMMERCE, DEPT. OF
National Oceanic and Atmospheric Administration, Western Administrative Support Ctr., Acquisition Management Division
7600 Sand Point Way NE, M/C WC3
Seattle, WA 98115-6349

Heide Sickles, Chief
Tel: (206) 526-6033 Fax: (206) 526-6025
Email: Heide.L.Sickles@noaa.gov
Web: www.ofa.noaa.gov

DEFENSE, DEPT. OF
Fleet & Industrial Supply Ctr.,
Puget Sound
467 W. St. M/C 04
Bremerton, WA 98314-5104
Peggy Williams, Small Business Specialist
Tel: (360) 476-2812 Fax: (360) 476-4121
Email: peggy_williams@puget.fisc.navy.mil
Web: www.puget.fisc.navy.mil

US Air Force, 62nd Contracting
Squadron, Small Business Office
P.O. Box 4178
McChord AFB, WA 98438-0178
Lori Houghton, Small Business Specialist
Tel: (253) 982-3890 Fax: (253) 982-5207
Email: Lori.Houghton@mcchord.af.mil
Web: public.mcchord.amc.af.mil

US Air Force, 92nd Air Refueling
Wing/LGC-Air Mobility Command, Small
Business Office
110 W. Ent St. #200
Fairchild AFB, WA 99011-9403
Marion Nelson, Small Business Specialist
Tel: (509) 247-4880 Fax: (509) 247-9870
Email: marion.nelson@fairchild.af.mil
Web: www.selltoairforce.org

ENERGY, DEPT. OF
Office of River Protection
2440 Stevens Dr. #2321
Richland, WA 99353
Cloette Ried, Small Business Program
Manager
Tel: (509) 373-6140 Fax: (509) 372-2781
Email: cloette_b_reid@rl.gov
Web: www.hanford.gov/orp/

Office of River Protection, CH2M Hill
Hanford Group
P.O. Box 1500, M/S IN H6-16
Richland, WA 99352
Leslie Wiberg, Small Business Program
Manager
Tel: (509) 372-3457 Fax: (509) 372-8036
Email: Leslie_d_Wiberg@rl.gov

Richland Operations Office
P.O. Box 550, A7-80
Richland, WA 99352
George Sanders, Small Business Program
Manager
Tel: (509) 372-1786 Fax: (509) 376-3703
Email: george_h_sanders@rl.gov
Web: www.hanford.gov/rl

Bechtel Hanford, Inc., 3370 George
Washington Way, M/S HO-04
Richland, WA 99352
Mary K. Funk, Small Business
Representative
Tel: (509) 372-9522 Fax: (509) 372-9049
Email: mkfunk@bhi-erc.com

Richland Operations Office, Fluor
Hanford, Supplier Advocacy Office
P.O. Box 1000, M/S H7-20
Richland, WA 99352
V.J. Meadows, Small Business Liaison
Tel: (509) 376-4697 Fax: (509) 376-1476
Email: valjeanne_b_meadows@rl.gov
Web: www.hanford.gov/rl/index.asp

Richland Operations Office, Office of
River Protection, Waste Treatment Plant
Bechtel National, Inc., 2435 Stevens Ctr.
Pl., M/S 14-3A
Richland, WA 99354

Carrie Brittain, Small Business Program
Manager
Tel: (509) 371-2338 Fax: (509) 371-2286
Email: cjbritta@bechtel.com
Web: www.bechtel.com

Richland Operations Office, Pacific
Northwest National Laboratory
P.O. Box 999, M/S J1-24
Richland, WA 99352
Andrea Melius , Small Business Program
Manager
Tel: (509) 376-4148 Fax: (509) 376-4149
Email: andrea.melius@pnl.gov
Web: www.pnl.gov/contracts

ENVIRONMENTAL PROTECTION AGENCY
Region X, Office of Small and
Disadvantaged Business Utilization
1200 6th Ave. (OMP-145)
Seattle, WA 98101
Marie McPeak, Officer
Tel: (206) 553-2894 Fax: (206) 553-4957
Email: www.epa.gov/osdbu

GENERAL SERVICES ADMINISTRATION
Regional Office of Small Business
Utilization
400 15th St. SW
Auburn, WA 98001-6599
Sheron Snyder, Small Business
Representative
Tel: (253) 931-7956 Fax: (253) 804-4887
Email: sheron.snyder@gsa.gov
Web: www.gsa.gov

HOMELAND SECURITY, DEPT. OF
US Coast Guard, Facilities Design &
Construction Ctr.
915 2nd Ave. #2664
Seattle, WA 98174-1011
Anita Repanich, Small Business Specialist
Tel: (206) 220-7426 Fax: (206) 220-7390
Email: arepanich@pacnorwest.uscg.mil
Web: www.uscg.mil/mlcpac/fdccp/

VETERANS AFFAIRS, DEPT. OF
Jonathan M. Wainwright Memorial VA
Medical Ctr. (629)
77 Wainright Dr.
Walla Walla, WA 99362
Daniel N. Turk, Small Business Specialist
Tel: (509) 525-5200 X22457
Fax: (509) 526-6209
Email: daniel.turk@med.va.gov
Web: www.va.gov/osdbu

VA Medical Ctr. (90C)
4815 N. Assembly St.
Spokane, WA 99205
Charles Marsden, Small Business Specialist
Tel: (509) 434-7224 Fax: (509) 434-7101
Email: charles.marsden@med.va.gov
Web: www.va.gov/osdbu

VA Puget Sound Healthcare System
(S138P&C)
1660 S. Columbian Way
Seattle, WA 98108
Maria Boelter, Small Business Specialist
Tel: (206) 762-1010
Email: maria.boelter@med.va.gov
Web: www.va.gov/osdbu

TREASURY, DEPT. OF THE
Bureau of the Public Debt
200 3rd St. UNB, 4rd Fl.

Parkersburg, WV 26101-1328
Jeff Stephenson, Small Business Specialist
Tel: (304) 480-7123 Fax: (304) 480-7203
Email: jstephenson@bpd.treas.gov
Web: www.treas.gov

Internal Revenue Service, Martinsburg
Computing Ctr.
250 Murall Dr. M/S 223
Kearneysville, WV 25430
Linda Miller, Small Business Specialist
Tel: (304) 264-5589 Fax: (304) 264-7008
Email: linda.k.miller@irs.gov
Web: www.treas.gov

VETERANS AFFAIRS, DEPT. OF
VA Medical Ctr.
1540 Spring Valley Dr.
Huntington, WV 25704
Mike Hughey, Small Business Specialist
Tel: (304) 429-6755 X2919
Fax: (304) 429-0275
Email: mike.hughey@med.va.gov
Web: www.va.gov/osdbu

VA Medical Ctr. (517/ASSL)
200 Veterans Ave.
Beckley, WV 25801
Sandra Herald, Small Business Specialist
Tel: (304) 255-2121 X4133
Fax: (304) 256-5498
Email: Sandra.Herald@med.va.gov
Web: www.va.gov/osdbu

AGRICULTURE, DEPT. OF
Forest Service, Forest Products
Laboratory
1 Gifford Pinchot Dr.
Madison, WI 53726
Shawn Lacina, Contract Specialist
Tel: (608) 231-9287 Fax: (608) 231-9585
Email: slacina@fs.fed.us
Web: www.fpl.fs.fed.us

Natural Resources Conservation
Service, Wisconsin State Office
8030 Excelsior Dr. #200
Madison, WI 53717
Beverly Bartek, Contracting Specialist
Tel: (608) 662-4422 X262
Fax: (608) 662-4430
Email: beverly.bartek@wi.usda.gov

COMMERCE, DEPT. OF
Minority Business Development
Agency, Wisconsin Minority Business
Opportunity Committee
Schlitz Business Park
Keghouse, 111 W. Pleasant St.
Milwaukee, WI 53212
Leni Siker, Executive Director
Tel: (414) 289-6767 Fax: (414) 289-8562
Email: leni@wi-brc.org
Web: www.wi-brc.org

DEFENSE, DEPT. OF
US Air Force, 440th AW/LGC-Air Force
Reserve Command, Small Business
Office
Gen. Mitchell IAP-ARS, 300 E. College Ave.
Milwaukee, WI 53207-6299
Lonna Jonas, Small Business Specialist
Tel: (414) 482-5273 Fax: (414) 482-5901
Email: ljonas@generalmitchell.af.mil
Web: www.selltoairforce.org

AGRICULTURE, DEPT. OF
Natural Resources Conservation
Service
Federal Bldg., 100 E. B St. #3124
Casper, WY 82601-1911
Joseph Kirkland, Contract Specialist
Tel: (307) 233-6787 Fax: (307) 233-6795
Email: joseph.kirkland@wy.usda.gov
Web: www.wy.nrcs.usda.gov

DEFENSE, DEPT. OF
US Air Force, 90th Contracting
Squadron/LGC-Air Force Space
Command, Small Business Office
7505 Marne Loop, Bldg. 208
Warren AFB, WY 82005-2860
Charles (Mel) Melvin, Director of Small
Business Operations
Tel: (307) 773-4737 Fax: (307) 773-3964
Email: Charles.Melvin@warren.af.mil
Web: www.warren.af.mil

ENERGY, DEPT. OF
Naval Petroleum Reserves
907 N. Poplar #150
Casper, WY 82601
Neil Hauglend, Small Business Program
Manager
Tel: (307) 261-5000 X5017
Fax: (307) 261-5817
Email: Neil.Hauglend@rmotc.doe.gov
Web: www.rmotc.com

Naval Petroleum Reserves in CO, UT &
WY
907 N. Poplar #150
Casper, WY 82601
Janet Boulanger, Small Business Program
Manager
Tel: (307) 261-5000 X5076
Fax: (307) 261-5817
Email: janet.boulanger@rmotc.doe.gov
Web: www.rmotc.com

VETERANS AFFAIRS, DEPT. OF
VA Medical Ctr.
2360 E. Pershing Blvd.
Cheyenne, WY 82001
Robert O. Baker, Small Business Specialist
Tel: (307) 778-7326 Fax: (307) 778-7361
Email: bob.baker@med.va.gov
Web: www1.va.gov

VA Medical Ctr. (90C)
1898 Fort Rd.
Sheridan, WY 82801
James C. Wiltse, Contracting Specialist
Tel: (307) 672-1679 Fax: (307) 672-1901
Email: james.wiltse@med.va.gov
Web: www.va.gov/osdbu

Private Sector Minority Business Opportunities
Oportunidades de negocios minoritarios en el sector privado

BANK ONE SERVICES CORPORATION
Supplier Diversity
Procurement Services/Supplier Diversity
AZ1-1260
Phoenix, AZ 85004-1260
Lupe Barto, Regional Supplier Diversity
Manager
Tel: (602) 221-4868 Fax: (602) 221-2727
Email: Lupe_A_Barto@bankone.com
Web: www.bankone.com

GRAND CANYON MINORITY SUPPLIER DEVELOPMENT COUNCIL
Development Council
802 N. 5th Ave.
Phoenix, AZ 85003
Ron Williams, Executive Director
Tel: (602) 495-9950 Fax: (602) 495-9943
Email: ronwilliams@qwest.net
Web: www.gcmsdc.org

HONEYWELL INTERNATIONAL
Global Sourcing
1300 W. Warner Rd.
Tempe, AZ 85284
Elton Beldock, Supplier Diversity Coordinator
Tel: (480) 592-3854 Fax: (480) 592-2554
Email: elton.beldock@honeywell.com
Web: www.honeywell.com

AEROJET
Supplier Diversity Program
P.O. Box 13222
Sacramento, CA 95813-6000
Jo Ann Hoffman, Administrator
Tel: (916) 355-3689 Fax: (916) 355-3926
Email: jo.hoffman@aerojet.com
Web: www.aerojet.com

AEROSPACE CORPORATION, THE
Small Business Office
P.O. Box 92957 M/S M2-357
2350 E. El Segundo Blvd.
El Segundo, CA 90245-4691
Michael J. Cryderman, SBLO
Tel: (310) 336-1198 Fax: (310) 336-2779
Email: michael.j.cryderman@aero.org
Web: www.aero.org

AEROTHERM CORPORATION
Advanced Engineering & Sciences Division
1735 Technology Dr. #8400
San Jose, CA 95110
Tel: (408) 392-8265 Fax: (408) 451-9204
Email: duane.baker@itt.com
Web: www.aerotherm.com

ALARIS MEDICAL SYSTEMS
10221 Wateridge Cr.
San Diego, CA 92121
Estan Molisdes, Sourcing Manager
Tel: (858) 458-7000 X6312
Fax: (858) 458-7760
Web: www.alarismed.com

APPLE COMPUTER, INC.
Attn: Procurement Business Office
1 Infinite Loop, M/S 35-PO
Cupertino, CA 95014
Tel: (408) 974-4176 Fax: (408) 253-5244
Email: supplierdiversity@apple.com
Web: www.apple.com/supplierdiversity

ARAMARK
Minority Business
115 N. 1st St.
Burbank, CA 91502
Jim Crosley, Director of Supply Chain
Management
Tel: (818) 973-3532 Fax: (818) 973-3886
Email: jim.crosley@uniform.aramark.com
Web: www.aramark.com

AT&T
Supplier Diversity Office
1657 Royal Blvd.
Glendale, CA 91207
Fred Lona, Supplier Diversity Manager
Tel: (818) 246-9018 Fax: (818) 551-0738
Email: flona@att.com
Web: www.att.com/supplier_diversity

BANK OF AMERICA
Supplier Diversity
1 S. Van Ness Ave.
San Francisco, CA 94103
Kim Vu, Supplier Diversity Manager
Tel: (415) 241-3428 Fax: (415) 241-5386
Email: kim.t.vu@bankofamerica.com
Web: www.bankofamerica.com/
supplierdiversity

C.E. WYLIE CONSTRUCTION COMPANY
Estimating Department
3777 Ruffin Rd.
San Diego, CA 92123-1894
Sharon Wylie, Marketing Manager
Tel: (858) 571-4911 Fax: (858) 571-4926
Email: cewylie@cewylie.com
Web: www.cewylie.com

CHEVRON TEXACO CORPORATION
Procurement, Supplier Diversity/Small Business Programs
6101 Bollinger Canyon Rd. #1304
San Ramon, CA 94583
Audrey Goins Brichi, Supplier Diversity
Manager
Tel: (866) 876-8793 Fax: (925) 790-3987
Email: smallbiz@chevrontexaco.com
Web: www.chevron.com

CISCO SYSTEMS, INC.
170 W. Tasman Dr.
San Jose, CA 95134
Diane Thelan, SBLO/MBE Outreach
Tel: (408) 526-4503 Fax: (408) 526-4100
Web: www.cisco.com

DUTRA CONSTRUCTION CORPORATION, INC.
Estimating Department
1000 Point San Pedro Rd.
San Rafael, CA 94901
Albert Joe, Estimator
Tel: (415) 258-6876 Fax: (415) 482-6617
Email: a.joe@dutragroup.com
Web: www.dutragroup.com

EDO/TSO
Business Operations
254 East Ave. #K-4
Lancaster, CA 93535
Brenda McQuiston, Contracts Manager
Tel: (661) 723-3886 X223
Fax: (661) 948-7003
Email: bmcquiston@edotso.com
Web: www.edotso.com

GENERAL ATOMICS AERONAUTICAL SYSTEMS, INC.
16761 Via Del Campo Ct.
San Diego, CA 92127
Armando Plascencia, SBLO
Tel: (858) 455-4572 Fax: (858) 455-4549
Email: armando.plascencia@ga.com
Web: www.ga.com

HEALTH NET FEDERAL SERVICES
Government Contracts
2025 Aerojet Rd.
Rancho Cordova, CA 95742
Donna Clausen, SBLO
Tel: (916) 351-5282 Fax: (916) 351-5295
Email: donna.clausen@health.net
Web: www.health.net

HENSEL PHELPS CONSTRUCTION CO.
2415 Campus Dr. #100
Irvine, CA 92612
Michael Verrastro, Chief Estimator
Tel: (949) 852-0111 Fax: (949) 852-0218
Email: mverrastro@henselphelps.com
Web: www.henselphelps.com

HEWLETT-PACKARD
Corporate Business Diversity Program
3000 Hanover St., M/S 20 DP
Palo Alto, CA 94304
Jo Ann Butler, Manager
Tel: (650) 857-3095 Fax: (650) 852-2920
Email: jo-ann-butler@hp.com
Web: www.hp.com

KAISER PERMANENTE
Business Diversity Department
1950 Franklin St., 10th Fl.
Oakland, CA 94612
Carida Pickens, Supplier Diversity Coordinator
Tel: (510) 987-4863 Fax: (510) 873-5048
Email: carida.pickens@kp.org
Web: www.kp.org

L3 COMMUNICATION
Purchasing
960 Industrial Rd.
San Carlos, CA 94070
Richard L. Greeno, SBLO
Tel: (650) 591-8411 Fax: (650) 594-9612
Email: rick.greeno@L-3com.com
Web: www.L-3com.com

MCKESSON CORPORATION
Small Business Liaison Office
1 Post St., 28th Fl.
San Francisco, CA 94104-5295
Susan Jee, SBLO
Tel: (415) 983-7574 Fax: (415) 983-8343
Email: susan.jee@mckesson.com
Web: www.mckesson.com

MONTGOMERY WATSON HARZA GLOBAL, INC. (MWH)
Contracts and Procurement Office
250 N. Madison Ave.
Pasadena, CA 911101
Pamela A. Taylor, Corp. Procurement
Manager/SBLO
Tel: (626) 568-6381 Fax: (626) 568-6512
Email: pamela.a.taylor@mwhglobal.com
Web: www.mwhglobal.com

NATIONAL SEMICONDUCTOR CORPORATION
2900 Semiconductor Dr. #A1-415
Santa Clara, CA 95051
Edward Sweeney, Senior VP, Human
Resources
Tel: (408) 721-5000 Fax: (408) 720-9574
Email: edward.sweeney@national.com
Web: www.national.com

NESTLÉ USA, INC.
Purchasing Department
800 N. Brand Blvd.
Glendale, CA 91203
DeLynne Ano, Supplier Diversity Development
Manager
Tel: (818) 549-7021 Fax: (818) 637-3317
Email: Delynne.ano@us.nestle.com
Web: www.nestle.com

NORTHROP GRUMMAN CORPORATION
1 Space Park Dr., Bldg. E1 #4021
Redondo Beach, CA 90278
Al Boldon, Small Business Program Director
Tel: (310) 814-0322 Fax: (310) 813-5599
Email: al.boldon@ngc.com
Web: www.northropgrumman.com

PACIFIC GAS & ELECTRIC CORPORATION
Purchasing
245 Market St. #N5D

San Francisco, CA 94177
Krystal Frank, Director
Tel: (415) 973-4436 Fax: (415) 973-8087
Email: klf3@pge.com
Web: www.pge.com

RALPH'S GROCERY COMPANY
Specialty Merchandising/HR
P.O. Box 54143
Los Angeles, CA 90054
Millie Smith, Director, Human Resources
Tel: (310) 884-9000 Fax: (310) 884-2571
Email: msmith@ralphs.com
Web: www.ralphs.com

RAYTHEON COMPANY
Supplier Diversity Program
1520 Hughes Way., Bldg. 01 M/S R280
Long Beach, CA 90810
Benita Fortner, Corporate SBLO
Tel: (310) 847-2312 Fax: (310) 847-2367
Email: bfortner@raytheon.com
Web: www.raytheon.com

SBC COMMUNICATIONS, INC.
Supplier Diversity Office
2600 Camino Ramon, #1E104
San Ramon, CA 94583
Joan Kerr, Executive Director
Tel: (925) 823-4527 Fax: (925) 901-0562
Email: jk1692@sbc.com
Web: www.sbcsuppliersdiversity.com

SILICON GRAPHICS, INC.
1600 Amphitheatre Pkwy. #30-2-725
Mountain View, CA 94043
John Fabia, SBLO
Tel: (650) 933-2441
Email: john.fabia@sgi.com
Web: www.sgi.com

SOUTHERN CALIFORNIA EDISON
Equal Opportunity Department
2244 Walnut Grove Ave. #380F G04
Rosemead, CA 91770
Frank Quevedo, VP
Tel: (626) 302-8802 Fax: (626) 302-4434
Email: frank.quevedo@sce.com
Web: www.sce.com

SOUTHERN CALIFORNIA GAS COMPANY
Diverse Business Enterprises
555 W. 5th St., M/S GT26F1
Los Angeles, CA 90013
Yolanda Padilla, Supplier Diversity Manager
Tel: (213) 244-5627 Fax: (213) 244-5621
Email: ypadilla@semprautilities.com
Web: www.supplierdiversity.sempra.com

THE BOEING COMPANY
Supplier Diversity Office
P.O. Box 2515 M/C 110-SC71
2201 Seal Beach Blvd., M/C 110-SC71
Seal Beach, CA 90740-8250
Barbara Taylor, Supplier Diversity Manager
Tel: (714) 896-3540
Web: www.boeing.com

TOWILL, INC.
5099 Commercial Cr. #100
Concord, CA 94520
Dennis Curtin, President
Tel: (925) 682-6976 Fax: (925) 682-6390
Email: dennis.curtin@towill.com
Web: www.towill.com

COLORADO

BALL CORPORATION
9300 W. 108th Cr.
Broomfield, CO 80031
Bea Valdez, Senior Buyer, Diversity Program
Administrator
Tel: (303) 460-5139 Fax: (303) 460-5170
Email: beavaldez@ball.com
Web: www.ball.com

CH2M HILL
9191 S. Jamaica St.
Englewood, CO 80112
Ren Freeman, Senior Diversity Specialist
Tel: (720) 286-2668 Fax: (720) 286-9340
Email: feedback@ch2m.com
Web: www.ch2mhill.com

LOCKHEED MARTIN SPACE SYSTEMS COMPANY
Astronautics Operations
P.O. Box 179
M/S DC9800
Denver, CO 80201-0179
Carol Trammell, SBLO
Tel: (303) 971-5439 Fax: (303) 971-2191
Email: carol.trammell@lmco.com
Web: www.lockheedmartin.com

STORAGE TECHNOLOGY CORPORATION (STORAGE TEK)
1 Storage Tek Dr., M/S 5236
Louisville, CO 80028
Rick Pelletier, Purchasing Manager
Tel: (303) 673-5151 Fax: (303) 673-4945
Email: richard_pelletier@storagetek.com
Web: www.storagetek.com

CONNECTICUT

AETNA- RETIREMENT SERVICES
Supplier Diversity Program
151 Farmington Ave., RW51
Hartford, CT 06156
Kristen Hickey, Manager
Tel: (860) 273-6541 Fax: (860) 273-4916
Email: hickeyk@aetna.com
Web: www.aetna.com

PITNEY BOWES, INC.
Global Diversity Leadership
1 Elmcroft Rd., M/S 64-15
Stamford, CT 06926-0700
Kevin Beirne, Manager of Business Diversity
Development
Tel: (203) 351-6555 Fax: (203) 351-6961
Email: Kevin.beirne@pb.com
Web: www.pb.com

SIKORSKY AIRCRAFT CORPORATION
Small Business Liaison Office
P.O. Box 9729
6900 Main St.
Stratford, CT 06615
Larry Wooten, Supplier Diversity Manager
Tel: (203) 386-6779 Fax: (860) 998-8037
Email: lwooten@sikorsky.com
Web: www.sikorsky.com

DELAWARE

DUPONT
Supplier Diversity Program
1007 Market St. #D5028
Wilmington, DE 19898
Paul Jones, Global Manager
Tel: (302) 774-7248 Fax: (302) 774-1688
Web: www.dupont.com/tempo

HERCULES, INC.
Energy and Support Svcs.
1313 N. Market St., Hercules Plz.
Wilmington, DE 19894-0001
Catherine Abernathy, Global Marketing Comm.
Manager
Tel: (302) 594-5000 Fax: (302) 594-5400
Email: cabernathy@herc.com
Web: www.hercules.com

DISTRICT OF COLUMBIA

AFFILIATED COMPUTER SERVICES
Small Business Liaison Office
400 K St. NW
Washington, DC 20005
Kent Miller, Director
Tel: (202) 414-3610 Fax: (202) 289-2685
Email: kent.miller@acs-inc.com
Web: www.acs-inc.com

AMTRAK
Supplier Diversity Office
60 Massachusetts Ave. NE #2E-120
Washington, DC 20002
Rodney P. Ruffin, Director
Tel: (202) 906-3600 Fax: (202) 906-2889
Email: ruffinr@amtrak.com
Web: www.amtrak.com

CITIBANK
1101 Pennsylvania Ave. NW #1100
Washington, DC 20004
Ernest Skinner, VP & Director Community
Relations
Tel: (202) 879-6870 Fax: (202) 879-6888
Email: ernest.skinner@citicorp.com
Web: www.citibank.com

EDISON ELECTRIC INSTITUTE
Human Resources
701 Pennsylvania Ave. NW
Washington, DC 20004
Trish Higgins, Secretary
Tel: (202) 508-5180 Fax: (202) 508-5503
Web: www.eei.org

FANNIE MAE
Contracting and Procurement
4000 Wisconsin Ave. NW
Washington, DC 20016
Mia Cole, Director of Customer Requirements
& Support
Tel: (202) 752-4336 Fax: (202) 752-0037
Email: mia_cole@fanniemae.com
Web: www.fanniemae.com

INTERNATIONAL FRANCHISE ASSOCIATION
Emerging Markets Department
1350 New York Ave. NW #900
Washington, DC 20005
Sonia Brathwaite, Director of Diversity
Tel: (202) 628-8000 Fax: (202) 628-0812
Email: sonia@franchise.org
Web: www.franchise.org

POTOMAC ELECTRIC POWER COMPANY (PEPCO) HOLDINGS INC.
Pepco Holdings, Supplier Diversity Department
701 9th St. NW, 9th Fl. #9209
Washington, DC 20068
Ronda J. Gebicke, Manager
Tel: (202) 872-3008 Fax: (202) 331-6655
Email: rjgebicke@pepco.com
Web: www.pepco.com

THE AMERICAN RED CROSS
2025 E. St. NW
Washington, DC 20006
Art Howard, Senior Director
Tel: (202) 303-4498
Web: www.redcross.org

TOM BROWN & COMPANY
1090 Vermont Ave. NW #800
Washington, DC 20005
Mona Brown, President
Tel: (202) 393-7755 Fax: (202) 393-7758

FLORIDA

AERO SIMULATION, INC.

Purchasing Department
4450 E. Adamo Dr. #501
Tampa, FL 33605-5941
Dennis Samuels, Purchasing Manager
Tel: (813) 628-4447 Fax: (813) 628-8404
Email: asi@aerosimulation.com
Web: www.aerosimulation.com

BURGER KING CORPORATION
Diversity Resources
5505 Blue Lagoon Dr.
Miami, FL 33126
Clyde Rucker, Senior VP
Tel: (305) 378-3000 Fax: (305) 378-3114
Web: www.burgerking.com

5505 Blue Lagoon Dr.
Miami, FL 33126
Sonia Pequignot, Specialist Supply Chain
Management
Tel: (305) 378-3219 Fax: (305) 378-3114
Email: spequignot@whopper.com
Web: www.burgerking.com

LOCKHEED MARTIN CORPORATION
Corporative Shared Services
8529 Southpark Cr. #410
Orlando, FL 32819
Michael A. Bush, Director, Supplier Diversity
Tel: (407) 254-5818 Fax: (407) 254-5849
Email: michael.a.bush@lmco.com
Web: www.lockheedmartin.com/suppliernet

RYDER SYSTEM, INC.
Small Business Opportunities
3600 NW 82nd Ave.
Miami, FL 33166
Merci Yepez, Supplier Diversity Director
Tel: (305) 500-3311 Fax: (305) 500-3261
Web: www.ryder.com

SOUTH FLORIDA WATER MANAGEMENT DISTRICT
Procurement Department
3301 Gun Club Rd.
West Palm Beach, FL 33406
Frank Hayden, Director
Tel: (561) 682-6604 Fax: (561) 681-6275
Email: fhayden@sfwmd.gov
Web: www.sfwmd.gov

SYSCO FOOD SERVICES
P.O. Box 130
200 W. Story Rd.
Ocoee, FL 34761
Scott Concelman, Director of Merchandising
Tel: (407) 877-1416 Fax: (407) 656-8977
Email: concelman.Scott@cfl.sycso.com
Web: www.sysco.com

WALT DISNEY ATTRACTIONS
Minority Business Development
P.O. Box 10000
Lake Buena Vista, FL 32830-1000
Eugene Cambell, Director
Tel: (407) 828-5871 Fax: (407) 828-4049
Email: eugene.campbell@disney.com
Web: www.disney.go.com

GEORGIA

BELLSOUTH CORPORATION
Supplier Diversity Office
675 W. Peachtree St. NE #39F50
Atlanta, GA 30375
Debbie Stone, Supplier Diversity Manager
Tel: (404) 420-8444 Fax: (404) 872-1326
Email: debbie.stone@bellsouth.com
Web: www.bellsouth.com

COCA-COLA COMPANY
Supplier Diversity
P.O. Box 1734

Atlanta, GA 30301
Johnnie B. Booker, Director
Tel: (404) 676-5767 Fax: (404) 515-2637
Email: jbooker@na.ko.com
Web: www.coke.net/supplierdiversity

COCA-COLA ENTERPRISES, INC.
Supplier Diversity Office
P.O. Box 723040
Atlanta, GA 31139
Craig Hardin, Manager, Supplier Diversity
Tel: (770) 989-3161 Fax: (770) 989-3062
Email: supplierdiversity@na.coke.com
Web: www.coke.net/supplierdiversity

IDAHO

BOISE CASCADE CORPORATION
Procurement Office
P.O. Box 50
Boise, ID 83728-0001
Lanse Richardson, Director
Tel: (208) 384-6161 Fax: (208) 287-1700
Email: lanse_richardson@bc.com
Web: www.bc.com

ILLINOIS

ABBOTT LABORATORIES
Supplier Diversity Office
200 Abbott Park Rd.,
Department 548, Bldg. AP51-3
Abbott Park, IL 60064-6223
Will J. Stewart, Manager
Tel: (847) 937-5052 Fax: (847) 938-5706
Email: will.stewart@abbott.com
Web: www.abbott.com

ARCHER DANIELS MIDLAND COMPANY
P.O. Box 1470
Decatur, IL 62525
John A. Taylor, Director, Corporate Supplier
Diversity
Tel: (217) 451-2709 Fax: (217) 451-4383
Web: www.admworld.com

BAXTER HEALTHCARE CORPORATION
1435 Lake Cook Rd., LC2-1N
Deerfield, IL 60015
Brian Kook, Supplier Diversity Manager
Tel: (847) 948-3593 Fax: (847) 948-2275
Web: www.baxter.com

BOISE OFFICE SOLUTIONS
150 E. Pierce Rd.
Itasca, IL 60143
Wanda M. Lewis, Manager, MWBD and
Supplier Diversity
Tel: (630) 438-8464 Fax: (630) 438-2446
Web: www.boiseoffice.com

BP
28100 Torch Pkwy., 5th Fl. North
Warrenville, IL 60555
Debra A. Jennings-Johnson, Director, Supplier
Diversity
Tel: (630) 836-6451 Fax: (630) 836-5519
Email: suppdiv@bp.com
Web: www.bp.com

**CARDINAL HEALTH, MEDICAL PRODUCTS
AND SERVICES GROUP**
1430 Waukegan Rd., MPBL4
McGaw Park, IL 60085
Martha Holmes, Director, Small Business
Development
Tel: (847) 578-6799 Fax: (847) 785-6166
Email: martha.holmes@cardinal.com
Web: www.cardinal.com

CATERPILLAR INC.
Global Purchasing
100 NE Adam St.
Peoria, IL 61629
Jerry L. Crayton, Supplier Diversity Manager
Tel: (309) 675-4866 Fax: (309) 578-1558
Email: crayton_jerry_l@cat.com
Web: www.caterpillar.com

CHICAGO TRANSIT AUTHORITY
P.O. Box 3555
Chicago, IL 60654
Paul Cerpa, Manager, Small Business
Development
Tel: (312) 664-7200 Fax: (312) 396-8516
Web: www.transitchicago.com

COMPASS GROUP
North America Division
2790 Ginger Woods Dr.
Aurora, IL 60504
Olivia B. Dorsey, Manager, Supplier Relations
Tel: (630) 417-2399 Fax: (630) 329-4102
Email: odorsey@msn.com
Web: www.compass-group.com

JOHN DEERE
Supplier Diversity Office
3400 80th St.
Moline, IL 61265-5886
Art Rowe, Manager
Tel: (309) 765-5525 Fax: (309) 749-0251
Email: rowearthurw@johndeere.com
Web: jdsupply.deere.com

KRAFT FOODS
Ethnic Marketing & Business Development
Three Lakes Dr.
Northfield, IL 60093
Christine Charliendo, Contact Person
Tel: (847) 646-2000 Fax: (847) 646-0392
Web: www.kraft.com

KRAFT FOODS, INC.
Procurement
9855 Woods Dr.
Skokie, IL 60077
Sharon H. Patterson, Supplier Diversity
Director
Tel: (847) 646-6218 Fax: (847) 646-6220
Email: spatterson@kraft.com
Web: www.kraft.com

MCDONALD'S CORPORATION
Diversity
1 Kroc Dr.
Oak Brook, IL 60523
Rudy R. Méndez, VP
Tel: (630) 623-3028 Fax: (630) 623-3600
Web: www.mcdonalds.com

MOTOROLA
Supplier Diversity
1301 E. Algonquin Rd.
Schaumburg, IL 60196
Kathy Ahillen, Manager
Tel: (847) 576-7073 Fax: (847) 538-2279
Email: kathy.ahillen@motorola.com
Web: www.motorola.com

OLIN CORPORATION
Purchasing Office
427 N. Shamrock St.
East Alton, IL 62024
Gregory A. Smith, Director
Tel: (618) 258-2817 Fax: (618) 258-2861
Email: gasmith2@olin.com
Web: www.olin.com

SEARS, ROEBUCK AND CO.
Supplier Diversity
3333 Beverly Rd. #707D B5-249B
Hoffman State, IL 60179
Carol Martin, Manager Supplier Diversity
Tel: (847) 286-6108 Fax: (847) 645-3819
Email: cmartin@sears.com
Web: www.sears.com

STATE FARM INSURANCE
Corporate Office
1 State Farm Plz. #SB-2
Bloomington, IL 61710
Leonard Bell, Supplier Diversity Manager
Tel: (309) 766-2311 Fax: (309) 735-8200
Web: www.statefarm.com

INDIANA

ITT CORPORATION
P.O. Box 731, 7310 Innovation Blvd.
Fort Wayne, IN 46801-0731
Linda Pope, Small Business Liaison Officer
Tel: (260) 451-5595 Fax: (260) 451-5628
Email: linda.pope@itt.com
Web: www.ittind.com

KANSAS

YELLOW CORPORATION
Supplier Diversity Office
10990 Roe Ave.
Overland Park, KS 66211
Diane Pacheco, Supplier Diversity
Tel: (913) 344-3000 Fax: (913) 344-4125
Email: pacheco@yellowcorp.com
Web: www.yellowcorp.com

KENTUCKY

YUM! BRANDS, INC.
Community Diversity Department
1441 Gardiner Ln.
Louisville, KY 40213
Richard Abraham Rugnao, Community
Diversity Manager
Tel: (502) 874-8926 Fax: (502) 874-8662
Email: richard.rugnao@yum.com
Web: www.yum.com

MAINE

BATH IRON WORKS
Small Business Office
700 Washington St., M/S 3220
Bath, ME 04530
Stepson Everett, Small Business Officer
Tel: (207) 442-3663 Fax: (207) 442-1156
Email: stepson.everett@biw.com
Web: www.gdbiw.com

MARYLAND

BALTIMORE GAS & ELECTRIC
Supplier Diversity Office
2900 Lord Baltimore Dr.
Baltimore, MD 21244
Anita Jackson, Supplier Diversity Manager
Tel: (410) 597-6870 Fax: (410) 597-6871
Web: www.bge.com

MCKESSON BIOSERVICES
14665 Rothgeb Dr.
Rockville, MD 20850
Joan O'Brien, Director of Contracts
Tel: (301) 838-9315 Fax: (301) 838-9320
Email: joan.obrien@mckessonbio.com
Web: www.mckessonbio.com

OCEANEERING INTERNATIONAL INC.
501 Prince George's Blvd.
Upper Marlboro, MD 20774
Robert McCauley, Purchasing Manager/SBLO
Tel: (301) 249-2457 Fax: (301) 249-4022
Email: rmccauley@oceaneering.com
Web: www.oceaneering.com

MASSACHUSETTS

CHADWICK'S OF BOSTON, LTD.
Purchasing Department
35 United Dr.
West Bridgewater, MA 02379
Procurement Coordinator
Tel: (508) 583-8110 X2085
Fax: (508) 583-6314
Email: mpeters@brylane.com
Web: www.chadwicks.com

**CLEAN HARBORS ENVIRONMENTAL
SERVICES, INC.**
1501 Washington St.
Braintree, MA 02185
Philip Bail, SBLO
Tel: (781) 849-1800 X5309
Fax: (781) 356-1363
Email: bail.philip@cleanharbors.com
Web: www.cleanharbors.com

COMPAQ
200 Forest St., M/S MR01 3/D1
Marlboro, MA 01752-3085
Daniel Dean, SBLO
Tel: (978) 493-9130
Web: www.compaq.com

**HOMEGOODS, (DIVISION OF THE TJX
COMPANIES, INC.)**
Supplier Diversity Program
770 Cochituate Rd., J2S
Framingham, MA 01701
Virginia Nelson, Manager, Community
Relations
Tel: (508) 390-3043 Fax: (508) 390-3963
Email: supplier_diversity@tjx.com
Web: www.tjx.com

**MARMAXX GROUP, (DIVISION OF THE TJX
COMPANIES, INC.)**
770 Cochituate Rd.
Framingham, MA 01701
Ruth Johnson, Supplier Diversity Manager
Tel: (508) 390-3043 Fax: (508) 390-2350
Email: supplier_diversity@tjx.com
Web: www.tjx.com

POLAROID CORPORATION
Purchasing Department, Supplier Diversity
1265 Main St. W3-3 Purchasing
Waltham, MA 02451
Roger L. Small, Senior Buyer & Small
Business Liaison Officer
Tel: (781) 386-8878 Fax: (781) 833-8878
Email: smallr@polaroid.com
Web: www.polaroid.com

REEBOK INTERNATIONAL, LTD.
Supplier Diversity Office
100 Technology Ctr. Dr.
Stoughton, MA 02072
Susan Simonelli, Supplier Diversity
Coordinator
Tel: (781) 401-7044 Fax: (781) 401-7042
Web: www.reebok.com

THE TJX COMPANIES, INC.
Community Relations Department
770 Cochituate Rd.
Framingham, MA 01701
Virginia Nelson, Assistant VP/Manager,
Community Relations
Tel: (508) 390-3043 Fax: (508) 390-2350
Email: supplier_diversity@tjx.com
Web: www.tjx.com

TITAN SYSTEMS CORPORATION
700 Technology Park Dr.
Billerica, MA 01821
Scott Mckervey, Operations Manager
Tel: (978) 663-6600 Fax: (781) 687-9217
Web: www.titansystemscorp.com

MICHIGAN

DAIMLER CHRYSLER CORPORATION
DaimlerChrysler Corporation
Auburn Hills, MI 48326
Jethro Joseph, Supplier Diversity Coordinator
Tel: (248) 576-5741 Fax: (248) 576-8393
Web: www.daimlerchrysler.com

FORD MOTOR COMPANY
Minority Supplier Diversity Development
Henry Ford II World Center-WHQ, #917-A6,
MD918, One American Rd.
Dearborn, MI 48126-2798
Ray M. Jensen, Director
Tel: (313) 594-7338 Fax: (313) 845-4713
Email: rjensen@ford.com
Web: www.ford.com

GENERAL MOTORS CORPORATION
Supplier Diversity Program
30009 Van Dyke Ave.
Warren, MI 48090-9015
V. Diane Freeman, Senior Manager
Tel: (586) 575-4100 Fax: (313) 556-5108
Web: www.gmsupplypower.com

K-MART CORPORATION
Supplier Diversity Office
3100 W. Big Beaver Rd.
Troy, MI 48084
Diane Perkins, Coordinator
Tel: (248) 463-5238 Fax: (248) 637-1771
Email: dperkins@bluelight.com
Web: www.bluelight.com

ROCKWELL AUTOMATION
Global Support
1849 W. Maple Rd.
Troy, MI 48084
Charles Montpas, Director
Tel: (248) 280-7073 Fax: (248) 280-0611
Email: camontpa@ra.rockwell.com
Web: www.rockwell.com

MINNESOTA

3M
Sourcing Operation
3M Center, Bldg. 214-1N-04
St. Paul, MN 55144
John R. Fischer, Supplier Diversity Program
Manager
Tel: (651) 736-2324 Fax: (651) 733-2969
Email: jrfischer@mmm.com
Web: www.mmm.com

CARGILL, INC.
P.O. Box 9300
Cargill Office Center
Minneapolis, MN 55440-9300
Gayl M. Bunes, Acting Director, Supplier
Diversity
Tel: (952) 742-2336 Fax: (952) 742-1006
Web: www.cargill.com

MISSISSIPPI

MISSISSIPPI SPACE SERVICES
Contracts Department
Bldg. 2108
Stennis Space Center, MS 39529
David Watson, Contracting Officer
Tel: (228) 688-6586 Fax: (228) 688-7834
Email: david.watson@ssc.nasa.gov
Web: www.mssfos.com

VERTEX AEROSPACE
Purchasing Department
555 Industrial Dr. South
Madison, MS 39110-9073
Bill Goss, Supplier Diversity Coordinator
Tel: (601) 607-6363 Fax: (601) 607-6486
Email: bgoss@vertexae.com
Web: www.vertexaerospace.com

MISSOURI

ANHEUSER-BUSCH COMPANIES, INC.
One Busch Pl.
St. Louis, MO 63118
Manager, Supplier Diversity
Tel: (314) 577-2236 Fax: (314) 577-2905
Web: www.a-bsupplierdiversity.com/main.asp

ANHEUSER-BUSCH, INC.
Corporate Purchasing Department
1 Busch Pl.
St. Louis, MO 63118
Marc Braeckel, Executive Assistance
Tel: (314) 577-2436
Web: www.anheuser-busch.com

AQUILA, INC.
20 W. 9th St.
Kansas City, MO 64105
Janet Preece, Manager, Supplier Diversity and
e-Business
Tel: (816) 737-7463 Fax: (816) 467-9954
Email: dsupplier@aquila.com
Web: www.aquila.com

HALLMARK CARDS, INC.
Supplier Diversity Office
2501 McGee St.
Kansas City, MO 64108
Mary Shanon, Supplier Diversity Program
Manager
Tel: (816) 274-5325 Fax: (816) 274-8008
Web: www.hallmark.com

STONE CONTAINER CORPORATION
18095 Edison Ave.
Chesterfield, MO 63005
David Rodriguez, Supplier Diversity Program
Manager
Tel: (636) 519-5323 Fax: (636) 519-5399
Email: drodriguez@smurfit.com
Web: www.smurfit-stone.com

NEBRASKA

CONAGRA FOODS, INC.
6 ConAgra Dr.
Omaha, NE 68102
Calvin Eakins, Manager, Supplier Diversity
Tel: (402) 595-6334 Fax: (402) 595-5304
Email: calvin-eakins@conagrafoods.com
Web: www.conagrafoods.com

NEW HAMPSHIRE

DARTMOUTH COLLEGE
Procurement Office
100 Tuck Hall
Hanover, NH 03755-9050
Gregory T. Husband, Director of Procurement
and Auxiliary Services
Tel: (603) 646-2811 Fax: (603) 646-3810
Email: gregory.t.husband@dartmouth.edu
Web: www.tuck.dartmouth.edu

NEW JERSEY

AFFILIATED COMPUTER SERVICES
300 Frank W. Burr Blvd.
Teaneck, NJ 07666
Eddie Quintanilla, Facilities & Administration
Coordinator
Tel: (201) 996-7000 Fax: (201) 692-0971
Email: eddie.quintanilla@acs-inc.com
Web: www.acs-inc.com

BECTON, DICKINSON & COMPANY
1 Becton Dr.
Franklin Lakes, NJ 07417-1883
James Swartz, Small Business Coordinator
Tel: (201) 847-6726
Email: james_swartz@bd.com
Web: www.bd.com

BRISTOL-MYERS SQUIBB COMPANY
Supplier Diversity
P.O. Box 4500
777 Scudders Mill Rd.
Plainsboro, NJ 08536
Ingrid M. Sheremeta, Associate Director,
Supplier Diversity
Tel: (609) 897-5348 Fax: (609) 897-5310
Email: ingrid.sheremeta@bms.com
Web: www.bms.com

CENDANT CORPORATION
One Campus Dr.
Parsippany, NJ 07054
Jeanine Brady, Manager, Supplier Diversity
Tel: (973) 496-6023 Fax: (973) 496-5161
Email: jeanine.brady@cendent.com
Web: www.cendant.com

HONEYWELL INTERNATIONAL
Global Diversity
101 Columbia Rd.
Morristown, NJ 07962
Roslyn Dickerson, Corporate VP
Tel: (973) 455-2000 Fax: (973) 455-4807
Web: www.honeywell.com

JOHNSON & JOHNSON
Strategic Sourcing
410 George St.
New Brunswick, NJ 08901
Ann Mullen, Supplier Diversity Manager
Tel: (732) 524-2983/1865
Fax: (732) 524-5225
Email: mwbe@corus.jnj.com
Web: www.jnj.com/supplier_resources/
supplier_diversity

JP MORGAN CHASE & COMPANY
Newport Ctr. 5,
575 Washington Blvd., 12th Fl.
Jersey City, NJ 07310
Harvey Butler, VP, Supplier Diversity Program
Director
Tel: (201) 595-5264 Fax: (201) 595-5220
Email: harvey.butler@jpmchase.com
Web: www.jpmorganchase.com

MERCK & COMPANY, INC.
Supplier Diversity Program
2 Merck Dr. #WS1W-53
Whitehouse Station, NJ 08889-0200
Vince Colarusso, SBLO
Tel: (908) 423-2851 Fax: (908) 735-1807
Email: supplier_diversity@merck.com
Web: www.merck.com/supplierdiversity

RICOH CORPORATION
Minority Vendor Program
5 Dedrick Place
West Caldwell, NJ 07006
Garry R. Kappmeier, Manager
Tel: (973) 808-7544 Fax: (973) 808-7643
Email: garry.kappmeier@ricoh-usa.com
Web: www.ricoh-usa.com

TOYOTA MOTOR SALES, USA
Supplier Development
Henderson Dr.
W. Caldwell, NJ 07006
Christine A. Adamcik
Tel: (973) 882-6227 Fax: (973) 575-1147
Email: supplier_diversity-tms@toyota.com
Web: www.toyota.com

VERIZON COMMUNICATIONS, INC.
Supplier Diversity
825 Rahway Ave.
Union, NJ 07083
Samuel Delgado, Director, Supplier Diversity
Tel: (732) 855-9988 Fax: (908) 964-8361
Email: samuel.a.delgado@verizon.com
Web: www.verizon.com/diversity/suppliers

NEW MEXICO

AEROJET
Supplier Diversity Program
604 Spring St.
Socorro, NM 87801
James Martin, Administrator
Tel: (505) 835-2071 X11
Fax: (505) 835-4911
Email: james.martin@aerojet.com
Web: www.aerojet.com

NEW YORK

ALTRIA CORPORATE SERVICES, INC.
Supplier Diversity Office
120 Park Ave.
New York, NY 10017
Keith Hines, Manager, Corporate Purchasing
Tel: (917) 663-3758 Fax: (917) 663-5317
Email: keith.hines@altria.com
Web: www.altria.com

AVON PRODUCTS, INC.
Global Supplier Development
1251 Ave. of the Americas
New York, NY 10020-0196
Donna L. Westerman, Director of Supplier
Diversity & Social Accountability
Tel: (212) 282-7352 Fax: (212) 282-6524
Email: donna.westerman@avon.com
Web: www.avon.com

AVON PRODUCTS, INC.
Global Supplier Development
Midland & Peck Ave.
Rye, NY 10580
Andrew Topp, Manager
Tel: (914) 935-2040 Fax: (914) 935-2335
Email: andrew.topp@avon.com
Web: www.avon.com

COLGATE-PALMOLIVE COMPANY
300 Park Ave.
New York, NY 10022
Jeannie Maddox, Program Manager
Tel: (212) 310-2449 Fax: (212) 310-2923
Web: www.colgate.com

CON EDISON
Minority & Women Business Enterprise
Program
4 Irving Pl. #1708
New York, NY 10003
Joy Crichlow, Director
Tel: (212) 460-3076 Fax: (212) 614-1899
Email: crichlowj@coned.com
Web: www.coned.com

EASTMAN KODAK COMPANY
Supplier Diversity Office
300 Weiland Rd.
Rochester, NY 14652-3674
Joyce M. Wichie, Director
Tel: (585) 477-4466 Fax: (585) 588-5520
Email: joyce.wichie@kodak.com
Web: www.kodak.com/go/supplierdiversity

**INTERNATIONAL BUSINESS MACHINES,
INC. (IBM)**
Global Supplier Diversity
Route 100, MD HTE1-2SOM

Somers, NY 10589
I. Javette Jenkins, Minority Supplier Programs Director
Tel: (914) 766-2376 Fax: (914) 766-9262
Email: javette@us.ibm.com
Web: www.ibm.com/procurement

METROPOLITAN LIFE INSURANCE CO.
Diversity Supplier Partnership
1 Metlife Plz.
Long Island City, NY 11101
Andrea Whittington
Tel: (212) 578-9554 Fax: (212) 578-9221
Web: www.metlife.com

PEPSI-COLA COMPANY
One Pepsi Way
Somers, NY 10589
J. Frederick Canady, Supplier Diversity Coordinator
Tel: (914) 767-7243 Fax: (914) 767-1248
Email: fred.canady@pepsi.com
Web: www.pepsi.com

PFIZER, INC.
Supplier Diversity Office
150 E. 42nd St., Mezzanine
New York, NY 10017
Gwen Turner, Manager
Tel: (212) 573-2656 Fax: (212) 573-1219
Email: gwendolyn.turner@pfizer.com
Web: www.pfizersupplierdiversity.com

PHILIP MORRIS MANAGEMENT CORPORATION
Supplier Diversity Office
120 Park Ave., 24th Fl.
New York, NY 10017
Tel: (212) 880-5000 Fax: (917) 663-2167
Web: www.philipmorris.com

PRAXAIR, INC.
Global People Excellence Office
P.O. Box 44
Tonawanda, NY 14151-0044
Kim Smith, Manager
Tel: (716) 879-7834 Fax: (716) 879-2344
Web: www.praxair.com

XEROX CORPORATION
Supplier Diversity Office
P.O. Box 1600
800 Phillips Rd.
Webster, NY 14580
Dan Robinson, Manager, Global Purchasing/ Market Access
Tel: (585) 422-2295
Email: Dan.Robinson@usa.xerox.com
Web: www.xerox.com

XEROX CORPORATION
Supplier Diversity Office
800 Phillips Rd., Bldg. 205-99P
Webster, NY 14580
Dan Robinson, Manager
Tel: (585) 422-2295 Fax: (585) 231-5895
Email: dan.robinson@usa.xerox.com
Web: www.xerox.com

NORTH CAROLINA

BANK OF AMERICA
Multicultural Supplier Development
525 N. Tryon St., 9th Fl.
Charlotte, NC 28255
Leonard Hilliard, Contact
Tel: (704) 386-8213
Email: leonard.hillard@bankofamerica.com
Web: www.bankofamerica.com/ supplierdiversity

BANK OF AMERICA CORPORATION
101 N. Tryon St., M/C NC1-022-15-02
Charlotte, NC 28255

Joseph D. Hill, Executive Vice President
Tel: (704) 387-2273 Fax: (704) 386-1668
Email: josephdhill@bankofamerica.com
Web: www.bankofamerica.com

BURLINGTON INDUSTRIES
3330 W. Friendly Ave.
Greensboro, NC 27410
David Kelly, Supplier Diversity Manager
Tel: (336) 379-2633 Fax: (336) 574-5401
Email: kelly.david@burlington.com
Web: www.burlington.com

COOPER TOOLS
P.O. Box 728
1000 Lufkin Rd.
Apex, NC 27502
C. Green, Manager, Government & Hardware Services
Tel: (919) 387-2305 Fax: (919) 387-2370
Email: c.green@cooperhandtools.com
Web: www.cooperhandtools.com

DUKE ENERGY COMPANY
P.O. Box 1244
526 S. Church St.
Charlotte, NC 28201
I. Alexander, Minority Business Development Program Director
Tel: (704) 382-7943 Fax: (704) 382-1995
Email: ialexander@duke-energy.com
Web: www.duke-energy.com

FIRST UNION BANK
Diversity Supplier Office
301 S. Tryon St.
Charlotte, NC 28288-1116
Lenny Springs, Director of Supplier Diversity
Tel: (704) 374-6807 Fax: (704) 383-6293
Email: lenny.springs@wachovia.com
Web: www.wachovia.com

GLAXOSMITHKLINE
Supplier Administration Group
P.O. Box 13398
Five Moore Dr.
Research Triangle Park, NC 27709
Tel: (800) 485-3030 Fax: (919) 315-0177
Email: ussupplierdiversity@gsk.com
Web: www.gsk.com

PHYAMERICA GOVERNMENT SERVICES, INC.
1000 Park 40 Plz., #500
Durham, NC 27713
Laura Williams, Office Manager
Tel: (919) 383-0355 Fax: (919) 383-0807
Email: laurawilliams@sterlinghealthcare.biz
Web: www.sterling-healthcare.com

OHIO

AMERICAN ELECTRIC POWER COMPANY
1 Riverside Plz.
Columbus, OH 43215-2372
Julie Sloat, Managing Director
Tel: (614) 716-1000 Fax: (614) 716-1823
Email: jsloat@aep.com
Web: www.aep.com

BORDEN CHEMICAL
180 E. Broad St.
Columbus, OH 43215
Bob Massey, Global Supply Leader
Tel: (614) 225-4127 Fax: (614) 225-4238
Email: loscoccopf@bordenchem.com
Web: www.bordenchem.com

CINCOM SYSTEMS, INC.
Purchasing Department
55 Merchant St.
Cincinnati, OH 45246
Donna Alig, Buyer
Tel: (513) 612-2300 Fax: (513) 612-2000
Email: dalig@cincom.com

Web: www.cincom.com

GENERAL ELECTRIC
GE Aircraft Engines
1 Newman Way, M/D A-86
Cincinnati, OH 45215
Mark K. Miller, Leader, Supplier Diversity Programs
Email: mark.mk.miller@ae.ge.com
Web: www.ge.com

GOODYEAR TIRE & RUBBER CORPORATION
Compliance Diversity and Worklife
1144 E. Market St.
Akron, OH 44316-0001
Jim McElroy, Manager
Tel: (330) 796-2121 Fax: (330) 796-2222
Web: www.goodyear.com

NCR CORPORATION
Supplier Diversity
1700 S. Patterson Blvd.
Daytona, OH 45479
Clairesse Jackson, Director
Tel: (937) 445-5000 Fax: (301) 212-5651
Email: cj125487@exchange.washington. ncr.com
Web: www.ncr.com

RUBBERMAID, INC.
Purchasing & Sourcing
3320 W. Market St.
Fairborn, OH 44333
Karl Harrison, VP of Purchasing
Tel: (330) 869-7100 Fax: (330) 202-5465
Web: www.rubbermaid.com

OREGON

LEVI STRAUSS & COMPANY
Shared Financial Services
3125 Chad Dr.
Eugene, OR 97408
Manuel Balesteri, Procurement Services Manager
Tel: (541) 242-7336 Fax: (541) 242-7555
Email: mbalesteri@levi.com
Web: www.levi.com

NIKE, INC.
One Bowerman Dr.
Beaverton, OR 97005-6453
Brenda R. Dizer, Supplier Diversity Manager
Tel: (503) 532-2719 Fax: (503) 671-2671
Email: brenda.dizer@nike.com
Web: www.nikesupplierdiversity.com

PENNSYLVANIA

ALUMINIUM COMPANY OF AMERICA, THE
201 Isabella St.
Pittsburgh, PA 15212
Franklin Thomas, Lead Director
Tel: (412) 553-4545 Fax: (412) 553-4498
Web: www.alcoa.com

ARAMARK CORPORATION
1101 Market St.
Philadelphia, PA 19107
Dennis Glen, V. President, Minority Business Development
Tel: (215) 238-6882 Fax: (215) 238-6848
Email: glen_dennis@aramark.com
Web: www.aramark.com

CONRAIL
2001 Market St., 29th Fl.
Philadelphia, PA 19103
Anthony Carlini, VP of Human Resources
Tel: (215) 209-5099 Fax: (215) 209-4819
Email: anthony.carlini@conrail.com
Web: www.conrail.com

GOVCON/VERTICALNET
5 Walnut Grove #320
Horsham, PA 19044
Tel: (215) 675-1800 Fax: (215) 675-4880
Email: info@govcon.com
Web: www.govcon.com

SAFEGUARD BUSINESS SYSTEMS
455 Maryland Dr.
Fort Washington, PA 19034
Tel: (215) 641-5000 Fax: (215) 641-2469
Email: rmason@gosafeguard.com
Web: www.gosafeguard.com

SHAW ENVIRONMENTAL
Procurement
2790 Mosside Blvd.
Monroeville, PA 15146
Deborah Borkovich, Director Procurement
Tel: (412) 372-7701 Fax: (412) 373-7135
Web: www.theitgroup.com

TENNESSEE

AEROJET
Supplier Diversity Program
1367 Old State Route 34
Jonesborough, TN 37659
Katherine Ramsey, Administrator
Tel: (423) 753-1257 Fax: (423) 753-1297
Email: katherine.ramsey@aerojet.com
Web: www.aerojet.com

AMERICAN PRESIDENT LINES, LTD.
6060 Primacy Pkwy. #300
Memphis, TN 38119
Sandra Elrod, SBLO
Tel: (901) 684-7876 Fax: (530) 685-7289
Email: sandra_elrod@apl.com
Web: www.apl.com

BECHTEL JACOBS COMPANY, LLC
Small Business Office
P.O. Box 4699
Bldg. K1007, M/S 7596
Oak Ridge, TN 37831-7596
McArthur Moore, Supplier Advocate Manager
Tel: (865) 576-3847 Fax: (865) 241-9330
Email: moorem1@bechteljacobs.org
Web: www.bechteljacobs.com

BECHTEL JACOBS COMPANY, LLC
Supplier Diversity Office
P.O. Box 4699
E. Tennessee Technology Park, Bldg. K1330, M/S 7020
Oak Ridge, TN 37831-7020
Mary Alice Douglass, Diversity Programs Representative
Tel: (865) 241-1167 Fax: (865) 574-6368
Email: dou@bechteljacobs.org
Web: www.bechteljacobs.com

BWXT Y-12, LLC
Socioeconomic Programs, Acquisitions and Asset Management
P.O. Box 2002 M/S 6501
Oak Ridge, TN 37831-6501
Spencer Rollins, Socio-Economic Programs Manager
Tel: (865) 576-2090 Fax: (865) 576-3664
Email: rollinsse@y12.doe.gov
Web: www.y12.doe.gov

FEDERAL EXPRESS
Diverse Supplier Development
3131 Democrat Rd. Bldg. D #0100
Memphis, TN 38118
Dennis Taylor, DSD Advisor
Tel: (901) 224-4877 Fax: (901) 224-5071
Email: dataylor5@fedex.com
Web: www.fedex.com/us

TEXAS

AIG-VALIC
2929 Allen Pkwy.
Houston, TX 77019
Chelton Skillern, Procurement Specialist
Tel: (713) 831-3100 Fax: (713) 831-6069
Web: www.aigvalic.com

AMERICAN AIRLINES
Diversity Supplier Program
4333 Amon Carter Blvd.
Ft. Worth, TX 76155
Luis Gomez, Manager Supplier Diversity
Tel: (817) 963-2620 Fax: (817) 931-6947
Email: nancy.l.walker@aa.com
Web: www.aa.com/supplierdiversity

US Hispanic National Organizations and Promotions
4255 Amon Carter Blvd. M/D 4413
Fort Worth, TX 76155
Juan J. Rios, Manager
Tel: (817) 931-4243
Email: juan.rios@aa.com
Web: www.aa.com

C CONSTRUCTION CO.
3212 Chandler Hwy.
Tyler, TX 75702
Crystal Smith, SBLO
Tel: (903) 597-1500 Fax: (903) 597-0567
Email: csmith@cconstruction.net
Web: www.cconstruction.net

COCA-COLA COMPANY
Supplier Diversity
2000 St. James Pl.
Houston, TX 77056-4198
Evette Blackman, Supplier Diversity Support Specialist
Tel: (404) 676-5767 Fax: (713) 888-5688
Email: supplierdiversity@na.ko.com
Web: www.coke.net/supplierdiversity

CONOCOPHILLIPS
P.O. Box: 2197
Houston, TX 77252
Hubert Jones, Supplier Diversity Director
Tel: (281) 293-1000 Fax: (281) 293-1440
Web: www.supplierdiversity.conocophillips.com

DELL COMPUTER
1 Dell Way
Round Rock, TX 78682
Fred Hayes, SBLO
Tel: (512) 338-4400 Fax: (512) 283-6161
Email: sblo@dell.com
Web: www.dell.com

DR. PEPPER / SEVEN-UP COMPANIES, INC.
Procurement Office
P.O. Box 869077
Plano, TX 75086-9077
Wade Hogle, Supplier Diversity Director
Tel: (972) 673-7000 Fax: (972) 673-7980
Email: consumer_relations@dpsu.com
Web: www.dpsu.com

ELECTRONIC DATA SYSTEMS CORPORATION
Supplier Diversity Office
5400 Legacy Dr.
Plano, TX 75024
Mike Muzzy, Supplier Diversity Coordinator
Tel: (972) 605-5072 Fax: (972) 797-5736
Email: info@eds.com
Web: www.eds.com

FLUOR CORPORATION
Fluor Global Sourcing & Supply
8101 W. Sam Houston Pkwy. South, #150
Houston, TX 77072
James A. Scotti, VP/COO
Tel: (713) 596-7607 Fax: (713) 596-7779

Email: supplier.diversity@fluor.com
Web: www.fluor.com

FRITO-LAY, INC.
Supplier Diversity
7701 Legacy Dr.
Plano, TX 75024
Jean Lacefield, Manager
Tel: (972) 334-2499 Fax: (972) 334-3861
Email: fritolay.supplier.diversity@fritolay.com
Web: www.fritolay.com

FUJITSU NETWORK COMMUNICATIONS
National Diversity Initiative
2801 Telecom Pkwy.
Richardson, TX 75082
Julie Crowner, Manager
Tel: (972) 479-6271 Fax: (972) 479-3377
Email: ndi@fnc.fujitsu.com
Web: www.fnc.fujitsu.com

HALLIBURTON
Global Supplier Diversity
4100 Clinton Dr.
Houston, TX 77020
Linda Holloway, Manager
Tel: (713) 753-3319 Fax: (713) 753-2224
Email: linda.holloway@halliburton.com
Web: www.halliburton.com

HUNT BUILDING CORPORATION
Estimating Department
4401 N. Mesa
El Paso, TX 79902
Robert Cabello, VP of Estimating
Tel: (915) 533-1122 Fax: (915) 533-0119
Email: robertc@huntbuilding.com
Web: www.huntbuilding.com

JC PENNEY COMPANY
Supplier Diversity Development
P.O. Box 10001
Dallas, TX 75301-6314
Art Avila, Manager
Tel: (972) 431-4339 Fax: (972) 431-3858
Email: aavila@jcpenney.com
Web: www.jcpenney.com

TEXAS INSTRUMENTS
Minority/Women Business Development
P.O. Box 650311 M/S 3935
Dallas, TX 75265
Shannon Suber, Director
Tel: (972) 917-2365 Fax: (972) 917-2516
Email: s-suber1@ti.com
Web: www.ti.com

THE BURLINGTON NORTHERN SANTA FE RAILWAY CORPORATION
Strategic Sourcing & Supply
2500 Lou Menk Dr. AOB-1
Forth Worth, TX 76131
Billlye Tolbert, DBE Coordinator
Tel: (817) 352-3909 Fax: (817) 352-2651
Web: www.bnsf.com

THE DOW CHEMICAL COMPANY
400 W. Sam Houston Pkwy., Sam Houston
DDC Operations Purchasing
Houston, TX 77042
Rosalie Brockman, Diversity Supplier Manager
Tel: (989) 636-1000 Fax: (989) 832-1556
Web: www.dow.com

VIRGINIA

BOOZ, ALLEN & HAMILTON
Small Business Office
8283 Greensboro Dr.
McLean, VA 22102
Nicole Lewis
Tel: (703) 902-5000 Fax: (703) 902-3333
Email: lewis_nicole@bah.com

Web: www.boozallen.com

CIRCUIT CITY STORES, INC.
Administrative Services
9960 Mayland Dr.
Richmond, VA 23233
Ron Jones, Assistant Vice President for Procurement and Supply Services
Tel: (804) 527-4000 Fax: (804) 967-8815
Web: www.circuitcity.com

COMPUTER SCIENCE CORPORATION
Supplier Diversity Office
45245 Business Ct.
Sterling, VA 20166
Addie Olsen, Manager
Tel: (703) 736-3773 Fax: (703) 736-5010
Email: aolsen2@csc.com
Web: www.csc.com

CONTRACTORS PAVING CORPORATION, INC.
3431 Trent Ave.
Norfolk, VA 23502
Ed Manley, VP & Estimator
Tel: (757) 340-1161 Fax: (757) 340-4582
Email: cteets@contractorspaving.com

DOMINION VIRGINIA POWER
Supplier Diversity Program
701 E. Cary St.
Richmond, VA 23219
Lowell B. Carrington, Director
Tel: (804) 771-3915 Fax: (866) 298-7864
Email: lowell_carrington@dom.com
Web: www.dom.com

DYNCORP
15000 Conference Ctr. Dr.
Chantilly, VA 20151
Diane Dempsey, SBLO
Tel: (703) 818-5671 Fax: (703) 818-4069
Email: diane.dempsey@dyncorp.com
Web: www.dyncorp.com

EG & G TECHNICAL SERVICES INC.
10687 Gaskins Way #101
Manassas, VA 20109
Laura Butler, Purchasing Manager
Tel: (703) 330-4275 Fax: (703) 330-4169
Email: lbutler@egg.com
Web: www.egginc.com

EXXONMOBIL CORPORATION
Supplier Diversity
3225 Gallows Rd.
Fairfax, VA 22037
Nancy Swartout, Supplier Diversity
Tel: (281) 870-6407 Fax: (703) 846-7376
Email: nancy.swartout@exxonmobil.com
Web: www.exxonmobil.com

FREDDIE MAC
Minority Business Development
8200 Jones Branch Dr.
McLean, VA 22102
Jay D. Inouye, Executive Administrator
Tel: (703) 902-7700
Email: j_inouye@freddiemac.com
Web: www.freddiemac.com

GOVERNMENT TECHNOLOGY SERVICES, INC.
3900 Stonecroft Blvd.
Chantilly, VA 20151-1010
Bridgette Atkinson, VP of Human Resources
Tel: (703) 631-3333 X2086
Fax: (703) 222-5240
Web: www.gtsi.com

MCI
701 S. 12th St.
Arlington, VA 22202
John Marshall, Program Director
Tel: (703) 886-4563 Fax: (703) 886-0740
Email: j.marshall@mci.com

MITRE CORPORATION
7515 Colshire Dr.
McLean, VA 22102
Bill Albright, Director of Quality Work LIfe and Benefits
Tel: (703) 883-6538 Fax: (703) 883-7211
Email: albright@mitre.org
Web: www.mitre.org

RAYTHEON SYSTEMS
7700 Arlington Blvd.
Falls Church, VA 22042-2900
Lee Wesner, SBLO
Tel: (703) 876-1983 Fax: (703) 280-4613
Email: lwesner@raytheon.com
Web: www.raytheon.com

TITAN SYSTEMS CORPORATION
Administrative Services
2740 Ellsmere Ave.
Norfolk, VA 23513
Bobbi Brown, Manager, Material/SBLO
Tel: (757) 963-1364 Fax: (757) 963-1357
Email: bbrown@titan.com
Web: www.titan.com

TURNER CONSTRUCTION CORPORATION
3865 Wilson Blvd. #200
Arlington, VA 22203
Deborah H. Cook
Tel: (703) 841-5200
Email: dcook@tcco.com
Web: www.turnerconstruction.com

UNYSIS CORPORATION
Supplier Diversity Program
8008 Westpark Dr.
McLean, VA 22102
Jean Gray, Small Business Liaison
Tel: (703) 556-5100 Fax: (703) 620-1442
Email: jean.gray@unisys.com
Web: www.unisys.com/sdp

WASHINGTON GAS
Supplier Diversity Office
6801 Industrial Rd. #270
Springfield, VA 22151
John Riley, Manager Procurement
Tel: (703) 750-5825 Fax: (703) 750-4424
Email: jriley@washgas.com
Web: www.washgas.com

WASHINGTON

MICROSOFT CORPORATION
One Microsoft Way
Redmond, WA 98052-6399
G. Winston Smith, Director Supplier Diversity
Tel: (425) 882-8080 Fax: (425) 706-7329
Web: www.microsoft.com/mscorp/procurement

THE BOEING COMPANY
Enterprise-Wide Supplier Diversity Program
P.O. Box 3707 M/C 2H-50
Seattle, WA 98168
Carrie L. Hill, Director, Enterprise Supplier Diversity
Tel: (206) 544-8463 Fax: (206) 544-3405
Email: carrie.l.hill@boeing.com
Web: www.boeing.com

WISCONSIN

MILLER BREWING COMPANY
Procurement Contracts & Supplier Diversity
P.O. Box 482, 3939 W. Highland Blvd.
Milwaukee, WI 53201-0482
Tina Kelly-Beckett, Manager
Tel: (414) 931-3754 Fax: (414) 931-2324
Email: tkelly-beckett@mbco.com

Interview

FERNANDO ESPUELAS

Fernando Espuelas is the Chairman and CEO of VOY, LLC, a company focused on building a cultural bridge between Latinos and the mainstream through media platforms including cable television, music, television programming, film, publishing, and internet. He is currently working on a pilot for a talk show called *"GO!"* that describes his recipe for success. VOY's core brand message is that self-empowerment and optimism are the keys to success and personal fulfillment. With a long history of building globally recognized brands and a strong advocate of empowering and connecting Latinos, Espuelas co-founded and was formerly Chairman and CEO of StarMedia Network, a pioneering internet media company for Spanish- and Portuguese- speaking audiences worldwide. At StarMedia, he was responsible for building a network that has broken national barriers to become the most recognized Internet brand in Latin America, serving twenty-five million people worldwide. Espuelas raised $500 million dollars for the company in a combination of private and public offerings.

AHHY As the Chairman & CEO of VOY, LLC, how do you leverage your experience and insight in order to be well positioned, and what is your vision of the company for the future?

Espuelas First of all, it starts with the vision for the future—what are we trying to create? Where are we going? How do we get there? Essentially, the process of building a company from scratch never obeys a pattern necessarily, but there are plenty of things you have to do and certain mind sets that you have to adopt in order to be successful. So having done this before and… I actually started my company in the 6th grade… I have done this over and over again. Hopefully, each time that you do it, you do it a little bit better. You can incorporate

Continued on 110

Fernando Espuelas on the set of *GO! with Fernando Espuelas.*

Interview, from 109

all the things you did right and all the things you did wrong and take it from there. For us, the vision for the future is to create an icon brand for the Latino market in the U.S. that is representative of the very aspirations of the community—a brand that doesn't describe a product or service, but a mind-set of optimism and self-empowerment, and can be rolled out across a series of businesses that are of unique appeal to Hispanics in the United States today.

…AHHY You said that you started something at a very young age?

Espuelas In the 6th grade, I started a bank—an insurance company. I had my friends invest in my company. We would insure books and pencils and pens and erasers and we would also lend money to kids… they would take out loans from our bank, which they would repay and so forth. It was a time when my mom and I had just come to the U.S. It was a way to make some sort of contribution to our finances and start that business.

…AHHY was it successful?

Espuelas It was very successful up to the point when we started to advertise (laughs) around the school, and the teachers got all freaked out about it because you know…they thought financial services in the 6th grade was a bit odd, but up to that point it was very successful. I mean it was a very simple observation, which was people

wanted these kinds of services and so I decided to do it.

…AHHY can you talk more about your vision for a Hispanic icon brand?

Espuelas When you look at the Hispanic market today, what you see is obviously a fast growing vibrant market…fastest growing demography in the United States, and today the income of Hispanics in this country is bigger than the gross domestic product in Brazil, believe it or not. So it is already the largest Latin economy in the world, but when you look at this economy, you realize that there are really no transcendental brands for the Hispanic market—there really are no brands that stand out for the experience of being Hispanic in the United States or for the aspirations of Hispanics in the U.S. So our vision is to create this brand that is representative of the new generation Hispanics and then attach this brand to very high quality media vehicles like a cable channel, a publishing company, a music company, etc…that can be part of a lifestyle that Hispanics can connect with.

AHHY VOY, LLC is focused on building a cultural bridge between Latinos and the mainstream through media platforms. Why did you decide to take this approach?

Espuelas I think that one of the interesting results of the success of Hispanics in the United States today is a bit of isolation, and isolation at many different levels—isolation from your culture back home if you are an early immigrant within families the generation gap is really important so that the mother might be watching Spanish language television and the kids are watching English language television. And there is also generational long-term alienation from Latin culture for so many years… really for almost the whole history of the United States. Being Hispanic in

the U.S. was not a good thing and so many families essentially Anglicized themselves and literally took the culture out of their lives. Yet today in 2005, I am convinced that millions and millions of Hispanics, that have essentially left the culture behind, are looking to connect back into Latin culture in a new way and want their children to connect back.

At the same time, I think that there is a very large group of non-Latinos in the United States that are either consciously or unconsciously consuming Latin culture—whether it is food, whether it is music, whether it is the movies they go to see—and this is the audience for Latin-themed media products. It is really a very large one in this country yet that very specific segmentation is absent. But the idea of the cultural bridge is literally media that connects people to each other and connects them back to the culture—in English—the possibility of those that have left the culture behind to reconnect with it or those that are discovering Latin culture for the first time to connect with it as well.

AHHY In your book, *Life in Action*, you describe VOY, LLC "as a vehicle for Latinos in the United States and Latin America to cross into the mainstream and achieve 'self-actualization.'" Can you provide an example of how VOY will help Hispanics achieve this?

Espuelas I think one of the realities of media is that media is not just simply a reflection of society, but it is one of the primary mechanisms by which society understands itself. So when you see on television that roughly eighty percent of the Hispanic characters on television are negative stereotypes… Hispanics will see themselves reflected that way and there is a natural reaction of feeling limited by that image and moreover non-Hispanics see those images as well and limits the ability of Hispanics to advance in society.

So by creating media products that seek to show the very best of our culture—that seek to essentially create a new image for Hispanics—not a new image in the true sense because there is already an image that exists in the community, but a new public interest as well… that this kind of media will serve as a catalyst for people to think of themselves differently, for people to think of the Hispanic community differently and to really start showing in media the range of possibilities that are open to us as individuals, but also open to us as an ethnic group in this country. So what we hope to do obviously through a variety of vehicles, whether they are television shows, or movies, or internet sites, is to show the new face of Hispanics as we are—as a vibrant energetic part of the American fabric and have…would be a mirror of our aspirations and at the same time, almost a presentation card to the rest of society who may have huge misperceptions as to what Hispanics are, can do or not do based on what popular media has decided to depict us as.

This is a key point and it is very emblematic of things. First of all in English language television, roughly eighty percent of Hispanic characters are depicted as domestic workers. Now, there are a lot of domestic workers who are Hispanics, but that is not the reality—it is not the essence of who we are. That is what you do when you are an immigrant to this country in order to have…like my mom worked as a housekeeper, so I could go to school, then I could go to college so I could be you know… be another American and that is played throughout the community, but not played out in the media.

Additionally, you have other things that are…for example, in Spanish language television, if you look at the…basically every soap opera you see a similar dynamic which is light skinned people are the masters and dark skinned people are the servants. This might be reflective of Latin American societies where there are tremendous amounts of racism, and a systemic approach of keeping people poor, but that is un-American you know… that will not play in the United States and it should not play with Hispanics either. We have an opportunity by being Americans who happen to be Latin to reject those kinds of racial stereotypes, to reject the imagery of subjugation, which unfortunately is a big part of Latin culture, and so now we should be through media—and obviously through many other forms. In our business, we should be articulating a positive American vision of society in which race has no bearing on anything and certainly no bearing in terms of your economic opportunity or your education or whatever. So our role, and obviously we are just one company, is to erase those stereotypes, to begin to show Latin culture for its richness and try to ameliorate some of the historical negatives coming out of the Latin American experience.

AHHY You are a strong advocate of empowering and creating community among Hispanics. In your opinion, what is the greatest challenge facing the Hispanic population?

Espuelas This is my perspective—it is a symptom of a bigger issue and that symptom is the lack of education among Hispanics. We have the low-est indices of any ethnic group in this country of high school and college graduation and that is objectively a tragedy for the community, but it is also a tragedy for the United States. In the next twenty years, roughly twenty-five percent of all American workers will retire and will be replaced by Hispanics and so what we are doing is transferring essentially a highly educated workforce with one—look at statistics today—that is going to be a lot less educated and that will create a huge social economic problem looking to the future.

But I see the symptom because I think, 'why do people not get a certain education if they could?' There are many many reasons for that. Education in the United States is political, so if you are living in a poor community, you are probably going to get a poor education. At the same time, I think we have to go back to some of the imagery that is available in the media to inspire or not inspire people and when you see that eighty percent of people who are just like you on television are cutting the grass or cleaning the house, it is very hard. You know, if you are in a poor situation or difficult situation or if your family just arrived and is trying to make ends meet, it is very hard to fight the temptation not to go to work.

I mean I started working when I was eleven years old, pumping gas in a gas station to help my mom. But at the same time, she made sure that I kept going to school, and I certainly understood that my past was not through being a gas attendant, but through finishing college. I think that kind of mindset shift and also, objective reality shift—in terms of helping people who just arrived, to be able to focus their lives on education and to create a culture of education where there are role models. Where, you know, now the Attorney General of the United States is Hispanic and everyone is going oh ah oh ah… but give me a break, why should that be

Fernando Espuelas on the set of *GO! with Fernando Espuelas.*

Continued on 112

Fernando Espuelas on the set of *GO! with Fernando Espuelas.*

at all dramatic? I mean, I think it is great. You know, we still are in this very silly situation where we are wondering, 'can a Hispanic be an Attorney General?' Well, sure I mean a Hispanic can be an officer, can be the president of the country, but we don't have that kind of stimula in the market place that would give kids the sense that they too can participate in the American dream. And so in the end, I think it does comes down to education and that is the biggest challenge from my perspective.

AHHY What lessons did you learn from the collapse of StarMedia Networks during the dotcom era? Is this what lead you to start VOY, LCC, and what new challenges have you faced? How have you been able to overcome these challenges?

Espuelas StarMedia still exists— we have millions of users all over the world and it is one of the main brands of the internet for Spanish speakers in the world. It is not like it collapsed, the stock (laughs) market collapsed, but anyway. StarMedia is and was for me up to this point, the greatest business experience I have ever had. It was the opportunity that I had to project my imagination on to the future and make it come true. When we started this company, no one believed that Hispanics would use the internet—no one had raised a single dollar of venture funding for the internet in Latin America. We were to be the catalyst literally for billions and billions of dollars of investments throughout Latin America and everything from computers to telephone networks to education frankly. So, it was one of these companies that is representative of an era and representative of what can happen when you connect high technology with the great energy of Latinos.

In terms of what I learned, part of it frankly was the end when the stock market basically collapsed when Argentina blew up and Latin America blew up—economically speaking—because it is in moments of extreme stress and difficulty, moments that you learn about yourself when you meet your true self and you finally answer the question whether you have the inner strength to be truly successful in life. Which truly successful in life from my perspective is not getting everything right, and you win everything, but rather you go from experience to experience to experience, growing with each experience and able to incorporate that learning into some sort of greater sense of knowledge about yourself or the universe or whatever.

VOY is very much its own company. It is informed by my experience. It is informed by a desire not to repeat either victories or defeats. It is really an opportunity for me to express my entrepreneurship in a totally different way.

AHHY How have your life experiences helped you understand the challenges that newcomers to our country encounter? How were you able to overcome these challenges, and what advice can you offer to young Hispanics looking to excel professionally?

Espuelas Well, once again, I arrived with my mom as a kid. We only had a hundred dollars and through my mom's tremendous energy and effort and dedication, we were able to survive and eventually thrive. And I think essentially that most immigrants have some version of that story because the U.S. is probably the only place in the world where you are not bound by the past. It doesn't matter if you were not born in that special family, it doesn't matter if you were not born in that special city. You basically start with the same level of opportunity as anybody else and then it is up to you to take it to the next level.

What I would say… I would give just one bit of advice… especially for an early arrival. There has to be almost a single-minded focus on education. And I mean everything around that. Everything from learning English as well as possible to really putting yourself on a college track that will define you going forward for the rest of your life. I think, you know, that as you look at the growth of the Hispanic market in the U.S. and all the companies that are been created towards that market place. Hispanic executives, Hispanic managers in particular, will have a disproportionate competitive advantage going forward, because these companies that are creating services that want to target the Hispanic market are looking for talented, educated Hispanics to run the show. And today there are very few, and hopefully tomorrow, there will be many more.

So someone who is interested in business or interested in anything else, I think that single-minded focus on education is the driver, and there are a lot of resources in this country that you can tap into There are lot of opportunities for education. I mean I had a full scholarship to college so I didn't… my first year tuition was twelve thousand dollars and my mom's income was seven thousand dollars, so if it wasn't for a full scholarship, I could never have gone to college. I think many people can get some scholarships. It is a matter of work and finding it and certainly a bit of luck, but it is there. That would be my primary advice.

Interview

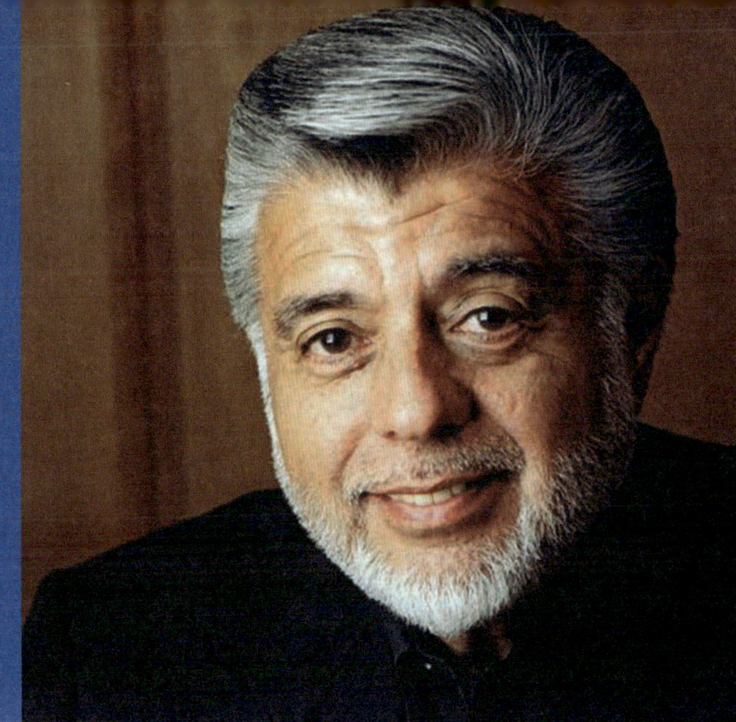

DAVID C. LIZÁRRAGA

David C. Lizarraga is a dynamic and visionary international leader who has always been deeply concerned about his community. He has long been an advocate of empowering people so that they may improve the quality of their lives. Born and raised in East Los Angeles, he began working with young, at-risk teens in East L.A. as a young man. Since that time, he has worked tirelessly to give economically disadvantaged families and young people access to the tools they need to pursue the American Dream, dedicating his life to rebuilding communities. For over 28 years, he has overseen TELACU (The East Los Angeles Community Union), a non-profit community development corporation founded in 1968. As president and CEO of TELACU and TELACU Millennium, LLC, he has created what is now the largest Hispanic business in the County of Los Angeles. Internationally recognized as one of the country's top Latino leaders, Lizarraga is often called on for his expertise in the fields of business, real estate development and community development. Lizarraga is also the Chairman of the United States Hispanic Chamber of Commerce (USHCC) and plans to focus on key issues that affect all Hispanic business men and women.

AHHY You are recognized as one of the nation's most successful Hispanic leaders. What challenges did you face when you founded TELACU (The East Los Angeles Community Union), and what do you attribute to the progress of TELACU as one of the most successful Hispanic community and economic development corporations in the nation?

Lizarraga How we are recognized is really not as significant as what we do. Recognition comes as a result of accomplishments, so I am going to talk about what we have done. I always talk in the framework of "we" because, like anything else, it is the people who comprise the TELACU team that make our organization successful and give me the opportunity to lead a pioneering institution. No one does it alone.

Continued on 114

The TELACU model works with communities to achieve positive results, and that is what people interpret as success. Positive results can be measured in dollars, they can be measured in people served, they can be measured in impact...there are infinite means of measuring success and positive results. But the challenges TELACU initially faced back in the late 60s and early 70s stemmed from the fact that few organizations had examined the whole issue of economic empowerment, and we hadn't looked at the possibility of creating this economic empowerment in a third world community.

Our country understands very well the needs of third world countries. We have historically provided aid to foreign countries, third world countries and developing nations, but we have never been successful in empowering and assisting our own domestic third world communities. TELACU originally began with the consideration that our community was an economically disadvantaged third world economy. What I mean by this is that people living in economically healthy communities seem to generate the ability to work, earn money, and spend money within that community, and to have that capital circulate within the local economy in such a manner that it has a multiplying, exponential impact. That was the missing element in East Los Angeles 40 years ago.

In East Los Angeles, we lived and slept in our community, but we worked and spent our hard earned money outside of our community. That pattern created disinvestment upon disinvestment upon disinvestment. Businesses left, jobs evaporated, hope vanished. So much so that the number one challenge we had was to believe that we, at TELACU, could make a difference at all.

I also had to admit that, initially, I was part of the problem. In my desire to create change by being an organizer in the community, I did my fair share of scaring some of those businesses away because I felt my community had been disempowered. As an organization, we felt that addressing issues of economic empowerment was too far from reality and that we shouldn't even be trying. But in those early years, we decided to look at the possibility of being

innovative, of thinking 'outside of the box' and utilizing grants ... minimal grants that were available ... in a manner that was not common at the time. We used those funds as equity and leveraged them, creating self-sustaining businesses to economically empower TELACU's services to the community. In effect, we did what every other business does. We harnessed the prospect of community and economic development to a business model aligned with the U.S. economy. We also came to an early realization that there are many things that TELACU as an organization and David Lizarraga as an individual did not know. When you know what you don't know, then you can surround yourself with people who do know, and you can utilize that talent and capability to build a team that possesses the skills necessary to succeed. We joined forces with other successful local business people so that we would not make the mistakes that young businesses often make. Leveraging and partnering are very common concepts now, but 35 years ago, they were very new concepts for people like us, when most community-based organizations were dependent on zero-based government grant funds to keep themselves alive. Our partners brought to the table capability and experience that allowed us to spread our risk. Unfortunately 35 years later, many of the dynamic institutions that serve our community today are still dependent on grants for their survival. This type of dependency is one that TELACU was not willing to accept.

AHHY Your career and community activities have been focused on empowering people and communities. What motivated or inspired you to take this approach, and what obstacles have you had to face in your business activities? How were you able to overcome these obstacles?

Lizarraga The process of empowerment is vital. You have to believe that people can and will respond positively to empowerment. You can only empower people if you are willing to take the time to teach, to inspire, and to provide people with the tools to move ahead. Empowerment isn't just something that is accomplished because you declare

that it will be done. Empowerment comes about as a result of giving people the tools that will allow them to be change agents in a community. So empowering people means that you are willing to participate in the process of generating, assisting, producing and creating collective power.

What inspired me to do this, quite honestly, is the fact that I believe God gave me a desire, a hunger to make a difference in my community. We are all placed in this world for just a moment, a blink of an eye, and while we are here we must make a difference. We have all been given a great responsibility to be contributors to a great society, a great country. We are very fortunate to be in the United States, to have the opportunity to penetrate and participate in the system, and to understand that we need to provide access to that system for our community.

As a young man, I was a militant leader wanting to force change within our community. Realizing that I needed to be prepared in order to bring about change from within the system itself, I needed not only to be an activist and an advocate, but I also had to do the research necessary to provide alternatives and possibilities that would result in solutions. It's pretty easy to be against something; it's much more difficult to have to provide alternative solutions as evidence of ideals that you stand for.

The road was not an easy one. Quite often as a young man, I tried very hard to break through barriers and break down doors. A person who had an important impact on my life one day asked me, "I see you David. You're leading these marches and filling up city hall and protesting...but what change have you created?" I said, "well, you know we are leading the marches and getting people organized and the newspapers are telling our story and the TV stations are there as well. We want to make sure the system understands they are not serving us properly and we're going to protest it!" And he said, "I understand that...but what change have you created?" And I said, "Well, we are getting in there and we are busting down the doors." Finally he said, "Have you ever tried turning the knob and walking in? And when you turn the knob and walk in, talking about everything that doesn't work, do you have anything that does work?"

It was an important time in my life because it meant that I needed not only to talk about what didn't work, but if I wanted to create change, I had to take time to do the analysis, study, research, and put together databases to advance creative concepts, ideas and possibilities so that we would have alternatives to discuss. We not only had a responsibility to talk about what didn't work, but we had to take advantage of the opportunity to talk about what could work. That meant we needed to do our homework.

AHHY As the Chairman of the U.S. Hispanic Chamber of Commerce, what do you hope to achieve on behalf of Hispanic businesses? What is your number one goal as Chairman of the USHCC?

Lizarraga What is really important to the U.S. Hispanic Chamber of Commerce is for it to grow. We represent 2 million businesses in the United States ... 2 million businesses owned and operated by Hispanic men and women. Our members represent first and foremost a very active, hardworking business community who needs a Chamber that is a national voice for that community. From our offices in Washington DC, we must advance an aggressive legislative agenda that will meet the needs of our membership nationwide; an agenda that works from the bottom up and not from the top down. We must increase our services so that our members receive real value for their participation. The Chamber must continue to maintain a commitment to be fiscally transparent, responsible and accountable in utilizing the financial resources received from our members and our corporate sponsors.

It also means that we are going to grow the organization by not only serving Hispanic business men and women, but also chambers that are Spanish-speaking. There are a number of immigrant-based, Spanish-speaking chambers in existence now that we are not serving. This presents a great opportunity for the USHCC.

In my state of California, Hispanics represent one-third of the entire population. That means that we represent one-third of California's economy, the fifth largest economy on planet Earth! And it is small- and medium-sized businesses that are impacting its economic growth. Most small- and medium-sized businesses in California are led by Latinos and Latinas that get up everyday, put together precious investment capital, and go about starting businesses that grow. I believe this is what is fueling the continued growth of California's economy. The Chamber itself is committed to better serving this small- and medium-sized business community, and to aligning our strategy not only to affect national change, but also to look at how we affect state and local legislation that impacts small businesses. It must be aligned from the nation's capitol to our states' capitols to our local city councils and on to our local communities.

We are really excited because we are also going to work at the national level to have an effective federal and corporate procurement strategy. We are implementing a procurement strategy that links corporate America with our small- and medium-sized business membership at the local, regional and national levels. We are establishing a system that will enable our members to have increased access to corporate and federal contract opportunities...opportunities that have for too long eluded us. We are excited because the Chamber is growing. We are excited because we are aligned. We are excited over the fact that we are going to have a very effective legislative conference right after spring break. We are going to work Capitol Hill with our members, meeting not only with Latino representatives, but also with members of Congress who have Latino constituencies throughout the United States. They need to be listening to our message.

AHHY In your opinion, what is the greatest challenge facing the Hispanic population?

Lizarraga We have many challenges and we can't take them on one at a time, we have to multi-track. If you are talking about the greatest challenge the Hispanic business community might have, I think it still is the issue of access to capital. The Hispanic business com-munity, if it is going to grow, will need access to capital; that is an area in which the Chamber must lead. How can we obtain access to capital for small businesses that want to become medium businesses, and medium businesses that want to become bigger businesses? Believe it or not, it is small- and medium-sized businesses, and Latina-owned businesses that are the fastest growing employers in the United States. They stimulate our economy, generating jobs and creating wealth. We must implement a plan to address the critical issue of access to capital.

AHHY What role will the Hispanic community play in shaping the general direction of the country?

Lizarraga One thing that is for certain is that our numbers continue to grow. This will continue as long as the United States shares this huge border with Mexico where you have a continuous flow of immigration. As long as we represent a refuge and an opportunity for a better life, we are going to have folks from the Caribbean, Central America, and South America wanting to come to this country. One thing we do when we come here, is that we become part of a very hard-working community. We pool our resources, invest our biggest asset which is the labor of our friends and family, and in so doing, we generate growth. Hispanics are the embodiment of the American Dream. We are a population that is shaping the future of this country. Any corporation in the United States that wants to grow will do so only if it finds a way of advancing their growth strategy by addressing the needs of the Hispanic community. If they don't, they simply are not going to grow. The Hispanic consumer base is the largest untapped segment of the United States economy, and that is where the greatest opportunity for corporate growth lies. Those that spend the time and resources necessary to effectively serve the Hispanic population are going to achieve great economic success. Our own Hispanic business people should be foremost among American entrepreneurs enjoying that success.

Business

According to the U.S. Census Bureau, the real median income of Hispanic households was $32,997 in 2003. According to projections from the Selig Center for Economic Growth at the University of Georgia, Hispanics will control about $686 billion in spending power in 2004.

The ten states with the largest Hispanic markets in 2004, according to the Selig Center, were California, Texas, Florida, New York, Illinois, New Jersey, Arizona, Colorado, New Mexico, and Georgia (Fig. 1). The rapid growth of the Hispanic population continues to increase the buying power of Hispanics, which represents the fastest-growing consumer market in the United States, according to the Latin Business Association. Better employment will also increase the buying power of the Hispanic population, in addition to a young Hispanic population entering the workforce for the first time.

Many Hispanics are starting their own businesses, and this should increase the growth of this consumer market. According to the most recent official numbers available from the U.S. Census Bureau, there were 1.2 million Hispanic-owned businesses that generated $186.3 billion in revenues in 1997. Sole proprietorship and incorporated businesses owned by individuals represented the largest number (one million) of Hispanic-owned businesses. California, Texas, Florida and New York accounted for seventy-three percent of Hispanic-owned businesses (Fig. 2). Mexicans owned the greatest number of Hispanic-owned firms (Fig. 3). According to HispanTelligence, the number of Hispanic-owned businesses are expected to reach two million and generate revenues totaling $273.81 billion in 2004, and grow fifty-five percent to 3.2 million by 2010.

FIG 1. Hispanic Buying Power (Billions of Dollars)

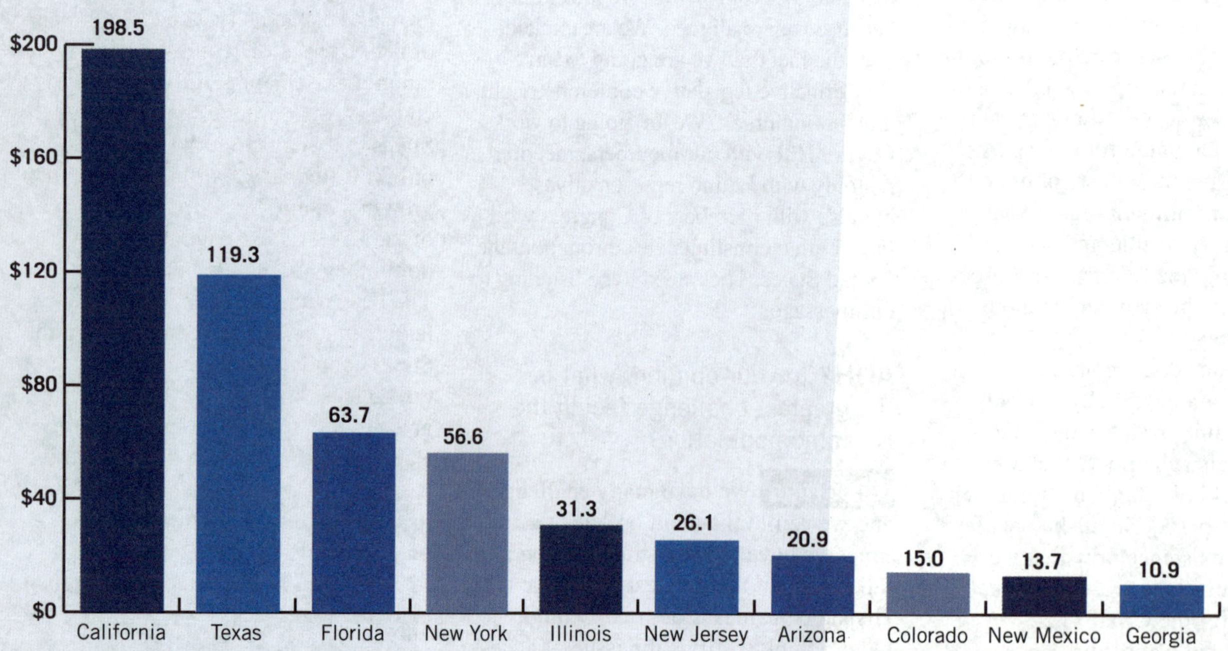

Source: Selig Center for Economic Growth, Terry College of Business, The University of Georgia, May 2004.

FIG 2. States with the Largest Number of Hispanic-Owned Firms: 1997

		Percent of total
U.S. total	1,199,900	
California	336,400	28.0
Texas	240,400	20.0
Florida	193,900	16.2
New York	104,200	8.7
New Jersey	36,100	3.0
Illinois	31,000	2.6
Arizona	28,900	2.4
New Mexico	28,300	2.4
Colorado	20,900	1.7
Virginia	13,700	1.1

Source: U.S. Census Bureau.

The information above is the most current data. The 2002 report will be released towards the end of August, 2005.

FIG 3. Hispanic-Owned Firms by Ethnic Group: 1997

	Firms	Receipts
Total	1,199,900	186,300
Mexican	472,000	73,700
Hispanic Latin American	287,000	41,000
Other Hispanic	188,500	20,700
Cuban	125,300	26,500

Source: U.S. Census Bureau.

According to the Pew Hispanic Center and Inter-American Development Bank, the remittance flow from the United States to Latin American in 2003, could approach $30 billion, and this would be the largest single remittance channel in the world. Based on the five countries studied, fourteen percent (in Ecuador) to twenty-eight percent of the adult population (in El Salvador) received remittances in 2003 (Fig. 4).

The most utilized method to send remittances by U.S. Hispanics was wire transfer (Fig. 5). Forty percent of adult, foreign Hispanics sent remittances on a regular basis, and two thirds of them remitted money at least once a month (Fig. 6). Fifty-six percent of remitters sent money between $100 and $300 at a time (Fig. 7) and forty-six percent of remitters who earned less than $30,000 sent money with a greater frequency (Fig. 8).

FIG 4. Percentage of Adults Receiving Remittances by Country

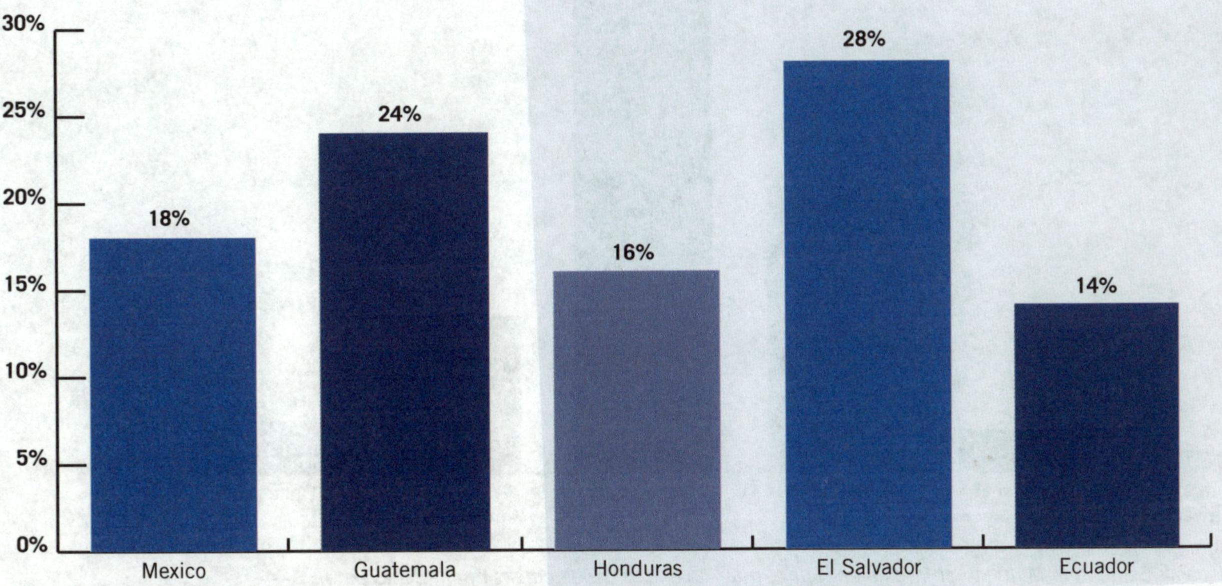

Source: Pew Hispanic Center and Multilateral Investment Fund, Inter-American Development Bank (2003 data).

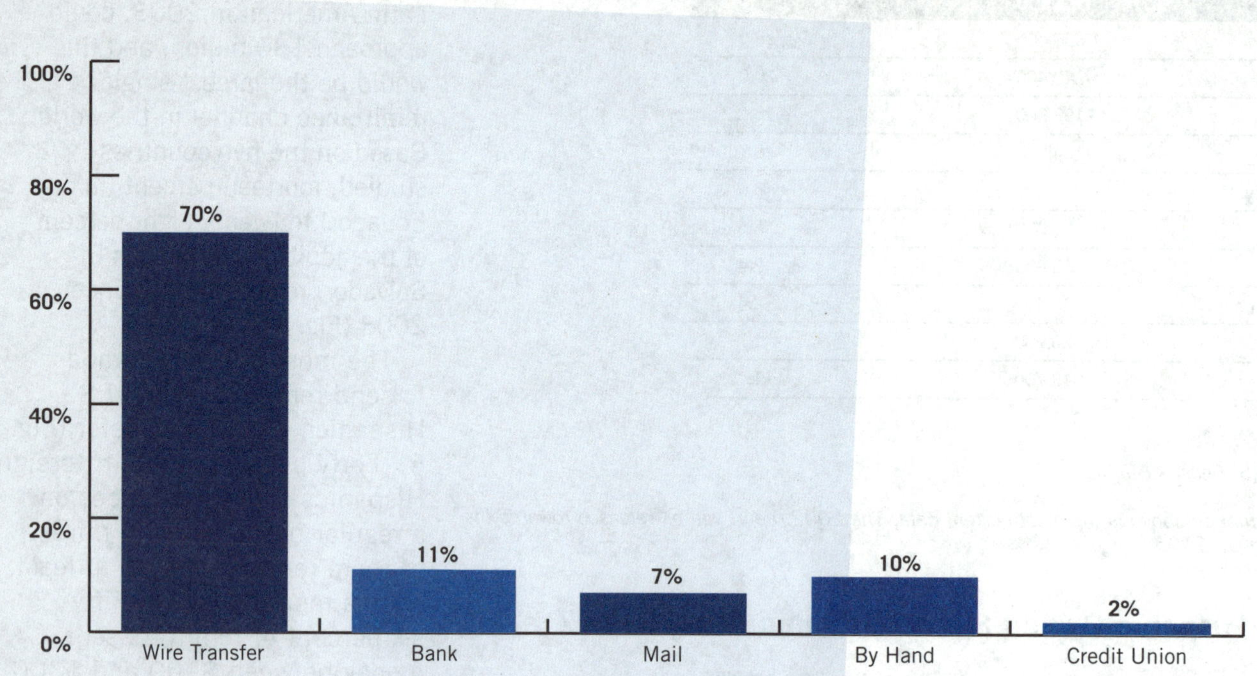

Source: Pew Hispanic Center (2003 data).

FIG 6. Frequency of Remittances to Countries of Origin by Hispanic Immigrants

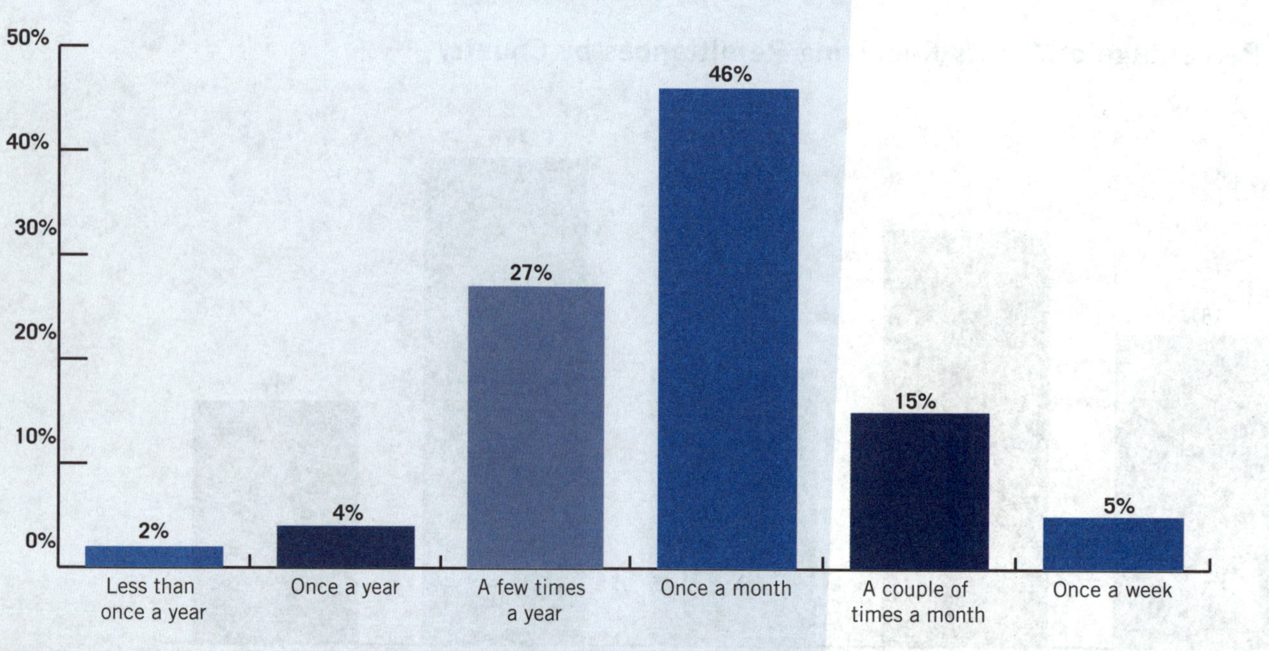

Source: Pew Hispanic Center and Multilateral Investment Fund, Inter-American Development Bank (2003 data).
Note: Forty-two percent of adult, foreign-born Latinos in the U.S. regularly send remittances to their country of origin.

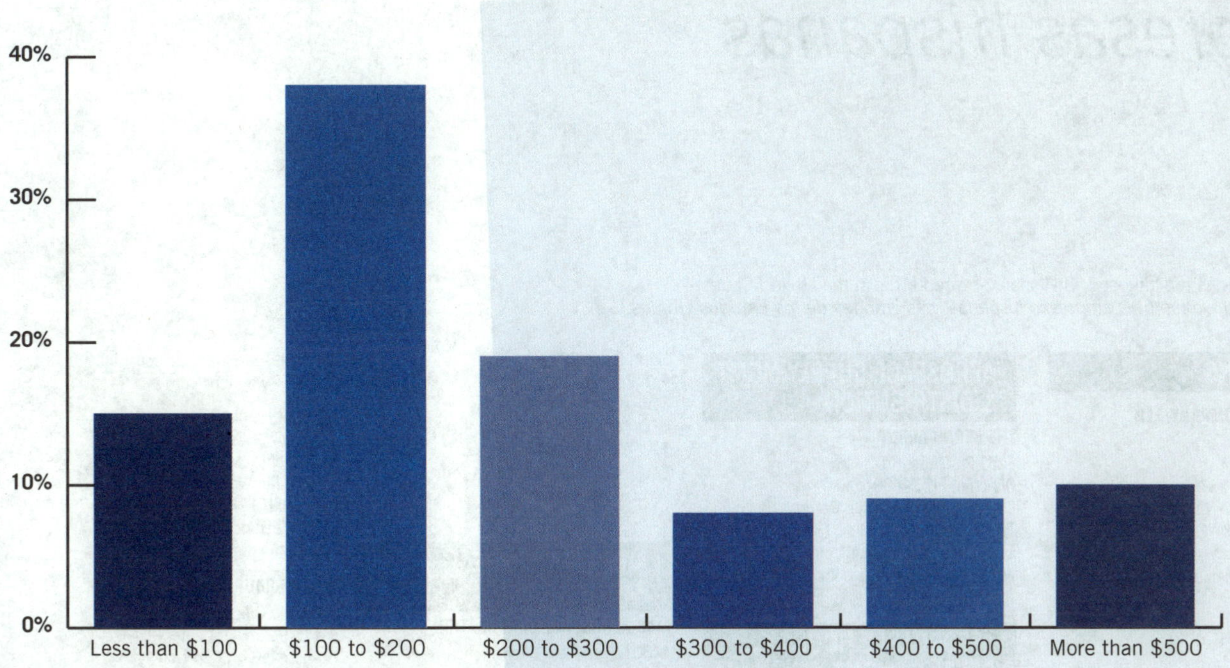

Source: Pew Hispanic Center (2003 data).

FIG 8. U.S. Foreign-Born Latinos: Percent of Remittance Senders by Income

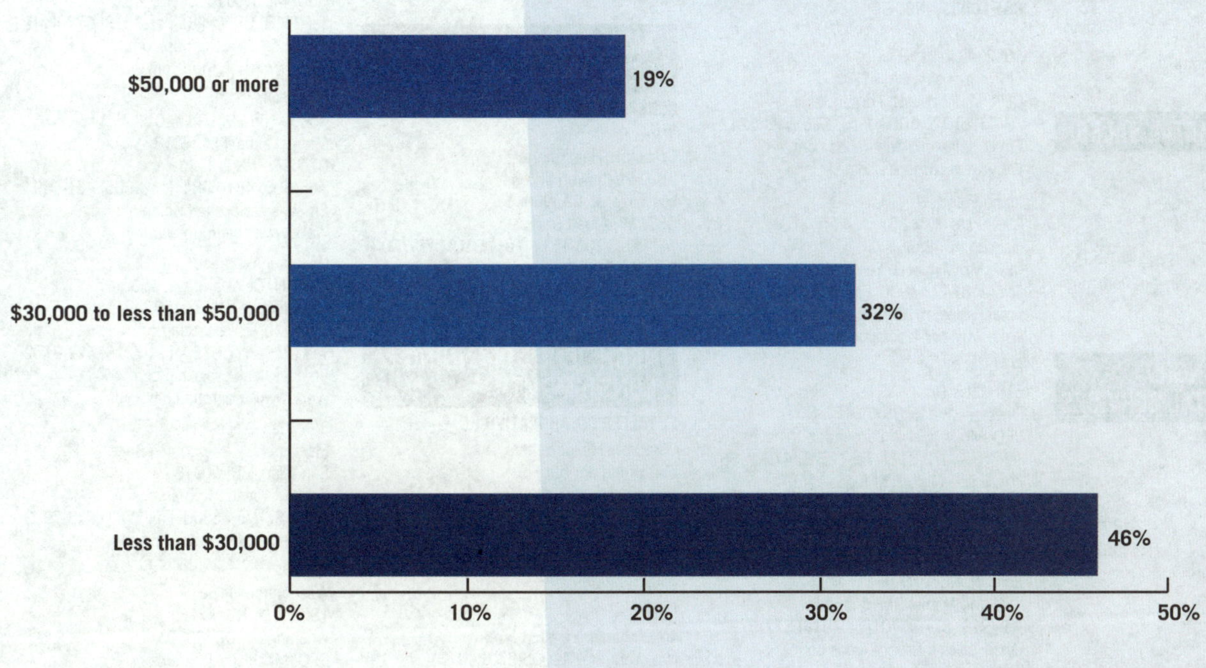

Source: Pew Hispanic Center (2003 data).

Hispanic Companies
Empresas hispanas

This listing includes the largest 500 Hispanic-owned firms in the United States.
Este listado incluye las 500 empresas hispanas más grandes de los Estados Unidos.

ACCOUNTING

MACIAS GINI & COMPANY, LLP
Head Office
3000 S St. #300
Sacramento, CA 95816
CEO: Mr. Kenneth A. Macias
Tel: (916) 928-4600 Fax: (916) 928-2755
Email: rgreen@maciasgini.com
Web: www.maciasgini.com

Fresno Office
2497 W. Shaw Ave. #107
Fresno, CA 93711
CEO: Mr. Kenneth A. Macias
Tel: (559) 229-2261 Fax: (559) 229-2271
Email: rgreen@maciasgini.com
Web: www.maciasgini.com

Los Angeles Office
515 S. Figueroa St. #325
Los Angeles, CA 90071
CEO: Mr. Kenneth A. Macias
Tel: (213) 612-0200 Fax: (213) 286-6426
Email: jgodsey@maciasgini.com
Web: www.maciasgini.com

Walnut Creek Office
2175 N. California Blvd. #645
Walnut Creek, CA 94596
CEO: Mr. Kenneth A. Macias
Tel: (925) 274-0190 Fax: (925) 274-3819
Email: kjo@maciasgini.com
Web: www.maciasgini.com

AEROSPACE METAL SALES

HURLEN CORPORATION
9841 Bell Ranch Dr.
Santa Fe Springs, CA 90670
CEO: Mr. Jay I. Hurtado
Tel: (562) 941-5330 Fax: (562) 941-4750
Email: info@hurlen.comsales@hurlen.com
Web: www.hurlen.com

AEROSPACE SNGR./ ENVIRONMENTAL SERVICES

AJT & ASSOCIATES, INC.
Corporate Headquarters
8910 Astronaut Blvd.
Cape Canaveral, FL 32920
CEO: Mr. Alfredo J. Teran
Tel: (321) 783-7989 Fax: (321) 784-4108
Email: ajt@ajt-assoc.com
Web: www.ajt-assoc.com

AEROSPACE SUPPLY MGMT. & DISTRIBUTION

THE BERND GROUP
1251 Pinehurst Rd.
Dunedin, FL 34698
CEO: Ms. Pilar Ricaurte- Bernd
Tel: (800) 346-8835 Fax: (800) 346-4717
Email: info@berndgroup.com
Web: www.berndgroup.com

AFFORDABLE HOUSING DEVEL. & MGMT.

THE COMMUNITIES GROUP
Head Office
1012 N St. Northwest
Washington, DC 20001
CEO: Mr. Jaime Bordenave
Tel: (202) 667-3002
(800) 226-9999 Fax: (202) 667-3035
Email: info@thecommunitiesgroup.com
Web: www.thecommunitiesgroup.com

AGRICULTURAL COMMODITIES WHSL.

C&F FOODS, INC.
Corporate Office
15620 E. Valley Blvd.
City of Industry, CA 91744
CEO: Mr. Miguel G. Fernandez
Tel: (626) 723-1000 Fax: (626) 723-1212
Email: sales-info@cnf-foods.com
Web: www.cnf-foods.com

Idaho Plant
22689 US Hwy. 30
Hansen, ID 83334
CEO: Mr. Miguel G. Fernandez
Tel: (208) 423-4900 Fax: (208) 423-4903
Email: sales-info@cnf-foods.com
Web: www.cnf-foods.com

Missouri Plant
515 Noles Dr.
Sikeston, MO 63801
CEO: Mr. Miguel G. Fernandez
Tel: (573) 472-5111 Fax: (573) 472-1966
Email: sales-info@cnf-foods.com
Web: www.cnf-foods.com

North Carolina Plant
5201 Departure Dr.
Raleigh, NC 27604
CEO: Mr. Miguel G. Fernandez
Tel: (919) 877-9770 Fax: (919) 877-9790
Email: sales-info@cnf-foods.com
Web: www.cnf-foods.com

North Dakota Plant
P.O. Box 55
Manvel, ND 58256
CEO: Mr. Miguel G. Fernandez
Tel: (701) 696-2040 Fax: (701) 696-2042
Email: sales-info@cnf-foods.com
Web: www.cnf-foods.com

AIRCRAFT SPARE PARTS WHSL.

MAC AEROSPACE CORPORATION
14301-I Sullyfield Circle
Chantilly, VA 20151-1630
CEO: Mr. Javier Rodriguez
Tel: (703) 502-8300 Fax: (703) 502-8303
Email: macero@macero.com
Web: www.macaerospace.com

AIRPORT CONCESS./OFFICE EQUIP. SALES

SOUTHWEST OFFICE SYSTEMS, INC.
P.O. Box 612248
Dallas-Ft. Worth, TX 75261-2248
CEO: Mr. Vince E. Puente, Sr.
Tel: (817) 318-7600 Fax: (817) 255-8640

AMPLIFIER & SEMICONDUCTOR WHSL.

GENERAL TRANSISTOR CORPORATION, INC.
Corporate Headquarters
5300 Beethoven St.
Los Angeles, CA 90066
CEO: Mr. Albert Barrios
Tel: (310) 306-1111 Fax: (310) 578-7200
Email: sales@gtcelectronics.com
Web: www.gtcelectronics.com

ARCH., ENG., PLANNING & CONST. MGMT.

EL TALLER COLABORATIVO PC
Corporate Headquarters
550 Broad St., 5th Fl.
Newark, NJ 07102-4531
CEO: Mr. Alex Garcia
Tel: (973) 424-6420 Fax: (973) 622-6030
Email: agarcia@etcpc.com
Web: www.etcpc.com

New York Office
40 Exchange Pl. #1311
New York, NY 10005-2701
CEO: Mr. Alex Garcia
Tel: (212) 952-1955 Fax: (212) 952-1928

Email: agarcia@etcpc.com
Web: www.etcpc.com

Pennsylvania Office
1008 W. 8th Ave., 2nd Fl.
King of Prussia, PA 19406-1344
CEO: Mr. Alex Garcia
Tel: (610) 768-0877 Fax: (610) 768-0879
Email: agarcia@etcpc.com
Web: www.etcpc.com

CSA GROUP
Atlanta Office
115 Perimeter Center Pl. NE #765
Atlanta, GA 30346
CEO: Mr. Jesus J. Suarez
Tel: (678) 320-9733 Fax: (678) 320-9734
Email: sales@csagroup.com
Web: www.csagroup.com

Chicago Office
311 Wacker Dr. #4550
Chicago, IL 60606
CEO: Mr. Jesus J. Suarez
Tel: (312) 697-4797 Fax: (513) 677-4442
Email: sales@csagroup.com
Web: www.csagroup.com

Corporate Office
8790 Governor's Hill Dr. #200
Cincinnati, OH 45249
CEO: Mr. Jesus J. Suarez
Tel: (513) 677-4440 Fax: (513) 677-4442
Email: sales@csagroup.com
Web: www.csagroup.com

Miami Office
15050 NW 79th Ct. #201
Miami Lakes, FL 33016
CEO: Mr. Jesus J. Suarez
Tel: (305) 461-5484 Fax: (305) 461-5494
Email: sales@csagroup.com
Web: www.csagroup.com

Philadelphia Office
1341 N. Delaware Ave. #500
Philadelphia, PA 19125
CEO: Mr. Jesus J. Suarez
Tel: (215) 427-8750 Fax: (215) 427-8752
Email: sales@csagroup.com
Web: www.csagroup.com

San Juan Office
Mercantil Plz. Mezzanine Suite
San Juan, PR 00918
CEO: Mr. Jesus J. Suarez
Tel: (787) 754-6800 Fax: (787) 753-7300
Email: sales@csagroup.com
Web: www.csagroup.com

Washington Office
1800 K St. NW #716
Washington, DC 20006
CEO: Mr. Jesus J. Suarez
Tel: (240) 401-1476
Email: sales@csagroup.com
Web: www.csagroup.com

ARCHITECTURE

WIDOM WIEN COHEN O'LEARY TERASAWA
Inland Empire
4280 Latham St. #H
Riverside, CA 92501
CEO: Mr. Adrian O. Cohen
Tel: (909) 682-0470 Fax: (909) 682-1801
Email: info@wwcot.com
Web: www.wwcot.com

Main Office
3130 Wilshire Blvd., 6th Floor
Santa Monica, CA 90403
CEO: Mr. Adrian O. Cohen
Tel: (310) 828-0040 Fax: (310) 453-9432
Email: info@wwcot.com
Web: www.wwcot.com

Palm Springs
490 S. Farell Dr.
Palm Springs, CA 92262
CEO: Mr. Adrian O. Cohen
Tel: (760) 320-1709 Fax: (760) 320-9336
Email: info@wwcot.com
Web: www.wwcot.com

Ventura County
5158 Goldman Ave. #F
Moorpark, CA 93021
CEO: Mr. Adrian O. Cohen
Tel: (805) 529-0296 Fax: (805) 552-0040
Email: info@wwcot.com
Web: www.wwcot.com

ARCHITECTURE DESIGN SERVICES

KELL MUÑOZ ARCHITECTS, INC.
Main Office
800 NW Loop 410 #700N
San Antonio, TX 78216
CEO: Mr. Henry R. Muñoz III
Tel: (210) 349-1163 Fax: (210) 525-1038
Email: debrag@kellmunoz.com
Web: www.kellmunozarchitects.com

ARCHITECTURE & ENG. SALES

BERMELLO AJAMIL & PARTNERS
Broward Office
1 E. Broward Blvd. #610
Fort Lauderdale, FL 33301
CEO: Mr. Luis Ajamil
Tel: (954) 467-1113 Fax: (954) 467-1116
Email: info@bamiami.com
Web: www.bamiami.com

Main Office
2601 S. Bayshore Dr., 10th Fl.
Miami, FL 33133
CEO: Mr. Luis Ajamil
Tel: (305) 859-2050 Fax: (305) 859-7835
Email: info@bamiami.com
Web: www.bamiami.com

ARCHITEC & ENG. SERVICES

GUTIERREZ-PALMENBERG, INC.
Corporate Office
2922 W. Clarendon Ave.
Phoenix, AZ 85017
CEO: Mr. Gilbert T. Gutierrez
Tel: (602) 234-0696 Fax: (602) 234-0699
Email: gill.g@gpimail.com
Web: www.gpieng.com

MOLZEN-CORBIN & ASSOCIATES
Head Office
2701 Miles Rd. Southeast
Albuquerque, NM 87106
CEO: Mr. Adelmo Archuleta
Tel: (505) 242-5700 Fax: (505) 242-0673
Email: hresources@molzencorbin.com
Web: www.molzencorbin.com

Carlsbad Office
101 N. Halagueno
Carlsbad, NM 88221
CEO: Mr. Adelmo Archuleta
Tel: (505) 628-0380
Email: hresources@molzencorbin.com
Web: www.molzencorbin.com

Las Cruces Office
1155 Commerce Dr. #F
Las Cruces, NM 88011
CEO: Mr. Adelmo Archuleta
Tel: (505) 522-0049 Fax: (505) 522-7884
Email: hresources@molzencorbin.com
Web: www.molzencorbin.com

WOLFBERG ALVAREZ & PARTNERS
1500 San Remo Ave. #300
Coral Gables, FL 33146
CEO: Mr. Julio Alvarez
Tel: (305) 666-5474 Fax: (305) 669-9875
Email: rcanals@wolfbergalvarez.com
Web: www.wolfbergalvarez.com

ART PRODUCTS DISTRIB.

INTERMARKET CORPORATION
7286 SW 48th St.
Miami, FL 33155
CEO: Mr. Manuel A. Alvarez
Tel: (305) 663-9400 Fax: (305) 663-0102
Email: sales@intermarketcorp.com
Web: www.intermarketcorp.com

AUDIO/VIDEO DESIGN & INSTALLATION SERVICES

PAQUITO & SONS, INC.
Corporate Office
225 Yellow Pl.
Rockledge, FL 32955
CEO: Mr. Carlos M. Gonzalez, Jr.
Tel: (321) 638-9966 X248
(888) 477-9966 X248
Fax: (321) 638-9977
Email: info@islandsys.net
Web: www.islandsys.net

AUTO INSURANCE

FRED LOYA INSURANCE
Vision Managing General Agency, Inc.,
Maverick Insurance Agency, Inc.
1800 Lee Trevino #201
El Paso, TX 79936
CEO: Mr. Fred Loya Jr.
Tel: (915) 590-5692
(800) 554-0595 Fax: (800) 387-8220
Email: info@fredloya.com
Web: www.fredloyainsurance.com

AUTO PAINT & BODY SHOP

1-DAY PAINT & BODY CENTERS, INC.
21801 S. Western Ave.
Torrance, CA 90501
CEO: Mr. Javier R. Uribe, Sr.
Tel: (310) 328-8900 Fax: (310) 328-3995
Web: www.1daypaint.com

AUTOMATED ID TRACKING SOLUTIONS MFG.

RETAIL SYSTEMS INTERNATIONAL, INC.
Corporate Headquarters
901 Lane Ave.
Chula Vista, CA 91914
CEO: Mr. Wolf Bielas
Tel: (619) 482-3013
(800) 466-8247 Fax: (619) 482-3168
Email: info@rsiidtech.com
Web: www.rsiidtech.com

AUTOMOTIVE

CHASTANG ENTERPRISES, INC.
6200 N. Loop East
Houston, TX 77026-1936
CEO: Mr. Joe Chastang
Tel: (713) 671-0101 Fax: (713) 671-9703
Email: wmichael@bayoucityford.com
Web: www.bayoucityford.com

AUTOMOTIVE DEALER

ALLAN VIGIL FORD, INC.
6790 Mt. Zion Blvd.
Morrow, GA 30260
CEO: Mr. M. Allan Vigil
Tel: (770) 968-0680 Fax: (678) 364-3908
Email: sales@vigilfordfleet.com
Web: www.vigilfordfleet.com

ANCIRA ENTERPRISES, INC.
6111 Bandera Rd.
San Antonio, TX 78238
CEO: Mr. Ernesto Ancira Jr.
Tel: (210) 681-4900 Fax: (210) 681-9413
Email: ancira@ancira.com
Web: www.ancira.com

BURT AUTOMOTIVE NETWORK
5200 S. Broadway
Englewood, CO 80113
CEO: Mr. Lloyd G. Chavez Jr.
Tel: (303) 761-0333
(800) 535-2878 Fax: (303) 789-6211
Email: autos@burt.com
Web: www.burt.com

DOTHAN CHRYSLER PLYMOUTH DODGE, INC.
4066 Ross Clark Cr.
Dothan, AL 36304
CEO: Mr. Dino Velazquez
Tel: (334) 794-0606 Fax: (334) 702-8951
Web: www.dothanchrysler.com

ELDER AUTOMOTIVE GROUP
Aston Martin Tampa
320 E. Fletcher Ave.
Tampa, FL 33612
CEO: Ms. Irma Elder
Tel: (813) 371-8200 Fax: (813) 371-8199
Email: info@elderford.com
Web: www.elderautomotivegroup.com

Aston Martin Troy
1815 Maplelawn
Troy, MI 48084
CEO: Ms. Irma Elder
Tel: (888) 224-7224 Fax: (248) 643-9261
Email: info@elderford.com
Web: www.elderautomotivegroup.com

Headquarters - Elder Ford
777 John R. Rd.
Troy, MI 48083
CEO: Ms. Irma Elder
Tel: (248) 585-4000 Fax: (248) 585-4039
Email: info@elderford.com
Web: www.elderautomotivegroup.com

Jaguar of Tampa
320 E. Fletcher Ave.
Tampa, FL 33612
CEO: Ms. Irma Elder
Tel: (813) 371-8200 Fax: (813) 371-8199
Email: info@elderford.com
Web: www.elderautomotivegroup.com

Jaguar of Troy
1815 Maplelawn
Troy, MI 48084
CEO: Ms. Irma Elder
Tel: (888) 224-7224 Fax: (248) 643-9261
Email: info@elderford.com
Web: www.elderautomotivegroup.com

Saab of Troy
1819 Maplelawn
Troy, MI 48084
CEO: Ms. Irma Elder
Tel: (248) 205-1333 Fax: (248) 205-1350
Email: info@elderford.com
Web: www.elderautomotivegroup.com

GARCIA AUTOMOTIVE GROUP
Garcia Honda
8301 Lomas Blvd. Northeast
Albuquerque, NM 87110
CEO: Mr. Edward Garcia
Tel: (505) 260-5000 Fax: (505) 260-5013
Email: info@garciacars.com
Web: garciahonda.com

Garcia Mitsubishi
8201 Lomas Blvd. NE
Albuquerque, NM 87110
CEO: Mr. Edward Garcia
Tel: (505) 260-5050 Fax: (505) 260-5070
Email: info@garciacars.com
Web: garciamitsubishi.com

Garcia Subaru
8100 Lomas Blvd. NE
Albuquerque, NM 87110
CEO: Edward Garcia
Tel: (505) 260-5155 Fax: (505) 260-5180
Email: info@garciacars.com
Web: garciasubaru.com

Garcia Subaru
1234 Renaissance Blvd. Northeast
Albuquerque, NM 87107
CEO: Mr. Edward Garcia
Tel: (505) 217-3000 Fax: (505) 217-3050
Email: info@garciacars.com
Web: garciainfiniti.com

GONZALES AUTOMOTIVE GROUP, INC.
Head Office
5800 E. Firestone Blvd.
South Gate, CA 90280
CEO: Mr. Silvestre Gonzales
Tel: (562) 776-2330 Fax: (562) 776-2331
Web: www.casadegonzalescpj.com

GREENWAY FORD, INC.
Headquarters
9001 E. Colonial Dr.
Orlando, FL 32817
CEO: Mr. Frank J. Rodriguez
Tel: (407) 275-3200 Fax: (407) 515-6499
Email: sales@greenwayford.dealerspace.com
Web: www.greenwayfordoforlando.com

HEADQUARTER TOYOTA
5895 NW 167th St.
Hialeah, FL 33015
CEO: Mr. Jeronimo M. Esteve
Tel: (305) 364-9800 Fax: (305) 827-0169
Email: sales@headquartertoyota.com
Web: www.headquartertoyota.com

HERITAGE FORD LINCOLN MERCURY
1115 E. Spring St.
Cookeville, TN 38501
CEO: Mr. Jaime R. Vergara

Tel: (931) 526-3325 Fax: (931) 525-6416
Email: heritageford@charter.net
Web: www.heritagefordlm.com

LOU SOBH AUTOMOTIVE
2473 Pleasant Hill Rd.
Duluth, GA 30096
CEO: Mr. Lou Sobh
Tel: (770) 232-0099 Fax: (770) 232-2695
Email: sales@lousobh.com
Web: www.lousobh.com

MIKE SHAW CHEV. BUICK PONTIAC SAAB GMC
1080 S. Colorado Blvd.
Denver, CO 80246
CEO: Mr. Michael J. Shaw
Tel: (303) 639-6398 Fax: (303) 639-6334
Email: sales@mikeshawauto.net
Web: www.mikeshawauto.com

1313 Motor City Dr.
Colorado Springs, CO 80906
CEO: Mr. Michael J. Shaw
Tel: (719) 866-1119 Fax: (719) 634-1058
Email: cssales@mikeshawauto.net
Web: www.mikeshawauto.com

OCEAN AUTO CENTER, INC.
9675 NW 12th St.
Miami, FL 33172
CEO: Mr. Juan M. Martinez
Tel: (786) 464-1100 Fax: (786) 464-1155
Email: sales@oceanmazda.com
Web: www.oceanmazda.com

POPULAR FORD SALES INC.
2505 Coney Island Ave.
Brooklyn, NY 11223
CEO: Mr. Steven Risso
Tel: (718) 376-5600 Fax: (718) 375-9691
Email: popularford@salespoint.
dealerconnection.com
Web: www.popularfordny.com

SUNLAND PARK PONTIAC-BUICK-GMC
955 Crockett Way
El Paso, TX 79922
CEO: Mr. Hector Rico
Tel: (915) 584-8419 Fax: (915) 581-9203
Web: www.sunlandparkonline.com

VARELA AUTO GROUP LLC
2929 S Loop 256
Palestine, TX 75801
CEO: Mr. Fernando Varela
Tel: (903) 729-2171 Fax: (903) 723-8954
Email: allstarford@earthlink.net
Web: www.allstarfordmercury.com

AUTOMOTIVE EQUIPMENT

UNI BORING COMPANY, INC.
2280 W. Grand River
Howell, MI 48843
CEO: Mr. Facundo Bravo
Tel: (517) 548-0500 Fax: (517) 548-1336
Email: ubci@uniboring.com
Web: www.uniboring.com

AUTOMOTIVE PARTS

HERKO INTERNATIONAL INC.
12975 SW 132nd St.
Miami, FL 33186
CEO: Mr. Juan C. Guiterrez
Tel: (305) 971-4997 Fax: (305) 971-4998
Email: sales@herko.com
Web: www.herko.com

AUTOMOTIVE SALES

ALVAREZ LINCOLN MERCURY, INC.
8051 Auto Dr.
Riverside, CA 92504
CEO: Mr. Ramon Alvarez
Tel: (909) 687-1212 Fax: (909) 687-1288
Email: bdd@alvarezlincoln-mercury.com
Web: www.alvarezlm.com

CHAPARRAL PONTIAC-BUICK-GMC TRUCK
3514 Bristol Hwy.
Johnson City, TN 37601
CEO: Alfredo R. Gonzalez
Tel: (423) 282-3871 Fax: (423) 282-9035

DOUGLASTON CHEVROLET, INC./ BAY CHEVROLET
24002 Northern Blvd.
Douglaston, NY 11362
CEO: Mr. Anthony L. Arciniaga
Tel: (718) 224-4400 Fax: (718) 224-7151
Email: baychevrolet@carbuyers.com

DOWNEY FORD, INC.
9500 Lakewood Blvd.
Downey, CA 90240
CEO: Mr. Bob Remy
Tel: (562) 861-6771 Fax: (562) 869-3072
Email: downeyford@salespoint.
dealerconnection.com
Web: www.downeyford.com

LOVE CHRYSLER, INC.
4331 S. Staples St.
Corpus Christi, TX 78411
CEO: Ms. Marion Luna Brem
Tel: (361) 857-2554 Fax: (361) 857-6323
Email: marionbrem@aol.com
Web: www.marionlunabrem.com

METRO FORD, INC.
9000 NW 7th Ave.
Miami, FL 33150
CEO: Mr. Lombardo Pérez
Tel: (800) 793-8176 Fax: (305) 757-4819
Email: kenny@metroford.com
Web: www.metroford.com

ROLLING HILLS FORD, INC.
1101 E. Hwy. 50
Clermont, FL 34711
CEO: Mr. Jay Rosario
Tel: (352) 394-6161
(877) 564-3673 Fax: (352) 394-1737
Email: dougc@rollinghillsford.com
Web: www.rollinghillsford.com

TAMIAMI AUTOMOTIVE GROUP
8250 SW 8th St.
Miami, FL 33144
CEO: Mr. Carlos Planas
Tel: (305) 266-5500 Fax: (305) 266-5604
Web: www.tamiami.fivestardealers.com

VICTOR BUICK GMC TRUCK, INC.
2525 Wardlow Rd.
Corona, CA 92882
CEO: Mr. Victor Covarrubias
Tel: (909) 737-2552 Fax: (909) 737-7866
Email: info@victorbuickgmc.com
Web: www.victorbuickgmc.com/en_US/

AUTOMOTIVE SALES & SCVS.

AZF AUTOMOTIVE GROUP, INC.
190 NW 42nd Ave.
Miami, FL 33126
CEO: Mr. Ivan G. Motta
Tel: (305) 477-2425 Fax: (305) 477-2930
Web: www.zonafranca-auto.com

DESERT SUN MOTORS, INC.
2600 N. White Sands Blvd.
Alamogordo, NM 88310
CEO: Mr. Robert Martinez
Tel: (505) 437-7530 Fax: (505) 434-2097
Email: sales@desertsunmotors.com
Web: www.desertsunmotors.com

LLOYD A. WISE, INC.
Head Office
10550 International Blvd.
Oakland, CA 94603
CEO: Mr. Anthony A. Batarse, Jr.
Tel: (510) 638-4800 Fax: (510) 430-8869
Email: info@lloydawiseinc.com
Web: www.lloydawiseinc.com

PONTIAC BUICK GMC OF ABILENE
2200 N. 1st St.
Abilene, TX 79603
CEO: Mr. Raymond A. Sisneros
Tel: (325) 691-6400 Fax: (325) 691-6414
Web: www.sisnerosabilene.com

SOUTH VALLEY AUTO PLAZA
P.O. Box 625
King City, CA 93930
CEO: Mr. Vincente Lopez
Tel: (831) 385-4865 Fax: (831) 385-3324
Email: vlopez@svap.net
Web: www.southvalleyautoplaza.com

AVIATION & COMPUTER CONSULTING

WASHINGTON CONSULTING GROUP INTERNATIONAL
4915 Auburn Ave. #301
Bethesda, MD 20814
CEO: Mr. Armando C. Chapelli, Jr.
Tel: (301) 656-2330 Fax: (301) 656-1996
Email: acchapelli@washcg.com
Web: www.washcg.com

BANKING SERVICES

THE BANK OF BELEN
19339 Hwy. 314
Belen, NM 87002-6383
CEO: Mr. Kenneth J. Carson Jr.
Tel: (505) 864-3301 Fax: (505) 864-2223
Email: info@bankofbelen.net
Web: www.bankofbelen.net

BANKING/FINANCE

E.J. DE LA ROSA & COMPANY, INC.
Head Office
11900 W. Olympic Blvd. #500
Los Angeles, CA 90064-1151
CEO: Mr. Edward J. De La Rosa
Tel: (310) 207-1975 Fax: (310) 207-1995
Email: edelarosa@ejdelarosa.com
Web: www.ejdelarosa.com

San Francisco Office
90 New Montgomery St. #414
San Francisco, CA 94105
CEO: Mr. Edward J. De La Rosa
Tel: (415) 495-8863 Fax: (415) 495-8864
Email: edelarosa@ejdelarosa.com
Web: www.ejdelarosa.com

FALCON INTERNATIONAL BANK
Laredo Downtown Branch
801 Matamoros
Laredo, TX 78041
CEO: Mr. Adolfo E. Gutierrez
Tel: (956) 723-9855
Web: www.falconbank.com

Laredo East Branch
204 Bob Bullock Loop
Laredo, TX 78043
CEO: Mr. Adolfo E. Gutierrez
Tel: (956) 723-2265 Fax: (956) 723-0841
Email: mail@falconbank.com
Web: www.falconbank.com

Laredo North Branch
7718 McPherson Rd.
Laredo, TX 78041
CEO: Mr. Adolfo E. Gutierrez
Tel: (956) 723-2265 Fax: (956) 723-0841
Email: mail@falconbank.com
Web: www.falconbank.com

Main Branch
5219 McPherson Rd.
Laredo, TX 78041
CEO: Mr. Adolfo E. Gutierrez
Tel: (956) 723-2265 Fax: (956) 723-0841
Email: mail@falconbank.com
Web: www.falconbank.com

San Antonio Stone Oak Branch
19230 Stone Oak Pkwy.
San Antonio, TX 78258
CEO: Mr. Adolfo E. Gutierrez
Tel: (210) 402-6143 Fax: (210) 495-7420
Email: mail@falconbank.com
Web: www.falconbank.com

INTERAMERICAN BANK
Hialeah Branch
4090 W.12th Ave.
Miami, FL 33012
CEO: Mr. Agustin Velasco
Tel: (305) 824-0001 Fax: (305) 827-6392
Email: hialeah@interamericanbank.com
Web: www.interamericanbank.com

Kendall Branch
12855 SW 88th St.
Miami, FL 33186
CEO: Mr. Agustin Velasco
Tel: (305) 380-0990 Fax: (305) 386-9101
Email: kendall@interamericanbank.com
Web: www.interamericanbank.com

Main Branch
9190 Coral Way
Miami, FL 33165
CEO: Mr. Agustin Velasco, Jr.
Tel: (305) 223-1434 Fax: (305) 223-0865
Email: ibank@interamericanbank.com
Web: www.interamericanbank.com

West Miami Branch
1350 Red Rd.
Miami, FL 33144
CEO: Mr. Agustin Velasco, Jr.
Tel: (305) 261-1413 Fax: (305) 262-9252
Email: wmiami@interamericanbank.com
Web: www.interamericanbank.com

West Palm Beach
2265 S. Congress Ave.
West Palm Beach, FL 33406
CEO: Mr. Agustin Velasco
Tel: (561) 439-4555 Fax: (561) 439-8654
Email: wpb@interamericanbank.com
Web: www.interamericanbank.com

INTERNATIONAL BANCSHARES CORPORATION
Commerce Bank
P.O. Box 2949
Laredo, TX 78044-2949
CEO: Mr. Dennis E. Nixon
Tel: (956) 724-1616 Fax: (956) 724-6518
Web: www.ibc.com

IBC Austin
9606 N. Mopac Expressway #110
Austin, TX 78759
CEO: Mr. Dennis E. Nixon
Tel: (512) 346-3900 Fax: (512) 343-2538
Web: www.ibc.com

IBC Brownsville
P.O. Box 1831
Brownsville, TX 78522
CEO: Mr. Dennis E. Nixon
Tel: (956) 547-1000 Fax: (956) 547-1006
Web: www.ibc.com

IBC Corpus Christi
P.O. Box 2648
Corpus Christi, TX 78403
CEO: Mr. Dennis E. Nixon
Tel: (361) 888-4000 Fax: (361) 888-5243
Web: www.ibc.com

IBC Eagle Pass
439 E. Main St.
Eagle Pass, TX 78852
CEO: Mr. Dennis E. Nixon
Tel: (830) 773-2313 Fax: (830) 773-6461
Web: www.ibc.com

IBC Houston
P.O. Box 6568
Houston, TX 77005
CEO: Mr. Dennis E. Nixon
Tel: (713) 526-1211 Fax: (713) 526-3930
Web: www.ibc.com

IBC Laredo
1200 San Bernardo Ave.
Laredo, TX 78042-1359
CEO: Mr. Dennis E. Nixon
Tel: (956) 722-7611 Fax: (956) 726-6637
Web: www.ibc.com

IBC McAllen
P.O. Box 579
McAllen, TX 78505-0579
CEO: Mr. Dennis E. Nixon
Tel: (956) 686-0263 Fax: (956) 632-3565
Web: www.ibc.com

IBC Oklahoma
3601 NW 63rd St.
Oklahoma City, OK 73116
CEO: Mr. Dennis E. Nixon
Tel: (405) 841-2100 Fax: (405) 841-2175
Web: www.ibc.com

IBC Port Lavaca
P.O. Box 228
Port Lavaca, TX 77979
CEO: Mr. Dennis E. Nixon
Tel: (361) 552-9771 Fax: (361) 552-8937
Web: www.ibc.com

IBC San Antonio
P.O. Box 47526
San Antonio, TX 78205
CEO: Mr. Dennis E. Nixon
Tel: (210) 518-2500 Fax: (210) 518-2590
Web: www.ibc.com

IBC Zapata
P.O. Box 1030
Zapata, TX 78076-1030
CEO: Mr. Dennis E. Nixon
Tel: (956) 765-8361 Fax: (956) 765-9593
Web: www.ibc.com

RANCHERS BANKS
Alameda Branch
7600 4th St. NW
Albuquerque, NM 87107
CEO: Mr. Henry Jaramillo
Tel: (505) 897-9464 Fax: (505) 897-9458
Email: info@ranchersbanks.com
Web: www.ranchersbanks.com

Edgewood Branch
150 State Rd. 344
Edgewood, NM 87015
CEO: Mr. Henry Jaramillo
Tel: (505) 286-3595 Fax: (505) 286-9432
Email: info@ranchersbanks.com
Web: www.ranchersbanks.com

Grants Branch
1129 N. 1st St.
Grants, NM 87020
CEO: Mr. Henry Jaramillo
Tel: (505) 287-4438 Fax: (505) 287-2027
Email: info@ranchersbanks.com
Web: www.ranchersbanks.com

Los Lunas Branch
328 W. Main St.
Los Lunas, NM 87031
CEO: Mr. Henry Jaramillo
Tel: (505) 865-4601 Fax: (505) 865-8164
Email: info@ranchersbanks.com
Web: www.ranchersbanks.com

Main Office
P.O. Box 545
Belen, NM 87002
CEO: Mr. Henry Jaramillo
Tel: (800) 801-3283
(505) 966-0400 Fax: (505) 966-0494
Email: info@ranchersbanks.com
Web: www.ranchersbanks.com

Moriarty Branch
1401 Route 66 Ave.
Moriarty, NM 87035
CEO: Mr. Henry Jaramillo
Tel: (505) 832-2300 Fax: (505) 832-0567
Email: info@ranchersbanks.com
Web: www.ranchersbanks.com

Rio Communities Branch
300 Rio Communities Blvd.
Belen, NM 87002
CEO: Mr. Henry Jaramillo
Tel: (505) 864-4459 Fax: (505) 864-1547
Email: info@ranchersbanks.com
Web: www.ranchersbanks.com

South Valley Branch
3801 Isleta Blvd. Southwest
Albuquerque, NM 87105
CEO: Mr. Henry Jaramillo
Tel: (505) 873-7333 Fax: (505) 873-3554
Email: info@ranchersbanks.com
Web: www.ranchersbanks.com

Valencia Branch
3453 Hwy. 47
Los Lunas, NM 87031
CEO: Mr. Henry Jaramillo
Tel: (505) 865-9622 Fax: (505) 865-8163
Email: info@ranchersbanks.com
Web: www.ranchersbanks.com

UNIBANK
Bird Road
9290 SW 40th St.
Miami, FL 33165
CEO: Mr. Joseph M. Guerra
Tel: (305) 552-1515 Fax: (305) 552-1358
Email: birdrd@unibank-usa.com
Web: www.unibank-usa.com

Coral Gables
1220 Ponce de Leon Blvd.
Coral Gables, FL 33134
CEO: Mr. Joseph M. Guerra
Tel: (305) 442-1220 Fax: (305) 443-1255
Email: cgables@unibank-usa.com
Web: www.unibank-usa.com

Deerfield Beach
1898-A W. Hillsboro Blvd.
Deerfield Beach, FL 33442
CEO: Mr. Joseph M. Guerra
Tel: (954) 571-9789 Fax: (954) 571-9795
Email: deerfield@unibank-usa.com
Web: www.unibank-usa.com

Executive Office and Lending Center
701 Brickell #1700
Miami, FL 33131
CEO: Mr. Joseph M. Guerra
Tel: (305) 577-6000 Fax: (305) 577-6083

Email: exec@unibank-usa.com
Web: www.unibank-usa.com

Margate
7220 W. Atlantic Blvd.
Margate, FL 33063
CEO: Mr. Joseph M. Guerra
Tel: (954) 973-1313 Fax: (954) 977-6911
Email: margate@unibank-usa.com
Web: www.unibank-usa.com

Operations Center
9795 S. Dixie Hwy.
Pinecrest, FL 33156
CEO: Mr. Joseph M. Guerra
Tel: (305) 740-9522 Fax: (305) 740-9523
Email: operations@unibank-usa.com
Web: www.unibank-usa.com

Orlando
1627 S. Conway Rd.
Orlando, FL 32812
CEO: Mr. Joseph M. Guerra
Tel: (407) 658-2800 Fax: (407) 658-1516
Email: orlando@unibank-usa.com
Web: www.unibank-usa.com

Pembroke Pines
204 S.Flamingo Rd.
Pembroke Pines, FL 33027
CEO: Mr. Joseph M. Guerra
Tel: (954) 392-4500 Fax: (954) 392-5997
Email: ppines@unibank-usa.com
Web: www.unibank-usa.com

St. Cloud
4001 13th St.
St. Cloud, FL 34769
CEO: Mr. Joseph M. Guerra
Tel: (407) 891-1414 Fax: (407) 891-6081
Email: exec@unibank-usa.com
Web: www.unibank-usa.com

Sunrise
10147-A W. Oakland Park Blvd.
Sunrise, FL 33351
CEO: Mr. Joseph M. Guerra
Tel: (954) 747-0999 Fax: (954) 747-0802
Email: sunrise@unibank-usa.com
Web: www.unibank-usa.com

West Kendall
15780 SW 72nd St.
Miami, FL 33193
CEO: Mr. Joseph M. Guerra
Tel: (305) 388-4044 Fax: (305) 388-7330
Email: kendall@unibank-usa.com
Web: www.unibank-usa.com

UNITED PANAM FINANCIAL CORPORATION
3990 Westerly Pl. #200
Newport Beach, CA 92660
CEO: Mr. Guillermo Bron
Tel: (949) 224-1917 Fax: (949) 224-1912
Web: www.upfc.com

BANKING/FINANCE SVCS.

STERLING FINANCIAL INVESTMENT GROUP
225 NE Mizner Blvd., 4th Fl.
Boca Raton, FL 33432
CEO: Mr. Charles P. Garcia
Tel: (561) 886-2200 Fax: (561) 886-2329
Email: info@mysterling.com
Web: www.mysterling.com

BEER DIST.

SILVER EAGLE DISTRIBUTORS, LTD.
1000 Park of Commerce Blvd.
Homestead, FL 33035
CEO: Mr. Ramon F. Oyarzun
Tel: (305) 230-2337 Fax: (305) 230-0333

Email: sales@buybud-sed.
comroyarzun@buybud-sed.com
Web: www.abwholesaler.com/
silvereagledistributors

BLDG. CONSTRUCTION

N.C. STURGEON, INC.
P.O. Box 60708
Midland, TX 79718
CEO: Mr. Chuck Sturgeon
Tel: (432) 563-5393 Fax: (432) 561-5210
Email: csturgeon@ncsturgeon.com
Web: www.ncsturgeon.com

BLDG. MATERIAL SALES

FLORIDA LUMBER COMPANY
2431 NW 20th St.
Miami, FL 33142
CEO: Mr. Ignacio Perez
Tel: (305) 635-6412 Fax: (305) 633-4054
Email: sales@floridalumber.com
Web: www.floridalumber.com

BLDG. MATERIAL WHSL.

GANCEDO LUMBER COMPANY, INC.
9300 NW 36th Ave.
Miami, FL 33147
CEO: Mr. Martin Perez
Tel: (305) 836-7030 Fax: (305) 836-1162

BOLT & NUT DISTRIB.

CORDOVA BOLT, INC.
5601 Dolly Ave.
Buena Park, CA 90621
CEO: Mr. Moses E. Cordova
Tel: (714) 739-7500
(800) 421-3435 Fax: (714) 994-2661
Email: cordova@deltanet.com
Web: www.cordovabolt.com

BUILDING MAINTENANCE SERVICES

PROFESSIONAL BUILDING MAINTENANCE
8523 Lankershim Blvd.
Sun Valley, CA 91352
CEO: Mr. Fernando Real
Tel: (818) 771-1100 Fax: (818) 771-1107

CANDLE MANUFACTURING

REED CANDLE COMPANY
1531 W. Poplar
San Antonio, 78207
CEO: Sister Schodts Reed
Tel: (210) 734-4243 Fax: (210) 734-2342

CAPITAL & HIGH TECH EQUIP. LEASING

SOMERSET CAPITAL GROUP, LTD.
1087 Broad St. #301
Bridgeport, CT 06604
CEO: Mr. Pedro E. Wasmer
Tel: (203) 394-6182 Fax: (203) 394-6192
Email: info@somersetcapital.com
Web: www.somersetcapital.com

CARPET, DRAPERY, TILE DISPLAY MFG.

WEST COAST SAMPLES, INC.
Corporate Office
14450 Central Ave.
Chino, CA 91710
CEO: Mr. Larry Barrios Jr.
Tel: (909) 464-1616 Fax: (909) 465-9982
Email: lbarrios@wcsample.com
Web: www.wcsample.com

CERAMIC, MARBLE & STONE TILES

IBERIA TILES CORPORATION
Coral Gables, FL
4221 Ponce De Leon Blvd.
Miami, FL 33146
CEO: Ms. Rosa Sugrañes
Tel: (305) 446-0222 Fax: (305) 446-3134
Email: info@iberiatiles.com
Web: www.iberiatiles.com

Main Office
2975 NW 77th Ave.
Miami, FL 33122
CEO: Ms. Rosa Sugrañes
Tel: (305) 591-3880 Fax: (305) 591-4341
Email: info@iberiatiles.com
Web: www.iberiatiles.com

4041 Kingston Ct. #A
Marietta, GA 30067
CEO: Ms. Rosa Sugrañes
Tel: (770) 818-0080 Fax: (770) 818-9009
Email: info@iberiatiles.com
Web: www.iberiatiles.com

1721 Oakbrook Dr.
Norcross, GA 30093
CEO: Ms. Rosa Sugrañes
Tel: (770) 840-9000 Fax: (770) 840-9800
Email: info@iberiatiles.com
Web: www.iberiatiles.com

1711 Powerline
Pompano Beach, FL 33069
CEO: Ms. Rosa Sugrañes
Tel: (954) 978-8453 Fax: (954) 978-2129
Email: info@iberiatiles.com
Web: www.iberiatiles.com

CHEM. PROTECTION GARMENTS/HEAT SEALING

VINYL TECHNOLOGY, INC.
200 Railroad Ave.
Monrovia, CA 91016-4643
CEO: Mr. Carlos A. Mollura, Sr.
Tel: (626) 443-5257 Fax: (626) 443-0531
Email: sales@vinyltechnology.com
Web: www.vinyltechnology.com

CHEMICALS DISTRIBUTION

SOLVENTS AND CHEMICALS, INC.
Corporate Headquarters/ Houston Branch
P.O. Box 490
Pearland, TX 77584
CEO: Mr. Gabriel Baizan
Tel: (713) 485-5377
(800) 622-3990 Fax: (713) 485-6129
Email: wayne_black@solvchem.com
Web: www.solvchem.com

Dallas-Ft. Worth Branch
881 Dividend Rd.
Midlothian, TX 76065
CEO: Mr. Gabriel Baizan
Tel: (972) 723-1574/(800) 977-7930

Email: Ron_Reeves@solvchem.com
Web: www.solvchem.com

Longview Branch
P.O. Box 220
Panola, TX 75685
CEO: Mr. Gabriel Baizan
Tel: (800) 717-6830 Fax: (903) 766-3440
Email: wayne_black@solvchem.com
Web: www.solvchem.com

CHEMICALS & FUEL WHSL.

MALACO INTERNATIONAL, INC.
1990 N. California Blvd. #608
Walnut Creek, CA 94596
CEO: Ms. Elizabeth Llama
Tel: (925) 280-8710 Fax: (925) 280-4580
Email: malaco1@aol.com

COMM. BLDG. CONSTRUCTION

CROSSLAND CONSTRUCTION COMPANY, INC.
Arkansas Division
2501 W. Hudson
Rogers, AR 72756
CEO: Mr. Ivan E. Crossland
Tel: (479) 631-7077 Fax: (479) 631-7080
Email: info@crosslandconstruction.com
Web: www.crosslandconstruction.com

Corporate Office
US Hwy. 69
Columbus, KS 66725
CEO: Mr. Ivan E. Crossland
Tel: (620) 429-1414 Fax: (620) 429-1412
Email: info@crosslandconstruction.com
Web: www.crosslandconstruction.com

Oklahoma Division
14149 E. Admiral Pl. North
Tulsa, OK 74116
CEO: Mr. Ivan E. Crossland
Tel: (918) 712-1441 Fax: (918) 712-2044
Email: info@crosslandconstruction.com
Web: www.crosslandconstruction.com

COMMERCIAL BANKING

CENTINEL BANK OF TAOS
Main Office
P.O. Box 828
Taos, NM 87571
CEO: Ms. Rebeca Romero Rainey
Tel: (505) 758-6700 Fax: (505) 758-6772
Email: centinel@centinelbank.com
Web: www.centinelbank.com

MotorBank
508 Paseo del Pueblo Norte
Taos, NM 87571
CEO: Ms. Rebeca Romero Rainey
Tel: (505) 758-6788
(505) 758-6789 Fax: (505) 758-6789
Email: centinel@centinelbank.com
Web: www.centinelbank.com

Northside Office
707 Paseo del Pueblo Norte
Taos, NM 87571
CEO: Ms. Rebeca Romero Rainey
Tel: (505) 758-6721 Fax: (505) 758-6760
Email: centinel@centinelbank.com
Web: www.centinelbank.com

Questa Office
1 State Rd. 38
Questa, NM 87556
CEO: Ms. Rebeca Romero Rainey
Tel: (505) 586-0577 Fax: (505) 586-1858

Email: centinel@centinelbank.com
Web: www.centinelbank.com

Red River Office
320 E. Main St.
Red River, NM 87558
CEO: Ms. Rebeca Romero Rainey
Tel: (505) 754-2351 Fax: (505) 754-2762
Email: centinel@centinelbank.com
Web: www.centinelbank.com

COMMERCIAL JANITORIAL SERVICES

PREFERRED BUILDING SERVICES INC.
772 Kearny Ave.
Kearny, NJ 07032
CEO: Mr. Francisco Hernandez
Tel: (201) 955-1770
(800) 644-1770 Fax: (201) 955-9007
Email: russells@preferredbuildingservice.com
Web: www.preferredbuildingservice.com

SPARKLE MAINTENANCE, INC.
Headquarters
5827 4th St. NW
Albuquerque, NM 87107
CEO: Mr. Carlo Lucero
Tel: (505) 345-5501/ (800) 794-5501
Fax: (505) 345-4901
Email: sparkle@sparklecorp.com
Web: www.sparklecorp.com

COMMERCIAL & OFFICE FURNITURE

CONTRACT ASSOCIATES, INC.
Albuquerque
800 20th St. Northwest
Albuquerque, NM 87104
CEO: Ms. Maria Griego-Raby
Tel: (505) 881-8070 Fax: (505) 888-7536
Email: jillg@contractassoc.com
Web: www.contractassoc.com

Los Alamos
134 Eastgate Dr. #A
Los Alamos, NM 87544
CEO: Ms. Maria Griego-Raby
Tel: (505) 662-9343 Fax: (505) 662-9327
Email: jillg@contractassoc.com
Web: www.contractassoc.com

Santa Fe
128 Grant Ave. #217
Santa Fe, NM 87501
CEO: Ms. Maria Griego-Raby
Tel: (505) 995-0557 Fax: (505) 995-0519
Email: jillg@contractassoc.com
Web: www.contractassoc.com

COMMERCIAL PEST CONTROL

ROACH BUSTERS OF AMERICA, INC.
5769 NW 7th St. #218
Miami, FL 33126
CEO: Mr. Juan A. Lopez
Tel: (800) 761-2847 Fax: (305) 448-8008
Email: bugzy@roachbusters.com
Web: www.roachbustersofamerica.com

COMMERCIAL PRINTING

ATLANTIC GRAPHIC SERVICES, INC.
57 Plain St.
Clinton, MA 01510
CEO: Mr. Ariel Schmidt
Tel: (978) 368-1262 Fax: (978) 365-6945

Email: info@atlanticgraphics.com
Web: www.atlanticgraphics.com

COMMERCIAL PRINTING SERVICES

ALBUQUERQUE PRINTING COMPANY
3838 Bogan Ave. Northeast
Albuquerque, NM 87109
CEO: Mr. Tony Fernandez
Tel: (505) 872-2200 Fax: (505) 872-4200
Web: www.abqprint.com

COMMERCIAL WEB PRINTING

BEST LITHO, INC.
6912 NW 46th St.
Miami, FL 33166-5604
CEO: Mr. Eduardo Garcia
Tel: (305) 592-7693 Fax: (305) 477-4692
Email: ed@bestlitho.com

COMMUNICATIONS WHSL.

BRIGHTSTAR CORPORATION
Headquarters
2010 NW 84th Ave.
Miami, FL 33122
CEO: Mr. R. Marcelo Claure
Tel: (305) 477-8676 Fax: (305) 477-8676
Email: marcelo.claure@brightstarcorp.com
Web: www.brightstarcorp.com

Vernon Hills Office
Technology Way
Libertyville, IL 60048
CEO: Mr. R. Marcelo Claure
Tel: (847) 573-2600 Fax: 1(877) 573-1041
Email: marcelo.claure@brightstarcorp.com
Web: www.brightstarcorp.com

COMPUTER HARDWARE DISTRIBUTION

EBC COMPUTER CORPORATION
1825 W. Research Way #B
Salt Lake City, UT 84119
CEO: Mr. Eduardo A. Bedoya
Tel: (801) 886-0100 Fax: (801) 886-0200
Email: csr@ebccomputers.com
Web: www.ebccomputers.com

1361 S. State St.
Orem, UT 84097
CEO: Mr. Eduardo A. Bedoya
Tel: (801) 932-0400 Fax: (801) 932-0200
Email: orem@ebccomputers.com
Web: www.ebccomputers.com

4089 Riverdale Rd.
Ogden, UT 84405
CEO: Mr. Eduardo A. Bedoya
Tel: (801) 395-0400 Fax: (801) 395-0600
Email: ogden@ebccomputers.com
Web: www.ebccomputers.com

COMPUTER NETWORK INSTALLATION

L&M TECHNOLOGIES, INC.
Corporate Office
4209 Balloon Park Rd. NE
Albuquerque, NM 87109-5802
CEO: Mr. Peter E. Harrod
Tel: (505) 343-0200 Fax: (505) 343-0300
Email: fred@lmtechnologies.com
Web: www.lmtechnologies.com

COMPUTER NETWORKING

NETWORK MANAGEMENT RESOURES, INC.
565 Benfield Rd., 3rd Fl.
Severna Park, MD 21146
CEO: Mr. David A. Garcia
Tel: (410) 544-4949 Fax: (410) 544-5300
Email: info@nmr1.com
Web: www.nmr1.com

COMPUTER PRODS. & SVCS.

NPA WEST, INC.
Corporate Headquarters
3835 N. Freeway Blvd. #140
Sacramento, CA 95834
CEO: Mr. Alan Rees
Tel: (916) 631-8007
(888) 933-6786 Fax: (916) 631-9009
Email: sales@npawest.com
Web: www.npawest.com

PCNET, INC.
100 Technology Dr.
Trumbull, CT 06611-1395
CEO: Mr. Camilo Soto
Tel: (203) 452-8500 Fax: (203) 452-8696
Email: camilos@pcnet-inc.com
Web: www.pcnet-inc.com

COMPUTER RETAILING

VANGUARD COMPUTERS, INC.
Head Office
13100 W. Lisbon Rd. #100
Brookfield, WI 53005
CEO: Mr. Steve Wangard
Tel: (262) 317-1900 Fax: (262) 317-1999
Email: sales@vanguardinc.com
Web: www.vanguardinc.com

Madison Area
2222 Evergreen Rd. #1
Middleton, WI 53562
CEO: Mr. Steve Wangard
Tel: (608) 227-7270 Fax: (608) 227-7277
Email: sales@vanguardinc.com
Web: www.vanguardinc.com

COMPUTER SALES & SVCS.

ANALYTICAL COMPUTER SERVICES
Austin Office
7950 Anderson Sq. #108
Austin, TX 78757
CEO: Mr. Frank H. Trifilio
Tel: (512) 459-0455 Fax: (512) 459-0266
Web: www.acstexas.com

Corporate Office
11500 NW Freeway #320
Houston, TX 77092
CEO: Mr. Frank H. Trifilio
Tel: (713) 681-0039 Fax: (713) 681-0057
Web: www.acstexas.com

Dallas Office
1901 Royal Ln. #102
Dallas, TX 75229
CEO: Mr. Frank H. Trifilio
Tel: (972) 247-4227 Fax: (972) 247-9874
Web: www.acstexas.com

Houston Office
4202 Directors Row #100
Houston, TX 77092
CEO: Mr. Frank H. Trifilio
Tel: (713) 290-2230 Fax: (713) 681-0056
Web: www.acstexas.com

INTERFACE COMPUTER COMMUNICATIONS INC.
Corporate Headquarters
633 S. Plymouth Ct. #1A
Chicago, IL 60605
CEO: Mr. David R. Andalcio
Tel: (312) 588-0737 Fax: (312) 588-5970
Email: info@iccfone.com
Web: www.iccfone.com

Philadelphia Office
3000 Valley Forge Cir. #250
King of Prussia, PA 19406
CEO: Mr. David R. Andalcio
Tel: (215) 825-7647 Fax: (877) 711-3556
Email: info@iccfone.com
Web: www.iccfone.com

NPA WEST, INC.
Los Angeles Office
5122 Bolsa Ave. #106
Huntington Beach, CA 92649
CEO: Mr. Alan Rees
Tel: (714) 892-5160 Fax: (714) 892-5170
Email: sales@npawest.com
Web: www.npawest.com

COMPUTER SVCS., MFG.

THE CENTECH GROUP, INC.
Corporate Headquarters
4600 N. Fairfax Dr. #400
Arlington, VA 22203
CEO: Mr. Fernando V. Galaviz
Tel: (703) 525-4444 Fax: (703) 525-2349
Email: marketing@centechgroup.com
Web: www.centechgroup.com

COMPUTER SYST. DEVEL. SERVICES

INFORMATION & COMPUTING SERVICES INC.
Head Office
4899 Belfort Rd. #200
Jacksonville, FL 32256
CEO: Mr. Jorge F. Morales
Tel: (904) 399-8500 Fax: (904) 398-7855
Email: info@icsfl.com
Web: www.icsfl.com

COMPUTER SYST. INTEGRATION

INFORMATIX, INC.
Main Office
649 Mission St. #400
San Francisco, CA 94105
CEO: Mr. Raul Ocazionez
Tel: (415) 365-1515 Fax: (415) 365-1517
Email: informatix@informatixinc.com
Web: www.informatixinc.com

COMPUTER SYST. VIA DIRECT MODEL

ALIENWARE CORPORATION
Corporate Headquarters
12400 SW 134th Court, Bay 8
Miami, FL 33186
CEO: Mr. Nelson Gonzalez
Tel: (305) 251-9797 Fax: (351) 259-9874
Email: info@alienware.com
Web: www.alienware.com

COMPUTER SYST. INTEGRATION

TRI-COR INDUSTRIES, INC.
Corporate Headquarters
4600 Forbes Blvd. #205
Lanham, MD 20706
CEO: Mr. Louis Gonzalez
Tel: (301) 731-6140 Fax: (301) 306-6740
Email: contactus@tricorind.com
Web: www.tricorind.com

San Antonio Branch
2929 Mossrock #125
San Antonio, TX 78230
CEO: Mr. Louis Gonzalez
Tel: (210) 348-9836 Fax: (210) 348-9838
Email: contactus@tricorind,com
Web: www.tricorind.com

Western Region
5800 E. Bannister Rd. #240
Kansas City, MO 64134
CEO: Mr. Louis Gonzalez
Tel: (816) 523-3984
(800) 711-9335 Fax: (816) 523-3968
Email: contactus@tricorind.com
Web: www.tricorind.com

Western Region
5 Eagle Ctr. #8
O'Fallon, IL 62269
CEO: Mr. Louis Gonzalez
Tel: (618) 632-9804 Fax: (618) 632-0445
Email: contactus@tricorind.com
Web: www.tricorind.com

CONCRETE FOUNDATION & CONSTRUCTION

E&M CONCRETE CONSTRUCTION, INC.
P.O. Box 50512
Oxnard, CA 93030
CEO: Mr. Edmundo Mendez Sr.
Tel: (805) 658-2888 Fax: (805) 650-9428
Email: emc@jetlink.net
Web: www.emconcrete.com

CONCRETE PROD. MFG.

PRE-CON PRODUCTS
P.O. Box 2109
Simi Valley, CA 93062-2109
CEO: Mr. David Zarraonandia
Tel: (805) 527-0841 Fax: (805) 584-0769
Email: karen@pre-conproducts.com
Web: www.pre-conproducts.com

Construction Office
7404 Morris St.
Riverside, CA 92503
CEO: Mr. David Zarraonandia
Tel: (909) 358-0463
Email: karen@pre-conproducts.com
Web: www.pre-conproducts.com

CONSTRUCTION

APACHE CONSTRUCTION COMPANY INC.
1933 Coors Blvd. SW
Albuquerque, NM 87121-4308
CEO: Mr. Mariano Chavez
Tel: (505) 877-7978 Fax: (505) 877-5301
Email: valyfenc@aol.com

CENTURY HOMEBUILDERS, LLC
7270 NW 12th St. #410
Miami, FL 33126
CEO: Mr. Sergio Pino
Tel: (305) 599-8100 Fax: (305) 470-1900
Email: bimmerman@centurypartners.com
Web: www.centuryhomebuilders.com

COMMUNITY ASPHALT CORPORATION
Main Office and Plant
14005 NW 186th St.
Hialeah, FL 33018
CEO: Mr. Jose L. Fernandez
Tel: (305) 829-0700 Fax: (305) 829-8772
Email: jose@cacorp.net
Web: www.cacorp.net

Vero Beach Office and Plant
5100 29th Ct.
Vero Beach, FL 32967
CEO: Mr. Jose L. Fernandez
Tel: (561) 770-3771 Fax: (561) 770-3707
Email: jose@cacorp.net
Web: www.cacorp.net

West Palm Beach Office and Plant
7795 Hooper Rd.
West Palm Beach, FL 33411
CEO: Mr. Jose L. Fernandez
Tel: (561) 790-6467 Fax: (561) 790-1073
Email: jose@cacorp.net
Web: www.cacorp.net

DAVID MONTOYA CONSTRUCTION, INC.
Corporate Office
315 Alameda Blvd. Northeast
Albuquerque, NM 87113
CEO: Mr. David J. Montoya
Tel: (505) 898-6330 Fax: (505) 898-4331
Email: info@montoyaconstruction.com
Web: www.montoyaconstruction.com

G.M. CONSTRUCTION, INC.
Corporate Office
6002 N. Michigan Rd.
Indianapolis, IN 46228
CEO: Mr. Charles J. Garcia
Tel: (317) 254-3240 Fax: (317) 254-3250
Email: info@gmconstruction.com
Web: www.gmconstruction.com

Georgia Office
1100 Circle 75 Pkwy. #800
Atlanta, GA 30339
CEO: Mr. Charles J. Garcia
Tel: (770) 984-3253 Fax: (770) 984-3256
Email: info@gmconstruction.com
Web: www.gmconstruction.com

KFOURY CONSTRUCTION GROUP, INC.
11307 Sunset Hills Rd.
Reston, VA 20190-5231
CEO: Mr. Jorge A. Kfoury
Tel: (703) 736-1000 Fax: (703) 736-0736
Email: jKfoury@Kfoury.com
Web: www.Kfoury.com

NORTHEAST REMSCO CONSTRUCTION, INC.
Corporate Office
1433 Hooper Ave. #121, Bayview Corporate Center
Toms River, NJ 08753
CEO: Mr. Juan Agustin Gutierrez
Tel: (732) 557-6100 Fax: (732) 370-1926
Email: afonso@northeastconstruction.com
Web: www.northeastconstruction.org

R.A. DURAN CONSTRUCTION CORPORATION
22901 Savi Ranch Pkwy. #A
Yorba Linda, CA 92887
CEO: Mr. Raymond A. Duran
Tel: (714) 283-1911 Fax: (714) 283-2107
Email: durancorp@aol.com

RAYCO CONSTRUCTION, INC.
933 Ave. J East
Grand Prairie, TX 75050
CEO: Mr. Ray Gomez
Tel: (972) 641-2266 Fax: (972) 641-8624
Email: raygomez@raycoinc.com
Web: www.raycoinc.com

ROBERT E. RIVERA CONSTRUCTION COMPANY
HCR 69 Box 735
Santa Rosa, NM 88435
CEO: Mr. Robert E. Rivera
Tel: (505) 472-3885 Fax: (505) 472-3892
Email: ygriego@aol.com

STAR PAVING COMPANY
Division of the Cruz Corporation
P.O. Box 12333
Albuquerque, NM 87195
CEO: Mr. Joe M. Cruz
Tel: (505) 877-0380 Fax: (505) 877-6655
Email: sales@starpaving.com
Web: www.starpaving.com

CONST. & ARCHITECT SVCS.

CSR CONSTRUCTION CORPORATION
139 Chestnut St.
Nutley, NJ 07110
CEO: Mr. Francisco J. Salas
Tel: (973) 667-1600 Fax: (973) 667-6461
Email: lcohen@csrgroup.com
Web: www.csrgroup.com

CONST. ENGINEERING

GEC ASSOCIATES, INC.
12208 SW 129th Ct.
Miami, FL 33186
CEO: Mr. Faustino J. Paredes
Tel: (305) 969-3031 Fax: (305) 969-0763
Email: info@gecassociates.com
Web: www.gecassociates.com

CONST. ENGINEERING SERVICES

THE CUBE CORPORATION
45665 Willow Pond Plz.
Sterling, VA 20164
CEO: Mr. Juan A. Mencia
Tel: (703) 481-9101 Fax: (703) 481-9193
Email: cubemail@cubecorp.com
Web: www.cubecorp.com

CONST. EQUIPMENT SALES & SERVICES

STEVE'S EQUIPMENT SERVICE, INC.
Facilities & Administrative Offices
1400 Powis Rd.
West Chicago, IL 60185
CEO: Mr. Stephen L. Martines
Tel: (630) 231-4840 Fax: (630) 231-4945
Email: info@sesequip
Web: www.sesequip.com

Service Center
6915 W. Chicago Ave.
Gary, IN 46406
CEO: Mr. Stephen L. Martines
Tel: (219) 949-9595 Fax: (219) 949-3533
Email: info@sesequip.comsales@sesequip.com
Web: www.sesequip.com

CONST. EQUIPMENT & SERVICES

GROWERS EQUIPMENT COMPANY
Ft. Lauderdale-Davie Office
2695 Davie Rd.
Davie, FL 33314
CEO: Mr. Norberto H. Lopez
Tel: (954) 916-1020 Fax: (954) 916-0080
Email: sales@growersford.com
Web: www.growersford.com

CONST. MGMT.

PACO GROUP, INC.
Corporate Office
261 5th Ave. #701
New York, NY 10016
CEO: Mr. Frank Otero
Tel: (212) 685-0578 Fax: (212) 685-1379
Email: fotero@pacogroup.com
Web: www.pacogroup.com

Miami Office
5001 SW 74th Ct. #203
Miami, FL 33155
CEO: Mr. Frank Otero
Tel: (305) 666-3456 Fax: (305) 666-8217
Email: fotero@pacogroup.com
Web: www.pacogroup.com

SUN EAGLE CORPORATION
461 N. Dean Ave.
Chandler, AZ 85226
CEO: Mr. Martin Alvarez
Tel: (480) 961-0004 Fax: (480) 940-9160
Email: info@suneaglecorporation.com
Web: www.suneaglecorporation.com

THOMAS A. MASON COMPANY, INC.
P.O. Box 511490
Milwaukee, WI 53203-0251
CEO: Mr. Thomas A. Mason
Tel: (414) 271-6688
(888) 258-6688 Fax: (414) 289-9363
Email: tamco@tamason.com
Web: www.tamason.com

CONST. MGMT., EDUCATIONAL FACILITIES

JASCO CONSTRUCTION COMPANY, INC.
13317 SW 124th St.
Miami, FL 33186
CEO: Mr. Esteban L. Suarez
Tel: (305) 234-6449 Fax: (305) 234-2892

CONST. REMEDIATION SVCS.

PANGEA GROUP
2604 S. Jefferson Ave.
St. Louis, MO 63118-1505
CEO: Mr. Michael Zambrana
Tel: (636) 519-4877 Fax: (636) 519-4876
Email: admin@pangea-group.com
Web: www.pangea-group.com

CONSUMER ELECTRIC, HOUSEWARE, WHSL.

PRECISION TRADING CORPORATION
1430 NW 88th Ave.
Miami, FL 33172
CEO: Mr. Israel Lapciuc
Tel: (305) 592-4500 Fax: (305) 593-6169
Email: simon@precisiontrading.com
Web: www.precisiontrading.com

CONTRACTING.

PACO GROUP, INC.
Carson Office
306 W. Torrance Blvd..
Carson, CA 90745
CEO: Mr. Euculed Thompson Jr.
Tel: (310) 834-5037 Fax: (310) 834-5019
Email: edteng@aol.com
Web: www.edteng.com

Headquarters
23341 Del Lago
Laguna Hills, CA 92653
CEO: Mr. Euculed Thompson Jr.
Tel: (949) 598-1900 Fax: (949) 598-1948
Email: edteng@aol.com
Web: www.edteng.com

New Jersey Office
164 Chapel Ave.
Jersey City, NJ 07305
CEO: Mr. Euculed Thompson Jr.
Tel: (201) 915-5183 Fax: (201) 333-7084
Email: edteng@aol.com
Web: www.edteng.com

HEGA CONSTRUCTION COMPANY, INC.
101 Q St. Northeast
Washington, DC 20002
CEO: Mr. Marco A. Hechavarria
Tel: (202) 269-0599 Fax: (202) 832-8115
Email: hega@juno.com

MAGNUM CONSTRUCTION MANAGEMENT CORPORATION
6201 SW 70th St., 2nd Fl.
Miami, FL 33143
CEO: Mr. Jorge Munilla
Tel: (305) 541-6869 Fax: (305) 541-9771
Email: webmaster@mcmcorp.com
Web: www.mcmcorp.com

R&W CONCRETE CONTRACTORS INC.
Corporate Office
1415 Indiana St.
San Francisco, CA 94107
CEO: Mr. Brian Rodrigues
Tel: (415) 401-6162 Fax: (415) 401-6161

CONSTRUCTION MGMT./ GENERAL CONTRACTING

CONSOLIDATED CONTRACTING SERVICES INC.
Orange County
181 Avenida La Plata #200
San Clemente, CA 92673
CEO: Mr. Jose A. Elias-Calles
Tel: (949) 498-7500 Fax: (949) 498-7992
Email: ccsi@consolidatedcontracting.com
Web: www.consolidatedcontracting.com

San Diego
624 Garrison St. #102
Oceanside, CA 92054
CEO: Mr. Jose A. Elias-Calles
Tel: (760) 967-7455 Fax: (760) 967-7045
Email: ccsi@consolidatedcontracting.com
Web: www.consolidatedcontracting.com

CONTRACTOR

ALLRIGHT DIVERSIFIED SERVICES, INC.
Headquarters
5591 N. Goldenstate Blvd. #102
Fresno, CA 93722
CEO: Ms. Olga Martinez
Tel: (559) 271-7254 Fax: (559) 271-7057

Email: info@allrightinc.com
Web: www.allrightinc.com

STRAIGHT LINE INDUSTRIES, INC.
5 Arrowhead Ln.
Cohoes, NY 12047
CEO: Ms. Pilar G. Dexter
Tel: (518) 220-2000 Fax: (518) 220-9993
Web: www.StraightLineIndustries.com

CORP., PERSONAL, BUSINESS INSURANCE

THE HOME AGENCY
210 Smith Ave.
Elwood, NE 68937
CEO: Mr. Jimmie Baldonado
Tel: (308) 785-2803 Fax: (308) 785-2560
Email: jbaldonaado@thehomeagency.com
Web: www.thehomeagency.com

COSMETICS & NUTRITIONAL PRODS. MFG.

COBE CHEMICAL COMPANY, INC.
8616 Slauson Ave.
Pico Rivera, CA 90660
CEO: Mr. Sergio Quiñones
Tel: (562) 942-2426 Fax: (562) 942-9985
Email: sales@cobechem.com
Web: www.cobechem.com

CUSTOM INJECTION MOLDED PLASTIC COMPNTS.

JMS PLASTICS, INC.
52275 Indiana State Route 933
South Bend, IN 46637
CEO: Mr. David M. Martinez
Tel: (574) 277-3228

DAIRY PROD. MFG. &WHSL.

MENDEZ DAIRY/TROPICAL CHEESE COMPANY
P.O. Box 1357
Perth Amboy, NJ 08862
CEO: Mr. Rafael Mendez
Tel: (732) 442-6337 Fax: (732) 442-8227
Email: r_mendez@ideadairy.com
Web: www.idealdairy.com

DESSERT/FOOD MFG.

LULU'S DESSERT CORP.
4383 Exchange Ave.
Vernon, CA 90058
CEO: Ms. Maria de Lourdes Sobrino
Tel: (323) 585-8804 Fax: (323) 277-2444
Email: alarson@lulusdessert.com
Web: www.lulusdessert.com

DIGITAL PRINT & FULFILLMENT

FULFILLMENT CORPORATION OF AMERICA
1035 NW 14th Ave.
Portland, OR 97209-2705
CEO: Mr. David P. Torres, Jr.
Tel: (503) 833-5421 Fax: (503) 224-6834
Email: info@fulfillmentcorp.com
Web: www.fulfillmentcorp.com

DIRECT-MAIL SERVICES

MINI-MAILERS, INC.
Irvine Spectrum
7 Cushing St.
Irvine, CA 92618-4220
CEO: Mr. William Rivera
Tel: (949) 655-1400 Fax: (949) 655-1420
Email: irvine@minimailers.com
Web: www.minimailers.com

Los Angeles
5700 Bandini Blvd.
Los Angeles, CA 90040-2809
CEO: Mr. William Rivera
Tel: (323) 724-6464 Fax: (323) 724-6330
Email: la@minimailers.com
Web: www.minimailers.com

DIRECT-MAIL SERVICES/ DATA PROCESSING

PRONTO POST, INC.
5300 NW 163 St.
Hialeah, FL 33014
CEO: Mr. J. Michael Vazquez
Tel: (305) 621-7900 Fax: (305) 620-9252
Email: mike@prontopost.
comInfo@prontopost.com
Web: www.prontopost.com

DIRECT MARKETING SVCS.

INKTEL DIRECT CORPORATION
Head Office
13975 NW 58th Ct.
Miami Lakes, FL 33014
CEO: Mr. J. Ricky Arriola
Tel: (305) 523-1110 Fax: (305) 827-0341
Web: www.inktel.com

Inktel Direct Chicago
1269 N. Wood Dale Rd.
Wood Dale, IL 60191
CEO: Mr. J. Ricky Arriola
Tel: (630) 694-7200 Fax: (630) 694-7245
Web: www.inktel.com

DISPLAY & PROMOTIONAL PACKAGING

CARTONCRAFT, INC.
500 N. Hough St.
Barrington, IL 60010
CEO: Mr. Felipe A. Reyes
Tel: (847) 842-0247 Fax: (847) 842-0258
Email: info@cartoncraftinc.com
Web: www.cartoncraftinc.com

DISTRIB. TAPES/ADHES., MFG. GASKETS/RUBBER

ABLE INDUSTRIAL PRODUCTS, INC.
2006 S. Baker Ave.
Ontario, CA 91761
CEO: Mr. Harold H. Martinez
Tel: (909) 930-1585/(800) 423-7008
Fax: (909) 930-1587
Email: haroldh@able123.com
Web: www.able123.com

DRYWALL & PAINTING

HERNANDEZ ENTERPRISES, INC.
Corporate Office
6824 Phillips Pkwy. Dr. South
Jacksonville, FL 32256

CEO: Mr. Jorge Hernandez
Tel: (904) 260-3462
Web: www.hei-usa.com

ELECTRIC CONSTRUCTION

MOUNTAIN POWER ELECTRICAL CONTRACTORS, INC.
4301 S. Country Club
Tucson, AZ 85714
CEO: Mr. Frank M. Siqueiros
Tel: (520) 294 1131 Fax: (520) 294-0355
Email: mtnpower@aol.com

ELECTRIC CONTRACTING ELECTRIC PRODS. WHSL.

MERCEDES ELECTRIC SUPPLY, INC.
8550 NW South River Dr.
Miami, FL 33166
CEO: Ms. Mercedes C. LaPorta
Tel: (305) 887-5550/(800) 636-5550
Fax: (305) 887-8761
Email: info@mercedeselectric
Web: www.mercedeselectric.com

ELECTRICAL CONTRACTING

ALMAN CONSTRUCTION SERVICES
Corporate Office
7677 Hunnicut Rd.
Dallas, TX 75228
CEO: Mr. Robert G. Guzman
Tel: (214) 388-1800/(877) 246-3724
Fax: (214) 388-1818
Email: alman@almanelec.com
Web: www.almanelec.com

DFW Jobsite Office
P.O. Box 612088
DFW Airport, TX 75261
CEO: Mr. Robert G. Guzman
Tel: (972) 574-2310 Fax: (972) 574-2351
Email: alman@almanelec.com
Web: www.almanelec.com

Fort Worth Office
2320 Oakland Blvd. #105
Fort Worth, TX 76103
CEO: Mr. Robert G. Guzman
Tel: (817) 535-0567 Fax: (817) 535-0193
Email: alman@almanelec.com
Web: www.almanelec.com

BARRI ELECTRIC COMPANY, INC.
1485 Bayshore Blvd.
San Francisco, CA 94124-3002
CEO: Mr. Ernie B. Ulibarri
Tel: (415) 468-6477
(888) 372-3045 Fax: (415) 468-7191
Email: barrielect@aol.com
Web: www.barrielectric.com

HONSHY ELECTRIC COMPANY, INC.
7345 SW 41st St.
Miami, FL 33155
CEO: Mr. Manuel G. Diaz
Tel: (305) 264-5500 Fax: (305) 266-3159
Email: honshy@mindspring.com

ELECTRICAL & HIGH-TECH EQUIP. LEASING

ONESOURCE DISTRIBUTORS, INC.
Corporate Office
3951 Oceanic Dr.
Oceanside, CA 92056

CEO: Mr. Robert S. Zamarripa
Tel: (760) 966-4500 Fax: (760) 966-4599
Email: bobz@1sourcedist.com
Web: www.1sourcedist.com

Downey Office
11899 S. Woodruff Ave.
Downey, CA 90241
CEO: Mr. Robert S. Zamarripa
Tel: (562) 803-1833 Fax: (562) 803-5590
Email: bobz@1sourcedist.com
Web: www.1sourcedist.com

El Centro Office
950 S. Hope St.
El Centro, CA 92243
CEO: Mr. Robert S. Zamarripa
Tel: (760) 352-1015 Fax: (760) 353-9236
Email: bobz@1sourcedist.com
Web: www.1sourcedist.com

Fullerton Office
619 S. Raymond Ave.
Fullerton, CA 92831
CEO: Mr. Robert S. Zamarripa
Tel: (714) 278-1660 Fax: (714) 680-4085
Email: bobz@1sourcedist.com
Web: www.1sourcedist.com

Irvine Office
1021 Duryea Ave.
Irvine, CA 92614
CEO: Mr. Robert S. Zamarripa
Tel: (949) 263-8900 Fax: (949) 263-6735
Email: bobz@1sourcedist.com
Web: www.1sourcedist.com

Miramar Office
9275 Carroll Park Dr.
San Diego, CA 92121
CEO: Mr. Robert S. Zamarripa
Tel: (858) 452-9001 Fax: (858) 546-0638
Email: bobz@1sourcedist.com
Web: www.1sourcedist.com

National City Office
2530 Southport Way
National City, CA 91950
CEO: Mr. Robert S. Zamarripa
Tel: (619) 336-0888 Fax: (619) 336-0897
Email: bobz@1sourcedist.com
Web: www.1sourcedist.com

Oxnard Office
2451 Eastman Ave. #1
Oxnard, CA 93030
CEO: Mr. Robert S. Zamarripa
Tel: (805) 485-3830 Fax: (805) 485-6548
Email: bobz@1sourcedist.com
Web: www.1sourcedist.com

Yuma Office
2166 S. Factor Ave.
Yuma, AZ 85364
CEO: Mr. Robert S. Zamarripa
Tel: (928) 782-4311 Fax: (928) 343-1958
Email: bobz@1sourcedist.com
Web: www.1sourcedist.com

ELECTRICAL TECHNOLOGY

PHILATRON INTERNATIONAL
Head Office
15315 Cornet Ave.
Santa Fe Springs, CA 90670
CEO: Mr. Phillip M. Ramos, Jr.
Tel: (562) 802-2570
(800) 421-3547 Fax: (562) 802-0264
Email: moreinfo@philatron.com
Web: www.philatron.com

TECHNICAL TELEPHONE SYSTEMS, INC.
14K Worlds Fair Dr.
Somerset, NJ 08873-1345
CEO: Mr. George Cruzado

Tel: (732) 563-6600 Fax: (732) 566-6240
Email: info@tts.com
Web: www.tts.com

ELECTRONIC COMPONENTS DISTRIB.

MAST DISTRIBUTORS, INC.
710-2 Union Pkwy.
Ronkonkoma, NY 11779
CEO: Mr. Jaime A. Santiago
Tel: (631) 471-4422
(800) 645-4420 Fax: (631) 471-2040
Email: info@mastd.com
Web: www.mastd.com

ELECTRONIC SUPPLY

TORRES ELECTRICAL SUPPLY COMPANY, INC.
Corporate Headquarters
P.O. Box 1908
Stuart, FL 34997
CEO: Mr. Oscar L. Torres
Tel: (772) 286-5049
(800) 433-8694 Fax: (772) 286-5496
Email: sales@torreselectrical.com
Web: www.torreselectrical.com

Palm Beach County
14255 US Hwy.1 #290
Juno Beach, FL 33408
CEO: Mr. Oscar L. Torres
Tel: (561) 624-1096 Fax: (561) 624-5513
Email: sales@torreselectrical.com
Web: www.torreselectrical.com

WESTERN SWITCHES AND CONTROLS, INC.
Canoga Park Office
6001 Canoga Ave.
Canoga Park, CA 91304
CEO: Mr. Leo Alonzo
Tel: (818) 947-7900 Fax: (818) 947-7918
Email: wscvn@westernswitches.com
Web: www.westernswitches.com

Corporate Office
750 Challenger St.
Brea, CA 92821
CEO: Mr. Leo Alonzo
Tel: (714) 482-4100 (800) 454-8144 Fax: (714) 482-4120
Email: wscsa@westernswitches.com
Web: www.westernswitches.com

Phoenix Office
3638 E. Southern Ave. #6
Phoenix, AZ 85040
CEO: Mr. Leo Alonzo
Tel: (602) 243-3888 Fax: (602) 243-0455
Email: wscaz@westernswitches.com
Web: www.westernswitches.com

Sunnyvale Office
544 Wendell Dr. #9
Sunnyvale, CA 94089
CEO: Mr. Leo Alonzo
Tel: (408) 743-9630 Fax: (408) 734-9743
Email: wscsa@westernswitches.com
Web: www.westernswitches.com

ELECTRONIC WARFARE MILITARY EQUIP.

TMC DESIGN CORP.
4325 Del Rey Blvd.
Las Cruces, NM 88012
CEO: Mr. Leroy C. Gomez

Tel: (505) 382-4600 Fax: (505) 523-8588
Email: tmcd@tmcdesign.com
Web: www.tmcdesign.com

EMPLOYMENT STAFFING

DIVERSE STAFFING, INC.
Corporate Office
211 E. Imperial Hwy. #201
Fullerton, CA 92835
CEO: Mr. Fred Flores
Tel: (714) 525-8477 Fax: (714) 525-8682
Email: fflores@dss-staffing.com
Web: www.dss-staffing.com

Los Angeles County
5900 SE Ave. #156
Commerce, CA 90040
CEO: Mr. Fred Flores
Tel: (323) 721-4461 Fax: (323) 721-0403
Email: fflores@dss-staffing.com
Web: www.dss-staffing.com

South Bay/Long Beach
455 S. Carson Plz. Dr. #G
Carson, CA 90746
CEO: Mr. Fred Flores
Tel: (310) 856-0869 Fax: (310) 856-0875
Email: fflores@dss-staffing.com
Web: www.dss-staffing.com

FUTURE FORCE PERSONNEL
Head Office
15800 NW 57th Ave.
Miami Lakes, FL 33014
CEO: Ms. Adela Gonzalez
Tel: (305) 557-4900 Fax: (305) 821-4095
Email: info@futureforcepersonnel.com
Web: www.futureforcepersonnel.com

South Dade
8410 W. Flagler St. #206B
Miami, FL 33144
CEO: Ms. Adela Gonzalez
Tel: (305) 226-0426 Fax: (305) 226-8601
Email: info@futureforcepersonnel.com
Web: www.futureforcepersonnel.com

G&A OUTSOURCING, INC.
Dallas Fort Worth Minority
Business Development Ctr.
545 E. John Carpenter Frwy. #100
Irving, TX 75062
CEO: Mr. Antonio R. Grijalva
Tel: (214) 688-1612 Fax: (214) 688-1753
Email: mmora@dmbdc.com
Web: www.gacompanies.com

Houston
5847 San Felipe #1181
Houston, TX 77057
CEO: Mr. Antonio R. Grijalva
Tel: (713) 784-1181 Fax: (713) 784-2705
Email: tgrijalva@gacompanies.com
Web: www.gacompanies.com

Houston Minority Business
Development Ctr.
2900 Woodridge #310
Houston, TX 77087
CEO: Mr. Antonio R. Grijalva
Tel: (713) 644-0821 Fax: (713) 644-3523
Email: mthibodeaux@gacompanies.com
Web: www.gacompanies.com

The University of Texas System - Bonding
and Technical Assistance
6900 Fannin FHB 103
Houston, TX 77030
CEO: Mr. Antonio R. Grijalva
Tel: (713) 794-4105 Fax: (713) 794-4117
Email: dsamuels@gacompanies.com
Web: www.gacompanies.com

Washington DC
8550 Lee Hwy. #450
Fairfax, VA 22031
CEO: Mr. Antonio R. Grijalva
Tel: (703) 208-3303 Fax: (703) 208-3305
Email: dvasquez@gacompanies.com
Web: www.gacompanies.com

EMPLOYMENT SERVICES & FACILITY MGMT.

RIOJAS ENTERPRISES, INC.
Headquarters
10 E. Cambridge Circle Dr. #120
Kansas City, KS 66103
CEO: Mr. Carlos Riojas
Tel: (913) 281-1600 Fax: (913) 281-2468
Email: riojas@rei-able.com
Web: www.riojas-able.com

ENERGY SVCS., HVAC ENG. SYSTEMS

PROTEC, INC.
6935 NW 50th St.
Miami, FL 33166
CEO: Mr. Alfredo Sotolongo
Tel: (305) 594-3684 Fax: (305) 477-2514
Email: protec@protecinc.com
Web: www.protecinc.com

ENGINEERING

GUTIERREZ-PALMENBERG, INC.
Phoenix Internet-Texas, Inc.
1401 Elm St. #1923
Dallas, TX 75202
CEO: Mr. Gilbert T. Gutierrez
Tel: (214) 231-0080
(817) 640-4375
(877) 530-2375 Fax: (214) 749-1292
Email: gill.g@gpimail.com
Web: www.gpieng.com

Sierra Vista Office
4116 Avenida Cochise #S
Sierra Vista, AZ 85635
CEO: Mr. Gilbert T. Gutierrez
Tel: (520) 458-7111 Fax: (520) 458-7109
Email: gill.g@gpimail.com
Web: www.gpieng.com

ENGINEERING, ARCHITECH., CONST. MGMT.

SUNLAND GROUP
Austin
1907 N. Lamar #220
Austin, TX 78705
CEO: Mr. Orlando J. Teran
Tel: (512) 494-0208 Fax: (414) 494-0406
Email: info@sunlandgrp.com
Web: www.sunlandgrp.com

Dallas
6060 N. Central Expressway #429
Dallas, TX 75206
CEO: Mr. Orlando J. Teran
Tel: (214) 800-2808 Fax: (214) 800-2868
Email: info@sunlandgrp.com
Web: www.sunlandgrp.com

Denver
110 16th St. #1400
Denver, CO 80202
CEO: Mr. Orlando J. Teran
Tel: (303) 626-0639
Email: info@sunlandgrp.com
Web: www.sunlandgrp.com

Houston
10497 Town & Country Way #550
Houston, TX 77024
CEO: Mr. Orlando J. Teran
Tel: (713) 467-8484 Fax: (713) 467-3353
Email: info@sunlandgrp.
commarketing@sunlandgrp.com
Web: www.sunlandgrp.com

San Antonio
110 Broadway #70
San Antonio, TX 78205
CEO: Mr. Orlando J. Teran
Tel: (210) 561-6170
Email: info@sunlandgrp.com
Web: www.sunlandgrp.com

ENGINEERING DESIGN & CONSTRUCTION MGMT.

J.L. PATTERSON & ASSOCIATES, INC.
Branch Office
1400 112th Ave. SE #100
Bellevue, WA 98004
CEO: Ms. Jacqueline L. Patterson
Tel: (425) 688-8694 Fax: (425) 646-7569
Email: info@jlpatterson.com
Web: www.jlpatterson.com

Main Office
725 W. Town & Country Rd. #300
Orange, CA 92868
CEO: Ms. Jacqueline L. Patterson
Tel: (714) 835-6355 Fax: (714) 835-6671
Email: info@jlpatterson.com
Web: www.jlpatterson.com

ENGINEERING & ENVIRONMENT SERVICES

CAPE ENVIRONMENTAL MANAGEMENT, INC.
Bellevue Office
1502 J.F. Kennedy Dr.
Bellevue, NE 68005
CEO: Mr. Fernando J. Rios
Tel: (402) 934-9243
Email: HR@capeenv.com
Web: www.capeenv.com

Corporate & Southern Regional Office
2302 Parklake Dr. #200
Atlanta, GA 30345-2907
CEO: Mr. Fernando J. Rios
Tel: (770) 908-7200 Fax: (770) 908-7219
Email: HR@capeenv.com
Web: www.capeenv.com

Denver Office
9035 Wadsworth Blvd. #3650
Westminster, CO 80021
CEO: Mr. Fernando J. Rios
Tel: (303) 940-7994
Email: HR@capeenv.com
Web: www.capeenv.com

Kansas City Office
12525 Hollingsworth Rd.
Kansas City, KS 66109
CEO: Mr. Fernando J. Rios
Tel: (913) 721-9955
Email: HR@capeenv.com
Web: www.capeenv.com

Midwest Regional Office
91 Noll St.
Waukegan, IL 60085
CEO: Mr. Fernando J. Rios
Tel: (847) 336-4341 Fax: (847) 336-4971
Email: HR@capeenv.com
Web: www.capeenv.com

Norfolk Office
6330 Newtown Rd. #309

Norfolk, VA 23502
CEO: Mr. Fernando J. Rios
Tel: (757) 461-5335
Email: HR@capeenv.com
Web: www.capeenv.com

Northeast Regional Office
180 Gordon Dr. #102
Exton, PA 19341
CEO: Mr. Fernando J. Rios
Tel: (610) 594-8606 Fax: (610) 594-8609
Email: HR@capeenv.com
Web: www.capeenv.com

Rome Office
303 W. Liberty, 2nd Fl.
Rome, NY 13440
CEO: Mr. Fernando J. Rios
Tel: (315) 336-6285
Email: HR@capeenv.com
Web: www.capeenv.com

San Antonio Office
12037 Starcrest Dr.
San Antonio, TX 78216
CEO: Mr. Fernando J. Rios
Tel: (210) 377-2008
Email: HR@capeenv.com
Web: www.capeenv.com

Warner Robins Office
603A Russell Pkwy.
Warner Robins, GA 31088
CEO: Mr. Fernando J. Rios
Tel: (478) 923-6788
Email: HR@capeenv.com
Web: www.capeenv.com

Washington, DC Office
9251 Hampton Overlook
Capital Heigths, MD 20743
CEO: Mr. Fernando J. Rios
Tel: (301) 324-1572
Email: HR@capeenv.com
Web: www.capeenv.com

Western Regional Office
2823 McGaw Ave.
Irvine, CA 92614
CEO: Mr. Fernando J. Rios
Tel: (949) 474-3090
Email: HR@capeenv.com
Web: www.capeenv.com

ENGINEERING, LOGISTICS & ADMIN. SERVICES

ADVANCED FEDERAL SERVICES CORP.
P.O. Box 1219
Madison, AL 35758-5219
CEO: Mr. Alfredo Bonilla III
Tel: (256) 772-7795 Fax: (256) 461-1927
Email: info@afscorp.com
Web: www.afscorp.com

ENGINEERING, PROJECT MGMT., CONSTRUCTION

AR UTILITY SPECIALISTS INC.
2840 S. 36th St. Bldg. E #5
Phoenix, AZ 85034-7238
CEO: Mr. Alejandro Reynoso
Tel: (602) 431-2175 Fax: (602) 431-2163
Email: alexreynoso@arusi.net
Web: www.arusi.net

ENGINEERING SAFETY & PROD. ASSURANCE, IT

MUÑIZ ENGINEERING, INC.
16903 Buccaneer Ln. #200
Houston, TX 77058

CEO: Mr. Edelmiro Muñiz
Tel: (281) 283-6200
(888) 895-3014 Fax: (281) 283-6170
Email: info@munizengineering.com
Web: www.munizengineering.com/

6478 S. Pike Dr.
Larkspur, CO 80118
CEO: Mr. Edelmiro Muñiz
Tel: (303) 681-2517 Fax: (303) 861-2127
Email: info@munizengineering.com
Web: www.munizengineering.com

7820 Pan American Frwy. NE #1
Albuquerque, NM 87109
CEO: Edelmiro Muñiz
Tel: (505) 858-0254 Fax: (505) 858-0354
Email: info@munizengineering.com
Web: www.munizengineering.com

ENGINEERING SERVICES

CNC ENGINEERING CO.
8 Corporate Park #100
Irvine, CA 92606
CEO: Mr. Clement N. Calvillo
Tel: (949) 863-0588 Fax: (949) 863-0589
Web: www.cnc-eng.com

INTUITIVE RESEARCH & TECHNOLOGY CORPORATION
Corporate Office
2100 N. Hwy. 360 #1201
Grand Prairie, TX 75050
CEO: Mr. A. R. "Rey" Almodovar
Tel: (972) 988-9500 Fax: (972) 786-0029
Email: rey.almodovar@irtc-hq.com
Web: www.irtc-hq.com

Main Office
6767 Old Madison Pike #240, Bldg. 2
Huntsville, AL 35806
CEO: Mr. A. R. "Rey" Almodovar
Tel: (256) 922-9300 Fax: (256) 922-1122
Email: rey.almodovar@irtc-hq.com
Web: www.irtc-hq.com

J.J. SOSA & ASSOC. INC.
5811 Memorial Hwy. #207
Tampa, FL 33615-5000
CEO: Mr. Jose J. Sosa
Tel: (813) 888-1285
Email: jjsa1@aol.com
Web: www.jjsosa.com

SEI GROUP, INC.
303 Williams Ave. #123
Huntsville, AL 35801
CEO: Mr. Eloy J. Torres
Tel: (256) 533-0500 X335
Fax: (256) 533-0589
Email: curtis.spurlings@seigroupinc.com
Web: www.seigroupinc.com

ENGINEERING SVCS. & SOFTWARE DEVELOPMENT

TRANDES CORPORATION
Chesapeake Office
600 B Greentree Rd.
Chesapeake, VA 23320
CEO: Mr. James A. Brusse
Tel: (757) 549-7760 Fax: (757) 549-7759
Email: jcarran@trandes.com
Web: www.trandes.com

Corporate Office
4601 Presidents Dr. #360
Lanham, MD 20706
CEO: Mr. James A. Brusse
Tel: (301) 459-0200 Fax: (301) 459-1069
Email: jcarran@trandes.com
Web: www.trandes.com

Lexington Park Office
23923 By the Mill Rd.
California, MD 20619
CEO: Mr. James A. Brusse
Tel: (301) 863-0106 Fax: (858) 863-0255
Email: jcarran@trandes.com
Web: www.trandes.com

Norfolk Electronic Maintenance Center
4601 Presidents Dr. #360
Lanham, MD 20706
CEO: Mr. James A. Brusse
Tel: (301) 459-0200 Fax: (301) 459-1069
Email: chall@trandes.com
Web: www.trandes.com

San Diego Office
9471 Ridgehaven Ct. #A
San Diego, CA 92123
CEO: Mr. James A. Brusse
Tel: (858) 268-4930 Fax: (858) 268-4603
Web: www.trandes.com

Vallejo Office
1422 Springs Rd. #A
Vallejo, CA 94591
CEO: Mr. James A. Brusse
Tel: (707) 648-2445 Fax: (707) 648-1035
Web: www.trandes.com

ENGINEERING & TECH SERVICES

SYMVIONICS, INC.
Alexandria, Virginia Office
2121 Eisenhower Ave. #200
Alexandria, VA 22314
CEO: Mr. Lawrence B. Barraza
Tel: (703) 549-8330 Fax: (703) 549-8120
Email: rweeks@symvionics.com
Web: www.symvionics.com

Camp Pendleton, California Office
NAWC TSD - MCAS Flight Simulator Bldg.
2394, Attn: ISEO
Camp Pendleton, CA 92055
CEO: Mr. Lawrence B. Barraza
Tel: (760) 725-4752 Fax: (760) 725-4095
Email: rweeks@symvionics.com
Web: www.symvionics.com

Charleston, South Carolina Office
222 W. Coleman Blvd. #202
Mt. Pleasant, SC 29464
CEO: Mr. Lawrence B. Barraza
Tel: (843) 881-5559 Fax: (843) 881-9359
Email: rweeks@symvionics.com
Web: www.symvionics.com

Corporate Office
488 E. Santa Clara St. #201
Arcadia, CA 91006
CEO: Mr. Lawrence B. Barraza
Tel: (626) 305-1400 Fax: (626) 305-8860
Email: rweeks@symvionics.com
Web: www.symvionics.com

Dayton, Ohio Office
P.O. Box 24297
Huber Heights, OH 45424
CEO: Mr. Lawrence B. Barraza
Tel: (937) 236-5079 Fax: (937) 236-5095
Email: rweeks@symvionics.com
Web: www.symvionics.com

Del Mar, California Office
13306 Roxton Cr.
San Diego, CA 92130
CEO: Mr. Lawrence B. Barraza
Tel: (858) 481-1238 Fax: (858) 481-4172
Email: rweeks@symvionics.com
Web: www.symvionics.com

Edwards Air Force Base, California Office
190 Sierra Ct. #A-3
Palmdale, CA 93550

CEO: Mr. Lawrence B. Barraza
Tel: (661) 273-7003 Fax: (661) 273-7144
Email: rweeks@symvionics.com
Web: www.symvionics.com

Fort Walton Beach, Florida Office
1813 John Sims Pkwy. #206
Niceville, FL 32578
CEO: Mr. Lawrence B. Barraza
Tel: (850) 897-3311 Fax: (850) 897-2201
Email: rweeks@symvionics.com
Web: www.symvionics.com

Holloman Air Force Base, New Mexico Office
550 Tabosa Attn: Housing Maintenance
Holloman AFB, NM 88330
CEO: Mr. Lawrence B. Barraza
Tel: (505) 572-5784 Fax: (505) 572-2449
Email: rweeks@symvionics.com
Web: www.symvionics.com

Hurlburt Field, Florida Office
505th Training Squadron 142 Hartson St.
Hurlburt Field, FL 32544-5225
CEO: Mr. Lawrence B. Barraza
Tel: (850) 884-6074 Fax: (850) 884-6998
Email: rweeks@symvionics.com
Web: www.symvionics.com

Lackland Air Force Base, Texas Office
1250 Arnold Cr. #1
Lackland Air Force Base, TX 78236
CEO: Mr. Lawrence B. Barraza
Tel: (210) 671-1815 Fax: (210) 671-0543
Email: rweeks@symvionics.com
Web: www.symvionics.com

Moffett Field, California Office
P.O. Box 159
Moffett Field, CA 94035
CEO: Mr. Lawrence B. Barraza
Tel: (650) 564-9490 Fax: (650) 564-9494
Email: rweeks@symvionics.com
Web: www.symvionics.com

NAS Jacksonville, Florida Office
5513 Roosevelt Blvd. PMB #192
Jacksonville, FL 32244
CEO: Mr. Lawrence B. Barraza
Tel: (904) 778-3608 Fax: (904) 778-3608
Email: rweeks@symvionics.com
Web: www.symvionics.com

NASA Dryden, California Flight Test Research Center
190 Sierra Ct. #A-3
Palmdale, CA 93550
CEO: Mr. Lawrence B. Barraza
Tel: (661) 273-7003 Fax: (661) 273-7144
Email: rweeks@symvionics.com
Web: www.symvionics.com

Nellis Air Force Base, Nevada Office
P.O. Box 9779
Las Vegas, NV 89191-0779
CEO: Mr. Lawrence B. Barraza
Tel: (702) 652-1857 Fax: (702) 643-7760
Email: rweeks@symvionics.com
Web: www.symvionics.com

NFESC Port Hueneme Office
1100 23rd Ave.
Port Hueneme, CA 93043
CEO: Mr. Lawrence B. Barraza
Tel: (805) 982-4028 Fax: (805) 982-1602
Email: rweeks@symvionics.com
Web: www.symvionics.com

Northrop Grumman, California Office
Military Aircraft Division, One Hornet Way
El Segundo, CA 90245
CEO: Mr. Lawrence B. Barraza
Tel: (310) 505-5498 Fax: (310) 335-3260
Email: rweeks@symvionics.com
Web: www.symvionics.com

Palmdale, California Office
190 Sierra #A-3

Palmdale, CA 93550
CEO: Mr. Lawrence B. Barraza
Tel: (661) 273-7003 Fax: (661) 273-7144
Email: rweeks@symvionics.com
Web: www.symvionics.com

Pensacola
4051-G Barrancas Ave. PMB #104
Pensacola, FL 32507
CEO: Mr. Lawrence B. Barraza
Tel: (850) 452-7034 Fax: (850) 452-2014
Email: rweeks@symvionics.com
Web: www.symvionics.com

San Diego North, California Office
7582 Clairemont Mesa Blvd.
San Diego, CA 92111
CEO: Mr. Lawrence B. Barraza
Tel: (858) 560-2979 Fax: (858) 560-2980
Email: rweeks@symvionics.com
Web: www.symvionics.com

San Diego South, California Office
6420 Federal Blvd. #G
Lemon Grove, CA 91945
CEO: Mr. Lawrence B. Barraza
Tel: (619) 287-1826 Fax: (619) 287-0258
Email: rweeks@symvionics.com
Web: www.symvionics.com

Virginia Beach, Virginia Office
1300 Diamond Springs Rd. #206
Virginia Beach, VA 23455
CEO: Mr. Lawrence B. Barraza
Tel: (757) 363-1777 Fax: (757) 363-2529
Email: rweeks@symvionics.com
Web: www.symvionics.com

Washington Navy Yard Office
1322 Patterson Ave. #100
Washington, DC 20374-5065
CEO: Mr. Lawrence B. Barraza
Tel: (202) 685-9377 Fax: (202) 685-1674
Email: rweeks@symvionics.com
Web: www.symvionics.com

ENGINEERING, ARCHITECTURAL SERVICES

CORZO CASTENA CARBALLO THOMPSON SALMAN P.A.
Coral Gables Office
901 Ponce De Leon Blvd. #900
Coral Gables, FL 33134
CEO: Mr. Jorge E. Corzo
Tel: (305) 445-2900 Fax: (305) 445-3366
Email: bcarballo@c3ts.com
Web: www.c3ts.com

Fort Lauderdale Office
3996 NW 9 Ave.
Fort Lauderdale, FL 33309
CEO: Mr. Jorge E. Corzo
Tel: (954) 565-2113 Fax: (954) 565-4079
Email: bcarballo@c3ts.com
Web: www.c3ts.com

ENVELOPE & LABEL MFG.

CONTINENTAL ENVELOPE COMPANY, INC.
404 Tonnelle Ave.
Jersey City, NJ 07306
CEO: Mr. Jose M. Perez
Tel: (201) 656-7800 Fax: (201) 656-8026
Email: donjose@aol.com

ENVIRONMENTAL CONSULTING SERVICES

HOLGUIN FAHAN & ASSOCIATES, INC.
Colton Office
1003 E. Cooley Dr. #201

Colton, CA 92324
CEO: Mr. Andrew R. Holguin
Tel: (909) 422-8988 Fax: (909) 422-8099
Email: Mark_Fahan@hfa.com
Web: www.hfa.com

Corporate Headquarters/ CA/MXT Program Office
143 S. Figueroa St.
Ventura, CA 93001
CEO: Mr. Andrew R. Holguin
Tel: (805) 652-0219 Fax: (805) 652-0793
Email: Mark_Fahan@hfa.com
Web: www.hfa.com

Orange Office
948 N. Lemon St.
Orange, CA 92867
CEO: Mr. Andrew Holguin
Tel: (714) 210-5971 Fax: (714) 210-5975
Email: Mark_Fahan@hfa.com
Web: www.hfa.com

Tempe Office
1215 S. Park Ln. #1
Tempe, AZ 85281
CEO: Mr. Andrew R. Holguin
Tel: (480) 505-3332 Fax: (480) 505-3336
Email: Mark_Fahan@hfa.com
Web: www.hfa.com

Vacaville Office
871 Cotting Ct. #C
Vacaville, CA 95688
CEO: Mr. Andrew R. Holguin
Tel: (707) 454-0156 Fax: (707) 454-0196
Email: Mark_Fahan@hfa.com
Web: www.hfa.com

ENVIRONMENTAL ENGINEERING

KEMRON ENVIRONMENTAL SERVICES, INC.

Analytical Laboratory
156 Starlite Dr.
Marietta, OH 45750
CEO: Mr. Juan J. Gutierrez
Tel: (740) 373-4071 Fax: (740) 373-4835
Email: ovl@kemron.com
Web: www.kemron.com

Atlanta Regional Office
1359-A Ellsworth Industrial Blvd.
Atlanta, GA 30319
CEO: Mr. Juan J. Gutierrez
Tel: (404) 636-0928
(800) 548-6939 Fax: (404) 636-7162
Email: atlanta@kemron.com
Web: www.kemron.com

Charleston Office
5 Craddock Way,
Rock Branch Industrial Park
Poca, WV 25159
CEO: Mr. Juan J. Gutierrez
Tel: (304) 755-0999
(888) 437-1133 Fax: (304) 755-0990
Email: charleston@kemron.com
Web: www.kemron.com

Chicago Regional Office
3155 Blackhawk Dr. # 17, Bldg. 379
Ft. Sheridan, IL 60037
CEO: Mr. Juan J. Gutierrez
Tel: (847) 266-1350
(847) 266-3584 Fax: (847) 266-3584
Web: www.kemron.com

Cleveland Regional Office
19501 Five Points Rd.
Cleveland, OH 44135
CEO: Mr. Juan J. Gutierrez
Tel: (216) 898-1251 Fax: (216) 898-1252
Web: www.kemron.com

Corporate Headquarters

8150 Leesburg Pike #1410
Vienna, VA 22182
CEO: Mr. Juan J. Gutierrez
Tel: (703) 893-4106
(800) 777-1042 Fax: (703) 893-1741
Email: vienna@kemron.com
Web: www.kemron.com

San Antonio Regional Office
5206 Casbury
San Antonio, TX 78249
CEO: Mr. Juan J. Gutierrez
Tel: (210) 649-5434
(800) 887-2990 Fax: (210) 694-5414
Email: sanantonio@kemron.com
Web: www.kemron.com

Tampa Office
P.O. Box 271524
Tampa, FL 33688
CEO: Mr. Juan J. Gutierrez
Tel: (813) 882-4998
Web: www.kemron.com

Treatability and Geotechnical Laboratory
1359-A Ellsworth Industrial Blvd.
Atlanta, GA 30318
CEO: Mr. Juan J. Gutierrez
Tel: (404) 636-0928 Fax: (404) 636-7162
Web: www.kemron.com

ENVIRONMENTAL & ENGINEERING CONSULTING SERVICES

GEO-MARINE, INC.

Atlantic Region - Virginia
11846 Rock Landing # C
Newport News, VA 23606
CEO: Mr. Ruben G. Garza
Tel: (757) 873-3702 Fax: (757) 873-3703
Email: rGarza@geo-marine.com
Web: www.geo-marine.com

Central Region
2700 NE Loop 410 #380
San Antonio, TX 78217-4810
CEO: Mr. Ruben G. Garza
Tel: (210) 930-3007 Fax: (210) 930-3777
Email: rGarza@geo-marine.com
Web: www.geo-marine.com

Corporate Headquarters
550 E. 15th St.
Plano, TX 75074
CEO: Mr. Ruben G. Garza
Tel: (972) 423-5480 Fax: (972) 422-2736
Email: rGarza@geo-marine.com
Web: www.geo-marine.com

Knoxville
146-E Market Pl. Blvd.
Knoxville, TN 37922
CEO: Mr. Ruben G. Garza
Tel: (865) 692-0084 Fax: (865) 692-0560
Email: rGarza@geo-marine.com
Web: www.geo-marine.com

Western Region - El Paso
3945 Doniphan Park Cir. #C
El Paso, TX 79922
CEO: Mr. Ruben G. Garza
Tel: (915) 585-0168 Fax: (915) 585-2153
Email: rGarza@geo-marine.com
Web: www.geo-marine.com

Western Region - Las Vegas
4336 Losee Rd. #9B
Las Vegas, NV 89030
CEO: Mr. Ruben G. Garza
Tel: (702) 597-3920 Fax: (702) 597-3922
Email: rGarza@geo-marine.com
Web: www.geo-marine.com

LOPEZ GARCIA GROUP

Main Office

1825 Market Ctr. Blvd. #150
Dallas, TX 75207
CEO: Ms. Wendy A. Lopez
Tel: (214) 741-7777 Fax: (214) 741-9413
Email: marketing@lopezgarciagroup.com
Web: www.lopezgarciagroup.com

ENVIRONMENTAL, HEALTH & SAFETY, OPS., SUPPORT

RCS CORPORATION

Headquarters
955 Colony Pkwy.
Aiken, SC 29803
CEO: Mr. Carlos F. Garcia
Tel: (803) 641-0100 Fax: (803) 641-7037
Email: mail@rcscorporation.com
Web: www.rcscorporation.com

South Carolina
2154 N. Ctr. St. #201
N. Charleston, SC 29406
CEO: Mr. Carlos F. Garcia
Tel: (843) 553-2220 Fax: (843) 553-4405
Email: mail@rcscorporation.com
Web: www.rcscorporation.com

Tennesse
P.O. Box 2501
Oak Ridge, TN 37831
CEO: Mr. Carlos F. Garcia
Tel: (865) 220-9692
Email: mail@rcscorporation.com
Web: www.rcscorporation.com

NAVARRO RESEARCH & ENGINEERING, INC.

669 Emory Valley Rd.
Oak Ridge, TN 37830
CEO: Ms. Susana Navarro-Velenti
Tel: (865) 220-9650 Fax: (865) 220-9651
Email: inquiries@navresearch.com
Web: www.navresearch.com

ENVIRONMENTAL REMEDIATION SERVICES

AMERICAN REMEDIAL TECHNOLOGIES INC.
P.O. Box 970
Lynwood, CA 90262
CEO: Mr. Mark Quinonez Patten
Tel: (323) 357-1900 Fax: (323) 357-1909
Email: mrq@americanremedial.com
Web: www.americanremedial.com

ENVIRONMENTAL SUPPORT SERVICES

NORTH WIND ENVIRONMENT, INC.

Corporate Office
545 Shoup Ave. #200
Idaho Falls, ID 83402
CEO: Ms. Sylvia M. Medina
Tel: (208) 528-8718 Fax: (208) 528-8714
Email: aarmstrong@nwindenv.com
Web: www.nwindenv.com

EQUIPMENT FOR HIGH TECH MANUFACTURING

CEIBA TECHNOLOGIES

Headquarters
410 N. Roosevelt Ave.
Chandler, AZ 85226
CEO: Mr. John Vargas
Tel: (480) 705-4541 Fax: (480) 705-5236
Email: cpardon@ceibatech.com
Web: www.ceibatech.com

EQUIPMENT & SERVICES

HUSCO INTERNATIONAL, INC.
World Headquarters
W. 239 N. 218 Pewaukee Rd.
Waukesha, WI 53188
CEO: Mr. Agustin A. Ramirez
Tel: (262) 513-4200 Fax: (262) 513-4514
Email: huswm@huscointl.com
Web: www.huscointl.com

ESPRESSO COFFEE MFG.

ROWLAND COFFEE ROASTERS, INC.
5605 NW 82nd Ave.
Miami, FL 33166
CEO: Mr. Jose Angel Souto
Tel: (305) 594-9039 Fax: (305) 594-7603
Email: jc@javacabana.com
Web: www.javacabana.com

EXCAVATION, GROUNDWORK

ORTIZ ENTERPRISES, INC.
Corporate Office
12 Mauchly, Bldg. J
Irvine, CA 92618
CEO: Mr. Patrick A. Ortiz
Tel: (949) 753-1414 Fax: (949) 753-1477
Email: oei@ortizent.com
Web: www.ortizent.com

EXEC. MGMT. CONSULTING

ENGINEERING MANAGEMENT & INTEGRATION
585 Grove St.
Herndon, VA 20170-4727
CEO: Mr. James Fitzwilliam Ortiz
Tel: (707) 742-0585 Fax: (707) 742-8034
Email: information@em-i.com
Web: www.em-i.com

FACILITIES SUPPORT & MANAGEMENT SERVICES

DSS SERVICES, INC.
613 NW Loop 410 #150
San Antonio, TX 78216
CEO: Mr. Vivian Spurlock
Tel: (210) 348-7820 Fax: (210) 348-9466
Email: sanantonio@dunhillstaff.com
Web: www.dunhillstaff.com

FARM INDUST. & ALLIED EQUIP. DISTRIBUTION

GROWERS EQUIPMENT COMPANY
Head Office
8501 NW 58th St.
Miami, FL 33166
CEO: Mr. Norberto H. Lopez
Tel: (305) 592-7890 Fax: (305) 477-1659
Email: sales@growersford.com
Web: www.growersford.com

FINANCIAL SERVICES

MENENDEZ FINANCIAL & INSURANCE SERVICES, INC.
555 5th St. #300
Santa Rosa, CA 95401
CEO: Mr. Michael J. Menendez
Tel: (707) 578-0675 Fax: (707) 578-4245
Email: patricia_oliver@glic.com
Web: www.menendezfinancial.com

THE ARENAS GROUP, INC.
9107 Wilshire Blvd. #500
Beverly Hills, CA 90210
CEO: Mr. Ruben Arenas
Tel: (310) 724-5230 Fax: (310) 388-5859
Email: info@thearenasgroup.com
Web: www.thearenasgroup.com

FINANCIAL SVCS.,REAL ESTATE DEVELOP.

TELACU INDUSTRIES, INC.
5400 E. Olympic Blvd. #300
Los Angeles, CA 90022
CEO: Mr. David C. Lizárraga
Tel: (323) 721-1655 Fax: (323) 721-3560
Email: info@telacu.com
Web: www.telacu.com

FIXED INCOME DEBT/ASSET MGMT.

SAMUEL A. RAMIREZ & CO., INC.
Chicago
120 N. LaSalle St. #1420
Chicago, IL 60602
CEO: Mr. Samuel A. Ramirez, Sr.
Tel: (312) 630-2002 Fax: (312) 630-2005
Web: www.ramirezco.com

Houston
2323 S. Shepherd #930
Houston, TX 77019
CEO: Mr. Samuel A. Ramirez, Sr.
Tel: (713) 526-0050 Fax: (713) 526-1503
Web: www.ramirezco.com

Los Angeles
444 S. Flower St. #4260
Los Angeles, CA 90071
CEO: Mr. Samuel A. Ramirez, Sr.
Tel: (213) 627-6120 Fax: (213) 627-6040
Web: www.ramirezco.com

Main Office
61 Broadway #2924
New York, NY 10006
CEO: Mr. Samuel A. Ramirez, Sr.
Tel: (212) 248-0500
(800) 888-4086 Fax: (212) 248-0528
Web: www.ramirezco.com

Miami
600 Brickell Ave. #301M
Miami, FL 33131
CEO: Mr. Samuel A. Ramirez, Sr.
Tel: (305) 347-6486 Fax: (305) 347-6488
Web: www.ramirezco.com

Oakland
410 14th St.
Oakland, CA 94612
CEO: Mr. Samuel A. Ramirez, Sr.
Tel: (510) 466-6320 Fax: (916) 424-0843
Web: www.ramirezco.com

San Antonio
1 Alamo Ctr. 106 S. St. Marys #230
San Antonio, TX 78205
CEO: Mr. Samuel A. Ramirez, Sr.
Tel: (210) 225-3900 Fax: (210) 255-5787
Web: www.ramirezco.com

San Juan
Banco Popular Ctr. 209 Munoz Rivera Ave.
Su Hato Rey, PR 00918
CEO: Mr. Samuel A. Ramirez, Sr.
Tel: (787) 759-8080 Fax: (787) 753-4071
Web: www.ramirezco.com

FLOOR COVERING

JJJ FLOOR COVERING, INC.
4831 Passons Blvd. #A
Pico Rivera, CA 90660
CEO: Mr. Jose Gutierrez
Tel: (562) 692-9008 Fax: (562) 692-5979

FOOD

GRANDE FOODS, A CALIFORNIA CORP.
671 N. Poplar St.
Orange, CA 92868-1011
CEO: Mr. Scott Gallegos
Tel: (714) 978-0061 Fax: (714) 978-0436

R.W. GARCIA COMPANY, INC.
San Jose Office
345 Phelan Ave.
San Jose, CA 95112
CEO: Mr. Robert Garcia
Tel: (408) 287-4616 Fax: (408) 287-7724
Email: mgarcia@rwgarcia.com
Web: www.rwgarcia.com

Tampa Office
6002 Benjamin Rd.
Tampa, FL 33634
CEO: Mr. Robert Garcia
Tel: (813) 886-3590 Fax: (813) 888-8064
Email: mgarcia@rwgarcia.com
Web: www.rwgarcia.com

RUIZ MEXICAN FOODS, INC.
2151 E. Francis St.
Ontario, CA 91761
CEO: Mr. Edward F. Ruiz
Tel: (909) 947-7811 Fax: (909) 947-2338

FOOD DIST. IMPORT., EXPORT.

QUIRCH FOODS COMPANY
7600 NW 82nd Pl.
Miami, FL 33166
CEO: Mr. Guillermo Quirch
Tel: (305) 691-3535 Fax: (305) 691-2015
Email: bill@quirchfoods.com
Web: www.quirchfoods.com

FOOD INDUSTRY EQUIPMENT

TAYLOR ULTIMATE SERVICE COMPANY
750 N. Blackhawk Blvd.
Rockton, IL 61072
CEO: Mr. Raul Piedra, Jr.
Tel: (815) 624-8333
(800) 255-0626 Fax: (815) 624-8000
Email: info@taylor-company.com
Web: www.taylor-company.com

FOOD PROD. DISTRIBUTION

DIAZ WHOLESALE & MANUFACTURING COMPANY, INC.
5501 Fulton Industrial Blvd.
Atlanta, GA 30336
CEO: Mr. Rene M. Diaz
Tel: (404) 344-5421
(800) 394-4639 Fax: (404) 344-3003
Email: diazfoods@diazfoods.com
Web: www.diazfoods.com

OLE MEXICAN FOODS, INC.
5385 Gateway Blvd.
Lakeland, FL 33815
CEO: Mr. Eduardo Moreno
Tel: (863) 680-3311 Fax: (863) 686-4327

Email: info@olemexicanfoods.net
Web: www.tortilla.net/

8140 NW 74th Ave. #17
Medley, FL 33166
CEO: Mr. Eduardo Moreno
Tel: (305) 887-5687 Fax: (305) 887-5698
Email: info@olemexicanfoods.net
Web: www.tortilla.net/

612 NE Tarboro St. E
Wilson, NC 27893
CEO: Mr. Eduardo Moreno
Tel: (252) 293-9885 Fax: (252) 293-9925
Email: info@olemexicanfoods.net
Web: www.tortilla.net/

3684 Centre Cr.
Fort Mill, SC 29715
CEO: Mr. Eduardo Moreno
Tel: (803) 802-5630 Fax: (803) 802-5634
Email: info@olemexicanfoods.net
Web: www.tortilla.net/

3200 Commerce Ctr. Pl.
Louisville, KY 40211
CEO: Mr. Eduardo Moreno
Tel: (502) 772-3334 Fax: (502) 772-3354
Email: info@olemexicanfoods.net
Web: www.tortilla.net/

4300 Windfern #200
Houston, TX 77041
CEO: Mr. Eduardo Moreno
Tel: (713) 939-7930 Fax: (713) 939-1494
Email: info@olemexicanfoods.net
Web: www.tortilla.net/

Corporate Office
6585 Crescent Dr.
Norcross, GA 30071
CEO: Mr. Eduardo Moreno
Tel: (770) 582-9200 Fax: (770) 582-9400
Email: info@olemexicanfoods.net
Web: www.tortilla.net/

ZMG, INC./ JOJO'Z ENTERPRISES
300 W. 28th St. #A
National City, CA 92050
CEO: Mr. Steve Gomez
Tel: (619) 474-8428 Fax: (619) 474-1263

FOOD PROD. MFG.

LA TORTILLA FACTORY INC.
Head Office
3635 Standish Ave.
Santa Rosa, CA 95407
CEO: Mr. Carlos Tamayo
Tel: (707) 586-4000 Fax: (707) 586-4017
Email: info@latortillafactory.com
Web: www.latortillafactory.com

FOODS WHSL.

LATIN FOOD GROUP
10800 NW 97th St.
Miami, FL 33178
CEO: Mr. José Salazar
Tel: (305) 597-4542 Fax: (305) 888-1107
Web: www.latinfood.com/

FRUIT EXPORTING

FRUIT PROS LLC
8515 Avenida de la Fuente
San Diego, CA 92154
CEO: Mr. Carlos A. Velarde
Tel: (619) 671-9100 Fax: (619) 671-9900
Email: carlos@fruitpros.com
Web: www.fruitpros.com

FRUIT JUICES

INDIA BEVERAGES OF FLORIDA, INC.
7091 NW 82nd Ave.
Miami, FL 33166
CEO: Mr. Fernando Martinez
Tel: (305) 592-6366

FURNITURE

EL DORADO FURNITURE CORPORATION
Calle Ocho Blvd.
2475 SW 8th St.
Miami, FL 33135
CEO: Mr. Luis Capo
Tel: (305) 642-4355 Fax: (305) 643-4544
Web: www.eldoradofurniture.com

Headquarters
4200 NW 167th St.
Miami, FL 33054
CEO: Mr. Luis Capo
Tel: (305) 624-2400 Fax: (305) 624-9700
Web: www.eldoradofurniture.com

Hialeah Blvd.
1940 W. 49th St.
Miami, FL 33142
CEO: Mr. Luis Capo
Tel: (305) 827-2233 Fax: (305) 827-5617
Web: www.eldoradofurniture.com

Kendall Outlet
12650 N. Kendall Dr.
Miami, FL 33186
CEO: Mr. Luis Capo
Tel: (305) 595-5970 Fax: (305) 598-7364
Web: www.eldoradofurniture.com

Miami Airport Blvd.
1260 NW 72nd Ave.
Miami, FL 33126
CEO: Mr. Luis Capo
Tel: (305) 592-1121 Fax: (305) 477-5813
Web: www.eldoradofurniture.com

Miami Airport Gallery
1201 NW 72nd Ave.
Miami, FL 33126
CEO: Mr. Luis Capo
Tel: (305) 477-1909 Fax: (305) 477-5813
Web: www.eldoradofurniture.com

New Kendall Blvd.
13755 N. Kendall Dr.
Miami, FL 33186
CEO: Mr. Luis Capo
Tel: (305) 752-3720 Fax: (305) 752-3738
Web: www.eldoradofurniture.com

Pembroke Pines Blvd.
12201 Pines Blvd.
Pembroke Pines, FL 33026
CEO: Mr. Luis Capo
Tel: (954) 436-7900 Fax: (954) 885-4103
Web: www.eldoradofurniture.com

Plantation
400 S. University Dr.
Plantation, FL 33324
CEO: Mr. Luis Capo
Tel: (954) 472-3200 Fax: (954) 472-4525
Web: www.eldoradofurniture.com

FURNITURE DISTRIBUTION

J.R., INC
Main Office
P.O. Box 2819
Universal City, TX 78148
CEO: Mr. Jesse Rodriguez
Tel: (210) 658-6364
(800) 683-0846 Fax: (210) 658-0329
Email: customerservice@jrinc.org
Web: www.jrinc.org

FURNITURE MFG.

CISCO BROTHERS CORPORATION
Warehouse
1933 W. 60th St.
Los Angeles, CA 90047
CEO: Mr. Francisco Pinedo
Tel: (323) 778-8612 Fax: (323) 778-9073
Email: cisco@ciscobrothers.com
Web: www.ciscobrothers.com

GAS STATIONS, CONVENIENCE STORES

GASETERIA OIL CORPORATION
364 Maspeth Ave.
Brooklyn, NY 11211
CEO: Mr. Oscar Porcelli
Tel: (718) 782-4200 Fax: (718) 782-5175
Web: www.gaseteria.com

GASOLINE STATIONS

THREE-PLUS, INC.
4101 California Ave.
Kenner, LA 70065
CEO: Ms. Diana Lopera Icaza
Tel: (504) 469-1213 Fax: (504) 469-1219

GENERAL CONSTRUCTION

ADT CONSTRUCTION GROUP INC.
1335 E. Sunset Rd. #J
Las Vegas, NV 89119-4935
CEO: Mr. Ruben G. Vasquez
Tel: (702) 262-1902 Fax: (702) 262-1957
Email: rvasquez@adtconstruction.com
Web: www.adtconstruction.com

AZTEC CONSULTANTS, INC.
2021 Omega Rd. #200
San Ramon, CA 94583
CEO: Mr. Edward R. Duarte
Tel: (925) 837-1050 Fax: (925) 837-1652
Email: aztec@azteccm.com
Web: www.azteccm.com

CAL, INC.
2040 Peabody Rd. #400
Vacaville, CA 95687
CEO: Mr. David Esparza
Tel: (707) 446-7996
(800) 359-4467 Fax: (707) 446-4906
Email: desparza@cal-inc.com
Web: www.cal-inc.com

CAMINO CONSTRUCTION L.P.
1208 Metro Park Blvd.
Lewisville, TX 75057
CEO: Mr. Rogelio T. Ayala
Tel: (972) 436-2868 Fax: (972) 436-2898

EXPLORE GENERAL INC.
Fresno Office
4321 N. West Ave.
Fresno, CA 93705
CEO: Mr. Jamie Gonzalez
Tel: (559) 227-7088 Fax: (559) 227-7087
Email: info@exploregeneral.com
Web: www.exploregeneral.com

Sacramento Office
5707 Dudley Blvd.
McClellan, CA 95652
CEO: Mr. Jamie Gonzalez
Tel: (916) 564-8866 Fax: (916) 564-8882
Email: info@exploregeneral.com
Web: www.exploregeneral.com

San Francisco Office
45 Lansing St. #102
San Francisco, CA 94105
CEO: Mr. Jamie Gonzalez
Tel: (415) 896-1925 Fax: (415) 896-1935
Email: info@exploregeneral.com
Web: www.exploregeneral.com

INTEGRATED CONTROL SYSTEMS, INC.
Colorado Office
14818 W. 6th Ave. #10-A
Golden, CO 80401
CEO: Mr. Steven B. Chavez
Tel: (303) 277-0708 Fax: (303) 277-0423
Email: schavez@icsicontrols.com
Web: www.icsicontrols.com

Head Office
4020 Vassar Dr. NE #H
Albuquerque, NM 87107
CEO: Mr. Steven B. Chavez
Tel: (505) 884-3503 Fax: (505) 883-0130
Email: schavez@icsicontrols.com
Web: www.icsicontrols.com

Phoenix Office
4050 E. Cotton Rd. #66
Phoenix, AZ 85040
CEO: Mr. Steven B. Chavez
Tel: (480) 491-6830 Fax: (480) 491-6847
Email: schavez@icsicontrols.com
Web: www.icsicontrols.com

MACRO-Z TECHNOLOGY
Main Office
841 E. Washington Ave.
Santa Ana, CA 92701
CEO: Mr. Bryan Zatica
Tel: (714) 564-1130
(800) 303-3240 Fax: (714) 564-1144
Email: BryanZ@MZTCO.com
Web: www.MZTCO.com

Regional Office - Boise
797 S. Orchard St.
Boise, ID 83705
CEO: Mr. Bryan Zatica
Tel: (208) 345-7070 Fax: (208) 433-1813
Email: BryanZ@MZTCO.com
Web: www.MZTCO.com

Regional Office - Renton
17233 140th Ave. SE
Renton, WA 98058
CEO: Mr. Bryan Zatica
Tel: (425) 271-1670 Fax: (425) 271-1679
Email: BryanZ@MZTCO.com
Web: www.MZTCO.com

Regional Office - Sausalito
10 Liberty Ship Way #150
Sausalito, CA 94965
CEO: Mr. Bryan Zatica
Tel: (415) 331-1257 Fax: (415) 331-1597
Email: BryanZ@MZTCO.com
Web: www.MZTCO.com

Regional Office - Tempe
1801 S. Jen Tilly Lane #D-18
Tempe, AZ 85281
CEO: Mr. Bryan Zatica
Tel: (480) 394-0610 Fax: (480) 394-0595
Email: BryanZ@MZTCO.com
Web: www.MZTCO.com

NEW ERA BUILDERS INC.
16126 St. Clair Ave.
Cleveland, OH 44110-3029
CEO: Mr. Joe Lopez
Tel: (216) 486-5520 Fax: (216) 486-2440
Email: newera@nls.netjoelopez@nls.net
Web: www.bxohio.com

R&W CONCRETE CONTRACTORS INC.
San Francisco Office
1423 San Mateo Ave.
South San Francisco, CA 94080
CEO: Mr. Brian Rodrigues

Tel: (650) 616-8885 Fax: (650) 616-8887

REYES CONSTRUCTION, INC.
Head Office
1383 S. Signal Dr.
Pomona, CA 91766
CEO: Mr. Joseph Reyes
Tel: (909) 622-2259 Fax: (909) 622-3053
Email: Jflores@reyesconstruction.com
Web: www.reyesconstruction.com

RGC CONSTRUCTION, INC.
320 S. Jones Blvd.
Las Vegas, NV 89107
CEO: Mr. Rolando A. Hernandez
Tel: (702) 258-7825 Fax: (702) 258-7682
Email: info@rgcinc.com
Web: www.rgcinc.com

ROGER & SONS CONSTRUCTION, INC.
P.O. Box 358
East Chicago, IN 46312
CEO: Mr. Rogelio Zepeda
Tel: (219) 397-8819 Fax: (219) 397-1010
Web: www.cafnwin.org/member_detail116.asp

SONAG COMPANY, INC.
Corporate Office
5510 W. Florist Ave.
Milwaukee, WI 53218
CEO: Mr. Brian L. Ganos
Tel: (414) 393-9911 Fax: (414) 393-9902
Email: postmaster@sonag.com
Web: www.sonag.com

T & G CONSTRUCTORS INC.
Corporate Headquarters
8623 Commodity Cir.
Orlando, FL 32819-9003
CEO: Mr. Rick Gonzalez
Tel: (407) 352-4443 Fax: (407) 514-3801
Email: info@t-and-g.com
Web: www.t-and-g.com

TIERRA LIMITED INC.
10325 S. Oxford Ave.
Chicago Ridge, IL 60415
CEO: Mr. Jesus Lopez
Tel: (708) 876-9090 Fax: (708) 424-8607
Web: www.tierralimited.com

GENERAL CONSTRUCTION/ MGMT. SERVICES

PERERA CONSTRUCTION & DESIGN, INC.
2890 Inland Empire Blvd. #102
Ontario, CA 91764
CEO: Mr. Henry Perera, Jr.
Tel: (909) 484-6350 Fax: (909) 484-3439
Email: Scotts@pererainc.com
Web: www.pererainc.com

GENERAL CONTRACTING & ENGINEERING

A. RUIZ CONSTRUCTION COMPANY & ASSOCIATION, INC.
1601 Courtland Ave.
San Francisco, CA 94110
CEO: Mr. Antonio Ruiz
Tel: (415) 647-4010 Fax: (415) 285-9243
Email: truiz@aruizconstruction.com
Web: www.aruizconstruction.com

GENERAL CONTRACTING SERVICES

IMPERIAL CONSTRUCTION GROUP, INC.
505 N. Broad St.
Elizabeth, NJ 07208
CEO: Mr. Francisco Dominguez
Tel: (908) 354-7400 Fax: (908) 354-7479
Email: louf@imperialconstruction.com
Web: www.imperialconstruction.com

PAUL J. SIERRA CONSTRUCTION, INC.
912 W. Martin Luther King Blvd.
Tampa, FL 33603
CEO: Mr. Paul J. Sierra
Tel: (813) 228-6661
(800) 409-5897 Fax: (813) 223-5328
Email: sierra@sierraconstruction.com
Web: www.sierraconstruction.com

GENERAL CONTRACTOR

ALLIANCE GENERAL CONTRACTORS, LLC
Main Office
5045 List Dr.
Colorado Springs, CO 80919
CEO: Mr. Wendel P. Torres
Tel: (719) 596-8114 Fax: (719) 596-5969
Email: info@agccolorado.com
Web: www.agccolorado.com

AMBRECO, INC.
703 N. Main St.
Belton, TX 76513
CEO: Mr. Robert Dominguez Jr.
Tel: (254) 939-5175 Fax: (254) 939-7888
Email: ambreco@ambreco.com
Web: www.ambreco.com

AZTECA ENTERPRISES, INC.
2518 Chalk Hill Rd.
Dallas, TX 75212
CEO: Mr. Luis Spinola
Tel: (214) 905-0612 Fax: (214) 905-0828
Email: azteca@azteca-omega.com
Web: www.azteca-omega.com

H & H CONSTRUCTION & MECHANICAL, INC.
Connecticut Office
191 Post Rd. West
Westport, CT 06680
CEO: Mr. Daniel R. Hernandez Jr.
Tel: (203) 221-2734 Fax: (203) 222-0527
Email: info@hsmechanical.com
Web: www.hsmechanical.com

Headquarters
721 Bayway Ave.
Elizabeth, NJ 07202
CEO: Mr. Daniel R. Hernandez Jr.
Tel: (908) 352-4345 Fax: (908) 352-0644
Email: info@hsmechanical.com
Web: www.hsmechanical.com

New York Office
W. Tower, 6th Fl.
Uniondale, NY 11556-0165
CEO: Mr. Daniel R. Hernandez Jr.
Tel: (516) 522-2697 Fax: (516) 522-0527
Email: info@hsmechanical.com
Web: www.hsmechanical.com

THOS. S. BYRNE LIMITED
Corporate Office
900 Summit Ave.
Fort Worth, TX 76102
CEO: Mr. John Avila, Jr.
Tel: (817) 335-3394 Fax: (817) 877-5507
Email: info@tsbyrne.com
Web: www.tsbyrne.com

ZURQUI CONSTRUCTION SERVICES
10421 NW 28th St.
Miami, FL 33172
CEO: Mr. Eddy Gonzalez Jr.
Tel: (305) 597-8869

VISTACON, INC.
1801 Wyoming #206
El Paso, TX 79902
CEO: Mr. Basilio A. Silva Jr.
Email: vistacon@vista-con.com

GENERAL ENG. CONSTRUCTION

GSE CONSTRUCTION COMPANY
1020 Shannon Ct.
Livermore, CA 94550
CEO: Mr. Orlando Gutierrez
Tel: (925) 447-0292 Fax: (925) 447-0962
Email: gse@gseconstruction.com
Web: www.gseconstruction.com

GENERAL ENG. & HEAVY CONSTRUCTION

BAY CITIES PAVING & GRADING, INC.
5029 Forni Dr.
Concord, CA 94520
CEO: Mr. Benjamin L. Rodriguez Jr.
Tel: (925) 687-6666 Fax: (925) 687-2122
Email: baycities@jps.net

GENERAL PRODUCTS

SUPERIOR TANK COMPANY, INC.
Bakersfield Office
19436 Colombo St.
Bakersfield, CA 93308
CEO: Mr. J.E. Marquez
Tel: (661) 392-0188 Fax: (661) 392-8770
Email: james@superiortank.com
Web: www.superiortank.com

GENERAL SERVICES

METRO PACKAGING & IMAGING, INC.
5 Haul Rd.
Wayne, NJ 07470
CEO: Mr. Manuel de Torres
Tel: (973) 709-9100 Fax: (973) 709-9477

GLASS & GLAZING

STANDARD GLASS & MIRROR, INC.
3714 Lapas Dr.
Houston, TX 77023
CEO: Mr. Bennie Romero Jr.
Tel: (713) 640-2233 Fax: (713) 640-2244

GLASS, PLASTIC EQUIPMENT DIST.

ALL AMERICAN CONTAINERS, INC.
All American Containers of Georgia
105 Forest Pkwy. #800
Forest Park, GA 30297
CEO: Ms. Remedios Diaz-Oliver
Tel: (770) 997-1992 Fax: (770) 997-0171
Email: larrym@allamericancontainers.com
Web: www.americancontainers.com

All American Containers of Tampa
2400 Gelman Pl.
Tampa, FL 33619
CEO: Ms. Remedios Diaz-Oliver

Tel: (813) 248-2023 Fax: (813) 248-1059
Email: sales@allamericancontainers.com
Web: www.americancontainers.com

American Packaging of Puerto Rico
Road 869, km 1.5, Royal Industrial Park,
Barrio Palmas
Catano, PR 00962
CEO: Ms. Remedios Diaz-Oliver
Tel: (787) 275-2670 Fax: (787) 275-2673
Email: carlosr@americanpackaging-pr.com
Web: www.americancontainers.com

Corporate Headquarters
9330 NW 110th Ave.
Miami, FL 33178
CEO: Ms. Remedios Diaz-Oliver
Tel: (305) 887-0797 Fax: (305) 888-4133
Email: info@americancontainers.com
Web: www.americancontainers.com

GOODS TRANSPORTATION

MCO TRANSPORT, INC.
Administrative Offices
P.O. Box 1320
Wilmington, NC 28402
CEO: Mr. Daniel F. Comas
Tel: (910) 343-8372 Fax: (910) 343-8003
Web: www.mcotransport.com/

Brunswick, GA Terminal
1400 W. 9th St. Administrative Bldg. Gate 1
Brunswick, GA 31512
CEO: Mr. Daniel F. Comas
Tel: (912) 264-6167 Fax: (912) 554-0639
Web: www.mcotransport.com/

Chareston, SC Terminal
P.O. Box 70208
Charleston, NC 29406
CEO: Mr. Daniel F. Comas
Tel: (843) 747-5949 Fax: (843) 745-9762
Web: www.mcotransport.com/

Savannah, GA Terminal
P.O. Box 7088
Garden City, GA 31408
CEO: Mr. Daniel F. Comas
Tel: (912) 966-0277 Fax: (912) 966-5113
Web: www.mcotransport.com/

Wilmington, NC Terminal
P.O. Box 1320
Wilmington, NC 28402
CEO: Mr. Daniel F. Comas
Tel: (910) 763-4531 Fax: (912) 763-0167
Web: www.mcotransport.com/

GRAPHIC DESIGN, PRINTING, MAILING

ORIGINAL IMPRESSIONS, LLC
12900 SW 89th Ct.
Miami, FL 33176
CEO: Mr. Roland B. Garcia, Sr.
Tel: (305) 233-1322
Email: roland@originalimpressions.com
Web: www.originalimpressions.com

HARDWARE & SOFTWARE SALES

GC MICRO CORPORATION
Corporate Headquarters
3910 Cypress Dr.
Petaluma, CA 94954
CEO: Ms. Belinda Guadarrama
Tel: (707) 789-0600 Fax: (707) 789-0700
Web: www.gcmicro.com

HEALTHCARE

CROWN MEDICAL, INC.
6785 SW 40th St.
Miami, FL 33155
CEO: Mr. Rafael Mendoza
Tel: (305) 740-4444 Fax: (305) 740-3488
Email: rmend222@aol.com
Web: www.expertsinveins.com

MOLINA HEALTHCARE, INC.
Corporate Office
1 Golden Shore Dr.
Long Beach, CA 90802
CEO: Mr. J. Mario Molina
Tel: (562) 435-3666 Fax: (562) 951-1514
Email: jmmolina@molinahealthcare.com
Web: www.molinahealthcare.com

Molina Healthcare of Michigan
100 W. Big Beaver Rd. #600
Troy, MI 48084
CEO: Mr. J. Mario Molina
Tel: (248) 925-1700 Fax: (248) 925-1709
Web: www.molinahealthcare.com

Molina Healthcare of New Mexico
P.O. Box 3887
Albuquerque, NM 87190
CEO: Mr. J. Mario Molina
Tel: (505) 342-4660 Fax: (505) 342-7411
Web: www.molinahealthcare.com

Molina Healthcare of Utah
P.O. Box 8543
Midvale, UT 84047
CEO: Mr. J. Mario Molina
Tel: (801) 858-0400 Fax: (801) 858-0409
Web: www.molinahealthcare.com

Molina Healthcare of Washington
P.O. Box 1469
Bothell, WA 98041
CEO: Mr. J. Mario Molina
Tel: (800) 869-7175
Web: www.molinahealthcare.com

Molina Healthcare of Washington
508 W. 6th Ave. #900
Spokane, WA 99204-2470
CEO: Mr. J. Mario Molina
Tel: (800) 423-9899 Fax: (425) 424-1161
Web: www.molinahealthcare.com

HEALTHCARE SERVICES

BEVERLY ONCOLOGY & IMAGING CENTERS, INC.
Beverly Hills Facility
150 N. Robertson #160
Beverly Hills, CA 90211
CEO: Ms. Ruth Lopez Norodor
Tel: (323) 930-1123 Fax: (310) 659-5460
Web: www.beverlyoncology.com

Los Angeles Facility
6200 Wilshire Blvd. #100
Los Angeles, CA 90048
CEO: Ms. Ruth Lopez Norodor
Tel: (323) 930-1123 Fax: (323) 930-1368
Web: www.beverlyoncology.com

Montebello Facility
120 W. Beverly Blvd.
Montebello, CA 90640
CEO: Ms. Ruth Lopez Norodor
Tel: (323) 724-8780 Fax: (323) 728-9936
Web: www.beverlyoncology.com

Montebello Facility
111 W. Beverly Blvd. #104
Montebello, CA 90640
CEO: Ms. Ruth Lopez Norodor
Tel: (323) 724-8755 Fax: (323) 727-7212
Web: www.beverlyoncology.com

Monterey Park Facility
605 N. Garfield Ave.
Monterey Park, CA 91754
CEO: Ms. Ruth Lopez Williams
Tel: (626) 571-6729 Fax: (626) 571-1170
Web: www.beverlyoncology.com

Pasadena Facility
2750 E. Washington Blvd. #100
Pasadena, CA 91107
CEO: Ms. Ruth Lopez Williams
Tel: (626) 794-2836 Fax: (626) 794-1697
Web: www.beverlyoncology.com

HEATING, COOLING, VENT., PLUMBING

QUALIFIED MECHANICAL CONTRACTORS, INC.
1001 S. Euclid Ave.
Tucson, AZ 85719
CEO: Mr. Santiago Nieto
Tel: (520) 624-8988 Fax: (520) 624-3716
Email: info@qualifiedmechanical.com
Web: www.qualifiedmechanical.com

HEATING SUPPLIES WHSL.

JORDA ENTERPRISES, INC.
Head Office
7591 NW 7th St.
Miami, FL 33126
CEO: Mr. Jorge Guisasola
Tel: (305) 262-0095 Fax: (305) 264-7679
Email: jordamech@aol.com

MECHANICAL HEATING SUPPLY, INC.
461 Timpson Pl.
Bronx, NY 10455
CEO: Mr. Frank Rivera
Tel: (718) 402-9765 Fax: (718) 585-1682

HEAVY AIR CARGO

CONTRANS LOGISTICS LLC
5255 Triangle Pkwy. #500
Norcross, GA 30092
CEO: Mr. William R. Cortez
Tel: (678) 969-9529 Fax: (678) 969-9065
Email: bcortez@contrans.com
Web: www.contrans.com

HEAVY CONSTRUCTION DEMOLITION

SBBI, INC.
P.O. Box 770
Sonoita, AZ 85637
CEO: Ms. Josephine Echeverria-Walker
Tel: (520) 455-5983 Fax: (520) 455-5984
Email: jewsonoita@aol.com

HEAVY CONSTRUCTION & SUPPORT SERVICES

CORNEJO & SONS, INC.
2060 E. Tulsa St.
Wichita, KS 67216
CEO: Mr. Ron Cornejo
Tel: (316) 522-5100 Fax: (316) 522-8187
Web: www.cornejocorp.com

HIGHWAY & RAIL TRANSIT CONSTRUCTION

AZTECA CONSTRUCTION, INC.
3871 Security Park Dr.

Rancho Cordova, CA 95742
CEO: Mr. Rafael M. Martin
Tel: (916) 351-0202 Fax: (916) 351-9270
Email: azteca@azteca-construction.com
Web: www.azteca-construction.com

HISPANIC FOOD MFG.

AZTECA FOODS, INC.
P.O. Box 427
Summit-Argo, IL 60501
CEO: Mr. Arthur Velasquez
Tel: (708) 563-6600 Fax: (708) 563-6644
Email: info@aztecafoods.com
Web: www.aztecafoods.com

HOMEOWNER & FLOOD INSURANCE

PROFESSIONAL CASUALTY INSURANCE
9212 SW 73rd Ave.
Pinecrest, FL 33156
CEO: Mr. Manny A. Varas
Tel: (305) 740-9787 Fax: (305) 663-0454
Email: info@professionalcasualty.com
Web: www.professionalcasualty.com

HOT ROLLED STEEL SVC. CTR./WAREHOUSE

FERRAGON CORPORATION
Corporate Office
11103 Memphis Ave.
Cleveland, OH 44144
CEO: Mr. Eduardo Gonzalez
Tel: (216) 671-6161 Fax: (216) 671-4078
Email: info@ferragon.com
Web: www.ferragon.com

Ferrolux Metals Co.
36263 Michigan Ave.
Wayne, MI 48184
CEO: Mr. Eduardo Gonzalez
Tel: (734) 727-6161 Fax: (734) 722-3251
Email: info@ferragon.com
Web: www.ferragon.com

Ferrousouth Headquarters
38 C.R. 370
Iuka, MS 38852
CEO: Mr. Eduardo Gonzalez
Tel: (662) 424-0115 Fax: (662) 424-0116
Email: info@ferragon.com
Web: www.ferragon.com

HUMAN RESOURCES

RMPERSONNEL, INC.
4707 Montana Ave.
El Paso, TX 79903
CEO: Ms. Ceci Miles Mulvihill
Tel: (915) 565-7674 Fax: (915) 565-7687
Email: info@RMPersonnel.com
Web: www.rmpersonnel.com

HUMAN RESOURCES, PAYROLL, BENEFITS, RISK-MGMT

RESOURCE MANAGEMENT, INC.
281 Main St. #5
Fitchburg, MA 01420
CEO: Mr. Reinaldo Lopez
Tel: (978) 343-0048 Fax: (978) 343-0719
Email: info@rmi-solutions.com
Web: www.rmi-solutions.com

HVAC

SAN BENITO HEATING & SHEETMETAL INC.
731 San Felipe Rd.
Hollister, CA 95023
CEO: Mr. Robert J. Rodriguez
Tel: (831) 637-1112 Fax: (831) 637-4068
Web: www.sanbenitoheating.com

HVAC CONTRACTOR

VARIO CONSTRUCTION COMPANY
207 S. Villa Ave. #105
Villa Park, IL 60181
CEO: Mr. Carlos E. Vargas
Tel: (630) 834-4600
(800) 834-4600 Fax: (630) 833-4175
Email: cvargas@variomechanical.com
Web: www.variomechanical.com

HVAC SVCS./MECHANICAL CONSTRUCTION

AIR FLOW SHEET METAL, INC.
21220 Commerce Point Dr.
Walnut, CA 91789
CEO: Mr. Augie D. Juarez
Tel: (909) 468-2600 Fax: (909) 468-2606
Email: afm@airflowmech.com

IMPORT, WHSL., DISTR. OF BLUE CRAB MEAT

JOHN KEELER & CO., INC.
OneCrab
3000 NW 109th Ave.
Miami, FL 33172
CEO: Mr. John R. Keeler
Tel: (305) 836-6858 Fax: (305) 836-6859
Email: info@onecrab.com
Web: www.onecrab.com

IMPORTERS & DISTR. OF FRESH PRODUCE

FRU-VEG MARKETING, INC.
Headquarters
2300 NW 102 Ave.
Miami, FL 33172
CEO: Ms. Conchita Espinosa
Tel: (305) 591-7766 Fax: (305) 591-7665
Email: info@fruveg.com
Web: www.fruveg.com

INDUSTRIAL/ MANUFACTURING

INJECTRONICS, INC.
Clinton Division
One Union St.
Clinton, MA 01510-2930
CEO: Mr. Carlos M. Baranano
Tel: (978) 368-8701 Fax: (978) 368-7941
Email: hr@injectronics.com
Web: www.injectronics.com

INFORMATION TECH.

FORCE 3, INC.
Corporate Headquarters
2147 Priest Bridge Dr.
Crofton, MD 21114

CEO: Mr. Rocky Cintron
Tel: (301) 261-0204 Fax: (410) 721-5624
Email: info@force3.com
Web: www.force3.com

San Antonio Operations
814 Arion Pkwy.
San Antonio, TX 78216
CEO: Mr. Rocky Cintron
Tel: (210) 979-0204 Fax: (210) 979-7801
Email: info@force3.com
Web: www.force3.com

INTEGRATED INFORMATION TECHNOLOGY CORPORATION
4725 S. Monaco St. #300
Denver, CO 80237
CEO: Mr. Francisco Garcia
Tel: (303) 796-8799 Fax: (303) 796-9506
Email: l.abram@iitc.net
Web: www.integrated-info.com

PROCEED TECHNICAL RESOURCE, INC.
2805 Network Blvd. #503
Frisco, TX 75034
CEO: Mr. Edward R. Garcia
Tel: (972) 769-0746 x19
Fax: (972) 543-0300
Email: egarcia@proceedtech.com
Web: www.proceedtech.com

TERRADIGM INC.
401 Alvarado Dr. SE #G
Albuquerque, NM 87108-2939
CEO: Mr. Michael A. Romero
Tel: (505) 265-5765 Fax: (505) 265-1265
Email: gcarmichael@terradigm.com
Web: www.terradigm.com

INFORMATION TECH. & ENG. SERVICES

ORION INTERNATIONAL TECHNOLOGIES, INC.
Corporate Office
2201 Buena Vista SE #211
Albuquerque, NM 87106
CEO: Mr. Miguel Rios, Jr.
Tel: (505) 998-4000 Fax: (505) 998-5060
Email: info@orionint.com
Web: www.orionint.com

East Coast Office
2000 N. 15th St. #507
Arlington, VA 22201
CEO: Mr. Miguel Rios, Jr.
Tel: (703) 276-1600 Fax: (703) 276-1603
Email: info@orionint.com
Web: www.orionint.com

INFRASTRUCTURE DEVELP./ SYST. INTEG.

CORDOBA CORPORATION
Corporate Headquarters
660 S. Figueroa St. #1170
Los Angeles, CA 90017
CEO: Mr. George L. Pla
Tel: (213) 895-0224 Fax: (213) 895-6677
Email: info@cordobacorp.com
Web: www.cordobacorp.com

San Francisco Bay Area
1300 Clay St. #840
Oakland, CA 94612
CEO: Mr. George L. Pla
Tel: (510) 208-0200 Fax: (510) 208-0206
Email: sales@cordobacorp.com
Web: www.cordobacorp.com

INSTITUTIONAL & RETAIL ENERGY BROKERAGE

CHOICE! ENERGY
5718 Westheimer Rd. #1300
Houston, TX 77057-5732
CEO: Mr. Enrique Javier Loya
Tel: (713) 334-0790
(800) 864-7470 Fax: (713) 613-0599
Web: www.choiceenergy.com

INSURANCE

BMI FINANCIAL GROUP, INC.
Corporate Headquarters
1320 S. Dixie Hwy., 6th Fl.
Coral Gables, FL 33146
CEO: Mr. Tony M. Sierra
Tel: (305) 443-2898 Fax: (305) 442-8486
Email: bmi@bmicos.com
Web: www.bmicos.com

INSURANCE AGENCY & BROKERAGE

INSURANCE MARKETERS, INC.
141 Almeria Ave.
Coral Gables, FL 33134
CEO: Mr. Evarist Milian Jr.
Tel: (305) 442-9507 Fax: (305) 447-8527
Email: info@insurancemrkt.com
Web: www.insurancemrkt.com

INSURANCE & FINANCIAL SERVICES

MANUEL LUJAN INSURANCE, INC.
P.O. Box 3727
Albuquerque, NM 87190
CEO: Mr. E. Larry Lujan
Tel: (505) 266-7771 Fax: (505) 255-8140
Email: info@mlins.com
Web: www.mlins.com

INSURANCE SALES

ESTRELLA GROUP HOLDING
P.O. Box 350037
Miami, FL 33135
CEO: Nicolas Estrella
Tel: (305) 443-2829 Fax: (305) 448-1816
Email: general@estrellainsurance.com
Web: www.estrellainsurance.com

INSURANCE SALES & SVCS.

FORTUN INSURANCE & FINANCIAL SERVICES GROUP
365 Palermo Ave.
Coral Gables, FL 33134-6607
CEO: Mr. Hector D. Fortun
Tel: (305) 445-3535 Fax: (305) 447-9478
Email: fortunhd@fortuninsurance.com
Web: www.fortuninsurance.com

INTERMODAL TRUCKING

CORAL TRUCKING CO.
Branch Office
3408 N. Graham St.
Charlotte, NC 28206
CEO: Mr. Jose A. Allende

Tel: (704) 347-5002
(877) 726-7257 Fax: (704) 347-5003
Email: jallende@coraltrucking.com
Web: www.coraltrucking.com

Corporate Office
8181 NW 36th St. #18
Miami, FL 33166
CEO: Mr. Jose A. Allende
Tel: (305) 513-9299
(877) 926-7259 Fax: (305) 513-9607
Email: jallende@coraltrucking.com
Web: www.coraltrucking.com

INTERNETWORKING SVCS. & HARDWARE

NETWORK ARCHITECHS
1720 Louisiana NE #301
Albuquerque, NM 87110
CEO: Mr. Mike French
Tel: (505) 256-9047
Web: www.netarch.com

221 N. Kansas #1103
El Paso, TX 79901
CEO: Mr. Mike French
Tel: (915) 533-6382
Web: www.netarch.com

INTERPRETATION/ TRANSLATION SERVICES

ALBORS & ASSOCIATES, INC.
Head Office
5971 Brick Ct. #200
Winter Park, FL 32792
CEO: Mr. René Albors
Tel: (407) 678-8634
(800) 785-8634 Fax: (407) 657-7004
Email: info@albors.com
Web: www.albors.com

INTERSTATE TRANSPORTATION SVCS.

PAN AMERICAN EXPRESS, INC.
Head Office
P.O. Box 3317
Laredo, TX 78044-3317
CEO: Mr. Ricardo Guardado
Tel: (956) 723-4848
(800) 874-7197 Fax: (956) 723-9979
Email: panamex@panamex-zero.com
Web: www.panamex-zero.com

Sales Office
P.O. Box 42260
Detroit, MI 48242
CEO: Mr. Ricardo Guardado
Tel: (734) 856-5533
(800) 446-6055 Fax: (734) 856-6633
Email: panamex@panamex-zero.com
Web: www.panamex-zero.com

INTL. FREIGHT TRANSPORTATION

AMERITRANS WORLD GROUP, INC.
7102 NW 50th St.
Miami, FL 33166-5636
CEO: Mr. Martin Roy Leon
Tel: (305) 599-2662 Fax: (305) 592-3916
Email: info@ameritransworld.com
Web: www.ameritransworld.com

IT CONSULTING

CAIRO CORPORATION
14900 Conference Ctr. Dr. #500
Chantilly, VA 20151
CEO: Mr. Alba M. Aleman
Tel: (703) 667-9420 Fax: (703) 667-9421
Email: info@cairocorp.com
Web: www.cairocorp.com

IT & ENG. SERVICES

PREFERRED SYSTEMS SOLUTIONS, INC.
3040 Williams Dr. #505
Fairfax, VA 22031
CEO: Mr. Robert J. Hisel Jr.
Tel: (703) 663-2777 Fax: (703) 663-2780
Web: www.pssfed.com

IT HARDWARE & SOFTWARE

WILDFLOWER INTERNATIONAL LTD.
Corporate Office
1500 S. Saint Francis Dr.
Santa Fe, NM 87505 -4040
CEO: Ms. Kimberly DeCastro
Tel: (505) 466-9111 Fax: (505) 466-9100
Email: info@wildflowerintl.com
Web: www.wildflowerintl.com

East Coast Branch Office
159 Mitchell Rd.
Oak Ridge, TN 37830
CEO: Ms. Kimberly DeCastro
Tel: (865) 483-9199 Fax: (865) 483-6737
Email: info@wildflowerintl.com
Web: www.wildflowerintl.com

IT SOLUTION PROVIDER

DYNAMIC SYSTEMS, INC.
Colorado Branch Office
10475 Park Meadows Dr. #600
Littleton, CO 80124
CEO: Mardi Norman
Tel: (720) 279-2353 Fax: (720) 279-2501
Email: lisa.jensen@dynasys.com
Web: www.dynasys.com

Corporate Office
5261 W. Imperial Hwy.
Los Angeles, CA 90045
CEO: Mardi Norman
Tel: (310) 337-4400 Fax: (310) 337-4423
Email: lisa.jensen@dynasys.com
Web: www.dynasys.com

New Mexico Branch Office
12127 N. Hwy. 14
Ceder Crest, NM 87008
CEO: Mardi Norman
Tel: (505) 720-4860 Fax: (949) 487-1106
Email: lisa.jensen@dynasys.com
Web: www.dynasys.com

Orange County Branch Office
31726 Rancho Viejo Rd.
San Juan Capistrano, CA 92675
CEO: Mardi Norman
Tel: (949) 487-1100 Fax: (949) 487-1106
Email: lisa.jensen@dynasys.com
Web: www.dynasys.com

Utah Office
670 W. Shepard #103
Farmington, UT 84025
CEO: Mardi Norman
Tel: (801) 447-3777 Fax: (801) 447-3778
Email: lisa.jensen@dynasys.com
Web: www.dynasys.com

IT SOLUTIONS DATABASE MGMT.

SYSTEMS RESEARCH GROUP, INC.
740 Wooten Rd. #108
Colorado Springs, CO 80915
CEO: Mr. Fredrick V. Garcia
Tel: (719) 596-0737 Fax: (719) 596-8635
Email: admin@srgcorp.com
Web: www.srgcorp.com

IT STAFFING

VISIONIT
3031 W. Grand Blvd. #695
Detroit, MI 48202
CEO: Mr. David H. Segura
Tel: (313) 664-5650
(877) 768-7222 Fax: (313) 664-5651
Email: info@visionitinc.com
Web: www.visioninfotech.com

IT STAFFING & HUMAN RESOURCES

SUPERIOR DESIGN INTERNATIONAL, INC.
Headquarters
6365 NW 6th Way #360
Fort Lauderdale, FL 33309-6162
CEO: Ms. Carmen Castillo
Tel: (954) 938-5400 Fax: (954) 772-5061
Email: information@sdintl.com
Web: www.sdintl.com

Atlanta Office
900 Circle 75 Pkwy. #690
Atlanta, GA 30339
CEO: Ms. Carmen Castillo
Tel: (770) 850-1109 Fax: (770) 850-1103
Email: information@sdintl.com
Web: www.sdintl.com

Buffalo Office
P.O. Box 9057
Williamsville, NY 14231-9057
CEO: Ms. Carmen Castillo
Tel: (716) 631-8310 Fax: (716) 633-2026
Email: information@sdintl.com
Web: www.sdintl.com

IT SUPPORT, SOFTWARE DEVELOPMENT

LINGUALLISTEK
9861 Broken Land Pkw. #300
Columbia, MD 21046
CEO: Ms. Elizabeth Rendon
Tel: (410) 953-0300/6777
Fax: (410) 953-8114
Email: lingualistek@lingualistek.com
Web: www.lingualistek.com

Texas Office
7323 Hwy. 90 W. #500
Antonio, TX 78227
CEO: Ms. Elizabeth Rendon
Tel: (210) 674-1155
Email: lingualistek@lingualistek.com
Web: www.lingualistek.com

IT SERVICES

POTOMAC MANAGEMENT GROUP
510 King St. #200
Alexandria, VA 22314
CEO: Mr. Dennis J. Garcia
Tel: (703) 836-1037 Fax: (703) 836-1388
Email: info@potomacmgmt.com
Web: www.potomacmgmt.com

JANITORIAL CLEANING & MGMT.

UNITED BUILDING MAINTENANCE, INC.
Chicago Office
225 W. Randolph
Chicago, IL 60606
CEO: Mr. James S. Cabrera
Tel: (312) 957-9080
Email: jcjr@ubm-usa.com
Web: www.ubm-usa.com

Corporate Office
165 Easy St.
Carol Stream, IL 60188
CEO: Mr. James S. Cabrera
Tel: (630) 653-4848 Fax: (630) 653-0660
Email: jcjr@ubm-usa.com
Web: www.ubm-usa.com

JANITORIAL, MAINT., LANDSCAPING SERVICES

SUPPORT SERVICE OF AMERICA INC.
12440 Firestone Blvd. #312
Norwalk, CA 90650
CEO: Mr. Alex E. Fortunati
Tel: (800) 564-0005
(562) 868-3550 Fax: (562) 868-7811
Email: alexf@supportservicesamerica.com
Web: www.supportservicesamerica.com

JANITORIAL SERVICES

A&A MAINTENANCE ENTERPRISE, INC.
Branch Office
3785 NW 82nd Ave. #203
Miami, FL 33166
CEO: Mr. Armando Rodriguez Jr.
Tel: (305) 640-2448 Fax: (305) 640-3054
Email: info@aamaintenance.com
Web: www.aamaintenance.com

Corporate Headquarters
200 Mamaroneck Ave.
White Plains, NY 10601
CEO: Mr. Armando Rodriguez Jr.
Tel: (914) 949-6676 Fax: (914) 949-9202
Email: info@aamaintenance.com
Web: www.aamaintenance.com

D&A BUILDING SERVICES, INC.
Head Office, A&C Window Cleaning
Services, Inc.
983 Explorer Cove
Altamonte Springs, FL 32701
CEO: Mr. Albert Sarabasa, Jr.
Tel: (407) 831-5388
(877) 326-3200 Fax: (407) 831-1377
Email: al@dabuildingservices.com
Web: www.dabuildingservices.com

EMPIRE MAINTENANCE CO., INC.
Arizona
841 W. Fairmont Dr. #4
Tempe, AZ 85282
CEO: Mr. Ruben Garcia
Tel: (602) 967-1201 Fax: (602) 967-1271
Email: ruben@empiremaintenance.com
Web: www.empiremaintenance.com

Corporate Headquarters
624 South Palm Ave.
Alhambra, CA 91803
CEO: Mr. Ruben Garcia
Tel: (626) 289-8755
(323) 283-6123 Fax: (626) 281-4263
Email: ruben@empiremaintenance.com
Web: www.empiremaintenance.com

Southern California
9187 Chesapeake Dr.

San Diego, CA 92123
CEO: Mr. Ruben Garcia
Tel: (619) 715-1574 Fax: (619) 715-1579
Email: ruben@empiremaintenance.com
Web: www.empiremaintenance.com

LANDSCAPE & IRRIGATION CONST./WHSL.

VILA & SON LANDSCAPE CORPORATION

Corporate Headquarters
20451 SW 216th St.
Miami, FL 33170
CEO: Mr. Juan C. Vila
Tel: (305) 255-9206 Fax: (305) 909-0046
Email: yordy@vila-n-son.com
Web: www.vila-n-son.com

Miami
13901 NW 118 Ave.
Medley, FL 33178
CEO: Mr. Juan C. Vila
Tel: (305) 805-0066 Fax: (305) 805-4270
Email: jorgeg@vila-n-son.com
Web: www.vila-n-son.com

Orlando
1900 Williams Rd.
Winter Garden, FL 34787
CEO: Mr. Juan C. Vila
Tel: (407) 654-9415 Fax: (407) 654-9417
Email: philipt@vila-n-son.com
Web: www.vila-n-son.com

West Palm Beach
1930 D. Rd.
Loxahatchee, FL 33470
CEO: Mr. Juan C. Vila
Tel: (561) 795-3070 Fax: (561) 795-3879
Email: philipt@vila-n-son.com
Web: www.vila-n-son.com

LANDSCAPE, LAWN MAINT., RETAIL SALES

MALDONADO NURSERY & LANDSCAPING, INC.

16348 Nacogdoches St.
San Antonio, TX 78247
CEO: Mr. Jerry Maldonado
Tel: (210) 599-1219 Fax: (210) 599-9736
Email: roy@mnlssa.com
Web: www.mnlsa.com

LAW FIRM

ADORNO & YOSS P.A.

Atlanta
2 Midtown Plz. 1349 W. Peachtree St. #1500
Atlanta, GA 30309
CEO: Mr. Henry N. Adorno
Tel: (404) 347-8300 Fax: (404) 347-8395
Email: info@adorno.com
Web: www.adorno.com

Boca Raton
700 S. Federal Hwy. #200
Boca Raton, FL 33432
CEO: Mr. Henry N. Adorno
Tel: (561) 393-5660 Fax: (561) 338-8698
Email: info@adorno.com
Web: www.adorno.com

Corporate Office
2601 S. Bayshore Dr. #1600
Miami, FL 33133
CEO: Mr. Henry N. Adorno
Tel: (305) 858-5555 Fax: (305) 858-4777
Email: info@adorno.com
Web: www.adorno.com

Delray Beach
200 Congress Park Dr. #210
Delray Beach, FL 33445
CEO: Mr. Henry N. Adorno
Tel: (561) 454-0301 Fax: (561) 454-0319
Email: info@adorno.com
Web: www.adorno.com

Fort Lauderdale North
350 E. Las Olas Blvd. #1700
Ft. Lauderdale, FL 33301
CEO: Mr. Henry N. Adorno
Tel: (954) 763-1200 Fax: (954) 766-7800
Email: info@adorno.com
Web: www.adorno.com

Fort Lauderdale South
880 SE 3rd Ave. #500
Ft. Lauderdale, FL 33335
CEO: Mr. Henry N. Adorno
Tel: (954) 523-5885 Fax: (954) 760-9531
Email: info@adorno.com
Web: www.adorno.com

Irvine
4 Park Plz. #1200
Irvine, CA 92614
CEO: Mr. Henry N. Adorno
Tel: (949) 955-6800 Fax: (949) 955-6899
Email: info@adorno.com
Web: www.adorno.com

Los Angeles
633 W. 5th St. #1150
Los Angeles, CA 90071
CEO: Mr. Henry N. Adorno
Tel: (213) 229-2400 Fax: (213) 229-2499
Email: info@adorno.com
Web: www.adorno.com

New York
80 Broad St., 32nd Fl.
New York, NY 10004
CEO: Mr. Henry N. Adorno
Tel: (212) 809-5700 Fax: (212) 809-5701
Email: info@adorno.com
Web: www.adorno.com

Tallahassee
301 Bronough St. #650
Tallahassee, FL 32301
CEO: Mr. Henry N. Adorno
Tel: (850) 222-5139
Email: info@adorno.com
Web: www.adorno.com

West Palm Beach
1551 Forum Pl., Bldg. 200 and 400
West Palm Beach, FL 33401
CEO: Mr. Henry N. Adorno
Tel: (561) 640-8000 Fax: (561) 640-6030
Email: info@adorno.com
Web: www.adorno.com

GARCES & GRABLER P.C.

235 Livinston Ave.
New Brunswick, NJ 08901
CEO: Mr. Guillermo Garces
Tel: (732) 249-1300 Fax: (732) 220-1555

LEGAL SERVICES

CREDITOR IUSTUS ET REMEDIUM LLP

Headquarters
8031 Linda Vista Rd.
San Diego, CA 92111
CEO: Mr. Felipe E. Becer
Tel: (800) 496-8909 Fax: (858) 496-5978
Email: attorney@cirlaw.com
Web: www.cirlaw.com

Los Angeles Office
1925 Century Park E. #500
Los Angeles, CA 90067
CEO: Mr. Felipe E. Becerra

Tel: (310) 226-6795 Fax: (310) 286-7285
Email: attorney@cirlaw.com
Web: www.cirlaw.com

SANCHEZ & DANIELS

Chicago Office
333 W. Wacker Dr. #500
Chicago, IL 60606
CEO: Mr. Manuel Sanchez
Tel: (312) 641-1555 Fax: (312) 641-3004
Email: sd@sanchezdaniels.com
Web: www.sanchezdaniels.com

Wheaton Office
2100 Manchester Rd., Bldg A #309
Wheaton, IL 60187
CEO: Mr. Manuel Sanchez
Tel: (630) 752-9880 Fax: (630) 752-9881
Email: sd@sanchezdaniels.com
Web: www.sanchezdaniels.com

LIGHTING & ELECTRICAL SALES

UNALITE ELECTRIC & LIGHTING CORPORATION

P.O. Box 770446
Woodside, NY 11377-0446
CEO: Mr. Israel Bulbank
Tel: (718) 898-5100 Fax: (718) 898-7957
Email: unalite@fcc.net
Web: www.unalite.com

LOGIS., ACQ. SUPPORT, IT SYSTEMS

TESSADA & ASSOCIATES, INC.

Corporate Head Office
8001 Forbes Pl. #310
Springfield, VA 22151
CEO: Mr. Enrique A. Tessada
Tel: (703) 564-1210 Fax: (703) 564-1225
Email: rtessada@tessada.com
Web: www.tessada.com

LONG DISTANCE TELECOMM.

LATIN NODE, INC.

7230 NW 31st St.
Miami, FL 33122
CEO: Mr. Jorge Granados
Tel: (305) 592-4848 Fax: (305) 592-4949
Email: sale@latinode.com
Web: www.latinode.com

LOOSELEAF PRODUCTS MFG.

CONTINENTAL BINDER & SPECIALTY CORPORATION

Arizona Regional Office
3625 N.16th St. #118
Phoenix, AZ 85016
CEO: Mr. Andrew H. Lisardi
Tel: (602) 222-2463 Fax: (602) 222-1119
Email: tomd@continentalbinder.com
Web: www.continentalbinder.com

Colorado Regional Office
2765 S. Colorado Blvd. #216
Denver, CO 80222
CEO: Mr. Andrew H. Lisardi
Tel: (303) 451-5871 Fax: (303) 568-9177
Email: densales@continentalbinder.com
Web: www.continentalbinder.com

Main Plant
407 W. Compton Blvd.
Gardena, CA 90248-1703
CEO: Mr. Andrew H. Lisardi
Tel: (310) 324-8227
(800) 872-2897 Fax: (310) 715-6740
Email: sales@continentalbinder.com
Web: www.continentalbinder.com

Texas Regional Office
5426 Gary Cooper Dr.
San Antonio, TX 78240
CEO: Mr. Andrew H. Lisardi
Tel: (210) 732-4888 Fax: (210) 684-4888
Email: sandyc@continentalbinder.com
Web: www.continentalbinder.com

MACHINE CASTING & FORGING MFG.

AZTEC MANUFACTURING CORPORATION

15378 Oakwood Dr.
Romulus, MI 48174
CEO: Mr. Francis Lopez
Tel: (734) 942-7433 Fax: (734) 942-9499
Email: flopez@aztecmfgcorp.com
Web: www.aztecmfgcorp.com

MAINTENANCE

EXCEL LANDSCAPE, INC.

710 Rimpau Ave. #108
Corona, CA 92879-5724
CEO: Mr. Jose Alfaro
Tel: (951) 735-9650 Fax: (951) 735-0469

MASONRY CONSTRUCTION

A.L.L. MASONRY CONSTRUCTION COMPANY

1414 W. Willow St.
Chicago, IL 60622
CEO: Mr. Luis Puig, Sr.
Tel: (773) 489-1280 Fax: (773) 489-0360

MATERIAL HANDLING

ROCKY DURON & ASSOCIATES INC.

9100 John Carpenter Fwy.
Dallas, TX 75247
CEO: Mr. Marciano Duron
Tel: (214) 358-3455
(800) 875-5457 Fax: (214) 358-5713
Email: info@rockyduron.com
Web: www.rockyduron.com

MEAT PACKING DIST.

H&H FOODS

P.O. Box 358
Mercedes, TX 78570
CEO: Mr. Liborio E. Hinojosa, Sr.
Tel: (956) 565-6363 Fax: (956) 565-4108
Email: liboriosr@hhfoods.com
Web: www.hhfoods.com

MEAT PROD. MFG.

LOPEZ FOODS, INC.

Head Office
6016 NW 120th Ct.
Oklahoma City, OK 73162
CEO: Mr. Eduardo Sanchez
Tel: (405) 603-7500 Fax: (405) 603-6009
Web: www.lopezfoods.com

Main Plant
9500 NW 4th St.

Oklahoma City, OK 73127
CEO: Mr. Ed Sanchez
Tel: (405) 789-7500 Fax: (405) 499-0114
Web: www.lopezfoods.com

FAR WEST MEATS
7759 Victoria Ave.
Highland, CA 92346
CEO: Mr. Thomas Serrato
Tel: (909) 864-1990
(800) 772-6328 Fax: (909) 864-0554
Email: sales@farwestmeats.com
Web: www.farwestmeats.com

MEAT, SEAFOOD, & DAIRY WHSL.

NORTHWESTERN MEAT, INC.
2100 NW 23rd St.
Miami, FL 33142
CEO: Mr. Elpidio Nuñez Ojeda
Tel: (305) 633-8112 Fax: (305) 633-6907
Email: numeat@bellsouth.net
Web: www.numeat.com

MEDICAL, SOCIAL SVCS., INFO. SYSTEM

PROFESSIONAL PERFORMANCE DEVELOPMENT GROUP, INC.
Corporate Office
5441 Babcock Rd. #200
San Antonio, TX 78240
CEO: Ms. Ana Maria Lecea
Tel: (210) 615-1117
(800) 460-7734 Fax: (210) 615-1158
Web: www.ppdg.com

MEN'S APPAREL DESIGN & WHSL.

SUPREME INTERNATIONAL, INC.
Corporate Headquarters
3000 NW 107th Ave.
Miami, FL 33172
CEO: Mr. George Feldenkreis
Tel: (305) 592-2830 Fax: (305) 594-2307
Email: info@perry.com
Web: www.supreme.com

METAL FRAMING, DRYWALL, PAINTING

W.G. VALENZUELA DRYWALL, INC.
4085 N. Highway Dr.
Tucson, AZ 85705
CEO: Mr. William G. Valenzuela
Tel: (520) 887-5652 Fax: (520) 887-8404

METAL STAMPING

ARANDA TOOLING, INC.
15301 Springdale St.
Huntington Beach, CA 92649
CEO: Mr. Pedro Aranda
Tel: (714) 379-6565 Fax: (714) 379-6570
Email: dan.aranda@arandatooling.com
Web: www.arandatooling.com

METAL STAMPING TOOLS & DIE MFG.

DIXIEN LLC
5286 Circle Dr.
Lake City, GA 30260
CEO: Mr. Juan R. Garcia

Tel: (404) 366-7427 Fax: (404) 366-2403
Email: info@dixien.com
Web: www.dixien.com

MEXICAN DELI & MARKET

LA AMAPOLA, INC.
7420 E. Florence Ave.
Downey, CA 90240
CEO: Mr. Carlos B. Galvan
Tel: (562) 776-0246 Fax: (562) 776-0296
Email: amapolamarket@earthlink.net
Web: www.amapolamarket.com

7223 S. Compton Ave.
Los Angeles, CA 90001
CEO: Mr. Carlos B. Galvan
Tel: (323) 587-7118 Fax: (323) 587-2889
Email: amapolamarket@earthlink.net
Web: www.amapolamarket.com

MEXICAN FOOD

RUIZ FOOD PRODUCTS, INC.
Head Office
P.O. Box 37
Dinuba, CA 93618
CEO: Mr. John Signorino
Tel: (800) 477-6474 Fax: (559) 591-1623
Email: contactus@ruizfoods.com
Web: www.ruizfoods.com

MEXICAN FOOD MFG.

PUENTES BROTHERS, INC.
3060 Industrial Way NE
Salem, OR 97303
CEO: Mr. George Puentes
Tel: (503) 370-9710 Fax: (503) 370-4482
Email: george@donpancho.com
Web: www.donpancho.com

MFG. ADVERTISING PRODUCTS

JARCO US CASTINGS CORP.
4409 Park Ave.
Union City, NJ 07087
CEO: Mr. Mario A. Herrera
Tel: (800) 433-1494
(201) 271-0003 Fax: (201) 271-0009
Email: info@jarcousa.com
Web: www.jarcousa.com

MFG., ENGINEERING SVCS., CONSULTING

GONZALEZ DESIGN GROUP
Corporate Headquarters
29401 Stephenson Hwy.
Madison Heights, MI 48071
CEO: Mr. Gary Gonzalez
Tel: (248) 548-6010 Fax: (248) 548-3160
Email: gondes1@gonzalez-group.com
Web: www.gonzalez-group.com

MFG. & INSTALLER OF WOOD STAIR RAILINGS

GENERAL STAIR CORP.
690 W. 83rd St.
Hialeah, FL 33014
CEO: Mr. Saby Behar
Tel: (305) 769-9900 Fax: (305) 824-1113
Email: info@generalstair.com
Web: www.generalstair.com

MANUFACTURING

MOVADO GROUP, INC.
650 From Rd.
Paramus, NJ 07652-3507
CEO: Mr. Efraim Grinberg
Tel: (201) 267-8000
Web: movadogroupinc.com

SUPERIOR TANK COMPANY, INC.
P.O. Box 3166
Santa Fe Springs, CA 90670
CEO: Mr. James E. Marquez
Tel: (562) 946-8804 Fax: (562) 941-1722
Email: james@superiortank.com
Web: www.superiortank.com

THOS. S. BYRNE LIMITED
Austin Office
1250 S. Capital of Texas Hwy, Three Cielo #395
Austin, TX 78746
CEO: Mr. John Avila, Jr.
Tel: (512) 347-1898 Fax: (512) 347-0950
Email: info@tsbyrne.com
Web: www.tsbyrne.com

Dallas Office
2777 Stemmons Frwy. #998
Dallas, TX 75207
CEO: Mr. John Avila, Jr.
Tel: (214) 267-0920 Fax: (214) 267-0926
Email: info@tsbyrne.com
Web: www.tsbyrne.com

San Antonio Office
9311 San Pedro Ave. #700
San Antonio, TX 78216
CEO: Mr. John Avila, Jr.
Tel: (210) 340-9080 Fax: (210) 340-9085
Email: info@tsbyrne.com
Web: www.tsbyrne.com

MFG. METAL PRODUCTS

MARISA INDUSTRIES, INC.
Design, Engineering and Assembly Facility
2965 Lapeer Rd.
Auburn Hills, MI 48326
CEO: Mr. Jesse M. Lopez
Tel: (248) 475-9600 Fax: (248) 475-9908
Email: jpogodzinsky@baeind.com
Web: www.marisaind.com

Manufacturing Facility
24400 Sherwood
Centerline, MI 48015
CEO: Mr. Jesse M. Lopez
Tel: (586) 754-3000 Fax: (586) 754-3007
Email: jpogodzinsky@baeind.com
Web: www.marisaind.com

MGMT. CONSULTING FIRM

THE VENTURA GROUP, INC.
8550 Lee Hwy. #450
Fairfax, VA 22031
CEO: Mr. Michael J. Sierra
Tel: (703) 208-3303 Fax: (703) 208-3305
Email: info@theventuragroup.com
Web: www.theventuragroup.com

MGMT. & ENGINEERING SERVICES

PRIORITY ONE SERVICES, INC.
6600 Fleet Dr.
Alexandria, VA 22310
CEO: Mr. Jose Figueroa
Tel: (703) 971-5505 Fax: (703) 719-6773
Email: pepe@priorityservices.com

Web: www.priorityoneservices.com

MGMT., TECH., IT, EDUCATIONAL SERVICES

ANALYTICAL SERVICES, INC.
Florida Office
5 Clifford Dr.
Shalimar, FL 32579
CEO: Ms. Irma L. Tuder
Fax: (850) 651-2565
Email: tuderi@asi-hsv.com
Web: www.asi-hsv.com

Headquarters
689 Discovery Dr. #300
Huntsville, AL 35806
CEO: Ms. Irma L. Tuder
Tel: (256) 890-0083 Fax: (256) 890-0242
Email: tuderi@asi-hsv.com
Web: www.asi-hsv.com

Mississippi Office
3532 Manor Dr. #3
Vicksburg, MS 39180
CEO: Ms. Irma L. Tuder
Tel: (601) 636-8440 Fax: (601) 636-8086
Email: tuderi@asi-hsv.com
Web: www.asi-hsv.com

Montgomery Office
124 W. Main St. #300
Prattville, AL 36067
CEO: Ms. Irma L. Tuder
Tel: (334) 358-6141 Fax: (334) 361-7671
Email: tuderi@asi-hsv.com
Web: www.asi-hsv.com

MGMT & TECHNOLOGY/ SERVICES

CREATIVE ASSOCIATES INTERNATIONAL, INC.
5301 Wisconsin Ave. NW #700
Washington, DC 20015
CEO: Ms. M. Charito Kruvant
Tel: (202) 966-5804 Fax: (202) 363-4771
Email: creative@cali-dc.com
Web: www.caii-dc.com

MKTG., PROD. & DISTRIB. OF FILMS

ARENAS ENTERTAINMENT
100 N. Crescent Dr. Garden Level
Beverly Hills, CA 90210
CEO: Mr. Santiago Pozo
Tel: (310) 385-4401 Fax: (310) 385-4402
Email: info@arenasgroup.com
Web: www.arenasgroup.com

MOVING, SHIPPING & STORAGE SERVICES

LA ROSA DEL MONTE EXPRESS, INC.
Connecticut
110 Austin St.
Bridgeport, CT 06604
CEO: Mr. Hiram Rodriguez
Tel: (800) 775-6452 Fax: (203) 333-3372
Email: info@larosadelmonte.com
Web: www.larosadelmonte.com

Illinois
4834 W. Armitage Ave.
Chicago, IL 60639
CEO: Mr. Hiram Rodriguez
Tel: (800) 643-6684 Fax: (773) 745-1608
Email: info@larosadelmonte.com
Web: www.larosadelmonte.com

Main Office
1133-35 Tiffany St.
Bronx, NY 10459
CEO: Mr. Hiram Rodriguez
Tel: (718) 991-3300
(800) 452-7672 Fax: (718) 893-1948
Email: info@larosadelmonte.com
Web: www.larosadelmonte.com

Massachusetts
471 Southbridge St.
Worcester, MA 01610
CEO: Mr. Hiram Rodriguez
Tel: (800) 752-4049 Fax: (508) 752-4019
Email: info@larosadelmonte.com
Web: www.larosadelmonte.com

Miami
7675 NW 66th St.
Miami, FL 33166
CEO: Mr. Hiram Rodriguez
Tel: (800) 599-5524
(305) 599-2590 Fax: (305) 599-0343
Email: info@larosadelmonte.com
Web: www.larosadelmonte.com

Ohio
3530 Ridge Rd.
Brooklyn, OH 44102
CEO: Mr. Hiram Rodriguez
Tel: (216) 961-8900 Fax: (216) 961-4152
Email: info@larosadelmonte.com
Web: www.larosadelmonte.com

Orlando
600-608 E. Landstreet Rd.
Orlando, FL 32824
CEO: Mr. Hiram Rodriguez
Tel: (888) 605-6262 Fax: (407) 826-4167
Email: info@larosadelmonte.com
Web: www.larosadelmonte.com

Philadelphia
2250-64 N. 5th St.
Philadelphia, PA 19133
CEO: Mr. Hiram Rodriguez
Tel: (800) 538-1372/(215) 203-8000
Fax: (215) 203-8129
Email: info@larosadelmonte.com
Web: www.larosadelmonte.com

Puerto Rico
Carretera #2, Km 19.6
Toa Baja, PR 00949
CEO: Mr. Hiram Rodriguez
Tel: (787) 780-5775
Email: info@larosadelmonte.com
Web: www.larosadelmonte.com

Texas
500 S. Belt Line Rd. #500
Irving, TX 75060
CEO: Mr. Hiram Rodriguez
Tel: (214) 492-6387 Fax: (214) 492-6389
Email: info@larosadelmonte.com
Web: www.larosadelmonte.com

MULTIMEDIA SERVICES

JARDON & HOWARD TECHNOLOGIES, INC.
13501 Ingenuity Dr. #300
Orlando, FL 32826
CEO: Mr. James E. Jardon II
Tel: (407) 381-7797 Fax: (407) 381-0017
Web: www.jht.com

Kennedy Space Center Office
United Space Alliance USK 179
Kennedy Space Center, FL 32899
CEO: Mr. James E. Jardon II
Tel: (321) 861-1100 Fax: (321) 861-1112
Web: www.jht.com

Pax River Office
23330 Cottonwood Pkwy. #350
California, MD 20619

CEO: Mr. James E. Jardon II
Tel: (240) 725-0727 X222
Web: www.jht.com

Pensacola Office
600 University Office Blvd. #12
Pensacola, FL 32504
CEO: Mr. James E. Jardon II
Tel: (850) 969-9601 Fax: (850) 969-9628
Web: www.jht.com

NATURAL GAS DISTRIB./ OFFSET PRINTING

PS ENERGY GROUP, INC.
2987 Clairmont Rd. #450
Atlanta, GA 30359
CEO: Ms. Livia Whisenhunt
Tel: (404) 321-5711
(800) 334-7548 Fax: (404) 321-3938
Email: info@psenergy.com
Web: www.psenergy.com

NON-METALLIC STRAPPING/ OFFSET PRINTING

DYNARIC, INC.
Head Office
5740 Bayside Rd.
Virginia Beach, VA 23455
CEO: Mr. Joseph Martinez
Tel: (757) 363-5851 Fax: (757) 363-8015
Email: gd@dynaric.com
Web: www.dynaric.com

OFFICE CONSTRUCTION & RENOVATION

TESORO CORPORATION
Head Office
520 S. Independence Blvd.
Virginia Beach, VA 23452
CEO: Mr. Dennis F. Gilbert
Tel: (757) 518-8491 Fax: (757) 518-8589
Email: info@tesorocorp.com
Web: www.tesorocorp.com

North Carolina Office
400 Front St. #11
Beaufort, NC 28516
CEO: Mr. Dennis F. Gilbert
Tel: (252) 728-5352 Fax: (252) 728-4959
Email: info@tesorocorp.com
Web: www.tesorocorp.com

South Carolina Office
2020 Hawthorne Dr. #9B
North Charleston, NC 29406
CEO: Mr. Dennis F. Gilbert
Tel: (843) 554-6144 Fax: (843) 554-6188
Email: info@tesorocorp.com
Web: www.tesorocorp.com

Yorktown Office
200A Commerce Cr.
Yorktown, VA 23693
CEO: Mr. Dennis F. Gilbert
Tel: (757) 873-3427 Fax: (757) 873-3468
Email: info@tesorocorp.com
Web: www.tesorocorp.com

OFFICE PRODUCTS

CONTACT OFFICE SOLUTIONS
Calabasas Office
2700 Agoura Rd. #195
Calabasas, CA 91301
CEO: Mr. Richard Gomez
Tel: (818) 878-3005 Fax: (818) 878-1507

Email: info@contactcopier.com
Web: www.contactcopier.com

Corporate Headquarters
18528 Dominguez Hills Dr.
Ranch Dominguez, CA 90220
CEO: Mr. Richard Gomez
Tel: (310) 381-3999 Fax: (310) 381-3989
Email: info@contactcopier.com
Web: www.contactcopier.com

Irvine Office
17767 Mitchell North
Irvine, CA 92614
CEO: Mr. Richard Gomez
Tel: (800) 281-8281 Fax: (310) 381-3989
Email: info@contactcopier.com
Web: www.contactcopier.com

SUPPLY SOURCE, INC.
Corporate Headquarters
2605 Reach Rd.
Williamsport, PA 17701
CEO: Ms. Ray Thompson
Tel: (570) 327-1500 Fax: (570) 327-1244
Email: info@officesupplysource.com
Web: www.officesupplysource.com

Harrisburg
2323 Woodlawn St.
Harrisburg, PA 17104
CEO: Ms. Ray Thompson
Tel: (717) 558-0682 Fax: (717) 558-0682
Email: info@officesupplysource.com
Web: www.officesupplysource.com

Johnstown Office
521 Napoleon St.
Johnstown, PA 15901
CEO: Ms. Ray Thompson
Tel: (814) 535-8271 Fax: (814) 536-3994
Email: info@officesupplysource.com
Web: www.officesupplysource.com

Lancaster
1860 Charter Ln. #101
Lancaster, PA 17601
CEO: Ms. Ray Thompson
Tel: (717) 299-7266 Fax: (717) 299-7243
Email: info@officesupplysource.com
Web: www.officesupplysource.com

State College
200 E. Calder Way
State College, PA 16801
CEO: Ms. Ray Thompson
Tel: (814) 237-2660 Fax: (814) 237-9155
Email: info@officesupplysource.com
Web: www.officesupplysource.com

OFFICE & SCHOOL SUPPLY EXPORTERS

A.M. CAPEN'S COMPANY, INC.
1255 Liberty Ave.
Hillside, NJ 07205
CEO: Mr. Camilo Fernandez
Tel: (908) 351-1520 Fax: (908) 351-9235
Email: amcapens@aol.com

OFFICE SUPPLIES & FURNITURE DEALER

FM OFFICE EXPRESS, INC.
2555-B Baird Rd.
Penfield, NY 14526-2390
CEO: Mr. Fabricio Morales
Tel: (585) 385-0810 Fax: (585) 385-4401
Email: dburger@fm-resources.com
Web: www.fm-resources.com

OFFICE SUPPLY DISRIB.

TEJAS OFFICE PRODUCTS, INC.
1225 W. 20th St.
Houston, TX 77008
CEO: Mr. Lupe Fraga
Tel: (713) 864-6004
(800) 593-6004 Fax: (713) 864-3933
(866) 637-3933
Email: tejas@tejasoffice.com
Web: www.tejasoffice.com

OFFICE SUPPLY & FURNITURE DISTRIB.

PROFTECH, LLC
200 Clearbrook Rd.
Elmsford, NY 10523
CEO: Mr. Jose R. Montiel
Tel: (800) 937-8354 Fax: (800) 937-8353
Email: admin@proftech.com
Web: www.proftech.com

OFFICE SUPPLY, MATERIAL HANDLING, JANITORIAL SUPPLY

QUINTANA SUPPLY
41 Rogers Rd.
Ward Hill, MA 01835
CEO: Mr. Michael Quintana
Tel: (800) 499-1000
(978) 679-4411 Fax: (978) 689-7674
Email: quintanaas@aol.com
Web: www.qaisupply.com

OFFICE SUPPLY SALES

OFFICE SOLUTIONS BUSINESS PRODUCTS & SERVICES
23303 La Palma Ave.
Yorba Linda, CA 92887
CEO: Mr. Robert J. Mairena
Tel: (714) 692-7412 Fax: (714) 692-7409
Email: sales@officesol.com
Web: www.officesol.com

OIL FIELD & INDUST. SUPPLIES WHSL.

PETRO AMIGOS SUPPLY, INC.
2620 Fountainview Dr. #225
Houston, TX 77057-7621
CEO: Mr. César Vasquez
Tel: (713) 977-9924 Fax: (713) 977-9935
Email: cvasquez@petroamigos.com

OIL FIELD CONSTRUCTION SERVICES

MED-LOZ LEASE SERVICE, INC.
P.O. Box 627
Zapata, TX 78076
CEO: Mr. Juan A. Medina
Tel: (956) 765-6029 Fax: (956) 765-9419

OPTICAL SECURITY/ATM NETWORK CONSULT.

TECHNICA CORPORATION
45245 Business Ct. #300
Dulles, VA 20166
CEO: Mr. Miguel Collado

Tel: (703) 662-2000 Fax: (703) 662-2001
Email: info@technicacorp.com
Web: www.technicacorp.com

PAINT, CHEM. EXPORTING

ANDES CHEMICAL CORPORATION
10850 NW 30th St.
Miami, FL 33172
CEO: Mr. Fernando Espinosa
Tel: (305) 591-5601 Fax: (305) 591-5607
Email: fernando.espinosa@andeschem.com
Web: www.andeschem.com

PAINTING SERVICES

BORBON, INC.
7312 Walnut Ave.
Buena Park, CA 90620
CEO: Mr. David Morales
Tel: (714) 994-0170 Fax: (714) 994-0641
Email: lus@borbon.net

PAINTING & WALLCOVERING SERVICES

MILAM & COMPANY PAINTING, INC.
4550 Allen St.
Houston, TX 77007
CEO: Mr. David K. Milam, Sr.
Tel: (713) 869-0225 Fax: (713) 869-9528

PAPER BAG MFG.

ENDPAK PACKAGING, INC.
7343 Paramount Blvd.
Pico Rivera, CA 90660
CEO: Mr. Edgar A. Garcia
Tel: (562) 801-0281 Fax: (562) 801-0542
Email: edgar@endpak.com

PAPER, PLASTIC & CLEANING SUPPLIES

TSN, INC.
Colorado Warehouse
P.O. Box 679
Frederick, CO 80530-0679
CEO: Mr. Israel Salazar
Tel: (303) 530-0600 Fax: (303) 530-1919
Email: tnelson@tsndist.com
Web: www.tsndist.com

Colorado Warehouse
P.O. Box 1799
Richmond, IN 47375
CEO: Mr. Israel Salazar
Tel: (765) 962-1283 Fax: (765) 962-7806
Email: tnelson@tsndist.com
Web: www.tsndist.com

PERSONNEL PLACEMENT, EXEC. PLACEMENT

DMDICKASON PERSONNEL SERVICES
4900 N. Mesa St.
El Paso, TX 79932
CEO: Don Dickason
Tel: (915) 532-9400 Fax: (915) 532-5830
Web: www.dmdickason.com

PETROCHEMICALS DISTRIB.

THE PLAZA GROUP, INC.
10375 Richmond Ave. #1620
Houston, TX 77042-4143
CEO: Mr. Randy E. Velarde
Tel: (713) 266-1059
(800) 876-3738 Fax: (713) 266-8660
Email: maryesquivel@theplazagrp.com
Web: www.theplazagrp.com

PETROLEUM PRODUCTS, FUELS, OILS

DELTA FUEL CO., INC.
P.O. Box 1810
Ferriday, LA 71334
CEO: Mr. Clinton L. Vegas
Tel: (318) 757-3975 Fax: (318) 757-6742
Web: www.deltafuel.com

PHARM. & MEDICAL EXPORT

FARMA INTERNATIONAL
9501 Old S. Dixie Hwy.
Miami, FL 33156
CEO: Mr. George Medina
Tel: (305) 670-4416 Fax: (305) 670-4417
Email: ulisesrodriguez@farmainternational.com
Web: www.farmainternational.com

PHARM. & MEDICAL SUPPLY

DAVILA PHARMACY, INC.
Main Office
1423 Guadalupe St. #108
San Antonio, TX 78207
CEO: Mr. Rudolfo Davila
Tel: (210) 226-5293 Fax: (210) 224-9257
Email: davilarx@texas.net
Web: www.davilapharmacy.com

Headquarters
3075 NW 107th Ave.
Miami, FL 33172-2134
CEO: Mr. Carlos M. de Cespedes
Tel: (305) 592-2324 Fax: (305) 591-9643
Email: claudiao@pharmed.com
Web: www.pharmed.com

PMG Group of Ohio
7905 Cochran Rd. #300
Glenwillow, OH 44139
CEO: Mr. Carlos M. de Cespedes
Tel: (440) 914-9800 Fax: (440) 914-9900
Web: www.pharmed.com

Tampa Florida
8130 Anderson Rd.
Tampa, FL 33634
CEO: Mr. Carlos M. de Cespedes
Tel: (800) 741-3836 Fax: (813) 884-6630
Web: www.pharmed.com

PKG., PAINTING SERVICES

GROUP O, INC.
Group O Direct
4905 77th Ave.
Milan, IL 61264
CEO: Mr. Robert Ontiveros
Tel: (309) 736-8100
(309) 736-8171 Fax: (309) 736-8171
Email: info@groupodirect.com
Web: www.groupo.com

PLASTIC CONTAINERS

CLASSIC CONTAINERS, INC.
Head Office
1700 S. Hellman Ave.
Ontario, CA 91761
CEO: Mr. Manny G. Hernandez
Tel: (909) 930-3610 Fax: (909) 930-3640
Email: mannysr@classiccontainers.com
Web: www.classiccontainers.com

PLASTIC EQUIPMENT SALES

PLASTEC USA, INC.
7752 NW 74th Ave.
Miami, FL 33166
CEO: Mr. Hector V. Sosa
Tel: (305) 887-6920 Fax: (305) 883-8254
Email: plastec@plastecusa.com
Web: www.plastecusa.com

PLASTIC LAMINATE CABINET & COUNTERS

LOZANO CASEWORKS, INC.
242 W. Hanna St.
Colton, CA 92324
CEO: Mr. David F. Lozano, Sr.
Tel: (909) 783-7530 Fax: (909) 783-0439
Email: davesr.lci@mpowercom.net

PLUMBING, HEATING, FIRE PROTECTION

PRIBUSS ENGINEERING, INC.
523 Mayfair Ave.
South San Francisco, CA 94080
CEO: Mr. Bayardo J. Chamorro
Tel: (650) 588-0447 Fax: (650) 588-8592
Email: mail@pribuss.com
Web: www.pribuss.com

PLUMBING & HVAC

MIDCONTINENT MECHANICAL, INC.
1640 Erie St.
North Kansas City, MO 64116
CEO: Mr. Joseph A. Hurtado
Tel: (816) 471-5758 Fax: (816) 471-5609
Email: joe@midcontinentmechanical.com
Web: www.midcontinentmechanical.com

PLUMBING, PIPING, HEATING, AC.

TREVINO & ASSOCIATES MECHANICAL, INC.
9806 Brockbank Dr.
Dallas, TX 75220
CEO: Mr. Mike Trevino, Sr.
Tel: (214) 358-2170 Fax: (214) 358-1594
Email: service@trevinomechanical.com
Web: www.trevinomechanical.com

POOL SERVICES

CALIFORNIA'S GUNITE, POOL PLASTERING
510 Greenville Rd.
Livermore, CA 94550
CEO: Mr. Manuel Rodriguez
Tel: (925) 606-6122 Fax: (925) 606-1961
Email: cgpp@sdcglobal.net

PORK RIND MANUFACTURER

EVANS FOOD GROUP LTD.
2240 6th St.
Ports Mouth, OH 45662
CEO: Mr. Alan F. Sussna
Tel: (740) 354-6654 Fax: (740) 353-2482
Email: sales@evansfood.com
Web: www.evansfood.com

615 N. Great SW Pkwy.
Arlington, TX 76011
CEO: Mr. Alan F. Sussna
Tel: (817) 640-5626 Fax: (817) 649-7832
Email: sales@evansfood.com
Web: www.evansfood.com

1920 Augusta Ct.
Ontario, CA 91761
CEO: Mr. Alan F. Sussna
Tel: (909) 947-3001 Fax: (909) 923-5383
Email: sales@evansfood.com
Web: www.evansfood.com

Corporate Office
4118 S. Halsted St.
Chicago, IL 60609
CEO: Mr. Alan F. Sussna
Tel: (773) 254-7400 Fax: (773) 254-7791
Email: sales@evansfood.com
Web: www.evansfood.com

PREPACKAGED FINANCIAL SOFTWARE DEVELOP.

TRADESTATION SECURITIES, INC.
8050 SW 10th St. #2000
Plantation, FL 33324
CEO: Mr. William R. Cruz/ Ralph L. Cruz
Tel: (800) 808-9336
(954) 652-7677
Email: Sales@TradeStation.com
Web: www.tradestation.com

PRINTING

INTERSTATE ENVELOPE MANUFACTURING COMPANY, LLC
56-15 55th Dr.
Maspeth, NY 11378
CEO: Mr. Ricardo Wilkowski
Tel: (718) 326-2424 Fax: (718) 894-1570
Email: rw@interstate-envelope.com
Web: www.interstate-envelope.com

PARAISO PUBLISHERS, INC.
2198 E. Anderson St.
Vernon, CA 90058
CEO: Mr. Manuel Dinovitzer
Tel: (323) 581-9850
(800) 373-1891 Fax: (323) 581-1775
Email: sales@paradisegreetings.com
Web: www.paradisegreetings.com

VISTA COLOR CORPORATION, LTD.
3401 NW 36th St.
Miami, FL 33142
CEO: Mr. Jesus Serrano
Tel: (305) 635-2000 Fax: (305) 635-1985
Email: prep@vistacolor.com
Web: www.vistacolor.com

PRINTING & MAILING SVCS.

ADVANCED XEROGRAPHICS IMAGING SYSTEMS, INC.
6851 TPC Dr.
Orlando, FL 32822-5141
CEO: Mr. David R. Salazar

Tel: (407) 351-0232 Fax: (407) 363-4586
Email: sales@axisorlando.comMHakimipour
@axisorlando.com
Web: www.axisorlando.com

PRINTING SERVICES

COLONIAL PRESS INTERNATIONAL INC.
3690 NW 50th St.
Miami, FL 33142
CEO: Mr. Jorge Gomez
Tel: (305) 633-1581
(800) 767-1581 Fax: (305) 638-8924
Web: www.colonialpressintl.com

COMMERCE PRINTING SERVICES
322 N. 12th St.
Sacramento, CA 95814
CEO: Mr. Giberto Caravantes
Tel: (916) 442-8100 Fax: (916) 448-2727
Email: customerservice@commerceprinting.
com
Web: www.commerceprinting.com

PRIVATE EQUITY FIRM

PALLADIUM EQUITY PARTNERS
Corporate Office
1270 Ave. of the Americas #2200
New York, NY 10020
CEO: Mr. Marcos A. Rodriguez
Tel: (212) 218-5150 Fax: (212) 218-5155
Email: palladium@palladiumequity.com
Web: www.palladiumequity.com

PRIVATE SECURITY SVCS.

ABC SECURITY SERVICES, INC.
1840 Embarcadero
Oakland, CA 94606
CEO: Ms. Ana Chretien
Tel: (510) 436-0666 Fax: (510) 436-0826
Email: anachretien@abcsecurityservices.
com

PRODUCE PROCESSING

FIELD FRESH FOODS, INC.
14805 S. San Pedro St.
Gardena, CA 90248
CEO: Mr. Emelio E. Castaneda
Tel: (310) 719-8422 Fax: (310) 719-8415
Email: customerservice@fieldfreshfoods.
com
Web: www.fieldfreshfoods.com

PROFESSIONAL EMPLOY. SERVICES

G&A OUTSOURCING, INC.
Austin
12920 Noyes Ln.
Austin, TX 78732
CEO: Mr. Antonio R. Grijalva
Tel: (512) 266-6707 Fax: (512) 266-9119
Email: robster@wt.net
Web: www.gacompanies.com

PROFESSIONAL SVCS. FOR GOV.

BRTRC, INC.
Corporate Headquarters
8260 Willow Oaks Corporate Dr. #800
Fairfax, VA 22031

CEO: Mr. Gerardo M. Sanz
Tel: (703) 204-9277/(800) 307-9277
Fax: (703) 204-9447
Email: business@brtrc.com
Web: www.brtrc.com

Fairborn, OH Office
3162 Presidential Dr.
Fairborn, OH 45324
CEO: Mr. Gerardo M. Sanz
Tel: (937) 429-9234 Fax: (937) 429-7051
Email: business@brtrc.com
Web: www.brtrc.com

Stafford, VA Office
306 Garrisonville Rd. #302
Stafford, VA 22554
CEO: Mr. Gerardo M. Sanz
Tel: (540) 657-1190 Fax: (540) 657-9557
Email: business@brtrc.com
Web: www.brtrc.com

PROGRAM & CONSTRUCTION MGMT.

PARAGON PROJECT RESOURCES INC.
7929 Brookriver Dr. #600
Dallas, TX 75247
CEO: Mr. William Correa
Tel: (214) 634-7060 Fax: (214) 634-0097
Email: info@2paragon.com
Web: www.2paragon.com

PROPERTY & CASUAL INSURANCE

GRANADA INSURANCE CO.
4075 SW 83rd Ave.
Miami, FL 33155-4200
CEO: Mr. Juan Diaz-Padron
Tel: (305) 554-0353
(800) 392-9966 Fax: (305) 662-3914
Web: www.granadainsurance.com

PUBLIC WORKS LANDSCAPING, IRRIGATION

RMT LANDSCAPE CONTRACTORS, INC.
520 Doolite Dr.
San Leandro, CA 94577
CEO: Rick De Herrera
Tel: (925) 552-0966

PUBLICATION

EL CLASIFICADO
1125 Goodrich Blvd.
Los Angeles, CA 90022
CEO: Ms. Martha de la Torre
Tel: (800) 242-2527
(323) 278-5310 Fax: (323) 278-5315
Email: elclasificado@elclasificado.com
Web: www.elclasificado.com

PUMPS & PROCESS EQUIP. SERVICES

ARROYO PROCESS EQUIPMENT, INC.
Head Office
13750 Automobile Blvd.
Clearwater, FL 33762
CEO: Mr. Frank Arroyo
Tel: (727) 573-5294/(800) 445-2630
Fax: (727) 573-0217

Email: sales@arroyoprocess.com
Web: www.arroyoprocess.com

Jacksonville
11105 N. Lane Ave.
Jacksonville, FL 32254
CEO: Mr. Frank Arroyo
Tel: (904) 783-6000/(800) 445-2630
Fax: (904) 781-0522
Email: sales@arroyoprocess.com
Web: www.arroyoprocess.com

Mulberry
1351 S.R. 60 West
Mulberry, FL 33860
CEO: Mr. Frank Arroyo
Tel: (863) 425-1145 Fax: (863) 425-2936
Email: sales@arroyoprocess.com
Web: www.arroyoprocess.com

RADIO SALES & DISTRIB.

BEAM RADIO, INC.
2200 NW 102nd Ave. #3
Miami, FL 33172
CEO: Mr. Manuel A. Alvarez
Tel: (305) 477-2326 Fax: (305) 477-6351
Email: beam@beamradio.com
Web: www.beamradio.com

RADIOPHARMACEUTICALS

BIOTECH PHARMACY, INC.
Albuquerque
3500 Comanche Rd. NE, Bldg. B
Albuquerque, NM 87107
CEO: Mr. Leroy Candelaria
Tel: (505) 830-9071 Fax: (505) 830-3227
Email: information@biotechpharmacy.com
Web: www.biotechpharmacy.com

El Paso
118 W. Castellano Rd.
El Paso, TX 79912
CEO: Mr. Leroy Candelaria
Tel: (901) 545-5095 Fax: (915) 545-5096
Email: information@biotechpharmacy.com
Web: www.biotechpharmacy.com

Las Vegas
3950 S. Eastern Ave. #140
Las Vegas, NV 89119
CEO: Mr. Leroy Candelaria
Tel: (702) 791-3608 Fax: (702) 791-5290
Email: information@biotechpharmacy.com
Web: www.biotechpharmacy.com

RAILCAR LEASING SVCS.

EXCEL RAILCAR CORP. & COS.
112 Water St.
Naperville, IL 60540
CEO: Mr. Eugene R. Constance
Tel: (630) 305-8500 Fax: (630) 305-8503
Email: creetz@excelrailcar.com
Web: www.excelrailcar.com

RAW MATERIALS WHSL.

RHO INDUSTRIES, INC.
5625 FM 1960 W. #406
Houston, TX 77069
CEO: Mr. Jorge de la Riva
Tel: (281) 880-6263 Fax: (281) 880-5354
Email: jorge@rhoind.com

READY-MIX CONCRETE SALES

ADONEL CONCRETE, PUMPING & FINISHING INC.
2101 NW 110th Ave.
Miami, FL 33172
CEO: Mr. Luis A. Garcia
Tel: (305) 392-5416 Fax: (305) 599-2827
Email: luisgarcia@adonelconcrete.com
Web: www.adonelconcrete.com

READY-MIX CONCRETE

CENTRAL CONCRETE SUPERMIX, INC.
Corporate Headquarters
4300 SW 74th Ave.
Miami, FL 33155-7520
CEO: Mr. Jose A. Cancio
Tel: (305) 262-3250 Fax: (305) 267-0698
Email: info@supermix.com
Web: www.supermix.com

SONAG READY MIX LLC
5510 W. Florist Ave.
Milwaukee, WI 53218
CEO: Mr. Brian L. Ganos
Tel: (262) 252-9911 Fax: (262) 252-9902
Email: postmaster@sonag.com
Web: www.sonag.com

REAL ESTATE/ DEVELOPMENT

PRIMESTOR PROPERTIES
228 S. Beverly Dr.
Beverly Hills, CA 90212-3805
CEO: Mr. Arturo Sneider
Tel: (310) 652-1177 Fax: (310) 652-3165
Email: arturo@primestor.com
Web: www.primestor.com

THE RELATED GROUP OF FLORIDA
Corporate Office
2828 Coral Way
Miami, FL 33145
CEO: Mr. Jorge M. Perez
Tel: (305) 460-9900 Fax: (305) 460-9911
Email: info@relatedgroup.com
Web: www.relatedgroup.com

RESELLER OF ENTERPRISE COMPUTING SOLUTIONS

MOBIUS PARTNERS SERVER SOLUTIONS
Dallas Office
5000 Quorum Dr. #110
Dallas, TX 75254
CEO: Mr. Jay Uribe
Tel: (469) 374-7666 Fax: (469) 374-7622
Email: jayu@mobiuspartners.com
Web: www.mobiuspartners.com

Headquarters
837 Isom Rd.
San Antonio, TX 78216
CEO: Mr. Jay Uribe
Tel: (210) 979-0380
(888) 834-5531 Fax: (210) 979-0381
Email: jayu@mobiuspartners.com
Web: www.mobiuspartners.com

RESIDENTIAL CONTRACTING & CONSTR.

REY GROUP, INC.
233 S. Semoran Blvd.
Orlando, FL 32807

CEO: Mr. Tony Rey
Tel: (407) 281-6666
Email: info@reyhomes.com
Web: www.reyhomes.com

RESTAURANT

CANCHOLA GROUP, INC.
200 N. Country Club Rd.
Tucson, AZ 85716
CEO: Mr. Roger M. Canchola
Tel: (520) 881-3838 Fax: (520) 325-4684
Email: cancholagroup@theriver.com

LOS RANCHOS RESTAURANTS, INC.
Bayside
401 Biscayne Blvd.
Miami, FL 33132
CEO: Mr. Julio Somoza
Tel: (305) 375-8188
Web: www.losranchossteakhouse.com

Cocowalk
3015 Grand Ave. #118
Coconut Grove, FL 33133
CEO: Mr. Julio Somoza
Tel: (305) 461-8222
Web: www.losranchossteakhouse.com

Coral Gables
2728 Ponce De Leon Blvd.
Coral Gables, FL 33134
CEO: Mr. Julio Somoza
Tel: (305) 446-0050
Web: www.losranchossteakhouse.com

Sweetwater
125 SW 107th Ave.
Miami, FL 33174
CEO: Mr. Julio Somoza
Tel: (305) 552-6767 Fax: (305) 551-3900
Web: www.losranchossteakhouse.com

The Falls
8888 SW 136th St.
Miami, FL 33176
CEO: Mr. Julio Somoza
Tel: (305) 238-6867
Web: www.losranchossteakhouse.com

RESTAURANT & FOOD DIST.

NORSAN GROUP
Head Office
P.O. Box 2148
Tucker, GA 30085
CEO: Mr. Norberto Sanchez
Tel: (770) 414-5026 Fax: (770) 414-5839
Email: info@norsangroup.com
Web: www.norsangroup.com
www.fronteramexmexgrill.com

RESTAURANT & FOOD MFG.

EL CHARRO CAFE
311 N. Ct. Ave.
Tucson, AZ 85701
CEO: Mr. Raymon Flores
Tel: (520) 622-1922
Email: catering@elcharrocafe.com
Web: www.elcharrocafe.com

RETAIL

PUENTE CONCESSIONS, INC.
P.O. Box 613136, DFW Airport
Dallas-Forth Worth Airport, TX 75261-3136
CEO: Ms. Gina Puente-Brancato
Tel: (972) 574-4351 Fax: (972) 574-4353
Email: gpuentebrancato@charter.net

RETAIL GASOLINE CENTERS

MID-ATLANTIC PETROLEUM PROPERTIES LLC.
12321 Middlebrook Rd. #110
Germantown, MD 20872-1591
CEO: Mr. Carlos Horcasitas
Tel: (301) 972-4116 Fax: (301) 972-3137

RETAIL HARDWARE & HOUSEWARE

GRACIOUS HOME
East Side Store
1217 & 1220 3rd Ave. at 70th St.
New York, NY 10021
CEO: Mr. Natan Wekselbaum
Tel: (212) 517-6300 Fax: (212) 249-1534
Email: info@gracioushome.com
Web: www.gracioushome.com

West Side Store
1992 Broadway at 67th St.
New York, NY 10023
CEO: Mr. Natan Wekselbaum
Tel: (212) 231-7800 Fax: (212) 875-9976
Email: info@gracioushome.com
Web: www.gracioushome.com

RETAIL PHARMACIES

NAVARRO DISCOUNT PHARMACIES
5959 NW 37th Ave.
Miami, FL 33142
CEO: Mr. Jose F. Navarro
Tel: (305) 633-3000 Fax: (305) 633-7755
Email: info@navarropharmacies.com
Web: www.navarropharmacies.com

RETAILING, SUPERMARKET & CATERING

ECO & SONS, INC.
161 Jefferson St.
Passaic, NJ 07055
CEO: Mr. Rafael E. Cueller
Tel: (973) 614-0052
Email: info@ecoandsons.com
Web: www.ecoandsons.com

ROOFING SERVICES

GARCIA ROOFING, INC.
201 Mount Vernon Ave.
Bakersfield, CA 93307-2741
CEO: Mr. Michael Garcia
Tel: (661) 325-5736 Fax: (661) 325-1226
Email: mgarcia49@hotmail.com
Web: www.garciaroofing.com

THL ENTERPRISES INC.
7371 Rowlett Park Dr.
Tampa, FL 33610
CEO: Mr. Thomas H. Lopez
Tel: (813) 236-7500 Fax: (813) 236-7510
Email: thlroof@earthlink.net

ROOFING & WATERPROOFING SVCS.

CABRAL ROOFING & WATERPROOFING CORPORATION
815 Olympic Blvd.
Montebello, CA 90640
CEO: Mr. Andrew H. Cabral
Tel: (323) 832-9100 Fax: (323) 832-9300

Email: contact@cabralroofing.com
Web: www.cabralroofing.com

RUBBER & PLASTIC PROD. MFG.

EBCO, INC.
1371 Brummel Ave.
Elk Grove, IL 60007
CEO: Mr. Bill Bernardo
Tel: (847) 956-7700 Fax: (847) 364-0364
Email: info@ebco-inc.com
Web: www.ebco-inc.com

RUBBER STAMPS

MARKMASTER, INC.
Head Office
11111 N. 46th St.
Tampa, FL 33617-2009
CEO: Mr. Ronald A. Govin
Tel: (813) 988-6000 Fax: (813) 985-6860
Email: rgovin@mmstamp.com
Web: www.mmstamp.com

SAFETY ENGINEERING & TECH. SERVICES

HERNANDEZ ENGINEERING, INC.
16055 Space Center Blvd. #725
Houston, TX 77062
CEO: Ms. Teresita Z. Hernandez
Tel: (281) 280-5159 Fax: (281) 480-7525
Email: inquire@hernandez-eng.com
Web: www.hernandez-eng.com

SEAFOOD IMPORTING

SURAM TRADING CORPORATION
Head Office
2655 LeJeune Rd. #1006
Coral Gables, FL 33134
CEO: Mr. Guido Adler
Tel: (305) 448-7165 Fax: (305) 445-7185

SECURE COMMUNICATIONS

TALISEN TECHNOLOGIES, INC.
12655 Olive Blvd. #500
St. Louis, MO 63141
CEO: Mr. George Brill
Tel: (314) 317-7700 Fax: (314) 317-7701
Email: info@talisentech.com
Web: www.talisentech.com

SECURITY GUARDS

ASSET PROTECTION & SECURITY SERVICES INC.
5502 Burnham Dr.
Corpus Christi, TX 78413
CEO: Mr. Charles S. Mandel
Tel: (361) 906-1552 Fax: (361) 906-1844
Email: assetmain@aol.com
Web: www.asset-security-pro.com

MONTERREY SECURITY CONSULTANTS, INC.
2232 S. Blue Island Ave.
Chicago, IL 60608
CEO: Mr. Juan Gaytan Jr.
Tel: (773) 843-0434 Fax: (773) 843-0435
Email: general@monterreysecurity.com
Web: www.monterreysecurity.com

SECURITY GUARDS/PRIV. INVESTIGATIONS

ALANTE SECURITY GROUP INC.
86 Garden St.
Westbury, NY 11590
CEO: Mr. Luis A. Lopez
Tel: (516) 997-8118 Fax: (516) 997-8855
Email: alantesecurity@prodigy.net
Web: www.alantesecurity.com

SECURITY & LIFESAFETY INTEGRATION

ACTCOM, INC.
Headquarters
100 Landmark Sq.
Virginia Beach, VA 23452
CEO: Mr. Ray Lorenzo
Tel: (757) 463-2034
(757) 460-2671
(877) 613-3580 Fax: (757) 463-2035
(757) 460-0076
Email: dlorenzo@actcom.org
Web: www.actcom.org

Metro Washington Office
7721 B Fullerton Rd.
Springfield, VA 22153
CEO: Mr. Ray Lorenzo
Tel: (571) 322-3200
(877) 613-3580 Fax: (571) 322-3202
Email: dlorenzo@actcom.org
Web: www.actcom.org

SECURITY MANAGEMENT SERVICES

MVM, INC.
1593 Spring Hill Rd. #700
Vienna, VA 22182
CEO: Dario O. Marquez, Jr.
Tel: (703) 790-3138 Fax: (703) 790-9526
Email: marquezdo@mvminc.com
Web: www.mvminc.com

SHIPPING CONTAINER MFG.

CANO CONTAINER CORPORATION
Corporate Headquarters
2300 N. Raddant Rd. #A
Aurora, IL 60504
CEO: Mr. Juventino Cano
Tel: (630) 585-7500 Fax: (630) 585-7501
Email: info@canocontainer.com
Web: www.canocontainer.com

SOFTWARE FOR HEALTHCARE ORG.

API SOFTWARE, INC.
310 N. Wilson Ave.
Hartford, WI 53027
CEO: Mr. Luis Garcia
Tel: (262) 673-6815 Fax: (262) 673-2650
Email: sales@apisoftwareinc.com
Web: www.api-wi.com

Puerto Rico Office
Medical Ophthalmic Plz. Office 203 Carr #2 Km. 11.9
Bayamon, PR 00959
CEO: Mr. Luis Garcia
Tel: (787) 787-4778 Fax: (787) 269-1214

Email: sales@apisoftwareinc.com
Web: www.api-wi.com

SOUND & LIGHTING EQUIPMENT SALES

TEI ELECTRONICS, INC.
750 W. 18th St.
Hialeah, FL 33010
CEO: Mr. Danilo Alonso
Tel: (305) 887-5197
(800) 327-8811 Fax: (305) 885-4950
Email: info@teilighting.com
Web: www.teilighting.com

SPANISH-LANGUAGE RADIO STATIONS

SPANISH BROADCASTING SYSTEMS, INC.
Corporate Office
2601 S. Bayshore Dr. PH II
Coconut Grove, FL 33133
CEO: Mr. Raul Alarcon Jr.
Tel: (305) 441-6901 Fax: (305) 446-5148
Email: arodriguez@sbsmiami.com
Web: www.spanishbroadcasting.com

SPICES & SEASONING

BADIA SPICES, INC.
P.O. Box 226497
Miami, FL 22172
CEO: Joseph Badia
Tel: (305) 629-8000 Fax: (305) 629-8100
Email: info@badia-spices.com
Web: badia-spices.com

STAFFING CONSTRUCTION JOBS

MA&O, INC.
Corporate Office
P.O. Box 29691
Atlanta, GA 30359
CEO: Miguel Candelaria
Tel: (770) 234-9912 Fax: (770) 234-9752
Email: info@MAOLabor.com
Web: www.maolabor.com

STAFFING & HUMAN RESOURCES

THE SITE GROUP, INC.
Site Personnel Services, Inc.
10979 Reed Hartman Hwy. #1030
Cincinnati, OH 45242
CEO: Mr. David W. Aragon III
Tel: (513) 793-7696 Fax: (513) 793-8027
Email: administrator@thesitegroup.com
Web: www.thesitegroup.com

Site Personnel Services, Inc.
7900 International Dr. #200
Minneapolis, MN 55425
CEO: Mr. David W. Aragon III
Tel: (952) 854-4113 Fax: (952) 854-4672
Email: administrator@thesitegroup.com
Web: www.thesitegroup.com

Site Personnel Services, Inc.
2602 American Dr.
Appleton, WI 54915
CEO: Mr. David W. Aragon III
Tel: (920) 739-6443 Fax: (920) 739-7167
Email: administrator@thesitegroup.com
Web: www.thesitegroup.com

Site Personnel Services, Inc.

2850 Thornhills Ave. #110
Grand Rapids, MI 49546
CEO: Mr. David W. Aragon III
Tel: (616) 949-3387 Fax: (616) 949-8544
Email: administrator@thesitegroup.com
Web: www.thesitegroup.com

Site Personnel Services, Inc.
28 E. Jackson Bldg. #S625, 10th Fl.
Chicago, IL 60604
CEO: Mr. David W. Aragon III
Tel: (312) 922-7574 Fax: (312) 922-7590
Email: administrator@thesitegroup.com
Web: www.thesitegroup.com

Site Personnel Services, Inc.
426 S. Archer Dr.
Pueblo West, CO 81007
CEO: Mr. David W. Aragon III
Tel: (719) 647-0252 Fax:
Email: administrator@thesitegroup.com
Web: www.thesitegroup.com

SITE Personnel Services, Inc./SITE Staffing, Inc./Executive Search/Management Alliance Programs, Inc. Corporate Offices
16550 W. Lisbon Rd.
Menomonee Falls, WI 53051
CEO: Mr. David W. Aragon III
Tel: (262) 783-5181 Fax: (262) 783-7905
Email: administrator@thesitegroup.com
Web: www.thesitegroup.com

Site Staffing, Inc.
816 W. National Ave.
Milwaukee, WI 53204
CEO: Mr. David W. Aragon III
Tel: (414) 383-8084 Fax: (414) 383-8143
Email: administrator@thesitegroup.com
Web: www.thesitegroup.com

Site Staffing, Inc.
10701 W. North Ave. #100
Milwaukee, WI 53226
CEO: Mr. David W. Aragon III
Tel: (414) 479-9023 Fax: (414) 479-1781
Email: administrator@thesitegroup.com
Web: www.thesitegroup.com

Site Staffing, Inc.
2929 W. Villard Ave.
Milwaukee, WI 53208
CEO: Mr. David W. Aragon III
Tel: (414) 438-4650 Fax: (414) 461-5284
Email: administrator@thesitegroup.com

SUPERIOR DESIGN INTERNATIONAL, INC.
Austin Office
11400 Burnet Rd. MD 0071L028
Austin, TX 78758
CEO: Ms. Carmen Castillo
Tel: (512) 823-6328 Fax: (413) 691-5541
Email: information@sdintl.com
Web: www.sdintl.com

Boston Office
18 Commerce Way #1850
Boston, MA 01801
CEO: Ms. Carmen Castillo
Tel: (781) 933-4095 Fax: (781) 933-4407
Email: information@sdintl.com
Web: www.sdintl.com

Chicago Office
1827 Walden Office Sq. #460
Schaumburg, IL 60173
CEO: Ms. Carmen Castillo
Tel: (847) 925-0423 Fax: (847) 925-0422
Email: information@sdintl.com
Web: www.sdintl.com

Cincinnati Office
9075 Centre Pointe Dr. #260
West Chester, OH 45069
CEO: Ms. Carmen Castillo
Tel: (513) 881-6960 Fax: (513) 881-6967
Email: information@sdintl.com

Web: www.sdintl.com
Houston Office
4747 Bellaire Blvd. #150
Bellaire, TX 77401
CEO: Ms. Carmen Castillo
Tel: (713) 660-6033 Fax: (713) 660-7052
Email: information@sdintl.com
Web: www.sdintl.com

New York Office
11 E. 44th St. #1800
New York, NY 10017
CEO: Ms. Carmen Castillo
Tel: (212) 883-0988 Fax: (212) 883-0391
Email: information@sdintl.com
Web: www.sdintl.com

Philadelphia Office
1 Plymouth Meeting #420
Plymouth Meeting, PA 19462-1308
CEO: Ms. Carmen Castillo
Tel: (610) 941-9350 Fax: (610) 941-9361
Email: information@sdintl.com
Web: www.sdintl.com

Phoenix Office
2255 N. 44th St. #170
Phoenix, AZ 85008-3278
CEO: Ms. Carmen Castillo
Tel: (602) 220-0877 Fax: (602) 220-0886
Email: information@sdintl.com
Web: www.sdintl.com

Raleigh Office
1 Copley Pkwy. #220
Morrisville, NC 27560
CEO: Ms. Carmen Castillo
Tel: (919) 380-8188 Fax: (919) 380-7757
Email: information@sdintl.com
Web: www.sdintl.com

San Jose Office
2635 N. 1st St. #114
San Jose, CA 95134
CEO: Ms. Carmen Castillo
Tel: (408) 570-0750 Fax: (408) 570-0711
Email: information@sdintl.com
Web: www.sdintl.com

Santa Monica Office
2800 28th St. #122
Santa Monica, CA 90405
CEO: Ms. Carmen Castillo
Tel: (310) 396-5771 Fax: (310) 396-5774
Email: information@sdintl.com
Web: www.sdintl.com

Seattle Office
22833 Bothell Everett Hwy. #156-2
Bothell, WA 98021
CEO: Ms. Carmen Castillo
Tel: (425) 489-9020 Fax: (425) 489-1989
Email: information@sdintl.com
Web: www.sdintl.com

STAMPING & SPRING MFG.

SOLAR SPRING & WIRE FORMS
345 Criss Cir.
Elk Grove Village, IL 60007-1291
CEO: Mr. Oscar Diaz
Tel: (847) 437-7838 Fax: (847) 437-6468
Email: odiaz@solarspring.com

STEEL FABRICATION & ERECTION

THE IDEAL GROUP, INC.
Headquarters
2525 Clark St.
Detroit, MI 48029
CEO: Mr. Frank Venegas Jr.

Tel: (313) 842-7290 Fax: (313) 842-7860
Email: sgucken@idealsteel.com
Web: www.idealsteel.com

Second Facility
10068 Industrial Dr.
Hamburg, MI 48139
CEO: Mr. Frank Venegas Jr.
Tel: (810) 231-1722 Fax: (810) 231-9568
Email: sgucken@idealsteel.com
Web: www.idealsteel.com

STEEL SALES & SERVICES

THE DIEZ GROUP
Delaco Steel
8111 Tireman
Dearborn, MI 48126
CEO: Mr. Gerald Diez
Tel: (313) 491-1200 Fax: (313) 491-6210
Email: diez@supremegear.com
Web: www.diezgroup.com

Lapeer Metal Stamping Companies, Inc.
930 S. Saginaw St.
Lapeer, MI 48446-2699
CEO: Mr. Gerald Diez, Sr.
Tel: (810) 664-8588 Fax: (810) 664-9810
Email: diez@supremegear.com
Web: www.lapeermetal.com

Supreme Gear Company
19024 Florida
Roseville, MI 48066
CEO: Mr. Gerald Diez
Tel: (586) 775-6325 Fax: (586) 775-1227
Email: diez@supremegear.com
Web: www.supremegear.com

STEEL & SPECIAL ALLOYS DISTRIB.

TUBE AMERICA, INC.
6550 Bingle Rd.
Houston, TX 77092
CEO: Mr. Cosme J. Salazar
Tel: (713) 690-9990 Fax: (713) 690-9991
Email: cosme@tubeamerica.com

STORAGE TANK MFG. & INSTALLATION

SUPERIOR TANK COMPANY, INC.
Houston Branch
4812 Old Richmond Rd.
Rosenberg, TX 77471
CEO: Mr. J.E. Marquez
Tel: (281) 342-0750 Fax: (281) 342-0751
Email: james@superiortank.com
Web: www.superiortank.com

Santa Fe Springs Branch Office
12450 Los Nietos Rd.
Santa Fe Springs, CA 90670
CEO: Mr. J.E. Marquez
Tel: (562) 946-8804 Fax: (562) 941-1722
Email: james@superiortank.com
Web: www.superiortank.com

SUPPLIER OF COLORANTS TO INK INDUSTRY

SPECTRA COLORS CORPORATION
25 Rizzolo Rd.
Kearny, NJ 07032
CEO: Mr. Luis B. Marrero
Tel: (201) 997-0606
(800) 527-8588 Fax: (201) 997-0504

Email: dyes@spectracolors.com
Web: www.spectracolors.com

SURVEYS & PROGRAM EVALUATION

AGUIRRE INTERNATIONAL

Corporate Headquarters
555 Airport Blvd. #400
Burlingame, CA 94010
CEO: Dr. Edward Aguirre
Tel: (650) 373-4900 Fax: (650) 348-0260
Email: aguirre@aiweb.com
Web: www.aguirreinternational.com

Washington, D.C. Office
1156 15th St. #1000 NW
Washington, DC 20005
CEO: Dr. Edward Aguirre
Tel: (202) 263-9260 Fax: (202) 296-6926
Email: aguirre@aintl.com
Web: www.aguirreinternational.com

Workforce Development Group
1156 15th St. NW #1000
Washington, DC 20005
CEO: Dr. Edward Aguirre
Tel: (202) 693-3660 Fax: (202) 296-2519
Email: onet@aintl.com
Web: www.aguirreinternational.com

SYSTEM ENG. & INFO SERVICES

FIORE INDUSTRIES, INC.

5301 Central Ave. #900
Albuquerque, NM 87108
CEO: Mr. Bill M. Miera
Tel: (505) 255-9797 Fax: (505) 255-8886
Email: info@fiore-ind.com
Web: www.fiore-ind.com

SYSTEM ENG., SYSTEM DESIGN & DEVEL.

CSSI, INC.

Corporate Headquarters
400 Virginia Ave. SW #710
Washington, DC 20024
CEO: Ms. Cynthia A. Castillo
Tel: (202) 863-2175 Fax: (202) 863-2398
Email: info@cssiinc.com
Web: www.cssiinc.com

CSSI, Inc. Maryland
21789 North Coral Dr. #2b
Lexington Park, MD 20653
CEO: Ms. Cynthia A. Castillo
Tel: (301) 866-2065 Fax: (301) 866-2067
Email: info@cssiinc.com
Web: www.cssiinc.com

CSSI, Inc. New Jersey
6712 Washington Ave. #106 Washington
Square East
Egg Harbor Twp., NJ 08234
CEO: Ms. Cynthia A. Castillo
Tel: (609) 569-0122 Fax: (609) 407-9356
Email: info@cssiinc.com
Web: www.cssiinc.com

CSSI, Inc. South Carolina
6650 Rivers Ave.
Charleston, SC 29406
CEO: Ms. Cynthia A. Castillo
Tel: (609) 569-0122 Fax: (609) 407-9356
Email: info@cssiinc.com
Web: www.cssiinc.com

TECH. & COMM. SVCS., IT & PR CONSULT.

AUTOMOTIVE SUPPORT GROUP, LLC

Dearborn, MI
22226 Garrison
Dearborn, MI 48124
CEO: Ms. Lizabeth Ardisana
Tel: (313) 565-4700 Fax: (313) 565-4701
Email: info@asgren.com
Web: www.asgren.com

TECH. INTEGRATION & OPERATION PROG. MGMT.

VISIONARY INTEGRATION PROFESSIONAL, INC.

Corporate Headquarters
80 Iron Point Cir. #100
Folsom, CA 95630
CEO: Ms. Jonna Ward
Tel: (916) 985-9625 Fax: (916) 985-9632
Email: info@vipincorp.com
Web: www.vipincorp.com

Denver Region
7524 S. Platteview Dr.
Littleton, CO 80128
CEO: Ms. Jonna Ward
Tel: (303) 973-6661 Fax: (303) 973-6662
Email: info@vipincorp.com
Web: www.vipincorp.com

New York City Region
1 Liberty Plz., 23rd Fl. #2337
New York, NY 10006
CEO: Ms. Jonna Ward
Tel: (212) 201-5422
Email: info@vipincorp.com
Web: www.vipincorp.com

Washington DC Region
1421 Prince St. #230
Alexandria, VA 22314
CEO: Ms. Jonna Ward
Tel: (703) 548-2255 Fax: (703) 548-2275
Email: info@vipincorp.com
Web: www.vipincorp.com

TECH. PROD. SALES

HOLMAN'S, INC.

Corporate Headquarters
6201 Jefferson St. Northeast
Albuquerque, NM 87109
CEO: Mr. A. Tony Trujillo
Tel: (505) 343-0007
(800) 545-0932 Fax: (505) 343-3509
Email: info@holmans.com
Web: www.holmans.com

Tempe Sales Office
1320 S. Priest Dr. #101
Tempe, AZ 85281
CEO: Mr. A. Tony Trujillo
Tel: (480) 967-0032
(800) 545-1062 Fax: (480) 967-8726
Email: az-info@holmans.com
Web: www.holmans.com

TECH./SERVICE

ADVANCIA CORPORATION

Anchorage, AK
801 B Ave. #400
Anchorage, AK 99501
CEO: Mr. Randy Alvarado
Tel: (907) 269-2542 Fax: (907) 269-1349

Email: info@advancia.com
Web: www.advancia.com

Arizona
9435 E. Placita La Rana
Tucson, AZ 85749-9210
CEO: Mr. Randy Alvarado
Tel: (520) 295-6941 Fax: (520) 749-6404
Email: info@advancia.com
Web: www.advancia.com

Corporate Headquarters
655 Research Pkwy., 4th Fl.
Oklahoma City, OK 73104
CEO: Mr. Randy Alvarado
Tel: (405) 996-3000 Fax: (405) 996-3100
Email: info@advancia.com
Web: www.advancia.com

Kansas City, MO
1125 Grand #2010
Kansas City, MO 64106
CEO: Mr. Randy Alvarado
Tel: (816) 480-3480 Fax: (816) 480-3488
Email: info@advancia.com
Web: www.advancia.com

Missouri
881 Historic Rt. 66 #3A
St. Robert, MO 65584
CEO: Mr. Randy Alvarado
Tel: (573) 336-8312 Fax: (573) 336-8314
Email: info@advancia.com
Web: www.advancia.com

Washington D.C.
1501 N. Lee Hwy. #101
Arlington, VA 22209
CEO: Mr. Randy Alvarado
Tel: (703) 243-6067 Fax: (703) 243-4173
Email: info@advancia.com
Web: www.advancia.com

GEMINI ASSOCIATES, INC.

Corporate Office
33 Musick
Irvine, CA 92618
CEO: Mr. Robert L. Manciet
Tel: (949) 830-8858 Fax: (949) 830-0858
Email: sales@federalsales.com
Web: www.federalsales.com

MIRATEK CORPORATION

Headquarters Office
8201 Lockheed #218
El Paso, TX 79925
CEO: Mr. Joe L. Diaz
Tel: (915) 772-2852 Fax: (915) 772-1764
Email: jdiaz@miratekcorporation.com
Web: www.miratekcorporation.com

Kirtland Air Force Base
3710 Trestle Rd.
Kirtland, Air Force Base, NM 87110
CEO: Mr. Jose L. Diaz
Tel: (505) 846-8727
Email: jdiaz@miratekcorporation.com
Web: www.miratekcorporation.com

New Mexico Office
1100 Main St. #14
Las Cruces, NM 88005
CEO: Mr. Jose L. Diaz
Tel: (505) 644-6808 Fax: (505) 373-3050
Email: jdiaz@miratekcorporation.com
Web: www.miratekcorporation.com

San Antonio Office
259 Eland Dr.
San Antonio, TX 78213
CEO: Mr. Jose L. Diaz
Tel: (210) 733-9208 Fax: (210) 734-4739
Email: jdiaz@miratekcorporation.com
Web: www.miratekcorporation.com

Washington D.C. Office
901 6th St. SW #406
Washington, DC 20024
CEO: Mr. Jose L. Diaz
Tel: (202) 484-2429 Fax: (202) 484-2469
Email: jdiaz@miratekcorporation.com
Web: www.miratekcorporation.com

TECH., SOFTWARE SERVICE

GEOLOGICS CORPORATION

Boston Office
100 Cummings Cr. #329A
Beverly, MA 01915
CEO: Mr. Fernando J. Arroyo
Tel: (978) 524-8152 Fax: (978) 524-8153
Email: farroyo@geologics.com
Web: www.geologics.com

Charleston Office
1007 Bankton Dr.
Hanahan, SC 29406-2925
CEO: Mr. Fernando J. Arroyo
Tel: (843) 744-4005 Fax: (843) 744-3005
Email: farroyo@geologics.com
Web: www.geologics.com

Denver Office
5250 E. Arapahoe Rd. #F7-230
Centennial, CO 80122
CEO: Mr. Fernando J. Arroyo
Tel: (303) 795-5842 Fax: (303) 797-8710
Email: farroyo@geologics.com
Web: www.geologics.com

Headquarters/ Geologics Environment/
Systems Engineering/ Networking &
Information Security/ Technical Services
5285 Shawnee Rd. #300
Alexandria, VA 22312
CEO: Mr. Fernando J. Arroyo
Tel: (703) 750-4000 Fax: (703) 750-4010
Email: farroyo@geologics.com
Web: www.geologics.com

Houston Office
1300 Hercules #150
Houston, TX 77058
CEO: Mr. Fernando J. Arroyo
Tel: (281) 480-2560 Fax: (281) 480-8927
Email: farroyo@geologics.com
Web: www.geologics.com

Los Angeles Office
25375 Orchard Village Rd. #102
Valencia, CA 91355
CEO: Mr. Fernando J. Arroyo
Tel: (661) 259-5767 Fax: (661) 255-8084
Email: farroyo@geologics.com
Web: www.geologics.com

TELECOMM. EQUIP.

MAYA TELECOM, INC.

255 Primera Blvd. #100
Lake Mary, FL 32746
CEO: Mr. Reynaldo Rodriguez
Tel: (407) 804-5577 Fax: (407) 804-9128
Email: reynaldor@mayatel.com
Web: www.mayatel.com

TELECOMM.

MCA COMMUNICATIONS, INC.

525 Northville
Houston, TX 77037
CEO: Mr. Richard Cortez
Tel: (281) 591-2434 Fax: (281) 591-6228
Email: mca@mcacom.com
Web: www.mcacom.com

WALKERCOM INC.
Corporate Office
2900 Woodridge #100
Houston, TX 77087
CEO: Mr. Richard Gonzalez
Tel: (800) 683-5326
(713) 880-4411 Fax: (713) 861-4067
Email: richardg@walkercom
Web: www.walkercom.com

TELECOMM. INFRASTRUCTURE

MASTEC, INC.
Corporate Office
800 Douglas Rd., 12th Fl.
Coral Gables, FL 33134
CEO: Mr. Austin Shanfelter
Tel: (305) 599-1800 Fax: (305) 406-1900
Email: services@mastec.com
Web: www.mastec.com

TELECOMM. PRODUCTS MFG. & DISTRIB.

TRINET COMMUNICATIONS, INC.
Chicago Office
5124 N. Pearl
Shiller Park, IL 60176-1051
CEO: Mr. Jon J. Fernandez
Tel: (847) 671-4522 Fax: (847) 671-4534
Email: sales@trinetmail.com
Web: www.trinetcommunications.com

Dallas Facility
1821 Diplomat Dr.
Dallas, TX 75234
CEO: Mr. Jon J. Fernandez
Tel: (972) 852-0538 Fax: (972) 852-0542
Email: sales@trinetmail.com
Web: www.trinetcommunications.com

Main Office
6567 Brisa St.
Livermore, CA 94450
CEO: Mr. Jon J. Fernandez
Tel: (925) 294-1720 Fax: (925) 449-9063
Email: sales@trinetmail.com
Web: www.trinetcommunications.com

TELECOMM. SALES & SVCS.

NEXXTWORKS INC.
Headquarters
30798 US Hwy. 19 North
Palm Harbor, FL 34684
CEO: Mr. Richard A. Cartagena
Tel: (727) 725-0400 Fax: (727) 723-0307
Email: info@nexxtworks.com
Web: www.nexxtworks.com

Northeasr Region
295 E. Swedesford Rd. #266
Wayne, PA 19087
CEO: Mr. Richard A. Cartagena
Tel: (610) 889-1599 Fax: (610) 889-1579
Email: info@nexxtworks.com
Web: www.nexxtworks.com

TELECOMM. SERVICES

SUNSTRAND ELECTRIC COMPANY, INC.
1616 Berkley St.
Elgin, IL 60123
CEO: Mr. Eugene W. Aguirre
Tel: (847) 742-0266 Fax: (847) 742-0268
Email: receptionist@sunstrand.com
Web: www.sunstrand.com

TEMPORARY EMPLOYMENT AGENCY

GONZALES LABOR SYSTEMS, INC.
Arlington Branch Service Center
3008 W. Division St. #D
Arlington, TX 76012
CEO: Mr. Cruz Gonzales
Tel: (817) 261-5005 Fax: (817) 261-0466
Email: info@glstemps.com
Web: www.glstemps.com

Corporate Office
3008 W. Division St. #A
Arlington, TX 76012
CEO: Mr. Cruz Gonzales
Tel: (817) 261-5005 Fax: (817) 261-0466
Email: info@glstemps.com
Web: www.glstemps.com

Dallas Office
1499 Regal Row #309
Dallas, TX 75247
CEO: Mr. Cruz Gonzales
Tel: (214) 638-5601 Fax: (214) 638-1674
Email: info@glstemps.com
Web: www.glstemps.com

Fort Worth Office
1523 Jacksboro Hwy.
Fort Worth, TX 76106
CEO: Mr. Cruz Gonzales
Tel: (817) 626-9880 Fax: (817) 626-9888
Email: info@glstemps.com
Web: www.glstemps.com

Garland Office
1436 Buckingham
Garland, TX 75042
CEO: Mr. Cruz Gonzales
Tel: (972) 205-0909 Fax: (972) 205-0783
Email: info@glstemps.com
Web: www.glstemps.com

THERMOFORMED PLASTIC PACKAGES

LION PLASTICS NORTH INC.
P.O. Box 2397
Clifton, NJ 07015
CEO: Mr. Diego G. De Leon
Tel: (973) 471-2071 Fax: (973) 471-0147
Email: diego@lionplastics.com
Web: www.lionplastics.com

TIRE & TUBE SALES

TIRE GROUP INTERNATIONAL, INC.
6695 NW 36th Ave.
Miami, FL 33147
CEO: Mr. Antonio R. Gonzales
Tel: (305) 696-0096 Fax: (305) 696-5926
Email: tgi@tiregroup.com
Web: www.tiregroup.com

TISSUE PROD. & PAPER BAG MFG.

ROSES SOUTHWEST PAPERS, INC.
1701 2nd St. Southwest
Albuquerque, NM 87102
CEO: Mr. Robert E. Espat
Tel: (505) 842-0134 Fax: (505) 242-0342
Email: rsespat@rosesnm.com
Web: www.rosessouthwest.com

TRAFFIC MGMT. SYST.

F.R. ALEMAN & ASSOCIATES, INC.
Corporate Headquarters
10305 NW 41st St. #200
Miami, FL 33178
CEO: Mr. Frank R. Aleman
Tel: (305) 591-8777 Fax: (305) 599-8749
Email: framiami@fr-aleman.com
Web: www.fr-aleman.com

Jacksonville Office
1279 Kingsley Ave. #111
Orange Park, FL 32073
CEO: Mr. Frank R. Aleman
Tel: (904) 269-3266 Fax: (904) 269-9111
Email: frajax@fr-aleman.com
Web: www.fr-aleman.com

Lake City Office
681 SE Baya Ave.
Lake City, FL 32025
CEO: Mr. Frank R. Aleman
Tel: (386) 719-6955 Fax: (386) 719-9155
Email: fralakecity@fr-aleman.com
Web: www.fr-aleman.com

Lake Worth Office
6178 Wauconda Way West
Lake Worth, FL 33463
CEO: Mr. Frank R. Aleman
Tel: (561) 641-4467 Fax: (561) 641-4467
Email: fralakew@fr-aleman.com
Web: www.fr-aleman.com

Orlando Office
1080 Woodcock Rd. #277
Orlando, FL 32803
CEO: Mr. Frank R. Aleman
Tel: (407) 894-5651 Fax: (407) 894-5255
Email: fraorl@fr-aleman.com
Web: www.fr-aleman.com

Tallahassee Office
1471 Timberlane Rd. #120-7
Tallahassee, FL 32312
CEO: Mr. Frank R. Aleman
Tel: (850) 893-9731 Fax: (850) 893-9732
Email: fratal@fr-aleman.com
Web: www.fr-aleman.com

Tampa Office
3014 US Highway 301N. #300
Tampa, FL 33619
CEO: Mr. Frank R. Aleman
Tel: (813) 621-3533 Fax: (813) 621-7083
Email: fratampa@fr-aleman.com
Web: www.fr-aleman.com

TRANSPORTATION

TRANSPORTATION ENGINEERING, INC.
Head Office
300 Primera Blvd. #200
Lake Mary, FL 32746
CEO: Mr. Andrés E. Núñez, Jr.
Tel: (407) 805-0355 Fax: (407) 805-0227
Email: hr@tei-fl.com
Web: www.tei-fl.com

TRAVEL AGENCY

CAPITOL TRAVEL & TOURS INTERNATIONAL
5420 16th Ave.
Hialeah, FL 33012
CEO: Mr. William Gonzales
Tel: (305) 884-5323
(800) 848-0329 Fax: (305) 827-4527
Email: capitol-travel@msn.com
Web: www.capitol-travel.com

THE ALAMO TRAVEL GROUP
Air National Gurad Way
Bldg. 9 #N105-N106
Tucson, AZ 85706
CEO: Ms. Patricia Pliego Stout
Tel: (520) 889-4966 Fax: (520) 889-4982
Email: pprewitt@alamotravel.com
Web: www.alamotravel.com

Barksdale AFB
460 Billy Mitchell Dr.
Barksdale AFB, LA 71110
CEO: Ms. Patricia Pliego Stout
Tel: (318) 741-3521 Fax: (318) 741-6992
Email: kdake@alamotravel.com
Web: www.alamotravel.com

Corporate Headquarters
9000 Wurzbach Rd.
San Antonio, TX 78240
CEO: Ms. Patricia Pliego Stout
Tel: (210) 593-0084 Fax: (210) 614-2448
Email: laguilera@alamotravel.com
Web: www.alamotravel.com

Holloman AFB
Bldg. 222 #214
Holloman AFB, NM 88330
CEO: Ms. Patricia Pliego Stout
Tel: (505) 479-4860 Fax: (505) 479-4866
Email: bdexter@alamotravel.com
Web: www.alamotravel.com

Lackland AFB
1561 Stewart St. #2 Bldg.5616
Lackland AFB, TX 78236
CEO: Ms. Patricia Pliego Stout
Tel: (210) 677-0400 Fax: (210) 677-0458
Email: tfriesenhahn@alamotravel.com
Web: www.alamotravel.com

Langley AFB
Bldg. 15 #114
Langley AFB, VA 23665
CEO: Ms. Patricia Pliego Stout
Tel: (757) 764-5989 Fax: (757) 766-1891
Email: jscarry@alamotravel.com
Web: www.alamotravel.com

Luke AFB
7383 N. Litchfield Rd., Bldg. 1150 #1122A
Luke AFB, AZ 85309
CEO: Ms. Patricia Pliego Stout
Tel: (623) 935-9514 Fax: (623) 935-9543
Email: nholyoke@alamotravel.com
Web: www.alamotravel.com

New Orleans
433 Gravier St.
New Orleans, LA 70130
CEO: Ms. Patricia Pliego Stout
Tel: (504) 528-9499 Fax: (504) 528-9535
Email: gheaps@alamotravel.com
Web: www.alamotravel.com

Security Hill
469 Moore St. #236, Bldg. 2169
Lackland AFB, TX 78243
CEO: Ms. Patricia Pliego Stout
Tel: (210) 928-2306 Fax: (210) 928-2315
Email: emartinez@alamotravel.com
Web: www.alamotravel.com

Texas A & M University
200 Discovery Dr.
College Station, TX 77845
CEO: Ms. Patricia Pliego Stout
Tel: (800) 633-5943 Fax: (979) 845-6407
Email: karla@fsis.tamu.edu
Web: www.alamotravel.com

Tinker AFB
D St., Bldg. 1 Door 7
Tinker AFB, OK 73145

CEO: Ms. Patricia Pliego Stout
Tel: (405) 739-5057 Fax: (405) 741-1984
Email: cwiegert@alamotravel.com
Web: www.alamotravel.com

University of the Incarnate Word
847 E. Hildebrand
San Antonio, TX 78212
CEO: Ms. Patricia Pliego Stout
Tel: (210) 805-5704 Fax: (210) 821-7129
Email: lbarneybey@alamotravel.com
Web: www.alamotravel.com

Wilford Hall Medical Center
2200 Berquist Dr. #6A65
Lackland AFB, TX 78236
CEO: Ms. Patricia Pliego Stout
Tel: (210) 674-7033 Fax: (210) 674-7053
Email: tfriesenhahn@alamotravel.com
Web: www.alamotravel.com

TRAVEL SERVICES

BUSINESS TRAVEL ADVISORS, INC.
3750 NW 87th Ave. #100
Miami, FL 33178
CEO: Mr. Sergio L. Barrera
Tel: (305) 594-2929
(800) 237-2929 Fax: (305) 593-0473
Email: info@bta-fla.com
Web: www.bta-fl.com

TRAMEX TRAVEL
Frito Lay/Pepsi On-Site
7701 Legacy Dr. MD 1B-153
Plano, TX 75024
CEO: Mr. Juan Portillo
Tel: (972) 334-5055 Fax: (972) 334-5973
Email: claytonking@tramex.com
Web: www.tramex.com

Northwest Hills (Headquarters)
4505 Spicewood Springs Rd. #200
Austin, TX 78759
CEO: Mr. Juan Portillo
Tel: (512) 343-2201
(800) 527-3039 Fax: (512) 343-0022
Email: claytonking@tramex.com
Web: www.tramex.com

Round Rock
2541 S. IH-35 #600
Round Rock, TX 78664
CEO: Mr. Juan Portillo
Tel: (512) 246-2015 Fax: (512) 246-9214
Email: claytonking@tramex.com
Web: www.tramex.com

Tarrytown
2727 Exposition Blvd. #128
Austin, TX 78703
CEO: Mr. Juan Portillo
Tel: (512) 473-8585 Fax: (512) 480-8551
Email: claytonking@tramex.com
Web: www.tramex.com

TRUCKING SERVICES

J. TORRES COMPANY, INC.
5810 S. Union Ave.
Bakersfield, CA 93307
CEO: Mr. Joe Torres, Jr.
Tel: (661) 832-2635 Fax: (661) 832-3980
Email: joe@jtccorp.com
Web: www.jtccorp.com

TRUCKING/ TRANSPORTATION

JESS DIAZ TRUCKING, INC.
P.O. Box 367
La Mirada, CA 90637
CEO: Mr. Dimas Diaz
Tel: (714) 522-4800

UNDERGROUND UTILITIES

VALVERDE CONSTRUCTION, INC.
10936 Shoemaker Ave.
Santa Fe Springs, CA 90670
CEO: Mr. Joe A. Valverde
Tel: (562) 906-1826 Fax: (562) 906-1918
Email: joev@valverdeconst.com
Web: www.valverdeconst.com

USED TRUCKS & EQUIP. SALES

RODY TRUCK CENTER CORPORATION
2479 NW 36th St.
Miami, FL 33142
CEO: Mr. Rodovaldo Gomez
Tel: (305) 638-3583 Fax: (305) 638-0957

UTILITY, COMMERCIAL, RESIDENTIAL TREE SVCS.

ARBOR TREE SURGERY, INC.
Corporate Headquarters
802 Paso Robles St.
Paso Robles, CA 93446
CEO: Mr. Steven G. Alvarez
Tel: (805) 239-1239
(800) 238-9494 Fax: (805) 239-3742
Web: www.arbortree.com

UTILITY COMPANY PRODUCTS MFG.

J&R CONCRETE PRODUCTS, INC.
440 W. Markham St.
Perris, CA 92571
CEO: Mr. Raul E. Ramirez
Tel: (909) 943-5855 Fax: (909) 940-9207
Email: sales@jr-concrete.com
Web: www.jr-concrete.com

VALUE ADDED RESELLER OF DC POWER EQUIP.

GEMINI POWER SYSTEMS, INC.
3985 Gateway Ctr. Blvd. #170
Pinnellas Park, FL 33782
CEO: Mr. Nelson Gonzalez
Tel: (727) 563-9770 Fax: (727) 578-2015
Email: ngonzalz@gps-us.com

VOICE & DATA CABLING SERVICES

SPECTRUM COMMUNICATIONS CABLING SERVICES, INC.
226 N. Lincoln Ave.
Corona, CA 92882
CEO: Mr. Robert Rivera
Tel: (909) 371-0549/(800) 319-8711
Fax: (909) 273-3114

Email: info@spectrumccsi.com
Web: www.spectrumccsi.com

450 California Ave. #434
Bakersfield, CA 93309
CEO: Mr. Robert Rivera
Tel: (800) 319-8711 Fax: (661) 325-9075
Email: info@spectrumccsi.com
Web: www.spectrumccsi.com

Colorado Office
2910 N. powers Blvd. #300
Colorado Springs, CO 80922
CEO: Mr. Robert Rivera
Tel: (719) 472-0433 Fax: (719) 472-0408
Email: info@spectrumccsi.com
Web: www.spectrumccsi.com

WAREHOUSE

PUBLIC LOGISTICS, INC.
3147 Progress Cr.
Mira Loma, CA 91752
CEO: Ms. Anna E. Aguiar
Tel: (909) 360-2450 Fax: (909) 360-2455
Email: info@publicinc.com
Web: www.publiclogistics.com

WASTE REMOVAL

UNITED PUMPING SERVICE, INC.
14000 E. Valley Blvd.
City of Industry, CA 91746
CEO: Mr. Eduardo T. Perry
Tel: (626) 961-9326 Fax: (626) 336-7734
Email: sales@unitedpumping.com
Web: www.unitedpumping.com

WASTE REMOVAL & RECYCLING

GALLEGOS SANITATION INC.
1106 W. Vine Dr.
Fort Collins, CO 80522
CEO: Mr. Gerald Gallegos
Tel: (970) 484-5556 Fax: (970) 484-0662

WATER FILTER & CONDITIONER MFG.

NATIONAL WATER PURIFIERS CORPORATION
1065 E. 14th St.
Hialeah, FL 33010
CEO: Ms. Judith Garcia
Tel: (305) 887-7065 Fax: (305) 887-6209

WHOLESALE

BARTLETT DAIRY, INC.
880 Alabama Ave.
Brooklyn, NY 11207
CEO: Mr. Thomas Malave
Tel: (718) 257-6000 Fax: (718) 257-8132
Email: tmalave@bartlettny.com
Web: www.bartlettny.com

WHOLESALE DISTRIBUTORS OF PET PRODUCTS

ELF CORPORATION
Headquarters
1155 Charles St. #115
Longwood, FL 32750
CEO: Mr. Ernesto Alvarez

Tel: (407) 332-1211
(800) 393-7387 Fax: (407) 332-8368
Email: elfcorp1@earthlink.net
Web: www.elfpetprod.com

WHOLESALE A/C & REFRIG. EQUIPMENT LEASING

REFRICENTER OF MIAMI, INC.
7101 NW 43rd St.
Miami, FL 33166
CEO: Mr. Jose C. Hernandez
Tel: (305) 477-8880 Fax: (305) 599-9323
Email: info@refricenter.net
Web: www.refricenter.net

WHOLESALE DISTRIBUTORS OF PET PRODUCTS

ELF CORPORATION
Satellite
2310 Sister Welcome Rd.
Lake City, FL 32025
CEO: Mr. Ernesto Alvarez
Tel: (800) 544-8470
(904) 755-9848 Fax: (904) 755-9883
Email: elfcorp1@earthlink.net
Web: www.elfpetprod.com

South Florida Warehouse
9014 NW 105th Way
Medley, FL 33178
CEO: Mr. Ernesto Alvarez
Tel: (800) 471-1888 Fax: (305) 887-5053
Email: elfcorp1@earthlink.net
Web: www.elfpetprod.com

WHOLESALE LIVESTOCK

AMETZA, LLC
1701 Bowker Rd.
El Centro, CA 92243
CEO: Mr. Felipe Irigoyen
Tel: (760) 352-5435 Fax: (760) 352-5460
Email: ametza@thegrid.net

WHOLESALE STEEL DISTRIBUTOR

EVERGLADES STEEL CORPORATION/ MEDLEY STEEL SUPPLY
P.O. Box 667510
Miami, FL 33166-7510
CEO: Mr. Orlando A. Gomez
Tel: (305) 591-9460 Fax: (305) 592-1037
Email: info@evergladessteel.com
Web: www.evergladessteel.com

WINDOWS, DOORS, GLASS RAILING MFG.

R.C. ALUMINUM INDUSTRIES, INC.
2805 NW 75th Ave.
Miami, FL 33122
CEO: Mr. Raul Casares
Tel: (305) 592-1515 Fax: (305) 592-2184
Email: rc@rcalum.com
Web: www.rcalum.com

Hispanic Conventions and Events 2005
Convenciones y eventos hispanos 2005

JANUARY

SOCIETY OF HISPANIC PROFESSIONAL ENGINEERS
2005 National Technical & Career Conference
January 5-9/Dallas, TX
Contact: Daun White
Tel: (323) 725-3970 Fax: (323) 725-0316
Email: daun.white@shpe.org
Web: www.shpe.org

MARYLAND HISPANIC CHAMBER OF COMMERCE
Fiesta Anual de Los Reyes Magos
January 6/Baltimore, MD
Contact: Gigi Guzman
Tel: (410) 558-3515 Fax: (410) 558-3513
Email: mdhcc@mdhcc.net
Web: www.mdhcc.net

NATIONAL LATINA BUSINESS WOMEN ASSOCIATION
2005 NLBWA-LA: Building your Business through Smart Networking
January 13/Hollywood, CA
Contact: Emily Robinson
Tel: (310) 699-9296 Fax: (310) 496-2865
Email: info@nlbwa-la.com
Web: www.nlbwa-la.com

CONGRESS OF RACIAL EQUALITY
King Holiday Celebration 2005
January 17/New York, NY
Contact: Ron Innis
Tel: (212) 598-4000 Fax: (212) 598-4141
Email: core@core-online.org
Web: www.core-online.org

US HISPANIC PUBLISHERS FEDERATION, INC.
10th International Hispanic Media Convention
January 17-19/Miami, FL
Contact: Manuel Toro
Tel: (407) 767-0070
Email: linamartinez@ushpf.org
Web: www.ushpf.org

NATIONAL ASSOCIATION FOR BILINGUAL EDUCATION
NABE Conference
January 19-22/San Antonio, TX
Contact: Carmella Baccari
Tel: (202) 898-1829 Fax: (202) 789-2866
Web: www.nabe.org

GREATER CARIBBEAN AMERICAN CHAMBER OF COMMERCE, INC.
11th Anniversary Banquet and Installation of Officers
January 22/Lauderhill, FL
Tel: (954) 730-8885 Fax: (954) 730-8875
Email: galarsvp@gcacc.com
Web: www.gcacc.com

STRATEGIC RESEARCH INSTITUTE (SRI)
11th Annual Marketing to US Hispanics and Latin America Conference
January 24-27/Miami Beach, FL
Contact: Rupa Ranganathan
Tel: (212) 967-0095 Fax: (212) 967-7973
Email: rranganathan@srinstitute.com
Web: www.srinstitute.com

TEXAS ASSOCIATION OF MEXICAN-AMERICAN CHAMBER OF COMMERCE
Legislative Leadership Awards & Gala
January 26/Houston, TX
Contact: Carlos T. Mendoza
Tel: (512) 444-5727 Fax: (512) 444-4929
Email: info@tamacc.org
Web: www.tamacc.org

THE CONFERENCE BOARD
2005 Logistics Conference
January 26-28/Ft. Lauderdale, FL
Contact: Michael Wheeler
Tel: (212) 339-0345 Fax: (212) 836-9740
Web: www.conference-board.org

NATIONAL NEWSPAPER PUBLISHERS ASSOCIATION
Mid-Winter Workshop/Educating and Empowering a Nation
January 26-30/Las Vegas, NV
Contact: Sunny Jills
Tel: (202) 588-8764 Fax: (202) 588-8960
Web: www.nnpa.org

WOW PRODUCTIONS
2005 National Multicultural Conference and Summit
January 27-28/Hollywood, CA
Contact: Wendy Anderson
Tel: (626) 683-8243
Email: wowproductions2@earthlink.net
Web: www.multiculturalsummit.org

THE CENTER FOR BUSINESS INTELLIGENCE
2005 Pharmaceutical Marketing Compliance Congress
January 31-February 1/Washington, DC
Tel: (781) 939-2400 Fax: (781) 939-2490
Email: register@cbinet.com
Web: www.cbinet.com

THE ADVERTISING CLUB, DIVERSITY COMMITTEE
A Showcase of ANA Multicultural Excellence Award Winners Reception
January TBA/New York City, NY
Contact: Kris Earley
Tel: (212) 533-8080 Fax: (212) 533-1929
Email: kris@theadvertisingclub.org
Web: www.theadvertisingclub.org

FEBRUARY

CUBAN AMERICAN NATIONAL COUNCIL
Cuban American Awards
February 4/Washington, DC
Contact: Cristina Santana
Tel: (305) 642-3484 X133
Fax: (305) 642-9122
Email: conference@cnc.org
Web: www.cnc.org

MEXICAN AMERICAN CHAMBER OF COMMERCE
2nd Annual Bilingual College Student Financial Aid Workshop
February 5/Stockton, CA
Contact: Alicia Arong
Tel: (209) 943-6117 Fax: (209) 943-0114
Email: arongal@earthlink.net
Web: www.ssjmacc.org

PUERTO RICAN/HISPANIC CHAMBER OF COMMERCE OF BROWARD COUNTY
5th Annual Anniversary, Gala and Shining Star Awards
February 5/Dania, FL
Contact: Evelyn L. Rios
Tel: (954) 274-4102
Email: prchamberonline@prchamberonline.com
Web: www.prchamberonline.com

NATIONAL LATINO CHILDREN'S INSTITUTE
3rd Bi-Annual National Conference
February 5-8/San Antonio, TX
Contact: Josie Garza
Tel: (210) 228-9997 Fax: (210) 228-9972
Email: nlci@nlci.org
Web: www.nlci.org

AMERICAN ADVERTISING FEDERATION
9th Annual Most Promising Minority Students Program
February 8-10/New York City, NY
Contact: Wally Snyder
Tel: (202) 898-0089 Fax: (202) 898-0159
Email: aaf@aaf.org
Web: www.aaf.org

CUBAN AMERICAN NATIONAL COUNCIL
CANC Conference
February 10/Orlando, FL
Contact: Christina Santana
Tel: (305) 642-3484 Fax: (305) 642-9122
Email: conference@cnc.org
Web: www.cnc.org

PUERTO RICAN/HISPANIC CHAMBER OF COMMERCE OF BROWARD COUNTY
4th Annual Puerto Rican Fiestas Patronales and Business Expo
February 10-13/Dania, FL
Contact: Evelyn L. Rios
Tel: (954) 274-4102
Email: prchamberonline@prchamberonline.com
Web: www.prchamberonline.com

DIVERSIFIED BUSINESS COMMUNICATIONS
Complementary & Alternative Healthcare Expo
February 12-13/New York, NY
Contact: Nancy Hasselback
Tel: (207) 842-5500 Fax: (207) 842-5503
Email: custserv@divcom.com
Web: www.divbusiness.com

AMERICAN COUNCIL ON EDUCATION
87th Annual Meeting
February 12-15/Washington, DC
Contact: Wendy Bresler
Tel: (202) 939-9410 Fax: (202) 833-4730
Email: annualmeeting@ace.nche.edu
Web: www.acenet.edu

NATIONAL MINORITY BUSINESS COUNCIL, INC.
NMBC's 25th Annual Awards Luncheon
February 16/New York, NY
Contact: John F. Robinson
Tel: (212) 997-4753 Fax: (212) 997-5102
Email: nmbc@msn.com
Web: www.nmbc.org

GLOBAL DIVERSITY, INC.
Business Exchange 2005 Tour for Success
February 17/Miami, FL
Tel: (410) 730-6906 Fax: (410) 730-6908
Email: registration@globaldiversitygroup.com
Web: www.mpbnetwork.com

NATIONAL ASSOCIATION OF HISPANIC JOURNALISTS
16th Annual Scholarship Banquet
February 17/New York, NY
Contact: Joe Torres
Tel: (202) 662-7145 Fax: (202) 662-7144
Email: nahj@nahj.org
Web: www.nahj.org

CEN-TEX HISPANIC CHAMBER OF COMMERCE
Hispanic Women's Conference
February 19/Waco, TX
Contact: Joe Rodriguez
Tel: (254) 754-7111 Fax: (254) 754-3456
Email: info@wacohispanicchamber.com
Web: www.wacohispanicchamber.com

THE NATIONAL HISPANIC MEDIA COALITION
8th Annual Impact Awards Gala
February 25/Los Angeles, CA
Contact: Claudia Flores
Tel: (213) 746-6988 Fax: (213) 746-1305
Email: info@nhmc.org
Web: www.nhmc.org

TALLER PUERTORRIQUENO
Arturo A. Schomburg Symposium
February 26/Philadelphia, PA
Contact: Carmen Febo-San Miguel
Tel: (215) 426-3311 Fax: (215) 426-5682
Email: cfebo@tallerpr.org
Web: www.tallerpr.org

NATIONAL HISPANIC BUSINESS ASSOCIATION
Leadership Conference 2005
Feburary 26-28/Washington, DC
Contact: Conrado Castillo
Tel: (512) 495-9511 Fax: (512) 495-9730
Web: www.nhba.org

MARCH

AMERICAN GI FORUM OF THE UNITED STATES
2005 Mid-Year Conference
March 2-5/Del Rio, TX
Contact: Marian Martinez
Tel: (303) 458-1700 Fax: (303) 458-1634
Email: info@agif.us
Web: www.agif.us

ORLANDO REGIONAL CHAMBER OF COMMERCE
Hispanic Summit
March 3-4/Orlando, FL
Contact: Vilma Quintana
Tel: (407) 835-2520
Email: vilma.quintana@orlando.org
Web: www.orlando.org

THE NEW YORK STATE ASSOCIATION FOR BILINGUAL EDUCATION
28th Annual Conference
March 3-6/Rye Brook, NY
Contact: Jean V. Mirvil
Email: jmirvil@nysabe.org
Web: www.nysabe.org

LATIN AMERICAN EDUCATIONAL FOUNDATION
LAEF's Gala 2005
March 5/Denver, CO
Contact: Carmen Mendoza

Tel: (303) 446-0541 Fax: (303) 446-0526
Email: carmen@laef.org
Web: www.laef.org

NATIONAL COUNCIL OF LA RAZA
NCLR Capital Awards
March 8/Washington, DC
Contact: Miguel Munguia
Tel: (202) 785-5384 Fax: (202) 776-1792
Email: mmunguia@nclr.org
Web: www.nclr.org

NATIONAL ASSOCIATION OF HISPANIC PUBLICATIONS
2005 Annual National Convention
March 9-12/Philadelphia, PA
Contact: Joe Carrillo
Tel: (202) 662-7250 Fax: (202) 662-7251
Email: joe@nahp.org
Web: www.nahp.org

UNITED STATES HISPANIC LEADERSHIP INSTITUTE
23rd National Conference of the US Hispanic Leadership Institute
March 10-13/Chicago, IL
Contact: Jessica Lilley
Tel: (312) 427-8683 Fax: (312) 427-5183
Email: ushli@aol.com
Web: www.ushli.com

SAN DIEGO LATINO FILM FESTIVAL
2005 San Diego Latino Film Festival
March 10-20/San Diego, CA
Contact: Ethan van Thillo
Tel: (619) 230-1938 Fax: (619) 230-1937
Email: sdlff@sdlatinofilm.com
Web: www.sdlatinofilm.com

HISPANIC NATIONAL BAR ASSOCIATION
Mid-Year CLE Conference and National Moot Court Competition
March 11-12/Dallas, TX
Contact: Jose Ortiz
Tel: (202) 223-4777 Fax: (202) 223-2324
Web: www.hnba.com

THE NATIONAL LEAGUE OF CITIES-HISPANIC ELECTED LOCAL OFFICIALS
2005 Annual Congressional City Conference
March 11-15/TBA,
Contact: Marsena Mitchell
Tel: (202) 626-3169 Fax: (202) 626-3043
Email: inet@nlc.org
Web: www.nlc.org

ALIANZA DOMINICANA, INC.
Dominican Women's Conference
March 12/New York, NY
Contact: Miriam Mejia
Tel: (212) 740-1960 Fax: (212) 740-1967
Email: mmejia@alianzadom.org
Web: www.alianzadom.org

LEAGUE OF UNITED LATIN AMERICAN CITIZENS
8th Annual Awards Gala
March 14/Washington, DC
Contact: Carlos Zapata
Tel: (202) 833-6130 Fax: (202) 833-6135
Email: czapata@lulac.org
Web: www.lulac.org

CENTER FOR DEMOCRATIC RENEWAL
International Day Against Racism
March 21/Atlanta, GA
Contact: C. Morgan
Tel: (404) 221-0025 Fax: (404) 221-0045
Email: info@thecdr.org
Web: www.thecdr.org

INTERNATIONAL QUALITY & PRODUCT CENTER
8th Annual Website Globalization Conference
March 22-24/San Francisco, CA
Contact: Michelle
Tel: (212) 885-2694

STUDENT NATIONAL MEDICAL ASSOCIATION
40th Annual Medical Education Conference
March 24-27/St. Louis, MO
Contact: Kara L. Odom Black
Tel: (202) 882-2881 Fax: (202) 882-2886
Email: snmamain@msn.com
Web: www.snma.org

U.S.-MEXICO CHAMBER OF COMMERCE
8th Annual U.S.-Mexico Border Conference
March 26/Washington, DC
Contact: Gerardo Funes
Tel: (202) 312-1525 Fax: (202) 312-1530
Email: gerardo@usmcoc.org
Web: www.usmcoc.org

CHICAGO MINORITY BUSINESS DEVELOPMENT COUNCIL
38th Annual Chicago Minority Business Opportunity Fair
March 29-30/Chicago, IL
Contact: Cynthia Jordan
Tel: (312) 755-8880 X19
Fax: (312) 755-8890
Email: cjordan@cmbdc.org
Web: www.cmbdc.org

NATIONAL HISPANIC CORPORATE COUNCIL
Annual Members Meeting
March 29-31/New Orleans, LA
Contact: Helen Trinidad
Tel: (703) 807-5137 Fax: (703) 807-0567
Email: htrinidad@nhcc-hq.org
Web: www.nhcc-hq.org

DIVERSITYBUSINESS.COM
5th National Multicultural Business Conference
March 30-31 & April 1/Mashantucket, CT
Contact: Bill Stokes
Tel: (203) 255-8966 Fax: (203) 255-8501
Email: wstokes@ccaii.com
Web: www.div2000.com

MANA-A NATIONAL LATINA ORGANIZATION
MANA Training Conference, Membership Annual Meeting and Latina Leadership Forum
March 31-April 3/San Antonio, TX
Contact: Alma Morales Riojas
Tel: (202) 833-0060 Fax: (202) 496-0588
Email: hermana2@aol.com
Web: www.hermana.org

LATINO EMPOWERMENT FOUNDATION & CONFERENCE
Imagine 2005 Latino Speaker's Success Forum
March TBA/Los Angeles, CA
Contact: Daniel Gutierrez
Tel: (800) 368-5415 Fax: (714) 844-9416
Email: info@acceptyourgreatness.com
Web: www.latinoempowerment.org

NATIONAL ASSOCIATION OF HISPANIC PUBLIC ADMINISTRATORS
10th Annual Conference
March TBA/Miami, FL
Contact: Maria De La Milera
Tel: (305) 375-5856
Email: info@nahpa.com
Web: www.nahpa.org

APRIL

NATIONAL HISPANIC MEDICAL ASSOCIATION
9th Annual Conference, Medical Practice for the 21st Century: Enhancing Quality Care and Health Literacy
April 1-3/Los Angeles, CA
Contact: Alexandra Jimenez
Tel: (202) 628-5895 Fax: (202) 628-5898
Email: nhma@nhmamd.org
Web: www.nhmamd.org

AMERICAN CANCER SOCIETY
2nd Annual Gala de la Vida
April 2/New York, NY
Contact: Lillibet Arizare
Tel: (212) 237-3854 Fax: (212) 237-3855
Web: www.cancer.org

HISPANIC ASSOCIATION OF COLLEGES AND UNIVERSITIES
HACU Capitol Forum
April 3-5/Washington, DC
Contact: Lilly Cardenas
Tel: (210) 692-3805 Fax: (210) 692-0823
Email: hacu@hacu.net
Web: www.hacu.net

AMERICAN DIABETES ASSOCIATION
9th Annual Rainbow Gala Fighting Diabetes Among Diverse Communities
April 3/Livingston, NJ
Contact: Diane Allen
Tel: (732) 469-7979 Fax: (732) 469-3906
Email: askada@diabetes.org
Web: www.diabetes.org

THE DMA DIRECTO: COUNCIL FOR HISPANIC MARKETING
12th Annual Directo Days Conference
April 4-5/New York, NY
Contact: Amy Maurer
Tel: (212) 768-7277 Fax: (212) 302-6714
Email: customerservice@the-dma.org
Web: www.the-dma.org/conferences

MFM GROUP
3rd Annual Innovations in Hispanic Marketing Conference
April 6-7/Miami, FL
Tel: (866) 636-7350 Fax: (305) 667-7840
Email: conference@mfmgroup.com
Web: www.trademeetings.com

NATIONAL ASSOCIATION OF HISPANIC FEDERAL EXECUTIVES, INC.
Hispanic Federal Executive Summit VII
April 7-8/Orlando, FL
Contact: Manuel Oliverez
Tel: (703) 787-0291 Fax: (703) 787-4675
Email: nahfe@cs.com
Web: www.nahfe.org

GLOBAL SOLUTIONS UNLIMITED
The ABC's of Multi-Cultural Competency
April 7/Fort Lauderdale, FL
Contact: TBA
Tel: (954) 584-1824

HISPANIC CHAMBER OF COMMERCE OF METRO ORLANDO
2005 Hispanic Business Expo
April 8-9/Orlando, FL
Contact: Myriam Cardama
Tel: (407) 428-5870 Fax: (407) 428-5871
Email: info@hispanicchamber.net
Web: www.hispanicchamber.net

YOUTH BUILD USA
Diversity Leadership: Healing and Dealing
April 11-13/Los Angeles, CA
Contact: Michelle Quinn-Davidson
Tel: (617) 741-1256   Fax: (617) 623-4331
Email: mquinn-davidson@youthbuild.org
Web: www.youthbuild.org

ASSOCIATION OF HISPANIC ADVERTISING AGENCIES
18th Semi Annual Conference
April 13-15/San Antonio, TX
Contact: Manuel E. Machado
Tel: (703) 610-9014   Fax: (703) 610-9005
Email: info@ahaa.org
Web: www.ahaa.org

AMERICAN ASSOCIATION FOR AFFIRMATIVE ACTION
31st AAAA Annual Conference
April 13-16/St. Louis, MO
Contact: Laura Garcia Hacek
Tel: (800) 252-8952 X4122   Fax: (703) 435-4390
Email: execdir@affirmativeaction.org
Web: www.affirmativeaction.org

NATIONAL ASSOCIATION OF MINORITY MEDIA EXECUTIVES (NAMME)
NAMME Annual Awards Banquet
April 14/Washington, DC
Contact: Toni F. Laws
Tel: (703) 893-2410   Fax: (703) 893-2414
Email: tlaws@namme.org
Web: www.namme.org

LATIN CHAMBER OF COMMERCE OF USA
XXV Hemispheric Congress of Latin Chambers of Commerce and Industry
April 14-17/Miami, FL
Contact: Waldo Castro Molleda
Tel: (305) 642-3870 x194
Web: www.camacol.org

MINORITIES IN BUSINESS MAGAZINE
Show me the Multicultural Money National Business Conference
April 16/Los Angeles, CA
Contact: Roger
Tel: (323) 933-0945   Fax: (323) 936-0249
Email: mib1@pacbell.net
Web: www.mibmagazine.net

LINKAGE, INC.
6th Annual Summit on Leading Diversity
April 19-21/Atlanta, GA
Contact: James Snow
Tel: (781) 402-5443   Fax: (781) 402-5556
Email: ljsnow@linkage-inc.com
Web: www.linkageinc.com

UNITED STATES HISPANIC CHAMBER OF COMMERCE
Legislative Conference
April 19-21/Washington, DC
Contact: Georgina Salguero
Tel: (202) 842-1212   Fax: (202) 842-3221
Email: ushcc@ushcc.com
Web: www.ushcc.com

MEXICAN AMERICAN OPPORTUNITY FOUNDATION
MAOF National Hispanic Women's Conference
April 20/Los Angeles, CA
Contact: Tatiana Villanueva
Tel: (323) 278-3603   Fax: (323) 890-9637
Email: tvillanueva@maof.org
Web: www.maof.org

THE COMMUNITY CHEST PRODUCTIONS
Minorities in Special Events Conference
April 20-22/Las Vegas, NV
Tel: (310) 330-0540   Fax: (310) 330-0540
Email: info@thecommunitychest.com
Web: www.minoritiesinspecialevents.com

NATIONAL ALLIANCE OF MARKET DEVELOPERS
53rd Annual Conference
April 21-24/Cleveland, OH
Contact: Clyde C. Allen
Tel: (908) 561-4062   Fax: (908) 561-6827
Email: allenpartner@earthlink.net
Web: www.namdntl.org

100 HISPANIC WOMEN, INC.
8th Anniversary Gala Celebration: Leading Latinas Towards Excellence in Leadership
April 21/New York, NY
Contact: Shirley Rodriguez Remeneski
Tel: (212) 239-1430   Fax: (212) 239-1431
Email: feedback@100hispanicwomen.org
Web: www.100hispanicwomen.org

NATIONAL HISPANIC EMPLOYEE ASSOCIATION
Workforce Leadership Summit
April 22-24/Washington, DC
Contact: Raul Araojo
Tel: (925) 939-3925   Fax: (415) 276-9385
Email: mentor@mentores.org
Web: www.mentores.org

FAMILIES FIRST, INC./CAPITAL AREA MOSAIC
Annual Family Forum
April 23/Atlanta, GA
Contact: Pamela Henry
Tel: (404) 853-2800   Fax: (404) 685-0203
Email: cvalley@familiesfirst.org
Web: www.familiesfirst.org

A. MILLER GROUP FOUNDATION & NATIONAL DIVERSITY COUNCIL
Diversity Events Planning: Best Practices for 2005 Seminar
April 25-27/Atlanta, GA
Contact: Allen Miller
Tel: (248) 395-4400   Fax: (248) 395-2850
Email: amillergroup@aol.com

PACIFICAMERICAS CONSULTING GROUP
Festival de la Familia
April 25/Sacramento, CA
Tel: (916) 326-5520
Web: www.pacficamericas.com

IQPC
Multicultural Branding
April 26-28/New York City, NY
Tel: (212) 885-2759
Email: info@iqpc.com
Web: www.iqpc.com

LATIN AMERICAN ASSOCIATION
Latino Summit 2005
April 27/College Park, GA
Contact: Gilda Pedraza
Tel: (404) 638-1800   Fax: (404) 638-1806
Email: gpedraza@latinaamericanassoc.org
Web: www.latinaamericanassoc.org

NATIONAL ASSOCIATION FOR MULTI-ETHNICITY IN COMMUNICATIONS
11th Anniversary Vision Awards
April 29/Beverly Hills, CA
Contact: Kathy Johnson
Tel: (714) 371-4077   Fax: (714) 371-2103
Email: info@namic.com
Web: www.namic.com

CEN-TEX HISPANIC CHAMBER OF COMMERCE
Cinco de Mayo
April 30-May 1/Waco, TX
Contact: Joe Rodriguez
Tel: (254) 754-7111   Fax: (254) 754-3456
Email: info@wacohispanicchamber.com
Web: www.wacohispanicchamber.com

MAY

ALL ACCESS ENTERTAINMENT
Fiesta Broadway
May 1/Los Angeles, CA
Contact: Peter Bellas
Tel: (310) 914-8308   Fax: (310) 914-8313
Email: info@allaccess.la
Web: www.fiestabroadway.la

CONEXION ARGENTINA
Festival Argentino en Miami
May 1/Miami, FL
Contact: Enrique Kogan
Tel: (305) 358-9911
Email: info@conexionargentina.com
Web: www.conexionargentina.com

EL AGUILA
Diversity Career Fair and Expo
May 5/White Plains, NY
Contact: Miguel Blanco
Tel: (914) 686-2598   Fax: (914) 686-2566
Email: aguilabrowser@aol.com
Web: www.elaguilanews.com

NEW YORK UNIVERSITY CENTER FOR MARKETING
Marketing to the New Majority: How to Reach the Multicultural Consumer
May 6-7/New York, NY
Contact: Lisa Skrilloff
Tel: (212) 992-3402   Fax: (212) 992-3650
Email: lisa@multicultral.com
Web: www.multicultural.com

THE FRIENDS OF SWEET AUBURN
Sweet Auburn SpringFest 2005
May 6-8/Atlanta, GA
Contact: Charles E. Johnson
Tel: (404) 886-4469   Fax: (678) 528-4545
Email: friends@sweetauburn.com
Web: www.friendsofsweetauburn.com

LATINAS CONTRA CANCER
Mother's Day Walk Against Cancer, Many Small Steps Making a Big Difference
May 9/San Jose, CA
Contact: Ysabel Duron
Tel: (408) 280-0811   Fax: (408) 280-0833
Email: lcc-ysabel@sbcglobal.net
Web: www.latinascontracancer.org

HISPANIC ASSOCIATION ON CORPORATE RESPONSIBILITY
2005 HACR Symposium
May 9-10/Los Angeles, CA
Contact: Rima Matsumoto
Tel: (202) 835-9672   Fax: (202) 457-0455
Email: symposium@hacr.org
Web: www.hacr.org

UNIVERSITY OF NORTH FLORIDA
Hispanic Professionals Conference
May 11th/Jacksonville, FL
Tel: (904) 620-4211
Web: www.unf.edu

LATINO LITERACY NOW
The Latino Book & Family Festival
May 15-16/San Diego, CA
Contact: Cecilia Amoros
Tel: (760) 434-4484   Fax: (760) 434-7476
Email: cecilia@latinofestivals.com
Web: www.latinofestivals.com

CORNELL'S DIVERSITY MANAGEMENT PROGRAM
Advanced Diversity Strategies
May 16-17/New York, NY
Contact: Christopher J. Metzler
Tel: (212) 340-2852   Fax: (212) 340-2890
Email: cm277@cornell.edu
Web: www.ilr.cornell.edu/mgmtprog/dm/certificates.html

CITYARTS
36th Annual Benefit & Awards Ceremony, Making a Difference through the Arts
May 18/New York, NY
Contact: Tsipi Ben-Haim
Tel: (212) 966-0377   Fax: (212) 966-0551
Email: info@cityarts.org
Web: www.cityarts.org

NATIONAL MULTICULTURAL INSTITUTE (NMCI)
Cultural Liberty: Championing Diversity, Equity and Human Rights
May 19-22/Bethesda, MD
Contact: Melinda Chow
Tel: (202) 483-0700 X232
Fax: (202) 483-5233
Email: nmci@nmci.org
Web: www.nmci.org

LATINA STYLE MAGAZINE
Latina Style Business Series
May 20/Miami, FL
Contact: Joy Hayes
Tel: (202) 955-7930   Fax: (202) 955-7934
Email: joy@latinastyle.com
Web: www.latinastyle.com

HISPANIC ASSOCIATION OF COLLEGES AND UNIVERSITIES
6th International Conference
May 22-24/Santa Fe, NM
Contact: Lilly Cardenas
Tel: (210) 692-3805   Fax: (210) 692-0823
Email: hacu@hacu.net
Web: www.hacu.net

JUNE

NIA ENTERPRISES
2005 Nia Enterprises Leadership Summit Series
June 4/Chicago, IL
Contact: Sheryl Huggins
Tel: (312) 222-0943   Fax: (312) 222-0944
Email: info@niaonline.com
Web: www.niaonline.com

THE LAGRANT FOUNDATION
6th Annual Recognition Reception/Awards Program
June 7/New York, NY
Contact: Kim L. Hunter
Tel: (323) 469-8680   Fax: (323) 469-8683
Email: kimhunter@lagrant.com
Web: www.lagrantfoundation.org

NEW AMERICA ALLIANCE
2005 Spring Conference & 4th Philanthropy Awards
June 9-11/San Diego, CA
Contact: Carmen Ortiz
Tel: (202) 772-4158 Fax: (202) 772-3374
Email: cmcghee@naaonline.org
Web: www.naaonline.org

NATIONAL ASSOCIATION OF HISPANIC JOURNALISTS
23rd Annual NAHJ Convention and Media & Career Expo
June 15-18/Forth Worth, TX
Contact: Joe Torres
Tel: (202) 662-7145 Fax: (202) 662-7144
Email: register@nahj.org
Web: www.nahj.org

NATIONAL HISPANIC CORPORATE COUNCIL & FLORIDA INTERNATIONAL UNIVERSITY CHAPMAN GRADUATE SCHOOL OF BUSINESS
The Future of Hispanic Marketing
June 16-18/Miami, FL
Contact: Ada Lucero
Tel: (703) 807-5137 Fax: (703) 807-0567
Email: alucero@nhcc-hq.org
Web: www.nhcc-hq.org

THE PUERTO RICAN FAMILY INSTITUTE
The Puerto Rican Family Institute Anniversary Gala
June 17/New York City, NY
Contact: Maria Elena Girone
Tel: (212) 924-6320 Fax: (212) 691-5635
Email: comments@prfi.org
Web: www.prfi.org

MODERN FREE AND ACCEPTED MASONS OF THE WORLD, INC.
Supreme Grand Council Session
June 18-25/New Orleans, LA
Contact: Billy Gaddis, Jr.
Tel: (706) 322-3326 Fax: (706) 322-3805
Email: webmaster@modernfree.com
Web: www.modernfree.com

SOCIETY OF HUMAN RESOURCES MANAGEMENT
2005 Annual Conference & Exposition
June 19-22/San Diego, CA
Contact: David B. Hutchins
Tel: (703) 548-3440 Fax: (703) 535-6490
Email: shrm@shrm.org
Web: www.shrm.org

NATIONAL ASSOCIATION OF LATINO ELECTED OFFICIALS
22nd Annual Conference
June 23-25/San Juan, PR
Contact: Luis Lopez
Tel: (213) 747-7606 Fax: (213) 747-7664
Email: llopez@naleo.org
Web: www.naleo.org

CEN-TEX HISPANIC CHAMBER OF COMMERCE
Annual Golf Tournament
June 24/Waco, TX
Contact: Joe Rodriguez
Tel: (254) 754-7111 Fax: (254) 754-3456
Email: info@wacohispanicchamber.com
Web: www.wacohispanicchamber.com

NATIONAL HISPANIC CORPORATE ACHIEVERS
22nd Annual National Awards
June 24/New York, NY
Contact: Daniel Ramos
Tel: (407) 330-9993 Fax: (407) 330-5993

Email: info@hispanicachievers.org
Web: www.hispanicachievers.com

LEAGUE OF UNITED LATIN AMERICAN CITIZENS
76th LULAC National Convention: Emerging Latino Communities, Strengthening America
June 27-July 2/Little Rock, AR
Contact: Carlos Zapata
Tel: (202) 833-6130 Fax: (202) 833-6135
Email: czapata@lulac.org
Web: www.lulac.org

NATIONAL PUERTO RICAN COALITION, INC.
NPRC National Policy Conference
June 29-July 1/San Juan, PR
Contact: Cecilia Shannon
Tel: (202) 223-3915 Fax: (202) 429-2223
Email: nprc@nprcinc.org
Web: www.bateylink.org

BRUNICO COMMUNICATIONS, INC.
Marketing to U.S. Hispanic Youth Conference
June TBA/Los Angeles, CA
Contact: Sonya Roberts
Tel: (416) 408-2300 x536
Web: www.kidscreen.com/hispanic_youth

HISPANIC COUNCIL ON INTERNATIONAL RELATIONS
7th Annual International Leadership Award Gala
June TBA/Washington, DC
Contact: Ruby Marcelo
Tel: (202) 776-1754 Fax: (202) 776-1790
Email: hispaniccouncil@hcir.org
Web: www.hcir.org

JULY

ASPIRA NATIONAL ASSOCIATION
ASPIRA's Youth Leadership Conference
July 8-11/Ellenville, NY
Contact: Carmen Nazario
Tel: (973) 484-7554 Fax: (973) 484-0184
Email: ctorres@nj.aspira.org
Web: www.aspira.org

CONFERENCE OF MINORITY TRANSPORTATION OFFICIALS
2005 National Meeting & Training Conference
July 9-13/Atlanta, GA
Contact: Julie A. Cunningham
Tel: (202) 530-0551 Fax: (202) 530-0617
Email: jcunningham@comto.org
Web: www.comto.org

NATIONAL COALITION AGAINST DOMESTIC VIOLENCE (NCADV)
NCADV National Conference
July 11-14/Denver, CO
Tel: (303) 839-1852 Fax: (303) 831-9251
Email: mainoffice@ncadv.org
Web: www.ncadv.org

NATIONAL COUNCIL OF LA RAZA
NCLR Annual Conference
July 16-19/Philadelphia, PA
Contact: Janet Murguia
Tel: (202) 785-1670 Fax: (202) 776-1792
Web: www.nclr.org

NATIONAL HISPANIC INSTITUTE
Lorenzo de Zavala Youth Legislative Session
July 17-24/Texas, TX
Contact: Ernesto Nieto
Tel: (512) 357-6137 Fax: (512) 357-2206

Email: info@nhimail.com
Web: www.nhi-net.org

NATIONAL ASSOCIATION OF HISPANIC NURSES
30th Annual Conference
July 20-22/Orlando, FL
Tel: (202) 387-2477 Fax: (202) 483-7183
Email: info@thehispanicnurses.org
Web: www.thehispanicnurses.org

MANA-A NATIONAL LATINA ORGANIZATION
Hermanitas Summer Program
July 21-24/Crystal City, VA
Contact: Alma Morales Riojas
Tel: (202) 833-0060 Fax: (202) 496-0588
Email: hermana2@aol.com
Web: www.hermana.org

ASSOCIATION OF PERSONS IN SUPPORTED EMPLOYMENT
16th Annual APSE Conference
July 24-27/Mobile, AL
Contact: Bob Niemiec
Tel: (804) 278-9187 Fax: (804) 278-9377
Email: apse@apse.org
Web: www.apse.org

TEXAS ASSOCIATION OF MEXICAN-AMERICAN CHAMBER OF COMMERCE
30th Annual Convention and Business Expo
July 27-30/Houston, TX
Contact: Carlos T. Mendoza
Tel: (512) 444-5727 Fax: (512) 444-4929
Email: info@tamacc.org
Web: www.tamacc.org

CUBAN AMERICAN NATIONAL FOUNDATION
CANF Annual Meeting
July TBA/Miami, FL
Contact: Alfredo Mesa
Tel: (305) 592-7768 Fax: (305) 592-7889
Email: hq@canf.org
Web: www.canf.org

AUGUST

ASSOCIATION OF LATINO PROFESSIONALS IN FINANCE AND ACCOUNTING
ALPFA National Convention
August 6-10/Miami, FL
Contact: Shanina Rivera
Tel: (213) 243-0004 Fax: (213) 243-0006
Email: convention@national.alpfa.org
Web: www.alpfa.org

FEDERATION OF SOUTHERN COOPERATIVES LAND ASSISTANCE FUND
38th Annual Meeting
August 19-20/Epes, AL
Contact: Ralph Paige
Tel: (404) 765-0991 Fax: (404) 765-9178
Email: fsc@mindspring.com
Web: www.federationsoutherncoop.com

LABOR COUNCIL FOR LATIN AMERICAN ADVANCEMENT
4th Annual National Latino Leadership Seminar
August 25-29/Albuquerque, NM
Contact: Karinne Hernandez
Tel: (202) 347-4223 Fax: (202) 347-5095
Email: headquarters@lclaa.org
Web: www.lclaa.org

SEPTEMBER

THE CONGRESSIONAL HISPANIC CAUCUS INSTITUTE
CHCI Conference
September 12-13/Washington, DC
Contact: Fatima Cuevas
Tel: (202) 543-1771 Fax: (202) 546-2143
Email: fcuevas@chci.org
Web: www.chci.org

THE CONGRESSIONAL HISPANIC CAUCUS INSTITUTE
28th Annual Gala
September 14/Washington, DC
Contact: Fatima Cuevas
Tel: (202) 543-1771 Fax: (202) 546-2143
Email: fcuevas@chci.org
Web: www.chci.org

U.S. HISPANIC CHAMBER OF COMMERCE
26th Annual USHCC Convention and Business Expo
September 14-17/Milwaukee, WI
Contact: Connie Valiente
Tel: (202) 842-1212 Fax: (202) 842-3221
Email: ushcc@ushcc.com
Web: www.ushcc.com

HISPANIC WOMEN'S CORPORATION
20th National Hispanic Women's Conference
September 15-16/Phoenix, AZ
Contact: Nellie Moreno
Tel: (602) 954-7995 Fax: (602) 954-7563
Web: www.hispanicwomen.org

BERT CORONA LEADERSHIP INSTITUTE
2nd Annual Migrant & Immigrant Youth Conference
September 19-22/Washington, DC
Contact: Wenndy Carrasco
Tel: (202) 723-7241 Fax: (202) 723-7246
Email: info@bcli.info
Web: www.bcli.info

LATINO BEHAVIORAL HEALTH INSTITUTE
2005 Annual Conference
September 21-23/Universal City, CA
Contact: Ambrose Rodriguez
Tel: (213) 738-2882 Fax: (213) 384-0729
Email: info@lbhi.org
Web: www.lbhi.org

INTERNATIONAL ECONOMIC DEVELOPMENT COUNCIL
2005 Annual Conference
September 25-28/Chicago, IL
Contact: Jeff Finkle
Tel: (202) 223-7800 Fax: (202) 223-4745
Email: jfinkle@iedconline.org
Web: www.iedconline.org

NATIONAL SOCIETY OF HISPANIC MBAS
16th Annual Conference & Career Expo
September 29-October 1/Anaheim, CA
Contact: Ana Herrera-Malone
Tel: (214) 596-9338 X226
Fax: (214) 596-9325
Email: aherrera@nshmba.org
Web: www.nshmba.org

LATIN BUSINESS ASSOCIATION
2005 Latin Business Expo
September 29-30/Los Angeles, CA
Contact: Martha Montoya
Tel: (323) 721-4000 Fax: (213) 628-8519
Email: mmontoya@lbausa.com
Web: www.lbausa.com

ABC RADIO NETWORKS & HEALTH AND HUMAN SERVICES
Take a Loved One to the Doctor Day
September TBA/Nationwide,
Tel: (800) 444-6472
Web: www.omhrc.gov

HISPANIC HERITAGE AWARDS FOUNDATION
2005 Hispanic Heritage Awards Ceremony
September TBA/Washington, DC
Contact: Jose Antonio Tijerino
Tel: (202) 861-9797 Fax: (202) 861-9799
Email: contact@hispanicheritageawards.org
Web: www.hispanicheritageawards.org

THE UNIVERSITY OF MEDICINE & DENTISTRY OF NEW JERSEY
Conference on Culturally Competent Care: A Mosaic for the New Millennium
September TBA/Philadelphia, PA
Contact: Barbara Hurley
Tel: (973) 972-3474 Fax: (973) 972-6196
Email: preislro@umdnj.edu
Web: www.umdnj.edu

OCTOBER

LATINO AND PUERTO RICAN AFFAIRS COMISSION
7th Annual Gala Awards Banquet
October 2/Uncasville, CT
Contact: Lucy Goicoechea-Hernandez
Tel: (860) 240-8330 Fax: (860) 240-0315
Web: www.cga.state.ct.us/lprac

LATIN AMERICAN COALITION
Annual Latin American Festival
October 3-9/Charlotte, NC
Contact: Angeles Ortega
Tel: (704) 531-3848 Fax: (704) 531-3850
Email: info@latinamericancoalition.org
Web: www.latinamericancoalition.org

DIALOGUE ON DIVERSITY
10th Annual Dialogue on Diversity Awards
October 6/Washington, DC
Contact: Cristina Caballero
Tel: (703) 631-0650 Fax: (703) 631-0617
Email: dialog.div@prodigy.net
Web: www.dialogueondiversity.org

HISPANIC SCHOLARSHIP FUND
2005 HSF Alumni Hall of Fame
October 6/Washington, DC
Contact: Chris Padula
Tel: (415) 808-2317 Fax: (415) 808-2302
Email: info@hsf.net
Web: www.hsf.net

HISPANIC COMMITTEE OF VIRGINIA
2005 HCV Gala & Fundraising
October 8/McLean, VA
Contact: Julie Rosenberg
Tel: (703) 671-5666 Fax: (703) 671-2325
Web: www.hispaniccommitteeofvirginia.org

AGUILAR PRODUCTIONS, INC.
2nd Annual Latino Family Festival & Mktg. Expo
October 9/St. Paul, MN
Contact: Richard J. Aguilar
Tel: (651) 665-0633 Fax: (651) 665-0129
Email: aguilarproductions@msn.com
Web: www.aguilarproductions.org

NATIONAL BANKERS ASSOCIATION
2005 Annual Conference
October 11-14/Los Angeles, CA
Contact: Evonne Holliday

Tel: (202) 588-5432 Fax: (202) 588-5443
Email: eholliday@nationalbankers.org
Web: www.nationalbankers.org

MEXICAN AMERICAN CULTURAL CENTER
National Publishers, Producers to Discuss Future Needs of Hispanic Catholics
October 12-14/San Antonio, TX
Contact: Sr. Toby Lardie
Tel: (210) 732-2156 Fax: (210) 732-9072
Email: tlardie@maccsa.org
Web: www.maccsa.org

NATIONAL ASSOCIATION OF HISPANIC REAL ESTATE PROFESSIONALS
2005 Hispanic Marketing Conference and Expo
October 14-17/New York City, NY
Contact: Elizabeth Lopez
Tel: (800) 964-5373 Fax: (619) 297-3229
Email: membership@nahrep.org
Web: www.nahrep.org

HISPANIC ASSOCIATION OF COLLEGES AND UNIVERSITIES
19th Annual Conference
October 15-18/Phoenix, AZ
Contact: Lilly Cardenas
Tel: (210) 692-3805 Fax: (210) 692-0823
Email: hacu@hacu.net
Web: www.hacu.net

HISPANIC ASSOCIATION OF COLLEGES AND UNIVERSITIES
HACU 19th Annual Conference
October 15-18/Phoenix, AZ
Contact: Lilly Cardenas
Tel: (210) 692-3805 Fax: (210) 692-0823
Email: hacu@hacu.net
Web: www.hacu.net

NATIONAL MINORITY SUPPLIER DEVELOPMENT COUNCIL, INC.
NMSDC Conference
October 23-26/Dallas, TX
Contact: Maureen Viaova
Tel: (212) 944-2430 Fax: (212) 719-9611
Web: www.nmsdcus.org

PUERTO RICAN LEGAL DEFENSE AND EDUCATION FUND
32nd Anniversary Banquet
October 24/New York, NY
Contact: Cesar a. Perales
Tel: (212) 219-3360 Fax: (212) 431-4276
Email: info@prldef.org
Web: www.prldef.org

CEN-TEX HISPANIC CHAMBER OF COMMERCE
Annual Banquet
October 27/Waco, TX
Contact: Joe Rodriguez
Tel: (254) 754-7111 Fax: (254) 754-3456
Email: info@wacohispanicchamber.com
Web: www.wacohispanicchamber.com

UNIVERSITY OF NORTH CAROLINA MATHEMATICS AND SCIENCE EDUCATION NETWORK
2005 Pre-College Leadership Retreat
October 29-30/Reidsville, NC
Contact: Verna L. Holoman
Tel: (919) 966-3256 Fax: (919) 962-1316
Email: holomanv@northcarolina.edu
Web: www.unc.edu/depts/msen

CALIFORNIA CHICANO NEWS MEDIA ASSOCIATION
2005 Annual Journalism Opportunities Conference
October TBA/Los Angeles, CA
Contact: Efrain Hernandez, Jr.

Tel: (213) 743-4960 Fax: (213) 743-4989
Email: ccnmainfo@ccnma.org
Web: www.ccnma.org

NOVEMBER

SOCIETY OF MEXICAN AMERICAN ENGINEERS AND SCIENTISTS
31st Annual International Symposium and Career Fair
November 1-6/San Jose, CA
Contact: Mark Perez
Tel: (281) 557-3677 Fax: (281) 557-3757
Email: symposium_2005@maes-bayarea.org
Web: www.maes-natl.org

ASSOCIATION OF NATIONAL ADVERTISERS
Multicultural Marketing Conference
November 6-8/South Beach, FL
Contact: Patricia Hanlon
Tel: (212) 697-5950 Fax: (212) 661-8057
Email: phanlon@ana.net
Web: www.ana.net

HISPANIC AMERICAN POLICE COMMAND OFFICERS ASSOCIATION
32nd National Training Conference
November 7-11/Las Vegas, NV
Contact: Jose Acosta
Tel: (703) 534-2895 Fax: (703) 534-2896
Email: info@hapcoa.org
Web: www.hapcoa.com

CHILDREN'S DEFENSE FUND
30th Anniversary Gala
November 11/New York, NY
Contact: David W. Hornbeck
Tel: (202) 628-8787 Fax: (202) 662-3510
Email: cdfinfo@childrensdefense.org
Web: www.childrensdefense.org

CONEXION ARGENTINA
II Rock en Miami
November 13/Miami, FL
Contact: Enrique Kogan
Tel: (305) 358-9911
Email: info@conexionargentina.com
Web: www.conexionargentina.com

DIVERSITY BEST PRACTICES
2005 Diversity and Women Summit & Gala
November 16-17/Washington, DC
Contact: Edie Fraser
Tel: (202) 466-8209 Fax: (202) 833-1808
Email: inquire@tpag.com
Web: www.diversitybestpractices.com

MINORITY CORPORATE COUNSEL ASSOCIATION (MCCA)
Creating Pathways to Diversity Conference
November 2/New York City, NY
Contact: Shawn Boynes
Tel: (202) 371-5909 Fax: (202) 216-9040
Email: info@mcca.com
Web: www.mcca.com

AMERICAN ANTHROPOLOGICAL ASSOCIATION
104th Annual Meeting
November 30-December 4/Washington, DC
Contact: Khara Minter
Tel: (703) 528-1902 Fax: (703) 528-3546
Web: www.aaanet.org

MEXICAN AMERICAN LEGAL DEFENSE AND EDUCATIONAL FUND
30th Anniversary Awards Gala
November TBA/Los Angeles, CA
Contact: Ray Ramirez

Tel: (213) 629-2512
Web: www.maldef.org

NATIONAL HISPANA LEADERSHIP INSTITUTE
2005 Leadership Training & Mujer Awards Gala
November TBA
Contact: Marisa Rivera-Albert
Tel: (703) 527-6007 Fax: (703) 527-6009
Email: nhli@aol.com
Web: www.nhli.org

DECEMBER

NATIONAL ORGANIZATION FOR THE ADVANCEMENT OF HISPANICS
20th Annual Membership Meeting & Awards Gala
December TBA/Fredericksburg, VA
Contact: Rosa Holseberg
Tel: (540) 372-3437
Email: noah-va@noah-va.org
Web: www.noah-va.org

TBA

HISPANIC BUSINESS MAGAZINE
3rd Annual Woman of the Year Awards Reception
Spring, 2005
Contact: Jesus Chavarria
Tel: (805) 964-4554 Fax: (805) 964-5539
Email: events@hbinc.com
Web: www.hispanicbusiness.com

MFM TRADE MEETINGS
2005 Hispanic Marketing Conference
Spring, 2005
Contact: Francois Fournier
Tel: (866) 636-7350 Fax: (305) 667-7840
Email: conference@mfmgroup.com
Web: www.trademeetings.com

MINORITY BUSINESS DEVELOPMENT AGENCY
National MED Week Conference
TBA/Washington DC
Contact: Alfonso Jackson
Tel: (215) 861-3597 Fax: (215) 861-3595
Email: help@mbda.gov
Web: www.mbda.gov

NATIONAL MEDICAL ASSOCIATION
2005 Annual Convention and Scientific Assembly
TBA/New York, NY
Contact: Kimberly Taylor
Tel: (202) 347-1895 Fax: (202) 898-2510
Web: www.nmanet.org

NATIONAL PAN-HELLENIC COUNCIL, INC.
NPHC Convention
TBA/Chicago, IL
Contact: Virginia LeBlanc
Tel: (812) 855-8820 Fax: (812) 856-5477
Email: execdirector@nphchq.org
Web: www.nphchq.org

Readership Survey
Encuesta entre nuestros lectores

TIYM Publishing Co., Inc.
6718 Whittier Ave., #130
McLean, VA 22101
Tel: (703) 734-1632
Fax: (703) 356-0787
E-mail: tiym@tiym.com

By completing this survey, you will automatically receive a free copy of the 2006/2007 YEARBOOK.

Name: ____

☐ Male ☐ Female

DOB: ____

Address: ____

City, State, Zip: _______________________________________

Phone (optional): ______________________________________

E-mail (optional): ______________________________________

Profession/Occupation: _________________________________

Salary (approximately): ☐ Under 24,000 ☐ 25-40,000 ☐ 41-55,000
        ☐ 56-75,000 ☐ 76-100,000 ☐ over 100,000

Educational Attainment: ☐ High School ☐ Undergraduate
        ☐ Graduate Degree ☐ Post-Graduate Degree
        ☐ Other

Languages: ____

I utilize the Yearbook to ________________________________

I think the Yearbook should include more information about ______________________
____

I learned about the Yearbook through:

☐ Library ☐ Bookstore ☐ Internet ☐ Friend ☐ Employer ☐ Conference/Convention
☐ Other ____

Please feel free to provide additional comments in the space below:
____
____
____

Thank you for your valuable feedback. Your participation allows us to continue improving the premier national reference guide for and about Hispanic Americans, the ANUARIO HISPANO-HISPANIC YEARBOOK.

Information Update
Actualice la información

TIYM Publishing Co., Inc.
6718 Whittier Ave., #130
McLean, VA 22101
Tel: (703) 734-1632
Fax: (703) 356-0787
E-mail: tiym@tiym.com

If your organization, agency, or publication has made changes during the past year, or if you know of one that does not appear within this edition, please take a few moments to let us know by filling out the form below. Fax to **(703) 356-0787**, or mail this form. Don't forget to include the correct postage. You may also e-mail the updated information to **tiym@tiym.com**. We appreciate your efforts in helping us keep the **ANUARIO HISPANO-HISPANIC YEARBOOK** as up-to-date and accurate as possible.

Please indicate listing preference:

- ☐ Career Opportunities for Hispanics: ☐ Federal/State ☐ Private Sector
- ☐ Minority Business Opportunities
- ☐ Institution Offering Scholastic Financial Aid
- ☐ Hispanic Company
- ☐ Hispanic Organization
- ☐ Hispanic Publication
- ☐ Hispanic Radio Station
- ☐ Hispanic TV Station
- ☐ Other

Agency/ Company/ Organization Name: _____________________________

Date Founded: ____________

If it is a ☐ Branch or ☐ Affiliate of a larger organization, What is the name of that organization?________________

Address: _____________________________

City: _______________ State: _________ Zip Code: _____________

Telephone 1: _______________ Telephone 2: _______________ Fax: _______________

E-mail: _______________ Web: _______________

Name of the Principal Contact: _______________

Title of the Principal Contact: _______________

Chief Purpose of the Organization (☐ attached is a separate sheet with a detailed description, or organization brochure): _______________

Publication/ Station Name: _______________

Circulation: _______________ Verified: _______________

No. of Members: _______ Most Important Meeting: _______________ Date Held: _______________

How often is the Publication Produced:

Language: ☐ Spanish ☐ English ☐ Other: _______________

Other Specifications: _______________

Thank you for helping us keep the **ANUARIO HISPANO-HISPANIC YEARBOOK** up-to-date.

A MESSAGE FROM THE COMMANDANT OF THE MARINE CORPS

The Marine Corps is proud to be a part of the 19th edition of the Hispanic Yearbook. The efforts by TIYM Publishing Company to highlight the accomplishments of Hispanic Americans continue to raise the consciousness of our diverse society.

The most fundamental functions of the Marine Corps are to make Marines and win battles. To this end, we must rely on the will and talents of highly skilled men and women from varied backgrounds and experiences.

Hispanic Marines have a long and distinguished legacy of contributing to the Corps; from Private France Silva, the first Hispanic Marine to earn the Medal of Honor, to Brigadier General Joseph Medina, the first Marine to command a Naval Expeditionary Strike Group. Marines of Hispanic descent continue to exemplify and embody the ideals that make the Corps great.

Congratulations to the leadership of TIYM Publishing Company for their initiative and vision. The Hispanic Yearbook serves as an outstanding guide that recognizes and celebrates the accomplishments of all Hispanics.

Best wishes for continued success.

Semper Fidelis,

M. W. Hagee
General, U.S. Marine Corps

The call "Send in the Marines!" has been sounded over 200 times since the end of World War II — an average of once every 90 days. Our nation's leaders have great confidence in the Marine Corps' ability to succeed anytime, anywhere, and in any situation. The warfighting excellence and warrior culture displayed by today's Marine Corps is part of a legacy that extends back 229 years.

United States Marines have defended and fought for the American people since before the Continental Congress approved the Declaration of Independence. Congress authorized the formation of two battalions of Marines on November 10, 1775 - the official birth date of the Marine Corps.

The foresight of Congress to mandate the existence of an always ready, combined–arms expeditionary force seems particularly discerning in light of the current Global War on Terrorism.

The ongoing Global War on Terrorism is different than any war America has ever fought, and the stakes are high. In this new kind of conflict our military must be responsive, agile, decisive and expeditionary in order to quickly respond to crises and conflict when needed.

Every Marine and Marine unit is trained and ready to rapidly task-organize and deploy from the United States or while stationed abroad. When crises erupt anywhere in the world, the nation may call upon the Marine Corps to rapidly carry out the Nation's foreign policy and security objectives. Throughout our history, the Marine Corps has been the force most ready when the nation is least ready.

Marines are warriors. We are comprised of smart, tough, highly adaptable men and women who serve as the nation's force-in-readiness. Ours is a smaller, more dynamic force than any other in the American arsenal, and the only forward-deployed force designed for expeditionary operations by air, land, or sea. It is our size and expertise that allow us to move faster and adapt to rapidly changing situations. Working to overcome disadvantage and turn conflict into victory, we accomplish great things, and we do so as a team.

While innovations and new technology are critical for improving readiness and combat and support capabilities, the Marine Corps never underestimates the importance and value of the individual Marine. We recognize that the individual Marine, with a diverse range of experiences and traditions, is the strength of our Corps.

Everyone who joins the Marine Corps has chosen an extremely challenging route. Marines – officer and enlisted – rise to challenges, becoming more innovative and creative when faced with problems. Each Marine is encouraged to maximize leadership potential through practice and evaluation, leading to better decisions in real-world situations.

The common denominator is leadership. Marines are required to be leaders and advance based on their potential leadership qualities. Our training is tough. It has to be as Marines take on responsibility well beyond their years.

As we move further into the 21st century, we face a rapidly changing world with complex situations. Our focus must be on training people to make sound decisions under rapidly changing conditions. The Marine Corps must be prepared for what may be called a "three-block war." On one block we may deliver humanitarian assistance to help people survive. Moments later, on the next block, we may be called upon to take a harder line as a peacekeeping force. Finally, if hostilities do erupt, we must be able to win mid-intensity battles on a third block. To effectively make the right decision for the situations we face on each block requires a sharp and agile mind, and the ability to take charge.

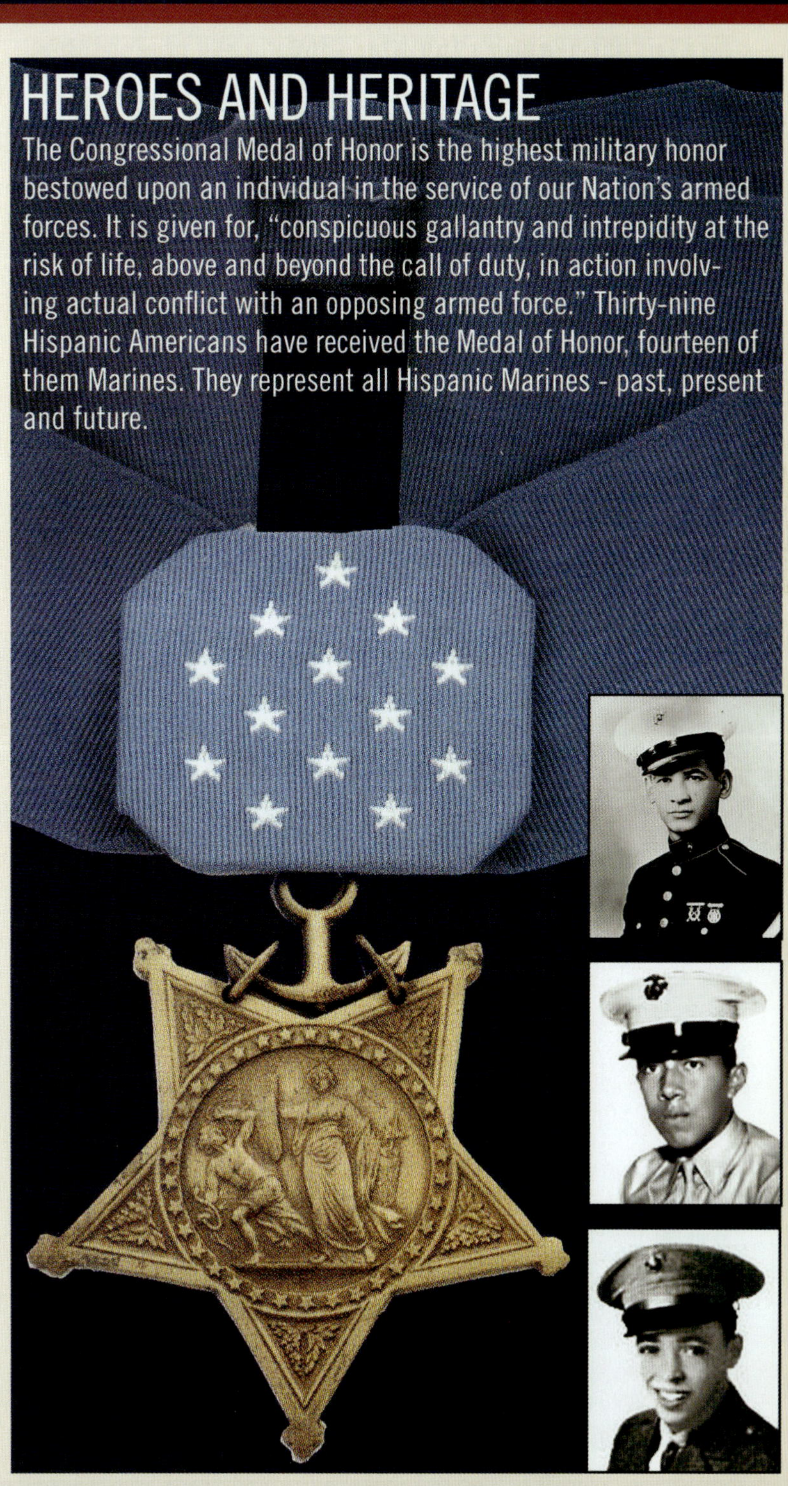

HEROES AND HERITAGE

The Congressional Medal of Honor is the highest military honor bestowed upon an individual in the service of our Nation's armed forces. It is given for, "conspicuous gallantry and intrepidity at the risk of life, above and beyond the call of duty, in action involving actual conflict with an opposing armed force." Thirty-nine Hispanic Americans have received the Medal of Honor, fourteen of them Marines. They represent all Hispanic Marines - past, present and future.

FORGING TODAY'S MARINES...

STAFF SERGEANT DANIEL V. VELIS JR.
RECRUITING STATION SALT LAKE CITY

Staff Sergeant Daniel Velis is a Marine recruiter in Salt Lake City. His mission is of the upmost importance, as he and more than 2,600 other recruiters enlist nearly 40,000 recruits each year to maintain the Corps' readiness. Velis' performance in another mission has brought him attention and honors. While serving with 3rd Battalion, 5th Marine Regiment in Iraq, Velis courageously led his squad, overcoming an ambush and fearlessly put himself in harms way to pull a wounded Marine to safety. For his actions, Velis received the Bronze Star with Valor.

MAJOR MARIA MARTE
II MARINE EXPEDITIONARY FORCE

In 2004, Major Maria Marte deployed to Afghanistan as part of the 22nd Marine Expeditionary Unit. Marte, an engineering officer, helped overcome cultural differences and aided in the effort to rebuild the war torn nation. While there, the unit maintained security and stability in the region.

CORPORAL JOSEPH B. PEREZ
3RD BATTALION, 5TH MARINE REGIMENT

Corporal Joseph Perez received the Marine Corps' second highest award, the Navy Cross, for extraordinary heroism. On April 4, 2003, in Iraq, Perez was the point man of his platoon on the forward edge of the battlefront. Encountering heavy fire, Perez led a charge against an entrenched enemy. Twice wounded, Perez took out an enemy bunker and continued to direct the fire of his fellow Marines, enabling them to overcome the enemy.

INTO LEADERS...

COLONEL ANGELA SALINAS
CHIEF OF STAFF, MARINE CORPS RECRUITING COMMAND

Colonel Angela Salinas is the highest ranking Hispanic female in the Marine Corps. She has been named one of the 100 Most Influential Hispanics by Hispanic Business Magazine. Salinas entered the Marine Corps in 1974 as an enlisted recruit at Parris Island. Receiving her officer commission in 1977, Salinas went on to become the first woman to command a Marine Corps Recruiting Station and a Recruiting District. She also commanded the 4th Recruit Training Battalion at Parris Island, guiding future Marines into the Corps.

BRIGADIER GENERAL JOSEPH V. MEDINA
COMMANDER, EXPEDITIONARY STRIKE GROUP THREE

Brigadier General Joseph V. Medina, commander of Expeditionary Strike Group Three, is the first Marine to command an Expeditionary Strike Group of six ships and one submarine. Medina is a 28-year Marine veteran. A 1976 graduate of the Naval Academy, Medina has commanded a battalion of Marines, was a distinguished graduate of the Marine Corps Command and Staff College, and commanded the 3rd Marine Regiment in Hawaii. Expeditionary Strike Group Three deployed for the first time in 2004 in direct support of Central Command and the Global War on Terrorism.

FIRST SERGEANT PATRICIA Y. HERNANDEZ
SERGEANT MAJOR, 1ST MEDICAL BATTALION

First Sergeant Patricia Hernandez joined the Marines in 1990 and quickly rose through the ranks becoming a first sergeant in just 13 years. She developed leadership experience on the drill field of Recruit Depot Parris Island, S.C., as a drill instructor. In 2002, she deployed to Kabul, Afghanistan as the public affairs chief of the Consolidated Press Information Center. Hernandez is also the first female Marine to graduate from Survival, Evasion, Resistance and Escape School.

MARINEOFFICER.COM

A MESSAGE FROM THE CHIEF OF NAVAL OPERATIONS TO THE ANUARIO HISPANO – HISPANIC YEARBOOK 2005

Please accept my warmest congratulations on the 19th edition of the Anuario Hispano-Hispanic Yearbook. The U.S. Navy is proud to be included in this important publication.

The United States Navy recognizes diversity as an important element in our ability to defend the nation. We value the contributions of our service members from rich and varied backgrounds, and we hold in high esteem the thousands of Hispanic Sailors who have served their country with honor and distinction.

Individuals with diverse skills, talents, and experiences create a bright future of inclusiveness and tolerance. The power of this yearbook is the tangible link it provides between the Hispanic community and organizations, like the Navy, that actively demonstrate their support of these principles.

My very best wishes for your continued success.

Sincerely,

VERN CLARK
Admiral, U.S. Navy

Hoy, él tiene la educación, el entrenamiento y la experiencia para lograr lo que quiere. Él es una persona con la que podemos contar, un Militar del U.S. Army.
1-800-USA-ARMY   GOARMY.COM

This is not just what we believe, it's who we are. It's what's imprinted in our 100 years of history. Like Henry Ford once said, "The foundations of society are the people and their means to grow things." That's why it's important for corporations and individuals to join their efforts so that stronger communities are built and quality of life is enhanced. For all you do for your community, we salute you.

Ford Motor Company

Cultivating communities is the best path to progress.

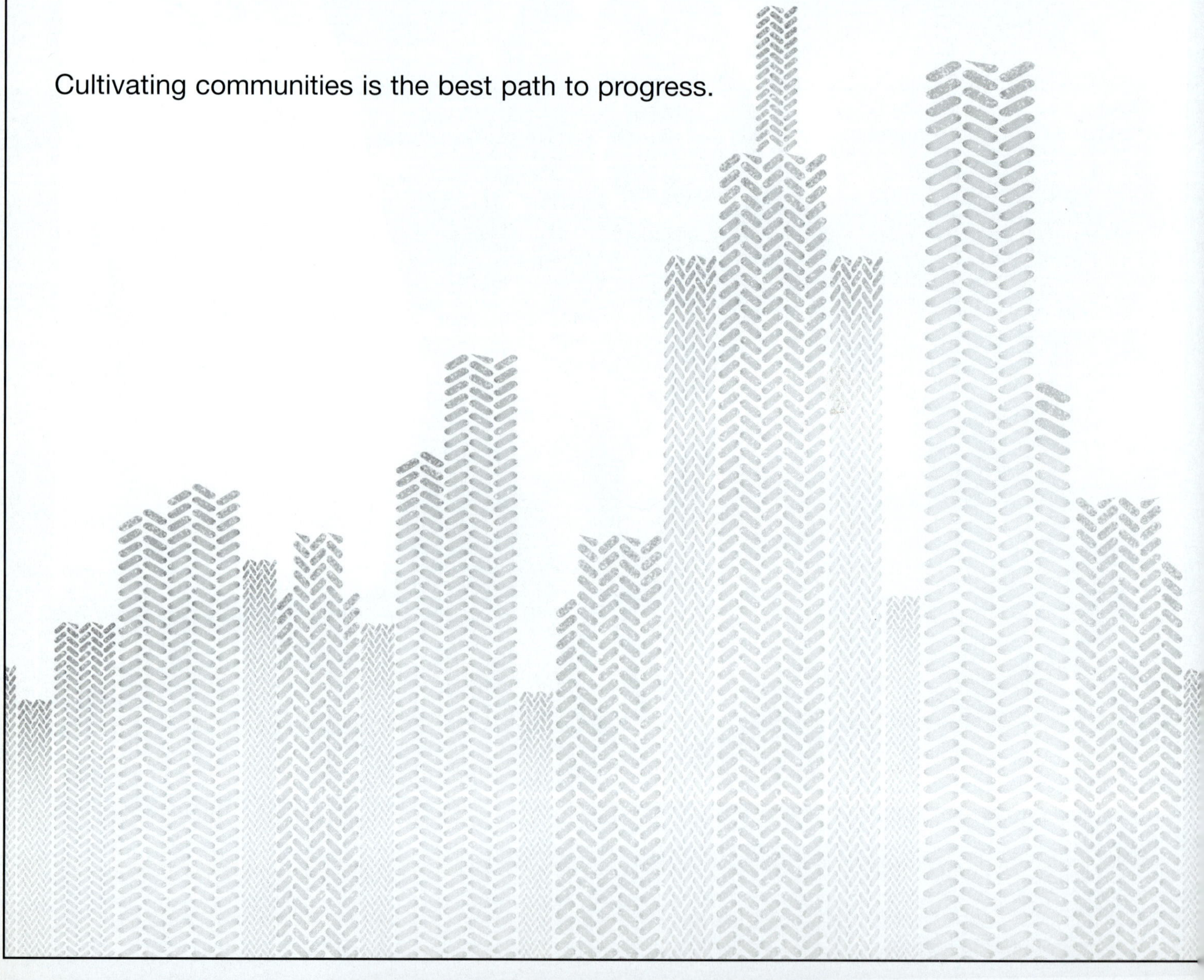

US Embassies and Consulates in Hispanic Countries
Embajadas y consulados de EUA en los países hispanos

ARGENTINA

BUENOS AIRES (E)
Av. Colombia #4300
Buenos Aires, C1425GMN Argentina
Tel: (54) (11) 5777-4533
Fax: (54) (11) 5777-4240
Web: usembassy.state.gov/buenosaires

AMB: Lino Gutierrez
DCM: Hugo Llorens
POL: Philip H. Egger
COM: Brian Brisson
CON: Gregory T. Frost
MGT: Gustavo A. Mejia
AGR: Robert Hoff
APHIS: Thomas Schissel
CLO: Heidi Inder
DAO: William A. Dalson
DEA: Anthony Greco, Jr.
ECO: Perry Ball
EST: Kathleen W. Barmon
FAA: Jose Ochoa
FMO: David H. Ball
GSO: William R. Wisell
IMO: vacant
IPO: Allan E. Richardson
ISSO: George Torres
LEGATT: Augustine Rodriguez
MLO: Michael R. Borders
PAO: Mark B. Krischik
RAMC: Charleston Finance Center

BOLIVIA

LA PAZ (E)
Av. Arce #2780
La Paz, Bolivia
Tel: (591) (2) 216-8000
Fax: (591) (2) 216-8111
Email: borgesrv@state.gov
Web: bolivia.usembassy.gov

AMB: David N. Greenlee
AMB OMS: Anne Kirlian
DCM: David M. Robinson
DCM OMS: Althena Aikens
POL/ECO: Todd C. Chapman
CON: David R. Dreher
MGT: Lawrence Hess
AID: Liliana Ayalde
CLO: M. Antonieta Romero
DAO: William P. Rushing
DEA: Alex Romero
EEO: Barbara A. Cordano
FMO: Tim A. Sears
GSO: Lawrence L. Hess
IMO: Kevin M. Byron
IPO: William D. Griffin
ISSO: Mark D. Wecker
MLO: Daniel Barreto

NAS: Carol S. Fuller
PAO: Thomas R. Genton
RSO: John M. Eustace

COCHABAMBA (CA)
Av. Oquendo #564, Torres Soffer,
Piso 6, Of. #601
Cochabamba, Bolivia
Tel: [591] (4) 116-313
Fax: [591] (4) 257-714

CA: William Scarborough
DEA: John Emerson
AID: Richard Fisher
NAS: Francisco Alvarez
PC: Remigio Ancalle

SANTA CRUZ (CA)
Calle Güemes #6, Zona Equipetrol
Santa Cruz, Bolivia
Tel: [591] (03) 363-842
Fax: [591] (03) 32-554

CA: Mary F. Telchi
DEA: James R. White
PC: Trevor Murray
NAS: Pedro T. Hernandez

BRAZIL

BRASILIA (E)
Av. das Nacoes, Quadra 801, Lote 3
Brasilia, DF, 70403-900 Brazil
Tel: (55) (61) 312-7000
Fax: (55) (61) 312-7676

AMB: John Danilovich
AMB OMS: Laura Bailey
DCM: Phillip Chicola
DCM OMS: Rosalyn Weise
POL: Dennis Hearne
CON: Simon Henshaw
MGT: Frank Manganiello
AID: Richard Goughnour
CLO: Larry Pete Davis
CUS: Julio Velez
DEA: Mark K. Edmondson
ECO: Roman Wasilewski
FCS: Janice Corbett
FMO: Lois Price
GSO: Dan Christenson
ICASS Chair: Janice Corbett
IMO: Fred Sadler
ISO: Karl Jarvis
ISSO: Kevin R. Lee
LEGATT: Daniel Clegg
MLO: Col. Antonio H. Rebelo
NAS: Mark Hoffman
RSO: Patrick Linehan
RSO: Tom Stocking

BELEM (CA)
Rua Oswaldo Cruz 165,
Bairro do Comercio
Belem, Para., 66017-019 Brazil
Tel: [55] (91) 242-7815
Fax: [55] (91) 223-0413

CA: Christine Serrao

FORTALEZA (CA)
Instituto Brasil-Estados Unidos,
Rua Nogueira Acioly, 891, Aldeota
Fortaleza, 6011-140 Brazil
Tel: [55] (85) 252-1539
Fax: [55] (85) 252-1539

CA: Patricia Cavin

MANAUS (CA)
Rua Recife 1010, Adrianopolis
Manaus, Amazonas, 69057-001 Brazil
Tel: [55] (92) 633-4907
Fax: [55] (92) 633-4907

CA: James R. Fish

PORTO ALEGRE (CA)
Agencia Consular Americana a/c Instituto
Cultural Brasileiro Norte Americano, Rua
Riachuelo 1257, Centro
Porto Alegre, RS, 90010-271 Brazil
Tel: [55] (51) 3225-2255/3226-3344
Fax: [55] (51) 3226-3344

CA: Debra T. Godoy

RECIFE (C)
Rua Goncalves Maia, 163, Boa Vista
Recife, 50070-060 Brazil
Tel: [55] (81) 3421-2441
Fax: [55] (81) 3231-1906

PO: Peter J. Swavely
CON: Maureen A. Smith

RIO DE JANEIRO (CG)
Av. Presidente Wilson, 147 Castelo,
Unit 3501
Rio de Janeiro, 20030-020 Brazil
Tel: [55] (21) 2292-7117
Fax: [55] (21) 2220-0439

CG: Mark Boulware
POL: Kathleen List
ECO: Erin McConaha
CON: Anthony Benesch
MGT: Hector E. Morales
RSO: Mark Hoffman
IRM: vacant
PAO: Catherine J. Jarvis
DAO: CDR Glenn Rosen
AGR: William Westman (res. Brasilia)
LOC: Pamela Howard-Reguindin
COM: James Cunningham

SALVADOR DA BAHIA (CA)
Ave. Tancredo Neves, Salvador Trade
Center, Edifico 1632, #1401
Salvador, Bahia, Brazil
Tel: [55] (71) 3113-2090/2091
Fax: [55] (71) 3113-2090

CA: Heather M. Marques

SAO PAULO (CG)
Rua Padre Joao Manoel 933
P.O. Box: 2489
Sao Paulo, 01411-001 Brazil
Tel: [55] (11) 3081-6511
Fax: [55] (11) 3062-5154
Web: www.consuladoamericanosp.org.br

CG: Patrick Duddy
POL/ECO: Milton Charlton
COM: Richard Lenahan
RSO: Arthur J. Balek
MGT: Dorothy Imwold
PAO: Michael Greenwald
FAS: Ronald Verdonk
LAB: Patrick Del Vecchio
IRS: Frederick Dulas (res. Mexico City)
DEA: Joseph Leszczynski
CON: Dennis Imwold

CHILE

SANTIAGO (E)
Av. Andres Bello #2800
Las Condes, Santiago, ASdfaS Chile
Tel: [56] (2) 232-2600
Fax: [56] (2) 330-3710
Web: www.usembassy.cl

AMB: Craig A. Kelly
AMB OMS: Linda Hartsock
DCM: Emi L. Yamauchi
DCM OMS: Melissa Magana
CG: Sean Murphy
CG OMS: Jackie Michell
PO: John Vance
POL: Andrew Chritton
COM: Americo Tadeu
CON: Paul M. Fermoile
MGT: Floyd S. Cable
AFSA: Ana Servent
AGR: Christine Sloop
APHIS: Eric Hoffman
CLO: Beverly Tadeu
DAO: David Cazares
DEA: James Kuykendall
ECO: Kevin Sullivan
FMO: Angela Sharpe
GSO: Robert Frazier
ICASS Chair: Christine Sloop
IMO: Brian W. Powers
ISO: Robin Byrd
LAB: Harry R. Kamian

Source: U.S. Department of State. www.foia.state.gov

LEGATT: Joseph Tipton
PAO: Judi Baroody
RSO: Joseph Castro

COLOMBIA

BOGOTA (E)

Calle 22D-BIS #47-51
Bogota, Colombia
Tel: [57] (1) 315-0811
Fax: [57] (1) 315-2197
Email: webb@state.gov
Web: usembassy.state.gov/posts/co1

AMB: William B. Wood
AMB OMS: Cherryl D. Busch
DCM: Milton K. Drucker
CG: Raymond G. McGrath
POL: Jeffrey Delaurentis
COM: Robert L. Farris
CON: Clarence Hudson
MGT: Paul E. Rowe
AFSA: Craig Conway
AGR: David Mergen
AID: Michael J. Deal
APHIS: John L. Shaw
ATF: Kenneth G. Engstrom
CLO: Jacqueline U. Keenan
CUS: Stephen Hayward
DAO: William Graves
DEA: David Gaddis
ECO: Francisco Fernandez
EEO: Elizabeth Mihm
FMO: Thomas Doherty
GSO: Mason S. Green
ICASS Chair: Phyllis M. Powers
IMO: Byron Leo Hudkins
IPO: Gregory S. Lee
IRS: vacant
ISO: Timothy J. McNamara
ISSO: Mike Brown
LEGATT: Wilfrid W. Meyer
MLO: Simeon Trombitas
NAS: Phyllis M. Powers
PAO: Anne T. Callaghan
RSO: Mark J. Hunter

COSTA RICA

SAN JOSE (E)

Pavas, San Jose Unit 2501
Costa Rica
Tel: (506) 519-2000
Fax: (506) 519-2305

DCM: Douglas Barnes
CG: Robin J. Morritz
POL: Frederick Kaplan
MGT: Scott D. McAdoo
AGR: Katherine Nishura
APHIS: John Stewart
CLO: Ana Morales
DEA: Dirk Lamagno
ECO: Whitney J. Witteman
FCS: James McCarthy
FMO: Carmen Castro
GSO: Panfilo Marquez
IMO: Jasper R. Daniels
IPO: Larry Helmich
PAO: Laurie Wietzenkorn
RSO: Michael E. Wilkins

CUBA

HAVANA (USINT)

Calzada between L & M St.
Vedado, Havana, Cuba
Tel: [53] (7) 833-3551/9
Fax: [53] (7) 833-2095
Web: usembassy.state.gov/havana

AMB: James C. Cason
DCM: Edward Alexander Lee
CG: Richard C. Beer
POL: Francisco D. Sainz
MGT: David S. Elmo
AFSA: Geoff Schradrack
CLO: Peggy Heffern
ECO: Francisco D. Sainz
FMO: Richard Heffern
GSO: Charles Sewall
ICASS Chair: Kelly Keiderling
IMO: Marc Beroud
INS: John Wallace Bird
IPO: Fred Reichard
PAO: Kelly Keiderling-Franz
RSO: Thomas Borisch

DOMINICAN REPUBLIC

SANTO DOMINGO (E)

Corner of Calle Cesar Nicolas Penson and
Calle Leopoldo Navarro
Santo Domingo, Dominican Republic
Tel: [809] 221-2171
Fax: [809] 686-7437
Web: www.usemb.gov.do

AMB: Hans H. Hertell
DCM: Lisa J. Kubiske
DCM OMS: Holly Hubler
CG: Mary B. Marshall
POL: Michael Meigs
COM: David Katz
MGT: Roland G. Estrada
AFSA: Jay Raman
AGR: David Salmon
AID: Elena Brineman
APHIS: Carolyn Cohen
CLO: Carmen Toca and Neil King
DAO: Acting Dao Ltc. Glenn R. Huber
DEA: Elias Lopez
ECO: Michael Meigs
EEO: Angela Kerwin
FMO: John Bredin
GSO: Robyn Hooker
ICASS Chair: Mary B. Marshall
IMO: Kenneth Hooks
INS: Bartolome Rodriguez
IPO: David Gilmore
ISSO: David Gilmore
LEGATT: Andrew Diaz
NAS: Richard S. Hawkins
PAO: Patricia Hawkins
RSO: Richard G. Saylor
State ICASS: Mary B. Marshall
ECO/POL 731-4335: AGR 227-0112

PUERTO PLATA (CA)

Calle Beller #51, 2nd Fl., Of. #6
Puerto Plata, Dominican Republic
Tel: [809] 586-4204

CA: William G. Kirkman

ECUADOR

QUITO (E)

Av. 12 de Octubre y Av. Patria
Quito, Ecuador
Tel: [593] (2) 256-2890
Fax: [593] (2) 250-2052
Web: www.usembassy.org.ec

AMB: Kristie A. Kenney
AMB OMS: Maria Beck
DCM: Arnold A. Chacon
DCM CHG: Ingeborg Steinmetz
POL: Erik Hall
COM: Jim Sullivan
CON: Patricia Johnson
MGT: Frank J. Ledahawsky

AGR: Melinda Sallyards
AID: Lars J. Klassen
CLO: A.J. Ketchem
DAO: Anita Domingo
DEA: William Hudson
ECO: Larry Memmott
EEO: Jim Sullivan
FMO: Pat Hamilton
GSO: Sarah Hall
ICASS Chair: Anita Domingo
IMO: James Davidson
INS: Salvador Briseno
IPO: Gordon E. Ward
ISSO: Gordon E. Ward
MLO: Kevin Saderup
NAS: Brian Doherty
PAO: Martha Estell
RSO: Frederick J. Ketchem

GUAYAQUIL (CG)

9 de Octubre y Garcia Moreno
Guayaquil, Ecuador
Tel: [593] (4) 232-3570
Fax: [593] (4) 232-5286

CG: Kevin Herbert
CON: Larry Huffman
MGT: Gayle Hamilton
IRM: Edwin Siasoco
HLS: (Vacant)
DEA: Anthony Petrino
INS: (Vacant)

EL SALVADOR

SAN SALVADOR (E)

Final Blvd. Santa Elena,
Antiguo Cuscatlan
El Salvador
Tel: (503) 278–4444
Fax: (503) 278–6011
Web: www.usinfo.org.sv

AMB: Hugh Douglas Barclay
AMB OMS: Sharon Propst
DCM: Philip C. French
DCM OMS: Debra Grau
CG: James W. Herman
POL: Annie E. Pforzheimer
CON: James W. Herman
MGT: Andrew Oltyan
AGR: Stephen Huete (Guatemala)
AID: Mark Silverman
APHIS: Elizabeth Davis (Guatemala)
CLO: Tina Pennel
DAO: Jerry Zayas
DEA: James Rose
ECO: Jessica Webster
EST: Jessica Webster
FAA: Ruben D. Quinones (Miami)
FAA CASLO: Victor Guardia (Miami)
FCS: Daniel Thompson
FMO: Philip Anstead
GSO: Michael Barrow
ICASS Chair: James Herman
IMO: Dale Rice
INS: Edward Sotomayor
IPO: Ron Dick
IRS: Frederick Dulas (Mexico, D.F.)
LAB: Philip Thompson
LEGATT: David Wattley (Panama)
MLO: Felix Santiago
PAO: Donna J. Roginski
RSO: John Root
State ICASS: Andrew W. Oltyan

GUATEMALA

GUATEMALA CITY (E)

Av. Reforma 7-01 Zona 10
Guatemala City, Guatemala

Tel: (502) 331-1541
Fax: (502) 331-6660
Web: usembassy.state.gov/guatemala

AMB: John R. Hamilton
AMB OMS: Dolores V. Appel
DCM: Bruce Wharton
DCM OMS: Maryann Hughes
CG: Michael Jacobsen
POL: Alexander Featherstone
COM: Mitchell G. Larsen
CON: Michael Jacobsen
MGT: Scott R. Heckman
AGR: Stephen Huete
AID: Glenn Anders
APHIS: Gordon Tween
CLO: Tracy Schmidt/Melissa Stoddard
DAO: Richard Nazario
DEA: Michael O'Brien
ECO: Steven S. Olson
EEO: Diane Corbin/Michael Rinker
FMO: Tor Petersen
GSO: Daniel O. Hamilton
ICASS Chair: Robert Schmidt
IMO: Michael Rinker
INS: Roy Hernandez
IPO: Stephen Wheelock
ISO: Linda Howard
LAB: Troy D. Fitrell
MLO: Mark S. Wilkins
NAS: Daniel P. Bellegarde
PAO: Mary Thompson-Jones
RSO: Michael Foster
State ICASS: Mary Thompson-Jones

HONDURAS

TEGUCIGALPA (E)

Av. La Paz
Tegucigalpa, Honduras
Tel: (504) 236-9320
Fax: (504) 236-9037
Web: www.usmission.hn

AMB: Larry Palmer
DCM: Roger Pierce
CG: Ian Brownlee
POL: Francisco Palmieri
COM: Mitch Larsen (res. Guatemala)
MGT: Jesse I. Coronado
AFSA: Derrick Olsen
AGR: Steve Huete (res.Guatemala)
AID: Paul Tuebner
CLO: Sigret Sanes
DAO: Derek R. Dickey, USAF
DEA: Ivan Rios (Acting)
ECO: Patrick Dunn
EEO: Calvin T. Watlington
FMO: Calvin Watlington
GSO: Ana P. Baide
ICASS Chair: Fred Kerzic
IMO: Mari Jain Womack
INS: Luis Figueroa
IPO: Monica Barreto
ISO: Scott Tatu
LAB: Derrick Olsen
LEGATT (res. Panama): David Wattley
MLO: Mario Mastrandrea
PAO: Melissa Cooper
RSO: Bruce Lizzi
State ICASS: Francisco Palmieri
JTF-B: COL Raymond Thomas

MEXICO

MEXICO CITY (E)

Paseo de la Reforma 305
Mexico, D.F., 06500 Mexico
Tel: [52] (55) 5080-2000
Fax: [52] (55) 5080-2005
Web: www.usembassy-mexico.gov

AMB: Antonio O. Garza, Jr.
AMB OMS: Antoinette D. Wilson
CM: Antonio O. Garza
CM OMS: Antoinette D. Wilson
DCM; Stephen R. Kelly
DCM OMS: Linda R. Ren
CG: Laura A. Clerici
CG OMS: Reyna M. Ramirez
POL: Leslie Ann Bassett
CON: Robyn M. Bishop
MGT: James Robertson
AFSA: Ali Jalili
AID: Edward L. Kadunc, Jr.
APHIS: Dale Maki
ATF: Ramon Bazan
ATO: Bruce Zanin
CLO: Dora Cuartas-Nazario
CUS: Luis M. Alvarez
DAO: Leocadio Muniz
DEA: Larry Holifield
ECO: James Heg
EEO: Ragini Gupta
EPA: Matthew Witosky
EST: Dana M. Weant
FCS: John Breidenstine
FMO: Stephen Garrett
GSO: Patricia Lacina
ICASS Chair: Oscar E. Lujan
IMO: Michael J. Kovich
INS: Oscar E. Lujan
IPO: Joe L. DeRoche
IRS: Angel G. Arroyo
ISO: Vincent J. Ryan
LAB: Alyce J. Tidball
MLO: Michael Rhea
NAS: James McAnulty
PAO: Jeff Brown
RSO: Patricia Hartnett-Kelly
State ICASS: Dana Weant

ACAPULCO (CA)

Hotel Acapulco Continental, Costera M.
Aleman 121-Local 14
Acapulco, Guerrero, 39580 Mexico
Tel: [52] (74) 81-1699
Fax: [52] (74) 84-0300
Email: consular@grol.telmex.net.mx

CA: Alexander Richards

CABO SAN LUCAS (CA)

Blvd. Marina y Pedregal #1, Local #3
Zona Centro Cabo San Lucas, Baja
California Sur, Mexico
Tel: (114) 33566
Fax: (114) 33566

CA: Michael J. Houston

CANCUN (CA)

Plaza Caracol Dos, 2do Nivel #320-323,
Cancun, Quitana Roo, 77500 Mexico
Tel: [52] (98) 83-2450
Fax: [52] (98) 83-1373

CA: Lynette Belt

CIUDAD JUAREZ (CG)

Av. Lopez Mateos 924 N.
Ciudad Juarez, Chihuahua, 32310 Mexico
Tel: [52] (656) 611-3000
Fax: [52] (656) 616-9056
Web: usembassy.state.gov/ciudadjuarez

CG: Maurice S. Parker
CON: Michael D. Puccetti
MGT: Kathy A. Johnson-Casares
RSO: James E. Heim
PD: Joanne Joria-Hooper
DEA: Michael Corbett
DHS/BICE: Benny C. Aguirre

COZUMEL (CA)

Av. Juarez #33,Local 8, Centro Commercial
"Villa Mar", Plaza Principal 2do. Nivel
Cozumel, Quitana Roo, 77600 Mexico
Tel: [52] (987) 245-74
Fax: [52] (987) 223-39
Email: anne@cozumel.net

CA: Anne R. Harris

GUADALAJARA (CG)

Progreso #175
Guadalajara, Jalisco, 44100 Mexico
Tel: [52] (33) 3825-2998/2700
Fax: [52] (33) 3826-6549
Web: www.usembassy-mexico.gov/
Guadalajara.htm

CG: Sandra J. Salmon
CON: Kevin Richardson
COM: Isabella G. Cascarano
MGT: Joanne Edwards
RSO: Peter Velazquez
BPAO: Angela B. Emerson
LEGATT: Andrew Diaz, Jr.
DEA: Michael Chavarria
USDA/APHIS: Yvette Perez-Marcano

HERMOSILLO (C)

Monterrey #141 Pte.
Hermosillo, Sonora, 83260 Mexico
Tel: [52] (662) 217-2375
Fax: [52] (662) 217-2578

PO: Marvin S. Brown
CON: Christian D. Bendsen
MGT: Michael A. Via
BCBP: Tom Bowles

IXTAPA (CA)

Local 9 Plaza Ambiente
Ixtapa, Zihuatanejo, Guerrero,
40880 Mexico
Tel: (52) (755) 3-1108
Fax: (52) (755) 4-6276
Email: lizwilliams@diplomats.com

CA: Elizabeth Williams

MATAMOROS (C)

Av. Primera 2002
Matamoros, Tamaulipas, 87330 Mexico
Tel: [52] (868) 812-4402
Fax: [52] (868) 816-2171

PO: John K. Naland
CON: Robert B. Waldrop
MGT: Susan M. Walsh

MAZATLAN (CA)

Hotel Playa Mazatlan, Rodolfo T. Loaiza
#202 Zona Dorada
Mazatlan, Sinaloa, 82100 Mexico
Tel: [52] (69) 165-889/134-444 x285
Email: mazagent@red2000.com.mx

CA: Patti K. Fletcher De Arteaga

MERIDA (C)

Paseo Montejo #453
Merida, Yucatan, 9700 Mexico
Tel: [52] (999) 925-5011
Fax: [52] (999) 925-6219

PO: Lisa A. Vickers
CON: Mauricio F. Glorioso
MGT: Jeannette M. Juricic
DEA: Pedro J. Janer

MONTERREY (CG)

Av. Constitucion #411 Pte.
Monterrey, Nuevo Leon, 64000 Mexico
Tel: [52] (81) 8345-2120
Fax: [52] (81) 8342-0177

Web: www.usembassy-mexico.gov/
Monterrey.html

CG: John A. Ritchie
MGT: Lynn M. Ferenc
CON: Peter E. Cozzens
RSO: Merrill C. Wohlman
COM: Ellen Lenny-Pessagno
PD: Indran Amirthanayagam
DHS/BICE: Esmerehildo Pardo
LEGATT: Luis A. Vasquez
BCBP: Laura M. Murphy
DEA: Guadalupe Flores
USDA/ATO: Daniel A. Martinez
USDA/APHIS/IS: Thomas J. Andre, Jr.

NOGALES, SONORA (C)

Calle San Jose s/n Fracc. Alamos
Nogales, Sonora, 84065 Mexico
Tel: [52] (631) 313-4820
Fax: [52] (631) 313-4652

PO: Kristin M. Hagerstrom
NGT: Jeanette Fogarty
CON: Benjamin R. Ousley

NUEVO LAREDO (C)

Tamps., Calle Allende #3330, Col. Jardin
Nuevo Laredo, Tamaulipas, 88260 Mexico
Tel: [52] (867) 714-0512
Fax: [52] (867) 714-7984

PO: Michael L. Yoder
CON: Joseph Demaria
MGT: Juan Aguero

OAXACA (CA)

Macedonio Alcala #201, Desp. 206
Oaxaca, Oaxaca, 68000 Mexico
Tel: [951] 43054
Fax: [951] 43054
Email: conagent@oax.1.telmex.net.mx

CA: Mark A. Leyes

PUERTO VALLARTA (CA)

Plaza Zaragoza 166,
Piso 2-18, Edif. Vallarta Plaza
Puerto Vallarta, Jalisco, 48300 Mexico
Tel: [52] (322) 2-00-69
Fax: [52] (322) 2-00-74

CA: Kelly A. Trainor

REYNOSA (CA)

Monterrey con Sinaloa #390,
Colonia Rodriguez
Reynosa, Tamaulipas, Mexico
Tel: [52] (899) 923-9331
Fax: [52] (899) 923-9245
Email: usconsularagent@hotmail.com

CA: Roberto Rodriguez

SAN LUIS POTOSI (CA)

Edif. Las Terrazas, Av. Venustiano Carranza
2076, Int.41, 40 Piso, Col. Polanco
San Luis Potosi, 78220 Mexico
Tel: [52] (48) 117-802
Fax: (52) (48) 117-803
Email: fercar@infosel.net.mx

CA: Carolyn Lazaro

SAN MIGUEL DE ALLENDE (CA)

Dr. Hernandez Macias #72
San Miguel de Allende, Guanajuato, Mexico
Tel: (415) 22357
Fax: (415) 21588
Email: coromar@unisono.net.mx

CA: COL Philip J. Maher

TIJUANA (CG)

Tapachula #96
Tijuana, Baja California Norte, 22420
Mexico
Tel: [52] (664) 622-7400
Fax: [52] (664) 681-8016
Web: www.usembassy-mexico.gov/Tijuana.
htm

CG: David C. Stewart
CON: Joyce A. Deshazo
ACS: Alfred B. Anzaldua
MGT: Jesse I. Coronado
RSO: Edward A. Brennan
PD: Elizabeth W. Davis
DEA: Alexander Toth
DHS/BICE: Scott L. Hatfield
BCBP: Juan Dania

USDA/AGR TRADE OFFICE (ATO)

Jaime Balmer #8-201, Col. Polanco
Mexico, DF, 11560 Mexico
Tel: [52] (55) 5280-5291/5277
Fax: [52] (55) 5281-6093

ATO: Bruce Zanin

NICARAGUA

MANAGUA (E)

Km. 4 1/2 Carretera Sur
Managua, Nicaragua
Tel: (505) 266-6010
Fax: (505) 266-3865
Email: embassyinfo@state.gov
Web: usembassy.state.gov/managua

AMB: Barbara C. Moore
AMB OMS: Patricia Brania
DCM: Peter M. Brennan
CG: Luis Espada-Platet
POL: Carlos Garcia
MGT: Paula M. Bravo
AFSA: Rafael Foley
AGR: Katherine Nishiura (res. San Jose)
AID: James Vermillion
APHIS: Steve Smith
CLO: Jan Von Schleh
DAO: Michael B. Rhea
DEA: Phillip Welcome
ECO: Janet R. Potash
FAA: Ruben Quinones (res. Miami)
FMO: W. Lee Thompson
GSO: Jill Thompson
IMO: Jose M. Ortiz
IPO: Greg Von Schleh
IRS: Frederick Dulas (res. Mexico City)
ISO: Warren C. Talley
ISSO: Greg Von Schleh
MLO: Hector Salinas
NAS: Eigil Hansen
PAO: Marcia Bosshardt
RSO: Michael Poehlitz

PANAMA

PANAMA CITY (E)

Apartado 0816-02561, Zona 5
Panama City, Panama
Tel: [507] 207-7000
Fax: [507] 225-0949
Email: panamaweb@state.gov
Web: usembassy.state.gov/panama

AMB: Linda Watt
AMB OMS: Elizabeth Selva
DCM: Christopher McMullen
DCM OMS: Rachel Landgraff
CG: Cmdr. Charles A. Richards
PO: Guillermo Soriano
POL: Richard Sacks

COM: Karla King
CON: Nereida Vazquez
MGT: Joseph Hilliard
AID: Leopoldo Garza
APHIS: Angel Cielo
CUS: Cristopher Martinez
DAO: Ronald McCammon
DEA: William Snyder
ECO: Andrew Bowen
EEO: Joseph Ortiz
FAA: Victor Tamariz (res. Miami)
FMO: Kati Osborne
GSO: James Gearhart
IMO: Robert Knott
INS: George Suhr
IPO: Joseph Ortiz
IRS: Frederick Dulas (res. Mexico City)
ISO: Bethany McDow
ISSO: Robert J. Knott
LEGATT: David Wattley
MLO: Cmdr. Ernest Hugh
NAS: Jon Danilowicz
PAO: Eugene Santoro
RSO: Timothy O'Brien

PARAGUAY

ASUNCION (E)

1776 Mariscal Lopez Av., A.P.
Asuncion, Paraguay
Tel: [595] (21) 213-715
Fax: [595] (21) 213-728

AMB: John F. Keane
DCM: Kevin M. Johnson
POL: James P. Merz
CON: Sonya M. Tsiros
MGT: A. Daniel Hernandez
AFSA: Linda B. Lee
AID: Wayne R. Nilsestuen
CLO: Lucita W. Daley
DAO: Frank P. Wagdalt
DEA: Gregory Beloney
ECO/COM: Patrick R. O'Reilly
EEO: Karen L. Williams
FMO: Harold E. Hodges
GSO: Graham L. Webster
ICASS Chair: Sonya Tsiros
IMO: Thomas W. Daley
LEGATT: Scott Thorley
PAO: Karen L. Williams
RSO: Theodore R. Carpenter
State ICASS: Sonya M. Tsiros

PERU

LIMA (E)

Av. La Encalada, Cuadra 17, Monterrico
Lima, Peru
Tel: [51] (1) 434-3000
Fax: [51] (1) 618-2397
Web: usembassy.state.gov/lima

AMB: J. Curtis Struble
AMB OMS: Maria Huscilowitc
DCM: John Caulfield
DCM OMS: Sarah Madrid
POL: Alex Margulies
COM: Margaret Hanson-Muse
CON: David Buentello
MGT: Robert Davis
AFSA: Kay Barton
AGR: Melinda Sallyards
AID: Hilda Arellano
APHIS: Gladys Solano
CLO: Tina Cruz-Hubbard
DAO: Raymond Anderson
DEA: Terry Parham
ECO: Timothy Stater
EEO: Janice Green
FMO: Roger Sullivan

GSO: Wesley Green
ICASS Chair: Raymond Anderson
IMO: Mark Abbey
INS: Alonso Gonzalez
IPO: Dennis Coriell
NAS: Susan Keogh
OMS: Ana Watts
PAO: Josie Shumake
RSO: Richard Watts

CUZCO (CA)

Avenida Tullumayo #125
Cuzco, Peru
Tel: [51] (84) 24-5102
Fax: [51] (84) 23-3541

CA: Olga Villagarcia

PORTUGAL

LISBON (E)

Av. Forcas Armadas
Lisbon, 1600-081 Portugal
Tel: [351] (21) 727-3300
Fax: [351] (21) 727-2354
Web: www.american-embassy.pt

AMB: John N. Palmer
DCM: Adrienne O'Neal
CG: Brian Oberle
POL: Robert Blau
COM: Greg Taevs
MGT: John Olson
AFSA: Carol Bryan
AGR: Steven Hammomd (res. Madrid)
CLO: Olga Alt
DAO: Col. Rick Villalobos
DEA: Alfredo Christlieb (res. Madrid)
ECO: Robert Blau
EEO: Audrey Huon-Dumentat (res. Paris)
FAA: Anthony F. Fazio (res. Paris)
FAA/CASLO: Mike Galvan (res. Madrid)
FMO: Christopher O'Connor
GSO: Chris Karber
IMO: Chris Gustavus
IRS: Frederick D. Pablo (res. Paris)
LEGATT: Ed Sanchez (res. Madrid)
MLO: Frank Winkle
PAO: Joao Ecsodi
RSO: Carol E. Gallo

FUNCHAL (CA)

Rua da Alfandega #10, 2nd Floor, #A&B
Funchal, Madeira, 9000-059 Portugal
Tel: [351] (291) 235-636
Fax: [351] (291) 229-360

CA: Edgar Potter

PONTA DELGADA (C)

Av. Infante D. Henrique, Box #3000
Sao Miguel, Azores, PSC 76 Portugal
Tel: [351] 296-282216
Fax: [351] 296-287216

PO: William R. Meara
VC: Robert Farquhar

SPAIN

MADRID (E)

Serrano #75
Madrid, 28006 Spain
Tel: [34] (1) 91587-2200
Fax: [34] (1) 91587-2303
Email: amemb@embusa.es
Web: www.embusa.es/

AMB: George L. Argyros
DCM: J. Robert Manzanares
DCM/CHG: J. Robert Manzanares

DCM OMS: Sally Camp
CG: Alcy Frelick
POL: Kathleen Fitzpatrick
MGT: Michael S. Hoza
AFSA: Robert Riley
AGR: Stephen Hammond
DAO: Capt. Daniel Wenceslao
DEA: Alfredo Christlieb
ECO: Whitney Baird
FAA/CASLO: Stephen Perez
FMO: Leticia Macapinlac
GSO: Margaret Kurtz-Randall
ICASS Chair: James Nealon
IMO: Stephen M. Widenhouse
INS: Dan Cadman
IPO: William T. Bonnett, II
ISO: Jerry W. Robertson
ISSO: Jerry W. Robertson
LEGATT: Eduardo Sanchez
PAO: James Nealon
RSO: Randall Bennett

BARCELONA (CG)

Paseo Reina Elisenda de Montcada #23
Barcelona, 08034 Spain
Tel: [34] (93) 280-2227
Fax: [34] (93) 205-5206
Web: www.embusa.es/barcelonaen.html

CG: Juan A. Alsace
MGT: David J. Cummings
CON: Linda L. Eichblatt
PA: William P. Francisco
USCS: David Hunter

FUENGIROLA (CA)

Av. Juan Gomez "Juanito" #8,
Edif. Lucia 1C
Malaga, 29640 Spain
Tel: [34] 952-474-891
Fax: [34] 952-465-189

CA: Roberta G. Aaron

LA CORUNA (CA)

Canton Grande #6-8E
La Coruna, 15003 Spain
Tel: [34] 981-213-233
Fax: [34] 981-228-808

CA: Marcelino Fuentes-Ramos

LAS PALMAS (CA)

Los Martinez De Escobar, 3 Of. #7
Las Palmas, 35007 Spain
Tel: [34] 928-271-259
Fax: [34] 8225-863

CA: Ana Maria Quintana

PALMA DE MALLORCA (CA)

Edif. Reina Constanza, c/Porto Piso #8-9D
Palma de Mallorca, 07015 Spain
Tel: [34] 971-403-905/707
Fax: [34] 971-403-971

CA: Bartolome Bestard

SEVILLE (CA)

Paseo de las Delicias #7
Seville, 41012 Spain
Tel: [34] (95) 423-1885
Fax: [34] (95) 423-2040

CA: Jerry L. Johnson

VALENCIA (CA)

Dr. Romagosa #1, 2da - Planta J
Valencia, 46002 Spain
Tel: [34] 96-351-6973
Fax: [34] 96-352-9565

CA: Mary Ann Garrity

URUGUAY

MONTEVIDEO (E)

Lauro Muller #1776
Montevideo, 11200 Uruguay
Tel: [598] (2) 418-7777
Fax: [598] (2) 418-8611
Email: webmastermvd@state.gov
Web: uruguay.usembassy.gov

AMB: Martin J. Silverstein
AMB OMS: Graciela L. Tift
DCM: James G. Williard
DCM OMS: Ruthe L. Fonfrias
POL: Oliver P. Griffith
CON: Stephen A. Barneby
MGT: David J. Savastuk
APHIS: Theresa L. Boyle
CLO: Renee Savastuk
CUS: Carlos M. Maza
DAO: Brian J. Butcher
ECO: James M. Perez
EEO: Cheryl L. Payne
FMO: Douglas L. DeMaggio
GSO: M. Katherine Stana
ICASS Chair: Stephen Barneby
IMO: Mark A. Hodgson
ISSO: Andrius F. Ciziunas
PAO: vacant
RSO: M. Jeremy Yamin
State ICASS: Stephen Barneby

VENEZUELA

CARACAS (E)

Calle F con Calle Suapure,
Colinas de Valle Arriba
Caracas, 1080 Venezuela
Tel: [58] (212) 975-6411
Fax: [58] (212) 907-2016
Email: embajada@state.gov
Web: embajadausa.org.ve/

AMB: William R. Brownfield
AMB OMS: Celestina M. Renteria
DCM: Stephen G. McFarland
DCM OMS: Michelle Nichols
POL: Abelardo A. Arias
COM: Sean Kelley
CON: Daniel F. Keller
MGT: Sandra M. Muench
AFSA: Harry B. Meyer
AGR: Bernardette Borris
AID: Miguel J. Reabold
CLO: Gail S. Arias
CUS: Gerardo Chavez
DAO: Lee C. Bauer
DEA: Paul Abosamra
ECO: Richard M. Sanders
EEO: Carlos I. Figueroa
FMO: Thomas N. Johnson
GSO: Joseph E. Davenport
ICASS Chair: Terry DeRouchey
IMO: George Escobedo
IPO: Roger Bjorkdahl
ISO: Barbara C. Kuehn
ISSO: Barbara C. Kuehn
LEGATT: Dennis C. Pierce
NAS: Alfred A. Smiley
PAO: Salome Hernandez
RSO: Daniel R. Garner

MARACAIBO (CA)

CEVAZ–Centro Venezolano-Americano del
Zulia, Calle 63 #3E60, Apartado #419
Maracaibo, Estado Zulia, Venezuela
Tel: [58] (61) 982-164/925-953
Fax: [58] (61) 921-098
Web: venezuela.usembassy.gov/

CA: George Quintero

ARGENTINA

EMBASSY OF THE ARGENTINE REPUBLIC
Chancery: 1600 New Hampshire Ave. NW
Washington, DC 20009
Tel: (202) 238-6400 Fax: (202) 332-3171
Web: www.embajadaargentinaeeuu.org
National Holiday: Independence Day,
May 25

Ambassador E. and P.
His Excellency Jose Octavio BORDON;
Mrs. Monica Gonzalez de Bordon
Minister (Deputy Chief of Mission)
Mr. Daniel CHUBURU;
Mrs. Araceli Mejica de Chuburu
Minister (Commercial)
Mrs. Cecilia Barrios BARON;
Mr. David T. Hollywood
Minister
Mr. Alejandro Luis CASIRO;
Mrs. Hyo Shin Kim De Casiro
Minister
Mr. Rodolfo Alberto CERVINO;
Mrs. Ana Maria Cerviño Curia
Minister
Mr. Marcelo CIMA
Minister (Financial)
Ms. Noemi C. E. LA GRECA
Minister (Agricultural)
Mr. Jose Domingo MOLINA;
Mrs. Mary Alice Troast
Counselor
Ms. Marta Victoria DE JONG
Counselor
Mrs. Patricia ESPADA;
Mr. Nelson F. Espada
Counselor
Mr. Roberto Carlos HERMIDA;
Mrs. Liliana Pintacola de Hermida
Counselor
Mr. Jose Luis SUTERA
Counselor
Mr. Jose Luis VILA; Mrs. Monica Nielsen
First Secretary
Mr. Mariano ENRICO
First Secretary
Mr. Marcelo Adrian MASSONI;
Mrs. Maria Catalina Olivero
Second Secretary
Mr. Julio Cesar MERCADO;
Mrs. Mariana Elizabeth Crespo
Attache (Administrative)
Mr. Luis Angel BARBERO;
Mrs. Rosa Alvarez de Barbero
Attache (Administrative)
Mr. Paula VALENZA

Assistant Attache
Lieutenant Colonel Antonio Agustin DUARTE;
Mrs. Maria Delfina Roquier de Duarte
Naval Attache
Rear Admiral Eduardo Luis AVILES;
Mrs. Maria de la Paz Dominguez
Naval Attache
Captain Javier Armando VALLADARES;
Mrs. Lilia Cristina Carmen Wiman
Air Attache & Assistant Defense Attache
Colonel Jorge Oscar RATTI;
Mrs. Judit Schoos
Assistant Military Attache
Colonel Raul Alberto SENORANS;
Mrs. Graciela Elvira Suller
Assistant Air Attache
Lieutenant Colonel Miguel Angel Alejandro
BEAN; Mrs. Maria Alejandro Vasallo
Assistant Air Attache
Colonel Hugo Alberto MORENO;
Mrs. Maria Cristina Garcia Taverna
Assistant Air Attache
Colonel Gabriel Fernando RODINO

Air Attache's Office
2405 I St. NW
Washington, DC 20037
Tel: (202) 452-8500

Consular Cultural, Accounting Offices
1811 Q. St. NW
Washington, DC 20009
Tel: (202)238-6460

Financial Attache's Office
1800 K St. NW #924
Washington, DC 20036
Tel: (202) 466-3031

Military Attache's Office
1810 Connecticut Ave. NW
Washington, DC 20009
Tel: (202) 667-4900

Naval Attache's Office
630 Indiana Ave. NW
Washington, DC 20004
Tel: (202) 626-2100

BOLIVIA

EMBASSY OF THE REPUBLIC OF BOLIVIA
Chancery: 3014 Massachusetts Ave. NW
Washington, DC 20008
Tel: (202) 483-4410 Fax: (202) 328-3712
Web: www.bolivia-usa.org
National Holiday: Independence Day,
August 6

Ambassador E. and P.
His Excellency Jaime APARICIO;
Mrs. Pamela Mota e Cunha de Aparicio

Minister-Counselor (Deputy Chief of Mission)
Mr. Roberto BARBERY;
Mrs. Carmina Barbery
Minister-Counselor
Mr. Oswaldo Cuevas GAETE;
Mrs. Mabel Armand Hugon de Cuevas
First Secretary & Consul
Mr. Carlos Hugo JIMENEZ;
Mrs. Sandra Iriarte
First Secretary (Legal)
Mr. Pablo Alejandro Montenegro ERNST;
Mrs. Alejandra M. Echazu de Montenegro
First Secretary (Economic)
Mrs. Claudia V. Querejazu VIDOVIC
Second Secretary
Miss Alejandra KEMPFF
Second Secretary & Vice Consul
Ms. Bernardete Villarroel RIVERO
Third Secretary & Consular Agent
Mrs. Kelly Ardaya DE LOPEZ;
Mr. Jorge Lopez Soria
Attache (Civil) & Consular Agent
Ms. Maria Nancy Gladis Escobar CLAROS
Attache (Civil)
Mrs. Sandra Danitza GARCIA
Attache (Police)
Colonel Antonio PARDO;
Mrs. Ximena Medrano EGUES
Attache (Civil)
Ms. Lilian R. Rocha PELAEZ
Attache (Administrative)
Ms. Aida Casanovas VALDIVIA
Attache (Commercial)
Mr. Jorge Velazquez GAINSBORG
Military Attache
Colonel Eduardo Paz Campero AMELUNGE;
Mrs. Maria T. Garcia De Paz Campero
Naval Attache
Captain Hans PINTO; Mrs. Emma Pinto
Air Attache
Lieutenant Colonel Walter ALVAREZ;
Mrs. Rosa Maria Alvarez
Assistant Military Attache
Lieutenant Rodrigo Rico TORO;
Mrs. Nancy Rico Toro
Assistant Air Attache
Captain Rene Carlos PINTO;
Mrs. Shirley Titze de Claros

BRAZIL

BRAZILIAN EMBASSY
Chancery: 3006 Massachusetts Ave. NW
Washington, DC 20008
Tel: (202) 238-2700 Fax: (202) 238-2827
Email:consular@brasilemb.org
Web: www.brasilemb.org
National Holiday: Independence Day,
September 7

Ambassador E. and P.
His Excellency Rubens BARBOSA;
Mrs. Maria Ignez Correa Barbosa
Minister-Counselor (Deputy Chief of Mission)
Mr. Marcos Bezerra Abbott GALVAO;
Mrs. Ana Maria Bueno Doria A. Galvao
Minister-Counselor
Mr. Evandro de Sampaio DIDONET;
Mrs. Susan Kleebank
Counselor
Mr. Joao Pedro C. COSTA;
Mrs. Telma Regina Pavarino Costa
Counselor
Mr. Vergniaud ELYSEU; Mrs. Virginia Elyseu
Counselor
Mrs. Susan KLEEBANK;
Mr. Evandro de Sampaio Didonet
Counselor
Mrs. Ana E. Pupo NETTO;
Mr. Paulo Cesar Pagi Chaves
Counselor
Mr. Fernando M. VIDAL;
Ms. Fatima I. Mourao
Counselor
Mr. Flavio MAREGA;
Mrs. Claudia Maria Marega
First Secretary
Mr. Breno de Souza Brasil Dias COSTA;
Mrs. Marilia A. Bulhoes
First Secretary
Mr. Nestor J. FORSTER Jr.;
Mrs. Maria Theresa D. Forster
First Secretary
Mr. Alexandre J. V. PORTO
Second Secretary
Mr. Carlos Da FONSECA;
Mrs. Marisa Von Bulow
Second Secretary
Mr. Roberto GOIDANICH;
Ms. Simoni P. Goidanich
Third Secretary
Mr. Murilo F. GABRIELLI;
Mrs. Silvia S. Martins
Third Secretary
Mr. Fernando Meirelles De A. PIMENTEL;
Mrs. Manuela Maria C.F. De A. Pimentel
Third Secretary
Mr. Carlos L. VILLANOVA;
Mrs. Eduarda A. Villanova
Attache
Ms. Andrea AZEVEDO
Attache
Mrs. Priscila C. BARROSO
Attache (Tax & Customs)
Mr. Luiz Henrique CASEMIRO;
Mrs. Maria Luiza Casemiro
Attache & Vice Consul
Mr. Francisco CAVALCANTI
Attache
Ms. Keila EVANGELISTA;
Mr. Joao Sergio Carneiro

Attache
Ms. Keila EVANGELISTA;
Mr. Joao Sergio Carneiro
Attache
Ms. Ana Patricia C. FRANCO
Attache
Mr. Orlando HENRIQUES;
Mrs. Maria Luz CARRETERO
Attache
Mr. Jose Menache NEISTEIN
Attache
Mr. Joao Amancio Queiroz NETO;
Mrs. Victoria M. Ferreira De Queiroz
Attache
Mr. Fabiano Rubio SCARANO;
Mrs. Marta Guedes Da C. Scarano
Attache & Vice Consul
Mrs. Simone Cristina DE DEUS SILVA;
Mr. Valerio Garcia De Deus
Defense & Air Attache
Major General Carlos Alberto FAGUNDES;
Mrs. Elza M.P. Fagundes
Military Attache
Major General Godofredo Jesus CORREA;
Mrs. Marta Francisca Sales Correa
Naval Attache
Rear Admiral Edison Lawrence M. DANTAS;
Mrs. Wanda Maria L.B. Dantas
Assistant Defense & Air Attache
Colonel Robinson Velloso FILHO;
Mrs. Heloise S.V. Velloso
Assistant Military Attache
Colonel Mauro Cesar Lourena CID;
Mrs. Agnes Barbosa Cid
Assistant Military Attache
Colonel Marcelo Lopes SERRANO;
Mrs. Yvana Lima Serrano
Assistant Naval Attache
Captain Archimedes F. DELGADO;
Mrs. Claudia J. Delgado
Assistant Naval Attache
Captain Gilberto Carlos PEDROSO;
Mrs. Lucia Harumi Pedroso
Assistant Air Attache
Colonel Antonio Franciscangeus NETO;
Mrs. Maria de Fatima Franciscangelis

Brazilian Aeronautical Commission
1701 22nd St. NW
Washington, DC 20008
Tel: (202) 483-4031

Brazilian Army Commission
4632 Wisconsin Ave. NW
Washington, DC 20016
Tel: (202) 244-5010

Brazilian Naval Commission
5130 Macarthur Blvd. NW
Washington, DC 20016-3344
Tel: (202) 244-3950

CHILE

EMBASSY OF THE REPUBLIC OF CHILE
Chancery: 1732 Massachusetts Ave. NW
Washington, DC 20036
Tel: (202) 785-1746 Fax: (202) 887-5579
Web: www.chile-usa.org
National Holiday: Independence Day,
September 18

Ambassador E. and P.
His Excellency Andres BIANCHI;
Mrs. Liliam Urdinola Uribe
Minister-Counselor (Deputy Chief of Mission)
Mr. Roberto Alonso BUDGE;
Mrs. Maria Alejandra Vergara
Minister-Counselor
Mr. Pablo Rodrigo GAETE;
Mrs. Maria Cristina Larrain Garcia
Minister-Counselor

Mr. Eduardo GALVEZ;
Mrs. Luisa Avendano de la Vega
Counselor
Mr. Javier Andres Becker MARSHALL;
Mrs. Ana Regina Gonzalez Molina
Counselor (Press)
Ms. Eliana Virginia JIMENEZ
Counselor (Technical Advisor)
Lieutenant Colonel Conrado Marco Pacheco
KUTZ; Mrs. Milagro Erices Fortunatti
Counselor
Mr. Luciano Parodi GAMBETTI;
Mrs. Renata Salvarani Pometto
Counselor (Agricultural)
Mr. Eduardo Alejandro SANTOS
First Secretary & Consul
Mr. Francisco del CAMPO LAGOS;
Mrs. Joyce Hein Martinez
First Secretary
Mr. Alejandro Arnaldo Marisio CUGAT;
Mrs. Maria Cecilia Beretta
Second Secretary (Economic)
Mr. Roberto E. MATUS;
Mrs. Consuelo Olavarria
Third Secretary
Mr. Ricardo J. BOSNIC;
Mrs. Ximena V. SALAZAR
Third Secretary
Ms. Beatriz DE LA FUENTE
Third Secretary & Consul
Mr. Ivan Andres FAVEREAU
Third Secretary
Mr. Andres Agustin LAMOLIATTE;
Mrs. Elisabeth Ursula Brauchle
Attache (Civil)
Mrs. Maria Hilda Bolvaran DE PINCUS;
Mr. Pedro E. Pincus
Assistant Attache
Ms. Silvia Mora MORALES;
Mr. Jorge Caceres Valencia
Defense & Naval Attache
Rear Admiral Daniel F. ARELLANO;
Mrs. Maria C. Schwarzenberg
Assistant Military Attache
Colonel Rodolfo I. Gonzalez PALANECK;
Mrs. Monica C. Munoz Aguirre
Assistant Naval Attache
Captain Claudio H. Gonzalez MAIER;
Mrs. Lidia E. Marentis Casanova

Air Attache Office
1029 Vermont Ave. #1100 NW
Washington, DC 20005
Tel: (202) 872-1334

Military Attache Office
2174 Wisconsin Ave. NW
Washington, DC 20007
Tel: (202) 785-2083

Naval Attache Office
1875 Connecticut Ave. #700 NW
Washington, DC 20009
Tel: (202) 667-7790

COLOMBIA

EMBASSY OF COLOMBIA
Chancery: 2118 Leroy Pl. NW
Washington, DC 20008
Tel: (202) 387-8338 Fax: (202) 232-8643
Email:emwas@colombiaemb.org
Web: www.colombiaemb.org
National Holiday: Independence Day,
July 20

Ambassador E. and P.
His Excellency Luis Alberto MORENO;
Mrs. Gabriela Febres Cordero
Minister (Deputy Chief of Mission)
Mr. Luis Bernardo Ortiz BRAVO;
Mrs. Maria Clara Sanchez Ballesteros

Minister-Counselor
Mr. Francisco J. ECHEVERRI;
Ms. Elizabeth Marian Winger
Minister-Counselor
Mrs. Maria Claudia GOMEZ;
Mr. Mauricio Camargo
Counselor
Ms. Josefina MARTINEZ;
Mr. Juan M. Estela
Counselor
Mr. Carlos MORALES; Mrs. Betty Leon
Counselor (Commercial)
Mrs. Mariana PACHECO
Counselor
Mr. Esteban Piedrahita URIBE
Counselor
Mr. Juan J. QUINTANA; Mrs. Maria P. Navia
Counselor
Ms. Sandra R. Sandoval VALDERRAMA
Second Secretary
Mrs. Ana Maria PUJANA;
Mr. Miguel Ceballos
Third Secretary
Ms. Alexandra Bardenheuer PIEDRAHITA
Third Secretary
Ms. Ana Maria Currea REINOSO
Third Secretary
Ms. Claudia Estrada OSORIO
Third Secretary
Mr. Andres Garay ACEVEDO
Third Secretary
Ms. Patricia Rojas ECHAVARRIA
Attache (Police)
Colonel Alvaro Caro MELENDEZ;
Mrs. Ana Clemencia Villamil Cortes
Attache (Commercial)
Mr. Harold Enrique EDER;
Ms. Maria Eugenia Lloreda
Military Attache
General Euclides SANCHEZ;
Mrs. Valentina Gonzalez
Naval Attache
Captain Edgar Enrico Cabrera LUNA;
Mrs. Doris Murillo
Air Attache
Colonel Carlos Alberto Ruales MORILLO;
Mrs. Constanza Echeverria Garzon

Commercial Attache Office
1901 L St. #700 NW
Washington, DC 20036
Tel: (202) 887-9000 FAX: (202) 223-0526

Consular Office
1901 L St. #700 NW
Washington, DC 20008
Tel: (202) 887-9000

COSTA RICA

EMBASSY OF COSTA RICA
Chancery: 2114 S St. NW
Washington, DC 20008
Tel: (202) 234-2945 Fax: (202) 265-4795
Email:consulate@costarica-embassy.org
Web: www.costarica-embassy.org
National Holiday: Independence Day,
September 15

Ambassador E. and P.
His Excellency Jaime DAREMBLUM;
Mrs. Gina Daremblum
Minister-Counselor (Deputy Chief of Mission)
Ms. Ana Villalobos ARRIETA
Minister-Counselor & Consul General
Mr. Alejandro Cedeno ULLOA
Minister-Counselor (Commercial & Economic)
Ms. Laura DACHNER
First Secretary
Ms. Pamela TREJOS

Attache
Ms. Maritza Chan VALVERDE
Attache
Mr. Christian MASSEY
Attache (Commercial)
Mr. Jose Carlos QUIRCE

Consular Office
2112 S St. NW
Washington, DC 20008
Tel: (202) 328-6628

CUBA

CUBAN INTERESTS SECTION
Chancery: Embassy of Switzerland,
2630 16th St. NW
Washington, DC 20009
Tel: (202) 797-8518 Fax: (202) 797-8521
Email:ofia@sicuw.org

Counselor
Mr. Dagoberto RODRIGUEZ BARRERA;
Mrs. Marisabel A. De Miguel Fernandez
Minister-Counselor (Deputy Chief of Mission)
Mr. Juan Manuel RODRIGUEZ VASQUEZ
First Secretary
Mr. Lazaro HERRERA MARTINEZ
First Secretary
Mrs. Ines FORS FERNANDEZ
First Secretary
Mr. Jose Ignacio BORGES NAVIA
First Secretary
Mr. Jose Alberto PIERO SANCHEZ
Second Secretary
Mr. Reinaldo Florentino RODRIGUEZ
LAVADO
Second Secretary
Mr. Cuauhtemoc Dario MACHADO FONT
Second Secretary
Mr. Jorge Francisco SOBERON LUIS
Second Secretary
Mr. Rafael Reyes ROBAINA
Third Secretary
Mr. Juan Carlos ARTOLA RODRIGUEZ
Attache
Mr. Carlos A. GUZMAN VAZQUEZ
Attache
Mr. Roberto PUPO ALFARO
Second Secretary (Administrative Affairs)
Mr. Angel Aurelio TORRES JAIME
Attache (Administrative Affairs)
Mr. Enrieque E. CLAVERO GONZALEZ
First Secretary & Consul General
Mr. Bernardo GUANCHE HERNANDEZ
Second Secretary & Vice Consul
Mr. Jesus Diosdado PERZ CALDERON
Third Secretary & Vice Consul
Mr. David DIAZ JIMENEZ
First Secretary (Economic Affairs)
Mr. Ernesto PLASENCIA ESCALANTE

DOMINICAN REPUBLIC

EMBASSY OF THE DOMINICAN REPUBLIC
Chancery: 1715 22nd St. NW
Washington, DC 20008
Tel: (202) 332-6280 Fax: (202) 265-8057
Email:embassy@us.serex.gov.do
Web: www.domrep.org
National Holiday: Independence Day,
February 27

Ambassador E. and P.
His Excellency Hugo M. Guilliani CURY;
Mrs. Milady D. Guilliani
Minister-Counselor (Deputy Chief of Mission)
Mrs. Judith Marcano WILLIAMS
Minister-Counselor
Mr. Francisco A. CARABALLO;

Mrs. Laura Amelia Yaryura De Caraballo
Minister-Counselor
Ms. Maria Teresa Guilliani CORONADO
First Secretary
Mr. Carlos ATILES
First Secretary
Mr. Jose A. Blanco CONDE;
Dr. Maria G. Caceres Caceres
First Secretary
Mr. Carlos Enrique Diaz WARDEN;
Mrs. Laura Urena Diaz
Defense, Military, Naval & Air Attache
Major General Hugo Rafael Gonzalez
BORRELL;
Mrs. Rossanna E. Dalmasi de Gonzalez
Assistant Defense, Military & Air Attache
Captain Abraham E. JORGE;
Mrs. Jenny R. Ramirez de Jorge

ECUADOR

EMBASSY OF ECUADOR
Chancery: 2535 15th St. NW
Washington, DC 20009
Tel: (202) 234-7200 Fax: (202) 667-3482
Email:mecuawaa@pop.erols.com
Web: www.ecuador.org
National Holiday: Independence Day,
August 10

Ambassador E. and P.
His Excellency Raul Gangotena
RIVADENEIRA; Mrs. Anne Patteet Denil
Minister
Mr. Santiago Chavez PAREJA;
Mrs. Monica Maria Hidalgo Chiriboga
Minister
Ms. Mae Montano VALENCIA
Counselor
Mr. Gustavo ANDA;
Mrs. Cristina Davalos Saenz
Counselor
Mr. Jorge A. ICAZA;
Mrs. Mariana Ruiz Salazar
Counselor & Consul General
Mr. Pablo F. YANEZ
Second Secretary
Mr. Juan Carlos Apunte FRANCO
Second Secretary
Ms. Myrian ELJURI
Second Secretary
Mr. Giovanny Gudino VITERI;
Mrs. Paulina Loor Navarro
Third Secretary
Mrs. Cristina Y. Camacho DEL CASTILLO;
Mr. Jorge Fabian Teran Garces
Attache (Civil)
Ms. Susan Garzon RAMIREZ;
Mr. Augusto Rodas Checa
Attache (Civil)
Ms. Allysson Lopez ALVAREZ
Attache (Police)
Colonel Luis Ordonez SANCHEZ;
Mrs. Amparito Pazmino Garzon
Attache (Civil)
Ms. Maria Victoria SALAZAR
Attache & Consular Agent
Ms. Janina SMITH
Assistant Attache
Colonel German FLORES; Mrs. Laura Arias
Assistant Attache (Police)
Major Nelson Villegas UBILLUS;
Mrs. Magdalena Perez Sanchez
Military Attache
Colonel Carlos Maldonado MOSQUERA;
Mrs. Gisela Serrano Marquez
Naval Attache
Captain Alano MOLESTINA;
Mrs. Delia Rosales
Air Attache
Colonel Patricio Zavala KAROLYS;

Mrs. Mariana Diaz Quinonez
Assistant Military Attache
Colonel Nelson Augusto Ramos ALBAN;
Mrs. Myrian Elizabeth Pena Vargas
Assistant Naval Attache
Commander Leopoldo PROCEL;
Mrs. Maria Mariduena

Air Attache Office
2535 15th St. NW
Washington, DC 20009
Tel: (202) 234-0601

Consular Affairs Office
2535 15th St. NW
Washington, DC 20009
Tel: (202) 234-7166

Military Attache Office
2535 15th St. NW
Washington, DC 20009
Tel: (202) 234-0647

Naval Attache Office
2535 15th St. NW
Washington, DC 20009
Tel: (202) 265-7674

Police Attache Office
2535 15th St. NW
Washington, DC 20009
Tel: (202) 464-9990 Fax: (202) 464-9988

EL SALVADOR

EMBASSY OF EL SALVADOR
Chancery: 2308 California St. NW
Washington, DC 20008
Tel: (202) 265-9671 Fax: (202) 234-3834
Email:correo@elsalvador.org
Web: www.elsalvador.org
National Holiday: Independence Day,
September 15

Ambassador E. and P.
His Excellency Rene A. LEON
Minister-Counselor (Deputy Chief of Mission)
Mrs. Carmen TOBAR
Minister-Counselor
Ms. Lina Maria CALDERON
Counselor (Political)
Mr. Luis Aparicio BERMUDEZ;
Mrs. Carmen De Aparicio
Counselor (Administrative)
Ms. Grace M. AWAD
Counselor (Political)
Mrs. Claudia Beatriz Beltran GALVEZ;
Mr. Daniel Palacios Marchesini
Counselor (Systems)
Mr. Carlos CORTEZ
Counselor (Press & Public Affairs)
Mrs. Claudia Nuset DE BARTOLINI;
Mr. Frank Paul Bartolini
Counselor (Community Affairs)
Ms. Vilma HERRERA
Counselor (Economic)
Mr. Werner M. ROMERO
Counselor (Economic)
Mr. Enilson SOLANO;
Mrs. Claudia Rivera Solano
Counselor & Consul General
Mr. Carlos Adrian Velasco NOVOA
Counselor
Ms. Flor Young BARAHONA
First Secretary
Mrs. Dora Maria DE AGUILAR;
Mr. Jose M. Aguilar
First Secretary
Mrs. Patricia Maria DE HERODIER
First Secretary & Vice Consul
Miss Mirian E. VARGAS
Attache (Commercial)
Mr. Francisco Javier CALLEJA;

Mrs. Maureen Calleja
Defense, Military, Naval & Air Attache
Colonel Jorge Barahona PINEDA

Consulate General
1724 20th St. NW
Washington, DC 20009
(202) 331-4032 Fax: (202) 331-4036

Counselor for Economic, Financial and
Commercial Affairs Office
2308 California St. NW
Washington, DC 20008
Tel: (202) 265-9671

Defense Attache Office
2308 California St. NW
Washington, DC 20008

GUATEMALA

EMBASSY OF GUATEMALA
Chancery: 2220 R St. NW
Washington, DC 20008
Tel: (202) 745-4952 Fax: (202) 745-1908
Email:info@guatemala-embassy.org
Web: www.guatemala-embassy.org
National Holiday: Independence Day,
September 15

Minister-Counselor (Charge da Affaires ad Interim)
Mr. Lionel Valentin MAZA
Counselor
Mr. George DE LA ROCHE;
Mrs. Alice Mary Newton
Counselor (Cultural)
Mrs. Maria Z. LANDIS
Counselor (Legal)
Mr. Rodrigo VIELMANN
First Secretary
Ms. Araceli Phe FUNCHAL
First Secretary & Consul
Miss Ivonne SANCHEZ
Second Secretary
Mrs. Maria C. HERNANDEZ;
Mr. Oscar Maynor Hernandez
Third Secretary
Mr. Jorge Eduardo CONTRERAS
Third Secretary
Miss Sandra Paola Godoy CABRERA
Third Secretary
Mr. Hector Palacios LIMA;
Mrs. Sonia Palacios
Attache (Commercial)
Miss Ana Maria GONZALEZ
Defense, Military, Naval & Air Attache
Brigadier General Carlos H. BUCARO;
Mrs. Maria M. Bucaro
Assistant Defense, Military & Air Attache
Lieutenant Colonel Jose I. PALACIOS;
Mrs. Mirna V. De Palacios

Commercial Attache Office
2220 R St. NW
Washington, DC 20008

Consular Section Office
2220 R St. NW
Washington, DC 20008

Defense, Military, Naval and
Air Attache Office
2220 R St. NW
Washington, DC 20008
Tel: (202) 232-2226

HONDURAS

EMBASSY OF HONDURAS
Chancery: 3007 Tilden St. NW #4-M
Washington, DC 20008

Tel: (202) 966-2604 Fax: (202) 966-9751
Email:embhondu@aol.com
Web: www.hondurasemb.org
National Holiday: Independence Day,
September 15

Ambassador E. and P.
His Excellency Mario Miguel CANAHUATI;
Mrs. Sandra de Canahuati
Minister (Deputy Chief of Mission)
Mr. Sergio Membreno CEDILLO;
Mrs. Brenda Membreno
Minister
Miss Maria Bennaton REGALADO
Minister
Mr. Ramon CUSTODIO;
Mrs. Mei Ling M. Lavecchia
Counselor (Legal)
Mr. David HERNANDEZ;
Mrs. Xochitl Noemi Salgado Alvarez
Counselor (Consular)
Mr. Leonardo Irias NAVAS;
Mrs. Norma Dolores Irias
Counselor
Mrs. Brenda MEMBRENO;
Mr. Sergio Membreno Cedillo
Counselor (Tourism)
Mrs. Sara Pineda DE MURPHY;
Mr. Charles Vincent Murphy
Counselor (Special Assistant to Ambassador)
Mr. Jose Benjamin ZAPATA;
Mrs. Susan Mary Zapata
First Secretary
Miss Graciamaria Aguero GUEVARA
First Secretary
Ms. Cynthia ROMERO
Attache (Commercial)
Miss Nuria Ortiz NAVARRO
Defense, Military, Naval & Air Attache
Colonel Carlos Humberto RAMOS;
Mrs. Ana Carolina Ramos

Consular Section
1528 K St. NW #200
Washington, DC 20005
Tel: (202) 737-2972 Fax: (202) 737-2907

MEXICO

EMBASSY OF MEXICO
Chancery: 1911 Pennsylvania Ave. NW
Washington, DC 20006
Tel: (202) 728-1600 Fax: (202) 728-1698
Web: www.embassyofmexico.org
National Holiday: Independence Day,
September 16

Ambassador E. and P.
His Excellency Juan Jose Bremer MARTINO;
Mrs. Maria Marcela Sanchez De Bremer
Minister (Deputy Chief of Mission)
Mr. Mario Chacon CARRILLO;
Mrs. Emilia Hernandez Martinez
Minister (Monetary Affairs)
Mr. Ariel Buira y SEIRA;
Mrs. Janet Margaret Clark de Buira
Minister
Mr. Luis Cabrera CUARON
Minister
Mr. Fernando Creixell NORIEGA;
Mrs. Griselda Escudero de Creixell
Minister (Cultural)
Mr. Ignacio Duran LOERA;
Mrs. Luz Elena Ruesga de Duran
Minister (Energy)
Mr. Saul Alejandro Feder SCHWARZ;
Mrs. Leliet Ivonne Huymans
Minister
Mr. Carlos Isauro Felix CORONA;
Mrs. Eun Hai Kim
Minister (Consular)
Mr. Edgardo Flores RIVAS;

Mrs. Lilia D. Carmen Bolivar y Sanchez
Minister (Tax & Customs)
Mr. Jose Martin Garcia SANJINES;
Mrs. Patricia Gomez de Garcia
Minister (Agriculture)
Mr. Enrique Lobo NIEMBRO;
Mrs. Maria Isabel Cruz de Lobo
Minister (Trade)
Mr. Hector Marquez SOLIS;
Mrs. Florina Martinez Vega
Minister (Economic Affairs)
Mr. Carlos Alberto MARTINEZ;
Mrs. Barbara Oliva
Minister (Environment & Natural Resources)
Mr. Teodoro Maus REISBAUM;
Mrs. Nicolette Reim Maus
Minister (Secretary of Interior)
Mr. Gerardo Olmos CRUZ;
Ms. Maria Teresa Guevara Lopez
Minister (Political Affairs)
Mr. Carlos Rico FERRAT;
Mrs. Maria Cruz Mateos de Rico
Counselor (Economic)
Mrs. Karen Nicole Antebi BENUZILLO;
Mr. William Goldfarb Legher
Counselor & Deputy Consul
Mr. Leocadio Beytia VEGA;
Mrs. Amada Olguin Valerio
Counselor
Mr. Juan Rodrigo Labardini FLORES;
Mrs. Norma Libia Ramirez de Labardini
Counselor (Press)
Mr. Jose Miguel Monterrubio CUBAS;
Mrs. Maria E. Bandera de Monterrubio
Counselor
Mr. Jaime Ortiz AUB;
Mrs. Lorena Ochoa Rodriguez
Counselor (Legal)
Mr. Carlos Quesnel MELENDEZ;
Mrs. Margarita Gonzalez de Quesnel
Counselor (Financial)
Ms. Cecilia Ramos AVILA
Counselor (Trade)
Mr. Sergio Soto NUNEZ;
Mrs. Thelma Ruth Orozco Rodriguez
Counselor (Trade)
Mr. Raul Urteaga TRANI; Ms. Julia Urteaga
First Secretary
Ms. Maria Elena Alcaraz VELAZQUEZ
First Secretary
Mr. Salvador Behar LAVALLE;
Mrs. Adriana Isabel Kado Segovia
First Secretary
Ms. Maria Cortina BORJA;
Mr. Robert Emerson Mcquiston
First Secretary (Trade Affairs)
Mr. Miguel Angel Narvaez FLORES;
Mrs. Marcela Gonzalez Ramirez
First Secretary
Mr. Heroldo E. Paredes BALDERAS;
Mrs. Judith Dominguez Curiel
First Secretary (Migration & Border)
Mr. Ricardo Pineda ALBARRAN;
Mrs. Silvia Esther Cruz Palma
First Secretary
Mr. Enrique Rojo STEIN
First Secretary (Secofi-Nafta)
Mrs. Marcia San Roman GARCIA;
Mr. Luis Albert Somersille Williams
First Secretary
Mr. Sergio Zapata LOZANO
First Secretary
Mr. Jose Alfonso Zegbe CAMARENA
Second Secretary
Ms. Norma ANG SANCHEZ
Second Secretary
Ms. Marcela Celorio MANCERA
Second Secretary
Ms. Fernanda Montano VALDES
Second Secretary
Mrs. Dolores Repetto ALVAREZ;
Mr. Alfredo Flores Alatorre Ortiz

Second Secretary
Mr. Ricardo F. Rojas GRANADOS
Second Secretary
Mr. Juan Manuel Saldivar CANTU
Second Secretary
Mr. Francisco Sandoval SAQUI
Third Secretary
Ms. Mireya Magana GALVEZ
Third Secretary
Ms. Lorena Montes DE OCA;
Mr. Rodrigo Salas MILES
Attache (Agricultural)
Mr. Hector Cortes Gomez RUEDA;
Mrs. Virginie Dezan
Attache (Office of Ambassador)
Mrs. Lea CORTI; Mr. Jesus Arturo Garcia
Attache (Agricultural Affairs)
Mr. Luis Alberto Cruz GARCIA
Attache (Legal)
Mr. Guillermo Fonseca LEAL;
Mrs. Maria Fernanda Alva Hernandez
Attache (Agricultural)
Mr. Froylan Gracia GALICIA;
Miss Mara Gabriela Yanez Zazueta

Agricultural and Forestry Minister Office
1911 Pennsylvania Ave. NW
Washington, DC 20006
Tel: (202) 728-1687 Fax: (202) 728-1728

Consular Office
2827 16th St. NW
Washington, DC 20009
Tel: (202) 736-1000

Defense, Military and Air Force Office
1911 Pennsylvania Ave. NW
Washington, DC 20006
Tel: (202) 728-1687 Fax: (202) 728-1741

Financial Counselor Office
1615 L St. #310 NW
Washington, DC 20005
Tel: (202) 338-9010 Fax: (202) 338-9244

Naval Attache Office
1911 Pennsylvania Ave. NW
Washington, DC 20006
Tel: (202) 728-1760 Fax: (202) 728-1767

Tourism Minister Office
1911 Pennsylvania Ave. NW
Washington, DC 20006
Tel: (202) 728-1687 Fax: (202) 728-1758

Trade Minister Office
1911 Pennsylvania Ave. NW
Washington, DC 20006
Tel: (202) 728-1687 Fax: (202) 728-1712

Trade Minister Office
1911 Pennsylvania Ave. NW
Washington, DC 20006
Tel: (202) 728-1687 Fax: (202) 728-1712

Trade Negotiations Office
1911 Pennsylvania Ave. NW
Washington, DC 20006
Tel: (202) 728-1687 Fax: (202) 296-4904

NICARAGUA

EMBASSY OF THE REPUBLIC OF NICARAGUA
Chancery: 1627 New Hampshire Ave. NW
Washington, DC 20009
Tel: (202) 939-6570 Fax: (202) 939-6545
National Holiday: Independence Day,
September 15

Ambassador E. and P.
His Excellency Salvador E. Stadthagen
ICAZA; Mrs. Analia Vargas de Stadthagen
Minister-Counselor
Ms. Carmen Marina Gutierrez SALAZAR
Minister-Counselor

Mr. Alcides J. Montiel BARILLAS
Minister-Counselor & Consul General
Mr. Harold Rivas REYES;
Mrs. Jeannette Rivas
Counselor & Consul
Mrs. Dinora Daria GUEVARA
Attache
Ms. Agnes M. ALVARADO
Attache (Consular)
Mrs. Martha E. Davila CISNEROS
Attache (Press)
Mr. Arturo Jose Wallace SALINAS
Defense, Military, Naval & Air Attache
Colonel Pedro L. Martinez MEJIA;
Mrs. Ruth Palacios Alvir

PANAMA

EMBASSY OF THE REPUBLIC OF PANAMA
Chancery: 2862 McGill Terr. NW
Washington, DC 20008
Tel: (202) 483-1407 Fax: (202) 483-8416
National Holiday: Independence Day,
November 3

Ambassador E. and P.
His Excellency Roberto Alfaro ESTRIPEAUT;
Mrs. Rossana Luigia Ameglio de Alfaro
Minister-Counselor
Mr. Carlos Raul de la Guardia PLATA;
Mrs. Yessamine Y. Donato de la Guardia
Counselor (Legal)
Ms. Maria Alejandra TULIPANO
Attache (Economic)
Mr. Carlos A. Gonzalez SANTAMARIA
Attache (Legal)
Ms. Maruquel Patricia ICAZA
Attache (Political) & Consul General
Mr. Juan Vasquez VERA
Attache
Miss Estelabel Joana Vieira PIAD

PARAGUAY

EMBASSY OF PARAGUAY
Chancery: 2400 Massachusetts Ave. NW
Washington, DC 20008
Tel: (202) 483-6960 Fax: (202) 234-4508
National Holiday: Independence Day,
May 14

Ambassador E. and P.
His Excellency James Spalding HELLMERS;
Mrs. Cecilia Coello de Spalding
Minister (Commercial)
Ms. Maria Guillermina Frizza ARCE
Counselor
Mr. Jose M. IBANEZ;
Mrs. Rossana Catalina Cardenas Monges
First Secretary
Miss Maria Leticia Casati CABALLERO;
Mr. Edgar Cubero Gomez
Second Secretary
Mr. Victor Luis Bernal LUGO
Second Secretary
Mr. Jorge Brizuela PEREZ
Second Secretary
Ms. Norma Cardozo SALDIVAR
Attache (Educational)
Mrs. Maria Graciela Meza MEZGOLITS
Attache
Mr. Ruben RAMOS
Attache
Ms. Annalisa VERDUN
Defense, Military, Naval & Air Attache
Brigadier General Pedro Villalba
ORTELLADO;
Mrs. Gladys Rufina Acosta de Villalba

Commercial and Economic Affairs Office

2400 Massachusetts Ave. NW
Washington, DC 20008

Defense Attache Office
2400 Massachusetts Ave. NW
Washington, DC 20008

Press and Information Affairs Office
2400 Massachusetts Ave. NW
Washington, DC 20008
Tel: (202) 483-6962

Visa and Consular Affairs Office
2400 Massachusetts Ave. NW
Washington, DC 20008
Tel: (202) 483-6960

PERU

EMBASSY OF PERU
Chancery: 1700 Massachusetts Ave. NW
Washington, DC 20036
Tel: (202) 833-9860 Fax: (202) 659-8124
Email:webadmin@embassyofperu.us
Web: www.peruvianembassy.us
National Holiday: Independence Day,
July 28

Ambassador E. and P.
His Excellency Eduardo Ferrero Costa
Minister (Deputy Chief of Mission)
Mr. Nestor Popolizio BARDALES
Minister & Consul General
Mr. Eduardo Salcedo PENARRIETA;
Mrs. Evelyne Bertorini de Salcedo
Minister-Counselor (Cultural)
Mr. Eloy ALFARO; Mrs. Diva Alfaro
Minister-Counselor (Administrative)
Mr. Jose Antonio GARCIA;
Mrs. Elizabeth Garcia
Minister-Counselor (Economic)
Mr. Alfredo Jose VALENCIA;
Mrs. Julia De Valencia
Counselor
Mr. Italo Acha PUERTAS;
Mrs. Fabiana Molla de Acha
Counselor (Political, Military & Narcotics)
Mr. Ignacio HIGUERAS; Mrs. Ena Higueras
Counselor (Press)
Mr. Rodolfo Pereira TERRONES
Counselor (Legal)
Mr. Jorge RAFFO; Mrs. Olga Raffo
Counselor (Economic & Trade)
Mr. Roberto RODRIGUEZ;
Mrs. Roxana Rodriguez
Counselor
Mr. Augusto E. Salamanca CASTRO;
Mrs. Maria Elena Paz Gutzalenko
First Secretary & Deputy Consul
Mr. Manuel A. Ruiz GUTIERREZ;
Mrs. Cecilia Retamal De Ruiz
First Secretary & Deputy Consul
Mr. German Vera ESQUIVEL
Second Secretary
Mr. Rodolfo CORONADO
Second Secretary & Vice Consul
Ms. Catherine Lovon BALTA
Second Secretary
Mr. Renzo Villa PRADO
Third Secretary
Mr. Jorge A. Izaguirre SILVA
Third Secretary
Mr. Jose Antonio Torrico OBANDO;
Mrs. Jessica Namihas de Torrico
Assistant Attache
Lieutenant Colonel Fernando Berrocal
CABRERA; Mrs. Elba Alcazar de Berrocal
Military Attache
Lieutenant General Jose M. Huerta
TORRES; Mrs. Ana M. Risco de Huerta
Naval Attache

Rear Admiral Pablo Camogliano PAZOS;
Mrs. Margarita Camogliano
Air Attache
Colonel Gonzalo TUEROS;
Mrs. Claudia Farfan de Tueros
Assistant Military Attache
Colonel Orlando E. Agreda PALOMINO;
Mrs. Maria Esther Tenorio de Agreda
Assistant Naval Attache
Captain Jorge M. Cochella MALDONADO;
Mrs. Adelina R. Cicirello de Cochella
Assistant Air Attache
Lieutenant Colonel Nerio Pineda Arce la
TORRE; Mr. Veronica Negri de Pineda Acre
Assistant Air Attache
Major Edgar Romainville VILLASANTE;
Mrs. Maria M. Latorre de Romainville

Air Attache Office
2141 Wisconsin Ave. #A
Washington, DC 20007
Tel: (202) 333-1528

Consulate General Office
1625 Massachusetts Ave. #605 NW
Washington, DC 20036
Tel: (202) 462-1081

Joint Fight Against Drugs Office
1511 K St.
Washington, DC 20005
Tel: (202) 737-5484

Military Attache Office
2141 Wisconsin Ave. #F NW
Washington, DC 20007
Tel: (202) 342-8127 Fax: (202) 333-7417

Naval Commissioner & Attache Office
2141 Wisconsin Ave. #J NW
Washington, DC 20007
Tel: (202) 337-6670

PORTUGAL

EMBASSY OF PORTUGAL
Chancery: 2125 Kalorama Rd. NW
Washington, DC 20008
Tel: (202) 328-8610 Fax: (202) 462-3726
Email:delegacao.s.francisco@iapmei.icep.pt
Web: www.portugalemb.org
National Holiday: Independence Day,
June 10

Ambassador E. and P.
His Excellency Pedro CATARINO;
Mrs. Cheryl Atarino
Minister-Counselor (Deputy Chief of Mission)
Ms. Josefina Reis CARVALHO
Minister-Counselor
Mr. Jose Alves Costa PEREIRA
Counselor (Education)
Mrs. Maria Da Graca Borges CASTANHO
Counselor (Political)
Mr. Nuno Vaultier MATHIAS
Counselor (Economic)
Mr. Mario S. MENEZES;
Mrs. Maria Margarida Menezes
Counselor (Press)
Mr. Manuel Silva PEREIRA;
Mrs. Anabela Lopes Garcia Abreu
First Secretary
Ms. Florbela PARAIBA
First Secretary
Mrs. Catarina RODRIGUES;
Mr. Pedro De Sa Da Bandeira
Attache & Vice Consul
Mrs. Maria Amelia Manso Nobre HILKER;
Mr. Douglas Gordon Hilker
Attache (Latin American Affairs)
Ms. Ana Maria Pires MONTEIRO
Defense & Air Attache
Major General Carlos Castro LEAL;

Mrs. Elvira Esperanca Costa Leal
Military Attache
Lieutenant Colonel Isidro de Morais
PEREIRA;
Mrs. Cecilia Goncalves Torres Pereira
Naval Attache
Captain Augusto Ferreira CARVALHO;
Mrs. Ana Isabel Carvalho

Consular Section
2310 Tracy Pl. NW
Washington, DC 20008
Tel: (202) 232-7632

Defense and Air Attache Office
2310 Tracy Pl. NW
Washington, DC 20008
Tel: (202) 234-5037

Military Attache Office
2310 Tracy Pl. NW
Washington, DC 20008
Tel: (202) 234-4483

Naval Attache Office
2310 Tracy Pl. NW
Washington, DC 20008
Tel: (202) 234-4483

SPAIN

EMBASSY OF SPAIN
Chancery: 2375 Pennsylvania Ave. NW
Washington, DC 20037
Tel: (202) 452-0100 Fax: (202) 362-3993
Web: www.spainemb.org
National Holiday: Independence Day,
October 12

Ambassador E. and P.
His Excellency Carlos WESTENDORP Y
CABEZA; Amaya de MIGUEL
Minister (Deputy Chief of Mission)
Mr. Felix VALDES;
Mrs. Maria Cristina Diago Brull
Minister & Consul General
Mr. Mariano Alonso Buron ABERASTURI
Minister (Cultural Affairs)
Mrs. Carmen G. de Amezua del PINO
Counselor (Economic & Commercial)
Mr. Jose Alberto Azcona OLIVERA;
Mrs. Maria Transito Abrain Rodriguez
Counselor
Mr. Juan J. Buitrago DE BENITO;
Mrs. Maria Victoria Pena Hernando
Counselor
Mr. Juan Pedro Chozas PEDRERO;
Mrs. Victoria Sumbera Calderon
Counselor
Mrs. Paloma Maria CONDE;
Mr. Miguel Ignacio Herreros de Tejada
Counselor (Financial)
Mr. Ubaldo Gonzalez DE FRUTOS
Counselor (Agriculture, Fisheries & Food)
Mr. Samuel J. JUAREZ;
Mrs. Maria Concepcion Lopez Diaz
Counselor (Education)
Dr. Miguel Martinez LOPEZ;
Mrs. Maria A. Lopez Saez
Counselor
Mr. Borja MONTESINO;
Mrs. Sonia Perez Mendez
Counselor (Economic & Commercial)
Mr. Manuel MORENO; Mrs. Estela Garcia
Counselor (Commercial)
Mr. Odon Palla SAGUES;
Mrs. Paz Valiente Calvo
Counselor (Economic & Administrative)
Mr. Dario POLO
Counselor
Mr. Ramon SANTOS;
Mrs. Carmen Ayllon Martinez

Counselor
Mr. Juan Ignacio SELL;
Mrs. Genoveva Fernandez
Counselor (Information)
Mr. Florentino SOTOMAYOR;
Mrs. Maria Teresa Suarez
First Secretary
Mr. Fernando Prieto RIOS;
Mrs. Maria Rios Gomez
Attache (Agricultural, Fisheries & Food)
Ms. Elena M. Cores GARCIA
Attache
Mr. Luis Manuel GARCIA;
Mrs. Marta Betolaza
Attache
Mr. Antonio Linos CASTELLS;
Mrs. Nuria Pallas Ruiz
Attache
Mr. Andres Otero PINARDO;
Mrs. Maria Lopez Salmon
Attache (Administrative)
Mr. Jose A. RIERA; Mrs. Maria Pia De-Luca
Attache (Commercial)
Ms. Adela RODRIGUEZ
Defense Attache
Rear Admiral Teodoro E. DE LESTE;
Mrs. Gabriela M. Ramirez
Military Attache
Colonel Angel Fernando Perez UTRILLA;
Mrs. Nieves Del Cojo
Naval Attache
Captain Francisco J. Gil DE SOLA;
Mrs. Marta Letang Benjumeda
Air Attache
Colonel Pablo Martinez DARVE;
Mrs. Matilde Sanz Arroita
Defense Cooperation Attache
Colonel Gonzalo De Riva GARCIA;
Mrs. Blanca Solla Santos
Assistant Defense Cooperation Attache
Major Luis Alberto Castilla GARCIA;
Mrs. Adela Gamboa Delgado
Assistant Defense Cooperation Attache
Lieutenant Colonel Fernando Martin NIETO;
Mrs. Maria Pilar Novas Castro
Assistant Defense Cooperation Attache
Lieutenant Colonel Jesus Romero GARCIA;
Mrs. Maria Clara Quesada Rivera

Air Attache Office
4801 Wisconsin Ave., 3rd Fl. NW
Washington, DC 20016
Tel: (202) 244-2166

Agricultural Office
2375 Pennsylvania Ave. NW
Washington, DC 20037
Tel: (202) 728-2339 Fax: (202) 728-2320

Consular Office
2375 Pennsylvania Ave. NW
Washington, DC 20037

Cultural Office
2375 Pennsylvania Ave. NW
Washington, DC 20037
Tel: (202) 728-2334 Fax: (202) 728-2312

Defense Attache Office
4801 Wisconsin Ave., 4th Fl. NW
Washington, DC 20016
Tel: (202) 244-0093

Defense Cooperation Attache Office
4801 Wisconsin Ave., 4th Fl. NW
Washington, DC 20016
Tel: (202) 244-0093

Economic and Commercial Office
2375 Pennsylvania Ave. NW
Washington, DC 20037
Tel: (202) 728-2368 Fax: (202) 466-7385

Education Office

2375 Pennsylvania Ave. NW
Washington, DC 20037
Tel: (202) 728-2335 Fax: (202) 728-2312

Financial Office
2375 Pennsylvania Ave. NW
Washington, DC 20037
Tel: (202) 728-2338 Fax: (202) 728-2318

Information Office
2375 Pennsylvania Ave. NW
Washington, DC 20037
Tel: (202) 728-2332 Fax: (202) 728-2308

Labor and Social Affairs Office
2375 Pennsylvania Ave. NW
Washington, DC 20037
Tel: (202) 728-2331 Fax: (202) 728-2304

Military Attache Office
4801 Wisconsin Ave., 3rd Fl. NW
Washington, DC 20016
Tel: (202) 244-6161 Fax: (202) 362-3993

Naval Attache Office
4801 Wisconsin Ave., 3rd Fl. NW
Washington, DC 20016
Tel: (202) 244-2166

URUGUAY

EMBASSY OF URUGUAY
Chancery: 1913 I St. NW
Washington, DC 20006
Tel: (202) 331-1313 Fax: (202) 331-8142
Email:uruwashi@uruwashi.org
Web: www.uruwashi.org
National Holiday: Independence Day,
August 25

Ambassador E. and P.
His Excellency Hugo Fernandez FAINGOLD;
Ms. Veronica C. Cortabarria Izquierdo
Minister-Counselor (Deputy Chief of Mission)
Mr. Ricardo Nario FAGUNDEZ;
Mrs. Laura Dupuy Lasserre
Minister (Financial)
Mr. Carlos C. STENERI;
Mrs. Maria M. Berro Steneri
Minister-Counselor (Agricultural Advisor)
Dr. Julio BAROZZI
Counselor (Economic, Trade & Tourism)
Ms. Marion Daniela Blanco ESPINO
Counselor
Mr. Carlos Gitto SPIGNOLA;
Mrs. Maria Del Rosario Croce Urbina
Counselor & Consul
Mr. Mario Liori SANCHEZ;
Mrs. Maria Del Rosario Gonzalez Moreno
FirstSecretary (Economic & Trade)
Mr. Alejandro GAROFALI;
Mrs. Irma Susanne Hummel Fors
First Secretary (Political)
Mr. Fernando Nestor Sandin TUSSO;
Mrs. Gabriela Paola Isnardi Gomez
Defense & Military Attache
General Angel Bertolotti NEUMAN;
Mrs. Maria Elena Buscasso Olmedo
Naval Attache
Captain Nelson Wander Olivera
FERNANDEZ; Mrs. Silvia Ortiz Silvera
Air Attache
Mr. Ernesto I. MARTINEZ;
Mrs. Mirta Graciela Martinez
Assistant Defense & Military Attache
Colonel Juan TROCHE;
Mrs. Aroma Arhancet Carrasco

continued on p 183

Hispanic Consulates in the US
Consulados hispanos en EUA

ARGENTINA

CALIFORNIA
Los Angeles (CG)
5055 Wilshire Blvd. #210
Los Angeles, CA 90036
Tel: (213) 739-5959

Consul General
Mr. Luis Maria KRECKLER
Deputy Consul General
Mr. Raul Ignacio GUASTAVINO
Deputy Consul
Mr. Roberto H. DIEZ
Deputy Consul
Mr. Leandro Federico FERNANDEZ SUAREZ
Deputy Consul
Mr. Roberto Carlos DUPUY
Consular Agent
Mrs. Claudia A. Bonicalzi de TABUYO
Consular Agent
Mr. Juan Carlos TOCE

Argentine Trade Office
3580 Wilshire Blvd. #1412
Los Angeles, CA 90010
Tel: (213) 623-3230

FLORIDA
Miami (CG)
800 Brickell Ave. Penthouse 1
Miami, FL 33131
Tel: (305) 373-7794

Consul General
Mr. Luis M. RICCHERI
Deputy Consul General
Mr. Alejandro Hector NIETO
Deputy Consul General
Mr. Miguel Edgardo REALMONTE
Deputy Consul
Mr. Guillermo RODRIGUEZ
Deputy Consul
Mr. Maximo E. GOWLAND
Deputy Consul
Mr. Ruben Omar HEGUILEIN
Deputy Consul
Mr. Hugo Esteban MASSUANI
Deputy Consul
Mr. Adrian Salvador MACIEL
Deputy Consul
Mr. Diego Alvarez RIVERA
Consular Agent
Mr. Juan Jose ALVAREZ
Consular Agent
Ms. Ester GARCIA
Consular Agent
Mr. Horacio Hugo RAVERA
Consular Agent
Mrs. Elsa Catalina Barone de LAMELA

Tourism Office
2655 Lejeune Rd. #F
Miami, FL 33134
Tel: (305) 442-1366

Consular Agent
Mr. Eduardo A. PIVA

GEORGIA
Atlanta (CG)
245 Peachtree Center Ave. #2101
Atlanta, GA 30303
Tel: (404) 880-0805

Consul General
Mr. Carlos LAYÚS

ILLINOIS
Chicago (CG)
205 N Michigan Ave. #4208/4209
Chicago, IL 60601
Tel: (301) 819-2620 Fax: (312) 819-2626

Consul General
Mr. Ernesto Manuel PAZ
Deputy Consul
Mr. Marcelo Pablo DI PACE
Consular Agent
Mr. Jorge Luis MANGHI

Argentine Trade Office
233 N Michigan Ave. #1408
Chicago, IL 60601
Tel: (312) 565-2466

NEW YORK
New York (CG)
12 W 56th St.
New York, NY 10019
Tel: (212) 603-0400

Consul General
Mr. Hector TIMERMAN
Deputy Consul General
Mr. Luis Pablo Maria BELTRAMINO
Deputy Consul General
Mr. Alejandro Antonio BERTOLO
Deputy Consul General
Mr. Fernando Tulio CERVETTO
Deputy Consul
Mr. Mario J.A. OYARZABAL
Deputy Consul
Mr. Ciro Luciano Ciliberto INFANTE
Deputy Consul
Mr. Carlos Alejandro POFFO
Consular Agent
Ms. Graciela Maria FINAURI

Argentine Trade Office
900 3rd Ave., 4th Fl.
New York, NY 10022
Tel: (212) 759-6477

TEXAS
Houston (CG)
3050 Post Oak Blvd. #1625
Houston, TX 77056
Tel: (713) 871-8935

Consul General
Mr. Ricardo GAUTHIER
Consular Agent
Mr. Armando David ALVAREZ

Argentine Trade Office
2000 Post Oak Blvd. #1810
Houston, TX 77056
Tel: (713) 871-8890

WASHINGTON, DC
Washington, DC (Consular Section)
1811 Q. St. NW
Washington, DC 20009
Tel: (202) 238-6460 Fax (202) 238-6471
Email: consular@embajadaargentinaeeuu.org

Head of Consular Affairs
Mr. Rodolfo CERVIÑO

BOLIVIA

ALABAMA
Mobile (HC)
3413 Canacee Dr.
Mobile, AL 36693
Tel: (334) 666-6969 Fax: (334) 661-2873

Honorary Consul
Mr. Thomas PURVIS

CALIFORNIA
San Francisco (CG)
870 Market St. #575
San Francisco, CA 94102
Tel: (415) 495-5173 Fax: (415) 399-8958

Consul General
Mr. Fernando Lazcano DUNN
Consul
Ms. Roxana W. Oller CATOIRA
Consular Agent
Mr. Gonzalo Alvestegui FLORES

DISTRICT OF COLUMBIA
Washington (EMB)
3014 Massachusetts Ave. NW
Washington, DC 20008
Tel: (202) 483-4410 Fax: (202) 328-3712

Vice Consul
Ms. Bernardete Villarroel RIVERO
Consular Agent
Ms. Maria Nancy Gladis Escobar CLAROS

Washington (HCG)
4339 Garfield St. NW
Washington, DC 20008
Tel: (202) 244-7648

Honorary Consul General
Mr. William R. JOYCE

Consulate of Bolivia
1819 H St. NW #240
Washington, DC 20006
Tel: (202) 232-4828 Fax: (202) 232-8017

Consul
Mr. Carlos Hugo JIMENEZ
Consular Agent
Mrs. Kelly Ardaya DE LOPEZ

FLORIDA
Miami (CG)
1101 Brickell Ave. #1103
Miami , FL 33131
Tel: (305) 358-6303 Fax: (305) 358-6305

Consul General
Mr. Moises Jarmusz LEVY
Consul
Miss Maria Isabel Carrasco de MAUBRAS
Consular Agent
Mr. Ramiro Herrera QUISPE

GEORGIA
Atlanta (HCG)
1401 Peachtree St. NE #240
Atlanta , GA 30309
Tel: (404) 522-0777 Fax: (404) 873-3335

Honorary Consul General
Mr. S. George HANDELSMAN

ILLINOIS
Chicago (HC)
1111 W Superior Unit #309
Melrose Park, IL 60160
Tel: (708) 343-1234 Fax: (708) 343-4290

Honorary Consul
Mr. Jaime ESCOBAR

MASSACHUSETTS
Boston (HCG)
85 Devonshire St. #1000
Boston, MA 02109
Tel: (617) 742-1500 Fax: (617) 742-9130

Honorary Consul General
Mr. Russell D. LEBLANG

MINNESOTA
Minneapolis (HC)
20550 Hackamore Rd.
Hamel, MN 55340
Tel: (763) 478-9495 Fax: (763) 478-6631

Honorary Consul
Mrs. Gloria STEINE

NEW YORK
New York (CG)
211 E 43rd St. #702

Source: US Department of State. www.state.gov

New York, NY 10017
Tel: (212) 687-0530 Fax: (212) 687-0532
Consul General
Mr. Jorge Edmundo Heredia CAVERO
Consul
Mrs. Teresa Pinto Roman Vda DE CASAP

OKLAHOMA
Oklahoma City (HC)
210 Park Ave.
Oklahoma City , OK 73102
Tel: (405) 239-7900 Fax: (405) 235-5852

Honorary Consul
Mr. Joe Ray SIMON

PUERTO RICO
San Juan (HC)
1409 Calle Lunchetti Unit
San Juan, PR 00914
Tel: (787) 722-5449 Fax: (787) 722-8457

Honorary Consul
Mr. Hugh Alanson ANDREWS

TEXAS
Dallas (HC)
1881 Sylvan Ave. #110
Dallas , TX 75208
Tel: (214) 571-6131

Honorary Consul
Ms. Maria URIOSTE

Houston (HCG)
800 Wilcrest Unit #100
Houston , TX 77042
Tel: (713) 977-2344 Fax: (713) 977-2362

Honorary Consul General
Mrs. Diana Galindo de WALKER
Honorary Consul
Mr. Juan Jose FRIAS
Honorary Vice Consul
Ms. Marilyn Harris BAUTISTA

WASHINGTON
Seattle (HC)
15215 52nd Ave. #100
Seattle , WA 98188
Tel: (206) 244-6696 Fax: (206) 243-3795

Honorary Consul
Mr. Rene Ricardo Antezana MONTANO

BRAZIL

ALABAMA
Birmingham (HC)
1901 6th Ave. North #2900
Birmingham , AL 35242
Tel: (205) 970-0714

Honorary Consul
Mr. Michael Hugh JOHNSON

ARIZONA
Scottsdale (HC)
9721 E Desert Cove Ave.
Scottsdale, AZ 85260
Tel: (480) 767-7639

Honorary Consul
Mr. Brad BRADOS

CALIFORNIA
Los Angeles (CG)
8484 Wilshire Blvd. #730, 711
Beverly Hills, CA 90211
Tel: (213) 651-2664

Consul General
Mr. Jose Vicente PIMENTEL

Deputy Consul General
Mr. Michael F. GEPP
Deputy Consul
Mr. Luis Fernando CARVALHO
Deputy Consul
Mrs. Marissol T. C. ROMARIS
Deputy Consul
Mr. Joao Alberto QUINTAES
Vice Consul
Mrs. Marisa Fuentes GONCALVES
Vice Consul
Mrs. Cristina Ribeiro ROCHA

San Diego (HC)
2380 Caminito Agrado
San Diego , CA 92107
Tel: (619) 224-1145

Honorary Consul
Mr. Nelson PEREIRA

San Francisco (CG)
300 Montgomery St. #900
San Francisco , CA 94104
Tel: (415) 981-8170

Consul General
Mr. Georges LAMAZIERE
Deputy Consul
Ms. Marcia Jabor CANIZIO
Deputy Consul
Mr. Roberto Teixeira de AVELLAR
Vice Consul
Mrs. Maria Ligia Ferreira VERDI

DISTRICT OF COLUMBIA
Washington (EMB)
3006 Massachusetts Ave. NW
Washington , DC 20008
Tel: (202) 238-2700 Fax: (202) 238-2827

Vice Consul
Mr. Francisco CAVALCANTI
Vice Consul
Mrs. Simone Cristina de DEUS SILVA

FLORIDA
Miami (CG)
2601 S Bayshore Dr. #800
Miami , FL 33133
Tel: (305) 285-6200

Consul General
Mr. Lucio Pires de AMORIM
Deputy Consul General
Mr. Jose Mauro COUTO
Deputy Consul General
Mr. Eduardo de Mattos HOSANNAH
Deputy Consul
Mr. Paulo de Mello VIDAL
Deputy Consul
Mr. Rui Antonio VASCONCELLOS
Deputy Consul
Mr. Hervelter de MATTOS
Vice Consul
Mr. Bernardo FELLER
Vice Consul
Mr. Jorge Luiz FRANCATO
Vice Consul
Mr. Michel Mont CORNIGLION

GEORGIA
Atlanta (HC)
1201 W Peachtree St.
Atlanta , GA 30309
Tel: (404) 881-7987

Honorary Consul
Mr. Timothy Sewell PERRY

Savannah (HC)
107 Prosperity Dr.
Savannah , GA 31408
Tel: (912) 964-0711 Fax: (912) 964-0771

Honorary Consul
Mr. James Robert MYRICK

HAWAII
Honolulu (HC)
345 Queen St. #400
Honolulu , HI 96813
Tel: (808) 235-0571

Honorary Consul
Mr. Eric Guimaraes CRISPIN

ILLINOIS
Chicago (CG)
401 N Michigan Ave., 30th Fl.
Chicago , IL 60611
Tel: (312) 464-0244 Fax: (312) 464-0299

Consul General
Mr. Alexandre Addor NETO
Deputy Consul General
Mr. Mario GRIECO
Consul
Mr. Miguel J. F. C. MAGALHAES
Consul
Mrs. Ellen Osthoff BARROS
Vice Consul
Ms. Elaine SERAFIM
Vice Consul
Mr. Rodrigo Silva MERHEB
Vice Consul
Ms. Maria Gemina QUEIROZ

LOUISIANA
Baton Rouge (HC)
1465 Ted Dunham Ave.
Baton Rouge , LA 70802
Tel: (504) 336-4143

Honorary Consul
Mr. Joseph Simon BROWN

MASSACHUSETTS
Boston (CG) & Brazilian Air Force Office
20 Park Plz. #810
Boston , MA 02116
Tel: (617) 542-4000 Fax: (617) 542-4318

Consul General
Mr. Mauricio E. Cortes COSTA
Vice Consul
Mr. Israel SANTOS
Vice Consul
Ms. Maria Josina Afonso RODRIGUES
Vice Consul
Mrs. Ricedla Maria Filgueira DIAS
Vice Consul
Mr. Andre Baker MEIO

MISSISSIPPI
Jackson (HC)
175 E Capitol St. #700
Jackson , MS 39201
Tel: (601) 961-2600

Honorary Consul
Mr. J. Kelly ALLGOOD

NEW YORK
New York (CG)
1185 Ave. of Americas, 21st Fl.
New York , NY 10036
Tel: (917) 777-7777

Consul General
Mr. Julio Cesar Gomes Dos SANTOS
Deputy Consul General
Mr. George Monteiro PRATA
Deputy Consul General
Mr. Claudio Frederico ARRUDA
Deputy Consul
Ms. Maria Cristina MARTINS
Deputy Consul
Mr. Andre GUIMARAES
Deputy Consul
Ms. Cecilia ISHITANI
Vice Consul
Mr. Dario V. CAMPOS

Vice Consul
Ms. Marizete ZARDO

Office of the Financial Counselor
565 5th Ave., 17th Fl.
New York, NY 10017
Tel: (212) 489-7930

Deputy Consul
Mrs. Mariana MOSCARDO
Deputy Consul
Mr. Henrique PINTO
Deputy Consul
Mr. Gilberto C. Paranhos VELLOSO
Deputy Consul
Mr. Sergio Ricoy PENA
Deputy Consul
Mr. Luiz Claudio THEMUDO

TENNESSEE
Memphis (HC)
1256 N McLean Blvd.
Memphis , TN 38108
Tel: (901) 272-6505

Honorary Consul
Mr. Edson P. PEREDO

TEXAS
Houston (CG)
1233 W Loop South #1150
Houston , TX 77027
Tel: (713) 961-3063

Consul General
Mr. Carlos Alberto Azevedo PIMENTEL
Deputy Consul General
Mr. Milton Torres SILVA
Vice Consul
Mr. Geroncio Jose DE SILVA
Vice Consul
Mrs. Flavia Regina PASSOS
Vice Consul
Ms. Carmen Castilho ALONSO
Vice Consul
Mr. Luciano Nascimento DE OLIVEIRA
Vice Consul
Ms. Selma Teles DA SILVA

VIRGINIA
Norfolk (HC)
625 Chesopeian Trail
Virginia Beach , VA 23452
Tel: (804) 340-5820

Honorary Consul
Mr. James Earnest THOMPSON

CHILE

CALIFORNIA
Los Angeles (CG)
6100 Wilshire Blvd. #1240
Los Angeles , CA 90048
Tel: (323) 933-3697 Fax: (323) 933-3842

Consul General
Mr. Rodrigo PEREZ
Consular Agent
Mr. Alejandro Norberto Moya ARAYA

San Diego (HC)
550 W. C St. #1820
San Diego, CA 92101-3509
Tel: (619) 232-6361 Fax: (619) 696-0991

Honorary Consul
Mr. George L. GILDRED

San Francisco (CG)
870 Market St. #1058
San Francisco , CA 94102
Tel: (415) 982-7662 Fax: (415) 982-2384

Consul General
Mr. Cesar Alberto Ruiz ASMUSSEN
Honorary Consul
Mr. Fernando ALEGRIA

Santa Clara (HCA)
1376 Johnson St.
Menlo Park , CA 94025
Tel: (650) 543-3847 Fax: (650) 322-6403

Honorary Consular Agent
Mr. Carlos LOPEZ

DISTRICT OF COLUMBIA
Washington (EMB)
1732 Massachusetts Ave. NW
Washington, DC 20036
Tel: (202) 785-1746 Fax: (202) 887-5579

Consul
Mr. Ivan Andres FAVEREAU
Consul
Mr. Francisco del CAMPO LAGOS
Consul
Mr. Alejandro Pablo ARRIARAN

FLORIDA
Miami (CG)
800 Brickell Ave. #1230
Miami , FL 33131
Tel: (305) 371-3219 Fax: (305) 374-4270

Consul General
Mr. Francisco Javier Perez WALKER
Consul
Mr. Carlos F. CORNEJO
Consular Agent
Mr. Gerardo Garcia HUIDOBRO

Commercial Office
1101 Brickell Ave. #M-103
Miami , FL 33133
Tel: (305) 599-2224

GEORGIA
Atlanta (HC)
2876 Sequoyah Dr. NW
Atlanta , GA 30327
Tel: (404) 355-7923

Honorary Consul
Mrs. Erika M. MONCKEBERG

HAWAII
Honolulu (HC)
1329 Lusitania St. #206
Honolulu , HI 96813
Tel: (808) 550-4985

Honorary Consul
Ms. Gladys VERNOY

ILLINOIS
Chicago (CG)
875 N Michigan Ave. #3352
Chicago , IL 60611
Tel: (312) 654-8780 Fax: (312) 654-8948

Consul General
Mr. Jorge Alejandro Rogers TARDEL

LOUISIANA
New Orleans (HC)
1350 Port of New Orleans Pl.
New Orleans , LA 70130
Tel: (504) 528-3364 Fax: (504) 524-4156

Honorary Consul
Mr. Angel Pelayo CARRERAS

MASSACHUSETTS
Boston (HC)
1 Bernardo O'Higgins Cir.
Brighton, MA 02135-7840

Tel: (617) 232-0416 Fax: (617) 232-0817
Honorary Consul
Mr. Paul William GARBER
Honorary Consul
Mr. Philip C. GARBER

MISSOURI
Kansas City (HC)
4153 Broadway
Kansas City, MO 64111
Tel: (816) 531-2345

Honorary Consul
Mr. Robert William EVANS

NEVADA
Las Vegas (HC)
9333 Canyon Mesa Dr.
Las Vegas, NV 89144
Tel: (702) 255-4035

Honorary Consul
Ms. Paulina Elena BIGGS

NEW YORK
New York (CG)
866 United Nations Plz. #601
New York , NY 10017
Tel: (212) 355-0612 Fax: (212) 688-5879

Consul General
Ambassador Oscar FUENTES
Consul
Mr. Jorge VALENZUELA
Consular Agent
Mr. Juan A. Somavia Santa CRUZ
Consular Agent
Mr. Patricio Balmaceda URETA
Honorary Consul
Ms. Elba FUENTES

PENNSYLVANIA
Philadelphia (CG)
446 6th & Chestnut St. #1030
Philadelphia , PA 19106
Tel: (215) 829-9520 Fax: (215) 829-0594

Consul General
Mr. Jose Luis Morales MOLYNEUX

PUERTO RICO
San Juan (CG)
1509 Lopez Landron #800
Santurce, PR 00911
Tel: (809) 725-6365 Fax: (809) 725-7295

Consul General
Mr. Francisco Ossa CONCHA

SOUTH CAROLINA
Charleston (HC)
948 Equestrian Dr.
Mount Pleasant, SC 29464
Tel: (843) 884-6224 Fax: (843) 792-3212

Honorary Consul
Mr. Carlos SALINAS

TEXAS
Dallas (HC)
3500 Oak Lawn Ave. #200
Dallas , TX 75219-4343
Tel: (214) 528-2731 Fax: (214) 522-7167

Honorary Consul
Ms. Dorothy J. REID

Houston (CG)
1360 Post Oak Blvd. #1330
Houston , TX 77056
Tel: (713) 963-9066 Fax: (713) 961-3910

Consul General
Mr. Carlos Vicente Charme SILVA

Consular Agent
Mr. Jaime M. Jana SAENZ

WASHINGTON
Olympia (HC)
700 Sleater-Kinney Rd. SE #B-261
Olympia, WA 98503
Tel: (360) 754-8747

Honorary Consul
Mr. Jorge D. GILBERT

COLOMBIA

CALIFORNIA
Los Angeles (CG)
8383 Wilshire Blvd. #420
Beverly Hills, CA 90211
Tel: (323) 653-9863

Consul General
Mrs. Myriam E. Beltran DE FORERO

San Francisco (CG)
595 Market St. #2130
San Francisco , CA 94105
Tel: (415) 795-7195

Consul General
Mr. Roger Enrique Taboada GARCIA
Vice Consul
Ms. Tania Margarita Corena BOSSA

DISTRICT OF COLUMBIA
Washington (CG)
1101 17th St. NW #1007
Washington, DC 20036
Tel: (202) 332-7476 Fax: (202) 332-7180

Consul
Ms. Maria De Los Angeles BARRAZA
Vice Consul
Ms. Jaqueline ESPITIA

FLORIDA
Miami (CG)
280 Aragon Ave.
Miami, FL 33134
Tel: (305) 448-5558

Consul General
Mrs. Carmenza JARAMILLO
Consul
Mrs. Marta Cecilia Tamara GARCIA
Vice Consul
Ms. Luz Estela PENA
Vice Consul
Mrs. Maria Daza CASTRO
Vice Consul
Mr. Alexander Terreros BONILLA
Vice Consul
Mr. Alfredo A. Saade DIAZGRANADOS

Trade Office
601 Brickell Key Dr. #801
Miami, FL 33131
Tel: (305) 374-3144

Deputy Consul General
Mr. Mauricio Gomez ORDONEZ
Consul
Mrs. Gladys E. Zambrano ARCINIEGAS

GEORGIA
Atlanta (CG)
5901 C Peachtree-Dunwoody Rd. #375
Atlanta, GA 30328
Tel: (770) 668-0451 Fax: (770) 668-0763

Consul General
Mr. Guillermo Salah ZULETA
Vice Consul
Mrs. Luz Marleny Acosta SUAREZ

ILLINOIS
Chicago (CG)
500 N Michigan Ave. #2040
Chicago, IL 60611
Tel: (312) 923-1196 Fax: (312) 923-1197

Consul General
Mrs. Priscila CEBALLOS
Consul
Mr. Francisco J. Vasquez GOMEZ

LOUISIANA
New Orleans (CG)
 2 Canal St. #2302
New Orleans, LA 70130
Tel: (504) 525-5580

MASSACHUSETTS
Boston (CG)
535 Boylston St., 3rd Fl.
Boston, MA 02116
Tel: (617) 303-4656 Fax: (617) 536-9372

Consul
Mr. Juan Ramon Villa GOMEZ
Vice Consul
Ms. Rosa Amalia Zuluaga CANO
Vice Consul
Ms. Adriana M. Gutierrez CASTANEDA

NEW YORK
New York (CG)
10 E 46th St.
New York, NY 10017
Tel: (212) 949-9898

Consul General
Mr. Jaime Buenahora FEBRES
Consul
Mr. Jose David Name CARDOZO
Consul
Mr. Roberto Castro Diaz GRANADOS
Consul
Mrs. Sara A. Rocio Prieto PARDO
Consul
Mrs. Nelsy Raquel Munar JARAMILLO
Consul
Mr. Ivan Dario Arias ARANZAZU
Consul
Mrs. Maria Patricia VEGALARA
Consul
Ms. Maria Carlota Velez DE MAYORAL
Consul
Ms. Maria Gisela Manrique DE BORRERO
Consular Attache
Ms. Marcela Manuela Gomez DURANA

Trade Office
277 Park Ave., 47th Fl.
New York, NY 10172
Tel: (212) 223-1120

Consul
Ms. Maria Cecilia Ruiseco GUTIERREZ

PUERTO RICO
San Juan (CG)
Ponce De Leon Ave. #814
Hato Rey, PR 00918
Tel: (809) 754-6885

Consul General
Mr. Luis Montoya MORENO
Vice Consul
Mr. Felipe Muriel AREVALO

Trade Office
1510 Esq. San Patricio Plz.
San Juan, PR 00968
Tel: (787) 273-1444 Fax: (787) 273-7006

TEXAS
Houston (CG)
5851 San Felipe Unit #300
Houston, TX 77057

Tel: (713) 527-8919

Consul General
Mr. Hernan Arizmendi POSADA
Consul
Mr. Luis Carlos Rodriguez GUTIERREZ

COSTA RICA

CALIFORNIA
Los Angeles (CG)
1605 W Olympic Blvd. #400
Los Angeles, CA 90015
Tel: (213) 380-7915 Fax: (213) 380-5639

Consul General
Mr. Ricardo Alberto Gonzalez DIAZ
Consul
Mr. Percy CALVO
Consul
Mr. Alexis Chacon VALVERDE
Consul
Ms. Brigida Cordero ARIAS
Consular Agent
Ms. Cynthia Solis LIZANO

San Francisco (CG)
870 Market St. #645
San Francisco, CA 94102
Tel: (415) 392-8488

COLORADO
Denver (HC)
3356 S Xenia St.
Denver, CO 80231-4542
Tel: (303) 696-8211 Fax: (303) 696-1110

Honorary Consul
Mr. Tito CHAVERRI

DISTRICT OF COLUMBIA
Washington (EMB)
2114 S St. NW
Washington , DC 20008
Tel: (202) 234-2945 Fax: (202) 265-4795

Consul General
Mr. Alejandro Cedeno ULLOA

FLORIDA
Miami (CG)
1101 Brickell Ave. #704
Miami , FL 33131
Tel: (305) 871-7485 Fax: (305) 871-0860

Consul General
Ms. Roxana PACHECO
Consul
Miss Maria A. FERNANDEZ
Consul
Mrs. Deidamia Maria MONGE
Consul
Miss Kattia J. Saborio CHAVERRI
Consul
Mr. Oscar Camacho RAMIREZ
Consular Agent
Mr. Carlos Alberto Paez PIZARRO

Tampa (CG)
2200 Barker Rd.
Tampa, FL 33605
Tel: (813) 248-6741 Fax: (813) 248-6741

Consul General
Mrs. Erica Salgado WINIKER

GEORGIA
Atlanta (CG)
1870 The Exchange Unit #100
Atlanta, GA 30339
Tel: (770) 951-7025 Fax: (770) 951-7073

Consul General
Ms. Emilia Maria Trejos CASTRO

Consul
Ms. Alejandra CHAVERRI

ILLINOIS
Chicago (CG)
203 N Wabash Ave. #1312
Chicago, IL 60601
Tel: (312) 263-2772 Fax: (312) 263-5807

Consul General
Mr. Juan SALAS
Honorary Consul
Mr. Carlos L. ROJAS

LOUISIANA
New Orleans (CG)
2 Canal St. #2334
New Orleans, LA 70130
Tel: (504) 581-6800 Fax: (504) 581-6850

Consul General
Mr. Gonzalo CALDERON

MASSACHUSETTS
Boston (HCG)
175 McClellan Hwy.
Boston, MA 02128-9114
Tel: (617) 561-2444 Fax: (617) 561-2461

Honorary Consul General
Mr. Leonard FLORENCE

MINNESOTA
Minneapolis (HC)
2424 Territorial Rd.
St. Paul, MN 55114
Tel: (651) 481-3616 Fax: (651) 645-4684

Honorary Consul
Mr. Anthony L. ANDERSEN

NEW MEXICO
Albuquerque (CG)
7033 Luella Anne Dr. NE
Albuquerque, NM 87109
Tel: (505) 822-1420

NEW YORK
New York (CG)
80 Wall St. #718-19
New York, NY 10005
Tel: (212) 509-3066 Fax: (212) 509-3068

Consul General
Mr. Otto Roberto VARGAS
Consul
Mr. Eric Chaves SALAS
Vice Consul
Miss Rebeca SIBAJA
Vice Consul
Mr. Eduardo Salgado RETANA
Consular Agent
Mr. Armando E. HEILBRON
Consular Agent
Ms. Maria Del Pilar MADRIGAL
Consular Agent
Mr. Eduardo HERNANDEZ
Consular Agent
Mr. Eliecer Feinzaig MINTZ
Honorary Consul
Mr. C. Joseph HALLINAN, JR.

NORTH CAROLINA
Durham (CG)
3516 University Dr. #A
Durham, NC 27707

PENNSYLVANIA
Philadelphia (CG)
1411 Walnut St. #200
Philadelphia, PA 19102
Tel: (800) 233-9894

PUERTO RICO
San Juan (CG)
1510 Ponce De Leon Ave.
Santurce, PR 00909
Tel: (787) 723-6227 Fax: (787) 723-6226

Consul General
Mr. Luis Roberto RAMIREZ

TEXAS
Austin (C)
1730 E O'Horf
Austin, TX 78741
Tel: (512) 445-0023

Dallas (HC)
7777 Forrest Ln. #B-445
Dallas, TX 75230
Tel: (972) 566-7020 Fax: (972) 566-7943

Honorary Consul
Mr. Jaime Abraham DAVIDSON

Houston (CG)
3000 Wilcrest Dr. #112
Houston, TX 77042
Tel: (713) 266-0484 Fax: (713) 266-1527

Consul General
Mrs. Cira M. Sanchez SIBAJA
Consul
Mrs. Maria Gabriela BOLANOS

San Antonio (CG)
6836 San Pedro #206-B
San Antonio, TX 78216
Tel: (210) 824-8474 Fax: (210) 824-8489

Consul
Ms. Marta Cecilia Rojas OROZCO

DOMINICAN REPUBLIC

ALABAMA
Mobile (C)
154 State St., 2nd Fl.
Mobile, AL 36603
Tel: (334) 433-8894

ALASKA
Anchorage (HC)
8101 Rovenna St.
Anchorage, AK 99518
Tel: (907) 336-6450

Honorary Consul
Mr. Francisco Del ROSARIO

CALIFORNIA
San Francisco (CG)
1516 Oak St. #321
Alameda, CA 94501
Tel: (415) 982-5144

FLORIDA
Jacksonville (CG)
1914 Beach Way Rd. #1-A
Jacksonville, FL 32207
Tel: (904) 346-0909 Fax: (904) 346-0919

Miami (CG)
1038 Brickell Ave.
Miami, FL 33131
Tel: (305) 358-3221

Vice Consul
Mr. Nelson Ahmed Chabebe BAEZ
Vice Consul
Mr. Marcos Jose Pereyra JORGE
Vice Consul
Mr. Diego Ramon Guerra NOUEL

GEORGIA
Atlanta (HC)
191 Peachtree St. #4600
Atlanta, GA 30303

Tel: (404) 572-4814

Honorary Consul
Mr. Horace Holden SIBLEY

LLINOIS
Chicago (CG)
1 Northfield Plz. #300
Northfield, IL 60093
Tel: (847) 441-1831 Fax: (847) 441-1833

Consul General
Mr. Remberto Mariano Vasquez ESCOTO

LOUISIANA
New Orleans (CG)
2 Canal St. #2100
New Orleans, LA 70130
Tel: (504) 522-1843 Fax: (504) 522-1007

Consul General
Mr. Joaquin A. Balaguer RICARDO

MARYLAND
Baltimore (HC)
11841 Sherbourne Dr.
Timonium, MD 21093
Tel: (410) 560-2101 Fax: (410) 561-9419

Honorary Consul
Mrs. Rita Hernandez DE DIAZ

MASSACHUSETTS
Boston (CG)
20 Park Plz. #601
Boston, MA 02116
Tel: (617) 482-8121 Fax: (617) 482-8133

Consul General
Mrs. Eladia Medina REYNOSO

MICHIGAN
Detroit (HC)
7311 Whittaker
Detroit, MI 48209
Tel: (313) 843-0389

Honorary Consul
Dr. Fernando COLON M.

MINNESOTA
Minneapolis (HCG)
120 S. 6th St. #1910
Minneapolis, MN 55402
Tel: (612) 339-7566 Fax: (612) 339-9055

Honorary Consul General
Mr. Ralph S. PARKER II

NEW YORK
New York (CG)
1501 Broadway #410
New York, NY 10036
Tel: (212) 768-2480 Fax: (212) 768-2677

Vice Consul
Ms. Delia FELIZ
Vice Consul
Mr. Henry Taveras QUIRICO

PENNSYLVANIA
Philadelphia (CG)
5th & Chestnut St. #216
Philadelphia, PA 19106
Tel: (215) 923-3006 Fax: (215) 923-3007

Vice Consul
Mr. Nelson CUELLO

PUERTO RICO
Mayaguez (CG)
30 Calle McKinley St., 2ndFl.
Mayaguez, PR 00680
Tel: (809) 833-0007

Consul General
Mr. Ernesto R. Castellanos DOMINGUEZ

Ponce (C)
Marginal
Ponce, PR 00731
Tel: (809) 842-9004

San Juan (CG)
1612 Avenida Ponce de Leon Unit, 7th Fl.
San Juan, PR 00907
Tel: (809) 725-9550

Consul General
Ms. Carmen Fantina Sosa CORDERO

TEXAS
Houston (HC)
3300 S Gessner Unit #113
Houston, TX 77063
Tel: (713) 266-0165

Honorary Consul
Ms. Ana Maria DIAZ

ECUADOR

CALIFORNIA
Los Angeles (CG)
8484 Wilshire Blvd. #540
Beverly Hills, CA 90211
Tel: (323) 658-6020

Deputy Consul General
Mr. Fernando ARIAS
Deputy Consul General
Mr. Marcelo Salcedo PAZMINO
Consul
Mrs. Grimaneza Montenegro SILVA
Vice Consul
Mr. Nestor Alejandro Landeta VARGAS
Consular Agent
Miss Maria Cristina PENLAND
Consular Agent
Mrs. Paulina Y. Mejia VASCONEZ
Consular Agent
Mr. Pablo R. SANDOVAL

San Francisco (CG)
235 Montgomery St. #944
San Francisco, CA 94104
Tel: (415) 957-5921 Fax: (415) 957-5923

Consul General
Mr. Gustavo Palacio URRUTIA
Consul
Mr. Enrique A. LASSO
Consul
Ms. Olimpia Vargas BORBUA
Honorary Consul
Mrs. Ximena Cordovez ANGOTTI

FLORIDA
Miami (CG)
1101 Brickell Ave. #M-102
Miami , FL 33131
Tel: (305) 539-8214 Fax: (305) 539-8313

Consul General
Mr. Leonardo Tamariz MEJIA
Deputy Consul General
Ms. Nancy Carmen Cely ICAZA
Consul
Ms. Carmen Sanchez MORAN
Consul
Mrs. Beatriz Zohrer PONTON
Consul
Mr. Leonardo Simon Nina RECALDE

Miami (Visa Office)
3785 NW 82nd Ave. #317
Miami, FL 33166
Tel: (305) 716-5252 Fax: (305) 716-9296

GEORGIA
Atlanta (HC)
5505 Roswell Rd. #350
Atlanta, GA 30342
Tel: (404) 252-2211 Fax: (404) 252-8580

Honorary Consul
Mrs. Patricia BOEZIO

ILLINOIS
Chicago (CG)
30 S Michigan Ave. #204
Chicago, IL 60603
Tel: (312) 338-1003 Fax: (312) 338-1004

Consul General
Mr. Galo Fernando Chaves DAVILA
Deputy Consul General
Dr. Carlos Bolivar Rojas PAZMINO
Consular Agent
Mrs. Yadira Asuncion Lopez FIGUEREDO
Consular Agent
Mr. Julio Alexis Pazos CARRILLO
Honorary Consul
Mr. Hernan Marcelo Vela HERVAS

LOUISIANA
New Orleans (CG)
2 Canal St. #2338
New Orleans, LA 70130
Tel: (504) 523-3229

Consul General
Mr. Alejandro CEVALLOS
Consul
Ms. Alicia C. Acosta NUNEZ
Consular Agent
Mr. Ider S. Rivadeneyra SALAZAR

MASSACHUSETTS
Boston (HC)
52 Cranberry Ln.
Needham, MA 02492
Tel: (781) 444-0213

Honorary Consul
Mrs. Beatriz STEIN

Boston (HC)
52 Cranberry Ln.
Needham, MA 02492
Tel: (781) 444-0213

Honorary Consul
Mrs. Beatriz STEIN

NEVADA
Las Vegas (HCG)
3500 Paradise Rd.
Las Vegas, NV 89109
Tel: (702) 735-8193

Honorary Consul General
Ms. Michele G. JARAMILLO

NEW JERSEY
Jersey City (CG)
30 Montgomery St. #1020
Jersey City, NJ 07302
Tel: (201) 985-1300

Consul General
Mr. Ivan Enrique Naranjo LOGRONO
Consul
Rear Admiral Gustavo Alfonso Jarrin AMPUDIA
Consular Agent
Mr. Carlos L. HERMOSA
Consular Agent
Ms. Silvia Chavez MURGEYTIO
Consular Agent
Mrs. Patricia Pelaez MORA

NEW YORK
New York (CG)
800 2nd Ave. #600
New York, NY 10017
Tel: (212) 808-0170

Consul General
Mr. David Alfredo Molina VIZCAINO
Consul
Ms. Gloria Espinel CHIRIBOGA
Consul
Ms. CONSUELOOTERO
Consul
Ms. Veronica Aguilar TORRES
Deputy Consul
Ms. Carol Jara ACOSTA
Vice Consul
Mr. Juan Granados PALADINES
Consular Agent
Mr. Marco Vinicio Bustillos VIERA
Consular Agent
Mr. Jorge Vallejo VILLARROEL
Consular Agent
Mr. Oscar Fuertes JIMENEZ

Commercial Office
399 Park Ave. #28-B
New York, NY 10022
Tel: (212) 888-7229

PENNSYLVANIA
Philadelphia (CG)
Independence Sq. #1015-1017
Philadelphia, PA 19106
Tel: (215) 925-9060

PUERTO RICO
San Juan (HC)
6 S Inf Calle Abad Veb Club Manor
Rio Piedros, PR 00924
Tel: (787) 999-5226 Fax: (787) 999-5243

Honorary Consul
Mr. Andres VITOLA

TEXAS
Houston (CG)
4200 Westheimer #218
Houston, TX 77027
Tel: (713) 622-1787

Consul General
Mr. Arturo Ontaneda LUCIANO
Consul
Captain Jorge Bassante GARCIA
Consul
Mr. Luis F. Tapia VARGAS
Consular Agent
Ms. Sofia Robalino AGUIRRE
Consular Agent
Ms. Maria ENCALADA
Consular Agent
Mr. Jose Bustos ZAPATA
Consular Agent
Mr. Jaime Eduardo Munoz AGUIRRE
Honorary Consul
Dr. Carlos E. ROMERO

Dallas (HC)
7510 Acorn Ln.
Frisco, TX 75034
Tel: (972) 712-9107 Fax: (253) 369-7475

Honorary Consul
Mr. Ricardo M. Bowen GRIMMER

UTAH
Salt Lake City (HC)
2530 S. West Temple Unit
Salt Lake City, UT 84115

Tel: (801) 631-0843

Honorary Consul
Mrs. Veronica Flores Van LEEUWEN

EL SALVADOR

ARIZONA
Phoenix (HC)
4521 E Charles Dr.
Paradise Valley, AZ 85253
Tel: (602) 948-4899

Honorary Consul
Mr. Tracy R. THOMAS

CALIFORNIA
Los Angeles (CG)
3450 Wilshire Blvd. #250
Los Angeles, CA 90010
Tel: (213) 383-8580

Consul General
Mr. Mauricio Enrique Ruano MARTINEZ
Vice Consul
Mr. Rafael Antonio Carballo LACAYO
Vice Consul
Miss Anna Maria de la GASCA
Honorary Consul
Mrs. Gina C. LEVY

San Francisco (CG)
870 Market St. #508
San Francisco, CA 94102
Tel: (415) 781-7924

Consul General
Mr. Hugo HERRERA
Vice Consul
Mr. Luis Roberto Castellanos ALVAREZ

Santa Ana (VC)
1212 N Broadway Ave. #100
Santa Ana, CA 92701

DISTRICT OF COLUMBIA
Washington (CG)
1724 20th St. NW
Washington , DC 20009
Tel: (202) 331-4032 Fax: (202) 331-4036

Consul General
Mr. Carlos Adrian Velasco NOVOA
Vice Consul
Miss Mirian E. Vargas CASTILLO

FLORIDA
Miami (CG)
300 Biscayne Blvd. Way #1020
Miami, FL 33131
Tel: (305) 371-8850

Consul General
Mr. Fernando Quinonez MEZA
Vice Consul
Mrs. Ana Maria ESERSKI
Vice Consul
Mr. Roberto Alas ENGELHARD
Vice Consul
Ms. Florence Kriete AVILA
Honorary Consul
Mr. Raul J. Valdes FAULI

ILLINOIS
Chicago (CG)
104 S Michigan Ave. #816
Chicago, IL 60603
Tel: (312) 332-1393 Fax: (312) 332-1393

Consul General
Ms. Patricia Maza PITTSFORD

LOUISIANA
New Orleans (HCG)
315 W David Pkwy.

Metairie, LA 70005
Tel: (504) 828-1727 Fax: (504) 831-7404

Honorary Consul General
Dr. Patricia Elena MOLINA

MASSACHUSETTS
Boston (CG)
20 Meridian St., 4th Fl.
Boston, MA 02128
Tel: (617) 567-8484

Consul General
Mr. Roberto F. ESCOBAR
Vice Consul
Mr. Pedro A. Angel ORELLANA

MISSOURI
Kansas City (HC)
608 W 101st St.
Kansas City, MO 64114
Tel: (816) 941-6648

Honorary Consul
Mr. John H. FISHER

St. Louis (HC)
7730 Forsyth #150
St. Louis, MO 63105
Tel: (314) 862-0300

Honorary Consul
Mr. Michael Jay BOBROFF

NEW YORK
New York (CG)
46 Park Ave.
New York, NY 10016
Tel: (212) 889-3608

Consul General
Ms. Lorena Sol De POOL
Consul
Mrs. Ana Vilma Avila De SOLER
Consul
Ms. Gilda VELASQUEZ

New York (CG)
1090 Suffolk Ave.
Brentwood, NY 11717
Tel: (631) 273-1355

Consul General
Mr. Luis Montes BRITO
Vice Consul
Mr. Oscar E. Landaverde CONTRERAS
Consular Agent
Ms. Elizabeth del Carmen HERRERA

PENNSYLVANIA
Philadelphia (HC)
119 Bleddyn Rd.
Ardmore, PA 19003

Honorary Consul
Mrs. Ana Maria KEENE

PUERTO RICO
Bayamon (HCG)
Caparra Office Ctr. #224
Guaynabo, PR 00968
Tel: (787) 793-7577 Fax: (787) 793-7578

Honorary Consul General
Ms. Maria Teresa DE ESTEVEZ

TEXAS
Dallas (CG)
1555 W Mockingbird Ln. #216
Dallas, TX 75235

Consul General
Mrs. Astrid S. ARIZ
Vice Consul
Mrs. Ana Maria Perez de LOPEZ

Houston (CG)

6420 Hillcroft St. #100
Houston, TX 77081
Tel: (713) 270-6239

Consul General
Mr. Luis Ernesto CARRANZA
Consul
Mr. Leocadio Jose J. Chacon CORADO
Vice Consul
Ms. Marlene E. Orantes de SALAZAR
Vice Consul
Mrs. Ana Silvia Arce de GALLO

UTAH
Salt Lake City (HC)
2530 S. West Temple Unit
Salt Lake City , UT 84115
Tel: (801) 631-0843

Honorary Consul
Mrs. Veronica Flores VAN LEEUWEN

GUATEMALA

ALABAMA
Montgomery (HC)
2153 Meadow Lane Dr.
Montgomery, AL 36106
Tel: (205) 269-2756

Honorary Consul
Mr. Jose Roberto ORTEGA-LOPEZ

CALIFORNIA
Los Angeles (CG)
1605 W Olympic Blvd. #422
Los Angeles, CA 90015
Tel: (213) 365-9251

Consul General
Mr. Fernando CASTILLO
Consul
Ms. Lissette ORDONEZ
Vice Consul
Ms. Maria E. FIGUEROA DE ALVARADO
Vice Consul
Mr. German Arnoldo CEREZO
Vice Consul
Ms. Patricia MEIGHAM
Vice Consul
Mrs. Guadalupe de MURGA
Vice Consul
Ms. Alma R. BOLANOS
Vice Consul
Mr. Javier Oscar JORDAN
Honorary Consul
Mr. John L. ULMEN

San Diego (HC)
10405 San Diego Mission Rd. #205
San Diego, CA 92108
Tel: (619) 282-8127

Honorary Consul
Mr. Eugene Herbert SAPPER

San Francisco (CG)
870 Market St. #667
San Francisco, CA 94102
Tel: (415) 788-5651

Consul General
Mrs. Erika PINEDA DE SHARRON
Vice Consul
Mr. Hugo Arnoldo BLANCO
Vice Consul
Mrs. Maria Delgado DE MORATAYA
Consular Agent
Miss Ana Maria Lucero BARAHONA
Honorary Consul
Mr. Carlos Armando AFRE

COLORADO
Denver (CG)
820 16th St. #615

Denver, CO 80202

Consul General
Mr. Alfredo Vasquez RIVERA
Consul
Mr. Fernando Molina NANNINI
Consular Agent
Mr. Percy Rolando Pena RILEY

DISTRICT OF COLUMBIA
Washington (EMB)
2220 R St. NW
Washington, DC 20008
Tel: (202) 745-4952 Fax: (202) 745-1908

Consul
Miss Ivonne SANCHEZ

FLORIDA
Ft. Lauderdale (HC)
2601 Oakland Park Blvd. #200
Ft. Lauderdale, FL 33306
Tel: (954) 467-1700 Fax: (954) 764-1700

Honorary Consul
Mr. John P. BAUER

Miami (CG)
1101 Brickell Ave. #1003-S
Miami, FL 33131
Tel: (305) 679-9945

Consul General
Ms. Cristy ANDRINO
Vice Consul
Ms. Ana Maria Corea VILLEDA
Vice Consul
Ms. Dunia MIRANDA
Vice Consul
Mr. Juan Pablo Riley PORTILLO
Consular Agent
Mr. Angel Manuel Salazar ANLEU
Consular Agent
Ms. Doris Quezada GUZMAN
Honorary Consul
Mr. George L. COMBALUZIER

GEORGIA
Atlanta (HC)
4772 E Conway Dr. NW
Atlanta, GA 30327
Tel: (404) 255-7019 Fax: (404) 255-0023

Honorary Consul
Mrs. Maria Teresa FRASER

ILLINOIS
Chicago (CG)
203 N Wabash Ave. #910
Chicago, IL 60601
Tel: (312) 332-1587 Fax: (312) 322-4256

Consul General
Ms. Shary Edith MIJANGOS DE THIEL
Vice Consul
Mrs. Miriam L. Suchini de ALVAREZ
Consular Agent
Ms. T. Roxana RIEPELE
Consular Agent
Mr. Serminio SANCHINEL
Honorary Vice Consul
Mrs. Lillian Gleason de MAGNUSON

KANSAS
Leavenworth (HC)
419 Delaware St.
Leavenworth, KS 66048
Tel: (913) 682-0342

LOUISIANA
Lafayette (HC)
735 Rue Jefferson
Lafayette, LA 70501
Tel: (318) 268-5474

Honorary Consul
Mr. Enrique Leonardo HERRERA

New Orleans (HC)
1001 Howard Ave. #2504
New Orleans, LA 70113
Tel: (504) 558-3777

Honorary Consul
Ms. Margarita Lourdes JEREZ

MINNESOTA
Minneapolis (HC)
2105 1st Ave. South
Minneapolis, MN 55404
Tel: (612) 870-3459

Honorary Consul
Mr. Alex Edmund S. DAHINTEN

MISSOURI
Kansas City (HC)
400 E Red Bridge Rd. #107
Kansas City, MO 64131
Tel: (816) 942-6990 Fax: (816) 942-4301

Honorary Consul
Dr. Joseph Peter SPALITTO

NEW YORK
New York (CG)
57 Park Ave.
New York, NY 10016
Tel: (212) 686-3837

Consul General
Ms. Rosa Maria Merida De MORA
Consul
Mrs. Maria Luz ZYRIEK
Consul
Ms. Sara Ivonne Mishaan ROSSELL
Vice Consul
Ms. Mara E. MEJIA
Vice Consul
Mrs. Margarita SIMEONIDIS
Vice Consul
Mr. Roberto ROSENBERG
Consular Agent
Mrs. Claudia DE FERNANDEZ
Consular Agent
Mr. Pedro TZUNUN
Consular Agent
Mrs. Claudia Gatica MORENO
Consular Agent
Mrs. Olga Leticia Recinos GONZALEZ
Consular Agent
Mrs. Dina Beatriz Mogollon VARGAS

OREGON
Portland (HC)
821 NW 11th Ave. #323
Portland, OR 97209
Tel: (503) 224-4193 Fax: (503) 224-4886

Honorary Consul
Mr. Serge D'ROVENCOURT

PENNSYLVANIA
Philadelphia (HC)
1245 Highland Ave. #301
Abington, PA 19001
Tel: (215) 885-5551

Honorary Consul
Dr. Roberto Rendon MALDONADO

Pittsburgh (HC)
709 Washington Dr.
Pittsburgh, PA 15229
Tel: (412) 366-7715

Honorary Consul
Mrs. Margarita WINIKOFF

PUERTO RICO
San Juan (HC)

530 Ponce de Leon, Atrium Office Ctr. Ave.
San Juan, PR 00901
Tel: (787) 289-7871 Fax: (787) 289-8779

Honorary Consul
Mr. Alberto M. Perez NEGRONI

RHODE ISLAND
Providence (HC)
11 Lancashire St.
Providence, RI 02908

Honorary Consul
Mrs. Zoila R. GUERRA

TENNESSEE
Memphis (HC)
147 Jefferson Ave.
Memphis, TN 38103
Tel: (901) 527-8466 Fax: (901) 527-8469

Honorary Consul
Mr. George E. WHITWORTH

TEXAS
Houston (CG)
3013 Fountain View Unit #210
Houston, TX 77057
Tel: (713) 953-9531

Consul General
Mr. Jose Barillas TRENNERT
Vice Consul
Mrs. Beatriz Fontana SCHIOZZI
Consular Agent
Mrs. Lizbeth Karina Pivaral ORTIZ
Honorary Consul
Dr. Carlos Hugo MONSANTO
Honorary Consul
Mr. Jose Rafael ESPADA

San Antonio (HC)
4840 Whirlwind
San Antonio, TX 78217

Honorary Vice Consul
Mr. Carlos Ferreyro LUCERO

WASHINGTON
Seattle (HC)
2100 5th Ave.
Seattle, WA 98121
Tel: (206) 728-5920

Consul General
Mr. Hector Palacios LIMA

HONDURAS

ARIZONA
Phoenix (CG)
2121 W University Dr. #124/7
Tempe, AZ 85281
Tel: (602) 595-9250

Consul General
Mr. Tulio Alberto Avila PINEDA

CALIFORNIA
San Diego (HC)
525 B St. #2002
San Diego, CA 92101
Tel: (619) 533-4515

Honorary Consul
Ms. Ella Isabel FLORES-PARIS

San Francisco (CG)
870 Market St. #449
San Francisco, CA 94102
Tel: (415) 392-0076

Consul
Mrs. Amalia Leticia HERNANDEZ
Vice Consul
Mr. Servio Tulio Chavez PETIT

Honorary Vice Consul
Mr. Henry Langenberg MC INTYRE

Los Angeles (CG)
3550 Wilshire Blvd. #410
Los Angeles, CA 90010
Tel: (213) 383-9244

Consul General
Miss Vivian Veronica Panting GALO
Vice Consul
Ms. Leydis Cristina Romero ZUNIGA
Consular Agent
Ms. Aissa Alejandra ANTUNEZ
Consular Agent
Mr. Luis Martinez IRIAS
Consular Agent
Mrs. Rafaela E. ACOSTA
Honorary Consul
Mr. George V. CHILINGAR
Honorary Vice Consul
Ms. Susana M. STEVENSON
Honorary Consular Agent
Mr. Oscar Artiles PONCE

FLORIDA
Jacksonville (C)
1914 Beachway Rd. #3-0
Jacksonville , FL 33207
Tel: (904) 348-3550

Consul
Mr. Antonio J. VALLADARES

Miami (CG)
7171 Coral Way #309
Miami, FL 33155
Tel: (305) 269-9399 Fax: (305) 269-9445

Consul General
Mr. Carlos A. Siercke MARTINEZ, SR.
Consul
Mrs. Miriam Bernarda YNESTROZA
Consular Agent
Mr. Jose J. Jalil SALOMON
Consular Agent
Mr. Manuel VILLEDA-TOLEDO
Consular Agent
Mr. Augustin GONZALEZ
Consular Agent
Mrs. Maria Gisela DE ZACAPA
Consular Agent
Ms. Virginia BUESO
Consular Agent
Captain Jose Eduardo Espinal PAZ
Consular Agent
Mr. Jimmy Roberto KAFIE
Consular Agent
Mr. Juan Carlos VASQUEZ
Consular Agent
Mr. Francisco Mejia GUEVARA
Honorary Consul
Mr. Federico Alberto SMITH
Honorary Consul
Mr. Owen S. FREED

Tampa (CG)
1107 E. Jackson St. #103
Tampa, FL 33602
Tel: (813) 209-2349

Consul General
Mr. Luis Alberto CASTILLO

GEORGIA
Atlanta (C)
600 Houze Way #3-A
Roswell, GA 30076
Tel: (770) 234-9560

Consul General
Dr. Cecilia WILSON

HAWAII
Honolulu (HC)

1734 Malanai St. #B
Honolulu, HI 96826
Tel: (808) 944-2811

Honorary Consul
Mrs. Lesby Perez BILLAM-WALKER

ILLINOIS
Chicago (CG)
4506 W Fullerton Ave.
Chicago, IL 60639
Tel: (773) 342-8281 Fax: (773) 342-8293

Consul General
Mr. Gregorio Irias NAVAS
Consular Agent
Mr. Lenyng Hernandez MATUTE
Honorary Vice Consul
Ms. Maura Rosa Alcerro PRUDOT

LOUISIANA
Baton Rouge (HC)
11017 N Oak Hills Pkwy.
Baton Rouge, LA 70810
Tel: (225) 766-4350 Fax: (225) 766-7334

Honorary Consul
Ms. Vilma Cabrera CALHOUN
Honorary Vice Consul
Mr. William HUMPHREYS

New Orleans (CG)
2 Canal St. #1641
New Orleans , LA 70130
Tel: (504) 522-3118

Consul General
Ms. Maria Eugenia Lobo CRESPO
Consular Agent
Ms. Glenda Marina Romero VALLADARES
Honorary Consul
Mr. Carlos David FLORES

MARYLAND
Baltimore (HCG)
5803 Loch Raven Blvd.
Baltimore, MD 21239
Tel: (301) 435-6233

Honorary Consul General
Mr. Rene Licona DUARTE

MASSACHUSETTS
Boston (C)
486 Beacon St. #2
Newton, MA 02115
Tel: (617) 247-2007

Consul
Ms. Graciela SUAREZ

MICHIGAN
Detroit (C)
3620 Shady Ln.
Detroit, MI 48216

MINNESOTA
Minneapolis (HC)
20 Cygnet Pl.
Long Lake, MN 55356
Tel: (612) 473-5376

Honorary Consul
Mr. Harold Joseph PANUSKA

MISSOURI
St. Louis (HC)
6241 Alexander Dr.
St. Louis, MO 63105
Tel: (314) 727-9179

Honorary Consul
Ms. Maria TAXMAN

NEVADA
Reno (HC)
5250 Neil Rd. #303
Reno, NV 89502-6503
Tel: (775) 829-1209

Honorary Consul
Dr. Rudolf GUNNERMAN

NEW YORK
New York (CG)
35 W 35th St., 6th Fl.
New York, NY 10001

Consul General
Ms. E. Antonieta MAXIMO
Consular Agent
Mr. Francisoco Quezada LOBO

PUERTO RICO
San Juan (CG)
Ponce de Leon Ave. #604
San Juan, PR 00918

Consular Agent
Ms. Gina Elisabeth Urcina RASKOFF

TEXAS
Houston (CG)
4151 SW Freeway #700
Houston , TX 77027
Tel: (713) 622-4572

Consul General
Mrs. Lastenia PINEDA
Consular Agent
Mrs. Maria Elena Torres de GOMEZ
Consular Agent
Mr. Eduardo FAASCH, SR.
Consular Agent
Mr. Oscar CASTANEDA
Consular Agent
Mr. Dax VENEGAS
Consular Agent
Ms. Elizabeth CRUZ
Consular Agent
Ms. Carol Leticia BARAHONA
Honorary Consular Agent
Mrs. Mayra O. SIMON

MEXICO

ALASKA
Anchorage (HC)
3000 Rosalind Pl.
Anchorage, AK 99507
Tel: (907) 223-5544 Fax: (907) 563-9152

Honorary Consul
Mrs. Lina B. Ruiz MARISCAL

ARIZONA
Nogales (CG)
571 N Grand Ave.
Nogales , AZ 85621
Tel: (602) 287-2521

Consul General
Mr. Carlos I. Gonzalez MAGALLON
Consul
Mr. Ruben Guido ASTORGA
Deputy Consul
Miss Miriam Villanueva AYON

Phoenix (CG)
1990 W Camelback Rd. #110
Phoenix , AZ 85015
Tel: (602) 249-2735

Consul General
Mr. Carlos Flores VIZCARRA
Deputy Consul
Mr. Fernando Vargas BRIONES
Vice Consul
Mr. Rigoberto Lizarraga RENDON

Tucson (C)
553 S Stone Ave.
Tucson , AZ 85701
Consul
Mr. Juan Manuel Calderon JAMES
Deputy Consul
Ms. Eugenia Cabrera MURILLO

Douglas (C)
1201 F St.
Douglas , AZ 85607
Tel: (520) 364-3142
Consul
Mr. Miguel Escobar VALDEZ
Deputy Consul
Mr. Roberto Campos PADILLA

Yuma (C)
600 W 16th St.
Yuma, AZ 85364
Tel: (928) 344-0066
Consul
Mr. Hugo Rene Oliva ROMERO
Deputy Consul
Mr. Juan Gabriel Morales MORALES

CALIFORNIA
Calexico (C)
408 Heber Ave.
Calexico, CA 92231
Tel: (619) 357-3863
Consul
Mr. Raul Cueto MARTINEZ
Consul
Mr. Luis Guillermo Romero PARRA
Deputy Consul
Mr. Miguel Eduardo Rea FALCON

Fresno (C)
2409 Merced St.
Fresno, CA 93721
Tel: (209) 233-4219
Consul
Mr. Jaime Paz y Puente GUTIERREZ
Consul
Mr. Jose Antonio Lagunas BORJA
Deputy Consul
Mrs. Juana Maria Ruiz MARTINEZ

Los Angeles (CG)
2401 W 6th St.
Los Angeles, CA 90057
Tel: (213) 351-6815 Fax: (213) 389-9186
Consul General
Mr. Ruben Alberto Beltran GUERRERO
Deputy Consul General
Mr. Salvador Jimenez MUNOZ
Consul
Mr. Alejandro R. Schiavon DELGADO
Consul
Mrs. Norma A. Ramirez Avila DE MOLINA
Consul
Mr. Ramon Carrillo DE ALBORNOZ
Consul
Mr. Jose Antonio Larios PONCE
Consul
Mr. Jesus Garcia LUNA
Consul
Mr. Mario Perez Ramirez ZAMORA
Consul
Mr. Alejandro Pelayo RANGEL
Consul
Mr. Agustin Emilio Pradillo CUEVAS
Consul
Mr. Carlos Alfonso Villeda TREJO
Consul
Mr. Alejandro Contreras CASTANEDA
Consul
Mrs. Maria de Nuria Marine GONZALEZ
Consul
Mr. Julian Adem Diaz DE LEON

Consul
Ms. Milagros Alejandra CANO
Consul
Mr. Enrique Esteban Zepeda VAZQUEZ
Consul
Mr. Alejandro Garza BOLADO
Consul
Mr. Reynaldo Cruz SERRANO
Vice Consul
Mr. Miguel Angel Peralta VELASCO
Vice Consul
Mrs. Patricia Bracho Soto RUIZ
Vice Consul
Mrs. Guadalupe Maria Bello MORIN

Commercial Office
350 S Figueroa St., 2nd Fl.
Los Angeles, CA 90021
Vice Consul
Mr. Herminio Hernandez RAMIREZ

Tourism Office
1801 Century Park East #1080
Los Angeles, CA 90067
Tel: (310) 203-8328
Vice Consul
Mr. Jorge Antonio Gamboa PATRON

Oxnard (C)
3151 W 5th St.
Oxnard, CA 93030
Tel: (805) 984-8738 Fax: (805) 984-8747
Consul
Mr. Fernando GAMBOA
Consul
Mr. Eduardo Giles MARTINEZ

Sacramento (CG)
1010 8th St.
Sacramento, CA 95814
Tel: (916) 329-3526 Fax: (916) 441-3147
Deputy Consul General
Mrs. Adriana Gonzalez CORREIA
Consul
Mr. Luis Enrique Castresana RUBIO

San Bernardino (C)
293 North D St.
San Bernardino, CA 92401
Tel: (714) 889-9836
Consul
Mr. Carlos Ignacio Giralt CABRALES
Deputy Consul
Mr. Ernesto Navarro BECERRA

San Diego (CG)
1549 India St.
San Diego, CA 92101
Tel: (619) 231-8414
Consul General
Mr. Luis Cabrera CUARON
Deputy Consul General
Mr. Francisco Javier Diaz DE LEON
Consul
Mr. Mario Cuevas ZAMORA
Consul
Mr. Alfonso Navarro BERNACHI
Consul
Mr. Jose Francisco Anza SOLIS
Consul
Mr. Alberto Lozano MERINO
Consul
Mr. Jose Juan Gutierrez CABELLO
Consul
Mr. Mario Ricardo Palmerin VELASCO
Consul
Mr. Miguel Angel Mendez Buenos AIRES
Consul
Mrs. Lydia Antonio DE LA GARZA
Vice Consul
Mrs. Laura E. Quintanilla CASAS

Office of Agriculture & Forestry Affairs
12625 High Bluff Dr.

San Diego, CA 92130

Office of Mexican Fisheries
2550 5th Ave. #101
San Diego, CA 92101

San Francisco (CG)
532 Folsom St.
San Francisco, CA 94105
Consul General
Mr. Alfonso de Maria y CAMPOS
Consul
Mr. Rene SANTILLAN
Consul
Mr. Bernardo Mendez LUGO
Consul
Mr. Jaime Arturo Martin SERRANO
Consul
Mr. Leobardo Sarabia QUIROZ
Deputy Consul
Mr. Fernando Sandoval FLORES
Vice Consul
Ms. Maria Rocio Schlaepfer PEDRAZZINI

San Jose (CG)
540 N 1st St.
San Jose, CA 95112
Tel: (408) 294-3414
Consul General
Mr. Bruno Figueroa FISCHER
Consul
Mr. Jeremias Guzman BARRERA
Consul
Ms. Maria Teresa Ceron VELEZ

Santa Ana (C)
828 N Broadway St.
Santa Ana, CA 92701
Consul
Mr. Luis Miguel Ortiz Haro AMIEVA
Deputy Consul
Mr. Alberto Bernal ACERO
Vice Consul
Mr. Luis Chao PRATT

Office of the Attorney General
3701 Wilshire Blvd. #1111
Los Angeles, CA 90010
Tel: (213) 351-6820
Consul
Mr. Gonzalo Villarreal GUERRA

COLORADO
Denver (CG)
48 Steele St.
Denver, CO 80206
Tel: (303) 331-1110
Deputy Consul General
Mr. Juan Roberto Gonzalez RAMIREZ
Consul
Mrs. Lucrecia Maria E. Barrera ROMERO
Consul
Mrs. Mariana Agustina Diaz NAGORE
Consul
Ms. Vanessa Calva RUIZ

DISTRICT OF COLUMBIA
Washington (EMB)
1911 Pennsylvania Ave. NW
Washington, DC 20006
Tel: (202) 728-1600 Fax: (202) 728-1698
Deputy Consul
Mr. Leocadio Beytia VEGA

FLORIDA
Miami (CG)
5975 SW 72nd St. #301
Miami, FL 33143
Tel: (786) 268-4900 Fax: (786) 268-4895
Consul General
Mr. Jorge Lomonaco TONDA

Consul
Ms. Sofia Garcia CEJA
Consul
Mr. Marco Arturo Ruiz VELASCO
Consul
Mr. Jaime Marquez Diez CANEDO
Consul
Mr. Jorge Valdes Diaz VELEZ
Consul
Mr. Miguel Alejandro Sandoval LARA
Consul
Mr. Rodrigo Arturo Ortega CAJIGAS
Vice Consul
Mr. Antonio Alfredo Lomeli ITURBE

Commercial Office
5975 SW 72nd St. #404
Miami, FL 33134
Consul
Mr. Jose Antonio Rivas HURTADO

Tourism Office
128 Aragon Ave.
Miami, FL 33156
Tel: (305) 443-9160
Vice Consul
Mrs. Maria T. Villarreal DE SAITCEVSKY

Orlando (C)
100 W Washington St.
Orlando, FL 32801
Consul
Mrs. Luz Elena Bueno ZIRION
Consul
Mr. Sergio Rivadeneyra MARTELL
Deputy Consul
Mr. Gilberto Velarde MEIXUEIRO
Vice Consul
Mrs. Maria Aurelia Morales GELAIN

GEORGIA
Atlanta (CG)
2600 Apple Valley Rd.
Atlanta, GA 30319
Tel: (404) 266-2233 Fax: (404) 266-2302
Consul General
Mrs. Remedios Gomez ARNAU
Consul
Ms. Carmen Dinorah Martin Rayo SOLIS
Consul
Mr. Juan Carlos Lara ARMIENTA
Consul
Mr. Jesus Diaz GONZALEZ
Consul
Ms. Maria Marisela Quijano HERRERO
Consul
Ms. Ana Maria Carrillo SOUBIC

Commercial Office
229 Peachtree St. NE #907
Atlanta, GA 30303

HAWAII
Honolulu (HC)
620 McCully St. #506
Honolulu, HI 96826
Tel: (808) 947-0828
Honorary Consul
Mrs. Laura Elena Angel GUZMAN

ILLINOIS
Chicago (CG)
204 S Ashland Ave.
Chicago , IL 60607
Tel: (312) 833-6331
Consul General
Mr. Carlos Manuel Sada SOLANA
Consul
Mrs. Selene Barcelo DE ALEXANDROU
Consul
Mr. Jose H. CASTRO

Consul
Mrs. Edurne Nerea Pineda AYERBE
Consul
Mr. Julio Cesar Huerta GARCIA
Consul
Mr. Felipe Ulises Cuellar SANCHEZ
Consul
Mrs. Rita Maria F. Vargas TORREGROSA
Consul
Mr. Bruno Hernandez PICHE
Consul
Mrs. Beatriz Margain CHARLES
Consul
Mr. Rodrigo Bustamante Riva PALACIO
Vice Consul
Mr. Emilio Carlos Bracho ARAGON
Vice Consul
Mr. Jacobo Tellez OCAMPO

Mexican Tourism Board
225 N Michigan Ave. #1850
Chicago , IL 60601
Tel: (312) 606-0069

Consul
Mrs. Martha VARELA
Vice Consul
Ms. Monica Garcia PLASCENCIA

Commercial Office
225 N Michigan Ave. #1800
Chicago, IL 60601
Tel: (312) 856-0316

Consul
Mr. Miguel Angel Leaman RIVAS

INDIANA
Indianapolis (C)
39 W Jackson Pl. #103
Indianapolis, IN 46225
Tel: (317) 951-0005

Consul
Mr. Sergio Aguilera BETETA
Consul
Mr. Jorge Cuauhtemoc Elizondo MEJIA
Deputy Consul
Mr. Felipe Luis Soria AYUSO
Vice Consul
Ms. Elsa Villa MATA

LOUISIANA
New Orleans (CG)
2 Canal St. #2240
New Orleans, LA 70130
Tel: (504) 522-3596

MASSACHUSETTS
Boston (CG)
20 Park Plz. #506
Boston, MA 02116
Tel: (617) 426-4942

Consul General
Mr. Porfirio Thierry Munoz LEDO
Consul
Mr. Rodrigo Marquez LARTIGUE
Consul
Mr. Eduardo R. De Olloqui GONZALEZ
Vice Consul
Ms. Taide Leticia Navarrete PELLICER
Vice Consul
Mr. German Murguia MIER

MICHIGAN
Detroit (C)
645 Griswold Ave., 43rd Fl.
Detroit, MI 48226
Tel: (313) 965-1868

Consul
Mr. Miguel Antonio Meza ESTRADA
Consul
Mrs. Mercedes Esquivel DE ANTUNES
Consul

Mr. Ranulfo Salvador Ramirez GAITAN
Consul
Mr. Antonio Ortega SAENZ
Deputy Consul
Mr. Oscar Antonio DE LA TORRE AMEZCUA

Commercial Office
2000 Town Ctr. #1900
Southfield, MI 48075

MISSOURI
Kansas City (C)
1600 Baltimore Unit #100
Kansas City, MO 64108
Tel: (816) 556-0800

Consul
Mr. Everardo Luis Suarez AMEZCUA
Consul
Mr. Fernando Gonzalez SANTOYO
Deputy Consul
Mrs. Maria Noemi Hernandez TELLEZ

NEBRASKA
Omaha (C)
3552 Dodge St.
Omaha, NE 68131
Tel: (402) 595-1841 Fax: (402) 595-1845

Consul
Mr. Jose Luis Cuevas HILDITCH
Deputy Consul
Mr. Luis Fernando Alva MARTINEZ

NEVADA
Las Vegas (C)
300 S 4th St.
Las Vegas, NV 89101
Tel: (702) 383-0623

Consul
Mrs. Berenice Rendon TALAVERA
Consul
Mrs. Maria Luisa SANTOS
Deputy Consul
Mr. Euclides Del Moral ARBONA

NEW MEXICO
Albuquerque (C)
1610 4th St. NW #0
Albuquerque, NM 87102
Tel: (505) 247-2139

Consul
Mr. Juan Manuel Solana MORALES
Consul
Mr. Ricardo F. Hernandez LECANDA
Deputy Consul
Mr. Benito Valdez VEGA
Deputy Consul
Mr. Raul Salvatore Ramirez COSSA

NEW YORK
New York (CG)
27-29 E 39th St.
New York , NY 10016
Tel: (212) 689-0456

Consul General
Mr. Arturo Sarukhan CASAMITJANA
Deputy Consul General
Mr. Francisco Javier Olavarria PATINO
Consul
Ms. Lucia Liceaga ARTEAGA
Consul
Mr. Norberto S. TERRAZAS
Consul
Mr. Gerardo Guerrero GOMEZ
Consul
Mr. Hugo Hiriart URDANIVIA
Consul
Mrs. Lourdes CHAVEZ
Consul

Mr. Gaspar Hernan Orozco RIOS
Consul
Ms. Leticia Maki Teramoto SAKAMOTO
Consul
Mrs. Paloma Marina Ojeda DE PUJALTE

Commercial Office
150 E. 58th St., 17th Fl.
New York , NY 10155

Tourism Office
21 E 63rd St.
New York , NY 10022
Tel: (212) 821-0314 Fax: (212) 821-0367

Mexican Foreign Trade Institute
375 Park Ave. #1905
New York , NY 10152
Tel: (212) 826-2916

Consul
Mr. Edmundo F. Gonzalez HERRERA
Consul
Mr. Rodrigo Esponda CASCAJARES
Vice Consul
Ms. Hortensia Guerrero SOTELO

NORTH CAROLINA
Charlotte (HC)
4424 Taggart Creek Rd.
Charlotte, NC 28208
Tel: (704) 394-2190

Honorary Consul
Mr. Wayne P. COOPER

Raleigh (C)
336 E Six Forks Rd.
Raleigh, NC 27606
Tel: (919) 754-0046 Fax: (919) 754-1726

Consul
Mr. Armando Ortiz ROCHA
Deputy Consul
Mr. Carlos Jesus Isunza CHAVEZ

OREGON
Portland (C)
1234 SW Morrison St.
Portland, OR 97205
Tel: (503) 274-1442

Consul
Mr. Martin ALCALA
Consul
Mrs. Martha Ortiz De ROSAS

PENNSYLVANIA
Philadelphia (C)
111 S Independence Mall Unit East, #310
Philadelphia, PA 19106
Tel: (215) 922-4262

Consul
Ms. Maria Del Rocio Vazquez ALVAREZ
Consul
Mr. Juan I. Zavala Gomez Del CAMPO

PUERTO RICO
San Juan (CG)
654 Avenida Munoz Rivera Unit #1837
San Juan, PR 00918
Tel: (809) 764-0258

Consul
Mr. Rodolfo Aguilar MELLADO
Deputy Consul
Mr. Francisco J. Valdes ROA

TEXAS
Brownsville (C)
724 E Elizabeth & 7th St.
Brownsville, TX 78520
Tel: (512) 542-4431

Consul
Mr. Juan Carlos Foncerrada BERUMER

Consul
Mr. Marco Antonio Cerritos MORENO
Deputy Consul
Mr. Hector Jose Aguilar MEZA

Dallas (CG)
8855 N. Stemmons Freeway
Dallas, TX 75247
Tel: (214) 522-9740

Consul General
Mr. Ezequiel Padilla COUTTOLENC
Deputy Consul General
Mr. Julian Jose Salgado SAAVEDRA
Consul
Mrs. Ana Feldman De MENDOZA
Consul
Ms. Patricia Amalia BELMAR
BUSTAMANTE
Consul
Mrs. Lorena LARIOS RODRIGUEZ
Consul
Ms. Maria F. Reynaud RODRIGUEZ
Consul
Ms. Ana Virginia Hernandez CARDENAS
Vice Conul
Ms. Laura PADILLA

Office of the Commercial Counselor
2777 Stemmons Frwy. Unit #1632
Dallas , TX 75258

Vice Consul
Ms. Concepcion Virginia Arteaga SANZ

Del Rio (C)
2398 Spur 239
Del Rio, TX 78840
Tel: (830) 774-5031

Consul
Mr. Roberto Canseco MARTINEZ
Vice Consul
Mr. Enrique Eliseo Montemayor SANCHEZ

Eagle Pass (C)
140 Adams St.
Eagle Pass, TX 78852
Tel: (512) 773-9255

Consul
Mr. Jorge Ernesto Espejel MONTES
Deputy Consul
Mr. Gerardo Javier Guiza VARGAS

El Paso (CG)
910 E San Antonio St.
El Paso, TX 79901
Tel: (915) 533-3644

Consul General
Mr. Juan Carlos Cue VEGA
Deputy Consul General
Mr. Victor Manuel Trevino ESCUDERO
Consul
Mr. Hector Raul Acosta FLORES
Consul
Mr. Jonathan Chait AUERBACH
Consul
Mr. Vicente Colmenares SUMANO
Consul
Mrs. Virginia S. Alvarado MARCOS
Vice Consul
Mr. Gustavo Ernesto Calderon MIRANDA
Vice Consul
Miss Ioana Navarrete PELLICER

Fort Worth (HC)
813 W Magnolia Ave.
Fort Worth, TX 76104
Tel: (817) 870-2270

Honorary Consul
Mr. Jerry MURAD, JR.

Houston (CG)

4507 San Jacinto St.
Houston, TX 77004
Tel: (713) 271-6800 Fax: (713) 271-3201
Consul General
Mr. Eduardo Ibarrola NICOLIN
Deputy Consul General
Mrs. Maria Luisa B. Lopez GARGALLO
Consul
Ms. Norma Edith Aguilar ANDRADE
Consul
Mr. Armando Camarena ARANDA
Consul
Mrs. Silvia Munoz De COATS
Consul
Mr. Luis Gabriel Ferrer ORTEGA
Consul
Mr. Jose Luis Avila SAAVEDRA
Consul
Ms. Cristina Oropeza ZORRILLA
Consul
Mr. Carlos Garcia DELGADO
Consul
Mrs. Soileh Padilla MAYER
Consul
Ms. Carolina Zaragoza FLORES
Consul
Mr. Hugo Juarez CARRILLO
Vice Consul
Mr. Daniel Gutierrez AGUIRRE
Vice Consul
Mr. Juan Arnulfo Reyes FIERRO

Tourism Office
2707 N Loop Unit #450
Houston, TX 77008

Trade Office
5065 Westheimer Rd. #707
Houston, TX 77056
Tel: (713) 965-0767

Laredo (CG)
1612 Farragut St.
Laredo, TX 78040
Tel: (512) 723-6369

Consul General
Mr. Daniel Hernandez JOSEPH
Deputy Consul General
Mr. Rene David Mejia QUINTANA
Deputy Consul
Mr. Miguel Angel REYES y SOTO
Vice Consul
Mrs. Alicia Beatriz Barberena HURTADO

McAllen (C)
600 S Broadway St.
McAllen, TX 78501
Tel: (512) 686-0243

Consul
Mr. Luis Manuel Lopez MORENO
Consul
Mr. Jose Luis Hernandez SALAZAR
Vice Consul
Mr. Arturo Javier Salgado BENITEZ
Vice Consul
Mr. Jose Luis Diaz Miron HINOJOSA

Midland (C)
511 W Ohio St. #121
Midland, TX 79701

Presidio (C)
67-17 Kelley Addition 1 Hwy.
Presidio, TX 79845
Tel: (915) 229-2788 Fax: (915) 229-2792

Consul
Mr. Justiniano Menchaca FUENTES
Vice Consul
Mr. Francisco Javier Jacobi DURAN

San Antonio (CG)
127 Navarro St.
San Antonio, TX 78205
Tel: (512) 227-9145

Consul General
Mrs. Martha Irene LARA
Consul
Mr. Yuri Sergio Camarillo MARTINEZ
Consul
Mr. Santiago Gabriel Garcia GONZALEZ
Consul
Mr. Agustin Rodriguez DE LA GALA
Consul
Mr. Eduardo Nino AVALOS
Deputy Consul
Mrs. Marta Beatriz Navarro-PARADA
Vice Consul
Mr. Heriberto Gonzalez ESCAMILLA
Mexican Cultural Institute
600 Hemisfair Plz. Way
San Antonio, TX 78205

Consul
Mr. Enrique Alberto Cortazar GAYTAN

Commercial Affairs Office
203 S St. Mary's St. #450
San Antonio, TX 78213

Office of Mexican Attorney General
613 NW Loop 410 Unit #610
San Antonio, TX 78216
Tel: (210) 344-1131

Consul
Mr. Fernando Morones GONZALEZ
Consul
Mr. Carlos Agusto Lazos CHAVEZ
Consul
Mr. Manuel Efren Campos ARMENDARIZ

Austin (CG)
800 Brazos St. #330
Austin, TX 78701

Consul General
Mr. Francisco Javier Alejo LOPEZ
Deputy Consul General
Mr. Vicente M. Sanchez VENTURA
Consul
Mrs. Angeles GOMEZ

Salt Lake City (C)
230 W 400 South, 2nd Fl.
Salt Lake City, UT 84101
Tel: (801) 521-8502

Consul
Mrs. Juana Maria P. Deluera CANCHOLA
Consul
Mr. Arturo Chavarria BALLEZA

VIRGINIA
Norfolk (HC)
51 E Virginia Beach Blvd.
Norfolk, VA 23502
Tel: (804) 461-4933

Honorary Consul
Mr. Roberto Rodriguez ITURRALDE

Richmond (HC)
2420 Pemberton Rd.
Richmond, VA 23233
Tel: (804) 747-9200

Honorary Consul
Mr. Walter W. REGIRER

WASHINGTON
Seattle (C)
2132 3rd Ave.
Seattle, WA 98121

Consul
Mr. Jorge Luis Madrazo CUELLAR
Deputy Consul
Mr. Roberto Ascencion Caldera ARROYO
Vice Consul
Mrs. M. Del Carmen Castaneda DE YUDIN
Vice Consul
Mrs. Sylvia E. Zenil DE MEEK

WISCONSIN
Madison (HC)
141 N Hancock St.
Madison , WI 53703
Tel: (608) 283-6000

Honorary Consul
Dr. Rudolph Caro HECHT

NICARAGUA

CALIFORNIA
San Francisco (CG)
870 Market St. #518
San Francisco, CA 94102
Tel: (415) 765-6821

Consul
Mrs. Mayra Centeno GADEA

Los Angeles (CG)
3303 Wilshire Blvd. #410
Los Angeles, CA 90010
Tel: (213) 252-1170

Honorary Consul
Ms. Mina NELSON

DISTRICT OF COLUMBIA
Washington (EMB)
1627 New Hampshire Ave. NW
Washington, DC 20009
Tel: (202) 939-6570 Fax: (202) 939-6545

Consul General
Mr. Harold Rivas REYES
Consul
Mrs. Dinora Daria GUEVARA

FLORIDA
Miami (CG)
8532 SW 8th St. #270
Miami , FL 33144
Tel: (305) 220-6900

Consul General
Mr. Jose Velasquez ESCOBAR
Consular Agent
Ms. Hilda Eulalia Sequeira CASTELLON

GEORGIA
Atlanta (HC)
3161 Lemons Ridge Dr.
Atlanta, GA 30339
Tel: (770) 319-1673

Honorary Consul
Mr. Joseph Thomas RATCHFORD, Jr.

LOUISIANA
New Orleans (CG)
2 Canal St. #1937
New Orleans, LA 70130
Tel: (504) 523-1507

Honorary Vice Consul
Mrs. Gertrudis R. Lacayo HASBUN

MASSACHUSETTS
Springfield (HC)
52 Mulberry St.
Springfield, MA 01105
Tel: (413) 781-5400

Honorary Consul
Dr. Sherman Edward FEIN

NEW YORK
New York (CG)
820 2nd Av. #802
New York, NY 10017
Tel: (212) 344-4491

Consular Agent
Mr. Cesar Antonio Mercado PAVON

Honarary Consul
Mrs. Maria Rogelia Urcuyo De ZARRUK

PENNSYLVANIA
Philadelphia (HC)
1201 N. 2nd St.
Philadelphia, PA 19122-4501
Tel: (215) 627-9414 Fax: (215) 627-0734

Honorary Consul
Mr. Alejandro Jose Gallardoq PRIO

Pittsburgh (HC)
Mobay Rd.
Pittsburgh, PA 15205
Tel: (412) 777-2000

Honorary Consul
Dr. Richard L. WHITE

PUERTO RICO
San Juan (HCG)
B1 Palma Sola Blvd.
Guaynabo, PR 00966
Tel: (787) 781-6530

Honorary Consul General
Mrs. Eva Luz Garcia De PICO

TEXAS
Houston (CG)
8989 Westheimer Rd. #103
Houston, TX 77063
Tel: (713) 789-2762 Fax: (713) 789-3164

Consul General
Mrs. Regina Emma Gonzalez SOLORZANO
Vice Consul
Mrs. Maria Mercedes BECK
Honorary Consul
Mr. Antonio Jose RENAZCO

WISCONSIN
Milwaukee (HC)
3521 W. National Ave.
Milwaukee , WI 53215

Honorary Consul
Mr. Alvaro ALEMAN

PANAMA

CALIFORNIA
Los Angeles (HC)
3137 W. Ball Rd. #104
Anaheim, CA 92804
Tel: (714) 816-1809

Honorary Consul
Mr. Fernando DALY

San Diego (HC)
2552 Chatsworth Blvd.
San Diego, CA 92106
Tel: (619) 225-8144

Honorary Consul
Mrs. Carolina Teran De MOURITZEN
Honorary Vice Consul
Mr. Adolfo Gonzalez Rubio BECKMANN

San Francisco (CG)
870 Market St. #551-553
San Francisco, CA 94102
Tel: (415) 391-4268 Fax: (415) 391-4269

Consul General
Mr. Oliver Enrique SERRANO
Honorary Deputy Consul General
Mr. Antonio CUCALON

DISTRICT OF COLUMBIA
Washington (EMB)
2862 McGill Terrace NW
Washington, DC 20008

Tel: (202) 483-1407 Fax: (202) 483-8416
Consul
Ms. Mylene Mayuly MARRONE

FLORIDA
Miami (CG)
2801 Ponce De Leon Blvd. #1050
Coral Gables, FL 33134
Tel: (305) 447-3700 Fax: (305) 447-4142

Consul General
Mr. Manuel COHEN
Consul
Mr. Franklin KARDONSKI
Consul
Mr. Yosef AVIAD CATTAN
Vice Consul
Ms. Gloriela De Los Angeles SAMUDIO
Vice Consul
Mrs. Monique GILINSKI
Vice Consul
Mrs. Irma G. Fonseca De TURCO
Vice Consul
Mrs. Zunilda Guevara De MARINA
Honorary Consul
Mr. Sylvan HOLTZMAN

Trade Development Institute
1477 S. Miami Ave., 2nd Fl.
Miami, FL 33130
Tel: (305) 374-8823 Fax: (305) 374-7822
Consul
Ms. Rosalinda Pinilla VALDES

Tampa (CG)
1101 Channelside Dr. #279
Tampa, FL 33602
Tel: (813) 283-0063 Fax: (813) 283-0064
Consul General
Mr. Eric Alberto Moreno ARAYA

GEORGIA
Atlanta (CG)
225 Peachtree St. #503 NE
Atlanta, GA 30303
Tel: (404) 522-4114 Fax: (404) 522-4120

Consul General
Mr. Jaime Bolivar Aleman ALEGRIA

HAWAII
Honolulu (HCG)
1352 S. Beretania St.
Honolulu, HI 96814
Tel: (808) 531-5483

Honorary Consul General
Mr. Truman William BROPHY

LLINOIS
Chicago (HCG)
9048 S. Commercial Ave.
Chicago, IL 60617-4303
Tel: (773) 933-0395

Honorary Consul General
Mrs. Lirella Jaen SANDOVAL
Honorary Consul
Mrs. Irma L. BLATCHFORD
Honorary Vice Consul
Mr. Jorge Eliezer MONCADA

LOUISIANA
New Orleans (CG)
2 Canal St.
New Orleans, LA 70130
Tel: (504) 525-3458 Fax: (504) 424-8960

Consul General
Mr. Gabriel Jose Bazan KODAT
Vice Consul
Ms. Maria del Pilar Pitty CORDOBA

MASSACHUSETTS
Boston (HCG)
22 Fox Run
East Sandwich, MA 02537
Tel: (508) 888-7311

Honorary Consul General
Prof. Ronald Thomas CARROLL

NEW YORK
New York (CG)
1212 Ave. of the Americas, 6th Fl.
New York, NY 10036
Tel: (212) 840-2450 Fax: (212) 840-2469

Consul General
Mrs. Rita Cecilia Garcia De FROCHAUX

Office of Maritime Safety
6 W. 48th St.
New York, NY 10036
Tel: (212) 869-6440 Fax: (212) 575-2285

OHIO
Cleveland (HC)
31300 Tuttle Dr.
Bay Village, OH 44140
Tel: (440) 835-8671

Honorary Consul
Mrs. Marie Antoinette FRASER

PENNSYLVANIA
Philadelphia (CG)
124 Chestnut St.
Philadelphia, PA 19106
Tel: (215) 574-2994 Fax: (215) 625-4876

Consul General
Mrs. Georgia ATHANASOPULOS

PUERTO RICO
San Juan (CG)
201 De Diego Ave.
San Juan, PR 00926
Tel: (787) 620-6593

Consul General
Ms. Bonnie Sara Garcia ALVARADO

TEXAS
Houston (CG)
24 Greenway Plz. #1307
Houston, TX 77046
Tel: (713) 622-4451 Fax: (713) 622-4468

Consul General
Mr. Carlos AROSEMENA
Vice Consul
Mr. Mario VILAR
Honorary Consul
Mrs. Miriam R. SERA
Honorary Vice Consul
Mr. Camilo Enrique DIAZ

PARAGUAY

CALIFORNIA
Los Angeles (CG)
6033 W Century Blvd. #985
Los Angeles, CA 90045
Tel: (310) 417-9500 Fax: (310) 417-9520

Consul General
Mr. Jose Antonio DOS SANTOS
Consular Agent
Mr. Sergio Enrique Rodriguez FRAGNAUD

FLORIDA
Miami (CG)
300 Biscayne Blvd. Way #907
Miami, FL 33131
Tel: (305) 374-9090

Consul General
Mr. Carlos Alberto Ortiz BAREIRO
Consul
Mr. Estanislao LEZCANO
Consul
Mr. Eduardo Victor Florentin BOLF
Consular Agent
Mr. Humberto Martinez SCHEMBORI

KANSAS
Kansas City (CG)
630 Minnesota Ave.
Kansas City, KS 66101
Tel: (913) 281-5252

LOUISIANA
New Orleans (CG)
611 Gravier St. #903
New Orleans, LA 70130

MICHIGAN
Detroit (HC)
27387 Parkview
Detroit, MI 48092

Honorary Consul
Mrs. Alice ROJAS

NEW YORK
New York (CG)
211 E 43rd St. #2101
New York, NY 10017

Consul General
Mr. Jose Emilio GOROSTIAGA
Consular Agent
Ms. Shirley MONGELOS

PUERTO RICO
San Juan (HC)
267 #5-C
San Juan, PR 00903

Honorary Consul
Mrs. Maria Elena DE HASZARD

PERU

CALIFORNIA
Los Angeles (CG)
3450 Wilshire Blvd. #800
Los Angeles, CA 90010
Tel: (213) 252-5910 Fax: (213) 252-8130

Consul General
Mrs. Liliana Tamara Cino DE SILVA
Deputy Consul
Mr. Alex CONTRERAS

San Francisco (CG)
870 Market St. #1067
San Francisco, CA 94102
Tel: (415) 362-7136

Consul General
Mr. Raul RIVERA
Consul
Mrs. Liliana TRELLES
Honorary Consul
Ms. Maria Isabel Wong VARGAS

COLORADO
Denver (CG)
1001 S. Monaco Pkwy. #210
Denver, CO 80224

Consul General
Ms. Maria Susan Landaveri PORTURAS
Vice Consul
Mr. Ramiro Maurice RIVERA

CONNECTICUT
Hartford (CG)
250 Main St. #D
Hartford, CT 06106

Consul General
Mr. Jose Arsenio Benzaquen PEREA

DISTRICT OF COLUMBIA
Washington (EMB)
1700 Massachusetts Ave. NW
Washington, DC 20036
Tel: (202) 833-9860 Fax: (202) 659-8124

Vice Consul
Ms. Catherine Lovon BALTA

FLORIDA
Miami (CG)
444 Brickell Ave. #M-135
Miami, FL 33131
Tel: (305) 374-8935

Consul General
Mrs. LUISAGAMIO
Deputy Consul General
Mr. Gustavo M. Gutierrez PIZARRO
Deputy Consul
Mr. Alfonso Paz SOLDAN
Deputy Consul
Mr. Jose Marcos Rodriguez CHACON
Consular Agent
Mr. Fernando ALBAREDA

Tampa (HC)
2106 W. Busch Bvld.
Tampa, FL 33612
Tel: (941) 923-7586

Honorary Consul
Mr. Julio Enrique VEGA GUANILO

GEORGIA
Atlanta (HC)
1401 Peachtree St. NE #240
Atlanta, GA 30309
Tel: (404) 299-8234

ILLINOIS
Chicago (CG)
180 N. Michigan Ave. #1830
Chicago, IL 60601
Tel: (312) 853-6173

Consul General
Mr. Efrain Saavedra BARRERA
Deputy Consul General
Mr. Jorge ROSADO
Vice Consul
Mr. Jaime ARROSPIDE

LOUISIANA
New Orleans (HC)
2308 World Trade Center
New Orleans, LA 70130
Tel: (504) 523-6496

Honorary Consul
Ms. Maria O'Byrne STEPHENSON

MASSACHUSETTS
Boston (CG)
20 Park Plz. #515
Boston, MA 02116-4399

Consul General
Mr. Mariano Garcia GODOS

MISSOURI
St. Louis (HC)
3 The Prado Unit
St. Louis, MO 63124
Tel: (314) 991-1750

Honorary Consul

Mrs. Rosa Ana SCHWARZ

NEW JERSEY
Paterson (CG)
100 Hamilton Plz. #1221
Paterson, NJ 07505
Tel: (201) 278-3324

Deputy Consul General
Mr. Gonzalo Enrique PAREDES
Deputy Consul General
Mr. Gonzalo E. PAREDES
Deputy Consul General
Ms. Amalia MARIATEGUI

NEW YORK
New York (CG)
241 E. 49th St.
New York, NY 10017
Tel: (212) 481-7419 Fax: (646) 735-3866

Consul General
Mr. Heli Adelfo Pelaez CASTRO
Deputy Consul General
Mr. Gabriel A. PACHECO
Deputy Consul General
Ms. Ana Maria Deustua CARAVEDO
Deputy Consul General
Mr. Alejandro Ugarte VELARDE
Vice Consul
Mr. Abel Antonio Cardenas TUPPIA

OKLAHOMA
Tulsa (HC)
2430 E. 41st St.
Tulsa, OK 74105
Tel: (918) 245-5911

Honorary Consul
Dr. Luis Alberto REINOSO

PUERTO RICO
San Juan (HCG)
E-2 Camino Las Rosas Unit
San Juan, PR 00926
Tel: (787) 283-6903

Honorary Consul General
Mr. Manuel Augusto Maurtua HELDEN

TEXAS
Dallas (HC)
306 N. Loop 288 #183
Denton, TX 76201
Tel: (940) 565-8569

Honorary Consul
Dr. Victor Raul Alvarez HOLLEMWEGUER

Houston (CG)
5177 Richmond Ave. #695
Houston, TX 77056
Tel: (713) 355-9571 Fax: (713) 355-9377

Consul General
Mr. Eduardo V. RIVOLDI
Deputy Consul General
Ms. Maria G. Porras ALOR
Honorary Consul
Mr. Bernardo TREISTMAN

WASHINGTON
Seattle (HC)
3717 NE 157th St. #100
Seattle, WA 98155
Tel: (206) 714-9037

Honorary Consul
Mr. Miguel Angel VELASQUEZ

PORTUGAL

CALIFORNIA
San Francisco (CG)
3298 Washington St.
San Francisco, CA 94115
Tel: (415) 346-3400

Consul General
Dr. Augusto Jose PEIXOTO
Consul
Mr. Jose Luis M. Ferreira DIAS

Commercial Office
88 Kearney St. #1770
San Francisco, CA 94108
Fax: (415) 391-7147

Los Angeles (C)
1801 Ave. of the Stars #400
Los Angeles, CA 90067
Tel: (310) 277-1491

CONNECTICUT
Waterbury (HC)
20 E. Main St. #220
Waterbury, CT 06702
Tel: (203) 755-4111

Consul
Dr. Abilio Lopez GOUVEIA

DISTRICT OF COLUMBIA
Washington (EMB)
2125 Kalorama Rd. NW
Washington, DC 20008
Tel: (202) 328-8610 Fax: (202) 462-3726

Vice Consul
Mrs. Maria Amelia Manso Nobre HILKER

FLORIDA
Miami (HC)
1901 Ponce De Leon Blvd., 2nd Fl.
Coral Gables, FL 33134
Tel: (305) 444-6311

Honorary Consul
Mr. Joseph T. THERIAGA

HAWAII
Honolulu (HC)
1585 Kapiolani Blvd. #728
Honolulu, HI 96814
Tel: (808) 523-4580

Honorary Consul
Mr. John Henry FELIX
Honorary Vice Consul
Mr. Ernest MORGADO

ILLINOIS
Chicago (HC)
21 S. Clark St.
Chicago, IL 60670-0947
Tel: (312) 259-9408

Honorary Consul
Mr. Nelson De CASTRO

LOUISIANA
New Orleans (HC)
201 St. Charles Ave.
New Orleans, LA 70170-5100
Tel: (504) 582-8272

Honorary Consul
Mr. William Hugh HINES

MASSACHUSETTS
Boston (CG)
One Exeter Pl., 7th Fl.
Boston, MA 02116
Tel: (617) 536-8740

Consul General
Mr. Americo Madeira BARBARA

New Bedford (C)
628 Pleasant St. #204/218
New Bedford, MA 02740
Tel: (508) 997-6151

Consul
Mr. Fernando Teles FAZENDEIRO

NEW JERSEY
Newark (CG)
1 Riverfront Plz.
Newark, NJ 07102
Tel: (973) 643-4200

Consul General
Mr. Paulo Neves POCINHO

NEW YORK
New York (CG)
630 5th Ave. #801
New York, NY 10111
Tel: (212) 246-4580

Consul General
Mr. Jose Carlos J. Cruz ALMEIDA
Consul
Mr. Frederico COSTA
Consul
Mr. Eduardo Souto De MOURA
Consul
Mr. Miguel A. J. Malheiro GARCIA

PENNSYLVANIA
Philadelphia (HC)
7950 Loretto Ave.
Philadelphia, PA 19111
Tel: (215) 745-2889

Honorary Consul
Mr. Carl Marques SANTUS

PUERTO RICO
San Juan (HC)
416 San Leandro
Rio Piedras, PR 00926
Tel: (809) 755-8556

Honorary Consul
Mr. Jose C. Duarte Da SILVEIRA

RHODE ISLAND
Providence (C)
56 Pine St., 6th Fl.
Providence, RI 02903
Tel: (401) 272-2003

Consul
Mr. Antonio Botelho De SOUSA
Vice Consul
Mr. Rogerio De Oliveira MEDINA

TEXAS
Houston (HC)
600 Travis St. #6700
Houston, TX 77002
Tel: (713) 759-1188

Honorary Consul
Mr. James H. WESTMORELAND

SPAIN

ALASKA
Anchorage (HVC)
14900 S. Windsor Cir.
Anchorage, AK 99516
Tel: (907) 345-8645

Honorary Vice Consul
Mr. Roberto Albacete GONZALEZ

ARIZONA
Phoenix (HC)
3134 E Camelback UN
Phoenix, AZ 85016
Tel: (602) 955-2055

Honorary Consul
Mr. Alfredo Jose MOLINA

CALIFORNIA
Los Angeles (CG)
5055 Wilshire Blvd. #860
Los Angeles , CA 90036
Tel: (323) 938-0158

Consul General
Mr. Jose Luis Dicenta BALLESTER

Commercial Office
660 S. Figueroa St. #1050
Los Angeles , CA 90017
Tel: (213) 627-5284 Fax: (213) 627-0883

Consul
Mr. Antonio Estevez MARIN

Education Office
6300 Wilshire Blvd. #830
Los Angeles, CA 90048
Tel: (323) 852-6997 Fax: (213) 852-0759

Consul
Mrs. Maria Del Mar Torres RUIZ

San Diego (HC)
10922 Anja Way
Lakeside, CA 92040-2717
Tel: (619) 448-7282

Honorary Consul
Mrs. Maria Angeles OLSON

San Francisco (CG)
1405 Sutter St.
San Francisco, CA 94109
Tel: (415) 922-2995

Consul General
Mr. Camilo Barcia Garcia VILLAMIL

CONSULAR ANNEX OF SPAIN
Los Angeles (CON)
8383 Wilshire Blvd. #960
Beverly Hills, CA 90211
Tel: (213) 658-7188

Consul
Mr. Ignacio DUCASSE

COLORADO
Denver (HC)
5740 Oak Creek La.
Greenwood Village, CO 80121
Tel: (303) 797-0656

Honorary Consul
Mr. Luis P. FONSECA

DISTRICT OF COLUMBIA
Washington (EMB)
2375 Pennsylvania Ave. NW
Washington, DC 20037
Tel: (202) 452-0100 Fax: (202) 833-5670

Consul General
Mr. Mariano Alonso Buron ABERASTURI

FLORIDA
Miami (CG)
2655 Le Jeune Rd. #203
Miami, FL 33134
Tel: (305) 446-5511

Consul General
Mr. Francisco Javier VALLAURE
Deputy Consul

Mr. Jose Ruiz ARBELOA

Commercial Office
2655 Le Jeune Rd. #1111&1114
Miami, FL 33134
Tel: (305) 446-4387

Consul
Mrs. Begona CRISTETO

Spanish Tourist
1221 Brickell Ave. #1850
Miami, FL 33131
Tel: (305) 358-1992

Consul
Ms. Beatriz Marco ARCE

Spanish Education
2655 Le Jeune Rd. #1008
Miami , FL 33134
Tel: (305) 448-2146 Fax: (305) 445-0508

Consul
Mr. Miguel Martinez LOPEZ

Pensacola (HVC)
100 Ingalls Dr.
Pensacola, FL 32506-5259
Tel: (904) 455-5360

Honorary Vice Consul
Ms. Maria D. DAVIS

GEORGIA
Atlanta (HVC)
1010 Huntcliff #2315
Atlanta, GA 30350
Tel: (404) 993-4883

Honorary Vice Consul
Mr. Ignacio Luis TABOADA

HAWAII
Honolulu (HVC)
5253 Kalanianaole Hwy.
Honolulu, HI 96821
Tel: (808) 377-8870 Fax: (808) 373-2469

Honorary Vice Consul
Mr. John Henry FELIX

IDAHO
Boise (HC)
999 Main St., 13th Fl.
Boise, ID 83702
Tel: (208) 389-7297

Honorary Consul
Ms. Adeliag SIMPLOT

ILLINOIS
Chicago (CG)
180 N. Michigan Ave. #1500
Chicago , IL 60601
Tel: (312) 782-4588

Consul General
Mr. Rodrigo Aguirre De CARCER
Vice Consul
Mr. Francisco J. Moreno FERNANDEZ

Nation Spanish Tourist Office
845 N. Michigan Ave. #915E
Chicago , IL 60611
Tel: (312) 642-1992

Consul
Mr. Julio Lopez ASTOR

Spanish Commercial Office
500 N. Michigan Ave. #1500
Chicago , IL 60611
Tel: (312) 644-1154

Consul
Ms. Josefina BELTRAN
Consul
Mr. Jose Manuel Rodriguez RANERO

LOUISIANA
New Orleans (CG)
2 Canal St.
New Orleans, LA 70130
Tel: (504) 525-4951

Consul General
Mr. Jose G. Nunez IGLESIAS

MASSACHUSETTS
Boston (CG)
545 Boylston St. #803
Boston , MA 02116
Tel: (617) 536-2506

Consul General
Mr. Enrique Iranzo ARQUES

MICHIGAN
Detroit (HVC)
2890 Lakewoods Ct.
Orchard Lake, MI 48324
Tel: (248) 683-9104

Honorary Vice Consul
Mr. Louis BETANZOS

MINNESOTA
Minneapolis (HVC)
824 Summit Ave.
Minneapolis, MN 55403
Tel: (612) 377-4228

Honorary Consul
Ms. Aurora O. I. RIOS-REXACH

MISSOURI
Kansas City (HC)
316 Avila Cir.
Kansas City , MO 64114
Tel: (816) 942-2649 Fax: (816) 942-2649

Honorary Consul
Mr. Eugene Francis GRAY

St. Louis (HVC)
5715 Manchester Ave.
St. Louis, MO 63110

Honorary Vice Consul
Mr. Jose L. MOLINA, Jr.

NEW JERSEY
Newark (HC)
249 University Ave.
Newark, NJ 07102

Honorary Consul
Mr. Arturo LOPEZ

NEW MEXICO
Santa Fe (HC)
300 Paseo de Peralta #101
Santa Fe, NM 87501
Tel: (505) 880-1455

Honorary Consul
Mr. Robert Oldham MOORE

NEW YORK
New York (CG)
150 E. 58th St., 30th & 31st Fl.
New York, NY 10155
Tel: (212) 355-4080

Consul General
Mr. Emilio CASSINELLO
Deputy Consul General
Mrs. Maria L. Huidobro MARTIN-LABORDA
Consul
Mr. LUISVELACSO
Consul
Mr. Antonio Manuel GARRIDO
Consul
Mr. Enrique Ojeda VILA

National Spanish Tourist Office

666 5th Ave., 35th Fl.
New York , NY 10103
Tel: (212) 265-8822

Consul
Mr. Alvaro RENEDO
Deputy Consul
Ms. Maria Teresa Ortiz MARIN

Spanish Commercial Office
405 Lexington Ave. 44th Fl.
New York , NY 10174
Tel: (212) 661-4959

Consul
Mr. Agustin M. MAINAR
Consul
Mr. Manuel VALLE
Deputy Consul
Mr. Ricardo Fernandez CALVO

Spanish Education Office
358 5th Ave. #1404
New York , NY 10011
Tel: (212) 629-4435 Fax: (212) 629-4438

Consul
Mr. Gustavo A. Martinez FERNANDEZ

NORTH CAROLINA
Durham (HVC)
600 Foster St.
Durham , NC 27701
Tel: (919) 667-1988

Honorary Vice Consul
Mr. Rafael Lopez BARRANTES

OHIO
Cincinnati (HVC)
2605 Burnet Ave.
Cinicinnati , OH 45219
Tel: (513) 961-3737

Honorary Vice Consul
Mr. Sidney L. KAUFMAN

PENNSYLVANIA
Philadelphia (HVC)
3410 Warden Dr.
Philadelphia, PA 19129

Honorary Vice Consul
Mr. Herminio MUNIZ

PUERTO RICO
San Juan (CG)
Edificio Mercantil Plz. #1101
Hato Rey , PR 00918
Tel: (787) 758-6090 Fax: (787) 763-0190

Consul General
Mr. Fernando Gonzalez CAMINO
Consular Agent
Mr. Gabino Iglesias FERNANDEZ

Spanish Commerical Office
239 Arterial Hostos Ave. #705
San Juan , PR 00918
Tel: (787) 758-6345 Fax: (787) 758-6948

Consul
Mr. Enrique Fontana LLOPIS

TEXAS
Corpus Christi (HC)
7517 Yorkshire Blvd.
Corpus Christi , TX 78413
Tel: (512) 994-7517

Honorary Consul
Mr. Fernando Moral IGLESIAS

Dallas (HC)
5499 Glen Lakes Dr. #209
Dallas, TX 75231
Tel: (214) 373-1200

Honorary Consul

Ms. Janet Pollman KAFKA

El Paso (HC)
420 Golden Springs Dr.
El Paso, TX 79912
Tel: (915) 534-0677

Honorary Consul
Mr. Arthur Sheldon HALL

Houston (CG)
1800 Bering Dr. #660
Houston , TX 77057
Tel: (713) 783-6200

San Antonio (HC)
8350 Delphian
San Antonio, TX 78148

Honorary Consul
Mrs. Isabel De Pedro MARIN

UTAH
Salt Lake City (HC)
5131 S. Morning Sun Dr.
Taylorsville, UT 84123
Tel: (801) 264-8321 Fax: (801) 293-8097

Honorary Consul
Mr. Baldomero LAGO

WASHINGTON
Seattle (HVC)
P.O. Box 3707 MS 65-68 N.
Seattle, WA 98124
Tel: (425) 237-9373

Honorary Vice Consul
Mr. Luis F. Esteban BERNALDEZ

URUGUAY

CALIFORNIA
Los Angeles (CG)
429 Santa Monica Blvd. #400
Santa Monica, CA 90401
Tel: (310) 394-5777

Consul General
Mr. Rodolfo INVERNIZZI

San Francisco (HC)
564 Market St. #221
San Francisco, CA 94104
Tel: (415) 981-1115

Honorary Consul
Mr. Mark RITCHIE

DISTRICT OF COLUMBIA
Washington (EMB)
1913 I St. NW
Washington, DC 20006
Tel: (202) 331-1313 Fax: (202) 331-8142

Consul
Mr. Mario Liori SANCHEZ

FLORIDA
Miami (CG)
1077 Ponce De Leon Blvd.
Coral Gables, FL 33134
Tel: (305) 443-9764 Fax: (305) 443-7802

Consul General
Mrs. Maria Lucia TRUCILLO
Deputy Consul General
Mr. Arturo V. Villarreal RODRIGUEZ
Consul
Mr. Jorge Angel Collazo UBOLDI
Honorary Consul
Mrs. Richard Peter STANHAM

HAWAII
Honolulu (HC)
1833 Kalakaua Ave. #710

Honolulu, HI 96815
Tel: (808) 947-2889
Honorary Consul
Mr. Luis Enrique ZANOTTA

ILLINOIS
Chicago (CG)
875 N. Michigan Ave. #1422
Chicago, IL 60611
Tel: (312) 642-3430 Fax: (312) 642-3470
Consul General
Dr. Olga Graziella REYES DE PRIETO
Honorary Consul
Mr. Carlos Guillermo RIZOWY

LOUISIANA
New Orleans (HC)
2 Canal St. #2002
New Orleans, LA 70130
Tel: (504) 525-8354
Honorary Consul
Mr. Julio E. Rios PENA

MASSACHUSETTS
Boston (HC)
67 Union St.
Natick, MA 01760
Tel: (617) 650-7936
Honorary Consul
Mr. Raul LAGUARDA

NEVADA
Reno (HC)
562 N. Maine St.
Fallon, NV 89406
Tel: (775) 423-6041
Honorary Consul
Dr. David Clement HENLEY

NEW YORK
New York (CG)
420 Madison Ave., 6th Fl.
New York, NY 10017
Tel: (212) 753-8581 Fax: (212) 753-1603
Consul General

Mr. Juan Jose Di SEVO
Deputy Consul General
Ms. Maria Del Barcelo DEBENEDETTI
Consul
Mr. Gerardo PRATO

PUERTO RICO
San Juan (HC)
254 Monterrey Urb.
San Juan, PR 00926
Honorary Consul
Ms. Josefina De HILLYER
Honorary Vice Consul
Mr. Ariel Alonso OROZ

UTAH
Salt Lake City (HC)
8300 S. 700th E. #B
Sandy, UT 84070
Tel: (801) 256-0182 Fax: (801) 256-0183
Honorary Consul
Mr. Giro Aroldo DARELLI

WASHINGTON
Seattle (HC)
420 Fifth Ave. #4100
Seattle, WA 99101
Tel: (804) 625-3658
Honorary Consul
Mr. Hartley PAUL

VENEZUELA

CALIFORNIA
San Francisco (CGI)
311 California St. #620
San Francisco, CA 94104
Tel: (415) 955-1982
Consul General
Mr. Domingo LLANOS
Consul
Mr. Gerardo COLL
Vice Consul
Mrs. Isis C. Cedeno GARCICA

Consular Agent
Mr. Alfonso Jose D'SANTIAGO

FLORIDA
Miami (CG)
1101 Brickell Ave. #901
Miami , FL 33131
Tel: (305) 577-4301
Consul General
Mr. Antonio Jose HERNANDEZ
Consul Agent
Mrs. Alexandra PERALES
Consular Agent
Mr. Jose A. Fernandez ESCALANTE

ILLINOIS
Chicago (CG)
20 N. Wacker Dr. #1925
Chicago, IL 60606
Tel: (312) 236-9658
Consul
Mrs. Isannia DELGADO
Consul
Ms. Ana M. Gonzalez AROCHA
Consular Agent
Mr. Alexi LEONES
Consular Agent
Mrs. Yasmely FLORES
Consular Agent
Mr. Richard Rivero ALEJOS

LOUISIANA
New Orleans (CG)
1006 World Trade Center #1908
New Orleans, LA 70130
Tel: (504) 522-3284
Consul General
Mrs. Maria Del Madriz BUSTAMANTE
Consular
Mrs. Maria Victoria LINARES
Consular Agent
Mrs. Martha A. LUCENA

MASSACHUSETTS
Boston (CG)
545 Boylston St., 3rd Fl.
Boston, MA 02116

Tel: (617) 266-9355
Consul
Mrs. Francisca C. CADENAS

NEW YORK
New York (CG)
7 E. 51st St.
New York, NY 10022
Tel: (212) 826-1660
Deputy Consul General
Mrs. Leonor Cecilia Osorio GRANADO
Consular Agent
Mrs. LUZZAMBRANO
Consular Agent
Mr. Tulio Francisco VIRQUEZ
Consular Agent
Mrs. Luz Mary ZAMBRANO RODRIGUEZ

PUERTO RICO
San Juan (CG)
Ponce De Leon Ave. #601, 6th Fl.
Hato Rey, PR 00936
Tel: (787) 766-4250
Consul General
Mr. Vinicio Jose Romero MARTINEZ
Deputy Consul General
Mrs. Marbella Marquez GARCIA

TEXAS
Houston (CG)
2925 Briar Park Dr. #900
Houston, TX 77042
Tel: (713) 961-5141
Consul General
Ms. Aura Mahuampi Rodriguez De ORTIZ
Consul
Ms. Elizabeth C. LEON
Consul
Ms. Teresa APONTE
Consul
Mr. Nabil MORA

Hispanic Embassies in the US continued from p 169

Financial Affairs Office
1025 Connecticut Ave. NW #902
Washington, DC 20036
Tel: (202) 223-9833 Fax: (202) 223-2119

Military, Naval and Air Attache Office
1913 I St., 3rd Fl. NW
Washington, DC 20006
Tel: (202) 466-3167

Trade Bureau
1030 15th St. NW #760
Washington, DC 20005
Tel: (202) 789-8225

VENEZUELA

EMBASSY OF THE BOLIVARIAN REPUBLIC OF VENEZUELA
Chancery: 1099 30th St. NW
Washington, DC 20007
Tel: (202) 342-2214 Fax: (202) 342-6820
Email:apaiva@embavenez-us.org
Web: www.embavenez-us.org
National Holiday: Independence Day, July 5

Ambassador E. and P.
His Excellency Bernardo Alvarez HERRERA;
Mrs. Margarete E. Hietzge De Alvarez
Minister-Counselor
Mrs. Sandra Violeta Franco DE PICO;
Mr. Efrain Pico Ponte
Minister-Counselor
Mr. Fadi KABBOUL;
Mrs. Marie Claire Massaad De Kabboul
Minister-Counselor
Mrs. Nancy Meza CUELLO
Counselor
Mrs. Gloria Teresa Arreaza RUBIN;
Mr. Antonio Enrique Rangel Barling
Counselor
Mrs. Irama Balza GODOY
Counselor (Press)
Mr. Andres Guillermo Izarra GARCIA
Counselor
Mr. Hector G. Quintero MONTIEL
First Secretary
Ms. Marie A. Borregales CHIRINOS
First Secretary
Mrs. Jeny Figueredo FRIAS
Second Secretary
Mr. Nestor Luis Fajardo ACOSTA;
Mrs. Xiomara J. Ibarra Perez

Second Secretary
Mrs. Karina Pacheco PARILLI;
Mr. Francisco J. Gilly Curiel
Attache (Cultural)
Ms. Dinorah Cecilia CARNEVALI
Attache
Mrs. Elizabeth C. HERNANDEZ;
Mr. Carlos A. Jimenez Perrone
Attache
Mr. Ramon KEY;
Mrs. Claudina C. Villarroel Galicia
Attache (Cultural)
Ms. Maria C. Marquez DE MASSIANI;
Mr. Felipe A. Massiani
Defense Attache
Major General Angel Federico Valecillos RIOS;
Mrs. Nancy J. Bohorquez de Valecillos
Military Attache
General Gerardo Jose Colmenares GOMEZ;
Mrs. Melvatais Colmenares
Naval Attache
Rear Admiral Pedro Jose Negrin RUIZ;
Mrs. Eros Maximiliana Lezama de Negrin
Air Attache
Brigadier General Cesar Jose Arteaga ARTEAGA;

Mrs. Miriam Coromoto Riut de Arteaga
Assistant Defense Attache
Colonel Juan Carlos Plaza PAREDES;
Mrs. Minerva Maria Plaza

Air Attache Office
2409 California St. NW
Washington, DC 20008
Tel: (202) 234-9132

Defense and Naval Attache Offices
2437 California St. NW
Washington, DC 20008
Tel: (202) 265-7323

Information Service Office
1099 30th St. NW
Washington, DC 20007

Military and Air Attache Offices
2409 California St. NW
Washington, DC 20008
Tel: (202) 234-3633

Naval Attache Office
2437 California St. NW
Washington, DC 20008
Tel: (202) 265-7323

Missions and Observers to the OAS
Misiones y observadores ante la OEA

ALGERIA

2118 Kalorama Rd. NW
Washington, DC 20008
Tel: (202) 265-2800 Fax: (202) 667-2174
Email: embalg.us@verizon.net

Ambassador Perm. Observer
vacant
Minister Counselor, Permanent Observer
Mr. Djamel MOKTEFI; Mrs. Sabah Moktefi
Counselor, Alternate Observer
Mr. Ameur BETKA; Mrs. Houria Betka

ANGOLA, PEOPLE'S REPUBLIC OF

2108 16th St. NW
Washington, DC 20009
Tel: (202) 785-1156 Fax: (202) 785-1258
Email: angola@angola.org

Ambassador Perm. Observer
Her Excellency Josefina Pitra DIAKITE

ANTIGUA AND BARBUDA

3216 New Mexico Ave. NW
Washington, DC 20016
Tel: (202) 362-5122 Fax: (202) 362-5225
Email: embantbar@aol.com

Ambassador Perm. Rep.
Her Excellency Deborah Mae LOVELL
Minister Counselor, Alternate Representative
Mr. Starret A. GREENE;
Mrs. Joycelyn V. Greene
First Secretary, Alternate Representative
Mrs. Ann-Marie Layne CAMPBELL;
Mr. Richard Campbell

ARGENTINA

1816 Corcoran St. NW
Washington, DC 20009
Tel: (202) 387-4142 Fax: (202) 328-1591
Email: argentin@oas.org

Ambassador Perm. Rep.
His Excellency Rodolfo Hugo GIL
Minister, Alternate Representative
Ms. Silvia Maria MEREGA
Counselor, Alternate Representative
Mr. Eduardo Acevedo DIAZ;
Mrs. Maria del Pilar Asua Mosso de
Acevedo Diaz
Counselor, Alternate Representative
Mr. Gerardo BOMPADRE;
Mrs. Silvia A. Behrens de Bompadre
Secretary, Alternate Representative
Mr. Sebastian MOLTENI;
Mrs. Mariela Analia Canepa de Molteni
Secretary, Alternate Representative
Mrs. Rosa Delia Gomez DURAN;

Mr. Carlos Gustavo Arguindequi
Air Attache
Colonel Jorge Oscar RATTI;
Mrs. Judit Schoos de Ratti
Naval Attache
Captain Javier VALLADARES;
Mrs. Lilia Wiman de Valladares
Military Attache
Colonel Ricardo ECHEGARAY;
Mrs. Beatriz Neme de Echegaray

ARMENIA

2225 R St. NW
Washington, DC 20008
Tel: (202) 319-1976 Fax: (202) 319-2982
Email: amembusadm@msn.com

Ambassador Perm. Observer
His Excellency Arman KIRAKOSSIAN;
Mrs. Susana Nazarian
Minister Counselor
Mr. Armen YEDIGARIAN;
Mrs. Irina Sarkissian

AUSTRIA

3524 International Ct. NW
Washington, DC 20008
Tel: (202) 895-6700 Fax: (202) 895-6750
Email: austrianembassy@washington.nu

Ambassador Perm. Observer
Her Excellency Eva NOWOTNY;
Prof. Thomas Nowotny
Minister, Deputy Chief of Mission, Alternate Observer
Mr. Harald GUENTHER
First Secretary (Political), Alternate Observer
Mr. Johann SATTLER;
Mrs. Himangi Zanpure-Sattler

AZERBAIJAN

2741 34th St. NW
Washington, DC 20008
Tel: (202) 337-3500 Fax: (202) 337-5911
Email: azerbaijan@azembassy.com

Ambassador Perm. Observer
His Excellency Hafiz Mir Jalal PASHAYEV;
Mrs. Rena Pashayeva
Second Secretary, Alternate Observer
Mr. Ilgar MOUKHTAROV;
Mrs. Nargiz Ragimkhanova

BAHAMAS, THE

2220 Massachusetts Ave. NW
Washington, DC 20008
Tel: (202) 319-2660 Fax: (202) 319-2668
Email: bahamas@oas.org

Ambassador Perm. Rep.

His Excellency Joshua SEARS;
Mrs. Michelle Sears
First Secretary, Alternate Representative
Mr. Eugene F. Torchon NEWRY;
Mrs. Yvette Pintard Newry
Second Secretary, Alternate Representative
Mrs. Monique D. VANDERPOOL;
Mr. Brent Vanderpool
Second Secretary, Alternate Representative
Ms. Betty GREENSLADE
Third Secretary, Alternate Representative
Ms. Chanelle P. BROWN

BARBADOS

2144 Wyoming Ave. NW
Washington, DC 20008
Tel: (202) 939-9200 Fax: (202) 332-7467
Email: barbados@oas.org

Ambassador Perm. Rep.
His Excellency Michael I. KING;
Mrs. Jacqueline King
Minister Counselor, Alternate Representative
Mr. David BULBULIA;
Mrs. Beverley Bulbulia
First Secretary, Alternate Representative
Ms. Donna Michelle FORDE
First Secretary, Alternate Representative
Mrs. Heidi M.R. MCLEOD;
Dr. Chrsitopher McLeod
Defense Attache, Alternate Representative
Lt. Colonel Atheline A. BRANCH
Attache
Ms. Felicia R. HACKETT
Attache
Ms. Angela S. APPLEWHAITE

BELGIUM

3330 Garfield St. NW
Washington, DC 20008
Tel: (202) 333-6900 Fax: (202) 333-3079
Email: washington@diplobel.org

Ambassador Perm. Observer
His Excellency Frans van DAELE;
Mrs. Christiane van Daele
First Political Counselor, Alternate Observer
Mrs. France CHAINAYE

BELIZE

2535 Massachusetts Ave. NW
Washington, DC 20008
Tel: (202) 332-9636 X228
Fax: (202) 332-6888
Email: belize@oas.org

Ambassador Perm. Rep.
Her Excellency Lisa SHOMAN
Minister Counselor, Alternate Representative
Mr. Nestor MENDEZ
Minister Counselor, Alternate Representative

Mr. Michael E. BEJOS
Second Secretary, Alternate Representative
Ms. Lauren Laverne QUIROS

BOLIVIA

1620 I St. NW #703
Washington, DC 20006
Tel: (202) 785-0218 Fax: (202) 296-0563
Email: bolivia@oas.org

Ambassador Perm. Rep.
Her Excellency Maria Tamayo ARNAL;
Mr. Enrique Arnal
Minister Counselor, Alternate Representative
Mr. Ricardo Martinez COBARRUBIAS
First Secretary, Alternate Representative
Mrs. Patricia Bozo DE DURAN;
Mr. Juan Carlos Duran
Civil Attache
Mrs. Norma A. PETERSON
Chief of Military Delegation
General Felix TORRICO;
Mrs. Graciela Vergara de Torrico
Military Attache Adviser
General Emilio Bayna MERCADO;
Mrs. Maria Adela Hurtado de Bayna
Naval Attache, Adviser
Col. Adm. Gustavo Zalles MEDRANO;
Mrs. Patricia Arrieta de Zalles

BOSNIA AND HERZEGOVINA

2109 E St. NW
Washington, DC 20037
Tel: (202) 337-1500 X229
Fax: (202) 337-1502
Email: info@bosnianembassy.org

Ambassador Perm. Observer
His Excellency Igor DAVIDOVIC

BRAZIL

2600 Virginia Ave. NW #412
Washington, DC 20037
Tel: (202) 333-4224 Fax: (202) 333-6610
Email: delbrasupa@delbrasupa.org

Ambassador Perm. Rep.
vacant
Interim Representative, Minister Counselor, Alternate Representative
Mr. Carlos Jose MIDDELDORF
Counselor, Alternate Representative
Mr. Jose Luiz Machado COSTA
First Secretary, Alternate Representative
Mrs. Marcia Maria Adorno Cavalcanti
RAMOS; Mr. José Ivan Cavalcanti Ramos
First Secretary, Alternate Representative
Mr. Silvio Jose Alburquerque E SILVA
Second Secretary, Alternate Representative

Mr. Paulo Eduardo de Azevedo RIBEIRO;
Mrs. Mariana Feres Nascimento de
Azevedo Ribeiro
Second Secretary, Alternate Representative
Mr. Gustavo Martins NOGUEIRA;
Mrs. Monica Alexandra dos Santos Cardoso
Third Secretary, Alternate Representative
Ms. Camile Nemitz FILIPPOZZI;
Mr. Scott David Mitchell
Attache
Ms. Clarissa Maria Flecha de Lima
ALVARES
Attache
Mr. Gilberto Cruz SILVA;
Mrs. Heliane Pires Ferreira Silva
Attache
Mrs. Marina Gurgel do Amaral VALENTE;
Mr. Eduardo Gurgel do Amaral Valente
Attache
Mrs. Maria Terezinha de Almeida
COUTINHO;
Mr. Cesar Clarimundo Coutinho
Attache
Mrs. Maria do Socorro Santos CONCEICAO;
Mr. Jose Edvaldo da Conceicao
Cultural Attache
Mrs. Laurentina Lima De Jesus SILVA;
Mr. Jose Mariano da Silva
Air Attache
Brig. Fernando Antonio Tacca de
ANDRADE; Mrs. Regiane da Silva Medeiros
Attache
Colonel Av Luis Eduardo Franca
MARINHO;
Mrs. Valeria Candida Barreto Marinho
Attache
Colonel Qema Joao Artur SANTOS;
Mrs. Vera Lucia dos Santos Santos
Attache
CMG Fernando Cesar da Silva MOTTA;
Mrs. Raquel Gomes Motta
Attache
Ten Col. Qema Jose Luiz Monteiro
GIANBARTHOLOMEI;
Mrs. Eloisa Helena Salta Giambartholomei

BULGARIA

1621 22nd St. NW
Washington , DC 20008
Tel: (202) 387-0174 Fax: (202) 234-7973
Email: office@bulgary-embassy.org

Ambassador Perm. Observer
Her Excellency Elena POPTODOROVA
Counselor, Alternate Observer
Mr. Hristo GUDJEV
First Secretary, Alternate Observer
Mr. Tihomir STOYTCHEV

CANADA

501 Pennsylvania Ave. NW
Washington, DC 20001
Tel: (202) 682-1768 Fax: (202) 682-7624
Email: wshdc-prmoas@dfait-maeci.gc.ca

Ambassador Perm. Rep.
His Excellency Paul D. DURAND;
Mrs. Patricia Fortier
Counselor, Alternate Representative
Mr. Douglas Gordon FRASER
Counselor, Alternate Representative
Mr. David MORRIS; Mrs. Ligia I. Monge
First Secretary, Alternate Representative
Ms. Catherine VEZINA; Mr. Antoine Chevrier
Second Secretary, Alternate Representative
Ms. Amanda SHELDRAKE
Alternate Representative
Ms. Basia M. MANITIUS;
Dr. Andrzej Z. Manitius

Military Adviser
Mr. Ian MACK; Mrs. Sue Mack
Military Advisor
Col. Rick RYAN; Mrs. Rose Ryan
Attache
Mrs. Yolande GAUTRON
Program Assistance
Mr. Andre PROVENCHER

CHILE

2000 L St. NW #720
Washington, DC 20036
Tel: (202) 887-5475 Fax: (202) 775-0713
Email: miscloea@chileoas.org

Ambassador Perm. Rep.
His Excellency Esteban TOMIC;
Mrs. Susanne Huneeus
**Minister Counselor, Permanent
Representative**
Mr. Eduardo GALVEZ
First Secretary, Alternate Representative
Mr. Patricio POWELL;
Mrs. Susan Roraff de Powell
Second Secretary, Alternate Representative
Mr. Rodrigo HUME;
Mrs. Paola Cadenasso de Hume
Third Secretary, Alternate Representative
Mrs. Carola MUNOZ; Mr. Ivan Favereau
Third Secretary, Alternate Representative
Mr. David QUIROGA;
Mrs. Nancy Palavecino de Quiroga
Attache
Mrs. Mónica LABARCA;
Mr. Charles Gebbert
Adviser
Brigadier General Jose Miguel PIUZZI;
Mrs. Maria Luisa Carvajal de Piuzzi
Rear Admiral
Commander Roberto CARVAJAL;
Mrs. Ana Maria Ramirez de Carvajal
Adviser
Colonel Luis ILI; Mrs. Alejandra Nuno de Ili

COLOMBIA

1609 22nd St. NW
Washington, DC 20008
Tel: (202) 332-8003 Fax: (202) 234-9781
Email: colombia@oas.org

Ambassador Perm. Rep.
vacant
**Interim Representative, Minister
Plenipotentiary**
Ms. Maria Clara Isaza MERCHAN
Second Secretary, Alternate Representative
Mr. Pedro VIVEROS
Second Secretary, Alternate Representative
Mr. Jorge Mario Echeverry CARDENAS;
Mrs. Nadia Dziewczapolski
Second Secretary, Alternate Representative
Mr. Andres Felipe VILLAMIZAR
First Secretary
Mrs. Margarita MANJARREZ;
Mr. Camilo Garcia
Counselor
Mrs. Pilar Gaitan POMBO;
Mr. Santiago Pombo

COSTA RICA

2112 S St. NW #300
Washington, DC 20008
Tel: (202) 234-9280 Fax: (202) 986-2274
Email: croea@hotmail.com

Ambassador Perm. Rep.
vacant
Ambassador, Interim Representative
His Excellency Luis Guardia MORA;

Mrs. Carmen de Guardia
Ambassador, Alternate Representative
His Excellency Agustin Castro SOLANO
Minister Counselor, Alternate Representative
Lic. Rodrigo Sotela ALFARO;
Mrs. Gabriela G. de Sotela
Minister Counselor, Alternate Representative
Mrs. Roxana Teran De de la CRUZ;
Mr. Antonio de la Cruz
Attache
Ms. Ana Leon-Paez SOTELA

CROATIA

2343 Massachusetts Ave. NW
Washington , DC 20008
Tel: (202) 588-5943 Fax: (202) 588-8937
Email: amboffice@croatiaemb.org

Ambassador Perm. Observer
His Excellency Neven JURICA;
Mrs. Dunja Jurica
Deputy Chief of Mission, Alternate Observer
Mr. Marijan GUBIC; Mrs. Suzana Gubic
Minister Counselor, Alternate Observer
Mr. Vice SKRACIC; Mrs. Helena Skracic

CYPRUS

2211 R St. NW
Washington, DC 20008
Tel: (202) 462-5772 Fax: (202) 483-6710
Email: info@cypressembassy.net

Ambassador Perm. Observer
His Excellency Euripides L. EVRIVIADES
Counselor, Alternate Observer
Mr. Havalombos KAFKARIDES
First Secretary, Alternate Observer
Mr. Basil POLEMETIS

CZECH REPUBLIC

3900 Spring of Freedom St. NW
Washington, DC 20008
Tel: (202) 274-9100 Fax: (202) 966-8540
Email: pol_washington@embassy.mzv.cz

Ambassador Perm. Observer
His Excellency Martin PALOUS
Deputy Chief of Mission, Alternate Observer
Mr. Vratislav JANDA
Press Secretary, Alternate Observer
Mr. Peter JANOUSEK

DENMARK

3200 Whitehaven St. NW
Washington, DC 20008
Tel: (202) 234-4300 Fax: (202) 328-1470
Email: wasamb@um.dk

Ambassador Perm. Observer
His Excellency Ulrik FEDERSPIEL;
Dr. Birgitte Federspiel
First Secretary, Alternate Observer
Ms. Lotte LUND; Mr. Mads Hansen

DOMINICA (THE COMMONWEALTH OF)

3216 New Mexico Ave. NW
Washington, DC 20016
Tel: (202) 364-6781 Fax: (202) 364-6791
Email: embdomdc@aol.com

Ambassador Perm. Rep.
His Excellency Swinburne A. S. LESTRADE;
Mrs. Annette Lestrade
Third Secretary, Alternate Representative
Ms. Judith Anne ROLLE

DOMINICAN REPUBLIC

1715 22nd St. NW
Washington, DC 20008
Tel: (202) 332-9142 Fax: (202) 232-5038
Email: republicadominicana@oas.org

Ambassador Perm. Rep.
vacant
Interim Representative, Minister Counselor
Ms. Mayerlyn CORDERO;
Mr. Mauricio Pastora
Minister Counselor, Alternate Representative
Mr. Jose Dantes DIAZ;
Mrs. Josefina Navarro
Minister Counselor, Alternate Representative
Mr. Victor TIRADO; Mrs. Liset Tirado
Minister Counselor, Alternate Representative
Ms. Wilma Medina LEAL
Minister Counselor, Alternate Representative
Mr. Francisco CRUZ
Minister Counselor, Alternate Representative
Mr. Juan Antonio MARTE;
Mrs. Lourdes Martes
Minister Counselor, Alternate Representative
Ms. Cristy RODRIGUEZ
Counselor, Alternate Representative
Mr. Flavio MEDINA; Mrs. Inova C. Medina
First Secretary
Ms. Karen HERRERA; Mr. Carlos Ferdinand
First Secretary, Alternate Representative
Mr. Ramon Revi MATOS
Military Attache
M. Gen. Hugo Gonzalez BORRELL;
Mrs. Rossanna E. Dalmasi de Gonzalez

ECUADOR

2535 15th St. NW
Washington, DC 20029
Tel: (202) 234-1494 Fax: (202) 234-3159
Email: ecuoea@ecuador.org

Ambassador Perm. Rep.
His Excellency Marcelo HERVAS;
Mrs. Luz Blanca de Hervas
Minister, Alternate Representative
Mr. Jaime Augusto Barberis MARTINEZ;
Mrs. Maria Amparo Aviles de Barberis
First Secretary, Alternate Representative
Mr. Efrain Baus PALACIOS;
Mrs. Carla Maria Davalos de Baus
First Secretary, Alternate Representative
Mr. Santiago Novoa ANDRADE;
Mrs. Fanny Isabel Caicedo de Noboa
Civil Attache
Mrs. Nelly ARMIJOS; Mr. Guillermo Freire

EGYPT

3521 International Ct. NW
Washington, DC 20008
Tel: (202) 895-5400 Fax: (202) 244-5131
Email: embassy@egyptembdc.org

Ambassador Perm. Observer
His Excellency M. Nabil FAHMY;
Mrs. Nermin Fahmy
Deputy Chief of Mission, Alternate Observer
Dr. Walid M. ABDELNASSER;
Mrs. Dahlia Mohamed Nazih M. Tawakol
Counselor, Alternate Observer
Mr. Hussein Abdel Karim MUBARAK;
Mrs. Hwaida Essam Abdel Ranman

EL SALVADOR

1211 Connecticut Ave. NW #401
Washington, DC 20036
Tel: (202) 467-0054 Fax: (202) 467-4261
Email: moeasv@covad.net

Ambassador Perm. Rep.
Her Excellency Abigail Castro DE PEREZ
Ambassador, Alternate Representative
His Excellency Luis Menendez Leal
CASTRO;
Mrs. Elvira Margarita de Menendez
Counselor, Permanent Representative
Lic. Luis Armando CALDERON
Counselor, Alternate Representative
Lic. Gabriela ZABLAH
Adviser
Mr. Pedro IRAHETA

EQUATORIAL GUINEA

2020 16th St. NW
Washington, DC 20009
Tel: (202) 518-5700 Fax: (202) 518-5252
Email: info@equatorialguinea.org

Ambassador Perm. Observer
His Excellency Teodoro Biyogo NSUE

ESTONIA

2131 Massachusetts Ave. NW
Washington , DC 20008
Tel: (202) 588-0101 Fax: (202) 588-0108
Email: info@estemb.org

Ambassador Perm. Observer
His Excellency Juri LUIK
Third Secretary, Alternate Observer
Mr. Priit MASING

EUROPEAN UNION

2300 M St. NW
Washington, DC 20037
Tel: (202) 862-9500 Fax: (202) 429-1766

Ambassador Perm. Observer
His Excellency Gunter BURGHARDT;
Mrs. Rita Burghardt
Minister, Alternate Observer
Mr. Gerard DEPAYRE
Political Counselor, Alternate Observer
Mr. Philippe COESSENS;
Mrs. Christine Lassey
Counselor, Alternate Observer
Ms. Elizabeth PAPE; Mr. Heinz Pape
Alternate Observer
Mrs. Despina MANOS; Mr. Elias Manos

FINLAND

3301 Massachusetts Ave. NW
Washington, DC 20008
Tel: (202) 298-5800 Fax: (202) 298-6030
Email: sanomat.was@formin.fi

Ambassador Perm. Observer
His Excellency Jukka VALTASAARI;
Mrs. Etel Valtasaari
Minister, Alternate Observer
Mr. Matti ANTTONEN; Mrs. Virve Anttonen
Minister Counselor, Alternate Observer
Ms. Ulla-Maija FINSKAS

FRANCE

4911 Loughboro Rd. NW
Washington, DC 20016
Tel: (202) 295-3802 Fax: (202) 244-9328
Email: france@oas.org

Ambassador Perm. Observer
Her Excellency Sylvie ALVAREZ
Counselor, Alternate Observer
Mr. Raymond QUEREILHAC;
Mrs. Mickaelle Merceron

GEORGIA

1101 15th St. NW #602
Washington , DC 20005
Tel: (202) 387-9151 Fax: (202) 393-4537
Email: embgeorgiausa@yahoo.com

Ambassador Perm. Observer
His Excellency Levan MIKELADZE;
Mrs. Lali Chikvaidze-Mikeladze
Minister, Alternate Observer
Mr. David SOUMBADZE;
Mrs. Inga Diasamidze-Soumbadze

GERMANY

4645 Reservoir Rd. NW
Washington, DC 20007
Tel: (202) 298-8140 Fax: (202) 298-4391
Email: ge-embus@lx.netcom.com

Ambassador Perm. Observer
His Excellency Wolfgang ISCHINGER;
Mrs. Jutta Falke-Ischinger
Minister (Deputy Chief of Mission), Alternate Observer
Mr. Peter GOTTWALD;
Mrs. Verena Gottwald
Minister (Political Affairs), Alternate Observer
Mr. Rolf W. NIKEL;
Mrs. Regine Francoise Nikel
First Secretary (Political Affairs), Alternate Observer
Mr. Daniel KRIENER; Mrs. Petra Kriener

GHANA

3512 International Dr. NW
Washington, DC 20008
Tel: (202) 686-4520 Fax: (202) 686-4527

Ambassador Perm. Observer
His Excellency Fritz Kwabena POKU;
Mrs. Nana Efua Salvo-Poku
Deputy Chief of Mission, Alternate Observer
Mr. Isaac AGGREY; Mrs. Gloria Agrrey
First Secretary (Consular), Alternate Observer
Mr. Chris OBENG

GREECE

2221 Massachusetts Ave. NW
Washington, DC 20008
Tel: (202) 939-1300 Fax: (202) 939-1324
Email: greece@greekembassy.org

Ambassador Perm. Observer
His Excellency George SAVVAIDES;
Mrs. Maria Savvaides
Minister, Alternate Representative
Mr. Eleftherios ANGHELOPOULOS;
Mrs. Anastasia Anthi
Second Secretary (Political), Alternate Observer
Mr. Dimitris ANGHELAKIS

GRENADA

1701 New Hampshire Ave. NW
Washington, DC 20009
Tel: (202) 265-2561 Fax: (202) 265-2468
Email: grenada@oas.org

Ambassador Perm. Rep.
His Excellency Denis G. ANTOINE
Counselor, Alternate Representative
Ms. Marguerite ST. JOHN
First Secretary, Alternate Representative
Ms. Patricia D.M. CLARKE

GUATEMALA

1507 22nd St. NW
Washington, DC 20037
Tel: (202) 833-4015 Fax: (202) 833-4011
Email: oea@minex.gob.gt

Ambassador Perm. Rep.
His Excellency Francisco Villagran DE LEON
Ambassador, Alternate Representative
His Excellency Juan LEON
Counselor, Alternate Representative
Mr. Otto PEREZ
Third Secretary, Alternate Representative
Mr. Jorge Eduardo Enrique CONTRERAS
Third Secretary, Alternate Representative
Ms. Elsa Liliana SAMAYOA

GUYANA

2490 Tracy Pl. NW
Washington, DC 20008
Tel: (202) 265-6900 Fax: (202) 232-1297
Email: guyanaembassydc@verizon.net

Ambassador Perm. Rep.
His Excellency Bayney R. KARRAN;
Mrs. Donna Karran
First Secretary, Alternate Representative
Ms. Deborah YAW
First Secretary, Alternate Representative
Mr. Forbes JULY; Mrs. Valentina July

HAITI

2311 Massachusetts Ave. NW
Washington, DC 20008
Tel: (202) 332-4090 Fax: (202) 518-8742
Email: haiti@oas.org

Ambassador Perm. Rep.
His Excellency Duly BRUTUS;
Mrs. Nerta Brutus
Minister Counselor, Alternate Representative
Mr. Jean Ricot DORMEUS;
Mrs. Marie Carmelle Dormeus
First Secretary, Alternate Representative
Mr. Pierre Daniel LAVIOLETTE;
Mrs. Diane S. Laviolette
First Secretary, Alternate Representative
Mr. Youri EMMANUEL;
Mrs. Sandra Sanchez Emmanuel

HOLY SEE

3339 Massachusetts Ave. N.W.
Washington, DC 20008
Tel: (202) 333-7121 Fax: (202) 337-4036
Email: nuntius@worldnet.att.net

Ambassador Perm. Observer
His Excellency Most Reverend Gabriel
MONTALVO

HONDURAS

5100 Wisconsin Ave. NW #403
Washington, DC 20016
Tel: (202) 362-9656 Fax: (202) 537-7170
Email: honduras@oas.org

Ambassador Perm. Rep.
His Excellency Salvador E. Rodezno
FUENTES; Mrs. Elizabeth Rodezno
Ambassador, Alternate Representative
His Excellency Mauricio Aguilar ROBLES
Counselor, Alternate Representative
Lic. Maria Guadalupe CARIAS
Attache, Adviser
Mrs. Rosario Zapata DE LASERNA;
Mr. Eduardo Laserna
Military Attache

Col. Rodolfo INTERIANO;
Mrs. Melida Interiano

HUNGARY

3910 Shoemaker St. NW
Washington, DC 20008
Tel: (202) 362-6730 Fax: (202) 966-8135
Email: office@huembwas.og

Ambassador Perm. Observer
His Excellency Andras SIMONYI;
Mrs. Nada Pejak-Simonyi
Counselor (Deputy Chief of Mission), Alternate Observer
Mr. Viktor SZEDERKENYI; Mrs. Adel Keleti
Counselor, Alternate Observer
Mrs. Terez Dehelan-DOROMBOZI

INDIA

2107 Massachusetts Ave. NW
Washington, DC 20008
Tel: (202) 939-7000 Fax: (202) 265-4351

Ambassador Perm. Observer
His Excellency Ranendra SEN;
Mrs. Kalpana Sen
Deputy Chief of Mission, Alternate Observer
Mr. Rakesh SOOD
Minister, Alternate Observer
Mr. Sunil JAIN; Mrs. Gargi Jain

IRELAND

2234 Massachusetts Ave. NW
Washington, DC 20008
Tel: (202) 462-3939 Fax: (202) 239-5993
Email: embirlus@aol.com

Ambassador Perm. Observer
His Excellency Noel FAHEY;
Mrs. Christine Fahey
First Secretary, Alternate Observer
Mr. Tim DOYLE

ISRAEL

3514 International Dr. NW
Washington, DC 20008
Tel: (202) 364-5590 Fax: (202) 364-5423
Email: ask@israelemb.org

Ambassador Perm. Observer
His Excellency Daniel AYALON;
Mrs. Ann Ayalon
Counselor, Alternate Observer
Mr. Reuven AZAR

ITALY

3000 Whitehaven St. NW
Washington, DC 20008
Tel: (202) 612-4466 Fax: (202) 518-2153
Email: lambertini@itwash.org

Ambassador Perm. Observer
His Excellency Gerolamo SCHIAVONI;
Mrs. Ana Patricia Schiavoni
First Counselor, Alternate Observer
Mr. Inigo LAMBERTINI;
Mrs. Maria Grazia Lambertini

JAMAICA

1520 New Hampshire Ave. NW
Washington, DC 20036
Tel: (202) 986-0121 Fax: (202) 452-9395
Email: jamaica@oas.org

Ambassador Perm. Rep.

His Excellency Gordon V. SHIRLEY
Minister, Alternate Representative
Ms. Delrose E. MONTAGUE

JAPAN

2520 Massachusetts Ave. NW
Washington, DC 20008
Tel: (202) 238-6812 Fax: (202) 265-9497
Email: hikeda@embjapan.org

Ambassador Perm. Observer
His Excellency Ryozo KATO;
Mrs. Hanako Kato

KAZAKHSTAN

1401 16th St. NW
Washington, DC 20036
Tel: (202) 232-5488 Fax: (202) 232-5845
Email: kazak@intr.net

Ambassador Perm. Observer
His Excellency Kanat B. SAUDABAYEV

KOREA

2450 Massachusetts Ave. NW
Washington, DC 20008
Tel: (202) 939-5600 Fax: (202) 387-0205
Email: shhong79@mofat.go.kr

Ambassador Perm. Observer
His Excellency Sung-Joo HAN;
Mrs. Song-Mi Han
Minister, Alternate Observer
Mr. Sung-lac WI; Mrs. Sang-hak Wi
Counselor, Alternate Observer
Mr. Seong-hoa HONG;
Mrs. Hyun-sook Hong

LATVIA

4325 17th St. NW
Washington, DC 20011
Tel: (202) 726-8213 Fax: (202) 726-6785
Email: embassy.usa@mfa.gov.lv

Ambassador Perm. Observer
His Excellency Maris RIEKSTINS;
Mrs. Irena Riekstina
Deputy Chief of Mission
Mr. Maris SELGA; Mrs. Marika Selga

LEBANON

2560 28th St. NW
Washington, DC 20008
Tel: (202) 939-6300 Fax: (202) 939-6324
Email: info@lebanonembassyus.org

Ambassador Perm. Observer
His Excellency Dr. Farid ABBOUD;
Mrs. Rim Abboud
Deputy Chief of Mission, Alternate Observer
Mr. Carla JAZZAR
First Secretary, Alternate Observer
Mr. Ziad ATALLAH
First Secretary, Alternate Observer
Ms. Rola NOUREDDINE

MEXICO

2440 Massachusetts Ave. NW
Washington, DC 20008
Tel: (202) 332-3663 Fax: (202) 234-0602
Email: mision.oea@sre.gob.mx

Ambassador Perm. Rep.
His Excellency Jorge Chen CHARPENTIER
Minister, Alternate Representative
Lic. Ernesto Campos TENORIO;
Mrs. Ana Isabel Rodriguez
Minister, Alternate Representative
Lic. Ricardo Tarcisio Navarrete Montes
DE OCA;
Mrs. Luz Maria Zurita Aguilar de Navarrete
Counselor, Alternate Representative
Lic. Juan Sandoval MENDIOLEA;
Mrs. Ana Isabel Tapuerca
Counselor, Alternate Representative
Lic. Jose Manuel Castaneda RESENDIZ;
Mrs. Maria Eugenia Alpizar
First Secretary, Alternate Representative
Lic. Marcelina Y. Cruz MIMILA;
Mr. Angel Alfonso Espejel
Third Secretary, Alternate Representative
Lic. Muan Iruegas NATIVIDAD
Third Secretary, Alternate Representative
Lic. Gabriel Morales MORALES;
Mrs. Maria Cristina Zorrilla Oropeza
Attache
Mrs. Margarita Montano PARDO
Attache
Mrs. Maria del Carmen Cecilia Davila
MARTINEZ
Attache
Mrs. Diana Emelit Arenas GUTIERREZ

MOROCCO

1601 21st St. NW
Washington, DC 20009
Tel: (202) 462-7979 Fax: (202) 462-7643
Email: embassy@embassyofmorocco.us

Ambassador Perm. Observer
His Excellency Aziz MEKOUAR;
Mrs. Maria Felice Cittadini Cesi
Minister (DCM), Alternate Observer
Mr. Mohammed ARIAD
First Secretary, Alternate Observer
Ms. Jamila ALAOUI

NETHERLANDS

4200 Linnean Ave. NW
Washington, DC 20008
Tel: (202) 244-5300 Fax: (202) 364-4213
Email: nlgovwas@netherlands-embassy.org

Ambassador Perm. Observer
His Excellency Boudewijn J. VAN
EENENNAAM
Minister, Alternate Observer
Mr. Wim J.P. GEERTS
**Minister Plenipotentiary for Aruba, Alternate
Observer**
Mr. Henry BAARH
**Minister Plenipotentiary for the Netherlands
Antilles, Alternate Observer**
Mr. Jeffrey CORION
Second Secretary, Alternate Observer
Mrs. Guusje KORTHALS ALTES

NICARAGUA

1627 New Hampshire Ave. NW
Washington, DC 20009
Tel: (202) 332-1643 Fax: (202) 745-0710
Email: nicaragua@oas.org

Ambassador Perm. Rep.
Her Excellency Carmen Marina Gutirrez
SALAZAR; Mr. Juan Carlos Rivers
Minister Counselor, Alternate Representative
Ms. Lila M. Bolanos CHAMORRO
Counselor, Alternate Representative
Mr. Arturo Harding TEFEL;
Mrs. Nolaska Harding
First Secretary, Alternate Representative
Ms. Julieta M. Blandon MIRANDA
Attache

Ms. Mariana Silva AMADOR
Defense Attache
Mr. Pedro Leonel MARTINEZ;
Mrs. Ruth Palacios de Martinez

NORWAY

2720 34th St. NW
Washington, DC 20008
Tel: (202) 333-6000 Fax: (202) 337-0870
Email: emb.washington@mfa.no

Ambassador Perm. Observer
His Excellency Knut VOLLEBAEK;
Mrs. Ellen Sofie Aa. Vollebaek
Minister Counselor, Alternate Observer
Mr. Morten AASLAND; Ms. Bente Weisser
First Secretary, Alternate Observer
Mr. Evan STORMOEN

PAKISTAN

3517 International Ct. NW
Washington, DC 20008
Tel: (202) 243-6500 Fax: (202) 686-1567

Ambassador Perm. Observer
His Excellency Jehangir KARAMAT
Deputy Chief of Mission, Alternate Observer
Mr. Mohammad SADIQ; Mrs. Sadia Sadiq
**Second Secretary, Officer Responsible for
the OAS**
Mr. Imran ALI

PANAMA

2201 Wisconsin Ave. NW #C-100
Washington, DC 20007
Tel: (202) 965-4826 Fax: (202) 965-4836
Email: panama@oas.org

Ambassador Perm. Rep.
His Excellency Aristides ROYO
Ambassador, Alternate Representative
His Excellency Ricardo Gonzalez DE MENA
Legal Counselor, Alternate Representative
Ms. Nisla Lorena Aparicio ROBLES;
Mr. Diego Grajales
Counselor, Alternate Representative
Mr. Resires VARGAS
Counselor, Alternate Representative
Mr. Milton RUIZ
Attache, Adviser
Ms. Esther TAYLOR

PARAGUAY

2022 Connecticut Ave. NW
Washington, DC 20008
Tel: (202) 244-3003 Fax: (202) 244-3005
Email: paraguay@oas.org

Ambassador Perm. Rep.
His Excellency Luis Enrique Chase PLATE
Minister, Alternate Representative
Mrs. Elisa Ruiz DIAZ
First Secretary, Alternate Representative
Mr. Jose Mendez VALL;
Mrs. Marina de Mendez
Second Secretary, Alternate Representative
Mrs. Sonia Quiroga DE ALVARENGA;
Mr. Nestor Alvarenga
Third Secretary
Ms. Carla Poletti SERAFINI
Attache
Mr. Jorge Ruiz DIAZ

PERU

1901 Pennsylvania Ave. NW #402
Washington, DC 20006
Tel: (202) 232-2281 Fax: (202) 466-3068

Ambassador Perm. Rep.
His Excellency Alberto Borea ODRIA;
Mrs. Sandra de Borea
Minister, Alternate Representative
Lic. Antonio Garcia REVILLA
Minister Counselor, Alternate Representative
Mrs. Ana Maria SANCHEZ; Mr. Edison Rios
Minister Counselor, Alternate Representative
Lic. Jorge WURST; Mrs. Claudia de Wurst
Counselor, Hemispheric Security Matters
Mr. Jaime Salinas SEDO;
Mrs. Isabel de Salinas
Counselor, Alternate Representative
Ms. Ana PENA
First Secretary, Alternate Representative
Mr. Ricardo SILVA-SANTISTEBAN;
Mrs. Angela de Silva-Santisteban
First Secretary, Alternate Representative
Mr. Augusto BAZAN;
Mrs. Patricia Gabaldoni de Bazan
First Secretary, Alternate Representative
Mr. Manuel RUIZ; Mrs. Cecilia de Ruiz
First Secretary
Mr. Alejandro BEOUTIS;
Mrs. Diana Buendia de Beoutis
Attache (Cultural Counselor)
Ambassador Antonio LULLI;
Mrs. Elvira de Lulli
Naval Attache
Rear Admiral Hector SOLDI;
Mrs. Rossana de Soldi
Military Attache
Colonel Hector BERTRAN;
Mrs. Rosario de Bertran
Military Attache
Colonel Victor Anibal VELAZCO;
Mrs. Martha de Velazco
Military Attache
Colonel Moises REJANOVINSHI

PHILIPPINES

1600 Massachusetts Ave. NW
Washington, DC 20036
Tel: (202) 467-9300 Fax: (202) 467-9417
Email: wdcpepolitical@aol.com

Ambassador Perm. Observer
His Excellency Albert F. DEL ROSARIO;
Mrs. Margaret Gretchen del Rosario
Deputy Chief of Mission, Alternate Observer
Mr. Evan P. GARCIA; Mrs. Jocelyn B. Garcia
Minister (Political), Alternate Observer
Ms. Lourdes O. YPARAGUIRRE

POLAND

2640 16th St. NW
Washington, DC 20009
Tel: (202) 234-3800 Fax: (202) 328-6271
Email: information@ioip.org

Ambassador Perm. Observer
His Excellency Przemyslaw GRUDZINSKI;
Mrs. Maria Grudzinska
Minister Counselor, Alternate Observer
Mr. Miroslaw LUCZKA;
Mrs. Malgorzata Orzechowska

PORTUGAL

2012 Massachusetts Ave. NW
Washington, DC 20036
Tel: (202) 350-5426 Fax: (202) 462-3726
Email: portugaloas@attglobal.net

Ambassador Perm. Observer
Her Excellency Josefina Reis CARVALHO
Attache, Alternate Observer
Ms. Ana Maria Pires MONTERO

QATAR

4200 Wisconsin Ave. #200
Washington, DC 20016
Tel: (202) 274-1600 Fax: (202) 237-0061

Ambassador Perm. Observer
His Excellency Bader O. AL-DAFA;
Mrs. Awatef Mohamed Al Dafa
Minister
Mr. Hamad M. AL-KHALITA

ROMANIA

1607 23rd St. NW
Washington, DC 20008
Tel: (202) 332-4852 Fax: (202) 232-4748
Email: office@roembus.org

Ambassador Perm. Observer
His Excellency Sorin Dumitru DUCARU;
Mrs. Carmen Ducaru
Minister Counselor, Alternate Observer
Mrs. Daniela GITMAN; Mr. Cristian Gitman
Third Secretary, Alternate Observer
Mr. Bogdan NEAGU; Mrs. Claudia Neagu

RUSSIAN FEDERATION

2650 Wisconsin Ave. NW
Washington, DC 20007
Tel: (202) 298-5755 Fax: (202) 298-5735
Email: russianembassy@mindspring.com

Ambassador Perm. Observer
His Excellency Yuri V. USHAKOV;
Mrs. Svetlana M. Ushakova
First Secretary, Alternate Observer
Mr. Vladimir A. PROSKURYAKOV;
Mrs. Ella N. Proskuryakova

SAINT LUCIA

3216 New Mexico Ave. NW
Washington, DC 20016
Tel: (202) 364-6792 Fax: (202) 364-6723
Email: eofsaintlu@aol.com

Ambassador Perm. Rep.
Her Excellency Sonia Merlyn JOHNNY;
Dr. Lloyd Jackson
Minister Counselor, Alternate Representative
Ms. Glenice JEROME
First Secretary, Alternate Representative
Ms. Yasmin Solitahe Solitahe ODLUM
Administrative Attache
Ms. Thais MEROE
Attache
Ms. Angela CHERRY
Attache
Ms. Melanie DOMINIQUE

SAINT VINCENT AND THE GRANADINES

3216 New Mexico Ave. NW
Washington, DC 20016
Tel: (202) 364-6730 Fax: (202) 364-6736
Email: ejohn@embsvg.com

Ambassador Perm. Rep.
His Excellency Ellsworth I.A. JOHN;
Mrs. Charmane John

Minister Counselor, Alternate Representative
Mr. Dwight Fitzgerald BRAMBLE
Counselor, Alternate Representative
Mr. Frank Montgomery CLARKE

SAUDI ARABIA, KINGDOM OF

601 New Hampshire Ave. NW
Washington, DC 20037
Tel: (202) 342-3800 Fax: (202) 944-6750

Ambassador Perm. Observer
His Excellency Ahmed A. KATAN
Minister, Alternate Observer
Mr. Rihab MASSOUD

SLOVAK REPUBLIC

3523 International Ct. NW
Washington, DC 20008
Tel: (202) 237-1054 Fax: (202) 237-6438
Email: info@slovakembassy-us.org

Ambassador Perm. Observer
His Excellency Rastislav KACER;
Mrs. Otilia Kacerova
Counselor, Alternate Observer
Mr. Miroslav WLACHOVSKY
Third Secretary, Alternate Observer
Ms. Miriam VYPALOVA

SPAIN

2915 Connecticut Ave. #102 NW
Washington, DC 20008
Tel: (202) 265-8365 Fax: (202) 332-6889
Email: espana@oas.org

Ambassador Perm. Observer
His Excellency Eduardo GUTIERREZ;
Mrs. Carmen Seoane
Minister, Alternate Observer
Mr. Enrique ASOREY;
Mrs. Eun-Sook Yang Ahn
Counselor, Alternate Observer
Mr. Juan Pedro CHOZAS;
Mrs. Victoria Julia Sumbera
Attache
Ms. Maria del Rocio ALBA

SRI LANKA

2148 Wyoming Ave. NW
Washington, DC 20008
Tel: (202) 483-4026 Fax: (202) 483-8017

Ambassador Perm. Observer
His Excellency Devinda Rohan
SUBASINGHE;
Mrs. Helga Wurzer-Subasinghe
Deputy Chief of Mission, Alternate Observer
Ambassador Janaka NAKKAWITA;
Mrs. Rohini Nakkawita
Second Secretary, Alternate Observer
Ms. Dayani MENDIS

ST. KITTS AND NEVIS

3216 New Mexico Ave. NW
Washington, DC 20016
Tel: (202) 686-2636 Fax: (202) 686-5740

Ambassador Perm. Rep.
His Excellency Dr. Izben C. WILLIAMS;
Mrs. Shirmel Williams
Minister Counselor, Alternate Representative
Mr. Kevin M. ISAAC
Counselor, Alternate Representative
Ms. Jasmine E. HUGGINS

SURINAME

4301 Connecticut Ave. NW #460
Washington, DC 20008
Tel: (202) 244-7488 Fax: (202) 244-5878
Email: esuriname@covad.net

Ambassador Perm. Rep.
His Excellency Henry Lothar ILLES;
Mrs. Margo Lizette Illes Deekman
Counselor, Alternate Representative
Mr. Rabinder LALA; Mrs. Carmelita P. Lala
First Secretary, Alternate Representative
Mr. Henry Leonard Leonard MACDONALD;
Mrs. Hyacinth S. MacDonald

SWEDEN

1501 M St. NW
Washington, DC 20005
Tel: (202) 467-2600 Fax: (202) 467-2699
Email: ambassaden.washington@foreign
ministry.es

Ambassador Perm. Observer
His Excellency Jan ELIASSON;
Mrs. Kerstin E. Eliasson
First Secretary, Alternate Observer
Mr. Gunnar ALDEN; Mrs. Sara Alden

SWITZERLAND

2900 Cathedral Ave. NW
Washington, DC 20008
Tel: (202) 745-7900 Fax: (202) 387-2564
Email: vertretung@was.rep.admin.ch

Ambassador Perm Observer
His Excellency Christian
BLICKENSTORFER;
Mrs. Susanne Blickenstorfer
Minister, Alternate Observer
Mr. Alexander WITTWER;
Mrs. Maya Wittwer
First Secretary, Alternate Observer
Mr. Arno WICKI

THAILAND

1024 Wisconsin Ave. NW
Washington, DC 20007
Tel: (202) 944-3600 Fax: (202) 944-3611

Ambassador Perm. Observer
His Excellency Kasit PIROMYA;
Mrs. Chintana Piromya
Minister and Deputy Chief of Mission, Alternate Observer
Mr. Chirachai PUNKRASIN;
Mrs. Kanyaratana Punkrasin
Second Secretary, Alternate Observer
Ms. Anintita VATCHARASIRITHAM

TRINIDAD AND TOBAGO

1708 Massachusetts Ave. NW
Washington, DC 20036-1903
Tel: (202) 467-6490 Fax: (202) 785-3130
Email: info@ttembwash.com

Ambassador Perm. Rep.
Her Excellency Marina Annette VALERE
Counselor, Alternate Representative
Mr. Mackisack LOGIE;
Mrs. Joy Cadogan-Logie
Counselor, Alternate Representative
Dr. Paul BYAM
Counselor, Alternate Representative
Ms. Jennifer MARCHAND
Defense Attache, Adviser

Lt. Colonel Anthony PHILLIPS-SPENCER;
Mrs. Joanne Phillips-Spencer
Immigration Attache
Mr. Deodath MAHARAJ;
Mrs. Jennifer Maharaj

TUNISIA

1515 Massachusetts Ave. NW
Washington, DC 20005
Tel: (202) 862-1850 Fax: (202) 862-1858
Email: at.washington@verizon.net

Ambassador Perm. Observer
His Excellency Hatem ATALLAH;
Mrs. Fayka Atallah
Deputy Chief of Mission, Alternate Observer
Mr. Tarek AZOUZ; Mrs. Raoudha Azouz

TURKEY

2525 Massachusetts Ave. NW
Washington, DC 20008
Tel: (202) 612-6700 Fax: (202) 612-6744
Email: contact@turkishembassy.org

Ambassador Perm Observer
His Excellency O. Faruk LOGOGLU;
Mrs. Mevhibe Logoglu
Minister Counselor, Alternate Observer
Mr. Engin SOYSAL; Mrs. Tulay Soysal
First Secretary, Alternate Observer
Mr. Oguzhan ERTUGRUL;
Mrs. Ozge Ertugrul

UKRAINE

3350 M St. NW
Washington, DC 20007
Tel: (202) 333-0606 Fax: (202) 333-0817

Ambassador Perm. Observer
His Excellency Mykhailo REZNYK
Counselor, Alternate Observer
Mr. Yurii KLYMENCO
First Secretary, Alternate Observer
Mr. Gennadiy SALYKIN

UNITED KINGDOM OF GREAT BRITAIN AND NORTHERN IRELAND

3100 Massachusetts Ave. NW
Washington, DC 20008
Tel: (202) 588-6528 Fax: (202) 588-7870
Email: rachel.edis@fco.gov.uk

Perm. Observer
Mr. Robert CULSHAW; Mrs. Elaine Culshaw
Minister, Alternate Observer
Mr. Alan CHARLTON; Mrs. Judy Charlton
Counselor, Alternate Observer
Mr. Sebastian WOOD; Mrs. Sirinat Wood
Second Secretary, Alternate Observer
Mrs. Rachel EDIS
Attache, Alternate Observer
Mrs. Sarah TURNER; Mr. David Turner

UNITED STATES

WHA/USOAS, Bureau of Western
Hemisphere Affairs,
Department of State #5914
Washington, DC 20520-6258
Tel: (202) 647-9376 Fax: (202) 647-6973

continued on p 192

Hispanic Missions to the UN
Misiones hispanas ante la ONU

The (UN) works to maintain peace and provide humanitarian assistance throughout the world. It was founded on October 24, 1945 and includes 189 member states.
La (ONU) lucha por el mantenimiento de la paz y presta de asistencia humanitaria a nivel universal. Fue fundada el 24 de octubre de 1945 y la integran 189 estados miembros.

ARGENTINA

PERMANENT MISSION OF ARGENTINA TO THE UNITED NATIONS

1 United Nations Plz., 25th Fl.
New York, NY 10017
Tel: (212) 688-6300 Fax: (212) 980-8395
Email: argentina@un.int
Web: www.un.int/argentina

Ambassador E. and P.
His Excellency César Mayoral;
Mrs. Virginia M. Silvestre de Mayoral
Minister Plenipotentiary, Deputy Permanent Representative
Mr. Alberto Pedro D'Alotto;
Mrs. Andrea Vázquez de D'Alotto
Counsellor
Mr. Ricardo Luis Bocalandro;
Mrs. Maria Elena Urriste de Bocalandro
Counsellor
Mr. Gustavo Eduardo Ainchil;
Mrs. Maria Fabiana Loguzzo
First Secretary
Mrs. Maria Fabiana Loguzzo;
Mr. Gustavo Eduardo Ainchil
First Secretary
Mrs. Gabriela Martinic; Mr. Mateo Estreme
First Secretary
Mr. Mateo Estreme; Mrs. Gabriela Martinic
First Secretary
Mr. Guillermo Kendall
First Secretary
Mr. Marcelo Gabriel Suarez Salvia;
Mrs. Evangelina d'Andrea de Suarez Salvia
Second Secretary
Mr. Federico Alejandro Barttfeld;
Mrs. Marina Michelutti de Barttfeld
Second Secretary
Mrs. Maria Josefina Martinez Gramuglia;
Mr. Diego M. Hofman
Attache
Mr. Jorge Luis Lavia;
Mrs. Isabel Salinas de Lavia
Attache
Mr. Adrian Antonio Vernis
Attache
Mr. Dario Fabian Ozan
Attache
Mr. Gustavo Alejandro Maggiora;
Mrs. Rossanna Cuesta de Maggiora
Attache, Military Adviser
Mr. Ricardo Jose Etchegaray
Attache, Deputy Military Adviser
Mr. Alberto Oscar Gabrielli;
Mrs. Jorgelina Gonzalez de Gabrielli
Attache, Civil Police Adviser
Mr. Alejandro A. Chmielewski
Attache
Mr. Raul Alberto Senorans

BOLIVIA

PERMANENT MISSION OF BOLIVIA TO THE UNITED NATIONS

211 E 43rd St., 8th Fl. #802
New York, NY 10017
Tel: (212) 682-8132 Fax: (212) 687-4642
Email: delgaliviaonu@hotmail.com
Web: www.bolivia-un.org

Ambassador E. and P.
His Excellency Ernesto Aranibar Quiroga;
Mrs. Maria Lucy Estenssoro de Aranibar
His Excellency/Deputy Permanent Representative
Mr. Erwin Ortiz Gandarillas;
Mrs. Renata W. de Ortiz
Minister Counsellor
Ms. Maria Alicia Terrazas Ontiveros
Counsellor
Ms. Ana Duran Ruiz
Second Secretary
Mr. Ruddy Flores Monterrey
Second Secretary
Mr. Gustavo Murillo Carrasco
Attache
Mr. Marco Macerez Camacho
Attache, Military Adviser
Colonel Carlos R. De La Fuente;
Mrs. Nury Meruvia De La Fuente

BRAZIL

PERMANENT MISSION OF BRAZIL TO THE UNITED NATIONS

747 3rd Ave., 9th Fl.
New York, NY 10017-2803
Tel: (212) 372-2600 Fax: (212) 371-5716
Email: delbrasonu@delbrasonu.org
Web: www.un.int/brazil

Ambassador E. and P.
His Excellency Ronaldo Mota Sardenberg;
Mrs. Celia De Nadai Silva Sardenberg
His Excellency/Ambassaddor E. and P./Deputy Permanent Representative
Mr. Henrique R. Valle;
Mrs. Joan Margaret Thompson-Valle
Minister Plenipotentiary
Mr. Frederico S. Duque Estrada Meyer
Minister Plenipotentiary
Mr. Paulo Roberto Campos Tarrisse de Fontoura;
Mrs. Maria Thereza Pereira de Araujo Tarrisse de Fontoura
Minister Plenipotentiary
Mr. Carlos Sergio Sobral Duarte;
Mrs. Monica Fernandes Guimaraes Duarte
Minister Plenipotentiary
Mr. Martin Garcia Moritan

Counsellor
Mrs. Lucia Maria Maiera;
Mr. Marcio Augusto Nunes
Counsellor
Ms. Irene Vida Gala
First Secretary
Mr. Alexandre Campello de Siqueira
First Secretary
Mr. Benedicto Fonseca, Filho;
Mrs. Solange Cristiane Faleiro Fonseca
First Secretary
Mr. Marcelo Baumbach
Second Secretary
Ms. Tatiana Rosito
Second Secretary
Ms. Gilda Motta Santos-Neves
Second Secretary
Mr. Marcelo Marotta Viegas;
Mrs. Maria Rafaela Bertucci Drummond de Mello Viegas
Second Secretary
Mr. Sidney Leon Romeiro;
Mrs. Eliane Isabelle de Carvalho
Second Secretary
Mr. Jao Marcelo Galvao de Queiroz;
Mrs. Luisa Fernanda Bonilla de Galvao de Queiroz
Second Secretary
Mr. Pedro Escosteguy Cardoso
Second Secretary
Mr. Elio de Almeida Cardoso;
Mrs. Kristine Kjaer Sorensen Cardoso
Second Secretary
Mr. Caio Mario Renault;
Mrs. Flavia de Figueiredo e Silva Renault
Second Secretary
Mr. Luis Guilherme Nascentes da Silva;
Mrs. Patricia Amaral de Oliveira da Silva
Attache
Ms. Adelia Maria da Rocha
Attache
Ms. Celia Del Bubba
Attache
Mr. Marcio Edward de Lima Goncalves
Attache
Mr. Carlos Augusto Veloso
Attache
Mr. Jucilton Salazar Pereira;
Mrs. Maria das Gracas Alexandre Pereira
Attache
Mr. Mauricio Teixeira Ramos;
Mrs. Neide Louback Carepa Ramos
Attache
Mr. Ronaldo da Silva Barros;
Mrs. Cristhiane Nunes Fernandes
Attache
Mrs. Rosa Maria dos Reis Nora;
Mr. Manoel Monteiro Nora
Attache
Mrs. Elcy dos Santos Oliveira;
Mr. Cesar Claudio Moreira Giraldes

Attache
Mrs. Jerusa Medeiros Silva Coutinho;
Mr. Walmar Coutinho Filho
Minister Counsellor, Military Adviser
General (Air Force) Reginaldo dos Santos;
Mrs. Eliane Moraes Monteiro dos Santos
First Secretary, Deputy Military Adviser
Lt. Colonel (Army) Pedro Aurelio de Pessoa;
Mrs. Alessandra Machado de Pessoa
First Secretary, Deputy Military Adviser
Commander (Navy) Marcos Lourenco de Almeida; Mrs. Noelia Cantarino da Costa
Second Secretary, Deputy Military Adviser
Major (Air Force) Mario Sergio Rodrigues da Costa;
Mrs. Graca Fabiane de Souza Santos Costa

CHILE

PERMANENT MISSION OF CHILE TO THE UNITED NATIONS

305 E 47th St., 10th & 11th Fl.
New York, NY 10017
Tel: (212) 832-3323 Fax: (212) 832-8714
Email: chile@un.int
Web: www.un.int/chile

Ambassador E. and P.
His Excellency Heraldo Muñóz;
Mrs. Pamela Q. Munoz
His Excellency/Ambassador/ Deputy Permanent Representative
Mr. Cristián Maquieira; Mrs. Julie A. White
Minister Counsellor
Mr. Jaime Acuña;
Mrs. Milagro Iturra de Acuna
Counsellor
Mr. Cristian A. Rehren;
Mrs. Norma Marincovich de Rehren
Counsellor
Mr. Claudio Rojas;
Mrs. Catalina Infante de Rojas
Counsellor
Mr. Armin E. Andereya;
Mrs. Sonia Correa de Andereya
Counsellor
Mr. Fernando Zalaquett
First Secretary
Mr. Ignacio Llanos;
Mrs. Paulina Echeverria de Llanos
Second Secretary
Mr. Rodrigo Donoso
Second Secretary
Mr. Andres E. Landerretche;
Mrs. Patricia Bustamante de Landerretche
Third Secretary
Mrs. Carla Serazzi; Mr. Sergio Chacon
Counsellor (Legal Affairs)
Ms. Maria Aida Rodriguez
Counsellor
Mr. Luis Antonio Lennon

Source: United Nations, Permanent Missions to the United Nations Vol. 292. August 2004.

Counsellor
Mrs. Rebeca Arredondo;
Mr. Nelson Alvarado
Attache (Press)
Mrs. Maria Isabel Seguel;
Mr. Luis Enrique Banales
Attache
Mrs. Maria Eugenia Suarez Cabello;
Mr. Emilio A. Farias
Attache, Military Adviser
Colonel Marcos Lopez;
Mrs. Ana Maria Valenzuela de Lopez
Attache, Deputy Military Adviser
Colonel Pedro Bustos

COLOMBIA

**PERMANENT MISSION OF COLOMBIA TO
THE UNITED NATIONS**
140 E 57th St., 5th Fl.
New York, NY 10022
Tel: (212) 355-7776 Fax: (212) 371-2813
Email: colombia@colombiaun.org
Web: www.colombia.un.org

Ambassador E. and P.
Her Excellency Maria Angela Holguin
**His Excellency/Ambassador/Deputy
Permanent Representative**
Mr. Jose Nicolas Rivas
**His Excellency/Ambassador/Deputy
Permanent Representative**
Mr. Gustavo Dajer;
Mrs. Oriana Carrera de Dajer
Minister Plenipotentiary
Mrs. Beatriz Patti Londono;
Mr. Hernando Castro
Minister Plenipotentiary
Mrs. Ana Carlina Plazas
Minister Counsellor
Mr. Alvaro Sandoval;
Mrs. Angela Cordero de Sandoval
Minister Counsellor
Mr. Carlos E. Jaramillo
First Secretary
Mr. Jorge Hernan Betancur;
Mrs. Paola Salazar de Betancur
Second Secretary
Mr. Pedro A. Roa Arboleda
Second Secretary
Mr. Alvaro J. Londono
Attache
Mr. Diego Alvear; Mrs. Martha L. Cifuentes
Attache
Ms. Anyul Molina

COSTA RICA

**PERMANENT MISSION OF COSTA RICA TO
THE UNITED NATIONS**
211 E 43rd St. #903
New York, NY 10017
Tel: (212) 986-6373 Fax: (212) 986-6842
Email: fobp@aol.com

Ambassador E. and P.
His Excellency Bruno Stagno Ugarte;
Mrs. Laetitia Bayle de Stagno
**Her Excellency/Ambassador/Deputy
Permanent Representative**
Mrs. Maria Elena Chassoul
Minister Counsellor
Mr. Antonio Alarcon
Minister Counsellor
Mr. Jorge Ballestero; Mrs. Nellda Ballestero
Counsellor
Mr. Carlos Fernando Diaz Paniagua
Counsellor
Ms. Marcela Calderon
Second Secretary

Ms. Cinthia Soto
Third Secretary
Mrs. Oriana Vargas de Mendiola;
Mr. Dionyssis Koutsoudimitropoulos
Attache
Mr. Frederic Bijou
Attache
Mrs. Sylvia Anderson
Her Excellency/Ambassador/Special Adviser
Mrs. Emilia Castro de Barish

CUBA

**PERMANENT MISSION OF CUBA TO THE
UNITED NATIONS**
315 Lexington Ave.
New York, NY 10016
Tel: (212) 689-7215 Fax: (212) 779-1697
Email: cuba@un.int

Ambassador E. and P.
His Excellency Orlando Requeijo Gual;
Mrs. Belkis Lima de Requeijo
**His Excellency/Ambassador E. and P./ Deputy
Permanent Representative**
Mr. Rodney Alejandro Lopez Clemente;
Mrs. Lourdes Diaz de Lopez
Counsellor
Mr. Yuri Ariel Gala Lopez;
Mrs. Yaima Gonzalez de Gala
Counsellor
Mr. Ricardo Tur Novo;
Mrs. Martha E. de la Concepcion de Tur
Counsellor
Mrs. Juana Elena Ramos Rodriguez;
Mr. Raul Gregorio Filgueiras Rivero
Counsellor
Mr. Raul Gregorio Filgueiras Rivero;
Mrs. Juana Elena Ramos de Filgueiras
Counsellor
Mr. Nelson Gregorio Fleitas Ravelo;
Mrs. Iris M. Hernandez de Fleitas
Counsellor
Mrs. Lourdes Diaz Fernandez;
Mr. Rodney Alejandro Lopez Clemente
First Secretary
Mr. Jorge Luis Bernaza Fernandez;
Mrs. Imara Llerandi de Bernaza
First Secretary
Mr. Bernardo Andres Toscano Sardinas;
Mrs. Barbara E. Roman de Toscano
First Secretary
Mr. Jorge Alberto Pena Argilagos;
Mrs. Lourdes Jova de Pena
Second Secretary
Mr. Yobany Gomez Gonzalez;
Mrs. Deborah Avila de Gomez
Second Secretary
Mr. Oscar Cornelio Oliva;
Mrs. Olga Lidia Gonzalez de Cornelio
Second Secretary
Mr. Jorge Cumberbach Miguen;
Mrs. Nadieska Navarro de Cumberbach
Second Secretary
Mrs. Nadieska Navarro Barro;
Mr. Jorge Cumberbach Miguen
Second Secretary
Mr. Jesus M. Aguiar Santos;
Mrs. Mercedes Basart de Aguiar
Second Secretary
Mr. Hector Ramirez Rodriguez;
Mrs. Livia Torriente de Ramirez
Third Secretary
Mr. Ovidio Roque Pedrera;
Mrs. Zudelis Cosano de Roque
Attache
Mr. Miguel Antonio Rodriguez Gonzalez;
Mrs. Alejandra Rodriguez de Rodriguez
Attache
Mr. Odilio H. Perez Martinez
Attache

Mr. Porfirio Blanco Diaz
Attache
Mr. Norberto Pena Torres
Attache
Mr. Patricio Alarcon Balboa
Attache
Mr. Pablo Luis Almora Bocourt
Attache
Mr. Teoclio Domingo Reyes Santana;
Mrs. Eufemia Caridad Rosario de Reyes
Attache
Mrs. Eufemia Caridad Rosario Martinez;
Mr. Teoclio Domingo Reyes Santana
Attache
Mr. Henry Solomon Gonzalez
Attache
Mr. Jorge Luis Machado Labanino
Attache
Mr. Adalberto Varona Grey
Attache
Mr. Jose Luis Miranda Cruz
Attache
Mr. Antonio Reinerio Acosta Garcia
Attache
Mr. Alberto G. Hernandez Pons;
Mrs. Aleida R. Guerra de Hernandez

DOMINICAN REPUBLIC

**PERMANENT MISSION OF THE DOMINICAN
REPUBLIC TO THE UNITED NATIONS**
144 E 44th St., 4th Fl.
New York, NY 10017
Tel: (212) 867-0833 Fax: (212) 986-4694
Email: drun@un.int

Ambassador E. and P.
Vacant
**His Excellency/Ambassador/Deputy
Permanent Representative**
Mr. Luis T. Graveley; Mrs. Edith de Graveley
**His Excellency/Ambassador/Deputy
Permanent Representative**
Mr. Ramon Osiris Blanco Dominguez;
Mrs. Gilda de Blanco
**His Excellency/Ambassador/Deputy
Permanent Representative**
Mr. Juan Ramon Gonzalez;
Mrs. Johanna de Gonzalez
**His Excellency/Ambassador/Deputy
Permanent Representative**
Mr. Manuel E. Felix
**His Excellency/Ambassador/Deputy
Permanent Representative**
Mr. Enriquillo A. del Rosario Ceballos;
Mrs. Audrey del Rosario
**His Excellency/Ambassador/Deputy
Permanent Representative**
Mr. Jose Felipe Rivera;
Mrs. Alba Collado de Rivera
Minister Counsellor
Mr. Francisco Tovar Morillo;
Mrs. Ruth Elizabeth Vargas de Tovar
Minister Counsellor
Mrs. Maria de Jesus Diaz de Cordova;
Mr. Emilio Manuel Cordova Roca
Minister Counsellor
Mr. Jose Miguel Sosa; Mrs. Doris de Sosa
Minister Counsellor
Mr. Manuel Bautista;
Mrs. Maria de Bautista
Minister Counsellor
Mr. Antonio Jaquez Cruz
Counsellor
Mr. Olivio Fermin
Counsellor
Mrs. Eusebia Margarita Nunez Pichardo;
Mr. Eduardo Pichardo
Counsellor
Mrs. Maria P. Pena Jimenez
Counsellor

Mrs. Obdulia Guzman; Mr. Gabriel Guzman
Counsellor
Mrs. Ilka Clarissa Mieses de Azcona;
Mr. David Azcona
Counsellor
Mrs. Dolores Bermudez Holbrook
First Secretary
Ms. Mariela Sanchez de Cruz
First Secretary
Mrs. Marlene A. Boves Arroyo;
Mr. Jose L. Arroyo
First Secretary
Mrs. Argentina Arias Macario
First Secretary
Mrs. Alexandra Arias Orlowska;
Mr. Hany Youhana
First Secretary
Mr. Jose Alfonso Blanco Conde;
Mrs. Maria Gabriela Caceres de Blanco
Third Secretary
Mrs. Loida Pujols; Mr. Alberto Pena
Attache, Military Adviser
General Luis Mariano Rodriguez Martinez;
Mrs. Fe E. Urbaez de Rodriguez

ECUADOR

**PERMANENT MISSION OF ECUADOR TO
THE UNITED NATIONS**
866 United Nations Plz. #516
New York, NY 10017
Tel: (212) 935-1680 Fax: (212) 935-1835
Email: ecuador@un.int
Web: www.ecuadoronu.com

Ambassador E. and P.
His Excellency Luis Gallegos Chiriboga;
Mrs. Fabiola Jaramillo de Gallegos
**His Excellency/Ambassador/Deputy
Permanent Representative**
Mr. Miguel Carbo
Minister
Mr. Eduardo Calderon;
Mrs. Amparo Saa-Jaramillo de Calderon
Minister
Mr. Benjamin F. Villacis;
Mrs. Ximena Ruales de Villacis
Minister
Mr. Humberto Jimenez;
Mrs. Liliana Valdez de Jimenez
First Secretary
Ms. Silvia Espindola
Second Secretary
Ms. Marisol Nieto
Second Secretary
Ms. Veronica Gomez
Attache
Mrs. Maritza Piedrahita; Mr. Mario Silva

EL SALVADOR

**PERMANENT MISSION OF EL SALVADOR
TO THE UNITED NATIONS**
46 Park Ave.
New York, NY 10016
Tel: (212) 679-1616 Fax: (212) 725-3467
Email: elsalvador@un.int

Ambassador E. and P.
Her Excellency Carmen Maria Gallardo
**His Excellency/Ambassador/Deputy
Permanent Representative**
Mr. Guillermo A. Meléndez-Barahona;
Mrs. Reina de Melendez
**Minister Counsellor, Deputy Permanent
Representative**
Mr. Carlos Enrique Garcia Gonzalez;
Mrs. Ines E. Oviedo de Garcia
Counsellor
Ms. Vanessa Eugenia Interiano

Second Secretary
Ms. Beatriz Alfaro
Second Secretary
Ms. M. Aracely Jovel
Third Secretary (Administrative Affairs)
Ms. Mirna D. Mena de Farfan
Third Secretary (Administrative Affairs)
Mr. Jesus Artiga Hernandez;
Mrs. Maria Leticia de Artiga
Third Secretary (Administrative Affairs)
Mr. Luis E. Alvarado Ramirez;
Mrs. Vicenta de Alvarado
Defense Attache
Colonel Hector E. Celarie;
Mrs. Ana Maria Landaverde de Celarie

GUATEMALA

**PERMANENT MISSION OF GUATEMALA TO
THE UNITED NATIONS**
57 Park Ave.
New York, NY 10016
Tel: (212) 679-4760 Fax: (212) 685-8741
Email: guatemala@un.int
Web: www.un.int/guatemala

Ambassador E. and P.
His Excellency Gert Rosenthal;
Mrs. Margit Uhlmann de Rosenthal
**Minister Plenipotentiary, Deputy Permanent
Representative**
Mr. Jose Alberto Briz Gutierrez
Minister Counsellor
Mr. Roberto Lavalle-Valdes;
Mrs. Tomoko Lavalle
Minister Counsellor
Ms. Connie Taracena Secaira
Counsellor
Ms. Karla Gabriela Samayoa-Recari
First Secretary
Ms. Monica Bolanos-Perez
Second Secretary
Mrs. Luisa Fernanda Bonilla Galvao de
Queiroz;
Mr. Joao Marcelo Galvao de Queiroz
Attache
Ms. Sonia Catalina Ovalle-Trabanino

HONDURAS

**PERMANENT MISSION OF HONDURAS TO
THE UNITED NATIONS**
866 United Nations Plz. #417
New York, NY 10017
Tel: (212) 752-3370 Fax: (212) 223-0498
Email: honduras_un@hotmail.com
Web: www.un.int/honduras

Ambassador E. and P.
His Excellency Manuel Acosta Bonilla;
Mrs. Anna Lucia Marchetti de Acosta
**His Excellency/Ambassador/Deputy
Permanent Representative**
Mr. Marco Antonio Suazo
**His Excellency/Ambassador/Deputy
Permanent Representative**
Mr. Jorge Flores Callejas
Counsellor
Mrs. Denise Vargas de Acosta;
Mr. Manuel Acosta
First Secretary
Mr. Carlos Roberto Quesada Lopez
First Secretary
Ms. Keny Maria Bendeck Vargas
Attache
Ms. Karla Patricia Garcia Lopez;
Mr. Armando A. Mejia
Attache
Mrs. Gloria Vega de Ochoa

MEXICO

**PERMANENT MISSION OF MEXICO TO THE
UNITED NATIONS**
2 United Nations Plz., 28th Fl.
New York, NY 10017
Tel: (212) 752-0220 Fax: (212) 688-8862
Email: mexico@un.int
Web: www.un.int/mexico

Ambassador E. and P.
His Excellency Enrique Berruga;
Mrs. Delia Sanchez de Berruga
**His Excellency/Ambassador/Deputy
Permanent Representative**
Mr. Juan Manuel Gomez Robledo;
Mrs. Elena Gomez Robledo
Minister
Mrs. Maria Angelica Arce de Jeannet;
Mr. Frederic-Yves Jeannet
Minister
Ms. Andrea Garcia Guerra
Counsellor
Mr. Leon Francisco Rodriguez Zahar
First Secretary
Ms. Amparo Anguiano Rodriguez
Second Secretary
Mr. Alfonso Ascencio;
Mrs. Lilli Ann Guzman de Ascencio
Second Secretary
Ms. Ana Paola Barbosa
Third Secretary
Mr. Diego Simancas
Third Secretary
Ms. Mariana Olivera
Third Secretary
Mr. Carlos G. Ruiz Massieu Aguirre
Third Secretary
Mr. Benito Jimenez Sauma
Third Secretary
Ms. Jennifer Feller
Attache
Mr. Manuel Matus Fuentes
Attache
Mr. Salvador Victoria Hernandez
Attache
Mrs. Maria Luisa Avalos
Attache
Mr. Jose Emilio Balderas Carvajal;
Mrs. Monica Puente de Balderas
Attache
Mrs. Noemi Sanchez Miranda;
Mr. Josue Dorantes

NICARAGUA

**PERMANENT MISSION OF NICARAGUA TO
THE UNITED NATIONS**
820 2nd Ave., 8th Fl.
New York, NY 10017
Tel: (212) 490-7997 Fax: (212) 286-0815
Email: nicaragua@un.int

Ambassador E. and P.
His Excellency Eduardo J. Sevilla Somoza;
Mrs. Beatriz Obregon de Sevilla
**His Excellency/Ambassador/Deputy
Permanent Representative**
Mr. Mario H. Castellon Duarte;
Mrs. Esperanza Escorcia de Castellon
**His Excellency/Ambassador/Deputy
Permanent Representative**
Mr. Ernesto Fernandez Holmann;
Mrs. Marta Regina de Fernandez
Minister Counsellor
Mr. Eugenio A. Cano;
Mrs. Linda Jannine Acevedo de Cano
Counsellor
Mr. Felix R. Parrales
First Secretary

Mr. Mauricio A. Solorzano;
Mrs. Elisa Noguera de Solorzano
Second Secretary
Mrs. Andrea Delgado de Morales;
Mr. Wilfredo Morales
Attache
Mrs. Yadira Blanco Walker;
Mr. Robert Carr Walker

PANAMA

**PERMANENT MISSION OF PANAMA TO
THE UNITED NATIONS**
866 United Nations Plz. #4030
New York, NY 10017
Tel: (212) 421-5420 Fax: (212) 421-2694
Email: emb@panama-un.org

Ambassador E. and P.
His Excellency Ricardo Alberto Arias;
Mrs. Maruquel Boyd de Arias
**Her Excellency/Ambassador/Deputy
Permanent Representative**
Mrs. Mary Morgan-Moss; Mr. Michael Moss
**His Excellency/Ambassador/Alternate
Permanent Representative**
Mr. Hernan Tejeira
**Counsellor, Alternate Permanent
Representative**
Mr. Tomas A. Guardia
Counsellor
Ms. Elena Ng
Attache
Mrs. María P. Sgro; Mr. John J. Sgro
Attache
Mr. Osvaldo Heilbron;
Mrs. Josefa de Heilbron
Attache
Mr. David Moreinis; Mrs. Vivian de Moreinis
Attache
Mrs. Karina C. Arias Fonseca;
Mr. Stephen Gianotti

PARAGUAY

**PERMANENT MISSION OF PARAGUAY TO
THE UNITED NATIONS**
211 E 43rd St. #400
New York, NY 10017
Tel: (212) 687-3490 Fax: (212) 818-1282
Email: paraguay@un.int

Ambassador E. and P.
His Excellency Eladio Loizaga;
Mrs. Elizabeth Franco de Loizaga
Minister, Deputy Permanent Representative
Mr. Juan Alfredo Buffa;
Mrs. Mercedes Ramirez de Buffa
Minister
Mrs. Terumi Matsuo de Claverol;
Mr. Jorge B. Claverol
First Secretary
Mr. Carlos Jose Ruckelshaussen Villarejo;
Mrs. Liza Del Vecchio de Ruckelshaussen
First Secretary
Ms. Doris Roman Gonzalez
Second Secretary
Ms. Lorena Patino

PERU

**PERMANENT MISSION OF PERU TO THE
UNITED NATIONS**
820 2nd Ave. #1600
New York, NY 10017
Tel: (212) 687-3336 Fax: (212) 972-6975
Email: onuper@aol.com

Ambassador E. and P.
His Excellency Oswaldo de Rivero;
Mrs. Juliette Horwood de Rivero
Minister, Deputy Permanent Representative
Mr. Marco Balarezo;
Mrs. Silvia Indacochea de Balarezo
Minister Counsellor
Mr. Alfredo Chuquihuara;
Mrs. Liliana Herrera de Chuquihuara
Counsellor
Mr. Jose Antonio Doig;
Mrs. Maria Alba de Doig
Counsellor
Ms. Romy Tincopa
Counsellor
Mr. Hugo Flores
First Secretary
Ms. Maria Arce de Gabay; Mr. Victor Gabay
First Secretary
Mr. Vitaliano Gallardo;
Mrs. Ljubinka Petkovich de Gallardo
First Secretary
Mr. Rolando Ruiz Rosas;
Mrs. Camila Valdeavellano de Ruiz
Second Secretary
Ms. Yella Zanelli
Third Secretary
Ms. Claudia Aleman

PORTUGAL

**PERMANENT MISSION OF PORTUGAL TO
THE UNITED NATIONS**
866 2nd Ave., 9th Fl.
New York, NY 10017
Tel: (212) 759-9444 Fax: (212) 355-1124
Email: portugal@un.int
Web: www.un.int/portugal

Ambassador E. and P.
His Excellency Goncalo Aires de Santa
Clara Gomes;
Mrs. Maria Laura de Santa Clara Gomes
**Minister Counsellor, Deputy Permanent
Representative**
Mr. Rui Macieira
Counsellor
Mrs. Sara Feronha Martins
Counsellor
Ms. Florbela Ferreira
First Secretary
Mr. Francisco Duarte;
Mrs. Margarida Pereira Martins
First Secretary
Mr. Miguel Graca
Second Secretary
Mr. Pedro Abecasis Costa Pereira
Counsellor (Legal Affairs)
Mr. Sebastiao Jose C. Povoas
Counsellor, Military Adviser
Lt. Colonel Jose Correia;
Mrs. Maria Gabriella Correia
Press Counsellor
Mr. Sebastiao Filipe Coelho Ferreira;
Mrs. Maria Luisa A. Mendes Coelho
Counsellor
Ms. Isabel Botelho Leal
Adviser
Ms. Mafalda Reynolds Dias
Adviser
Ms. Clotilde Mesquita
Adviser
Ms. Vanessa Gomes
Adviser
Ms. Catarina Carvalho
Attache (Administrative Affairs)
Mrs. Maria Lizette Esteves das Neves;
Mr. Carlos Alberto Casquilho das Neves
Attache (Administrative Affairs)
Mrs. Maria Arcelina Condesso

SPAIN

PERMANENT MISSION OF SPAIN TO THE UNITED NATIONS

823 United Nations Plz.,
345 E 46th St., 9th Fl.
New York, NY 10017
Tel: (212) 661-1050 Fax: (212) 949-7247
Email: spain@spainun.org
Web: www.spainun.org

Ambassador E. and P.
His Excellency Juan Antonio Yanez-Barnuevo;
Mrs. Isabel Sampedro de Yanez-Barnuevo
His Excellency/Ambassador/Deputy Permanent Representative
Mr. Inigo de Palacio Espana;
Mrs. Sonsoles Cano de Palacio
Counsellor, Military Adviser
Mr. Gabriel de la Cruz;
Mrs. Maria Angeles Fortun de la Cruz
Counsellor
Mr. Roman Oyarzun;
Mrs. Begona Allendesalazar de Oyarzun
Counsellor
Mr. Faustino Diaz;
Mrs. Teresa Guelbenzu de Diaz
Counsellor
Mr. Jorge Romeu
Counsellor
Mr. Alfonso Barnuevo;
Mrs. Ana Maria de Artinano de Barnuevo
Counsellor
Mr. Javier Garcia de Viedma;
Mrs. Pilar Gonzalez-Vidaurreta
Counsellor
Mr. Gonzalo M. Quintero
Counsellor
Ms. Caridad Batalla

Counsellor
Ms. Paloma Duran
Counsellor
Mr. Francisco Barrios de Tiedra;
Mrs. Marina Casasus de Barrios
Counsellor
Mr. Arturo Relanzon;
Mrs. Pilar Orozco de Relanzon
First Secretary
Mr. Daniel Soto Gurpide
First Secretary
Mr. David Carriedo
First Secretary
Mr. Pablo Sanz
First Secretary
Ms. Ana Jimenez
First Secretary
Mr. Gabriel Cremades;
Mrs. Marina Izquierdo de Cremades
First Secretary, Deputy Military Adviser
Mr. Francisco L. Monedero
First Secretary
Mr. Javier Colomina;
Mrs. Paloma Gonzalez de Colomina
Attache
Mr. Jorge Revilla;
Mrs. Ana Isabel Alvarez de Revilla

URUGUAY

PERMANENT MISSION OF URUGUAY TO THE UNITED NATIONS

866 United Nations Plz. #322
New York, NY 10017
Tel: (212) 752-8240 Fax: (212) 593-0935
Email: uruguay@un.int
Web: www.un.int/uruguay

Ambassador E. and P.
His Excellency Felipe Paolillo
Minister, Deputy Permanent Representative
Ms. Susana Rivero
Minister Counsellor
Mr. Enrique Loedel;
Mrs. Mercedes de Loedel
Minister Counsellor
Mrs. Nury Bauzan de Senes;
Mr. Giovanni Senes
First Secretary
Mr. Santiago Wins
Attache (Press)
Mr. Jorge Reiner
Attache
Mr. Edison N. Wibmer
Attache, Military Adviser
Colonel Alvaro Picabea
Attache, Military Adviser
Colonel Jorge Jackson
Attache, Military Adviser
Captain Daniel Cleffi;
Mrs. Laura A. Ferrando de Cleffi

VENEZUELA

PERMANENT MISSION OF VENEZUELA TO THE UNITED NATIONS

335 E 46th St.
New York, NY 10017
Tel: (212) 557-2055 Fax: (212) 557-3528
Email: venezuela@un.int

Ambassador E. and P.
His Excellency Fermin Toro Jimenez;
Mrs. Beatriz Trujillo de Toro
Her Excellency/Ambassador/Deputy Permanent Representative
Ms. Adriana P. Pulido Santana

Her Excellency/Ambassador/Deputy Permanent Representative
Mrs. Imeria Nunez de Odreman;
Mr. Jose Manuel Odreman Aparicio
Minister Counsellor
Ms. Eleyda Garcia-Matos;
Mr. Williams Gimenez Ramos
Minister Counsellor
Ms. Marly L. Cedeno Reyes
Counsellor
Mr. Marcos Fuenmayor-Contreras
Counsellor
Ms. Pui Leong
First Secretary
Mr. Carlos Armando Lazo-Garcia
First Secretary
Mr. Franklin Rangel
First Secretary
Mr. Asdrubal Pulido Leon
Second Secretary
Ms. Laila Taj El Dine
Second Secretary
Ms. Zully Gonzalez-Urdaneta
Second Secretary
Mrs. Julia Lopez Camacaro
Second Secretary
Mr. Domingo Blanco;
Mrs. Jennifer de Blanco
Third Secretary
Ms. Raquel Escobar-Gomez
Third Secretary
Mr. Alonso Herrera de Abreu
Attache
Mr. Jhon Osman Valles Egurrola
Minister Counsellor, Military Adviser
Brigadier General Juan Roa-Gomez;
Mrs. Nora Sanchez de Roa
Attache, Assistant Military Adviser
Captain Oscar Luis Cabello Guerra;
Mrs. Noritza Torrealba de Cabello

Missions and Observers to the OAS continued from p 188

Ambassador Perm. Rep.
His Excellency John F. MAISTO;
Ms. Maria Consuelo Maisto
Ambassador, Deputy Permanent Representative
His Excellency Timothy J. DUNN;
Mrs. Denise Dunn
Ambassador, Secretary's of State's Special Coordinator
His Excellency Ronald D. GODARD;
Mrs. Wesley Ann Godard
Counselor, Alternate Representative
Ms. Margarita RIVA-GEOGHEGAN
Counselor, Alternate Representative
Mr. Earl M. IRVING;
Mrs. Jeanne Frances Irving
Alternate Representative
Mr. Giovanni A. SNIDLE;
Mrs. Rebecca K. Blood
Alternate Representative
Mr. David SULLIVAN;
Mrs. Deana Jordan Sullivan
Alternate Representative
Mr. Daniel MARTINEZ;
Mrs. Carolina Gabaldon Martinez
Alternate Representative
Ms. Therese TRACY-BAIER;
Mr. Patrick Baier
Alternate Representative
Mr. Mark SIGLER
Alternate Representative
Mr. Fernando J. ROJAS
Alternate Representative
Mr. Daniel W. CENTO;

Mrs. Carmen L. Cento
Alternate Representative
Ms. Wendy SNEFF
Alternate Representative
Mr. Douglas WRAY; Mrs. Ann Wary
Alternate Representative
Mr. Stacy WILLIAMS;
Mrs. Lemoiquel Williams
Alternate Representative
Mr. Sergio GARCIA;
Mrs. Adriana C. Quiroga-Garcia
Alternate Representative
Mr. James C. TODD; Mrs. Evelyne J. Todd
Alternate Representative
Ms. Catherine NEWLING
Alternate Representative
Mr. Steve LISTON; Mrs. Susan Liston
Alternate Representative
Mr. Eli SUGARMAN
Alternate Representative
Mr. David HULTS
Alternate Representative
Mr. David SILVERMAN
Adviser
Mr. Steven LEBENS
Adviser
Rear Admiral William D. SULLIVAN;
Mrs. Patricia Dunn

URUGUAY

2801 New Mexico Ave. NW #1210
Washington, DC 20007

Tel: (202) 333-0588 Fax: (202) 337-3758
Email: uruoea@erols.com

Ambassador Perm. Rep.
His Excellency Juan Enrique FISCHER;
Mrs. Eva Fischer
Minister Counselor, Alternate Representative
Dr. Jorge A. SERE STURZENEGGER;
Mrs. María Mercedes Ponce de León
Minister Counselor, Alternate Representative
Mrs. Cristina CARRION;
Mr. Gustavo Rodriguez
Secretary, Alternate Representative
Lic. Laura Dupuy LASSERRE;
Dr. Ricardo Nario

VENEZUELA

1099 30th St., 2nd Fl. NW
Washington, DC 20007
Tel: (202) 342-5837 Fax: (202) 625-5657
Email: missionvene@venezuela-oas.org

Ambassador Perm. Rep.
His Excellency Jorge Valero BRICENO;
Mrs. Zulay de Valero
Ambassador, Alternate Representative
His Excellency Nelson Pineda PRADA;
Mrs. Carmen Pineda
Minister Counselor, Alternate Representative
Mrs. Ilenia MEDINA; Mr. Armando Arce
Minister Counselor, Alternate Representative
Mr. Salvador Hernandez VELA

Minister Counselor, Alternate Representative
Mrs. Stefania MOSCA
Counselor, Alternate Representative
Mr. Mario A. Aguzzi DURAN
Counselor, Alternate Representative
Mr. Mario VARGAS
Second Secretary, Alternate Representative
Mrs. Magaly SAAVEDRA;
Mr. Jesus Mendoza
Second Secretary, Alternate Representative
Mrs. Moira MENDEZ
Cultural Attache
Mr. Nelson RODRIGUEZ

YEMEN

2319 Wyoming Ave. NW
Washington, DC 20008
Tel: (202) 965-4760 Fax: (202) 337-2017

Ambassador Perm Observer
His Excellency Abdulwahab AL-HAJJRI
Principal Information and Outreach Officer, Alternate Observer
Mr. Mohammed AL-BASHA

YUGOSLAVIA

2134 Kalorama Rd. NW
Washington, DC 20008

Ambassador, Perm. Observer
Vacant

US Citizenship and Immigration Services
Servicios estadounidenses de inmigración y ciudadanía

Contact information for the US Citizenship and Immigration Services (USCIS) within the Department of Homeland Security (DHS) is listed below.

ALABAMA

BIRMINGHAM RESIDENT AGENT

5900 Airport Hwy. #A-17
Birmingham, AL 35212
Tel: (800) 375-5283
Web: http://uscis.gov

BIRMINGHAM APPLICATION SUPPORT CENTER (ASC)

Beacon Ctr., 529 Beacon Pkwy. West
#101/106
Birmingham, AL 35209
Tel: (800) 375-5283
Web: http://uscis.gov
Please, be sure to have an appointment letter to appear for fingerprinting.

TALLADEGA DETENTION FACILITY

565 E. Renfroe Rd., C/O Federal
Corrections Institute
Talledega, AL 35160-4811
Tel: (800) 375-5283
Web: http://uscis.gov

ALASKA

ANCHORAGE APPLICATION SUPPORT CENTER (ASC)

620 E. 10th Ave. #7
Anchorage, AK 99501
Tel: (800) 375-5283
Web: http://uscis.gov
Please, be sure to have an appointment letter to appear for fingerprinting.

ANCHORAGE DISTRICT OFFICE

620 E. 10th Ave. #102
Anchorage, AK 99501
Bernadette Nocerino-Doody, District Director
Tel: (800) 375-5283
Web: http://uscis.gov
Service area: State of Alaska. The Anchorage District Office has offices at the ports-of-entry located in Ketchikan, Juneau, Fairbanks, Dutch Harbor, and Kodiak.

ARIZONA

PHOENIX APPLICATION SUPPORT CENTER (ASC)

2545 E. Thomas Rd.
Phoenix, AZ 85016
Tel: (800) 375-5283
Web: http://uscis.gov
Please, be sure to have an appointment letter to appear for fingerprinting.

PHOENIX DISTRICT OFFICE

2035 N. Central Ave.
Phoenix, AZ 85004
Stephen L. Fickett, District Director
Tel: (800) 375-5283
Web: http://uscis.gov
Service area: with respect to the submission of application for service benefits, the Phoenix District Office has jurisdiction over all counties in Arizona with the exception of Cochise, Pima, Santa Cruz, Graham and Pinal, which are served by the Tucson Sub Office. To speak with an Immigration Information Officer, you may make an appointment via the Internet at www.infopass.uscis.gov.

TUCSON APPLICATION SUPPORT CENTER (ASC)

1835 S. Alvernon #216/217
Tucson, AZ 85711
Tel: (800) 375-5283
Web: http://uscis.gov
Please, be sure to have an appointment letter to appear for fingerprinting.

TUCSON SUB OFFICE

6431 S. Country Club Rd.
Tucson, AZ 85706-5907
William N. Johnston, Officer in Charge
Tel: (800) 375-5283
Web: http://uscis.gov
Service area: the Tucson Sub Office serves Southern Arizona: Pima, Santa Cruz, Cochise, Graham, and Pinal Counties. To speak with an Immigration Information Officer, obtain a ticket at Window #1.

YUMA APPLICATION SUPPORT CENTER (ASC)

3250 S. 4th Ave. #E
Yuma, AZ 85365
Tel: (800) 375-5283
Web: http://uscis.gov
Please, be sure to have an appointment letter to appear for fingerprinting.

ARKANSAS

FORT SMITH APPLICATION SUPPORT CENTER (ASC)

4977 Old Greenwood Rd.
Fort Smith, AR 72903
Tel: (800) 375-5283
Web: http://uscis.gov
Please, be sure to have an appointment letter to appear for fingerprinting.

FORT SMITH SUB OFFICE

4977 Old Greenwood Rd.
Fort Smith, AR 72903
Tel: (800) 375-5283
Web: http://uscis.gov
Service Area: Western Arkansas. Immigration Information Officer(s) are available for assistance on a first-come, first-served basis in the lobby of the office.

CALIFORNIA

BAKERSFIELD APPLICATION SUPPORT CENTER (ASC)

4701 Planz Rd. A12
Bakersfield, CA 93309
Tel: (800) 375-5283
Web: http://uscis.gov
Please, be sure to have an appointment letter to appear for fingerprinting.

BELLFLOWER APPLICATION SUPPORT CENTER (ASC)

Bellflower Plz. 17610 Bellflower Blvd. #A-110
Bellflower, CA 90706
Tel: (800) 375-5283
Web: http://uscis.gov
Please, be sure to have an appointment letter to appear for fingerprinting.

BUENA PARK APPLICATION SUPPORT CENTER (ASC)

8381 La Palma Ave. #A
Buena Park, CA 90620
Tel: (800) 375-5283
Web: http://uscis.gov
Please, be sure to have an appointment letter to appear for fingerprinting.

CALEXICO APPLICATION SUPPORT CENTER (ASC)

16 Heffernan Ave.
Calexico, CA 92231
Tel: (800) 375-5283
Web: http://uscis.gov
Please, be sure to have an appointment letter to appear for fingerprinting.

CALIFORNIA SERVICE CENTER

P.O. Box 30111
Laguna Niguel, CA 92607-0111
Donald Neufeld, Service Center Director
Tel: (800) 375-5283
Web: http://uscis.gov
Service area: the CSC accepts and processes certain applications and petitions from people residing in the following jurisdictions: California, Nevada, Arizona, Hawaii, and the Territory of Guam.

CHULA VISTA CUSTOMER SERVICE CENTER

1261 3rd Ave. #A
Chula Vista, CA 91911
Tel: (800) 375-5283
Web: http://uscis.gov
Adjustment of Status Applications (I-485) are accepted at the Chula Vista Customer Service Center and the Imperial County Satellite Office, and the filing should only be done in person.

EL MONTE APPLICATION SUPPORT CENTER (ASC)

Golden Vista Plz. 9251 Garvey Ave. #Q
South El Monte, CA 91733
Tel: (800) 375-5283
Web: http://uscis.gov
Please, be sure to have an appointment letter to appear for fingerprinting.

FAIRFAX APPLICATION SUPPORT CENTER (ASC)

5949 W. Pico Blvd.
Los Angeles, CA 90035
Tel: (800) 375-5283
Web: http://uscis.gov
Please, be sure to have an appointment letter to appear for fingerprinting.

FRESNO APPLICATION SUPPORT CENTER (ASC)

4893 E. Kings Canyon
Fresno, CA 93727
Tel: (800) 375-5283
Web: http://uscis.gov
Please, be sure to have an appointment letter to appear for fingerprinting.

FRESNO SUB OFFICE

1177 Fulton Mall
Fresno, CA 93721-2816
Don Riding, Officer in Charge
Tel: (800) 375-5283
Web: http://uscis.gov
Service area: Fresno, Inyo, Kern, Kings, Madera, Mariposa, Merced, Mono, and Tulare counties.

GARDENA APPLICATION SUPPORT CENTER (ASC)

15715 Crenshaw Blvd. #B-112
Gardena, CA 90249
Tel: (800) 375-5283
Web: http://uscis.gov
Please, be sure to have an appointment letter to appear for fingerprinting.

GOLETA APPLICATION SUPPORT CENTER (ASC)

6831-B Hollister Ave.
Goleta, CA 93117
Tel: (800) 375-5283
Web: http://uscis.gov
Please, be sure to have an appointment letter to appear for fingerprinting.

Source: U.S. Department of Homeland Security, Citizenship and Immigration Services (USCIS).

LOS ANGELES ASYLUM OFFICE

290 S. Anaheim Blvd.
Anaheim, CA 92805
Robert V. Looney, Asylum Office Director
Tel: (800) 375-5283 Fax: (714) 635-8707
Web: http://uscis.gov
Service area: the Asylum Office in Los Angeles has jurisdiction over the States of Arizona and Hawaii, the Territory of Guam, the following counties in the State of California: Los Angeles, Orange, Riverside, San Bernardino, San Luis Obispo, Santa Barbara, Ventura, Imperial, and San Diego, and that southern portion of the State of Nevada currently within the jurisdiction of the Las Vegas Sub Office.

LOS ANGELES DISTRICT OFFICE

300 N. Los Angeles St. #1001
Los Angeles, CA 90012
Jane Arellano, Director
Tel: (800) 375-5283
Web: http://uscis.gov
Service area: the Los Angeles District includes Los Angeles, Orange, Riverside, San Bernardino, Santa Barbara, San Luis Obispo, and Ventura counties. To speak with an Immigration Information Officer, you may make an appointment via the Internet at www.infopass.uscis.gov.

LOS ANGELES WILSHIRE APPLICATION SUPPORT CENTER (ASC)

888 Wilshire Blvd.
Los Angeles, CA 93117
Tel: (800) 375-5283
Web: http://uscis.gov
Please, be sure to have an appointment letter to appear for fingerprinting.

MODESTO APPLICATION SUPPORT CENTER (ASC)

901 N. Carpenter Rd. #14
Modesto, CA 95351
Tel: (800) 375-5283
Web: http://uscis.gov
Please, be sure to have an appointment letter to appear for fingerprinting.

OAKLAND APPLICATION SUPPORT CENTER (ASC)

2040 Telegraph Ave.
Oakland, CA 94612
Tel: (800) 375-5283
Web: http://uscis.gov
Please, be sure to have an appointment letter to appear for fingerprinting.

OAKLAND CITIZENSHIP OFFICE

Oakland Federal Bldg., 1301 Clay St. #380 North
Oakland, CA 94612
Tel: (800) 375-5283
Web: http://uscis.gov
The Oakland Citizenship Office serves only those with appointments. The Oakland office does not provide information or forms.

OXNARD APPLICATION SUPPORT CENTER (ASC)

Carriage Sq. Shopping Ctr.
250 Citrus Grove Ln. #100
Oxnard, CA 93036
Tel: (800) 375-5283
Web: http://uscis.gov
Please, be sure to have an appointment letter to appear for fingerprinting.

POMONA APPLICATION SUPPORT CENTER (ASC)

435 W. Mission Blvd. #110
Pomona, CA 91766
Tel: (800) 375-5283

Web: http://uscis.gov
Please, be sure to have an appointment letter to appear for fingerprinting.

RIVERSIDE APPLICATION SUPPORT CENTER (ASC)

10082 Magnolia Ave.
Riverside, CA 92503
Tel: (800) 375-5283
Web: http://uscis.gov
Please, be sure to have an appointment letter to appear for fingerprinting.

SACRAMENTO APPLICATION SUPPORT CENTER (ASC)

731 K St. #100
Sacramento, CA 95814
Tel: (800) 375-5283
Web: http://uscis.gov
Please, be sure to have an appointment letter to appear for fingerprinting.

SACRAMENTO SUB OFFICE

650 Capitol Mall
Sacramento, CA 95814
Susan Curda, Officer in Charge
Tel: (800) 375-5283
Web: http://uscis.gov
Service area: the Sacramento Sub Office serves the counties of: Alpine, Amador, Butte, Calaveras, Colusa, El Dorado, Nevada, Placer, Plumas, Sacramento, San Joaquin, Sierra, Sutter, Tuolumne, Yolo, and Yuba. To speak with an Immigration Information Officer, you may make an appointment via the Internet at www.infopass.uscis.gov.

SALINAS APPLICATION SUPPORT CENTER (ASC)

Santa Rita Plz. 1954 N. Main St.
Salinas, CA 93906
Tel: (800) 375-5283
Web: http://uscis.gov
Please, be sure to have an appointment letter to appear for fingerprinting.

SAN BERNARDINO SUB OFFICE

655 W. Rialto Ave.
San Bernardino, CA 92410-3327
Irene Martin, Officer in Charge
Tel: (800) 375-5283
Web: http://uscis.gov
Service area: Riverside and San Bernardino Counties. To speak with an Immigration Information Officer, you may make an appointment via the Internet at www.infopass.uscis.gov.

SAN DIEGO APPLICATION SUPPORT CENTER (ASC)

2509 El Cajon Blvd.
San Diego, CA 92104
Tel: (800) 375-5283
Web: http://uscis.gov
Please, be sure to have an appointment letter to appear for fingerprinting.

SAN DIEGO DISTRICT OFFICE

880 Front St. #4254
San Diego, CA 92101
Adoption/Orphan Officer
Tel: (800) 375-5283 Fax: (619) 557-6790
Web: http://uscis.gov

880 Front St. #1234
San Diego, CA 92101
Debra A. Rogers, District Director
Tel: (800) 375-5283
Web: http://uscis.gov
Service area: the San Diego District Office serves San Diego and Imperial counties. To speak with an Immigration Information Officer, you may make an appointment via the Internet at www.infopass.uscis.gov.

SAN FRANCISCO APPLICATION SUPPORT CENTER (ASC)

250 Broadway
San Francisco, CA 94111
Tel: (800) 375-5283
Web: http://uscis.gov
Please, be sure to have an appointment letter to appear for fingerprinting.

SAN FRANCISCO ASYLUM OFFICE

75 Hawthorne St. #303S
San Francisco, CA 94107
Emilia Bardini, Asylum Office Director
Tel: (800) 375-5283
Web: http://uscis.gov
Service area: the Asylum Office in San Francisco has jurisdiction over the following counties in the State of California: Alameda, Alpine, Amador, Butte, Calaveras, Colusa, Contra Costa, Del Norte, El Dorado, Fresno, Glenn, Humboldt, Inyo, Kern, Kings, Lake, Lassen, Madera, Marin, Mariposa, Mendocino, Merced, Modoc, Mono, Monterey, Napa, Nevada, Placer, Plumas, Sacramento, San Benito, San Francisco, San Joaquin, San Mateo, Santa Clara, Santa Cruz, Shasta, Sierra, Siskiyou, Solano, Sonoma, Stanislaus, Sutter, Tehama, Trinity, Tulare, Tuolumne, Yolo, and Yuba. The Asylum Office in San Francisco also has jurisdiction over the portion of Nevada currently under the jurisdiction of the Reno Sub Office, and the States of Oregon, Washington and Alaska.

SAN FRANCISCO DISTRICT OFFICE

444 Washington St.
San Francisco, CA 94111
David N. Still, District Director
Tel: (800) 375-5283
Web: http://uscis.gov
Service area: the San Francisco District Office serves Alameda, Contra Costa, Del Norte, Lake, Marin, Mendocino, Napa, San Francisco, San Mateo, Somona and Trinity counties. To speak with an Immigration Information Officer, you may make an appointment via the Internet at www.infopass.uscis.gov.

SAN JOSE APPLICATION SUPPORT CENTER (ASC)

122 Charcot Ave.
San Jose, CA 95131-1101
Tel: (800) 375-5283
Web: http://uscis.gov
Please, be sure to have an appointment letter to appear for fingerprinting.

SAN JOSE SUB OFFICE

1887 Monterey Rd.
San Jose, CA 95112
Warren Janssen, Officer in Charge
Tel: (800) 375-5283
Web: http://uscis.gov
Service area: the San Jose Sub Office serves the following counties: Santa Clara, Santa Cruz, San Benito, and Monterey. To speak with an Immigration Information Officer, you may make an appointment via the Internet at www.infopass.uscis.gov.

SANTA ANA APPLICATION SUPPORT CENTER (ASC)

1666 N. Main St. #100-A
Santa Ana, CA 92701
Tel: (800) 375-5283
Web: http://uscis.gov
Please, be sure to have an appointment letter to appear for fingerprinting.

SANTA ANA SUB OFFICE

34 Civic Ctr. Plz. Federal Bldg.
Santa Ana, CA 92701

Marta Salgado-Nino, Officer in Charge
Tel: (800) 375-5283
Web: http://uscis.gov
Service area: all of Orange County and a portion of South Los Angeles County. To speak with an Immigration Information Officer, you may make an appointment via the Internet at www.infopass.uscis.gov.

SANTA ROSA APPLICATION SUPPORT CENTER (ASC)

1401 Guerneville Rd. #100
Santa Rosa, CA 95403
Tel: (800) 375-5283
Web: http://uscis.gov
Please, be sure to have an appointment letter to appear for fingerprinting.

VAN NUYS APPLICATION SUPPORT CENTER (ASC)

14515 Hamlin St., 2nd Fl. #200
Van Nuys, CA 91411
Tel: (800) 375-5283
Web: http://uscis.gov
Please, be sure to have an appointment letter to appear for fingerprinting.

VISTA APPLICATION SUPPORT CENTER (ASC)

727 W. San Marcos Blvd. #101-102
San Marcos, CA 92069
Tel: (800) 375-5283
Web: http://uscis.gov
Please, be sure to have an appointment letter to appear for fingerprinting.

COLORADO

DENVER APPLICATION SUPPORT CENTER (ASC)

15037 E. Colfax Ave. #G
Aurora, CO 80011
Tel: (800) 375-5283
Web: http://uscis.gov
Please, be sure to have an appointment letter to appear for fingerprinting.

DENVER DISTRICT OFFICE

4730 Paris St.
Denver, CO 80239
Mario Ortiz, District Director
Tel: (800) 375-5283
Web: http://uscis.gov
Service area: the Denver District serves the states of Colorado, Wyoming and Utah. The Denver District Office has a Sub Office in Salt Lake City, Utah; and a Satellite Office in Casper, Wyoming. To speak with an Immigration Information Officer, you may make an appointment via the Internet at www.infopass.uscis.gov.

GRAND JUNCTION APPLICATION SUPPORT CENTER (ASC)

2454 Hwy. 6 and 50 Valley Plz. #115
Grand Junction, CO 81505
Tel: (800) 375-5283
Web: http://uscis.gov
Please, be sure to have an appointment letter to appear for fingerprinting.

CONNECTICUT

HARTFORD APPLICATION SUPPORT CENTER (ASC)

249 Pearl St.
Hartford, CT 06103
Tel: (800) 375-5283
Web: http://uscis.gov
Please, be sure to have an appointment letter to appear for fingerprinting.

HARTFORD SUB OFFICE

450 Main St., 4th Fl.
Hartford, CT 06103-3060
Ethan Enzer, Officer in Charge
Tel: (800) 375-5283
Web: http://uscis.gov
Service area: the State of Connecticut. To speak with an Immigration Information Officer, you may make an appointment via the Internet at www.infopass.uscis.gov.

DELAWARE

DOVER APPLICATION SUPPORT CENTER (ASC)

Blue Hen Corporate Ctr.,
655 S. Bay Rd. #4E
Dover, DE 19901-4699
Tel: (800) 375-5283
Web: http://uscis.gov
Please, be sure to have an appointment letter to appear for fingerprinting.

DOVER SATELLITE OFFICE

1305 McD Dr.
Dover, DE 19901
Donald Monica, District Director
Tel: (800) 375-5283
Web: http://uscis.gov
Service area: State of Delaware. Customers are taken on a first-come, first-served basis.

FLORIDA

FT. LAUDERDALE APPLICATION SUPPORT CENTER (ASC)

11690 State Rd. 84
Davie, FL 33325
Tel: (800) 375-5283
Web: http://uscis.gov
Please, be sure to have an appointment letter to appear for fingerprinting.

HIALEAH APPLICATION SUPPORT CENTER (ASC)

Westland Promenade,
3700 W. 18th Ave. #110
Hialeah, FL 33012
Tel: (800) 375-5283
Web: http://uscis.gov
Please, be sure to have an appointment letter to appear for fingerprinting.

JACKSONVILLE APPLICATION SUPPORT CENTER (ASC)

4121 Southpoint Blvd.
Jacksonville, FL 32216
Tel: (800) 375-5283
Web: http://uscis.gov
Please, be sure to have an appointment letter to appear for fingerprinting.

JACKSONVILLE SUB OFFICE

4121 Southpoint Blvd.
Jacksonville, FL 32216
Louise Germain, Officer in Charge
Tel: (800) 375-5283
Web: http://uscis.gov
Service area: for immigration-related matters, this office serves the following counties: Alachua, Baker, Bay, Bradford, Calhoun, Clay, Columbia, Dixie, Duval, Escambia, Franklin, Gadsden, Gilchrist, Gulf, Hamilton, Holmes, Jackson, Jefferson, Lafayette, Leon, Levy, Liberty, Madison, Nassau, Okaloosa, Putnam, Santa Rosa, St. Johns, Suwanee, Taylor, Union, Wakulla, Walton, and Washington. To speak with an Immigration Information Officer, you may make an appointment via the Internet at www.infopass.uscis.gov.

MIAMI APPLICATION SUPPORT CENTER (ASC)

11865 SW 26th St. (Coral Way) #J-6
Miami, FL 33175
Tel: (800) 375-5283
Web: http://uscis.gov
Please, be sure to have an appointment letter to appear for fingerprinting.

MIAMI ASYLUM OFFICE

77 SE 5th St., 3rd Fl.
Miami, FL 33131
Erich J. Cauller, Asylum Office Director
Tel: (800) 375-5283
Web: http://uscis.gov
Service area: the Asylum Office in Miami has jurisdiction over the State of Florida, the Commonwealth of Puerto Rico, and the United States Virgin Islands.

MIAMI - BISCAYNE APPLICATION SUPPORT CENTER (ASC)

Biscayne Plz. 521 NE. 81st St. Bay 11
Miami, FL 33138
Tel: (800) 375-5283
Web: http://uscis.gov
Please, be sure to have an appointment letter to appear for fingerprinting.

MIAMI DISTRICT OFFICE

7880 Biscayne Blvd.
Miami, FL 33138
Jack Bulger, Director
Tel: (800) 375-5283
Web: http://uscis.gov
Service area: State of Florida. To speak with an Immigration Information Officer, you may make an appointment via the Internet at www.infopass.uscis.gov.

MIAMI INFORMATION OFFICE

6445 NE 7th Ave.
Miami, FL 33138
Tel: (800) 375-5283
Web: http://uscis.gov

MIAMI NATURALIZATION OFFICE

77 SE 5th St., 2nd Fl.
Miami, FL 33131
Tel: (800) 375-5283/(305) 415-6500
Web: http://uscis.gov
The Naturalization Office provides information on naturalization to persons in the Miami area. Scheduled naturalization interviews are conducted at this office.

ORLANDO APPLICATION SUPPORT CENTER (ASC)

Terracotta Business Ctr., 5449 S. Semoran Blvd. #18C
Orlando, FL 32822
Tel: (800) 375-5283
Web: http://uscis.gov
Please, be sure to have an appointment letter to appear for fingerprinting.

ORLANDO SUB OFFICE

9403 Tradeport Dr.
Orlando, FL 32827
Tel: (800) 375-5283
Web: http://uscis.gov
Service area: the Orlando Sub Office serves the counties of Orange, Osceola, Seminole, Lake, Brevard, Flagler, Volusia, Marion, and Sumter. To speak with an Immigration Information Officer, you may make an appointment via the Internet at www.infopass.uscis.gov.

TAMPA APPLICATION SUPPORT CENTER (ASC)

9280 Bay Plz. Blvd. #726
Tampa, FL 33619
Tel: (800) 375-5283

Web: http://uscis.gov
Please, be sure to have an appointment letter to appear for fingerprinting.

TAMPA SUB OFFICE

5524 W. Cypress St.
Tampa, FL 33607-1708
Kathy Redman, Officer in Charge
Tel: (800) 375-5283
Web: http://uscis.gov
Service area: the Tampa Sub Office serves the counties of Citrus, Hernando, Pasco, Pinellas, Hillsborough, Polk, Hardee, Manatee, Sarasota, De Soto, Charlotte, and Lee. To speak with an Immigration Information Officer, you may make an appointment via the Internet at www.infopass.uscis.gov.

WEST PALM APPLICATION SUPPORT CENTER (ASC)

2711 Exchange Ct.
West Palm Beach, FL 33401
Tel: (800) 375-5283
Web: http://uscis.gov
Please, be sure to have an appointment letter to appear for fingerprinting.

WEST PALM BEACH SATELLITE OFFICE

326 Fern St.
West Palm Beach, FL 33401
John Damone, Officer in Charge
Tel: (800) 375-5283
Web: http://uscis.gov
Service area: Palm Beach, Martin, St. Lucie, Indian River, Okeechobee, Hendry, Glades, and Highland Counties. To speak with an Immigration Information Officer, you may make an appointment via the Internet at www. infopass.uscis.gov.

GEORGIA

ATLANTA APPLICATION SUPPORT CENTER (ASC)

3523 Buford Hwy. #100
Atlanta, GA 30329
Tel: (800) 375-5283
Web: http://uscis.gov
Please, be sure to have an appointment letter to appear for fingerprinting.

ATLANTA DISTRICT OFFICE

Martin Luther King Jr. Federal Bldg., 77 Forsyth St. SW
Atlanta, GA 30303
Rosemary L. Melville, District Director
Tel: (800) 375-5283
Web: http://uscis.gov
Service area: Alabama, North Carolina, South Carolina, and Georgia. To speak with an Immigration Information Officer, you may make an appointment via the Internet at www. infopass.uscis.gov.

GUAM

AGANA APPLICATION SUPPORT CENTER (ASC)

Sirena Plz. #100, 108 Hernan Cortez Ave.
Hagatna, GU 96910
Tel: (800) 375-5283
Web: http://uscis.gov
Please, be sure to have an appointment letter to appear for fingerprinting.

AGANA SUB OFFICE

Sirena Plz. #100, 108 Hernan Cortez Ave.
Hagatna, GU 96910
Robert E. Johnson, Officer in Charge
Tel: (800) 375-5283

Web: http://uscis.gov
Service area: Guam and the Northern Mariana Islands. To speak with an Immigration Information Officer, you must obtain a ticket, available on a first-come, first-served basis in the lobby of the office.

HAWAII

HONOLULU APPLICATION SUPPORT CENTER (ASC)

677 Ala Moana Blvd. #102/103
Honolulu, HI 96813
Tel: (800) 375-5283
Web: http://uscis.gov
Please, be sure to have an appointment letter to appear for fingerprinting.

HONOLULU DISTRICT OFFICE

595 Ala Moana Blvd.
Honolulu, HI 96813
David Gulick, District Director
Tel: (800) 375-5283
Web: http://uscis.gov
Service area: the Honolulu District Office serves the entire state of Hawaii, Territory of Guam, Commonwealth of Northern Marianas. To speak with an Immigration Information Officer, you may make an appointment via the Internet at www.infopass.uscis.gov.

IDAHO

BOISE APPLICATION SUPPORT CENTER (ASC)

1185 S. Vinnell Way
Boise, ID 83709
Tel: (800) 375-5283
Web: http://uscis.gov
Please, be sure to have an appointment letter to appear for fingerprinting.

BOISE SUB OFFICE

1185 S. Vinnell Way
Boise, ID 83709
Robert Mather, Officer in Charge
Tel: (800) 375-5283
Web: http://uscis.gov
Service area: the Boise Sub Office serves Southwest and South Central Idaho covering the counties of Ada, Gooding, Adams, Jerome, Blaine, Lincoln, Boise, Minidoka, Camas, Owyhee, Canyon, Payette, Cassia, Twin Falls, Elmore, Valley, Gem, and Washington. To speak with an Immigration Information Officer, you may make an appointment via the Internet at www.infopass.uscis.gov.

IDAHO FALLS APPLICATION SUPPORT CENTER (ASC)

1820 E. 17th St. #190
Idaho Falls, ID 83404
Tel: (800) 375-5283
Web: http://uscis.gov
Please, be sure to have an appointment letter to appear for fingerprinting.

ILLINOIS

BROADWAY APPLICATION SUPPORT CENTER (ASC)

4853 N. Broadway
Chicago, IL 60640
Tel: (800) 375-5283
Web: http://uscis.gov
Please, be sure to have an appointment letter to appear for fingerprinting.

CHICAGO APPLICATION SUPPORT CENTER (ASC)
888 S. Route 59 #124
Naperville, IL 60540
Tel: (800) 375-5283
Web: http://uscis.gov
Please, be sure to have an appointment letter to appear for fingerprinting.

CHICAGO ASYLUM OFFICE
401 S. La Salle St., 8th Fl.
Chicago, IL 60605
Robert W. Esbrook, Asylum Office Director
Tel: (800) 375-5283/(312) 353-9607
Web: http://uscis.gov
Service area: the Asylum Office in Chicago has jurisdiction over the States of Illinois, Indiana, Michigan, Wisconsin, Minnesota, North Dakota, South Dakota, Kansas, Missouri, Ohio, Iowa, Nebraska, Montana, Idaho, and Kentucky.

CHICAGO DISTRICT OFFICE
10 W. Jackson Blvd.
Chicago, IL 60604
Michael Comfort, District Director
Tel: (800) 375-5283
Web: http://uscis.gov
Service area: the Chicago District includes the states of Illinois, Indiana, and Wisconsin. The Chicago Office serves the state of Illinois and the following counties in Northwest Indiana: Lake, Porter, LaPorte and St. Joseph. To speak with an Immigration Information Officer, you may make an appointment via the Internet at www.infopass.uscis.gov.

CHICAGO-NORRIDGE APPLICATION SUPPORT CENTER (ASC)
4701 N. Cumberland Ave. #1-3 BCD
Chicago, IL 60706
Tel: (800) 375-5283
Web: http://uscis.gov
Please, be sure to have an appointment letter to appear for fingerprinting.

PULASKI APPLICATION SUPPORT CENTER (ASC)
Super Mall, Space 101 5160 S. Pulaski Ave.
Chicago, IL 60632
Tel: (800) 375-5283
Web: http://uscis.gov
Please, be sure to have an appointment letter to appear for fingerprinting.

WAUKEGAN APPLICATION SUPPORT CENTER (ASC)
25 S. Greenbay Rd.
Waukegan, IL 60085
Tel: (800) 375-5283
Web: http://uscis.gov
Please, be sure to have an appointment letter to appear for fingerprinting.

INDIANA

HAMMOND APPLICATION SUPPORT CENTER (ASC)
Indianapolis Blvd. (RT. 41) 7852 Interstate Plz. Dr.
Hammond, IN 46324
Tel: (800) 375-5283
Web: http://uscis.gov
Please, be sure to have an appointment letter to appear for fingerprinting.

INDIANAPOLIS APPLICATION SUPPORT CENTER (ASC)
950 N. Meridian St. #400
Indianapolis, IN 46204-3915
Tel: (800) 375-5283

Web: http://uscis.gov
Please, be sure to have an appointment letter to appear for fingerprinting.

INDIANAPOLIS SUB OFFICE
950 N. Meridian St. #400
Indianapolis, IN 46204-3915
Donald Ferguson, Officer in Charge
Tel: (800) 375-5283
Web: http://uscis.gov
Service area: the State of Indiana except Lake, Porter, LaPorte, and St. Joseph counties in Northwest Indiana. Residents of these four counties are served by the Chicago District Office. To speak with an Immigration Information Officer, you may make an appointment via the Internet at www.infopass.uscis.gov.

IOWA

DES MOINES APPLICATION SUPPORT CENTER (ASC)
210 Walnut St. #371
Des Moines, IA 50309
Tel: (800) 375-5283
Web: http://uscis.gov
Please, be sure to have an appointment letter to appear for fingerprinting.

DES MOINES OFFICE
210 Walnut St. #369
Des Moines, IA 50309
Tel: (800) 375-5283
Web: http://uscis.gov

KANSAS

WICHITA APPLICATION SUPPORT CENTER (ASC)
271 W. 3rd St. North #1050
Wichita, KS 67202
Tel: (800) 375-5283
Web: http://uscis.gov
Please, be sure to have an appointment letter to appear for fingerprinting.

WICHITA SATELLITE OFFICE
271 W. 3rd St. North #1050
Wichita, KS 67202-1212
Sheffeld Trendel, Officer in Charge
Tel: (800) 375-5283
Web: http://uscis.gov
Service area: the Wichita Satellite Office serves the western two thirds of the state of Kansas. To speak with an Immigration Information Officer, you may make an appointment via the Internet at www.infopass.uscis.gov.

KENTUCKY

CHANGE OF ADDRESS
P.O. Box 7134
London, KY 40742-7134
Tel: (800) 375-5283
Web: http://uscis.gov
Services: Form AR-11, Change of address.

1084-I S. Laurel Rd.
London, KY 40744
Tel: (800) 375-5283
Web: http://uscis.gov
Services: Form AR-11, Change of address. For commercial overnight or fast freight services.

LOUISVILLE APPLICATION SUPPORT CENTER (ASC)
601 W. Broadway #22
Louisville, KY 40202-2250
Tel: (800) 375-5283
Web: http://uscis.gov
Please, be sure to have an appointment letter to appear for fingerprinting.

LOUISVILLE SUB OFFICE
Gene Snyder US Courthouse & Customhouse #390, 601 W. Broadway
Louisville, KY 40202
Tel: (800) 375-5283
Web: http://uscis.gov
Service area: Kentucky for all applications.

LOUISIANA

NEW ORLEANS APPLICATION SUPPORT CENTER (ASC)
701 Loyola Ave. #T-8011
New Orleans, LA 70113
Tel: (800) 375-5283
Web: http://uscis.gov
Please, be sure to have an appointment letter to appear for fingerprinting.

NEW ORLEANS DISTRICT
701 Loyola Ave., 8th Fl.
New Orleans, LA 70113
M. Stella Jarina, District Director
Tel: (800) 375-5283
Web: http://uscis.gov
Service area: New Orleans District Office: State of Louisiana and Southern Mississippi (Hancock, Harrison, Jackson, George, Stone and Pearl River counties). To speak with an Immigration Information Officer, you may make an appointment via the Internet at www.infopass.uscis.gov.

MAINE

HOULTON APPLICATION SUPPORT CENTER (ASC)
Port Of Entry at end of Interstate 95, POB 189
Houlton, ME 04730
Tel: (800) 375-5283
Web: http://uscis.gov
Please, be sure to have an appointment letter to appear for fingerprinting.

PORTLAND APPLICATION SUPPORT CENTER (ASC)
176 Gannett Dr.
South Portland, ME 04106
Tel: (800) 375-5283
Web: http://uscis.gov
Please, be sure to have an appointment letter to appear for fingerprinting.

PORTLAND DISTRICT
176 Gannett Dr.
South Portland, ME 04106
Rodolfo "Rudy" Lara, District Director
Tel: (800) 375-5283
Web: http://uscis.gov
Service area: the Portland District serves the States of Maine and Vermont and the Pittsburgh, NH Port of Entry. To speak with an Immigration Information Officer, you may make an appointment via the Internet at www.infopass.uscis.gov.

MARYLAND

BALTIMORE APPLICATION SUPPORT CENTER (ASC)
George H. Fallon Federal Bldg., 31 Hopkins Plz.
Baltimore, MD 21201
Tel: (800) 375-5283
Web: http://uscis.gov
Please, be sure to have an appointment letter to appear for fingerprinting.

BALTIMORE DISTRICT
George H. Fallon Federal Bldg., 31 Hopkins Plz.
Baltimore, MD 21201
Richard Caterisano, District Director
Tel: (800) 375-5283
Web: http://uscis.gov
Service area: the Baltimore District serves the state of Maryland. To speak with an Immigration Information Officer, you may make an appointment via the Internet at www.infopass.uscis.gov.

GLENMONT APPLICATION SUPPORT CENTER (ASC)
Glenmont Plz. 12331-C Georgia Ave.
Wheaton, MD 20906
Tel: (800) 375-5283
Web: http://uscis.gov
Please, be sure to have an appointment letter to appear for fingerprinting.

SALISBURY APPLICATION SUPPORT CENTER (ASC)
119 W. Naylor Mill Rd. #11
Salisbury, MD 21801
Tel: (800) 375-5283
Web: http://uscis.gov
Please, be sure to have an appointment letter to appear for fingerprinting.

MASSACHUSETTS

BOSTON APPLICATION SUPPORT CENTER (ASC)
170 Portland St.
Boston, MA 02114
Tel: (800) 375-5283
Web: http://uscis.gov
Please, be sure to have an appointment letter to appear for fingerprinting.

BOSTON DISTRICT OFFICE
John F. Kennedy Federal Bldg., Government Ctr.
Boston, MA 02203
Denis Riordan, Director
Tel: (800) 375-5283
Web: http://uscis.gov
Service area: the Boston District Office services the state of Massachusetts. To speak with an Immigration Information Officer, you may make an appointment via the Internet at www.infopass.uscis.gov.

MICHIGAN

DETROIT APPLICATION SUPPORT CENTER (ASC)
2652 E. Jefferson Ave.
Detroit, MI 48207
Tel: (800) 375-5283
Web: http://uscis.gov
Please, be sure to have an appointment letter to appear for fingerprinting.

DETROIT DISTRICT OFFICE
333 Mt. Elliot

Detroit, MI 48207
Carol Jenifer, District Director
Tel: (800) 375-5283
Web: http://uscis.gov
Service area: the Detroit District services the State of Michigan including the Upper Peninsula. To speak with an Immigration Information Officer, you may make an appointment via the Internet at www.infopass.uscis.gov.

GRAND RAPIDS APPLICATION SUPPORT CENTER (ASC)
4484 Breton Rd.
Kentwood, MI 49508
Tel: (800) 375-5283
Web: http://uscis.gov
Please, be sure to have an appointment letter to appear for fingerprinting.

SAULT ST. MARIE APPLICATION SUPPORT CENTER (ASC)
International Bridge Plz.
Sault St. Marie, MI 49783
Tel: (800) 375-5283
Web: http://uscis.gov
Please, be sure to have an appointment letter to appear for fingerprinting.

MINNESOTA

DULUTH APPLICATION SUPPORT CENTER (ASC)
208 Federal Bldg., 515 W. 1st St.
Duluth, MN 55802
Tel: (800) 375-5283
Web: http://uscis.gov
Please, be sure to have an appointment letter to appear for fingerprinting.

ST. PAUL APPLICATION SUPPORT CENTER (ASC)
1360 University Ave. #103
St. Paul, MN 55104
Tel: (800) 375-5283
Web: http://uscis.gov
Please, be sure to have an appointment letter to appear for fingerprinting.

ST. PAUL DISTRICT
2901 Metro Dr. #100
Bloomington, MN 55425
Denise Frazier, District Director
Tel: (800) 375-5283
Web: http://uscis.gov
Service area: the St. Paul District serves Minnesota, North Dakota, and South Dakota. The following Wisconsin counties are serviced by the St. Paul USCIS office: Adams, Ashland, Barron, Bayfield, Buffalo, Burnett, Chippewa, Clark, Douglas, Dunn, Eau Claire, Iron, Jackson, Juneau, La Crosse, Lincoln, Marathon, Monroe, Oneida, Pepin, Pierce, Polk, Portage, Price, Rusk, Sawyer, St. Croix, Taylor, Trempealeau, Vernon, Vilas, Washburn, and Wood. To speak with an Immigration Information Officer, you may make an appointment via the Internet at www.infopass.uscis.gov.

MISSISSIPPI

JACKSON APPLICATION SUPPORT CENTER (ASC)
McCoy Federal Bldg.,
100 W. Capitol St. #B8
Jackson, MS 39269
Tel: (800) 375-5283
Web: http://uscis.gov
Please, be sure to have an appointment

letter to appear for fingerprinting. Please note that this location cannot collect digital information for customers who wish to file their applications electronically.

JACKSON SATELLITE OFFICE
Dr. A. H. McCoy Federal Bldg., 100 W. Capitol St. #B-8
Jackson, MS 39269
M. Stella Jarina, District Director
Tel: (800) 375-5283
Web: http://uscis.gov
Service area: the Jackson office is responsible for the greater central area of Mississippi. All people living in areas south of Highway 8 (which traverses the state in an east-west latitude) should go to the Jackson office for service and/or benefits related issues. People residing in Hancock, Harrison, Jackson, George, Stone and Pearl River counties fall under the jurisdiction of the New Orleans District Office and should go to that office for services and benefits related issues. Persons residing North of Highway 8 fall under the jurisdiction of the Memphis, Tennessee Office.

MISSOURI

KANSAS CITY APPLICATION SUPPORT CENTER (ASC)
9747 NW Conant Ave.
Kansas City, MO 64153
Tel: (800) 375-5283
Web: http://uscis.gov
Please, be sure to have an appointment letter to appear for fingerprinting.

KANSAS CITY DISTRICT OFFICE
9747 NW Conant Ave.
Kansas City, MO 64153
Michael Jaromin, District Director
Tel: (800) 375-5283
Web: http://uscis.gov
Service area: the Kansas City District includes the states of Missouri and Kansas. The Kansas City District Office serves western Missouri and eastern Kansas. To speak with an Immigration Information Officer, you may make an appointment via the Internet at www.infopass.uscis.gov.

ST. LOUIS APPLICATION SUPPORT CENTER (ASC)
1222 Spruce St. #1.100
St. Louis, MO 63103
Tel: (800) 375-5283
Web: http://uscis.gov
Please, be sure to have an appointment letter to appear for fingerprinting.

ST. LOUIS SUB OFFICE
Robert A. Young Federal Bldg.
1222 Spruce St. #1.100
St. Louis, MO 63103-2815
Chester Moyer, Officer in Charge
Tel: (800) 375-5283
Web: http://uscis.gov
Service area: the St. Louis Sub Office services eastern Missouri, which encompasses the Eastern Judicial District of the Federal District Court. To speak with an Immigration Information Officer, you must obtain a ticket, available on a first-come, first-served basis in the lobby of the office.

MONTANA

HELENA APPLICATION SUPPORT CENTER (ASC)
2800 Skyway Dr.
Helena, MT 59602
Tel: (800) 375-5283
Web: http://uscis.gov
Please, be sure to have an appointment letter to appear for fingerprinting.

HELENA DISTRICT OFFICE
2800 Skyway Dr.
Helena, MT 59602
Alan Puckett, District Director
Tel: (800) 375-5283
Web: http://uscis.gov
Service area: the Helena District Office services the states of Montana and Idaho (except for the ten northernmost counties of Idaho, which fall under the jurisdiction of the Seattle District), and the Canadian Provinces of Alberta and Saskatchewan. The Helena District Office also manages the ports of entry into the US at the following Montana locations: Sweetgrass, Chief Mountain, Del Bonita, Wild Horse, Willow Creek, Piegan, Roosville, Whitlash, Raymond, Morgan, Opheim, Scobey, Turner, and Whitetail. To speak with an Immigration Information Officer, you may make an appointment via the Internet at www.infopass.uscis.gov.

NEBRASKA

INFORMATION OFFICE
13824 T Plz. (Millard Plz.)
Omaha, NE 68137
Tel: (800) 375-5283
Web: http://uscis.gov
Services: Employment Authorization Documents (work cards) and extensions are provided to eligible applicants from 8:00 AM to 12:00 PM at this office.

NEBRASKA SERVICE CENTER
P.O. Box 87102
Lincoln, NE 68501-7102
Tel: (800) 375-5283
Web: http://uscis.gov
Services: Form I-102, Application for Replacement/Initial Nonimmigrant Arrival/Departure Document.

P.O. Box 87129
Lincoln, NE 68501-7129
Tel: (800) 375-5283
Web: http://uscis.gov
Services: Form I-129, Petition for Nonimmigrant Worker (Non-Premium Processing)

P.O. Box 87103
Lincoln, NE 68501-7103
Tel: (800) 375-5283
Web: http://uscis.gov
Services: Form I-129, Petition for Nonimmigrant Worker (Premium Processing)

P.O. Box 87130
Lincoln, NE 68501-7130
Tel: (800) 375-5283
Web: http://uscis.gov
Services: Form I-129F, Petition for Fiance(e) (Not eligible for Premium Processing) and Form I-130, Petition for Alien Relative (note: those I-130s filed with an I-485 should be sent to the USCIS local office having jurisdiction over your place of residence.)

P.O. Box 87131
Lincoln, NE 68501-7131

Tel: (800) 375-5283
Web: http://uscis.gov
Services: Form I-131, Application for Travel Document (Note: If you are submitting Form I-131 and/or Form I-765 with your Form I-485, please send the entire package to the P.O. Box listed for Form I-485. If you are submitting Form I-485, Form I-131, and/or Form I-765 with your Form I-140, please send the entire package to the P.O. Box listed for concurrent filings for Form I-140.)

P.O. Box 87245
Lincoln, NE 68501-7245
Tel: (800) 375-5283
Web: http://uscis.gov
Services: Form I-131, Application for Travel Document (Haitian Refugee Immigration Fairness Act (HRIFA) application for advance parole for dependents outside the US only); and Form I-485 - (HRIFA only)

P.O. Box 87485
Lincoln, NE 68501-7485
Tel: (800) 375-5283
Web: http://uscis.gov
Services: Form I-140, Immigrant Petition for Alien Worker (if filed concurrently with Form I-485); Form I-485, Application to Register Permanent Residence or to Adjust Status.

P.O. Box 87140
Lincoln, NE 68501-7140
Tel: (800) 375-5283
Web: http://uscis.gov
Services: Form I-140, Immigrant Petition for Alien Worker (if filed alone); Form I-905, Application for Authorization to Issue Certification for Health Care Workers.

P.O. Box 87290
Lincoln, NE 68501-7290
Tel: (800) 375-5283
Web: http://uscis.gov
Services: Form I-290, (Appeals & Motions)

P.O. Box 87360
Lincoln, NE 68501-7360
Tel: (800) 375-5283
Web: http://uscis.gov
Services: Form I-360, Petition for Amerasian, Widow(er), or Special Immigrant (NOTE: Please see Form I-360 more information on where to file this petition.)

P.O. Box 87400
Lincoln, NE 68501-7400
Tel: (800) 375-5283
Web: http://uscis.gov
Service area: Alaska. Form N-400, Application for Naturalization

P.O. Box 87209
Lincoln, NE 68501-7209
Tel: (800) 375-5283
Web: http://uscis.gov
Services: Form I-485, (Refugee only)

P.O. Box 87589
Lincoln, NE 68501-7589
Tel: (800) 375-5283
Web: http://uscis.gov
Services: Form I-589, Application for Asylum and Withholding of Deportation Fees.

P.O. Box 87698
Lincoln, NE 68501-7698
Tel: (800) 375-5283
Web: http://uscis.gov
Services: Form I-694, Notice of Appeal of Decision; Form I-695, Application for Replacement of Form I-688A, Employment Authorization; or Form I-688, Temporary Resident Card (Under Public Law 99-603); Form I-698, Application to Adjust Status from Temporary to Permanent Resident (Under Section 245A of Public Law 99-603).

P.O. Box 87730
Lincoln, NE 68501-7730
Tel: (800) 375-5283
Web: http://uscis.gov
Services: Form I-730, Refugee/Asylee
Relative Petition.

P.O. Box 87751
Lincoln, NE 68501-7751
Tel: (800) 375-5283
Web: http://uscis.gov
Services: Form I-751, Petition to Remove
Conditions on Residence.

P.O. Box 87765
Lincoln, NE 68501-7765
Tel: (800) 375-5283
Web: http://uscis.gov
Services: Form I-765, Application for
Employment Authorization (NOTE: If you are
submitting Form I-765 with another form, mail
your applications to the P.O. Box for the other
(principal) form. If you are submitting Form I-
131 and/or Form I-765 with your Form I-485,
or with your concurrently filed Forms I-140
and I-485, please send the entire package
to the P.O. Box listed for concurrent filings
for Form I-140.)

P.O. Box 87817
Lincoln, NE 68501-7817
Tel: (800) 375-5283
Web: http://uscis.gov
Services: Form I-817, Application for Voluntary
Departure under the Family Unity Program.

P.O. Box 87821
Lincoln, NE 68501-7821
Tel: (800) 375-5283
Web: http://uscis.gov
Services: Form I-821, Application for
Temporary Protected Status. (ONLY for
applicants from El Salvador, Honduras, and
Nicaragua; all other TPS applicants must file
with the local USCIS office having jurisdiction
over your place of residence.)

P.O. Box 87824
Lincoln, NE 68501-7824
Tel: (800) 375-5283
Web: http://uscis.gov
Services: Form I-824, Application for Action
on an Approved Application/Petition (NOTE:
If you are submitting Form I-824 with another
form, mail your package to the P.O. Box for
the other (principal) form.)

P.O. Box 87864
Lincoln, NE 68501-7864
Tel: (800) 375-5283
Web: http://uscis.gov
Services: Form I-864 Affidavit of Support

P.O. Box 87865
Lincoln, NE 68501-7865
Tel: (800) 375-5283
Web: http://uscis.gov
Services: Form I-865, Sponsor's Notice of
Change of Address and all other Change of
Address Requests.

P.O. Box 87426
Lincoln, NE 68501-7426
Tel: (800) 375-5283
Web: http://uscis.gov
Services: Form N-426, Request for
Certification of Military or Naval Service.

P.O. Box 87373
Lincoln, NE 68501-7373
Attn: E-Filed (Form #)
Tel: (800) 375-5283
Web: http://uscis.gov
Services: Form E-Filing, When sending
supporting documentation for forms filed
electronically.

P.O. Box 82521
Lincoln, NE 68501-2521
Tel: (800) 375-5283
Web: http://uscis.gov
Services: General Correspondence (Inquiries)
(Sending applications or petitions to this
address will only delay their processing)

**OMAHA APPLICATION SUPPORT CENTER
(ASC)**
Millard Plz., 13822 - 30 T Plz.
Omaha, NE 68137-4154
Tel: (800) 375-5283
Web: http://uscis.gov
Please, be sure to have an appointment letter
to appear for fingerprinting.

OMAHA DISTRICT OFFICE
3736 S. 132nd St.
Omaha, NE 68144
Gerard Heinauer, District Director
Tel: (800) 375-5283
Web: http://uscis.gov
Service area: the Omaha District serves the
states of Iowa and Nebraska. To speak with
an Immigration Information Officer, you may
make an appointment via the Internet at www.
infopass.uscis.gov.

NEVADA

**LAS VEGAS APPLICATION SUPPORT
CENTER (ASC)**
6175 S. Pecos Rd.
Las Vegas, NV 89120
Tel: (800) 375-5283
Web: http://uscis.gov
Please, be sure to have an appointment letter
to appear for fingerprinting.

LAS VEGAS SUB OFFICE
3373 Pepper Ln.
Las Vegas, NV 89120-2739
Karen D. Dorman, Officer in Charge
Tel: (800) 375-5283
Web: http://uscis.gov
Service area: the Las Vegas office serves the
Nevada counties of Clark, Esmeralda, Nye,
and Lincoln. All other counties in Nevada are
serviced by the Reno office.

RENO SUB OFFICE
1351 Corporate Blvd.
Reno, NV 89502
Jerry Garcia, Officer in Charge
Tel: (800) 375-5283
Web: http://uscis.gov
Service area: the Reno Sub Office serves
people residing in Carson, Churchill, Douglas,
Elko, Eureka, Humboldt, Lander, Lyon,
Mineral, Pershing, Storey, Washoe and White
Pine counties.

NEW HAMPSHIRE

**MANCHESTER APPLICATION SUPPORT
CENTER (ASC)**
803 Canal St.
Manchester, NH 03101
Tel: (800) 375-5283
Web: http://uscis.gov
Please, be sure to have an appointment letter
to appear for fingerprinting.

MANCHESTER SATELLITE OFFICE
803 Canal St.
Manchester, NH 03101
Carole Donovan, Officer in Charge
Tel: (800) 375-5283

Web: http://uscis.gov
Service area: the State of New Hampshire.
To speak with an Immigration Information
Officer, you may make an appointment via the
Internet at www.infopass.uscis.gov.

NEW JERSEY

CHERRY HILL SUB OFFICE
1886 Greentree Rd.
Cherry Hill, NJ 08003
Tel: (800) 375-5283
Web: http://uscis.gov
Service area: Atlantic, Burlington, Camden,
Cape May, Cumberland, Gloucester, Mercer,
Monmouth, Ocean, and Salem Counties.
To speak with an Immigration Information
Officer, you may make an appointment via the
Internet at www.infopass.uscis.gov.

**HACKENSACK APPLICATION SUPPORT
CENTER (ASC)**
116 Kansas St. Main Fl.
Hackensack, NJ 07601
Tel: (800) 375-5283
Web: http://uscis.gov
Please, be sure to have an appointment letter
to appear for fingerprinting.

NEWARK ASYLUM OFFICE
1200 Wall St. West, 4th Fl.
Lyndhurst, NJ 07071
Susan Raufer, Asylum Office Director
Tel: (800) 375-5283
Web: http://uscis.gov
Service area: the Newark Asylum Office
in Lyndhurst, New Jersey, has jurisdiction
over the State of New York within the
boroughs of Manhattan and the Bronx in
the City of New York; the Albany Sub Office;
jurisdiction of the Buffalo District Office;
the State of Pennsylvania, excluding the
jurisdiction of the Pittsburgh Sub Office; and
the States of Connecticut, Delaware, Maine,
Massachusetts, New Hampshire, New Jersey,
Rhode Island, and Vermont.

NEWARK DISTRICT OFFICE
Peter Rodino, Jr. Federal Bldg.,
970 Broad St.
Newark, NJ 07102
Andrea Quarantillo, District Director
Tel: (800) 375-5283
Web: http://uscis.gov
Service area: Bergen, Essex, Hudson,
Hunterdon, Middlesex, Morris, Passaic,
Somerset, Sussex, Union, and Warren
Counties. To speak with an Immigration
Information Officer, you may make an
appointment via the Internet at www.infopass.
uscis.gov.

NEW MEXICO

**ALBUQUERQUE APPLICATION SUPPORT
CENTER (ASC)**
1605 Isleta Blvd. SW #C
Albuquerque, NM 87105
Tel: (800) 375-5283
Web: http://uscis.gov
Please, be sure to have an appointment letter
to appear for fingerprinting.

ALBUQUERQUE SUB OFFICE
1720 Randolph Rd. SE
Albuquerque, NM 87106
Betty Garcia, Officer in Charge
Tel: (800) 375-5283
Web: http://uscis.gov

Service area: in Northern New Mexico, the
counties of: Bernalillo, Catron, Cibola, Colfax,
Curry, De Baca, Guadalupe, Harding, Los
Alamos, McKinley, Mora, Quay, Rio Arriba,
Roosevelt, San Miguel, Sandoval, San Juan,
Santa Fe, Socorro, Taos, Torrance, Valencia,
and Union. All other counties in New Mexico
fall under the direct jurisdiction of the El Paso
District Office.

NEW YORK

**ALBANY APPLICATION SUPPORT CENTER
(ASC)**
1086 Troy-Schenectady Rd.
Latham, NY 12110
Tel: (800) 375-5283
Web: http://uscis.gov
Please, be sure to have an appointment letter
to appear for fingerprinting.

ALBANY SUB OFFICE
1086 Troy-Schenectady Rd.
Latham, NY 12110
Gary Hale, Officer in Charge
Tel: (800) 375-5283
Web: http://uscis.gov
Service area: the Albany Sub Office serves the
following counties in New York State: Albany,
Broome, Chenango, Clinton, Columbia,
Delaware, Essex, Franklin, Fulton, Greene,
Hamilton, Herkimer, Madison, Montgomery,
Oneida, Otsego, Rensselaer, Saint Lawrence,
Saratoga, Schenectady, Schoharie, Tioga,
Warren, and Washington. To speak with an
Immigration Information Officer, you may
make an appointment via the Internet at www.
infopass.uscis.gov.

BUFFALO DISTRICT OFFICE
Federal Ctr., 130 Delaware Ave.
Buffalo, NY 14202
M. Frances Holmes, District Director
Tel: (800) 375-5283
Web: http://uscis.gov
Service area: all of New York State with the
exception of the following counties: Bronx,
Kings (Brooklyn), New York City (Manhattan),
Queens, Staten Island, Richmond, Nassau,
Suffolk, Dutchess, Orange, Putnam,
Rockland, Sullivan, Ulster, and Westchester.
To speak with an Immigration Information
Officer, you may make an appointment via the
Internet at www.infopass.uscis.gov.

NEW YORK ASYLUM OFFICE
1 Cross Island Plz., 3rd Fl.
Rosedale, NY 11422
Patricia Jackson, Asylum Office Director
Tel: (800) 375-5283
Web: http://uscis.gov
Service area: the Asylum Office in New York
has jurisdiction over the State of New York
excluding the jurisdiction of the Albany Sub
Office, the Buffalo District Office, and the
boroughs of Manhattan and the Bronx.

NEW YORK CITY DISTRICT OFFICE
26 Federal Plz.
New York City, NY 10278
Mary Ann Gantner, District Director
Tel: (800) 375-5283
Web: http://uscis.gov
Service area: New York City, they serve
the following counties and 5 Boroughs:
(Manhattan, Bronx, Brooklyn, Queens,
Staten Island), Nassau, Orange, Suffolk,
Westchester, Putnam, Rockland, Dutchess,
Ulster, and Sullivan. To speak with an
Immigration Information Officer, you may

make an appointment via the Internet at www.infopass.uscis.gov.

NORTH CAROLINA

CHARLOTTE APPLICATION SUPPORT CENTER (ASC)

4801 Chastain Ave. Bldg. 10, #175
Charlotte, NC 28217
Tel: (800) 375-5283
Web: http://uscis.gov
Please, be sure to have an appointment letter to appear for fingerprinting.

CHARLOTTE SUB OFFICE

6130 Tyvola Ctr. Dr.
Charlotte, NC 28217
Richard Gottlieb, Officer in Charge
Tel: (800) 375-5283
Web: http://uscis.gov
Service area: North Carolina. To speak with an Immigration Information Officer, you may make an appointment via the Internet at www.infopass.uscis.gov.

NORTH DAKOTA

FARGO APPLICATION SUPPORT CENTER (ASC)

657 2nd Ave. #104
North Fargo, ND 58102
Tel: (800) 375-5283
Web: http://uscis.gov
Please, be sure to have an appointment letter to appear for fingerprinting.

OHIO

CINCINNATI APPLICATION SUPPORT CENTER (ASC)

550 Main St. #1524
Cincinnati, OH 45202
Tel: (800) 375-5283
Web: http://uscis.gov
Please, be sure to have an appointment letter to appear for fingerprinting.

CINCINNATI SUB OFFICE

J.W. Peck Federal Bldg.,
550 Main St. #4001
Cincinnati, OH 45202
Helaine Tasch, Officer in Charge
Tel: (800) 375-5283
Web: http://uscis.gov
Service area: Adams, Brown, Butler, Champaign, Clark, Clermont, Clinton, Darke, Greene, Hamilton, Highland, Lawrence, Miami, Montgomery, Preble, Scioto, Shelby, and Warren. To speak with an Immigration Information Officer, you may make an appointment via the Internet at www.infopass.uscis.gov.

CLEVELAND APPLICATION SUPPORT CENTER (ASC)

A.J.C. Federal Bldg., 1240 E. 9th St. #1259
Cleveland, OH 44199
Tel: (800) 375-5283
Web: http://uscis.gov
Please, be sure to have an appointment letter to appear for fingerprinting.

CLEVELAND DISTRICT OFFICE

A.J.C. Federal Bldg., 1240 E. 9th St. #501
Cleveland, OH 44199
Mark B. Hansen, District Director
Tel: (800) 375-5283
Web: http://uscis.gov

Service area: the Cleveland District Office has jurisdiction over the entire state of Ohio. The office services the following counties: Allen, Ashland, Ashtabula, Auglaize, Carroll, Columbiana, Crawford, Cuyahoga, Defiance, Erie, Fulton, Geauga, Hancock, Hardin, Henry, Holmes, Huron, Lake, Lorain, Lucas, Mahoning, Marion, Medina, Mercer, Ottawa, Paulding, Portage, Putnam, Richland, Ross, Sandusky, Seneca, Stark, Summit, Trumbull, Tuscarawas, Union, Van Wert, Wayne, Williams, Wood, and Wyandot. To speak with an Immigration Information Officer, you may make an appointment via the Internet at www.infopass.uscis.gov.

COLUMBUS APPLICATION SUPPORT CENTER (ASC)

Leveque Towers, 50 W. Broad St. #321
Columbus, OH 43215
Tel: (800) 375-5283
Web: http://uscis.gov
Please, be sure to have an appointment letter to appear for fingerprinting.

COLUMBUS SATELLITE OFFICE

Leveque Tower, 50 W. Broad St. #306
Columbus, OH 43215
Cheryl Gallegos, Officer in Charge
Tel: (800) 375-5283
Web: http://uscis.gov
Service area: Athens, Belmont, Coshocton, Delaware, Fairfield, Fayette, Franklin, Gallia, Guernsey, Harrison, Hocking, Jackson, Jefferson, Knox, Licking, Logan, Madison, Meigs, Monroe, Morgan, Morrow, Muskingum, Noble, Perry, Pickaway, Pike, Ross, Union, Vinton, and Washington.

OKLAHOMA

OKLAHOMA CITY APPLICATION SUPPORT CENTER (ASC)

4400 SW 44th St. #A
Oklahoma City, OK 73119
Tel: (800) 375-5283
Web: http://uscis.gov
Please, be sure to have an appointment letter to appear for fingerprinting.

OKLAHOMA CITY SUB OFFICE

4400 SW 44th St. #A
Oklahoma City, OK 73119-2800
Barry C. Royce, Officer in Charge
Tel: (800) 375-5283
Web: http://uscis.gov
Service area: the Oklahoma City Sub Office serves all of Oklahoma.

OREGON

PORTLAND APPLICATION SUPPORT CENTER (ASC)

721 SW 14th Ave.
Portland, OR 97205
Tel: (800) 375-5283
Web: http://uscis.gov
Please, be sure to have an appointment letter to appear for fingerprinting.

PORTLAND, OREGON DISTRICT OFFICE

511 NW Broadway
Portland, OR 97209
William McNamee, District Director
Tel: (800) 375-5283
Web: http://uscis.gov
Service area: the Portland District services the entire state of Oregon. To speak with an

Immigration Information Officer, you may make an appointment via the Internet at www.infopass.uscis.gov.

PENNSYLVANIA

PHILADELPHIA APPLICATION SUPPORT CENTER (ASC)

120 N. 8th St.
Philadelphia, PA 19107
Tel: (800) 375-5283
Web: http://uscis.gov
Please, be sure to have an appointment letter to appear for fingerprinting.

PHILADELPHIA DISTRICT OFFICE

1600 Callowhill St.
Philadelphia, PA 19130
Donald Monica, District Director
Tel: (800) 375-5283
Web: http://uscis.gov
Service area: the States of: Pennsylvania, Delaware, and West Virginia. The Philadelphia District Office serves the state of Delaware and the eastern Pennsylvania counties of: Adams, Berks, Bucks, Cameron, Carbon, Centre, Chester, Clinton, Columbia, Cumberland, Dauphin, Delaware, Franklin, Fulton, Huntingdon, Juniata, Lackawanna, Lancaster, Lebanon, Lehigh, Luzerne, Lycoming, Mifflin, Monroe, Montgomery, Montour, Northampton, Northumberland, Perry, Philadelphia, Pike, Potter, Schuykill, Snyder, Sullivan, Susquehanna, Tioga, Union, Wayne, Wyoming, and York. To speak with an Immigration Information Officer, you may make an appointment via the Internet at www.infopass.uscis.gov.

PITTSBURGH APPLICATION SUPPORT CENTER (ASC)

800 Penn Ave. #101
Pittsburgh, PA 15222
Tel: (800) 375-5283
Web: http://uscis.gov
Please, be sure to have an appointment letter to appear for fingerprinting.

PITTSBURGH SUB OFFICE

3000 Sidney St. #241
Pittsburgh, PA 15203
Debra Zamberry, Officer in Charge
Tel: (800) 375-5283
Web: http://uscis.gov
Service area: the Pittsburgh Sub Office serves the State of West Virginia and the western Pennsylvania counties of: Allegheny, Armstrong, Beaver, Bedford, Blair, Bradford, Butler, Cambria, Clarion, Clearfield, Crawford, Elk, Erie, Fayette, Forest, Greene, Indiana, Jefferson, Lawrence, McKean, Mercer, Somerset, Venango, Warren, Washington, and Westmoreland. To speak with an Immigration Information Officer, you may make an appointment via the Internet at www.infopass.uscis.gov.

YORK APPLICATION SUPPORT CENTER (ASC)

3400 Concord Rd.
York, PA 17402
Tel: (800) 375-5283
Web: http://uscis.gov
Please, be sure to have an appointment letter to appear for fingerprinting.

PUERTO RICO

SAN JUAN DISTRICT OFFICE

San Patricio Office Ctr.,
7 Tabonuco St. #100
Guaynabo, PR 00968
Maria Del Mar Arana, District Director
Tel: (800) 375-5283
Web: http://uscis.gov
Service area: the San Juan District Office serves the entire island of Puerto Rico and the US Virgin Islands. To speak with an Immigration Information Officer, you may make an appointment via the Internet at www.infopass.uscis.gov.

SAN JUAN, PR APPLICATION SUPPORT CENTER (ASC)

458 Ing. Jose Canals St.
San Juan, PR 00918
Tel: (800) 375-5283
Web: http://uscis.gov
Please, be sure to have an appointment letter to appear for fingerprinting.

RHODE ISLAND

PROVIDENCE SUB OFFICE

200 Dyer St.
Providence, RI 02903
Jeffrey Trecartin, Officer in Charge
Tel: (800) 375-5283
Web: http://uscis.gov
Service area: the State of Rhode Island. To speak with an Immigration Information Officer, you may make an appointment via the Internet at www.infopass.uscis.gov.

PROVIDENCE/CRANSTON, RI APPLICATION SUPPORT CENTER (ASC)

Cross Roads Office Park,
105 Sockanosset Cross Rd. #210
Cranston, RI 02920
Tel: (800) 375-5283
Web: http://uscis.gov
Please, be sure to have an appointment letter to appear for fingerprinting.

SOUTH CAROLINA

CHARLESTON APPLICATION SUPPORT CENTER (ASC)

170 Meeting St. 5th Fl.
Charleston, SC 29403
Tel: (800) 375-5283
Web: http://uscis.gov
Please, be sure to have an appointment letter to appear for fingerprinting. Please note that this location cannot collect digital information for customers who wish to file their applications electronically.

CHARLESTON OFFICE

170 Meeting St., 5th Fl.
Charleston, SC 29401
Jerri Adair, Officer in Charge
Tel: (800) 375-5283
Web: http://uscis.gov
Service area: together with the satellite office in Greer, South Carolina, the Charleston Office services the entire state of South Carolina. To speak with an Immigration Information Officer, you must obtain a ticket, available on a first-come, first-served basis in the lobby of the office.

GREER, SC - SATELLITE OFFICE
142D W. Phillips Rd.
Greer, SC 29650
Tel: (800) 375-5283
Web: http://uscis.gov
Services: Greer, SC - Satellite office (serves the "up-state" of South Carolina)

SOUTH DAKOTA

RAPID CITY APPLICATION SUPPORT CENTER (ASC)
1675 Samco Rd.
Rapid City, SD 57702
Tel: (800) 375-5283
Web: http://uscis.gov
Please, be sure to have an appointment letter to appear for fingerprinting.

SIOUX FALLS APPLICATION SUPPORT CENTER (ASC)
Riverside Station, 300 E. 8th St.
Sioux Falls, SD 57104
Tel: (800) 375-5283
Web: http://uscis.gov
Please, be sure to have an appointment letter to appear for fingerprinting.

TENNESSEE

MEMPHIS APPLICATION SUPPORT CENTER (ASC)
1341 Sycamore View Rd. #100
Memphis, TN 38134
Tel: (800) 375-5283
Web: http://uscis.gov
Please, be sure to have an appointment letter to appear for fingerprinting.

MEMPHIS SUB OFFICE
1341 Sycamore View Rd. #100
Memphis, TN 38134
Tel: (800) 375-5283
Web: http://uscis.gov
Service area: Arkansas (Eastern half), Mississippi (Northern half), Tennessee. Immigration Information Officers are available in the lobby of the office on a first-come, first-served basis.

NASHVILLE APPLICATION SUPPORT CENTER (ASC)
247 Venture Cr.
Nashville, TN 37228
Tel: (800) 375-5283
Web: http://uscis.gov
Please, be sure to have an appointment letter to appear for fingerprinting.

TEXAS

BROWNSVILLE APPLICATION SUPPORT CENTER (ASC)
Southwind Shopping Ctr., 943 N. Expressway 77 #23
Brownsville, TX 78520
Tel: (800) 375-5283
Web: http://uscis.gov
Please, be sure to have an appointment letter to appear for fingerprinting.

DALLAS APPLICATION SUPPORT CENTER (ASC)
Village at Bachman Lake, 3701 W. Northwest Hwy. #211
Dallas, TX 75220
Tel: (800) 375-5283
Web: http://uscis.gov

Please, be sure to have an appointment letter to appear for fingerprinting.

DALLAS DISTRICT OFFICE
8101 N. Stemmons Fwy.
Dallas, TX 75247
Angela Barrows, District Director
Tel: (800) 375-5283
Web: http://uscis.gov
Service area: the Dallas District Office serves all of Dallas, Fort Worth, Irving, North Central Texas (Panhandle and North of Waco). Except for emergencies and distant travelers, this office will no longer accept walk-ins.

EL PASO APPLICATION SUPPORT CENTER (ASC)
10500 Montwood Dr.
El Paso, TX 79935
Tel: (800) 375-5283
Web: http://uscis.gov
Please, be sure to have an appointment letter to appear for fingerprinting.

EL PASO DISTRICT OFFICE
1545 Hawkins Blvd. #167
El Paso, TX 79925
Raymond Adams, District Director
Tel: (800) 375-5283
Web: http://uscis.gov
Service area: the El Paso District's area of operation includes the City and County of El Paso, 15 adjacent West Texas counties (Brewster, Crane, Culberson, Ector, Hudspeth, Jeff Davis, Loving, Midland, Pecos, Presidio, Reeves, Terrell, Upton, Ward and Winkler), and the state of New Mexico. To speak with an Immigration Information Officer, you may make an appointment via the Internet at www.infopass.uscis.gov.

FT. WORTH APPLICATION SUPPORT CENTER (ASC)
Ft. Worth Town Ctr. Mall,
4200 S. Fwy. #1309
Ft. Worth, TX 76115
Tel: (800) 375-5283
Web: http://uscis.gov
Please, be sure to have an appointment letter to appear for fingerprinting.

HARLINGEN DISTRICT OFFICE
1717 Zoy St.
Harlingen, TX 78552
Alfonso R. Deleon, District Director
Tel: (800) 375-5283
Web: http://uscis.gov
Service area: the Harlingen District has jurisdiction over the following counties located in the southernmost tip of the state of Texas: Brooks, Cameron, Hidalgo, Kennedy, Kleberg, Starr, and Willacy. To speak with an Immigration Information Officer, you may make an appointment via the Internet at www.infopass.uscis.gov.

HOUSTON APPLICATION SUPPORT CENTER (ASC)
Corum Plz. 8505-D Gulf Fwy.
Houston, TX 77017
Tel: (800) 375-5283
Web: http://uscis.gov
Please, be sure to have an appointment letter to appear for fingerprinting.

HOUSTON ASYLUM OFFICE
16630 Imperial Valley Dr. #200
Houston, TX 77060
Tel: (800) 375-5283/(281) 774-4830
Web: http://uscis.gov
Service area: this Asylum Office serves the States of Louisiana, Arkansas, Mississippi, Tennessee, Texas, Oklahoma, New Mexico,

Colorado, Utah, and Wyoming. Application status cannot be checked on a walk-in basis. Please submit your request in writing.

HOUSTON DISTRICT OFFICE
126 Northpoint
Houston, TX 77060
Hipolito Acosta, District Director
Tel: (800) 375-5283
Web: http://uscis.gov
Service area: 30 counties in southeastern Texas: Angelina, Austin, Brazoria, Chambers, Colorado, Fort Bend, Galveston, Grimes, Hardin, Harris, Jasper, Jefferson, Liberty, Madison, Matagorda, Montgomery, Nacogdoches, Newton, Orange, Polk, Sabine, San Augustine, San Jacinto, Shelby, Trinity, Tyler, Walker, Waller, Washington (for all services except Naturalization), and Wharton. To speak with an Immigration Information Officer, you may make an appointment via the Internet at www.infopass.uscis.gov.

HOUSTON NW APPLICATION SUPPORT CENTER (ASC)
10555 NW Fwy. #150
Houston, TX 77092
Tel: (800) 375-5283
Web: http://uscis.gov
Please, be sure to have an appointment letter to appear for fingerprinting.

LAREDO APPLICATION SUPPORT CENTER (ASC)
707 E. Calton Rd. #301
Laredo, TX 78041
Tel: (800) 375-5283
Web: http://uscis.gov
Please, be sure to have an appointment letter to appear for fingerprinting.

LUBBOCK APPLICATION SUPPORT CENTER (ASC)
3502 Slide Rd. #A-24
Lubbock, TX 79414
Tel: (800) 375-5283
Web: http://uscis.gov
Please, be sure to have an appointment letter to appear for fingerprinting.

MCALLEN APPLICATION SUPPORT CENTER (ASC)
220 S. Bicentennial #C
McAllen, TX 78501
Tel: (800) 375-5283
Web: http://uscis.gov
Please, be sure to have an appointment letter to appear for fingerprinting.

SAN ANTONIO APPLICATION SUPPORT CENTER (ASC)
Randolph Blvd. 5121 Crestway Dr. #112
San Antonio, TX 78239
Tel: (800) 375-5283
Web: http://uscis.gov
Please, be sure to have an appointment letter to appear for fingerprinting.

SAN ANTONIO DISTRICT OFFICE
8940 Fourwinds Dr.
San Antonio, TX 78239
Kenneth Pasquarell, District Director
Tel: (800) 375-5283
Web: http://uscis.gov
Service area: 78 counties of Central and South Texas, which includes major cities such as San Antonio, Austin, Waco, San Angelo, College Station/Bryan, Victoria, Corpus Christi, Kerrville, Uvalde, Del Rio, Eagle Pass, and Laredo. To speak with an Immigration Information Officer, you may make an appointment via the Internet at www.infopass.uscis.gov.

SOUTH DALLAS APPLICATION SUPPORT CENTER (ASC)
7334 S. Westmoreland Rd.
Dallas, TX 75237
Tel: (800) 375-5283
Web: http://uscis.gov
Please, be sure to have an appointment letter to appear for fingerprinting.

SW HOUSTON APPLICATION SUPPORT CENTER (ASC)
Fondren Rd. Plz. 7086 Bissonnet St.
Houston, TX 77074
Tel: (800) 375-5283
Web: http://uscis.gov
Please, be sure to have an appointment letter to appear for fingerprinting.

TEXAS SERVICE CENTER
P.O. Box 851488
Mesquite, TX 75185-1488
Tel: (800) 375-5283
Web: http://uscis.gov
Service area: the Texas Service Center accepts and processes certain applications and petitions from individuals residing in the following states: Alabama, Arkansas, Florida, Georgia, Kentucky, Louisiana, Mississippi, New Mexico, North Carolina, South Carolina, Oklahoma, Tennessee, and Texas.

P.O. Box 851204
Mesquite, TX 75185-1204
Tel: (800) 375-5283
Web: http://uscis.gov
Service area: Alabama. Form N-400, Naturalization.

P.O. Box 851182
Mesquite, TX 75185-1182
Tel: (800) 375-5283
Web: http://uscis.gov
Services: Form I-131, Application for Travel Document; Form I-824, Application for Action on an Approved Application/Petition; Form I-102, Application for Replacement/Initial Nonimmigrant Arrival-Departure Document; I-539, Application to Extend/Change Nonimmigrant.

P.O. Box 850997
Mesquite, TX 75185-0997
Tel: (800) 375-5283
Web: http://uscis.gov
Services: Form I-765, Application for Employment; Form I-821, Application for Temporary Protected Status (El Salvador)

P.O. Box 853062
Mesquite, TX 75185-3062
Tel: (800) 375-5283
Web: http://uscis.gov
Services: Form I-765, Application for Employment; Form I-821, Application for Temporary Protected Status (Mitch)

P.O. Box 851041
Mesquite, TX 75185-1041
Tel: (800) 375-5283
Web: http://uscis.gov
Services: Form I-765, Application for Employment

P.O. Box 852401
Mesquite, TX 75185-2401
Tel: (800) 375-5283
Web: http://uscis.gov
Services: Form I-765, E-Filing Application for Employment.

continued on p 214

Es una satisfacción para Castilla y León, estar presente en el Anuario Hispano, una de las publicaciones de gran prestigio y mayor consulta entre los empresarios y la sociedad del Estado de Florida ya que constituye un documento de referencia para las actividades económicas y el intercambio comercial.

Los vínculos históricos y afectivos que mantiene Castilla y León con el continente americano y sobre todo con la comunidad hispana, vienen reflejados no sólo por compartir el mismo idioma, lo que nos facilita la comunicación con otros 400 millones de habitantes hispano parlantes, sino por compartir raíces culturales y una cercanía y entendimiento entre nuestros pueblos.

Desde estas breves líneas, quisiera invitar a los empresarios lectores de esta publicación a que conozcan las ventajas competitivas de nuestra Región como un lugar idóneo para desarrollar sus actividades económicas.

Castilla y León reúne unas inmejorables condiciones para la inversión y el desarrollo de proyectos empresariales con un firme compromiso por parte del gobierno regional en apoyar las actividades productivas más innovadoras. La Junta de Castilla y León pone a disposición de los inversores y empresarios un conjunto de incentivos financieros, recursos humanos altamente cualificados e infraestructuras tecnológicas que dan soporte científico a sectores como ciencias de la salud, biotecnología, aeronáutica y tecnologías de la información y comunicación, sectores ya presentes en nuestra Comunidad y en los que nos encontramos trabajando con especial interés.

El gobierno de Castilla y León está especialmente implicado para que nuestro tejido productivo más consolidado afronte el reto de internacionalizarse y dé el salto hacia al mercado americano. Este reto internacional nos ha llevado a posicionar centros de negocios en las ciudades de Nueva York y Miami, entre otros, con el fin de canalizar los intereses del empresariado norteamericano hacia Castilla y León, atender de forma directa y personalizada las necesidades de nuestros empresarios, facilitando el intercambio comercial y ayudándoles a posicionarse en los mercados internacionales.

Castilla y León, en definitiva, ofrece rentabilidad económica a las inversiones y a sus empresarios, competitividad y posicionamiento internacional así como seguridad, tranquilidad y calidad de vida a sus ciudadanos.

Tomás Villanueva Rodríguez
Vicepresidente segundo y Consejero de Economía y Empleo
Junta de Castilla y León

It is a great satisfaction for the Region of Castilla y León to be present in the Anuario Hispano/Hispanic Yearbook, one of the most prestigious and frequently consulted publications among businesspersons and the general public in Florida and a point of reference for economic activity and commercial exchanges.

The historical and sentimental ties maintained by Castilla y León with the American continent, and especially with the Hispanic community, are evident not only in a common language which enables us to communicate with another 400,000,000 Spanish-speaking people, but also in shared cultural roots and a closeness and understanding between our nations.

In these few lines, I would like to invite the businesspersons who read this publication to learn about the competitive advantages of our region as an ideal location in which to develop their economic activity.

Castilla y León combines the best conditions for investment and for the development of business projects. The regional government is firmly committed to supporting the most innovative production activity. The Council of Castilla y León makes available to investors and businessmen a combination of financial incentives, highly qualified human resources, and technological infrastructures which provide scientific support to sectors in our community such as health sciences, biotechnology, aeronautics, and information and communication technology—areas in which we work with special enthusiasm.

The government of Castilla y León is especially committed to having our most consolidated production network meet the challenge of entering the international arena and take the plunge into the American market. This international challenge has led us to establish business centers in the cities of New York and Miami, among others, with the object of channeling the interest of North American businesspersons toward Castilla y León and serving the needs of our businesspersons in a direct and personal way by facilitating commercial exchanges and helping them to establish themselves in international markets.

In the final analysis, Castilla y León offers profitability to investors and its businesspersons; competitiveness and international standing; and safety, tranquility, and quality of life to its citizens.

 **Universidad de León, España**

Constituye para mi un motivo de satisfacción y de orgullo realizar, de nuevo, esta carta de presentación de la Universidad de León (ULE), de la que soy Rector elegido en el año 2000 y reelegido en el año 2004, para su publicación en la 19ª edición del Anuario Hispano.

La ULE es una institución pública de enseñanza superior que une a la juventud y pujanza de alguna de sus titulaciones establecidas en los últimos treinta años, la consolidada experiencia de otras, como Educación y Veterinaria, cuyos orígenes hay que buscarlos en el siglo XIX.

Nuestra oferta académica abarca un total de 55 titulaciones de diplomatura y licenciatura distribuidas en los campos de las ciencias sociales y jurídicas, de las humanidades, de las ciencias experimentales y de la salud y de las enseñanzas técnicas que son cursadas por unos 15.000 estudiantes. Esta oferta se amplia además con una treintena de programas de doctorado que son cursados por unos dos mil alumnos. Creo conveniente destacar que los aspectos agropecuarios, biotecnológicos y medioambientales representan las señas de identidad de nuestra Universidad.

Nuestra Universidad posee dos campus ubicados en las ciudades de León y de Ponferrada. Las ciudades de León, ciudad milenaria fundada por los romanos y en la que se ubica el campus principal, y de Ponferrada, de origen medieval, conservan importantes monumentos y joyas artísticas del pasado. Ambas se encuentran situadas sobre el Camino de Santiago y tienen un tamaño que permite el desarrollo de una vida sosegada y segura, muy adecuada para el desarrollo del pensamiento y del conocimiento.

Los estudiantes europeos, americanos y asiáticos, que representan un porcentaje creciente cada año, encuentran en nuestra Universidad y en nuestras ciudades un medio adecuado para ampliar sus conocimientos profesionales y sobre la cultura y civilización españolas en un ambiente afable y distendido en el que las actividades culturales y de ocio programadas por la Universidad juegan un papel destacado.

Ángel Penas Merino
Rector

Productos de Castilla y León, Calidad de España

PASIÓN POR EL VINO

La historia y la importancia de los vinos de Castilla y León se mezcla con la vida en la región; más allá de una actividad económica, la elaboración de vino se ha convertido a lo largo del tiempo en un modo de vida.

Desde la Edad Media, la producción de vino ha inculcado una cultura particular en cada una de las distintas zonas vinícolas de Castilla y León, una cultura que se ve reflejada tanto en las costumbres populares de la región como en sus tradicionales herramientas de trabajo, como son las bodegas y las prensas.

Castilla y León ocupa un lugar privilegiado en el mapa vitivinícola español. Cinco Denominaciones de Origen y ocho comarcas de Vinos de la Tierra perfilan las zonas de producción de vinos de calidad de la región.

A la hora de analizar cada uno de los diferentes vinos de Castilla y León, cobra vital importancia la consideración de las peculiaridades geográficas, geológicas y climáticas de las distintas regiones vinícolas, que se extienden a lo largo de 90.000 hectáreas.

Todo el abanico de vinos de calidad se produce en la región. Desde los tintos de guarda, de largo envejecimiento, los crianzas y reservas del Duero, hasta vinos jóvenes, ligeros y frutales, pasando por blancos de marcado carácter varietal, cada uno tiene su hueco. Sin olvidar elaboraciones de espumosos, licores y aguardientes, que completan una oferta vinícola que se funde con la rica cocina.

Las Denominaciones de Origen Ribera del Duero, Rueda, Cigales, Toro y Bierzo acogen a más de 400 bodegas productoras de vinos de calidad, amparadas por los consejos reguladores de cada zona.

Las comarcas de Vinos de la Tierra, que aglutinan a otros dos centenares de bodegas, se reparten prácticamente por toda la geografía regional y se enmarcan en espacios de gran valor histórico cultural.

El Duero es el río español de vinos por naturaleza. Nace en las montañas de Urbión, en la Comunidad de Castilla y León, y muere en Oporto (Portugal). Es el río de los grandes vinos de calidad de moda en España. Es el padre de los tintos de la región de Castilla y León. El "Durii" como le llamaron los romanos hace dos mil años, es hoy, como ayer, la savia de las uvas (de las Denominaciones de Origen Ribera del Duero, Toro, Rueda y Cigales y, a su paso, riega al resto de las comarcas vitivinícolas de la región con mayor diversidad de tipos de vinos de la Península Ibérica.

La variedad tempranillo es la gran cepa española que se dedica exclusivamente a la elaboración de vinos de calidad en una buena parte de las comarcas vitivinícolas de la nación de vinos situada más al sur de Europa. Es en Castilla y León, donde adquiere carta de naturaleza en los vinos tranquilos de corto y largo envejecimiento. Vinos de mucho color, gran estructura, potencial aromático, muy frutales y apropiados para el envejecimiento, y criados en robles nuevos seleccionados de distintas procedencias. Los vinos tintos del Duero son, sin duda, la vanguardia que se ajusta a los gustos del consumidor moderno, que busca este tipo de vinos de calidad en los mercados internacionales.

La historia de los grandes vinos tintos del Duero nació hace más de 140 años de la mano de la legendaria bodega española Vega Sicilia, situada en Castilla y León, a orillas del Duero, junto a la villa medieval de Peñafiel, en la provincia de Valladolid. Los referentes culturales del vino, no sólo por la historia del cultivo de la vid, sino también por los elementos que caracterizan su arquitectura tradicional, pues las galerías subterráneas y cavidades horadadas en roca o tierra -donde se guardan y envejecen los vinos- son muy frecuentes en Castilla y León. Hoy, las modernas bodegas irrumpen con diseños vanguardistas y arquitectos de la fama de Richard Rogers, Norman Foster o Rafael Moneo dirigen proyectos de bodegas en Burgos y Valladolid... es decir, en el Duero.

Junto a la variedad tempranillo, origen de los célebres tintos de Ribera de Duero y Toro, se cultiva la uva blanca verdejo, que en estos momentos está considerada como una de las mejores variedades para vinificar vinos blancos en España. Sus dos cualidades más importantes son la extraordinaria potencia en aromas, muy personales y con sensaciones garantizadas en aromas de series frutales-florales arropadas por una vigorosa estructura en boca. Otra de sus grandes virtudes es la capacidad para envejecer. En el siglo pasado fue utilizada para la elaboración de vinos generosos (similares al Jerez-Serry) pero hoy se ha convertido en una magnífica cepa capaz de evolucionar muy bien en las fermentaciones en barricas nuevas y en el envejecimiento en madera. Otra característica que ha logrado posicionar en los mercados los vinos blancos de Rueda elaborados con uva verdejo es que han alcanzado un digna posición entre los mejores vinos blancos españoles en relación calidad-precio.

La cercanía a Asturias y Galicia de la comarca de El Bierzo, con las que hace frontera, dotan a este espacio de una vegetación característica diferente a la del resto de la Comunidad de Castilla y León. Un microclima donde las zonas de viñas conviven con árboles frutales, pastizales e inmensos bosques de castaños y robles. Los vinos de la Denominación de Origen Bierzo tienen un cimiento varietal: la mencía. Es la variedad reina del denominado "volcán del Noroeste" de la viticultura española.

El despertar de la enología y el desarrollo de la viticultura de Castilla y León posibilita la creación de rutas de interés turístico. El paisaje de viñedos, salpicado por profusos testimonios de arquitectura popular de bodegas y del rico patrimonio histórico-artístico que atesora la región, muestra un rasgo genuino de la tradición del vino en Castilla y León.

Para más información pueden contactar:

EXCAL, S.A.
Recondo s/n
47007 Valladolid (SPAIN)
Phone: +34 983 293 966
Fax: +34 983 209 803
E-mail: alimentacion@excal.es
Web: www.excal.es

EXCAL USA
Empire State Building
350 Fifth Ave, Room 2600
New York, 10118 NY
Phone: 212 967 2170
Fax: 212 564 1415
E-mail: newyork@excal.es

JAMÓN IBÉRICO DE GUIJUELO, COMPLEMENTO PERFECTO

El cerdo ha sido el gran protagonista dentro de la gastronomía y cultura de España, sobre todo en la España rural, donde ha sido parte fundamental de la dieta cárnica. Es el único animal del que se aprovecha absolutamente todo. El jamón es la pieza más importante de todos los productos de chacinería que se extraen del cerdo ibérico.

La cantidad y composición de la grasa son factores determinantes en la calidad final de los productos cárnicos y, en especial, del jamón, apreciada a través de las vetas blancas que presenta y que le proporcionan jugosidad. La elaboración del jamón se inicia por un proceso de curación, para eliminar humedad y conseguir la fusión natural de las grasas, durante la maduración, en la que aparecen los aromas y sabores característicos del jamón.

Según el modo de alimentación al que se someta el cerdo ibérico se distinguen tres tipos:
- **Jamón Ibérico de Bellota:** Procede de cerdos alimentados con bellotas y hierbas campeando por las dehesas.
- **Jamón Ibérico de Recebo:** De cerdos alimentados con bellotas en dehesas pero que también han tenido una alimentación suplementaria con piensos debidamente autorizados.
- **Jamón Ibérico de Pienso:** De cerdos alimentados en las dehesas exclusivamente con piensos autorizados.

Al sureste de la provincia de Salamanca, a una altitud superior a los mil metros, Guijuelo presta su nombre y resonancia a la comarca española más importante en la artesanía chacinera del cerdo ibérico. La industria del jamón nace en Guijuelo, por los años 1880, como consecuencia de los beneficios que la compra de jamones, recogidos por las tierras de Sayago y Benavente (Zamora) proporcionaban a los arrieros de Guijuelo, que intercambiaban embutidos y perniles por productos deficitarios en esta comarca (trigo o sal). La conjunción de unas condiciones climáticas adecuadas y la proximidad de dehesas en las que se aprovechaban la proximidad de la montaña fue la causa de que se fuera consolidando aquí esa tradición jamonera.

Aprender Español en León, España

LOS CURSOS DE ESPAÑOL

La Universidad de León ofrece Cursos de Lengua y Cultura Españolas en todos los niveles. Desde 1956 son ya casi cincuenta años de actividad que acreditan a nuestra institución como una de las pioneras en este campo. Los Cursos se imparten en el Centro de Idiomas, edificio clásico situado en el corazón de la ciudad y al que se ha dotado en los dos últimos años de nuevas aulas, sala de informática, biblioteca y todos los medios audiovisuales de última generación, adecuados para la enseñanza de idiomas.

Nuestra oferta es variada y se adapta a las necesidades de todo tipo de alumnado:

- Cursos Regulares (octubre a junio)
- Cursos de Verano (julio y agosto)
- Cursos Trimestrales (octubre a diciembre; marzo a mayo)
- Cursos de Formación para Profesores de Español (julio y agosto)
- Curso de Preparación DELE (mayo y noviembre)
- Curso Intensivo para Estudiantes ERASMUS (enero y septiembre)
- Cursos a medida para grupos (cualquier época del año)
- Cursos "en línea" AVE (octubre a junio)

Los Cursos de Lengua y Cultura Españolas para estudiantes extranjeros han ido evolucionando y adaptándose a las necesidades del momento, pero siempre manteniendo sus principios fundamentales: el cuidado esmerado de todos los aspectos relacionados con la enseñanza y la atención individualizada que se dispensa a los estudiantes. El objetivo es siempre garantizar las mejores condiciones de aprendizaje en todos los niveles. Información sobre nuestros cursos de español en: www.unileon.es/spanish Información sobre la Universidad de León en www.unileon.es

LA CIUDAD Y LA PROVINCIA DE LEÓN

León es una ciudad fundada hace 2000 años, enclave y encrucijada del Camino de Santiago, situada en la zona noroeste de España, bien comunicada por autopistas, tren y avión con el resto de España.

Con una población de 150.000 habitantes, la ciudad se convierte en marco y complemento adecuado para el aprendizaje de la lengua española y de la cultura que la sustenta. León, centro administrativo y comercial de la provincia del mismo nombre, es una ciudad acogedora y amable que ofrece al visitante un equilibrio perfecto entre la ciudad medieval antigua y la parte moderna, con un gran patrimonio histórico y artístico. La seguridad y la tranquilidad son también aspectos destacables de nuestra ciudad.

León es una ciudad que se puede recorrer fácilmente caminando, lo que permite al viajero conocer sus calles y sus gentes. La oferta es amplia y variada, tanto desde el aspecto cultural (auditorio para conciertos de música clásica y ópera; museos y centros de arte), como desde el ámbito de celebraciones festivas, algunas de reconocimiento internacional como la Semana Santa. Ciudad referente a nivel de España para la celebración de convenciones y congresos es, igualmente, uno de los destinos más significados del turismo cultural por la importancia de sus monumentos. De ahí que disponga de una amplia oferta de hoteles y restaurantes y de que determinadas zonas de la ciudad tengan un encanto especial. Es el caso, por ejemplo, del llamado "Barrio Húmedo", en la parte antigua de la ciudad, que ofrece al visitante la posibilidad de disfrutar de numerosos locales de hostelería muy animados a últimas horas de la tarde, y otros lugares, más tranquilos si los prefiere, como zonas de cafés, propicios para la charla reposada, o modernos locales con los más diversos ambientes.

Tanto la ciudad como la provincia de León reúnen excelentes condiciones para disfrutar de su patrimonio artístico, de su riqueza y variedad de paisajes y también de la hospitalidad y cordialidad de su gente. El clima es continental, con veranos secos y soleados (temperaturas máximas durante el día entre 25 y 30 grados y mínimas nocturnas en torno a los 15 grados) e inviernos fríos y rigurosos.

Más información sobre la ciudad y la provincia de León en:

www.aytoleon.com (páginas del Ayuntamiento de la ciudad de León)
www.dipuleon.com (páginas de la Diputación Provincial de León)

Learn Spanish in León, Spain

SPANISH COURSES

The University of León offers courses in Spanish Language and Culture at all levels. Our institution, which has been in operation for nearly 50 years (since 1956), is recognized as one of the pioneers in this field. The courses are given in the Language Center, a classic-style building located in the heart of the city. In the past two years, the Center has gained new classrooms, a computer room, a library, and all the latest audiovisual media geared to language teaching.

Our courses are varied and adaptable to the needs of all types of students:

- Regular Courses (October to June)
- Summer Courses (July and August)
- Quarterly Courses (October to December and March to May)
- Training Courses for Spanish Professors (July and August)
- DELE Preparation Course (May and November)
- ERASMUS Intensive Course For Students (January and September)
- Courses Designed for Individual Groups (all year)
- Online AVE Courses (October to June)

The Spanish Language and Culture courses for foreign students have been evolving and becoming more adaptable to current needs while maintaining their fundamental principles: conscientious attention to all aspects of teaching, and individual attention to students. Our objective is to always guarantee the best learning conditions at all levels.

For information on our Spanish courses, visit www.unileon.es/spanish
For information on the University of León, visit www.unileon.es

THE CITY AND PROVINCE OF LEÓN

The city of León, founded 2,000 years ago, is an enclave and a crossroads of the Road to Santiago. It is located in the northwestern part of Spain, and is very accessible to the rest of Europe by car, train, and plane.

With a population of 150,000, the city offers an ideal setting for learning the Spanish language and its underlying culture. Welcoming and friendly, León is the administrative and commercial center of the province of León. Visitors will find a perfect balance between the medieval and modern parts of the city , as well as a great historical and artistic heritage. A safe and tranquil environment also add to our city's appeal.

It is easy to get around León on foot, which allows travelers to become familiar with its streets and people. The city's activities are extensive and varied: culture is found in the concert hall for classical music and opera, and in museums and art centers; and there are holiday celebrations—some known internationally, such as Holy Week (Semana Santa). León is a focal point in Spain for conventions and conferences, and its important monuments make it one of the most significant destinations for cultural tourism. This has resulted in a wide array of hotels and restaurants and has added a special charm to certain parts of the city. For example, there is the so-called "Wet District" (Barrio Húmedo), in the old part of the city, where one can visit a group of local hotels late in the day. There are also more tranquil areas with cafés which lend themselves to relaxed conversation, or modern locations with a wide variety of atmospheres.

The city and province of León combine excellent conditions that make it possible to enjoy their artistic heritage as well as the richness and variety of their natural scenery and the hospitality and cordiality of their people. The climate is continental, with dry, sunny summers (highest daytime temperatures between 25 and 30 degrees Celsius and lowest nighttime temperatures around 15 degrees) and cold and rigorous winters.

More information on the city and province of León can be found at:

www.aytoleon.com (website for the City Hall of the city of León)
www.dipuleon.com (website for the Provincial Council of León)

Translation of the letter from the President of Spain

Here in Spain, we have been following with much interest and satisfaction the ongoing development of the Anuario Hispano-Hispanic Yearbook. I send my sincere congratulations to those of you who are responsible for bringing the Yearbook to us. This indispensable publication provides a complete inventory of a vital Hispanic community in the United States, a community to which Spain naturally feels very connected.

We Spaniards feel close to all that is Hispanic. We are the Hispanics on the other side of the Atlantic—the European Hispanics.

Many factors connect Spain to the United States. Of the many reasons which motivate us to enrich and expand our relations in all areas, one of the most compelling is the existence in the United States of a community with which Spaniards share a common language, culture, and history.

It is Spain's desire to expand its relations with the Hispanic community in the United States, to become better acquainted with this community and to undertake joint projects for our mutual benefit. Such projects would not be solely of an economic nature, but would also include the areas of education, culture, and science.

Latin America and Spain made a qualitative leap in their relations many years ago. History and culture are no longer the only factors which unite our two societies; economic relations now also play a prominent role. Today, Spain is the second largest foreign investor in Latin America and has combined its own prosperity with the equity development of the Continent.

Of course, the United States should be part of the expansion of Spain's relations with the hemisphere. Within the United States, these growing relations should include an emerging Hispanic population which has been progressively assuming functions of higher responsibility in the government and society of that great country and which is also an integral part of the worldwide Hispanic family.

In addition to observing the quantitative growth of the Hispanic community, we are interested in learning more about the new dynamics it has created, such as the affirmation of Hispanic values, the community's continuing relationship with its countries of origin, and the very relevant role the Hispanic community can play in the relations among the United States, Latin America, and Spain.

Today we celebrate the extraordinary contribution made by the Yearbook. This is evident in the latest edition, which affirms the vitality of the Hispanic community. The Yearbook is an indispensable tool for all of us who desire to work closely with this community. Many thanks to you for all your efforts.

José Luis Rodríguez Zapatero

Association of American Chambers of Commerce in Latin America (AACCLA)
Asociación de Cámaras Americanas de Comercio en América Latina

ARGENTINA

AMERICAN CHAMBER OF COMMERCE IN ARGENTINA

Viamonte 1133, Piso 8
Buenos Aires, Argentina 1053
Felix Zumelzu, CEO
Tel: (54)11-4371-4500
Fax: (54) 11-4371-8400
Email: amcham@amchamar.com.ar
Web: www.amchamar.com.ar

US Mailing Address
8307 NW 68th St. #1423, Miami
Commercial Center
Miami, FL 33102-5743

BOLIVIA

AMERICAN CHAMBER OF COMMERCE OF BOLIVIA

P.O. Box 8268 #3
Av. 6 de Agosto, entre Bellisaria Salinas y
Pedro Zalizar, Edificio Hilda
La Paz, Bolivia
Ana María Galindo de Paz, General Manager
Tel: (59) 12-244-3939
Fax: (59) 12-244-3972
Email: a.m.galindo@amchambolivia.com
Web: www.amchambolivia.com

BRAZIL

AMERICAN CHAMBER OF COMMERCE FOR BRAZIL

Rio de Janeiro
Caixa Postal 916
Praça Pio X-15, 5th Fl.
Rio de Janeiro, Brazil 20040
Sergio Raposo, CEO
Tel: (55) 21-2203-2477
Fax: (55) 21-2223-0438
Email: foxtrail@amchamrio.com.br
Web: www.amchamrio.com.br

Sao Paulo
Rua da Paz 1431, Chácara Santo Antonio
São Paulo, Brazil 04713-001
Arthur Vasconcellos, Executive Director
Tel: (55) 11-5180-3804
Fax: (55) 11-5180-3777
Email: vasco@amcham.com.br
Web: www.amcham.com.br

CHILE

CHILEAN - AMERICAN CHAMBER OF COMMERCE

P.O. Box Casilla 82, Santiago 34

Av. Pdte. Kennedy 5735,
Oficina 201, Las Condes
Santiago, Chile
Jaime Bazán, CEO
Tel: (56) 2-290-9700
Fax: (56) 2-212-0515
Email: amcham@amchamchile.cl
Web: www.amchamchile.cl

COLOMBIA

COLOMBIAN - AMERICAN CHAMBER OF COMMERCE

Apartado Aereo 8008
Calle 98 #22-64, Oficina 1209
Bogotá, Colombia
Joseph Finnin, CEO
Tel: (57) 1-621-5042
Fax: (57) 1-621-6838
Email: direct@amchamcolombia.com.co
Web: www.amchamcolombia.com.co

Cali
Apartado Aereo 5943
Av. 5AN #17N-98 Edificio Nucleo
Professional, Oficina 503
Cali, Colombia
Ana Lucía Jaramillo V., Executive Director
Tel: (57) 2-667-2993
Fax: (57) 2-667-2992
Email: amcham-dir@uniweb.net.co
Web: www.amchamcolombia.com.co

Cartagena
Av. 1 Norte #3N-97
Cartagena, Colombia
Jaime Borda Martelo, President
Tel: (57) 5-667-2993
Fax: (57) 5-667-2992
Email: amcham-dir@uniweb.net.co
Web: www.amchamcolombia.com.co

Medellín
Apartado Aereo 66655
Calle 4 Sur #43A-195, Oficina 163, Centro
Ejecutivo el Poblado
Medellin, Colombia
Nicolás de Zubiría G., CEO
Tel: (57) 4-268-7491
Fax: (57) 4-268-3198
Email: Administrativa@amchambemed.com
Web: www.amchambermed.com

COSTA RICA

COSTA RICAN - AMERICAN CHAMBER OF COMMERCE

P.O. Box 4946
San Jose, Costa Rica 1000
Lynda Solar, CEO
Tel: (50) 6-220-2200

Fax: (50) 6-220-2300
Email: chamber@amcham.co.cr
Web: www.amcham.co.cr

US Mailing Address
P.O. Box 025216, SJO 1576
Miami, FL 33102-5216

DOMINICAN REPUBLIC

AMERICAN CHAMBER OF COMMERCE OF THE DOMINICAN REPUBLIC

Apartado Postal 95-2
Av. Sarasota #25, Torre Empresarial, Piso 6
Santo Domingo, Dominican Republic
William Malamud, CEO
Tel: (80) 9-381-0777
Fax: (80) 9-381-0303
Email: amcham@codetel.net.do
Web: www.amcham.org.do

US Mailing Address
P.O. Box 02-5256, EPS A-528
Miami, FL 33102

ECUADOR

ECUADORIAN - AMERICAN CHAMBER OF COMMERCE

Cuenca
Av. Octavio Chacon 1-55, Centro Comercial
Parque Industrial, 2do. Piso 2 #303-304
Cuenca, Ecuador
Geovany Osorio, CEO
Tel: (59) 3-786-1873
Fax: (59) 3-780-6512
Email: cceasecu@etapaonline.net.ec
Web: www.ecamcham.com

Guayaquil
Cdla. Kennedy Norte, Av. Francisco de
Orellana, Edificio Centrum, Piso 6
Guayaquil, Ecuador
Jorge Farah, CEO
Tel: (59) 34-269-3470
Fax: (59) 34-269-3465
Email: director@amchamecuador.org
Web: www.amchamecuador.org

Manta
Edif. Banco del Pichincha, 3er. Piso #302
Manta, Ecuador
Ana Lucía Cedeño, CEO
Tel: (59) 3-562-7386
Fax: (59) 3-562-7386
Email: camameri@interactive.net.ec
Web: www.ecamcham.com

Quito
La Niña y Av. 6 de Diciembre, Edificio
Multicentro, Piso 4

Quito, Ecuador
Roque Miño, CEO
Tel: (59) 32-250-7450
Fax: (59) 32-250-4571
Email: info@ecamcham.com
Web: www.ecamcham.com

EL SALVADOR

AMERICAN CHAMBER OF COMMERCE OF EL SALVADOR

Edificio World Trade Center II Tercer Nivel
89 Avenida Norte, Col. Escalon
San Salvador, El Salvador
Enzo Bettaglio, CEO
Tel: (50) 3-264-9494
Fax: (50) 3-263-9393
Email: ebettaglio@amchamsal.com
Web: www.amchamsal.com

GUATEMALA

AMERICAN CHAMBER OF COMMERCE IN GUATEMALA

5a Av. 5-55, zona 14,
Europlaza Torre I, Nivel 5
Guatemala City, Guatemala 01014
Carolina Castellanos, CEO
Tel: (50) 2-333-3899
Fax: (50) 2-368-3536
Email: director@amchamguate.com
Web: www.amchamguate.com

US Mailing Address
P.O. Box 440999, ID07-0120
Miami, FL 33126-1009

HAITI

AMERICAN CHAMBER OF COMMERCE & INDUSTRY IN HAITI

18, Rue Moise
Pétion-Ville, Haiti
Tel: (50) 9-511-3024
Email: info@amchamhaiti.org
Web: www.amchamhaiti.org

US Mailing address
P.O. Box 13486-Delmas
Port-au-Prince, Haiti

HONDURAS

HONDURAN - AMERICAN CHAMBER OF COMMERCE

Apartado Postal 1838
Hotel Honduras Maya
Tegucigalpa, Honduras
Patricia López, CEO

Source: Association of American Chambers of Commerce in Latin America. www.aaccla.org

Tel: (50) 4-232-6035
Fax: (50) 4-232-2031
Email: amcham1@honduras.quik.com
Web: www.amchamhonduras.org

San Pedro Sula
Edificio Park Plaza, Barrio Guamilito, 5 y 6
Calle 11 Ave. N.O. Local # 12
San Pedro Sula, Honduras
Tel: (50) 4-557-6402
Fax: (50) 4-557-7634
Email: amchamservices@sulanet.net
Web: www.amcham.hn2.com

JAMAICA

AMERICAN CHAMBER OF COMMERCE OF JAMAICA

Jamaica Pegasus Hotel #127,
81 Knutsford Blvd.
Kingston 5, Jamaica
Becky Stockhausen, Executive Director
Tel: (87) 6-929-7866
Fax: (87) 6-929-8597
Email: amcham@cwjamaica.com
Web: www.amchamjamaica.org

MEXICO

AMERICAN CHAMBER OF COMMERCE OF MEXICO

Guadalajara
Av. Moctezuma 442,
Col. Jardines del Sol, Zapopan
Jalisco, Mexico 45050
Tel: (52) 33-3634-6606
Fax: (52) 33-3634-7374
Email: direccion_gdl@amcham.com.mx
Web: www.amcham.com.mx

Mexico D.F.
Lucerna 78-4
Mexico D.F., Mexico 06600

Jack Sweeney, EVP and CEO
Tel: (52) 55-5141-3800
Fax: (52) 55-5703-3908
Email: amchammx@amcham.com.mx
Web: www.amcham.com.mx

Monterrey
Río Manzanarez 434 Oriente, Col. del Valle
Garza Garcia, N.L., Mexico 66220
Tel: (52) 81-8114-2000
Fax: (52) 81-8114-2100
Email: socios_mty@amcham.com.mx
Web: www.amcham.com.mx

US Mailing Address
P.O. Box 60326
Houston, TX 77205-0326

NICARAGUA

AMERICAN CHAMBER OF COMMERCE OF NICARAGUA

Apartado Postal 2720
Managua, Nicaragua
Marcia Salazar, CEO
Tel: (50) 5-267-3099
Fax: (50) 5-267-3098
Email: amcham@amchamnic.org.ni
Web: www.amchamnic.org.ni

PANAMA

AMERICAN CHAMBER OF COMMERCE & INDUSTRY OF PANAMA

Apartado Postal 168 Estafeta Balboa
Panama, Panama
David Hunt, CEO
Tel: (50) 7-269-3881
Fax: (50) 7-223-3508
Email: amcham@panamcham.com
Web: www.panamcham.com

PARAGUAY

PARAGUAYAN - AMERICAN CHAMBER OF COMMERCE

Gral. Díaz 521, Piso 4, Edificio El Faro International
Asuncion, Paraguay
Gerald McCulloch, CEO
Tel: (595) (21) 442-135/6
Fax: (59) 52-144-2135
Email: pamchamb@conexion.com.py
Web: www.pamcham.com.py

Ciudad del Este
Av. Boqueron 803, 2do. Piso
Ciudad del Este, Paraguay
Tel: (59) 56-151-2287
Fax: (59) 56-151-2228
Web: www.pamcham.com.py

PERU

AMERICAN CHAMBER OF COMMERCE OF PERU

Av. Ricardo Palma 836, Miraflores
Lima 18, Peru
Aldo Defilippi, CEO
Tel: (51) 1-241-0708
Fax: (51) 1-241-0709
Email: adefilippi@amcham.org.pe
Web: www.amcham.org.pe

TRINIDAD & TOBAGO

AMERICAN CHAMBER OF COMMERCE OF TRINIDAD & TOBAGO

Hilton Trinidad and Conference Center
#350-352, Lady Young Rd.
Port of Spain, Trinidad & Tobago

Lisa Chamely-Aqui, CEO
Tel: (86) 8-627-8570
Fax: (86) 8-627-7405
Email: lchamley@amchamtt.com
Web: www.amchamtt.com

URUGUAY

CHAMBER OF COMMERCE URUGUAY - USA

Plaza Independencia 831, Oficina 209,
Edificio Plaza Mayor
Montevideo, Uruguay 11100
Magdalena Aonzo, CEO
Tel: (59) 82-908-9186
Fax: (59) 82-908-9187
Email: maonzo@ccuruguayusa.com
Web: www.ccuruguayusa.com

VENEZUELA

VENEZUELAN - AMERICAN CHAMBER OF COMMERCE & INDUSTRY

Apartado 5181
Torre Credival, Piso 10, 2da Av. de Campo Alegre, Campo Alegre
Caracas, Venezuela 1010-A
Antonio Herrera-Vaillant, CEO
Tel: (58) 221-263-0833
Fax: (58) 212-263-1829
Email: aherrera@venamcham.org
Web: www.venamcham.org

US Mailing Address
P.O. Box 020010, S-522
Jet International C.A.
Miami, FL 33102-0010

Spanish Chambers of Commerce
Cámaras de comercio españolas

A CORUÑA
Cámara de Comercio, Industria y Navegación
C/ Alameda, 30-32 - 1º
Apartado de Correos 201
A Coruña, 15003
D. José Antonio Quiroga y Piñeyro, Presidente
D. Gonzalo Ortíz Amor, Director General/
Secretario General
Tel: (981) 216-074 Fax: (981) 225-208
Email: ccincoruna@camaras.org
Web: www.camaracoruna.com

ALAVA (VICTORIA)
Cámara de Comercio e Industria
C/ Eduardo Dato, 38
Apartado de Correos: 298
Alava, 01005
D. Josu de Lapatza Urbiola, Presidente
D. Lorenzo Bergareche Capa, Secretario
General
Tel: (945) 141-800 Fax: (945) 143-156
Email: cocia@camaradealava.com

ALBACETE
Cámara de Comercio e Industria
C/ Tesifonte Gallego, 22
Albacete, 02002
D. Vicente Muñoz Chacón, Presidente
D. Esteban Villanueva Soriano, Secretario
General
Tel: (967) 590-093 Fax: (967) 235-345
Email: ccialbacete@camaras.org
Web: www.camaranet.com/albacete/

ALCOY (ALICANTE)
Cámara de Comercio e Industria
C/ Sant Francesc, 10
Alcoy, 03801
D. Enrique Rico Ferrer, Presidente
Dª Ana Mª Moltó Anduix, Secretaria General
en Funciones
Tel: (965) 549-100 Fax:: (965) 549-099
E.mail: camara@camaraalcoy.net

ALICANTE
Cámara de Comercio, Industria y Navegación
C/ San Fernando, 4
Alicante, 03002
D. Antonio Fernández Valenzuela, Presidente
D. Andrés Sevila Castelló, Secretario General
Tel: (965) 201-133 Fax: (965) 201-457
Email: general@camara-alc.es
Web: www.camaralicante.com

ALMERIA
Cámara de Comercio, Industria y Navegación
C/ Conde Ofalia, 22 - Entlo.
Almeria, 04001
D. José Antonio Flores Rubio, Presidente

D. José María Cosano Pérez, Secretario
General
Tel: (950) 234-433 Fax: (950) 234-850
Email: info@camaradealmeria.es
Web: www.camaradealmeria.es

ANDUJAR, JAÉN
Cámara de Comercio e Industria
C/ San Francisco, 7-2º
Andujar, Jaén, 23740
D. Eduardo Criado García, Presidente
Da Ma José Moreno Díaz, Secretaria Adjunta
en Funciones
Tel: (953) 500-890 Fax: (953) 500-890

AREVALO, AVILA
Cámara de Comercio e Industria
Plaza El Salvador, 2-2º D
Arevalo, Avila, 05200
D. Angel Partearroyo Losada, Presidente
Da Ma del Rocío López Muñoyerro, Secretaria
Interina
Tel: (920) 300-072 Fax: (920) 303-723
Email: camara@arevalociudad.com
Web: www.arevalociudad.com

ASTORGA, LEÓN
Cámara de Comercio e Industria
Padres Redentoristas, 26
Astorga, León, 24700
D. Victorino González Ochoa, Presidente
D. Enrique García Tomassoni, Secretario
General
Tel: (987) 602-423 Fax: (987) 618-709
Email: secretaria@camaraastorga.com
Web: www.astorga.com/empresa/ccomerci.htm

AVILA
Cámara de Comercio e Industria
C/ Eduardo Marquina, 6
Avila, 05001
D. José Angel Domínguez González,
Presidente
D. Ignacio Alberto Jiménez Muñoz, Secretario
General
Tel: (920) 352-300 Fax: (920) 255-159
Email: ca0500@camaras.org
Web: www.camaradeavila.com

AVILÉS, ASTURIAS
Cámara de Comercio, Industria y Navegación
Plaza de Camposagrado, 1
Avilés, Asturias, 33400
D. Antonio Sabino y García-González,
Presidente
D. Carlos Rodríguez de la Torre Rodríguez,
Secretario General
Tel: (985) 544-111 Fax: (985) 541-528
Email: ccinaviles@camaras.org
Web: www.avilescamara.com

AYAMONTE, HUELVA
Cámara de Comercio, Industria y Navegación
Muelle de Portugal, 41- 2º
Apartado de Correos 58
Ayamonte, Huelva, 21400
D. Javier González Hernández, Presidente
Da Carmen Ma Bañez Jiménez, Secretaria
General en Funciones
Tel: (959) 320-050 Fax: (959) 320-050
Web: www.camara-ayamonte.com

BADAJOZ
Cámara de Comercio e Industria
Avda. Europa, 4
Badajoz, 06004
D. Fernando Herrera Tabares, Presidente
D. Matias Sánchez Pocostales, Secretario
General
Tel: (924) 234-600 Fax: (924) 243-853
Email: camarabadajoz@camaras.org
Web: www.camarabadajoz.org

BARCELONA
**Consejo de Cámaras Oficiales de Comercio,
Industria y Navegación de Cataluña**
Avda. Diagonal, 452-454
Barcelona, 08006
D. Miquel Valls Maseda, Presidente
D. Xavier Carbonell Roura, Director Gerente
Dª Mª Dolors Colomer Pous, Secretaria General
Tel: (934) 169-300 Fax: (934) 169-301
Email: consell@cambrescat.es
Web: www.cambrescat.es

BEJAR, SALAMANCA
Cámara de Comercio e Industria
C/ Colón, 33, 1
Bejar, Salamanca, 37700
D. Manuel Bruno Nevado, Presidente
D. Eduardo Miralles Soria, Secretario Interino
Tel: (923) 400-610 Fax: (923) 403-783
Email: cocibejar@zentro.com
Web: www.cocicyl.es/e-index_
DirectorioCamaras_Bejar.html

BILBAO
Cámara de Comercio, Industria y Navegación
Gran Vía, 13
Bilbao, 48001
D.Ignacio Ma Echeberría Monteberría,
Presidente
D. Juan Luis Laskurain Argarate, Director
General
D. Juan Carlos Landeta Basterrechea,
Secretario General
Tel: (944) 706-500 Fax: (944) 436-171
Email: info@camarabilbao.com
Web: www.camarabilbao.com

BRIVIESCA, BURGOS
Cámara de Comercio e Industria
C/ Medina, 2
Briviesca, Burgos, 09240
D. José Ramón Temiño Santaolalla, Presidente
D. José María Menor Monasterio, Secretario
General
Tel: (947) 590-243 Fax: (947) 592-700
Email: camarabriviesca@ctv.es
Web: www.cocicyl.es/e-index_
DirectorioCamaras_Briviesca.html

BURGOS
Cámara de Comercio e Industria
C/ San Carlos, 1-1o
Apartado de Correos 186
Burgos, 09003
D. Antonio Miguel Méndez Pozo, Presidente
D. José Ma Vicente Domingo, Secretario
General
Dª Mª Jesús Martínez Urrutia, Vicesecretaria
General
Tel: (947) 257-420 Fax: (947) 263-626
Email: correo@camaraburgos.com
Web: www.camaraburgos.com

CÁCERES
Cámara de Comercio e Industria
Plaza del Doctor Durán, 2
Apartado de Correos: 100
Cáceres, 10003
D. José Jarones Santos, Presidente
D. Teófilo Amores Mendoza, Secretario General
Tel: (927) 627-108 Fax: (927) 627-109
Email: correo@camaracaceres.es
Web: www.camaracaceres.es

CÁDIZ
Cámara de Comercio, Industria y Navegación
C/ Antonio López, 4
Cádiz, 11004
D. Ángel Juan Pascual, Presidente
D. Adolfo González-Santiago Cabadas,
Secretario General
Tel: (956) 010-000 Fax: (956) 250-710
Email: secretariocadiz@camaranet.com
Web: www.camaracadiz.com

CAMPO DE GIBRALTAR, ALGECIRAS
Cámara de Comercio, Industria y Navegacón
Avda. Virgen del Carmen, 15-1o
Campo de Gibraltar, Algeciras, 11201
D. Carlos Enrique Fenoy Rico, Presidente
D. Manuel Tinoco Tinoco, Secretario General
Tel: (956) 655-811 Fax: (956) 655-960
Email: camara@camaracampodegibraltar.com
Web: www.camaracampodegibraltar.com

CANTABRIA, SANTANDER
Cámara de Comercio, Industria y Navegación
Plaza de Velarde, 5
Cantabria, Santander, 39001
D. Modesto Piñeiro García-Lago, Presidente
Da Mar Cervera Pérez, Secretaria General en
Funciones
Tel: (942) 318-000 Fax: (942) 314-310
Email: ccincantabria@camaracant.es
Web: www.camaracantabria.com

CARTAGENA, MURCIA
Cámara de Comercio, Industria y Navegación
Muelle Alfonso XII, s/n
Apartado de correos: 132
Cartagena, Murcia, 30201
D. Manuel Pérez de Lema Gómez, Presidente
D. Ramiro Alonso Gutiérrez, Secretario General
Tel: (968) 507-050/54/58 Fax: (968) 122-692
Email: admin@cocin-cartagena.es
Web: www.cocin-cartagena.es

CASTELLON
Cámara de Comercio, Industria y Navegación
Avda. Hermanos Bou, 79
Castellon, 12003
D. Salvador Martí Huguet, Presidente
D. Vicente Casañ, Secretario General en
Funciones
Tel: (964) 356-500 Fax: (964) 356-510
Email: fgarcia@camaracs.es
Web: www.camaracs.es

CEUTA
Cámara de Comercio, Industria y Navegación
C/ Dueñas, 2
Ceuta, 51001
D. Luis Moreno Naranjo, Presidente
Da. María del Rosario Espinosa Suárez,
Secretaria General Accidental
Tel: (956) 509-590 Fax: (956) 509-589
Email: cocinceuta@camaras.org
Web: www.camaraceuta.org

CIUDAD REAL
Cámara de Comercio e Industria
C/ Lanza, 2
Apartado Correos: 306
Ciudad, 13004
D. Juan Antonio León Triviño, Presidente
D. Gunther Lorenz, Director General
D. Jose Cano Martinez, Secretario General
Tel: (926) 274-444 Fax: (926) 253-813
Email: info@camaracr.org
Web: www.camaracr.org

CORDOBA
Cámara de Comercio e Industria
C/ Peréz de Castro, 1
Cordoba, 14003
D. Luis Carreto Clavo, Presidente
D. Luis Díaz Alonso, Director-Gerente
D. José Enriquez Fernandéz de Castillejo y
Cerezo, Secretario General
Tel: (957) 296-199 Fax: (957) 202-106
Email: camaracordoba@telefonica.net

CUENCA
Cámara de Comercio e Industria
C/ Calderón de la Barca, 30
Apartado Correos: 25
Cuenca, 16001
D. Agustín M. Tello Arcas, Presidente
D. Carlos Martínez García, Secretario General
Tel: (969) 222-351 Fax: (969) 228-923
Email: correo@camaracuenca.org
Web: www.camaracuenca.org

FERROL, A CORUÑA
Cámara de Comercio, Industria y Navegación
Recinto Ferial de Punta Arnela - A Malata, s/n
Ferrol, A Coruña, 15405
D. Francisco Cruz Senra, Presidente
D. Antonio González Lago, Secretario General
Tel: (981) 333-165 Fax: (981) 333-096
Email: info@camaraferrol.org
Web: www.camaraferrol.org

GIJÓN
Cámara de Comercio, Industria y Navegación
Carretera Piles al Infanzón, 652
Gijón, 33202
D. Guillermo Quirós Pintado, Presidente
Da Macarena García Fernández-Nespral,
Secretaria General
Tel: (985)180-180 Fax: (985) 180-106
Email: infocamara@camaragijon.com
Web: www.camaragijon.com

GIRONA
Cámara de Comercio, Industria y Navegación
C/ Gran Via Jaume I, 46
Apartado Correos 150
Girona, 17001
D. Antonio Hostench i Figueras, Presidente
D. Eduard Torrent Pairó, Director Gerente
D. Santiago Coquard Oriol, Secretario General
Tel: (972) 418-500 Fax: (972) 418-501
Email: girona@cambrescat.es
Web: www.cambra.gi

GRANADA
Cámara de Comercio, Industria y Navegación
C/ Paz, 18
Apartado de Correos 291
Granada, 18002
D. Antonio Robles Lizancos, Presidente
D. Jaime Parra Parra, Gerente
D. Fernando Mir Gómez, Secretario General
Tel: (958) 536-152 Fax: (958) 536-292
Email: ccigranada@camaras.org
Web: www.camaragranada.org

GUADALAJARA
Cámara de Comercio e Industria
C/ Mayor, 28
Guadalajara, 19001
D. Manuel Jiménez Moya, Presidente
D. Carlos A. García Llorente, Secretario
General en Funciones
Tel: (949) 247-032 Fax: (949) 247-245
Email: mailto:cciguadalajara@camaras.org
Web: www.camaranet.com/guadalajara

GUIPÚZCOA (SAN SEBASTIÁN)
Cámara de Comercio, Industria y Navegación
Avda. Tolosa, 75
Guipúzcoa, 20018
D. José Mª Echarri Campo, Presidente
D. Félix Iraola Escrihuela, Director Gerente
Tel: (943) 000-300 Fax: (943) 000-266

HUELVA
Cámara de Comercio, Industria y Navegación
C/ Sor Angela de la Cruz, 1
Huelva, 21003
D. Antonio Ponce Fernández, Presidente
D. Arsenio Martínez Barea, Secretario General
en Funciones

Tel: (959) 245-900/43 Fax: (959) 245-699
Email: registro@camarahuelva.com
Web: www.camarahuelva.com

HUESCA
Cámara de Comercio e Industria
C/ Santo Angel de la Guarda, 7
Huesca, 22005
D. Antonio Ruspira Morraja, Presidente
D. Jose Luis Melendez Perez, Director Gerente
Tel: (974) 218-899 Fax: (974) 229-644
Email: camarahuesca@camarahuesca.com
Web: www.camarahuesca.com

JAEN
Cámara de Comercio e Industria
C/ Hurtado, 29,
Apartado Correos: 18
Jaen, 23001
D. Miguel Angel López Barea, Presidente
D. Manuel Luis Fernández Ruiz, Secretario
General
Tel: (953) 247-950 Fax: (953) 240-738
Email: secgeneral@camarajaen.com
Web: www.camarajaen.com

JEREZ DE LA FRONTERA, CÁDIZ
Cámara de Comercio e Industria
C/ Cádiz, 5,
Apartado Correos: 149
Jerez de la Frontera, Cádiz, 11407
D. Jesús Medina Cachero, Presidente
D. José Manuel Perea Rosado, Secretario
General
Tel: (956) 340-791 Fax: (956) 344-965
Email: camara@camarajerez.com
Web: www.camaraenaccion.com

LA RIOJA, LOGROÑO
Cámara de Comercio e Industria
C/ Portales, 12
La Rioja, Logroño, 26001
D. Jose Mª Ruiz-Alejos Herrero, Presidente
D. Luis Maraver Alonso, Secretario General
Tel: (941) 248-500 Fax: (941) 239-965
Email: camararioja@camararioja.com

LAS PALMAS
Cámara de Comercio, Industria y Navegación
C/ León y Castillo, 24
Las Palmas, 35003
D. José Miguel Suárez Gil, Presidente
Da Pilar Alcaide Azcona, Directora General
D. Luis Padrón López, Secretario General
Tel: (928) 391-045 Fax: (928) 362-350
Email: info@camaralp.es
Web: www.camaralaspalmas.org

LEÓN
Cámara de Comercio e Industria
C/ Fajeros, 1
Apartado Correos: 287
León, 24002
D. Manuel Lamelas Viloria, Presidente
D. Antonio Miguel Díaz Carro, Secretario
General
Tel: (987) 224-400/04 Fax: (987) 222-451
Email: ccileon@camaraleon.com
Web: www.camaraleon.com

LINARES, JAÉN
Cámara de Comercio e Industria
C/ Sagunto, 1
Apartado Correos: 143
Linares, Jaén, 23700

D. Alfonso L. Navarro Conde, Presidente
D. Manuel Valenzuela Villarrubia, Secretario
Interino
D. Raúl J. Caro Menéndez, Gerente
Tel: (953) 606-063 Fax: (953) 695-511
Email: camara@camaradelinares.org
Web: www.camaradelinares.org

LORCA, MURCIA
Cámara de Comercio e Industria
Plaza del Caño, 3
Apartado de Correos: 92
Lorca, Murcia, 30800
D. Eusebio Abellán Martínez, Presidente
D. Joaquín Gómez Quetglas, Secretario
General
Tel: (968) 477-488 Fax: (968) 477-416
Email: coci-lorca@cocin-murcia.es
Web: www.camaracomlorca.es

LUGO
Cámara de Comercio, Industria y Navegación
C/ Avda. de Ramón Ferreiro, 18
Lugo, 27002
D. Alfredo H. Mosteirín Castañer, Presidente
D. Alberto Fernández Piñeiro, Director General
D. Vicente Silva Meilán, Secretario General
Tel: (982) 284-300 Fax: (982) 244-301
Email: camara@camaralugo.com
Web: www.camaralugo.com

LL

LLEIDA
Cámara de Comercio e Industria
C/ Anselm Clave, 2
Lleida, 25007
D. Joan Simo Burgués, Presidente
D. Salvador Roig Bonet, Secretario General
Tel: (973) 236-161 Fax: (973) 247-467
Email: lleida@cambrescat.es
Web: www.cambralleida.com

M

MADRID
Cámara de Comercio e Industria
Ribera del Loira, 56-58
Madrid, 28042
D. Fernando Fernández-Tapias Román,
Presidente
D. José María Isardo Agüero, Director General
D. Alberto Durán Ruiz de Huidobro, Secretario
General
Tel: (91) 538-3500 Fax: (91) 538-3677
Email: cpd2@camaramadrid.es
Web: www.camaramadrid.es

MALAGA
Cámara de Comercio, Industria y Navegación
C/ Cortina de Muelle, 23 - Palacio de
Villalcazar
Malaga, 29015
D. Jerónimo Pérez Casero, Presidente
D. Agustín Palacios Luque, Secretario General
Tel: (951) 010-800 Fax: (952) 229-894
Email: info@camaramalaga.com
Web: www.camaramalaga.com

MANRESA
Cámara de Comercio e Industria
Plaza Pedregar, 1
Manresa, 08240
D. Jorge Santasusana Codina, Presidente
D. Joseph Ribera y Ferrer, Secretario General
Tel: (93) 872-4222 Fax: (93) 872-7766

Email: manresa@cambrescat.es
Web: www.cambramanresa.com

MELILLA
Cámara de Comercio, Industria y Navegación
C/ Miguel de Cervantes, 7
Melilla, 52001
Dª Margarita López Alméndariz, Presidenta
Dª Margarita Cerezo Fernández, Secretaria
General en Funciones
Tel: (952) 684-840 Fax: (952) 683-119
Email: ccinmelilla@camaras.org

MIRANDA DE EBRO, BURGOS
Cámara de Comercio e Industria
C/ Ronda del Ferrocarril, 31- 1º
Miranda de Ebro, Burgos, 09200
D. Ginés Clemente Ortíz, Presidente
Dna. Eva Lapera Ruíz, Secretaria General en
Funciones
Tel: (947) 335-200 Fax: (947) 313-593
Email: contactar@camaramiranda.com
Web: www.camaramiranda.com

MOTRIL, GRANADA
Cámara de Comercio, Industria y Navegación
C/ Catalanes, 4, bajo
Motril, Granada, 18600
D. José Luis Estévez López, Presidente
D. Antonio Rojas Ciurana, Secretario General
Tel: (958) 821-160 Fax: (958) 609-136
Email: ccimotril@camaras.org

MURCIA
Cámara de Comercio, Industria y Navegación
Plaza de San Bartolomé, 3
Murcia, 30004
D. Pedro García-Balibrea Martínez, Presidente
D. Enrique Torres Tortosa, Secretario General
en Funciones
Tel: (968) 229-400 Fax: (968) 229-424
Email: jperez@cocin-murcia.es
Web: www.cocin-murcia.es

O

ORIHUELA, ALICANTE
Cámara de Comercio e Industria
Avda. de la Vega, 22 - Entlo.
Orihuela, Alicante, 03300
D. Juan Fco. Cerdán Martínez, Presidente
D. Luciano Costa Andreu, Secretario General
Tel: (96) 674-3502 Fax: (96) 673-6730
Email: camaraor@dip-alicante.es

OURENSE
Cámara de Comercio e Industria
Avda. de la Habana, 30 bis
Ourense, 32003
D. Ovidio Fernández Ojea, Presidente
Dna. Covadonga Toca Carús, Secretaria
General en Funciones
Tel: (988) 233-116 Fax: (988) 233-088
Email: camara@camaraourense.com
Web: www.camaraourense.com

OVIEDO
Cámara de Comercio, Industria y Navegación
C/ Quintana, 32
Oviedo, 33009
D. Severino García Vigón, Presidente
D. Fernando Villabella Patallo, Secretario
General en Funciones
D. Javier Cuesta Menéndez, Director General
Tel: (985) 207-575 Fax: (985) 207-200
Email: correo@camara-ovi.es

Web: www.camara-ovi.es

P

PALAMOS, GIRONA
Cámara de Comercio, Industria y Navegación
Plaza de la Murada, 1
Palamos, Girona, 17230
D. José Colomer Trias, Presidente
D. David Sánchez Vencells, Secretario
Accidental
Tel: (972) 314-077 Fax: (972) 318-810
Email: palamos@cambrescat.es
Web: www.cambrescat.es/palamos/p-01.htm

PALENCIA
Cámara de Comercio e Industria
Plaza Pío XII, 7
Palencia, 34005
D. Vicente Villagrá Blanco, Presidente
D. Juan Carlos Garrán García, Secretario
General
Tel: (979) 165-051 Fax: (979) 730-970
Email: general@cocipa.es
Web: www.cocipa.es

PALMA DE MALLORCA
Cámara de Comercio, Industria y Navegación, Mallorca, Eivissa i Formentera
C/ Estudio General, 7
Palma de Mallorca, 07001
D. Miguel Lladó Oliver, Presidente
D. Antonio Grimalt Llofriu, Secretario General
Tel: (971) 710-188 Fax: (971) 726-302
Email: ccinmallorca@camaras.org
Web: www.cambresbalears.com

PAMPLONA, NAVARRA
Cámara de Comercio e Industria
C/ General Chinchilla, 4
Pamplona, Navarra, 31002
D. Francisco J. Taberna Jimenez, Presidente
D. Ignacio Galañena Sainz, Secretario General
Dna. Marta Vera Janín, Directora General
Tel: (948) 077-070 Fax: (948) 077-080
Email: comunicacion@camaranavarra.com
Web: www.camaranavarra.com

PONTEVEDRA
Cámara de Comercio, Industria y Navegación
C/ Jardines Vicenti, 4-2º
Pontevedra, 36001
D. Manuel Durán Couto, Presidente
Dna. María del Rosario Lorenzo Pontevedra,
Secretaria General
Tel: (986) 866-303 Fax: (986) 862-643
Email: ccinpontevedra@camaras.org
Web: www.camaras.org/pontevedra

R

REUS, TARRAGONA
Cámara de Comercio e Industria
C/ Boule, 2
Reus, Tarragona, 43201
D. Francesc Cabré Masdeu, Presidente
D. Juan José Sardá Arasa, Secretario General
Tel: (977) 338-080 Fax: (977) 315-810
Email: reus@cambrescat.es
Web: www.cambrareus.org

S

SABADELL
Cámara de Comercio e Industria
C/ Alfonso XIII, 45
Sabadell, 08202

D. Antonio Peñarroya Trench, Presidente
D. Eduard Borras Finestres, Secretario General
D. Jaime Bercial Casbas, Director Gerente
Tel: (937) 451-255 Fax: (937) 451-256
Email: sabadell@cambrescat.es
Web: www.cambrasabadell.org

SALAMANCA
Cámara de Comercio e Industria
Plaza de Sexmeros, 2
Salamanca, 37001
D. José Luis Zarza Sánchez, Presidente
D. Gabriel Hortal Castaño, Secretario General
Tel: (923) 211-797 Fax: (923) 280-146
Email: secretaria@camarasalamanca.com
Web: www.camarasalamanca.com

SANT FELIU DE GUIXOLS, GIRONA
Cámara de Comercio, Industria y Navegación
Paseo del Mar, 40
Sant Feliu de Guixols, Girona, 17220
D. Joan Puig i Valls, Presidente
D. Martín Rondos Casas, Secretario General
Tel: (972) 320-884 Fax: (972) 325-450
Email: stfeliu@cambrescat.es
Web: www.cambrescat.es/stfeliu/p-01.htm

SANTA CRUZ DE TENERIFE
Cámara de Comercio, Industria y Navegación
Plaza de la Candelaria, 6
Santa Cruz de Tenerife, 38003
D. Ignacio González Martín, Presidente
D. Rafael Espejo Castro, Secretario General
D. Vicente Dorta Antequera, Director General
Tel: (922) 100-400 Fax: (922) 245-270
Email: info@camaratenerife.com
Web: www.camaratenerife.com

SANTIAGO DE COMPOSTELA, A CORUNA
Cámara de Comercio, Industria y Navegación
C/ San Pedro de Mezonzo, 44 - bajo
Santiago de Compostela, A Coruna, 15701
D. Jesús Asorey Carril, Presidente
D. Fernando Barros Fornos, Secretario General
Adjunto
D. Filomena Casal Gomez, Secretaria General
Tel: (981) 596-800/50 Fax: (981) 590-322
Email: ccinsantiago@camaras.org
Web: www.camaranet.com/santiago

SEGOVIA
Cámara de Comercio e Industria
C/ San Francisco, 32
(Ed. Casa del Sello de Panos)
Segovia, 40001
D. Jesús Postigo Quintana, Presidente
D. Rafael Aznar Mendiola, Secretario General
D. Carlos Besteiro Rivas, Director General
Tel: (921) 432-300/11 Fax: (921) 430-563
Email: raznar@camaras.org
Web: www.camarasegovia.org

SEVILLA
Cámara de Comercio, Industria y Navegación
Plaza de la Contratación, 8
Sevilla, 41004
D. Ramón Contreras Ramos, Presidente
D. Antonio Mª Fernández Palacios, Secretario
General
D. Salvador Fernandez Sala, Gerente
Tel: (954) 211-005 Fax: (954) 225-619
Email: ccinsevilla@camaras.org
Web: www.camaradesevilla.com

SORIA
Cámara de Comercio e Industria
C/ Venerable Carabantes, 1C - 1º
Soria, 42003
D. Jesús Moya Moya, Presidente
D. Jose Ignacio Diez Garcia, Secretario General
Accidental

Tel: (975) 213-944 Fax: (975) 228-619
Email: ccisoria@camarasoria.com
Web: www.camarasoria.com

T

TARRAGONA
Cámara de Comercio, Industria y Navegación
Avenida Pau Casals, 17
Tarragona, 43003
D. Javier Artal Morillo, Presidente
D. José Ramón Gispert Magarolas, Secretario
General
Tel: (977) 219-676 Fax: (977) 240-900
Email: tarragona@cambrescat.es
Web: www.bambratgn.com

TARREGA, LLEIDA
Cámara de Comercio e Industria
Plaza Mayor, 4
Tarrega, Lleida, 25300
Dª. Silvia Falip Tolo, Presidenta
Dª Mª Jesús Grau Martínez, Secretaria General
Tel: (973) 314-327 Fax: (973) 314-355
Email: tarrega@cambrescat.es
Web: www.cambratarrega.com

TERRASSA, BARCELONA
Cámara de Comercio e Industria
C/ Blasco de Garay, 29/49
Terrassa, Barcelona, 08224
D. Alberto Vilardell Figueras, Presidente
D. Josep Prats i Llopart, Director Gerente
Dª Marta Torrents i Fenoy, Secretaria General
en Funciones
Tel: (937) 339-833 Fax: (937) 891-165
Email: info@cambraterrassa.es
Web: www.cambraterrassa.es

TERUEL
Cámara de Comercio e Industria
C/ Amantes, 17
Teruel, 44001
D. Florencio Muñoz Rodríguez, Presidente
D. Santiago Ligros Mancho, Secretario General
Tel: (978) 618-191 Fax: (978) 618-192
Email: camara.teruel@jet.es
Web: www.camarateruel.com

TOLEDO
Cámara de Comercio e Industria
Plaza de San Vicente, 3
Toledo, 45001
D. Fernando Jerez Alonso, Presidente
D. Jose M Calvo Cirujano, Secretario General
D. Joaquin Echevarria Cuesta, Director General
Tel: (925) 280-111 Fax: (925) 280-004
Email: ccitoledo@infonegociio.com
Web: www.camaranet.com/toledo

TORRELAVEGA, CANTABRIA
Cámara de Comercio e Industria
C/ Ruíz Tagle, 6
Torrelavega, Cantabria, 39300
D. Ramón González Rosalía, Presidente
D. Emilio Laborda Valle, Secretario General
D. Enrique Portilla Alonso, Secretario Adjunto
Tel: (942) 890-162 Fax: (942) 884-083
Email: coci.torrelavega@tsai.es
Web: www.camaratorrelavega.com

TORTOSA, TARRAGONA
Cámara de Comercio, Industria y Navegación
C/ Cervantes, 7
Tortosa, Tarragona, 43500
D. Valetín Faura Sanmartín, Presidente
D. Jaume Sabaté Verge, Secretario General
D. Francesc Minguell Panisello, Director
Gerente

Tel: (977) 441-537 Fax: (977) 444-370
Email: tortosa@cambrescat.es
Web: www.cambratortosa.com

TUY, PONTEVEDRA
Cámara de Comercio, Industria y Navegación
C/ Augusto González Besada, 15 - 1° Derecha.
Tui, Pontevedra, 36700
D. Carlos Dagá Escribano, Presidente
D. Francisco Javier Pérez Alves, Secretario
General
Tel: (986) 600-216 Fax: (986) 601-512
Email: camaratui@camaratui.com
Web: www.camaratui.com

VALENCIA
Cámara de Comercio, Industria y Navegación
C/ Poeta Querol, 15
Valencia, 46002
D. Arturo Virosque Ruiz, Presidente
D. Antonio Rico Gil, Secretario General
D. Fernando Zárraga Quintana, Director
Tel: (963) 103-900 Fax: (963) 516-349
Email: info@camaravalencia.com
Web: www.camaravalencia.com

VALLADOLID
Cámara de Comercio e Industria
Avda. Ramón Pradera, s/n
Valladolid, 47009
D. Vicente Garrido Capa, Presidente
D. Federico Sanz Rubiales, Secretario General
D. Arturo Rodríguez-Monsalve Garrigós,
Director General
Tel: (983) 370-400 Fax: (983) 370-660
Email: camaravalladolid@camaravalladolid.
com
Web: www.camaravalladolid.com

VALLADOLID
Consejo Regional de Cámaras de Comercio e
Industria de Castilla y León
Plaza San Juan Bautista de la Salle, 2
- Entreplanta
Valladolid, 47006
D.Manuel Vidal Gutiérrez, Presidente
D. Valentín Fernández-Soto Vélez , Director
Tel: (983) 374-859/12 Fax: (983) 374-969
Email: camarasclm@teleline.es
Web: www.cocicyl.es

VALLS
Cámara de Comercio e Industria
C/ Jacint Verdaguer, 1, 2n
Valls, 43800

D. Marcelli Morera Figuerola, Presidente
D. Rafael Castells Paris, Secretario General
Tel: (977) 600-909 Fax: (977) 606-456
Email: valls@cambrescat.es
Web: www.cambravalls.com

VIGO
Cámara de Comercio, Industria y Navegación
C/ Velazquez Moreno, 29 - 3 y 4 (Galerias
Duran)
Vigo, 36202
D. José García Costas, Presidente
D. Manuel Fernández Pool, Secretario General
Accidental
D. José Manuel García Orois, Director General
Tel: (986) 432-533 Fax: (986) 435-659
Email: camaravigo@camaravigo.com
Web: www.camaravigo.com

VILAGARCIA DE AROUSA, PONTEVEDRA
Cámara de Comercio, Industria y Navegación
Avda. Doctor Tourón, 48
Vilagarcia de Arousa, Pontevedra, 36600
D. Carlos Oubiña Portas, Presidente
D. Emilio Cores Arenaz, Secretario General
Tel: (986) 565-286 Fax: (986) 500-621

Email: camaravilagarcia@camaravilagarcia.
com

Z

ZAMORA
Cámara de Comercio e Industria
C/ Pelayo, 6
Zamora, 49014
D. Manuel Vidal Gutiérrez, Presidente
D. Francisco J. Díaz Rincón, Secretario
General
Tel: (980) 530-050 Fax: (980) 518-594
Email: general@camarazamora.com

ZARAGOZA
Cámara de Comercio e Industria
C/ Isabel Católica, 2 (antigua Feria de
Muestras)
Zaragoza, 50009
D. Manuel Teruel Izquierdo, Presidente
D. Luis Fernandez Ordonez, Secretario General
D. Jose Miguel Sanchez Munoz, Director
General
Tel: (976) 306-161 Fax: (976) 357-945
Email: cci@camarazaragoza.com
Web: www.camarazaragoza.com

US Citizenship and Immigration Services continued from p 200

continued from p 200

P.O. Box 851804
Mesquite, TX 75185-1804
Tel: (800) 375-5283
Web: http://uscis.gov
Services: Form I-485, Application to Register
Permanent Residence or to Adjust Status;
I-181, Adjustment

P.O. Box 852211
Mesquite, TX 75185-2211
Tel: (800) 375-5283
Web: http://uscis.gov
Services: Form I-129, Non-Immigrant
Petition

P.O. Box 850919
Mesquite, TX 75185-0919
Tel: (800) 375-5283
Web: http://uscis.gov
Services: Form I-130, Alien Relative Petition

P.O. Box 851892
Mesquite, TX 75185-1892
Tel: (800) 375-5283
Web: http://uscis.gov
Services: Form I-589, Application For Asylum,
I-213, FD258

P.O. Box 852939
Mesquite, TX 75185-2939
Tel: (800) 375-5283
Web: http://uscis.gov
Services: Form I-140 Immigrant Petition
for Alien Worker (if concurrently filed with
I-485)

P.O. Box 852135
Mesquite, TX 75185-2135
Tel: (800) 375-5283
Web: http://uscis.gov
Services: Form I-140, Immigrant Petition
for Alien Worker (if filed alone); I-290
A&B, Notice of Appeal to the Administrative
Appeals Unit (AAU); Form I-360, Petition for
Amerasian, Widow(er), or Special Immigrant;
Form I-526, Immigrant Petition By Alien
Entrepreneur; Form I-829, Petition by
Entrepreneur to Remove Conditions.

P.O. Box 851443
Mesquite, TX 75185-1443
Tel: (800) 375-5283
Web: http://uscis.gov
Services: Form I-90, Application to Replace
Permanent Resident.

P.O. Box 851983
Mesquite, TX 75185-1983
Tel: (800) 375-5283
Web: http://uscis.gov
Services: Form I-90, Application to Replace
Permanent Resident - E-Filing

P.O. Box 850965
Mesquite, TX 75185-0965
Tel: (800) 375-5283
Web: http://uscis.gov
Services: Form I-129F, Petition for Alien
Fiance(e); Form I-212, Application for
Permission to Reapply for Admission into
the US. After Deportation or Removal;
Form I-612, Application for Waiver of the
Foreign Residence Requirement; Form I-
751, Petition to Remove the Conditions on
Residence; I-817, Application for Family Unity
Benefits; All I-72 and RFE Responses.

P.O. Box 279030
Dallas, TX 75227-0930
Tel: (800) 375-5283
Web: http://uscis.gov
Services: Premium Processing

P.O. Box 850891
Mesquite, TX 75185-0891
Tel: (800) 375-5283
Web: http://uscis.gov
Services: Address and Attorney Change
Notification

P.O. Box 851488
Mesquite, TX 75185-1488
Tel: (800) 375-5283
Web: http://uscis.gov
Services: General Correspondence

UTAH

SALT LAKE CITY APPLICATION SUPPORT
CENTER (ASC)
5536 South 1900 W. St. #C
Taylorsville, UT 84118
Tel: (800) 375-5283
Web: http://uscis.gov
Please, be sure to have an appointment letter
to appear for fingerprinting.

SALT LAKE CITY SUB OFFICE

5272 S. College Dr. #100
Murray, UT 84123
Allan Speirs, Officer in Charge
Tel: (800) 375-5283
Web: http://uscis.gov
Service area: the Salt Lake City Sub Office serves the entire State of Utah. To speak with an Immigration Information Officer, you must obtain a ticket, available on a first-come, first-served basis in the lobby of the office.

VERMONT

ST. ALBANS APPLICATION SUPPORT CENTER (ASC)

64 Gricebrook Rd.
St. Albans, VT 05478
Tel: (800) 375-5283
Web: http://uscis.gov
Please, be sure to have an appointment letter to appear for fingerprinting.

ST. ALBANS SUB OFFICE

64 Gricebrook Rd.
Saint Albans, VT 05478
Tel: (800) 375-5283
Web: http://uscis.gov
An Immigration Information Officer is located at the front counter. It is not necessary to take a number for assistance.

VERMONT SERVICE CENTER

75 Lower Welden St.
Saint Albans, VT 05479
Paul Novak, Director
Tel: (800) 375-5283
Web: http://uscis.gov
VSC no longer has a public information window available for walk-in questions.

VIRGIN ISLANDS

CHARLOTTE AMALIE SUB OFFICE

Nisky Ctr., #1A 1st Fl. South
Charlotte Amalie, St. Thomas, VI 00802
Jerome Kettles, Officer in Charge
Tel: (800) 375-5283
Web: http://uscis.gov
Service area: the Charlotte Amalie Sub Office serves St. Thomas and St. John, US Virgin Islands.

ST. CROIX APPLICATION SUPPORT CENTER (ASC)

Sunny Isles Shopping Ctr.
Christiansted, St. Croix, VI 00823
Tel: (800) 375-5283
Web: http://uscis.gov
Please, be sure to have an appointment letter to appear for fingerprinting. Please note that this location cannot collect digital information for customers who wish to file their applications electronically.

ST. CROIX SUB OFFICE

Sunny Isle Shopping Ctr.
Christiansted, St. Croix, VI 00820
Carol Harry, Officer in Charge
Tel: (800) 375-5283
Web: http://uscis.gov

Service area: the St. Croix Sub Office serves the entire island of St. Croix, US Virgin Islands.

ST. THOMAS APPLICATION SUPPORT CENTER (ASC)

Nisky Ctr., #1A 1st Fl. South
Charlotte Amalie, St. Thomas, VI 00802
Tel: (800) 375-5283
Web: http://uscis.gov
Please, be sure to have an appointment letter to appear for fingerprinting.

VIRGINIA

ALEXANDRIA APPLICATION SUPPORT CENTER (ASC)

8850 Richmond Hwy.
Alexandria, VA 22309-1586
Tel: (800) 375-5283
Web: http://uscis.gov
Please, be sure to have an appointment letter to appear for fingerprinting.

ARLINGTON ASYLUM OFFICE

1525 Wilson Blvd. #300
Arlington, VA 22209
Marla J. Belvedere, Asylum Office Director
Tel: (800) 375-5283
Web: http://uscis.gov
Service area: the Asylum Office in Arlington has jurisdiction over the District of Columbia, the western portion of the State of Pennsylvania currently within the jurisdiction of the Pittsburgh Sub Office, and the States of Maryland, Virginia, West Virginia, North Carolina, Georgia, Alabama, and South Carolina.

NORFOLK SUB OFFICE

5280 Henneman Dr.
Norfolk, VA 23513
Tel: (800) 375-5283
Web: http://uscis.gov
Service area: the Norfolk Sub Office serves the residents of southeastern Virginia including the cities and/or counties of Chesapeake, Fredericksburg, Richmond, Prince Edwards, Rockville, Williamsburg, Hampton Roads, Accomack, and Mecklenburg.

WASHINGTON DISTRICT OFFICE

4420 N. Fairfax Dr.
Arlington, VA 22203
Phyllis Howard, District Director
Tel: (800) 375-5283
Web: http://uscis.gov
Service area: the District of Columbia and the Commonwealth of Virginia. This office is responsible for processing most immigration benefit applications (such as legal residence and naturalization), and enforcing US immigration law, for the entire state of Virginia and the District of Columbia. To speak with an Immigration Information Officer, you may make an appointment via the Internet at www.infopass.uscis.gov.

WASHINGTON

RICHLAND APPLICATION SUPPORT CENTER (ASC)

825 Jadwin Ave. #165
Richland, WA 99352

Tel: (800) 375-5283
Web: http://uscis.gov
Please, be sure to have an appointment letter to appear for fingerprinting.

SEATTLE APPLICATION SUPPORT CENTER (ASC)

457 SW 148 St. #101
Burien, WA 98166
Tel: (800) 375-5283
Web: http://uscis.gov
Please, be sure to have an appointment letter to appear for fingerprinting.

SEATTLE DISTRICT OFFICE

815 Airport Way South
Seattle, WA 98134
Robert J. Okin, District Director
Tel: (800) 375-5283
Web: http://uscis.gov
Service area: Western Washington. To speak with an Immigration Information Officer, you may make an appointment via the Internet at www.infopass.uscis.gov.

SPOKANE APPLICATION SUPPORT CENTER (ASC)

920 W. Riverside #691
Spokane, WA 99201
Tel: (800) 375-5283
Web: http://uscis.gov
Please, be sure to have an appointment letter to appear for fingerprinting.

SPOKANE SUB OFFICE

US Courthouse, 920 W. Riverside #691
Spokane, WA 99201
Diana Wolder, Officer in Charge
Tel: (800) 375-5283
Web: http://uscis.gov
Service area: includes the following counties: In Washington: Adams, Benton, Chelan, Asotin, Columbia, Douglas, Ferry, Franklin, Garfield, Grant, Lincoln, Okanogan, Pend O'reille, Spokane, Stevens, Walla Walla, and Whitman. To speak with an Immigration Information Officer, you may make an appointment via the Internet at www.infopass.uscis.gov.

YAKIMA APPLICATION SUPPORT CENTER (ASC)

415 N. 3rd St.
Yakima, WA 98901
Tel: (800) 375-5283
Web: http://uscis.gov
Please, be sure to have an appointment letter to appear for fingerprinting.

YAKIMA SUB OFFICE

415 N. 3rd St.
Yakima, WA 98901
Keith Brown, Officer in Charge
Tel: (800) 375-5283
Web: http://uscis.gov
Service area: Kittitas, Klickitat, and Yakima counties. To speak with an Immigration Information Officer, you may make an appointment via the Internet at www.infopass.uscis.gov.

WEST VIRGINIA

CHARLESTON APPLICATION SUPPORT CENTER (ASC)

210 Kanawha Blvd. West
Charleston, WV 25302

Tel: (800) 375-5283
Web: http://uscis.gov
Please, be sure to have an appointment letter to appear for fingerprinting.

CHARLESTON, WV SATELLITE OFFICE

210 Kanawha Blvd. West
Charleston, WV 25302
Debra Zamberry, Officer in Charge
Tel: (800) 375-5283
Web: http://uscis.gov
Service area: the Charleston, WV Satellite office serves the State of West Virginia. It provides forms and information to the public and conducts naturalization interviews. To speak with an Immigration Information Officer, you may make an appointment via the Internet at www.infopass.uscis.gov.

WISCONSIN

MILWAUKEE APPLICATION SUPPORT CENTER (ASC)

310 E. Knapp, 1st Fl.
Milwaukee, WI 53202
Tel: (800) 375-5283
Web: http://uscis.gov
Please, be sure to have an appointment letter to appear for fingerprinting.

MILWAUKEE SUB OFFICE

310 E. Knapp St.
Milwaukee, WI 53202
Kay Leopold, Officer in Charge
Tel: (800) 375-5283
Web: http://uscis.gov
Service area: Brown, Calumet, Columbia, Crawford, Dane, Dodge, Door, Florence, Fond Du Lac, Forest, Grant, Green, Green Lake, Iowa, Jefferson, Kenosha, Kewaunee, Lafayette, Langlade, Manitowoc, Marinette, Marquette, Menominee, Milwaukee, Oconto, Outgamie, Ozaukee, Racine, Richland, Rock, Sauk, Shawano, Sheboygan, Walworth, Washington, Waukesha, Waupaca, Waushara, and Winnebago.

WYOMING

CASPER APPLICATION SUPPORT CENTER (ASC)

150 E. B St. #1014
Casper, WY 82601
Tel: (800) 375-5283
Web: http://uscis.gov
Please, be sure to have an appointment letter to appear for fingerprinting.

Wondering how to pay for college?

The Coast Guard has the money to help.

Coast Guard Academy:

A free college education and guaranteed job after graduation as a Coast Guard officer.

College Student Pre-Commissioning Initiative:

Receive full tuition for your junior and senior years, books and educational fees, a monthly stipend of approximately $2,000, plus guaranteed job after graduation as a Coast Guard officer

Active Duty Montgomery GI Bill:

Up to $1004 per month for 36 months.

Reserve Montgomery GI Bill:

Up to $288 per month for 36 months.

Tuition Assistance:

Up to $250 per semester hour, up to $4,500 per year.

Coast Guard Foundation Grant:

$250 per student per year for books and other education-related expenses

Coast Guard Mutual Assistance:

Grants of $100 per student per year for the cost of college textbooks, plus interest free loans loans are available.

Servicemember's Opportunity College Coast Guard:

An affiliation of colleges, that assists members in earning an associate degree or a bachelor's degree, and allow Coast Guard members to transfer college credits between schools and reduce their requirements for residency.

For more information, call us toll-free at

1-877-NOW-USCG (1-877-669-8724).

or visit:

Active Duty & Reserve	Civilian
www.gocoastguard.com	www.uscg.mil.civilian jobs

These programs may have additional requirements for participation. Amounts and availability of programs are subject to change. Contact your local Coast Guard recruiter for more information.

A MESSAGE FROM THE COMMANDANT OF THE COAST GUARD

Congratulations on the nineteenth edition of the Hispanic American Yearbook. This publication is a valued resource for people throughout the United States.

The Coast Guard serves multiple roles. We are simultaneously a military service, a law enforcement agency and a federal regulatory agency. Our vast array of missions range from national defense and homeland security to rescuing people at sea and protecting our marine environment. No other agency or service has the wide range of authorities and responsibilities that the Coast Guard manages every day.

How can we perform so many missions so well? The answer is simple: the Coast Guard is comprised of the best people our country has to offer. One example is Chief Petty Officer Diego Herrera. In the aftermath of 9-11, Chief Herrera was chosen to expand our fledgling canine program into a full-fledged, nation-wide program. Highly trained animals and their handlers complete a rigorous 15-week training program and now search out explosives and illegal drugs in ports around the country. Our canine units are successful in large part because of the skill and experience of Chief Herrera.

Or, consider LT Angelina Hidalgo. A graduate of the Coast Guard Academy, LT Hidalgo served as the Weapons Officer on CG Cutter *Dauntless* for two years. She then became the first Hispanic woman to command a Coast Guard patrol boat when she took command of CG Cutter *Kingfisher*. Under her guidance, *CGC Kingfisher* conducted 11 search and rescue cases and 135 law enforcement boardings, and executed security zone enforcement for three NASA Space Shuttle launches.

Auxiliarist Jose Martin, a private pilot, commands 25 aircraft and 100 aircrew. His unit's weekly harbor patrols provide surveillance for terrorists, oil spills, and illegal maritime activity. These volunteers transport vital equipment and personnel, and even provide surveillance for Navy ice experts. Additionally, this Spanish-born American has helped rescue mariners in distress.

The Coast Guard hires civilian employees as well. Dr. Jose Gonzalez, a native of El Salvador, is a highly accomplished author and teacher. He is Professor of English at the U.S. Coast Guard Academy. Dr. Gonzalez is highly decorated in the state of Connecticut and in New England for both his teaching skills and his poetry. He is the co-editor of <u>Latino Boom: An Anthology of Modern Latino Literature</u>, the first Latino literature anthology to use extensive resources for readers, and has published poetry and other creative and critical works.

These four Hispanic Americans epitomize the Coast Guard's core values of honor, respect, and devotion to duty. They, and thousands like them, are what make the Coast Guard great. Join us and be one of the people who makes America's Coast Guard the best maritime service in the world.

Semper Paratus - Always Ready.

THOMAS H. COLLINS
Admiral, United States Coast Guard

Interview

JOSEFINA CARBONELL

Josefina G. Carbonell was appointed by the President and sworn in as Assistant Secretary for Aging at the U.S. Department of Health and Human Services (HHS) on August 8, 2001. The Administration on Aging (AoA) is the federal focal point and advocacy agency for older Americans and their concerns. As the Assistant Secretary for Aging, Ms. Carbonell is dedicated to preparing America to meet the challenges and to maximize the opportunities presented by the longevity of its people. Her priorities include ensuring that the U.S. Administration on Aging and the Aging Services Network continue to play a leadership role in shaping our evolving health and long term care system on behalf of older people; helping older people to stay active and healthy; supporting families in their efforts to care for their loved ones at home and in the community; and ensuring the rights of older people. Prior to joining HHS, Ms. Carbonell was President and CEO of the largest Hispanic geriatric health and human service organization in the nation – Little Havana Activities & Nutrition Centers (LHANC) in Dade County, Florida. Josefina Carbonell is nationally recognized as a person of compassion and action and is the recipient of numerous awards, including one of the Hispanic Business Most Influential Hispanic Women in 2003.

AHHY The Administration on Aging is the federal focal point and advocacy agency for older Americans and their health concerns. As the Assistant Secretary for Aging at the US Department of Health and Human Services (HHS), how do you ensure that the nearly 3 million Hispanics over 60 years of age have equal access to services and support?

Carbonell The key to AoA's success in reaching the at-risk elderly population is the investments we've made in the local community providers. These providers are developing culturally appropriate programs and services that are responsive to the diverse needs of older Hispanic American adults and their families. Many of our 29,000 community-based organizations and seniors centers are Hispanic administered organizations and others that are located in targeted ethnic communities. According to our most recent data, 6.1 % of the Older Americans Act recipients were Hispanic, although Hispanics currently make up 5.5% of the older population. We are proud that Hispanic adult participation has increased 43% in three years. Hispanics have equal access to our core services, such as meals, transportation, and home and community-based supports that allow frail elders to remain at home for as long as possible.

In addition, we have enhanced the ability of the Eldercare Locator and the Alzheimer's Call Center to provide information and assistance in Spanish. We are also focusing on the needs of Hispanics caring for loved ones with Alzheimer's Disease by ensuring that one quarter of the grants under our Alzheimer's program specifically serve Hispanic families.

Finally, we are investing in evidence-based health promotion services specifically targeted to Hispanics. These projects will demonstrate effective ways that local community service providers can implement culturally appropriate nutrition and physical activity programs that will help Hispanic seniors and their loved ones control chronic diseases like diabetes and remain healthier longer.

AHHY You began your advocacy career as a volunteer when you feared that service agencies were bypassing immigrants. As the founder of Little Havana Activities and Nutrition Centers, what challenges and obstacles did you face as the largest agency providing social services for elderly Hispanics? What were the benefits to the Hispanic Community?

Carbonell We began as most new organizations do, as a small storefront operation that grew with the community we served. As the first provider serving Hispanics in Miami, we faced all the challenges that growing organizations do: having the staff and the ability to provide good quality services to a growing clientele. We did everything a little bit at a time. We started out with funding from the United Way and other private organizations, then gained the capacity to access federal funds. We learned from experience. As we saw pockets of need, we expanded to fill them. For example, we got into child care because the seniors attending the meal sites brought their grandchildren with them, so we started an intergenerational child care center.

AHHY The Hispanic population in the US represents 12 percent of the total population, of which 5 percent are people over 60 years of age. What initiative has the Department implemented to reach out to Hispanics so that they are aware of the importance of maintaining a healthy lifestyle at an earlier age? In particular, how have you addressed the huge disparities in health coverage and status among Hispanics?

Carbonell At the US Department of Health and Human Services, we are committed to reducing health disparities by supporting research to understand and reduce differences in health outcomes, by providing better "access" to health care, by arming people with prevention tools that will prevent disease and disability later in life, through enhanced benefits such as those offered by the Medicare Modernization Act, and by getting these messages out to communities in a culturally appropriate manner.

We are also helping people seek access to care through community health centers, which provide critical health care services to those who lack health insurance. The Department of Health and Human Services continues to expand the number of community health centers, so that every county that needs a health center can support one.

AoA also recognizes the importance of helping older Americans lead a healthier lifestyle. In August 2004, we launched the You Can! Campaign, which promotes physical activity and good nutrition among older adults. Our goal is to partner with 2000 community organizations to reach 2 million people in 2 years. We are already well on our way. To date, we have enrolled 1880 organizations, and enroll more everyday. Our materials are available in English and in Spanish.

We are also helping Hispanics to maintain a healthy lifestyle through our evidence-based disease prevention program. We are demonstrating how our aging services provider organizations can effectively deliver low-cost interventions that have proven to be effective in reducing the risk of disease and disability. We are giving special attention to Hispanic elders under this program.

Most importantly, we are working with trusted community-based organizations throughout the country to educate Medicare beneficiaries in their own communities about the benefits now available to them under the Medicare program. Medicare serves almost 3 million Hispanics with important benefits, including preventive benefits, like cardiovascular and diabetes screenings, and access to prescription drugs, which address key health risks in Hispanic communities.

AHHY How have your life experiences helped you understand the challenges that newcomers to our country encounter? How were you able to overcome these challenges?

Carbonell My family came to the United States as refugees from Cuba. That experience taught me how to make every challenge an opportunity; to have strength in the face of adversity.

AHHY In your opinion, what is the greatest challenge facing the Hispanic population?

Carbonell We need to take better care of ourselves. We need to practice healthy behaviors.

We also need to recognize the value and strengths of our unique experience. We have the best of both worlds – the best of two cultures, the best of two languages. We need to ensure that young Hispanics are equipped to use that to their advantage in a global economy. That is why the Department of Health and Human Services has embarked upon a major effort to recruit Hispanics into the sciences, into the health professions and into human services.

AHHY What role will the Hispanic community play in shaping the general direction of the country?

Carbonell We will play a unique role in the Americas as we see technology, communications, and travel take us into a more global economy. We have the power to unite the entire hemisphere.

Interview

CRISTINA SARALEGUI

Cristina Saralegui is a 30-year veteran journalist who is recognized as the most influential role model for today's Hispanic woman. She is strong-willed, successful, savvy and committed to making a difference. An icon to millions worldwide, a 2001 *People en Español* Hispanic Opinion Tracker (HOT) poll found that Hispanic Americans named Cristina as their favorite female talk show host. Cristina sees her #1 role in media and in life as a "motivator."

AHHY You are the first and only Hispanic woman to have a successful radio show "Cristina Opina," a widely circulated magazine "Cristina la Revista," and a most-watched talk show "Cristina," all at the same time. What do you attribute to your success, and what challenges have you encountered? How were you able to overcome these challenges?

Saralegui Hard work, perseverance and coordinating skills. My biggest challenge has been time management and finding the right people that I can depend on to delegate the many different tasks that my company must accomplish at any given time, after all a big part of what we do is based on teamwork.

AHHY Your show is considered innovative due to your assertive style and honest discussions on issues traditionally considered taboo in the Hispanic community. Why did you decide to take this approach?

Saralegui I am now on my 16th year of production. Back when we started, the general consensus was that Hispanics would not open up and share their stories, but time proved otherwise, and thanks to the generosity of all the guests that shared their stories with us, the Cristina show became a big success. As far as my style is concerned, talk shows are nothing more than a reflection of its hosts' approach to a particular topic. I am a very direct person, and I say things as I see them. This way of being has gotten me into trouble but helped me with the show.

AHHY Throughout your career, you have been dedicated to bringing the interests and opinions of the Hispanic community to mainstream media. In your opinion, what is the greatest challenge facing the Hispanic community in the United States? What changes have you observed in South Florida's Hispanic community over the past 5 or 10 years?

Saralegui Education is still a big challenge for our community. Without education, reaching the higher levels of power and opinion-making is nearly impossible. Even though we have seen some improvements there is still room to grow here. South Florida has become Latin America's favorite business capital. This is where people want to make deals and live. It's bilingual and it's convenient with a great infrastructure. We have become one of the most international capitals of the world.

AHHY As a successful professional woman who started her own media empire, what advice would you give to young Hispanic women aspiring to excel in any business?

Saralegui Dare to dream, we are what we think about. Write down your goals, make task lists, check

them everyday, work hard, work smart, and create a circle of friends and colleagues that share your enthusiasm for your goals. Be positive, stay away from negativism, do not take shortcuts, do not deceive your principles and success will always follow you.

AHHY How have your life experiences helped you understand the challenges that newcomers to our country encounter?

Saralegui The exile mentality is a good thing if you keep fresh in your mind that you have been given a great opportunity to live and succeed in one of the greatest countries that has existed. It is up to you to make things work.

HISPANIC AMERICAN Education

In 2003, fifty-seven percent of Hispanics age twenty-five years and over had a high school diploma or higher, while 11.4 percent had a bachelor's degree or more (Fig. 1). This was the lowest among any race or ethnic group in the country. Foreign-born Hispanics had a smaller proportion of students with a bachelor's degree than their native-born counterparts. The low educational attainment of foreign-born Hispanics (who make up more than fifty percent of the Hispanic population) was a contributing factor to the overall low level of educational attainment of the entire Hispanic population (Fig. 2).

According to the U.S. Department of Education, minority enrollment in elementary and secondary schools has risen recently due to the growth in the number of Hispanic students. Between 1972 and 2000, Hispanic students in public schools increased by eleven percent and the overall percentage of minority students increased by seventeen percent. By comparison, Black students increased by about two percent between the same time (Fig. 3). From 1980–2000, Hispanic enrollment in colleges and universities also increased, but a smaller proportion of Hispanics complete college compared to non-Hispanic Whites and Blacks (Fig. 4).

Educational attainment varies among Hispanics. Among Latinos twenty-five years and older, other Hispanics, Cubans, Puerto Ricans, and Central and South Americans were more likely to have at least graduated from high school and college than Mexicans (Fig. 5).

FIG 1. Educational Attainment of the Population 25 Years and Over by Race, Hispanic Origin, and Age: 2003

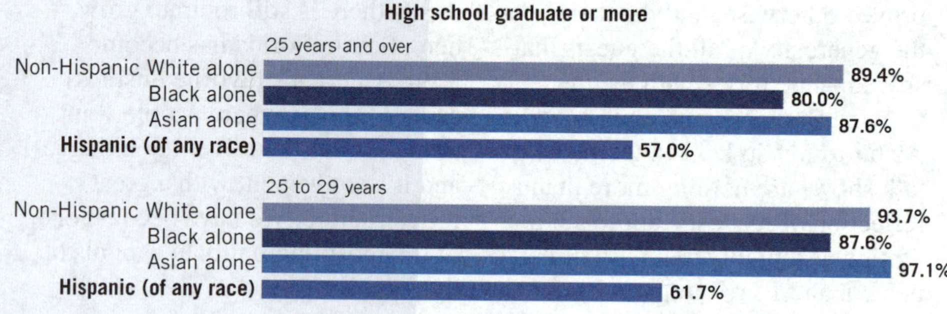

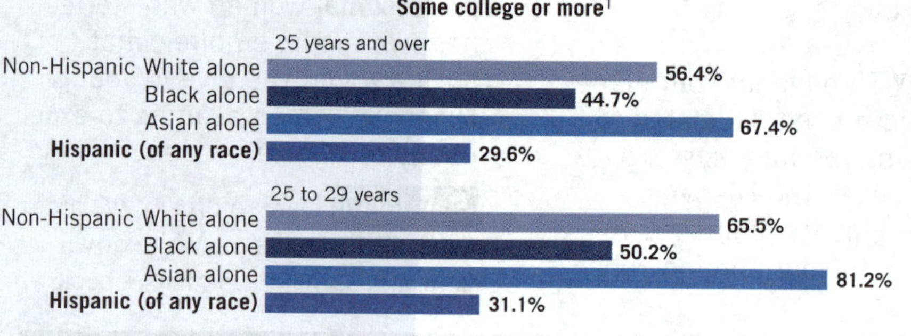

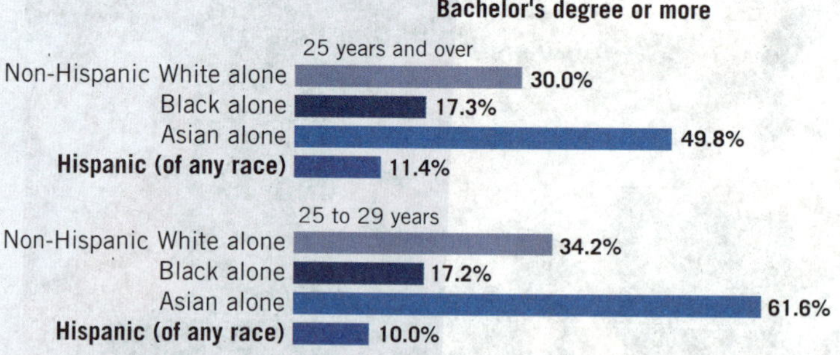

Source: U.S. Census Bureau, Current Population Survey, Annual Social and Economic Supplement, 2003.

[1] *Some college includes respondents who have completed some college, but have no degree and those who have completed an associate's degree.*

FIG 2. Educational Attainment of the Population 25 Years and Over by Nativity, Race, and Hispanic Origin: 2003 (In percent)

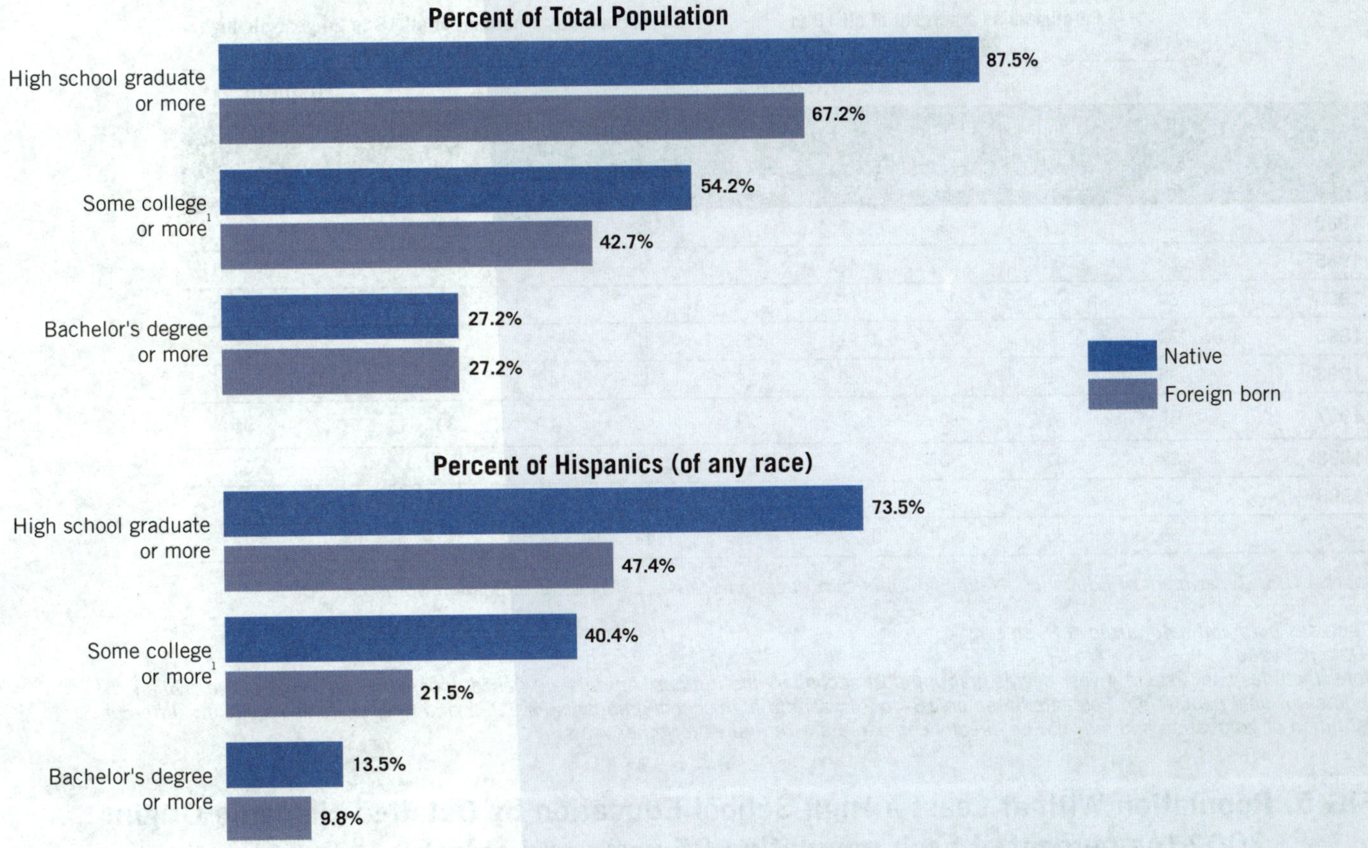

Percent of Total Population

High school graduate or more
Native: 87.5%
Foreign born: 67.2%

Some college[1] or more
Native: 54.2%
Foreign born: 42.7%

Bachelor's degree or more
Native: 27.2%
Foreign born: 27.2%

Native
Foreign born

Percent of Hispanics (of any race)

High school graduate or more
Native: 73.5%
Foreign born: 47.4%

Some college[1] or more
Native: 40.4%
Foreign born: 21.5%

Bachelor's degree or more
Native: 13.5%
Foreign born: 9.8%

Source: U.S. Census Bureau, Current Population Survey, Annual Social and Economic Supplement, 2003.

[1] *Some college includes respondents who have completed some college, but have no degree and those who have completed an associate's degree.*

FIG 3. Percent of Public School Students Enrolled in Grades K-12 Who Where Minorities, by Race/Etnicithy: 1972-2000

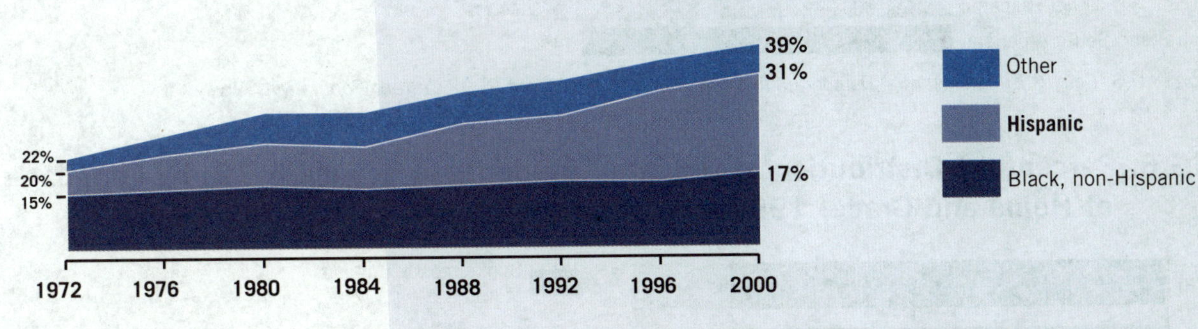

Source: U.S. Department of Education, National Center for Education Statistics, Digest of Education Statistics, The Condition of Education, 2002, based on U.S. Department of Commerce, Bureau of the Census, October Current Population Surveys, 1972-2000.

| Year | Enrollment as a percent of all 18 to 24 year-olds | | | | | Enrollment as a percent of all 18 to 24 year-old high school completers | | | | |
| | | | | Hispanic | | | | | Hispanic | |
	Total	White, non-Hispanic	Black, non-Hispanic	Total	U.S. Citizens[1]	Total	White, non-Hispanic	Black, non-Hispanic	Total	U.S. Citizens[1]
1980	26	27	19	16	-	32	32	28	30	-
1985	28	30	20	17	-	34	35	26	27	-
1990	32	35	25	16	-	39	40	33	29	-
1995	34	38	27	21	26	42	44	35	35	36
1996	36	39	27	20	26	43	45	36	34	38
1997	37	41	30	22	28	45	47	39	36	40
1998	37	41	30	20	26	45	47	40	34	36
1999	36	39	30	19	24	44	45	39	32	34
2000	36	39	31	22	31	43	44	39	36	43

Source: U.S. Department of Education, National Center for Education Statistics, Digest of Education Statistics, 2001.

[1] *Includes born and naturalized U.S. citizens.*
- Data not valid.
Note: Includes both 2- and 4-year degree-granting post-secondary institutions. All data are based upon sample surveys of the civilian noninstitutional population. Percents based on 18- to 24-year-old high school graduates for 1992 and later years use a slightly different definition of graduation and may not be directly comparable with figures for other years.

FIG 5. Population With at Least a High School Education by Detailed Hispanic Origin: 2002 (As percent of each population 25 years and older)

Source: U.S. Census Bureau, Annual Demographic Supplement to the March 2002 Current Population Survey.

FIG 6. Percentage Distribution of Hispanic Students in Grades K-12, by Language Spoken at Home and Grade: 1999

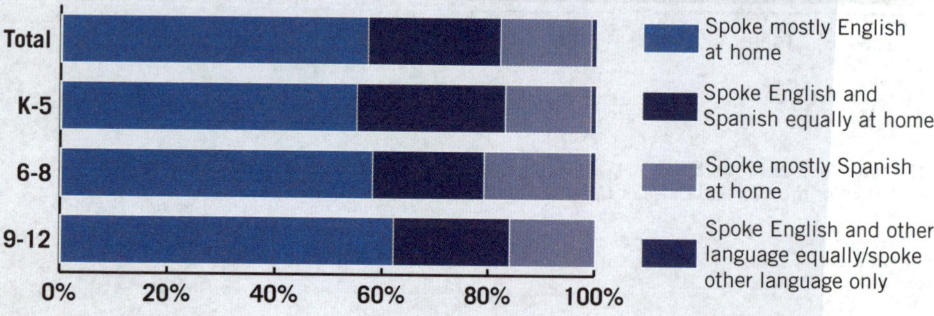

Source: U.S. Department of Education, National Center for Education Statistics, Digest of Education Statistics, 2000.

HISPANICAMERICAN
Health

There are large disparities in health coverage and health status among Hispanics. Hispanics are more likely to lack employer coverage for health insurance than Whites. Nationally, Hispanics have the lowest rate of health insurance coverage in comparison to other racial groups. This is largely due to their place of employment not providing them with health coverage. Between 2002 to 2003, forty percent of non–elderly Hispanics had employer coverage compared to sixty-nine percent of non–elderly Whites. With Medicare coverage, five percent of Hispanics were covered compared to eighty-three percent of Whites (Fig. 1 – 3). Health care coverage varies among Hispanics. According to the Pew Hispanic Center, one fifth of native–born Hispanics lack coverage compared with a quarter of foreign–born Hispanics who are naturalized and about fifty-five percent of foreign–born Hispanics who do not have U.S. citizenship (Fig. 4). Many Hispanics, with or without health care coverage face various obstacles to health care due to language, transportation, childcare, immigration status, and cultural beliefs. This causes significant barriers to reliable and consistent health care that can detect and prevent diseases on time.

Heart disease, for example, is the leading cause of death among Hispanics (Fig. 5), accounting for approximately twenty-four percent of all Hispanic deaths. Similarly, Mexican Americans suffer in

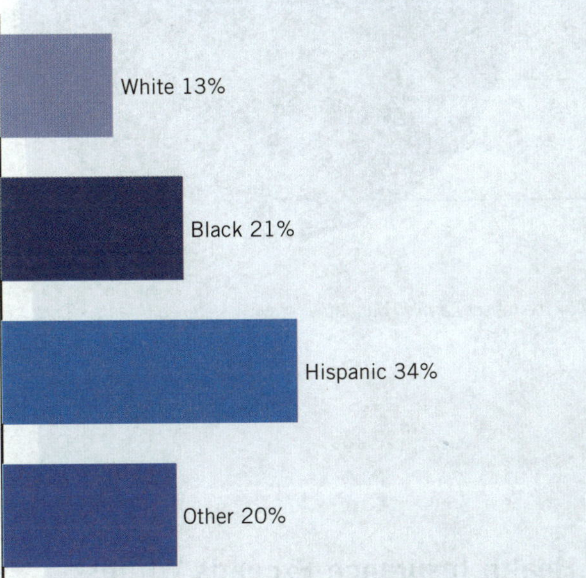

FIG 1. United States Rate of Nonelderly Uninsured by Race/Ethnicity, 2002–2003

Source: State Health Facts published by the Kaiser Family Foundation at www.statehealthfacts.kff.org.

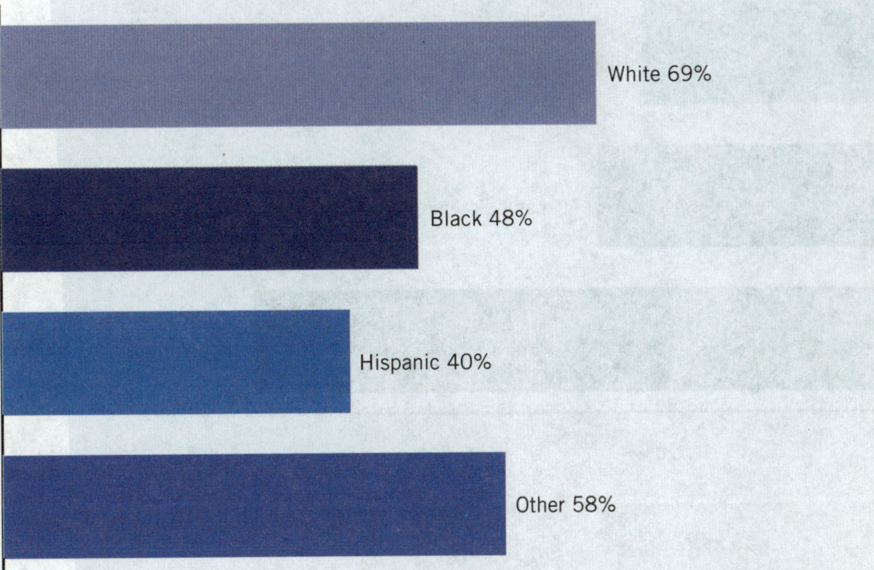

FIG 2. United States Rate of Nonelderly with Employer Coverage by Race/Ethnicity, 2002–2003

Source: State Health Facts published by the Kaiser Family Foundation at www.statehealthfacts.kff.org.

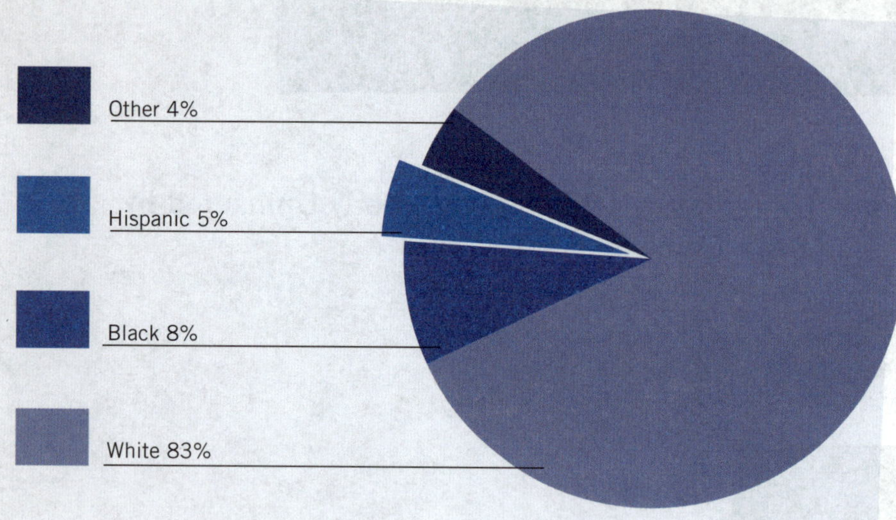

Source: State Health Facts published by the Kaiser Family Foundation at www.statehealthfacts.kff.org.

FIG 4. Latino Lack of Health Insurance Exceeds Whites

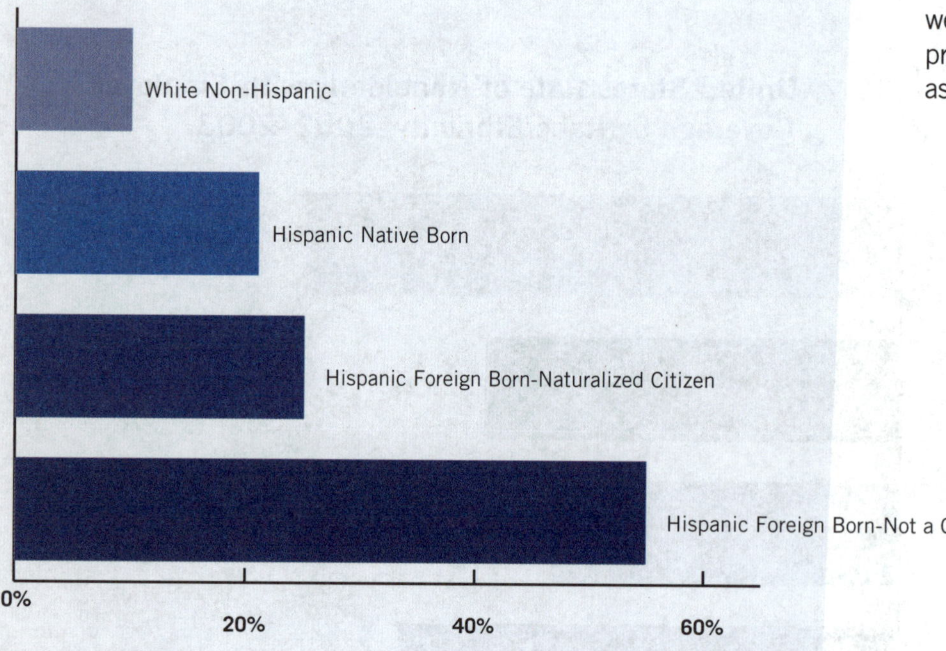

Source: Pew Hispanic Center, January 2002.

greater numbers from obesity and overweight rates, two of the leading risk factors for heart disease. According to the Kaiser Family Foundation in 2002, 57.6 percent of Hispanics were overweight and obese (Fig. 6). Diabetes is also a risk factor for cardiovascular disease, and it is the fifth leading cause of death among Hispanics and more prevalent in Hispanics age 50 and over. According to the American Diabetes Association, two million or 8.2 percent of all Hispanics aged twenty years and older have diabetes.

In 2003, Hispanic children were more likely to be uninsured than non–Hispanic White children— twenty-one percent compared with 7.4 percent. In addition, the likelihood of health insurance coverage for children in poverty was lower than for the population of all children (Fig. 7).

Between 2000 and 2003, the number of Hispanics who were uninsured increased from 11.8 million to 13.2 million. At the same time, the number of Hispanics who were covered by government and private health insurance increased as well (Fig. 8).

FIG 5. 10 Leading Causes of Death for Hispanics and Latinos, 2001 (per 100,000 deaths)

Hispanics/Latinos All Ages/Both Sexes	Hispanic/Latino Males All Ages	Hispanic/Latina Females All Ages
Heart Diseases	Heart Diseases	Heart Diseases
27,090	14,195	12,895
Cancer	Cancer	Cancer
22,371	11,825	10,546
Accidents	Accidents	Stroke
9,523	7,157	3,434
Stroke	Stroke	Diabetes
6,416	2,982	3,073
Diabetes	Homicide	Accidents
5,663	2,756	2,366
Homicide	Diabetes	Influenza and pneumonia
3,331	2,590	1,413
Chronic liver disease and cirrhosis	Chronic liver disease and cirrhosis	Chronic lower respiratory diseases
3,301	2,410	1,350
Chronic lower respiratory disease	Suicide	Kidney Diseases
2,832	1,576	965
Influenza and pneumonia	Chronic lower respiratory disease	Certain conditions originating in the perinatal period
2,722	1,482	959
Certain conditions originating in the perinatal period	Human immunodeficiency virus (HIV)	Chronic liver disease and cirrhosis
2,227	1,437	891

Source: Office of Minority Health (OMH), DATA2010...the Healthy People 2010 Database–April 2004 Edition.

FIG 6. United States Overweight and Obesity Rate by Race/Ethnicity, 2002

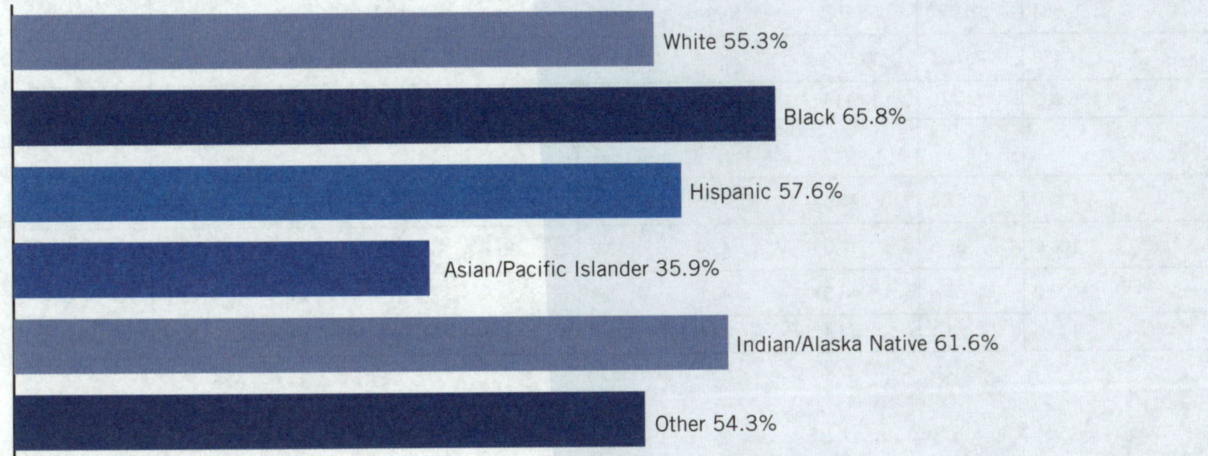

Source: State Health Facts published by the Kaiser Family Foundation at www.statehealthfacts.kff.org.

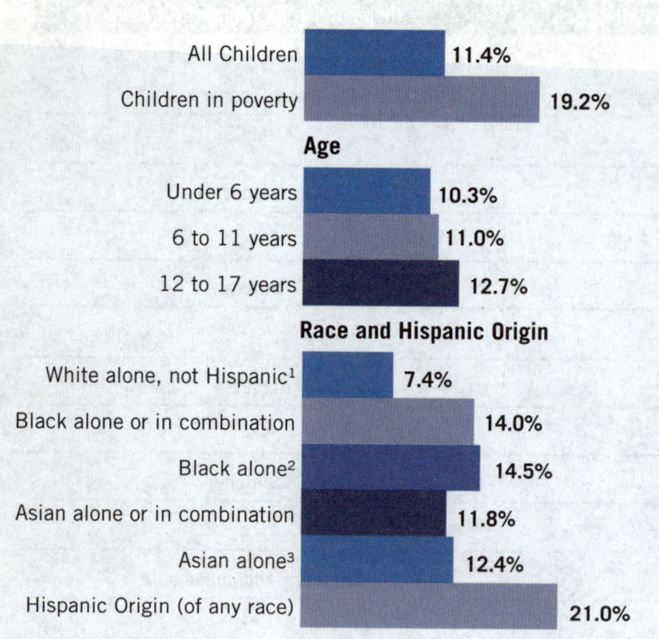

Source: U.S. Census Bureau, Current Population Survey, 2004 Annual Social and Economic Supplement.

[1] *The 2003 CPS asked respondents to choose one or more races. White Alone refers to people who reported White and did not report any other race. The use of this single–race population does not imply that it is the preferred method of presenting or analyzing data. The Census Bureau uses a variety of approaches. More than one race was reported for about four percent of children in Census 2000.*

[2] *Black alone refers to people who reported Black and did not report any other race category.*

[3] *Asian alone refers to people who reported Asian and did not report any other race category.*

FIG 8. Health Insurance Coverage by Race and Hispanic Origin: 2000 to 2003

Race and Hispanic Origin and Year	Total people	Covered by private or government health insurance								Not covered
		Total	Private health insurance			Government health insurance				
			Total	Employment based	Direct purchase	Total	Medicaid	Medicare	Military health care	
HISPANIC (of any race) **Numbers**										
2003	40,425	27,188	18,183	16,788	1,551	10,716	8,505	2,462	639	13,237
2002	39,384	26,627	18,108	16,714	1,469	10,280	7,946	2,535	724	12,756
2001	37,438	25,021	17,322	15,965	1,390	9,227	7,074	2,295	704	12,417
2000	36,093	24,210	17,114	15,893	1,337	8,566	6,552	2,141	682	11,883
Percents										
2003	100.0	67.3	45.0	41.5	3.8	26.5	21.0	6.1	1.6	32.7
2002	100.0	67.6	46.0	42.4	3.7	26.1	20.2	6.4	1.8	32.4
2001	100.0	66.8	46.3	42.6	3.7	24.6	18.9	6.1	1.9	33.2
2000	100.0	67.1	47.4	44.0	3.7	23.7	18.2	5.9	1.9	32.9

Source: U.S. Census Bureau, Current Population Survey, 2000 to 2003 Annual Social and Economic Supplements.

ScholarSite.com Financial Aid
Ayudas financieras en ScholarSite.com

Approximately 100 student financial aid opportunities are listed below. They were selected for their focus on Hispanic American students at the undergraduate level. For more detailed information on conditions and restrictions for these and thousands of other opportunities, please visit TIYM's financial aid website, www.scholarsite.com.

Assistantship

U

UNIVERSITY OF FLORIDA
Knight Center for Scholarships, Placement and Multicultural Affairs
P.O. Box 118400
2070 Weimer Hall
Gainesville, FL 32611-8400

Karl and Madira Bickel Minority Student Assistantship
Web: www.ufl.edu
Requirements: This assistantship is available to minority students who work 10 hours per week in the College of Journalism and Communications.
Disciplines: Communications
Award: $1,800
Eligible Inst.: University of Florida

Award

A

AMERICAN DENTAL HYGIENISTS' ASSOCIATION
444 N. Michigan Ave. #3400
Chicago, IL 60611

ADHA Institute for Oral Health Scholarship Program
Tel: (312) 440-8900
Email: mail@adha.net
Web: www.adha.org
Requirements: Scholarships are available to certificate/associate, baccalaureate, or graduate degree candidates who have: completed a minimum of one year in a dental hygiene program; a minimum dental hygiene grade point average of 3.0 (on a 4.0 scale); and demonstrated a financial need of at least $1,500 (not necessary for certain scholarships). There are also scholarships available for applicants who demonstrate one of the following requirements: member of a minority group (including African Americans, Asians, Hispanics, Native Americans, and males); academic excellence (must have a 3.5 gpa on a 4.0 scale); leadership potential; a desire to become a dental hygiene educator; a strong potential to serve in the public or community health care arena.
Disciplines: Dental Hygiene
Award: varies
Eligible Inst.: US schools
Deadline: May 1

THE AMERICAN PHYSIOLOGICAL SOCIETY
9650 Rockville Pike
Bethesda, MD 20814

NIDDK Minority Travel Awards
Tel: (301) 530-7132 Fax: (301) 571-8305
Requirements: The APS is offering travel awards for underepresented minorities to attend the yearly APS Meeting. The awards are open to graduate students, postdoctoral students, and advanced undergraduate students. Students who obtained their undergraduate education in Minority Biomedical Research Programs (MBRS) and Minority Access to Research Career (MARC)-eligible institutions as well as students in the APS Porter development program, are encouraged to apply.
Disciplines: Natural Sciences, Medical Sciences, Medical Research
Award: Transportation, meals & lodging
Eligible Inst.: US schools
Deadline: December 8

O

OHIO UNIVERSITY
Office of Admissions
120 Chubb Hall
Athens, OH 45701

King-Chavez-Parks Award
Sylvester James Aji
Tel: (740) 593-9376 Fax: (740) 593-0560
Email: diversity@ohio.edu
Web: www.ohio.edu
Requirements: These scholarship awards are designed to help undergraduate students from underrepresented populations. Recipient must maintain at least a 3.4 GPA and earn 48 credit hours per year to renew this scholarship.
Disciplines: Any
Award: tuition
Eligible Inst.: US schools
Deadline: February 1

U

UNIVERSITY OF MISSOURI-KANSAS CITY
Financial Aid and Scholarships Office
101 Administrative Ctr., 5100 Rockhill Rd.
Kansas City, MO 64110-2499

Chancellor's Historically Under-Represented Minority Award
Pat McTee, Director of Financial Aid
Tel: (816) 235-1154 Fax: (816) 235-5511
Email: finaid@umkc.edu
Web: www.umkc.edu/finaid
Requirements: This scholarship is available to newly enrolled non-resident students of Black, Hispanic or Native Amerian descent. Applicants must indicate their minority status on their admissions application and must be native-born U.S. citizens.
Disciplines: Any
Award: Varies
Eligible Inst.: University of Missouri-Kansas City

Fellowship

A

ACADEMY FOR EDUCATIONAL DEVELOPMENT
1825 Connecticut Ave. NW
Washington, DC 20009-5721

Public Policy and International Affairs Fellowship (PPIA) Program
Tel: (202) 884-8632 Fax: (202) 884-8407
Email: ppia@aed.org
Web: www.ppiaprogram.org
Requirements: The PPIA Fellowship Program was designed to prepare students, primarily from historically underrepresented groups, for graduate studies in public and/or international affairs and groom them for professional roles in public service. There is an array of opportunities under the Fellowship which span a period of development from the junior year of college to beyond the completion of a graduate degree.
Disciplines: Public Policy, International Relations

C

COMMITTEE ON INSTITUTIONAL COOPERATION
Minorities Fellowship Program
Kirkwood Hall 114, Indiana University
Bloomington, IN 47405

CIC Minorities Fellowship in the Natural Sciences
Tel: (800) 457-4420
Requirements: Applicant must not currently be enrolled in a graduate program at a CIC university.
Disciplines: Natural Sciences
Award: full tuition
Eligible Inst.: US schools

E

ENTOMOLOGICAL FOUNDATION
Education & Training Committee
9332 Annapolis Rd. #210
Lanham, MD 20706

Stan Beck Fellowship
Melodie Dziduch, Awards Coordinator
Tel: (301) 459-9082 Fax: (301) 459-9084
Email: melodie@entfdn.org
Web: www.entfdn.org
Requirements: This fellowship is available to undergraduate and graduate students with need. Consideration will be given to physical limitations or economic, minority or environmental conditions. Minority students and women are strongly encouraged to apply for this award.
Disciplines: Biology, Zoology
Award: varies
Eligible Inst.: US & Intl. schools
Deadline: July 1

H

HISPANIC LINK NEWS SERVICE
1420 N St. NW
Washington, DC 20005

Hispanic Link Journalism Foundation Reporting Fellowship
Charles Ericksen
Tel: (202) 234-0280 Fax: (202) 234-4090
Email: zapotec@aol.com
Requirements: This is a grant opportunity for Hispanic aspiring journalist. The intern will spend one year with Hispanic Link News services, writing on issues that affect the Hispanic community, by covering all branches of the federal government.
Disciplines: Journalism
Award: $21,000
Eligible Inst.: US schools

N

NATIONAL PHYSICAL SCIENCE CONSORTIUM
Student Recruitment Office
P.O. Box 30001
Las Cruces, NM 88003-8001

National Physical Science Consortium Graduate Fellowships
Gene Bailey
Tel: (800) 952-4118 Fax: (505) 646-6097
Email: npsc@npsc.org
Web: www.npsc.org
Requirements: National Physical Science Consortium Graduate Fellowships in the Physical Sciences for Minorities and Women programs offer up to 6 yr. funding, including tuition & fees; stipends of $12,500 in year 1-4 and $15,000 in years 5-6 plus 2 summers of paid research internship. Must have the ability to pursue graduate work at an NPSC member institution. Applicants must be undergraduates with at least a 3.0 GPA, or be completing a

Master's at an institution that does not have a Ph.D. program in your discipline, or possess a degree and have been out of school at least one year.
Disciplines: Physical Education, Engineering
Award: $156,000-$200,000
Eligible Inst.: US schools
Deadline: November 5

R

ROBERT WOOD JOHNSON FOUNDATION
P.O. Box 2316
Princeton, NJ 08543-2316

Summer Medical Education Program
Lois Bergeisen
Tel: (609) 452-8701 Fax: (716) 597-6036
Email: fields@robers.edu
Web: www.rwjf.org
Requirements: To be eligible for SMEP, an applicant must: be a U.S. citizen or hold a permanent resident visa; have completed at least one year of college (in addition, qualified post-baccalaureate applicants are also eligible); have an overall GPA of 3.00, with 2.75 in the sciences; and have a combined SAT score of at least 950 or ACT score of at least 20.
Disciplines: Any
Award: $1,000
Eligible Inst.: US schools
Deadline: April 15

Grant

A

ARKANSAS DEPARTMENT OF HIGHER EDUCATION
Financial Aid Division
114 E. Capitol St.
Little Rock, AR 72201-3818

Freshman/Sophomore Minority Grant Program
Judy McAnish, Coordinator
Tel: (501) 371-2050 Fax: (501) 324-9308
Email: finaid@adhe.arknet.edu
Web: www.arscholarships.com
Requirements: Minority students who are full-time freshmen or sophomores in college and interested in teacher education programs are eligible. Students must perform pre-service internships in public school settings and sign a statement of interest in teaching. For more information, applicants should contact the College of Education Office or Dean of Students on the campus they plan to attend.
Disciplines: Education
Award: $1,000
Eligible Inst.: US schools

M

MICHIGAN TECHNOLOGICAL UNIVERSITY
Financial Aid Office
1400 Townsend Dr.
Houghton, MI 49931-1295

Minority Grants
Tel: (906) 487-2622 Fax: (906) 487-3343
Requirements: All accepted students are automatically considered for merit-based scholarships for which they are eligible, a special application form is not required. This scholarship is renewable provided the recipient meets the renewal criteria.
Disciplines: Any

Award: $1,000-$15,000
Eligible Inst.: Michigan Technological University
Deadline: February 15

P

PRESBYTERIAN CHURCH (USA)
Office of Financial Aid for Studies
100 Witherspoon St.
Louisville, KY 40202-1396

Racial Ethnic Supplemental Grant
Frances Cook
Tel: (502) 569-5776 Fax: (502) 569-5018
Email: fcook@ctr.pcusa.org
Web: www.pcusa.org
Requirements: Studying full-time in a PC(USA) seminary or accredited theological institution approved by the student's Committee on Preparation for Ministry. M.Div. students must be enrolled as an inquirer or candidate by a PC(USA) presbytery prior to the application deadline date eligible for the award a maximum of two years as an Inquirer,eligible for the award in their third/final year as a Candidate, MACE students must be seeking a degree to pursue a church occupation.Recommended by the financial aid officer at theological institution. Funding allocated for first professional degree for a church occupation. Students already awarded an M.Div. or MACE will not be considered for grants, but may apply for a theological student loan. For African American, Alaska Native, Asian American, Hispanic American, or Native American students who have been awarded the Presbyterian Study Grant and have remaining need.
Disciplines: Religion & Theology
Award: $500-$1,000
Eligible Inst.: US schools

W

WAYNE STATE UNIVERSITY
Center of Chicano-Boricua Studies
Faculty Administration Bldg. #324
Detroit, MI 48202

Latino En Marcha Grant
Tel: (313) 577-4378 Fax: (313) 577-1274
Email: admissions@wayne.edu
Web: www.wayne.edu
Requirements: This grant is available to qualified Latino students in the Center for Chicano-Boricua Studies Program. Awards are based on academic merit and financial need.
Disciplines: Any
Award: Varies
Eligible Inst.: Wayne State University

Internship

H

HISPANIC YOUTH FOUNDATION
600 Pennsylvania Ave. SE #300
Washington, DC 20003

Summer in Washington Internship
Grace Ramos
Tel: (202) 543-3619
Email: hyf@webtv.net
Requirements: The HYF invites Hispanic students to apply for an eight week summer internship in the nations capital. Hispanic students will take part in political education activities while gaining valuable experience. To qualify, you must be a full time student

enrolled in a college or university and have a demonstrated interest in political science or other social studies related to government and public service. The student must enclose a completed application, a resume, one reference letter, unofficial transcript of grades, two essays, typed, double spaced, 250 words, one about how have you demonstrated a passion for public service, and one about what do you believe is one of the most serious issues facing Hispanics in the country today.
Disciplines: Political Science, Public Services
Award: varies
Eligible Inst.: US schools
Deadline: April 1

N

NATIONAL ASSOCIATION OF LATINO ELECTED & APPOINTED OFFICIALS
514 C St. NE
Washington, DC 20002

Shell Legislavite Internship Program
Marina Martinez
Tel: (202) 546-2536 Fax: (202) 546-4121
Web: www.naleo.org
Disciplines: Public Relations
Award: $4,500
Eligible Inst.: US schools

U

UNIVERSITY OF MICHIGAN, SCHOOL OF PUBLIC HEALTH
M3226 School of Public Health II
Ann Arbor, MI 48109-2029

Summer Enrichment Program for Minority Undergraduates
Dr. Richard Liechtenstein
Tel: (734) 936-3296
Email: um_sep@umich.edu
Web: www.sph.umich.edu/hmp/sep_hmp.html
Requirements: The ultimate goal of the program is to increase minority participation in a career area in which minorities have been underrepresented. Interns work in a hospital or other health organizations in the Detroit/Ann Arbor area.
Disciplines: Any
Award: $3,000

Loan

T

TENNESSEE STUDENT ASSISTANCE CORPORATION
404 James Robertson Pkwy. #1950
Nashville, TN 37243-0820

Minority Teaching Fellows Program
Michael Roberts, Executive Director
Tel: (615) 741-1346 X102
Fax: (615) 741-6101
Email: michael.roberts@state.tn.us
Web: www.state.tn.us/tsac/grants/
Requirements: This program is available to entering freshmen with a minimum GPA of 2.75 or continuing college student with a college GPA of 2.5. Applicants must score at least 18 on the ACT or 850 on the SAT or be in the top 25% of their high school class. Recipients must agree to teach at a K-12 level in a Tennessee public school one year for each year the award is received. Applicant must be enrolled full-time at a two-year or four-year institution or university in Tennessee and be a

resident of Tennessee. In addition, applicant must submit an essay, references, test scores, transcripts, and a completed application.
Disciplines: Education
Award: $5,000
Eligible Inst.: US schools
Deadline: April 15

Scholarship

A

AMERICAN LIBRARY ASSOCIATION
50 E. Huron St.
Chicago, IL 60611

Spectrum Initiative Scholarship
Tel: (312) 280-4270
Email: diversity@ala.org
Web: www.ala.org
Requirements: The Spectrum Initiative's major drive is to recruit applicants and award scholarships to American Indian/Alaska Native, Asian, Black/African American, Hispanic/Latino or Native Hawaiian/Other Pacific Islander students for graduate programs in library and information science. To be eligible for a Spectrum Scholarship: Applicant must be a citizen or permanent resident of the U.S. or Canada; Applicant must be American Indian/Alaska Native, Asian, Black/African American, Hispanic/Latino or Native Hawaiian/Other Pacific Islander; Applicant must attend an ALA-accredited graduate program in library and information studies or an ALA-recognized NCATE School Library Media program: ALA Office for Accreditation Directory of Institutions offering accredited programs. National Council for the Accreditation Of Teacher Education (NCATE); Applicant shall have completed no more than a third of the credit requirements toward her/his MLIS or school library media degree at the time of award; Applicant must be enrolled in an accredited program and begin school no later than September 1st or the Fall Semester immediately following the award; Applicants may have full or part time status.
Disciplines: Library Science
Award: $5,000
Eligible Inst.: US schools
Deadline: March 1

ARKANSAS DEPARTMENT OF HIGHER EDUCATION
Financial Aid Division
114 E. Capitol St.
Little Rock, AR 72201-3818

Minority Teachers Scholarship
Judy McAnish, Coordinator
Tel: (501) 371-2050 Fax: (501) 371-2001
Email: finaid@adhe.arknet.edu
Web: http://arscholarships.com
Requirements: This scholarship is available to minority college students enrolled full-time who have completed at least 60 semester credit hours. Applicants must have been admitted to an approved program resulting in teacher certification; and have at least a 2.5 cumulative GPA. After graduation, teachers are required to teach full-time in a public school in Arkansas for 5 years to receive full loan forgiveness. The teaching requirement is 3 years for guidance counseling, teaching in one of the 42 Arkansas Delta counties, math, science, foreign language, or for African-American males teaching at the elementary level.
Disciplines: Education
Award: $5,000
Eligible Inst.: US schools
Deadline: June 1

ASSOCIATION OF HISPANIC PROFESSIONALS FOR EDUCATION

Cal State Fullerton-Student Academic Services
P.O. Box 340
Fullerton, CA 92634-9480

Corporate Scholarship

Gary Jimenez
Tel: (714) 278-2288 Fax: (714) 449-4195
Requirements: This scholarship is available to students with clear career goals and potential. Applicants must have a minimum GPA of 3.0 with 30 semester units or 45 quarter units of college or university work. Applicants must demonstrate a commitment to community service.
Disciplines: Any
Award: $500-$700
Eligible Inst.: US schools
Deadline: February 1

B

BIOLA UNIVERSITY

Office of Admissions
13800 Biola Ave.
La Mirada, CA 90639-4652

Scholarships for Underrepresented Groups of Ethnicity (SURGE)

Scholarship Administrator
Tel: (562) 903-4752
Web: www.biola.edu
Requirements: These scholarships are available to underrepresented students not eligible for Academic Scholarships. Awards are based on GPA and are renewable. A separate application is required.
Disciplines: Any
Award: $2,500/yr
Eligible Inst.: Biola University
Deadline: April 1

C

CALIFORNIA ADOLESCENT NUTRITION AND FITNESS PROGRAM

2140 Shattuck Ave. #610
Berkeley, CA 94704

California Adolescent Nutrition and Fitness (CANFIT) Program Scholarship

Leena Kamat, Administrative Assistant
Tel: (510) 644-1533 Fax: (510) 644-1535
Email: info@canfit.org
Web: www.canfit.org
Requirements: Undergraduate and graduate scholarships are available for African American, American Indian/Alaska Native, Asian/Pacific Islander or Latino/Hispanic students expressing financial need to study nutrition, physical education, or culinary arts in the state of California. By providing undergraduate and graduate scholarships, the CANFit Program hopes to encourage more students to consider careers that will improve adolescent nutrition and fitness. Enrollment in an approved masters level or doctoral graduate program in Nutrition, Public Health Nutrition, or Physical Education; or American Dietetic Association Approved Pre professional Practice Program at an accredited university in California 12-15 units of graduate course work completed and verified with an official copy of university transcript and a 3.0 or better GPA (cumulative) Minority student affiliation (see list above)
Disciplines: Dietetics & Nutrition, Education, Physical Education, Health Care, Public Services
Award: varies

Eligible Inst.: US schools
Deadline: March 31

COCA COLA CORPORATION

Shorter College, 315 Shorter Ave. SW
Rome, GA 30165-4267

Coca Cola Minority Scholarship

Susan Tate
Tel: (703) 233-7228 Fax: (703) 233-7314
Email: state@shorter.edu
Web: www.uncf.org
Requirements: Students must complete a Free Application for Federal Student Aid (FAFSA) and request that the Student Analysis Report (SAR) be sent to the financial aid office at their college or university.
Disciplines: Any
Award: $5,000
Eligible Inst.: Shorter College

CUBAN-AMERICAN TEACHERS' ASSOCIATION

12037 Peoria St.
Sun Valley, CA 91352

Cuban-American Teachers' Association Scholarship

Alberto C. Del Calvo
Tel: (818) 768-2669
Requirements: Applicants should display an interest in Cuban heritage and the Cuban-American community. Must be active students and have at least a 3.0 GPA. Students should also speak "acceptable" spanish.
Disciplines: Any
Award: $300-$500
Eligible Inst.: US schools
Deadline: April 1

D

DOW JONES NEWSPAPER FUND

P.O. Box 300
Princeton, NJ 08543-0300

Dow Jones Newspaper Fund Minority Business Reporting Program

Linda Waller, Deputy Director
Tel: (609) 520-5929 Fax: (609) 520-5804
Email: linda.waller@dowjones.com
Web: http://djnewspaperfund.dowjones.com
Requirements: The Business Reporting Program is specifically intended for minority sophomores and juniors. These interns cover business and consumer news at daily newspapers and news services. They attend a one-week training seminar at New York University's Department of Journalism and Mass Communication in Manhattan. Applicants must submit the application form, a resume, three to five recently published clips, a list of courses with grades and a 500-word essay. The test should be completed no later than Dec. 1. Minority is defined as African-American, Hispanic, Asian American/Pacific Islander or American Indian/Alaskan Native.
Disciplines: Business
Award: $1,000
Eligible Inst.: US schools
Deadline: November 1

E

EMERSON COLLEGE

Office of Admission
100 Beacon St.
Boston, MA 02116

RKO General, Inc. Endowed Minority Scholarship

Tel: (617) 824-8500 Fax: (617) 824-8619

Email: admiss@emerson.edu
Web: www.emerson.edu
Requirements: To be awarded to minority residents of the Commonwealth of Massachusetts majoring in one or more areas of communication to the public (radio/television, film or print/broadcast journalism). Scholarships are awarded to students who demonstrate academic achievement, with preference ot those students who show financial need.
Disciplines: Communications
Eligible Inst.: Emerson College
Deadline: January 15

WCVB-TV Scholarship

Tel: (617) 824-8500 Fax: (617) 824-8619
Email: admiss@emerson.edu
Web: www.emerson.edu
Requirements: The WCVB-TV Scholarship provides funds for tuition, fees, and books to a student in broadcast communication who is considered disadvantaged. Preference is given to AHANA (African, Hispanic, Asian, Native American) students. The Scholarship is awarded to a student enrolled in either the junior or senior year, or in a graduate program. the recipient must be an American citizen or satisfactorily demonstrate that he or she plans to remain in the United States for his or her life work. Emerson College has sole responsibility to select the recipient.
Disciplines: Broadcasting
Eligible Inst.: Emerson College
Deadline: January 15

William Randolph Hearst Scholarship

Tel: (617) 824-8500 Fax: (617) 824-8619
Email: admiss@emerson.edu
Web: www.emerson.edu
Requirements: Awarded to AHANA (African, Hispanic, Asian, Native American) students on the basis of financial need.
Disciplines: Performing Arts
Eligible Inst.: Emerson College
Deadline: January 15

F

FORT HAYS STATE UNIVERSITY

Office of Student Financial Assistance
Custer Hall #306
Hays, KS 67601

Foundation for the Care of Mexican Children Scholarship

Tel: (785) 628-5666
Email: tigers@fhsu.edu
Web: www.fhsu.edu
Requirements: This scholarship is available to students of Mexican descent, either citizens of Mexico or the U.S.
Disciplines: Any
Award: Varies
Eligible Inst.: Fort Hays State University
Deadline: December 15, February 15

G

GOVERNMENT FINANCE OFFICERS ASSOCIATION

Scholarship Committee
180 N. Michigan Ave. #800
Chicago, IL 60601

Minorities in Government Finance Scholarship

Jeffrey L. Esser, Executive Director
Tel: (312) 977-9700 Fax: (312) 977-4806
Email: scholarships@gfoa.org
Web: www.gfoa.org
Requirements: This scholarship recognizes

outstanding performance by minority students preparing for careers in state and local government finance. Applicants must be one of the following groups (as defined by the U.S. Census Bureau): Black Indian, Eskimo, Aleut, Asian or Pacific Islander, and Hispanic. Juniors and Seniors are eligible to apply. Applicants must plan to pursue a career in state or local government finance. Undergraduates must submit a transcript.
Disciplines: Public Administration, Accounting, Political Science, Economics, Business Administration
Award: $5,000
Eligible Inst.: US schools
Deadline: February 19

H

HISPANIC COLLEGE FUND, INC.

1717 Pennsylvania Ave. # 460
Washington, DC 20006

H.I.S. Program

Tatiana Pham, Program Manager
Tel: (202) 296-5400 Fax: (202) 296-3774
Email: hcf-info@hispanicfund.org
Web: www.hispanicfund.org
Requirements: Applicant must be a freshman, sophomore, junior, or senior in the fall of 2004. Also must plan to enroll as a full-time undergraduate student (registered for at least 12 credits per semester) from the fall 2004 to the spring 2005. Apply to or be enrolled in a college or university in the fifty states or Puerto Rico. To apply for this program, you need to apply to the general Hispanic College Fund Scholarship Program and to INROADS Internship Program.
Disciplines: Business Administration, Accounting, Business, Banking/Finance, Economics, Engineering
Eligible Inst.: US schools
Deadline: April 15

The Sallie Mae Fund First in My Family Scholarship Program

Tatiana Pham, Program Manager
Tel: (800) 644-4223 Fax: (202) 296-3774
Email: hcf-info@hispanicfund.org
Web: www.hispanicfund.org
Requirements: Applicant must be the first in the family to attend college. Applicant must also be Hispanic, Latin American/Caribbean, Mexican, Nicaraguan, or Spanish and enrolled full-time at a two-year or four-year institution or university and be both studying and a resident of Arizona, California, Florida, New York, or Texas. In addition, applicant must submit an essay, financial need analysis, resume, references, test scores, transcript, college acceptance letter, copy of taxes, copy of SAR, and a completed application.
Disciplines: Agriculture, Business, Chemical Engineering, Computer & Information Science, Economics, Electrical Engineering
Award: $1,000-$5,000
Eligible Inst.: US schools
Deadline: April 30

HISPANIC HEALTH COUNCIL, INC

175 Main St.
Hartford, CT 06106

Maria Borrero Scholarship

Jeannette B. De Jesus, Executive Director
Tel: (860) 527-0856 Fax: (860) 724-0437
Email: jeannetted@hispanichealth.com
Web: www.hispanichealth.com
Requirements: This scholarship is available to Hispanic students.
Disciplines: Health Care

Award: $500
Eligible Inst.: US schools

HISPANIC LEAGUE OF THE PIEDMONT TRIAD

Scholarship Chair
P.O. Box 30651
Winston-Salem, NC 27130-0651

Hispanic League of The Piedmont Triad Scholarship

Tel: (336) 775-4578 Fax: (336) 475-9671
Email: hlpt@yahoo.com
Web: www.hlpt.org
Requirements: Academic Achievement and financial need are considerations for these scholarships. For complete listing of criteria please contact our administrators: Hispanic League of the Piedmont Triead Scholarship Program P.O. Box 1465 Taylor, SC 29687-1465 or write to fssp@greenville.infi.net.
Disciplines: Any
Award: varies
Eligible Inst.: US schools
Deadline: February 15

HISPANIC SCHOLARSHIP FUND

55 2nd St. #1500
San Francisco, CA 94105

HSF/Toyota Foundation Scholarship Program

Tel: (877) 473-4636 Fax: (415) 808-2302
Email: highschool@hsf.net
Web: www.hsf.net/scholarship/Special.htm
Requirements: To be eligible for a scholarship, you must: Be of Hispanic heritage (one parent fully Hispanic or each parent half Hispanic); Be a U.S. citizen or legal permanent resident with a permanent resident card or passport stamped I-551 (not expired) residing in Puerto Rico; Be a graduating high school senior, in Puerto Rico; Be enrolled full-time in a degree-seeking program at a four-year college or university in Puerto Rico; Have an interest in majoring in a field pertaining to the environment; Have a minimum cumulative grade point average (GPA) of 3.5 on a 4.0 scale (or the equivalent).
Disciplines: Environmental Science
Award: $2,500
Eligible Inst.: US schools
Deadline: May 17

K

KANSAS BOARD OF REGENTS

1000 SW Jackson St. #520
Topeka, KS 66612-1368

Kansas Ethnic Minority Scholarship Program

Diane Lindeman, Director of Student Financial Aid
Tel: (785) 296-3421 Fax: (785) 296-0983
Email: dlindeman@ksbor.org
Web: www.kansasregents.org
Requirements: The Kansas Ethnic Minority Scholarship program is designed to assist financially needy, academically competitive students who are identified as members of any of the following ethnic/racial groups: African American, American Indian or Alaskan Native; Asian or Pacific Islander; or Hispanic.
Disciplines: Any
Award: $1,850
Eligible Inst.: US schools
Deadline: May 1

L

LANGSTON UNIVERSITY

P.O. Box 728
Langston, OK 73050

Non-Black Scholarship

Addie Jones
Tel: (405) 466-3282 Fax: (405) 466-2986
Email: financial@lunet.edu
Web: www.lunet.edu
Requirements: As a predominantly black college Langston University has established this scholarship to attract Hispanics, Asian Americans and Anglos to their campus. Applicants must be full time students carrying at least a 12 hour study load. Transfer students must have at least a 2.5 cumulative GPA.
Disciplines: Any
Award: $600
Eligible Inst.: Langston University
Deadline: May 1

LEAGUE OF UNITED LATIN AMERICAN CITIZENS

2000 L St. NW #610
Washington, DC 20036

LULAC National Scholarship Fund

Lorena Garrido, Scholarship Coordinator
Tel: (202) 835-9646 Fax: (202) 835-9685
Email: lnescaward@aol.com
Web: www.lnesc.org
Requirements: Must be a minority student pursuing full-time studies leading to a bachelor's degree at a college approved by LULAC and GM. Must have a college grade point average of at least 3.2 on a 4.0 scale or the equivalent, or for entering freshman, must have a high school grade point average of at least 3.5 on a 4.0 scale or the equivalent. Entering freshman must have also scored at least 23 on the ACT test (composite) or at least 970 on the SAT test (verbal & math). Must major in courses leading to a professional career in engineering.
Disciplines: Engineering
Award: $2,000
Eligible Inst.: US schools
Deadline: July 15

LEWIS-CLARK STATE COLLEGE

Financial Aid Office
500 8th Ave.
Lewiston, ID 83501

Avista Corporation Minority Scholarship

Tel: (208) 799-2224
Email: finaid@lcsc.edu
Web: www.lcsc.edu
Requirements: This scholarship is available to minority students; one scholarship will be awarded to a Native American student and one scholarship will be awarded to a minority student. Applicants must have a minimum GPA of 2.5. To be eligible students must be majoring in one of the following approved fields of study: accounting, biology/chemistry, business, communications, computer science/technology, economics, environmental science, engineering, mathematics, natural resources, political science, statistics or technology.
Disciplines: Any
Award: $1,000
Eligible Inst.: Lewis-Clark State College
Deadline: March 1

Minority and At Risk Student Scholarship

Tel: (208) 799-2224
Email: finaid@lcsc.edu
Web: www.lcsc.edu
Requirements: This scholarship is available to talented students who may be at risk of failing to realize their ambitions because of their cultural, economic, or physical circumstances. Applicants must be Idaho residents, graduates of an Idaho high school, and must meet at least three of the following criteria: be a first-generation college student; be disabled; be a migrant farm worker or other seasonal farm worker or the dependent of a migrant farm worker or other seasonal farm worker; have substantial financial need; or be a minority person, i.e., a black non-Hispanic, a Hispanic, a Native American, or a member of another ethnic group whose members have participated in higher education at a rate lower than their occurrence in the general population. A separate application is required.
Disciplines: Any
Award: Varies
Eligible Inst.: Lewis-Clark State College
Deadline: March 1

M

MANA-A NATIONAL LATINA ORGANIZATION

1725 K St. NW #501
Washington, DC 20006

Rita Dimartino Scholarship in Communications

Elisa Sanchez
Tel: (202) 833-0060 Fax: (202) 496-0588
Email: hermana2@aol.com
Web: www.hermana.org
Requirements: This scholarship is available to Latina undergraduate or graduate students in the field of communications. To order an application by mail, send a self-addressed, stamped envelope.
Disciplines: Communications
Award: $200-$1,000
Eligible Inst.: US schools
Deadline: April 1

MEXICAN AMERICAN WOMEN'S NATIONAL ASSOCIATION, NATIONAL LATINA ORGANIZATION

1725 K St. NW #501
Washington, DC 20006

MANA National Scholarship Program

Liliana Lopez
Tel: (202) 833-0060 Fax: (202) 496-0588
Email: hermana2@aol.com
Web: www.hermana.org
Requirements: Applicants must be outstanding students, a proven leader in extracurricular activities and community involvement. There website has a down loadable application and details about individual programs.
Disciplines: Any
Award: $1,000-$5,000
Eligible Inst.: US schools
Deadline: April 1

MEXICAN-AMERICAN GROCER'S ASSOCIATION

405 N. San Fernando Rd.
Los Angeles, CA 90031

Mexican-American Grocer's Association Scholarships

Jackie Solis
Tel: (323) 227-1565
Requirements: The Mexican-American Grocer's Association offers scholarships to first year hispanic college students. Scholarships are awarded on the basis of overall academic performance, financial need, and extracurricular activities.
Disciplines: Business
Award: $500-$1,500

Eligible Inst.: US schools
Deadline: July 31

MICHIGAN STATE UNIVERSITY

305 Communications Arts & Sciences
East Lansing, MI 48824

Hispanics in Journalism Scholarships

Dr. Stan Soffin
Tel: (517) 353-6430 Fax: (517) 355-7710
Web: www.msu.edu
Requirements: This scholarship program is for undergraduate and graduate students currently enrolled at the University of Michigan for more information please refer to their website.
Disciplines: Journalism
Award: $200-$1,000
Eligible Inst.: Michigan State University

MICHIGAN TECHNOLOGICAL UNIVERSITY

Financial Aid Office
1400 Townsend Dr.
Houghton, MI 49931-1295

Minority Academic Scholarship

Tel: (906) 487-2622 Fax: (906) 487-3343
Requirements: All accepted students are automatically considered for merit-based scholarships for which they are eligible, a special application form is not required. This scholarship is renewable provided the recipient meets the renewal criteria.
Disciplines: Any
Award: $15,000
Eligible Inst.: Michigan Technological University
Deadline: February 15

N

NATIONAL ASSOCIATION FOR CAMPUS ACTIVITIES EDUCATIONAL FOUNDATION

13 Harbison Way
Columbia, SC 29212-3401

Multicultural Scholar Program

Dionne Blakeney
Tel: (803) 732-6222 Fax: (803) 749-1047
Email: dionneb@naca.org
Web: www.naca.org
Requirements: The Multicultural Scholarship Program is part of the NACA Educational Foundation's affirmative action effort to increase the participation of ethnic minorities in the field of campus activities. They offer multiple scholarships throughout the year for undergraduate and graduate college students.
Disciplines: Any
Award: varies
Eligible Inst.: US schools
Deadline: May 1

NATIONAL ASSOCIATION OF HISPANIC JOURNALISTS

1193 National Press Bldg.
Washington, DC 20045-2100

Cox Enterprises Committee

Ana Carrion
Tel: (202) 662-7483 Fax: (202) 662-7144
Email: nahj@nahj.org
Web: www.nahj.org
Requirements: These scholarships are intended for students that plan on pursuing careers in the media. Every year scholarships ranging from $1,000 to $5,000 are awarded. For more information please consult their web site.
Disciplines: Journalism
Award: $1,000-$5,000
Eligible Inst.: US schools

**NATIONAL ASSOCIATION OF
MINORITY ENGINEERING PROGRAM
ADMINISTRATORS, INC.**
National Scholarship Selection Committee
Chair, NAMEPA, Inc.
1133 W. Morse Blvd. #201
Winter Park, FL 32789

NAMEPA Scholarship Fund
Tel: (407) 647-8839 Fax: (407) 629-2502
Email: namepa@namepa.org
Web: www.namepa.org
Requirements: Applicant must be Native
American or Eskimo, African American, or
Hispanic and enrolled full-time at a two-year
or four-year institution or university. For
freshman applicant, they are required to have
been approved for admission and designated
as an engineering major. In addition, the
applicant's ACT/SAT score, and an official
copy of the candidate's high school transcript.
Applicant must attend a NAMEPA member
institution. Candidates must submit a one page
essay expressing their reasons for choosing
engineering, why they think they should be
selected, and an overview of their future
aspirations as an engineer. Also, a completed
recommendation form from a science/math
teacher, counselor, or MEP official who is
familiar with the candidate should be enclosed
with the application. For a transfer student
everything is same as an freshman applicant
except they need to submit official college
transcript.
Disciplines: Engineering, Aerospace Science,
Chemical Engineering, Civil Engineering,
Computer & Information Science,
Mechanical Engineering
Award: $1,000
Eligible Inst.: US schools
Deadline: March 30

**NATIONAL STUDENT NURSES'
ASSOCIATION, INC.**
555 W. 57th St. #1327
New York City, NY 10019

**Breakthrough to Nursing Scholarships for
Ethnic People of Color**
Susan Wong
Tel: (212) 581-2215 Fax: (212) 581-2368
Email: nsna@nsna.org
Web: www.nsna.org
Requirements: The NSNA has developed
this program to improve diversity in the
nursing fields. This program was designed to
assist under represented students with their
financial needs.
Disciplines: Nursing
Award: $1,000-2,500
Eligible Inst.: US schools
Deadline: February 1

O

OHIO UNIVERSITY
Office of Admissions
120 Chubb Hall
Athens, OH 45701

Templeton Scholars Program
Sylvester James Aji
Tel: (740) 593-9376 Fax: (740) 593-9196
Email: diversity@ohio.edu
Web: www.ohio.edu
Requirements: These scholarship awards are
designed to help undergraduate students from
underrepresented populations. Recipient must
maintain at least a 3.4 GPA and earn 48 credit
hours per year to renew this scholarship.
Disciplines: Any
Award: tuition

Eligible Inst.: Ohio University
Deadline: February 1

R

RUST COLLEGE
Financial Aid Office
150 Rust Ave.
Holly Springs, MS 38635

**United Methodists Ethnic Minority
Scholarships**
Helen Street
Tel: (601) 252-8000 Fax: (610) 252-6107
Requirements: Hispanics, Native Americans,
Pacific Islanders, Asians, and Africans who
are active members of the United Methodists
Church for at least 1 year prior to application
are eligible.
Disciplines: Any
Award: $400-$600
Eligible Inst.: Rust College
Deadline: April 30

S

SACRAMENTO BEE
Community Relations Department
P.O. Box 15779
Sacramento, CA 95852

Minority Media Scholarship
Cathy Rodriguez
Tel: (916) 321-1880 Fax: (916) 321-1783
Web: www.sacbee.com
Requirements: Students must reside in the
counties of Sacramento, Placer, Eldorado,
and Yolo to qualify for this program. This is
not a renewable program. For an application
send a business size self addressed stamped
envelope.
Disciplines: Mass Communications & Public
Relations
Award: $1,500-$2,500
Eligible Inst.: US schools
Deadline: January 31

**SALVADORAN AMERICAN LEADERSHIP AND
EDUCATIONAL FUND**
1625 W. Olympic Blvd. #706
Los Angeles, CA 90015

"Fulfilling Our Dreams" Scholarship Fund
Mayra A. Soriano
Tel: (213) 480-1052 Fax: (213) 487-2530
Email: m.soriano@salef.org
Web: www.salef.org
Requirements: The Salvadoran American
Leadership and Educational Fund is a great
opportunity for any graduating high school
student, or currently enrolled college student.
These scholarships can be used nationally in
any school for any major. The award committee
considers community involvement a large
factor in evaluating an application.
Disciplines: Any
Award: $500-$5,000
Eligible Inst.: US schools
Deadline: June 28

**SOCIETY OF HISPANIC PROFESSIONAL
ENGINEER'S FOUNDATION**
5400 E. Olympic Blvd. #306
Los Angeles, CA 90022

**Society of Hispanic Professional
Engineer's Scholarships**
Kathy Borunda
Tel: (323) 888-2080
Web: www.shpe.org
Requirements: The Society of Hispanic
Professional Engineer's Foundation program

---

encourages high school graduating seniors,
undergraduate, and graduate college students
to apply for thier program on the internet. The
web address is www.shpe.org. Applicants are
also required to attach a copy of thier resume
to thier application.
Disciplines: Engineering
Award: $500-$7,000
Eligible Inst.: US schools
Deadline: April 15

T

TAYLOR UNIVERSITY
236 W. Reade Ave.
Upland, IN 46989

Ethnic Student Scholarship
Tel: (765) 998-5358
Email: admissions_u@tayloru.edu
Web: www.tayloru.edu
Requirements: This scholarship is available to
students who have the ability to demonstrate
exceptional leadership skills or who contribute
to cultural diversity.
Disciplines: Any
Award: 25% Tuition
Eligible Inst.: Taylor University

U

U.S. HISPANIC CHAMBER OF COMMERCE
1030 15th St. NW #206
Washington, DC 20005

**U.S. Hispanic Chamber of Commerce
Scholarship**
Guillermo Castano
Tel: (202) 842-1212 Fax: (202) 842-3221
Web: www.ushcc.com
Requirements: This scholarship is available
to Hispanic students enrolled in vocational
programs and undergraduate and graduate
programs at colleges and universities. Awards
are based on achievement, community
involvement, and financial need. Applicants
must have U.S. citizenship, a minimum GPA
of 3.0, and a declared business major.
Disciplines: Business
Award: $1,000
Eligible Inst.: US schools
Deadline: November 1

**UNITED STATES HISPANIC LEADERSHIP
INSTITUTE**
431 S. Dearborn St. #1203
Chicago, IL 60605

**Dr. Juan Andrade, Jr. Scholarship for Young
Hispanic Leaders**
Jessica Lilley, Youth Leadership
Development Coordinator
Tel: (312) 427-8683 Fax: (312) 427-5183
Email: ushli@aol.com
Web: www.ushli.com
Requirements: Applicant must be a citizen
or legal resident, enrolled or accepted for
enrollment as a full-time in a four-year college/
university (undergraduate) in the US or US
territories, and demonstrate a verifiable need
for financial support. At least one parent must
be of Hispanic ancestry.
Disciplines: Any
Award: varies
Eligible Inst.: US schools
Deadline: July 16

UNIVERSITY OF ARIZONA
UA Hispanic Alumni Association
1111 N. Cherry Ave.
Tucson, AZ 85721-0069

**Rigulo Cuesta Memorial Scholarships for
Hispanics**
Rose Garcia
Tel: (520) 626-9327 Fax: (520) 621-9030
Email: uaha@al.arizona.edu
Requirements: Preference is shown to students
with Cuban-American heritage.
Disciplines: Education
Award: $100-$300
Eligible Inst.: University of Arizona
Deadline: May 15

UNIVERSITY OF FLORIDA
Knight Center for Scholarships, Placement
and Multicultural Affairs
P.O. Box 118400
2070 Weimer Hall
Gainesville, FL 32611-8400

General Electric Scholarships
Tel: (352) 392-1365
Web: www.ufl.edu
Requirements: Applicants must have a 3.0
GPA and display leadership potential and
interest in mechanical, electrical or industrial
engineering and systems, or computer and
information sciences.
Disciplines: Engineering
Award: $5,000
Eligible Inst.: University of Florida

UNIVERSITY OF IDAHO
Student Financial Aid Services
Moscow, ID 83844-2431

Diversity Out-of-State Tuition Waiver
Shawna Lindquist, Associate Director for
Scholarships
Tel: (208) 885-6312 Fax: (208) 885-5592
Email: finaid@uidaho.edu
Web: www.uidaho.edu
Requirements: To be eligible to receive a
University of Idaho Multicultural Scholarship
this is one of many you first need to fill out the
financial aid forms and also the UI application
for admissions.
Disciplines: Any
Award: $1,500-$6,000
Eligible Inst.: University of Idaho
Deadline: February 15

Emma McAllister Novel Scholarship
Tel: (319) 335-1450 Fax: (319) 335-3060
Email: financial-aid@uiowa.edu
Web: www.uiowa.edu
Requirements: This scholarship is available
to undergraduate or graduate minority
students.
Disciplines: Arts
Award: $1,000
Eligible Inst.: University of Iowa
Deadline: February 1

College of Business Administration
108 Pappajohn Business Administration
Bldg. #W160
Iowa City, IA 52242

Oeffner Minority Scholarship
Tel: (319) 335-1450 Fax: (319) 335-3060
Email: financial-aid@uiowa.edu
Web: www.uiowa.edu
Requirements: This scholarship is available to
undergraduates in good academic standing
who belong to an ethnic or racial group
underrepresented within the College of
Nursing. Financial need is considered.
Disciplines: Nursing
Award: $3,000/sem
Eligible Inst.: University of Iowa

Office of Student Financial Aid
208 Calvin Hall
Iowa City , IA 52242

Robert Vernon Family Memorial Fund
Director of Financial Aid
Tel: (319) 335-1450 Fax: (319) 335-3060
Email: financial-aid@uiowa.edu
Web: www.uiowa.edu
Requirements: This scholarship is available to undergraduate U.S. citizens with preference given to American Indian, Black, and female minority students showing financial need. No application is required. Qualified students will automatically be considered from Special Support Services and admission records.
Disciplines: Any
Award: Varies
Eligible Inst.: University of Iowa

UNIVERSITY OF MISSOURI-KANSAS CITY
School of Nursing
2220 Holmes
Kansas City, MO 64110-2499

George Hedgepeth Trust Scholarship Fund
Tel: (816) 235-1154 Fax: (816) 235-5511
Web: www.umkc.edu
Requirements: Undergraduates and graduates; preference to minorities; 3.0 GPA or above.
Disciplines: Nursing
Award: Varies
Eligible Inst.: University of Missouri-Kansas City

Financial Aid and Scholarships Office
101 Administrative Ctr., 5100 Rockhill Rd.
Kansas City, MO 64110-2499

Greater Kansas City Hispanic Scholarship
Pat McTee, Director of Financial Aid
Tel: (816) 235-1154 Fax: (816) 235-5511
Email: finaid@umkc.edu
Web: www.umkc.edu/finaid
Requirements: This scholarship is available to U.S. citizens or permanent residents who are of Hispanic descent. Applicants must be accepted or enrolled in a college or university and must be residents of the metropolitan Kansas City area.
Disciplines: Any
Award: Varies
Eligible Inst.: University of Missouri-Kansas City
Deadline: March 1

Conservatory of Music
Grant Hall, 5228 Charlotte
Kansas City, MO 64110-2499

Hazel Browne Williams Scholarship
Tel: (816) 235-1154 Fax: (816) 235-5511
Web: www.umkc.edu
Requirements: Minority students seeking education degree at undergraduate or graduate level.
Disciplines: Education
Award: $1,000
Eligible Inst.: University of Missouri-Kansas City
Deadline: February 28

UNIVERSITY OF TEXAS AT ARLINGTON
Scholarships & Financial Aid
P.O. Box 19199
Arlington, TX 76019-0199

Alliance for Minority Participation Scholarship
Chris Woodyard
Tel: (817) 272-2197 Fax: (817) 272-3555
Email: schol@uta.edu
Web: www.uta.edu
Requirements: The Alliance for Minority Participation Scholarship is funded by the National Science Foundation and entails a 12 month research project. Selection is based on merit and academic performance. Students may apply no later than their junior year in anticipation of completing the research project in the senior and graduation year. This scholarship program is intended only for students planning to attend University of Texas at Arlington. For further information please consult their website.
Disciplines: Engineering
Award: $6,000
Eligible Inst.: University of Texas at Arlington
Deadline: June 1

Hispanic Scholarship
Chris Woodyard
Tel: (817) 272-2197 Fax: (817) 272-3555
Email: schol@uta.edu
Web: www.uta.edu
Requirements: Applicants for the UTA Hispanic Scholarship must be of Hispanic origin and have a minimum of 15 hours completed at UTA with at least a 2.5 GPA. Co-founded by the Alumni Association and the Association of Mexican American Students (AMAS), financial need, demonstrated leadership ability and potential for success will be considerations in the selection process. This scholarship program is intended only for students planning to attend University of Texas at Arlington. For further information please consult their website.
Disciplines: Any
Award: $250
Eligible Inst.: University of Texas at Arlington
Deadline: June 1

UNIVERSITY OF TEXAS-PAN AMERICAN
Office of Financial Aid
1201 W. University Dr. SSB 186
Edinburg, TX 78539-2999

Adolph Coors Scholarship
Tel: (210) 381-2501 Fax: (210) 381-2392
Web: www.panam.edu/finaid
Requirements: This scholarship is intended to increase the number of minority college graduates with management and leadership potential. Juniors and senior are eligible to apply. Selection is based on academic achievement. The UTPA Scholarship Application may be used to apply.
Disciplines: Business
Award: $300/yr
Eligible Inst.: University of Texas-Pan American
Deadline: January 14

URBAN LEAGUE OF METROPOLITAN DENVER
5900 E. 39th St.
Denver, CO 80206

Gil Mosley Scholarship
Erin Knight
Tel: (303) 388-5861 Fax: (303) 388-3523
Web: www.denverurbanleague.org
Requirements: The Gil Mosley Scholarship is for undergraduate minority students. All applicants should send in their transcripts, letters of recommendation, and have a minimum GPA of 2.5 on a 4.0 scale. For an application students should call 1-888-839-0467.
Disciplines: Any
Award: $1,000
Eligible Inst.: US schools
Deadline: May 16

URBAN SCHOLARSHIP FUND

Urban Scholarship Fund
Email: submissions@urbanscholarshipfund.com
Web: http://www.blacknews.com/UrbanScholarshipFund.com/
Requirements: The Urban Scholarship Fund is open to minority students who attend or plan to attend a school in the United States in the fall. In order to apply, one or both of your parents must be African-American, Hispanic American or Asian American. You must submit an 800-word essay on a designated topic.
Disciplines: Any
Award: $500
Eligible Inst.: US schools
Deadline: August 31

V

VANDERBILT UNIVERSITY
Office of Undergraduate Admissions
2305 W. End Ave.
Nashville, TN 37203-1727

Chancellor's Scholarships
Tel: (615) 322-2561 Fax: (615) 343-7765
Email: admissions@vanderbilt.edu
Web: www.vanderbilt.edu/admissions
Requirements: Are full tuition scholarships awarded on the basis of academic merit to minority students with outstanding academic records. These scholarships also include a stipend for a summer of study or research in a Vanderbilt program either in Nashville or overseas after the sophomore or junior year.
Disciplines: Any
Award: Tuition
Eligible Inst.: Vanderbilt University

VETERANS OF FOREIGN WARS
3981 Colman
San Diego, CA 95051

U.S. VFW Mexican Ancestry Scholarship
Gilbert Castorena
Tel: (619) 690-0907
Requirements: To be eligible for this scholarship, applicants must be Hispanics, have a financial needs and good grades.
Disciplines: Any
Award: $500
Eligible Inst.: US schools
Deadline: April 30

VIRGINIA SOCIETY OF CPAS EDUCATIONAL FOUNDATION
P.O. Box 4620
Glen Allen, VA 23058-4620

Minority Undergraduate Accounting Scholarship
Tracey Zink, Public Relations Coordinator
Tel: (804) 270-5344 Fax: (804) 273-1741
Email: tzink@vscpa.com
Web: www.cpastudentzone.com
Requirements: This scholarship is available to U.S. citizens who are members of one of the VSCPA-defined minority groups (African American, Hispanic America, American Indian, or Asian Pacific American). Applicants must be accounting majors with at least 12 hours of accounting and a minimum GPA of 3.0 in accounting (an official transcript is required).
Disciplines: Accounting
Award: $22,000
Eligible Inst.: US schools
Deadline: July 1

W

WALSH UNIVERSITY
Financial Aid Office
2020 Easton St. NW
North Canton, OH 44720-3396

Timken Foundation Endowed Scholarship
Tel: (216) 490-7165 Fax: (216) 490-7165
Email: admissions@alex.walsh.edu
Web: www.walsh.edu
Requirements: This scholarship is available to minority students enrolled full-time.
Disciplines: Any
Award: Varies
Eligible Inst.: Walsh University

WASHINGTON EDUCATION FOUNDATION
1605 NW Sammamish Rd. #100
Issaquah, WA 98027

Costco Scholarship Fund
Tel: (877) 655-4097 Fax: (425) 416-2001
Email: info@waedfoundation.org
Web: www.waedfoundation.org
Requirements: Applicants must be US citizens who are African American, Latino or Native American, Latino or Native American. High School grade point average of 3.0 or better and register for full time enrollment at Seattle University. The scholarship will be renewed each year, for four years, provided the student maintains satisfactory academic progress. Must complete 36 credits per academic year with a GPA of 2.0. The Scholarships are awarded during admissions process to Seattle University. To apply the student must complete the Undergraduate Application for Admission and the Free Application for Federal Student Aid (FAFSA).
Disciplines: Any
Award: $7,000
Eligible Inst.: Seattle University
Deadline: February 15

WAYNE STATE UNIVERSITY
Engineering Building
5050 Anthony Wayne Dr.
Detroit, MI 48202

Chrysler Corporation Minority Scholarship
Tel: (313) 577-3780
Email: admissions@wayne.edu
Web: www.wayne.edu
Requirements: Minority students in Mechanical Engineering, Electrical Engineering, Industrial Management or Business Administration. The student must also demonstrate financial need, outstanding scholastic achievement and leadership qualities.
Disciplines: Mechanical Engineering, Electrical Engineering, Business Administration
Award: Varies depending on funds available.
Eligible Inst.: Wayne State University

Office of Scholarships and Financial Aid
Student Services Ctr., 3 West
Detroit , MI 48202

Ford EEOC Scholarship
Kevin J. Culler, Interim Director of Financial Aid
Tel: (313) 577-3378 Fax: (313) 577-6648
Email: admissions@wayne.edu
Web: www.wayne.edu
Requirements: This scholarship is available to minority or female students who are either a Ford Motor Company employee, or a spouse or child of a Ford Motor Company employee; certification of Ford employment required.
Disciplines: Any
Award: Varies depending on funds available.
Eligible Inst.: Wayne State University
Deadline: April 28

Hispanic Serving Institutions (HSI)
Instituciones al servicio de los hispanos

ARIZONA

ARIZONA WESTERN COLLEGE
P.O. Box 929
Yuma, AZ 85366
Dr. Don Schoening, President
Tel: (928) 317-6000 Fax: (928) 344-7730
Web: www.azwestern.edu

CENTRAL ARIZONA COLLEGE
Signal Peak
8470 N. Overfield Rd.
Coolidge, AZ 85228
Dr. Terry A. Calaway, President
Tel: (520) 426-4444 Fax: (520) 426-4234
Web: www.centralaz.edu

COCHISE COLLEGE
Douglas
4190 W. Hwy. 80
Douglas, AZ 85607
Dr. Karen A. Nicodemus, President
Tel: (520) 364-7943 Fax: (520) 417-4006
Web: www.cochise.edu

ESTRELLA MOUNTAIN COMMUNITY COLLEGE
3000 N. Dysart Rd.
Avondale, AZ 85323
Dr. Homero Lopez, President
Tel: (623) 935-8000 Fax: (623) 935-8008
Web: www.emc.maricopa.edu

INTERNATIONAL INSTITUTE OF THE AMERICAS
5242 W. Camelback Rd.
Glendale, AZ 85301
Dr. Logan P. Bauer, President
Tel: (623-849-7830 Fax: (623-849-7839
Web: www.iia.edu

PHOENIX COLLEGE
1202 W. Thomas Rd.
Phoenix, AZ 85013
Dr. Corina Gardea, President
Tel: (602) 264-7433 Fax: (602) 285-7832
Web: www.phoenixcollege.edu

PIMA COUNTY COMMUNITY COLLEGE DISTRICT
District Office
4905 E. Broadway Blvd. #C-232
Tucson, AZ 85709
Dr. Roy Flores, Chancellor
Tel: (520) 206-4747 Fax: (520) 206-4990
Web: www.pima.edu

SOUTH MOUNTAIN COMMUNITY COLLEGE
7050 S. 24th St.
Phoenix, AZ 85042
Dr. Ken Atwater, President
Tel: (602) 243-8150 Fax: (602) 243-8108
Web: www.southmountaincc.edu

UNIVERSITY OF ARIZONA SOUTH
1140 N. Colombo
Sierra Vista, AZ 85635
Dr. Randall H. Groth, Associate Vice President and Dean
Tel: (520) 458-8278 Fax: (520) 458-5823
Web: www.uas.arizona.edu

CALIFORNIA

ALLAN HANCOCK COLLEGE
800 S. College Dr.
Santa Maria, CA 93454
Dr. Ann Foxworthy, Superintendent/President
Tel: (805) 922-6966 Fax: (805) 347-9896
Web: www.hancockcollege.edu

ALLIANT INTERNATIONAL UNIVERSITY
10455 Pomerado Rd.
San Diego, CA 92131-1799
Dr. Judith E.N. Albino, President
Tel: (858) 635-4000 Fax: (858) 693-4884
Web: www.alliant.edu

ANTELOPE VALLEY COLLEGE
3041 W. Ave. K
Lancaster, CA 93536
Dr. Jackie Fisher, Superintendent/President
Tel: (661) 722-6300 Fax: (661) 722-6324
Web: www.avc.edu

BAKERSFIELD COLLEGE
1801 Panorama Dr.
Bakersfield, CA 93305
Dr. Lincoln Hall, Interim President
Tel: (661) 395-4211 Fax: (661) 395-4698
Web: www.bakersfieldcollege.edu

CALIFORNIA STATE POLYTECHNIC UNIVERSITY
Pomona
3801 W. Temple Ave.
Pomona, CA 91768
Dr. J. Michael Ortiz, President
Tel: (909) 869-2290 Fax: (909) 869-4535
Web: www.csupomona.edu

CALIFORNIA STATE UNIVERSITY
Bakersfield
9001 Stockdale Hwy.
Bakersfield, CA 93311
Dr. Horace Mitchell, President
Tel: (661) 664-2011 Fax: (661) 664-3194
Web: www.csub.edu

Dominguez Hills
1000 E. Victoria St.
Carson, CA 90747
Dr. James E. Lyons, President
Tel: (310) 243-3301 Fax: (310) 243-3858
Web: www.csudh.edu

Fresno
5241 N. Maple Ave., M/S TA48
Fresno, CA 93740
Dr. John D. Welty, President
Tel: (559) 278-2324 Fax: (559) 278-4715
Web: www.csufresno.edu

Fullerton
800 N. State College
Fullerton, CA 92834
Dr. Milton A. Gordon, President
Tel: (714) 278-3456 Fax: (714) 278-2649
Web: www.fullerton.edu

Long Beach
1250 Bellflower Blvd.
Long Beach, CA 90840
Dr. Robert C. Maxson, President
Tel: (562) 985-4121 Fax: (562) 985-5419
Web: www.csulb.edu

Los Angeles
5151 State University Dr.
Los Angeles, CA 90032
Dr. James M. Rosser, President
Tel: (323) 343-3000 Fax: (323) 343-6424
Web: www.calstatela.edu

Monterey Bay
100 Campus Center, Bldg. 1
Seaside, CA 93955
Dr. Peter Smith, President
Tel: (831) 582-3680 Fax: (831-582-3558
Web: www.csumb.edu

Northridge
18111 Nordhoff St.
Northridge, CA 91330-8230
Dr. Jolene Koester, President
Tel: (818) 677-2121 Fax: (818) 677-2254
Web: www.csun.edu

San Bernardino
5500 University Pkwy.
San Bernardino, CA 92407
Dr. Albert K. Karnig, President
Tel: (909) 880-5002 Fax: (909) 880-7007
Web: www.csusb.edu

Stanislaus
801 W. Monte Vista Ave.
Turlock, CA 95382
Dr. Marvalene Hughes, President
Tel: (209) 667-3964 Fax: (209) 678-3206
Web: www.csustan.edu

CAÑADA COLLEGE
4200 Farm Hill Blvd.
Redwood City, CA 94061
Ms. Rosa G. Perez, President
Tel: (650) 306) 3238 Fax: (650) 306-3144
Web: www.canadacollege.edu

CERRITOS COLLEGE
11110 Alondra Blvd.
Norwalk, CA 90650
Dr. Noelia Vela, President
Tel: (562) 860-2451 X2204
Fax: (562) 860-1104
Web: www.cerritos.edu

CHAFFEY COLLEGE
5885 Haven Ave.
Rancho Cucamonga, CA 91737
Dr. Marie Kane, Superintendent/President
Tel: (909-941-2157 Fax: (909) 941-2783
Web: www.chaffey.edu

CITY COLLEGE OF SAN FRANCISCO
Phelan
50 Phelan Ave., E200
San Francisco, CA 94112
Dr. Philip R. Day, Chancellor
Tel: (415) 239-3303 Fax: (415) 239-3918
Web: www.ccsf.edu

COLLEGE OF THE DESERT
43-500 Monterey Ave.
Palm Desert, CA 92260
Dr. Maria C. Sheehan, Superintendent/President
Tel: (760) 773-2500 Fax: (760) 341-9732
Web: www.collegeofthedesert.edu

COLLEGE OF THE SEQUOIAS
915 S. Mooney Blvd.
Visalia, CA 93277
Dr. Kamiran S. Badrkhan, Superintendent/President
Tel: (559) 730-3731 Fax: (559) 730-3894
Web: www.cos.edu

EAST LOS ANGELES COLLEGE
1301 Avenida Cesar Chavez
Monterey Park, CA 91754
Mr. Ernest H. Moreno, President
Tel: (323) 265-8650 Fax: (323) 265-8763
Web: www.elac.edu

EL CAMINO COMMUNITY COLLEGE
16007 Crenshaw Blvd.
Torrance, CA 90506
Dr. Thomas M. Fallo, Superintendent/President
Tel: (310) 660-3471 Fax: (310) 660-6024
Web: www.elcamino.edu

FRESNO CITY COLLEGE
1101 E. University Ave.
Fresno, CA 93741
Dr. Ned Doffoney, President
Tel: (559) 442-8251 Fax: (559) 265-5777
Web: www.fresnocitycollege.edu

FULLERTON COLLEGE
321 E. Chapman Ave.
Fullerton, CA 92832
Dr. Kathleen Hodge, President
Tel: (714) 992-7038 Fax: (714) 992-7519
Web: www.fullcoll.edu

GAVILAN COLLEGE
5055 Santa Teresa Blvd.
Gilroy, CA 95020
Dr. Steven M. Kinsella, Superintendent/
President
Tel: (408) 848-4712 Fax: (408) 847-5102
Web: www.gavilan.edu

GLENDALE COMMUNITY COLLEGE
1500 N. Verdugo Rd.
Glendale, CA 91208
Dr. John A. Davitt, President
Tel: (818) 240-1000 Fax: (818) 549-9436
Web: www.glendale.edu

HARTNELL COLLEGE
156 Homestead Ave.
Salinas, CA 93901
Dr. Edward Valeau, President/
Superintendent
Tel: (831) 755-6900 Fax: (831) 753-7941
Web: www.hartnell.cc.ca.us

HEALD COLLEGE
Administrative Office
670 Howard St.
San Francisco, CA 94105
Ms. Amy McCombs, President
Tel: (415) 808-1430 Fax: (415) 808-1594
Web: www.heald.edu

IMPERIAL VALLEY COLLEGE
380 E. Aten Rd.
Imperial, CA 92251
Dr. Paul Pai, Superintendent/President
Tel: (760) 355-6219 Fax: (760) 355-6461
Web: www.imperial.edu

LONG BEACH CITY COLLEGE
4901 E. Carson St.
Long Beach, CA 90808
Dr. E. Jan Kehoe, Superintendent/President
Tel: (562) 938-4123 Fax: (562) 938-4098
Web: www.lbcc.edu

LOS ANGELES CITY COLLEGE
855 N. Vermont Ave.
Los Angeles, CA 90029
Dr. Doris Pichon Givens, President
Tel: (323) 953-4010 Fax: (323) 953-4013
Web: www.lacitycollege.edu

LOS ANGELES COUNTY COLLEGE OF NURSING AND ALLIED HEALTH
1237 N. Mission Rd.
Los Angeles, CA 90033
Ms. Katherine Eaves, Provost
Tel: (323) 226-4911 Fax: (323) 226-6343
Web: www.ladhs.org/lacusc/lacnah

LOS ANGELES MISSION COLLEGE
13356 Eldridge Ave.
Sylmar, CA 91342
Dr. Adriana D. Barrera, President
Tel: (818) 364-7795 Fax: (818) 364-7826
Web: www.lamission.edu

LOS ANGELES TRADE-TECHNICAL COLLEGE
400 W. Washington Blvd.
Los Angeles, CA 90015
Dr. Daniel A. Castro, President
Tel: (213) 763-7040 Fax: (213) 763-5367
Web: www.lattc.edu

MODESTO JUNIOR COLLEGE
435 College Ave.
Modesto, CA 95350
Dr. James H. Williams, President
Tel: (209) 575-6067 Fax: (209) 575-6630
Web: www.mjc.yosemite.cc.ca.us

MT. SAN ANTONIO COLLEGE
1100 N. Grand Ave.
Walnut, CA 91789
Dr. Christopher C. O'Hearn, President
Tel: (909) 594-5611 Fax: (909) 598-2303
Web: www.mtsac.edu

MT. SAN JACINTO COLLEGE
1499 N. State St.
San Jacinto, CA 92583
Dr. Richard J. Giese, Superintendent/
President
Tel: (909) 487-6752 Fax: (909) 654-9712
Web: www.msjc.edu

NATIONAL HISPANIC UNIVERSITY
14271 Story Rd.
San Jose, CA 95127
Dr. David P. Lopez, President
Tel: (408) 273-2697 Fax: (408) 254-7629
Web: www.nhu.edu

OXNARD COLLEGE
4000 S. Rose Ave.
Oxnard, CA 93033
Dr. Lydia Ledesma-Reese, President
Tel: (805) 986-5808 Fax: (805) 986-5908
Web: www.oxnardcollege.edu

PALO VERDE COMMUNITY COLLEGE
One College Dr.
Blythe, CA 92225
Dr. James W. Hottois, Superintendent/
President
Tel: (760) 921-5500 Fax: (760) 921-5590
Web: www.paloverde.edu

PALOMAR COLLEGE
1140 W. Mission Rd.
San Marcos, CA 92069-1487
Mr. Robert P. Deegan, Superintendent/
President
Tel: (760) 744-1150 X2105
Fax: (760) 591-0698
Web: www.palomar.edu

PASADENA CITY COLLEGE
1570 E. Colorado Blvd.
Pasadena, CA 91106
Dr. James Kossler, President/
Superintendent
Tel: (626) 585-7071 Fax: (626) 585-7915
Web: www.pasadena.edu

REEDLEY COLLEGE
995 N. Reed Ave.
Reedley, CA 93654
Dr. Barbara Hioco, President
Tel: (559) 638-3641 Fax: (559) 638-0305
Web: www.reedleycollege.edu

RIO HONDO COLLEGE
3600 Workman Mill Rd.
Whittier, CA 90601
Dr. Rose Marie Joyce, Superintendent/
President
Tel: (562) 908-3403 Fax: (562) 908-3463
Web: www.riohondo.edu

RIVERSIDE COMMUNITY COLLEGE
4800 Magnolia Ave.
Riverside, CA 92506
Dr. Salvatore G. Rotella, President
Tel: (909) 222-8800 Fax: (909) 222-8035
Web: www.rcc.edu

SAN BERNARDINO COMMUNITY COLLEGE DISTRICT
114 S. Del Rosa Dr.
San Bernardino, CA 92408
Dr. Donald F. Averill, Chancellor
Tel: (909) 382-4090 Fax: (909) 382-0152
Web: www.sbccd.cc.ca.us

SAN BERNARDINO VALLEY COLLEGE
701 S. Mount Vernon Ave.
San Bernardino, CA 92410
Mrs. Denise Whittaker, President
Tel: (909) 384-8298 Fax: (909) 885-6438
Web: www.sbccd.cc.ca.us/sbvc

SAN DIEGO STATE UNIVERSITY
Imperial Valley
720 Heber Ave.
Calexico, CA 92231
Dr. Stephen B.W. Roeder, Dean of the
Campus
Tel: (760) 768-5515 Fax: (760) 768-5632
Web: www.ivcampus.sdsu.edu

SANTA MONICA COLLEGE
1900 Pico Blvd.
Santa Monica, CA 90405
Dr. Piedad F. Robertson, Superintendent/
President
Tel: (310) 434-4200 Fax: (310) 434-4386
Web: www.smc.edu

SOUTHWESTERN COLLEGE
900 Otay Lakes Rd.
Chula Vista, CA 91910
Ms. Norma L. Hernandez, Superintendent/
President
Tel: (619) 482-6301 Fax: (619) 421-0346
Web: www.swc.cc.ca.us

UNIVERSITY OF LA VERNE
1950 Third St.
La Verne, CA 91750
Dr. Stephen Morgan, President
Tel: (909) 593-3511 X4398
Fax: (909) 593-0965
Web: www.ulv.edu

VENTURA COLLEGE
4667 Telegraph Rd.
Ventura, CA 93003
Dr. Mike Gregoryk, Acting President
Tel: (805) 654-6400 Fax: (805) 654-6466
Web: www.venturacollege.edu

VICTOR VALLEY COLLEGE
18422 Bear Valley Rd.
Victorville, CA 92392
Dr. Patricia Spencer, President
Tel: (760) 245-4271 X2414
Fax: (760) 245-9744
Web: www.vvc.edu

WEST HILLS COMMUNITY COLLEGE
9900 Cody St.
Coalinga, CA 93210
Dr. Frank Gornick, Chancellor
Tel: (559) 934-2107 Fax: (559) 934-2810
Web: www.westhillscollege.com

WEST LOS ANGELES COLLEGE
9000 Overland Ave.
Culver City, CA 90230
Dr. Frank Quiambao, President
Tel: (310) 287-4325 Fax: (310) 253-9067
Web: www.wlac.edu

WHITTIER COLLEGE
P.O. Box 634
Whittier, CA 90608
Ms. Janice A. Legosa, Interim President
Tel: (562) 907-4201 Fax: (562) 907-4242
Web: www.whittier.edu

WOODBURY UNIVERSITY
7500 Glenoaks Blvd.
Burbank, CA 91510
Dr. Kenneth R. Nielsen, President
Tel: (818) 767-0888 X302
Fax: (818) 767-3470
Web: www.woodbury.edu

COLORADO

ADAMS STATE COLLEGE
208 Edgemont Blvd.
Alamosa, CO 81102
Dr. Richard A. Wueste, President
Tel: (719) 587-7341 Fax: (719) 587-7547
Web: www.adams.edu

COLORADO STATE UNIVERSITY
Pueblo
2200 Bonforte Blvd.
Pueblo, CO 81001
Dr. Ronald L. Applbaum, President
Tel: (719) 549-2100 Fax: (719) 549-2650
Web: www.colostate-pueblo.edu

COMMUNITY COLLEGE OF DENVER
P.O. Box 173363
Denver, CO 80217
Dr. Christine Johnson, President
Tel: (303) 556-2411 Fax: (303) 556-3586
Web: www.ccd.edu

OTERO JUNIOR COLLEGE
1802 Colorado Ave.
La Junta, CO 81050
Mr. Jim Rizzuto, President
Tel: (719) 384-6831 Fax: (719) 384-6947
Web: www.ojc.edu

PUEBLO COMMUNITY COLLEGE
900 W. Orman
Pueblo, CO 81004
Dr. Michael Davis, President
Tel: (719) 549-3213 Fax: (719) 549-3333
Web: www.pueblocc.edu

TRINIDAD STATE JUNIOR COLLEGE
600 Prospect
Trinidad, CO 81082
Dr. Frank Armijo, President
Tel: (719) 846-5541 Fax: (719) 846-5667
Web: www.trinidadstate.edu

CONNECTICUT

CAPITAL COMMUNITY COLLEGE
950 Main St.
Hartford, CT 6103
Dr. Booker T. Devaughn, Interim President
Tel: (860) 906-5100 Fax: (860) 906-5115
Web: www.ccc.commnet.edu

FLORIDA

BARRY UNIVERSITY
11300 NE Second Ave.
Miami Shores, FL 33161
Sister Linda Bevilacqua, President
Tel: (305) 899-3010 Fax: (305) 899-3018
Web: www.barry.edu

BROWARD COMMUNITY COLLEGE
District Administrative Offices
225 E. Las Olas Blvd.
Fort Lauderdale, FL 33301
Dr. Larry A. Calderon, President

Tel: (954) 201-7401 Fax: (954) 201-7576
Web: www.broward.edu

CARLOS ALBIZU UNIVERSITY
Miami
2173 NW 99th Ave.
Miami, FL 33172
Dr. Salvador Santiago-Negron, President
Tel: (305) 593-1223 Fax: (305) 592-7930
Web: www.mia.albizu.edu

FLORIDA INTERNATIONAL UNIVERSITY
University Park
Miami, FL 33199
Dr. Modesto Maidique, President
Tel: (305) 348-2111 Fax: (305) 348-3660
Web: www.fiu.edu

MIAMI DADE COLLEGE
District Administration
300 NE 2nd Ave.
Miami, FL 33132
Dr. Eduardo J. Padron, College President
Tel: (305) 237-3316 Fax: (305) 237-3109
Web: www.mdc.edu

Homestead
500 College Terrace
Homestead, FL 33030
Dr. Richard B. Schinoff, Campus President
Tel: (305) 237-5006 Fax: (305) 237-5002
Web: www.mdc.edu/homestead

Kendall
11011 Southwest 104th St.
Miami, FL 33176
Dr. Wasim Shomar, Kendall Campus
President
Tel: (305) 237-2245 Fax: (305) 237-2658
Web: www.mdc.edu/kendall

Medical Center
950 NW 20th St.
Miami, FL 33127
Dr. Castell V. Bryant, Campus President
Tel: (305) 237-4025 Fax: (305) 237-4170
Web: www.mdc.edu

North Campus
11380 NW 27th Ave.
Miami, FL 33167
Dr. Jose A. Vicente, North Campus
President
Tel: (305) 237-1153 Fax: (305) 237-1899
Web: www.mdcc.edu/north

Wolfson
300 NE 2nd Ave. #1301
Miami, FL 33132
Dr. Rolando Montoya, Wolfson Campus
President
Tel: (305) 237-3310 Fax: (305) 237-3724
Web: www2.mdc.edu/wolfson

NOVA SOUTHEASTERN UNIVERSITY
3301 College Ave.
Fort Lauderdale, FL 33314-7796
Mr. Ray Ferrero, President
Tel: (954) 262-7300 Fax: (954) 262-3800
Web: www.nova.edu

ST. THOMAS UNIVERSITY
16401 NW 37th Ave.
Miami Gardens, FL 33054
Rev. Franklyn M. Casale, President
Tel: (305) 628-6663 Fax: (305) 628-6511
Web: www.stu.edu

UNIVERSITY OF MIAMI
Coral Gables
230 Ashe Building
Coral Gables, FL 33124
Dr. Donna E. Shalala, President

Tel: (305) 284-4104 Fax: (305) 284-4875
Web: www.miami.edu

VALENCIA COMMUNITY COLLEGE
Osceola
1800 Denn John Ln.
Kissimmee, FL 34744
Dr. Silvia C. Zapico, Campus Provost
Tel: (407) 299-5000 Fax: (407) 582-4858
Web: www.valenciacc.edu

ILLINOIS

MACCORMAC COLLEGE
29 E. Madison St.
Chicago, IL 60602
Dr. Leo Loughead, President
Tel: (312) 922-1884 Fax: (312) 922-4286
Web: www.maccormac.edu

MALCOLM X COLLEGE
City Colleges of Chicago
1900 W. Van Buren
Chicago, IL 60612
Dr. Zerrie D. Campbell, President
Tel: (312) 850-7000 Fax: (312) 850-7039
Web: www.ccc.edu/malcolmx

MORTON COLLEGE
3801 S. Central Ave.
Cicero, IL 60804
Dr. Brent Knight, President
Tel: (708) 656-8000 Fax: (708) 656-3186
Web: www.morton.edu

NEERN ILLINOIS UNIVERSITY
5500 N. Saint Louis Ave.
Chicago, IL 60625-4699
Dr. Salme H. Steinberg, President
Tel: (773) 442-5400 Fax: (773) 442-5070
Web: www.neiu.edu

RICHARD J. DALEY COLLEGE
City Colleges of Chicago
7500 S. Pulaski Rd.
Chicago, IL 60652
Dr. Sylvia Ramos, President
Tel: (773) 838-7511 Fax: (773) 838-7985
Web: www.ccc.edu/daley

ROBERT MORRIS COLLEGE
Chicago
401 S. State St. #410
Chicago, IL 60605
Mr. Michael P. Viollt, President/CEO
Tel: (312) 935-6600 Fax: (312) 935-6656
Web: www.robertmorris.edu

ST. AUGUSTINE COLLEGE
1345 W. Argyle
Chicago, IL 60640
Dr. Z. Clara Brennan, President
Tel: (773) 878-8756 Fax: (773) 878-7067
Web: www.staugustinecollege.edu

WILBUR WRIGHT COLLEGE
City Colleges of Chicago
4300 N. Narragansett Ave.
Chicago, IL 60634
Dr. Charles P. Guengerich, President
Tel: (773) 481-8183 Fax: (773) 481-8185
Web: www.ccc.edu/wright

KANSAS

DONNELLY COLLEGE
608 N. 18th St.
Kansas City, KS 66102
Dr. Kenneth R. Gibson, President

Tel: (913) 621-6070 Fax: (913) 621-8719
Web: www.donnelly.edu

NEW JERSEY

HUDSON COUNTY COMMUNITY COLLEGE
70 Sip Ave.
Jersey City, NJ 7306
Dr. Glen E. Gabert, President
Tel: (201) 360-4001 Fax: (201) 714-2136
Web: www.hccc.edu

NEW JERSEY CITY UNIVERSITY
2039 Kennedy Blvd.
Jersey City, NJ 7305
Dr. Carlos Hernandez, President
Tel: (201) 200-3113 Fax: (201) 200-2352
Web: www.njcu.edu

PASSAIC COUNTY COMMUNITY COLLEGE
Paterson
One College Blvd.
Paterson, NJ 7505
Dr. Steven M. Rose, President
Tel: (973) 684-5900 Fax: (973) 684-1925
Web: www.pccc.edu

SAINT PETER'S COLLEGE
2641 Kennedy Blvd.
Jersey City, NJ 7306
Rev. James N. Loughran, President
Tel: (201) 915-9014 Fax: (201) 451-3515
Web: www.spc.edu

UNION COUNTY COLLEGE
1033 Springfield Ave.
Cranford, NJ 7016
Dr. Thomas H. Brown, President
Tel: (908) 709-7100 Fax: (908) 709-0527
Web: www.ucc.edu

NEW MEXICO

ALBUQUERQUE TECHNICAL VOCATIONAL INSTITUTE
525 Buena Vista Southeast
Albuquerque, NM 87106
Mr. Michael J. Glennon, President
Tel: (505) 224-4433 Fax: (505) 224-4430
Web: www.tvi.edu

CLOVIS COMMUNITY COLLEGE
417 Schepps Blvd.
Clovis, NM 88101
Dr. Beverlee J. McClure, President
Tel: (505) 769-4001 Fax: (505) 769-4011
Web: www.clovis.edu

COLLEGE OF SANTA FE
1600 St. Michael's Dr.
Santa Fe, NM 87505
Dr. Linda N. Hanson, President
Tel: (505) 473-6011 Fax: (505) 473-6125
Web: www.csf.edu

COLLEGE OF THE SOUTHWEST
6610 Lovington Hwy.
Hobbs, NM 88240
Mr. Gary A. Dill, President
Tel: (505) 392-6561 Fax: (505) 392-6006
Web: www.csw.edu

EASTERN NEW MEXICO UNIVERSITY
Station #1
Portales, NM 88130
Dr. Steven G. Gamble, President
Tel: (505) 562-2121 Fax: (505) 562-2980
Web: www.enmu.edu

EASTERN NEW MEXICO UNIVERSITY
Roswell
P.O. Box 6000
Roswell, NM 88202-6000
Dr. Judy Armstrong, Provost
Tel: (505) 624-7112 Fax: (505) 624-7119
Web: www.roswell.enmu.edu

LUNA COMMUNITY COLLEGE
P. O. Box 1510
Las Vegas, NM 87701
Mr. Leroy Sanchez, President
Tel: (505) 454-2500 Fax: (505) 454-2520
Web: www.luna.cc.nm.us

MESALANDS COMMUNITY COLLEGE
911 S. Tenth St.
Tucumcari, NM 88401
Dr. Phillip O. Barry, President
Tel: (505) 461-4413 X108
Fax: (505) 461-1901
Web: www.mesalands.edu

NEW MEXICO HIGHLANDS UNIVERSITY
National Ave.
Las Vegas, NM 87701
Mr. Manny M. Aragon, President
Tel: (505) 454-3269 Fax: (505) 454-3069
Web: www.nmhu.edu

NEW MEXICO JUNIOR COLLEGE
5317 Lovington Hwy.
Hobbs, NM 88240
Dr. Steve McCleery, President
Tel: (505) 392 4510 Fax: (505) 392-2526
Web: www.nmjc.edu

NEW MEXICO STATE UNIVERSITY
Alamogordo Branch Community College
2400 N. Scenic Dr.
Alamogordo, NM 88310
Dr. Roger Bates, Campus Executive Officer
Tel: (505) 439-3696 Fax: (505) 439-3749
Web: alamo.nmsu.edu

Carlsbad Branch Community College
1500 University Dr.
Carlsbad, NM 88220
Dr. Melvin M. Vuk, Campus Executive Officer
Tel: (505) 234 9210 Fax: (505) 885-4951
Web: www.cavern.nmsu.edu

Doña Ana Branch Community College
3400 S. Espina St., MSC 3DA
Las Cruces, NM 88003
Dr. Margie Huerta, Campus Executive Officer
Tel: (505-527-7500 Fax: (505) 527-7515
Web: www.nmsu.edu

P.O. Box 30001, MSC 3Z
Las Cruces, NM 88003
Dr. Michael V. Martin, President
Tel: (505) 646-2035 Fax: (505) 646-6334
Web: www.nmsu.edu

NORTHERN NEW MEXICO COMMUNITY COLLEGE
921 Paseo de Onate
Espanola, NM 87532
Dr. Jose - Griego, President
Tel: (505) 747-2140 Fax: (505) 747-2170
Web: www.nnmcc.edu

SANTA FE COMMUNITY COLLEGE
6401 Richards Ave.
Santa Fe, NM 87508
Mr. James N. McLaughlin, President
Tel: (505) 428-1000 Fax: (505) 428-1237
Web: www.sfccnm.edu

UNIVERSITY OF NEW MEXICO
Main
Scholes Hall, Room 160
Albuquerque, NM 87131
Mr. Louis Caldera, President
Tel: (505) 277-2626 Fax: (505) 277-5965
Web: www.unm.edu

Valencia
280 La Entrada Rd.
Los Lunas, NM 87031
Dr. Alice Letteney, Executive Director
Tel: (505) 925-8500 Fax: (505) 925-8501
Web: www.unm.edu

WESTERN NEW MEXICO UNIVERSITY
Main
P.O. Box 680
Silver City, NM 88062
Dr. John E. Counts, President
Tel: (505) 538-6238 Fax: (505) 538-6364
Web: www.wnmu.edu

NEW YORK

BORICUA COLLEGE
3755 Broadway
New York, NY 10032
Dr. Victor G. Alicea, President
Tel: (212) 694-1000 Fax: (212) 694-1015
Web: www.boricuacollege.edu

BOROUGH OF MANHATTAN COMMUNITY COLLEGE
City University of New York
199 Chambers St.
New York, NY 10007
Dr. Antonio Pérez, President
Tel: (212) 220-8000 Fax: (212) 220-1244
Web: www.bmcc.cuny.edu

BRONX COMMUNITY COLLEGE
City University of New York
University Ave. and West 181st St.
Bronx, NY 10453
Dr. Carolyn G. Williams, President
Tel: (718) 289-5151 Fax: (718) 289-6011
Web: www.bcc.cuny.edu

CITY COLLEGE OF NEW YORK
City University of New York
Convent Ave. and 138th St.
New York, NY 10031
Dr. Gregory H. Williams, President
Tel: (212) 650-7285 Fax: (212) 650-7680
Web: www.ccny.cuny.edu

COLLEGE OF MOUNT SAINT VINCENT
6301 Riverdale Ave.
Bronx, NY 10471-1093
Dr. Charles L. Flynn, President
Tel: (718) 405-3200 Fax: (718) 405-3748
Web: www.mountsaintvincent.edu

EUGENIO MARIA DE HOSTOS COMMUNITY COLLEGE
City University of New York
475 Grand Concourse
Bronx, NY 10451
Dr. Dolores M. Fernández, President
Tel: (718) 518-4300 Fax: (718) 518-4294
Web: www.hostos.cuny.edu

JOHN JAY COLLEGE OF CRIMINAL JUSTICE
City University of New York
899 Tenth Ave.
New York, NY 10019
Dr. Jeremy Travis, President

Tel: (212) 237-8884 Fax: (212) 237-8957
Web: www.jjay.cuny.edu

LA GUARDIA COMMUNITY COLLEGE
City University of New York
31-10 Thomson Ave. #E-513
Long Island City, NY 11101
Dr. Gail O. Mellow, President
Tel: (718) 482-5050 Fax: (718) 482-5036
Web: www.lagcc.cuny.edu

LEHMAN COLLEGE
City University of New York
250 Bedford Park Blvd. West
Bronx, NY 10468
Dr. Ricardo R. Fernández, President
Tel: (718) 960-8000 Fax: (718) 960-8935
Web: www.lehman.cuny.edu

NEW YORK CITY COLLEGE OF TECHNOLOGY
City University of New York
300 Jay St.
Brooklyn, NY 11201
Dr. Russell K. Hotzler, President
Tel: (718) 260-5400 Fax: (718) 260-5406
Web: www.citytech.cuny.edu

VAUGHN COLLEGE OF AERONAUTICS AND TECHNOLOGY
86-01 23rd Ave.
Flushing, NY 11369
Dr. John C. Fitzpatrick, President
Tel: (866) 682-8446 Fax: (718) 429-0671
Web: www.aero.edu

PUERTO RICO

AMERICAN UNIVERSITY OF PUERTO RICO
Bayamón
P.O. Box 2037
Bayamon, PR 00960-2037
Prof. Juan B. Nazario Negrón, President
Tel: (787) 620-2040 #1032
Fax: (787) 785-7377
Web: www.aupr.edu

ATLANTIC COLLEGE
P.O. Box 1774
Guaynabo, PR 970
Dr. Teresa De Dios-Unanue, President
Tel: (787) 720-1022 Fax: (787) 720-1092
Web: www.atlanticcollege-pr.com

CARIBBEAN UNIVERSITY
Bayamón
P.O. Box 493
Bayamon, PR 00960-0493
Prof. Ana E. Cucurella, President & CEO
Tel: (787) 780-0070 X501
Fax: (787) 785-0101
Web: www.caribbean.edu

COLEGIO UNIVERSITARIO DE SAN JUAN
Tres Monjitas Industrial Park
San Juan, PR 918
Dr. Tomás Flores-Navarro, Chancellor
Tel: (787) 250-7111 X2227
Fax: (787) 250-7395
Web: www.cunisanjuan.edu

CONSERVATORY OF MUSIC OF PUERTO RICO
Calle Rafael Lamar 350 Esq. F.D. Roosevelt
San Juan, PR 918
Prof. María del Carmen Gil, Chancellor
Tel: (787) 751-0160 X274
Fax: (787) 758-8268
Web: www.cmpr.edu

ESCUELA DE ARTES PLÁSTICAS DE PUERTO RICO
P.O. Box 9021112
San Juan, PR 00902-1112
Ms. Marimar Benítez, Chancellor
Tel: (787) 725-8120 Fax: (787) 725-8111
Web: www.eap.edu

INTER AMERICAN UNIVERSITY OF PUERTO RICO
Aguadilla
Box 20000
Aguadilla, PR 605
Dr. Juan Aníbal Aponte, Chancellor
Tel: (787) 891-0925 X2205
Fax: (787) 882-3020
Web: www.aguadilla.inter.edu

Arecibo
P.O. Box 4050
Arecibo, PR 00614-4050
Dr. Jean Marie González, Chancellor
Tel: (787) 878-5104 Fax: (787) 880-1624
Web: www.arecibo.inter.edu

Ponce
104 Parque Industrial Turpó, Rd. One
Mercedita, PR 00715-1602
Dr. Vilma E. Colón-Acosta, Director of
Education & Social Sciences Department
Tel: (787) 284-1912 X2042
Fax: (787) 284-1925
Web: www.ponce.inter.edu

San Germán
P.O. Box 5100
San German, PR 683
Prof. Agnes Mojica, Chancellor
Tel: (787) 264-1912 X7330
Fax: (787) 892-6350
Web: www.sg.inter.edu

System Central Office
P.O. Box 363255
San Juan, PR 00936-3255
Lic. Manuel J. Fernos, President
Tel: (787) 766-1912 Fax: (787) 751-3375
Web: www.inter.edu

PONTIFICAL CATHOLIC UNIVERSITY OF PUERTO RICO
Ponce
2250 Las Americas Ave. #564
Ponce, PR 717
Prof. Marcelina Velez de Santiago,
President
Tel: (787) 841-2000 Fax: (787) 651-2034
Web: www.pucpr.edu

SISTEMA UNIVERSITARIO ANA G. MÉNDEZ
Central Administration
P.O. Box 21345
San Juan, PR 00928-1345
Mr. José F. Méndez, President
Tel: (787) 751-0178 Fax: (787) 766-1706
Web: www.suagm.edu

UNIVERSIDAD ADVENTISTA DE LAS ANTILLAS
P.O. Box 118
Mayagüez, PR 681
Dr. Myrna Costa, President
Tel: (787) 834-9595 Fax: (787) 834-9597
Web: www.uaa.edu

UNIVERSIDAD CENTRAL DEL CARIBE
P.O. Box 60327
Bayamon, PR 00960-6032
Dr. Nilda Candelario, President
Tel: (787) 798-3001 Fax: (787) 798-6836
Web: www.uccaribe.edu

UNIVERSIDAD DEL ESTE
P.O. Box 2010
Carolina, PR 984
Dr. Alberto Maldonado Ruiz, Chancellor
Tel: (787) 257-7373 Fax: (787) 776-1220
Web: www.suagm.edu/cue

UNIVERSIDAD DEL TURABO
Estación Universidad, P. O. Box 3030
Gurabo, PR 778
Dr. Dennis Alicea, Chancellor
Tel: (787) 746-0717 Fax: (787) 744-5394
Web: www.suagm.edu

UNIVERSIDAD METROPOLITANA
P.O. Box 21150
San Juan, PR 928
Dr. Federico M. Matheu, Chancellor
Tel: (787) 766-1717 X6400
Fax: (787) 759-7663
Web: www.suagm.edu/umet/default.htm

UNIVERSIDAD POLITÉCNICA DE PUERTO RICO
Hato Rey
P.O. Box 192017
San Juan, PR 919
Mr. Ernesto Vazquez-Barquet, President
Tel: (787) 754-8000/(787) 622-8000
Fax: (787) 763-8919
Web: www.pupr.edu

UNIVERSITY OF PUERTO RICO
Aguadilla
P.O. Box 250160
Aguadilla, PR 00604-0160
Prof. Pablo Rodríguez, Chancellor
Tel: (787) 890-1265 Fax: (787) 891-3455
Web: www.uprag.edu

Arecibo
P.O. Box 4010
Arecibo, PR 00614-4010
Dr. Edwin Hernández-Vera, Chancellor
Tel: (787) 815-0000 Fax: (787) 880-2245
Web: www.upra.clu.edu

Bayamón
Industrial Minillas
Bayamon, PR 959
Dr. Andrés Rodríguez Rubio, Chancellor
Tel: (787) 786-2885 Fax: (787) 798-1595
Web: www.uprb.edu

Carolina
P.O. Box 4800
Carolina, PR 00984-4800
Dr. Victor Borrero Aldahondo, Chancellor
Tel: (787) 276-0226 Fax: (787) 750-7940
Web: www.uprc.edu

Cayey
Antonio R. Barceló Ave. #205
Cayey, PR 736
Dr. Rafael Aragunde, Chancellor
Tel: (787) 738-2161 X2121
Fax: (787) 738-8039
Web: www.cayey.upr.edu

Central Administration
Jardín Botánico Sur
San Juan, PR 00926-1117
Lic. Antonio García Padilla, Interim
President
Tel: (787) 250-0000 X2000
Fax: (787) 759-6917
Web: www.upr.edu

Humacao
100 Rd. 908, Station 100
Humacao, PR 791

Dra. Hilda M. Colón Plumey, Chancellor
Tel: (787) 850-9374 Fax: (787) 852-4638
Web: www.webmail.uprh.edu

Mayagüez
P.O. Box 9000
Mayagüez, PR 00681-9000
Dr. Jorge I. Vélez-Arocho, Chancellor
Tel: (787) 265-3878 Fax: (787) 834-3031
Web: www.uprm.edu

Medical Sciences Center
P.O. Box 365067
San Juan, PR 00936-5067
Dr. Jose Carlo-Izquierdo, Chancellor
Tel: (787) 758-2525 Fax: (787) 767-0755
Web: www.rcm.upr.edu

Río Piedras
P.O. Box 23300
San Juan, PR 00931-3300
Dr. Gladys Escalona-DeMotta, Chancellor
Tel: (787) 763-3877 Fax: (787) 764-8700
Web: www.rrp.upr.edu

UNIVERSITY OF THE SACRED HEART
P.O. Box 12383
San Juan, PR 914
Dr. José Jaime Rivera, President
Tel: (787) 728-1515 X1225
Fax: (787) 728-1692
Web: www.sagrado.edu

TEXAS

ALAMO COMMUNITY COLLEGE DISTRICT
201 W. Sheridan
San Antonio, TX 78204-1429
Dr. J. Terence Kelly, Chancellor
Tel: (210) 208-8020 Fax: (210) 208-8149
Web: www.accd.edu

AMARILLO COLLEGE
P. O. Box 447
Amarillo, TX 79178-0001
Dr. Steven Jones, President
Tel: (806) 371-5123 Fax: (806) 371-5370
Web: www.actx.edu

COASTAL BEND COLLEGE
3800 Charco Rd.
Beeville, TX 78102
Dr. John M. Brockman, President
Tel: (361) 358-2838 X2200
Fax: (361) 358-3971
Web: www.coastalbend.edu

DEL MAR COLLEGE
101 Baldwin Blvd.
Corpus Christi, TX 78404
Mr. José Alaniz, Acting President
Tel: (361) 698-1203 Fax: (361) 698-1559
Web: www.delmar.edu

EL CENTRO COLLEGE
801 Main St.
Dallas, TX 75202
Dr. Wright L. Lassiter, President
Tel: (214) 860-2010 Fax: (214) 860-2335
Web: www.elcentrocollege.edu

EL PASO COMMUNITY COLLEGE
P.O. Box 20500
El Paso, TX 79998
Dr. Richard Rhodes, President
Tel: (915) 831-6511 Fax: (915) 831-6507
Web: www.epcc.edu

HOUSTON COMMUNITY COLLEGE SYSTEM
3100 Main St., 12th Fl.
Houston, TX 77266-7517

Dr. Bruce Leslie, Chancellor
Tel: (713) 718-5059 Fax: (713) 718-2232
Web: www.hccs.edu

LAREDO COMMUNITY COLLEGE
Main
W. End Washington St.
Laredo, TX 78040
Dr. Ramon H. Dovalina, President
Tel: (956) 722-0521 Fax: (956) 721-5381
Web: www.laredo.edu

MIDLAND COLLEGE
3600 N. Garfield
Midland, TX 79705
Dr. David E. Daniel, President
Tel: (432) 685-4520 Fax: (432) 685-4522
Web: www.midland.edu

MOUNTAIN VIEW COLLEGE
4849 W. Illinois Ave.
Dallas, TX 75211
Mr. Felix Zamora, President
Tel: (214) 860-8700 Fax: (214) 860-8734
Web: www.mvc.dcccd.edu

NW VISTA COLLEGE
3535 N. Ellison Dr.
San Antonio, TX 78251
Dr. Jacqueline Claunch, President
Tel: (210) 348-2001 Fax: (210) 348-2004
Web: www.accd.edu/nvc

OUR LADY OF THE LAKE UNIVERSITY
411 Southwest 24th St.
San Antonio, TX 78207
Dr. Tessa Martinez Pollack, President
Tel: (210) 431-3950 Fax: (210) 431-4055
Web: www.ollusa.edu

PALO ALTO COLLEGE
1400 W. Villaret Blvd.
San Antonio, TX 78224-2499
Dr. Ana M. Guzmán, President
Tel: (210) 921-5260 Fax: (210) 921-5385
Web: www.accd.edu/pac/pacmain/pachp.htm

SAN ANTONIO COLLEGE
1300 San Pedro
San Antonio, TX 78212
Dr. Robert E. Zeigler, President
Tel: (210) 733-2190 Fax: (210) 733-2204
Web: www.accd.edu/sac/sacmain/sac.htm

SAN JACINTO COLLEGE NORTH
5800 Uvalde Rd.
Houston, TX 77049
Dr. Charles Grant, President
Tel: (281) 459-7100 Fax: (281) 459-7132
Web: www.sjcd.cc.tx.us

SOUTH PLAINS COLLEGE
1401 S. College Ave.
Levelland, TX 79336
Dr. Gary D. McDaniel, President
Tel: (806) 894-9611 Fax: (806) 894-6880
Web: www.southplainscollege.edu

SOUTH TEXAS COMMUNITY COLLEGE
P.O. Box 9701
McAllen, TX 78502
Dr. Shirley A. Reed, President
Tel: (956) 618-8366 Fax: (956) 618-8368
Web: www.stcc.cc.tx.us

SOUTHWEST TEXAS JUNIOR COLLEGE
2401 Garner Field Rd.
Uvalde, TX 78801
Dr. Ismael Sosa, President
Tel: (830) 278-4401 Fax: (830) 591-7354
Web: www.swtjc.net

ST. EDWARD'S UNIVERSITY
3001 S. Congress Ave.
Austin, TX 78704
Dr. George E. Martin, President
Tel: (512) 448-8417 Fax: (512) 448-8687
Web: www.stedwards.edu

ST. MARY'S UNIVERSITY
1 Camino Santa Maria
San Antonio, TX 78228-8572
Dr. Charles L. Cotrell, President
Tel: (210) 436-3722 Fax: (210) 431-2226
Web: www.stmarytx.edu

ST. PHILIP'S COLLEGE
1801 Martin Luther King Dr.
San Antonio, TX 78203
Dr. Angie S. Runnels, President
Tel: (210) 531-3591 Fax: (210) 531-3590
Web: www.accd.edu/spc

SUL ROSS STATE UNIVERSITY
Hwy. 90 E., Campus Box 114
Alpine, TX 79832
Dr. R. Vic Morgan, President
Tel: (432) 837-8032 Fax: (432) 837-8334
Web: www.sulross.edu

TEXAS A&M INTERNATIONAL UNIVERSITY
5201 University Blvd.
Laredo, TX 78041
Dr. Ray M. Keck, President
Tel: (956) 326-2320 Fax: (956) 326-2319
Web: www.tamiu.edu

TEXAS A&M UNIVERSITY
Corpus Christi
6300 Ocean Dr.
Corpus Christi, TX 78412
Dr. Robert R. Furgason, President
Tel: (361) 825-2612 Fax: (361) 825-2614
Web: www.tamucc.edu

Kingsville
700 University Blvd., MSC 101
Kingsville, TX 78363
Dr. Rumaldo Z. Juarez, President
Tel: (361) 593-3207 Fax: (361) 593-3218
Web: www.tamuk.edu

TEXAS STATE TECHNICAL COLLEGE
Harlingen
1902 N. Loop 499
Harlingen, TX 78550
Dr. J. Gilbert Leal, President
Tel: (800) 852-8784 Fax: (956) 364-5100
Web: www.harlingen.tstc.edu

UNIVERSITY OF HOUSTON
Downtown
1 Main St. #990-S
Houston, TX 77002
Dr. Max Castillo, President
Tel: (713) 221-8001 Fax: (713) 221-8075
Web: www.uhd.edu

UNIVERSITY OF ST. THOMAS
3800 Montrose Blvd.
Houston, TX 77006
Dr. Robert Ivany, President
Tel: (713) 525-2160 Fax: (713) 525-2161
Web: www.stthom.edu

UNIVERSITY OF TEXAS
Pan American
1201 W. University Dr.
Edinburg, TX 78541
Dr. Blandina Cardenas, President
Tel: (956) 381-2100 Fax: (956) 381-2150
Web: www.panam.edu

UNIVERSITY OF TEXAS AT BROWNSVILLE AND TEXAS SOUTHMOST COLLEGE
80 Fort Brown
Brownsville, TX 78520
Dr. Juliet V. Garcia, President
Tel: (956) 544-8200 Fax: (956) 548-0020
Web: www.utb.edu

UNIVERSITY OF TEXAS AT EL PASO
500 W. University Ave.
El Paso, TX 79968-0500
Dr. Diana Natalicio, President
Tel: (915) 747-5555 Fax: (915) 747-5069
Web: www.utep.edu

UNIVERSITY OF TEXAS AT SAN ANTONIO
6900 N. Loop 1604 West
San Antonio, TX 78249
Dr. Ricardo Romo, President
Tel: (210) 458-4011 Fax: (210) 458-5959
Web: www.utsa.edu

UNIVERSITY OF TEXAS HEALTH SCIENCE CENTER AT SAN ANTONIO
7703 Floyd Curl Dr.
San Antonio, TX 78229-3900
Dr. Francisco G. Cigarroa, President
Tel: (210) 567-2000 Fax: (210) 567-2025
Web: www.uthscsa.edu

UNIVERSITY OF TEXAS OF THE PERMIAN BASIN
4901 E. University Blvd.
Odessa, TX 79762
Dr. W. David Watts, President
Tel: (432) 552-2020 Fax: (432) 552-2109
Web: www.utpb.edu

UNIVERSITY OF THE INCARNATE WORD
4301 Broadway
San Antonio, TX 78209
Dr. Louis J. Agnese, President
Tel: (210) 829-6000 Fax: (210) 829-6096
Web: www.uiw.edu

VICTORIA COLLEGE
2200 E. Red River
Victoria, TX 77901
Dr. Jimmy Goodson, President
Tel: (361) 573-3291 Fax: (361) 582-2564
Web: www.victoriacollege.edu

WASHINGTON

COLUMBIA BASIN COLLEGE
2600 N. 20th Ave.
Pasco, WA 99301
Dr. Lee R. Thornton, President
Tel: (509) 547-0511 Fax: (509) 546-0404
Web: www.cbc2.org

HERITAGE UNIVERSITY
3240 Fort Rd.
Toppenish, WA 98948
Dr. Kathleen Ross, President
Tel: (509) 865-8500 Fax: (529) 865-4469
Web: www.heritage.edu

State Health Departments
Departamentos estatales de salud

ALABAMA

ALABAMA DEPARTMENT OF PUBLIC HEALTH
P.O. Box 303017
Montgomery, AL 36130-3017
Tel: (334) 206-5200
Web: www.adph.org

ALASKA

ALASKA DEPARTMENT OF HEALTH AND SOCIAL SERVICES
P.O. Box 110601
Juneau, AK 99811-0610
Tel: (907) 465-3030
Web: www.hss.state.ak.us

AMERICAN SAMOA

AMERICAN SAMOA GOVERNMENT
Department of Health
Pago Pago, AS 96799
Tel: (684) 633-4606
Web: www.asg-gov.com/departments/doh.asg.htm

ARIZONA

ARIZONA DEPARTMENT OF HEALTH SERVICES
150 N. 18th Ave.
Phoenix, AZ 85007
Tel: (602) 542-1025
Web: www.hs.state.az.us

ARKANSAS

ARKANSAS DEPARTMENT OF HEALTH
4815 W. Markham St.
Little Rock, AR 72205
Tel: (501) 661-2000
Web: www.healthyarkansas.com

CALIFORNIA

CALIFORNIA DEPARTMENT OF HEALTH SERVICES
P.O. Box 942732
Sacramento, CA 94234-7320
Tel: (916) 440-7400
Web: www.dhs.ca.gov

COLORADO

COLORADO DEPARTMENT OF PUBLIC HEALTH AND ENVIRONMENT
Turning Point Office
4300 Cherry Creek Dr. South
Denver, CO 80246-1530
Tel: (303) 692-2000
Web: www.cdphe.state.co.us

CONNECTICUT

CONNECTICUT DEPARTMENT OF PUBLIC HEALTH
P.O. Box 340308
410 Capitol Ave.
Hartford, CT 06134-0308
Tel: (860) 509-8000
Web: www.dph.state.ct.us

DELAWARE

DELAWARE HEALTH AND SOCIAL SERVICES
1901 N. DuPont Hwy., Main Bldg.
New Castle, DE 19720
Tel: (302) 255-9040
Web: www.state.de.us/dhss

DISTRICT OF COLUMBIA

DISTRICT OF COLUMBIA DEPARTMENT OF HEALTH
825 N. Capitol St. NE
Washington, DC 20002
Tel: (202) 442-5999
Web: www.dchealth.dc.gov

FLORIDA

FLORIDA DEPARTMENT OF HEALTH
4052 Bald Cypress Way #A00
Tallahassee, FL 32399-1700
Tel: (850) 245-4321
Web: www.doh.state.fl.us

GEORGIA

GEORGIA DIVISION OF PUBLIC HEALTH
2 Peachtree St. NW
Atlanta, GA 30303-3186
Tel: (404) 657-2700
Web: www.health.state.ga.us

HAWAII

HAWAII STATE DEPARTMENT OF HEALTH
1250 Punchbowl St.
Honolulu, HI 96813
Tel: (808) 586-4400
Web: www.hawaii.gov/health

IDAHO

IDAHO DEPARTMENT OF HEALTH AND WELFARE
P.O. Box 83720
450 W. State St.
Boise, ID 93720-0036
Tel: (208) 334-5500
Web: www.healthandwelfare.idaho.gov

ILLINOIS

ILLINOIS DEPARTMENT OF PUBLIC HEALTH
535 W. Jefferson St.
Springfield, IL 62761
Tel: (217) 782-4977
Web: www.idph.state.il.us

INDIANA

INDIANA STATE DEPARTMENT OF PUBLIC HEALTH
2 N. Meridian St.
Indianapolis, IN 46204
Tel: (317) 233-1325
Web: www.statehealth.in.gov

IOWA

IOWA DEPARTMENT OF PUBLIC HEALTH
321 E. 12th St.
Des Moines, IA 50319
Tel: (515) 281-5787
Web: www.idph.state.ia.us/

KANSAS

KANSAS DEPARTMENT OF HEALTH AND ENVIRONMENT
1000 SW Jackson #300
Charles Curtis State Office Bldg.
Topeka, KS 66612-1365
Tel: (785) 296-1500
Web: www.kdhe.state.ks.us

KENTUCKY

KENTUCKY CABINET FOR HEALTH AND FAMILY SERVICES
Department for Public Health, Division of Local Health Department Operations
275 E. Main St. #HS1W-C
Frankfort, KY 40621
Tel: (502) 564-4990
Web: www.chs.state.ky.us

LOUISIANA

LOUISIANA DEPARTMENT OF HEALTH AND HOSPITALS
Office of Public Health
1201 Capitol Access Rd. #4
Baton Rouge, LA 70802
Tel: (225) 342-8093
Web: www.oph.dhh.state.la.us

MAINE

MAINE DEPARTMENT OF HUMAN SERVICES
Bureau of Health
286 Water St., Station 11
Augusta, ME 04333
Tel: (207) 287-8016
Web: www.state.me.us/dhs/boh/index.htm

MARYLAND

MARYLAND DEPARTMENT OF HEALTH AND MENTAL HYGIENE
201 W. Preston St.
Baltimore, MD 21201
Tel: (410) 767-6860
Web: www.dhmh.state.md.us

MASSACHUSETTS

MASSACHUSETTS DEPARTMENT OF PUBLIC HEALTH
250 Washington St.
Boston, MA 02108-4619
Tel: (617) 624-6000
Web: www.state.ma.us/dph/

MICHIGAN

MICHIGAN DEPARTMENT OF HEALTH
Lewis Cass Bldg., 6th Fl., 320 S. Walnut St
Lansing, MI 48913
Tel: (517) 373-3500
Web: www.michigan.gov/mdch

MINNESOTA

MINNESOTA DEPARTMENT OF HEALTH
P.O. Box 64975
St. Paul, MN 55164-0975
Tel: (651) 215-5800
Web: www. health.state.mn.us

MISSISSIPPI

MISSISSIPPI STATE DEPARTMENT OF HEALTH
P.O. Box 1700
Jackson, MS 39215-1700
Tel: (601) 576-7400
Web: www.msdh.state.ms.us/msdhsite/index.cfm

MISSOURI

MISSOURI DEPARTMENT OF HEALTH AND SENIOR SERVICES
P.O. Box 570
Jefferson City, MO 65102
Tel: (573) 751-6400
Web: www.dhss.state.mo.us

MONTANA

MONTANA DEPARTMENT OF PUBLIC HEALTH AND HUMAN SERVICES
P.O. Box 4210
Helena, MT 59604-4210
Tel: (406) 444-5622
Web: www.dphhs.state.mt.us

NEBRASKA

NEBRASKA DEPARTMENT OF HEALTH AND HUMAN SERVICES
P.O. Box 95044
Lincoln, NE 68509-5044
Tel: (402) 471-2306
Web: www.hhs.state.ne.us

NEVADA

NEVADA STATE HEALTH DIVISION
505 E. King St. #201
Carson City, NV 89701
Tel: (775) 684-4200
Web: www.health2k.state.nv.us

NEW HAMPSHIRE

NEW HAMPSHIRE DEPARTMENT OF HEALTH AND HUMAN SERVICES
129 Pleasant St.
Concord, NH 03301
Tel: (603) 271-4958
Web: www.dhhs.state.nh.us

NEW JERSEY

NEW JERSEY DEPARTMENT OF HEALTH AND SENIOR SERVICES
P.O. Box 360
Trenton, NJ 08625-0360
Tel: (609) 292-7837
Web: www.state.nj.us/health

NEW MEXICO

NEW MEXICO DEPARTMENT OF HEALTH
1190 S. St. Francis Dr.
Santa Fe, NM 87502-6110
Tel: (505) 827-2613
Web: www.health.state.nm.us

NEW YORK

NEW YORK STATE DEPARTMENT OF HEALTH
Empire State Plz., Corning Tower
Albany, NY 12237
Tel: (518) 474-2011
Web: www.health.state.ny.us

NORTH CAROLINA

NORTH CAROLINA DEPARTMENT OF HEALTH AND HUMAN SERVICES
Office of Citizen Services
2001 Mail Service Ctr.
Raleigh, NC 27699-2001
Tel: (919) 733-4261
Web: www.dhhs.state.nc.us

NORTH DAKOTA

NORTH DAKOTA DEPARTMENT OF HEALTH
600 E. Boulevard Ave.
Bismarck, ND 58505-0200
Tel: (701) 328-2372
Web: www.health.state.nd.us

OHIO

OHIO DEPARTMENT OF HEALTH
P.O. Box 118, 246 N. High St.
Columbus, OH 43216-0118
Tel: (614) 466-3543
Web: www.odh.state.oh.us

OKLAHOMA

OKLAHOMA STATE DEPARTMENT OF HEALTH
1000 NE 10th St.
Oklahoma City, OK 73117
Tel: (405) 271-5600
Web: www.health.state.ok.us

OREGON

OREGON DEPARTMENT OF HUMAN SERVICES
Health Division
800 NE Oregon St.
Portland, OR 97232
Tel: (503) 731-4000
Web: www.ohd.hr.state.or.us

PENNSYLVANIA

PENNSYLVANIA DEPARTMENT OF HEALTH
Health and Welfare Bldg.,
8th Fl. West, 7th and Foster Sts.
Harrisburg, PA 17120
Tel: (877) 724-3258
Web: www.health.state.pa.us

PUERTO RICO

HEALTH DEPARTMENT OF PUERTO RICO
P.O. Box 70184
San Juan, PR 00936
Tel: (787) 274-7676
Web: www.salud.gov.pr

RHODE ISLAND

RHODE ISLAND DEPARTMENT OF HEALTH
3 Capitol Hill
Providence, RI 02908
Tel: (401) 222-2231
Web: www.health.state.ri.us

SOUTH CAROLINA

SOUTH CAROLINA DEPARTMENT OF HEALTH AND ENVIRONMENT CONTROL
2600 Bull St.
Columbia, SC 29201
Tel: (803) 898-3432
Web: www.scdhec.net

SOUTH DAKOTA

SOUTH DAKOTA DEPARTMENT OF HEALTH
600 E. Capitol
Pierre, SD 57501-2536
Tel: (605) 773-3361
Web: www.state.sd.us/doh/index.htm

TENNESSEE

TENNESSEE DEPARTMENT OF HEALTH
Commissioner's Office
425 5th Ave. North,
Cordell Hull Bldg., 3rd Fl.
Nashville, TN 37247
Tel: (615) 741-3111
Web: www2.state.tn.us/health

TEXAS

TEXAS DEPARTMENT OF HEALTH
1100 W. 49th St.
Austin, TX 78756-3199
Tel: (512) 458-7111
Web: www.tdh.state.tx.us

UTAH

UTAH DEPARTMENT OF HEALTH
P.O. Box 141010
Salt Lake City, UT 84114-1010
Tel: (801) 538-6101
Web: www.health.utah.gov

VERMONT

VERMONT DEPARTMENT OF HEALTH
P.O. Box 70, 108 Cherry St.
Burlington, VT 05402-0070
Tel: (802) 863-7200
Web: www.healthyvermonters.info

VIRGIN ISLANDS

DEPARTMENT OF HEALTH
48 Sugar Estate
Charlotte Amalie, VI 00802
Tel: (340) 774-0117
Web: www.usvi.org/health

VIRGINIA

VIRGINIA DEPARTMENT OF HEALTH
P.O. Box 2448
Richmond, VA 23218-2448
Tel: (804) 864-7000
Web: www.vdh.state.va.us

WASHINGTON

WASHINGTON STATE DEPARTMENT OF HEALTH
Office of Health Consumer Assistance
P.O. Box 47890
Olympia, WA 98504-7890
Tel: (360) 236-4052
Web: www.doh.wa.gov

WEST VIRGINIA

WEST VIRGINIA DEPARTMENT OF HEALTH AND HUMAN RESOURCES
State Capitol Complex, Bldg. 3 #206
Charleston, WV 25305
Tel: (304) 558-0684
Web: www.wvdhhr.org

WISCONSIN

WISCONSIN DEPARTMENT OF HEALTH AND FAMILY SERVICES
1 W. Wilson St. #650
Madison, WI 53702
Tel: (608) 266-1865
Web: www.dhfs.wisconsin.gov

WYOMING

WYOMING DEPARTMENT OF HEALTH
2300 Capitol Ave. #117
Cheyenne, WY 82002
Tel: (307) 777-7656
Web: www.wdhfs.state.wy.us/wdh/index.htm

Hispanic Organizations
Organizaciones hispanas

ALABAMA

SOUTH REGIONS MINORITY BUSINESS COUNCIL, INC.
4715 Alton Ct.
Burmingham, AL 35210
Scott Vowels, Executive Director
Tel: (205) 957-1882 Fax: (205) 957-2114
Email: info@srmbc.org
Web: www.srmbc.org

ALABAMA HISPANIC CHAMBER OF COMMERCE
P.O. Box 55505
Birmingham, AL 35255
Sigfredo Rubio, President
Tel: (205) 326-2226 Fax: (205) 328-9669
Email: sigfredo@bellsouth.net
Web: www.alabamahispanicchamber.com

ALABAMA HISPANIC ASSOCIATION
1595 Slaughter Rd. #A
Madison, AL 35758
Margaret Rotger, President
Tel: (256) 325-4242
Email: aha@alabamahispanicassociation.org
Web: www.alabamahispanicassociation.org

PERUVIAN AMERICAN MEDICAL SOCIETY
Southeast Region Chapter
617 Princess Ln.
Bessemer, AL 35023
Dr. Fernando L. Franco, President
Tel: (205) 759-0657
Email: piurano@wwisp.com
Web: www.pamsnational.org

ARCHDIOCESE OF MOBILE
Hispanic Pastoral Ministry
712 Dauphin Island Pkwy.
Mobile, AL 36606
Rev. Christopher J. Viscardi, SJ, Coordinator for Hispanic Affairs
Tel: (251) 478-3737 Fax: (251) 478-9990
Email: hispanicaom@wordnet.att.net

CATHOLIC DIOCESE OF BIRMINGHAM
Hispanic Ministry Office
P.O. Box 12047
Birmingham, AL 35202-2047
Candelaria Hernandez, Director
Tel: (205) 838-8308 Fax: (205) 836-1910

Email: chernandez@bhmdiocese.org
Web: www.bhmdiocese.org

HOTEL EMPLOYEES AND RESTAURANT EMPLOYEES INTERNATIONAL UNION
Local 719 Huntsville
102 Mossy Springs Trail
Madison, AL 35757
Vickie Burks, Secretary/Treasurer
Tel: (256) 498-2744
Email: info@hereunion.org
Web: www.hereunion.org

CONSTRUCTORES PARA CRISTO
P.O. Box 661406
Birmingham, AL 35266-1406
Diane Davis, Executive Director
Tel: (205) 979-8552
Email: paz1111@aol.com
Web: www.cpcmexico.org

THE HISPANIC INTEREST COALITION OF ALABAMA
P.O. Box 320668
Birmingham, AL 35232
Bart Thau, Chair
Tel: (205) 591-5545 Fax: (205) 591-5743
Email: info@hispanicinterest.org
Web: www.hispanicinterest.org

AUBURN LATINO ASSOCIATION OF STUDENTS
Auburn University
Foy Student Union
Auburn, AL 36849
Jana Gutierrez, Advisor
Tel: (334) 844-6387
Email: oronall@auburn.edu
Web: www.auburn.edu/student_info/latino_association/

ALASKA

CONSEJO DE LATINOAMERICANOS EN ALASKA PARA SERVICIOS ESPECIALES
1565 S. Bragaw St.
Anchorage, AK 99508
Agustin Francis, President
Tel: (907) 222-3710 Fax: (907) 222-3710
Email: infoclase@alaska.com

ARCHDIOCESE OF ANCHORAGE
Our Lady of Guadeloupe, Hispanic Ministry Office

811 W 6th Ave.
Anchorage, AK 99501
Fr. Paul Scanlon, Director for Hispanic Ministry
Tel: (907) 276-3455 Fax: (907) 258-9785
Email: holyfamilycathedral@alaska.com
Web: www.holyfamilycathedral.org

HOTEL EMPLOYEES AND RESTAURANT EMPLOYEES INTERNATIONAL UNION
Local 878 Anchorage
P.O. Box 1005640
530 E. 4th Ave.
Anchorage, AK 99510
Marvin Jones, President
Tel: (907) 272-6591 Fax: (907) 277-8595
Email: local878@worldnet.att.net
Web: www.union878.com

ARIZONA

MOVIMIENTO ARTISTICO DEL RIO SALADO, INC.
P.O. Box 548
Phoenix, AZ 85001
Ralph Cordova, Director
Tel: (602) 253-3541 Fax: (602) 253-3550
Email: gallery@mars-artspace.org
Web: www.mars-artspace.org

ACCION INTEGRATED MARKETING
439 W Comstock Ct.
Gilbert, AZ 85233
Norma Armenta, Director/Producer
Tel: (480) 390-2969 Fax: (480) 471-8590
Email: norma@accionim.com
Web: www.accionim.com

ARIZONA-MEXICO COMMISSION
1700 W. Washington #180
Phoenix, AZ 85007
Victor Flores, President
Tel: (602) 542-1345 Fax: (602) 542-1411
Email: info@azmc.org
Web: www.azmc.org

BORDER TRADE ALLIANCE
111 W. Monroe #510
Phoenix, AZ 85003
Maria Luisa O'Connell, President
Tel: (602) 266-7427 Fax: (602) 266-9826
Email: mlo@thebta.org
Web: www.thebta.org

GRAND CANYON MINORITY SUPPLIER DEVELOPMENT COUNCIL
802 N. 5th Ave.
Phoenix, AZ 85003
Ron Williams, President
Tel: (602) 495-9950 Fax: (502) 495-9943

Email: grandcanyoncouncil@gcmsdc.org
Web: www.gcmsdc.org

NATIONAL SOCIETY OF HISPANIC MBAS
Phoenix Chapter
P.O. Box 11315
Tempe, AZ 85284
Leeann Maldonado, Chapter President
Tel: (480) 213-7269
Email: general@phoenix.nshmba.org
Web: http://phoenix.nshmba.org

ARIZONA HISPANIC CHAMBER OF COMMERCE
Affiliate of NCLR
255 E Osborn St. #201
Phoenix, AZ 85012
Harry Garewal, President/CEO
Tel: (602) 279-1800 Fax: (602) 279-8900
Email: info@azhcc.com
Web: www.azhcc.com

NOGALES-SANTA CRUZ COUNTY CHAMBER OF COMMERCE
123 W. Kino Pkwy.
Nogales, AZ 85621
Dan Doyle, Chairman
Tel: (520) 287-3685 Fax: (520) 287-3688
Email: info@nogaleschamber.com
Web: www.nogaleschamber.com

TUCSON HISPANIC CHAMBER OF COMMERCE
823 E. Speedway Blvd.
Tucson, AZ 85712
Fred Orozco, President/CEO
Tel: (520) 620-0005 Fax: (602) 620-9685
Email: president@thcc.us
Web: www.hispanicchambertucson.org

MULTI-CULTURAL AFFAIRS
Glendale Community College
6000 W. Olive Ave.
Glendale, AZ 85302
José Mendoza, Program Coordinator
Tel: (623) 845-3079 Fax: (623) 845-3329
Email: jose.mendoza@gcmail.maricopa.edu
Web: www.gc.maricopa.edu

NATIONAL LATINO PEACE OFFICERS ASSOCIATION
Arizona State
P.O. Box 1551
Phoenix, AZ 85001
Frank Balkcom, State President
Tel: (602) 440-5601
Email: fbalkcom@aznlpoa.com
Web: www.aznlpoa.com

MULTI-PURPOSE

AMIGOS DE LAS AMERICAS
Tucson Chapter
3150 N. Bear Canyon Rd.
Tucson, AZ 85749
Leslie Willingham, President
Tel: (520) 749-0448
Email: info@amigostucson.org
Web: www.amigostucson.org

ARIZONA LATINO MEDIA ASSOCIATION
P.O. Box 1168
Phoenix, AZ 85001
Anita Luera, President
Email: info@almaweb.org
Web: www.almaweb.org

CENTRO ADELANTE CAMPESINO
P.O. Box 1338
Surprise, AZ 85374
Richard Miranda, Executive Director
Tel: (623) 583-9830 Fax: (623) 583-3422
Email: centro@campesino.net

CHICANOS POR LA CAUSA, INC.
1112 E. Buckeye Rd.
Phoenix, AZ 85034-4043
Edmundo Hidalgo, Chief Operating Officer
Tel: (602) 257-0700 Fax: (602) 256-2740
Email: edmundo.hidalgo@cplc.org
Web: www.cplc.org

FRIENDLY HOUSE, INC.
Adult Education Department
802 S. 1st Ave.
Phoenix, AZ 85003
Luis Enriquez, Director of Adult Education
Tel: (602) 257-1870 X219 Fax: (602) 257-8278
Email: luise@friendlyhouse.org
Web: www.friendlyhouse.org

HISPANIC LEADERSHIP INSTITUTE
Valle del Sol, Inc.
4117 N. 17th St.
Phoenix, AZ 85016
Luz Sarmina-Gutierrez, CEO
Tel: (602) 248-8101 Fax: (602) 248-8113
Email: info@valledelsol.com
Web: www.valledelsol.com

LEAGUE OF UNITED LATIN AMERICAN CITIZENS
State of Arizona
P.O. Box 2443
Tucson, AZ 85719
Samuel Esquivel, State Director
Tel: (520) 903-2838 Fax: (520) 792-6388
Email: samuel.esquivel@med.va.gov
Web: www.azlulac.org

Youth Leadership Conference
P.O. Box 2443
Tucson, AZ 85702
Enrique Perez Gomez, District Three Director
Tel: (520) 206-6790 Fax: (520) 206-6071
Email: info@sazlulacylc.org
Web: www.sazlulacylc.org

POLITICAL ACTION

SOUTHWEST VOTER REGISTRATION EDUCATION PROJECT
Arizona Regional Office
31 E. Southern Ave. #1
Phoenix, AZ 85042
Adelita Villegas, Field Organizer
Tel: (602) 268-8683 Fax: (602) 305-7936
Email: avillegas@svrep.org
Web: www.svrep.org

PROFESSIONAL

ASSOCIATION OF LATINO PROFESSIONALS IN FINANCE AND ACCOUNTING
Phoenix Chapter
KPMG, LLP, 1 Arizona Center, 400 E. Van Buren #1100
Phoenix, AZ 85004-2207
Eduardo Gonzalez, Chapter President
Tel: (602) 250-8163
Email: eagonzalez@kpmg.com
Web: www.alpfa.org

HISPANIC NATIONAL BAR ASSOCIATION
300 W Washington, Division 504
Phoenix, AZ 85003
Francisca Cota, Judicial Council Co-Liaison
Tel: (602) 261-8524 Fax: (602) 495-5744
Email: francisca.cota@phoenix.gov
Web: www.hnba.com

NATIONAL ASSOCIATION OF HISPANIC NURSES
Valle del Sol Chapter
P.O. Box 67545
Phoenix, AZ 85082
Teresa Rojas, President
Tel: (602) 628-5215
Email: tereroja@hotmail.com
Web: www.nahnphx.org

RELIGIOUS

COMUNIDAD HISPANA SHILOH
Shiloh Community Church
1902 N. 32nd St.
Phoenix, AZ 85050
Rev. Benjamin Vega, Pastor
Tel: (602) 569-0311 Fax: (602) 569-3723
Email: benjaminvega@shilohcc.net
Web: www.shilohcc.net

DIOCESE OF PHOENIX
Hispanic Ministry
400 Este Calle Monroe
Phoenix, AZ 85004
José Robles, Director for Hispanic Ministry
Tel: (602) 354-2043 Fax: (602) 354-2432
Email: jrobles@diocesephoenix.org
Web: www.diocesephoenix.org

NATIONAL CATHOLIC COUNCIL FOR HISPANIC MINISTRY
3131 E Camelback Rd. #200
Phoenix, AZ 85016
Rev. Kenneth G. Davis, Interim President
Tel: (602) 266-8623 Fax: (602) 606-5705
Email: ncchm1@aol.com
Web: www.ncchm.com

RESEARCH

CENTER FOR LATIN AMERICAN STUDIES
Arizona State University
P.O. Box 874502
Tempe, AZ 85287-4502
Tod Swanson, Director
Tel: (480) 965-5127 Fax: (480) 965-6679
Email: latam.studies@asu.edu
Web: www.asu.edu/clas/latin/

CHICANO RESEARCH COLLECTION
Arizona State University
P.O. Box 871006
Tempe, AZ 85287-1006
Christine Marin, Archivist
Tel: (480) 965-3145 Fax: (480) 965-0776
Web: www.asu.edu/lib/archives

HISPANIC RESEARCH CENTER
Arizona State University
P.O. Box 872702
Tempe, AZ 85287-2702
Gary D. Keller, Director
Tel: (480) 965-3990 Fax: (480) 965-0315
Email: gary.keller@asu.edu
Web: www.asu.edu/clas/hrc

MEXICAN AMERICAN STUDIES & RESEARCH CENTER
University of Arizona
Cesar E Chavez Bldg., #208
Tucson, AZ 85721-0023
Dr. Antonio Estrada, Director
Tel: (520) 621-7551 Fax: (520) 621-7966
Email: masrc@u.arizona.edu
Web: http://fp.arizona.edu/masrc

NATIONAL LAW CENTER FOR INTER-AMERICAN FREE TRADE
440 N. Bonita Ave.
Tucson, AZ 85745-2747
Boris Kozolchyk, Director/Founder
Tel: (520) 622-1200 Fax: (520) 622-0957
Email: natlaw@natlaw.com
Web: www.natlaw.com

SPEC. INT., AIDS

SOUTHERN ARIZONA AIDS FOUNDATION
Salud es Poder, Latino Men's Health Project
375 S. Euclid Ave.
Tucson, AZ 85719
Susan Banes, Secretary
Tel: (520) 628-7223 Fax: (520) 628-7222
Email: info@saaf.org
Web: www.saaf.org/latino.htm

SPEC. INT., ALCOHOL/DRUG CENTER

CASA DE VIDA, INC.
1900 W. Speedway Blvd.
Tucson, AZ 85745-2215
Joseph Parker, Director
Tel: (520) 792-0591
Email: jparker@lafrontera.org

SPEC. INT., CHILD CARE

CASA DE LOS NIÑOS
1101 N 4th Ave.
Tucson, AZ 85705
Dee-Dee Samet, Esq., President
Tel: (520) 624-5600 Fax: (520) 623-2443
Email: info@casadelosninos.org

RANCHO FELIZ CHARITABLE FOUNDATION, INC.
6910 E. 5th Ave.
Scottsdale, AZ 85251
Heather Josowigz, Administrative Assistant
Tel: (480) 949-7144 Fax: (480) 946-9000
Email: heather@gillenwater.biz
Web: www.ranchofeliz.com

SPEC. INT., EDUCATION

ARIZONA HISPANIC SCHOOL ADMINISTRATORS ASSOCIATION
P.O. Box 16023
Tucson, AZ 85711
Dr. Kent Paredes Scribner, President
Tel: (602) 455-6701
Email: kent.scribner@ahsaa.net
Web: www.ahsaa.net

CENTER FOR LATIN AMERICAN STUDIES
University of Arizona
P.O. Box 210158-B
Tucson, AZ 85721-0158
Dr. William H. Beezley, Interim Director
Tel: (520) 626-7242 Fax: (520) 626-7248
Email: laac@u.arizona.edu
Web: http://las.arizona.edu

CHICANA AND CHICANO STUDIES DEPARTMENT
Arizona State University
Lattie F. Coor Hall #6635
Tempe, AZ 85287
Cordelia Candelaria, Professor/Chair
Tel: (480) 965-5091 Fax: (480) 965-7165
Email: ccscronica@asu.edu
Web: www.asu.edu/clas/chicana

ESPIRITU COMMUNITY DEVELOPMENT CORPORATION
NFL YET Academy
4848 S. Second St.
Phoenix, AZ 85040
Fernando Ruiz, Executive Director
Tel: (602) 305-5012 Fax: (602) 243-7799
Email: fruiz@espiritu.org
Web: www.espiritu.org

HISPANIC MOTHER-DAUGHTER PROGRAM
Arizona State University
P.O. Box 871112
Tempe, AZ 85287-1112
Angelica Sanchez, Director
Tel: (480) 965-5838 Fax: (480) 727-7592
Email: Angelica.Sanchez@asu.edu
Web: www.asu.edu/studentlife/msc/hmdp.html

LOS DIABLOS ALUMNI ASSOCIATION
Arizona State University
P.O. Box 873702
Tempe, AZ 85287-3702
Guadalupe Sosa Valencia, President
Tel: (602) 926-3382
Email: guadalupe50@msn.com
Web: www.asu.edu

MEXICAYOTL ACADEMY, INC.
Affiliate of NCLR
850 N. Morley Ave.
Nogales, AZ 85621
Baltazar Garcia, Director
Tel: (520) 287-6790 Fax: (520) 287-0037
Email: durias@extremezone.com

PROJECT 1000
Arizona State University
P.O. Box 875305
c/o Graduate College
Tempe, AZ 85287-5305
Michael J. Sullivan, Director
Tel: (800) 327-4893 Fax: (480) 965-8309
Email: project1000@asu.edu
Web: www.mati.eas.asu.edu/p1000/

REFORMA
Central Arizona Chapter
Ironwood Library, 4354 E. Ft. Lowell Rd.
Tucson, AZ 85712
Donie Gignac, Chapter President
Tel: (520) 791-4580
Email: dgignac@ci.tuscon.az.us
Web: www.sir.arizona.edu/reforma/

REFORMA
Tucson Chapter
P.O. Box 27473
Tucson, AZ 85726-7473
Anna Sanchez, Chapter President
Tel: (520) 791-4393 Fax: (520) 791-5249
Email: anna.sanchez@tucsonaz.gov
Web: www.reforma.org

SPEC. INT., EMPLOYMENT

SER-JOBS FOR PROGRESS OF SOUTHERN ARIZONA, INC.
Affiliate of SER-Jobs for Progress National, Inc.
40 W. 28th St.
Tucson, AZ 85713
Ernest Urias, Executive Director
Tel: (520) 624-8629 Fax: (520) 623-5754
Email: ser1@qwest.net
Web: www.ser-national.org

SPEC. INT., HEALTH SERVICES

ARIZONA LATIN-AMERICAN MEDICAL ASSOCIATION
P.O. Box 24152
Tempe, AZ 85285-4152
Adolfo Echevesde, Executive Director
Tel: (480) 491-2042 Fax: (480) 491-2060
Email: alma@latinohealthonline.com
Web: www.latinohealthonline.com/alma/

CONCILIO LATINO DE SALUD
546 E Osborn Rd. #22
Phoenix, AZ 85012
Elisabeth Valdez, Director
Tel: (602) 285-0959 Fax: (602) 285-0980
Email: conciliolts@aol.com

ESPERANCA
1911 W. Earll Dr.
Phoenix, AZ 85015
Raul Espericueta, President/CEO
Tel: (602) 252-7772 Fax: (602) 340-9197
Email: raul@esperanca.org
Web: www.esperanca.org

LUZ SOCIAL SERVICES, INC.
Tucson Office
2797 N. Introspect Dr.
Tucson, AZ 85745
Ricardo M. Jasso, Executive Director
Tel: (520) 882-6216 Fax: (520) 623-9291
Email: rjasso@luzsocialservices.org
Web: www.luzsocialservices.org

ASSOCIATION OF COMMUNITY ORGANIZATIONS FOR REFORM NOW
Arizona Chapter
1018 W Roosevelt St.
Phoenix, AZ 85007
Helene O'Brien, National Field Director
Tel: (602) 254-8356 Fax: (602) 258-7143
Email: fielddirect@acorn.org
Web: www.acorn.org

HOUSING AMERICA CORPORATION
Affiliate of NCLR
P.O. Box 600
Somerton, AZ 85350
Laurie G. Senko, Executive Director
Tel: (928) 627-4221 Fax: (928) 627-4213
Email: housingamerica@hacorp.org
Web: www.hacorp.org

HOUSING FOR MESA INC.
P.O. Box 4457
Mesa, AZ 85211
John R. Smith, President/CEO
Tel: (480) 649-1335
Email: info@housingformesa.org
Web: www.housingformesa.org

HOTEL EMPLOYEES AND RESTAURANT EMPLOYEES INTERNATIONAL UNION
Local 631 Phoenix
1841 N. 24th St. #5
Phoenix, AZ 85008
Jose Encino, Secretary/Treasurer
Tel: (602) 306-1848 Fax: (602) 306-1832
Email: here631@worldnet.att.net
Web: www.hereunion.org

LA FRONTERA CENTER, INC.
Latino Services
260 S Scott Ave.
Tucson, AZ 85701
Richard Popy, Supervisor
Tel: (520) 884-8470 Fax: (520) 620-0434
Web: www.lafrontera.org

MANOS DE AYUDA, INC.
2851 N. Melpomene Way
Tucson, AZ 85749
Rebecca Garfunkel, Volunteer Coordinator
Tel: (520) 760-8645 Fax: (520) 760-3311
Email: mda_volunteers@cox.net
Web: www.manosdeayuda.org

ORGANIZATION LATINOS UNITED
6929 N Hayden Rd. #C4, PMB #625
Scottsdale, AZ 85252
Sonia M. de Falcone, President/Founder
Tel: (480) 609-1635 Fax: (480) 609-1639

Email: lizconlin@hotmail.com
Web: www.oluorg.org

TUCSON MEXICO TRADE OFFICE
City of Tucson
P.O. Box 27210
Tucson, AZ 85726-7210
Augustine Garcia, Director
Tel: (520) 791-5199 Fax: (520) 791-5752
Email: augustine.garcia@tucsonaz.gov
Web: www.cityoftucson.org/tmto

AMERICAN BEGINNINGS
2215 S 8th Ave.
Yuma, AZ 85366-4596
Fernando Quiros, Executive Director
Tel: (928) 783-5794 Fax: (928) 783-2410

FRIENDLY HOUSE, INC.
Immigration Services for Latinos
802 S 1st Ave.
Phoenix, AZ 85003
Marianne Gonko, Director/Immigration Services
Tel: (602) 257-1870 Fax: (602) 257-8278
Email: marianneg@friendlyhouse.org
Web: www.friendlyhouse.org

CENTRO DE AMISTAD, INC.
Affiliate of NCLR
8202 S. Avenida del Yaqui
Guadalupe, AZ 85283
Santino Bernasconi, President/CEO
Tel: (480) 839-2926 Fax: (480) 839-9985
Email: santinob@centrodeamistad.org

CHICANOS POR LA CAUSA
Tucson Chapter
200 N Stone Ave.
Tucson, AZ 85701
Tel: (520) 882-0018 Fax: (520) 884-9007
Email: cplc.tucson@cplc.org
Web: www.cplctucson.org

FRIENDLY HOUSE, INC.
Academia del Pueblo, Youth Center
201 E. Durango St.
Phoenix, AZ 85004
Desiree Castillo, Principal
Tel: (602) 416-7302
Email: desireec@friendlyhouse.org
Web: www.friendlyhouse.org

GOLDEN GATE COMMUNITY CENTER
1625 N. 39th Ave.
Phoenix, AZ 85009
Tony Banegas, Director
Tel: (602) 223-0017 Fax: (602) 269-1234
Email: tbanegas@arizonaschildren.org
Web: www.goldengatecenter.org

LEAGUE OF UNITED LATIN AMERICAN CITIZENS
Southern Arizona Institute for Leadership-Council 1057
2202 S. March Pl.
Tucson, AZ 85703
Alberto Soto, Council President
Tel: (520) 624-0595 X18 Fax: (520) 792-6388

NOSOTROS, INC.
440 N Grande St.
Tucson, AZ 85745
Frank Romero, Executive Director
Tel: (520) 623-3489 Fax: (520) 624-7999
Email: nosotros2@qwest.com

VALLE DEL SOL, INC.
Affiliate of NCLR
1209 S 1st Ave.
Phoenix, AZ 85003

Maria Elena Ochoa, Senior Programs Officer
Tel: (602) 248-8101 Fax: (602) 254-7121
Email: mariaelenao@valledelsol.com
Web: www.valledelsol.com

HISPANIC WOMEN'S CORPORATION
4545 N 36th St. #207
Phoenix, AZ 85018-3474
Linda Mazon Gutierrez, President
Tel: (602) 954-7995 Fax: (602) 954-7563
Email: hwc@inetmail.att.net
Web: www.hispanicwomen.org

CHICANO/LATINO LAW STUDENT ASSOCIATION
Arizona State University
P.O. Box 873001
Memorial Union #340
Tempe, AZ 85287-3001
Jessica Sanchez, President
Tel: (480) 965-2255 Fax: (480) 965-7311
Email: jessica.sanchez.1@asu.edu

EL CONCILIO
Arizona State University
P.O. Box 873001
Tempe, AZ 85287-3001
David Virgil, President
Tel: (490) 965-2255
Email: el_concilio_asu@yahoo.com
Web: www.asu.edu

HISPANIC BUSINESS STUDENT ASSOCIATION
University of Arizona
1130 E Helen #2045
Tucson, AZ 85721
Stacey Lippert, Advisor
Tel: (520) 621-2782 Fax: (520) 621-6147
Email: staceys@eller.arizona.edu
Web: http://clubs.asua.arizona.edu/~hbsa

HISPANIC SCHOLARSHIP FUND
University of Arizona
1201 E Drachman St. #204
Tucson, AZ 85719
Paul Cervant, President
Tel: (520) 621-2782 Fax: (520) 621-6147
Email: pcervant@email.arizona.edu
Web: www.arizona.edu

JUNTOS
University of Arizona
1110 E. North Campus
Tucson, AZ 85721
Elizabeth Primero, President
Tel: (520) 621-2782 Fax: (520) 621-6147
Email: eprimero@email.arizona.edu
Web: www.arizona.edu

KAPPA DELTA CHI SORORITY
University of Arizona
P.O. Box 41676
Tucson, AZ 85717
Rebecca Covarrubias, President
Tel: (520) 621-8046
Email: rebeccac@u.arizona.edu
Web: http://clubs.asua.arizona.edu/~kdchi/

LA RAZA-HISPANIC NATIONAL BAR ASSOCIATION
University of Arizona
U of A College of Law #176
Tucson, AZ 85721
Christina Vejar, President
Tel: (520) 621-2782 Fax: (520) 621-6147
Email: christina.vejar@law.arizona.edu
Web: www.arizona.edu

MOVIMIENTO ESTUDIANTIL CHICANO DE AZTLAN
Arizona State University College of Liberal Arts and Sciences
P.O. Box 873001
Tempe, AZ 85287-3001
F. Arturo Rosales, Advisor
Tel: (480) 965-2255 Fax: (480) 965-2110
Email: mecha@asu.edu

MOVIMIENTO ESTUDIANTIL CHICANO DE AZTLAN
Gateway Community College
108 N. 40th St.
Phoenix, AZ 85034
Denise Menchaca, Advisor
Tel: (602) 286-8125
Email: Denise.Menchaca@gcumail.maricopa.edu

MOVIMIENTO ESTUDIANTIL CHICANO DE AZTLAN
University of Arizona
1110 E. North Campus
Tucson, AZ 85721
Vanessa Gallego, Co-Chair
Tel: (520) 621-2782 Fax: (520) 621-6147
Email: gnightryder32@hotmail.com
Web: http://clubs.asua.arizona.edu/~mecha/

OMEGA DELTA PHI FRATERNITY
University of Arizona
P.O. Box 43392
Tucson, AZ 85733
Mario Calderon, Advisor
Tel: (520) 621-2782 Fax: (520) 621-6147
Email: calderonm@arizona.edu

RITMOS LATINOS
University of Arizona
2002 E. River Rd. #L8
Tucson, AZ 85718
Alejandra Valdez, President
Tel: (520) 621-2782 Fax: (520) 621-6147
Email: avaldez@email.arizona.edu
Web: http://clubs.asua.arizona.edu/~ritmos

SOCIETY OF HISPANIC PROFESSIONAL ENGINEERS
Arizona State University
P.O. Box 873001
Tempe, AZ 85287-3001
Daniel Ferrer, President
Tel: (480) 965-2255
Email: shpe@shpe.eas.asu.edu
Web: http://shpe.eas.asu.edu/shpe/

SPANISH CLUB
University of Arizona
1423 E. University Blvd. M LNG 545
Tucson, AZ 85721
Giuliana Donnelly, Advisor
Tel: (520) 621-2782 Fax: (520) 621-6147
Email: gdonnell@u.arizona.edu
Web: www.arizona.edu

ARKANSAS

ARKANSAS REGIONAL MINORITY SUPPLIER DEVELOPMENT COUNCIL
P.O. Box 2242
300 Spring Bldg. #415
Little Rock, AR 72201
Charles King, Jr., Executive Director
Tel: (501) 374-7026 Fax: (501) 371-0409
Email: info@armsdc.org
Web: www.armsdc.org

ARKANSAS DEMOCRATIC HISPANIC CAUCUS
170 Santa Fe
Hot Springs, AR 71913
Jorge L. Garcia, President

Tel: (501) 664-5262
Email: jgarcia1@cablelynx.com
Web: www.arkdhc.org

RELIGIOUS

DIOCESE OF LITTLE ROCK
Hispanic Ministry Office
2500 N Tyler St.
Little Rock, AR 72217
Mickey Espinoza, Director for Hispanic Ministry
Tel: (501) 664-0340 Fax: (501) 664-9075
Email: mespinoza@dolr.org
Web: www.dolr.org

SPEC. INT., EDUCATION

LATIN AMERICAN STUDIES PROGRAM
University of Arkansas
425 Kimpel Hall
Fayetteville, AR 72701
Steven Bell, Director
Tel: (479) 575-2951 Fax: (479) 575-6795
Email: sbell@uark.edu
Web: www.uark.edu/depts/lastinfo

SPEC. INT., HOUSING

ASSOCIATION OF COMMUNITY ORGANIZATIONS FOR REFORM NOW
Arkansas
2101 S. Main St.
Little Rock, AR 72206
Zach Polett, Political Director
Tel: (501) 376-7151 Fax: (501) 376-3952
Email: poldirect@acorn.org
Web: www.acorn.org

CALIFORNIA

ARTISTIC

AZTECA RECORDS
P.O. Box 65766
Los Angeles, CA 90065-0766
Cesar C. Cantú, President
Tel: (323) 221-6800

THE BARRIO SYMPHONY/LA SINFÓNICA DEL BARRIO
P.O. Box 26306
Los Angeles, CA 90026-0306
Peter A. Quesada, Founder/Music Director
Tel: (323) 466-4425 Fax: (323) 962-1664
Email: cndc@aol.com

BAYVIEW OPERA HOUSE
4705 3rd St.
San Francisco, CA 94124
Shelley Bradford-Bel, Executive Director
Tel: (415) 824-0386 Fax: (415) 824-7124
Email: bvoh@pacbell.net
Web: www.bayviewoperahouse.org

BOWERS MUSEUM OF CULTURAL ART
2002 N. Main St.
Santa Ana, CA 92706
Vickie Byrd, vice President
Tel: (714) 567-3600
Email: vbyrd@bowers.org
Web: www.bowers.org

CINE ACCIÓN
346 9th St., 2nd Fl.
San Francisco, CA 94103
Ronald Ponce, President
Tel: (415) 553-8135 Fax: (415) 553-8137
Web: www.cineaccion.com

CUADRATURA DEL CIRCULO POETICO IBEROAMERICANO
P.O. Box 54
Santa Monica, CA 90406-0054
Pedro Izquierdo-Tejido, President
Tel: (310) 829-2694

EL TEATRO CAMPESINO
National Headquarters
P.O. Box 1240
San Juan Bautista, CA 95045
Luis Valdéz, Director
Tel: (831) 623-2444
Email: luis@elteatrocampesino.com
Web: www.elteatrocampesino.com

FRANCISCO MARTINEZ DANCE THEATRE
6723 Matilija Ave.
Valley Glen, CA 91405
David Allen Jones, Executive Director
Tel: (818) 988-2192 Fax: (818) 988-2192
Email: info@fmdt.org
Web: www.fmdt.org

HISPANICS FOR LOS ANGELES OPERA
135 N Grand Ave.
Los Angeles, CA 90012
Orlando Ortega, Chair
Tel: (213) 368-9600 Fax: (213) 972-3007
Email: info@hispanicsforlaopera.org
Web: www.hispanicsforlaopera.org

INNER CITY ARTS
720 Kohler St.
Los Angeles, CA 90021
Cynthia Harnisch, Executive Director
Tel: (213) 627-9621 Fax: (213) 627-6469
Email: info@inner-cityarts.org
Web: www.inner-cityarts.org

LOS ANGELES MUSIC AND ART SCHOOL
3630 E. 3rd St.
Los Angeles, CA 90063
Isela Sotelo, Executive Director
Tel: (323) 262-7734 Fax: (323) 262-2805
Email: isotelo@lamusart.org/ stayintune@lamusart.org
Web: www.lamusart.org

LOS DANZANTES DE AZTLÁN
California State University
Chicano/Latin American Studies, 5340 N. Campus Dr., M/S SS97
Fresno, CA 93740-8019
Juan Felipe Herrera, Chair
Tel: (559) 278-2848 Fax: (209) 278-6468
Email: juanh@csufresno.edu
Web: http://cls.csufresno.edu/

MARIACHI USA FOUNDATION
1 W. California Blvd. #228
Pasadena, CA 91105-3033
Oralia Michel, President
Tel: (626) 568-0902 Fax: (626) 568-1021
Email: info@mariachiusa.org
Web: www.mariachiusa.org

NATIONAL ASSOCIATION OF LATINO INDEPENDENT PRODUCERS
West Coast Office
P.O. Box 1247
Santa Monica, CA 90406
Kathryn Galan, Executive Director
Tel: (310) 395-8880
Email: info@nalip.org
Web: www.nalip.org

NEIGHBORHOOD MUSIC SCHOOL ASSOCIATION
Boyle Heights & Los Angeles
358 S. Boyle Ave.
Los Angeles, CA 90033
Terry Castaneda, President
Tel: (323) 268-0762 Fax: (323) 269-2992
Email: neighbormusic@cs.com

PLAZA DE LA RAZA
School of Performing and Visual Arts
3540 N. Mission Rd.
Los Angeles, CA 90031
Rose Marie Cano, Executive Director
Tel: (323) 223-2475 Fax: (213) 223-1804
Email: information@plazadelaraza.org
Web: www.plazadelaraza.org

PROFESSIONAL MUSICIANS, LOCAL 47, AFM
817 N. Vine St.
Hollywood, CA 90038-3779
Hal Espinosa, President
Tel: (323) 462-2161 Fax: (323) 461-3090
Email: local47@afm.org
Web: www.afm.org/47/ www.promusic47.org

SELF HELP GRAPHICS AND ART, INC.
3802 Cesar E. Chavez Ave.
Los Angeles, CA 90063
Tomas Benitez, Director
Tel: (323) 881-6444 Fax: (323) 881-6447
Email: info@selfhelpgraphics.com
Web: www.selfhelpgraphics.com

BUSINESS

APPLE HISPANIC ASSOCIATION
1 Infinite Loop, M/S 60-ITMS
Cupertino, CA 95014
Grelia Reiber, President
Tel: (408) 974-2665

GUATEMALAN TRADE CENTER
1138 Wilshire Blvd. #300
Los Angeles, CA 90017
Byron Vásquez, Director
Tel: (213) 250-3416 Fax: (213) 250-3705

INSTITUTE OF THE AMERICAS
University of California, San Diego
10111 N. Torrey Pines Rd.
La Jolla, CA 92037
Jeffrey Davidow, President
Tel: (858) 453-5560 Fax: (858) 453-2165
Email: support@iamericas.org
Web: www.iamericas.org

LATIN BUSINESS ASSOCIATION
120 S. San Pedro St. #530
Los Angeles, CA 90012
Ray Durazo, Chairman of the Borad
Tel: (213) 628-8510 Fax: (213) 628-8519
Email: ray@durazo.com
Web: www.lbausa.com

LATINO BUSINESS ASSOCIATION
Pajaro Valley Chamber of Commerce
P.O. Box 1748
444 Main St.
Watsonville, CA 95076
Jorge Ruegerin, Chair
Tel: (831) 724-3900 Fax: (831) 728-5300
Email: info@pajarovalleychamber.com
Web: www.pajarovalleychamber.com

MEXICAN AMERICAN GROCERS ASSOCIATION
405 N San Fernando Rd.
Los Angeles, CA 90031
Steven A. Soto, President/CEO
Tel: (323) 227-1565 Fax: (323) 227-6935
Email: maga727@sbcglobal.net
Web: www.maga-inc.org

NATIONAL SOCIETY OF HISPANIC MBAS
San Diego Chapter
P.O. Box 9284841
San Diego, CA 92192
Liliana Zuniga-Avila, Chapter President
Email: general@sandiego.nshmba.org
Web: http://sandiego.nshmba.org

San Francisco Chapter
P.O. Box 26618
San Francisco, CA 94126-6618
Mariela Perez - Rea, Chapter President
Email: general@sanfrancisco.nshmba.org
Web: http://sanfrancisco.nshmba.org

San Jose Chapter
3964 Rivermark Plz. #260
Santa Clara, CA 95054
Eddie Correa, Chapter President
Tel: (408) 853-8514
Email: general@sanjose.nshmba.org
Web: http://sanjose.nshmba.org

NORTHERN CALIFORNIA SUPPLIER DEVELOPMENT COUNCIL
1999 Harrison St. #655
Oakland, CA 94612
Michael Ruiz, President
Tel: (510) 587-0636 Fax: (510) 587-0649
Email: info@ncsdc.org
Web: www.ncsdc.org

SOUTHERN CALIFORNIA MINORITY BUSINESS DEVELOPMENT COUNCIL, INC.
515 S. Flower St. #1301
Los Angeles, CA 90071
John W. Murray, Jr., President
Tel: (213) 689-6960 Fax: (213) 689-1707
Email: info@scmbdc.org
Web: www.scmbdc.org

USA-CENTRAL AMERICAN TRADE EXPO CORPORATION
3333 Wilshire Blvd. #612
Los Angeles, CA 90010
Hugo W. Merida, CEO
Tel: (213) 389-5025 Fax: (213) 389-5775
Email: info@usacatradeexpo.com
Web: www.usacatradeexpo.com

CHAMBER OF COMMERCE

ANTELOPE VALLEY HISPANIC CHAMBER OF COMMERCE
38434 9th St. E. #J
Palmdale, CA 93550
Tel: (661) 538-0607 Fax: (661) 538-1057
Email: acosta@qnet.com

THE BOLIVIAN-AMERICAN CHAMBER OF COMMERCE
P.O. Box 56104
San Jose, CA 95156
Tel: (408) 272-2494 Fax: (408) 272-9424

CALIFORNIA HISPANIC CHAMBER OF COMMERCE
770 L St.
Sacramento, CA 95814
Melinda Guzman, Chairperson
Tel: (916) 444-2221 Fax: (916) 669-2870
Email: canetej@cahcc.com
Web: www.cahcc.com

CALIFORNIA MEXICAN AMERICAN CHAMBER OF COMMERCE
3586 E. Olympic Blvd.
Los Angeles, CA 90023
Frank C. Moreno, President
Tel: (323) 269-4092 Fax: (323) 269-4175
Email: mexamoreno@aol.com

CÁMARA DE COMERCIO NICARAGUENSE-AMERICANA DE CALIFORNIA
P.O. Box 92345
City of Industry, CA 91715-2345
Tito Lagos, President
Tel: (626) 814-1012 Fax: (626) 814-1772
Email: caconaca@camarasdecomercio.us
Web: http://camarasdecomercio.com/nicaragua

CENTRAL CALIFORNIA HISPANIC CHAMBER OF COMMERCE
National Headquarters
2331 Fresno St.
Fresno, CA 93721
Rojelio Vasquez, President
Tel: (559) 485-6640 Fax: (559) 495-4811
Email: directorlorena@cchcc.com
Web: www.cchcc.com

COACHELLA VALLEY MEXICAN AMERICAN CHAMBER OF COMMERCE
P.O. Box 1874
Indio, CA 92202
Jacqueline Lopez, PresidentPresident
Tel: (760) 342-9402 Fax: (760) 406-4288
Email: info@cvmacc.org
Web: www.cvmacc.org

ECUADORIAN AMERICAN CHAMBER OF COMMERCE OF LOS ANGELES
701 N. Alvarado St.
Los Angeles, CA 90026
Franklin Figueroa, President
Tel: (323) 939-6568 Fax: (323) 938-2520
Email: franklinfigueroa@hotmail.com

EL MONTE CHAMBER OF COMMERCE
P.O. Box 5866
El Monte, CA 91734-1866
Richard Nichols, Executive Director
Tel: (626) 443-0180 Fax: (818) 443-0463
Email: chamber@ksb8.com
Web: www.emsem.com

FONTANA HISPANIC CHAMBER OF COMMERCE
P.O. Box 3944
Fontana, CA 92334
Tel: (909) 428-6797 Fax: (909) 428-6797
Email: fontanahcc@sbcglobal.net

FRESNO AREA HISPANIC CHAMBER OF COMMERCE
1456 W Shaw Ave.
Fresno, CA 93711
Antonio Valtierra, President
Tel: (559) 222-8705 Fax: (559) 222-8706
Email: webmaster@wattleweb.com
Web: www.fahcc.org

GILROY HISPANIC CHAMBER OF COMMERCE
P.O. Box 1312
Gilroy, CA 95021
Tel: (408) 225-5053 Fax: (408) 846-6598

GREATER CORONA HISPANIC CHAMBER OF COMMERCE
119 E. 4th St.
Corona, CA 92879-1406
Dr. George Beloz, President
Tel: (909) 737-0955 Fax: (909) 737-5668
Email: gbeloz@aol.com
Web: www.gchcc.com

THE GREATER MORENO VALLEY HISPANIC CHAMBER OF COMMERCE
24371 Sunnymead Blvd. #C
Moreno Valley, CA 92553
Tel: (909) 485-8170 Fax: (909) 485-6918

GREATER RIVERSIDE HISPANIC CHAMBER OF COMMERCE
P.O. Box 5872
Riverside, CA 92517
Damain Castillo, President
Tel: (951) 682-7422 Fax: (951) 784-1587
Email: info@grhcc.org
Web: www.grhcc.org

GREATER SAN JOSÉ HISPANIC CHAMBER OF COMMERCE
84 W Santa Clara St. #100
San Jose, CA 95113
Carlos Figueroa, President
Tel: (408) 494-0296 Fax: (408) 494-0291
Email: info@gsjhcc.org
Web: www.gsjhcc.org

GREATER STOCKTON HISPANIC CHAMBER OF COMMERCE
343 E. Main St. #806
Stockton, CA 95202
Alicia Arong, President
Tel: (209) 943-6117 Fax: (209) 943-0114
Email: arongal@earthlink.net
Web: www.ssjmacc.org

HIGH DESERT HISPANIC CHAMBER OF COMMERCE
P.O. Box 2157
14455 Park Ave. #A
Victorville, CA 92392
Rudy Cabriales, President
Tel: (760) 241-6661 Fax: (202) 318-7328
Email: hdhcc.victorville@verizon.net
Web: www.hdhcc.com

HISPANIC CHAMBER OF COMMERCE OF ALAMEDA COUNTY
1840 Embarcadero St. #101
Oakland, CA 94606
Ron Silva, President
Tel: (510) 536-4477 Fax: (510) 536-4320
Email: info@hccac.com
Web: www.hccac.com

HISPANIC CHAMBER OF COMMERCE OF CONTRA COSTA COUNTY
P.O. Box 23964
Pleasant Hill, CA 94523
Pedro Babiak, President
Tel: (925) 281-2623 Fax: (925) 281-2623
Email: info@h5c.org
Web: www.h5c.org

HISPANIC CHAMBER OF COMMERCE OF MARIN
P.O. Box 4423
San Rafael, CA 94913
Raul Lara, President
Tel: (415) 721-9686 Fax: (415) 479-4587
Email: latinocoun@aol.com
Web: www.hccm.net

HISPANIC CHAMBER OF COMMERCE OF MONTERREY COUNTY
5 E. Gabilan St. #214
Salinas, CA 93901
Tel: (831) 757-1251 Fax: (831) 757-1246

HISPANIC CHAMBER OF COMMERCE OF ORANGE COUNTY
2323 N. Broadway St. #305
Santa Ana, CA 92706-1640
Joel Ayala, President & CEO
Tel: (714) 953-4289 Fax: (714) 953-0273
Email: mail@hcoc.org
Web: www.hcoc.org

HISPANIC CHAMBER OF COMMERCE OF SILICON VALLEY
696 E Santa Clara St. #106
San Jose, CA 95112
Miguel A. Olivo, Chair
Tel: (408) 213-0320 Fax: (408) 213-0329
Email: info@hccsv.org
Web: www.hccsv.org

HISPANIC CHAMBER OF COMMERCE OF SONOMA COUNTY
P.O. Box 11392
Santa Rosa, CA 95406
Maria Lemus, President
Tel: (707) 577-7129 Fax: (707) 577-7075
Email: execdirectorhccsc@hotmail.com
Web: www.hccsc.com

HISPANIC CHAMBER OF COMMERCE OF YOLO COUNTY
P.O. Box 1232
117 W. Main St. #22-C
Woodland, CA 95695
Jennifer Pearson-Cruickshank, President
Tel: (530) 666-5335 Fax: (530) 406-8880
Email: jennifercruickshank@hotmail.com
Web: www.dcn.davis.ca.us/YoloLINK/programs/pHispanChambeCommer-4516.html

HISPANIC CHAMBER OF COMMERCE SANTA CLARA COUNTY
696 E. Santa Clara St. #106
San Jose, CA 95112
Dennis King, Executive Director
Tel: (408) 213-0320 Fax: (408) 213-0329
Email: info@hccsv.org
Web: www.hccsv.org

INLAND EMPIRE HISPANIC CHAMBER OF COMMERCE
320 North E St. #211
San Bernardino, CA 92401
Rita Arias, President
Tel: (909) 888-2188 Fax: (909) 888-1151
Email: members@iehcc.org
Web: www.iehcc.org

INSTITUTO DE EDUCACION POPULAR DEL SUR DE CALIFORNIA
Cypress Park Community Job Center
2055 N Figueroa St.
Los Angeles, CA 90065
Lamberto Castillo, Coordinator
Tel: (323) 223-2021
Email: lamberto@idepsca.org
Web: www.idepsca.org

KERN COUNTY HISPANIC CHAMBER OF COMMERCE
1401 19th St. #110
Bakersfield, CA 93301
Lou Gomez, Executive Director
Tel: (661) 633-5495 Fax: (661) 633-5499
Email: lgomez@kchcc.org
Web: www.kernhispanicchamber.com

LATINO CHAMBER OF COMMERCE OF COMPTON
P.O. Box 449
Compton, CA 90221
Josie Maruffo, President
Tel: (310) 639-4455 Fax: (310) 639-4455
Email: josie@latinoccc.org
Web: www.latinoccc.org

LATINO CHAMBER OF COMMERCE OF POMONA VALLEY
142 E 3rd St.
Pomona, CA 91766
Mike Suarez, President
Tel: (909) 469-0995 Fax: (909) 469-0760
Email: pomonalatinochamber@yahoo.com

LINCOLN HEIGHTS CHAMBER OF COMMERCE
2716 N. Broadway #210
Los Angeles, CA 90031
Steven Kesten, President
Tel: (323) 221-6571 Fax: (323) 221-1513

LOS ANGELES METRO HISPANIC CHAMBER OF COMMERCE
3333 Wilshire Blvd. #607
Los Angeles, CA 90010
Angel Diaz, Chairman
Tel: (213) 739-7016 Fax: (213) 389-5775
Email: chamber@lahispanicc.org
Web: www.lahispanicc.org

MADERA HISPANIC CHAMBER OF COMMERCE
11110 El Capitan Dr.
Madera, CA 93638
Stephen Rico, President
Tel: (559) 674-8821 Fax: (559) 674-9084
Email: mhcc123@madnet.net
Web: www.madera-hcc.org

MERCED COUNTY HISPANIC CHAMBER OF COMMERCE
1640 N St. #220
Merced, CA 95340
Chris Tafoya, President
Tel: (209) 384-9537 Fax: (209) 723-5051
Email: info@mercedhcc.com
Web: www.mercedhcc.com

MEXICAN AMERICAN CHAMBER OF COMMERCE AND INDUSTRY
P.O. Box 65766
Los Angeles, CA 90065
César C. Cantú, President
Tel: (323) 221-6800

MORENO VALLEY HISPANIC CHAMBER OF COMMERCE
P.O. Box 246
Moreno Valley, CA 92556
Jaime C. Hurtado, President
Tel: (951) 485-8170 Fax: (951) 685-8185
Email: info@mvhcc.com
Web: www.mvhcc.com

THE NORTHEAST SAN FERNANDO VALLEY CHAMBER OF COMMERCE
601 S. Brand Blvd.

San Fernando, CA 91340
Ramiro Estrada, Executive Director
Tel: (818) 361-1184 Fax: (818) 898-1986
Email: mail@nesfvcc.org
Web: www.nesfvcc.org

POMONA VALLEY LATINO CHAMBER OF COMMERCE OF COMPTON
142 E. 3rd St.
Pomona, CA 91766
Tel: (909) 469-0702 Fax: (909) 469-0604
Email: camlat@gte.net

PORTUGUESE CHAMBER OF COMMERCE OF CALIFORNIA
84 W. Santa Clara St.
San Jose, CA 95113-1815
Maria Alice Jensen, President
Tel: (408) 288-7655 Fax: (408) 288-6182
Email: help@portuguesechamber.com
Web: www.portuguesechamber.com

REGIONAL HISPANIC CHAMBER OF COMMERCE
1 World Trade Ctr. #420
Long Beach, CA 90831
Sandy L. Cajas, President/CEO
Tel: (562) 597-7298 Fax: (562) 597-7298
Email: reghispaniccc@verizon.net
Web: www.regionalhispaniccc.org

SACRAMENTO HISPANIC CHAMBER OF COMMERCE
2848 Arden Way #230
Sacramento, CA 95825
E. Dennis Trinidad, President/CEO
Tel: (916) 486-7708 Fax: (916) 486-7728
Email: dennis@sachcc.org
Web: www.sachcc.org

SAN BENITO COUNTY HISPANIC CHAMBER OF COMMERCE
449 San Benito St. #28
Hollister, CA 95023
Tel: (831) 638-1163 Fax: (831) 638-1026
Email: rornelas@hollinet.com

SAN DIEGO COUNTY HISPANIC CHAMBER OF COMMERCE
1250 6th Ave. #550
San Diego, CA 92101
Paola Hernandez, Chair
Tel: (619) 702-0790 Fax: (619) 696-3282
Email: sdchcc@sdchcc.com
Web: www.sdchcc.com

SAN FRANCISCO HISPANIC CHAMBER OF COMMERCE
703 Market St. #611
San Francisco, CA 94103
Fernando Rivera, President
Tel: (415) 278-9611
Email: info@sfhcc.com
Web: www.sfhcc.com

SAN MATEO COUNTY HISPANIC CHAMBER OF COMMERCE
812 Palm Ave.
Redwood City, CA 94061
Tel: (650) 839-1369 Fax: (650) 839-2009
Email: lizquiros@aol.com

SANTA BARBARA HISPANIC CHAMBER OF COMMERCE
P.O. Box 6592
Santa Barbara, CA 93160-6592
Luis Villegas, President/CEO
Tel: (888) 630-9757 Fax: (888) 560-1686
Email: lvillegas@sbhcc.com
Web: www.sbhcc.com

SOLANO/NAPA COUNTY HISPANIC CHAMBER OF COMMERCE
P.O. Box 2723
Fairfield, CA 94533
Karla Velez, President
Tel: (707) 643-5037 Fax: (707) 557-9844
Email: info@hccsolanonapa.org
Web: www.hccsolanonapa.org

SOUTH BAY LATINO CHAMBER OF COMMERCE
13545 S. Hawthorne Blvd. #201
Los Angeles, CA 90045
Mr. Candy Saenz, President/CEO
Tel: (310) 676-2568
Email: candy@sblcc.net
Web: www.sblcc.net

SOUTH SAN JOAQUIN HISPANIC CHAMBER OF COMMERCE
P.O. Box 475
Manteca, CA 95336
Teresa Clarck, President
Tel: (209) 239-4424 Fax: (209) 825-7162
Email: tac610@aol.com

STANISLAUS COUNTY HISPANIC CHAMBER OF COMMERCE
1114 J St.
Modesto, CA 95354
Tel: (209) 571-6480 Fax: (209) 549-1140
Email: hispanicchamber@sdcglobalnet

STOCKTON SAN JOAQUIN COUNTY MEXICAN-AMERICAN CHAMBER OF COMMERCE
343 E. Main St. #806
Stockton, CA 95202
Alicia Arong, President
Tel: (209) 943-6117 Fax: (209) 943-0114
Email: arongal@earthlink.net
Web: www.ssjmacc.org

TULARE KINGS HISPANIC CHAMBER OF COMMERCE
711 N. Court St. #C
Visalia, CA 93291
Vincent Salinas, President
Tel: (559) 734-6020 Fax: (559) 734-6021
Email: tkhcc@aol.com
Web: www.tkhcc.com

UNITED STATES-MEXICO CHAMBER OF COMMERCE
California Pacific Chapter
2450 Colorado Ave. #400-E
Santa Monica, CA 90404
Marlen Marroquin Gati, Executive Director
Tel: (310) 586-7901 Fax: (310) 586-7800
Email: info@usmcocca.org
Web: www.usmcocca.org

USA-CENTRAL AMERICAN TRADE EXPO CORPORATION
Headquarters
3333 Wilshire Blvd. #612
Los Angeles, CA 90010
Hugo W. Mérida, CEO
Tel: (213) 389-5025 Fax: (213) 389-5775
Email: info@usacatradeexpo.com
Web: www.usacatradeexpo.com

CALIFORNIA CHICANO NEWS MEDIA ASSOCIATION
Central Valley Chapter
P.O. Bin 440
Bakersfield, CA 93302-0440
Rosario Ortiz, Chapter President
Tel: (661) 395-7458 Fax: (661) 395-7519
Email: rortiz@bakersfield.com
Web: www.ccnma.org

Headquarters
300 S Grand Ave. #3950
Los Angeles, CA 90071-8110
Julio Moran, Executive Director
Tel: (213) 437-4408 Fax: (213) 437-4423
Email: ccnmainfo@ccnma.org
Web: www.ccnma.org

Inland Empire Chapter
474 W Esplanade Ave.
San Jacinto, CA 92504
Mark Acosta, Chapter President
Tel: (909) 763-3453 Fax: (909) 763-3450

Email: macosta@pe.com
Web: www.ccnma.org

Los Angeles Chapter
202 W. 1st St.
Los Angeles, CA 90012
Efrain Hernandez, Jr., Chapter President
Tel: (213) 237-7389 Fax: (213) 237-2199
Email: efrain.hernandez.jr@latimes.com
Web: www.ccnma.org

Sacramento Chapter
1710 Arden Way
Sacramento, CA 95815
Pablo Espinoza, Chapter President
Tel: (916) 614-1971 Fax: (916) 614-1906
Email: pespinoza@univision.net
Web: www.ccnma.org

San Jose Chapter
750 Ridder Park Dr.
San Jose, CA 95190
Sam Diaz, Chapter President
Tel: (408) 920-5021 Fax: (408) 884-2324
Email: sdiaz@sjmercury.com
Web: www.ccnma.org

Tri-County Chapter
P.O. Box 7142
Ventura, CA 93006-7142
Frank Moraga, Chapter President
Tel: (805) 645-1052 Fax: (805) 650-2950
Email: fmoraga@venturacountystar.com
Web: www.home.earthlink.net/~fmoraga/

HISPANIC PUBLIC RELATIONS ASSOCIATION
National Headquarters
660 S. Figueroa St. #1140
Los Angeles, CA 90071
Sandra Bernardo, President
Tel: (951) 272-1888
Email: sandra.bernardo@eurorscq.com
Web: www.hpra-usa.org

LATINO PRINT NETWORK
National Association of Hispanic Publications
27777 Jefferson St. #200
Carlsbad, CA 92008
Kirk Whisler, Sales Coordinator
Tel: (760) 434-7474 Fax: (760) 434-7476
Email: kirk@whisler.com
Web: www.latinoprintnetwork.com

NATIONAL HISPANIC MEDIA COALITION
National Office
2514 S. Grand Ave.
Los Angeles, CA 90007
Alex Nogales, President & CEO
Tel: (213) 746-6988 Fax: (213) 746-1305
Email: info@nhmc.org
Web: www.nhmc.org

NATIONAL LATINO COMMUNICATIONS CENTER
303 S. Loma Dr. South Wing
Los Angeles, CA 90017
Jay Rodriguez, President
Tel: (213) 484-1009 Fax: (213) 483-7848
Web: www.nlcc.com

ASOCIACIÓN DE INTELECTUALES HISPANOS
P.O. Box 65766
Los Angeles, CA 90065
César C. Cantú, President
Tel: (323) 221-6800

ASOCIACIÓN ECUATORIANA
4530 S Deland Ave.
Pico Rivera, CA 90660
León Hi Fong, President
Tel: (562) 692-6115

BARAHONA CENTER FOR STUDY OF BOOKS IN SPANISH FOR CHILDREN AND ADOLESCENTS
California State University San Marcos
333 S. Twin Oaks Valley Rd.
San Marcos, CA 92096-0001
Dr. Isabel Schon, Director
Tel: (760) 750-4070 Fax: (760) 750-4073
Email: ischon@csusm.edu
Web: www.csusm.edu/csb/

BILINGUAL FOUNDATION OF THE ARTS
National Headquarters
421 N. Ave. #19
Los Angeles, CA 90031
Carmen Zapata, President
Tel: (323) 225-4044
Email: bfa99@earthlink.net
Web: www.bfatheatre.org

CARPINTERIA VALLEY HISTORICAL SOCIETY AND MUSEUM OF HISTORY
956 Maple Ave.
Carpinteria, CA 93013
David W. Griggs, Director
Tel: (805) 684-3112 Fax: (805) 684-4721
Web: www.caohwy.com/c/cavamuhi.htm

CASA DE LA CULTURA DE LONG BEACH
2418 E. Anaheim St.
Long Beach, CA 90804
Carlos O. Pallares, President
Tel: (562) 438-1134 Fax: (562) 438-7030
Email: copallares@earthlink.net

CASA DE LA CULTURA GUATEMALA
1138 Wilshire Blvd. #300
Los Angeles, CA 90017
Byron Vásquez, President
Tel: (213) 250-9090 Fax: (213) 250-3705

CENTRO ARTÍSTICO CULTURAL - BOHEMIA DE LOS ANGELES
P.O. Box 73110
Los Angeles, CA 90003
George De Aztlan, President
Tel: (213) 230-4868 Fax: (323) 778-0984
Email: BOHEMIA2000@webtv.net

CENTRO CULTURAL CENTER FOR LATINO ARTS
2868 Mission St.
San Francisco, CA 94110
Jennie E. Rodriguez, Executive Director
Tel: (415) 821-1155
Email: jennie@missionculturalcenter.org
Web: www.missionculturalcenter.org

CENTRO CULTURAL DE LA RAZA
2125 Park Blvd.
San Diego, CA 92101
Aida Macias, President
Tel: (619) 235-6135 Fax: (619) 595-0034
Email: centro@centroraza.com
Web: www.centroraza.com

CLUB AMBATO - ECUADOR
640 N. Hobart Blvd.
Los Angeles, CA 90004
Ruben Arcos, President
Tel: (323) 665-4581 Fax: (323) 662-8906

CLUB BUENA VOLUNTAD
Centro Maravilla
4716 Cesar Chavez Ave.
Los Angeles, CA 90022
Margarita Calderon, President
Tel: (323) 260-2804

CLUB HERMANDAD NICARAGUENSE AMERICANA
5712 Fountain Ave.
Los Angeles, CA 90028
Manuel Salazar, President

Tel: (323) 467-4813 Fax: (323) 669-1029
Email: y_calderon@msn.com

COMITE DE FESTEJOS SALVADORENO
501 S. Manhattan Pl. #102
Los Angeles, CA 90020
Bianca Alvarenga, Director of Public Relations
Tel: (213) 487-2950
Email: boardofdirectors@cofesal.org
Web: www.cofesal.org

COMUNIDADES MEXICANAS
2409 Merced St.
Fresno, CA 93721
Erika Martinez, Coordinator
Tel: (559) 445-2615 Fax: (559) 495-0535
Email: comunidades@consulmexfresno.net

DANZA FLORICANTO/USA
4032 S Overcrest Dr.
Whittier, CA 90601
Gema Sandoval, Executive Director
Tel: (562) 695-3546 Fax: (562) 695-3546
Email: floricanto@earthlink.net
Web: www.danzafloricantousa.com

EL PUEBLO DE LOS ANGELES HISTORICAL MONUMENT
Administrative Office
125 Paseo de la Plz.
Los Angeles, CA 90012
Rushmore Cervantes, Interim General Manager
Tel: (213) 485-6855 Fax: (213) 485-8238
Web: www.ci.la.ca.us/ELP/

FRESNO ART MUSEUM
2233 N. 1st St.
Fresno, CA 93703
Carlos Martinez, Director
Tel: (559) 441-4221 Fax: (559) 441-4227
Email: carlos@fresnoartmuseum.org
Web: www.fresnoartmuseum.org

FUNDACIÓN ECUADOR USA
P.O. Box 555564
Los Angeles, CA 90055
Franklin Figueroa, Sr., President
Tel: (323) 939-6568 Fax: (323) 938-2520
Email: franklinfigueroasr@hotmail.com

GALERÍA DE LA RAZA
2857 24th St.
San Francisco, CA 94110
Carolina Ponce de León, Executive Director
Tel: (415) 826-8009
Email: info@galeriadelaraza.org
Web: www.galeriadelaraza.org

HISPANIC FESTIVITIES COMMITTEE, LOS ANGELES COUNTY
USC Medical Center
1200 N State St. #1112K
Los Angeles, CA 90033
Adelaida de la Cerda, Public Relations
Tel: (323) 226-6899 Fax: (323) 226-6696
Email: adelacerda@alcusc.org

HISTORIC MISSION SAN LUIS REY MUSEUM
4050 Mission Ave.
Oceanside, CA 92057
Pete Litrenta, Director of Development
Tel: (760) 757-3651 Fax: (760) 757-4613
Web: www.sanluisrey.org

HOLLENBECK RECREATION CENTER
Department of Recreation and Parks
415 S. St. Louis St.
Los Angeles, CA 90033
Jon Kirk Mukri, General Manager
Tel: (323) 261-0113 Fax: (323) 526-3975
Email: hollenbeckrc@rap.lacity.org
Web: www.laparks.org

INLAKECH CULTURAL ARTS CENTER
937 W. 5th St.

Oxnard, CA 93033
Javier Gomez, Founder & Artistic Director
Tel: (805) 486-7063 Fax: (805) 486-7468
Email: anahuacq@aol.com
Web: www.inlakechculturalartscenter.org

INSTITUTO CULTURAL MEXICANO DE SAN DIEGO
1549 India St.
San Diego, CA 92101
Tel: (619) 231-8414 Fax: (619) 231-4802
Email: mexicons@electricity.com
Web: www.consulmexsd.org

INSTITUTO LITERARIO Y CULTURAL HISPANICO
8452 Furman Ave.
Westminster, CA 92683
Juana A. Arancibia, President
Tel: (714) 892-8285 Fax: (714) 892-8285
Email: ilchja@aol.com

LA CASA DE LA RAZA
601 E. Montesido
Santa Barbara, CA 93103
Raquel Lopez, Director
Tel: (805) 965-8581 Fax: (805) 965-6451
Email: casa@hotmail.com

LA RAZA GALERIA POSADA
1421 R St.
Sacramento, CA 95814
Zenaida Lopez, Director
Tel: (916) 446-5133
Email: info@galeriaposada.org
Web: www.galeriaposada.org

LAKEWOOD PAN AMERICAN FESTIVAL
Recreation and Community Services Department, Lakewood City Hall
5050 Clark Ave.
Lakewood, CA 90712
Joan Biegel, Director of Recreation & Community Services
Tel: (562) 866-9771 X2408 Fax: (562) 866-0505
Web: www.lakewoodcity.org

LATIN AMERICAN MUSICIANS UNION
2765 Willow Pl.
South Gate, CA 90280
María Graciela, President
Tel: (323) 564-2016
Email: lamusa20@aol.com

LATINO FACULTY, STAFF AND STUDENT ASSOCIATION
Cal Poly Pomona
Cultural Ctr., 3801 W. Temple Ave.
Pomona, CA 91768
Steve Quintero, President
Tel: (909) 869-2841
Email: sfquintero@csupomona.edu

LINCOLN HEIGHTS SENIOR CITIZEN CENTER
Club Hispano del Pueblo
2323 Workman St.
Los Angeles, CA 90031
Alicia Martinez, President
Tel: (323) 225-9339 Fax: (323) 226-0994

LOS CALIFORNIANOS
P.O. Box 600522
San Diego, CA 92160-0522
Boyd Ellis de Larios, President
Email: latejedora@loscalifornianos.org
Web: www.loscalifornianos.org

LOS CENZONTLES MEXICAN ARTS CENTER
13108 San Pablo Ave.
San Pablo, CA 94805
Eugene Rodriguez, Founder
Tel: (510) 233-8015
Email: contact@loscenzontles.com
Web: www.loscenzontles.com

MEXICA MOVEMENT
P.O. Box 5088
Huntington Park, CA 90255-9088
Olin Tezcatlipoca, Director
Tel: (323) 981-0352
Email: cuicatl@earthlink.net
Web: www.mexica-movement.org

MEXICAN CULTURAL INSTITUTE OF LOS ANGELES
125 Paseo de la Plaza #300
Los Angeles, CA 90012
Susana S. Bautista, Executive Director
Tel: (213) 624-3660 Fax: (213) 624-9387
Email: info@mexicanculturalinstitute.org

MEXICAN HERITAGE CORPORATION OF SAN JOSE
1700 Alum Rock Ave.
San Jose, CA 95116
Marcela Aviles, Executive Director
Tel: (408) 928-5500 Fax: (408) 928-5550
Web: www.mhcviva.org

MEXICAN HERITAGE CULTURAL BOARD
P.O. Box 65766
Los Angeles, CA 90065
Cesar C. Cantú, Chairman
Tel: (323) 221-6800

MEXICAN MOTHER OF THE YEAR ASSOCIATION
St. Mary's Parish Church
216 Casa Grande Ave.
Montebello, CA 90640-2733
Carmen M. Sandoval, Secretary
Tel: (323) 722-4275 Fax: (323) 629-1951

THE MEXICAN MUSEUM
Fort Mason Center, Bldg. D
San Francisco, CA 94123
William Moreno, Executive Director
Tel: (415) 202-9700 Fax: (415) 441-7683
Email: info@mexicanmuseum.org
Web: www.mexicanmuseum.org

MEXICAN-AMERICAN HISTORICAL FOUNDATION
5060 Mt. Helena Ave.
Los Anegeles, CA 90041
Fernando Del Río, Consultant
Tel: (323) 255-3079 Fax: (323) 255-2620
Email: websalsa@pacbell.net

MULTI-ETHNIC STUDENT ALLIANCE
Azusa Pacific University
P.O. Box 7000
Azusa, CA 91702-7000
Joy Hoffman, Director
Tel: (626) 815-6000 x3720 Fax: (626) 815-3800
Email: jhoffman@apu.edu
Web: www.apu.edu/mep/

MUSEUM OF LATIN AMERICAN ART
628 Alamitos Ave.
Long Beach, CA 90802
Robert Gumbiner, Chairman/Founding Director
Tel: (562) 437-1689 Fax: (562) 437-7043
Email: gregorio@molaa.com
Web: www.molaa.com

PEÑA ANDALUZA EN CALIFORNIA
1628 Fern St.
San Diego, CA 92102
Charo Monge, President
Tel: (619) 234-7897 Fax: (619) 231-1942
Email: andalus@wans.net
Web: www.andaluza-usa.com

SANTA BARBARA HISTORICAL MUSEUM
136 E. De la Guerra St.
Santa Barbara, CA 93101
Michael Redmon, Director of Research
Tel: (805) 966-1601 Fax: (805) 966-1603
Email: mredmon@sbhistorical.org
Web: www.santabarbaramuseum.com

VIVA PANAMA ORGANIZATION
444 Chestnut Ave. #10
Long Beach, CA 90802
Victor Grimaldo, Director
Tel: (818) 915-2121
Email: VGrimaldo@vivapanama.org
Web: www.vivapanama.org/HomePage.htm

MUNDO LATINO PRODUCTIONS
P.O. Box 65766
Los Angeles, CA 90065-0766
Cesar C. Cantú, President
Tel: (323) 221-6800

NOSOTROS, INC.
650 N. Bronson Ave. #102
Hollywood, CA 90004
Jerry G. Velasco, President
Tel: (323) 466-8566 Fax: (323) 466-8540
Email: info@nosotros.org
Web: www.nosotros.org

CALIFORNIA HIGHWAY PATROL HISPANIC ADVISORY COMMITTEE
California Highway Patrol
411 N Central Ave. #410
Glendale, CA 91203
Manny Padilla, Chief
Tel: (818) 240-8200 Fax: (818) 240-5962
Web: www.chp.ca.gov

HISPANIC AMERICAN POLICE COMMAND OFFICERS ASSOCIATION
Los Angeles Chapter
P.O. Box 802467
Santa Clarita, CA 91380-2467
Richard L. Castro, President
Tel: (866) 731-7181
Email: carrasco@hapcoa.org
Web: www.hapcoa.org/losangeles

LATINO PEACE OFFICERS ASSOCIATION
Orange County Chapter
P.O. Box 6773
Fullerton, CA 92834-6773
Rudy Sanchez, President
Tel: (714) 672-9429
Email: parrami@sbcglobal.net
Web: www.nlpoa.org/Orange_Chapter

NATIONAL LATINO PEACE OFFICERS ASSOCIATION
133 SW B1#B
Rohnert Park, CA 94928
Felipe A Ortiz, National President
Tel: (877) 657-6200
Web: www.nlpoa.com

Alameda Chapter
P.O. Box 17083
Oakland, CA 94601
Art Bautista, President
Email: artbautista@aol.com
Web: www.nlpoa.com

California Chapter
P.O. Box 4411
Montebello, CA 90640
Hank Aguilar, President
Tel: (877) 657-6200
Email: agy777@aol.com
Web: www.nlpoa.com

Coachella Valley Chapter
80-352 Corte El Dorado
Indio, CA 92201
Mark Barfknecht, President
Tel: (877) 657-6200
Email: lpoa1@juno.com
Web: www.nlpoa.com

East Los Angeles Chapter
P.O. Box 1525
Montebello, CA 90640
Gil Carrillo, President
Tel: (877) 657-6200
Email: gil187@aol.com
Web: www.nlpoa.com

Fresno Chapter
5869 E Dwight Ave.
Fresno, CA 93727
Felipe Martinez, President
Tel: (877) 657-6200
Email: mtz808@netzero.net
Web: www.nlpoa.com

Kings County Chapter
P.O. Box 122
Corcoran, CA 93212
San Ramirez, Chapter President
Tel: (877) 657-6200 Fax: (415) 897-3961
Email: sammyr@onemain.com
Web: www.nlpoa.org/Kings_Chapter.htm

Monterey County Chapter
P.O. Box 4608
Salinas, CA 93912-4609
Ruben Sanchez, President
Tel: (877) 657-6200
Email: rsanchez@ultimanet.com
Web: www.nlpoa.com

National Office
351 E. Washington St.
Petaluma, CA 94952
Rene Lopez, Chapter President
Tel: (877) 657-6200 Fax: (707) 782-0767
Email: donrene007@comcast.net
Web: www.nlpoa.com

North San Diego Chapter
P.O. Box 460241
Escondido, CA 92046
Art Lopez, President
Tel: (877) 657-6200
Email: sdnccnlpoa@juno.com
Web: www.nlpoa.com

North Santa Barbara Chapter
2121 S Centerpoint Pkwy.
Santa María, CA 93455
Ed Torres, President
Tel: (877) 657-6200
Email: torrese@co.santa-barbara.ca.us
Web: www.nlpoa.com

Orange County Chapter
P.O. Box 6773
Fullerton, CA 92834
Rudy Sanchez, President
Tel: (877) 657-6200
Email: parrami@sbcglobal.net
Web: www.nlpoa.com

Sacramento Chapter
P.O. Box 58065
Elk Groove, CA 95758
Jose Sais, Chapter President
Tel: (877) 657-6200
Email: jsais2001@yahoo.com
Web: www.nlpoasacramento.org

San Bernardino/Riverside Chapter
25612 Barton Rd. #222
Loma Linda, CA 92354
Larry Gonzalez, Chapter President
Tel: (877) 657-6200 Fax: (909) 798-8365
Email: lgspy4u@aol.com
Web: www.nlpoa.com

San Diego County Chapter
P.O. Box 122708
San Diego, CA 92112
David Ardilla, President
Tel: (877) 657-6200
Email: president@nlpoasandiegocounty.com
Web: www.nlpoasandiegocounty.com

San Diego Metro Chapter
P.O. Box 128025
San Diego, CA 92112
Jose J. Cuervo, President
Tel: (877) 657-6200
Email: president@nlpoasandiegometro.com
Web: www.nlpoasandiegometro.com

San Francisco Chapter
P.O. Box 410692
San Francisco, CA 94140-6921
Michael Serujo, President
Tel. (415) 681-6177 Fax. (415) 681-3768
Email: newsmakermedia@cs.com
Web: www.nlpoa.com

San Francisco County Chapter
35 Gilbert St.
San Francisco, CA 94103
Nelson A. Martinez, President
Tel: (877) 657-6200
Email: sfconlpoa@yahoo.com
Web: www.geocities.com/sfconlpoa

San Gabriel Valley Chapter
P.O. Box 2422
Irwindale, CA 91706
Art Acevedo, President
Tel: (310) 871-3376
Email: haacevedo1@aol.com
Web: www.nlpoa.com

San Joaquin Chapter
P.O. Box 2142
Stockton, CA 95201
Chuck Arellano, President
Tel: (877) 657-6200
Email: socheese@aol.com
Web: www.nlpoa.com

Santa Clara County Founding Chapter
765 Story Rd. #150
San Jose, CA 95112
Noe Longoria, Chapter President
Tel: (408) 289-1057
Email: noe@longoria.net
Web: www.latinopoa.org

Sonoma Chapter
P.O. Box 7142
Santa Rosa, CA 95407-0142
Ronald Perez, President
Email: blueron@aol.com
Web: www.nlpoa.org

Tulare Chapter
P.O. Box 3835
Visalia, CA 93278
Juan Morales, President
Tel: (877) 657-6200
Web: www.geocities.com/lpoa2001

Ventura Chapter
P.O. Box 6075
Oxnard, CA 93031
Ralph Nieves, President
Email: ralfnjil@adelphia.net
Web: www.nlpoa.org

MULTI-PURPOSE

AID FOR BAJA CALIFORNIA
P.O. Box 367
Pico Rivera, CA 90660-0367
Fernando Almanza, Jr., President
Tel: (562) 692-8630 Fax: (562) 692-1790
Email: falmanza@aidforbajacalifornia.com
Web: www.aidforbajacalifornia.com

AMERICAN GI FORUM OF UNITED STATES
California Chapter
P.O. Box 1312
Morgan Hill, CA 95038
Felipe Flores, State Commander
Tel: (408) 360-8831
Web: www.agif.org

ASSOCIATION OF MERCHANTS & COMMERCE
Bell Gardens
6006 Shull St.
Bell Gardens, CA 90201
Ronald V. Garcia, President
Tel: (562) 806-2355 Fax: (562) 806-1585
Email: bellgardens1@earthlink.net
Web: www.bellgardenschamber.org

AZTLAN ACADEMY
Administrative Office
1179-A Sherwood Ave.
San Jose, CA 95126
Javier H. Salazar, Artistic Director
Tel: (408) 984-0342 Fax: (408) 984-0352
Email: aztlanacademy@lycos.com
Web: www.aztlanacademy.org

BILINGUAL & CITIZENSHIP CENTER
Los Angeles Southwest College
1600 W. Imperial Hwy.
Los Angeles, CA 90047
Linda Larson, Counselor
Tel: (323) 241-5281 Fax: (323) 241-5469
Web: www.lasc.cc.ca.us/sprog/bilin.html

CALIFORNIA MISSION STUDIES ASSOCIATION
P.O. Box 3357
Bakersfield, CA 93385
Rose Marie Beebe, President
Tel: (408) 266-7427
Email: cmsa@lightspeed.net
Web: www.ca-missions.org

CALIFORNIA TOMORROW
1904 Franklin St. #300
Oakland, CA 94612
Laurie Olsen, Executive Director
Tel: (510) 496-0220 Fax: (510) 496-0225
Email: ct411@californiatomorrow.org
Web: www.californiatomorrow.org

CASA FAMILIAR, INC.
Main Office
119 W. Hall Ave.
San Ysidro, CA 92173
Andrea Skorepa, Executive Director
Tel: (619) 428-1115 Fax: (619) 428-2802
Email: admin@casafamiliar.org
Web: www.casafamiliar.org

CÉSAR E. CHAVEZ FOUNDATION
National Chavez Center
P.O. Box 62
Keene, CA 93531
Andres F. Irlando, President
Tel: (661) 823-6134 Fax: (661) 823-6246
Email: chavezcenter@cecfmail.org
Web: www.ufw.org

CHARO COMMUNITY DEVELOPMENT CORPORATION
4301 E. Valley Blvd.
Los Angeles, CA 90032
Cynthia Amador, President/CEO
Tel: (323) 269-0751 Fax: (323) 266-4326
Email: webmaster@charocorp.com
Web: www.charocorp.com

THE CITY OF WEST COVINA
P.O. Box 1440
West Covina, CA 91793
Roger Hernandez, Council Member
Tel: (626) 939-8400 Fax: (626) 939-8406
Email: roger.hernandez@westcovina.org
Web: www.westcov.org

DELHI COMMUNITY CENTER
505 E Central Ave.
Santa Ana, CA 92707
Irene Martinez, Executive Director
Tel: (714) 481-9600 Fax: (714) 481-9699
Email: delhi1997@aol.com

DOLORES HUERTA FOUNDATION
P.O.Box 9189
Bakersfield, CA 93309
Lori De Leon, Assistant Program Developer
Tel: (661) 322-3033 Fax: (661) 322-3171
Email: mail@doloreshuerta.org
Web: www.doloreshuerta.org

THE EAST LOS ANGELES COMMUNITY UNION
Headquarters
5400 E. Olympic Blvd.
Los Angeles, CA 90022
David C. Lizarraga, President & CEO
Tel: (323) 721-1655 Fax: (323) 724-3372

Email: info@telacu.com
Web: www.telacu.com

EAST LOS ANGELES NEIGHBORHOOD SERVICE CENTER
133 N. Sunol Dr.
Los Angeles, CA 90063
Cathy Garcia, Director
Tel: (323) 260-2801 Fax: (323) 266-6457

EASTMONT COMMUNITY CENTER
Affiliate of NCLR
701 S. Hoefner Ave.
East Los Angeles, CA 90022
Teresa Palacios, Contact
Tel: (323) 726-7998 Fax: (323) 726-9237
Email: eastmontcenter1@aol.com

ESPERANZA COMMUNITY HOUSING CORPORATION
2337 S. Figueroa St.
Los Angeles, CA 90007
Sister Diane Donoghue, Executive Director
Tel: (213) 748-7285 Fax: (213) 748-9630
Email: info@esperanzachc.org
Web: www.esperanzachc.org

FAMILIA CENTER
711 E. Cliff Dr.
Santa Cruz, CA 95060
Yolanda Henry, Executive Director
Tel: (831) 423-5747 Fax: (831) 423-5922
Web: www.familiacenter.org

FAMILIAS UNIDAS
205-39th St.
Richmond, CA 94805
Marco Gonzales, President
Tel: (510) 412-5930
Email: lhuerta@familias-unidas.org
Web: www.familias-unidas.org

GUADALUPE CENTER
21600 Hart St.
Canoga Park, CA 91303
Margaret Pontius, Director
Tel: (818) 340-2050 Fax: (818) 883-4122
Email: margaretpontius@sbcglobal.net

HISPANIC CLUSTER GROUP
291 S. La Cienaga Blvd. #308
Beverly Hills, CA 90211
Richard Cervantes, President
Tel: (310) 652-6449 Fax: (310) 652-5462
Email: rccbeth@aol.com

HISPANIC OUTREACH TASKFORCE
13215 E. Penn St. #310
Whittier, CA 90602
Mary Romero, President
Tel: (562) 789-0550 Fax: (562) 789-0559
Email: hot.viz@verizon.net
Web: www.hotoutreach.org

HOUSE OF PUERTO RICO SAN DIEGO
P.O. Box 81982
San Diego, CA 92138
Tel: (619) 234-3445
Email: hprsd@houseofpuertorico.com
Web: www.houseofpuertorico.com

INSTITUTO DE EDUCACION POPULAR DEL SUR DE CALIFORNIA
Downtown Community Job Center
109 W. 14th Pl.
Los Angeles, CA 90015
Elena Marmol, Coordinator
Tel: (213) 747-2064
Email: downtowncjc@idepsca.org
Web: www.idepsca.org
Harbor City Day Labor Site
25716 S. Vermont
Harbor City, CA 90710
Bertha Gomez, Coordinator
Tel: (310) 325-3268 Fax: (310) 325-2890
Email: bertha@idepsca.org
Web: www.idepsca.org

Hollywood Community Job Center

5545 Virginia Ave.
Los Angeles, CA 90038
Mark Jimenez, Coordinator
Tel: (323) 469-9002
Email: hollywood@idepsca.org
Web: www.idepsca.org

La Escuela de la Comunidad
363 E. Villa St. #208
Pasadena, CA 91101
Susana Zamorano, Coordinator
Tel: (626) 796-7618
Email: la_escuelita@idepsca.org
Web: www.idepsca.org

Main Office
1565 W. 14th St.
Los Angeles, CA 90015
Raul Anorve, Executive Director
Tel: (213) 252-2952 Fax: (213) 252-2953
Email: infoidepsca@idepsca.org
Web: www.idepsca.org

Pasadena Community Job Center
500 N. Lake Ave.
Pasadena, CA 91101
Hector Catepotzo, Coordinator
Tel: (626) 440-0112 Fax: (626) 440-0113
Email: pasajobcenter@idepsca.org
Web: www.idepsca.org

West Los Angeles Community Job Center
11299 W. Exposition Blvd.
Los Angeles, CA 90064
Flor Herbach, Coordinator
Tel: (310) 231-1179 Fax: (310) 231-0242
Email: westlajc@idepsca.org
Web: www.idepsca.org

INTERNATIONAL INSTITUTION OF LOS ANGELES
435 S. Boyle Ave.
Los Angeles, CA 90033
Stephen Boss, President
Tel: (323) 264-6217 Fax: (323) 264-6418
Web: www.iilosangeles.org

LA RAZA CENTRO LEGAL
474 Valencia St. #295
San Francisco, CA 94103
Ana Maria Loya, Executive Director
Tel: (415) 575-3500 Fax: (415) 255-7593
Email: analoya@pacbell.net
Web: www.lrcl.org

LATINO ALUMNI ASSOCIATION
University of California, Los Angeles
James West Alumni Center, Box 951397
Los Angeles, CA 90095-1397
Danielle Campos, President
Tel: (310) 206-5058 Fax: (310) 825-8678
Email: danielle.campos@bankofamerica.com

LEAGUE OF UNITED LATIN AMERICAN CITIZENS
National Executive Committee
17439 Bellflower Blvd.
Bellflower, CA 90706
José R. Pacheco, VP for Far west
Tel: (562) 867-4910
Web: www.lulac.org

Orange County Chapter
12671 Willow Wood Ave.
Garden Grove, CA 92840
Ricardo Mendoza, President
Tel: (714) 740-1779
Web: www.lulac.org

LINCOLN HEIGHTS RECREATION CENTER
2303 Workman St.
Los Angeles, CA 90031
Trish Heuer, Director
Tel: (323) 225-2838 Fax: (323) 225-7497

LOS ANGELES MISSION
P.O. Box 55900
303 E. 5th St.
Los Angeles, CA 90013

Marshall McNott, President
Tel: (213) 629-1227 Fax: (213) 629-0036
Email: jlewis@lamission.net
Web: www.losangelesmission.org

LOS BOMBEROS
Los Angeles Fire Department
P.O. Box 532727
Los Angeles, CA 90053
Benjamin Flores, President
Tel: (213) 225-5946
Email: info@losbomberos.com
Web: www.losbomberos.com

LULAC NATIONAL EDUCATIONAL SERVICE CENTERS, INC.
4788 Mission St.
San Francisco, CA 94112
Rosie Flamenco, Director
Tel: (415) 206-1114 Fax: (415) 206-1129
Email: infosan@lnesc-sanfran.org
Web: www.lnesc-sanfran.org

Los Angeles Satellite Office
5339 Olympic Blvd.
Los Angeles, CA 90022
María Vanegas, Director
Tel: (323) 838-0091 Fax: (323) 838-0094
Email: infopom@lnesc-pomona.org
Web: www.lnesc-pomona.org

Pomona Headquarters
360 E. Holt Ave.
Pomona, CA 91767
María Vanegas, Director
Tel: (909) 623-0588 Fax: (909) 620-5488
Email: infopom@lnesc-pomona.org
Web: www.lnesc-pomona.org

LULAC STATE COUNCIL & DISTRICT OFFICES
5340 Circulo Nuevo
Yorba Linda, CA 92887
Cory A. Aguirre, President
Tel: (714) 777-6810 Fax: (714) 773-0986
Web: www.lulac.org

MANNY MOTA INTERNATIONAL FOUNDATION
1653 W. Colorado Blvd.
Los Angeles, CA 90041
Cecilia Mota-Molina, Executive Director
Tel: (323) 255-6682 Fax: (323) 255-1098
Email: ccmota@aol.com
Web: www.mannymotafoundation.org

MARAVILLA FOUNDATION
5729 E. Union Pacific
Commerce, CA 90022
Alex Sotomayor, Director
Tel: (323) 263-4188 Fax: (323) 721-0356
Web: www.infoline-la.org/fsc.html

MINORITY APARTMENT OWNERS ASSOCIATION
11215 S. Western Ave.
Los Angeles, CA 90047
Ruth Haylas, Executive Director
Tel: (323) 754-2818 Fax: (323) 754-0540
Email: maoa87@aol.com

NATIONAL CONFERENCE FOR COMMUNITY AND JUSTICE
Los Angeles Region
1055 Wilshire Blvd. #1615
Los Angeles, CA 90017
Fran Spears, Executive Director
Tel: (213) 250-8787 Fax: (213) 250-8799
Email: losangeles@nccj.org
Web: www.nccjla.org

NATIONAL IMAGE, INC.
P.O. Box 1368
Bonita, CA 91908-1368
John Griego, Chairman
Tel: (619) 934-5277
Web: www.nationalimageinc.org

PARTIDO NACIONAL LA RAZA UNIDA
National Office

P.O. Box 13
San Fernando, CA 91340
Xenaro Ayala, Director
Tel: (818) 365-6534
Email: partido_nacional@yahoo.com
Web: www.pnlru.org

San Diego Chapter
P.O. Box 4265
Chula Vista, CA 91909-4265
Xenaro Ayala, Director
Tel: (619) 987-8063 Fax: (619) 934-4561
Email: pnlrusd@hotmail.com
Web: www.pnlru.org

PROFESSIONAL HISPANICS IN ENERGY
20505 Yorba Linda Blvd. #324
Yorba Linda, CA 92886-7109
Cynthia Verdugo-Peralta, President
Tel: (714) 777-7729 Fax: (714) 777-7728
Email: info@phie.org
Web: www.phie.org

PROYECTO PASTORAL AT DOLORES MISSION
Headquarters
135 N. Mission Rd.
Los Angeles, CA 90033-3307
Patricia Ortíz, Operations Director
Tel: (323) 881-0018 Fax: (323) 268-7228
Email: admin@proyectopastoral.org
Web: www.proyectopastoral.org

REGIS HOUSE COMMUNITY CENTER
11346 Iowa Ave.
West Los Angeles, CA 90025
Albertina Morales, Executive Director
Tel: (310) 477-8168 Fax: (310) 479-6146

SAINT JOSEPH CENTER
204 Hampton Dr.
Venice, CA 90291-8633
Rhonda Meister, Executive Director
Tel: (310) 396-6468 Fax: (310) 392-8402
Email: executiveidrector@stjosephctr.org/
info@stjosephctr.org
Web: www.stjosephctr.org

SAN FERNANDO VALLEY INTERFAITH COUNCIL
10824 Topanga Canyon Blvd. #7
Chatsworth, CA 91311
Barry Smedberg, Executive Director
Tel: (818) 718-6460 Fax: (818) 718-0734
Email: info@vic-la.org
Web: www.sfvic.org

SANTA FE SPRINGS NEIGHBORHOOD MULTIPURPOSE SENIOR CENTER
9255 Pioneer Blvd.
Santa Fe Springs, CA 90670
Maricela Balberas, Director
Tel: (562) 692-0261 Fax: (562) 695-8620
Email: social_services@santafesprings.org.

SOCIETY OF MEXICAN AMERICAN ENGINEERS AND SCIENTISTS
Bay Area Chapter
P.O. Box 15424
Fremont, CA 94539
Mark Perez, President
Email: president@maes-bayarea.org
Web: www.maes-bayarea.org

Long Beach Chapter
4427 Candlewood St. Box 179
Lakewood, CA 90712-1726
Tatiane Espinoza, President
Email: espt@chevrontexaco.com
Web: www.maeslongbeach.org

Orange County Chapter
PMB #403-C, 16585-C Von Karman
Irvine, CA 92606
Hugo Lira, President
Email: hugo.a.lira@boeing.com
Web: www.orangecountymaes.org

SPANISH SPEAKING CITIZENS' FOUNDATION
1470 Fruitvale Ave.
Oakland, CA 94601
José Arredondo, Executive Director
Tel: (510) 261-7839 Fax: (510) 261-2968
Email: josea@sscf.org
Web: www.sscf.org

STANFORD CHICANO/LATINO ALUMNI ASSOCIATION OF NORTHERN CALIFORNIA
Stanford Alumni Association
P.O. Box 19811
Stanford, CA 94309
Perla Rodriguez, President
Tel: (650) 725-0689
Email: prodriguez@univision.net
Web: http://e.stanfordalumni.org/Clubs/sclaa-nc/index.asp

US/MEXICO SISTER CITIES ASSOCIATION, INC.
P.O. Box 3193
South El Monte, CA 91733-3608
Tel: (626) 448-2655 Fax: (626) 448-2655
Email: webmaster@usmsca.org
Web: http://home.earthlink.net/~tohancuff/

YMCA OF METROPOLITAN OF LOS ANGELES
625 S. New Hampshire Ave.
Los Angeles, CA 90005
Larry Rosen, President
Tel: (213) 380-6448 Fax: (213) 251-9720
Web: www.ymcala.org

ALPHA 66
P.O. Box 6434
Torrance, CA 90504
Miguel Talleda, California Coordinator
Tel: (310) 324-8778
Email: lvalpha66cal@earthlink.net
Web: www.alpha66.org

CALIFORNIA DEMOCRATIC COUNCIL
8124 W. 3rd St. #207
Los Angeles, CA 90048
Chris Stampolis, President
Tel: (800) 446-9709 Fax: (408) 296-1470
Email: califdems@aol.com
Web: www.cdc-ca.org

CALIFORNIA LEAGUE OF CONSERVATION VOTERS EDUCATION FUND
10780 Santa Monica Blvd. #210
Los Angeles, CA 90025
Luis Cabrales, Director of Community Programs
Tel: (310) 441-4162 X306 Fax: (310) 441-1685
Email: lcabrales@ecovote.org
Web: www.clceducationfund.org

CALIFORNIA REPUBLICAN NATIONAL HISPANIC ASSEMBLY
34671 Daela Dr.
Winchester, CA 92596
Uvaldo Martinez, Jr., State Chairman
Tel: (619) 709-4147
Email: staternha@aol.com
Web: www.carnha.org

COMMITTEE IN SOLIDARITY WITH THE PEOPLE OF EL SALVADOR
P.O. Box 57337
Los Angeles, CA 90057
Don White, Coordinator
Tel: (323) 852-0721 Fax: (323) 913-1881
Email: lacispes@igc.org
Web: www.cispes.org

EAST LOS ANGELES, MINORITY BUSINESS DEVELOPMENT CENTER
5271 E Beverly Blvd.
Los Angeles, CA 90022
Sal Carlos
Tel: (323) 726-7734 Fax: (323) 721-9794
Email: bpidesign@aol.com
Web: www.lacity.org

LABOR COUNCIL FOR LATIN AMERICAN ADVANCEMENT
Los Angeles Chapter
774 Valencia St.
Los Angeles, CA 90017
Rey España, Chapter President
Tel: (213) 483-7811 Fax: (213) 483-4808
Web: www.lclaa.org

LATINO ISSUES FORUM
National Headquarters
160 Pine St. #700
San Francisco, CA 94111
Luis Arteaga, Executive Director
Tel: (415) 284-7228
Email: larteage@lif.org
Web: www.lif.org

MEXICAN AMERICAN LEGAL DEFENSE AND EDUCATIONAL FUND
Sacramento Satellite Office
926 J St. #422
Sacramento, CA 95814
Rita Durgin, Legislative Secretary
Tel: (916) 443-7531 Fax: (916) 443-1541
Email: maldef@tomatoweb.com
Web: www.maldef.org

MEXICAN AMERICAN POLITICAL ASSOCIATION
National Headquarters
310 N. Soto St.
Los Angeles, CA 90033
Nativo Vigil Lopez, President
Tel: (323) 269-1575 Fax: (323) 260-8015
Email: nativolopez@sbcglobal.net
Web: www.mapa.org

NATIONAL ASSOCIATION OF LATINO ELECTED AND APPOINTED OFFICIALS
Los Angeles Chapter
1122 W. Washington Blvd. 3rd Fl.
Los Angeles, CA 90015
Arturo Vargas, Executive Director
Tel: (213) 747-7606 Fax: (213) 747-7664
Email: epullenayegam@naleo.org
Web: www.naleo.org

NATIONAL ORGANIZATION FOR MEXICAN AMERICAN RIGHTS
San Diego Chapter
P.O. Box 180283
Coronado, CA 92178-0283
Marlow Martínez, President
Tel: (619) 545-4217 Fax: (619) 545-6515
Email: marlow.martinez@navy.mil
Web: www.nomarinc.org

PUERTO RICO FEDERAL AFFAIRS ADMINISTRATION
Western States Regional Office
650 Town Center Dr. #680
Costa Mesa, CA 92626
Ana Carricchi Lopez, Sr. Community Officer
Tel: (714) 556-4490 Fax: (714) 556-7295
Email: info@prfaa.com
Web: www.prfaa.com

SOUTHWEST VOTER REGISTRATION EDUCATION PROJECT
California Regional Office
2914 N. Main St., 2nd Fl.
Los Angeles, CA 90031
Sofia Torres, Field Organizer
Tel: (323) 343-9299 Fax: (323) 343-9100
Email: sofia.torres@svrep.org
Web: www.svrep.org

TOMÁS RIVERA POLICY INSTITUTE
University of Southern California, School of Policy, Planning, and Development
Ralph & Goldie Lewis Hall, 650 Child's Way #102
Los Angeles, CA 90089-0626
Harry Pachón, President
Tel: (213) 821-5615 Fax: (213) 821-1976
Email: info@trpi.org
Web: www.trpi.org

WILLIAM C. VELASQUEZ INSTITUTE
California Office
2914 N Main St., 1st Fl.
Los Angeles, CA 90031
Antonio González, President
Tel: (323) 222-2217 Fax: (323) 222-2011
Email: agonzalez@wcvi.org
Web: www.wcvi.org

PROFESSIONAL

ASSOCIATION OF LATINO PROFESSIONALS IN FINANCE AND ACCOUNTING
Los Angeles Chapter
c/o Manzano & Associates, 2162 Tulane Ave.
Long Beach, CA 90815
Jose Manzano, Chapter President
Tel: (562) 547-5990
Email: joselmanzano@aol.com
Web: www.alpfa.org

National Headquarters
510 W. 6th St. # 400
Los Angeles, CA 90014
Shanina Rivera, VP of Administration
Tel: (213) 243-0004 Fax: (213) 243-0006
Email: info@national.alpfa.org
Web: www.alpfa.org

San Diego Chapter
Qualcomm Inc., 5775 Morehouse Al-107B10
San Diego, CA 92121
Alejandro M. Barraza, Chapter President
Tel: (858) 480-6219 Fax: (858) 658-4678
Email: alejandro.barraza@pyxis.com
Web: www.alpfa.org

San Francisco Chapter
Ernst & Young, LLP, 1331 N. California Blvd. #200
Walnut Creek, CA 94596
Michael Canul, Chapter President
Tel: (925) 977-3973 Fax: (925) 977-2994
Email: sfpresident@alpfabayarea.org
Web: www.alpfa.org

HISPANIC ASSOCIATION OF REAL ESTATE PROFESSIONALS SILICON VALLEY
2530 Berryessa Rd. #434
San Jose, CA 95132
Rebecca Gallardo-Serrano, President
Tel: (408) 718-6562
Email: contact@harepofsv.com
Web: www.harepofsv.com

HISPANIC NETWORK
1125 E Broadway #138
Glendale, CA 91205
Carlos Rodríguez, President
Tel: (818) 956-0555 Fax: (818) 956-8001
Email: incaman@aol.com

LA RAZA LAWYERS OF CALIFORNIA
P.O. Box 30
San Jose, CA 95103
Miguel Marquez, President
Email: miguel.marquez@stanfordalumni.org
Web: www.larazalawyers.net

NATIONAL ASSOCIATION OF HISPANIC NURSES
Orange County Chapter
23232 Peralta Dr. #215
Laguna Hills, CA 92653
Martha Drennan, President
Tel: (949) 460-7701 Fax: (949) 460-7704
Email: zoila13@aol.com
Web: http://hispanicnurses.org

NATIONAL ASSOCIATION OF HISPANIC REAL ESTATE PROFESSIONALS
404 Camino del Rio South #602
San Diego, CA 92108
John U. Sepulveda, CEO
Tel: (619) 686-4050 Fax: (619) 297-3229
Email: membership@nahrep.org
Web: www.nahrep.org

NATIONAL SOCIETY OF HISPANIC MBAS
Los Angeles Chapter
P.O. Box 55301
Santa Clarita, CA 91385
Al Escobar, Chapter President
Tel: (661) 251-8811 Fax: (661) 244-4943
Email: general@losangeles.nshmba.org
Web: http://losangeles.nshmba.org/

Orange County Chapter
P.O. Box 52918
Irvine, CA 92686
Jemma Draper, Chapter President
Email: general@orangecounty.nshmba.org
Web: www.nshmba.org

PERUVIAN AMERICAN MEDICAL SOCIETY
San Diego, California Chapter
277 Church Ave.
Chula Vista, CA 91910
Dr. Luis F. Sanchez, President
Tel: (619) 426-9610
Web: www.pamsnational.org

Southern California Chapter
16395 Las Cumbres
Whittier, CA 90603
Dr. Alejandro Aguilar, President
Tel: (562) 947-7514
Web: www.pamsnational.org

SAN FRANCISCO LA RAZA LAWYERS
P.O. Box 192241
San Francisco, CA 94119
Victor M. Marquez, President
Tel: (415) 354-2880
Email: victor@marquezgonzaleslaw.com
Web: www.larazalawyers.org/index.htm

SOCIETY OF HISPANIC PROFESSIONAL ENGINEERS
800 N State College Blvd.
Fullerton, CA 92834
Manuel Gutirrez, President
Tel: (714) 278-3879 Fax: (714) 278-4171
Email: officers@shpe.ecs.fullerton.edu

Fresno Professional Chapter
P.O. Box 5531
Fresno, CA 93755-5531
Robert Navarro, President
Tel: (559) 230-3142
Email: robert_navarro@dot.ca.gov
Web: http://fresno.shpe.us

San Diego Professional Chapter
P.O. Box 910131
San Diego, CA 92191
Roman Diaz, Jr., Chapter President
Tel: (858) 484-1803 Fax: (858) 484-6394
Email: president@shpesd.org
Web: http://reg2.shpe.org/shpesd/

Ventura County Professional Chapter
P.O. Box 2397
Camarillo, CA 93011
Gustavo Perez, President
Email: shpevcc@yahoo.com
Web: http://reg2.shpe.org/vcc/

WOMEN LAWYERS ASSOCIATION OF LOS ANGELES
634 S. Spring St. #617
Los Angeles, CA 90014
Judith Seeds Miller, President
Tel: (213) 892-8982 Fax: (213) 892-8948
Email: info@wlala.org
Web: www.wlala.org

RELIGIOUS

ALL PEOPLES CHRISTIAN CENTER
822 E. 20th St.
Los Angeles, CA 90011
Julio Ramos, Administrative Director
Tel: (213) 747-6357 Fax: (213) 747-0541
Email: jramos@allpeoplescc.org
Web: www.allpeoplescc.org

ARCHDIOCESE OF LOS ANGELES
3424 Wilshire Blvd.
Los Angeles, CA 90010-2202
Graciela Villalobos, Contact
Tel: (213) 637-7561 Fax: (213) 637-6280
Email: info@la-archidocese.org
Web: www.la-archdiocese.org

ARCHDIOCESE OF SAN FRANCISCO
Hispanic Ministry Office
One Peter Yorke Way
San Francisco, CA 94109
Rev. Msgr. Jose Rodriguez, Vicar for Spanish Speaking
Tel: (415) 614-5500
Email: rodriguezj@sfarchdiocese.org
Web: www.sfarchdiocese.org

CALIFORNIA CATHOLIC CONFERENCE DIVISION FOR HISPANIC AFFAIRS
1119 K St., 2nd Fl.
Sacramento, CA 95814-3904
Al Hernandez, Associate Director
Tel: (916) 443-4851 Fax: (916) 443-5629
Web: www.cacatholic.org

CHURCH OF JESUS CHRIST OF LATTER-DAY SAINTS
Los Angeles California Temple Visitors' Center
10777 W. Santa Monica Blvd.
Los Angeles, CA 90025
Elder Simpson, Director
Tel: (310) 474-1549 Fax: (310) 474-0651
Web: www.lds.org

CHURCH OF JESUS CHRIST OF LATTER-DAY SAINTS
Oakland California Temple Visitors' Center
4766 Lincoln Ave.
Oakland, CA 94602
Elder Simpson, Director
Tel: (510) 531-1475 Fax: (510) 531-7625
Web: www.lds.org

COMBONI MISSIONARIES OF SOUTHERN CALIFORNIA
645 S Aldenville Ave.
Covina, CA 91723
Angelo Biancalana, Director
Tel: (626) 339-1914 Fax: (626) 974-4238
Email: admin@comboni.org
Web: www.comboni.org

THE CUBA-AMERICA JEWISH MISSION
1442A Walnut St. #224
Berkeley, CA 94709
June Safran, Executive Director
Email: mission@thecajm.org
Web: www.thecajm.org

DIOCESE OF FRESNO
Campesino Ministry
1550 N. Fresno St.
Fresno, CA 93703-3788
Zeferino González, Coordinator
Tel: (559) 488-7455
Email: martin@dioceseoffresno.org
Web: www.dioceseoffresno.org

DIOCESE OF MONTEREY
Hispanic Ministry
485 Church St.
Monterey, CA 93940
Sister Lydia Schneider, Director for Hispanic Ministry
Tel: (831) 373-1335 Fax: (831) 424-3351
Email: hispanic@dioceseofmonterey.org
Web: www.dioceseofmonterey.org

DIOCESE OF OAKLAND
Hispanic Ministry Office
3014 Lake Shore Ave.
Oakland, CA 94610-3697
Héctor Medina, Director
Tel: (510) 496-7224 Fax: (510) 273-4982
Email: hmedina@oakdiocese.org
Web: www.oakdiocese.org/espanol/latino.htm

DIOCESE OF ORANGE
Hispanic Ministry
2811 E Villa Real Dr.
Orange, CA 92867-1999
Olivia Cornejo, Director of Hispanic Affairs
Tel: (714) 282-3064 Fax: (714) 282-3029
Email: ocornejo@rcbo.org
Web: www.rcbo.org

DIOCESE OF SACRAMENTO
Hispanic Apostolate
2110 Broadway
Sacramento, CA 95818
Deacon Germán A. Toro, Director
Tel: (916) 733-0177 Fax: (916) 733-0195
Email: gtoro@diocese-sacramento.org
Web: www.diocese-sacramento.org

DIOCESE OF SAN BERNARDINO
Hispanic Affairs
1201 E Highland Ave.
San Bernardino, CA 92404-4641
Petra Alexander, Coordinator
Tel: (909) 475-5451 Fax: (909) 475-5155
Email: palexander@sbdiocese.org
Web: www.sbdiocese.org

DIOCESE OF SAN DIEGO
Hispanic Affairs
3888 Paducah Dr.
San Diego, CA 92117
Enrique Méndez, Director of Hispanic Affairs
Tel: (858) 490-8249 Fax: (858) 490-8272
Email: emendez@diocese-sdiego.org
Web: www.diocese-sdiego.org

DIOCESE OF SANTA ROSA
Hispanic Ministry
P.O. Box 178
Napa, CA 94559
Rev. Oscar Diaz, Director of Hispanic Ministry
Tel: (707) 226-9379 Fax: (707) 254-9262
Web: www.santarosacatholic.org

DIOCESE OF STOCKTON
Hispanic Ministry Office
1125 N Lincoln St.
Stockton, CA 95203
Digna Ramírez, Director
Tel: (209) 466-0636 Fax: (209) 463-5937
Web: www.stocktondiocese.org

FIRST FUNDAMENTAL BIBLE CHURCH
2301 Findlay Ave.
Monterey Park, CA 91754
Alex D. Montoya, Pastor
Tel: (323) 728-3897 Fax: (323) 728-0257
Email: info@ffbc.net
Web: www.ffbc.net

DIOCESE OF MONTERRY
Hispanic Ministry Department
485 Church St.
Monterey, CA 93940
Sr. Lydia Schneider, Director
Tel: (831) 373-1335 Fax: (831) 424-3351
Email: hispanic@dioceseofmonterey.org

DIOCESE OF SAN JOSE
Hispanic Youth & Adults
900 Lafayette St. #301
Santa Clara, CA 95050
Antonio Ojeda, Associate
Tel: (408) 983-0134
Email: ojeda@dsj.org
Web: www.dsj.org

ISLAMIC CENTER OF SOUTHERN CALIFORNIA
434 S. Vermont Ave.
Los Angeles, CA 90020
Martha Gelagri, Head of Latino Services
Tel: (213) 382-9200 Fax: (213) 384-4572
Email: icsc@islamctr.org
Web: www.islamctr.org

PRESBYTERIAN HISPANIC CHURCH
112 E. Beach St.
Watsonville, CA 95076-4704
Carmen Rosales, Pastor
Tel: (831) 728-8653

SACRED HEART CATHOLIC CHURCH
Hispanic Ministry
12704 Foothill Blvd.
Rancho Cucamonga, CA 91739-9764
Robert Cardenas, Deacon
Tel: (909) 899-1049 x145 Fax: (909) 899-3229

SAINT BENEDICT CHURCH
Club Guadalupano
1022 W. Cleveland Ave.
Montebello, CA 90640
Leticia Cangas, President
Tel: (323) 278-1124 Fax: (323) 721-5075

SAN CARLOS BORROMÉO DE CARMELO MISSION
3080 Rio Rd.
Carmel, CA 93923
Sir Richard Menn, Mission Curator
Tel: (831) 624-3600 Fax: (831) 624-0658
Email: sirrichard@carmelmission.org
Web: www.carmelmission.org

SOUTHERN CALIFORNIA ECUMENICAL COUNCIL
54 N. Oakland Ave.
Pasadena, CA 91101-2086
Rev. Albert G. Cohen, Executive Director
Tel: (626) 578-6371 Fax: (626) 578-6358

ST. DOMINICS CHURCH
Hispanic Action Group
2002 Merton Ave.
Los Angeles, CA 90041
Felipe Barrientos, President
Tel: (323) 254-2519 Fax: (323) 255-3067

SYNOD OF SOUTHERN CALIFORNIA & HAWAII
Hispanic Commission
1501 Wilshire Blvd.
Los Angeles, CA 90017-2205
Rev. Ernesto Hernandez, Coordinator
Tel: (213) 483-3840 X226 Fax: (213) 483-4275
Email: erhdez@yahoo.com
Web: www.synod.org

RESEARCH

APPLIED RESEARCH CENTER
3781 Broadway
Oakland, CA 94611
Gary Delgado, Executive Director
Tel: (510) 653-3415 Fax: (510) 653-3427
Email: arc@arc.org
Web: www.arc.org

CENTER FOR CHICANO STUDIES
University of California, Santa Barbara
South Hall #4518
Santa Barbara, CA 93106-6040
Carlos Morton, Director
Tel: (805) 893-3895 Fax: (805) 893-4446
Web: http://www.research.ucsb.edu/ccs/

CENTER FOR IBERIAN AND LATIN AMERICAN STUDIES
University of California, San Diego
9500 Gilman Dr.
La Jolla, CA 92093-0528
Charles Briggs, Director
Tel: (858) 534-6050 Fax: (858) 534-7175
Email: latamst@ucsd.edu
Web: http://cilas.ucsd.edu

CENTER FOR LATIN AMERICAN STUDIES
University of California, Berkeley
2334 Bowditch St.
Berkeley, CA 94720
Harley Shaiken, Chair
Tel: (510) 642-2088 Fax: (510) 642-3260
Email: clas@berkeley.edu
Web: http://ist-socrates.berkeley.edu:7001/

CENTER FOR LATINO STUDIES IN THE AMERICAS
University of San Francisco
2130 Fulton St., Harney 240
San Francisco, CA 94117-1080
Gerardo Marín, Executive Director
Tel: (415) 422-2940 Fax: (415) 422-2346
Email: celasa@usfca.edu
Web: www.usfca.edu/celasa

CENTER FOR THE STUDY OF LATINO HEALTH AND CULTURE
UCLA School of Medicine
924 Westwood Blvd. #730
Los Angeles, CA 90024
David E. Hayes-Bautista, Director
Tel: (310) 794-0663 Fax: (310) 794-2862
Email: cesla@ucla.edu
Web: www.cesla.med.ucla.edu

CENTER FOR U.S. MEXICAN STUDIES
University of California, San Diego
9500 Gilman Dr. #0510
La Jolla, CA 92093-0510
Chris Woodruff, Director
Tel: (858) 534-4503 Fax: (858) 534-6447
Email: usmex@ucsd.edu
Web: www.usmex.ucsd.edu

CHICANO RESOURCE CENTER
East Los Angeles Library
4837 E. 3rd St.
Los Angeles, CA 90022
Antonio Lopez, Adult Reference Librarian
Tel: (323) 263-5087 Fax: (323) 264-5465
Web: www.colapublib.org/libs/eastla/chicano.html

CHICANO STUDIES PROGRAM
California State University, Sacramento
Amador Hall, CSU
Sacramento, CA 95819
Prof. Sam Rios, Program Interim Director
Tel: (916) 278-6344 Fax: (916) 278-5156
Email: srios@csus.edu
Web: www.csus.edu/chicano

CHICANO STUDIES RESEARCH CENTER
University of California, Los Angeles
193 Haines Hall
Los Angeles, CA 90095-1544
Chon A. Noriega, Director
Tel: (310) 825-2363 Fax: (310) 206-1784
Email: csrcinfo@chicano.ucla.edu
Web: www.sscnet.ucla.edu/csrc

GENEALOGICAL SOCIETY OF HISPANIC AMERICA
Southern California Chapter
P.O. Box 2472
Santa Fe Springs, CA 90670-0472
Donie Nelson, SC Secretary
Email: doniegsha@earthlink.net
Web: www.scgsgenealogy.com

THE HENRY J. KAISER FAMILY FOUNDATION
Headquarters
2400 Sand Hill Rd.
Menlo Park, CA 94025
Marsha Lillie-Blanton, VP, Race/Ethnicity & Health Care
Tel: (650) 854-9400 Fax: (650) 854-4800
Web: www.kff.org

LATIN AMERICAN CENTER
University of California, Los Angeles
10343 Bunche Hall , 405 Hilgard Ave., Box 951447
Los Angeles, CA 90095-1447
Carlos Alberto Torres, Director
Tel: (310) 825-4571 Fax: (310) 206-6859
Email: latinamctr@international.ucla.edu
Web: www.international.ucla.edu/lac

LATIN AMERICAN STUDIES PROGRAM
California State University, Fullerton
P.O. Box 6846
Fullerton, CA 92834-6846
Sandra Perez-Linggi, Program Coordinator
Tel: (714) 278-3161 Fax: (714) 278-5944
Email: splinggi@fullerton.edu
Web: http://hss.fullerton.edu/latinamerican

LATINO MENTAL HEALTH RESEARCH PROGRAM
University of California, San Francisco/San Francisco General Hospital
1001 Portero Ave. #7M6
San Francisco, CA 94110
Ricardo F. Munoz, Director
Tel: (415) 206-5214
Email: munoz@itsa.ucsf.edu
Web: http://medschool.ucsf.edu/latino/

NATIONAL LATINO RESEARCH CENTER
Cal State San Marcos
333 S. Twin Oaks Valley Rd.
San Marcos, CA 92096-0001
Gerardo Gonzalez, Director
Tel: (760) 750-3500 Fax: (760) 750-3510
Email: nlrc@csusm.edu
Web: www.csusm.edu/nlrc

SAN JOSE PUBLIC LIBRARY
Biblioteca Latinoamericana
921 S. First St.
San Jose, CA 95110
John A. Ramos, President
Tel: (408) 294-1237
Email: bla.sjpl@ci.sj.ca.us
Web: www.labla.org

SOCIETY OF HISPANIC HISTORICAL AND ANCESTRAL RESEARCH
P.O. Box 490
Midway City, CA 92655-0490
Mimi Lozano, President
Tel: (714) 894-8161 Fax: (714) 898-7063
Email: mimilozano@aol.com
Web: www.shhar.org

UC LINGUISTIC MINORITY RESEARCH INSTITUTE
University of California
4722 S. Hall
Santa Barbara, CA 93106-3220
Beverly Bavaro Leaney, Assistant Editor
Tel: (805) 893-2250
Email: beverly@lmri.ucsb.edu
Web: http://lmri.ucsb.edu/

SPEC. INT., AIDS

AIDS SERVICE CENTER
1030 S. Aroyo Pkwy.
Pasadena, CA 91105
Yvonne C. Benson, Executive Director
Tel: (626) 441-8495 X222 Fax: (626) 799-6253
Email: ycb@aidssc.org
Web: www.aidsservicecenter.org

BIENESTAR
Hollywood Center
4955 W Sunset Blvd.
Los Angeles, CA 90027
Oscar De La O, President/CEO
Tel: (323) 660-9680 Fax: (323) 660-6279
Email: odelao@bienestar.org
Web: www.bienestar.org

BLACK-LATINO AIDS PROJECT
University of California, Los Angeles
160 Kerckhoff Hall, 308 Westwood Plz.
Los Angeles, CA 90024
Amilcar Rizzo, Director
Tel: (310) 825-0068
Email: blaidsproject@hotmail.com
Web: www.studentgroups.ucla.edu/blaids

CENTER FOR AIDS PREVENTION STUDIES
University of California, San Francisco
74 New Montgomery #600
San Francisco, CA 94105
Barbara Marin, Director
Tel: (415) 597-9100 Fax: (415) 597-9213
Email: capsweb@psg.uscf.edu
Web: www.caps.ucsf.edu

IMANI UNIDOS AIDS PROJECT
1713 W 108th St.

Los Angeles, CA 90047
Mother Velma Miller, Administrative Council
Tel: (323) 754-8453 Fax: (323) 754-1506
Email: info@faithumcc.org
Web: www.faithumcc.org

INSTITUTO FAMILIAR DE LA RAZA
2837 Mission St.
San Francisco, CA 94110
Maria Cahabela Sanchez, Volunteer Coordinator
Tel: (415) 647-4141 x301 Fax: (415) 647-3662

MAYVIEW COMMUNITY HEALTH CENTER
Palo Alto
270 Grant Ave.
Palo Alto, CA 94306
Maria Solis, Assistant Director
Tel: (650) 327-1223 Fax: (650) 327-8572
Email: mayview1@earthlink.net
Web: www.mayview.org

MINORITY AIDS PROJECT
5149 W. Jefferson Blvd.
Los Angeles, CA 90016
Elder Claude Bowen, Director Human Resources
Tel: (323) 936-4949 Fax: (323) 936-4973
Email: aids101@map-usa.org
Web: www.map-usa.org

PACTO LATINO
P.O. Box 86793
San Diego, CA 92138
Tel: (619) 725-0946 Fax: (619) 725-0950
Email: info@pactolatino.org
Web: www.pactolatino.org

PROYECTO CONTRA SIDA POR VIDA
2973 16th St.
San Francisco, CA 94103
Prado Gomez, Executive Director
Tel: (415) 864-7278 Fax: (415) 575-1645
Email: prado@pcpv.org
Web: www.pcpv.org

SPEC. INT., ALCOHOL/DRUG CENTER

AL-ALANON
Hispanic Office
11627 E. Telegraph Rd. #150
Santa Fe Springs, CA 90670
Sofia Carrillo, Coordinator
Tel: (562) 948-2190 Fax: (562) 948-2122

CALIFORNIA HISPANIC COMMISSION ON ALCOHOL AND DRUG ABUSE
Administrative Office
2101 Capital Ave.
Sacramento, CA 95816
James Hernandez, Executive Director
Tel: (916) 443-5473 Fax: (916) 443-1732
Web: www.chcada.org

9842 W 13th St. #B
Garden Grove, CA 92844
Frank Luna, Office Manager
Tel: (714) 531-4624 Fax: (714) 531-1189
Web: www.chcada.org

CLARE FOUNDATION
Adult Recovery Home
1871 9th St.
Santa Monica, CA 90404
Sandy Chapin, Director
Tel: (310) 314-6200 Fax: (310) 396-6974
Email: info@clarefoundation.org
Web: www.clarefoundation.org

EAST LOS ANGELES ALCOHOLISM COUNCIL
916 S. Atlantic Blvd.
Los Angeles, CA 90022
Charles García, Executive Director
Tel: (323) 268-9344 Fax: (323) 268-9348
Email: info@eastlaalcoholcouncil.com
Web: http://64.33.85.89

EL CENTRO DE LIBERTAD
Main Office
1230-A Hopkins

Redwood, CA 94062
Maggie Cuadros, President
Tel: (650) 599-9955 Fax: (650) 599-9273
Email: recovery@elcentrodelibertad.org
Web: www.elcentrodelibertad.org

EL CENTRO SUBSTANCE ABUSE TREATMENT
2130 E 1st St. #350
Los Angeles, CA 90033
Raul Astrada, Director
Tel: (323) 265-9228 Fax: (323) 265-7166

LATINO FAMILY ALCOHOL AND DRUG ABUSE CENTER
5801 E Beverly Blvd.
Los Angeles, CA 90022
John Robles, Director
Tel: (323) 722-4529 Fax: (323) 722-4450
Email: jrobles@chcada.org

LATINO RECOVERY HOME
California Hispanic Commission on Alcohol and Drug Abuse, Inc.
2436 Wabash Ave.
Los Angeles, CA 90033
Henry Alonzo, Assistant Director
Tel: (323) 780-8756 Fax: (616) 813-0928
Email: cquiroga@chcada.org

MEXICAN AMERICAN ALCOHOLISM PROGRAMS, INC.
4241 Florin Rd. #65
Sacramento, CA 95823-2535
Barbara Weiss, Director
Tel: (916) 394-2320
Email: barbaraweiss@elkgrove.net
Web: www.elkgrove.net/maap

NATIONAL COUNCIL ON ALCOHOLISM AND DRUG DEPENDENCY, INC.
1245 E. Walnut St. #117
Pasadena, CA 91106
Frank Melendez, Latino Outreach Worker
Tel: (626) 795-9127 Fax: (626) 795-0979
Email: pasadena.ca@ncadd.org
Web: www.ncadd.org

UNIDOS
9842 W. 13th St. #B
Garden Grove, CA 92844
Frank Luna, Office Manager
Tel: (714) 531-4624 Fax: (714) 531-1189
Email: sruiz@chcada.org
Web: www.chcada.org/unidos

VICTORY OUTREACH INTERNATIONAL
P.O. Box 3760
San Dimas, CA 91773
Pastor Sonny Arguinzoni, Executive Director
Tel: (909) 599-4437 Fax: (909) 599-6244
Email: info@victoryoutreach.org
Web: www.victoryoutreach.org

ZONA SECA, INC.
Santa Barbara Branch
26 W. Figueroa St.
Santa Barbara, CA 93101
Frank Banales, Executive Director
Tel: (805) 963-8961 Fax: (805) 963-8964
Email: fbanales@zonaseca.com
Web: www.zonaseca.com

SPEC. INT., CHILD CARE

AYUDA AL NIÑO BOLIVIANO
9219 Trailhead Pt.
Riverside, CA 92509
Tel: (951) 681-6771 Fax: (951) 685-0814
Email: ayuda@ayuda.org
Web: www.ayuda.org

CASA BLANCA CHILD CARE CENTER
3020 Madison St. #8
Riverside, CA 92504
Art Cabrera, Director
Tel: (951) 689-7891
Email: consilio.casablanca@msn.com

CENTRO DE NIÑOS
4850 E Cesar Chavez
Los Angeles, CA 90022
Sandra Serrano Sewell, Executive Director
Tel: (323) 268-4600 Fax: (323) 526-9068

CHILDREN OF THE AMERICAS
Mexico Programs
67 Gingham St.
Trabuco Canyon, CA 92679
W.O. Mills III, President
Tel: (949) 709-0673
Email: dave@americaschildren.org
Web: www.americaschildren.org

EAST LOS ANGELES SKILLS CENTER
3921 Selig Pl.
Los Angeles, CA 90031
Pete Fernandez, Principal
Tel: (213) 227.0018 Fax: (213) 222-2351
Email: info@lausd.k12.us.elasc
Web: www.lausd.k12.ca.us

FOUNDATION FOR THE CHILDREN OF THE CALIFORNIAS
12680 High Bluf Dr. #200
San Diego, CA 92130
María Luisa Bojorquez, Office Manager
Tel: (858) 720-0381 Fax: (858) 720-0384
Email: mariab@usfcc.org
Web: www.usfcc.org

FUTURO INFANTIL HISPANO
2227 E. Garvey Ave. North
West Covina, CA 91791
Oma Velasco, Director
Tel: (626) 339-1824 Fax: (626) 915-4148
Web: www.futuroinfantil.org

GOOD BEGINNINGS EARLY CHILDHOOD EDUCATION PROGRAM
University of Southern California
1839 S. Hoover St.
Los Angeles, CA 90006
Mary Helen Barajas, Program Director
Tel: (213) 747-6254 Fax: (213) 747-7256
Email: mbarajas@lacorps.org
Web: www.lacorps.org

LIFE STEPS FOUNDATION, INC.
Infant Development Projects
12555 W. Jefferson Blvd. #275
Los Angeles, CA 90066
Virginia Franco, Founder/CEO
Tel: (800) 530-5433
Web: www.lifestepsfoundation.org

MAR VISTA FAMILY CENTER
5070 Slauson Ave.
Culver City, CA 90230
Lucía Díaz, Director
Tel: (310) 390-9607 Fax: (310) 390-4888
Email: marvistain@aol.com

NINOS LATINOS UNIDOS
Headquarters
10016 Pioneer Blvd. #123
Sante Fe Springs, CA 90670
Pedro V. Travieso, Director of Programs & Operation
Tel: (562) 801-5454 Fax: (562) 942-8955
Email: travieso@nlu.org
Web: www.nlu.org

REFUGIO DE CRISTO
8050 Lloyd Ave.
North Hollywood, CA 91605
Hugo Fraga, Vice President
Tel: (818) 909-0005 Fax: (818) 785-7309
Email: hugofazzi@aol.com

SALVATION ARMY DAY CARE CENTER
836 Stanford Ave.
Los Angeles, CA 90021
Sara Varela, Director
Tel: (213) 623-9022 Fax: (213) 623-9093

VILLA DE NIÑOS
9999 Feron Blvd. #B

Rancho Cucamanga, CA 91730
Andrea Figueroa, Supervisor
Tel: (909) 484-1903 Fax: (909) 481-0051
Email: afiguroa@verizon.com

SPEC. INT., COUNSELING

ABOUT FACE DOMESTIC VIOLENCE INTERVENTION PROJECT
3407 W. 6th St. #700
Los Angeles, CA 90020
Sandra G. Baca, Director
Tel: (213) 384-7084 Fax: (213) 384-7653
Web: /www.aboutfacela.com

AMANECER COMMUNITY COUNSELING SERVICES
1200 Wilshire Blvd. #208
Los Angeles, CA 90017
Amy Wilson, Acting Director
Tel: (213) 481-7464 Fax: (213) 481-7147
Email: awilson@ccsla.org
Web: www.ccsla.org

COMMUNITY COUNSELING SERVICES
1200 Wilshire Blvd., 2nd Fl. #100
Los Angeles, CA 90017
Jorge Simich, Executive Director
Tel: (213) 481-1347 Fax: (213) 482-9466

EAST LOS ANGELES WOMEN CENTER
1255 S. Atlantic Blvd.
Los Angeles, CA 90022
Stella Montoya, Board President
Tel: (323) 526-5819 Fax: (323) 526-5822
Email: forraza@aol.com

FAMILY VIOLENCE PREVENTION FUND
San Francisco
383 Rhode Island St. #304
San Francisco, CA 94103-5133
Esta Soler, President
Tel: (415) 252-8900 Fax: (415) 252-8991
Email: info@endabuse.org
Web: www.fvpf.org

LA FAMILIA COUNSELING SERVICE
26801 Mocine Ave.
Hayward, CA 94544
Héctor E. Méndez, Executive Director
Tel: (510) 881-5921 Fax: (510) 881-5925
Email: lfcs2000@aol.com
Web: www.lafamiliaUSA.org

SPEC. INT., EDUCATION

ACADEMIA SEMILLAS DEL PUEBLO
4736 Huntington Dr. South
Los Angeles, CA 90032
Maria Martinez, President
Tel: (323) 225-4549 Fax: (323) 987-1240
Email: info@dignidad.org
Web: www.dignidad.org/english/welcome.html

ALFONSO B. PEREZ SCHOOL SPECIAL EDUCATION CENTER
4540 Michigan Ave.
Los Angeles, CA 90022
Beverly Feinstein, Principal
Tel: (323) 269-0681 Fax: (323) 262-7781
Email: perez-school@lausd.k12.ca.us

BARRIO LOGAN COLLEGE INSTITUTE
1807 Main St.
San Diego, CA 92113
Berenice Jau Gil, Elementary Program Director
Tel: (619) 232-4686 Fax: (919) 232-4689
Email: berenice@blci.org
Web: www.blci.org

BASIC ADULT SPANISH EDUCATION
7009 Owensmouth Ave. #101
Canoga Park, CA 91303
Virginia G. Rafelson, Executive Director
Tel: (818) 348-4771 Fax: (818) 883-5834
Email: virginiar@baseedu.org
Web: www.baseedu.org

CALIFORNIA ASSOCIATION FOR BILINGUAL EDUCATION
16033 E San Bernardino Rd.
Covina, CA 91722-3900
María S. Quezada, Executive Director
Tel: (626) 814-4441 Fax: (626) 814-4640
Email: info@bilingualeducation.org
Web: www.bilingualeducation.org

CALIFORNIA ASSOCIATION OF EDUCATIONAL OFFICE PROFESSIONALS
2001 Point West Way
Sacramento, CA 95815
Linda Quattlebaum, Treasurer
Tel: (909) 765-5100 Fax: (909) 765-5119
Email: scallaha@hemetusd.k12.ca.us
Web: www.caeop.org

CALIFORNIA MINI-CORP PROGRAM
California State University, Bakersfield
9001 Stockdale Hwy.
Bakersfield, CA 93311-1099
Rocio Munoz, Coordinator
Tel: (661) 664-2429 Fax: (661) 665-6745
Email: rmunoz@csubak.edu

CAMINO NUEVO CHARTER ACADEMY
635 S. Harvard Blvd.
Los Angeles, CA 90005
Ana Ponce, Executive Director
Tel: (213) 736-5542 x106
Email: aponce@caminonuevo.org
Web: www.caminonuevo.org

CENTER FOR LATIN AMERICAN STUDIES
San Diego State University
Storm Hall 146
San Diego, CA 92182-4446
James Gerber, Director
Tel: (619) 594-1103 Fax: (619) 594-8748
Email: jgerber@mail.sdsu.edu
Web: www-rohan.sdsu.edu/~latamweb

Stanford University
Bolivar House, 582 Alvarado Row
Stanford, CA 94305
Herbert S. Klein, Director
Tel: (650) 723-4444 Fax: (650) 723-9822
Email: hklein@stanford.edu
Web: www.stanford.edu/group/las

CENTER FOR THE STUDY OF BOOKS IN SPANISH FOR CHILDREN & ADOLESCENTS
California State University San Marcos
5th Fl., 333 S Twin Oaks Valley Rd.
San Marcos, CA 92096-0001
Dr. Isabel Schon, Director
Tel: (760) 750-4070 Fax: (760) 750-4073
Email: ischon@csusm.edu
Web: www.csusm.edu/csb

CENTRO CULTURAL PLACITA
P.O. Box 531734
Los Angeles, CA 90053-1734
José Cohen, Executive Director
Tel: (323) 343-0994

CENTRO JUAN MONTALVO
5300 Santa Monica Blvd. #310
Los Angeles, CA 90029
Ana Lucia Jaramillo, Director
Tel: (323) 463-2945

CENTRO LATINO DE EDUCACION POPULAR
1709 West 8th St. #A
Los Angeles, CA 90017
Melanie Stephens, Executive Director
Tel: (213) 483-7753 Fax: (213) 483-7973
Email: melanie@centrolatinoliteracy.org
Web: www.centrolatinoliteracy.org

CHICANA AND CHICANO STUDIES DEPARTMENT
California State University
800 N. State College Blvd. H314
Fullerton, CA 92831
Isaac Cárdenas, Chairman
Tel: (714) 278-48-15 Fax: (714) 278-33
Email: icardenas@fullerton.edu
Web: http://hss.fullerton.edu/chicano

CHICANO BILINGUAL/BICULTURAL STUDIES PROGRAM
University of California, Riverside
3600 HMNSS Bldg.
Riverside, CA 92521
Adalberto Aguirre, Jr., Chair/Professor
Tel: (951) 827-4577 Fax: (951) 827-4344
Email: adalberto.aguirre@ucr.edu
Web: www.chicanobbstudies.ucr.edu

CHICANO STUDIES PROGRAM
University of California, Berkeley
506 Barrows Hall #2570
Berkeley, CA 94720-2570
Alfred Arteaga, Coordinator
Tel: (510) 643-0796 Fax: (510) 642-6456
Email: arteaga@socrates.berkeley.edu
Web: http://ist-socrates.berkeley.edu/~ethnicst

CHICANO-LATINO EDUCATION COMMITTEE
United Teachers Los Angeles
3303 Wilshire Blvd., 10th Fl.
Los Angeles, CA 90010
Richard Lieb
Tel: (213) 487-5560 Fax: (213) 487-1618
Web: www.utla.net

CHICANO/LATINO GRADUATE STUDENT ASSOCIATION
Stanford University
El Centro Chicano, Bldg. #590-F, Old Union
Stanford, CA 94305-3044
Frances Morales, Assistant Dean/Director
Tel: (650) 723-5397 Fax: (650) 725-6487
Email: fmorales@stanford.edu
Web: www.stanford.edu/group/cgsa/

CHICANO/LATINO STUDENT AFFAIRS CENTER
Smith Campus Center, 170 E. 6th St. #228
Claremont, CA 91711
Maria Aguiar Torres, Dean of Student Affairs
Tel: (909) 621-8044 Fax: (909) 621-8981
Email: maria_torres@cucmail.claremont.edu
Web: www.cuc.claremont.edu/chicano

COLEGIO POPULAR
2839 Mariposa
Fresno, CA 93721
Tomás González, Director
Tel: (559) 441-7131 Fax: (559) 441-7155
Email: tomas@romero.com

COLLEGE ASSISTANCE MIGRANT PROGRAM
California State University, Sacramento
River Front Center 1, 6000 J St.
Sacramento, CA 95819-6108
Miguel Servantez, Chair
Tel: (916) 278-7241 Fax: (916) 278-5193
Email: mservantez@csus.edu
Web: www.csus.edu/camp

COUNCIL OF MEXICAN-AMERICAN ADMINISTRATORS OF THE LOS ANGELES UNIFIED SCHOOL DISTRICT
Middleton Elementary School
6537 Malabar St.
Hunington Park, CA 90255
Javier Miranda, President
Tel: (323) 582-6387 Fax: (323) 587-7006

DEPARTMENT OF CHICANA AND CHICANO STUDIES
University of California at Santa Barbara
1713 S Hall #1714
Santa Barbara, CA 93106-4120
Chela Sandoval, Chair
Tel: (805) 893-5546 Fax: (805) 893-4076
Web: www.chicst.ucsb.edu

DEPARTMENT OF EDUCATIONAL RESEARCH, ADMINISTRATION, AND FOUNDATIONS
California State University, Fresno
5005 N. Maple Ave. M/S ED 303
Fresno, CA 93740
Alfredo Cuellar, President

Tel: (559) 278-0391
Email: alfredoc@csufresno.edu
Web: www.csufresno.edu

DOLORES MISSION ALTERNATIVE SCHOOL
Proyecto Pastoral at Dolores Mission
135 N. Mission Rd.
Los Angeles, CA 90033
Manuel Dominguez, Director
Tel: (323) 264-9143 Fax: (213) 268-7228
Email: dma@proyectopastoral.org
Web: www.proyectopastoral.org

EL CENTRO CHICANO
University of Southern California
817 W. 34th St. #300
Los Angeles, CA 90089-2991
Gabriela Lopez, Interim Director
Tel: (213) 740-1480 Fax: (213) 745-6721
Email: ecc@usc.edu
Web: www.usc.edu/student-affairs/elcentro

ESCUELA ARGENTINA DE LOS ANGELES
P.O. Box 5332
Whittier, CA 90607-5332
Elba D. Bonini, Board of Director
Tel: (562) 946-3076

ESCUELA DE LA RAZA UNIDA
Affiliate of NCLR
P.O. Box 910
Blythe, CA 92226
Rigoberto Garnica, Executive Director
Tel: (760) 922-2582 Fax: (760) 921-3261
Email: j72eru@aol.com

GOLDEN STATE MINORITY FOUNDATION
419 N. Larchmont Blvd. #98
Los Angeles, CA 90004
Ivan Houston, President
Tel: (323) 751-5101   Fax: (323) 751-5114
Email: gsmf@earthlink.net
Web: www.gsmf.org

THE HISPANIC CAUCUS AMERICAN ASSOCIATION FOR HIGHER EDUCATION
California State University, San Bernadino
5500 University Pkwy.
San Bernadino, CA 92407
Juan Delgado, Secretary
Tel: (909) 880-5826 Fax: (909) 880-7086
Email: jdelgado@csusb.edu
Web: http://hcaucus.csusb.edu/exec.html

HISPANIC EDUCATION ENDOWMENT FOUNDATION
Orange County Community Foundation
30 Corporate Park #410
Irvine, CA 92606
Rose Armengol Garris, Program Director
Tel: (949) 553-4202 x23
Email: ragarris@heef.org
Web: www.heef.org

HISPANIC ENGINEER NATIONAL ACHIEVEMENT AWARDS CONFERENCE
3900 Whiteside St.
Los Angeles, CA 90063
Anna Park, Executive Director
Tel: (323) 262-0997 Fax: (323) 262-0946
Email: info@henaac.org
Web: www.henaac.org

HISPANIC SCHOLARSHIP FUND
National Headquarters
55 Second St. #1500
San Francisco, CA 94105
Sara Martínez Tucker, President
Tel: (415) 808-2300 Fax: (415) 808-2301
Email: info@hsf.net
Web: www.hsf.net

LATIN AMERICAN AND IBERIAN STUDIES
University of California at Santa Barbara
Phelps Hall 4206
Santa Barbara, CA 93106-4150

Sarah Cline, Director
Tel: (805) 893-3161 Fax: (805) 893-8341
Email: laisdirector@lais.ucsb.edu
Web: www.lais.ucsb.edu

LATIN AMERICAN AND LATINO STUDIES DEPARTMENT
University of California, Santa Cruz
1156 High St.
Santa Cruz, CA 95064
Gabriela F. Arredondo, Assistant Professor
Tel: (831) 459-4284 Fax: (831) 459-3125
Email: lals@ucsc.edu
Web: http://lals.ucsc.edu

LATIN AMERICAN CIVIC ASSOCIATION
340 Parkside Dr.
San Fernando, CA 91340
Guille Gaeta, Secretary to the Director
Tel: (818) 361-8641 Fax: (818) 361-1546

LATIN AMERICAN STUDIES CENTER
California State University, Los Angeles
5151 State University Dr.
Los Angeles, CA 90032
Marjorie Bray, Director
Tel: (323) 343-2180 Fax: (323) 343-5485
Email: mbray@calstatela.edu

LATIN BUSINESS ASSOCIATION
Elan International
620 Newport Center Dr., 11th Fl.
Newport Beach, CA 92660
Lucia de Garcia, President/CEO
Tel: (949) 721-6644 Fax: (949) 653-9855
Email: lucia.degarcia@cox.net
Web: www.lbausa.com

LATINOS IN ENGLISH
3911 Roderick Rd.
Los Angeles, CA 90065
Rose Sánchez, Director
Tel: (323) 256-6603 Fax: (323) 845-1773
Email: qbnwriter@aol.com

LOS ANGELES COUNTY BILINGUAL DIRECTORS ASSOCIATION
Los Angeles County Office of Education
9300 E. Imperial Hwy. #109
Downey, CA 90242
Darline P. Robles, Superintendent
Tel: (562) 922-6111 Fax: (562) 922-6768
Email: Robles.Darline@lacoe.edu
Web: www.lacoe.edu

METROPOLITAN SKILLS CENTER
2801 W. 6th St.
Los Angeles, CA 90010
Cynthia Moore, Principal
Tel: (213) 386-7269 Fax: (213) 252-9435

MEXICAN AMERICAN ALUMNI ASSOCIATION
University of Southern California
University Park Campus, Student Union Bldg. #203
Los Angeles, CA 90089-4890
Raul Vargas, Director
Tel: (213) 740-4735 Fax: (213) 740-7250
Email: maaa@usc.edu
Web: www.usc.edu/maaa

MEXICAN AMERICAN STUDIES DEPARTMENT
San José State University
1 Washington Sq.
San José, CA 95192-0118
Louis Holscher, Chair
Tel: (408) 924-5760
Email: holscher@sjsu.edu
Web: www2.sjsu.edu/depts/SocialWork/depts/mexamer

NATIONAL ASSOCIATION FOR CHICANA AND CHICANO STUDIES
P.O. Box 720052
San Jose, CA 95172-0052
Reynaldo Macias, Chair

Tel: (310) 206-4573
Email: naccs@naccs.org
Web: www.naccs.org

NATIONAL HISPANIC UNIVERSITY
14271 Story Rd.
San Jose, CA 95127-9989
Edward M. Alvarez, Chair
Tel: (408) 254-6900 Fax: (408) 254-1369
Email: webmaster@nhu.edu
Web: www.nhu.edu

PARENT INSTITUTE FOR QUALITY EDUCATION
Affiliate of NCLR
4010 Morena Blvd. #200
San Diego, CA 92117
Saul Sanchez, Contact
Tel: (858) 483-4499 Fax: (858) 483-4646
Email: sanchezsaul@yahoo.com
Web: www.piqe.org

PUENTE LEARNING CENTER
People United to Enrich the Neighborhood
501 S Boyle Ave.
Los Angeles, CA 90033
Sister Jennie Lechtenberg, Founder/Executive Director
Tel: (323) 780-8900 Fax: (323) 780-0359
Web: www.puente.org

PUENTE PROJECT
300 Lakeside Dr., 7th Fl.
Oakland, CA 94612
Yanira Guzman, Mentor
Tel: (510) 987-9548 Fax: (510) 834-0737
Email: puente@ucop.edu
Web: www.puente.net

SALVADORAN AMERICAN LEADERSHIP AND EDUCATION FUND
1625 W Olympic Blvd. #718
Los Angeles, CA 90015
Carlos Antonio H. Vaquerano, Executive Director
Tel: (213) 480-1052 Fax: (213) 487-2530
Email: info@salef.org
Web: www.salef.org

SCIENCE CAREERS OPPORTUNITY PROGRAM
California State University at Fresno, School of Sciences and Mathematics
2555 E. San Ramon Ave., M/S SB90
Fresno, CA 93740-8034
Frank Castro, Director
Tel: (559) 278-5751 Fax: (209) 278-7804
Email: frankyc@csufresno.edu
Web: www.csufresno.edu

SOCIETY FOR THE ADVANCEMENT OF CHICANOS AND NATIVE AMERICANS IN SCIENCE
P.O. Box 8526
Santa Cruz, CA 95061-8526
Marigold Linton, President-elect
Tel: (831) 459-0170 Fax: (831) 459-0194
Email: info@sacnas.org
Web: www.sacnas.org

SPANISH RESOURCE CENTER
University of Southern California
3375 S Hoover St. #F204
Los Angeles, CA 90089-0031
Ana Isabel Sánchez Salmerón, Education Advisor
Tel: (213) 740-5896 Fax: (213) 821-2304
Email: ana.sanchez.usa@correo.mec.es
Web: www.sgci.mec.es/usa

STANFORD LITERACY IMPROVEMENT PROJECT
Stanford University
El Centro Chicano, Bldg. 590-F, Old Union
Stanford, CA 94305-3044
Chris Gonzalez Clarke, Assistant Director
Tel: (650) 723-2089 Fax: (650) 725-6487
Email: chris.clarke@stanford.edu
Web: www.stanford.edu/dept/elcentro/

WASTE WATCHERS, INC.
P.O. Box 3535
Fremont, CA 94539
Richard Ahern, Vice President
Tel: (510) 791-7964 Fax: (510) 793-9627
Email: rgahern@aol.com
Web: http://hometown.aol.com/rgahern/myhomepage/index.html

SPEC. INT., EMPLOYMENT

ARRIBA JUNTOS
1850 Mission St.
San Francisco, CA 94103
Dalila Ahumada, Executive Director
Tel: (415) 487-3240 Fax: (415) 863-9314
Email: info@arribajuntos.org
Web: www.arribajuntos.org

CALEXICO COMMUNITY ACTION COUNCIL
2151 Rockwood Ave. #166
Calexico, CA 92231
Steve F. Rivera, Executive Director
Tel: (760) 357-6464 Fax: (760) 357-6614
Email: riveras@ccac.vtc.us
Web: www.ccac-vtc.org

CENTER FOR TRAINING AND CAREERS, INC.
1600 Las Plumas Ave.
San Jose, CA 95133
Rose A. Amador, President & CEO
Tel: (408) 251-3165 Fax: (408) 251-4978
Email: roseamador@aol.com
Web: www.ctcsj.org

CHICANO SERVICES
315 W 9th St.
Los Angeles, CA 90015
Sofia Esparza, CEO
Tel: (213) 253-5959 Fax: (213) 930-0657

EAST LOS ANGELES OCCUPATIONAL CENTER
2100 Marengo St.
Los Angeles, CA 90033
Ruberto Ceja, Principal
Tel: (323) 223-1283 Fax: (323) 223-6365
Email: east-la-oc@lausd.k12.ca.us
Web: www.elaoc.org

EL CENTRO/SER-JOBS FOR PROGRESS, INC.
155 W. Main St.
El Centro, CA 92243
Rubén García, Executive Director
Tel: (760) 352-8514 Fax: (760) 352-5790
Email: serlatinos@yahoo.com
Web: www.ser-national.org

FRESNO/SER-JOBS FOR PROGRESS, INC.
407 S. Clozis Ave. #109
Fresno, CA 93721
Rebecca Mendibles, Executive Director
Tel: (559) 452-0881 Fax: (559) 452-8038
Email: becki.m@nsbcglobal.net
Web: www.ser-national.org

GLOBAL EDUCATION PARTNERSHIP
San Francisco Bay Area
310 8th St. #303
Oakland, CA 94607
Tom Parker, Office Manager
Tel: (510) 834-7255 Fax: (510) 834-7256
Email: tparker@globaledpartnership.org
Web: www.geponline.org

INSTITUTO LABORAL DE LA RAZA
2947 16th St.
San Francisco, CA 94117
Sarah M. Shaker, Director
Tel: (415) 431-7522 Fax: (415) 431-4846
Email: info@ilaboral.org
Web: www.ilaboral.org

JOBS FOR PROGRESS, INC./SER SOUTH BAY
14411 Santa Anita Ave.
El Monte, CA 91733
Charles Villanueva, Executive Director
Tel: (626) 444-6204 Fax: (626) 823-6494
Email: charlesv4u@yahoo.com
Web: www.ser-national.org

JOBS FOR PROGRESS, INC./SER-SOUTH BAY
Affiliate of SER-Jobs for Progress National, Inc.
12440 E. Firestone Blvd. #1001
Norwalk, CA 90650
Rick D. Sánchez, Executive Director
Tel: (562) 863-6464 Fax: (626) 823-6494
Email: rds_sobay@hotmail.com
Web: www.ser-national.org

LOS ANGELES COUNTY HISPANIC MANAGERS ASSOCIATION
P.O. Box 94262
City of Industry, CA 91715
Andy Martinez, President
Tel: (323) 343-8298
Email: information@lachma.com
Web: www.lachma.com

LOS ANGELES COUNTY WORKFORCE
350 S. Bixel St. #160
Los Angeles, CA 90017
Alma Salazar, Contact
Tel: (562) 438-4474 Fax: (562) 438-4474
Email: asalazar@unitela.com
Web: www.laworkforce.org

ORANGE COUNTY/SER-JOBS FOR PROGRESS, INC.
1243 E. Warner Ave.
Santa Ana, CA 92705
Ronald W. Puente, Executive Director
Tel: (714) 556-8741 Fax: (714) 556-0640
Email: seroccal@aol.com
Web: www.ser-national.org

PACOIMA SKILLS CENTER
13545 Van Nuys Blvd.
Pacoima, CA 91331
Andres Ameigeiras, Principal
Tel: (818) 896-9558 Fax: (818) 899-7087
Email: pacoima-skills-ctr@lausd.k12.ca.us
Web: www.lausd.k12.ca.us/pacoima_skills_ctr/

SALUDOS HISPANOS
5400 E. Olympic Blvd. #120
Los Angeles, CA 90022
Kim Solomon, Coordinator
Tel: (800) 748-6426
Email: kim@saludos.com
Web: www.saludos.com

SAN DIEGO/SER-JOBS FOR PROGRESS, INC.
3355 Mission Ave. #123
Oceanside, CA 92054
George López, President/CEO
Tel: (760) 754-6500 Fax: (760) 967-6357
Email: georgelopez@nctimes.net
Web: www.ser-national.org

UNITED STATES EQUAL EMPLOYMENT OPPORTUNITY COMMISSION
Los Angeles District Office
255 E.Temple, 4th Fl.
Los Angeles, CA 90012
Olophius E. Perry, District Director
Tel: (213) 894-1000 Fax: (213) 894-1118
Web: www.eeoc.gov/losangeles

SPEC. INT., FAMILY PLANNING

AVANCE, INC.
Los Angeles Office
2208 E. 4th St.
Los Angeles, CA 90033
Carlos Guevara, Program Director
Tel: (323) 260-8080 Fax: (323) 260-8084
Email: cguevara@avance.org
Web: www.avance.org

COUNTY OF LOS ANGELES DEPARTMENT OF CHILDREN AND FAMILY SERVICES
Adoptions Division
695 S. Vermont Ave.
Los Angeles, CA 90005
Sari Grant, Program Manager
Tel: (888) 811-1121 X2
Email: adoptions@dcfs.co.la.ca.us
Web: http://dcfs.co.la.ca.us/Adoptions/main.htm

FAMILY SERVICE OF LONG BEACH
Administrative Office
1041 Pine Ave.
Long Beach, CA 90813
Russell Brammer, Executive Director
Tel: (562) 436-9893
Email: info@fslb.org
Web: www.fslb.org

LA COLONIA ANAHEIM INDEPENDENCIA FAMILY RESOURCE CENTER
10841 Garza Ave.
Anaheim, CA 92804
Rosa Rentieria, Center Manager
Tel: (714) 826-9070 Fax: (714) 826-2732
Email: info@factoc.org
Web: www.factoc.org/collaboratives/indep.asp

LATINO FAMILY INSTITUTE
1501 W. Cameron Ave. #240
West Covina, CA 91790
Jorge Jaramillo, Board of Director
Tel: (800) 294-9161
Email: info@latinoadoptions.com
Web: www.latinoadoptions.com

NATIONAL LATINO FATHERHOOD AND FAMILY INSTITUTE
5252 E Beverly Blvd.
Los Angeles, CA 90022
Tel: (323) 728-7770 Fax: (323) 728-8666
Web: www.nlffi.org

PLAZA COMMUNITY CENTER, INC.
Family Support Center
4018 City Terrace Dr.
Los Angeles, CA 90063
Gloria Ornelas, Program Director
Tel: (323) 268-3219 Fax: (323) 268-2578
Email: pcc@vfnet.com
Web: www.vfnet.com

PREGNANCY COUNSELING CENTER
San Fernando Valley
10211 Sepulveda Blvd.
Mission Hills, CA 91345
Jule Bill, Director
Tel: (818) 895-8441 Fax: (818) 895-2921
Email: pccofsfv@earthlink.com
Web: www.pccofsfv.com

SOMOS FAMILIA, PLAZA FAMILY PRESERVATION NETWORK
3700 Princeton St.
Los Angeles, CA 90023
John Stuart, Program Director
Tel: (323) 261-0414 Fax: (323) 261-9178
Email: familyprez@plazacc.org
Web. www.plazacc.org

SPEC. INT., GAY&LESBIAN

FAMILIA DE STANFORD
Stanford University Office of Student Activities
Bldg. 590-F, The Nitery
Stanford, CA 95305-3044
Yvonne Yarbro-Bejarano, Chair
Tel: (650) 723-5397 Fax: (650) 725-6487
Email: familia@lists.stanford.edu
Web: www.stanford.edu/group/familia

SPEC. INT., HEALTH SERVICES

ALTAMED HEALTH SERVICES CORPORATION
AltaMed Drug Treatment Program
1701 Zonal Ave.
Los Angeles, CA 90033
Castulo de la Rocha, President/CEO
Tel: (323) 223-6189
Email: info@altamed.org
Web: www.altamed.org

AltaMed Medical Groups
5425 E. Pomona Blvd.
Los Angeles, CA 90022
Castulo de la Rocha, President/CEO

Tel: (323) 720-9950
Email: info@altamed.org
Web: www.altamed.org

AltaMed Medical Groups
10454 E. Valley Blvd.
El Monte, CA 91731
Castulo de la Rocha, President/CEO
Tel: (626) 453-8466
Email: info@altamed.org
Web: www.altamed.org

AltaMed Medical Groups
9436 E. Slauson Ave.
Pico Rivera, CA 90660
Castulo de la Rocha, President/CEO
Tel: (562) 949-6069
Email: info@altamed.org
Web: www.altamed.org

Corporate Office/Affiliate of NCLR
500 Citadel Dr. #490
Los Angeles, CA 90040
Castulo de la Rocha, President/CEO
Tel: (323) 725-8751 Fax: (323) 889-7399
Email: info@altamed.org
Web: www.altamed.org

HIV Services
204 1/2 W. 6th St.
Los Angeles, CA 90012
Castulo de la Rocha, President/CEO
Tel: (213) 629-0962
Email: info@altamed.org
Web: www.altamed.org

HIV Services
5255 E. Pomona Blvd. # 4, 9 &11A/B
Los Angeles, CA 90033
Castulo de la Rocha, President/CEO
Tel: (323) 890-8767
Email: info@altamed.org
Web: www.altamed.org

HIV Services
5427 E. Whittier Blvd.
Los Angeles, CA 90022
Castulo de la Rocha, President/CEO
Tel: (323) 869-5450
Email: info@altamed.org
Web: www.altamed.org

Senior Services
512 S. Indiana St.
Los Angeles, CA 90063
Castulo de la Rocha, President/CEO
Tel: (323) 980-4000
Email: info@altamed.org
Web: www.altamed.org

Senior Services
701 Cesar E. Chavez Ave. #201
Los Angeles, CA 90012
Castulo de la Rocha, President/CEO
Tel: (213) 229-3685
Email: info@altamed.org
Web: www.altamed.org

Senior Services
5425 E. Pomona Blvd.
Los Angeles, CA 90022
Castulo de la Rocha, President/CEO
Tel: (323) 728-0411
Email: info@altamed.org
Web: www.altamed.org

Senior Services
6330 Rugby Ave. #200
Huntington Park, CA 90255
Castulo de la Rocha, President/CEO
Tel: (323) 277-7678
Email: info@altamed.org
Web: www.altamed.org

Teen Programs
249 E. Pomona Ave.
Monterey Park, CA 91755

Castulo de la Rocha, President/CEO
Tel: (323) 722-8300
Email: info@altamed.org
Web: www.altamed.org

Teen Programs
2476 S. Atlantic Blvd.
Commerce, CA 90040
Castulo de la Rocha, President/CEO
Tel: (323) 980-3061
Email: info@altamed.org
Web: www.altamed.org

ARTHRITIS FOUNDATION
Southern California Chapter
4311 Wilshire Blvd. #530
Los Angeles, CA 90010-3775
Robert J. King, Chapter President
Tel: (323) 954-5750 Fax: (323) 954-5790
Email: info.sca@arthritis.org
Web: www.arthritis.org

CALIFORNIA HEALTHCARE FOUNDATION
476 Ninth St.
Oakland, CA 94607
Dr. Mark D. Smith, President/CEO
Tel: (510) 238-1040 Fax: (510) 238-1388
Web: www.chcf.org

CALIFORNIA LATINO MEDICAL ASSOCIATION
2550 Corporate Pl. #C202
Monterey Park, CA 91754
Margaret Juarez, President
Email: info@calma.org
Web: www.calma.ws

CALIFORNIA LATINO PSYCHOLOGICAL ASSOCIATION
University of California, Irvine
Counseling Center, 202 Student Services I
Irvine, CA 92697
Miguel E. Gallardo, President
Tel: (949) 824-6457 Fax: (949) 824-6586
Email: mgallard@uci.edu
Web: www.latinopsych.org

CHILDREN'S MEDICAL SERVICES
CHDP Program and CCS Program
P.O. Box 1489
San Luis Obispo, CA 93406
Greg Thomas, Public Health Director
Tel: (805) 781-5502 Fax: (805) 781-4492
Web: www.slopublichealth.org

CLINICA MONSEÑOR OSCAR A. ROMERO
123 S. Alvarado St.
Los Angeles, CA 90057
Roland Palencia, Executive Director
Tel: (213) 989-7700 Fax: (213) 989-7701
Email: ropalencia@clinicaromero.com
Web: www.clinicaromero.com

CLINICA MONSEÑOR OSCAR A. ROMERO
2032 Marengo St.
Los Angeles, CA 90033
Eduardo Gonzalez, Executive Director
Tel: (323) 987-1030 Fax: (323) 221-4528
Email: egonzalez@clinicaromero.com
Web: www.clinicaromero.com

CLINICA TEPATI
1500 C St.
Sacramento, CA 95814
Horacio Lemus, Executive Administrator
Tel: (916) 874-5303 Fax: (530) 752-2996
Email: hzlemus@ucdavis.edu
Web: http://cim.ucdavis.edu/clinics/Clinica_Tepat

CLINICA TEPATI
UC Davis School of Medicine
Department of Family Practice, TB 152
Davis, CA 95616
Michael Onstad, Co-Director
Tel: (530) 752-7028 Fax: (530) 752-2696
Email: maonstad@ucdavis.edu
Web: http://cim.ucdavis.edu/clinics/clinica_tepati

CLINICAS DE SALUD DEL PUEBLO, INC.
Affiliate of NCLR
1166 K St.
Brawley, CA 92227
Dr. Gus Escalindo, Executive Director
Tel: (760) 344-9951 Fax: (760) 344-5840

EL FUERTE SINALOA
1910 W. Verdugo Ave.
Burbank, CA 91506
Cuquita Reyna, President
Tel: (818) 845-0353

EL MONTE COMPREHENSIVE HEALTH CENTER
Los Angeles County, Department of Health Services
10953 Ramona Blvd.
El Monte, CA 91731
Hugo Almeida, Administrator
Tel: (626) 579-8302 Fax: (626) 448-6210
Email: halmeida@dhs.co.la.ca.us
Web: www.ladhs.org/programs

HISPANIC AMERICAN ALLERGY AND IMMUNOLOGY ASSOCIATION
4644 Lincoln Blvd. #410
Marina del Rey, CA 90292
Jorge Quel, Executive Director
Tel: (310) 823-6766 Fax: (310) 823-6966
Email: email@haama.org
Web: www.haama.org

LA CLÍNICA DE LA RAZA
Affiliate of NCLR
1515 Fruitvale Ave.
Oakland, CA 94601
Jane García, CEO
Tel: (510) 535-4017 Fax: (510) 535-4189
Email: mtorres@laclinica.org
Web: www.laclinica.org

LA CLÍNICA DE LA RAZA
Clinica Alta Vista/The Teen Clinic
3022 International Blvd. #100
Oakland, CA 94610
Tina Simeon, Site Manager
Tel: (510) 535-4230 Fax: (510) 535-4019
Email: webadmin@laclinica.org
Web: www.laclinica.org

LA CLÍNICA DE LA RAZA
San Antonio Neighborhood Health Center
1030 International Blvd.
Oakland, CA 94606
Renata Fineburg, Site Manager
Tel: (510) 238-5400 Fax: (510) 238-5437
Web: www.laclinica.org

LAS ISABELAS
P.O. Box 90627
San Jose, CA 95109
Mary Rose Delgadillo, Interim Executive Director
Tel: (408) 287-4890 Fax: (408) 287-4892
Email: lasisabelas@sbcglobal.net
Web: www.lasisabelas.org

LATIN AMERICAN DENTAL STUDENTS
UCLA
102 Men's Gym Bldg.
Los Angeles, CA 90065
Tim Ngubeni
Tel: (310) 825- 2420 Fax: (310) 206- 3175
Email: tngubeni@saonet.ucla.edu

LATINO COALITION FOR A HEALTHY CALIFORNIA
1225 8th St. #500
Sacramento, CA 95814
Lupe Alonzo-Diaz, Executive Director
Tel: (916) 448-3234 Fax: (916) 448-3248
Email: lupe@lchc.org
Web: www.lchc.org

LATINO HEALTH ACCESS
1717 N. Broadway
Santa Ana, CA 92706
America Bracho, President & CEO

Tel: (714) 542-7792 Fax: (714) 542-4853
Email: info@latinohealthaccess.org
Web: www.latinohealthaccess.org

MINORITY ORGAN TISSUE TRANSPLANT EDUCATION PROGRAM OF LOS ANGELES
National Kidney Foundation of Southern California
5777 W. Century Blvd. #1450
Los Angeles, CA 90045
Elivey Jimenez, Patient & Community Services Director
Tel: (310) 641-8152
Email: ejimenez@kidneysocal.org
Web: www.kidneysocal.org

MULTICULTURAL AREA HEALTH EDUCATION CENTER
5051 E. 3rd St.
Los Angeles, CA 90022
Luis Mata, President/CEO
Tel: (323) 780-7640 Fax: (323) 780-7646
Email: mahec@msn.com
Web: www.mahec-la.com

ORTHOPEDIC HOSPITAL-INTERNATIONAL CHILDREN'S PROGRAM
2400 S Flower St.
Los Angeles, CA 90007
María Aguilar, Coordinator
Tel: (213) 742-1339 Fax: (213) 742-1078

PUBLIC HEALTH FOUNDATION ENTERPRISES, INC.
13200 Crossroads Pkwy. N. #135
City of Industry, CA 91746
Gerald R. Solomon, President & CEO
Tel: (562) 699-7320 Fax: (562) 699-8856
Email: gsolomon@phfe.org/info@phfe.org
Web: www.phfe.org

RANCHO LOS AMIGOS MEDICAL CENTER
7601 E. Imperial Hwy.
Downey, CA 90242
Consuelo C. Diaz, CEO
Tel: (562) 401-7111 Fax: (562) 803-0056
Email: admission@rancho.org
Web: www.rancho.org

SALUD PARA LA GENTE
204 E. Beach St.
Watsonville, CA 95076
Arcadio Viveros, CEO
Tel: (831) 728-8250
Web: www.saludparalagente.org

SEIU - UNITED HEALTHCARE WORKERS
Local 399
5480 Ferguson Dr.
Los Angeles, CA 90022
Jorge Rodriguez, Executive VP
Tel: (323) 734-8399 Fax: (323) 721-3538
Web: www.seiu399.org

ASOCIACIÓN CAMPESINA LAZARO CARDENAS
Affiliate of NCLR
315 N San Joaquin St.
Stockton, CA 95202
Carol J. Ornelas, Executive Director
Tel: (209) 466-6811 Fax: (209) 466-3465
Email: cornelas@aclc.org
Web: www.aclc.org

CABRILLO ECONOMIC DEVELOPMENT CORPORATION
11011 Azahar St.
Saticoy, CA 93004
Rodney Fernández, Executive Director
Tel: (805) 659-3791 Fax: (805) 659-3195
Email: rfernandez@cabrilloedc.org
Web: www.ruralisc.org/cedc.htm

CHICANA SERVICE ACTION CENTER, INC.
Homeless Assistance Program and Transitional Housing

315 W 9th St. #101
Los Angeles, CA 90015
Alicia Reyes, Social Service Coordinator
Tel: (213) 629-5800 Fax: (213) 430-0657

COALITION FOR ECONOMIC SURVIVAL
1296 N. Fairfax Ave.
Los Angeles, CA 90046
Larry Gross, Executive Director
Tel: (323) 656-4410 Fax: (323) 656-4416
Email: contactces@net
Web: www.CESinAction.org

FAIR HOUSING FOUNDATION OF HUNTINGTONG PARK
3600 Long Beach Blvd. #302
Long Beach, CA 90807
Barbara Shull, Executive Director
Tel: (562) 989-1206 Fax: (562) 989-1836
Email: barbara@fhfla.com
Web: www.fhfla.com

GUADALUPE HOMELESS PROJECT
Proyecto Pastoral at Dolores Mission
171 S. Gless St.
Los Angeles, CA 90033
Elias Puentes, Director
Tel: (323) 881-0032
Email: ghp@proyectopastoral.org
Web: www.proyectopastoral.org

NEIGHBORHOOD HOUSING SERVICES OF ORANGE COUNTY
198 W. Lincoln Ave., 2nd Fl.
Anaheim, CA 92805
Glenn Hayes, Executive Director
Tel: (714) 490-1250 Fax: (714) 490-1263
Email: nhs@aol.com
Web: www.nhsoc.org

NEW ECONOMICS FOR WOMEN
303 S. Loma Dr.
Los Angeles, CA 90017
Magie Cervantes, President
Tel: (213) 483-2060 Fax: (213) 483-7848
Email: info@neweconomicsforwomen.org
Web: www.neweconomicsforwomen.org

RURAL COMMUNITY ASSISTANCE CORPORATION
Affiliate of NCLR
3120 Freeboard Dr. #201
West Sacramento, CA 95691
William French, Executive Director
Tel: (916) 447-2854 Fax: (916) 447-2878
Email: mail@rcac.org
Web: www.rcac.org

TELACU
LINC Partners
5400 E. Olympic Blvd.
Los Angeles, CA 90022
David C. Lizarraga, President & CEO
Tel: (323) 721-1655 Fax: (323) 724-3372
Email: info@telacu.com
Web: www.telacu.com

CALIFORNIA COUNCIL FOR THE HUMANITIES
315 W. 9th St. #702
Los Angeles, CA 90015
Felicia Harmer Kelley, Senior Program Manager
Tel: (213) 623-5993 Fax: (213) 623-6833
Email: fkelley@calhum.org
Web: www.calhum.org

CALIFORNIA HUMAN DEVELOPMENT CORPORATION
Farm Worker Services Program
3315 Airway Dr.
Santa Rosa, CA 95403
Mike Mitcithie, Executive Director
Tel: (707) 523-1155 Fax: (707) 523-3776
Web: www.chdcorp.org

CHICANO FEDERATION OF SAN DIEGO COUNTY, INC.
P.O. Box 40508
San Diego, CA 92164-0508
Raymond Uzeta, President/CEO
Tel: (619) 285-5600 Fax: (619) 285-5614
Web: www.chicanofederation.org

CITY OF LOS ANGELES HUMAN RELATIONS COMMISSION
200 N. Spring St., City Hall #1625
Los Angeles, CA 90012
Rabbi Allen I. Freehling, Executive Director
Tel: (213) 978-1660 Fax: (213) 978-1668
Email: rabbiallenf@mailbox.facility.org
Web: www.ci.la.ca.us/hra

COALITION FOR HUMANE IMMIGRANT RIGHTS OF LOS ANGELES
2533 W. 3rd St. #101
Los Angeles, CA 90057
Angelica Salas, Executive Director
Tel: (213) 353-1333 Fax: (213) 353-1344
Email: info@chirla.org
Web: www.chirla.org

COMUNIDAD EN MOVIMIENTO
Proyecto Pastoral at Dolores Mission
135 N. Mission Rd.
Los Angeles, CA 90033
Claudia Martinon, Director
Tel: (323) 881-0019
Email: cem@proyectopastoral.org
Web: www.proyectopastoral.org

HISPANIC AGENTS AND BROKERS ASSOCIATION
2175 John S Gibson Blvd.
San Pedro, CA 90731
Paul Pesqueira, President
Tel: (310) 548-7601 Fax: (310) 548-2656

LOS ANGELES COUNTY BAR ASSOCIATION
P.O. Box 55020
Los Angeles, CA 90055
John J. Collins, President
Tel: (213) 627-2727 Fax: (213) 896-6500
Email: jcollins@ccmslaw.com
Web: www.lacba.org

LOS BOMBEROS OF NORTHERN CALIFORNIA
765 Story Rd. #150
San Jose, CA 95112
Albert N. Olmos, President
Tel: (408) 294-7679
Email: losbomberospres@sbcglobal.net
Web: www.latinofirefighters.org

605 CITIZENSHIP PROJECT
10016 Pioneer Blvd. #107
Santa Fe Springs, CA 90670
Nelly Paredes-Walsborn, Director/Founder Member
Tel: (209) 848-0396
Email: nanawals@cs.com
Web: www.csulb.edu/projects/tad/

CATHOLIC CHARITIES OF LOS ANGELES
Immigration And Refugee Division
P.O.Box 15095
1531 James M. Wood Blvd.
Los Angeles, CA 90015-0095
Ronald G. Lopez, CEO
Tel: (213) 251-3400 Fax: (213) 380-4603
Email: rlopez@ccharities.org
Web: www.catholiccharitiesla.org

NATIONAL NETWORK FOR IMMIGRANT & REFUGEE RIGHTS
310 8th St. #303
Oakland, CA 94607
Catherine Tactaquin, Executive Director
Tel: (510) 465-1984 Fax: (510) 465-1885
Email: nnirr@nnirr.org
Web: www.nnirr.org

POMONA VALLEY CENTER FOR COMMUNITY DEVELOPMENT
1041 S. White Ave.
Pomona, CA 91766
Tomas Ursua, Executive Director
Tel: (909) 629-4649 Fax: (909) 629-1714

SAN JUAN MACIAS ORIENTATION IMMIGRANT CENTER
9766 N Canyon Blvd.
Pacoima, CA 91331
Mike S. Garcia, Executive Director
Tel: (818) 896-1156 Fax: (818) 896-1157

EL SANTO NIÑO COMMUNITY CENTER
601 E 23rd St.
Los Angeles, CA 90011
Fiona Gibson, Director
Tel: (213) 748-5246 Fax: (213) 748-9006

HOMELESS OUTREACH PROGRAM
333 S. Central Ave.
Los Angeles, CA 90013
Mike Neely, Director
Tel: (213) 621-2800 Fax: (213) 621-4119
Email: hopl@earthlinknet.net

REFORMA
Orange County Chapter
P.O. Box 4150
California State University, Pollak Library
Fullerton, CA 92834-4150
Barbara Miller, Chapter President
Tel: (714) 278-4460
Email: bmiller@fullerton.edu
Web: http://atm-info.com/reformaoc/

BUENA FE MEDIATION SERVICES
4716 Cesar Chavez Ave., Bldg B
Los Angeles, CA 90022
Nusun Mohammed, Director
Tel: (323) 260-2855 Fax: (323) 415-0804

CALIFORNIA RURAL LEGAL ASSISTANCE
Central Office
631 Howard St. #300
San Francisco, CA 94105-3907
Jose R. Padilla, Executive Director
Tel: (415) 777-2752
Web: www.crla.org

CONSUMER ACTION/ACCIÓN PRO CONSUMIDOR
717 Market St. #310
San Francisco, CA 94103
Joe Ridout, Consumer Advice Counselor
Tel: (415) 777-9648 Fax: (415) 777-5267
Email: hotline@consumer-action.org
Web: www.consumer-action.org

HERMANDAD MEXICANA LATINOAMERICANA
Affiliate of NCLR
611 W Civic Center Dr.
Santa Ana, CA 92701
Francisco Roman, President
Tel: (714) 541-0250 Fax: (714) 541-2460
Email: info@hermandadmexicana.com
Web: www.hermamdadmexicana.com

HISPANIC NATIONAL BAR ASSOCIATION
402 W. Broadway #810
San Diego, CA 92101
Yuri Calderon, Treasurer
Tel: (619) 615-6672 Fax: (619) 615-6673
Email: ycalderon@bwslaw.com
Web: www.hnba.com

HISPANIC NATIONAL BAR ASSOCIATION OF ORANGE COUNTY
P.O. Box 17777
Irvine, CA 92623-7777

Tel: (949) 440-6700 x253
Email: contact@ochba.org
Web: www.ochba.org

LEGAL AID FOUNDATION OF LOS ANGELES
Main Office
1102 S. Crenshaw Blvd.
Los Angeles, CA 90019
Bruce Iwasaki, Executive Director
Tel: (323) 801-7989 Fax: (323) 801-7921
Web: www.lafla.org

LOS ANGELES COUNTY BAR ASSOCIATION
Lawyer Referral and Information Service
P. O. Box 55020
Los Angeles, CA 90055-2020
Patricia Holt, Directing Attorney
Tel: (213) 627-2727 Fax: (213) 896-6500
Email: Iris@lacba.org
Web: www.smartlaw.org

MEXICAN AMERICAN LEGAL DEFENSE AND EDUCATIONAL FUND
National Headquarters
634 S. Spring St., 11th Fl.
Los Angeles, CA 90014
Ann Marie Tallman, President
Tel: (213) 629-2512 Fax: (213) 629-0266
Email: info@maldef.org
Web: www.maldef.org

MEXICAN-AMERICAN BAR ASSOCIATION
1301 W. 2nd St. #101
Los Angeles, CA 90026
Silvia Morgan, Administrator
Tel: (213) 481-2889 Fax: (213) 481-1273
Email: mabalaco@earthlink.net
Web: www.mabalawyers.org

PROTECCION LEGAL FEMENINA
5300 E Beverly Blvd. #D
Los Angeles, CA 90022-2187
Terry Garcia Hitomi, Director
Tel: (323) 721-9882 Fax: (323) 721-7731

EAST LOS ANGELES MENTAL HEALTH SERVICES
Affiliate of NCLR
1436 Goodrich Blvd.
City of Commerce, CA 90022
Alfredo Larios, Vice President
Tel: (323) 725-1337 Fax: (323) 278-5344
Web: http://dmh.co.la.ca.us/scripts/cervices/sa7.html

INTERCOMMUNITY CHILD GUIDANCE CENTER
8106 Broadway Ave.
Whittier, CA 90606
Charlene Dimas Peinado, Associate Director
Tel: (562) 692-0383 Fax: (562) 692-0380
Email: icgc@vfnet.com
Web: www.vfnet.com

LAMP COMMUNITY
527 S. Crocker St.
Los Angeles, CA 90013
Shannon Murray, Director
Tel: (213) 488-0031 Fax: (213) 488-4934
Web: www.lampcommunity.org

PACIFIC CLINICS
Latino Services
800 S. Santa Anita Ave.
Arcadia, CA 91006
Susan Mandel, Executive Director
Tel: (562) 942-8256 Fax: (562) 949-4807
Email: latinoservices@pacificclinics.org
Web: www.pacificclinics.org

TRI-CITY MENTAL HEALTH CENTER
Adults Services/Children's Outpatient
2008 N. Garey Ave.
Pomona, CA 91766
Luann Martenson, Ph.D., CEO
Tel: (909) 623-6131 Fax: (909) 865-9281

Email: Info@tricitymhs.org
Web: www.tricitymhs.org

TRI-CITY MENTAL HEALTH CENTER
Youth & Family Services Center
790 E. Bonita Ave.
Pomona, CA 91767
Stephany Barone, Program Manager
Tel: (909) 447-3400 Fax: (909) 447-3401
Email: Info@tricitymhs.org
Web: www.tricitymhs.org

ASSOCIATION FOR HISPANIC ELDERLY
National Headquarters/Project Ayuda
234 E. Colorado Blvd. #300
Pasadena, CA 91101
Carmela G. Lacayo, President/CEO
Tel: (626) 564-1988 Fax: (626) 564-2659
Email: support@anppm.org
Web: www.anppm.org

CASA SANTA MARIA
7551 Orangethorpe Ave.
Buena Park, CA 90621
Walter Warg, Manager
Tel: (714) 994-1404

CENTRO LATINO DE SAN FRANCISCO
Affiliate of NCLR
1655 15th St.
San Francisco, CA 94103
Gloria Bonilla, Executive Director
Tel: (415) 861-8168 Fax: (415) 861-8799
Web: www.centrolatinosf.org

GREATER EAST LOS ANGELES SENIOR CITIZENS ORGANIZATION
133 N. Sunol Dr.
Los Angeles, CA 90063
Kathy Garcia, Director
Tel: (323) 260-2801 Fax: (323) 266-6457
Email: elacsc133n@aol.com

HISPANO-AMERICANO CLUB
El Monte Senior Center
3120 N Tyler Ave.
El Monte, CA 91731
Lupe Blanco, President
Tel: (626) 580-2210 Fax: (626) 444-5056

MEXICAN AMERICAN SENIOR CITIZENS SOCIAL CLUB OF PICO RIVERA
4632 Orange St.
Pico Rivera, CA 90660
Steve Moreno, President
Tel: (562) 696-8849

NATIONAL ASSOCIATION FOR HISPANIC ELDERLY
Pasadena Office
234 E. Colorado Blvd. #300
Pasadena, CA 91101
Carmela G. Lacayo, President
Tel: (626) 564-1988 Fax: (626) 564-2659
Email: anppm@aol.com
Web: www.anppm.org

SPANISH SPEAKING SENIOR CENTER
Affiliate to Chicano Fed. of San Diego Co., Inc.
3751 Boston Ave.
San Diego, CA 92113
Peggy de la Peña, Manager
Tel: (619) 263-7785 Fax: (619) 263-7786

ACADEMY OF LATINO LEADERS IN ACTION
821 W Whittier Blvd. #200-A
Montebello, CA 90640
Marta Sámano, President
Tel: (323) 725-0640 Fax: (323) 725-7264
Email: alla@azteca.net

AGUA PARA LA VIDA
2311 Webster St.
Berkeley, CA 94705
Gilles Corcos, Director
Tel: (510) 643-8003 Fax: (510) 643-5571
Email: aplv@aplv.org
Web: www.aplv.org

BARRIOS UNIDOS
1817 Soquel Ave.
Santa Cruz, CA 95062
Nane Alejandrez, Executive Director
Tel: (831) 457-8208 Fax: (831) 457-0389
Email: nane@barriosunidos.net
Web: www.barriosunidos.net

CALIFORNIA COUNCIL FOR THE HUMANITIES
312 Sutter St. #601
San Francisco, CA 94108
Jim Quay, Executive Director
Tel: (415) 391-1474 Fax: (415) 391-1312
Email: info@calhum.org
Web: www.calhum.org

614 5th Ave. #C
San Diego, CA 92101
Amy Rouillard, Senior Program Officer
Tel: (619) 232-4020 Fax: (619) 232-4095
Email: info@calhum.org
Web: www.calhum.org

CAMPESINOS UNIDOS, INC.
P.O. Box 39
Brawley, CA 92227
José M. López, Executive Director
Tel: (760) 344-6300 Fax: (760) 344-0322
Email: cuijml@brawleyonline.com

CASA ECUADOR
1322 Longwood Ave.
Los Angeles, CA 90019
Luis Bermeo, President
Tel: (323) 934-2310

CASAL DELS CATALANS DE CALIFORNIA
P.O. Box 91142
Los Angeles, CA 90009
Carme Royg, President
Tel: (310) 374-4952 Fax: (310) 640-8847
Email: pete@balsel.com
Web: www.casalcalifornia.org

CATHOLIC CHARITIES OF ORANGE COUNTY
1800 E. McFadden
Santa Ana, CA 92705
Theresa Montminy, Executive Director/CEO
Tel: (714) 347-9600 Fax: (714) 662-1861
Email: ccocinfo@ccoc.org
Web: www.ccoc.org

CENTER FOR EMPLOYMENT TRAINING
701 Vine St.
San Jose, CA 95110
Max Martinez, Communications Director
Tel: (408) 287-7924
Email: maxm@cet2000.org
Web: www.cetweb.org

CENTRO DE ASISTENCIA SOCIAL GUATEMALTECO
1138 Wilshire Blvd. #300
Los Angeles, CA 90017
Byron Vásquez, Executive Director
Tel: (213) 250-3416 Fax: (213) 250-3705

CENTRO MARAVILLA SERVICE CENTER
4716 Cesar Chavez Ave.
Los Angeles, CA 90022
Nusun Muhammad, Director
Tel: (323) 260-2805 Fax: (323) 780-7986

CHARO COMMUNITY DEVELOPMENT CORPORATION
4301 E Valley Blvd.
Los Angeles, CA 90032
Cynthia Amador, President/CEO
Tel: (323) 269-0751 Fax: (323) 266-4326
Email: webmaster@charocorp.com
Web: www.charocorp.com

CHICANO ALUMNI ASSOCIATION
California State University, Fresno
5241 N. Maple Ave.
Fresno, CA 93740
Manuel Olgin, President
Tel: (559) 278-2999 Fax: (559) 278-9011
Email: info@chicanoalumni.com
Web: www.chicanoalumni.com

CHICANO CORRECTIONAL WORKERS ASSOCIATION
P.O. Box 3680
Visalia, CA 93278-3680
Suzanna Aguilera Marrero, President
Email: pres@ccwa.net
Web: www.ccwa.net

CHICANO CULTURAL CENTER
Bakersfield College
1801 Panorama Dr.
Bakersfield, CA 93305
Juan Gutierrez, Publication Information Specialist
Tel: (661) 395-4265

CHICANO/LATINO FACULTY & STAFF ASSOCIATION
California State University, Fullerton
P.O. Box 4150
Fullerton, CA 92834-6830
Janette L. Hyder, President
Tel: (714) 278-3920
Email: jhyder@fullerton.edu
Web: www.fullerton.edu/deanofstudents/CLFSA/

CHICANO/LATINO STUDIES STUDENTS ASSOCIATION
California State University, Long Beach
1250 Bellflower Blvd.
Long Beach, CA 90840
Dr. Victor M. Rodriguez, Chair
Tel: (562) 985-4111 Fax: (562) 985-4631
Email: vrodrig5@csulb.edu
Web: www.csulb.edu/depts/chls/

CLUB COJUMATLAN
2714 Humbert Ave.
South El Monte, CA 91733
Mr. Juan Anaya, Director
Tel: (626) 575-0149

COLOMBIA VISION
P.O. Box 18166
Anaheim, CA 92817
Alba Ramirez, President
Tel: (714) 404-2465
Email: alba@colombiavision.org
Web: www.colombiavision.org

COMITE DE BENEFICENCIA MEXICANA
2900 Calle Pedro Infante
Los Angeles, CA 90066
Marta Soriano, President
Tel: (323) 264-1428 Fax: (323) 264-4962

COMMUNITIES ACTIVELY LIVING INDEPENDENT AND FREE
849 S. Broadway, #M-100
Los Angeles, CA 90014
Lillibeth Navarro, Executive Director
Tel: (213) 627-0477 Fax: (213) 627-0535
Email: info@calif-ilc.org

CUBAN-AMERICAN ALLIANCE EDUCATION FUND
P.O. Box 5113
San Luis Obispo, CA 93403
Delvis Fernandez, Executive Director
Tel: (805) 627-1959
Email: caaef@direcway.com
Web: www.cubamer.org

EL CENTRO DE AMISTAD
6800 Owens Mouth Ave. #310
Canoga Park, CA 91303
Ed Viramontes, Executive Director
Tel: (818) 347-8565 Fax: (818) 347-0506
Email: ed.v@elcentrodeamistad.org

EL CONCILIO DEL CONDADO DE VENTURA
301 South C St.
Oxnard, CA 93030
Yvonne R. Gutierrez, Executive Director
Tel: (805) 486-9777 Fax: (805) 486-9881
Email: ygutierrez@elconcilioventura.org
Web: www.elconcilioventura.org

EL CONCILIO OF SAN MATEO COUNTY
1419 Burlingame Ave. #N
Burlingame, CA 94010
Ortensia López, Executive Director
Tel: (650) 373-1087 Fax: (650) 373-1090
Email: or10sia@aol.com
Web: www.el-concilio.com

EL CONCILIO/COUNCIL FOR SPANISH
Affiliate of NCLR
308 N. California St.
Stockton, CA 95202
Jose Rodriguez, Executive Director
Tel: (209) 547-2855 Fax: (209) 547-2870
Email: jrod@elconcilio.org
Web: www.elconcilio.org

EL PROYECTO DEL BARRIO, INC.
Affiliate of NCLR
8902 Woodman Ave.
Arleta, CA 91331
Corinne Sánchez, President/CEO
Tel: (818) 830-7133 Fax: (818) 830-7280
Email: corinnesa@aol.com

EL RESCATE
1313 W 8th St. #200
Los Angeles, CA 90017
Ricardo Mendez, Executive Director
Tel: (213) 387-3284 Fax: (213) 387-9189
Web: www.elrescate.org

EL SERENO RECREATION CENTER
4721 Klamath St.
Los Angeles, CA 90032
Santiago Cuevas, Director
Tel: (323) 225-3517 Fax: (323) 226-0946

FIESTA EDUCATIVA, INC.
3839 Selig Pl.
Los Angeles, CA 90031
Irene Martinez
Tel: (323) 221-6696 Fax: (323) 221-6699
Email: info@fiestaeducativa.org
Web: www.fiestaeducativa.org

FORMER STUDENTS AND PROFESSORS OF THE JOSE MARTI INSTITUTE IN LA HABANA
4778 N. Peck Rd.
El Monte, CA 91732
Dr. Roberto Román, President
Tel: (626) 350-3917 Fax: (626) 350-5259

HEBER PUBLIC UTILITY DISTRICT
P.O. Box H
Heber, CA 92249
John Jordan, General Manager
Tel: (760) 482-2440 Fax: (760) 353-9951

HISPANIC FOUNDATION OF SILICON VALLEY
P.O. Box 720591
San José, CA 95172
Angie Aguirre, Project Coordinator
Tel: (408) 278-2210 Fax: (408) 278-0280
Email: aguirre@hispanicfoundation-sv.org
Web: www.hispanicfoundation-sv.org

HISPANIC URBAN LEAGUE
1201 E 1st St.
Los Angeles, CA 90033
Rosie Rosales, Director
Tel: (323) 264-4494 Fax: (323) 621-0937

HISPANICS IN PHILANTHROPY
Headquarters
200 Pine St. #700
San Francisco, CA 94104
Marithe Miller, Executive Assistant
Tel: (415) 837-0427 Fax: (415) 837-1074
Email: marithe@hiponline.org
Web: www.hiponline.org

HOTEL EMPLOYEES AND RESTAURANT EMPLOYEES, INTERNATIONAL UNION
Local 11 Los Angeles
675 S. Park View St.
Los Angeles, CA 90057
María Elena Durazo, President
Tel: (213) 738-8180 Fax: (213) 758-5049
Email: local11@aol.com
Web: www.herelocal11.org

Local 19 San Jose
1415 Koll Cir. #105
San Jose, CA 95112-4615
Enrique Fernandez, Business Manager
Tel: (408) 437-1061 Fax: (408) 437-1068
Email: here19@worldnet.att.net
Web: www.hereunion.org

INSTITUTO FAMILIAR DE LA RAZA
Administrative Office
2919 Mission St.
San Francisco, CA 94110
Concepcion Salcedo, Director
Tel: (415) 229-0500 Fax: (415) 647-3662
Email: csalcedo@instituto-sf-ca.org
Web: www.instituto-sf-ca.org

INTERNATIONAL RESCUE COMMITTEE, INC.
San Diego
4535 30th St. #110
San Diego, CA 92116
Brianna Arentz, Job Developer
Tel: (619) 641-7510 X239 Fax: (619) 641-7520
Email: irc@sd.theirc.org
Web: www.theirc.org/sandiego

LA CLINICA DEL PUEBLO
1547 N Avalon Blvd.
Wilmington, CA 90744
Patricia Powell, Executive Director
Tel: (310) 830-0100 Fax: (310) 830-0187

LA RAZA COMMUNITY RESOURCE CENTER
474 Valencia St. #100
San Francisco, CA 94103
Melba Maldonado, Executive Director
Tel: (415) 863-0764 Fax: (415) 863-1690
Email: info@larazacrc.com
Web: www.larazacrc.org

LA VOZ LIBRE - THE FREE VOICE SPANISH NEWSPAPER
P.O. Box 20599
Los Angeles, CA 90006
Angel Prada, President
Tel: (213) 388-4639 Fax: (213) 388-2053
Email: amprada@pacbell.net

LAS FAMILIAS
307 E 7th St.
Los Angeles, CA 90014
Alice Calaghan, Director
Tel: (213) 614-1745 Fax: (213) 614-2046

LATINO COMMUNITY FOUNDATION
225 Bush St. #500
San Francisco, CA 94104
Marcela Medina, Chair
Tel: (415) 733-8591 Fax: (415) 981-8422
Email: info@latinocf.org
Web: www.latinocf.org

LATINO RESOURCE ORGANIZATION
610 California Ave.
Venice, CA 90291
Joseph Soto, Executive Director
Tel: (310) 578-6069 Fax: (310) 578-0490
Email: latinoresource@msn.com

LIGA DE ASISTENCIA CUBANA
1824 W Sunset Blvd. #202
Los Angeles, CA 90026-6503
Abel Pérez, President
Tel: (213) 483-4890 Fax: (213) 483-6474
Email: mayo20@aol.com
Web: www.20demayo.org

LOS ANGELES MOTHERS AGAINST DRUNK DRIVING
P.O. Box 451217
5757 W. Century Blvd. #615
Westchester, CA 90045
Jan St. Michel, President
Tel: (310) 215-2905 Fax: (310) 215-2908
Email: info@maddlosangeles.org
Web: www.maddlosangeles.org

MADRES DEL ESTE DE LOS ANGELES - SANTA ISABEL
924 S Mott St.
Los Angeles, CA 90023-1412
Juana B. Gutiérrez, President
Tel: (323) 263-8191

MEXICAN AMERICAN COMMUNITY SERVICES AGENCY, INC.
130 N. Jackson Ave.
San Jose, CA 95116
Olivia Soza Mendiola, CEO
Tel: (408) 928-1122
Email: olivia@macsa.org
Web: www.macsa.org

MEXICAN AMERICAN OPPORTUNITY FOUNDATION
Headquarters
401 N. Garfield Ave.
Montebello, CA 90640
Martin Castro, President/CEO
Tel: (323) 890-9600 Fax: (323) 890-9632
Email: maofinfo@maof.org
Web: www.maof.org

NATIONAL CENTER FOR MISSING & EXPLOITED CHILDREN
California
18111 Irvine Blvd. #C
Tustin, CA 92780-3403
Shirley Goins, Director
Tel: (714) 508-0150 Fax: (714) 508-0154
Email: sgoins@ncmec.org
Web: www.missingkids.com

NATIONAL COUNCIL OF LA RAZA
Los Angeles Office
523 W. 6th St. #801
Los Angeles, CA 90014
Monica Lozano, Chair
Tel: (213) 489-3428 Fax: (213) 489-1167
Web: www.nclr.org

OCCIDENTAL COLLEGE LATINO ALUMNI ASSOCIATION
Occidental College
1600 Campus Rd.
Los Angeles, CA 90041-3314
Patty Salgado, President
Tel: (323) 724-9770
Email: patty2deesee@aol.com
Web: www.oclaa.org

SAINT FRANCIS CENTER
1835 S. Hope St
Los Angeles, CA 90015
Christine Carley, Director of Community Partnerships
Tel: (213) 747-5347 Fax: (213) 765-8915
Email: ccarley@stfranciscenterla.org
Web: www.stfranciscenterla.org

SALVADORAN-AMERICAN LEADERSHIP AND EDUCATIONAL FUND
1625 W. Olympic Blvd. #718
Los Angeles, CA 90015
Carlos H. Vaquerano, Executive Director
Tel: (213) 480-1052 Fax: (213) 487-2530
Email: chvaquerano@salef.org
Web: www.salef.org

SAN DIEGO COUNTY LATINO ASSOCIATION
P.O. Box 12104
San Diego, CA 92112-3104
Gustavo Godoy, President
Tel: (858) 694-3029
Email: gustavo.godoy@sdcounty.ca.gov
Web: www.sdcla.com

SANTA ROSA COMMUNITY CENTER
Loaves and Fishes III
511 Kalisher St.
San Fernando, CA 91340
Gabriel Hernandez, Director
Tel: (818) 365-3194 Fax: (818) 365-4645

SHARE FOUNDATION
National Office
598 Bosworth St. #1
San Francisco, CA 94131
José Artiga, Executive Director
Tel: (415) 239-2595 Fax: (415) 239-0785
Email: sharesf@share-elsalvador.org
Web: www.share-elsalvador.org

SOUTHWEST MINORITY ECONOMIC DEVELOPMENT ASSOCIATION
1601 W. 2nd St.
Santa Ana, CA 92703
John Collins, President
Tel: (714) 547-4073 Fax: (714) 543-8933
Email: smeda@aol.com

THE SPANISH SPEAKING UNITY COUNCIL OF ALAMEDA COUNTY
1900 Fruitvale Ave. #2A
Oakland, CA
Arabella Martinez, CEO
Tel: (510) 535-6900 Fax: (510) 534-7771
Web: www.unitycouncil.org

TASK FORCE ON MINORITY ALUMNI RELATIONS
Stanford University
Frances C. Arrillaga Alumni Center, 326 Galvez St.
Stanford, CA 94305-6105
Charles J. Ogletree, Jr., Chair
Tel: (650) 736-8140 Fax: (650) 725-8676
Email: minoritytaskforce@stanford.edu
Web: http://minoritytaskforce.stanford.edu/index.shtml

UNIDAD ESPAÑOLA LA PEÑA
150 N Willow Ave.
City of Industry, CA 91746
José Mazaira, President
Tel: (626) 961-9800 Fax: (626) 961-8530

UNIFICATION OF DISABLED LATIN AMERICANS
3727 W. 6th St. #511
Los Angeles, CA 90020
Rubén B. Hernández, President & Founder
Tel: (213) 388-8352 Fax: (213) 388-3802
Email: udla10@aol.com
Web: www.udlaonline.org

UNITED FARM WORKERS
National Farm Workers Service Center, Inc.
634 S. Spring St. #400
Los Angeles, CA 90014
Paul F. Chavez, President/Chairman
Tel: (213) 362-0260 Fax: (213) 362-0265
Email: hed@nfwscmail.com
Web: www.ufw.org

UNITED FARM WORKERS
Political Legislative Office
5313 E. Beverly Blvd.
Los Angeles, CA 90022
Christine Chavez-Delgado, CA political Director
Tel: (323) 722-0118 Fax: (323) 722-8263
Email: ufwofamer@aol.com
Web: www.ufw.org

UNITED FARM WORKERS OF AMERICA
National Headquarters
P.O. Box 62
Keene, CA 93531
Arturo S. Rodriguez, President
Tel: (661) 822-5571 X105 Fax: (661) 822-6103
Email: execoffice@ufwmail.com
Web: www.ufw.org

THE UNITY COUNCIL
3411 E. 12th St. #200
Oakland, CA 94601

Arabella Martinez, CEO
Tel: (510) 535-6900 Fax: (510) 534-3894
Email: info@unitycouncil.org
Web: www.unitycouncil.org

VISIÓN UNIDA
P.O. Box 15856
San Luis Obispo, CA 93406-5856
Gil Apodaca, President
Tel: (805) 546-2633
Email: info@visionunidaslo.org
Web: www.visionunidaslo.org

VOLUNTEERS FOR INTER-AMERICAN DEVELOPMENT ASSISTANCE
6251 Hollis St.
Emeryville, CA 94608
Peter Smith Klemens, Managing Director
Tel: (510) 655-8432 Fax: (510) 655-8281
Email: info@vidausa.org
Web: www.vidausa.org

WATTS CENTURY LATINO ORGANIZATION
10360 Wilmington Ave.
Los Angeles, CA 90002
Arturo Ybarra, President
Tel: (323) 564-9140 Fax: (323) 564-2737
Email: wclo@sbcglobal.net

AMATEUR ATHLETIC FOUNDATION OF LOS ANGELES
2141 W. Adams Blvd.
Los Angeles, CA 90018
Anita L. DeFrantz, President
Tel: (323) 730-4600 Fax: (323) 730-9637
Email: info@aafla.org
Web: www.aafla.org

MEXICAN AMERICAN BOWLING ORGANIZATION
8309 Honeycomb Way
Sacramento, CA 95828-6657
Tel: (888) 682-8362 Fax: (916) 688-4681
Email: info@mambo.org
Web: www.mambo.org

CENTRAL CITY EAST BOYLE HEIGHTS LIONS CLUB
4249 Abbott Rd.
Lynwood, CA 90262
Louis Garcia, President
Tel: (323) 569-6149 Fax: (323) 569-6149
Email: guapamusic@aol.com

COMMUNITY SERVICE OFFICE
Los Angeles Harbor College
1111 Figueroa Pl.
Wilmington, CA 90744
Carla Mussa-Muldoon, Director
Tel: (310) 233-4251 Fax: (310) 233-4686
Web: www.lahc.edu

UNITED LATINO FUND
315 W. 9th St. #709
Los Angeles, CA 90015
Tel: (213) 236-2929 Fax: (213) 236-2930
Email: info@unitedlatinofund.us
Web: www.unitedlatinofund.us

ASOCIACIÓN INTERNACIONAL DE MUJERES SALVADOREÑAS
501 W Whittier Blvd.
Montebello, CA 90640
Anita Jobian, Vice President
Tel: (323) 728-6655 Fax: (323) 728-2338
Email: aimsa@aimsausa.org
Web: www.aimsausa.org

CHICANA SERVICE ACTION CENTER, INC.
P.O. Box 23309

Los Angeles, CA 90023
Alicia Reyes, Coordinator
Tel: (323) 268-7564 Fax: (213) 430-0658
Email: alicia.reyes@lacsac.com

CHICANA SERVICE ACTION CENTER, INC.
Corporate and Administrative Offices
315 W. 9th St. #101
Los Angeles, CA 90015
Sophia Esparza, Executive Director
Tel: (213) 629-5800 Fax: (213) 430-0658
Email: bernice.rubio@lacsac.com

Downtown One-Stop Workforce Employment and Training
315 W. 9th St. #101
Los Angeles, CA 90015
Sophia Esparza, Director
Tel: (213) 629-5800 Fax: (213) 430-0657

CHICANA SERVICE ACTION CENTER, INC.
Pomona Employment and Education Center
630 N. Park Ave.
Pomona, CA 91768
Sophia Esparza, Executive Director
Tel: (909) 620-0383 Fax: (909) 629-3171

CHICANA SERVICE ACTION CENTER, INC.
Youth Comprehensive Training Centers
315 W. 9th St. #101
Los Angeles, CA 90015
Sophia Esparza, Executive Director
Tel: (213) 629-5800 Fax: (213) 430-0658

CHICANA/LATINA FOUNDATION
1419 Burlingame Ave. #N
Burlingame, CA 94010
Olga Talamante, Executive Director
Tel: (650) 373-1083 Fax: (650) 373-1090
Email: info@chicanalatina.org
Web: www.chicanalatina.org

CHICANA/LATINA RESEARCH CENTER
University of California, Davis
Social Sciences and Humanities #2223, 1 Shields Ave.
Davis, CA 95616-8706
Ines Hernandez-Avila, Director
Tel: (530) 752-8882 Fax: (530) 754-8622
Email: clrc@ucdavis.edu
Web: www.ucdavis.edu

COMISIÓN FEMENIL MEXICANA NACIONAL
New Economics for Women
303 S. Loma Dr.
Los Angeles, CA 90017
Maggie Cervantes, Executive Director
Tel: (213) 483-2060 Fax: (213) 483-7848
Email: info@neweconomicsforwomen.org
Web: www.neweconomicsforwomen.org

COMMUNITY MOTHERS CLUB
Neighborhood Center
9255 Pioneer Blvd.
Santa Fe Springs, CA 90670
Angelina Lopez, President
Tel: (562) 692-0261 Fax: (562) 695-8620

DOLORES MISSION WOMEN'S COOPERATIVE CHILD CARE CENTER
Proyecto Pastoral at Dolores Mission
157 S. Gless St.
Los Angeles, CA 90033
Lorraine Gutierrez, Director
Tel: (323) 881-0011
Email: dmwc@proyectopastoral.org
Web: www.proyectopastoral.org

HISPANAS ORGANIZED FOR POLITICAL EQUALITY
634 S. Spring St. #920
Los Angeles, CA 90014
Helen I. Torres, Executive Director
Tel: (213) 622-0606
Email: latinas@latinas.org
Web: www.latinas.org

LA CASA DE LAS MADRES
1850 Mission St. #B

San Francisco, CA 94103
Kathy Black, Executive Director
Tel: (415) 503-0500
Email: info@lacasa.org
Web: www.lacasa.org

LATINA ASSOCIATION, INC.
P.O. Box 550
San Diego, CA 92112
Fanny Miller, President
Tel: (619) 426-1491 Fax: (619) 426-3206
Email: fanny@ellatino.net

LATINA HEALTH ORGANIZATION
P.O. Box 7567
Oakland, CA 94601
Luz Alvarez Martinez, Executive Director
Tel: (510) 534-1362 Fax: (510) 534-1364
Email: questions@latinahealth.org
Web: www.latinahealth.org

LOS ANGELES BUSINESS WOMEN TRADE
501 W. Whittier Blvd.
Monte Bello, CA 90640
Anita Jobian, Vice President
Tel: (323) 728-6655 Fax: (323) 728-2338
Email: info@labwtexpo.com
Web: www.labwtexpo.com

MANA- A NATIONAL LATINA ORGANIZATION
Sonoma County Chapter
P.O. Box 2845
Santa Rosa, CA 95405
Laura Martell, Chapter President
Tel: (707) 641-7211 Fax: (707) 641-7055
Email: lem@sonic.net
Web: www.hermana.org

Imperial Valley Chapter
P.O.Box 73
El Centro, CA 92244
Linda Valenzuela, Chapter President
Tel: (760) 353-2840 Fax: (760) 353-3613
Email: lvalenzuela@girlscoutssdi.org
Web: www.hermana.org

Orange County Chapter
P.O. Box 4081
Santa Ana, CA 92702-4081
Lucy Santana, Chapter President
Tel: (714) 563-6262
Email: manadeorangecounty@earthlink.net

San Diego Chapter
P.O. Box 81364
San Diego, CA 92138-1364
Melody Vela, Chapter President
Tel: (619) 225-9594 Fax: (619) 225-0500
Email: sdmanaprez@sbcglobal.net
Web: www.sdmana.org

MARGARET CRUZ LATINA BREAST CANCER FOUNDATION
7 Joost Ave. #101
San Francisco, CA 94131
Olivia Fe, Executive Director
Tel: (415) 584-3444 Fax: (415) 584-3455
Email: latinabca@hotmail.com
Web: www.latinabca.org

MISS LATIN WORLD BEAUTY PAGEANT
P.O. Box 65766
Los Angeles, CA 90065-0766
César C. Cantú, President
Tel: (323) 221-6800

NATIONAL LATINA ALLIANCE
633 W. 5th St. #1150
Los Angeles, CA 90071
Angela Weimer, President
Tel: (323) 980-7992
Email: info@nationallatinaalliance.org
Web: www.nationallatinaalliance.org

BARRIO STATION
2175 Newton Ave.

San Diego, CA 92113
Rachel Ortiz, Executive Director
Tel: (619) 238-0314 Fax: (619) 238-0331
Email: oortiz@barriostation.sdcoxmail.com
Web: www.barrio-station.org

BIENVENIDOS FOSTER FAMILY AGENCY
421 S Glendora Ave.
West Covina, CA 91790
Brian Fernandez, Program Director
Tel: (626) 919-3579 Fax: (626) 919-2660
Email: ffa@bienvenidos.org
Web: www.bienvenidos.org

BIG BROTHERS BIG SISTERS
San Luis Obispo County
880 Industrial Way
San Luis Obispo, CA 93401
J.J. Lynch, Recruiting Coordinator
Tel: (805) 781-3226 Fax: (805) 781-3029
Email: info@slobigs.org
Web: www.slobigs.org

CASA LIBRE- FREEDOM HOUSE
845 S. Lake St.
Los Angeles, CA 90057
Peter A. Schey, Executive Director
Tel: (213) 637-5814
Email: pschey@centerforhumanrights.org
Web: www.casa-libre.org/

CASA YOUTH SHELTER
P.O. Box 216
Los Alamitos, CA 90720
Luciann Maulhardt, Executive Director
Tel: (562) 594-6825 Fax: (562) 594-9185
Email: agency@casayouthshelter.org
Web: www.casayouthshelter.org

CHICANO LATINO YOUTH LEADERSHIP PROJECT, INC.
P.O. Box 16566
Sacramento, CA 95816
Tel: (916) 446-1640 Fax: (916) 446-2899
Email: contactus@clylp.com
Web: www.clylp.com

THE CHILDREN'S COLLECTIVE, INC.
5870 W. Jefferson Blvd. Unit C
Los Angeles, CA 90016
Jackie Kimbrough, Director
Tel: (310) 733-4388 Fax: (310) 733-4320
Email: info@childrenscollective.org
Web: www.childrenscollective.org

CLUB DE DAMAS ORQUIDEAS COSTARRICENSES
6449 Triton Dr.
Pico Rivera, CA 90660
Nelly Orona, Founder
Tel: (562) 949-6868
Email: ronel145@aol.com

DANGERMAN EDUCATION FOUNDATION INC.
11684 Ventura Blvd. #368
Studio City, CA 91604
Roger Tinsley, President
Tel: (818) 752-3952 Fax: (818) 752-7145
Email: superhero@thedangerman.com
Web: www.thedangerman.com

EAST LOS ANGELES BOYS AND GIRLS CLUB
324 N. McDonnell Ave.
Los Angeles, CA 90022
Anna Araujo, Executive Director
Tel: (323) 263-4955 Fax: (323) 263-6814
Email: elabgc@aol.com
Web: www.elabgc.org

FUTURE LEADERS OF AMERICA INC.
2021 Sperry Ave. #11
Ventura, CA 93003
Christopher Martinez, Executive Director
Tel: (805) 642-6208 Fax: (805) 642-6483
Email: flainfo@latinoleaders.org
Web: www.latinoleaders.org

THE GARY CENTER
341 Hillcrest St.

La Habra, CA 90631
Martha Lester, Executive Director
Tel: (562) 691-3263 Fax: (562) 690-5063
Email: gary@garycenter.org
Web: www.garycenter.org

GRUPO JUVENIL FUERZA NUEVA
407 S Chicago St.
Los Angeles, CA 90033
Ricardo Garcia, Youth Minister
Tel: (323) 268-7432 Fax: (323) 268-8076

HOLLENBECK YOUTH CENTER
Administrative Office
2015 E 1st St.
Los Angeles, CA 90033
Danny Hernandez, Executive Director
Tel: (323) 881-6562 Fax: (323) 415-6898
Email: hollenbeckpbc@yahoo.com
Web: www.hollenbeckyouthcenter.org

IMPACTO LEADERSHIP CHALLENGE
Proyecto Pastoral at Dolores Mission/ Elementary Site
1401 E. 1st St.
Los Angeles, CA 90033
Angelica Solis, Director
Tel: (323) 269-7552
Email: asolis@proyectopastoral.org
Web: www.proyectopastoral.org

JOVENES, INC.
1208 Pleasant Ave.
Los Angeles, CA 90033
Richard Estrada, Executive Director
Tel: (323) 260-8035 Fax: (323) 260-8046
Email: jovenesinc@aol.com

KEDREN HEAD START
710 E.111th Pl.
Los Angeles, CA 90059
Robert Owens, Director
Tel: (323) 299-9742 Fax: (323) 777-6208

LOS ANGELES BOYS AND GIRLS CLUB
2635 Pasadena Ave.
Los Angeles, CA 90031
June Aiello, Executive Director
Tel: (323) 221-9111 Fax: (213) 223-9846
Web: www.labgc.org

LOS ANGELES TIMES SUMMER CAMP FUND
202 W. First St.
Los Angeles, CA 90012
Raul Bustillos, Grants Director
Tel: (213) 237-5763 Fax: (213) 237-4609
Email: raul.bustillos@latimes.com
Web: www.latimes.com/extras/summercamp

LOS NIÑOS
287 G St.
Chula Vista, CA 91910
Elisa Sabatini, Executive Director
Tel: (619) 426-9110 Fax: (619) 426-6664
Email: info@losninosinternational.org
Web: www.losninosinternational.org

LATINO/A COLLEGE LEADERSHIP INSTITUTE
1055 Wilshire Blvd. #1615
Los Angeles, CA 90017
Sergio Marin, Institute Coordinator
Tel: (213) 250-8787 Fax: (213) 250-8799
Email: losangeles@nccj.org
Web: www.nccjla.org

NUEVO AMANECER LATINO CHILDREN SERVICES
5400 Pomona Blvd.
Los Angeles, CA 90022
Norma Duque Acosta, President/CEO
Tel: (323) 720-9951 Fax: (323) 720-9953
Email: nalffa@aol.com

PARA LOS NIÑOS
845 E 6th St.
Los Angeles, CA 90021
Miki Jordan, President/CEO
Tel: (213) 623-8446 Fax: (213) 623-8716
Web: www.paralosninos.org

SALESIAN BOYS AND GIRLS CLUB OF LOS ANGELES
3218 Wabash Ave.
Los Angeles, CA 90063
Bill Schafer, Executive Director
Tel: (323) 263-7519 Fax: (323) 263-8558
Email: bscfaser@salesianclub.la.org

SALINAS BARRIOS UNIDOS
P.O. Box 9441
Salinas, CA 93915
Tel: (831) 751-9054 Fax: (831) 751-9011
Email: info@barriosunidos.org
Web: www.barriosunidos.org

SOCIEDAD PRO NIÑOS SALVADOREÑOS
850 N. Hobart Blvd.
Los Angeles, CA 90029
Gelma Castro, President
Tel: (323) 665-6937 Fax: (323) 664-0754

VARIETY BOYS AND GIRLS CLUB
2530 Cincinnati St.
East Los Angeles, CA 90033
Judy Zdravje, Executive Director
Tel: (323) 269-3177 Fax: (323) 269-3268
Email: judyzdrvje@hotmail.com
Web: www.vbgc.org

YOUNG LATINO LEADERS
2600 Middlefield Rd.
Redwood City, CA 94063
Paul Vega, Executive Director
Tel: (650) 780-7522 Fax: (650) 298-8184
Email: paulvega@sbcglobal.net
Web: www.younglatinoleaders.org

YOUTH OPPORTUNITIES UNLIMITED
8419 S. Vermont Ave.
Los Angeles, CA 90044
James L. Watson, Director
Tel: (323) 789-4977 Fax: (323) 789-4975
Email: youinc@pacbell.net

ARGENTINOS EN STANFORD
Stanford University Office of Student Activities
Tresidder Memorial Union 459 Lagunita Dr. #9
Stanford, CA 94305
Ernesto Staroswiecki, President
Tel: (650) 723-2300
Email: ernestos@stanford.edu
Web: http://argentina.stanford.edu

BALLET FOLKLÓRICO AT UCR
UC Riverside
094 Costo Hall
Riverside, CA 92521
Jennifer Sandoval, Director
Tel: (951) 827-1012
Email: sandoval_jennifer@hotmail.com
Web: www.students.ucr.edu

BALLET FOLKLORICO DE STANFORD
Stanford University
El Centro Chicano, The Nitery #590F, Old Union
Stanford, CA 94305
Simon Escobedo, Co-Chair
Tel: (650) 723-2089
Web: www.stanford.edu/group/folklorico

BARRIO ASSISTANCE
Stanford University
El Centro Chicano, Bldg. 590-F, Old Union
Stanford, CA 94305
Angelica Amador, Coordinator
Tel: (650) 723-2089
Email: aamador@stanford.edu
Web: www.stanford.edu/group/ba

BARRIO YOUTH ALTERNATIVES
University of California, Los Angeles
220 Westwood Blvd. #105
Los Angeles, CA 90024
Daisy D. Alfaro, Director
Tel: (310) 825-5969 Fax: (310) 206-3175
Email: bayaucla@yahoo.com

BERKELEY LA RAZA LAW JOURNAL
Boalt Hall School of Law, University of California
858 Simon Hall
Berkeley, CA 94720
Daniel Castro, Editor in Chief
Tel: (510) 642-9351 Fax: (510) 643-6171
Email: larazajournal@law.berkeley.edu
Web: www.boalt.org/LRLJ/

BRAZILIAN STUDENT ASSOCIATION
Stanford University
Student Affairs Office
Redwood City, CA 94062
Hector Chang, Financial Officer
Tel: (650) 723-3542 Student Affair's Office
Email: hc10@stanford.edu
Web: www.stanford.edu/group/brazil

CALIFORNIA CHICANO AND LATINO MEDICAL STUDENTS ASSOCIATION
David Geffen School of Medicine at UCLA
Office of Academic Enrichment, 13-154 CHS
Los Angeles, CA 90095-6990
Joel Ramirez, Co-Chair
Tel: (310) 794-9574
Web: www.medstudent.ucla.edu/cmsa

CHICANO & LATINO ENGINEERS AND SCIENTISTS SOCIETY
University of California, Davis
Student Programs & Activities Ctr., 1 Shields Ave.
Davis, CA 95616-8706
Angelina Padilla, President
Tel: (530) 752-2027
Email: angpadilla@ucdavis.edu
Web: http://engineering.ucdavis.edu/

CHICANO LATINO LAW REVIEW
University of California, Los Angeles
UCLA School of Law, Box 951476
Los Angeles, CA 90095
Scott Carter, Advisor
Tel: (310) 825-2894
Email: cllr@lawnet.ucla.net

CHICANOS FOR CREATIVE MEDICINE
University of California, Irvine
11805 Mollyknoll Ave.
Whittier, CA 90604
Abraham Palomares, President
Tel: (562) 587-6593
Email: uciccm@hotmail.com
Web: www.uci.edu

CHICANOS IN LAW
California State University, Fresno
5150 N. Maple Ave., M/S JA62
Fresno, CA 93740-8026
Tony Garduque, Advisor
Tel: (559) 278-5351 Fax: (559) 278-2323
Email: tonyg@csufresno.edu
Web: www.csufresno.edu

CHICANOS-LATINOS IN HEALTH EDUCATION
University of California, Davis
Student Programs & Activities Center,
1 Shields Ave.
Davis, CA 95616-8706
Manuel Tapia, President
Tel: (530) 752-2027 Fax: (530) 752-4951
Email: mtapia@ucdavis.edu
Web: www.ucdavis.edu

CHICANOS/LATINOS FOR COMMUNITY MEDICINE
California State University, Long Beach
1212 Bellflower Blvd.
Long Beach, CA 90815
Brian Sandoval, President
Tel: (562) 985-4181
Email: bsandov2@csulb.edu
Web: www.csulb.edu/org/clcm/

EL CENTRO CHICANO
Stanford University
Old Union, Bldg. F-590
Stanford, CA 94305-3044
Dr. Frances Morales, Assistant Dean/Director
Tel: (650) 723-2089 Fax: (650) 725-6487
Email: fmorales@stanford.edu
Web: www.stanford.edu/dept/elcentro/main.html

EL CENTRO LEGAL
University of California, Los Angeles
UCLA School of Law #2243
Los Angeles, CA 90095
Mike Kockler, Advisor
Tel: (310) 825-4891
Email: elcentro@lawnet.ucla.edu

EXTENDED OPPORTUNITY PROGRAMS AND SERVICES
Santa Ana College
SAC U-101 Johnson Center
Santa Ana, CA 92706
Irma Archuleta, Director
Tel: (714) 564-6232 Fax: (714) 564-6239
Email: saceops@sac.edu
Web: www.sac.edu

HERMANAS UNIDAS DE CSUF
California State University, Fullerton
TSU-246, Mailbox 18
Fullerton, CA 92834
Maria Escobar, Co-Chair
Tel: (714) 458-4847
Email: futuredrmariaescobar@hotmail.com

HISPANIC BUSINESS STUDENT ASSOCIATION
California State University, Fresno
5141 N. Cedar #201
Fresno, CA 93710
Alicia Gonzales, President
Tel: (559) 916-3343
Email: amgonzales@csufresno.edu
Web: www.hbsa.net

HISPANIC BUSINESS STUDENT ASSOCIATION
San Diego State University
5500 Campanile Dr. BA336
San Diego, CA 92182-7748
Gabriela Magana, President
Email: hbsa1@hotmail.com
Web: www.hbsa.sdsu.edu

HISPANIC STUDENT BUSINESS ASSOCIATION
California State University, Long Beach
P.O. Box 15947
Long Beach, CA 90815
Kali Merideth, President
Tel: (562) 985-7630
Email: csulbhsba@yahoo.com
Web: www.csulb.edu/hsba

INTERNATIONAL STUDENTS ASSOCIATION
Santa Barbara City College
721 Cliff Dr.
Santa Barbara, CA 93109
Frederico Peinado, Advisor
Tel: (805) 965-0581 X2489 Fax: (805) 965-0781
Email: peinado@sbcc.edu
Web: www.sbcc.edu

LA RAZA LAW STUDENT ASSOCIATION
University of California, Los Angeles
3222 Law Bldg.
Los Angeles, CA 90095-1476
Gladdys Uribe, President
Tel: (310) 206-5158
Email: laraza@lawnet.ucla.edu

LA RAZA STUDENT ASSOCIATION
California State University
University Student Union #206
1250 Bellflower Blvd.
Long Beach, CA 90840-0604
Anna Nazarian, Advisor
Tel: (562) 985-4181
Web: www.csulb.edu/web/org/studentlife/index.html

LA UNION ESTUDIANTIL DE LA RAZA
UC Riverside Chicano Student Program
177 Costo Hall
Riverside, CA 92521
Gabriel Mendoza, Advisor
Tel: (951) 827-1012
Email: Gabriel.Mendoza@ucr.edu
Web: www.uer-inc.com

LATIN AMERICAN DENTAL ASSOCIATION
University of California, Los Angeles
10833 Le Conte Ave.
Los Angeles, CA 90024
Iris Kesara Han, President
Tel: (310) 794-7971
Email: lilmissiris@yahoo.com

LATIN AMERICAN STUDENT ASSOCIATION
University of California, Los Angeles
308 Westwood Plz., Kerckhoff Hall 146
Los Angeles, CA 90024
Tony Gutierrez, President
Tel: (310) 206-2631
Email: lasa@ucla.edu
Web: www.bol.ucla.edu/~lasa/

LATINA LEADERSHIP NETWORK
Gavilan College
5055 Santa Teresa Blvd.
Gilroy, CA 95020
Celia S. Marquez, Advisor
Tel: (408) 848-4777
Email: cmarquez@gavilan.edu

LATINIC SOCIETAS UNITAS
UC Riverside, Chicano Students Program
145 Costo Hall
Riverside, CA 92521
Rosa Maria Mesa, President
Tel: (951) 827-1012
Email: rosa.mesa@email.ucr.edu
Web: www.lsu1992.com

LATINO BUSINESS ASSOCIATION
California State University, Northridge
College of Business, Administration and Economics, 18111 Nordhoff St.
Northridge, CA 91330-8245
Rosie Licea, President
Tel: (818) 386-5907
Email: president@csunlba.org
Web: www.csunlba.org

LATINO BUSINESS STUDENT ASSOCIATION
Loyola Marymount University
1 LMU Dr.
Los Angeles, CA 90045
Jonathan D. Gomez, Co-President
Tel: (310) 338-5808
Email: lbsa@lion.lmu.edu
Web: http://aslmu.lmu.edu/lbsa/Home.html

UC Riverside
008 Costo Hall
Riverside, CA 92521
Guillermo Trobado
Tel: (714) 342-5122
Email: guillermo.trabado@email.ucr.edu
Web: www.careers.ucr.edu/lbsa

University of California, Los Angeles
Box 951573
Los Angeles, CA 90095-1573
Mike Cohn, Advisor
Tel: (310) 206-1932
Email: uclalbsa@yahoogroups.com
Web: www.uclalbsa.com

Cal State Polytechnic University, Pomona
3801 W. Temple Ave.
Pomona, CA 91768
Hector Campos, President
Tel: (909) 869-4672
Email: hcampos@lbsapomona.com
Web: http://lbsapomona.com/CMS/index.php

LATINO CENTER
Santa Monica College
1900 Pico Blvd.
Santa Monica, CA 90405
Maria Martinez, Coordinator
Tel: (310) 434-4452 Fax: (310) 434-4324
Web: www.smc.edu/latino

LATINO MEDICAL STUDENT ASSOCIATION
David Geffen School of Medicine at UCLA
Office of Acadmeic Enrichment, 13-154 CHS
Los Angeles, CA 90095-6990
Katherine Revoredo, Co-Chairman
Tel: (310) 794-9574
Web: www.medstudent.ucla.edu/cmsa

University of California, San Francisco
Student Activity Ctr., 500 Parnassus Ave. Box 0376
San Francisco, CA 94143-0376
Rocio Medina, President
Tel: (415) 260-0405
Email: rmedina@itsa.ucsf.edu

LATINO PARENTS ASSOCIATION
USC El Centro Chicano
817 W 34th St., 3rd Fl.
Los Angeles, CA 90089-2991
Adriana Pulido, Coordinator
Tel: (213) 740-1480 Fax: (213) 745-6721
Web: www.usc.edu/student-affairs/elcentro

LATINO STUDENTS ASSOCIATION
Citrus Community College
1000 W. Foothill Blvd.
Glendora, CA 91741-1899
Ricardo, President
Tel: (626) 914-8610

LATINOS IN SCIENCE
UC Riverside Chicano Student Programs
023 Costo Hall
Riverside, CA 92521
Claudia Rico, Director
Tel: (951) 827-1012
Email: crico001@student.ucr.edu
Web: www.students.ucr.edu

LATINOS IN TECHNICAL CAREERS
California State University, Chico
400 W. 1st St.
Chico, CA 95929
Eduardo Espinoza, President
Email: ltc_president@yahoo.com
Web: www.csuchico.edu/ltc

LATINOS UNIDOS
College of San Mateo
1700 W. Hillsdale Blvd.
San Mateo, CA 94402
Karina Orocio, President
Tel: (650) 574-6161 Fax: (650) 574-6167

LOS HERMANOS DE STANFORD
Stanford University
El Centro Chicano, Bldg. #590F, Old Union
Stanford, CA 94305
Raymond Belarmino, President
Tel: (650) 723-2089
Web: www.stanford.edu/group/hermanos

LOS INGENIEROS
UC Santa Barbara
College of Engineering
Santa Barbara, CA 93106
Aaron Ramirez, Co-Chair
Tel: (805) 893-4512
Email: aramirez@umail.ucsb.edu
Web: www.engineering.ucsb.edu/~li2000/

MINI-CORPS
Stanislaus University
510 Bercut Dr. #Q
Sacramento, CA 95814
Fernando Peña, Coordinator
Tel: (209) 667-3259 Fax: (209) 667-3333
Email: fpena@ben.bcoe.butte.k12.ca.us
Web: www.csustan.edu/teachered/minicorps

MOVIMIENTO ESTUDIANTIL CHICANO DE AZTLAN
California State University Hayward
25800 Carlos Bee Blvd.
Hayward, CA 94542-3056
Norma Gugierrez, Co-Chair
Tel: (510) 885-3657
Email: mecha@csuhayward.edu
Web: www.csuhayward.edu/studorgs/Mecha/index.html

California State University, San Marcos
Office of Student Activities, Craven Hall, #4116
San Marcos, CA 92096
Irene Gomez, President
Tel: (760) 750-4970
Email: gomez031@csusm.edu
Web: http://public.csusm.edu/student_orgs/mecha/

Chapman University
1 University Dr.
Orange, CA 92866
Cruz Ruiz, President
Tel: (714) 997-6761 Fax: (714) 744-7021
Email: salce100@chapman.edu
Web: www.chapman.edu/lead/clubsorgs/ethnic/

Citrus Community College
1000 W. Foothill Blvd.
Glendora, CA 91741-1899
Nancy Acevedo, President
Tel: (626) 914-8610
Web:

San Diego City College
D106 1313 Park Blvd.
San Diego, CA 92101
Monica Larragoitia, President
Tel: (619) 388-3695

San Joaquin Delta Community College
5151 Pacific Ave.
Stockton, CA 95207
Mario Moreno, Advisor
Tel: (209) 954-5566

San Jose State University
1 Washington Sq., Box 64
San José, CA 95192-0038
Alejandro Ramirez, Co-Chair
Tel: (408) 705-0676
Email: raidersbondo@aol.com

University of California, Davis
Student Programs & Activities Center, Box #177
1 Shields Ave.
Davis, CA 95616-8706
Elizabeth Paniagua, President
Tel: (530) 752-2027
Email: ePaniagua@ucdavis.edu
Web: www.ucdavis.edu

University of California, Los Angeles
407 Kerckhoff Hall, 308 Westwood Plz.
Los Angeles, CA 90024
nicolas Patino, President
Tel: (323) 343-3000
Email: mechadeucla@yahoo.com

University of California, Riverside
229 Costo Hall
Riverside, CA 92521
Alex Rico, Co-Chair
Tel: (951) 924-1693
Email: rico_mecha@hotmail.edu

NU ALPHA KAPPA FRATERNITY, INC
Founding Chapter/California Polytechnic State University
P.O. Box 12102
San Luis Obispo, CA 93406
Tony Tejada, President
Email: slonak@yahoogroups.com
Web: www.naknet.org/founding

PROJECT MOTIVATION
Stanford University
P.O. Box 590-I
The Nitery
Stanford, CA 94305
Jay Saldivar, Co-Chair
Tel: (650) 725-2659
Email: yvejay@stanford.edu
Web: www.stanford.edu/group/promo

RAZA RECRUITMENT AND RETENTION CENTER
University of California, Berkeley
500 Eshelman Hall
Berkeley, CA 94720
Tel: (510) 642-1322
Web: www.Berkeleyraza.org

SIGMA DELTA PI -NATIONAL SPANISH HONORARY SOCIETY
Mount St. Mary's College
12001 Chalon Rd.
Los Angeles, CA 90049
Montserrat Reguant, Chair of the Department of Modern Languages
Tel: (310) 954-4270
Email: mreguant@msmc.la.edu

UCLA Dept. of Spanish and Portuguese
P.O. Box 951532
5310 Rolfe Hall
Los Angeles, CA 90095
Ruth Budd, Advisor
Tel: (310) 825-1036 Fax: (310) 206-4757
Email: rbudd@longwood.edu
Web: www.lwc.edu/staff/lgoetz/modlang/sigmadeltapi.html

SOCIETY OF HISPANIC PROFESSIONAL ENGINEERS
California Institute of Technology
1200 E. California Blvd.
Pasadena, CA 91125
Cristina Thomas, President
Tel: (626) 395-6208 Fax: (626) 683-1392
Email: cathomas@its.caltech.edu
Web: www.ugcs.caltech.edu/~clases/

California State University, Fresno
Student Activities 5280 N. Jackson M/S SU36
Fresno, CA 93740-8028
Angeles Torres, President
Tel: (559) 278-2976 Fax: (559) 278-4517
Email: angeles07@excite.com
Web: www.csufresno.edu/shpe/

California State University, Sacramento
Student Activities Box 172, 6000 J St.
Sacramento, CA 95819
Miguel Ramirez, Co-President
Tel: (916) 278-5957 Fax: (916) 278-7086
Email: sacshpe@yahoo.com

Loyola Marymount University
7900 Loyola Blvd.
Los Angeles, CA 90045
Jose Saez, Advisor
Tel: (310) 338-2877 Fax: (310) 338-5976
Email: shpe@lion.lmu.edu
Web: http://aslmu.lmu.edu/shpe/

SHPE National Headquarters
5400 E. Olympic Blvd. #210
Los Angeles, CA 90022
Daun E. White, Executive Director
Tel: (323) 725-3970 Fax: (323) 725-0316
Email: daun.white@shpe.org
Web: www.shpe.org

SOCIETY OF LATINO ENGINEERS AND SCIENTISTS
San Jose State University
1 Washington Sq.
San Jose, CA 95192
Michelle Urquhart, President
Email: vivintage44@yahoo.com

University of California, Los Angeles
Los Angeles, CA 90022
Terry Saunders, Advisor
Tel: (310) 825-7041
Email: soles@seas.ucla.edu

STANFORD LATINO LAW STUDENTS ASSOCIATION
Stanford University Law School
559 Nathan Abbott Way
Stanford, CA 94305-8610
Alexis Amezcua, President
Tel: (650) 723-3087
Email: amezcua@stanford.edu
Web: http://sllsa.stanford.edu

STANFORD RAZA MEDICAL ASSOCIATION
Stanford University Office of Students Affairs
251 Campus Dr. M/S/O/B 341
Stanford, CA 94305
Anne Miranda
Tel: (650) 725-1437
Email: amiranda@stanford.edu

STANFORD MINORITY MEDICAL ALLIANCE
Stanford University School of Medicine
251 Campus Dr. MSOB #341
Stanford, CA 94305-5404
Mike Molina, Coordinator
Tel: (650) 725-1437 Fax: (650) 725-5538
Email: molina@stanford.edu
Web: http://med.stanford.edu/osa/summa

TEATRO QUINTO SOL
UC Riverside Chicano Student Program
229 Costo Hall
Riverside, CA 92521
Graciela Larios, President
Tel: (951) 827-1012
Email: graciela.larios@email.ucr.edu

COLORADO

CHICANO HUMANITIES AND ARTS COUNCIL
772 Santa Fe Dr.
Denver, CO 80204
Crystal O'Brien, Executive Director
Tel: (303) 571-0440
Email: CHAC2515@aol.com
Web: www.chacweb.org

EL CENTRO SU TEATRO
4725 High St.
Denver, CO 80216
Anthony García, Executive Director
Tel: (303) 296-0219 Fax: (303) 296-4614
Email: elcentro@suteatro.org
Web: www.suteatro.org

HISPANIC CONTRACTORS OF COLORADO
1114 W. 7th Ave.
Denver, CO 80204-4432
Helga Grunerud, Executive Director
Tel: (303) 893-3893 Fax: (303) 893-2877
Email: hcocolorado@qwest.net
Web: www.hispanic-contractors.org

SANTA FE DRIVE REDEVELOPMENT CORPORATION
1029 Santa Fe Dr.
Denver, CO 80204
Veronica Barela, Executive Director
Tel: (303) 534-8342 X102 Fax: (303) 534-7418
Email: vbarela@newsed.org
Web: www.newsed.org

DENVER HISPANIC CHAMBER OF COMMERCE
924 W. Colfax Ave. #201
Denver, CO 80204
Greg Lopez, President
Tel: (303) 534-7783 Fax: (303) 595-8977

Email: glopez@qwest.net
Web: www.dhc.com

HISPANIC CHAMBER OF COMMERCE OF COLORADO SPRINGS
P.O. Box 2014
Colorado Springs, CO 80901
Lionel Rivera, President
Tel: (719) 635-5001 Fax: (719) 635-6311
Email: infodesk@coshcc.com
Web: www.coshcc.com

LATINO CHAMBER OF COMMERCE OF PUEBLO
215 S. Victoria Ave.
Pueblo, CO 81003
Sandy Gutierrez, President/CEO
Tel: (719) 542-5513 Fax: (719) 542-4657
Email: info@pueblolatinochamber.com
Web: www.pueblolatinochamber.com

CENTRO CULTURAL MEXICANO
Denver Office
48 Steel St.
Denver, CO 80206
Marcela De Lamar, Executive Director
Tel: (303) 331-1870 Fax: (303) 331-0169
Email: culture@terapath.com

CLUB PERÚ DENVER
1060 S. Foothill Dr.
Lakewood, CO 80228
Ana Rios de Morrow, President
Tel: (303) 985-5382 Fax: (303) 763-5796
Email: info@clubperudenver.com
Web: www.clubperudenver.com

COLORADO SOCIETY OF HISPANIC GENEALOGY
924 W. Colfax Ave. #104L
Denver, CO 80204-2629
Armando Atencio, President
Email: valsena@msn.com
Web: www.hispanicgen.org

MUSEO DE LAS AMERICAS
861 Santa Fe Dr.
Denver, CO 80204
José Aguayo, Executive Director
Tel: (303) 571-4401 Fax: (303) 607-9761
Email: shannabl@museo.org
Web: www.museo.org

TRINIDAD HISTORY MUSEUM
P.O. Box 377
Trinidad, CO 81082
Paula Manini, Director
Tel: (719) 846-7217 Fax: (719) 845-0117
Email: paulamanini@hotmail.com
Web: www.coloradohistory.org

AMERICAN GI FORUM OF UNITED STATES
2870 N. Speer Blvd. #102
Denver, CO 80211
David Rodriguez, National Commander
Tel: (303) 458-1700 Fax: (303) 458-1634
Email: info@agif.us
Web: www.agif.org

AMIGOS DE LA COMUNIDAD
309 W. 1st Ave.
Denver, CO 80223
Tara Bradley
Tel: (303) 722-5150 Fax: (303) 722-5118
Email: tbradley@larasa.org

HISPANIC ANNUAL SALUTE
P. O. Box 40720
Denver, CO 80204
Dan Sandos, Board President
Tel: (303) 699-0715
Email: dcsandos@aol.com
Web: www.hispanicannualsalute.org

LEAGUE OF UNITED LATIN AMERICAN CITIZENS
Council #3043
530 Santa Fe Dr.
Pueblo, CO 81006
Angelina Najar, President
Tel: (719) 542-6475
Email: angelina.najar@hotmail.com

NATIONAL IMAGE, INC.
Image de Denver
1746 Grove St.
Denver, CO 80204
Lorenzo Cervantes, President
Tel: (303) 236-6467
Email: Lorenzo_Cervantes@blm.gov
Web: www.nationalimageinc.org

LATINO INITIATIVE
Colorado Democratic Party
777 Santa Fe Dr.
Denver, CO 80204
Margaret Atencio, Director
Tel: (303) 623-4762 Fax: (303) 623-2443
Email: info@coloradodems.org

ASSOCIATION OF LATINO PROFESSIONALS
Denver Chapter
707 17th St. #2700
Denver, CO 80202-3499
Kathy Garcia, Chapter President
Tel: (303) 382-7153 Fax: (303) 295-8829
Email: president@denver.alpfa.org
Web: www.alpfa.org

NATIONAL SOCIETY OF HISPANIC MBAS
Denver Chapter
8027 S Kalispell Way
Denver, CO 80207
Nayeli Solorzano, Chapter President
Tel: (303) 707-7515 Fax: (303) 707-7448
Email: general@denver.nshmba.org
Web: http://denver.nshmba.org

AMERICAN JEWISH COMMITTEE
Latino Jewish Dialogue
950 S. Cherry #418
Denver, CO 80246
Gale Kahn, Director
Tel: (303) 320-1742 Fax: (303) 320-1742
Email: colorado@ajc.org

ARCHDIOCESE OF DENVER
Hispanic Ministry Office
2830 Lawrence St.
Denver, CO 80205
Maria del Mar Munoz-Visoso, Director
Tel: (303) 295-9470 Fax: (303) 295-9471
Email: mar.munoz-visoso@archden.org
Web: www.archden.org

DIOCESE OF PUEBLO
Hispanic Affairs Office
1001 Grand Ave.
Pueblo, CO 81003-2948
Ronald Roybal, Director of Pastoral Outreach
Tel: (719) 544-9861 Fax: (719) 544-1220

DEPARTMENT OF ETHNIC STUDIES
University of Colorado at Boulder
Campus Box 339, Ketchum 30
Boulder, CO 80309-0339
Ward Churchill, Chair
Tel: (303) 492-8852 Fax: (303) 492-7799
Email: ethnic.studies@colorado.edu
Web: www.colorado.edu/EthnicStudies/

THE GENEALOGY SOCIETY OF HISPANIC AMERICA
Trinidad Chapter
P.O. Box 9606
Denver, CO 80209-0606
Vickie Arellano, President
Email: vickie450@msn.com
Web: www.gsha.net

THE LATINO/A RESEARCH & POLICY CENTER
University of Colorado at Denver
1380 Lawrence St. #1100
Denver, CO 80204
Estevan Flores, Ph.D., Executive Director
Tel: (303) 352-3700 Fax: (303) 352-3715
Email: contact@lrpc.cudenver.edu
Web: www.itera.cudenver.edu/lrpc

BUENO CENTER FOR MULTICULTURAL EDUCATION
University of Colorado at Boulder
UCB 247, School of Education
Boulder, CO 80309-0249
Leonard Baca, Executive Director
Tel: (303) 492-5416
Email: buenoctr@colorado.edu
Web: www.colorado.edu/education/BUENO/

CESAR CHAVEZ CULTURAL CENTER
501 20th St.
Greeley, CO 80639
Priscilla Falcon, Director
Tel: (970) 351-2424 Fax: (970) 351-2360
Email: priscilla.falcon@unco.edu
Web: www.unco.edu/cccc

COLORADO ASSOCIATION FOR BILINGUAL EDUCATION
P.O. Box 33120
Northglenn, CO 80233
Jorge Garcia, President
Tel: (303) 447-5073
Email: cabe@cobilingual.org
Web: www.cobilingual.org

COLORADO DEPARTMENT OF EDUCATION
English Language Acquisition
201 E. Colfax Ave.
Denver, CO 80203-1799
Bernie Martinez, Project Director
Tel: (303) 866-6870 Fax: (303) 866-6857
Email: martinez_b@cde.state.co.us
Web: www.cde.state.co.us/

DENVER PUBLIC SCHOOLS
Hispanic Education Advisory Council
900 Grant St. #400
Denver, CO 80203
Flor Amaro, Staff Liaison
Tel: (720) 423-3433 Fax: (720) 423-3732
Email: flor_amaro@dpsk12.org
Web: www.dpsk12.org

EL CENTRO STUDENT SERVICES
Colorado State University
178 Lory Student Ctr.
Fort Collins, CO 80523
Guadalupe Salazar, Director
Tel: (970) 491-1926 Fax: (970) 491-2534
Email: gsalazar@lamar.colostate.edu
Web: www.colostate.edu/depts/elcentro

ESCUELA TLATELOLCO CENTRO DE ESTUDIOS
2949 N. Federal Blvd.
Denver, CO 80211
Nita J. Gonzales, President/CEO
Tel: (303) 964-8993 Fax: (303) 964-9795
Email: et@escuelatlatelolco.org
Web: www.escuelatlatelolco.org

HISPANIC ADVISORY COUNCIL AWARDS
Brighton School District
630 S. 8th Ave.
Brighton, CO 80601
Magdalena Del Villar, Director
Tel: (303) 655-2757
Email: mdelvillar@brightonps27jk12.co.us

HISPANIC EDUCATION INC.
8685 Aspen Cir.
Parker, CO 80134
Joseph C'de Baca, Coordinator
Tel: (303) 766-1942
Email: hispaniced@aol.com
Web: www.hispaniceducation.org

HISPANIC EDUCATIONAL FOUNDATION
P.O. Box 2102
Longmont, CO 80502
Tom Garcia, Treasurer
Tel: (303) 776-6237

INROADS, INC.
Colorado Office
4601 DTC Blvd. #150A
Denver, CO 80237
Hollis E. Booker, Managing Director
Tel: (303) 607-0385 Fax: (303) 607-0474
Email: hbooker@inroads.org
Web: www.inroads.org

LATIN AMERICAN EDUCATIONAL FOUNDATION
National Headquarters
924 W. Colfax Ave. #103
Denver, CO 80204
Elisa Zuniga Ramirez, President
Tel: (303) 446-0541 Fax: (303) 446-0526
Email: carmen@laef.org
Web: www.laef.org

LATIN AMERICAN SUPPORT ORGANIZATION
Denver Water Department
1600 W 12th Ave.
Denver, CO 80204
Patricia Salazar, Sales Administrator
Tel: (303) 628-6346 Fax: (303) 628-6046
Email: patsalazar@denverwater.org
Web: www.water.denver.co.gov

LULAC NATIONAL EDUCATIONAL SERVICE CENTERS, INC.
Colorado Headquarters
720 N Main St. #455
Pueblo, CO 81003
Steve García, Director
Tel: (719) 542-9074 Fax: (719) 543-7287
Email: infocol@lnesc-colo.org
Web: www.lnesc-colo.org

Colorado Springs Office
829 N Circle Dr. #101
Colorado Springs, CO 80909-5008
Steve Garcia, Director
Tel: (719) 637-0037 Fax: (719) 637-0038
Email: infocol@lnesc-colo.org
Web: www.lnesc-colo.org

Denver Colorado Office
715 Galapago St. #1
Denver, CO 80204
Eddie L. Duarte, Counselor
Tel: (303) 893-0100
Email: infocol@lnesc-colo.org
Web: www.lnesc-colo.org

MINORITY ARTS & SCIENCES PROGRAM
University of Colorado at Boulder
Campus Box 347
Boulder, CO 80309-0347
Maria Ruiz-Jargon, Advisor
Tel: (303) 492-8229 Fax: (303) 492-6554
Email: masp@colorado.edu
Web: www.colorado.edu/masp/

MULTICULTURAL RESOURCE CENTER
Community College of Denver
P.O. Box 173363
Campus Box 209
Denver, CO 80217
Michael Johnson, Chair
Tel: (303) 556-4963 Fax: (303) 556-2599
Email: michael.johnson@ccd.edu
Web: www.ccd.edu/mrc/

PUEBLO HISPANIC EDUCATION FOUNDATION
2200 Bonfire Blvd. #325

Pueblo, CO 81001
Gloria Gutierrez, Interim Executive Director
Tel: (719) 549-2564
Email: phef@colostate-pueblo.edu
Web: www.phet.net

SOCIETY OF SPANISH AND SPANISH-AMERICAN STUDIES
University of Colorado at Boulder
Department of Spanish and Portuguese, 134
McKenna Languages Bldg. 278 UCB
Boulder, CO 80309-0278
Luis T. Gonzalez-del-Valle, Director
Tel: (303) 492-5900 Fax: (303) 492-3699
Email: gonzalezl@colorado.edu
Web: www.colorado.edu/spanish/sssas/index.htm

UNITED MEXICAN-AMERICAN STUDENTS
University of Colorado-Boulder
Campus Box 207, UMC 321
Boulder, CO 80309
Teresa Estrada
Tel: (303) 492-6571
Email: teresa.estrada@colorado.edu
Web: www.Colorado.EDU/StudentGroups/UMAS-MECHA/UMAS.html

HISPANIC ADVISORY COALITION OF EMPLOYEES RESOURCES
1740 Broadway, MAC C7300-494
Denver, CO 80274
Ron Timm, Chair
Tel: (303) 863-5009 Fax: (303) 863-5693
Email: ron.k.timm@wellsfargo.com

NATIONAL EMPLOYMENT LAW INSTITUTE
1601 Emerson St.
Denver, CO 80218
Esq. David K. Fram, Director ADA/EEO
Tel: (303) 861-5600 Fax: (303) 861-5665
Email: neli@neli.org
Web: www.neli.org

ROCKY MOUNTAIN/SER-JOBS FOR PROGRESS, INC.
Affiliate of SER-Jobs for Progress National, Inc.
1016 West Ave. #5
Alamosa, CO 81101
Leon Ortega, Senior Field Representative
Tel: (719) 589-5821 Fax: (719) 589-0344
Email: lortega@cwfc.net
Web: www.ser-national.org

Affiliate of SER-Jobs for Progress National, Inc.
1931 E Bridge St.
Brighton, CO 80601
Lourdies Villa, Field Representative
Tel: (303) 659-5128 Fax: (303) 659-2940
Email: lvilla@co.adams.co.us
Web: www.ser-national.org

Affiliate of SER-Jobs for Progress National, Inc.
405 E Olive St.
Lamar, CO 81052
Jacob Jaramillo, Field Representative
Tel: (719) 336-9019 Fax: (719) 336-2259
Email: jjaramillo@cwfc.net
Web: www.ser-national.org

Affiliate of SER-Jobs for Progress National, Inc.
528 Main St.
Walsenburg, CO 81089
Mary Anderson, Senior Field Representative
Tel: (719) 738-3004 Fax: (719) 738-3616
Email: manderson@cwfc.net
Web: www.ser-national.org

Affiliate of SER-Jobs for Progress National, Inc.
201 N Weber
Colorado Springs, CO 80903
Lynn Dyatt, Senior Field Representative
Tel: (719) 578-5444 Fax: (719) 578-9752
Email: rmser6587@qwest.net
Web: www.ser-national.org

Affiliate of SER-Jobs for Progress National, Inc.

3555 Pecos St., 2nd Fl.
Denver, CO 80211
Charles Tafoya, Executive Director
Tel: (303) 433-3118 Fax: (303) 480-9214
Email: chuck@rmser.org
Web: www.ser-national.org

Affiliate of SER-Jobs for Progress National, Inc.
P.O. Box 1010
Alamosa, CO 81101
Leon Ortega, Senior Field Representative
Tel: (719) 589-5821 Fax: (719) 589-0344
Web: www.ser-national.org

SOCIETY OF HISPANIC HUMAN RESOURCE PROFESSIONALS
P.O. Box 173361
1380 Lawrence #610, Box B
Denver, CO 80217-3361
LeRoy Romero, Co-Chair
Email: vivaleroy@comcast.net
Web: www.shhrp.org

SPEC. INT., FAMILY PLANNING

CHELTENHAM RAZALOGIA PARENT EMPOWERMENT PROGRAM
1580 Julian St.
Denver, CO 80204
Claudia Beck, Principal
Tel: (303) 825-3323 Fax: (303) 825-3826
Email: claudia_beck@dpsk12.org
Web: http://cheltenham.dpsk12.org

LATIN AMERICAN RESEARCH AND SERVICE AGENCY
309 W 1st Ave.
Denver, CO 80223
Miguel Barragan, Community Relations
Tel: (303) 722-5150 X110 Fax: (303) 722-5118
Email: larasa@larasa.org
Web: www.larasa.org

TU CASA, INC.
P.O. Box 473
Alamosa, CO 81101
Lynn M. Johnson, Executive Director
Tel: (719) 589-2465 Fax: (719) 589-1465
Email: tucasa@fone.net

SPEC. INT., HEALTH SERVICES

CLINICA TEPEYAC
3617 Kalamath St.
Denver, CO 80211
Rosanna Reyes, Executive Director
Tel: (303) 458-5302 Fax: (303) 433-7452
Email: rreyes@clinicatepeyac.org
Web: www.clinicatepeyac.org

COLORADO MIGRANT HEALTH PROGRAM
903 S. 12th St.
Rocky Ford, CO 81067
Mitt Garcia, Director
Tel: (719) 254-6481 Fax: (719) 254-5112

P. O. Box G
707 Elberta Ave.
Palisade, CO 81526
Tony Merot, Clinic Manager
Tel: (970) 464-5862 Fax: (970) 464-7352
Email: fwhs@acsol.net

La Clinica Campesina Rural Health Clinic
2000 W. South Boulder
Lafayette, CO 80026
Esther Burke, President
Tel: (303) 665-9310 Fax: (303) 926-0363
Web: www.clinicacampesina.org

Pueblo Community Health Center
310 Colorado Ave.
Pueblo, CO 81004
Byron Geer, Case Manager
Tel: (719) 543-8711 Fax: (719) 543-5340
Web: www.cchn.org/health_centers

Valley-Wide Health Services

186 N. Hurt St.
Center, CO 81125
Antonia Romero, Clinic Manager/Migrant Health Coordinator
Tel: (719) 754-2778 Fax: (719) 754-2166
Email: romeroan@vwhs.org
Web: www.vwhs.org

LA CASA QUICK NEWTON FAMILY HEALTH CENTER
4545 Navaho St.
Denver, CO 80211
Pat Jacobson, Manager
Tel: (303) 436-8700 Fax: (303) 436-8609

LA MARIPOSA HEALTH CLINIC
1020 W 11th Ave.
Denver, CO 80204
Tina Quitana, Practice Manager
Tel: (303) 572-4782 Fax: (303) 572-4786
Email: tina.quintana00@dhha.org

NATIONAL LATINO BEHAVIORAL HEALTH ASSOCIATION
P.O. Box 387
506 Welch St. #B
Berthoud, Co 80513
Marie Sanchez, Executive Director
Tel: (970) 532-7210 Fax: (970) 532-7209
Email: Marie.sanchez@prodigy.net
Web: www.nlbha.org

PLAN DE SALUD DEL VALLE
Brighton Salud
30 S. 20th St. #A
Brighton, CO 80601
Stanley J.Brasher, Executive Director
Tel: (303) 659-4000 Fax: (303) 659-9306
Email: jbrasher@saludclinic.org
Web: www.saludclinic.org

Commerce City Salud
6075 Pkwy. Dr. #160
Commerce City, CO 80022
Stanley J.Brasher, Executive Director
Tel: (303) 286-8900 Fax: (303) 286-8260
Email: jbrasher@saludclinic.org
Web: www.saludclinic.org

Estes Park Salud
600 S. Saint Vrain #2
Estes Park, CO 80517
Stanley J.Brasher, Executive Director
Tel: (970) 586-9230 Fax: (303) 586-0292
Email: jbrasher@saludclinic.org
Web: www.saludclinic.org

Fort Collins Salud
114 Bristlecone Dr.
Fort Collins, CO 80524
Stanley J.Brasher, Executive Director
Tel: (970) 494-4040 Fax: (303) 494-4076
Email: jbrasher@saludclinic.org
Web: www.saludclinic.org

Fort Morgan Salud
909 E. Railroad Ave.
Fort Morgan, CO 80701
Stanley J.Brasher, Executive Director
Tel: (970) 867-0300 Fax: (303) 867-7607
Email: jbrasher@saludclinic.org
Web: www.saludclinic.org

Frederick Salud
P.O. Box 189
630 Main
Frederick, CO 80530
Stanley J.Brasher, Executive Director
Tel: (303) 833-2050 Fax: (303) 825-7664
Email: jbrasher@saludclinic.org
Web: www.saludclinic.org

Headquarters
1115 2nd St.
Fort Lupton, CO 80621
Stanley J.Brasher, Executive Director
Tel: (303) 892-6401 Fax: (303) 892-1511
Email: jbrasher@saludclinic.org
Web: www.saludclinic.org

Longmont Salud
231 E. 9th Ave.
Longmont, CO 80501
Stanley J.Brasher, Executive Director
Tel: (303) 776-3250 Fax: (303) 682-9269
Email: jbrasher@saludclinic.org
Web: www.saludclinic.org

Sterling Salud
1410 S. 7th Ave.
Sterling, CO 80722
Stanley J.Brasher, Executive Director
Tel: (970) 526-2589 Fax: (303) 526-0244
Email: jbrasher@saludclinic.org
Web: www.saludclinic.org

SERVICIOS DE LA RAZA, INC.
Affiliate of NCLR
4055 Tejon St.
Denver, CO 80211
José R. Mondragón, Executive Director
Tel: (303) 458-5851 Fax: (303) 455-1332
Email: serviciosdelaraza@lycos.com
Web: http://serviciosdelaraza.tripod.com/

SPEC. INT., HOUSING

COLORADO RURAL HOUSING
3621 W. 73rd Ave. #C
Westminster, CO 80030
Jerry Harkins, President
Tel: (303) 428-1448
Email: sales@crhdc.org
Web: http://crhdc.org

DEL NORTE NEIGHBORHOOD DEVELOPMENT CORPORATION
2926 Zuni St. #202
Denver, CO 80211
Marvin Kelly, Executive Director
Tel: (303) 477-4774 X11
Email: mkelly@delnortendc.org
Web: www.delnortendc.org

SPEC. INT., HUMAN RELATIONS

NATIONAL COALITION AGAINST DOMESTIC VIOLENCE
National Headquarters
P.O. Box 18749
Denver, CO 80218
Rita Smith, Executive Director
Tel: (303) 839-1852 X105 Fax: (303) 831-9251
Email: sbaca@ncadv.ord
Web: www.ncadv.org

PROJECT SALVADOR
Box 300105
Denver, CO 80203-0105
Carolyn Long, Board Member
Tel: (303) 964-3488
Email: luchando@juno.com
Web: www.projectsalvador.org

SPEC. INT., INFORMATION REFERRAL

REFORMA
Colorado Chapter
P.O. Box 8523
Denver, CO 80201-8523
Orlando Archibeque, Chapter President
Tel: (303) 556-3482
Email: orlando.archibeque@cudenver.edu
Web: www.reforma.org

SPEC. INT., LEGAL ASSISTANCE

COLORADO HISPANIC BAR ASSOCIATION
P.O. Box 189
1550 Larimer St.
Denver, CO 80202
Lorenzo A. Trujillo, President
Tel: (303) 460-9891
Email: LAT_Esq@msn.com
Web: www.chba.net

COLORADO LEGAL SERVICES, INC.
Denver Office
1905 Sherman St. #400
Denver, CO 80203
John Asher, Executive Director
Tel: (303) 837-1313 Fax: (303) 830-7860
Web: www.coloradolegalservices.org

COLORADO LEGAL SERVICES, INC.
Durango Office
1474 Main Ave. #200
Durango, CO 81301-5140
Arthur Jacobs, Managing Attorney
Tel: (970) 247-0266 Fax: (970) 385-8515
Web: www.coloradolegalservices.org

Grand Junction Office
200 N. 6thSt. #203
Grand Junction, CO 81501
Joel Smith, Manager
Tel: (970) 243-7817 Fax: (970) 243-7814
Web: www.coloradolegalservices.org

Greeley Office
800 8th Ave. #202
Greeley, CO 80631-1122
Mario Rivera, Managing Attorney
Tel: (970) 353-7554 Fax: (970) 353-7557
Web: www.coloradolegalservices.org

La Junta Office
207 1/2 Colorado St.
La Junta, CO 81050
Larry Davis, Managing Attorney
Tel: (719) 384-5438 Fax: (719) 384-8676
Web: www.coloradolegalservices.org

HISPANIC NATIONAL BAR ASSOCIATION
455 Sherman St.
Denver, CO 80203
Maria "Tish" Antill, Vice President
Tel: (303) 861-2744 Fax: (303) 861-0040
Email: antillmt@qwest.com
Web: www.hnba.com

SPEC. INT., MENTAL HEALTH

MENTAL HEALTH CORPORATION OF DENVER
Centro de las Familias
75 Meade St.
Denver, CO 80219
Diane Guerrero, Program Director
Tel: (303) 504-1900 Fax: (303) 935-0294
Web: www.mhcd.org

SPEC. INT., SOCIAL INTEREST

CUMBRES PROGRAM
University of Northern Colorado
Carter Hall 3005
Greeley, CO 80639
Linda Carbajal, Director
Tel: (970) 351-2410
Email: lcarbajal@yahoo.com
Web: http://www.univnorthco.edu/cumbres

EL COMITÉ DE LONGMONT
455 Kimbart St.
Longmont, CO 80501
Ed Navarro, President
Tel: (303) 651-6125 Fax: (303) 702-0314
Email: elcomite@qwest.net
Web: www.elcomitedelongmont.org

NEWSED COMMUNITY DEVELOPMENT CORPORATION
1029 Santa Fe Dr.
Denver, CO 80204
Veronica Barela, CEO
Tel: (303) 534-8342 Fax: (303) 534-7418
Email: vbarela@newsed.org
Web: www.newsed.org

SPANISH RESPONSE PROGRAM
Denver Victims Service Center
P.O. Box 18975
Denver, CO 80218

Marian Mosquera, Spanish Response Counselor
Tel: (303) 860-0660 Fax: (303) 831-7282
Email: momosquera@denvervictims.org
Web: www.denvervictims.org

AZTLAN RECREATION CENTER
4435 Navajo St.
Denver, CO 80211
Rosmary Ornalez, Recreation Director
Tel: (303) 458-4899 Fax: (303) 458-4887
Web: www.denvergov.com

LA ALMA RECREATION CENTER
1325 W 11th Ave.
Denver, CO 80204
David Rodríguez, Recreation Director
Tel: (303) 534-9282 Fax: (303) 572-4660

LA FAMILIA RECREATION CENTER
65 S Elati St.
Denver, CO 80223
Sid Schuck, Recreation Director
Tel: (303) 698-4995 Fax: (303) 698-5512

COLORADO ORGANIZATION FOR LATINA OPPORTUNITY AND REPRODUCTIVE RIGHTS
P.O. Box 201061
Denver, CO 80220-1061
Melanie Herrera Bortz, President
Tel: (303) 393-0382

MI CASA RESOURCE CENTER FOR WOMEN, INC.
Affiliate of NCLR
360 Acoma St.
Denver, CO 80223
Carmen Carrillo, CEO
Tel: (303) 573-1302 Fax: (303) 595-0422
Email: info@micasadenver.org
Web: www.micasadenver.org

GIRLS INCORPORATED OF METRO DENVER
1499 Julian St.
Denver, CO 80204
Colleen Colarelli, President/CEO
Tel: (303) 893-4363 Fax: (303) 893-4352
Email: ccolarelli@girlsincdenver.org
Web: www.girlsincdenver.org

LATIN AMERICAN SUPPORT ORGANIZATION
Denver Water Department Chapter
1600 W 12th Ave.
Denver, CO 80204-3412
Carlos E. Sanchez, President
Tel: (303) 628-6097 Fax: (303) 628-6034
Email: carlos.sanchez@denverwater.org

EL CENTRO STUDENT SERVICES
Colorado State University
178 Lory Student Center
Fort Collins, CO 80523
Guadalupe Salazar, Director of El Centro
Tel: (970) 491-5722 Fax: (970) 491-2534
Email: gsalazar@lamar.colostate.edu
Web: www.colostate.edu/Depts/elcentro/

EL PARNASO, SPANISH CLUB
Adams State College
208 Edgemont Ave.
Alamosa, CO 81102
Eva Rayas-Ihm, Assistant Professor
Tel: (719) 587-7852 Fax: (719) 587-7171
Email: erihm@adams.edu
Web: http://languages.adams.edu/f

LAMBDA THETA NU
Metropolitan State College of Denver
P.O. Box 173362

Campus Box Club HUB
Denver, CO 80204
Mitchelle Joromello, President
Tel: (303) 556-2595 Fax: (30) 556-2596

LATIN AMERICAN STUDENT ORGANIZATION
El Centro, Colorado State University
178 Lory Student Ctr.
Fort Collins, CO 80523-8033
Guadalupe Salazar, Director of El Centro
Tel: (970) 491-5722 Fax: (970) 491-2534
Web: www.colostate.edu/depts/elcentro

LATINO FACULTY AND STAFF ASSOCIATION
Metropolitan State College of Denver
P.O. Box 173362
Denver, CO 80217
Maria Castro, President
Tel: (303) 556-4419 Fax: (303) 556-4297
Email: castrom@mscd.edu
Web: www.mscd.edu/~lfsa

MULTI-ETHNIC FACULTY AND STAFF CAUCUS
Colorado State University
213A Student Services
Fort Collins, CO 80523
Valerie Gallegos, Co-Chair
Tel: (970) 491-3745
Email: Valerie.Gallegos@ColoState.edu
Web: www.admin.colostate.edu/caucus/index.html

SIGMA LAMBDA BETA FRATERNITY
University of Colorado, Boulder/Lambda Chapter
UMC 420 CB 207
Boulder, CO 80309
Stefan Galicia, Membership Educator
Tel: (303) 735-1082
Email: lambdabetas@lists.colorado.edu
Web: www.colorado.edu/Greeks/SLB/

SIGMA LAMBDA BETA INTERNATIONAL FRATERNITY
El Centro, Colorado State University
178 Lory Student Center
Fort Collins, CO 80523-8033
Nathan Castillo, Member
Tel: (970) 491-5722
Email: betas@lamar.colostate.edu
Web: http://lamar.colostate.edu/~betas

CONNECTICUT

AETNA HISPANIC NETWORK
Aetna Inc.
151 Farmington Ave.
Hartford, CT 06156
Teodoro Mercado-Perez, Diversity Programs Manager
Tel: (860) 273-2464 Fax: (860) 273-7232

NATIONAL SOCIETY OF HISPANIC MBAS
Hartford Chapter
P.O. Box 231712
Hartford, CT 06123-1712
Yvonne Zayas, Chapter President
Email: general@connecticut.nshmba.org
Web: www.nshmba.org

SPANISH AMERICAN MERCHANTS ASSOCIATION OF CONNECTICUT
Hartford
95 Park St.
Hartford, CT 06106
Julio Mendoza, Executive Director
Tel: (860) 278-5825   Fax: (860) 241-9000
Email: julio_mendoza@samact.org
Web: www.samact.org

GREATER STANFORD HISPANIC CHAMBER OF COMMERCE, INC.
P.O. Box 4153
465 Canal St.
Stamford, CT 06907

Eva A. Maldonado, President
Tel: (203) 359-2050 Fax: (203) 359-4153
Email: evamaldonado1@yahoo.com
Web: www.gshccinc.org

HISPANIC CHAMBER OF COMMERCE OF GREATER WATERBURY, INC.
451 Meriden Rd.
Waterbury, CT 06705
Joel Rosario, President
Tel: (203) 759-0939 X108 Fax: (203) 596-2276
Email: joelrosario1@aol.com

GUAKIA, INC.
235 Wethersfield Ave.
Hartford, CT 06114
Barbara Fernandez, Executive Director
Tel: (860) 548-9555 Fax: (860) 548-9117
Email: barbara.fernandez@guakia.org
Web: www.guakia.org

HISPANIC CENTER
87 West St.
Danbury, CT 06810
María Cinta Lowe, Executive Director
Tel: (203) 798-2855 Fax: (203) 798-6337
Email: hispaniccenter@aol.com

THE PORTUGUESE FOUNDATION OF CONNECTICUT
86 New Park Ave.
Hartford, CT 06106
Gabriel R. Serrano, President
Tel: (860) 236-5514
Email: info@pfict.org
Web: www.pfict.org

PUERTO RICAN/LATIN AMERICAN CULTURAL CENTER
University of Connecticut
360 Fairfield Rd. #U-2188
Storrs, CT 06269
Mayte Perez-Franco, Director
Tel: (860)-486-1135 Fax: (860) 486-4642
Email: Mayte.Perez-Franco@uconn.edu
Web: www.latino.uconn.edu

SPANISH AMERICAN CULTURAL ORGANIZATION
Centro de la Comunidad, Inc.
109 Blinman St.
New London, CT 06320
Alejandro Cooper, Director
Tel: (860) 442-4463 Fax: (860) 443-4391

NATIONAL LATINO PEACE OFFICERS ASSOCIATION
Connecticut Chapter
1 Union Ave.
New Haven, CT 06519
Francisco Ortiz, President
Tel: (877) 657-6200
Email: fortiz@newhavenct.net
Web: www.nlpoa.com

CENTRO DE SAN JOSE
290 Grand Ave.
New Haven, CT 06513
Ed Bonilla, Executive Director
Tel: (203) 777-6771 Fax: (203) 777-5290
Email: centrosanjose@cccfs.org

CONNECTICUT ASSOCIATION FOR UNITED SPANISH ACTION
555 Windsor St.
Hartford, CT 06120
Carmen Sierra, Executive Director
Tel: (860) 424-0077 Fax: (860) 560-0396
Email: mail@causainc.org
Web: www.causainc.org

HISPANIC SERVICES PROGRAM
Goodwill Industries, Inc.
165 Ocean Terrace
Bridgeport, CT 06605
Marisol Vazquez, Director
Tel: (203) 368-6511 Fax: (203) 335-9326

LEAGUE OF UNITED LATIN AMERICAN CITIZENS
375 James St.
New Haven, CT 06513
Lynn Hopson, Director
Tel: (203) 777-7501 Fax: (203) 773-9320
Email: info@lulac.org
Web: www.lulac.org

SAN JUAN CENTER, INC.
180 Pleasant St.
Hartford, CT 06103
George Cruz, Executive Director
Tel: (860) 525-0360 Fax: (860) 525-0571

SPANISH COMMUNITY OF WALLINGFORD, INC.
284 Washington St.
Wallingford, CT 06492
Blanca Santana, Executive Director
Tel: (203) 265-5866 Fax: (203) 294-2256
Email: spanish.cntr@snet.net

UNITED HISPANIC ACTION OF NORWALK
P.O. Box 628
Norwalk, CT 06856-0628
Jose A. Bermudez, President
Tel: (203) 866-5369
Email: bermudez.jose@sbcglobal.net

LATINO AND PUERTO RICAN AFFAIRS COMMISSION
State of Connecticut
18-20 Trinity St.
Hartford, CT 06106
Fernando Betancourt, Executive Director
Tel: (860) 240-8330 Fax: (860) 240-0315
Email: fbetancourt@yahoo.com
Web: www.cga.ct.gov/lprac/Index.htm

PUERTO RICO FEDERAL AFFAIRS ADMINISTRATION
Connecticut Regional Office
100 Pearl St.
Hartford, CT 06103
Edna Negron, Regional Director
Tel: (860) 522-2434 Fax: (860) 522-2579
Email: info@prfaa.com
Web: www.prfaa.com

REPUBLICAN NATIONAL HISPANIC ASSEMBLY
RNHA-Connecticut
CT Republicans, 97 Elm St. Rear
Hartford, CT 06106
Pat Longo, State Chairman
Tel: (860) 547-0589
Email: info@rnha.org
Web: www.rnha.org

ASSOCIATION OF LATINO PROFESSIONALS IN FINANCE AND ACCOUNTING
Hartford Chapter
c/o AETNA, 1000 Middle St. MC4P
Middletown, CT 06457
Carlota Grate, Chapter President
Tel: (860) 636-0802
Email: gratec@aetna.com
Web: www.alpfa.org

HISPANIC POLICE ASSOCIATION OF WATERBURY, CT, INC.
P.O. Box 127
Waterbury, CT 06720
Raymond Batista, President
Emaisl: titob99@sbcglobal.net
Web: www.waterburyhpa.com

SOCIETY OF HISPANIC PROFESSIONAL ENGINEERS
Connecticut-Hartford Professional Chapter
1028 W. Blvd. #235
West Hartford, CT 06119
Jose L. Martinez, Jr., Chapter President
Email: info@shpect.com
Web: www.shpect.com

RELIGIOUS

ARCHDIOCESE OF HARTFORD
Hispanic Ministry Office
467 Bloomfield Ave.
Bloomfield, CT 06002
Lucy Yuniz, Director for Hispanic Ministry
Tel: (860) 243-0940 Fax: (860) 286-2797
Email: hispanic.evnglztn@snet.net
Web: www.archdioceseofhartford.org

DIOCESE OF BRIDGEPORT
St. Peter Parish
695 Colorado Ave.
Bridgeport, CT 06605-1699
Monsignor Aniceto Villamide, Pastor
Tel: (203) 366-5611 Fax: (203) 335-1924

DIOCESE OF NORWICH
Hispanic Ministry
61 Club Rd.
Windham, CT 06280-1007
Sr. Mary Jude Lazarus, SCMC, Director for Hispanic Ministry
Tel: (860) 423-8617

PROGRAMA DE MINISTERIOS HISPANOS
77 Sherman St.
Hartford, CT 06105
Heidi Hadsell, President
Tel: (860) 509-9500 Fax: (860) 509-9509
Email: info@hartsem.edu
Web: www.hartsem.edu

SPEC. INT., AIDS

AIDS PROJECT HARTFORD
110 Bartholomew Ave.
Hartford, CT 06106
Sandy D'Amato, Office Manager
Tel: (860) 951-4833 Fax: (860) 951-4779
Email: mail@aidsprojecthartford.org
Web: www.aidsprojecthartford.org

LATINOS CONTRA SIDA
184 Wethersfield Ave.
Hartford, CT 06114
Edna Berestain, Executive Director
Tel: (860) 296-6400 Fax: (860) 728-3782
Email: edna.berenstain@latinoscontrasida.org
Web: www.latinoscontrasida.org

SPEC. INT., ALCOHOL/DRUG CENTER

CHEMICAL ABUSE SERVICES AGENCY
690 Artic St.
Bridgeport, CT 06690
Asher Delerme, Executive Director
Tel: (203) 339-4112 Fax: (203) 339-4115
Email: casa690@aol.com

HOGAR CREA INTERNATIONAL OF CONNECTICUT, INC.
18 New Park Ave.
Hartford, CT 06106
Edwin Rivera Pacheco, Director
Tel: (860) 232-7353 Fax: (860) 223-4733
Email: hogarcreact@aol.com
Web: www.hogarcrea.org

SPEC. INT., EDUCATION

ASPIRA OF CONNECTICUT, INC.
1600 State St.
Bridgeport, CT 06605
Alma Maya, Executive Director
Tel: (203) 336-5762 Fax: (203) 366-5803

Email: amaya@ct.aspira.org
Web: www.ctaspira.org

BRIDGE ACADEMY
P.O. Box 2267
510 Barnum Ave.
Bridgeport, CT 06608
Felipe Reinoso, Principal
Tel: (203) 336-9999 Fax: (203) 336-9852
Email: felipereinoso@hotmail.com

CENTER FOR LATIN AMERICAN & CARIBBEAN STUDIES
University of Connecticut
83 Bolton Rd. #1161
Storrs, CT 06269-1161
Tricia Gabany-Guerrero, Director
Tel: (860) 486-4964 Fax: (860) 486-2963 .
Email: latinamerica@uconn.edu
Web: http://clacs.uconn.edu

CENTRO DE LA COMUNIDAD
109 Blinman St.
New London, CT 06320
Alejandro Melendez-Cooper, Executive Director
Tel: (860) 442-4463 Fax: (860) 443-4391
Email: centrodelacomunidad@yahoo.com

COUNCIL ON LATIN AMERICAN AND IBERIAN STUDIES
Yale University
P.O. Box 208206
New Haven, CT 06520
Enrique Mayer, Director
Tel: (203) 432-3422 Fax: (203) 432-5963
Email: latin.america@yale.edu
Web: www.yale.edu/las

INSTITUTE OF PUERTO RICAN AND LATINO STUDIES
University of Connecticut
354 Mansfield Rd. Unit 2137
Storrs, CT 06269-2137
Blanca G. Silvestrini, Director
Tel: (860) 486-3997 Fax: (860) 486-2906
Email: prladm02@uconnvm.uconn.edu
Web: www.oralhistory.uconn.edu/~prladm02

SPANISH SPEAKING CENTER OF NEW BRITAIN, INC.
29 Cedar St.
New Britain, CT 06051
Mary Sanders, Executive Director
Tel: (860) 224-2651 Fax: (860) 225-1713
Email: spanishspeakingctr@yahoo.com

SPEC. INT., HEALTH SERVICES

HISPANIC HEALTH COUNCIL
175 Main St.
Hartford, CT 06106
Dominick Cristofaro, President
Tel: (860) 527-0856 Fax: (860) 724-0437
Email: info@hispanichealth.com
Web: www.hispanichealth.com

HISPANOS UNIDOS
116 Sherman Ave.
New Haven, CT 06511
Luz Gonzales, Executive Director
Tel: (203) 781-0226 Fax: (203) 781-0229
Email: hunidos@yahoo.com
Web: www.hispanos-unidos.org

SPEC. INT., HOUSING

CASA OTOÑAL, INC.
135 Sylvan Ave.
New Haven, CT 06519
Patricia McCann, Executive Director
Tel: (203) 773-1847 Fax: (203) 773-3045

SPEC. INT., HUMAN RELATIONS

CATHOLIC CHARITIES MIGRATION AND REFUGEE SERVICES
125 Market St.

Hartford, CT 06103
Sr. Dorothy Strelchun, Director
Tel: (860) 548-0059 Fax: (860) 549-8697

CONNECTICUT ASSOCIATION FOR UNITED SPANISH ACTION, INC.
555 Windsor St.
Hartford, CT 06120
Carmen Sierra, Executive Director
Tel: (860) 424-0077 Fax: (860) 560-0396
Email: mail@causainc.org
Web: www.causainc.org

LA CASA DE PUERTO RICO
48 Main St.
Hartford, CT 06106
Rosaida Rosario, Executive Director
Tel: (860) 522-7296 Fax: (860) 246-6070

SPEC. INT., LEGAL ASSISTANCE

HISPANIC NATIONAL BAR ASSOCIATION
Region I
2 Union Plz.
New London, CT 06320
Santa Mendoza, Regional President
Tel: (860) 271-2224 Fax: (860) 443-8131
Email: smendoza@sswbgg.com
Web: www.hnba.com

SANTIAGO LAW GROUP
One Constitution Plaza #900
Hartford, CT 06103
Rafael Santiago, Managing Member
Tel: (860) 547-1331 Fax: (860) 713-8905
Email: rsantiago@santiagolawgroup.com
Web: www.santiagolawgroup.com

SPEC. INT., MENTAL HEALTH

INSTITUTE FOR THE HISPANIC FAMILY
80 Jefferson St.
Hartford, CT 06106
Waldemar Gracia, Director
Tel: (860) 527-1124 Fax: (860) 724-2539
Email: wgracia@cccss.org

LATINO COMMUNITY SERVICES PROGRAM
Sonia Center
1125 Main St.
Willimantic, CT 06226
Jane Perry, Division Manager
Tel: (860) 423-8667 Fax: (860) 450-7297

SPEC. INT., SENIORS

LA CASA BIENVENIDA SENIOR CENTER
135 E. Liberty St.
Waterbury, CT 06706
Lydia Ochoa, Project Director
Tel: (203) 754-5684

SPANISH SENIOR CENTER
1057 E. Main St.
Bridgeport, CT 06608
Miguel Cardozo, Program Director
Tel: (203) 333-9332

SPEC. INT., SOCIAL INTEREST

CONNECTICUT PUERTO RICAN FORUM, INC.
95 Park St.
Hartford, CT 06106
Calixto Torres, Executive Director
Tel: (860) 247-3227 Fax: (860) 549-5761
Email: ctforum@ctpuertoricanforum.org
Web: www.ctpuertoricanforum.org

HISPANIC CENTER OF GREATER DANBURY
87 West St.
Danbury, CT 06810
María-Cinta Lowe, Executive Director
Tel: (203) 798-2855 Fax: (203) 798-6337
Email: hispaniccenter@aol.com
Web: www.hispaniccenterofdanbury.org

HUMANIDAD, INC.
Affiliate of NCLR
1800 Silas Deane Hwy. #159
Rocky Hill, CT 06067-1317
Evens Jacobs, Jr., Executive Director
Tel: (860) 563-6103 Fax: (860) 721-7215
Email: info@humanidad.us
Web: www.humanidad.us

INSTITUTE FOR LIFE COPING SKILLS INC.
Sistema Adkins for Latino/Hispanic Clients
141 Franklin St.
Stamford, CT 06901
Caroline Manuele Adkins, Vice President
Tel: (800) 783-2577 Fax: (203) 353-0699
Email: info@adkinslifeskills.org
Web: www.adkinslifeskills.org

JUNTA FOR PROGRESSIVE ACTION, INC.
169 Grand Ave.
New Haven, CT 06513
Cheila Serrano, Administrative Assistant
Tel: (203) 787-0191 Fax: (203) 787-4934
Email: cheila.serrano@juntainc.org
Web: www.juntainc.org

NEW HAVEN-LEON SISTER CITY PROJECT
608 Whitney Ave.
New Haven, CT 06511
Patricia Nuelsen, Administrative Director
Tel: (203) 562-1607 Fax: (203) 624-1683
Email: nh@newhavenleon.org
Web: www.newhavenleon.org

SONIA CENTER
1125 Main St.
Willimantic, CT 06226
Rebecca Soto, Program Coordinator
Tel: (860) 423-8667 Fax: (860) 450-7297

STUDENT ORGANIZATION

ASSOCIATION OF LATINO AMERICAN STUDENTS
Housatonic Community College
900 Lafayette Blvd.
Bridgeport, CT 06604
Hernan Yepes, Advisor
Tel: (203) 332-5017
Email: HYepes@hcc.commnet.edu
Web: www.hcc.commnet.edu/student/clubs.html

THE CENTER FOR LATIN AMERICAN & CARIBBEAN STUDIES
University of Connecticut
843 Bolton Rd. #1131
Storrs, CT 06269-1161
Peter Kingstone, Director
Tel: (860) 486-4964 Fax: (880) 486-2963
Email: LatinAmerica@uconn.edu
Web: http://clacs.uconn.edu/index.html

DESPIERTA BORICUA
301 Crown St.
New Haven, CT 06520
Email: ariana.gallisa@yale.edu
Web: www.yale.edu/db/welcome.html

LA CASA CULTURAL
Yale University
301 Crown St.
New Haven, CT 06511
Rosalinda Garcia, Director
Tel: (203) 432-0856
Email: rosalinda.garcia@yale.edu
Web: www.yale.edu/centro/

LAMBDA THETA PHI, LATIN FRATERNITY
University of Connecticut/Lambda Chapter
233 Glenbrook Rd. #4121
Storrs, CT 06269
Eduardo Colon, President
Tel: (860) 486-2000 Fax: (860) 486-1194
Email: lambdas@studentorgs.uconn.edu
Web: www.lambdachapter.com

DELAWARE

MULTI-PURPOSE

LATIN AMERICAN COMMUNITY CENTER
403 N. Van Buren St.
Wilmington, DE 19805
María Matos, Executive Director
Tel: (302) 655-7338 Fax: (302) 655-7334
Email: matoslacc@yahoo.com
Web: www.thelatincenter.org

POLITICAL ACTION

CITY OF WILMINGTON, MINORITY BUSINESS ENTERPRISE OFFICE
City Council
800 N. French St., 9th Fl., Louis L. Redding
City/County Bldg.
Wilmington, DE 19801-3537
Theodore Blunt
Tel: (302) 576-2140 Fax: (302) 576-4071
Email: cbarnes@ci.wilmington.de.us
Web: www.ci.wilmington.de.us

SPEC. INT., HUMAN RELATIONS

TELAMON CORPORATION
26351 Patriots Way
Georgetown, DE 19947
Doris Gonzalez, State Head Start Director
Tel: (302) 934-1642 Fax: (302) 934-9697
Email: dgonzalez@telamon.org
Web: www.telamon.org

Central Sussex Head Start Center
211 N. Race St.
Georgetown, DE 19947
Nada Kimball, Center Aide
Tel: (302) 677-1885 Fax: (302) 677-1889
Web: www.telamon.org

Colonial Gardens Head Start Center
1000 Hayes Dr.
Dover, DE 19904
Sylvia Durant, Center Director
Tel: (302)741-2490 Fax: (302) 741-2499
Email: sdurant@telamon.org
Web: www.telamon.org

Georgetown Annex Head Start Center
308 N. Railroad Ave.
Georgetown, DE 19947
Nada Kimball, Center Aide
Tel: (302) 855-0325 Fax: (302) 934-9697
Web: www.telamon.org

Harrington Head Start Center
112 East St.
Harrington, DE 19952
Lurys Fuhrman, Director
Tel: (302) 398-9196 Fax: (302) 398-9252
Email: lfuhrman@telamon.org
Web: www.telamon.org

Smyrna Head Start Center
204 George's Alley
Smyrna, DE 19977
Sodonia Worthy, Center Director
Tel: (302) 653-5499 Fax: (302) 653 3862
Email: sworthy@telamon.org
Web: www.telamon.org

State Head Start Office
204 George's Alley
Smyrna, DE 19977
Esther Graham, State Head Start Director
Tel: (302) 659-5092 Fax: (302) 659-5106
Email: egraham@telamon.org
Web: www.telamon.org

State Office
504 N. Dupont Hwy.
Dover, DE 19901
Aurea Garcia, Case Manager
Tel: (302)734-1903 Fax: (302)734-0382

Email: agarcia@telamon.org
Web: www.telamon.org

White Oak Head Start Center
195 Willis Rd.
Dover, DE 19901
Sherry Bell, Center Director
Tel: (302) 736-5933 Fax: (302) 736-5932
Email: sbell@telamon.org
Web: www.telamon.org

SPEC. INT., SOCIAL INTEREST

DELAWARE GOVERNOR'S ADVISORY COUNCIL ON HISPANIC AFFAIRS
1901 N. Dupont Hwy., DE Health & Services
Campus
New Castle, DE 19720
Wanda Lopez, Director
Tel: (302) 292-1447 Fax: (302) 255-4463
Email: wandalopezwml@comcast.net

DELMARVA RURAL MINISTRIES, INC.
26 Wyoming Ave.
Dover, DE 19904
Debra Singletary, CEO
Tel: (302) 678-3652 Fax: (302) 678-0545
Email: dsingletary@drminc.org
Web: www.drminc.org

LA ESPERANZA, INC.
216 N. Race St.
Georgetown, DE 19947
Marissa C. Vonville, Executive Director
Tel: (302) 854-9262 Fax: (302) 854-9277
Email: laesperanza@dmv.com
Web: www.laesperanza.org

OFICINA DE LA FAMILIA Y DE LOS NIÑOS
301 N. Harrison St.
Wilmington, DE 19805
Carlos Dipres, Team Leader
Tel: (302) 655-6486 Fax: (302) 655-9815
Email: carlosdipres@cssde.org

DISTRICT OF COLUMBIA

ARTISTIC

ALMA BOLIVIANA
1510 31st St. NW
Washington, DC 20007
Maria de Martinez, President
Tel: (202) 338-2522 Fax: (202) 338-2522

EL MUSEO FONDO DEL SOL
2112 R St. NW
Washington, DC 20008
Marcos Zuver, Program Director
Tel: (202) 265-9235 Fax: (202) 265-1078

EL TEATRO DE DANZA CONTEMPORÁNEA DE EL SALVADOR
3420 38th St. NW #416B
Washington, DC 20016
Miya Hisaka Silva, Artistic Director
Tel: (202) 362-4218 Fax: (202) 362-4218
Email: miyahisaka@aol.com

GRUPO DE ARTISTAS LATINOAMERICANOS THEATRE
P.O. Box 43209
Washington, DC 20010
Hugo Medrano, Artistic Director
Tel: (202) 234-7174 Fax: (202) 332-1247
Email: info@galatheatre.org
Web: www.galatheatre.org

NATIONAL HISPANIC FOUNDATION FOR THE ARTS
Water Front Center
1010 Wisconsin Ave. NW #210
Washington, DC 20007
Richard Rodriguez, Executive Director
Tel: (202) 293-8330 Fax: (202) 965-5252
Email: info@hispanicarts.org
Web: www.hispanicarts.org

TEATRO DE LA LUNA
4020 Georgia Ave. NW
Washington, DC 20011
Mario Marcel, Executive Director
Tel: (202) 882-6227 Fax: (202) 291-2357
Email: info@teatrodelaluna.org
Web: www.teatrodelaluna.org

BUSINESS

ASSOCIATION OF AMERICAN CHAMBERS OF COMMERCE IN LATIN AMERICA
1615 H St. NW
Washington, DC 20062-2000
James Fendell, President
Tel: (202) 463-5485 Fax: (202) 463-3126
Email: info@aaccla.org
Web: www.aaccla.org

GREATER AMERICA BUSINESS COALITION
Ronald Reagan Building
1300 Pennsylvania Ave. NW #G0003
Washington, DC 20004-3021
Albert Zapanta, Chairman
Tel: (301) 986-0300 Fax: (301) 986-8803
Email: information@greateramerica.org
Web: www.greateramerica.org

LATIN AMERICAN MANAGEMENT ASSOCIATION
National Headquarters
419 New Jersey Ave. SE
Washington, DC 20003
Stephen Denlinger, CEO
Tel: (202) 546-3803 Fax: (202) 546-3807
Email: lamausa@bellatlantic.net
Web: www.lamausa.com

LATINO ECONOMIC DEVELOPMENT CORPORATION
2316 18th St. NW
Washington, DC 20009
Juan J. Patlan, Executive Director
Tel: (202) 588-5102 Fax: (202) 588-5204
Email: juanpatlan@aol.com
Web: www.ledcdc.org

NATIONAL ASSOCIATION OF MINORITY CONTRACTORS
National Headquarters
666 11th St. NW #520
Washington, DC 20001
Owen Tonkins, Executive Director
Tel: (202) 347-8259 Fax: (202) 628-1876
Email: owen_tonkins@namcline.org
Web: www.namcline.org

NATIONAL SOCIETY OF HISPANIC MBAS
Washington DC Chapter
P.O. Box 65087
Washington, DC 20035-5087
Maria Carrasquillo, Chapter President
Email: president@washingtondc.nshmba.org
Web: www.nshmba.org

NEW AMERICA ALLIANCE
1050 Connecticut Ave. NW #1000
Washington, DC 20036
María del Pilar Avila, Executive Director
Tel: (202) 772-4158 Fax: (202) 772-3374
Email: pavila@naaonline.org
Web: www.naaonline.org

UNITED STATES-PANAMA BUSINESS COUNCIL
1300 Pennsylvania Ave. NW #G-0003
Washington, DC 20004-3021
Margaret de Sosa, Executive Vice President
Tel: (202) 312-1645 Fax: (202) 312-1646
Email: info@us-panama.org
Web: www.us-panama.org

CHAMBER OF COMMERCE

GREATER WASHINGTON IBERO AMERICAN CHAMBER OF COMMERCE
1112 16th St. NW #340

Washington, DC 20036
Fernando Barrueta, President
Tel: (202) 728-0352 Fax: (202) 728-0355
Email: info@iberochamber.org
Web: www.iberochamber.org

UNITED STATES HISPANIC CHAMBER OF COMMERCE
National Headquarters
1300 Pennsylvania Ave. NW #270
Washington, DC 20004
Armando Ojeda, President /CEO
Tel: (202) 842-1212 Fax: (202) 842-3283
Email: info@usmcoc.org
Web: www.ushcc.com

UNITED STATES-MEXICO CHAMBER OF COMMERCE
Binational Offices
1300 Pennsylvania Ave. NW #270
Washington, DC 20004-3021
Albert Zapanta, President & CEO
Tel: (202) 312-1520 Fax: (202) 312-1530
Email: zapantaz@usmcoc.org
Web: www.usmcoc.org

VENEZUELAN-AMERICAN CHAMBER OF COMMERCE AND INDUSTRY
1615 L St. NW #430
Washington, DC 20036
Antonio Herrera-Vaillant, President
Tel: (202) 822-0711 Fax: (202) 429-3231
Email: aherrera@venamcham.org
Web: www.venamcham.org

COMMUNICATIONS

HISPANIC LINK
1420 N St. NW
Washington, DC 20005
Héctor Ericksen-Mendoza, Executive Director
Tel: (202) 234-0280 Fax: (202) 234-4090
Email: hector@hispaniclink.org
Web: www.hispaniclink.org

NATIONAL ASSOCIATION OF HISPANIC JOURNALISTS
National Headquarters
100 National Press Bldg., 529 14th St. NW
Washington, DC 20045-2001
Veronica Villafañe, President
Tel: (202) 662-7145 Fax: (202) 662-7144
Email: nahj@nahj.org
Web: www.nahj.org

NATIONAL ASSOCIATION OF HISPANIC PUBLICATIONS
National Headquarters
529 14th St. NW #1085
Washington, DC 20045
Alec Andrade, Projects, Communications & Productions
Tel: (202) 662-7250 Fax: (202) 662-7251
Email: alec@nahp.org
Web: www.nahp.org

WALTER KAITZ FOUNDATION
1724 Massachusetts Ave. NW
Washington, DC 20036
Debbie A. Smith, Executive Director
Tel: (202) 775-3611 Fax: (202) 775-1059
Email: info@walterkaitz.org
Web: www.walterkaitz.org

CULTURAL

ART MUSEUM OF THE AMERICAS
Affiliate of Organization of American States
1889 F St. NW
Washington, DC 20006
Charo Marroquin, Administrative Officer
Tel: (202) 458-6016 Fax: (202) 458-6021
Email: cmarroquin@oas.org
Web: www.museum.oas.org/index.html

ASOCIACIÓN COSTA RICA, INC.
P.O. Box 53331
Washington, DC 20009

Illiana Navarro, President
Tel: (202) 623-3825
Email: asociacion_costarica@hotmail.com

BRAZILIAN AMERICAN CULTURAL INSTITUTE
4719 Wisconsin Ave. NW
Washington, DC 20016-4609
José Neistein, Director
Tel: (202) 362-8334 Fax: (202) 362-8337
Email: info@bacidc.org
Web: www.bacidc.org

ESPACIO CULTURAL SALVADOREÑO
c/o General Consulate of El Salvador
1724 20th St. NW
Washington, DC 20009
Mario Cader-Frech, Director
Tel: (202) 256-6542 Fax: (202) 332-7642
Email: culturaSal@aol.com
Web: www.rree.gob.sv/sitio%5Csitio.nsf/pages/
espaciocultural

HISPANIC HERITAGE AWARDS FOUNDATION
2600 Virginia Ave. NW #406
Washington, DC 20037
Jose Antonio Tijerino, President/CEO
Tel: (202) 861-9797 Fax: (202) 861-9799
Email: contact@hispanicheritageawards.org
Web: www.hispanicheritageawards.org

MEXICAN CULTURAL INSTITUTE
Washington Office
2829 16th St. NW
Washington, DC 20009
Alejandro Negrin, Director
Tel: (202) 728-1628 Fax: (202) 462-7241
Email: altirado@erols.com

SISTER CITIES INTERNATIONAL
1301 Pennsylvania Ave. NW #850
Washington, DC 20004
Tim Honey, Executive Director
Tel: (202) 347-8630 X8631 Fax: (202) 393-6524
Email: thoney@sister-cities.org
Web: www.sister-cities.org

SMITHSONIAN CENTER FOR LATINO INITIATIVES
900 Jefferson Dr. SW #1479, MRC 448
Washington, DC 20560-0448
Ana Cabral, Director
Tel: (202) 633-1240 Fax: (202) 786-2477
Email: cabrala@si.edu
Web: http://latino.si.edu

WASHINGTON DC METROPOLITAN POLICE DEPARTMENT
Latino Liaison Unit
1800 Columbia Rd. NW
Washington, DC 20001
Sgt. Juan Espinal, Member
Tel: (202) 673-4445 Fax: (202) 673-4466
Web: http://mpdc.dc.gov/about/units/llu.shtm

ALLIANCE FOR RESPONSIBLE CUBA POLICY FOUNDATION
700 12th St. NW #1100
Washington, DC 20005
Albert A. Fox, Jr., President
Tel: (202) 624-3330 Fax: (202) 624-3331
Web: www.responsiblecubapolicy.org

AMERICAS GLOBAL FOUNDATION
930 M St. NW #609
Washington, DC 20001
Victor Pinzon, President & Founder
Tel: (202) 371-9696 Fax: (202) 216-9550
Email: vicpinzon@theamericas.org
Web: www.theamericas.org

CASA DEL PUEBLO
National Headquarters
1459 Columbia Rd. NW

Washington, DC 20009
John Makwalu
Tel: (202) 332-1082 Fax: (202) 667-7783
Email: mithika@yahoo.com

CUBAN-AMERICAN NATIONAL COUNCIL, INC.
Legislative Policy and Government Affairs Office
1444 I St. NW #800
Washington, DC 20005
Alicia Diaz, Director
Tel: (202) 898-4880 Fax: (202) 835-3613
Email: adiaz@cnc.org
Web: www.cnc.org

DOMINICAN AMERICAN NATIONAL ROUNDTABLE
Head Office
1050 17th St. NW #600
Washington, DC 20036
Cid Wilson, President
Tel: (202) 238-0097 Fax: (202) 238-9078
Email: info@danr.org
Web: www.danr.org

HISPANIC SUPPORT GROUP
3900 Wisconsin Ave.
Washington, DC 20016
Judy M. Majors, Chairperson
Tel: (202) 752-7587 Fax: (202) 752-4230
Email: judy_major@fanniemae.com
Web: www.efanniemae.com

INTER-AMERICAN BAR ASSOCIATION
1211 Connecticut Ave. NW #202
Washington, DC 20036
Richard Osborne, Coordinator
Tel: (202) 466-5944 Fax: (202) 466-5946
Email: iaba@iaba.org
Web: www.iaba.org

THE INTER-AMERICAN DIALOGUE
1211 Connecticut Ave. NW #510
Washington, DC 20036
Peter Hakim, President
Tel: (202) 822-9002 Fax: (202) 822-9553
Email: iad@thedialogue.org
Web: www.thedialogue.org

LA CASA
Drug and Medical Treatment Program
1436 Irving St. NW
Washington, DC 20010
Anthony Lugo, Director
Tel: (202) 673-3592 Fax: (202) 462-5669
Email: NetTony355@netscape.net
Web: www.dccfh.org

NATIONAL COMMUNITY FOR LATINO LEADERSHIP, INC.
1701 K St. NW #301
Washington, DC 20006
Alfred Ramirez, President
Tel: (202) 721-8290 Fax: (202) 721-8296
Email: ncll@latinoleadership.org
Web: www.latinoleadership.org

NATIONAL MULTICULTURAL INSTITUTE
National Headquarters
3000 Connecticut Ave. NW #438
Washington, DC 20008-2556
Elizabeth P. Salett, President
Tel: (202) 483-0700 Fax: (202) 483-5233
Email: nmci@nmci.org
Web: www.nmci.org

CARIBBEAN/LATIN AMERICAN ACTION
1818 N St. NW #310
Washington, DC 20036
Federico Sacasa, Executive Director
Tel: (202) 466-7464 Fax: (202) 822-0075
Email: fsacasa@c-caa.org
Web: www.claa.org

CITIZENS' EDUCATIONAL FOUNDATION-US
513 Capitol Ct. NE #200
Washington, DC 20002

Jose E. Aponte, Executive Director
Tel: (202) 546-3060 Fax: (202) 546-3380
Email: contactcef@cefus.net
Web: www.cefus.net

CONGRESSIONAL HISPANIC CAUCUS
Washington Office
1527 Longworth HOB
Washington, DC 20515
Alejandro Perez, Executive Director
Tel: (202) 225-2410 Fax: (202) 225-2016
Web: www.house.gov/reyes/chc

CONGRESSIONAL HISPANIC CAUCUS INSTITUTE, INC.
911 2nd St. NE
Washington, DC 20002
Esther Aguilera, Executive Director
Tel: (202) 543-1771 Fax: (202) 546-2143
Email: chci@chci.org
Web: www.chci.org

COUNCIL OF LATINO AGENCIES
2437 15th St. NW
Washington, DC 20009
MIchelle Guzman, Office Manager
Tel: (202) 328-9451 Fax: (202) 667-6135
Email: mguzman@consejo.org
Web: www.consejo.org

COUNCIL ON HEMISPHERIC AFFAIRS
1250 Connecticut Ave. NW #1C
Washington, DC 20036
Lawrence Birns, Director
Tel: (202) 223-4975 Fax: (202) 223-4979
Email: coha@coha.org
Web: www.coha.org

CUBAN AMERICAN NATIONAL FOUNDATION
Washington DC Office
1822 Jefferson Pl. NW
Washington, DC 20063
Camila Ruiz, Director
Tel: (202) 530-1894 Fax: (202) 530-2444
Email: hq@canf.org
Web: www.canfnet.org

GUATEMALA HUMAN RIGHTS COMMISSION
3321 12th St. NE
Washington, DC 20017-4008
Patricia Davis, Interim Executive Director
Tel: (202) 529-6599 Fax: (202) 526-4611
Email: pdavis@ghrc-usa.org
Web: www.ghrc-usa.org

HISPANIC AMERICAN LEADERSHIP COUNCIL
Democratic National Committee
430 S. Capitol St. SE
Washington, DC 20003
Alice Travis Germond, Secretary
Tel: (202) 863-8000 Fax: (202) 863-8174
Email: halc@dnc.org
Web: www.democrats.org/leadershipcouncils/halc.
html

HISPANIC COUNCIL ON INTERNATIONAL RELATIONS
National Headquarters
1111 19th St. NW #403
Washington, DC 20036
Marco Aguilar, Executive Director
Tel: (202) 785-5884 Fax: (202) 785-0265
Email: hispaniccouncil@hcir.org
Web: www.hcir.org

HISPANIC ELECTED LOCAL OFFICIALS CAUCUS
National Headquarters
1301 Pennsylvania Ave. NW #550
Washington, DC 20004
Mary Gordon, Manager, Constituency Services
Tel: (202) 626-3169 Fax: (202) 626-3043
Email: gordon@nlc.org
Web: www.nlc.org

INTER-AMERICAN DEFENSE BOARD
Affiliate of Organization of American States
2600 16th St. NW
Washington, DC 20441-0002

Keith Huber, Chairman
Tel: (202) 939-6041
Email: info@jid.org
Web: www.jid.org

LABOR COUNCIL FOR LATIN AMERICAN ADVANCEMENT
National Office
888 16th St. NW #640
Washington, DC 20006
Jesse Rios, Executive Director
Tel: (202) 347-4223 Fax: (202) 347-5095
Email: headquarters@lclaa.org
Web: www.lclaa.org

LATIN AMERICA WORKING GROUP
110 Maryland Ave. NE, Box 15
Washington, DC 20002
Lisa Haugaard, Executive Director
Tel: (202) 546-7010 Fax: (202) 543-7647
Email: lisah@lawg.org
Web: www.lawg.org

MAYOR'S OFFICE ON LATINO AFFAIRS
2000 14th St. NW, 2nd Fl.
Washington, DC 20009
Gustavo Velasques, Executive Director
Tel: (202) 671-2825 Fax: (202) 673-4557
Email: Gustavo.Velasques@dc.gov
Web: www.dc.gov

NATIONAL ASSOCIATION OF LATINO ELECTED & APPOINTED OFFICIALS
Washington Office
311 Massachusetts Ave. NE
Washington, DC 20002
Larry Gonzalez, Director
Tel: (202) 546-2536 Fax: (202) 546-4121
Email: lgonzalez@naleo.org
Web: www.naleo.org

NATIONAL HISPANIC CAUCUS OF STATE LEGISLATORS
National Headquarters
444 N. Capitol St. NW #404
Washington, DC 20001
Elizabeth Burgos, Executive Director
Tel: (202) 434-8070 Fax: (202) 434-8072
Web: www.nhcsl.com

NATIONAL PUERTO RICAN COALITION, INC.
National Headquarters
1901 L St. NW #802
Washington, DC 20036
Manuel Mirabal, President & CEO
Tel: (202) 223-3915 Fax: (202) 429-2223
Email: nprc@nprcinc.org
Web: www.bateylink.org

NATIONAL REPUBLICAN SENATORIAL COMMITTEE
Ronald Reagan Republican Center
425 2nd St. NE
Washington, DC 20002
Mark Stevens, Director
Tel: (202) 675-6000 Fax: (202) 675-4730
Email: mstevens@nrsc.org
Web: www.nrsc.org

PAN-AMERICAN DEVELOPMENT FOUNDATION
Affiliate of Organization of American States
1889 F St. NW
Washington, DC 20006
Amy Coughenour Betancourt, Deputy Director
Tel: (202) 458-3969 Fax: (202) 458-6316
Email: padf-dc@padf.org
Web: www.padf.org

PUERTO RICO FEDERAL AFFAIRS ADMINISTRATION
1100 17th St. NW #800
Washington, DC 20036
Mari Carmen Aponte, Executive Director
Tel: (202) 778-0710 Fax: (202) 778-0721
Email: info@prfaa.com
Web: www.prfaa.com

REPUBLICAN NATIONAL COMMITTEE
GOP Outreach

310 1st St. SE
Washington, DC 20003
Claudia E. Jaquez, Outreach Coordinator
Tel: (202) 863-8600 Fax: (202) 863-8808
Email: info@gop.com
Web: www.rnc.org

REPUBLICAN NATIONAL HISPANIC ASSEMBLY OF THE US

P.O. Box 1882
Washington, DC 20013-1882
Massey Villarreal, National Chairman
Tel: (202) 544-6700 Fax: (202) 544-6869
Email: info@rnha.org
Web: www.rnha.org

WASHINGTON OFFICE ON LATIN AMERICA

1630 Connecticut Ave. NW #200
Washington, DC 20009
Joy Olson, Executive Director
Tel: (202) 797-2171 Fax: (202) 797-2172
Email: wola@wola.org
Web: www.wola.org

PROFESSIONAL

ASSOCIATION OF LATINO PROFESSIONALS

441 G St. NW
Washington, DC 20548
Elizabeth Martinez, Chapter President
Tel: (202) 512-9230
Email: martinez@gao.gov
Web: www.alpfa.org

HISPANIC BAR ASSOCIATION OF THE DISTRICT OF COLUMBIA

P.O. Box 1011
Washington, DC 20013-1011
Brigida Benitez, President
Tel: (202) 388-4990
Email: info@hbadc.org
Web: www.hbadc.org

NATIONAL ASSOCIATION OF HISPANIC NURSES

1501 16th St. NW
Washington, DC 20036
Rudy Valenzuela, President
Tel: (202) 387-2477 Fax: (202) 483-7183
Email: info@thehispanicnurses.org
Web: www.thehispanicnurses.org

NATIONAL ASSOCIATION OF HISPANIC PUBLICATIONS FOUNDATION

1085 National Press Bldg.
Washington, DC 20045
Thomas L. Oliver, Executive Director
Tel: (202) 662-7250 Fax: (202) 662-7254
Email: tomoliver@nahp.org
Web: www.nahp.org

RELIGIOUS

ARCHDIOCESE OF WASHINGTON

Spanish Catholic Center
P.O. Box 11450
5001 Eastern Ave.
Washington, DC 20008-0650
Rev. Donald F. Lippert, Executive Director
Tel: (301) 853-4566 Fax: (301) 853-7671
Email: padredonato@capuchin.com
Web: www.centrocatolicohispano.org

BRAZILIAN BAPTIST CHURCH

5671 Western Ave. NW
Washington, DC 22191
Rev. Carlos Mendes, Pastor
Tel: (202) 537-7280 Fax: (202) 537-9406
Email: igreja@ibbwdc.com
Web: www.ibbwdc.com

HISPANIC APOSTOLATE

Cathedral of St. Matthews
1725 Rhode Island Ave. NW
Washington, DC 20036
Rev. Msgr. Ronald Jameson, Rector
Tel: (202) 347-3215 Fax: (202) 347-7184
Email: cathstmatt@stmatthewscathedral.org

SACRED HEART COMMUNITY CENTER

3211 Sacred Heart Way NW
Washington, DC 20010-3354
Sonia M. Aquino, Coordinator
Tel: (202) 234-8000 Fax: (202) 234-9159
Email: hleonzo@shrineofthesacred.org
Web: www.shrineofthesacredheart.org

SECRETARIATE FOR HISPANIC AFFAIRS

National Conference of Catholic Bishops
3211 4th St. NE
Washington, DC 20017-1194
Ronaldo M. Cruz, Executive Director
Tel: (202) 541-3150 Fax: (202) 722-8717
Email: hispanicaffairs@usccb.org
Web: www.usccb.org/hispanicaffairs

SHRINE OF THE SACRED HEART

3211 Sacred Heart Way NW
Washington, DC 20010
Fr. Estaban Carter, Pastor
Tel: (202) 234-8000 Fax: (202) 234-9159
Email: hceonzo@shrineofthesacredheart.org
Web: www.shrineofthesacredheart.org

ST. THOMAS THE APOSTLE

2665 Woodley Rd. NW
Washington, DC 20008
Rev. Mark Brennan, Pastor
Tel: (202) 234-1488 Fax: (202) 234-1480
Email: stawdc@aol.com
Web: www.parishes.org/stthomasapostle.html

UNITED STATES CATHOLIC CONFERENCE/ HISPANIC AFFAIRS

3211 4th St. NE
Washington, DC 20017
Ronaldo Crúz, Executive Director Hispanic Affairs
Tel: (202) 541-3000 Fax: (202) 722-8717
Email: hispanicaffairs@usccb.org
Web: www.usccb.org/hispanicaffairs

RESEARCH

CENTER FOR IMMIGRATION STUDIES

1522 K St. NW #820
Washington, DC 20005-1202
Mark Krikorian, Director
Tel: (202) 466-8185 Fax: (202) 466-8076
Email: center@cis.org
Web: www.cis.org

FOUNDATION FOR THE ADVANCEMENT OF HISPANIC AMERICANS, INC.

National Headquarters
P.O. Box 66012
Washington, DC 20035
Pedro De Mesones, President
Tel: (703) 866-1578 Fax: (703) 455-4709
Email: pdemesones@msn.com

INTER-UNIVERSITY PROGRAM FOR LATINO RESEARCH

University of Notre Dame
1608 Rhode Island Ave. NW #244
Washington, DC 20036
Olga Herrera, Program Coordinator
Tel: (202) 974-6282 Fax: (202) 728-4076
Email: oherrera@nd.edu
Web: www.nd.edu/~iuplr

THE LATINO COALITION

707 5th St. SE
Washington, DC 20003
Roberto G. de Posada, President
Tel: (202) 546-0008 Fax: (202) 546-0807
Email: rdeposada@hbrt.org
Web: www.thelatinocoalition.com

MEXICO-NORTH RESEARCH NETWORK, INC.

231 F St. NE
Washington, DC 20002
Greta de Leon, Executive Director
Tel: (202) 546-0801 Fax: (202) 546-0801
Email: mexnor@mexnor.org
Web: www.mexnor.org

SPEC. INT., AIDS

NATIONAL MINORITY AIDS COUNCIL

National Headquarters
1931 13th St. NW
Washington, DC 20009-4432
Paul Akio Kawata, Executive Director
Tel: (202) 483-6622 X321 Fax: (202) 483-1135
Email: pkawata@nmac.org
Web: www.nmac.org

WHITMAN WALKER CLINIC

Latino Services
1734 14th St. NW
Washington, DC 20020
Gerald Filbin, Secretary
Tel: (202) 939-7881 Fax: (202) 678-8099
Email: latino@wwc.org
Web: www.wwc.org

SPEC. INT., ALCOHOL/DRUG CENTER

ADAMS MILL ABSTINANCE CENTER

1808 Adams Mill Rd. NW
Washington, DC 20009
Larry Ricks, Clinic Manager
Tel: (202) 673-6618 Fax: (202) 673-2037
Email: lricks@dchealth.com

ANDRÓMEDA - CENTRO HISPANO DE SALUD MENTAL

1400 Decatur St. NW
Washington, DC 20011
Dr. Ricardo Galbis, Executive Director, MD
Tel: (202) 291-4707 Fax: (202) 723-4560
Email: andromeda@andromedahealthcenter.org
Web: www.andromedahealthcenter.org

LATINO COUNCIL ON ALCOHOL AND TOBACCO

1616 P St. NW #430
Washington, DC 20036
Diana Rodriguez-Algra, President
Tel: (202) 265-8054 Fax: (202) 265-8056
Email: lcat@nlcatp.org
Web: www.nlcatp.org

SALOMON ZELAYA REHABILITATION CENTER

1345 Newton St. NW
Washington, DC 20010
Pablo M. Sánchez, Executive Director
Tel: (202) 745-7719 Fax: (202) 745-0244
Email: aa_sanchez@msn.com

SPEC. INT., CHILD CARE

BARBARA CHAMBERS CHILDREN'S CENTERS

1470 Irving St. NW
Washington, DC 20010
Maribel Torres, Executive Director
Tel: (202) 387-6755 Fax: (202) 319-9066
Email: bccc@barbarachambers.org
Web: www.barbarachambers.org

E. MAZIQUE PARENT/CHILD RESOURCE CENTER

1719 13th St. NW, 3rd Fl.
Washington, DC 20009
Leslie A. Johnson, Executive Director
Tel: (202) 462-3375 Fax: (202) 939-8696
Email: ecmpcco31@aol.com

MARY'S CENTER

Affiliate of NCLR
2333 Ontario Rd. NW
Washington, DC 20009
Guadalupe Pacheco, Chair
Tel: (202) 483-8196 Fax: (202) 797-2628
Email: info@maryscenter.org
Web: www.maryscenter.org

ROSEMOUNT CENTER

125 Michigan Ave. NE
Washington, DC 20017
Carmen Herrara, Office Manager
Tel: (202) 265-9885 Fax: (202) 265-2636
Email: info@rosemountcenter.com
Web: www.rosemountcenter.com

VILLAGE DAY CARE CENTER

2900 14th St. NW
Washington, DC 20009
Stephanie Tindal, Director
Tel: (202) 234-3855 Fax: (202) 399-7291

SPEC. INT., EDUCATION

AMERICAN ASSOCIATION FOR HIGHER EDUCATION HISPANIC CAUCUS

1 DuPont Cr. NW #360
Washington, DC 20036-1143
Diane Dade, Executive Assistant
Tel: (202) 293-6440 X767 Fax: (202) 293-0073
Email: ddade@aahe.org
Web: www.aahe.org

ASPIRA ASSOCIATION, INC.

National Headquarters
1444 Eye St. NW #800
Washington, DC 20005
John Villamil-Cassanova, Executive Vice President
Tel: (202) 835-3600 X123 Fax: (202) 835-3613
Email: info@aspira.org
Web: www.aspira.org/Nat_Office1.htm

BELL MULTICULTURAL HIGH SCHOOL

MCIP SER
3145 Hiatt Pl. NW
Washington, DC 20010
María Tukeva, Principal
Tel: (202) 673-7314 Fax: (202) 673-7581
Email: mcipoffice@yahoo.com
Web: www.mcip.org

CARLOS ROSARIO INTERNATIONAL CAREER CENTER & PUBLIC CHARTER SCHOOL

c/o Lincoln Middle School
1100 Harvard St. NW
Washington, DC 20009
Sonia Gutierrez, Executive Director
Tel: (202) 797-4700 Fax: (202) 232-6442
Email: info@carlosrosario.org
Web: www.carlosrosario.org

CENTER FOR ADVANCEMENT OF RACIAL AND ETHNIC EQUITY

American Council on Education
1 DuPont Cr. NW #800
Washington, DC 20036
William B. Harvey, Vice President & Director
Tel: (202) 939-9395 Fax: (202) 785-2990
Email: caree@ace.nche.edu
Web: www.acenet.edu

CENTER OF ARGENTINE STUDENTS AND GRADUATES IN THE UNITED STATES

P.O. Box 32247
Washington, DC 20007
Emilio Bunge, President
Tel: (202) 276-5804
Email: e_bunge@red-argentina.net
Web: www.centroargentino.org

CENTRONÍA

1420 Columbia Rd. NW
Washington, DC 20009
Eileen Wasow, Deputy Executive Director
Tel: (202) 332-4200 X160 Fax: (202) 745-2562
Email: ewasow@centronia.org
Web: www.cbmlc.org

DEVELOPING HISPANIC-SERVING INSTITUTIONS PROGRAM

1990 K St. NW. 6th Fl.
Washington, DC 20006-8512
Josephine Hamilton, Team Leader
Tel: (202) 502-7777 Fax: (202) 502-7861
Email: title.five@ed.gov
Web: www.ojc.edu/titlev/titlev.asp

EDUCATIONAL VIDEO IN SPANISH

3039 4th St. NE
Washington, DC 20017
Arturo Salcedo Martínez, Executive Director
Tel: (202) 635-2606 Fax: (202) 635-2603
Email: evs@evstv.org
Web: www.evstv.org

ENGAGING LATINO COMMUNITIES FOR EDUCATION
1400 20th St. NW #G-1
Washington, DC 20036
Alex Chough, Associate Director
Tel: (202) 530-1135 Fax: (202) 530-0809
Email: alex_chough@edpartnerships.org
Web: www.edpartnerships.org

HIGHER ACHIEVEMENT PROGRAM
19 I St. NW
Washington, DC 20001
Isadora Carreras, Development Director
Tel: (202) 842-5116 Fax: (202) 842-5123
Email: icarreras@higherachievement.org
Web: www.higherachievement.org

HISPANIC ASSOCIATION OF COLLEGES AND UNIVERSITIES
National Internship Program (HNIP)
1 Dupont Cr. NW #605
Washington, DC 20036
William Gil, Executive Director
Tel: (202) 467-0893 Fax: (202) 496-9177
Email: wgil@hacu.net
Web: www.hacu.net

HISPANIC ASSOCIATION OF COLLEGES & UNIVERSITIES
1 DuPont Cir. NW #605
Washington, DC 20036
Luis Maldonado, Executive Director
Tel: (202) 833-8361 Fax: (202) 833-8367
Email: govrel@hacu.net
Web: www.hacu.net

HISPANIC COLLEGE FUND, INC.
1717 Pennsylvania Ave. NW #460
Washington, DC 20006
Fernando Barrueta, President & CEO
Tel: (202) 296-5400 Fax: (202) 296-3774
Email: hcf-info@hispanicfund.org
Web: www.hispanicfund.org

HISPANIC SCHOLARSHIP FUND INSTITUTE
1001 Connecticut Ave. NW #632
Washington, DC 20036
Sara Martinez Tucker, President/CEO
Tel: (202) 296-0009 Fax: (202) 296-3633
Email: info@hsfi.org
Web: www.hsfi.org

INSTITUTE FOR LANGUAGES AND CULTURES OF THE AMERICAS
1411 K St. NW #500
Washington, DC 20005
Hernándo Caicedo, Executive Director
Tel: (202) 637-7065 Fax: (202) 637-7091
Email: info@ilcawca.org
Web: www.ilcawca.org

J. F. OYSTER BILINGUAL ELEMENTARY SCHOOL
2801 Calvert St. NW
Washington, DC 20008
Marta Guzman, Principal
Tel: (202) 671-3111 Fax: (202) 671-3087
Email: marta.guzman@k12.dc.us
Web: www.k12.dc.us/schools/oyster/oyster.html

JOHN QUINCY ADAMS COMMUNITY SCHOOL
2020 19th St. NW
Washington, DC 20009
Juanita Gray, Principal
Tel: (202) 673-7311 Fax: (202) 673-6500
Email: cnorris@blupit-tech.com
Web: www.blupit-tech.com/adams

LATIN AMERICAN CENTER FOR GRADUATE STUDIES IN MUSIC
Catholic University of America
Benjamin T. Rome School of Music
Washington, DC 20064
Dr. Grayson Wagstaff, Director
Tel: (202) 319-5835 Fax: (202) 319-6280
Email: wagstaff@cua.edu
Web: http://lamc.cua.edu

LATIN AMERICAN STUDIES PROGRAM
George Washington University
1957 E St. NW #501-M
Washington, DC 20052
James Ferrer, Jr., Director
Tel: (202) 994-4060 Fax: (202) 994-5477
Email: lasp@gwu.edu
Web: www2.gwu.edu/~lasp

LATINO STUDENT FUND
P.O. Box 5403
Washington, DC 20016
Rosalia G-H Miller, President
Tel: (202) 244-3438 Fax: (202) 244-3757
Email: director@latinostudentfund.org
Web: www.latinostudentfund.org

LOS MANOS DE APA- HANDS OF MY FATHER CENTER
Academy for Educational Development
1825 Connecticut Ave. NW
Washington, DC 20009-5721
Sharon Yandian, Coordinator
Tel: (202) 884-8000 Fax: (202) 884-8400
Email: communicationsmail@aed.org
Web: www.aed.org

LULAC NATIONAL EDUCATIONAL SERVICE CENTERS, INC.
League of United Latin American Citizens
2000 L St. NW #610
Washington, DC 20036
Lorena Garrido, National Secretary
Tel: (202) 835-9646 Fax: (202) 835-9685
Email: inforg@lnesc.org
Web: www.lnesc.org

NATIONAL ASSOCIATION FOR BILINGUAL EDUCATION
National Headquarters, Affiliate of NCLR
1030 15th St. NW #470
Washington, DC 20005
James Crawford, Executive Director
Tel: (202) 898-1829 Fax: (202) 789-2866
Email: nabe@nabe.org
Web: www.nabe.org

NATIONAL CLEARINGHOUSE FOR ENGLISH LANGUAGE ACQUISITION
George Washington University
2121 K St. NW #260
Washington, DC 20037
Dr. Nancy Zelasko, Director
Tel: (800) 321-6223 Fax: (202) 467-4283
Email: askncela@ncela.gwu.edu
Web: www.ncela.gwu.edu

QUALITY EDUCATION FOR MINORITIES NETWORK
1818 N St. NW #350
Washington, DC 20036
Sherly McBay, President
Tel: (202) 659-1818 Fax: (202) 659-5408
Email: qemnetwork@qem.org
Web: http://qemnetwork.qem.org

SPANISH EDUCATIONAL DEVELOPMENT CENTER
Affiliate of NCLR
1848 Kalorama Rd. NW
Washington, DC 20009
Martha Egas, Executive Director
Tel: (202) 462-8848 Fax: (202) 462-6886
Email: info@sedcenter.com
Web: www.sedcenter.com

TEACHING FOR CHANGE
P.O. Box 73038
Washington, DC 20056
Deborah Menkart, Director
Tel: (202) 588-7204 Fax: (202) 238-0109
Email: necadc@aol.com
Web: www.teachingforchange.org

WHITE HOUSE INITIATIVE ON EDUCATIONAL EXCELLENCE FOR HISPANIC AMERICANS
400 Maryland Ave. SW #5E110
Washington, DC 20202-3601
Adam Chavarria, Executive Director
Tel: (202) 401-1411 Fax: (202) 401-8377
Email: whitehouseforhispaniceducation@ed.gov
Web: www.yesican.gov

HISPANIC ASSOCIATION ON CORPORATE RESPONSIBILITY
National Headquarters
1444 I St. NW #850
Washington, DC 20005
Alfonso E. Martinez, President & CEO
Tel: (202) 835-9672 X204 Fax: (202) 457-0455
Email: hacr@hacr.org
Web: www.hacr.org

NATIONAL COUNCIL OF HISPANIC EMPLOYMENT PROGRAM MANAGERS
Washington, DC
Jeffrey Vargas, Contact
Tel: (202) 747-5051 Fax: (202) 747-5051
Email: chair@nationalcouncilhepm.com
Web: www.nationalcouncilhepm.com

FAMILY AND CHILD SERVICES OF WASHINGTON DC, INC.
929 L St. NW
Washington, DC 20001
Charlotte L. McConnell, Executive Director
Tel: (202) 289-1510
Email: cmconnell@fcsdc.com
Web: www.familyandchildservices.org

PLANNED PARENTHOOD
1108 16th St. NW
Washington, DC 20036
Rick Clark, Director
Tel: (202) 347-8500 Fax: (202) 783-3219
Web: www.ppmw.org

"LLEGO" THE NATIONAL LATINA/O LESBIAN, GAY, BISEXUAL AND TRANSGENDER ORGANIZATION
1420 K St. NW #400
Washington, DC 20005
Robert de Leon, Executive Assistant
Tel: (202) 408-5380 Fax: (202) 408-8478
Email: info@llego.org
Web: www.llego.org

DIABETES COLLABORATIVE INFORMATION
Unity Health Care, Inc.
3020 14th St. NW #401
Washington, DC 20009
Amy Simmons, Coordinator
Tel: (202) 296-1890
Email: asimmons@nachc.com
Web: www.unityhealthcare.org/diabetes_PR.htm

FARMWORKER HEALTH SERVICES
1221 Massachusetts Ave. NW #5
Washington, DC 20005
Oscar Gomez, Executive Director
Tel: (202) 347-7377 Fax: (202) 347-6385
Email: oscar@farmworkerhealth.org
Web: www.farmworkerhealth.org

THE HENRY J. KAISER FAMILY FOUNDATION
Washington, DC Office
1330 G St. NW
Washington, DC 20005
Dr. Drew E. Altman, President/CEO
Tel: (202) 347-5270 Fax: (202) 347-5274
Web: www.kff.org

HISPANIC AND MULTICULTURAL AFFAIRS
Howard University Hospital
2041 Georgia Ave. NW
Washington, DC 20060
Cathrene Uzoma, Director
Tel: (202) 865-5284 Fax: (202) 865-3245
Web: www.huhosp.org/patient_care/hispanic_affairs.htm

HISPANIC-SERVING HEALTH PROFESSIONS SCHOOLS
1120 Connecticut Ave. #260
Washington, DC 20036
Alenin Perez-Dushku, Executive Director
Tel: (202) 293-2701 Fax: (202) 293-2704
Email: hshps@hshps.com
Web: www.hshps.com

INTER-AMERICAN COLLEGE OF PHYSICIANS AND SURGEONS
1101 Pennsylvania Ave. NW #820
Washington, DC 20004
Dr. Rene F. Rodriguez, President
Tel: (202) 467-4756 Fax: (202) 467-4758
Email: info@icps.org
Web: www.icps.org

LA CLÍNICA DEL PUEBLO
2831 15th St. NW
Washington, DC 20009-4607
Juan Romagoza, Executive Director
Tel: (202) 462-4788 Fax: (202) 667-3706
Email: jromagoza@lcdp.org
Web: www.lcdp.org

NATIONAL ALLIANCE FOR HISPANIC HEALTH
National Headquarters
1501 16th St. NW
Washington, DC 20036
Jane Delgado, President/CEO
Tel: (202) 387-5000
Email: alliance@hispanichealth.org
Web: www.hispanichealth.org

NATIONAL ASSOCIATION OF HISPANIC NURSES
National Headquarters
1501 16th St. NW
Washington, DC 20036
Rudy Valenzuela, President
Tel: (202) 387-2477 Fax: (202) 483-7183
Email: info@thehispanicnurses.org
Web: www.thehispanicnurses.org

NATIONAL HISPANIC MEDICAL ASSOCIATION
1411 K St. NW #1100
Washington, DC 20005
Dr. Elena Rios, President
Tel: (202) 628-5895 Fax: (202) 628-5898
Email: nhma@nhmamd.org
Web: www.nhmamd.org

NATIONAL LATINA HEALTH NETWORK
National Office
1680 Wisconsin Ave., NW
Washington, DC 20007
Jeanette Beltran, National Director of Special Programs
Tel: (202) 965-9633 Fax: (202) 965-9637
Email: nlhn.dc@verizon.net
Web: www.nlhn.net

NATIONAL MINORITY ORGAN TISSUE TRANSPLANT EDUCATION PROGRAM
Ambulatory Care Center
2041 Georgia Ave. NW #3100
Washington, DC 20060
Suzanne Marshall, Program Coordinator
Tel: (202) 865-4888 Fax: (202) 865-4880
Email: smarshall@nationalmottep.org
Web: www.mottep.org

PAN-AMERICAN HEALTH ORGANIZATION
Affiliate of Organization of American States
525 23rd St. NW
Washington, DC 20037
Maritza La Cruz-Llanos, Administrator
Tel: (202) 974-3000
Email: info@paho.org
Web: www.paho.org

THE SPANISH OUTREACH DIABETES MANAGEMENT PROGRAM
Washington Free Clinic
1525 Newton St. NW
Washington, DC 20010
Jordan Davis, Volunteer Coordinator
Tel: (202) 667-1106 Fax: (202) 328-2652
Email: wfclinicv@hotmail.com
Web: www.wfclinic.org

MARY'S HOUSE
4303 13th St. NE
Washington, DC 20017
Sharon Murphy, Deputy Director
Tel: (202) 635-9025 Fax: (202) 529-5793
Email: casademary@aol.com
Web: www.maryhouse.org

MI CASA, INC.
1769 Lanier Pl. NW
Washington, DC 20009
Fernando Lemos, Executive Director
Tel: (202) 232-1375 Fax: (202) 232-7649
Email: micasa@micasa-inc.org
Web: www.micasa-inc.org

LEAGUE OF UNITED LATIN AMERICAN CITIZENS
2000 L St. NW #610
Washington, DC 20036
Brent A. Wilkes, National Executive Director
Tel: (202) 833-6130 Fax: (202) 833-6135
Email: bwilkes@lulac.org
Web: www.lulac.org

MEXICAN AMERICAN LEGAL DEFENSE AND EDUCATIONAL FUND
Washington, DC Regional Office
1717 K St. NW #311
Washington, DC 20036
Hector Villagra, Regional Counsel
Tel: (202) 293-2828 Fax: (202) 293-2849
Email: mdemeo@maldef.org
Web: www.maldef.org

NETWORK IN SOLIDARITY WITH THE PEOPLE OF GUATEMALA
1830 Connecticut Ave. NW
Washington, DC 20009
Tel: (202) 518-7638 Fax: (202) 223-8221
Email: nisgua@igc.org
Web: www.nisgua.org

NICARAGUA NETWORK
1247 E St. SE
Washington, DC 20003
Chuck Kaufman, Program Coordinator
Tel: (202) 544-9355 Fax: (202) 544-9359
Email: nicanet@afgj.org
Web: www.nicanet.org

BERT CORONA LEADERSHIP INSTITUTE
1500 Farragut St. NW
Washington, DC 20011
E. Francisco Lopez, President & CEO
Tel: (202) 723-7241 Fax: (202) 723-7246
Email: info@bcli.info
Web: www.bcli.info

CATHOLIC CHARITIES IMMIGRATION LEGAL SERVICES
924 G St. NW
Washington, DC 20001-4532
Edward J. Orzechowski, President
Tel: (202) 772-4356 Fax: (202) 737-4409
Email: holthoffk@catholiccharitiesdc.org
Web: www.catholiccharitiesdc.org

CENTRAL AMERICAN RESOURCE CENTER
Affiliate of NCLR
1459 Columbia Rd. NW
Washington, DC 20009
Saúl Solórzano, Executive Director
Tel: (202) 328-9799 Fax: (202) 328-0023
Email: SSolorzano@carecendc.org
Web: www.dccarecen.org

HISPANIC SERVICE CENTER, INC.
1805 Belmont Rd. NW #205
Washington, DC 20009
Marta E. Bustos, Manager
Tel: (202) 234-3435 Fax: (202) 328-6218
Email: mbustos@erols.com

PEW HISPANIC CENTER
1919 M St. NW #460
Washington, DC 20036
Roberto Suro, Director
Tel: (202) 452-1702 Fax: (202) 785-8282
Email: info@pewhispanic.org
Web: www.pewhispanic.org

AYUDA, INC.
National Headquarters Affiliate of NCLR
1736 Columbia Rd. NW
Washington, DC 20009
Barbara Laur, Executive Director
Tel: (202) 387-4848 Fax: (202) 387-0324
Web: www.ayudainc.org

HISPANIC NATIONAL BAR ASSOCIATION
National Headquarters
815 Connecticut Ave. NW #500
Washington, DC 20006
Carmen M. Feliciano, Executive Director
Tel: (202) 223-4777
Email: info@hnba.com
Web: www.hnba.com

MIGRANT LEGAL ACTION PROGRAM
1001 Connecticut Ave. NW #915
Washington, DC 20036
Roger Rosenthal, Executive Director
Tel: (202) 775-7780 Fax: (202) 775-7784
Email: mlap@mlap.org
Web: www.mlap.org

MINORITY FELLOWSHIP PROGRAM
American Psychological Association
750 1st St. NE
Washingotn, DC 20002-4242
James Jones, Director
Tel: (202) 336-6127 Fax: (202) 336-6012
Web: www.apa.org/mfp

EDUCATIONAL ORGANIZATION FOR UNITED LATIN AMERICANS, INC.
Spanish Senior Center
1842 Calvert St. NW
Washington, DC 20009
Julia Diaz Asper, President
Tel: (202) 483-5800 Fax: (202) 588-5806
Email: info@eofula.org
Web: www.eofula.org

EOFULA - SPANISH SENIOR CENTER
1832 Calvert St.
Washington, DC 20009
Angel Luis Irene, Director
Tel: (202) 483-5800 Fax: (202) 588-5806
Email: info@eofula.org
Web: www.eofula.com

NATIONAL ASSOCIATION FOR HISPANIC ELDERLY
Washington DC Office/Project Ayuda
1015 18th St. NW #401
Washington, DC 20036-5214
Julia Neidecker-Gonzales, Project Coordinator
Tel: (202) 293-9329 Fax: (202) 466-9028
Email: nahedc@email.com

NATIONAL HISPANIC COUNCIL ON AGING
1341 Connecticut Ave. NW #42
Washington, DC 20036
Yanira Cruz, President/CEO
Tel: (202) 429-0787 Fax: (202) 429-0789
Email: nhcoa@nhcoa.org
Web: www.nhcoa.org

ACCIÓN INTERNATIONAL
Washington Office
733 15th St. NW #700
Washington, DC 20005
María Otero, President/CEO
Tel: (202) 393-5113 Fax: (202) 393-5115
Email: info@accion.org
Web: www.accion.org

AMERICAN CENTER FOR INTERNATIONAL LABOR SOLIDARITY
1925 K St. NW #300
Washington, DC 20006
Teresa Casertano, Coordinator for the Americans
Tel: (202) 659-6300 Fax: (202) 778-6344
Email: tcasertano@solidaritycenter.org
Web: www.solidaritycenter.org

AMERICAN SOCIETY FOR PUBLIC ADMINISTRATION
1120 G St. NW #700
Washington, DC 20005
Antoinette Samuel, Executive Director
Tel: (202) 393-7878 Fax: (202) 638-4952
Email: tsamuel@aspanet.org
Web: www.aspanet.org

ASOCIACIÓN DE DAMAS PARAGUAYAS
3545 16th St. NW
Washington, DC 20010
Rosita Becker, President
Tel: (202) 387-0654 Fax: (202) 387-0654

ASSOCIATION OF COMMUNITY ORGANIZATIONS FOR REFORM NOW
District of Columbia
739 8th St. SE
Washington, DC 20003
Mat Mayers, Legislative Director
Tel: (202) 547-2500 Fax: (202) 546-2483
Email: natacorndc@acorn.org
Web: www.acorn.org

CATHOLIC CHARITIES
924 G St. NW
Washington, DC 20001
Edward J. Orzechowski, President
Tel: (202) 526-4100 Fax: (202) 526-1829
Email: holthoffk@catholiccharitiesdc.org
Web: www.catholiccharitiesdc.org

CATHOLICS FOR A FREE CHOICE
1436 U St. NW #301
Washington, DC 20009-3997
Frances Kissling, President
Tel: (202) 986-6093 Fax: (202) 332-7995
Email: cffc@catholicsforchoice.org
Web: www.catholicsforchoice.org

THE CENTER FOR NATIVE LANDS
Environmental Law Institute
1616 P St. NW #200
Washington, DC 20036
Bill Threlkeld, Program Manager
Tel: (202) 939-3800 Fax: (202) 939-3868
Web: www.nativelands.org

CHANGE, INC.
1413 Park Rd. NW
Washington, DC 20010
Grace Rolling, Executive Director
Tel: (202) 387-3725 Fax: (202) 387-3729
Email: changeinc@hotmail.com

CHILEAN AMERICAN FOUNDATION
P.O. Box 34295
Washington, DC 20043-4295
Miriam Israel, President
Tel: (202) 638-2002
Email: caf@chileusfoundation.org
Web: www.chileusfoundation.org

CONGRESSIONAL HISPANIC CONFERENCE
313 Cannon HOB
Washington, DC 20515
Marlo H. Lopez, Executive Director
Tel: (202) 225-2778

CONGRESSIONAL HISPANIC LEADERSHIP INSTITUTE
1825 I St. NW #400
Washington, DC 20006
Octavio Hinojosa, Executive Director
Tel: (202) 429-2033 Fax: (202) 429-9574
Email: ohinojosa@chli.org
Web: www.chli.org

CUBAN-AMERICAN ALLIANCE EDUCATION FUND
1010 Vermont Ave. NW #620
Washington, DC 20005
Delvis Fernandez Levy, President
Tel: (805) 627-1959 Fax: (805) 627-1959
Email: caaef@igc.org
Web: www.cubamer.org

ECUMENICAL PROGRAM ON CENTRAL AMERICA AND THE CARIBBEAN
1470 Irving St. NW
Washington, DC 20010
Olivia Burlingame Goumbri, Coordinator
Tel: (202) 332-0292 Fax: (202) 332-1184
Email: epicainfo@epica.org
Web: www.epica.org

HISPANIC WAR VETERANS OF AMERICA
1300 Pennsylvania Ave. NW #G0003
Washington, DC 20004-3021
Jess Quintero, President
Tel: (703) 971-3241 Fax: (703) 971-4642
Web: www.hwva.org

INTERNATIONAL FOUNDATION FOR ELECTION SYSTEMS
1101 15th St., NW
Washington, DC 20005
William J. Hybl, Chairman
Tel: (202) 828-8507 Fax: (202) 452-0804
Email: info@ifes.org
Web: www.ifes.org

LUTHERAN SOCIAL SERVICES
Washington, DC
4406 Georgia Ave. NW
Washington, DC 20011-7124
Katherine Miller-Holland, Volunteer Coordinator
Tel: (202) 723-3000 Fax: (202) 723-3303
Email: hollandk@lssnca.org
Web: www.lssnca.org

NATIONAL COUNCIL OF LA RAZA
Raul Yzaguirre Bldg., 1126 16th St., 6th Fl. NW
Washington, DC 20036
M. Janet Murguia, President/CEO
Tel: (202) 785-1670 Fax: (202) 776-1792
Web: www.nclr.org

NEIGHBORS' CONSEJO
3118 16th St. NW
Washington, DC 20010
Najiya Shana'-Salvador, Executive Director
Tel: (202) 234-6855 Fax: (202) 234-4863
Email: info@neighborsconsejo.org
Web: www.neighborsconsejo.org

OFFICE ON LATINO AFFAIRS
District of Columbia Government
2000 14th St. NW., 2nd Fl.
Washington, DC 20009
Gustavo Velasquez, Director
Tel: (202) 671-2825 Fax: (202) 673-4557
Email: ola@dc.gov
Web: http://ola.dc.gov/ola/site/default.asp

REFUGEE SERVICE CENTER
Catholic Charities of the Archdiocese of Washington
1501 Columbia Rd. NW
Washington, DC 20009
Jane Strom, Program Administrator
Tel: (202) 667-9000 Fax: (202) 667-3420
Email: strom@catholiccharitiesdc.org
Web: www.catholiccharitiesdc.org

SELF RELIANCE FOUNDATION - ACCESO HISPANO
1101 Pennsylvania Ave. NW, 6th Fl.
Washington, DC 20045
Arturo Vásquez, Executive Director
Tel: (202) 637-8800 Fax: (202) 637-8801
Web: www.selfreliancefoundation.org

SHARE FOUNDATION
Washington DC Office
415 Michigan Ave. NE
Washington, DC 20017
Dave Johnson, Policy Office Director
Tel: (202) 319-5540 Fax: (202) 319-5541
Email: sharedc@share-elsalvador.org
Web: www.share-elsalvador.org

SPANISH CATHOLIC CENTER/CENTRO CATÓLICO HISPANO
1618 Monroe St. NW
Washington, DC 20010
Javier Garcete, President
Tel: (202) 939-2400 Fax: (202) 232-1970
Web: www.centrocatolicohispano.org

SPEC. INT., SPORTS

FUTURE OF NICARAGUA FOUNDATION
2440 M St. NW #205
Washington, DC 20037
Steven B. Hopping, Co-Chair
Tel: (202) 828-7017 Fax: (202) 828-9677
Web: www.futureofnicaragua.org

SPEC. INT., VOLUNTARY SERVICE

HERMANOS Y HERMANAS MAYORES
Latino Chapter of Big Brothers Big Sisters of the National Capital Area
666 11th St. NW, Mezzanine Level
Washington, DC 20001
Jorge Bustíos, Coordinator
Tel: (202) 783-5585 Fax: (202) 783-5169
Email: jbustios@bbbsnca.org
Web: www.bbbsnca.org

PARTNERS OF THE AMERICAS
1424 K St. NW #700
Washington, DC 20005
Malcolm Butler, President/CEO
Tel: (202) 628-3300 Fax: (202) 628-3306
Email: info@partners.net
Web: www.partners.net

SPEC. INT., WOMEN

DIALOGUE ON DIVERSITY
1000 Connecticut Ave. #600
Washington, DC 20036
Cristina C. Caballero, President/CEO
Tel: (703) 631-0650 Fax: (703) 631-0617
Email: Dialog.Div@prodigy.net
Web: www.Dialogueondiversity.org

INTER-AMERICAN COMMISSION OF WOMEN
Affiliate of Organization of American States
WHA/USOAS #5914, Department of State
Washington, DC 20520
Carmen Lomelin, Executive Secretary
Tel: (202) 647-9907 Fax: (202) 647-0911
Email: clomellin@oas.org
Web: www.oas.org/cim

INTERNATIONAL ASSOCIATION OF WOMEN JUDGES
901 15th St. NW #550
Washington, DC 20005
Joan D. Winship, Executive Director
Tel: (202) 354-3847 Fax: (202) 354-3853
Email: office@iawj.org
Web: www.iawj.org

MANA-A NATIONAL LATINA ORGANIZATION
National Headquarters
1725 K St. NW #501
Washington, DC 20006
Alma Morales Riojas, President/CEO
Tel: (202) 833-0060 Fax: (202) 496-0588
Email: hermana2@aol.com
Web: www.hermana.org

MY SISTER'S PLACE
Latino Services and Program
P.O. Box 29596
Washington, DC 20017
Judith Bennette-Sattler, Executive Director
Tel: (202) 529-5991 Fax: (202) 529-5984
Email: abrookover@mysistersplacedc.org
Web: www.mysistersplacedc.org

NATIONAL CONFERENCE OF PUERTO RICAN WOMEN, INC.
National Headquarters
5 Thomas Cr. NW
Washington, DC 20005
Vanny Marreno, National President
Tel: (202) 387-4716 Fax: (202) 885-6558
Email: vannym@erols.com
Web: www.nacoprw.org

NATIONAL WOMEN'S POLITICAL CAUCUS
1634 Eye St. NW #310
Washington, DC 20006
Llenda Jackson-Leslie, President
Tel: (202) 785-1100 Fax: (202) 785-3605
Email: info@nwpc.org
Web: www.nwpc.org

SPEC. INT., YOUTH

HISPANIC/LATINO OUTREACH PROGRAM
Girl Scout Council of the Nation's Capital
4301 Connecticut Ave. NW #M-2
Washington, DC 20008
Maria Cotto, Linguistic Outreach Specialist
Tel: (202) 237-1670 x586 Fax: (202) 274-2161
Email: mcotto@gscnc.org
Web: www.gscnc.org/outreach/hispanic/default.php

YOUTH DEVELOPMENT AND OUTREACH PROGRAM (IDB)
IDB Youth Network
1300 New York Ave. NW, Stop B-570
Washington, DC 20057
Elena Suarez, Chief of Section
Tel: (202) 623-1060 Fax: (202) 623-1402
Email: Bidjuventud@iadb.org
Web: www.iadb.org/EXR/mandates/youth/index.htm

LATIN AMERICAN YOUTH CENTER
1419 Columbia Rd. NW
Washington, DC 20009
Alex Wilson, Chair
Tel: (202) 319-2225 Fax: (202) 462-5696
Email: info@layc-dc.org
Web: www.layc-dc.org

LATINO OUTREACH PROGRAM
Girl Scout Council of the Nation's Capital
4301 Connecticut Ave. NW #M-2
Washington, DC 20008
Glorimar Ortiz-Rios, Director
Tel: (202) 237-1670 X579 Fax: (202) 274-2161
Email: gortiz@gscnc.org
Web: www.gscnc.org

NATIONAL DISSEMINATION CENTER FOR CHILDREN WITH DISABILITIES
P.O. Box 1492
Washington, DC 20013-1492
Susan Ripley, Director
Tel: (202) 884-8200 Fax: (202) 884-8441
Email: nichcy@aed.org
Web: www.nichcy.org

STUDENT ORGANIZATION

LATIN AMERICAN GRADUATE ORGANIZATION
Georgetown University
ICC484, Georgetown University
Washington, DC 20057
Emily Gereffi, President
Tel: (202) 687-0140 Fax: (202) 687-0141
Email: lago@georgetown.edu
Web: www.georgetown.edu/sfs/programs/clas/lago.html

LATIN AMERICAN LAW STUDENT ASSOCIATION
Catholic University of America
3600 John McCormack Rd.
Washington, DC 20064
José Garza, President
Tel: (202) 319 5140
Email: joeytxas@yahoo.com

SPANISH CLUB
Catholic University of America
208 McMahon Hall
Washington, DC 20064
Dr. Joan Grimbert, Chair
Tel: (202) 319-5240 Fax: (202) 319-6077
Email: grimbert@cua.edu
Web: www.cua.edu

FLORIDA

ARTISTIC

COCONUT GROVE PLAYHOUSE
3500 Main Hwy.
Miami, FL 33133
K. William Kerlin, Director
Tel: (305) 442-2662 Fax: (305) 444-6437
Email: bkerlin@cgplayhouse.org
Web: www.cgplayhouse.com

HISPANIC-AMERICAN LYRIC THEATER
9130 SW 123rd Ave. Ct.
Miami, FL 33186-7185
George Mattox, Executive Director
Tel: (305) 596-5352
Email: tmattox@aol.com

LATIN ACADEMY OF RECORDING ARTS & SCIENCES, INC.
Florida Chapter
311 Lincoln Rd. #301
Miami Beach, FL 33139
Neil Crilly, Executive Director
Tel: (305) 672-4060 Fax: (305) 672-2076
Email: florida@grammy.com
Web: www.grammy.com/latin_academy/

NEW THEATER, INC.
4120 Laguna St.
Coral Gables, FL 33134
Eilene Suarez, Managing Director
Tel: (305) 443-5909 Fax: (305) 443-1642
Email: eilenesuarez@new-theater.org
Web: www.new-theater.org

SOCIEDAD ARGENTINA DE AUTORES Y COMPOSITORES
825 Brickell Bay Dr. #2047
Miami, FL 33131
Hernán Beillard, General Manager
Tel: (305) 381-9326 Fax: (305) 358-2502
Email: sadaicmia@aol.com
Web: www.sadaicmia.com

BUSINESS

AMERICAN VENEZUELAN BUSINESS LEAGUE
10773 NW 58th St. #124
Miami, FL 33178
Tel: (305) 894-4811 Fax: (305) 436-7698
Email: rlp@amvefound.org

ASOCIACION HISPANOAMERICANA DE MUJERES PROFESIONALES Y DE NEGOCIOS
P.O. Box 2964
Orlando, FL 32802
Tel: (407) 977-6722

CUBAN AMERICAN CPA ASSOCIATION, INC.
P.O. Box 442061
Miami, FL 33144
Gloria Lopez, President
Tel: (305) 220-3771 Fax: (305) 220-2363
Email: cacpa@cacpa.org
Web: www.cacpa.org

FLORIDA REGIONAL MINORITY PURCHASING COUNCIL
Main Office
600 NW 79th Ave. #388
Miami, FL 33126-4018
Beatrice Louissaint, President & CEO
Tel: (305) 260-9901 Fax: (305) 260-9902
Email: frmbc@frmbc.org
Web: www.frmbc.org

HISPANIC BUSINESS INITIATIVE FUND
1101 Channelside Dr.
Tampa, FL 33602
Tel: (813) 864-6517

HISPANIC BUSINESS INITIATIVE FUND OF GREATER ORLANDO, INC.
315 E Robinson St. #190
Orlando, FL 32801
Kirsten Palacios, President
Tel: (407) 428-5872 Fax: (407) 428-5873
Email: jfranchi@hbiforl.org
Web: www.hbiforl.org

HISPANIC MARKETING AND COMMUNICATION ASSOCIATION
P.O. Box 565891
Miami, FL 33256-5891
Elena del Valle, President
Tel: (305) 648-2848
Email: hmca@hmca.org
Web: www.hmca.org

INTER-AMERICAN BUSINESSMEN ASSOCIATION
2925 Salcedo St. #1D
Coral Gables, FL 33134
Delo Trejo, President
Tel: (305) 442-8038 Fax: (305) 442-8039
Email: aihe@bellsouth.net

LATIN BUILDERS ASSOCIATION
782 NW Le Jeune Rd. #450
Miami, FL 33126
William J. Delgado, Executive Vice President
Tel: (305) 446-5989 X25 Fax: (305) 446-0901
Email: lba@latinbuilders.org
Web: www.latinbuilders.org

NATIONAL MINORITY SUPPLIER DEVELOPMENT COUNCIL OF FLORIDA
6880 Lake Ellenor Dr. #104A
Orlando, FL 32809
Malik Ali, Executive Director
Tel: (407) 245-6062 Fax: (407) 857-8647
Email: info@fmsdc.org
Web: www.nmsdcfl.com

NATIONAL SOCIETY OF HISPANIC MBAS
Orlando Chapter
P.O. Box 4755
Winter Park, FL 32793
Gloria Esteban, President
Tel: (407) 823-0082
Email: general@orlando.nshmba.org
Web: www.nshmba.org

South Florida Chapter
P.O. Box 226206
Miami, FL 33122
William Somerville, Chapter President
Email: general@southflorida.nshmba.org
Web: http://southflorida.nshmba.org

Tampa Bay Chapter
P.O. Box 20626
Tampa, FL 33622-0626
Maria Elena Elisalde, Chapter President
Email: general@tampabay.nshmba.org
Web: http://tampabay.nshmba.org

PUERTO RICO CONVENTION BUREAU
10544 NW 26th St. #E-203
Miami, FL 33172
Karla Mora, Sales Coordinator
Tel: (800) 875-4765 Fax: (305) 471-0209
Email: kmora@prcb.org

CHAMBER OF COMMERCE

AMERICAN CHAMBER OF COMMERCE IN GUATEMALA
P.O. Box 440999
Miami, FL 33126-1009
Email: director@amchamguate.com
Web: www.amchamguate.com

AMERICAN CHAMBER OF COMMERCE OF THE DOMINICAN REPUBLIC
P.O. Box 025256
Miami, FL 33102
Email: amcham@verizon.net.do
Web: www.amcham.org.do

ARGENTINE-FLORIDA CHAMBER OF COMMERCE
2666 Brickell Ave., 3rd Fl.
Miami, FL 33129
Edgardo De Fortuna, President
Tel: (305) 858-1516 Fax: (305) 858-3767
Email: afcc@argentinaflorida.com
Web: www.argentinaflorida.com

BRAZILIAN-AMERICAN CHAMBER OF COMMERCE
Florida Office
P.O. Box 310038
Miami, FL 33231-0038
Mary B. Arnaud, Executive Director
Tel: (305) 579-9030 Fax: (305) 579-9756
Email: baccf@brazilchamber.org
Web: www.brazilchamber.org

CHILE-UNITED STATES CHAMBER OF COMMERCE
801 Brickell Ave. #900
Miami, FL 33131
Juan Pablo Cuevas, President
Tel: (305) 789-6690 Fax: (305) 372-0189
Email: camara@chileus.org
Web: www.chileus.org

CHILE-UNITED STATES CHAMBER OF COMMERCE
Miami-Dade Chapter
801 Brickell Ave. #900
Miami, FL 33131
Juan Pablo Cuevas, President
Tel: (305) 789-6690 Fax: (305) 372-0189
Email: camara@chileus.org
Web: www.chileus.org

COLOMBIAN AMERICAN CHAMBER OF COMMERCE
312 Minorca Ave.
Coral Gables, FL 33134
Carolina Coulson, Executive Director
Tel: (305) 446-2542 Fax: (305) 398-0545
Email: usa@colombiachamber.com
Web: www.colombiachamber.com

COSTA RICAN-AMERICAN CHAMBER OF COMMERCE
P.O. Box 025216
Miami, FL 33102-5216
Email: chamber@amcham.co.cr
Web: www.amcham.co.cr

FIRST COAST HISPANIC CHAMBER OF COMMERCE
5121 Bowden #103
Jacksonville, FL 32216
Clark Vargas, President

Tel: (904) 731-3173 Fax: (904) 732-9333
Email: cvargas@cvaltd.com
Web: www.fchcc.com

FLORIDA STATE HISPANIC CHAMBER OF COMMERCE
13876 SW 56th St. #466
Jacksonville, FL 33175
Tel: (786) 221-2199 Fax: (786) 221-2199
Email: jf_fshcc@bellsouth.net

GREATER MIAMI CHAMBER OF COMMERCE
Hispanic Business Group
1601 Biscayne Blvd.
Miami, FL 33132
George Foyo, President
Tel: (305) 350-7700 Fax: (305) 371-8255
Email: chamber1@greatermiami.com
Web: www.greatermiami.com

GULF COAST LATIN CHAMBER OF COMMERCE
P.O. Box 3311
8051 N. Tamiami Trail #37
Sarasota, FL 34243
Jaime Delgado, Chairman
Tel: (941) 358-7065 Fax: (941) 358-7584
Email: info@latinchamber.org
Web: www.latinchamber.org

HIALEAH HISPANIC CHAMBER OF COMMERCE
4410 W. 16th Ave. #62
Hialeah, FL 33012
Vicente P. Rodriguez, President
Tel: (305) 557-5060 Fax: (305) 556-7333

HIALEAH LATIN CHAMBER OF COMMERCE & INDUSTRIES
1840 W. 49th St. #700
Hialeah, FL 32012
Daniel Hernández, President
Tel: (305) 828-9898 Fax: (305) 828-9777
Email: emma@hialeahchamber.com
Web: www.hialeahchamber.com

HISPANIC CHAMBER OF COMMERCE OF METRO FLORIDA
315 E Robinson St. #190
Orlando, FL 32801
Ramon Ojeda, President
Tel: (407) 428-5870 Fax: (407) 428-5871
Email: ramon@hispanicchamber.net
Web: www.hispanicchamber.net

HISPANIC CHAMBER OF COMMERCE OF PALM BEACH COUNTY, INC.
420 Clematis St., 2nd Fl.
West Palm Beach, FL 33401
Judy Dunn, Administrator
Tel: (561) 832-1986 Fax: (561) 832-1891
Email: info@palmbeachhispanicchamber.com
Web: www.palmbeachhispanicchamber.com

LATIN AMERICAN CHAMBER OF COMMERCE OF LOWER KEY WEST
P.O. Box 629
Key West, FL 33041
Arturo Espínola Arnau, President
Tel: (305) 294-6156

LATIN CHAMBER OF COMMERCE OF BROWARD COUNTY
8320 W. Sunrise Blvd. #206
Plantation, FL 33322
Jose Lopez, President
Tel: (954) 625-6616 Fax: (954) 625-6693
Email: lccb@latinchamberbroward.com
Web: www.latinchamberbroward.com

LATIN CHAMBER OF COMMERCE OF UNITED STATES
National Headquarters
1417 W. Flagler St.
Miami, FL 33135
William Alexander, President
Tel: (305) 642-3870 Fax: (305) 642-0653
Email: info@camacol.org
Web: www.camacol.org

MIAMI BEACH LATIN CHAMBER OF COMMERCE
510 Lincoln Rd.
Miami Beach, FL 33139
Maria Diez, Chairwoman
Tel: (305) 674-1414 Fax: (305) 674-9052
Email: info@miamibeach.org
Web: www.miamibeach.org

NAPLES HISPANIC CHAMBER OF COMMERCE
2740 Bayshore Dr. #5
Naples, FL 34112
Paul G. Finizio, Chairman
Tel: (239) 774-4300 Fax: (239) 774-9293
Email: nhcc2004@hotmail.com
Web: www.napleshispanicchamber.org

NICARAGUAN AMERICAN CHAMBER OF COMMERCE
175 Fountainbleau Blvd. #1R-10
Miami, FL 33172
Arturo Chamorro, President
Tel: (305) 599-2737 Fax: (305) 220-1841
Email: nacc@fdn.com
Web: www.nacc-miami.com

PERUVIAN AMERICAN CHAMBER OF COMMERCE
9737 NW 41st St. PMB 348
Miami, FL 33178
Ivan F. Garcia, President
Tel: (305) 471-9434 Fax: (305) 471-9605
Email: ivan@usaperu.org
Web: www.peruvianchamber.org

PUERTO RICAN CHAMBER OF COMMERCE OF BROWARD COUNTY
7321 Taylor St.
Hollywood, FL 33024
Frank Nieves, President
Tel: (954) 965-2491
Email: prchamberonline@prchamberonline.com
Web: www.prchamberonline.com

PUERTO RICAN CHAMBER OF COMMERCE OF SOUTH FLORIDA
3550 Biscayne Blvd. #306
Miami, FL 33137
Joseph Lopez, Chairperson
Tel: (305) 571-8006 Fax: (305) 571-8007
Email: ldr@infi.net
Web: www.puertoricanchamber.com

SOUTH BEACH HISPANIC CHAMBER OF COMMERCE OF GREATER MIAMI
301 Arthur Godfry Rd. #304
Miami Beach, FL 33140
Liliam López, President
Tel: (305) 534-1903 Fax: (305) 534-8365
Email: llopez@floridahispanicchamber.com
Web: www.floridahispanicchamber.com

SOUTHWEST FLORIDA HISPANIC CHAMBER OF COMMERCE
10051 McGregor Blvd. #204
Ft. Myers, FL 33919
Leonardo Garcia, Executive Director
Tel: (239) 418-1441 Fax: (239) 418-1475
Email: hispanicchamber.lg@earthlink.net
Web: www.swflhispanicchamber.org

SPAIN UNITED STATES CHAMBER OF COMMERCE
1221 Brickell Ave. #1000
Miami, FL 33131
Jose Luis Esteve, President
Tel: (305) 358-5988 Fax: (305) 358-6844
Email: info@spainchamber.org
Web: www.spainuscc.org

TAMPA BAY CHAMBER OF COMMERCE
4023 N. America Ave. #101
Tampa, FL 33607
Kim Scheeler, President
Tel: (813) 414-9411 Fax: (813) 414-9411
Email: tampabayhischacom@aol.com

UNITED STATES-MEXICO CHAMBER OF COMMERCE
Inter-American Chapter
703 Waterford Way #700
Miami, FL 33126
Elba Hentschel, Regional Executive Director
Tel: (305) 728-6175 Fax: (305) 261-8121
Email: usmcoc@bellsouth.net
Web: www.usmcoc.org

VENEZUELAN AMERICAN CHAMBER OF COMMERCE
2332 Galiano St. #236
Coral Gables, FL 33134
Luis José Vicentini, President
Tel: (305) 728-7042 Fax: (305) 728-7043
Email: info@venezuelanchamber.org
Web: www.venezuelanchamber.org

COMMUNICATIONS

LA PRENSA NEWSPAPER
685 S. Ronald Raegan Blvd.
Longwood, FL 32750
Manuel A. Toro, Director
Tel: (407) 767-0070 Fax: (407) 767-5478
Email: laprensa@laprensaorlando.com
Web: www.laprensaorlando.com

NATIONAL FEDERATION OF HISPANIC OWNED NEWSPAPERS
685 S. Ronald Reagan Blvd.
Longwood, FL 32750
Manuel A. Toro, Executive Director
Tel: (407) 767-0070 Fax: (407) 767-5478
Web: www.nfhon.org

CULTURAL

ASOCIACIÓN ARGENTINA DE FLORIDA CENTRAL
5454 Hoffner Ave. #106
Orlando, FL 32822
Matilda T. Mal, President
Tel: (407) 275-0207
Email: mtm5931@terra.com

CASA DE PUERTO RICO
6908-C Easter St.
Winter Park, FL 32792
Rafael Birriel, President
Tel: (407) 679-8842 Fax: (407) 679-8842

CENTRO CULTURAL ESPAÑOL DE COOPERACIÓN IBEROAMERICANA
800 Douglas Rd. # 170
Coral Gables, FL 33134
Maria Del Valle, Director
Tel: (305) 448-9677 Fax: (305) 448-9676
Email: cce@ccemiami.org
Web: www.ccemiami.org

CÍRCULO CUBANO DE TAMPA
2010 Avenida República de Cuba
Tampa, FL 33605
Jorge Díaz, President
Tel: (813) 248-2954 Fax: (813) 247-4400
Email: jdiaz8@tampabay.rr.com
Web: www.cubanclub.org

COLONIAL SPANISH QUARTER MUSEUM
P.O. Box 210
St. Augustine, FL 32085-0210
Charles Dale, Director
Tel: (904) 825-6830 Fax: (904) 825-6874
Email: sqmuse@aug.com
Web: www.historicstaugustine.com

CUBAN AMERICAN HERITAGE FESTIVAL INC.
5570 3rd Ave.
Key West, FL 33040
Tel: (305) 295-9665 Fax: (305) 294-7207
Web: www.cubanfest.com

CUBAN MUSEUM INC.
214 Giralda Ave.
Coral Gables, FL 33134
Tel: (305) 529-5400

HISPANIC HERITAGE COUNCIL, INC.
5040 NW 7th St. #690
Miami, FL 33126
Eduardo Mendoza, Executive Director
Tel: (305) 461-1014 Fax: (305) 461-1015
Email: info@hispanicfestival.com
Web: www.hispanicfestival.com

LATIN AMERICAN FIESTA ASSOCIATION
P.O. Box 4557
Tampa, FL 33677
Roseann Favata, Executive Director
Tel: (813) 238-9584

MEXICAN AMERICAN COUNCIL, INC.
P.O. Box 343546
Florida City, FL 33034-0546
Maria C. Garza, President
Tel: (305) 245-5865 Fax: (305) 248-7997

MUNICIPIOS DE CUBA EN EL EXILIO
4610 NW 7th St.
Miami, FL 33126
Jesus Herrera, President
Tel: (305) 447-8866 Fax: (305) 442-4206
Email: herrerajesus@bellsouth.net

MUSEUM OF ARTS AND SCIENCES' CUBAN MUSEUM
Smithsonian Institute
1040 Museum Blvd.
Daytona Beach, FL 32114
Bonnie Tremblay, Member Services Manager
Tel: (386) 255-0285 Fax: (386) 255-5040
Email: betty@moas.org
Web: www.moas.org

MUSEUM OF FLORIDA HISTORY
500 S. Bronough St.
Tallahassee, FL 32399-0250
Frederick Gaske, Director
Tel: (850) 245-6400 Fax: (850) 245-6833
Email: fgaske@dos.state.fl.us
Web: http://dhr.dos.state.fl.us/museum

NORTH FLORIDA HISPANIC ASSOCIATION
P.O. Box 37361
Tallahassee, FL 32315-7361
William Torres, President
Tel: (850) 216-6049
Email: WTorres@tnfha.org
Web: www.tnfha.org

SOCIEDAD CUBANA DE ORLANDO, INC.
5088 Hoffner Ave.
Orlando, FL 32812
Raul Pino, President
Tel: (407) 856-4105 Fax: (407) 856-4111

ST. AUGUSTINE HISTORICAL SOCIETY
271 Charlotte St.
St. Augustine, FL 32084
Overton G. Ganong, Executive Director
Tel: (904) 824-2872 Fax: (904) 824-2569
Email: oldhouse@aug.com
Web: www.oldesthouse.org

TOURIST OFFICE OF SPAIN
1395 Brickell Ave. #1130
Miami, FL 33131
Beatriz Marco, Director
Tel: (305) 358-1992 Fax: (305) 358-8223
Email: oetmiami@tourspain.es
Web: www.spain.info

ENTERTAINMENT

MIAMI LATIN FILM FESTIVAL
10700 SW 88th Ct.
Miami, FL 33176
Jamie Angulo, Founder/President/Executive Director
Tel: (305) 279-1809
Email: jangulo@hispanicfilm.com
Web: www.hispanicfilm.com

LAW ENFORCEMENT

LATINO OFFICERS ASSOCIATION FLORIDA
P.O. Box 44-0581
Miami, FL 33144
Alexander Martinez, President
Tel: (305) 785-6740
Email: information@loafla.org
Web: www.loafla.org

NATIONAL LATINO PEACE OFFICERS ASSOCIATION
Miami-Dade Chapter
P.O. Box 668354
Miami, FL 33166
Jeff Mallow, Chapter President
Email: nlpoa@bellsouth.net
Web: www.nlpoa.com

UNITED CORRECTIONAL OFFICERS FEDERATION, INC.
Park Pl. II 12952 SW 133 Ct. #B
Miami, FL 33186
Edgar Nieves, President
Tel: (305) 270-4844 Fax: (305) 274-2757
Email: ucofmail@aol.com
Web: www.ucof.net

MULTI-PURPOSE

AYUDA: LATIN YOUTH
Happy Kids
7118 Byron Ave.
Miami Beach, FL 33141
Jeannette Egozi, Executive Director
Tel: (305) 864-2273
Email: ayuda-miami@aol.com
Web: www.ayudamiami.org

CUBAN CENTER FOR CULTURAL, SOCIAL & STRATEGIC STUDIES, INC.
P.O. Box 651806
Miami, FL 33265
Tel: (305) 270-8779 Fax: (305) 595-1883
Email: mailbox@cubancenter.org
Web: www.cubancenter.org

HISPANIC COALITION, INC.
5659 W. Flagler St.
Miami, FL 33134
Rosa E. Kasse, President & CEO
Tel: (305) 262-0060 Fax: (305) 262-0518
Email: hispacoal@aol.com

HISPANIC FOUNDATIONS INC.
3601 Tampa Cr. E
Tampa, FL 33629
Tel: (813) 835-3838 Fax: (813) 831-2444
Email: Info@HispanicFoundations.org
Web: www.hispanicfoundations.org

HISPANIC UNITY OF FLORIDA, INC.
5840 Johnson St.
Hollywood, FL 33021
Josie Bacallao, President/CEO
Tel: (954) 964-8884 Fax: (954) 964-8646
Web: www.hispanicunity.org

LULAC NATIONAL EDUCATIONAL SERVICES CENTER, INC.
7100 SW 99th Ave. #104
Miami, FL 33173
Dulce Diaz Vega, Director
Tel: (305) 270-0063 Fax: (305) 270-7869
Email: infomia@lnesc-miami-fla.org
Web: www.lnesc-miami-fla.org

PUERTO RICAN PROFESSIONAL ASSOCIATION
South Florida Chapter
P.O. Box 524288
Miami, FL 33152
Luis Torres, Chairman
Tel: (305) 981-5513 Fax: (305) 629-3906
Email: ltorres5@bellsouth.net
Web: www.profesa.org

SOCIETY OF HISPANIC PROFESSIONAL ENGINEERS
Central Florida Professional Chapter
440 Sawgrass Corporate Pkwy. #112
Sunrise, FL 33325
Jesus Mustafa, Chapter President
Tel: (954) 846-0009 Fax: (954) 846-1090
Email: jesus_Mustafa@hotmail.com
Web: www.shpe.org

POLITICAL ACTION

ALPHA 66
1714 W. Flagler St.
Miami, FL 33135
Gerardo Rosales, Clerk
Tel: (305) 541-5433 Fax: (305) 324-5909

CONSEJO DEMOCRATA COLOMBO-AMERICANO
12205 SW 71 Ct.
Miami, FL 33156-5449
Carlos A. Cabrera, President
Tel: (305) 665-7278 Fax: (305) 661-2577
Email: cacabrera@aol.com

CUBA FREE PRESS, INC.
Proyecto Cuba Prensa Libre
9451 SW 97th St.
Miami, FL 33176
Juan A. Granados, President
Tel: (305) 270-8779 Fax: (305) 595-1883
Email: mailbox@cubafreepress.org
Web: www.cubafreepress.org

CUBA INDEPENDIENTE Y DEMOCRÁTICA
10020 SW 37th Terrace
Miami, FL 33165
Huber Matos, Secretary General
Tel: (305) 551-8484 Fax: (305) 599-9365
Email: rmatos@cfl.rr.com
Web: www.cubacid.com

CUBAN COMMITTEE FOR DEMOCRACY INC.
600 Brickell Ave. #301H
Miami, FL 33131
Marlene Arzola, Outreach Coordinator
Tel: (305) 373-4754 Fax: (305) 373-4755
Email: ccd@ccdusa.org
Web: www.ccdusa.org

CUBAN-AMERICAN NATIONAL FOUNDATION
National Headquarters
1312 SW 27th Ave.
Miami, FL 33145
Francisco Hernández, President
Tel: (305) 592-7768 Fax: (305) 592-7889
Email: hq@canf.org
Web: www.canfnet.org

CUBANET NEWS, INC.
145 Madeira Ave. #207
Coral Gables, FL 33134
Jose Alberto Hernández, M.D., President
Tel: (305) 774-1887
Email: cubanet@cubanet.org
Web: www.cubanet.org

DIRECTORIO REVOLUCIONARIO DEMOCRATICO CUBANO
P.O. Box 110235
Hialeah, FL 33011
Javier de Céspedes, President
Tel: (305) 279-4416
Email: info@directorio.org
Web: www.directorio.org

GOVERNMENT OF PUERTO RICO OFFICE
Orlando Regional Office
400 S. Orange Ave., 9th Fl.
Orlando, FL 32802
Dr. Sylvia T. Caceres, Regional Director
Tel: (407) 423-4422 Fax: (407) 423-0330
Web: www.prfaa.com

HERMANOS AL RESCATE/P.O. Box 430846
Miami, Fl 33243-0846
Tel: (305) 477-1868 Fax: (305) 663-9510

Email: brothers@hermanos.com
Web: www.hermanos.org

HISPANIC AFFAIRS ADVISORY BOARD
Miami-Dade County
Stephen P. Clark Center, 111 NW 1st St. #620
Miami, FL 33128-1989
Maria Lazo, Director
Tel: (305) 375-2104 Fax: (305) 375-5715
Email: m55@miamidade.gov
Web: http://miamidade.gov/

PUERTO RICO FEDERAL AFFAIRS ADMINISTRATION
South Florida Regional Office
800 Douglas Rd. #149
Coral Gables, FL 33134
Manuel Benítez-Gorbea, Regional Director
Tel: (305) 448-5145 Fax: (305) 448-7184
Email: info@prfaa.com
Web: www.prfaa.com

Southern States Regional Office
400 S. Orange Ave., 9th Fl.
Orlando, FL 32801
Sylvia Caceres, Regional Director
Tel: (407) 423-4422 Fax: (407) 423-0330
Email: info@prfaa.com
Web: www.prfaa.com

REPUBLICAN NATIONAL HISPANIC ASSEMBLY
RNHA-Florida
14622 SW 52nd St.
Miami, FL 33175
Antonio de la Luz, State Chairman
Tel: (305) 220-9417 Fax: (305) 220-9417
Email: ortueta98@aol.com
Web: www.rnhacentralflorida.org/pages/1/index.htm

SPANISH AMERICAN LEAGUE AGAINST DISCRIMINATION
900 SW 1st St. #201
Miami, FL 33130
Jaime Perez, Executive Director
Tel: (305) 326-8585 Fax: (305) 324-4482
Email: osvaldosalad@aol.com

UNION IBEROAMERICANA DE MUNICIPALISTAS
National Headquarters
6822 SW 34th Ct.
Miramar, FL 33023
Lilly Guzmán, Chair
Tel: (954) 987-5969 Fax: (954) 964-2698
Email: uim@eurosur.org
Web: www.uimunicipalistas.org

PROFESSIONAL

ASSOCIATION OF LATINO PROFESSIONALS IN FINANCE AND ACCOUNTING
1111 Brickell Ave. #2801
Miami, FL 33131
Zameer Upadhya, Chapter President
Tel: (305) 420-8091 Fax: (305) 374-1135
Email: president@miami.alpfa.org
Web: www.alpfa.org

Orlando Chapter
200 S. Orange Ave. #2210
Orlando, FL 32801
Loha Pereira, Chapter President
Tel: (407) 650-1738 X2215
Email: president@orlando.alpfa.org
Web: www.alpfa.org

NATIONAL SOCIETY FOR HISPANIC PROFESSIONALS
8260 N. Bayshore Dr.
Miami, FL 33138
Xiomara A. Sosa, President/CEO
Tel: (305) 832-7928
Email: xasosa@nshp.org
Web: www.nshp.org

PERUVIAN AMERICAN MEDICAL SOCIETY
Central Florida Chapter
1403 Medical Plaza Dr. #101
Sanford, Fl 32771
Dr. Gonzalo Huamán, President
Tel: (407) 322-0090
Email: gonny105@aol.com
Web: www.pamsnational.org

South Florida Chapter
2473 SW 132nd Way
Davie, FL 33325
Dr. Luis A. Espinoza, President
Tel: Fax: (954) 236-0507
Email: espinosa@medscape.com
Web: www.pamsnational.org

Tampa Bay, Florida Chapter
4700 N. Habana, #702
Tampa, FL 33614
Dr. Pedro Mendez, President
Tel: (813) 872-0613
Email: ernmen@hotmail.com
Web: www.pamsnational.org

SOCIETY OF HISPANIC PROFESSIONAL ENGINEERS
Central Florida Professional Chapter
201 E. Pine St. #1000
Orlando, FL 32801
Tatiana Hernandez, Chapter President
Tel: (407) 839-3955
Email: txhernan@yahoo.com
Web: www.shpe.org

RELIGIOUS

AMIGOS EN CRISTO, INC.
25999 Old 41 Rd.
Bonita Springs, FL 34125
Rev. Bob Selle, Pastor
Tel: (239) 437-6727
Email: bobselle@aol.com
Web: www.amigoscenter.org

ARCHDIOCESE OF MIAMI
Hispanic Ministry Office
9401 Biscayne Blvd.
Miami Shores, FL 33138
Felipe Eftevez, Bishop
Tel: (305) 762-1091 Fax: (305) 758-2027
Email: bpfernan@mail.miamiarch.org
Web: www.miamiarch.org

CATHOLIC DIOCESE OF VENICE
Hispanic Affairs
P.O. Box 2006
Venice, FL 34284
John J. Nevins, D.D., Bishop
Tel: (941) 484-9543 Fax: (941) 484-1121
Email: information@dioceseofvenice.org
Web: www.dioceseofvenice.org

CUBAN HEBREW CONGREGATION OF MIAMI
1700 Michigan Ave.
Miami, FL 33139
Fabio Nick, President
Tel: (305) 534-7213 Fax: (305) 534-5143
Email: bethshmuel@bellsouth.net

DIOCESAN HISPANIC MINISTRY COORDINATOR
9401 Biscayne Blvd.
Miami Shores, FL 33138
Felipe Estevez, Bishop
Tel: (305) 757-6241 Fax: (305) 754-1797
Email: information@miamiarch.org
Web: www.miamiarch.org

DIOCESE OF ORLANDO
Hispanic Ministry
P.O. Box 1800
Orlando, FL 32802-1800
Rev. Jose Bautista, Director for Hispanic Ministry
Tel: (407) 246-4930 Fax: (407) 246-4939
Email: hispmin@orlandodiocese.org
Web: www.orlandodiocese.org

DIOCESE OF PALM BEACH
Hispanic Ministry
9995 N. Military Trail
Palm Beach Gardens, FL 33410
Sister Vivian Gonzalez, Director for Hispanic Ministry
Tel: (561) 775-9544 Fax: (561) 775-9556
Email: info@diocesepb.org
Web: www.diocesepb.org

DIOCESE OF PENSACOLA-TALLAHASSEE
Hispanic Ministry
P.O. Box 17329
Pensacola, FL 32522
Sr. Maria Ramos, Director for Hispanic Ministry
Tel: (850) 435-3500 Fax: (850) 436-6424
Email: ramosa@ptdiocese.org
Web: www.ptdiocese.org

DIOCESE OF ST. AUGUSTINE
Multicultural Ministry
134 E. Church St.
Jacksonville, FL 32202-3130
Alba M. Orozco, Coordinator
Tel: (904) 353-3243 Fax: (904) 353-0630
Email: amorozco@ccbjax.org

DIOCESE OF ST. PETERSBURG
Hispanic Affairs
P.O. Box 40200
St. Petersburg, FL 33743
Sandra Bonilla, Director
Tel: (727) 344-1611 Fax: (727) 345-2143
Email: SMB@dosp.org
Web: www.dioceseofstpete.org

IGLESIA EPISCOPAL DE SAN SIMÓN
10950 SW 34th St.
Miami, FL 33165
Rev. Carlos Sandoval, Rector
Tel: (305) 221-4753 Fax: (305) 220-2678
Email: info@stsimons.org
Web: www.stsimons.org

JOVENES DE MIAMI EN ACCION
P.O. Box 172472
Hialeah, FL 33017
William Betancur, Director
Tel: (305) 638-7884
Email: jovenesenaccion@aol.com
Web: www.jovenesdemiami.com

LATIN AMERICAN CHRISTIAN CENTER
980 SW 81st Ave.
North Lauderdale, FL 33068
Nicolas Rivera, Pastor
Tel: (954) 720-4467
Email: centrolatinoamer@aol.com

LATIN AMERICAN MISSION
P.O. Box 52-7900
Miami, FL 33152-7900
Tel: (305) 884-8400 Fax: (305) 884-8649
Email: info@lam.org
Web: www.lam.org

SOUTH AMERICA MISSION
5217 S. Military Trail
Lake Worth, FL 33463
William Ogden, Executive Director
Tel: (561) 965-1833 Fax: (561) 439-8950
Email: samusa2@southamericamission.org
Web: www.southamericamission.org

SOUTHEAST PASTORAL INSTITUTE
Hispanic Ministry
7700 SW 56th St.
Miami, FL 33155
Rev. Mario Vizcaino, Director
Tel: (305) 279-2333 Fax: (305) 279-0925
Email: sepimiami@aol.com
Web: www.sepimiami.org

SPANISH CHURCH HOUSE OF PRAYER
3220 N. Carl G Rose Hwy.
Hernando, FL 34442
Tel: (352) 341-5100

SPANISH EVANGELICAL PUBLISHERS ASSOCIATION
1370 NW 88th Ave.
Miami, Fl 33172-3020
Pablo Vera, Executive Assistant
Tel: (305) 592-6136 Fax: (786) 331-7720
Email: sepa@bmsi.com
Web: www.sepalit.org

RESEARCH

CENTER FOR LATIN AMERICAN STUDIES
University of Florida
P.O. Box 115530
319 Grinter Hall
Gainesville, FL 32611-5530
Carmen Diana Deere, Director
Tel: (352) 392-0375 Fax: (352) 392-7682
Email: deere@latam.ufl.edu
Web: www.latam.ufl.edu

CUBAN RESEARCH INSTITUTE
Florida International University
DM 353, University Park
Miami, FL 33199
Uva de Aragon, Associate Director
Tel: (305) 348-2894 Fax: (305) 348-3593
Email: lacc@fiu.edu
Web: http://lacc.fiu.edu/cri/

LATIN AMERICAN AND CARIBBEAN CENTER
Florida International University
University Park, DM 353
Miami, FL 33199
Eduardo A. Gamarra, Director
Tel: (305) 348-2894 Fax: (305) 348-3593
Email: lacc@fiu.edu
Web: http://lacc.fiu.edu

SPEC. INT., AIDS

LEAGUE AGAINST AIDS
3050 Biscayne Blvd. #509
Miami, FL 33137
Dr. Manuel M. Vega, Executive Director
Tel: (305) 576-1000 Fax: (305) 576-4097
Email: casemanagement@leagueagainstaids.com
Web: www.leagueagainstaids.com

UNION POSITIVA, INC.
1901 SW 1st St. 3rd Fl.
Miami, FL 33135
Doralba Munoz, Executive Director
Tel: (305) 644-0667 Fax: (305) 644-0636
Email: unionpositiva@aol.com
Web: www.unionpositiva.org

SPEC. INT., CHILD CARE

KIDCO CHILD CARE
Miami Satellite Office
3630 NE 1st Ct.
Miami, FL 33137
Nilsa M. Velázquez, President/CEO
Tel: (305) 576-6990 Fax: (305) 576-5321
Email: info@kidcochildcare.org
Web: www.kidco-childcare.org

ROSA VALDEZ CENTER
1802 N. Albany Ave.
Tampa, FL 33607
Lisa Lockhart, Manager
Tel: (813) 253-3853 Fax: (813) 259-9581
Email: tumccmr@tampabay.rr.com

SPEC. INT., COUNSELING

FAMILY COUNSELING SERVICES OF GREATER MIAMI
Central Office
10651 N. Kendall Dr. #100
Miami, FL 33176
Josie Diaz, Director
Tel: (305) 271-9800 Fax: (305) 270-3330
Web: www.familycounseling.org

South Office
10700 Caribbean Blvd. #207
Miami, FL 33189
Josie Diaz, Director
Tel: (305) 232-1610 Fax: (305) 238-5054
Web: www.familycounseling.org

SPEC. INT., EDUCATION

ADVANCED TECHNICAL CENTERS
5600 NW 36th St.
Miami, FL 33122
Yolanda Ruiz, Director
Tel: (305) 649-7500 X115 Fax: (305) 871-5643
Email: yruiz@advancedtechnicalcenters.com
Web: www.advancedtechnicalcenters.com

ASPIRA OF FLORIDA, INC.
3650 N. Miami Ave.
Miami, FL 33127
Raúl Martínez, President
Tel: (305) 576-8494 Fax: (305) 576-6217
Email: rmartinez@fl.aspira.org
Web: http://fl.aspira.org

CENTRO EDUCACIONAL BILINGUE
1040 SW 27th Ave.
Miami, FL 33135
Diana Gonzáles, Manager
Tel: (305) 649-4600 Fax: (305) 649-1049

CUBA FOR KIDS FOUNDATION
P.O. Box 432804
South Miami, FL 33243
Dr. Ismael Roque-Velasco, Author/Producer
Tel: (305) 667-6230 Fax: (305) 740-6724
Email: info@cubaforkids.com
Web: www.cubaforkids.com

HISPANIC SERVICES COUNCIL
802 E. Baker St.
Plant City, FL 33563
Tel: (813) 659-8566

INSTITUTE FOR CUBAN AND CUBAN-AMERICAN STUDIES
University of Miami
P.O. Box 248174
Coral Gables, FL 33124-3010
Dr. Jaime Suchlicki, Director
Tel: (305) 284-2822 Fax: (305) 284-4875
Email: iccas@miami.edu
Web: www.miami.edu/iccas

INTER-AMERICAN PRESS ASSOCIATION
1801 SW 3rd Ave., Jules Dubois Bldg.
Miami, FL 33129
Julio Muñoz, Executive Director
Tel: (305) 634-2465 Fax: (305) 635-2272
Email: jmunoz@sipiapa.org
Web: www.sipiapa.org

LATIN AMERICAN AND CARIBBEAN AFFAIRS
Rollins College
1000 Holt Ave., Box 2761
Winter Park, FL 32789
Pedro A. Pequeno, Director
Tel: (407) 646-2370 Fax: (407) 646-2325
Email: ppequeno@rollins.edu
Web: www.rollins.edu/laca

LATIN AMERICAN STUDIES PROGRAM
University of Miami
P.O. Box 248093
Ashe Administrative Bldg. #505
Coral Gables, FL 33124-4650
Dr. Rebecca Biron, Program Director
Tel: (305) 284-1854 Fax: (305) 284-2068
Email: las@miami.edu
Web: www.as.miami.edu/lasp

LATINA AND LATINO CRITICAL LEGAL THEORY, INC.
Coral Gables, FL
Prof. Berta Hernandez-Truyol, Co-Chair
Tel: (305) 284-5432 Fax: (305) 284-6506
Email: latcrit@law.miami.edu
Web: www.latcrit.org

LINCOLN-MARTI
National Headquarters
904 SW 23rd Ave.
Miami, FL 33135
Demetrio Pérez Jr., Principal/President
Tel: (305) 643-4888 Fax: (305) 649-2767
Email: info@lincoln-marti.com
Web: www.lincoln-marti.com

NATIONAL ASSOCIATION OF CUBAN AMERICAN EDUCATORS
National Headquarters
P.O. Box 226951
Miami, FL 33132
Gaston Fernández de la Torriente, Executive Director
Tel: (305) 593-2555 Fax: (305) 471-7616

NATIONAL ASSOCIATION OF HISPANIC PUBLIC ADMINISTRATORS
P.O. Box 142171
Coral Gables, FL 33114-2171
Suzanne Salichs, President
Tel: (305) 638-6800
Email: info@nahpa.com
Web: www.nahpa.com

SALVADORAN AMERICAN HUMANITARIAN FOUNDATION
2050 Coral Way #600
Miami, FL 33145
Jose Eduardo Siman, President
Tel: (800) 992-8858 Fax: (305) 860-1415
Email: contact@sahf.org
Web: www.sahf.org

ACCIÓN USA
111 SW 5th Ave.
Miami, FL 33130
William Mateo, Contact
Tel: (305) 548-3360 Fax: (305) 548-3348
Email: miamiloans@accion.org
Web: www.accionusa.org

COALITION OF FLORIDA FARMWORKER ORGANIZATIONS, INC.
778 W. Palm Dr.
Florida City, FL 33034
Arturo López, Executive Director
Tel: (305) 246-0357 Fax: (305) 246-2445
Email: coffo@algxmail.com
Web: www.coffo.org

21 S. Krome Ave.
Homestead, FL 33030
Harold Jean Baptist, Outreach Coordinator
Tel: (305) 247-4779 Fax: (305) 242-0701
Web: www.coffo.org

Belle Glade
425 SW 4th St.
Belle Glade, FL 33430
Pedro Narezo III, Chairperson
Tel: (561) 992-0603 Fax: (561) 992-8618
Email: farmworker@earthlink.net
Web: www.coffo.org

Florida City
778 W. Palm Dr.
Florida City, FL 33034
Arturo Lopez, Executive Director
Tel: (305) 246-0357 Fax: (305) 246-2445
Email: coffo@algxmail.com
Web: www.coffo.org

Multi-Service Office
P.O. Box 1969
Immokalee, FL 34143
Arturo Lopez, Executive Director
Tel: (239) 657-7272 Fax: (239) 657-6909
Email: coffo@algxmail.com
Web: www.coffo.org

COALITION OF IMMOKALEE WORKERS
P.O. Box 603
Immokalee, FL 34143
Lucas Benitez, Co-Director
Tel: (239) 657-8311 Fax: (239) 657-8311
Email: workers@ciw-online.org
Web: www.ciw-online.org

FLORIDA SER-JOBS FOR PROGRESS, INC.
Affiliate of SER-Jobs for Progress National, Inc.
P.O. Box 661597
Miami Springs, FL 33266-1597
Jose L. Cela, President
Tel: (305) 871-2820 Fax: (305) 871-5643
Email: jlcela@serflorida.org
Web: www.serflorida.org

NATIONAL HISPANIC CORPORATE ACHIEVERS
445 Douglas Ave. #2005-16
Altamonte Springs, FL 32714
Daniel Ramos, Chairman
Tel: (407) 330-9993 Fax: (407) 330-5993
Email: info@hispanicachievers.org
Web: www.hispanicachievers.com

AMERICAN CANCER SOCIETY HISPANIC OUTREACH SUBCOMMITTEE
3407 NW 9th Ave. #100
Ft. Lauderdale, FL 33309
Jodie Kennell, Director
Tel: (954) 564-0880 X127 Fax: (954) 561-8072
Email: josephien.kennell@cancer.org
Web: www.cancer.org

CUBAN MEDICAL ASSOCIATION IN EXILE
P.O. Box 141016
Coral Gables, FL 33114-1016
Dr. Enrique Huertas, President
Tel: (305) 445-1429 Fax: (305) 445-9310

HISPANIC HEALTH INITIATIVES INC.
P.O. Box 1925
202 Live Oaks Blvd.
Casselberry, FL 32707
Josephine Nercado, Director
Tel: (407) 339-2001 Fax: (407) 339-1700
Email: hhi2001@aol.com

HISPANO DANDO ESPERANZA HISPANICS GIVING HOPE
Marrow Donor Program
10100 Dr. Martin Luther King Jr., St. North
St. Petersburg, FL 33716-2806
Ivan D. Mangual, Recruitment Specialist
Tel: (727) 568-2115 Fax: (727) 568-2175
Email: imangual@fvsblood.org
Web: www.marrow.org

LEAGUE AGAINST CANCER/LIGA CONTRA EL CANCER
2180 SW 12th Ave.
Miami, FL 33129
Luis Villa, Jr., President
Tel: (305) 856-4914 Fax: (305) 856-8172
Email: info@ligacontraelcancer.org
Web: www.ligacontraelcancer.org

EVERGLADES COMMUNITY ASSOCIATION, INC.
P.O. Box 343529
Homestead, FL 33034-0529
Steven C. Kirk, Executive Director
Tel: (305) 242-2142 Fax: (305) 242-2143
Email: tomneibaur@farmworker.org

AMERICAN-NICARAGUAN FOUNDATION
848 Brickell Ave. #604
Miami, FL 33131
Carmen C. Narvaez
Tel: (305) 374-3391 Fax: (305) 374-5993
Email: carmenn@aidnicaragua.org
Web: www.aidnicaragua.org

ASOCIACION DOMINICANA USA
P.O. Box 1715
Coral Gables, FL 33134
Nelcida Hanley de Chakoff, Executive Director
Tel: (305) 444-6864 Fax: (305) 661-8480
Email: nelcidah@yahoo.com

HISPANIC HUMAN RESOURCES COUNCIL, INC.
1427 S. Congress Ave.
West Palm Beach, FL 33406
Judy Pierman, Deputy Director
Tel: (561) 641-7400 Fax: (561) 641-3607
Email: carmenhhrc@aol.com
Web: www.hhrcinc.com

MUNICIPIO DE SANTIAGO DE CUBA EN EXILIO
845 SW 14th Ave.
Miami, FL 33135
Antonio Gonzalez Montoya, President
Tel: (305) 858-6739 Fax: (305) 856-6090

VOLUSIA COUNTY HISPANICS ASSOCIATION
766 Deltona Blvd. #A
Deltona, FL 32725
Zenaida Denizac, President
Tel: (386) 860-1128
Email: contact@volusiahispanics.com
Web: www.volusiahispanics.com

LATIN AMERICAN IMMIGRATION AND REFUGEE ORGANIZATION, INC.
4623 Forest Hill Blvd. #108
West Palm Beach, FL 33415
Tel: (561) 966-4515 Fax: (561) 966-4660

CUBAN AMERICAN DEFENSE LEAGUE
142 Beacom Blvd.
Miami, FL 33135
Tel: (305) 649-4993

HISPANIC NATIONAL BAR ASSOCIATION
P.O. Box 3373
Tampa, FL 33601
John Cain, Regional Director
Tel: (813) 221-0200 Fax: (813) 221-8558
Email: jnc@manfitzlaw.com
Web: www.hnba.com

Region VIII (FL)
Angones, Hunter, McClure, et al. Concord Bldg., 8th Fl., 44 W. Flagler St.
Miami, FL 33130
Carlos Singh, Regional President
Tel: (305) 371-5000 Fax: (305) 371-3948
Email: hnba@verizon.net
Web: www.hnba.com

ACTION COMMUNITY CENTER, INC.
970 SW 1st St. #304
Miami, FL 33130
María P. Albo, Program Director
Tel: (305) 545-9298 Fax: (305) 545-0203
Email: actioncm@bellsouth.net

DE HOSTOS SENIOR CENTER
2902 NW 2nd Ave.
Miami, FL 33127
Esther Couvierter, Executive Director
Tel: (305) 573-6220 Fax: (305) 573-2193
Email: vhscenter@aol.com
Web: www.geocities.com/dehostosmiami

ALIANZA FRATERNAL JOSE MARTI, INC.
444 SW 64th Ct.
Miami, FL 33144

Miriam E. Quiros, President
Tel: (305) 267-4187 Fax: (305) 262-0778
Email: luz@baltero.com

ASOCIACIÓN ARGENTINA DE LA BAHÍA DE TAMPA
P.O. Box 11137
St. Petersburg, FL 33733
Osvaldo Laino, President
Tel: (813) 251-8601 Fax: (813) 254-1109
Email: jolaino@ad7.com

CANAAN INTERNATIONAL'S CITIES OF REFUGE
P.O. Box 290345
Tampa, FL 33617
Steve Concepcion
Tel: (813) 985-3598
Email: info@canaaninternational.org
Web: www.canaaninternational.org

CENTRO CAMPESINO FARMWORKER CENTER, INC.
P.O. Box 343449
Florida City, FL 33034
Tel: (305) 245-7738 Fax: (305) 247-2619
Email: info@centrocampesino.org
Web: www.centrocampesino.org

CENTRO CAMPESINO-FARMWORKER CENTER, INC.
35801 SW 186th Ave.
Florida City, FL 33034
Steven Mainster, Executive Director
Tel: (305) 245-7738 Fax: (305) 247-2619
Email: info@centrocampesino.org
Web: www.centrocampesino.org

CHARITY IN ACTION, INC.
149 Ponce de Leon Blvd.
Coral Gables, FL 33134
Alicia A. Kehrhahn, President
Tel: (305) 444-4332 Fax: (305) 444-4332

COLOMBIAN AMERICAN COALITION OF FLORIDA
12205 71st Ct. SW
Miami, FL 33156-5449
Carlos A. Cabrera, President
Tel: (305) 665-7278 Fax: (305) 661-2577
Email: cacabrera@aol.com

COLOMBIAN AMERICAN SERVICE ASSOCIATION
8500 SW 8th St. #218
Miami, FL 33144
Esperanza Martinez, Executive Director
Tel: (305) 448-2272 Fax: (305) 448-0178
Email: casamiami@aol.com
Web: www.casa-usa.org

CUBAN AMERICAN NATIONAL COUNCIL, INC.
1223 SW 4th St.
Miami, FL 33135
Guarione M. Diaz, President
Tel: (305) 642-3484 X101 Fax: (305) 642-9122
Email: gmd@cnc.org
Web: www.cnc.org

FARMWORKER ASSOCIATION OF FLORIDA, INC.
815 S. Park Ave.
Apopka, FL 32703
Catalino Frias, President
Tel: (407) 886-5151 Fax: (407) 884-6644
Email: apopkafwaf@aol.com
Web: www.thefarmworkerassociationofflorida.org

FOOD FOR THE POOR, INC.
550 SW 12th Ave., Dept. 9662
Deerfield Beach, FL 33442
Tel: (954) 427-2222
Email: donorservice@foodforthepoor.org
Web: www.foodforthepoor.org

THE GUATEMALAN-MAYA CENTER
110 N. F St.
Lake Worth, FL 33460

Lucio Perez-Reynozo, Executive Director
Tel: (561) 586-6446 Fax: (561) 586-6446

KIWANIS CLUB COLOMBIAN-AMERICAN OF MIAMI-DADE
1915 W 8th Ave.
Hialeah, FL 33010-2303
Alvaro Lozano, President
Tel: (305) 883-6004 Fax: (305) 883-8622
Email: lozano@ambassadorbeverages.com

LATINO INTEGRATION FOR DEVELOPMENT ORGANIZATION
1583 E. Silver Star Rd. 317 Forrest Crest Ct.
Ocoee, FL 34761
Esperanza Elliott, Co-Founder
Tel: (407) 532-3572 Fax: (407) 532-3572
Email: lift@ix.netcom.com

LATINO LEADERSHIP, INC.
615-A Herndon Ave.
Orlando, FL 32803
Marytza Sanz, Executive Director
Tel: (407) 893-6424 Fax: (407) 893-6423
Web: www.latino-leadership.org

NATIONAL CENTER FOR MISSING & EXPLOITED CHILDREN
Florida
9176 Alternate A1A #100
Lake Park, FL 33403-1445
Tel: (561) 848-1900 Fax: (561) 848-0308
Web: www.missingkids.com

PANAMA CANAL SOCIETY, INC.
7985 113th St. #334
Seminole, FL 33772-4787
Tel: (727) 391-4359 Fax: (727)-319-8593
Email: office@pancanalsociety.org
Web: www.pancanalsociety.org

REDLANDS CHRISTIAN MIGRANT ASSOCIATION
Affiliate of NCLR
402 W. Main St.
Immokalee, FL 34142-3933
Judy Brill, Community Relations
Tel: (239) 658-3560 Fax: (239) 658-3571
Email: info@rcma.org
Web: www.rcma.org

SOUTHWEST SOCIAL SERVICES, INC.
25 Tamiami Blvd.
Miami, FL 33144
Cristina Pinedo, Executive Director
Tel: (305) 261-6202 Fax: (305) 266-8110
Email: swss@bbsector.net

GUADALUPE CENTER, INC.
211 S 9th St.
Immokalee, FL 34142
Janie Bidaurri, Assistant Director
Tel: (239) 657-4361 Fax: (239) 657-6816

LATINAS UNIDAS, INC.
P.O. Box 90-1603
Homestead, FL 33090
Tel: (786) 243-3933

MANA- A NATIONAL LATINA ORGANIZATION
646 Ocoee Commerce Pkwy.
Ocoee, FL 34761-2918
Olivia Triana, President
Tel: (407) 877-4501 Fax: (407) 877-4595
Email: olivia.triana.bhfe@statefarm.com
Web: www.hermana.org

YOUTH CO-OP
Main Office
3525 NW 7th St.
Miami, FL 33125

María Rodríguez, Executive Director
Tel: (305) 643-6730 X21 Fax: (305) 643-2739
Email: MRODRIGUEZ@YCOOP.ORG

ARGENTINE TANGO CLUB
University of Florida
Gainesville, FL 32611
Ana Cristina Siqueria, President
Tel: (352) 375-7730
Email: anasique@soc.ufl.edu

BRAZILIAN STUDENT ASSOCIATION
University of Florida
Gainesville, FL 32611
Claudia Kusano, President
Tel: (352) 846-4215
Email: brasapresident@yahoo.com
Web: http://grove.ufl.edu/~brasa/

BRAZILIAN-PORTUGUESE CLUB
University of Florida
Gainesville, FL 32611
Mary Risner, Faculty Advisor
Tel: (352) 392-0375
Email: maryr@ufl.edu
Web: http://grove.ufl.edu/~bpc/

CUBAN-AMERICAN STUDENT ASSOCIATION
University of Florida
315 JWRU
Gainesville, FL 32611
Reynaldo Jimenez, Faculty Advisor
Tel: (352) 392-2463
Email: jimenez@rll.ufl.edu
Web: http://grove.ufl.edu/~ufcasa/

DOMINICAN STUDENTS ASSOCIATION
University of Florida
Gainesville, FL 32611
Lenny Flores, President
Tel: (352) 870-6141
Email: dsa@grove.ufl.edu
Web: http://grove.ufl.edu/~dsa

ECUADORIAN STUDENT ASSOCIATION
University of Florida
Gainesville, FL 32611
Ramon Espinel, faculty Advisor
Tel: (352) 392-1391 x23
Email: respinel@ifas.ufl.edu
Web: http://grove.ufl.edu/~ecuasa/

FEDERACION DE ESTUDIANTES CUBANOS
University of Miami
University Center #205
Coral Gables, FL 33146
Silia Sagre, President
Tel: (305) 284-6290
Email: silia32@aol.com
Web: www.miami.edu/studorgs/fec

HISPANIC AMERICAN MEDICAL STUDENT ASSOCIATION
University of Florida
Gainesville, FL 32611
Carlos A. Montes, President
Tel: (352) 256-0522
Email: cmontes@ufl.edu

HISPANIC ASSOCIATION OF BILINGUAL ASSISTANCE
University of Florida
Gainesville, FL 32611
Stephanie Hise, President
Tel: (407) 687-8188
Email: shise18@hotmail.com

HISPANIC CHI ALPHA
University of Florida
Gainesville, FL 32611
Wilnaliz Irizarry, President
Tel: (352) 371-0853
Email: hispanicchialpha@hotmail.com

HISPANIC COMMUNICATORS ASSOCIATION
University of Florida
Reitz Union #324

Gainesville, FL 32611
Diana Delgado, Secretary
Tel: (352) 271-2046
Email: hcauf@yahoogroups.com
Web: http://grove.ufl.edu/~hcagator

HISPANIC GRADUATE STUDENT ASSOCIATION
University of Florida
303 Weil Hall
Gainesville, FL 32611-2083
Deborah Townsend, President
Tel: (352) 271-6607
Email: hgsauf@yahoo.com
Web: http://grove.ufl.edu/~hgsa

HISPANIC STUDENT ASSOCIATION
University of Florida
Reitz Union, 3rd Fl., #34
Gainesville, FL 32611
Daniel Sanchez, President
Tel: (352) 392-3261
Email: hsapresidentuf@yahoo.com
Web: http://grove.ufl.edu/~hsauf

INSTITUE OF HISPANIC -LATINO CULTURES, "LA CASITA"
University of Florida
1504 W. University Ave.
Gainesville, FL 32611
Leticia Martinez, Director
Tel: (352) 392-1261
Email: leticiacm@dso.ufl.edu
Web: www.dso.ufl.edu/multicultural/lacasita/

MEXICAN-AMERICAN STUDENT ASSOCIATION
University of Florida
Gainesville, FL 32611
Greg Moreland, Faculty Advisor
Tel: (352) 392-2016 x240
Email: moreland@rll.ufl.edu
Web: http://grove.ufl.edu/~masa/

MEXICANS IN GAINESVILLE
University of Florida
Gainesville, FL 32611
Sebastian Galindo-Gonzalez, President
Tel: (352) 846-5137
Email: galindo@animal.ufl.edu
Web: http://grove.ufl.edu/~mexicano/

NICARAGUAN STUDENT ASSOCIATION
University of Florida
Gainesville, FL 32611
Philip Williams, Faculty Advisor
Tel: (352) 392-8127
Email: pjw@polisci.ufl.edu
Web: http://grove.ufl.edu/~nisas/

SOCIETY OF HISPANIC PROFESSIONAL ENGINEERS
University of Central Florida
P.O. Box 162993
Orlando, FL 32816
Nicolas Zamora, President
Tel: (407) 823-2220
Email: contact@shpeucf.org
Web: http://pegasus.cc.ucf.edu/~shpeucf

SPANISH AMERICAN LAW STUDENTS ASSOCIATION
University of Florida
University of Florida, Bruton-Geer Student Organization Office
Gainesville, FL 32611
Noemar Castro, Faculty Advisor
Tel: (352) 392-0421
Email: castro@law.ufl.edu

STUDENT ASSOCIATION OF LATIN AMERICAN STUDIES
University of Florida
310 Grinter
Gainesville, FL 32611
Anouk St-Arnaud, President
Tel: (352) 377-9054
Email: gslean@yahoo.com

SUMMIT OF THE AMERICAS CENTER
Florida International University
University Park DM 353
Miami, FL 33199
Carl Cira, Director
Tel: (305) 348-2894 Fax: (305) 348-3593
Email: cirac@fiu.edu
Web: www.americasnet.net

VENEZUELAN STUDENT ASSOCIATION
University of Florida
University of Florida, HSA Office- Reitz Union
Gainesville, FL 32611
Rosa Elena Pacanins, President
Tel: (352) 362-6490
Email: repl@ufl.edu
Web: http://grove.ufl.edu/~vensa/

GEORGIA

DIAZ FOODS
5501 Fulton Industrial Blvd.
Atlanta, GA 30336
Rene Diaz, President/CEO
Tel: (404) 344-5421 Fax: (404) 344-3003
Email: diazfoods@diazfoods.com
Web: www.diazfoods.com

BRAZILIAN AMERICAN CHAMBER OF COMMERCE OF GEORGIA, ATLANTA
P.O. Box 93411
Atlanta, GA 30377
Alessandra Coppola, President
Tel: (404) 880-1551
Email: baccga1@aol.com
Web: www.bacc-ga.com

GEORGIA HISPANIC CHAMBER OF COMMERCE
2801 Buford Hwy. #500
Atlanta, GA 30329
Sara J. Gonzalez, President/CEO
Tel: (404) 929-9998 Fax: (404) 929-9908
Email: sgonzalez@ghcc.org
Web: www.ghcc.org

METRO-ATLANTA CHAMBER OF COMMERCE
235 Andrew Young International Blvd. NW
Atlanta, GA 30303
Sam Williams, President
Tel: (404) 586-8524 Fax: (404) 586-8427
Email: samwilliams@macoc.com
Web: www.metroatlantachamber.com

CLUB ARGENTINO DE ATLANTA
1076 Greenbriar Cr.
Decatur, GA 30033
Susana Macri Brady, Coordinator
Tel: (404) 296-1363 Fax: (404) 296-1363
Email: susanamb@aol.com

THE MEXICAN CENTER OF ATLANTA
5195 Jimmy Carter Blvd. #222
Norcross, GA 30093
Consuelo Luna, Regional Director
Tel: (770) 416-0969 Fax: (770) 416-0974
Email: mexictr@bellsouth.net
Web: www.mexicancenteratlanta.org

ALFA CENTRO HISPANO
Doraville Center
3609 Shallowford Rd. #B-501
Doraville, GA 30340
Luz Cediel, Executive Director
Tel: (770) 455-4416

Forest Park Center
4584 Jonesboro Rd. #A

Forest Park, GA 30297
Luz Cediel, Executive Director
Tel: (404) 608-8459

Smyrna Center
675 Windy Hill Rd.
Smyrna, GA 30080
Luz Cediel, Executive Director
Tel: (770) 333-9603 Fax: (770) 333-0953
Email: alfaluz@aol.com

LATIN AMERICAN ASSOCIATION
Clayton Office
2750 Buford Hwy.
Atlanta, GA 30324
Frank Ros, Chair
Tel: (404) 638-1800 Fax: (404) 638-1806
Email: main@latinamericanassoc.org
Web: www.latinamericanassoc.org

Cobb County Office #1
490 Windy Hill Rd. #2426
Smyrna, GA 30082
Frank Ros, Chair
Tel: (770) 420-6556 Fax: (678) 213) 0500
Email: galarragam@latinamericanassoc.org
Web: www.latinamericanassoc.org

Cobb County Office #2
861 Franklin Rd.
Marietta, GA 30067
Frank Ros, Chair
Tel: (404) 396-7478 Fax: (678) 213-0360
Email: cobboffice@latinamericanassoc.org
Web: www.latinamericanassoc.org

Gwinnett Office
1250 Old Norcross Tucker Rd.
Tucker, GA 30084
Frank Ros, Chair
Tel: (770) 934-3513 Fax: (770) 339-9154
Email: ndyste@latinamericanassoc.org
Web: www.latinamericanassoc.org

LEAGUE OF UNITED LATIN AMERICAN CITIZENS
Southeast Region-Georgia
P.O. Box 12104
Atlanta, GA 30355
Arturo Ordoqui, President
Tel: (770) 924-3440 Fax: (770) 638-1806
Email: stratisy@earthlink.net

NATIONAL IMAGE, INC.
Image de Atlanta
P.O. Box 1512
Atlanta, GA 30301
Sylvia Sánchez, President
Tel: (404) 266-1956 Fax: (404) 266-1956
Email: sylviasanchez00@aol.com
Web: www.nationalimageinc.org

ASSOCIATION OF LATINO PROFESSIONALS IN FINANCE AND ACCOUNTING
191 Peachtree St. NE #1500
Atlanta, GA 30303-1924
Jose Velaz, Chapter President
Tel: (404) 220-1759
Email: jvelaz@deloitte.com
Web: www.alpfa.org

NATIONAL SOCIETY OF HISPANIC MBAS
5195 Jimmy Carter Blvd. #200
Norcross, GA 30093
Grace Williams, President
Tel: (770) 448-6020 Fax: (770) 448-6077
Email: general@atlanta.nshmba.org
Web: http://atlanta.nshmba.org

ARCHDIOCESE OF ATLANTA
Hispanic Apostolate Office
680 W Peachtree St. NW
Atlanta, GA 30308-1984

Jose Duvan Gonzalez, Director Tel: (404) 888-7839 Fax: (404) 885-7479
Email: jdgonzalez@archatl.com
Web: www.archatl.com

DIOCESE OF SAVANNAH
Hispanic Ministry Office
601 E Liberty St.
Savannah, GA 31401-5196
Sr. Pat Brown, Director for Hispanic Ministry
Tel: (912) 201-4100 Fax: (912) 201-4101
Web: www.diosav.org

HERMANDAD DE SAN MARTÍN DE PORRES
6017 Western Hills Dr. #101
Norcross, GA 30071
Eduardo Ezeta, President
Tel: (770) 409-9710 Fax: (770) 409-0456
Email: eezeta@bellsouth.net

LA PRIMERA IGLESIA BAUTISTA HISPANA
810 S. College Ave.
Douglas, GA 31534
Tel: (912) 389-1000
Web: www.igbautista.org

VENEZUELA NOW, INC.
14656 Cooper Gap Rd.
Suches, GA 30572-3216
Virgil Allmond, President
Tel: (770) 617-0581
Email: virgilallmond@yahoo.com
Web: www.venezuelamissions.com

AID ATLANTA
Hispanic Outreach Program
1438 W. Peachtree St. NW #100
Atlanta, GA 30309-2955
Kim Anderson, Executive Director
Tel: (404) 870-7775
Email: kim.anderson@aidatlanta.org
Web: www.aidatlanta.org/education/education_programs.shtml#hispanic

GRUPO JÓVENES DE ATLANTA
1864 Atlanta Hwy.
Gainesville, GA 30504
Tel: (770) 297-8537

CIUDAD DE ANGELES
5240 Roswell Rd. NE
Marietta, GA 30062
Gary Gardner, Director
Tel: (770) 416-1598
Email: director@ciudaddeangeles.org
Web: www.ciudaddeangeles.org

CENTER FOR LATIN AMERICAN AND CARIBBEAN STUDIES
University of Georgia
290 S Hull St.
Athens, GA 30602-1778
Brent Berlin, Director
Tel: (706) 542-9079 Fax: (706) 542-8432
Email: clacs@uga.edu
Web: www.clacs.uga.edu

LATIN AMERICAN AND CARIBBEAN STUDIES
Emory University
1385 Oxford Rd.
Atlanta, GA 30322
F. Rebeca Quintana, Program Administrative Assistant
Tel: (404) 727-6562 Fax: (404) 727-6724
Email: lacs@emory.edu
Web: www.lacsp.emory.edu

LATINO INSTITUTE FOR EXCELLENCE, INC.
379 Pat Mell Rd. #411
Marietta, GA 30060
Dr. Wilson Triviño, Executive Director
Tel: (404) 918-1774 Fax: (770) 426-9977
Email: win@life-usa.org
Web: www.life-usa.org

CLINICA DE LA SALUD HISPANA
3652 Chamblee Dunwoody Rd. #4
Chamblee, GA 30341
Omar Velez, Manager
Tel: (770) 451-0662
Email: OmarV@clinicadelasaludhispana.com
Web: www.clinicadelasaludhispana.com

DÍA DE LA MUJER LATINA, INC.
3605 Sandy Plains Rd. #240-402
Marietta, GA 30066-3066
Venus Ginés, CEO/Founder
Tel: (678) 494-8879 Fax: (678) 494-8879
Email: venus2004@diadelamujerlatina.org
Web: www.diadelamujerlatina.org

TELAMON CORPORATION
Blacksherar Office
P.O. Box 413
3351 W. Hwy 84
Blackshear, GA 31516
Analicia Perez, Manager
Tel: (912) 449-3016 Fax: (912) 449-4579
Email: aperez@telamon.org
Web: www.telamon.org

Douglas Office
P.O. Box 966
Douglas, GA 31534
Myrtice Moore, Regional Manager
Tel: (912) 384-8856 Fax: (912) 384-8929
Email: mmoore@telamon.org
Web: www.telamon.org

Glennville Office
P.O. Box 815
111 Oliver Ln.
Glennville, GA 30427
Billie Fuller, Director
Tel: (912) 654-2182 Fax: (912) 654-2190
Email: bfuller@telamon.org
Web: www.telamon.org

Kiddie Kastle III Office
P.O. Box 469
133 Serena Dr.
Norman Park, GA 31771
Mary Williams, Center Director
Tel: (912) 769-3627 Fax: (912) 769-3182
Email: mwilliams@telamon.org
Web: www.telamon.org

Lyons Office
120 E. Liberty Ave.
Lyons, GA 30436
Paulette Burnside, Regional Coordinator
Tel: (912) 526-3094 Fax: (912) 526-5906
Email: pburnside@telamon.org
Web: www.telamon.org

Lyons Office (2)
684 N. Washington St.
Lyons, GA 30436
Ivey Murphy, Director
Tel: (912) 526-9556 Fax: (912) 526-3424
Email: imurphey@telamon.org
Web: www.telamon.org

Statesboro Office
P.O. Box 645
105 Elm St.
Statesboro, GA 30458
Elsie Tretheway, Regional Manager
Tel: (912) 764-6169 Fax: (912) 489-6516

Email: etretheway@telamon.org
Web: www.telamon.org

Valdosta Office
200 E. Mary St.
Valdosta, GA 31601
Carmen Wilkinson, Regional Manager
Tel: (912) 244-4920 Fax: (912) 244-0907
Email: cwilkinson@telamon.org
Web: www.telamon.org

HISPANIC NATIONAL BAR ASSOCIATION
Region VII (AL, GA, MS)
c/o Alston & Bird LLP, One Atlantic Ctr., 1201 W. Peachtree St.
Atlanta, GA 30309-3424
Luis Aguilar, Regional President
Tel: (404) 881-7396 Fax: (404) 881-7777
Email: laguilar@alston.com
Web: www.hnba.com

MEXICAN AMERICAN LEGAL DEFENSE AND EDUCATIONAL FUND
41 Marietta St. #1000
Atlanta, GA 30303
Tisha Tallman, Regional Counsel
Tel: (678) 559-1071 Fax: (678) 559-1079
Web: www.maldef.org

ENRICHMENT SERVICES PROGRAM, INC.
DHR-DCA Head Start
P.O. Box 788
900 Linwood Blvd.
Columbus, GA 31902
Justino López, Jr., Community Services Housing Director
Tel: (706) 649-1606 Fax: (706) 649-1603

GEORGIA HISPANIC NETWORK
P.O. Box 421812
Atlanta, GA 30342
Priscilla Nieves, President
Email: info@georgiahispanicnetwork.org
Web: www.georgiahispanicnetwork.org

HONDURAS OUTREACH, INC.
150 E. Ponce de Leon Ave. #270
Decatur, GA 30030
Beth Barnwell, Executive Director
Tel: (404) 378-0919 Fax: (404) 378-8429
Email: askhoi@hoi.org
Web: www.hoi.org

SOUTHEAST GEORGIA COMMUNITIES PROJECT, INC.
300 S. State St.
Lyons, GA 30436
Andrea H. Cruz, Co-Founder/Executive Director
Tel: (912) 526-5451 Fax: (912) 526-0089
Email: southeastgeorgia@bellsouth.net

HISPANIC STUDENT ASSOCIATION
University of Georgia
404 Memorial Hall
Athens, GA 30602
Robert Bryant, Advisor
Tel: (706) 542-5773 Fax: (706) 542-8478
Email: hsa@uga.edu
Web: www.uga.edu/hsa

SPANISH SPEAKING ORGANIZATION
Georgia Tech
Service Bldg. #123-ISSP Office
Atlanta, GA 30332-0284
Alex Escudero, President
Tel: (404) 894-2000 Fax: (404) 894-9862
Email: sso@gatech.edu
Web: http://cyberbuzz.gatech.edu/sso/

HAWAII

CHAMBER OF COMMERCE

HAWAII HISPANIC CHAMBER OF COMMERCE
P.O. Box 235263
Honolulu, HI 96823
Susana Geng Ho, President
Tel: (808) 545-4344 Fax: (808) 521-1496
Email: hhcc1992@yahoo.com

MULTI-PURPOSE

UNITED PUERTO RICAN ASSOCIATION OF HAWAII, INC.
1249 N. School St.
Honolulu, HI 96817
Angel Santiago, President
Tel: (808) 847-2751

RELIGIOUS

DIOCESE OF HONOLULU
Hispanic Ministry Office
1184 Bishop St.
Honolulu, HI 96813
Gary Secor, Delegate for Clergy
Tel: (808) 533-1791 Fax: (808) 521-8428

SPEC. INT., SOCIAL INTEREST

HISPANIC CENTER OF HAWAII
2044 S Beretania St. #2
Honolulu, HI 96826
Nancy Ortiz, Executive Director
Tel: (808) 941-5216 Fax: (808) 941-1594
Email: centrohispano1@aol.com

SPEC. INT., WOMEN

MUJERES AL EXITO
P.O. Box 893234
Mililani, HI 96789
Vicky Ramirez, President
Tel: (808) 550-8616 Fax: (808) 585-7404
Email: vr_financialsvcs@yahoo.com
Web: www.womenforsuccess.com

IDAHO

BUSINESS

HISPANIC BUSINESS ASSOCIATION
315 Stampede Dr.
Nampa, ID 83687
Tel: (208) 463-4226 Fax: (208) 442-6801
Email: info@hbaonline.org
Web: www.hbaonline.org

CULTURAL

OFFICE OF MULTICULTURAL AFFAIRS
University of Idaho
P.O. Box 443177
Moscow, ID 83844-3177
Francisco Salinas, Director
Tel: (208) 885-7716 Fax: (208) 885-9494
Email: fsalinas@uidaho.edu
Web: www.students.uidaho.edu/oma/

MULTI-PURPOSE

IMAGE DE IDAHO DEL SUDESTE
P.O. Box 1341
Pocatello, ID 83204
Andy Guerra, Secretary
Tel: (208) 232-1549 Fax: (208) 232-1549
Email: andres@dcdi.net

RELIGIOUS

CATHOLIC MIGRANT FARMWORKER NETWORK
1915 University Dr.
Boise, ID 83706
Celine Caufield, Director
Tel: (208) 384-1778
Email: cmfncc@stpaulboise.org
Web: www.cmfn.org

DIOCESE OF BOISE
Cultural Ministries Office
303 Federal Way
Boise, ID 83705
Lina Oropeza, Secretary
Tel: (208) 342-1311 Fax: (208) 342-0224
Email: loropeza@rcdb.org
Web: www.catholicidaho.org/multicultural.cfm

SPEC. INT., SOCIAL INTEREST

IDAHO COMMISSION ON HISPANIC AFFAIRS
5460 W Franklin Rd. #B
Boise, ID 83705
Margie Gonzalez, Executive Director
Tel: (208) 334-3776 Fax: (208) 334-3778
Email: mgonzalez@icha.state.id.us
Web: www.state.id.us/icha/

IDAHO MIGRANT COUNCIL, INC.
317 Happy Day Blvd. #250
Caldwell, ID 83607
Alfred Pacheco, Executive Director
Tel: (208) 454-1652 Fax: (208) 459-0448
Email: apacheco@imcmail.org

ILLINOIS

ARTISTIC

BALLET FOLKLORICO
Back of the Yard Neighborhood Council
1751 W. 47th St., 2nd Fl.
Chicago, IL 60609-3889
Salvador Cisneros, Director
Tel: (773) 523-4416 Fax: (773) 254-3525
Email: scisneros@bync.org
Web: www.bync.org/folklorico/index.cfm

MEXICAN FOLKLORIC DANCE COMPANY OF CHICAGO
3842 S. Archer Ave.
Chicago, IL 60632-1014
Henry A. Roa, Executive Director
Tel: (773) 247-1522 Fax: (773) 247-1502
Email: mexfolroa@ameritech.net
Web: www.mexfoldanco.org

MOVIMIENTO ARTÍSTICO CHICANO, INC.
P.O. Box 2890
Chicago, IL 60690
Carlos Cumpián, Director
Tel: (773) 539-9638 Fax: (773) 539-0013
Email: marczim@uic.edu
Web: www.marchabrazo.org

PEOPLE'S MUSIC SCHOOL
931 W Eastwood Ave.
Chicago, IL 60640
Mary Ellen McGarry, Executive Dirrector
Tel: (773) 784-7032 Fax: (773) 784-7134
Email: marye@peoplesmusicschool.org
Web: www.peoplesmusicschool.org

BUSINESS

CHICAGO MINORITY BUSINESS DEVELOPMENT COUNCIL
1 E. Wacker Dr. #1200
Chicago, IL 60601
Tracye E. Smith, Executive Director
Tel: (312) 755-8880 Fax: (312) 775-8890
Email: tsmith@cmbdc.org
Web: www.cmbdc.org

CULTURAL ENTERPRISE OPPORTUNITY PROJECT
Jane Addams Center/Small Business Development Unit
4520 N. Beacon St.
Chicago, IL 60640
Tom Ullmann, Specialist
Tel: (773) 561-3500 Fax: (773) 561-3506
Email: croeschley@hullhouse.org
Web: www.hullhouse.org

KRAFT FOODS HISPANIC EMPLOYEE COUNCIL
Philip Morris/Kraft Foods
801 Waukegan Rd.
Glenview, IL 60025
Celso Bejarano, President
Tel: (847) 646-2000 Fax: (847) 646-3864
Web: www.kraft.com

MIDWEST ASSOCIATION OF HISPANIC ACCOUNTANTS
DePaul University Student Chapter
1 E. Jackson Blvd.
Chicago, IL 60604
Fabiola Salcedo, Chapter President
Tel: (312) 362-5058 Fax: (312) 362-6208
Email: maha@condor.depaul.edu
Web: http://condor.depaul.edu/~maha

NATIONAL SOCIETY OF HISPANIC MBAS
P.O. Box 1204
Chicago, IL 60690-1204
Roxanne Vergara, Chapter President
Tel: (312) 409- 5628
Email: general@chicago.nshmba.org
Web: www.nshmba.org

CHAMBER OF COMMERCE

47TH STREET CHAMBER OF COMMERCE
1646 W. 47th St.
Cicero, IL 60609
Tel: (773) 579-1200 Fax: (773) 579-1986
Email: daautorepair@hotmail.com

AURORA HISPANIC CHAMBER OF COMMERCE
P.O. Box 7111
Aurora, IL 60507
Zaida Chapa, President
Tel: (630) 264-2422 Fax: (630) 892-8013
Email: Zchapa@aol.com
Web: www.ahcc-il.com

THE CHAMBER OF COMMERCE OF NORTHERN ILLINOIS
5483 Cheyenne Dr.
Rockford, IL 61109
Tel: (815) 873-8581
Email: mariahawley3@yahoo.com.mx

CICERO CHAMBER OF COMMERCE
5801 W. Cermak Rd., 2nd Fl.
Cicero, IL 60804
Donna Renzi, Executive Director
Tel: (708) 863-6000 Fax: (708) 863-8981
Email: sales@midwaydoor.com

COSMOPOLITAN CHAMBER OF COMMERCE
560 W. Lake St., 5th Fl.
Chicago, IL 60661
Gloria Bell, Executive Director
Tel: (312) 786-0212 Fax: (312) 786-9079
Email: glbell1455@yahoo.com
Web: www.cosmochamberevents.org

CUBAN AMERICAN CHAMBER OF COMMERCE OF ILLINOIS
3330 N. Ashland Ave.
Chicago, IL 60657
Erio Montenegro, President
Tel: (773) 248-2400 Fax: (773) 248-6437

GUATEMALAN CHAMBER OF COMMERCE
2814 N Kedzie Ave.
Chicago, IL 60618
Rene Noriega, President
Tel: (773) 227-7330 Fax: (773) 227-7379
Email: guatemala2001@aol.com

ILLINOIS HISPANIC CHAMBER OF COMMERCE
33 N LaSalle St.
Chicago, IL 60602
Juan A. Ochoa, President/CEO
Tel: (312) 372-3010 Fax: (312) 372-3403
Email: info@ihccbusiness.net
Web: www.ihccbusiness.net

LATIN AMERICAN CHAMBER OF COMMERCE
3512 W. Fullerton Ave.
Chicago, IL 60647
Antonio Guillen, President
Tel: (773) 252-5211 Fax: (773) 252-7065
Email: lacc@latinamericanchamberofcommerce.com
Web: www.latinamericanchamberofcommerce.com

3610 W. 26th St., 2nd Fl.
Chicago, IL 60623
Martha De La Vega, Executive Director
Tel: (773) 521-5387 Fax: (773) 521-5252
Email: info@lavillitachamber.com
Web: www.lavillitachamber.com

PUERTO RICAN CHAMBER OF COMMERCE OF ILLINOIS
2450 W. Division St.
Chicago, IL 60622
Minerva Santiago, Executive Director
Tel: (773) 486-1331 Fax: (773) 486-1340
Email: info@prcci.com
Web: www.prcci.com

UNITED STATES-MEXICO CHAMBER OF COMMERCE
Mid-America Chapter
130 E. Randolph Dr., 36th Fl.
Chicago, IL 60601
Leroy Allala, Executive Director
Tel: (312) 729-1355 Fax: (312) 729-1354
Email: leroy@usmcoc.org
Web: www.usmcoc.org

COMMUNICATIONS

THE SAN JOSE GROUP
625 N. Michigan Ave. 16th Fl.
Chicago, IL 60611
Katherine Key, VP Client Services
Tel: (312) 751-8500 Fax: (312) 751-9080
Email: sanjose@sjadv.com
Web: www.sanjosegroup.com

SPANISH-AMERICAN LANGUAGE NEWSPAPER AGENCY
55 E. Jackson Blvd. #1820
Chicago, IL 60604-4196
John Conley, Genreal Manager
Tel: (312) 368-4840 Fax: (312) 427-7829

CULTURAL

ALDO CASTILLO GALLERY
233 W. Huron Ave.
Chicago, IL 60610
Aldo Castillo, President
Tel: (312) 337-2536 Fax: (312) 337-3627
Email: info@artaldo.com
Web: www.artaldo.com

BRAZILIAN CULTURAL CENTER OF CHICAGO
1436 W. Jonquil
Chicago, IL 60626
Maria Dell, President
Tel: (773) 465-3717
Email: mariadell@brazilianculturalcenter.org
Web: www.brazilianculturalcenter.org

INSTITUTO MEXICANO DE CULTURA Y EDUCACIÓN DE CHICAGO
Chicago Office
702 N. Wells
Chicago, IL 60610
Manuel J. Medina, President
Tel: (312) 255-1556 Fax: (312) 255-9294
Web: www.geocities.com/Athens/Academy/1107/index.html

INTERNATIONAL LATINO CULTURAL CENTER OF CHICAGO
Colmbia College Chicago
600 S. Michigan Ave.
Chicago, IL 60605-1996
Rose Mary Bombela, Chair
Tel: (312) 431-1330 Fax: (312) 344-8030
Email: info@latinoculturalcenter.org
Web: www.latinoculturalcenter.org

LATIN AMERICAN STUDIES PROGRAM
University of Illinois, Chicago
P.O. Box 4348
Chicago, IL 60608
Frances Aparicio, Director
Tel: (312) 996-2445 Fax: (312) 996-1796
Email: franapar@uic.edu
Web: www.uic.edu/las/latamst

MEXICAN FINE ARTS CENTER MUSEUM
Pilsen-Little Village
1852 W. 19th St.
Chicago, IL 60608
Carlos Tortolero, Director
Tel: (312) 738-1503 Fax: (312) 738-9740
Email: rachel@mfacmchicago.org
Web: www.mfacmchicago.org

ORGANIZATION OF LATIN AMERICAN STUDENTS
Elgin Community College
1700 Spartan Dr.
Elgin, IL 60123
Connie Zapata, Advisor
Tel: (847) 697-1000
Email: czapata@elgin.edu

PUERTO RICAN CULTURAL CENTER
2739-41 W. Division St.
Chicago, IL 60622
Jose Lopez, Executive Director
Tel: (773) 342-8023 Fax: (773) 342-6609
Email: info@prcc-chgo.org
Web: www.prcc-c.fatcow.com

PUERTO RICAN PARADE COMMITTEE OF CHICAGO
1237 N. California
Chicago, IL 60622
Miguel Sanchez, President
Tel: (773) 292-1414 Fax: (773) 292-1860
Email: prparade@sbcglobal.net
Web: www.prparadechicago.com

SEGUNDO RUIZ BELVIS CULTURAL CENTER
1632 N. Milwaukee
Chicago, IL 60647
Pablo Medina, Board Member
Tel: (773) 235-3988 Fax: (773) 235-8080
Email: info@ruizbelvis.org
Web: www.ruizbelvis.org

ENTERTAINMENT

COMMUNITY TV NETWORK
2418 W. Bloomingdale
Chicago, IL 60647
Denise Zaccardi, Executive Director
Tel: (773) 278-8500 Fax: (773) 278-8635
Email: ctvnchicago@yahoo.com
Web: www.ctvnetwork.org

LAW ENFORCEMENT

HISPANIC AMERICAN POLICE COMMAND OFFICERS ASSOCIATION
Midwest Chapter
P.O. Box 4865
Chicago, IL 60680-4865
Frank Limon, Chapter President
Tel: (773) 788-9093
Email: limon@hapcoa.org
Web: www.hapcoa.org

HISPANIC ILLINOIS STATE LAW ENFORCEMENT ASSOCIATION
P.O. Box 470086
Chicago, IL 60647-0086
Luis Gutierrez, President
Tel: (708) 342-1910 Fax: (708) 342-1910
Email: info@hislea.org
Web: www.hislea.org

LATIN AMERICAN POLICE ASSOCIATION
P.O. Box 4551
Chicago, IL 60680-4551
Jerry Negrete, Jr., President
Tel: (773) 767-4201 Fax: (773) 767-4381
Email: info@lapa1961.org
Web: www.lapa1961.org

MULTI-PURPOSE

ADVISORY COUNCIL ON LATINO AFFAIRS
Chicago Commission on Human Relations
740 N. Sedgwick #300
Chicago, IL 60610
Clarence N. Wood, Chairman
Tel: (312) 744-4111 Fax: (312) 744-1081
Email: cwood@aol.com
Web: www.cityofchicago.org/humanrelations/

ALBANY PARK COMMUNITY CENTER
Administrative Office
3403 W. Lawrence Ave. #300
Chicago, IL 60625
Diane M. Yost, Executive Director
Tel: (773) 583-5111 Fax: (773) 583-5062
Email: info@albanyparkcommunitycenter.org
Web: www.albanyparkcommunitycenter.org

AMERICAN GI FORUM OF THE UNITED STATES
Illinois Chapter
1117 Genessee St.
Waukegan, IL 60085
Louis Rodriguez, Illinois State Commander
Tel: (847) 336-1004 X225 Fax: (630) 953-1326
Email: jrodriguez@serlake.org
Web: www.agif.us/IL.htm

ASSOCIATION HOUSE OF CHICAGO
1116 N. Kedzie Ave.
Chicago, IL 60651
Harriet Sadauskas, Executive Director
Tel: (773) 772-7170 Fax: (773) 384-0560
Email: info@associationhouse.org
Web: www.associationhouse.org

CASA AZTLAN
1831 S. Racine St.
Chicago, IL 60608
Carlos Aranjo, Executive Director
Tel: (312) 666-5508 Fax: (312) 666-7829
Web: www.neiu.edu/~casaaztl/Main.htm

CATHOLIC CHARITIES OF THE ARCHDIOCESE OF CHICAGO
Immigration Services
126 N. Desplaines St.
Chicago, IL 60661
Rev. Michael M. Boland, Administrator
Tel: (312) 655-7000 Fax: (312) 427-3130
Web: www.catholiccharities.net

CENTRO SIN FRONTERAS-UNITED METHODIST CHURCH
4811 W. Armitage
Chicago, IL 60639
Ema Lozano, Director
Tel: (773) 836-8383 Fax: (773) 836-8388
Email: sinfronteras1205@aol.com
Web: www.pueblosinfronteras.org

CORDI-MARIAN CENTER
1100 S. May
Chicago, IL 60607
Fran Fister, Director
Tel: (312) 666-3787

EL VALOR CORPORATION
1850 W. 21st St.
Chicago, IL 60608
Vincent A. Allocco, President/CEO
Tel: (312) 666-4511 Fax: (312) 666-6677
Email: vallocco@elvalor.net
Web: www.elvalor.org

FAMILY AND RESCUE
P.O. Box 17528
Chicago, IL 60617
Joyce M. Coffee, Executive Director
Tel: (773) 375-1918 Fax: (773) 734-1245
Email: administration@familyrescueinc.org
Web: www.familyrescueinc.org

FIESTA DEL SOL
2026 S. Blue Island Ave.
Chicago, IL 60608
Juan F. Soto, Executive Director
Tel: (312) 666-2663 Fax: (312) 666-4661
Email: jfsoto@fiestadelsol.org
Web: www.fiestadelsol.org

HISPANIC/LATINO STUDENT SERVICES
Northwestern University
1936 Sheridan Rd. Multicultural Center
Evanston, IL 60208
Ronnie Rios, Director
Tel: (847) 467-7337 Fax: (847) 491-3128
Email: hispanic-latino@northwestern.edu
Web: www.northwestern.edu/latino/

INSTITUTE FOR LATINO PROGRESS
2570 S. Blue Island Ave.
Chicago, IL 60608
Juan Salgado, Executive Director
Tel: (773) 890-0055 Fax: (773) 890-1537
Email: juan@idpl.org
Web: www.idpl.org

LULAC NATIONAL EDUCATIONAL SERVICE CENTERS, INC.
4355 W. 26th St. #3
Chicago, IL 60623
Ernestina Bobe, Director
Tel: (773) 277-2513 Fax: (773) 277-3930
Email: infochi@lnesc-chicago.org
Web: www.lnesc-chicago.org

METROPOLITAN FAMILY SERVICES
14 E. Jackson Blvd.
Chicago, IL 60604
Richard L. Jones, President/CEO
Tel: (312) 986-4000
Email: webadmin@metrofamily.org
Web: www.metrofamily.org

MEXICAN CIVIC COMMITTEE
3934 W. 26th St.
Chicago, IL 60623
Marshall Del Rio, Director
Tel: (773) 521-2700 Fax: (773) 521-7908

NATIONAL COUNCIL OF LA RAZA
203 N. Wabash Ave. #918
Chicago, IL 60601
Simón López, Senior Workforce Coordinator
Tel: (312) 269-9250 Fax: (312) 269-9260
Email: chicago@nclr.org
Web: www.nclr.org

PILSEN-LITTLE VILLAGE
Administrative Office
2319 S. Damen Ave.
Chicago, IL 60608
Francisco Cisneros, Executive Director
Tel: (773) 579-0832 Fax: (773) 579-0762
Email: fcisneros@pilsenmh.org
Web: www.pilsenmh.org

RAFAEL CINTRON-ORTIZ LATINO CULTURAL CENTER
University of Illinois, Chicago
803 S. Morgan St., Lecture Center B2
Chicago, IL 60607-7028
Rodrigo Carramiñana, Director
Tel: (312) 996-3095 Fax: (312) 996-9092

Email: rodrigoc@uic.edu
Web: www.uic.edu/depts/lcc

RENACER BOLIVIANO, INC.
P.O. Box 1184
Chicago, IL 60690-1184
Alberto Olivera, President
Email: albolitej@renacer.org
Web: http://renacer.org

THE RESURRECTION PROJECT
1818 S. Paulina St.
Chicago, IL 60608
Raúl I. Raymundo, CEO
Tel: (312) 666-1323 Fax: (312) 942-1123
Email: info@resurrectionproject.org
Web: www.resurrectionproject.org

SOCIAL AND EDUCATIONAL SERVICES
5244 N. Lakewood St.
Chicago, IL 60640
Elida Scalfi, Executive Director
Tel: (773) 878-6035 Fax: (773) 878-6037

SOCIETY OF HISPANIC PROFESSIONAL ENGINEERS
Midwest Regional Chicago Professional Chapter
P.O. Box 2330
Chicago, IL 60690-2330
Doris A. Williams, President
Tel: (312) 220-2169
Email: dd4685@sbc.com
Web: www.enteract.com/~shpe/

SPANISH CENTER, INC.
309 N. Eastern Ave.
Joliet, IL 60432
Lois Nelson, Executive Director
Tel: (815) 727-3683 Fax: (815) 727-9459
Email: loisn22@comcast.net
Web: www.spanishcenter.org

POLITICAL ACTION

CUBAN-AMERICAN NATIONAL FOUNDATION
Chicago Chapter
1727 W. 21st St.
Chicago, IL 60608
Iván H. Fernández, Area Director
Tel: (708) 544-4491 Fax: (312) 829-6657
Email: ferdelpro@aol.com

LA CASA CULTURAL LATINA
University of Illinois at Urbana Champaign
1203 W. Nevada St.
Urbana, IL 61801
Geraldo Rosales, Director
Tel: (217) 333-4950 Fax: (217) 244-4513
Email: grosales@uiuc.edu
Web: www.odos.uiuc.edu/lacasa/

MEXICO SOLIDARITY NETWORK
4834 N. Springfield
Chicago, IL 60625
Tom Hansen, Director
Tel: (773) 583-7728 Fax: (773) 583-7738
Email: msn@mexicosolidarity.org
Web: www.mexicosolidarity.org

REPUBLICAN NATIONAL HISPANIC ASSEMBLY
RNHA-Illinois
P.O. Box 788
McHenry, IL 60051
Gregory Rodriguez, ViceChairman
Tel: (847) 274-2229 Fax: (847) 288-1628
Email: ilchairmanrnha@aol.com
Web: www.rnha.org/grassroots/#state

U.S. HISPANIC LEADERSHIP INSTITUTE
431 S. Dearborn St. #1203
Chicago, IL 60605
Juan Andrade Jr., President
Tel: (312) 427-8683 Fax: (312) 427-5183
Email: ushli@aol.com
Web: www.ushli.com

PROFESSIONAL

THE CHICAGO ASSOCIATION OF MINORITY STUDENTS
P.O. Box A3139
Chicago, IL 60690
Fred Evans, President
Email: fred.evans5471@sbcglobal.net
Web: www.camr.net

HISPANIC AMERICAN CONSTRUCTION INDUSTRY ASSOCIATION
901 W. Jackson Blvd
Chicago, IL 60607
Cesar A. Santoy, Executive Director
Tel: (312) 666-5910 Fax: (312) 666-5692
Email: info@haciaworks.org
Web: www.haciaworks.org

HISPANIC LAWYERS ASSOCIATION OF ILLINOIS
321 S Plymouth Ct. #600
Chicago, IL 60604
Homero Tristan, President
Tel: (312) 345-9200 Fax: (312) 345-1533
Email: htristan@tristanports.com
Web: www.hlai.org

MIDWEST ASSOCIATION OF HISPANIC ACCOUNTANTS
DePaul University Student Chapter
1 E Jackson Blvd., School of Accountancy & MIS #6011
Chicago, IL 60604
Lizett Corral, President
Tel: (312) 362-5058 Fax: (312) 362-6208
Email: maha@condor.depaul.edu
Web: http://condor.depaul.edu/~maha

PERUVIAN AMERICAN MEDICAL SOCIETY
Illinois - Indiana Chapter
555 Warren Terrace
Hinsdale, IL 60521
Dr. Juan Angelats, President
Tel: (630) 325-9136
Email: angelats@sbcglobal.net
Web: www.pamsnational.org

SOCIETY OF HISPANIC PROFESSIONAL ENGINEERS
P.O. Box 318
Prospect Heights, IL 60070
Amilcar Guzman, President
Tel: (847) 808-7389 Fax: (847) 542-0898
Email: aguzman@shpechicago.org
Web: www.shpechicago.org

RELIGIOUS

ARCHDIOCESE OF CHICAGO
Hispanic Affairs
1850 S. Throop
Chicago, IL 60608
Rev. Claudio Diaz, Director for Hispanic Ministry
Tel: (312) 738-1080 Fax: (312) 243-3459
Email: cdiaz@archchicago.org
Web: www.archchicago.org

DIOCESE OF BELLEVILLE
Hispanic Ministry Office
2620 Lebanon Ave.
Belleville, IL 62221
Sr. Cecilia Hellmann, Coordinator for Hispanic Ministry
Tel: (618) 235-9601 X129 Fax: (618) 235-7115
Email: chellmann@diobelle.org
Web: www.diobelle.org

DIOCESE OF JOLIET
Hispanic Affairs/St. Charles Borromeo Pastoral Center
402 S. Independence Blvd.
Romeoville, IL 60446-2264
Miguel Moreno, Director
Tel: (815) 834-4037
Email: mmoreno@dioceseofjoliet.org
Web: www.dioceseofjoliet.org/ohm

DIOCESE OF ROCKFORD
Centro Sembrador
921 W. State St.
Rockford, IL 61102-2808
Rev. William Schuessler, Vic. Hispanic Ministries
Tel: (815) 962-8042 Fax: (815) 968-2808

DIOCESE OF SPRINGFIELD IN ILLINOIS
P.O. Box 3187
1615 W. Washington St.
Springfield, IL 62702
Sr. Jane Boos, SSND, Contact Hispanic Ministry
Tel: (217) 698-8500 Fax: (217) 698-0802
Email: osc@dio.org
Web: www.dio.org

DIOCESE OF ROCKFORD
HispanicCatholic MinistryY
555 Colman Center Drive
Rockford, IL 61125
Very Rev. Archimedes Vallejo J.C.D., Chairman
Tel: (815) 399-4300

DIOCESE OF PEORIA
HispanicCatholic MinistryY
613 NE Jefferson Ave.
Peoria, IL 61603
Msgr. Brian Rejsek, Director
Tel: (309) 671-1568 x222

RESEARCH

CENTER FOR LATIN AMERICAN AND CARIBBEAN STUDIES
University of Illinois, Urbana-Champaign
910 S. 5th St., 201 International Studies Bldg.
Champaign, IL 61820
Nils Jacobsen, Director
Tel: (217) 333-3182 Fax: (217) 244-7333
Email: clacs@uiuc.edu
Web: www.uiuc.edu/unit/lat

CENTER FOR LATIN AMERICAN STUDIES
University of Chicago
5848 S. University Ave., Kelly Hall 310
Chicago, IL 60637
Dain Borges, Director
Tel: (773) 702 8420 Fax: (773) 702-1755
Email: clas@uchicago.edu
Web: clas.uchicago.edu

CENTER FOR LATINO RESEARCH
DePaul University
2320 N. Kenmore Ave. #5A08
Chicago, IL 60614
Dr. Felix Masud-Piloto, Director
Tel: (773) 325-4818 Fax: (773) 325-7166
Email: clr@depaul.edu
Web: www.depaul.edu/~laltinos

PUERTO RICAN STUDIES ASSOCIATION
University of Illinois at Urbana-Champaign
1108 W. Stoughton Ave.
Urbana, IL 61801
Pedro A. Caban, President
Tel: (217) 244-0188 Fax: (217) 333-8122
Email: prsa@uiuc.edu
Web: www.puertorican-studies.org

SPEC. INT., AIDS

CALOR-A DIVISION OF ANIXTER CENTER
3220 W. Armitage Ave.
Chicago, IL 60647
Omar López, Executive Director
Tel: (773) 235-3161 Fax: (773) 772-0484
Email: askcalor@anixter.org
Web: www.calor.org

MIDWEST HISPANIC AIDS COALITION
53 W. Jackson Blvd. #1322
Chicago, IL 60604
Patricia Canessa, Executive Director
Tel: (312) 913-3001 Fax: (312) 913-3003
Email: pcanessa@mhhcsalud.org
Web: www.mhhcsalud.org

VIDA/SIDA
2703 W. Division
Chicago, IL 60622
Dr. Roberto Sanabria
Tel: (773) 278-6737 Fax: (773) 278-6753
Web: www.vidasida.org

SPEC. INT., ALCOHOL/DRUG CENTER

LATINO TREATMENT CENTER
54 S. Grove Ave.
Elgin, IL 60120
Ernest Pujals, Director
Tel: (847) 695-9175 Fax: (847) 695-9194
Email: latino86@msn.com

Chicago Facility
2608 W. Peterson
Chicago, IL 60659
Adriana Pujals, Assistant Director
Tel: (773) 465-1161 Fax: (773) 465-1693
Email: adri1631@aol.com

SPEC. INT., CHILD CARE

LA ESPERANZA DEL FUTURO
Child Abuse Unit for Studies, Education, and Services
1009 W. Wellington Ave.
Chicago, IL 60657
Richard LaBrie, Executive Director
Tel: (773) 248-5500 Fax: (773) 248-5688
Email: causes1@aol.com
Web: www.causesforchildren.org

LA PROGRESIVA PRE-SCHOOL
2609 N. Kimball
Chicago, IL 60647
Norma Reyes, Director
Tel: (773) 342-6690 Fax: (773) 235-8885

LUGAR PARA MADRES
ChildServ/Lake County Family Service Center
1103 Greenwood Ave.
Waukegan, IL 60087
Maria Elena Jonas, Supervisor
Tel: (847) 263-2200 Fax: (847) 662-0663
Email: mejonas@childserv.org
Web: www.childserv.org

SPEC. INT., COUNSELING

COUNSELING CENTER OF LAKEVIEW
3225 N. Sheffield Ave.
Chicago, IL 60657
Gelsys Rubio, Program Director
Tel: (773) 549-5886 Fax: (773) 549-3265
Web: www.epagecity.com/site/epage/9508_373.htm

SPEC. INT., EDUCATION

ASPIRA OF ILLINOIS, INC.
2435 N. Western Ave.
Chicago, IL 60647
José Rodríguez, Executive Director
Tel: (773) 252-0970 Fax: (773) 252-0994
Email: info@il.aspira.org
Web: www.aspirail.org

ASSOCIATION OF LATINO INFORMATION TECHNOLOGY PROFESSIONALS
P. O. Box 0440
Chicago, IL 60609
Jaime Viteri, President
Email: alitp_chicago@hotmail.com
Web: www.alitp.org

CASA LATINA CULTURAL CENTER
Western Illinois University
1 University Cr.
Macomb, IL 61455
Tel: (309) 298-3379 Fax: (309) 298-2567
Email: A-Godines@wiu.edu
Web: www.student.services.wiu.edu/casa/

CENTER FOR LATINO AND LATIN AMERICAN STUDIES
Northern Illinois University
515 Garden Rd.
DeKalb, IL 60115
Michael J. Gonzales, Director
Tel: (815) 753-1531 Fax: (815) 753-1651
Email: gonzales@niu.edu
Web: www.clas.niu.edu/latino

CENTRO LATINO UNIVERSIDAD POPULAR
1510 N. Rockwell
Chicago, IL 60622
Olivia Flores Godinez, Director
Tel: (773) 772-0836 Fax: (773) 772-0837
Email: upopular@prodigy.net

HISPANIC CENTER OF EXCELLENCE
University of Illinois
Department of Medical Education, 990 College of Medicine East 808, S. Wood St. M/C 591
Chicago, IL 60612
Jorge A. Girotti, Director
Tel: (312) 996-4493 Fax: (312) 996-9922
Email: jorgeg@uic.edu
Web: www.uuic.edu/depts/mcam/hcoe

INROADS, INC.
Chicago Office
25 E. Washington Ave. #801
Chicago, IL 60602
Michael E. Jackson, Managing Director
Tel: (312) 553-5053 Fax: (312) 553-5065
Email: mjackson@inroads.org
Web: www.inroads.org

LATIN AMERICAN RECRUITMENT AND EDUCATIONAL SERVICES
University of Illinois, Chicago
2640 Student Services Bldg., 1200 W. Harrison St.
Chicago, IL 60607
Leonard Ramirez, Director
Tel: (312) 996-3356

LATINO INITIATIVES FOR THE NEXT CENTURY
205 N. Michigan #2315
Chicago, IL 60601
Rudy J. Mulder, Chairman/Founder
Tel: (877) 510-5462 Fax: (312) 946-0501
Email: admin@linc-usa.org
Web: www.linc-usa.org

LEAGUE OF UNITED LATIN AMERICAN CITIZENS
LULAC Chapter 5226
10437 S. Ave. G
Chicago, IL 60617
Cynthia Madrigal, Secretary
Tel: (312) 464-3500
Email: cynmad@yahoo.com

MINORITY ACCESS PROGRAM
Illinois Institute of Technology
3300 S. Federal St.
Chicago, IL 60616-3793
Irma Dobbins, Director
Tel: (312) 567-5249 Fax: (312) 567-5114
Email: dobbins@iit.edu
Web: www.iit.edu/~cmp

OUR LADY OF GUADALUPE PARISH
3200 E. 91st St.
Chicago, IL 60617
Fr. Edmundo Andres, Associate Pastor
Tel: (773) 768-0793 Fax: (773) 768-3245
Email: jfm@claret.org
Web: www.parishesonline.net

SOCIEDAD HONORARIA HISPÁNICA
P.O. Box 5318
Buffalo Grove, IL 60089-5318
Carol Kearns, President
Tel: (847) 550-0455
Email: sociedad@comcast.net
Web: www.sociedadhonorariahispanica.org

SPEC. INT., EMPLOYMENT

CENTRAL STATES SER-JOBS FOR PROGRESS, INC.
3948 W. 26th #213
Chicago, IL 60623
Rachel McDonald, Executive Director
Tel: (773) 542-9030 Fax: (773) 542-9213
Email: rmcdonald@centralstatesser.org
Web: www.ser-national.org

GRACIELA KENIG AND ASSOCIATES-CAREER DEVELOPMENT SPECIALISTS FOR HISPANICS
4334 Ivy Dr.
Glenview, IL 60026
Graciela Kenig, President/Founder
Tel: (847) 699-1817 Fax: (847) 699-1864
Email: info@careersforlatinos.com
Web: www.careersforlatinos.com

HISPANIC ALLIANCE FOR CAREER ENHANCEMENT
25 E. Washington #1500
Chicago, IL 60602
Abe Tomas Hughes, Chairman
Tel: (312) 435-0498 Fax: (312) 435-1494
Email: abetomas@hace-usa.org
Web: www.hace-usa.org

ILLINOIS ASSOCIATION OF HISPANIC STATE EMPLOYEES
P.O. Box 641526
Chicago, IL 60664-1526
Jose Javier Lopez, President
Tel: (312) 814-8942 Fax: (312) 814-8538
Email: iahse@mail.state.il.us
Web: www.iahse.org

ILLINOIS MIGRANT COUNCIL
28 E. Jackson Blvd. #1600
Chicago, IL 60604
Eloy Salazar, Executive Director
Tel: (312) 663-1522 Fax: (312) 663-1994
Email: info@illinoismigrant.org
Web: www.illinoismigrant.org

SER-JOBS FOR PROGRESS, INC. OF LAKE COUNTY
117 N Genesee St.
Waukegan, IL 60085
Katherine A. Harris, Executive Director
Tel: (847) 336-1004 Fax: (847) 336-1435
Email: kharris@serlake.org
Web: www.ser-lake.org

SPANISH COALITION FOR JOBS, INC.
2011 W. Pershing Rd.
Chicago, IL 60609
Victor Herrera, Recruitment Coordinator
Tel: (773) 247-0707 Fax: (773) 247-3924
Email: vherrera@scj-usa.org
Web: www.scj-usa.org

1737 W. 18th St.
Chicago, IL 60608
Mary Gonzalez-Koenig, President/CEO
Tel: (312) 243-3030 Fax: (312) 243-9109
Email: scj@scj-usa.org
Web: www.scj-usa.org

SPEC. INT., FAMILY PLANNING

CASA CENTRAL SOCIAL SERVICES CORPORATION
1343 N. California Ave.
Chicago, IL 60622
Ann R. Alvarez, President/CEO
Tel: (773) 645-2300
Email: inforequest@casacentral.org
Web: www.casacentral.org

SPEC. INT., GAY&LESBIAN

ASSOCIATION OF LATINO MEN FOR ACTION
P.O. Box 13159
Chicago, IL 60613
Julio Rodriguez, President
Tel: (773) 929-7688
Email: info@almachicago.org
Web: www.almachicago.org

SPEC. INT., HEALTH SERVICES

ADVOCATE HEALTH CARE
2025 Windsor Dr.
Oak Brook, IL 60523-1586
Daniel Parker, Vice President, Public Relations
Tel: (800) 3-ADVOCATE
Email: dan.parker@advocatehealth.com
Web: www.advocatehealth.com

ALIVIO MEDICAL CENTER
IPHCA Member
966 W. 21st St.
Chicago, IL 60608
Carmen Velásquez, Executive Director
Tel: (773) 650-1224 Fax: (773) 650-1226
Email: msanchez@aliviomedical.org
Web: www.aliviomedicalcenter.org

ALZHEIMER'S ASSOCIATION
National Office
225 N. Michigan Ave., Fl. 17
Chicago, IL 60601-7633
Kent Barnheiser, President & CEO
Tel: (312) 335-8700 Fax: (312) 335-1110
Email: info@alz.org
Web: www.alz.org/hispanic/overview.asp

BOLIVIAN-AMERICAN MEDICAL ASSOCIATION
1111 W. Superior St. #309
Melrose Park, IL 60160
Dr. Jaime Escobar, President
Tel: (708) 343-0420 Fax: (708) 343-4290

CHICANO HISPANIC HEALTH COALITION
Chicago Dept. of Public Health, DePaul Center
333 S. State St. #2144
Chicago, IL 60604
Esther Sciammarella, MS, Director
Tel: (312) 747-8820 Fax: (312) 747-9694
Email: sciammarella_esther@cdph.org

ERIE FAMILY HEALTH CENTER
1701 W. Superior St.
Chicago, IL 60622
Minerva Carlos, Secretary
Tel: (312) 666-3494 Fax: (312) 666-6228
Email: info@eriefamilyhealth.org
Web: www.eriefamilyhealth.org

HEALTH & DISABILITY ADVOCATES
205 W Monroe St., 3rd Fl.
Chicago, IL 60606
Barbara Otto, Executive Director
Tel: (312) 223-9600 Fax: (312) 223-9518
Email: hda@hdadvocates.org
Web: www.hdadvocates.org

HEALTHCARE ALTERNATIVE SYSTEMS, INC.
2755 W. Armitage Ave.
Chicago, IL 60647
Marco E. Jacome, Executive Director
Tel: (773) 252-3100 X118 Fax: (773) 252-8945
Email: info@hascares.org
Web: www.hascares.org

DuPage Outpatient
799 Roosevelt Rd., Bldg. 6, #312
Glen Ellyn, IL 60137
Marco E. Jacome, Executive Director
Tel: (630) 942-9720 Fax: (630) 942-9725
Email: mjacome@hascares.org
Web: www.hascares.org

Outpatient Services South
4534 S. Western Ave.
Chicago, IL 60609
Marco E. Jacome, Executive Director
Tel: (773) 254-5141 Fax: (773) 254-5753
Email: mjacome@hascares.org
Web: www.hascares.org

188 W. Randolph St. #415
Chicago, IL 60601
R. Ivan Lugo, President
Tel: (312) 577-4013 Fax: (312) 577-0052
Email: hispanicdental@hdassoc.org
Web: www.hdassoc.org

HISPANOCARE, INC.
836 W. Wellington Ave.
Chicago, IL 60657
Estella Espinoza, Office Coordinator
Tel: (773) 296-7157 Fax: (773) 327-8208
Email: estella.espinoza@advocatehealth.com

SPEC. INT., HOUSING

HISPANIC HOUSING DEVELOPMENT CORPORATION
205 W. Wacker Dr. #2300
Chicago, IL 60606
Hipolito P. Roldán, President/CEO
Tel: (312) 443-1360 Fax: (312) 443-1058
Email: proldan@hhdevcorp.com

LATIN UNITED COMMUNITY HOUSING ASSOCIATION
3541 W. North Ave. #210
Chicago, IL 60647
Juan Rivera, Executive Director
Tel: (773) 276-5338
Web: www.lucha.org

LITTLE MEXICO
115 W Wolt Rd.
Wheeling, IL 60090
Sr. Teresa María Martínez, Director
Tel: (847) 419-8935

SPANISH COALITION FOR HOUSING
4035 W. North Ave.
Chicago, IL 60639
Ofelia Navarro, Executive Director
Tel: (773) 342-7575 Fax: (773) 342-8528
Email: onavarro@spanishcoalitionforhousing.com
Web: www.state.il.us/dhr/housenet/private/spanish

EASTER SEALS METROPOLITAN CHICAGO
Executive Office
14 E. Jackson Blvd. #900
Chicago, IL 60604
Timothy Muri, President & CEO
Tel: (312) 939-5115 Fax: (312) 939-0283
Email: info@eastersealchicago.org
Web: www.chicago.easterseals.com

Head Start Program
2345 W. North Ave.
Chicago, IL 60647
Adrienne Hamilton, Program Manager
Tel: (773) 276-4000 Fax: (773) 276-5653
Email: ahamilton@easterealschicago.org
Web: www.chicago.easterseals.com

SPEC. INT., IMMIGRATION

CATHOLIC CHARITIES OF THE ARCHDIOCESE OF CHICAGO
Immigration and Naturalization Services
126 N. Desplaines St.
Chicago, IL 60661
Nancy Gabilanes, Program Director
Tel: (312) 427-7078 Fax: (312) 427-3130
Web: www.catholiccharities.net

HEARTLAND ALLIANCE FOR HUMAN NEEDS & HUMAN RIGHTS
208 S. LaSalle St. #1818
Chicago, IL 60604
Rev. Dr. Sid L. Mohn, President

Tel: (312) 660-1300 Fax: (312) 660-1500
Email: moreinfo@heartlandalliance.org
Web: www.heartlandalliance.org

SPEC. INT., LEGAL ASSISTANCE

CHICAGO LEGAL CLINIC, INC.
Immigration Program
2938 E. 91st. St.
Chicago, IL 60617
Carrie Huff, Secretary
Tel: (773) 731-1762 Fax: (773) 731-4264
Email: info@clclaw.org
Web: www.clclaw.org

MEXICAN AMERICAN LEGAL DEFENSE AND EDUCATIONAL FUND
Chicago Regional Office
188 W. Randolph St. #1405
Chicago, IL 60601
Maria Valdez, Regional Counsel
Tel: (312) 782-1422 Fax: (312) 782-1428
Web: www.maldef.org

SPEC. INT., MENTAL HEALTH

ESPERANZA COMMUNITY SERVICES SCHOOL
520 N. Marshfield
Chicago, IL 60622
Barbara Fields, Executive Director
Tel: (312) 243-6097
Web: www.esperanzacommunityservices.org

SPEC. INT., SENIORS

CENTER HOME FOR HISPANIC ELDERLY
1401 N. California Ave.
Chicago, IL 60222
Ann R. Alvarez, President/CEO
Tel: (773) 782-8700
Web: www.centerhome.org

SPEC. INT., SOCIAL INTEREST

ADAS MCKINLEY COMMUNITY SERVICES, INC.
Agency Administrative Office
725 S. Wells #1A
Chicago, IL 60607
George Jones Jr., Executive Director
Tel: (312) 554-0600
Email: info@adasmckinley.org
Web: www.adasmckinley.org

CENTRO CRISTO REY
115 N. State St.
Aurora, IL 60505
Margarita Rodriguez, Area Coordinator
Tel: (630) 851-1890 Fax: (630) 851-3625

CENTRO DE INFORMACIÓN Y PROGRESO
28 N Grove Ave. #200
Elgin, IL 60120
Audry Reed, Director
Tel: (847) 695-9050 Fax: (847) 931-7991
Email: centro@centrodeinformacion.org
Web: www.centrodeinformacion.org

CENTRO ROMERO
6216 N. Clark St.
Chicago, IL 60660
Daisy J. Funes, Executive Director
Tel: (773) 508-5300 Fax: (773) 508-5399
Email: info@centroromero.org

EL CENTRO DE LA CAUSA
731 W. 17th St.
Chicago, IL 60616
Felipe Ayala, Director
Tel: (312) 243-8508 Fax: (312) 243-8414

EL VALOR
1850 W. 21st St.
Chicago, IL 60608
Vincent Allocco, Executive Director
Tel: (312) 666-4511 Fax: (312) 666-6677
Email: vallocco@elvalor.org

Web: www.elvalor.org

ELGIN HISPANIC NETWORK
P.O. Box 1554
Elgin, IL 60121
Gilbert Feliciano
Email: ehn_il@yahoo.com
Web: www.elginhispanicnetwork.org

ERIE NEIGHBORHOOD HOUSE
Youth, Adult, and Technology Programs
1347 W. Erie St.
Chicago, IL 60622
Esther Nieves, Executive Director
Tel: (312) 666-3430 Fax: (312) 666-3955
Web: www.eriehouse.org

FIESTA HISPANA
P.O. Box 142
Rockford, IL 61105
Laura Ortiz, President
Tel: (815) 332-5924 Fax: (815) 332-9501
Email: fiestahispana@aol.com
Web: www.fiestahispana.com

GADS HILL CENTER
1919 W. Cullerton St.
Chicago, IL 60608
Barbara Castellan, CEO
Tel: (312) 226-0963 Fax: (312) 226-2248
Email: dceniceros@gadshillcenter.org
Web: www.gadshillcenter.org

HISPANIC AMERICAN LABOR COUNCIL
2538 S. Christiana Ave.
Chicago, IL 60623
August Sallas, President
Tel: (773) 762-4726

HISPANIC SOCIAL SERVICE AGENCY
3859 W. 26th St.
Chicago, IL 60623
Cristina Quintana, Program Coordinator
Tel: (773) 277-7330 Fax: (773) 277-7340

LA VOZ LATINA
412 Market St.
Rockford, IL 61107
Marco T. Lenis, President/CEO
Tel: (815) 965-5784 Fax: (815) 965-5935
Email: matulenis@lavozlatina-rkfd.org
Web: www.lavozlatina-rkfd.org

LATINO BUSINESS ASSOCIATION OF WILL COUNTY
1256 W Jefferson #207
Joliet, IL 60435
Tony Marquez, President
Tel: (815) 744-9998
Email: tonmarquez@netzero.com
Web: www.el-lba.org

MCCORMICK TRIBUNE YMCA IN LOGAN SQUARE
1834 N Lawndale
Chicago, IL 60647
Jeannette Feliciano, Executive Director
Tel: (773) 235-2525 Fax: (773) 235-9193
Email: jeannette_feliciano@ymcachgo.org
Web: www.ymcachgo.org

MUJERES LATINAS EN ACCIÓN
1823 W. 17th St.
Chicago, IL 60608
Maria S. Pesqueira, Executive Director
Tel: (773) 226-1544 Fax: (312) 226-2720
Email: mujeresmail@mujereslat.org
Web: www.mujereslatinasenaccion.org

NATIONAL CENTER FOR LATINOS WITH DISABILITIES, INC.
Affiliate of NCLR
1921 S. Blue Island Ave.
Chicago, IL 60608
Maria Elena Rodriguez-Sullivan, Executive Director
Tel: (312) 666-3393 Fax: (312) 666-1787
Email: ncld@ncld.com
Web: www.ncld.com

NATIONAL PUERTO RICAN FORUM, INC.
Chicago Office
1000 N. Milwaukee Ave. 4th Fl.
Chicago, IL 60622-4000
Monica Brown, Regional Director
Tel: (773) 395-1666 Fax: (773) 395-1999
Email: monicab@nprf.org
Web: www.nprf.org

THE OFFICE OF MINORITY AFFAIRS
Eastern Illinois University
600 Lincoln Ave.
Charleston, IL 61920
Mona Davenport, National President
Tel: (217) 581-6692 Fax: (217) 581-7300
Email: csmyd@eiu.edu
Web: www.eiu.edu/~minoraff/

PILSEN-LITTLE VILLAGE
1801 S. Ashland Ave.
Chicago, IL 60608
Claudia G. Martinez, Executive Director
Tel: (312) 829-6189 Fax: (312) 829-6192
Email: claudia@pilsenlittlevillage.org
Web: www.pilsenlittlevillage.org

PUERTO RICAN CULTURAL CENTER
2739-41 W. Division St.
Chicago, IL 60622
José E. López, Executive Director
Tel: (773) 342-8023 Fax: (773) 342-6609
Web: www.prcc-chgo.org

ROTARY CLUB INTERNATIONAL
1560 Sherman Ave., 1 Rotary Ctr.
Evanston, IL 60201
Paul Harris Award, Program Manager
Tel: (847) 866-3000 Fax: (847) 328-8554
Email: rotaract@rotaryintl.org
Web: www.rotary.org

SEGUNDO RUIZ BELVIS CULTURAL CENTER
1632 N. Milwaukee Ave.
Chicago, IL 60647
Andres Briganti, Board Member
Tel: (773) 235-3988 Fax: (773) 235-8080
Email: info@ruizbelvis.org
Web: www.ruizbelvis.org

SPANISH ACTION COMMITTEE OF CHICAGO
2452 W. Division St.
Chicago, IL 60622
Leoncio Vazquez, Executive Director
Tel: (773) 292-1052 Fax: (773) 292-1073
Email: mail@spanishaction.com
Web: www.sacchicago.com

UNITED NEIGHBORHOOD ORGANIZATION
954 W. Washington Blvd., 3rd Fl.
Chicago, IL 60607
Juan Rangel, President
Tel: (312) 432-6301
Email: jrangel@uno-online.org
Web: www.uno-online.org

WEST TOWN CONCERNED CITIZENS COALITION
3501 W. Armitage Ave.
Chicago, IL 60647
Tito Vargas, Executive Director
Tel: (773) 235-2144 Fax: (773) 235-2159
Email: westtowncoalition@yahoo.com
Web: www.neiu.edu/~westtown/

YMCA
Metropolitan Headquarters
801 N. Dearborn St.
Chicago, IL 60610
Stephen S.Cole, President & CEO
Tel: (312) 932-1200 Fax: (312) 932-1318
Email: contactus@ymcachgo.org
Web: www.ymcachgo.org

South Chicago
3039 E. 91st. St.
Chicago, IL 60617
Dominic Martin, Executive Director
Tel: (773) 721-9100 Fax: (773) 721-9330

Email: dominic_martin@ymcachgo.org
Web: www.ymcachgo.org

SPEC. INT., VOLUNTARY SERVICE

MISSION HONDURAS
P.O. Box 56007
Chicago, IL 60656-0007
Joan Fabiano, Financial Coordinator
Tel: (773) 631-2916 Fax: (773) 631-2916
Email: mhonduraschgo@sbcglobal.net
Web: www.missionhonduras.com

SPEC. INT., WOMEN

CHICAGO ABUSED WOMEN COALITION
P.O. Box 477916
Chicago, IL 60647-7916
Olga Becker, Executive Director
Tel: (773) 278-4566 Fax: (773) 489-6111
Email: cawcadmin@mindspring.com
Web: www.cawc.org

LA LECHE LEAGUE INTERNATIONAL
P.O. Box 4079
1400 N. Meacham Rd.
Schaumburg, IL 60168-4079
Hedy Nuriel, Executive Director
Tel: (847) 519-7730 Fax: (847) 519-0035
Email: lllibod@llli.org
Web: www.lalecheleague.org

RAINBOW HOUSE/ARCO IRIS
20 E Jackson
Chicago, IL 60604
Berta Powell, Shelter Director
Tel: (773) 762-6611 Fax: (773) 762-7903
Email: rainbowhouse@igc.apc.org
Web: www.rainbow-house.org

SOCIETY OF WOMEN ENGINEERS
Executive Offices
230 E. Ohio St. #400
Chicago, IL 60611-3265
Violettee Vi Brown, Executive Director
Tel: (312) 596-5223 Fax: (312) 596-5252
Email: president@swe.org/hq@swe.org
Web: www.swe.org

SPEC. INT., YOUTH

ADA S. MCKINLEY COMMUNITY SERVICES, INC.
South Chicago Neighborhood House
8458 S Mackinaw Ave.
Chicago, IL 60617
Miguel Alvarado, Program Coordinator
Tel: (773) 731-8187 Fax: (773) 731-8130
Email: malvarado@adasmckinley.org
Web: www.adasmckinley.org

BOYS AND GIRLS CLUBS OF CHICAGO
Corporate Headquarters
550 W. van Buren St. #350
Chicago, IL 60610
Andrea Hynes, Contact
Tel: (312) 235-8000 Fax: (312) 427-4110
Email: webmaster@bgcc.org
Web: www.bgcc.org

BROADER URBAN INVOLVEMENT LEADERSHIP DEVELOPMENT, INC.
1223 N. Milwaukee Ave.
Chicago, IL 60622
David Wax, President
Tel: (773) 227-2880 Fax: (773) 227-3012
Email: info@buildchicago.org
Web: www.buildchicago.org

CENTRO NUESTRO/YOUTH CENTER
3208 W. North Ave.
Chicago, IL 60647
Terri Lynn Jones, Executive Director
Tel: (773) 489-3157 Fax: (773) 489-3417
Email: tjones@cyccn.org

CHICAGO BOYS & GIRLS CLUB
General Wood Unit
2950 W. 25th St.
Chicago, IL 60623
Victor Ceballos, Director
Tel: (773) 247-0700 Fax: (773) 927-4599
Email: vceballos@bgcc.org
Web: www.bgcc.org

Little Villa Unit
2801 S Ridgeway
Chicago, IL 60623
Roberto Cepeda, Director
Tel: (773) 277-1800 Fax: (773) 277-4777

EL HOGAR DEL NIÑO
2325 S California Ave.
Chicago, IL 60608
Jane M. Garza Mancillas, Founder
Tel: (773) 523-1629 X2 Fax: (773) 523-8230
Email: janemgarza@comcast.net

GIRL SCOUTS OF CHICAGO
222 S. Riverside Plz. #2120
Chicago, IL 60606
Veronica Aguinaga, Field Executive
Tel: (312) 416-2500 X224 Fax: (312) 416-2932
Email: info@girlscouts-chicago.org
Web: www.girlscouts-chicago.org

LATINO YOUTH, INC.
The Kenilworth Union Church
2200 S. Marshall Blvd.
Chicago, IL 60623
Carmen Aviles, Executive Director
Tel: (773) 277-0400 Fax: (773) 277-0401
Email: emont15709@aol.com

PILSEN YMCA
YMCA of Metropolitan Chicago
801 N. Dearborn St.
Chicago, IL 60610
Jim Sifuentes, Executive Director
Tel: (312) 932-1200 Fax: (312) 738-1915
Email: jim_sifuentes@ymcachicago.org
Web: www.ymcachgo.org

YOUTH GUIDANCE
122 S. Michigan Ave. #1510
Chicago, IL 60603
Floyd S. Keene, President
Tel: (312) 253-4900 Fax: (312) 253-4917
Email: ctoole@youth-guidance.org
Web: www.youth-guidance.org

YOUTH OUTREACH SERVICES
6417 W. Irving Park Rd.
Chicago, IL 60634
Rick Velasquez, Executive Director
Tel: (773) 777-7112 Fax: (773) 777-7611
Email: info@yos.org
Web: www.yos.org

YOUTH SERVICE PROJECT, INC.
3942 W. North Ave.
Chicago, IL 60647
Hector J. Villafan, Executive Director
Tel: (773) 772-6270 Fax: (773) 772-8755
Email: info@youthserviceproject.org
Web: www.youthserviceproject.org

YOUTH SERVICES- NUEVOS FUTUROS
Chicago Commons Association
3645 W. Chicago Ave.
Chicago, IL 60651-3934
Frank Schell III, President/CEO
Tel: (773) 638-5600 Fax: (773) 722-5045
Email: info@chicagocommons.org
Web: www.chicagocommons.org

STUDENT ORGANIZATION

ALPHA PSI LAMBDA, INC.
Zeta Chapter
University of Illinois at Chicago
Chicago, IL 60612
Emilio Padilla, President
Email: epadil2@uic.edu
Web: www2.uic.edu/stud_orgs/greek/apl/index.htm

EL CENTRO
Northeastern Illinois University
3119 N. Pulaski Rd.
Chicago, IL 60641-5667
Daniel Lopez, Jr., Assistant Dean
Tel: (773) 777-9955 Fax: (773) 685-1393
Email: elcentro@neiu.edu
Web: www.neiu.edu/~elcentro/

HISPANIC AMERICAN LEADERSHIP ORGANIZATION
Morton College
3801 S Central Ave.
Cicero, IL 60804
Victor Cornejo, Vice President
Tel: (708) 656-8000 X262 Fax: (708) 656-3297

LA CASA CULTURAL LATINA
University of Illinois, Urbana-Champaign
1203 W Nevada St.
Urbana, IL 61801
Giraldo Rosales, Director
Tel: (217) 333-4950 Fax: (217) 244-4513
Email: lacasa@uiuc.edu
Web: www.odos.uiuc.edu/lacasa

LATIN AMERICAN STUDENT ORGANIZATION
Eastern Illinois University
Student Union, 600 Lincoln Ave.
Charleston, IL 61920
Kary Brito, Advisor
Tel: (217) 581-2219 Fax: (217) 581-6764

LATINO AMERICAN CULTURAL CENTER
University of Illinois, Chicago
LC B2 604 M/C 218 803 S. Morgan St.
Chicago, IL 60607
Rodrigo Carraminana, Director
Tel: (312) 996-3095 Fax: (312) 996-9092
Email: rodrigoc@uic.edu
Web: www.uic.edu/depts/lcc/

LATINO ASSOCIATION OF BUSINESS STUDENTS
University of Illinois, Chicago
UIC Campus Programs
Chicago, IL 60607-3525
Javier Atristain
Tel: (847) 372-4561
Email: japris1@uic.edu
Web: www.vcsa.uic.edu

ORGANIZATION OF LATIN AMERICAN STUDENTS
5706 S. University Ave. #001
Chicago, IL 60637
Carina Elizabeth Sanchez, President
Tel: (773) 702-8787 Fax: (773) 702-7718
Web: http://olas.uchicago.edu/

Chicago State University
9501 S. King Dr.
Chicago, IL 60628
Leticia Carrillo, Advisor
Tel: (773) 995-3763
Email: lcarrillo@csu.edu

Olive-Harvey College
10001 S. Woodlawn Ave.
Chicago, IL 60628
Tel: (773) 291-6337

PUERTO RICAN STUDENT ASSOCIATION
University of Illinois, Chicago
UIC Campus Programs, M/C 118, Chicago Cr. Ctr.
Office #516, 750 S. Halstead
Chicago, IL 60607
Luis Duarte, Advisor
Tel: (312) 355-0501
Email: luisd@uic.edu
Web: www2.uic.edu/stud_orgs/cultures/prsa/main.html

SIGMA LAMBDA BETA
Mighty Xi Chapter
University of Illinois at Chicago
Chicago, IL 60607
Israel Urbina, President

Tel: (312) 413-5070
Web: www.sigmalambdabeta.com/xi

SIGMA LAMBDA BETA FRATERNITY
Sigma Alpha Chapter
DePaul University, 1 E. Jackson
Chicago, IL 60604
Miguel Ayala, President
Email: mayala1@shrike.depaul.edu
Web: http://condor.depaul.edu/~betas/contents.html

Western Illinois University - Beta Chapter
P.O. Box 6053
Macomb, IL 61455-6053
Edward Virage, President
Tel: (309) 836-3390
Email: chin0latin0@yahoo.com
Web: www.sigmalambdabeta.com/beta/home.html

SIGMA LAMBDA BETA INTERNATIONAL FRATERNITY, INC.
Illinois State University
Office of Student Life, Campus Box 2700
Normal, IL 61790-2700
Sue Payne, Advisor
Tel: (309) 438-8968 Fax: (309) 438-5593
Email: smpayne@ilstu.edu
Web: www.members.tripod.com/paranoid75

SOCIETY OF HISPANIC PROFESSIONAL ENGINEERS
University of Illinois, Chicago
Campus Programs (M/C 118), #306CCC, 750 S. Halsted
Chicago, IL 60607
Nora Rincon, President
Tel: (312) 996-7000
Email: nrinco1@uic.edu
Web: www2.uic.edu/stud_orgs/prof/shpe/

University of Illinois, Urbana-Champaign
1308 W. Green St. #103A Engineering Hall
Urbana, IL 61801
Maria Barajas, President
Tel: (217) 244-8899
Email: mabaraja@uiuc.edu

UNION FOR PUERTO RICAN STUDENTS
Northeastern Illinois University
5500 N. St. Louis Ave.
Chicago, IL 60625
Yvonne Nieves, President
Tel: (773) 583-4050 X4660 Fax: (773) 442-4665

INDIANA

LATIN AMERICAN MUSIC CENTER
Indiana University
School of Music
Bloomington, IN 47405
Carmen Téllez, Director
Tel: (812) 855-2991
Email: lamc@indiana.edu
Web: www.music.indiana.edu/som/lamc

INDIANA REGIONAL MINORITY SUPPLIER DEVELOPMENT COUNCIL
2126 N. Meridian St.
Indianapolis, IN 46202
Reginald K. Henderson, President
Tel: (317) 923-2110 Fax: (317) 923-2204
Email: irmsdc@indy.net
Web: www.irmsdc.com

NATIONAL SOCIETY OF HISPANIC MBAS
Indianapolis Chapter
P.O. Box 1501
Indianapolis, IN 46206-1501
Steve A. Ramos, Chapter President
Tel: (317) 767-9265
Email: general@indianapolis.nshmba.org
Web: http://indianapolis.nshmba.org

GREATER FORT WAYNE HISPANIC CHAMBER OF COMMERCE
826 Ewing St.
Ft. Wayne, IN 46806
Tel: (260) 422-6697 Fax: (260) 426-7372
Email: rosawheeler@cs.com
Web: www.fwhispanicchamber.com

INDIANA STATE HISPANIC CHAMBER OF COMMERCE
2511 E. 46th St.
Indianapolis, IN 46205
Tel: (317) 547-0200 Fax: (317) 547-0210
Email: mjgm@iishcc.com
Web: www.ishcc.com

INDIANAPOLIS HISPANIC CHAMBER OF COMMERCE
111 Monument Cir. #1950
Indianapolis, IN 46204
Tom O'Neil, President
Tel: (317) 464-2254 Fax: (317) 464-2217
Email: info@indyhispanicchamber.com
Web: www.indyhispanicchamber.com

MICHIANA HISPANIC CHAMBER OF COMMERCE
401 E. Colfax Ave. #310
South Bend, IN 46634
Tel: (219) 289-6846 Fax: (219) 289-6873

BRAZILIAN ASSOCIATION AT INDIANA UNIVERSITY
La Casa/ 715 E. 7th St.
Bloomington, IN 47401
Marlene Andrade Martins, Coordinator
Tel: (812) 855-0174 Fax: (812) 855-9788
Email: baiu@indiana.edu
Web: www.indiana.edu/~baiu/

LATINO GRADUATE STUDENT ASSOCIATION
Indiana University- La Casa/Latino Cultural Center
715 E. 7th St.
Bloomington, IN 47408
Marlene Medrano, President
Tel: (812) 855-0174 Fax: (812) 855-9788
Email: bmedrano@indiana.edu

ALSE CLEMENTE CENTER, INC.
3616 Elm St.
Chicago, IN 46312
Gloria Balerini, Executive Director
Tel: (219) 391-8485 Fax: (219) 391-8394
Email: rclemente24@hotmail.com

DIOCESE OF EVANSVILLE
Hispanic Affairs
908 Clay St.
Jasper, IN 47546
Rev. Gene Heerdink, Coordinator of the Ministry to the Spanish Speaking
Tel: (812) 634-7206 Fax: (812) 634-7809
Email: gheerdink@evansville-diocese.org

DIOCESE OF FORT WAYNE-SOUTH BEND
Hispanic Affairs
1103 S. Calhoun St.
Fort Wayne, IN 46801
Father Robert C. Schulte, Chancellor
Tel: (260) 422-4611
Email: fhogan@fw.diocesefwsb.org
Web: www.diocesefwsb.org

DIOCESE OF GARY
Hispanic Ministry Office
P.O. Box 3027

East Chicago, IN 46312
Adelina Torres, Director for Hispanic Ministry
Tel: (219) 397-2125 Fax: (219) 397-2168
Email: atorres@dcgary.org
Web: www.dcgary.org

EL CENTRO GUADALUPE
317 N Washington St.
Huntingburg, IN 47542
Gene Heerdink, Coordinator of Ministry to Spanish Affairs
Tel: (812) 683-5212 Fax: (812) 683-9012
Email: gheerdink@evansville-diocese.org

IGLESIA DE SANTA MARIA
317 N. New Jersey St.
Indianapolis, IN 46204
Rev. Michael O'mara, Pastor
Tel: (317) 637-3999 Fax: (317) 637-0111
Email: parish@stmarysindy.org
Web: www.stmarysindy.org

INTER-UNIVERSITY PROGRAM FOR LATINO RESEARCH
University of Notre Dame
P.O. Box 764
Notre Dame, IN 46556-0764
Gilberto Cardenas, Executive Director
Tel: (574) 631-3481 Fax: (574) 631-3884
Email: iuplr@nd.edu
Web: www.nd.edu/~iuplr

LATINO STUDIES PROGRAM
Indiana University
1033 E. 3rd St., Sycamore Hall 046
Bloomington, IN 47405
Dr. Jorge Chapa, Director
Tel: (812) 856-1795 Fax: (812) 855-9997
Email: latino@indiana.edu
Web: www.indiana.edu/~latino

CENTER FOR LATIN AMERICAN AND CARIBBEAN STUDIES
Indiana University
1125 E Atwater Ave.
Bloomington, IN 47401
Jeffrey Gould, Director
Tel: (812) 855-9097 Fax: (812) 855-5345
Email: clacs@indiana.edu
Web: www.indiana.edu/~clacs

HISPANIC EDUCATION CENTER
580 E. Stevens St. #2A
Indianapolis, IN 46203
Sister Marikay Duffy, Executive Director
Tel: (317) 634-5022 Fax: (317) 634-0442
Email: heclaura@hotmail.com
Web: www.hispaniceducationcenter.org

INSTITUTE FOR LATINO STUDIES
University of Notre Dame
230 McKenna Hall
Notre Dame, IN 46556
Gilbert Cardenas, Contact
Tel: (574) 631-3819 Fax: (574) 631-3522
Email: cardenas7@nd.edu

HISPANIC CENTER/EL CENTRO HISPANO
Hispanic AIDS Prevention Program in Indiana
617 E. North St.
Indianapolis, IN 46204
Carmen Berucha, Director
Tel: (317) 636-6551 Fax: (317) 686-6500
Email: cberucha@elcentrohispano.org

EL CENTRO HISPANO
617 E. North St.
Indianapolis, IN 46204

Carmen Derusha, Director
Tel: (317) 636-6551 Fax: (317) 686-6500
Email: cderusha@elcentrohispano.org

TRANSITION RESOURCES CORPORATION
IN01-Indiana State Office
5809 N. Post Rd.
Indianapolis, IN 46216
L. Diane Swift, State Director
Tel: (317) 547-1924 X205 Fax: (317) 547-6594
Email: ldswift@transitionresources.org
Web: www.transitionresources.org

IN02-Kokomo
P.O. Box 307
709 S. Reed Rd.
Kokomo, IN 46903-0307
Guadalupe Chavez, Regional Manager
Tel: (765) 459-0571 X3068 Fax: (765) 457-5202
Email: gchavez@transitionresources.org
Web: www.transitionresources.org

IN03-Madison
620 Green Rd.
Madison, IN 47250-2142
Vicky Germano, Regional Manager
Tel: (812) 273-5451 Fax: (812) 273-1881
Email: vgermano@transitionresources.org
Web: www.transitionresources.org

IN05-South Bend
851 S. Marietta #800
South Bend, IN 46601
Andres Valtierra, Regional Manager
Tel: (574) 237-9407 Fax: (574) 237-9408
Email: avaltierra@transitionresources.org
Web: www.transitionresources.org

IN06-Vincennes
214 Buntin St. #204
Vincennes, IN 47591
Nancy Vargas, Regional Manager
Tel: (812) 886-0783 Fax: (812) 886-0875
Email: nvargas@transitionresources.org
Web: www.transitionresources.org

IN07-Logansport
P.O. Box 7014
2835 E. Market St.
Logansport, IN 46947-7014
Elsie Baker, Deputy State Director
Tel: (574) 722-6652 X17 Fax: (574) 753-8653
Email: ebaker@transitionresources.org
Web: www.transitionresources.org

IN12-Peru
P.O. Box 82
14 S. Wabash St.
Peru, IN 46970-2209
Scott Burns, Regional Manager
Tel: (765) 472-3562 Fax: (765) 473-8654
Email: sburns@transitionresources.org
Web: www.transitionresources.org

IN15-New Albany
3303 Plaza Dr. #2
New Albany, IN 47150
Rhonda Kidd, Deputy State Director
Tel: (812) 981-0154 Fax: (812) 981-0158
Email: rkidd@transitionresources.org
Web: www.transitionresources.org

IN16-Jeffersonville
1613 E. 8th St.
Jeffersonville, IN 47130
Jeremy Riley, Case Manager
Tel: (812) 338-4983 Fax: (812) 283-6835
Email: jriley@transitionresources.org
Web: www.transitionresources.org

IN18-Corydon
725 Quarry Rd.
Corydon, IN 47112
Tana Sillings, Case Manager
Tel: (812) 738-8811 Fax: (812) 738-8873
Email: tsillings@transitionresources.org
Web: www.transitionresources.org

IN19-Paoli
1075 Sandy Hook Rd.
Paoli, IN 47454
Donna Jennings, Case Manager
Tel: (812) 723-4206 Fax: (812) 723-4240
Email: djennings@transitionresources.org
Web: www.transitionresources.org

IN20-Scottsburg
1092 Community Way
Scottsburg, IN 47170
Melodie Rutledge, Case Manager
Tel: (812) 752-3886 Fax: (812) 752-5197
Email: mrutledge@transitionresources.org
Web: www.transitionresources.org

IN21-Salem
P.O. Box 47
190 Becks Mills Rd.
Salem, IN 47167
Karen Bruce, Case Manager
Tel: (812) 883-2283 Fax: (812) 883-1544
Email: kbruce@transitionresources.org
Web: www.transitionresources.org

**LATIN AMERICAN COMMUNITY ALLIANCE
FOR SUPPORT ASSISTANCE**
Main Office
4433 Broadway Ave.
Gary, IN 46409
Lawrence E. Sharp, Executive Director
Tel: (219) 980-4636 Fax: (219) 980-3244
Email: lsharp1457@aol.com
Web: www.IILC.org

**NATIONAL LEAGUE OF CUBAN AMERICAN
COMMUNITY-BASED CENTERS**
Educational Opportunities Center
3000 S. Wayne Ave.
Fort Wayne, IN 46807
Willa Kilne, Director
Tel: (260) 745-5421 Fax: (219) 744-1363
Email: staff@fwtrio.com
Web: www.fwtrio.com

**PASCUAL RODRIGUEZ LATIN AMERICAN
SOFTBALL LEAGUE**
6815 Kennedy Ave.
Hammond, IN 46323
Agustin Igartua, Jr., Commissioner
Tel: (219) 845-3333 Fax: (219) 845-2088

**NATIONAL CONFERENCE OF PUERTO RICAN
WOMEN, INC.**
Indiana Chapter
P.O. Box 524
Hammond, IN 46325
Sylvia Morrisroe, President
Email: nacoprw@verizon.net
Web: http://mysite.verizon.net/res1u8rq/

DELTA PHI MU
1001 Stewart Ctr., Box 631
West Lafayette, IN 47907
Yasmin Fuentes, President
Tel: (765) 430-1392
Email: yfuentes@purdue.edu
Web: www.purdue.edu/dphi

ECUADORIAN STUDENT ASSOCIATION
Purdue University
Purdue University
West Lafayette, IN 47907
Andres Maldonado, President
Tel: (765) 714-3480
Email: armaldon@purdue.edu
Web: http://web.ics.purdue.edu/~galapago/

**GAMMA PHI OMEGA SORORITY OF INDIANA
UNIVERSITY**
Alpha Chapter/Indiana University, Bloomington
715 E. 7th St.
Bloomington, IN 47408
Angelica Anaya
Tel: (812) 855-0174 Fax: (812) 855-9788
Email: aanaya@indiana.edu
Web: http://php.indiana.edu/~aanaya/alpha.html

LA CASA/LATINO CULTURAL CENTER
Indiana University
715 E. 7th St.
Bloomington, IN 47408
Lillian Casillas, Director
Tel: (812) 855-0174 Fax: (812) 855-9788
Email: asd@indiana.edu
Web: www.indiana.edu/~lacasa

LATINO LAW STUDENT ASSOCIATION
Indiana University, Bloomington
La Casa/Latino Cultural Center, 715 E. 7th St.
Bloomington, IN 47408
Lucelly Duenas, President
Tel: (812) 855-0174 Fax: (812) 855-9788

LATINOS UNIDOS OF INDIANA UNIVERSITY
La Casa, 715 E. 7th St.
Bloomington, IN 47405
Paul Rodriguez, President
Tel: (812) 855-0174 Fax: (812) 855-9788
Email: luiu@indiana.edu
Web: www.indiana.edu/~luiu

**MULTICULTURAL OUTREACH RECRUITMENT
EDUCATORS**
Indiana University, Bloomington
300 N. Jordan Ave.
Bloomington, IN 47405-1106
Lori Patton, Advisor
Tel: (812) 855-1678
Email: Lpatton@indiana.edu
Web: http://mypage.iu.edu/~more/

**PUERTO RICAN STUDENT ASSOCIATION OF
INDIANA UNIVERSITY**
P.O. Box 3462
La Casa/Latino Cultural Ctr., 715 E. 7th St.
Bloomington, IN 47405
Lillian Casillas, Director
Tel: (812) 855-0174 Fax: (812) 855-9788
Email: mlcasill@indiana.edu
Web: www.lacaralatina.org

**SIGMA LAMBDA BETA FRATERNITY OF
INDIANA UNIVERSITY**
Indiana University
La Casa, 715 E. 7th St.
Bloomington, IN 47405
Jason Cuadrado, Secretary
Tel: (812) 855-0174
Email: jcuadrad@indiana.edu

**SOCIETY OF HISPANIC PROFESSIONAL
ENGINEERS**
Purdue University, Calumet
2200 169th St.
Hammond, IN 46323-2094
Ismael Nieves, President
Tel: (219) 845-2105
Email: shpe@hotmail.com
Web: www.shpe.org

IOWA

LATIN AMERICAN STUDIES
**Iowa State University/College of Liberal Arts
and Sciences**
326 Pearson Hall, Department of Foreign
Languages and Literatures
Ames, IA 50011
Kathy S. Leonard, Director
Tel: (515) 294-5344
Email: kleonard@iastate.edu
Web: www.las.iastate.edu/Latin_American/home.
shtml

LOS AMIGOS CLUB
909 Daniels Dr. St. NE
Cedar Rapids, IA 52402-4616
Pat Arenas, Secretary
Tel: (319) 362-7606

MEXICAN FIESTA COMMITTEE
1231 32nd St.
Ft. Madison, IA 52627
Aaron Prado, President
Tel: (319) 372-9537

**QUAD CITIES MEXICAN AMERICAN
ORGANIZATION, INC.**
Col Ballroom
P.O. Box 2557
1012 W. 4th St.
Davenport, IA 52802
Michael Cervantes, Operations Manager
Tel: (563) 322-4431 Fax: (563) 322-1448

IOWA DIVISION OF LATINO AFFAIRS
Department of Human Rights
Lucas State Office Bldg., 321 E. 12th St.
Des Moines, IA 50319
John-Paul Chaisson-Cardenas, Administrator
Tel: (515) 281-4080 Fax: (515) 242-6119
Email: john.chaisson@iowa.gov
Web: www.state.ia.us/dhr/ia

LA CASA LATINA, INC.
223 10th St.
Sioux City, IA 51103
Christy Nicholson, Director
Tel: (712) 252-4259 Fax: (712) 252-5655

LATINOS UNIDOS OF IOWA, INC.
4119 27th St.
Des Moines, IA 50310
Lena Robinson, Founder
Tel: (515) 279-6840
Email: iowalatina@aol.com
Web: www.latinosunidosofiowa.com

**LEAGUE OF UNITED LATIN AMERICAN
CITIZENS**
Council #304
1424 36th St.
Ft. Madison, IA 52627
Alexandria Lozano, President
Tel: (319) 372-4252
Web: www.lulac.org

ARCHDIOCESE OF DUBUQUE
Hispanic Ministries
320 Mulberry St.
Waterloo, IA 50703
Rev. Msgr. Leon L. Connolly, Vicar for Hispanic
Ministry
Tel: (319) 287-6414

**DES MOINES LATINO SERVICE PROVIDERS
COALITION**
1446 Martin Luther King Jr. Pkwy.
Des Moines, IA 50314
Chris Villalobos, Co-Chair
Tel: (515) 471-2341 Fax: (515) 243-5879
Email: frankdunn40@hotmail.com

DIOCESAN HISPANIC MINISTRY
12 W. Linn St.
Marshalltown, IA 50158
Christina Feagan, Director of Hispanic Ministry
Tel: (641) 753-7815 Fax: (641) 752-6277

DIOCESE OF DAVENPORT
Hispanic Affairs
2706 N. Gaines St.
Davenport, IA 52804
Rev. Rudolph Juarez, Coordinator for Hispanic
Ministry
Tel: (319) 324-1911 Fax: (319) 324-5842

DIOCESE OF DAVENPORT
Hispanic Ministry Office
2706 N Gaines St.
Davenport, IA 52804-1998
Fr. Rudolph Juarez, Vicar for Hispanic Ministry
Tel: (563) 324-1911 Fax: (563) 324-5811
Email: juarez@davenportdiocese.org

DIOCESE OF SIOUX CITY
Hispanic Ministry
1821 Jackson St.
Sioux City, IA 51105
Juan Garcia, Associate
Tel: (712) 255-7933
Email: juang@scdiocese.org

DIOCESE OF DEN MOINES
Hispanic Outreach Program
601 Grand Ave.
Des Moines, IA 50309
Adriana Cardona, Outreach Promoter
Tel: (515) 244-3761

LAS GUADALUPANAS
Chapel of Our Lady of Guadalupe
801 SE Scott
Des Moines, IA 50309
Fr. Tom Pfeffer, Pastor
Tel: (515) 266-6695

LATIN AMERICAN STUDIES PROGRAM
252 International Ctr.
Iowa City, IA 52242-1802
Claire Fox, Chair
Tel: (319) 335-0096 Fax: (319) 335-0280
Email: claire-fox@uiowa.edu

LATINO LEADERSHIP PROJECT
2507 University Ave.
Des Moines, IA 50311
Warren Morron, Executive Director
Tel: (515) 271-4633 Fax: (515) 271-4010
Email: llp@grinnell.edu
Web: www.llp.20m.com

MIDWEST EDUCATIONAL RESOURCE DEVELOPMENT FUND, INC.
962 40th St.
West Des Moines, IA 50265
Ila R. Plasencia, President
Tel: (515) 225-6865 Fax: (515) 261-7270
Email: irplasencia@peoplepc.com

MINORITY STUDENT AFFAIRS
Iowa State University
2224 Student Services Bldg. #2080
Ames, IA 50011-2224
Leonard Perry, Director
Tel: (515) 294-6338 Fax: (515) 294-6397
Email: ldperry@iastate.edu
Web: www.dso.iastate.edu/dept/msa/

US LATINO STUDIES PROGRAM
402 Catt Hall
Ames, IA 50011
Dr. Hector Avalos, Director
Tel: (515) 294-0051 Fax: (515) 294-0780
Email: havalos@iastate.edu
Web: www.public.iastate.edu/~latinostudies

HISPANIC EDUCATIONAL RESOURCES, INC.
828 Scott Ave.
Des Moines, IA 50309
Andria Macias-Castillo, Executive Director
Tel: (515) 282-6542 Fax: (515) 282-0260
Email: andria@herdm.com
Web: www.herdm.com

YOUNG WOMENS COUNSELLING ASSOCIATION
425 Lafayette St.
Waterloo, IA 50703
Dulce Culpepper
Tel: (319) 234-1909 Fax: (319) 234-3462
Email: ywca@ywcabhc.org
Web: www.ywcabhc.org

HISPANIC/LATINO STUDENT UNION
RDC 110
Cedar Falls, IA 50613
Lorena Knight, President
Tel: (319) 273-2333
Email: lori973@uni.edu

MEXICAN-AMERICAN YOUNG ACHIEVERS SOCIETY
644 Squaw Creek Dr. #18
Ames, IA 50010
Brenda Vargas, President
Tel: (515) 232-2634
Email: mayas@iastate.edu
Web: www.stuorg.iastate.edu/mayas

SIGMA LAMBDA BETA FRATERNITY, INC.
University of Iowa
145 Iowa Memorial Union
Iowa City, IA 52242-1317
Jim Trigglio, Assistant Executive Director
Tel: (888) 486-2382 Fax: (319) 353-2245
Email: headquarters@sigmalambdabeta.com
Web: www.sigmalambdabeta.com

SOCIETY OF HISPANIC PROFESSIONAL ENGINEERS
110 Marston Hall
Ames, IA 50011
Guadalupe Vera, Advisor
Tel: (515) 294-1516
Email: lupevera@iastate.edu
Web: www.shpe.org

KANSAS

WICHITA HISPANIC CHAMBER OF COMMERCE
1150 N Broadway #700
Wichita, KS 67212
Charlie Rivera, President
Tel: (316) 265-6334 Fax: (316) 264-9965
Email: mparks@wichita.org
Web: www.wichitahispanicchamber.org

NATIONAL LATINO PEACE OFFICERS ASSOCIATION
Topeka Chapter
320 S Kansas Ave. #100
Topeka, KS 78245
Michael Padilla, President
Tel: (877) 657-6200
Email: mpadilla@topeka.org
Web: www.nlpoa.com

Wichita-Sedgwick Co.-Kansas Chapter
P.O. Box 49502
Wichita, KS 67201-9502
Eddie Melon, Chapter President
Tel: (316) 259-7586
Email: eddieshark@sbcglobal.net
Web: www.nlpoa.com

AMERICAN GI FORUM OF THE UNITED STATES
Kansas City Chapter
1000 Cheyenne
Ulysses, KS 67880
Jose Olivas, Commander
Tel: (620) 356-4070
Email: jolivas@ummam.org
Web: www.agif.us/KA.htm

EL CENTRO DE SERVICIOS PARA HISPANOS
134 NE Lake
Topeka, KS 66616
Manuel Perez, Administrator
Tel: (785) 232-8207 Fax: (785) 232-8834
Email: cyndip@sbcglobal.net

HISPANIC SOCIAL SERVICES
Catholic Charities, Inc./Diocese of Wichita
437 N. Topeka
Wichita, KS 67202
David Osio, Director
Tel: (316) 264-8344 x290 Fax: (316) 262-5356
Email: dosio@wkscatholiccharities.org
Web: www.wkscatholiccharities.org

KANSAS HISPANIC AND LATINO AMERICAN AFFAIRS COMMISSION
900 Jackson
Topeka, KS 66612
Elias Garcia, Executive Director
Tel: (785) 296-3465
Email: info@khlaac.org
Web: www.khlaac.org

UNITED METHODIST MEXICAN-AMERICAN MINISTRIES
Liberal Care Center
P.O. Box 1815
Liberal, KS 67901
Dora Ponce, Community Developer
Tel: (620) 624-6865 Fax: (620) 624-4723
Email: dponce@ummam.org
Web: www.ummam.org

UNITED METHODIST WESTERN KANSAS MEXICAN-AMERICAN MINISTRIES
P.O. Box 766
Garden City, KS 67846
Isela Lerma, Community Developer
Tel: (620) 275-1766 Fax: (620) 275-4729
Email: ilerma@ummam.org
Web: www.ummam.org

708 Avenue H
Dodge City, KS 67801
Elva Dominguez, Community Developer
Tel: (620) 225-0625 Fax: (620) 225-2422
Email: edominguez@ummam.org
Web: www.ummam.org

321 W Grant
Ulysses, KS 67880
Jose Olivas, Community Developer
Tel: (620) 356 -4079 Fax: (620) 356-1195
Email: jolivas@ummam.org
Web: www.ummam.org

REPUBLICAN NATIONAL HISPANIC ASSEMBLY
RNHA-Kansas, Organizing Chapter
901 N. Broadway
Wichita, KS 67214
Richard Macias, State Coordinator
Tel: (316) 265-5245 Fax: (316) 265-3953
Email: rmacias@kscable.com
Web: www.rnha.org

DIOCESE OF SALINA
P.O. Box 1038
103 N. 9th St.
Salina, KS 67402
Rev. Paul S. Coakley, Bishop
Tel: (785) 827-8746 Fax: (785) 827-6133
Email: chancery@salinadiocese.org
Web: www.salinadiocese.org

DIOCESE OF WICHITA
Hispanic Affairs
437 N Topeka
Wichita, KS 67202
Rev. Charles Seiwert, Hispanic Ministry Director
Tel: (316) 269-3919 Fax: (316) 269-5852

UNITED METHODIST MEXICAN-AMERICAN MINISTRIES
P.O. Box 766
Garden City, KS 67846
Penney Schwab, Executive Director
Tel: (620) 275-4970 Fax: (620) 275-4729
Email: pschwab@ummam.org
Web: www.ummam.org

CENTER OF LATIN AMERICAN STUDIES
University of Kansas
1440 Jayhawk Blvd., 320 Bailey Hall
Lawrence, KS 66045-7574
Judy Farmer, Office Manager
Tel: (785) 864-4213 Fax: (785) 864-3800
Email: latamst@ku.edu
Web: www.ku.edu/~latamst

HISPANIC EDUCATION FOUNDATION
1000 N. Cheyenne
Ulysses, KS 67880
Barbara Olivas, Director
Tel: (620) 356-4070
Email: Cacfp@pld.com

LATIN AMERICAN STUDIES PROGRAM
Kansas State University
215 Eisenhower Hall
Manhattan, KS 66506-1004
Bradley Shaw, Director
Tel: (785) 532-1988 Fax: (785) 532-7004
Email: ias@ksu.edu
Web: www.ksu.edu/ias/lassec

SER-CORPORATION OF KANSAS, INC.
1020 N. Main St. #B
Wichita, KS 67203
Richard López, CEO
Tel: (316) 264-5372 Fax: (316) 264-0194
Email: relopez@sercorp.com
Web: www.ser-national.org

GUADALUPE CLINIC
940 S St. Francis
Wichita, KS 67211
Marlene Dreiling, Director
Tel: (316) 264-8974 Fax: (316) 262-4938
Email: guadalupe@guadalupe.kscoxmail.com

LA FAMILIA SENIOR COMMUNITY CENTER
841 W 21st St. North
Wichita, KS 67203
Carolyn Benitez, Executive Director
Tel: (316) 267-1700 Fax: (316) 267-7112
Email: lafamiliasenior@msn.com

EL CENTRO, INC.
Administration
650 Minnesota Ave.
Kansas City, KS 66101
Ian Bautista, Executive Director
Tel: (913) 677-0100 Fax: (913) 362-8250
Email: ibautista@elcentroinc.com
Web: www.elcentroinc.com

HARVEST AMERICA CORPORATION
Dodge City Office
236 San Jose Dr., Hennessy Hall #135
Dodge City, KS 67801-0693
Teresa Fuentes, Area Director
Tel: (620) 227-7882 Fax: (620) 227-7559
Email: teresafuentes@hotmail.com
Web: www.harvestamerica.org
Garden City Office

116 E. Chestnut St. #102
Garden City, KS 67846
Ashley Furtado, SW Program Assistant
Tel: (620) 275-1619 Fax: (620) 275-1762
Email: afurtado@harvestamerica.org
Web: www.harvestamerica.org

Goodland Office
P.O. Box 752
212 N. 17th St.
Goodland, KS 67735-0752
Barbara Fernandez-Ayala, Area Director
Tel: (785) 899-3878 Fax: (785) 899-3878
Email: harvestamerica@harvestamerica.org
Web: www.harvestamerica.org

Great Bend Office
2604 19th St.
Great Bend, KS 67530-2318
Isabel Bojorquez, Area Director
Tel: (620) 792-7070 Fax: (620) 792-7353
Email: harvestamerica@harvestamerica.org
Web: www.harvestamerica.org

Hays Office
P.O. Box 659
Hays, KS 67601-0659
Isabel Bojorquez, Area Director
Tel: (785) 625-5654 Fax: (785) 625-0092
Email: harvestamerica@harvestamerica.org
Web: www.harvestamerica.org

Headquarters
14th and Metropolitan
Kansas, KS 66103
Alfred Kayhill, Director
Tel: (913) 342-2121 Fax: (913) 342-2861
Email: harvestamerica@harvestamerica.org
Web: www.harvestamerica.org

Liberal Office
1801 N. Kansas
Liberal, KS 67901-4193
Teresa Fuentes, Area Director
Tel: (620) 629-2791 Fax: (620) 624-3355
Email: teresafuentes@hotmail.com
Web: www.harvestamerica.org

National Headquarters
14th and Metropolitan St.
Kansas City, KS 66103-1084
Tel: (913) 342-2121 Fax: (913) 342-2861
Email: harvestamerica@harvestamerica.org
Web: www.harvestamerica.org

KANSAS HISPANIC AND LATINO AFFAIRS COMMISSION
900 SW Jackson Dr.
Topeka, KS 66612
Elias Garcia, Executive Director
Tel: (785) 296-3465 Fax: (785) 296-8118
Email: khlaac@khlaac.org
Web: www.khlaac.org

SPEC. INT., WOMEN

MANA-A NATIONAL LATINA ORGANIZATION
Topeka Chapter
P.O. Box 703
Topeka, KS 66601
Michelle Cuevas-Stubblefield, Chapter President
Tel: (785) 286-3960 (h)
Email: info@manatopeka.org
Web: www.manatopeka.org

STUDENT ORGANIZATION

HISPANIC AMERICAN LEADERSHIP ORGANIZATION
Wichita State University
1845 N Fairmount, Box 66
Wichita, KS 67260
Erika Sandoval, President
Tel: (316) 978-2699
Email: wsuhalo@hotmail.com
Web: http://webs.wichita.edu/halo

KAPPA DELTA CHI SORORITY, INC.
Alpha Alpha Chapter
Wichita State University, 1845 Fairmount, Box 66
Wichita, KS 67260
Emily Johnson, President
Email: kdxalpha_alpha@yahoo.com
Web: http://webs.wichita.edu/kdx

SIGMA LAMBDA BETA LATINO FRATERNITY INC.
1845 Fairmount, Box 66
Wichita, KS 67207
Alex Castellanos, President
Tel: (316) 990-1839
Email: support@rhobeta.org
Web: http://webs.wichita.edu/slb

HISPANIC AMERICAN LEADERSHIP ORGANIZATION
Kansas State University/224 Anderson Hall
Manhattan, KS 66506
Naureen Kazi, President
Tel: (785) 532-6276 Fax: (785) 532-6339
Email: nmkazi@ksu.edu
Web: www.ksu.edu/halo/Halo1.html

KENTUCKY

BUSINESS

KENTUCKIANA MINORITY BUSINESS COUNCIL
614 W. Main St. #5500
Louisville, KY 40202
Derwin Webb, President & CEO
Tel: (502) 625-0138 Fax: (502) 625-0082
Email: dwebb@kmbc.biz
Web: www.kmbc.biz

PROFESSIONAL

NATIONAL ASSOCIATION OF HISPANIC NURSES
Kentucky Chapter
1400 S 1st St.
Louisville, KY 40201
Haydee N. Canovas, President
Tel: (502) 637-2546 X24
Email: kentuckynahn@yahoo.com
Web: www.quepasaenlouisville.com/KNAHN.htm

RELIGIOUS

DIOCESE OF COVINGTON
Office of Hispanic Ministry
947 Donaldson Rd.
Erlanger, KY 41018
Luis Fernando Poppe, Director for Hispanic Ministry
Tel: (859) 283-6200
Email: fpoppe@dioofcovky.org

DIOCESE OF LEXINGTON
Hispanic Affairs
1310 W. Main St.
Lexington, KY 40508-2048
Sr. Sandra Delgado, OP, Director for Hispanic
Tel: (859) 253-1993 Fax: (859) 254-6284
Email: sdelgado@cdlex.org
Web: http://hispanic.cdlex.org

NICARAGUAN PRISON MINISTRY, INC.
P.O. Box 4560
Lexington, KY 40544
Rodney Brown, President
Email: president@npmi.org
Web: www.npmi.org

DIOCESE OF OWENSBORO
Office of Wowensboro
600 Locust St.
Owensboro, KY 42301
Patti Murphy, Director
Tel: (270) 683-1545 x142
Email: Patricia.Murphy@pastoral.org
Web: www.owensborodio.org/hispanic

ARCHIDIOCESE OF LOUISVILLE
Office of Multicultural Ministry
1200 S. Shelby St.
Louisville, KY 40203-2600
Annette Turner, Director
Tel: (502) 636-0296 Fax: (502) 636-2379
Email: aruiz@omm@archlou.org

LOUISIANA

CHAMBER OF COMMERCE

HISPANIC CHAMBER OF COMMERCE OF LOUISIANA
P.O. Box 5985
Metairie, LA 70009-5985
Manuel Blanco, President
Tel: (504) 885-4262 Fax: (504) 887-5422
Email: info@hccl.biz
Web: www.hccl.biz

CULTURAL

UNIDAD HISPANOAMERICANA
3600 Airline Hwy.
Metairie, LA 70001
Oscar Rivas, President
Tel: (504) 834-2020 Fax: (504) 834-2029
Email: unidashispanoamericana@msn.com

MULTI-PURPOSE

NICARAGUAN INDEPENDENT COMMITTEE FOR ASSISTANCE
P.O. Box 640103
Kenner, LA 70064
Giovanna Icaza, Chairman
Tel: (504) 455-9700 Fax: (504) 454-3601
Web: www.orgsites.com/la/nica/

RELIGIOUS

DIOCESE OF ALEXANDRIA
Hispanic Ministry Office
P.O. Box 7417
Alexandria, LA 71306-0417
Rev. P. Pedro J. Sierra Posada, Director for Hispanic Ministry
Tel: (318) 445-2401
Email: frpsierra@diocesealex.org
Web: www.diocesealex.org

DIOCESE OF BATON ROUGE
Hispanic Ministry Office
5850 Florida Blvd. #B
Baton Rouge, LA 70806-4247
Rev. Rafael Juantorena, Director for Hispanic Ministry
Tel: (225) 927-8700 Fax: (225) 927-8787
Email: apostolado@diobr.org

DIOCESE OF LAFAYETTE
Hispanic Ministry
1408 Carmel Dr.
Lafayette, LA 70501
Rev. Arturo Lozano, S.J., Director for Hispanic Ministry
Tel: (337) 261-5544 Fax: (337) 261-5560
Email: arturo@dol-louisiana.org
Web: www.dol-louisiana.org

DIOCESE OF LAKE CHARLES
Hispanic Ministry Office
2333 E Broad St.
Lake Charles, LA 70602
Rev. Edward Lavine, Director Hispanic Ministry
Tel: (337) 439-7436 Fax: (337) 439-7435
Email: dlcemcs@aol.com

DIOCESE OF SHREVEPORT
Hispanic Affairs
3500 Fairfield Ave.
Shreveport, LA 71104-4108
Elisa Milazzo, Coordinator for Hispanic Ministry
Tel: (318) 221-5296

DIOCESE OF HOUMA-THIBODAUX
Hispanic Ministry
P.O. Box 505
Schriever, LA 70395
Rhona Clement, Program Specialist
Tel: (985) 850-3137 Fax: (985) 868-7727
Web: www.htdiocese.org

DIOCESE OF SHREVEPORT
Hispanic Ministry
3500 Fairfield Ave.
Shreveport, LA 71104
Rev. Padre Rigoberto Betancurt, Coordinator for Hispanic Ministry
Tel: (318) 221-0238 x4

ST. PHILLIP NERI CATHOLIC CHURCH
Hispanic Affairs
P.O. Box 146
Kinder, LA 70648
Rev. Carlos A. Garcia Cardona, Director for Hispanic Ministry
Tel: (337) 738-5612 Fax: (337) 738-2728
Email: carlospeto@hotmail.com

RESEARCH

STONE CENTER FOR LATIN AMERICAN STUDIES
Tulane University
100 Jones Hall
New Orleans, LA 70118
Thomas F. Reese, Executive Director
Tel: (504) 865-5164 Fax: (504) 865-6719
Email: rtsclas@tulane.edu
Web: www.tulane.edu/~clas

SPEC. INT., EDUCATION

ALUMNI OF THE DIVISION DE SALUD OF THE UNIVERSIDAD DEL VALLE, INC.
4712 Richland Ave.
New Orleans, LA 70002
Dr. Fred Husserl, MD, President
Tel: (504) 842-3930 Fax: (504) 842-3676
Email: fhusserl@ochsner.org
Web: www.adsuv.8m.com

SPEC. INT., HEALTH SERVICES

HISPANIC AMERICAN MEDICAL ASSOCIATION OF LOUISIANA
P.O. Box 1812
Harvey, LA 70059
Juan Gershanik, Member
Tel: (504) 891-6156

SPEC. INT., HOUSING

ASSOCIATION OF COMMUNITY ORGANIZATIONS FOR REFORM NOW
1024 Elysian Fields Ave.
New Orleans, LA 70117
Wade Rathke, Chief Organizer
Tel: (504) 943-0044 Fax: (504) 943-3842
Email: laacorn@acorn.org
Web: www.acorn.org

SPEC. INT., LEGAL ASSISTANCE

ASOCIACIÓN DE ABOGADOS HISPANOS DE LOUISIANA
3632 Canal St.
New Orleans, LA 70119-6111
César Bulgors, President
Tel: (504) 488-3722 Fax: (504) 482-8525
Email: cburgos@burgosevans.com
Web: www.burgosevans.com

SPEC. INT., SENIORS

NATIONAL ASSOCIATION FOR HISPANIC ELDERLY
New Orleans Office/Project Ayuda
4321 Magnolia St.

New Orleans, LA 70115
Alfredo Sánchez, Project Coordinator
Tel: (504) 899-2707 Fax: (504) 891-8226

SPEC. INT., SOCIAL INTEREST

HISPANIC CONNECTION, INC.
17555 S. Harrell's Ferry Rd.
Baton Rouge, LA 70816
Maria Edwards, Recruiting Division Director
Tel: (225) 756-4123 Fax: (225) 756-4670
Email: hispanicconnection@cox.net
Web: www.hispanicconnection.org

SPEC. INT., VOLUNTARY SERVICE

COLOMBIAN VOLUNTEERS OF NEW ORLEANS
4712 Richland Ave.
Metairie, LA 70002
Diego Pereira, President
Tel: (504) 455-5339 Fax: (504) 885-2231
Email: maconrh@aol.com

STUDENT ORGANIZATION

ALIANZA DEL DERECHO
Tulane University
Law School Weinmann Hall, 6329 Freret St.
New Orleans, LA 70118
Alejandro Rodriguez, President
Tel: (504) 862-8843
Email: arodrigu@law.tulane.edu

BRAZILIAN ASSOCIATION
Louisiana State University
122 Johnston Hall
Baton Rouge, LA 70803
Andrea Angee, President
Tel: (225) 383-3669
Email: aagee1@lsu.edu
Web: www.lsu.edu/student_organizations/
brazilian/

LATIN AMERICAN STUDENT ASSOCIATION
Tulane University Office of Multicultural Affairs
6823 St. Charles Ave., #102 Central Bldg.
New Orleans, LA 70118
Luther Buie, Advisor
Tel: (504) 865-5181 Fax: (504) 862-8795
Web: http://oma.tulane.edu

SOCIETY OF HISPANIC PROFESSIONAL ENGINEERS
Louisiana State University
Dept. of Electrical & Computer Engineering,
3304 CEBA
Baton Rouge, LA 70803-5901
Raquel Ortega, Coordinator
Tel: (225) 288-2410
Email: shpelsu@yahoo.com
Web: http://appl003.lsu.edu/slas/csli.nsf/index

MAINE

RELIGIOUS

DIOCESAN HISPANIC MINISTRY COORDINATOR SACRED HEART/ST. DOMINIC PARISH
80 Sherman St.
Portland, ME 04101
Padre Felipe M. Tracy
Tel: (207) 772-6501 Fax: (207) 772-9615
Email: tsacredh@maine.rr.com
Web: www.shsdp.org

ST. PIUS X CHURCH
492 Ocean Ave.
Portland, ME 04103
Rev. Arthur Pare, SJ, Pastor
Tel: (207) 775-3032 Fax: (207) 874-7514
Email: parish@stpiusx-parish.org
Web: www.stpiusx-parish.org

SPEC. INT., EDUCATION

NATIONAL ASSOCIATION OF HISPANIC AND LATINO STUDIES
New England University
P.O. Box 325
Biddesord, ME 04005-0325
Dr. Lemuel Berry, Jr., Executive Director
Tel: (207) 283-8004 X2678 Fax: (207) 839-3776
Email: naaasgrp@webcom.com
Web: www.naaas.org

MARYLAND

ARTISTIC

GRUPO FOLKLORICO DE PANAMA
1613 Billman Ln.
Silver Spring, MD 20902
Norma Small Warren, Director
Tel: (301) 933-6764 Fax: (202) 806-5792
Email: nsmall-warren@howard.edu
Web: www.panamaencounters.netfirms.com

GRUPO FOLKLORICO LATINOAMERICANO
105 Aspenwood Way. #E
Baltimore, MD 21237
José Moreno, President
Tel: (410) 987-1791
Web: http://folkloric.20m.com/

NATIONAL COUNCIL FOR THE TRADITIONAL ARTS
National Headquarters
1320 Fenwick Ln. #200
Silver Spring, MD 20910
Joseph Wilson, Chairman
Tel: (301) 565-0654 X13 Fax: (301) 565-0472
Email: info@ncta.net
Web: www.ncta.net

ZIVA'S SPANISH DANCE ENSEMBLE
2505 Oakenshield Dr.
Potomac, MD 20854
Ziva Cohen, Artistic Director
Tel: (301) 424-1355 Fax: (301) 251-4125
Email: spanish_dance@hotmail.com
Web: www.zivasspanishdanceensemble.org

CHAMBER OF COMMERCE

BALTIMORE HISPANIC CHAMBER OF COMMERCE
601 Alluvion St.
Baltimore, MD 21230
Roberto N. Allen, President
Tel: (410) 685-3700 Fax: (410) 685-3706
Email: rallen@saul.com
Web: www.baltimorehcc.org

HISPANIC CHAMBER OF COMMERCE OF MONTGOMERY COUNTY
150 Maryland Ave.
Rockville, MD 20850
Carmen Ortiz Larsen, President
Tel: (301) 654-4000 Fax: (301) 654-4004
Email: clarsen@aquasinc.com
Web: www.hccmc.org

107 Fleet St.
Rockville, MD 20850
Tel: (301) 933-7600 Fax: (301) 933-7713

MARYLAND HISPANIC CHAMBER OF COMMERCE
149 N Luzerne Ave.
Baltimore, MD 21224
Dick Colon, President
Tel: (410) 558-3515 Fax: (410) 558-3513
Web: www.mdhcc.net

CULTURAL

ASOCIACIÓN MEXICANA DE MARYLAND, INC.
8806 Bel Air Rd.

Baltimore, MD 21236
Petra P. Piñeyro, President
Tel: (410) 931-1640 Fax: (410) 931-1640

CLUB PUERTO RICO OF MARYLAND
9004 Hamor Rd.
Randallstown, MD 21133
Jesus Manuel Miranda, President
Tel: (410) 786-7628
Email: jmiranda@cms.hhs.gov

CORAL CANTIGAS
P.O. Box 2212
Rockville, MD 20847
Ana Astrid Molina, Executive Director
Tel: (301) 424-8296 Fax: (301) 424-0471
Email: coralcantigas@comcast.net
Web: www.cantigas.org

LATIN AMERICAN FOLK INSTITUTE
3800-A 34th St.
Mount Rainier, MD 20712-2045
Carlos Giménez, Director of Programs
Tel: (301) 887-9331 Fax: (301) 887-0308
Email: info@lafi.org
Web: www.lafi.org

MONTGOMERY COUNTY DEPARTMENT OF PUBLIC LIBRARIES
Multicultural Services
100 Maryland Ave.
Rockville, MD 20850
Barbara Mcnally, Executive Director
Tel: (240) 777-6670 Fax: (240) 777-6672
Email: barbara.mcnally@montgomerycountymd.gov
Web: www.montgomerylibrary.org

PANAMANIAN ASSOCIATION OF METROPOLITAN WASHINGTON DC
3036 Schubert Dr.
Silver Spring, MD 20904
Al Lovell, Coordinator
Tel: (301) 890-9113

MULTI-PURPOSE

CASA DE MARYLAND, INC.
Germantown Office
12900 Middlebrook
Germantown, MD 20874
Gustavo Torres, Executive Director
Tel: (240) 777-3499 Fax: (301) 217-3401
Email: yotagri@casamd.org
Web: www.casademaryland.org

CENTRO DE LA COMUNIDAD, INC.
3021 Eastern Ave.
Baltimore, MD 21224
Carmen L. Nieves, Executive Director
Tel: (410) 675-8906 Fax: (410) 675-3146
Email: cnieves_centro@verizon.net
Web: www.centrodelacomunidad.org

FEDERATION OF HISPANIC ORGANIZATIONS OF THE BALTIMORE METROPOLITAN AREA, INC.
P.O. Box 25915
Baltimore, MD 21224
Maria Rodriguez, President
Tel: (410) 931-1640
Email: MRodADMD@aol.com

SPANISH SPEAKING COMMUNITY OF MARYLAND, INC.
8519 Piney Branch Rd.
Silver Spring, MD 20901
Emilio P. Rivas, Director
Tel: (301) 587-7217 Fax: (301) 322-3381

POLITICAL ACTION

BALTIMORE COUNTY OFFICE OF FAIR PRACTICES AND COMMUNITY AFFAIRS
400 Washington Ave. #124
Towson, MD 21204
James T. Smith, County Executive

Tel: (410) 887-5557 Fax: (410) 769-8914
Email: jimsmith@co.ba.md.us
Web: www.co.ba.md.us

GOVERNOR'S COMMISSION ON HISPANIC AFFAIRS
Maryland Department of Human Resources
311 W Saratoga St. #272
Baltimore, MD 21201
Hector L. Torres, Executive Director
Tel: (800) 714-8813 Fax: (410) 333-6555
Email: hispanic@dhr.state.md.us
Web: www.dhr.state.md.us/hispanic

MARYLAND HISPANIC BAR ASSOCIATION
27 Wood Ln., 2nd Fl.
Rockville, MD 20850
Marianne C. Cordier, President
Tel: (240) 268-0230
Email: maccordier@aol.com
Web: www.hispanicbar.com

MAYOR'S OFFICE OF HISPANIC AFFAIRS
100 N Holliday St. #221
Baltimore, MD 21202
José Ruiz, Mayor's Hispanic Liaison
Tel: (410) 396-3100 Fax: (410) 545-6535
Email: jose.ruiz@baltimorecity.gov
Web: www.baltimorecity.gov

OFFICE OF MINORITY AFFAIRS
State of Maryland
6 Saint Paul St.
Baltimore, MD 21202
Sharon R. Pinder, Director
Tel: (410) 767-8232 Fax: (410) 333-7568
Email: info@oma.state.md.us
Web: www.oma.state.md.us

RELIGIOUS

ARCA DE REPUFIO CASA DE ADORACION
738 University Dr.
Waldorf, MD 20602
Angel Serrano, Pastor
Tel: (800) 483-2610 Fax: (301) 396-8025
Email: aserrano@ewmortagage.com

ARCHDIOCESE OF BALTIMORE
Office of Hispanic Ministry
320 Cathedral St.
Baltimore, MD 21201
María T.P. Johnson, Director
Tel: (410) 547-5423 Fax: (410) 625-8485
Email: hispanicministry@archbalt.org

BILINGUAL CHRISTIAN CHURCH
6000 Erdman Ave.
Baltimore, MD 21205
Angel Nuñez, Contact
Tel: (410) 675-7256 Fax: (410) 483-0295
Email: spanishch@aol.com
Web: www.angelnunezministries.org

CENTRO CRISTIANO VIDA NUEVA
Instituto de Musica Hispano
8508 Adelphi Rd.
Adelphi, MD 20783
Rev. Carlos Santiago, Pastor
Tel: (301) 422-2029 Fax: (240) 358-8634
Email: vidanueva2000@netzero.net
Web: www.ccvn.turincon.com

CHRIST THE KING
Hispanic Ministry
2300 East-West Hwy.
Silver Spring, MD 20910
Rev. John Plans, Pastor
Tel: (301) 589-8616 Fax: (301) 587-1929
Email: christ-the-king@juno.com

CHURCH OF JESUS CHRIST OF LATTER-DAY SAINTS
Washington DC Visitor Center
9900 Stoneybrook Dr.
Kensington, MD 20895
Elder Salsbury, Director

Tel: (301) 588-0650 Fax: (301) 588-0653
Email: dcstake@washingtonlds.org
Web: www.washingtonlds.org

FIRST BAPTIST CHURCH OF LAUREL
811 5th St.
Laurel, MD 20707-5195
Rev. Segumundo Mir, Pastor
Tel: (301) 725-1688
Email: pastormir@aol.com

IGLESIA LUTERANA "CRISTO SENOR DE LA VIDA"/ CENTRO HISPANO LUTERANO
Affiliate of Lutheran Church Missouri Synod
3799 East-West Hwy.
Hyattsville, MD 20782
Manny Tadeo, Contact
Tel: (301) 277-4729 Fax: (301) 699-0071
Email: manny.tadeo@verizon.com

MINISTERIO HISPANO DE BALTIMORE
1660 Bank St.
Baltimore, MD 21231
Fidel Compres, Pastor
Tel: (410) 276-1660 Fax: (410) 276-1660
Email: bhministerio@earthlink.net

MISSION HELPERS OF THE SACRED HEART
1001 W. Joppa Rd.
Baltimore, MD 21204
Sister Judy Waldt, President
Tel: (410) 823-8585 Fax: (410) 823-6355
Email: missionhelpercenter@missionhelpers.org
Web: www.missionhelpers.org

MOTHER SETON
19951 Father Hurley Blvd.
Germantown, MD 20874
Rev. Robert Gessetto, Pastor
Tel: (301)924-3838 Fax: (301) 428-4951
Email: mspps@aol.com
Web: www.mothersetonparish.org

OUR LADY OF LOURDES
Hispanic Fellowship Lunch
7500 Pearl St.
Bethesda, MD 20814
Eufemia Leon, Coordinator
Tel: (301) 681-0966 Fax: (301) 986-8716
Email: info@bethesdalourdes.org
Web: www.bethesdalourdes.org

OUR LADY OF SORROWS
1006 Larch Ave.
Takoma Park, MD 20912
Rev. Raymond Wadas, Pastor
Tel: (301) 891-3500 Fax: (301) 891-1523
Web: www.angelfire.com/md2/olos

ST. BARTHOLOMEW
7212 Blacklock Rd.
Bethesda, MD 20817
Rev. Luis Salcedo, Pastor
Tel: (301) 229-7933 Fax: (301) 229-7998
Web: www.parishes.org/bartholomew.html

ST. BERNARD
5700 St. Bernard's Dr.
Riverdale, MD 20737
Rev. John McKay, Pastor
Tel: (301) 277-1000 Fax: (301) 277-3464

ST. BERNARDINE
2400 Brooks Dr.
Suitland, MD 20746-1144
Ligia Rojas, Coordinator
Tel: (301) 736-0707 Fax: (301) 736-2984
Email: st.bernardine@erols.com

ST. CAMILLUS
1600 St. Camillus Dr.
Silver Spring, MD 20903
Sister Cathy McConnel, Incharge of Spanish Services
Tel: (301) 434-8400 Fax: (301) 434-8041
Web: www.rc.net/washington/st_camillus

ST. CATHERINE LABOURE
Coro Hispano

11801 Claridge Rd.
Wheaton, MD 20902
Evaristo Gonzalez, Director
Tel: (301) 946-3636 Fax: (301) 946-5064

ST. MARK'S
7501 Adelphi Rd.
Hyattsville, MD 20783
Rev. John T. Dakes, Pastor
Tel: (301) 422-8300 Fax: (301) 422-2313
Email: pastor@www.stmarkhyattsville.org
Web: www.stmarkhyattsville.org

ST. MARTIN'S CATHOLIC CHURCH
201 S. Frederick Ave.
Gaithersburg, MD 20877
Isabel Andrade, Secretary
Tel: (301) 840-1830 Fax: (301) 990-7538
Email: chruchfox@yahoo.com
Web: www.stmartinsweb.com

ST. MICHAEL THE ARCHANGEL
824 Pershing Dr.
Silver Spring, MD 20910
Rev. Eddie Tolentino, Pastor
Tel: (301) 589-1155 Fax: (301) 589-3470
Email: pastor@stmichaelarchangel.net
Web: www.parishes.org/michaelarchangel.html

ST. PETER, OLNEY
2900 Sandy Spring Rd.
Olney, MD 20832
Thomas M. Kalita, Pastor
Tel: (301) 924-3774 Fax: (301) 774-5259
Web: www.stpetersolney.org

ST. PETER'S PARISH
3320 St. Peter's Dr.
Waldorf, MD 20601
Rev. Msgr. Henry Otero, Pastor
Tel: (301) 843-8916 Fax: (301) 843-3163
Web: www.stpeterswaldorf.org

ST. RAPHAEL
Hispanic Ministry Office
1590 Kimblewick Rd.
Rockville, MD 20854-6198
Luisa Duarte, Hispanic Coordinator
Tel: (301) 762-2143 Fax: (301) 762-0719

LATIN AMERICAN PAPER MONEY SOCIETY
3304 Milford Mill Rd.
Baltimore, MD 21244
Arthur C. Matz, President
Tel: (410) 655-3109
Email: matzlansa@aol.com
Web: www.crosswinds.net/~lansa

NATIONAL INSTITUTE OF MENTAL HEALTH
Division of Mental Disorders, Behavioral Research and AIDS
6001 Executive Blvd., Room 6217, MSC 9621
Bethesda, MD 20892-9621
Ellen Stover, Ph.D., Director
Tel: (301) 443-9700
Email: estover@mail.nih.gov
Web: www.nimh.nih.gov

Division of Extramural Activities
6001 Executive Blvd., Rm. 6154, MSC 9609
Bethesda, MD 20892-9609
Jane A. Steinberg, Ph.D., Director
Tel: (301) 443-3367
Email: jsteinbe@nih.gov
Web: www.nimh.nih.gov/dea/index.htm

Division of Intramural Research Programs
6001 Executive Blvd., Bldg. 10, Room 4N222
Bethesda, MD 20892-1381
Maxine Steyer, Program Specialist
Tel: (301) 496-4183 Fax: (301) 480-8348
Email: steyerm@intra.nimh.nih.gov
Web: http://intramural.nimh.nih.gov/

Division of Neuroscience and Basic Behavioral Science
6001 Executive Blvd., MSC 9645, Neuroscience Center, Room 7204
Bethesda, MD 20892-9645
Steve Foote, Ph.D., Director
Tel: (301) 443-3563 Fax: (301) 443-1731
Email: sfoote@mail.nih.gov
Web: www.nimh.nih.gov/diva/index.htm

Services Research and Clinical Epidemiology Branch
6001 Executive Blvd.Room 7146, MSC 9631
Bethesda, MD 20892-9631
Junius Gonzales, M.D., Chief
Tel: (301) 443-3364 Fax: (301) 443-4045
Email: jgonzale@mail.nih.gov
Web: www.nimh.nih.gov/srceb/index.cfm

The Behavioral and Integrative Neuroscience Research Branch
6001 Executive Blvd. # 7172, MSC 9637
Bethesda, MD 20892-9637
Kevin J. Quinn, Ph.D, Chief
Tel: (301) 443-1576 Fax: (301) 443-4822
Email: kquinn@mail.nih.gov
Web: www.nimh.nih.gov/bn/bnindex.cfm

PUERTO RICAN-AMERICAN RESEARCH INSTITUTE
P.O. Box 2274
Gaithersburg, MD 20886
Ernest Acosta, Jr., President
Tel: (301) 216-1380
Email: ernest377@juno.com
Web: www.prari.org

ALCOHOLICOS ANÓNIMOS HISPANOS DE MARYLAND
Oficina de Información
P.O. Box 8584
Silver Spring, MD 20910
Tel: (301) 587-6191
Web: www.lsiaa.org

CENTRO NACIONAL PARA INFORMACIÓN DE ALCOHOL Y DROGAS DE SAMHSA
P.O. Box 2345
Rockville, MD 20852
Charles G. Curie, Administrator
Tel: (301) 468-2600 Fax: (301) 468-6433
Email: info@health.org
Web: www.health.org

AMIGOS EN ACCION
114 W Montgomery Ave.
Rockville, MD 20850
Mónica Barberis-Young, Director
Tel: (301) 309-8775 Fax: (301) 762-2939
Email: fia@communityministrymc.org
Web: www.communityministrymc.org

CENTER FOR THE ADVANCEMENT OF HISPANICS IN SCIENCE AND ENGINEERING EDUCATION
George Washington University
8100 Corporate Dr. #401
Landover, MD 20785
Charles E. Vela, President
Tel: (301) 918-1014 Fax: (301) 918-1087
Email: cahsee@seas.gwu.edu
Web: www.cahsee.org

CONEXIONES, INC.
P.O. Box 433
Columbia, MD 21045
Dr. Murray Simon, President
Tel: (410) 997-7702 Fax: (410) 997-7702
Email: simonjuana@aol.com

ESCUELA ARGENTINA, INC.
P.O. Box 59937
Rockville, MD 20859-9937
Angela Torchia-Estrada, Administrative Assistant
Tel: (301) 365-0955 Fax: (301) 299-4813
Email: aestrada@escuelaargentinaonline.org
Web: www.escuelaargentinaonline.org

LATIN AMERICAN STUDIES CENTER
University of Maryland
0128-B Holzapfel Hall
College Park, MD 20742
Saul Sosnowski, Director
Tel: (301) 405-6459 Fax: (301) 405-3665
Email: lasc@umd.edu
Web: www.inform.umd.edu/LAS

MULTICULTURAL INSTITUTE
Towson University
Administration Bldg., 8000 York Rd. #215
Towson, MD 21252
Dr. Joanna Basuray, Director
Tel: (410) 704-3931 Fax: (410) 704-6093
Email: jbasuray@towson.edu
Web: wwwnew.towson.edu/multiculturalinstitute/

PROGRAM IN LATIN AMERICAN STUDIES
Johns Hopkins University
Greenhouse 003-Basement Level, 3400 N Charles St.
Baltimore, MD 21218
Alicia Lewis, Administrator
Tel: (410) 516-6166 Fax: (410) 516-5515
Email: alewis22@jhu.edu
Web: www.jhu.edu/~plas

CALIDAD EN SALUD
University Research Co., LLC
7200 Wisconsin Ave. #600
Bethesda, MD 20814
Kerisha King, Project Coordinator
Tel: (301) 654-8338 Fax: (301) 941-8427
Email: kking@urc-chs.com
Web: www.urc-chs.com/services/health/calidadII.htm

DIVISION OF REHABILITATION SERVICES
Baltimore City
1515 W. Mt. Royal Ave.
Baltimore, MD 21217
Bob Burns, Director
Tel: (410) 333-6119 Fax: (410) 333-3134
Email: region3@dors.state.md.us
Web: www.dors.state.md.us

ST. JOSEPH MEDICAL CENTER AUXILIARY
7601 Ausler Dr.
Towson, MD 21204
John K. Tolmie, President
Tel: (410) 337-1000

ALIANZA DE MESAS REDONDAS PANAMERICANAS/ALLIANCE OF PAN-AMERICAN ROUNDTABLES
8019 Thornley Ct.
Bethesda, MD 20817
Fabiola Chiriboga, President
Tel: (301) 365-5299 Fax: (301) 365-4967
Email: fabiche2@aol.com
Web: www.alianzamrp.org

CASA DE MARYLAND, INC.
734 University Blvd. East
Silver Spring, MD 20903
Gustavo Torres, Executive Director
Tel: (301) 431-4185 Fax: (301) 431-4179
Email: yotagri@casamd.org
Web: www.casademaryland.org

Main Office
310 Tulip Ave.
Takoma Park, MD 20912
Gustavo Torres, Executive Director

Tel: (301) 270-3609 Fax: (301) 270-8659
Email: info@casamd.org
Web: www.casademaryland.org

HISPANIC ALLIANCE OF MONTGOMERY
4874 Chevy Chase Blvd.
Chevy Chase, MD 20815-5340
Fernando Cruz-Villalba, President
Tel: (301) 657-3542
Email: vilacruz@erols.com

HISPANIC UNITED OF MONTGOMERY
15831 Crabbs Branch Way
Rockville, MD 20855
Galo A. Correa Sr., President
Tel: (240) 386-0191
Email: galo_a_correa@yahoo.com

**SPANISH SPEAKING COMMUNITYSilver
Spring Office**
8519 Piney Branch Rd.
Silver Spring, MD 20901
Emilio P. Rivas, Director
Tel: (301) 587-7217 Fax: (301) 589-1397

TELAMON CORPORATION
Maryland State Office
917 Mt. Hermon Rd. #2
Salisbury, MD 21804
Karen Webster, State Director
Tel: (410) 546-4604 Fax: (410) 546-0566
Email: kwebster@telamon.org
Web: www.telamon.org

VOCES VS. VIOLENCIA
1000 Twinbrook Pkwy.
Rockville, MD 20851
Mindi Kensinger, Director
Tel: (301) 424-0656 Fax: (301) 738-1030
Email: mkensinger@mhamc.org
Web: www.mhamc.org

**APOSTOLADO HISPANOImmigration Legal
Services**
430 S Broadway St., 3rd Fl.
Baltimore, MD 21231
Evelyn Rosario, Coordinator of Services
Tel: (410) 522-2668 Fax: (410) 675-1451
Email: erosario@catholiccharities-md.org
Web: www.catholiccharities-md.org

FOREIGN BORN INFORMATION5999 Harpers
Farm Rd. #E-200
Columbia, MD 21044
Don Downy, Volunteer Coordinator
Tel: (410) 992-1923 Fax: (410) 730-0113
Email: info@firnonline.org
Web: www.firnonline.org

UNITED WAY OF CENTRAL MARYLAND
100 S. Charles St., 5th Fl.
Baltimore, MD 21203-1576
Bernard A. Cook, Chair
Tel: (410) 547-8000 Fax: (410) 547-8289
Email: info@uwcm.org
Web: www.uwcm.org

ADULT BEHAVIOR HEALTH PROGRAM
2424 Reedie Dr.
Wheaton, MD 20902
Viviana Azar, Family Therapist
Tel: (240) 777-1323 Fax: (240) 777-3226
Email: viviana.azar@co.mo.ma.us
Web: www.montgomerycountymd.gov

**AMIGOS DE LA CULTURA HISPANO-
AMERICANA**
705 Camellia Rd.
Salisbury, MD 21804

Mayra Elassal, President
Tel: (410) 749-2115

CASA DE MARYLAND
734 E. University Blvd.
Silver Spring, MD 20903
Alma Archila, Receptionist
Tel: (301) 431-4185 Fax: (301) 431-4179
Email: info@casamd.org
Web: www.casademaryland.org

**HISPANIC ORGANIZATIONS LEADERSHIP
ALLIANCE**
P.O. Box 11107
Takoma Park, MD 20913
Rudy Arredondo, President
Tel: (301) 270-3112
Email: hola_5@hotmail.com
Web: www.ruralco.org

MAYOR'S OFFICE OF THE HISPANIC AFFAIRS
Community Outreach Office
3411 Bank St.
Baltimore, MD 21224
José Ruiz, Mayor's Hispanic Liaison
Tel: (410) 545-6532 Fax: (410) 545-6535
Email: jose.ruiz@baltimorecity.gov
Web: www.baltimorecity.gov

MCIL RESOURCES FOR INDEPENDENT LIVING
Hispanic Department
3011 Montebello Terr.
Baltimore, MD 21214
Camilo Quintero, Director
Tel: (410) 444-1400 Fax: (410) 444-0825
Email: camiloq@mcil-md.org
Web: www.mcil-md.org

SHARE DC-METRO, INC.
P.O. Box 768
Bladenburg, MD 20710
German R. Rodriguez, Hispanic Outreach Coord.
Tel: (301) 864-9815 Fax: (301) 864-5370
Email: rodriguezg@catholiccharitiesdc.org
Web: www.sharedc.org

**SPANISH CATHOLIC CENTER /CENTRO
CATÓLICO HISPANO**
Gaithersburg Branch
13-15 E. Deer Park Dr.
Gaithersburg, MD 20877
Celia Rivas, LLM, Coordinator
Tel: (301) 417-9113 Fax: (301) 417-9895
Email: sccdc@erols.com
Web: www.centrocatolicohispano.org

**SPANISH CATHOLIC CENTER/CENTRO
CATÓLICO HISPANO**
Langley Park
1015 University Blvd. East
Silver Spring, MD 20903
Alvina Longvalentin, Coordinator
Tel: (301) 434-3999
Email: volunteerscc@yahoo.com
Web: www.centrocatolicohispano.org

**NATIONAL CONFERENCE OF PUERTO RICAN
WOMEN, INC.**
Maryland Chapter
P.O. Box 3294
Wheaton, MD 20902
Argelia Leon, Treasurer
Tel: (301) 649-6396

CLUB AMIGOS DEL NIÑO COLOMBIANO
2901 Boston St. #218
Baltimore, MD 21224
Bertha Albornoz, President
Tel: (410) 563-4967 Fax: (410) 563-4967
Email: albornozruizj@aol.com

EDUCATION BASED LATINO OUTREACH
606 S Ann St.
Baltimore, MD 21231

Jessica Robinson, Program Coordinator
Tel: (410) 563-3160 Fax: (410) 563-0097
Email: volunteer@eblo.org
Web: www.eblo.org

NIÑOS UNIDOS DE MONTGOMERY COUNTY
644 Lakeworth Dr.
Gaithersburg, MD 20878
Elizabeth Jaramillo, President
Tel: (301) 947-4300 Fax: (301) 519-1968
Email: ninosunidos@aol.com

TEEN CHALLENGE OF MARYLAND, INC.
Hispanic Outreach
13919 Baltimore Ave.
Laurel, MD 20707
Rev. Manuel Baerga, Executive Director
Tel: (301) 617-4956 Fax: (301) 617-4958
Email: tcusa@teenchallengeusa.com
Web: www.teenchallenge.com/maryland

LATINO STUDENT UNION
University of Maryland
3101 Stamp Student Union
College Park, MD 20742
Oscar Trejo, Vice President, Public Relations
Tel: (301) 314-8327
Email: darawkus8@hotmail.com
Web: www.studentorg.umd.edu/lsu/index.html

MARYLAND BRAZILIAN SOCIETY
University of Maryland
College Park, MD 20742
Amarildo DaMata, President
Email: mdbraziliansociety@yahoo.com
Web: www.studentorg.umd.edu/mbs

ORGANIZACION LATINA ESTUDIANTIL
Johns Hopkins University
Mattin Center #210, 3400 N. Charles St.
Baltimore, MD 21218
Raquel Bracho, President
Tel: (410) 516-2224 Fax: (410) 516-4703
Email: ole@jhu.edu
Web: http://webhost5.nts.jhu.edu/ole/

MASSACHUSETTS

MUSICAMADOR
199 Pemberton St.
Cambridge, MA 02140
Rosi Amador, Director
Tel: (617) 492-1515 Fax: (617) 492-1515
Email: mail@musicamador.com
Web: www.musicamador.com

NEW WORLD THEATER
University of Massachusetts
100 Hicks Way #16, Curry Hicks
Amherst, MA 01003
Dennis Conway, Director
Tel: (413) 545-1972 Fax: (413) 545-4414
Email: nwt@admin.umass.edu
Web: www.newworldtheater.org

ACCIÓN INTERNATIONAL
56 Roland St. #300
Boston, MA 02129
William W. Burrus, President/CEO
Tel: (617) 625-7080 Fax: (617) 625-7020
Email: info@accionusa.org
Web: www.accionusa.org

NATIONAL SOCIETY OF HISPANIC MBAS
Boston Chapter
P.O. Box 130151
Boston, MA 02113
Raul Medina, Chapter President
Tel: (617) 481-0230
Email: general@boston.nshmba.org
Web: http://boston.nshmba.org

**NEW ENGLAND MINORITY SUPPLIER
DEVELOPMENT COUNCIL**
100 Huntington Ave.
Boston, MA 02116
Deborah Cousins-Messier, Chairperson
Tel: (617) 578-8900
Email: info@nemsdc.org
Web: www.nemsdc.org

**HISPANIC-AMERICAN CHAMBER OF
COMMERCE**
780 Dudlet St.
Boston, MA 02125
Gerardo Villacres, Executive Director
Tel: (617) 261-4222 Fax: (617) 261-6333
Email: hacc@hacc.com
Web: www.hacc.com

**MASSACHUSETTS HISPANIC CHAMBER OF
COMMERCE**
1628 Main St.
Springfield, MA 01103
Tel: (413) 272-2221 Fax: (413) 731-5399
Email: latinochamber@lcc1.com
Web: www.lcc1.com

P.O. Box 16542
Worcester, MA 01601
Jose Luiz Garcia, President
Tel: (508) 393-8600 Fax: (508) 919-0007
Email: jose@spanishmarketing.com

PUERTO RICAN CULTURAL CENTER, INC.
38 School St.
Springfield, MA 01105
Eva Gomez, Director
Tel: (413) 737-7450
Web: www.prccma.org

AMIGOS DE LAS AMERICAS
Boston Chapter
P.O. Box 490
Belmont, MA 02178
Sigrid Bergenstein, President
Tel: (781) 237-4204
Email: sigridb@comcast.net
Web: http://io.amigoslink.org/~boston

CASA LATINA, INC.
National Headquarters
140 Pine St.
Florence, MA 01062
Lillian Torres, Co-Director
Tel: (413) 586-1569 Fax: (413) 586-1597
Email: casa1@map.com

**COMMUNITY MINORITY CULTURAL CENTER,
INC.**
298 Union St. 2nd Fl.
Lynn, MA 01901
Abner Darby, Co-Executive Director
Tel: (781) 477-7090 Fax: (781) 477-0419
Email: cmccstaff@verizon.net
Web: www.cmcc.citymax.com/page/page/500262.
htm

CONCILIO HISPANO DE CAMBRIDGE, INC.
Affiliate of NCLR
105 Windsor St.
Cambridge, MA 02139
Sylvia Saavedra-Keber, Executive Director
Tel: (617) 661-9406 Fax: (617) 661-8008
Email: concilio@conciliohispano.org
Web: www.conciliohispano.org

EL CENTRO DEL CARDENAL
76 UNION PARK ST.
Boston, MA 02118
James McCarthy, Executive Director
Tel: (617) 542-9292 Fax: (617) 542-6912

EL INSTITUTO DE LA FAMILIA, INC.
2383 Main St.
Springfield, MA 01107
Barbara Rivera, Director
Tel: (413) 746-4885 Fax: (413) 737-2321
Email: brivera@newnotrhcc.org
Web: www.newnorthcc.org

HARVARD JOURNAL OF HISPANIC POLICY
John F. Kennedy School of Governemnt
Harvard University, 79 JFK St.
Cambridge, MA 02138
Adrian Rodriguez, Editor
Tel: (617) 496-8655 Fax: (617) 384-9555
Email: hjhp@ksg.harvard.edu
Web: www.ksg.harvard.edu/latino/

HISPANIC OFFICE OF PLANNING AND EVALUATION, INC.
165 Brookside Ave., Extension
Jamaica Plain, MA 02130
Jose Duran, Executive Director
Tel: (617) 524-8888 Fax: (617) 524-4939
Email: rrodriguez@hopemass.org

LEAGUE OF UNITED LATIN AMERICAN CITIZENS
Northeast Region-Massachusetts
P.O. Box 146
Jamaica Plain, MA 02130
Regla Gonzalez, State Director
Tel: (617) 327-6760 Fax: (617) 323-4181
Email: reglag@aol.com
Web: www.lulacboston.org

MULTICULTURAL EDUCATION TRAINING & ADVOCACY
240 A Elm St. #22
Somerville, MA 02144
Roger Rice, Co-Director
Tel: (617) 628-2226 Fax: (617)628-0322
Email: rlr@shore.net

NUEVA ESPERANZA, INC.
401 Main St.
Holyoke, MA 01040
Carlos Vega, Director
Tel: (413) 533-9442 Fax: (413) 533-2661
Email: nuevesp@rcn.com

STATE OFFICE OF MINORITY AND WOMEN BUSINESS ASSISTANCE
State of Massachusetts
10 Park Plz.
Boston, MA 02116-3740
Robert Fortes, Director
Tel: (617) 973-8692 Fax: (617) 973-8637
Email: wsomwba@state.ma.us
Web: www.somwba.state.ma.us/

WOBURN COUNCIL OF SOCIAL CONCERN, INC. - HISPANIC PROGRAM
2 Merrimac St.
Woburn, MA 01801-1606
Dean A. Solomon, Director
Tel: (781) 935-6495 Fax: (781) 935-1923
Email: dean@socialconcern.com
Web: www.socialconcern.com

MAURICIO GASTÓN INSTITUTE FOR LATINO COMMUNITY DEVELOPMENT AND PUBLIC POLICY
University of Massachusetts
100 Morrissey Blvd.
Boston, MA 02125-3393
Andrés Torres, Director
Tel: (617) 287-5790 Fax: (617) 287-5788
Email: gaston.institute@umb.edu
Web: www.gaston.umb.edu

PUERTO RICO FEDERAL AFFAIRS ADMINISTRATION
Northern New England Regional Office
31 St. James Ave. #570
Boston, MA 02116
Jose Masso, Regional Director

Tel: (617) 350-6400 Fax: (617) 350-6582
Email: info@prfaa.com
Web: www.prfaa.com

Western Massachusetts Satellite Office
38 School St.
Springfield, MA 01105
Jaime Cotto, Community Officer
Tel: (413) 737-7450 Fax: (413) 737-1305
Email: info@prfaa.com
Web: www.prfaa.com

ASSOCIATION OF LATINO PROFESSIONALS IN FINANCE AND ACCOUNTING
Massachusetts Chapter
Sovereign Bank, 75 State St., 3rd Fl.
Boston, MA 02109
Eduardo Tobon, Chapter President
Tel: (617) 757-5588
Email: etobon@sovereignbank.com
Web: www.alpfa.org

LATINO PROFESSIONAL NETWORK
P.O. Box 6019
Boston, MA 02209
Richard B. Colón, Board President
Tel: (617) 247-1818 Fax: (617) 743-5272
Email: info@lpn.org
Web: www.lpn.org

ARCHDIOCESE OF BOSTON
Hispanic Apostolate Office
2121 Commonwealth Ave.
Boston, MA 02135-3193
Sr. Nancy Charlesworth, Director
Tel: (617) 746-5816 Fax: (617) 783-4564
Email: sister_nancy_charlesworth@rcab.org
Web: www.rcab.org

BLESSED SACRAMENT
Diocesan Hispanic Ministry
445 Plainfield St.
Springfield, MA 01107
Rev. Juan Garcia, Director
Tel: (413) 736-8208 Fax: (413) 731-0962
Email: juanfgarcia@comcast.net

CENTRO DE LA FAMILIA SAN ANDRES
171 Amory St.
Jamaica Plain, MA 02130
Luis Enrique Benavides, Pastor
Tel: (617) 522-1535
Email: lbenavides@msn.com

DIOCESE OF FALL RIVER
Hispanic Apostolate
233 County St.
New Bedford, MA 02740
Rev. Richard D. Wilson, Director
Tel: (508) 992-9408 Fax: (508) 990-0575
Email: rdw@dioc-fr.org

P.O. Box 2577
Fall River, MA 02722
Rev. Richard Wilson, Director
Tel: (508) 675-1311   Fax: (508) 679-9220

DIOCESE OF SPRINGFIELD
Blessed Sacrament
35 Harriet St.
Springfirld, MA 01107
Rev. Juan F. Garcia, Administrator
Tel: (413) 736-8208
Web: www.diospringfield.org/sc/clmpe.html

Holy Family Parish
235 Eastern Ave.
Springfield, MA 01109
Rev. Msgr. Richard S. Sniezyk, Pastor
Tel: (413) 732-1422
Email: m.dupont@diospringfield
Web: www.diospringfield.org/sc/clmpe.html

LA VIDA, INC.
40 Green St.
Lynn, MA 01902
Frances Martinez, Executive Director
Tel: (781) 586-0193 Fax: (781) 586-0196
Web: www.la-vida.org

MINISTERIO COSECHA
644 Middle St., PMB 397
Weymouth, MA 02189
Rev. Sergio Perez, Pastor
Tel: (781) 335-4696
Email: sergiovision@aol.com

NUESTRA SEÑORA DE GUADALUPE
233 County St.
New Bedford, MA 02740
Rev. Richard Wilson, Pastor
Tel: (508) 996-5862 Fax: (508) 992-2208
Email: rdwilson1@comcast.net

DAVID ROCKEFELLER CENTER FOR LATIN AMERICAN STUDIES
Harvard University
61 Kirkland St.
Cambridge, MA 02138
John Coatsworth, Director
Tel: (617) 495-3366 Fax: (617) 496-2802
Email: drclas@fas.harvard.edu
Web: www.fas.harvard.edu/~drclas

HARVARD FAMILY RESEARCH PROJECT
Harvard Graduate School of Education
3 Garden St.
Cambridge, MA 02138
Stacey Miller, Publications/Communications Manager
Tel: (617) 495-9108 Fax: (617) 495-8594
Email: hfrp@gse.harvard.edu
Web: www.hfrp.org

INSTITUTE FOR ECONOMIC DEVELOPMENT
Boston University
264 Bay State Rd.
Boston, MA 02215
Dilip Mookherjee, Director
Tel: (617) 353-4030 Fax: (617) 353-4143
Email: ied@bu.edu
Web: www.bu.edu/econ/ied

CASA ESPERANZA
P.O. Box 191540
Roxbury, MA 02119
Ricardo Quiroga, Executive Director
Tel: (617) 445-7411 x12 Fax: (617) 541-0844
Email: rquiroga@casaesperanza.org
Web: www.casaesperanza.org

HIGHER EDUCATION INFORMATION CENTER
Boston Public Library
700 Boylston St.
Boston, MA 02116
Jane Hurton, Director of CounselingTel: (617) 536-0200 Fax: (617) 536-4737
Web: www.edinfo.org

Iglesia Evangelica Hispana
61-A Warren St.
Lawrence, MA 01841
David Zagunis, Director
Tel: (978) 975-7622 Fax: (978) 975-8976

LASPAU
Harvard University
25 Mt. Auburn St.
Cambridge, MA 02138
Ned Strong, Executive Director
Tel: (617) 495-5255 Fax: (617) 495-8990
Email: ned_strong@harvard.edu
Web: www.laspau.harvard.edu/

LATIN AMERICAN & LATINO/A STUDIES
Smith College
Seelye Hall #210
Northampton, MA 01063
Kathleen E. Gauger, Adm. Asst.
Tel: (413) 585-3591
Email: kgauger@email.smith.edu
Web: www.smith.edu/las/index.html

LATIN AMERICAN SCHOLARSHIP PROGRAM
25 Mt. Auburn St.
Cambridge, MA 02138-6095
Judith Adler, Senior Program Officer
Tel: (617) 495-5255 Fax: (617) 495-8990
Email: judith_adler@harvard.edu
Web: www.laspau.harvard.edu

LATIN AMERICAN STUDIES PROGRAM
Brandeis University
Olin-Sang 206, M/S 036
Waltham, MA 02454
Silvia Arrom, Director
Tel: (781) 736-2290 Fax: (781) 736-2273
Email: arrom@brandeis.edu
Web: www.brandeis.edu/departments/latinam

OFFICE OF MINORITY EDUCATION
Massachusetts Institute of Technology
77 Massachusetts Ave.., Bldg. 4-113
Cambridge, MA 02139
Kim Beamon, Associate Dean/Associate Director
Tel: (617) 253-5010 Fax: (617) 253-9899
Email: ome@mit.edu
Web: http://web.mit.edu/ome/

TERI COLLEGE ACCESS
Higher Education Information Center
31 St. James Ave., 4th Fl.
Boston, MA 02116
Arturo U. Iriarte, Ph.D, Executive Director
Tel: (617) 535-6825 Fax: (617) 422-8805
Email: iriarte@teri.org
Web: www.edinfo.org

SOUTHEASTERN MASSACHUSETTS/SER-JOBS FOR PROGRESS, INC..
164 Bedford St.
Fall River, MA 02720
M. Paula Raposa, Executive Director
Tel: (508) 676-1916 Fax: (508) 676-2330
Email: admin@ser-jobs.com
Web: www.ser-national.org

GAY AND LESBIAN LATINO ORGANIZATION
Graper Valley Health Center
405 Grove St.
Worcester, MA 01605
Leo Negron, Representative
Tel: (508) 854-3260 Fax: (508) 854-3265
Email: gallo@hascm.org

GANDARA HEALTH CENTER
333 E Columbus Ave.
Springfield, MA 01105
Henry East-Trou, Executive Director
Tel: (413) 736-8329 Fax: (413) 788-8098

HARVARD PILGRIM HEALTH CARE
1600 Crown Colony Dr.
Quincy, MA 02169
Tel: (800) 421-3590
Web: www.harvardpilgrim.org

LATIN AMERICAN HEALTH INSTITUTE
Brockton Office
157 Centre St.
Brockton, MA 02301
Daniel Velez-Rivera, President
Tel: (508) 941-0005 Fax: (508) 427-6915
Email: brockton@lhi.org
Web: www.lhi.org

Lowell Office
144 Merrimack St.
Lowell, MA 01852
Daniel Velez-Rivera, President
Tel: (978) 459-3366 Fax: (978) 446-0817
Email: lowell@lhi.org
Web: www.lhi.org

LATINO HEALTH INSTITUTE
95 Berkeley St.
Boston, MA 02116
Dora Gutierrez, Director of Community Health
Tel: (617) 350-6900
Email: dora@lhi.org
Web: www.lhi.org

NATIONAL ASSOCIATION OF HISPANIC NURSES
Western Massachusetts Chapter
8 Anthony Dr.
Rutland, MA 01543-1719
Sandra Lawless
Email: sjlv63@msn.com
Web: www.thehispanicnurses.org

SPANISH AMERICAN UNION, INC.
2335 Main St.
Springfield, MA 01107
Robert Bailey, Executive Director
Tel: (413) 734-7381 Fax: (413) 734-8293
Email: fiscal@lacasahispana.org
Web: www.lacasahispana.org

COALITION FOR A BETTER ACRE, INC.
517 Moody St., 3rd Fl.
Lowell, MA 01854
Laura Buxbaum, Interim Director
Tel: (978) 452-7523 Fax: (978) 452-4923
Email: laura.buxbaum@cbacre.org

NEW ENGLAND FARM WORKERS' COUNCIL
Affiliate of Corporation for Public Management
1628-1640 Main St.
Springfield, MA 01103
Heriberto Flores, Executive Director
Tel: (413) 781-2145 Fax: (413) 781-5928
Email: eanefwc@aol.com
Web: www.partnersforcommunity.org

LA ALIANZA HISPANA
409 Dudley St.
Roxbury, MA 02119
Rosa Bastiam, Administrative Assistant
Tel: (617) 427-7175 Fax: (617) 442-2259
Email: info@laalianza.org
Web: www.laalianza.org

LEAGUE OF UNITED LATIN AMERICAN CITIZENS
Northeast Region - Massachusetts
41 Eden St.
Framingham, MA 01702
Laura Medrano, Vice President
Tel: (617) 957-1462
Email: lauramedrano@lulac.org
Web: www.lulac.org

CENTRO PRESENTE, INC.
54 Essex St., 2nd Fl.
Cambridge, MA 02139
María Elena Letona, Director
Tel: (617) 497-9080 Fax: (617) 497-7247
Email: centro@cpresente.org
Web: www.cpresente.org

GREATER LAWRENCE COMMUNITY ACTION COUNCIL, INC.
Spanish Community Services

305 Essex St.
Lawrence, MA 01840
Isabel Melendez, Program Director
Tel: (978) 681-4905 Fax: (978) 681-4979
Email: spanish@glcac.org
Web: www.glcac.org

HARVARD LATINO LAW REVIEW
Harvard Law School
1541 Massachusetts Ave.
Cambridge, MA 02138
Angela Johnson, Editor
Tel: (6170 496-8282
Email: hllr@law.harvard.edu
Web: www.ksg.harvard.edu/latino

ASSOCIATION OF COMMUNITY ORGANIZATIONS FOR REFORM NOW
Massachusetts
1486 Dorchester Ave.
Boston, MA 02122
Joyce Campbell, Director
Tel: (617) 436-7100 Fax: (617) 436-4878
Email: natacornma@acorn.org
Web: www.acorn.org

ASSOCIATION SAN MARTIN DE PORRES CENTRO HISPANO
155 Crescent St.
Brockton, MA 02403
Enrique Marrero, Director
Tel: (508) 584-2241

CASA MYRNA VAZQUEZ, INC.
P.O. Box 180019
Boston, MA 02118
Shiela Y. Moore, Executive Director
Tel: (617) 521-0100
Email: smoore@casamyrna.org
Web: www.casamyrna.org

CENTRO LAS AMERICAS
11 Sycamore St.
Worcester, MA 01608
Orlando Rodriguez, Executive Director
Tel: (508) 798-1900 Fax: (508) 798-1908
Email: info@centrolasamericas.org
Web: www.centrolasamericas.org

CENTRO LATINO DE CHELSEA, INC.
267 Broadway
Chelsea, MA 02150
Juan Vega, Executive Director
Tel: (617) 884-3238 Fax: (617) 884-4646
Email: jvega@centrolatino.org
Web: www.centrolatino.org

ENERSOL ASSOCIATES, INC.
55 Middlesex St. #221
N. Chelmsford, MA 01863
Richard Hansen, President
Tel: (978) 251-1828 Fax: (978) 251-5291
Email: enersol@igc.org
Web: www.enersol.org

INQUILINOS BORICUAS EN ACCIÓN, INC.
405 Shawmut Ave.
Boston, MA 02118
Lisa Morales, Executive Assistant
Tel: (617) 927-1707 Fax: (617) 536-5816
Email: lmorales@iba-etc.org
Web: www.iba-etc.org

LA FAMILIA HISPANA, INC.
P.O. Box 6550
Holyoke, MA 01041-6550
Marisella Cartagena, Board of Director
Tel: (413) 532-4496 Fax: (413) 532-8035
Email: dilen@hge.net
Web: www.lafamiliahispana.org

NEW BEDFORD DEPARTMENT OF HUMAN SERVICES
Office of Cultural Affairs

133 William St. #219
New Bedford, MA 02740
Adonis Ferreira, Coordinator
Tel: (508) 979-1516 Fax: (508) 991-6148
Email: adonisf@ci.new-bedford.ma.us
Web: www.ci.new-bedford.ma.us

SPANISH AMERICAN CENTER, INC.
112 Spruce St.
Leominster, MA 01453
Neddy Latima, Director
Tel: (978) 534-3145 Fax: (978) 534-5146
Email: neddyl@choice1mail.com

LA ALIANZA HISPANA, INC.
Affiliate of SER-Jobs for Progress National, Inc.
409 Dudley St.
Roxbury, MA 02119
Willie Rodriguez, Executive Director
Tel: (617) 427-7175 Fax: (617) 442-2259
Email: arabia61@yahoo.com
Web: www.laalianza.org

MUJERES UNIDAS EN ACCION
15 Medway St.
Dorchester, MA 02124
Felisa White, Director
Tel: (617) 296-3016 Fax: (617) 296-3998
Email: mujeresuni@hotmail.com

WOMANSHELTER/COMPANERAS
P.O. Box 1099
Holyoke, MA 01041
Karen Boyle Cavanaugh, Director
Tel: (413) 538-9717 Fax: (413) 538-9411
Email: kbcavanaugh@womanshelter.org
Web: www.womanshelter.org

ROCA, INC.
101 Park St.
Chelsea, MA 02150
Molly Baldwin, Executive Director
Tel: (617) 889-5210 X221 Fax: (617) 889-2145
Email: baldwinm@rocainc.com
Web: www.rocainc.com

ASSOCIATION OF PUERTO RICAN STUDENTS
Massachussetts Institute of Technology
Massachussetts Institute of Technology
Cambridge, MA 02139
Felix Santiago, President
Email: fxo33@mit.edu
Web: web.mit.edu/apr/www/home.htm

CHICANO CAUCUS OF AMHERST
Amherst College
Dean of Students Office, Box 105
Amherst, MA 01002-5000
Ron Espiritu, Co-chair
Tel: (413) 542-2000
Email: rdespiritu@amherst.edu
Web: www.amherst.edu/~chicano

CONCILIO LATINO
Harvard University
c/o Harvard University Dean of Students, 4 University Hall
Cambridge, MA 02138
Martha Casillas, Executive Co-Chair
Email: concilio@hcs.harvard.edu
Web: www.hcs.harvard.edu/~concilio/

LA CAUSA
Amherst College
P.O. Box 1836
Amherst, MA 01002-5000
Eduardo Garcia, Chair

Email: egarcia@amherst.edu
Web: www.amherst.edu/~lacausa

LA FUERZA
Boston University
One Sherbon St.
Boston, MA 02215
Robert Trevino, Co-Chair
Tel: (617) 353-2000
Email: lafuerza@bu.edu
Web: http://people.bu.edu/lafuerza/index.htm

LATIN BUSINESS CLUB
MIT-Sloan School of Management
50 Memorial Dr.
Cambridge, MA 02142
Jose Siade, Board Member
Tel: (617) 253-1000 Fax: (617) 253-9899
Email: jsiade@mit.edu
Web: http://web.mit.edu/clublatino/www/index.html

MEZCLA
Wellesley College
Snyder Ctr., 106 Central St.
Wellesley, MA 02181
Tel: (781) 283-2489 Fax: (781) 283-3674
Email: Mezclamail@wellesley.edu

MINORITY FACULTY DEVELOPMENT PROGRAM
Harvard Medical School
164 Longwood Ave. 2nd Fl.
Boston, MA 02115-5818
Joan Y. Reede, Dean
Tel: (617) 432-2413 Fax: (617) 432-3834
Email: joan_reede@hms.harvard.edu
Web: www.mfdp.med.harvard.edu/contact/

MICHIGAN

BALLET OF MARIA VALDEZ
531 Ash St.
Lansing, MI 48906
Maria Valdez, Director
Tel: (517) 372-3023 Fax: (517) 372-3023
Email: valdezm1@msu.edu

HISPANIC BUSINESS ALLIANCE
645 Griswold St. #1500
Detroit, MI 48226
Frederick Feliciano, President
Tel: (313) 963-4700
Email: treasurer@hbaweb.org
Web: www.hbaweb.org

MICHIGAN MINORITY BUSINESS DEVELOPMENT COUNCIL
Michigan Headquarters
3011 W Grand Blvd. #230
Detroit, MI 48202
E. Delbert Gray, President
Tel: (313) 873-3200 Fax: (313) 873-4783
Email: mail@mmbdc.com
Web: www.mmbdc.com

NATIONAL SOCIETY OF HISPANIC MBAS
Detroit Chapter
P.O. Box 43201
Detroit, MI 48243
Antonio Ochoa, Chapter President
Tel: (248) 363-1898
Email: general@detroit.nshmba.org
Web: www.nshmba.org

GREATER LANSING HISPANIC CHAMBER OF COMMERCE
300 E. Michigan Ave. #300
Lansing, MI 48933

J. R. Rios, President
Tel: (517) 487-6340 Fax: (517) 484-6910
Email: rtrent@lansingchamber.org

MICHIGAN HISPANIC CHAMBER OF COMMERCE
24445 Northwestern Hwy. #206
Southfield, MI 48075
Tel: (248) 208-9915 Fax: (248) 208-9936
Email: jknott@mhcc.org
Web: www.mhcc.org

NATIONAL HISPANIC MEDIA COALITION
Michigan
3544 Eastham Rd.
Dearborn, MI 48120
Fern Espino, Chair
Tel: (313) 336-6868
Email: fernespino@cs.com
Web: www.nhmc.org

CASA DE UNIDAD
1920 Scotten
Detroit, MI 48209
Veronica Paiz, Executive Director
Tel: (313) 843-9598 Fax: (313) 843-7307
Web: www.casadeunidad.org

MARIACHI AMERICA
1433 Campbell
Detroit, MI 48209
Manuel Zaragoza, Director
Tel: (313) 849-1914

SPANISH SPEAKING INFORMATION CENTER
202 E. Blvd. Dr. #320
Flint, MI 48503
Lily Tamez Kehoe, Executive Director
Tel: (810) 239-4417 Fax: (810) 239-4419
Email: centro4417@aol.com
Web: http://www.geocities.com/spanishspeakin
ginfocenter/

AMERICAN GI FORUM OF THE UNITED STATES
Michigan Chapter
704 Trumbull
Bay City, MI 48708
Henry Martinez, Commander
Tel: (989) 893-4823
Web: www.agif.us/MI.htm

COMMUNITY ACTION AGENCY
1214 Greenwood
Jackson, MI 49203
Kate Martin, Director of Development
Tel: (517) 784-4800 Fax: (517) 784-5188
Email: kmartin@caajlh.org
Web: www.caajlh.org

DETROIT HISPANIC DEVELOPMENT CORPORATION
1211 Trumbull
Detroit, MI 48216
Hector Cruz, Chair
Tel: (313) 967-4880 Fax: (313) 967-4884
Web: www.dhdc1.org

FAMILY INDEPENDENCE AGENCY
Allegan County
3255 122nd #300
Allegan, MI 49010
Susan Bailey Carman, Director
Tel: (269) 673-7700 Fax: (269) 673-7795
Email: fiaweb@michigan.gov
Web: www.michigan.gov/fia

Alpena County
711 W. Chisholm
Alpena, MI 49707
Douglas McCombs, Director

Tel: (989) 354-7200 Fax: (989) 534-7242
Email: fiaweb@michigan.gov
Web: www.michigan.gov/fia

Benzie County 10- Zone 2
P.O. Box 114
Beulah, MI 49617
Doug Lapham, Director
Tel: (231) 882-1330 Fax: (231) 882-9078
Email: fiaweb@michigan.gov
Web: www.michigan.gov/fia

Grand Traverse County 28- Zone 2
701 S Elmwood #19
Traverse City, MI 49684-3185
Mary Marois, Director
Tel: (231) 941-3900 Fax: (231) 941-0037
Email: fiaweb@michigan.gov
Web: www.michigan.gov/fia

Huron County 32- Zone 4
1911 Sand Beach Rd.
Bad Axe, MI 48413
Thomas Dillon, Director
Tel: (989) 269-9201 Fax: (989) 269-9875
Email: fiaweb@michigan.gov
Web: www.michigan.gov/fia

Ingham County 33- Zone 3
5303 S Cedar St.
Lansing, MI 48909
Douglas Williams, Director
Tel: (517) 887-9400 Fax: (517) 887-9500
Email: fiaweb@michigan.gov
Web: www.michigan.gov/fia

Ionia County 34- Zone 3
P.O. Box 506
Ionia, MI 48846
Philip L. Larson, Director
Tel: (617) 527-5200 Fax: (617) 527-1849
Email: fiaweb@michigan.gov
Web: www.michigan.gov/fia

Leelanau County
701 S. Elmwood #19
Traverse City, MI 49684-3185
Mary L. Marois, Director
Tel: (231) 941-3900 Fax: (231) 941-0037
Email: fiaweb@michigan.gov
Web: www.michigan.gov/fia

Lenawee County
1040 S. Winter St. #3013
Adrian, MI 49221
Joseph A. Satterelli, Director
Tel: (517) 264-6300 Fax: (517) 264-6357
Email: fiaweb@michigan.gov
Web: www.michigan.gov/fia

Manistee County
1672 US 31 South
Manistee, MI 49660
Dean Van Natter, Chair
Tel: (231) 723-8375 Fax: (231) 398-2106
Web: www.mfia.state.mi.us

Michigan National Headquarters
P.O. Box 30037
Lansing, MI 48909
Douglas E. Howard, Director
Tel: (517) 373-2035 Fax: (517) 335-6101
Email: fiaweb@michigan.gov
Web: www.michigan.gov/fia

Tuscola County
1365 Cleaver Rd.
Caro, MI 48723
Thomas Dillon, Director
Tel: (989) 673-9100 Fax: (989) 673-9209
Email: fiaweb@michigan.gov
Web: www.michigan.gov/fia

Van Buren County
P. O. Box 7
57150 C. R. 681
Hartford, MI 49057
Marc Del Mariani, Director

Tel: (269) 621-2800 Fax: (269) 621-2927
Email: fiaweb@michigan.gov
Web: www.michigan.gov/fia

HISPANIC BAR ASSOCIATION OF MICHIGAN
P.O. Box 776
Royal Oak, MI 48067
Diana Trivax-Levy, President
Tel: (586) 263-0003
Email: dbtdlt@aol.com
Web: www.michbar.org/localbars/hispanic/
content.html

INTERFAITH COUNCIL FOR PEACE AND JUSTICE
Latin America Task Force
730 Tappan
Ann Arbor, MI 48104
Chuck Warpehoski, Director
Tel: (734) 663-1870 Fax: (734) 663-9458
Email: info@icpj.net
Web: www.icpj.net

LATIN AMERICAN SERVICES
121 Franklin St. SE
Grand Rapids, MI 49507
Gloria Zamarripa, Director
Tel: (616) 336-4018 Fax: (616) 336-4012
Email: Zamarripag@nwd.org

LATIN AMERICANS FOR SOCIAL AND ECONOMIC DEVELOPMENT, INC.
4138 W. Vernor
Detroit, MI 48209
Jane Garcia, Executive Director
Tel: (313) 554-2025 Fax: (313) 554-2242

MIGRANT PROGRAM
Arenac County, State of Michigan
3709 Deep River Rd.
Standish, MI 48658
Rick Joels, Director
Tel: (989) 846-4551 Fax: (989) 846-4365
Email: joelsr@michigan.gov
Web: www.michigan.gov

NORTHWEST MICHIGAN MIGRANT
1209 S. Garfield Ave. #C
Traverse City, MI 49686
Kevin Benson, Agriculture Employment Specialist
Tel: (231) 922-3729 Fax: (231) 922-3737
Email: bensonk@mihigan.gov
Web: www.michaglabor.org

PERUVIAN AMERICAN MEDICAL SOCIETY
6488 Tamerlane Dr.
West Bloomfield, MI 48322-2379
Nora del Busto, President
Email: delbustonora_md@hotmail.com
Web: www.pamsnational.org

MICHIGAN COMMISSION ON SPANISH SPEAKING AFFAIRS
201 N Washington Sq., 3rd Fl.
Lansing, MI 48913
Marylou Olivarez-Mason, Executive Director
Tel: (517) 373-8339 Fax: (517) 373-0176
Email: masonm1@michigan.gov
Web: www.michigan.gov/mdcd

REPUBLICAN NATIONAL HISPANIC ASSEMBLY
1317 Giddings Ave. SE
Grand Rapids, MI 49506
Francisco M. Vega, State Chairman
Tel: (616) 245-5924
Web: www.rnha.org

PERUVIAN AMERICAN MEDICAL SOCIETY
Midwest Region Chapter
201 Orchard St.
Alma, MI 48801
Dr. Victor V. Rozas, President
Tel: (989) 463-4805

Email: vrozas@voyager.net
Web: www.pamsnational.org

SOCIETY OF HISPANIC PROFESSIONAL ENGINEERS
Detroit Professional Chapter
P.O. Box 8494
Royal Oak, MI 48068
Theo Moreno, President
Tel: (586) 492-8901
Email: theo.l.moreno@gm.com
Web: www.shpe-detroit.org

ARCHDIOCESE OF DETROIT
Hispanic Affairs
305 Michigan Ave. GRB 10th Fl.
Detroit, MI 48226-2605
Raúl Feliciano, Director for Hispanic Ministry
Tel: (313) 237-5934 Fax: (313) 237-5869

CRISTO REY CHURCH
201 W Miller Rd.
Lansing, MI 48910
Rev. Federico Thelen, Pastor
Tel: (517) 394-4639 Fax: (517) 394-8090
Email: veronicam@cristoreychurch.com
Web: www.cristoreychurch.com

DIOCESE OF KALAMAZOO
Hispanic Ministry Office
215 N Westnedge Ave.
Kalamazoo, MI 49007
Fanny Tabares, Director for Hispanic Ministry
Tel: (269) 349-8714 X236
Email: ftabares@dioceseofkalamazoo.org
Web: www.dioceseofkalamazoo.org

DIOCESE OF LANSING
Hispanic Ministry Office
300 W Ottawa St.
Lansing, MI 48933
Serapio Hernández, Director for Hispanic Ministry
Tel: (517) 342-2498 Fax: (517) 342-2468
Email: sherna@dioceseoflansing.org
Web: www.dioceseoflansing.com

DIOCESE OF MARQUETTE
Hispanic Affairs
P.O. Box 550
Marquette, MI 49855
Mary Jeske, Secretary
Tel: (906) 227-9111 Fax: (906) 225-0437
Email: mjeske@dioceseofmarquette.org
Web: www.dioceseofmarquette.org

DIOCESE OF SAGINAW
Hispanic Ministry
5800 Weiss St.
Saginaw, MI 48603-2799
Maria D. Cepeda, Director for Hispanic Ministry
Tel: (989) 797-6646 Fax: (989) 797-6670
Email: maria@dioceseofsaginaw.org
Web: www.dioceseofsaginaw.org

DIOCESE OF GAYLORDS
Hispanic Ministry Office
720 2nd St.
Traverse City, MI 49684
Sylvia Cortez, Director
Tel: (231) 946-1205
Web: www.dioceseofgaylord.org/searchindex.html

SAINT JOSEPH CATHOLIC CHURCH
Hispanic Ministry
61 N 23rd St.
Battle Creek, MI 49015
Rev. John Sleckstein, Pastor
Tel: (269) 962-0165 Fax: (269) 962-5937
Email: springer@voyager.net
Web: www.stjoseph-battlecreek.org

ST. GABRIEL CHURCH
8118 W Vernor
Detroit, MI 48209
Jaime Hinojos, Deacon
Tel: (313) 841-0753 Fax: (313) 841-0916
Email: stgabriel-det@rc.net

RESEARCH

CENTER FOR LATIN AMERICAN AND CARIBBEAN STUDIES
Michigan State University
300 Delia Koo International Academic Center
East Lansing, MI 48824
Scott Whiteford, Director
Tel: (517) 353-1690 Fax: (517) 432-7471
Email: clacs@msu.edu
Web: www.isp.msu.edu/clacs/

SPEC. INT., ALCOHOL/DRUG CENTER

FAMILY SERVICES AND CHILDREN AID
142 E Maumee St.
Adrian, MI 49221
Carol Zawacki, Acting Supervisor
Tel: (517) 263-2625 Fax: (517) 263-7369

MID-MICHIGAN TEEN CHALLENGE
Saginaw Center
818 S Michigan Ave.
Saginaw, MI 48602-1531
Salvador Flores, Executive Director
Tel: (989) 249-8818 Fax: (989) 791-6628
Email: mmteench@hotmail.com
Web: www.teenchallenge.com

SPEC. INT., CHILD CARE

OSMAN HOPE, INC.
P.O. Box 1327
Brighton, MI 48116
Pete Borg, Vice President
Email: info@osmanhope.org
Web: www.osmanhope.org

SPEC. INT., COUNSELING

EL CENTRO "LA FAMILIA"
Easter Seals
35 W. Huron #200
Pontiac, MI 48342
Dr. Sonya Acosta, Director
Tel: (248) 858-5320 Fax: (248) 858-1604
Email: sacosta@essmichigan.org
Web: www.essmichigan.org

SPEC. INT., EDUCATION

ALANA
Michigan State University
116 Linton Hall
East Lansing, MI 48824-1113
Yevonne Smith, Associate Dean
Tel: (517) 353-3262 Fax: (517) 353-3355
Web: www.grad.msu.edu/alana.htm

CAPITOL AREA LITERACY COALITION
1028 E Saginaw
Lansing, MI 48906
Lois Bader, Director
Tel: (517) 485-4949 Fax: (517) 485-1924
Email: mail@thereadingpeople.org
Web: www.thereadingpeople.org

CENTER FOR CHICANO-BORICUA STUDIES
Wayne State University
656 W. Kirby #3326
Detroit, MI 48202
Dr. Andre Furtado, Director
Tel: (313) 577-4378 Fax: (313) 993-4073
Email: a.furtado@wayne.edu
Web: www.cbs.wayne.edu

CHICANO/LATINO STUDIES
Michigan State University
442 Berkey Hall
East Lansing, MI 48824
Theresa Meléndez, Director
Tel: (517) 432-7187 Fax: (517) 353-8685
Email: tmelende@msu.edu
Web: www.msu.edu/~cls

COMMISSION ON SPANISH SPEAKING AFFAIRS
Department of Career Development
210 N. Washington Sq., 3rd Fl.
Lansing, MI 48913
Marylou Olivarez-Mason, Executive Director
Tel: (517) 373-8339 Fax: (517) 373-0176

HISPANIC JOURNALISM PROGRAM
Michigan State University, School of Journalism
305 Communication Arts Bldg.
East Lansing, MI 48824-1212
Rosa Morales, Director
Tel: (517) 353-3859
Web: www.msu.edu/~prattdou/jschool/

INTERNATIONAL INSTITUTE OF METROPOLITAN DETROIT, INC.
111 E Kirby Rd.
Detroit, MI 48202
Wojciech Zolnowski, Executive Director
Tel: (313) 871-8600 Fax: (313) 817-1651
Email: ydubaisi@iimd.org
Web: www.iimd.org

JULIAN SAMORA RESEARCH INSTITUTE
Michigan State University
301 Nisbet Bldg., 1407 S Harrison
East Lansing, MI 48823-5286
Israel Cuéllar, Professor/Director
Tel: (517) 432-1317 Fax: (517) 432-2221
Email: info@jsri.msu.edu
Web: www.jsri.msu.edu

LATIN AMERICAN AND CARIBBEAN STUDIES
University of Michigan
1080 S University St.
Ann Arbor, MI 48109-1106
Sueann Caufield, Acting Director
Tel: (734) 763-0553 Fax: (734) 615-8880
Email: lacs.office@umich.edu
Web: www.umich.edu/~iinet/lacs

LATIN AMERICAN STUDIES PROGRAM
Grand Valley State University
105 Student Bldg.
Allendale, MI 49401
Russell Rhoads, Director
Tel: (616) 331-3898 Fax: (616) 331-3899
Email: rhoadsr@gvsu.edu
Web: www4.gvsu.edu/las

MICHIGAN EDUCATION ASSOCIATION
Bilingual/Migrant Education Program
P.O. Box 2573
East Lansing, MI 48826-2573
Linda Keway, PD/HR Consultant
Tel: (800) 292-1934 Fax: (517) 337-5587
Email: lkeway@mea.org
Web: www.mea.org

MULTI-ETHNIC STUDENT AFFAIRS
University of Michigan
2202 Michigan Union, 530 State St.
Ann Arbor, MI 48108-1349
Angela Munoz, Latino Coordinator
Tel: (734) 763-9044 Fax: (734) 615-6842
Email: munoza@umich.edu

OFFICE OF INTERNATIONAL STUDENT SERVICES
Western Michigan University
1903 W Michigan Ave., A411 Ellsworth Hall
Kalamazoo, MI 49008-5246
Barbara Shouse, Director
Tel: (269) 387-5865 Fax: (269) 387-5899
Email: oiss.info@wmich.edu
Web: www.wmich.edu/oiss

OFFICE OF MULTICULTURAL AFFAIRS
Madonna University
36600 Schoolcraft Rd.
Livonia, MI 48066
Osvaldo Rivera, Director
Tel: (734) 432-5541 Fax: (734) 432-5393
Email: orivera@madonna.edu
Web: www.madonna.edu

SPEC. INT., EMPLOYMENT

SER METRO DETROIT, JOBS FOR PROGRESS, INC.
9301 Michigan Ave.
Detroit, MI 48210
Ignacio Salazar, CEO
Tel: (313) 846-2240 Fax: (313) 846-2247
Email: isalazar@detroitnwa.org
Web: www.sermetro.org

SPEC. INT., FAMILY PLANNING

CHILD AND FAMILY SERVICES OF WESTERN MICHIGAN, INC.
Hispanic/Latino Services- Allegan Office
217 Hubbard
Allegan, MI 49010
Julio Rios, Program Supervisor
Tel: (616) 673-1896
Email: allegan@cfswm.org
Web: www.cfswm.org

LATINO FAMILY SERVICES
3815 W. Fort St.
Detroit, MI 48216
Alicia Villarreal, Executive Director
Tel: (313) 841-7380 Fax: (313) 841-3730
Email: a.villareal@latinofamilyservices.org
Web: www.latinofamilyservices.org

SPEC. INT., HEALTH SERVICES

ALCONA HEALTH CENTER
P.O. Box 279
Lincoln, MI 48742
Christine Baumgardner, Executive Director
Tel: (989) 736-8658 Fax: (989) 736-8380
Email: cbaumgardner@mpca.net

AMERICAN RED CROSS
Ottawa County Chapter
270 James St.
Holland, MI 49424
Sindee Maxwell, Executive Director
Tel: (616) 396-6545 Fax: (616) 396-3921
Email: jmiller@ottawaredcross.org
Web: www.ottawaredcross.org

FAMILY MEDICAL CENTER OF MICHIGAN
8765 Lewis Ave.
Temperance, MI 48182
Ed Larkin, Executive Director
Tel: (734) 847-3802 Fax: (734) 847-3418
Email: elarkin@mpca.net

INTERCARE COMMUNITY HEALTH NETWORK
285 James St.
Holland, MI 49424
Maria D. Sibella, Manager
Tel: (616) 399-0200 Fax: (616) 399-5055
Email: maria@intercare.org
Web: www.intercare.org

697 Weld St.
Benton Harbor, MI 49022
Timothy Radabaugh, Manager
Tel: (269) 927-5400 Fax: (269) 927-5493
Email: timothy@intercare.org
Web: www.intercare.o

6270 W Main St.
Eau Claire, MI 49111
Zully Westrate, Manager
Tel: (269) 461-6927 Fax: (269) 461-3068
Email: zully@intercare.org
Web: www.intercare.org

Bangor Office
308 Charles St.
Bangor, MI 49013
Georgette Peterson, Manager
Tel: (269) 427-7967 Fax: (269) 427-7574

Email: georgette@intercare.org
Web: www.intercare.org

Pullman Health Center
5498 109th Ave.
Pullman, MI 49450
Sharon Stevensen, Director
Tel: (269) 236-5021 Fax: (269) 236-0505
Web: www.intercare.org

JUNCTION HEALTH CENTER
4771 Michigan Ave.
Detroit, MI 48210
John Cawacki, Director
Tel: (313) 897-2600 Fax: (313) 897-2424

MICHIGAN PRIMARY CARE ASSOCIATION
2525 Jolly Rd. #280
Okemos, MI 48864
Kim Sibilsky, Executive Director
Tel: (517) 381-8000 Fax: (517) 381-8008
Email: ksibilsky@mpca.net
Web: www.mpca.net

MIGRANT HEALTH PROMOTION
224 W Michigan Ave.
Saline, MI 48176
Kimberly Kratz, Executive Director
Tel: (734) 944-0244 Fax: (734) 944-1405
Email: info@migranthealth.org
Web: www.migranthealth.org

NORTHWEST MICHIGAN HEALTH SERVICES, INC.
Affiliate of NCLR
10767 Traverse Hwy. #B
Traverse City, MI 49684
Ann Avery, Interim Executive Director
Tel: (231) 947-1112 Fax: (231) 947-7739
Email: avery49068@aol.com

SPEC. INT., HUMAN RELATIONS

CRISTO REY COMMUNITY CENTER
1717 N High St.
Lansing, MI 48906
John Roy Castillo, Executive Director
Tel: (517) 372-4700 Fax: (517) 372-8499
Email: cristorey@earthlink.net
Web: www.cristo-rey.com

TELAMON CORPORATION
Bay City Office
111 Washington Ave.
Bay City, MI 48708
Jose Costilla, Regional Manager
Tel: (989) 894-8941 Fax: (989) 894-8944
Email: jcostilla@telamon.org
Web: www.telamon.org

Employment & Resources Centers
232 E Michigan Ave.
Paw Paw, MI 49079
Marcos Flores, Regional Manager
Tel: (269) 655-9916 Fax: (269) 655-9507
Email: mflores@telamon.org
Web: www.telamon.org

Job Connection Office
710 Chicago #310
Holland, MI 49423
Martha Cerda, Case Manager
Tel: (616) 396-5160 Fax: (616) 396-6992
Email: mcerda@telamon.org
Web: www.telamon.org

SCMWC Office
1040 S Winter St. #1014
Adrian, MI 49221
Maryellen Salazar, Regional Manager
Tel: (517) 263-6825 Fax: (517) 265-3286
Email: msalazar@telamon.org
Web: www.telamon.org

Sparta Migrant Head Start
347 Evergreen
Sparta, MI 49345
Sergio Rodriguez, Center Director
Tel: (616) 887-0663 Fax: (616) 887-2590
Email: srodriguez@telamon.org
Web: www.telamon.org

State Office
6350 W Michigan Ave.
Lansing, MI 48917
Sam Garcia, State Director
Tel: (517) 323-7002 Fax: (517) 323-9840
Email: sgarcia@telamon.org
Web: www.telamon.org

Traverse City Office
10767 Traverse Hwy. #A
Traverse City, MI 49684
Nancy Sanchez, Case Manager
Tel: (231) 941-5300 Fax: (231) 941-0924
Email: nsanchez@telamon.org
Web: www.telamon.org

SOUTHWEST COUNSELING AND DEVELOPMENT SERVICES
Waterman Center
1700 Waterman St.
Detroit, MI 48209
John Van Camp, President/CEO
Tel: (313) 841-8900 Fax: (313) 841-4470
Web: http://comnet.org/swcds/

CAPITAL AREA COMMUNITY SERVICES, INC.
101 E Willow St.
Lansing, MI 48906
Ivan W. Love, Jr., Director
Tel: (517) 482-6281 Fax: (517) 482-7747
Email: ksnow1327@hotmail.com

CHILD AND FAMILY SERVICES OF WESTERN MICHIGAN, INC.
Hispanic/Latino Services
412 Century Ln.
Holland, MI 49423
Julio Rios, Hispanic Program Supervisor
Tel: (616) 396-2301 Fax: (616) 396-8070
Email: cfswm@cfswm.org
Web: www.cfswm.org

COMMUNITY ACTION AGENCY
Lenawee Office
400 W South St.
Adrian, MI 49221
Burt Fenby, Director
Tel: (517) 263-7861 Fax: (517) 263-6531
Email: bfenby@caajlh.org
Web: www.caajlh.org

CORRECTIONAL ASSESSMENT & TREATMENT SERVICES
Ingham County Sheriff's Office
630 N. Cedar St.
Mason, MI 48854
Gene L. Wriggelsworth, Sheriff
Tel: (517) 676-2431 X4 Fax: (517) 676-8236
Email: gwriggelsworth@ingham.org
Web: www.ingham.org

HISPANIC CENTER OF WESTERN MICHIGAN
Affiliate of NCLR
730 Grandville Ave.
Grand Rapids, MI 49503
Emily Aleman, Executive Director
Tel: (616) 742-0200 Fax: (616) 742-0205
Email: hcwm@iserv.net

HISPANIC INTERNAL REVENUE EMPLOYEES
27277 Martinsville Rd.
New Boston, MI 48164
Barbara R. Parra-Vasquez, President
Tel: (313) 234-1205 Fax: (313) 234-1293
Email: barbara.vasquez@irs.gov

HISPANIC SERVICE CENTER
270 N. Cedar st
Imlay City, MI 48444
Norma Young, Executive Director
Tel: (810) 724-3665 Fax: (810) 924-7731
Email: imlayhsc@yahoo.com

MEXICANTOWN COMMUNITY DEVELOPMENT CORPORATION
2810 W Vernor
Detroit, MI 48216
Maria-Elena Rodriguez, President
Tel: (313) 967-9898 Fax: (313) 967-9903
Email: info@mexicantown.org
Web: www.mexicantown.org

NEW DETROIT, INC.
Affiliate of NCLR
3011 W Grand Blvd. #1200
Detroit, MI 48202-3013
Horacio Vargas, Director
Tel: (313) 664-2000 Fax: (313) 664-2071
Web: www.newdetroit.org

CASA MARIA FAMILY SERVICE CENTER
1500 Trumbull Ave.
Detroit, MI 48216
Ken Brown, Program Coordinator
Tel: (313) 962-4230 Fax: (313) 962-4251

DELTA TAU LAMBDA SORORITY, INC.
Alpha Chapter, University of Michigan
P.O. Box 7714
Ann Arbor, MI 48107
Darilis Garcia-McMillan, President/Founder
Tel: (734) 673-9879
Email: dtl-info@deltataulambda.org
Web: www.deltataulambda.org

LA VOZ LATINA
University of Michigan
Multi-Ethnic Student Affairs, 2202 Michigan Union
Ann Arbor, MI 48109
Harlyn Pacheco, President
Tel: (734) 763-9044 Fax: 734) 615-6842
Email: lavoz.latina@umich.edu
Web: www.umich.edu/~lavoz

LAMBDA THETA PHI, FRATERNIDAD LATINA, INC.
University of Michigan Alpha Omicron Chapter
610 S. Forest #5
Ann Arbor, MI 48104
Edgar Garza, President
Tel: (734) 789-1064
Email: egarza@umich.edu
Web: www.umich.edu/~ltpao/first.html

LATIN AMERICAN AND NATIVE AMERICAN MEDICAL ASSOCIATION
University of Michigan
University of Michigan
Ann Arbor, MI 48109
Lori Burke, President
Email: burkel@umich.edu
Web: www.umich.edu/~lanama

LATINO LAW STUDENTS ASSOCIATION
University of Michigan
Hutchins Hall, Legal Research 102A
Ann Arbor, MI 48109
Michelle Echeverria, Chair
Tel: (734) 763-0285
Email: llsa@umich.edu
Web: www.law.umich.edu/journalsandorgs/llsa/

NATIVE AMERICA & HISPANIC BUSINESS STUDENTS
Michigan State University
415 Eppley Ctr.
East Lansing, MI 48824-1121
Jose De La Maza, Advisor
Tel: (517) 353-3524

Email: delamaza@msu.edu
Web: www.msu.edu/~nahbs

PUERTO RICAN ASSOCIATION
University of Michigan
1206 Washtenaw Ct. #2
Ann Arbor, MI 48104
Celimar Valentin
Tel: (734) 883-4180
Email: cvalenti@umich.edu
Web: www.umich.edu/~pra/

SOCIETY OF HISPANIC PROFESSIONAL ENGINEERS
University of Michigan
1211 Beal Ave.
Ann Arbor, MI 48104
Lander Coronado-Garcia, President
Tel: (734) 763-3240 Fax: (734) 647-7126
Email: shpe@umich.edu
Web: www.engin.umich.edu/soc/shpe

MINNESOTA

NATIONAL SOCIETY OF HISPANIC MBAS
Minneapolis-St. Paul Chapter
P.O. Box 2911
Minneapolis, MN 55402
Harold Lockheimer, Chapter President
Tel: (612) 630-8052
Email: general@msp.nshmba.org
Web: http://msp.nshmba.org

RIVERVIEW ECONOMIC DEVELOPMENT ASSOCIATION
176 Concord St.
St. Paul, MN 55107
Mike DeTomaso, Executive Director
Tel: (651) 222-6347 Fax: (651) 222-8398
Email: md@districtdelsol.com
Web: www.districtdelsol.com/contact.html

CENTRO
1915 Chicago Ave.
Minneapolis, MN 55404
Tel: (612) 874-1412 Fax: (612) 874-8149
Email: centro@qwest.net
Web: www.centromn.org

NATIONAL LATINO PEACE OFFICERS ASSOCIATION
Minnesota State Chapter
P.O. Box 1223
Minnetonka, MN 55345
Bill Martinez, President
Tel: (877) 657-6200
Email: bill.martinez@ci.stpaul.mn.us
Web: www.nlpoa.org

HISPANOS EN MINNESOTA
HIV/AIDS Prevention Program
155 S. Wabasha St. #128
St. Paul, MN 55107
Jerry Guevara, Executive Director
Tel: (651) 227-0831 Fax: (651) 227-0834
Email: heminnesota1@qwset.net
Web: www.hispanosenMinnesota.org

CHICANO LATINO AFFAIRS COUNCIL
555 Park St.
St. Paul, MN 55103
Heladio F. Zavala, Chair
Tel: (651) 296-9587 Fax: (651) 297-1297
Email: clac.desk@state.mn.us
Web: www.clac.state.mn.us

SOCIETY OF HISPANIC PROFESSIONAL ENGINEERS
Minneapolis/St. Paul Professional Chapter
P.O. Box 28098
Woodbury, MN 55128
Elda Garcia Bloemendal, President
Tel: (651) 736-7576 Fax: (651) 733-2840
Email: etgarcia@mmm.com
Web: www.shpe.org

ARCHDIOCESE OF ST. PAUL & MINNEAPOLIS
Hispanic Ministry
1723 Bryant Ave. North
Minneapolis, MN 55411
Anne Attea, Director for Hispanic Ministry
Tel: (612) 529-7700 Fax: (612) 529-7618
Email: hispanicministry@archspm.org
Web: www.archspm.org

CATHOLIC CHARITIES OF ST. PAUL & MINNEAPOLIS
Hispanic Outreach
490 Hall Ave.
St. Paul, MN 55107
Fr. Larry Snyder, Executive Director
Tel: (612) 224-0799 Fax: (612) 224-1513
Email: ljohnson@ccspm.org
Web: www.ccspm.org

DIOCESE OF CROOKSTON
Hispanic Ministry Office
1200 Memorial Dr.
Crookston, MN 56716
Sr. Leona Ulewicz, CDP, Coordinator for Hispanic Affairs
Tel: (218) 281-4533 Fax: (218) 281-3328
Email: lulewicz@crookston.org
Web: www.crookston.org

DIOCESE OF WINONA
Hispanic Ministry
Box 588
Winona, MN 55987
Juan Valencia, Director for Hispanic Ministry
Tel: (507) 387-5587 Fax: (507) 457-3027
Email: jvalencia@ccwinona.org

DIOCESE OF NEW ULM
Hispanic Service Ministry
1400 6th St. North
New Ulm, MN 56073
Fr. Anthony Stubeda, Director
Tel: (507) 359-2966
Email: dnu@dnu.org

OUR LADY OF GUADALUPE CATHOLIC CHURCH
401 Concord St.
St. Paul, MN 55107
Martin Jaques, Deacon
Tel: (651) 228-0506 X12 Fax: (651) 224-5162

LIFE-WORK PLANNING CENTER
201 N. Broad St. #100
Mankato, MN 56001
Jane Hanson,Administrative Assistant
Tel: (507) 345-1577 Fax: (507) 345-1469
Email: janehan@hickorytech.net
Web: www.lwpc.org

DEPARTMENT OF CHICANO STUDIES
University of Minnesota Twin Cities Campus
2 Scott Hall, 72 Pleasant St. SE
Minneapolis, MN 55455
Louis Mendoza, Department Chair
Tel: (612) 624-6309 Fax: (612) 626-7904
Email: chicstud@tc.umn.edu
Web: www.cla.umn.edu/chicano

LA OPORTUNIDAD, INC.
2700 E. Lake St. #3100
Minneapolis, MN 55406
Eloisa Echavez, Executive Director
Tel: (612) 872-6165 Fax: (612) 872-0964
Email: oportunidad@oportunidad.org
Web: www.oportunidad.org

LATIN AMERICAN STUDIES PROGRAM
Carleton College
Leighton Hall 229
Northfield, MN 55057
Jay Levi, Director
Tel: (507) 646-4110 Fax: (507) 646-4044
Email: jlevi@carleton.edu
Web: http://webapps.acs.carleton.edu/curricular/
ltam

**PROGRAM FOR CULTURAL COOPERATION
SPAIN-USA**
University of Minnesota
Global Campus, 230 Heller Hall #271,19th
Ave. S.
Minneapolis, MN 55455
Holly Zimmerman, Coordinator
Tel: (612) 625-9888 Fax: (612) 626-8009
Email: zimme001@umn.edu
Web: www.umabroad.umn.edu/pub/pcc/pcc.html

JOB SERVICE SECURITY
Department of Economic Security
12 Civic Ctr. Plz. #1600A
Mankato, MN 56001
Janie Sandoval, Migrant Labor Representative
Tel: (507) 389-6723 Fax: (507) 389-2708
Email: jsandova@ngwmail.des.state.mn.us
Web: www.mnworks.org

MIGRANT HEALTH SERVICE, INC.
810 4th Ave. South
Moorhead, MN 56560
Joan Altanbernd, Director
Tel: (218) 236-6502 Fax: (218) 236-6507
Email: jaltenbernd@fargocity.com

CASA DE ESPERANZA
P.O. Box 75177
St. Paul, MN 55175
Marcela Soto, Chair
Tel: (651) 646-5553 Fax: (651) 646-5999
Email: info@casadeesperanza.org
Web: www.casadeesperanza.org

MIGRANT LEGAL SERVICES-SOUTHERN
Minnesota Regional Legal Services
46 E. 4th St. #700 Minesota Bldg.
St. Paul, MN 55101
Jennifer Stohl, Director
Tel: (651) 291-2837 X133 Fax: (651) 228-9450
Email: jennifer.stohl@smrls.org
Web: www.legalassist.org

SOUTHERN MINNESOTA LEGAL SERVICES
12 Civic Ctr. Plz. #3000
Mankato, MN 56002
Rosa Mooney, Paralegal
Tel: (507) 387-5588 Fax: (507) 387-2321
Email: mankato@smrls.org

CENTRO DE CRISIS
203 W. Clark St.
Albert Lea, MN 56007
Rose Homestead, Assistant Supervisor
Tel: (507) 373-2223 Fax: (507) 377-5505

CHICANOS LATINOS UNIDOS EN SERVICIO
Minneapolis Office
2700 E. Lake St. #1160
Minneapolis, MN 55406
Martina Mendez, Executive Assistant
Tel: (612) 746-3500 Fax: (612) 871-1058
Email: mmendez@clues.org
Web: www.clues.org

Elder Wellness Office
401 Concord St.
St. Paul, MN 55107
Cori Bruno, Manager
Tel: (651) 291-8174
Email: cbruno@clues.org
Web: www.clues.org

St. Paul Office
797 E. 7th St.
St. Paul, MN 55104
Mauren Acosta, Director of Fund Development
Tel: (651) 379-4200 Fax: (651) 292-0347
Email: macosta@clues.org
Web: www.clues.org

CLOUDFOREST INITIATIVES
P.O. Box 40207
St. Paul, MN 55104
Shelley Sherman, US Coordinator
Tel: (651) 592-4143
Email: cloudforest@hwpics.com
Web: www.cloudforestmexico.org

COMMON HOPE
P.O. Box 14298
St. Paul, MN 55114
Jim McDonald, President
Tel: (651) 917-0917 Fax: (651) 917-7458
Email: info@mn.commonhope.org
Web: www.commonhope.org

**LATIN AMERICAN-MEXICAN ASSOCIATION
FOR NETWORKING AND OPPORTUNITY**
P.O. Box 3373
Mankato, MN 56002-3373
Victoria Salas, Director
Tel: (507) 344-8361 Fax: (507) 344-8590
Email: lamano@gotocrystal.net
Web: www.la-mano.org

**MINNESOTA DEPARTMENT OF HUMAN
RIGHTS**
190 E. 5th St. #700
St. Paul, MN 55101
Jeff Holman, Communications Officer
Tel: (651) 296-5663
Email: Jeff.Holman@state.mn.us
Web: www.humanrights.state.mn.us

NEIGHBORHOOD HOUSE
179 Robie St. East
St. Paul, MN 55107-2360
Keri Kowski, Communications Associate
Tel: (651) 227-9291 Fax: (651) 227-8734
Email: kkowski@neighb.org
Web: www.neighb.org

NEIGHBORHOOD JUSTICE CENTER
500 Laurel Ave.
St. Paul, MN 55102
Joy Bartscher, Executive Director
Tel: (651) 222-4703 Fax: (651) 222-0931
Email: jbartscher@NJCinc.org
Web: www.njcinc.org

**BLACK, INDIAN, HISPANIC, AND ASIAN
WOMEN IN ACTION**
1830 James Ave. North
Minneapolis, MN 55417
Alice O. Lynch, Executive Director
Tel: (612) 521-2986 Fax: (612) 529-6745
Email: aolynch@biha.org
Web: www.biha.org

CADA HOUSE
P.O. Box 466

Mankato, MN 56002
Judy Anderson, Coordinator
Tel: (507) 625-7233 Fax: (507) 625-9431
Email: cada@ic.mankato.mn.us

MUJERES UNIDAS
55 8th St. South, Box 254
St. James, MN 56081
Laura Araka, Advocates
Tel: (507) 375-5770 Fax: (507) 375-5049
Web: www.inspire-hope.org

**CHICANO-LATINO YOUTH LEADERSHIP
INSTITUTE**
Region Nine Development Commission
P.O. Box 3367
410 E. Jackson St.
Mankato, MN 56001
Theresa Eckstein, Outreach Worker
Tel: (800) 450-5643 Fax: (507) 387-7105
Email: theresa.eckstein@juno.com
Web: www.rndc.org/programs/chyli/

LA RAZA STUDENT CULTURAL CENTER
University of Minnesota
300 Washington Ave. SE #211
Minneapolis, MN 55455
Nubia Esparza, Board Member
Tel: (612) 625-2995 Fax: (612) 627-7680
Email: laraza@umn.edu
Web: http://www.tc.umn.edu/~laraza/

LATINO LAW STUDENT ALLIANCE
University of Minnesota
22919th Ave. South
Minneapolis, MN 55455
Juan Vega, President
Tel: (612) 625-1000
Email: vega0026@umn.edu

SPANISH CLUB
University of St. Thomas
2115 Summit Ave. M/S 4102
St. Paul, MN 55105-1096
Dr. Jane Tar, Advisor
Tel: (651) 962-5152
Email: jdtar@stthomas.edu

MISSISSIPPI

DIOCESE OF BILOXI
Hispanic MInistry
720 E. Beach Blvd.
Long Beach, MS 39560
Rev. Louis Lohan, Director
Tel: (228) 863-1810

DIOCESE OF JACKSON
Office of Hispanic Ministry
P.O. Box 2248
Jackson, MS 39225-2248
Bro. Ted Dausch, Director of Hispanic Ministry
Tel: (601) 949-6931 Fax: (601) 960-8455
Email: ted.dausch@jacksondiocese.org
Web: www.jacksondiocese.org

ST. JAMES CATHOLIC CHURCH
El Ministerio Hispanic
845 Lakeshire Dr.
Tupelo, MS 38804
Elquin Gonzales, Coordinator
Tel: (662) 842-4881 Fax: (662) 844-0327
Email: spanish_st_james@bellsputh.net

MISSISSIPPI HISPANIC ASSOCIATION
P.O. Box 7138
Jackson, MS 39282
Paco Rosales, President

Tel: (601) 371-9009
Email: pacobev@aol.com
Web: www.mshispanicassociation.org

MISSOURI

ST. LOUIS CULTURAL FLAMENCO SOCIETY
P.O. Box 21818
St. Louis, MO 63109
Marisel Salascruz, Artistic Director
Tel: (314) 781-1537 Fax: (314) 781-6263
Email: marisel@stlflamenco.org
Web: www.stlflamenco.org

WARA BOLIVIAN FOLKLORIC DANCES
59 Forum Ctr.
Chesterfield, MO 63017
Carol Quick, Director
Tel: (314) 878-3033
Email: carolquick@yahoo.com

**HISPANIC ECONOMIC DEVELOPMENT
CORPORATION**
1427 W. 9th St. #201
Kansas City, MO 64101
Carlos E. Salazar, Director
Tel: (816) 221-3442 Fax: (816) 221-6458
Email: hedc@kchedc.org
Web: www.kchedc.org

NATIONAL SOCIETY OF HISPANIC MBAS
Kansas City Chapter
P.O. Box 45264
Kansas City, MO 64171
Julio F. Suarez, Chapter President
Tel: (913) 568-6823
Email: general@kansascity.nshmba.org
Web: http://kansascity.nshmba.org

**HISPANIC CHAMBER OF COMMERCE OF
GREATER KANSAS CITY**
1600 Baltimore #250
Kansas City, MO 64108
CiCi Rojas, President
Tel: (816) 472-6767 Fax: (816) 472-1252
Email: info@hispanicchamberofkc.com
Web: www.hispanicchamberofkc.com

**HISPANIC CHAMBER OF COMMERCE OF
METROPOLITAN ST. LOUIS**
P.O. Box 78386
St. Louis, MO 63178-8386
Maria Zywiciel, President
Tel: (314) 771-4788 Fax: (314) 771-4790
Email: hccstlmo@sbcglobal.net
Web: www.hccstl.com

AMISTAD HISPANO HABLANTE
3957 Geraldine Ave. #A
St. Ann, MO 63074
Tomas Diaz, President
Tel: (314) 427-4390
Email: tomas.diaz@sbcglobal.net

ARGENTINE SOCIETY OF ST. LOUIS
P.O. Box 6063
Chesterfield, MO 63006-6063
Cristina Santa Cruz, Founder/Editor
Tel: (636) 230-5044 Fax: (636) 230-5044
Email: ctraboulsi@aol.com

GRUPO ATLANTICO FROM COLOMBIA
1111 Dunston Dr.
St. Louis, MO 63146
Carmen S. Dence, Director
Tel: (314) 362-8425
Email: dencec@mir.wustl.edu

HISPANIC ARTS COUNCIL OF ST. LOUIS
#3 The Prado
St. Louis, MO 63130
Virginia Braxs, Vice President
Tel: (314) 863-0570
Email: mvbraxs@wustl.edu

HISPANIC CULTURAL DANCERS
2484 Pontchartrain Dr.
Florissant, MO 63033
Elisa Hillberg, Director
Tel: (314) 837-5746 Fax: (314) 837-5746
Email: apbender@yahoo.com

HISPANIC LEADERS OF GREATER ST. LOUIS
P.O. Box 1576
St. Louis, MO 63188
Jaime Torres Rivera, Chairman
Tel: (314) 539-5176 Fax: (314) 539-5489
Email: hlgstl@hotmail.com
Web: www.hispanicstlouis.com

PANAMENIAN SOCIETY OF ST. LOUIS
3752 St. Kevin Park Dr.
St. Ann, MO 63074
Janice Sheffer, President
Tel: (314) 428-0523
Email: sheffer90@hotmail.com

SPANISH SOCIETY OF ST. LOUIS
7107 Michigan
St. Louis, MO 63111-2841
Larry Arnowitz, President
Tel: (314) 351-2232

ENTERTAINMENT

FESTIVAL HISPANIC, INC.
2484 Pontchartrain Dr.
Florissant, MO 63033
Elisa Hillberg, Director
Tel: (314) 837-5746 Fax: (314) 837-5746
Email: hispanicfest@aol.com
Web: www.hispanicfestivalstl.com

LAW ENFORCEMENT

NATIONAL LATINO PEACE OFFICERS ASSOCIATION
Kansas City Chapter
P.O. Box 15078
Kansas City, MO 64106
Bill Aguirre, President
Tel: (877) 657-6200
Email: lpoaginovigil@hotmail.com
Web: www.nlpoa.org

MULTI-PURPOSE

CENTRO LATINO DE SALUD, EDUCACION Y CULTURA
601 Business Loop, 70 W. #208
Columbia, MO 65203
Alejandra Gudino, President
Tel: (573) 449-9442
Web: http://centrolatino.missouri.org

POLITICAL ACTION

HISPANIC ORGANIZATION FOR JUSTICE AND EQUALITY
5811 E Truman Rd. #108
Kansas City, MO 64126
Frank Perez, Executive Director
Tel: (816) 231-4400 Fax: (816) 231-4418
Email: hoje@sbcglobal.net

PROFESSIONAL

PERUVIAN AMERICAN MEDICAL SOCIETY
Missouri Chapter
322 Gascony Way
Warson Woods, MO 63122
Dr. Aníbal V. Zambrano, President
Email: akzambrano@hotmail.com
Web: www.pamsnational.org

RELIGIOUS

DIOCESE OF JEFFERSON CITY
Hispanic Ministry Office
P.O. Box 417
Jefferson City, MO 65102
Sr. Joyce Schramm, Coordinator for Hispanic Ministry
Tel: (573) 635-9127 Fax: (573) 635-0386
Email: hispanicmin@diojeffcity.org
Web: www.diojeffcity.org

DIOCESE OF KANSAS CITY & ST. JOSEPH
Hispanic Ministry Office
P.O. Box 419037
Kansas City, MO 64141-6037
Dale J. Mooney, Coordinator for Hispanic Ministry
Tel: (816) 756-1858 X241 Fax: (816) 756-0878
Email: mooney@diocesekcsj.org
Web: www.diocesekcsj.org

ARCHDIOCESE OF ST. LOUIS
Hispanic Ministry
20 Archbishop May Dr.
St. Louis, MO 63119
Hector Antonio Molina, Jr., Director
Tel: (314) 792-7890 Fax: (314) 792-7898
Email: hmolina@archstl.org
Web: www.archstl.org/offices/hispanic.htm

Diocese of Jefferson City
P.O. Box 417
605 Clark St.
Jeffersson City, MO 65102
Sr. Joyce Schramm, Coordinator
Tel: (573) 635-9127 Fax: (573) 635-0386
Email: hispanicmin@diojeffcity.org
Web: www.diojeffcity.org/hispanicmin.htm

DIOCESE OF SPRINGFIELD-CAPE GIRARDEAU
Office of Hispanic Ministry
601 S. Jefferson Ave.
Springfield, MO 65806
Milagros Calvetti, Hispanic Ministry Director
Tel: (417) 866-0841
Email: mcalvetti@dioscg.org

SPEC. INT., CHILD CARE

LATIN AMERICA CHILDCARE
1445 N. Boonville Ave.
Springfield, MO 65802
Ken Dahlager, Director
Tel: (800) 289-7071 Fax: (417) 862-3301
Email: office@latinamericachildcare.org
Web: www.latinamericachildcare.org

SPEC. INT., COUNSELING

GUADALUPE CENTER, INC.
Casa Feliz Counseling Center
2600 Belleview St.
Kansas City, MO 64108
Chris Medina, Executive Director
Tel: (816) 531-6911
Email: crmedina@guadalupecenters.org
Web: www.guadalupecenters.org

MATTIE RHODES COUNSELING & ART CENTER
Affiliate of NCLR
1740 Jefferson St.
Kansas City, MO 64108
Mary Lou Jaramillo, Executive Director
Tel: (816) 471-2536 Fax: (816) 471-2521
Email: mattie@crn.org
Web: www.mattierhodes.org

SPEC. INT., EDUCATION

CONSORTIUM FOR GRADUATE STUDY IN MANAGEMENT
5585 Pershing #240
St. Louis, MO 63112-4621

Peter J. Andrada III, Executive Director
Tel: (314) 877-5500 Fax: (314) 877-5505
Email: arandap@cgsm.org
Web: www.cgsm.org

DON BOSCO COMMUNITY CENTER, INC.
ESL Program
526 Campbell
Kansas City, MO 64106
David Holsclaw, Director
Tel: (816) 691-2832 Fax: (816) 221-8862
Email: holsclaw@donbosco.org
Web: www.donbosco.org

GUADALUPE CENTER, INC.
Alta Vista Charter High School
1722 Holly St.
Kansas City, MO 64108
Chris Medina, Executive Director
Tel: (816) 471-2582 Fax: (816) 471-2139
Email: crmedina@guadalupecenters.org
Web: www.guadalupecenters.org

LULAC NATIONAL EDUCATIONAL SERVICE CENTERS, INC.
301 E. Amour Blvd. #460
Kansas City, MO 64111
Yvonne Vasquez Rangel, Director
Tel: (816) 561-0227 Fax: (816) 561-8319
Email: infokan@lñesc-kansas.org
Web: www.lnesc-kansas.org

MINORITY ENGINEERING & SCIENCE PROGRAM
University of Missouri, Rolla
1870 Miner Cir., 212 Engineering Research Laboratory
Rolla, MO 65409
Jacques P. Fransaw, Coordinator
Tel: (573) 341-4212 Fax: (573) 341-4890
Email: mep@umr.edu
Web: http://campus.umr.edu/mep

SPEC. INT., EMPLOYMENT

RURAL MISSOURI, INC.
1014 Northeast Dr.
Jefferson City, MO 65109
Ken Lueckenotte, Executive Director
Tel: (573) 635-0136 Fax: (573) 635-5636
Email: ken@rmiinc.org
Web: www.rmiinc.org

SPEC. INT., HEALTH SERVICES

CABOT WESTSIDE CLINIC
1810 Summit St.
Kansas City, MO 64108
John V. Villanueva, Executive Director
Tel: (816) 471-0900 Fax: (816) 471-3150
Email: johnv@cabot.org
Web: www.hauw.org/cabot.htm

GUADALUPE CENTER, INC.
Health & Social Services
2641 Belleview
Kansas City, MO 64108
Chris Medina, Executive Director
Tel: (816) 561-6885 Fax: (816) 561-7009
Email: crmedina@guadalupecenters.org
Web: www.guadalupecenters.org

LA CLÍNICA
3646 Fairview Ave.
St. Loius, MO 63116
William Chignolli, President
Tel: (314) 664-5565 Fax: (314) 773-0709
Email: info@laclinica-stl.org
Web: www.laclinica-stl.org

SPEC. INT., HOUSING

ASSOCIATION OF COMMUNITY ORGANIZATIONS FOR REFORM NOW
Kansas City Office

6301 Rockhill Rd. #412
Kansas City, MO 64131
Roosvelt Johnson, Director
Tel: (816) 931-6611 Fax: (816) 931-6614
Email: moacornkcro@acorn.org
Web: www.acorn.org

WESTSIDE HOUSING ORGANIZATION
919 W 24th St.
Kansas City, MO 64108
Gerald Shechter, Executive Director
Tel: (816) 421-8048 Fax: (816) 421-8131
Email: whodidit@crn.org
Web: www.westsidehousing.org

SPEC. INT., SOCIAL INTEREST

ACCION SOCIAL COMUNITARIA
3646 Fairview Ave.
St. Louis, MO 63116
C. William Chignoli, Executive Director
Tel: (314) 664-5465 Fax: (314) 773-0709
Email: info@accionsocialcomunitaria.org
Web: www.accionsocialcomunitaria.org

NATIONAL CENTER FOR MISSING & EXPLOITED CHILDREN
Kansas City
1018 W. 39th St. #B
Kansas City, MO 64111
Steve McBride, Director
Tel: (816) 756-5422 Fax: (816) 756-1804
Email: kcbranch@ncmec.org
Web: www.missingkids.com

SPEC. INT., WOMEN

MANA-A NATIONAL LATINA ORGANIZATION
Kansas City Chapter
2100 Metropolitan
Kansas City, MO 66106
Elida Cardenas, Chapter President
Tel: (816) 361-9068
Email: ecardenas@kc.rr.com
Web: www.hermana.org

SPEC. INT., YOUTH

CAMP FIRE USA
National Headquarters
4601 Madison Ave.
Kansas City, MO 64112-1278
Stewart J. Smith, CEO
Tel: (816) 756-1950 Fax: (816) 756-0258
Email: info@campfireusa.org
Web: www.campfireusa.org

GUADALUPE CENTER, INC.
Our Lady of Guadalupe Elementary School
2310 Madison
Kansas City, MO 64108
Chris Medina, Executive Director
Tel: (816) 221-2539
Email: crmedina@guadalupecenters.org
Web: www.guadalupecenters.org

GUADALUPE CENTER, INC.
Plaza de Niños Pre-School
1711 Broadway
Kansas City, MO 64108
Chris Medina, Executive Director
Tel: (816) 472-5108 Fax: (816) 472-1735
Email: crmedina@guadalupecenters.org
Web: www.guadalupecenters.org

Sacred Heart Youth Center
814 W 26th St.
Kansas City, MO 64108
Chris Medina, Executive Director
Tel: (816) 221-5226 Fax: (816) 221-5347
Email: crmedina@guadalupecenters.org
Web: www.guadalupecenters.org

MONTANA

RURAL EMPLOYMENT OPPORTUNITIES
Billings Office
1739 Grand Ave. #A
Billings, MT 59102
Louis Brandt, District Manager
Tel: (406) 256-1140 Fax: (406) 256-8411
Email: info@reomontana.org
Web: www.reomontana.org

National Headquarters
P.O. Box 831
Helena, MT 59624
Bruce Day, Executive Director
Tel: (406) 442-7850 Fax: (406) 442-7855
Email: info@reomontana.org
Web: www.reomontana.org

MONTANA MIGRANT COUNCIL, INC.
3318 3rd Ave. N.#100
Billings, MT 59101
Claudia Stephens, Research & Development
Coordinator
Tel: (406) 248-3149 Fax: (406) 245-6636
Email: cstephens@180com.net

NEBRASKA

EL MUSEO LATINO
4701 S 25th St.
Omaha, NE 68107
Tel: (402) 731-1137 Fax: (402) 733-7012
Email: webmaster@elmuseolatino.org
Web: www.elmuseolatino.org

NATIONAL LATINO PEACE OFFICERS
ASSOCIATION
Omaha Chapter
P.O. Box 7164
Omaha, NE 68107
Mark Martinez, President
Tel: (877) 657-6200
Email: pepelpoa@msn.com
Web: www.nlpoa.com

AMERICAN GI FORUM OF UNITED STATES
3318 Jason Dr.
Bellevue, NE 68123
Al Garcia, Commander
Tel: (402) 291-6620
Web: www.agif.us/NE.htm

CHICANO AWARENESS CENTER
4821 S. 24th St.
Omaha, NE 68107-2704
Rebecca Valdez, Executive Director
Tel: (402) 733-2720 Fax: (402) 733-6720
Email: aramos@cacinc.org
Web: www.cacinc.org

MEXICAN-AMERICAN COMMISSION
P.O. Box 94965
Lincoln, NE 68509-4965
Cecilia Olivarez Huerta, Executive Director
Tel: (402) 471-2791 Fax: (402) 471-4381
Email: mac01@nol.org
Web: www.mex-amer.state.ne.us

NAF MULTICULTURAL HUMAN DEVELOPMENT
CORPORATION
306 E 6th St.
North Platte, NE 69101
Ella Ochoa, Executive Director
Tel: (308) 534-2630 Fax: (308) 534-9451
Web: www.nafmhdc.org

Grand Island Regional Office
1306 W 3rd St.
Grand Island, NE 68801
Silvester Juanez, Office Manager
Tel: (308) 385-5021 Fax: (308) 385-6029
Web: www.nafmhdc.org

Lexington Regional Office
1308 N Adams
Lexington, NE 68850-0616
Penny Ruiz, Office Manager
Tel: (308) 324-4266 Fax: (308) 324-3267
Email: pruiz@atcjet.net
Web: www.nafmhdc.org

Lincoln Regional Office
941 O St. #201
Lincoln, NE 68508
Federico Torres, Regional Director
Tel: (402) 434-2821 Fax: (402) 435-4803
Email: ftorres@alltel.net
Web: www.nafmhdc.org

Scottsbluff Regional Office
3305 N 10th St.
Gering, NE 69341-0552
Mona Alonzo, Regional Director
Tel: (308) 632-5831 Fax: (308) 632-3771
Email: egurrola@actcom.net
Web: www.nafmhdc.org

ARCHDIOCESE OF OMAHA
Hispanic Affairs
3216 N. 60th St.
Omaha, NE 68104
Angela Erevia, Director for Hispanic Ministry
Tel: (402) 558-3134 Fax: (402) 551-3050
Email: amerevia@archomaha.org
Web: www.archomaha.com

Juan Diego Center
5211 S 31st St.
Omaha, NE 68107
Ana Barrios, Program Director
Tel: (402) 731-5413 Fax: (402) 731-5865
Email: anab@ccomaha.org
Web: www.ccomaha.org

DIOCESE OF GRAND ISLAND
Hispanic Ministry Office
P.O. Box 651
214 W. 5th St.
North Platte, NE 69103
Rev. Paul J. Colling, Associate Director
Tel: (308) 324-4647 Fax: (308) 532-3574

LATINO AND LATIN AMERICAN STUDIES
University of Nebraska-Lincoln
420 University Terr.
Lincoln, NE 68588-0686
Miguel A. Carranza, Associate Professor
Tel: (402) 472-9983
Email: mcarranza1@unl.edu
Web: www.unl.edu/unlies/latino/latino.htm

OFFICE OF LATINO AND LATIN AMERICAN
University of Nebraska at Omaha
Arts and Sciences Hall #307
Omaha, NE 68182
Dr. Lourdes Gouveia, Director
Tel: (402) 554-3358
Email: lgouveia@mail.unomaha.edu
Web: http://avalon.unomaha.edu/ollas

HISPANIC COMMUNITY CENTER
2300 O St.
Lincoln, NE 68510
Holly Burns, Executive Director
Tel: (402) 474-3950 Fax: (402) 474-3842
Email: centrohispano@hispaniconline.com

NAF MULTICULTURAL HUMAN DEVELOPMENT
CORPORATION
Omaha Regional Office
4826 S. 24th St.
Omaha, NE 68107
Rose Herrera, Instructor
Tel: (402) 734-4100 Fax: (402) 734-4103

MEXICAN LADIES ASSOCIATION
3216 Rodeo Rd.
North Platte, NE 69101
Peggy Nila Mata, President
Tel: (308) 534-2494

NEVADA

HISPANIC CHAMBER OF COMMERCE OF
NORTHERN NEVADA
425 E Taylor
Reno, NV 89502
Eduardo Wagner, Executive Director
Tel: (775) 786-4100 Fax: (775) 786-4112
Email: ewagner@hccnn.org
Web: www.hccnn.org

LAS VEGAS LATIN CHAMBER OF COMMERCE
300 N 13th St.
Las Vegas, NV 89101
Otto Merida, Executive Director
Tel: (702) 385-7367 Fax: (702) 385-2614
Email: otto@lvlcc.com
Web: www.lasvegaslatincc.com

LATIN CHAMBER OF COMMERCE OF NEVADA
P.O. Box 7500
Las Vegas, NV 89125-2500
Otto Merida, Executive Director
Tel: (702) 385-7367 Fax: (702) 385-2614
Email: otto@lvlcc.com
Web: www.lasvegaslatincc.com

SOCIEDAD CULTURAL HISPANA, INC.
2065 Wagonwheel Ave.
Las Vegas, NV 89119
Fidel Torea, President
Tel: (702) 736-3881

NATIONAL LATINO PEACE OFFICERS
ASSOCIATION
Las Vegas Chapter
P.O. Box 15322
Las Vegas, NV 89114
José Montoya, Chapter President
Email: j3501m@lvmpd.com
Web: www.nlpoa.com

Nevada State Chapter
P.O. Box 1717
Las Vegas, NV 89125
Roberto Juarez, State President
Email: made4amerc@aol.com
Web: www.nlpoa.com

Reno Chapter
P.O. Box 7789
Reno, NV 89510-7789
Sgt. Modesto Reyes, Chapter President
Tel: (775) 329-8845
Email: modestoreyes2061@hotmail.com
Web: www.nlpoa.com

LEAGUE OF UNITED LATIN AMERICAN
CITIZENS
Farwest Region-Nevada
P.O. Box 20267

San Valley, NV 89433
Nickolas Martinez, State Director
Tel: (775) 747-1847 Fax: (775) 674-1889
Email: statedirector@nvlulac.org
Web: www.nvlulac.org

NEVADA ASSOCIATION OF LATIN
AMERICANS, INC.
National Headquarters
323 N. Maryland Pkwy.
Las Vegas, NV 89101
Terri Del Latorre, Executive Director
Tel: (702) 382-6252 Fax: (702) 383-7021

NEVADA HISPANIC SERVICES, INC.
National Headquarters
3905 Neil Rd. #02
Reno, NV 89502
Jesse Gutierrez, Executive Director
Tel: (775) 826-1818 Fax: (775) 826-1819
Email: office@nhs.reno.nv.us
Web: www.nhsreno.org

DIOCESE OF LAS VEGAS
Hispanic Ministry Office
P.O. Box 18316
Las Vegas, NV 89114-8316
Teresa Ruiz, Director for Hispanic Ministry
Tel: (702) 735-3500 Fax: (702) 735-8941
Email: ruiz@dioceseoflasvegas.org
Web: www.lasvegas-diocese.org

DIOCESE OF RENO
Hispanic Affairs
290 S Arlington Ave.
Reno, NV 89501-1211
Maripaz Ramos, Director for Hispanic Affairs
Tel: (775) 329-9274 Fax: (775) 384-8619
Email: dioceseofreno@catholicreno.org
Web: www.catholicreno.org

REFORMA
Nevada Chapter
Nevada State College, 1125 Nevada State Dr.
Henderson, NV 89012
Gregory Robinson, Chapter President
Email: gregory_robinson@nsc.nevada.edu
Web: www.reforma.org

LATINOS UNIDOS CELEBRANDO SALUD
Clark County Health District, 400 Shadow Ln. #A
Las Vegas, NV 89106
Gail Muniz, Facilitator
Tel: (702) 385-1924 Fax: (702) 759-1416
Email: muniz@cchd.org

EAST LAS VEGAS COMMUNITY
DEVELOPMENT CORPORATION
3320 Sunrise Ave. #108
Las Vegas, NV 89101
Margarita V. Rebollal, Executive Director
Tel: (702) 307-1710 Fax: (702) 307-1712
Email: getthefacts@elvcdc.org

GUATEMALAN UNITY COMMITTEE OF
NEVADA
3220 Sandy Ln.
Las Vegas, NV 89115
Israel Fuentes, President
Tel: (702) 385-1991 Fax: (702) 385-1949
Email: israelstrans@aol.com

STUDENT ORGANIZATION OF LATINOS
4505 Maryland Pkwy. Box 2023
Las Vegas, NV 89154-2023
Chelsie Campbell, President
Tel: (702) 895-4165 Fax: (702) 895-4996
Email: solunlv@yahoo.com
Web: http://sol.unlv.edu

NEW HAMPSHIRE

LATIN AMERICAN CENTER
521 Maple St.
Manchester, NH 03045
Greg Schinder, Director
Tel: (603) 669-5661 Fax: (603) 669-5265
Email: mvelasquez@snhs.org
Web: www.snhs.org

DIOCESE OF MANCHESTER
Hispanic Ministry
383 Beech St.
Manchester, NH 03103
Sr. Maria Luz Cervantes, Director
Tel: (603) 625-5655 Fax: (603) 626-1517
Web: www.catholicchurchnh.org

LATIN AMERICAN, LATINO, AND CARIBBEAN STUDIES
Dartmouth College
304-B Silsby Hall
Hanover, NH 03755-1804
Sheila Laplante, Program Administrator
Tel: (603) 646-1640 Fax: (603) 646-3050
Email: sheila.laplante@dartmouth.edu
Web: www.dartmouth.edu/~lalacs

HABLEMOS DE DIABETES
New Hampshire Minority Health Coalition
P.O. Box 3992
Manchester, NH 03105
Jeanie Holt, Director
Tel: (603) 627-7703 Fax: (603) 627-8527
Web: www.nhhealthequity.org/pro_diabetes.html

HUMAN LEUKOCYTE ANTIGENS
New England Satellite
171 Londonderry Rd.
Windham, NH 03087
Jackie McLoon, Recruitment Coordinator
Tel: (603) 437-9683 Fax: (603) 437-9685
Email: hlanewengland@att.net
Web: www.hlaregistry.org

LATIN AMERICAN CENTER
521 Maple St.
Manchester, NH 03104
Eileen Phinney, Program Coordinator
Tel: (603) 669-5661
Email: ephinney04@aol.com

NEW JERSEY

COMITE DE APOYO A LOS TRABAJADORES AGRICOLAS
P.O. Box 510
4 S. Delsea Dr.
Glassboro, NJ 08028
Nelson Carrasquillo, Executive Director

Tel: (856) 881-2507 Fax: (856) 881-2027
Email: cata@cata-farmworkers.org
Web: www.cata-farmworkers.org

LATIN AMERICAN ECONOMIC DEVELOPMENT ASSOCIATION, INC.
Affiliate of NCLR
129 N. Broadway #300
Camden, NJ 08102
Alfonso Castillo, Executive Director
Tel: (856) 338-1177 Fax: (856) 365-7205
Email: acastillo@laeda.com
Web: www.laeda.com

SPANISH MERCANTILE FEDERATION
4113 Palisade Ave.
Union City, NJ 07087
Manuel Fernandez, Director
Tel: (201) 865-1570 Fax: (201) 865-1570
Email: elsie@elespecial.com

CAMARA DE COMERCIO LATINA DE ELIZABETH
605 Elizabeth Ave.
Elizabeth, NJ 07206
Manuel Perez, President
Tel: (908) 289-0677 Fax: (908) 289-6833

ECUADORIAN-AMERICAN CHAMBER OF COMMERCE
61 Hudson St.
Hackensack, NJ 07601
Kley Peralta, President
Tel: (201) 342-5741 Fax: (201) 457-1683
Email: gizmet98@aol.com

GREATER NEW BRUNSWICK HISPANIC CHAMBER OF COMMERCE
P.O. Box 346
New Brunswick, NJ 08903
Harry Ayala, President
Tel: (732) 745-5120 Fax: (732) 565-7532
Email: harryayala@aol.com

HISPANIC AMERICAN CHAMBER OF COMMERCE OF ESSEX COUNTY
P.O. Box 9146
Newark, NJ 07104
Alex Garcia, Vice President
Tel: (973) 484-5441 Fax: (973) 350-9238
Email: jcallas@etcpc.com
Web: www.haccf.org

HUDSON COUNTY HISPANIC CHAMBER OF COMMERCE
6000 Madison St.
West New York, NJ 07093
Hilda Sosa, President
Tel: (201) 662-0052 Fax: (201) 662-8485
Email: hilda1118@aol.com

MORRIS COUNTY HISPANIC CHAMBER OF COMMERCE
P.O. Box 834M
Morristown, NJ 07960
Willie Montano, President
Tel: (973) 644-3093 Fax: (973) 984-3360
Email: wmontano@mchacc.org
Web: www.mchacc.org

PERTH AMBOY CHAMBER OF COMMERCE
P.O. Box 1546
Perth Amboy, NJ 08861
Gary Rumpf, President
Tel: (732) 442-7400 Fax: (732) 442-7450
Email: email@perthamboychamber.com
Web: www.perthamboychamber.com

STATEWIDE HISPANIC CHAMBER OF COMMERCE OF NEW JERSEY
150 Warren St. #110
Jersey City, NJ 07302
Daniel H. Jara, President/CEO
Tel: (201) 451-9512 Fax: (201) 451-9547
Email: djara@att.net
Web: www.shccnj.org

ALBORADA SPANISH DANCE THEATRE
55 Piersoll Rd.
Old Bridge, NJ 08857
Eva Lucena, Executive Director
Tel: (732) 255-4071
Email: alboradadance@aol.com
Web: www.alboradadance.org

SOCIEDAD CULTURAL BORINCANA, INC.
225 Market St., PMB 78
Patterson, NJ 07505
José A. Villalongo, Sr., President
Tel: (862) 571-2661 Fax: (973) 742-2710
Email: Villalongo@aol.com
Web: http://scborincana.tripod.com

CENTRO COMUNAL BORINCANO
832 S. 4th St.
Camden, NJ 08103
Sonia Plaza, Director
Tel: (856) 541-0179
Email: elcentro1211@aol.com

EL CLUB DEL BARRIO
76 Clinton Ave.
Newark, NJ 07114
Mercedes Valle, Secretary
Tel: (973) 624-4222 Fax: (973) 624-2932
Email: office@elclubdelbarrio.org
Web: www.elclubdelbarrio.org

FOCUS-HISPANIC CENSOR FOR COMMUNITY DEVELOPMENT, INC.
441-443 Broad St.
Newark, NJ 07102
Loyza Rivera, Public Relations Director
Tel: (973) 624-2528 Fax: (973) 624-6450
Email: info@focus411.org
Web: www.focus411.org

HOPE AND SEASON, INC.
211 S St.
Morristown, NJ 07960
Esperanza Porras-Field, President
Tel: (973) 267-8990 Fax: (973) 984-3360
Email: hopeseason@aol.com

LA CASA DE DON PEDRO INC.
Executive Office/Day Care Center
75 Park Ave.
Newark, NJ 07104
Raymond Ocasio, Executive Director
Tel: (973) 482-8312 Fax: (973) 482-1883
Email: lc.donpedro@aol.com
Web: www.lacasanwk.org

MERCER COUNTY HISPANIC ASSOCIATION
200 E State St., 2nd Fl., Bank of America Bldg.
Trenton, NJ 08607
Luisa Robinson, Executive Director
Tel: (609) 392-2446 Fax: (609) 695-7618
Email: lrobinson@njmecha.org

PUERTO RICAN ACTION BOARD
P.O. Box 240
New Brunswick, NJ 08903
Guillermo Beytagh Maldonado, Executive Director
Tel: (732) 828-4510 Fax: (732) 828-4546
Email: prabinc@aol.com
Web: www.prab.org

PUERTO RICAN CONGRESS OF NEW JERSEY, INC.
230 1st St.
Lakewood, NJ 08701
Lydia Valencia, Executive Director
Tel: (732) 905-7217 Fax: (732) 905-7969
Email: prci@prcongress.org

PUERTORRIQUEÑOS ASOCIADOS FOR COMMUNITY ORGANIZATION, INC.
390 Manila Ave.
Jersey City, NJ 07302

Elio Rivera, Executive Director
Tel: (201) 963-8282 Fax: (201) 653-5229
Email: info@pacoagency.com
Web: www.pacoagency.com

CENTRO HISPANO DE SERVICIOS SOCIALES
P.O. Box 2248
Willingboro, NJ 08046
Jose Ramos, Executive Director
Tel: (609) 835-1111 Fax: (609) 835-4366
Email: jramos@sascanj.org

SPANISH SPEAKING PEOPLES' COMMUNITY CENTER
Eastern Division
3900 Ventnor Ave.
Atlantic City, NJ 08401
Lydia Muñoz, Director
Tel: (609) 345-1249 Fax: (609) 345-8533

AMERICAN SPANISH COMMITTEE
P.O. Box 42
Leonia, NJ 07605-0042
Anthony F. Gonzalez, Chairman
Tel: (201) 567-7417 Fax: (201) 816-9727
Email: conquistadera1492@yahoo.com

CAMDEN COUNTY OFFICE OF HISPANIC AFFAIRS AND COMMUNITY DEVELOPMENT
520 Market St. #306
Camden, NJ 08102
Israel Nieves, Director
Tel: (856) 225-5312 Fax: (856) 225-5591
Email: hispanic@camdencounty.com

PUERTO RICO FEDERAL AFFAIRS ADMINISTRATION
New Jersey Regional Office
744 Broad St.
Newark, NJ 07102-3802
Gloria Soto, Regional Director
Tel: (973) 824-6030 Fax: (973) 824-6130
Email: info@prfaa.com
Web: www.prfaa.com

ASSOCIATION OF LATINO PROFESSIONALS IN FINANCE AND ACCOUNTING
Newark Chapter
P.O. Box 400034
Newark, NJ 07104
Alfredo Rivera, Chapter President
Tel: (201) 723-1241
Email: born2speak@aol.com
Web: www.alpfa.org

HISPANIC DIRECTORS ASSOCIATION OF NEW JERSEY
P.O. Box 25
New Brunswick, NJ 08903-0025
Daniel Santo Pietro, Executive Director
Tel: (732) 828-7606 Fax: (732) 828-7526
Email: dspietro@optonline.net
Web: www.hdanj.org

ARCHDIOCESE OF NEWARK
Hispanic Apostolate
171 Clifton Ave.
Newark, NJ 07104-0500
Maricela Quintana, Director
Tel: (973) 497-4334
Web: www.rcan.org

DIOCESE OF CAMDEN
Hispanic Ministry Office
15 N 7th St.
Camden, NJ 08102
Victor S. Muro, Director for Hispanic Ministry
Tel: (856) 756-7900 Fax: (856) 756-0297
Web: www.camdendiocese.org

DIOCESE OF METUCHEN
Our Lady of The Most Holy Rosary
625 Florida Grove Rd.
Perth Amboy, NJ 08861
Rev. Msgr. Glenn J. Comandini, Director for
Hispanic Ministry
Tel: (732) 826-2771 Fax: (732) 826-0320
Web: http://parishesonline.com

DIOCESE OF TRENTON
St. Mary's Cathedral
151 N Warren St.
Trenton, NJ 08608
Rev. John K. Bermond, Vicar for Hispanic Ministry
Tel: (609) 396-8445 Fax: (609) 396-5624

DIOCESE OF PATERSON
Office of Ministry Among Hispanics
777 Valley Rd.
Clifton, NJ 07013
Rev. Terrence Moran, CSSR, Director Tel: (973)
777-8818 X239
Email: tmoran@patersondiocese.org

**CENTER FOR HISPANIC POLICY, RESEARCH
AND DEVELOPMENT**
Department of Community Affairs
P.O. Box 800
Trenton, NJ 08625-0800
Angie Armand-Leon, Director
Tel: (609) 984-3223 Fax: (609) 984-0821
Email: chprd@dca.state.nj.us
Web: www.nj.gov/dca/chprd

**THE HISPANIC INSTITUTE FOR RESEARCH
AND DEVELOPMENT OF BERGEN COUNTY**
Administrative Office
17 Arcadian Ave.
Paramus, NJ 07652
Emilio S. Fandiño, Executive Director
Tel: (201) 368-1414 Fax: (201) 368-8985
Email: info@hird.org
Web: www.hird.org

**PUERTO RICAN ASSOCIATION FOR
COMMUNITY ORGANIZATION**
390 Manila Ave.
Jersey City, NJ 07302
Eliu Rivera, Executive Director
Tel: (201) 963-8282 Fax: (201) 653-5229

CURA, INC.
729 E. Landis Ave.
Vineland, NJ 08360
Magdalia Centeno, Director
Tel: (856) 696-7335 Fax: (856) 696-7334
Email: intake@curainc.org
Web: www.curainc.org

HISPANIC FAMILY CENTER, INC
2700 Westfield Ave.
Camden, NJ 08105
Cathy Saxton, Director
Tel: (856) 365-7393 Fax: (856) 365-1862
Email: cathysaxton@aol.com

**CHILDREN OF NICARAGUA FABRETTO
FOUNDATION**
426 Wesley Ave. 2nd Fl.
Ocean City, NJ 08226
Francis J. Rienzo, President
Tel: (609) 399-1534 Fax: (609) 399-1596
Email: francis@fabretto.org
Web: wwww.fabretto.org

NUESTROS NIÑOS DAY CARE CENTER, INC.
301 Garden St.
Hoboken, NJ 07030

Linda Lorence, Director
Tel: (201) 656-8317 Fax: (201) 656-3797
Email: nuestrosni@aol.com

PLAINFIELD BILINGUAL DAY CARE CENTER
225 W 2nd St.
Plainfield, NJ 07060
Eva J. Rosas-Amirault, Director
Tel: (908) 753-3124 Fax: (908) 753-3123
Email: eva.rosas@verizon.net
Web: www.plainfield.com/biling.htm

**PUERTO RICAN COMMUNITY DAY CARE
CENTER**
223 Perrry St.
Trenton, NJ 08618
Alma Garcia, Executive Director
Tel: (609) 392-8787 Fax: (609) 392-7905
Email: almagarcia@puertoricandaycare.org
Web: www.puertoricandaycare.org

ASPIRA OF NEW JERSEY, INC.
Executive Office
390 Broad St.
Newark, NJ 07104
Ivan Quervalu, President
Tel: (973) 484-7554 Fax: (973) 484-0184
Email: iquervalu@nj.aspira.org
Web: www.aspira.org

HISPANIC AFFAIRS OFFICE
Rutgers University
311 N 5th St.
Camden, NJ 08102
Miguel Greenup, Director
Tel: (609) 225-1766 Fax: (609) 225-6049
Email: greenup@camden.rutgers.edu
Web: www.rutgers.edu

LATIN AMERICAN STUDIES PROGRAM
Rutgers University
105 George St., Cook/Douglas Campus
New Brunswick, NJ 08901-1414
Tomás Eloy Martinez, Director
Tel: (732) 932-9323 Fax: (732) 932-2069
Email: eloy@rci.rutgers.edu
Web: www.rci.rutgers.edu/~rulas

PROGRAM IN LATIN AMERICAN STUDIES
Princeton University
58 Prospect Ave.
Princeton, NJ 08544
Deborah Yashar, Director
Tel: (609) 258-4148 Fax: (609) 258-0113
Email: plas@princeton.edu
Web: www.princeton.edu/~plas

**HISPANIC AFFAIRS & RESOURCES CENTER
OF MONMOUTH COUNTY**
913 Cewall Ave.
Ashbury Park, NJ 07712
Fatima Potente, Executive Director
Tel: (732) 774-3282 Fax: (732) 502-8955
Email: harc@monmouth.com

PUERTO RICAN UNITY FOR PROGRESS, INC.
Affiliate of SER-Jobs for Progress National, Inc.
427 Broadway St.
Camden, NJ 08103
Carmen D. Perez, Executive Director
Tel: (856) 541-1418 Fax: (856) 541-1476
Email: prupcm@aol.com

**PARENTS AND CHILDREN TOGETHER
ORGANIZED FOR FAMILY LEARNING**
P.O. Box 114
Allentown, NJ 08501
José Oliva, Director
Tel: (609) 259-7177
Email: pacto1983@aol.com

**HISPANIC FAMILY CENTER OF SOUTHERN
NEW JERSEY, INC.**
35 Church St.
Camden, NJ 08105
Elsa Candelario, Director
Tel: (856) 541-6985 Fax: (856) 963-2663
Email: hscfnj@aol.com
Web: www.hispanicfamilycenter.com

**HISPANIC FAMILY CENTER OF SOUTHERN
NEW JERSEY, INC.**
The Women's Resource Center
2700 Westfield Ave.
Camden, NJ 08105
Cathy Saxton, Director
Tel: (856) 365-7393 Fax: (856) 365-1862
Email: hscfnj@aol.com

HUMAN LEUKOCYTE ANTIGENS
800 Kinderkamack Rd. #300
Oradell, NJ 07649
Elie Katz, Ph.D., D.Sc., Founder
Tel: (201) 705-1799 Fax: (201) 265-2032
Email: danielleo@bcrbc.org
Web: www.communitybloodservices.org

THE PUERTO RICAN FAMILY INSTITUTE, INC.
New Jersey Clinic
40 Journal Sq. #302
Jersey City, NJ 07306
Nelida Arancibia, Director
Tel: (201) 610-1446 Fax: (201) 610-9426
Web: www.prfi.org

LATINO COMMUNITY LAND TRUST
206 E Hanover St.
Trenton, NJ 08608
David Baldes, President
Tel: (609) 695-1401 Fax: (609) 695-0710

**PUERTORRIQUENOS ASOCIADOS FOR
COMMUNITY ORGANIZATIONS, INC.**
180 4th St.
Jersey City, NJ 07302
Eliu Rivera, Executive Director
Tel: (201) 798-1446 Fax: (201) 798-0363
Email: info@pacoagency.com
Web: www.pacoagency.com

**BERGEN COUNTY COMMUNITY ACTION
PROGRAM, INC.**
241 Moore St.
Hackensack, NJ 07601
Robert F. Halsch, Jr., Executive Director
Tel: (201) 968-0200 Fax: (201) 968-0240
Email: rhalsch@bergencap.org
Web: www.bergencap.org

HISPANIC NATIONAL BAR ASSOCIATION
Region III (NJ)
c/o 650 Blvd. East #4E
West New York, NJ 07093-3932
Ramon de la Cruz, Regional President
Tel: (201) 869-0483 Fax: (201) 869-0483
Email: abogado@verizon.net
Web: www.hnba.com

EL PRIMER PASO, LTD.
29 Segur St.
Dover, NJ 07801
Amy Singeret, Director
Tel: (973) 361-0880 Fax: (973) 361-8033
Email: eppdir@attglobal.net

**FOCUS HISPANIC CENTER FOR COMMUNITY
DEVELOPMENT, INC.**
441-443 Broad St.
Newark, NJ 07102
Casto Maldonado, President & CEO
Tel: (973) 624-2528
Email: info@focus411.org
Web: www.focus411.org

**HISPANIC INFORMATION CENTER OF
PASSAIC, INC.**
186 Gregory Ave.
Passaic, NJ 07055
Lorenzo T. Hernandez, Executive Director
Tel: (973) 779-0260 Fax: (973) 779-0453
Email: hicpassaic@aol.com

HISPANIC MULTI-PURPOSE SERVICE CENTER
911 E. 23rd St.
Paterson, NJ 07513
Maria Magda O'Keese, Director
Tel: (973) 357-1006 Fax: (973) 684-7442

LA CASA DE DON PEDRO, INC.
75 Park Ave.
Newark, NJ 07104
Raymond Ocasio, Executive Director
Tel: (973) 482-8312 Fax: (973) 482-1883
Email: rocasio@lacasanwk.org
Web: www.lacasanwk.org

Community Improvement Center
317 Roseville Ave.
Newark, NJ 07107
Norma Sessa, Director
Tel: (973) 485-0701 Fax: (973) 485-7555
Email: nssesa@lacasanwk.org

PUERTO RICAN ACTION COMMITTEE, INC.
P.O. Box 444
Penns Grove, NJ 08069
David Rodriguez, Director
Tel: (856) 299-5800 Fax: (856) 299-3276
Email: drprac@verizon.net

PUERTO RICAN INSTITUTE
Seton Hall University
400 S. Orange Ave.
South Orange, NJ 07079
Sonia Ford, Bilingual Secretary
Tel: (973) 761-9422 Fax: (973) 275-2383
Email: picharel@shu.edu
Web: http://academic.shu.edu/pri/

**PUERTO RICAN ORGANIZATION FOR
COMMUNITY EDUCATION AND ECONOMIC
DEVELOPMENT , INC.**
1126 Dickinson St.
Elizabeth, NJ 07201
Teresa Soto Vega, Executive Director
Tel: (908) 351-7727 Fax: (908) 353-5185
Email: info@proceedinc.com
Web: www.proceedinc.com

RURAL OPPORTUNITIES, INC.
New Jersey Division
78 W Landis Ave.
Vineland, NJ 08360
Patricia Constantino, Executive Director
Tel: (856) 696-1000 Fax: (856) 696-4892
Email: pconstantino@ruralinc.org
Web: www.ruralinc.org

SPANISH SPEAKING PEOPLE
303 Sumner St.
Landisville, NJ 08326
Lydia Muñoz, Director
Tel: (856) 697-2967 Fax: (856) 697-0061
Email: spanishcommunitycenter@yahoo.com

LATINO INTERNATIONAL SKATING COALITION
353 W. Graisbury Ave.
Audubon, NJ 08106-2034
Arsenette Reiter, President
Email: LISC@snip.net
Web: www.latinoskating.org

NATIONAL ASSOCIATION OF CUBAN-AMERICAN WOMEN OF THE U.S.A
National Headquarters
308 38th St.
Union City, NJ 07087
Ziomara Sánchez, National President
Tel: (201) 271-9308 Fax: (201) 223-0035
Email: nacawcc@aol.com

NATIONAL WOMEN'S POLITICAL HISPANIC CAUCUS
New Jersey Chapter
P.O. Box 1546
Highland Park, NJ 08904-1546
Carmen Delia Díaz, Regional Representative
Tel: (732) 985-3967 Fax: (732) 393-0295
Email: carmen.diaz@att.net
Web: www.nwpc.org

NORTH HUDSON COMMUNITY ACTION-HEAD START PROGRAM
535 41st Ave.
Union City, NJ 07087
Lauren Johnson, Director
Tel: (201) 617-0901 Fax: (201) 601-0137

ASSOCIATION OF LATIN AMERICAN STUDENTS
Kean University
1000 Morris Ave.
Union, NJ 07083
Arcangela Cabrera, President
Tel: (908) 737-5197
Web: www.studentorg-ku.org/alas.html

LAMBDA SIGMA UPSILON LATINO FRATERNITY, INC.
National Headquarters
P.O. Box 645
Hoboken, NJ 07030
Freddy P. Rambay, President
Tel: (800) 578-1155 Fax: (800) 224-0654
Email: info@lsu79.org
Web: www.lsu79.org/one.htm

LAMBDA THETA ALPHA LATIN SORORITY, INC.
Bloomfield College/Beta Chapter
467 Franklin St.
Bloomfield, NJ 07003
Linda Cervantes, President
Tel: (973) 748-9000
Email: LTA.Cervantes@verizon.net
Web: www.lambdalady.org

LATIN AMERICAN SERVICE ORGANIZATION
St. Peter's College
2641 Kennedy Blvd.
Jersey City, NJ 07306
Idalia Borges, President
Tel: (201) 915-9000 Fax: (201) 915-9038
Email: laso@spc.edu

LATIN AMERICAN STUDENT ORGANIZATION
Montclair State University
Student Center, Annex #100
Upper Montclair, NJ 07043
Orville Morales, President
Tel: (973) 655-4440 Fax: (973) 655-7433
Email: l_a_s_o@hotmail.com

MOVIMIENTO ESTUDIANTIL CHICANO DE AZTLAN
National Headquarters
P.O. Box 1331
Trenton, NJ 08607
Luisa Robinson, Director
Tel: (609) 392-2446 Fax: (609) 695-7618
Email: lrobinson@comcast.net
Web: www.angelfire.com/sd/mcdsd/MEChALinks.html

NATIONAL BORICUA LATINO HEALTH ORGANIZATION
UMDNJ-Robert Wood Johnson Medical School
675 Hoes Ln.
Piscataway, NJ 08854
Cynthia Ferrer, Program Administrator
Tel: (732) 235-4684 Fax: (732) 235-3972
Email: ferrercl@umdnj.edu
Web: www2.umdnj.edu/saludweb

UNITED LATINO ASSOCIATION
Rowan Univesity
201 Mullica Hill Rd.
Glassboro, NJ 08028
Nancy Rosario, President
Email: rosari34@students.rowan.edu
Web: www.rowan.edu/open/clubs/ula/index.htm

NEW MEXICO

INSTITUTE FOR SPANISH ARTS
P.O. Box 8418
Santa Fe, NM 87504-8418
Maria Benitez, Director
Tel: (505) 955-8562
Email: flamenco@mariabenitez.com
Web: www.mariabenitez.com

LOS REYES DE ALBUQUERQUE FOUNDATION
1205 Lester Dr. NE
Albuquerque, NM 87112
Roberto Martinez, Director
Tel: (505) 299-3055

MILLICENT ROGERS MUSEUM
P.O. Box A
Taos, NM 87571
Shelby Tisdale, Executive Director
Tel: (505) 758-2462 Fax: (505) 758-5751
Email: stisdale@newmex.com
Web: www.millicentrogers.org

SPANISH COLONIAL ARTS SOCIETY, INC.
P.O. Box 5378
Santa Fe, NM 87502-5378
Stuart Ashman, Executive Director
Tel: (505) 982-2226 Fax: (505) 982-4585
Email: info@spanishcolonial.org
Web: www.spanishcolonial.org

TANGO CLUB OF ALBUQUERQUE
Lloyd Shaw Dance Center
5506 Coal Ave.
Albuquerque, NM 87108
Paul Akmajian, President
Email: tango_abq@yahoo.com
Web: www.geocities.com/tango_abq/

ASOCIACION DE COMERCIANTES LATINOS DE ALBUQUERQUE
202 Central Ave. SE
Albuquerque, NM 87102
Tel: (505) 247-9222 Fax: (505) 247-2557
Email: jdelgadillo@comcast.net

ASSOCIATION OF LATINO PROFESSIONALS IN FINANCE AND ACCOUNTING
Albuquerque Chapter
Internal Revenue Service-CI, 5338 Montgomery NE #301
Albuquerque, NM 87109
Katrina Lucero Romero, CPA, Chapter President
Tel: (505) 827-0354 Fax: (505) 837-9039
Web: www.alpfa.org

NEW MEXICO MINORITY BUSINESS ASSOCIATION
718 Central Ave. SW
Albuquerque, NM 87102
Tel: (505) 843-7114 Fax: (505) 242-2030
Email: info@nedainc.net

SIETE DEL NORTE
P.O. Box 400
Embudo, NM 87531
Amos A. Atencio, President
Tel: (505) 579-4217 Fax: (505) 579-4206
Email: amosatencio@cybermesa.com

ALBUQUERQUE HISPANO CHAMBER OF COMMERCE
1309 4th St. SW
Albuquerque, NM 87102
Alex O. Romero, President/CEO
Tel: (505) 842-9003 Fax: (505) 764-9664
Email: alex@ahcnm.org
Web: www.ahcnm.org

CLOVIS CURRY COUNTY HISPANIC AMERICAN CHAMBER OF COMMERCE
1404 N Lea
Clovis, NM 88101
Tel: (505) 762-5365 Fax: (505) 769-8236

HISPANO CHAMBER OF COMMERCE DE LAS CRUCES
P.O. Box 1964
Las Cruces, NM 88005
Gabe Ruiz, President
Tel: (505) 523-2681 Fax: (505) 523-4639
Email: gruiz@pnm.com
Web: www.lascruceshispanochamber.org

MEXICANO/CHICANO CHAMBER OF COMMERCE
1912 N Alabama St.
Silver City, NM 88061
Tel: (505) 388-8201 Fax: (505) 538-5598

NEW MEXICO HISPANO CHAMBER OF COMMERCE DEL NORTE
943 Don Cubero Ave.
Santa Fe, NM 87501
Andrés Romero, President
Tel: (505) 982-3094 Fax: (505) 982-3094

RATON COLFAX COUNTY HISPANO CHAMBER OF COMMERCE
P.O. Box 1041
Raton, NM 87740
Arturo Cruz, President
Tel: (505) 445-8242 Fax: (505) 445-8242
Email: rchcc@hotmail.com

ROSWELL HISPANIC CHAMBER OF COMMERCE
327 N. Main St.
Roswell, NM 88201
Melissa Urban, Executive Director
Tel: (505) 624-0889 Fax: (505) 624-0538
Email: info@roswellhcc.com
Web: www.roswellhcc.com

ASPECTOS CULTURALES
1219 Luisa St. #2
Santa Fe, NM 87505
Roberto Mondragón, Director
Tel: (800) 657-0366 Fax: (505) 986-1499
Email: cultura@aspectosculturales.com
Web: www.aspectosculturales.com

EL RANCHO DE LAS GOLONDRINAS
334 Los Pinos Rd.
Santa Fe, NM 87507
George B. Paloheimo, Director
Tel: (505) 471-2261 Fax: (505) 471-5623
Email: mail@golondrinas.org
Web: www.golondrinas.org

GUADALUPE HISTORIC FOUNDATION
Santuario de Guadalupe
100 S Guadalupe St.
Santa Fe, NM 87501
Leo Kahn, President
Tel: (505) 988-2027

MARTINEZ HACIENDA
Taos Historic Museums
P.O. Drawer CCC
Taos, NM 87571
Karen Young, Director
Tel: (505) 758-1000 Fax: (505) 758-0330
Email: thm@taoshistoricmuseums.com
Web: www.taoshistoricmuseums.com

MUSEUM OF INTERNATIONAL FOLK ART
P.O. Box 2087
Santa Fe, NM 87504-2087
Dr. Joyce Ice, Director
Tel: (505) 476-1204 Fax: (505) 476-1300
Email: info@moifa.org
Web: www.moifa.org

NATIONAL HISPANIC CULTURAL CENTER
1701 4th St. SW
Albuquerque, NM 87102
Tomas Chavez, Director
Tel: (505) 246-2261 Fax: (505) 246-2613
Web: www.nhccnm.org

NATIONAL HISPANIC CULTURAL CENTER FOUNDATION
1701 4th St. SW
Albuquerque, NM 87102
Mary Peña-Noskin, President
Tel: (505) 766-9858 Fax: (505) 766-9665
Email: mpnoskin@nhccnm.org
Web: www.hcfoundation.org

NEW MEXICO HISPANIC CULTURE PRESERVATION LEAGUE
P.O. Box 7956
Albuquerque, NM 87194
Conchita Lucero, President
Email: jrlmcl@qwest.net
Web: www.nmhcpl.com

SPANISH CLUB
Eastern New Mexico University
Station #19
Portales, NM 88130
Dr. Mary Ayala, Director
Tel: (505) 562-2451 Fax: (505) 562-2142
Email: mary.ayala@enmu.edu

HISPANIC AMERICAN POLICE COMMAND OFFICERS ASSOCIATION
Albuquerque Chapter
P.O. Box 883
Albuquerque, NM 87103-0883
Gilbert Najar, Chapter President
Email: najar@hapcoa.org
Web: www.hapcoa.org

AMERICAN GI FORUM OF UNITED STATES
New Mexico Chapter
3301 Mountain Rd. NW
Albuquerque, NM 87104
Louis Tellez, State Commander
Tel: (505) 242-5440 Fax: (505) 247-2993
Email: americangif@earthlink.net
Web: www.agif.us/NM.htm

AMIGOS DE LAS AMERICAS
Albuquerque Chapter
5901-J Wyoming, NE #118
Albuquerque, NM 87109
Dan Kutvirt, President
Tel: (505) 822-9870
Email: info@amigosabq.org
Web: http://amigosabq.org/

HANDS ACROSS CULTURES
P.O. Box 2215
Espanola, NM 87532
Harry Montoya, President/CEO
Tel: (505) 747-1889 Fax: (505) 747-1623
Email: hmontoya@aol.com
Web: www.HACC95.org

HISPANIC ROUND TABLE OF NEW MEXICO
P.O. Box 1275
Albuquerque, NM 87125
Juan Jose Pena, Chairperson
Tel: (505) 348-2092 Fax: (505) 248-8124
Email: jjp3000@aol.com
Web: www.hrtnm.org

HOME EDUCATION LIVELIHOOD PROGRAM,
5101 Copper NE
Albuquerque, NM 87108
John Martinez, Executive Director
Tel: (505) 265-3717 Fax: (505) 265-5412

LULAC NATIONAL EDUCATIONAL SERVICE CENTERS, INC.
500 2nd St. NW #500
Albuquerque, NM 87102
Frances A. Gandara, Director
Tel: (505) 243-3787 Fax: (505) 243-7850
Email: infoabq@lnesc-abq-nm.org
Web: www.lnesc-abq-nm.org

PARTIDO NACIONAL LA RAZA UNIDA
Albuquerque Chapter
P.O. Box 40376
Albuquerque, NM 87196
Xenaro Ayala, Director
Tel: (505) 255-9312
Email: pnlrunm@yahoo.com
Web: www.pnlru.org

INTERHEMISPHERIC RESOURCE CENTER
Albuquerque Office
P.O. Box 4506
Albuquerque, NM 87196
Tom Barry, Policy Director
Tel: (505) 842-8288 Fax: (505) 388-0619
Email: irc@irc-online.org
Web: www.irc-online.org

Silver City Office
P.O. Box 2178
Silver City, NM 88062
Laura Carlsen, Americas Program Director
Tel: (505) 388-0208 Fax: (505) 388-0619
Email: laura@irc-online.org
Web: www.irc-online.org

ARCHDIOCESE OF SANTA FE
Hispanic Affairs
4000 St. Joseph Pl. NW
Albuquerque, NM 87120
Deacon Juan Barajas, Director of Hispanic Ministry
Tel: (505) 831-8152 Fax: (505) 831-8206
Email: evangelization@archidiocesesantafe.org
Web: www.archidiocesesantafe.org

DIOCESE OF GALLUP
Hispanic Ministry Office
217 E Wilson Ave.
Gallup, NM 87301
Magda L. Garcia, HNSG, Hispanic Ministry Coordinator
Tel: (505) 722-5511 Fax: (505) 863-0075
Email: quadalupesjfrs@cnet.com
Web: www.dioceseofgallup.org

DIOCESE OF LAS CRUCES
Hispanic Ministry
1280 Med Park
Las Cruces, NM 88005
Carlos Corral, Vicar for Hispanic Ministry
Tel: (505) 523-7577 Fax: (505) 524-3874
Email: ccorral@dioceseoflascruces.org
Web: www.dioceseoflascruces.org

OUR LADY OF GUADALUPE PARISH
P.O. Box 288
Peralta, NM 87042
Albert Gallegos, Pastor
Tel: (505) 869-2189

CENTER FOR LATIN AMERICAN STUDIES
New Mexico State University
1200 University Ave. Box 3LAS
Las Cruces, NM 88003
Dr. Neil Harvey, Director
Tel: (505) 646-2842 Fax: (505) 646-2842
Email: nharvey@nmsu.edu

HISPANIC GENEALOGICAL RESEARCH CENTER OF NEW MEXICO
P.O. Box 51088
Albuquerque, NM 87181
Ronaldo Miera, President
Tel: (505) 836-5438
Email: hgrc@hgrc-nm.org
Web: www.hgrc-nm.org

LATIN AMERICAN AND IBERIAN INSTITUTE
University of New Mexico
801 Yale NE, MSC02 1690
Albuquerque, NM 87131-0001
Dr. Cynthia Radding, Director
Tel: (505) 277-2961 Fax: (505) 277-5989
Email: info@laii.unm.edu
Web: www.unm.edu/~laiinfo

SOUTHWEST HISPANIC RESEARCH INSTITUTE
University of New Mexico
University of New Mexico
Albuquerque, NM 87131
Margaret Montoya, Interim Director
Tel: (505) 277-2965
Email: montoya@law.umn.edu
Web: www.umn.edu/~shri

SPANISH COLONIAL RESEARCH CENTER
University of New Mexico
Zimmerman Library, MSC05 3020
Albuquerque, NM 87131-0001
Joseph P. Sánchez, Editor
Tel: (505) 277-1370 Fax: (505) 277-4603
Email: clahr@unm.edu
Web: www.unm.edu/~clahr

RIO GRANDE CENTER
P.O. Box 310
Embudo, NM 87531
Arturo Rangel, Executive Director
Tel: (505) 579-4251 Fax: (505) 579-4016
Email: riograndeinc@hotmail.com

HOME EDUCATION LIVELIHOOD PROGRAM,
Child Development Division
1252 Barker Rd.
Las Cruces, NM 88005
Gloria López, Director
Tel: (505) 523-2411 Fax: (505) 523-6646
Email: glopez@helpcdd.com
Web: www.helpcdd.com

EL CENTRO DE LA RAZA
The University of New Mexico
1153 Mesa Vista Hall, MSC06 3830
Albuquerque, NM 87131-0001
Verónica Méndez Cruz, Director
Tel: (505) 277-5020 Fax: (505) 277-5182
Email: vmcruz@unm.edu
Web: www.unm.edu/~elcentro/

HISPANIC EDUCATORS ASSOCIATION
New Mexico State University
Las Cruces, NM 88003-8001
Laura Morales, President
Tel: (505) 644-7059
Email: beyputt@aol.com
Web: www.nmsu.edu/~activ/Organizations/HispanicEA.html

HISPANIC ENGINEERING AND SCIENCE ORGANIZATION
University of New Mexico
Diversity Programs in School of Engineering, MSC 01-1080
Albuquerque, NM 87131-1381
Pedro A. Ramos, President
Tel: (505) 277-9046 Fax: (505) 277-9676
Email: hesorg@unm.edu
Web: www.unm.edu/~hesorg

NEW MEXICO ALLIANCE FOR HISPANIC EDUCATION
P.O. Box 25806
Albuquerque, NM 87125-5806
Edward Dobbs, President
Tel: (505) 342-3504
Email: information@nmalliance.org
Web: www.nmalliance.org

NEW MEXICO MATHEMATICS, ENGINEERING SCIENCE ACHIEVEMENT, INC.
2808 Central SE #122
Albuquerque, NM 87106
Michael R. Garcia, Executive Director
Tel: (505) 366-2500 Fax: (505) 366-2529
Email: pjc@NMMESA.NMT.EDU
Web: http://nmmesa.nmt.edu

REFORMA
1209 Camino Carlos Rey
Santa Fe, NM 87507
Leslie Monsalve-Jones, Chapter President
Tel: (505) 476-9718
Email: leslie@stlib.state.nm.us
Web: http://lib.nmsu.edu/reforma/

LAS CRUCES/SER-JOBS FOR PROGRESS, INC.
P.O. Box 2795
Las Cruces, NM 88004
Elvira Tobias, Executive Director
Tel: (505) 524-1946 Fax: (505) 524-1946
Email: etobias@ser-national.org
Web: www.ser-national.org

SER DE NEW MEXICO
1931 San Mateo NE
Albuquerque, NM 87110
Pete Salazar, Executive Director
Tel: (505) 268-4500 Fax: (505) 268-4499
Email: info@serdenm.org
Web: http://www.serdenm.org/

SER, SANTA FE JOBS FOR PROGRESS, INC..
2516 Cerillos Rd.
Santa Fe, NM 87505
Alex A. Martínez, Executive Director
Tel: (505) 473-0428 Fax: (505) 438-4813
Email: amartinez@hq.sersantafe.org
Web: www.ser-national.org

HOMEWISE
1570 Pacheco St. #A-1
Santa Fe, NM 87505
Michael Loftin, Executive Director
Tel: (505) 983-6214 Fax: (505) 983-4655
Email: info@homewise.org
Web: www.homewise.org

HISPANIC NATIONAL BAR ASSOCIATION
Region XV (NM, UT)
P.O. Box 27198
Albuquerque, NM 87125
Rosalie Fragoso, Regional President
Tel: (505) 841-6042 Fax: (505) 841-6009
Email: rfragoso@state.nm.us
Web: www.hnba.com

SOUTHERN NEW MEXICO LEGAL SERVICES
300 N Downtown Mall
Las Cruces, NM 88001

Ismael Alvarez, Deputy Director
Tel: (505) 526-4451 Fax: (505) 541-4840
Email: snmls@htg.net

AMIGOS DE BOLIVIA Y PERU
P.O. Box 901
Flora Vista, NM 87415
Ken Rustad, Steering Coordinator
Tel: (505) 325-9194
Email: peruybolivia@earthlink.net
Web: www.amigosdeboliviayperu.org

FUNDACION DE TIERRA PRESERVADA
369 Montezuma Ave. #277
Santa Fe, NM 87501-2626
Sarae T. Leuckel, Founder
Tel: (505) 757-8907 Fax: (505) 989-7381
Web: www.tierrapreservada.org

NMSU HISPANIC CAUCUS
New Mexico State University
P.O. Box 30001
Las Cruces, NM 88003-8001
Eric Lopez, Chair
Tel: (505) 646-2402
Email: leric@nmsu.edu
Web: www.nmsu.edu/hispanic-caucus

MANA- A NATIONAL LATINA ORGANIZATION
Albuquerque Chapter
5707 Morgan Ln. NW
Albuquerque, NM 87120
Evangeline Sandoval Trujillo, Chapter President
Tel: (505) 899-0761 Fax: (505) 792-8129
Email: estrujillo@yahoo.com
Web: www.hermana.org

Santa Fe Chapter
P.O. Box 9236
Santa Fe, NM 87504-9236
Sandra Rodriguez, Chapter President
Email: srodriguez@csf.edu
Web: http://www.hermana.org/chapfrm.htm

YOUTH DEVELOPMENT, INC.
516 1st St. NW
Albuquerque, NM 87102
Chris Baca, President/CEO
Tel: (505) 242-7306 Fax: (505) 843-7727
Email: cbaca@ydinm.org
Web: www.ydinm.org

ASSOCIATION OF LATINO PROFESSIONALS IN FINANCE AND ACCOUNTING
University of New Mexico
Anderson Schools of Management, MSC05 3090
Albuquerque, NM 87131
Robert Butler, President
Tel: (505) 255-3753
Email: rbutler@unm.edu
Web: www.unm.edu/~alpfa

BILINGUAL EDUCATION STUDENT
Eastern New Mexico University
ENMU Station 39, 1500 S Ave. K
Portales, NM 88130
Gloria Tapia, President
Tel: (505) 562-2995 Fax: (505) 562-2523
Email: gloria.tapia@enmu.edu

BRAZIL CLUB
University of New Mexico
Student Activities Box 8, MSC03 2210
Albuquerque, NM 87131
Michael Gradoville, President
Tel: (505) 681-4724
Email: onecanreachme@yahoo.com
Web: www.unm.edu/~brazil/

CAPOEIRA CLUB
University of New Mexico
Student Activities Box 130, MSC 03 2210
Albuquerque, NM 87131
Eric Bierke, President
Tel: (505) 710-0070
Email: ejbierke@yahoo.com
Web: www.unm.edu/~sac/ethnic.html

DESTINO
University of New Mexico
Student Activities Box 26, MSC03 2210
Albuquerque, NM 87131
Eva Gonzales, President
Tel: (505) 907-4494
Email: evag@unm.edu
Web: www.destinounm.org

EL CENTRO DE LA RAZA
University of New Mexico
1153 Mesa Vista Hall, MSC06 3830
Albuquerque, NM 87131-0001
Andrew Gonzalez, Coordinator
Tel: (505) 277-5020 Fax: (505) 277-5182
Email: andrew@unm.edu
Web: www.unm.edu/~elcentro

HISPANIC BUSINESS STUDENT ASSOCIATION
New Mexico State University
Chicano Programs, MSC 4188
Las Cruces, NM 88003
Berta Morales, President
Tel: (505) 646-4206 Fax: (505) 646-1962
Email: atreb143@aol.com
Web: www.nmsu.edu/~hbsa

University of New Mexico
Anderson Schools of Management, MSC05 3090
Albuquerque, NM 87131
Juan Sedillo, President
Tel: (505) 379-7975
Email: nauj_lobo@yahoo.com
Web: www.unm.edu/~hbsa

HISPANIC HONOR SOCIETY
University of New Mexico
Student Activities Ctr., Box 111 M/S/C 032210
Albuquerque, NM 87131-0001
Carmella Scorcia, President
Tel: (505) 266-2558
Email: carmella44@hotmail.com
Web: www.unm.edu/~hhonor

HISPANIC STUDENT ASSOCIATION
Clovis Community College
417 Schepps Blvd.
Clovis, NM 88101
Sandra Reyes Garcia, Co-Chair
Tel: (505) 769-4771 Fax: (505) 769-4190
Email: sandra.garcia@clovis.edu
Web: www.clovis.edu

LAMBDA THETA PHI LATIN FRATERNITY, INC.
University of New Mexico
Student Activities Ctr., Student Union 1018, Box 99 M/S/C 032210
Albuquerque, NM 87131
Ray Campos, President
Tel: (505) 277-4706
Email: lambda75@unm.edu
Web: www.unm.edu/~lambda75/

MEXICAN AMERICAN LAW STUDENT ASSOCIATION
University of New Mexico
117 Stanford NE, MSC11 6070
Albuquerque, NM 87131-0001
Denise M. Chanez, President
Tel: (505) 277-2146
Email: unm-malsa@law.unm.edu
Web: http://lawschool.unm.edu/organizations/malsa

MOVIMIENTO ESTUDIANTIL CHICANO DE AZTLAN
New Mexico State University
New Mexico State University
Las Cruces, NM 88003

Miguel de la Cruz, President
Tel: (505) 646-4206
Email: myleader17@hotmail.com

University of New Mexico
Student Activities Box 4, MSC03 2210
Albuquerque, NM 87131
Santiago Servizio, Chair
Tel: (505) 620-9616
Email: sservizi@unm.edu
Web: www.unm.edu/~mecha

RAZA GRADUATE STUDENT ASSOCIATION
University of New Mexico
1153 Mesa Vista Hall, El Centro de la Raza, MSC06 3830
Albuquerque, NM 87131
Joseph Garcia
Tel: (505) 277-5020
Email: mboravi@unm.edu
Web: www.unm.edu/~rgsa

SOCIETY OF HISPANIC PROFESSIONAL ENGINEERS
New Mexico State University
Las Cruces, NM 88003
Veronia Bunn, President
Tel: (505) 646-2510
Email: vbunn@nmsu.edu
Web: www.nmsu.edu/~activ/Organizations/SocietyHPE.html

STUDENT ORGANIZATION FOR LATIN AMERICAN STUDIES
University of New Mexico
Latin American Studies MSC 02 1690
Albuquerque, NM 87131
Sandra Ortsman, President
Tel: (505) 277-6847
Email: sandrita@unm.edu
Web: www.unm.edu/~sac

NEW YORK

ALMA SOLANA BALLET
45 Alto Ave.
Port Chester, NY 10573
John Mecca, Director
Tel: (914) 939-2409

AMERICAN SPANISH DANCE THEATER, INC.
Andrea Del Conte Danza España
144 E 24th St. #4A
New York, NY 10010-3730
Andrea del Conte, Executive Director
Tel: (212) 674-6725 Fax: (212) 674-6725
Email: adelconte@aol.com
Web: www.delconte-danza.com

THE AMERICAS SOCIETY
680 Park Ave.
New York, NY 10021
Veronica Clemens, Program Assistant
Tel: (212) 249-8950
Email: inforequest@as-coa.org
Web: www.americas-society.org

AMIGOS DE LA ZARZUELA
141 Strattford Rd.
New Hyde Park, NY 11040
Carmen B. Lombas-García, Executive Director
Tel: (212) 222-2655 Fax: (516) 742-4298

ANNABELLA GONZALEZ DANCE THEATER, INC.
4 E. 89th St. #P-C
New York, NY 10128-0645
Annabella González, Artistic/Executive Director
Tel: (212) 722-4128 Fax: (212) 722-4128
Email: agdt@mindspring.com
Web: www.agdt.org

ASSOCIATION OF HISPANIC ARTS
220 E. 106 St. #35

New York, NY 10029
William Aguado, Chairman
Tel: (212) 876-1242 Fax: (212) 876-1285
Email: ahanews@latinoarts.org
Web: www.latinoarts.org

BALLET HISPANICO
167 W. 89th St.
New York, NY 10024
Antonio Ortiz, Marketing Director
Tel: (212) 362-6710 X38 Fax: (212) 362-7809
Email: info@ballethispanico.org
Web: www.ballethispanico.org

BRONX COUNCIL ON THE ARTS, INC.
Main Office
1738 Hone Ave.
Bronx, NY 10461-1486
William Aguado, Executive Director
Tel: (718) 931-9500 Fax: (718) 409-6445
Email: bronxart@bronxarts.org
Web: www.bronxarts.org

BRONX MUSEUM OF THE ARTS
1040 Grand Concourse, 165th St.
Bronx, NY 10456-3999
Robert Sancho, Chair
Tel: (718) 681-6000 Fax: (718) 681-6181
Email: rsancho@bxma.org
Web: www.bxma.org

CAPOEIRA FOUNDATION/DANCE BRAZIL
246 W. 38th St., 8th Fl.
New York, NY 10018
Jelon Vieira, Artistic Director
Tel: (212) 382-0555 Fax: (212) 278-8555
Web: www.dancebrazil.org

EL PUENTE
Arts and Cultural Council for Youth
211 S. 4th St.
Brooklyn, NY 11211
Frances Lucerna, Executive Director
Tel: (718) 387-0404 Fax: (718) 387-6816
Email: flucerna@elpuente.us
Web: www.elpuente.us

EN FOCO, INC.
32 E. Kingsbridge Rd.
Bronx, NY 10468
Charles Biasiny-Rivera, Executive Director
Tel: (718) 584-7718 Fax: (718) 584-7718
Email: info@enfoco.org
Web: www.enfoco.org

FLAMENCO VIVO CARLOTA SANTANA
481 8th Ave. #744
New York, NY 10001
Ann Stuart, General Manager
Tel: (212) 736-4499 Fax: (212) 736-1326
Email: santana@flamenco-vivo.org
Web: www.flamenco-vivo.org

FOTOGRAFICA
484 W. 43rd St. #22T
New York, NY 10036
Perla de León, Director
Tel: (212) 244-5182 Fax: (212) 244-5182
Email: perlafotografica@aol.com

THE INSTITUTE FOR SPANISH ARTS
201 E 37th St. #3G
New York, NY 10016
Maria Benitez, Director
Tel: (212) 867-7338 Fax: (212) 867-7338
Email: flamenco@mariabenitez.com
Web: www.mariabenitez.com

INTAR HISPANIC-AMERICAN ARTS CENTER
P.O. Box 756
New York, NY 10036
Max Ferra, Artistic Director
Tel: (212) 695-6134 Fax: (212) 268-0102
Email: intarnewyork@aol.com

LATIN AMERICAN THEATER EXPERIMENT & ASSOCIATED, INC.
107 Suffolk St. #200
New York, NY 10002

Nelson Landrieu, Executive Director
Tel: (212) 529-1948 Fax: (212) 529-7362
Email: info@teatrolatea.com
Web: www.teatrolatea.com

MIND BUILDERS CREATIVE ARTS CENTER
3415 Olinville Ave.
Bronx, NY 10467
Madaha Kinsey-Lamb, Assistant Director
Tel: (718) 652-6256 Fax: (718) 652-7324
Email: mindbuilders@hotmail.com

NATIONAL ASSOCIATION OF LATINO INDEPENDENT PRODUCERS
East Coast Office
32 Broadway, 14th Fl.
New York, NY 10004
Edwin Pagan, President
Tel: (646) 336-6333 Fax: (212) 727-0549
Email: paganimage@aol.com
Web: www.nalip.org/newyork

NUYORICAN POETS CAFE
236 E. 3rd St.
New York, NY 10009
Carmen Pietri-Diaz, Executive Director
Tel: (212) 505-8183 Fax: (212) 475-6541
Email: nuyorican@mindspring.com
Web: www.nuyorican.org

PREGONES THEATER
571-575 Walton Ave.
Bronx, NY 10451·
Rosalba Rolón, Artistic Director
Tel: (718) 585-1202 Fax: (718) 585-1608
Email: info@pregones.org
Web: www.pregones.org

PUERTO RICAN TRAVELING THEATER COMPANY, INC.
141 W. 94th St.
New York, NY 10025
Miriam Colón Valle, Executive Artistic Director
Tel: (212) 354-1293 Fax: (212) 307-6769
Email: prttmy@aol.com

SOCIEDAD GENERAL DE AUTORES Y EDITORES
30 Copper Sq., 4th Fl.
New York, NY 10003
Emilio Garcia, Executive Director
Tel: (212) 752-7230 Fax: (212) 754-4378
Email: egarcia@sgae.org
Web: www.sgae.es

SPANISH THEATER REPERTORY COMPANY, LTD.
138 E. 27th St.
New York, NY 10016
Gilberto Zaldivar, Executive Producer
Tel: (212) 889-2850 Fax: (212) 225-9085
Email: repertorio@mindspring.com
Web: www.repertorio.org

TAHUANTINSUYO
P.O. Box 2340
Astoria, NY 11102
Guillermo Guerrero, President
Tel: (718) 728-1793 Fax: (718) 728-1793
Email: tawawan@aol.com
Web: http://hometown.aol.com/tawawan/myhomepage/index.html

TALLER BORICUA/PUERTO RICAN WORKSHOP
1680 Lexington Ave.
New York, NY 10029
Fernando Salicrup, Director
Tel: (212) 831-4333 Fax: (212) 831-6274
Email: info@tallerboricua.org
Web: www.tallerboricua.org

THALIA SPANISH THEATRE
P.O. Box 4368
41-17 Greenpoint Ave.
Long Island City, NY 11104
Kathrun Giaimo, Administrative Director
Tel: (718) 729-3880 Fax: (718) 729-3388
Email: info@thaliatheatre.org
Web: www.thaliatheatre.org

BUSINESS

ACCION NEW YORK
115 E. 23rd St.
New York, NY 10010
Robert Espaillat, President & CEO
Tel: (212) 387-0494 Fax: (212) 387-0277
Email: info@accionnewyork.org
Web: www.accionnewyork.org

ASOCIACION DE COMERCIANTES HISPANO
217-A Smith St.
Brooklyn, NY 11201
Ana Soreano, President
Tel: (718) 875-1214 Fax: (718) 875-1280

ASSOCIATION OF HISPANICS ORGANIZED TO RAISE AWARENESS
American Express Co.
World Financial Center, 200 Vesey St.
New York, NY 10285
Lourdes Sierra, Membership Director
Tel: (212) 640-1941 Fax: (212) 619-8610
Email: lourdes.sierra@aexp.com

ASSOCIATION OF YOUNG LATINO ENTREPRENEURS
P.O. Box 746
New York, NY 10029
Rey Hollingsworth, National Chair
Tel: (212) 828-8775
Email: info@ubslic.net
Web: www.ayle.org

AUDUBON PARTNERSHIP FOR ECONOMIC DEVELOPMENT LDC
Affiliate of NCLR
513 W. 207th St.
New York, NY 10034
Walther G. Delgado, Executive Director
Tel: (212) 544-2400 Fax: (212) 544-0248
Email: wdelgado@audubonpartnership.org
Web: www.audubonpartnership.org

COLOMBIAN AMERICAN ASSOCIATION, INC.
30 Vesey St. #506
New York, NY 10007
Linda Calvet, Executive Director
Tel: (212) 233-7776 Fax: (212) 233-7779
Email: andean@nyct.net
Web: www.colombianamerican.org

COUNCIL OF THE AMERICAS
680 Park Ave.
New York, NY 10021
Roselyn Nunez, Administrative Assistant
Tel: (212) 628-3200 Fax: (212) 249-1880
Email: inforequest@as-coa.org
Web: www.counciloftheamericas.org

CUBAN-AMERICAN ASSOCIATES
142-05 Roosevelt Ave. #324
Flushing, NY 11354
George Balbi, Director
Tel: (718) 762-1432 Fax: (718) 762-1432
Email: gbalbi@aol.com

DELI & GROCERY STORE OWNERS ASSOCIATION OF US
513 W 179th St.
New York, NY 10033
Tel: (212) 928-0252

MINORITY BUSINESS DEVELOPMENT AGENCY
New York Region
26 Federal Plz. #3720
New York, NY 10278
Heyward B. Davenport, Regional Director
Tel: (212) 264-3262 Fax: (212) 264-0725
Email: nyro-info@mbda.gov
Web: www.mbda.gov

MULTICULTURAL MARKETING RESOURCES INC.
286 Spring St. #201
New York, NY 10013
Lisa Skriloff, President
Tel: (212) 242-3351 Fax: (212) 691-5969
Email: pr@multicultural.com
Web: www.inforesources.com/

NATIONAL HISPANIC BUSINESS GROUP
7 W 51st St., 3rd Fl.
New York, NY 10019
Alexander Roca, Board Member
Tel: (212) 265-2664 Fax: (212) 265-2675
Email: info@nhbg.org
Web: www.nhbg.org

NATIONAL SUPERMARKETS ASSOCIATION
17-20 Whitestone Expressway #302
Whitestone, NY 11357
Tel: (718) 747-2860 Fax: (718) 747-2859
Email: nsa17200@aol.com

PUERTO RICAN/LATINO BUSINESS DEVELOPMENT CENTER
Empire State Development Corporation
633 3rd Ave., 32nd Fl.
New York, NY 10017
Martha Otero, Director
Tel: (212) 803-3227
Email: motero@empire.state.ny.us
Web: www.empire.state.ny.us

PUERTO RICO TOURISM COMPANY
666 5th Ave.
New York, NY 10103
Narciso Moreno, Director of Operations
Tel: (212) 586-6262 Fax: (212) 586-1212
Web: www.gotopuertorico.com

VENEZUELAN AMERICAN ASSOCIATION OF THE UNITED STATES, INC.
30 Vesey St. #506
New York, NY 10007
Alfredo González, President
Tel: (212) 233-7776 Fax: (212) 233-7779
Email: andean@nyct.net
Web: www.venezuelanamerican.org

CHAMBER OF COMMERCE

ARGENTINE-AMERICAN CHAMBER OF COMMERCE
630 5th Ave., 25th Fl.
New York, NY 10111
Alan Stoga, President
Tel: (212) 698-2238 Fax: (212) 698-2239
Email: argentinechamber@argentinechamber.org
Web: www.argentinechamber.org

BRAZILIAN AMERICAN CHAMBER OF COMMERCE
509 Madison Ave. #304
New York, NY 10022
Jennifer Sprance, Contact
Tel: (212) 751-4691 Fax: (212) 751-7692
Email: info@brazilcham.com
Web: www.brazilcham.com

BRONX HISPANIC CHAMBER OF COMMERCE
P.O. Box 5400-57
Bronx, NY 10454
Lorena Evia, President
Tel: (917) 213-3324
Email: l_evia@bronxhcc.org

CAMARA DE COMERCIO SALVADOREÑA USA
P.O. Box 4077
Garden City, NY 11531
Patricia Avalos, Vice President
Tel: (516) 680-2517 Fax: (516) 481-9693
Email: avalospat@aol.com

CARIBBEAN AMERICAN CHAMBER OF COMMERCE & INDUSTRY
63 Flushing Ave., Bldg. #5BNY
Brooklyn, NY 11205
Roy A. Hastick, Sr., President
Tel: (718) 834-4544 Fax: (718) 834-9774
Email: rahastick@msn.com
Web: www.cacci.org

DOMINICAN CHAMBER OF COMMERCE
110 E Burnside Ave.
Bronx, NY 10453
Leo V. Martinez, President
Tel: (718) 583-1900 Fax: (718) 583-8021
Email: reachlvm@netzero.net

DOMINICAN-AMERICAN CHAMBER OF COMMERCE OF NEW YORK, INC.
825 3rd Ave., 11th Fl.
New York, NY 10022
Eliezer Diaz, President
Tel: (212) 709-0218 Fax: (212) 269-2383
Email: info@dacc-ny.com
Web: www.dacc-ny.com

EAST HARLEM CHAMBER OF COMMERCE
186 E 116th St.
New York, NY 10029
Tel: (212) 996-2288 Fax: (212) 996-2283
Email: eastharlemchamber@aol.com

EL BARRIO CHAMBER OF COMMERCE
1665 Lexington Ave.
New York, NY 10029
Luis Malave, President
Tel: (212) 860-2455 Fax: (212) 876-5079
Email: malave39@msn.com

HISPANIC CHAMBER OF COMMERCE QUEENS
76-11 37th Ave. #203
Jackson Heights, NY 11372
Edwardo Giraldo, President
Tel: (718) 899-4418 X206 Fax: (718) 899-5998
Email: egiraldo@aol.com

LONG ISLAND HISPANIC CHAMBER OF COMMERCE
15 Atlantic Ave., 2nd Fl.
Lynbrook, NY 11563
Celeste M. Hernandez, Executive Director
Tel: (516) 256-2483 Fax: (516) 256-2463
Email: lihcc@optonline.net
Web: www.lihcc.com

MANHATTAN HISPANIC CHAMBER OF COMMERCE
P.O. Box 3494, Grand Central Station
New York, NY 10163
Maria Alvarez Castro, President/CEO
Tel: (212) 683-5955 Fax: (212) 683-5999
Email: manhattanhcc@aol.com
Web: www.nycmhcc.com

MEXICAN AMERICAN CHAMBER OF COMMERCE OF NORTHEAST USA
2710 Broadway, 2nd Fl.
New York, NY 10025
Jaime Lucero, President
Tel: (212) 531-0552 Fax: (212) 531-0064
Email: casapuebla@aol.com

NEW YORK STATE FEDERATION OF HISPANIC CHAMBERS OF COMMERCE
130 William St. 9th Fl.
New York, NY 10038
Lorraine Cortes-Vazquez, President
Tel: (212) 233-8955 Fax: (212) 233-8996
Email: info@hispanicfederation.org
Web: www.hispanicfederation.org

2710 Broadway
New York, NY 10025
Tel: (212) 222-8300 Fax: (212) 222-8412
Email: mnunez@sbbt.org

THE SPAIN-UNITED STATES CHAMBER OF COMMERCE
350 5th Ave. #2600
New York, NY 10118
Lidia del Pozo, Executive Director
Tel: (212) 967-2170 Fax: (212) 564-1415
Email: info@spainuscc.org
Web: www.spainuscc.org

UNITED STATES-MEXICO CHAMBER OF COMMERCE
380 Lexington Ave., 48th Fl.
New York, NY 10168
Eduardo Ramos-Gomez, Executive Director
Tel: (212) 471-4704 Fax: (212) 471-4701
Email: northeast@usmcoc.org
Web: www.usmcocne.org

WESTCHESTER HISPANIC CHAMBER OF COMMERCE
P.O. Box 80
White Plains, NY 10603
Felix Sanchez, President
Tel: (914) 328-7181 Fax: (914) 681-1978
Email: afrederico@unionstate.com

COMMUNICATIONS

CENTER FOR CUBAN STUDIES
124 W. 23rd St.
New York, NY 10011
Sandra Levinson, Executive Director
Tel: (212) 242-0559 Fax: (212) 242-1937
Email: cubanccr@igc.org
Web: www.cubaupdate.org

COMMUNICATIONS CAREERS FOR LATINOS, INC.
300 Park Ave. #1700
New York, NY 10022
Arthur Navarro, Founder
Tel: (212) 572-4861 Fax: (212) 572-4861
Email: anava95734@aol.com
Web: www.alct.org

HISPANIC INFORMATION AND TELECOMMUNICATIONS NETWORK
449 Broadway, 3rd Fl.
New York, NY 10013
José Luis Rodríguez, President
Tel: (212) 966-5660 Fax: (212) 966-5725
Email: pr@hitn.org
Web: www.hitn.org

NATIONAL ASSOCIATION OF MINORITIES IN COMMUNICATIONS
336 W. 37th St. #302
New York, NY 10018
Kathy A. Johnson, Executive Vice President
Tel: (212) 594-5985 Fax: (212) 594-8391
Email: kathy.johnson@namic.com
Web: www.namic.com

NATIONAL HISPANIC MEDIA COALITION
Puerto Rican Legal Defense and Education
99 Hudson St., 14th Fl.
New York, NY 10013-2815
Marta García, Founder & Co-Chair
Tel: (212) 965-9758 Fax: (212) 625-3768
Email: mediacoalition@aol.com
Web: www.nhmc.org

CULTURAL

THE AMERICAS SOCIETY, INC.
680 Park Ave.
New York, NY 10021
Daniel Shapiro, Director of Literature
Tel: (212) 249-8950 Fax: (212) 249-5868
Email: dshapiro@as-coa.org
Web: www.americas-society.org

BOYS AND GIRLS HARBOR
Conservatory for the Performing Arts and Raices Latin Music Collection
1 E. 104th St.
New York, NY 10029
Ramon Rodriguez, Director
Tel: (212) 427-2244 x573 Fax: (212) 427-3969
Web: www.harborconservatory.org

BRAZILIAN AMERICAN CULTURAL CENTER
16 W 46th St., 2nd Fl.
New York, NY 10036
Maria Sanchez, Executive Director
Tel: (800) 222-2746 X307 Fax: (212) 869-2685

CARIBBEAN CULTURAL CENTER
408 W. 58th St.
New York, NY 10019

Melady Capote, Executive Director
Tel: (212) 307-7420 Fax: (212) 315-1086
Email: mail@caribecenter.org
Web: www.caribecenter.org

CENTRO CIVICO CULTURAL AGUADILLANO, INC.
656 Willoughby Ave.
Brooklyn, NY 11206
Eva Martin, Director
Tel: (718) 443-2900 Fax: (718) 443-2905

CENTRO CULTURAL BALLET QUISQUEYA, INC.
2153 Amsterdam Ave. #11
New York, NY 10032
Normandía Maldonado, Executive Director
Tel: (212) 795-0107 Fax: (212) 795-0107

CENTRO CULTURAL MEXICANO
New York Office
27 E. 39th St.
New York, NY 10016
Generoso Villareal, Director
Tel: (212) 217-6421 Fax: (212) 217-6425
Email: info@lavitrina.com
Web: www.lavitrina.com

CHARAS, INC.
P.O. Box 2258
New York, NY 10009
Carlos García, Executive Director
Tel: (212) 534-2666 Fax: (212) 534-8988
Email: charas65@yahoo.com
Web: www.charas.org

CLEMENTE SOTO VELEZ CULTURAL & EDUCATIONAL CENTER
107 Suffolk St.
New York, NY 10002
Jude Figueroa, Interim Executive Director
Tel: (212) 260-4080 Fax: (212) 353-3707
Email: info@csvcenter.org

COMITE NOVIEMBRE
c/o Institute for Puerto Rican/Hispanic Elderly
105 E. 22nd St. #615
New York, NY 10010
Suleika Cabrera, Chair
Tel: (212) 677-4181 Fax: (212) 777-5106
Email: iprhe@aol.com

EL MUSEO DEL BARRIO
1230 5th Ave.
New York, NY 10029
Monica Armendariz, Public Relations
Tel: (212) 831-7272 Fax: (212) 831-7927
Email: info@elmuseo.org
Web: www.elmuseo.org

THE HISPANIC SOCIETY OF AMERICA
613 W. 155th St.
New York, NY 10032
Mencia Figuerora, Public Relation Coordinator
Tel: (212) 926-2234 Fax: (212) 690-0743
Email: figuerora@hispanicsociety.org
Web: www.hispanicsociety.org

HOSTOS CENTER FOR THE ARTS AND CULTURE
Hostos Community College
450 Grand Concourse Ave.
Bronx, NY 10451
Wallace I. Edgecombe, Director
Tel: (718) 518-6700 Fax: (718) 518-6690
Email: wedgecombe@hostos.cuny.edu

INSTITUTO CERVANTES AT AMSTER YARD
211-215 E. 49th St.
New York, NY 10017
Tel: (212) 308-7720 Fax: (212) 308-7721
Email: cenny@cervantes.es
Web: www.cervantes.org

LA CASA HERENCIA CULTURAL PUERTORRIQUEÑA, INC.
1230 5th Ave. #458
New York, NY 10029
Otilio Diaz, Executive Director
Tel: (212) 722-2600 Fax: (212) 722-3033

QUEEN SOFIA SPANISH INSTITUTE
684 Park Ave.
New York, NY 10021
Guillermo Salgado, Class Program Coordinator
Tel: (212) 628-0420 Fax: (212) 734-4177
Email: information@spanishinstitute.org
Web: www.spanishinstitute.org

SOCIEDAD PUERTORRIQUEÑA DE QUEENS, INC.
P. O. Box 6282
Long Island City, NY 11106
Betsy Dávila, President
Tel: (718) 204-9035 Fax: (718) 204-9035

THE SPANISH INSTITUTE
684 Park Ave.
New York, NY 10021
Inmaculada de Habsburgo, President/CEO
Tel: (212) 628-0420 Fax: (212) 734-4177
Email: information@spanishinstitute.org
Web: www.spanishinstitute.org

HISPANIC ORGANIZATION OF LATIN ACTORS
107 Suffolk St. #302
New York, NY 10002
Manny Alfaro, Executive Director
Tel: (212) 253-1015 Fax: (212) 253-9651
Email: holagram@hellohola.org
Web: www.hellohola.org

LOS PLENEROS DE LA 21
1680 Lexington Ave. #209
New York, NY 10029-4603
Juan Gutierrez, Director
Tel: (212) 427-5221 Fax: (212) 427-5339
Email: pleneros21@aol.com
Web: www.losplenerosdela21.org

ZONA DESIGN, INC.
Empire State Bldg., 350th Ave. #321
New York, NY 10118
Zoa Martines, President & Creative Director
Tel: (212) 244-2900 Fax: (212) 244-3101
Email: zmartinez@zonadesign.com
Web: www.zonadesign.com

HISPANIC AUXILIARY POLICE ASSOCIATION
4240 Hutchinson River Pkwy.
Bronx, NY 10475
Dolores Roque, President
Tel: (718) 320-5357

HISPANIC COURT OFFICERS SOCIETY OF THE STATE OF NEW YORK, INC.
National Headquarters
215 E 161st St.
Bronx, NY 10451
Bryan Negron, President
Tel: (718) 590-2920 Fax: (718) 590-0405

NATIONAL LATINO OFFICERS ASSOCIATION OF AMERICA
P.O. Box 02-0120
Brooklyn, NY 11201
Anthony Miranda, Executive Chairman
Tel: (866) 579-5809
Email: stmpfs@aol.com
Web: www.nloaus.org

ALIANZA DOMINICANA, INC.
La Plaza Beacon School/Affiliate of NCLR
515 W 182nd St.
New York, NY 10033
Moisés Pérez, Director
Tel: (212) 928-4992 Fax: (212) 795-8590
Email: mperez@alianza.org

BANANA KELLY, INC.
863 Prospect Ave.

Bronx, NY 10459
Orlando Marin, Chairman
Tel: (718) 328-1086
Web: www.synergos.org/usa/banana1.html

CITY OF WHITE PLAINS SERVICE OFFICE
65 Mitchell Pl.
White Plains, NY 10601
Martha Guarini, Assistant Officer
Tel: (914) 422-1255 Fax: (914) 422-1295

CLAREMONT NEIGHBORHOOD CENTERS, INC.
489 E 169th St.
Bronx, NY 10456
Rachel Spivey, Executive Director
Tel: (718) 588-1000 Fax: (718) 681-0736

COMMUNITY ACTION COUNCIL, INC.
Port Washington Office
382 Main St.
Port Washington, NY 11050
Mario Martínez, Director
Tel: (516) 883-3201 Fax: (516) 883-2467

COMMUNITY ASSOCIATION OF PROGRESSIVE DOMINICANS
3940 Broadway, 2nd Fl.
New York, NY 10032
Víctor Morisete, Executive Director
Tel: (212) 781-5500 Fax: (212) 927-6089
Email: vmorisete@acdp.org

COMPREHENSIVE COMMUNITY DEVELOPMENT CORPORATION
731 White Plains Rd.
Bronx, NY 10473
Pedro Espada, President
Tel: (718) 589-8771 Fax: (718) 893-7775
Email: nortiz@soundviewhealth.net

COUNCIL OF BROOKLYN ORGANIZATIONS, INC.
278 Broadway
Brooklyn, NY 11211
Leo Litvinichuck, Director
Tel: (718) 782-2832 Fax: (718) 782-2832

EAST SIDE HOUSE SETTLEMENT
337 Alexander Ave.
Bronx, NY 10454-1108
John A. Sánchez, Director
Tel: (718) 665-5250 Fax: (718) 585-1433
Email: jsanchez@eastsidehouse.org
Web: www.eastsidehouse.org

ESPERANZA DOMINICAN RELIEF
2152 Rathbun Rd.
Oneonta, NY 13820
L.J. Olivia, Founder/CEO
Email: info@esperanzadr.com
Web: www.esperanzadr.com

GODDARD RIVERSIDE COMMUNITY CENTER
593 Columbus Ave.
New York, NY 10024
Stephan Russo, Executive Director
Tel: (212) 873-6600 Fax: (212) 595-6498
Email: srusso@goddard.org
Web: www.goddard.org

GROSVENOR NEIGHBORHOOD HOUSE
176 W 105th St.
New York, NY 10025
Emily Lopez, Director
Tel: (212) 749-8500 Fax: (212) 749-4060

HAMILTON-MADISON HOUSE
50 Madison St.
New York, NY 10038
Frank T. Modica, Executive Director
Tel: (212) 349-3724 Fax: (212) 791-7540
Email: hmh100@hmh100.com
Web: www.hmh100.com

HARTLEY HOUSE
413 W 46th St.
New York, NY 10036
Mary Follet, Executive Director

Tel: (212) 246-9885 Fax: (212) 246-9855
Email: info@hartleyhouse.org
Web: www.hartleyhouse.org

HISPANIC SUPPORT ORGANIZATION
Verizon Communications
P.O. Box 2196
New York, NY 10008-2924
Alex Toro, President
Tel: (212) 395-1222 Fax: (212) 597-2697

HUDSON GUILD
441 W 26th St.
New York, NY 10001
Janice McGuire, Executive Director
Tel: (212) 760-9804 Fax: (212) 268-9983
Email: info@hudsonguild.org
Web: www.hudsonguild.org

IBERO-AMERICAN ACTION LEAGUE, INC.
Affiliate of United Way
911 E. Main St.
Rochester, NY 14605-2722
Julio Vázquez, President & CEO
Tel: (585) 256-8900 Fax: (585) 256-0120
Web: www.iaal.org

JOINT NEIGHBORHOOD PROJECT, INC.
532 E 2nd St.
Jamestown, NY 14701
Carmen Lydell, Coordinator for Spanish Outreach
Tel: (716) 664-7101 Fax: (716) 664-7103
Email: jnp@madbbs.com

LINCOLN SQUARE NEIGHBORHOOD CENTER
250 W 65th St.
New York, NY 10023
Stephanie Pinder, Executive Director
Tel: (212) 874-0860 Fax: (212) 799-6574
Email: spinder_lsnc@yahoo.com

NATIONAL CONGRESS OF PUERTO RICAN VETERANS, INC.
2434 E. Tremont Ave.
Bronx, NY 10461
Hector Cruz, Executive Officer
Tel: (718) 822-8077

NEW YORK CITY MISSION SOCIETY
105 E. 22nd St.
New York, NY 10010-5494
Stephanie Palmer, Executive Director
Tel: (212) 674-3500 Fax: (212) 979-5764
Email: advancement@nycmissionsociety.org
Web: www.nycmissionsociety.org

PROMESA
1776 Clay Ave.
Bronx, NY 10457-7239
Ruben Medina, Executive Director
Tel: (718) 299-1100 Fax: (718) 716-7822
Email: info@promesa.org
Web: www.promesa.org

RIDGEWOOD BUSHWICK SENIOR CITIZENS COUNCIL, INC.
Hope Gardens Multi-Service Center
195 Linden St.
Brooklyn, NY 11221
Anna Gonzalez, Director
Tel: (718) 455-1100 Fax: (718) 919-4705
Email: hopegardens@rbscc.org
Web: www.rbscc.org

SOUTH BRONX ACTION GROUP, INC.
384 E 149th St. #220
Bronx, NY 10455
Carmen Allende, Executive Director
Tel: (718) 993-5869 Fax: (718) 993-7904
Email: sbaginc@aol.com

SOUTH BRONX COMMUNITY CORPORATION
441 E 155th St.
Bronx, NY 10455
Maria Aguirre, Executive Director
Tel: (718) 585-5234 Fax: (718) 401-0154
Email: sbccmaguirre@aol.com

SPANISH ACTION COALITION
821 N Clinton Ave.
Rochester, NY 14605
Carlos Santana, Director
Tel: (585) 232-4050 Fax: (585) 232-3594
Email: cspanishaction@rochester.rr.com

UNITED BRONX PARENTS, INC.
La Escuelita
773 Prospect Ave.
Bronx, NY 10455
Lorraine Montenegro, Executive Director
Tel: (718) 991-7100 Fax: (718) 991-7643
Email: ubpexec@aol.com
Web: ubpinc.org

POLITICAL ACTION

COMMONWEALTH OF PUERTO RICO
Department of Puerto Rican Community Affairs
475 Park Ave., 7th Fl. South
New York, NY 10016
Laura M. Irizarry-Huertas, Regional Director
Tel: (212) 252-7300 Fax: (212) 726-9957
Web: www.prfaa.com

HISPANIC POLICY DEVELOPMENT PROJECT
National Headquarters
122 E. 42nd St., 42nd Fl.
New York, NY 10168
Siobhan Oppenheimer Nicolau, President
Tel: (646) 723-0750 Fax: (646) 723-0752
Email: siobhan96@aol.com

**NATIONAL ASSOCIATION OF LATINO ELECTED
AND APPOINTED OFFICIALS**
New York Chapter
60 E. 42nd St. #2222
New York, NY 10165
Enrique Ortiz, Director
Tel: (646) 227-0797 Fax: (646) 227-0897
Email: eortiz@naleo.org
Web: www.naleo.org

NATIONAL HISPANIC AMERICAN AGENDA
10-93 Jackson Ave. #3RR
Long Island City, NY 11101
Peter Fontanes, Chairman
Tel: (646) 721-0984
Email: email@hispanicsummit.org
Web: www.hispanicagendasummit.org

**NEW YORK STATE BLACK AND PUERTO
RICAN AND HISPANIC LEGISLATIVE CAUCUS**
Legislative Office Bldg. #442A
Albany, NY 12248
Adriano Espaillat, Chairman
Tel: (518) 455-5347 Fax: (518) 455-4535
Email: bpcaucus@assembly.state.ny.us
Web: www.assembly.state.ny.us

INSTITUTE FOR PUERTO RICAN POLICY
Affiliate of PRLDEF
99 Hudson St., 14th Fl.
New York, NY 10013
Cesar Perales, President/General Counsel
Tel: (212) 219-3360 Fax: (212) 431-4276
Email: cesar_perales@prldef.org
Web: www.prldef.org

**REPUBLICAN NATIONAL HISPANIC
ASSEMBLY**
RNHA-New York
148 E. Madison St.
East Islip, NY 11573
Larry Meneses, State Coordinator
Tel: (516) 381-3466 Fax: (631) 277-5701
Email: elrepublicano@mindspring.com
Web: www.rnha.org

SOMOS EL FUTURO, INC.
826 Legislative Office Bldg.
Albany, NY 12248
Peter Rivera, Chair
Tel: (518) 455-5102 Fax: (518) 455-3693
Email: info@somoselfuturo.org
Web: www.somoselfuturo.org

PROFESSIONAL

**ASSOCIATION OF LATINO PROFESSIONALS IN
FINANCE AND ACCOUNTING**
New York
1177 Ave. of the Americas, 18th Fl.
New York, NY 10036
Steven Mendez, Chapter President
Tel: (646) 471-1031
Email: president@newyork.alpfa.org
Web: www.alpfany.org

**INTERAMERICAN COLLEGE OF PHYSICIANS
AND SURGEONS**
New York Office
233 Broadway #771
New York, NY 10279
Rene F. Rodriguez, President
Tel: (212) 777-3642 Fax: (212) 267-5394
Email: info@icps.org
Web: www.icps.org

**NATIONAL ACTION COUNCIL FOR MINORITIES
IN ENGINEERING**
440 Hamilton Ave. #302
White Plains, NY 10601-1813
John Brooks Slaughter, President/CEO
Tel: (914) 539-4010 Fax: (914) 539-4032
Email: jslaughter@nacme.org
Web: www.nacme.org

NATIONAL SOCIETY OF HISPANIC MBAS
New York Chapter
P.O. Box 3328
New York, NY 10017
Marcela Solano, Chapter President
Tel: (212) 439-8054
Email: general@newyork.nshmba.org
Web: www.nshmba.org

PERUVIAN AMERICAN MEDICAL SOCIETY
New York, New Jersey & Connecticut Chapter
66 Waldord Ct.
Brooklyn, NY 11230
Dr. Ernesto A. Mendoza, President
Tel: (718) 421-4287
Web: www.pamsnational.org

THE PUERTO RICAN BAR ASSOCIATION
10 E. 40th St. #3702
New York, NY 10016
Dolly Caraballo, Esq., President
Tel: (212) 213-8860 Fax: (212) 213-1064
Email: dollycaraballo@aol.com
Web: www.prba.net

**SOCIETY OF HISPANIC PROFESSIONAL
ENGINEERS**
New York City Professional Chapter
Giampolo Rivera, Chapter President
Email: info@shpe-nyc.org
Web: www.shpe-nyc.org

Rochester New York Professional Chapter
P.O. Box 23643
Rochester, NY 14692
Aracelis Feliciano, Chapter President
Tel: (585) 422-0677
Email: rochester@reg4.shpe.org
Web: http://shperoc.speedhost.com

RELIGIOUS

ARCHDIOCESE OF NEW YORK
Hispanic Affairs
1011 1st Ave.
New York, NY 10022
Juan L. Blanchard, Director of Hispanic Ministry
Tel: (212) 371-1000 X2982 Fax: (212) 317-9429
Email: juan.blanchard@archny.org
Web: www.archny.org

**ASSOCIATION OF SPANISH SPEAKING
AMERICAN BAPTIST CHURCHES OF NEW
YORK METROPOLITAN AREA**
475 Riverside Dr. #432
New York, NY 10115

Hilda Rio, President
Tel: (212) 870-3195 Fax: (212) 870-3228

CATHOLIC DIOCESE OF ROCHESTER
Hispanic Ministry
1150 Buffalo Rd.
Rochester, NY 14624
Nemecio Martinez, Interim Coordinator
Tel: (585) 328-3210 X1358 Fax: (585) 328-3149
Email: martinez@dor.org
Web: www.dor.org

CENTRO CARISMATICO CATÓLICO HISPANO
826 E. 166th St.
Bronx, NY 10459
Josu Iriondo, Executive Director
Tel: (718) 378-1734 Fax: (718) 378-1819

DIOCESE OF ALBANY
Hispanic Outreach
801 Stanley St.
Schenectady, NY 12207
Kim Green, Director of Hispanic Outreach
Tel: (518) 382-2004 Fax: (518) 382-2695
Email: hosschenectadyng@choice1mail.com

DIOCESE OF ALBANY
Hispanic Outreach
40 N. Main Ave.
Albany, NY 12203
Anne Tranelli, Director
Tel: (518) 453-6677 Fax: (518) 453-6793
Email: anne.tranelli@rcda.org
Web: www.rcda.org

DIOCESE OF BROOKLYN
Hispanic Ministry
7200 Douglaston Pkwy.
Douglaston, NY 11362
Sonia Casanova, Director for Hispanic Ministry
Tel: (718) 229-8001 Fax: (718) 229-2658
Email: scasanova@iccdob.org

DIOCESE OF BUFFALO
Hispanic Affairs
795 Main St.
Buffalo, NY 14203-1215
Msgr. David M. Gallivan, Director
Tel: (716) 847-2217 Fax: (716) 847-2206
Email: dgallivan@buffalodiocese.org
Web: www.buffalodiocese.org

DIOCESE OF ROCKVILLE CENTRE
Hispanic Affairs
P.O. Box 9023
Rockville Centre, NY 11571-9023
Deacon Manuel J. Ramos, DirectorTel: (516)
678-5800 X618 Fax: (516) 678-1786
Email: mramos@drvc.org
Web: www.drvc.org

DIOCESE OF ROCKVILLE CENTRE
Hispanic Ministry
P.O. Box 9023
Rockville Centre, NY 11571-9023
Deacon Manuel J. Ramos, Director for Hispanic
Ministry
Tel: (516) 489-3675 Fax: (516) 485-8371
Email: mramos@drvc.org
Web: www.drvc.org

DIOCESE OF SYRACUSE
Spanish Apostolate
170 Seymour St.
Syracuse, NY 13202-3207
Rev. Robert D. Chryst, Director for Spanish
Apostolate
Tel: (315) 422-9390 Fax: (315) 422-9390
Web: www.syrdio.org

FIRST SPANISH PRESBYTERIAN CHURCH
161 S. 3rd St.
Brooklyn, NY 11211
Daniele Rivera, Pastor
Tel: (718) 388-0700

HOLY CROSS ASISTENCIA SOCIAL
600 Soundview Ave.
Bronx, NY 10473

Aubrey McNeil, Pastor
Tel: (718) 893-5550 Fax: (718) 378-3655

IGLESIA EVANGELICA ESPAÑOLA
800 E 156th St.
Bronx, NY 10455
Miguel Diaz, Pastor
Tel: (718) 993-1260 Fax: (718) 993-8378
Email: ieeb@verizon.net

LATINO AMERICAN DAWAH ORGANIZATION
P.O. Box 735
Bronx, NY 10465
Samantha Sanchez, President
Email: lado@latinodawah.org
Web: www.latinodawah.org

NORTHEAST HISPANIC CATHOLIC CENTER
Episcopal Regions I,II,III & IV
1011 1st Ave. #1616
New York, NY 10022-4134
Rudy Vargas, IV, Executive Director
Tel: (212) 751-7045 Fax: (212) 753-5321
Email: nhcc1011@aol.com

NORTHEAST PASTORAL CENTER
Hispanic Affairs Office
1753 1st Ave. #1233
New York, NY 10022
Juan Blanchard, Director
Tel: (212) 371-1000 X2982 Fax: (212) 753-9429
Email: haoffice@archny.org

DIOCESE OF RECOKVILLE CENTRE
Hispanic Ministry Office
50 N. Park Ave.
Rockville Centre, NY 11570
Manuel J. Ramos, Director
Tel: (516) 678-5800 x618
Email: mramos@drvc.org
Web: www.drvc.org/oldsite/departments/spanish.htm

ROMAN CATHOLIC DIOCESE OF ROCHESTER
Hispanic Apostolate Office
1150 Buffalo Rd.
Rochester, NY 14624
Nemesio Martinez, Interim Coordinator
Tel: (585) 328-3210 Fax: (716) 328-4142
Email: nmartinez@dor.org
Web: www.dor.org

RESEARCH

**CENTER FOR LATINO, LATIN AMERICAN, AND
CARIBBEAN STUDIES**
University at Albany, SUNY
SS-247, University at Albany, SUNY
Albany, NY 12222
Edna Acosta-Belen, Director
Tel: (518) 442-4590 Fax: (518) 442-4790
Email: lrr@albany.edu
Web: www.albany.edu/celac/

CENTER FOR PUERTO RICAN STUDIES
Hunter College of City University of New York
695 Park Ave.
New York, NY 10021
Dr. Felix Matos-Rodriguez, Director
Tel: (212) 772-5686 Fax: (212) 650-3673
Email: felix.matos@hunter.cuny.edu
Web: www.centropr.org

DEPARTMENT OF PUERTO RICAN STUDIES
John Jay College of Criminal Justice
1552 N Hall
New York, NY 10019
Jose Louis Morin, Director
Tel: (212) 237-8749 Fax: (212) 237-8742
Web: www.jjay.cuny.edu

INSTITUTE OF LATIN AMERICAN STUDIES
Columbia University
420 W. 118th St., 18th Fl.
New York, NY 10027
Albert Fishlow, Director
Tel: (212) 854-4643 Fax: (212) 854-4607
Email: af594@columbia.edu
Web: www.columbia.edu/cu/ilas

LATIN AMERICAN & CARIBBEAN STUDIES CENTER
State University of New York, Stony Brook
N-333 Social & Behavioral Sciences Bldg.
Stony Brook, NY 11794 -4345
Kathleen Vernon, Associate Professor
Tel: (631) 632-7569 Fax: (631) 632-9432
Email: kvernon@notes.cc.sunysb.edu
Web: http://naples.cc.sunysb.edu/CAS/lacc.nsf

LATIN AMERICAN STUDIES PROGRAM
Cornell University
190 Uris Hall
Ithaca, NY 14853
John Henderson, Director
Tel: (607) 255-3345 Fax: (607) 255-8919
Email: jsh6@cornell.edu
Web: www.einaudi.cornell.edu/latinamerica

LATINO STUDIES PROGRAM
Columbia University
660 Schermerhorn Ext., 1200 Amsterdam Ave.
New York, NY 10027
Prof. Francisco Rivera-Batiz, Director
Tel: (212) 854-0507 Fax: (212) 854-0500
Email: lsp@columbia.edu
Web: www.columbia.edu/cu/latino/mags/index3.htm

PUERTO RICAN HISPANIC GENEALOGICAL SOCIETY, INC.
P.O. Box 260118
Bellerose, NY 11426-0118
Miguel J. Hernandez, President
Tel: (914) 941-4920
Email: miguel.hernandez14@verizon.net
Web: www.rootsweb.com/~prhgs

TOMÁS RIVERA POLICY INSTITUTE
New York Office
Columbia University, 420 W. 118th St. M/C 3320
New York, NY 10227-7213
Rodolfo de la Garza, Vice President of Research
Tel: (212) 854-2292 Fax: (212) 222-0598
Email: info@trpi.org
Web: www.trpi.org

SPEC. INT., AIDS

AIDS COMMUNITY RESOURCES, INC.
627 W Genesee St.
Syracuse, NY 13204
Michael Crinnin, Executive Director
Tel: (315) 475-2430 Fax: (315) 472-6515
Email: info@aidscommunityresources.com
Web: www.aidscommunityresources.com

AIDS ROCHESTER, INC.
1350 University Ave.
Rochester, NY 14607
Paula Silvestrone, Executive Director
Tel: (585) 442-2220 Fax: (585) 442-5049
Email: info@aidsrochester.org
Web: www.aidsrochester.org

AMERICAN RED CROSS MINORITY OUTREACH
HIV/AIDS Services
786 Delaware Ave.
Buffalo, NY 14209
Nancy Blaschak, Director
Tel: (716) 886-7500 Fax: (716) 878-2220
Web: www.redcross.org/ny/buffalo

BIASHELP OF LONG ISLAND
P.O. Box 20369
Huntington Station, NY 11746
Jeffrey L. Reynolds, Chief Operating Officer
Tel: (631) 385-2451 (LIAAC) Fax: (631) 271-5200 (LIAAC)
Email: biaslpli@aol.com
Web: www.biashelp.org

BRONX AIDS SERVICES, INC.
540 E Fordham Rd.
Bronx, NY 10458
Sarageon Avery, Executive Director

Tel: (718) 295-5605 Fax: (718) 733-3429
Email: info@basnyc.org
Web: www.basnyc.org

CENTRO CIVICO OF AMSTERDAM, INC.
143-145 E. Main St.
Amsterdam, NY 12010
Ladan Alomar, Executive Director
Tel: (518) 842-3762 Fax: (518) 842-9139
Email: civico@telenet.net

HISPANIC AIDS FORUM
213 W 35th St., 12th Fl.
New York, NY 10001
Heriberto Sanchez Soto, Executive Director
Tel: (212) 563-4500 Fax: (212) 868-6237
Email: nyc2@hafnyc.org
Web: www.hafnyc.org

LATINO COMMISSION ON AIDS
24 W 25th St., 9th Fl.
New York, NY 10010
Dennis de León, President
Tel: (212) 675-3288 Fax: (212) 675-3466
Email: ddeleon@latinoaids.org
Web: www.latinoaids.org

LATINO RELIGIOUS LEADERSHIP PROJECT
Latino Commission on AIDS
24 W. 25th St., 9th Fl.
New York, NY 10010
Guillermo Chacon, Vice President
Tel: (212) 675-3288 Fax: (212) 675-3466
Email: gchacon@latinoaids.org
Web: www.latinoaids.org

MÚSICA AGAINST DRUGS, INC.
622 Broadway
Brooklyn, NY 11206
Alma Villegas, Executive/Artistic Director
Tel: (718) 218-7640 Fax: (718) 218-7650
Email: galeriamm@aol.com

SOUTHERN TIER AIDS PROGRAM, INC.
122 Baldwin St.
Johnson City, NY 13790
John Barry, Deputy Director
Tel: (607) 798-1706 Fax: (607) 798-1977
Email: info@stapinc.org
Web: www.stapinc.org

UNITED BRONX PARENTS, INC.
Casita Esperanza
974 Prospect Ave.
Bronx, NY 10459
Valentina Di Tomasso, Director
Tel: (718) 893-6555 Fax: (718) 893-2850
Web: www.ubpinc.org

UNITED BRONX PARENTS, INC.
Mrs. A's Place
966 Prospect Ave.
Bronx, NY 10459
Lorraine Montenegro, Executive Director
Tel: (718) 617-6060 Fax: (718) 589-2986
Web: www.ubpinc.org

SPEC. INT., ALCOHOL/DRUG CENTER

ALCOHOL AND DRUG DEPENDENCY SERVICES, INC.
291 Elm St.
Buffalo, NY 14203
Richard J. Gallager, Executive Director
Tel: (716) 854-2977 Fax: (716) 854-1223

ARMS ACRES, INC.
75 Seminary Hill Rd.
Carmel, NY 10512
Patrice Wallace-Moore, Executive Director
Tel: (845) 225-3400 Fax: (845) 228-5465
Email: pwallace-moore@libertymgt.com
Web: www.armsacres.com

1841 Broadway #300
New York, NY 10023
Trish Attia, Director
Tel: (212) 399-6902 Fax: (212) 399-6906
Web: www.armsacres.com

CARVER COMMUNITY COUNSELING SERVICES
846 State St.
Schenectady, NY 12307
Guido Iovinella, Program Director
Tel: (518) 382-7838 Fax: (518) 382-1641

CATHOLIC FAMILY CENTER RESTART
55 Troup St.
Rochester, NY 14608
Dawn Holman, Administrative Assistant
Tel: (585) 546-3046 Fax: (585) 546-2607
Email: dholman@cfcrochester.org
Web: www.cfcrochester.org

COMMUNITY ACTION ORGANIZATION/DART
1237 Main St.
Buffalo, NY 14209
Kenneth Bossert, Program Administrator
Tel: (716) 884-9101 Fax: (716) 884-7703

EL COMIENZO ALCOHOL PROGRAM
951 Niagara St.
Buffalo, NY 14213
Mildred Colon, Director
Tel: (716) 883-5344 Fax: (716) 884-1758

EL REGRESO, INC.
North Brooklyn Communities of Williamsburg-Bushwick-Greenpoint
189-191 S 2nd St.
Brooklyn, NY 11211
Carlos Pagan, Executive Director
Tel: (718) 384-6400 Fax: (718) 384-0540
Email: elregreso@aol.com

HUNTS POINT MULTI-SERVICE CENTER
Drug Abuse Center
754 E 151st St.
Bronx, NY 10455
Manuel Colon, Acting Director
Tel: (718) 401-5420 Fax: (718) 665-9782
Email: dcolon@hpmsc.org

INWOOD COMMUNITY SERVICE
651 Academy St., 3rd Fl.
New York, NY 10034
Charly Corliss, Program Director
Tel: (212) 942-0043 Fax: (212) 567-9476
Email: inwoodsvc@aol.com

SOUTH BRONX MENTAL HEALTH COUNCIL, INC.
Alcoholism Out Patient Clinic
1241 Lafayette Ave.
Bronx, NY 10474
Albert Negron, Program Director
Tel: (718) 378-6500 Fax: (718) 842-3846

VIDA FAMILY SERVICES, INC.
127 E 105th St.
New York, NY 10029
Olga Vazquez, CEO
Tel: (212) 289-1004 Fax: (212) 427-3433
Email: vidafamilysvces@aol.com

SPEC. INT., CHILD CARE

AGUADILLA DAY CARE CENTER
656 Willoughby Ave.
Brooklyn, NY 11206
Laticia Vega, Administrator
Tel: (718) 443-2900 Fax: (718) 443-2905
Email: jomimeal@aol.com

AMISTAD CHILD DAY CARE CENTER
110-15 164th Pl.
Jamaica, NY 11433
Jennie Campanelli, Executive Director
Tel: (718) 526-5911 Fax: (718) 526-1527

CONCILIO PUERTO RICO DAY CARE CENTER
180 Suffolk St.
New York, NY 10002
Cecilia M. Abrilla, Executive Director
Tel: (212) 674-6730 Fax: (212) 253-7110

DAWNING VILLAGE DAY CARE CENTER
2090 1st Ave.
New York, NY 10029
Conmstance Mavrovitis, Director
Tel: (212) 369-5313 Fax: (212) 369-5850
Email: dawningvillage@yahoo.com

DR. RICHARD GREEN DAY CARE CENTER
450 Castle Hill Ave.
Bronx, NY 10473
Milagros del Marrero, Director
Tel: (718) 904-1689 Fax: (718) 904-1833

HAVERSTRAW ECUMENICAL PROJECT/DAY CARE CENTER
34 1st St.
Haverstraw, NY 10927
Daysi Rivera, Administrator
Tel: (845) 429-5263 Fax: (845) 429-0507
Email: hepkids@aol.com

HUNTS POINT MULTI-SERVICE CENTER
Family Day Care
630 Jackson Ave.
Bronx, NY 10455
Sandra Stone, Director
Tel: (718) 993-3004 Fax: (718) 292-3317

LA PUERTA ABIERTA
2864 W 21st St.
Brooklyn, NY 11224
Jayne Doyle, Administrator
Tel: (718) 373-1100 Fax: (718) 449-0538

LITTLE SHEPHERDS DAY CARE CENTER
2260 Andrews Ave.
Bronx, NY 10468
Dexter Cruzado, Executive Director
Tel: (718) 295-2740 Fax: (718) 364-6706

NUESTROS NIÑO DAY CARE CENTER
384 S. 4th St.
Brooklyn, NY 11211
Mirian L. Cruz, Director
Tel: (718) 963-1555 Fax: (718) 963-0240
Email: nuestrosninoscds@aol.com

PAMELA C. TORRES DAY CARE CENTER, INC.
161 Saint Anns Ave.
Bronx, NY 10454
Nilza Cruz, Director
Tel: (718) 585-2540 Fax: (718) 585-2421
Email: nilzan@aol.com

PARK SLOPE FAMILY DAY CARE
333 14th St.
Brooklyn, NY 11215
Lucia B. Ferraz, Director
Tel: (718) 788-7803 Fax: (718) 788-0631

PEQUEÑOS SOULS DAY CARE CENTER
114-34 E 122nd St.
New York, NY 10035
Esther L. Smith, Director
Tel: (212) 427-7644 Fax: (212) 427-7645
Email: psdcc@aol.com

SHIRLEY CHISHOLM DAY CARE CENTER
333 14th St.
Brooklyn, NY 11215
Philip David, Director
Tel: (718) 499-7154 Fax: (718) 832-3880
Email: s.shirleydcc2@verizon.net

STAGG STREET CENTER FOR CHILDREN
77-83 Stagg St.
Brooklyn, NY 11206
Cecilie Newton, Education Director
Tel: (718) 388-1395 Fax: (718) 599-6053
Email: daycarecenter77@aol.com

TREMONT CROTONA DAY CARE CENTER
1600 Crotona Park East
Bronx, NY 10460
Patrick Rodriguez, Executive Director
Tel: (718) 378-5600 Fax: (718) 589-1766

UNITED BRONX PARENTS, INC.
Day Care Center #1

888 Westchester Ave.
Bronx, NY 10459
Irene Castro, Education Director
Tel: (718) 378-5000 Fax: (718) 378-2395
Web: www.ubpinc.org

UNITED COMMUNITY OF WILLIAMSBURG DAY CARE CENTER
152 Manhattan Ave.
Brooklyn, NY 11206
Anna Butler, Director
Tel: (718) 388-4298 Fax: (718) 388-5590

WASHINGTON HEIGHTS CHILD CARE
610-614 W 175th St.
New York, NY 10033
Nettie Hill, Executive Director
Tel: (212) 781-6910 Fax: (212) 781-2472

SPEC. INT., COUNSELING

CENTER FOR FAMILY LIFE IN SUNSET PARK
345 43rd St.
Brooklyn, NY 11232
Julie Stein Brokway, CSW, Co-Director
Tel: (718) 788-3500 Fax: (718) 788-2275
Web: www.cflsp.org

HISPANIC COUNSELING CENTER, INC.
344 Fulton Ave.
Hempstead, NY 11550
Gladys Serrano, Executive Director
Tel: (516) 538-2613 Fax: (516) 538-2515
Email: hispaniccc@hotmail.com
Web: www.hispaniccounseling.com

SPEC. INT., EDUCATION

A BETTER CHANCE
National Office
240 W 35th Fl., 9th Fl.
New York, NY 10001-2506
Colin Lord, Director of the College Preparatory
Schools Program
Tel: (646) 346-1310 Fax: (646) 346-1311
Email: clord@abetterchance.org
Web: www.abetterchance.org

ACADEMIA NORTEAMERICANA DE LA LENGUA ESPAÑOLA
Correspondiente de la Real Academia Española
P.O. Box 349
New York, NY 10116
Dr. Odón Betanzos Palacios, Director
Tel: (718) 761-0556 Fax: (718) 761-0556
Email: acadnorteamerica@aol.com
Web: www.georgetown.edu/academia

AESTHETIC REALISM FOUNDATION
141 Greene St.
New York, NY 10012
Margot Carpenter, Executive Director
Tel: (212) 777-4490 Fax: (212) 777-4426
Email: mcarpenter@aestheticrealism.org
Web: www.aestheticrealism.org

ASPIRA OF NEW YORK
Bronx Office
2488 Grand Concourse #424
Bronx, NY 10458
Alex Betancourt, Deputy Executive Director
Tel: (718) 508-0013 Fax: (718) 508-0017
Email: abetancourt@ny.aspira.org
Web: http://nyaspira.org

ASPIRA OF NEW YORK, INC.
Administrative Office
520 8th Ave., 22nd Fl.
New York, NY 10018
Hector Gesualdo, Executive Director
Tel: (212) 564-6880 X102 Fax: (212) 564-7152
Email: HGesualdo@NY.aspira.org
Web: www.nyaspira.org

BANK STREET COLLEGE OF EDUCATION
Bilingual Education Program
610 W. 112th St.
New York, NY 10025

Luisa Costa Garro, Ph.D., Coordinator of the
Language Series
Tel: (212) 875-4689 Fax: (212) 875-4753
Email: lgarro@bnkst.edu
Web: www.bnkst.edu

THE BILINGUAL SCHOOL, PUBLIC SCHOOL 25
811 E 149th St.
Bronx, NY 10455
Miriam Diaz, Principal
Tel: (718) 292-2995 Fax: (718) 292-2997

BILINGUAL STUDIES PROGRAM
Kingsboro Community College
2001 Oriental Blvd.
Brooklyn, NY 11235
Diego Colón, Director
Tel: (718) 265-5343
Email: DColon@Kingsborough.edu
Web: www.kbcc.cuny.edu/SpecialPrograms/
Kccbe.htm

CARIBBEAN RESEARCH CENTER
CUNY Medgar Evers College
1150 Carroll St.
Brooklyn, NY 11225
Dr. J.A. George Irish, Executive Director
Tel: (718) 270-6082 Fax: (718) 270-6916
Email: caribbeanrescenter@yahoo.com
Web: www.caribbeanrescenter.org

CENTER FOR LATIN AMERICAN AND CARIBBEAN STUDIES
New York University
53 Washington Square South, 4th Fl.
New York, NY 10012
George Yudice, Director
Tel: (212) 998-8686 Fax: (212) 995-4163
Email: clacs.info@nyu.edu
Web: www.nyu.edu/gsas/dept/latin

CENTRO DE ESTUDIOS PUERTORRIQUEÑOS
Hunter College, City University of New York
695 Park Ave.
New York, NY 10021
Félix V. Matos Rodríguez Ph.D., Director
Tel: (212) 772-5688 Fax: (212) 650-3673
Email: felix.matos@hunter.cuny.edu
Web: www.centropr.org

CHILDREN'S ART & SCIENCE WORKSHOPS
300 Ft. Washington Ave. #1H
New York, NY 10032
Yokasta Morales, Executive Director
Tel: (212) 923-7766 Fax: (212) 795-5901
Email: ymorales@caswkids.org
Web: www.caswkids.org

DEPARTMENT OF AFRICANA AND PUERTO RICAN-LATINO STUDIES
Hunter College of City University of New York
1711 HW
New York, NY 10021
Dr. Ehiedul Iweriebor, Chair
Tel: (212) 772-5035 Fax: (212) 650-3596
Email: eiedor@hunter.cuny.edu
Web: www.hunter.cuny.edu/blpr

DEPARTMENT OF LATIN AMERICAN AND CARIBBEAN STUDIES
University of Albany, SUNY
1400 Washington Ave., SS-250
Albany, NY 12222
Edna Acosta-Belén, Department Chair
Tel: (518) 442-4890 Fax: (518) 442-4790
Email: eab@albany.edu
Web: www.albany.edu/lacs

DEPARTMENT OF LATIN AMERICAN & PUERTO RICO STUDIES
Lehman College
250 Bedford Park Blvd. West
Bronx, NY 10468
Dr. Forrest Colburn, Chair
Tel: (718) 960-8280 Fax: (718) 960-7804
Email: laprs@lehman.cuny.edu
Web: www.lehman.edu/lehman/departments

DEPARTMENT OF SPANISH AND PORTUGUESE
Columbia University
612 W. 116th St.
New York, NY 10027
Patricia Grieve, Chair
Tel: (212) 854-4187 Fax: (212) 854-5322
Email: peg1@columbia.edu
Web: www.columbia.edu/cu/spanish/index.html

DOMINICAN STUDIES INSTITUTE
City College of New York
Convent Ave. & 138th St.
New York, NY 10031-9198
Ramona Hernandez, Director
Tel: (212) 650-7496 Fax: (212) 650-7489
Email: rahernandez@ccny.cuny.edu
Web: www.ccny.cuny.edu/dsi

EAST HARLEM COLLEGE & CAREER COUNSELING PROGRAM
1 E 104th St.
New York, NY 10029
Paula J. Martin, Executive Director
Tel: (212) 348-9200 Fax: (212) 831-8202
Email: pmartin@harlemctred.org
Web: www.harlemctred.com

ESCUELA ARGENTINA EN NUEVA YORK
6813 Nansen St.
Forest Hills, NY 11375
Martha Liboreiro
Tel: (718) 268-3235 Fax: (718) 268-3144

ESCUELA HISPANA MONTESSORI
18th Ave. D
New York, NY 10009
Diomedes Rosario, Executive Director
Tel: (212) 982-6650 Fax: (212) 674-0978

INSTITUTE FOR URBAN AND MINORITY EDUCATION
P.O. Box 75, Teacher's College, Columbia
University
New York, NY 10027
Erwin Flaxman, Director
Tel: (212) 678-3433 Fax: (212) 678-4137
Email: iume@tc.columbia.edu
Web: http://iume.tc.columbia.edu/

INTERNATIONAL INSTITUTE OF BUFFALO, NEW YORK, INC.
864 Delaware Ave.
Buffalo, NY 14209
Hinke Boot, Executive Director
Tel: (716) 883-1900 Fax: (716) 883-9529
Email: iib@iibuff.org
Web: www.iibuff.org

JANEY PROGRAM IN LATIN AMERICAN STUDIES
New School University
65 5th Ave. #425
New York, NY 10003
Courtney Jung, Assistant Professor
Tel: (212) 229-5905 Fax: (212) 807-1669
Email: jung@newschool.edu
Web: www.newschool.edu/gf/centers/programs.
htm

LADIES COMMITTEE PUERTO RICAN CULTURAL, INC.
1495 Herkimer St.
Brooklyn, NY 11233
Alicia Ponce de León, Executive Director
Tel: (718) 345-4775 Fax: (718) 485-0086
Email: aponce1318@aol.com

LATIN AMERICAN AND HISPANIC CARIBBEAN STUDIES
City College of New York
138th St. & Convent Ave. #108, NAC 6th Fl.
New York, NY 10031
Iris Lopez, Chairperson
Tel: (212) 650-6763 Fax: (212) 650-6635
Email: irislopez@yahoo.com
Web: www.cuny.edu

LATINO STUDIES PROGRAM
Cornell University
434 Rockefeller Hall
Ithaca, NY 14853
Mary Pat Brady, Director
Tel: (607) 255-3197 Fax: (607) 255-2433
Email: mpb23@cornell.edu
Web: http://latino.lsp.cornell.edu

LITERACY VOLUNTEERS OF AMERICA-WESTCHESTER COUNTY AFFILIATE, INC.
85 Executive Blvd.
Elmsford, NY 10523
Patricia P. Rajala, Executive Director
Tel: (914) 592-2656 Fax: (914) 592-1456
Email: wchester@aol.com

MID-BRONX YOUTH SKILLS
489 St. Paul's Pl.
Bronx, NY 10456
Sandra Atwell, Executive Director
Tel: (718) 590-0655 Fax: (718) 681-2411
Email: sad57@aol.com

NATIONAL URBAN FELLOWS, INC.
102 W 38th St. #700
New York, NY 10018
Luis Benitez, Program Director
Tel: (212) 730-1700 Fax: (212) 730-1823
Email: lbenitez@nuf.org
Web: www.nuf.org

NEW YORK STATE ASSOCIATION FOR BILINGUAL EDUCATION
502 Genessee St.
Buffalo, NY 14204
David Mauricio, President
Email: DAVIDMAURICIO1@cs.com
Web: www.nysabe.org

NYC TEACHING FELLOWS
65 Court St. #322
Brooklyn, NY 11201
Tania Caraballo-Catus, Director of Marketing &
Recruitment
Tel: Fax: (718) 935-4185
Email: fellows@nycboe.net
Web: www.nycteachingfellows.org

OFFICE OF MULTICULTURAL AFFAIRS
41 Park Row #907
New York, NY 10038
Denise Belen Santiago, Director
Tel: (212) 346-1546
Email: dsantiago@pace.edu
Web: http://appserv.pace.edu/execute/page.
cfm?doc_id=2554

PUERTO RICAN AND LATINO STUDIES
Brooklyn College
1205 Boylan Hall, 2900 Bedford Ave.
Brooklyn, NY 11210-2889
Maria Perez y Gonzalez, Department Chair
Tel: (718) 951-5561 Fax: (718) 951-4183
Email: mariapg@brooklyn.cuny.edu
Web: www.brooklyn.cuny.edu/bc/depts/ug/prs.
shtml

PUERTO RICAN EDUCATIONAL & CULTURAL CENTER
24 Van Sinderen Ave.
Brooklyn, NY 11207
Alicia Ponce de León, Executive Director
Tel: (718) 345-4775 Fax: (718) 485-0086

PUERTO RICAN EDUCATORS ASSOCIATION
P.O. Box 534
Bronx, NY 10462
Alejandrina Hendrick, President
Tel: (212) 860-5887 Fax: (212) 828-3587
Email: wrknmom50@aol.com

ROCHESTER EDUCATIONAL OPPORTUNITY CENTER
305 Andrews St.
Rochester, NY 14604
Dr. Melva Brown, Executive Director
Tel: (585) 232-2730 Fax: (585) 546-7824
Web: www.rochestereoc.com

SOCIETY OF SPANISH ENGINEERS, PLANNERS AND ARCHITECTS, INC.
308 Pleasant Ave.
New York, NY 10035
Raymond Plume, Board Member
Tel: (212) 410-4931 Fax: (212) 410-3721

SPONSORS FOR EDUCATIONAL OPPORTUNITY
30 W. 21st St. #900
New York, NY 10038
Rafael Brana, Director SEO Career Program
Tel: (646) 435-9550
Email: rbrana@seo-usa.org
Web: www.seo-usa.org

C.A.S.E.S.
346 Broadway, 3rd Fl.
New York, NY 10013
Joel Copperman, President/CEO
Tel: (212) 732-0076 Fax: (212) 553-6508
Email: jcopperman@cases.org
Web: www.cases.org

CENTER FOR FAMILY LIFE EMPLOYMENT SERVICES
443 39th St., 3rd Fl.
Brooklyn, NY 11232
María Ferreira, Coordinator
Tel: (718) 633-4823 Fax: (718) 633-6729
Email: mferreira@cflsp.org
Web: www.cflsp.org

EVERYWOMAN OPPORTUNITY CENTER, INC.
Headquarters Office
237 Main St. #330
Buffalo, NY 14203
Myrna F. Young, Executive Director
Tel: (716) 847-1120 Fax: (716) 847-1550
Email: myoung@everywoman.org
Web: www.everywoman.org

FARM WORKERS COMMUNITY CENTER
P.O. Box 607
Goshen, NY 10924
Stash Grajewski, Director
Tel: (845) 651-4272 Fax: (845) 651-4399
Email: dhealamo@alamo.net

FEDERATION EMPLOYMENT & GUIDANCE SERVICE
315 Hudson St.
New York, NY 10013
Alfred Miller, EVP/CEO
Tel: (212) 366-8401 Fax: (212) 366-8441
Email: kscaccia@fegs.org
Web: www.fegs.org

LIGA DE ACCION HISPANA
700 Oswego St.
Syracuse, NY 13204
Matriza Alvado, Director
Tel: (315) 475-6153 Fax: (315) 474-5767
Web: www.laligaonline.com

NATIONAL PUERTO RICAN FORUM, INC.
National Headquarters
1946 Webster Ave., 3rd Fl.
Bronx, NY 10457-4249
Gladys Padro-Soler, Executive Director
Tel: (646) 792-0440 Fax: (646) 792-1020
Email: gladysps@nprf.org
Web: www.nprf.org

OPPORTUNITIES FOR A BETTER TOMORROW
783 4th Ave.
Brooklyn, NY 11232
Sister Mary Franciscus, Executive Director
Tel: (718) 369-0303 Fax: (718) 369-1518
Email: sistermaryobt@erols.com
Web: www.obtjobs.com
Email: yolanda.delosreyes@labor.state.ny.org

RURAL OPPORTUNITIES, INC.
Affiliate of NCLR
400 East Ave.
Rochester, NY 14607
Stuart J. Mitchell, President/CEO

Tel: (585) 340-3368 Fax: (585) 340-3335
Email: smitchell@ruralinc.org
Web: www.ruralinc.org

SER OF WESTCHESTER, INC.
171 E. Post Rd. #201
White Plains, NY 10601
Diana Campos, Executive Director
Tel: (914) 681-0996 Fax: (914) 681-1978
Email: serwestchester@aol.com
Web: www.serwestchester.org

SPANUSA, EXECUTIVE RECRUITERS OF SPANISH-SPEAKING PROFESSIONALS
1415 Boston Post Rd.
Larchmont, NY 10538
Manuel Boado, President
Tel: (914) 381-5555 Fax: (914) 381-0811
Email: info@spanusa.net
Web: www.spanusa.net

WILDCAT SERVICE CORPORATION
17 Battery Pl.
New York, NY 10004
Amalia V. Betanzos, President/CEO
Tel: (212) 209-6000 Fax: (212) 635-3876
Email: abetanzos@wildcatatwork.org
Web: www.wildcatatwork.org

ALIANZA DOMINICANA, INC.
Family Center/Affiliate of NCLR
715 W 179th St.
New York, NY 10033
Moisés Pérez, Director
Tel: (212) 795-4226 Fax: (212) 795-4285
Web: www.alianzadom.org

LATIN AMERICA PARENTS ASSOCIATION
P.O. Box 339-340
Brooklyn, NY 11234
Joe Tartaglia, President
Tel: (718) 236-8689
Email: info@lapa.com
Web: www.lapa.com

LOWER EAST SIDE FAMILY UNION COOPERATION
Executive Office
84 Stanton St.
New York, NY 10002
Ralph DuMont, Executive Director
Tel: (212) 260-0040 Fax: (212) 529-3422
Email: info@lesfu.org
Web: www.lesfu.org

PUERTO RICAN ASSOCIATION FOR COMMUNITY AFFAIRS
245 E. 111th St.
New York, NY 10029
Yolanda Sánchez, Executive Director
Tel: (212) 423-9010 Fax: (212) 996-8134

THE PUERTO RICAN FAMILY INSTITUTE, INC.
Adolescent Day Treatment Program
145 W. 15th St.
New York, NY 10011
Grace Velasquez, Program Coordinator
Tel: (212) 229-6960 Fax: (212) 414-7825
Email: gvelasquez@prfi.org
Web: www.prfi.org

THE PUERTO RICAN FAMILY INSTITUTE, INC.
Brooklyn Mental Health Clinic
217 Havemeyer St., 4th Fl.
Brooklyn, NY 11211
Abigail Juárez-Karic, Program Director
Tel: (718) 963-4430 Fax: (718) 963-1776
Web: www.prfi.org

Home Based Crisis Intervention Program
217 Havemeyer St., 4th Fl.
Brooklyn, NY 11211
Abigail Karic, Program Director
Tel: (718) 388-8934 Fax: (718) 963-0814
Web: www.prfi.org
Intermediate Care Facility #1
3050 Laconia Ave.

Bronx, NY 10469
Angelina Rivera, Residence Manager
Tel: (718) 231-6532 Fax: (718) 405-2044
Web: www.prfi.org

National Office
145 W. 15th St.
New York, NY 10011
María Elena Girone, Executive Director
Tel: (212) 414-7800 Fax: (212) 691-5635
Email: comments@prfi.org
Web: www.prfi.org

Queens Mental Health Clinic
97-45 Queens Blvd. #503
Rego Park, NY 11375
Eva Morales, Program Director
Tel: (718) 275-0983 Fax: (718) 275-7973
Web: www.prfi.org

ANTHONY L. JORDAN HEALTH CENTER
82 Holland St.
Rochester, NY 14605
Daniel T. Day, President
Tel: (585) 423-5800 Fax: (585) 423-2806
Email: dday@westsidehealth.net

ARGENTINE AMERICAN MEDICAL SOCIETY
854 Jefferson St.
Baldwin harbor, NY 11510
Mara J. Fiorentino, President
Tel: (516) 771-0580 Fax: (516) 771-0580
Email: aamssecret@msn.com
Web: www.aams.us

BETANCES HEALTH UNIT, INC.
280 Henry St.
New York, NY 10002
Wanda Evans, Executive Director
Tel: (212) 227-8401 Fax: (212) 227-8842
Email: info@betances.org
Web: www.betances.org

BORIKEN NEIGHBORHOOD HEALTH CENTER
2253 3rd Ave., 3rd Fl.
New York, NY 10035
Thomas Vance, Public Relations/Outreach Director
Tel: (212) 289-6650 Fax: (212) 360-6149
Email: elliborinquen@cs.com

CENTRO CIVICO HISPANOAMERICANO, INC.
230 Green St.
Albany, NY 12202
Cecilia Sanz, Executive Director
Tel: (518) 465-1145 Fax: (518) 465-1138
Email: frc@centrocivicoalbany.org

CENTRO MEDICO DOMINICANO DE DIAGNOSTICO Y TRATAMIENTO
629 W. 185th St.
New York, NY 10033
Jacquelin Almonte, Administration
Tel: (212) 928-3900 Fax: (212) 795-0478

CLINICA CENTRAL DE DIAGNOSTICO Y TRATAMIENTO SERVICIOS MEDICOS HISPANOS
8209 Roosevelt Ave., 2nd Fl.
Jackson Heights, NY 11372
Amanda Martínez, Executive Director
Tel: (718) 507-8000 Fax: (718) 205-0871

COMMUNITY HEALTHCARE NETWORK
Bronx Health Center
975 Westchester Ave.
Bronx, NY 10459
Lillian Kestler, Executive Director
Tel: (718) 991-9250 Fax: (718) 991-3829
Web: www.chnnyc.org

EAST HARLEM COUNCIL FOR HUMAN SERVICES, INC.
2253 3rd Ave., 3rd Fl.
New York, NY 10035
Elizabeth Sánchez, Executive Director
Tel: (212) 289-6650 Fax: (212) 360-6149

FIRST SATURDAY IN OCTOBER, INC.
198 E 161st St. #201
Bronx, NY 10451
Carmen Feliciano, President
Tel: (718) 590-7789 Fax: (718) 590-5814

THE HEALTH ASSOCIATION
Esperanza Latina
235 N Clinton Ave.
Rochester, NY 14605
Lillian Ayala, Director
Tel: (585) 325-7987 Fax: (585) 325-4673
Email: information@thehealthassociation.org
Web: www.thehealthassociation.org

HEALTH INDUSTRY RESOURCES ENTERPRISES, INC.
989 Ave. of the Americas
New York, NY 10018
Dr. Rosa Gil, Executive Director
Tel: (212) 219-1618 Fax: (212) 219-2087

HUNTS POINT MULTI-SERVICE CENTER
Health Clinic
754 E 151st St.
Bronx, NY 10455
Manuel Rosas, Director
Tel: (718) 402-2800 Fax: (718) 665 -9782
Email: marosa@worldnet.att.net
Web: www.hpmsc.org

JOURNAL OF THE HISPANO AMERICAN BIOMEDICAL ASSOCIATION
130 W. 42nd St. #608
New York, NY 10036
J. Ricardo Loret de Mola, President
Tel: (212) 997-9624 Fax: (212) 997-9615
Email: habausa@hotmail.com
Web: www.americadrs.com

LATINO ORGANIZATION FOR LIVER AWARENESS
P.O. Box 842
Throggs Neck Station
Bronx, NY 10465
Gladys Moreira, Director of Operations
Tel: (718) 892-8697 Fax: (718) 918-0527
Web: www.lola-national.org

LINCOLN WIC PROGRAM
234 E 149th St.
Bronx, NY 10451
Lorena Drago, Executive Director
Tel: (718) 579-5398 Fax: (718) 579-4604

MOBILIZATION FOR YOUTH HEALTH SERVICES, INC.
199 Ave. B
New York, NY 10009
Willie Zayerz, Director
Tel: (212) 254-1456 Fax: (212) 505-8437
Email: mfyhs@yahoo.com

NATIONAL MEDICAL FELLOWSHIPS, INC.
Headquarters
5 Hanover Square, 15th Fl.
New York, NY 10004
Vivian Fox, President
Tel: (212) 483-8880 Fax: (212) 483-8897
Email: info@nmfonline.org
Web: www.nmf-online.org

NEW YORK FOUNDING HOSPITAL
590 Ave. of the Americas
New York, NY 10011
Virginia Keim, Director of Development and Public Relations
Tel: (212) 633-9300 Fax: (212) 491-9563
Email: ginnyk@nyfoundling.org
Web: www.nyfoundling.org

THE PUERTO RICAN FAMILY INSTITUTE, INC.
Adult Supportive Care Management
145 W. 15th St., 7th Fl.
New York, NY 10011
David Ortiz, Program Director
Tel: (212) 924-6320 Fax: (212) 414-7827
Web: www.prfi.org

THE PUERTO RICAN FAMILY INSTITUTE, INC.
Intermediate Care Facility #2
1668 Grand Ave.
Bronx, NY 10453
Carmen López, Residence Manager
Tel: (718) 731-8434 Fax: (718) 731-8442
Email: clopez@prfi.org
Web: www.prfi.org

THE PUERTO RICAN FAMILY INSTITUTE, INC.
Manhattan Child Placement Prevention Program
145 W. 15th St.
New York, NY 10011
Yolanda Alicea, Director
Tel: (212) 229-6950 Fax: (212) 924-4404
Email: yalicea@prfi.org
Web: www.prfi.org

New Arrivals Program
145 W. 15th St.
New York, NY 10011
Daisy Vazquez, Program Director
Tel: (212) 229-6910 Fax: (212) 414-7833
Email: dvazquez@prfi.org
Web: www.prfi.org

Partial Hospitalization Program
217 Havemeyer St., 3rd Fl.
Brooklyn, NY 11211
Ann Rimey, Program Coordinator
Tel: (718) 963-1655 Fax: (718) 963-1776
Web: www.prfi.org

Placement Prevention Program for Juveniles on Probation
145 W. 15th St.
New York, NY 10011
Sonia Acobo Morales, Program Director
Tel: (212) 229-6906 Fax: (212) 414-7831
Email: smorales@prfi.org
Web: www.prfi.org

ROBERTO CLEMENTE CENTER
540 E. 13th St.
New York, NY 10009
Jaime Inclan, Director
Tel: (212) 387-7400 Fax: (212) 387-7432
Email: j14@nyu.com

RYAN NENA COMMUNITY HEALTH CENTER
279 E 3rd St.
New York, NY 10009
Kathy Gruben, Project Director
Tel: (212) 477-8500 Fax: (212) 473-4970
Email: info@ryan-nena.org
Web: www.ryancenter.org

SEGUNDO RUIZ BELVIS DIAGNOSTICS AND TREATMENT CENTER
545 E. 142nd St.
Bronx, NY 10454
Elizabeth Rodriguez, Executive Director
Tel: (718) 579-1765 Fax: (718) 579-5024
Email: elizabeth.rodriguez@newyorkcityhhc.org

SHARE, SELF-HELP FOR WOMEN WITH BREAST OR OVARIAN CANCER
Latina SHARE Program
1501 Broadway #704A
New York, NY 10036
Ivis Sampayo, Director
Tel: (212) 719-0364 Fax: (212) 869-3431
Email: Isampayo@sharecancersupport.org
Web: www.sharecancersupport.org

SOUTHVIEW HEALTH CENTER, INC.
731 White Plains Rd.
Bronx, NY 10473
Pedro Espada, Jr., President
Tel: (718) 589-2232 Fax: (718) 378-2880
Email: info@soundviewhealth.net
Web: www.soundviewhealth.net

URBAN HEALTH PLAN, INC.
El Nuevo San Juan
1065 Southern Blvd.
Bronx, NY 10459
Paloma Hernandez, President/CEO

Tel: (718) 589-2440 Fax: (718) 589-4793
Email: information@urbanhealthplan.org
Web: www.urbanhealthplan.org

AQUINAS HOUSING CORPORATION
1945 Vyse Ave.
Bronx, NY 10460
Michael Brennan, Executive Director
Tel: (718) 842-6440 Fax: (718) 542-4223
Email: aquineshob@aol.com

ASSOCIATION OF COMMUNITY ORGANIZATIONS FOR REFORM NOW
New York Office
88 3rd Ave.
Brooklyn, NY 11217
Steve Kest, Executive Director
Tel: (718) 246-7900 Fax: (718) 246-7939
Email: nyacorn@acorn.org
Web: www.acorn.org

COOPER SQUARE COMMITTEE, INC.
61 E 4th St.
New York, NY 10003
Steven Herrick, Director
Tel: (212) 228-8210 Fax: (646) 602-2260
Email: coopersquarecomm@aol.com
Web: www.coopersquare.org

EL BARRIO'S OPERATION FIGHT BACK, INC.
413 E 120th St. #403
New York, NY 10035
Gustavo Rosado, Executive Director
Tel: (212) 410-7900 Fax: (212) 410-7997
Email: ebofb413@aol.com

ERIE REGIONAL HOUSING DEVELOPMENT COOPERATION
104 Maryland Ave.
Buffalo, NY 14201
Donna Rice, Executive Director
Tel: (716) 845-0485 Fax: (716) 845-0486

FIFTH AVENUE COMMITTEE, INC.
621 DeGraw St.
Brooklyn, NY 11217
Michelle De la Uz, Executive Director
Tel: (718) 237-2017 Fax: (718) 237-5366
Email: fac@fifthhave.org
Web: www.fifthave.org

MANHATTAN VALLEY DEVELOPMENT CORPORATION
73 W 108th St.
New York, NY 10025
Donna Gibbons, Executive Director
Tel: (212) 678-4410 Fax: (212) 666-4770
Email: info@mvdc.org
Web: www.mvdc.org

NEIGHBORHOOD ASSOCIATION FOR INTER-CULTURAL AFFAIRS
1055 Grand Concourse
Bronx, NY 10452
Eduardo Lagurre, Chief Executive Director
Tel: (718) 538-3344 Fax: (718) 537-3195
Email: naica981@cs.com

NUEVO EL BARRIO PARA LA REHAB DE LA VIVIENDA Y LA ECONOMIA
18 E 116th St.
New York, NY 10029
Roberto Anazagasti, General Manager
Tel: (212) 427-0555 Fax: (212) 427-0875
Email: ranerve1@aol.com

PUEBLO EN MARCHA
c/o St. Pius
401 E. 145th St.
Bronx, NY 10454
Maximino Rivera, Executive Director
Tel: (718) 665-7375 Fax: (718) 866-0044
Email: pueblomarcha2@aol.com

SOUTH BRONX MENTAL HEALTH COUNCIL,
Bronx III Intensive Supportive Apartment Program
932 Kelly St.
Bronx, NY 10459
Michael Lopez, Director
Tel: (718) 542-0880 Fax: (718) 993-0647

SOUTH SIDE UNITED HOUSE DEVELOPMENT FUND CORPORATION (LOS SURES), INC.
213 S 4th St.
Brooklyn, NY 11211
David Pagan, Executive Director
Tel: (718) 387-2418 Fax: (718) 387-4683

SUNSET PARK REDEVELOPMENT COMMITTEE, INC.
5101 4th Ave.
Brooklyn, NY 11220
Nelson Ramos, Director
Tel: (718) 492-8580 Fax: (718) 439-0961

ADELANTE OF SUFFOLK COUNTY, INC.
10 3rd Ave.
Brentwood, NY 11717
Miriam Garcia, Executive Director
Tel: (631) 434-3481 Fax: (631) 434-3496
Email: adelante2@juno.com
Web: www.adelantesc.org

ALIANZA DOMINICANA, INC.
2410 Amsterdam Ave., 4th Fl.
New York, NY 10033
Moisés Pérez, Executive Director
Tel: (212) 740-1960 Fax: (212) 740-1967
Email: mperez@alianzadom.org
Web: www.alianzadom.org

ASSOCIATION OF LATINO SPEAKERS
85 4th Ave. #JJ
New York, NY 10003
Alberto O. Cappas, President
Tel: (212) 866-0125 Fax: (212) 353-9114
Email: acappas@yahoo.com

CASITA MARIA, INC.
928 Simpson St.
Bronx, NY 10459
Lue Ann Eldar, Executive Director
Tel: (718) 589-2230 Fax: (718) 589-5714
Email: info@casita.us
Web: www.casita.us

CENTER FOR MIGRATION STUDIES OF NEW YORK, INC.
209 Flagg Pl.
Staten Island, NY 10304-1199
Rev. Joseph Fugolo, Executive Director
Tel: (718) 351-8800 Fax: (718) 667-4598
Email: offices@cmsny.org
Web: www.cmsny.org

CÍRCULO DE LA HISPANIDAD, INC.
62 W. Park Ave.
Long Beach, NY 11561
Gil Bernardino, Executive Director
Tel: (516) 889-3869 Fax: (516) 889-4572
Email: gbernardino@cdlh.org
Web: www.cdlh.org

COALITION FOR HISPANIC FAMILY SERVICES
315 Wyckoff Ave., 4th Fl.
Brooklyn, NY 11237
Denise Rosario, Executive Director
Tel: (718) 497-6090 Fax: (718) 497-9495
Email: drosario@hispanicfamilyservicesny.org
Web: www.hispanicfamilyservicesny.org

ECUADOREAN AMERICAN ASSOCIATION, INC.
30 Vesey St. #506
New York, NY 10007-2914
Montserrat Hernández, Director
Tel: (212) 732-4333 Fax: (212) 723-0660
Email: andean@nyct.net
Web: www.theamericasfoundation.org

HISPANIC FEDERATION OF NEW YORK CITY
130 William St., 9th Fl.
New York, NY 10038
Lillian Rodriguez-Lopez, President
Tel: (212) 233-8955 Fax: (212) 233-8996
Email: info@hispanicfederation.org
Web: www.hispanicfederation.org

HISPANIC OUTREACH SERVICES
Troy Outreach Office
1915 5th Ave.
Troy, NY 12180
Jessica Escabales, Site Coordinator
Tel: (518) 273-7869 Fax: (518) 273-6089
Email: hostroyje@choiceonemail.com
Web: www.hispanicoutreachservices.org

HISPANICS UNITED OF BUFFALO
254 Virginia St.
Buffalo, NY 14201
Paula Rosner, Executive Director
Tel: (716) 856-7110 Fax: (716) 856-9617
Email: hispanicsunitedofbuffalo@hotmail.com

INTERNATIONAL RESCUE COMMITTEE, INC.
122 E 42nd St., 11th Fl.
New York, NY 10168
Lang Ngan, Media Relations Manager
Tel: (212) 551-3106 Fax: (212) 551-3101
Email: lngan@theirc.org
Web: www.theirc.org

LA FUERZA UNIDA DE GLEN COVE, INC.
14 Glen St. #305
Glen Cove, NY 11542
Pascual Blanco, Executive Director
Tel: (516) 759-0788 Fax: (516) 759-3465
Email: lafuerzaunida@aol.com

LOISAIDA, INC.
710 E. 9th St.
New York, NY 10009
Antonio Santana, President
Tel: (212) 353-0272
Email: loisaidabenefit@aol.com
Web: www.loisaidainc.org

MAMARONECK OPPORTUNITY CENTER
134 Center Ave.
Mamaroneck, NY 10543
Beverly Brewer Villa, Director
Tel: (914) 698-7140 Fax: (914) 698-6964

NATIONAL ASSOCIATION OF PUERTO RICAN/ HISPANIC SOCIAL WORKERS
P.O. Box 651
Brentwood, NY 11717
Luis Valenzuela, President
Tel: (631) 864-1536 Fax: (631) 864-1536
Email: sonia@naprhsw.com
Web: www.naprhsw.com

CARIBBEAN AMERICAN CENTER OF NEW YORK
195 Cadman Plz., West, 1st Fl.
Brooklyn, NY 11201
Jean Alexander, Executive Director
Tel: (718) 625-1515 Fax: (718) 625-0717
Email: jeanpalexander@hotmail.com

HERGO SERVICE CENTER, INC.
82-19 Roosevelt Ave., 2nd Fl.
Jackson Heights, NY 11372
Ron Katirare, Executive Director
Tel: (718) 507-4646 Fax: (718) 779-6361

HERMANOS FRATERNOS DE LOIZA ALDEA,
1702 Lexington Ave.
New York, NY 10029
Blanca Irizarry, Executive Director
Tel: (212) 410-4220 Fax: (212) 831-8722
Email: hfdla@aol.com

HISPANIC BROTHERHOOD OF ROCKVILLE CENTER, INC.
59 Clinton Ave.
Rockville Center, NY 11570

Margarita Grasing, Executive Director
Tel: (516) 766-6610 Fax: (516) 776-6040

IMMIGRATION AND REFUGEE PROGRAM
Church World Service
475 Riverside Dr. #700
New York, NY 10115
Joe Roberson, Director
Tel: (212) 870-2061 Fax: (212) 870-3523
Email: bchassler@churchworldservice.org
Web: www.churchworldservice.org

LATIN AMERICAN INTEGRATION CENTER
49-06 Skillman Ave.
Woodside Queens, NY 11377
Ana María Archila, Executive Director
Tel: (718) 565-8500 Fax: (718) 565-0646
Email: ana@lightnyc.org

NEW YORK ASSOCIATION FOR NEW AMERICANS, INC.
17 Battery Pl.
New York, NY 10004-1102
Jose Valencia, President/CEO
Tel: (212) 425-2900 Fax: (212) 344-1621
Web: www.nyana.org

NORTHERN MANHATTAN COALITION FOR IMMIGRANTS RIGHTS
665 W. 182 St.
New York, NY 10033
Tel: (212) 781-0355 Fax: (212) 781-0943

SOUTHSIDE COMMUNITY MISSION, INC.
250 Hooper St.
Brooklyn, NY 11211
Kathryn Walsh, Program Coordinator
Tel: (718) 387-3803 Fax: (718) 387-3739

COORDINATING AGENCY FOR SPANISH AMERICANS
40 Main St.
Hempstead, NY 11550
Marianela Jordan, Executive Director
Tel: (516) 572-0750 Fax: (516) 572-0756
Email: marianela.jordan@mail.co.naffau.ny.us

NORTH AMERICAN CONGRESS ON LATIN AMERICA
38 Greene St., 4th Fl.
New York, NY 10013
Marshall Beck, Editor
Tel: (646) 613-1440 Fax: (646) 613-1443
Email: mbeck@nacla.org
Web: www.nacla.org

REFORMA
Northeast Chapter (CT, MA, NJ, NY, PA, RI)
New York Public Library, 11 W 40th St. #213
New York, NY 10018
Maricella Nunez, President
Tel: (212) 930-0045 Fax: (212) 869-3567
Email: lightt1198@yahoo.com
Web: www.reforma-northeast.org

SPANISH COMMUNITY PROGRESS
204 Hawthorne Ave.
Yonkers, NY 10705
Wilda Mejias, Director
Tel: (914) 969-5400 Fax: (914) 969-5890
Email: scpf1970@optonline.net

CENTRAL AMERICAN LEGAL ASSISTANCE
240 Hooper St.
Brooklyn, NY 11211
Anne Pilsbury, Director
Tel: (718) 486-6800 Fax: (718) 486-5287

MOREIRA LAW FIRM
130 W. 42nd St. #501
New York, NY 10036
Dr. Jorge Moreira, President
Tel: (212) 398-8600 Fax: (212) 398-9425
Email: morlawfirm@aol.com

NASSAU/SUFFOLK LAW SERVICES COMMITTEE, INC.
1757 Veterans Hwy. #50
Islandia, NY 11749
Jeffrey Segel, Executive Director
Tel: (631) 232-2400 Fax: (631) 232-2489
Email: nslsl@earthlink.net
Web: www.nslawservices.org

NORTHERN MANHATTAN IMPROVEMENT CORPORATION
76 Wadsworth Ave.
New York, NY 10033
Barbara Lowry, Executive Director
Tel: (212) 822-8300 Fax: (212) 928-4180
Email: info@nmic.org
Web: www.nmic.org

PUERTO RICO FEDERAL AFFAIRS ADMINISTRATION
475 Park Ave. S., 7th Fl.
New York, NY 10016
Laura M. Irizarry-Huertas, Regional Director
Tel: (212) 252-7300 Fax: (212) 726-9957
Email: info@prfaa.com
Web: www.prfaa.com

CENTRO SOCIAL LA ESPERANZA
21 Audubon Ave.
New York, NY 10032
James Malley, Executive Director
Tel: (212) 928-5810 Fax: (212) 740-2053
Email: esperanza@hotmail.com

CHILDREN AND ADOLESCENT SERVICES, INC.
781 E 142nd St., 3rd Fl.
Bronx, NY 10454
Julio Ortega, Director
Tel: (718) 993-1400 Fax: (718) 993-0647

CONTINUING DAY TREATMENT PROGRAM
781 E 142nd St., 3rd Fl.
Bronx, NY 10454
Nancy Faunt, Director
Tel: (718) 993-1400 Fax: (718) 993-0647

FEDERATION OF PUERTO RICAN ORGANIZATIONS, INC.
2 Van Sinderen Ave., 2nd Fl.
Brooklyn, NY 11207
Brenda Whitaker, President
Tel: (718) 345-9500 Fax: (718) 498-1779
Email: info@fmcp-ny.org
Web: www.fmcp-ny.org

LAKE SHORE BEHAVIORAL HEALTH
254 Franklin St.
Buffalo, NY 14202
Howard K. Hitzel, President
Tel: (716) 842-0440 Fax: (716) 842-4069
Email: hhitzel@lake-shore.org
Web: www.lake-shore.org

METROPOLITAN CENTER FOR MENTAL HEALTH
Hispanic Family Services
1090 St. Nicholas Ave.
New York, NY 10033
Francine Ruskin, HFS Director
Tel: (212) 543-2379 Fax: (212) 543-2378
Email: fruskin@metropolitancenter.com
Web: www.metropolitancenter.com

MICA CONTINUING TREATMENT PROGRAM
1241 Lafayette Ave.
Bronx, NY 10474
Blanca Rosa Gayoso, Director
Tel: (718) 378-6500 Fax: (718) 842-3846

THE PUERTO RICAN FAMILY INSTITUTE, INC.
Bronx Mental Health Clinic
4123 3rd Ave.
Bronx, NY 10457
Lourdes Sanchez, Program Director
Tel: (718) 299-3045 Fax: (718) 716-2605
Email: lsanchez@prfi.org
Web: www.prfi.org

THE PUERTO RICAN FAMILY INSTITUTE, INC.
Manhattan Mental Health Clinic
145 W 15th St.
New York, NY 10011
Yolanda Alicea-Yinn, Program Director
Tel: (212) 229-6950 Fax: (212) 924-4404
Email: yayinn@prfi.org
Web: www.prfi.org

ROCHESTER REHAB CENTER, INC.
1000 Elmwood Ave. #600
Rochester, NY 14620
George Gieselman, President
Tel: (585) 271-2520 Fax: (585) 271-1198
Email: rehabadmin@rochesterrehab.org
Web: www.rochesterrehab.org

SCHOOL SITE MENTAL HEALTH PROGRAM, INC.
781 E 142nd St.
Bronx, NY 10451
Julio Ortega, Director
Tel: (718) 993-1400 Fax: (718) 993-0647
Email: sbmhc@msn.com

SOUTH BRONX MENTAL HEALTH COUNCIL, INC.
781 E 142nd St.
Bronx, NY 10454
Dr. Humberto L. Martínez, Executive Director
Tel: (718) 993-1400 Fax: (718) 993-0647
Email: sbmhc@msn.com
Web: www.sbmhc.org

52 Anderson Ave.
Bronx, NY 10452
Michael Lopez, Director
Tel: (718) 588-4770 Fax: (718) 588-2518
Email: sbmhc@msn.com

UNITAS THERAPEUTIC COMMUNITY, INC.
940 Garrison Ave.
Bronx, NY 10474
Dr. Ian S. Amritt, Executive Director
Tel: (718) 589-0551 Fax: (718) 328-4265
Email: unitastc@aol.com
Web: www.unitastc.com

BETANCES SENIOR CITIZENS CENTER
401 St. Anns Ave.
Bronx, NY 10454
Maria Canales, Director
Tel: (718) 292-4922 Fax: (718) 292-7437

CABS NURSING HOME CO., INC.
270 Nostrand Ave.
Brooklyn, NY 11205-4991
David Wieder, Administrator
Tel: (718) 638-0500 Fax: (718) 857-3200
Email: dwieder@cabsnursing.com

CARVER COMMUNITY CENTER
55 E 102nd St.
New York, NY 10029
Diana Ayala, Director
Tel: (212) 289-2708 Fax: (212) 360-1947
Email: carversenior@yahoo.com

CASA BORICUA SENIOR CITIZEN'S CENTER
910 E 172nd St.
Bronx, NY 10460
Abigail Serrano, Director
Tel: (718) 542-0222 Fax: (718) 378-7630

CONSUMER ACTION PROGRAM OF BEDFORD STUYVESANT
545 Broadway
Brooklyn, NY 11206
Adolfo G. Alayon, President
Tel: (718) 388-1601 Fax: (718) 388-4143

ELMCOR SENIOR CENTER
98-19 Astoria Blvd.
East Elmhurst, NY 11369
Ann Henderson, Director
Tel: (718) 457-9757 Fax: (718) 898-4600

Email: info@elmcor.org
Web: www.elmcor.org

GRAND STREET SETTLEMENT
Grand Coalition of Seniors
80 Pitt St.
New York, NY 10002
Margarita Rosa, Executive Director
Tel: (212) 674-1740 Fax: (212) 979-8677
Email: info@grandstreet.org
Web: www.grandstreet.org

INSTITUTE FOR THE PUERTO RICAN/ HISPANIC ELDERLY
105 E. 22nd St. #615
New York, NY 10010
Suleika Cabrera Drinane, Executive Director
Tel: (212) 677-4181 Fax: (212) 777-5106
Email: iprhe@aol.com

LATINO GERONTOLOGICAL CENTER
75 Maiden Ln. #208
New York, NY 10038
Mario E. Tapia, President
Tel: (212) 402-5474
Email: info@gerolatino.org
Web: www.gerolatino.org

MANHATTAN VALLEY GOLDEN AGE
Senior Citizen Center
135 W 106th St.
New York, NY 10025
Anna Nary Cox, Director
Tel: (212) 749-7015 Fax: (212) 749-8611

MILLBROOK SENIOR CITIZENS CENTER
211 St. Anns Ave.
Bronx, NY 10454
Rey Colón, Assistant Director
Tel: (718) 401-4901 Fax: (718) 401-4084

NEW YORK FOUNDATION FOR SENIOR CITIZENS
11 Park Pl., 14th Fl.
New York, NY 10007-2801
Linda R. Hoffman, President
Tel: (212) 962-7559 Fax: (212) 227-2952
Email: nyfscinc@aol.com
Web: www.nyfsc.org

PROGRAMA DE CUIDADORES DE BROOKLYN
Institute for the Puerto Rican/Hispanic Elderly
1368 Fulton St., 3rd Fl.
Brooklyn, NY 11216
Marian M. Inguanzo, Social Work Supervisor
Tel: (718) 230-5838 Fax: (718) 230-7522
Email: marian.inguanzo@iprhe.org

PUERTO RICAN HOME ATTENDANT SERVICE
564 Southern Blvd.
Bronx, NY 10455
Juan Hernández, Assistant Director
Tel: (718) 292-8770 Fax: (718) 585-2114
Email: prhas.jhernandez@verizon.net

RIDGEWOOD BUSHWICK SENIOR CITIZENS COUNCIL, INC.
280 Wyckoff Ave.
Brooklyn, NY 11237
Paula Griffiths, Assistant Executive Director
Tel: (718) 821-0254 Fax: (718) 417-9056
Email: pgriffiths@rbscc.org
Web: www.rbscc.org

Atlantic Senior Center
70 Pennsylvania Ave.
Brooklyn, NY 11207
Alfreida Luis, Director
Tel: (718) 345-7994 Fax: (718) 345-0560
Email: atlanticcenter@rbscc.org
Web: www.rbscc.org

Borinquen Senior Center
80 Siegel St.
Brooklyn, NY 11206
Ilza Rodriguez, Director
Tel: (718) 782-6334 Fax: (718) 782-0901
Email: borinquen@rbscc.org
Web: www.rbscc.org

Buena Vida Continuing Care and Rehabilitation Center
48 Cedar St.
Brooklyn, NY 11206
Lillian Abreu, Director, Community Affairs and Volunteers
Tel: (718) 455-6200 Fax: (718) 452-7681
Email: community@buenavidacenter.org
Web: www.buenavidacenter.org

Diana H. Jones Senior Center
741 Flushing Ave.
Brooklyn, NY 11206
Narcisa Ruiz, Director
Tel: (718) 782-3601 Fax: (718) 782-3604
Email: dianajones@rbscc.org
Web: www.rbscc.org

Queens Multi-Service Center
76-01 Myrtle Ave.
Glendale, NY 11385
Rosann Rosario, director
Tel: (718) 366-0200 Fax: (718) 366-1281
Email: queens@rbscc.org
Web: www.rbscc.org

Respite Center
59-04 Decatur St.
Ridgewood, NY 11385
Ann Mickitch, Director
Tel: (718) 366-5591 Fax: (718) 366-8874
Email: respite@rbscc.org
Web: www.rbscc.org

SOUTH BRONX SENIOR TRANSPORTATION NETWORK
910 E 172nd St.
Bronx, NY 10460
Nelson Pena, Director
Tel: (718) 589-4295 Fax: (718) 589-0751

SPANISH SPEAKING AGENCY COUNCIL RAICES, INC.
30 3rd Ave. #617
Brooklyn, NY 11217
Jose Ortiz, Executive Director
Tel: (718) 643-0232 Fax: (718) 643-8257
Email: jortiz@ssecraices.org

SUNSET PARK SENIOR CITIZEN CENTER, INC.
4520 4th Ave.
Brooklyn, NY 11220
María Cardona, Director
Tel: (718) 492-9370 Fax: (718) 492-5042

UNITED BRONX PARENTS, INC.
Centro Esperanza
603 Prospect Ave.
Bronx, NY 10455
Milly Figueroa, Program Director
Tel: (718) 402-5142 Fax: (718) 991-7643
Web: www.ubpinc.org

AGUSTIN PUCHO OLIVENCIA COMMUNITY CENTER
261 Swan St.
Buffalo, NY 14204
Carlos Olivencia, President
Tel: (716) 852-1648 Fax: (716) 852-1648

AVON HISPANIC NETWORK
Avon Products, Inc.
1345 6th Ave., 27th Fl.
New York, NY 10105
Ana Maria Vitek, President
Tel: (212) 282-5610 Fax: (212) 282-6086

BRAZIL FOUNDATION
225 W. 86th St. #1109
New York, NY 10024
Leona S. Forman, President/CEO
Tel: (212) 595-6995 Fax: (212) 877-2325
Email: newyork@brazilfoundation.org
Web: www.brazilfoundation.org

BRAZILIAN RAINBOW GROUP
119 W. 24th St. 6th Fl.
New York, NY 10011
Eryck Duran, Executive Director
Tel: (212) 367-1471
Email: info@brgny.org
Web: www.brgny.org

BROOKLYN UNIDOS
Ridgewood Bushwick Senior Citizens Council, Inc.
217 Wyckoff Ave.
Brooklyn, NY 11237
Christiana M. Fisher, CEO
Tel: (718) 821-0254 Fax: (718) 417-9056
Email: rbscc@rbscc.org
Web: www.rbscc.org

CATHOLIC CHARITIES OF MONTGOMERY COUNTY
1 Kimball St.
Amsterdam, NY 12010
John Nasso, Executive Director
Tel: (518) 842-4202 Fax: (518) 842-4245
Email: jnasso@catholiccharitiesmc.org
Web: www.catholiccharitiesmc.org

THE CENTER FOR MULTICULTURAL EXPERIENCES
State University of New York, Oneonta
Lee Hall, Oneonta State
Oneonta, NY 13820
Mary H. Bonderoff, Program Coordinator
Tel: (607) 436-2617
Email: bonderm@oneonta.edu
Web: www.oneonta.edu/development/cme/

CENTRO CRISTIANO DE BAY RIDGE
Mission of Mercy-Mision Miscricordi
6324 7th Ave.
Brooklyn, NY 11220
Iris Sanchez, Executive Director
Tel: (718) 745-5204 Fax: (718) 921-4005
Email: brcc@bayridgechristian.org
Web: www.bayridgechristian.org

CHRISTIAN COMMUNITY IN ACTION, INC.
910 E 172nd St., 4th Fl.
Bronx, NY 10460
Luis Alejandro, Executive Director
Tel: (718) 542-5900 Fax: (718) 378-6886

CITIZENS ADVICE BUREAU
2054 Morris Ave.
Bronx, NY 10453
Carolyn McLaughlin, Executive Director
Tel: (718) 365-0910 Fax: (718) 365-0697
Email: cmclaughlin@cabny.org
Web: www.cabny.org

CNY LATINO
1529 Woodmancy Rd.
Tully, NY 13159-9791
Hugo Acosta, Owner/Publisher
Tel: (315) 415-8593 Fax: (315) 696-0146
Email: info@cnylatino.com
Web: www.cnylatino.com

COLONY-SOUTH BROOKLYN HOUSES
297 Dean St.
Brooklyn, NY 11217
Balaguru Cacarla, Executive Director
Tel: (718) 625-3810 Fax: (718) 875-8719

COMMUNITY ACTION ORGANIZATION
70 Harvard Pl.
Buffalo, NY 14209
L. Nathan Hare, Executive Director
Tel: (716) 881-5150 Fax: (716) 881-2927
Email: lnhare@caoec.org
Web: www.caoec.org

COMMUNITY PLACE OF GREATER ROCHESTER
57 Central Park
Rochester, NY 14605
Sherry Walker-Cowart, Executive Director
Tel: (585) 327-7200 Fax: (585) 546-3230

Email: info@communityplace.org
Web: www.communityplace.org

DAVIDSON COMMUNITY CENTER
2038 Davidson Ave.
Bronx, NY 10453
Angel Caballero, Executive Director
Tel: (718) 731-6360 Fax: (718) 731-8580
Email: angel.dcc@verizon.net

EASTCHESTER COMMUNITY ACTION PROGRAM
142-144 Main St.
Tuckahoe, NY 10707
Vivian T. Yancy, Director
Tel: (914) 337-7768 Fax: (914) 337-2751
Email: vyancy@westcop.org
Web: www.westcop.org

FAMILY OF ELLENVILLE
221 Canal St.
Ellenville, NY 12428
Lisa Cavanaugh, Program Director
Tel: (845) 647-2443 Fax: (845) 647-2460
Email: info@familyofwoodstockinc.org
Web: www.familyofwoodstockinc.org

FOREST HILLS COMMUNITY HOUSE
108-25 62nd Dr.
Forest Hills, NY 11375
O. Lewis Harris, Executive Director
Tel: (718) 592-5757 Fax: (718) 592-2933
Email: oharris@fhch.org
Web: www.fhch.org

HEMPSTEAD HISPANIC CIVIC ASSOCIATION
236 Main St.
Hempstead, NY 11550
Agnes M. Rodríguez, Executive Director
Tel: (516) 292-0007 Fax: (516) 292-0026
Email: hhcany@hotmail.com

THE HISPANIC FEDERATION
130 William St., 9th Fl.
New York, NY 10038
Lillian Rodriguez-Lopez, President/CEO
Tel: (212) 233-8955 Fax: (212) 233-8996
Email: info@hispanicfederation.org
Web: www.hispanicfederation.org

HISPANIC OUTREACH SERVICES
Administrative Office
40 N. Main Ave.
Albany, NY 12203
Sister Anne Tranelli, CSJ, Executive Director
Tel: (518) 453-6655 Fax: (518) 453-6792
Email: anne.tranelli@rcda.org
Web: www.hispanicoutreachservices.org

Albany Office
130 Ontario St.
Albany, NY 12206
Sister Anne Tranelli, CSJ, Executive Director
Tel: (518) 463-1217 Fax: (518) 463-1218
Email: hosalbanydo@choiceonemail.com
Web: www.hispanicoutreachservices.org

Amsterdam Outreach Office
1 Kimball St.
Amsterdam, NY 12010
Sister Anne Tranelli, CSJ, Executive Director
Tel: (518) 843-0004 Fax: (518) 843-0005
Email: hosamsterdamcr@choiceonemail.com
Web: www.hispanicoutreachservices.org

Schenectady Outreach Office
801 Stanley St.
Schenectady, NY 12307
Sister Anne Tranelli, CSJ, Executive Director
Tel: (518) 382-2004 Fax: (518) 382-2695
Email: hosschenectadyng@choiceonemail.com
Web: www.hispanicoutreachservices.org

LA GUARDIA MEMORIAL HOUSE
307 E 116th St.
New York, NY 10029
Luis Zuchman, Executive Director
Tel: (212) 534-7800 Fax: (212) 534-6068

Email: lewz@scanny.org
Web: www.scanny.org

LAMBERT HOUSES COMMUNITY DEVELOPMENT
1005 E 179th St.
Bronx, NY 10460
Rosmary Ordinar, Director
Tel: (718) 542-9377 Fax: (718) 542-0381
Email: rordonez@phippsny.org

LATINO OUTREACH PROGRAM
Learning Disabilities Association of New York
27 W. 20th St. #303
New York, NY 10011
Francisa Whisnant, Coordinator
Tel: (212) 645-6730 Fax: (212) 924-8896
Email: ldanyc@verizon.net
Web: www.ldanyc.com

LOWER WESTSIDE HOUSEHOLD SERVICES COOPERATION
250 W 57th St. #1511
New York, NY 10107
Lucia Pons, Executive Director
Tel: (212) 307-7107 Fax: (212) 956-2308

NATIONAL CENTER FOR MISSING & EXPLOITED CHILDREN
New York
275 Lake Ave.
Rochester, NY 14608-1042
Ellen Hagelberg, President
Tel: (585) 242-0900 Fax: (585) 242-0717
Email: nybranch@ncmec.org
Web: www.missingkids.com

NATIONAL CENTER FOR MISSING & EXPLOITED CHILDREN
New York/Mohawk Valley
934 York St.
Utica, NY 13502
Kathy Harm, Director
Tel: (315) 732-7233 Fax: (315) 624-7134
Email: kharm@ncmec.org
Web: www.missingkids.com

NATIONAL LATINO ALLIANCE FOR THE ELIMINATION OF DOMESTIC VIOLENCE
P.O. Box 672
New York, NY 10035
Adelita M. Medina, Exxecutive Director
Tel: (646) 672-1404 Fax: (646) 672-0360
Email: amedina@dvalianza.org
Web: www.dvalianza.org

NUEVO EL BARRIO PARA LA REBILITACION DE LA VIVIENDA Y ECONOMIA
18 E. 116th St.
New York, NY 10029
Roberto Anazagasti, Manager
Tel: (212) 427-0555 Fax: (212) 427-0875
Email: ranerve1@aol.com

OFFICE FOR HISPANIC AFFAIRS
Westchester County Government
148 Martine Ave. #911
White Plains, NY 10601
Martha Lopez-Hanratty, Program Administrator
Tel: (914) 995-2476
Email: mal6@westchestergov.com
Web: www.westchestergov.com/hispanicaffairs/

PRONTO OF LONG ISLAND, INC.
128 Pineaire Dr.
Bay Shore, NY 11706
Ruth V. Negron-Gaines, Executive Director
Tel: (631) 231-8290 Fax: (631) 231-8390
Email: prontolieoptonline.net

RURAL OPPORTUNITIES, INC.
Central Administrative Offices
400 E. Ave.
Rochester, NY 14607
Stuart J. Mitchell, President/CEO
Tel: (585) 340-3369 Fax: (585) 340-3337
Email: smitchell@ruralinc.org
Web: www.ruralinc.org

SOUTHSIDE COMMUNITY MISSION, INC.
280 Marcy Ave.
Brooklyn, NY 11211
John Mulhurn, Supervisor
Tel: (718) 782-8181 Fax: (718) 388-2702
Email: ffcmny@aol.com

TINKER FOUNDATION, INC.
55 E. 59th St.
New York, NY 10022
Martha Twitchell Muse, Chairman
Tel: (212) 421-6858 Fax: (212) 223-3326
Email: tinker@tinker.org
Web: http://fdncenter.org/grantmaker/tinker

**UNION OF NEEDLETRADES INDUSTRIAL &
TEXTILE EMPLOYEES**
Headquarters Office
275 7th Ave.
New York, NY 10001-6708
Chris Chafe, Political Action Coordinator
Tel: (212) 265-7000
Email: cchafe@unitehere.org
Web: www.uniteunion.org

UNITED BRONX PARENTS, INC.
La Casita
834 E 156th St.
Bronx, NY 10455
Olga Ambert, Director
Tel: (718) 292-9808 Fax: (718) 665-5778
Web: www.ubpinc.org

La Casita #3
1006 151st St.
Bronx, NY 10455
Myrlen Banks, Assistant Director
Tel: (718) 742-0082 Fax: (718) 742-9367

**UNITED PUERTO RICAN ORGANIZATION OF
SUNSET PARK**
166-A 22nd St.
Brooklyn, NY 11232
Elizabeth C. Yeampierre, Executive Director
Tel: (718) 492-9307 Fax: (718) 492-9030
Email: uprise99@aol.com

WESTCHESTER HISPANIC COALITION
46 Waller Ave.
White Plains, NY 10605
Graciela Heymann, Executive Director
Tel: (914) 948-8466 Fax: (914) 948-0311
Email: whc10605@aol.com

**WESTERN NEW YORK HISPANICS AND
FRIENDS CIVIC ASSOCIATION**
429 W Delavan Ave.
Buffalo, NY 14213
Andrés García, President
Tel: (716) 859-4100 Fax: (716) 859-4109
Email: agarcia@kaleadahelp.org

HENRY STREET SETTLEMENT
265 Henry St.
New York, NY 10002
Verona Jeter, Executive Director
Tel: (212) 766-9200 Fax: (212) 791-5710
Email: info@henrystreet.org
Web: www.henrystreet.org

THE HUMANIST CENTER OF CULTURES
43-13 47th St. #E36
Long Island City, NY 11104
Nicole Myers, Director
Tel: (212) 501-0118
Email: nicole@newhumanist.net
Web: www.centerofcultures.org

100 HISPANIC WOMEN, INC.
358 5th Ave. #504
New York, NY 10001
Shirley Rodriguez Remeneski, President
Tel: (212) 239-1430 Fax: (212) 239-1431
Email: feedback@100hispanicwomen.org
Web: www.100hispanicwomen.org

**DOMINICAN WOMEN'S DEVELOPMENT
CENTER**
519 W. 189th St., Ground Fl.
New York, NY 10040
Rosita M. Romero, Executive Director
Tel: (212) 994-6060 Fax: (212) 994-6065
Email: el.centro@verizon.net

**EDWIN GOULD SERVICES FOR CHILDREN OF
UNITED FAMILIES OF EAST HARLEM**
1968 2nd Ave.
New York, NY 10029
Gerald Weeks, Director
Tel: (212) 876-0367 Fax: (212) 876-0874
Email: newyork1971@dfaalstate.ny.us

LATIN WOMEN IN ACTION
103-06 39th Ave.
Corona, NY 11368
Hadee Zambrana, CEO
Tel: (718) 478-2972
Web: www.mujereslatinasenaccion.com

**NATIONAL LATINA INSTITUTE FOR
REPRODUCTIVE HEALTH**
50 Broad St. #1825
New York, NY 10004
Silivia Henriquez, Executive Director
Tel: (212) 422-2553 Fax: (212) 422-2556
Email: nlirh@latinainstitute.org
Web: www.latinainstitute.org

**NONTRADITIONAL EMPLOYMENT FOR
WOMEN**
243 W 20th St.
New York, NY 10011
Anne Rascon, Executive Director
Tel: (212) 627-6252 Fax: (646) 486-2293
Email: new@new-nyc.org
Web: www.new-nyc.org

PRO MUJER INTERNATIONAL
120 Wall St., 20th Fl.
New York, NY 10005
Lynne Patterson, Executive Director
Tel: (212) 952-0181
Email: promujer@promujer.org
Web: www.promujer.org

WOMEN'S COMMUNITY HEALTH CLINIC
975 Westchester Ave.
Bronx, NY 10459
Lillian Kestler, Center Director
Tel: (718) 991-9250 Fax: (718) 991-3829
Web: www.chnnyc.org

WOMEN'S PRISON ASSOCIATION
110 2nd Ave.
New York, NY 10003
Ann L. Jacobs, Executive Director
Tel: (212) 674-1163 Fax: (212) 677-1981
Email: ajacobs@wpaonline.org
Web: www.wpaonline.org

ASOCIACIONES DOMINICANAS, INC.
510 W 145th St.
New York, NY 10031
Sukhwant Walia, Executive Director
Tel: (212) 690-3290 Fax: (212) 368-2677

**BRONX CHILDREN CENTER COMMUNITY
PROGRAM**
4215 3rd Ave.
Bronx, NY 10457
Dr. John Litt, Director
Tel: (718) 299-2304 Fax: (718) 583-6090

**BRONX ORGANIZATION FOR THE LEARNING
DISABLED**
1180 Rev. James Polite Ave.
Bronx, NY 10459
M. Egan, Director
Tel: (718) 589-7379 Fax: (718) 589-2052
Email: boldny@aol.com

**COMMITTEE FOR HISPANIC CHILDREN AND
FAMILIES, INC.**
Affiliate of NCLR
140 W. 22nd St. #301
New York, NY 10011
Elba Montalvo, Executive Director
Tel: (212) 206-1090 Fax: (212) 206-8093
Email: chcfinc@chcfinc.org
Web: www.chcfinc.org

**EASTER SEALS CHILD DEVELOPMENT
CENTER**
1180 Rev. James Polite Ave.
Bronx, NY 10459
Gloria Altieri, Director
Tel: (718) 378-1370 Fax: (718) 378-1370
Email: galtieri@eastersealsny.org

ELMCOR YOUTH ADULT ACTIVITIES, INC.
Women and Child
107-20 Northern Blvd.
Corona, NY 11368
Paula Mostossky, Clinical Supervisor
Tel: (718) 651-0096 Fax: (718) 457-3932
Email: info@elmcor.org
Web: www.elmcor.org

**FAMILY COUNSELING SERVICE OF THE
FINGER LAKES, INC.**
Hispanic Youth Program
671 S Exchange St.
Geneva, NY 14456
Maria Bizardi, Hispanic Youth Program
Coordinator
Tel: (315) 789-2613 Fax: (315) 789-2524
Email: familycounselingservice@yahoo.com

**GLENN E. HINES MEMORIAL BOYS AND
GIRLS CLUB OF NEWBURGH**
285 Liberty St.
Newburgh, NY 12550
Nelson McAllister, Chief Professional Officer
Tel: (845) 561-4936 Fax: (845) 561-5288
Email: nmcal285@aol.com
Web: www.bgcnewburghny.net

**LA ASOCIACIÓN BENEFICA CULTURAL PADRE
BILLINI**
25-28 89th St.
Jackson Heights, NY 11370
Ana López, Executive Director
Tel: (718) 651-8427 Fax: (718) 651-5572
Email: fba4000@hotmail.com

**NEIGHBORHOOD ASSOCIATION FOR PUERTO
RICAN AFFAIRS**
1997 Bathgate Ave.
Bronx, NY 10457
Carmen Bermúdez, Executive Director
Tel: (718) 583-3220 Fax: (718) 731-4096
Email: naprainc@aol.com

NEIGHBORHOOD YOUTH & FAMILY SERVICES
601 E Tremont Ave.
Bronx, NY 10457
Lizette H. Tait, Executive Director
Tel: (718) 299-2340 Fax: (718) 299-2343
Email: nyfs1@aol.com

**NEW YORK COUNCIL ON ADOPTABLE
CHILDREN**
589 8th Ave., 15th Fl.
New York, NY 10018
Ernesto Loperena, Executive Director
Tel: (212) 475-0222 Fax: (212) 714-2838
Email: coac@erols.com
Web: www.coac.org

**NYC BRONX TASK FORCE CHILD ABUSE
PREVENTION**
Headquarters
1551 Parker St.
Bronx, NY 10462
Dominick J. Masullo, Chief of Department
Tel: (718) 863-1882 Fax: (718) 863-2810
Email: infor@bxtfcap.org
Web: www.bxtfcap1.org

THE PUERTO RICAN FAMILY INSTITUTE, INC.
Bronx Child Placement Prevention Program
384 E 149th St. #622
Bronx, NY 10455
Luis A. Rivera, Program Director
Tel: (718) 665-0005 Fax: (718) 665-1282
Web: www.prfi.org

Children's Intensive Care Management Program
175 Remsen St., 11th Fl.
Brooklyn, NY 11201
Beverly Christie, Senior Program Leader
Tel: (718) 596-1320 Fax: (718) 596-1250
Web: www.prfi.org

**THE PUERTO RICAN YOUTH DEVELOPMENT
AND RESOURCE CENTER, INC.**
997 N. Clinton Ave.
Rochester, NY 14621
Nancy Padilla, Executive Director
Tel: (585) 325-3570 Fax: (585) 325-3767
Email: pryd@fpryd.org
Web: www.pryd.org

**RIDGEWOOD BUSHWICK SENIOR CITIZENS
COUNCIL, INC.**
Youth and Education Department
1474 Gates Ave.
Brooklyn, NY 11237
Lucy Belardo, Coordinator
Tel: (718) 381-9653 Fax: (718) 381-9680
Email: youthandeducation@rbscc.org
Web: www.rbscc.org

SINERGIA, INC.
15 W. 65th St., 6th Fl.
New York, NY 10023
Donald Lasa, Executive Director
Tel: (212) 496-1300 Fax: (212) 496-5608
Email: intake@sinergiany.org
Web: www.sinergiany.org

CENTER FOR MULTICULTURAL AFFAIRS
SUNY College at Fredonia
E-125 Thompson Hall
Fredonia, NY 14063
Averl Otis, Director
Tel: (716) 673-3398 Fax: (716) 673-3765
Email: averl.otis@fredonia.edu
Web: www.fredonia.edu/department/maffairs/
index.asp

CHI UPSILON SIGMA LATIN SORORITY, INC.
Grand Chapter Board
99 Park Ave. #278A
New York, NY 10016
Militza Diaz, President
Tel: (212) 969-0793 Fax: (212) 867-7904
Email: president@justbecus.org
Web: www.justbecus.org

CUBAN AMERICAN STUDENT ASSOCIATION
Cornell University
434 Rockefeller Hall
Ithaca, NY 14853
Maria Christina Garcia, Advisor
Tel: (607) 255-3197 Fax: (607) 255-2433
Email: mcg20@cornell.edu
Web: http://latino.lsp.cornell.edu

DOMINICAN STUDENT ASSOCIATION
Cornell University
434 Rockefeller Hall
Ithaca, NY 14853
Hector Velez, Advisor
Tel: (607) 255-3197 Fax: (607) 255-2433
Email: velez@ithaca.edu
Web: www.rso.cornell.edu/quisqueya

DOMINICANS 2000
The City College of New York, North Academic Ctr. 3/201, Convent Ave. at 138th St.
New York, NY 10031
Ydanis Rodríguez, Chair
Tel: (212) 650-5008 Fax: (212) 650-5035
Email: kirsys@hotmail.com

FUERZA LATINA
University at Albany, State University of New York
1400 Washington Ave., Campus Ctr. #349
Albany, NY 12222
Raquel Mendoza, President
Tel: (518) 442-5679 Fax: (518) 442-3908
Email: fuerza@csc.albany.edu
Web: www.albany.edu/~fuerza

HERMANDAD DE SIGMA IOTA ALPHA, INC.
Headquarters
P.O. Box 237
New York, NY 10012
Jessica Anne Mayorga, national President
Email: neb@hermandad-sia.org
Web: www.hermandad-sia.org

LA ASOCIACIÓN LATINA
Cornell University
434 Rockefeller Hall
Ithaca, NY 14853
Melanie Castro, Co-Chair
Tel: (607) 255-3197 Fax: (607) 255-2433
Email: mrc35@cornell.edu
Web: http://latino.lsp.cornell.edu

LA LUCHA
Cornell University
434 Rockefeller Hall
Ithaca, NY 14853-1601
Danette Danield, President
Tel: (607) 255-3197 Fax: (607) 255-2433
Email: dld27@cornell.edu
Web: http://latino.lsp.cornell.edu

LA UNIDAD LATINA, LAMBDA UPSILON FRATERNITY, INC.
Albany University
Campus Center 130, 1400 Washington Ave.
Albany, NY 12206
Oliver Labastida, President
Email: LUL@albany.edu
Web: www.albany.edu/~lul

Cornell University
722 University Ave., 434 Rockefeller Hall
Ithaca, NY 14850
Hector Velez, Advisor
Tel: (607) 255-3197 Fax: (607) 255-2433
Email: velez@ithaca.edu
Web: www.rso.cornell.edu/lambdas

National Office
PMB #39, 511 6th Ave.
New York, NY 10011
Jason Torres, President
Tel: Fax: (707) 215-0538
Email: president@launidadlatina.org
Web: www.launidadlatina.org

LAMBDA ALPHA UPSILON
National Headquarters
29 John St., PMB 181
New York, NY 10038
Anthony Munoz, National Executive Director
Email: collegiate@lambdas.com
Web: www.lambdas.com

LAMBDA THETA PHI, FRATERNIDAD LATINA, INC.
Cornell University
434 Rockefeller Hall
Ithaca, NY 14853-1601
Terrell Buckner, Chapter President
Tel: (607) 255-3197 Fax: (607) 255-2433
Email: tb77@cornell.edu
Web: www.rso.cornell.edu/lambda

LATIN AMERICAN LAW STUDENTS ASSOCIATION
Columbia University Law School
435 W. 116th St. #108
New York, NY 10027
Francesco Noero
Tel: (212) 854-2395
Email: fn2109@columbia.edu
Web: www.law.columbia.edu

LATIN AMERICAN SOCIETY
St. Francis College
180 Remsen St.
Brooklyn, NY 11201
Enildo Garcia, Director
Tel: (718) 522-2300 X4895239

LATIN AMERICAN STUDENT ORGANIZATION
State University of New York, Stony Brook
Student Activities Ctr. #202
Stony Brook, NY 11794-2800
Elizabeth Guerra, President
Tel: (646) 732-9339
Web: www.ic.sunysb.edu/Clubs/laso/

LATIN AMERICAN STUDENTS ASSOCIATION
Mercy College
555 Broadway
Dobbs Ferry, NY 10522
Tel: (914) 674-7236 Fax: (914) 693-9455

LATINAS PROMOVIENDO COMUNIDAD/ LAMBDA PI CHI SORORITY, INC.
Cornell University
434 Rockefeller Hall
Ithaca, NY 14853-1601
Imasul Villarreal, President
Tel: (607) 255-3197 Fax: (607) 255-2433
Email: iv25@cornell.edu
Web: www.rso.cornell.edu/lpcalpha

LATINO MALE AND FEMALE INITIATIVE
Borough of Manhattan Community College
199 Chambers St. #S-326
New York, NY 10007
Dr. Pedro Pérez, Counselor/Asst. Professor
Tel: (212) 220-8154 Fax: (212) 220-1298
Email: pperez@bmcc.cuny.edu

LATINO STUDIES PROGRAM
Cornell University
434 Rockefeller Hall
Ithaca, NY 14853
Mary Pat Brady, Director
Tel: (607) 255-3197 Fax: (607) 255-2433
Email: mpb23@cornell.edu
Web: http://latino.lsp.cornell.edu

MOVIMIENTO ESTUDIANTIL CHICANO DE AZTLAN
Cornell University
434 Rockefeller Hall
Ithaca, NY 14853
Elisa Cruz, Co-Chair
Email: pachanga2004@cornell.edu
Web: www.rso.cornell.edu/mecha

NATIONAL ASSOCIATION OF LATINO FRATERNAL ORGANIZATIONS, INC.
320 Quinby Rd.
Rochester, NY 14623-1226
Jeffrey Vargas, Chair
Email: jvargas@launidadlatina.org
Web: www.nalfo.org

OMEGA PHI BETA SORORITY, INC.
Gamma Chapter
P.O. Box 3352
Grand Central Station
New York, NY 10163
Nicole Jarvis, President
Email: gamma@omegaphibeta.org
Web: www.omegaphibeta.org

PHI IOTA ALPHA FRATERNITY
State University of New York at New Paltz SUNY
75 S Manheim Blvd., Student Activities Office
New Paltz, NY 12561
Marvin James, President
Tel: (914) 257-4845 Fax: (845) 257-3695
Web: www.phiota.org

PUERTO RICAN STUDENT ASSOCIATION
Cornell University
434 Rockefeller Hall
Ithaca, NY 14853-1601
Nilsa Maldonado, Advisor
Tel: (607) 255-3197 Fax: (607) 255-2433
Email: nbm4@cornell.edu
Web: http://latino.lsp.cornell.edu

SABOR LATINO DANCE ENSEMBLE
Cornell University
434 Rockefeller Hall
Ithaca, NY 14853
Marihug Cedeno, President
Tel: (607) 255-3197
Web: http://latino.lsp.cornell.edu

SANGRE TAINA
Cornell University
434 Rockefeller Hall
Ithaca, NY 14853
Nilsa Maldonado, Advisor
Tel: (607) 255-3197 Fax: (607) 255-2433
Email: nbm4@cornell.edu
Web: http://latino.lsp.cornell.edu

SCIENCE ORGANIZATION OF LATINOS
Cornell University
434 Rockefeller Hall
Ithaca, NY 14853-1601
Laurel Southhard, Advisor
Tel: (607) 255-3197 Fax: (607) 255-2433
Email: les3@cornell.edu
Web: http://latino.lsp.cornell.edu

SIGMA LAMBDA UPSILON/SENORITAS LATINAS UNIDAS SORORITY, INC.
Cornell University
434 Rockefeller Hall
Ithaca, NY 14853
Daisy Torres, President
Tel: (607) 255-3197 Fax: (607) 255-2433
Email: dt69@cornell.edu
Web: http://latino.lsp.cornell.edu

SOCIETY OF HISPANIC PROFESSIONAL ENGINEERS
Cornell University Student Chapter
167 Olin Hall
Ithaca, NY 14853
Jackie Romero, President
Tel: (607) 255-4896 Fax: (607) 255-2433
Email: shpe@cornell.edu
Web: www.rso.cornell.edu/shpe/sponsors.php

TEATROTALLER
Cornell University
434 Rockefeller Hall
Ithaca, NY 14853
Debra Castillo, Advisor
Tel: (607) 255-3197 Fax: (607) 255-2433
Email: dac9@cornell.edu
Web: http://latino.lsp.cornell.edu

NORTH CAROLINA

LATIN AMERICAN CHAMBER OF COMMERCE OF CHARLOTTE, INC.
2938 Whet Meadow Ln.
Charlotte, NC 28270
Carlos E. Sanchez, Chairman
Tel: (704) 806-0106 Fax: (704) 510-7470
Email: info@lacccharlotte.com
Web: www.lacccharlotte.com

NORTH CAROLINA HISPANIC CHAMBER OF COMMERCE
150 Fayetteville St. Mall #110
Raleigh, NC 27601
Federico van Gelderen, President
Tel: (919) 828-6087
Email: info@nchcc.org
Web: www.nchcc.org

ESPANOL MARKETING AND COMMUNICCATIONS, INC.
2000 CentreGreen Way #140
Cary, NC 27513
Eva May, Managing Director
Tel: (919) 678-6133 Fax: (919) 678-6134
Email: hola@espanolmarketing.com
Web: www.espanolmarketing.com

CENTRO HISPANO/LATINO
222 B Hay St.
Fayetteville, NC 28301
Janice Holden, President
Tel: (910) 321-1492 Fax: (910) 321-1495
Email: hlcenter@mindspring.com

THE HISPANIC/LATINO CENTER, INC.
222 B Hay St.
Fayettesville, NC 28301
Janis Holden, President
Tel: (910) 321-1492 Fax: (910) 321-1495
Email: hlcenter@mindspring.com

NATIONAL LATINO PEACE OFFICERS ASSOCIATION
North Carolina - La Calle Chapter
P.O. Box 528
Greenville, NC 27835
John Garcia, President
Tel: (877) 657-6200
Email: hispanicoutreach@wilsonnc.org
Web: www.nlpoa.org

EL VINCULO HISPANO
105 E. 2nd St.
Siler City, NC 27344
Vince Sanabria, Executive Director
Tel: (919) 742-1448 Fax: (919) 742-1451
Email: sanabria@pinehurst.net

LATINO COMMUNITY DEVELOPMENT CENTER
201 W. Main St.
Durham, NC 27701
Ivan Kohar Parra, Executive Director
Tel: (919) 225-1673
Email: kmparra@aol.com

MI CASA SU CASA CENTRO DE RECURSOS
6030 Albemarle Rd.
Charlotte, NC 28212
Tel: (704) 536-9845 Fax: (704) 536-9876
Email: micasa@dasia.net
Web: www.micasasucasa.org

EL PUEBLO, INC.
4 N. Blount St.
Raleigh, NC 27601
Andrea Bazan-Manson, Executive Director
Tel: (919) 835-1525 Fax: (919) 835-1526
Email: elpueblo@elpueblo.org
Web: www.elpueblo.org

NORTH CAROLINA SOCIETY OF HISPANIC PROFESSIONALS
P.O. Box 1557
Apex, NC 27502-3557
Marco Zarate, President
Tel: (919) 654-4516
Email: mailbox@thencshp.org
Web: www.thencshp.org

RELIGIOUS

CATHOLIC SOCIAL SERVICES
Programa Esperanza
1123 S Church St.
Charlotte, NC 28203-4003
Teresa Villamarin, Social Worker, Outreach, Hispanic Services
Tel: (704) 370-3235 Fax: (704) 370-3377
Email: tivillamarin@charlottediocese.org
Web: www.cssnc.org

DIOCESE OF CHARLOTTE
Hispanic Affairs
6212 Tuckaseegee Rd.
Charlotte, NC 28214
Rev. Vincent Finnerty, CM, Director for Hispanic Ministry
Tel: (704) 391-3732

DIOCESE OF CHARLOTTE
Hispanic Affairs
1123 S. Church St.
Charlotte, NC 28203-4003
Sr. Andrea Inkrott, OSF, Director Hispanic Ministry
Tel: (704) 370-3269
Web: www.charlottediocese.org

DIOCESE OF RALEIGH
Hispanic Affairs
715 Nazareth St.
Raleigh, NC 27606
Rev. Fernando Torres, Vicar for Hispanic Ministry
Tel: (919) 821-9738 Fax: (919) 821-9705
Email: torres@raldioc.org
Web: www.dioceseofraleigh.org

DIOCESE OF RALEIGH
Hispanic Ministry
715 Nazareth St.
Raleigh, NC 27606-2187
Teresa Aldahondo, Coordinator
Tel: (919) 821-9764 Fax: (919) 821-8140
Email: alda@raldioc.org
Web: www.dioceseofraleigh.org

SEMINARIO DE GRACIA
P.O. Box 91627
Raleigh, NC 27675
Daniel White, President
Tel: (919) 414-2947
Email: danglowhite@mindspring.com
Web: www.seminariodegracia.org

ST. JULIA CATHOLIC CHURCH
210 Harold Hart Rd.
Siler City, NC 27344-8346
Michael Lorentsen, OFM Conv., Pastor
Tel: (919) 742-5584 Fax: (919) 742-4917

SPEC. INT., AIDS

AMERICAN SOCIAL HEALTH ASSOCIATION
P.O Box 13827
Research Triangle Park, NC 27709
James R. Allen, President/CEO
Tel: (919) 361-8400 Fax: (919) 361-8425
Web: http://www.ashastd.org

SPEC. INT., CHILD CARE

CHILD CARE NETWORKS, INC.
Latino Program
P.O. Box 1531
117 E. Salisbury St.
Pittsboro, NC 27312
Florence Simán, Latino Project Coordinator

Tel: (919) 542-6644 Fax: (919) 542 0902
Email: Florence@childcarenetwroks.org
Web: www.childcarenetworks.org

SPEC. INT., EDUCATION

CENTER FOR LATIN AMERICAN & CARIBBEAN STUDIES
Duke University
2114 Campus Dr.
Durham, NC 27708-0255
John French, Director
Tel: (919) 681-3980 Fax: (919) 681-7966
Web: www.duke.edu/web/las

DIAMANTE, INC.
106 Lochwood East Dr.
Cary, NC 27511
Lizette Cruz-Watko, Executive Director
Tel: (919) 852-0075 Fax: (919) 852-0075
Email: latinodiamante@mindspring.com
Web: http://latinodiamante.home.mindspring.com

INSTITUTE OF LATIN AMERICAN STUDIES
University of North Carolina at Chapel Hill
223 E Franklin St., Campus Box 3205
Chapel Hill, NC 27599-3205
Arturo Escobar, Director
Tel: (919) 966-1484 Fax: (919) 962-0398
Email: ilas@email.unc.edu
Web: www.unc.edu/depts/ilas/front.html

SPEC. INT., FAMILY PLANNING

NETWORK EN ESPAÑOL
Family Health International
P.O. Box 13950
Research Triangle Park, NC 27709
Marina McCune, Editor
Tel: (919) 544-6979 X444 Fax: (919) 544-7261
Email: mmccune@fhi.org
Web: www.fhi.org

SPEC. INT., HUMAN RELATIONS

CASA INTERNACIONAL
322 Hawthorne Ln.
Charlotte, NC 28204
Jose Hernandez Paris, Executive Director
Tel: (704) 333-8099 Fax: (704) 334-2423
Email: info@ihclt.org
Web: www.ihclt.org

THE HISPANIC TASK FORCE OF LEE COUNTY
1817 Lee Ave.
Sanford, NC 27330
Meribel Diaz, Executive Director
Tel: (919) 775-5447 Fax: (919) 777-5295

INTERNATIONAL HOUSE
322 Hawthorne Ln.
Charlotte, NC 28204
José Hernández-Paris, Executive Director
Tel: (704) 333-8099 Fax: (704) 334-2423
Email: info@ihclt.org
Web: www.ihclt.org

TELAMON CORPORATION
Hendersonville Head Start Center 13
2 Sugar Hill Dr.
Hendersonville, NC 28792
Shawn Wolff, Center Director
Tel: (828) 697-8266 Fax: (828) 697-9132
Email: shawnwolff@telamon.org
Web: www.telamon.org

St. Martin Migrant Head Start Center 17
3201 Easy St.
Dunn, NC 28334
Josie Lorenzo, Center Director
Tel: (910) 567-5510 Fax: (910) 567-5519
Email: jlorenzo@telamon.org
Web: www.telamon.org

- **State Office 1**
4917 Waters Edge Dr. #220

Raleigh, NC 27606
Thom Myers, State Director
Tel: (919) 851-6141 X221 Fax: (919) 851-2605
Email: tmyers@telamon.org
Web: www.telamon.org

State Office 11
P.O. Box 1626
Whiteville, NC 28472
Margie Atkinson, Regional Manager
Tel: (910) 642-8229 Fax: (910) 642-8555
Email: matkinson@telamon.org
Web: www.telamon.org

State Office 12
P.O. Box 7074
Wilson, NC 27893
Faye Lucas, Regional Manager
Tel: (252) 291-1203 Fax: (252) 291-6859
Email: flucas@telamon.org
Web: www.telamon.org

State Office 2
P.O. Box 37
Ahoskie, NC 27910
Brenda Chamblee, Regional Manager
Tel: (252) 332-4381 Fax: (252) 332-3260
Email: bchamblee@telamon.org
Web: www.telamon.org

State Office 22
5300 Foxfire Rd.
Fayetteville, NC 28303
Karina Fonseca, Regional Coordinator
Tel: (910) 826-1185 Fax: (910) 828-9583
Email: kfonseca@telamon.org
Web: www.telamon.org

State Office 4
1314 N Main St. #B
Hendersonville, NC 28792
Jairo Mercado-Estay, Regional Manager
Tel: (828) 692-0593 Fax: (828) 698-0282
Email: jmercado@telamon.org
Web: www.telamon.org

State Office 6
302 E Church St.
Benson, NC 27504
Enrique Torres, Regional Manager
Tel: (919) 207-5813 Fax: (919) 207-1914
Email: etorres@telamon.org
Web: www.telamon.org

State Office 7
220 Wintergreen Dr. #F, North Court Sq.
Lumberton, NC 28358
Patsy Jacobs, Regional Manager
Tel: (910) 671-0504 Fax: (910) 671-0190
Email: pjacobs@telamon.org
Web: www.telamon.org

Telamon Corporate Office 99
P.O. Box 33315
Raleigh, NC 27636-3315
Richard A. Joanis, Executive Director
Tel: (919) 851-7611 X201 Fax: (919) 851-1139
Email: djoanis@telamon.org
Web: www.telamon.org

W.W. Newman Head Start Center 18
P.O. Box 129
Prospect Hill, NC 27314
Denise Pierce, Center Director
Tel: (336) 562-5737 Fax: (336) 562-5739
Email: dpierce@esinc.net
Web: www.telamon.org

SPEC. INT., INFORMATION REFERRAL

OFFICE OF CITIZEN SERVICES
North Carolina Department of Health and Human Services
2012 Mail Service Ctr.
Raleigh, NC 27699-2012
Rogelio Valencia, Hispanic Ombudsman
Tel: (919) 855-4401 Fax: (919) 715-8174

Email: care.line@ncmail.net
Web: www.dhhs.state.nc.us/ocs

SPEC. INT., LEGAL ASSISTANCE

HISPANIC NATIONAL BAR ASSOCIATION
Region VI (NC, SC)
P.O. Box 2760
c/o Sara Lee Branded Apparel
Winston-Salem, NC 27102
Francisco Velasco, President
Tel: (336) 519-5686
Email: francisco.velasco@saralee.com
Web: www.hnba.com

SPEC. INT., SOCIAL INTEREST

CENTRO HISPANO
201 W. Main St. #100
Durham, NC 27701
Angelina Schiavone, Executive Director
Tel: (919) 687-4635 Fax: (919) 687-0401
Email: aschiavone@elcentronc.org

COALICIÓN LATINOAMERICANA/LATIN AMERICAN COALITION
5471 Central Ave. #A
Charlotte, NC 28212
Angeles Ortega Moore, Executive Director
Tel: (704) 531-3848 Fax: (704) 531-3850
Email: info@latinamericancoalition.org
Web: www.latinamericancoalition.org

CULTURAS UNIDAS
975 Walnut St. #104
Cary, NC 27511
Sara Nienow, President
Tel: (919) 467-6696 Fax: (919) 467-6042
Email: info@culturasunidas.org
Web: www.culturasunidas.org

FARMWORKER PROJECT
P.O. Box 352
Benson, NC 27504
Mercedes Hernandez, Administrator
Tel: (919) 894-7406 Fax: (919) 894-7406
Email: mercedessp@earthlink.net

HIGH COUNTRY AMIGOS, INC.
820 State Farm Rd. #E
Boone, NC 28607
Yolanda Otero Dillard, President
Tel: (828) 264-2930
Email: amigos@goboone.net
Web: www.highcountryamigos.org

LATIN AMERICAN RESOURCE CENTER
P.O. Box 31871
Raleigh, NC 27622-1871
Aura Camacho-Maas, Executive Director
Tel: (919) 839-7200
Email: auracm@thelarc.org
Web: www.thelarc.org

PROGRAMA ESPERANZA
Catholic Social Services/Diocese of Charlotte
1123 S. Church St.
Charlotte, NC 28203
Carmen Cruz, Social Worker/Hispanic Services
Tel: (704) 370-3236 Fax: (704) 370-3377
Email: cmcruz@charlottediocese.org
Web: www.cssnc.org/Esperanza

UNITED WAY OF CENTRAL CAROLINAS, INC.
301 S Brevard St.
Charlotte, NC 28202
Gloria King, Director
Tel: (704) 377-1100 Fax: (704) 342-4482
Email: info@uwcentralcarolinas.org
Web: www.uwcentralcarolinas.org

STUDENT ORGANIZATION

CAROLINA HISPANIC ASSOCIATION
University of North Carolina, Chapel Hill
Carolina Union, Box 25, FPG Student Union, CB
Chapel Hill, NC 27599

Juan Gonzalez-Espitia, Advisor
Tel: (919) 962-1024
Email: jcge@email.unc.edu
Web: www.unc.edu/student/orgs/chispa

HISPANIC LAW STUDENTS ASSOCIATION
Duke University
School of Law
Durham, NC 27708
Ana Maria Navia, President
Tel: (919) 613-7007
Email: Ana.Navia@law.duke.edu

LATINAS PROMOVIENDO COMUNIDAD/ LAMBDA PI CHI SORORITY, INC.
Kappa Chapter, Duke University
1 Office of University Life, 01-3 Bryan Ctr., Box 90834
Durham, NC 27708
Adrianna Domingos, President
Tel: (619) 684-8111
Email: LPC_kappa@egroups.com
Web: www.duke.edu/web/lpc/

MI GENTE, ASOCIACION DE ESTUDIANTES LATINOS
Duke University
Durham, NC 27708
Tomas Lopez, Co-President
Tel: (919) 613-7007
Email: tl2@duke.edu
Web: www.duke.edu/web/migente

NORTH DAKOTA

SPEC. INT., LEGAL ASSISTANCE

MIGRANT LEGAL SERVICES
North Dakota Office
118 Broadway #616
Fargo, ND 58102
Arabella Demetario, Supervisor
Tel: (701) 232-8872 Fax: (701) 232-8366
Email: arabella.demetario@smrls.org
Web: www.smrls.org

OHIO

ARTISTIC

ALMA DE MEXICO
4603 Willow Ave.
Lorain, OH 44055
Vanessa Villa, Director
Tel: (440) 277-4676
Email: volleysaint2@yahoo.com

BUSINESS

COLUMBUS MINORITY CONTRACTORS AND BUSINESS ASSISTANCE PROGRAM
1393 E Broad St., 2nd Fl.
Columbus, OH 43205-1534
Frank Watson, President
Tel: (614) 252-8005 Fax: (614) 258-9667
Email: mcbap@comba.com
Web: www.comba.com

NATIONAL SOCIETY OF HISPANIC MBAS
Cincinnati Chapter
P.O. Box 8124
Cincinnati, OH 45208-0124
Ramon Rodriguez, Chapter President
Email: general@cincinnati.nshmba.org
Web: http://cincinnati.nshmba.org

SOUTH CENTRAL OHIO MINORITY BUSINESS COUNCIL
Headquarters Office
37 N. High St.
Columbus, OH 43215
Cathy Mock, President
Tel: (614) 225-6959 Fax: (614) 221-1669
Web: www.scombc.org

CHAMBER OF COMMERCE

GREATER DAYTON HISPANIC CHAMBER OF COMMERCE
1 Chamber Plz.
Dayton, OH 45402-2400
Philip Parker, President
Tel: (937) 226-8209 Fax: (937) 226-8254
Email: president@gd-hcc.org
Web: www.gd-hcc.org

HISPANIC CHAMBER OF COMMERCE FOR OHIO
4115 Bridge Ave. #107
Cleveland, OH 44113
Rick Zamora, Chairman
Tel: (216) 281-4422 Fax: (216) 281-4222
Email: hba@hbahcco.org
Web: www.hbahcco.org

HISPANIC CHAMBER OF COMMERCE OF GREATER CINCINNATI
3805 Edwards Rd. #555
Cincinnati, OH 45209-1948
Lori Wall, Office Manager
Tel: (513) 458-6649 Fax: (513) 458-6610
Email: hccgcrt@hispanicccgc.com
Web: www.hispanicccgc.com

HISPANIC CHAMBER OF COMMERCE OF GREATER COLUMBUS
2950 E. Main St.
Columbus, OH 43209-2615
Cecilia Roman, President
Tel: (614) 231-4744
Email: allvideo@ameritech.net

92 N Woods Blvd.
Columbus, OH 43235
Ezra Escudero, President
Tel: (614) 570-7701

CULTURAL

BUREAU OF CULTURAL AFFAIRS
216 N Main St.
Dayton, OH 45402
Pamela Harrington, Artist Curator
Tel: (937) 223-2489 Fax: (937) 223-0795

DAMAS LATINAS Y AMIGOS, INC.
P.O. Box 184
Columbus, OH 43085
Patricia Houston, President
Tel: (614) 841-1958
Email: dlatinasorg@mail.com

MEXICAN MUTUAL SOCIETY
Covain-Ohio
1820 E. 28th St.
Lorain, OH 44055
Joel Aredondo, President
Tel: (440) 277-7375

MEXICO CLUB OF GREATER DAYTON
8365 State Route 202
Tipp City, OH 45371
Philip Morones, President
Tel: (937) 667-5145 Fax: (937) 669-9996
Email: pmorones@woh.rr.com

LAW ENFORCEMENT

NATIONAL LATINO PEACE OFFICERS ASSOCIATION
Ohio Chapter
P.O. Box 351024
Toledo, OH 43635
Tom Gonzales, President
Tel: (877) 657-6200
Email: nlpoaohio@aol.com
Web: www.nlpoa.com

MULTI-PURPOSE

AMIGOS DE LAS AMERICAS
Ohio Chapter
P.O. Box 126
Kent, OH 44240
Nancy Grim, President
Tel: (330) 678-0727
Email: ngrim@sbcglobal.net
Web: http://io.amigoslink.org/~ohio/index.html

INTERNATIONAL FAMILY RESOURCE CENTER
Travelers Aid International of Greater Cincinnati
200 McFarland St.
Cincinnati, OH 45202
Naomi Sims Satterwhite, Executive Director
Tel: (513) 721-7660 Fax: (513) 354-8559
Email: ifrc@fsmail.org
Web: www.servingfamilies.org

LORAIN COUNTY URBAN LEAGUE
401 Broad St. #B
Elyria, OH 44035
Fred Wright, President/CEO
Tel: (440) 323-3364 Fax: (440) 323-5299
Email: fwright@lcul.org
Web: www.lcul.org

OFFICE OF HISPANIC STUDENT SERVICES
Ohio State University/Multicultural Center
4th Fl., Ohio Union, 1739 N. High St.
Cloumbus, OH 43210
Carmen Breckenridge, Coordinator
Tel: (614) 688-8449
Web: http://multiculturalcenter.osu.edu/hispanic/

OHIO HISPANIC COALITION
6161 Busch Blvd. #311
Columbus, OH 43229
Julia Arbini-Carbonell, President
Tel: (614) 840-9934 Fax: (614) 840-9935
Email: julia@ohiohispaniccoalition.org
Web: www.ohiohispaniccoalition.org

ORGANIZACION CIVICA Y CULTURAL HISPANA AMERICANA
3660 Shirley Rd.
Youngstown, OH 44502
Mary Isa Garayua, Director
Tel: (330) 781-1808 Fax: (330) 781-0885
Email: occha@sbcglobal.net
Web: http://youngstownoccha.org

UNIVERSITY-WIDE COUNCIL OF HISPANIC ORGANIZATIONS
Ohio State University
1739 N. High St. #211
Columbus, OH 43210
Maria de Cambra, Chair
Tel: (614) 292-9334
Email: de-cambra.1@osu.edu
Web: http://ucho.org.ohio-state.edu/

POLITICAL ACTION

OHIO HISPANIC DEMOCRATIC ORGANIZATION
271 E State St.
Columbus, OH 43215
Todd Rensi, Director
Tel: (614) 221-6563 Fax: (614) 221-0721
Email: todd@ohiodems.org
Web: www.ohiodems.org

PUERTO RICO FEDERAL AFFAIRS ADMINISTRATION
Ohio Satellite Office
5415 Lorain Ave.
Cleveland, OH 44102
Angel Pagan, Senior Community Officer
Tel: (216) 939-1722 Fax: (216) 939-1728
Email: info@prfaa.com
Web: www.prfaa.com

RELIGIOUS

ARCHDIOCESE OF CINCINNATI
Hispanic Ministries Office
115 W. Seymour Ave.
Cincinnati, OH 45216
Rev. William J. Jansen, MCCJ, Hispanic Coordinator
Tel: (513) 948-1760 Fax: (513) 521-7221
Email: wjanmccj@fuse.net

ARCHDIOCESE OF CINCINNATI
Hispanic Ministry Office St. Charles
115 W Seymour Ave.
Cincinnati, OH 45216
Rev. William Jansen, Director
Tel: (513) 948-1760 Fax: (513) 948-1823
Email: wjansen@catholiccincinnati.org
Web: www.catholiccincinnati.org

COMMISSION ON CATHOLIC COMMUNITY ACTION
7800 Detroit Ave.
Cleveland, OH 44102
Len Calabrese, Executive Director
Tel: (216) 281-3839 Fax: (216) 281-3850
Web: www.catholic-action.org

DIOCESE OF CLEVELAND
Office of Hispanic Ministry
1031 Superior Ave.
Cleveland, OH 44114-2519
Sr. Alicia Alvarado,, Director
Tel: (216) 696-6525 X2530 Fax: (216) 781-8243
Email: aalvarado@dioceseofcleveland.org
Web: www.dioceseofcleveland.org/hispanicministry

DIOCESE OF COLUMBUS
Hispanic Ministry Office
143 E Patterson Ave.
Columbus, OH 43202
Angela Johnston, Director for Hispanic Ministry
Tel: (614) 262-7992 Fax: (614) 263-6882
Email: cathlatinocntr@aol.com
Web: www.colsdioc.org

DIOCESE OF STEUBENVILLE
Hispanic Ministry Office
P.O. Box 969
Steubenville, OH 43952-5969
Linda A.Nichols, Contact
Tel: (740) 282-3631 Fax: (740) 282-3327
Email: lnichols@diosteub.org
Web: www.diosteub.org

DIOCESE OF TOLEDO
Hispanic Ministry Office
1933 Spielbusch Ave.
Toledo, OH 43697-0985
Misael Mayorga, Director for Hispanic Ministry
Tel: (419) 244-6711 Fax: (419) 244-4791
Email: mmyorga@toledodiocese.org
Web: www.toledodiocese.org

DIOCESE OF TOLEDO
Ministerial Leadership Formation
P.O. Box 985
Toledo, OH 43697-0985
Alfredo Díaz, Associate Secretary
Tel: (419) 244-6711 Fax: (419) 244-4791
Email: adiaz@toledodiocese.org
Web: www.toledodiocese-spl.org

DIOCESE OF YOUNGSTOWN
St. Rose of Lima
50 Struthers-Coitsville Rd.
Youngstown, OH 44505
Rev. Charles Poore, Pastor
Tel: (330) 755-3633
Email: chancery@doy.org
Web: www.doy.org

IGLESIA UNIDA DE CRISTO BUENAS NUEVAS
4401 Clark Ave.
Cleveland, OH 44102
Rev. Edward Rivera-Santiago, Pastor
Tel: (216) 961-9798

SPANISH EVANGELICAL CHURCH
P.O. Box 897
Youngstown, OH 44506
Rev. Rolando Rojas, Senior Pastor
Tel: (330) 746-6034
Email: spanishevangelical@sbcglobal.net
Web: www.spanishevangelical.org

ST. BERNARD HISPANIC COMMUNITY
St. Bernard Parish
44 University Ave.
Akron, OH 44308-1609
Ada Gelpi, Hispanic Office Coordinator
Tel: (330) 253-5364 Fax: (330) 253-6949
Email: stbernardchurch@aol.com

CATHOLIC CHARITY SERVICES OF CUYAHOGA COUNTY
2012 W 25th St. #507
Cleveland, OH 44113
Ramonita Rodriguez Johnson, Director
Tel: (216) 696-2197 Fax: (216) 696-2088
Email: hisctr25@dioceseofcleveland.org
Web: www.dioceseofcleveland.org

HISPANIC URBAN MINORITY ALCOHOLISM DRUG ABUSE
3305 W. 25th St.
Cleveland, OH 44109
Andres González, Executive Director
Tel: (216) 459-1222 Fax: (216) 459-2696
Email: humadaop@aol.com

LORAIN URBAN MINORITY ALCOHOLISM AND DRUG ABUSE OUTREACH PROGRAM
Affiliate of NCLR
2314 Kelly Pl.
Lorain, OH 44052
Ruth Williams-Clark, Executive Director
Tel: (440) 246-4616 Fax: (440) 246-1997
Web: www.umadaops.com

YOUNGSTOWN URBAN MINORITY ALCOHOLISM AND DRUG ABUSE OUTREACH PROGRAM
496 Glenwood Ave. #120
Youngstown, OH 44502
Darryl Alexander, Executive Director
Tel: (330) 743-2772 Fax: (330) 743-2238
Email: yumadaop@aol.com
Web: www.yumadaop.org

CENTER FOR LATIN AMERICAN STUDIES
Ohio State University
306 Oxley Hall, 1712 Neil Ave.
Columbus, OH 43210
Fernando Unzueta, Director
Tel: (614) 688-3963 Fax: (614) 292-7726
Email: unzueta.1@osu.edu
Web: http://oia.osu.edu/clas

DEPARTMENT OF SPANISH & PORTUGUESE
Ohio State University
298 Hagerty Hall, 1775 College Rd.
Columbus, OH 43210
Melinda Robinson, Secretary/Receptionist
Tel: (614) 292-4958 Fax: (614) 292-7726
Email: spanport@osu.edu
Web: http://sppo.osu.edu/

ESPERANZA, INC.
4115 Bridge Ave. #108
Cleveland, OH 44113
Barbara Esperon, Interim Director
Tel: (216) 651-7178 Fax: (216) 651-7183
Email: hope@esperanzainc.com
Web: www.esperanzainc.com

LATIN AMERICAN STUDIES
Ohio University
Yamada International House, 56 E Union St.
Athens, OH 45701-2979
Dr. Brad Jokisch, Director
Tel: (740) 593-1840 Fax: (740) 593-1837

Email: latstudy@ohio.edu
Web: www.ohio.edu/latinamerican

QUEEN OF APOSTLES SCHOOL
235 Courtland Ave.
Toledo, OH 43609
Sr. Brenda Haynes, Principal
Tel: (419) 241-7829 Fax: (419) 241-4180
Email: smbhaynes@yahoo.com
Web: www.cyss.org/Schools/ElePages/Schools/11.html

EL CENTRO DE SERVICIOS SOCIALES, INC.
1888 E. 31st St.
Lorain, OH 44055
Yolanda Fernandez, Chairperson
Tel: (440) 277-8235 Fax: (440) 277-9236
Email: avelez@elcentro.org

FARM LABOR ORGANIZING COMMITTEE, AFL-CIO
Affiliate of NCLR
1221 Broadway St.
Toledo, OH 43609-2007
Baldemar Velásquez, Director
Tel: (419) 243-3456 Fax: (419) 243-5655
Email: info@floc.com
Web: www.floc.com

ADVOCATES FOR BASIC LEGAL EQUALITY, INC.
Lucas County
520 Madison Ave. #740, Spitzer Bldg.
Toledo, OH 43604-1373
Joe Tafelski, Executive Director
Tel: (419) 255-0814 Fax: (419) 259-2880
Email: jtafelski@ablelaw.org
Web: www.ablelaw.org

HISPANIC NATIONAL BAR ASSOCIATION
Region X (KY, OH, TN)
3631 Perkins Ave.
Cleveland, OH 44114
Alexander Sanchez, Regional President
Tel: (216) 391-3028 Fax: (216) 391-6206
Email: ASanchez@unca.org
Web: www.hnba.com

NORD CENTER
6140 S Broadway
Lorain, OH 44053-3891
Dr. Rubén Ocasio, Director
Tel: (440) 233-7232 Fax: (440) 233-4466
Email: rocasio@nordcenter.org
Web: www.nordcenter.org

HISPANIC SENIOR CENTER
7800 Detroit Ave.
Cleveland, OH 44102
Edna Fuentes Casiano, Director
Tel: (216) 631-3599 Fax: (216) 631-3654

CENTRO SAN JOSÉ
1500 Market Ave. North
Canton, OH 44714
Sr. Teresa Ann Wolf, Coordinator/Pastoral Care
Tel: (330) 454-2220 Fax: (330) 454-2255
Email: srteresawolf@msn.com

EL BARRIO, INC.
2001 W. 65th St.
Cleveland, OH 44102
Tel: (216) 281-0109 Fax: (216) 281-6465
Email: info@elbarrioinc.org
Web: www.elbarrioinc.org

HISPANIC FUND
Community Foundation of Greater Lorain County
1865 N. Ridge Rd. E. #A
Lorain, OH 44055
Michael Ferrer, President
Tel: (440) 277-0142 Fax: (440) 277-6955
Email: foundation@cfglc.org
Web: http://cfglc.org/hisfd.html

MEXICAN AMERICAN CITIZENS CLUB
2938 Randall St.
Lorain, OH 44052
Paulie P. García, President
Tel: (440) 288-0719 Fax: (440) 288-0719

OFFICE OF MINORITY AFFAIRS AND COMMUNITY RELATIONS
Cleveland State University
2121 Euclid Ave., Rhodes Tower 1227
Cleveland, OH 44114
Maritza L. Perrez, Multicultural Programming Coordinator
Tel: (216) 687-9394 Fax: (216) 687-5442
Email: omacr@csuohio.edu
Web: www.csuohio.edu/omacr/

OHIO COMMISSION ON HISPANIC/LATINO AFFAIRS
77 S. High St. 18th Fl.
Columbus, OH 43215
Ezra C. Escudero, Executive Director
Tel: (614) 466-8333 Fax: (614) 995-0896
Email: ezra.escudero@ochla.state.oh.us
Web: www.state.oh.us/spa/

SOUTH LORAIN COMMUNITY DEVELOPMENT CORPORATION
P.O. Box 1351
Lorain, OH 44055
Patrick Metzge, Executive Director
Tel: (440) 277-6142 Fax: (440) 277-7097
Email: pmslcdc@kellnet.com
Web: www.kellnet.com/slcdc

SPANISH AMERICAN COMMITTEE FOR A BETTER COMMUNITY
4407 Lorain Ave.
Cleveland, OH 44113
Leo Serrano, Executive Director
Tel: (216) 961-2100 Fax: (216) 961-3305
Email: sac@spanishamerican.org
Web: www.spanishamerican.org

GOLDEN ACRES MIGRANT MINISTRANT CENTER
8365 State Rte. 202
Tipp City, OH 45371-9471
Philip Morones, President
Tel: (937) 667-5145 Fax: (937) 669-9996
Email: pmorones@earthlink.net

WOMEN'S CENTER OF GREATER CLEVELAND
6209 Storer Ave.
Cleveland, OH 44102
Mary Jane Chichester, Executive Director
Tel: (216) 651-1450 Fax: (216) 651-4351
Email: mpower@womensctr.org
Web: www.womensctr.org

EL CENTRO DE SERVICIOS SOCIALES, INC.
Youth Center
1910 E. 28th St.
Lorain, OH 44055
Victor Leandry, Executive Director
Tel: (440) 277-4711 Fax: (440) 277-9236
Email: vleandry@elcentro.org

ALPHA PSI LAMBDA, INC.
Ohio State University

Ohio State University
Columbus, OH 43210
Armando Flores, President
Email: flores.62@osu.edu
Web: http://apl.org.ohio-state.edu/

ALPHA PSI LAMBDA NATIONAL, INC.
P.O. Box 163788
Columbus, OH 43216
Melissa Cardenas, National President
Email: cardenas@frognet.net
Web: www.alpha-psi-lambda.org

HISPANIC GRADUATE STUDENT ORGANIZATION
Ohio State University
Columbus, OH 43210
Lisette Garcia, President
Tel: (614) 292-8763
Email: garcia.161@sociology.osu.edu
Web: www.service.ohio-state.edu/students/hgo/

HISPANIC LAW STUDENTS ORGANIZATION
Ohio State University, College of Law
Columbus, OH 43210
Terea Molina, President
Email: molina.27@osu.edu

LA ALIANZA IBEROAMERICANA
Case Western Reserve University
10900 Euclid Ave., Sears 470
Cleveland, OH 44106-7062
Judith Olson-Fallon, Educational Services for Students
Tel: (216) 368-5230 Fax: (216) 368-8826
Email: jko2@case.edu
Web: www.cwru.edu/studentorgs/

LATINO STUDENT UNION
Bowling Green State University
Bowling Green State University
Bowling Green, OH 43403
Raquel Colon, President
Tel: (419) 372-8325
Email: craquel@bgnet.bgsu.edu
Web: www.bgsu.edu/studentlife/organizations/lsu/main.html

LATINOS EN ACCION
University of Cincinnati
P.O. Box 210136
Cincinnati, OH 45221-0136
Evan Susarret, President
Tel: (513) 556-4185
Email: evan@writeme.com
Web: www.uc.edu/groups/lea/html_files/general/englishmain.html

LATINOS UNIDOS
Cleveland State University
2121 Euclid Ave.
Cleveland, OH 44115
Jamie Vega, Advisor
Tel: (216) 687-3742

LOS UNIDOS
Lorain County Community College
1005 N. Abbe Rd.
Elyria, OH 44035
Antonio Barrios, Advisor
Tel: (440) 366-4036 Fax: (440) 365-6519
Email: los_unidos@yahoo.com
Web: www.lorainccc.org

OKLAHOMA

GREATER OKLAHOMA CITY HISPANIC CHAMBER OF COMMERCE
4316 S Walker
Oklahoma City, OK 73109
Tel: (405) 616-5031 Fax: (405) 616-0600

GREATER TULSA HISPANIC CHAMBER OF COMMERCE
10802 E 31st St. #A
Tulsa, OK 74147
Fred Ramos, President

Tel: (918) 664-5326 Fax: (918) 384-0096
Email: admin@tulsahispanicchamber.com
Web: www.tulsahispanicchamber.com

MULTI-PURPOSE

AMERICAN GI FORUM OF THE UNITED STATES
Oklahoma Chapter
P.O. Box 94725
Oklahoma City, OK 73143
J. Marty Martinez, State Commander
Tel: (405) 209-1405
Email: jmartinez16@cox.net
Web: www.agif.us/OK.htm

MULTI-PURPOSE HUMAN RELATIONS

COALITION OF LATIN AMERICAN (HUMAN AND CIVIL) RIGHTS ADVOCATES
3015 NW 31st
Oklahoma City, OK 73112
Iris Santos Rivera, Coordinator
Tel: (405) 943-8684

RELIGIOUS

ARCHDIOCESE OF OKLAHOMA CITY
Office for Hispanic Ministry
P.O. Box 32180
Oklahoma City, OK 73123
Rosario Martinez, Director for Hispanic Ministry
Tel: (405) 721-5651 Fax: (405) 721-5210
Email: rmartinez@catharchdioceseokc.org
Web: www.catharchdioceseokc.org

DIOCESE OF TULSA
Hispanic Ministry
1541 E Newton Pl.
Tulsa, OK 74106
Rev. Patrick M. Brankin, Director for Hispanic Ministry
Tel: (918) 584-2424 Fax: (918) 584-2421
Email: info@dioceseoftulsa.org
Web: www.dioceseoftulsa.org

SPEC. INT., EDUCATION

LATIN AMERICAN STUDIES PROGRAM
University of Oklahoma
729 Elm St., Hester Hall 207
Norman, OK 73129-0535
Robert H. Cox, Director
Tel: (405) 325-1584 Fax: (405) 325-7402
Email: rhcox@ou.edu
Web: www.ou.edu/cas/ias/Latam/LATINAM.htm

SPEC. INT., EMPLOYMENT

OKLAHOMA RURAL OPPORTUNITIES DEVELOPMENT CORPORATION
308 SW 25th St.
Oklahoma City, OK 73109
José Angel Gómez, President/CEO
Tel: (405) 840-7077 Fax: (405) 634-7077
Email: jagomez@orodevcorp.org
Web: www.orodevcorp.org

SER OKLAHOMA, INC.
Affiliate of SER-Jobs for Progress National, Inc.
12310 E. 21st St.
Tulsa, OK 74129
Julian Rodriguez, Executive Director
Tel: (918) 437-2590
Email: julian@rodznews.com
Web: www.ser-national.org

SPEC. INT., SOCIAL INTEREST

LATINO COMMUNITY DEVELOPMENT AGENCY
420 SW 10th St.
Oklahoma City, OK 73109-5610
Patricia B. Fennell, Executive Director

Tel: (405) 236-0701 Fax: (405) 236-0737
Email: execdir@latinoagencyokc.org
Web: www.latinoagencyokc.org

STUDENT ORGANIZATION

LATIN DANCING & CULTURAL CLUB
Oklahoma State University
060 Student Union
Stillwater, OK 74078
Stefanie Peterson, Coordinator
Tel: (405) 744-6482
Email: ldcc_osu@hotmail.com
Web: www.osudance.org/

OREGON

BUSINESS

LATIN AMERICAN TRADE COUNCIL OF OREGON
5475 SW Arrowwood Ln.
Portland, OR 97225
Tom Miles, Representative
Tel: (503) 292-2919
Email: info@latco.org
Web: www.latco.org

NIKE HISPANIC NETWORK
Nike Inc.
One Bowerman Dr.
Beaverton, OR 97005
Vance Muñoz, Chair
Tel: (503) 671-6453 Fax: (503) 671-6306

CHAMBER OF COMMERCE

HISPANIC METROPOLITAN CHAMBER OF COMMERCE OF OREGON
P.O. Box 1837
Portland, OR 97207
Roman Hernandez, President
Tel: (503) 222-0280 Fax: (503) 243-5597
Email: hmcc@qwest.net
Web: www.hmccoregon.com

ROGUE VALLEY HISPANIC CHAMBER OF COMMERCE
2311 Voorhies Rd.
Medford, OR 97501
Tel: (541) 535-6277 Fax: (541) 779-7669

CULTURAL

CENTRO CULTURAL CÉSAR CHÁVEZ
Oregon State University Campus
1969 A St.
Corvalis, OR 97331
Luis Palacios, Office Assistant
Tel: (541) 737-3790 Fax: (541) 737-7504
Email: ccc@mu.orst.edu
Web: www.mu.oregonstate.edu/cesarchavez/

MIRACLE THEATRE GROUP
425 SE 6th Ave.
Portland, OR 97214
Jose Gonzalez, President
Tel: (503) 236-7253
Web: www.milagro.org

PORTLAND GUADALAJARA SISTER CITY ASSOCIATION
1200 SE Morrison St.
Portland, OR 97214
Shelli Romero, President
Tel: (503) 232-7550
Email: pgsca.president@cincodemayo.org
Web: www.cincodemayo.org

MULTI-PURPOSE

OREGON COMMISSION ON HISPANIC AFFAIRS
777 Pearl St. #105A
Eugene, OR 97401

Francisca Leyva-Johnson, Chair
Tel: (541) 912-9083 Fax: (541) 682-5894
Email: francisca.e.johnson@ci.eugene.or.us
Web: http://oregonhispanic.org/

RELIGIOUS

ARCHDIOCESE OF PORTLAND IN OREGON
Hispanic Ministry
2838 E Burnside St.
Portland, OR 97214
Raúl Velázquez, Director for Hispanic Ministry
Tel: (503) 233-8325 Fax: (503) 234-2545
Email: rvelazquez@archdpdx.org
Web: www.archdpdx.org

CANBY HISPANIC FOURSQUARE CHURCH
420 N. Knights Bridge Rd.
Canby, OR 97013
Rev. Emilio Ortiz, Pastor
Tel: (503) 266-2481

DIOCESE OF BAKER
Hispanic Ministry Office
P.O. Box 5999
Bend, OR 97708
Gustavo Ruiz, Director for Hispanic Ministry
Tel: (541) 388-4004 Fax: (541) 388-2566
Email: gart@dioceseofbaker.org
Web: www.dioceseofbaker.org

HISPANIC MINISTRY OFFICE
Diocese of Portland in Oregon
2838 E. Burnside St.
Portland, OR 97214
Raul Velazquez, Director
Tel: (503) 233-8325 Fax: (503) 234-2545
Email: rvelazquez@archdpdx.org

SPRINGFIELD SPANISH FOURSQUARE CHURCH
2030 E St.
Springfield, OR 97477
Rev. Adrian Torrescano, Pastor
Tel: (541) 741-8544 Fax: (541) 746-8667
Email: elcaminochurch@juno.com

SPEC. INT., AIDS

MULTICULTURAL HIV/AIDS ALLIANCE OF OREGON
P.O. Box 5913
Portland, OR 97208
Alfie Linn-Ortiz, Executive Director
Tel: (503) 408-6993 Fax: (503) 408-6999
Email: Alfie.linn@mhaao.org
Web: www.mhaao.org

SPEC. INT., ALCOHOL/DRUG CENTER

OREGON CHICANO CONCILIO
St. Michael's House
1704 NE 43rd Ave.
Portland, OR 97213
Luis Polanco, Director
Tel: (503) 284-7141

SPEC. INT., CHILD CARE

CHILD AID
917 SW Oak St. #301
Portland, OR 97205
Catie Coman, Executive Director
Tel: (503) 223-3008
Web: www.child-aid.org

SPEC. INT., EDUCATION

FOREST GROVE CITY LIBRARY
2114 Pacific Ave.
Forest Grove, OR 97116
Colleen Winters, Director
Tel: (503) 992-3247 Fax: (503) 992-3201
Web: www.ci.forest-grove.or.us/library

WOODBURN PUBLIC LIBRARY
280 Garfield St.
Woodburn, OR 97071
Linda Sprauer, Library Director
Tel: (503) 982-5252 Fax: (503) 982-2808
Email: woodburn@ccrls.org
Web: www.ccrls.org/woodburn/

SPEC. INT., EMPLOYMENT

OREGON HUMAN DEVELOPMENT CORPORATION
Gresham Branch
18448 SE Pine
Gresham, OR 97233
Angelique Kauffman, Coordinator
Tel: (503) 666-3009 Fax: (503) 492-8463
Email: akauffman@ohdc.org
Web: www.ohdc.org

Klamath Falls Branch
829 Klamath Ave.
Klamath Falls, OR 97601-6162
Erlinda Reyes, Coordinator
Tel: (541) 883-7186 Fax: (541) 883-7187
Email: ereyes@ohdc.org
Web: www.ohdc.org

Ontario Branch
2880 SW 4th Ave. #8
Ontario, OR 97914-1874
Cynthia Castillo, Trainer
Tel: (541) 881-1491 Fax: (541) 881-8592
Email: ccastillo@ohdc.org
Web: www.ohdc.org

Regional Service Office
233 SE Washington St.
Hillsboro, OR 97123
Daniel Ornelas, Coordinator
Tel: (503) 640-5496 Fax: (503) 844-6585
Email: dornelas@ohdc.org
Web: www.ohdc.org

SPEC. INT., HEALTH SERVICES

VALLEY HEALTH CARE, MIGRANT HEALTH CLINIC
Nyssa Office
17 S 3rd St.
Nyssa, OR 97913
Hugh Philips, Manager
Tel: (541) 372-5738 Fax: (541) 372-5732
Email: hphilips@vfhc.org

YAKIMA VALLEY FARM WORKERS CLINIC
Salud Medical Center
P.O. Box 66
Woodburn, OR 97071
Silvia Arroyo, Director
Tel: (503) 982-2000 Fax: (503) 981-5839
Web: www.yvfwc.com

SPEC. INT., MENTAL HEALTH

NUESTRA COMUNIDAD SANA
P.O. Box 1217
Hood River, OR 97031
Ed Medina, President
Tel: (541) 386-4880 Fax: (541) 386-5802
Email: ncs@gorge.net
Web: http://community.gorge.net/ncs/

SPEC. INT., SOCIAL INTEREST

CENTRO HISPANO OF SOUTHERN OREGON
P.O. Box 1236
Medford, OR 97501
Milo Salgado, President
Tel: (541) 772-7760
Email: chso@jeffnet.org
Web: www.chso.org

CENTRO LATINOAMERICANO
944 W. 5th Ave.
Eugene, OR 97402
Carmen Urbina, Executive Director
Tel: (541) 687-2667 Fax: (541) 687-7841
Email: carmen@cla1.org

OREGON ASSOCIATION OF MINORITY ENTREPRENEURS
4134 N. Vancouver
Portland, OR 97217
Samuel Brooks, Chairman
Tel: (503) 249-7744 Fax: (503) 249-2027
Web: www.oame.org

OREGON HUMAN DEVELOPMENT CORPORATION
Central Office
9620 SW Barbur Blvd. #110
Portland, OR 97219
Joe Lyons, Support Specialist
Tel: (503) 245-2600 Fax: (503) 245-9602
Email: ohdc@ohdc.org
Web: www.ohdc.org

Hispanic Program
901 SE Oak St. #106
Portland, OR 97214
Catalina Coz, Manager
Tel: (503) 236-9670 Fax: (503) 236-9684
Web: www.ohdc.org

Woodburn Branch
120 E. Lincoln #125
Woodburn, OR 97071
Frances Alvarado, Supervisor
Tel: (503) 982-5100 Fax: (503) 980-6789
Email: falvarado@ohdc.org
Web: www.ohdc.org

PINEROS Y CAMPESINOS UNIDOS DEL NOROESTE
300 Young St.
Woodburn, OR 97071
Ramon Ramirez, President
Tel: (503) 982-0243 X201 Fax: (503) 982-1031
Email: farmworkerunion@pcun.org
Web: www.pcun.org

SPEC. INT., SPORTS

OREGON DEMOCRATIC LATINO CAUCUS
4445 SW Barbur Blvd.
Portland, OR 97239-0001
Susan Castillo, Member
Tel: (503) 234-5365 Fax: (503) 236-2352
Web: www.dpo.org/latino

SPEC. INT., YOUTH

OREGON COUNCIL FOR HISPANIC ADVANCEMENT
108 NW 9th Ave. #201
Portland, OR 97209
Steffeni Mendoza Gray, Executive Director
Tel: (503) 228-4131 Fax: (503) 228-0701
Email: s.mendozagray@ocha-nw.org
Web: www.ocha-nw.org

OREGON HUMAN DEVELOPMENT CORPORATION
Youth Center
233 SE Washington St.
Hillsboro, OR 97123
Jose Estrada, Manager
Tel: (503) 640-6349 Fax: (503) 844-6585
Email: jestrada@ohdc.org
Web: www.ohdc.org

PENNSYLVANIA

ARTISTIC

ASOCIACIÓN DE MÚSICOS LATINO AMERICANOS
P.O. Box 50296

2726 N. 6th St.
Philadelphia, PA 19133
Jesse Bermudez, Founder/Executive Director
Tel: (215) 223-3060 Fax: (215) 223-3299
Email: amla@amla.org
Web: www.amla.org

DANZANTE
200 Crescent St.
Harrisburg, PA 17104
Maria Vaga, Vice President
Tel: (717) 232-2615 Fax: (717) 232-2616
Email: danzante@paonline.com
Web: www.danzante.org

MINORITY ARTS RESOURCE COUNCIL
1421 W Girard Ave.
Philadelphia, PA 19130
Curtis E. Brown, Executive Director
Tel: (215) 236-2688 Fax: (215) 236-4255

BUSINESS

BORINQUEN CREDIT UNION
629 W Erie Ave.
Philadelphia, PA 19140
Anet Cruz, Manager
Tel: (215) 228-4180 Fax: (215) 228-5110
Email: bfcu629@aol.com

HISPANIC ASSOCIATION OF CONTRACTORS AND ENTERPRISES, INC.
167 W. Allegheny Ave. #200
Philadelphia, PA 19140-5846
Bill Salas, Jr., President
Tel: (215) 426-8025 Fax: (215) 426-9122
Email: gsalas@hacecdc.org
Web: www.HACE@cdc.org

NATIONAL SOCIETY OF HISPANIC MBAS
Philadelphia Chapter
P.O. Box 96
Montgomeryville, PA 18936-0096
Vanessa Vega, Chapter President
Email: general@philadelphia.nshmba.org
Web: http://philadelphia.nshmba.org

CHAMBER OF COMMERCE

DELAWARE VALLEY HISPANIC CHAMBER OF COMMERCE
P.O. Box 263
Olyphant, PA 18447
Tel: (617) 856-8201

GREATER PHILADELPHIA HISPANIC CHAMBER OF COMMERCE
200 S Broad St. #700
Philadelphia, PA 19102
Luis Cruz, President
Tel: (215) 790-3723 Fax: (215) 790-3600
Email: gphcc@philachamber.com
Web: www.philahispanicchamber.org

HISPANIC CHAMBER OF COMMERCE IN WESTERN PENNSYLVANIA, INC.
2323 D. Main St.
Pittsburgh, PA 15215
Cameil D. Williams, Executive Director
Tel: (412) 628-8394
Web: www.pmahcc.org

PENNSYLVANIA LATINO CHAMBER OF COMMERCE
P.O. Box 11545
Harrisburg, PA 17108
Daniel Bentancourt, President
Tel: (717) 920-9920 Fax: (717) 920-9921

PITTSBURGH METROPOLITAN AREA HISPANIC CHAMBER OF COMMERCE
425 6th Ave. #1360
Pittsburgh, PA 15219
Tel: (412) 628-8394
Email: joe.manich@ansys.com

CULTURAL

CASA DEL CARMEN
4400 N. Reese St.
Philadelphia, PA 19140
Giovanni Morante, Director
Tel: (215) 329-5660 Fax: (215) 329-6722

INSTITUTO INTERNACIONAL DE LITERATURA IBEROAMERICANA
University of Pittsburgh
1312 Cathedral of Learning
Pittsburgh, PA 15260
Erika Braga, Communication Specialist II
Tel: (412) 624-3359 Fax: (412) 624-0829
Email: iili@pitt.edu
Web: www.pitt.edu/~hispan/iili

LATIN AMERICAN CULTURAL UNION
P.O. Box 19403
Pittsburgh, PA 15213
Brent Rondon, President
Tel: (412) 362-7730
Email: rondon@duq.edu
Web: www.lacunet.org

LATIN FIESTA, INC.
564 Wartman St.
Philadelphia, PA 19128
Pedro Jimenez
Tel: (215) 482-2191 Fax: (215) 204-5528
Email: latinfiestainc@aol.com
Web: www.latinfiestainc.com

RAICES CULTURALES LATINOAMERICANAS
P.O. Box 60662
Philadelphia, PA 19133
Yolanda Alcorta, Executive Director
Tel: (215) 425-1390
Email: raicesnews@aol.com
Web: www.raicesculturales.org

TALLER PUERTORRIQUEÑO
2721 N. 5th St.
Philadelphia, PA 19123
Carmen Febo-San Miguel, Executive Director
Tel: (215) 426-3311 Fax: (215) 426-5682
Email: cfebo@tallerpr.org
Web: www.tallerpr.org

YORK SPANISH AMERICAN CENTER
200 E. Princess St.
York, PA 17403
Alex Ramos, Director
Tel: (717) 846-9434 Fax: (717) 843-5722
Email: alexramos123@aol.com

MULTI-PURPOSE

COMMUNITY ACTION COMMISSION
1514 Derry St.
Harrisburg, PA 17104
Linda Figueroa, Executive Director
Tel: (717) 232-9757 Fax: (717) 234-2227
Email: info@cactricounty.org
Web: www.cactricounty.org

COMMUNITY ACTION DEVELOPMENT CORPORATION OF BETHLEHEM
705 E 4th St.
Bethlehem, PA 18015
Ellen Larmer, Project Director
Tel: (610) 807-9337 Fax: (610) 807-9313

COUNCIL OF SPANISH SPEAKING ORGANIZATIONS, INC.
705-09 N. Franklin St.
Philadelphia, PA 19123
Roberto Santiago, Executive Director
Tel: (215) 627-3100 Fax: (215) 627-7440
Email: cancilio@elconcilio.net
Web: www.elconcilio.net

COUNCIL OF SPANISH SPEAKING ORGANIZATIONS OF LEHIGH VALLEY, INC.
520 E. 4th St.
Bethlehem, PA 18015
Sis-Obed Torres Cordero, Executive Director
Tel: (610) 868-7800 Fax: (610) 868-4096
Email: cssolb@aol.com

CROSSROADS COMMUNITY CENTER
2916-18 N 6th St.
Philadelphia, PA 19133
Ruth Hunsberter, Administrator
Tel: (215) 223-7897 Fax: (215) 223-0800
Email: crossroadscommunitycenter@juno.com
Web: www.crossroadscc.mennonite.net

HISPANIC AMERICAN COUNCIL OF ERIE
554 E. 10th St.
Erie, PA 16503
Joe Tuzynski, Executive Director
Tel: (814) 455-0212 Fax: (814) 453-2363
Email: hace@velocity.net
Web: www.eriehispaniccouncil.org

HISPANIC AMERICAN ORGANIZATION, INC.
136 S. 4th St.
Allentown, PA 18102
Lupe Pearce, Executive Director
Tel: (610) 435-5334 Fax: (610) 435-2131
Email: hao4paz@aol.com

HISPANIC CENTER OF READING AND BERKS COUNTY, INC.
501 Washington St., 1st Fl.
Reading, PA 19601
Jonathan Encarnacion, Executive Director
Tel: (610) 376-3748 Fax: (610) 372-2619
Email: jona324@earthlink.net
Web: www.centrohispano.org

LATINO LEADERSHIP ALLIANCE OF BUCKS COUNTY
229 Mill St.
Bristol, PA 19007
Margarita Marengo, Executive Director
Tel: (215) 788-4452 Fax: (215) 788-4623
Email: latinos@llabc.org
Web: www.llabc.org

LULAC NATIONAL EDUCATIONAL SERVICE CENTERS, INC.
Philadelphia
2501 Kensington Ave. #111
Philadelphia, PA 19125
Jessica Rivera, Director
Tel: (215) 423-4811 Fax: (215) 423-4819
Email: riveraj_us@yahoo.com
Web: www.lnesc-philly.org

NORRIS SQUARE CIVIC ASSOCIATION
149 W Susquehanna Ave.
Philadelphia, PA 19122
Patricia De Carlo, Director
Tel: (215) 426-8723 Fax: (215) 426-5822
Email: padeca10@amazon.com

NUEVA ESPERANZA, INC.
4261 N. 5th St.
Philadelphia, PA 19140
Rev. Luis Cortés, Executive Director
Tel: (877) 574-5322 Fax: (215) 324-2542
Email: lcortes@nueva.org
Web: www.esperanza.us

PENNSYLVANIA ASSOCIATION OF LATINO ORGANIZATIONS
P.O. Box 675
Harrisburg, PA 17101
Dr. Jesus Sierra, President
Tel: (866) 854-7256 Fax: (717) 920-4728
Email: info@paloweb.org
Web: www.paloweb.org

SPANISH AMERICAN CIVIC ASSOCIATION, INC.
545 Pershing Ave.
Lancaster, PA 17602
Carlos Graupera, Executive Director
Tel: (717) 397-6267 Fax: (717) 295-7762
Email: cegraupera@aol.com
Web: www.sacapa.org

POLITICAL ACTION

GOVERNOR'S ADVISORY COMMISSION ON LATINO AFFAIRS
506 Finance Bldg.

Harrisburg, PA 17120
Norman Bristol Colon, Executive Director
Tel: (717) 783-3877 Fax: (717) 705-0791
Email: gacla@state.pa.us
Web: www.gacla.state.pa.us

LATIN AMERICA/CARIBBEAN PEACEBUILDING PROGRAM
American Friends Service
1501 Cherry St.
Philadelphia, PA 19102
Natalie Cardona, Assistant Coordinator
Tel: (215) 241-7162 Fax: (215) 241-7177
Email: ncardona@afsc.org
Web: www.afsc.org/latinamerica/peace/Default.htm

PENNSYLVANIA STATEWIDE LATINO COALITION
1211 N. 2nd St.
Philadelphia, PA 19122
Loida Esbri, Chairperson
Tel: (215) 425-7752 Fax: (215) 425-7338
Email: pslc2004c@aol.com
Web: www.pslconline.org

PUERTO RICO FEDERAL AFFAIRS ADMINISTRATION
Pennsylvania
1211 N. 2nd St.
Philadelphia, PA 19112
Maria D. Quiñones, Regional Director
Tel: (215) 851-9930 Fax: (215) 851-9931
Email: mquinones@prfaa.com
Web: www.prfaa.com

REPUBLICAN NATIONAL HISPANIC ASSEMBLY
RNHA-Pennsylvania
4683 Stafford Ave.
Bethlehem, PA 18020
Timothy Cuevas, Contact
Tel: (610) 614-0757 Fax: (610) 614-0757
Email: tcuvas@ibius.jnj.com
Web: www.rnha.org

NATIONAL ASSOCIATION OF HISPANIC NURSES
Philadelphia Chapter
P.O. Box 60825
Philadelphia, PA 19133
Marisol Valle-Ortiz, President
Email: hispanicnurses@nahnphiladelphia.org
Web: www.nahnphiladelphia.org

SOCIETY OF HISPANIC PROFESSIONAL ENGINEERS
Great Philadelphia Chapter
P.O. Box 1497
Philadelphia, PA 19105
Andrea Martinez-Ayala, President
Tel: (267) 625-6968
Email: president@shpegpc.org
Web: www.shpegpc.org

ARCHDIOCESE OF PHILADELPHIA
Hispanic Affairs
222 N. 17th St.
Philadelphia, PA 19103-1299
Anna C. Vega, Director for Hispanic Ministry
Tel: (215) 587-3786 Fax: (215) 587-3561
Web: hispaniccatholics@adphila.org

CHRISTIAN CHURCHES UNITED/LA CASA DE AMISTAD MINISTRY
Affiliate of NCLR
P.O. Box 60750
Harrisburg, PA 17106
Jackie Rucker, Director
Tel: (717) 236-3279 Fax: (717) 238-1916

DIOCESE OF ALLENTOWN
Office of Hispanic Affairs
900 S. Woodward St.
Allentown, PA 18103-4179
Sis. Patricia Kennedy, Director for Hispanic Ministry
Tel: (610) 289-4900 Fax: (610) 289-7917
Email: pkennedy@allentowndiocese.org

DIOCESE OF SCRANTON
Hispanic Ministry
300 Wyoming Ave.
Scranton, PA 18503
David Clarke, Director of Hispanic Ministry
Tel: (570) 207-2213 Fax: (570) 207-2204
Email: david-clarke@dioceseofscranton.org
Web: www.dioceseofscranton.org

IGLESIA SINAI-ASAMBLEAS DE DIOS
2806 N 5th St.
Philadelphia, PA 19133
Rev. Sergio Martinez, Senior Pastor
Tel: (215) 229-1656 Fax: (215) 228-0243
Email: information@iglesiasinai.org
Web: www.iglesiasinai.org

INCARNATION OF OUR LORD
Hispanic Ministry
5105 N 5th St.
Philadelphia, PA 19120
Rev. Geraldo J. Pinero, Pastor
Tel: (215) 329-2320 Fax: (215) 329-6149
Email: office@incarnationparish.net

NATIONAL MINISTRIES
Hispanic Ministries
P.O. Box 851
Valley Forge, PA 19482-0851
Rev. Eddie Cruz, Director
Tel: (800) 222-3872 X2421 Fax: (610) 768-2453
Email: eddie.cruz@abc-usa.org
Web: www.nationalministries.org

PRIMERA IGLESIA CRISTIANA HISPANA
P.O. Box 467
Harrisburg, PA 17108-0467
Emilio Martínez, Pastor
Tel: (717) 233-1588 Fax: (717) 233-6828
Email: bcchurch@juno.com

ROMAN CATHOLIC DIOCESE OF PITTSBURGH
Hispanic Catholic Community
3201 Craft Pl.
Pittsburgh, PA 15213
Francisco Carballido, Community Council President
Tel: (412) 362-5596
Email: dondaniele@juno.com
Web: www.diopitt.org

SACRED HEART OF JESUS
336 N 4th St.
Allentown, PA 18102
Rev. John Grabish, Pastor
Tel: (610) 434-5171 Fax: (610) 434-2441

SIERVAS MISIONERAS DE LA SANTÍSIMA TRINIDAD
3501 Solly Ave.
Philadelphia, PA 19136
Deborah Wilson, General Custodian
Tel: (215) 335-7500 Fax: (215) 335-7511
Email: voc@msbt.org
Web: www.msbt.org

ST. BONIFACE
Hispanic Ministry
174 W Diamond St.
Philadelphia, PA 19122
Father James Cassio, Pastor
Tel: (215) 739-6376 Fax: (215) 739-5102

ST. FRANCIS OF ASSIS CHURCH
Hispanic Ministry
1439 Market St.
Harrisburg, PA 17103
Father Daniel Mitzel, Pastor

Tel: (717) 232-1003 Fax: (717) 232-4536
Email: cfagan@hbgdiocese.org
Web: www.hbgdiocese.org

ST. JOHN BOSCO CHURCH
Hispanic Ministry
235 E County Line Rd.
Hatboro, PA 19040
Rev. Charles Kennedy, Pastor
Tel: (215) 672-7280 Fax: (215) 672-1105
Web: www.saintjohnbosco.org

ST. MARK
Hispanic Ministry
921 Radcliffe St.
Bristol, PA 19007
Adolfo Crespo, Pastor
Tel: (215) 788-2319 Fax: (215) 785-4121
Email: fathermooney@stmarkschurch.net

ST. PETER THE APOSTLE CHURCH
Hispanic Ministry
1019 N 5th St.
Philadelphia, PA 19123
Thomas Gavigan, Pastor
Tel: (215) 627-2386 Fax: (215) 627-3296
Web: www.stjohnneumann.org

GAY AND LESBIAN LATINO AIDS EDUCATION INITIATIVE
1233 Locust St., 3rd Fl.
Philadelphia, PA 19107
Gloria Casarez, Executive Director
Tel: (215) 985-3382 Fax: (215) 985-3388
Email: gloria@galaei.org
Web: www.critpath.org/galaei

MINORITY HEALTH CARE COMMUNICATIONS, INC.
7720 Main St.
Fogelsville, PA 18051-1630
K. Mary Hess, President
Tel: (610) 417-5844
Web: www.minority-healthcare.org

GREATER ERIE COMMUNITY ACTION COMMITTEE
Latino Outreach
87 W 8th St.
Erie, PA 16501
Rafael Rodriguez, Director
Tel: (814) 459-4581 Fax: (814) 456 -0161
Web: www.gecac.org

HOGAR CREA
1409 Pembroke Rd.
Bethlehem, PA 18017
Haydee Santiago, Executive Director
Tel: (610) 866-3442 Fax: (610) 866-5490

Philadelphia Office
2018 E Cumberland St.
Philadelphia, PA 19605
Miguel Gonzalez, Supervisor
Tel: (215) 739-1479 Fax: (215) 739-1558
Web: www.hogarcreapr.org

HOGAR CREA INTERNATIONAL OF PENNSYLVANIA
314 Hanover Ave.
Allentown, PA 18019
Nydia Ramos, Administrator
Tel: (610) 820-8200 Fax: (610) 820-8300

HOGAR CREA, LANCASTER
26 Green St.
Lancaster, PA 17602
Wayne Wright, Director
Tel: (717) 397-8633 Fax: (717) 397-0285
Email: hclancaster@hotmail.com

HISPANIC AMERICAN ORGANIZATION, INC.
Los Niños Learning Center
136 S 4th St.
Allentown, PA 18102
Melissa Owens, Director
Tel: (610) 435-3968 Fax: (610) 435-2131

THE LIGHTHOUSE
152 W Lehigh Ave.
Philadelphia, PA 19133
Johnny Irizarry, CEO
Tel: (215) 425-7800 Fax: (215) 425-6091
Email: jirizarry@lighthse.net

HOUSE OF COUNSELING AND INTEGRAL HEALTH, INC.
213 W Allegheny Ave.
Philadelphia, PA 19133
Birma Montes, Executive Director
Tel: (215) 634-3259 Fax: (215) 634-1234

THE AMERICAN ASSOCIATION OF TEACHERS OF SPANISH AND PORTUGUESE
423 Exton Commons
Exton, PA 19341-2451
Emily Spinelli, President
Tel: (610) 363-7005 Fax: (610) 363-7116
Email: corporate@aatsp.org
Web: www.aatsp.org

ASPIRA OF PENNSYLVANIA, INC.
4322 N. 5th St.
Philadelphia, PA 19140
Alfredo Calderon, Executive Director
Tel: (215) 455-1300 Fax: (215) 455-6310
Email: info@aspirapa.org
Web: www.aspirapa.org

CENTER FOR LATIN AMERICAN STUDIES
University of Pittsburgh
4E04 Wesley W. Posvar Hall
Pittsburgh, PA 15260
Kathleen M. DeWalt, Director
Tel: (412) 648-7392 Fax: (412) 648-2199
Email: clas@pitt.edu
Web: www.ucis.pitt.edu/clas/

LATIN AMERICAN AND LATINO STUDIES PROGRAM
University of Pennsylvania
3624 Market St. #1E-164
Philadelphia, PA 19104-2615
Ann Farnsworth-Alvear, Director
Tel: (215) 898-9919 Fax: (215) 573-2318
Email: lals@sas.upenn.edu
Web: www.sas.upenn.edu/lals

LATIN AMERICAN STUDIES ASSOCIATION
University of Pittsburgh
946 William Pitt Union
Pittsburgh, PA 15260
Marysa Navarro, President
Tel: (412) 648-7929 Fax: (412) 624-7145
Email: lasa@pitt.edu
Web: http://lasa.international.pitt.edu/

Albright College
P.O. Box 15234
Reading, PA 19612-5234
Elizabeth Kiddy, Director
Tel: (610) 921-7810 Fax: (610) 921-7683
Email: betsyk@alb.edu
Web: www.albright.edu/academics/depts/latin-american-studies.html

LATIN AMERICAN STUDIES PROGRAM
Bucknell University
103 Coleman Hall
Lewisburg, PA 17837
John Peeler, Director

Tel: (570) 577-1540 Fax: (570) 577-3536
Email: peeler@bucknell.edu
Web: www.bucknell.edu/academics/academic_
programs/latin_american_studies

LEAGUE OF UNITED LATIN AMERICAN CITIZENS
LULAC National Educational Service Center
2501 Kensington Ave. #111
Philadelphia, PA 19125
Jessica Rivera, Program Coordinator
Tel: (215) 423-4811 Fax: (215) 423-4819
Email: riveraj_us@yahoo.com

LITERACY COUNCIL OF LANCASTER-LEBANON
1 Cumberland St.
Lebanon, PA 17042
Cathy Roth, Coordinator
Tel: (717) 274-3461 Fax: (717) 270-2943
Email: cathy@adultlit.org
Web: www.adultlit.org

PUERTO RICAN LATIN ASSOCIATION
804 Franklin St.
Reading, PA 19602
Eli Velasquez, President
Tel: (610) 478-4140 Fax: (610) 404-4312

MANPOWER
1891 Santa Barbara Dr. #108
Lancaster, PA 17601
Serife Norfleat, Director
Tel: (717) 581-0700 Fax: (717) 581-3420
Email: norfleat.pa@na.manpower.com
Web: www.us.manpower.com

SOUTHCENTRAL EMPLOYMENT COOPERATION
2643 N 3rd St.
Harrisburg, PA 17110
Gary Hober, Executive Director
Tel: (717) 236-7931 Fax: (717) 236-9016
Web: www.pacareerlink.state.pa.us

AMERICAN CANCER SOCIETY, INC.
Southeast Region
1626 Locus St.
Philadelphia, PA 19103
Deirdre Whitfield, Cancer Control Specialist
Tel: (215) 985-5400 Fax: (215) 985-5406
Email: deirdre.whitfield@cancer.org
Web: www.cancer.org

CHOICE, INC.
1233 Locust St. #301
Philadelphia, PA 19107
Trina Johnston, Executive Director
Tel: (215) 985-3355 Fax: (215) 985-2838
Email: info@choice-phila.org
Web: www.choice-phila.org

DELAWARE VALLEY COMMUNITY HEALTH
Maria de los Santos Health Center
452 W Allegheny Ave.
Philadelphia, PA 19130
Patricia Deitch, CEO
Tel: (215) 291-2500 Fax: (215) 291-2587
Email: dvch@dvch.org
Web: www.dvch.org

ESPERANZA HEALTH CENTER
Parkview Medical Office Bldg., 1331 E. Wyoming Ave.
Philadelphia, PA 19124
Bryan R. Hollinger, Medical Director
Tel: (215) 831-1100 X2232 Fax: (215) 831-0500
Email: dw@esperanzahealth.com
Web: www.esperanzahealthcenter.org

HEALTH PROMOTION COUNCIL OF SOUTHEASTERN PENNSYLVANIA
Latino Health Projects
260 S. Broad St.
Philadelphia, PA 19102

Lina Castro, Coordinator
Tel: (215) 731-6192
Email: lina@phmc.org
Web: www.hpcpa.org

KOINONIA CHRISTIAN MINISTRIES
Spanish Health Ministry
205 E State St.
Kennett Square, PA 19348
Dona J. Sensenig, Director
Tel: (610) 444-1972 Fax: (610) 444-8815
Email: shm@kenneth.net
Web: www.koinoniaministry.org

LA SALUD HISPANA, INC.
Lancaster
40 E. Orange St.
Lancaster, PA 17602
Flor Santaló Sherbahn, Executive Director
Tel: (717) 396-1155 Fax: (717) 396-1224
Email: salud40@aol.com

MULTICULTURAL HEALTH EDUCATION DEVELOPMENT
2928 Peach St.
Erie, PA 16508
Agnes Piscaro, Director
Tel: (814) 453-6229 Fax: (814) 456-3731
Email: mhederie@yahoo.com

SOUTH EAST HEALTH CENTER
800 Washington Ave.
Philadelphia, PA 19147
Amy Villanova, Office Manager
Tel: (215) 339-5100 Fax: (215) 271-6835

CONCILIO DE VIVIENDA JUSTA MONTGOMERY COUNTY
105 E Glenside Ave. #E
Glenside, PA 19038
Elizabeth Albert, Executive Director
Tel: (215) 576-7711 Fax: (215) 576-1509
Email: balbert@fairhousingmontco.org
Web: www.fairhousingmontco.org

LUDLOW SOCIAL SERVICE CENTER
1653 N 8th St.
Philadelphia, PA 19122
Marvin Lewis, Director
Tel: (215) 232-1615 Fax: (215) 232-9519

SACA DEVELOPMENT CORPORATION
Affiliate of NCLR
545 Pershing Ave.
Lancaster, PA 17602
Mayra Guevara, President/CEO
Tel: (717) 397-6267 Fax: (717) 431-4009
Web: www.sacapa.org

THE HISPANIC CENTER, INC.
800 Allegheny Ave. #127
Pittsburgh, PA 15233
Andy Rind, Interim Executive Director
Tel: (866) 772-8329 Fax: (412) 237-3195
Email: arind@ccac.edu
Web: www.pghhispaniccenter.org

NATIONAL IMAGE, INC.
Image de Bucks County
209 Westbury Dr.
Warminster, PA 18974
Ada Tuleja, Chapter President
Tel: (215) 674-4216
Email: adatuleja@mailcity.com
Web: www.nationalimageinc.org

COMMUNITY LEGAL SERVICES, INC.
1424 Chestnut St.
Philadelphia, PA 19102
Pamela Mooney, Office Manager
Tel: (215) 981-3700 Fax: (215) 981-4434

Email: pmooney@clsphila.org
Web: www.clsphila.org

ASOCIACIÓN DE PUERTORRIQUEÑOS EN MARCHA
National Headquarters
2147 N. 6th St.
Philadelphia, PA 19122
Luis Cabrera, Executive Director
Tel: (215) 235-6788 Fax: (215) 232-9450

CENTRO DE SERVICIOS PARA HISPANOS
2742 N. 5th St.
Philadelphia, PA 19133
Carmen Dominguez, Social Worker
Tel: (215) 427-3400 Fax: (215) 427-3420

NATIONAL ASSOCIATION FOR HISPANIC ELDERLY
3150 N. Mascher St. #100
Philadelphia, PA 19133
Gladys Lleuvat, Project Coordinator
Tel: (215) 426-1212 Fax: (215) 426-6313

NORRIS SQUARE SENIOR CITIZEN CENTER
2121 N Howard St.
Philadelphia, PA 19122
Maria Freiser, Director
Tel: (215) 423-7241 Fax: (215) 634-7751

ACTION COMUNIDAD LATINO AMERICA OF MONTGOMERY COUNTY
515 Walnut St.
Pottstown, PA 19464
Adamino Ortíz, Executive Director
Tel: (610) 970-2134 Fax: (610) 970-2135
Email: adamino@aclamo.org

Main Office
512 W. Marshall St.
Norristown, PA 19401
Adamino Ortíz, Executive Director
Tel: (610) 277-2570 Fax: (610) 277-6434
Email: adamino@aclamo.org

CASA GUADALUPE CENTER
143 Linden St.
Allentown, PA 18102
Margie Maldonado, Executive Director
Tel: (610) 435-9902 Fax: (610) 439-9032
Email: casa@casalv.org

CENTRO PEDRO CLAVER
3565 N. 7th St.
Philadelphia, PA 19140-4401
Roger Zepernick, Executive Director
Tel: (215) 227-7111 Fax: (215) 227-7105
Email: centro@libertynet.org
Web: www.centroclaver.com

CHAMBERSBURG HISPANIC CENTER
252 S. Main St.
Chambersburg, PA 17201
Diana Martes, Director
Tel: (717) 262-2480 Fax: (717) 264-0115
Email: chc@internet.net

CONGRESO DE LATINOS UNIDOS, INC.
Main Office
216 W. Somerset St.
Philadelphia, PA 19133
Nick Torres, Executive Director
Tel: (215) 763-8870 Fax: (215) 291-0561
Email: webmaster@congreso.net
Web: www.congreso.net

HISPANIC OUTREACH PROGRAM
1012 Brock Dr.
Lebanon, PA 17046
Lucy Flecha, Coordinator
Tel: (717) 273-8901 Fax: (717) 273-8942
Email: lflecha@lebanoncountyhousing.com

LATINO AMERICAN ALLIANCE OF NORTHEASTERN PENNSYLVANIA
62 Analomink St.
East Stroudburg, PA 18301
Alberto Candelle, President
Tel: (570) 420-3725 Fax: (570) 420-3730
Email: laanepa@localnet.com
Web: www.laanepa.org

MT. PLEASANT HISPANIC AMERICAN CENTER
301 S. 13th St.
Harrisburg, PA 17104
Sol Vasquez, Director
Tel: (717) 232-7691 Fax: (717) 233-7227

NATIONAL IMAGE, INC.
Image of Philadelphia
6391 Oxford Ave. #233
Philadelphia, PA 19111
Carlos Deno, President
Tel: (215) 737-5738 Fax: (215) 737-2520
Email: prcd15@msn.com
Web: www.nationalimageinc.org

RURAL OPPORTUNITIES, INC.
1500 N 2nd St. #11
Harrisburg, PA 17102
Kay Washington, Director
Tel: (717) 234-6616 Fax: (717) 234-6692
Email: kwashington@ruralinc.org
Web: www.ruralinc.org

RURAL OPPORTUNITIES, INC.
415 McFarlan Rd. #108
Kennett Square, PA 19348
Nita O. Agostino, Director of State Operations
Tel: (610) 925-5600 Fax: (610) 925-5906
Email: nagostino@ruralinc.org
Web: www.ruralinc.org

US-CUBA SISTER CITIES ASSOCIATION
National Office
320 Lowenhill St.
Pittsburgh, PA 15216
Lisa Valanti, President
Tel: (412) 563-1519 Fax: (412) 563-1945
Email: USCSCA@aol.com
Web: www.uscsca.org

BERKS COMMUNITY ACTION PROGRAM
631 Washington St.
Reading, PA 19603
Bill Richardson, Director
Tel: (610) 376-6571 Fax: (610) 376-6575

INTERNATIONAL LATINO WOMEN'S CONGRESS
209 Westbury Dr.
Warminster, PA 18974
Ada L. Tuleja, CEO & Chairperson of the Board
Tel: (215) 674-4216 Fax: (215) 674-3314
Email: ada.tuleja@latinowomeninc.org
Web: www.latinowomeninc.org

LATINA MOBILE PROJECT
100 E. Lehigh Ave. #107A
Philadelphia, PA 19125
JoAnne Fischer, Executive Director
Tel: (215) 707-1010 Fax: (215) 739-8604
Email: mcc@momobile.org
Web: www.momobile.org

NATIONAL CONFERENCE OF PUERTO RICAN WOMEN, INC.
Philadelphia
P.O. Box 125
Philadelphia, PA 19103
Iris Violeta Colon Torres, President
Tel: (215) 901-2661
Email: vopoeta@aol.com
Web: www.nacoprwphila.org

SPEC. INT., YOUTH

AMPARO DE LA NIÑEZ, INC.
107-109 E Luray St.
Philadelphia, PA 19120
Felipe Castro, Executive Director
Tel: (215) 324-2919 Fax: (215) 324-4350
Email: alc@childrensafeharbor.org
Web: www.childrensafeharbor.org

CASA CAMINO BROINQUENO ARDIENTE
1241 E 26th St.
Erie, PA 16504
Wilfredo Velez, Founder
Tel: (814) 874-6761 Fax: (814) 874-6756
Email: wvelez@eriesd.iu5.org

STUDENT ORGANIZATION

LA CASA LATINA
University of Pennsylvania
3601 Locust Walk
Philadelphia, PA 19104-6224
Anamaria Cobo, Director
Tel: (215) 746-6043 Fax: (215) 746-6045
Email: lacasa@pobox.upenn.edu
Web: www.vpul.upenn.edu/lacasa

LATIN AMERICAN JEWISH STUDIES ASSOCIATION
Swarthmore College
500 College Ave.
Swarthmore, PA 19081
Leo Spitzer, President
Tel: (610) 328-8682 Fax: (610) 328-7769
Email: lajsa@swarthmore.edu
Web: www.acad.swarthmore.edu/lajsa

LATIN AMERICAN STUDENT ASSOCIATION
Penn State University
200 Bradley Ave. #30
State College, PA 16801
Oscar J. Barbosa, President
Tel: (814) 883-5392
Email: oscarjb@psu.edu
Web: http://www.clubs.psu.edu/up/lasa/main.htm

LATINO CAUCUS
Pennsylvania State University
020 HUB/Robeson Center
University Park, PA 16802
Jennifer Moreno, President
Tel: (814) 865-3776
Email: jpm338@psu.edu
Web: www.clubs.psu.edu/latinocaucus

LATINO CELEBRATION
Millersville University
P.O. Box 1002
Millersville, PA 17551
Aida Ceara, Chair
Tel: (717) 872-3258 Fax: (717) 871-2632

PUERTO RICO

ARTISTIC

CONSERVATORY OF MUSIC OF PUERTO RICO
Rafael Lamar #350, F.D. Roosevelt Ctr.
San Juan, PR 00918-2199
Maria del Carmen Gil, Chancellor
Tel: (787) 751-0160 Fax: (787) 758-8268
Email: mcgil@cmpr.gopeirno.pr
Web: www.cmpr.edu

ESCUELA DE ARTES PLASTICAS DE PUERTO RICO
P.O. Box 9021112
San Juan, PR 00902-1112
Marimar Benitez, Rectora
Tel: (787) 725-8120 Fax: (787) 725-8111
Email: eap@coqui.net

LIGA DE ESTUDIANTES DE ARTE DE SAN JUAN
Apartado 9066221
San Juan, PR 00906-6221
Elsa Costas, Director
Tel: (787) 722-4468 Fax: (787) 722-4468
Email: ligadearte@centenialpr.net

PUERTO RICO FILM COMMISSION
P.O. Box 362350
San Juan, PR 00936-2350
Laura Velez, Director
Tel: (787) 758-4747 X2251 Fax: (787) 756-5706
Email: lavelez@pridco.com
Web: www.puertoricofilm.com

BUSINESS

ASOCIACIÓN DE AGENCIAS PUBLICITARIAS DE PUERTO RICO, INC.
P.O. Box 195239
San Juan, PR 00919-5239
Rachelle M. Whitten Ryan, Executive Director
Tel: (787) 764-9906 Fax: (787) 764-6956
Email: aap@centennialpr.net
Web: www.agenciaspublicitarias.com

ASOCIACIÓN DE BANCOS DE PUERTO RICO
208 Ave. Ponce de Leon #1014
San Juan, PR 00918-1002
Arturo Carrión, Executive Vice President
Tel: (787) 753-8630 Fax: (787) 754-6022
Email: info@abpr.com
Web: www.abpr.com

ASOCIACIÓN DE COMERCIANTES DE MATERIALES DE CONSTRUCCIÓN, INC.
P.O. Box 9020800
San Juan, PR 00902-0800
Fernando Quygano, President
Tel: (787) 721-4872 Fax: (787) 721-7359

ASOCIACIÓN DE CONTRATISTAS GENERALES DE AMERICA
Puerto Rico Chapter
Calle Perseo 501 #211
San Juan, PR 00920
Jorge J. Fuentes, President
Tel: (787) 781-2200 Fax: (787) 782-3480
Email: agcpr@agcpr.com
Web: www.agcpr.com

ASOCIACIÓN DE DETALLISTAS DE GASOLINA DE PUERTO RICO, INC.
P.O. Box 193652
San Juan, PR 00919
Efrain Reyes, President
Tel: (787) 726-0961 Fax: (787) 268-3035

ASOCIACIÓN DE ENFERMERIA VISITANTE GREGORIA AUFANT, INC.
114 Eleanor Roosevelt St.
San Juan, PR 00918-3105
Carmén Martino, Executive Director
Tel: (787) 759-7036 Fax: (787) 753-4399/8095
Email: madeline.garcia@aevga.org
Web: www.aevga.org

Ave. Campo Rico 784, Urbanización Country Club
Rio Piedras, PR 00924
Carmen Martino, Director
Tel: (787) 762-7666 Fax: (787) 762-7715
Web: www.aevga.org

3ra. Sección-Urbanización Lomas Verdes
Lomas Berdes X-48 Carlos Andaluz Ave.
Bayamón, PR 00956
Carmen Santana, Supervisor
Tel: (787) 780-4010 Fax: (787) 787-5787

ASOCIACIÓN DE HOSPITALES DE PUERTO RICO, INC.
Villanevares Professional Bldg. #101
San Juan, PR 00927
Sr. Juan Rivera, Executive Vice President
Tel: (787) 764-0290 Fax: (787) 753-9748
Email: asohospr@asociacionhosppr.org
Web: www.asociacionhosppr.org

ASOCIACIÓN DE INDUSTRIALES DE PUERTO RICO
P.O. Box 195477
San Juan, PR 00919-5477
Reynaldo Encarnacion, President
Tel: (787) 759-9445 Fax: (787) 756-7670
Email: prma@i-lan.com
Web: www.i-lan.com

ASOCIACIÓN DE MERCADEO, INDUSTRIA Y DISTRIBUCIÓN DE ALIMENTOS
Edificio Plz. Triple-S, #902-A Ave. FD Roosevelt, #1510
Guaynabo, PR 00968
Tel: (787) 792-7575 Fax: (787) 792-8085
Email: mida@coqui.net

ASOCIACIÓN DE NOTARIOS DE PUERTO RICO
P.O. Box 363613
San Juan, PR 00936-3613
Licienciado Dennis D. Martinez Colon, President
Tel: (787) 758-2773 Fax: (787) 759-6703
Email: asociacionde@notariosdepr.org
Web: www.anota.org

ASOCIACIÓN PRODUCTOS DE PUERTO RICO
P.O. Box 363631
San Juan, PR 00936-3631
Francisco Martinez, President
Tel: (787) 753-8484 Fax: (787) 753-0855
Email: rdelafuente@hechoenpr.com
Web: www.hechoenpr.com

CENTRO UNIDO DE DETALLISTAS DE PUERTO RICO
P.O. Box 190127
San Juan, PR 00919-0127
Enid Toro de Báez, President
Tel: (787) 641-8413 Fax: (787) 763-8406
Email: mhernandez@centrounido.org
Web: www.centrounido.futuroeusa.com

COMERCIANTES DE PLAZA LAS AMERICAS, INC.
P.O. Box 363268
San Juan, PR 00936-3268
Franklin Domensh, General Manager
Tel: (787) 767-1558 Fax: (787) 282-6458
Email: wlozano@plazalasamericas.net
Web: www.plazalasamericas.net

ECONOMIC DEVELOPMENT BANK FOR PUERTO RICO
P.O. Box 2134
San Juan, PR 00922-2134
Antonio F. Faría, President
Tel: (787) 641-4300 Fax: (787) 721-1443
Email: afaria@bde.gobierno.pr
Web: www.bdepr.org

FEDERACION DE ASOCIACIONES PECUARIAS DE PUERTO RICO, INC.
P.O. Box 2635
Mayagüez, PR 00681
David A. Gimenez, President
Tel: (787) 834-9191 Fax: (787) 833-1055
Email: pecuaria@coqui.net

NATIONAL SOCIETY OF HISPANIC MBAS
Puerto Rico Chapter
P.O. Box 1389
Vega Baja, PR 00694-1389
Irvin Cortés, President
Tel: (787) 345-9315 Fax: (787) 858-7284
Email: general@puertorico.nshmba.org
Web: www.puertorico.nshmba.org

PUERTO RICO BANKS ASSOCIATION
208 Ave. Ponce de León #1014
San Juan, PR 00918-1002
Arturo L. Carrión, Executive Vice President
Tel: (787) 753-8630 Fax: (787) 754-6022
Email: info@abpr.com
Web: www.abpr.com

PUERTO RICO HOTEL AND TOURISM ASSOCIATION
954 Ave. Ponce de Leon, Miramar Plz. #702
San Juan, PR 00907-3605
Erin Benítez, Executive Vice President
Tel: (787) 725-2901 Fax: (787) 725-2913
Email: ebenitez@prhta.org
Web: www.prhta.org

PUERTO RICO MANUFACTURERS ASSOCIATION
P.O. Box 195477
San Juan, PR 00919-5477
William Riefkohl, Executive Vice President
Tel: (787) 759-9445 Fax: (787) 756-7670
Email: williamriefkohl@prma.com
Web: www.prma.com

TRABAJADORES UNIDOS DE LA AUTORIDAD METROPOLITANA DE AUTOBUSES
Graneia 1378 Urb. Santiago Iglesias
San Juan, PR 00921
Antonio R. Diaz, President
Tel: (787) 781-7405 Fax: (787) 783-0345

UNION DE TRABAJADORES DE LA AUTORIDAD DE CARRETERAS
P.O. Box 11085
Fernandez Juncos Station
San Juan, PR 00910
Néstor Gasparini Torres, President
Tel: (787) 723-0550

UNION GASTRONOMICA DE PUERTO RICO
P.O. Box 13037
San Juan, PR 00908-3037
Rebeca Morales, President
Tel: (787) 725-2030 Fax: (787) 725-2033

CHAMBER OF COMMERCE

CAMARA DE COMERCIANTES MAYORISTAS DE PUERTO RICO
625 Ponce de Leon Ave.
San Juan, PR 00901
Tel: (787) 754-6262 Fax: (787) 754-2620

CAMARA DE COMERCIO DE PONCE Y SUR DE PUERTO RICO
P.O. Box 7455
Ponce, PR 00732-7455
Hector Lopez, Executive Director
Tel: (787) 844-4400 Fax: (787) 844-4705
Email: camarasur@trtc.net
Web: http://camarasur.org/

CAMARA DE COMERCIO DEL OESTE DE PUERTO RICO
Calle Mendez Vigo Doral, Bank Plz. Piso 9 #905
Mayaguez, PR 00681
Rafael Molina, President
Tel: (787) 832-3749 Fax: (787) 832-4287
Email: oeste@ccopr.org
Web: www.ccopr.org

CAMARA DE COMERCIO MEXICANA DE PUERTO RICO
P.O. Box 41241, Minillas Station
Santurce, PR 00907
Tel: (787) 728-8109

CAMARA OFICIAL ESPANOLA DE COMERCIO EN PUERTO RICO
P.O. Box 9020894
San Juan, PR 00902-0894
Sr. Jose Luis Rivera, President
Tel: (787) 728-0082 Fax: (787) 728-0084
Email: camacoespr@tld.net
Web: www.camaraespanola.com

CHAMBER OF COMMERCE OF PUERTO RICO/ CÁMARA DE COMERCIO DE PUERTO RICO
P.O. Box 9024033
San Juan, PR 00902-4033
Leonardo Cordero Suria, President
Tel: (787) 721-6060 Fax: (787) 723-1891
Email: camarapr@camarapr.net
Web: www.camarapr.org

CULTURAL

SOCIEDAD CORAL DE PUERTO RICO, INC.
International Federation of Choral Music
P.O. Box 21663
San Juan, PR 00931
Luis Olivieri, Executive Coordinator
Tel: (787)758-9014
Email: coral8000@aol.com

MULTI-PURPOSE

CASA DE TODOS
Affiliate of Fondos Unidos de Puerto Rico
Box 6128
Juncos, PR 00777-9710
Magdalia Martinez, Director
Tel: (787) 734-5511 Fax: (787) 734-4565

CASA PROTEGIDA JULIA DE BURGOS
Affiliate of Fondos Unidos de Puerto Rico
P.O. Box 362433
San Juan, PR 00936-2433
Sra. Gloria Cruz Rivera, Director
Tel: (787) 723-3500 Fax: (787) 725-8580
Email: casajulia@coqui.net
Web: www.casajuliadeburgos.org

CRUZ ROJA AMERICANA
Capítulo de Puerto Rico
P.O. Box 902067
San Juan, PR 00902-1067
Pedro L. Negron Ramirez, Executive Director
Tel: (787) 758-8150 Fax: (787) 758-6086

FOUNDATION FOR COMMUNITY DEVELOPMENT OF PUERTO RICO, INC.
P.O. Box 6300
Caguas, PR 00726-6300
Norberto Menéndez, Executive Director
Tel: (787) 258-5162 Fax: (787) 743-7658

HOGAR DEL NIÑO EL AVE MARÍA
Affiliate of Fondos Unidos de Puerto Rico
P.O. Box 607061
Bayamón, PR 00960
Flor Florencia, Director
Tel: (787) 279-3003

LEAGUE OF UNITED LATIN AMERICAN CITIZENS
Puerto Rico Chapter
ME 44, Las Bahias Ave.
Catano, PR 00962
Carmen Cruz, State Director
Tel: (787) 788-6741 (h) Fax: (787) 788-6741
Email: ccruz3172@brtc.net
Web: www.lulac.org

MISIÓN RESCATE
Centro de Arecibo
Calle A Buzón 92 Interior
Arecibo, PR 00612
Juan de Jesus, Director
Tel: (787) 879-3625

NATIONAL COUNCIL OF LA RAZA
Puerto Rico Office
201 Diego Ave. Plaza San Francisco #221
San Juan, PR 00927
Sonia Perez, Vice President
Tel: (787) 641-0546 Fax: (787) 641-0545
Email: nclr-pr@ncllr.org
Web: www.nclr.org

OFICINA PARA LA PROMOCIÓN Y DESARROLLO HUMANO, INC.
Affiliate of Fondos Unidos de Puerto Rico
Apartado 353, Ave. Luis Llorens Torres #242
Arecibo, PR 00613
Sister Roberta, Director
Tel: (787) 817-6951 Fax: (787) 817-7597
Email: opdh@_inc@hotmail.com
Web: www.utuadoweb.com/opdh

PROGRAMA DE APOYO Y ENLACE COMUNITARIO, INC.
P.O. Box 9000
#629
Aguada, PR 00602
Maria A. Hernandez, Director
Tel: (787) 252-3439 Fax: (787) 252-3439
Email: programapaec@hotmail.com

YMCA DE PONCE
Affiliate of Fondos Unidos de Puerto Rico
7843 Nazaret Urb. Santa Maria
Ponce, PR 00717
José A. Ortiz, Director
Tel: (787) 843-1870 Fax: (787) 843-1811
Email: ymca@ymcaponce.org
Web: www.ymcaponce.org

YMCA DE SAN JUAN
Affiliate of Fondos Unidos de Puerto Rico
P.O. Box 360590
San Juan, PR 00936-0590
Sra. Vivian Dávila, Executive Director
Tel: (787) 728-7200 Fax: (787) 728-0643
Email: ymcasj@coqui.net

POLITICAL ACTION

ASOCIACIÓN DE ALCALDES DE PUERTO RICO, INC.
P.O. Box 9066565
San Juan, PR 00906-6565
Jaime Garcia, Executive Director
Tel: (787) 724-1939 Fax: (787) 721-8333
Email: jgarcia@alcaldespr.com

PROFESSIONAL

PERUVIAN AMERICAN MEDICAL SOCIETY
Puerto Rico Chapter
104 Ave. Arterial Hostos #61
San Juan, PR 00918
Dr. Luis Flores-Vilar, President
Tel: (787) 763-7328
Email: joflores@coqui.net
Web: www.pamsnational.org

RELIGIOUS

ASOCIACIÓN ADVENTISTA DEL ESTE
P.O. Box 29027
San Juan, PR 00929
Pastor Pedro Canales, President
Tel: (787) 758-8282 Fax: (787) 759-6812

ASOCIACIÓN DE FRAILES CAPUCHINOS, INC.
P.O. Box 21350
Rio Piedras, PR 00928-1350
Jorge Macias, Director
Tel: (787) 764-3090 Fax: (787) 764-4070
Email: pochi0926@hotmail.com

CONSORCIO DE CENTROS CRISTIANOS DE PUERTO RICO, INC.
Calle Marginal, Vista Hermosa B-1, Urb. Forest Hill
Bayamón, PR 00959
Marta Soto, Director
Tel: (787) 786-9407 Fax: (787) 787-8417

IGLESIA DE DIOS PENTECOSTAL
Movimiento Internacional-Región Puerto Rico
P.O. Box 13324
Santurce, PR 00908
Moisés Flores, General Manager
Tel: (787) 758-8562 Fax: (787) 999-1560
Email: triufo96@yahoo.com
Web: www.radiotriunfo.com

MISIONALES PONTIFICIAS
Asociación de la Santa Infancia
P.O. Box 191882
San Juan, PR 00919-1882
Wanda Gonzalez, National Delegate
Tel: (787) 754-0995 Fax: (787) 754-0749

RESEARCH

FUNDACIÓN DR. GARCÍA RINALDI
Affiliate of Fondos Unidos de Puerto Rico
P.O. Box 8816
San Juan, PR 00910-0816
Teresita Ibarra, Director
Tel: (787) 725-4065 Fax: (787) 725-4319
Email: info@fundaciongarciarinaldi.org
Web: www.fundaciondrgarciarinaldi.org

FUNDACIÓN PUERTORRIQUEÑA DE CONSERVACIÓN
Urb. Sagrado Corazón, 382 Ave. San Claudio
PMB 97
San Juan, PR 00926-4107
Esther M. Rojas, Executive Director
Tel: (787) 760-2115 Fax: (787) 761-3889
Email: erojas@prcf.org
Web: www.fundacionpr.org

SOCIEDAD DE INVESTIGACION CIENTIFICA, INC.
P.O. Box 33060
Veterans Plz. Station
San Juan, PR 00933-0060
Blanca Lebrón, Executive Director
Tel: (787) 641-7582 X10148 Fax: (787) 641-8359
Email: lebron.blanca@med.va.gov

SOCIEDAD ESPELEOLOGICA DE PUERTO RICO, INC.
P.O. Box 31074
San Juan, PR 00929
Julio Rodriguez, President
Tel: (787) 269-9639
Email: presi@sepri.org
Web: www.sepri.org

ZENOBIA AND JUAN RAMON JIMENEZ ROOM
University of Puerto Rico
P.O. Box 22933
San Juan, PR 00931-2933
Elsa E. Rodriguez, Professor
Tel: (787) 764-0000 x 5170

SPEC. INT., AIDS

ALBERGUE LA PROVIDENCIA, INC.
P.O. Box 10142
Ponce, PR 00732-0142
Padre Francisco Garcia Director
Tel: (787) 841-2119 Fax: (787) 840-6642

ASOCIACIÓN DE CENTROS DE SALUD PRIMARIA DE PUERTO RICO
Affiliate of NCLR
Ed. Euskalduna 3er. Piso, Calle Navarro #56
Hato Rey, PR 00918-4419
Alicia Suárez, Acting Executive Director
Tel: (787) 758-3411 Fax: (787) 758-1736
Email: acsppr@coqui.net

BILL'S KITCHEN, INC.
Affiliate of Fondos Unidos de Puerto Rico
P.O. Box 195678
San Juan, PR 00919-5678
Sandra I. Torres Rivera, Executive Director
Tel: (787) 754-6525 Fax: (787) 754-6589
Email: guardiola@spiderlink.net

COAI, INC.
P.O. Box 8634
San Juan, PR 00910-0634
Jose Mulinelli, Executive Director
Tel: (787) 793-7530 Fax: (787) 793-7530
Email: coai@yunque.net

ESTANCIA CORAZON, INC.
P.O. Box 3309 Marina Station
Carretera #2-Centro Medico de Mayagüez-Casa de Salud- 4to. Piso
Mayagüez, PR 00681
Ivonne Santiago Nieves, Executive Director
Tel: (787) 831-5095 Fax: (787) 265-2650
Email: ecorazon@coqui.net

INICIATIVA COMUNITARIA DE INVESTIGACIÓN

Affiliate of Fondos Unidos de Puerto Rico
P.O. Box 366535
San Juan, PR 00936-6535
José Vargas Vidot, Director
Tel: (787) 250-8629 X300 Fax: (787) 753-4454
Email: iniciativa@hotmail.com

SPEC. INT., ALCOHOL/DRUG CENTER

CENTRO RENACER, INC.
Affiliate of Fondos Unidos de Puerto Rico
P.O. Box 3772
Guaynabo, PR 00970-3772
Rev. Félix Cabrera, Director
Tel: (787) 720-0235 Fax: (787) 731-8747

HOGAR POSADA LA VICTORIA
Affiliate of Fondos Unidos de Puerto Rico, Santa Rosa Unit
P.O. Box 6789
Bayamón, PR 00960
Gladys Colón de Vázquez, Executive Director
Tel: (787) 870-2379 Fax: (787) 870-5314
Email: posadalavictoria@prtc.net

HOGAR RESURRECCIÓN, INC.
Affiliate of Fondos Unidos de Puerto Rico
P.O. Box 8606
Caguas, PR 00726
Raul Hernandez, Executive Director
Tel: (787) 747-1393 Fax: (787) 747-1319

HOGAR SANTÍSIMA TRINIDAD
Affiliate of Fondos Unidos de Puerto Rico
P.O. Box 607061, BMS 326
Bayamon, PR 00960-7061
Padre Pedro Gorena, Administrator
Tel: (787) 799-6208 Fax: (787) 799-1977
Email: trinita@prtc.net

SPEC. INT., CHILD CARE

ASOCIACIÓN PADRES PRO BIENESTAR NIÑOS CON IMPEDIDOS, INC.
P.O. Box 21280
San Juan, PR 00928-1280
Carmen Selles Vila, Executive Director
Tel: (787) 763-4665 Fax: (787) 765-0345
Email: centroinfo@apnipr.org
Web: www.apnipr.org

CENTRO MI ESCUELITA INFANTIL
Calle 37 Block 40 #7 Cierrabayamon
Bayamón, PR 00961
Carmen Boyef, President
Tel: (787) 787-8322 Fax: (787) 787-8322

CENTRO SANTA LUISA, INC.
Affiliate of Fondos Unidos de Puerto Rico
RR #6
San Juan, PR 00926
Sor. Catalina Sanchez, Director
Tel: (787) 720-2764 Fax: (787) 731-7795
Email: centrosantaluisa@yahoo.com
Web: www.geocities.com/centrosantaluisa

CINDERELLA NURSERY DAY CARE
Calle Coqui #720
Mayagüez, PR 00680
Luz González, Director
Tel: (787) 834-3770 Fax: (787) 834-3770

HOGAR DE GRUPO SALEM, INC.
P.O. Box 2270
Arecibo, PR 00613
Evelin Toledo, Director
Tel: (787) 878-2272

MUNDO DE LOS NIÑOS
P.O. Box 6173
Caguas, PR 00726
Minerva Carro, Director
Tel: (787) 739-5824 Fax: (787) 739-5824

NILDA SANTIAGO CHILD CARE
Calle C-3, Rep. San Juan
Arecibo, PR 00612

Nilda Santiago, Director
Tel: (787) 879-3256

POSADA DE AMOR, INC.
P.O Box 1552
Quebradillas, PR 00678
Carmen Lydia Vives, Director
Tel: (787) 895-5519 Fax: (787) 895-5519

PROYECTO CHILD CARE
Municipio San Sebastián
P.O. Box 1603
San Sebastián, PR 00685
Verónica Vélez, Director
Tel: (787) 896-6825 Fax: (787) 896-6825

TERCERA IGLESIA PRESBITERIANA
P.O. Box 3901
Aguadilla, PR 00605
Alicia Medina, Executive Director
Tel: (787) 882-2075 Fax: (787) 997-1103

SPEC. INT., COUNSELING

INSTITUTO DE ORIENTACIÓN Y TERAPIA FAMILIAR
Affiliate of Fondos Unidos de Puerto Rico
P.O. Box 861
Caguas, PR 00726
Rosa Luz Ramírez, Director
Tel: (787) 746-5756 Fax: (787) 746-3080

SPEC. INT., EDUCATION

ASOCIACIÓN DE MAESTROS DE PUERTO RICO
P.O. Box 191088
San Juan, PR 00919-1088
Aida Diaz, President
Tel: (787) 765-3995 Fax: (787) 754-8874
Email: adiaz@amprnet.org

ASOCIACIÓN DE PSYCOLOGIA DE PUERTO RICO
P.O. Box 363435
San Juan, PR 00936-3435
David Pérez-Jiménez, Ph.D., President
Tel: (787) 751-7100 Fax: (787) 758-6467
Email: appr@coqui.net
Web: www.asppr.org

ASPIRA OF PUERTO RICO, INC.
P.O. Box 29132
San Juan, PR 00929-0132
Hilda Maldonado, Executive Director
Tel: (787) 641-1985 Fax: (787) 257-2725
Email: hmaldonado@pr.aspira.org
Web: http://pr.aspira.org

ASSOCIACIÓN DE ANTIGUOS ALUMNOS COLEGIO SAN IGNACIO DE LOYOLA
Urb. Santa Maria, 1940 Calle Sauco
San Juan, PR 00927-6718
Luis F. Gonzales, President
Tel: (787) 767-0022 Fax: (787) 767-0022
Email: nitonito@yahoo.com
Web: www.aacsi.org

ATENEO PUERTORRIQUEÑO
P.O. Box 9021180
San Juan, PR 00902
Eduardo Morales Coll, President
Tel: (787) 722-4839 Fax: (787) 725-3873
Email: ateneopr@caribe.net
Web: www.ateneopr.com

BRIDGES FOR PEACE, INTERNATIONAL
Centro de Recursos Hispanos
PMB 133, 100 Gran Blvd. #112
San Juan, PR 00926-5955
Teri Riddering, Coordinator
Tel: (787) 782-0868 Fax: (787) 782-0868
Email: bfp@isla.net
Web: www.puentesparalapaz.org

CENTRO ESPERANZA, INC.
P.O. Box 482
Calle 1 Esquina 4 Parcelas Vieques

Loiza, PR 00772
Sor Carmen Gloria Alayón, HC, Director
Tel: (787) 876-1545 Fax: (787) 876-1545
Email: cesperanza@coqui.net

CIUDADANOS DEL KARSO
497 Calle E. Pol #94
San Juan, PR 00926-5636
Abel Vale, President
Tel: (787) 760-2100 Fax: (787) 760-2070
Email: avale@cdk-pr.org
Web: www.cdk-pr.org

COLUMBIA COLLEGE
Centro de Yauco
P.O. Box 3062
Yauco, PR 00698
Carmen L. Martinez, Director
Tel: (787) 856-0845 Fax: (787) 267-2335
Email: cmartinez@columbiaco.edu
Web: www.columbiaco.edu

DEPARTAMENTO DE EDUCACION
Instituto Tecnologico de Puerto Rico Recinto de Ponce
P.O. Box 7284
Ponce, PR 00732-7284
Louis Rodriguez, Director
Tel: (787) 843-1305 Fax: (787) 812-5630

ESCUELA DE MEDICINA SAN JUAN BAUTISTA
P.O. Box 4968
Caguas, PR 00726-4968
Juan Rodriguez del Valle, President
Tel: (787) 743-3038 Fax: (787) 746-3093
Email: jrodriguez@sanjuanbautista.edu
Web: www.sanjuanbautista.edu

HISPANIC EDUCATIONAL TELECOMMUNICATIONS SYSTEM
Inter American University of Puerto Rico
P.O. Box 363255
San Juan, PR 00936-3255
Dr. Nitza M. Hernandez Lopez, Executive Director
Tel: (787) 766-1912 X2221 Fax: (787) 250-7984
Email: n_hernandez@upr.edu
Web: www.hets.org

INTER AMERICAN UNIVERSITY OF PUERTO RICO, GUAYAMA CAMPUS
Call Box 10004
Guayama, PR 00785
Prof. Carlos E. Colon-Ramos, Chancellor
Tel: (787) 864-2222 Fax: (787) 864-8232
Email: ccolon@interedu

JANE STERN DORADO COMMUNITY LIBRARY
Affiliate of Fondos Unidos de Puerto Rico
P.O. Box 609
Dorado, PR 00646
Carmen Teresa Arroyo, Director
Tel: (787) 796-3675 Fax: (787) 796-1227
Email: jsdcl@coqui.net
Web: http://home.coqui.net/jsdcl

JUAN DOMINGO EN ACCIÓN, INC.
Affiliate of Fondos Unidos de Puerto Rico
Calle Robles #55 (Interior)
Guaynabo, PR 00966
Natividad Montalvo, Director
Tel: (787) 783-4034 Fax: (787) 783-4034
Email: jdomingo@coqui.net

LULAC NATIONAL EDUCATIONAL SERVICE CENTERS, INC.
Bayamon Puerto Rico Headquarters
Calle Maceo #29
Bayamon, PR 00961
Zaida Vazquez, Director
Tel: (787) 785-8080 X31 Fax: (787) 786-6933
Email: infobay@lnesc-bayamon-pr.org
Web: www.lnesc-bayamon-pr.org

REFORMA
Puerto Rico Chapter
Veterans Hospital Library, 10 Casia St.
San Juan, PR 00921-3201
Carmen Sierra, Chapter President

Tel: (787) 641-7582
Email: carmen.sierra-ramirez@med.va.gov
Web: www.reforma.org

SEMINARIO EVANGELICO DE PUERTO RICO
776 Ave. Ponce de León
San Juan, PR 00925
Sergio Ojeda Carcamo, President
Tel: (787) 763-6700 Fax: (787) 751-0847
Email: drsojeda@seminarioevangelicopr.org
Web: www.seminarioevangelicopr.org

SPEC. INT., EMPLOYMENT

SER-JOBS FOR PROGRESS, INC. OF PUERTO RICO
Affiliate of SER-Jobs for Progress National, Inc.
P.O. Box 364583
San Juan, PR 00936-4583
Jose E. Ramos Delgado, Executive Director
Tel: (787) 707-7545 Fax: (787) 771-4602
Email: hspresbi@coqui.net
Web: www.ser-national.org

SINDICATO PUERTORRIQUEÑO DE TRABAJADORES. INC.
1813 Caso las Colosias Conspanpias
Ponce, PR 00717
Roberto Pagan, President
Tel: (787) 843-6850 Fax: (787) 842-5771
Email: spt_seiu@prtc.net
Web: www.sptseiu.org

UNION DE PERIODISTAS
P.O. Box 364302
San Juan, PR 00936-4302
Israel Rodriguez, Secretary Treasurer
Tel: (787) 781-8500 Fax: (787) 749-4839
Email: upagra@caribe.net

VETELBA
P.O. Box 29030
PMB Departamento 484 HC-01
Caguas, PR 00725-8900
Elba Bonilla, Director
Tel: (787) 258-6534 Fax: (787) 258 -6533
Email: vetelba@coqui.net

SPEC. INT., FAMILY PLANNING

INSTITUTO DEL HOGAR CELIA Y HARRIS BUNKER
Affiliate of Fondos Unidos de Puerto Rico
P.O. Box 20155
San Juan, PR 00928-0155
Yasiris Febles, Director
Tel: (787) 765-7895 Fax: (787) 767-4904
Email: institutohogar@geocities.com
Web: www.geocities.com/Heartland/Trail/2771

SPEC. INT., HEALTH SERVICES

AMERICAN CANCER SOCIETY / SOCIEDAD AMERICANA DEL CANCER
Caguas
P.O. Box 1368
Caguas, PR 00726
Miriam Diaz, Director
Tel: (787) 743-4040 Fax: (787) 744-4336
Web: www.cancer.org

ASHFORD PRESBYTERIAN COMMUNITY HOSPITAL
Damas Voluntarias
P.O. Box 9020032
San Juan, PR 00902
Pedro J. Gonzalez, Executive Director
Tel: (787) 721-2160 Fax: (787) 721-6976
Web: www.presbypr.com

ASOCIACIÓN DE ALZHEIMER Y DESÓRDENES RELACIONADOS DE PUERTO RICO
P.O. Box 362026
San Juan, PR 00936-2026
Aracelis Abreu, Director

Tel: (787) 727-4151 Fax: (787) 727-4890
Email: alzheimerpr@alzheimerpr.org
Web: www.alzheimerpr.org

ASOCIACIÓN DE LA DISTROFIA MUSCULAR, INC.
Capitulo de Puerto Rico
Ave. Ponce de Leon 431, Edif. Nacional Plz. #705
Hato-Rei, PR 00917
Helda Rosado, Director
Tel: (787) 751-4088 Fax: (787) 250-4414
Email: puertoricodistric@mdausa.org
Web: www.mdausa.org

ASOCIACIÓN MEDICA DE PUERTO RICO, INC.
P.O. Box 9387
San Juan, PR 00908-9387
Rafael Alicea, Executive Director
Tel: (787) 721-6969 Fax: (787) 722-1191/724-5208
Email: asocmed@coqui.net

ASOCIACIÓN PUERTORRIQUEÑA DE DIABETES
P.O. Box 190842
San Juan, PR 00919-0842
Elba Blanes, Executive Director
Tel: (787) 281-0617 Fax: (787) 281-7175
Email: diabetes@coqui.net
Web: www.diabetespr.org

ASOCIACIÓN PUERTORRIQUEÑA DE PARKINSON
Affiliate of Fondos Unidos de Puerto Rico
P.O. Box 7579
Carolina, PR 00986-7579
Sra. Carmen Orobitg, Director
Tel: (787) 768-5565 Fax: (787) 752-0650
Email: asocparkinsonpr@aol.com
Web: www.parkinson.org

CENTRO DE ADULTOS Y NINOS CON IMPEDIMENTOS, INC.
Affiliate of Fondos Unidos de Puerto Rico
Calle Dr. Gonzalez #133
Isabela, PR 00662
Sonia M. Ramos Velasquez, Director
Tel: (787) 872-5565 Fax: (787) 872-4111
Email: canii@coqui.net
Web: www.caniipr.org

CONSEJO RENAL DE PUERTO RICO, INC.
1008 Avenida Americo Miranda, Centro Comercial Metropolitano #208-C
San Juan, PR 00921
Dra. Mary Molina, President
Tel: (787) 764-8689 Fax: (787) 250-0360
Email: marymo@coqui.net
Web: www.consejorenal.com

CUERPO VOLUNTARIO DE SERVICIOS MÉDICOS DE EMERGENCIA, INC.
Affiliate of Fondos Unidos de Puerto Rico
P.O. Box 1290
Hatillo, PR 00659
Sr. Angel L. Crespo, Director
Tel: (787) 262-1686 Fax: (787) 262-1686
Email: cusme911@coqui.net

EL CENTRO DE AYUDA Y TERAPIA AL NIÑO CON IMPEDIMENTO
#140 Calle Monseñor José Torres
Moca, PR 00676
Migdalia Gonzalez Lugo, Director
Tel: (787) 877-4213 Fax: (787) 877-2022
Email: ayani@prpc.net

HOGAR SAN GERARDO, INC.
MSC 250, Winston Church Ave.
San Juan, PR 00926
Dr. Lorenzo Bosque, Director
Tel: (787) 761-8383 Fax: (787) 748-2065

PUERTO RICO LUPUS SUPPORT GROUP
P.O. Box 50817
Levittown, PR 00950
Sallie Valcárcel, President
Tel: (787) 795-3942 Fax: (630) 982-6537
Email: prlupus@usa.net
Web: /www.lupus.org

SOCIEDAD AMERICANA DEL CÁNCER
Division de Puerto Rico
P.O. Box 366004
San Juan, PR 00936-6004
Dr. Lillian Santos, Executive Director
Tel: (787) 764-2295 Fax: (787) 764-0553
Email: lsantos@cancer.org
Web: www.cancer.org

SOCIEDAD AMERICANA DEL CANCER DE PUERTO RICO, INC.
Hospital Doctor Manuel Figueroa
P.O. Box 140456
Arecibo, PR 00614-0456
Carlos Hernàndez, Director
Tel: (787) 879-0656 Fax: (787) 817-0556
Email: Carlos.Hernàndez@cancer.org
Web: www.cancer.org

SOCIEDAD AMERICANA DEL CANCER UNIDAD OESTE, INC.
Urbanization Ramires de Arellano Calle J
Campeche #38
Mayagüez, PR 00682
Mildred J. Carrero-Mercado, Director
Tel: (787) 833-3320 Fax: (787) 833-3320
Web: www.cancer.org

SOCIEDAD DE EDUCACIÓN Y REHABILITACIÓN DE PUERTO RICO
Affiliate of Fondos Unidos de Puerto Rico
P.O. Box 360325
San Juan, PR 00936-0325
Nilda Morales, Executive Director
Tel: (787) 767-6710 Fax: (787) 758-0950
Email: info@serpr.org
Web: www.serpr.org

SPEC. INT., HUMAN RELATIONS

CORPORACIÓN PARA EL DESARROLLO ECONÓMICO Y SOCIAL DE SAN SEBASTIÁN
Affiliate of Fondos Unidos de Puerto Rico
P.O. Box 845
San Sebastian, PR 00685
Myrian Torres, Executive Director
Tel: (787) 896-3645 Fax: (787) 896-3645
Email: codesance@coqui.net

HOGAR RUTH, INC.
Affiliate of Fondos Unidos de Puerto Rico
P.O. Box 538
Vega Alta, PR 00692
Ileana Aymat Ríos, Administrator
Tel: (787) 883-1884
Email: hogarruth@hotmail.com

HOGAR SANTA MARIA EUFRASIA, INC.
P.O. Box 1909
Arecibo, PR 00613
Hna. Francisca Torres, Director
Tel: (787) 878-5166 Fax: (787) 880-2632
Web: www.buonpastoreint.org

NATIONAL ASSOCIATION OF SOCIAL WORKERS
Puerto Rico Chapter
P.O. Box 192051
San Juan, PR 00919-2051
Antonio S. Rodriguez, Executive Director
Tel: (787) 758-3588 Fax: (787) 281-8433
Email: naswprc@caribe.net
Web: www.naswdc.org

NATIONAL PUERTO RICO FORUM, INC.
Puerto Rico Office
1059-1061 Calle Gonzalez
Rio Piedras, PR 00925
Priscilla M. Ramos, Regional Director
Tel: (787) 282-8331 Fax: (787) 282-7152
Email: kofb@nprf.org
Web: www.nprf.org

SPEC. INT., LEGAL ASSISTANCE

MCCONNELL VALDES
270 Munoz Rivera Ave.
Hato Rey, PR 00918
Arturo J. García, Managing Partner
Tel: (787) 759-9292 Fax: (787) 759-9225
Email: ajg@mcvpr.com
Web: www.mcvpr.com

SPEC. INT., MENTAL HEALTH

MENTAL HEALTH AND ANTI-ADDICTION SERVICES ADMINISTRATION
Puerto Rico Chapter
P.O. Box 21414
San Juan, PR 00928-1414
Dr. Rosa Pereze, Administrator
Tel: (787) 764-3670 Fax: (787) 765-5888
Email: info@mentalhealth.org/dalilaag@afssmca.gobierno.pr
Web: www.mentalhealth.org

SPEC. INT., SENIORS

CENTRO COMUNIDAD PARA ENVEJECIENTES PERLA DEL SUR
4645 Paquito Moncatnem Per. del Sur
Ponce, PR 00731
Lidia Echeverria R., Director
Tel: (787) 843-0436 Fax: (787) 841-3727

CENTRO DE ACTIVIDADES MÚLTIPLES SANTA LUISA
Affiliate of Fondos Unidos de Puerto Rico
RR 6 BOX 9492
San Juan, PR 00962
Sor Catalina Sánchez, Director
Tel: (787) 720-2764 Fax: (787) 731-7795
Email: centrosantaluisa@yahoo.com

CENTRO DE ANCIANOS - LA NUEVA AURORA
Apartado 588 Mameyal
Dorado, PR 00646
Kydian Y. Cardona Maldonado, Director
Tel: (787) 796-2469 Fax: (787) 796-3660

CENTRO DE CUIDADO DIURNO MUNICIPAL HOCONUCO BAJO
P.O. Box 85
San German, PR 00683
Gloria Martoro, Director
Tel: (787) 892-7150 Fax: (787) 892-7150

CENTRO DE ENVEJECIENTES CORAZONES UNIDOS
Proyecto Hope
P.O. Box 1452
Orocovis, PR 00720
Maria Gonzalez, Director
Tel: (787) 867-2240 Fax: (787) 867-2240

CENTRO DE ENVEJECIENTES DE TOA ALTA
P.O. Box 82
Toa Alta, PR 00954
David Oterro, Director
Tel: (787) 870-3808 Fax: (787) 870-6883

CENTRO DE ENVEJECIENTES EDAD DE ORO
Calle Santiago Iglesias #51
San Lorenzo, PR 00754
Carmen Rlta Pujoles, Director
Tel: (787) 736-8374 Fax: (787) 736-8374

CENTRO DE ENVEJECIENTES JULIO PEREZ IRIZARRY, INC.
P.O. Box 1661
Hormigueros, PR 00660-5661
Harry Candelario, Director
Tel: (787) 849-2626 Fax: (787) 849-4680

CENTRO DE ENVEJECIENTES MANUEL ACEVEDO ROSARIO
P.O. Box 633
Bo. Puente Peña
Camuy, PR 00627
Ninsa Rosa, Director
Tel: (787) 898-2190

CENTRO DE ENVEJECIENTES-SAN MARTIN
HC-03 Box 14303-Caguanas
Utuado, PR 00641
Luz N. Ruiz, Director
Tel: (787) 894-7463

CENTRO DE ENVEJECIMIENTO LOS APRINES
Calle Ca. Lebrim #449
Vieques, PR 00765
Maria S. Bonew, Director
Tel: (787) 741-2262 Fax: (787) 741-2262
Email: cemim@prtc.net

CENTRO GERIATRICO EL REMANSO
Affiliate of Fondos Unidos de Puerto Rico
RR11 Box 4103
Bayamón, PR 00956
Sister Teresita Rivera, Director
Tel: (787) 797-5083 Fax: (787) 279-0963
Email: centroremanso@yahoo.com

HOGAR CARMEN PIMENTEL
Calle Alejo Cruzado #1037
Rio Piedras, PR 00924
Carmen Pimentel, Director
Tel: (787) 752-7788

HOGAR DE ANCIANOS BETZAIDA
Bo. Ceiba Baja-HC-02- Box 8976
Aguadilla, PR 00603
Carmala Arce, Director
Tel: (787) 882-9004

HOGAR DE ANCIANOS EL EDEN
Km. 1 Barrio Sonadora - Ramal 792
Aguas Buenas, PR 00703
Noelocasio Rivera, Director
Tel: (787) 732-8520 Fax: (787) 732-8520

HOGAR DE ANCIANOS REMANZO DE LA VEJEZ
Calle Hospital, #13
Lares, PR 00669
José Villegas, Director
Tel: (787) 897-2400

HOGAR REMEMBRANZA
Carr. 806 Km 0.3
Toa Alta, PR 00953
Carmen E. Rivera, Director
Tel: (787) 870-3227 Fax: (787) 798-3097

HOGAR RETIRO LAS MARIAS
Calle Mayagüez 18
Hato Rey, PR 00917
Evelyn Gonzalez, Director
Tel: (787) 758-4368 Fax: (787) 758-4368

HOGAR RIDER
Hospital Rider Memorial
Call Box 859
Humacao, PR 00792
Lydia Abreu, Director
Tel: (787) 852-0768 Fax: (787) 852-0157

HOGAR SANTA TERESA DE JORNET
P.O. Box 21012
San Juan, PR 00928-1012
Carmen Vasques, Director
Tel: (787) 761-5805 Fax: (787) 755-5575

HOGAR SUSTITUTO RODRIGUEZ ORTIZ
P.O. Box 1314
Carolina, PR 00986
Evelyn Rodriguez, Director
Tel: (787) 750-6219 Fax: (787) 750-6219

JESUS DE SANTA MARIA
Carr. 785-HC-02-Box 34127
Caguas, PR 00725
Gloria E. Hernández, Director
Tel: (787) 747-7546 Fax: (787) 747-7546

LYDIA'S HOME CARE
715 Carr. 349
Mayagüez, PR 00680
Lydia Casilla, Director
Tel: (787) 833-7882

MARRERO-ORTIZ
P.O. Box Box 231
Villalba, PR 00766

Luz Ortiz Alvarado, Director
Tel: (787) 867-5332

PERSONAS DE EDAD AVANZADA LAS MONJAS
Calle Santiago Iglesias esq. Uruguay
San Juan, PR 00917
Elsie Dazila, Director
Tel: (787) 754-7844 Fax: (787) 765-9322

REMANSO DE LA VEJEZ
Calle Hospital #13
Lares, PR 00669
José Villegas, Director
Tel: (787) 897-2400

SPEC. INT., SOCIAL INTEREST

APOYO EMPRESARIAL PENÍNSULA DE CANTERA, INC.
Affiliate of Fondos Unidos de Puerto Rico
P.O. Box 7187
San Juan, PR 00916-7187
Sandra Fuentes, Director
Tel: (787) 268-3138 Fax: (787) 727-0278

BANCO DE ALIMENTOS DE PUERTO RICO
Affiliate of Fondos Unidos de Puerto Rico
P.O. Box 2989
Bayamón, PR 00960-2989
Angela Menchaca, Executive Director
Tel: (787) 740-3663 Fax: (787) 786-8810
Email: bdadpr@prtc.net

CENTRO DE AYUDA SOCIAL
Affiliate of Fondos Unidos de Puerto Rico
Bo. Obrero Station-P.O. Box 7093
Santurce, PR 00916-7093
Rev. Aurea Martinez Villar, Executive Director
Tel: (787) 781-3965 Fax: (787) 781-2333
Email: ccnaanae@coqui.net

CHRISTIAN COMMUNITY CENTER
Affiliate of Fondos Unidos de Puerto Rico
P.O. Box 30024
San Juan, PR 00929
Isabel Martinez, Director
Tel: (787) 789-8758 Fax: (787) 789-8758
Email: cccenter@coqui.net

FIDEICOMISO DE CONSERVACIÓN DE PR
P.O. Box 9023554
San Juan, PR 00902-3554
Fernando Lloveras, Executive Director
Tel: (787) 722-5834 Fax: (787) 722-5872

PUERTO RICO COMMUNITY FOUNDATION
P.O. Box 70362
San Juan, PR 00936-8362
Nelson I. Colón, President
Tel: (787) 721-1037 Fax: (787) 721-1673
Email: fcpr@fcpr.org
Web: www.fcpr.org

TRAVELERS AID OF PUERTO RICO
Travelers Aid International
P.O. Box 38017
Airport Station
San Juan, PR 00937-1017
Mildred Sosa, Executive Director
Tel: (787) 791-1034 Fax: (787) 791-1054
Email: taidofpr@prtc.net

VIEQUES CONSERVATION & HISTORICAL TRUST
Calle Flamboyán, #138
Vieques, PR 00765
Sandra I. Ortiz, Office Administrator
Tel: (787) 741-8850 Fax: (787) 741-2844
Email: vcht@coqui.net
Web: www.vcht.org

SPEC. INT., SPORTS

FEDERACION PUERTORRIQUEÑA DE BOXEO AFICIONADO, INC.
P.O. Box 9065964 - Puerta de Tierra Station
San Juan, PR 00906-5964
Pedro R. Aponte, President

Tel: (787) 721-5575 Fax: (787) 721-4252
Email: fpba@pucpr.edu

FEDERACION PUERTORRIQUEÑA DE CICLISMO
P.O Box 194674
San Juan, PR 00919-4674
Alexis Cruz Maldonado, President
Tel: (787) 721-8755 Fax: (787) 723-0140
Email: fecipur@yahoo.com
Web: www.federacionciclismopr.com

FEDERACION PUERTORRIQUEÑA DE VOLEIBOL
P.O. Box 363711
San Juan, PR 00936-3711
Ramon Luis Carrasquillo, Executive Director
Tel: (787) 282-7524
Email: fpvbremsa@yahoo.com

PUERTO RICO GOLF ASSOCIATION
58 Caribe St.
San Juan, PR 00907
Sidney Wolf, President
Tel: (787) 721-7742 Fax: (787) 723-5670
Email: swolf@prga.org
Web: www.prga.org

SALON DE LA FAMA DEL DEPORTE RIO PEDRENSE
P.O. Box 191184
San Juan, PR 00919-1184
Isaura Diaz, Manager
Tel: (787) 765-9470 Fax: (787) 751-2762

CENTRO DE VOLUNTARIOS DE FONDOS UNIDOS
Affiliate of Fondos Unidos de Puerto Rico
P.O. Box 191914
San Juan, PR 00914-1914
Sra. Carmen L. Rodríguez, Director
Tel: (787) 728-8500 Fax: (787) 728-7099
Email: c.rodriguez@fundusunadus.com

VOLUNTARY SERVICE OPTOMETRIC ASSOCIATION
Inter American University of Puerto Rico
P.O. Box 191049
School of Optometry
San Juan, PR 00919-1049
Grace Gomez, Director for Student Affairs Office
Tel: (787) 765-1915 Fax: (787) 767-3920
Email: ggomez@inter.edu
Web: www.optonet.inter.edu

CARIBE GIRL SCOUTS COUNCIL
500 Eliza Colberg 15th Stop
Santurce, PR 00907
Maritza Gomez, President
Tel: (787) 721-5771 Fax: (787) 721-6291
Email: cgsdirejec@coqui.net

CASA PENSAMIENTO DE MUJER DEL CENTRO, INC.
P.O. Box 2002
Aibonito, PR 00705
Charity Rivera, Executive Director
Tel: (787) 735-6698 Fax: (787) 735-3200
Email: casapens@promocomercio.com

CENTRO DE FORTALECIMIENTO E.S.C.A.P.E.
Affiliate of Fondos Unidos de Puerto Rico
P.O. Box 2598
Guaynabo, PR 00970-2598
Yatira Pizarro, Director
Tel: (787) 287-6161 Fax: (787) 287-6110
Email: escape@caribe.net
Web: http://slaq.prw.net/abusos/centro.htm

HISPANIC BUSINESS WOMEN'S ALLIANCE
530 Ponce de Leon Ave.
San Juan, PR 00901-2304
Lourdes Aponte-Rosario, President

Tel: (787) 760-7196 Fax: (787) 289-8779
Email: laponte@hbwa.net
Web: www.hbwa.net

HOGAR FÁTIMA
P.O. Box 4228
Bayamon Gardens Station
Bayamón, PR 00958-4228
María Saez, Director
Tel: (787) 787-2580 Fax: (787) 787-2580
Email: fatima001@prpc.net

TALLER SALUD, INC.
Affiliate of Fondos Unidos de Puerto Rico
P.O. Box 524
Loiza, PR 00772
Laura Colon Martinez, General Coordinator
Tel: (787) 876-8704 Fax: (787) 876-3440
Email: tsalud@caribe.net

ASOCIACIÓN PRO JUVENTUD Y COMUNIDAD DEL BARRIO PALMAS
Affiliate of Fondos Unidos de Puerto Rico
Barrio Palmas, 257 Cucharilla
Cataño, PR 00962
Sra. Gloria Maldonado, Director
Tel: (787) 788-5105 Fax: (787) 788-6269
Email: apjcatano@hotmail.com

BOY SCOUTS OF AMERICA
Affiliate of Fondos Unidos de Puerto Rico
P.O. Box 70181
San Juan, PR 00936
Harold Hernandez, Director
Tel: (787) 790-0323 Fax: (787) 793-0357
Email: hpagan@bsamail.org
Web: www.bsapr.org

BOYS AND GIRLS CLUB DE MAYAGÜEZ
Affiliate of Boys and Girls Club de Puerto Rico
P.O. Box 9300665
San Juan, PR 00936-0665
Julio Montalvo Feliciano, Director
Tel: (787) 805-3855 Fax: (787) 805-3855
Email: jmontalvo@bgcpr.org
Web: www.bgcpr.org

BOYS AND GIRLS CLUB DE PUERTO RICO
Affiliate of Fondos Unidos de Puerto Rico
P.O. Box 9300665
San Juan, PR 00930-0665
Jose Campos Fuste, Executive Director
Tel: (787) 268-4504 Fax: (787) 268-4504
Email: jcampos@bgcpr.org
Web: www.bgcpr.org

CENTRO MARGARITA, INC.
Affiliate of Fondos Unidos de Puerto Rico
P.O. Box 1640
Cidra, PR 00739
Mario Otero, Director
Tel: (787) 739-6030 Fax: (787) 739-0808
Email: centromar@centromargarita.org
Web: www.centromargarita.org

EL HOGAR DEL NIÑO
Affiliate of Fondos Unidos de Puerto Rico
P.O. Box 20667
San Juan, PR 00928-0667
Mary Martin, Director
Tel: (787) 761-2805 Fax: (787) 283-1345
Email: elhogarnino@prtc.net

EXITO A LOS SEIS/SUCCESS BY SIX
Affiliate of Fondos Unidos de Puerto Rico
P.O. Box 191914
San Juan, PR 00919-1914
William J. Perez, President/CEO
Tel: (787) 728-8500 Fax: (787) 728-7099
Email: info@fondosunidos.org
Web: www.fondosunidos.com/en/services/successbysix.htm

HOGAR ALBERGUE PARA NIÑOS JESÚS DE NAZARET, INC.
Affiliate of Fondos Unidos de Puerto Rico
P.O. Box 1147
Mayagüez, PR 00681
Olga Ortíz Valentín, Contact
Tel: (787) 831-6161 Fax: (787) 831-4226
Email: childnom@coqui.net

HOGAR FORJADORES DE ESPERANZA
Affiliate of Fondos Unidos de Puerto Rico
P.O. Box 4181, Bayamón Gardens Station
Bayamón, PR 00958
Damaris Rivera de Seijo, Director
Tel: (787) 730-0200 Fax: (787) 730-0909
Web: www.icdc.org/Organizaciones/forjadores_de_esperanza.htm

HOGARES TERESA TODA
Affiliate of Fondos Unidos de Puerto Rico
P.O. Box 868
Canóvanas, PR 00729
Hna. Inés Peña, Director
Tel: (787) 886-2060 Fax: (787) 886-2075
Email: htodapr@isla.net

INSTITUTO DE FORMACIÓN SANTA ANA
Affiliate of Fondos Unidos de Puerto Rico
P.O. Box 554
Adjuntas, PR 00601
Hna. Ismaela Castro, Director
Tel: (787) 829-2504 Fax: (787) 829-2504
Web: http://home.coqui.net/isahogar/isa_2.htm

MAKE-A-WISH FOUNDATION
San Jorge Children's Hospital, Affiliate of Fondos Unidos de Puerto Rico
Suite 112 MSC 476, 100 Grand Blvd. Paseo
San Juan, PR 00926-5955
Luis Caraballo, Executive Director
Tel: (787) 283-7915 Fax: 787-283-7930
Email: info@makeawishpr.org
Web: www.makeawishpr.org

PROGRAMA DE EDUCACIÓN COMUNAL DE ENTREGA Y SERVICIOS, INC.
Affiliate of Fondos Unidos de Puerto Rico
P.O. Box 647
Punta Santiago, PR 00741
Hna. Nancy Madden George, Director
Tel: (787) 285-4135 Fax: (787) 285-0696
Email: peces@coqui.net
Web: www.tendenciaspr.com/PECES.html

AMERICAN MEDICAL STUDENT ASSOCIATION
Universidad de Puerto Rico, Cayey
Avenida Antonio R. Barcelo
Cayey, PR 00736
Gloridee Rosario, Director
Tel: (787) 738-2162 X2206 Fax: (787) 263-0676
Email: gloridee@hotmail.com
Web: www.upr.clu.edu

ASOCIACIÓN ESTUDIANTES DE ENFERMERÍA
Universidad del Sagrado Corazón
P.O. Box 12383
Programa de Enfermería
San Juan, PR 00914-0383
Keina Alcantra Vicente, Member
Tel: (787) 728-1515 X2427/2430
Email: aee@sagrado.edu
Web: www.sagrado.edu

BETA SIGMA KAPPA SOCIETY
Inter American University of Puerto Rico
P.O. Box 191049
School of Optometry
San Juan, PR 00919-1049
Grace Gomez, Director for Student Affairs Office
Tel: (787) 765-1915 Fax: (787) 767-3920
Email: ggomez@inter.edu
Web: www.optonet.inter.edu

CAPÍTULO ESTUDIANTIL DE MICROBIOLOGÍA
Universidad del Sagrado Corazón

P.O. Box 12383
Departamento de Ciencias Naturales
San Juan, PR 00914-0383
Mayra Rolón, Advisor
Tel: (787) 728-1515
Email: mrolon@sagrado.edu
Web: www.sagrado.edu

NATIONAL OPTOMETRIC STUDENT ASSOCIATION
Inter American University of Puerto Rico
P.O. Box 191049
San Juan, PR 00919-1049
Dick Robles Rodríguez, Director
Tel: (787) 765-1915 Fax: (787) 767-3920
Email: drobles@inter.edu
Web: www.optonet.inter.edu

PUERTO RICO OPTOMETRIC STUDENT ASSOCIATION
Inter American University of Puerto Rico
P.O. Box 191049
School of Optometry
San Juan, PR 00919-1049
Grace Gomez, Director for Student Affairs Office
Tel: (787) 765-1915 Fax: (787) 767-3920
Email: ggomez@inter.edu
Web: www.optonet.inter.edu

RHODE ISLAND

MULTICULTURAL FOODSERVICE & HOSPITALITY ALLIANCE
65 Weybosset St. #60
Providence, RI 02903
Daniel Halpern, President/CEO
Tel: (401) 751-8883 Fax: (401) 751-8333
Email: mfhainfo@mfha.net
Web: www.mfha.net

HISPANIC AMERICAN CHAMBER OF COMMERCE OF RHODE ISLAND
545 Royal Little Dr.
Providence, RI 02904
Tel: (401) 331-2615 Fax: (401) 331-2822
Email: juanahorton@earthlink.com
Web: www.haccri.com

LYDIA PEREZ & YORUBA
209 Maryland Ave.
Warwick, RI 02888
Lydia Perez, Director
Tel: (401) 737-0751 Fax: (401) 737-0751
Email: yorubapr@earthlink.net
Web: www.prfdance.org/yoruba2.htm

PUERTO RICAN INSTITUTE FOR ARTS AND ADVOCACY
P.O. Box 8168
Warwick, RI 02888
Lydia Perez, Exucutive Director
Tel: (401) 737-0751 Fax: (401) 737-0751
Email: yorubapr@earthlink.net

RHODE ISLAND COMMISSION FOR HUMAN RIGHTS
180 Westminster St., 3rd Fl.
Providence, RI 02903
Michael Evora, Executive Director
Tel: (401) 222-2661 Fax: (401) 222-2616
Web: www.richr.ri.gov

PROGRESO LATINO
626 Broad St.

Central Falls, RI 02863
Edwin Cancel, Executive Director
Tel: (401) 728-5920 Fax: (401) 724-5550
Email: progresolatino@earthlink.net

RELIGIOUS

DIOCESE OF PROVIDENCE
Hispanic Affairs
184 Broad St.
Providence, RI 02903-3695
Aida Hidalgo, Director for Hispanic Affairs
Tel: (401) 421-7833 Fax: (401) 453-6135
Email: ahidalgo@dioceseofprovidence.org
Web: www.dioceseofprovidence.org

IGLESIA BAUTISTA HISPANA EL CALVARIO
747 Broad St.
Providence, RI 02907
Orlando Irizarry, Pastor
Tel: (401) 461-7507 Fax: (401) 785-8275
Web: www.calbaptist.org

IGLESIA CATOLICA ESPIRITU SANTO
472 Atwells Ave.
Providence, RI 02909
Taticio Bagatin, Pastor
Tel: (401) 421-3551 Fax: (401) 421-3557

OUR LADY OF MOUNT CARMEL
12 Spruce St.
Providence, RI 02903
Hilda Lopez, Pastor Assistant
Tel: (401) 274-2113 Fax: (401) 453-1221

ST. JOSEPH CATHOLIC CHURCH
854 Providence St.
West Warwick, RI 02893
Charles Downing, Pastor
Tel: (401) 821-4072 Fax: (401) 821-2408
Email: downing@dioceseofprovidence.org
Web: www.dioceseofprovidence.org

ST. MICHAEL CHURCH
239 Oxford St.
Providence, RI 02905
Rev. Raymond Malm, Pastor
Tel: (401) 781-7210 Fax: (401) 461-6164

RESEARCH

CENTER FOR THE STUDY OF RACE AND ETHNICITY IN AMERICA
Brown University
P.O. Box 1886
Providence, RI 02912
Evelyn Hu-DeHart, Director
Tel: (401) 863-3080 Fax: (401) 863-7589
Email: evelyn_hu-dehart@brown.edu

DEPARTMENT OF PORTUGUESE AND BRAZILIAN STUDIES
Brown University
Box 0
Providence, RI 02912
Luiz Valente, Director
Tel: (401) 863-3042 Fax: (401) 863-7261
Email: Luiz_Valente@brown.edu
Web: http://www.brown.edu/Departments/
Portuguese_Brazilian_Studies/

SPEC. INT., AIDS

RHODE ISLAND PROJECT AIDS
232 W Exchange St.
Providence, RI 02903
Magali Garcia, Latino Outreach Coordinator
Tel: (401) 831-5522 Fax: (401) 454-0299
Email: magali@aidsprojectri.org
Web: www.aidsprojectri.org

SPEC. INT., EDUCATION

CENTER FOR LATIN AMERICAN STUDIES
Brown University
111 Thayer St., Box 1970

Providence, RI 02912
Julio Ortega, Director
Tel: (401) 863-2106 Fax: (401) 863-2121
Web: www.watsoninstitute.org/clas

PUBLIC SCHOOL DEPARTMENT
Language and Culture
650 Prairie Ave.
Providence, RI 02905
Jose Gonzalez, Director
Tel: (401) 456-9297 Fax: (401) 278-2831
Email: jose.gonzalez@ppsd.org
Web: www.providenceschools.org

SPEC. INT., EMPLOYMENT

SER-JOBS FOR PROGRESS, INC.
Affiliate of SER-Jobs for Progress National, Inc.
101 Main St. #302
Pawtucket, RI 02860
Lissa Dreyer, Executive Director
Tel: (401) 724-1820 Fax: (401) 724-8490
Email: ser4@mindspring.com
Web: www.ser-national.org

SPEC. INT., HUMAN RELATIONS

CITY HALL OF PAWTUCKET
137 Roosevelt Ave.
Pawtucket, RI 02860
James E. Doyle, Mayor
Tel: (401) 728-0500 Fax: (401) 723-8620
Web: www.pawtucketri.com

SPEC. INT., LEGAL ASSISTANCE

INTERNATIONAL INSTITUTE OF RHODE ISLAND
Administrative Office
645 Elmwood Ave.
Providence, RI 02907
William Shuey, Executive Director
Tel: (401) 461-5940 Fax: (401) 467-6530
Email: bshuey@iiri.org
Web: www.iiri.org

SPEC. INT., SOCIAL INTEREST

CENTER FOR HISPANIC POLICY AND ADVOCACY
421 Elmwood Ave.
Providence, RI 02907
Miriam Wysong, Executive Director
Tel: (401) 467-0111 Fax: (401) 467-2507
Email: chispa@chispa.org
Web: www.chispa.org

HELPLINE OF TRAVELERS AID SOCIETY
Llamenos/United Way
160 Broad St.
Providence, RI 02903
Christina Alcedeo, Director of Community Services
Tel: (401) 351-6500 Fax: (401) 421-7410
Email: calcedeo@crossroadsri.org
Web: www.crossroadsri.org

PROYECTO ESPERANZA
400 Dexter St.
Central Falls, RI 02863
John Barry, Executive Director
Tel: (401) 728-0515 Fax: (401) 728-2330

STUDENT ORGANIZATION

FEDERACIÓN DE ESTUDIANTES PUERTORRIQUEÑOS
Brown University
Campus Box 2311
Providence, RI 02912
Ayana Morales, Co-Chair
Email: Ayana_Morales@brown.edu
Web: www.brown.edu/Students/FEP/index.html

LATIN AMERICAN STUDENTS ORGANIZATION
Brown University
P.O. Box 1930
Providence, RI 02912
Lissette M. Jimenez, Co Chair
Tel: (401) 863-2341 Fax: (401) 863-1090
Email: lissette_jimenez@brown.edu
Web: www.brown.edu/students/Latin_American_
Students_Organization/

SOUTH CAROLINA

MULTI-PURPOSE

ACERCAMIENTO HISPANO/HISPANIC OUTREACH, INC.
5808 E Shakespeare Rd.
Columbia, SC 29223
Irma Santana, Board Director
Tel: (803) 714-0085 Fax: (803) 714-0474
Email: info@schispanicoutreach.org
Web: www.schispanicoutreach.org

RELIGIOUS

DIOCESE OF CHARLESTON
Hispanic Ministry Office
P.O. Box 290515
Columbia, SC 29229-0009
Rev. Filemon Juya, Vicar for Hispanic Ministry
Tel: (803) 779-7584
Email: fileajuyab@aol.com
Web: www.catholic-doc.org

SPEC. INT., EDUCATION

HISPANIC ASSISTANCE FUND
Box 34555
Greenville, SC 29614
Dr. Juan Teruel, Chairman
Tel: (864) 770-1312 Fax: (864) 770-1314
Email: hafund@hafund.org
Web: www.hafund.org

LATIN AMERICAN & CARIBBEAN STUDIES
College of Charleston
66 George St.
Charleston, SC 29424
Douglas Friedman, Director
Tel: (843) 953-5701 Fax: (843) 953-8140
Email: lacs@cofc.edu
Web: www.cofc.edu/~friedman/lastud/latina.html

LATIN AMERICAN STUDIES PROGRAM
University of South Carolina
408 Gambrell Hall
Columbia, SC 29208
Ann Kingsolver, Interim Director
Tel: (803) 777-0437 Fax: (803) 777-0568
Email: kingsolver@sc.edu
Web: www.cla.sc.edu/LASP

SPEC. INT., HEALTH SERVICES

SOUTH CAROLINA HISPANIC/LATINO HEALTH COALITION
P.O. Box 722
Columbia, SC 29202-0722
Edena Meetze, Chair
Email: edena@schlhc.org
Web: www.schlhc.org

SPEC. INT., HUMAN RELATIONS

TELAMON CORPORATION
South Carolina State Office 1
P.O. Box 12217
Columbia, SC 29211-2217
Barbara Coleman, State Director
Tel: (803) 256-7411 Fax: (803) 256-8528
Email: bcoleman@telamon.org
Web: www.telamon.org

TELAMON CORPORATION
South Carolina State Office 10
400 Lexington Ave.
Kingstree, SC 29556
Wayne Rogers, Director
Tel: (843) 354-5708 Fax: (843) 354-5749
Email: wrogers@telamon.org
Web: www.telamon.org

TELAMON CORPORATION
South Carolina State Office 2
127 Greenville St. SW
Aiken, SC 29802
Nancy Pennington, Case Manager
Tel: (803) 648-9037 Fax: (803) 649-9447
Email: npennington@telamon.org
Web: www.telamon.org

TELAMON CORPORATION
South Carolina State Office 4
P.O. Box 31545
North Charleston, SC 29417
Deborah Johnson, Regional Manager
Tel: (843) 574-1872 Fax: (843) 766-3260
Email: djohnson@telamon.org
Web: www.telamon.org

TELAMON CORPORATION
South Carolina State Office 5
P.O. Box 1172
Florence, SC 29503
Anita White, Regional Manager
Tel: (843) 667-4664 Fax: (843) 667-9434
Email: awhite@telamon.org
Web: www.telamon.org

TELAMON CORPORATION
South Carolina State Office 6
P.O. Box 2252
Orangeburg, SC 29116
Patricia Crawford, Case Manager
Tel: (803) 534-6444 Fax: (803) 534-1802
Email: pcrawford@telamon.org
Web: www.telamon.org

TELAMON CORPORATION
South Carolina State Office 7
P.O. Box 5291
Spartanburg, SC 29304
Carmen Bowers, Regional Manager
Tel: (864) 573-8783 Fax: (864) 573-6342
Email: cbowers@telamon.org
Web: www.telamon.org

SPEC. INT., SOCIAL INTEREST

NATIONAL CENTER FOR MISSING & EXPLOITED CHILDREN
South Carolina
2008 Marion St. #I
Columbia, SC 29201-2151
Margaret Friroson, Director
Tel: (803) 254-2326 Fax: (803) 254-4299
Web: www.missingkids.com

SOUTH DAKOTA

SPEC. INT., EMPLOYMENT

MIGRANT AND SEASONAL FARMWORKERS PROGRAM
South Dakota Office
221 S Central
Pierre, SD 57501
Bill Podhradsky, State Director
Tel: (605) 224-0454 Fax: (605) 224-8320
Email: bpodhradsky@tie.net

TENNESSEE

BUSINESS

HISPANIC BUSINESS ALLIANCE
7845 US Hwy. 64 #331

Memphis, TN 38133
Tel: (901) 266-2999 Fax: (901) 379-0825
Email: hba@matcu.com

CHAMBER OF COMMERCE

NASHVILLE AREA HISPANIC CHAMBER OF COMMERCE
4050 Nolensville Rd. #211
Nashville, TN 37211
Yuri Cunza, President
Tel: (615) 332-9777
Email: nashvillehispanicchamber@yahoo.com
Web: www.nashvillehispanicchamber.com

TENNESSEE HISPANIC CHAMBER OF COMMERCE
P.O. Box 69
Hermitage, TN 37076
Greg Rodriguez, Jr., President
Tel: (615) 251-3585 Fax: (615) 251-3599
Email: greg@tnhispanic.com
Web: www.tnhispanic.com

RELIGIOUS

DIOCESE OF MEMPHIS
Hispanic/Multicultural Ministries
5825 Shelby Oaks Dr.
Memphis, TN 38134-7389
Rev. Tony Clark, Director for Multicultural Ministries
Tel: (901) 373-1284 Fax: (901) 373-1269
Email: tony.clark@cc.cdom.org
Web: www.cdom.org

DIOCESE OF NASHVILLE
Hispanic Ministry
10682 Old Nashville Hwy.
Smyrna, TN 37167
Rev. Richard Gagnnon, Director for Hispanic Ministry
Tel: (615) 459-3046 Fax: (615) 459-3989

RESEARCH

BRAZILIAN STUDIES ASSOCIATION
Vanderbilt University
VU Station B 350031, 2301 Vanderbilt Pl.
Nashville, TN 37235-0031
Timothy J.Power, President
Tel: (615) 322-2527 Fax: (615) 343-6002
Email: brasa@vanderbilt.edu
Web: www.brasa.org

CENTER FOR LATIN AMERICAN AND IBERIAN STUDIES
Vanderbilt University
VU Station B #351806, 2301 Vanderbilt Pl.
Nashville, TN 37235-1806
Norma Antillon
Tel: (615) 322-2527 Fax: (615) 322-2305
Email: norma.g.antillon@vanderbilt.edu
Web: http://sitemason.vanderbilt.edu/clais

SPEC. INT., CHILD CARE

CASA DE SARA
P.O. Box 30306
Knoxville, TN 37930
Lori Santoro, Executive Director
Tel: (865) 690-3323
Email: lsantoro@casadesara.org
Web: www.casadesara.org

SPEC. INT., HUMAN RELATIONS

TELAMON CORPORATION
Alamo Migrant Head Start Center 5
P.O. Box 266
Alamo, TN 38001
Phyllis Olley, Center Director
Tel: (731) 696-3536 Fax: (731) 696-3538
Email: polley@telamon.org
Web: www.telamon.org

Bybee Migrant Head Start Center 4
P.O. Box 769
Newport, TN 37821
Pauline Raines, Director
Tel: (423) 623-0703 Fax: (423) 623-0721
Email: praines@telamon.org
Web: www.telamon.org

State Head Start Office 1
4709 Papermill Rd. #103, Bldg. 1
Knoxville, TN 37909
J. Davis, Director
Tel: (865) 212-4011 Fax: (865) 212-3631
Email: jdavis@telamon.org
Web: www.telamon.org

Summer City Migrant Head Start Center 3
P.O. Box 707
Dayton, TN 37321
Vicki Chacon, Center Director
Tel: (423) 447-3228 Fax: (423) 447-3430
Email: vchacon@telamon.org
Web: www.telamon.org

Unicoi Migrant Head Start Center 2
P.O. Box 9
Unicoi, TN 37692
Silvia Fregoso, Center Director
Tel: (423) 743-2028 Fax: (423) 743-5496
Email: sfregoso@telamon.org
Web: www.telamon.org

SPEC. INT., SOCIAL INTEREST

CASA MARIA
North American Sisters of the Good Shepherd
4083 Hemingway
Memphis, TN 38128
Sr. Linda Larkman, Coordinator
Tel: (901) 373-7456
Email: goodshpvol@aol.com
Web: www.goodshepherdsistersna.com

TEXAS

ARTISTIC

LA PEÑA
227 Congress Ave. #300
Austin, TX 78701
Cynthia Perez, Executive Director
Tel: (512) 477-6007 Fax: (512) 477-0758
Email: lapena@igc.apc.org
Web: www.lapena-austin.org

NATIONAL ASSOCIATION OF LATINO ARTS AND CULTURE
1204 Buena Vista St.
San Antonio, TX 78207
Tel: (210) 432-3982 Fax: (210) 432-3934
Email: info@nalac.org
Web: www.nalac.org

PUERTO RICAN FOLKLORIC DANCE & CULTURAL DANCE
15228 Quiet Pond Ct.
Austin, TX 78728
Dr. Ana Maria Maynard, Director
Tel: (512) 251-8122
Email: dance@prfdance.org
Web: www.prfdance.org

RODRIGUEZ ACADEMY OF DANCE
9403 Richmond Ave.
Houston, TX 77063
Rogelio Rodriguez, Owner
Tel: (713) 780-1796 Fax: (713) 780-0798
Email: rodriguez@rodriguezacademy.com
Web: www.rodriguezacademy.com

TEATRO DALLAS
1331 Record Crossing Rd.
Dallas, TX 75235
Cora Cardona, Artistic Director/Founder
Tel: (214) 689-6492
Email: teatro@airmail.net
Web: http://web2.airmail.net/teatro

TEXAS TALENT MUSICIANS ASSOCIATION
P.O. Box 681266
San Antonio, TX 78268-1266
Robert Arellano, President
Tel: (210) 222-8862 Fax: (210) 224-7592
Email: info@tejanomusicawards.com
Web: www.tejanomusicawards.com

BUSINESS

ADELANTE
Frito-Lay Inc.
7701 Legacy Dr.
Plano, TX 75024
Angel Rodriguez
Tel: (972) 334-7000

ASSOCIATION OF LATINO PROFESSIONALS IN FINANCE AND ACCOUNTING
San Antonio Chapter
6800 Park Ten Blvd. #191W
San Antonio, TX 78213
Carmen Garcia, Chapter President
Tel: (210) 732-7701 Fax: (210) 732-8715
Email: carmen@ccgarcia.com
Web: www.alpfa.org

HISPANIC CONTRACTORS ASSOCIATION DE TEJAS
115 E Travis St. #1500
San Antonio, TX 78205
Tel: (210) 825-0910 Fax: (210) 227-2779

HISPANIC CONTRACTORS ASSOCIATION-GREATER HOUSTON AREA, INC.
P.O. Box 41908
Austin, TX 77241-1908
Joe L. Morales, Vice Chair
Tel: (713) 320-1193 Fax: (281) 856-8051
Email: hca.gha@mordata.net
Web: www.hca-houston.com

MEXICAN AMERICAN NETWORK OF ODESSA
1609 W 10th St.
Odessa, TX 79763
Mary Martha Arana, President/CEO
Tel: (432) 335-0250 Fax: (432) 337-6266
Email: mano@manochamber.org
Web: www.manochamber.org

NATIONAL BUSINESS ASSOCIATION
National Headquarters
5151 Beltline Rd. #1150
Dallas, TX 75254
Raj Nisankarao, President
Tel: (800) 456-0440 Fax: (972) 960-9149
Email: info@nationalbusiness.org
Web: www.nationalbusiness.org

NATIONAL HISPANIC BUSINESS ASSOCIATION
National Headquarters
1712 E. Riverside Dr. #208
Austin, TX 78741
Anissa Gonzales-Wieck, President
Tel: (512) 495-9511 Fax: (512) 495-9730
Email: agonzalezweick@nhba.org
Web: www.nhba.org

NATIONAL SOCIETY OF HISPANIC MBAS
Dallas/Fort Worth Chapter
P.O. Box 224568
Dallas, TX 75222-4568
Isaac Rodriguez, Chapter President
Email: president@dfw.nshmba.org
Web: http://dfw.nshmba.org/home.asp

NATIONAL SOCIETY OF HISPANIC MBAS
McAllen Chapter
2112 W University Dr. #334
Edinburg, TX 78539
Lourdes Servantes, Chapter President
Tel: (956) 381-2284 Fax: (956) 381-2244
Email: general@mcallen.nshmba.org
Web: http://mcallen.nshmba.org

National Office
1303 Walnut Hill Ln. #300
Irving, TX 75038
Ana Herrera Malone, Marketing & Dev. Director
Tel: (877) 467-4622 Fax: (214) 596-9325
Email: aherrera@nshmba.org
Web: www.nshmba.org

CHAMBER OF COMMERCE

AMERICAN CHAMBER OF COMMERCE OF MEXICO, A.C.
P.O. Box 60326
Houston, TX 77205-0326
Email: amchammx@amcham.com.mx
Web: www.amcham.com.mx

ARLINGTON HISPANIC CHAMBER OF COMMERCE
301 S Center St. #400
Arlington, TX 76010
Willie Rodriguez, President
Tel: (817) 461-8815 Fax: (817) 795-9499
Email: info@hispanic-chamber.org
Web: www.hispanic-chamber.org

BEE COUNTY AREA HISPANIC CHAMBER OF COMMERCE
1400 W Corpus Christi St. #15
Beeville, TX 78102
Katherine Cantu Ramires, President
Tel: (361) 592-3315 Fax: (361) 592-3315
Email: kathyr@dbs.tech.com

CAMARA DE COMERCIO HISPANA DE AMARILLO
P.O. Box 1861
Amarillo, TX 79105
John D. Cruz, President
Tel: (806) 379-8800 Fax: (806) 376-7873
Email: cacha@cacha.org
Web: www.cacha.org

CÁMARA DE EMPRESARIOS LATINOS DE HOUSTON
6420 Hillcroft #305
Houston, TX 77081
Adan G. Vega, President
Tel: (713) 774-5002 Fax: (713) 774-1534
Email: info@empresarioslatinos.org
Web: www.empresarioslatinos.org

CENTEX HISPANIC CHAMBER OF COMMERCE
501 Franklin Ave. #806
Waco, TX 76701
Patrick Contreras, President
Tel: (254) 754-7111 Fax: (254) 754-3456
Email: info@wacohispanicchamber.com
Web: www.wacohispanicchamber.com

COLLIN COUNTY HISPANIC CHAMBER OF COMMERCE
P.O. Box 7
Melissa, TX 75454
San Miguel Grill, President
Tel: (972) 801-2717 Fax: (972) 838-4572
Email: info@cchchamber.org
Web: www.cchchamber.org

CORPUS CHRISTI HISPANIC CHAMBER OF COMMERCE
P.O. Box 1515
Corpus Christi, TX 78403
Patricia Cardenas, Chair Elect
Tel: (361) 885-6124 Fax: (361) 881-5157
Email: patricia@pocca.com
Web: www.cchispanicchamber.org

DENTON HISPANIC CHAMBER OF COMMERCE
P.O. Box 2536
Denton, TX 76202
D. Jorge Urbina, Chair

Tel: (940) 565-1919 Fax: (940) 565-1917
Email: dentonhcoc@hotmail.com
Web: www.dentonhcoc.org

EAGLE PASS HISPANIC CHAMBER OF COMMERCE
P.O. Box 3040
Eagle Pass, TX 78853
Raul Mendez, President
Tel: (830) 757-2704 Fax: (830) 757-2703
Email: recalderon@sbcglobal.net

EL PASO HISPANIC CHAMBER OF COMMERCE
201 E Main #100
El Paso, TX 79901
Cindy Ramos-Davidson, CEO
Tel: (915) 566-4066 Fax: (915) 566-9714
Email: epncc01@whc.net
Web: www.ephcc.org

FORT WORTH HISPANIC CHAMBER OF COMMERCE
1327 N Main St.
Fort Worth, TX 76106
Dan C. Villegas, Chairman
Tel: (817) 625-5411 Fax: (817) 625-1405
Email: daniel.c.villegas@chase.com
Web: www.fwhcc.org

GOLDEN TRIANGLE HISPANIC CHAMBER OF COMMERCE
3046 Proctor St. #A
Port Arthur, TX 77651
Edna Gonzalez, President
Tel: (409) 983-1169 Fax: (409) 963-2329
Email: egonzalez1@gthcc.org
Web: www.gthcc.org

GRAND PRAIRIE HISPANIC CHAMBER OF COMMERCE
114 NE 4th St.
Grand Prairie, TX 75050
Tel: (972) 642-2621 Fax: (972) 642-4116

GREATER AUSTIN HISPANIC CHAMBER OF COMMERCE
3000 S IH 35 #305
Austin, TX 78704
Rosie Mendoza, Chair
Tel: (512) 476-7502 Fax: (512) 476-6417
Email: dmg@hispanicaustin.com
Web: www.hispanicaustin.com

GREATER DALLAS HISPANIC CHAMBER OF COMMERCE
Maple Office
4622 Maple Ave. #207
Dallas, TX 75219
Arturo Violante, Interim President
Tel: (214) 521-6007 Fax: (214) 520-1687
Email: gdhcc@gdhcc.com
Web: www.gdhcc.com

GREATER HISPANIC CHAMBER OF COMMERCE OF CORNAL COUNTY
904 River Oak Dr.
Seguin, TX 78155-7044
Tel: (830) 606-1805
Email: ghccnbtx@aol.com

GREATER VICTORIA HISPANIC CHAMBER OF COMMERCE
P.O. Box 2465
Victoria, TX 77902-2465
Pete Munoz, President
Tel: (361) 573-5277 Fax: (361) 573-5911

HARLINGEN HISPANIC CHAMBER OF COMMERCE
2309 N Ed Carey
Harlingen, TX 78550
Manny Vela, Chairman
Tel: (956) 421-2400 Fax: (956) 364-1879
Email: hhcoc@sbcglobal.net
Web: www.harlingenchamber.com

HISPANIC CHAMBER OF COMMERCE OF GREATER BAYTOWN
1300 Rolling Brooke #502
Baytown, TX 77522
Mary Hernandez, President
Tel: (281) 422-6908 Fax: (281) 427-8988
Email: hccgb@juno.com

HOUSTON HISPANIC CHAMBER OF COMMERCE
2900 Woodridge Dr. #312
Houston, TX 77087-2506
Iris Correa, President/CEO
Tel: (713) 644-7070 Fax: (713) 644-7377
Email: icorrea@houstonhispanicchamber.com
Web: www.houstonhispanicchamber.com

KLEBERG HISPANIC CHAMBER OF COMMERCE
111 N 5th St.
Kingsville, TX 78363
Daniel Garza, President
Tel: (361) 592-2708 Fax: (361) 592-8540
Email: khcc111@gcol.com

LAREDO HISPANIC CHAMBER OF COMMERCE
P.O.Box 790
Laredo, TX 78042
Miguel Conchas, President/CEO
Tel: (956) 722-9895 Fax: (956) 791-4503
Email: chamber@laredochamber.com
Web: www.laredochamber.com

LUBBOCK HISPANIC CHAMBER OF COMMERCE
1302 Main St. #102
Lubbock, TX 79401
Alex Martinez, Chair
Tel: (806) 762-5059 Fax: (806) 763-2124
Email: lhcc@lubbockhispanic.org
Web: www.lubbockhispanic.org

MCALLEN HISPANIC CHAMBER OF COMMERCE
P.O. Box 721025
McAllen, TX 78504
Cynthia Sakulenzki, President
Tel: (956) 928-0060 Fax: (956) 928-0073
Email: info@mhcc.net
Web: www.mhcc.net

MIDLAND HISPANIC CHAMBER OF COMMERCE
208 S Marienfeld
Midland, TX 79701
Jose Zertuche, President
Tel: (432) 682-2960 Fax: (432) 687-3972
Email: bo@midlandhcc.com
Web: www.midlandhcc.com

SAN ANTONIO HISPANIC CHAMBER OF COMMERCE
318 W Houston St. #300, Casa de Mexico International Bldg.
San Antonio, TX 78205
A.J. Rodriguez, President
Tel: (210) 225-0462 Fax: (210) 225-2485
Email: president@sahcc.org
Web: www.sahcc.org

SAN MARCOS HISPANIC CHAMBER OF COMMERCE
215 W San Antonio St. #112
San Marcos, TX 78666
Richard Garza, President
Tel: (512) 353-1103 Fax: (512) 353-2175
Email: yg@sanmarcoshispanic.com
Web: www.sanmarcoshcc.com

SEGUIN-GUADALUPE COUNTY HISPANIC CHAMBER OF COMMERCE
971 W Court
Seguin, TX 78155
Edward Dabila, President
Tel: (830) 372-3151 Fax: (830) 372-9499
Email: shcc@axs4u.net

TEXAS ASSOCIATION OF MEXICAN-AMERICAN CHAMBERS OF COMMERCE
National Headquarters
3000 S IH 35 #210
Austin, TX 78704-6536
Carlos T. Mendoza, President/CEO
Tel: (512) 444-5727 Fax: (512) 444-4929
Email: carlosm@tamacc.org
Web: www.tamacc.org

DALLAS-FORT WORTH NETWORK OF HISPANIC COMMUNICATORS
P.O. Box
Dallas, TX 75222
Ana Barerra, President
Email: dfwhispanic@hotmail.com
Web: www.dfwhispanic.org

LATINO USA
University of Texas, Austin
Communication Bldg. B #3.142
Austin, TX 78712
Alex Avila, Senior Producer
Tel: (512) 471-1817 Fax: (512) 475-6873
Email: avila@mail.utexas.edu
Web: www.latinousa.org

NATIONAL ASSOCIATION OF HISPANIC JOURNALISTS
Region 5
P.O. Box 2171
San Antonio, TX 78297
Nora López, Region Director
Tel: (210) 250-3000 Fax: (210) 250-3150
Email: nlopez@express-news.net
Web: www.nahj.org

US HISPANIC PUBLISHERS FEDERATION, INC.
National Headquarters
6065 Hillcroft #400B
Houston, TX 77081
Lina Martínez, President
Tel: (713) 272-0100 Fax: (713) 272-0011
Email: linamartinez@ushpf.org
Web: www.ushpf.org

ADAIR MARGO GALLERY
415 E. Yandell Dr.
El Paso, TX 79902
Adair Margo, President
Tel: (915) 533-0048 Fax: (915) 496-8550
Email: amargo@adairmargo.com
Web: www.adairmargo.com

CASA ARGENTINA DE HOUSTON
4740 Ingersoll #104
Houston, TX 77027
Maria Ines Sicardi, President
Tel: (713) 622-2212 Fax: (713) 622-2212
Email: tesorero@casaargentina.org
Web: www.casaargentina.org

CENTRO CULTURAL MEXICANO EN EL VALLE DE TEXAS
307 S. Broadway
McAllen, TX 78501
Maria Del Carmen Austin, Director
Tel: (956) 972-1223
Email: mexcultura@aol.com

EL PASO MUSEUM OF ART
1 Arts Festival Plz.
El Paso, TX 79901
Sandra Rodriguez, Receptionist
Tel: (915) 532-1707 Fax: (915) 532-1010
Email: RodriguezSX2@elpasoartmuseum.org
Web: www.elpasoartmuseum.org

GUADALUPE CULTURAL ARTS CENTER
1300 Guadalupe St.
San Antonio, TX 78207
Noah Garcia, Chairman

Email: info@guadalupeculturalarts.org
Web: www.guadalupeculturalarts.org

INSTITUTE OF HISPANIC CULTURE OF HOUSTON
3315 Sul Ross
Houston, TX 77098
Dionel Aviles, President
Tel: (713) 528-6358 Fax: (713) 529-1992
Email: info@ihch.org
Web: www.ihch.org

INSTITUTO CULTURAL MEXICANO
San Antonio Chapter
600 Hemisfair Plz.
San Antonio, TX 78205
Dr. Enrique Cortazar, Director
Tel: (210) 227-0123 Fax: (210) 223-1978
Email: ecortqazar@imexicano.org

MEXIC-ARTE MULTICULTURAL WORKS
P.O. Box 2273
Austin, TX 78768
Sylvia Orozco, Executive Director
Tel: (512) 480-9373 Fax: (512) 480-8626
Email: info@mexic-artemuseum.org
Web: www.mexic-artemuseum.org

MEXICAN AMERICAN CULTURAL CENTER
National Headquarters
3115 W. Ashby Pl.
San Antonio, TX 78228
María E. González, RSM, President
Tel: (210) 732-2156 Fax: (210) 732-9072
Email: macc@maccsa.org
Web: www.maccsa.org

MEXICO INSTITUTE
2904 Floyd St. #A2
Dallas, TX 75204
Clara Borja Hinojosa, Director
Tel: (214) 442-1680 Fax: (214) 442-1644
Email: clara.hinojosa@worldnet.att.net

SAN ANGELO MUSEUM OF FINE ARTS
One Love St.
San Angelo, TX 76903
Howard Taylor, Director
Tel: (325) 653-3333 Fax: (935) 658-6800
Email: museum@samfa.org
Web: www.samfa.org

TEJANO ARTIST MUSIC MUSEUM, INC.
2908 Overdale Rd.
Austin, TX 78723
Marcelo Tafoya, President
Tel: (512) 928-3122 Fax: (512) 928-1797
Email: musica_usa@hotmail.com

AMIGOS EN AZUL
Austin Hispanic Police Officers Association
P.O. Box 685123
Austin, TX 78768-5123
Hank Moreno, President
Tel: (512) 736-2848
Email: hdm45@sbcglobal.net
Web: www.amigosenazul.com

HISPANIC AMERICAN POLICE COMMAND OFFICERS ASSOCIATION
South Central Texas Chapter
P.O. Box 831544
San Antonio, TX 78283-1544
Ruben Garcia, President
Email: rgarcia@hapcoa.org
Web: www.hapcoa.org/sanantonio

NATIONAL LATINO PEACE OFFICERS ASSOCIATION
Fort Worth Chapter
P.O. Box 4858
Fort Worth, TX 76164
Lt. C. Ramirez, President
Tel: (877) 657-6200
Email: cramirezfam@aol.com
Web: www.nlpoa.org/Fort_Worth_Chapter.htm

Greater Dallas Chapter
P.O. Box 22641
Dallas, TX 75222-6411
George Aranda, President
Tel: (214) 428-1710 Fax: (214) 428-1717
Email: lpoa@dallaslpoa.com
Web: www.dallaslpoa.com

Southeast Harris County Chapter
P.O. Box 660
Pasadena, TX 77501
Raymond Garivey, President
Tel: (713) 765-9155
Email: info@southeastharriscounty.com
Web: www.southeastharriscounty.com

MULTI-PURPOSE

AMERICAN GI FORUM OF THE UNITED STATES
Texas Chapter
P.O. Box 5910
Corpus Christi, TX 78405
Ram Chavez, Commander
Tel: (361) 992-1434 Fax: (361) 808-7026
Email: ramchavez@sbcglobal.net
Web: www.agif.us/TX.htm

AMIGOS DE LAS AMERICAS
Houston Chapter
5618 Star Ln.
Houston, TX 77057
Tom Ren, Chair
Tel: (800) 231-7796 Fax: (713) 782-9267
Email: info@amigoslink.org
Web: www.amigoslink.org

ASSOCIATION FOR THE ADVANCEMENT OF MEXICAN AMERICANS
6001 Gulf Fwy. #B1
Houston, TX 77023
Dr. Rudy Ramos, Board Chair
Tel: (713) 926-4756 Fax: (713) 926-8035
Email: AAMA@aamainc.us
Web: www.aamainc.com

AVENIDA GUADALUPE ASSOCIATION, INC.
1327 Guadalupe St.
San Antonio, TX 78207
Theresa De La Haya, Interim President
Tel: (210) 223-3151 Fax: (210) 223-4405
Email: aga@satx.rr.com
Web: www.agatx.org

GULF OF MEXICO FOUNDATION
5403 Everhart, PMB 51
Corpus Christi, TX 78411
John LaRue, President
Tel: (361) 882-3939 Fax: (361) 882-1262
Email: info@gulfmex.org
Web: www.gulmex.org

HARLINGEN INFORMATION & SOCIAL SERVICES ORGANIZATION
Affiliate of NCLR
804 N. Commerce St.
Harlingen, TX 78550
Antonio Ramirez, Director
Tel: (956) 423-5200

HISPANIC ENTREPRENEUR RESOURCE ORGANIZATION AND EXECUTIVE SERVICES
14927 James River Ln.
Houston, TX 77084
Rosemary Acosta-Clark, President
Tel: (281) 859-0564 Fax: (281) 859-3014
Email: rosemaryclark@4heroes.org
Web: www.4heroes.org

HOUSTON HISPANIC FORUM
Institute of Hispanic Culture Bldg., 3315 Sul Ross
Houston, TX 77098
Rey Gonzales, President
Tel: (713) 522-8077 Fax: (713) 522-6249
Email: hhf@airmail.net
Web: www.hispanicforum.org

LEAGUE OF UNITED LATIN AMERICAN CITIZENS
8th District
5207 Airline Dr. #100
Houston, TX 77022
Sylvia Gonzalez, District Director
Tel: (713) 695-5980 Fax: (713) 697-1012
Email: d8mgr@lulac.org
Web: www.lulac.org

Texas LULAC District 15
101 W. Husache
San Antonio, TX 78201
Lourdes Rodriguez, District Director
Tel: (210) 857-8315 (c) Fax: (210) 212-4860
Email: lourdesbr@sbcglobal.net
Web: www.txlulac.org/Locations/district15_html

Texas LULAC District 4
704 Feliz
El Paso, TX 79905
Carlos Veloz, District Director
Tel: (915) 772-0392 (h)
Email: cveloz@elp.rr.com
Web: www.txlulac.org/Locations/district4_html

LULAC NATIONAL EDUCATIONAL SERVICE CENTERS, INC.
2220 Broadway
Houston, TX 77012
Rose Ann Blanco, Director
Tel: (713) 641-2463 Fax: (713) 641-2484
Email: infohou@lnesc-houston.org
Web: www.lnesc-houston.org

400 Mann St. #513
Corpus Christi, TX 78401
Feliberto Valdez, Director
Tel: (361) 883-5134 Fax: (361) 883-8749
Email: infocor@lnesc-cctx.org
Web: www.lnesc-cctx.org

345 S. Edgefield Ave.
Dallas, TX 75208
Renato de los Santos, Director
Tel: (214) 943-2528 Fax: (214) 943-3298
Email: infodal@lnesc-dallas.org
Web: www.lnesc-dallas.org

1011 S. Brazos
San Antonio, TX 78207
Tel: (210) 226-2772
Web: www.lnesc.org/lnesc_san_antonio.htm

109 N. Oregon #416
El Paso, TX 75208
César Garcia, Director
Tel: (915) 351-1133 Fax: (915) 351-1135
Email: infoelp@lnesc-elpaso.org
Web: www.lnesc-elpaso.org

MEXICAN AMERICAN LEGAL DEFENSE AND EDUCATIONAL FUND
Houston Ripley House Office
4410 Navigation #229
Houston, TX 77011
Mary Alice Escobedo, Program Office Assistant
Tel: (713) 315-6494 Fax: (713) 315-6404
Web: www.maldef.org

MEXICAN AMERICAN UNITY COUNCIL, INC.
National Headquarters
2300 W. Commerce St. #200
San Antonio, TX 78207
Frances Teran, President
Tel: (210) 978-0500 Fax: (210) 978-0547
Email: info@mauc.org
Web: www.mauc.org

NATIONAL COUNCIL OF LA RAZA
San Antonio Office
405 N. Saint Mary St. #500
San Antonio, TX 78205
Sandra Ponce-Jones, Administrative Assistant
Tel: (210) 212-4454 Fax: (210) 212-4459
Web: www.nclr.org

NATIONAL IMAGE, INC.
Image de Austin
P. O. Box 27803
Austin, TX 78755
Alfredo Garcia, Chapter President
Tel: (512) 345-7567 Fax: (512) 345-2191
Email: donalfredogarcia@yahoo.com
Web: www.nationalimageinc.org

PERUVIAN AMERICAN MEDICAL SOCIETY
Houston, Texas Chapter
11678 Arrowood Cr.
Houston, TX 77063
Dr. Luis T. Campos, President
Tel: (713) 827-9525
Web: www.pamsnational.org

SOCIETY OF MEXICAN AMERICAN ENGINEERS AND SCIENTISTS
Austin Chapter
P.O. Box 20364
Austin, TX 78720
Lorena Schaible, President
Email: timlorena@yahoo.com
Web: www.maes-texas.org

SOCIETY OF MEXICAN AMERICAN ENGINEERS AND SCIENTISTS
National Office
711 W. Bay Area Blvd. #206
Webster, TX 77598-4051
Rafaela Schwan, Executive Director
Tel: (281) 557-3677 Fax: (557) 3757
Email: execdir@maes-natl.org
Web: www.maes-natl.org

SOUTHWEST KEY PROGRAM, INC.
3000 S IH-35 #410
Austin, TX 78704
Juan J. Sánchez, President
Tel: (512) 462-2181 Fax: (512) 462-2028
Email: info@swkey.org
Web: www.swkey.org

SPECIAL MISSIONS FOUNDATION
P.O. Box 1925
Georgetown, TX 78627-1925
Sandra Romero de Thompson, Special Missions HQ
Tel: (877) 930-9720
Email: srt@specialmissions.org
Web: www.specialmissions.org

TEJANO CENTER FOR COMMUNITY CONCERNS, INC.
6901 Brownwood
Houston, TX 77020
Richard Farias, President/CEO
Tel: (713) 673-1080 Fax: (713) 673-1304
Email: farias.r@tccc-ryss.org
Web: www.tccc-ryss.org

TEJANO CENTER FOR COMMUNITY CONCERNS, INC.
Administrative Office/Affiliate of NCLR
2950 Broadway
Houston, TX 77017
Richard Farias, President & CEO
Tel: (713) 644-2340 Fax: (713) 641-1853
Email: farias.r@tccc-ryss.org
Web: www.tccc-ryss.org

POLITICAL ACTION

NALEO EDUCATIONAL FUND
Houston Office
1314 Texas Ave. #1630
Houston, TX 77002
Rafael Palafox, Director
Tel: (713) 228-6400 Fax: (713) 228-0606
Email: info@naleo.org
Web: www.naleo.org

PUERTO RICO FEDERAL AFFAIRS ADMINISTRATION
Texas Satellite Office
One Riverway #1700
Houston, TX 77056

Nick Rivera, Senior Community Officer
Tel: (714) 871-0200 Fax: (714) 871-0201
Email: info@prfaa.com
Web: www.prfaa.com

SOUTHWEST VOTER REGISTRATION EDUCATION PROJECT
National Administrative Office
206 Lombard St., 2nd Fl.
San Antonio, TX 78226
Antonio González, President
Tel: (210) 922-0225 Fax: (210) 932-4055
Email: agonzalez@svrep.org
Web: www.svrep.org

TEJANO DEMOCRATS
Headquarters
1110 S. Closner St.
Edinburg, TX 78539
Rep. Aaron Peña, Chairman
Tel: (956) 383-5555 Fax: (956) 381-0001
Email: aaronpenajr@aol.com
Web: www.tejanodemocrats.org

PROFESSIONAL

ASSOCIATION OF LATINO PROFESSIONALS IN FINANCE AND ACCOUNTING
Austin Chapter
c/o Optimum Group Services, 9430 Research Blvd. #400
Austin, TX 78759
Manuel Azuara, Chapter President
Tel: (512) 343-4501
Email: manuel@ogsweb.com
Web: www.alpfa.org

Dallas Chapter
c/o Abbott Laboratories, 1921 Hurd Dr.
Irving, TX 75038
Maria Torres, Chapter President
Tel: (972) 518-7502 Fax: (752) 518-0932
Email: maria.torres@abbott.com
Web: www.alpfa.org

El Paso Chapter
Robert Half International, 4110 Rio Bravo #220
El Paso, TX 79902
E. Denise Pacillas, Chapter President
Tel: (915) 546-4060
Email: denise.pacillas@rhi.com
Web: www.alpfa.org

Houston Chapter
210 Westcott
Houston, TX 77007
Maximilliano Jambrina, Chapter President
Tel: (713) 213-1238 Fax: (713) 869-3707
Email: maxi_jambrina@jambrina.com
Web: www.alpfa.org

HISPANIC CONTRACTORS ASSOCIATION OF DFW
2818 Ruder St.
Dallas, TX 75212
Elizabeth Sauceda, President
Tel: (214) 954-1088 Fax: (214) 954-1098
Email: elizabeth@hcadfw.org
Web: www.hcadfw.org

INTERNATIONAL ASSOCIATION OF HISPANIC MEETING PROFESSIONALS
1120 NASA Pkwy. #405
Houston, TX 77058
Margaret G. Gonzalez, President
Tel: (281) 333-1552 Fax: (281) 333-1996
Email: mgvragency@aol.com
Web: www.hispanicmeetingprofessionals.com

NATIONAL ASSOCIATION OF HISPANIC FIREFIGHTERS
2821 McKinney Ave. #7
Dallas, TX 75204
Edward Davis, President
Tel: (214) 631-0025 Fax: (214) 969-0357
Email: info@nahf.org

Web: www.nahf.org

NATIONAL ASSOCIATION OF HISPANIC NURSES
Houston Chapter
P.O. Box 355
Tomball, TX 77377-0355
Jackie Perry, President
Email: jperry5415@aol.com
Web: www.nahnhouston.org

San Antonio Chapter
P.O. Box 15762
San Antonio, TX 78215
Bessie Prado, President
Tel: (210) 736-3858 Fax: (210) 736-3858
Email: bprado@nahnsa.com
Web: www.nahnsa.org

NATIONAL HISPANIC PROFESSIONAL ORGANIZATIONS
Houston Chapter
12303 Gulf Frwy. #2602
Houston, TX 77034
Ben Mendez, President
Tel: (713) 813-9158 Fax: (281) 464-0607
Email: houston@nhpo.us
Web: www.nhpo.us

NATIONAL HISPANIC PROFESSIONAL ORGANIZATIONS
Valley Chapter
4600 W Military Hwy. #1300
McAllen, TX 78503
Julian Mendez, President
Tel: (956) 630-1877 Fax: (956) 683-9565
Email: valley@nhpo.us
Web: www.nhpo.us

NATIONAL SOCIETY OF HISPANIC MBAS
Austin Chapter
1316 Strickland
Austin, TX 78748
Daniel Estrada, Chapter President
Tel: (512) 297-5270
Email: general@austin.nshmba.org
Web: http://austin.nshmba.org/

Houston Chapter
PMB 299, 1302 Waugh Dr.
Houston, TX 77019-3908
Kornel G. Rost, Chapter President
Email: general@houston.nshmba.org
Web: http://houston.nshmba.org/

San Antonio Chapter
P.O. Box 5131
San Antonio, TX 78201
Laura Tolic, Chapter President
Tel: (210) 431-4043
Email: general@sanantonio.nshmba.org
Web: http://sanantonio.nshmba.org/

SOCIETY OF HISPANIC PROFESSIONAL ENGINEERS
Austin Professional Chapter
P.O. Box 2630
Austin, TX 78768
Ernesto Gonzalez, Chapter President
Tel: (512) 797-9101
Email: info@shpeaustin.org
Web: www.shpeaustin.org

Dallas Chapter
P.O. Box 59614
Dallas, TX 75229
Richard Medina, Chapter President
Email: shpe_dfw@comcast.net
Web: www.shpedfw.org

Texas Bay Area Professional Chapter
P.O. Box 590091
Houston, TX 77259-0091
Oscar Alvarado, Chapter President
Tel: (409) 945-1254
Email: alvarao@bp.com
Web: www.shpetbac.org

SOCIETY OF MEXICAN-AMERICAN ENGINEERS AND SCIENTISTS
San Antonio Chapter
P.O. Box 27131
San Antonio, TX 78227
Reynaldo Treviño, Chapter President
Tel: (210) 977-2847 Fax: (210) 977-2159
Email: trevino3311@sbcglobal.net
Web: www.maes-satx.org

ASOCIACIÓN NACIONAL DE SACERDOTES HISPANOS EN EE.UU.
St. Philip of Jesus Church
9700 Villita St.
Houston, TX 77013
Rev. Miguel Solorzano, Pastor
Tel: (713) 672-6141 Fax: (713) 672-8675
Email: info@ansh.org
Web: www.ansh.org

ASOCIACIÓN PARA LA EDUCACION TEOLÓGICA HISPANA
100 E 27th St.
Austin, TX 78705-5711
Daniel Dávila, Executive Director
Tel: (512) 708-0660 Fax: (512) 708-0671
Email: office@aeth.org
Web: www.aeth.org

CASAS POR CRISTO
P.O. Box 3726
El Paso, TX 79923
Sarah Berkbigler, Director of Development
Tel: (915) 565-7800 Fax: (915) 565-6958
Email: staff@casasporcristo.org
Web: www.casasporcristo.org

DIOCESE OF AUSTIN
Hispanic Ministry Office, Pastoral Center
1625 Rutherford Ln.
Austin, TX 78754-5105
Gil Leija, Director
Tel: (512) 873-7771 Fax: (512) 873-8338
Email: gil-leija@austindiocese.org
Web: www.austindiocese.org

DIOCESE OF BEAUMONT
Hispanic Ministry Office
P.O. Box 3948
Beaumont, TX 77704
Sister Augustine Serrano, Director for Hispanic Ministry
Tel: (409) 838-0451 X153 Fax: (409) 838-4511
Email: aserrano@dioceseofbmt.org
Web: www.dioceseofbmt.org

DIOCESE OF DALLAS
Hispanic Ministry Office
P.O. Box 190507
Dallas, TX 75219-0507
Rita Gracia, Director for Hispanic Ministry
Tel: (214) 528-2240 X330 Fax: (214) 523-2429
Email: rgracia@cathdal.org
Web: www.cathdal.org

DIOCESE OF FORT WORTH
Hispanic Pastoral Services
800 W. Loop 820 South
Fort Worth, TX 76108-2919
Andrés Aranda, Director
Tel: (817) 560-2452 x258 Fax: (817) 244-8839
Email: aaranda@fwdioc.org
Web: www.fwdioc.org

DIOCESE OF GALVESTON-HOUSTON
Hispanic Ministry Office
2403 E Holcomb Blvd.
Houston, TX 77021
Jorge A. Delgado, Director for Hispanic Ministry
Tel: (713) 741-8727 Fax: (713) 747-9206
Email: jdelgado@diogh.org
Web: www.diocese-gal-hou.org

DIOCESE OF LAREDO
Laredo Pastoral Center
1901 Corpus Christi St.
Laredo, TX 78044
James A. Tamayo, Bishop
Tel: (956) 727-2140 Fax: (956) 727-2777
Email: info@dioceseoflaredo.org
Web: www.dioceseoflaredo.org

DIOCESE OF TYLER
Hispanic Ministry Office
1015 ESE Loop #323
Tyler, TX 75701-9663
Lupe Natera, Director
Tel: (903) 534-1077 Fax: (903) 534-1370
Email: lnatera@dioceseoftyler.org
Web: www.dioceseoftyler.org

NATIONAL ASSOCIATION OF HISPANIC PRIESTS
1120 52nd St.
Lubbock, TX 79412
Rosa Garcia, Secretary
Tel: (806) 744-1136 Fax: (806) 741-1915
Email: info@ansh.org
Web: www.ansh.org

OUR LADY OF GUADALUPE CATHOLIC CHURCH
Austin
1206 E. 9th St.
Austin, TX 78702
Viola Ruiz, Administrative Assistant
Tel: (512) 478-7955 Fax: (512) 478-8377
Email: viola@olgaustin.org
Web: www.olgaustin.org

UNION BAPTIST ASSOCIATION
2916 West T.C. Jester #200
Houston, TX 77018-7006
Gloria Londono, Administrative Assistant
Tel: (713) 957-2000 Fax: (713) 957-1478
Email: glorialondono@ubahouston.org
Web: www.ubahouston.org

WORLD GOSPEL OUTREACH
P.O. Box 14348
Humble, TX 77347-4348
Allen Danforth, Founder
Tel: (281) 548-7222 Fax: (281) 548-7224
Email: wgoadmin@juno.com
Web: www.wgoreach.org

CENTER FOR MEXICAN-AMERICAN STUDIES
University of Texas, Austin
West Mall Bldg. #5.102, M/C F9200
Austin, TX 78712
José Limón, Director
Tel: (512) 471-4557 Fax: (512) 471-9639
Email: cmas@uts.cc.utexas.edu
Web: www.utexas.edu/depts/cmas

CHICANO STUDIES
University of Texas, El Paso
Graham Hall #104
El Paso, TX 79968
Dennis Bixier-Marquez, Director
Tel: (915) 747-6578 Fax: (915) 747-6501
Email: dbixlerm@utep.edu
Web: http://academics.utep.edu/Default.aspx?alias=academics.utep.edu/chicano

INTERCULTURAL CANCER COUNCIL
6655 Travis #322
Houston, TX 77030-1312
Pamela Jackson, Director of Outreach Programs
Tel: (713) 798-4617 Fax: (713) 798-6222
Email: pjackson@bcm.tmc.edu
Web: www.iccnetwork.org

LATIN AMERICAN STUDIES
Baylor University
One Bear Pl.
Waco, TX 76798-7206
Dr. Lizbeth Souza-Fuertes, Director
Tel: (254) 710-4531 Fax: (2540 710-3799
Email: lilly_fuertes@baylor.edu
Web: www.baylor.edu/latin_american

LOZANO LONG INSTITUTE OF LATIN AMERICAN STUDIES
University of Texas
One University St. D0800, SRH 1.310
Austin, TX 78712-0331
Nicolas Shumway, Director
Tel: (512) 471-5551
Email: ilas@uts.cc.utexas.edu
Web: www.utexas.edu/cola/llilas/

WILLIAM C. VELASQUEZ INSTITUTE
National Office
206 Lombard St., 1st Fl.
San Antonio, TX 78226
Antonio González, President
Tel: (210) 922-3118 Fax: (210) 922-7095
Email: agonzalez@wcvi.org
Web: www.wcvi.org

OFICINA INTERGRUPAL HISPANA
Dallas AA Central Office
6162 E Mockingbird Ln. #213
Dallas, TX 75214
Jane Jones, Director
Tel: (214) 887-6699 Fax: (214) 887-0443
Email: aa@dallas-aa.org
Web: www.dallas-aa.org

BRAZIL MISSION SOCIETY
P.O. Box 5086
Georgetown, TX 78627
Dr. Bill Thompson, President/Executive Director
Tel: (512) 869-7929
Email: billthompson@ulbrausa.com
Web: www.brazilmissionsociety.com

MI ESCUELITA PRESCHOOL, INC.
4231 Maple Ave.
Dallas, TX 75219
Carolyn Strickland, Director
Tel: (214) 526-0220 Fax: (214) 528-0966
Web: www.miescuelita.org

ADELANTE! US EDUCATIONAL LEADERSHIP FUND
8415 Datapoint Dr. #400
San Antonio, TX 78229
Xochitl Hayes, Controller
Tel: (210) 692-1971 Fax: (210) 692-1951
Email: info@adelantefund.org
Web: www.adelantefund.org

AMERICA-MEXICO FOUNDATION, INC.
827 Union Pacific, PMB 078-380
Laredo, TX 78045-9452
Mary Ellis, President
Tel: (322) 222-1478
Email: becasvallarta@yahoo.com
Web: www.pvnet.com.mx/amf

CENTER FOR MEXICAN AMERICAN STUDIES
University of Texas at Austin
W. Mall Bldg. #5.102, M/C F9200
Austin, TX 78712
José E. Limón, Director
Tel: (512) 471-4557 Fax: (512) 471-9639
Email: cmas@uts.cc.utexas.edu
Web: www.utexas.edu/depts/cmas/

HISPANIC ASSOCIATION OF COLLEGES AND UNIVERSITIES
National Headquarters
8415 Datapoint Dr. #400
San Antonio, TX 78229
Antonio R. Flores, President &CEO
Tel: (210) 692-3805 Fax: (210) 692-0823
Email: hacu@hacu.net
Web: www.hacu.net

INTERCULTURAL DEVELOPMENT RESEARCH ASSOCIATION
5835 Callaghan Rd. #350
San Antonio, TX 78228-1190
Maria Robledo Montecel, Executive Director
Tel: (210) 444-1710 Fax: (210) 444-1714
Email: cmontecl@idra.org
Web: www.idra.org

LA LLAMADA
Our Lady of the Lake University
411 SW 24th St.
San Antonio, TX 78207
Gloria Urrabazo, Executive Director
Tel: (210) 434-6711
Web: www.ollusa.edu/StudentLife/La_Llamada/default.htm

LATIN AMERICAN AND IBERIAN STUDIES PROGRAM
Texas Tech University
P.O. Box 42071
Lubbock, TX 79409
Alberto Julian Perez, Director
Tel: (806) 742-1562
Email: julian.perez@ttu.edu
Web: www3.tltc.ttu.edu/Perez/default.htm

LATIN AMERICAN STUDIES PROGRAM
Baylor University
1 Bear Pl. #97206
Waco, TX 76798-7206
Dr. Lizbeth Souza-Fuertes, Director
Tel: (254) 710-4531 Fax: (254) 710-3799
Email: lilly_fuertes@baylor.edu
Web: www.baylor.edu/latin_american

LATINO LEARNING CENTER, INC.
3522 Polk Ave.
Houston, TX 77003
Joe Sedera, Executive Director
Tel: (713) 223-1391 Fax: (713) 222-2338
Email: llcorg@hotmail.com
Web: www.latinolearning.org

LEARN, INC.
2161 50th St.
Lubbock, TX 79412
Eddie Anaya, Executive Director
Tel: (806) 763-4256 Fax: (806) 763-0791
Email: eanaya@learnprograms.org
Web: www.learnprograms.org

MEXICAN AMERICAN SCHOOL BOARD MEMBERS ASSOCIATION
P.O. Box 160098
San Antonio, TX 78280
Tomas Molina, Executive Director
Tel: (210) 844-8698

MULTICULTURAL EDUCATION AND COUNSELING TO THE ARTS
1900 Kane St.
Houston, TX 77007
Alice E. Valdez, Executive Director
Tel: (713) 802-9370 Fax: (713) 802-9403
Email: alicevaldez@yahoo.com
Web: www.meca-houston.org

NATIONAL HISPANIC INSTITUTE
P.O. Box 220
Maxwell, TX 78656
Marcie Longoria, Associate of Public Relations
Tel: (512) 357-6137 Fax: (512) 357-2206
Email: info@nhimail.com
Web: www.nhi-net.org

OFFICE OF BILINGUAL EDUCATION
University of Texas, Austin
1 University Station #D6200
Austin, TX 78712-0387
Alba A. Ortiz, Director
Tel: (512) 471-6244 Fax: (512) 471-5550
Email: alba.ortiz@mail.utexas.edu

REFORMA
ARRIBA (Southeast Texas) Chapter
1103 Hackney
Houston, TX 77023
Diana Morales, Chapter President
Tel: (713) 923-6856
Email: dmorales@hpl.lib.tx.us
Web: www.reforma.org

REFORMA
El Corazon de Tejas (Austin/Central Texas)
Palmer Lane Elementary Library, 1806 Palmer Ln.
Austin, TX 78727
Maribel Garza, Chapter President
Tel: (512) 594-4000 Fax: (512) 594-4005
Email: aweebawubba@yahoo.com
Web: www.main.org/reforma/

REFORMA
Rio Trinidad Chapter
P.O. Box 7496
Dallas, TX 75209-7496
Ramiro Salazar, Chapter President
Email: rsalazar@dallaslibrary.org
Web: www.reforma.org

REFORMA
San Antonio Chapter
San Antonio Public Library, 600 Soledad
San Antonio, TX 78205
Robert Briseno, Chapter President
Tel: (210) 207-2681 Fax: (210) 207-2553
Email: rbriseno@sanantonio.gov

REFORMA
Tarrant County Chapter
4300 E. Berry St.
Fort Worth, TX 76105
Daniel Berdaner, Interim President
Tel: (817) 536-1945
Email: dberdaner@hotmail.com
Web: www.reforma.org

STAY, INC.
700 S Zarzamora #103
San Antonio, TX 78207
Oscar Hernández, Director
Tel: (210) 433-9307 Fax: (210) 435-0711

STUDENT ALTERNATIVES PROGRAM, INC.
Affiliate of NCLR
P.O. Box 15644
San Antonio, TX 78212
Eduardo Gutierrez, Chairman
Tel: (210) 227-0295 Fax: (210) 227-7879
Email: stdtalt@aol.com
Web: www.stdsapi.com

TEXAS ALLIANCE FOR MINORITIES IN ENGINEERING, INC.
University of Texas, Austin
10100 Burnet Rd. #10
Austin, TX 78758
Shari Getz, Executive Director
Tel: (512) 471-6100
Email: tame@engr.utexas.edu
Web: www.tame.org

TEXAS ASSOCIATION FOR BILINGUAL EDUCATION
6323 Sovereign Dr. #178
San Antonio, TX 78229
Sandra Acosta, President
Tel: (800) 822-3930 Fax: (210) 979-6485
Email: acostas@tabe.org
Web: www.tabe.org

TEXAS MIGRANT COUNCIL, INC.
P.O. Box 2579
Laredo, TX 78041
Mary Capello, CEO
Tel: (956) 722-5174 Fax: (956) 725-0907

UTPA GEAR UP PROJECT
University of Texas Pan American
1201 W University Dr. #112
Edinburg, TX 78541-2999
Cindy Valdez, Interim Director
Tel: (956) 292-7501 Fax: (956) 292-7503
Email: valdezc@panam.edu
Web: www.panam.edu/dept/gearup

SPEC. INT., EMPLOYMENT

ELADIO R. MARTÍNEZ LEARNING CENTER
Affiliate of SER-Jobs for Progress National, Inc.
4500 Bernal Dr.
Dallas, TX 75212
Rosa L. Peña, Principal
Tel: (972) 794-6900 Fax: (972) 794-6901
Email: ropena@dallasisd.org
Web: www.ser-national.org

FORT WORTH SER-JOBS FOR PROGRESS, INC.
Affiliate of SER-Jobs for Progress National, Inc.
303 W. Central Ave.
Fort Worth, TX 76106
Andrew Mantecon, Executive Director
Tel: (817) 624-3260 Fax: (817) 624-3765
Email: andrewmantecon@yahoo.com
Web: www.fwser.com

GRAND PRAIRIE SER-JOBS FOR PROGRESS, INC.
Affiliate of SER-Jobs for Progress National, Inc.
401 W. Marshall Dr. #419
Grand Prairie, TX 75051
Sondra Banks, Executive Director
Tel: (972) 237-9300 Fax: (972) 237-7915
Email: sondrabanks@hotmail.com
Web: www.ser-national.org

NATIONAL ORGANIZATION FOR MEXICAN-AMERICAN RIGHTS, INC.
P.O. Box 681205
San Antonio, TX 78268-1205
Dan J. Solis, Chairman
Tel: (210) 520-1831 Fax: (210) 520-1831
Email: chairman@nomarinc.org
Web: www.nomarinc.org

RMPERSONNEL, INC.
4707 Montana Ave.
El Paso, TX 79903
Ceci Miles Mulvihill, President
Tel: (915) 565-7674 Fax: (915) 565-7687
Email: cecim@rmpersonnel.com
Web: www.rmpersonnel.com

SER CHILD DEVELOPMENT CENTER
Affiliate of SER-Jobs for Progress National, Inc.
1525 W. Mockingbird Ln. #300
Dallas, TX 75235
Alice Escobar, Executive Director
Tel: (214) 637-8307 Fax: (214) 637-8313
Email: aescobar@serkids.org
Web: www.ser-national.org

SER-JOBS FOR PROGRESS NATIONAL, INC.
National Headquarters
5215 N. O'Connor Blvd. #2550
Irving, TX 75039
Ignacio Salazar, President/CEO
Tel: (972) 506-7815 Fax: (972) 506-7832
Web: www.ser-national.org

SER-JOBS FOR PROGRESS OF SAN ANTONIO, INC.
Affiliate of SER-Jobs for Progress National, Inc.
1499 Hillcrest
San Antonio, TX 78228
Linda Rivas, Executive Director
Tel: (210) 438-0586 Fax: (210) 438-8058
Email: linda.rivas@twc.state.tx.us
Web: www.ser-national.org

SER-JOBS FOR PROGRESS OF SOUTHWEST TEXAS, INC.
Affiliate of SER-Jobs for Progress National, Inc.
4605 Maher Ave.
Laredo, TX 78041
Jose Cardenas, Executive Director
Tel: (956) 724-1844 Fax: (956) 724-1831
Email: cardenas@serjobs.org
Web: www.ser-national.org

SER-JOBS FOR PROGRESS OF THE TEXAS GULF COAST, INC.
Affiliate of SER-Jobs for Progress National, Inc.
6615 Rookin St.
Houston, TX 77074
Jesse Castaneda, Executive Director
Tel: (713) 773-6000 Fax: (713) 773-6010
Email: jesse.castaneda@serhouston.org
Web: www.serhouston.org

SOUTH TEXAS VETERANS HEALTHCARE SYSTEM
Audie L. Murphy Division (136P)
7400 Merton Minter Blvd. #003-A
San Antonio, TX 78229
Virginia Clingan, EEO Assistant
Tel: (210) 617-5300 X5815 Fax: (210) 949-3356
Email: virginia.clingan@med.va.gov
Web: www.vasthcs.med.va.gov

SPEC. INT., FAMILY PLANNING

AVANCE, INC.
Austin Officec
3000 S. IH-305 #205
Austin, TX 78704
Rosalia Castaneda, Executive Director
Tel: (512) 326-9335 Fax: (512) 326-1033
Email: rcstaneda.aus@avance.org
Web: www.avance.org

AVANCE, INC.
Dallas Office
2816 Swiss Ave.
Dallas, TX 75204
Lisa Oglesby Rocha, Executive Director
Tel: (214) 887-9907 Fax: (214) 887-9159
Email: loglesby.dal@avance.org
Web: www.avance-dallas.org

AVANCE, INC.
El Paso Office
720 Arizona Ave.
El Paso, TX 79902
Sanjay Mathur, Executive Director
Tel: (915) 351-2419 Fax: (915) 351-2457
Email: smathur.elp@avance.org
Web: www.avance-elpaso.org

AVANCE, INC.
Houston Office
4281 Dacoma
Houston, TX 77092
Sylvia Garcia, Executive Director
Tel: (713) 812-0033 Fax: (713) 912-9829
Email: sgarcia.hou@avance.org
Web: www.avance.org

AVANCE, INC.
National Headquarters
2300 W Commerce #304
San Antonio, TX 78207-3839
Rebecca Cervantez, Executive Director
Tel: (210) 220-1788 Fax: (210) 220-3795
Email: varriola@avancesa.org
Web: www.avancesa.org

AVANCE, INC.
Rio Grande Valley Office
1205 Galveston
McAllen, TX 78501
Raquel Oliva, Executive Director
Tel: (956) 618-1642 Fax: (956) 618-1698
Email: roliva.rgv@avance.org
Web: www.avancergv.org

AVANCE, INC.
San Antonio Office
2300 W. Commerce
San Antonio, TX 78207
Rebecca Cervantez, Executive Director
Tel: (210) 220-1788 Fax: (210) 220-3795
Email: rcervantez.sa@avance.org

Web: www.avancesa.org

SPEC. INT., GAY&LESBIAN

AUSTIN LATINO LESBIAN AND GAY ORGANIZATION
701 Tillery St. Box 4
Austin, TX 78702
Lorenzo Herrera, Executive Director
Tel: (512) 472-2001 Fax: (512) 472-6301
Email: lorenzo@allgo.org
Web: www.allgo.org

SPEC. INT., HEALTH SERVICES

CENTER FOR HEALTH POLICY DEVELOPMENT, INC.
6905 Alamo Down Pkwy.
San Antonio, TX 78238
Charlene Doria-Ortiz, Executive Director
Tel: (210) 520-8020 Fax: (210) 520-9522
Email: chpdonline@chpdonline.org
Web: www.chpdonline.org

CENTRO DE SALUD FAMILIAR LA FE, INC.
TACHC Member
608 S. Saint Vrain St.
El Paso, TX 79901-3007
Salvador Balcorta, Executive Director
Tel: (915) 534-7979 Fax: (915) 534-7601
Email: balcorta@mail.htg.net

COMUNIDADES UNIDAS PRO SALUD
1701 N. 8 #B26
McAllen, TX 78501
Luisa Flippin, Director
Tel: (96) 686-7456
Email: cups7456@sbcglobal.net

MIGRANT HEALTH PROMOTION
P.O. Box 337
Progreso, TX 78579
Rebecca Garza, Associate Director
Tel: (956) 565-0002 Fax: (956) 565-0136

NATIONAL CENTER FOR FARMWORKER HEALTH
National Headquarters
1770 FM 967
Buda, TX 78610
E. Roberta Ryder, CEO
Tel: (512) 312-2700 Fax: (512) 312-2600
Email: ryder@ncfh.org
Web: www.ncfh.org

NUESTRA CLINICA DEL VALLE
1203 E Ferguson
Pharr, TX 78577
Lucy Ramirez, Executive Director
Tel: (956) 787-0787 Fax: (956) 787-2021

OFFICE OF MINORITY HEALTH INITIATIVES AND CULTURAL COMPETENCY
1100 W. 49th St.
Austin, TX 78756
Randy Fritz, Chief Operating Officer
Tel: (512) 458-7629 Fax: (512) 458-7713
Email: OMH@tdh.state.tx.us
Web: www.tdh.state.tx.us/minority

PAN AMERICAN HEALTH ORGANIZATION
5400 Suncrest Dr. #C-4
El Paso, TX 79912
Norma Green, Executive Secretary
Tel: (915) 845-5950 Fax: (915) 845-4361
Email: mail@fep.paho.org
Web: www.fep.paho.org

SU CLINICA FAMILIAR
TACHC Member
2018 Pease St.
Harlingen, TX 78550
Dr. Alberto Vasquez, Member
Tel: (956) 428-4171 Fax: (956) 412-3054
Email: doctorv860@pol.net

UNITED STATES-MEXICO BORDER HEALTH ASSOCIATION
5400 Suncrest Dr. #C-5
El Paso, TX 79912
Dr. Miguel A. Escobedo, President
Tel: (915) 581-6450 Fax: (915) 833-7840
Email: mail@usmbha.org
Web: www.usmbha.org

SPEC. INT., HOUSING

COLONIAS DEL VALLE, INC.
1203 E. Ferguson St. #225
Pharr, TX 78577
Aida Gonzales, Executive Director
Tel: (956) 787-9903 Fax: (956) 782-1016
Email: colonias2002@hotmail.com

HOUSTON ESPERANZA
Affiliate of NCLR
P.O. Box 230457
Houston, TX 77223
Paul Ramirez, President
Tel: (713) 926-2794 Fax: (281) 481-2360
Email: pramirez@houston.rr.com

LA GLORIA DEVELOPMENT CORPORATION
Affiliate of NCLR
615 Cadena St.
El Cenizo, TX 78046
Juan Idrogo, President
Tel: (956) 791-3034 Fax: (956) 791-6997
Email: lagloria@netscorp.net

SPARKS HOUSING DEVELOPMENT CORPORATION
Affiliate of NCLR
106 Payton Rd.
El Paso, TX 79928
Frank Desales, Executive Director
Tel: (915) 852-2245 Fax: (915) 852-1737
Email: sparkshousing@msn.com

TEXAS ENTERPRISE FOR HOUSING DEVELOPMENT, INC.
Affiliate of NCLR
3316 N Stewart Rd.
Mission, TX 78572
Reyes L. Cortéz, Executive Director
Tel: (956) 585-4447 Fax: (956) 585-4447

VECINOS UNIDOS
3603 N. Winnetka Ave.
Dallas, TX 75212
Rosa López, Director
Tel: (214) 761-1086 Fax: (214) 761-0838
Email: relopez@vecinosunidos.com
Web: www.vecinosunidos.com

SPEC. INT., HUMAN RELATIONS

ESPERANZA, PEACE AND JUSTICE CENTER
922 San Pedro
San Antonio, TX 78212
Graciela Sánchez, Director
Tel: (210) 228-0201 Fax: (210) 228-0000
Email: esperanza@esperanzacenter.org
Web: www.esperanzacenter.org

THE MEXICAN AMERICAN LEGISLATIVE CAUCUS
1005 Congress Ave. #420
Austin, TX 78701
Sabine Romero, Executive Director
Tel: (512) 236-8410 Fax: (512) 236-8402
Email: info@malc.org
Web: www.malc.org

TEXAS ASSOCIATION OF CHICANOS IN HIGHER EDUCATION
San Antonio Chapter
NW Vista College, G 161, 3535 N. Ellison Dr.
San Antonio, TX 78251
Tomas Larralde, Chapter President
Tel: (210) 348-2387 Fax: (210) 348-2348
Email: tlarrald@accd.edu

Web: www.geocities.com/tachistas/main.html

TEXAS FIESTA EDUCATIVA, INC.
Satellite Office
530 S. Texas #J
Weslaco, TX 78596
Yvette Hinojosa, Director
Tel: (956) 969-3611 Fax: (956) 969-8761
Email: yvette@tfepoder.org
Web: www.tfepoder.org

SPEC. INT., IMMIGRATION

CASA DE PROYECTO LIBERTAD
113 N. 1st St.
Harlingen, TX 78550
Rogelio Nunez, Executive Director
Tel: (956) 425-9552 Fax: (956) 425-8249
Email: nrogelio@aol.com

HOUSTON COMMUNITY SERVICES - CENTRO AZTLAN
Affiliate of NCLR
5115 Harrisburg Blvd.
Houston, TX 77011
Edward M. Castillo, Executive Director
Tel: (713) 926-8771 Fax: (713) 926-8771
Email: hcsaztlan@sbcglobal.net

SPEC. INT., INFORMATION REFERRAL

BOLIVIAN CHARITY FOUNDATION
P.O. Box 79332
Houston, TX 77279-9332
Fernando Garnica, President
Email: bcf@bolivia.com
Web: www.boliviancharity.com

INFORMATION REFERRAL RESOURCE ASSISTANCE, INC.
Affiliate of SER-Jobs for Progress National, Inc.
618 N McColl St.
McAllen, TX 78502
Aguie Peña, Executive Director
Tel: (956) 682-3436 Fax: (956) 687-6062
Email: apena@irra.org
Web: www.ser-national.org

INFORMATION REFERRAL RESOURCE ASSISTANCE, INC./CREATIVE ACADEMIC ACHIEVEMENT
Children of the Sun Charter School
1205 S 7th St.
Raymondville, TX 78580
Aguie Peña, Superintendent/CEO
Tel: (956) 689-3300 Fax: (956) 690-0370
Email: aguiepena@hotmail.com
Web: www.irra.com

INFORMATION REFERRAL RESOURCE ASSISTANCE, INC./CREATIVE ACADEMIC ACHIEVEMENT
One Stop Multi-Service Charter School
115 S Mayberry Ave.
Mission, TX 78572
Aguie Peña, Superintendent/CEO
Tel: (956) 519-2227 Fax: (956) 519-1685
Email: aguiepena@hotmail.com
Web: www.irra.com

INFORMATION REFERRAL RESOURCE ASSISTANCE, INC./CREATIVE ACADEMIC ACHIEVEMENT
One Stop Multi-Service Charter School
4737 S Sugar Rd.
Edinburg, TX 78539
Aguie Peña, Superintendent/CEO
Tel: (956) 380-6616 Fax: (956) 380-6916
Email: aguiepena@hotmail.com
Web: www.irra.com

INFORMATION REFERRAL RESOURCE ASSISTANCE, INC./CREATIVE ACADEMIC ACHIEVEMENT
One Stop Multi-Service Charter School
317 S Missouri Ave.
Weslaco, TX 78596

Aguie Peña, Superintendent/CEO
Tel: (956) 969-2600 Fax: (956) 969-1191
Email: aguiepena@hotmail.com
Web: www.irra.com

SPEC. INT., LEGAL ASSISTANCE

DALLAS HISPANIC BAR ASSOCIATION
2101 Ross Ave.
Dallas, TX 75201
Scott Sullivan, President
Email: mail@dallashispanicbar.com
Web: www.dallashispanicbar.com

HISPANIC NATIONAL BAR ASSOCIATION
Region XII (AR, LA, OK, TX)
US Dept. of Education Office for Civil Rights, 1999 Bryan St. #2600
Dallas, TX 75201
Jose Ortiz, Regional President
Tel: (214) 880-2426 Fax: (214) 880-3082
Email: ortizjag@yahoo.com
Web: www.hnba.com

MEXICAN AMERICAN LEGAL DEFENSE AND EDUCATIONAL FUND
San Antonio Regional Office
140 E. Houston St. #300
San Antonio, TX 78205
Nina Perales, Regional Counsel
Tel: (210) 224-5476 Fax: (210) 224-5382
Email: maldefsa@aol.com
Web: www.maldef.org

SPEC. INT., SENIORS

AMIGOS DEL VALLE, INC.
1116 N. Conway Ave.
Mission, TX 78572
Isaias Aguayo, Executive Director
Tel: (956) 581-9494 Fax: (956) 581-2210
Email: iaguayo@amigos.dcci.com

DENVER HARBOR SENIORS
6402 Market St.
Houston, TX 77020
Richard Caldwell, Executive Director
Tel: (713) 672-6395 Fax: (713) 672-1295
Email: rcaldwell04@sbcglobal.net

LA VOZ DEL ANCIANO
3316 Sylvan Ave.
Dallas, TX 75212
Triny Garcia, Executive Director
Tel: (214) 741-5700
Email: info@lavozdelanciano.org
Web: www.lavozdelanciano.org

LATINO EDUCATION PROJECT
1045 Airline Rd. #2
Corpus Christi, TX 78412
Frances Pawlik, Executive Director
Tel: (361) 980-0361 Fax: (361) 980-0951
Email: info@latinoeducationproject.org
Web: www.latinoeducationproject.org

ASOCIACIÓN PRO SERVICIOS SOCIALES, INC.
Affiliate of NCLR
406 Scott St.
Laredo, TX 78040
Alberto Luera, Executive Director
Tel: (956) 724-6244 Fax: (956) 724-5458
Email: centro_ashtlan@hotmail.com

BAPTIST MISSION CENTERS
Administrative Office
P.O. Box 30417
Houston, TX 77249
Ginger Smith, Executive Director
Tel: (713) 227-0304 Fax: (713) 224-0611
Email: gks@bmchouston.org
Web: www.bmchouston.org

CHICANOS UNIDOS-CAMPESINOS, INC.
216 E Ave. D
Muleshoe, TX 79347
Juan Chavez, President

Tel: (806) 272-4700

DALLAS CONCILIO OF HISPANIC SERVICES ORGANIZATIONS
4800 Harry Hines Blvd.
Dallas, TX 75235
Cecilia McKay, Executive Director
Tel: (214) 818-0481 Fax: (214) 818-0485
Email: concilio@dallasconcillo.org
Web: www.dallasconcilio.org

GUADALUPE COMMUNITY CENTER
1801 W. Durango
San Antonio, TX 78207
Elvia F. Gonzales, Executive Director
Tel: (210) 226-6178
Email: gcc@stic.net

HISPANIC UNITED CHARITIES
18170 Hillcrest Rd.
Dallas, TX 75252
Lorenzo Aguilar, Chairman
Tel: (972) 596-0755 Fax: (972) 596-0017
Email: info@hispanicunitedcharities.org
Web: www.ekeda.com/portfolio/huc/index.htm

LA ROSA FAMILY SERVICES
P.O. Box 16042
Houston, TX 77222-6042
Candelaria Perez Johnson, Executive Director
Tel: (713) 699-3974 Fax: (713) 699-0385
Email: candy@larosafamilyservices.org
Web: www.larosafamilyservices.org

LIFTING BURDENS, INC.
P.O. Box 4503
McAllen, TX 78502
Jorge Gatica, President
Tel: (956) 648-3416
Email: mkgatica@yahoo.com
Web: www.liftingburdens.org

NATIONAL IMAGE, INC.
San Antonio Chapter
5302 Arrowhead Dr.
San Antonio, TX 78228
Mary Espiritu, President
Tel: (210) 434-9656 Fax: (210) 434-9656
Web: www.nationalimageinc.org

NATIONAL ORGANIZATION OF PROFESSIONAL HISPANIC
Natural Resources Conservation Service Employees
4100 Piedras Dr. East #253
San Antonio, TX 78228
Bertha T. Venegas, President
Tel: (210) 735-3391 Fax: (210) 735-3392
Email: bertha.venegas@tx.usda.gov
Web: www.nrcs.usda.gov/intranet/hispanic/

NEIGHBORHOOD CENTERS, INC.
Ripley House- Ripley Campus
4410 Navigation Blvd.
Houston, TX 77011
Margie Pena, Area Manager
Tel: (713) 315-6400 Fax: (713) 315-6404
Email: margie.pena@neighborhood-centers.org
Web: www.neighborhood-centers.org

PROYECTO ORGANIZATIVO SIN FRONTERAS
201 E. 9th Ave.
El Paso, TX 79901
Carlos Marentes, Executive Director
Tel: (915) 532-0921 Fax: (915) 532-4822

SANTA MARIA FOUNDATION
3355 Coral Grove
San Antonio, TX 78247-4822
Rick Jones, Executive Director
Tel: (210) 545-4083
Email: info@santamariafoundation.org
Web: www.santamariafoundation.org

TEXAS ASSOCIATION OF CHICANOS IN HIGHER EDUCATION
P.O. Box 986
Austin, TX 78767-0986

Dr. Ellias Villareal, President
Tel: (361) 698-1903
Email: info@tache.org
Web: www.tache.org

WESLEY COMMUNITY CENTER, INC.
1410 Lee St.
Houston, TX 77009-8299
Ruth Palmer, Executive Director
Tel: (713) 223-8131 Fax: (713) 225-3449
Email: info@wesleyhousehouston.org
Web: www.wesleyhousehouston.org

ALAMO AREA COUNCIL OF GOVERNMENTS
8700 Tesoro Dr. #700
San Antonio, TX 78217
Al J. Notzon III, Executive Director
Tel: (210) 362-5200 Fax: (210) 225-5937
Email: mail@aacog.com
Web: www.aacog.com

HISPANIC WOMEN'S NETWORK OF TEXAS
Austin Chapter
P.O. Box 1356
Austin, TX 78767-1356
Velia Saenz Williams, President
Email: president@hwntaustin.org
Web: www.hwntaustin.org

LATINA MAMI
P.O. Box 140674
Austin, TX 78714
Gloria Perez-Walker, Founder
Tel: (512) 494-7758
Email: info@latinamami.org
Web: www.latinamami.org

MANA-A NATIONAL LATINA ORGANIZATION
San Antonio
P.O. Box 691453
San Antonio, TX 78269
Evangeline Elizondo, President
Tel: (210) 690-0803 Fax: (210) 690-0803
Email: manadesa@aol.com
Web: www.hermana.org

ANY BABY CAN
Child and Family Resource Center
1121 E 7th St.
Austin, TX 78702
Tel: (800) 672-0238 Fax: (512) 454-0205
Email: info@abcaus.org
Web: www.abcaus.org

CHICANO FAMILY CENTER
7524 Ave. E
Houston, TX 77012
Elena Vergara, Executive Director
Tel: (713) 923-2316 Fax: (713) 923-4243
Email: elenav@swbell.net

GULF COAST COUNCIL OF LA RAZA, INC.
Affiliate of NCLR
4129 Greenwood
Corpus Christi, TX 78416
María Luisa Garza, Executive Director
Tel: (361) 881-9988 Fax: (361) 881-9994
Email: drgarzaml@gcclr.esc2.net

NATIONAL LATINO CHILDREN'S INSTITUTE
1325 N. Flores #114
San Antonio, TX 78212
Rebeca M. Barrera, President
Tel: (210) 228-9997 Fax: (210) 228-9972
Email: nlci@nlci.org
Web: www.nlci.org

COALITION OF HISPANIC-AMERICAN STUDENTS
P.O. Box 519
Prairie View, TX 77446
Elma Gonzalez, Advisor
Tel: (936) 857-2014 Fax: (936) 857-2255
Email: elma_gonzalez@pvamu.edu
Web: www.pvamu.edu

HISPANIC ASSOCIATION FOR CULTURAL ENRICHMENT AT RICE
Rice University
6100 Main St.
Houston, TX 77251-1892
Victor Castillo, President
Tel: (713) 348-3886 Fax: (713) 348-5618
Email: hacer@rice.edu
Web: www.ruf.rice.edu/~hacer

HISPANIC HERITAGE CLUB
P.O. Box 2007
8060 Spencer Hwy., San Jacinto College Central Campus
Pasadena, TX 77505-2007
Rosie Flores, Adviser
Tel: (281) 476-1877 Fax: (281) 478-2743
Email: rosie.flores@sjcd.edu

HISPANIC PRESIDENTS COUNCIL
Texas A&M University
Texas A&M University
College Station, TX 77843
Sarah Ann Pena, President
Tel: (361) 726-9640
Email: spena05@tamu.edu
Web: http://hpc.tamu.edu

HISPANIC STUDENT ASSOCIATION
Baylor University
1 Bear Pl. #85628
Waco, TX 76798
Rebecca Medina, President
Tel: (210) 363-5002
Email: hsa@baylor.edu
Web: www.baylor.edu/~hsa

HISPANIC STUDENT ORGANIZATION
Galveston College
4015 Ave. Q
Galveston, TX 77550
Maria Eliaz, Advisor
Tel: (409) 763-6551 X336 Fax: (409) 944-1500

INSTITUTE OF LATIN AMERICAN STUDIES ASSOCIATION
University of Texas at Austin
1 University Station D0800, SRH 1.310
Austin, TX 78712-0331
Andrés Manosalva, Interim President
Tel: (512) 471-5551 Fax: (512) 471-3090
Email: andresabril24@yahoo.com
Web: www.utexas.edu/cola/llilas/students/studentgroups/ilassa/index.html

KAPPA DELTA CHI SORORITY, INC.
National Headquarters
P.O. Box 4317
Lubbock, TX 79409
Ruby Alvarado, Executive Director
Email: info@kappadeltachi.org
Web: www.kappadeltachi.org

LA SOCIEDAD HISPANA CULTURAL
Our Lady of the Lake University
411 SW 24th St. #FH 214
San Antonio, TX 78207-4666
Dr. Maribel Larraga, Director
Tel: (210) 434-6711 X8164 Fax: (210) 431-4025
Email: larrm@lake.ollusa.edu

LA UNIDAD LATINA, LAMBDA UPSILON FRATERNITY, INC.
Alpha Theta Chapter
411 SW 24th St.
San Antonio, TX 78207
Albert Moreno
Email: lulat@lake.ollusa.edu

Web: www.launidadlatina.org/chapters/alpha_theta

LATIN AMERICAN STUDENT SERVICES ORGANIZATION
University of Houston-Downtown, Student Activities
One Main St., 280 South
Houston, TX 77002
Eddie Garza, President
Tel: (713) 291-0003
Email: uhdlasso@hotmail.com
Web: www.uhd.edu

LEAGUE OF UNITED LATIN AMERICAN CITIZENS
University of Houston-Downtown, Student Activities
1 Main St.
Houston, TX 77002
Ubaldo Rodriguez, President
Tel: (713) 454-3500
Email: ubaldo_rodriguez13@yahoo.com
Web: www.uhd.edu/campus/activities/organizations/Lulac/luframe.html

MIDLAND COLLEGE HISPANIC STUDENT ASSOCIATION ("M" CLASS)
Midland College
3600 N. Garfield
Midland, TX 79705
Lupe Daniels, Sponsor
Tel: (432) 685-5510
Email: JDaniels@midland.edu

MOVIMIENTO ESTUDIANTIL CHICANO DE AZTLAN
University of Texas, El Paso
Graham Hall 104, 500 W. University
El Paso, TX 79968
Dennis Bixler-Marquez, Advisor
Tel: (915) 747-5462 Fax: (915) 747-6501
Email: mecha@utep.edu

SOCIETY OF HISPANIC PROFESSIONAL ENGINEERS
Texas Tech University
P.O. Box 42013
College of Engineering, M/S 3111
Lubbock, TX 79409
Nestor Vidales, President
Tel: (806) 742-3451 Fax: (806) 742- 3493
Email: nestor.c.vidales@ttu.edu
Web: www.coe.ttu.edu/shpe

SOCIETY OF HISPANIC PROFESSIONAL ENGINEERS
University of Texas, Austin
College of Engineering, ECJ - 2.102
Austin, TX 78712
Rene Grado, President
Tel: (512) 471-7112
Email: shpeofficer@lists.cc.utexas.edu
Web: www.engr.utexas.edu/shpe

SOCIETY OF HISPANIC PROFESSIONAL ENGINEERS
University of Texas, El Paso
College of Engineering, 500 W. University Ave.
El Paso, TX 79968
William Davis, President
Tel: (915) 747-5460 Fax: (915) 747-5616
Email: maesshpe@eng.utep.edu
Web: http://eng.utep.edu/maesshpe/

SOCIETY OF MEXICAN-AMERICAN ENGINEERS AND SCIENTISTS
Southwest Texas State University
601 University Dr., Science Bldg. #142/142-A
San Marcos, TX 78666
Carlos Gutierrez, Advisor
Tel: (512) 245-3647 Fax: (512) 245-8233
Email: maes@txstate.edu
Web: www.studentorgs.txstate.edu/maes

SOCIETY OF MEXICAN-AMERICAN ENGINEERS AND SCIENTISTS
University of Texas, El Paso

College of Engineering, 500 W University
El Paso, TX 79968
William Davis, President
Tel: (915) 747-5460 Fax: (915) 747-5616
Email: maesshpe@eng.utep.edu
Web: http://eng.utep.edu/maesshpe

SPANISH CLUB
University of Dallas
1845 E. Northgate Dr.
Irving, TX 75062
Javier Andreau, President
Tel: (972) 721-5323
Email: javi_andreu@yahoo.com
Web: www.udallas.edu/studentlife/clubs.cfm

**TEXAS ASSOCIATION OF MEXICAN
AMERICAN COLLEGE STUDENTS**
Tarrant County College
WSTU #2811
Arlington, TX 76018
Vesta Wheatley, Student Activities Director
Tel: (817) 515-7795
Email: vesta.wheatley@tccd.edu

**THE TEXAS UNION - MEXICAN AMERICAN
CULTURE COMMITTEE**
University of Texas
P.O. Box 7338
Austin, TX 78713-7338
Julio Vela, Chairperson
Tel: (512) 475-6630 Fax: (512) 475-6414
Email: studentevents@union.utexas.edu

**UNITED LATIN AMERICAN MEDICAL
STUDENTS**
UT Health Science Ctr. at San Antonio, 7703
Floyd Curl Dr.
San Antonio, TX 78284
Elizeth De Leon, Member
Tel: (210) 567-2654 Fax: (210) 567-2644
Email: deleone@uthscsa.edu
Web: http://studentservices.uthscsa.edu

UTAH

HISPANIC PROGRAM MANAGERS
US Forest Service
324 25th St.
Ogden, UT 84401
Sherill Neil, Director
Tel: (801) 625-5401 Fax: (801) 625-5722

UTAH HISPANIC CHAMBER OF COMMERCE
P.O. Box 1805
Salt Lake City, UT 84110
Robert Rendon, Chairman
Tel: (801) 532-3308 Fax: (801) 532-3309
Email: info@utahhcc.com
Web: www.utahhcc.com

HISPANIC STUDENT SENATOR
Weber State University
Services for Multicultural Students, 1116
University Cr.
Ogden, UT 84408
Rebeca LaMar, Student Senator
Tel: (801) 626-7331 Fax: (801) 626-7635
Email: celestevilchis@mail.weber.edu
Web: www.weber.edu/x5843.xml#lchss

**NATIONAL LATINO PEACE OFFICERS
ASSOCIATION**
Utah Chapter
P.O. Box 22113
Salt Lake City, UT 84122

John M. Cardona, President
Tel: (801) 580-6381 Fax: (801) 313-0121
Email: louie.muniz@ci.slc.ut.us
Web: www.nlpoa.org

OFFICE OF HISPANIC AFFAIRS
**Utah Department of Community and Economic
Development**
324 S. State St. #500
Salt Lake City, UT 84111
Tony Yapias, Director
Tel: (801) 538-8755 Fax: (801) 538-8678
Email: tyapias@utah.gov
Web: http://dced.utah.gov/hispanic/index.html

UTAH COALITION OF LA RAZA
National Headquarters
P.O. Box 389
Salt Lake City, UT 84110
Jorge Arce-Larreta
Tel: (801) 359-8922
Email: jarcelarreta@hotmail.com

UTAH REPUBLICAN HISPANIC ASSEMBLY
8928 S. Wasatch Blvd.
Sandy, UT 84093
Marco Díaz, Jr., State Chairman
Tel: (801) 947-8696
Email: marcohdiaz@yahoo.com

**CHURCH OF JESUS CHRIST OF LATTER-DAY
SAINTS**
Park City Family Tree Visitors' Center
531 Historic Main St.
Park City, UT 84060
Steve Peterson, Director
Tel: (435) 940-9502 Fax: (435) 940-9503
Web: www.lds.org

**CHURCH OF JESUS CHRIST OF LATTER-DAY
SAINTS**
St. George Utah Visitor Center
490 S 300 East
St. George, UT 84770
Elder Martin, Director
Tel: (435) 673-5181 Fax: (435) 652-9589
Web: www.lds.org

DIOCESE OF SALT LAKE CITY
Hispanic Ministry
27 C St.
Salt Lake City, UT 84103
Maria Cruz Gray, Director for Hispanic Ministry
Tel: (801) 328-8641 X361 Fax: (801) 328-9680
Email: maria.cruz.gray@dioslc.org
Web: www.dioslc.org

CENTER FOR ETHNIC STUDENT AFFAIRS
University of Utah
200 S. Central Campus Dr. #318
Salt Lake City, UT 84112
Karen Kwan, Advisor
Tel: (801) 581-8151 Fax: (801) 581-7119
Email: kwan@sa.utah.edu
Web: www.utah.edu/cesa/

ETHNIC STUDIES PROGRAM
University of Utah
380 S 1400 East #112
Salt Lake City, UT 84112-0310
Lisa Flores, Director
Tel: (801) 581-5206 Fax: (801) 581-8437
Email: lisa.flores@ed.utah.edu
Web: www.ethnic.utah.edu

REFORMA
Reforma de Utah
P.O. Box 521271
Salt Lake City, UT 84152-1271
Tessa Epstein, President
Tel: (801) 594-8640
Email: tepstein@slcpl.lib.ut.us
Web: www.reforma.org

SERVICES FOR MULTICULTURAL STUDENTS
Weber State University
1116 University Cir.
Ogden, UT 84408-1116
Ruth Patino Stubbs, Latin Students Counselor
Tel: (801) 626-7330 Fax: (801) 626-7635
Email: rstubbs@weber.edu
Web: http://weber.edu/sms.xml

**HISPANIC EMPLOYMENT PROGRAM COUNCIL
OF UTAH**
6009 Wardleigh Rd., Bldg. 1209
Hill AFB, UT 84056-5838
Barbara Garcia, Contact
Tel: (801) 775-2258
Email: barbara.garcia@hill.af.mil
Web: www.hepcu.org

**CENTRO DE LA FAMILIA DE UTAH/INSTITUTE
OF HUMAN RESOURCE DEVELOPMENT**
Affiliate of NCLR
3780 SW Temple
Salt Lake City, UT 84115
Graciela Italiano Thomas, Executive Director
Tel: (801) 521-4473 Fax: (801) 521-6242
Email: centro@la-familia.org
Web: www.la-familia.org

FRATERNIDAD HISPANA
3098 W. 5685 South
Taylors Ville, UT 84118
Elizabeth Robertson, Director
Tel: (801) 966-7294 Fax: (801) 966-7294
Email: hrobertson@utah-inter.net

COMMUNITY ACTION AGENCY
815 S Freedom Blvd. #100
Provo, UT 84601
Myla Dutton, Executive Director
Tel: (801) 373-8200 Fax: (801) 373-8228
Email: mdutton@unitedwayuc.org
Web: www.communityactionprovo.org

OFFICE OF HISPANIC AFFAIRS
State of Utah
324 S. State St. #500
Salt Lake City, UT 84111
Elizabeth Balcazar, Program Coordinator
Tel: (801) 538-8755 Fax: (801) 538-8678
Email: ebalcazar@utah.gov
Web: http://dced.utah.gov/hispanic

ESTUDIANTES UNIDOS
Weber State University
Services for Multicultural Students, 1116
University Cr.
Ogden, UT 84408
Maria Parrilla De Kokal, Advisor
Tel: (801) 626-7622 Fax: (801) 626-7635
Web: www.weber.edu/x5843.xml#lchss

HISPANIC AREA COUNCIL
Weber State University
Services for Multicultural Students, 1116
University Cr.

Ogden, UT 84408
Rebeca LaMar, Student Senator
Tel: (801) 626-7331 Fax: (801) 626-7635
Web: www.weber.edu/x5843.xml#lchss

MINORITY LAW CAUCUS
S.J. Quinney College of Law
332 S. 1400 E. Front
Salt Lake City, UT 84112
Yelena Ayrapetova, President
Email: mlc@law.utah.edu
Web: http://clubs.asuu.utah.edu/mlc

**MOVIMIENTO ESTUDIANTIL CHICANA/O DE
AZTLAN**
Weber State University
Services for Multicultural Students, 1116
University Cr.
Ogden, UT 84408
Maria Parrilla De Kokal, Advisor
Tel: (801) 626-7622 Fax: (801) 626-7635
Web: www.weber.edu/x5843.xml#lchss

VIRGINIA

FOUNDATION FOR THE PERFORMING ARTS
Wolf Trap
1645 Trap Rd.
Vienna, VA 22182
Tarrence D. Jones, President/CEO
Tel: (703) 255-1920 Fax: (703) 255-1905
Email: wolftrap@wolftrap.org
Web: www.wolf-trap.org

SOCIEDAD LITERARIA VENEZOLANA
4343 Lee Hwy. #505
Arlington, VA 22207
Simon R. Contreras Velásquez, Director
Tel: (703) 528-4094 Fax: (703) 228-5813
Email: sr-contreras@yahoo.com

**ASSOCIATION OF HISPANIC ADVERTISING
AGENCIES**
National Headquarters
8201 Greensboro Dr., 3rd Fl.
McLean, VA 22102
Horacio Gavilan, Executive Director
Tel: (703) 610-9014 Fax: (703) 610-9005
Email: info@ahaa.org
Web: www.ahaa.org

NATIONAL HISPANIC CORPORATE COUNCIL
1530 Wilson Blvd. #110
Arlington, VA 22209
Carlos Soto, President/CEO
Tel: (703) 807-5137 Fax: (703) 807-0567
Email: csoto@nhcc-hq.org
Web: www.nhcc-hq.org

**AMERICAN PERUVIAN CHAMBER OF
COMMERCE**
313 N. Glebe Rd. #200-A
Arlington, VA 22203
Ricardo M. Gaitan, President
Tel: (703) 914-4797 Fax: (703) 525-2903
Email: gaitanricardo@aol.com
Web: www.peruchamber.com

**PENINSULA TIDEWATER HISPANIC CHAMBER
OF COMMERCE**
445 Grafton Dr.
Yorktown, VA 23693
Gaby Lopez Rengifo, President
Tel: (757) 890-6203 Fax: (757) 890-0596
Email: gaby.rengifo@pthcc.org
Web: www.pthcc.org

VIRGINIA HISPANIC CHAMBER OF COMMERCE
Headquarters Office
10700 Midlothian Turnpike #200
Richmond, VA 23235
Michel Zajur, President/CEO
Tel: (804) 378-4099 Fax: (804) 379-1727
Email: info@vahcc.com
Web: www.vahcc.com

COMMUNICATIONS

NATIONAL ASSOCIATION OF MINORITY MEDIA EXECUTIVES
1921 Gallows Rd. #600
Vienna, VA 22182-3900
Toni F. Lewis, Executive Director
Tel: (888) 968-7658 Fax: (703) 893-2410
Email: tlaws@namme.org
Web: www.namme.org

UNITY: JOURNALISTS OF COLOR, INC.
1601 N. Kent St. #1003
Arlington, VA 22209
Anna M. Lopez, Executive Director
Tel: (703) 469-2100 Fax: (703) 469-2108
Email: info@unityjournalists.org
Web: www.unityjournalists.org

COMMUNICATIONSSOCIAL INTEREST

UNITED COMMUNITY MINISTRIES, INC.
Main Office
7511 Fordson Rd.
Alexandria, VA 22306
Cheri Zeman, Executive Director
Tel: (703) 768-7106 Fax: (703) 768-4788
Email: executivedirector@ucmagency.org
Web: www.ucmagency.org

CULTURAL

ASOCIACIÓN SALVADOREÑA AMERICANA DE VIRGINIA
859 N. Larrimore St.
Arlington, VA 22205
J. Walter Tejada, President
Tel: (703) 538-5909
Email: jtejada@gmu.edu

LAW ENFORCEMENT

HISPANIC AMERICAN POLICE COMMAND OFFICERS ASSOCIATION
National Chapter
6055 A Arlington Blvd.
Falls Church, VA 22044
Lee Ray Villareal, Acting Executive Director
Tel: (703) 534-2895 Fax: (703) 534-2896
Email: info@hapcoa.org
Web: www.hapcoa.org

MULTI-PURPOSE

AMERICAN GI FORUM OF THE UNITED STATES
Washington DC Chapter
P.O. Box 4247
Alexandria, VA 22301
Librado M. Rivas, Vice Commander
Tel: (703) 325-2063
Email: libradorivas@hoffman.army.mil
Web: www.agif.us/DC.htm

LEAGUE OF UNITED LATIN AMERICAN CITIZENS
Northern Virginia
P.O. Box 5290
Arlington, VA 22205-0499
Yolanda Smingler, President
Email: lulacnva@lycos.com
Web: http://lulacnva.tripod.com

MARCELINO PAN Y VINO, INC.
P.O. Box 8523
Falls Church, VA 22041
Rev. José E. Hoyos, Honorary President & Founder
Email: marcelinpanyvino@hotmail.com
Web: www.mapavi.org

NATIONAL HISPANIC ENVIRONMENTAL COUNCIL
106 N. Fayette St.
Alexandria, VA 22314
Roger Rivera, President
Tel: (703) 683-3956 Fax: (703) 683-5125
Web: www.nheec.org

PARENT EDUCATIONAL ADVOCACY TRAINING CENTER
6320 Augusta Dr. #1200
Springfield, VA 22150
Ana Avanzini, Latino Outreach Information Specialist
Tel: (703) 923-0010 Fax: (703) 923-0030
Email: partners@peatc.org
Web: www.peatc.org

ST. JOHN THE EVANGELIST CATHOLIC CHURCH
Haiti/Dominican Republic Outreach Mission
271 Winchester St.
Warrenton, VA 20186-2819
Bernie Ragan, Deacon
Tel: (540) 347-9680
Email: info@stjohntheevangelist.org
Web: www.stjohntheevangelist.org/organizations/organization.php?org=109

POLITICAL ACTION

DEMOCRATIC LATINO ORGANIZATION OF VIRGINIA
6355 Lakeview Dr.
Falls Church, VA 22041
Philip D. Vasquez, Chair
Tel: (703) 731-4396 Fax: (703) 333-2757
Email: pvasquez@cox.net
Web: www.dlov.org

REPUBLICAN NATIONAL HISPANIC ASSEMBLY
RNHA- Virginia
4246 Chain Bridge Rd.
Fairfax, VA 22030
Federico G. Morales, State Chairman
Tel: (703) 354-2465 Fax: (703) 354-2465
Email: rhava@webtv.net
Web: www.rnha.org

PROFESSIONAL

NATIONAL ASSOCIATION OF HISPANIC FEDERAL EXECUTIVES, INC.
P.O. Box 469
Herndon, VA 20172-0469
Manuel Oliverez, President/CEO
Tel: (703) 787-0291 Fax: (703) 787-4675
Email: nahfe@cs.com
Web: www.nahfe.org

RELIGIOUS

ALL SAINTS CATHOLIC CHURCH
Hispanic Ministry
9300 Stonewall Rd.
Manassas, VA 20110
Rev. John Mosimann, Pastor
Tel: (703) 368-4500 Fax: (703) 257-9299
Web: www.rc.net/arlington/all_saints

ARLINGTON UNITED METHODIST CHURCH/ IGLESIA METODISTA HISPANA UNIDA DE ARLINGTON
716 S Glebe Rd.
Arlington, VA 22204
Rev. Daniel Mejía, Pastor

Tel: (703) 920-8076 Fax: (703) 979-7051
Email: pastordaniel@arlingtonumc.com
Web: www.arlingtonumc.com

CATHEDRAL OF ST. THOMAS MOORE
3901 Cathedral Ln.
Arlington, VA 22203
Rev. Matthew Zuberbueler, Pastor
Tel: (703) 525-1300 Fax: (703) 528-5760

COLUMBIA BAPTIST CHURCH
103 W. Columbia St.
Falls Church, VA 22046
Daniel Carro, Pastor Hispanic Congregation
Tel: (703) 534-5700 Fax: (703) 536-6757
Email: webmaster@columbiabaptist.org
Web: www.columbiabaptist.org

CULMORE UNITED METHODIST CHURCH/ IGLESIA METODISTA HISPANA UNIDA DE CULMORE
5901 Leesburg Pike
Falls Church, VA 22041
Rev. Grace Ellen Rice, Senior Pastor
Tel: (703) 820-5131 Fax: (703) 820-4386
Web: www.culmoreumc.org

DIOCESE OF ARLINGTON
Hispanic Apostolate
80 N. Glebe Rd.
Arlington, VA 22203
Rev. Ovidio Pecharromán, Director for Hispanic Apostolate
Tel: (703) 524-2122 Fax: (703) 524-4261

FAIRFAX BAPTIST TEMPLE
6401 Missionary Ln.
Fairfax Station, VA 22039
Troy R. Calvert, Pastor Spanish Church
Tel: (703) 323-8100 Fax: (703) 250-8660
Email: troycalvert@fbtministries.org
Web: www.fbtministries.org

FLORIS UNITED METHODIST CHURCH
Floris Neighbors Program
2730 Centreville Rd.
Herndon, VA 20171
Libby Fielder, Coordinator
Tel: (703) 793-0026 Fax: (703) 793-0028
Email: lfielder@florisumc.org
Web: www.florisumc.org

GREENBRIER BAPTIST CHURCH/ GLESIA BAUTISTA GREENBRIER
5401 7th Rd. South
Arlington, VA 22204
Rob Tennant, Pastor
Tel: (703) 671-6688 Fax: (703) 379-2996
Email: revtennant@hotmail.com

HISPANIC APOSTOLATE
Diocese of Richmond
811 Cathedral Pl.
Richmond, VA 23220
Elisa Montalvo, Director
Tel: (804) 359-5661 Fax: (804) 358-9159
Email: emontalvo@richmonddiocese.org
Web: www.richmonddiocese.org

MISION HISPANA CRISTO SALVA
First Baptist Church of Woodbridge
P.O. Box 6788
Woodbridge, VA 22195
Rev. Luiggi Reggiardo, Hispanic Pastor
Tel: (703) 494-4848
Email: lreggiardo@fbcwoodbridge.org
Web: www.fbcwoodbridge.org

OUR LADY OF ANGELS CATHOLIC CHURCH
13752 Mary's Way
Woodbridge, VA 22191
Father Lange, Pastor
Tel: (703) 494-2444 Fax: (703) 494-0005
Web: www.olacc.org

OUR LADY OF LOURDES
830 S 23rd St.
Arlington, VA 22202

Rev. John M. O'Donohue, Pastor
Tel: (703) 684-9261 Fax: (703) 684-9261
Email: ol@erols.com
Web: www.olol-arlington.org

OUR LADY QUEEN OF PEACE
2700 S 19th St.
Arlington, VA 22204
Fr. Joseph Nangle, Ministerio Latino
Tel: (703) 979-5580 Fax: (703) 979-5590
Email: olqp.office@verizon.net
Web: www.ourladyqueenofpeace.org

PAGINAS HISPANAS
Good Shepherd
8710 Mt. Vernon Hwy.
Alexandria, VA 22309
Lia Tenorio, Hispanic Ministry Coordinator
Tel: (703) 780-4055 Fax: (703) 360-5385
Email: lia@gs-cc.org
Web: www.gs-cc.org/hispanic/index.html

QUEEN OF APOSTLES CATHOLIC CHURCH
4329 Sano St.
Alexandria, VA 22312-1538
Rev. Daniel L. Mode, Pastor
Tel: (703) 354-8711 Fax: (703) 354-0766
Web: www.queenofapostles.org

SOCIAL MINISTRIES OFFICE, OUR LADY QUEEN OF PEACE
2700 S. 19th St.
Arlington, VA 22204
Gene Betit, Social Ministries Director
Tel: (703) 979-5580 Fax: (703) 979-5590
Email: olqp.office@verizon.net
Web: www.ourladyqueenofpeace.org

ST. AGNES CATHOLIC CHURCH
1914 N Randolph St.
Arlington, VA 22207
Rev. Tarcisio Buitriago, Pastor
Tel: (703) 525-1166 Fax: (703) 243-2840
Web: www.saintagnes.org

ST. CHARLES BORROMEO
Latin American Community
3304 N. Washington Blvd.
Arlington, VA 22201
Neyda Jara, Parish Council Representative
Tel: (703) 527-5500 Fax: (703) 527-5505
Email: njara@edrs.com

ST. LEO THE GREAT CATHOLIC CHURCH
3700 Old Lee Hwy.
Fairfax, VA 22030
Fr. John Kelly, Pastor
Tel: (703) 273-5369 Fax: (703) 273-2371
Web: www.stleos.com

ST. PHILIP CATHOLIC CHURCH
7500 St. Philip Ct.
Falls Church, VA 22042
Barbara Ostander, Secretary
Tel: (703) 573-3809 Fax: (703) 560-8832
Email: st.philips@erols.com

ST. RITA CATHOLIC CHURCH
3815 Russell Rd.
Alexandria, VA 22305
Rev. Denis M. Donahue, Pastor
Tel: (703) 836-1640 Fax: (703) 836-7825
Web: www.strita-parish.org

RESEARCH

HISPANIC AMERICAN CENTER FOR ECONOMIC RESEARCH
4084 University Dr. #103
Fairfax, VA 22030
Alejandro Chafuen, President/CEO
Tel: (703) 934-6969
Email: info@hacer.org
Web: www.hacer.org

SPEC. INT., CHILD CARE

ENTERPRISES FOR HISPANIC YOUTH FOUNDATION
3951 Pender Dr. #120
Fairfax, VA 22030
Raul Almeida, President/CEO
Tel: (703) 383-7225 Fax: (703) 383-7222
Email: Raul.almeida@ehyfmail.org
Web: www.ehyf.org

HIGHER HORIZONS DAY CARE CENTER
5920 B Summers Ln.
Falls Church, VA 22041
Mary Ann Cornish, Director
Tel: (703) 820-2457 Fax: (703) 820-1578
Email: maryann.cornish@fairfaxcounty.gov
Web: www.higherhorizons.org

SEXUAL ASSAULT VICTIMS' ADVOCACY SERVICE
13928 Jefferson Davis Hwy. #C
Woodbridge, VA 22191
Bonnie Kilgore, Executive Director
Tel: (703) 497-1192 Fax: (703) 497-1195
Email: savas_youtheducatoroutreachcoor@yahoo.com
Web: savasofprvc.com

ESCUELA BOLIVIA
P.O. Box 100066
Arlington, VA 22210-0066
Natalia Salazar, Director
Tel: (703) 205-0268
Email: info@escuelabolivia.org
Web: www.escuelabolivia.org

OFFICE OF DIVERSITY PROGRAMS AND SERVICES - GEORGE MASON UNIVERSITY
Organization for Hispanic Leadership in America
MSN: 2F6
4400 University Dr.
Fairfax, VA 22030
Jessica Ranero, Assistant Director
Tel: (703) 993-2700 Fax: (703) 993-4022
Email: jranero@gmu.edu
Web: www.gmu.edu/student/msaf

SPANISH FOR EDUCATORS
816 S Walter Reed Dr.
Arlington, VA 22204
Simón R. Contreras, Instructor
Tel: (703) 228-5813 Fax: (703) 228-5813
Email: hquinone@arlington.k12.va.us

ABLE LABOR
P.O. Box 6104
Fort Belvoir, VA 22060
Paul Leach, President
Tel: (703) 799-8395 Fax: (703) 777-0441

EAST COAST MIGRANT HEAD START PROJECT
4245 N Fairfax Dr. #800
Arlington, VA 22203
Rafael Guerra, CEO
Tel: (703) 243-7522 Fax: (703) 243-1259
Email: guerra@ecmhsp.org
Web: www.ecmhsp.org

HISPANIC EMPLOYMENT PROGRAM
P.O. Box 230294
Centreville, VA 20120-0294
Tel: Fax: (703) 266-9055
Email: hepm@aol.com
Web: www.hepm.org

HISPANIC ORGANIZATIONS LEADERSHIP ALLIANCE
USDA Chapter

813 Sledgehammer Dr.
Fredericksburg, VA 22405
Carmen Nordlund, President
Tel: (703) 305-7480 Fax: (540) 899-3887
Email: carmen.nordlund@fns.usda.gov

HISPANOS UNIDOS DE VIRGINIA
Affiliate of NCLR
5400-B Seven Corners Pl.
Falls Church, VA 22044
Johnny N. Simancas, Executive Director
Tel: (703) 533-9300 Fax: (703) 533-9369
Email: jsimancas@aol.com

INTERNATIONAL MEDICAL SERVICES FOR HEALTH
45449 Severn Way #161
Sterling, VA 20166
Linda Pfeiffer, President
Tel: (703) 444-4477 Fax: (703) 444-4471
Email: contact@inmed.org
Web: www.inmed.org

NORTHERN VIRGINIA FAMILY SERVICE
Main Office
10455 White Granit Dr. #100
Oakton, VA 22124
Dorothy Moga, Chair
Tel: (703) 385-3267
Email: info@nvfs.org
Web: www.nvfs.org

HISPANIC COMMITTEE OF VIRGINIA/ COMITE HISPANO DE VIRGINIA
National Headquarters
5827 Columbia Pike #200
Falls Church, VA 22041
Jorge E. Figueredo, Executive Director
Tel: (703) 671-5666 Fax: (703) 671-2325
Email: info@hcva.com
Web: www.hispaniccommitteeofvirginia.org

NATIONAL ORGANIZATION FOR THE ADVANCEMENT OF HISPANICS
National Headquarters
2217 Princess Anne St. #205-1
Fredericksburg, VA 22401
Jose Osegueda II, President
Tel: (540) 372-3437 Fax: (540) 372-3437
Email: noah-va@noah-va.org
Web: www.noah-va.org

TELAMON CORPORATION
Virginia HOPE III Housing Office 10
P.O. Box 500
Gretna, VA 24557
Robert Gilbert, Homeownership Project Coordinator
Tel: (434) 656-8357 Fax: (434) 656-8356
Email: rgilbert@telamon.org
Web: www.telamon.org

Virginia Housing Services Office 8
P.O. Box 444
South Hill, VA 23970
Carolyn Walker, Housing Program Manager
Tel: (434) 447-2744 Fax: (434) 447-5877
Email: cwalker@telamon.org
Web: www.telamon.org

Virginia Office 1
4913 Fitzhugh Ave. #202
Richmond, VA 23230
Sharon Saldarriaga, State Director
Tel: (804) 355-4676 Fax: (804) 355-6407
Email: ssaldarriaga@telamon.org
Web: www.telamon.org

Virginia Office 12
1 Solutions Way #103

Waynesboro, VA 22980
Melissa Wender, Regional Manager
Tel: (540) 941-8432 Fax: (540) 941-2402
Email: mwender@telamon.org
Web: www.telamon.org

Virginia Office 2
1332-D Piney Forest Rd.
Danville, VA 24540
Kathy Bullano, Regional Manager
Tel: (434) 836-9071 Fax: (434) 836-9072
Email: kbullano@telamon.org
Web: www.telamon.org

Virginia Office 3
P.O. Box 908
Exmore, VA 23350
Pauline James, Regional Manager
Tel: (757) 442-2002 Fax: (757) 442-7392
Email: pjames@telamon.org
Web: www.telamon.org

Virginia Office 5
316 Main St.
South Boston, VA 24592
Wanda Jenkins, Regional Manager
Tel: (434) 572-8993 Fax: (434) 572-8613
Email: wjenkins@telamon.org
Web: www.telamon.org

Virginia Office 6
120 W Danville St.
South Hill, VA 23970
Carolyn Walker, Housing Program Manager
Tel: (434) 447-2744 Fax: (434) 447-5877
Email: cwalker@telamon.org
Web: www.telamon.org

Virginia Office 7
20 E Piccadilly St. #15
Winchester, VA 22601
Gwendolyn Puryear, Regional Manager
Tel: (540) 722-2507 Fax: (540) 722-3366
Email: gpuryear@telamon.org
Web: www.telamon.org

UNIDOS POR EL PERÚ
4600 37th St.
Arlington, VA 22207
Abad Ramirez, President
Tel: (703) 533-7321 Fax: (703) 533-2227
Email: aramirez@starpower.net

HISPANIC COMMITTEE OF VIRGINIA/COMITÉ HISPANO DE VIRGINIA
Arlington Office
2049 N 15th St. #100
Arlington, VA 22201
Jorge Figueredo, Executive Director
Tel: (703) 243-3033 Fax: (703) 243-2297
Email: info@hcva.com
Web: www.hcva.com

HOGAR HISPANO
Catholic Charities of the Diocese of Arlington
6201 Leesburg Pike #307
Falls Church, VA 22044
Nancy Jane Shestack, Program Director
Tel: (703) 534-9805 Fax: (703) 534-9809
Web: www.ccda.net

CENTER FOR MULTICULTURAL HUMAN SERVICES
701 W. Broad St. #305
Falls Church, VA 22307
Dr. Lisa Karlisch, Director of Program Operations
Tel: (703) 533-3302 X210 Fax: (703) 237-2083
Email: dhunt@cmhsweb.org
Web: www.cmhsweb.org

FAIRFAX AREA AGENCY ON AGING
12011 Government Center Pkwy. #708
Fairfax, VA 22035-1104
Grace Starbird, Director
Tel: (703) 324-5411 Fax: (703) 449-8689
Email: fairfax-aaa@fairfaxcounty.gov
Web: www.co.fairfax.va.us/service/aaa/homepage.html

ASSOCIATION OF NAVAL OFFICERS
P.O. Box 10951
Arlington, VA 22210
Capt. Willam Nieto, Jr., President & CEO
Tel: (202) 619-7135
Email: William_Nieto_Jr@nps.org
Web: www.ansomil.org

FRIENDS OF THE DOMINICAN REPUBLIC, INC.
4512 Park Rd.
Alexandria, VA 22312
Roger Weiss, Membership Director
Tel: (360) 354-0907
Web: www.fotdr.org

INSURANCE INSTITUTE FOR HIGHWAY SAFETY
1005 N Glebe Rd.
Arlington, VA 22201
Brian O'Neil, President
Tel: (703) 247-1500 Fax: (703) 247-1586
Web: www.highwaysafety.org

INTER-AMERICAN FOUNDATION/ GRASSROOTS DEVELOPMENT
901 N. Stuart St.10th Fl.
Arlington, VA 22003
Paula Durbin, Public Affairs Specialist
Tel: (703) 306-4301 Fax: (703) 306-4365
Email: pdurbin@iaf.gov
Web: www.iaf.gov

MISSION OF HOPE, BOLIVIA
P.O. Box 4001
Charlottesville, VA 22903
Cindy Thacker, Executive Director
Tel: (434) 977-4748 Fax: (434) 977-4748
Email: cindytha@cstone.net
Web: www.missionofhopebolivia.org

NATIONAL CENTER FOR MISSING & EXPLOITED CHILDREN
Ministry Outreach Program
Charles B. Wang Intl. Childrens Bldg.,
699 Prince St.
Alexandria, VA 22314-3175
Herb Jones, Special Assistant to the NCMEC President Director, MOP
Tel: (703) 838-8384 Fax: (703) 274-2222
Email: hjones@ncmec.org
Web: www.ncmec.org

TENANTS AND WORKERS SUPPORT COMMITTEE
P.O. Box 2327
3801 Mt. Vernon Ave. #5
Alexandria, VA 22305
Amalia Ruiz, President
Tel: (703) 684-5697 Fax: (703) 684-5714
Web: www.twsc.org

DAMAS DEL SUR
8340 Greensboro Dr. #1001
McLean, VA 22102
Angie Zapata, President

LATINAS UNIDAS: VOZ Y PRESENCIA
6001 Arlington Blvd. #209
Falls Church, VA 22044
Luz M. Diago, President

Tel: (703) 578-0687 Fax: (703) 578-0687
Email: ldiago@msn.com

NATIONAL COUNCIL OF HISPANIC WOMEN
1300 Crystal Dr. #1610
Arlington, VA 22202
Litizia Ramirez Erickson, National Secretary
Tel: (310) 822-2739
Email: joy7@onebox.com
Web: www.go.to/nchw

NATIONAL HISPANA LEADERSHIP INSTITUTE
1901 N Moore St. #206
Arlington, VA 22209
Marisa Rivera-Albert, President
Tel: (703) 527-6007 Fax: (703) 527-6009
Email: nhli@aol.com
Web: www.nhli.org

RAPE AGGRESSION DEFENSE PROGRAM
498-A Wythe Creek Rd.
Poquoson, VA 23662
Kathy Wright, Executive Board Member
Tel: (757) 868-4400 Fax: (757) 868-4401
Email: wright@rad-systems.com
Web: www.rad-systems.com

WOMEN'S CENTER OF NORTHERN VIRGINIA
133 Park St. NE
Vienna, VA 22180
Clara M. Conti, CEO
Tel: (703) 281-2657
Email: twc@thewomenscenter.org
Web: www.thewomenscenter.org

CENTER FOR CHILD WELFARE
George Mason University- Research Center
Thompson Hall #207D, M/S 2E8, Fairfax Campus
Fairfax, VA 22030-4444
Dennis Ritchie, Director
Tel: (703) 993-1951 Fax: (703) 993-1970
Email: dritchi1@gmu.edu
Web: www.gmu.edu/acadexcel

IVY INTER-AMERICAN FOUNDATION
P.O. Box 248
Ivy, VA 22945
Anabella Jordan , President
Tel: (434) 295-4698 Fax: (434) 296-8330
Email: ivyinteram@aol.com
Web: www.ivyinteramericanfoundation.org

WASHINGTON

BALLET FOLKLORICO "OLLIN"
Olympia
913 E. Dundee Rd. NW
Olympia, WA 98502-4419
Cathy Shultz Reyes, Business Manager
Tel: (360) 786-8567 Fax: (360) 943-5354
Email: ballerollin@thurston.com
Web: www.paradisewest.com

**NATIONAL MINORITY SUPPLIER
DEVELOPMENT COUNCIL, INC.**
Northwest Minority Business Council
320 Andover Park East #205
Tukwila, WA 98188-7635
Victor Valdez, MIM, Executive Director
Tel: (206) 575-7748 Fax: (206) 575-7783
Email: vfvaldez@nmbc.biz
Web: www.nmbc.biz

**HISPANIC CHAMBER OF COMMERCE OF
GREATER YAKIMA**
P.O. Box 2712
Yakima, WA 98907
Velma Perez, President
Tel: (509) 453-2050 Fax: (509) 453-5165
Email: delnorte@nwinfo.net
Web: www.yakimahispanicchamber.com

**HISPANIC CHAMBER OF COMMERCE OF
YAKIMA COUNTY**
P.O. Box 11146
Yakima, WA 98909
Velma Perez, President
Tel: (509) 453-2050 Fax: (509) 453-5165
Email: redr@charter.net
Web: www.yakimahispanicchamber.com

**NORTH CENTRAL WASHINGTON HISPANIC
CHAMBER OF COMMERCE**
P.O. Box 2001
Wenatchee, WA 98807-2001
Mario Reyes, President
Tel: (509) 662-2116 Fax: (509) 663-2022
Email: informacion@ncwhcc.org
Web: www.ncwhcc.org

**OTHELLO HISPANIC CHAMBER OF
COMMERCE**
646 S 3rd St.
Othello, WA 99344
Tel: (509) 989-1147 Fax: (509) 488-3857
Email: rag71@gosi.net

**RED MOUNTAIN CULTURAL CHAMBER OF
COMMERCE**
P.O. Box 373
Benton City, WA 99320
Tel: (509) 588-4443 Fax: (509) 588-5402

**TRI-CITIES HISPANIC CHAMBER OF
COMMERCE**
118 N 5th Ave.
Pasco, WA 99301
Tel: (509) 542-0933 Fax: (509) 545-2085
Email: lavoz@bmi.net

US-MEXICO CHAMBER OF COMMERCE
Northwest Chapter
2200 Alaskan Way #430
Seattle, WA 98121-1684
Michael Alvarez, President
Tel: (206) 625-0868 Fax: (206) 443-3828
Email: info@usmcocnw.org
Web: www.usmcocnw.org

**WASHINGTON STATE HISPANIC CHAMBER
OF COMMERCE**
P.O. Box 21925
Seattle, WA 98111-3925
Cesar Caycedo, President
Tel: (206) 441-8894 Fax: (206) 441-9503
Email: president@wshcc.com
Web: www.wshcc.com

**NATIONAL LATINO PEACE OFFICERS
ASSOCIATION**
Seattle Chapter
P.O. Box 23296
Federal Way, WA 98093
Yvonne Gallegos, President
Email: y_gallegos@msn.com
Web: www.nlpoa.com

CENTRO CULTURAL HISPANO AMERICANO
3631 Brookside Way W.
University Place, WA 98466-1401
Nelida Mendoza, Executive Director
Tel: (253) 210-0134
Email: nelida@centroculturalha.org

Web: www.centroculturalha.org

**CHELAN-DOUGLAS COMMUNITY ACTION
COUNCIL**
620 Lewis St.
Wenatchee, WA 98801
Janice Soder, Deputy Director
Tel: (509) 662-6156 Fax: (509) 662-1737
Email: janices@cdcac.org

MANO CON MANO HEALTH REACH
2350 10th Ave. E #207
Seattle, WA 98102-4074
Susan Jones, Board Member
Email: manoconmano@aol.com
Web: www.manoconmano.org

NATIONAL IMAGE, INC.
Washington State Chapter
9725 Moran Rd. NE
Bainbridge Island, WA 98110
Fidel Alvarez, Regional Director
Tel: (206) 684-7576 Fax: (206) 470-6937
Email: fidel.alvarez@seattle.gov
Web: www.nationalimageinc.com

SISTER ISLAND PROJECT
P.O. Box 1413
Langley, WA 98260
Victoria Santos, Co-Director
Tel: (360) 321-4012
Email: sisterisland@mail2world.com
Web: www.sisterislandproject.org

**REPUBLICAN NATIONAL HISPANIC
ASSEMBLY**
Washington State RNHA
P.O. Box 298
Redmond, WA 98073-0298
E. R. Chavez, State Chairman
Tel: (425) 898-8615
Email: chair@wrnha.org
Web: www.rnhanm.homestead.com

**WASHINGTON STATE COMMISSION ON
HISPANIC AFFAIRS**
P.O. Box 40924
Olympia, WA 98504-0924
Antonio M. Ginatta, Executive Director
Tel: (360) 753-3159 Fax: (360) 753-0199
Email: hispanic@cha.wa.gov
Web: www.cha.wa.gov

ARCHDIOCESE OF SEATTLE
Hispanic Affairs Office
910 Marion St.
Seattle, WA 98104-1299
Isacc Govea, Assistant Director to Cultural and
Ethnic Communities
Tel: (206) 382-4825 Fax: (206) 382-2069
Email: isaccg@seattlearch.org
Web: www.seattlearch.org

CASHMERE SPANISH FOURSQUARE CHURCH
6710 Stein Hill Rd.
Cashmere, WA 98815
Rev. Martin Hernandez, Pastor
Tel: (509) 782-1115

CHELAN SPANISH FOURSQUARE CHURCH
P.O. Box 341
Chelan, WA 98816
Rev. Guadalupe Ramirez, Pastor
Tel: (509) 682-9008

DIOCESE OF SPOKANE
Hispanic Ministry
P.O. Box 1453
Spokane, WA 99210
Sr. Mryta Iturriaga, Consultant for Hispanic
Ministry
Tel: (509) 358-7315 Fax: (509) 358-7302

Email: miturriaga@dioceseofspokane.org
Web: www.dioceseofspokane.org

DIOCESE OF YAKIMA
Hispanic Ministry Formation
5301-B Tieton Dr.
Yakima, WA 98908
Maria Elena Trevino-Ponce, Director
Tel: (509) 965-7110 Fax: (509) 966-0596
Email: mponce@yakimadiocese.org
Web: www.yakimadiocese.org

DIOCESE OF YAKIMA
Hispanic Ministry Office
5301-B Teton Dr.
Yakima, WA 98908
Rev. Pedro Romo, Director for Hispanic Ministry
Tel: (509) 965-7117 Fax: (509) 966-0596

DRYDEN SPANISH FOURSQUARE CHURCH
P.O. Box 54
Dryden, WA 98821
Rev. Jose J. Perez, Pastor
Tel: (509) 665-2497

**MILL CREEK HISPANIC FOURSQUARE
CHURCH**
16620 Ashway
Lynwood, WA 98037
Rev. Jose Monterroso, Pastor
Tel: (425) 742-3366 Fax: (425) 743-6410
Email: jmonterroso@mc4square.org

QUINCY SPANISH FOURSQUARE CHURCH
P.O. Box 1043
Quincy, WA 98848
Rev. Norberto Garcia, Pastor
Tel: (509) 787-4182
Email: lafuente@crcwnet.com

SAN JUAN DIEGO
1880 Summitview Rd.
Cowiche, WA 98923
Fr. Tony Casteneda, Pastor
Tel: (509) 678-4164

SEATTLE SPANISH FOURSQUARE CHURCH
11452 26th SW
Seattle, WA 98146
Rev. Guillermo Lopez, Pastor
Tel: (206) 248-4250

SPANISH ASSEMBLY OF GOD
501 W 2nd St.
Wapato, WA 98951
Juan Baez, Pastor
Tel: (509) 877-2377

**ST. FRANCIS DE SALES ROMAN CATHOLIC
CHURCH**
P.O. Box 1089
Chelan, WA 98816-1089
Father Daniel Dufner, Director of Hispanic
Ministry
Tel: (509) 682-2433 Fax: (509) 682-9147

ST. MARY'S CHURCH
Hispanic Ministry Office
611 20th Ave. South
Seattle, WA 98144
Guidelia Alejo, Pastoral Associate
Tel: (206) 324-7100 X16 Fax: (206) 329-4596
Email: guidella_alejo@hotmail.com

TONASKET HISPANIC FOURSQUARE CHURCH
P.O. Box 1038
Tonasket, WA 98855
Rev. Raul Martinez, Pastor
Tel: (509) 486-2000

**VIDA NUEVA- NORTHWEST HISPANIC
MINISTRIES**
701 W. Blackburn Rd.

Mt. Vernon, WA 98274
Jose Strong, Pastor
Tel: (360) 424-9215 Fax: (360) 336-2405
Email: jose_strong@yahoo.com
Web: www.crchurches.net/vidanueva/

YAKIMA SPANISH FOURSQUARE CHURCH
P.O. Box 362
Yakima, WA 98902
Rev. Reynaldo Roman Rodriguez, Pastor
Tel: (509) 453-9879

SPEC. INT., CHILD CARE

FRIENDS OF THE ORPHANS NORTHWEST
1607 116th NE #105
Bellevue, WA 98004
Karen Langenwalter, Executive Director
Tel: (425) 646-3935 Fax: (425) 646-7886
Email: fotonw@fotonw.org
Web: www.fotonw.org

MID COLUMBIA COALITION FOR CHILDREN
Affiliate of NCLR
P.O. Box 2715
Pasco, WA 99302
Terry Fleischmen, Executive Director
Tel: (509) 547-8826 Fax: (509) 545-6294

SPEC. INT., EDUCATION

CHICANO EDUCATION PROGRAM
203 Monroe Hall
Cheney, WA 99004
Carlos Maldonado, Director
Tel: (509) 359-2404 Fax: (509) 359-2310

CHICANO STUDIES PROGRAM
American Ethnic Studies Department, University
of Washington
P.O. Box 354380
13521 Padelford Hall #B505
Seattle, WA 98195-4380
Stephen H. Sumida, Chair
Tel: (206) 543-5401 Fax: (206) 616-4071
Email: aes@u.washington.edu
Web: http://depts.washington.edu/aes/

HEADSTART
1901 Rock Island Rd.
Wenatchee, WA 98801
Lucio Perea, Director
Tel: (509) 884-2435 Fax: (509) 884-1383

LATIN AMERICAN STUDIES
Central Washington University
400 E University Way
Ellensburg, WA 98926
Michael Ervin, Interim Program Director
Tel: (509) 963-3347
Email: ervinm@cwu.edu
Web: www.cwu.edu/~la_studies

LATIN AMERICAN STUDIES PROGRAM
University of Washington
P.O. Box 353650
Seattle, WA 98195
Max Savishinsky, Assistant Director
Tel: (206) 685-3435 Fax: (206) 685-0668
Email: lasuw@u.washington.edu
Web: http://jsis.artsci.washington.edu/programs/
latinam/

MIDCOLUMBIA LIBRARIES
Kennewick Branch
1620 S. Union
Kennewick, WA 99338
Tom Moak, Branch Manager
Tel: (509) 783-7878
Web: www.mcl-lib.org

MIGRANT EDUCATIONAL PROGRAM
Yakima Regional Office-ESD 105
33 S. 2nd Ave.
Yakima, WA 98902
Thomas Romero, Executive Director
Tel: (509) 575-2885 Fax: (509) 575-2918
Email: Thomasr@esd105.wednet.edu

Web: www.esd105.wednet.edu

Northwest ESD 189
1601 R Ave.
Anacortes, WA 98221
Leann Swanson, Board of Director
Tel: (360) 299-4000 Fax: (360) 299-4070
Email: info@esd189.org
Web: www.esd189.org

MIGRANT STUDENT DATA & RECRUITMENT
1110-B S. 6th St.
Sunnyside, WA 98944
Lee Campos, Director
Tel: (509) 837-2712
Email: lcampos@msdr.org
Web: www.msdr.org

MULTICULTURAL STUDENT SERVICES
Washington State University
P.O. Box 647206
CUB #51
Pullman, WA 99164-7206
J. Manuel Acevedo, Director
Tel: (509) 335-7852 Fax: (509) 335-1525
Email: mss@wsu.edu
Web: www.wsu.edu/multicultural/

OFFICE OF MINORITY AFFAIRS
University of Washington
1410 NE Campus Pkwy. Box 355845
Seattle, WA 98195-5845
Dr. Nancy Barcelo, Vice President
Tel: (206) 543-6598
Email: vpoma@u.washington.edu
Web: http://depts.washington.edu/oma/home.php

WHATCOM HISPANIC ORGANIZATION
P.O. Box 5601
Bellingham, WA 98227
Pedro Perez, President
Tel: (360) 676-8911 Fax: (360) 671-2231
Email: info@whatcomhispanic.org
Web: www.whatcomhispanic.org

SPEC. INT., EMPLOYMENT

CENTRO LATINO SER-JOBS FOR PROGRESS, INC.
Affiliate of SER-Jobs for Progress National, Inc.
1208 S 10th St.
Tacoma, WA 98405
Alfonso Montoya, Executive Director
Tel: (253) 572-7717 Fax: (253) 572-7837
Email: amontoya@centrolatino-ser.org
Web: www.centrolatino-ser.org

OKANOGAN FARMWORKERS CLINIC
Hispanic Office
P. O. Box 1340
Okanogan, WA 98840
Ann Featherly, Executive Assistant
Tel: (509) 422-5700 Fax: (509) 422-1320
Email: afeatherly@myfamilyhealth.org

WASHINGTON FARMWORKERS INVESTMENT PROGRAM
Yakima Valley OIC
815 Fruitvale Blvd.
Yakima, WA 98902
Gilbert Alaniz, Program Director
Tel: (509) 248-6751 Fax: (509) 575-0482
Email: galaniz@yvoic.org
Web: www.yvoic.org

SPEC. INT., HEALTH SERVICES

COMMUNITY HEALTH CENTER LA CLÍNICA
Affiliate of NCLR
515 W Court St.
Pasco, WA 99301-1323
John Troidl, Executive Director
Tel: (509) 547-2204 Fax: (509) 547-9329

SEA-MAR COMMUNITY HEALTH CENTER
Bellingham Medical/Dental Center

800 E. Chestnut St.
Bellingham, WA 98225
Sharon Dowes, Executive Director
Tel: (360) 671-3225

SEA-MAR COMMUNITY HEALTH CENTER
Mt. Vernon
1400 La Venture Rd.
Mt. Vernon, WA 98273
Mary Lou Martinez, Director
Tel: (360) 428-4075 Fax: (360) 428-5813
Email: maryloumartinez@seamarchc.org

SPEC. INT., HUMAN RELATIONS

EL CENTRO DE LA RAZA
2524 16th Ave. South
Seattle, WA 98144-5104
Roberto Maestas, Executive Director
Tel: (206) 329-9442 Fax: (206) 329-0786
Web: www.elcentrodelaraza.com

SPEC. INT., LEGAL ASSISTANCE

NORTHWEST IMMIGRANT RIGHTS PROJECT
Eastern Washington Office
P.O. Box 270
121 Sunnyside Ave.
Granger, WA 98932
Karen Summers, President
Tel: (509) 854-2100
Web: www.nwirp.org

SPEC. INT., SOCIAL INTEREST

WASHINGTON STATE MIGRANT COUNCIL
Administrative Office
105 S 6th St. #B
Sunnyside, WA 98944
Carlos M. Diaz, Executive Director
Tel: (509) 839-9762 Fax: (509) 839-7689
Email: cdiaz@wsmconline.org
Web: www.wsmconline.org

SPEC. INT., SOCIAL SERVICES

CENTRO LATINO
1208 S. 10th St.
Tacoma, WA 98405
Alfonso Montoya, Executive Director
Tel: (253) 572-7717 Fax: (253) 572-7837
Email: reception@centrolatino-ser.org
Web: www.centrolatino-ser.org

STUDENT ORGANIZATION

MECHA DE UW
University of Washington
HUB Box 352238 #204T
Seattle, WA 98195-2238
Francesca Barajas, Co-Chair
Tel: (206) 543-9244
Email: mecha@u.washington.edu
Web: http://students.washingtotn.edu/mecha/

MOVIMIENTO ESTUDIANTIL CHICANO DE AZTLAN
Eastern Washington University
203 Monroe Hall
Cheney, WA 99004
Yesica Gutierrez, President
Tel: (509) 922-7991
Email: yesicagutierres@hotmail.com

O EME TE, LATINO BROTHERHOOD
Eastern Washington University
PUB 326
Cheney, WA 99004
Omar Torres, President
Tel: (359) 235-8156
Email: torres_ewu@hotmail.com

SOCIETY OF HISPANIC PROFESSIONAL ENGINEERS
University of Washington

207 Loew, Box 352180
Seattle, WA 98195-2180
David Mendez, Vice President
Tel: (206) 427-4250 Fax: (206) 685-0666
Web: http://students.washington.edu/shpe

SOCIETY OF LATINO ENGINEERS AND SCIENTISTS
Washington State University
P.O. Box 642713
Pullman, WA 99164-2713
Chrlena Grimes, Academic Coordinator
Tel: (509) 335-1584 Fax: (509) 335-9608

WEST VIRGINIA

SPEC. INT., HUMAN RELATIONS

TELAMON CORPORATION
West Virginia State Office 1
129 S Queen St.
Martinsburg, WV 25401
Karen Hoff, State Director
Tel: (304) 263-0916 Fax: (304) 263-4809
Email: khoff@telamon.org
Web: www.telamon.org

West Virginia State Office 2
60 W Sioux Ln.
Romney, WV 26757
Carol Mcgowan, Deputy State Director
Tel: (304) 822-4514 Fax: (304) 822-4515
Email: cmcgowan@telamon.org
Web: www.telamon.org

West Virginia State Office 5
283 Monroe St., Berkeley Plz.
Martinsburg, WV 25401
Tammy Keel, Case Manager
Tel: (304) 596-2255 Fax: (304) 596-2259
Email: tkeel@telamon.org
Web: www.telamon.org

WISCONSIN

BUSINESS

HISPANIC BUSINESS & PROFESSIONALS ASSOCIATION, INC.
833 Lombard Dr.
Racine, WI 53402
Tel: (262) 681-9730 Fax: (262) 681-9730
Email: grendon@wi.net

HISPANIC PROFESSIONALS OF GREATER MILWAUKEE
1000 N Water St.
Milwaukee, WI 53202
Tel: (414) 291-7957 Fax: (414) 291-5458
Email: amelia.macareno@hotmail.com

CHAMBER OF COMMERCE

HISPANIC CHAMBER OF COMMERCE OF WISCONSIN
816 W National Ave.
Milwaukee, WI 53204
Maria Monreal-Cameron, President/CEO
Tel: (414) 643-6963 Fax: (414) 643-6994
Email: mcameron@hccw.org
Web: www.hccw.org

CULTURAL

MEXICAN FIESTA INTERNACIONAL
1220 W Windlake
Milwaukee, WI 53215
Oscar Cervera, Executive Director
Tel: (414) 383-7066
Email: info@mexicanfiesta.org
Web: www.mexicanfiesta.org

LAW ENFORCEMENT

NATIONAL LATINO PEACE OFFICERS ASSOCIATION
Milwaukee Chapter
P.O. Box 370031
Milwaukee, WI 53237
Luis Gonzales, President
Email: lpoawisc@wi.rr.com
Web: www.nlpoa.org

MULTI-PURPOSE

CENTRO DE LA COMUNIDAD UNIDA / UNITED COMMUNITY CENTER
1028 S. 9th St.
Milwaukee, WI 53204
Dr. Bacardo Diaz, Executive Director
Tel: (414) 384-3100 Fax: (414) 645-0165
Web: www.unitedcc.org

CENTRO HISPANO OF DANE COUNTY
Affiliate of NCLR
835 W. Badger Rd.
Madison, WI 53713
Reynaldo Morales, Team Member
Tel: (608) 255-3018 Fax: (608) 255-2975
Email: reynaldo@centrohispanomadison.org
Web: www.centrohispanomadison.org

COUNCIL FOR THE SPANISH SPEAKING INC.
Milwaukee
614 W. National Ave.
Milwaukee, WI 53204
Rosa M. Dominguez, President/CEO
Tel: (414) 384-3700 Fax: (414) 384-7622
Email: jimenez@execpc.com

ESPERANZA UNIDA, INC.
1329 W. National Ave.
Milwaukee, WI 53204
Isabella Reyes, President
Tel: (414) 649-2570
Email: info@esperanzaunida.org
Web: www.esperanzaunida.org

LA CASA DE ESPERANZA, INC.
410 Arcadian Ave.
Waukesha, WI 53186
Anselmo Villareal, Executive Director
Tel: (262) 547-0887 Fax: (262) 547-0735
Email: info@lacasadeesperanza.org
Web: www.lacasadeesperanza.org

LATINOS UNITED FOR CHANGE AND ADVANCEMENT, INC.
P.O. Box 2033
Madison, WI 53701-2033
Alfonso Zepeda-Capistran, President
Tel: (262) 227-5632 Fax: (608) -0364
Email: president@madisonlucha.org
Web: www.madison.com/communities/madisonlucha

Headquarters
2607 S. 5th St.
Milwaukee, WI 53207
Lupe Martínez, President/CEO
Tel: (414) 389-6000 Fax: (414) 671-4833
Web: www.umos.org

Hills Buildiing
1673 S. 9th St.
Milwaukee, WI 53204
Lupe Martínez, President/CEO
Tel: (414) 389-6600
Web: www.umos.org

Job Center South
1644 S. 9th St.
Milwaukee, WI 53204
Lupe Martínez, President/CEO
Tel: (414) 389-6400 Fax: (414) 645-8968
Web: www.umos.org

Outback Building
1663 S. 9th St.
Milwaukee, WI 53204
Lupe Martínez, President/CEO

Tel: (414) 383-5063
Web: www.umos.org

POLITICAL ACTION

COLOMBIA SUPPORT NETWORK
P.O. Box 1505
Madison, WI 53701
Cecilia Zarate Laun, Program Director
Tel: (608) 257-8753 Fax: (608) 255-6621
Email: csn@igc.org
Web: www.colombiasupport.net

PROFESSIONAL

PERUVIAN AMERICAN MEDICAL SOCIETY
Wisconsin Chapter
2025 W. Oklahoma Ave. #112
Milwaukee, WI 53215
Dr. Eduardo Paz, President
Tel: (414) 383-6776
Email: pazepaz@aol.com
Web: www.pamsnational.org

RELIGIOUS

ARCHDIOCESE OF MILWAUKEE
Hispanic Ministry
P.O. Box 070912
Milwaukee, WI 53207-0912
Pedro Martinez, Director for Hispanic Ministry
Tel: (414) 769-3393 Fax: (414) 769-3408
Web: www.archmil.org

DIOCESE OF GREEN BAY
Hispanic Ministry
P.O. Box 23825
1825 Riverside Dr.
Green Bay, WI 54305-3825
Rudy Pineda, Director
Tel: (920) 437-7531 X8247 Fax: (920) 437-0694
Email: rpineda@gbdioc.org
Web: www.gbdioc.org

OFFICE OF HISPANIC MINISTRY
Diocese of Madison
P.O. Box 44983
Madison, WI 53744-4983
Rev. Robert C. Morlino, Bishop
Tel: (608) 821-3092 Fax: (608) 821-3139
Email: hispanicministry@straphael.org
Web: www.madisondiocese.org/ohm/index.html

RESEARCH

LATIN AMERICAN, CARIBBEAN, AND IBERIAN STUDIES PROGRAM
University of Wisconsin, Madison
1155 Observatory Dr., 209 Ingraham Hall
Madison, WI 53706
Guido Podesta, Program Director
Tel: (608) 262-2811 Fax: (608) 265-5851
Email: gpodesta@wisc.edu
Web: http://polyglot.lss.wisc.edu/laisp

SPEC. INT., EDUCATION

AURORA WEIER EDUCATIONAL CENTER
2669 N Richards St.
Milwaukee, WI 53212
Emilio Lopez, Executive Director
Tel: (414) 562-8398 Fax: (414) 562-8494

CENTER FOR LATIN AMERICAN AND CARIBBEAN STUDIES
University of Wisconsin-Milwaukee
P.O. Box 413
Milwaukee, WI 53201-0413
Kristin Ruggiero, Director
Tel: (414) 229-4401 Fax: (414) 229-2879
Email: clacs@uwm.edu
Web: www.uwm.edu/Dept/CLACS

PARTNERS FOR COMMUNITY DEVELOPMENT
1407 S 13th St.

Sheboygan, WI 53081
Lucio Fuentez, President
Tel: (920) 459-2780 Fax: (920) 459-2782
Email: lucio@partners4cd.com
Web: www.partners4cd.com

ROBERTO HERNANDEZ CENTER
University of Wisconsin Milwaukee
P. O. Box 413
Bolton Hall #272
Milwaukee, WI 53201-0413
Camila Alvarez, Outreach Specialist
Tel: (414) 229-3663 Fax: (414) 229-2250
Email: camila@uwm.edu
Web: www.hernandezcenter.uvm.edu

SPEC. INT., EMPLOYMENT

MILWAUKEE SER-JOBS FOR PROGRESS, INC.
Affiliate of SER-Jobs for Progress National, Inc.
1020-30 W. Mitchell
Milwaukee, WI 53204
Abel R. Ortíz, Executive Director
Tel: (414) 649-2640 Fax: (414) 649-2644
Email: valdez@milwaukeeser.org
Web: www.ser-national.org

SPEC. INT., SENIORS

LA GUADALUPANA SENIOR CENTER
1028 S 9th St.
Milwaukee, WI 53204
Walter Sava, Executive Director
Tel: (414) 384-2301 Fax: (414) 649-4411

LATINO AGING NETWORK
Milwaukee County Department on Aging
235 W. Galena St. #180
Milwaukee, WI 53212
Estaphani Sustien, Executive Director
Tel: (414) 289-5950 Fax: (414) 289-8525
Email: info@milwaukeecounty.com
Web: www.milwaukeecounty.com

SPEC. INT., SOCIAL INTEREST

LA CAUSA, INC.
P.O. Box 04188
Milwaukee, WI 53204-0188
Hugo Cardona, President & CEO
Tel: (414) 902-1500 Fax: (414) 647-5974
Email: lacausa@lacausa.org
Web: www.lacausa.org

LA UNION AMERICANA DE DERECHOS CIVILES DE WISCONSIN
207 E Buffalo St. #325
Milwaukee, WI 53202-5774
Laurence Dupuis, Legal Director
Tel: (414) 272-4032 Fax: (414) 272-0182
Email: liberty@aclu-wi.org
Web: www.aclu-wi.org

STUDENT ORGANIZATION

CHICANO & LATINO STUDIES CERTIFICATE STUDENT ASSOCIATION
University of Wisconsin-Madison
312 Ingraham Hall, 1155 Observatory Dr.
Madison, WI 53706
Gilberto Corral
Tel: (608) 658-1517
Email: gcorral@wisc.edu

EDUCATED LATINA LEADERS ASSOCIATION
University of Wisconsin-Madison
1402 Regent St. #422
Madison, WI 53711
Mariluz Gonzalez
Tel: (608) 661-5029
Email: mgonzalez5@wisc.edu

LA COLECTIVA
University of Wisconsin-Madison

MSC, 2nd Fl. Red Gym
Madison, WI 53706
Angelina Orozco, Co-President
Tel: (773) 615-6001
Email: la_colectiva_cosas@yahoo.com

LATINO BALL PLANNING COMMITTEE
University of Wisonsin-Madison
1 Langdon St. #412
Madison, WI 53703
Dominic Ledesma
Tel: (608) 213-8127
Email: latinoball@hotmail.com

LATINO MEN'S GROUP
University of Wisconsin-Madison
716 Langdon MSC, 2nd Fl.
Madison, WI 53706
Gerardo Mancilla
Tel: (773) 710-4374
Email: latinomensgroup@yahoo.com

LATINOS UNIDOS ORGANIZATION
University of Wisconsin, Parkside, Multicultural Affairs, WYLL D182
900 Wood Rd. Box 2000
Kenosha, WI 53141-2000
Carmen Ireland, Co-Advisor
Tel: (262) 595-2073 Fax: (262) 595-2393
Email: carmen.ireland@uwp.edu
Web: www.uwp.edu/clubs/latinos.unidos/info/info.htm

MEXICAN STUDENTS ASSOCIATION
University of Wisconsin-Madison
716 Langdon St., 2nd Fl., Red Gym
Madison, WI 53706
Norman Mercado-Silva
Tel: (608) 260-0312
Email: mexsa@lists.services.wisc.edu
Web: http://mexsa.rso.wisc.edu/

SOCIETY OF HISPANIC PROFESSIONAL ENGINEERS
University of Wisconsin-Madison
1550 Engineering Dr. #1084
Madison, WI 53706
John Miles
Tel: (608) 658-9236
Email: shpe@cae.wisc.edu
Web: http://shpemadison.org

UNIÓN PUERTORRIQUEÑA
University of Wisconsin-Madison
716 Langdon St., 2nd Fl.
Madison, WI 53706-1495
Joshua Toro, President
Tel: (608) 262-5132
Email: jatoro@wisc.edu
Web: www.wisc.edu/msc/

WYOMING

SPEC. INT., EDUCATION

CHICANO STUDIES PROGRAM
University of Wyoming
1000 E University Ave.
Laramie, WY 82070
Dr. Ed A. Munoz, Director
Tel: (307) 766-4127
Email: chicano_studies@uwyo.edu
Web: http://uwadmnweb.uwyo.edu/chicanostudies

Hispanic Publications
Publicaciones hispanas

1-2 ISSUES/YEAR

BOLETÍN APOYO
Asociación para la Conservación del Patrimonio Cultural de las Américas
P.O. Box 76932
Washington, DC 20013
Amparo R. de Torres, Editor
Tel: (202) 707-1120 **Fax:** (202) 707-1525
Email: ator@loc.gov
Web: http://apoyo.solinet.net/
Circ.: 4,500
Price: Free
Publication description: Boletín APOYO is the publication on conservation issues in Spanish reaching wide audiences.
Date established: 1990

2 ISSUES/YEAR

AZTLAN, A JOURNAL OF CHICANO STUDIES
UCLA Chicano Studies Research Center
193 Haines Hall, Box 951544
Los Angeles, CA 90095-1544
Wendy Belcher, Publications Coordinator
Tel: (310) 825-2363 **Fax:** (310) 206-1784
Email: aztlan@csrc.ucla.edu
Web: www.sscnet.ucla.edu/csrc
Circ.: 1,000
Subscription: $30.00 /year
Publication description: The UCLA Chicano Studies research center supports interdisciplinary, collaborative, and policy-oriented research on issues critical to the Chicano community the center's publication unit disseminates books, working papers and the peer-reviewed Aztlan; a journal of Chicano studies.
Date established: 1970

GASTÓN REPORT, THE
Mauricio Gaston Institute for Latino Community Development and Public Policy
University of Massachusetts, 100 Morrissey Blvd.
Boston, MA 02125
Andrés Torres, Director
Tel: (617) 287-5790 **Fax:** (617) 287-5788
Email: gaston.institute@umb.edu
Web: www.gaston.umb.edu
Circ.: 12,000
Price: Free
Publication description: Newsletter.
Date established: 1989

LATIN AMERICAN MUSIC REVIEW
University of Texas Press
P.O. Box 7819
Austin, TX 78713-7819
Dr. Gerard Behague, Editor
Tel: (512) 471-0373 **Fax:** (512) 471-7836
Email: gbehague@mail.utexas.edu
Web: www.utexas.edu/utpress
Circ.: 500
Price: $17.00 **Subscription:** $30.00/year
Publication description: LAMR examines all aspects of the musical traditions of Latin America such as primitive, folk, popular, and art music, including Hispanic-American music in North American.
Date established: 1980

NHLI NEWS
National Hispanic Leadership Institute
1901 N. Moore St. #206
Arlington, VA 22209
Marisa Rivera-Albert, Editor-in-Chief
Tel: (703) 527-6007 **Fax:** (703) 527-6009
Email: nhli@aol.com
Web: www.nhli.org
Circ.: 2,000
Price: Free
Publication description: English publication for 230 Members

LALRP JOURNAL
Latin American Literary Review Press
P.O. Box 17660
Pittsburgh, PA 15235
Ivette Miller, Editor
Tel: (412) 824-7903 **Fax:** (412) 824-7909
Email: latin@angstrom.net
Web: www.lalrp.org
Circ.: 1,200
Subscription: $26.00/year
Publication description: Audience: mainly academic.
Date established: 1972

REVIEW: LATIN AMERICAN LITERATURE & ARTS OF THE AMERICAS
The Americas Society, Inc.
680 Park Ave.
New York, NY 10021
Daniel Shapiro, Director of Literature
Tel: (212) 249-8950 **Fax:** (212) 249-5868
Email: dshapiro@as-coa.org
Web: www.americas-society.org
Circ.: 2,000
Subscription: $35.00/year
Publication description: The Americas Society promotes the understanding of the political, economic, and cultural issues that define and challenge the Americas today.
Date established: 1968

VISIÓN NEWSLETTER
Mexican-American Cultural Center
3115 W. Ashby Pl.
San Antonio, TX 78228
María Elena Gonzalez, President
Tel: (210) 732-2156 **Fax:** (210) 732-9072
Email: macce@maccsa.org
Web: www.maccsa.org
Circ.: 15,000
Price: Free
Publication description: Newsletter.
Date established: 1972

VISIONES NEWSLETTERS
Alternativas para Latinas en Autosuficiencia
1398 Valencia St.
San Francisco, CA 94110
Julie Abrams, Executive Director
Tel: (415) 826-5090 **Fax:** (415) 826-1885
Email: oficina@womensinitiative.org
Web: www.womensinitiative.org
Price: Free
Publication description: Visiones are a semester publication of the Project WINGS.
Date established: 1998

ZIVA'S SPANISH DANCE ENSEMBLE'S NEWSLETTER
Ziva's Spanish Dance Ensemble
2505 Oakenshield Dr.
Potomac, MD 20854
Víctor Cohen, Business Manager
Tel: (301) 424-1355 **Fax:** (301) 251-4125
Email: spanish_dance@hotmail.com
Web: www.members.tripod.com/~spanishdance
Circ.: 500
Price: Free
Publication description: Newsletter.
Date established: 1995

3 ISSUES/YEAR

BILINGUAL RESEARCH JOURNAL
National Association for Bilingual Education
1030 15th St. NW #470
Washington, DC 20005
Josue M. Gonzalez, Editor
Tel: (202) 898-1829 **Fax:** (202) 789-2866
Email: nabe@nabe.org
Web: www.nabe.org
Circ.: 3,000
Price: $13.00 **Subscription:** $40.00/year
Publication description: National English journal.
Date established: 1975

CEPAL REVIEW
The United Nations
2 United Nations Plz. #DC2-853
New York, NY 10017
Tel: (212) 963-8302 **Fax:** (212) 963-3489
Email: publications@un.org
Web: www.un.org/publications
Price: $15.00
Publication description: Cepal Review is the leading journal for the study of economic and social development issues in Latin America and the Caribbean.

ECOS DEL SUR
Argentine Society of Saint Louis
P.O. Box 6063
Chesterfield, MO 63006
Cristina Santa Cruz, Founder of the Society/Editor
Tel: (636) 230-5044 **Fax:** (636) 230-5044
Email: ctraboulsi@aol.com
Circ.: 400-500
Price: Free **Subscription:** $10.00/year.
Date established: 1991

JOURNAL OF LATIN AMERICAN STUDIES
Cambridge University Press
40 W. 20th St.
New York, NY 10011
Professor Paul Cammack, Editor
Tel: (212) 924-3900 **Fax:** (212) 691-3239
Email: paul.cammack@man.ac.uk
Web: www.cup.org
Circ.: 1,900
Price: $80.00
Publication description: Journal of Latin American Studies presents recent research in the field of Latin American studies in economics, geography, politics, international relations, sociology, social anthropology, economic history and cultural history.
Date established: 1969

MUSEO DEL BARRIO, EL
El Museo del Barrio
1230 5th Ave.
New York, NY 10029
Monica Armendariz, Public Relations Coordinator
Tel: (212) 831-7272 **Fax:** (212) 831-7927
Email: info@elmuseo.org
Web: www.elmuseo.org
Circ.: 10,000
Price: Free
Publication description: Bilingual newsletter for members only

NETWORKEN ESPANOL
Family Health International/Network
P.O. Box 13950
Research Triangle Park, NC 27709
Marina Mccune, Editor
Tel: (919) 544-7040 **Fax:** (919) 544-7261
Email: mmccune@fhi.org
Web: www.fhi.org
Circ.: 33,000
Subscription: $25.00/year
Publication description: FHI publications provide practical, evidence-based information for policy and community leaders, program managers, health care providers, educators and others on HIV/AIDS prevention and care, sexually transmitted infections, reproductive health, maternal health, adolescent health, contraceptive technology and gender issues.

NUEVA LUZ PHOTOGRAPHIC JOURNAL

En Foco, Inc.
32 E. Kingsbridge Rd.
Bronx, NY 10468
Charles Biasiny-Rivera, Executive Director
Tel: (718) 584-7718 **Fax:** (718) 584-7718
Email: info@enfoco.org
Web: www.enfoco.org
Circ.: 10,000
Price: $7.00 **Subscription:** $30.00/year
Publication description: To promote photographers of color, Hispanic, African American, Asian and other minorities.
Date established: 1974

PUEBLO NEWS, EL

El Pueblo, Inc.
4 N. Blount St., 2nd Fl.
Raleigh, NC 27601
Andrea Bazan Manson, Executive Director
Tel: (919) 835-1525 **Fax:** (919) 835-1526
Email: elpueblo@elpueblo.org
Web: www.elpueblo.org
Circ.: 9,000
Price: Free .
Date established: 1994

¿QUÉ TAL? NEWSLETTER

Latin America Parents Association
P.O. Box 339-340
Brooklyn, NY 11234
Maria Giuliani, Editor
Tel: (718) 236-8689
Email: info@lapa.com
Web: www.lapa.com
Circ.: 2,000
Price: Free
Publication description: Spanish newsletter for members only.

REVISTA EXEGESIS

Universidad de Puerto Rico en Humacao
Estación Postal CUH
Humacao, PR 00791-4300
Marcos Reyes-Davila, Director
Tel: (787) 850-9370 **Fax:** (787) 850-0492
Email: mf_reyes@webmail.uprh.edu
Web: cuhwww.upr.clu.edu/exegesis
Circ.: 1,500
Subscription: $12.00/year
Publication description: Local/regional Spanish journal. Academic and Creative purpose.
Date established: 1986

REVISTA INTERAMERICANA DE BIBLIOGRAFÍA

Organization of American States
1889 F St. NW
Washington, DC 20006-4499
Sara Meneses, Director
Tel: (202) 458-3140 **Fax:** (202) 458-6115
Email: smeneses@oas.org
Web: www.oas.org/culture
Circ.: 1,000
Subscription: $36.00/year
Publication description: International English newsletter.
Date established: 1951

TORRE DE PAPEL

University of Iowa
111 Phillips Hall
Iowa City, IA 52242
Jaime Orrego, Editor
Tel: (312) 335-0487 **Fax:** (319) 335-2990
Email: torredepapel@uiowa.edu
Web: www.uiowa.edu/~spanport/
Circ.: 150
Price: $10.00 **Subscription:** $21.00/year
Publication description: Includes articles on the arts of Latin American and the Caribbean.
Date established: 1990

3-4 ISSUES/YEAR

EVALUATION EXCHANGE, THE

Harvard Graduate School of Education
3 Garden St.
Cambridge, MA 02138
Stacey Miller, Publications/Communications Manager
Tel: (617) 495-9108 **Fax:** (617) 495-8594
Email: stacey_miller@harvard.edu
Web: www.hfrp.org
Circ.: 13,000
Price: Free
Publication description: Harvard Family Research Project (HFRP) publishes research on early childhood care and education, family, school and community partnerships, evaluation and accountability, and professional development, related to Hispanics.
Date established: 1995

4 ISSUES/YEAR

INFORMACIÓN

Hispanic Committee of Virginia
5827 Columbia Pike #200
Falls Church, VA 22041
Jorge Figueredo, Executive Director
Tel: (703) 671-5666 **Fax:** (703) 671-2325
Email: executivedirector@hcva.org
Web: www.hcva.org
Circ.: 2,000
Price: Free
Publication description: Newsletter.
Date established: 1998

NETWORK NEWSLETTER

Council of Latino Agencies
2437 15th St. NW
Washington, DC 20009
Rodrigo Lelva, Editor
Tel: (202) 328-9451 **Fax:** (202) 667-6135
Email: rlelva@consejo.com
Web: www.consejo.org
Circ.: 500
Price: Free .
Date established: 1977

5 ISSUES/YEAR

NOTICIAS DE NUESTRAS RAICES

Genealogical Society of Hispanic America
Southern California Chapter
P. O. Box 9606
Denver, CO 80209-0606
Pauline Salazar, Editor
Tel: (310) 204-6808 **Fax:** (310) 839-3985
Email: flora03@adelphia.net
Web: www.gsha.net
Circ.: 130
Price: Free **Subscription:** $10.00 /year
Publication description: Newsletter promotes Hispanic genealogical and historical research with a focus on California, southwestern United States and Mexico.
Date established: 1992

6 ISSUES/YEAR

CRITICAS

360 Park Ave. South
New York, NY 10010
Adriana Lopez, Editor
Tel: (646) 746-6826
Email: adlopez@reedbusiness.com
Circ.: 55,000
Subscription: $39.95/year
Publication description: Criticas is the comprehensive review of the latest in Spanish-language publishing - written in English.

RES

Editorial Televisa - USA
6355 NW 36th St.
Miami, FL 33166
Patrick Holmes, Senior Advertiser/Sales Executive
Tel: (305) 871-6400 **Fax:** (305) 871-5026
Email: pholmes@editorialtelevisa.com
Web: www.buyeditorialtelevisa.com
Circ.: 178,398
Publication description: International Spanish magazine. Because of its concept, editorial content, modern design and quality, ERES® is the leading magazine for young people. ERES® knows how to talk with its readers because it speaks their own language about their favorite artists, music, TV, fashion, beauty, amusements, sports, exercise, love, psychology, health, nutrition and other topics of interest. Throughout the year, the publication provides special issues dedicated to themes such as male/female relationships, beauty, music, the ERES® awards and the blockbuster anniversary special. ERES® is the ideal magazine to reach young women and men. .
Date established: 1997

FREEDOM SOCIALIST NEWSPAPER

Freedom Socialist Party/Radical Women
5018 Rainier Ave. South, New Freeway Hall
Seattle, WA 98118
Andrea Bauer, Managing Editor
Tel: (206) 722-2453 **Fax:** (206) 723-7691
Email: fsnews@mindspring.com
Web: www.socialism.com
Price: $0.75 **Subscription:** $8.00/year
Publication description: Socialist Feminist political party dedicated to eradicating injustice and inequality and bigotry for all people.
Date established: 1965

HORA DE CIERRE

Instituto de Prensa, Sociedad Interamericana de Prensa
1801 SW 3rd Ave.
Miami, FL 33129
Horacio Ruiz, Publisher
Tel: (305) 634-2465 **Fax:** (305) 635-2272
Email: info@sipiapa.org
Web: www.institutodeprensa.com
Circ.: 10,000
Price: Free
Publication description: International Spanish magazine.
Date established: 1992

HOY DÍA

Scholastic, Inc.
557 Broadway
New York, NY 10012
Richard Robinson, President/CEO
Tel: (212) 343-6636 **Fax:** (212) 343-6727
Email: custserv@scholastic.com
Web: www.scholastic.com
Subscription: $7.75/year
Publication description: Scholastic Inc., the global children's publishing and media company's corporate mission, which is supported through all of its divisions, is to instill the love of reading and learning for lifelong pleasure in all children.
Date established: 1991

LION EN ESPAÑOL

Lions Clubs International
300 W. 22nd St.
Oak Brook, IL 60523-8842
Fernando Fernández, Editor
Tel: (630) 571-5466 **Fax:** (630) 571-8890
Email: rkleinfe@lionsclubs.org
Web: www.lionsclubs.org
Circ.: 70,000
Subscription: $6.00/year.
Date established: 1940

LVCC NEWSLETTER

Little Village Chamber of Commerce
3610 W. 26th St., 2nd Fl.
Chicago, IL 60623
Martha De La Vega, Executive Director
Tel: (773) 521-5387 **Fax:** (773) 521-5252
Email: mdelavega@lavillitachamber.com
Web: www.lavillitachamber.com
Circ.: 1,000
Price: Free
Publication description: Newsletter of Little Village Chamber of Commerce

NABE NEWS

National Association for Bilingual Education (NABE)
1030 15th St. NW #470
Washington, DC 20005
Alicia Sosa, Director of Membership and Publications
Tel: (202) 898-1829 **Fax:** (202) 789-2866
Email: nabe_news@nabe.org
Web: www.nabe.org
Circ.: 4,500
Price: $5.00
Publication description: NABE's official news magazine is published eight times annually and distributed free of charge to its members. .
Date established: 1975

NACLA REPORT ON THE AMERICAS

North American Congress on Latin America
38 Greenen St., 4th Fl.
New York, NY 10013
Marshall Beck, Editor
Tel: (646) 613-1440 **Fax:** (646) 613-1443
Email: nacweb@nacla.org
Web: www.nacla.org
Circ.: 8,000
Price: $5.45 **Subscription:** $36.00/year
Publication description: The core of NACLA's work is its bimonthly magazine NACLA Report on the Americas, the most widely read English language publication on Latin America. .
Date established: 1967

PETRÓLEO INTERNACIONAL

Keller International Publishing Corp.
150 Great Neck Rd.
Great Neck, NY 11021
Victor Prieto, Editor
Tel: (516) 829-9210 X114
Fax: (516) 829-5414
Email: vprieto@kellerpubs.com
Web: www.kellerpubs.com
Circ.: 10,314
Publication description: Distributed in the United Estates and throughout Latin America as well. The premier Spanish-Language magazine for top level and technical management decision-makers in the oil, gas and petrochemical industry.
Date established: 1943

PORTADA

Contenido LLC
P.O. Box 20526, Park West Station
New York, NY 10025
Marcos Baer, Publisher

Tel: (212) 340-4774
Email: marcos@portada-online.com
Web: www.portada-online.com
Circ.: 1,500
Subscription: $109.00/year
Publication description: Produces news, analysis and insights to foster the development of the print media sector (newspapers and magazines) for Spanish speaking audiences.
Date established: 2002

QUE TAL
Scholastic, Inc.
557 Broadway
New York, NY 10012
Richard Robinson, President/CEO
Tel: (212) 343-6636 **Fax:** (212) 343-6727
Email: custserv@scholastic.com
Web: www.scholastic.com
Subscription: $7.75/year
Publication description: Scholastic Inc., the global children's publishing and media company's corporate mission, which is supported through all of its divisions, is to instill the love of reading and learning for lifelong pleasure in all children.
Date established: 1991

REVISTA AÉREA LATINOAMERICANA
Strato Publishing Co.
405 E. 56th St. #4E
New York, NY 10022
Elaine Asch, Editor
Tel: (212) 371-7392 **Fax:** (212) 371-1224
Email: revistaaerea@revistaaerea.com
Web: www.revistaaerea.com
Circ.: 11,200
Price: Free
Publication description: Latin American Aviation Trade magazine .
Date established: 1937

SOL, EL
Scholastic, Inc.
557 Broadway
New York, NY 10012
Richard Robinson, President/CEO
Tel: (212) 343-6636 **Fax:** (212) 343-6727
Email: custserv@scholastic.com
Web: www.scholastic.com
Subscription: $7.75/year
Publication description: Scholastic Inc., the global children's publishing and media company's corporate mission, which is supported through all of its divisions, is to instill the love of reading and learning for lifelong pleasure in all children.
Date established: 1991

SUPER ONDA
Hispanic Business, Inc.
425 Pine Ave.
Santa Barbara, CA 93117
Leslie Dinaberg, Managing Editor
Tel: (805) 964-4554 X212
Fax: (805) 964-5539
Email: leslie.dinaberg@hbinc.com
Web: www.superonda.com
Circ.: 100,000
Price: $3.99
Publication description: Focuses on the booming hispanic youth market.
Date established: 1999

7 ISSUES/YEAR

BLACK DIASPORA
Black Diaspora Comm., Ltd.
350 5th Ave. #3304
New York, NY 10118

Tel: (212) 268-8348 **Fax:** (212) 268-8370
Email: blackdias@earthlink.net
Price: $4.95 **Subscription:** $28.85/year
Publication description: Hispanic and African American publication.
Date established: 1979

8 ISSUES/YEAR

ESTYLO MAGAZINE
Mandalay Publications, Inc.
3600 Wilshire Blvd. #1903
Los Angeles, CA 90010
Daniel E. Wolfus, Publisher
Tel: (213) 383-6300 **Fax:** (213) 383-2666
Email: info@estylo.com
Web: www.estylo.com
Circ.: 162,000
Price: $2.95 **Subscription:** $9.95/year
Publication description: Bilingual; Hispanic fashion, beauty, celebrity, music, travel, food, lifestyle.
Date established: 1997

8-10 ISSUES/YEAR

PROYECTO MAGAZINE
Latin Builders Association
782 NW Le Jeune Rd. #405
Miami, FL 33126
Carmen Rodriguez, Editor
Tel: (786) 287-3362 **Fax:** (305) 446-0901
Email: proyecto@latinbuilders.org
Web: www.proyecto.org
Circ.: 1,000
Price: Free
Publication description: Local/regional Spanish magazine.
Date established: 1974

9 ISSUES/YEAR

REVISTA MARYKNOLL
Maryknoll Fathers & Brothers
P.O. Box 308
Maryknoll, NY 10545
Linda Unger, Editor
Tel: (914) 941-7590 X2438
Fax: (914) 945-0670
Email: revista@maryknoll.org
Web: www.maryknoll.org
Circ.: 75,000
Subscription: $15.00/year
Publication description: Shares the rich, spiritual experiences of the missionaries and the people with whom they work.
Date established: September 1980

10 ISSUES/YEAR

CONNECTION TO THE AMERICAS
Resource Center of the Americas
3019 Minnehaha Ave. South
Minneapolis, MN 55406
Chip Mitchell, Editor
Tel: (612) 276-0788 **Fax:** (612) 276-0898
Email: webeditor@americas.org
Web: www.americas.org
Circ.: 2,200
Price: Free
Publication description: English newsletter

IDRA NEWSLETTER
Intercultural Development Research Assoc.
5835 Callaghan Rd. #350
San Antonio, TX 78228

Maria R. Montece, Ph.D., Executive Director
Tel: (210) 444-1710 **Fax:** (210) 444-1714
Email: contact@idra.org
Web: www.idra.org
Circ.: 10,000
Price: Free
Publication description: Founded on the principle that all children deserve equal educational opportunity, the organization is dedicated to eliminating educational injustice through involvement in the areas of training, technical assistance and research.
Date established: 1973

LATIN BEAT MAGAZINE
Latin Beat Magazine
15900 Crenshaw Blvd. #223
Gardena, CA 90249
Rudolph Mangual, Editor
Tel: (310) 516-6767 **Fax:** (310) 516-9916
Email: info@latinbeatmagazine.com
Web: www.latinbeatmagazine.com
Circ.: 50,000
Price: $2.50 **Subscription:** $35.00/year
Publication description: National English magazine.
Date established: 1991

NICARAGUA MONITOR NEWSLETTER
Nicaragua Network Education Fund
1247 E St. SE
Washington, DC 20003
Katherine Hoyt, Editor
Tel: (202) 544-9355 **Fax:** (202) 544-9359
Email: nicanet@afgj.org
Web: www.nicanet.org
Circ.: 1,000
Subscription: $20.00/year
Publication description: Includes the latest news about Nicaragua and the U.S. solidarity movement along with background information on economic and environmental issues, action alerts, and book reviews. .
Date established: 1989

VOZ DE ESPERANZA, LA
Esperanza Center
922 San Pedro
San Antonio, TX 78212
Gloria Ramirez, Editor
Tel: (210) 228-0201 **Fax:** (210) 228-0000
Email: esperanza@esperanzacenter.org
Web: www.esperanzacenter.org
Circ.: 5,000
Subscription: $12.00/year

20 ISSUES/YEAR

SOUTHEAST CHICAGO OBSERVER
Southeast Chicago Development Commission
9204 S. Commercial Ave. #307
Chicago, IL 60617
Jerome A. Jajchik, Editor
Tel: (773) 768-4386 **Fax:** (773) 768-4394
Email: jjajchik@southeastchicagoobserver.com
Web: www.southeastchicagoobserver.com
Circ.: 20,000
Price: Free **Subscription:** $27.00/year
Publication description: To inform residents, promote business and encourage community growth and development.

26 ISSUES/YEAR

HISPANIC OUTLOOK IN HIGHER EDUCATION MAGAZINE, THE
The Hispanic Outlook in Higher Education
210 Route 4 East #310
Paramus, NJ 07652
Susan Lopez, Editor
Tel: (201) 587-8800 **Fax:** (201) 587-9105
Email: pub@hispanicoutlook.com
Web: www.hispanicoutlook.com
Circ.: 28,000
Price: $2.75 **Subscription:** $29.95/year
Publication description: The Hispanic Outlook in Higher Education Magazine is the Hispanic journal on tofday's college campus that reaches a broad cultural audience of educators, administrators, students, student service and community based organizations, plus corporations.
Date established: 1990

ANNUALLY

A REPORT OF THE NATIONAL TASK FORCE ON MINORITY HIGH ACHIEVEMENT
College Entrance Examination Board
45 Columbus Ave.
New York, NY 10023
Tel: (212) 713-8000 **Fax:** (212) 713-8304
Web: www.collegeboard.com
Price: $12.00
Publication description: This report describes the scope of the shortage of academically very successful Black, Latino, and Native American students and examines its implications from the perspective of the changing demographics.
Date established: 1999

AAMC DIRECTORY OF AMERICAN MEDICAL EDUCATION
Association of American Medical Colleges
2450 N St. NW
Washington, DC 20037
Laly May Johnson, Editor
Tel: (202) 828-0416 **Fax:** (202) 828-1123
Email: publications@aamc.org
Web: www.aamc.org
Subscription: $85.00/year
Publication description: The AAMC Directory of American Medical Education lists administrators, department and division chairs for all the accredited medical schools in the United States, Canada and Puerto Rico.
Date established: 1995

AGENDA DE DECORACIÓN
Casiano Communications
1700 Ave. Fernández Juncos
San Juan, PR 00909-2938
Elena Menéndez, Editor
Tel: (787) 728-3000 **Fax:** (787) 728-5948
Email: agendasedit@casiano.com
Web: www.casiano.com
Circ.: 40,000
Price: $18.25
Publication description: Puerto Rico's leading Guide for home decorating and remodeling.
Date established: 1996

AGENDA PARA LA NOVIA
Casiano Communications
1700 Ave. Fernández Juncos
San Juan, PR 00909-2938
Elena Menéndez, Editor
Tel: (787) 728-3000 **Fax:** (787) 728-5948
Email: agendasedit@casiano.com
Web: www.casiano.com
Circ.: 40,000

Price: $18.25
Publication description: Puerto Rico's Leading Wedding Planning Guide.
Date established: 1991

AGENDA PARA MAMÁ
Casiano Communications
1700 Ave. Fernández Juncos
San Juan, PR 00909-2938
Elena Menéndez, Editor
Tel: (787) 728-3000 x2450
Fax: (787) 268-1001
Email: agendasedit@casiano.com
Web: www.casiano.com
Circ.: 40,000
Price: $18.25
Publication description: The perfect publication for future parents and other family members. .
Date established: 1994

AL PRINCIPIO
Epsilon Beta Chapter of Sigma Delta Pi, The National Collegiate Hispanic Honor Society, Southwest Texas State University
Department of Modern Languages
San Marcos, TX 78666
Dr. Roberto A. Galván, Contact
Tel: (512) 245-2360 **Fax:** (512) 245-8298
Email: rg07@txstate.edu
Web: www.txstate.edu/academics
Price: $500.00
Publication description: To disseminate the Hispanic culture.
Date established: 1962

ANALES DE LA LITERATURA ESPAÑOLA CONTEMPORÁNEA
Society of Spanish and Spanish-American Studies
Department of Spanish and Portuguese, University of Colorado 134 McKenna Languages Bldg. UCB 278
Boulder, CO 80309-0278
Marilyn G. Ratciff Mensing, Publications Administrative Assistant
Tel: (303) 492-5900 **Fax:** (303) 492-3699
Email: sssas@colorado.edu
Web: www.colorado.edu/spanish/sssas/index.htm
Circ.: 2,000
Price: $30.00 .
Date established: 1975

ANUARIO DE LA COMISIÓN DE DERECHO INTERNACIONAL
The United Nations
2 United Nations Pl. #DC2-853
New York, NY 10017
Miguel Marzullo, Contact - Spanish Language Publications
Tel: (212) 963-8302 **Fax:** (212) 963-3489
Email: publications@un.org
Web: www.un.org/publications
Price: $60.00

ANUARIO DE LA COMISIÓN DE LAS NACIONES UNIDAS
The United Nations
2 United Nations Pl. #DC2-853, Dept. I004
New York, NY 10017
Miguel Marzullo, Contact - Spanish Language Publications
Tel: (212) 963-8302 **Fax:** (212) 963-3489
Email: publications@un.org
Web: www.un.org/publications
Price: $65.00

ANUARIO DE LAS NACIONES UNIDAS SOBRE DESARME
The United Nations
2 United Nations Pl. #DC2-853, Dept. I004
New York, NY 10017

Miguel Marzullo, Contact - Spanish Language Publications
Tel: (212) 963-8302 **Fax:** (212) 963-3489
Email: publications@un.org
Web: www.un.org/publications
Price: $55.00

ANUARIO HISPANO-HISPANIC YEARBOOK
TIYM Publishing Co., Inc.
6718 Whittier Ave. #130
McLean, VA 22101
Angela E. Zavala, Editor
Tel: (703) 734-1632 **Fax:** (703) 356-0787
Email: hispanicyearbook@tiym.com
Web: www.hispanicyearbook.com
Circ.: 150,000
Price: $29.95
Publication description: Annual international bilingual publication.
Date established: 1985

ANUARIO JURÍDICO DE LAS NACIONES UNIDAS
The United Nations
2 United Nations Pl. #DC2-853, Dept. I004
New York, NY 10017
Miguel Marzullo, Contact - Spanish Language Publications
Tel: (212) 963-8302 **Fax:** (212) 963-3489
Email: publications@un.org
Web: www.un.org/publications
Price: $60.00

BIENVENIDOS MAGAZINE
Coral Publications
2000 Carr. 8177 #26 PMB 145
Guaynabo, PR 00966-3762
Addie Coral Romero, Editor
Tel: (787) 720-1848 **Fax:** (787) 720-1848
Email: aromero@coral-publications.com
Web: www.coral-publications.com
Circ.: 45,000
Price: Free **Subscription:** $4.00/year
Publication description: English Magazine with editorial content focusing on tourism in Puerto Rico.
Date established: 1990

BIG BOOK OF MINORITY OPPORTUNITIES: THE DIRECTORY OF SPECIAL PROGRAMS FOR MINORITY GROUP MEMBERS
Garrett Park Press, Inc.
P.O. Box 190
Garrett Park, MD 20896-0190
Willis L. Johnson, Editor
Tel: (301) 946-2553 **Fax:** (301) 949-3955
Circ.: 500
Price: $39.95
Publication description: National English publication contains listings of career information services, employment skills banks, and financial aid sources for minorities.
Date established: 1997

BOOK OF LIST, THE
Casiano Communications
1700 Ave. Fernández Juncos
San Juan, PR 00909-2938
Loreil Albanese, Editor
Tel: (787) 728-3000 **Fax:** (787) 268-1626
Email: wpages@casiano.com
Web: www.casiano.com
Circ.: 35,000
Price: $19.30
Publication description: The leading Annual Industry Ranking Directory in Puerto Rico.
Date established: 1989

CAMARASUR ALULUAL, EL
Cámara de Comercio de Ponce y Sur de Puerto Rico
P.O. Box 7455
Ponce, PR 00732-7455

Dr. Ernesto Cordova, President
Tel: (787) 844-4400 **Fax:** (787) 844-4705
Email: camarasur@prtc.net
Web: http://ponce.inter.edu/proyecto/wtic/camara/camara.html
Circ.: 2,500
Price: Free
Publication description: Newsletter.
Date established: 1994

CARIBBEAN BUSINESS WHITE PAGES
Casiano Communications
1700 Ave. Fernández Juncos
San Juan, PR 00909-2938
Loreil Albanase, Editor
Tel: (787) 728-3000 X3410
Fax: (787) 268-1001
Email: wpedit@casiano.com
Web: www.casiano.com
Circ.: 35,000
Price: $28.75
Publication description: The leading most complete and up-to-date, business, commercial and industrial directory in Puerto Rico and the Caribbean.
Date established: 1988

CARIBBEAN YELLOW PAGES
Caribbean Publishing Co.
815 NW 57th Ave.
Miami, FL 33126
Mark Ercolin, Editor
Tel: (305) 442-4205 **Fax:** (305) 442-8329
Email: mia-sales@caribpub.com
Web: www.caribpub.com
Circ.: 50,000
Price: $35.00
Publication description: Local/regional English Yellow Pages.
Date established: 1980

CARIBBEAN/LATIN AMERICA PROFILE
Caribbean Publishing Co.
815 NW 57th Ave. #125
Miami, FL 33126
Jim Runyon, Editor
Tel: (305) 442-4205 **Fax:** (305) 442-8329
Email: mia-sales@caribpub.com
Web: www.latinamericaprofile.com
Circ.: 50,000
Price: $39.95 .
Date established: 1980

CENTER FOR LATIN AMERICAN STUDIES NEWSLETTER
Arizona State University
P.O. Box 872401
Social Sciences Bldg. #213
Tempe, AZ 85287-4502
Tod Swanson, Director
Tel: (480) 965-5127 **Fax:** (480) 965-6679
Email: latam.studies@asu.edu
Web: www.asu.edu/clas/latin/
Circ.: 200
Price: Free
Publication description: English newsletter.
Date established: 1965

CÍRCULO POÉTICO
Círculo de Cultura Panamericano
P.O. Box 469
Cedar Grove, NJ 07009-0469
Dr. Octavio de la Suaree, Editor
Tel: (973) 239-3125 **Fax:** (973) 239-3125
Email: ccp_circulo@aol.com
Web: www.circulodeculturapanamericano.org
Circ.: 700
Price: $15.00
Publication description: Contains poetry from Hispanic poets residents in the United States and from Spain, Central and South America.
Date established: 1963

CÍRCULO: REVISTA DE CULTURA
Círculo de Cultura Panamericano
P.O. Box 469
Cedar Grove, NJ 07009-0469
Elio Alba-Buffill, Editor
Tel: (973) 239-3125 **Fax:** (201) 239-3125
Email: ccpcirculo@aol.com
Web: www.circulodeculturapanamericano.org
Circ.: 650
Price: $20-40.00
Publication description: Contains scholarly works in Spanish American and Spanish literature and culture, and reviews on recently published books.
Date established: 1970

DE HECHO NEWSPAPER
Solid Future Publishing
6425 W. 52nd Ave. #1
Denver, CO 80002
German Gonzalez, Editor
Tel: (303) 975-1142 **Fax:** (303) 975-1858
Email: dehecho@solidfuture.net
Web: www.solidfuture.net
Circ.: 15,000
Price: Free
Publication description: Spanish weekly newspaper .
Date established: 1999

DELAWARE HISPANIC YELLOW PAGES
P.O. Box 423, Historic New Castle
New Castle, DE 19720
Nancy Bastidas, President/CEO
Tel: (302) 598-4344
Email: dhc@delawarehispanic.com
Web: www.delawarehispanic.com
Circ.: 10,000
Publication description: Yellow Pages for the Hispanic Community.
Date established: 1988

DESARROLLO MÁS ALLÁ DE LA ECONOMÍA
Inter-American Development Bank
External Relations Office,
1300 New York Ave. NW
Washington, DC 20577
Rafael Cruz, Senior Editor
Tel: (202) 623-1154 **Fax:** (202) 623-3531
Email: idb-books@iadb.org
Web: www.iadb.org
Price: $24.95
Publication description: Financial Publication.

DIMENSIÓN INTERNACIONAL DE LOS DERECHOS HUMANOS, LA
Inter-American Development Bank
External Relations Office, 1300 New York Ave. NW
Washington, DC 20577
Rafael Cruz, Senior Editor
Tel: (202) 623-1108 **Fax:** (202) 623-1709
Email: idb-books@iadb.org
Web: www.iadb.org
Price: $24.95
Publication description: Written by Diego RodriguezPinzón, Claudia Martin and Tomás Ojeda Quintana

DIRECTORIO COMERCIAL
SBJ Publishing Co.
P.O. Box 16783
Seattle, WA 98116
Ramón Rodríguez, Publisher
Tel: (206) 297-8532 **Fax:** (206) 706-3082
Email: rraasbj@aol.com
Web: www.latinointeraction.com
Circ.: 25,000
Price: Free .
Date established: 1998

DIRECTORIO DE AGENCIAS PARTICIPANTES Y SERVICIOS

Fondos Unidos de Puerto Rico
P.O. Box 191914
San Juan, PR 00919-1914
María Elena Lampaya, VP of Communications Department
Tel: (787) 728-8500 **Fax:** (787) 728-7099
Email: me.lampaya@fondosunidos.org
Web: www.fondosunidos.com
Circ.: 1,500
Price: Free

DIRECTORIO HISPANO

12005 NE 12th St. #26
Bellevue, WA 98005
Raúl Pérez-Calleja, Publisher
Tel: (425) 646-8846 **Fax:** (425) 646-8823
Email: raulperez@elsietedias.com
Web: www.elsietedias.com
Circ.: 25,000
Price: Free
Publication description: Telephone directory of businesses and organizations .
Date established: 1992

DIRECTORIO HISPANO

Latino Publishing, Inc.
5665 Columbia Pike
Falls Church, VA 22041
Segundo Morillo, President
Tel: (703) 671-4000 **Fax:** (703) 671-8886
Email: dhispano@hotmail.com
Web: www.latinopub.com
Circ.: 100,000
Price: Free
Publication description: Spanish Yearbook.
Date established: 1995

DIRECTORIO HISPANO DE LA FLORIDA CENTRAL

La Prensa Inc.
685 S. Roland Reagan Blvd.
Longwood, FL 32750-6403
Manuel Toro, Director
Tel: (407) 767-0070 **Fax:** (407) 767-5478
Email: laprensa@laprensaorlando.com
Web: www.laprensaorlando.com
Circ.: 65,000
Price: Free **Subscription:** $12.00/year
Publication description: Local/regional Spanish newspaper.
Date established: 1991

DIRECTORIO HISPANO DE LOUISIANA

Raices, Inc.
P.O. Box 8399
New Orleans, LA 70182
Ada Cossio, Editor
Tel: (504) 467-6023 **Fax:** (504) 286-1700
Circ.: 15,000
Price: Free
Publication description: Spanish directory of Louisiana businesses and services.
Date established: 1989

DIRECTORIO HISPANO, EL

685 S Ronald Reagan Blvd.
Longwood, FL 32750
Manuel Toro, Editor
Tel: (407) 767-0070 **Fax:** (407) 215-7214
Email: directoriohispano@laprensaorlando.com
Circ.: 65,000
Price: Free
Publication description: Local/regional Spanish publication; Audience: 135,000 readers (mercado latino).
Date established: 1985

DIRECTORIO LATINO

A.B.M. Enterprises, Inc.
P.O. Box 7360
Omaha, NE 68107

Marcos Mora, Editor
Tel: (402) 734-0279 **Fax:** (402) 934-0709
Email: abm@abm-enterprises.com
Web: www.abm-enterprises.com
Circ.: 25,000
Price: Free
Publication description: The only Spanish Yellow Pages Telephone Directory in the state of Nebraska that provides business and public service information to the Spanish speaking community. Its mission is to increase awareness and interaction between both the Spanish speaking consumer and the business community.
Date established: 1999

DIRECTORIO LATINO

Spanish Marketing
P.O. Box 252
Northborough, MA 01532
Jose Luis Garcia, Manager
Tel: (508) 393-8600 **Fax:** (508) 393-5457
Email: info@spanishmarketing.com
Web: www.eldirectoriolatino.com
Circ.: 24,000
Price: Free
Publication description: The best Spanish Yellow Pages Directory.
Date established: 1993

DIRECTORY OF PUERTO RICAN OFFICIALS

National Puerto Rican Coalition, Inc.
1901 L St. NW #802
Washington, DC 20036
Manuel Mirabal, Editor
Tel: (202) 223-3915 **Fax:** (202) 429-2223
Email: nprc@nprcinc.org
Web: www.bateylink.org
Circ.: 1,000
Price: Free .
Date established: 1994

DIRECTORY ON NATIONAL FELLOWSHIPS, INTERNSHIPS AND SCHOLARSHIPS FOR LATINO YOUTH

Congressional Hispanic Caucus Institute, Inc.
911 2nd St. NE
Washington, DC 20002
Carmen Joge, Editor
Tel: (202) 543-1771 **Fax:** (202) 546-2143
Email: cjoge@chci.org
Web: www.chci.org
Publication description: CHCI's third edition of the National Directory of Scholarships, Internships, and Fellowships for Latino Youth includes very important and useful information for Latino students and young professionals wishing to finance their higher education and enhance their educational and professional experience with leadership development opportunities.
Date established: 2000

ENTERTAINMENT

Entertainment Publications of Puerto Rico, Inc.
Bldg. 11, Calle 107, Ground Fl.,
Metro Office Park
Guaynabo, PR 00968
Alexandra Exposipo, Account Coordinator
Tel: (787) 781-7272 **Fax:** (787) 781-5464
Email: cucpr@coqui.net
Circ.: 20,000
Price: $40.00 .
Date established: 1994

ESCRIBANO, EL

St. Augustine Historical Society
271 Charlotte St.
St. Augustine, FL 32084
Overton G. Ganong, Executive Director
Tel: (904) 824-2872 **Fax:** (904) 824-2569
Email: oldhouse@aug.com

Web: www.oldesthouse.org
Circ.: 1,000
Price: $19.95 .
Date established: 1883

ESPERANZA NEWSLETTER, LA

La Esperanza, Inc.
216 N. Race St.
Georgetown, DE 19947
Marissa VonVille, Executive Director
Tel: (302) 854-9262 **Fax:** (302) 854-9277
Email: laesperanza@dmv.com
Web: www.laesperanza.org
Price: Free
Publication description: La Esperanza is grounded in a faith-based calling to provide hospitality and service to strangers in our midst who have migrated to Sussex County, Delaware.
Date established: 1996

ETHNIC GENEALOGY: A RESEARCH GUIDE

Greenwood Publishing Group
88 Post Rd. West
Westport, CT 06881
David Wilfinger, Product Coordinator
Tel: (203) 226-3571 X3385
Fax: (203) 750-9790
Email: dwilfing@greenwood.com
Web: www.greenwood.com
Price: $84.95
Publication description: This book will be useful to librarians, to genealogists, and to persons searching American Indian, Asian-American, black American, and Hispanic-American ancestries.
Date established: 1983

GOVERNMENT FINANCE STATISTICS YEARBOOK

International Monetary Fund
Publication Services,
700 19th St. NW #12-607
Washington, DC 20431
Tel: (202) 623-7430 **Fax:** (202) 623-7201
Email: publications@imf.org
Web: www.imf.org
Subscription: $80.00
Publication description: Government Finance Statistical Yearbook; Financial statistics

GRASSROOTS DEVELOPMENT (DESARROLLO DE BASE)

Inter-American Foundation(IAF)
901 N. Stuart St. 10th Fl.
Arlington, VA 22003
Paula Durbin, Public Affairs Specialist
Tel: (703) 306-4301 **Fax:** (703) 306-4365
Email: publications@iaf.gov
Web: www.iaf.gov
Circ.: 8,000
Price: Free
Publication description: The journal of IAF reports on the experiences of IAF grantees and analyzes development issues of concern to the IAF. The journal is published in English, Spanish, and Portuguese.
Date established: 1977

GUÍA HISPANIC YELLOW PAGES

Cinco Estrellas International, Inc.
4724 W. Lawrence Ave.
Chicago, IL 60630
Jordan Lichtenstain, Editor
Tel: (773) 725-4959 **Fax:** (773) 725-8075
Email: guia@chicagoguia.com
Web: www.chicagoguia.com
Circ.: 300,000
Price: Free
Publication description: Local/regional Spanish Yellow Pages.
Date established: 1979

GUIA, LA

AIDS Treatment Data Network
611 Broadway #613
New York, NY 10012
Ken Fornataro, Executive Director
Tel: (212) 260-8868 **Fax:** (212) 260-8869
Email: network@atdn.org
Web: www.atdn.org
Circ.: Variable
Price: Free
Publication description: La Guia is the Spanish language edition of The Experimental Treatment Guide.

GUIA SPANISH YELLOW PAGES

GUIA
4724 W. Lawrence Ave.
Chicago, IL 60630
Alan Bresloft, General Manager
Tel: (773) 725-4959 **Fax:** (773) 725-8075
Email: albresloft@sbcglobal.net
Web: www.chicagoguia.com
Circ.: 250,000
Price: Free
Publication description: Spanish Yellow pages directory supports an important and rapidly expanding market segment.
Date established: 1980

HACR CORPORATE BEST PRACTICES

Hispanic Association for Corporate Responsiblity
1444 I St. NW #850
Washington, DC 20005
Omar Velarde-Wong, National Director of Marketing and Communications
Tel: (202) 835-9672 **Fax:** (202) 457-0455
Email: hacr@hacr.org
Web: www.hacr.org
Circ.: 6,000
Price: Free **Subscription:** $100.00/year.
Date established: 1991

HACR HISPANICS TODAY

Hispanic Association for Corporate Responsiblity
1444 I St. NW #850
Washington, DC 20005
Omar Velarde-Wong, National Director of Marketing and Communications
Tel: (202) 835-9672 X206
Fax: (202) 457-0455
Email: hacr@hacr.org
Web: www.hacr.org
Circ.: 6,000
Price: Free **Subscription:** $100.00/year.
Date established: 1991

HEALTH IN THE AMERICAS

Pan American Health Organization
525 23rd St. NW
Washington, DC 20037
Mirta Roses Periago, Director
Tel: (202) 974-3000 **Fax:** (202) 974-3663
Email: nodarene@paho.org
Web: www.paho.org
Circ.: 8,000
Price: $60.00 .
Date established: 1997

HISPANIC AMERICAN PERIODICALS INDEX

UCLA Latin American Center
10343 Bunche Hall, 405 Hilgard Ave., Box 951447
Los Angeles, CA 90095-1447
Barbara G. Valk, Editor
Tel: (310) 825-6634 **Fax:** (310) 206-6859
Email: lacpubs@international.ucla.edu
Web: www.isop.sscnet.ucla.edu/lac/
Price: $425.00
Publication description: Hispanic American Periodicals Index (HAPI) is an annual

publication listing citations to articles, documents, reviews, bibliographies, original literary works, and other items appearing in the nearly three hundred journals published throughout the world which regularly contain information on Latin America.

HISPANIC COMMUNITY RESOURCE DIRECTORY

Washington State Commission
on Hispanic Affairs
P.O. Box 40924
Olympia, WA 98504-0924
Antonio M. Ginatta, Executive Director
Tel: (360) 753-3159 **Fax:** (360) 753-0199
Email: hispanic@cha.wa.gov
Web: www.cha.wa.gov
Circ.: 1,000
Price: Free .
Date established: 1971

HISPANIC CULTURE REVIEW JOURNAL

George Mason University
Modern and Classical Languages, MSN
3E5, 4400 University Dr.
Fairfax, VA 22030-4444
Liliana Caballero, Editor
Tel: (703) 993-2904
Email: hcr@gmu.edu
Web: www.gmu.edu/org/hcr
Circ.: 1,000
Subscription: $6.00/year
Publication description: Journal published one time a year by students of George Mason University. HCR has introduced essays, fiction and poetry written in English or Spanish focusing on topics related to the Hispanic world. .
Date established: 1991

HISPANIC SCHOLARSHIP DIRECTORY

The National Hispanic Press Foundation & WPR Publishing
941 National Press Bldg.
Washington, DC 20045
Thomas Oliver, Executive Director
Tel: (202) 662-7250
Email: tomoliver@nahponline.org
Web: www.scholarshipsforhispanics.org
Circ.: 12,000,000
Price: Free
Publication description: Hispanic Scholarship Directory is the America's leading source of scholarship and grant information for Hispanic Americans.
Date established: 1996

HISPANIC YELLOW PAGES

Hispanic Yellow Pages, Inc.
Corp 5700 Memorial Hwy. #208
Tampa, FL 33615
Ileana De Leon Devin, President
Tel: (813) 886-4787 **Fax:** (813) 881-1515
Email: jdevin@tampabay.rr.com
Web: www.buscaloenespanol.com
Circ.: 105,000
Price: Free
Date established: 1989

HISPANIC YELLOW PAGES

Hispanic Yellow Pages, Inc.
5553 Rising Sun Ave.
Philadelphia, PA 19120
Arturo Suárez, President
Tel: (215) 457-2101 **Fax:** (215) 329-6260
Email: javierhyp@hotmail.com
Circ.: 35,000
Price: Varies
Publication description: Pages for Southeatern and South Jersey State.
Date established: 1993

HISPANIC YELLOW PAGES CONNECTICUT & WESTERN MASSACHUSETTS

Connecticut Hispanic Yellow Pages, Inc.
P.O. Box 2203
Hartford, CT 06145
Héctor Torres, Editor/Publisher
Tel: (860) 560-8713 **Fax:** (860) 560-8699
Circ.: 145,000
Price: free
Publication description: Local/regional Spanish publications. There are three publications with the same name in Hartford, in Fairfield County and in Western Massachusetts.
Date established: 1989

HISPANIC YELLOW PAGES OF UTAH

Hispanic Media Services
P.O. Box 9434
Salt Lake City, UT 84109
Bruce Fereday, President
Tel: (801) 274-8814 **Fax:** (801) 274-8815
Email: sales@paginasamarillasdeutah.com
Web: www.paginasamarillasdeutah.com
Circ.: 85,000
Price: Free
Publication description: The Hispanic Yellow Pages of Utah is a locally owned telephone directory that targets the Spanish speaking population of Utah, published by Hispanic Media Services, Inc.
Date established: 1992

HISPANIC YELLOW PAGES, THE

The Hispanic Yellow Pages, Inc.
1420 Valwood Pkwy. #170
Carrollton, TX 75006
Jim Macdonald, General Manager
Tel: (214) 217-2000 **Fax:** (214) 217-2002
Email: hyp@hyptexas.com
Web: www.hyptexas.com
Circ.: 100,000
Price: Free .
Date established: 1997

INTERNATIONAL FINANCIAL STATISTICS YEARBOOK

International Monetary Fund
Publication Services, 700 19th St. NW #12-607
Washington, DC 20431
Tel: (202) 623-7430 **Fax:** (202) 623-7201
Email: publications@imf.org
Web: www.imf.org
Subscription: $95.00/year
Publication description: Financial statistics

LARASA DIRECTORY LATINO ORGANIZATIONS IN COLORADO

Latin American Research and Service Agency
309 W. 1st Ave.
Denver, CO 80223
Polly Baca, Executive Director
Tel: (303) 722-5150 **Fax:** (303) 722-5118
Email: larasa@larasa.org
Web: www.larasa.org
Circ.: 500
Subscription: $30.00 /year
Publication description: Directory for organizations/businesses, serving large proportion of latinos and government agencies.
Date established: 1964

LATINO'S YELLOW PAGES

First Latino Yellow Pages, Inc.
140 Little Falls St. #206
Falls Church, VA 22046
Rosario Hernandez, Editor
Tel: (703) 534-6050 **Fax:** (703) 534-6090
Email: latinosyp@webcombo.net
Web: www.latinosyellowpages.net

Circ.: 100,000
Price: Free
Publication description: Spanish Yellow Pages.
Date established: 1996

LIDER/LEADER POLITICAL NEWSLETTER

P.O. Box 423, Historic New Castle
New Castle, DE 19720
Nancy Bastidas, President/CEO
Tel: (302) 598-4344
Email: delaware@delawarehispanic.com
Web: www.delawarehispanic.com
Circ.: 10,000
Price: $3.00 .
Date established: 1988

MEMBERSHIP RESOURCE DIRECTORY

Latino Chamber of Commerce of Pueblo, Inc.
215 S Victoria Ave.
Pueblo, CO 81003
Sandy Gutiérrez, Executive Director
Tel: (719) 542-5513 **Fax:** (719) 542-4657
Email: info@pueblolatinochamber.com
Web: www.pueblolatinochamber.com
Circ.: 1,000
Price: Free .
Date established: 1995

MIAMI TRADENUMBERS

WorldCity, Inc.
Baltimore Executive Center, 1200 Anastasia Ave. #200
Coral Gables, FL 33134
Ken Roberts, Publisher
Tel: (305) 441-2244 **Fax:** (305) 441-9888
Email: kroberts@worldcityweb.com
Web: www.worldcityweb.com
Circ.: 5,000
Price: $49.00
Publication description: Primarily distributed in the Miami area, compiles data of Miami's trade with the rest of the world.
Date established: 1998

MICHIGAN HISPANIC DIRECTORY

Sanchez Communications
4124 W Vernor
Detroit, MI 48209
Dolores Sanchez, Publisher
Tel: (313) 841-0100 **Fax:** (313) 841-0155
Email: elcentral1@aol.com
Circ.: 15,000
Price: Free .
Date established: 1991

MINORITIES IN HIGHER EDUCATION ANNUAL STATUS REPORT

American Council of Education
1 DuPont Cir. NW #800
Washington, DC 20036
Wendy Bresler, Director of Publications
Tel: (202) 939-9380 **Fax:** (202) 939-9302
Email: pubs@ace.nche.edu
Web: www.acenet.edu
Price: $29.95
Publication description: Minorities in Higher Education Annual Status Report summarizes the most recent data on the progress of African Americans, Hispanics, Asian Americans, and American Indians in US higher education. The reports examines rates of college participation, degree attainment, higher education employment, and other trends.

MINORITY BUSINESS INFORMATION RESOURCES DIRECTORY

Diversity Information Resources, Inc.
2105 Central Ave. NE
Minneapolis, MN 55418
Leslie Bonds, Executive Director

Tel: (612) 781-6819 **Fax:** (612) 781-0109
Email: info@diversityinforesources.com
Web: www.diversityinforesources.com
Circ.: 6,000
Price: $65.00
Publication description: National English publication.
Date established: 1992

MUNDO HISPÁNICO YELLOW PAGES

Mundo Hispánico, Inc.
1927 Piedmont Cir.
Atlanta, GA 30324
Lino H. Domínguez, Publisher
Tel: (404) 881-0441 **Fax:** (404) 881-6085
Email: editorial@mundohispanico.com
Web: www.mundohispanico.com
Circ.: 64,000
Price: Free **Subscription:** $100.00/year
Publication description: Spanish newspaper.
Date established: 1979

NACME JOURNAL

National Action Council for Minorities in Engineering
440 Hamilton Ave. #302
White Plains, NY 10601-1813
Alex A. Johnson, Administrator
Tel: (914) 539-4010 **Fax:** (914) 539-4032
Email: ajohnson@nacme.org
Web: www.nacme.org
Circ.: 15,000
Price: Free
Publication description: NACME has provided leadership and support for the national effort to increase the representation of successful African American, American Indian and Latino women and men in engineering and technology, math- and science-based careers.
Date established: 1974

NATIONAL DIRECTORY OF LATINO ELECTED OFFICIALS

National Association of Latino Elected Officials Educational Fund, Inc.
1122 W. Washington Blvd., 3rd Fl.
Los Angeles, CA 90015
Erica Bernal, Director of Communications
Tel: (213) 747-7606 **Fax:** (213) 747-7664
Email: info@naleo.org
Web: www.naleo.org
Circ.: 2,500
Price: $35.00
Publication description: The directory is the most comprehensive listing of Latino elected officials.
Date established: 1984

NATIONAL MINORITY AND WOMEN-OWNED BUSINESS DIRECTORY

Diversity Information Resources, Inc.
2105 Central Ave. NE
Minneapolis, MN 55418
Leslie Bonds, Executive Director
Tel: (612) 781-6819 **Fax:** (612) 781-0109
Email: info@diversityinforesources.com
Web: www.diversityinforesources.com
Circ.: 6,000
Price: $115.00 .
Date established: 1969

PADF ANNUAL REPORT

Pan American Development Foundation (PADF)
1889 F St. NW 2nd Fl.
Washington, DC 20006
Amy Coughenour, Deputy Director
Tel: (202) 458-3969 **Fax:** (202) 458-6316
Email: padf-dc@padf.org
Web: www.padf.org
Circ.: 2,000
Price: Free

Publication description: International bilingual newsletter.
Date established: 1962

PAGINAS AMARILLAS DE COLORADO

6795 E. Tennessee Ave. #355
Denver, CO 80224
Martha Rubí, Managing Partner
Tel: (303) 377-6664 **Fax:** (303) 377-6665
Email: m_rubi@paginasadc.com
Web: www.paginasadc.com
Circ.: 60,000
Price: Free
Publication description: Spanish.
Date established: 1996

PÁGINAS AMARILLAS HISPANAS-HISPANIC YELLOW PAGES

Casablanca Publishing, Inc.
P. O. Box 191033
Atlanta, GA 31119
Zaida González, Editor
Tel: (404) 844-0600 **Fax:** (404) 844-0626
Email: info@paginasamarillas-atl.com
Web: www.paginasamarillas-atl.com
Circ.: 80,000
Price: Free
Publication description: Local/regional Spanish Yellow Pages.
Date established: 1989

PARTNERS OF THE AMERICAS ANNUAL REPORT

Partners of the Americas
1424 K St. NW #700
Washington, DC 20005
Claudia C. Calderón, Publications Coordinator
Tel: (202) 628-3300 X225
Fax: (202) 628-3306
Email: info@partners.net
Web: www.partners.net
Price: Free
Publication description: Annual report

PLACES TO GO

Coral Publications
2000 Carr. 8177 #26 PMB 145
Guaynabo, PR 00966-3762
Addie Coral Romero, Publisher/Editor-in-Chief
Tel: (787) 720-1848 **Fax:** (787) 720-1848
Email: aromero@coral-publications.com
Web: www.coral-publications.com
Circ.: 300,000
Price: Free
Publication description: Places to Go is a full color, practical carry-around pocket guide. .
Date established: 1998

PROGRESO, POBREZA Y EXCLUSIÓN

Inter-American Development Bank
1300 New York Ave. NW
Washington, DC 20577
Rafael Cruz, Senior Editor
Tel: (202) 623-1108 **Fax:** (202) 623-1709
Email: idb-books@iadb.org
Web: www.iadb.org
Price: $24.95

PUBLICATIONS CATALOG

Pan American Health Organization
525 23rd St. NWt
Washington, DC 20037
Dr. Mirta Roses, Director
Tel: (202) 974-3086 **Fax:** (202) 338-0869
Web: www.paho.org
Price: Free
Publication description: Publications Catalog contains information and description of the technologies.

PUERTO RICO OFFICIAL INDUSTRIAL DIRECTORY

Direct Marketing & Media Group
P.O. Box 9024182
San Juan, PR 00902-4182
Lilia Molina Ruiz, President
Tel: (787) 268-1111 **Fax:** (787) 268-7044
Email: lmolina@dmmgonline.com
Circ.: 5,000
Price: $167.54
Publication description: The most comprehensive, in-depth database profiling nearly 420,000 businesses and 1,200,000 executives by name and title.
Date established: 1966

RAZA YELLOW PAGES, LA

Rossi Publications, Inc.
6001 N. Clark St.
Chicago, IL 60660
Robert J. Armband, Associate Publisher
Tel: (773) 273-2900 **Fax:** (773) 273-2927
Email: info@laraza.com
Web: www.laraza.com
Price: Free
Publication description: La Raza Yellow Pages is Chicago's leading Spanish Language yellow pages.
Date established: 1997

SER AMERICA

Ser-Jobs for Progress
5215 N. O'Connor Rd. #2550
Irving, TX 75039
Raul Santa, Editor
Tel: (972) 506-7815 X317
Fax: (972) 506-7832
Web: www.ser-national.org
Price: Free

SOLUCIÓN, HISPANIC YELLOW PAGES, LA

Solid Future Publishing
6425 W. 52nd Ave. #1
Denver, CO 80002
Al Mc Gregor, President
Tel: (303) 975-1142 **Fax:** (303) 975-1858
Email: almc@solidfuture.net
Web: www.solidfuture.net
Circ.: 50,000
Price: Free
Publication description: Spanish Yellow Pages Directory for the Denver Metro Area.
Date established: 1996

SOURCE BOOK OF MULTICULTURAL EXPERTS, THE

Multicultural Marketing Resources, Inc.
286 Spring St. #201
New York, NY 10013
Lisa Skriloff, Publisher/Editor
Tel: (212) 242-3351 **Fax:** (212) 691-5969
Email: lisa@multiculturalmarketingresources.com
Web: www.multiculturalmarketingresources.com
Circ.: 11,000
Price: $59.95
Publication description: The Source Book of Multicultural Experts is a desktop reference guide to experts on many different cultural and lifestyle markets such as Hispanic, Asian American, African American, women, and gay/lesbian.
Date established: 1998

SOUTHWEST DETROIT BUSINESS DIRECTORY

Latino Press Media, Inc.
1494 Junction St.
Detroit, MI 48209
Elías M. Gutiérrez, Publisher
Tel: (313) 841-9333 **Fax:** (313) 841-2950

Email: marketing@latinodetroit.com
Web: www.latinodetroit.com
Circ.: 30,000
Price: Free
Publication description: Newspaper with a Hispanic-Latino audience .
Date established: 2001

SPANISH INSTITUTE ANNUAL REPORT, THE

The Spanish Institute
684 Park Ave.
New York, NY 10021
Inmaculada Habsburgo, President
Tel: (212) 628-0420 **Fax:** (212) 734-4177
Email: information@spanishinstitute.org
Web: www.spanishinstitute.org
Price: Free

SPANISH TELEPHONE DIRECTORY

Spanish Publications, Inc.
6601 Tarnef St. #200
Houston, TX 77074
Marion Dueñas, Editor
Tel: (713) 774-4652 **Fax:** (713) 774-4666
Circ.: 125,000
Price: Free
Publication description: Dedicated to providing the Hispanic community with timely, accurate, objective, and complete information pertinent to the community. .
Date established: 1993

SPANISH YELLOW PAGES/ LAS PÁGINAS AMARILLAS EN ESPAÑOL

13343 SE Stark
Portland, OR 97233
Victoria Lewis, Marketing/Sales Manager
Tel: (503) 257-2333 **Fax:** (503) 257-2449
Email: info@myspanishyellowpages.com
Web: www.myspanishyellowpages.com
Circ.: 100,000
Price: Free
Publication description: Spanish directory.
Date established: 1994

STATISTICAL ABSTRACT OF LATIN AMERICA

UCLA Latin American Center
10343 Bunche Hall, 405 Hilgard Ave., Box 951442
Los Angeles, CA 90095-1447
James W. Wilkie, Editor
Tel: (310) 825-6634 **Fax:** (310) 206-6859
Email: lacpubs@international.ucla.edu
Web: www.isop.ucla.edu/lac/sala.asp
Circ.: 1,096
Price: $325.00
Publication description: Statistical Abstract of Latin America publishes current reliable statistics on the societies, economics, and politics of Latin America and guides users to additional quantitative publications and statistical sources on the region.

TRADEAMERICAS

WorldCity, Inc.
Baltimore Executive Ctr.,
1200 Anastasia Ave. #200
Coral Gables, FL 33134
Ken Roberts, Publisher
Tel: (305) 441-2244 **Fax:** (305) 441-9888
Email: kroberts@worldcityweb.com
Web: www.worldcityweb.com
Circ.: 15,000
Price: $99.00 **Subscription:** $72.00/year
Publication description: Hemispheric distribution; guide to trade, investment and business in the western hemisphere.
Date established: 1998

VEGA HISPANIC YELLOW PAGES

Vega & Associates
2721 Prosperity Ave. #200
Fairfax, VA 22031
Francisco Vega, Jr., President/CEO
Tel: (703) 908-9600 **Fax:** (703) 908-9400
Email: fvega@vegapages.com
Web: www.vegapages.com
Circ.: 160,000
Price: Free **Subscription:** $50.00/year
Publication description: Spanish-language yellow pages directory.
Date established: 1985

VIVA DIRECTORY

Albuquerque Hispanic Chamber of Commerce
1309 4th St. SW
Albuquerque, NM 87102
Loretta Armenta, President
Tel: (505) 842-9003 **Fax:** (505) 764-9664
Email: loretta_armenta@ahcnm.org
Web: www.ahcnm.org
Circ.: 5,000
Price: Free
Publication description: Local/regional English membership directory.
Date established: 1993

WORLD DEVELOPMENT REPORT

The World Bank Bookstore
P.O. Box 960
Herndon, VA 20172
Tel: (800) 645-7247 **Fax:** (703) 661-1501
Email: books@worldbank.org
Web: www.worldbank.org/publications
Circ.: 50,000
Price: $26.00
Publication description: World Development Report examines, over a 50 year period, the relationship between competing policy objectives of reducing poverty, maintaining growth, improving social cohesion, and protecting the environment.
Date established: 1978

YEARBOOK OF LABOUR STATISTICS

International Labor Office
1828 L St. NW #600
Washington, DC 20036
Marjorie Crow, Marketing Assistant
Tel: (202) 653-7652 **Fax:** (202) 653-7687
Email: crow@ilo.org
Web: www.us.ilo.org
Price: $184.00
Publication description: Anuario de Estadísticas del Trabajo. This publication is distributed around the world and is one of the most renowned publications by the ILO.
Date established: 1936

YEARBOOK OF THE UNITED NATIONS

The United Nations
2 United Nations Pl. #DC2-853
New York, NY 10017
Tel: (212) 963-8302 **Fax:** (212) 963-3489
Email: publications@un.org
Web: www.un.org/publications
Price: $150.00
Publication description: The Yearbook of the United Nations, comprehensive and reliable, is the primary reference work on the United Nations.

YELLOW PAGES IN SPANISH

Eventos Premium
6101 Idlewild Rd. #328
Charlotte, NC 28212
Hilda Gurdian, Publisher
Tel: (704) 568-6966 **Fax:** (704) 568-8936
Email: hgurdian@lanoticia.com
Web: www.lanoticia.com

Circ.: 26,000
Price: Free **Subscription:** $52.00/year
Publication description: An annual guide containing information on businesses interested in serving the Latin American market in the Charlotte region.
Date established: 1997

BIANNUALLY

CENTRO: JOURNAL OF THE CENTER FOR PUERTO RICAN STUDIES

Center for Puerto Rican Studies,
Hunter College
695 Park Ave., 14th Fl.
New York, NY 10021
Xavier F. Totti, Editor
Tel: (212) 772-5686 **Fax:** (212) 650-3673
Email: centro-journal@hunter.cuny.edu
Web: www.centropr.org
Circ.: 750
Price: $35.00
Publication description: The journal is a multi- and interdisciplinary, bilingual, referred publication of the center for Puerto Rican Studies. It contains Scholarly articles in the humanities, and the social and natural sciences, as well as interpretative essays, interviews, fiction, book reviews, and art work that address the Puerto Rican experience in the island and throughout the Diaspora.
Date established: 1987

DIÁLOGO MAGAZINE

Center for Latino Research,
DePaul University
2320 N. Kenmore Ave. #563
Chicago, IL 60614
Dr. Felix Masud-Piloto, Director
Tel: (773) 325-7316 **Fax:** (773) 325-7166
Email: clr@depaul.edu
Web: www.depaul.edu/~dialogo
Circ.: 6,000
Price: Free
Publication description: Diálogo is a multilingual publication that strives to provide an inclusive forum by publishing articles, essays, interviews, and creative work concerning Latino communities in the United States and their connections to Latin America.
Date established: 1985

IBERO'S VOICE NEWSLETTER

Ibero American Action League, Inc.
911 E. Main St.
Rochester, NY 14605-2722
Eugenio Marlin, Editor
Tel: (585) 256-8900 **Fax:** (585) 256-0120
Email: eamarlin@iaal.org
Web: www.iaal.org
Circ.: 5,000
Price: Free
Publication description: Provides services to empower and to find opportunities, to enable the latino community and others to reach for a better life.
Date established: 1995

LATINO(A) RESEARCH REVIEW JOURNAL

Center for Latino, Latin American and Caribbean Studies (CELAC)
CELAC, SS-247, University at Albany, SUNY
Albany, NY 12222
Dr. Edna Acosta-Belén, Editor
Tel: (518) 442-4590 **Fax:** (518) 442-4790
Email: lrr@albany.edu
Web: http://albany.edu/celac/index.html
Circ.: 1,000
Subscription: $25.00/year.
Date established: 1995

LATINO ELECTION HANDBOOK

National Association of Latino Elected and Appointed Officials Educational Fund
5800 S. Eastern Ave. #365
Los Angeles, CA 90040
Erica Bernal, Communications Director
Tel: (323) 720-1932 **Fax:** (323) 720-9519
Email: info@naleo.org
Web: www.naleo.org
Circ.: 2,500
Price: $15.00
Publication description: Reports how many Latinos voted in the elections.
Date established: 1984

MINORITY STUDENT OPPORTUNITIES IN UNITED STATES MEDICAL SCHOOLS

Association of American Medical Colleges
2450 N St. NW
Washington, DC 20037
Laly May Johnson, Editor
Tel: (202) 828-0416 **Fax:** (202) 828-1123
Email: publications@aamc.org
Web: www.aamc.org
Circ.: 500
Price: $12.00
Publication description: The data published show the number of minority applicants, the number offered an acceptance, the number of matriculants, and the number of graduates by gender and racial/ethnic groups.
Date established: 1987

NATIONAL DIRECTORY OF HISPANIC ORGANIZATIONS

Congressional Hispanic Caucus Institute, Inc.
911 2nd St. NE
Washington, DC 20002
DeAnna Vasquez, Operations Director
Tel: (202) 543-1771 **Fax:** (202) 546-2143
Email: dvasquez@chci.org
Web: www.chci.org
Circ.: 20,000
Price: $5.00
Publication description: Directory of Hispanic non-profit organizations.
Date established: 1990

PLUMA FRONTERIZA

Chicano Studies Program University of Texas at El Paso
Graham Hall #104
El Paso, TX 79968-0563
Raymundo E. Rojas, Editor
Tel: (915) 747-5462 **Fax:** (915) 747-6501
Email: chicstds@utep.edu
Web: www.utep.edu/chicano
Price: Free
Publication description: A publication dedicated to Chicano and Latino writers.

PODER NEWSLETTER

Texas Fiesta Educativa, Inc.
1017 N. Main Ave. #207
San Antonio, TX 78212
Yvette Hinojosa, Project Director
Tel: (210) 222-2637 **Fax:** (210) 475-9283
Email: poder@tfepoder.org
Web: www.tfepoder.org
Circ.: NA
Price: Free .
Date established: 1988

PROMESA DE UN FUTURO BRILLANTE, LA

National Latino Children's Institute
1325 N. Flores #114
San Antonio, TX 78212
Rebeca María Barrera, President
Tel: (210) 228-9997 **Fax:** (210) 228-9972
Email: nlci@nlci.org
Web: www.nlci.org
Circ.: 5,000

Price: Free .
Date established: 1997

RAZA LAW JOURNAL, LA

La Raza Law Students Association,
UC Berkeley
440 N. Addition Boat Hall, School of Law,
University of California
Berkeley, CA 94720
Kira Abrams, Publications Coordinator
Tel: (510) 642-9351 **Fax:** (510) 643-6171
Email: kabrams@law.berkeley.edu
Web: www.boalt.org/lrlj/
Circ.: 500
Price: $27.00 **Subscription:** $53.00/year
Publication description: The Berkeley La Raza Law Journal is celebrating its twentieth anniversary as the longest continually published legal academic journal devoted to Latina/o issues.
Date established: 1988

SOUTHERN NEVADA HISPANIC YELLOW PAGES

Southern Nevada Hispanic Yellow Pages
1051 Northeastern Ave.
Las Vegas, NV 89101
Eddie Escobedo, Jr., Associate Publisher
Tel: (702) 639-9300 **Fax:** (702) 639-9400
Email: vendo@aol.com
Web: www.elmundo.net/pages/eng/yellowpages.html
Circ.: 25,000
Price: Free
Publication description: Yellow Pages

SPAIN: THE BUSINESS LINK

The Spain-U.S. Chamber of Commerce
350 5th Ave. #2029, The Empire State Bldg.
New York, NY 10118
John Whitman, Editor
Tel: (212) 967-2170 X21
Fax: (212) 564-1415
Email: info@spainuscc.org
Web: www.spainuscc.org
Circ.: 2,000
Price: $8.00 **Subscription:** $20.00/year
Publication description: A bi-annual business journal that delivers business news with a uniquely Spanish perspective.
Date established: 1959

TALLER PUERTORRIQUEÑO CALENDAR OF EVENTS

Taller Puertorriqueño
2721 N. 5th St.
Philadelphia, PA 19133
Dora Viacava, Outreach Coordinator
Tel: (215) 426-3311 **Fax:** (215) 426-5682
Email: dviacava@tallerpr.org
Web: www.tallerpr.org
Price: Free
Publication description: To preserve, develop and promote Puerto Rican artistic and cultural traditions, as well as to support a better understanding of other Latin American Cultures.
Date established: 1974

UNITE MAGAZINE

Union of Needletrades Industrial and Textile Employees
275 7th Ave.
New York, NY 10001
Leyla Vurao, Editor
Tel: (212) 265-7000 **Fax:** (212) 765-9541
Email: webmaster@uniteunion.org
Web: www.uniteunion.org
Circ.: 400,000
Price: Free
Publication description: A new chapter in the history of the U.S. labor movement began in 1995 with the founding of UNITE (Union of Needletrades, Industrial and Textile Employees). The new union was formed by the merger of two of the nation's oldest unions, the International Ladies' Garment Workers' Union (ILGWU) and the Amalgamated Clothing and Textile Workers Union (ACTWU). Also, published in Spanish.
Date established: 1995

VENTANA, LA

Hispanic Education Center
580 E. Stevens St. #2A
Indianapolis, IN 46203
Meriam Davis, Executive Director
Tel: (317) 634-5022 **Fax:** (317) 634-0442
Email: heclaura@hotmail.com
Web: www.hispaniceducationcenter.org
Circ.: 700
Price: Free
Publication description: La Ventana is a newsletter of Hispanic Education Center.
Date established: 1988

BIMONTHLY

BIABOARD, AEROPOSTAL

HCP/Aboard In-flight, A Division of Biscayne Bay Publishing, Inc.
1 Herald Plz., 4th Fl.
Miami, FL 33132
Garry Duell, Publisher
Tel: (305) 376-2735 **Fax:** (305) 995-8108
Email: adsbyemail@herald.com
Web: www.aboardpublishing.com
Price: Free **Subscription:** $24.95/year.
Date established: 1998

ABOARD, ECUATORIANA

HCP/Aboard In-flight, A Division of Biscayne Bay Publishing, Inc.
1 Herald Plz., 4th Fl.
Miami, FL 33132
Garry Duell, Publisher
Tel: (305) 376-2735 **Fax:** (305) 995-8108
Web: www.aboardpublishing.com
Price: Free **Subscription:** $24.95/year.
Date established: 1998

ABOARD, GRUPO TACA (COSTA RICA, EL SALVADOR, HONDURAS, GUATEMALA, NICARAGUA)

HCP/Aboard In-flight, A Division of Biscayne Bay Publishing, Inc.
1 Herald Plz., 4th Fl.
Miami, FL 33132
Garry Duell, Publisher
Tel: (305) 376-2735 **Fax:** (305) 995-8108
Web: www.aboardpublishing.com
Price: Free **Subscription:** $24.95/year
Publication description: International bilingual magazine.
Date established: 1981

ABOARD, LADECO

HCP/Aboard In-flight, A Division of Biscayne Bay Publishing, Inc.
1 Herald Plz., 4th Fl.
Miami, FL 33132
Garry Duell, Publisher
Tel: (305) 376-2735 **Fax:** (305) 995-8108
Web: www.aboardpublishing.com
Price: Free **Subscription:** $24.95/year.
Date established: 1998

ABOARD, LAN-CHILE

HCP/Aboard In-flight, A Division of Biscayne Bay Publishing, Inc.
1 Herald Plz., 4th Fl.
Miami, FL 33132
Garry Duell, Publisher
Tel: (305) 376-2735 **Fax:** (305) 995-8108

Web: www.aboardpublishing.com
Price: Free **Subscription:** $24.95/year.
Date established: 1976

ABOARD, LLOYD AEREO BOLIVIANO
HCP/Aboard In-flight, A Division of
Biscayne Bay Publishing, Inc.
1 Herald Plz., 4th Fl.
Miami, FL 33132
Garry Duell, Publisher
Tel: (305) 376-2735 **Fax:** (305) 995-8108
Web: www.aboardpublishing.com
Price: Free **Subscription:** $24.95/year.
Date established: 1998

ABOARD, PLUNA
HCP/Aboard In-flight, A Division of
Biscayne Bay Publishing, Inc.
1 Herald Plz., 4th Fl.
Miami, FL 33132
Garry Duell, Publisher
Tel: (305) 376-2735 **Fax:** (305) 995-8108
Web: www.aboardpublishing.com
Price: Free **Subscription:** $24.95/year.
Date established: 1998

AMÉRICAS MAGAZINE
Organization of American States
17th St. Constitution Ave. NW
Washington, DC 20006
James Patrick Kiernan, Editor
Tel: (202) 458-3000 **Fax:** (202) 458-3171
Email: americasmagazine@oas.org
Web: www.americas.oas.org
Circ.: 55,000
Price: $3.50/ **Subscription:** $18.00/year
Publication description: International bilingual
magazine.
Date established: 1949

ARTE AL DÍA INTERNATIONAL MAGAZINE
American Art Corporation
2150 Coral Way #6B
Miami, FL 33145
Hernan Carrara, Marketing Director
Tel: (305) 854-3050 **Fax:** (305) 854-0760
Email: hcarrara@artealdia.com
Web: www.artealdia.com
Circ.: 25,000
Price: $7.00 **Subscription:** $48.00/year
Publication description: Diffusion of
contemporary Latin American art.
Date established: 1980

ARTE AL DÍA NEWSPAPER
American Art Corporation
2150 Coral Way #6B
Miami, FL 33145
Diego Costa Peuser, Editor
Tel: (305) 854-3050 **Fax:** (305) 854-0760
Email: diegocostapeuser@artealdia.com
Web: www.artealdia.com
Circ.: 25,000
Price: $7.00 **Subscription:** $48.00/year.
Date established: 1980

BOLETÍN INFORMATIVO
Centro Español de Washington, DC
P.O. Box 9485
Washington, DC 20016
Guadalupe de la Portilla, President
Tel: (703) 803-7187
Web: www.cewdc.org
Price: Free **Subscription:** 30.00/year
Publication description: Boletín Informativo
compiles information on Spanish current
events and upcoming activities of the Centro
Español de Washington, DC and other
Spanish cultural centers, along with articles
and photographs from recent center events.
Date established: 1996

BRAZILIAN PAPER, THE
P.O. Box 970458
Coconut Creek, FL 33097
Marcus César, Editor
Tel: (954) 782-6464 **Fax:** (954) 753-5054
Email: paper98@bellsouth.net
Web: www.brazilianpaper.net
Circ.: 15,000
Price: Free .
Date established: 1995

CARISMA Y VIDA CRISTIANA
Strang Communications
600 Rinehart Rd.
Lake Mary, FL 32746
Lydia Morales, Editor
Tel: (407) 333-0600 **Fax:** (407) 333-7100
Email: vida@strang.com
Web: www.vidacristiana.com
Circ.: 30,000
Price: $2.50 **Subscription:** $12.98/year.
Date established: 1995

**CASA & ESTILO INTERNACIONAL
MAGAZINE**
Linda International Publishing
12182 SW 128th St.
Miami, FL 33186
José Alfonso Niño, Editor in Chief
Tel: (305) 378-4466 **Fax:** (305) 378-9951
Email: janino@casayestilo.com
Web: www.casaestilo.com,www.estilonet.
com
Circ.: 60,000
Price: $19.00 **Subscription:** $17.00/year
Publication description: National bilingual
publication.
Date established: 1995

CATALINA MAGAZINE
CDK Media, LLC
1230 Ave. of Americas, 7th Fl.
New York, NY 10020
Cathy Areu Jones, Publisher/Editorial
Director
Tel: (212) 745-1363 **Fax:** (212) 202-7608
Email: info@catalinamagazine.com
Web: www.catalinamagazine.com
Circ.: 30,000
Price: $2.95 **Subscription:** $10.00/year
Publication description: English-language,
national lifestyle magazine targeting Hispanic
American women.
Date established: 2001

CRÓNICA DE HOLLYWOOD, LA
Alexander Pillin Communications
4913 Melrose Ave.
Los Angeles, CA 90029
Tracey Alexander, Publisher
Tel: (323) 464-0515 **Fax:** (323) 469-9979
Email: traceyandboris@aol.com
Circ.: 6,000
Price: Free
Publication description: Teach art and culture
to the Hispanic American public.
Date established: 1988

EAST TENNESSEE CATHOLIC, THE
Diocese of Knoxville
P.O. Box 11127
Knoxville, TN 37939-1127
John A. Kramer, Jr., Director
Tel: (865) 584-3307 **Fax:** (865) 584-8124
Email: postmaster@etcatholic.com
Web: www.etcatholic.com
Circ.: 18,700
Price: Free
Publication description: Catholic Social
Services newsletter.
Date established: 1993

ESTRELLA DE NICARAGUA, LA
P.O. Box 16-1094
Miami, FL 33116-1094
Nicolás López-Maltez, Editor
Tel: (305) 386-6491 **Fax:** (305) 386-7591
Email: nicolas@estrelladenicaragua.com
Web: www.estrelladenicaragua.com
Circ.: 35,000
Price: Free
Publication description: Local/regional
Spanish newspaper.
Date established: 1986

EXPLOSIÓN, LA
La Explosión Publication
P.O. Box 5744
Valdosta, GA 31603
Rita Palomba, Editor/Owner
Tel: (229) 245-0572 **Fax:** (229) 245-7791
Email: laexplo@surfsouth.com
Circ.: 10,000
Price: Free
Publication description: Bilingual tabloid.
To assist Hispanics in connecting with
merchants for all their needs and vice versa.
Also, to give them news and entertainment
from their particular country.
Date established: 1998

GACETA IBEROAMERICANA
P.O. Box 4213
Gaithersburg, MD 20885
Raúl Miranda Rico, Director/Editor
Tel: (301) 926-7848 **Fax:** (301) 926-7848
Email: editor@gacetaiberoamericana.com
Web: www.gacetaiberoamericana.com
Circ.: 10,000
Subscription: $25.00/year
Publication description: Gaceta de actualidad
literaria y cultural.
Date established: 1988

HHCC NEWSLETTER
Houston Hispanic Chamber of Commerce
2900 Woodridge Dr. #312
Houston, TX 77087
Iris Correa, President/CEO
Tel: (713) 644-7070 **Fax:** (713) 644-7377
Email: icorrea@houstonhispanicchamber.
com
Web: www.houstonhispanicchamber.com
Circ.: Price: Free

HISPANIC CHAMBER NEWS
Hispanic Chamber of Commerce of
Louisiana
P.O. Box 5985
Metairie, LA 70009
Cynthia Ceballos, Editor
Tel: (504) 885-4262 **Fax:** (504) 887-5422
Web: www.hccl.biz
Circ.: 250
Price: Free
Publication description: Bilingual newsletter
for members only.
Date established: 1988

HOLA BERKS
Reading Eagle Company
P.O. Box 582
Reading, PA 19603-0582
Félix Alfonso Peña, Editor
Tel: (610) 371-5038 **Fax:** (610) 371-5098
Email: holaberks@readingeagle.com
Web: www.holaberks.com
Circ.: 15,000
Price: Free
Publication description: Spanish tabloid.
Date established: 1999

HOMBRE MAGAZINE
Hombre Publishing Group
244 5th Ave. #2073
New York, NY 10001
Robert Dominguez, Editor
Tel: (212) 340-1345 **Fax:** (212) 591-6401
Email: robert@hombremagazine.com
Web: www.hombremagazine.com
Subscription: $12.00/6 issues
Publication description: Spanish Magazine
for the men.

IMPACTO
Impacto Newspaper
P.O. Box 544
Annandale, VA 22003
Julio C. Durán G., Editor/Publisher
Tel: (703) 916-0238 **Fax:** (703) 914-6648
Email: jduran@usalatino.zzn.com
Circ.: 15,000
Price: Free **Subscription:** $24.00/year
Publication description: Local/regional
Spanish tabloid.
Date established: 1986

INFO CAMERA FLORIDA NEWSLETTER
Southwest Florida Hispanic
Chamber of Commerce
10051 McGregor Blvd. #204
Fort Myers, FL 33919
Leonardo Garcia, Executive Director
Tel: (239) 418-1441 **Fax:** (239) 418-1475
Email: hispanicchamber.lg@earthlink.com
Web: www.swflhispanicchamber.org
Circ.: 600
Price: Free .
Date established: 1989

INFORMATIVO LATINO
Latin American Coalition
5471-A Central Ave.
Charlotte, NC 28212
Angeles Ortega Moore, Executive Director
Tel: (704) 531-3848 **Fax:** (704) 531-3850
Email: newsletter@latinamericancoalition.
org
Web: www.latinamericancoalition.org
Circ.: 500
Price: Free .
Date established: 1990

INTÉRPRETE MAGAZINE, EL
United Methodist Communications
P.O. Box 320
Nashville, TN 37202
Amanda Bachus, Editor
Tel: (615) 742-5113 **Fax:** (615) 742-5460
Email: abachus@umcom.org
Web: www.umcom.org
Circ.: 6,000
Subscription: $7.00/year
Publication description: National Spanish
magazine.
Date established: 1958

LATIN BUSINESS MAGAZINE
P.O. Box 573
Woodland Hills, CA 91365
Greg McComb, Editor/Publisher
Tel: (818) 703-1999 **Fax:** (818) 703-8182
Email: info@latinbusinessmag.com
Web: www.latinbusinessmag.com
Circ.: 150,000
Price: $4.00 **Subscription:** $15.00/year
Publication description: Latin Business
Magazine is a publication covering Latin
business, achievement and people in the
USA.
Date established: 2004

LATIN LONG ISLAND

P.O. Box 1012
Melville, NY 11747
Maria Morales-Prieto, Managing Editor
Tel: (631) 425-1300 **Fax:** (631) 425-1414
Email: mp@latinlongislandmagazine.com
Web: www.latinlongislandmagazine.com
Price: $3.95 **Subscription:** $20.70/year
Publication description: Only English language magazine covering the interests and issues of Hispanics on Long Island.
Date established: 2000

LATINA STYLE

1730 Rhode Island Ave. NW #1207
Washington, DC 20036
Robert Bard, Publisher
Tel: (202) 955-7930 **Fax:** (202) 955-7934
Email: info@latinastyle.com
Web: www.latinastyle.com
Circ.: 150,000
Price: $2.00-2.95 **Subscription:** $ 20.00/2 years
Publication description: National English magazine.
Date established: 1995

LATINO JOURNAL

Fuerza Latina
1400 Washington Ave., Campus Center #349
Albany, NY 12222
Raquel Mendoza, President
Tel: (518) 442-5679 **Fax:** (518) 442-3908
Email: fuerza@csc.albany.edu
Web: www.albany.edu/~fuerza
Price: Free
Publication description: Latino Journal is the newsletter of Fuerza Latina.
Date established: 1971

LATINO LEADERS

Ferraez Publications of America, Corp.
4229 Hunt Dr. #3910
Carrollton, TX 75010
Wendy Pedrero, Editor
Tel: (888) 528-4532 **Fax:** (525) 651-5722
Email: editors@latinoleaders.com
Web: www.latinoleaders.com
Circ.: 100,000
Price: $2.95 **Subscription:** $9.90/year
Publication description: Latino Leaders is a bimonthly publication with national distribution in the United States. Latino Leaders targets an educated and informed Latino readership, with articles featuring interviews with major Latino players in all fields of expertise. .
Date established: 2000

LULAC NEWS

League of United Latin American Citizens
2000 L St. NW #610
Washington, DC 22036
Lorraine Quiroga Mullaly, Editor
Tel: (202) 833-6130 **Fax:** (202) 408-0064
Email: LQuiroga@lulac.com
Web: www.lulac.org
Circ.: 15,000
Price: $4.50 **Subscription:** $24.00/year

MAHAGANY/LATIN HAWAII MAGAZINE

Ron Glo & Associates
P.O. Box 1521
Pearl City, HI 96782
Ron Williams, Publisher
Tel: (808) 486-0163 **Fax:** (808) 486-8061
Email: ronglo@hawaii.rr.com
Circ.: 50,000
Price: Free **Subscription:** $20.00/year.
Date established: 1988

MINORITY BUSINESS ENTREPRENEUR-MBE MAGAZINE

Minority Business Entrepreneur
3528 Torrance Blvd. #101
Torrance, CA 90503-4826
Christen Liebenberg, Editor
Tel: (310) 540-9398 **Fax:** (310) 792-8263
Email: cliebenberg@mbemag.com
Web: www.mbemag.com
Circ.: 40,000
Price: $5.00 **Subscription:** $18.00/year
Publication description: MBE is a bimonthly publication for and about minority and women business owners.
Date established: 1985

MULTICULTURAL MARKETING NEWS

Multicultural Marketing Resources, Inc.
286 Spring St. #201
New York, NY 10013
Lisa Skriloff, President
Tel: (212) 242-3351 **Fax:** (212) 691-5969
Email: pr@multicultural.com
Web: www.multicultural.com
Circ.: 3,500
Subscription: $125.00/year
Publication description: Marketing Resources (MMR) is a public relations and marketing company that represents corporations with multicultural and diversity news and the nation's leading experts in marketing to Hispanic, Asian American, African American, women, lesbian and other cultural and lifestyle markets. They also represent minority- and women-owned businesses and specialize in promoting multicultural marketing news.
Date established: 1994

NUESTRA GENTE MAGAZINE

Independent Publishers Representatives
1187 Coast Village Rd. #1
Santa Barbara, CA 93108
Michelle Markman, Editor
Tel: (805) 969-9766 **Fax:** (805) 969-9718
Email: info@ipr-hispanic.com
Web: www.ipr-hispanic.com/nuestragente
Circ.: 865,000
Price: Free
Publication description: Nuestra Gente magazine is written as a mass market family magazine that targets the Hispanic woman and her family living in the United States.

OYE MAGAZINE - OPEN YOUR EYES

Tlahtoani Media Group, LLC
6380 Wilshire Blvd. #1113
Los Angeles, CA 90048
César E. Recendez, Publisher
Tel: (323) 651-2064 **Fax:** (323) 651-2607
Email: editorial@oyemag.com
Web: www.oyemag.com
Circ.: 50,000
Price: $3.50 **Subscription:** $19.95/year
Publication description: Magazine.
Date established: 1999

PARA TODOS

33565 Via de Agua
San Juan Capistrano, CA 92675
Silvia Ichar, Editor
Tel: (949) 493-1492 **Fax:** (949) 493-5268
Email: paratodos@paratodos.com
Web: www.paratodos.com
Circ.: 50,000
Price: Free **Subscription:** $6.00/year.
Date established: 1995

PHYSICIANS & PATIENTS

The Journal of the Hispano American Biomedical Association
130 W. 42nd St. #608
New York, NY 10036

George D. Falus, Publisher
Tel: (212) 997-9624 **Fax:** (212) 997-9615
Email: habausa@hotmail.com
Web: www.americadrs.com
Circ.: 40,000
Price: Free
Publication description: Helping health care professionals provide better health services to Hispanic patients.
Date established: 2003

REAL VOICES MAGAZINE

National Association of Hispanic Real Estate Professionals
404 Camino del Rio South #602
San Diego, CA 92108
Moises Vela, Executive Director
Tel: (619) 209-4760 **Fax:** (619) 297-3229
Email: membership@nahrep.org
Web: www.nahrep.org
Circ.: 20,000
Price: Free
Publication description: To increase Hispanic homeownership by empowering the real state professionals that serve the Hispanic community.
Date established: 1999

ROSWELL HISPANO CHAMBER OF COMMERCE NEWSLETTER

Roswell Hispano Chamber of Commerce
327 N. Main St.
Roswell, NM 88201
Frances Medrano, President
Tel: (505) 624-0889 **Fax:** (505) 624-0538
Email: info@roswellhcc.com
Web: www.roswellhcc.com
Circ.: 100
Price: Free
Publication description: Local/regional English newsletter.
Date established: 1983

SALUD HISPANA HEALTH MAGAZINE, LA

La Salud Hispana, Inc.
185 Bridge Plz. #200
Fort Lee, NJ 10021
Dr. Rodrigo Cárdenas, President/CEO
Tel: (201) 947-0101 **Fax:** (201) 947-4177
Email: drcardenas@lasaludhispana.com
Web: www.lasaludhispana.com
Circ.: 125,000
Price: $1.95 **Subscription:** $12.99/year
Publication description: Health magazine.
Date established: 1989

SHPE MAGAZINE

Society of Hispanic Professional Engineers
5400 E. Olympic Blvd. #210
Los Angeles, CA 90022
Daun E. White, Executive Director
Tel: (323) 725-3970 X106
Fax: (323) 725-0316
Email: daun.white@shpe.org
Web: www.shpe.org
Circ.: 15,000
Publication description: SHPE magazine contains articles on important issues and developments in engineering, science, and major activities in SHPE.
Date established: 1974

SOUTH TEXAS CATHOLIC NEWSPAPER

Diocese of Corpus Christi
620 Lipan St.
Corpus Christi, TX 78401
Paula Goldapp, Editor
Tel: (361) 882-6191 **Fax:** (361) 883-2556
Email: stc@diocesecc.org
Web: www.goccn.org
Circ.: 21,000
Subscription: $12.00/year.
Date established: 1966

T.Q.S. REVIEW

T.Q.S. Publications
P.O. Box 9275
Berkeley, CA 94709
Octavio I. Romano V, Editor-in-Chief
Tel: (510) 655-8036 **Fax:** (510) 601-6938
Email: tqs@tqsbooks.com
Web: www.tqsbooks.com
Circ.: 500
Price: Free **Subscription:** $18.00/year
Publication description: Bilingual.
Date established: 1967

TECOLOTE, EL

Acción Latina
2958 24th St.
San Francisco, CA 94110
Pedro Tuyub, Managing Editor
Tel: (415) 648-1045 **Fax:** (415) 648-1046
Email: accionlatina@accionlatina.org
Web: http://news.eltecolote.org
Circ.: 10,000
Price: Free **Subscription:** $22.00/year
Publication description: Seeks to provide a vehicle of information and organization to the Chicano/Latino communities of the Bay Area, articulating its social, cultural, political and economic needs through ongoing and timely coverage of issues.
Date established: 1970

TEXTILES PANAMERICANOS

Billian Publishing
2100 Powers Ferry Rd. #300
Atlanta, GA 30339
German Garcia, Editor
Tel: (770) 955-5656 **Fax:** (770) 952-0669
Email: editor@textileindustries.com
Web: www.textilespanamericanos.com
Circ.: 17,000
Price: $10.00 **Subscription:** $50.00/year
Publication description: International Spanish magazine.
Date established: 1941

URBAN LATINO

735 2nd Ave. #Penthouse
New York, NY 10016
Rodrigo Salazar, Editor-in-Chief
Tel: (212) 681-2491 **Fax:** (212) 681-2487
Email: mail@urbanlatino.com
Web: www.urbanlatino.com
Circ.: 350,000
Subscription: $16.00/year
Publication description: A nationally distributed bi-monthly publication for today's Latino, offering competitive CPMs and special opportunities designed to assist with marketing goals.
Date established: 1995

VENEZUELA AL DÍA

6955 NW 77th Ave. #309
Miami, FL 33166
Manuel Corao, Director Editor
Tel: (305) 805-0245 **Fax:** (305) 805-0245
Email: venedia@venezuelaaldia.com
Web: www.venezuelaaldia.com
Circ.: 31,000
Price: Free

VOZ ETERNA MAGAZINE, LA

La Voz Eterna
P.O. Box 15218
Houston, TX 77220-4809
Harris Goodwin, Editor
Tel: (713) 674-7172 **Fax:** (713) 674-6545
Email: lavozeterna@aol.com
Web: www.lavozeterna.org
Circ.: 17,000
Price: $8.50

Publication description: International Spanish magazine.
Date established: 1963

VOZ HISPANA, LA
La Voz Hispana
P.O. Box 1328
Lancaster, PA 17608-1328
Enelly Betancourt, Editor
Tel: (717) 399-6610 **Fax:** (717) 399-6507
Web: www.lancasteronline.com
Circ.: 5,400
Price: Free
Publication description: La Voz Hispana is a tabloid-sized newspaper published for Lancaster County's Hispanic population.

VOZ, LA
1020 Kipling Rd.
Elizabeth, NJ 07208
Abel Garcia Berry, Editor
Tel: (908) 352-6654 **Fax:** (908) 352-9735
Email: lavoznj@aol.com
Circ.: 38,000
Price: Free **Subscription:** $15.00/year
Publication description: The Spanish newspaper of New Jersey.
Date established: 1969

BIWEEKLY

ACENTO LATINO
Dickson Press, Inc.
P.O. Box 35395
Fayetteville, NC 28303
Liliana Parker, Editor
Tel: (910) 486-2760 **Fax:** (910) 486-2761
Email: liliana@acentolatino.com
Web: www.acentolatino.com
Circ.: 15,000
Price: Free **Subscription:** $30.00/year
Publication description: Spanish articles written by Hispanic editors. Also includes advertisements.
Date established: 1928

ACHEI USA NEWSPAPER
3660 NE 18th Terrace #202
Pompano Beach, FL 33064
Jose Nunez, Editor
Tel: (954) 788-2959 **Fax:** (954) 788-2960
Email: achei@bellsouth.net
Web: www.acheiusa.com
Circ.: 8,000
Price: Free .
Date established: 1964

AGUILA NEWS, EL
2 Williams St. #401
White Plains, NY 10601
Norma Maximo, Publisher
Tel: (914) 686-2598 **Fax:** (914) 686-2566
Email: info@elaguilanews.com
Web: www.elaguilanews.com
Circ.: 30,000
Price: Free
Publication description: Covers news and community happenings of all Latinos, with Latin American news section. To inform the Westchester Hispanic community with the latest news.
Date established: 1997

¡AL BORDE! MAGAZINE
P.O. Box 2227280
Los Angeles, CA 90022
Alicia Monsalve, Editor
Tel: (888) 264-1487 **Fax:** (323) 278-5315
Email: alicia@alborde.com
Web: www.alborde.com
Circ.: 32,000

Subscription: $35.00/24 Editions.
Date established: 1997

AMÉRICA ECONOMÍA
Dow Jones
1201 Brickell Ave. #350
Miami, FL 33131
Nils Strandberg, President/Publisher
Tel: (305) 341-1270 **Fax:** (305) 341-1278
Email: nils@aeconomia.com
Web: www.americaeconomia.com
Circ.: 79,000
Price: $4.95 **Subscription:** $120.00/year
Publication description: To Empower our readers through Knowledge by providing corporate leaders and policymakers insightful cross-border business coverage and commentary required to stay ahead of the competition in a relentlessly changing marketplace.
Date established: 1987

ANGELES ALTERNATIVE PRESS, LOS
L.A. Alternative Press
P.O. Box 41170
Los Angeles, CA 90041
Martin Albornoz, Publisher
Tel: (323) 767-1010 **Fax:** (323) 255-8885
Email: info@laalternativepress.com
Web: www.laalternativepress.com
Circ.: 60,000
Price: Free
Publication description: Los Angeles Alternative Press is locally owned newspaper.
Date established: 2002

ART DECO TROPICAL NEWSPAPER
Miami Beach Art Deco Publishing
221 Meridian Ave. #410
Miami Beach, FL 33139
Mirta Pestana, Editor
Tel: (305) 534-3884 **Fax:** (305) 674-3491
Email: martdeco@bellsouth.net
Circ.: 5,000
Price: Free
Publication description: Local/regional Spanish newsletter.
Date established: 1991

BIENVENIDOS A MIAMI MAGAZINE
Publishing Group
1751 NE 162nd St.
Miami, FL 33162
Tina Kaplan, Editor
Tel: (305) 944-9444 **Fax:** (305) 949-0544
Email: tina@welcomemag.com
Circ.: 15,000
Price: Free .
Date established: 1975

CATHOLIC SUN, THE
Catholic Diocese of Phoenix
P.O. Box 13549
Phoenix, AZ 85002-3549
Robert DeFrancesco, Editor
Tel: (602) 257-5565 **Fax:** (602) 258-6404
Email: info@catholicsun.org
Web: www.catholicsun.org
Circ.: 110,000
Subscription: $10.00/year
Publication description: Spanish & English publication; Audience: Catholics in Arizona.

Date established: 1985

DEFENSOR CHIEFTAIN, EL
200 Winkler SW
Socorro, NM 87801
Dana Bowley, Editor
Tel: (505) 835-0520 **Fax:** (505) 835-1837
Email: editorial@dchieftain.com
Web: www.dchieftain.com
Circ.: 3,800

Price: $0.50 **Subscription:** $28.00/year
Publication description: Local/regional English tabloid.
Date established: 1950

ENFOQUE 3 MAGAZINE
Metropolitan News
P.O. Box 65-0833
Miami, FL 33265
Silvio Mancha, Editor
Tel: (305) 223-8637 **Fax:** (305) 225-6719
Email: m3news@bellsouth.net
Web: www.enfoque3.com
Circ.: 10,000
Price: Free .
Date established: 1993

FURIA LATINA
1494 Junction St.
Detroit, MI 48209
Elias M. Gutierrez, Publisher
Tel: (313) 841-9333 **Fax:** (313) 841-2950
Email: furia@latinodetroit.com
Web: www.latinodetroit.com
Circ.: 10,000
Price: Free .
Date established: 2002

FURIA MUSICAL
Editorial Televisa - USA
6355 NW 36th St.
Miami, FL 33166
Patrick Holmes, Senior Advertiser/Sales Executive
Tel: (305) 871-6400 **Fax:** (305) 871-5026
Email: pholmes@editorialtelevisa.com
Web: www.buyeditorialtelevisa.com
Circ.: 24,370
Subscription: $26.00/year
Publication description: International Spanish magazine.
Date established: 1993

HIGHBRIDGE HORIZON
Highbridge Community Life Center
979 Ogden Ave.
Bronx, NY 10452
Denae Brewer, Editor
Tel: (718) 293-4352 **Fax:** (718) 588-1965
Email: denae@highbridgehorizon.com
Web: www.highbridgehorizon.com
Price: Free **Subscription:** $25.00/year
Publication description: Seeks to encourage residents to become involved in improvement projects in their neighborhood and provide a forum for residents to learn and develop viable skills.
Date established: 1999

IAC NEWSLETTER
The Greater Washington Ibero American Chamber of Commerce
1420 16th St. #240
Washington, DC 20036
Raul Cano-Rogers, President
Tel: (202) 728-0352 **Fax:** (202) 728-0355
Email: iberocham@aol.com
Web: www.iberochamber.org
Circ.: 1,500
Price: Free
Publication description: Newsletter for members.
Date established: 1976

IDAHO UNIDO
Idaho Unido
201 S. 10th Ave.
Pocatello, ID 83201
Farhana Hibbert, Publisher
Tel: (208) 234-7383
Email: idaho@unido.com
Web: www.unido.com
Circ.: 10,000

Subscription: $50.00/year
Publication description: Provides information in a bilingual English-Spanish format.
Date established: 1995

IMF SURVEY MAGAZINE
International Monetary Fund
Publication Services,
700 19th St. NW Box XS700
Washington, DC 20431
Laura Wallace, Editor
Tel: (202) 623-7430 **Fax:** (202) 623-7201
Email: imfsurvey@imf.org
Web: www.imf.org
Price: Free **Subscription:** $79.00/year
Publication description: IMF Survey Magazine provides topical coverage of the IMF's activities, policies and research in the context of global economic & financial developments.
Date established: 1945

INLAND EMPIRE HISPANIC NEWS
Hispanic Communication and Development Corporation
1558 N. Waterman Ave. #D
San Bernardino, CA 92404
Graciano Gomez, Publisher
Tel: (909) 381-6259 **Fax:** (909) 384-0419
Email: hispanic_news@eee.org
Circ.: 15,000
Price: Free .
Date established: 1987

KANSAS CITY HISPANIC NEWS
Arce Communications
1911 Baltimore
Kansas City, MO 64108
Joé M. Arce, Publisher/Editor
Tel: (816) 472-5246 **Fax:** (816) 472-6397
Email: kchnews@swbell.net
Circ.: 20,000
Price: Free **Subscription:** $20.00/year
Publication description: Local English newspaper.
Date established: 1996

LATIN STYLE
6860 Lexington Ave.
Los Angeles, CA 90038
Walter Martínez, Editor
Tel: (323) 462-4409 **Fax:** (323) 462-0842
Email: latinstyle@artnet.net
Web: www.latinstylemag.com
Circ.: 120,000
Subscription: $24.00/year
Publication description: National English magazine.
Date established: 1994

LATINO MID WEST NEWS
Latino Mid West News, Inc.
4180 W. Broadway #2A
Robbinsdale, MN 55422
Fernando Duque, Marketing Director
Tel: (763) 535-3373 **Fax:** (763) 537-5200
Email: latinomidwestnews@usa.net
Web: www.latinomidwestnews.com
Circ.: 20,000
Price: Free **Subscription:** $35.00/year
Publication description: Latino Mid West News strives to provide the local, regional, national and international news.
Date established: 1999

LATINO NEWS NEWSPAPER
Latino News, Inc.
P.O. Box 28
Gadsden, AL 35902
Jairo Vargas, Publisher
Tel: (256) 442-0372 **Fax:** (256) 442-8914
Email: sales@latino-news.com
Web: www.latino-news.com

Price: Free
Publication description: Latino News Newspaper provides the Hispanic community with important information, transmitting the latest news at local, national and international levels.
Date established: 1997

LUSO-AMERICANO NEWSPAPER

88 Ferry St.
Newark, NJ 07105
Fernando Santos, Editor
Tel: (973) 589-4600 **Fax:** (973) 589-3848
Email: fsantos@lusoamericano.com
Web: www.lusoamericano.com
Circ.: 30,000
Price: $0.50 **Subscription:** $60.00/year
Publication description: Portuguese-American Newspaper.
Date established: 1928

NACIONAL, EL

304 SW 25th St.
Oklahoma City, OK 73109
Randy Quiroga King, Editor
Tel: (405) 632-4531 **Fax:** (405) 632-4533
Email: nacional@swbell.net
Web: www.elnacionalnews.com
Circ.: 21,500
Price: Free **Subscription:** $49.00/year
Publication description: Local/regional Spanish newspaper.
Date established: 1988

NOTICIAS & ECONOMIC DEVELOPMENT NEWSLETTER

Greater Austin Hispanic Chamber of Commerce
3000 S. IH 35 #305
Austin, TX 78704
Gina L. Lopez, Media/Publications Specialist
Tel: (512) 476-7502 **Fax:** (512) 476-6417
Email: news@hispanicaustin.com
Web: www.hispanicaustin.com
Circ.: 1,000
Price: Free

NOTICIERO, EL

2613 Davie Blvd.
Fort Lauderdale, FL 33312
Tel: (954) 792-8019 **Fax:** (954) 792-2881
Email: elnot12@aol.com
Price: Free

NUEVA PRENSA, LA

P.O. Box 1333
Lafayette, CA 94549
Roberto Castellón, Director
Tel: (925) 210-1107 **Fax:** (925) 210-1108
Email: robercaste@aol.com
Circ.: 13,000
Price: Free
Publication description: Spanish tabloid.
Date established: 1980

PAGINAS AMARILLAS, LAS

304 SW 25th St.
Oklahoma City, OK 73109
Randy Quiroga King, Editor
Tel: (405) 632-4531 **Fax:** (405) 632-4533
Email: nacional@swbell.net
Web: www.contactookc.com
Circ.: 12,500
Price: Free
Publication description: Oklahoma's Spanish yellow pages.
Date established: 1988

POPULAR, EL

Laureti Publishing, Inc.
P.O. Box 190359
Miami Beach, FL 33119
Marco Laureti, Publisher

Tel: (305) 673-5875 **Fax:** (305) 673-0507
Email: info@elpopular.com
Web: www.elpopular.com
Circ.: 60,000
Price: Free
Publication description: A bi-weekly publication targeting young Hispanics and Latin Americans in South Florida. This publication delivers complete entertainment updates and commentaries on music, celebrity interviews, concerts, restaurants, night clubs, dining, events, and high tech products. The publication has an audited circulation of over 50,000 copies which are distributed at over 1,700 locations. The distribution base includes places such as music stores, restaurants, coffee shops, cigar stores, book stores, latin American consulates, travel agencies, condominiums, convenience stores, electronics stores, hotels, video stores, liquor stores, hospitals, clinics, etc.
Date established: 1998

PRENSA SPANISH NEWSPAPER, LA

La Prensa Spanish Newspaper
P.O. Box 65661
Salt Lake City, UT 84165
Ingrid Quiroz, Editor
Tel: (801) 905-1051/52/53
Fax: (801) 905-1054
Email: laprensa@quik.com
Circ.: 18,000
Price: Free
Publication description: La Prensa is the oldest Spanish-language newspaper about the Hispanic Community in Utah, with an emphasis on the concerns and interests of this community.
Date established: 1992

PROGRESO HISPANO NEWSPAPER, EL

11101 Tyvola Rd. #105
Charlotte, NC 28217
Lcdo. Jose Herrera, Editor/President
Tel: (704) 529-6728 **Fax:** (704) 525-2328
Email: contact@elprogresohispano.com
Web: www.elprogresohispano.com
Circ.: 60,000
Price: Free **Subscription:** $37.50/year
Publication description: Spanish tabloid.
Date established: 1991

SOL DE SAN DIEGO, EL

El Sol de San Diego
P.O. Box 13447
San Diego, CA 92170
Julie J. Rocha, Editor
Tel: (619) 233-8496 **Fax:** (619) 233-5017
Email: elsolsd@aol.com
Web: www.elsoldesandiego.com
Circ.: 21,000
Price: Free
Publication description: San Diego's most awarded Latino publication.
Date established: 1987

SOL, EL

P.O. Box 81091
Salinas, CA 93912
Silvia Sansen, Editor
Tel: (831) 757-8118 **Fax:** (831) 757-1006
Email: ssansen@elsolsalinas.com
Web: www.californianonline.com/news/elsol/index.html
Circ.: 15,000
Price: Free **Subscription:** $50.00/year.
Date established: 1968

SOL LATINO, EL

P. O. Box 126
Lubbock, TX 79408
Damiam P. Morales, Editor

Tel: (806) 741-1956 **Fax:** (806) 740-0045
Email: elsollatino@nts.online.net
Web: www.elsollatino.com
Circ.: 30,000
Price: Free **Subscription:** $39.95/year
Publication description: Features general information, local, national, international news, local events, biographies, music news and more.
Date established: 1993

SOONER CATHOLIC, THE

Archdiocese of Oklahoma City, Office for Hispanic Ministry
P.O. Box 32180
Oklahoma City, OK 73123
Carmen Vasquez, Member for Hispanic Ministry
Tel: (405) 721-1810 **Fax:** (405) 721-5210
Email: rdyer@catharchdioceseokc.org
Web: www.catharchdioceseokc.org
Circ.: 20
Subscription: $20.00/year
Publication description: Publication dedicated to priests to aid them to conduct Mass.
Date established: 1993

TEXAS CATHOLIC NEWSPAPER, THE

Diocese of Dallas
P.O. Box 190347
Dallas, TX 75219
Bronson Havard, Editor
Tel: (214) 528-8792 **Fax:** (214) 528-3411
Email: texascatholic@msn.com
Web: www.cathdal.org
Circ.: 53,100
Subscription: $15.00/year
Publication description: Local/regional English newspaper.
Date established: 1952

TODAY'S CATHOLIC

Archdiocese of San Antonio
P.O. Box 28410
San Antonio, TX 78228-0410
Jordon McMorrough, Editor
Tel: (210) 734-2620 X128
Fax: (210) 734-2939
Email: jmcmorrough@archdiosa.org
Web: www.satodayscatholic.com
Circ.: 24,385
Subscription: $12.00/year
Publication description: Today's Catholic is the official publication of Archdiocese of San Antonio and provides the Catholic perspective on daily life for the Archdiocese.
Date established: 1892

TV Y NOVELAS

Editorial Televisa - USA
6355 NW 36th St.
Miami, FL 33166
Patrick Holmes, Senior Advertisers/Sales Executive
Tel: (305) 871-6400 **Fax:** (305) 871-5026
Email: pholmes@editorialtelevisa.com
Web: www.buyeditorialtelevisa.com
Circ.: 120,000
Subscription: $26.00/year
Publication description: International Spanish magazine.
Date established: 1982

UPDATE

Guatemala Human Rights Commission-USA
3321 12th St. NE
Washington, DC 20017-4008
Patricia Davis, President
Tel: (202) 529-6599 **Fax:** (202) 526-4611
Email: ghrc-usa.org@ghrc-usa.org
Web: www.ghrc-usa.org
Subscription: $15.00 -50.00/year
Publication description: Researches,

documents and publishes human rights violations in Guatemala. Publishes quarterly human rights reports to the Guatemalan community.
Date established: 1982

VANIDADES

Editorial Televisa - USA
6355 NW 36th St.
Miami, FL 33166
Patrick Holmes, Senior Advertiser/Sales Executive
Tel: (305) 871-6400 **Fax:** (305) 871-5026
Email: pholmes@editorialtelevisa.com
Web: www.buyeditorialtelevisa.com
Circ.: 110,000
Subscription: $26.00/year
Publication description: Editorial Televisa is the largest publisher of Spanish-language magazines in the world and the leader in Latin America and the U.S. Hispanic Markets. The company publishes 42 titles, most of them the leaders in their respective categories, including such titles as Vanidades, Cosmopolitan en español, Marie Claire en español, Harper's Bazaar en español, National Geographic en español, Men's Health en español and several other Spanish-language publications.
Date established: 1961

VIDA & SABOR

Latino Communications Network
2019 E. Lake St. #7
Minneapolis, MN 55407
Alberto Monserrate, President/CEO
Tel: (612) 729-5900 **Fax:** (612) 729-5999
Email: alberto@lcnmedia.com
Web: www.lcnmedia.com
Circ.: 15,000
Publication description: Vida & Sabor is an edgy, alternative entertainment guide that appeals to the younger latino reader.
Date established: 2000

VOZ HISPANA DE CONNECTICUT, LA

La Voz Hispana Newsprint, Inc.
35 Elm St.
New Haven, CT 06510
Abelardo King, Editor
Tel: (203) 865-2272 **Fax:** (203) 787-4023
Email: lavozhispana@hotmail.com
Circ.: 25,000
Price: Free **Subscription:** $52.00/year
Publication description: Bilingual newspaper.
Date established: 1993

WEST NEBRASKA REGISTER

Hispanic Ministry Office,
Diocese of Grand Island
P.O. Box 651
North Platte, NE 69103
Mary Parlin, Editor
Tel: (308) 532-2707 **Fax:** (308) 532-3574
Email: wnr@gidiocese.org
Web: www.gidiocese.org/offices/hispanicministry/index.htm
Circ.: 17,096
Price: $0.50 **Subscription:** $20.00/year
Publication description: West Nebraska Register gives information about the Diocese of Grand Island.
Date established: 1996

DAILY

AL DIA

Belo Interactive, Inc.
508 Young St., 2nd Fl.
Dallas, TX 75202

Robert Bailon, Editor
Tel: (469) 977-3600 **Fax:** (469) 977-3601
Email: gbailon@aldiatx.com
Web: www.aldiatx.com
Circ.: 40,000
Price: $0.25 **Subscription:** $36.00/year
Publication description: Al Dia is a Spanish-
language newspaper for North Texas.

DIARIO, EL
Editora Paso del Norte
425 N. Kansas St.
El Paso, TX 79901
Osvaldo Rodríguez, Publisher
Tel: (915) 838-1550 **Fax:** (915) 838-1551
Email: jbrown5246@aol.com
Web: www.diario.com.mx
Circ.: 96,334
Subscription: $243.94/year
Publication description: Local/regional
Spanish broadsheet.
Date established: 1976

DIARIO EL DÍA
Cuatro Comunicaciones
6120 Tarnef St. #110
Houston, TX 77074
Sergio R. Budini, Editor
Tel: (713) 772-8900 **Fax:** (713) 774-3362
Email: newsdesk@eldiausa.com
Web: www.eldiausa.com
Circ.: 45,000
Price: $0.25
Publication description: Local/regional
Spanish tabloid.
Date established: 1995

DIARIO LA ESTRELLA
400 W. 7th St.
Fort Worth, TX 76102
Javier J. Aldape, Publisher
Tel: (817) 390-7180 **Fax:** (817) 390-7280
Email: jaldape@diariolaestrella.com
Web: www.diariolaestrella.com
Circ.: 32,950
Price: Free
Publication description: Diario La Estrella is
a leading Spanish-language newspaper in
Dallas/Fort Worth.
Date established: 1994

DIARIO LAS AMÉRICAS
The Americas Publishing Co.
2900 NW 39th St.
Miami, FL 33142
Horacio Aguirre, Editor
Tel: (305) 633-3341 **Fax:** (305) 635-4002
Email: diario@ix.netcom.com
Web: www.diariolasamericas.com
Circ.: 70,000
Price: $0.35 **Subscription:** $73.49/year
Publication description: Spanish newspaper.
Date established: 1953

DIARIO LATINO
Healy Media, Inc.
637 3rd Ave. #A-1
Chula Vista, CA 91910
Jose S. Healy, General Director
Tel: (619) 409-1777 **Fax:** (619) 409-1771
Email: director@diariolatino.com
Web: www.diariolatino.com
Circ.: 15,000
Price: $0.25 **Subscription:** $48.00/year
Publication description: To connect Spanish-
speaking people, organizations and advertisers
with the Latino world.
Date established: 2003

DIARIO-LA PRENSA, EL
Latin Communications Group
345 Hudson St., 13th Fl.
New York, NY 10014

Pedro Rojas, Editor in Chief
Tel: (212) 807-4600 **Fax:** (212) 807-4705
Email: production@eldiariolaprensa.com
Web: www.eldiariony.com
Circ.: 57,550
Price: $0.50 **Subscription:** $46.80/year
Publication description: Newspaper.
Date established: 1913

HOY
Tribune Company
330 W. 34th St., 17th Fl.
New York, NY 10001
Armando Varela, Editor-in-Chief
Tel: (917) 339-0800 **Fax:** (212) 971-4413
Web: www.holahoy.com
Circ.: 65,768
Price: $0.25
Publication description: Hoy is the nation's
fastest growing Spanish newspaper, serving
the New York and Chicago metropolitan
areas.
Date established: 1999

LAREDO MORNING TIMES-TIEMPO, EL
Hearst Corp.
111 Esperanza Dr.
Laredo, TX 78041
Odie Arambula, Executive Editor
Tel: (956) 728-2555 **Fax:** (956) 723-1227
Email: odie@lmtonline.com
Web: www.lmtonline.com
Circ.: 26,000
Price: $0.50 **Subscription:** $117.00/year
Publication description: Spanish newspaper.
Date established: 1994

MAÑANA, EL
Editorial Argo
5901 McPherson St. #12
Laredo, TX 78040-5935
Ramón Cantú-Deandar, Editor
Tel: (956) 712-1122 **Fax:** (956) 717-5091
Email: elmanana@elmanana.com.mx
Web: www.elmanana.com.mx
Circ.: 50,000
Price: $0.75 **Subscription:** $150.00/year
Publication description: Spanish tabloid.
Date established: 1932

MEXICANO, EL
International Media Reps.
4045 Bonita Rd. #209
Bonita, CA 91902
Enrique Sanchez Diaz, Editor
Tel: (619) 267-6010 **Fax:** (619) 267-5965
Email: publicidad@el-mexicano.com.mx
Web: www.el-mexicano.com.mx
Circ.: 100,000
Price: $0.75
Publication description: Spanish newspaper.
Date established: 1959

NACIÓN, LA
La Voz Communication, Inc.
2615-A Shirlington Rd.
Arlington, VA 22206
Jesús Sánchez-Cañete, Chairman/
President/CEO
Tel: (703) 979-4156 **Fax:** (703) 979-5194
Email: advertising@lanacionusa.com
Web: www.lanacionusa.com
Circ.: 22,500
Price: Free **Subscription:** $60.00/year
Publication description: Spanish tabloid.
Date established: 1991

NACIONAL NEWSPAPER, EL
660 W 178th St. #1A
New York, NY 10033
Abalberto Dominguez, Editor
Tel: (212) 781- 1915 **Fax:** (212) 740-1299
Email: elnacional@nyc.rr.com

Web: www.elnacional.com
Circ.: 44,000
Price: $1.50
Publication description: This newspaper is
produced in the Dominican Republic and
arrives to New York the same day.
Date established: 1966

NUEVO DÍA, EL
El Día, Inc.
P.O. Box 9067512
San Juan, PR 00906-7512
Maria E. Ferre Rangel, President
Tel: (787) 273-7600 **Fax:** (787) 641-3924
Email: meferre@elnuevodia.com
Web: www.elnuevodia.net
Circ.: 205,000
Price: $0.45
Publication description: Spanish newspaper.
Date established: 1970

NUEVO HERALD, EL
The Miami Herald
1 Herald Plz.
Miami, FL 33132-1693
Loisa Ferrera, Advertising Manager
Tel: (305) 376-3535 **Fax:** (305) 376-2207
Email: lferrera@herald.com
Web: www.elherald.com
Circ.: 91,915
Price: $0.35
Publication description: Local/regional
Spanish newspaper.
Date established: 1989

NUEVO HERALDO, EL
1135 E. Van Buren St.
Brownsville, TX 78520
Santos Garcia, Editor
Tel: (956) 982-6612 **Fax:** (956) 542-0840
Email: tbhletters@link.freedom.com
Web: www.brownsvilleherald.com
Circ.: 33,000
Subscription: $96.00/year .
Date established: 1934

OPINIÓN, LA
700 S. Flower St. #3100
Los Angeles, CA 90017
Ruben Keoseyan, Editor
Tel: (213) 896-2333 **Fax:** (213) 896-2077
Email: marketing@laopinion.com
Web: www.laopinion.com
Circ.: 126,628
Price: $0.25 **Subscription:** $246.81/year
Publication description: Spanish
Newspaper.
Date established: 1926

PASO TIMES, EL
El Paso Times, Inc.
300 N. Campbell St.
El Paso, TX 79901
Don Flores, Editor
Tel: (915) 456-6260 **Fax:** (915) 546-6415
Email: elpasonews@elpasotimes.com
Web: www.elpasotimes.com
Circ.: 75,000
Price: $0.40 **Subscription:** $153.00/year.
Date established: 1881

RUMBO
Meximerica Media
115 E. Travis, 8th Fl.
San Antonio, TX 78205
Edward Schumacher-Matos, Editorial
Director
Tel: (210) 581-3500 **Fax:** (210) 581-3669
Email: info@diariosrumbo.com
Web: www.diariosrumbo.com
Circ.: 90,000
Price: $0.25
Publication description: Rumbo is a Spanish

newspaper that delivers useful information for
the Latino reader.

SAN JUAN STAR, THE
The Star Media Network
P.O. Box 364187
San Juan, PR 00936-4187
Garry Angulo, Publisher
Tel: (787) 782-4200 **Fax:** (787) 782-0310
Web: www.thesanjuanstar.com
Circ.: 104,000
Publication description: The San Juan Star
owns the Star Media Network.
Date established: 1959

SENTINEL, EL
200 E. Las Olas Blvd.
Ft. Lauderdale, FL 33301
Deborah Ramírez, Editor
Tel: (954) 749-4652 **Fax:** (954) 356-4582
Email: rdramirez@sun-sentinel.com
Web: www.sun-sentinel.com/elsentinel
Circ.: 95,000
Price: Free **Subscription:** Free
Publication description: Spanish language
newspaper serving Florida's Broward
County.
Date established: 2002

SOL DE TIJUANA, EL
Mucho Media Marketing
589 Vance St.
Chula Vista, CA 91910
Kathleen Girard, Executive Director
Tel: (619) 427-8291 **Fax:** (619) 427-8340
Circ.: 65,000
Price: $.75 .
Date established: 1989

VISIÓN DE GEORGIA, LA
CHL Communications, Inc.
195 W. Pike St. #201
Lawrenceville, GA 30045
Paco Elzaurdia, Editor
Tel: (770) 963-7521 **Fax:** (770) 963-7218
Email: editor@lavisiononline.com
Web: www.lavisiononline.com
Circ.: 60,200
Price: $0.50
Publication description: Bilingual
publication.
Date established: 2000

VOCERO DE PUERTO RICO, EL
Caribbean International News
P.O. Box 9067515
San Juan, PR 00906-7515
Gaspar Roca, Editor
Tel: (787) 721-2300 **Fax:** (787) 722-0131
Email: opinion@vocero.com
Web: www.vocero.com
Circ.: 220,000
Subscription: $240.00/year
Publication description: Local/regional
Spanish newspaper also distributed in
New York.
Date established: 1984

VOZ DE CUBA LIBRE, LA
La Voz De Cuba Libre Educational
Foundation
4826 Oakwood Ave.
Los Angeles, CA 90004
José Luis Fernandez, Director
Tel: (323) 463-9353 **Fax:** (323) 463-9363
Email: lavozdecubalibre@aol.com
Web: www.lavozdecubalibre.com
Circ.: 7,000
Price: Free
Publication description: Provides information
about Cuba and its people.
Date established: 1996

MONTHLY

90:00 MINUTES SOCCER MAGAZINE
Soccer Development of America
3803 Mission Blvd. #290
San Diego, CA 92109
Yan Skwara, Publisher
Tel: (858) 488-7775 **Fax:** (858) 488-2828
Email: info@soccerdev.com
Web: www.90soccer.com
Price: Free **Subscription:** $29.95/year
Publication description: 90:00 Minutes Soccer focuses on the players and lifestyles that surrounds the world's most popular sport.
Date established: 2002

ACENTO MAGAZINE
1444 N. Milwaukee Ave.
Chicago, IL 60622
Claudia Zuno Ramirez, General Manager
Tel: (773) 772-2707 **Fax:** (773) 772-7057
Email: mail@acentomagazine.com
Circ.: 10,000
Price: $2.00 **Subscription:** $19.99/year
Publication description: Dedicated to the Spanish reading community of the Chicago land area.
Date established: 1999

ACTUALIDAD CUBANA
Cuban American National Foundation
1312 SW 27th Ave.
Miami, FL 33145
Omar Lopez, Editor
Tel: (305) 592-7768 **Fax:** (305) 592-7889
Email: hq@canf.org
Web: www.canf.org
Circ.: 6,000
Price: Free
Publication description: The official news brief for member of the CANF.
Date established: 2000

AFFIRMATIVE ACTION REGISTER
Affirmative Action, Inc.
8356 Olive Blvd.
St. Louis, MO 63132
Joyce R. Green, Editor
Tel: (314) 991-1335 **Fax:** (314) 997-1788
Email: aareeo@concentric.net
Web: www.aar-eeo.com
Circ.: 67,000
Price: Free **Subscription:** $15.00/year
Publication description: The national Equal Employment Opportunity(EEO) recruitment publication directed to females, minorities, veterans, and disabled persons, as well as to all employment candidates.
Date established: 1974

AL DÍA NEWSLETTER
Chicano Latino Affairs Council
555 Park St. #210
St. Paul, MN 55103
Gladys Zelaya, Administrative Assistant
Tel: (651) 296-9587 **Fax:** (651) 297-1297
Email: clac.desk@state.mn.us
Web: www.clac.state.mn.us
Circ.: 900
Price: Free
Publication description: Eight page newsletter distributed the first week of every month.
Date established: 1970

ANTENNA MAGAZINE
Antenna Publishing
110 S. A St. #D
Oxnard, CA 93030
Sergio Cisneros, Editor
Tel: (805) 483-0344 **Fax:** (805) 483-0347
Email: info@revistaantenna.com
Web: www.revistaantenna.com

Circ.: 7,500
Price: $10.41 **Subscription:** $125.00/year
Publication description: National Spanish magazine.
Date established: 1986

AQUÍ LLEGÓ
The National Latina/o Lesbian, Gay, Bisexual & Transgender Organization
1420 K St. NW #400
Washington, DC 20005
Benjamin Sheppard, Editor
Tel: (202) 408-5380 **Fax:** (202) 408-8478
Email: publications@llego.org
Web: www.llego.org
Circ.: 3,000
Price: Free
Publication description: Devoted to representing Latino lesbian, gay, bisexual and transgender communities and to advocating on behalf of their needs on issues ranging from civil rights and social justice to health and human services.
Date established: 1989

ARCHITECTURAL DIGEST EN ESPAÑOL
Conde Nast Americas
1101 Brickell Ave.,15th Fl.
Miami, FL 33131
Madelin Bosakewich, Publisher
Tel: (305) 371-9393 **Fax:** (305) 371-9392
Email: adelapaz@condenastamericas.com
Circ.: 200,000
Price: $3.50 **Subscription:** $42.00/year
Publication description: Architectural Digest en Español is the world's most prestigious magazine of architecture and interior design.
Date established: 2000

ARGENTINO, EL-MERCOSUR NEWSPAPER
P.O. Box 351651
Miami, FL 33135
Alberto A. Micheli, Editor
Tel: (305) 532-6710 **Fax:** (305) 672-8511
Email: director@elargentino.com
Web: www.elargentino.com
Circ.: 10,000
Subscription: $22.00/year.
Date established: 1987

ARTES GRÁFICAS MAGAZINE
Carvajal International
901 Ponce de León Blvd. #601
Coral Gables, FL 33134
Alfredo Domador, Publisher
Tel: (305) 448-6875 **Fax:** (305) 448-9942
Email: adomador@b2bportales.com
Web: www.artesgraficas.com
Circ.: 22,000
Price: Free
Publication description: International Spanish magazine.
Date established: 1967

AUTOMUNDO MAGAZINE
Automundo Productions, Inc.
2960 SW 8th St., 2nd Fl.
Miami, FL 33135
Jorge Koechlin, President
Tel: (305) 541-4198 **Fax:** (305) 541-5138
Email: art@automundo.com
Web: www.automundo.com
Circ.: 55,000
Price: $2.95 **Subscription:** $19.95/year
Publication description: National Spanish magazine.
Date established: 1980

AVANCE HISPANO
Avance Hispano, Inc.
2601 Mission St. #500
San Francisco, CA 94110

Vanessa Carias, Publisher
Tel: (415) 285-6444 **Fax:** (415) 585-1398
Email: avancemagazine@aol.com
Web: www.avancehispano.com
Circ.: 50,000
Price: Free **Subscription:** $25.00/year.
Date established: 1989

BANDA ORIENTAL LATINOAMERICANA NEWSPAPER
321 Rahway Ave.
Elizabeth, NJ 07202
Julia Moreira, Editor/Publisher
Tel: (908) 965-0909 **Fax:** (908) 965-1724
Email: bandao@aol.com
Circ.: 30,000
Price: Free **Subscription:** $36.00/year
Publication description: Local/regional Spanish tabloid.
Date established: 1983

BARRIO LATINO NEWSPAPER
The Latino Media Group
3024 W. 25th St. #149
Cleveland, OH 44113
Angel Ramos, Editor
Tel: (216) 344-9922 **Fax:** (216) 344-9929
Email: latinobarrio@latinomediagroup.com
Web: www.latinomediagroup.com
Circ.: 10,000
Price: Free
Publication description: Spanish Newspaper.
Date established: 1998

BOTTOM LINE NEWSLETTER, THE
National Society of Hispanic MBA's (NSHMBA)
1303 Walnut Hill Ln. #300
Irving, TX 75247-4067
Ana Herrera-Malone, Marketing /Development Director
Tel: (214) 596-9338 X226
Fax: (214) 596-9325
Email: aherrera@nshmba.org
Web: www.nshmba.org
Circ.: 6,000
Price: Free
Publication description: English newsletter.

BRASILIANS, THE
The Brasilians Press and Publications, Inc.
21 W 46th St. #203
New York, NY 10036
Edilberto Luciano Mendes, Editor
Tel: (212) 398-6464
Email: editor@thebrasiliansonline.com
Web: www.thebrasiliansonline.com
Circ.: 60,000
Subscription: $10.00/year
Publication description: Monthly Portuguese/ English newspaper promoting and reporting on Brazil Abroad.
Date established: 1972

BRAZZIL MAGAZINE
P.O. Box 50536
Los Angeles, CA 90050
Rodney Mello, Publisher/Editor
Tel: (323) 255-8062 **Fax:** (323) 257-3487
Email: brazzil@brazzil.com
Web: www.brazzil.com
Circ.: 12,000
Subscription: $3.00/year
Publication description: Explaining Brazil and its multiracial culture to those who cannot speak Portuguese.
Date established: 1989

BUENA VIDA MAGAZINE
Casiano Communications
1700 Ave. Fernández Juncos
San Juan, PR 00909-2938

Karen Sloan, Editor
Tel: (787) 728-2687 **Fax:** (787) 728-5948
Email: buenavida@casiano.com
Web: www.casiano.com
Circ.: 63,000
Price: $2.75 **Subscription:** $19.00/year
Publication description: Informative articles on nutrition, beauty, health, exercise, family affairs, entertainment and more make this magazine the perfect guide to improve your quality of life.
Date established: 1990

BUENHOGAR
Editorial Televisa - USA
6355 NW 36th St.
Miami, FL 33166
Patrick Holmes, Senior Advertiser/Sales Executive
Tel: (305) 871-6400 **Fax:** (305) 871-5026
Email: pholmes@editorialtelevisa.com
Web: www.buyeditorialtelevisa.com
Circ.: 30,617
Subscription: $12.00/year
Publication description: Buenhogar features recipes and cooking, nutrition, home decoration, child rearing, psychology and education, health, medicine, beauty and fashion, culture, horoscopes and interviews with international personalities.
Date established: 1966

BUSINESS MATTERS NEWSLETTER
East Los Angeles Chamber of Commerce
P.O. Box 63220
Los Angeles, CA 90063
Ricardo Gonzales, Executive Director
Tel: (323) 722-2005 **Fax:** (323) 722-2405
Email: elacoc@pacbell.net
Web: www.elachamber.com
Circ.: 600
Price: Free
Publication description: English newsletter.
Date established: 1988

BUSINESS REVIEW NEWSLETTER
Albuquerque Hispanic Chamber of Commerce
1309 4th St. SW
Albuquerque, NM 87102
Loretta Armenta, President/CEO
Tel: (505) 842-9003 **Fax:** (505) 764-9664
Email: loretta_armenta@ahcnm.org
Web: www.ahcnm.org
Circ.: 5,000
Price: Free
Publication description: Local/regional English membership directory.
Date established: 1993

CAA NEWSLETTER
Colombian American Association, Inc.
30 Vesey St. #506
New York, NY 10007
Robert A. Gray, President
Tel: (212) 233-7776 **Fax:** (212) 233-7779
Email: andean@nyct.net
Web: www.colombianamerican.org
Price: Free .
Date established: 1927

CAMACOL
Latin Chamber of Commerce of USA
1417 W. Flagler St.
Miami, FL 33135
William Alexander, President
Tel: (305) 642-3870 **Fax:** (305) 642-0653
Email: info@camacol.org
Web: www.camacol.org
Circ.: 4,000
Price: Free

Publication description: Local/regional Spanish magazine.
Date established: 1965

CAMPESTRE, EL
International Media Reps
4045 Bonita Rd. #209
Bonita, CA 91902
Demetrio Carrasco, Owner
Tel: (619) 267-6010 **Fax:** (619) 267-5965
Circ.: 12,000
Price: Free .
Date established: 1985

CARIBBEAN CONTACT USA, THE
Archipelago Publications, Inc.
9010 SW 137th Ave. #248
Miami, FL 33186
Jerry Nahee, President/CEO
Tel: (305) 388-7440 **Fax:** (305) 388-7540
Email: caribnewsusa@aol.com
Circ.: 30,000
Price: Free **Subscription:** $35.00/year
Publication description: To be a vehicle of communication for the Caribbean American community in South Florida and throughout the area; to provide and disseminate information regarding business, culture, education, entertainment, sport, health and more.
Date established: 1994

CARIBBEAN TODAY
P.O.Box 6010
Miami, FL 33116-6010
Peter A. Webley, Publisher
Tel: (305) 238-2868 **Fax:** (305) 252-7843
Email: caribtoday@earthlink.net
Web: www.caribbeantoday.com
Circ.: 39,000
Price: Free **Subscription:** $35.00/year.
Date established: 1989

CASA MAGAZINE
Solid Future Publishing
6425 W. 52nd Ave. #1
Arvada, CO 80002
Al McGregor, President
Tel: (303) 975-1142 **Fax:** (303) 975-1858
Email: almc@solidfuture.net
Web: www.solidfuture.net
Circ.: 15,000
Price: Free
Publication description: Real Estate magazine

CENTRO UNIDO EN ACCIÓN
Centro Unido de Detallistas de Puerto Rico
P.O. Box 190127
San Juan, PR 00919-0127
Enid Toro de Baez, President
Tel: (787) 641-8413 **Fax:** (787) 641-8408
Email: etoro@centrounido.com
Web: www.centrounido.org
Circ.: 45,000
Price: $1.25
Publication description: Advocate of the small and medium size entrepreneur of Puerto Rico.
Date established: 1891

CHAMBER AT A GLANCE
El Paso Hispanic Chamber of Commerce
201 E. Main St. #100
El Paso, TX 79901
Cindy Ramos-Davidson, CEO
Tel: (915) 566-4066 **Fax:** (915) 566-9714
Email: ephcc@whc.net
Web: www.ephcc.org
Price: Free
Publication description: Promotes businesses in the community.

CHICAGO CATÓLICO NEWSPAPER
New World Publications - Archdiocese of Chicago
721 N. LaSalle St.
Chicago, IL 60610
Thomas H. Sheridan, Editor/General Manager
Tel: (312) 655-7777 **Fax:** (312) 642-7310
Email: mail@catholicnewworld.com
Web: www.catholicnewworld.com
Circ.: 12,000
Subscription: $25.00/year
Publication description: Local/regional Spanish newsletter.
Date established: 1985

CNY LATINO NEWSPAPER
Tennex Media Group
1529 Woodmancy Rd.
Tully, NY 13159-9791
Hugo Acosta, Publisher/Owner
Tel: (315) 415-8593 **Fax:** (315) 696-0146
Email: info@cnylatino.com
Web: www.cnylatino.com
Circ.: 8,000
Price: Free
Publication description: Hispanic oriented newspaper in the Central New York area. CNY Latino is a monthly periodical dedicated to the Hispanic population, but prepared to be read by any culture, since it is written in both "English and Spanish.".
Date established: 2004

COLOMBIANO USA, EL
1161 N. Maclay Ave. #D
San Fernando, CA 91340
Ben Bustillo, Editor/Publisher
Tel: (818) 361-3020 **Fax:** (818) 361-6539
Email: benbustillo@yahoo.com
Web: www.elcolombianousa.com
Publication description: This newspaper provide information to the Hispanic community that lives in the US

COMERCIO Y PRODUCCIÓN
Cámara de Comercio de Puerto Rico
P.O. Box 9024033
San Juan, PR 00902-4033
Leonardo Suria Lamb, President
Tel: (787) 721-6060 **Fax:** (787) 723-1891
Email: camarapr@camarapr.net
Web: www.camarapr.org
Circ.: 2,500
Price: Free
Publication description: Newsletter; internal circulation. Only for members of the Chamber of Commerce.
Date established: 1961

COMUNICÁNDOSE CON LA CÁMARA
Hispanic Chamber of Commerce of Wisconsin
816 W. National Ave.
Milwaukee, WI 53204
María Monreal-Cameron, President/CEO
Tel: (414) 643-6963 **Fax:** (414) 643-6994
Email: mcameron@hccw.org
Web: www.hccw.org
Circ.: 875
Price: Free
Publication description: Gives information about business and social interest to the Hispanic Chamber of Commerce of Wisconsin members .
Date established: 1993

CONEXIÓN ARGENTINA
905 S. Basyshore Dr. #822
Miami, FL 33131
Enrique Kogan, Publisher
Tel: (305) 358-9911 **Fax:** (305) 358-1986

Email: info@conexionargentina.com
Web: www.conexionargentina.com
Circ.: 35,000
Price: Free
Publication description: Spanish magazine.
Date established: 1998

CONSTRUCCIÓN PAN-AMERICANA
International Construction Publishing
4913 SW 75th Ave.
Miami, FL 33155-4440
Guido Castellanos, Editor
Tel: (305) 668-4999 **Fax:** (305) 668-7774
Email: info@cpa-mpa.com
Web: www.cpa-mpa.com
Circ.: 12,880
Price: Free **Subscription:** Free
Publication description: International Spanish magazine.
Date established: 1972

CONTACTO MAGAZINE
1317 N. San Fernando Blvd. #PMB-246
Burbank, CA 91504
Jesús Hernández Cuéllar, Editor
Tel: (818) 842-3308 **Fax:** (818) 557-6251
Email: editor@contactomagazine.com
Web: www.contactomagazine.com
Circ.: 25,000
Price: Free
Publication description: Contacto Magazine is an independent publication on current affairs.
Date established: 1994

COSMOPÓLITAN
Editorial Televisa - USA
6355 NW 36th St.
Miami, FL 33166
Patrick Holmes, Senior Advertiser/Sales Executive
Tel: (305) 871-6400 **Fax:** (305) 871-5026
Email: pholmes@editorialtelevisa.com
Web: www.buyeditorialtelevisa.com
Circ.: 130,000
Subscription: $12.00/year
Publication description: International Spanish magazine. The independent Latin woman's magazine for 24 years, COSMOPOLITAN en español® is published as part of a joint venture with The Hearst Corporation. It is tailored for young women who are getting ahead in their jobs as well as their personal lives. Strong emphasis is placed on beauty, fashion and looking your best. There are self-help articles on personal relationships and career-orientation, as well as regular sections on home entertaining, cooking, decorating and people.
Date established: 1973

CRISTINA LA REVISTA
Editorial Televisa - USA
6355 NW 36th St.
Miami, FL 33166
Patrick Holmes, Senior Advertiser/Sales Executive
Tel: (305) 871-6400 **Fax:** (305) 871-5026
Email: pholmes@editorialtelevisa.com
Web: www.buyeditorialtelevisa.com
Circ.: 87,000
Subscription: $12.00/year
Publication description: International Spanish magazine. The print version of the top-rated domestically-produced Spanish-language TV show in the U.S., Cristina la Revista is a complete magazine with regular sections on people, current events, self-help, decorating, fashion & beauty.
Date established: 1991

DE MUJER A MUJER
Latino Press Media, Inc.
1494 Junction St.
Detroit, MI 48209
Elías M. Gutiérrez, Publisher
Tel: (313) 841-0805 **Fax:** (313) 841-2950
Email: president@latinodetroit.com
Web: www.latinodetroit.com/mujer
Circ.: 15,000
Price: Free
Publication description: Newspaper with a Hispanic-Latino audience.
Date established: 2001

DE NORTE A SUR NEWSPAPER
De Norte a Sur, Inc.
250-05 Elkmont Ave.
Bellerose, NY 11426
Hebert Bonilla, Publisher
Tel: (718) 343-5829 **Fax:** (718) 343-5821
Email: denorteasur@denorteasur.com
Web: www.denorteasur.com
Circ.: 30,000
Subscription: $36.00/year
Publication description: This newpaper is distributed around the US with several offices in major cities, each having its own edition.
Date established: 1980

DIÁLOGO MAGAZINE
University of Puerto Rico
P.O. Box 364984
San Juan, PR 00936-4984
Armindo Nuñez Miranda, Editor
Tel: (787) 763-1370 **Fax:** (787) 250-8729
Email: a_nunez@upr1.upr.clu.edu
Circ.: 40,000
Price: $1.50 **Subscription:** $16.00/year
Publication description: Spanish tabloid.
Date established: 1996

DISIDENTE UNIVERSAL DE PUERTO RICO
Comisión Cubana de Derechos Humanos y Reconciliación Nacional
P.O. Box 360889
San Juan, PR 00936-0889
Jose Vilasuso Rivero, Editor
Tel: (787) 762-9853 **Fax:** (787) 762-3301
Email: disidenteuniversal@yahoo.com
Web: www.disidenteuniversal.org
Circ.: 5,000
Price: Free
Publication description: Promote Human Rights inside Cuba.
Date established: 1986

DIVERSITYINC
317 George St. #420
New Brunswick, NJ 08901-2008
Luke Visconti, Partner/Co-founder
Tel: (732) 509-5200 **Fax:** (732) 509-5225
Email: editor@diversityinc.com
Web: www.diversityinc.com
Date established: 1998

DIVINO MAGAZINE
DIVINO
76-26 Grand Central Pkwy.
Forest Hill, NY 11375
Cristian Farinola, Editor
Tel: (718) 793-1110
Email: divino@verizonmail.com
Price: Free
Publication description: Divino is a monthly rock, pop, and Latino cinema magazine written in Spanish for US Latinos.
Date established: 2002

DOMINICAN TIMES MAGAZINE
22-19 41st Ave., 2nd Fl.
Long Island, NY 11101
Juan Guillen, Publisher

Tel: (718) 472-5538 **Fax:** (718) 472-5587
Email: jguillen@dominicantimes.com
Web: www.dominicantimes.com
Subscription: $19.00/year

ECO LATINO NEWSPAPER
6779 Memphis Ave. #8
Brooklyn, OH 44144
Victor De La Cruz, Publisher
Tel: (216) 485-0924 **Fax:** (216) 485-0978
Email: ecolatino1@sbcglobal.net
Circ.: 30,000

ESTRELLA DE ESPERANZA, LA (STAR OF HOPE)
Editorial Vara y Cayado
P.O. Box 3, 14193 Hwy. 172
Crockett, KY 41413
John Martin, Manager
Tel: (606) 522-4348 X154
Fax: (606) 522-4896
Circ.: 8,000
Price: Free **Subscription:** $4.15/year
Publication description: International Spanish magazine.
Date established: 1967

EVANGELISTA PENTECOSTAL, EL
Iglesia de Dios Pentecostal, Movimiento Internacional-Región Puerto Rico.
P.O. Box 13324
Santurce, PR 00908
Moisés Flores, General Manager
Tel: (787) 758-8562 **Fax:** (787) 999-1560
Web: www.radiotriunfo.com
Circ.: 25,000
Price: Free
Publication description: To evangelize, edifying and restore thru our gospel music and the word of god.
Date established: 1980

EXPERIENCE IN DEMOCRACY NEWSLETTER
Bert Corona Leadership Institute
1500 Farragut St. NW
Washington, DC 20011
Wendy Carrasco, Deputy Director
Tel: (202) 723-7241 **Fax:** (202) 723-7246
Email: expdemocracy1@aol.com
Web: www.bcli.info
Price: Free **Subscription:** $150.00/year.
Date established: 1991

EXPORT MAGAZINE COMPRAR
Finocchiaro Enterprises
2921 Coral Way
Miami, FL 33145
Justin Finocchiaro, Editor
Tel: (305) 529-0142 **Fax:** (305) 529-9217
Email: mail@comprarmag.com
Web: www.comprarmag.com
Circ.: 50,000
Price: Free **Subscription:** $35.00/year
Publication description: Local/regional Spanish magazine.
Date established: 1976

FAMA MAGAZINE
Osmus Publishing Group Inc.
331 W. 57th St. #282
New York, NY 10019
Al Vazquez, Editor
Tel: (212) 633-9975 **Fax:** (212) 633-9976
Email: al@famaweb.com
Web: www.famaweb.com
Circ.: 120,000
Price: $2.79 **Subscription:** $19.99/year
Publication description: National distribution.
Date established: 1997

FAMILIA SENIOR COMMUNITY CENTER NEWSLETTER, LA
La Familia Senior Community Center
841 W 21st St. North
Wichita, KS 67203
Irma Allagar, Executive Director
Tel: (316) 267-1700 **Fax:** (316) 267-7112
Email: lafamiliasenior@msn.com
Circ.: 500
Price: Free .
Date established: 1989

FÉ EN MARCHA, LA
Ministerio Cristo Viene
P.O. Box 949
Camuy, PR 00627
Yiye Avila, Director
Tel: (787) 898-5120 **Fax:** (787) 820-4496
Email: cartas@yiyeavila.org
Web: www.yiyeavila.org
Price: Free

FLORIDA REVIEW MAGAZINE
905 Brickel Bay Dr. Lobby #2CL23
Miami, FL 33131
Mirtha Arriaran, Publisher/President
Tel: (305) 374-5235 **Fax:** (305) 358-9456
Email: mirtha@floridareview.com
Web: www.floridareview.com
Circ.: 20,000
Price: Free
Publication description: Brazilian publication.
Date established: 1985

FRONTLINES NEWSLETTER
U.S. Agency for International Development
RRB, #6.10
Washington, DC 20523-6100
USAID, Publisher
Tel: (202) 712-4810 **Fax:** (202) 216-3035
Email: frontlines@usaid.gov
Web: www.usaid.gov/pubs/frontlines
Circ.: 1,000
Price: Free
Publication description: A periodic general interest publication that highlights USAID-funded activities around the world, USAID staff accomplishments, and other items of interest to anyone involved in foreign economic and humanitarian assistance activities.
Date established: 1983

GLAMOUR EN ESPAÑOL
Conde Nast Americas
1101 Brickell Ave., 15th Fl.
Miami, FL 33131
Madelin Bosakewich, Publisher
Tel: (305) 371-9393 **Fax:** (305) 371-9392
Email: adelapaz@condenastamericas.com
Circ.: 200,000
Price: $2.95 **Subscription:** $35.40/year
Publication description: Glamour en Español goes-in-depth on issues relevant to women-challenging its readers to assume a bold attitude.
Date established: 2000

GUÍA DEL GOLFO
TV Net Productions, Inc.
6455 Gateway Ave. #A
Sarasota, FL 34231
Luis Eduardo Barón, Editor
Tel: (941) 923-0273 **Fax:** (941) 923-6483
Email: revista@guiadelgolfo.com
Web: www.guiadelgolfo.com
Circ.: 16,000
Price: Free .
Date established: 2000

HARPER'S BAZAAR
Editorial Televisa - USA
6355 NW 36th St.
Miami, FL 33166
Patrick Holmes, Senior Advertiser/Sales Executive
Tel: (305) 871-6400 **Fax:** (305) 871-5026
Email: pholmes@editorialtelevisa.com
Web: www.buyeditorialtelevisa.com
Circ.: 38,000
Subscription: $21.95/year
Publication description: International Spanish magazine. Harper's Bazaar en español® is the ultra avant-garde magazine for the upscale young Latin woman, supported by the prestige that has made it one of the most important fashion publications in the world. Published as part of a joint venture with The Hearst Corporation, Harper's Bazaar® caters to the needs and desires of the sophisticated, discriminating, high class woman with purchasing power. She makes her own decisions and is completely conscious of the importance of a good image. Harper's Bazaar® readers are creative, authentic, self-sufficient and elegant.
Date established: 1980

HAWAII HISPANIC NEWS
303-C Mananai Pl.
Honolulu, HI 96816
José Villa, Publisher/Editor
Tel: (808) 351-8013
Email: editor@hawaiihispanicnews.com
Web: www.hawaiihispanicnews.com
Price: Free
Publication description: The Hawaii Hispanic News On-Line started as a one-page newsletter in March of 1994, evolved into a community newspaper for Hawaii's 100,000 Hispanic residents, and has continued its evolution into cyberspace.
Date established: 1994

HERALDO CATÓLICO NEWSPAPER, EL
Catholic Diocese of Sacramento
5890 Newman Ct.
Sacramento, CA 95819
Deacon Ricardo Olvera, Editor
Tel: (916) 452-3691 **Fax:** (916) 452-2945
Email: Elheraldocatolico@aol.com
Web: www.diocese-sacramento.org/elheraldo.html
Circ.: 36,000
Price: Free .
Date established: 1979

HEROES MAGAZINE
Hispanic Entrepreneur Resource Organization & Executive Services
P.O. Box 842002
Houston, TX 77284-2002
Rosemary Acosta-Clark, Editor
Tel: (281) 859-0564 **Fax:** (281) 859-2636
Email: rosemaryclark@4heroes.org
Web: www.4heroes.org
Circ.: 2,000
Price: Free
Publication description: Informative Spanish/English tabloid-magazine.
Date established: 1999

HISPANIC BUSINESS
Hispanic Business, Inc.
425 Pine Ave.
Santa Barbara, CA 93117
Jesus Chavarria, Editor/Publisher
Tel: (805) 964-4554 **Fax:** (805) 964-5539
Email: editorial@hbinc.com
Web: www.hispanicbusiness.com
Circ.: 155,000
Price: $3.99 **Subscription:** $19.97/year

Publication description: National English magazine.
Date established: 1977

HISPANIC BUSINESS JOURNAL
Grupo Bogotá
198 W. Chew Ave.
Philadelphia, PA 19120
Ricardo Hurtado, Director
Tel: (215) 424-1200 **Fax:** (215) 424-6064
Email: rhurtado@elsoln1.com
Web: www.elsoln1.com
Price: $2.50
Publication description: Hispanic Business Journal

HISPANIC BUSINESS JOURNAL
Hispanic Chamber of Commerce of Silicon Valley
696 E. Santa Clara St. #106
San Jose, CA 95112
Dennis King, Executive Director
Tel: (408) 213-0320 **Fax:** (408) 213-0329
Email: info@hccsv.com
Web: www.hccsv.com
Circ.: 5,000
Price: Free
Publication description: Disseminates useful information and knowledge about the various levels of the Hispanic market to the Silicon Valley business community.
Date established: 1995

HISPANIC HOTLINE
Hispanic Hotline
P. O. Box 163510
Sacramento, CA 95816
Tony Vásquez, Publisher
Tel: (916) 448-7594 **Fax:** (916) 989-4742
Email: hispanic@jps.net
Web: www.careersnow-online.com/hispanic.html
Circ.: 8,000
Price: Free .
Date established: 1984

HISPANIC JOURNAL
Hispanic Journal, LLC
P.O. Box 810650
Dallas, TX 75381
Denise M. Nuño, Editor
Tel: (214) 350-4774 **Fax:** (214) 358-0018
Email: info@hispanicjournal.com
Web: www.hispanicjournal.com
Circ.: 210,000
Subscription: $24.00/year
Publication description: Hispanic Journal meets the unique needs of the Hispanic business and professional community in Texas.
Date established: 1994

HISPANIC MAGAZINE
Hispanic Publishing Group
999 Ponce de León Blvd. #600
Coral Gables, FL 33134
Joe Vidueira, Editor
Tel: (305) 442-2462 **Fax:** (305) 774-3578
Email: jvidueira@hisp.com
Web: www.hispanicmagazine.com
Circ.: 250,000
Price: $3.50 **Subscription:** $10.00/year
Publication description: English magazine.
Date established: 1988

HISPANIC NETWORK NEWSLETTER
Kern County Hispanic Chamber of Commerce
1401 19th St. #110
Bakersfield, CA 93301
Lou Gomez, Executive Director
Tel: (661) 633-5495 **Fax:** (661) 323-9619
Email: lgomez@kchcc.org

Web: www.kernhispanicchamber.com
Circ.: 650
Price: Free
Publication description: Hispanic Network Newsletter tells about what is happening in the business world and it provides information about business activities in Kern County.
Date established: 1985

HISPANIC PR MONITOR, THE
Hispanic PR Wire
13205 SW 137th Ave. #229
Miami, FL 33186
Manny Ruiz, President/CEO
Tel: (305) 971-2622 **Fax:** (305) 971-5955
Email: mruiz@hispanicprwire.com
Web: www.hispanicprwire.com
Circ.: 2,000
Price: Free .
Date established: 2000

HISPANIC PROFESSIONAL MAGAZINE
National Society of Hispanic MBA's (NSHMBA)
8204 Elmbrook #235
Dallas, TX 75247-4067
Ana Herrera-Malone, Marketing and Development Director
Tel: (877) 462-4622 **Fax:** (214) 267-1626
Email: editorialhmba@nshmba.org
Web: www.nshmba.org
Circ.: 15,000
Price: Membership
Publication description: English newsletter.
Date established: 2000

HISPANIC TRENDS
Hispanic Publishing Group - USHCC
999 Ponce de Leon #600
Coral Gables, FL 33134
Joe Vidueira, Editor
Tel: (305) 442-2462 **Fax:** (305) 774-3578
Email: jvidueira@hisp.com
Web: www.hispanictrends.com
Circ.: 50,000
Price: Free
Publication description: A magazine for all Hispanics with the largest national circulation of any Latino publication. It covers news, events, and issues of interest to the Hispanic community nationwide.
Date established: 1985

HISPANIDADES UPDATE
Hispanidades
4343 Lee Hwy. #505
Arlington, VA 22207
Simón R. Contreras, Coordinator
Tel: (703) 528-4094 **Fax:** (703) 228-5813
Email: sr_contreras@yahoo.com
Circ.: 1,000
Price: Free
Publication description: To promote the cultures of the spanish-speaking world through dancing.
Date established: 1981

HOLA HAWAII NEWSPAPER
Hola Hawaii Productions, Inc.
620 McCully St. #506
Honolulu, HI 96826
Laura E. Angel Guzman, President
Tel: (808) 947-0828 **Fax:** (808) 947-0828
Email: guzmanf002@hawaii.rr.com
Circ.: 10,000
Price: Free **Subscription:** $25.00/year
Publication description: To inform the Hispanic community regarding local and national Hispanic news.
Date established: 1999

HOY EN DELAWARE
Mundo Graphics
P.O. Box 593
Georgetown, DE 19947
Jose Somalo, Publisher
Tel: (302) 947-9199 **Fax:** (302) 947-9299
Email: hoy@del.net
Circ.: 8,000
Price: Free **Subscription:** $11.00/year
Publication description: To provide a positive publication for the betterment of all people in Delaware.
Date established: 1996

IDBAMÉRICA MAGAZINE
Inter-American Development Bank
External Relations Office,
1300 New York Ave. NW #B-0560
Washington, DC 20577
Roger Hamilton, Editor
Tel: (202) 623-1379 **Fax:** (202) 312-4201
Email: editor@iadb.org
Web: www.iadb.org
Circ.: N/A
Price: Free
Publication description: Magazine of the Inter-American Development Bank.
Date established: 1964

IDEAS
Editorial Televisa - USA
6355 NW 36th St.
Miami, FL 33166
Patrick Holmes, Senior Advertiser/Sales Executive
Tel: (305) 871-6400 **Fax:** (305) 871-5026
Email: pholmes@editorialtelevisa.com
Web: www.buyeditorialtelevisa.com
Circ.: 203,906
Subscription: $12.00/year
Publication description: International Spanish magazine. Ideas para su hogar® is a fun guide for women who enjoy decorating and other home projects. Food and cooking make up a substantial portion of the magazine. Ideas® goes beyond decorating into handicrafts, toys, furniture, gardening, knitting and sewing. A free pattern is included in each issue. It is specially designed for the Latin woman who takes pride in her home and her family.
Date established: 1978

IMAGEN
Casiano Communications
1700 Ave. Fernández Juncos
San Juan, PR 00909-2938
Annette Olivaras, Editor
Tel: (787) 728-8727 **Fax:** (787) 728-5948
Email: imagen@casiano.com
Web: www.casiano.com
Circ.: 70,000
Price: $2.95 **Subscription:** $20.00/year
Publication description: Puerto Rico's leading Women's family lifestyle magazine.
Date established: 1986

IMAGEN ARGENTINA MAGAZINE
P.O. Box 5175, Meadowview Station
North Bergen, NJ 07047
Carlos Novotny, Editor
Tel: (201) 662-0347 **Fax:** (201) 662-1041
Email: imagenargentina@aol.com
Circ.: 12,000
Price: Free **Subscription:** $30.00/year.
Date established: 1986

IMAGEN - REFLECTIONS OF TODAY'S LATINO
P.O. Box 7487
Albuquerque, NM 87194
José Armas, Editor
Tel: (505) 889-4088 **Fax:** (505) 889-4206

Email: armas@swcp.com
Web: www.imagenmag.com
Circ.: 25,000
Price: $24.00
Publication description: Imagen spotlights New Mexico's Latinos in news, arts and entertainment, leadership, heritage, sports, education, and business. .
Date established: 2000

INDUSTRIA AVÍCOLA
Watt Publishing Co.
122 S. Wesley Ave.
Mt. Morris, IL 61054
Chris Wright, Editor
Tel: (815) 734-4171 **Fax:** (815) 734-5679
Web: www.wattnet.com
Circ.: 14,005
Price: Free
Publication description: International Spanish magazine.
Date established: 1952

INFORME NEWSLETTER
Hispanic Chamber of Commerce
1250 6th Ave. #550
San Diego, CA 92101
Miguel Reza, Editor
Tel: (619) 702-0790 **Fax:** (619) 696-3282
Email: sdchcc@sdchcc.com
Web: www.sdchcc.com
Circ.: 2,000
Price: Free
Publication description: Local/regional English newsletter.
Date established: 1997

INSTITUTO DE MEXICO NEWSLETTER
Instituto Cultural Mexicano
600 HemisFair Plaza
San Antonio, TX 78240
Enrique Cortazar, Director
Tel: (210) 227-0123 **Fax:** (210) 223-1978
Email: mthomas@imexicano.org
Circ.: 3,500
Price: Free
Publication description: Spanish newsletter for members only.
Date established: 1984

INTER-AMERICAN TRADE REPORT
The National Law Center for Inter-American Free Trade
2 E. Congress St. #500
Tucson, AZ 85701-1728
Mina Goldberg, Editor
Tel: (520) 622-1200 **Fax:** (520) 622-0957
Email: natlaw@natlaw.com
Web: www.natlaw.com
Price: $50.00 **Subscription:** $695.00/year
Publication description: Inter-American Trade Report delivers monthly coverage of trade, commerce, and legal developments, important legislation and regulations, and relevant court decisions from across Latin America.

LAREDOS, A JOURNAL OF THE BORDERLANDS
ShuString Productions, Inc.
1812 Houston St.
Laredo, TX 78040
María Eugenia Guerra, CEO & Publisher
Tel: (956) 791-9950 **Fax:** (956) 791-4737
Email: laredos@swbell.net
Web: www.laredosnews.com
Circ.: 10,000
Price: Free **Subscription:** $36.00/year
Publication description: Covers Public information issues.
Date established: 1984

LATIN TRADE MAGAZINE
95 Merrick Way #600
Coral Gables, FL 33134
Michael Zellner, Editor
Tel: (305) 358-8373 **Fax:** (305) 579-9752
Email: mgallo@latintrade-inc.com
Web: www.latintrade.com
Circ.: 16,868
Subscription: $44.00/year
Publication description: National Spanish magazine.
Date established: 1993

LATINA
Latina Publications, LLC
1500 Broadway #700
New York, NY 10036
Christy Haubegger, Publisher
Tel: (212) 642-0200 **Fax:** (212) 997-2553
Email: editor@latina.com
Web: www.latina.com
Circ.: 300,000
Price: $2.50 **Subscription:** $12.97/year
Publication description: Magazine.
Date established: 1996

LATINFINANCE MAGAZINE
Latin American Financial Publications, Inc.
2121 Ponce de Leon Blvd. #1020
Coral Gables, FL 33134
John Barham, Editor
Tel: (305) 448-6593 **Fax:** (305) 448-0718
Email: johnb@latinfinance.com
Web: www.latinfinance.com
Circ.: 31,940
Price: $21.50 **Subscription:** $235.00/year
Publication description: LatinFinance covers business, finance, cross-border investment and capital markets in Latin America through good times and bad.
Date established: 1987

LATINO NEWSPAPER
Latino News, Inc.
P.O. Box 28
Gadsden, AL 35902
Jairo Vargas, Publisher
Tel: (256) 442-8914 **Fax:** (256) 442-0372
Email: sales@latino-news.com
Web: www.latino-news.com
Circ.: 20,000
Price: Free
Publication description: Spanish Newspaper.
Date established: 1997

LOFT MAGAZINE
Zoom Media Group
309 23rd St. #212
Miami Beach, FL 33139
David Yanovich, Editor
Tel: (305) 535-3125 **Fax:** (305) 535-3126
Email: david@zoommediagroup.com
Web: www.zoommediagroup.com
Circ.: 80,000
Price: $3.95 **Subscription:** $7.99/11 issues.
Date established: 2000

MAGAZINE
Mexican American Grocers Association
405 N. San Fernando Rd.
Los Angeles, CA 90031
Jerome Wilson Lloyd, Editor
Tel: (323) 227-1565 **Fax:** (323) 227-6935
Email: maga727@sbcglobal.net
Web: www.maga-inc.org
Circ.: 7,000
Price: Free **Subscription:** $100.00/year
Publication description: Local/regional English publication.
Date established: 1987

MARIE CLAIRE
Editorial Televisa - USA
6355 NW 36th St.
Miami, FL 33166
Patrick Holmes, Senior Advertiser/Sales
Executive
Tel: (305) 871-6400 **Fax:** (305) 871-5026
Email: pholmes@editorialtelevisa.com
Web: www.buyeditorialtelevisa.com
Circ.: 27,849
Subscription: $19.95/year
Publication description: International Spanish
magazine. The beauty and fashion magazine
for the sophisticated Latin American woman.
The Spanish-language Marie Claire® is
published under license from Marie Claire
Album. It is tailored to the concerns of
today's multifaceted woman: sensitive and
romantic, yet intelligent, practical and socially
responsible. Each issue includes a story of
a famous woman, past or present. There
are regular sections on decorating, gourmet
cooking, travel and health. .
Date established: 1990

**MARKETING TO THE EMERGING
MAJORITIES**
EPM Communications, Inc.
160 Mercer St., 3rd Fl.
New York, NY 10012-3212
Ira Mayer, President & Publisher
Tel: (212) 941-0099 **Fax:** (212) 941-1622
Email: info@epmcom.com
Web: www.epmcom.com
Subscription: $325.00/year
Publication description: Publish information
on marketing to Black, Hispanic and Asian
Americans.
Date established: 1988

MAXIM EN ESPAÑOL
Editorial Televisa - USA
6355 NW 36th St.
Miami, FL 33166
Patrick Holmes, Senior Advertiser/Sales
Executive
Tel: (305) 871-6400 **Fax:** (305) 871-5026
Email: pholmes@editorialtelevisa.com
Web: www.buyeditorialtelevisa.com
Circ.: 50,000
Subscription: $12.00/year
Publication description: Editorial Televisa is
the largest publisher of Spanish-language
magazines in the world and the leader
in Latin America and the U.S. Hispanic
Markets. The company publishes forty-two
titles, most of them the leaders in their
respective categories, including such titles
as Vanidades, Cosmopolitan en español,
Marie Claire en español, Harper's Bazaar en
español, National Geographic en español,
Men's Health en español and several other
Spanish-language publications.
Date established: 2001

MECÁNICA POPULAR
Editorial Televisa - USA
6355 NW 36th St.
Miami, FL 33166
Patrick Holmes, Senior Advertiser/Sales
Executive
Tel: (305) 871-6400 **Fax:** (305) 871-5026
Email: pholmes@editorialtelevisa.com
Web: www.buyeditorialtelevisa.com
Circ.: 171,332
Publication description: International Spanish
magazine. Published as part of a joint venture
with the Hearst Corporation Mecánica
Popular® is the Spanish language version
of Popular Mecanics® . Providing detailed
and easy to read information, it keeps the
contemporary Latin American male well

informed about topics of interest that are part
of his lifestyle. Mecánica Popular® features
up-to-date information on automobiles
science and technology, consumer
electronics, photography, computers and
accessories, as well as do-it- yourself
projects. Detailed articles on the latest
products and technological advancements
are complemented with full-color photographs
and descriptive illustrations.
Date established: 1968

MEDICINA Y CULTURA
Mundo Medico USA, Inc.
24 Club Way
Hartsdale, NY 10530
Robert A. Massa, Sales Contact
Tel: (914) 723-4092 **Fax:** (914) 723-4092
Email: rammedia@msn.com
Web: www.grupomundomedico.com
Circ.: 34,000.
Date established: 1992

MEDICO INTERAMERICANO MAGAZINE
Interamerican College of Physicians &
Surgeons
233 Broadway #771
New York, NY 10279
Javier Martinez, Editor
Tel: (212) 777-3642 **Fax:** (212) 777-5000
Email: info@icps.org
Web: www.icps.org
Circ.: 39,000
Price: Free .
Date established: 1981

MEN'S HEALTH EN ESPAÑOL
Editorial Televisa - USA
6355 NW 36th St.
Miami, FL 33166
Patrick Holmes, Senior Advertiser/Sales
Executive
Tel: (305) 871-6400 **Fax:** (305) 871-5026
Email: pholmes@editorialtelevisa.com
Web: www.buyeditorialtelevisa.com
Circ.: 35,000
Subscription: $12.00/year
Publication description: Published as a
joint venture with Rodale Press, Men's
Health en espanol® covers a wide range of
topics, including exercise, fitness, muscle
toning, vitality and strength, sex, healthy
foods, and beverages, dietary information,
nutrition, medical remedies, managing stress
and many other matters relating to good
health maintenance. Its articles provide the
necessary information to help today's young
men stay healthy and physically fit. Every
month there is a feature highlighting new
products that promote a healthy lifestyle
for men.
Date established: 1994

MENSAJERO, EL
Spanish Fiesta, Inc.
205 E. Joppa Rd. #2502
Towson, MD 21286
Dr. Eva Ramos Queral, President
Tel: (410) 823-7948 **Fax:** (410) 823-7117
Email: lquera@prodigy.net
Circ.: 9,000
Price: Free **Subscription:** None
Publication description: A community
organization serving the Hispanic community
of Maryland for 28 years.
Date established: 1973

MERCADO MAGAZINE
Solid Future Publishing
6425 W. 52 Ave. #1
Denver, CO 80002
Al McGregor, President

Tel: (303) 975-1142 **Fax:** (303) 975-1858
Email: almc@solidfuture.net
Web: www.solidfuture.net
Circ.: 15,000
Price: Free
Publication description: Savings magazine

MI GENTE MAGAZINE
Mi Gente Publications
418 N. Michigan Ave.
Saginaw, MI 48602
Larry J. Rodarte, Publisher/ Editor-in-Chief
Tel: (989) 753-1999 **Fax:** (989) 753-1927
Email: info@migentemag.com
Web: www.migentemag.com
Circ.: 15,000
Price: Free **Subscription:** $20.00/year
Publication description: In Spanish & English;
jrmigente@aol.com.
Date established: 1995

MIGRANT EDUCATION NEWS
Migrant Legal Action Program
P.O. Box 53308
Washington, DC 20009
Roger Rosenthal, Executive Director
Tel: (202) 462-7744 **Fax:** (202) 462-7914
Email: mlap@mlap.org
Web: www.mlap.org
Circ.: 1,000
Price: Free
Publication description: Migrant Education
News is a newsletter of Migrant Legal Action
Program .
Date established: 1998

MINORITY BUSINESS NEWS USA
TexCorp Communications, Inc.
11333 N. Central Expwy. #201
Dallas, TX 75243
Carol Foster, Editor
Tel: (214) 369-3200 **Fax:** (214) 265-9393
Email: carol@mbnews.com
Web: www.minoritybusinessnews.com
Circ.: 157,116
Subscription: $18.00/year
Publication description: National English
tabloid; news about minority and women
business enterprise in corporate America.
Date established: 1988

NATIONAL GEOGRAPHIC EN ESPAÑOL
Editorial Televisa - USA
6355 NW 36th St.
Miami, FL 33166
Patrick Holmes, Senior Advertiser/Sales
Executive
Tel: (305) 871-6400 **Fax:** (305) 871-5026
Email: pholmes@editorialtelevisa.com
Web: www.buyeditorialtelevisa.com
Circ.: 30,129
Subscription: $24.00/year
Publication description: Provides outstanding
photographs and precise articles; National
Geographic en español® is published
under license from the National Geographic
Society, a nonprofit organization whose
mission is to increase and diffuse geographic
knowledge. Impactive photography and
detailed illustrations enhance the diverse
articles on culture, people, natural marvels,
the animal world, science and technology.
National Geographic en español® transforms
its readers into adventurers of the world. It is
truly The Diary of a Planet.
Date established: 1997

NEWSLETTER
Hispanic Chamber of Commerce of Greater
Cincinnati
3805 Edwards Rd. #555
Cincinnati, OH 45209-1948

Robert P. Peraza, President
Tel: (513) 458-6649 **Fax:** (513) 458-6610
Email: president@hispanicccgc.com
Web: www.hispanicccgc.com
Circ.: 1,200
Price: Free
Publication description: Publication of
Membership.
Date established: 1996

NORTE DE AUSTIN NEWSPAPER, EL
P.O. Box 2181
Austin, TX 78768-2181
Gloria Montelongo Aguilar, Editor
Tel: (512) 448-1023 **Fax:** (512) 448-9962
Email: elnortedeaustin@earthlink.net
Circ.: 27,000
Price: Free .
Date established: 1996

NOSOTROS MAGAZINE
TeleGuía, Inc.
3114 Austin Blvd.
Cicero, IL 60804
Rose Montes, Publisher
Tel: (708) 656-9800 **Fax:** (708) 656-6679
Email: impanews@aol.com
Circ.: 14,000
Price: Free

NOSOTROS NEWS
Nosotros
650 N. Bronson Ave. #102
Hollywood, CA 90004
Jerry G. Velasco, President
Tel: (323) 466-8566 **Fax:** (323) 466-8540
Email: info@nosotros.org
Web: www.nosotros.org
Circ.: 10,000
Price: Free
Publication description: The Nosotros News
is the link to the entertainment world both in
English and Spanish.
Date established: 1970

NOTICIAS NEWSLETTER
Latino Chamber of Commerce of Pueblo,
Inc.
215 S. Victoria Ave.
Pueblo, CO 81003
Sandy Gutierrez, President/CEO
Tel: (719) 542-5513 **Fax:** (719) 542-4657
Email: info@pueblolatinochamber.com
Web: www.pueblolatinochamber.com
Circ.: 700
Price: Free
Publication description: Newsletter.
Date established: 1979

NOTICUBA BULLETIN
Cuba Independiente y Democrática
10020 SW 37 Terrace
Miami, FL 33165
Huber Matos, Secretary General
Tel: (305) 551-8484 **Fax:** (305) 559-9365
Email: rmatos@cfl.rr.com
Web: www.cubacid.com
Price: Free .
Date established: 1990

NUESTRA PARROQUIA NEWSLETTER
Claretian Publications
205 West Monroe
Chicago, IL 60606
Carmen Aguinaco, Editor
Tel: (312) 236-7782 **Fax:** (312) 236-8207
Email: aguinaco@claretianpubs.org
Web: www.claretianpubs.org
Circ.: 2,500
Subscription: $48.00/year
Publication description: Claretian Publications
also publishes other literature that relates
to the Hispanic Catholic Community in the

United States: Amigos de Jesus, and De Buena Fé.
Date established: 1997

NUESTRO MUNDO NEWSPAPER
3661 Davenport St.
Omaha, NE 68131
Benito Salazar, Editor
Tel: (402) 731-6210 **Fax:** (402) 731-6210
Email: nuestromundonewspaper@cox.net
Circ.: 7,000
Price: Free **Subscription:** $35.00/year
Publication description: Local/regional bilingual tabloid.
Date established: 1990

PAMPAS NEWSLETTER
8370 Greensboro Dr. #1007
McLean, VA 22101

PC MAGAZINE
Editorial Televisa - USA
6355 NW 36th St.
Miami, FL 33166
Patrick Holmes, Senior Advertiser/Sales Executive
Tel: (305) 871-6400 **Fax:** (305) 871-5026
Email: pholmes@editorialtelevisa.com
Web: www.buyeditorialtelevisa.com
Circ.: 161,857
Publication description: International Spanish magazine.
Date established: 1988

PEOPLE EN ESPAÑOL
The Time Inc. Magazine Company
1271 6th Ave.
New York, NY 10020
Jacqueline Hernandez-Fallous, Editor
Tel: (212) 522-4988 **Fax:** (212) 467-4845
Email: espanol@people.com
Web: www.peopleenespanol.com
Circ.: 250,000
Price: $2.49 **Subscription:** $19.97/year
Publication description: People en Español has grown to be the best selling Spanish-language magazine in the country with an estimated 3 million readers.
Date established: 1996

PERIODICO CAMINO LUZ Y VIDA, EL PERIODICO DEL PUEBLO CRISTIANO
P.O.Box 810128
Carolina, PR 00981
Luis Oscar Torres, President/Editor
Tel: (787) 413-4196
Web: www.caminoluzyvida.com
Subscription: $19.00/year
Publication description: Publishes Christian news and themes.
Date established: 2004

PERSPECTIVA MUNDIAL MAGAZINE
410 West St.
New York, NY 10014
Martin Koppel, Editor
Tel: (212) 594-1014 **Fax:** (212) 594-1018
Email: themilitant@verizon.net
Web: www.perspectivamundial.com
Circ.: 2,000
Price: $2.50 **Subscription:** $17.00/year
Publication description: Una revista socialista que defiende los intereses de pueblo trabajador.
Date established: 1977

PLAYERO, EL
Playeros, Inc.
P.O. Box 1508
Melbourne, FL 32902
Anselmo Baldonado, Editor
Tel: (321) 777-9225 **Fax:** (321) 777-1384
Email: elplayero@earthlink.net

Circ.: 10,000
Price: Free **Subscription:** $28.00/year
Publication description: Spanish newspaper in Brevard County.
Date established: 1993

PODER
Zoom Media Group
309 23rd St. #212
Miami Beach, FL 33139
David Yanovich, Editor
Tel: (305) 535-3125 **Fax:** (305) 535-3126
Email: david@zoommediagroup.com
Web: www.revistapoder.com
Circ.: 90,000
Price: $3.99 **Subscription:** $7.99/year.
Date established: 2000

PR TACTICS NEWSPAPER
Public Relations Society of America
33 Irving Place
New York, NY 10003
John Elsasser, Editor
Tel: (212) 460-1419 **Fax:** (212) 995-5024
Email: john.elsasser@prsa.org
Web: www.prsa.org
Circ.: 28,000
Price: $7.00 **Subscription:** $100.00/year
Publication description: Publishes news, trends, and how-to information about the practice of public relations.
Date established: 1994

PRENSA NUEVA ORLEANS, LA
111 Veterans Blvd. #1800
Metairie, LA 70005
Marietta Gonzalez, Editor
Tel: (504) 832-3555 **Fax:** (504) 378-0000
Email: laprensa@mcmediallc.com
Circ.: 15,000
Price: Free **Subscription:** $9.95/year
Publication description: Spanish-English publication.
Date established: 1995

PRESENCIA PANAMEÑA E HISPANA NEWSPAPER
Morgan's Owne. Asociación de Panameños Residentes en NY
P.O. Box 73-0757
Corona, NY 11372
Lic. Antonio Roberto Morgan, Publisher
Tel: (718) 592-3002 **Fax:** (718) 592-3002
Email: panamapost@aol
Web: www.panamausa.com/ourcomm.htm
Circ.: 20,000
Price: Free **Subscription:** $50.00/year
Publication description: Spanish-English newspaper.
Date established: 1994

PRIMERA, LA
Mark V Press
140 NE 32nd Ct.
Oakland Park, FL 33334
Gustavo Baner, Director
Tel: (954) 563-2505 **Fax:** (954) 563-2506
Email: redaccion@revistalaprimera.com
Web: www.revistalaprimera.com
Circ.: 10,000
Price: Free
Publication description: Publication for the Spanish-Speaking Jewish Community of South Florida.
Date established: 2003

PRODUCCÍON & DISTRIBUCIÓN
Izarra Publishing Group
37 NE 28th St.
Miami, FL 33187
Andrea Nieto, Editor
Tel: (305) 256-6774 x314
Fax: (305) 256-8487

Email: info@produ.com
Web: www.izarra.com,www.produ.com
Circ.: 7,000
Subscription: $99.00/year
Publication description: International Spanish magazine.
Date established: 1989

PRODUCCÍON & DISTRIBUCIÓN NIÑOS
Izarra Publishing Group
37 NE 28th St.
Miami, FL 33137
Andrea Nieto, Editor
Tel: (305) 256-6774 **Fax:** (305) 256-8487
Email: info@produ.com
Web: www.produ.com
Circ.: 5,000
Subscription: $99.00/year
Publication description: International Spanish magazine.
Date established: 1989

PRODUCTORES DE HORTALIZAS
Meister Publishing
37733 Euclid Ave.
Willoughby, OH 44094-5992
Katie O'Keeffe-Swank, Editor
Tel: (440) 942-2000 **Fax:** (440) 942-0662
Email: pdhca.circ@meistermedia.com
Web: www.meisterpro.com .
Circ.: 10,000
Price: $3.00 **Subscription:** $70.00/year
Publication description: International Spanish magazine.
Date established: 1992

PUBLICIDAD & COMERCIALES
Izarra Publishing Group
37 NE 28th St.
Miami, FL 33137
Andrea Nieto, Editor
Tel: (305) 256-3219 **Fax:** (305) 256-8487
Email: info@produ.com
Web: www.izarra.com,www.produ.com
Circ.: 6,000
Subscription: $99.00/year
Publication description: International Spanish magazine.
Date established: 1994

PUEBLO CATÓLICO, EL
Archdiocese of Denver
1300 S. Steele St.
Denver, CO 80210
Rossana Goñi, Editor
Tel: (303) 715-3219 **Fax:** (303) 715-2045
Email: elpueblo@archden.org
Web: www.archden.org/pueblo/
Circ.: 12,000
Price: Free **Subscription:** $ 10.00/year
Publication description: Spread Catholic faith among Hispanics in Northern Colorado. Promote values and help Hispanics to improve their lives in the United States. .
Date established: 1997

RAZATECA MAGAZINE
RazaTeca Publications
P.O. Box 611870
San Jose, CA 95161-1870
RazaTeca Publications, Publisher
Tel: (408) 971-6162
Email: RazaTeca@tdl.com
Web: www.tdl.com/~razateca
Circ.: 10,000
Price: $4.50 **Subscription:** $21.00/6 Issues
Publication description: RazaTeca is a bilingual (English/Spanish) magazine founded in 1996. It is the product of a grassroots efforts of Chicano/Latino community activists, students and professionals who volunteer their time as writers, editors and artists.
Date established: 1996

REFLEJOS BILINGUAL JOURNAL
155 E. Algonquin Rd.
West Dundee, IL 60118
Roberto Baeza, Editor
Tel: (847) 806-1111 **Fax:** (847) 806-1112
Email: jcampagna@reflejos.com
Web: www.reflejos.com
Circ.: 100,000
Price: Free .
Date established: 1990

REVISTA PANAMERICANA DE LA SALUD PÚBLICA
Pan American Health Organization (PAHO)
525 23rd St. NW
Washington, DC 20037
Maria Luisa Clark, Editor
Tel: (202) 974-3000 **Fax:** (202) 338-0869
Email: publiper@paho.org
Web: www.publications.paho.org
Circ.: 12,000
Price: $13.00 **Subscription:** $82.00/year
Publication description: This Health magazine is the most cited and consulted peer-reviewed journal in Latin America.
Date established: 1997

SA HISPANO
4000 Blanco Rd.
San Antonio, TX 78212
Winston Samuel Ojeda, President
Tel: (210) 735-4668 **Fax:** (210) 735-6724
Email: usa@sahispano.com
Web: www.sahispano.com
Circ.: 25,000.
Date established: 2003

SELECTA MAGAZINE
Selecta Magazine, Inc.
232 Andalusia Ave. #200
Coral Gables, FL 33134
Yadira Ortega, Editor
Tel: (305) 446-3305 **Fax:** (305) 446-5842
Email: yortega@revistaselecta.com
Web: www.revistaselecta.com
Circ.: 40,000
Price: $3.00 **Subscription:** $26.00/year
Publication description: Local/regional bilingual magazine.
Date established: 1984

SENSACIONAL
275 Fountain Blue Blvd. #168
Miami, FL 33172
Marta Ramos, Editor
Tel: (305) 220-5023 **Fax:** (305) 552-5807
Email: sensacio@bellsouth.net
Web: www.sensacional.net
Circ.: 35,000
Price: Free
Publication description: Local/regional Spanish newspaper.
Date established: 1991

SMALL BUSINESS JOURNAL
SBJ Publishing Co.
P.O. Box 16783
Seattle, WA 98116
Ramón Rodríguez, Editor
Tel: (206) 241-5854 **Fax:** (206) 241-5942
Email: rraasbj@aol.com
Circ.: 10,000
Price: Free
Publication description: Spanish special issues.
Date established: 1989

SOCCER AMERICA MAGAZINE
P.O. Box 23704
Oakland, CA 94623-0704
Mike Woitalla, Managing Editor
Tel: (510) 528-5000 **Fax:** (510) 528-5177

Email: mike@socceramerica.com
Web: www.socceramerica.com
Circ.: 40,000
Subscription: $79.00/year
Publication description: Bilingual magazine.
Date established: 1971

SOUTH FLORIDA CEO

The Americas Publishing Group
200 SE First St. #601
Miami, Fl 33131
Ron Mann, Publisher
Tel: (305) 379-1118
Email: mann@southfloridaceo.com
Web: www.southfloridaceo.com
Price: $29.95
Publication description: The Business magazine of Miami-Dade, Broward & The Palm Beaches

TACDC UPDATE

Texas Association of Community Development Corporations
1021 E. 7th St. #104
Austin, TX 78702
Courtney Enriquez, Membership Coordinator
Tel: (512) 457-8232 **Fax:** (512) 479-4090
Email: courtney@tacdc.org
Web: www.tacdc.org
Price: Free
Publication description: The TACDC Update is a monthly publication distributed to members via e-mail. The Update provides information to members on TACDC activities and advocacy efforts as well as upcoming trainings and funding opportunities.

TANGO REPORTER

La Prensa de Los Angeles
8033 Sunset Blvd. #704
Los Angeles, CA 90046
Carlos G. Groppa, Editor
Tel: (323) 654-6268
Email: tango4yoy@aol.com
Web: www.webcom.com
Circ.: 10,000
Subscription: $30.00/year
Publication description: Local/regional Spanish newsletter.
Date established: 1995

TEJANO HISPANIC COMMUNITY MONTHLY MAGAZINE, EL

El Tejano
2505 Sarita St.
Corpus Christi, TX 78405
Elizabeth M. Cuellar, Editor
Tel: (361) 884-2238 **Fax:** (361) 888-7703
Email: eltejano@aol.com
Circ.: 235,000
Price: Free **Subscription:** $25.00/year
Publication description: Spanish magazine.
Date established: 1996

TELE REVISTA

P.O. Box 145175
Coral Gables, FL 33114-5170
Ana Pereiro, Editor
Tel: (305) 445-1755 **Fax:** (305) 445-3907
Email: ana@telerevista.com
Web: www.telerevista.com
Circ.: 75,000
Price: $2.49 **Subscription:** $19.95/year
Publication description: National Spanish magazine.
Date established: 1992

TIPS THAT WORK AT WORK

Spanish at Work/Language Training
4343 Lee Hwy. #505
Arlington, VA 22207
Simón R. Contreras, Coordinator

Tel: (703) 528-4094 **Fax:** (703) 228-5813
Email: sr_contreras@yahoo.com
Circ.: 1,000
Price: Free
Publication description: To train office personnel in the Spanish language in the work place.
Date established: 1998

TODAY'S GROCER IN ESPAÑOL

Florida Grocer Publishing Co.
161 NE 97th St.
Miami Shores, FL 33138
Dennis M. Kane, Editor
Tel: (305) 758-2590 **Fax:** (305) 758-3429
Email: contact@todaysgrocer.com
Web: www.todaysgrocer.com
Circ.: 16,000
Price: $3.50 **Subscription:** $39.95/year
Publication description: Local/regional Spanish newspaper; Spanish section of Todays Grocer.
Date established: 1975

TRAJANO

Department of Foreign Languages, Adams State College
208 Edgemont Blvd.
Alamosa, CO 81102
Dr.Eva E. Rayas-Ihm, Department Head
Tel: (719) 587-7011 **Fax:** (719) 587-7176
Email: erihm@adams.edu
Web: http://languages.adams.edu/
Circ.: 200
Price: Free
Publication description: To encourage reading and the use of the Spanish Language among Hispanic Communities and anybody interested in Spanish Culture & Language.
Date established: 2001

TRAVEL & LEISURE EN ESPAÑOL

Editorial Televisa - USA
6355 NW 36th St.
Miami, FL 33166
Patrick Holmes, Senior Advertiser/Sales Executive
Tel: (305) 871-6400 **Fax:** (305) 871-5026
Email: pholmes@editorialtelevisa.com
Web: www.buyeditorialtelevisa.com
Circ.: 40,069
Subscription: $24.00/year
Publication description: Editorial Televisa is the largest publisher of Spanish-language magazines in the world and the leader in Latin America and the U.S. Hispanic Markets. The company publishes 42 titles, most of them the leaders in their respective categories, including such titles as Vanidades, Cosmopolitan en español, Marie Claire en español, Harper's Bazaar en español, National Geographic en español, Men's Health en español and several other Spanish-language publications.
Date established: 2002

TU

Editorial Televisa - USA
6355 NW 36th St.
Miami, FL 33166
Patrick Holmes, Senior Advertiser/Sales Executive
Tel: (305) 871-6400 **Fax:** (305) 871-5026
Email: pholmes@editorialtelevisa.com
Web: www.buyeditorialtelevisa.com
Circ.: 477,141
Publication description: International Spanish magazine. Centering on personal advice articles that help teenage readers cope with everyday problems, Tú is the relevant and fun magazine for adolescent women. Its sections and articles have been created and

designed to entertain and help her improve physically and intellectually. The latest trends in beauty and fashion are featured in a lively, hip style. Always of interest are the articles on the entertainment world and its leading personalities.
Date established: 1981

U.S. PORTUGAL BRASIL

P.O. Box 367
New York, NY 10024-0367
Frederico Ziotto, Editor
Tel: (212) 579-4750 **Fax:** (212) 579-4761
Email: brasil@pipeline.com
Circ.: 70,000
Subscription: $20.00/year
Publication description: A cultural focus covering education and community events.

URBAN LATINO WEST NEWS, THE

3288 21st. St. #9
San Francisco, CA 94110
Gail Neira, Publisher
Tel: (415) 821-4452 **Fax:** (415) 821-4452
Email: gail.neira@chi.org
Circ.: 20,000
Price: Free
Publication description: Local/regional Spanish newspaper.
Date established: 1995

UTAH CATÓLICO/INTERMOUNTAIN CATHOLIC NEWSPAPER-OFFICIAL NEWSPAPER

The Diocese of Salt Lake City
P.O. Box 2489
Salt Lake City, UT 84110
Barbara Lee, Editor
Tel: (801) 328-8641 **Fax:** (801) 537-1667
Email: icnews@icnp.com
Web: www.icnp.com
Circ.: 14,000
Price: Free **Subscription:** $20.00/year
Publication description: Official newspaper of the Diocese of Salt lake City.
Date established: 1899

VAA NEWSLETTER

Venezuelan American Association, Inc.
30 Vesey St. #506
New York, NY 10007
Alfredo J. Gonzalez, President
Tel: (212) 233-7776 **Fax:** (212) 233-7779
Email: andean@nyct.net
Web: www.venezuelanamerican.org
Price: Free
Publication description: Economic Newsletter.
Date established: 1927

VALIENTE MAGAZINE

6000 Custer Rd., Bldg. #9
Plano, TX 75023
Gavin Wallace, Publisher
Tel: (972) 517-2700 **Fax:** (469) 429-0020
Email: gavin@valientemagazine.com
Web: www.valientemagazine.com
Circ.: 35,000
Price: $2.95 **Subscription:** $12.00/year
Publication description: A premier Latino magazine in the North Texas region. Published monthly in English, Valiente is dedicated to acclaiming success in the lives of Latinos. Editorial content reflects issues concerning people, places, and communities in feature articles, profiles, and departments in fashion, entertainment, cuisine, business, health, culture, the arts, and more, together with chic and sophisticated photography that offers advertisers quality, value, and an excellent record of customer service.

VISTA MAGAZINE

Vista Publishing Corp.
1201 Brickell Ave. #360
Miami, FL 33131
Carmen Roiz, Editor
Tel: (305) 416-4644 **Fax:** (305) 416-4344
Email: croiz@vistamagazine.com
Web: www.vistamagazine.com
Circ.: 1,000,000
Price: Free
Publication description: A magazine for all Hispanics with the largest national circulation of any Latino publication. It covers news, events, and issues of interest to the Hispanic community nationwide.
Date established: 1984

VIVA NEW YORK MAGAZINE

R. Paniagua, Inc.
450 W. 33rd St., 3rd Fl.
New York, NY 10001
Neil Perlich Poter, Managing Editor
Tel: (212) 210-2100 **Fax:** (212) 326-4096
Email: vivanewyork@nyc.rr.com
Web: www.nydailynews.com
Circ.: 400,000
Price: Free
Publication description: Local /regional bilingual lifestyles magazine is published in conjunction with the New York Daily News.
Date established: 1991

VOGUE EN ESPAÑOL

Conde Nast Americas
1101 Brickell Ave., 15th Fl.
Miami, FL 33131
Madelin Bosakewich, Publisher
Tel: (305) 371-9393 **Fax:** (305) 371-9392
Email: adelapaz@condenastamericas.com
Circ.: 200,000
Price: $3.50 **Subscription:** $42.00
Publication description: Vogue en Español is a fashion magazine.
Date established: 2000

VOICE OF HISPANIC HIGHER EDUCATION, THE

The Hispanic Association of Colleges & Universities (HACU)
8415 Datapoint Dr. #400
San Antonio, TX 78229
Cynthia Vela, Office Manager
Tel: (210) 692-3805 X3231
Fax: (210) 692-0823
Email: jvalenzuela@hacu.net
Web: www.hacu.net
Circ.: 2,000
Price: $12.00/year $20/2years
Publication description: Spanish/English publication.
Date established: 1986

VOZ CATÓLICA, LA

Archdiocese of Miami
9401 Biscayne Blvd.
Miami, FL 33138-2970
Dora Amador, Editor
Tel: (305) 762-1201 **Fax:** (305) 762-1223
Email: redaccion@miamiarch.org
Web: www.vozcatolica.org
Circ.: 162,000
Price: Free **Subscription:** $24.00/year
Publication description: Local/regional Spanish newspaper; Audience: Hispanic.
Date established: 1982

VOZ HISPANIA, LA

National Organization for the Advancement of Hispanics
2217 Princess Anne St. #205-1
Fredericksburg, VA 22401
Rosa Holseberg, Executive Director

Tel: (540) 372-3437 Fax: (540) 372-3437
Email: noah-va@noah-va.org
Web: www.noah-va.org
Circ.: 500
Price: Free
Publication description: NOAH publishes the newsletter to keep the Hispanic Community in touch about its activities and services.
Date established: 1985

YO! YOUTH OUTLOOK

Pacific News Service
275 9th St.
San Francisco, CA 94103
Kevin Weston, Editor
Tel: (415) 503-4170 Fax: (415) 503-0970
Email: kweston@pacificnews.org
Web: www.youthoutlook.org
Circ.: 25,000
Subscription: $15.00/year
Publication description: YO! Youth Outlook is a literary journal of youth life in the Bay Area.

YSAC NEWSLETTER

York Spanish American Center
200 E. Princess St.
York, PA 17403
Alex Ramos, Director
Tel: (717) 846-9434 X1
Fax: (717) 843-5722
Email: spanishcenter@yahoo.com
Circ.: 100
Price: Free
Publication description: Annual local/regional English publication.
Date established: 2000

ZONA COMERCIAL

Direct Marketing & Media Group
P.O. Box 9024182
San Juan, PR 00902-4182
Lilia Molina Ruiz, President
Tel: (787) 268-1111 Fax: (787) 268-7044
Email: lmolina@dmmgonline.com
Web: www.zonacomercial.net
Circ.: 10,000
Subscription: $48.00/year.
Date established: 1914

ZOPILOTE NEWS

El Quinto Sol
824 S. Mill Ave. #219
Tempe, AZ 85281
Marco A. Albarran, Executive Director
Tel: (480) 557-7195
Email: zopilote1@mindspring.com
Web: www.elquintosol.org
Circ.: 10,000
Price: $3.50 Subscription: $18.00/year
Publication description: To promote the cultural and environmental diversities in relation to the positive development of ethnic communities.
Date established: 1993

PERIODICALLY

BRAIN QUEST HISPANIC AMERICA

Workman Publishing Conpany
708 Broadway
New York, NY 10003-9555
Jorge Ochoa, Editor
Tel: (212) 254-5900 Fax: (212) 254-8098
Email: info@workman.com
Web: www.workman.com
Circ.: 311,000
Price: $10.95
Publication description: Brain Quest Hispanic America is a English language title targeting Hispanic American kids ages 9-12. The book/trivia game includes 850 questions and answers on Hispanic history and cultural heritage.

CARTA INFORMATIVA STUDENT NEWSLETTER, LA

La Casa Cultural Latina at U of IL-Urbana-Champaign
1203 W. Nevada
Urbana, IL 61801
Giraldo Rosales, Director
Tel: (217) 333-4950 Fax: (217) 244-4513
Email: lacasa@uiuc.edu
Web: www.odos.uiuc.edu/lacasa
Price: Free .
Date established: 1972

LIBROS DE LA SEPAL

The United Nations
2 United Nations Pl. #DC2-853, Dept. I004
New York, NY 10017
Miguel Marzullo, Contact - Spanish Language Publications
Tel: (212) 963-8302 Fax: (212) 963-3489
Email: publications@un.org
Web: www.un.org/publications
Price: $20.00

SALUD EN LAS AMÉRICAS, LA

Pan American Health Organization (PAHO)
525 23rd St. NW
Washington, DC 20037
PAN American Health Organization, Publisher
Tel: (202) 974-3000 Fax: (202) 974-3663
Email: publiper@paho.org
Web: http://publications.paho.org
Circ.: 6,015
Subscription: $54.00.
Date established: 1993

QUARTERLY

AAMA NEWS

Association for the Advancement of Mexican Americans
6001 Gulf Freeway, Bldg. B-1
Houston, TX 77023
Maria Alanis, Director of Public Relations
Tel: (713) 926-4756 Fax: (713) 926-8035
Email: AAMA@aamainc.com
Web: www.aamainc.com
Circ.: 2000
Price: Free
Publication description: AAMA is committed to advancing the lives of at-risk and disadvantaged youth and families through an array of innovative programs of excellence in the areas of education, Health and Human Services and Community Development.
Date established: 1970

ACCIÓN LATINA

Latin American Community Center
403 N. Van Buren St.
Wilmington, DE 19805
Carlos De Los Ramos, Editor
Tel: (302) 655-7338 Fax: (302) 655-7334
Email: dlosramos@hotmail.com
Web: www.thelatincenter.org
Circ.: 2,000
Price: Free
Publication description: Improves the quality of life of the Hispanic community by developing resources to promote its advancement.
Date established: 1969

ADELANTE!

National Puerto Rican Coalition, Inc.
1901 L. St. NW #802
Washington, DC 20036
Keri Nunez, Managing Editor

Tel: (202) 223-3915 X309
Fax: (202) 429-2223
Email: nprc@nprcinc.org
Web: www.bateylink.org
Circ.: 600
Price: Free
Publication description: Newsletter.
Date established: 1977

AGENDA MAGAZINE

National Council of la Raza
17563 W. 158th Terrace
Olathe, KS 66062-6777
Sarah Chavez, Editor
Tel: (913) 397-7850 Fax: (913) 397-0890
Email: schavez @latinpointe.com
Web: www.latinpointe.com
Circ.: 20,000
Price: Free
Publication description: Agenda Magazine is the publication of National Council of la Raza.
Date established: 2002

AGUILA, EL

Hispanic American Police Command Officers Association
6055A Arlington Blvd.
Falls Church, VA 22044-2721
Elvin Crespo, Editor
Tel: (703) 534-2895 Fax: (703) 534-2896
Email: info@hapcoa.org
Web: www.hapcoa.org
Circ.: 1,000
Price: Free
Publication description: The newsletter of Hispanic American Police Command Officers Association.
Date established: 1973

AHA! HISPANIC ARTS NEWS

Association of Hispanic Arts, Inc.
250 W. 26th St., 4th Fl.
New York, NY 10001
Sandra Pérez, Editor
Tel: (212) 727-7227 Fax: (212) 727-0549
Email: ahanews@latinoarts.org
Web: www.latinoarts.org
Circ.: 18,000
Price: $4.00 Subscription: $20.00/year
Publication description: The newsletter includes commentary on topics, issues and trends of interest to the arts community and the general public.
Date established: 1975

ALBUQUERQUE

Albuquerque Convention and Visitors Bureau
PO Box 26866
Albuquerque, NM 87125
Shamaine Giannini, Director of Leisure Sales & Services
Tel: (505) 842-9918
Email: giannini@itsatrip.org
Web: www.itsatrip.org
Price: Free
Publication description: The official Albuquerque Visitors Guide and Vacation Planner.

ALLIANCE NEWSLETTER, THE

Hispanic Alliance for Career Enhancement
25 E. Washington St. #1500
Chicago, IL 60602
Ramiro Marquez, Director
Tel: (312) 435-0498 Fax: (312) 435-1494
Email: haceorg@hace-usa.org
Web: www.hace-usa.org
Circ.: 10,000
Price: Free

Publication description: Newsletter for the Hispanic Alliance for Career Enhancement.
Date established: 1982

ALLIANCE REPORTER, THE

National Alliance for Hispanic Health
1501 16th St. NW
Washington, DC 20036
Dr. Jane L. Delgado, President/CEO
Tel: (202) 797-4335 Fax: (202) 797-4353
Email: alliance@hispanichealth.org
Web: www.hispanichealth.org
Circ.: 5,000
Price: Free .
Date established: 1973

ANDAR MAGAZINE, EL

El Andar Media Corporation
P.O. Box 7745
Santa Cruz, CA 95060
Jorge Chino, Publisher
Tel: (831) 457-8353 Fax: (831) 457-8354
Email: Info@elandar.com
Web: www.elandar.com
Circ.: 50,000
Price: $4.95 Subscription: $18.00/year
Publication description: Local/regional bilingual newspaper.
Date established: 1989

ARIZONA REPORT, THE

Mexican American Studies & Research Ctr.
University of Arizona,
Cesar E. Chavez Bldg. #208
Tucson, AZ 85721-0023
Thomas Gelsimon, Managing Editor
Tel: (520) 621-7551 Fax: (520) 621-7966
Email: masrc@emailarizona.edu
Web: www.masrc.arizona.edu
Circ.: 2,000
Price: Free
Publication description: A quarterly newsletter that includes articles and essays on issues concerning Latinos, Center events, and information on the activities of Mexican American faculty at the University of Arizona.
Date established: 1996

ASOCIACIÓN ALZHEIMER PUERTO RICO

Asociación Alzheimer Puerto Rico
P.O. Box 362026
San Juan, PR 00936-2026
Aracelis Abreu, Director
Tel: (787) 727-4151 Fax: (787) 727-4890
Email: alzheimerpr@alzheimerpr.org
Web: www.alzheimerpr.org
Price: Free
Publication description: To give education, service and orientation to the community regarding Alzheimer's disease.
Date established: 1983

ASPIRA NEWS

Aspira Association, Inc. National Office
1444 & I St. NW #800
Washington, DC 20005
Johnny Villamil-Casanova, Executive Vice-President & CIO
Tel: (202) 835-3600 Fax: (202) 835-3613
Email: info@aspira.org
Web: www.aspira.org
Circ.: 3,000
Subscription: $10.00/year
Publication description: Newsletter.
Date established: 1961

AUTOMOVIL

Editorial Televisa - USA
6355 NW 36th St.
Miami, FL 33166
Patrick Holmes, Senior Advertiser/Sales Executive

Tel: (305) 871-6400 **Fax:** (305) 871-5026
Email: pholmes@editorialtelevisa.com
Web: www.buyeditorialtelevisa.com
Circ.: 41,517
Publication description: The top quality collectible magazine for the Hispanic auto enthusiast.
Date established: 1995

BERT CORONA LEADERSHIP INSTITUTE NEWSLETTER

Bert Corona Leadership Institute
1500 Farragut St. NW
Washington, DC 20011
Wendy Carrasco, Deputy Director
Tel: (202) 723-7241 **Fax:** (202) 723-7246
Email: expdemocracy1@aol.com
Web: www.bcli.info
Price: Free **Subscription:** $150.00/year.
Date established: 1991

BIHA NEWSLETTER

Black, Indian, Hispanic, and Asian Women in Action
1830 James Ave. North
Minneapolis, MN 55417
Alice O. Lynch, Executive Director
Tel: (612) 521-2986 **Fax:** (612) 529-6745
Email: info@biha.org
Web: www.biha.org
Circ.: 1,000
Price: Free
Publication description: BIHA was created to provide education, information and advocacy for and by Communities of Color and to serve as a forum for translating current concerns (family violence, racism, ageism, AIDS, chemical abuse) within communities of color for presentation to society as a whole.
Date established: 1983

BUILDING BLOCKS

Rural Opportunities, Inc.
400 East Ave.
Rochester, NY 14607
Sturt J. Mitchell, President/CEO
Tel: (585) 340-3300 **Fax:** (585) 340-3335
Email: smitchell@ruralinc.org
Web: www.ruralinc.org
Circ.: 4,000
Price: Free .
Date established: 1969

BULLETIN OF EXPERIMENTAL TREATMENTS FOR AIDS (BETA)

San Francisco AIDS Foundation
P.O. Box 426182
San Francisco, CA 94142
Leslie Hanna, Editor
Tel: (415) 487-8060 **Fax:** (415) 487-8069
Email: beta@sfaf.org
Web: www.sfaf.org/espanol.html
Circ.: 6,000
Price: Free
Publication description: Gives information about the AIDS

CALVARY BILINGUAL MULTICULTURAL LEARNING CENTER NEWSLETTER

Calvary Bilingual Multicultural Learning Ctr.
1420 Columbia Rd. NW
Washington, DC 20009
Julia Howell Barros, Development Director
Tel: (202) 332-4200 **Fax:** (202) 745-2562
Email: info@centronia.org
Web: www.cbmlc.org
Price: Free
Publication description: Newsletter of Calvary Bilingual Multicultural Learning Center.
Date established: 1995

CAMPUS POINTS

Spring Institute for International Studies
1610 Emerson St.
Denver, CO 80218
Myrna Ann Adkins, President
Tel: (303) 863-0188 **Fax:** (303) 863-0178
Email: spring@springinstitute.com
Web: www.spring-institute.org
Circ.: 2,500
Price: Free
Publication description: Newsletter.
Date established: 1979

CASA NEWS

Casa de los Niños
1101 N. 4th Ave.
Tucson, AZ 85705
Susie Huhn, Executive Director
Tel: (520) 624-5600 **Fax:** (520) 623-2443
Email: info@casadelosninos.org
Web: www.casadelosninos.org
Price: Free
Publication description: Casa News is the official publication of Casa de los Ninos center for children

CAUSA NEWSLETTER, LA

Chicanos Por La Causa, Inc.
1112 E. Buckeye Rd.
Phoenix, AZ 85034-4043
Annette White, Corporate Marketing Director
Tel: (602) 257-0700 **Fax:** (602) 256-2740
Email: annette.white@cplc.org
Web: www.cplc.org
Circ.: 2,500
Price: Free
Publication description: A statewide community development corporation committed to build strong, healthier communities as a lead advocate coalition builder and direct service provider.
Date established: 1969

CHCI NEWS

Congressional Hispanic Caucus Institute, Inc.
911 2nd St. NE
Washington, DC 20002
Rolando Rodriguez, Editor
Tel: (202) 543-1771 **Fax:** (202) 546-2143
Email: rgandara@chci.org
Web: www.chci.org
Price: Free
Publication description: CHCI News promotes and disseminates joint activities of the Institute with our corporate sponsors.

CLAVE

Latin American Folk Institute
3800A 34th St.
Mount Rainier, MD 20712
Luis Rumbaut, Editor
Tel: (301) 887-9331 **Fax:** (301) 887-0308
Email: info@lafi.org
Web: www.lafi.org
Circ.: 1,500
Price: $2.00 **Subscription:** $19.95/year
Publication description: Publishes interviews with artists, musicians, and other personalities, and reviews of their work, including music reviews of new albums.
Date established: 1997

COLONIAL LATIN AMERICAN HISTORICAL REVIEW

Spanish Colonial Research Center,
University of New Mexico
Zirnmerman Library MSC05 3020 1
University of New Mexico
Albuquerque, NM 87131
Joseph P. Sánchez, Editor

Tel: (505) 277-1370 **Fax:** (505) 277-4603
Email: clahr@unm.edu
Web: www.unm.edu/~clahr
Circ.: 1,000
Price: $9.00 **Subscription:** $35.00/year
Publication description: CLAHR is a source of information for those interested in colonial Luso-Hispano America. It promotes the study of colonial Luso-Hispano America and provides a greater understanding of the common heritage between north, central and south America and the Caribbean.
Date established: 1992

COLORLINES MAGAZINE

Applied Research Center
4096 Piedmont Ave. PMB 319
Oakland, CA 94611
Tram Nguyen, Executive Editor
Tel: (510) 653-3415 **Fax:** (510) 653-3427
Email: colorlines@arc.org
Web: www.colorlines.com
Circ.: 5,000
Price: $3.50 **Subscription:** $16.00/year
Publication description: ColorLines is the first national, multiracial magazine devoted to covering the politics and creations of communities of color.
Date established: 1998

COMERCIO NEWSLETTER

Georgia Hispanic Chamber of Commerce
2801 Buford Hwy. #500
Atlanta, GA 30329
Jordi Vinas, Director, Office Operations
Tel: (404) 929-9998 **Fax:** (404) 929-9908
Email: jvinas@ghcc.org
Web: www.ghcc.org
Circ.: 800
Price: Free .
Date established: 1984

CONEXIONES NEWSLETTER

National Lutheran Secretariat of Via de Cristo
1780 NW 82nd Ave.
Pembrook Place, FL 21045
Judy Laabs-Foss, Editor
Tel: (954) 432-4090 **Fax:** (953) 437-8141
Email: jer2911@comcast.net
Web: www.viadecristo.org
Circ.: 500
Price: Free
Publication description: Conexiones is the official publication of the National Lutheran Secretariat of Via de Cristo.
Date established: 1971

CORPORATE OBSERVER NEWSLETTER

Hispanic Association for Corporate Responsibility
1444 I St. NW #850
Washington, DC 20005
Omar Velarde-Wong, Editor-in-Chief
Tel: (202) 835-9672 **Fax:** (202) 457-0455
Email: hacr@hacr.org
Web: www.hacr.org
Circ.: 5,000
Price: Free
Publication description: Its mission is to promote enhanced opportunities in corporate America for the Hispanic community.
Date established: 1991

COUNCIL LETTER, THE

Cuban American National Council, Inc.
1225 SW 4th St.
Miami, FL 33135
Guarioné M. Díaz, President
Tel: (305) 642-3484 **Fax:** (305) 642-9122
Email: bfraga@cnc.org
Web: www.cnc.org

Circ.: 10,000
Price: Free
Publication description: Newsletter.
Date established: 1972

CROSSCURRENTS - ENLACE

Washington Office on Latin America
1630 Connecticut Ave. NW #200
Washington, DC 20009
Kimberly Stanton, Editor
Tel: (202) 797-2171 **Fax:** (202) 797-2172
Email: kstanton@wola.org
Web: www.wola.org
Circ.: 1,000
Price: $2.50 **Subscription:** $35.00/year
Publication description: Newsletters in English & in Spanish.
Date established: 1991

CUBA UPDATE NEWSLETTER

Center for Cuban Studies
124 W. 23rd St.
New York, NY 10011
Sandra Levinson, Editor
Tel: (212) 242-0559 **Fax:** (212) 242-1937
Email: cubanctr@igc.org
Web: www.cubaupdate.org
Circ.: 1,000
Price: $10.00 **Subscription:** $40.00/year
Publication description: Covers mainly politics, economics and the arts, with an emphasis on U.S.-Cuba relations.
Date established: 1973

CULTURAL PROGRAM BULLETIN

Instituto Cervantes
211-215 E. 49th St.
New York, NY 10017
Munoz Molina Antonio, Executive Director
Tel: (212) 308-7720 **Fax:** (212) 308-7721
Email: cenny@cervantes.es
Web: www.cervantes.org
Circ.: 15,000
Price: Free
Publication description: Cultural Program Bulletin gives information about the cultural activities to the members.
Date established: 1991

DESTINOS NEWSLETTER

Latin American Educational Foundation
924 W. Colfax Ave. #103
Denver, CO 80204
Larry Romero, Executive Director
Tel: (303) 446-0541 **Fax:** (303) 446-0526
Email: carmen@uswest.net
Web: www.laef.org
Circ.: 2,000
Price: Free
Publication description: English newsletter.
Date established: 1949

DIALOGUE/DIÁLOGO NEWSLETTER

Inter-American Dialogue
1211 Connecticut Ave. NW #510
Washington, DC 20036
Joan Caivano, Editor
Tel: (202) 822-9002 **Fax:** (202) 822-9553
Email: iad@thedialogue.org
Web: www.thedialogue.org
Price: Free
Publication description: Internet newsletter

DIALOGUE ON DIVERSITY NEWSLETTER

Dialogue on Diversity, Inc.
1000 Connecticut Ave. NW #600
Washington, DC 20036
Maria Cristina Caballero, President
Tel: (703) 631-0650 **Fax:** (703) 631-0617
Email: dialog.div@prodigy.net
Web: www.dialogueondiversity.org
Circ.: 2,500
Price: Free

Publication description: Quarterly newsletter, annual reports, briefs, Voices of American Diversity, key legislative issues and executive summaries of conferences. Audience: professional and business women

EDUCATIONAL QUARTERLY (EQ)

Congressional Hispanic Caucus Institute, Inc.
911 2nd St. NE
Washington, DC 20002
Carmen Joge, Programs Director
Tel: (202) 543-1771 **Fax:** (202) 546-2143
Email: cjoge@chci.org
Web: www.chci.org
Circ.: 25,000
Price: Free
Publication description: The Educational Quarterly (EQ) is a newsletter distributed to more than 25,000 high school students, parents, and educators throughout the United States.
Date established: 1978

EMPRESA NEWSLETTER, LA

Michigan Hispanic Chamber of Commerce
24445 Northwestern Hwy. #206
Southfield, MI 48075
Armando Ojeda, Executive Director
Tel: (248) 208-9915 **Fax:** (248) 208-9936
Email: info@mhcc.org
Web: www.mhcc.org
Circ.: 1,500.
Date established: 1989

EN MARCHA! NEWSLETTER

National Conference of Catholic Bishops, Secretariat for Hispanic Affairs
3211 4th St. NE
Washington, DC 20017
Rosalva Castañeda, Editor
Tel: (202) 541-3150 **Fax:** (202) 722-8717
Email: rcastaneda@nccbuscc.org
Web: www.usccb.org/hispanicaffairs/enmarcha.shtml
Circ.: 7,500
Price: Free
Publication description: It focuses on issues and events in the areas of evangelization, catechesis, immigration, pastoral ministries, demographics, and others which affect the lives of Hispanic Catholics in the United States.
Date established: 1980

ENCUENTRO NEWSLETTER

Asociación para la Educación Teológica Hispana
100 E. 27th St.
Austin, TX 78705
Daniel Davila, Executive Director
Tel: (404) 708-0660 **Fax:** (404) 708-0671
Email: office@aeth.org
Web: www.AETH.org
Circ.: 3,000
Price: Free
Publication description: The newsletter informs its membership regarding Hispanic theological education.
Date established: 1991

ENFOQUE NEWSLETTER

Center of U.S.-Mexican Studies
University of California-San Diego, 9500 Gilman Dr. M/C 0510
La Jolla, CA 92093-0510
Sandra del Castillo, Publications Distributor
Tel: (858) 534-4503 **Fax:** (858) 534-6447
Email: usmex@ucsd.edu
Web: www.usmex.ucsd.edu
Circ.: 5,000
Price: Free

Publication description: National English newsletter.
Date established: 1985

EPOCA NEWSLETTER, LA

Ohio Commission on Hispanic/Latino Affairs
77 S. High St., 18 Fl.
Columbus, OH 43215-6108
Ezra C. Escudero, Executive Director
Tel: (614) 466-8333 **Fax:** (614) 995-0896
Email: juan.lara@ochla.state.oh.us
Web: www.state.oh.us/spa/
Price: Free
Publication description: Provides information and commentary in areas of interest and concern to Hispanics through publication of a news bulletin, providing access to time-sensitive materials, and a quarterly newsletter which promotes Hispanic unity and awareness throughout Ohio.
Date established: 1977

EQUAL OPPORTUNITY, HISPANIC CAREER WORLD, ET. AL.

Equal Opportunity Publications
445 Broad Hollow Rd. #425
Melville, NY 11747
John R. Miller, Publisher
Tel: (631) 421-9421 **Fax:** (631) 421-0359
Email: info@eop.com
Web: www.eop.com
Circ.: 10,500
Subscription: $13.00/year
Publication description: is the recruitment link between students and professionals ant the companies that seek to hire them. each edition includes career guidance columns, news and trends, and feature articles that profile Hispanics.
Date established: 1968

EQUIDAD

Inter-American Development Bank
External Relations Office, 1300 New York Ave. NW
Washington, DC 20577
IDB Bookstore, Publisher
Tel: (202) 623-1154 **Fax:** (202) 623-3531
Email: idb-books@iadb.org
Web: www.iadb.org
Circ.: N/A
Price: Free
Publication description: Equidad features brief articles about poverty and inequality in Latin America and the Caribbean and highlights research activities, events and publications.
Date established: 1964

ETHNICITY AND DISEASE JOURNAL

ISHIB, International Society of Hypertension in Blacks, Inc.
100 Auburn Ave. #401
Atlanta, GA 30303
Keith C. Norris, Editor-in-Chief
Tel: (404) 880-0343 **Fax:** (404) 880-0347
Email: ethndis@ishib.org
Web: www.ishib.org
Price: $115.00
Publication description: Dedicated to improving the health and life expectancy of Ethnic Minority population around the world.
Date established: 1986

FINANCE & DEVELOPMENT MAGAZINE

International Monetary Fund
700 19th St. NW Box FD-101
Washington, DC 20431
Laura Wallace, Editor
Tel: (202) 623-7430 **Fax:** (202) 623-7201
Email: publications@imf.org
Web: www.imf.org

Price: Free
Publication description: Presents articles and book reviews on a wide variety of topics in international economics and finance, as well as economic development.

FINANCIAL STATEMENTS OF THE IMF

International Monetary Fund
Publication Services, 700 19th St. NW
Washington, DC 20002
International Monetary Fund, Publisher
Tel: (202) 473-7430 **Fax:** (202) 623-7201
Email: publications@imf.org
Web: www.imf.org
Price: Free
Publication description: International Spanish publication

FLC NEWSLETTER

Family Learning Center
3164 34th St.
Boulder, CO 80301
Brenda Lyle, Executive Director
Tel: (303) 442-8979 **Fax:** (303) 442-0901
Email: flc@flcboulder.org
Web: www.flcboulder.org
Price: Free
Publication description: Bilingual newsletter.
Date established: 1980

FLEXO ESPAÑOL

Flexographic Technical Association
900 Marconi Ave.
Ronkonkoma, NY 11779
Graciela I. Gilbride, Editor
Tel: (631) 737-6023 X17
Fax: (631) 737-6813
Email: ggilbride@flexography.org
Web: www.flexography.org
Circ.: 20,000
Price: Free .
Date established: 1986

FLORIDA HISPANO MAGAZINE

Albors Publishing, Inc.
5971 Brick Ct. #200
Winter Park, FL 32792
Jose G. Cestero Moscoso, Editor-in-Chief
Tel: (407) 678-8634 **Fax:** (407) 657-7004
Email: jose@albors.com
Circ.: 20,000
Subscription: $12.00/year
Publication description: The mission of the Florida Hispano is to inform Florida Hispanics of current issues impacting their communities in the fields of business, education, social reform, medicine, art, culture, entertainment and sports.
Date established: 1996

GLOBALIZACIÓN, CRECIMIENTO Y POBREZA: CONSTRUYENDO UNA ECONOMÍA MUNDIAL INCLUYENTE

The World Bank Bookstore
P.O. Box 960
Herndon, VA 20172
The World Bank, InfoShop
Tel: (800) 645-7247 **Fax:** (703) 661-1501
Email: books@worldbank.org
Web: www.worldbank.org/publications
Price: $25.00
Publication description: Globalization is already a powerful force for poverty reduction as societies and economies around the world are becoming more integrated.

HDA NEWS & REPORT NEWSLETTER

Hispanic Dental Association
188 W. Randolph St. #415
Chicago, IL 60601
Sandy Reed, Executive Director
Tel: (312) 577-4013 **Fax:** (312) 577-0052
Email: hispanicdental@hdassoc.org

Web: www.hdassoc.org
Circ.: 15,000
Price: Free
Publication description: HDA News & Report Newsletter brings the membership and the wider dental community up-to-date on HDA activities and achievements, interactions with state and federal government bodies, and programs designed to benefit the Hispanic population.
Date established: 1990

HERENCIA MAGAZINE, LA

P.O. Box 22576
Santa Fe, NM 87502
Ana Pacheco, Editor
Tel: (505) 474-2800 **Fax:** (505) 474-2828
Email: herencia@herencia.com
Web: www.herencia.com
Circ.: 20,000
Subscription: $19.99/year
Publication description: Local/regional bilingual magazine highlights New Mexico Hispanic culture both past and present. The magazine is targeted to Hispanics who communicate in both languages.
Date established: 1994

HISPANIA

AATSP
423 Exton Commons
Exton, PA 19341-2451
Janet Perez, Editor
Tel: (610) 363-7005 **Fax:** (610) 363-7116
Email: janet.perez@ttu.edu
Web: www.aatsp.org
Circ.: 14,000
Subscription: $75.00/year
Publication description: Includes scholarly articles on Hispanic and Luso-Brazilian literature and language that are judged to be of interest to specialists in the subject areas as well as to a diverse readership of teachers of Spanish and Portuguese.
Date established: 1917

HISPANIC AMERICAN HISTORICAL REVIEW

University of Maryland, 2115 Francis Scott Key Hall
College Park, MD 20742-7315
Barbara Weinstein, Senior Editor
Tel: (301) 405-7941 **Fax:** (301) 314-9193
Email: hahr@umail.umed.edu
Web: www.hahr.umd.edu
Circ.: 1,000
Subscription: $40.00/year
Publication description: Per-reviewed journal covering Latin American history.

HISPANIC HEALTH CARE INTERNATIONAL

National Association of Hispanic Nurses
1501 16th St. NW
Washington, DC 20036
Sara Torres, Editor-in-Chief
Tel: (202) 387-2477 **Fax:** (202) 483-7183
Email: info@thehispanicnurses.org
Web: www.thehispanicnurses.org
Circ.: 1,000
Price: Free
Publication description: Hispanic Health Care International is a bilingual journal.
Date established: 2002

HISPANIC MEDIA & MARKETS

SRDS, Inc.
1700 Higgins Rd.
Des Plains, IL 60018
Debi Dunklebenger, Editor
Tel: (847) 375-5000 **Fax:** (847) 375-5002
Email: aspan@srds.com
Web: www.srds.com
Circ.: 579

Subscription: $271.00/year
Publication description: Over 2,200 detailed information listings of Hispanic radio, television, daily and weekly newspapers, consumer and business publications, outdoor advertising companies, direct mail advertising opportunities and special events.
Date established: 1988

HISPANIC MEETINGS & TRAVEL MAGAZINE

GVR Public Relations Agency, Inc.
242 St. Cloud Dr.
Friendswood, TX 77546
Ángela González Rowe, Executive Editor
Tel: (281) 992-9639 **Fax:** (281) 996-7490
Email: angela.rowe@hispanicmeetingstravel.com
Web: www.hispanicmeetingstravel.com
Circ.: 15,000
Price: $8.50 **Subscription:** $34.00/year
Publication description: English.
Date established: 1994

HISPANIC NETWORK MAGAZINE

Olive Tree Publishing, Inc.
6845 Indiana Ave. #200
Riverside, CA 92506
Tricia Lawrence, Editor
Tel: (800) 433-WORK **Fax:** (951) 276-1700
Email: publisher@hnmagazine.com
Web: www.hnmagazine.com
Circ.: 100,000
Price: $3.50 **Subscription:** $18.00/year
Publication description: The Hispanic Network Magazine is one of the fastest growing Employment Publications in the United States. English magazine; Alt. contact: Andrea Castro

HISPANIC ORGANIZATION OF LATIN ACTORS (HOLA)

107 Suffolk St. #302
New York, NY 10002
Manny Alfaro, Editor
Tel: (212) 253-1015 **Fax:** (212) 253-9651
Email: holagram@hellohola.org
Web: www.hellohola.org
Circ.: 1,500
Subscription: 65.00
Publication description: The Hispanic Organization of Latin Actors (HOLA) is an arts service organization founded in 1976 to expand the presence of Hispanic actors in both the Latino and mainstream entertainment and communications media by facilitating industry access to employing professional and emerging Hispanic actors. HOLA members represent the full spectrum of Latino cultures, reflecting the nation's growing Hispanic population. .
Date established: 1975

HISPANIC TODAY MAGAZINE

EM Publishing Enterprises, Inc.
13351 Riverside Dr. #514
Sherman Oaks, CA 91423
Pam Peterson, Editor
Tel: (818) 654-0870 **Fax:** (818) 654-0874
Email: editor@hispanic-today.com
Web: www.hispanic-today.com
Circ.: 17,000
Price: Free
Publication description: The Hispanic Today Magazine is a career and education resource for the Hispanics.
Date established: 1981

HISPANIC TRENDS

United States Hispanic Chamber of Commerce
2175 K St. NW #100
Washington, DC 20037

Virginia Cueto, Editor
Tel: (202) 842-1212 **Fax:** (202) 842-3221
Email: vcueto@hisp.com
Web: www.ushcc.com
Circ.: 75,000
Price: Free
Publication description: USHCC National Magazine.
Date established: 2002

HUMAN RIGHTS MONITOR

Cuban American National Foundation
1822 Jefferson Pl. NW
Washington, DC 20036
Dennis Hays, Editor
Tel: (202) 530-1894 **Fax:** (202) 530-2444
Email: hq@canf.org
Web: www.canf.org
Circ.: 5,000
Price: Free .
Date established: 1984

IBERO INQUIRER

Ibero American Action League, Inc.
911 E Main St.
Rochester, NY 14605-2722
Eugenio Marlin, Editor
Tel: (585) 256-8900 **Fax:** (585) 256-0120
Email: eamarlin@iaal.org
Web: www.iaal.org
Price: Free
Publication description: Bilingual newsletter for members only.
Date established: 1988

INFORME, EL

Michigan Commission on Spanish Speaking Affairs
201 N. Washington Square, 3rd Fl.
Lansing, MI 48913
Marylou Olivarez-Mason, Executive Director
Tel: (517) 373-8339 **Fax:** (517) 373-0176
Email: masonm1@michigan.gov
Web: www.michigan.gov/mdcd
Circ.: 1,500
Price: Free
Publication description: The purpose of the Commission is to develop a unified policy and plan of action to serve the needs of Michigan's Hispanic people. .
Date established: 1977

KHLAAC LINK NEWSLETTER

Kansas Hispanic and Latino American Affairs Commission
900 SW Jackson #100
Topeka, KS 66612
Elias Garcia, Executive Director
Tel: (785) 296-3465 **Fax:** (785) 296-8118
Email: tracy.seybert@gov.state.ks.us
Web: www.khlaac.org
Circ.: 2,000
Price: Free .
Date established: 1992

LAEDA NEWSLETTER

Latin American Economic Development Association
129 N. Broadway #300
Camden, NJ 08102
Alfonso D. Castillo, Executive Director
Tel: (856) 338-1177 **Fax:** (856) 365-7205
Email: laeda@laeda.com
Web: www.laeda.com
Circ.: 900
Price: Free
Publication description: Bilingual newsletter.
Date established: 1987

LATIN AMERICA EVANGELIST

Latin America Mission, Inc.
5465 NW 36th St.
Miami, FL 33166

David R. Befus, President and Publisher
Tel: (305) 884-8400 X28/(800) 275-8410
Fax: (305) 885-8649
Email: evangelist@lam.org
Web: www.lam.org
Circ.: 15,000
Price: Free **Subscription:** $10.00/year
Publication description: International English magazine.
Date established: 1921

LATIN HEAT MAGAZINE

Latin Heat Entertainment
P.O. Box 27
West Covina, CA 91793
Bel Hernandez, Editor
Tel: (626) 917-2160 **Fax:** (626) 917-2160
Email: info@latinheat.com
Web: www.latinheat.com
Circ.: 30,000
Price: $2.95 **Subscription:** $19.95/year
Publication description: National English newsletter.
Date established: 1992

LATINO JOURNAL

112 J St. #300
Sacramento, CA 95814
Jose L. Perez, Publisher/CEO
Tel: (916) 492-9163 **Fax:** (916) 492-9418
Email: info@latinojournal.net
Web: www.latinojournal.net
Circ.: 16,000
Price: $5.00
Publication description: Print media.
Date established: October 1996

LATINOS IN THE UNITED STATES: A RESOURCE GUIDE FOR JOURNALISTS

National Association of Hispanic Journalists
529 14th St. NW, Bldg1000
Washington, DC 20045-2100
Joseph Torres, Communications Director
Tel: (202) 662-7145 **Fax:** (202) 662-7144
Email: nahj@nahj.org
Web: www.nahj.org
Circ.: 2,300
Price: $8.50
Publication description: English newsletter.
Date established: 1984

LATINOS ON WHEELS MAGAZINE (LOW)

On Wheels, Inc.
585 E. Larned St. #100
Detroit, MI 48226
Randi Payton, Publisher/President/CEO
Tel: (313) 963-2209 **Fax:** (313) 963-7778
Email: Publisher@onwheelsinc.com
Web: www.onwheelsinc.com/lowmagazine/default.asp
Circ.: 500,000
Subscription: $ 6.00/year
Publication description: Latinos magazine serves as a consumer magazine featuring auto-related lifestyle trends, a guide to the historical contributions of latinos to the auto industry, and a guide to the automotive products, personnel and related industries.
Date established: 2001

LBA MAGAZINE

Latin Business Association
120 S. San Pedro St. #530
Los Angeles, CA 90012
Veronica Sanchez, Editor
Tel: (323) 721-4000 x227 **Fax:** (323) 722-5050
Email: vsanchez@lbausa.co
Web: www.lbausa.com
Circ.: 172,000
Subscription: $10.00/year
Publication description: English newsletter.
Date established: 1979

LCAT NEWS

National Latino Council on Alcohol & Tobacco Prevention
1616 P st. NW #430
Washington, DC 20036
Juan Carlos Vega, Editor
Tel: (202) 265-8054 **Fax:** (202) 265-8056
Email: jcvega@nlcatp.org
Web: www.nlcatp.org
Circ.: 1,400
Price: Free .
Date established: 1992

LCC CHAMBER NEWSLETTER

Latin Chamber of Commerce of Nevada
P.O. Box 7500
Las Vegas, NV 89125-7500
Otto Merida, Executive Director
Tel: (702) 385-7367 **Fax:** (702) 385-2614
Email: lvlchamber@aol.com
Web: www.lasvegaslatincc.com
Circ.: 3,000
Price: Free
Publication description: English publication for members.
Date established: 1976

LECTURA Y VIDA

International Reading Association
800 Barksdale Rd., P.O. Box 8139
Newark, DE 19714-8139
MaryEllen Vogt, President
Tel: (302) 731-1600 **Fax:** (302) 731-1057
Email: lecturayvida@ira.com.ar
Web: www.reading.org
Circ.: 1,500
Subscription: $61.00/year
Publication description: Lectura y Vida is the International Reading Association's Spanish-language quarterly. Published through our offices in Argentina, it is of particular interest to those working in Latin America and elsewhere in the Spanish-speaking world.
Date established: 1979

LULAC ON THE MOVE

League of United Latin American Citizens (Southern Arizona Institute for Leadership)
P.O.Box 162
Tucson, AZ 85702
Linda Lecthoman, Board Member
Tel: (520) 903-2838 **Fax:** (520) 792-6388
Email: fimbres@aol.com
Web: www.lulac.org
Circ.: 350
Price: $3.00
Publication description: LULAC is a non profit educational organization dedicated to advancing the education of Hispanic and disadvantage youth in Arizona.
Date established: 2003

MAAC NEWS

MAAC Project
22 W 35th St. #100
National City, CA 91950
Connie Ojeda Hernandez, CEO
Tel: (619) 426-3595 **Fax:** (619) 426-2173
Email: chernandez@maacproject.org
Web: www.maacproject.org
Circ.: 3,000
Price: Free
Publication description: Local/regional English newsletter.
Date established: 1991

MAC NEWSLETTER

Mexican American Commission
P.O. Box 94965
Lincoln, NE 68509-4965
Cecilia Olivares Huerta, Executive Director
Tel: (402) 471-2791 **Fax:** (402) 471-4381

Email: mac01@nol.org
Web: www.mex-amer.state.ne.us/
commissioner.html
Circ.: 6,500
Price: Free
Publication description: Local/regional English newsletter

MALDEF NEWSLETTER

Mexican American Legal Defense &
Educational Fund (MALDEF)
634 S. Spring St.
Los Angeles, CA 90014
J.C. Flores, National Director of
Communications
Tel: (213) 629-2512 **Fax:** (213) 629-3120
Email: info@maldef.org
Web: www.maldef.org
Price: Free
Publication description: MALDEF'S latest newsletter featuring information on: Education, Employment, Immigrants' Rights, Political Access, Voting Rights, Public Resource Equity and our recent and coming Events. .
Date established: 1969

MANA NEWSLETTER

MANA - A National Latina Organization
1725 K St. NW #501
Washington, DC 20006
Alma Morales Riojas, Editor
Tel: (202) 833-0060 **Fax:** (202) 496-0588
Email: HerMANA2@aol.com
Web: www.herMANA.org
Circ.: 5,000
Price: Free
Publication description: Newsletter for the empowerment of Latinas.
Date established: 1974

MATICES

Center for Hispanic Policy, Research and
Development
P.O. Box 800
Trenton, NJ 08625-0800
Shelly Matos, Editor
Tel: (609) 984-3223 **Fax:** (609) 984-0821
Email: chprd@dca.state.nj.us
Web: www.nj.gov/dca/chprd
Price: Free
Publication description: Matices conveys the message that there are different cultures within the Hispanic community, each unique with traits and traditions, all of which together form that beautiful fabric proudly call "Hispanidad". Matices is the CHPRD's mechanism for enlightening those who are not aware of the many successes, contribution, culture, traditions and other treasurers of the Hispanic community.
Date established: 1975

MI CASA NEWSLETTER

Mi Casa Resource Center for Women
360 Acoma St.
Denver, CO 80223
Carmen Carrillo, Executive Director
Tel: (303) 573-1302 **Fax:** (303) 595-0422
Email: info@micasadenver.org
Web: www.micasadenver.org
Price: Free
Publication description: Newsletter.
Date established: 1977

MINERIA PAN-AMERICANA

International Construction Publishing
4913 SW 75th Ave.
Miami, FL 33155-4440
Guido Castellanos, Editor
Tel: (305) 668-4999 **Fax:** (305) 668-7774
Email: info@cpa-mpa.com
Web: www.cpa-mpa.com

Circ.: 9,194
Price: Free **Subscription:** Free
Publication description: International Spanish magazine.
Date established: 1987

MULTICULTURAL REVIEW

The Goldman Group
14497 N. Dale Mabry Hwy. #205N
Tampa, FL 33618
Lyn Miller-Lachmann, Editor-in-Chief
Tel: (813) 264-2772 **Fax:** (813) 264-2343
Email: editor@mcreview.com
Web: www.mcreview.com
Circ.: 5,000
Price: $25.00 **Subscription:** $29.95/year
Publication description: Journal for teachers at all levels, college professors, librarians, administrators, and anyone else interested in new developments and trends in the field of cultural diversity.
Date established: 1992

MUNDO ALIMENTICIO

Asociación de Mercadeo Industria y
Distribución de Alimentos
Edificio Plaza Triple-S, #902-A. Ave. FD
Roosevelt, #1510
Guaynabo, PR 00968
Edwin Colón Pérez, Executive Vice-
President
Tel: (787) 792-7575 **Fax:** (787) 792-8085
Email: info@midapr.com
Web: www.midapr.com
Circ.: 10,000
Price: Free
Publication description: Mundo Alimenticio is a tabloid publish to promote the improvement of the food industry.
Date established: 1980

NAFTA IN THE NEW MILLENNIUM

Center of U.S.-Mexican Studies
University of California-San Diego, 9500
Gilman Dr. M/C 0510
La Jolla, CA 92093-0510
Prof. Peter Smith, Editor
Tel: (858) 534-4503 **Fax:** (858) 534-6447
Email: usmex@ucsd.edu
Web: www.usmex.ucsd.edu
Circ.: 5,000
Price: $26.95
Publication description: National English newsletter.
Date established: 1985

NECLAS NEWSLETTER

New England Council of Latin American
Studies, Inc.
Smith College, Seelye Hall #210
Northampton, MA 01063
Joy Renjilian-Burgy, President
Tel: (413) 585-3591 **Fax:** (413) 585-3593
Email: kgauger@email.smith.edu
Circ.: 600
Price: Free
Publication description: New England Council of Latin American Studies newsletter.
Date established: 1970

NEIGHBORHOOD HOUSE NEWSLETTER

Neighborhood House
179 Robie St. East
St. Paul, MN 55107
Dan H. Hoxworth, President
Tel: (651) 227-9291 **Fax:** (651) 227-8734
Email: Kkowski@neighb.org
Web: www.neighb.org
Circ.: 10,000
Price: Free
Publication description: Neighborhood House Newsletter is a newsletter of Neighborhood

House is a multicultural, multilingual community center with programming for all ages and open doors for all people and is often a first stop for new immigrants and refugees.
Date established: 1897

NETWORK

Family Health International
P.O. Box 13950
Research Triangle Park, NC 27709
Kim Best, Managing Editor
Tel: (919) 544-7040 **Fax:** (919) 544-7261
Email: Publications@fhi.org
Web: www.fhi.org
Price: Free
Publication description: Clinical reseach work

NETWORK NEWS MAGAZINE

National Network for Immigrant & Refugee
Rights
310 8th St. #307
Oakland, CA 94607
Catherine Tactaquin, Executive Director
Tel: (510) 465-1984 **Fax:** (510) 465-1885
Email: nnirr@nnirr.org
Web: www.nnirr.org
Circ.: 5,000
Price: Free **Subscription:** $25.00/year
Publication description: The Network News Magazine provides timely analysis, action, and commentary from activists, organizers, community leaders, and policy advocates from the immigrant and refugee rights movements.
Date established: 1987

NEWS & VIEWS NEWSLETTER

Long Island Hispanic Chamber of
Commerce
15 Atlantic Ave., 2nd Fl.
Lynbrook, NY 11563
Celeste M. Hernandez, Executive Director
Tel: (516) 256-2483 **Fax:** (516) 256-2463
Email: lihcc@optonline.net
Web: www.lihispanicchamber.com
Circ.: 300
Price: Free .
Date established: 1989

NHCC NEWSLETTER

National Hispanic Corporate Council
1911 N. Fort Myer Dr.
Arlington, VA 22209
Ada Lucero, Manager
Tel: (703) 807-5137 **Fax:** (703) 807-0567
Email: alucero@nhcc-hq.org
Web: www.nhcc-hq.org
Circ.: 600
Price: free
Publication description: Newsletter, English

NHCOA NOTICIAS OF HISPANIC ISSUES AND NEWS

National Hispanic Council on Aging
(NHCOA)
1341 Connecticut Ave. NW #4.2
Washington, DC 20036
Marta Sotomayor, Editor
Tel: (202) 429-0787 **Fax:** (202) 429-0789
Email: nhcoa@nhcoa.org
Web: www.nhcoa.org
Circ.: 3,000
Subscription: $25.00/year
Publication description: National English newsletter. Audience: persons and organizations interested in the field of gerontology.
Date established: 1983

NIÑOS NEWS, LOS

Los Niños
287 G St.
Chula Vista, CA 91910
Elisa Sabatini, Executive Director
Tel: (619) 426-9110 **Fax:** (619) 426-6664
Email: info@losninosinternational.org
Web: www.losninosinternational.org
Circ.: 5,000
Price: Free .
Date established: 1974

NOTIKITOS

Lozano Enterprises & Los Kitos
Entertainment LLC
1833 E. 17th St. #210
Santa Ana, CA 92705
Martha Montoya, Editor
Tel: (714) 542-7787 **Fax:** (714) 542-7612
Email: martham@loskitos.com
Web: www.loskitos.com
Circ.: 35,000
Price: Free
Publication description: Bilingual news for Hispanic kids.
Date established: 1995

NOVEDADES

The National Law Center for Inter-American
Free Trade
440 N. Bonita Ave.
Tucson, AZ 85745-2747
Mina Goldberg, Editor
Tel: (520) 622-1200 **Fax:** (520) 622-0957
Email: natlaw@natlaw.com
Web: www.natlaw.com/novedades.htm
Circ.: 6,000
Price: Free
Publication description: NOVEDADES is published by the National Law Center for Inter-American Free Trade, a non-profit research and educational corporation whose purpose is to facilitate trade and investment in the Western Hemisphere.
Date established: 1981

NUESTRAS RAICES

Genealogical Society of Hispanic America
P. O. Box 9606
Denver, CO 80209-0606
Deborah Jeppson, Editor
Tel: (310) 204-6808 **Fax:** (310) 893-3985
Email: djeppson@ida.net
Web: www.gsha.net
Circ.: 400
Subscription: $20.00/year
Publication description: Nuestras Raices is a quarterly Journal. Audience: Hispanic genealogists.
Date established: 1988

NUEVA VIDA

The Resurrection Project
1818 S. Paulina
Chicago, IL 60608
Lupe Esparza, Editing Staff
Tel: (312) 666-1323 **Fax:** (312) 942-1123
Email: info@resurrectionproject.org
Web: www.resurrectionproject.org
Circ.: 10,000
Price: Free
Publication description: Spanish newsletter.
Date established: 1992

ORGANIZACIÓN DE DAMAS LATINAS

Damas Latinas y Amigos, Inc.
P.O. Box 184
Columbus, OH 43085
Aireen Aguilar, President
Tel: (614) 841-1958
Fax: (614) 841-1958 X51

Email: dlatinasorg@mail.com
Circ.: 150,000
Price: Free .
Date established: 1995

PARTNERS NEWSLETTER

Partners of the Americas
1424 K St. NW #700
Washington, DC 20005
Claudia C. Calderón, Publications
Coordinator
Tel: (202) 628-3300 X225
Fax: (202) 628-3306
Email: info@partners.net
Web: www.partners.net
Circ.: 20,000
Price: Free .
Date established: 1975

PASTORAL NEWSLETTER, LA/ UNIVERSE BULLETIN NEWSPAPER (ENGLISH)

Hispanic Ministry Diocese of Cleveland
1027 Superior Ave.
Cleveland, OH 44114
Robert Tayek, Director of Media &
Communications
Tel: (216) 696-6525 x2530 **Fax:** (216) 781-8243
Email: rtayek@dioceseofcleveland.org.
Web: www.dioceseofcleveland.org, www.catholicuniversebulletin.org
Circ.: 2,000
Price: Free
Publication description: Hispanic Catholic formation and leadership development at all levels.
Date established: 1970

PENSAMIENTO

Casa Pensamiento de Mujer del Centro, Inc.
P.O. Box 2002
Aibonito, PR 00705
Amárilis Pagán Jiménez, Executive Director
Tel: (787) 735-6698 **Fax:** (787) 735-3200
Email: casapens@coqui.net
Circ.: 1,000
Price: Free
Publication description: To promote the development of women in society.
Date established: 1990

PLAZA

Plaza De La Raza
3540 N. Mission Rd.
Los Angeles, CA 90031
María Jiménez Torres, Editor
Tel: (323) 223-2475 **Fax:** (323) 223-1804
Email: admin@plazaraza.org
Web: www.plazadelaraza.org
Circ.: 5,000
Price: Free
Publication description: Local/regional bilingual newsletter.
Date established: 1983

PRINCIPLES AND PRACTICES OF SAM BOOKLET

South America Mission
5217 South Military Trail
Lake Worth, FL 33463-6099
Jeff Orcutt, Editor
Tel: (561) 965-1833 **Fax:** (561) 439-8950
Email: samusa@samlink.org
Web: www.samlink.org
Price: Free
Publication description: Principles and Practices of SAM Booklet outlines the principles and practices of SAM.
Date established: 1989

PUBLIC RELATIONS STRATEGIST, THE

Public Relations Society of America
33 Maiden Ln., 11th Fl.
New York, NY 10038-5150
John Elsasser, Editor
Tel: (212) 460-1459 **Fax:** (212) 995-0757
Email: john.elsasser@prsa.org
Web: www.prsa.org
Subscription: $100/year
Publication description: The Strategist aims to present fresh perspectives and new ideas related to the strategic importance of effective public relations at the management level.

PUENTE, EL

National Latino Peace Officers Association
P.O. Box 17132
Arlington, VA 22216
Rafel Segarra, Editor
Tel: (703) 351-5565 **Fax:** (703) 351-7555
Email: rsegarra@newhavenct.net
Web: www.nlpoa.com
Price: Free
Publication description: Promotes equality and professionalism in law enforcement, education and career advancement, mentoring, and a strong commitment to community service.
Date established: 1998

PUETO RICO TRAVEL AND TOURISM

Casiano Communications
1700 Ave. Fernández Juncos
San Juan, PR 00909-2938
Ronald C. Flores, Editor
Tel: (787) 728-3000 X3537
Fax: (787) 728-8577
Email: ronaldf@casiano.com
Web: www.casiano.com
Circ.: 75,000
Price: Free **Subscription:** $7.50/year
Publication description: Pueto Rico Travel and Tourism combines the best features of a tourism guide. .
Date established: 2000

QUIPU

AIDS Project Rhode Island
232 W. Exchange St.
Providence, RI 02903-1024
Magali Garcia, Latino Outreach Coordinator
Tel: (401) 831-5522 **Fax:** (401) 454-0299
Email: magali@aidsprojectri.org
Web: www.aidsprojectri.org
Circ.: 5,000
Price: Free
Publication description: Spanish newsletter.
Date established: 1989

REFORMA NEWSLETTER

National Association to Promote Library & Information Services to Latinos and the Spanish Speaking
P.O. Box 832
Anaheim, CA 92815-0832
Pedro Reynoso, Editor
Tel: (909) 607-1298
Email: reformanews@myway.com
Web: www.reforma.org
Circ.: 1,000
Price: Membership
Publication description: To promot library and information services to latinos and the Spanish-speaking in the U.S.
Date established: 1971

REGINE MAGAZINE

Regine Magazine, LLC
P.O. Box 1930
New York, NY 10025
Regine Lopez-Pierre, Editor-In-Chief
Tel: (212) 531-3109

Email: reginemagazine@aol.com
Web: www.reginemagazine.com
Circ.: 25,000
Price: $6.00 **Subscription:** $48.00/year
Publication description: Regine is a lifestyle magazine that will celebrate the achievements and charitable work of the affluent African-American and Hispanics in New York, New Jersey and Connecticut. .
Date established: 2001

REPORT ON GUATEMALA

Network in Solidarity with the People of Guatemala
1830 Connecticut Ave. NW
Washington, DC 20009
Sarah Aird, Executive Director
Tel: (202) 518-7638 **Fax:** (202) 223-8221
Email: nisgua@igc.org
Web: www.nisgua.org
Subscription: $25.00/year
Publication description: The publication provides activists, scholars, and concerned citizens with in depth analyses of Guatemalan currents events and history.
Date established: 1981

RESTAURANTE MEXICANO, EL

Maiden Name Press, LLC
P.O. Box 2249
Oak Park, IL 60303
Kathleen Furore, Editor
Tel: (800) 407-5845 **Fax:** (708) 445-9477
Email: kfurore@restmex.com
Web: www.restmex.com
Circ.: 28,000
Subscription: $18.00/year
Publication description: El Restaurante Mexicano is the bilingual, audited-circulation U.S. magazine for Mexican, Tex-Mex, Southwestern and Latino restaurants .
Date established: 1997

REVISTA DE LA INDIERRA TAINA NEWSLETTER, LA

The Taino Inter-Tribal Council Inc.
P.O. Box 210
Vineland, NJ 08362
Roy Cibabo McClellan, Editor
Tel: (856) 690-1565 **Fax:** (856) 690-1312
Email: public-relations@taino-tribe.org
Web: www.taino-tribe.org
Circ.: 1,000
Price: Free
Publication description: La Revista De La Indierra Taina Newsletter is a bilingual newsletter of The Taino Inter-Tribal Council Inc. .
Date established: 1993

REVISTA IBEROAMERICANA

Instituto Nacional de Literatura Iberoamericana
1312 Cathedral of Learning, University of Pittsburgh
Pittsburgh, PA 15260
Mabel Morana, Director of Publication
Tel: (412) 624-3359 **Fax:** (412) 624-0829
Email: iili@pitt.edu
Web: www.pitt.edu/~hispan/iili/
Circ.: 2,500
Subscription: $65.00/year
Publication description: International Spanish journal; Audience: Latin Americanists, scholars. Literary criticism. Latin America.
Date established: 1998

SACNAS NEWS

Society for the Advancement of Chicanos and Native Americans in Science
P.O. Box 8526
Santa Cruz, CA 95061-8526

Jenny Kurzweil, Editor
Tel: (831) 459-0170 **Fax:** (831) 459-0194
Email: jenny@sacnas.org
Web: www.sacnas.org
Circ.: 6,000
Price: Free
Publication description: The Sacnas News explores current issues within the minority scientific community , celebrates the achievements and contributions of members, and provides resources for academic and professional development.
Date established: 1998

SALUD - A LATINA'S GUIDE TO TOTAL HEALTH

National Alliance for Hispanic Health
1501 16th St. NW
Washington, DC 20036
Dr. Jane L. Delgado, Publisher
Tel: (202) 797-4335 **Fax:** (202) 797-4353
Email: publications@hispanichealth.org
Web: www.hispanichealth.org
Price: $19.95
Publication description: Salud is the only health book written by and for Hispanic women.
Date established: 1997

SALUD COMUNAL

Asociacion de Salud Primaria de PR, Inc.
Edificio La Euskalduna, Calle Navarro # 56
Esquina Peñuelas
Hato Rey, PR 00918-0000
Sandra V. Garcia, Executive Director
Tel: (787) 758-3411 **Fax:** (787) 758-1736
Email: acsppr@coqui.net
Circ.: 700
Price: Free
Publication description: Magazine.
Date established: 1986

SALUDOS HISPANOS

United Council of Spanish Speaking People
73-121 Fred Waring Dr. #100
Palm Desert, CA 92260
Rosemarie Garcia-Solomon, Publisher
Tel: (323) 726-2188 **Fax:** (800) 730-3560
Email: info@saludos.com
Web: www.saludos.com
Circ.: 45,000
Subscription: $12.00/year
Publication description: Provides Hispanic youth with career, education and motivational information.
Date established: 1967

SER NEWS

Ser-Jobs for Progress
5215 N. O' Connor Blvd. #2550
Irving, TX 75039
Raul Santa, Editor
Tel: (972) 506-7815 X310
Fax: (972) 506-7832
Email: rsanta@ser-national.org
Web: www.ser-national.org
Price: Free .
Date established: 1964

SOL, EL

California Chicano News Media Association
USC Annenberg School of Journalism 300 S. Grand Ave. #3950
Los Angeles, CA 90071-8110
Luz Villarreal, President
Tel: (213) 437-4408 **Fax:** (213) 437-4423
Email: info@ccnma.org
Web: www.ccnma.org
Price: Free
Publication description: Newsletter of the California Chicano News Media Association.
Date established: 1972

SPANISH CATHOLIC CENTER
Spanish Catholic Center
1618 Monroe St. NW
Washington, DC 20010
Rev. Donald F. Lippert, O.F.M. Cap,
Executive Director
Tel: (202) 939-2437 **Fax:** (202) 234-7323
Email: infoscc@yahoo.com
Web: www.centrocatolicohispano.org
Circ.: 9,000
Price: Free
Publication description: Its principal purpose is to assist the Hispanic community of the metropolitan Washington area in the process of adaptation and integration into North American society.
Date established: 1967

STOCKTON SAN JOAQUIN COUNTY MEXICAN AMERICAN CHAMBER OF COMMERCE
Stockton San Joaquin County Mexican American Chamber of Commerce
343 E. Main St. #806
Stockton, CA 95202
Alicia Arong, President
Tel: (209) 943-6117 **Fax:** (209) 943-0114
Email: arongal@earthlink.net
Web: www.ssjmacc.org
Circ.: 300
Price: Free
Publication description: Business Journal designed to inform and educate issues of interest to the Hispanic business community.
Date established: 1972

TAMACC TIMES
Texas Association of Mexican American Chambers of Commerce
3000 S. IH-35 #210
Austin, TX 78704
Monica Loera, Editor
Tel: (512) 444-5727 **Fax:** (512) 444-4929
Email: monical@tamacc.org
Web: www.tamacc.org
Circ.: 11,500
Price: Free
Publication description: English newsletter for members only.
Date established: 1986

TECHNICA
Mellcom, Inc.
3900 Whiteside
Los Angeles, CA 90063
Ray Mellado, President
Tel: (323) 262-5545 **Fax:** (323) 262-0946
Email: adm9@mellcom.com
Web: www.mellcom.com
Circ.: 20,000
Price: Free
Publication description: English publication promotes engineering, science and technology careers for Hispanics of all ages.
Date established: 1999

TEL-A-SCOUT
Girl Scout Council of Orange County
P.O. Box 3739
Costa Mesa, CA 92628-3739
Jeannie Burns, Executive Director & CEO
Tel: (714) 979-7900 **Fax:** (714) 850-1299
Email: girlscouts@gscoc.org
Web: www.gscoc.org/index5a.html
Price: Free
Publication description: In partnership with trained and dedicated leaders, girls develop qualities that will serve them all of their lives, such as strong values, a social conscience, and the conviction of their own potential and self-worth.

TEXAS COMMUNITY DEVELOPER
Texas Association of Community Development Corporations
1021 E. 7th St. #104
Austin, TX 78702
Reymundo Ocañas, Executive Director
Tel: (512) 457-8232 **Fax:** (512) 479-4090
Email: info@tacdc.org
Web: www.tacdc.org
Circ.: 2,000
Price: Free

TODAY'S LATINO MAGAZINE
Today's Latino Magazine
217 N. Broad St.
Middletown, DE 19709
Milton Delgado, Editor & COO
Tel: (302) 376-1129 **Fax:** (302) 981-5131
Email: info@todayslatino.com
Web: www.todayslatino.com
Circ.: 6,000
Subscription: $9.95/year
Publication description: A Literary forum which empowers the latino heritage to the public at large.
Date established: 2002

TREATMENT REVIEW
AIDS Treatment Data Network
611 Broadway #613
New York, NY 10012
Ken Fornataro, Executive Director
Tel: (212) 260-8868 **Fax:** (212) 260-8869
Email: network@atdn.org
Web: www.atdn.org
Circ.: Variable
Price: Free
Publication description: Information bulletin

TRIBUNE NEWSLETTER, THE
International Women's Tribune Center
777 United Nations Plaza, 3rd Floor
New York, NY 10017
Vicki Semler, Director
Tel: (212) 687-8633 **Fax:** (212) 661-2704
Email: iwtc@iwtc.org
Web: www.iwtc.org
Circ.: 12,000
Price: Free
Publication description: It features issues as diverse as technology, violence, women's rights, indigenous knowledge, environment, microenterprise.
Date established: 1985

U.N. CHRONICLE
The United Nations
2 United Nations Pl. ##DC2-853
New York, NY 10017
The United Nations, Editor
Tel: (212) 963-8302 **Fax:** (212) 963-3489
Email: publications@un.org
Web: www.un.org/publications
Price: $8.00
Publication description: A must-read for every concerned world citizen, the United Nations Chronicle is a quarterly, easy-to-read report on the work of the United Nations and its agencies.

UNIVERSITY NEWSPAPER-POLITÉCNICO, EL
Universidad Politécnica de Puerto Rico
P.O. Box 192017
San Juan, PR 00919-2017
Prof. Ernesto Vazquez-Barquet, President
Tel: (787) 754-8000 x419 **Fax:** (787) 767-5343
Web: www.pupr.edu
Circ.: 6,000
Price: Free
Date established: 1991

USAID YELLOW BOOK
U.S. Agency for International Development
Ronald Regan Bldg., #6.10
Washington, DC 20523
USAID, Publisher
Tel: (202) 712-4810 **Fax:** (202) 216-3035
Email: frontlines@usaid.gov
Web: www.usaid.gov
Circ.: 1,000
Price: Free
Publication description: USAID Yellow Book is USAID's comprehensive directory of contracts, grants and cooperative agreements with universities, firms and non-profit institutions.
Date established: 1983

VARIOUS PUBLICATIONS
AIDS Treatment Data Network
611 Broadway #613
New York, NY 10012
Ken Fornataro, Executive Director
Tel: (212) 260-8868 **Fax:** (212) 260-8869
Email: network@atdn.org
Web: www.atdn.org/lared/index.html
Circ.: Variable
Price: Free

VENEZUELA UP-TO-DATE
Embassy of Venezuela-Press Office
1099 30th St. NW
Washington, DC 20007
José Emilio Castellanos, Editor
Tel: (202) 342-2214 **Fax:** (212) 342-6820
Web: www.embavenez-us.org
Price: Free

VISIÓN
Hispanic-American Chamber of Commerce
67 Broad St., 4th Fl.
Boston, MA 02109
Gerardo Villacres, Executive Director
Tel: (617) 261-4222 **Fax:** (617) 261-6333
Email: hacc@hacc.com
Web: www.hacc.com
Circ.: 2,500
Price: Free
Publication description: Publication that promotes the economic success of Hispanic Owned business in NE in order to improve the financial advancement to those that are employed by these business.
Date established: 1992

VISIÓN NEWSLETTER
Corpus Christi Hispanic Chamber of Commerce
P.O. Box 5523
Corpus Christi, TX 78465
Bob Vela, Director of Membership/Marketing
Tel: (361) 887-7408 **Fax:** (361) 888-9473
Email: rvela@ciris.net
Web: www.cchispanicchamber.org
Circ.: 900
Price: Free
Publication description: Newsletter.
Date established: 1939

VISTAS DEL VALLE NEWSLETTER
Valle del Sol
4117 N. 17th St.
Phoenix, AZ 85032
Carlos Galindo-Elvira, Editor
Tel: (602) 248-8101 x158 **Fax:** (602) 248-8113
Email: carlosg@valledelsol.com
Web: www.valledelsol.com
Circ.: 3,000
Price: Free
Publication description: Valle del Sol Newsletter.

VOCES UNIDAS MAGAZINE
Southwest Community Resources
211 10th St. SW
Albuquerque, NM 87102
Karlos Schmieder, Communications Organizer
Tel: (505) 247-8832 **Fax:** (505) 247-9972
Email: swop@swop.net
Web: www.swop.net
Circ.: 10,000
Price: Free **Subscription:** $10.00/year
Publication description: National English tabloid.
Date established: 1993

VOICE OF LA PUENTE, THE
La Puente Home Shelter
913 State Ave.
Alamosa, CO 81101
Lance Cheslock, Executive Director
Tel: (719) 589-5909 **Fax:** (719) 587-0810
Email: info@lapuente.net
Web: www.lapuente.net
Circ.: 3,000
Price: Free
Publication description: The Voice of La Puente provides an opportunity for the staff and guests to share their stories and reflections.
Date established: 1980

VOZ DEL PUEBLO TAINO NEWS JOURNAL, LA
The United Confederation of Taino People
P.O. Box 4515
New York, NY 10163
Roger Atihuibancex Hernandez, Chief Editor
Tel: (212) 604-4186 **Fax:** (775) 640-1358
Email: la_voz_taino@yahoo.com
Web: www.uctp.org
Circ.: 2,000
Price: Free **Subscription:** $12.00/year
Publication description: La Voz del Pueblo Taino News Journal is the official news journal of The United Confederation of Taino People.
Date established: 1998

VOZ, LA
Latin American Center
521 Maple St.
Manchester, NH 03104
Eileen Phinney, Program Coordinator
Tel: (603) 669-5661 **Fax:** (603) 669-5265
Email: ephinney04@aol.com
Circ.: 900
Price: Free
Publication description: La Voz is the newsletter of Latin American Center that provides professional assistance for the Latin community including; outreach and home visits, bilingual assistance, information and referrals, housing advocacy and assistance.
Date established: 1972

VOZ LATINA NEWSLETTER, LA
Labor Council of Latin American Advancement (LCLAA)
888 16th St. NW #640
Washington, DC 20006
Cefar Moreno, Editor
Tel: (202) 347-4223 **Fax:** (703) 347-5095
Email: headquarters@lclaa.org
Web: www.lclaa.org
Circ.: 15,000
Price: Free
Publication description: La Voz Latina Newsletter is the official newsletter of Labor Council of Latin American Advancement.
Date established: 1973

VS NEWSLETTER
Victim Services 2000
303 W. Colfax Ave. #1300
Denver, CO 80204
Ana Soler, Director
Tel: (720) 913-9090 **Fax:** (720) 913-9921
Email: asoler@vs2000.org
Web: www.vs2000.org
Circ.: 1,500
Price: Free
Publication description: English Newsletter.
Date established: 1987

WINDOWS ON SOUTH AMERICA
South America Mission
5217 South Military Trail
Lake Worth, FL 33463-6099
Jeff Orcutt, Editor
Tel: (561) 965-1833 **Fax:** (561) 439-8950
Email: samusa@samlink.org
Web: www.samlink.org
Circ.: 7,000
Price: Free
Publication description: English newsletter.
Date established: 1989

WORLD BANK ANNUAL REPORT, THE
The World Bank Bookstore
P.O. Box 960
Herndon, VA 20172
The World Bank, InfoShop
Tel: (800) 645-7247 **Fax:** (703) 661-1501
Email: books@worldbank.org
Web: www.worldbank.org/publications
Price: Free
Publication description: The Annual Report is prepared by the Executive Directors of the International Bank for Reconstruction and Development (IBRD) and the International Development Association (IDA) in accordance with the by-laws of the two institutions.

VARIES

BASIC FACTS
Inter-American Development Bank
External Relations Office, 1300 New York Ave. NW
Washington, DC 20577
IDB Bookstore, Publisher
Tel: (202) 623-3657 **Fax:** (202) 623-3531
Email: idb-books@iadb.org
Web: www.iadb.org
Price: Free
Publication description: National English newsletter

COMO PREPARAR LA DECLARACIÓN DE IMPUESTO FEDERAL, PUB. 579SP
US Internal Revenue Service (IRS)
P. O. Box 85074, Distribution Center
Richmond, VA 23261-5074
Tel: (800) 829-3676
Web: www.irs.gov/espanol/index.html
Price: Free .
Date established: 1990

CONNECTIONS NEWSLETTER
Archdiocese of Detroit - Catholic Youth Organization
305 Michigan Ave.
Detroit, MI 48226
Suzanne Heath, Executive Director
Tel: (313) 963-7172 **Fax:** (313) 963-7179
Email: info@cyodetroit.org
Web: www.cyodetroit.org
Price: Free
Publication description: Newsletter of Archdiocese of Detroit - Catholic Youth Organization.
Date established: 1933

CRÉDITO POR INGRESO DEL TRABAJO, PUB. 596SP
US Internal Revenue Service (IRS)
P. O. Box 85074, Distribution Center
Richmond, VA 23261-5074
Tel: (800) 829-1040
Web: www.irs.gov/pub/irs-pdf/p596sp.pdf
Price: Free .
Date established: 1992

DERECHOS DEL CONTRIBUYENTE, PUB. 1SP
US Internal Revenue Service (IRS)
P. O. Box 85074, Distribution Center
Richmond, VA 23261-5074
US Internal Revenue Service (IRS), Publisher
Tel: (800) 829-1040
Web: www.irs.gov/espanol
Price: Free .
Date established: 1991

DIRECTORY OF MINORITY ARTS AND ORGANIZATIONS
National Endowment for the Arts
Civil Rights Division, 1100 Pennsylvania Ave. NW #219
Washington, DC 20506
Carol Ann Huston, Editor
Tel: (202) 682-5454 **Fax:** (202) 602-5553
Email: webmgr@arts.endow.gov
Web: www.arts.endow.gov
Circ.: 2,000
Price: Free
Publication description: The publication includes a list of national arts service organizations with leadership and constituencies that are predominantly Asian-American, Afro-American, Hispanic, Native American, or multiracial.
Date established: 1982

EAST FLORIDA GAZETTE
St. Augustine Historical Society
271 Charlotte St.
St. Augustine, FL 32084
Overton G. Ganong, Executive Director
Tel: (904) 824-2872 **Fax:** (904) 824-2569
Email: oldhouse@aug.com
Web: www.oldesthouse.org
Price: Free .
Date established: 1883

FINANCIAL AID FOR HISPANIC AMERICANS
Reference Service Press
El Dorado Hills Business Park, 5000 Windplay Dr. #4
El Dorado Hills, CA 95762
Gail A. Schlachter, Editor
Tel: (916) 939-9620 **Fax:** (916) 939-9626
Email: Findaid@aol.com
Web: www.rspfunding.com
Price: $40.00
Publication description: The Financial Aid for Hispanic Americans includes more than 1,300 funding programs open to Americans of Mexico, Puerto Rico, Central American, or other Latin American heritage. .
Date established: 1985

FINANCIAL AID FOR MINORITIES
Garrett Park Press, Inc.
P.O. Box 190
Garrett Park, MD 20896
Robert Calver, Editor
Tel: (301) 946-2553 **Fax:** (301) 949-3955
Web: www.finaid.org
Price: $5.95 ea.
Publication description: Five issues each time.
Date established: 1968

GLOSARIO INGLÉS - ESPAÑOL DE TERMINOLOGIA TRIBUTARIA, PUB 850
US Internal Revenue Service (IRS)
P. O. Box 85074, Distribution Center
Richmond, VA 23261-5074
US Internal Revenue Service (IRS), Publisher
Tel: (800) 829-1040
Web: www.irs.gov/espanol
Price: Free .
Date established: 1989

GUIDE TO THE HISPANIC AMERICAN HISTORICAL REVIEW
Duke University Press
P.O. Box 90660
Durham, NC 27708-0660
Duke University Press, Customer Service
Tel: (919) 684-3600 **Fax:** (919) 688-4574
Email: orders@dukepress.edu
Web: www.dukeupress.edu
Circ.: 1,000
Price: $64.95
Publication description: National English journal.
Date established: 1980

INFORMACIÓN SOBRE PROGRAMS DE AYUDA CON LOS IMPUESTOS QUE OFRECE EL IRS, PUB. 2053-B
US Internal Revenue Service (IRS)
P. O. Box 85074. Distribution Center
Richmond, VA 23261-5074
US Internal Revenue Service (IRS), Publisher
Tel: (800) 829-1040
Web: www.irs.gov/espanol
Price: Free .
Date established: 1990

MOMENTO CATÓLICO, EL
Claretian Publications
205 W. Monroe
Chicago, IL 60606
Carmen Aguinaco, Editor
Tel: (312) 236-7782 **Fax:** (312) 236-8207
Email: aguinaco@claretianpubs.org
Web: www.claretianpubs.org
Circ.: 300,000
Price: Free .
Date established: 1990

PAPEL PERIÓDICO
Colegio Nacional de Periodistas de Cuba en el Exilio
900 SW 1st St.
Miami, FL 33130
Luis Felipe Marsans, Editor
Tel: (305) 324-6066
Web: www.cnpexilio.org
Circ.: 1,000
Price: Free .
Date established: 1962

SALALM NEWSLETTER
Seminar on the Acquisition of Latin American Library Materials
Sid Richardson Hall #1.109, SALALM Secretariat, Univ. of Texas
Austin, TX 78713
Laura Gutierrez-Witt, Executive Secretary
Tel: (512) 495-4471 **Fax:** (512) 495-4488
Email: LauraGW@mail.utexas.edu
Web: www.library.cornell.edu/colldev/salalmhome.html
Circ.: 500
Price: Free **Subscription:** $25.00/year
Publication description: The SALALM Newsletter provides a vehicle to keep members informed of happenings in the organization, activities of the members, and news and events in the field. It also can serve as the "public face" of the organization to non-members

SED NEWS
Spanish Education Development Center
1840 Kalorama Rd. NW
Washington, DC 20009
José González, Editor
Tel: (202) 462-8848 **Fax:** (202) 462-6886
Email: info@sedcenter.com
Web: www.sedcenter.com
Circ.: 1,000
Price: Free

TEATRO NOTES
Teatro Campesino
P.O. Box 1240
San Juan Bautista, CA 95045
Luis Valdez, Chairman
Tel: (831) 623-2444 **Fax:** (831) 623-4127
Email: info@elteatrocampesino.com
Web: www.elteatrocampesino.com
Price: Free
Publication description: National English newsletter.
Date established: 1994

TECOLOTE, EL
Hispanic Association for Cultural Enrichment at Rice
Rice University, M/S 526, P.O. Box 1892
Houston, TX 77251-1892
Philip Hernandez, Editor
Tel: (713) 348-3886 **Fax:** (713) 348-5618
Email: Hacer@rice.edu
Web: www.ruf.rice.edu/~hacer
Price: Free

TRASTORNO DE PÁNICO
National Institute of Mental Health
6001 Executive Blvd. #8184 MSC9663
Bethesda, MD 20892-9663
National Institute of Mental Health, Publisher
Tel: (301) 443-4513 **Fax:** (301) 443-4279
Email: nimhinfo@nih.gov
Web: www.nimh.nih.gov
Price: Free
Publication description: An easy to read booklet on panic disorder that explains what it is, when it starts, how long it lasts, and how to get help.
Date established: 1996

WATCH ON WASHINGTON
Latin American Management Association
419 New Jersey Ave. SE
Washington, DC 20003
Stephen Denlinger, President/CEO
Tel: (202) 546-3803 **Fax:** (202) 546-3807
Email: lamausa@bellatlantic.net
Web: www.lama-usa.com
Circ.: 2,500
Price: Free
Publication description: Bulletin.
Date established: 1973

WEEKLY

20 DE MAYO SPANISH
20 de Mayo
1824 W. Sunset Blvd. #202
Los Angeles, CA 90026-6503
Abel Pérez, Editor/Publisher
Tel: (213) 483-8511 **Fax:** (213) 483-6474
Email: Mayo20@aol.com
Web: www.20demayo.org
Circ.: 25,000
Subscription: $50.00/year
Publication description: Local/regional Spanish newspaper designed to serve

the interest of the Hispanic Community in Southern California. It also reaches Hispanics throughout the United States via paid subscriptions.
Date established: 1969

A SU SALUD
2500 W 8th St. #103
Amarillo, TX 79106
Dr. Ramón Godoy, Publisher/Editor
Tel: (806) 371-7084 **Fax:** (806) 371-7090
Email: lmensajero@aol.com
Web: www.elmensajero-ama.com
Circ.: 10,000
Price: Free **Subscription:** $45.00/year.
Date established: 1997

ACTUALIDAD NEWSPAPER, LA (ECO DEL VALLE DELAWARE)
La Actualidad
4953 N. 5th St.
Philadelphia, PA 19120
José A. Rivera, Editor
Tel: (215) 324-3838 **Fax:** (215) 457-4931
Email: laactual@aol.com
Circ.: 20,000
Price: $0.25 **Subscription:** $52.00/year
Publication description: Local/regional Spanish newspaper.
Date established: 1973

AHORA
Ahora Spanish-English Newspaper
743 S. Virginia St.
Reno, NV 89501
Sheila Sepulveda, Publisher
Tel: (775) 323-6811 **Fax:** (775) 323-6995
Email: ahoranewspaper@hotmail.com
Web: www.ahoranews.com
Circ.: 15,000
Price: Free
Publication description: Ahora is Reno, Nevada's Spanish- English newspaper.
Date established: 1983

AL DÍA
Al Día Newspaper, Inc.
211 N 13th St. #704
Philadelphia, PA 19107
Hernán Guaracao Calderón, Publisher
Tel: (215) 569-4666 **Fax:** (215) 569-3271
Email: editor@aldiainc.com
Web: www.aldiainc.com
Circ.: 50,000
Price: $0.50 **Subscription:** $70.00/year
Publication description: Local/Regional Spanish tabloid.
Date established: 1992

ALIANZA METROPOLITAN NEWS
Alianza Metropolitan News
P.O. Box 730275
San Jose, CA 95173-0275
Marcela Anzoategui, Editor
Tel: (408) 272-9394 **Fax:** (408) 272-9395
Email: saita@alianzanews.com
Web: www.alianzanews.com
Circ.: 40,000
Price: $1.06 **Subscription:** $55.00/year
Publication description: Provides Bay area regional bilingual Hispanic newsletter.
Date established: 1989

ARRIBA ART & BUSINESS NEWS
P.O. Box 12865
Austin, TX 78711
Romeo Rodríguez, Publisher
Tel: (512) 479-6397 **Fax:** (512) 479-6721
Email: arribanews@ccfi.com
Circ.: 8,500
Subscription: $50.00/year

Publication description: Local/regional bilingual tabloid.
Date established: 1980

AVISADOR MAGAZINE, EL
A1 Ruiz & Son
1722 Junction Ave. #E
San Jose, CA 95112
Orlando Ruiz-Gessa, Editor
Tel: (408) 437-0909 **Fax:** (408) 437-1114
Email: el_avisador@sbcglobal.net
Circ.: 5,500
Price: $0.50
Publication description: Spanish magazine

AVISO MAGAZINE, EL
El Aviso de Ocasion, Inc
6728 Seville Ave.
Huntington Park, CA 90255
José Ramiro Zepeda, President
Tel: (323) 983-2000 **Fax:** (323) 589-9395
Email: elaviso@aol.com
Web: www.elaviso.com
Circ.: 150,000
Price: Free
Publication description: Spanish weekly magazine & TV guide delivered home-to-home in Spanish-speaking neighborhoods.
Date established: 1989

AZTECA NEWS
Azteca News
P.O. Box 207
Santa Ana, CA 92701
Fernando Velo, Editor
Tel: (714) 972-9912 **Fax:** (714) 973-8117
Email: aztecanews@aol.com
Circ.: 42,000
Price: Free **Subscription:** $52.00/year
Publication description: Local/regional Spanish newspaper. Non-Spanish language ads are accepted. Translations into Spanish are available.
Date established: 1980

BAJO EL SOL
Freedom Press
851 N. Main St.
San Luis, AZ 85349
Maria Chavoya, Editor
Tel: (928) 627-5081 **Fax:** (928) 627-5048
Email: mchavoya@bajoelsol.com
Web: www.bajoelsol.com
Circ.: 21,000
Price: Free **Subscription:** $6.60/year
Publication description: Local news, sports, education, economic, health, family, and cultural issues

BEAT WITHIN, THE
Pacific News Service
275 9th St.
San Francisco, CA 94103
David Inocencio, Editor-in-Chief
Tel: (415) 503-4170 **Fax:** (415) 503-0970
Email: mmelamed@pacificnews.org
Web: www.thebeatwithin.org
Price: Free
Publication description: A weekly newsletter of writing and art from writing workshops in Bay Area juvenile halls.
Date established: 1996

BELL GARDENS SUN, THE
Eastern Group Publications, Inc.
2500 S. Atlantic Blvd., Bldg. A
Los Angeles, CA 90040
Jonathan Sanchez, Representative
Tel: (323) 263-5743 **Fax:** (323) 263-9169
Email: service@esp.com
Web: www.egpnews.com
Circ.: 7,000
Price: Free

Publication description: Bilingual tabloid.
Date established: 1995

BOHEMIO NEWS, EL
El Bohemio News, Inc.
4178 Mission St.
San Francisco, CA 94112
Fernando Rosado, Editor
Tel: (415) 469-9579 **Fax:** (415) 469-9481
Email: bohemio@ix.netcom.com
Web: www.elbohemio.com
Circ.: 45,000
Price: Free **Subscription:** $60.00/year
Publication description: First Spanish Newspaper.
Date established: 1971

BOLETÍN DE PUERTO RICO
Boletín de Puerto Rico
P.O. Box 361716
San Juan, PR 00936-1716
Humberto García, President
Tel: (787) 268-3733 **Fax:** (787) 268-3988
Email: boletinpr@boletinpr.com
Web: www.boletinpr.com
Circ.: 1,000
Price: $3.65 **Subscription:** $189.00/year.
Date established: 1978

BUENA SUERTE SPANISH NEWS
Información Publishing Co., Inc.
6065 Hillcroft Ave. #401-B
Houston, TX 77081
Emilio S. Martínez, President
Tel: (713) 272-0101 **Fax:** (713) 272-0011
Email: circulation@periodicobuenasuerte
Web: www.periodicobuenasuerte.com
Circ.: 92,000
Price: Free
Publication description: Local/regional Spanish newspaper.
Date established: 1986

CAMPEON, EL
4104 Live Oak St.
Dallas, TX 75204
Francisco Rayo, Publisher
Tel: 214-827-9700 **Fax:** 214-827-8200
Email: ellie@elheraldonews.com
Web: www.elheraldonews.com
Circ.: 35,000
Price: Free
Publication description: Insert of El Heraldo News.
Date established: 1992

CARIB NEWS
Carib News Corp.
7 W. 36th St.
New York, NY 10018
Karl Rodney, Publisher
Tel: (212) 944-1991 **Fax:** (212) 944-2089
Email: caribnews@worldnet.att.net
Web: www.nycaribnews.com
Circ.: 67,000
Price: $.50 **Subscription:** $40.00/year
Publication description: The weekly voice of the Caribbean American community.
Date established: 1981

CARIBBEAN BUSINESS NEWSPAPER
Casiano Communications
1700 Ave. Fernández Juncos
San Juan, PR 00909-2938
Francisco J. Cimadevilla, Esq., Editor
Tel: (787) 728-9300 **Fax:** (787) 268-1626
Email: cbusiness@casiano.com
Web: www.casiano.com
Circ.: 45,000
Subscription: $45.00/year
Publication description: Financial newspaper.
Date established: 1975

CARRIZO SPRINGS JAVELIN
Carrizo Springs Javelin
P.O. Box 1046
Carrizo Springs, TX 78834
Claudia McDaniel, Editor
Tel: (830) 876-2318 **Fax:** (830) 876-2620
Email: csjavelin@yahoo.com
Circ.: 2,000
Price: $.50 **Subscription:** $30.50/year
Publication description: Local/regional English broadsheet.
Date established: 1884

CATHOLIC NORTHWEST PROGRESS, THE
Archdiocese of Seattle
910 Marion St.
Seattle, WA 98104
Stephen Kent, Editor
Tel: (206) 382-4850 **Fax:** (206) 382-3487
Email: cathnwprogress@seattlearch.org
Web: www.seattlearch.org
Circ.: 18,000
Subscription: $27.50/year
Publication description: Local/regional English tabloid.
Date established: 1897

CATHOLIC SENTINEL
Oregon Catholic Press
P.O. Box 18030
Portland, OR 97218
Rocio Rios Niño, Editor
Tel: (503) 281-1191 **Fax:** (503) 460-5496
Email: sentinel@ocp.org
Web: www.sentinel.org
Circ.: 15,000
Price: Free **Subscription:** $28.00/year
Publication description: Local/regional English newspaper which conects the Catholic Hispanic community and to serve the Hispanics around the state.
Date established: 1870

CENTRAL HISPANIC NEWS, EL
Sanchez Communications
4124 W. Vernor
Detroit, MI 48209
Dolores Sanchez, Publisher
Tel: (313) 841-0100 **Fax:** (313) 841-0155
Email: elcentral1@aol.com
Circ.: 14,000
Price: Free **Subscription:** $37.00/year
Publication description: Hispanic Tabloid.
Date established: 1988

CHAMBER
United States Hispanic Chamber of Commerce
2175 K St. NW #100
Washington, DC 20037
Armando Ojeda, President/CEO
Tel: (202) 842-1212 **Fax:** (202) 842-3221
Email: chamberweekly@ushcc.com
Web: www.ushcc.com
Circ.: 2,000
Price: Free
Publication description: The newsletter provides up-to-the-minute information about USHCC, upcoming events and new opportunities for members chambers and Hispanic business owners.

CHICAGO DEPORTIVO
Chicago Deportivo
3748 S Cleveland Ave.
Brookfield, IL 60513
Julio Parrales, Editor
Tel: (708) 387-0380 **Fax:** (708) 485-4969
Email: Cdeportivo@aol.com
Circ.: 30,000
Price: Free

Publication description: Local/regional Spanish newspaper.
Date established: 1988

CHICANO, EL

Inland Empire Community Newspaper
P.O. Box 6247
San Bernadino, CA 92412
Diana Harrison, Editor
Tel: (909) 381-9898 Fax: (909) 384-0406
Email: iecn@gte.net
Circ.: 8,000
Price: Free Subscription: $93.00/year
Publication description: Bilingual newspaper.
Date established: 1969

CITY TERRACE COMET

Eastern Group Publications, Inc.
2500 S. Atlantic Blvd., Bldg. A
Los Angeles, CA 90040
Jonathan Sanchez, Representative
Tel: (323) 263-5743 Fax: (323) 263-9169
Email: service@esp.com
Web: www.egpnews.com
Circ.: 3,000
Price: Free
Publication description: Bilingual tabloid.
Date established: 1979

CLAMOR, EL

Valley Multimedia, Corp.
1300 N. 10th St. #460
McAllen, TX 78501
José Mario Flores, Publisher
Tel: (956) 994-3996 Fax: (956) 994-3989
Email: vmmedia@elclamor.com
Web: www.elclamor.com
Circ.: 15,000
Price: Free
Publication description: Spanish weekly newspaper.
Date established: 1981

CLARÍN, EL (WEEKLY SHOPPER)

BCC-Bugle Communications Corporation
P.O. Box 832677
Miami, FL 33283-2677
Jose R. Noboa, President
Tel: (305) 270-3333 Fax: (305) 270-2272
Email: custserv@elclarin.com
Web: www.elclarin.com
Circ.: 160,000
Price: Free Subscription: $21.00/year
Publication description: Local/regional Spanish newspaper.
Date established: 1980

CLASIFICADO, EL

1125 Goodrich Blvd.
Los Angeles, CA 90022
Martha C. de la Torre, Publisher
Tel: (323) 278-5310 Fax: (323) 278-5315
Email: elclasificado@elclasificado.com
Web: www.elclasificado.com
Circ.: 200,000
Price: Free
Publication description: El Clasificado is published to serve the shopping needs of the Spanish speaking community of Southern California.
Date established: 1988

COLOMBIANO NEWSPAPER, EL

Latinwork Publishing Corporation
15751 Sheridan St. #186
Fort Lauderdale, FL 33331
Alfredo Mantilla, Editor
Tel: (954) 430-1090 Fax: (954) 438-4418
Email: editor@elcolombiano.net
Web: www.elcolombiano.net
Circ.: 35,000
Price: Free

Publication description: Colombian news.
Date established: 1995

COMERCIO, EL

P.O. Box 10077
Manassas, VA 20108
Ronald Virto, Director General
Tel: (703) 393-6388 Fax: (703) 393-7910
Email: elcomerciodemanassas@msn.com
Web: www.elcomercionewspaper.com
Circ.: 35,000
Price: Free Subscription: $65.00/year
Publication description: Spanish language Newspaper In Metro Area.

COMMERCE COMET

Eastern Group Publications, Inc.
2500 S. Atlantic Blvd., Bldg. A
Los Angeles, CA 90040
Jonathan Sanchez, Representative
Tel: (323) 263-5743 Fax: (323) 263-9169
Email: service@esp.com
Web: www.egpnews.com
Circ.: 6,500
Price: Free
Publication description: Bilingual tabloid.
Date established: 1994

CONEXIÓN, LA

La Conexión, Inc.
916 W. Morgan St.
Raleigh, NC 27603
Mike Leary, Publisher
Tel: (919) 832-1225/(888) 739-4911
Fax: (919) 856-0164
Email: conectese@laconexionusa.com
Web: www.laconexionusa.com
Circ.: 20,000
Subscription: $75.00/year
Publication description: Spanish language weekly newspaper.
Date established: 1995

CONQUISTADOR LATINO NEWS SOURCE, EL

Conquistador Communications, LLC.
3220 W. National Ave.
Milwaukee, WI 53215
Victor Huyke, Editor
Tel: (414) 383-1000 Fax: (414) 383-8885
Email: conquistador@bizwi.rr.com
Circ.: 10,000
Price: Free Subscription: $55.00/year
Publication description: Bilingual tabloid.
Date established: 1998

CONQUISTADOR NEWSPAPER, EL

El Conquistador
229 W. Ilinois Ave., 1st Fl.
Aurora, IL 60506
Beatriz Jacobo, Editor
Tel: (630) 892-9691 Fax: (630) 892-9697
Email: editor@elconquistador.us
Web: www.conquistadornewspaper.com
Circ.: 15,000
Price: Free Subscription: $60.00/year
Publication description: Local/regional bilingual newspaper.
Date established: 1992

CONTRACT

Governor's Office of Minority Affairs-State of Maryland
6 Saint Paul St. #1502
Baltimore, MD 21202
Sharon Roberson Pinder, Special Secretary
Tel: (410) 767-8232 Fax: (410) 333-7568
Email: info@oma.state.md.us
Web: www.oma.state.md.us
Subscription: $125.00/year
Publication description: OMA 's mission is to assist minority firms in Maryland who are seeking contract and procurement opportunities with the state.

DENVER CATHOLIC REGISTER NEWSPAPER

Denver Catholic Diocese
1300 S Steele St.
Denver, CO 80210
Roxanne King, Editor
Tel: (303) 715-3215 Fax: (303) 715-2045
Email: editor@archden.org
Web: www.archden.org/dcr
Circ.: 93,000
Price: $.35 Subscription: $25.00/year
Publication description: Local/regional English newspaper.
Date established: 1900

DÍA NEWSPAPER, EL

El Día Publications
5718 W. Cermak Rd.
Cicero, IL 60804
Jorge A. Montes de Oca, Publisher
Tel: (708) 652-6397 Fax: (708) 652-6653
Email: eldianews@pop.net
Web: www.eldianews.com
Circ.: 45,000
Price: Free Subscription: $63.00/year
Publication description: Newspaper. The publication policy of EL DIA is to publish a weekly community newspaper serving the Hispanic communities of Chicago and other areas of Illinois and Wisconsin.
Date established: 1985

DIARIO METRO NEWSPAPER

Diario Metro, Inc.
P.O. Box 9142
Santurce, PR 00908
Wilfredo Umpierre, General Manager
Tel: (787) 791-7208 Fax: (787) 791-7304
Email: diariometro@yahoo.com
Web: www.diariometro.com
Circ.: 70,000
Price: $0.25 Subscription: $39.00/year
Publication description: Puerto Rican news and to educate the Puerto Rican American citizens.
Date established: 1993

DOS MOUNDS

902-A Southwest Blvd.
Kansas City, MO 64108-2358
Clara Reyes, Publisher
Tel: (816) 221-4747 Fax: (816) 221-4894
Email: creyes@dosmundos.com
Web: www.dosmundos.com
Circ.: 25,000
Subscription: $35.00/year
Publication description: Local/regional bilingual newspaper.
Date established: 1981

EAGLE PASS BUSINESS JOURNAL

P.O. Box 2160
Eagle Pass, TX 78853
Ricardo E. Caldron, Publisher
Tel: (830) 757-2705 Fax: (830) 757-2703
Email: epbj@sbcglobal.net
Circ.: 5,000
Price: $0.50 Subscription: $52.00/year.
Date established: 1994

EAST L.A-BROOKLYN-BELVEDERE COMET

Eastern Group Publications, Inc.
2500 S. Atlantic Blvd., Bldg. A
Los Angeles, CA 90040
Jonathan Sanchez, Representative
Tel: (323) 263-5743 Fax: (323) 263-9169
Email: service@esp.com
Web: www.egpnews.com
Circ.: 3,000
Price: Free
Publication description: Bilingual tabloid.
Date established: 1979

ECO DE VIRGINIA, EL

101 W. Plume St., 4th Fl.
Norfolk, VA 23510
Augusto Ratti-Angulu, Editor/Publisher
Tel: (757) 625-1341 Fax: (757) 625-1327
Email: elecodeva@yahoo.com
Circ.: 30,000
Price: Free
Publication description: Bilingual educational Hispanic weekly newspaper serving Hampton Roads, Williamsburg, Richmond, parts of northern Virginia and parts of North Carolina

ECUADOR NEWS

64-03 Roosevelt Ave., 2nd Fl.
Woodside, NY 11377
Dr. Marcello Arboleda, General Director
Tel: (718) 205-7014 Fax: (718) 205-6580
Email: ecuanews@inch.com
Web: www.ecuadornews.net
Circ.: 42,000
Price: Free
Publication description: The objective of Ecuador News is to provide the Ecuadorian and Latino-American communities with respectable, and trustworthy news.
Date established: 1996

EDITOR NEWSPAPER, EL

Amigo Publications
1502 Ave. M
Lubbock, TX 79401
Bidal Agüero, Editor
Tel: (806) 763-3841 Fax: (806) 741-1110
Email: eleditor@llano.net
Circ.: 12,195
Subscription: $14.00-22.00/year.
Date established: 1977

ELECTRONICS SUPPLY AND MANUFACTURING

CMP Media LLC
600 Community Dr.
Manhasset, NY 11030
Bruce Rayner, Editor-in-Chief
Tel: (516) 562-5000 Fax: (516) 562-5995
Email: brayner@cmp.com
Web: www.ebnonline.com, www.cmp.com
Circ.: 40,000
Price: Free
Publication description: CMP Media LLC is a leading high-technology business-to-business multimedia company that provides essential information and integrated marketing services to the technology and healthcare professionals worldwide.
Date established: 1973

EMPLEOS/JOBS

Spanish Communicators, Inc.
P.O. Box 660346
Birmingham, AL 35266
Sara Urdaneta, Communications Director
Tel: (202) 591-7119 Fax: (205) 591-7119
Email: spanishclassifieds@bham.rr.com
Circ.: 25,000
Price: 1996 Subscription: $30.00/year
Publication description: Features selling, buying, renting, trading and hiring opportunities within Alabama's Hispanic community.
Date established: 1985

ESPECIAL, EL/ESPECIALITO, EL

El Especial, Inc. - Headquarters
3510 Bergenline Ave.
Union City, NJ 07087
Jose Sibaja, Editor
Tel: (201) 348-1959 Fax: (201) 348-3385
Email: espadsny@aol.com
Web: www.elespecial.com

Circ.: 111,000
Price: $0.50
Publication description: Local/regional Spanish newspaper.
Date established: 1985

ESPECIAL NEWSPAPER, EL
El Especial, Inc.
175 Fontainebleau Blvd. #1F
Miami, FL 33172
Mercy Oliva/John Ibarria, Manager
Tel: (305) 225-3742 **Fax:** (305) 223-6049
Email: espadsmia@aol.com
Web: www.elespecial.com
Circ.: 111,000
Price: Free
Publication description: Local/regional Spanish newspaper.
Date established: 1989

ESTADIO NEWSPAPER
Estadio, Inc.
6431 S. Norcross-Tucker Rd.
Tucker, GA 30084
Henry Higuita, Editor
Tel: (770) 414-1107 **Fax:** (770) 414-4115
Email: director@estadiosports.com
Web: www.estadiosports.com
Circ.: 18,000
Price: Free
Publication description: Sports newspaper.
Date established: 1997

ESTRELLA DE PUERTO RICO, LA
La Estrella de Puerto Rico
165 Calle París, Urb. Floral Park
Hato Rey, PR 00917
Javier Medina, Editor
Tel: (787) 754-4440 **Fax:** (787) 754-4457
Email: javier.medina@estrelladepr.com
Web: www.estrelladepr.com
Circ.: 123,300
Price: Free **Subscription:** $80.00/year
Publication description: Local/regional Spanish newspaper.
Date established: 1983

EXCÉLSIOR
523 N. Grand Ave.
Santa Ana, CA 92701
Ron Gonzales, Editor
Tel: (714) 796-4310 **Fax:** (714) 796-4316
Web: www.ocexcelsior.com
Circ.: 89,000
Price: Free
Publication description: Spanish newspaper for Orange County, a division of the Orange County Register; Elizabeth Corbin, sales manager.
Date established: 1992

ÉXITO DEPORTIVO
Spanish Sports Productions
11636 Spry St.
Norwalk, CA 90650
Rafael Ramirez, Publisher
Tel: (562) 929-3802 **Fax:** (562) 929-3842
Email: info@exitodeportivo.com
Web: www.exitodeportivo.com
Circ.: 50,000
Price: Free
Publication description: Bilingual tabloid.
Date established: 1983

EXTRA MÁS NOTICIAS
Extra Más Noticias, Inc.
P.O. Box 2472
Norcross, GA 30091
José Galván, Editor
Tel: (770) 416-8692 **Fax:** (770) 242-6974
Email: extramasnoticias@bellsouth.net
Circ.: 7,500
Price: Free

Publication description: Tabloid, Spanish.
Date established: 1996

FARANDULA USA
Velazquez Publishing, Inc.
2025 S. Main St.
Santa Ana, CA 92707
Maribel Gonzalez, Editor
Tel: (714) 668-1010 **Fax:** (714) 668-1013
Email: miniondas@aol.com
Web: www.farandulausa.com
Circ.: 45,000
Price: Free **Subscription:** $110.00
Publication description: Spanish newspaper.
Date established: 1988

FEATURETTES
North American Precis Syndicate, Inc.
350 5th Ave. #6500
New York, NY 10118
Walter Villalta, Media Relations
Tel: (800) 222-5551 X121
Fax: (800) 990-4329
Email: wvillalta@napset.com
Web: www.napsnet.com
Publication description: NAPS distributes releases for most Fortune 500 companies, over 150 associations and government information offices and more than 100 PR firms including all of the 12 largest.

GACETA, LA
La Gaceta Publishing, Inc.
3210 E. 7th Ave.
Tampa, FL 33603
Patrick Manteiga, Editor/Publisher
Tel: (813) 248-3921 **Fax:** (813) 247-5357
Email: amanteiga@lagacetanewspaper.com
Web: www.lagacetanewspaper.com
Circ.: 18,000
Price: $0.50 **Subscription:** $25.00/year
Publication description: Trilingual newspaper, Italian, Spanish and English.
Date established: 1923

GAZETA BRAZILIAN NEWS
4390 N. Federal Hwy. #207
Fort Lauderdale, FL 33308
Fernanda Cirinos, Editor
Tel: (954) 938-9292 **Fax:** (954) 938-9227
Email: news@gazetanews.com
Web: www.gazetanews.com

GENTE DE MINNESOTA
Latino Communications Network
2019 E. Lake St. #7
Minneapolis, MN 55407
Juan Carlos Alanis, Publisher
Tel: (612) 729-5900 **Fax:** (612) 729-5999
Email: juancarlos@lcnmedia.com
Web: www.gentedeminnesota.com
Circ.: 15,000
Price: Free **Subscription:** $90.00/year
Publication description: Spanish Newspaper.
Date established: 1997

GOL USA INTERNACIONAL
69-10 Woodside Ave., 2nd Fl.
Woodside, NY 11377
Jorge Garcia, Editor
Tel: (718) 565-1818 **Fax:** (718) 565-0263
Email: golusa@attglobal.net
Web: www.golusa.net
Circ.: 73,900
Price: $1.00 **Subscription:** $24.00/year
Publication description: It is the only Spanish-Language publication in the US that covers the world of international soccer on a weekly basis.
Date established: 1993

GOLAZO DEPORTIVO
5881 NE 21st Dr.
Fort Lauderdale, FL 33308
Carlos Simaldone, Editor
Tel: (800) 444-1027 **Fax:** (954) 267-0599
Email: editor@golazodeportivo.com
Web: www.golazodeportivo.com
Circ.: 25,000
Price: Free
Publication description: Spanish sports newspaper.
Date established: 1986

GRAM NEWSPAPER, EL
2543 Del Rio Blvd.
Eagle Pass, TX 78852
Ruben Carrillo, Editor
Tel: (830) 773-8610 **Fax:** (830) 773-1641
Email: elgram@hilconet.com
Circ.: 5,000
Price: $.25 **Subscription:** $13.00/year
Publication description: Hispanic Newspaper.
Date established: 1995

GUÍA FAMILIAR, LA
Latin Publications, Inc.
7453 Woodley Ave.
Van Nuys, CA 91406
Victor Fields, Editor
Tel: (818) 882-9200 **Fax:** (818) 882-7200
Email: ads@latinpublications.com
Web: www.latinpublications.com
Circ.: 246,000
Price: Free .
Date established: 1979

HERALDO DE BROWARD, EL
El Heraldo de Broward, Inc.
1975 E. Sunrise Blvd. #810
Ft. Lauderdale, FL 33304
Elaine M. Vázquez, Editor
Tel: (954) 527-0627 **Fax:** (954) 792-7402
Email: elheraldobroward@aol.com
Web: www.elheraldo.com
Circ.: 18,000
Price: Free **Subscription:** $35.00/year.
Date established: 1995

HERALDO NEWS, EL
El Heraldo News
4104 Live Oak St.
Dallas, TX 75204
Ellie Byrd, Marketing Director
Tel: (214) 827-9700 X102
Fax: (214) 827-8200
Email: ellie@elheraldonews.com
Web: www.elheraldonews.com
Circ.: 55,000
Price: Free
Publication description: Spanish newspaper.
Date established: 1992

HISPANIA NEWS
Con Fé Communications, Ltd.
P.O. Box 15116
Colorado Springs, CO 80935
Robert L. Armendariz, Editor
Tel: (719) 540-0220 **Fax:** (719) 540-0599
Email: editor@hispanianews.com
Web: www.hispanianews.com
Circ.: 25,000
Price: Free **Subscription:** $28.00/year
Publication description: The only Hispanic newspaper on the web in the state of Colorado.
Date established: 1987

HISPANIC LINK NEWSLETTER
Hispanic Link News Service, Inc.
1420 N St. NW #101
Washington, DC 20005
Fresia Rodriguez, Editor

Tel: (202) 234-0280 **Fax:** (202) 234-4090
Email: editor@hispaniclink.org
Web: www.hispaniclink.org
Circ.: 1,300
Subscription: $140/year
Publication description: National English newsletter.
Date established: 1980

HISPANIC MARKET
Hispanic Market Weekly, Inc.
2625 Ponce de Leon Blvd. #285
Coral Gables, FL 33134
Arturo Villar, Publisher
Tel: (305) 448-5838 **Fax:** (305) 448-6573
Email: info@hmweekly.com
Web: www.hmweekly.com
Circ.: 10,000
Price: $1.08 **Subscription:** $397.00/year
Publication description: Hispanic Market Weekly is the source of the latest and most important information about the U.S. Hispanic market, the agencies, the advertisers, the media and the people who move them.

HISPANIC NEWS, EL
Padilla & Associates
1200 SE Morrison St.
Portland, OR 97214
Clara Padilla-Andrews, Publisher
Tel: (503) 228-3139 **Fax:** (503) 228-3384
Email: hispnews@hispnews.com
Web: www.hispnews.com
Circ.: 20,000
Subscription: $35.00/year
Publication description: Local regional bilingual newspaper. A minority business enterprise dedicated to the service of the Hispanic and Spanish speaking communities of the Northwest. clara@hispnews.com.
Date established: 1981

HISPANO DE TULSA
Zapata Multimedia
P.O. Box 52054
Tulsa, OK 74152
Margarita Treviño, Editor
Tel: (918) 622-8258 **Fax:** (918) 384-0096
Email: hispano@mail.gorilla.net
Web: www.hispanodetulsa.com
Circ.: 7,000
Price: Free **Subscription:** $52.00/year
Publication description: Provides information for the Hispanic community and role models for young adults.
Date established: 1993

HISPANO, EL
Larenas Publishing Co, Inc.
1903 21st St.
Sacramento, CA 95814
Bill Larenas, Editor
Tel: (916) 442-0267 **Fax:** (916) 442-2818
Circ.: 20,000
Price: Free **Subscription:** $65.00/year
Publication description: Local/regional bilingual newspaper.
Date established: 1979

HISPANO, EL
López Publications, Inc.
8605 W. Chester Pike
Upper Darby, PA 19082
Aaron López, Publisher/Editor
Tel: (610) 789-5512 **Fax:** (610) 789-5524
Email: alopez5268@aol.com
Web: www.el-hispano.com
Circ.: 48,000
Price: $0.50
Publication description: Spanish newspaper.
Date established: 1976

HISPANO NEWS, EL

El Hispano News
900 Park Ave. SW
Albuquerque, NM 87103
Lizette Collado, Editor
Tel: (505) 243-6161 **Fax:** (505) 842-5464
Circ.: 10,000
Price: $0.25
Subscription: $12.00-14.00/year
Publication description: Spanish Newspaper.
Date established: 1966

HISPANO NEWS, EL

El Hispano News
2102 Empire Central
Dallas, TX 75235
Fernando Zapata, Editor
Tel: (214) 357-2186 **Fax:** (214) 357-2195
Email: editor@elhispanonews.com
Web: www.elhispanonews.com
Circ.: 35,000
Price: Free
Publication description: Local/regional Spanish newspaper.
Date established: 1986

HISPANO NEWS, EL

Graph-ads Printing
1451 Grandville SW
Grand Rapids, MI 49509
Jaime Malone, Editor
Tel: (616) 452-1511 **Fax:** (616) 452-1542
Email: hnewsgr@aol.com
Circ.: 15,000
Price: Free
Date established: 1991

HISPANOS UNIDOS NEWSPAPER

Hispanos Unidos Newspaper
P.O. Box 462016
Escondido, CA 92046-2016
Ana Hannegan, Publisher & President
Tel: (760) 740-9561 **Fax:** (760) 737-3035
Email: info@hispanosnews.com
Web: www.hispanosnews.com
Circ.: 26,000
Price: Free **Subscription:** $30.00/year
Publication description: Weekly Broad-Sheet Spanish Newspaper.
Date established: 1987

HOY

Chicago Tribune
435 N. Michigan Ave., 3rd Fl.
Chicago, IL 60611
Alejandro Escalona, Editor
Tel: (312) 527-8400 **Fax:** (312) 527-8471
Email: exito@tribune.com
Web: www.holahoy.com
Circ.: 100,000
Price: Free
Publication description: Spanish tabloid.
Date established: 1993

IMPACTO LATIN NEWS

20 W. 22nd St. #807
New York, NY 10010
Carlos Carrillo, Publisher
Tel: (212) 807-0400 **Fax:** (212) 807-0408
Email: impacto@usa.com
Web: www.impactolatinnews.com
Circ.: 57,000
Price: $0.50 **Subscription:** $30.00/year
Publication description: Hispanic owned newspaper.
Date established: 1992

IMPACTO USA

Los Angeles Newspaper Group
21221 Oxnard St.
Woodland Hills, CA 91367
Fernando Paramo, Publisher
Tel: (562) 499-1415 **Fax:** (562) 499-1484
Email: fernando.paramo@impactousa.com
Web: www.impactousa.com
Circ.: 250,000
Price: Free
Publication description: Impacto USA is the Los Angeles area's largest home delivered Spanish language newspaper.
Date established: 1992

IMPARCIAL NEWSPAPER, EL

TeleGuía, Inc.
3116 S. Austin Blvd.
Cicero, IL 60804
Rose Montes, Publisher
Tel: (708) 656-9800 **Fax:** (708) 656-6679
Email: impanews@aol.com
Web: www.elimparcial.us
Circ.: 20,000
Price: Free **Subscription:** $39.00/year.
Date established: 1987

INDEPENDIENTE, EL

Spanish Sports Productions
11636 Spry St.
Norwalk, CA 90650
Rafael Ramirez, Publisher
Tel: (562) 929-3802 **Fax:** (562) 929-3842
Email: info@exitodeportivo.com
Web: www.exitodeportivo.com
Circ.: 50,000
Price: Free
Publication description: Bilingual tabloid.
Date established: 1983

INFORMACIÓN NEWSPAPER, LA

Información Publishing Co., Inc.
P.O. Box 20726
Houston, TX 77081
Emilio Martínez Paula, Editor
Tel: (713) 272-0100 **Fax:** (713) 272-0011
Email: lina.martinez@lainformacion.us
Web: www.lainformacion.us
Circ.: 10,000
Price: Free **Subscription:** $25.00/year
Publication description: Local/regional Spanish newspaper.
Date established: 1979

INFORMADOR DE DALTON, EL

Thompson Newspapers Corporation
308 S. Thornton Ave.
Dalton, GA 30720
Juan Varela, Editor
Tel: (706) 272-7725 **Fax:** (706) 272-7713
Email: juanvarela@daltoncitizen.com
Web: www.daltoncitizen.com
Circ.: 10,500
Price: Free **Subscription:** $138.00/year
Publication description: Spanish tabloid.
Date established: 1995

INFORMADOR DEL VALLE, EL

44075 N. Jackson St. #G
Indio, CA 92201
Hector Felix, Publisher
Tel: (760) 342-7558 **Fax:** (760) 342-2918
Email: elinform@gte.net
Circ.: 14,000
Price: Free **Subscription:** $224.00/year
Publication description: Spanish newspaper.
Date established: 1987

INFORMADOR HISPANO, EL

Garcia Publications
3722 Decatur Ave.
Fort Worth, TX 76161
Hilda Manrique, Editor
Tel: (817) 626-8624 **Fax:** (817) 626-1855
Email: elinformador@elinformadorhispano.net
Web: www.elinformadorhispano.com
Circ.: 30,000
Price: Free

Publication description: Local/regional Spanish tabloid.
Date established: 1987

LATINO, EL

Latina & Associates, Inc.
1550 Broadway St. #U
Chula Vista, CA 91911
Diane Cervantes, Editor
Tel: (619) 426-1491 **Fax:** (619) 426-3206
Email: sales@ellatinoonline.com
Web: www.ellatinoonline.com
Circ.: 90,500
Price: Free **Subscription:** $60.00/year
Publication description: Newspaper.
Date established: 1988

LATINO INTERNATIONAL

672 N. Semoran Blvd. #304
Orlando, FL 32807
Rudolph Perez, Jr., Editor
Tel: (407) 381-9119 **Fax:** (407) 381-9925
Email: latinointl@aol.com
Web: www.latinointlnews.com
Circ.: 55,000
Date established: 1990

LATINO PRESS

Latino Press, Inc.
1494 Junction St.
Detroit, MI 48209
Elias M. Gutierrez, Publisher
Tel: (313) 841-9333 **Fax:** (313) 841-2950
Email: president@latinodetroit.com
Web: www.latinodetroit.com
Circ.: 17,500
Price: Free
Publication description: Newspaper. Audience: Hispano-latinos.
Date established: 1993

LATINO PRESS

Latino Press Media, Inc.
1494 Junction St.
Detroit, MI 48209
Elías M. Gutiérrez, Publisher
Tel: (313) 841-9333 **Fax:** (313) 841-2950
Email: president@latinodetroit.com
Web: www.latinodetroit.com
Circ.: 17,500
Price: Free
Publication description: Hispanic newspaper.
Date established: 1993

LATINO SEMANAL, EL

El Latino Semanal/ Palm Beach Latino
4325 Georgia Ave.
West Palm Beach, FL 33405
Jose R. Uzal, Editor
Tel: (561) 835-4913 **Fax:** (561) 655-5059
Email: uzal@msn.com
Web: www.ellatinosales.com
Circ.: 36,000
Price: Free **Subscription:** $35.95/year
Publication description: Spanish newspaper.
Date established: 1975

LAWNDALE NEWS

The Lawndale News
5416 W 25th St.
Cicero, IL 60804
Daniel Nardini, Editor
Tel: (708) 656-6400 **Fax:** (708) 656-2433
Email: info@lawndalenews.com
Web: www.lawndalenews.com
Circ.: 200,000
Price: Free **Subscription:** $50.00/year
Publication description: Bilingual tabloid; Sunday circulation: 50,000.
Date established: 1940

LIBRE

Libre, LLC
904 SW 23rd Ave.
Miami, FL 33135-4926
Demetrio Pérez, Jr., Publisher
Tel: (305) 643-4200 **Fax:** (305) 649-2767
Email: demetrioperezjr@libreonline.com
Web: www.libreonline.com
Circ.: 5,000
Price: Free **Subscription:** $19.99/52 issues
Publication description: To unite the South Florida community by providing fair and balanced information.
Date established: 1966

MANHATTAN TIMES

5000 Broadway #A
New York, NY 10034
Luis Maranda, Publisher
Tel: (212) 569-5800 **Fax:** (212) 544-9545
Email: manhattantimes@aol.com
Circ.: 10,000
Price: Free .
Date established: 2000

MENSAJE NEWSLETTER

Latin American News and Book, Corp.
P.O. Box 2109
Elizabeth, NJ 07207
Jose Tenreiro-Napoles, Editor
Tel: (908) 355-8835 **Fax:** (908) 527-9160
Email: mensaje@verizon.com
Circ.: 52,000
Price: Free **Subscription:** $80.00/year
Publication description: Local/regional Spanish newspaper; Distributed to New York, New Jersey. Main Office: 614 Franklin St., Elizabeth, NJ 07206.
Date established: 1980

MENSAJERO, EL

2500 W. 8th St. #103
Amarillo, TX 79106
Ramón Godoy, Editor
Tel: (806) 371-7084 **Fax:** (806) 371-7090
Email: elmensajero@aol.com
Web: www.elmensajero-ama.com
Circ.: 10,000
Price: $0.50 **Subscription:** $55.00/year
Publication description: Spanish Newspaper.
Date established: 1989

MENSAJERO, EL

Cardenas Publications, Inc.
2760 Mission St.
San Francisco, CA 94110
José del Castillo, Publisher
Tel: (415) 206-7230 **Fax:** (415) 206-7238
Email: editorial@elmensajero.com
Web: www.elmensajero.com
Circ.: 112,139
Price: Free **Subscription:** $70.00/year
Publication description: Bilingual newspaper with a Bay Area readership.
Date established: 1987

MÉXICO LINDO

P.O. Box 1747
Gainesville, GA 30503
Dave Anderson, Editor
Tel: (770) 983-6394 **Fax:** (770) 983-6399
Email: mexico2@earthlink.com
Web: www.mexicolindo.com
Circ.: 1,300
Subscription: $50.00/year
Publication description: Bilingual.
Date established: 1990

MIAMI TODAY NEWSPAPER

Today Enterprises Inc.
P.O. Box 1368
Miami, FL 33101

Michael Lewis, Editor
Tel: (305) 358-2663 **Fax:** (305) 358-4811
Email: whatisok@aol.com
Web: www.miamitodaynews.com
Circ.: 34,000
Price: $2.00 **Subscription:** $80.00/year
Publication description: Newsletter; Audience: executive market.
Date established: 1983

MINIONDAS NEWSPAPER
2025 S. Main St.
Santa Ana, CA 92707
Sergio Velasquez, Editor
Tel: (714) 668-1010 **Fax:** (714) 668-1013
Email: miniondas@aol.com
Web: www.Miniondas.com
Circ.: 45,000
Price: Free **Subscription:** $110.00/year
Date established: 1975

MINNESOTA-IOWA HISPANIC DIRECTORY
Latino Communications Network
2019 E. Lake St. #7
Minneapolis, MN 55407
Alberto Monserrate, President/CEO
Tel: (612) 729-5900 **Fax:** (612) 729-5999
Email: alberto@lcnmedia.com
Web: www.lcnmedia.com
Circ.: 30,000
Publication description: The directory is targeted at latino families. It contains information regarding education, health care, legal information, emergency numbers and the Hispanic organizations .
Date established: 1997

MONTEBELLO COMET
Eastern Group Publications, Inc.
2500 S. Atlantic Blvd., Bldg. A
Los Angeles, CA 90040
Jonathan Sanchez, Representative
Tel: (323) 263-5743 **Fax:** (323) 263-9169
Email: service@esp.com
Web: www.egpnews.com
Circ.: 16,000
Price: Free
Publication description: Bilingual tabloid.
Date established: 1979

MONTEREY PARK COMET
Eastern Group Publications, Inc.
2500 S. Atlantic Blvd., Bldg. A
Los Angeles, CA 90040
Jonathan Sanchez, Representative
Tel: (323) 263-5743 **Fax:** (323) 263-9169
Email: service@esp.com
Web: www.egpnews.com
Circ.: 8000
Price: Free
Publication description: Bilingual tabloid.
Date established: 1979

MUNDO HISPÁNICO
Mundo Hispánico, Inc.
1927 Piedmont Cr.
Atlanta, GA 30324
Freira Rodriquez, Sales Manager
Tel: (404) 881-0441 **Fax:** (404) 881-6085
Email: sales@mundohispanico.com
Web: www.mundohispanico.com
Circ.: 45,000
Price: Free **Subscription:** $100.00/year
Publication description: Spanish newspaper.
Date established: 1979

MUNDO L.A. NEWSPAPER
Latin Publications, Inc.
P.O. Box 9190
Van Nuys, CA 91406
Victor Fields, Editor
Tel: (818) 882-9200 **Fax:** (818) 882-7200
Email: pr@latin.com

Web: www.mundola.net
Circ.: 540,000
Price: Free .
Date established: 1979

MUNDO NEWSPAPER, EL
El Mundo
2116 E. César Chavez St.
Austin, TX 78702
Roberto Angulo, Publisher
Tel: (512) 476-8636 **Fax:** (512) 476-6402
Email: elmundotx@aol.com
Web: www.elmundonewspaper.com
Circ.: 35,000
Price: $0.25 **Subscription:** $45.00/year
Publication description: Spanish newspaper.
Date established: 1991

MUNDO NEWSPAPER, EL
El Mundo
760 N. Eastern Ave. #110
Las Vegas, NV 89101
Eddie Escobedo, Sr., Publisher
Tel: (702) 649-8553 **Fax:** (702) 649-7429
Email: elmundo@ureach.com
Web: www.elmundo.net
Circ.: 30,000
Price: Free
Publication description: Hispanic weekly newspaper.
Date established: 1980

NEWS EN ESPAÑOL, THE
1648 West Olive Ave.
Porterville, CA 93257
César Girón, Editor
Tel: (559) 783-1258 **Fax:** (559) 783-1866
Email: espanews@sosinet.net
Circ.: 18,000
Price: Free .
Date established: 1993

NORTE DE ATLANTA, EL-WEEKEND MAGAZINE
239 Ezzard St.
Lawrenceville, GA 30046
Filberto Prieto, General Manager
Tel: (770) 237-9897 **Fax:** (770) 237-8769
Email: ventas/sales@radiomex610atlanta.com
Web: www.radiomex610atlanta.com
Circ.: 10,000
Price: Free
Publication description: Newspaper/Magazine.
Date established: 1999

NORTHEAST SUN
Eastern Group Publications, Inc.
2500 S. Atlantic Blvd., Bldg. A
Los Angeles, CA 90040
Jonathan Sanchez, Representative
Tel: (323) 263-5743 **Fax:** (323) 263-9169
Email: service@esp.com
Web: www.egpnews.com
Circ.: 18,500
Price: Free
Publication description: Bilingual tabloid.
Date established: 1945

NOTICIA, LA
Eventos Premium
6101 Idlewild Rd. #328
Charlotte, NC 28212
Maribel Bastidas, Editor
Tel: (704) 568-6966 **Fax:** (704) 568-8936
Email: mbastidas@lanoticia.com
Web: www.lanoticia.com
Circ.: 26,000
Price: Free **Subscription:** $78.00/year
Publication description: Spanish language newspaper.
Date established: 1997

NOTICIA HISPANOAMERICANA
636 Seaman Ave.
Baldwin, NY 11510
William Diaz, Director & Publisher
Tel: (516) 223-5678 **Fax:** (516) 377-6551
Email: noticia@optonline.net
Web: www.noticiahispanoamericana.com
Circ.: 40,000
Price: Free **Subscription:** $25.00/year
Publication description: Local/regional Spanish tabloid.
Date established: 1991

NOTICIAS DE FORT BEND, LAS
Las Noticias de Fort Bend County, Inc.
924 3rd St. #4
Rosenberg, TX 77471
Joe R. Morales, Editor
Tel: (806) 220-2869 **Fax:** (281) 789-6185
Email: noticiasdefb@aol.com
Circ.: 10,000
Price: Free .
Date established: 1975

NOTICIERO COLOMBIANO HISPANO
P.O. Box 972
Elizabeth, NJ 07207
Adriana Maya García, Editor
Tel: (908) 351-9390 **Fax:** (908) 351-9370
Email: Editorial@www.noticierohispano.com
Web: www.www.noticierohispano.com
Circ.: 60,000
Price: Free **Subscription:** $79.00/year
Publication description: Weekly Spanish Newspaper.
Date established: 1983

NOTICIERO SEMANAL
Freedom Communications
115 E. Oak Ave.
Porterville, CA 93257
Miguel Vaez, Editor
Tel: (559) 784-5000 **Fax:** (559) 784-5245
Email: miguel_vaez@link.freedom.com
Circ.: 20,000
Price: Free .
Date established: 1999

NOVEDADES
Lancer Productions, Inc.
10153 Riverside Dr. #114
Toluca Lake, CA 91602
Armando Gaitan, Editor
Tel: (323) 881-6515 **Fax:** (323) 881-6524
Email: teleguiausa@aol.com
Circ.: 50,000
Price: Free .
Date established: 1992

NOVEDADES
Novedades News, Inc.
121 S. Zang Blvd. #101
Dallas, TX 75208
Sergio A. Puerto, Editor
Tel: (214) 943-2932 **Fax:** (214) 943-7352
Email: spuerto@novedades-news.com
Web: www.novedades-news.com
Circ.: 38,000
Subscription: $130.00/year
Publication description: Local/regional Spanish newsletter.
Date established: 1989

NUESTRO MUNDO-PEOPLE'S WEEKLY WORLD NEWSPAPER
Long View Publishing Co.
235 W. 23rd St.
New York, NY 10011
Tim Wheeler, Editor
Tel: (212) 924-2523 **Fax:** (212) 645-5436
Email: pww@pww.org
Web: www.cpusa.org, www.pww.org

Circ.: 25,000
Subscription: $30.00/year.
Date established: 1969

NUEVO COQUI, EL
258 Clifton Ave.
Newark, NJ 07104
Irving Linares, Editor
Tel: (973) 481-3233 **Fax:** (973) 481-6807
Email: glorin@online.com
Circ.: 15,000
Price: Free **Subscription:** $60.00/year
Publication description: Weekly Newspaper.
Date established: 1977

NUEVO MUNDO
San Jose Mercury News
750 Ridder Park Dr.
San Jose, CA 95190
Marina Hinestrosa, Editor
Tel: (408) 920-5843 **Fax:** (408) 271-3732
Email: contacto@nuevomundo.com
Web: www.nuevomundo.com
Circ.: 50,000
Price: Free
Publication description: Spanish tabloid.
Date established: 1996

NUEVO SIGLO NEWSPAPER
7137 N. Armenia Ave. #B
Tampa, FL 33604-5250
Neris Ramón Palacios, Editor
Tel: (813) 932-7181 **Fax:** (813) 932-8202
Email: n.siglo@verizon.net
Circ.: 20,000
Price: Free
Publication description: Local/regional Spanish tabloid newspaper.
Date established: 1990

NUEVO SIGLO NEWSPAPER
E & L Communications
2644 W. 47th St.
Chicago, IL 60632
Ezequiel Banda Sifuentes, Editor
Tel: (773) 890-1656 **Fax:** (773) 890-2467
Email: ns@nuevosiglonews.com
Web: www.nuevosiglonews.com
Circ.: 30,000
Subscription: $30.00/year.
Date established: 1996

OBSERVADOR, EL
El Observador Publications, Inc.
P.O. Box 1990
San Jose, CA 95109
Hilbert Morales, Publisher/President
Tel: (408) 938-1700 **Fax:** (408) 938-1705
Email: hmorales@el-observador.com
Web: www.el-observador.com
Circ.: 76,000
Price: Free **Subscription:** $36.00/year
Publication description: To provide Latino community with Festival, Timely Information on multiple issues and education, politics, real estate, and local issues.
Date established: 1980

OELA NEWSLINE
The National Clearinghouse for English Language Acquisition & Language Instruction Education Programs
2121 K St. NW #260
Washington, DC 20037
Nancy Zelasko, Director
Tel: (202) 467-0867 **Fax:** (202) 467-4283
Email: askncela@ncela.gwu.edu
Web: www.ncela.gwu.edu
Circ.: N/A
Price: Free
Publication description: OELA Newsline is NCELA's email news bulletins.
Date established: 1993

OFERTA REVIEW, LA
La Oferta
1376 N. 4th St.
San Jose, CA 95112
Mary J. Andrade, Co-Publisher & Editor
Tel: (408) 436-7850 **Fax:** (408) 436-7861
Email: mary@laoferta.com
Web: www.laoferta.com
Circ.: 66,000
Price: Free
Publication description: Seeks to be the leading bilingual newspaper in the South Bay by serving its target market with a quality product and providing advertisers with the highest value; offers award-winning editorial and reporting, and is committed to increasing its market readership and circulation growth.
Date established: 1978

OLA, LA
Wave Community Newspapers, Inc.
4201 Wilshire Blvd. #600
Los Angeles, CA 90010
Yurina Rico, Editor
Tel: (323) 556-5720 **Fax:** (323) 556-5704
Email: yrico@wavenewspapers.com
Web: www.wavenewspapers.com
Circ.: 150,000
Price: Free **Subscription:** $89.00/year
Publication description: Bilingual weekly multi-cultural community newspaper; covers the Westside market of LA.
Date established: 1932

OPINIÓN NEWSPAPER, LA
La Opinión Company, Inc.
402 College Ave.
Jacksonville, TX 75766
Judith B. Cantúa, Editor
Tel: (903) 586-0827 **Fax:** (903) 586-7016
Email: opinion@ballistic.com
Circ.: 10,000
Price: $0.25 **Subscription:** $96.00/year
Publication description: Local/regional Spanish newspaper.
Date established: 1989

ORIENTAL, EL
Periodico El Oriental, Inc.
36 Ave. Cruz Ortiz Stella
Humacao, PR 00791
Vicente Pierantoni Pérez, Founder
Tel: (787) 852-1496 **Fax:** (787) 852-3405
Email: eloriental@centennial.pr.net
Circ.: 50,000
Price: Free
Publication description: Local/regional Spanish newspaper.
Date established: 1978

ORLANDO SENTINEL
633 N. Orange Ave.
Orlando, FL 32802-2833
Mercy Rodriguez, Publisher
Tel: (407) 420-5050 **Fax:** (407) 420-6212
Email: merodriguez@orlandosentinel.com
Web: www.orlandosentinel.com
Circ.: 60,000
Price: Free **Subscription:** Free
Publication description: Spanish language newspaper serving Orlando.
Date established: 2000

PAGINAS HISPANAS
Zapata Multimedia
P.O. Box 52054
Tulsa, OK 74152
Margarita Treviño, Editor
Tel: (918) 622-8258 **Fax:** (918) 262-4431
Email: editor@hispanodetulsa.com
Web: www.hispanodetulsa.com
Circ.: 7,000

Price: Free **Subscription:** $52.00/year
Publication description: Provides information for the Hispanic community and role models for young adults.
Date established: 1993

PAMPAS NEWSLETTER
8370 Greensboro Dr. #1007
McLean, VA 22102
Ana Eliza, Editor
Email: capilladelmonte@aol.com
Circ.: 30,000
Price: Free .
Date established: 1990

PERIODICO LA CORDILLERA
P.O. Box 1834
Cidra, PR 00739
Maria del Rosario Pagan, President
Tel: (787) 739-3094 **Fax:** (787) 739-1854
Email: lacordi@coqui.net
Circ.: 50,000
Price: Free **Subscription:** $52.00/year
Publication description: Spanish Publication.
Date established: 1992

PERIÓDICO USA, EL
Newspapers and Directories, Inc.
1016 Ivy Ave.
McAllen, TX 78501
José Luis B. Garza, Editor
Tel: (956) 631-5628 **Fax:** (956) 631-0832
Email: usa1@sc2000.net
Circ.: 25,000
Price: Free **Subscription:** $36.00/year
Publication description: Local/regional Spanish newspaper.
Date established: 1986

PERIODICO VISIÓN
Periodico Visión
P.O. Box 719
Mayaguez, PR 00681
Olga Marty, Editor
Tel: (787) 834-6829 **Fax:** (787) 833-0722
Email: pvision@coqui.net
Circ.: 54,000
Price: Free **Subscription:** $109.20/year
Publication description: Community newspaper.
Date established: 1985

PERLA DEL SUR, LA
La Perla del Sur
P.O. Box 8212
Ponce, PR 00732-8212
Omar Alfonso, Editor
Tel: (787) 842-5866 **Fax:** (787) 842-5823
Email: laperrla@periodicolaperla.com
Web: www.periodicolaperla.com
Circ.: 76,000
Price: Free **Subscription:** $52.00/year
Publication description: Spanish tabloid.
Date established: 1982

POPULAR BAKERSFIELD, EL
El Popular Spanish Newspaper
212 Goodman St.
Bakersfield, CA 93305
Raul R. Camacho, Sr., Publisher
Tel: (661) 398-1000 **Fax:** (661) 325-1351
Email: pub@elpopularnews.com
Web: www.elpopularnews.com
Circ.: 24,000
Price: $0.25
Publication description: 100% minority-owned Spanish newspaper.
Date established: 1983

PREGONERO, EL
Carroll Publishing Company
145 Taylor St. NE
Washington, DC 20017

Oscar Reyes, Vice President
Tel: (202) 281-2440 **Fax:** (202) 281-2408
Email: oscar@elpreg.org
Web: www.elpreg.org
Circ.: 28,450
Price: Free **Subscription:** $15.00/year
Publication description: Local/regional Spanish newspaper.
Date established: 1977

PREGONES AL DÍA
Pregones Theater
571-575 Walton Ave.
Bronx, NY 10451
Priscilla Aguilar, Program Manager
Tel: (718) 585-1202 **Fax:** (718) 585-1608
Email: info@pregones.org
Web: www.pregones.org
Circ.: 10,000
Price: Free
Publication description: The bilingual Newsletter of Pregones Theater.
Date established: 2001

PRENSA DE MINNESOTA, LA
Hispanic Publishing Inc.
3000 N. 2nd St.
Mpls, MN 55411
Lorena E. Duarte, Editor
Tel: (612) 312-1760 **Fax:** (612) 312-1769
Email: news@laprensa-mn.com
Web: www.laprensa-mn.com
Circ.: 15,000
Price: Free **Subscription:** $75.00/year
Publication description: Local/regional Spanish broadsheet.
Date established: 1991

PRENSA DE SAN DIEGO, LA
La Prensa de San Diego
1950 5th Ave. #1
San Diego, CA 92101-2309
Daniel L. Muñoz, Editor
Tel: (619) 231-2873 **Fax:** (619) 231-9180
Email: laprensa@ix.netcom.com
Web: www.laprensa-sandiego.org
Circ.: 35,000
Price: Free **Subscription:** $45-65.00/year
Publication description: La Prensa de San Diego is the MexicanAmerican newspaper.
Date established: 1976

PRENSA DEL NOROESTE DE ARKANSAS, LA
EZ Spanish Media
2323-D S. Old Missouri Rd.
Springdale, AR 72764
Edward J. Vega, General Manager
Tel: (479) 756-8686 **Fax:** (479) 756-8687
Email: info@ezspanishmedia.com
Web: www.ezspanishmedia.com
Circ.: 10,000
Price: Free
Publication description: To educate and inform the hispanic community of new NW Arkansas and SE Missouri.
Date established: 1998

PRENSA GRÁFICA, LA
Prensa Gráfica News
P.O. Box 350-895
Miami, FL 33135
Dr. Raúl R. Oliva, Editor
Tel: (305) 649-6267 **Fax:** (305) 649-6300
Circ.: 28,000
Price: Free
Publication description: Local/regional Spanish tabloid.
Date established: 1988

PRENSA, LA
318 S. Flores St.
San Antonio, TX 78204
Tino Duran, Publisher

Tel: (210) 242-7900 **Fax:** (210) 242-7901
Email: tduran@laprensa.com
Web: www.laprensa.com
Circ.: 100,000
Price: Free **Subscription:** $85.00/year
Publication description: Bilingual Newspaper.
Date established: 1989

PRENSA, LA
La Prensa Publications, Inc.
P.O. Box 6504
Austin, TX 78762
Cathy Vasques-Revilla, Publisher
Tel: (512) 478-3090 **Fax:** (512) 478-3137
Email: laprensanews.com
Web: www.laprensatexas.com
Circ.: 20,000
Price: Free **Subscription:** $75.00/year
Publication description: Local/regional bilingual broadsheet.
Date established: 1986

PRENSA LATINA, LA
995 S. Yates St. #3
Memphis, TN 38117
Hector Mendoza, Editor
Tel: (901) 751-2100 **Fax:** (901) 751-1202
Email: laprensalatina@laprensalatina.com
Web: www.laprensalatina.com
Circ.: 43,000
Price: Free .
Date established: 1998

PRENSA NEWSPAPER, LA
La Prensa Inc.
685 S. County Rd. #427
Longwood, FL 32750-6403
Dora Casanova, Editor
Tel: (407) 767-0070 **Fax:** (407) 767-5478
Email: laprensa@laprensaorlando.com
Web: www.laprensaorlando.com
Circ.: 30,000
Price: Free **Subscription:** $80.00/year
Publication description: Local/regional Spanish newspaper.
Date established: 1981

PROVIDENCE VISITOR EN ESPAÑOL, THE
The Providence Visitor
184 Broad St.
Providence, RI 02903
Michael Brown, Editor
Tel: (401) 272-1010 **Fax:** (401) 421-8418
Email: mkbrown@intop.net
Web: www.providencevisitor.com
Circ.: 2,000
Price: Free **Subscription:** $25.00/year
Publication description: Newspaper.
Date established: 1992

QUÉ ONDA! MAGAZINE - DALLAS FT. WORTH
Hispanic News & Entertainment
1415 N. Loop West, #950
Houston, TX 77008
J. Gabriel Esparza, Publisher
Tel: (713) 880-1133 **Fax:** (713) 880-2322
Email: gabriel@queondamagazine.com
Web: www.queondamagazine.com
Circ.: 65,000
Price: Free **Subscription:** $60.00/year.
Date established: 1993

QUÉ ONDA! MAGAZINE - HOUSTON
Hispanic News & Entertainment
1415 N. Loop West, #950
Houston, TX 77008
J. Gabriel Esparza, Publisher
Tel: (713) 880-1133 **Fax:** (713) 880-2322
Email: gabriel@queondamagazine.com
Web: www.queondamagazine.com
Circ.: 65,000

Price: Free **Subscription:** $60.00/year.
Date established: 1993

QUÉ ONDA! MAGAZINE-SAN ANTONIO
Hispanic News & Entertainment
1415 N. Loop West, #950
Houston, TX 77008
J. Gabriel Esparza, Publisher
Tel: (713) 880-1133 **Fax:** (713) 880-2322
Email: gabriel@queondamagazine.com
Web: www.queondamagazine.com
Circ.: 65,000
Price: Free **Subscription:** $35.00/year.
Date established: 1993

QUÉ PASA NEWSPAPER-CHARLOTTE
Latino Communications, Inc.
4425 Randolph Rd. #100
Charlotte, NC 28211
Luis Matta, Editor
Tel: (704) 319-5044 **Fax:** (704) 319-5040
Email: lmatta@quepasamedia.com
Web: www.quepasamedia.com
Circ.: 25,000
Price: Free .
Date established: 2000

QUÉ PASA NEWSPAPER-GREENBORO
Latino Communications, Inc.
3808 High Pont Rd. #C
Greensboro, NC 27407
Tel: (336) 854-5777 **Fax:** (336) 854-1692
Email: fcamara@quepasamedia.com
Web: www.quepasamedia.com
Circ.: 25,000
Price: Free .
Date established: 2000

QUÉ PASA NEWSPAPER-RALEIGH
Latino Communications, Inc.
150 Fayetteville St. Mall #110
Raleigh, NC 27601
Henando Pineros, Editor
Tel: (919) 645-1680 **Fax:** (919) 645-1699
Email: hpineros@quepasamedia.com
Web: www.quepasamedia.com
Circ.: 25,000
Price: Free .
Date established: 2000

QUÉ PASA NEWSPAPER-WINSTON-SALEM
Latino Communications, Inc.
3025 Waughtown St. #G
Winston-Salem, NC 27107
Francisco Camara, Executive Editor
Tel: (336) 784-9004 **Fax:** (336) 784-8337
Email: fcamara@quepasamedia.com
Web: www.quepasamedia.com
Circ.: 25,000
Price: Free **Subscription:** $150.00/year.
Date established: 1994

RAZA NEWSPAPER, LA
Rossi Publications, Inc.
6001 N. Clark St.
Chicago, IL 60660
Robert J. Armband, CEO
Tel: (773) 273-2900 **Fax:** (773) 273-2926
Email: info@laraza.com
Web: www.laraza.com
Circ.: 190,000
Price: $0.50
Publication description: Hispanic
newspaper.
Date established: 1970

REPORTERO, EL/THE REPORTER
2601 Mission St., 9th Fl.
San Francisco, CA 94110
Marvin J. Ramírez, Publisher
Tel: (415) 648-3711 **Fax:** (415) 648-3721
Email: lreportero@aol.com
Web: www.elreporterosf.com

Circ.: 20,000
Price: Free
Publication description: Local/regional
bilingual newspaper; Audience: Hispanic
Market.
Date established: 1991

**REPUBLICAN NATIONAL HISPANIC
ASSEMBLY WEEKLY NEWSLETTER**
Republican National Hispanic Assembly of
the US (RNHA)
P.O. Box 1882
Washington, DC 20013-1882
Marta R. Metelko, Executive Director
Tel: (202) 544-6700 **Fax:** (202) 544-6869
Email: info@rnha.org
Web: www.rnha.org
Circ.: 5,000
Price: Free
Publication description: Republican National
Hispanic Assembly Newsletter is a official
newsletter of Republican National Hispanic
Assembly of the US (RNHA).
Date established: 1974

RESUMEN NEWSPAPER
69-08 Roosevelt Ave.
Woodside, NY 11377-2934
Fernando F. Rojas, Chief Editor
Tel: (718) 899-8603 **Fax:** (718) 899-7616
Email: rojas123@aol.com
Circ.: 32,000
Price: $.50 **Subscription:** $14.50/year
Publication description: To serve and inform
the Hispanic community around N.Y. city and
Northern N.J.
Date established: 1971

RUMORES
517 N. Bristal St.
Santa Ana, CA 92703
Abel S. Torres, Editor
Tel: (714) 547-8283 **Fax:** (714) 547-3674
Email: editorial@rumoresnews.com
Web: www.rumoresnews.com
Circ.: 30,000
Price: Free
Publication description: Local/regional
Spanish newspaper.
Date established: 1985

SALVADOR DÍA A DÍA, EL
2797 W Pico Blvd. #1
Los Angeles, CA 90006
Eber Huezo, Editor
Tel: (323) 737-7910 **Fax:** (323) 737-1917
Email: elsalvadordiadia@aol.com
Web: www.diaadia.us
Circ.: 35,000
Price: Free .
Date established: 1989

SANTA ROSA NEWS
Santa Rosa News
P.O. Box 505
Santa Rosa, NM 88435-0505
Sherry Flanagan, Publisher
Tel: (505) 472-5454 **Fax:** (505) 472-5453
Email: sflanagan@plateautel.net
Circ.: 2,000
Price: $0.50 **Subscription:** $25.00/year
Publication description: Local/regional
English newspaper; 90% of the readers are
Hispanics.
Date established: 1924

SEMANA, LA
903 Albany St.
Boston, MA 02119
Pedro Nicolas Cuenca, Editor
Tel: (617) 427-6212 **Fax:** (617) 427-6227
Email: wcea2000@aol.com
Web: www.lasemanacuencavision.com

Circ.: 15,000
Price: Free **Subscription:** $100.00/year
Publication description: Local/regional
Spanish tabloid.
Date established: 1978

SEMANA NEWSPAPER
Spanish Publications, Inc.
6601 Tarnef St. #200
Houston, TX 77074
Raul Duenis, Publications Manager
Tel: (713) 774-4652 **Fax:** (713) 774-4666
Email: editorial@semananews.com
Web: www.semananews.com
Circ.: 125,000
Price: Free
Publication description: Dedicated to providing
the Hispanic community with timely, accurate,
objective, and complete information pertinent
to the community. .
Date established: 1993

SOL DE TEXAS, EL
1927 E. Beltline Rd. #164
Carollton, TX 75006
Rogelio Santillán, Publisher/General
Director
Tel: (972) 416-3800 **Fax:** (972) 416-7026
Email: sales@elsoldetexas.com
Web: www.elsoldetexas.com
Circ.: 28,000
Price: Free **Subscription:** $55.00/year
Publication description: Spanish newspaper.
Date established: 1966

SOL, EL
1325 H St.
Modesto, CA 95352
Olivia Ruiz, Editor
Tel: (209) 238-4634 **Fax:** (209) 238-4641
Email: elsolnews@yahoo.com
Circ.: 30,000
Price: Free
Publication description: Spanish tabloid.
Date established: 1993

SOL LATINO NEWSPAPER, EL
Grupo Bogotá Inc.
198 W. Chew Ave.
Philadelphia, PA 19120
Ricardo Hurtado, President
Tel: (215) 424-1200 **Fax:** (215) 424-6064
Email: rhurtado@elsoln1.com
Web: www.elsoln1.com
Circ.: 45,000
Price: Free **Subscription:** $52.00/year
Publication description: El Sol Latino is a
weekly publication targeted to the Hispanic
market in Philadelphia and the Delaware
Valley. .
Date established: 1991

SOLO AUTOS
Spanish Publications, Inc.
6601 Tarnef St. #200
Houston, TX 77074
Ralv Aro, Production Manager
Tel: (713) 774-4652 **Fax:** (713) 774-4666
Email: ads@soloautos.com
Circ.: 41,000
Price: Free
Publication description: Dedicated to providing
the Hispanic community with timely, accurate,
objective, and complete information pertinent
to the community. .
Date established: 1993

SPANISH TIMES
425 W. National Ave.
Milwaukee, WI 53204
Tony Kalil, Publisher
Tel: (414) 672-0929 **Fax:** (414) 672-9900
Circ.: 20,000

Price: Free
Publication description: The Spanish Times
is the voice of Latin America, maintaining the
concept of free expression and a respect for
diverse opinions.
Date established: 1979

TAOS NEWS, THE
The Taos News
P.O. Box U
Taos, NM 87571
Eric Hedlund, Editor
Tel: (505) 758-2241 **Fax:** (505) 758-9647
Email: circ@taosnews.com
Web: www.taosnews.com
Circ.: 10,730
Price: $0.75 **Subscription:** $30.00/year
Publication description: Spanish section in
The Taos News.
Date established: 1950

TIEMPO LATINO, EL
Farragut Media Group
1916 Wilson Blvd. #204
Arlington, VA 22201
Alberto Auendawo, Associate Publisher
Tel: (703) 527-7860 **Fax:** (703) 527-0369
Email: zulema@eltiempolatino.com
Web: www.eltiempolatino.com
Circ.: 36,000
Price: Free
Publication description: A weekly Spanish
Language newspaper serving the needs of
the Hispanic Community of the Washington
DC metro area .
Date established: 1991

TIEMPO LIBRE, EL
Las Vegas Review-Journal
P.O. Box 70
Las Vegas, NV 89125
Ruben Hofliger, Editor
Tel: (702) 387-2976 **Fax:** (702) 251-0736
Email: rhofliger@eltiempolibre.com
Web: www.eltiempolibre.com
Circ.: 32,000
Price: Free
Publication description: Spanish tabloid.
Date established: 1995

TIEMPO NEWSPAPER
Record Journal
11 Crown St.
Meriden, CT 06450
Daniel Román, Editor
Tel: (203) 317-2335 **Fax:** (203) 235-4048
Email: tiempo@record-journal.com
Web: www.tiempo.com
Circ.: 18,000
Price: Free **Subscription:** $20.00/year
Publication description: Local/regional
Spanish newspaper.
Date established: 1992

TIEMPOS DEL MUNDO
Tiempos del Mundo
38-42 9th St.
Long Island City, NY 11101
Jose Cardinali, Editor
Tel: (718) 786-4343 **Fax:** (718) 609-2676
Email: TDMNY@aol.com
Web: www.tdm.com
Circ.: 50,000
Subscription: $39.00/year
Publication description: Newspaper covering
the Western Hemisphere with the latest news
in Latin America.
Date established: 1996

TIEMPOS DEL MUNDO
Tiempos, USA Corp.
3600 New York Ave. NE
Washington, DC 20002

Jose Emilio Castellanos, Editor
Tel: (202) 636-8849 **Fax:** (202) 269-3206
Email: tdmeditor@huskynet.com
Web: www.tdm.com
Circ.: 10,000
Price: $0.75 **Subscription:** 39.00/year
Publication description: Newspaper covering the Western Hemisphere with the latest news in Latin America.
Date established: 1999 in Washington, DC

TIEMPOS USA, LOS
6521 Arlington Blvd. #214
Falls Church, VA 22042
Gonzalo Canales E., President /Publisher
Tel: (703) 536-9001 **Fax:** (703) 536-9848
Email: lostiemposusa@aol.com
Circ.: 20,000
Price: Free **Subscription:** $80.00/year
Publication description: Weekly Newspaper.
Date established: 2002

TRIBUNA HISPANA USA, LA
48 Main St.
Hempstead, NY 11550
Luis Aguilar, Editor
Tel: (516) 486-6457 **Fax:** (516) 292-3972
Email: editorial@latribunahispana.com
Web: www.latribunahispana.com
Circ.: 256,675
Price: Free
Publication description: La Tribuan Hispana newspaper has several offices throughout the Eastern part of the U.S. It has offices in NY, NJ and FL.
Date established: 1988

VENEZOLANO, EL
Editorial Tricolor
2300 NW 94th Ave. #206
Miami, FL 33172
Oswaldo Muñoz, Editor
Tel: (305) 717-3206 **Fax:** (305) 717-3250
Email: editor@el-venezolano.com
Web: www.el-venezolano.net
Circ.: 20,000
Price: Free
Publication description: National Spanish newspaper.
Date established: 1992

VIDA ACTUAL
Casiano Communications
1700 Ave. Fernández Juncos
San Juan, PR 00909-2938
Elsa Fernandez Miralles, Editor
Tel: (787) 728-3000 X3514
Fax: (787) 268-0135
Email: editora@casiano.com
Web: www.casiano.com
Circ.: 94,000
Subscription: $12.00/year
Publication description: Vida Actual is a Spanish-language newspaper filled with highly useful tips and general-interest information that will make life easier for its readers.
Date established: 2000

VIDA EN EL VALLE
The Fresno Bee
1626 E. St.
Fresno, CA 93786
John Esparza Loera, Editor
Tel: (559) 441-6780 **Fax:** (559) 441-6790
Email: jesparza@vidaenelvalle.com
Web: www.vidaenelvalle.com
Circ.: 59,919
Price: Free **Subscription:** $56.00/year
Publication description: Local/regional Spanish broadsheet.
Date established: 1990

VIDA NEWSPAPER
130 Palm Dr.
Oxnard, CA 93030
Carlos Olea, Editor
Tel: (805) 483-1008 **Fax:** (805) 483-6233
Email: escorp@aol.com
Circ.: 35,000
Price: Free
Publication description: Local/regional Spanish newspaper.
Date established: 1983

VIDA NUEVA
Hispanic Catholic Archdiocese of Los Angeles
3424 Wilshire Blvd.
Los Angeles, CA 90010
Mike Nelson, Editor
Tel: (213) 637-7360 **Fax:** (213) 637-6360
Email: mnelson@the-tidings.com
Web: www.the-tidings.com
Circ.: 65,000
Price: Free **Subscription:** $20.00/year
Publication description: Southern California Catholic weekly.
Date established: 1991

VIERNES
El Nuevo Herald
1 Herald Plz.
Miami, FL 33132
Andres Reynaldo, Editor
Tel: (305) 376-3535 **Fax:** (305) 376-2139
Email: areynaldo@herald.com
Web: www.miami.com
Circ.: 82,000
Price: $1.20 **Subscription:** $442.00/year.
Date established: 1989

VISIÓN LATINA, LA
A.B.M. Enterprises, Inc.
2312 M St.
Omaha, NE 68107
Marcos Mora, Editor
Tel: (402) 734-0279 **Fax:** (402) 934-0709
Email: elchuy007@aol.com
Web: www.latinocentral.com
Circ.: 25,000
Price: Free
Publication description: Heartland's only bilingual magazine designed to educate both the English and Spanish speaking communities; integrating the positive aspects of each culture into articles about education, history, entertainment, arts, people, health and community. .
Date established: 1999

VISITANTE, EL
El Vistante de Puerto Rico
Pumarada 1704
Santurce, PR 00940-1305
Carmen A. Flores, Advertising Coordinator
Tel: (787) 728-3710 **Fax:** (787) 268-1748
Email: anuncio@elvisitante.biz
Web: www.elvisitante.biz
Circ.: 65,000
Price: $0.25 **Subscription:** $25.00/year
Publication description: El Visitante is a weekly catholic newspaper.
Date established: 1974

VISTAZO NEWSPAPER, EL
1376 N. 4th St.
San Jose, CA 95112
Mary J. Andrade, Editor
Tel: (408) 436-7850 **Fax:** (408) 436-7861
Email: mary@el-vistazo.com
Web: www.elvistazo.com
Circ.: 36,490
Price: Free

Publication description: Bilingual newspaper serving the San Benito and Monterey Counties.
Date established: 1994

VIVA SPANISH NEWSPAPER
P.O. Box 511
Toppenish, WA 98948
Jim Flint, Publisher
Tel: (509) 865-4055 **Fax:** (509) 865-2655
Email: flintpub@yahoo.com
Circ.: 15,000
Price: Free .
Date established: 1984

VOCERO HISPANO, EL
1438 Eastern SE
Grand Rapids, MI 49509
Andrés Abreu, Owner
Tel: (616) 246-6023 **Fax:** (616) 246-1228
Email: elvocero@aol.com
Web: www.elvoceromi.com
Circ.: 25,000
Subscription: $32.00/year
Publication description: El Vocero Hispano committed to helping raise public awareness in the hispanic community.
Date established: 1993

VOCERO HISPANO NEWSPAPER
Vocero Hispano Newspaper, Inc.
390 Main St. #947
Worcester, MA 01608
Sergio Rivera, Jr., Editor
Tel: (508) 792-1942 **Fax:** (508) 792-1608
Email: voceronews@aol.com
Web: www.vocerohispano.com
Circ.: 26,000
Price: Free **Subscription:** $32.00/year
Publication description: Audience: Hispanic.
Date established: 1990

VOZ DE COLORADO, LA
Santa Fe Publishing Co., Inc.
4785 Tejon St. #202
Denver, CO 80211
Wanda M. Padilla, Publisher
Tel: (303) 936-8556 **Fax:** (720) 889-2455
Email: news@lavozcolardo.com
Circ.: 33,000
Price: $0.25 **Subscription:** $30.00/year
Publication description: Local/regional bilingual newspaper serving Colorado's Hispanic community.
Date established: 1973

VOZ DE HOUSTON, LA
La Voz de Houston
6101 SW Fwy. #127
Houston, TX 77057
Olga Ordóñez, Publisher
Tel: (713) 664-4404 **Fax:** (713) 664-4414
Email: editorial@lavozdehouston.com
Web: www.lavozdehouston.com
Circ.: 100,000
Price: Free
Publication description: Local/regional Spanish newspaper.
Date established: 1979

VOZ DE LA CALLE, LA
The Voice Publishing Co., Inc.
P.O. Box 3187
Hialeah, FL 33013
Vicente P. Rodríguez, Editor
Tel: (305) 687-5555 **Fax:** (305) 681-0500
Circ.: 25,000
Price: Free **Subscription:** $25.00/year.
Date established: 1980

VOZ DE MEXICO, LA
4159 74th St. #2b
Elmhurst, NY 11373

Veronica Rosendo, Publisher
Tel: (718) 505-1121 **Fax:** (718) 505-1127
Email: vozmexico@aol.com
Circ.: 10,000
Price: $0.50
Publication description: Presents a new alternative for Mexicans and Hispanics in New York, the five boroughs, plus certain areas of Westchester, Connecticut, Long Island, New Jersey, Pennsylvania, Chicago, IL. Los Angeles, CA and Puebla, Mexico.
Date established: 1992

VOZ HISPANA, LA
Casa Publications
159 E. 116th St.
New York, NY 10029
Joaquin del Rio, Editor
Tel: (212) 348-8270 **Fax:** (212) 348-4469
Email: Discomund@aol.com
Circ.: 68,000
Price: $0.50
Publication description: Spanish tabloid.
Date established: 1977

VOZ, LA
1460 E. Holt Blvd. #120
Pomona, CA 91767
Dr. Jerry Livesey, Executive Director/ Publisher
Tel: (909) 629-2292 **Fax:** (909) 629-7644
Email: lavoz1981@earthlink.net
Web: www.lavoz.net
Circ.: 15,000
Price: $1.10 **Subscription:** $39.00/year.
Date established: 1981

VOZ, LA
Ashland Media Group
800 N 1st Ave.
Phoenix, AZ 85003
Luis Manuel Ortiz, Editor
Tel: (602) 252-5331/(602) 443-4300
Fax: (602) 253-9022
Email: luismanuel@ashlandmedia.com
Web: www.lavozinternet.com
Circ.: 50,000
Subscription: $52.00/year.
Date established: 2000

WASHINGTON HISPANIC
2701 Ontario Rd. NW, 2nd Fl.
Washington, DC 20009
Alex Ormaza, Editor
Tel: (202) 667-8881 **Fax:** (202) 667-8902
Email: info@washingtonhispanic.com
Web: www.washingtonhispanic.com
Circ.: 35,000
Price: Free **Subscription:** $70.00/year
Publication description: Local/regional Spanish/English newspaper.
Date established: 1994

WEEKLY ISSUE/EL SEMANARIO, THE
5075 Leetsdale Dr. #F
Denver, CO 80246
Chris M. Fresquez, Publisher/Editor
Tel: (303) 672-0800 **Fax:** (303) 298-8654
Email: semanario@aol.com
Circ.: 18,500
Price: Free
Publication description: English/Spanish tabloid.
Date established: 1989

WEST TEXAS HISPANIC NEWS
P.O. Box 24
Lubbock, TX 79408
Ernest Barton, Publisher
Tel: (806) 747-3467 **Fax:** (806) 747-3524
Email: ebarton@westtexashispanicnews.com
Circ.: 4,000

Price: Free
Publication description: Local/regional bilingual broadsheet.
Date established: 1979

WYVERNWOOD CHRONICLE

Eastern Group Publications, Inc.
2500 S. Atlantic Blvd., Bldg. A
Commerce, CA 90040
Jonathan Sanchez, Representative
Tel: (323) 263-5743 **Fax:** (323) 263-9169
Email: service@esp.com
Web: www.egpnews.com
Circ.: 2,000
Price: Free
Publication description: Tabloid, Bilingual.
Date established: 1979

WEEKLY-FRIDAY

MUNDO HISPANO NEWSPAPER

Falcon Enterprise
9131 S. Monroe St. #C
Sandy, UT 84070
Sandra González, Marketing Director
Tel: (801) 569-3338 **Fax:** (801) 352-9638
Email: sandra@munhispano.com
Web: www.munhispano.com
Circ.: 10,000
Price: Free **Subscription:** $50.00/year
Publication description: To keep the Hispanic community informed on international & local issues. Also, to serve as an effective tool to businesses to penetrate the Hispanic market.
Date established: 1993

WEEKLY-THURSDAY

AHORA NOW

Ahora Now
601 E San Ysidro Blvd. #180
San Ysidro, CA 92173
Bertha Alicia González, Editor
Tel: (619) 428-2277 **Fax:** (619) 428-0871
Email: ahoranow@ix.netcom.com
Web: www.ahoranow.com
Circ.: 20,000
Price: Free
Publication description: Bilingual tabloid

COMPRADOR MEXICANO, EL

Aegle Enterprises
501 S Escondido Blvd.
Escondido, CA 92025
Lili Negrete, Asst. Manager
Tel: (760) 743-4450 **Fax:** (760) 743-3398
Email: spanishshoppers@aol.com
Circ.: 5,000
Price: Free
Publication description: Local/regional bilingual Spanish newspaper in San Diego, CA.
Date established: 1985

EASTSIDE SUN

Eastern Group Publications, Inc.
2500 S. Atlantic Blvd., Bldg. A
Commerce, CA 90040
Jonathan Sanchez, Representative
Tel: (323) 263-5743 **Fax:** (323) 263-9169
Email: service@esp.com
Web: www.egpnews.com
Circ.: 24,000
Price: Free
Publication description: Bilingual tabloid.
Date established: 1979

EXTRA NEWS

Tell-Cliff Corp.
3908 W. North Ave.
Chicago, IL 60647
Casey Sanchez, Editor
Tel: (773) 252-3534/(773) 252-6031
Fax: (773) 252-4073
Email: noticias@extranews.net
Web: www.extranews.net
Circ.: 71,205
Price: Free **Subscription:** $45.00/year
Publication description: Bilingual tabloid.
Date established: 1981

EXTRA SPANISH NEWSPAPER, EL

El Extra Newspaper
P.O. Box 27043
Dallas, TX 75227
Emmy Silva, Publisher/ Editor
Tel: (214) 309-0990 **Fax:** (214) 309-0204
Web: www.elextranewspaper.com
Circ.: 28,000
Price: Free **Subscription:** $1.52 /issue
Publication description: Provides an informative and entertaining Spanish newspaper of the highest quality on a weekly basis for the Hispanic community of Dallas/Fort Worth, Texas, thereby creating an excellent medium for the national and local advertisers in reaching the ever important and continually increasing Hispanic market of this area.
Date established: 1987

MEXICALO, EL

El Mexicalo
931 Niles St.
Bakersfield, CA 93305
Tony Monzano, Editor
Tel: (661) 323-9334 **Fax:** (661) 323-6951
Email: elmexicalo@sbcglobal.net
Circ.: 15,000
Price: $0.25 **Subscription:** $35.00
Publication description: Assist in transmitting, informing and educating the Hispanic community by the goods and services provided by the public and private sectors by developing better consumers, citizens and readership to the greatest extent possible.
Date established: 1980

MEXICAN AMERICAN SUN

Eastern Group Publications, Inc.
2500 S. Atlantic Blvd., Bldg. A
Los Angeles, CA 90040
Jonathan Sanchez, Representative
Tel: (323) 263-5743 **Fax:** (323) 263-9169
Email: service@esp.com
Web: www.egpnews.com
Circ.: 16,000
Price: Free
Publication description: Bilingual tabloid.
Date established: 1979

MUNDO, EL

Caribe Communications
408 S. Huntington Ave.
Boston, MA 02130-4814
Maximo Torres, Editor/Publisher
Tel: (617) 522-5060 **Fax:** (617) 524-5886
Email: elmundonews@aol.com
Circ.: 30,000
Price: $0.25 **Subscription:** $65.00/year
Publication description: Local/regional Spanish newspaper.
Date established: 1972

MUNDO, EL

El Mundo
P.O. Box 2231
Wenatchee, WA 98807
Jim Tiffany, Managing Editor
Tel: (509) 663-5737 **Fax:** (509) 663-6957
Email: elmundo1@nwi.net
Web: www.elmundocom.net
Circ.: 22,000
Price: Free
Publication description: Publish a high quality Spanish language newspaper that will serve as a vehicle for communicating with the Hispanic community of the State of Washington.
Date established: 1989

NUEVO HUDSON, EL

30 Journal Sq.
Jersey City, NJ 07306
Armando Bermúdez, Editor
Tel: (201) 217-2425 **Fax:** (201) 963-5854
Email: armando.bermudez@elnuevohudson.com
Web: www.elnuevohudson.com
Circ.: 70,000
Price: Free **Subscription:** $120.00/year
Publication description: Spanish tabloid.
Date established: 1995

NUEVO PATRIA, EL

El Nuevo Patria Publishing Co.
P. O. Box 2, Jose Martí Station
Miami, FL 33135-0002
Eladio José Armesto, Publisher
Tel: (305) 530-8787 **Fax:** (305) 577-8989
Email: patrianews@aol.com
Circ.: 30,000
Price: $0.50 **Subscription:** $24.00/year
Publication description: The oldest Hispanic community news, art, and entertainment newspaper in South Florida.
Date established: 1959

OPINION, LA

700 S. Flower St.
Los Angeles, CA 90017
Antonio Mejias, Editor
Tel: (213) 896-2333 **Fax:** (213) 896-2077
Email: marketing@laopinion.com
Web: www.laopinion.com/lavibra
Circ.: 135,000
Price: $0.25 **Subscription:** $140.00/year
Publication description: Spanish newspaper.
Date established: 1926

SPANISH JOURNAL

Spanish Journal
152 W Wisconsin Ave. #613
Milwaukee, WI 53203
Robert Miranda, Editor
Tel: (414) 271-5683 **Fax:** (414) 271-5994
Email: spanishj@spanishjournal.com
Web: www.spanishjournal.com
Circ.: 20,000
Price: Free
Publication description: Local/regional bilingual tabloid.
Date established: 1979

TELE GUÍA DE CHICAGO

TeleGuía, Inc.
3116 S. Austin Blvd.
Cicero, IL 60804
Rose Montes, Editor
Tel: (708) 656-6666 **Fax:** (708) 222-6822
Email: TeleGuia@aol.com
Web: www.teleguia.us
Circ.: 24,000
Price: $0.30 **Subscription:** $15.00/year
Publication description: A colorful Magazine for the TV and Radio media and entertainment.
Date established: 1985

TODO, EL

P.O. Box 10846
Bayamón, PR 00960
Benjamin Rodriguez, Editor
Tel: (787) 787-6011 **Fax:** (787) 740-0022
Email: redaccion@eltodo.net
Web: www.eltodo.net
Circ.: 75,000
Price: Free
Publication description: Newspaper.
Date established: 1972

VOZ, LA

Palacios-Rios Communications
102 W Cuyler St.
Dalton, GA 30720
Ricardo Rios, President
Tel: (706) 272-0436 **Fax:** (706) 272-0442
Email: lavoz@dalton.net
Web: www.lavoz.net
Circ.: 16,000
Price: Free
Publication description: Spanish tabloid.
Date established: 1999

WEEKLY-WEDNESDAY

FLYER, THE

The Flyer Publishing Co.
11900 SW 128th St.
Miami, FL 33186
Carlos Guzmán, President
Tel: (305) 232-4115 **Fax:** (305) 251-5261
Email: cguzman@theflyer.com
Web: www.theflyer.com
Circ.: 1,000,000
Price: Free
Publication description: Local/regional English newspaper.
Date established: 1981

LATINO NEWSPAPER, EL

El Latino
3284 23rd St.
San Francisco, CA 94110
Ricardo Ron, Editor
Tel: (415) 648-1670 **Fax:** (415) 648-3385
Email: sales@sflatino.com
Web: www.sflatino.com
Circ.: 40,000
Price: Free
Publication description: Spanish language newspaper that provides information in three areas: health, education, and immigration that affects Latinos in the USA.
Date established: 1992

PRENSA HISPANA

Prensa HIspana
809 E. Washington #209
Phoenix, AZ 85034
Manny Garcia, President/Director General
Tel: (602) 256-2443 **Fax:** (602) 256-2644
Email: prensahispana@qwest.net
Web: www.prensahispanaaz.com
Circ.: 65,000
Price: Free **Subscription:** $45.00/year
Publication description: Spanish weekly newspaper.
Date established: 1991

SIETE DIAS LATINO NEWSPAPER

12005 NE 12th St. #26
Bellevue, WA 98005
Raúl Pérez-Calleja, Publisher
Tel: (425) 646-8846 **Fax:** (425) 646-8823
Email: raulperez@elsietedias.com
Web: www.elsietedias.com
Circ.: 7,000
Price: Free
Publication description: Informative and educational news journal.
Date established: 1992

Hispanic Radio Stations
Estaciones de radio hispanas

KSKA-FM (91.1 MHZ)
Alaska Public Telecommunications, Inc.
3877 University Dr.
Anchorage, AK 99508
Bede Trantina, Station Manager
Tel: (907) 561-1161 Fax: (907) 273-9192
Web: www.kska.org

KASA-AM (1540 KHZ)
KASA Network
1445 W. Baseline Rd.
Phoenix, AZ 85041
Moisés Herrera, General Manager
Tel: (602) 276-4241 Fax: (602) 276-8119
Email: radiokasa@hotmail.com
Web: www.radiokasa.org

KCEC-FM (104.5 MHZ)
La Campesina Network
670 E. 32 St. #12A
Yuma, AZ 85364
Rosella Lopez, General Manager
Tel: (928) 782-5995 Fax: (928) 782-3879
Email: kcec1045fm@campesina.com
Web: www.campesina.com

KCKY-AM (1150 KHZ)
KASA Network
1445 W. Baseline Rd.
Phoenix, AZ 85041
Moisés Herrera, General Manager
Tel: (602) 276-4241 Fax: (602) 276-8119
Email: radiokasa@hotmail.com
Web: www.radiokasa.org

KDVA-FM (106.9 MHZ)
Entravision Communications Corporation
1641 E. Osborn Rd. #8
Phoenix, AZ 85016
Tom Duran, General Manager
Tel: (602) 266-2005 Fax: (602) 279-2921
Web: www.entravision.com

KEVT-AM (1030 KHZ)
2919 E. Broadway #230
Tucson, AZ 85016
Mario Calis, General Manager
Tel: (520) 889-8904 Fax: (520) 889-8573
Email: mcalis@kevtradio.com
Web: www.kevtradio.com

KHOT-FM (105.9 MHZ)
Univision Communications, Inc.
4745 N. 7th St. #140
Phoenix, AZ 85014
Steve Virissimo, General Manager
Tel: (602) 308-7900 Fax: (602) 308-7979
Web: www.univision.com

KHOV-FM (105.3 MHZ)
Univision Communications, Inc.
4745 N. 7th St. #140
Phoenix, AZ 85014
Steve Virissimo, General Manager
Tel: (602) 308-7900 Fax: (602) 308-7979
Web: www.univision.com

KLNZ-FM (103.5 MHZ)
Entravision Communications Corporation
1641 E. Osborn Rd. #8
Phoenix, AZ 85016
Tom Duran, General Manager
Tel: (602) 266-2005 Fax: (602) 279-2921
Web: www.entravision.com

KMIA-AM (710 KHZ)
Entravision Communications Corporation
1641 E. Osborn Rd. #8
Phoenix, AZ 85016
Tom Duran, General Manager
Tel: (602) 266-2005 Fax: (602) 279-2921
Web: www.entravision.com

KMRR-FM (100.3 MHZ)
Univision Communications, Inc.
4745 N. 7th St. #140
Phoenix, AZ 85014
Steve Virissimo, General Manager
Tel: (602) 308-7900 Fax: (602) 308-7979
Web: www.univision.com

KNAI-FM (88.3 MHZ)
La Campesina Network
3602 West Thomas St. #6
Phoenix, AZ 85019
Michael Nowakowski, General Manager
Tel: (602) 269-3121 Fax: (602) 269-3020
Email: knai883fm@campesina.com
Web: www.campesina.com

KNOG-FM (91.1 MHZ)
Radio Cadena Manantial
150 W. 1st St.
Nogales, AZ 85621
Marcos Romero, General Manager
Tel: (520) 287-5206 Fax: (520) 287-3606
Email: knog91fm@aol.com

KOMR-FM (106.3 MHZ)
Univision Communications, Inc.
4745 N. 7th St. #140
Phoenix, AZ 85014
Steve Virissimo, General Manager
Tel: (602) 308-7900 Fax: (602) 308-7979
Web: www.univision.com

KPHX-AM (1480 KHZ)
La Super X - Continental Broadcasting Corporation
824 E. Washington St.
Phoenix, AZ 85034
Jonathan Molina, General Manager
Tel: (602) 257-1351 Fax: (602) 256-0741

KQTL-AM (1210 KHZ)
Radio Unica
2955 E. Broadway Blvd.
Tucson, AZ 85716
Gabier Zazueta, General Manager
Tel: (520) 628-1200 Fax: (520) 326-4927

KRIT-FM (99.3 MHZ)
La Campesina Network
1301 Arizona Ave. #4
Parker, AZ 85344
Paco Jacobo, Program Director
Tel: (928) 669-9507 Fax: (928) 669-9513
Email: krcw993@campesina.com
Web: www.campesina.com

KRMB-FM (90.1 MHZ)
Radio Cadena Manantial
P.O. Box 2520
Douglas, AZ 85608
Warren Griffin, Office Administrator
Tel: (520) 364-5392 Fax: (520) 364-5392
Email: krmc91fm@juno.com
Web: www.radiomanantial.com

KRMC-FM (91.7 MHZ)
Radio Cadena Manantial
P.O. Box 2520
Douglas, AZ 85608
Warren Griffin, Office Administrator
Tel: (520) 364-5392 Fax: (520) 364-5392
Email: krmc91fm@juno.com
Web: www.radiomanantial.com

KSUN-AM (1400 KHZ)
Radio Fiesta, Inc.5
714 N. 3rd St.
Phoenix, AZ 85004
Peter Marquez, General Manager
Tel: (602) 252-0030 Fax: (602) 252-4211
Email: huracan@radiofiesta.net
Web: www.radiofiesta.net

KTZR -AM (1450 KHZ)
Clear Channel Communications
889 W. El Puente Ln.
Tucson, AZ 85713
Kent Cooper, General Manager
Tel: (520) 623-6429 Fax: (520) 622-2680
Email: Kentcooper@clearchannel.com
Web: www.clearchannel.com

KVVA-FM (107.1 MHZ)
Entravision Communications Corporation
1641 E. Osborn Rd. #8
Phoenix, AZ 85016
Tom Duran, General Manager
Tel: (602) 266-2005 Fax: (602) 279-2921
Web: www.entravision.com

KXEW-AM (1600 KHZ)
Clear Channel Communications
889 W. El Puente Ln.
Tucson, AZ 85713
Kent Cooper, General Manager
Tel: (520) 623-6429 Fax: (520) 622-2680
Email: Kentcooper@clearchannel.com
Web: www.clearchannel.com

KZLZ-FM (105.3 MHZ)
Entravision Communications Corporation
2959 E. Grant Rd.
Tucson, AZ 85716
Sonia Tabanico, General Manager
Tel: (520) 325-3054 Fax: (520) 325-3495
Web: www.entravision.com

KZNO-FM (98.3 MHZ)
Entravision Communications Corporation
2959 E. Grant Rd.
Tucson, AZ 85716
Sonia Tabanico, General Manager
Tel: (520) 325-3054 Fax: (520) 325-3495
Web: www.entravision.com

KDQN-FM (92.1 KHZ)
Bunyard Broadcasting
P.O. Box 311
De Queen, AR 71832
Victor Rojas, General Manager
Tel: (870) 642-2446 Fax: (870) 642-2442
Email: numberonecounty@yahoo.com
Web: www.kdqn.net

KREB-FM (99.5 MHZ)
EZ Spanish Media
2323-D S. Old Missouri Rd.
P.O. Box 335
Springdale, AR 72764
Edward J. Vega, General Manager
Tel: (479) 756-8686 Fax: (479) 756-8687
Email: evega@ezspanishmedia.com
Web: www.ezspanishmedia.com

KZAR-AM (1390 KHZ)
EZ Spanish Media
2323-D S. Old Missouri Rd.
P.O. Box 335
Springdale, AR 72765
Edward J. Vega, General Manager
Tel: (479) 756-8686 Fax: (479) 756-8687
Email: info@ezspanishmedia.com
Web: www.ezspanishmedia.com

CALIFORNIA

KAFY-AM (1100 KHZ)
Z Spanish Radio Network
1412 17th St.
Bakersfield, CA 93301
Rene Mora, General Manager
Tel: (661) 323-5239
Email: lafavorita@lafavorita.net
Web: www.lafavorita.net

KAFY-FM (95.9 MHZ)
KAFY, Inc.
4043 Geer Rd.
P.O. Box 1039
Hughson, CA 95326
Nelson Gomez, General Manager
Tel: (209) 883-8760 Fax: (209) 883-8769
Email: lafavorita@lafavorita.net
Web: www.lafavorita.net

KAZA-AM (1290 KHZ)
Radio KAZA
P.O. Box 1290
San Jose, CA 95108
Verónica Sibhu, General Manager
Tel: (408) 881-1290 Fax: (408) 881-1292
Email: kaza@kaza.com

KBHH-FM (95.3 MHZ)
La Campesina Network
2502 Merced St.
Fresno, CA 93721
Paco Jacobo, Program Director
Tel: (661) 837-0745 Fax: (661) 837-1612
Email: campesina@network.com
Web: www.campesina.com

KBKO-AM (1490 KHZ)
Clear Channel Communications
414 E. Cota St.
Santa Barbara, CA 93101
Richard Marsh, General Manager
Tel: (805) 965-1490 Fax: (805) 879-8434
Web: www.clearchannel.com

KBMB-FM (103.5 MHZ)
Entravision Communications Corporation
660 J St. #215
Sacramento, CA 95814
Larry Lemanski, General Manager
Tel: (916) 440-9500 Fax: (916) 447-3924
Web: www.1035thebomb.com

KBRG-FM (100.3 MHZ)
Entravision Communications Corporation
655 Campbell Technology Pkwy. #225
Campbell, CA 95008
Michael Murphy, General Manager
Tel: (408) 540-5683 Fax: (408) 540-5678
Email: mmurphy@entravision.com
Web: www.entravision.com

KBTW-FM (104.5 MHZ)
Lazer Broadcasting Corporation
1950 S. Sunwest Ln. #302
San Bernardino, CA 92408
Vicki Bails, General Manager
Tel: (909) 825-5020 Fax: (909) 884-5844
Email: aquipuro@radiolazer.com
Web: www.radiolazer.com

KBUE-FM (105.5 & 94.3 MHZ)
Liberman Broadcasting
1845 Empire Ave.
Burbank, CA 91504
Leonard Liberman, Owner
Tel: (323) 461-9300 Fax: (818) 729-5683
Web: www.aquisuena.com

KBYN-FM (95.9 MHZ)
KBYN, Inc.
4043 Geer Rd.
P.O. Box 1039
Hughson, CA 95326
Nelson Gomez, General Manager
Tel: (209) 883-8760 Fax: (209) 883-8769
Email: lafavorita@lafavorita.net
Web: www.lafavorita.net

KCAL-AM (1410 KHZ)
Lazer Broadcasting Corporation
1950 S. Sunwest Ln. #302
San Bernardino, CA 92408
Vicki Bails-Leth, General Manager
Tel: (909) 825-5020 Fax: (909) 884-5844
Email: vb@radiolazer.com
Web: www.radiolazer.com

KCBQ-AM (1170 KHZ)
KCDQ Radio
9255 Towne Centre Dr. #535
San Diego, CA 92121
Mark Larson, General Manager
Tel: (800) 873-1210 Fax: (619) 535-1212
Email: info@kcbq.com
Web: www.kcbq.com

KCCL-FM (101.9 MHZ)
Entravision Communications Corporation
1436 Auburn Blvd.
Sacramento, CA 95815
Larry Lemanski, General Manager
Tel: (916) 646-4000 Fax: (916) 646-3237
Web: www.entravision.com

KCFA-FM (106.1 MHZ)
KCFA, Inc.
4043 Geer Rd.
P.O. Box 1039
Hughson, CA 95326
Nelson Gomez, General Manager
Tel: (209) 883-8760 Fax: (209) 883-8769
Email: lafavorita@lafavorita.net
Web: www.lafavorita.net

KCHJ-AM (1010 AM)
Spanish Radio Group
5200 Standard St.
Bakersfield, CA 93308
Mike Allen, General Manager
Tel: (661) 327-9711 Fax: (661) 327-0797
Email: info@thespanishradio.com
Web: www.thespanishradio.com

KCVR-AM (1570 KHZ)
Entravision Communications Corporation
6820 Pacific Ave., Fl 3A
Stockton, CA 95207
Lisa Sunday, General Manager
Tel: (209) 474-0154 Fax: (209) 474-0316
Email: lsunday@entravision.com
Web: www.entravision.com

KCVR-FM (98.9 MHZ)
Entravision Communications Corporation
6820 Pacific Ave., Fl 3A
Stockton, CA 95207
Lisa Sunday, General Manager
Tel: (209) 474-0154 Fax: (209) 474-0316
Email: lsunday@entravision.com
Web: www.entravision.com

KDBV-AM (980 KHZ)
Wolfhouse Radio Group, Inc.
548 East Alisal St.
Salinas, CA 93905
Ron Stevens, General Manager
Tel: (831) 757-1910 Fax: (831) 771-1685
Email: wolfhouseradio@yahoo.es

KDIF-AM (1440 KHZ)
Clear Channel Communications
1465 Spruce St. #A
Riverside, CA 92507
Gilberto Esquivel, General Manager
Tel: (909) 784-4210 Fax: (909) 784-4213
Web: www.clearchannel.com

KDLD-FM (103.1 MHZ)
Entravision Communications Corporation
5700 Wilshire Blvd. #250
Los Angeles, CA 90036
Karl Meyer, General Manager
Tel: (323) 900-6300 Fax: (323) 900-6400
Web: www.indie1031.fm/main.html

KDLE-FM (103.1 MHZ)
Entravision Communications Corporation
5700 Wilshire Blvd. #250
Los Angeles, CA 90036
Karl Meyer, General Manager
Tel: (323) 900-6300 Fax: (323) 900-6400
Web: www.indie1031.fm/main.html

KESQ-AM (1400 KHZ)
Gulf-California Broadcasting Co.
42650 Melani Pl.
Palm Desert, CA 92211
Martin Serna, General Manager
Tel: (760) 568-6830 Fax: (760) 568-3984

KEYQ-AM (980 KHZ)
Radio Nueva Vida Network
2310 Ponderosa Dr. #28
Camarillo, CA 93010
Mary Guthrie, General Manager
Tel: (805) 482-4797 Fax: (805) 388-5202
Email: info@nuevavida.com
Web: www.nuevavida.com

KEZY-AM (1240 KHZ)
Radio Nueva Vida Network
2310 Ponderosa Dr. #28
Camarillo, CA 93010
Mary Guthrie, General Manager
Tel: (805) 482-4797 Fax: (805) 388-5202
Email: info@nuevavida.com
Web: www.nuevavida.com

KFVR-AM (1310 KHZ)
La Nueva
3560 Hillras Way
Fortune, CA 95540
Mario R. Meza, General Manager
Tel: (707) 725-9363 Fax: (707) 726-0446
Email: kncr@lanueva1090.com
Web: www.mcmedia.llc.com

KGEN-AM (1370 KHZ)
Azteca Broadcasting
P.O. Box 2040
Tulare, CA 93275
Margarita Hernández, General Manager
Tel: (559) 686-1370 Fax: (559) 685-1394
Email: kgen@sbcglobal.net

KGEN-FM (94.5 MHZ)
Azteca Broadcasting
P.O. Box 2040
Tulare, CA 93275
Margarita Hernández, General Manager
Tel: (559) 686-1370 Fax: (559) 685-1394
Email: kgen@sbcglobal.net

KGZO-FM (90.9 MHZ)
Radio Nueva Vida Network
2310 Ponderosa Dr. #28
Camarillo, CA 93010
Mary Guthrie, General Manager
Tel: (805) 482-4797 Fax: (805) 388-5202
Email: info@nuevavida.com
Web: www.nuevavida.com

KHDC-FM (90.9 MHZ)
Radio Bilingüe, Inc.
161 Main St.
Salinas, CA 93901
Delia Saldivar, General Manager
Tel: (831) 757-3216 Fax: (831) 757-9854
Web: www.radiobilingue.org

KHDV-FM (93.9 MHZ)
Wolfhouse Radio Group, Inc.
548 East Alisal St.
Salinas, CA 93905
Ron Stevens, General Manager
Tel: (831) 757-1910 Fax: (831) 771-1685
Email: wolfhouseradio@yahoo.es

KHJ-AM (930 KHZ)
Liberman Broadcasting
1845 Empire Ave.
Burbank, CA 91504
Leonard Liberman, Owner
Tel: (323) 461-9300 Fax: (323) 461-9946
Email: webmaster@aquisuena.com
Web: www.aquisuena.com

KICO-AM (1490 KHZ)
Hanson Broadcasting Company of California
695 Hwy. #111
Calexico, CA 92231
George Telleria, General Manager
Tel: (760) 357-5055 Fax: (760) 357-4168
Email: kicokqvo@trianglevision.com

KICO-AM (1490 KHZ)
Hanson Broadcasting Company of California
695 Hwy. 111
Calexico, CA 92231
Horge Telleria, Traffic Manager
Tel: (760) 357-5055 Fax: (760) 357-4168
Email: horge@kico.com

KIDI-FM (105.5 MHZ)
Emerald Wave Media
104 W. Chapel St.
Santa Maria, CA 93458
August Ruiz, General Manager
Tel: (805) 928-4334 Fax: (805) 349-2765
Email: labuenatv@aol.com

KIGS-AM (620 KHZ)
KIGS-AM
6165 E. Lacey Blvd.
Hanford, CA 93230
John Pereira, Owner
Tel: (559) 582-0361 Fax: (559) 582-3981
Email: info@kigs.com
Web: www.kigs.com

KIWI-FM (102.9 FM)
Spanish Radio Group
5200 Standard St.
Bakersfield, CA 93308
Mike Allen, General Manager
Tel: (661) 327-9711 Fax: (661) 327-0797
Email: info@thespanishradio.com
Web: www.thespanishradio.com

KJDJ-AM (1030-AM)
KJDJ-AM
604 E Chapel St.
Santa Maria, CA 93454
Manuel Salvador, Pastor
Tel: (805) 473-8728 Fax: (805) 352-1024

KLAX-FM (97.9 MHZ)
Spanish Broadcasting System
10281 W. Pico Blvd.
Los Angeles, CA 90064
David Haymore, General Manager
Tel: (310) 203-0900 Fax: (310) 203-8989

Email: dhaymore@sbslosangeles.com
Web: www.spanishbroadcasting.com

KLBS-AM (1330 KHZ)
Ethnic Radio, Inc.
401 Pacheco Blvd.
Los Banos, CA 93635
Alvaro Aguiar, Program Director
Tel: (209) 826-0578 Fax: (209) 826-1906
Email: pr@klbs.com
Web: www.klbs.com

KLNV-FM (106.5 MHZ)
Univision Communications, Inc.
600 W. Broadway #2150
San Diego, CA 92101
Peter Moore, General Manager
Tel: (619) 235-0600 Fax: (619) 744-4300
Web: www.univision.com

KLOB-FM (94.7 MHZ)
Entravision Communications Corporation
41601 Corporate Way
Palm Dessert, CA 92260
Tony Billett, General Manager
Tel: (760) 341-5837 Fax: (760) 341-0951
Web: www.entravision.com

KLOK-AM (1170 KHZ)
Entravision Communications Corporation
655 Campbell Technology Pkwy. #225
Campbell, CA 95008
Michael Murphy, General Manager
Tel: (408) 540-5683 Fax: (408) 540-5678
Email: mmurphy@entravision.com
Web: www.entravision.com

KLOK-FM (99.5 MHZ)
Entravision Communications Corporation
67 Garden Ct.
Monterey, CA 93940
Alejandro Sanchez, General Manager
Tel: (831) 333-9735 Fax: (831) 333-9750
Web: www.entravision.com

KLOQ-FM (98.7 MHZ)
Merced Radio
1020 W. Main St.
Merced, CA 95340
Yolanda Navarro, Program Director
Tel: (209) 723-2191 Fax: (209) 383-2950
Email: ynavarro@radiomerced.com
Web: www.radiomerced.com

KLQV-FM (102.9 MHZ)
Univision Communications, Inc.
600 W. Broadway #2150
San Diego, CA 92101
Peter Moore, General Manager
Tel: (619) 235-0600 Fax: (619) 744-4300
Email: pmoore@univision.com
Web: www.univision.com

KLTX-AM (1390 KHZ)
Radio Nueva Vida Network
2310 Ponderosa Dr. #28
Camarillo, CA 93010
Mary Guthrie, General Manager
Tel: (805) 482-4797 Fax: (805) 388-5202
Email: info@nuevavida.com
Web: www.nuevavida.com

KLVE-FM (107.5 MHZ)
Univision Communications, Inc.
655 N. Central Ave. #2500
Glendale, CA 91203
Thomas J. McSweeny, General Manager
Tel: (818) 500-4500 Fax: (818) 500-4480
Web: www.univision.com

KLYY-FM (97.5 MHZ)
Entravision Communications Corporation
5700 Wilshire Blvd. #250
Los Angeles, CA 90036

Karl Meyer, General Manager
Tel: (323) 900-6300 Fax: (323) 900-6400
Web: www.superestrella.com

KMBX-AM (700 KHZ)
Entravision Communications Corporation
67 Garden Ct.
Monterey, CA 93940
Alejandro Sanchez, General Manager
Tel: (831) 333-9735 Fax: (831) 333-9750
Web: www.entravision.com

KMIX-FM (100.9 MHZ)
Entravision Communications Corporation
6820 Pacific Ave., Fl 3A
Stockton, CA 95207
Lisa Sunday, General Manager
Tel: (209) 474-0154 Fax: (209) 474-0316
Email: lsunday@entravision.com
Web: www.entravision.com

KMJV-FM (106.3 MHZ)
Wolfhouse Radio Group, Inc.
548 East Alisal St.
Salinas, CA 93905
Ron Stevens, General Manager
Tel: (831) 757-1910 Fax: (831) 771-1685
Email: wolfhouseradio@yahoo.es

KMPG-AM (1520 KHZ)
Promo Radio Corporation
P.O. Box 369
Hollister, CA 95024
Rafel Regalado, General Manager
Tel: (831) 637-7994 Fax: (831) 637-4031

KMPO-FM (88.7 MHZ)
Radio Bilingüe, Inc.
5005 E. Belmont Ave.
Fresno, CA 93727
Lupita Carrasco, General Manager
Tel: (559) 455-5777 Fax: (559) 455-5778
Email: gpecarrasco@radiobilingue.org
Web: www.radiobilingue.org

KMRO-FM (90.3 MHZ)
Radio Nueva Vida Network
2310 E. Ponderosa Dr. #28
Camarillo, CA 93010
Mary Guthrie, General Manager
Tel: (805) 482-4797 Fax: (805) 388-5202
Email: info@nuevavida.com
Web: www.nuevavida.com

KMXX-FM (99.3 MHZ)
Entravision Communications Corporation
1803 N. Imperial Ave.
El Centro, CA 92243
Eric Chavez, General Manager
Tel: (760) 482-7777 Fax: (760) 352-1430
Web: www.entravision.com

KMYX-FM (92.5 MHZ)
La Campesina Network
6313 Schirra Ct.
Bakersfield, CA 93313
Arnulfo Rivas, Program Director
Tel: (661) 837-0745 Fax: (661) 837-1612
Email: kmyx925fm@campesina.com
Web: www.campesina.com

KNCR-AM (1090 KHZ)
La Nueva
3560 Hillras Way
Fortune, CA 95540
Mario R. Meza, General Manager
Tel: (707) 725-9363 Fax: (707) 726-0446
Email: kncr-am@lanueva1090.com
Web: www.mcmedia.llc.com

KNTO-FM (93.3 MHZ)
KNTO, Inc.
4043 Geer Rd.
Hughson, CA 95326

Nelson Gomez, General Manage
Tel: (209) 883-8760 Fax: (209) 883-8769
Email: lafavorita@lafavorita.net
Web: www.lafavorita.net

KOOR-AM (790 KHZ)
Infinity Broadcasting
1071 W. Shaw Ave.
Fresno, CA 93711
Chris Pacheco, General Manager
Tel: (559) 490-1019 Fax: (559) 490-5889
Email: clpacheco@cbs.com
Web: www.infinityradio.com

KOQO-FM (101.9 MHZ)
Infinity Broadcasting
1071 W Shaw Ave.
Fresno, CA 93711
Richard Hart, General Sales Manager
Tel: (559) 490-1019 Fax: (559) 490-5889
Email: richard.hart@infinitybroadcasting.com
Web: www.romance106.com

KOQO-FM (101.9 MHZ)
Infinity Broadcasting
1071 W. Shaw Ave.
Fresno, CA 93711
Chris Pacheco, General Manager
Tel: (559) 490-1019 Fax: (559) 490-4187
Email: clpacheco@cbs.com
Web: www.koqo.com

KOXR-AM (910 KHZ)
Lazer Broadcasting Corporation
418 S. A St., 4th Fl.
Oxnard, CA 93030
Jose Placencia, General Manager
Tel: (805) 487-0444 Fax: (805) 854-3738
Email: produccion@radiolazer.com
Web: www.radiolazer.com

KPFA-FM (94.1 MHZ)
1929 Martin Luther King, Jr. Way
Berkeley, CA 94704
Jim Bennett, General Manager
Tel: (510) 848-6767 Fax: (510) 848-3812
Email: info@kpfa.org
Web: www.kpfa.org

KPRZ-AM (1210 KHZ)
KRPZ Radio
9255 Towne Centre Dr. #535
San Diego, CA 92121
Mark Larson, General Manager
Tel: (800) 535-1210 Fax: (619) 535-1212
Email: kprz@kprz.com
Web: www.kprz.com

KPSL-FM (92.1 MHZ)
Spanish Radio Group
5200 Standard St.
Bakersfield, CA 93308
Mike Allen, General Manager
Tel: (661) 327-9711 Fax: (661) 327-0797
Email: info@thespanishradio.com
Web: www.thespanishradio.com

KPTI-FM (92.7 MHZ)
Spanish Broadcasting System
10281 W. Pico Blvd.
Los Angeles, CA 90064
David Haymore, General Manager
Tel: (310) 203-0900 Fax: (310) 203-8989
Email: dhaymore@sbslosangeles.com
Web: www.spanishbroadcasting.com

KRAY-FM (103.5 MHZ)
Wolfhouse Radio Group, Inc.
548 East Alisal St.
Salinas, CA 93905
Ron Stevens, General Manager
Tel: (831) 757-1910 Fax: (831) 771-1685
Email: wolfhouseradio@yahoo.es

KRCD-FM (103.9 MHZ)
Univision Communications, Inc.
655 N. Central Ave. #2500
Glendale, CA 91203
Thomas J. McSweeny, General Manager
Tel: (818) 500-4500 Fax: (818) 500-4480
Web: www.univision.com

KRCD-FM (98.3 MHZ)
Univision Communications, Inc.
655 N. Central Ave. #2500
Glendale, CA 91203
Thomas J. McSweeny, General Manager
Tel: (818) 500-4500 Fax: (818) 500-4480
Web: www.univision.com

KRCX-FM (99.9 MHZ)
Entravision Communications Corporation
1436 Auburn Blvd.
Sacramento, CA 95815
Larry Lemanski, General Manager
Tel: (916) 646-4000 Fax: (916) 646-3237
Web: www.entravision.com

KRKC-AM (1490 KHZ)
Radio Del Rey
1134 San Antonio Dr.
King City, CA 93930
Bill Gittler, General Manager
Tel: (831) 385-5421 Fax: (831) 385-0635
Email: krkc@dedot.com
Web: www.krkc.com

KRKC-FM (102.1 MHZ)
Radio Del Rey
1134 San Antonio Dr.
King City, CA 93930
Bill Gittler, General Manager
Tel: (831) 385-5421 Fax: (831) 385-0635
Email: krkc@dedot.com
Web: www.krkc.com

KRNC-FM (105.9 MHZ)
Infinity Broadcasting
1071 W. Shaw Ave.
Fresno, CA 93711
Chris Pacheco, General Manger
Tel: (559) 490-1019 Fax: (559) 490-5889
Email: clpacheco@cbs.com
Web: www.infinityradio.com

KRQK-FM (LA LEY 100.3 MHZ)
American General Media
2325 Skyway Dr.
Santa Maria, CA 93455
Rich Watson, General Manager
Tel: (805) 922-1041 Fax: (805) 928-3069

KRRE-FM (104.3 MHZ)
Entravision Communications Corporation
1436 Auburn Blvd.
Sacramento, CA 95815
Larry Lemanski, General Manager
Tel: (916) 646-4000 .Fax: (916) 646-3237
Web: www.entravision.com

KRRS-AM (1460 KHZ)
Moon Broadcasting
1410 Neotomas Ave. #104
P.O. Box 2277
Santa Rosa, CA 95405
Magie LeClerc, General Manager
Tel: (707) 545-1460 Fax: (707) 545-0112
Email: krrs1460@sonic.com
Web: www.krrs1460.com

KSCA-FM (101.9 MHZ)
Univision Communications, Inc.
655 N. Central Ave. #2500
Glendale, CA 91203
Thomas J. McSweeny, General Manager
Tel: (818) 500-4500 Fax: (818) 500-4480
Web: www.univision.com

KSDO-FM (106.9 MHZ)
Radio Nueva Vida Network
2310 E. Ponderosa Dr. #28
Camarillo, CA 93010
Mary Guthrie, General Manager
Tel: (805) 482-4797 Fax: (805) 388-5202
Email: info@nuevavida.com
Web: www.nuevavida.com

KSDO-FM (95.9 MHZ)
Radio Nueva Vida Network
2310 Ponderosa Dr. #28
Camarillo, CA 93010
Mary Guthrie, General Manager
Tel: (805) 482-4797 Fax: (805) 388-5202
Email: info@nuevavida.com
Web: www.nuevavida.com

KSDO-FM (91.3 MHZ)
Radio Nueva Vida Network
2310 Ponderosa Dr. #28
Camarillo, CA 93010
Mary Guthrie, General Manager
Tel: (805) 482-4797 Fax: (805) 388-5202
Email: info@nuevavida.com
Web: www.nuevavida.com

KSDO-FM (89.5 MHZ)
Radio Nueva Vida Network
2310 Ponderosa Dr. #28
Camarillo, CA 93010
Mary Guthrie, General Manager
Tel: (805) 482-4797 Fax: (805) 388-5202
Email: info@nuevavida.com
Web: www.nuevavida.com

KSDO-FM (90.1 MHZ)
Radio Nueva Vida Network
2310 Ponderosa Dr. #28
Camarillo, CA 93010
Mary Guthrie, General Manager
Tel: (805) 482-4797 Fax: (805) 388-5202
Email: info@nuevavida.com
Web: www.nuevavida.com

KSDO-FM (90.3 MHZ)
Radio Nueva Vida Network
2310 Ponderosa Dr. #28
Camarillo, CA 93010
Mary Guthrie, General Manager
Tel: (805) 482-4797 Fax: (805) 388-5202
Email: info@nuevavida.com
Web: www.nuevavida.com

KSDO-FM (91.7 MHZ)
Radio Nueva Vida Network
2310 Ponderosa Dr. #28
Camarillo, CA 93010
Mary Guthrie, General Manager
Tel: (805) 482-4797 Fax: (805) 388-5202
Email: info@nuevavida.com
Web: www.nuevavida.com

KSDO-FM (106.9 MHZ)
Radio Nueva Vida Network
2310 Ponderosa Dr. #28
Camarillo, CA 93010
Mary Guthrie, General Manager
Tel: (805) 482-4797 Fax: (805) 388-5202
Email: info@nuevavida.com
Web: www.nuevavida.com

KSDO-FM (98.1 MHZ)
Radio Nueva Vida Network
2310 Ponderosa Dr. #28
Camarillo, CA 93010
Mary Guthrie, General Manager
Tel: (805) 482-4797 Fax: (805) 388-5202
Email: info@nuevavida.com
Web: www.nuevavida.com

KSDO-FM (90.9 MHZ)
Radio Nueva Vida Network
2310 Ponderosa Dr. #28
Camarillo, CA 93010
Mary Guthrie, General Manager
Tel: (805) 482-4797 Fax: (805) 388-5202
Email: info@nuevavida.com
Web: www.nuevavida.com

KSDO-FM (95.9 MHZ)
Radio Nueva Vida Network
2310 Ponderosa Dr. #28
Camarillo, CA 93010
Mary Guthrie, General Manager
Tel: (805) 482-4797 Fax: (805) 388-5202
Email: info@nuevavida.com
Web: www.nuevavida.com

KSDO-FM (95.7 MHZ)
Radio Nueva Vida Network
2310 Ponderosa Dr. #28
Camarillo, CA 93010
Mary Guthrie, General Manager
Tel: (805) 482-4797 Fax: (805) 388-5202
Email: info@nuevavida.com
Web: www.nuevavida.com

KSDO-FM (90.1 MHZ)
Radio Nueva Vida Network
2310 Ponderosa Dr. #28
Camarillo, CA 93010
Mary Guthrie, General Manager
Tel: (805) 482-4797 Fax: (805) 388-5202
Email: info@nuevavida.com
Web: www.nuevavida.com

KSDO-FM (90.3 MHZ)
Radio Nueva Vida Network
2310 Ponderosa Dr. #28
Camarillo, CA 93010
Mary Guthrie, General Manager
Tel: (805) 482-4797 Fax: (805) 388-5202
Email: info@nuevavida.com
Web: www.nuevavida.com

KSDO-FM (91.3 MHZ)
Radio Nueva Vida Network
2310 Ponderosa Dr. #28
Camarillo, CA 93010
Mary Guthrie, General Manager
Tel: (805) 482-4797 Fax: (805) 388-5202
Email: info@nuevavida.com
Web: www.nuevavida.com

KSEA-FM (107.9 FM)
La Campesina Network
229 Pajaro St. #302-D
Salinas, CA 93901
Jorge L, Guizar, General Manager
Tel: (831) 754-1469 Fax: (831) 754-1563
Email: ksea1079fm@campesina.com
Web: www.campesina.com

KSEH-FM (94.5 MHZ)
Entravision Communications Corporation
1803 N. Imperial Ave.
El Centro, CA 92243
Eric Chavez, General Manager
Tel: (760) 482-7777 Fax: (760) 352-1430
Web: www.entravision.com

KSES-FM (107.1 MHZ)
Entravision Communications Corporation
67 Garden Ct.
Monterey, CA 93940
Alejandro Sanchez, General Manager
Tel: (831) 333-9735 Fax: (831) 333-9750
Web: www.entravision.com

KSJV-FM (91.5 MHZ)
Radio Bilingüe, Inc.
5005 E. Belmont Ave.
Fresno, CA 93727
Lupita Carrasco, General Manager
Tel: (559) 455-5777 Fax: (559) 455-5778
Email: gpecarrasco@radiobilingue.org
Web: www.radiobilingue.org

KSKD-FM (95.9 MHZ)
KSKD, Inc.
4043 Geer Rd.
P.O. Box 1039
Hughson, CA 95326
Nelson Gomez, General Manager
Tel: (209) 883-8760 Fax: (209) 883-8769
Email: lafavorita@lafavorita.net
Web: www.lafavorita.net

KSOL-FM (98.9 MHZ)
Univision Communications, Inc.
750 Battery St. #200
San Francisco, CA 94111
Michelle Hohman, General Manager
Tel: (415) 989-5765 Fax: (415) 733-5766
Email: estereosol989@univision.com
Web: www.univision.com

KSPE-FM (94.5 MHZ)
Clear Channel Communications
414 E. Cota St.
Santa Barbara, CA 93103
Richard Marsh, General Manager
Tel: (805) 965-1490 Fax: (805) 879-8434
Web: www.clearchannel.com

KSSC-FM (107.1 MHZ)
Entravision Communications Corporation
5700 Wilshire Blvd. #250
Los Angeles, CA 90036
Karl Meyer, General Manager
Tel: (323) 900-6300 Fax: (323) 900-6400
Web: www.superestrella.com

KSSD-FM (107.1 MHZ)
Entravision Communications Corporation
5700 Wilshire Blvd. #250
Los Angeles, CA 90036
Karl Meyer, General Manager
Tel: (323) 900-6300 Fax: (323) 900-6400
Web: www.superestrella.com

KSSE-FM (107.1 MHZ)
Entravision Communications Corporation
5700 Wilshire Blvd. #250
Los Angeles, CA 90036
Karl Meyer, General Manager
Tel: (323) 900-6300 Fax: (323) 900-6400
Web: www.superestrella.com

KSTN-AM (1420 MHZ)
San Joaquin Broadcasting
2171 Ralph Ave.
Stockton, CA 95206
Knox LaRue, General Manager
Tel: (209) 948-5786
Web: www.kstn.net

KTAP-AM (1600 KHZ)
Emerald Wave Media
104 W. Chapel
Santa María, CA 93458
Guisela Esparza, General Manager
Tel: (805) 928-4334 Fax: (805) 349-2765
Email: labuenatv@aol.com

KTGE-AM (1570 KHZ)
Wolfhouse Radio Group, Inc.
548 East Alisal St.
Salinas, CA 93905
Ron Stevens, General Manager
Tel: (831) 757-1910 Fax: (831) 771-1685
Email: wolfhouseradio@yahoo.es

KTNQ-AM (1020 KHZ)
Univision Communications, Inc.
655 N. Central Ave. #2500
Glendale, CA 91203
Thomas J. McSweeny, General Manager
Tel: (818) 500-4500 Fax: (818) 500-4480
Web: www.univision.com

KTOB-AM (1490 KHZ)
Moon Broadcasting
1410 Neotomas Ave. #104
P.O. Box 2277
Santa Rosa, CA 95405
Magie LeClerc, General Manager
Tel: (707) 545-1460 Fax: (707) 545-0112
Email: krrs1460@sonic.com
Web: www.krrs1460.com

KTQX-FM (91.5 MHZ)
Radio Bilingüe, Inc.
5005 E. Belmont Ave.
Fresno, CA 93727
Lupita Carrasco, General Manager
Tel: (559) 455-5777 Fax: (559) 455-5778
Email: gpecarrasco@radiobilingue.org
Web: www.radiobilingue.org

KTSE-FM (97.1 MHZ)
Entravision Communications Corporation
6820 Pacific Ave., Fl 3A
Stockton, CA 95207
Lisa Sunday, General Manager
Tel: (209) 479-0154 Fax: (209) 474-0316
Email: lsunday@entravision.com
Web: www.entravision.com

KUBO-FM (88.7 MHZ)
Radio Bilingüe, Inc.
P.O. Box 71
El Centro, CA 92243
Ana Lilia Barraza, General Manager
Tel: (760) 337-8053 Fax: (760) 337-8519
Web: www.radiobilingue.org

KUFW-FM (90.5 FM)
La Campesina Network
3106 S. Mooney Ave. #K
Visalia, CA 93277
Francisco Armenta, General Manager
Tel: (559) 622-9401 Fax: (559) 622-9521
Email: kufw905fm@campesina.com
Web: www.campesina.com

KUNA-FM (96.7 MHZ)
Gulf California Broadcasting Co.
42650 Melani Pl.
Palm Desert, CA 92211-5170
Martin Serna, General Manager
Tel: (760) 568-6830 Fax: (760) 568-3984
Email: meserna@kunamundo.comcom

KUTY-AM (1470 KHZ)
High Desert Broadcasting
570 E. Ave. #Q-9
Palmdale, CA 93550
Vicki Connor, General Manager
Tel: (661) 947-3107 Fax: (661) 272-5688
Email: vconnor@hdbav.com
Web: www.hdbav.com

KWAC-AM (1490 AM)
Spanish Radio Group
5200 Standard St.
Bakersfield, CA 93308
Mike Allen, General Manager
Tel: (661) 327-9711 Fax: (661) 327-0797
Email: info@thespanishradio.com
Web: www.thespanishradio.com

KWIZ-FM (96.7 MHZ)
Liberman Broadcasting
3101 W. 5th St.
Santa Ana, CA 92703

Winnie Coombs, General Manager
Tel: (714) 554-5000 Fax: (714) 554-9362
Web: www.sonido967.com

KWKW-AM (1330 KHZ)
Lotus Communications
3301 Barham Blvd. #201
Los Angeles, CA 90068
Jim Kalmenson, General Manager
Tel: (323) 851-5959 Fax: (323) 512-7460
Email: mrivera@kwkw1330.com
Web: www.kwkw1330.com

KWRM-AM (1370 KHZ)
Major Market Stations, Inc.
P.O. Box 100
Corona, CA 92878-100
Steve Cruz, General Manager
Tel: (951) 737-1370 Fax: (951) 735-9572
Email: kwrm@major-market.com
Web: www.major-market.com

KWRN-AM (1550 KHZ)
Major Market Stations, Inc.
15165 7th St. #D
Victorville, CA 92392
Iris Ivette Gutierrez, Sales/Marketing Director
Tel: (760) 955-8722 Fax: (760) 955-5751
Email: iris@major-market.com
Web: www.kwrn1550am.com

KWRU-AM (940 KHZ)
Radio Unica
4910 E. Clinton Ave. #107
Fresno, CA 93727
Alberto Felix, Program Director
Tel: (559) 452-0940 Fax: (559) 452-0948
Email: afelix@radiounica.com
Web: www.radiounica.com

KWST-AM (94.5 MHZ)
Entravision Communications Corporation
1803 N. Imperial Ave.
El Centro, CA 92243
Eric Chavez, General Manager
Tel: (760) 482-7777 Fax: (760) 352-1430
Web: www.entravision.com

KXEX-AM (1550 KHZ)
Rak Communications
139 W. Olive Ave.
Fresno, CA 93728
Albert R. Perez, General Manager
Tel: (559) 233-8803 Fax: (559) 233-8871
Email: rak@computermail.net

KXLM-FM (102.9 KHZ)
Lazer Broadcasting Corporation
200 SA. St. #400
Oxnard, CA 93030
Salvador Prieto, Program Director
Tel: (805) 240-2070 Fax: (805) 240-5960
Email: produccion@radiolazer.com
Web: www.radiolazer.com

KXOL-FM (96.3MHZ)
Spanish Broadcasting System
10281 W. Pico Blvd.
Los Angeles, CA 90064
David Haymore, General Manager
Tel: (310) 203-0900 Fax: (310) 203-8989
Email: dhaymore@sbslosangeles.com
Web: www.spanishbroadcasting.com

KXRS-FM (105.7 MHZ)
Lazer Broadcasting Corporation
1950 S. Sunwest Ln. #302
San Bernardino, CA 92408
Vicki Bails, General Manager
Tel: (909) 825-5020 Fax: (909) 884-5844
Email: aquipuro@radiolazer.com
Web: www.radiolazer.com

KXSB-FM (101.7 MHZ)
Lazer Broadcasting Corporation
1950 S. Sunwest Ln. #302
San Bernardino, CA 92408
Vicki Bails, General Manager
Tel: (909) 825-5020 Fax: (909) 884-5844
Email: aquipuro@radiolazer.com
Web: www.radiolazer.com

KZAB/KZBR-FM (93.5 MHZ)
Spanish Broadcasting System
10281 W. Pico Blvd.
Los Angeles, CA 90064
David Haymore, General Manager
Tel: (310) 203-0900 Fax: (310) 203-8989
Email: dhaymore@sbslosangeles.com
Web: www.spanishbroadcasting.com

KZOL-FM (107.9 MHZ)
Univision Communications, Inc.
1981 N. Gateway #101
Fresno, CA 93727
Robert Torres, General Manager
Tel: (559) 465-4000 Fax: (559) 251-9555
Email: rtorres@univision.com
Web: www.univision.com

QUE ONDA-FM (92.1 MHZ)
Univision Communications, Inc.
1981 N. Gateway #101
Fresno, CA 93727
Robert Torres, General Manager
Tel: (559) 465-4000 Fax: (559) 251-9555
Email: rtorres@univision.com
Web: www.univision.com

VIVA-FM (105.7 MHZ)
Univision Communications, Inc.
750 Battery St. #200
San Francisco, CA 94111
Michelle Hohman, General Manager
Tel: (415) 989-5765 Fax: (415) 733-5766
Email: viva1057@correo.univision.com
Web: www.univision.com

XEMO-AM (860 KHZ)
Uniradio Corp.
5030 Camino de la Siesta, #403
San Diego, CA 92108
Ing. Luis Carlos Astiazaran, Director General
Tel: (619) 497-0600 Fax: (619) 497-1019
Email: contactus@unimedios.com.mx
Web: www.uniradio.com

XERCN-AM (1470 KHZ)
Uniradio
5030 Camino De La Siesta #403
San Diego, CA 92108
Luis Carlos Astiazaran, General Manager
Tel: (619) 497-0600 Fax: (619) 497-1019
Email: contactus@unimedios.com.mx
Web: www.uniradio.com

XHA - RADIO AMOR (94.5 MHZ)
Uniradio Corp.
5030 Camino de la Siesta #403
San Diego, CA 92108
Ing. Luis Carlos Astiazaran, Director General
Tel: (619) 497-0600 Fax: (619) 497-1019
Email: contactus@unimedios.com.mx
Web: www.uniradio.com

XHFG PULSAR (107.3 MHZ)
Uniradio Corp.
5030 Camino de la Siesta #403
San Diego, CA 92108
Ing. Luis Carlos Astiazaran, Director General
Tel: (619) 497-0600 Fax: (619) 497-1019
Email: contactus@unimedios.com.mx
Web: www.uniradio.com

XHTY-FM (99.7 MHZ)
Uniradio Corp.
5030 Camino de la Siesta, #S-403
San Diego, CA 92108
Ing. Luis Carlos Astiazaran, Director General
Tel: (619) 497-0600 Fax: (619) 497-1019
Email: contactus@unimedios.com.mx
Web: www.uniradio.com

XLTN-FM (104.5 MHZ)
Califormula Broadcasting
1690 Frontage Rd.
Chula Vista, CA 91911
Alex Diaz, VP
Tel: (619) 575-9090 Fax: (619) 423-1818
Web: www.radiolatina.com

COLORADO

KBNO-AM (1280 KHZ)
Latino Communications LLC.
600 Grant #600
Denver, CO 80203
Michael Ferrufino, National Sales Mgr.
Tel: (303) 733-5266 Fax: (303) 733-5242
Email: kbno@kbno.net
Web: www.radioquebueno.com

KFTM-AM (1400 KHZ)
KRDZ Broadcasters, Inc.
P.O. Box 430
Ft. Morgan, CO 80701
Candy Trujillo, Spanish Program Director
Tel: (970) 867-5674 Fax: (970) 542-1023
Email: kftm@kci.net
Web: www.kftm.net

KGNU-FM (88.5 MHZ)
Boulder Community Broadcasting Association, Inc.
4700 Walnut St.
Boulder, CO 80301
Sam Fuqua, Public Affairs Dir.
Tel: (303) 449-4885
Email: music@kgnu.org
Web: www.kgnu.org

KJMN-FM (92.1 MHZ)
Entravision Communications Corporation
777 Grant St. #500
Denver, CO 80203
Mario Carrera, General Manager
Tel: (303) 832-0050 Fax: (303) 832-3410
Web: www.entravision.com

KLMR-AM (920 KHZ)
Commonwealth Communications
P.O. Box 890
Lamar, CO 81052
Ubaldo Reyes, Program Director
Tel: (719) 336-2206 Fax: (719) 336-7973
Email: klmr@cminet.net

KMXA-AM (1090 KHZ)
Entravision Communications Corporation
777 Grant St. #500
Denver, CO 80203
Mario Carrera, General Manager
Tel: (303) 832-0050 Fax: (303) 832-3410
Web: www.entravision.com

KNKN-AM (690 KHZ)
Metropolitan City, Inc.
30 N. Electronic Dr.
Pueblo West, CO 81007
Lupe Brown, General Manager
Tel: (719) 547-0411 Fax: (719) 547-9301
Email: radiolobo@amigo.net

KNKN-FM (107.1 MHZ)
Metropolitan City, Inc.
30 North Electronic Dr.
Pueblo West, CO 81007
Lupe Brown, General Manager
Tel: (719) 547-0411 Fax: (719) 547-9301
Email: radiolobo@amigo.net

KPVW-AM (107.1KHZ)
Entravision Communications Corporation
20 Sunset Dr. #6-A
Basalt, CO 81621
Mario Carrera, General Manager
Tel: (970) 927-7600 Fax: (970) 927-8001
Web: www.entravision.com

KRMX-AM (690 KHZ)
Metropolitan City, Inc.
30 N. Electronic Dr.
Pueblo West, CO 81007
Lupe Brown, General Manager
Tel: (719) 547-0411 Fax: (719) 547-9301
Email: radiolobo@amigo.net

KRZA-FM (88.7 MHZ)
Equal Representation of Media Advocacy Corporation
528 9th St.
Alamosa, CO 81101
Deannette Jacquez-Avila, Program Director
Tel: (719) 589-8844 Fax: (719) 587-0032
Email: krza@krza.org
Web: www.krza.org

KSLV-AM (1240 KHZ)
San Luis Valley Broadcasting, Inc.
P.O. Box 631
Monte Vista, CO 81144
Jerry Medina, Spanish Program Director
Tel: (719) 852-3581 Fax: (719) 852-3583
Email: kslv@amigo.com
Web: www.kslvradio.com

KUVO-FM (89.3 MHZ)
Denver Educational Broadcasting
P.O. Box 2040
Denver, CO 80201-2040
Florence Hernandez-Ramos, General Manager
Tel: (303) 480-9272x18 Fax: (303) 291-0757
Email: info@kuvo.org
Web: www.kuvo.org

KVVS-AM (1170 KHZ)
Rodriguez Gallegos Broadcasting Corporation
P.O. Box 698
Windsor, CO 80550
Rodriguez Gallegos, General Manager
Tel: (970) 686-1170 Fax: (970) 686-7700

KXPX-FM (96.5 MHZ)
Entravision Communications Corporation
777 Grant St. #500
Denver, CO 80203
Mario Carrera, General Manager
Tel: (303) 832-0050 Fax: (303) 832-3410
Web: www.entravision.com

CONNECTICUT

WCUM-AM (1450 KHZ)
Radio Cumbre Broadcasting
P.O. Box 3975
Bridgeport, CT 06605
Allison Sheahan, General Manager
Tel: (203) 335-1450 Fax: (203) 337-1220
Email: radiocumbre1450@aol.com
Web: www.radiocumbre.com

WLAT-AM (910 KHZ)
Mega Communications
330 Main St.
Hartford, CT 06106
Melvin Sanchez, General Manager
Tel: (860) 524-0001 Fax: (860) 548-1922

WNEZ-AM (1230 KHZ)
Mega Communications
330 Main St.
Hartford, CT 06106
Melvin Sanchez, General Manager
Tel: (860) 524-0001 Fax: (860) 548-1922

WPRX-AM (1120 KHZ)
Nievesquez Corporation
20-28 Sargeant St.
Hartford, CT 06105
Oscar Nieves, President
Tel: (860) 727-0844 Fax: (860) 727-0849
Email: wprx1120@aol.com
Web: www.members.aol.com/wprx1120

WRYM-AM (840 KHZ)
Hartford County Broadcasting
1056 Willard Ave.
Newington, CT 06111
Walter Martinez, Vice President
Tel: (860) 666-5646 Fax: (860) 666-5647

DISTRICT OF COLUMBIA

The Hispanic Radio Network, Inc., La Red Hispana
1101 Pennsylvania Ave. Northwest, 6th Fl.
Washington, DC 20004
Arturo Vasquez, CEO
Tel: (202) 637-8800 Fax: (202) 637-8801
Email: arturo@hrn.org
Web: www.hispanicradio.com

FLORIDA

WACC-AM (830 KHZ)
Archdiocese of Miami
1779 NW 28 St.
Miami, FL 33142
Father Alberto R. Cutié, General Director
Tel: (305) 638-9729 Fax: (305) 636-4571
Email: informacion@radiopaz.org
Web: www.paxcc.org

WAFC-AM (590 KHZ)
Glades Media
530 E. Alverdez Ave.
Clewiston, FL 33440
Robbie Castellanos, General Manager
Tel: (863) 983-5900 Fax: (863) 983-6109
Email: robbie@gladesmedia.com
Web: www.radiofiesta.com

WAFZ-FM (92.1 MHZ)
Glades Media
2105 W. Immokalee Dr.
Immokalee, FL 34142
Gary Holloway, General Manager
Tel: (239) 658-1490 Fax: (239) 658-6109
Email: gary@gladesmedia.com
Web: www.radiofiesta.com

WAMR-FM (107.5 MHZ)
Univision Communications, Inc.
800 Douglas Rd. #111
Coral Gables, FL 33134
Claudia Puig, General Manager
Tel: (305) 447-1140 Fax: (305) 643-1075
Email: sales@correo.univision.com
Web: www.univision.com

WAQI-AM (710 KHZ)
Univision Communications, Inc.
800 Douglas Rd. #111
Gables Coral, FL 33134
Claudia Puig, General Manager
Tel: (305) 447-1140 Fax: (305) 442-7676
Email: sales@correo.univision.com
Web: www.univision.com

WAUC-AM (1310 KHZ)
Marvina Enterprise
1310 S. Florida Ave.
Wauchula, FL 33873
Roberto Ayala, General Manager
Tel: (863) 773-5008 Fax: (863) 773-2032
Email: waucradiostation@earthlink.net

WCMQ-FM (92.3 MHZ)
Spanish Broadcasting System, Inc.
1001 Ponce de Leon Blvd.
Coral Gables, FL 33134
Jackie Nosti-Combo, VP/General Manager
Tel: (305) 444-9292 Fax: (305) 461-4466
Email: arodriguez@sbsmiami.com
Web: www.clasica92fm.com

WCRM-AM (1350 KHZ)
Manna Christian Mission, Inc.
3448 Canal St.
Fort Myers, FL 33916
Salvador Santana, General Manager
Tel: (239) 332-1350 Fax: (239) 332-8890
Email: manantial1350am@aol.com
Web: www.shoutcast.com

WDNA-FM (88.9 MHZ)
Bascomb Memorial Broadcasting Foundation, Inc.
4848 SW 74 Ct.
Miami, FL 33155
Margarita Pelleya, General Manager
Tel: (305) 662-8889 Fax: (305) 662-1975
Email: feedback@wdna.org
Web: www.wdna.org

WHSR-AM (980 KHZ)
Beasley Broadcast Group, Inc.
6699 N. Federal Hwy. #200
Boca Raton, FL 33487
Bob Morency, General Manager
Tel: (561) 997-0074 Fax: (561) 997-0476
Email: iynstyne@aol.com
Web: www.whsrentertainmentradio.com

WKIZ-AM (1500 KHZ)
Radio Tropical
527 Southard St.
Key West, FL 33040
Tel: (305) 293-9536
Email: wkizradio@aol.com
Web: www.wkizradio.com

WLCC-AM (760 KHZ)
Mega Communications, LLC
1915 N. Dale Marby Hwy. #200
Tampa, FL 33607
Cecilia Uebel, General Manager
Tel: (813) 871-1819 Fax: (813) 871-1155
Email: cecilia@megastations.net

WLQY-AM (1320 KHZ)
Entravision Communications Corporation
10800 Biscayne Blvd. #810
North Miami, FL 33161
Rick Santos, General Manager
Tel: (305) 891-1729 Fax: (305) 891-1583
Web: www.entravision.com

WMGG-AM (820 KHZ)
Mega Communications, LLC
1915 N. Dale Marby Hwy. #200
Tampa, FL 33607

Cecilia Uebel, General Manager
Tel: (813) 871-1819 Fax: (813) 871-1155
Email: cecilia@megastations.net

WNUE-FM (98.1 MHZ)
Mega Communications, LLC
337 S. North Lake Blvd. #1024
Altamonte Springs, FL 3321701
Rafael Grullon, General Manager
Tel: (407) 331-1777 Fax: (407) 830-6223
Email: steve@lanueva981.com
Web: www.mega981.com

WPSP-AM (1190 KHZ)
Q Broadcasting, Inc.
5730 Corporate Way #210
W. Palm Beach, FL 33407
Lissette M. Diaz, General Manager
Tel: (561) 681-9777 Fax: (561) 687-3398
Email: diaz1190am@aol.com

WQBA-AM (1140 KHZ)
Univision Communications, Inc.
800 Douglas Rd. #111
Coral Gables, FL 33134
Claudia Puig, General Manager
Tel: (305) 447-1140 Fax: (305) 441-2452
Email: sales@correo.univision.com
Web: www.univision.com

WQQZ-FM (88.7 KHZ)
Hispanic Broadcasting
4540 Curry Ford Rd.
Orlando, FL 32812
Daniel Ponce, General Manager
Tel: (407) 208-0333 Fax: (407) 208-0633
Email: wqqzfm@aol.com
Web: www.laqqz.com

WRHC-AM (1550 KHZ)
Fenix Broadcasting Corporation
330 SW 27th Ave., 2nd Fl.
Miami, FL 33135
Jorge Rodríguez, President/CEO
Tel: (305) 541-3300 Fax: (305) 541-7470
Email: ana670@aol.com
Web: www.cadenaazul.com

WRMA-FM (106.7 MHZ)
Spanish Broadcasting System, Inc.
1001 Ponce de Leon Blvd.
Coral Gables, FL 33134
Jackie Nosti-Cambo, General Manager
Tel: (305) 444-9292 Fax: (305) 461-4466
Email: arodriguez@sbsmiami.com
Web: www.romance106fm.com

WRMD-AM (680 KHZ)
ZGS Broadcasting of Tampa
402 N. Rio #218
Tampa, FL 33609
Maria Chacon, General Manager
Tel: (813) 319-5757 Fax: (813) 319-0029
Email: rumba680@tucontacto.net

WRMQ-AM (1140 KHZ)
Q Broadcasting, Inc.
1033 E. Semoran Blvd. #253
Casselberry, FL 32707
George Arroyo, General Manager
Tel: (407) 830-0800 Fax: (407) 260-6100
Email: mannyarroyo@salsa1030.com

WRNE-AM (980 KHZ)
Media One
312 E. 9 Mile Rd. #29
Pensacola, FL 32514
Robert Hill, General Manager
Tel: (850) 478-6000 Fax: (850) 484-8080
Eemail: hill@wrne980.com
Web: www.wrne980.com

WRTO-FM (98.3 MHZ)
Univision Communications, Inc.
800 Douglas Rd. #111
Coral Gables, FL 33134
Claudia Puig, General Manager
Tel: (305) 447-1140 Fax: (305) 443-4701
Email: sales@correo.univision.com
Web: www.univision.com

WSIR-AM (1490 KHZ)
Anscombe Broadcasting Group, Ltd.
665 Lake Howard Dr. SW
Winter Haven, FL 33880
Joe Fisher, General Manager
Tel: (863) 295-9411 Fax: (863) 401-9365
Email: info@rejoice1490.com
Web: www.rejoice1490.com

WSUA-AM (1260 KHZ)
Caracol Radio
2100 Coral Way #200
Miami, FL 33145
Tomas Martinez, General Manager
Tel: (305) 285-1260 Fax: (305) 858-5907
Email: admin@caracolusa.com
Web: www.caracolusa.com

WUNA-AM (1480 KHZ)
Way Broadcasting, Inc.
749 S. Bluford Ave.
Ocoee, FL 34761
Juan Nieves, General Manager
Tel: (407) 656-9823 Fax: (407) 656-2092

WVCG-AM (1080 KHZ)
Radio One, Inc.
2828 W. Flagler St.
Miami, FL 33135
Michael Silva, General Manager
Tel: (305) 644-0800 Fax: (305) 644-0038
Email: msilva@radio-one.com
Web: www.radio-one.com

WWFE-AM (670 KHZ)
Fenix Broadcasting Corporation
330 SW 27th Ave., 2nd Fl.
Miami, FL 33135
Jorge Rodríguez, President/CEO
Tel: (305) 541-3300 Fax: (305) 541-7470
Email: info@lapoderosa.com
Web: www.lapoderosa.com

WWRF-AM (1380 KHZ)
Glades Media
2326 S. Congress Ave. #2A
West Palm Beach, FL 33406
Jesus Lobo, General Manager
Tel: (561) 721-9951 Fax: (561) 721-9973
Email: jesus@gladesmedia.com
Web: www.radiofiesta.com

WXDJ-FM (95.7 MHZ)
Spanish Broadcasting System, Inc.
1001 Ponce de Leon Blvd.
Coral Gables, FL 33134
Jackie Nosti-Cambo, General Manager
Tel: (305) 444-9292 Fax: (305) 461-4466
Email: arodriguez@sbsmiami.com
Web: www.elzol.com

WZMQ-FM (106.3 MHZ)
South Broadcasting System
1001 Ponce de Leon Blvd.
Coral Gables, FL 33134-3319
Raul Rodriguez, Sr., General Manager
Tel: (305) 444-9292 Fax: (305) 461-9994
Email: sbssales@bellsouth.net
Web: www.grancadena.com

GEORGIA

CNN Radio Noticias
One CNN Center #0410A
P.O. Box 105366
Atlanta, GA 30303
Maria Asuncion Desax-Guerrero, Director
Tel: (404) 827-1220 Fax: (404) 878-5598
Email: maria.guerrero@cnn.com
Web: www.cnn.com

The Good News Network
P.O. Box 510
Appling, GA 30802
C. T. Barinouski, President
Tel: (800) 926-4669 Fax: (706) 309-9669
Email: CTBARINOUSKI@.comcest.net
Web: www.gnnradio.org

WAOS-AM (1600 KHZ)
La Favorita, Inc.
5815 Westside Rd.
Atlanta, GA 30106
Samuel Zamarrón, General Manager
Tel: (770) 944-0900 Fax: (770) 944-9794
Email: sammy@radiolafavorita.com
Web: www.radiolafavorita.com

WAOS-AM (1600 KHZ)
La Favorita, Inc.
5815 West Side Rd.
Austell, GA 30168
Samuel Zamarron, General Manager
Tel: (770) 944-0900 Fax: (770) 944-9794
Email: sammy@radiolafavorita.com
Web: www.radiolafavorita.com

WAZX-AM (1550 KHZ and 101.9KHZ)
GA-Mex Broadcasting, Inc.
2460 N. Atlanta Rd.
Smyrna, GA 30080
Humberto Izquierdo, General Manager
Tel: (770) 436-6171 Fax: (770) 436-0100
Email: izquierdo9@yahoo.com
Web: www.radiolaquebuena.com

WBLR-AM (1430 KHZ)
The Good News Network
2278 Wortham Ln.
Grovetown, GA 30813
C.T. Barinowski, General Manager
Tel: (706) 309-9610 Fax: (706) 309-9669
Email: ctbarinowski@comcast.net
Web: www.gnnradio.org

WDAL-AM (1430 KHZ)
Clear Channel Communications
613 Silver Circle
Dalton, GA 30721
Mark Cooper, General Manager
Tel: (706) 278-5511 Fax: (706) 278-9917
Email: markcooper@clearchannel.com
Web: www.clearchannel.com

WKSP (96.3 FM)
Clear Channel Communication
2743 Perimeter Pkwy. Bldg. 100 #200
Augusta, GA 30909
Barry Kaye, General Manager
Tel: (706) 396-6000 Fax: (706) 396-6010
Web: www.clearchannel.com

WKTM-FM (106.1 MHZ)
The Good News Network
2278 Wortham Ln.
Grovetown, GA 30813
C.T. Barinowski, General Manager
Tel: (706) 309-9610 Fax: (706) 309-9669
Email: ctbarinowski@comcast.net
Web: www.gnnradio.org

WLBA-AM (1130 KHZ)
La Favorita, Inc.
311 Green St., #200A
Gainsville, GA 30501
Ariel Zamarrón, General Manager
Tel: (770) 532-6331 Fax: (770) 532-2672
Email: lamexicana@mindspring.com
Web: www.radiolafavorita.com

WPBC-AM (1310 KHZ)
La Invasora
3684 Stewart Rd. #3
Atlanta, GA 30340
Daniel King, General Manager
Tel: (770) 986-9500 Fax: (770) 986-4113

WPLO-AM (610 KHZ)
Prieto Communications
239 Ezzat St.
Lawrenceville, GA 30246
Teresa Esquivel, General Manager
Tel: (770) 237-9897 Fax: (770) 237-8769
Email: tesquivel@radiomexonline.com
Web: www.radiomex610atlanta.com

WPRW (107.7 FM)
Clear Channel Communication
2743 Perimeter Parkway Bldg. 100 #200
Augusta, GA 30909
Barry Kaye, General Manager
Tel: (706) 396-6000 Fax: (706) 396-6010
Web: www.clearchannel.com

WQRX-AM (870 KHZ)
The Good News Network
2278 Wortham Ln.
Grovetown, GA 30813
C.T. Barinowski, General Manager
Tel: (706) 309-9610 Fax: (706) 309-9669
Email: ctbarinowski@comcast.net
Web: www.gnnradio.org

WWWE-AM (1100 KHZ)
Beasley Broadcast Group, Inc.
1465 Northside Dr. #218
Atlanta, GA 30318
Julia Jolian, General Manager
Tel: (404) 355-8600 Fax: (404) 355-4156
Web: www.bbgi.com

HAWAII

KWAI-AM (1080 AM)
100 N. Beretania St. #401
Honolulu, HI 96817
Barry Wagenvoord, General Manager
Tel: (808) 524-1080 Fax: (808) 531-6532
Email: kwai@aloha.net

IDAHO

KJOY-FM (101.9 MHZ)
KJHY-FM
P.O. Box 1600
Nampa, ID 83653
Steve Sumner, General Manager
Tel: (208) 322-3437

KWAL-AM (620 KHZ)
Silver Valley Broadcasting
120 First St.
Osburn, ID 83849
Paul Robinson, General Manager
Tel: (208) 752-1141 Fax: (208) 753-5111

KWEI-AM (1260 KHZ)
Treasure Valley Broadcasting Co.
1156 N. Orchard St.
Boise, ID 83706
Randy Williamson, General Manager
Tel: (208) 367-1859 Fax: (208) 383-9170

KWEI-FM (99.5 MHZ)
Treasure Valley Broadcasting Co.
1156 N. Orchard St.
Boise, ID 83706
Randy Williamson, General Manager
Tel: (208) 367-1859 Fax: (208) 383-9170

ILLINOIS

LA QUE BUENA-FM (105.1 MHZ)
Univision Communications, Inc.
625 N. Michigan Ave. #300
Chicago, IL 60611
Jerry Ryan, General Manager
Tel: (312) 642-1051 Fax: (312) 981-1850
Web: www.univision.com

PASION-FM (106.7 MHZ)
Univision Communications, Inc.
625 N. Michigan Ave. #300
Chicago, IL 60611
Jerry Ryan, General Manager
Tel: (312) 751-5566 Fax: (312) 981-1850
Web: www.univision.com

VIVA-FM (93.5 MHZ)
Univision Communications, Inc.
625 N. Michigan Ave. #300
Chicago, IL 60611
Jerry Ryan, General Manager
Tel: (312) 266-9848 Fax: (312) 981-1850
Web: www.univision.com

VIVA-FM (103.1 MHZ)
Univision Communications, Inc.
625 N. Michigan Ave. #300
Chicago, IL 60611
Jerry Ryan, General Manager
Tel: (312) 266-9848 Fax: (312) 981-1850
Web: www.univision.com

WDEK-FM (92 MHZ)
Spanish Broadcasting System
150 N. Michigan Ave. #1040
Chicago, IL 60601
Mario Paez, General Manager
Tel: (312) 920-9500 Fax: (312) 920-9514
Email: mpaez@sbschicago.com
Web: www.spanishbroadcasting.com

WIND-AM (560 KHZ)
Univision Communications, Inc.
625 N. Michigan Ave. #300
Chicago, IL 60611
Jerry Ryan, General Manager
Tel: (312) 981-1800 Fax: (312) 981-1820
Web: www.univision.com

WKIE-FM (92.5 MHZ)
Spanish Broadcasting System
150 N. Michigan Ave. #1040
Chicago, IL 60601
Mario Paez, General Manager
Tel: (312) 920-9500 Fax: (312) 981-1820
Email: mpaez@sbschicago.com
Web: www.spanishbroadcasting.com

WKIF-FM (92.7 MHZ)
Spanish Broadcasting System
150 N. Michigan Ave. #1040
Chicago, IL 60601
Mario Paez, General Manager
Tel: (312) 920-9500 Fax: (312) 920-9514
Email: mpaez@sbschicago.com
Web: www.spanishbroadcasting.com

WLEY-FM (107.9 MHZ)
Spanish Broadcasting System
150 N. Michigan Ave. #1040
Chicago, IL 60601
Mario Paez, General Manager
Tel: (312) 920-9500 Fax: (312) 920-9514
Email: mpaez@sbschicago.com
Web: www.spanishbroadcasting.com

WMBI-AM (1110 MHZ)
Moody Broadcasting
820 N. La Salle Blvd.
Chicago, IL 60610
Gerson García, General Manager
Tel: (312) 329-4281 Fax: (312) 329-8989
Email: radio.esperanza@MOODY.EDU
Web: www.radiomoody.com

WOJO-FM (105.1 MHZ)
Univision Communications, Inc.
625 N. Michigan Ave. #300
Chicago, IL 60611
Jerry Ryan, General Manager
Tel: (312) 981-1800 Fax: (312) 981-1820
Email: jerryryan@hispanicbroadcasting.com
Web: www.univision.com

WONX-AM (1590 KHZ)
Kovas Communications
2100 Lee St.
Evanston, IL 60202
Frank Kovas, General Manager
Tel: (847) 475-1590 Fax: (773) 273-1590

WRTO-AM (1200 KHZ)
Univision Communications, Inc.
625 N. Michigan Ave. #300
Chicago, IL 60611
Jerry Ryan, General Manager
Tel: (312) 981-1800 Fax: (312) 981-1820
Web: www.univision.com

WVIV-FM (103.1 MHZ)
Univision Communications, Inc.
625 N. Michigan Ave. #300
Chicago, IL 60611
Jerry Ryan, General Manager
Tel: (312) 981-1800 Fax: (312) 981-1820
Email: jerryryan@hispanicbroadcasting.com
Web: www.univision.com

WVIX-FM (93.5 MHZ)
Univision Communications, Inc.
625 N. Michigan Ave. #300
Chicago, IL 60611
Jerry Ryan, General Manager
Tel: (312) 981-1800 Fax: (312) 981-1820
Web: www.univision.com

INDIANA

WEDJ-FM (107.1 MHZ)
1800 N. Meridian St. #605
Indianapolis, IN 46202
Dwight Barnett, General Manager
Tel: (317) 924-1071 Fax: (317) 924-7766
Email: dwight@wedjfm.com
Web: www.wedjfm.com

IOWA

KDFR-FM (91.3 MHZ)
Family Radio Stations
2350 NE 44th Ct.
Des Moines, IA 50317
Larry Vavroch, Operations Manager
Tel: (515) 262-0449
Email: kdfr@familyradio.com
Web: www.familyradio.com

KANSAS

KYUU-AM (1470 MHZ)
Waitt Radio
224 N. Kansas Ave.
Liberal, KS 67901
Steve Schiffner, General Manager
Tel: (620) 624-8157 Fax: (620) 624-4606
Email: sschiffner@waittmedia.com
Web: www.waittmedia.com

LOUISIANA

WFNO-AM (830 KHZ)
MC Media, Inc.
111 Veterans Blvd., 18th Fl.
Metairie, LA 70005
Todd Matherne, CEO
Tel: (504) 832-3255 Fax: (504) 378-3555
Email: info@mcmediallc.com
Web: www.mcmediallc.com

MARYLAND

WACA-AM (1540 KHZ)
Radio America - AC Acquisitions LLC.
11141 Georgia Ave. # 310
Wheaton, MD 20902
Alejandro Carrasco, President
Tel: (301) 942-3500 Fax: (301) 942-7798
Email: alex@radioamerica.net
Web: www.radioamerica.net

WBBS-FM (94.3 MHZ)
Mega Communications
8121 Georgia Avenue, 10th Fl.
Silver Spring, MD 20910
Mary Elena Verdugo, General Manager
Tel: (301) 588-6200 Fax: (301) 588-6129
Email: info@megasepega.com
Web: www.megasepega.com

WBZS-FM (92.7 MHZ)
Mega Communications
8121 Georgia Avenue, 10th Fl.
Silver Spring, MD 20910
Mary Elena Verdugo, General Manager
Tel: (301) 588-6200 Fax: (301) 588-6129
Email: info@megasepega.com
Web: www.megasepega.com

WILC-AM (900 KHZ)
Radio Viva-900 - WILC Corporation
13499 Baltimore Ave. #200
Laurel, MD 20725
Wendy Thompson, General Manager
Tel: (301) 419-2122 Fax: (301) 419-2409

WKDV-AM, WZHF, WKDM, WKCW (1460 KHZ)
Way Broadcasting/ Multicultural Radio
12216 Parklawn Dr. #203
Rockville, MD 20852
Bill Parris, General Manager
Tel: (301) 424-9292

WWGB-AM (1030 AM)
WWGB
5210 Auth Rd. #500
Suitland, MD 20746
Ruth Salmeron, General Manager
Tel: (301) 899-1444 Fax: (301) 899-7244
Email: info@@wwgb.com
Web: www.wwgb.com

MASSACHUSETTS

WACM-AM (1490 KHZ)
Davidson Media Group, LLC
34 Sylvan St.
West Springfield, MA 01089
Peter Davidson, President
Tel: (413) 781-5200 Fax: (413) 734-2240

WAMG-AM (890 KHZ)
Mega Communications, LLC.
529 Main St. #200
Charlestown, MA 02129
David Collins, Director General
Tel: (617) 242-1800 Fax: (617) 241-0017
Web: www.lamegasepega.com

WCCN-AM (1110 KHZ)
Costa Eagle Radio Partners, Ltd.
462 Merrimack St.
Mithuen, MA 01844
Pat Costa, Station Manager
Tel: (978) 686-9966 Fax: (978) 687-1180

WCUW-FM (91.3 MHZ)
910 Main St.
Worcester, MA 01610
Joe Cutroni, General Manager
Tel: (508) 753-1012
Email: wcuw@wcuw.com
Web: www.wcuw.com

WJIB-AM (740 KHZ)
443 Concord Ave.
Cambridge, MA 02138
Bob Bettner, General Manager
Tel: (617) 868-7400

WLLH-AM (1400 KHZ)
Mega Communications, LLC.
529 Main St. #200
Charlestown, MA 02129
David Collins, General Manager
Tel: (617) 242-1800 Fax: (617) 242-0017
Web: www.lamegasepega.com

WNNW-AM (800 KHZ)
Costa Eagle Radio Partners Ltd.
462 Merrimack St.
Methuen, MA 01844
Johnny Mckenzie, General Manager
Tel: (978) 686-9966 Fax: (978) 687-1180
Email: contact@power800am.com
Web: www.power800am.com

WRCA-AM (1330 KHZ)
Beasley Broadcast Group, Inc.
552 Massachusetts Ave. #201
Cambridge, MA 02139
Stu Fink, General Manager
Tel: (617) 492-3300 Fax: (617) 492-2800
Web: www.bbgi.com

WSPR-AM (1270 KHZ)
Davidson Media Group, LLC
34 Sylvan St.
West Springfield, MA 01089
Peter Davidson, President
Tel: (413) 781-5200 Fax: (413) 734-2240

WUNR-AM (1600 KHZ)
Champion Broadcasting
160 N. Washington St.
Boston, MA 02114
Steve Lalli, General Manager
Tel: (617) 367-9003 Fax: (617) 367-2265

MICHIGAN

WCAR-AM (1090 KHZ)
WCAR Radio
32500 Park Lane
Garden City, MI 48135
Janice Zavistoski, Office Manager
Tel: (734) 525-1111 Fax: (734) 525-3608
Email: jgk@catholicradio.org
Web: www.catholicradio.org

WNWZ-AM (1410 KHZ)
Reaching Communications
50 Monroe Ave. NW #3500
Grand Rapids, MI 49503
Phil Catlett, General Manager
Tel: (616) 451-4800 Fax: (616) 451-9595
Web: www.1410lamaquina.com

WNZK-AM (690 / 680 KHZ)
Birach Broadcasting Corporation
21700 Northwestern Hwy. #1190
Southfield, MI 48075
Sima Birach, General Manager
Tel: (248) 557-3500 Fax: (248) 557-2950
Email: sima@birach.com
Web: www.wnzk.com

MINNESOTA

KSMM-AM (1530 KHZ)
Las Americas, Inc.
1107 Hazeltine Blvd. #520
Chaska, MN 55318
Paul Sadek, General Manager
Tel: (952) 361-0019 Fax: (952) 361-5529
Email: ksmm@relevantradio.com
Web: www.ksmm.com

KYSM-FM (103.5 MHZ)
Clear Channel Radio
1807 Lee Blvd.
North Mankato, MN 56003
Terry Cooley, Program Director
Tel: (507) 345-4673 Fax: (507) 345-4675
Email: terrycooley@clearchannel.com
Web: www.kysmradio.com

MISSOURI

KFUO-AM (850 KHZ)
Lutheran Church of Missouri Synod
85 Founder's Lane
St. Louis, MO 63105
Chuck Rather, Program Director
Tel: (314) 505-7800 Fax: (314) 725-2538
Email: crathert@kfuo.org
Web: www.kfuo.org

NEBRASKA

KBBX-FM (97.7 MHZ)
Journal Broadcast Group
5030 N. 72nd St.
Omaha, NE 68134
Steve Wexler, General Manager
Tel: (402) 592-5300 Fax: (402) 592-6605
Email: wexler@journalbroadcastgroup.com
Web: www.journalbroadcastgroup.com

NEVADA

KISF-FM (103.5 MHZ)
Univision Communications, Inc.
6767 W. Tropicana Ave. #102
Las Vegas, NV 89103
Dana Demerjian, General Manager
Tel: (702) 284-6400 Fax: (702) 284-6403
Email: ddemejrin@univision.com
Web: www.univision.com

KLAV-AM (1230 MHZ)
Gore Overguard, Inc.
1810 Weldon Pl.
Las Vegas, NV 89104
Peggy Merrill, Station Manager
Tel: (702) 796-1230 Fax: (702) 796-7433
Email: peggyklav@aol.com
Web: www.klav1230am.com

KLSQ-AM (870 KHZ)
Univision Communications, Inc.
6767 W. Tropicana Ave. #102
Las Vegas, NV 89103
Dana Demerjian, General Manager
Tel: (702) 284-6400 Fax: (702) 284-6403
Email: ddemejrin@univision.com
Web: www.univision.com

KQLO-AM (1590 KHZ)
KQLO
101 Locust St.
Reno, NV 89501
Lariano Chávez, General Manager
Tel: (775) 322-0847 Fax: (775) 322-0927
Email: radiouniversal1590an@yahoo.com
Web: www.kqlo.com

KQMR-FM (99.3 MHZ)
Univision Communications, Inc.
6767 W. Tropicana Ave. #102
Las Vegas, NV 89103
Dana Demerjian, General Manager
Tel: (702) 284-6400 Fax: (702) 284-6403
Email: ddemejrin@univision.com
Web: www.univision.com

KQRT-FM (105.1 MHZ)
Entravision Communications Corporation
500 Pilot Rd. #D
Las Vegas, NV 89119
Gabriel Quiroz, General Manager
Tel: (702) 597-3070 Fax: (702) 507-1084
Web: www.entravision.com

KRNV-FM (102.1 MHZ)
Entravision Communications Corporation
300 S. Wells Ave. #12
Reno, NV 89502
Viola Cody, General Manager
Tel: (775) 333-1017 Fax: (705) 333-9047
Web: www.entravision.com

KRRN-FM (92.7 MHZ)
Entravision Communications Corporation
500 Pilot Rd. #D
Las Vegas, NV 89119
Gabriel Quiroz, General Manager
Tel: (702) 597-3070 Fax: (702) 507-1084
Web: www.entravision.com

NEW JERSEY

WMIZ-AM (1270 KHZ)
Clear Channel Communications
632 Maurice River Pkwy.
P.O. Box 689
Vineland, NJ 08360
Carl Hemple, General Manager
Tel: (856) 692-8888 Fax: (856) 696-2568
Email: chemple@wmizradio.com
Web: www.wmizradio.com

WWRV-AM (1330 KHZ)
Radio Vision Christiana Mgmt.
419 Broadway
P.O. Box 2908
Paterson, NJ 07509

Jose Lastra, General Manager
Tel: (973) 881-8700 Fax: (973) 881-8324
Email: radiovision@radiovision.net
Web: www.radiovision.net

NEW MEXICO

COYOTE-FM (102.5 MHZ)
Univision Communications, Inc.
8009 Marble NE
Albuquerque, NM 87110
Chuck Morgan, General Manager
Tel: (505) 262-1142 Fax: (505) 262-9211
Web: www.univision.com

KANW-FM (89.1 MHZ)
Albuquerque Public Schools
2020 Coal Ave. Southeast
Albuquerque, NM 87106
Michael Brasher, General Manager
Tel: (505) 242-7163
Email: brasher@aps.edu
Web: www.kanw.com

KARS-AM (860 KHZ)
American General Media, Inc.
208 N. 2nd St.
Belen, NM 87002
Loco Larry, Spanish DJ
Tel: (505) 864-7447 Fax: (505) 864-2719
Email: nmgold@nmgold.com

KCRX-AM (1430 KHZ)
Radio Exitos
P.O. Box 2052
Roswell, NM 88202
Rosendo Casarez, Jr., Manager
Tel: (505) 622-7677 Fax: (505) 622-1432

KDCE-AM (950 KHZ)
RLG Broadcasting, Inc.
403 W. Pueblo Dr.
Española, NM 87532
Casey Gallegos, General Manager
Tel: (505) 753-8131 Fax: (505) 753-8685
Email: kdce@zeane.net
Web: www.kdce.net

KFMQ-FM (106.1 MHZ)
Clear Channel, Inc
1632 S. 2nd St.
Gallup, NM 87301
Blas Saucedo, Program Director
Tel: (505) 863-9391 Fax: (505) 863-9393

KFUN-AM (1230 KHZ)
KFUN and KFUS, Inc.
Number One Radio Heights
P.O. Box 700
Las Vegas, NM 87701
Joseph Baca, General Manager
Tel: (505) 425-6766 Fax: (505) 425-6767
Email: jbaca1946@yahoo.com

KINF-AM (1020 KHZ)
Roswell Radio, Inc.
P.O. Box 670
Roswell, NM 88202
John M. Dunn, General Manager
Tel: (505) 622-6450 Fax: (505) 622-9041
Email: kinf@roswellradio.org
Web: www.roswellradio.org

KISS-FM (97.3 MHZ)
Univision Communications, Inc.
8009 Marble Northeast
Albuquerque, NM 87110
Chuck Morgan, General Manager
Tel: (505) 262-1142 Fax: (505) 262-9211
Web: www.univision.com

KJFA-FM (101.3 MHZ)
Univision Communications, Inc.
8009 Marble NE
Albuquerque, NM 87110
Ozzie Sattler, General Manager
Tel: (505) 262-1142 Fax: (505) 262-9211
Web: www.univision.com

KKYC-FM (102.3 MHZ)
Broadcasting Entertainment
1000 Sycamore St.
Clovis, NM 88101
Ron Pierson, General Manager
Tel: (505) 762-6200 Fax: (505) 762-8800

KLMA-FM (96.5 MHZ)
Ojeda Broadcasting, Inc.
108 S. Willow
P.O. Box 457
Hobbs, NM 88241
Hermilo Ojeda, Owner
Tel: (505) 391-9650 Fax: (505) 397-9373
Email: klmaradio@leaco.net
Web: www.klmaradio.com

KNFT-AM (950 KHZ)
Runnels Broadcasting
P.O. Box 1320
Silver City, NM 88062
Max Murillo, Program Director
Tel: (505) 388-1958 Fax: (505) 388-5000
Email: silvercity@snmradio.com
Web: www.snmradio.com

KPZA-FM (103.7 MHZ)
Noalmark broadcasting
619 N. Turner
Hobbs, NM 88240
Paul Starr, General Manager
Tel: (505) 393-1103 Fax: (505) 393-4310
Email: mail@1radiosquare.com
Web: www.1radiosquare.com

KRDD-AM (1320 KHZ)
Trini B Espinoza
170 Red Bridge Rd.
P.O. Box 1615
Roswell, NM 88201
Carlos Espinoza, General Manager
Tel: (505) 623-8111

KRZY-AM (1450 KHZ)
Entravision Communications Corporation
3451 Candelaria Northeast
Albuquerque, NM 87107
Margarita Wilder, General Manager
Tel: (505) 342-4141 Fax: (505) 344-8714
Email: KRZY1059@aol.com
Web: www.entravision.com

KRZY-FM (105.9 MHZ)
Entravision Communications Corporation
3451 Candelaria Northeast
Albuquerque, NM 87107
Margarita Wilder, General Manager
Tel: (505) 342-4141 Fax: (505) 344-8714
Email: KRZY1059@aol.com
Web: www.entravision.com

KSSR-AM (1340 KHZ)
Room 66 Broadcasting, Inc.
2818 Will Rogers Dr.
P.O. Box 78
Santa Rosa, NM 88435
Joe Esquivel, General Manager
Tel: (505) 472-5777 Fax: (505) 472-5777
Email: kssrradio@yahoo.com

KSWV-AM (810 KHZ)
Qué Suave
102 Kause St.
P.O. Box 1088
Santa Fe, NM 87501

Anthony Gonzáles, General Manager
Tel: (505) 989-7441 Fax: (505) 989-7607
Email: kswvanthonygonzales@yahoo.com

KUNM-FM (89.9 MHZ)
University of New Mexico
MSC06 3520, Oñate Hall, 1 University of
New Mexico
Albuquerque, NM 87131
Richard S.Towne, General Manager
Tel: (505) 277-4806 Fax: (505) 277-8004
Email: kunm@kunm.org
Web: www.kunm.org

KVVF-FM (101.7 MHZ)
Univision Communications, Inc.
8009 Marble NE
Albuquerque, NM 87110
Chuck Morgan, General Manager
Tel: (505) 260-4400 Fax: (505) 262-9211
Web: www.univision.com

THE RANGE-FM (105.1 MHZ)
Univision Communications, Inc.
8009 Marble NE
Albuquerque, NM 87110
Ozzie Sattler, General Manager
Tel: (505) 260-4400 Fax: (505) 262-9211
Web: www.univision.com

NEW YORK

LATINIOMIX-FM (105.9 MHZ)
Univision Communications, Inc.
485 Madison Ave., 3rd Fl.
New York, NY 10022
Stephanie McNamara, General Manager
Tel: (212) 310-6000 Fax: (212) 310-6095
Web: www.univision.com

LATINIOMIX-FM (92.7MHZ)
Univision Communications, Inc.
485 Madison Ave., 3rd Fl.
New York, NY 10022
Stephanie McNamara, General Manager
Tel: (212) 310-6000 Fax: (212) 310-6095
Web: www.univision.com

WADO-AM (1280 KHZ)
Univision Communications, Inc.
485 Madison Ave., 3rd Fl.
New York, NY 10022
Stephanie McNamara, General Manager
Tel: (212) 310-6000 Fax: (212) 310-6095
Web: www.univision.com

WCAA-FM (105.9 KHZ)
Univision Communications, Inc.
485 Madison Ave.,3rd Fl.
New York, NY 10022
Stephanie McNamara, General Manager
Tel: (212) 310-6000 Fax: (212) 888-3694
Email: latinomix@univisionradio.com
Web: www.univision.com

WHCR-FM (90.3 MHZ)
The City College of New York
138th & Convent Ave., Nac Bldg. #1515
New York, NY 10031
Angela Harden, General Manager
Tel: (212) 650-7481 Fax: (212) 650-7480
Email: whcr903fm@yahoo.com
Web: www.whcr.org

WNSW-AM (1430 KHZ)
Multicultural Broadcasting, Inc.
449 Broadway, 2nd Fl.
New York, NY 10013
Gene Heinemeyer, General Manager
Tel: (212) 966-1059 Fax: (212) 966-9580

WPAT-AM (930 KHZ)
Multicultural Broadcasting, Inc.
449 Broadway, 2nd Fl.
New York, NY 10013
Gene Heinemeyer, General Manager
Tel: (212) 966-1059 Fax: (212) 966-9580

WPAT-FM (93.1 MHZ)
Spanish Broadcasting System
26 W. 56th St.
New York City, NY 10019
Frank Floris, General Manager
Tel: (212) 541-9200 Fax: (212) 541-9295
Email: floris@sbsnewyork.com
Web: www.spanishbroadcasting.com

WSKQ-FM (97.9 MHZ)
Spanish Broadcasting System
26 W. 56th St.
New York City, NY 10019
Frank Floris, General Manager
Tel: (212) 541-9200 Fax: (212) 541-9239
Email: ffloris@sbsnewyork.com
Web: www.lamega.com

WVOX-AM (1460 KHZ)
Whitney Radio
1 Broadcast Forum
New Rochelle, NY 10801
William O'Shaughnessy, President &
Editorial Director
Tel: (914) 636-1460 Fax: (914) 636-2900
Email: info@wvox.com
Web: www.wvox.com

WWRU-AM (1660 KHZ)
Radio Unica
51 E. 25th St., 7th FL
New York, NY 10010
Alejandro Sanchez, General Manager
Tel: (212) 679-5005 Fax: (212) 679-7823
Email: asanchez@radiounica.com
Web: www.radiounica.com

NORTH CAROLINA

GREENSBORO WWBG (1470 KHZ)
Que Pasa Radio/Latino Communications
3808 High Pont Rd. #C
Greensboro, NC 27408
Margarita Fernandez, RadioTraffic Manager
Tel: (336) 854-5777 Fax: (336) 854-1692
Email: radiotraffic@quepasamedia.com
Web: www.quepasamedia.com

RALEIGH/DURHAM WFTK (1030 KHZ)
Que Pasa Radio/Latino Communications
150 Fayeteville St. Mall #110
Raleigh, NC 27601
Margarita Fernandez, RadioTraffic Manager
Tel: (919) 645-1680 Fax: (919) 645-1699
Email: radiotraffic@quepasamedia.com
Web: www.quepasamedia.com

WGOS-AM (1070 KHZ)
6223 Old Mendenhall Rd.
High Point, NC 27263
Simon Ritchy, President/General Manager
Tel: (336) 434-5024 Fax: (336) 434-6018
Email: wgosradio@triad.rr.com
Web: www.wgos.net

WINSTON SALEM WTOB (1380 KHZ)
Que Pasa Radio/Latino Communications
3025 Waughtown St. #G
Winston-Salem, NC 27107
Margarita Fernandez, RadioTraffic Manager
Tel: (336) 784-9004 Fax: (336) 784-8337
Email: radiotraffic@quepasamedia.com
Web: www.quepasamedia.com

WNCT-AM (1070 KHZ)
Beasley Broadcast Group, Inc.
P.O. Box 7167
Greenville, NC 27835
Brad Hood, General Manager
Tel: (252) 757-0011 Fax: (252) 757-0286
Email: brad@oldies1079.com
Web: www.oldies1079.com

WNOW-AM (1030 KHZ)
Charlotte Metro radio
4201-J Stewart Andrew Blvd.
P.O. Box 19448
Charlotte, NC 28208
Russ Jones, General Manager
Tel: (704) 665-9355 Fax: (208) 545-9888
Email: ann@wnow.com
Web: www.wnow.com

WRRZ-AM (880 KHZ)
WRRZ
2164 SE Blvd.
P.O. Box 378
Clinton, NC 28329
Victor Sanchez, Program Director
Tel: (910) 592-2165 Fax: (910) 592-8556

OHIO

WDLW-AM (1380 KHZ)
Latino Media Group
3024 W. 25th St. #149
Cleveland, OH 44113
Angel Ramos, General Manager
Tel: (216) 631-9922 Fax: (216) 274-9119
Email: angel@latinomediagroup.com
Web: www.latinomediagroup.com

WEOL-AM (930 KHZ)
Elyria Lorain Broadcasting
538 Broad St.
P.O. Box 4006
Elyria, OH 44036
Gary Kneisley, President
Tel: (440) 322-3761 Fax: (440) 322-1536
Email: gkneisley@weol.com
Web: www.weol.com

OKLAHOMA

KTLR-AM (890 KHZ)
Tyler Broadcasting, Inc.
5101 S. Shields Blvd.
Oklahoma City, OK 73129
Tony Tyler, General Manager
Tel: (405) 616-5509 Fax: (405) 616-5505
Email: tony@ktlr.com
Web: www.tylermedia.com

KTUZ-FM (106.7 MHZ)
Tyler Broadcasting Corporation
5101 S. Shields Blvd.
Oklahoma City, OK 73129-3217
Amando Rubio, General Manager
Tel: (405) 616-5500 Fax: (405) 616-0328
Email: armando.r@tylermedia.com
Web: www.tylermedia.com

KZUE-AM (1460 KHZ)
La Tremenda
2715 S. Radio Rd.
El Reno, OK 73036
Nancy Galván, General Manager
Tel: (405) 262-1460 Fax: (405) 262-1886
Email: kzue@aol.com

OREGON

KRTA-AM (610 KHZ)
OPUS Broadcasting
511 Rossanley
Medford, OR 97501
Dean Flock, General Manager
Tel: (541) 772-0322 Fax: (541) 772-4233

KUIK-AM (1360 KHZ)
Dolphing Radio Inc.
3355 NE Cornell
P.O. Box 566
Hillsboro, OR 97124
Alvaro Gongora, Program Director
Tel: (503) 640-1360 Fax: (503) 640-6108
Email: amradio@kuik.com
Web: www.kuik.com

KWBY-AM (940 KHZ)
Radio Fiesta
1665 James St.
Woodburn, OR 97071
Donald Coss, General Manager
Tel: (503) 981-9400 Fax: (503) 981-3561
Web: www.lapantera940.com

KWIP-AM (880 KHZ)
P.O. Box 469
Dallas, OR 97338
Diane Burns, General Manger
Tel: (503) 623-0245 Fax: (503) 623-6733
Email: dburns@kwip.com

PENNSYLVANIA

WEMG-FM (104.9 KHZ)
Mega Communications
1341 N. Delaware Ave.
Philadelphia, PA 19125
Kevin Jones, General Manager
Tel: (215) 426-1900 Fax: (215) 426-1550
Email: kjones@megastations.net
Web: www.megastations.net

WHOL-AM (1600 KHZ)
Omega
1125 Colorado St.
Allentown, PA 18103
Mathew Braccili, General Manager
Tel: (610) 434-4801 Fax: (484) 223-0088
Web: www.whol1600.com

WLCH-FM (91.3 MHZ)
SACA Broadcasting
30 N. Ann St.
Lancaster, PA 17602
Enid Vazquez-Pereira, General Manager
Tel: (717) 295-7996 Fax: (717) 295-7759
Email: radiocentr@aol.com
Web: www.sacapa.org

WPHE-AM (690 KHZ)
Salvacion Broadcasting Company
321 W. Sedgley Ave.
Philadelphia, PA 19140
Sarrail Salva, General Manager
Tel: (215) 291-7532 Fax: (215) 739-1337
Email: rs@radiosalvacion.com
Web: www.radiosalvacion.com

PUERTO RICO

VIDA-AM (1400 KHZ)
Primera Iglesia Bautista de Carolina
P.O. Box 188
Carolina, PR 00986
Federico Iglesias, General Manager
Tel: (787) 757-1773 Fax: (787) 769-4103
Email: radiovida@cadenaradiovida.com
Web: www.cadenaradiovida.com

VIDA-FM (90.5 MHZ)
Primera Iglesia Bautista de Carolina
P.O. Box 188
Carolina, PR 00986
Federico Iglesias, General Manager
Tel: (787) 757-1773 Fax: (787) 769-4103
Email: radiovida@cadenaradiovida.com
Web: www.cadenaradiovida.com

WABA-AM (850 KHZ)
Aguadilla Radio & TV Corporation
P.O.Box 188
Aguadilla, PR 00605
Rosa Pellot, General Manager
Tel: (787) 882-0320 Fax: (787) 882-2282
Email: wabaradio@hotmail.com
Web: www.waba850.com

WAEL-AM (600 KHZ)
WAEL, Inc.
P.O. Box 1370
Mayaguez, PR 00681
Luis Pirallo, Program Director
Tel: (787) 832-0600 Fax: (787) 792-3140
Email: pd@waelfm96.com
Web: www.waelfm96.com

WAEL-FM (96.1 MHZ)
WAEL, Inc.
P.O. Box 1370
Mayaguez, PR 00681
Luis Pirallo, Program Director
Tel: (787) 832-0600 Fax: (787) 792-3140
Email: pd@waelfm96.com
Web: www.waelfm96.com

WALO-AM (1240 KHZ)
Ochoa Broadcasting Corporation
P.O. Box 9230
Humacao, PR 00792
Efrain Archilla-Roig, General Manager
Tel: (787) 852-1240 Fax: (787) 852-1280
Email: wlo@prtc.net

WBMJ-AM (1190 KHZ)
Calvary Evangelistic Mission, Inc.
P.O. Box 367000
San Juan, PR 00936-7000
Janet Luttrell, VP
Tel: (787) 724-1190 Fax: (787) 723-9633
Email: radio@therockradio.org
Web: www.therockradio.org

WBQN-AM (1160 KHZ)
WBQN Radio Borinquen, Inc.
P.O. Box 1625
Manati, PR 00674
Luis R. Rivera Caban, Manager
Tel: (787) 854-2450 Fax: (787) 854-3738
Email: wbqn@iturf.com

WBRQ-FM (97.7 MHZ)
New Life Broadcasting
P.O. Box 6715
Caguas, PR 00726
Orlando Mercado, General Manager
Tel: (787) 745-9700 Fax: (787) 745-9777
Email: nuevavida@nuevavidafm.com
Web: www.nuevavidafm.com

WCGB-AM (1060 KHZ)
Calvery Evangelistic Mission
P.O. Box 1414
Juana Díaz, PR 00795
Lawrence Trumbower, General Manager
Tel: (787) 837-1060 Fax: (787) 260-1060
Email: wcgbam@prtc.net
Web: www.therockradio.com

WCMA-FM (96.5 MHZ)
Spanish Broadcasting System of Puerto Rico, Inc.
Frances St. Lot 42 Amelia Industrial Park
P.O. Box 949
Guaynabo, PR 00968-0949
Sixto Pabon, General Manager
Tel: (787) 622-9700 Fax: (787) 622-9477

WCMN-AM (1500 KHZ)
P.O. Box 436
Arecibo, PR 00613
Byron Mitchell, General Manager
Tel: (787) 878-0070 Fax: (787) 880-1112
Email: wcmn@xsn.net

WCMN-AM (1280 KHZ)
Uno Radio Group
P.O. Box 100
Yabucoa, PR 00767
Maria Mitchell, General Manager
Tel: (787) 896-3065 Fax: (787) 850-4055
Email: wcmn@xsn.net
Web: www.notiuno.com

WCMN-FM (107.3 MHZ)
Caribbean Broadcasting Corporation
P.O. Box 436
Arecibo, PR 00613
Byron Mitchell, General Manager
Tel: (787) 878-0070 Fax: (787) 880-1112
Email: wcmn@xsn.net

WCRP-FM (88.1 MHZ)
Radio Revelacion
P.O. Box 344
Guayama, PR 00785-9905
Carmen Rivera, General Manager
Tel: (787) 864-3658 Fax: (787) 864-6780
Email: revelacion@rpc.net
Web: www.radiorevelacion.com

WDGT-FM (97.3)
Arzuaga Radio Group
P.O. Box 1553
Quebradillas, PR 00678
José J. Arzuaga, Owner
Tel: (787) 895-0000 Fax: (787) 895-4198
Email: magic973@prtc.net

WEGM-FM (95.1 MHZ)
Spanish Broadcasting System of Puerto Rico, Inc.
Frances St. Lot 42 Amelia Industrial Park
P.O. Box 949
Guaynabo, PR 00968-0949
Sixto Pabon, General Manager
Tel: (787) 622-9700
Fax: (787) 622-9477/78
Web: www.spanishbroadcasting.com

WEXS-AM (610 KHZ)
Community Broadcasting
P.O. Box 640
Patillas, PR 00723
Enrique García Cruz, General Manager
Tel: (787) 839-0610 Fax: (787) 839-0960

WFID-FM (95.7 MHZ)
Uno Radio Group
P.O. Box 363222
San Juan, PR 00926-3222
Luis A. Soto, President
Tel: (787) 744-3131 Fax: (787) 767-9343
Email: lsoto@unoradio.com
Web: www.unoradio.com

WGDL-AM (1200 KHZ)
Lares Broadcasting Corporation
P.O. Box 872
Lares, PR 00669
Pedro Hernández, General Manager
Tel: (787) 897-3889 Fax: (787) 897-7821

WHOY-AM (1210 KHZ)
Colón Radio Corporation
P.O. Box 1148
Salinas, PR 00751
Martín Colón, General Manager
Tel: (787) 824-3420 Fax: (787) 824-3420

WIAC-FM (102.5 MHZ)
Bestov Broadcast Group
P.O. Box 9023916
Bayamon, PR 00902-3916
Luis Mejia, General Manager
Tel: (787) 798-7878 Fax: (787) 798-9613
Email: info@sistema102.com
Web: www.sistema102.com

WIAC-AM (740 KHZ)
Bestov Broadcasting, Inc.
P.O. Box 9023916
San Juan, PR 00902-3916
Luis Mejia, General Manager
Tel: (787) 798-7878 Fax: (787) 798-9613

WIAC-FM (102.5 MHZ)
Cadena Radio
P.O. Box 9023916
San Juan, PR 00902-3916
Alan Mejia, General Manager
Tel: (787) 620-9898 Fax: (787) 620-0720
Web: www.sistema102.com

WIBS-AM (1540 KHZ)
International Broadcasting Corporation
Bori 1554
San Juan, PR 00927-6113
Pedro Roman Collazo, President
Tel: (787) 274-1800 Fax: (787) 281-9758

WIDI-FM (98.3 MHZ)
Arzuaga Radio Group
P.O. Box 1553
Quebradillas, PR 00678
José J. Arzuaga, Owner
Tel: (787) 895-0000 Fax: (787) 895-4198
Email: magic973@prtc.net

WIOA-FM (99.9 MHZ)
Spanish Broadcasting System of Puerto Rico, Inc.
Frances St. Lot 42 Amelia Industrial Park
P.O. Box 949
Guaynabo, PR 00968-0949
Ismael Nieves, General Manager
Tel: (787) 622-9700
Fax: (787) 622-9477/78
Web: www.spanishbroadcasting.com

WIOB-FM (97.5 MHZ)
Spanish Broadcasting System of Puerto Rico, Inc.
Frances St. Lot 42 Amelia Industrial Park
P.O. Box 949
Guaynabo, PR 00968-0949
Sixto Pabon, General Manager
Tel: (787) 622-9700
Fax: (787) 622-9477/78
Web: www.spanishbroadcasting.com

WIOC-FM (105.1 MHZ)
Spanish Broadcasting System of Puerto Rico, Inc.
Frances St. Lot 42 Amelia Industrial Park
P.O. Box 949
Guaynabo, PR 00968-0949
Sixto Pabon, General Manager
Tel: (787) 622-9700
Fax: (787) 622-9477/78
Web: www.spanishbroadcasting.com

WISA-AM (1390 KHZ)
Isabela Broadcasting, Inc.
P.O. Box 750
Isabela, PR 00662

David Mercado, General Manager
Tel: (787) 872-2030 Fax: (787) 872-0802

WIVA-FM (100.3 MHZ)
Uno Radio Group
P.O. Box 7213
Ponce, PR 00732-7213
Luis A. Soto, President
Tel: (787) 744-3131 Fax: (787) 743-0252
Email: lsoto@unoradio.com
Web: www.unoradio.com

WIVV-AM (1370 KHZ)
Calvary Evangelistic Mission, Inc.
P.O. Box 367000
San Juan, PR 00936-7000
Janet Luttrell, General Manager
Tel: (787) 724-1190 Fax: (787) 741-8717
Email: radio@therockradio.org
Web: www.therockradio.org

WKAQ-AM (580 KHZ)
Hispanic Broadcasting Corporation
P.O. Box 364668
San Juan, PR 00936
Huberto Biaggi, General Manager
Tel: (787) 758-5000 Fax: (787) 756-5220
Email: wkaq580@yahoo.com
Web: www.hispanicbroadcasting.com

WKAQ-FM (104.7 MHZ)
Hispanic Broadcasting Corporation
P.O. Box 364668
San Juan, PR 00936
Huberto Biaggi, General Manager
Tel: (787) 758-5800 Fax: (787) 763-1854
Web: www.hispanicbroadcasting.com

WKFE-AM (1550 KHZ)
Media Power Group
P.O. Box 260
Yauco, PR 00698
Joe Pagan, General Manager
Tel: (787) 856-1320 Fax: (787) 856-4420

WKJB-AM (710 KHZ)
Empresas Bechara
P.O. Box 1293
Mayaguez, PR 00681
Jose A. Bechara, President
Tel: (787) 834-6666 Fax: (787) 831-6925
Email: wkjb_wpra@yahoo.com

WKSA-FM (101.5 MHZ)
Bestov Broadcasting, Inc.
P.O. Box 750
Isabela, PR 00662
David Mercado Nieves, General Manager
Tel: (787) 872-2030 Fax: (787) 721-0733

WKVM-AM (810 KHZ)
Arquidiocesis de San Juan
Calle Carbonell, #415
Hato Rey, PR 00918
Alberto Perez Negroni, General Manager
Tel: (787) 751-1018 Fax: (787) 758-9967

WLEO-AM (1490 KHZ)
Uno Radio Group
P.O. Box 487
Caguas, PR 00726-0487
Jesus Soto, President
Tel: (787) 744-3131 Fax: (787) 743-0252
Email: lsoto@unoradio.com
Web: www.unoradio.com

WLRP-AM (1460 KHZ)
Las Raices Pepinianas
P.O. Box 1670
San Sebastian, PR 00685
Alfredo Pérez, General Manager
Tel: (787) 896-1460 Fax: (787) 896-8100

WLUZ-AM (1600 KHZ)
Marketing Promotion Network
P.O. Box 9394
San Juan, PR 00908
Tony Trelles, President
Tel: (787) 785-1600 Fax: (787) 785-2094

WMDD-AM (1480 KHZ)
Pan Caribbean Broadcasting Corporation
P.O. Box 948
Fajardo, PR 00738
Angel L. Vazquez, Program Director
Tel: (787) 863-0202 Fax: (787) 863-0166

WMEG-FM (106.9 MHZ)
Spanish Broadcasting System of Puerto Rico, Inc.
Frances St. Lot 42 Amelia Industrial Park
P.O. Box 949
Guaynabo, PR 00968-0949
Sixto Pabon, General Manager
Tel: (787) 622-9700
Fax: (787) 622-9477/78
Web: www.spanishbroadcasting.com

WMIA-AM (1070 KHZ)
Abacoa Radio Corporation
P.O. Box 1055
Arecibo, PR 00613-1055
Epifanio Rodríguez Velez, General Manager
Tel: (787) 878-1275

WMSW-AM (1120 KHZ)
Aurora Broadcasting Corporation
P.O. Box 140961
Arecibo, PR 00614
Archie Velez, General Manager
Tel: (787) 879-4094 Fax: (787) 880-0441
Email: radioonce@hotmail.com

WMTI-AM (1580 KHZ)
International Broadcasting Corporation
Bori 1554
San Juan, PR 00927-6113
Pedro Roman Collazo, President
Tel: (787) 274-1800 Fax: (787) 281-9758

WNIK-AM (1230 KHZ)
Kelly Broadcasting System Corporation
P.O. Box 556
Arecibo, PR 00613
Raúl Santiago, General Manager
Tel: (787) 880-2607 Fax: (787) 879-1011
Email: superk1065@hotmail.com

WNIK-FM (106.5 MHZ)
Kelly Broadcasting System Corporation
P.O. Box 556
Arecibo, PR 00613
Raúl Santiago, General Manager
Tel: (787) 880-2607 Fax: (787) 879-1011

WNNV-FM (91.7 MHZ)
West Coast Broadcasting
P.O. Box 847
Mayaguez, PR 00681
Aureo Matos, President
Tel: (787) 833-7100 Fax: (787) 833-7940

WNOD-FM (94.1 MHZ)
Spanish Broadcasting System of Puerto Rico, Inc.
Frances St. Lot 42 Amelia Industrial Park
P.O. Box 949
Guaynabo, PR 00968-0949
Sixto Pabon, General Manager
Tel: (787) 622-9700
Fax: (787) 622-9477/78
Web: www.spanishbroadcasting.com

WNOZ-AM (1340 KHZ)
Caribbean Broadcasting Corporation
Barrio Palmer
Aguadilla, PR 00605

Luis Ortiz, General Manager
Tel: (787) 826-8072 Fax: (787) 872-1040
Web: www.notiuno.com

WNRT-FM (96.9 MHZ)
Iglesia de Dios Pentecostal
P.O. Box 13324
Santurce, PR 00907
Moisés Flores, General Manager
Tel: (787) 758-8562 Fax: (787) 758-8833
Web: www.radiotriunfo.com

WODA-FM (94.7 MHZ)
Spanish Broadcasting System of Puerto Rico, Inc.
Frances St. Lot 42 Amelia Industrial Park
P.O. Box 949
Guaynabo, PR 00968-0949
Sixto Pabon, General Manager
Tel: (787) 622-9700
Fax: (787) 622-9477/78
Web: www.onda94.com

WOHA-AM (1080 KHZ)
Uno Radio Group
P.O. Box 487
Caguas, PR 00726-0487
Luis A. Soto, President
Tel: (787) 744-3131 Fax: (787) 743-0252
Email: lsoto@unoradio.com
Web: www.unoradio.com

WOIZ-AM (1130 KHZ)
Radio Antillas
P.O. Box 561130
Guayanilla, PR 00656
Luis Adán Rodríguez, General Manager
Tel: (787) 835-3130 Fax: (787) 835-3130
Email: radioantillas@yahoo.com

WORO-FM (92.5 MHZ)
Arquidiocesis de San Juan
Calle Carbonell, #415
P.O. Box 9021967
San Juan, PR 00902-1967
Alberto Perez- Negroni, General Manager
Tel: (787) 751-1380 Fax: (787) 758-9967
Email: radiooro@arquidiocesisdesanjuan.org

WOSO-AM (1030 KHZ)
Sherman Broadcasting
P.O. Box 9023940
San Juan, PR 00902-3940
Sergio Fernández, General Manager
Tel: (787) 724-4242 Fax: (787) 723-9676
Email: info@woso.com
Web: www.woso.com

WOYE-FM (94.1)
Spanish Broadcasting System
P.O. Box 1718
Mayaguez, PR 00681
Raul Alarcon, President
Tel: (787) 834-1094 Fax: (787) 295-4090

WPAB-AM (550 KHZ)
P.O. Box 7243
Ponce, PR 00732-7243
Jose Elias Torres, Program Director
Tel: (787) 840-5550 Fax: (787) 842-7174
Email: noticias@wpabradio.com
Web: www.wpabradio.com

WPPC-AM (1570 KHZ)
P.O. Box 9064
Ponce, PR 00732
Carlos Morales, General Manager
Tel: (787) 836-1570 Fax: (787) 840-7105
Email: radiofelicidad@yahoo.com
Web: www.radiofelicidad.org

WPRA-AM (990 KHZ)
Empresas Bechara
P.O. Box 1293
Mayaguez, PR 00681
Jose A. Bechara, President
Tel: (787) 834-6666 Fax: (787) 831-0925
Email: wkjb_wpra@yahoo.com

WPRM-FM (98.5 MHZ)
Uno Radio Group
P.O. Box 487
Caguas, PR 00726-0487
Luis A. Soto, President
Tel: (787) 744-3131 Fax: (787) 743-0252
Email: lsoto@unoradio.com
Web: www.salsoul.com

WPRP-AM (910 KHZ)
Radio Kadena Informativa, Inc.
P.O. Box 7771
Ponce, PR 00732
Carlos Morales, General Manager
Tel: (787) 844-0910 Fax: (787) 843-9770

WPRP-AM (910 KHZ)
Radio Kadena Informativa, Inc.
P.O. Box 7771
Ponce, PR 00732
Normando Valentin, Program Director
Tel: (787) 844-0910 Fax: (787) 843-9770

WQBS-AM (870 KHZ)
Aerco Broadcasting Corporation
Calle Bori 1508, Urb. Antonsanti
San Juan, PR 00927
Angel Romandez, General Manager
Tel: (787) 756-8700 Fax: (787) 765-2965
Web: www.aercobroadcasting.com

WQQZ-FM (88.7 MHZ)
Arzuaga Radio Group
P.O. Box 1553
Quebradillas, PR 00678
José J. Arzuaga, Owner
Tel: (787) 895-0000 Fax: (787) 895-4198
Email: sonorama@isla.net

WRIO-FM (101.1 MHZ)
Uno Radio Group
P.O. Box 7213
Ponce, PR 00732-7213
Luis A. Soto, President
Tel: (787) 284-8101 Fax: (787) 841-5184
Email: lsoto@unoradio.com
Web: www.salsoul.com

WRSS-AM (1410 MHZ)
Radio Progreso
P.O. Box 1410
San Sebastian, PR 00685
Cesar Vera, General Manager
Tel: (787) 896-2121 Fax: (787) 896-5753
Email: caribe@prpc.net
Web: www.prpc.net

WRTU-FM (89.7 MHZ)
Radio Universidad de Puerto Rico
P.O. Box 21305 University Station
San Juan, PR 00931-1305
Laura Candelas, General Manager
Tel: (787) 763-4699 Fax: (787) 763-5205
Email: lcandelas@wrtu.org
Web: www.wrtu.org

WTIL-AM (1300 KHZ)
Bestov Broadcast Group
P.O. Box 489
Mayaguez, PR 00681
Francisco Acosta, General Manager
Tel: (787) 834-1290 Fax: (787) 834-9845
Email: wtil@prtc.com

WTPM-FM (92.9 MHZ)
Asociacion Adventista del Septimo Día del Oeste
P.O. Box 1629
Mayaguez, PR 00681
Pastor Daniel A. Ponce, General Manager
Tel: (787) 831-9200 Fax: (787) 831-9292
Email: wtpm@eleden.net
Web: www.wtpm.org

WUKQ-AM (1420 KHZ)
Hispanic Broadcasting Corporation
P.O. Box 364668
San Juan, PR 00936
Huberto Biaggi, General Manager
Tel: (787) 758-5800 Fax: (787) 763-1854
Web: www.hispanicbroadcasting.com

WUKQ-FM (99.1 MHZ)
Hispanic Broadcasting Corporation
P.O. Box 364668
San Juan, PR 00936
Huberto Biaggi, General Manager
Tel: (787) 758-5800 Fax: (787) 763-1854
Web: www.hispanicbroadcasting.com

WUNO-AM (630 KHZ)
Uno Radio Group
P.O. Box 363222
San Juan, PR 00936-3222
Luis Gonzales, General Manager
Tel: (787) 758-1300 Fax: (787) 765-8557
Email: lsoto@unoradio.com
Web: www.notiuno.com

WUPR-AM (1530 KHZ)
Central Broadcasting, Inc.
P.O. Box 868
Utuado, PR 00641
José Martínez Giraud, General Manager
Tel: (787) 894-2460 Fax: (787) 894-4955
Email: wupr@coqui.net

WVOZ-AM (1520 KHZ)
International Broadcasting Corporation
Bori 1554
San Juan, PR 00927-6113
Pedro Roman Collazo, President
Tel: (787) 274-1800 Fax: (787) 281-9758

WVOZ-FM (107.7 MHZ)
International Broadcasting Corporation
Bori 1554
San Juan, PR 00927-6113
Pedro Roman Collazo, President
Tel: (787) 274-1800 Fax: (787) 281-9758

WXEW-AM (840 KHZ)
Caribbean Broadcasting Corporation
P.O. Box 6
Manati, PR 00674
Víctor Calderón, General Manager
Tel: (787) 850-0840 Fax: (787) 893-3065
Email: info@victoria.com
Web: www.radiovictoria.com

WZAR-FM (101.9 MHZ)
Uno Radio Group
P.O. Box 7213
Ponce, PR 00732-7213
Luis A. Soto, President
Tel: (787) 744-3131 Fax: (787) 743-0252
Email: lsoto@unoradio.com
Web: www.unoradio.com

WZET-FM (92.1 MHZ)
Spanish Broadcasting System of Puerto Rico, Inc.
Frances St. Lot 42 Amelia Industrial Park
P.O. Box 949
Guaynabo, PR 00968-0949

Sixto Pabon, General Manager
Tel: (787) 622-9700
Fax: (787) 622-9477/78
Web: www.spanishbroadcasting.com

WZMT-FM (93.3 MHZ)
Spanish Broadcasting System of Puerto Rico, Inc.
Frances St. Lot 42 Amelia Industrial Park
P.O. Box 949
Guaynabo, PR 00968-0949
Sixto Pabon, General Manager
Tel: (787) 622-9700
Fax: (787) 622-9477/78
Web: www.spanishbroadcasting.com

WZNT-FM (93.7 MHZ)
Spanish Broadcasting System of Puerto Rico, Inc.
Frances St. Lot 42 Amelia Industrial Park
P.O. Box 949
Guaynabo, PR 00968-0949
Sixto Pabon, General Manager
Tel: (787) 622-9700
Fax: (787) 622-9477/78
Web: www.spanishbroadcasting.com

WZUR-AM (1170 KHZ)
Uno Radio Group
P.O. Boc 487
Caguas, PR 00726-0487
Luis A. Soto, President
Tel: (787) 744-3131 Fax: (787) 743-0252
Email: lsoto@unoradio.com
Web: www.unoradio.com

RHODE ISLAND

WRIB-AM (1220 KHZ)
La Inconfundible
200 Water St.
East Providence, RI 02914
John Pierce, General Manager
Tel: (401) 434-0406 Fax: (401) 434-0409
Email: hasalsa9@aol.com

TEXAS

KAMA-AM (750 KHZ)
Univision Communications, Inc.
2211 E. Missouri Ave. #S-300
El Paso, TX 79903
Domingo Lopez, General Manager
Tel: (915) 544-9797 Fax: (915) 544-1247
Email: dlopez@univision.com
Web: www.univision.com

KAMV-AM (107.7 MHZ)
Univision Communications, Inc.
10801-2 Mopac Expresway #110 & 250
Austin, TX 78759
Tim McCoy, General Manager
Tel: (512) 419-1077 Fax: (512) 419-9328
Email: timmccoy@univisionradio.com
Web: www.univision.com

KANM-AM (1690 KHZ)
Texas A&M University
1236 TAMU
College Station, TX 77843-1236
Curtis Riddle, Program Director
Tel: (979) 862-2516 Fax: (979) 847-8854
Email: pd@kanm.tamu.edu
Web: http://kanm.tamu.edu

KBDR-FM (100.5 MHZ)
Sendero Multimedia
1 S. Main Ave.
Laredo, TX 78040

Steve Stevenson, General Manager
Tel: (956) 725-1000 Fax: (956) 686-8415
Web: www.lamonline.com

KBFM-FM (104.1 MHZ)
Clear Channel Communications, Inc.
901 E. Pike St.
Weslaco, TX 78596
Tim Thomas, General Manager
Tel: (956) 973-9202 Fax: (956) 973-9355
Email: timthomas@clearchannel.com
Web: www.clearchannel.com, www.b104.net

KBIC-FM (105.7 MHZ)
Christian Ministiies
P.O. Box 1290
Weslaco, TX 78599
Enrique Garza, General Manager
Tel: (956) 968-7777 Fax: (956) 968-5143
Email: egarza@radiovida.com
Web: www.radiovida.com

KBIV-AM (1650 KHZ)
Entravision Communications Corporation
5426 N. Mesa St.
El Paso, TX 79912
David Candelaria, General Manager
Tel: (915) 581-1126 Fax: (915) 585-4613
Email: Dcandelaria@entravision.com
Web: www.entravision.com

KBNA-FM (97.5 MHZ)
Univision Communications, Inc.
2211 E. Missouri Ave. #S-300
El Paso, TX 79903
Domingo Lopez, General Manager
Tel: (915) 544-9797 Fax: (915) 544-1247
Email: dlopez@univision.com
Web: www.univision.com

KBNL-FM (89.9 MHZ)
World Radio Network
P.O. Box 2425
Laredo, TX 78044
Arthuro Lozano, General Manager
Tel: (956) 724-9090 Fax: (956) 724-9919
Email: kbnl@hcjb.org
Web: www.hcjb.org

KBNR-FM (88.3 MHZ)
Radio Cadena Manantial
P.O. Box 5480
Brownsville, TX 78523-5480
Moisés Flores, General Manager
Tel: (956) 542-6933 Fax: (956) 542-0523
Email: kbnrfm88@aol.com
Web: www.radiokbnr.org

KBOR-AM (1600 KHZ)
La Nueva KBOR, Inc.
1050 McIntosh Dr.
Brownsville, TX 78521
Edgar Treviño, General Manager
Tel: (956) 544-1600 Fax: (956) 544-6106
Email: kborbuendia@aol.com

KBZO-AM (1460 KHZ)
Entravision Communications Corporation
1220 Broadway #500
Lubbock, TX 79401
Jose Sauceda, General Manager
Tel: (806) 763-6051 Fax: (806) 744-8363
Web: www.entravision.com

KCOM-AM (1550 KHZ)
Texas West Media
105 N. Sand
P.O. Box 9
Comanche, TX 76442
Bill Cole, General Manager
Tel: (915) 356-2558 Fax: (915) 356-5757
Email: kcom@comanchetx.com

KCOR-FM (95.1 MHZ)
Univision Communications, Inc.
1777 NE Loop 410 #400
San Antonio, TX 78217
Dan Wilson, General Manager
Tel: (210) 821-6548 Fax: (210) 804-7820
Email: dwilson@univision.com
Web: www.univision.com

KCZO-FM (92.1 MHZ)
Paulino Bernal Evangelism, Inc.
P.O. Box 252
McAllen, TX 78505
Paulino Bernal, General Manager
Tel: (956) 781-5528 Fax: (956) 686-2999

KDHN-AM (1470 KHZ)
704 W. Cleveland St.
Dimmitt, TX 79027
Wayne Collins, Program Director
Tel: (806) 647-4161 Fax: (806) 647-4715

KEDA-AM (1540 KHZ)
D & E Broadcasting Company
510 S. Flores St.
San Antonio, TX 78204
Alberto Dávila, General Manager
Tel: (210) 226-5254 Fax: (210) 227-7937
Email: kedakid@aol.com

KEDT-FM (90.3 MHZ)
South Texas Public Broadcasting Systems, Inc.
4455 S. Padre Island Dr. #38
Corpus Christi, TX 78411-4481
Stuart Jacoby, Program Director
Tel: (361) 855--2213 Fax: (361) 855-3877
Email: stewartjacoby@kedt.org
Web: www.kedt.org

KEDT-FM (90.7 MHZ)
South Texas Public Broadcasting Systems, Inc.
4455 S. Padre Island Dr. #38
Corpus Christi, TX 78411-4481
Stewart Jacoby, Program Director
Tel: (361) 855-2213 Fax: (361) 855-3877
Email: stewartjacoby@kedt.org
Web: www.kedt.org

KEJS-FM (106.5 MHZ)
Barton Company
1607 13th St.
Lubbock, TX 79401
Ernesto Barton, General Manager
Tel: (806) 747-5951 Fax: (806) 747-3524
Email: gesparza@kejsfm.com

KELG-AM (1440 KHZ)
Garcia Communications
7524 N. Lamar Blvd. #200
Austin, TX 78752
Joe José García, General Manager
Tel: (512) 453-1491 Fax: (512) 458-0700
Email: kelg@austinteias.com
Web: www.kelg.com

KELP-AM (1590 KHZ)
6900 Commerce Ave.
El Paso, TX 79915
Arnie McClatchey, General Manager
Tel: (915) 779-0016 Fax: (915) 779-6641
Email: info@kelpradio.com
Web: www.kelpradio.com

KEPS-AM (1270 KHZ)
Eagle Radio Network
127 Kilowat Dr.
P.O. Box 1123
Eagle Pass, TX 78853

Rosa T. de la Garza, General Manager
Tel: (830) 773-9246 Fax: (830) 773-9500

KEPX-FM (89.5 MHZ)
World Radio Network
P.O. Box 873
Eagle Pass, TX 78853
Amado Rodriguez, General Manager
Tel: (830) 757-0895 Fax: (830) 757-8950
Email: kepx@hcjb.org

KERB-AM (600 KHZ)
Paulino Bernal Evangelism, Inc.
P.O. Box 252
McAllen, TX 78505
Paulino Bernal, General Manager
Tel: (956) 781-5528 Fax: (956) 686-2999

KERB-FM (106.3 MHZ)
Paulino Bernal Evangelism, Inc.
P.O. Box 252
McAllen, TX 78505
Paulino Bernal, General Manager
Tel: (956) 781-5528 Fax: (956) 686-2999

KESS-FM (107.9 MHZ)
Univision Communications, Inc.
7700 John Carpenter Frwy.
Dallas, TX 75247
Frank Carter, General Manager
Tel: (214) 525-0400 Fax: (214) 631-1196
Email: fcarter@univision.com
Web: www.univision.com

KEYH-AM (850 KHZ)
Liberman Broadcasting
11767 Katy Fwy #1170
Houston, TX 77056
Winter Horton, General Manager
Tel: (281) 493-2900 Fax: (281) 596-9608

KFIT-AM (1060 KHZ)
Martin Broadcasters
P.O. Box 160158
Austin, TX 78716-0158
Terri Lewis, General Manager
Tel: (512) 328-8400 Fax: (512) 328-8437
Email: kfit@texas.net
Web: www.kfitam.com

KFRQ-FM (94.5 MHZ)
Entravision Communications Corporation
801 Jackson Rd.
McAllen, TX 78501
Larry Safir, General Manager
Tel: (956) 661-6000 Fax: (956) 661-6082
Email: lsafir@entravision.com
Web: www.kkps.com, www.entravision.com

KGBT-AM (1530 KHZ)
Univision Communications, Inc.
200 S. 10th St. #600
McAllen, TX 78501
Jose Morales, General Manager
Tel: (956) 631-5499 Fax: (956) 631-0090
Web: www.univision.com

KGBT-FM (98.5 MHZ)
Univision Communications, Inc.
200 S. 10th St. #600
McAllen, TX 78501
Joe Morales, General Manager
Tel: (956) 631-5499 Fax: (956) 631-0090
Email: jmorales@univision.com
Web: www.univision.com

KGOL-AM (1180 KHZ)
Entravision Communications Corporation
5821 SW Fwy. #600
Houston, TX 77057
Carmen Aguilar, General Manager
Tel: (713) 349-9880 Fax: (713) 349-0647
Web: www.entravision.com

KGRW-FM (94.7 MHZ)
Rodriguez Communications
3639 Wolfin Ave.
Amarillo, TX 79102
Israel Salazar, General Manager
Tel: (806) 355-1044 Fax: (806) 352-6525
Email: bsalazar@rodcom.com
Web: www.rodcom.com

KHER-FM (94.3 MHZ)
P.O. Box 707
Carrizo Springs, TX 78834
Sylpia Mijarez, General Manager
Tel: (830) 374-5730 Fax: (830) 374-9658

KHHL-FM (98.9 MHZ)
Amigo Broadcasting
2211 S. IH 35 #401
Austin, TX 78741
Rudy Ramos, Coordinator
Tel: (512) 416-1100 Fax: (512) 416-8205
Web: www.bmpradio.com

KHMC-FM (95.9 MHZ)
114 Jason Circle
Victoria, TX 77901
Homer Lopez, General Manager
Tel: (361) 575-9533 Fax: (361) 575-9502
Email: info@majic95.com
Web: www.majic95.com

KHOS-AM (980 KHZ)
P.O. Box 523
Merkel, TX 79536
Zacarias Serrato, General Manager
Tel: (915) 928-3060 Fax: (915) 928-4683

KHOY-FM (88.1 MHZ)
Catholic Telecommunications Center
1901 Corpus Christi
Laredo, TX 78040
Benett McBride, General Manager
Tel: (956) 722-4167 Fax: (956) 722-4467
Email: khoy@khoy.org
Web: www.khoy.org

KHRO-FM (94.7 MHZ)
Entravision Communications Corporation
5426 N. Mesa St.
El Paso, TX 79912
David Candelaria, General Manager
Tel: (915) 581-1126 Fax: (915) 585-4613
Email: Dcandelaria@entravision.com
Web: www.entravision.com

KILM-FM (102.1 MHZ)
BMP Radio
One Paseo Del Prado, Bldg. 102
Edinburg, TX 78539
Rudy Ramos, Coordinator
Tel: (956) 686-8170 Fax: (956) 686-8470
Email: info@bmpradio.com
Web: www.bmpradio.com

KIMP-AM (960 KHZ)
East Texas Broadcasting
P.O. Box 990
Mount Pleasant, TX 75456
Bud Kitchen, General Manager
Tel: (903) 572-8726 Fax: (903) 572-7232
Web: www.easttexasradio.com

KINE-AM (1330 KHZ)
P.O. Box 270547
Corpus Christi, TX 78427
Carlos López, General Manager
Tel: (361) 289-8877 Fax: (361) 389-7722

KINL-FM (92.7 MHZ)
Eagle Radio Network
127 Kilowat Dr.
P.O. Box 1123
Eagle Pass, TX 78853

Rosa T. de la Garza, General Manager
Tel: (830) 773-9246 Fax: (830) 773-9500
Email: Kinlkepf@wcsonline.com

KINT-FM (93.9 MHZ)
Entravision Communications Corporation
5426 N. Mesa St.
El Paso, TX 79912
David Candelaria, General Manager
Tel: (915) 581-1126 Fax: (915) 585-4613
Email: Dcandelaria@entravision.com
Web: www.entravision.com

KIRT-AM (1580 KHZ)
Bravo Broadcasting Co.
608 S. 10th St.
McAllen, TX 78501
Humberto Pedraza, General Manager
Tel: (956) 686-2111 Fax: (956) 668-0370
Email: kirtradio@aol.com

KJAV-FM (104.9 MHZ)
Paulino Bernal Evangelism, Inc.
P.O. Box 252
McAllen, TX 78505
Paulino Bernal, General Manager
Tel: (956) 781-5528 Fax: (956) 686-2999

KJBZ-FM (98.1 MHZ)
Guerra Enterprises
902 E. Calton Rd.
Laredo, TX 78041
Belinda Guerra, General Manager
Tel: (956) 726-9393 Fax: (956) 724-9915
Web: www.kjbz93.com

KJOJ-AM (880 KHZ)
Liberman Broadcasting
11767 Katy Fwy #1170
Houston, TX 77056
Winter Horton, General Manager
Tel: (281) 493-2900 Fax: (281) 596-9608

KJOJ-FM (103.3 MHZ)
Liberman Broadcasting
11767 Katy Fwy #1170
Houston, TX 77056
Winter Horton, General Manager
Tel: (281) 493-2900 Fax: (281) 596-9608

KKDL-FM (106.7 MHZ)
Entravision Communications Corporation
5307 E. Mockingbird Ln. #500
Dallas, TX 75206
Scott Savage, General Manager
Tel: (214) 887-9107 Fax: (214) 841-4215
Web: www.entravision.com

KKHR-FM (106.3 MHZ)
Powell Meredith Communications
402 Cypress St. #709
Abilene, TX 79601
Ben Gonzalez, Program Director
Tel: (325) 695-9898 Fax: (325) 695-9968
Email: star106@camalott.com
Web: www.star106.com

KKLB-FM (92.5 MHZ)
Garcia Broadcasting
7524 N. Lamar Blvd. #200
Austin, TX 78752
Joe José García, General Manager
Tel: (512) 453-1491 Fax: (512) 458-0700
Email: jjgarcia@kklb.com
Web: www.kklb.com

KKPS-FM (99.5 MHZ)
Entravision Communications Corporation
801 Jackson Rd.
McAllen, TX 78501
Larry Safir, General Manager
Tel: (956) 661-6000 Fax: (956) 661-6082

Email: lsafir@entravision.com
Web: www.kkps.com, www.entravision.com

KKUB-AM (1300 KHZ)
Brownfield Broadcasting, LLP.
Dios Llega al Hombre Ministries
1722 Tahoka Rd.
Brownfield, TX 79316
C. Torres, Program Director
Tel: (806) 637-4531 Fax: (806) 637-4610

KKYN-FM (106.9 MHZ)
Equicom Radio, Inc.
3218 N. Quincy St.
P.O. Box 1420
Plainview, TX 79073
Tom Hall, Operations Manager
Tel: (806) 296-2771 Fax: (806) 293-5732
Email: Jerrylarsen2000@hotmail.com
Web: www.kkyn.net

KLAR-AM (1300 KHZ)
P.O. Box 2517
Laredo, TX 78044
Héctor Patiño, General Manager
Tel: (956) 723-1300 Fax: (956) 723-9539

KLAT-AM (1010 KHZ)
Univision Communications, Inc.
1415 N. Loop W. 610 North
Houston, TX 77008
Mark Masepohl, General Manager
Tel: (713) 407-1415 Fax: (713) 407-1400
Email: mmasepohl@univision.com
Web: www.univision.com

KLEY-FM (94.1 KHZ)
Spanish Broadcasting System
7800 IH-10 W. #330
San Antonio, TX 78230
Peggy McCormick, General Manager
Tel: (210) 340-1234 Fax: (210) 366-1680
Email: pmccormick@sbssanantonio.com
Web: www.spanishbroadcasting.com

KLFB-AM (1420 KHZ)
Ballard Broadcasting Co.
2700 Marshall St.
Lubbock, TX 79415
Shirley Ballard, General Manager
Tel: (806) 765-8114 Fax: (806) 763-0428
Email: dj1040@webtv.net

KLHB-FM (98.3 FM)
Amigo Broadcasting
1300 Antelope St.
Corpus Christi, TX 78401
Eddi Alonso, General Manager
Tel: (361) 883-9830 Fax: (361) 888-5685

KLNO-FM (94.1 MHZ)
Univision Communications, Inc.
7700 John Carpenter Frwy.
Dallas, TX 75247
Frank Carter, General Manager
Tel: (214) 525-0400 Fax: (214) 631-1196
Email: fcarter@hunivision.com
Web: www.univision.com

KLSR-FM (105.3 MHZ)
Davis Broadcast Co., Inc.
P.O. Box 400
Memphis, TX 79245
Fernando Garcia, Spanish Program Director
Tel: (806) 259-3511 Fax: (806) 259-2397

KLTN-FM (102.9 FM)
Univision Communications, Inc.
1415 N. Loop W. #610 North
Houston, TX 77008
Mark Masepohl, General Manager
Tel: (713) 407-1415 Fax: (713) 407-1400

Email: mmasepohl@univision.com
Web: www.univision.com

KMIL-AM (1330 KHZ)
Malam Broadcasting Company
901 E. First St.
P.O. Box 832
Cameron, TX 76520
Joe Smitherman, General Manager
Tel: (254) 697-6633 Fax: (254) 697-6330
Email: kmil@tlab.net
Web: www.kmil.com

KMIQ-FM (105.1 MHZ)
P.O. Box 270547
Corpus Christi, TX 78427
Carlos López, General Manager
Tel: (361) 289-8877 Fax: (361) 389-7722

KMJR-FM (105.5 MHZ)
Amigo Broadcasting
1300 Antelope St.
Corpus Christi, TX 78401
Eddi Alonso, General Manager
Tel: (361) 883-9830 Fax: (361) 883-9303

KMUL-AM (1380 KHZ)
Broadcast Entertainment
600 W. 8th St. #486
Muleshoe, TX 79347
Elias Noe Anzaldoa, General Manager
Tel: (806) 272-4273 Fax: (806) 272-5067

KMXO-AM (1500 KHZ)
P.O. Box 523
Merkel, TX 79536
Zacarias Serrato, General Manager
Tel: (915) 928-3060 Fax: (915) 928-4683

KNDA-FM (102.9 KHZ)
Guerra Entertainment
2001 Saratoga Blvd #B
Corpus Christi, TX 78417
Patricia Rodriguez, General Manager
Tel: (361) 814-1030 Fax: (361) 814-1036
Email: littlericharddabomb@aol.com

KNEX-FM (106.1 MHZ)
BMP Radio, LP
505 Houston St.
Laredo, TX 78040
Steve Stevenson, General Manager
Tel: (956) 725-1491 Fax: (956) 725-3424
Email: studio@radioknext.com
Web: www.radioknext.com

KNON-FM (89.3 MHZ)
5353 Maple Ave.
Dallas, TX 75235
Tunde A. Obazee, National Programing
Director
Tel: (214) 637-1893
Email: npd@knon.org
Web: www.knon.org

KNTU-FM (88.1 MHZ)
University of North Texas
P.O. Box 310881
Denton, TX 76203
Mark Lambert, Operations Director
Tel: (940) 565-2435 Fax: (940) 565-2518
Email: kntu@unt.edu
Web: www.kntu.fm

KOFX-FM (92.3 MHZ)
Entravision Communications Corporation
5426 N. Mesa St.
El Paso, TX 79912
David Candelaria, General Manager
Tel: (915) 581-1126 Fax: (915) 585-4613
Email: Dcandelaria@entravision.com
Web: www.entravision.com

KOIR-FM (88.5 MHZ)
Río Grande Bible Institute
4300 S. Business Hwy. #281
Edinburg, TX 78539
Gerardo Lorenzo, General Manager
Tel: (956) 380-8100
Email: glorenzo@radioesperanza.com
Web: www.radioesperanza.com

KOKE-AM (1660 KHZ)
Amigo Broadcasting
2211 S. IH 35 #401
Austin, TX 78741
Rudy Ramos, Coordinator
Tel: (512) 416-1100 Fax: (512) 416-8205
Web: www.bmpradio.com

KOOP-FM (91.7 MHZ)
University of Texas
P.O. Box 2116
Austin, TX 78768-2116
Amy Wright, Station Manager
Tel: (512) 472-1369 Fax: (512) 472-6149
Email: info@koop.org
Web: www.koop.org

KOPY-FM (92.1 KHZ)
Sendro Multimedia, Inc.
P.O. Box 731
Alice, TX 78333
Bobby Peña, General Manager
Tel: (361) 664-1884 Fax: (361) 664-1886
Email: y92bobbypena@2fords.net

KOVE-FM (106.5 MHZ)
Univision Communications, Inc.
1415 N. Loop W. 610 North
Houston, TX 77008
Mark Masepohl, General Manager
Tel: (713) 407-1415 Fax: (713) 407-1400
Email: mmasepohl@univision.com
Web: www.univision.com

KOYE-FM (96.7 MHZ)
Waller Broadcasting
P.O. Box 1648
Jacksonville, TX 75766
Jessie Duron, Program Director
Tel: (903) 586-2527 Fax: (903) 589-0677
Email: jessied@wallerbroadcasting.com
Web: www.koye967.com

KPAN-AM (860 KHZ & 106.3 MHZ)
KPAN Radio Stations
218 E. 5th St.
Hereford, TX 79045
Chip Formby, General Manager
Tel: (806) 364-1860 Fax: (806) 364-5814
Email: kpan@kpanradio.com
Web: www.kpanradio.com

KPAN-FM (106.3 MHZ)
KPAN Radio Stations
218 E. 5th St.
Hereford, TX 79045
Chip Formby, General Manager
Tel: (806) 364-1860 Fax: (806) 364-5814
Email: kpan@kpanradio.com
Web: www.kpanradio.com

KPAS-FM (103.1 MHZ)
P.O. Box 371010
El Paso, TX 79937
Algie Folder, General Manager
Tel: (915) 851-3382 Fax: (915) 851-4360

KPSO-FM (106.3 MHZ)
Brooks Broadcasting Corporation
304 E. Rice St.
Falfurrias, TX 78355-3624
Raymond Creeley, General Manager
Tel: (361) 325-2112 Fax: (361) 325-2112

KQBU-FM (93.3 MHZ)
Univision Communications, Inc.
1415 N. Loop W. #400
Houston, TX 77008
Mark Masepohl, General Manager
Tel: (713) 407-1415 Fax: (713) 407-1400
Email: mmasepohl@univision.com
Web: www.univision.com

KQFX-FM (104.3 MHZ)
Rodriguez Communications
3639 Wolfin Ave.
Amarillo, TX 79102
Israel Salazar, General Manager
Tel: (806) 355-1044 Fax: (806) 352-6525
Email: bsalazar@rodcom.com
Web: www.rodcom.com

KQLM-FM (107.9 MHZ)
Mesa Entertainment
1100 S. Grant Ave.
Odessa, TX 79763
Benjamin Velasquez, President
Tel: (432) 333-1227 Fax: (432) 333-1227
Email: benjaminv@kqlm.com
Web: www.q108fm.com

KQQK-FM (107.9 MHZ)
Liberman Broadcasting
3000 Bering Dr.
Houston, TX 77057
Winter Horton, General Manager
Tel: (713) 3905100 Fax: (713) 315-3506
Web: www.xoradio.com

KQQK-FM (96.9 MHZ)
Liberman Broadcasting
11767 Katy Fwy #1170
Houston, TX 77079
Winter Horton, General Manager
Tel: (281) 493-2900 Fax: (281) 596-9608
Web: www.xoradio.com

KQUE-AM (1230 KHZ)
Liberman Broadcasting
11767 Katy Fwy #1170
Houston, TX 77056
Winter Horton, General Manager
Tel: (281) 493-2900 Fax: (281) 596-9608

KQXX-AM (1700 KHZ)
La Nueva KBOR, Inc.
1050 McIntosh Dr.
Brownsville, TX 78523
Edgar Treviño, General Manager
Tel: (956) 544-1600 Fax: (956) 544-6106
Email: kborbuendia@aol.com

KRDF-FM (98.3 MHZ)
P.O. Box 307
Spearman, TX 79081
Carolyn Cummings, General Manager
Tel: (806) 659-2529 Fax: (806) 659-3421

KRGE-AM (1290 KHZ)
Christian Ministries
P.O. Box 1290
Weslaco, TX 78599
Enrique Garza, General Manager
Tel: (956) 968-7777 Fax: (956) 968-5143
Email: egarza@radiovida.com
Web: www.radiovida.com

KRIO-AM (910 KHZ)
Río Grande Bible Institute
4300 S. Business Hwy. #281
Edinburg, TX 78539
Gerardo Lorenzo, General Manager
Tel: (956) 380-8100
Email: glorenzo@radioesperanza.com
Web: www.radioesperanza.com

KROM-FM (92.9 MHZ)
Univision Communications, Inc.
1777 NE Loop 410 #400
San Antonio, TX 78217
Dan Wilson, General Manager
Tel: (210) 821-6548 Fax: (210) 804-7820
Email: dwilson@univision.com
Web: www.univision.com

KRTX-AM (980 KHZ)
Univision Communications, Inc.
1415 N. Loop W. #610 North
Houston, TX 77008
Mark Masepohl, General Manager
Tel: (713) 407-1415 Fax: (713) 407-1400
Email: mmasepohl@univision.com
Web: www.univision.com

KSAB-FM (99.9 MHZ)
Clear Channel Communications
501 Tupper Ln.
Corpus Christi, TX 78417
Dan Pena, Program Director
Tel: (361) 289-0111 Fax: (631) 289-5035
Email: danpena@clearchannel.com
Web: www.clearchannel.com

KSAH-AM (720 KHZ)
Spanish Broadcasting System
7800 IH-10 West #330
San Antonio, TX 78230
Peggy McCormick, General Manager
Tel: (210) 340-1234 Fax: (210) 366-1680
Email: pmccormick@sbssanantonio.com
Web: www.spanishbroadcasting.com

KSEV-AM (700 KHZ)
Liberman Broadcasting
11451 Katy Fwy #125
Houston, TX 77079
Winter Horton, General Manager
Tel: (281) 588-4800 Fax: (281) 358-8409
Web: www.ksevradio.com

KSEY TESANO 1230 AM (1230 KHZ)
Southwest Broadcast Associates
1st National Bldg., 700 8th St. #210
Wichita Falls, TX 76301
Mark Aulabaugh, President
Tel: (940) 767-0011 Fax: (940) 767-0011
Email: kseytejano1230am@aol.com

KSHU-FM (90.5 MHZ)
Sam Houston State University
P.O. Box 2207
Huntsville, TX 77341
Adam Spry, Program Director
Tel: (936) 294-3939 Fax: (936) 294-1888
Email: cyscokyd@mailcity.com
Web: www.kshu.org

KSJT-FM (107.5 MHZ)
La Unica Broadcasting Company
209 W. Beauregard Ave.
San Angelo, TX 76903
Armando Martínez, General Manager
Tel: (915) 655-1717 Fax: (915) 657-0601
Email: ksjt@verizon.net

KSLR-AM (630 KHZ)
Salem Communications
9601 McAllister Fwy. #1200
San Antonio, TX 78216
David Ziebell, General Manager
Tel: (210) 344-8481 Fax: (210) 340-1213
Email: davidz@kslr.com
Web: www.kslr.com

KSML-AM (1260 KHZ)
Yates Broadcasting
121 Cotton Sq.
Lufkin, TX 75901

Generoso Lopez, Program Director
Tel: (936) 634-4584 Fax: (936) 632-5772
Email: generoso@ksml.net
Web: www.yatesbroadcasting.com

KSRU-AM (900 KHZ)
Sul Ross State University
SRSU Box C-22
Alpine, TX 79832
Keith West, Program Director
Tel: (915) 837-8416 Fax: (915) 837-8376
Email: ksru@sulross.edu
Web: www.sulross.edu/~finearts

KSRU-FM (90.1 MHZ)
Sul Ross State University
P.O. Box C-114
Alpine, TX 79832
Keith West, Program Director
Tel: (915) 837-8011 Fax: (915) 837-8376
Email: ksru@sulross.edu
Web: www.sulross.edu/~finearts

KSTV-AM (1510 KHZ)
P.O.Box 289
Stephenville, TX 76401
Robert Elliott, General Manager
Tel: (254) 968-2141 Fax: (254) 968-6221
Email: be@kstvfm.com
Web: www.kstvfm.com

KSVE-AM (1150 KHZ)
Entravision Communications Corporation
5426 N. Mesa St.
El Paso, TX 79912
David Candelaria, General Manager
Tel: (915) 581-1126 Fax: (915) 585-4613
Email: Dcandelaria@entravision.com
Web: www.entravision.com

KSYM-FM (90.1 MHZ)
San Antonio College
1300 San Pedro Ave.
San Antonio, TX 78212
Roberto Flores, Program Director
Tel: (210) 733-2787 Fax: (210) 733-2801
Email: ksym@accd.edu
Web: www.ksym.org

KTCY-FM (101.7 MHZ)
Entravision Communications Corporation
5307 E. Mockingbird Ln. #500
Dallas, TX 75206
Scott Savage, General Manager
Tel: (214) 887-9107 Fax: (214) 841-4215
Email: www.superestrella.com
Web: www.entravision.com

KTEP-FM (88.5 MHZ)
University of Texas at El Paso
500 W. University Ave.
Cotton Memorial #203
El Paso, TX 79968
Patrick Piotrowski, General Manager
Tel: (915) 747-5152 Fax: (915) 747-5641
Email: patrickp@utep.edu
Web: www.ktep.org

KTJK-AM (1230 KHZ)
P.O. Box 1489
Del Rio, TX 78841-1489
Jay Gonzalez, Program Director
Tel: (830) 775-9583 Fax: (830) 774-4009
Email: jay@ktjk.com
Web: www.ktjk.com

KTJM-FM (98.5 MHZ)
Liberman Broadcasting
11767 Katy Fwy #1170
Houston, TX 77056
Winter Horton, General Manager
Tel: (281) 493-2900 Fax: (281) 596-9608

KTJN-FM (106.3 KHZ)
La Nueva KBOR, Inc.
1050 McIntosh Dr.
Brownsville, TX 78521
Edgar Treviño, General Manager
Tel: (956) 544-1600 Fax: (956) 544-0311
Email: kborbuendia@aol.com

KTXZ-AM (1560 KHZ)
Garcia Communications
7524 N. Lamar Blvd. #200
Austin, TX 78752
Joe José García, General Manager
Tel: (512) 453-1491 Fax: (512) 458-0700
Email: ktxz@austintejas.com
Web: www.ktxz.com

KUHD-AM (1150 KHZ)
Vision Latina Broadcasting
419 Stadium Rd.
Port Arthur, TX 77642
Araceli Rabago, Program Director
Tel: (409) 983-4256 Fax: (409) 983-5858

KUKA-FM (105.9 MHZ)
Ideal Media, Inc.
810 Alviar St.
Alice, TX 78332
Teo Peña, General Manager
Tel: (361) 668-6666 Fax: (361) 668-6661
Email: info@kukafm.com
Web: www.kukafm.com

KUNO-AM (1400 KHZ)
Clear Channel Communications, Inc.
501 Tupper Ln.
Corpus Christi, TX 78417
Nick Rodriguez, Program Director
Tel: (361) 289-0111 Fax: (361) 289-5035
Email: nickrodriguez@clearchannel.com
Web: www.clearchannel.com

KUOL-AM (1470 KHZ)
Paulino Bernal Evangelism, Inc.
P.O. Box 252
McAllen, TX 78505
Paulino Bernal, General Manager
Tel: (956) 781-5528 Fax: (956) 686-2999

KUVA-FM (102.3 MHZ)
Rhattigan Broadcasting
P.O. Box 758
Uvalde, TX 78802
Richard Morris, News Director
Tel: (830) 278-2555 Fax: (830) 278-9461
Email: uvalderadio@uvalderadio.com
Web: www.uvalderadio.com

KVER (91.1 MHZ)
Christian Radio Station in Spanish
P.O. Box 12008
El Paso, TX 79913-0008
Alci Rengifo, Manager
Tel: (915) 544-9192 Fax: (915) 544-9193
Email: kver@hcjb.org
Web: www.kver.org

KVER-FM (91.1 MHZ)
Radio Cadena Manantial
4126 N. Mesa St.
El Paso, TX 79902
Alci Rengifo, General Manager
Tel: (915) 544-9192 Fax: (915) 544-9190
Email: kver91fm@aol.com

KVIV-AM (1340 KHZ)
Companerismo Christianiano
4900 Montana Ave.
El Paso, TX 79903
Alfonso Cabrera, General Manager
Tel: (915) 565-2999 Fax: (915) 562-3156

KVJY-AM (840 KHZ)
Radio Unica
3900 N. 10th St., 7th Fl.
McAllen, TX 78501
Rick Cruz-Aedo, NSM
Tel: (956) 668-8585 Fax: (956) 668-9996
Email: rossumberto-c@hotmail.com
Web: www.radiounica.com

KVLU-FM (91.3 MHZ)
P.O. Box 10064
Beaumont, TX 77710
Byron Balentine, Program Director
Tel: (409) 880-8164
Email: kvlu@hal.lamar.edu
Web: www.kvlu.org

KVLY-FM (107.9 MHZ)
Entravision Communications Corporation
801 Jackson Rd.
McAllen, TX 78501
Larry Safir, General Manager
Tel: (956) 661-6000 Fax: (956) 661-6082
Email: lsafir@entravision.com
Web: www.kkps.com, www.entravision.com

KVPA-FM (101.1 MHZ)
Entravision Communications Corporation
801 Jackson Rd.
McAllen, TX 78501
Larry Safir, General Manager
Tel: (956) 661-6000 Fax: (956) 661-6082
Email: lsafir@entravision.com
Web: www.kkps.com, www.entravision.com

KVRP-AM (1400 KHZ)
Rolling Plains Broadcasting Corporation
P.O. Box 1118
Haskell, TX 79521
Gary Barrett, General Manager
Tel: (940) 864-8505 Fax: (940) 864-8001
Email: sales@kvrp.com
Web: www.kvrp.com

KVWG-FM (95.3 MHZ)
Pearshell Radio Works
1581 Oilfield Rd.
Pearsall, TX 78061
Jesús Sifuentes, General Manager
Tel: (830) 334-8900 Fax: (830) 334-3488

KWCB-FM (89.7 MHZ)
Wilson County Public Radio
1905 10th St.
Floresville, TX 78114
Cissy Gonzalez, Program Director
Tel: (830) 393-6116 Fax: (830) 393-3817
Email: kwcb89fm@yahoo.com
Web: www.wcn-online.com/kwcb

KWOW-FM (104.1 MHZ)
Amigo Broadcasting
6401 Cobbs Dr.
Waco, TX 76710
Jaime Martinez, Program Director
Tel: (254) 772-6104 Fax: (254) 776-0642

KWRW-FM (97.7 MHZ)
EH Whitehead
P.O. Box 475
Rusk, TX 75785
Robert Gonzalez, Program Director
Tel: (903) 683-2257 Fax: (903) 683-5104
Email: kwrw@mediactr.com

KXOX-AM (1240 KHZ)
Stein Broadcasting, Inc.
1801 Hoyt Ln.
P. O. Box 570
Sweet Water, TX 79556
Lily Gutiérrez, Program Director
Tel: (915) 236-6655 Fax: (915) 235-4391
Web: http://kxox.tripod.com

KXTN-AM (1310 KHZ)
Univision Communications, Inc.
1777 NE Loop 410 #400
San Antonio, TX 78217
Dan Wilson, General Manager
Tel: (210) 829-1075 Fax: (210) 804-7820
Email: dwilson@univision.com
Web: www.univision.com

KXTN-FM (107.5 MHZ)
Univision Communications, Inc.
1777 NE Loop 410 #400
San Antonio, TX 78217
Dan Wilson, General Manager
Tel: (210) 829-1075 Fax: (210) 804-7820
Email: dwilson@univision.com
Web: www.univision.com

KXTQ-FM (93.7 MHZ)
Ramar Communications
P.O. Box 3757
Lubbock, TX 79452
Connie Jayes, Local Sales Mgr.
Tel: (806) 745-3434 Fax: (806) 748-1949
Web: www.magic937fm.com

KXXS-FM (104.9 MHZ)
Amigo Broadcasting
2211 S. IH 35 #401
Austin, TX 78741
Rudy Ramos, Coordinator
Tel: (512) 416-1100 Fax: (512) 416-8205
Web: www.bmpradio.com

KXYL-AM (1240 KHZ)
Watts Communications
600 Fisk Ave.
P.O. Box 100
Brownwood, TX 76804
Cathy Marie Hail, General Manager
Tel: (325) 646-3535 Fax: (324) 646-5347
Email: cathymarie@web-acess.net
Web: www.wattsradio.net/kxylam.htm

KXYZ-AM (1320 KHZ)
Radio Unica
7322 SW Freeway #1500
Houston, TX 77074
Ellen Cavenaugh, General Manager
Tel: (713) 334-1320 Fax: (713) 334-5150
Email: ecavanaugh@radiounica.com
Web: www.radiounica.com

KYND-AM (1520 KHZ)
P.O. Box 19886
Houston, TX 77224-9886
Bill Turner, General Manager
Tel: (281) 373-1520 Fax: (281) 373-5599
Email: kynd@infolife.net

KYST-AM (920 MHZ)
7322 SW Fwy. #500
Houston, TX 77074
Cruz Velázquez, General Manager
Tel: (713) 779-9292 Fax: (713) 779-1651
Email: c.velasquez@radio-noticias.com
Web: www.radio-noticias.com

KYZZ-FM (100.1 MHZ)
2824 Sherwood Way
San Angelo, TX 76901
Jason Meza, Program Director
Tel: (325) 949-3333 Fax: (325) 949-0851
Email: jason_meza@excite.com

KZIP-AM (1310 KHZ)
Rodriguez Communications
3639 Wolfin Ave.
Amarillo, TX 79102
Bert Zuniga, Program Director
Tel: (806) 355-1044 Fax: (806) 352-6525

KZMP-AM (1540 KHZ)
Entravision Communications Corporation
5307 E. Mockingbird Lane #500
Dallas, TX 75206
Scott Savage, General Manager
Tel: (214) 887-9107 Fax: (214) 841-4215
Web: www.entravision.com

KZMP-FM (104.9 MHZ)
Entravision Communications Corporation
5307 E. Mockingbird Lane #500
Dallas, TX 75206
Scott Savage, General Manager
Tel: (214) 887-9107 Fax: (214) 841-4215
Web: www.entravision.com

XEKD-AM (1010 KHZ)
205 San Felipe Ave.
Del Rio, TX 78840
Monica J. Martinez, General Manager
Tel: (830) 774-4866 Fax: (830) 774-2840
Email: ultimatetejanojamzz@msn.com

XHEM-AM (800 KHZ)
ABC, Inc.
2100 Trawood Dr.
El Paso, TX 79903
Francisco Aguirre, General Manager
Tel: (915) 542-2969 Fax: (915) 542-2958

XHHAC/UTJ-FM (100.7 MHZ)
205 San Felipe Ave.
Del Rio, TX 78840
Monica J. Martinez, General Manager
Tel: (830) 774-4866 Fax: (830) 774-2840
Email: ultimatetejanojamzz@msn.com

XHIM-FM (105.1 MHZ)
ABS, Inc.
2200 Trawood Dr.
El Paso, TX 79935
María Elena Lazo, General Manager
Tel: (915) 542-2969 Fax: (915) 542-2958
Web: www.hitfmradio.com

XHNZ-FM (107.5 MHZ)
ABC, Inc.
2100 Trawood Dr.
El Paso, TX 79903
Francisco Aguirre, General Manager
Tel: (915) 542-2969 Fax: (915) 542-2958

XHRG-FM (95.5 MHZ)
205 San Felipe Ave.
Del Rio, TX 78840
Monica J. Martinez, General Manager
Tel: (830) 774-4866 Fax: (830) 774-2840
Email: ultimatetejanojamzz@msn.com

UTAH

KBJA-AM (1640 KHZ)
Radio Unica, Utah
525 S. 300 W. #1
Salt Lake City, UT 84101

David C. Kifuri, General Manager
Tel: (801) 596-1640 Fax: (801) 229-0009
Email: d_kifuri@hotmail.com

KRCL-FM (90.9 MHZ)
Listeners Community Radio of Utah
1971 W. North Temple
Salt Lake City, UT 84116
Donna Land Maldonado, Station Manager
Tel: (801) 363-1818 Fax: (801) 533-9136
Email: mailman@krcl.org
Web: www.krcl.org

KSGO-AM (1600 KHZ)
Grande Broadcasting
80 S. Redwood Rd. #211
North Salt Lake City, UT 84054
Jesus Tovar, General Manager
Tel: (801) 936-9300 Fax: (801) 936-0686
Email: radiofiesta@aol.com

KSVN-AM (730 KHZ)
La Mejicana Azteca
4215 W. 4000 S.
West Heaven, UT 84401
Alex Collantes, Station Manager
Tel: (801) 292-1799 Fax: (801) 731-4445
Email: ksvn@aol.com

WASHINGTON

KDNA-FM (91.9 MHZ)
Northwest Communities Education Center
121 Sunnyside Ave.
P.O. Box 800
Granger, WA 98932
Ricardo Garcia, General Manager
Tel: (509) 854-1900 Fax: (509) 854-2223
Email: webjefe@radiokdna.org
Web: www.kdna.org

KRCW-FM (96.3 MHZ)
La Campesina Network
508 W. Lewis St.
Pasco, WA 99301
Armando Vega, General Manager
Tel: (509) 545-0700 Fax: (509) 543-4100
Email: krcw969fm@campesina.com
Web: www.campesina.com

KRSC-AM (1400 KHZ)
128 S. First Ave.
Otello, WA 99344
D.C. Hart, General Manager
Tel: (509) 488-0606 Fax: (509) 488-0909

KUOW-FM (94.9 MHZ)
University of Washington
P.O. Box 353750
Seattle, WA 98195
Lisa Levi, Program Director
Tel: (206) 543-2710 Fax: (206) 543-2720
Email: letters@kuow.org
Web: www.kuow.org

KYXE-AM (1020 KHZ)
**Butterfield Broadcasting, Radio Zorro and
La Mexicana**
706 Butterfield Rd.
P.O. Box 2888
Yakima, WA 98901
Bob Berry, General Manager
Tel: (509) 457-1000 Fax: (509) 452-0541

KZHR-FM (92.5 MHZ)
P.O. Box 2623
Pasco, WA 99302
Scott Smith, General Manager
Tel: (509) 546-0313 Fax: (509) 546-2678
Email: kona@konaradio.com

KZTA-FM (96.9 MHZ)
**Butterfield Broadcasting, Radio Zorro and
La Mexicana**
706 Butterfield Rd.
P.O. Box 2888
Yakima, WA 98901
Bob Berry, General Manager
Tel: (509) 457-1000 Fax: (509) 452-0541

KZTB-FM (96.7 MHZ)
Butterfield Broadcasting
P.O. Box 2888
Yakima, WA 98907
Bob Berry, General Manager
Tel: (509) 457-1000 Fax: (509) 452-0541

KZTS-AM (1210 KHZ)
**Butterfield Broadcasting, Radio Zorro and
La Mexicana**
706 Butterfield Rd.
P.O. Box 2888
Yakima, WA 98901
Bob Berry, General Manager
Tel: (509) 457-1000 Fax: (509) 452-0541

KZZM-FM (101.9 MHZ)
**Butterfield Broadcasting, Radio Zorro and
La Mexicana**
706 Butterfield Rd.
P.O. Box 2888
Yakima, WA 98901
Bob Berry, General Manager
Tel: (509) 457-1000 Fax: (509) 452-0541

WYOMING

KLEN-FM (106.3 MHZ)
Clear Channel Communications
1912 Capital Ave. #300
Cheyenne, WY 82001
Dave Chassin, Program Director
Tel: (307) 632-4400 Fax: (307) 632-1818
Email: klenfm@clearchannel.com
Web: www.1063klen.com

Hispanic Television Stations
Estaciones de televisión hispanas

ARIZONA

KDRX CHANNEL 48
Apogee Company
4625 S 33rd Pl.
Phoenix, AZ 85040
Tel: (602) 470-0507 Fax: (602) 470-0810

KHRR-TV CHANNEL 40
Apogee Company
2919 E Broadway, Garden Level
Tucson, AZ 85716
Araceli De-Leon, General Manager
Tel: (520) 322-6888 Fax: (520) 321-4224
Email: araceli@khrr.com

KQBN-TV CHANNEL 40
Apogee Company
2919 E Broadway, Garden Level
Tucson, AZ 85716
vacant, General Manager
Tel: (520) 322-6888 Fax: (520) 881-7926

KTVW-TV CHANNEL 33
Univision Television Group
6006 S 30th St.
Phoenix, AZ 85042
Ramon Pineda, General Manager
Tel: (602) 243-3333 Fax: (602) 276-8658
Email: rpineda@univision.net
Web: www.univision.net

KUVE CHANNEL 52
Univision Television Group
2301 N Forbes Blvd. #103
Tucson, AZ 85745
Ramon Pineda, General Manager
Tel: (520) 204-1246 Fax: (520) 204-1247
Email: rpineda@univision.net
Web: www.univision.net

CALIFORNIA

KVER CHANNEL 12
Entravision Communications Corporation
41601 Corporate Way
Palm Desert, CA 92260
Tony Billett, General Manager
Tel: (760) 341-5837 Fax: (760) 341-0951
Email: tbillett@entravision.com
Web: www.entravision.com

KTAS-TV CHANNEL 7
R & C Enterprises
1138 W Church St.
Santa Maria, CA 93458
Sandi Keefer, General Manager
Tel: (805) 928-7700 Fax: (805) 928-8606
Email: ktaf-tv@fix.net

KO9UF CHANNEL 9
R & C Enterprises
1138 W Church St.
Santa Maria, CA 93458
Sandi Keefer, General Manager
Tel: (805) 928-7700 Fax: (805) 928-8606
Email: ktaf-tv@fix.net

KABE CHANNEL 39
Univision Broadcast Center
5801 Truxtun Ave.
Bakersfield, CA 93309
Teresa Ford, General Manager
Tel: (661) 325-3939 Fax: (661) 325-3971
Email: tford@univision.net
Web: www.univision.net

KBNT-TV CHANNEL 17
Entravision Communications Corporation
5770 Ruffin Rd.
San Diego, CA 92123
Alberto Mier y Teran, General Manager
Tel: (858) 576-1919 Fax: (858) 715-1919
Web: www.entravision.com

KCSO-TV CHANNEL 33
Sainte Partners II, LP
142 N 9th St. #8
Modesto, CA 95350
Paul Schafer, General Manager
Tel: (209) 572-3400 Fax: (209) 575-4547
Email: pschafer@kcso33.com
Web: www.kcso33.com

KCU CHANNEL 15
Telemundo Group, Inc.
2450 N 1st St.
San Jose, CA 95131
Eduardo Dominguez, General Manager
Tel: (408) 944-4848 Fax: (408) 432-4420
Web: www.telemundo.com

KDTV CHANNEL 14
Univision Television Group
50 Fremont St., 41st Fl.
San Francisco, CA 94105
Marcela Medina, General Manager
Tel: (408) 392-6900 Fax: (408) 538-8053
Email: mmedina@univision.net
Web: www.univision.net

KDTV CHANNEL 28
Univision Television Group
50 Fremont St., 41st Fl.
San Francisco, CA 94105
Marcela Medina, General Manager
Tel: (408) 392-6900 Fax: (408) 538-8053
Email: mmedina@univision.net
Web: www.univision.net

KFTV-TV CHANNEL 21
Univision Television Group
3239 W Ashlan Ave.
Fresno, CA 93722
Maria Gutierrez, General Manager
Tel: (559) 222-2121 Fax: (559) 222-2890
Email: mlgutierrez@univision.net
Web: www.univision.net

KJLA CHANNEL 57
Costa de Oro Television
2323 Corinth Ave.
West Los Angeles, CA 90064
Francis Wilkinson, General Manager
Tel: (310) 943-5288 Fax: (310) 943-5299
Email: fwilkinson@kjla.com
Web: www.kjla.com

KMEX-TV CHANNEL 34
Univision Television Group
5999 Center Dr.
Los Angeles, CA 90045
Jorge Delgado, General Manager
Tel: (310) 216-3434 Fax: (310) 348-3413
Email: jdelgado@univision.net
Web: www.kmex.com

KMSG-TV CHANNEL 59
Sanger Telecaster
5111 E McKinley Ave.
Fresno, CA 93727
Charlie Pfaff, General Manager
Tel: (559) 435-5900 Fax: (559) 255-9626

KSMS-TV CHANNEL 67
Entravision Communications Corporation
67 Garden Ct.
Monterey, CA 93940
Alejandro Sanchez, General Manager
Tel: (831) 373-6767 Fax: (831) 373-6700
Web: www.entravision.com

KSTS CHANNEL 48
Telemundo Group, Inc.
2450 N 1st St.
San Jose, CA 95131
Eduardo Dominguez, General Manager
Tel: (408) 944-4848 Fax: (408) 432-4420
Web: www.telemundo.com

KTAS-TV CHANNEL 33
R &C Enterprises
1138 W Church St.
Santa Maria, CA 93458
Sandy Keefer, General Manager
Tel: (805) 928-7700 Fax: (805) 928-8606
Email: ktastv@fix.net

KUNA CHANNEL 15
Gulf California Broadcast Company
42-650 Melanie Pl.
Palm Desert, CA 92211-5170
Martin Serna, General Manager
Tel: (760) 568-6830 Fax: (760) 568-3984
Email: mserna@kunamundo.com

KUVS CHANNEL 19
Univision Television Group
1710 Arden Way
Sacramento, CA 95815
Diego Ruiz, General Manager
Tel: (916) 927-1900 Fax: (916) 614-1902
Email: kuvsnews@univision.net

KVEA-TV CHANNEL 52
3000 W Alamera Ave.
Fairbanks, CA 91523
Manuel Abud, General Manager
Tel: (818) 260-5700 Fax: (818) 260-5730
Email: noticiero52@kvea.com
Web: www.telemundola.com

KVER-TV CHANNEL 4
Entravision Communications Corporation
41601 Corporate Way
Palm Desert, CA 92260
Tony Billett, General Manager
Tel: (760) 341-5837 Fax: (760) 341-0951
Email: tbillett@entravision.com
Web: www.entravision.com

KWHY-TV CHANNEL 22
Telemundo Group, Inc.
1100 Air Way Ave.
Glendale, CA 91201
Manuel Abud, General Manager
Tel: (818) 409-5200 Fax: (818) 409-5205
Web: www.kwhy.com

XEWT CHANNEL 12
Energy Communications
637 3rd Ave. #B
Chula Vista, CA 91910
Patricia Alvarez, General Manager
Tel: (619) 585-9398 Fax: (619) 585-9463

XHAS-TV CHANNEL 33
Entravision Communications Corporation
5770 Ruffin Dr.
San Diego, CA 92123
Carlos Sanchez, General Manager
Tel: (858) 874-3320 Fax: (858) 874-3321
Email: csanchez@telemundo33.com
Web: www.telemundo33.com

XHUA CHANNEL 57
Energy Communications
637 3rd Ave. #B
Chula Vista, CA 91910
Patricia Alvarez, General Manager
Tel: (619) 585-9398 Fax: (619) 585-9463

KDTV CHANNEL 14
Univision Television Group
50 Fremont St., 41st Fl.
San Francisco, CA 94105
Marcela Medina, General Manager
Tel: (408) 392-6900 Fax: (408) 538-8053
Email: mmedina@univision.net
Web: www.univision.net

KESE CHANNEL 35
Telemundo
724 W Main St.
El Centro, CA 92243
Chris Gallu, General Manager
Tel: (760) 353-9990 Fax: (760) 352-2169
Email: ctgallu@hotmail.com

KUCO CHANNEL 27
Sainte Partners ii, Ip
300 Main St.
Chico, CA 95928
Doug Holroyd, General Sales Manager
Tel: (530) 893-1234 Fax: (530) 893-1266
Web: www.fox30.com

COLORADO

KCEC-TV CHANNEL 50
Entravision Communications Corporation
777 Grant St., 5th Fl.
Denver, CO 80203
Mario M. Carrera, General Manager
Tel: (303) 832-0050 Fax: (303) 832-3410
Web: www.entravision.com

KGHB CHANNEL 14
Entravision Communications Corporation
777 Grant St., 5th Fl.
Denver, CO 80203
Mario M. Carrera, General Manager
Tel: (303) 832-0050 Fax: (303) 832-3410
Web: www.entravision.com

KMAS-TV CHANNEL 63/67
Telemundo Network
1120 Lincoln St. #800
Denver, CO 80203
Giovanni Mercia, General Manager
Tel: (303) 832-0402 Fax: (303) 832-0777
Email: gmercia@telemundo.com
Web: www.telemundo.com

KTFP CHANNEL 14
Entravision Communications Corporation
777 Grant St., 5th Fl.
Denver, CO 80203
Mario M. Carrera, Vice President/General
Manager
Tel: (303) 832-0050 Fax: (303) 832-3410
Web: www.entravision.com

CONNECTICUT

WDMR-TV CHANNEL 65
ZGS Group
886 Maple Ave.
Hartford, CT 06114
Ivon Rodriguez, General Manager
Tel: (860) 956-1303 Fax: (860) 956-6834
Email: irodriguez@zgsgroup.com

WRDM-TV CHANNEL 13
ZGS Group
886 Maple Ave.
Hartford, CT 06114
Ivon Rodriguez, General Manager
Tel: (860) 956-1303 Fax: (860) 956-6834
Email: irodriguez@zgsgroup.com

DISTRICT OF COLUMBIA

APTN-LATIN AMERICAN DESK
Associated Press Television News (APTN)
1825 K St. #800
Washington, DC 20006
Will Stebbins, Deputy Editor/Latin America
Tel: (202) 736-9596 Fax: (202) 736-9579

Email: wstebbins@ap.org
Web: www.aptn.com

AMERICANS DESK
Associated Press Television News (APTN)
1825 K St. #800
Washington, DC 20006
Christina Mursa, Planning Editor
Tel: (202) 736-9580 Fax: (202) 736-9619
Web: www.aptn.com

FLORIDA

WEYS CHANNEL 22
TV-Hola
527 Southard St.
Key West, FL 33040
Lucho Monje, General Manager
Tel: (305) 296-4969 Fax: (305) 296-1669
Email: a.albertomonje@wdlptv.com
Web: www.wdlptv.com

WLTV CHANNEL 23
Univision Television Group
9405 NW 41st St.
Miami, FL 33178
Luis Fernandez Rocha, General Manager
Tel: (305) 471-3900 Fax: (305) 471-3995
Email: lfrocha@univision.net
Web: www.univision.com

WSCV-TV CHANNEL 51
WSCV Telemundo 51
15000 SW 27th St.
Miramar, FL 33027
Michael Rodriguez, General Manager
Tel: (954) 622-7002 Fax: (954) 622-7003
Email: michael.rodriguez@telemundo.com
Web: www.t51.com

WTMO-TV CHANNEL 40
ZGS Broadcasting of Orlando, inc.
1650 Sand Lake Rd. #340
Orlando, FL 32809
Roberto Viscon, General Manager
Tel: (407) 888-2288 Fax: (407) 888-3486
Email: rviscon@zgsgroup.com
Web: www.telemundo.com

WVEA-HP CHANNEL 62
Entravision Communications Corporation
2610 W Hillsborough Ave.
Tampa, FL 33614
Lilly Gonzalez, General Manager
Tel: (813) 872-6262 Fax: (813) 998-3600
Email: lgonzalez@entravision.com
Web: www.entravision.com

WVEN-TV CHANNEL 26
Entravision Communications Corporation
523 Douglas Ave.
Altamonte Springs, FL 32714
Antonio Guernica, General Manager
Tel: (407) 774-2626 Fax: (407) 774-3384
Email: aguemica@entravision.com
Web: www.entravision.com

WFTT-HP CHANNEL 50
Entravision Communications Corporation
2610 W Hillsborough Ave.
Tampa, FL 33614
Lilly Gonzalez, General Manager
Tel: (813) 998-3634 Fax: (813) 998-3600
Email: lgonzalez@entravision.com
Web: www.entravision.com

WRMD-TV CHANNEL 49
ZGS Group
402 N Reo St. #218A
Tampa, FL 33609
Wendy Thompson, Vice President
Tel: (813) 319-4949 Fax: (813) 319-5758

Email: wthompson@zgsgroup.com
Web: www.telemundo.com

GEORGIA

CNN EN ESPAÑOL
CNN
1 CNN Ctr., 12 S Tower
Atlanta, GA 30303
Cristina Ruiz, Marketing Director
Tel: (404) 827-2594 Fax: (404) 878-0030
Web: www.cnnenespanol.com

IDAHO

CHANNEL 12 COMMUNITY TELEVISION
City of Pocatello
911 N 7th Ave.
Pocatello, ID 83201
Enrique Hank Gonzalez, Producer
Tel: (208) 234-6280 Fax: (208) 234-6296

ILLINOIS

WFBT CHANNEL 23
Weigel Broadcasting
26 N Halsted St.
Chicago, IL 60661
Peter Zomaya, General Manager
Tel: (312) 705-2623 Fax: (312) 705-2666
Email: pzomaya@wciu.com

WGBO CHANNEL 66
Univision Television Group
541 N Fairbanks Ct. #1100
Chicago, IL 60611
Bert Medina, General Manager
Tel: (312) 670-1000 Fax: (312) 494-6491
Email: bmedina@univision.net
Web: www.univision.net

WSNS-TV CHANNEL 44
Telemundo Group, Inc.
454 N Columbus
Chicago, IL 60611
Eduardo Fernandez, General Manager
Tel: (312) 836-3000 Fax: (312) 836-3034
Email: wsns44community@telemundo.com
Web: www.wsns44.com

MARYLAND

WMDO-TV CHANNEL 37
Entravision Communications Corporation
962 Wayne Ave. #900
Silver Spring, MD 20910
Rudy Guernica, General Manager
Tel: (301) 589-0030 Fax: (301) 495-9556
Email: rguernica@wmdotv.com
Web: www.entravision.com

MASSACHUSETTS

WCEA CHANNEL 58
Cuenca Enterprises of America
903 Albany St.
Boston, MA 02119
Peter N. Cuenca, General Manager
Tel: (617) 427-6212 Fax: (617) 427-6227
Email: wcea2000@aol.com

WTMU CHANNEL 32
ZGS Group
529 Main St. #124
Charlestown, MA 02129

Patricia Domeniconi, General Manager
Tel: (617) 242-4606 Fax: (617) 242-4540
Email: pdomeniconi@zgsgroup.com

WUNI-TV CHANNEL 27
Entravision Communications
33 4th Ave.
Needham, MA 02494
Alex Von Lichtenberg, General Manager
Tel: (781) 433-2727 Fax: (781) 433-2750
Email: feedback@wunitv.com
Web: www.wunitv.com

WRIW CHANNEL 50
ZGS Group
529 Main St. #124
Charlestown, MA 02129
Patricia Dominiconi, General Manager
Tel: (617) 242-4606 Fax: (617) 242-4540
Email: pdominiconi@zgsgroup.com
Web: www.zgsgroup.com

NEVADA

KBLR-TV CHANNEL 39
Telemundo
73 Spectrum Blvd.
Las Vegas, NV 89101
Scott Gentry, General Manager
Tel: (702) 258-0039 Fax: (702) 258-0556
Email: sgentry@kblr39.com
Web: www.kblr39.com

KINC CHANNEL 15
Entravision Communications Corporation
500 Pilot Rd. #D
Las Vegas, NV 89119
Chris Roman, General Manager
Tel: (702) 434-0015 Fax: (702) 434-0527
Email: croman@univision.com
Web: www.entravision.com

KUVR-TV CHANNEL 46
Pappas Telecasting
940 Matly Ln. #15
Reno, NV 89502
Leo Ramos, General Manager
Tel: (775) 333-2727 Fax: (775) 327-6827

NEW JERSEY

WNJU-TV CHANNEL 47
Telemundo Group, Inc.
2200 Fletcher Ave., 6th Fl.
Fort Lee, NJ 07024
Manuel Martinez, General Manager
Tel: (201) 969-4247 Fax:
Email: redaccion@noticiero47.net
Web: www.noticiero47.com

WXTV-TV CHANNEL 41
Univision Communications, Inc.
500 Frank W Burr Blvd., 6th Fl.
Teaneck, NJ 07666
Christina Schwarz, General Manager
Tel: (201) 287-4141 Fax: (201) 287-9422
Email: cschwarz@univision.net
Web: www.univision.com

WFTY-TV CHANNEL 68
Univision Communications, Inc.
500 Frank W Burr Blvd., 6th Fl.
Teaneck, NJ 07666
Christina Schwarz, General Manager
Tel: (201) 287-4141 Fax: (201) 287-9422
Email: cschwarz@univision.net
Web: www.univision.com

WFUT-TV CHANNEL 68
Univision Communications, Inc.
500 Frank W Burr Blvd., 6th Fl.
Teaneck, NJ 07666
Christina Schwarz, General Manager
Tel: (201) 287-4141 Fax: (201) 287-9422
Email: cschwarz@univision.net
Web: www.univision.com

NEW MEXICO

KTEL-TV CHANNEL 53
Ramar Communications, Inc.
P.O. Box 30068
Albuquerque, NM 87110
Gabriel Zavala, Account Executive
Tel: (505) 884-5353 Fax: (505) 889-8390
Email: gzavala@ramarcom.com

KLUZ-TV CHANNEL 41
Entravision Communications Corporation
2725 Broadbent Pkwy. #F NE
Albuquerque, NM 87107
Margarita Wilder, General Manager
Tel: (505) 342-4141 Fax: (505) 344-8714
Web: www.entravision.com

KTFA-TV CHANNEL 14
Entravision Communications Corporation
2725 Broadbent Pkwy. #F NE
Albuquerque, NM 87107
Margarita Wilder, General Manager
Tel: (505) 342-4141 Fax: (505) 344-8714
Web: www.entravision.com

NEW YORK

HITN-TV CHANNEL 9401
Hispanic Information Telecommunications Network
449 Broadway, 3rd Fl.
New York, NY 10013
José Luis Rodríguez, President
Tel: (212) 966-5660 Fax: (212) 966-5725
Email: hitn@hitn.org
Web: www.hitn.org

R-NEWS CHANNEL 9 - R-NEWS EN ESPAÑOL
Time Warner Cable
71 Mount Hope Ave.
Rochester, NY 14620
Benjamin Herrera, Producer/News Anchor
Tel: (585) 756-2424 Fax: (585) 756-1673
Email: bherrera@rnews.com
Web: www.rnews.com

WNET-TV CHANNEL 13
Thirteen WNET New York
450 W 33rd St.
New York, NY 10001
William S. Baker, General Manager
Tel: (212) 560-2000 Fax: (212) 560-1314
Email: programming@thirteen.org
Web: www.thirteen.org

WXTV-TV CHANNEL 41
Univision Television Group
605 3rd Ave., 12th Fl.
New York, NY 10158
Christina Schwarz, General Manager
Tel: (212) 455-5400 Fax: (212) 867-6710
Email: cschwarz@univision.net
Web: www.univision.com

WXXI-TV CHANNEL 21
WXXI Public Broadcasting Council
280 State St.
Rochester, NY 14614
Mike Catuto, Producer/Reporter

Tel: (585) 325-7500 Fax: (585) 258-0330
Email: mcatuto@wxxi.org
Web: www.wxxi.org

AIM Tell-A-Vision
201 E 16th St., 5th Fl.
New York, NY 10003
Robert Rose, President/CEO
Tel: (212) 627-3192 Fax: (212) 255-9232
Email: info@aimtv.tv
Web: www.aimtv.tv

OREGON

KKEI CHANNEL 38
Univision Television Group
1628 NW Everett St.
Portland, OR 97209
Steve Hale, Operations Manager
Tel: (503) 241-2411 Fax: (503) 226-3557
Email: watchtvmail@comcast.net
Web: www.univision.com

KABH CHANNEL 15
Watch TV Inc.
1628 NW Everett St.
Portland, OR 97209
Gregory Herman, Gen. Mgr.
Tel: (503) 241-2411 Fax: (503)226-3557
Email: watchtvinc@aol.com

KWWA CHANNEL 49
Watch TV Inc.
1628 NW Everett St.
Portland, OR 97209
Steve Hale, Operations Manager
Tel: (503) 241-2411 Fax: (503)226-3557
Email: watchtvmail@comcast.net

PENNSYLVANIA

WWSI CHANNEL 62
Telemundo
1341 N Delaware Ave. #408
Philadelphia, PA 19125
Jimmy Rivera, General Manager
Tel: (215) 634-8862 Fax: (215) 425-2683
Email: j.rivera@wwsi-tv.com
Web: www.wwsi-tv.com

PUERTO RICO

WAPA-TV CHANNEL 4
Lyn Television
P.O. Box 362050
San Juan, PR 00936-2050
Joe Ramos, General Manager
Tel: (787) 792-4444 Fax: (787) 782-4420
Email: alba.rivera@guapatv.com

WIPN CHANNEL 3
Corporación de Puerto Rico para la Difusión Pública
P.O. Box 190-909
San Juan, PR 00919-0909
Jorge Iserni, General Manager
Tel: (787) 766-0505 Fax: (787) 753-9846
Web: www.tutv.puertorico.pr

WIPR CHANNEL 6
Corporación de Puerto Rico para la Difusión Pública
P.O. Box 190-909
San Juan, PR 00919-0909
Jorge Iserni, General Manager
Tel: (787) 766-0505 Fax: (787) 753-9846
Web: www.tutv.puertorico.pr

WKAQ-TV CHANNEL 2
Telemundo Group, Inc.
383 Roosevelt Ave.
Hato Rey, PR 00918
Luis Roldan, General Manager
Tel: (787) 758-2222 Fax: (787) 641-2175
Web: www.telemundo.com

WLII-TV CHANNEL 11
Univision Puerto Rico
P.O. Box 10000
San Juan, PR 00908-1000
Larry Sands, General Manager
Tel: (787) 620-1111 Fax: (787) 721-4685
Email: univision@centennialpr.net
Web: www.univision.centennialpr.net

WMTJ-TV CHANNEL 40
Sistema Universitario Ana G. Mendez
P.O. Box 21345
San Juan, PR 00928-1345
Migdalia Torres, Vice President
Tel: (787) 766-2600 Fax: (787) 250-8546
Web: www.suagm.edu

WOLE-TV CHANNEL 12
Western Broadcasting Corporation
P.O.Box 1200
Mayaguez, PR 00681
Luis A. Morales, General Manager
Tel: (787) 833-1200 Fax: (787) 831-6330
Email: woletv@coqui.net

WPRV CHANNEL 13
Arzobispado de San Juan
P.O. Box 9021967
San Juan, PR 00902-1967
Juan Miguel Muñiz, General Manager
Tel: (787) 276-1300 Fax: (787) 276-1307
Email: juanmiguel@teleorotv.com

WSTE CHANNEL 7
Siete Grande Televisión
P.O. Box 15096
San Juan, PR 00902
Wanda Costanzo, General Manager
Tel: (787) 724-7777 Fax: (787) 725-5870
Email: wconstanzo@supersiete.com

WSUR-TV CHANNEL 9
Univision Puerto Rico
P.O. Box 10000
San Juan, PR 00908-1000
Larry Sands, General Manager
Tel: (787) 620-1111 Fax: (787) 721-4685
Email: univision@centennialpr.net
Web: www.univision.centennialpr.net

WORA-TV CHANNEL 5
Univision Puerto Rico
P.O. Box 10000
San Juan, PR 00908-1000
Larry Sands, General Manager
Tel: (787) 620-1111 Fax: (787) 721-4685
Email: univision@centennialpr.net
Web: www.univision.centennialpr.net

TEXAS

K57IG CHANNEL 44
Caballero Television Texas, LLC
3310 Keller Springs Rd. #105
Carrollton, TX 75006
Eduardo Caballero, CEO
Tel: (972) 503-6800 Fax: (972) 503-6801
Email: e_caballero@masmusicateve.com
Web: www.masmusicateve.com

KLEG CHANNEL 44
Teleamerica Spanish Network
2700 N Stommone Fwy. #1100
Dallas, TX 75207

Blanca Estrada, General Manager
Tel: (214) 887-1900 Fax: (214) 887-1100
Email: teleamerica44@msn.com

KAJA-TV CHANNEL 68
KAJA Communications
P.O. Box 840
Corpus Christi, TX 78403
Tim Noble, General Manager
Tel: (361) 886-6101 Fax: (361) 887-6666
Email: tnoble@kristv.com
Web: www.kristv.com

KBZO-LP CHANNEL 51
Entravision Communications Corporation
1220 Broadway #600
Lubbock, TX 79401
Jose Sauceda, General Manager
Tel: (806) 763-6051 Fax: (806) 744-8363
Email: jsauceda@entravison.com
Web: www.entravision.com

KGBT-TV CHANNEL 4
Cosmos Broadcasting
9201 W Express, 83
Harlingen, TX 78552
Coby Cooper, General Manager
Tel: (956) 421-4444 Fax: (956) 366-4490
Email: ccooper@team4news.com
Web: www.team4news.com

KGMM CHANNEL 58
Caballero Television Texas, LLC
3310 Keller Springs Rd. #105
Carrollton, TX 75006
Eduardo Caballero, CEO
Tel: (972) 503-6800 Fax: (972) 503-6801
Email: e_caballero@masmusicateve.com
Web: www.masmusicateve.com

KHMM CHANNEL 14
Caballero Television Texas, LLC
3310 Keller Springs Rd. #105
Carrollton, TX 75006
Eduardo Caballero, CEO
Tel: (972) 503-6800 Fax: (972) 503-6801
Email: e_caballero@masmusicateve.com
Web: www.masmusicateve.com

KINT-TV CHANNEL 26
Entravision Communications Corporation
5426 N Mesa St.
El Paso, TX 79912
David Candelaria, General Manager
Tel: (915) 581-1126 Fax: (915) 585-4613
Email: dcandelaria@entravision.com
Web: www.entravision.com

KLDO-TV CHANNEL 27
Entravision Communications Corporation
222 Bob Bullock Loop
Laredo, TX 78043
Terry Elena Ordaz, General Manager
Tel: (956) 727-0027 Fax: (956) 727-2673
Email: telena@entravision.com
Web: www.entravision.com

KMMA CHANNEL 41
Caballero Television Texas, LLC
3310 Keller Springs Rd. #105
Carrollton, TX 75006
Eduardo Caballero, CEO
Tel: (972) 503-6800 Fax: (972) 503-6801
Email: e_caballero@masmusicateve.com
Web: www.masmusicateve.com

KZMM CHANNEL 7
Caballero Television Texas, LLC
3310 Keller Springs Rd. #105
Carrollton, TX 75006
Eduardo Caballero, CEO
Tel: (972) 503-6800 Fax: (972) 503-6801
Email: e_caballero@masmusicateve.com

Web: www.masmusicateve.com

KMMD CHANNEL 3
Caballero Television Texas, LLC
3310 Keller Springs Rd. #105
Carrollton, TX 75006
Eduardo Caballero, CEO
Tel: (972) 503-6800 Fax: (972) 503-6801
Email: e_caballero@masmusicateve.com
Web: www.masmusicateve.com

KMMW CHANNEL 47
Caballero Television Texas, LLC
3310 Keller Springs Rd. #105
Carrollton, TX 75006
Eduardo Caballero, CEO
Tel: (972) 503-6800 Fax: (972) 503-6801
Email: e_caballero@masmusicateve.com
Web: www.masmusicateve.com

KMUM CHANNEL 15
Caballero Television Texas, LLC
3310 Keller Springs Rd. #105
Carrollton, TX 75006
Eduardo Caballero, CEO
Tel: (972) 503-6800 Fax: (972) 503-6801
Email: e_caballero@masmusicateve.com
Web: www.masmusicateve.com

KNVO-TV CHANNEL 48
Entravision Communications Corporation
801 N Jackson Rd.
McAllen, TX 78501
Larry Safir, General Manager
Tel: (956) 687-4848 Fax: (956) 687-7784
Web: www.entravision.com

KORO-TV CHANNEL 28
Univision & Telefutura
102 N Mesquite St.
Corpus Christi, TX 78401
Anita Saenz-Carvalho, General Manager
Tel: (361) 883-2823 Fax: (361) 883-2262

KQMM CHANNEL 14
Caballero Television Texas, LLC
3310 Keller Springs Rd. #105
Carrollton, TX 75006
Eduardo Caballero, CEO
Tel: (972) 503-6800 Fax: (972) 503-6801
Email: e_caballero@masmusicateve.com
Web: www.masmusicateve.com

KTLM-TV CHANNEL 40
Sunbelt Multimedia
3900 N 10th St., 7th Fl.
McAllen, TX 78501
Bill Jorn, General Manager
Tel: (956) 686-0040 Fax: (956) 686-0770
Email: wjorn@ktlm-tv.com
Web: www.ktlm-tv.com

KTMD-TV CHANNEL 47
Telemundo Group, Inc.
3903 Stoney Brook Dr.
Houston, TX 77063
Roel Medina, General Manager
Tel: (713) 974-4848 Fax: (713) 974-5875
Email: t48gm@ktmd.com
Web: www.ktmd.com

KTXS CHANNEL 12
Lanco Communications
4420 N Clack
Abilene, TX 79601
Jackie Rutledge, General Manager
Tel: (325) 677-2281 Fax: (325) 676-9231
Email: rutledge@ktxs.com

KUVN-TV CHANNEL 23
Univision Television Group
2323 Bryan St. #1900
Dallas, TX 75201
Rebecca Muñoz-Diaz, General Manager

Tel: (214) 758-2300 Fax: (214) 758-2338
Email: bmdiaz@univision.net
Web: www.univision.net

KVAW CHANNEL 16
Hispanic Television Network
2524 Loop 431
Eagle Pass, TX 78852
Ignacio Trujillo, Station Manager
Tel: (830) 773-3668 Fax: (830) 773-3668
Email: ignacio78852@yahoo.com

KVDA-TV CHANNEL 60
Telemundo Group, Inc.
6234 San Pedro Ave.
San Antonio, TX 78216
Clara Rivas, General Manager
Tel: (210) 340-8860 Fax: (210) 341-3962
Web: www.telemundo.com

KVYE-TV CHANNEL 7
Entravision Communications Corporation
1803 N Imperial Ave.
El Centro, TX 92243
Eric Chavez, General Manager
Tel: (760) 337-8707 Fax: (760) 482-0099

KWEX-TV CHANNEL 41
Univision
411 E Durango Blvd.
San Antonio, TX 78204
Steve Giust, General Manager
Tel: (210) 227-4141 Fax: (210) 227-0469
Email: sgiust@univision.net
Web: www.univision.net

KXLN-TV CHANNEL 45
Univision Television Group
9440 Kirby Dr.
Houston, TX 77054
Craig Bland, General Manager
Tel: (713) 662-4545 Fax: (713) 668-9054
Web: www.univision.net

KXTQ-TV CHANNEL 46
Ramar Communications, Inc.
P.O. Box 3757
Lubbock, TX 79452
Chuck Heinz, General Manager
Tel: (806) 748-2400 Fax: (806) 748-1949
Email: cheinz@ramarcom.com

XERV CHANNEL 9
COX Communications
4909 N McColl Rd.
McAllen, TX 78501
Emmett Wells, General Sales Manager
Tel: (956) 972-1117 Fax: (956) 972-0476
Email: emmett.wells@cox.com
Web: www.cox.com

XHAB CHANNEL 7
COX Communications
4909 N McColl Rd.
McAllen, TX 78501
Emmett Wells, General Sales Manager
Tel: (956) 972-1117 Fax: (956) 972-0476
Email: emmett.wells@cox.com
Web: www.cox.com

XHBR CHANNEL 11
COX Communications
4909 N McColl Rd.
McAllen, TX 78501
Emmett Wells, General Sales Manager
Tel: (956) 972-1117 Fax: (956) 972-0476
Email: emmett.wells@cox.com
Web: www.cox.com

XHIJ-TV CHANNEL 44
International Communications
5925 Cromo Dr.
El Paso, TX 79912
Sergio Cabada, General Manager

Tel: (915) 585-6344 Fax: (915) 585-6333
Web: www.canal44.com

XHPN CHANNEL 3
COX Communications
4909 N McColl Rd.
McAllen, TX 78501
Emmett Wells, General Sales Manager
Tel: (956) 972-1117 Fax: (956) 972-0476
Email: emmett.wells@cox.com
Web: www.cox.com

KCRP-TV CHANNEL 41
Univision & Telefutura
102 N Mesquite St.
Corpus Christi, TX 78401
Anita Saenz-Carvalho, General Manager
Tel: (361) 883-2823 Fax: (361) 883-2262

KTES CHANNEL 40
Lanco Communications
4420 N Clack
Abilene, TX 79601
Jackie Rutledge, General Manager
Tel: (325) 677-2281 Fax: (325) 672-6621
Email: rutledge@ktxs.com

KTMO CHANNEL 36
Adlente television
P.O. Box 10
Amarillo, TX 79105-0010
Mike Lee, General Manager
Tel: (806) 383-1010 Fax: (806) 381-9859
Email: mikelee@newschannel10.com
Web: www.newschannel10.com

KXTX CHANNEL 39
Telemundo Communications Group
3900 Harry Hines Blvd.
Dallas, TX 75219
Jose Valle, General Manager
Tel: (214) 521-3900 Fax: (214) 523-5916
Web: www.telemundodallas.com

KTDO CHANNEL 48
Council Tree Communications
10033 Carnegie
El Paso, TX 79925
Art Olivas, General Manager
Tel: (915) 591-9595 Fax: (915) 591-9896
Email: aolivas@zgsgroup.com

KTLE CHANNEL 60
Midessa Television
11320 County Rd. 127 West
Midland, TX 79711
Rick Wood, General Manager/General Sales Manager
Tel: (432) 567-9999 Fax: (432) 567-9992
Email: rwood@kwes.com

KTLD CHANNEL 49
Midessa Television
11320 County Rd. 127 West
Midland, TX 79711
Rick Wood, General Manager/General Sales Manager
Tel: (432) 567-9999 Fax: (432) 567-9992
Email: rwood@kwes.com

KUNU CHANNEL 21
Saga Communications
3808 N Navarro
Victoria, TX 77901
Jeff Pryor, General Manager
Tel: (361) 575-2500 Fax: (361) 575-2255
Email: jpryor@kavu-tv.com

KVTX CHANNEL 45
Saga Communications
3808 N Navarro
Victoria, TX 77901
Jeff Pryor, General Manager
Tel: (361) 575-2500 Fax: (361) 575-2255

Email: jpryor@kavu-tv.com

TM25 CHANNEL 25
Drewy Communications
1909 S New Rd.
Waco, TX 76711
Jerry Pursley, General Manager
Tel: (254) 754-2525 Fax: (254) 757-1119
Email: jpursley@kxxv.com
Web: www.kxxv.com

KMUM CHANNEL 15
Caballero Television Texas, LLC
3310 Keller Springs Rd. #105
Carrollton, TX 75006
Eduardo Caballero, CEO
Tel: (972) 503-6800 Fax: (972) 503-6801
Email: e_caballero@masmusicateve.com
Web: www.masmusicateve.com

XHLAR CHANNEL 57
COX Communications
4909 N McColl Rd.
McAllen, TX 78501
Emmett Wells, General Sales Manager
Tel: (956) 972-1117 Fax: (956) 972-0476
Email: emmett.wells@cox.com
Web: www.cox.com

K40SW CHANNEL 40
International Communications
5925 Cromo Dr.
El Paso, TX 79912
Sergio Cabada, General Manager
Tel: (915) 585-6344 Fax: (915) 585-6333

XHPNT CHANNEL 46
COX Communications
4909 N McColl Rd.
McAllen, TX 78504
Emmett Wells, General Sales Manager
Tel: (956) 972-1117 Fax: (956) 972-0476
Email: emmett.wells@cox.com
Web: www.cox.com

XNPNH CHANNEL 52
COX Communications
4909 N McColl Rd.
McAllen, TX 78504
Emmett Wells, General Sales Manager
Tel: (956) 972-1117 Fax: (956) 972-0476
Email: emmett.wells@cox.com
Web: www.cox.com

XEW CHANNEL 2
COX Communications
4909 N McColl Rd.
McAllen, TX 78504
Emmett Wells, General Sales Manager
Tel: (956) 972-1117 Fax: (956) 972-0476
Email: emmett.wells@cox.com
Web: www.cox.com

XHGO CHANNEL 7
COX Communications
4909 N McColl Rd.
McAllen, TX 78504
Emmett Wells, General Sales Manager
Tel: (956) 972-1117 Fax: (956) 972-0476
Email: emmett.wells@cox.com
Web: www.cox.com

XEQ CHANNEL 9
COX Communications
4909 N McColl Rd.
McAllen, TX 78504
Emmett Wells, General Sales Manager
Tel: (956) 972-1117 Fax: (956) 972-0476
Email: emmett.wells@cox.com
Web: www.cox.com

continued on p 400

Hispanic Web Sites
Sitios en Internet Hispanos

BUSINESS

AVISO NET
www.aviso.net/dir/usa/hispanic
The fastest way to find Hispanic American business pages online.

GREATER WASHINGTON IBERO-AMERICAN CHAMBER OF COMMERCE
www.iberochamber.org
Improving commercial and business conditions of Hispanic-owned businesses located in the Greater Washington, DC metropolitan area.

HISPANIC ASSOCIATION ON CORPORATE RESPONSABILITY
www.hacr.org
Ensures that there is an equitable participation of the Hispanic community in Corporate America.

HISPANIC BUSINESS, INC.
www.hispanicbusiness.com
A dynamic link for today's Hispanic Executives and Professionals with reports on the latest corporate news.

HISPANIC YEARBOOK
www.hispanicyearbook.com
A database driven site containing exclusive information for and about the U.S. Hispanic/Latino community.

LATIN BUSINESS ASSOCIATION
www.lbausa.com
Promotes the growth of Latino-owned businesses by fostering development opportunities, providing educational workshops, and fomulating effective advocacy programs.

LATIN CHAMBER OF COMMERCE OF USA
www.camacol.org
One of the largest Hispanic business associations in the State of Florida.

LATIN TRADE
www.latintrade.com
A website containing information about international trade and a business directory for Latin America.

NATIONAL HISPANIC BUSINESS ASSOCIATION
www.nhba.org
To promote the development of undergraduate Hispanic business students through educational, professional, and networking opportunities to foster diversity, higher education, and the improvement of the Hispanic community.

NATIONAL HISPANIC CORPORATE COUNCIL
www.nhcc-hq.org
Helps increase employment, leadership, and business opportunities for Hispanics in Corporate America.

U.S. HISPANIC CHAMBER OF COMMERCE
www.ushcc.com
Facilitates the success of Hispanic business in the U.S.

U.S.-MEXICO CHAMBER OF COMMERCE
www.usmcoc.org
A coalition created to promote trade, investment and joint ventures on both sides of the border.

COMMUNITY & POLICY

ASPIRA ASSOCIATION
www.aspira.org
A national nonprofit organization devoted solely to the education and leadership development of Puerto Rican and other Latino youth.

CENTRAL AMERICAN RESOURCE CENTER
www.carecen-la.org
Dedicated to the empowerment of Central Americans in Los Angeles, CA.

CUBAN AMERICAN NATIONAL COUNCIL, INC.
www.cnc.org
Provides education, housing and community development services to Hispanic groups and other minorities.

HISPANIC COUNCIL ON INTERNATIONAL AFFAIRS
www.hcir.org
Dedicated to increasing the voice of U.S. Hispanics in foreign affairs, especially towards the Americas.

LABOR COUNCIL FOR LATIN AMERICAN ADVANCEMENT
www.lclaa.org
A national Latino trade union association representing Latino working men and women.

LATINO ISSUES FORUM
www.lif.org
Focuses on issues such as access to higher education, economic development, health care, citizenship, telecommunications and regulatory issues.

LEAGUE OF UNITED LATIN AMERICAN CITIZENS
www.lulac.org
Helps advance the economic condition, political influence, educational attainment, health and civil rights of the Hispanic population in the U.S.

MANA - A NATIONAL LATINA ORGANIZATION
www.hermana.org
Empowers Latinas through leadership development, community service, and advocacy.

MEXICAN AMERICAN LEGAL DEFENSE & EDUCATIONAL FUND
www.maldef.org
The premier Latino civil rights organization in the United States.

MIGENTE.COM
www.migente.com
The fastest growing online community targeting English-speaking Latinos to have his/her voice heard.

NATIONAL HISPANIC COUNCIL ON AGING
www.nhcoa.org
The voice for the elderly Hispanic community since 1983.

NATIONAL HISPANIC INSTITUTE
www.nhi-net.org
Provides high achieving Latino youth in high school and college with key learning experiences that hone their skills as future leaders in the Latino community.

U.S. COMMISSION ON CIVIL RIGHTS
www.usccr.gov
Investigates complaints alleging that citizens are being deprived of their right to vote by reason of their race, color, religion, sex, age, disability, or national origin.

UNITED STATES HISPANIC LEADERSHIP INSTITUTE
www.ushli.com
To fulfill the promises and principles of democracy by empowering minorities and similarly disenfranchised groups.

WILLIAM C. VELASQUEZ INSTITUTION
www.wcvi.org
To conduct research aimed at improving the level of political and economic participation in Latino and other underrepresented communities.

CULTURAL & ARTS

ASSOCIATION OF HISPANIC ARTS
www.latinoarts.org
Dedicated to the advancement of Latino arts and artists in the United States.

BILINGUAL FOUNDATION OF THE ARTS
www.bfatheatre.org
Founded for the purpose of presenting Hispanic world drama to an audience of English- and Spanish-speaking people.

EL CASTELLANO
www.el-castellano.com
An excellent guide to discover all about the Spanish language theories and practices.

FESTIVALS
www.festivals.com
This site contains worldwide festivals and events; it has a comprehensive list of festivals by country of origin.

HISPANIC SOCIETY OF AMERICA
www.hispanicsociety.org
Addresses all aspects of the Spanish culture as well as the culture of Portugal and Latin America.

JOE VILLARREAL
www.joevartist.com
Provides a large collection of artwork by renown cultural artist, Joe Villarreal.

NATIONAL HISPANIC FOUNDATION FOR THE ARTS
www.hispanicarts.org
Contains contributions of the Hispanic community to the arts in the United States.

THE HISPANIC CULTURE FOUNDATION
www.hcfoundation.org
The leading institution supporting Hispanic arts and humanities.

THE MEXICAN MUSEUM
www.mexicanmuseum.org
The soul and the spirit of the arts and cultures of Mexico and the Americas.

THE SMITHSONIAN CENTER FOR LATINO INITIATIVES
http://latino.si.edu
Established to help advance the knowledge and understanding of the Latino contributions to U.S. history, culture, and society.

EDUCATION

CALIFORNIA CHICANO NEWS MEDIA ASSOCIATION
www.ccnma.org
Provides scholarships and educational programs for Latinos pursuing careers in the news media.

HISPANIC ASSOCIATION OF COLLEGES & UNIVERSITIES
www.hacu.net
HACU helps improve access to post-secondary education for Hispanic students by creating special programs.

HISPANIC COLLEGE FUND, INC.
www.hispanicfund.org
HCF awards scholarships to Hispanic students wishing to pursue a career in business.

HISPANIC LINK
www.hispaniclink.org
Dedicated to the advancement of Hispanics

interested in pursuing media and journalism careers through fellowships, internships and scholarships.

HISPANIC SCHOLARSHIP FUND
www.hsf.net
The largest Hispanic scholarship granting organization in the nation.

HISPANO MUNDO
www.hispanomundo.com
The history and culture of Hispanic Americans.

LATIN AMERICAN EDUCATIONAL FOUNDATION
www.laef.org
A leader in meeting the higher education needs of Hispanic students.

LINCOLN-MARTI PRIVATE SCHOOLS
www.lincoln-marti.com
An institution dedicated to educating the future of our community, both academically and socially.

NATIONAL ASSOCIATION FOR BILINGUAL EDUCATION
www.nabe.org
The only national organization exclusively concerned with the education of language-minority students in American schools.

NATIONAL CAUCUS OF HISPANIC SCHOOL BOARD MEMBERS
www.nsba.org/caucus/hispanic/
Promotes quality education for all students with emphasis placed on the specific challenges faced by the Spanish/Hispanic students.

SCHOLARSITE.COM
www.scholarsite.com
The premier bilingual site in the area of student financial aid.

SOCIETY OF HISPANIC PROFESSIONAL ENGINEERS FOUNDATION
www.shpefoundation.org
Provides scholarship funds and educational support system for engineering and science students of Hispanic background.

EMPLOYMENT

IHISPANO.COM
www.ihispano.com
One of the leading career sites for Hispanic and bilingual professionals.

HIRE DIVERSITY
www.hirediversity.com
The leading online service for diversity recruitment.

HISPANIC EMPLOYMENT PROGRAM MANAGERS
www.hepm.org
Established to focus specific attention on the needs of Hispanic Americans in all areas of federal employment.

JOB CENTRO
www.jobcentro.com
The official career site of the U.S. Hispanic Chamber of Commerce.

JOB LATINO
www.joblatino.com
Offers employment opportunities for Hispanics in the Southwest region of the U.S.

LATINO PROFESSIONAL NETWORK
www.lpn.org
Creating career, educational and social opportunities for Latinos in Massachusetts and throughout the nation.

LATPRO
www.latpro.com
The leading employment resource for Hispanics in the Americas.

SALUDOS HISPANOS
www.saludos.com
Hispanic employment service for jobs.

SER NATIONAL
www.ser-national.org
National employment and training organization for Hispanics in the U.S.

SPANUSA
www.spanusa.net
An executive search firm specializing in the placement of bilingual professionals in the U.S. and Latin America.

ENTERTAINMENT

HITS TV
www.htv.com
International Latin music TV channel.

LA MUSICA
www.lamusica.com
A bilingual Latin music and entertainment site, guided towards the U.S. Hispanic market.

LATINO USA
www.latinousa.org
The only national, English-language radio program produced from a Latino perspective.

MTV NETWORKS LATIN AMERICA
www.mtvla.com
The best music entertainment programming in Spanish.

SISTEMA UNIDO DE RETRANSMISION
www.canalsur.com
TV network with programming about countries from Latin America for U.S. Hispanics.

SPANISH BROADCASTING SYSTEM
www.spanishbroadcasting.com
The largest Hispanic radio broadcasting company in the United States.

TELEMUNDO NETWORK GROUP
www.telemundo.com
The largest growing TV network in Spanish in the U.S.

UNIVISION COMMUNICATIONS, INC.
www.univision.com
The leading Spanish-language TV network in the U.S.

GENEALOGY

HISPANIC GENEALOGY CENTER
www.hispanicgenealogy.com
Helps people recapture Hispanic culture and find out about their historical past.

HISPANIC GENEALOGY RING
http://elanillo.com
Gives access to multiple sources about Hispanic genealogy.

INTERNET SERVICE PROVIDER

AMERICATEL CORPORATION
www.123.com
The Internet of the Hispanics.

AMERICA ONLINE LATIN AMERICA
www.aola.com
The #1 ISP in the world in Spanish.

TERRA NETWORKS, S.A.
www.terralycos.com
Global Internet company and ISP for Latin America and the U.S. Hispanic market.

YUPI INTERNET, INC.
www.yupimsn.com
An ISP for U.S. Hispanics. A joint venture of Telmex and Microsoft.

LITERARY

ARTE PUBLICO PRESS
www.arte.uh.edu
The oldest and largest publisher of U.S. Hispanic literature.

DOWNTOWN BROWN
www.downtownbrown.com
A selection of books, posters and documents related to Latinos in the U.S.

LAS MUJERES
www.lasmujeres.com
Information about the lives of politicians, entrepreneurs, writers, singers, painters, actresses, educators, and others.

THE LIBRARY OF CONGRESS - HISPANIC READING ROOM
http://lcweb.loc.gov/rr/hispanic/
The Hispanic Reading Room serves as the primary access point for research relating to U.S. Hispanics and Latinos.

MEDICAL & HEALTH

CLINICA TEPATI - UC DAVIS SCHOOL OF MEDICINE
http://cim.ucdavis.edu/clinics/Clinica_Tepati/
Addresses the needs for healthcare of the Latino community in Sacramento, CA.

HEALTH FINDER
www.healthfinder.gov/espanol/
A very useful guide to medicine in Spanish.

INTERAMERICAN COLLEGE OF PHYSICIANS AND SURGEONS
www.icps.org
The largest and oldest National Hispanic Medical Society in the United States.

LATIN AMERICAN HEALTH INSTITUTE
www.lhi.org
The premier Latino public health organization in New England.

LATINO MEDICAL
www.latinomedical.com
A non-profit organization working towards the betterment of the Latino Community through the field of medicine.

NATIONAL ALLIANCE FOR HISPANIC HEALTH
www.hispanichealth.org
Serves as a resource center for Hispanic-oriented health in the community.

NATIONAL ASSOCIATION OF HISPANIC NURSES
www.thehispanicnurses.org
The only organization representing Hispanic nurses in the U.S. designed to improve the quality of health of the Latino community.

NATIONAL HISPANIC MEDICAL ASSOCIATION
www.nhmamd.org
A representative for the 26,000 licensed physicians and 1,800 full time Hispanic medical

faculty.

NATIONAL LATINO/A LESBIAN, GAY, BISEXUAL & TRANSGENDER ORGANIZATION
www.llego.org
Seeks to provide social, health and political assistance to the gay and lesbian community.

THE HISPANIC FEDERATION
www.hispanicfederation.org
Helps build and strengthen community-based organizations which provide Latinos health care services, and other related services.

NEWS & MEDIA

AUTO MUNDO PRODUCTIONS, INC.
www.automundo.com
The #1 Spanish automotive publication in the U.S.

BUSINESS NEWS AMERICAS LTDA.
www.bnamericas.com
News website focusing on important events occurring in Latin America.

CNN EN ESPANOL
http://cnnenespanol.com
All the latest news around the world, U.S. and Latin America.

GRUPO DE DIARIOS AMERICA
www.gda.com
A unique consortium of the 12 most influential newspapers in Latin America.

HISPANIC NETWORK MAGAZINE
www.hnmagazine.com
Established to create business and employment opportunities.

HISPANIC PUBLISHING GROUP
www.hispaniconline.com
Offers a variety of information and entertainment for the U.S. Hispanic market.

HISPANIC PR WIRE, INC.
www.hispanicprwire.com
Dedicated to the distribution of news, public relations and information to other media and leaders of the Hispanic community.

HISPANIC VISTA
www.hispanicvista.com
A comprehensive site that covers information affecting U.S. Hispanics.

LATINA STYLE MAGAZINE
www.latinastyle.com
Hispanic cultural, career business news devoted to the contemporary Hispanic woman.

NATIONAL ASSOCIATION OF HISPANIC PUBLICATIONS
www.nahponline.org
To promote Hispanic print, the most effective medium to reach the Hispanic population.

NATIONAL LATINO COMMUNICATIONS CENTER
www.nlcc.com
Established itself as the single largest supplier of Latino TV programming.

ZOOM MEDIA GROUP
www.revistapoder.com
The latest news for business leaders in Latin America and Hispanics in the U.S.

POLITICAL ACTION

CONGRESSIONAL HISPANIC CAUCUS INSTITUTE
www.chci.org

To strengthen the Federal commitment to Hispanic citizens and heighten the Hispanic community's awareness of the operations and functions of the American political system.

CUBAN AMERICAN NATIONAL FOUNDATION
www.canfnet.org

To engage, support, and empower the Cuban people in ways that do not aid or legitimize the Castro regime.

NATIONAL ASSOCIATION OF HISPANIC FEDERAL EXECUTIVES
www.nahfe.org

Dedicated to the excellence, professionalism and integrity of the Hispanic American Federal executive's public service contributions to our nation.

NATIONAL ASSOCIATION OF LATINO ELECTED OFFICIALS
www.naleo.org

Promoting the participation of Latinos in the American political process.

NATIONAL COUNCIL OF LA RAZA
www.nclr.org

The nation's largest Hispanic civil rights organization

NATIONAL HISPANA LEADERSHIP INSTITUTE
www.nhli.org

Helps develop Hispanas as ethical leaders through training and professional development.

THE TOMAS RIVERA POLICY INSTITUTE
www.trpi.org

Helps close the gap that exists among policymakers and political leaders regarding the complexities that characterize the U.S. Latino population.

PORTAL

BUSCAPIQUE NETWORK - LA RED LATINA
www.buscapique.com

Search engine in Spanish to the world.

HISPANIA NETWORK, INC.
www.hispanianet.com

A bilingual portal for the Hispanic-Latino community.

LATIN WORLD
www.latinworld.com

The premier search engine for Iberoamerica and the Caribbean.

MUNDO LATINO
www.mundolatino.com

An interesting and informative website about the Latin American Community.

RED MUNDO LATINO
www.mundolatino.org

Your language, your people, your culture, your Internet community search engine.

PROFESSIONAL

ASSOCIATION OF HISPANIC ADVERTISING AGENCIES
www.ahaa.org

Lists all the Hispanic marketing-advertising companies in the U.S.

ASSOCIATION OF LATINO PROFESSIONALS IN FINANCE AND ACCOUNTING
www.alpfa.org

Dedicated to enhancing opportunities for Latinos in accounting and finance.

HISPANIC BUSINESS WOMEN'S ALLIANCE
www.hbwa.net

An on-line community of Hispanic women entrepreneurs, professionals, consultants, executives, and investors located throughout North America, Latin America, the Caribbean, and Spain.

HISPANIC NATIONAL BAR ASSOCIATION
www.hnba.com

Increases professional opportunities for Hispanics in the legal profession, and addresses issues of concern to the national Hispanic community.

NATIONAL ASSOCIATION OF HISPANIC JOURNALISTS
www.nahj.org

Dedicated to the recognition of Hispanics in the news industry.

NATIONAL SOCIETY OF HISPANIC MBA'S
www.nshmba.org

Fostering Hispanic leadership through graduate management education and professional development.

SOCIETY OF HISPANIC PROFESSIONAL ENGINEERS
www.shpe.org

Created to serve as role models in the Hispanic community.

MEXICAN AMERICAN ENGINEERS AND SCIENTISTS
www.maes-natl.org

Created to increase the number of Mexican Americans and other Hispanics in the technical and scientific fields.

RELIGIOUS

CENTRAL DE SERMONES
www.centraldesermones.com

A Christian portal for the Hispanic community in the U.S.

MINISTERIO EL NUEVO PACTO
http://elnuevopacto.com

Offers complete information about the Christian religion.

U.S. CONFERENCE FOR CATHOLIC BISHOPS - SECRETARIAT FOR HISPANIC AFFAIRS
www.nccbuscc.org/hispanicaffairs

Helps build a religious community of U.S. Hispanics.

SHOPPING

DE REMATE
www.deremate.com

The Spanish version of eBay. Targeting U.S. Hispanics and Latin America.

YAHOO! EN ESPANOL SHOPPING
http://espanol.shopping.yahoo.com/

Online shopping in Spanish.

SPORTS

ESPN DEPORTES
http://espndeportes.espn.go.com

The #1 leader in sports news.

FOX SPORTS LATIN AMERICA
www.foxsportsla.com

All of the latest news about Latin American soccer and the rest of the world.

FOX SPORTS WORLD ESPAÑOL
www.terra.com/fox

Your world of sports in Spanish.

MAJOR LEAGUE SOCCER
www.mlsnet.com/MLS/espanol

All of the lateste news about the U.S. professional soccer league in Spanish.

SOCCERTV
www.soccertv.com

The ultimate guide to televised soccer.

TECHNOLOGY

100CIA
http://100cia.com

Provides information about the latest news in science and technology.

ALLIANCE FOR LATINO COMMUNITY TECHNOLOGY
www.alct.org

Dedicated to preparing Latinos to acquire the skills of technology literacy.

AMES RESEARCH CENTER - OFICINA DE ASUNTOS PUBLICOS
http://amesnews.arc.nasa.gov/index_span.html

Information about NASA in Spanish.

IMPACTO, INFLUENCIA, CAMBIO
www.smithsonianeducation.org

Science, technology and invention in Latin America and the United States.

Hispanic Television Stations continued from p 397

KEUS-TV CHANNEL 31
Univision
40 W Twohig #101
San Angelo, TX 76903
James E.F. Riley, Station Manager
Tel: (325) 482-9277 Fax: (325) 481-3272
Email: jriley@entravision.com

KANG-TV CHANNEL 41
Telefutura
40 W Twohig #101
San Angelo, TX 76903
James E. F. Riley, Station Manager
Tel: (325) 482-9277 Fax: (325) 481-3272
Email: jriley@entravision.com

UTAH

KEJT CHANNEL 50
Telemundo
453 Simoron Dr.
Ogden, UT 84404

John Terrill, General Manager
Tel: (801) 393-0012 Fax: (801) 393-1105
Email: j.terrill@worldnet.att.net
Web: www.telemundo.com

KULX CHANNEL 51
Telemundo
453 Simoron Dr.
Ogden, UT 84404
John Terrill, General Manager
Tel: (801) 393-0012 Fax: (801) 393-1105
Email: j.terrill@worldnet.att.net
Web: www.telemundo.com

KUTF CHANNEL 3
Telefutura
525 S 300 West #1
Salt Lake City, UT 84101
Arlene Urias, General Manager
Tel: (801) 519-9784 Fax: (801) 519-9785
Email: aurias@ebcorp.net
Web: www.univision.net

KUTH CHANNEL 12
Univision
525 S 300 West #1
Salt Lake City, UT 84101
Arlene Urias, General Manager
Tel: (801) 519-9784 Fax: (801) 519-9785
Email: aurias@ebcorp.net
Web: www.univision.net

VIRGINIA

WZDC-TV CHANNEL 64
ZGS Communications, Inc.
2000 N 14th St. #400
Arlington, VA 22201
Ronald Gordon, Owner
Tel: (703) 528-5656 Fax: (703) 528-6566
Email: rgordon@zgsgroup.com

WZDC TELEMUNDO CHANNEL 64
2775 S Quincy St. #100
Arlington, VA 22206

Julissa Marenco, General Manager
Tel: (703) 820-8333 Fax: (703) 820-9686
Web: www.telemundo.com

WASHINGTON

KCJT CHANNEL 17
Hispanavision
713 W Yakima Ave.
Yakima, WA 98902
Ron Bevins, Owner/General Manager
Tel: (509) 452-8817 Fax: (509) 248-7499

WISCONSIN

WYTU CHANNEL 63
Weigel Broadcasting
809 S 60th St.
Milwaukee, WI 53214
Peter Zomaya, General Manager
Tel: (312) 705-2623 Fax: (312) 705-2666
Email: pzomaya@wciu.com